FINANCIAL MANAGEMENT

Text, Problems and Cases

EIGHTH EDITION

About the Authors

M. Y. Khan is a former Professor of Finance, Department of Financial Studies, University of Delhi. He has served as the Head of Department of Financial Studies and Dean Faculty of Business, University of Delhi. He has also been the Head, Department of Commerce, University of Delhi. Professor Khan has more than 40 years of teaching and research experience and has authored/co-authored about a dozen books. Some of his other major publications are *Basic Financial Management, Management Accounting, Cost Accounting* (co-authored with Professor Jain), *Indian Financial System* and *Financial Services*. Most of these books have run through several editions/reprints; two of these have seen more than 60 reprints and six editions.

Professor Khan has several research papers, published in journals of national and international repute, to his credit which are widely cited in the academic literature. Having guided more than a dozen Ph.D. students in the area of finance and accounting, he has published several research studies and completed many research projects. Professor Khan has also held several positions as a member on the boards of banks, mutual funds, academic institutions and so on. He has been Director of the Indian Bank and a Trustee of the PNB Mutual Fund. He has also been a member of the Board of Governors of the National Institute of Bank Management (RBI) and National Institute of Financial Management (Government of India). Enjoying the reputation of being an excellent teacher, he has been invited by several institutions as a Visiting Professor. The select list includes Indian Institute of Foreign Trade (IIFT), New Delhi, and Indian Institute of Technology (IIT) Delhi. He has organised several Management Development Programmes (MDPs) both for public and private sector executives in the areas of financial management, financial and cost analysis, profit planning and cost control, investment decisions, etc. His contributions in the field of finance have been recognised at national and international level and he has been recipient of several awards and recognitions.

P. K. Jain is Emeritus Professor of Finance in the Department of Management Studies, IIT Delhi. He earlier served as the Head of Department of Management Studies and Coordinator of Dalmia Research Programme on Management in Asia. He was Modi Foundation Chair Professor as well as Dalmia Chair Professor. With a varied teaching experience of more than four decades, Professor Jain taught subject areas of management accounting, financial management, financial analysis, cost analysis and cost control. Earlier, he taught at the Foundation for Technical Institute, Basrah and University of Basrah, Iraq. He was Visiting Faculty at the University of Paris I, School of Management, Asian Institute of Technology, Bangkok and Howe School of Technology Management, Stevens Institute of Technology, New Jersey. He has also been Visiting Faculty at International Centre for Promotion of Enterprises, Ljubljana, Slovenia, to teach finance in its MBA (International) programme (since 1997 till 2010) and has been conferred the title of Honorary Visiting Professor by the Faculty of Economics, Ljubljana, Slovenia. He has been conferred the best teacher award by IIT Delhi in January 2012.

He has authored/co-authored more than 10 textbooks. The select list includes *Basic Financial Management, Management Accounting, Cost Accounting, International Financial Management, Financial Management Practices: An Empirical Study of Indian Corporates, Financial Management Practices in Select Private Corporate Enterprises: A Comparative Study of India, Thailand and Singapore, IFCI: A Study in Financial Management, Economic Crisis in South East Asia*. He has published more than 200 research papers in journals of national and international repute and has published 15 research books/ monographs. Having guided 25 Ph.D. students in the area of finance and accounting, Professor Jain has also been associated with several research projects and consultancy in the field of finance. He is on the boards of many academic institutions and has organised several Management Development Programmes (MDPs)/Continuing Education Programmes (CEPs) for both public and private sector executives. His contributions in the field of finance have been recognised at national and international level and several awards and recognition have been conferred on him.

FINANCIAL MANAGEMENT

Text, Problems and Cases

EIGHTH EDITION

M Y KHAN
Former Professor of Finance
Department of Financial Studies
University of Delhi
Delhi

P K JAIN
Formerly Professor of Finance and Head,
Department of Management Studies Indian
Institute of Technology,
Delhi

McGraw Hill Education (India) Private Limited

Published by McGraw Hill Education (India) Private Limited,
Registered Office: Anjana Complex No: 5/90 A, Butt Road, St. Thomas Mount, Chennai – 600016, Tamil Nadu, India.

Financial Management, 8e

Seventh reprint 2025

Print Edition
ISBN-13: 978-93-5316-218-4
ISBN-10: 93-5316-218-1

eBook Edition
ISBN-13: 978-93-5316-219-1
ISBN-10: 93-5316-219-X

08 09 10 11 12 RAJ 29 28 27 26 25

Typeset at Pee-Gee Graphics, A-6/95, Sector 15, Rohini, Delhi 110085, and Printed and bound in India at
Rajkamal Electric Press, Plot No. 2, Phase-IV, Kundli, Haryana

Cover Designer: APS Compugraphics
Cover Image Source: ElenaBs / Alamy Stock Vector

Visit us at: www.mheducation.co.in
Toll free in India: 1800 103 5875
Write to us at: support.india@mheducation.com
CIN: U80302TN2010PTC111532

Preface to the Eighth Edition

We are pleased to place before the readers this thoroughly revised edition of our highly successful reference-cum-text book: **Financial Management—Text, Problems and Cases**. The focus continues on equipping the readers with theories, concepts, and techniques that can be applied to corporate decision-making including strategic, analytical or simply routine decisions.

New Features in the Eighth Edition

Numerous changes distinguish this edition from the earlier edition.

Updated Chapter Contents The thrust is primarily on incorporating updates in the field of financial management as well as the regulatory and policy developments therein. The important chapter-wise updates are as follows:

Chapter	*Addition/Inclusion/Rewriting/Pruning/ Deletion*
4	Addition of equity returns in India
5	Updated cash flow statement of Reliance Industries Limited (RIL).
6	(i) Updated Financial Statement Analysis of RIL. (ii) Inclusion of two cases on ratio analysis: (a) Tata Motors Ltd and (b) ITC Limited
11	Updated treatment of dividend payment tax in India
17	The framework relating to factoring in India completely rewritten
18	Updated DOL, DFL and DCL of RIL
19	Addition of Indian practices relating to pecking-order theory
29	Deletion of Chapter 29 relating to corporate governance
30	Updation of (i) Bonus ratio of select companies, (ii) Split ratio of select companies, (iii) Shares buyback of select companies, (iv) Equity dividend, EPS, DPS, and retention per share of RIL and (v) Inclusion of shares repurchase practices in India
32	(i) The SEBI framework relating to acquisition/takeover completely rewritten and (ii) Inclusion of Mergers and Acquisitions practices in India
35	The framework of External Commercial Borrowings completely rewritten

Pedagogical Features

The time-tested pedagogical features of the text are listed below.

Learning Objectives Each chapter begins with a number of learning objectives to ensure broad understanding of the concepts, theories and techniques of financial management.

Mini Cases Another distinct feature is the inclusion of a large number of **mini cases**. These chapter-end cases can be used by the readers to synthesise and apply related concepts, theories, and techniques.

Multiple Choice Questions Multiple choice questions with answers is yet another distinct feature of the new edition.

Web Supplements Inclusion of comprehensive cases, additional solved problems, solutions to all numerical review questions, power point presentation and a guide for instructors, among others, is an important feature of new edition.

Spreadsheet/Excel-Application Spreadsheet solutions have been provided in a large number of chapters.

Special Features

To further develop the readers' ability of applying various financial principles and techniques, following special features have been added in this edition:

Up-to-date Comprehensive Coverage The book is structured around financial decision-making and comprehensively covers objectives of financial management, organisation of finance function, time value of money, valuation of bonds and shares, risk and return, option valuation, financial analysis, profit planning and cost control, capital budgeting decisions, cost of capital, capital structure decisions, dividend policy decisions, working capital management, business valuation, corporate restructuring, foreign exchange markets, foreign exchange risk management techniques, international financial management, risk management, corporate governance, Indian corporate practices related to corporate objectives and financial decision making.

Analytical Approach and Decisional Focus Consistent with the aim of the book, a careful and thorough presentation of the financial consequences of management decision is the underlying theme. The orientation is managerial with emphasis on identification and solution of financial problems confronting business enterprises.

Chapter Organisation Each chapter is related to the managerial decision-making perspective. We have not merely described a concept but have also related it to the overall goal of wealth maximisation. After describing a concept, its application is illustrated with the help of step-by-step examples to improve clarity. In the preparation of the text, we have kept readability constantly in mind and have accordingly used a clear and concise, and by and large, non-mathematical writing style, especially in the treatment of concepts requiring the use of mathematics.

Numerous Illustrations/Solved Problems and Review Questions A comprehensive set of real-life solved problems, at the end of each chapter, are intended to serve as a review guide to test the readers' understanding of the subject. Numerous end-of-chapter review questions are included together with answers to help them prepare detailed solutions.

Rearrangement of Solved Problems/Review Questions have been rearranged in order of level of difficulty, namely, easy, medium and difficult.

Reorganisation of chapter-contents in terms of **learning objectives** in place of section-wise presentation.

Procedural Orientation, Practice Discussion and Cases To enable the readers to understand the real world of finance, contemporary industry practices as also procedural aspects have been included at relevant places in reasonable detail. About 15 integrated (comprehensive) cases and 40 mini cases form the part of this edition, for this purpose.

Financial Tables and Bibliography A complete set of financial tables is included as a ready reckoner. A select bibliography would be of special interest to teachers/advance students of the subject.

Target

The book is primarily targeted at teachers/students of finance, management, commerce, accounting and related professional disciplines/courses. Practitioners/professionals would also find it an invaluable text.

The financial management discipline is constantly changing. It is both stimulating and far reaching. We hope that the eighth edition of this book with its comprehensive and up-to-date coverage would contribute to a better understanding of corporate finance. We sincerely look forward to the same overwhelming response from readers to this edition as to the previous edition.

Acknowledgements

We would express our intellectual debt of gratitude to the numerous authors who have enriched the stream of literature in finance on which we have liberally drawn. Some of the more specific references are indicated in the text itself.

Professor Jain would like to place on record his deep sense of gratitude to the encouragement by Prof. V. Ramgopal Rao, Director, IIT Delhi. His colleagues, Dr. R. K. Arora (International Management Institute, New Delhi), Dr. Alok Dixit (IIM Lucknow) and Dr. MV Shivaani (IIM, Nagpur) have helped in several ways, in particular, in contributing the spreadsheet solutions included in various chapters of the book. We gratefully acknowledge their contribution. We also thank Ms. Anita Sharma who has developed Excel-based templates for students (available on the OLC) for easier understanding and gaining experience using spreadsheets.

Our thanks are also due to our student friends, Dr. Chhavi Mehta, Dr. Vandana Bhama, Dr. Sadaf Anwar and Ms Samta Jain. The authors record a word of appreciation for Professor Surendra S. Yadav's contribution. The authors have also a word of appreciation for the excellent support from Mrs. Vibha Mahajan, Mr. Nikhil Wadhera, Mr. Shivkant Singhal, Ms. Malvika Shah and Mr. Atul Gupta of McGraw Hill Education India for the speedy and excellent publication of the book.

A special word of thanks and appreciation is due to Sanya Nadeem, 9-year Boston-based grand-daughter of Professor Khan.

Authors

Preface to the First Edition

This book, in a sense, is an outgrowth of our teaching experience. In our academic interaction with teachers, postgraduate students and practising financial executives, we have found that they face considerable difficulty in using the available foreign books in this growing academic discipline. The present volume, in a way, represents a modest attempt to provide a solution to their problems.

It is intended primarily for postgraduate students in commerce and chartered and cost accountancy. Those doing similar courses in business management or appearing in the restructured civil services and other competitive examinations will hopefully find it equally useful. Its usefulness, however, is not confined to academicians alone. It may also be of special interest to the practitioners in the field.

In keeping with the aims of the book, we have attempted to present the text in a lucid and simple style; the treatment is comprehensive and by and large non-mathematical. Another notable feature of this volume is that the discussions of the concepts and theories are invariably followed by exhaustive illustrative problems. To test the understanding of the readers as also to enable them to have sufficient practice, a large number of exercises have also been given at the end of the chapters. A select bibliography at the end of the book would be of special interest to the teachers of the subject.

The theme of Financial Management is structured round the decision-making in the three inter-related financial areas: investment—long-term as well as current assets; financing; and dividend policy. Also included are the important tools of financial planning and management. The main discussion is divided into six parts comprising twenty chapters.

Part I of the book, which provides the setting to the detailed discussions that follow subsequently, contains two chapters. Chapter 1 outlines the *nature* of financial management in terms of its emerging and contemporary scope and objectives. The concern of Chapter 2 is with the time value of money, i.e. compounding and discounting or present value techniques and their practical applications in financial decision-making, particularly capital budgeting.

Part II, comprising two chapters, is devoted to the tools of analysis in financial management. While Chapter 3 explains and illustrates the statement of changes in financial position (funds flow and cash flow), the financial statement analysis (ratio analysis) is described in Chapter 4.

The subsequent discussions relate to the important decision-making areas in financial management. Thus, Part III focusses on the first and the most important aspect, namely, the long-term investment decision or capital budgeting. It consists of five chapters. The first of these (Chapter 5) presents the general principles of capital budgeting with particular reference to the type of information required (cash flow) and its essential ingredients. This is followed in Chapter 6 by a detailed account of the capital budgeting evaluation techniques, traditional as well as time-adjusted or discounted cash flow. The incorporation of risk and uncertainty into the capital budgeting exercise is elaborated in Chapter 7. Chapter 8 attempts to develop the concept and measurement of cost of capital—the most controversial element in financial management. The last chapter of this part (Chapter 9) dwells on the Indian corporate practices pertaining to capital expenditure decision-making in both the public and private sectors.

The second important decision involved in financial management (financing decision) is covered in the three chapters of Part IV. The discussions in Chapter 10 pertaining to the two inter-related aspects, i.e. operating and financial leverage, set the framework for the capital structure decisions of a firm. The capital structure theories, reflecting the controversy in the financial literature regarding the theoretical relationship between capital structure, cost of capital and value of a firm are examined in Chapter 11. In the light of the conclusions of this chapter, the considerations having a bearing on the designing of an appropriate capital structure are highlighted in the next chapter (Chapter 12).

Part V of the volume is devoted to the relevant dimensions of dividend policy decision. The first aspect, viz, the controversy in the academic literature as regards the relevance of dividend policy to the value of the enterprise, is the subject matter of Chapter 13. It is against the background of this theoretical discussion that Chapter 14 dwells on the determinants of an appropriate dividend policy.

Finally, Part VI of the book focusses on the management of current assets, more popularly designated as working capital management. The first three chapters of this part between them provide an overview of working capital management and deal respectively with the theory of working capital management in terms of the basic strategies for efficient management of current assets and current liabilities (Chapter 15), the planning and determinants of working capital (Chapter 16) and the financing and control of working capital in India with particular reference to the report of the Tandon Committee (Chapter 17). The next three chapters look into the management of the individual components of current assets. While cash management is the theme of Chapter 18, the various dimensions of receivables management are explained in Chapter 19. The last chapter (Chapter 20) discusses the relevant aspects of inventory management.

Detailed solutions of all the exercises included in each chapter of this book are provided in our book: *Management Accounting* and *Financial Management—Problems and Solutions*.

In the preparation of this book we have received encouragement and support from various quarters. In particular we would like to thank Mr. H.C. Jain, Librarian of the University South Campus Library for the excellent library support he provided to us at short notice. Mr. Subhash Chander deserves our thanks for speedy and accurate typing of the final draft.

Finally, we would be failing in our duty if we do not acknowledge the deep debt of gratitude that we owe to the various authors whose writings have provided an insight into the intricacies of the subject.

M Y Khan
P K Jain

Contents

Preface to the Eighth Edition *v*
Preface to the First Edition *ix*
Visual Walkthrough *xxii*

PART 1
FOUNDATION OF FINANCE

1. **Financial Management: An Overview** **1.3–1.26**
   Finance Function *1.3*
   Finance and Related Disciplines *1.4*
   Scope of Financial Management *1.7*
   Objectives of Financial Management *1.10*
   Agency Problem *1.19*
   Organisation of Finance Function *1.20*
   Emerging Role of Finance Managers in India *1.22*
   An Overview of the Book *1.23*
   Summary *1.24*
   References *1.25*
   Review Questions *1.25*

2. **Time Value of Money** **2.1–2.36**
   Introduction *2.1*
   Rationale of Time Value of Money *2.2*
   Compounding Technique *2.3*
   Present Value or Discounting Technique *2.11*
   Practical Applications of Compounding and Present Value Techniques *2.18*
   Summary *2.29*
   Solved Problems *2.31*
   Review Questions *2.33*
   Answers *2.34*

3. Risk and Return **3.1–3.43**

Introduction *3.1*
Risk and Return *3.2*
Risk and Return of a Single Asset *3.2*
Risk and Return of Portfolio *3.6*
Portfolio Selection *3.12*
Capital Asset Pricing Model (CAPM) *3.19*
Extended CAPM *3.25*
Arbitrage Pricing Theory *3.28*
Summary 3.29
References 3.30
Solved Problems 3.31
Mini Cases 3.36
Review Questions 3.40
Answers 3.43

4. Valuation of Bonds and Shares **4.1–4.23**

Introduction *4.1*
Basic Valuation Model *4.2*
Valuation of Bonds/Debentures *4.3*
Valuation of Preference Shares *4.8*
Valuation of Ordinary Shares *4.8*
Other Approaches to Valuation of Shares *4.12*
Relationship Among Financial Decisions, Return, Risk and Share Values *4.13*
Summary 4.15
References 4.16
Solved Problems 4.16
Mini Cases 4.20
Review Questions 4.22
Answers 4.23

PART 2
FINANCIAL ANALYSIS, PROFIT PLANNING AND CONTROL

5. Statement of Cash Flows **5.3–5.45**

Meaning *5.4*
Sources and Uses of Cash *5.4*
Usefulness of Statement of Cash Flows *5.4*
Preparation of Statement of Cash Flows *5.5*
AS-7: Statement of Cash Flows *5.13*
Summary 5.22
References 5.22

Solved Problems 5.22
Review Questions 5.41
Answers 5.45

6. Financial Statements Analysis **6.1–6.93**
Introduction *6.1*
Ratio Analysis—Meaning and Rationale *6.2*
Liquidity Ratios *6.3*
Leverage/Capital Structure Ratios *6.11*
Profitability Ratios *6.18*
Activity/Efficiency Ratios *6.26*
Integrated Analysis of Ratios *6.31*
Common Size Statements *6.40*
Importance of Ratio Analysis *6.42*
Limitations of Ratio Analysis *6.44*
Summary 6.45
References 6.48
Solved Problems 6.48
Mini Cases 6.71
Review Questions 6.86
Answers 6.92

7. Volume-Cost-Profit Analysis **7.1–7.27**
Introduction *7.1*
Break-Even Analysis *7.2*
Break-Even Analysis Applications *7.5*
Cash Break-Even Point *7.14*
Summary 7.16
References 7.18
Solved Problems 7.18
Mini Cases 7.22
Review Questions 7.24
Answers 7.27

8. Budgeting and Profit Planning **8.1–8.20**
Introduction *8.1*
Planning Process *8.1*
Budget—Definition, Meaning and Purpose *8.2*
Preparation/Types of Budgets *8.5*
Summary 8.13
References 8.14
Solved Problems 8.15
Review Questions 8.18
Answers 8.20

PART 3
LONG-TERM INVESTMENT DECISION

9. Capital Budgeting I: Principles and Techniques **9.3–9.77**
Introduction *9.3*
Nature of Capital Budgeting *9.3*
Data Requirement: Identifying Relevant Cash Flows *9.7*
Evaluation Techniques *9.27*
Summary 9.44
References 9.46
Solved Problems 9.47
Mini Cases 9.64
Review Questions 9.75
Answers 9.77

10. Capital Budgeting II: Additional Aspects **10.1–10.53**
Introduction *10.1*
NPV, IRR, Profitability Index Methods — A Comparison *10.1*
Project Selection Under Capital Rationing *10.12*
Inflation and Capital Budgeting *10.15*
Summary 10.19
References 10.20
Solved Problems 10.21
Mini Cases 10.42
Review Questions 10.51
Answers 10.53

11. Concept and Measurement of Cost of Capital **11.1–11.52**
Introduction *11.1*
Importance and Concept *11.2*
Cost of Debt *11.5*
Cost of Preference Shares *11.9*
Cost of Equity Capital *11.11*
Cost of Retained Earnings *11.17*
Computation of Overall Cost of Capital *11.18*
Summary 11.25
References 11.27
Solved Problems 11.28
Mini Cases 11.44
Review Questions 11.50
Answers 11.52

12. Analysis of Risk and Uncertainty **12.1–12.50**
Introduction *12.1*
Description and Measurement of Risk *12.2*

Precise Measures of Risk: Standard Deviation and Coefficient of Variation *12.9*
Risk Evaluation Approaches *12.11*
Risk and Real Optoins *12.24*
Summary 12.26
References 12.28
Solved Problems 12.28
Review Questions 12.45
Answers 12.48

PART 4
CURRENT ASSETS MANAGEMENT

13. Working Capital Management: An Overview **13.3–13.38**
Introduction *13.3*
Nature of Working Capital *13.3*
Planning of Working Capital *13.10*
Summary 13.20
References 13.22
Solved Problems 13.23
Mini Cases 13.31
Review Questions 13.35
Answers 13.38

14. Management of Cash and Marketable Securities **14.1–14.44**
Introduction *14.1*
Motives for Holding Cash *14.2*
Objectives of Cash Management *14.4*
Factors Determining Cash Balances *14.5*
Determining Cash Need *14.6*
Cash Management: Basic Strategies *14.16*
Cash Management Techniques/Processes *14.19*
Marketable Securities *14.23*
Summary 14.29
References 14.31
Solved Problems 14.31
Mini Cases 14.37
Review Questions 14.42
Answers 14.44

15. Receivables Management **15.1–15.30**
Introduction *15.1*
Objectives *15.2*
Credit Policies *15.3*
Credit Terms *15.8*
Collection Policies *15.12*

Summary *15.15*
References *15.16*
Solved Problems *15.16*
Mini Cases *15.25*
Review Questions *15.28*
Answers *15.30*

16. Inventory Management **16.1–16.26**
Introduction *16.1*
Objectives *16.2*
Techniques *16.5*
Just-in Time Inventory/Production *16.14*
Summary *16.16*
References *16.17*
Solved Problems *16.17*
Review Questions *16.24*
Answers *16.26*

17. Working Capital Financing **17.1–17.32**
Trade Credit *17.1*
Bank Credit *17.3*
Commercial Papers *17.9*
Certificate of Deposits (CDs) *17.13*
Factoring *17.14*
Summary *17.24*
Solved Problems *17.27*
Mini Cases *17.28*
Review Questions *17.30*
Answers *17.32*

PART 5
FINANCING DECISION

18. Operating, Financial and Combined Leverage **18.3–18.51**
Introduction *18.3*
Operating Leverage *18.4*
Financial Leverage *18.7*
Combined Leverage: Total Risk *18.20*
Summary *18.21*
References *18.23*
Solved Problems *18.23*
Mini Cases *18.43*
Review Questions *18.48*
Answers *18.51*

19. Capital Structure, Cost of Capital and Valuation **19.1–19.48**
Introduction *19.1*
Assumptions, Definitions and symbols *19.2*
Capital Structure Theories *19.4*
Summary 19.31
References 19.33
Solved Problems 19.33
Mini Cases 19.41
Review Questions 19.46
Answers 19.48

20. Designing Capital Structure **20.1–20.32**
Introduction *20.1*
Key factors *20.2*
Profitability Aspect: Earnings Before Interest and Tax (EBIT) – Earnings per Share (EPS) Analysis *20.2*
Liquidity Aspect: Cash Flow Analysis *20.4*
Other Factors *20.9*
Tax Planning *20.13*
Summary 20.15
References 20.16
Solved Problems 20.17
Mini Cases 20.22
Review Questions 20.30
Answers 20.32

PART 6
LONG-TERM FINANCING

21. Capital Markets **21.3–21.16**
Financial System *21.3*
Relationship Between New Issue Market and Stock Exchange *21.5*
Functions of Stock/Secondary Markets/ Exchanges *21.7*
Functions of New Issues/Primary Market *21.9*
Summary 21.14
References 21.15
Review Questions 21.16

22. Equity/Ordinary Shares **22.1–22.15**
Introduction *22.1*
Fundamentals of Equity Shares *22.1*
Issue Procedures *22.4*
Summary 22.11

Solved Problems *22.12*
Review Questions *22.13*
Answers *22.15*

23. Term Loans, Debentures/Bonds and Securitisation **23.1–23.27**
Introduction *23.1*
Term Loans *23.2*
Debentures/Bonds/Notes *23.7*
Securitisation *23.16*
Summary *23.22*
Solved Problems *23.23*
Review Questions *23.26*
Answers *23.27*

24. Hybrid Financing/Instruments **24.1–24.16**
Introduction *24.1*
Preference Share Capital *24.1*
Convertible Debentures/Bonds *24.4*
Warrants *24.7*
Options *24.10*
Summary *24.11*
Solved Problems *24.12*
Review Questions *24.14*
Answers *24.16*

25. Lease Financing and Hire-Purchase Finance **25.1–25.58**
Introduction *25.1*
Lease Financing *25.1*
Financial Evaluation of Leasing *25.10*
Hire-Purchase Finance *25.21*
Summary *25.28*
Solved Problems *25.29*
Mini Cases *25.47*
Review Questions *25.54*
Answers *25.58*

26. Venture Capital Financing **26.1–26.34**
Introduction *26.1*
Theoretical Framework *26.2*
Indian Venture Capital Scenario *26.16*
Summary *26.27*
References *26.33*
Review Questions *26.33*

PART 7
RISK MANAGEMENT

27. Option Valuation **27.3–27.29**

Introduction *27.3*
Option: Concept and Types *27.3*
Option Payoffs *27.9*
Call Option Boundaries *27.10*
Factors Influencing Option Valuation *27.12*
The Black-Scholes Option Pricing Model *27.17*

Summary 27.21
References 27.22
Solved Problems 27.23
Review Questions 27.27
Answers 27.29

28. Derivatives: Managing Financial Risk **28.1–28.19**

Introduction *28.1*
Forward Contracts *28.2*
Futures/Future Contracts *28.3*
Options/Options Contracts *28.8*

Summary 28.15
Solved Problems 28.16
Review Questions 28.17
Answers 28.19

PART 8
DIVIDEND DECISION

29. Dividend and Valuation **29.3–29.31**

Introduction *29.3*
Irrelevance of Dividends *29.4*
Relevance of Dividends *29.13*

Summary 29.19
References 29.21
Solved Problems 29.21
Review Questions 29.29
Answers 29.31

30. Determinants of Dividend Policy **30.1–30.40**

Introduction *30.1*
Factors Affecting Dividend Policy *30.1*
Bonus Shares (Stock Dividend) and Stock (Share) Splits *30.13*

Share Repurchase (Share Buyback) *30.17*
Legal, Procedural and Tax Aspects *30.23*
Summary 30.27
References 30.28
Solved Problems 30.29
Mini Cases 30.35
Review Questions 30.37
Answers 30.39

PART 9
VALUATION AND CORPORATE RESTRUCTURING

31. Business Valuation **31.3–31.46**
Introduction *31.3*
Conceptual Framework of Valuation *31.3*
Approaches/Methods of Valuation *31.6*
Other Approaches to Value Measurement *31.20*
Summary 31.23
References 31.25
Solved Problems 31.25
Mini Cases 31.32
Review Questions 31.43
Answers 31.45

32. Corporate Restructuring **32.1–32.98**
Introduction *32.1*
Conceptual Framework *32.1*
Financial Framework *32.5*
Tax Aspects of Amalgamation, Merger and Demergers *32.18*
Legal and Procedural Aspects of Mergers/Amalgamations and Acquisition/Takeovers *32.22*
Other Forms of Corporate Restructuring *32.55*
Summary 32.61
References 32.68
Solved Problems 32.68
Mini Cases 32.89
Review Questions 32.95
Answers 32.98

PART 10
INTERNATIONAL FINANCE

33. Foreign Exchange Markets and Dealings **33.3–33.29**
Introduction *33.3*
Foreign Exchange Markets *33.3*

Foreign Exchange Dealings *33.4*
Determinants and Select Theories of Exchange Rates *33.13*

Summary 33.16
References 33.17
Solved Problems 33.17
Review Questions 33.27
Answers 33.29

34. Foreign Exchange Exposure and Risk Management **34.1–34.34**

Introduction *34.1*
Types of Exposure *34.1*
Foreign Exchange Risk Management—External Techniques *34.5*
FIrm—Internal Hedging Techniques *34.11*

Summary 34.17
References 34.19
Solved Problems 34.19
Mini Cases 34.30
Review Questions 34.31
Answers 34.34

35. International Financial Management **35.1–35.47**

Introduction *35.1*
Multinational Capital Budgeting Decisions *35.2*
Cost of Capital *35.10*
Adjusted Present Value Approach *35.20*
Multinational Working Capital Management *35.20*
External Commercial Borrowings (ECBs) *35.23*
Euro Issues *35.29*
Foreign Currency Exchangeable Bonds *35.33*

Summary 35.35
References 35.38
Solved Problems 35.38
Review Questions 35.45
Answers 35.47

Appendices **A.1-A.8**
Select Bibliography **B.1-B.2**
Index **I.1-I.10**

VISUAL

Part Preview

Each part begins with an overview that provides a glimpse of the contents in its chapters.

PART
1

FOUNDATION OF FINANCE

Chapter 1 **FINANCIAL MANAGEMENT—AN OVERVIEW** *Chapter 2* **TIME VALUE OF MONEY** *Chapter 3* **RISK AND RETURN** *Chapter 4* **VALUATION OF BONDS AND SHARES**	This part of the book dwells on the foundations of finance. Chapter 1 gives an overview of financial management in terms of its relationship with related disciplines, scope, objectives, agency problems, organisation of finance functions in a typical organisation and the organisation of finance function in India. Chapter 2 discusses a basic financial concept, namely, time value of money. It explains and illustrates the basic compounding and discounting techniques as well as their applications. While risk and return including multivariate and factor valuation is analysed in Chapter 3, Valuation of bonds and shares is covered in Chapter 4.

CHAPTER
1
Financial Management—An Overview

LEARNING OBJECTIVES

LO 1.1	Define finance and describe its major areas—financial management/managerial finance/ corporate finance and financial services
LO 1.2	Differentiate financial management from the closely-related disciplines of accounting and economics
LO 1.3	Describe the scope of financial management and identify the key activities of the financial manager
LO 1.4	Explain why wealth/value maximisation, rather than profit/EPS maximisation, is the goal of financial management and how economic value added (EVA) and focus on shareholders relate to its achievement and summarise the major objectives of corporate finance by Indian corporates
LO 1.5	Discuss the agency problem/issue and measure to resolve it
LO 1.6	Outline the organisation of finance function and the emerging role of finance managers in India
LO 1.7	Outline the emerging role of finance managers in India
LO 1.8	Present an overview of the book

LO 1.1 FINANCE FUNCTION

Finance may be defined as the art and science of managing money. The major areas of finance are: **(1)** financial services and **(2)** managerial finance/corporate finance/financial management. While **financial services** is concerned with the design and delivery of advice and financial products to individuals, businesses and governments within the areas of banking and related institutions, personal financial planning, investments, real estate, insurance and so on, **financial management** is concerned with the duties of the financial managers in the business firm. **Financial managers** actively manage the financial affairs of any type of business, namely, financial and non-financial, private and public, large and small, profit-seeking and not-for-profit.

Finance is an art and science of managing money.

Financial management is concerned with the duties of the financial managers in the business firm.

Financial services is concerned with the design and delivery of advice and financial products to individuals, businesses and governments.

Learning Objectives

At the beginning of each chapter, the learning objectives outline what all the reader has to know when the chapter is completed.

WALKTHROUGH

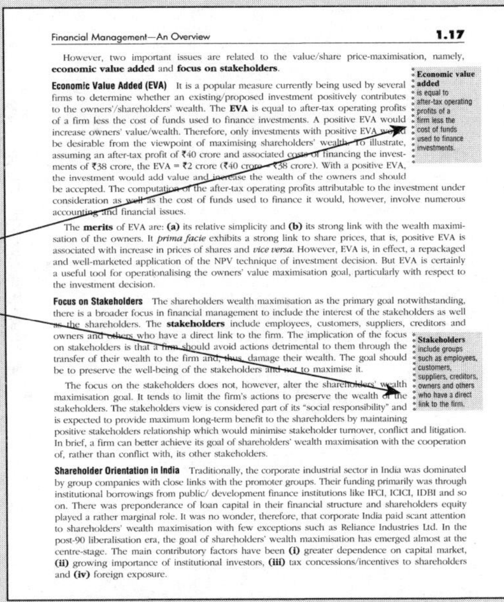

Financial Management—An Overview **1.17**

However, two important issues are related to the value/share price-maximisation, namely, **economic value added** and **focus on stakeholders**.

Economic Value Added (EVA) It is a popular measure currently being used by several firms to determine whether an existing/proposed investment positively contributes to the owners'/shareholders' wealth. The **EVA** is equal to after-tax operating profits of a firm less the cost of funds used to finance investments. A positive EVA would increase owners' value/wealth. Therefore, only investments with positive EVA would be desirable from the viewpoint of maximising shareholders' wealth. To illustrate, assuming an after-tax profit of ₹40 crore and associated costs of financing the investments of ₹38 crore, the EVA = ₹2 crore (₹40 crore – ₹38 crore). With a positive EVA, the investment would add value and increase the wealth of the owners and should be accepted. The computation of the after-tax operating profits attributable to the investment under consideration as well as the cost of funds used to finance it would, however, involve numerous accounting and financial issues.

Economic value added is equal to after-tax operating profits of a firm less the cost of funds used to finance investments.

The **merits** of EVA are: **(a)** its relative simplicity and **(b)** its strong link with the wealth maximisation of the owners. It *prima facie* exhibits a strong link to share prices, that is, positive EVA is associated with increase in prices of shares and *vice versa*. However, EVA is, in effect, a repackaged and well-marketed application of the NPV technique of investment decision. But EVA is certainly a useful tool for operationalising the owners' value maximisation goal, particularly with respect to the investment decision.

Focus on Stakeholders The shareholders wealth maximisation as the primary goal notwithstanding, there is a broader focus in financial management to include the interest of the stakeholders as well as the shareholders. The **stakeholders** include employees, customers, suppliers, creditors and owners and others who have a direct link to the firm. The implication of the focus on stakeholders is that a firm should avoid actions detrimental to them through the transfer of their wealth to the firm and, thus, damage their wealth. The goal should be to preserve the well-being of the stakeholders and not to maximise it.

Stakeholders include groups such as employees, customers, suppliers, creditors, owners and others who have a direct link to the firm.

The focus on the stakeholders does not, however, alter the shareholders' wealth maximisation goal. It tends to limit the firm's actions to preserve the wealth of the stakeholders. The stakeholders view is considered part of its "social responsibility" and is expected to provide maximum long-term benefit to the shareholders by maintaining positive stakeholders relationship which would minimise stakeholder turnover, conflict and litigation. In brief, a firm can better achieve its goal of shareholders' wealth maximisation with the cooperation of, rather than conflict with, its other stakeholders.

Shareholder Orientation in India Traditionally, the corporate industrial sector in India was dominated by group companies with close links with the promoter groups. Their funding primarily was through institutional borrowings from public/ development finance institutions like IFCI, ICICI, IDBI and so on. There was preponderance of loan capital in their financial structure and shareholders equity played a rather marginal role. It was no wonder, therefore, that corporate India paid scant attention to shareholders' wealth maximisation with few exceptions such as Reliance Industries Ltd. In the post-90 liberalisation era, the goal of shareholders' wealth maximisation has emerged almost at the centre-stage. The main contributory factors have been **(i)** greater dependence on capital market, **(ii)** growing importance of institutional investors, **(iii)** tax concessions/incentives to shareholders and **(iv)** foreign exposure.

Margin Notes

Important concepts and key terms are briefly summarised in the notes given in the margins.

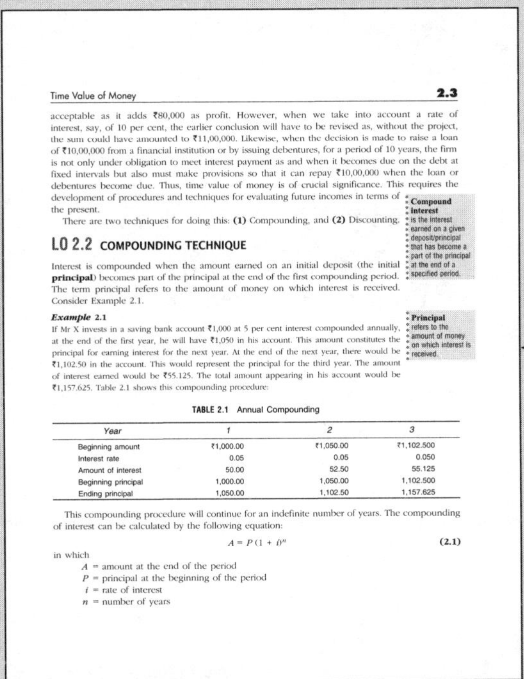

Time Value of Money **2.3**

acceptable as it adds ₹80,000 as profit. However, when we take into account a rate of interest, say, of 10 per cent, the earlier conclusion will have to be revised as, without the project, the sum could have amounted to ₹11,00,000. Likewise, when the decision is made to raise a loan of ₹10,00,000 from a financial institution or by issuing debentures, for a period of 10 years, the firm is not only under obligation to meet interest payment as and when it becomes due on the debt at fixed intervals but also must make provisions so that it can repay ₹10,00,000 when the loan or debentures become due. Thus, time value of money is of crucial significance. This requires the development of procedures and techniques for evaluating future incomes in terms of the present.

There are two techniques for doing this: **(1)** Compounding, and **(2)** Discounting.

Compound interest is the interest earned on a given deposit/principal that has become a part of the principal at the end of a specified period.

LO 2.2 COMPOUNDING TECHNIQUE

Interest is compounded when the amount earned on an initial deposit (the initial **principal**) becomes part of the principal at the end of the first compounding period. The term principal refers to the amount of money on which interest is received. Consider Example 2.1.

Principal refers to the amount of money on which interest is received.

***Example* 2.1**

If Mr X invests in a saving bank account ₹1,000 at 5 per cent interest compounded annually, at the end of the first year, he will have ₹1,050 in his account. This amount constitutes the principal for earning interest for the next year. At the end of the next year, there would be ₹1,102.50 in the account. This would represent the principal for the third year. The amount of interest earned would be ₹55.125. The total amount appearing in his account would be ₹1,157.625. Table 2.1 shows this compounding procedure:

TABLE 2.1 Annual Compounding

Year	*1*	*2*	*3*
Beginning amount	₹1,000.00	₹1,050.00	₹1,102.500
Interest rate	0.05	0.05	0.050
Amount of interest	50.00	52.50	55.125
Beginning principal	1,000.00	1,050.00	1,102.500
Ending principal	1,050.00	1,102.50	1,157.625

This compounding procedure will continue for an indefinite number of years. The compounding of interest can be calculated by the following equation:

$$A = P(1 + i)^n \quad (2.1)$$

in which

A = amount at the end of the period
P = principal at the beginning of the period
i = rate of interest
n = number of years

Examples

Solved examples help in the better understanding of concepts.

VISUAL

Boxed Items

Concepts and procedures can be better understood with the help of examples from the Indian financial sector, highlighted as boxed items in the text.

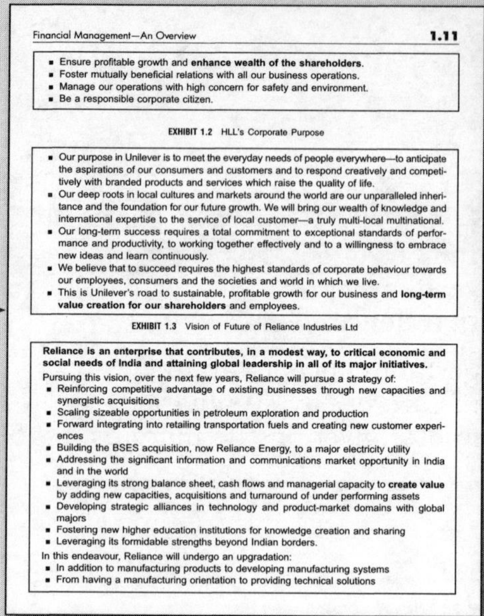

Financial Management—An Overview **1.11**

- Ensure profitable growth and **enhance wealth of the shareholders**.
- Foster mutually beneficial relations with all our business operations.
- Manage our operations with high concern for safety and environment.
- Be a responsible corporate citizen.

EXHIBIT 1.2 HLL's Corporate Purpose

- Our purpose in Unilever is to meet the everyday needs of people everywhere—to anticipate the aspirations of our consumers and customers and to respond creatively and competitively with branded products and services which raise the quality of life.
- Our deep roots in local cultures and markets around the world are our unparalleled inheritance and the foundation for our future growth. We will bring our wealth of knowledge and international expertise to the service of local customer—a truly multi-local multinational.
- Our long-term success requires a total commitment to exceptional standards of performance and productivity, to working together effectively and to a willingness to embrace new ideas and learn continuously.
- We believe that to succeed requires the highest standards of corporate behaviour towards our employees, consumers and the societies and world in which we live.
- This is Unilever's road to sustainable, profitable growth for our business and **long-term value creation for our shareholders** and employees.

EXHIBIT 1.3 Vision of Future of Reliance Industries Ltd

Reliance is an enterprise that contributes, in a modest way, to critical economic and social needs of India and attaining global leadership in all of its major initiatives.

Pursuing this vision, over the next few years, Reliance will pursue a strategy of:

- Reinforcing competitive advantage of existing businesses through new capacities and synergistic acquisitions
- Scaling sizeable opportunities in petroleum exploration and production
- Forward integrating into retailing transportation fuels and creating new customer experiences
- Building the BSES acquisition, now Reliance Energy, to a major electricity utility
- Addressing the significant information and communications market opportunity in India and in the world
- Leveraging its strong balance sheet, cash flows and managerial capacity to **create value** by adding new capacities, acquisitions and turnaround of under performing assets
- Developing strategic alliances in technology and product-market domains with global majors
- Fostering new higher education institutions for knowledge creation and sharing
- Leveraging its formidable strengths beyond Indian borders.

In this endeavour, Reliance will undergo an upgradation:

- In addition to manufacturing products to developing manufacturing systems
- From having a manufacturing orientation to providing technical solutions

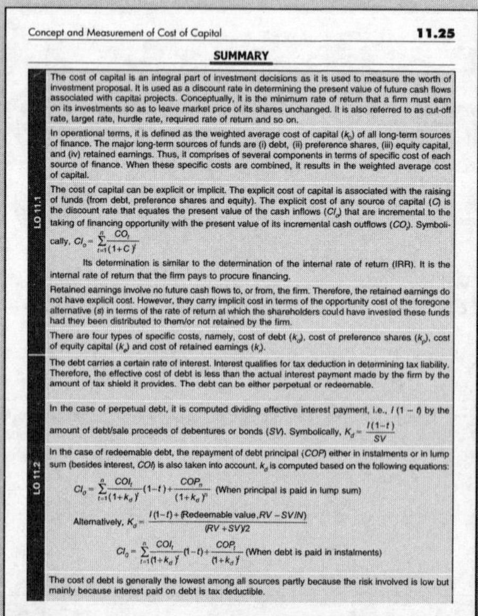

Concept and Measurement of Cost of Capital **11.25**

SUMMARY

LO 11.1

The cost of capital is an integral part of investment decisions as it is used to measure the worth of investment proposal. It is used as a discount rate in determining the present value of future cash flows associated with capital projects. Conceptually, it is the minimum rate of return that a firm must earn on its investments so as to leave market price of its shares unchanged. It is also referred to as cut-off rate, target rate, hurdle rate, required rate of return and so on.

In operational terms, it is defined as the weighted average cost of capital (k_0) of all long-term sources of finance. The major long-term sources of funds are (i) debt, (ii) preference shares, (iii) equity capital, and (iv) retained earnings. Thus, it comprises of several components in terms of specific cost of each source of finance. When these specific costs are combined, it results in the weighted average cost of capital.

The cost of capital can be explicit or implicit. The explicit cost of capital is associated with the raising of funds (from debt, preference shares and equity). The explicit cost of any source of capital (C) is the discount rate that equates the present value of the cash inflows (CI_o) that are incremental to the taking of financing opportunity with the present value of its incremental cash outflows (CO_t). Symbolically, $CI_o = \sum_{t=1}^{n} \frac{CO_t}{(1+C)^t}$

Its determination is similar to the determination of the internal rate of return (IRR). It is the internal rate of return that the firm pays to procure financing.

Retained earnings involve no future cash flows to, or from, the firm. Therefore, the retained earnings do not have explicit cost. However, they carry implicit cost in terms of the opportunity cost of the foregone alternative (*s*) in terms of the rate of return at which the shareholders could have invested these funds had they been distributed to them/or not retained by the firm.

There are four types of specific costs, namely, cost of debt (k_d), cost of preference shares (k_p), cost of equity capital (k_e) and cost of retained earnings (k_r).

LO 11.2

The debt carries a certain rate of interest. Interest qualifies for tax deduction in determining tax liability. Therefore, the effective cost of debt is less than the actual interest payment made by the firm by the amount of tax shield it provides. The debt can be either perpetual or redeemable.

In the case of perpetual debt, it is computed dividing effective interest payment, i.e., $I(1-t)$ by the amount of debt/sale proceeds of debentures or bonds (SV). Symbolically, $K_d = \frac{I(1-t)}{SV}$

In the case of redeemable debt, the repayment of debt principal (COP) either in instalments or in lump sum (besides interest, COI) is also taken into account. k_d is computed based on the following equations:

$$CI_0 = \sum_{t=1}^{n} \frac{COI_t}{(1+k_d)^t}(1-t) + \frac{COP_n}{(1+k_d)^n} \text{ (When principal is paid in lump sum)}$$

$$\text{Alternatively, } K_d = \frac{I(1-t) + (\text{Redeemable value}, RV - SV/N)}{(RV+SV)/2}$$

$$CI_0 = \sum_{t=1}^{n} \frac{COI_t}{(1+k_d)^t}(1-t) + \frac{COP_t}{(1+k_d)^t} \text{ (When debt is paid in instalments)}$$

The cost of debt is generally the lowest among all sources partly because the risk involved is low but mainly because interest paid on debt is tax deductible.

Summary

Each chapter ends with a summary—a series of bulleted statements that restates the most important points that have been mentioned in the chapter. This feature will aid the readers in recapitulating what they have learnt earlier in the chapter.

Walkthrough

Solved Problems

A number of solved problems at the end of every chapter will help the reader understand how to apply to problems the concepts discussed in the chapter.

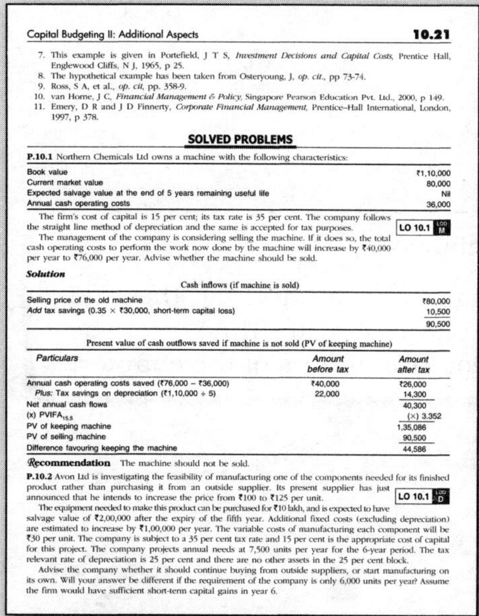

Capital Budgeting II: Additional Aspects **10.21**

7. This example is given in Portefield, J T S, *Investment Decisions and Capital Costs*, Prentice Hall, Englewood Cliffs, N J, 1965, p 25.
8. The hypothetical example has been taken from Osteryoung, J, *op. cit.*, pp 73-74.
9. Ross, S A, et al., *op. cit*, pp. 358-9.
10. van Horne, J C, *Financial Management & Policy*, Singapore Pearson Education Pvt. Ltd., 2000, p 149.
11. Emery, D R and J D Finnerty, *Corporate Financial Management*, Prentice–Hall International, London, 1997, p 378.

SOLVED PROBLEMS

P.10.1 Northern Chemicals Ltd owns a machine with the following characteristics:

Book value	₹1,10,000
Current market value	80,000
Expected salvage value at the end of 5 years remaining useful life	Nil
Annual cash operating costs	36,000

The firm's cost of capital is 15 per cent; its tax rate is 35 per cent. The company follows the straight line method of depreciation and the same is accepted for tax purposes.

LO 10.1 M

The management of the company is considering selling the machine. If it does so, the total cash operating costs to perform the work now done by the machine will increase by ₹40,000 per year to ₹76,000 per year. Advise whether the machine should be sold.

Solution

Cash inflows (if machine is sold)

Selling price of the old machine	₹80,000
Add tax savings (0.35 × ₹30,000, short-term capital loss)	10,500
	90,500

Present value of cash outflows saved if machine is not sold (PV of keeping machine)

Particulars	*Amount before tax*	*Amount after tax*
Annual cash operating costs saved (₹76,000 – ₹36,000)	₹40,000	₹26,000
Plus: Tax savings on depreciation (₹1,10,000 ÷ 5)	22,000	14,300
Net annual cash flows		40,300
(x) $PVIFA_{15,5}$		(×) 3.352
PV of keeping machine		1,35,086
PV of selling machine		90,500
Difference favouring keeping the machine		44,586

Recommendation The machine should not be sold.

P.10.2 Avon Ltd is investigating the feasibility of manufacturing one of the components needed for its finished product rather than purchasing it from an outside supplier. Its present supplier has just announced that he intends to increase the price from ₹100 to ₹125 per unit.

LO 10.1 D

The equipment needed to make this product can be purchased for ₹10 lakh, and is expected to have salvage value of ₹2,00,000 after the expiry of the fifth year. Additional fixed costs (excluding depreciation) are estimated to increase by ₹1,00,000 per year. The variable costs of manufacturing each component will be ₹30 per unit. The company is subject to a 35 per cent tax rate and 15 per cent is the appropriate cost of capital for this project. The company projects annual needs at 7,500 units per year for the 6-year period. The tax relevant rate of depreciation is 25 per cent and there are no other assets in the 25 per cent block.

Advise the company whether it should continue buying from outside suppliers, or start manufacturing on its own. Will your answer be different if the requirement of the company is only 6,000 units per year? Assume the firm would have sufficient short-term capital gains in year 6.

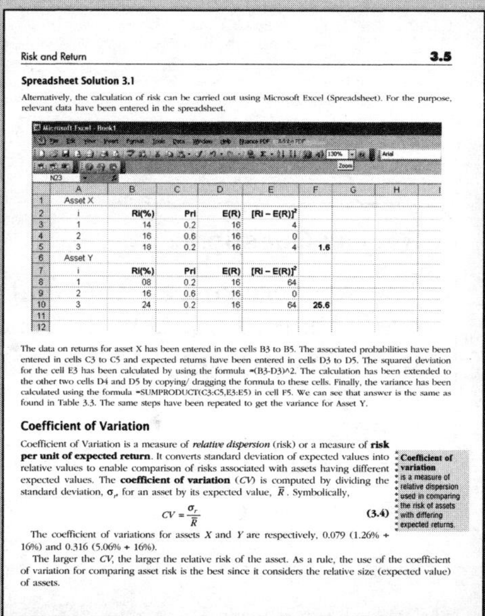

Risk and Return **3.5**

Spreadsheet Solution 3.1

Alternatively, the calculation of risk can be carried out using Microsoft Excel (Spreadsheet). For the purpose, relevant data have been entered in the spreadsheet.

	A	B	C	D	E	F	G	H
1	Asset X							
2	i	Ri(%)	Pri	E(R)	[Ri – E(R)]^2			
3	1	14	0.2	16	4			
4	2	16	0.6	16	0			
5	3	18	0.2	16	4	1.6		
6	Asset Y							
7	i	Ri(%)	Pri	E(R)	[Ri – E(R)]^2			
8	1	08	0.2	16	64			
9	2	16	0.6	16	0			
10	3	24	0.2	16	64	25.6		
11								
12								

The data on returns for asset X has been entered in the cells B3 to B5. The associated probabilities have been entered in cells C3 to C5 and expected returns have been entered in cells D3 to D5. The squared deviation for the cell E3 has been calculated by using the formula =(B3-D3)^2. The calculation has been extended to the other two cells D4 and D5 by copying/ dragging the formula to these cells. Finally, the variance has been calculated using the formula =SUMPRODUCT(C3:C5,E3:E5) in cell F5. We can see that answer is the same as found in Table 3.3. The same steps have been repeated to get the variance for Asset Y.

Coefficient of Variation

Coefficient of Variation is a measure of ***relative dispersion*** (risk) or a measure of **risk per unit of expected return**. It converts standard deviation of expected values into relative values to enable comparison of risks associated with assets having different expected values. The **coefficient of variation** (*CV*) is computed by dividing the standard deviation, σ_r, for an asset by its expected value, $\bar{R}$. Symbolically,

Coefficient of variation is a measure of relative dispersion used in comparing the risk of assets with differing expected returns.

$$CV = \frac{\sigma_r}{\bar{R}} \quad (3.4)$$

The coefficient of variations for assets *X* and *Y* are respectively, 0.079 (1.26% ÷ 16%) and 0.316 (5.06% ÷ 16%).

The larger the *CV*, the larger the relative risk of the asset. As a rule, the use of the coefficient of variation for comparing asset risk is the best since it considers the relative size (expected value) of assets.

Excel Spreadsheet Solutions

A large number of problems have also been solved with the help of Excel spreadsheets.

VISUAL

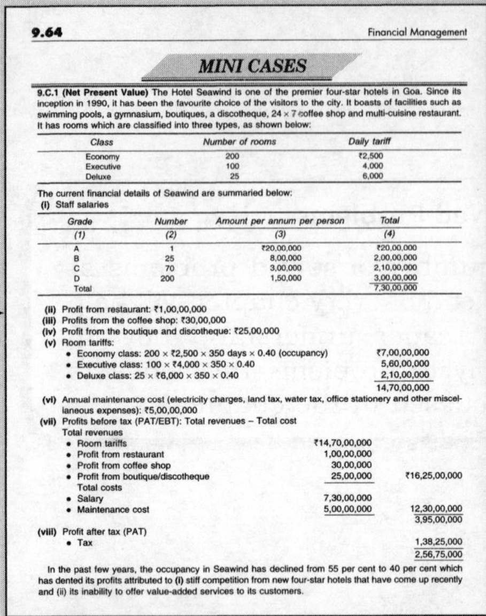

9.64 Financial Management

MINI CASES

9.C.1 (Net Present Value) The Hotel Seawind is one of the premier four-star hotels in Goa. Since its inception in 1990, it has been the favourite choice of the visitors to the city. It boasts of facilities such as swimming pools, a gymnasium, boutiques, a discotheque, 24 × 7 coffee shop and multi-cuisine restaurant. It has rooms which are classified into three types, as shown below:

Class	*Number of rooms*	*Daily tariff*
Economy	200	₹2,500
Executive	100	4,000
Deluxe	25	6,000

The current financial details of Seawind are summaried below:

(i) Staff salaries

Grade	*Number*	*Amount per annum per person*	*Total*
(1)	*(2)*	*(3)*	*(4)*
A	1	₹20,00,000	₹20,00,000
B	25	8,00,000	2,00,00,000
C	70	3,00,000	2,10,00,000
D	200	1,50,000	3,00,00,000
Total			7,30,00,000

(ii) Profit from restaurant: ₹1,00,00,000

(iii) Profits from the coffee shop: ₹30,00,000

(iv) Profit from the boutique and discotheque: ₹25,00,000

(v) Room tariffs:

• Economy class: 200 × ₹2,500 × 350 days × 0.40 (occupancy)	₹7,00,00,000
• Executive class: 100 × ₹4,000 × 350 × 0.40	5,60,00,000
• Deluxe class: 25 × ₹6,000 × 350 × 0.40	2,10,00,000
	14,70,00,000

(vi) Annual maintenance cost (electricity charges, land tax, water tax, office stationery and other miscellaneous expenses): ₹5,00,00,000

(vii) Profits before tax (PAT/EBT): Total revenues – Total cost

Total revenues		
• Room tariffs	₹14,70,00,000	
• Profit from restaurant	1,00,00,000	
• Profit from coffee shop	30,00,000	
• Profit from boutique/discotheque	25,00,000	₹16,25,00,000
Total costs		
• Salary	7,30,00,000	
• Maintenance cost	5,00,00,000	12,30,00,000
		3,95,00,000

(viii) Profit after tax (PAT)

• Tax	1,38,25,000
	2,56,75,000

In the past few years, the occupancy in Seawind has declined from 55 per cent to 40 per cent which has dented its profits attributed to (i) stiff competition from new four-star hotels that have come up recently and (ii) its inability to offer value-added services to its customers.

Mini Case

Small case studies at the end of chapter will illustrate the theoretical inputs of the chapter.

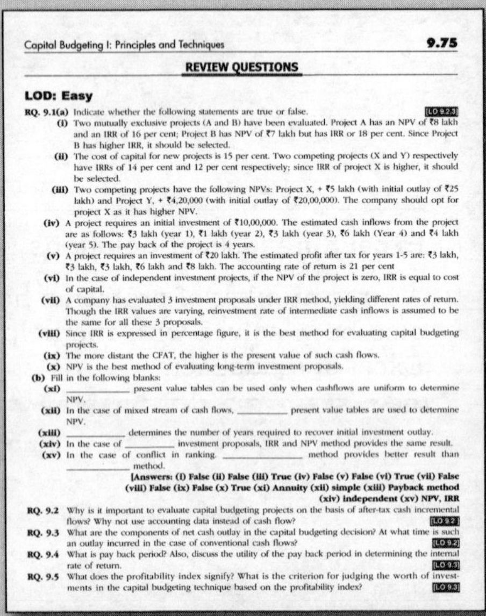

Capital Budgeting I: Principles and Techniques 9.75

REVIEW QUESTIONS

LOD: Easy

RQ. 9.1(a) Indicate whether the following statements are true or false. [LO 9.2,3]

(i) Two mutually exclusive projects (A and B) have been evaluated. Project A has an NPV of ₹8 lakh and an IRR of 16 per cent; Project B has NPV of ₹7 lakh but has IRR or 18 per cent. Since Project B has higher IRR, it should be selected.

(ii) The cost of capital for new projects is 15 per cent. Two competing projects (X and Y) respectively have IRRs of 14 per cent and 12 per cent respectively; since IRR of project X is higher, it should be selected.

(iii) Two competing projects have the following NPVs: Project X, + ₹5 lakh (with initial outlay of ₹25 lakh) and Project Y, + ₹4,20,000 (with initial outlay of ₹20,00,000). The company should opt for project X as it has higher NPV.

(iv) A project requires an initial investment of ₹10,00,000. The estimated cash inflows from the project are as follows: ₹3 lakh (year 1), ₹1 lakh (year 2), ₹3 lakh (year 3), ₹6 lakh (Year 4) and ₹4 lakh (year 5). The pay back of the project is 4 years.

(v) A project requires an investment of ₹20 lakh. The estimated profit after tax for years 1-5 are: ₹3 lakh, ₹3 lakh, ₹3 lakh, ₹6 lakh and ₹8 lakh. The accounting rate of return is 21 per cent

(vi) In the case of independent investment projects, if the NPV of the project is zero, IRR is equal to cost of capital.

(vii) A company has evaluated 3 investment proposals under IRR method, yielding different rates of return. Though the IRR values are varying, reinvestment rate of intermediate cash inflows is assumed to be the same for all these 3 proposals.

(viii) Since IRR is expressed in percentage figure, it is the best method for evaluating capital budgeting projects.

(ix) The more distant the CFAT, the higher is the present value of such cash flows.

(x) NPV is the best method of evaluating long-term investment proposals.

(b) Fill in the following blanks:

(xi) ____________ present value tables can be used only when cashflows are uniform to determine NPV.

(xii) In the case of mixed stream of cash flows, __________ present value tables are used to determine NPV.

(xiii) ____________ determines the number of years required to recover initial investment outlay.

(xiv) In the case of __________ investment proposals, IRR and NPV method provides the same result.

(xv) In the case of conflict in ranking. ______________ method provides better result than ____________ method.

[Answers: (i) False (ii) False (iii) True (iv) False (v) False (vi) True (vii) False (viii) False (ix) False (x) True (xi) Annuity (xii) simple (xiii) Payback method (xiv) independent (xv) NPV, IRR

RQ. 9.2 Why is it important to evaluate capital budgeting projects on the basis of after-tax cash incremental flows? Why not use accounting data instead of cash flow? [LO 9.2]

RQ. 9.3 What are the components of net cash outlay in the capital budgeting decision? At what time is such an outlay incurred in the case of conventional cash flows? [LO 9.2]

RQ. 9.4 What is pay back period? Also, discuss the utility of the pay back period in determining the internal rate of return. [LO 9.3]

RQ. 9.5 What does the profitability index signify? What is the criterion for judging the worth of investments in the capital budgeting technique based on the profitability index? [LO 9.3]

Review Questions

These exercises at the end of every chapter will help the reader in brushing up the concepts and revising the contents of the chapter.

WALKTHROUGH

Index

A comprehensive index would aid the readers in locating the entries in the right context in an accurate manner.

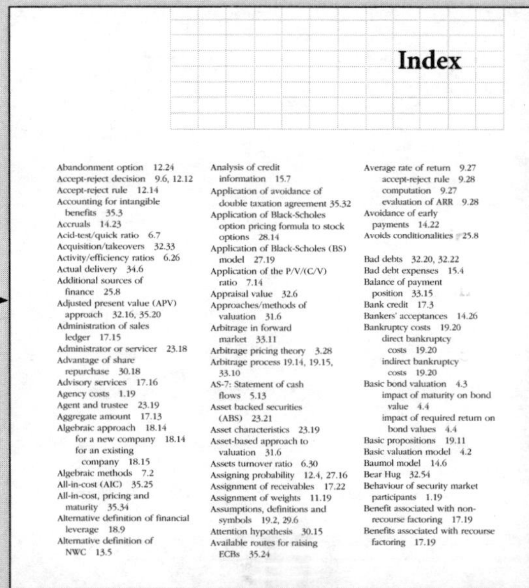

Index

Abandonment option 12.24
Accept-reject decision 9.6, 12.12
Accept-reject rule 12.14
Accounting for intangible benefits 35.3
Accruals 14.23
Acid-test/quick ratio 6.7
Acquisition/takeovers 32.33
Activity/efficiency ratios 6.26
Actual delivery 34.6
Additional sources of finance 25.8
Adjusted present value (APV) approach 32.16, 35.20
Administration of sales ledger 17.15
Administrator or servicer 23.18
Advantage of share repurchase 30.18
Advisory services 17.16
Agency costs 1.19
Agent and trustee 23.19
Aggregate amount 17.13
Algebraic approach 18.14
for a new company 18.14
for an existing company 18.15
Algebraic methods 7.2
All-in-cost (AIC) 35.25
All-in-cost, pricing and maturity 35.34
Alternative definition of financial leverage 18.9
Alternative definition of NWC 13.5
Analysis of credit information 15.7
Application of avoidance of double taxation agreement 35.32
Application of Black-Scholes option pricing formula to stock options 28.14
Application of Black-Scholes (BS) model 27.19
Application of the P/V/(C/V) ratio 7.14
Appraisal value 32.6
Approaches/methods of valuation 31.6
Arbitrage in forward market 33.11
Arbitrage pricing theory 3.28
Arbitrage process 19.14, 19.15, 33.10
AS-7: Statement of cash flows 5.13
Asset backed securities (ABS) 23.21
Asset characteristics 23.19
Asset-based approach to valuation 31.6
Assets turnover ratio 6.30
Assigning probability 12.4, 27.16
Assignment of receivables 17.22
Assignment of weights 11.19
Assumptions, definitions and symbols 19.2, 29.6
Attention hypothesis 30.15
Available routes for raising ECBs 35.24
Average rate of return 9.27
accept-reject rule 9.28
computation 9.27
evaluation of ARR 9.28
Avoidance of early payments 14.22
Avoids conditionalities 25.8

Bad debts 32.20, 32.22
Bad debt expenses 15.4
Balance of payment position 33.15
Bank credit 17.3
Bankers' acceptances 14.26
Bankruptcy costs 19.20
direct bankruptcy costs 19.20
indirect bankruptcy costs 19.20
Basic bond valuation 4.3
impact of maturity on bond value 4.4
impact of required return on bond values 4.4
Basic propositions 19.11
Basic valuation model 4.2
Baumol model 14.6
Bear Hug 32.54
Behaviour of security market participants 1.19
Benefit associated with non-recourse factoring 17.19
Benefits associated with recourse factoring 17.19

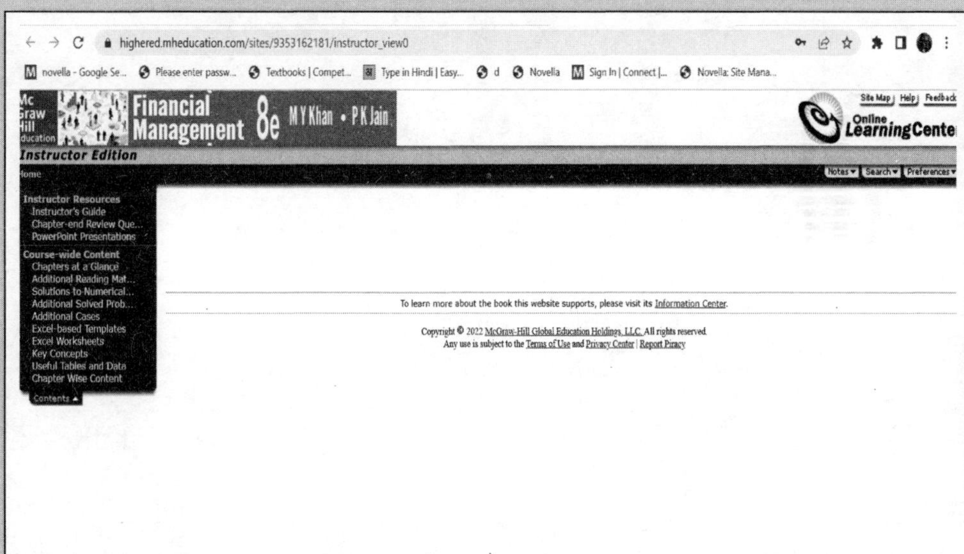

OLC (Online Learning Centre)

The OLC of the book contains additional resources for students as well as teachers.

PART 1

FOUNDATION OF FINANCE

Chapter 1
FINANCIAL MANAGEMENT: AN OVERVIEW

Chapter 2
TIME VALUE OF MONEY

Chapter 3
RISK AND RETURN

Chapter 4
VALUATION OF BONDS AND SHARES

This part of the book dwells on the foundations of finance. Chapter 1 gives an overview of financial management in terms of its relationship with related disciplines, scope, objectives, agency problems, organisation of finance functions in a typical organisation and the organisation of finance function in India. Chapter 2 discusses a basic financial concept, namely, time value of money. It explains and illustrates the basic compounding and discounting techniques as well as their applications. While risk and return including multivariate and factor valuation is analysed in Chapter 3, Valuation of bonds and shares is covered in Chapter 4.

CHAPTER 1

Financial Management: An Overview

LEARNING OBJECTIVES

LO 1.1	Define finance and describe its major areas—financial management/managerial finance/ corporate finance and financial services
LO 1.2	Differentiate financial management from the closely-related disciplines of accounting and economics
LO 1.3	Describe the scope of financial management and identify the key activities of the financial manager
LO 1.4	Explain why wealth/value maximisation, rather than profit/EPS maximisation, is the goal of financial management and how economic value added (EVA) and focus on shareholders relate to its achievement and summarise the major objectives of corporate finance by Indian corporates
LO 1.5	Discuss the agency problem/issue and measure to resolve it
LO 1.6	Outline the organisation of finance function in India
LO 1.7	Outline the emerging role of finance managers in India
LO 1.8	Present an overview of the book

LO 1.1 FINANCE FUNCTION

Finance is an art and science of managing money.

Finance may be defined as the art and science of managing money. The major areas of finance are: **(1)** financial services and **(2)** managerial finance/corporate finance/financial management. While **financial services** is concerned with the design and delivery of advice and financial products to individuals, businesses and governments within the areas of banking and related institutions, personal financial planning, investments, real estate, insurance and so on, **financial management** is concerned with the duties of the financial managers in the business firm. **Financial managers** actively manage the financial affairs of any type of business, namely, financial and non-financial, private and public, large and small, profit-seeking and not-for-profit.

Financial management is concerned with the duties of the financial managers in the business firm.

Financial services is concerned with the design and delivery of advice and financial products to individuals, businesses and governments.

They perform such varied tasks as budgeting, financial forecasting, cash management, credit administration, investment analysis, funds management and so on. In recent years, the changing regulatory and economic environments coupled with the globalisation of business activities have increased the complexity as well as the importance of the financial managers' duties. As a result, the financial management function has become more demanding and complex. The main elements of the financial management function are:

Financial managers actively manage the financial affairs of any type of business, namely, financial and non-financial, private and public, large and small, profit-seeking and not-for-profit.

- Relationship of finance and related disciplines
- Scope of financial management
- Goal/objectives of financial management
- Agency problem
- Organisation of the finance function
- Emerging role of finance managers in India

LO 1.2 FINANCE AND RELATED DISCIPLINES

Financial management, as an integral part of overall management, is not a totally independent area. It draws heavily on related disciplines and fields of study, such as economics, accounting, marketing, production and quantitative methods. Although these disciplines are interrelated, there are key differences among them. In this Section, we discuss these relationships.

Finance and Economics

The relevance of economics to financial management can be described in the light of the two broad areas of economics: macroeconomics and microeconomics.

Macroeconomics is concerned with the overall institutional environment in which the firm operates. It looks at the economy as a whole. Macroeconomics is concerned with the institutional structure of the banking system, money and capital markets, financial intermediaries, monetary, credit and fiscal policies and economic policies dealing with, and controlling level of, activity within an economy. Since business firms operate in the macroeconomic environment, it is important for financial managers to understand the broad economic environment. Specifically, they should **(1)** recognise and understand how monetary policy affects the cost and the availability of funds; **(2)** be versed in fiscal policy and its effects on the economy; **(3)** be aware of the various financial institutions/financing outlets; **(4)** understand the consequences of various levels of economic activity and changes in economic policy for their decision environment and so on.

Marginal analysis suggests that financial decisions should be made on the basis of comparison of marginal revenues and marginal costs/ added benefits exceed added costs.

Microeconomics deals with the economic decisions of individuals and organisations. It concerns itself with the determination of optimal operating strategies. In other words, the theories of microeconomics provide for effective operations of business firms. They are concerned with defining actions that will permit the firms to achieve success. The concepts and theories of microeconomics relevant to financial management are, for instance, those involving **(1)** supply and demand relationships and profit maximisation strategies, **(2)** issues related to the mix of productive factors, 'optimal' sales level and product pricing strategies, **(3)** measurement of utility preference, risk and the determination of value, and **(4)** the rationale of depreciating assets. In addition, the primary principle that applies in financial management is **marginal analysis**; it suggests that financial decisions should be made on the basis of comparison of marginal revenue and marginal cost. Such decisions will lead to an increase in profits of the firm. It is, therefore, important that financial managers must be familiar with basic microeconomics.

To illustrate, the financial manager of a department store is contemplating to replace one of its online computers with a new, more sophisticated one that would both speed up processing time and handle a large volume of transactions. The new computer would require a cash outlay of ₹8,00,000 and the old computer could be sold to net ₹2,80,000. The total benefits from the new computer and the old computer would be ₹10,00,000 and ₹3,50,000 respectively. Applying marginal analysis, we get:

Benefits with new computer	₹10,00,000	
Less: Benefits with old computer	3,50,000	
Marginal benefits **(a)**		₹6,50,000
Cost of new computer	8,00,000	
Less: Proceeds from sale of old computer	2,80,000	
Marginal cost **(b)**		5,20,000
Net benefits [**(a)** – **(b)**]		1,30,000

As the store would get a net benefit of ₹1,30,000, the old computer should be replaced by the new one.

Thus, a knowledge of economics is necessary for a financial manager to understand both the financial environment and the decision theories which underline contemporary financial management. He should be familiar with these two areas of economics. Macroeconomics provides the financial manager with an insight into policies by which economic activity is controlled. Operating within that institutional framework, the financial manager draws on microeconomic theories of the operation of firms and profit maximisation. A basic knowledge of economics is, therefore, necessary to understand both the environment and the decision techniques of financial management.

Finance and Accounting

The relationship between finance and accounting, conceptually speaking, has two dimensions: **(i)** they are closely related to the extent that accounting is an important input in financial decision making; and **(ii)** there are key differences in viewpoints between them.

Accounting function is a necessary input into the finance function. That is, accounting is a subfunction of finance. Accounting generates information/data relating to operations/activities of the firm. The end-product of accounting constitutes financial statements such as the balance sheet, the income statement (profit and loss account) and the statement of changes in financial position/sources and uses of funds statement/cash flow statement. The information contained in these statements and reports assists financial managers in assessing the past performance and future directions of the firm and in meeting legal obligations, such as payment of taxes and so on. Thus, accounting and finance are functionally closely related. Moreover, the finance (treasurer) and accounting (controller) activities are typically within the control of the vice-president/director (finance)/chief financial officer (CFO) as shown in Fig. 1.2. These functions are closely related and generally overlap; indeed, financial management and accounting are often not easily distinguishable. In small firms the controller often carries out the finance function and in large firms many accountants are intimately involved in various finance activities.

But there are two key differences between finance and accounting. The first difference relates to the treatment of funds, while the second relates to decision making.

Treatment of Funds The viewpoint of accounting relating to the funds of the firm is different from that of finance. The measurement of funds (income and expenses) in accounting is based on the **accrual principle/system**. For instance, revenue is recognised at the point of sale and not when collected. Similarly, expenses are recognised when they are incurred rather than when actually paid. The accrual-based accounting data do not reflect fully the financial circumstances of the firm. A firm may be quite profitable in the accounting sense in that it has earned profit (sales less expenses) but it may not be able to meet current obligations owing to shortage of liquidity due to uncollectable receivables, for instance. Such a firm will not survive regardless of its levels of profits.

Accrual method recognises revenue at the point of sale and expenses when they are incurred.

The viewpoint of finance relating to the treatment of funds is based on **cashflows**. The revenues are recognised only when actually received in cash (i.e. cash inflow) and expenses are recognised on actual payment (i.e. cash outflow). This is so because the financial manager is concerned with maintaining solvency of the firm by providing the cashflows necessary to satisfy its obligations and acquiring and financing the assets needed to achieve the goals of the firm. Thus, cashflow-based returns help financial managers avoid insolvency and achieve the desired financial goals.

Cashflow method recognises revenues and expenses only with respect to actual inflows and outflows of cash.

To illustrate, total sales of a trader during the year amounted to ₹10,00,000 while the cost of sales was ₹8,00,000. At the end of the year, it has yet to collect ₹8,00,000 from the customers. The accounting view and the financial view of the firms performance during the year are given below.

Accounting view (Income statement)		*Financial view (Cash flow statement)*	
Sales	₹10,00,000	Cash inflow	₹2,00,000
Less: Costs	8,00,000	*Less*: Cash outflow	8,00,000
Net profit	2,00,000	Net cash outflow	(6,00,000)

Obviously, the firm is quite profitable in accounting sense, it is a financial failure in terms of actual cash flows resulting from uncollected receivables. Regardless of its profits, the firm would not survive due to inadequate cash inflows to meet its obligations.

Decision Making Finance and accounting also differ in respect of their purposes. The purpose of accounting is collection and presentation of financial data. It provides consistently developed and easily interpreted data on the past, present and future operations of the firm. The financial manager uses such data for financial decision making. It does not mean that accountants *never* make decisions or financial managers *never* collect data. But the primary focus of the functions of accountants is on collection and presentation of data while the financial manager's major responsibility relates to financial planning, controlling and decision making. Thus, in a sense, finance begins where accounting ends.

Finance and Other Related Disciplines

Apart from economics and accounting, finance also draws—for its day-to-day decisions—on supportive disciplines such as marketing, production and quantitative methods. For instance, financial managers should consider the impact of new product development and promotion plans made in marketing area since their plans will require capital outlays and have an impact on the projected cash flows. Similarly, changes in the production process may necessitate capital expenditures which the financial managers must evaluate and finance. And, finally, the tools of analysis developed in the quantitative methods area are helpful in analysing complex financial management problems.

The marketing, production and quantitative methods are, thus, only indirectly related to day-to-day decision making by financial managers and are supportive in nature while economics and accounting are the primary disciplines on which the financial manager draws substantially.

The relationship between financial management and supportive disciplines is depicted in Fig 1.1.

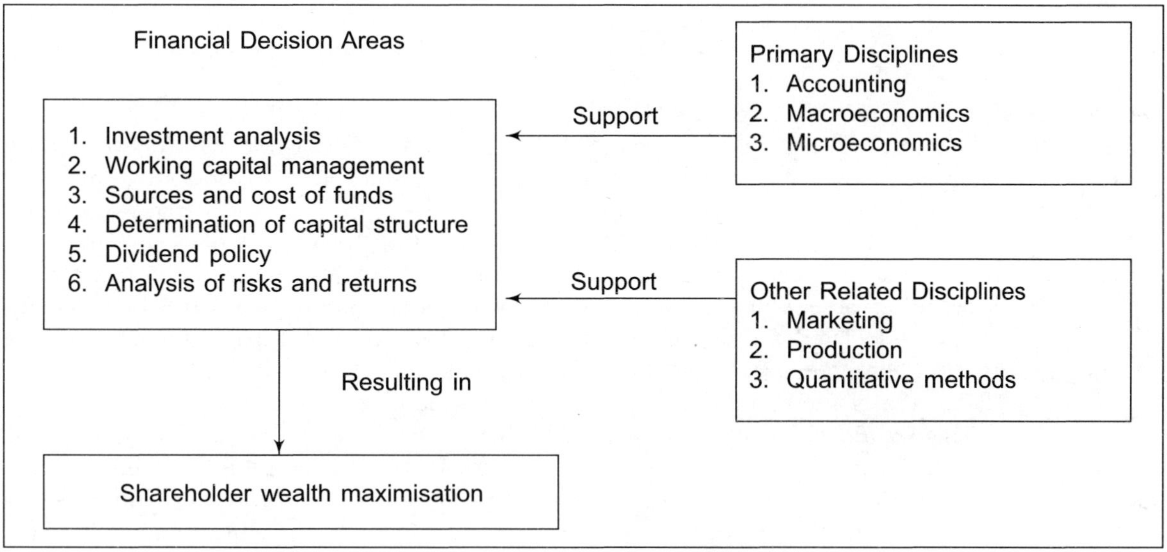

FIGURE 1.1 Impact of Other Disciplines on Financial Management

LO 1.3 SCOPE OF FINANCIAL MANAGEMENT

Financial management provides a normative, conceptual and analytical framework for financial decision making. The finance function covers both acquisition of funds as well as their allocations. Thus, apart from the issues involved in acquiring external funds, the main concern of financial management is the efficient and wise allocation of funds to various uses. Defined in a broad sense, it is viewed as an integral part of overall management.

The financial management framework is an analytical way of viewing the financial problems of a firm. The main contents of this approach are:[1] What is the total volume of funds an enterprise should commit? What specific assets should an enterprise acquire? How should the funds required be financed? Alternatively, the principal contents of the modern approach to financial management can be said to be: **(i)** How large should an enterprise be, and how fast should it grow? **(ii)** In what form should it hold assets? and **(iii)** What should be the composition of its liabilities?

The three questions posed above cover between them the major financial problems of a firm. In other words, the financial management, according to the new approach, is concerned with the solution of three major problems relating to the financial operations of a firm, corresponding to the three questions of investment, financing and dividend decisions. Thus, financial management, in the modern sense of the term, can be broken down into three major decisions as functions of finance: **(i)** The investment decision, **(ii)** The financing decision, and **(iii)** The dividend policy decision.

Investment Decision The **investment decision** relates to the selection of assets in which funds will be invested by a firm. The assets which can be acquired fall into two broad groups: **(i)** long-term assets which yield a return over a period of time in future, **(ii)** short-term or current assets, defined as those assets which in the normal course of business are convertible into cash without diminution in value, usually within a year. The first of these involving the first category of assets is popularly known in financial literature as **capital budgeting**. The aspect of financial decision making with reference to current assets or short-term assets is popularly termed as **working capital management**.

Investment decision relates to the selection of assets.

Capital Budgeting Capital budgeting is probably the most crucial financial decision of a firm. It relates to the selection of an asset or investment proposal or course of action whose benefits are likely to be available in future over the lifetime of the project. The long-term assets can be either new or old/existing ones. The *first* aspect of the capital budgeting decision relates to the choice of the new asset out of the alternatives available or the reallocation of capital when an existing asset fails to justify the funds committed. Whether an asset will be accepted or not will depend upon the relative benefits and returns associated with it. The measurement of the worth of the investment proposals is, therefore, a major element in the capital budgeting exercise. This implies a discussion of the methods of appraising investment proposals.

Capital budgeting relates to the selection of an asset whose benefits would be available over the project's life.

The *second* element of the capital budgeting decision is the analysis of risk and uncertainty. Since the benefits from the investment proposals extend into the future, their accrual is uncertain. They have to be estimated under various assumptions of the physical volume of sale and the level of prices. An element of risk in the sense of uncertainty of future benefits is, thus, involved in the exercise. The returns from capital budgeting decisions should, therefore, be evaluated in relation to the risk associated with it.

Finally, the evaluation of the worth of a long-term project implies a certain norm or standard against which the benefits are to be judged. The requisite norm is known by different names such as **cut-off rate**, **hurdle rate**, **required rate**, **minimum rate of return** and so on. This standard is broadly expressed in terms of the cost of capital. The concept and measurement of the cost of capital is, thus, another major aspect of capital budgeting decision. In brief, the main elements of capital budgeting decisions are: **(i)** the long-term assets and their composition, **(ii)** the business risk complexion of the firm, and **(iii)** the concept and measurement of the cost of capital.

Working Capital Management Working capital management is concerned with the management of current assets. It is an important and integral part of financial management as short-term survival is a prerequisite for long-term success. One aspect of working capital management is the trade-off between profitability and risk (liquidity). There is a conflict between profitability and liquidity. If a firm does not have adequate working capital, that is, it does not invest sufficient funds in current assets, it may become illiquid and consequently may not have the ability to meet its current obligations and, thus, invite the risk of bankruptcy. If the current assets are too large, profitability is adversely affected. The key strategies and considerations in ensuring a trade-off between profitability and liquidity is one major dimension of working capital management. In addition, the individual current assets should be efficiently managed so that neither inadequate nor unnecessary funds are locked up. Thus, the management of working capital has two basic ingredients: **(1)** an overview of working capital

Working capital management is concerned with the management of current assets.

management as a whole, and **(2)** efficient management of the individual current assets such as cash, receivables and inventory.

Financing Decision The second major decision involved in financial management is the financing decision. The investment decision is broadly concerned with the asset-mix or the composition of the assets of a firm. The concern of the financing decision is with the financing-mix or capital structure or leverage. The term **capital structure** refers to the proportion of debt (fixed-interest sources of financing) and equity capital (variable-dividend securities/source of funds). The financing decision of a firm relates to the choice of the proportion of these sources to finance the investment requirements. There are two aspects of the financing decision. *First*, the theory of capital structure which shows the theoretical relationship between the employment of debt and the return to the shareholders. The use of debt implies a higher return to the shareholders as also the financial risk. A proper balance between debt and equity to ensure a trade-off between risk and return to the shareholders is necessary. A capital structure with a reasonable proportion of debt and equity capital is called the **optimum capital structure**. Thus, one dimension of the financing decision whether there is an optimum capital structure and in what proportion should funds be raised to maximise the return to the shareholders? The second aspect of the financing decision is the determination of an appropriate capital structure, given the facts of a particular case. Thus, the financing decision covers two interrelated aspects: **(1)** the capital structure theory, and **(2)** the capital structure decision.

Financing decision relates to the choice of the proportion of debt and equity sources of financing.

Dividend Policy Decision The third major decision area of financial management is the decision relating to the dividend policy. The dividend decision should be analysed in relation to the financing decision of a firm. Two alternatives are available in dealing with the profits of a firm: **(i)** they can be distributed to the shareholders in the form of dividends or **(ii)** they can be retained in the business itself. The decision as to which course should be followed depends largely on a significant element in the dividend decision, the **dividend-pay out ratio**, that is, what proportion of net profits should be paid out to the shareholders. The final decision will depend upon the preference of the shareholders and investment opportunities available within the firm. The second major aspect of the dividend decision is the factors determining dividend policy of a firm in practice.

To conclude, the traditional approach to the functions of financial management had a very narrow perception and was devoid of an integrated conceptual and analytical framework. It had rightly been discarded in the academic literature. The modern approach to the scope of financial management has broadened its scope which involves the solution of three major decisions, namely, investment, financing and dividend. These are interrelated and should be jointly taken so that financial decision making is optimal. The conceptual framework for optimum financial decisions is the objective of financial management. In other words, to ensure an optimum decision in respect of these three areas, they should be related to the objectives of financial management. The goals/objectives of financial management are discussed in Section 3.

Key Activities of the Financial Manager

The primary activities of a financial manager are: **(i)** performing financial analysis and planning, **(ii)** making investment decisions and **(iii)** making financing decisions.

Performing Financial Analysis and Planning The concern of financial analysis and planning is with **(a)** transforming financial data into a form that can be used to monitor financial condition, **(b)** evaluating the need for increased (reduced) productive capacity and **(c)** determining the additional/reduced financing required. Although this activity relies heavily on accrual-based financial statements, its underlying objective is to assess cash flows and develop plans to ensure adequate cash flows to support achievement of the firm's goals.

Making Investment Decisions Investment decisions determine both the mix and the type of assets held by a firm. The mix refers to the amount of current assets and fixed assets. Consistent with the mix, the financial manager must determine and maintain certain optimal levels of each type of current assets. He should also decide the best fixed assets to acquire and when existing fixed assets need to be modified/replaced/liquidated. The success of a firm in achieving its goals depends on these decisions.

Making Financing Decisions Financing decisions involve two major areas: *first,* the most appropriate mix of short-term and long-term financing; *second,* the best individual short-term or long-term sources of financing at a given point of time. Many of these decisions are dictated by necessity, but some require an in-depth analysis of the available financing alternatives, their costs and their long-term implications.

LO 1.4 OBJECTIVES OF FINANCIAL MANAGEMENT

To make wise decisions a clear understanding of the objectives which are sought to be achieved is necessary. The objective provide a framework for optimum financial decision making. In other words, they are concerned with designing a method of operating the internal investment and financing of a firm. The term 'objective' is used in the sense of a goal or **decision criterion** for the three decisions involved in financial management. It implies that what is relevant is not the overall objective or goal of a business but a operationally useful criterion by which to judge a specific set of mutually interrelated business decisions, namely, investment, financing and dividend policy. Moreover, it provides a normative framework. That is, the focus in financial literature is on what a firm should try to achieve and on policies that should be followed if certain goals are to be achieved. The implication is that these are not necessarily followed by firms in actual practice. They are rather employed to serve as a basis for theoretical analysis and do not reflect contemporary empirical industry practices. Thus, the term is used in a rather narrow sense of what a firm *should attempt* to achieve with its investment, financing and dividend policy decisions.

Firms in practice state their vision, mission and values in broad terms and are also concerned about technology, leadership, productivity, market standing, image, profitability, financial resources, employees satisfaction and so on. Some illustrations of mission and values/corporate purpose/vision for future are depicted in Exhibits 1.1 to 1.3.

EXHIBIT 1.1 Ranbaxy's Missions and Values

MISSION

To become a research-based International Pharmaceutical Company.

VALUES

- Achieving customer satisfaction is fundamental to our business.
- Provide products and services of the highest quality.
- Practice dignity and equity in relationships and provide opportunities for our people to realise their full potential.

- Ensure profitable growth and **enhance wealth of the shareholders**.
- Foster mutually beneficial relations with all our business operations.
- Manage our operations with high concern for safety and environment.
- Be a responsible corporate citizen.

EXHIBIT 1.2 HLL's Corporate Purpose

- Our purpose in Unilever is to meet the everyday needs of people everywhere—to anticipate the aspirations of our consumers and customers and to respond creatively and competitively with branded products and services which raise the quality of life.
- Our deep roots in local cultures and markets around the world are our unparalleled inheritance and the foundation for our future growth. We will bring our wealth of knowledge and international expertise to the service of local customer—a truly multi-local multinational.
- Our long-term success requires a total commitment to exceptional standards of performance and productivity, to working together effectively and to a willingness to embrace new ideas and learn continuously.
- We believe that to succeed requires the highest standards of corporate behaviour towards our employees, consumers and the societies and world in which we live.
- This is Unilever's road to sustainable, profitable growth for our business and **long-term value creation for our shareholders** and employees.

EXHIBIT 1.3 Vision of Future of Reliance Industries Ltd

Reliance is an enterprise that contributes, in a modest way, to critical economic and social needs of India and attaining global leadership in all of its major initiatives.

Pursuing this vision, over the next few years, Reliance will pursue a strategy of:

- Reinforcing competitive advantage of existing businesses through new capacities and synergistic acquisitions
- Scaling sizeable opportunities in petroleum exploration and production
- Forward integrating into retailing transportation fuels and creating new customer experiences
- Building the BSES acquisition, now Reliance Energy, to a major electricity utility
- Addressing the significant information and communications market opportunity in India and in the world
- Leveraging its strong balance sheet, cash flows and managerial capacity to **create value** by adding new capacities, acquisitions and turnaround of under performing assets
- Developing strategic alliances in technology and product-market domains with global majors
- Fostering new higher education institutions for knowledge creation and sharing
- Leveraging its formidable strengths beyond Indian borders.

In this endeavour, Reliance will undergo an upgradation:

- In addition to manufacturing products to developing manufacturing systems
- From having a manufacturing orientation to providing technical solutions

- From being an intermediate goods producer to being a final goods and services provider
- From being a margin energy player to being a global energy major
- In addition to vertical integration in hydrocarbon energy markets to horizontal integration over diverse energy markets
- From licensing technology to developing technology
- From being an intellectual property user to an intellectual property creator
- In addition to operating in India to being a global company
- From building financial equity to fostering social equity

This change will entail creating new organisational competencies such as:

- Creating a customer-centric organisation
- Developing new products and technologies
- Exploring and producing oil and gas in demanding geological conditions
- Fostering and sustaining globally-oriented management talent
- Managing customer-oriented supply chains
- Developing and protecting intellectual capital
- Managing strategic technology and product-market relationships

Managing diversity in businesses, technologies, export markets and people is the primary challenge for Reliance, as it marches ahead in realising its vision.

This vision is the legacy of Shri Dhirubhai Ambani to all of us.

We are committed to pursue it with commitment and conviction.

Reliance is driven by his vision and continues to pursue a trajectory of growth, productivity and global leadership.

We discuss in this Section the alternative approaches in financial literature. There are two widely-discussed approaches: **(i)** Profit (total)/Earning Per Share (EPS) maximisation approach, and **(ii)** Wealth maximisation approach.

Profit/EPS Maximisation Decision Criterion

According to this approach, actions that increase profits (total)/EPS should be undertaken and those that decrease profits/EPS are to be avoided. In specific operational terms, as applicable to financial management, the profit maximisation criterion implies that the investment, financing and dividend policy decisions of a firm should be oriented to the maximisation of profits/EPS.

The term 'profit' can be used in **two** senses. As a *owner-oriented concept*, it refers to the *amount* and *share of national income* which is *paid to the owners of business*, that is, those who supply equity capital. As a *variant*, it is described as **profitability**. It is an operational concept[2] and signifies economic efficiency. In other words, profitability refers to a situation where output exceeds input, that is, the value created by the use of resources is more than the total of the input resources. Used in this sense, profitability maximisation would imply that a firm should be guided in financial decision making by one test; select assets, projects and decisions which are profitable and reject those which are not. In the current financial literature, there is a general agreement that profit maximisation is used in the second sense.

The rationale behind profitability maximisation, as a guide to financial decision making, is simple. Profit is a test of economic efficiency. It provides the yardstick by which economic performance can be judged. Moreover, it leads to efficient allocation of resources, as resources tend to be directed to uses which in terms of profitability are the most desirable. Finally, it ensures maximum social welfare. The individual search for maximum profitability provides the famous 'invisible hand' by which total economic welfare is maximised. Financial management is concerned with the efficient use of an important economic resource (input), namely, capital. It is, therefore, argued that profitability maximisation should serve as the basic criterion for financial management decisions.

The profit maximisation criterion has, however, been questioned and criticised on several grounds. The reasons for the opposition in academic literature fall into two broad groups: **(1)** those that are based on misapprehensions about the workability and fairness of the private enterprise itself, and **(2)** those that arise out of the difficulty of applying this criterion in actual situations. It would be recalled that the term objective, as applied to financial management, refers to an explicit operational guide for the internal investment and financing of a firm and not the overall goal of business operations. We, therefore, focus on the second type of limitations to profit maximisation as an objective of financial management.[3] The *main technical flaws* of this criterion are **ambiguity, timing of benefits,** and **quality of benefits**.

Ambiguity One practical difficulty with profit maximisation criterion for financial decision making is that the term profit is a vague and ambiguous concept. It has no precise connotation. It is amenable to different interpretations by different people. To illustrate, profit may be short-term or long-term; it may be total profit or rate of profit; it may be before-tax or after-tax; it may return on total capital employed or total assets or shareholders' equity and so on. If profit maximisation is taken to be the objective, the question arises, which of these variants of profit should a firm try to maximise? Obviously, a loose expression like profit cannot form the basis of operational criterion for financial management.

Timing of Benefits A more important technical objection to profit maximisation, as a guide to financial decision making, is that it ignores the differences in the time pattern of the benefits received over the working life of the asset, irrespective of when they were received. Consider Table 1.1.

TABLE 1.1 Time-Pattern of Benefits (Profits)

Time	*Alternative **A** (₹ in lakh)*	*Alternative **B** (₹ in lakh)*
Period **I**	150	50
Period **II**	100	100
Period **III**	50	150
Total	300	300

It can be seen from Table 1.1 that the total profits associated with the alternatives, A and B, are identical. If the profit maximisation is the decision criterion, both the alternatives would be ranked equally. But the returns from both the alternatives differ in one important respect, while alternative A provides higher returns in earlier years, the returns from alternative B are larger in later years. As a result, the two alternative courses of action are not strictly identical. This is primarily because a basic dictum of financial planning is **the earlier the better** as benefits received sooner are more valuable than benefits received later. The reason for the superiority of benefits now over benefits later lies in the fact that the former can be reinvested to earn a return. This is referred to as time value of money. The profit maximisation criterion does not consider the distinction between returns received in different time periods and treats all benefits irrespective of the timing, as equally valuable. This is not true in actual practice as benefits in early years should be valued more highly than equivalent benefits in later years. The assumption of equal value is inconsistent with the real world situation.

Quality of Benefits Probably the most important technical limitation of profit maximisation as an operational objective, is that it ignores the quality aspect of benefits associated with a financial course of action. The term **quality** here refers to the degree of certainty with which benefits can be expected. As a rule, the more certain the expected return, the higher is the quality of the benefits. Conversely, the more uncertain/fluctuating is the expected benefits, the lower is the quality of the benefits. An uncertain and fluctuating return implies **risk** to the investors. It can be safely assumed that the investors are **risk-averters**, that is, they want to avoid or at least minimise risk. They can, therefore, be reasonably expected to have a preference for a return which is more certain in the sense that it has smaller variance over the years.

Quality refers to the degree of certainty with which benefits can be expected.

Risk is the chance that actual outcomes may differ from those expected.

Risk-averters want to avoid risk.

The problem of uncertainty renders profit maximisation unsuitable as an operational criterion for financial management as it considers only the size of benefits and gives no weight to the degree of uncertainty of the future benefits. This is illustrated in Table 1.2.

TABLE 1.2 Uncertainty About Expected Benefits (Profits)

	Profit (₹ crore)	
State of Economy	*Alternative **A***	*Alternative **B***
Recession (Period I)	90	0
Normal (Period II)	100	100
Boom (Period III)	110	200
Total	300	300

It is clear from Table 1.2 that the total returns associated with the two alternatives are identical in a normal situation but the range of variations is very wide in case of alternative B, while it is narrow in respect of alternative A. To put it differently, the earnings associated with alternative B are more uncertain (risky) as they fluctuate widely depending on the state of the economy. Obviously, alternative A is better in terms of risk and uncertainty. The profit maximisation criterion fails to reveal this.

To conclude, the profit maximisation criterion is inappropriate and unsuitable as an operational objective of investment, financing and dividend decisions of a firm. It is not only vague and ambiguous but it also ignores two important dimensions of financial analysis, namely, risk, and time value of money. It follows from the above that an appropriate operational decision criterion for financial management should **(i)** be precise and exact, **(ii)** be based on the **'bigger the better'** principle, **(iii)** consider both quantity and quality dimensions of benefits, and **(iv)** recognise the time value of money. The alternative to profit maximisation, that is, wealth maximisation is one such measure.

Wealth Maximisation Decision Criterion

This is also known as value maximisation or net present worth maximisation. In current academic literature value maximisation is almost universally accepted as an appropriate operational decision criterion for financial management decisions as it removes the technical limitations which characterise the earlier profit maximisation criterion. Its operational features satisfy all the three requirements of a suitable operational objective of financial course of action, namely, exactness, quality of benefits and the time value of money.

The value of an asset should be viewed in terms of the benefits it can produce. The worth of a course of action can similarly be judged in terms of the value of the benefits it produces less the cost of undertaking it. A significant element in computing the value of a financial course of action is the precise estimation of the benefits associated with it. The wealth maximisation criterion is based on the concept of cash flows generated by the decision rather than accounting profit which is the basis of the measurement of benefits in the case of the profit maximisation criterion. Cash-flow is a precise concept with a definite connotation. Measuring benefits in terms of cash flows avoids the ambiguity associated with accounting profits. This is the first operational feature of the net present worth maximisation criterion.

The second important feature of the wealth maximisation criterion is that it considers both the quantity and quality dimensions of benefits. At the same time, it also incorporates the time value of money. The operational implication of the uncertainty and timing dimensions of the benefits emanating from a financial decision is that adjustments should be made in the cash-flow pattern, firstly, to incorporate risk and, secondly, to make an allowance for differences in the timing of benefits. The value of a stream of cash flows with value maximisation criterion is calculated by discounting its element back to the present at a capitalisation rate that reflects both time and risk. The value of a course of action must be viewed in terms of its worth to those providing the resources necessary for its undertaking. In applying the value maximisation criterion, the term **value** is used in terms of worth to the owners, that is, ordinary shareholders. The **capitalisation (discount) rate** that is employed is, therefore, the rate that reflects the time and risk preferences of the owners or suppliers of capital. As a measure of quality (risk) and timing, it is expressed in decimal notation. A discount rate of, say, 15 per cent is written as 0.15. A large capitalisation rate is the result of higher risk and longer time period. Thus, a stream of cash flows that is quite certain might be associated with a rate of 10 per cent, while a very risky stream may carry a 15 per cent discount rate.

For the above reasons, the net present value maximisation is superior to the profit maximisation as an operational objective. As a decision criterion, it involves a comparison of value to cost. An action that has a discounted value—reflecting both time and risk—that exceeds its cost can be said to create value. Such actions should be undertaken. Conversely, actions, with less value than cost, reduce wealth and should be rejected. In the case of mutually exclusive alternatives, when only one has to be chosen, the alternative with the greatest net present value should be selected. In the words of Ezra Solomon,[4]

> The gross present worth of a course of action is equal to the capitalised value of the flow of future expected benefit, discounted (or captialised) at a rate which reflects their certainty or uncertainty. Wealth or net present worth is the difference between gross present worth and the amount of capital investment required to achieve the benefits being discussed. Any financial action which creates wealth or which has a net present worth above zero is a desirable one and should be undertaken. Any financial action which does not meet this test should be rejected. If two or more desirable courses of action are mutually exclusive (i.e. if only one can be undertaken), then the decision should be to do that which creates most wealth or shows the greatest amount of net present worth.

Using Ezra Solomon's symbols and methods, the net present worth can be calculated as shown below:

(i) $$W = V - C \tag{1.1}$$

Where W = Net present worth

V = Gross present worth

C = Investment (equity capital) required to acquire the asset or to purchase the course of action

(ii) $$V = E/K \tag{1.2}$$

Where E = Size of future benefits available to the suppliers of the input capital

K = The capitalisation (discount) rate reflecting the quality (certainty/uncertainty) and timing of benefits attached to E

(iii) $$E = G - (M + I + T) \tag{1.3}$$

Where G = Average future flow of gross annual earnings expected from the course of action, before maintenance charges, taxes and interest and other prior charges like preference dividend

M = Average annual reinvestment required to maintain G at the projected level

T = Expected annual outflow on account of taxes

I = Expected flow of annual payments on account of interest, preference dividends and other prior charges

The operational objective of financial management is the maximisation of W in Eq. (1.1). Alternatively, W can be expressed symbolically by a short-cut method as in Eq. (1.4). Net present value (worth) or wealth is

$$W = \frac{A_1}{(1+K)} + \frac{A_2}{(1+K)^2} + \ldots + \frac{A_n}{(1+K)^n} - C \tag{1.4}$$

where $A_1, A_2, \ldots A_n$ represents the stream of cash flows expected to occur from a course of action over a period of time;

K is the appropriate discount rate to measure risk and timing; and

C is the initial outlay to acquire that asset or pursue the course of action.

It can, thus, be seen that in the value maximisation decision criterion, the time value of money and handling of the risk as measured by the uncertainty of the expected benefits is an integral part of the exercise. It is, moreover, a precise and unambiguous concept, and therefore, an appropriate and operationally feasible decision criterion for financial management decisions.

It would also be noted that the focus of financial management is on the value to the owners or suppliers of equity capital. The wealth of the owners is reflected in the market value of shares. So wealth maximisation implies the maximisation of the market price of shares. In other words, net present value maximisation (as a decision criterion in investment decisions), is the operational substitute for maximisation of the market price of shares.

In brief, what is relevant is not the overall goal of a firm but a decision criterion which should guide the financial course of action. Profit/EPS maximisation was initially the generally accepted theoretical criterion for making efficient economic decisions, using profit as an economic concept and defining profit maximisation as a criterion for economic efficiency. In current financial literature, it has been replaced by the wealth maximisation decision criterion because of the shortcomings of the former as an operational criterion, as **(i)** it does not take account of uncertainty of risk, **(ii)** it ignores the time value of money, and **(iii)** it is ambiguous in its computation. Owing to these technical limitations, profit maximisation cannot be applied in real world situations. Its modified form is the value maximisation criterion. It is important to note that value maximisation is simply extension of profit maximisation to a world that is uncertain and multiperiod in nature. Where the time period is short and degree of uncertainty is not great, value maximisation and profit maximisation amount to essentially the same thing.[5]

However, two important issues are related to the value/share price-maximisation, namely, **economic value added** and **focus on stakeholders**.

Economic value added is equal to after-tax operating profits of a firm less the cost of funds used to finance investments.

Economic Value Added (EVA) It is a popular measure currently being used by several firms to determine whether an existing/proposed investment positively contributes to the owners'/shareholders' wealth. The **EVA** is equal to after-tax operating profits of a firm less the cost of funds used to finance investments. A positive EVA would increase owners' value/wealth. Therefore, only investments with positive EVA would be desirable from the viewpoint of maximising shareholders' wealth. To illustrate, assuming an after-tax profit of ₹40 crore and associated costs of financing the investments of ₹38 crore, the EVA = ₹2 crore (₹40 crore – ₹38 crore). With a positive EVA, the investment would add value and increase the wealth of the owners and should be accepted. The computation of the after-tax operating profits attributable to the investment under consideration as well as the cost of funds used to finance it would, however, involve numerous accounting and financial issues.

The **merits** of EVA are: **(a)** its relative simplicity and **(b)** its strong link with the wealth maximisation of the owners. It *prima facie* exhibits a strong link to share prices, that is, positive EVA is associated with increase in prices of shares and *vice versa*. However, EVA is, in effect, a repackaged and well-marketed application of the NPV technique of investment decision. But EVA is certainly a useful tool for operationalising the owners' value maximisation goal, particularly with respect to the investment decision.

Focus on Stakeholders The shareholders wealth maximisation as the primary goal notwithstanding, there is a broader focus in financial management to include the interest of the stakeholders as well as the shareholders. The **stakeholders** include employees, customers, suppliers, creditors and owners and others who have a direct link to the firm. The implication of the focus on stakeholders is that a firm should avoid actions detrimental to them through the transfer of their wealth to the firm and, thus, damage their wealth. The goal should be to preserve the well-being of the stakeholders and not to maximise it.

Stakeholders include groups such as employees, customers, suppliers, creditors, owners and others who have a direct link to the firm.

The focus on the stakeholders does not, however, alter the shareholders' wealth maximisation goal. It tends to limit the firm's actions to preserve the wealth of the stakeholders. The stakeholders view is considered part of its "social responsibility" and is expected to provide maximum long-term benefit to the shareholders by maintaining positive stakeholders relationship which would minimise stakeholder turnover, conflict and litigation. In brief, a firm can better achieve its goal of shareholders' wealth maximisation with the cooperation of, rather than conflict with, its other stakeholders.

Shareholder Orientation in India Traditionally, the corporate industrial sector in India was dominated by group companies with close links with the promoter groups. Their funding primarily was through institutional borrowings from public/ development finance institutions like IFCI, ICICI, IDBI and so on. There was preponderance of loan capital in their financial structure and shareholders equity played a rather marginal role. It was no wonder, therefore, that corporate India paid scant attention to shareholders' wealth maximisation with few exceptions such as Reliance Industries Ltd. In the post-90 liberalisation era, the goal of shareholders' wealth maximisation has emerged almost at the centre-stage. The main contributory factors have been **(i)** greater dependence on capital market, **(ii)** growing importance of institutional investors, **(iii)** tax concessions/incentives to shareholders and **(iv)** foreign exposure.

With the gradual decline in the significance of the development/public financial/term lending institutions over the years and their disappearance from the Indian financial scene recently (as a result of their conversion into banks) and the consequent emergence of the capital market as the main source of corporate financing, shareholders' wealth maximisation is emerging as the prime goal of corporate financial management. Secondly, as a result of the institutionalisation of savings, institutional investors such as mutual funds, insurance organisations, foreign institutional investors and so on dominate the structure of the Indian capital market. To cater to the requirements of these institutional investors, corporates are pursuing more shareholder-friendly policies as reflected in their efforts to focus on shareholders' wealth maximisation. Thirdly, the abolition of wealth tax on equity shares and other financial assets coupled with tax exemption on dividends in recent years has provided an incentive to corporates to enhance share prices and, thus, focus on shareholders' wealth. Finally, the family-owned corporates are also undergoing major transformation. The scions of most business families are acquiring higher professional education in India and abroad. With the foreign exposure, they also appreciate the importance of shareholders' wealth. Thus, shareholder orientation is unmistakably visible in the corporate India.

PRIMARY OBJECTIVE OF CORPORATE MANAGEMENT

The major objective of corporate finance by Indian corporates are summarised as follows:

- The two most important objectives of management decision making in corporate finance in India are: **(i)** maximisation of earnings before interest and tax (EBIT) and earnings per share (EPS) (85 per cent) and **(ii)** maximisation of the spread between return on assets (ROA) and weighted average cost of capital (WACC), that is, economic value added (EVA) (76 per cent).
- Large firms (on the basis of sales, assets and market capitalisation), high growth firms and firms with high exports significantly focus on maximising EVA than small, low growth and low exports firms respectively.
- There is no significant difference in the EVA as a corporate finance objective followed by the firms in public and private sectors.
- The spread between cash flow return on investment (CFROI) and the WACC, that is, cash value added (CVA) is the third most important objective (54 per cent) of corporate finance management for large firms based on market capitalisation.
- Yet another important objective is the maximisation of market capitalisation. The MVA (market value added) objective is more likely to be followed by public sector units than by private sector firms.
- The overwhelming majority of corporates (70 per cent) consider maximising per cent return on investment in assets as the most important.
- Another perferred goal is desired growth rate in EPS/maximise aggregate earnings.
- Wealth maximisation/maximisation of share prices is the least preferred goal of the sample corporates.

Source: Jain, P K and Surendra S Yadav, "Financial Management Practices in India, Singapore and Thailand—A Comparison", *Management & Accounting Research*, Vol. 3, No. 4, 2000 pp 55-103. Also Anand, Manoj, "Corporate Finance Practices in India, a Survey", *Vikalpa*, Vol. 27, No. 4, 2003, pp 29-56.

LO 1.5 AGENCY PROBLEM

A characteristic feature of corporate enterprise is the separation between ownership and management as a corollary of which the latter enjoys substantial autonomy in regard to the affairs of the firm. With widely-diffused ownership, scattered and ill-organised shareholders hardly exercise any control/influence on management which may be inclined to act in its own interest rather than those of the owners. However, shareholders as owners of the enterprise have the right to change the management. Due to the threat of being dislodged/dismissed for poor performance, the management would have a natural inclination to achieve a minimum acceptable level of performance to satisfy the shareholders' requirements/goals, while focusing primarily on their own personal goals. Thus, in furtherance of their objective of survival, management would aim at **satisfying** instead of **maximising** shareholders' wealth.

Resolving the Agency Problem

From this conflict of management objective of survival (personal goals) and maximising owners value arises the agency problem, that is, the likelihood that managers may place personal goals ahead of corporate goals. The **agency problem** can be prevented/minimised by acts of **(i)** market forces and **(ii)** agency costs.

> **Agency problem** is the likelihood that managers may place personal goals ahead of corporate goals.

Market Forces Market forces act to prevent/minimise agency problems in two ways: **(1)** behaviour of security market participants and **(2)** hostile takeovers.

Behaviour of Security Market Participants The security market participants/ shareholders in general and large institutional investors like mutual funds, insurance organisations, financial institutions and so on which hold large blocks of shares of corporates, in particular, actively participate in management. To ensure competent management and minimise agency problems, they have in recent years actively exercised their voting rights to replace more competent management in place of under-performing management. In addition to exercising their legal voting rights, the large institutional shareholders also from time to time communicate with, and exert pressure on, corporate management to perform or face replacement.

> **Hostile takeover** is the acquisition of the firm (target) by another firm (the acquirer) that is not supported by management.

Hostile Takeovers Another market force that has in recent years threatened corporate management to perform in the best interest of the owners/shareholders is the possibility of a **hostile** takeover, that is, the acquisition of the (target) firm by another firm/group (i.e. acquirer) that is not supported by management. Such takeovers typically occur when the acquirer is of the view that the target firm is undevalued due to poor management and that its acquisition at its current low price may result in the enhancement of its value (i.e. share price) through restructuring its management, operations and financing. The constant threat of a takeover would motivate management to act in the best interests of the owners despite the fact that techniques are available to defend against a hostile takeover.

> **Agency costs** are costs borne by shareholders to prevent/minimise agency problems as to contribute to maximise owners wealth.

Agency Costs To respond to potential market forces by preventing/maximising agency problems and contributing to the maximisation of owners' wealth/value, the shareholders/owners have to incur four types of costs: **(i)** monitoring, **(ii)** bonding, **(iii)** opportunity and **(iv)** structuring.

Monitoring Expenditures Such expenditures relate to monitoring the activities of the management (agents) to prevent a **satisfying** in contrast to **share price maximising** behaviour by them. The monitoring outlays relate to payment for audit and control procedures to ensure that managerial behaviour is tuned to actions that tend to be in the best interest of the shareholders.

Fidelity bond is a contract in which a bonding company agrees to re-imburse a firm upto a stated amount for financial losses caused by dishonest acts of managers.

Bonding Expenditures They protect the owners against the potential consequences of dishonest acts by management/managers. The firm pays to obtain a **fidelity bond** from a third-party bonding company to the effect that the latter will compensate the former up to a specified amount for financial losses caused by dishonest acts of manager(s).

Opportunity Costs Such costs result from the inability of large corporates from responding to new opportunities. Due to the organisational structure, decision hierarchy, and control mechanism, the management may face difficulties in seizing upon profitable investment opportunities quickly.

Incentive plans tie anagement compensation to share price.

Stock options allow management to purchase shares at a special/concessional price.

Structuring Expenditure The structuring expenditures are the most popular, powerful and expensive agency costs incurred by corporates. They relate to structuring managerial compensation to correspond with share price maximisation. The objective is to offer incentives/compensation to management to act in the best interests of the owners. The restructured higher compensation packages to managers also enable corporates to hire the best available managers. The management compensation plans fall into two groups: **(a)** incentive plans and **(b)** performance plans.

Incentive Plans They tie management compensation to share price. The most widely-used incentive plan is **stock options** which confer on management the right to acquire shares of the corporate at a special/concessional price. A higher future price would result in larger management compensation. However, share prices may be affected by economic and behavioural "market forces" over which management may have no control. Despite positive management performance, market prices may decline.

Performance plans compensate management on the basis of proven performance.

Performance shares are given to management for meeting the stated performance goals.

Performance Plans These plans compensate management on the basis of its proven performance measured by EPS, growth in EPS and other ratios related to return. Based on these, performance shares may be given to management for meeting the stated performance goals. Another form of performance-based compensation is cash bonuses, that is, cash payments tied to the achievement of certain performance goals.

In brief, unconstrained managers may have other goals in addition to share price maximisation, but there are enough evidence to suggest that due to agency costs and market forces, share price maximisation is the primary goal of most firms.

LO 1.6 ORGANISATION OF FINANCE FUNCTION

The responsibilities for financial management are spread throughout the organisation in the sense that financial management is, to an extent, an integral part of the job for the managers involved in planning, allocation of resources and control. For instance, the production manager (engineer) shapes the investment policy (proposal of a new plant); the marketing manager/analyst provides inputs in forecasting and planning; the purchase manager influences the level of investment in inventories; and the sales manager has a say in the determination of receivables policy.

Nevertheless, financial management is highly specialised in nature and is handled by specialists. Financial decisions are of crucial importance. It is, therefore, essential to set up an efficient organisation for financial management functions.

Since finance is a major/critical functional area, the ultimate responsibility for carrying out financial management functions lies with the top management, that is, board of directors/managing director/ chief executive or the committee of the board. However, the exact nature of the organisation of the financial management function differs from firm to firm depending upon factors such as size of the firm, nature of its business, type of financing operations, ability of financial officers and the financial philosophy, and so on. Similarly, the designation of the chief executive of the finance department also differs widely in case of different firms. In some cases, they are known as finance managers while in others as vice-president (finance), director (finance), and financial controller and so on. He reports directly to the top management. Various sections within the financial management area are headed by managers such as controller and treasurer.

Figure 1.2 depicts the organisation of the financial management function in a large typical firm.

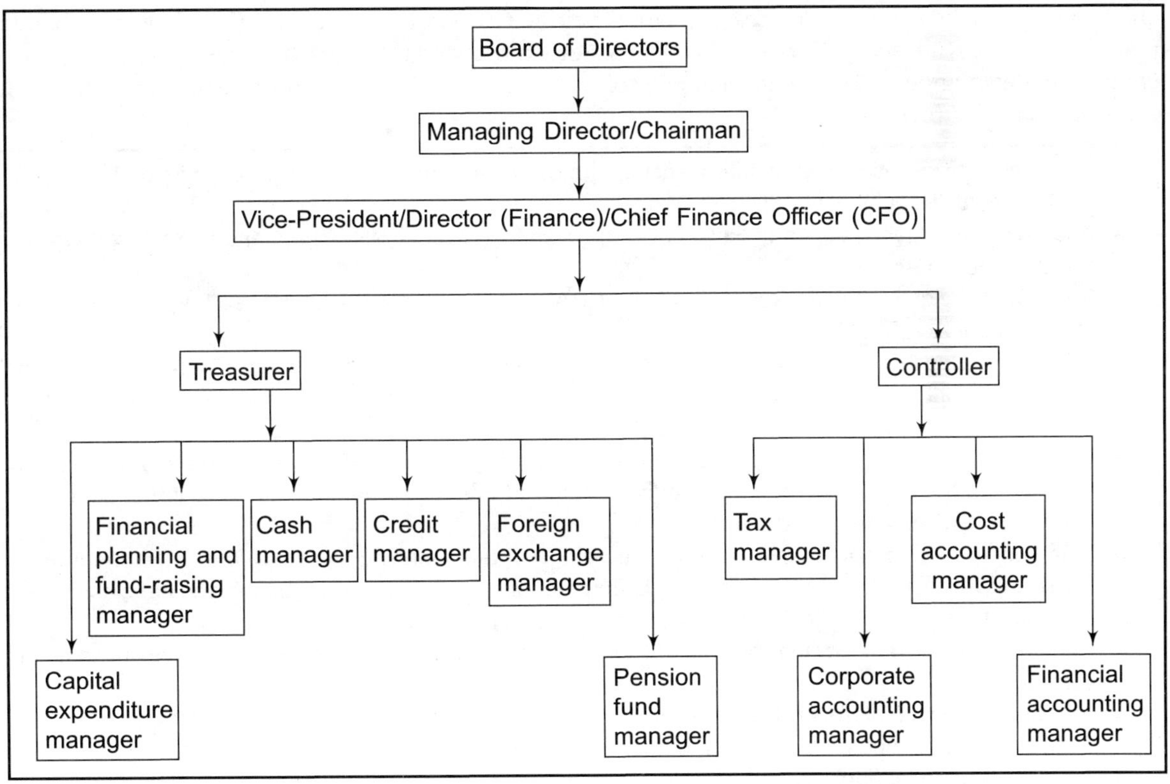

FIGURE 1.2 Organisation of Financial Management Function

The *job of the chief financial executive* does not cover only routine aspects of finance and accounting. As a member of top management, he is closely associated with the formulation of policies as well as decision making. Under him are controllers and treasurers, although they may be known by different designations in different firms. The tasks of financial management and allied areas like accounting are distributed between these two key financial officers. Their functions are described below.

The main concern of the treasurer is with the financing activities of the firm.

The **main concern of the treasurer** is with the financing activities of the firm. Included in the range of his functions are: **(i)** obtaining finance, **(ii)** banking relationship, **(iii)** investor relationship, **(iv)** short-term financing, **(v)** cash management, **(vi)** credit administration, **(vii)** investments, and **(viii)** insurance.

The functions of the controller are related mainly to accounting and control.

The **functions of the controller** are related mainly to accounting and control. The typical functions performed by him include: **(i)** financial accounting, **(ii)** internal audit, **(iii)** taxation, **(iv)** management accounting and control, **(v)** budgeting, planning and control, and **(vi)** economic appraisal and so on.

LO 1.7 EMERGING ROLE OF FINANCE MANAGERS IN INDIA

Reflecting the emerging economic and financial environment in the post-liberalisation era, the role/job of financial managers in India has become more important, complex and demanding. The key challenges are, *inter-alia*, in the areas specified below: **(a)** financial structure, **(b)** foreign exchange management, **(c)** treasury operations, **(d)** investor communication, **(e)** management control and **(f)** investment planning. The main elements of the changed economic and financial environment, *inter alia*, are the following:

- Considerable relaxation in industrial licensing framework in terms of the modifications in the Industries Development (Regulations) Act;
- Abolition of the Monopolies and Restrictive and Trade Practices (MRTP) Act and its replacement by the Competition Act;
- Repeal of Foreign Exchange Regulation Act (FERA) and enactment of a liberalised Foreign Exchange Management Act (FEMA);
- Abolition of Capital Issues (Control) Act and the setting-up of the Securities and Exchange Board of India (SEBI) under the SEBI Act for the regulation and development of the securities market and the protection of investors;
- Enactment of the Insurance Regulatory and Development Authority (IRDA) Act and the setting-up of the IRDA for the regulation of the insurance sector and the consequent dismantling of the monopoly of LIC and GIC and its subsidiaries;
- Emergence of the capital market at the centre-stage of the financing system and the disappearance of the erstwhile development/public financial/term lending institutions from the Indian financial scene;
- Emergence of a highly articulate and sophisticated money market;
- Globalisation, convertibility of rupee, liberalised foreign investments in India, Indian foreign investment abroad;
- Market-determined interest rate, emergence of highly innovative financial instruments;
- Growth of mutual funds; credit rating, other financial services;
- Rigorous prudential norms, credit risk management framework for banks and financial institutions;
- Access to Euro-issues, American Depository Receipts (ADRs);
- Privatisation/disinvestment of public sector undertakings.

LO 1.8 AN OVERVIEW OF THE BOOK

This book discusses the theory of financial management, outlines the relevant tools and techniques for analysing financial decisions, presents information about environment relevant for corporate finance in India and assesses the managerial finance practices by Indian corporates. Each major decision area is presented in terms of both return and risk factors and their potential impact on the owners wealth as reflected in share prices. Each chapter begins with a number of learning goals/ issues to ensure a broad understanding of the theories, concepts, techniques and practices of managerial finance. At the end of each chapter, there are chapter summaries, review questions, solved problems and self-test problems that can be used to test the readers' understanding of each key theory, concept, technique and practice. The chapter-end mini and comprehensive cases can be used to synthesize and apply related concepts and techniques. The activities of the financial managers are described in ten separate but related parts briefly outlined below.

Part 1 Foundation of Finance Chapter 1 provides an overview of financial management/corporate finance/managerial finance. Chapter 2 dwells on time value of money in terms of compounding and discounting and their applications. Chapter 3 explains the risk and return concepts. Chapter 4 discusses the valuation of bonds and shares.

Part 2 Financial Analysis, Profit Planning and Control Chapter 5 focuses on preparation of cash-flow statement. The techniques of financial statement analysis are covered in Chapter 6. The volume-cost-profit analysis is explained in Chapter 7. Chapter 8 presents various tools of budgeting and profit planning.

Part 3 Long-Term Investment Decision Chapter 9 analyses the general principles and techniques of capital budgeting. Chapter 10 explores some complex issues in capital budgeting. Chapter 11 explains cost of capital. Chapter 12 dwells on risk and uncertainty in capital budgeting.

Part 4 Current Assets Management Chapter 13 provides an overview of working capital management. Chapter 14 presents the tool for cash management. Chapter 15 discusses the important aspects of receivables/credit management. Chapter 16 dwells on the various facets of inventory management. Chapter 17 describes the various sources of financing working capital.

Part 5 Financing Decision Chapter 18 covers operating, financial and combined leverage. Capital structure theories and capital structure decisions are discussed in Chapters 19 and 20 respectively.

Part 6 Long-Term Finance Chapter 21 examines capital markets. Chapter 22 discusses equity share financing. Chapter 23 explains analytical issues relating to debt financing. Chapter 24 discusses hybrid financing in terms of preference shares, convertibles, warrants and options. Chapter 25 analyses lease financing and hire-purchase financing. Chapter 26 covers venture capital financing.

Part 7 Risk Management Chapter 27 deals with option valuation. Chapter 28 is devoted to a discussion of derivatives as a tool for managing financial risk.

Part 8 Dividend Decision Chapter 29 analyses the relationship between dividend and valuation. Chapter 30 discusses the various practical aspects of dividend policy.

Part 9 Valuation and Corporate Restructuring Chapter 31 explains the various approaches to business valuation. Chapter 32 explains corporate restructuring in detail.

Part 10 International Finance Chapters 33-35 discuss foreign exchange markets, foreign exchange risk management and international financial management.

SUMMARY

LO 1.1	Financial management/corporate finance/managerial finance is concerned with the duties of the finance manager in a business firm. He performs such varied tasks as budgeting, financial forecasting, cash management, credit administration, investment analysis and funds procurement. The recent trends towards globalisation of business activity has created new demands and opportunities in managerial finance.
LO 1.2	Finance is closely related to both macroeconomics and microeconomics. Macroeconomics provides an understanding of the institutional structure in which the flow of finance takes place. Microeconomics provides various profit maximisation strategies based on the theory of the firm. A financial manager uses these to run the firm efficiently and effectively. Similarly, he depends on accounting as a source of information/data relating to the past, present and future financial position of the firm. Despite this interdependence, finance and accounting differ in that the former is concerned with cash flows, while the latter provides accrual-based information; and the focus of finance is on the decision making but accounting concentrates on collection of data.
LO 1.3	The financial management function covers decision making in three inter-related areas, namely, investment including working capital management, financing and dividend policy. The three key activities of the financial manager are **(1)** performing financial analysis; **(2)** making investment decisions and **(3)** making financing decisions.
LO 1.4	The goal of the financial manager is to maximise the owners/shareholders wealth as reflected in share prices rather than profit/EPS maximisation because the latter ignores the timing of returns, does not directly consider cash flows and ignores risk. As key determinants of share price, both return and risk must be assessed by the financial manager when evaluating decision alternatives. The EVA is a popular measure to determine whether an investment positively contributes to the owners wealth. However, the wealth maximising action of the finance managers should be consistent with the preservation of the wealth of stakeholders, that is, groups such as employees, customers, suppliers, creditors, owners and others who have a direct link to the firm. Corporate India paid scant attention to the goal of shareholders wealth maximisation till the eighties. In the post-liberaliastion era, it has emerged at the centre-stage of corporate financial practices, the contributory factors being greater dependence on capital market, growing importance of institutional investors and foreign exposure.
LO 1.5	An agency problem results when managers as agents of owners place personal goals ahead of corporate goals. Market forces and the threat of hostile takeover tend to act to prevent/minimise agency problems. In addition, firms incur agency costs in the form of monitoring and bonding expenditures, opportunity costs and structuring expenditures which involve both incentive and performance-based compensation plans to motivate management to act in the best interest of the shareholders.
LO 1.6	The importance of the finance function depends on the size of the firm. Financial management is an integral part of the overall management of the firm. In small firms, the finance functions are generally performed by the accounting departments. In large firms, there is a separate department of finance headed by a specialist known by different designations such as vice-president, director of finance, chief finance officer and so on.

LO 1.7

Reflecting the emerging economic and financial environment in the post-liberalisation era since the early nineties, the role/job of finance managers in India has become more important, complex and demanding. The key challenges are in the areas of **(1)** financial structure, **(2)** foreign exchange management, **(3)** treasury operations, **(4)** investor communication, **(5)** management control and **(6)** investment planning.

REFERENCES

1. Solomon, E, Theory of Financial Management, Columbia University Press (New York), 1969, p 8.
2. *Ibid.*, p 17.
3. For a comprehensive account of the first category of shortcomings please refer to Solomon, E and J J Pringle, *An Introduction to Financial Management,* Good Year Publishing Company, (Santa Monica, Calif), 1977, pp 8-9. Also Solomon E, *op. cit.*, pp 15-16; Johnson, R W, Financial Management, Allyn and Bacon, (Boston), 1971, pp 8-10.
4. Solomon, E, *op. cit.*, p 20. Reprinted by permission of Columbia University Press, New York.
5. Solomon, E and Pringle J J, *op. cit.*, p 13.

REVIEW QUESTIONS

LOD: Easy

RQ.1.1 **(a)** Indicate whether the following statements are True or False. **[LO 1.3, 4, 5, 6]**

(i) Financial management deals with two major decisions, namely, investment and financing decisions.

(ii) Profit/EPS maximization is the sole objective of financial management.

(iii) Agency problem occurs when the management tries to fulfil its own interests at the cost of value of the firm.

(iv) Agency cost consists of **(a)** monitoring **(b)** binding **(c)** opportunity and **(d)** structuring cost such as stock options and cash bonuses, etc.

[Answers: (i) False (ii) False (iii) True (iv) True]

(b) In the following multiple choice questions select the correct answers.

(i) The only viable goal of financial management is
(a) profit maximization **(b)** wealth maximization
(c) sales maximization **(d)** assets maximization.

(ii) The basic objective of financial management is
(a) maximisation of profits
(b) maximisation of shareholder's wealth
(c) ensuring financial discipline in the organization
(d) none of the above.

(iii) Finance function involves
(a) procurement of finance only
(b) expenditure of funds only
(c) safe custody of funds only
(d) procurement and effective utilization of funds.

(iv) The goal of wealth maximization takes into consideration
(a) risk related to uncertainty of returns **(b)** timing of expected returns
(c) amount of returns expected **(d)** all the above.

(v) Financial management is mainly concerned with
  (a) arrangement of funds
  (b) all aspects of acquiring and utilizing means of financial resources for firm's activities
  (c) efficient management of every business
  (d) none of the above.

[Answers: (i) b (ii) b (iii) d (iv) d (v) b]

RQ.1.2 Briefly explain the three key activities of the financial manager. [LO 1.3]

RQ.1.3 Briefly describe the three basic reasons why profit/EPS maximisation fails to be consistent with wealth maximisation. [LO 1.4]

RQ.1.4 What is economic value added (EVA)? How is it used? [LO 1.4]

RQ.1.5 Describe the three broad areas of financial decision making. [LO 1.3]

RQ.1.6 What are the primary objectives of corporate management in India? [LO 1.4]

LOD: Medium

RQ.1.7 Describe the close relationship between finance and economics and explain why the finance manager should possess a basic knowledge of economics. What is the primary economic principle used in managerial finance? [LO 1.2]

RQ.1.8 What are the major differences between accounting and finance with respect to **(a)** emphasis on cash flows and **(b)** decision making? [LO 1.2]

RQ.1.9 What is the goal of the firm? Discuss how to measure achievement of this goal. [LO 1.4]

RQ.1.10 What is the agency problem? How do market forces act to prevent/minimise this problem? [LO 1.5]

RQ.1.11 Define agency costs and explain why firms incur them. Describe and differentiate between incentives and performance compensation plans. [LO 1.5]

RQ.1.12 Comment on the emerging role of the finance manager in India. [LO 1.7]

RQ.1.13 How is the finance function typically organised in a large organisation? [LO 1.6]

LOD: Difficult

RQ.1.14 Who are a firm's stakeholders and what consideration is often given to them in pursuing the firm's goal? Why? [LO 1.4]

RQ.1.15 "Value maximisation is smiply extension of profit maximisation to a world that is uncertain and multiperiod in nature." Elucidate the Statement with appropriate examples. [LO 1.4]

RQ.1.16 Outline the factors behind Indian companies according greater importance to the goal of shareholders wealth maximisation. [LO 1.4]

CHAPTER

2

Time Value of Money

LEARNING OBJECTIVES

LO 2.1	Discuss the role/rationale of time value of money in finance particularly future (compound) value and present (discounted) value
LO 2.2	Understand the concept of future value, its calculation for a single amount, compounding of interest more frequently than annually and find the future value of annuities
LO 2.3	Explain the concept of present value, its calculation for a single amount and determine the present value of a mixed stream of cashflows, an annuity and a perpetuity
LO 2.4	Describe procedures involved in determining deposits to accumulate a future sum, loan amortisation, computation of growth rates as well as develop further aspects of application of compounding and discounting techniques, namely, effective and nominal rates of interest and discount, present value of an annuity payable monthly/quarterly/half-yearly, and effective and flat rates of interest

INTRODUCTION

The object of this Chapter is to illustrate the basics of the mathematics of finance, that is, the time value of money. Recognition of the time value of money in financial decision making is extremely important. It was observed in Chapter 1 that wealth maximisation, as an objective of financial management, is superior to profit maximisation because, among other things, the former incorporates the timing of benefits received while the latter ignores it. Given the objective of wealth maximisation, much of the subject-matter of financial management is future-oriented. A financial decision taken today has implications for a number of years, that is, it spreads into the future. For example, firms have to acquire fixed assets for which they have to pay a certain sum of money to the vendors. The benefits arising out of the acquisition of such assets will be spread over a number of years in the future, till the working life of the assets. On the other hand, funds have to be procured from different sources such as raising of capital through new issues, bank borrowings, term loans from financial institutions, sale of debentures and so on. These involve a cash inflow at the time of raising funds as well as an obligation to pay interest/dividend and return the principal in future. It is on the basis of a comparison of the cash outflows (outlays) and the benefits (cash inflows) that financial decisions are made. For a meaningful comparison, the two variables must be strictly comparable. One basic requirement of comparability is the incorporation of the time element in the calculations. In other words, in order to have a logical and meaningful comparison between cash flows that accrue in different time periods, it is necessary to convert the sums of money to a common point of time. This chapter is devoted to a discussion of the techniques for doing so. The chapter explains the meaning of, and rationale underlying, the time value of money. The technique employed in adjusting the timing aspect of financial decision making through compounding and discounting is explained subsequently. The important applications of these techniques are also demonstrated. The effective rates of interest and discount, nominal rates of interest and discount, present value of annuity payable for the period less than a year (PTHLY), loan repayment schedule and effective flat rates of interest are discussed in *Appendix 2-A*. Finally, the main points are recapitulated in the summary.

LO 2.1 RATIONALE OF TIME VALUE OF MONEY

Conceptually, 'time value of money' means that the value of a unit of money is different in different time periods. The value of a sum of money received today is more than its value received after some time. Conversely, the sum of money received in future is less valuable than it is today. In other words, the present worth of a rupee received after some time will be less than a rupee received today. Since a rupee received today has more value, rational investors would prefer current receipt to future receipts. The time value of money can also be referred to as **time preference for money**.

Time value of money means that the value of a unit of money is different in different time periods.

The main reason for the time preference for money is to be found in the reinvestment opportunities for funds which are received early. The funds so invested will earn a rate of return; this would not be possible if the funds are received at a later time. The time preference for money is, therefore, expressed generally in terms of a rate of return or more popularly as a discount rate. The expected rate of return as also the time value of money will vary from individual to individual depending, *inter alia*, on his perception. The time value of money can be illustrated using a simple example.

> Suppose, Mr X is given the choice of receiving ₹1,000 either now or one year later. His choice would obviously be for the first alternative as he can deposit the amount in his saving bank account and earn a nominal rate of interest, say, five per cent. At the end of the year, the amount will accumulate to ₹1,050. In other words, the choice before Mr X is between ₹1,050 and ₹1,000 at the end of the year. As a rational person, Mr X should be expected to prefer the larger amount (i.e. ₹1,050 here). Here we say that the time value of money, that is, the rate of interest is five per cent. It may, thus, be seen that future cash flows are less valuable because of the investment opportunities of the present cash flows.

What applies to an individual applies equally, if not in greater measure, to a business firm. It is because business firms make decisions which have ramifications extending beyond the period in which they were taken. For instance, the capital budgeting decision generally involves the current cash outflows in terms of the amount required for purchasing a new machine or launching a new project and the execution of the scheme generates future cash inflows during its useful life. Let us assume that the project cost (current cash outflows) is ₹10,00,000. To keep the illustration simple, it is assumed that the project has a useful life of only one year in which it is estimated to have cash inflows of ₹10,80,000 (at the end of the first year). The project appears to be *prima facie* acceptable as it adds ₹80,000 as profit. However, when we take into account a rate of interest, say, of 10 per cent, the earlier conclusion will have to be revised as, without the project, the sum could have amounted to ₹11,00,000. Likewise, when the decision is made to raise a loan of ₹10,00,000 from a financial institution or by issuing debentures, for a period of 10 years, the firm is not only under obligation to meet interest payment as and when it becomes due on the debt at fixed intervals but also must make provisions so that it can repay ₹10,00,000 when the loan or debentures become due. Thus, time value of money is of crucial significance. This requires the development of procedures and techniques for evaluating future incomes in terms of the present.

There are two techniques for doing this: **(1)** Compounding, and **(2)** Discounting.

Compound interest is the interest earned on a given deposit/principal that has become a part of the principal at the end of a specified period.

LO 2.2 COMPOUNDING TECHNIQUE

Interest is compounded when the amount earned on an initial deposit (the initial **principal**) becomes part of the principal at the end of the first compounding period. The term principal refers to the amount of money on which interest is received. Consider Example 2.1.

Principal refers to the amount of money on which interest is received.

***Example* 2.1**

If Mr X invests in a saving bank account ₹1,000 at 5 per cent interest compounded annually, at the end of the first year, he will have ₹1,050 in his account. This amount constitutes the principal for earning interest for the next year. At the end of the next year, there would be ₹1,102.50 in the account. This would represent the principal for the third year. The amount of interest earned would be ₹55.125. The total amount appearing in his account would be ₹1,157.625. Table 2.1 shows this compounding procedure:

TABLE 2.1 Annual Compounding

Year	*1*	*2*	*3*
Beginning amount	₹1,000.00	₹1,050.00	₹1,102.500
Interest rate	0.05	0.05	0.050
Amount of interest	50.00	52.50	55.125
Beginning principal	1,000.00	1,050.00	1,102.500
Ending principal	1,050.00	1,102.50	1,157.625

This compounding procedure will continue for an indefinite number of years. The compounding of interest can be calculated by the following equation:

$$A = P(1 + i)^n \tag{2.1}$$

in which

A = amount at the end of the period

P = principal at the beginning of the period

i = rate of interest

n = number of years

The amount of money in the account at the end of various years is calculated by using Eq. 2.1.

Amount at the end of year 1 = ₹1,000 (1 + .05) = ₹1,050

2 = ₹1,050 (1 + .05) = ₹1,102.50

3 = ₹1,102.50 (1 + .05) = ₹1,157.625

The amount at the end of year 2 can be ascertained by substituting ₹1,000 (1 + .05) for ₹1,050, that is, ₹1,000 (1 + .05) (1 + .05) = ₹1,102.50. Similarly, the amount at the end of year 3 can be determined in the following way: ₹1,000 (1 + .05) (1 + .05) (1 + .05) = ₹1,157.625.

Thus, after substituting the actual figures for the investment of ₹1,000 in the formula $A = P(1 + i)^n$, we arrive at the same result as in Table 2.1. This is the fundamental equation of compound interest. The formula is useful as it can be applied quite readily for wide ranges of i and n. However, the calculations involved will be tedious and time-consuming if the number of years involved is large, say, 15 years or 20 years. To find the compound value of ₹1,000, assuming the rate of interest to be 5 per cent, the compounding factor 1.05 is to be raised to fifteenth power or twentieth power. In order to simplify the compound interest calculations, compound interest tables for values $(1 + i)^n$ for wide ranges of i and n have been compiled. Table A-1 given in *Appendix I* at the end of the book gives compound value interest factor of one rupee at different rates of interest for different time periods. The compounded values can be readily calculated with the help of Table A-1. For instance, if Mr X wishes to find out how much his savings, ₹1,000, will accumulate to in 15 years at 5 per cent rate of interest, application of the formula will require solving 1.05 raised to the power of fifteen: ₹1,000 $(1.05)^{15}$ = A

Using Table A-1, we find that the compound value interest factor (CVIF) of ₹1 at 5 per cent interest rate for 15 years is 2.079. Multiplying the initial principal (₹1,000) by 2.079, we obtain ₹2,079. With the help of the table, it is possible to calculate the compounded value for any combination of interest rate, i and number of years, n. Let us take another illustration.

The compound interest phenomenon is most commonly associated with various savings institutions. These institutions emphasise the fact that they pay compound interest on savings deposited with them. If an investor deposits ₹20,000 with a bank which is paying interest at 8 per cent on a 15-year time deposit, we consult Table A-1 and read the relevant value in the 15th row (time period) in the column of 8 per cent (rate of interest). This value is 3.172. Multiplying this factor by the actual deposit of ₹20,000, we find his savings will accumulate to ₹63,440.

Two important observations can be made from the Table A-1 for the sum of ₹ one. The first is that as the interest rate increases for any given year, the compound interest factor also increases. Thus, the higher the interest rate, the greater is the future sum. The second point is that for a given interest rate, the future sum of a rupee increases with the passage of time. Thus, the longer the period of time, the higher is the compound interest factor. However, it should be borne in mind that for an interest rate of zero per cent, the compound interest factor always equals 1 and, therefore, the future amount always equals the initial principal.

Alternatively, the calculation of the compounded value can be carried out using Microsoft Excel (Spreadsheet).

Spreadsheet Solution 2.1

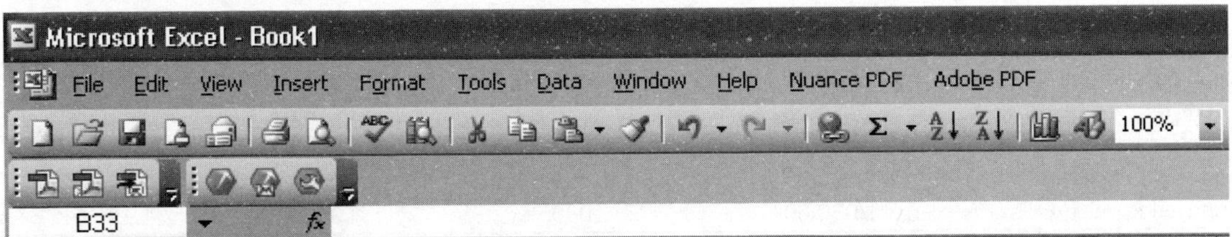

	A	B	C	D	E	F	G	H	I
1	Interest rate	0.05							
2	Time	0	1	2	3				
3	Cash flow	–1,000							
4	Future value		1,050	1,102.50	1,157.63				
5									

Interest rate is entered in cell B1 as a decimal number 0.05. Periods for the time line are entered in row 2. Instead of entering values in all the cells in row 2, you can enter 0 in cell B2, the formula B2+1 in cell C2 and then copy the formula in the remaining cells of row 2. Cash flows are entered in row 3. The single cash flow in this example has been shown in cell B3. The formula in equation 2.1 has been entered in cell C4 as =-$B3*(1+$B1)^C2. The minus sign is used in the formula because the cash flow in cell B3 bears a negative sign. The formula is then copied in cells D4 and E4. Cell E4 shows that the future value of ₹1,000, compounded for 3 years at 5 per cent per year is ₹1,157.625.

Future Value can also be found using the function wizard in Microsoft Excel. The equation of this function in Excel format is FV (Rate, Nper, Pmt, Pv, Type). In this equation, Rate stands for rate of interest per period; Nper stands for number of payment periods; Pmt stands for payment made each period and Pv is the present value, or the lump-sum amount that a series of future payments is worth right now. If Pv is omitted, it is assumed to be 0 (zero), and you must include the Pmt argument. A Type code is to be entered to indicate the time at which the payments are due. The code is 0 if the payments are due at the end of the period and 1 if the payments are due in the beginning of the period.

To use the function wizard, put the cursor on cell E2 and click; click the function wizard, a window 'insert function' will appear; choose 'Financial' from the category of functions, a list of financial functions will appear; scroll down to FV and then click OK, you will see the FV dialogue box. Enter 0.05 or $B1 for Rate, C2 for Nper, 0 or leave blank for Pmt as there are no periodic payments, -1,000 or $B3 for Pv and 0 or leave blank to indicate that payments occur at the end of the period. When you click OK after entering the data, you get the future value of ₹1,050 after 1 period. Copy the formula of cell E2 in cells E3 and E4 to get the FV values for the years 2 and 3 respectively.

Semi-annual and Other Compounding Periods In the above examples, we have assumed annual compounding of interest at the end of the year. Very often the interest rates are compounded more than once in a year. Savings institutions, particularly, compound interests semi-annually, quarterly and even monthly.

> **Semi-annual compounding** means two compounding periods within a year.

Semi-annual Compounding means that there are *two compounding periods* within the year. Interest is actually paid after every six months at a rate of one-half of the annual (stated) rate of interest.

***Example* 2.1**

Assume Mr X places his savings of ₹1,000 in a two-year time deposit scheme of a bank which yields 6 per cent interest compounded semi-annually. He will be paid 3 per cent interest compounded over four periods—each of six months' duration. Table 2.2 presents the calculations of the amount Mr X will have from the time deposit after two years.

TABLE 2.2 Semi-annual Compounding

Year	*6 months*	*1 Year*	*18 months*	*2 years*
Beginning amount	₹1,000.00	₹1,030.00	₹1,060.90	₹1,092.73
Interest rate	0.03	0.03	0.03	0.03
Amount of interest	30.00	30.90	31.83	32.78
Beginning principal	1,000.00	1,030.00	1,060.90	1,092.73
Ending principal	1,030.00	1,060.90	1,092.73	1,125.51

Table 2.2 reveals that his savings will amount to ₹1,060.90 and ₹1,125.51 respectively at the end of the first and second years.

Spreadsheet Solution 2.2

In line with the earlier spreadsheet application, the spreadsheet can be straight away applied to solve the Example 2.1.

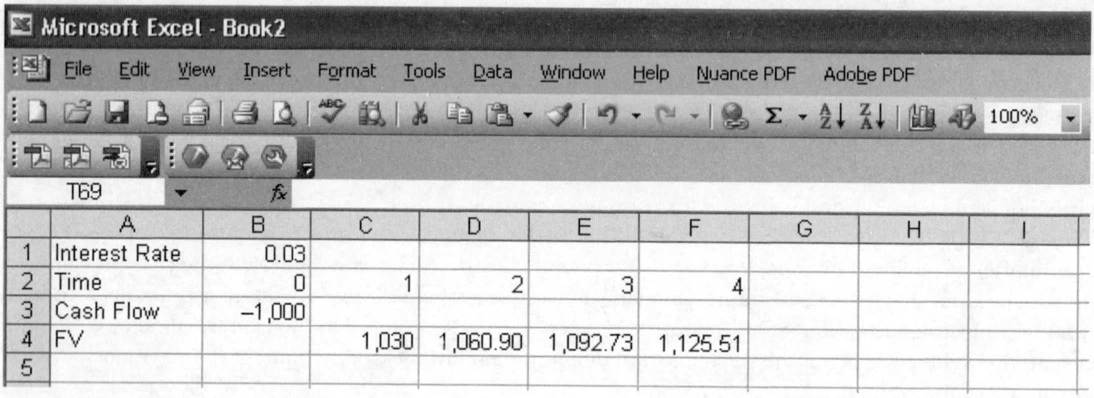

	A	B	C	D	E	F	G	H	I
1	Interest Rate	0.03							
2	Time	0	1	2	3	4			
3	Cash Flow	–1,000							
4	FV		1,030	1,060.90	1,092.73	1,125.51			
5									

Quarterly Compounding means that there are *four compounding periods* within the year. Instead of paying the interest once a year, it is paid in four equal instalments after every three months. Using the above illustration, there will be eight compounding periods and the rate of interest for each compounding period will be 1.5 per cent, that is (1/4 of 6 per cent).

Quarterly compounding means four compounding periods in a year.

Table 2.3 presents the relevant calculations regarding the amount he will have at the end of two years, when interest is compounded quarterly. At the end of the first year, his savings will accumulate to ₹1,061.363 and at the end of the second year he will have ₹1,126.49.

TABLE 2.3 Quarterly Compounding

Period (months)	*Beginning amount*	*Interest factor*	*Amount of interest*	*Beginning principal*	*Ending principal*
3	₹1,000.000	0.015	₹15.000	₹1,000.000	₹1,015.000
6	1,015.000	0.015	15.225	1,015.000	1,030.225
9	1,030.225	0.015	15.453	1,030.225	1,045.678
12	1,045.678	0.015	15.685	1,045.678	1,061.363
15	1,061.363	0.015	15.920	1,061.363	1,077.283

(Contd.)

(*Contd.*)

18	1,077.283	0.015	16.159	1,077.283	1,093.442
21	1,093.442	0.015	16.401	1,093.442	1,109.843
24	1,109.843	0.015	16.647	1,109.843	1,126.490

Table 2.4 presents a comparative picture of Mr X's savings at the end of two years when they are compounded annually, half-yearly and quarterly. The table warrants the generalisation that the more frequently the interest is compounded, the greater is the amount of money accumulated. This is primarily because interest is earned more frequently.

Spreadsheet Solution 2.3

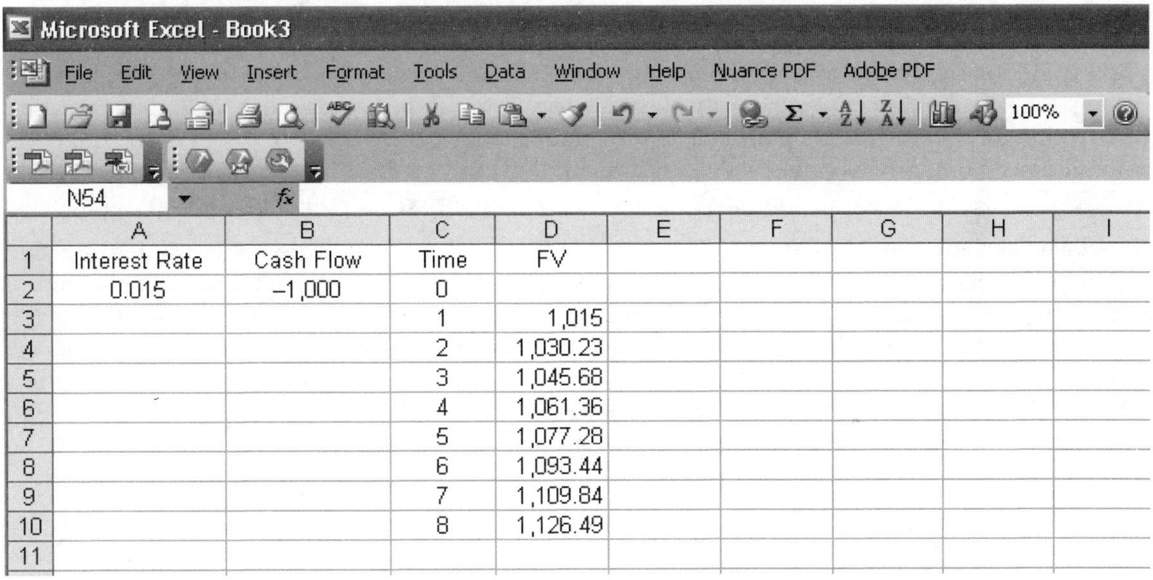

	A	B	C	D	E	F	G	H	I
1	Interest Rate	Cash Flow	Time	FV					
2	0.015	–1,000	0						
3			1	1,015					
4			2	1,030.23					
5			3	1,045.68					
6			4	1,061.36					
7			5	1,077.28					
8			6	1,093.44					
9			7	1,109.84					
10			8	1,126.49					
11									

TABLE 2.4 Comparison of Annual, Semi-annual and Quarterly Compounding

	Compounding period		
End of year	*Annual*	*Half-yearly*	*Quarterly*
1	₹1,060.00	₹1,060.90	₹1,061.36
2	1,123.60	1,125.51	1,126.49

The effect of compounding more than once a year can also be expressed in the form of a formula. Equation 2.1 can be modified as Eq. 2.2.

$$P\left\{1+\frac{i}{m}\right\}^{mn} = A \tag{2.2}$$

in which m is the number of times per year compounding is made. For semi-annual compounding, m would be 2, while for quarterly compounding it would equal 4 and if interest is compounded monthly, weekly and daily, would equal 12, 52 and 365 respectively.

The general applicability of the formula can be shown as follows, assuming the same figures of Mr X's savings of ₹1,000:

1. For semi-annual compounding, ₹1,000 $\left\{1+\frac{0.06}{2}\right\}^{2\times 2}$ = ₹1,000 (1 + 0.03)^4 = ₹1,125.51

2. For quarterly compounding, ₹1,000 $\left\{1+\frac{0.06}{4}\right\}^{4\times 2}$ = ₹1,000 (1 + 0.015)^8 = ₹1,126.49

The table of the sum of ₹1 (Table A-1) can also be used to simplify calculations when compounding occurs more than once a year. We are required simply to divide the interest rate by the number of times compounding occurs, that is ($i \times m$) and multiply the years by the number of compounding periods per year, that is, ($m \times n$). In our example, we have to look at Table A-1 for the sum of rupee one under the 3 per cent column and in the row for the fourth year when compounding is done semi-annually, the respective rate and year figures would be 1.5 per cent and the eighth year in quarterly compounding.

The compounding factor for 3 per cent and 4 years is 1.126 while the factor for 1.5 per cent and 8 years is 1.127. Multiplying each of the factors by the initial savings deposit of ₹1,000, we find ₹1,126 (₹1,000 × 1.126) for semi-annual compounding and ₹1,127 (₹1,000 × 1.127) for quarterly compounding. The corresponding values found by the long method are ₹1,125.51 and ₹1,126.49 respectively. The difference can be attributed to the rounding off of values in Table A-1.

Future/Compounded Value of a Series of Payments So far we have considered only the future value of a single payment made at time zero. In many instances, we may be interested in the future value of a series of payments made at different time periods. For simplicity, we assume that the compounding time period is one year and payment is made at the end of each year. Suppose, Mr X deposits each year ₹500, ₹1,000, ₹1,500, ₹2,000 and ₹2,500 in his saving bank account for 5 years. The interest rate is 5 per cent. He wishes to find the future value of his deposits at the end of the 5th year. Table 2.5 presents the calculations required to determine the sum of money he will have.

TABLE 2.5 Annual Compounding of a Series of Payments

End of year	*Amount deposited*	*Number of years compounded*	*Compounded interest factor from Table A-1*	*Future value (2) × (4)*
1	*2*	*3*	*4*	*5*
1	₹500	4	1.216	₹608.00
2	1,000	3	1.158	1,158.00
3	1,500	2	1.103	1,654.50
4	2,000	1	1.050	2,100.00
5	2,500	0	1.000	2,500.00
				8,020.50

Column 3 of Table 2.5 indicates that since the deposits are made at the end of the year, the first deposit will earn interest for four years, the second for three years and so on. The last payment of ₹2,500 comes at the end of the fifth year and, therefore, the future value remains ₹2,500. The future value of the entire stream of payments is the sum of the individual future values, that is, ₹8,020.50. The graphic presentation of these values is shown in the following time scale diagram which shows the equivalence of money sums (Fig. 2.1).

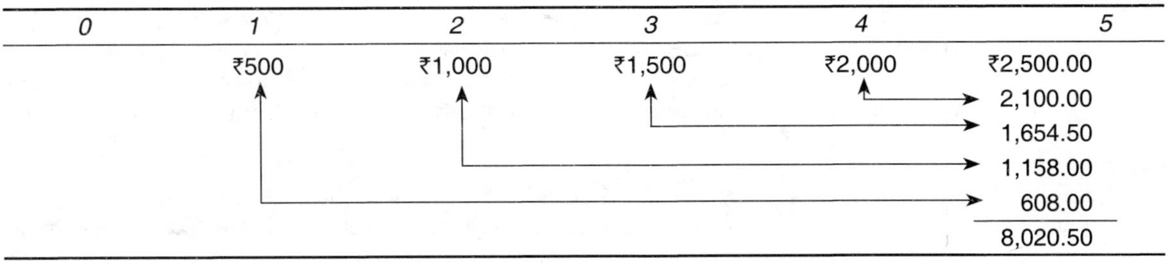

FIGURE 2.1 Graphic Illustration of Compounding Values

It may be noted here that we are making use of the compound interest formula for each payment separately. For instance, ₹500 put in at the end of the first year compounds for four years, and has a future value of ₹608 at 5 per cent interest [₹500$(1 + 0.05)^4$]. Similarly, ₹1,000 deposited at $n = 2$ compounds for 3 years and amounts to ₹1,158 [₹1,000$(1 + 0.05)^3$] and so on.

Future value of a series of payments can be calculated using the formula

$$FV_n = \sum_{t=1}^{n} CF_t(1 + i)^{n-t} \quad \textbf{(2.2A)}$$

Where CF_t is the cash flow occurring at time t, i is the interest rate per period and n is the number of periods.

Spreadsheet Solution 2.4

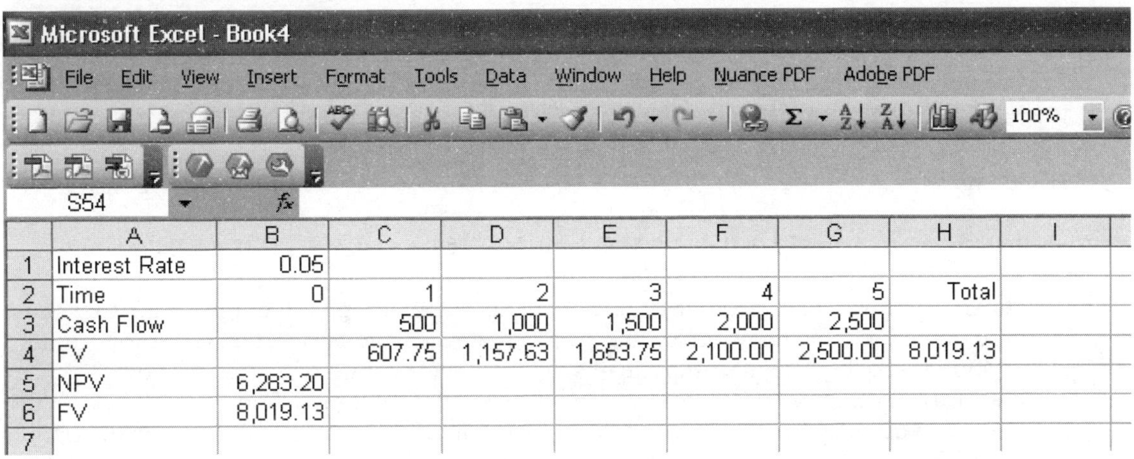

	A	B	C	D	E	F	G	H	I
1	Interest Rate	0.05							
2	Time	0	1	2	3	4	5	Total	
3	Cash Flow		500	1,000	1,500	2,000	2,500		
4	FV		607.75	1,157.63	1,653.75	2,100.00	2,500.00	8,019.13	
5	NPV	6,283.20							
6	FV	8,019.13							
7									

In cell C4 of the spreadsheet, enter the formula =C3*(1+$B1)^($G2-C2). Copy this formula in cells D4 to G4. The sum of future values of each year's cash flow is calculated in cell H4 by entering the function =SUM(C4:G4).

The difference in the future value as per the numerical solution and as per the spreadsheet solution is due to approximations in the manual calculations.

Future value of a series of payments can also be calculated in an alternate way. First, the NPV of the cash flows is calculated using the NPV function from the function wizard. To use this function, there is a need to specify the interest rate and the series of payments. In the cell B5, enter the function =NPV(B1,C3:G3) to get the NPV. Then, the future value of the series of payments can be computed using the formula =NPV$(1+i)^n$. This step has been performed in cell B6 using the function =B5*(1+B1)^G2.

Compound Sum of an Annuity An **annuity** is a stream of equal annual cash flows. Annuities involve calculations based upon the regular periodic contribution or receipt of a fixed sum of money. The calculations required to find the sum of an annuity on which interest is paid at a specified rate compounded annually are illustrated in Example 2.3.

Annuity is a stream of equal annual cash flows.

***Example* 2.3**

Mr X deposits ₹2,000 at the end of every year for 5 years in his saving account paying 5 per cent interest compounded annually. He wants to determine how much sum of money he will have at the end of the 5th year.

Solution

Table 2.6 presents the relevant calculations.

TABLE 2.6 Annual Compounding of Annuity

End of year	Amount deposited	Number of years compounded	Compounded interest factor from Table A-1	Future value (2) × (4)
1	2	3	4	5
1	₹2,000	4	1.216	₹2,432
2	2,000	3	1.158	2,316
3	2,000	2	1.103	2,206
4	2,000	1	1.050	2,100
5	2,000	0	1.000	2,000
				11,054

The calculations in this case can be cut short and simplified since the compound interest factor is to be multiplied by the same rupee amount (₹2,000) each year as shown in the following calculations:

Amount at the end of 5 years = ₹2,000 (1.216) + ₹2,000 (1.158) + ₹2,000 (1.103) + ₹2,000 (1.050) + ₹2,000 (1.000)

Taking out the common factor ₹2,000, = ₹2,000 (1.216 + 1.158 + 1.103 + 1.050 + 1.000)
= ₹2,000 (5.527) = ₹11,054.

From the above, it follows that in order to find the sum of the annuity, the annual amount must be multiplied by the sum of the appropriate **compound interest factor** annuity (CVIFA). Such calculations are available for a wide range of i and n. They are given in Table A-2, labelled as the sum of an annuity table. To find the answer to the annuity question of Example 2.3, we are required to look for the 5 per cent column and the row for the fifth year and multiply the factor by the annuity amount of ₹2,000. From the table we find that the sum of annuity of ₹1 deposited at the end of each year for 5 years is 5.526 (CVIFA). Thus, when multiplied by ₹2,000 annuity (A) we find the total sum as ₹11,052.

Compound/ future interest factor for an annuity is the multiplier used to calculate the future/ compound value of an annuity at a specified rate over a given period of time.

Symbolically, $Sn = CVIFA \times A$

where A is the value of annuity, and $CVIFA$ represents the appropriate factor for the sum of the annuity of ₹1 and Sn represents the compound sum of an annuity. The answer which we get from the long method was ₹11,054. This discrepancy can be attributed to the rounding off of values in Table A-2. Moreover, it may be noted that the sum of an annuity is always larger than the number of years the annuity runs, unless of course, when interest rate is zero; in the latter case it will equal the number of years.

Spreadsheet Solution 2.5

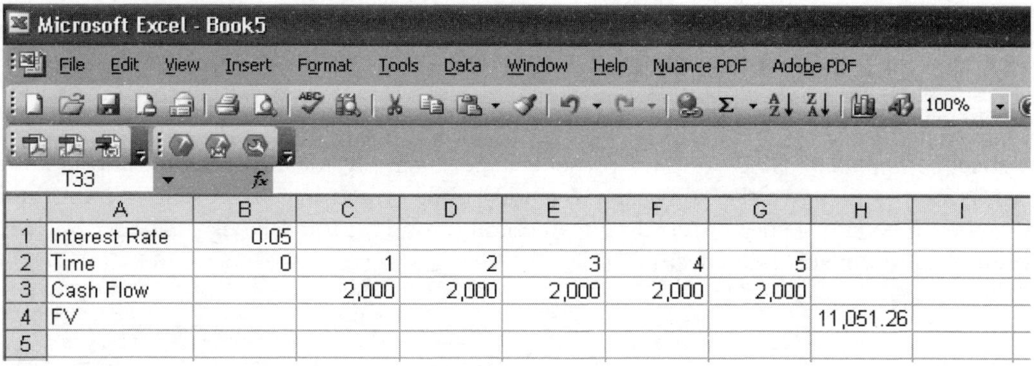

	A	B	C	D	E	F	G	H	I
1	Interest Rate	0.05							
2	Time	0	1	2	3	4	5		
3	Cash Flow		2,000	2,000	2,000	2,000	2,000		
4	FV							11,051.26	
5									

In Microsoft Excel, there is an inbuilt function, FV, for finding the future value of an annuity. The function has already been explained in Example 2.1. In cell H4, enter the function =FV(B1,G2,-2000,0,0) to get the future value of the annuity. The difference in future value as per the spreadsheet solution and as per the numerical solution is due to approximations.

Annuity tables are of great help in the field of investment banking as they guide the depositors and investors as to what sum an amount (X) paid for number of years, *n*, will accumulate to at a stated rate of compound interest. Let us illustrate. Mr X wishes to know the sum of money he will have in his saving account which pays 5 per cent interest at the end of 12 years if he deposits ₹.1,000, at the end of each year for the next twelve years. The appropriate factor for the sum of a twelve-year annuity at 5 per cent as given in Table A-2 is 15.917. Multiplying this factor by ₹1,000 deposit, we find the resultant sum to be ₹15,917.

LO 2.3 PRESENT VALUE OR DISCOUNTING TECHNIQUE

The concept of the present value is the exact opposite of that of compound value. While in the latter approach money invested now appreciates in value because compound interest is added, in the former approach (present value approach) money is received at some future date and will be worth less because the corresponding interest is lost during the period. In other words, the present value of a rupee that will be received in the future will be less than the value of a rupee in hand today. Thus, in contrast to the compounding approach where we convert present sums into future sums, in **present value** approach future sums are converted into present sums. Given a positive rate of interest, the present value of future rupees will always be lower. It is for this reason, therefore, that the procedure of finding present values is commonly called **discounting**. It is concerned with determining the present value of a future amount, assuming that the decision maker has an opportunity to earn a certain return on his money. This return is designated in financial literature as the discount rate, the cost of capital or an opportunity cost. These concepts are elaborated in Chapter 11. Let us illustrate the discounting procedure by an example (2.4).

> **Present value** is the current value of a future amount. The amount to be invested today at a given interest rate over a specified period to equal the future amount.

> **Discounting** is determining the present value of a future amount.

***Example* 2.4**

Mr X has been given an opportunity to receive ₹1,060 one year from now. He knows that he can earn 6 per cent interest on his investments. The question is: what amount will he be prepared to invest for this opportunity?

To answer this question, we must determine how many rupees must be invested at 6 per cent today to have ₹1,060 one year afterwards.

Let us assume that P is this unknown amount, and using Eq. 2.1 we have: $P(1 + 0.06) = ₹1,060$

Solving the equation for P, $P = \dfrac{₹1{,}060}{1.06} = ₹1{,}000$

Thus, ₹1,000 would be the required investment to have ₹1,060 after the expiry of one year. In other words, the present value of ₹1,060 received one year from now, given the rate of interest of 6 per cent, is ₹1,000. Mr X should be indifferent to whether he receives ₹1,000 today or ₹1,060 one year from today. If he can either receive more than ₹1,060 by paying ₹1,000 or ₹1,060 by paying less than ₹1,000, he would do so.

Mathematical Formulation Since finding present value is simply the reverse of compounding, the formula for compounding of the sum can be readily transformed into a present value formula. As shown in the preceding section, according to the compounding formula, $A = P(1 + i)^n$. Therefore, the present value equation becomes:

$$P = \frac{A}{(1+i)^n} = A\left\{\frac{1}{(1+i)^n}\right\} \tag{2.3}$$

Present value interest factor is the multiplier used to calculate at a specified discount rate the present value of an amount to be received in a future period.

in which P is the present value for the future sum to be received or spent; A is the sum to be received or spent in future; i is interest rate, and n is the number of years. Thus, the present value of money is the reciprocal of the compounding value.

Present Value Tables In order to simplify the present value calculations, tables are readily available for various ranges of i and n. Table A-3 in the Appendix gives the **present value interest factors** (PVIF) for various discount rates and years. Since the factors in Table A-3 give the present value of one rupee for various combinations of i and n, we can find the present value of the future lump sum by multiplying it with the appropriate present value interest factor (PVIF) from Table A-3.

In terms of a formula, it will be:

$$P = A(PVIF) \tag{2.4}$$

***Example* 2.5**

Mr X wants to find the present value of ₹2,000 to be received 5 years from now, assuming 10 per cent rate of interest. We have to look in the 10 per cent column of the fifth year in Table A-3. The relevant PVIF as per Table A-3 is 0.621.

Therefore, present value = ₹2,000 (0.621) = ₹1,242

Spreadsheet Solution

Microsoft Excel - Book1

C8 =

	A	B	C	D	E	F	G	H	I
1	Interest Rate	0.1							
2	Time	0	1	2	3	4	5		
3	Cash Flow						2,000		
4	Present Value	1,241.84							

Present value of a future cash flow can be found using the formula in equation 2.3. This formula has been entered in cell B4 as =G3/(1+B1)^G2. Cell B4 shows that the present value of ₹2,000, discounted for 5 years at 10 per cent per year is ₹1,241.84. (This value is different from the value in the numerical solution due to approximations). Present Value can also be found using the PV function in Microsoft Excel. The inputs required by the PV function are similar to those of the FV function. The only difference is that there is need to provide present value (FV) instead of future value (PV).

Some points may be noted with respect to present values. First, the expression for the present value factor for n years at i per cent, $1/(1 + i)^n$ is the reciprocal or inverse of the compound interest factor for n years at i per cent, $(1 + i)^n$. This observation can also be confirmed by finding out the reciprocal of the relevant present value factor of Example 2.5. The reciprocal of 0.621 is 1.610. The compound interest factor from Table A-1 for 5 years at 10 per cent is 1.611. The difference is due to rounding off of values in Table A-1.

In other words, in Example 2.5, the sum of ₹1,242 will be compounded to ₹2,000 in five years at 10 per cent rate of interest [₹1,242 × 1.611) = ₹2,000.862]. The difference of ₹0.862 is attributable to the fact that the table values are rounded figures. This indicates that both the methods, compounding and discounting of adjusting time value of money, yield identical results. Second, Table A-3 shows that the farther in the future a sum is to be received, the lower is its present value. See, for instance, the following extract from Table A-3:

Time (years)	*2*	*4*	*6*	*8*	*10*
5 per cent discount factor	0.907	0.823	0.711	0.677	0.614

Finally, the perusal of Table A-3 also reveals that the greater is the discount rate, the lower is its present value. Observe in this connection the following:

Discount rate	*4*	*8*	*12*	*16*	*20*
5 years time period	0.822	0.681	0.567	0.476	0.402

Thus, the higher the discount rate, the lower is the present value factor; and the longer the period of time, and correspondingly, the lower is the present value factor and *vice versa.* At the discount rate of zero per cent, the present value factor always equals one and, therefore, the future value of the funds equals their present value. But this aspect is only of academic importance as in actual practice the business firms can rarely, if ever, obtain the resources (capital) at zero rate of interest.

Present Value of a Series of Cash Flows So far we have considered only the present value of a single receipt at some future date. In many instances, especially in capital budgeting decisions, we may be interested in the present value of a series of receipts received by a firm at different time periods. Like compounding, in order to determine the present value of such a **mixed stream** of cash inflows, all that is required is to determine the present value of each future payment and then to aggregate them to find the total present value of the stream of cash flows. Symbolically,

Mixed stream is a stream of cashflows that reflects no particular pattern.

$$P = \frac{C_1}{(1+i)} + \frac{C_2}{(1+i)^2} + \frac{C_3}{(1+i)^3} + \ldots + \frac{C_n}{(1+i)^n} = \sum_{t=1}^{n} \frac{C_t}{(1+i)^t} \quad \textbf{(2.5)}$$

in which P = the sum of the individual present values of separate cash flows; C_1, C_2, C_3 ... C_n, refer to cash flows in time periods 1, 2, 3 ... n.

This is the general form of the present value formula. To put the formula in a more practical perspective, we will have

$$P = C_1(IF_1) + C_2(IF_2) + C_3(IF_3) + \ldots + C_n(IF_n) = \sum_{t=1}^{n} C_t(IF_t) \quad \textbf{(2.6)}$$

in which IF_1, IF_2, IF_3, ... IF_n represents relevant present value factors in different time periods, 1,2, 3 ... n.

If the time value of money is 10 per cent, we can easily find the present value of the following series of yearly payments (Example 2.6).

***Example* 2.6**

Year	*Cash flows*
1	₹500
2	1,000
3	1,500
4	2,000
5	2,500

In order to solve this problem, the present value of each individual cash flow discounted at 10 percent for the appropriate number of years is to be determined. The sum of all these individual values is then calculated to get the present value of the total stream. The present value factors required for the purpose are obtained from Table A-3. The results are summarised in Table 2.7.

TABLE 2.7 Present Value of a Mixed Stream of Cash Flows

Year end	*Cash flows*	*Present value factor (2) × (3)*	*Present value*
1	*2*	*3*	*4*
1	₹500	0.909	₹454.50
2	1,000	0.826	826.00
3	1,500	0.751	1,126.50
4	2,000	0.683	1,366.00
5	2,500	0.621	1,552.50
			5,325.50

Spreadsheet Solution 2.6

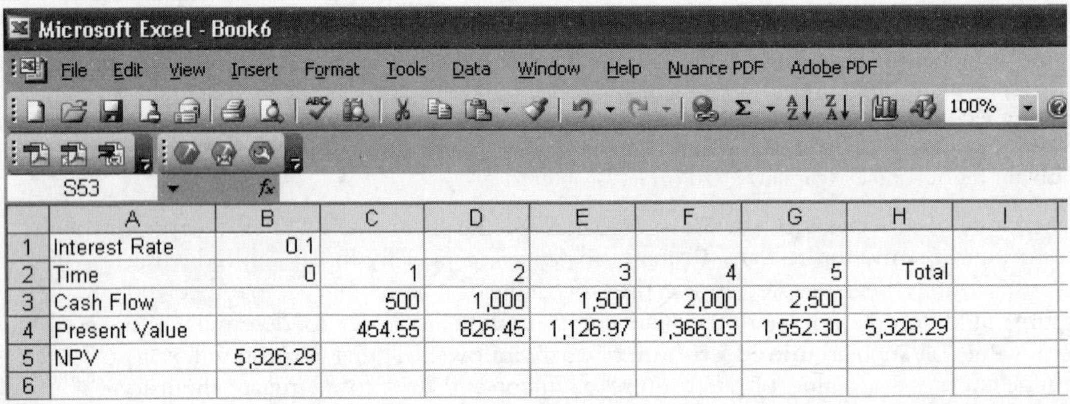

	A	B	C	D	E	F	G	H	I
1	Interest Rate	0.1							
2	Time	0	1	2	3	4	5	Total	
3	Cash Flow		500	1,000	1,500	2,000	2,500		
4	Present Value		454.55	826.45	1,126.97	1,366.03	1,552.30	5,326.29	
5	NPV	5,326.29							
6									

In cell C4 of the spreadsheet, enter the formula =C3/(1+B1)^C2. Copy this formula in cells D4 to G4. The sum of present values of each year's cash flow is calculated in cell H4 by entering the function =SUM(C4:G4). Present value of a series of payments can also be calculated by using the NPV function of Microsoft Excel. The function is entered in the cell B5. The results in cells H4 and B5 are identical.

Annuity We have already defined an annuity as a series of equal cash flows of an amount each time. Due to this nature of an annuity, a short cut is possible. Example 2.7 clarifies this method.

***Example* 2.7**

Mr X wishes to determine the present value of the annuity consisting of cash inflows of ₹1,000 per year for 5 years. The rate of interest he can earn from his investment is 10 per cent.

Solution

Table 2.8 shows the required calculations:

TABLE 2.8 Long Method for Finding Present Value of an Annuity of ₹1,000 for Five Years

Year end	*Cash flows*	*Present value factor*	*Present value (2) × (3)*
1	*2*	*3*	*4*
1	₹1,000	0.909	₹909.00
2	1,000	0.826	826.00
3	1,000	0.751	751.00
4	1,000	0.683	683.00
5	1,000	0.621	621.00
			3,790.00

Table 2.8 shows the long way of determining the present value of annuity. This method is the same as the one adopted for mixed stream. This procedure yields a present value of ₹3,791. However, calculations can be greatly cut short as the present value factor for each year is to be multiplied by the annual amount of ₹1,000. This method of calculating the present value of the annuity can also be expressed as an equation:

P = ₹1,000 (0.909) + ₹1,000 (0.826) + ₹1,000 (0.751) + ₹1,000 (0.683) + ₹1,000 (0.621)
= ₹3,790.

Simplifying the equation by taking out 1,000 as common factor outside the equation,

P = ₹1,000 (0.909 + 0.826 + 0.751 + 0.683 + 0.621) = ₹1,000 (3.790) = ₹3,790

Thus, the present value of an annuity can be found by multiplying the annuity amount by the sum of the present value factors for each year of the life of the annuity. Such ready-made calculations are available in Table A-4. This table presents the sum of present values for an annuity (PVIFA)/annuity discount factor (ADF) of ₹1 for wide ranges of interest rates, i, and number of years, n. From Table A-4 the sum ADF for five years at the rate of 10 per cent is found to be 3.791. Multiplying this factor by annuity amount (C) of ₹1,000 in this example gives ₹3,791. This answer is the same as the one obtained from the long method.

Present value interest factor for an annuity is the multiplier to calculate the present value of an annuity at a specified discount rate over a given period of time.

Now we can write the generalised formula to calculate the present value of an annuity:

$$P = \frac{C_1}{(1+i)} + \frac{C_2}{(1+i)^2} + \frac{C_3}{(1+i)^3} + \ldots + \frac{C_n}{(1+i)^n}$$

$$= C\left\{\frac{1}{(1+i)} + \frac{1}{(1+i)^2} + \frac{1}{(1+i)^3} + \ldots + \frac{1}{(1+i)^n}\right\} = C\left\{\sum_{t=1}^{n}\frac{1}{(1+i)^t}\right\} \quad \textbf{(2.7)}$$

The expression within brackets gives the appropriate annuity discount factor. Therefore, in more practical terms the method of determining present value is

$P = C\,(ADF)$ = ₹1,000 (3.791) = ₹3,791

It may be noted that the interest factor for the present value of an annuity is always less than the number of years the annuity runs, whereas in case of compounding the relevant factor is larger than the number of years the annuity runs. The facts given in Example 2.7 can be shown graphically (Fig. 2.2).

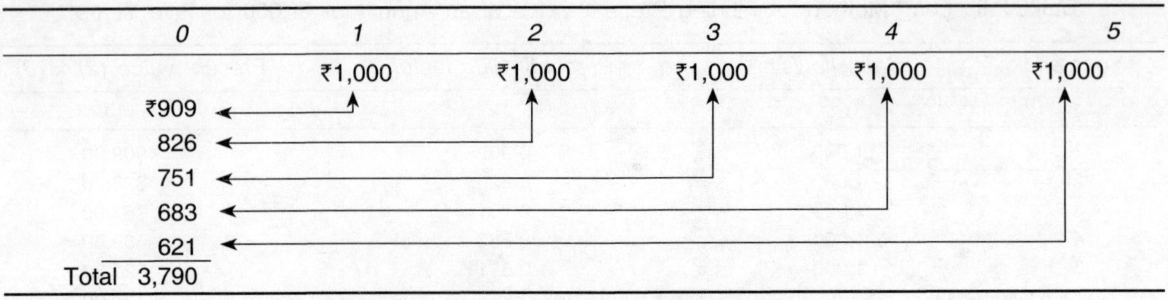

FIGURE 2.2 Graphic Illustration of Present Values

Spreadsheet Solution 2.7

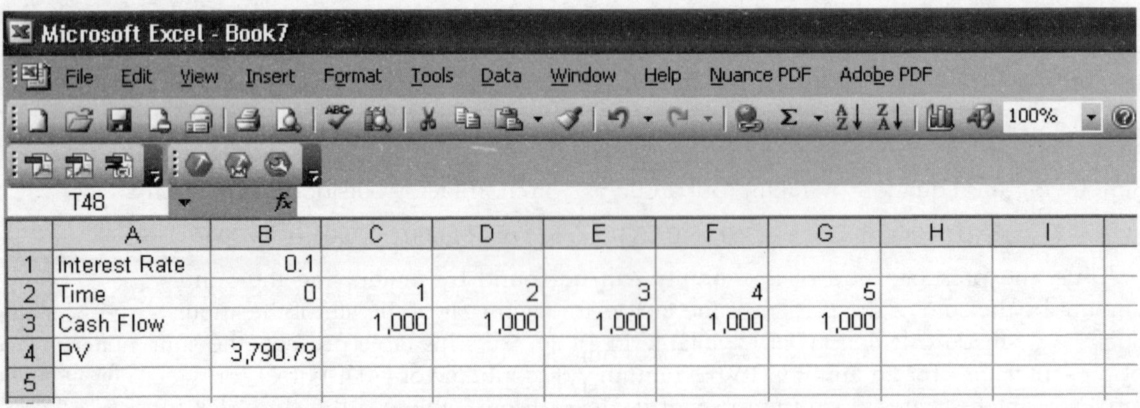

In Microsoft Excel, there is an inbuilt function, PV, for finding the present value of an annuity. In cell B4, enter the function =PV(B1,G2,-1000,0,0) to get the present value of the annuity.

Table A-4 can be easily applied to other problems relating to annuity also as shown in Example 2.8.

***Example* 2.8**

The ABC company expects to receive ₹1,00,000 for a period of 10 years from a new project it has just undertaken. Assuming a 10 per cent rate of interest, how much would be the present value of this annuity?

Solution

The appropriate ADF (annuity discount factor) of a 10 year annuity at 10 per cent is to be found from the 10th row (representing time period) against the 10 per cent interest column from Table A-4. This value is 6.145. Multiplying this factor by the annuity amount of ₹1,00,000, we find that the sum of the present value of annuity is ₹6,14,500.

Let us take an example to clarify how the problems involving varying cash inflows are to be worked out (Example 2.9).

***Example* 2.9**

If ABC company expects cash inflows from its investment proposal it has undertaken in time period zero, ₹2,00,000 and ₹1,50,000 for the first two years respectively and then expects annuity payment of ₹1,00,000 for the next eight years, what would be the present value of cash inflows, assuming a 10 per cent rate of interest?

Solution

We can solve the problem by applying the long method of finding the present values for each year's amount by consulting Table A-3. But we would like to apply the short-cut procedure as most of the payments are part of an annuity. Table 2.9 presents the relevant calculations:

TABLE 2.9 Present Value of Uneven Cash Inflows Having Annuity

1. Present value of ₹2,00,000 due in year 1 = (₹2,00,000 × 0.909)[a]	= ₹1,81,800
Present value of ₹1,50,000 due in year 2 = (₹1,50,000 × 0.826)[a]	= ₹1,23,900
2. Present value of eight year annuity with ₹1,00,000 receipts:	
(A) Present value at the beginning of year 3 = ₹1,00,000 (5.335)[b]	= ₹5,33,500
(B) Present value at the beginning of year 1 = ₹5,33,500 (0.826)	= ₹4,40,671[c]
3. Present value of total series = ₹7,46,371	

[a] Present value factor at 10 per cent from Table A-3.

[b] Present value factor at 10 per cent from Table A-4.

[c] (6.145 – 1.736) × ₹1,00,000

It may be noted that the present values (PV) of ₹2,00,000 and ₹1,50,000 (uneven cash flows) received at the end of the first and second years respectively are to be determined with reference to Table A-3. The present value of subsequent cash inflows of ₹1,00,000 each for 8 years is found in Table A-4. The value of an annuity of ₹1,00,000 for 8 years is found to be ₹5,33,500. The most important point to note here is that ₹5,33,500 is the present value at the beginning of the third year (end of year 2). Therefore, its present worth in time period zero would obviously be less than ₹5,33,500. This amount would have to be discounted back for two years at 10 percent. The present value factor for 2 years at 10 per cent discount is 0.826. Multiplying this sum by ₹5,33,500 we get ₹4,40,671. When the present values of the first two payments are added to the present value of the annuity component, we obtain the sum of the present value of the entire investment. For a better understanding of the problem, a graphic representation of the procedure of calculating the present value (PV) of such a problem has been given in Fig. 2.3.

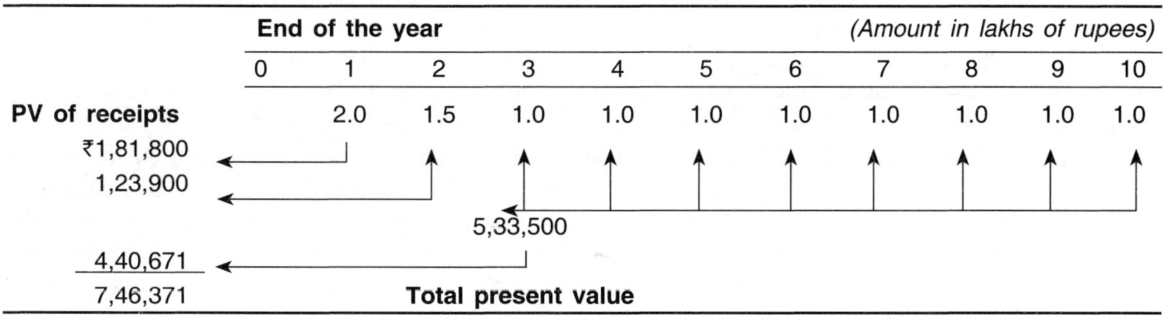

FIGURE 2.3 Graphic Presentation of Present Value of Mixed Streams

Spreadsheet Solution 2.8

Microsoft Excel - Book1

N21

	A	B	C	D	E	F	G	H
1	Interest Rate	0.1						
2	Time	0	1	2	3 to 10	Total		
3	Cash Flow		2,00,000	1,50,000	1,00,000			
4	PV at the end of year 2				5,33,492.62			
5	PV a the end of year 0		1,81,818.18	1,23,966.94	4,40,902.99	7,46,688.12		
6								

The problem is solved in two steps. First, the present values of cash flows for years 3 to 10 is found in cell E4 using the function =PV(B1,8, -100000,0,0). In the next step, the present value of this cash flow is found at the end of year 0 using the formula =E4/(1+B1)^2 in cell E5. The present values of cash flows in year 1 is found using the formula =C3/(1+B1)^C2 in cell C5. This formula is then copied to cell D5. Finally, the total present value is found in cell F5 using the formula =SUM(C5:E5).

Perpetuity is an annuity with an indefinite life, making continuous annual payments.

Present Value of an Infinite Life Annuity (Perpetuities) An annuity that goes on for ever is called a **perpetuity**. The present value of a perpetuity of ₹C amount is given by the formula:

$$C/i \tag{2.8}$$

This is because as the length of time for which the annuity is received increases, the annuity discount factor also increases but if the length goes on extending, this increase in the annuity factor slows down. In fact, as annuity life becomes infinitely long ($n \to \Phi$), the annuity discount factor approaches an upper limit. Such a limit is $1/i$. In other words, the appropriate factor is found by merely dividing 1 by the discount rate. The validity of this method can be seen by looking at the facts in Table A-4 for discount rates of 8, 12, 16 and 20 percent for a period of 50 years. As the number of years approaches 50, the value of these factors approaches, 12.23, 8.31, 6.25 and 5.00 respectively. Substituting 0.08, 0.12, 0.16 and 0.20 into our upper discount limit formula of $1/i$, we find the factors for finding the present value of perpetuities at these rates as 12.5, 8.33, 6.25 and 5.00.

***Example* 2.10**

Mr X wishes to find out the present value of investments which yield ₹500 in perpetuity, discounted at 5 per cent. The appropriate factor can be calculated by dividing 1 by 0.05. The resulting factor is 20. That is to be multiplied by the annual cash inflow of ₹500 to get the present value of the perpetuity, that is, ₹10,000. This should, obviously, be the required amount if a person can earn 5 per cent on investments. It is so because if the person has ₹10,000 and earns 5 per cent interest on it each year, ₹500 would constitute his cash inflow in terms of interest earnings, keeping intact his initial investments of ₹10,000.

LO 2.4 PRACTICAL APPLICATIONS OF COMPOUNDING AND PRESENT VALUE TECHNIQUES

In the preceding sections we have outlined compounding and discounting techniques. These techniques have a number of important applications, relevant to the task of the financial manager and investors. Some of these are illustrated here.

1. A financial manager is often interested in determining the size of annual payments to accumulate a future sum to repay an existing liability at some future date or to provide funds for replacement of an existing machine/asset after its useful life. Consider Example 2.11.

***Example* 2.11**

Company XYZ is establishing a sinking fund to retire ₹5,00,000, 8 per cent debentures, 10 years from today. The company plans to put a fixed amount into the fund each year for 10 years. The first payment will be made at the end of the current year. The company anticipates that the funds will earn 6 per cent a year. What equal annual contributions must be made to accumulate ₹5,00,000, 10 years from now?

Solution

The solution to this problem is closely related to the process of finding the compounded sum of an annuity. Table A-2 indicates that the annuity factor for 10 years at 6 per cent is 13.181. That is, one rupee invested at the end of each year for 10 years will accumulate to ₹13.181 at the end of the 10th year. In order to have ₹5,00,000 the required amount would be ₹5,00,000 ÷ 13.181 = ₹37,933.39. If ₹37,933.39 is deposited at the end of each year for ten years, there will be ₹5,00,000 in the account.

Spreadsheet Solution 2.9

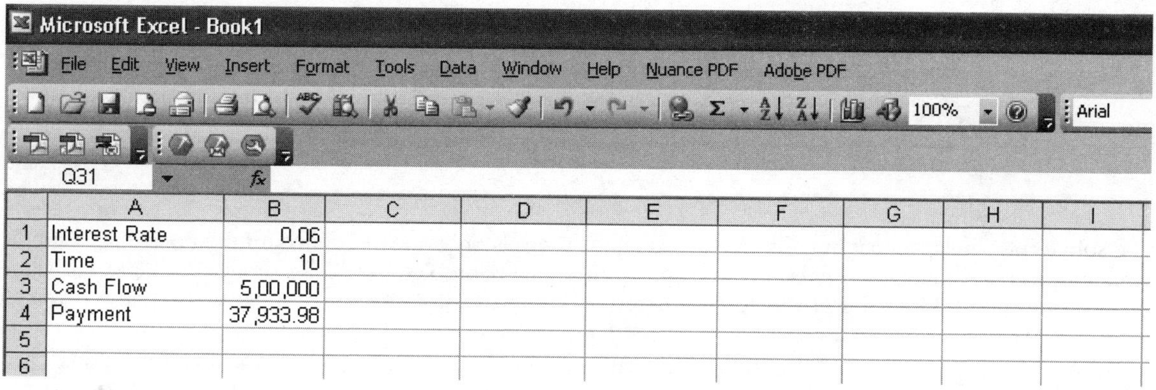

	A	B	C	D	E	F	G	H	I
1	Interest Rate	0.06							
2	Time	10							
3	Cash Flow	5,00,000							
4	Payment	37,933.98							
5									
6									

To find out the sinking fund payment, Excel function PMT can be used. The equation of this function in Excel format is PMT (rate, nper, PV, FV, type). Enter the rate of interest in cell B1, number of years in cell B2, and the amount to be accumulated in cell B3. In cell B4 enter the function =PMT(B1,B2,0,-B3,0). Since sinking fund accumulation represents a future value, the PV is to be entered as 0 and the sum to be accumulated is entered as FV. The result would be the amount of the sinking fund payment.

2. When the amount of loan taken from financial institutions or commercial banks is to be repaid in a specified number of equal annual instalments, the financial manager will be interested in determining the amount of the annual instalment. Consider Example 2.12.

***Example* 2.12**

A limited company borrows from a commercial bank ₹10,00,000 at 12 per cent rate of interest to be paid in equal annual end-of-year instalments. What would the size of the instalment be? Assume the repayment period is 5 years.

Solution

The problem relates to loan amortisation. The loan amortisation process involves finding out the future payments over the term of the loan whose present value at the interest rate just equals the initial principal borrowed. In this case, the company has borrowed ₹10,00,000 at 12 per cent. In order to determine the size of the payments, the 5-year annuity discounted at 12 per cent that has a present value of ₹10,00,000 is to be determined.

Present value, P, of an n year annuity of amount C is found by multiplying the annual amount, C, by the appropriate annuity discount factor (ADF) from Table A-4, that is, $P = C$ (ADF), or $C = P$/ADF in which P is the amount of loan, that is, (₹10,00,000), ADF is the present value of an annuity factor corresponding to 5 years and 12 per cent. This value is 3.605 as seen from Table A-4. Substituting the values, we have

$$C = ₹10,00,000/3.605 = ₹2,77,393$$

Thus, ₹2,77,393 is to be paid at the end of each year for 5 years to repay the principal and interest on ₹10,00,000 at the rate of 12 per cent.

Spreadsheet Solution 2.10

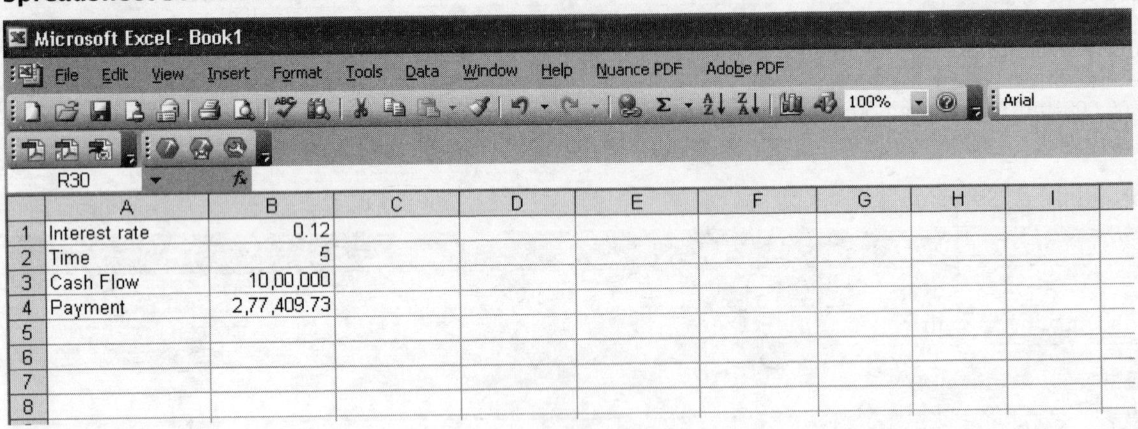

	A	B
1	Interest rate	0.12
2	Time	5
3	Cash Flow	10,00,000
4	Payment	2,77,409.73

The solution is similar to that in the previous example. There is only one difference. In the preceding example, the sum to be accumulated represented a future value. In this problem, the loan represents a present value. While using the PMT function, PV is to be entered as B3 and FV is to be entered as 0. The entry in cell B4 will be =PMT(B1,B2,-B3,0,0). The result would be the amount of annual installment.

3. An investor may often be interested in finding the rate of growth in dividend paid by a company over a period of time. It is because growth in dividends has a significant bearing on the price of the shares. In such a situation compound interest tables are used. Let us illustrate it by an Example (2.13).

***Example* 2.13**

Mr X wishes to determine the rate of growth of the following stream of dividends he has received from a company:

Year	*Dividend (per share)*	
1	₹2.50	
2	2.60 }	1
3	2.74 }	2
4	2.88 }	3
5	3.04 }	4

Solution

Growth has been experienced for four years. In order to determine this rate of growth, the amount of dividend received in year 5 has been divided by the amount of dividend received in the first year. This gives us a compound factor which is 1.216 (₹3.04 ÷ ₹2.50). Now, we have to look at Table A-1 which gives the compounded values of ₹1 at various rates of interest (for our purpose the growth rate) and number of years. We have to look to the compound factor 1.216 against fourth year in the row side. Looking across year 4 of Table A-1 shows that the factor for 5 per cent is exactly 1.216; therefore, the rate of growth associated with the dividend stream is 5 per cent.

Spreadsheet Solution 2.11

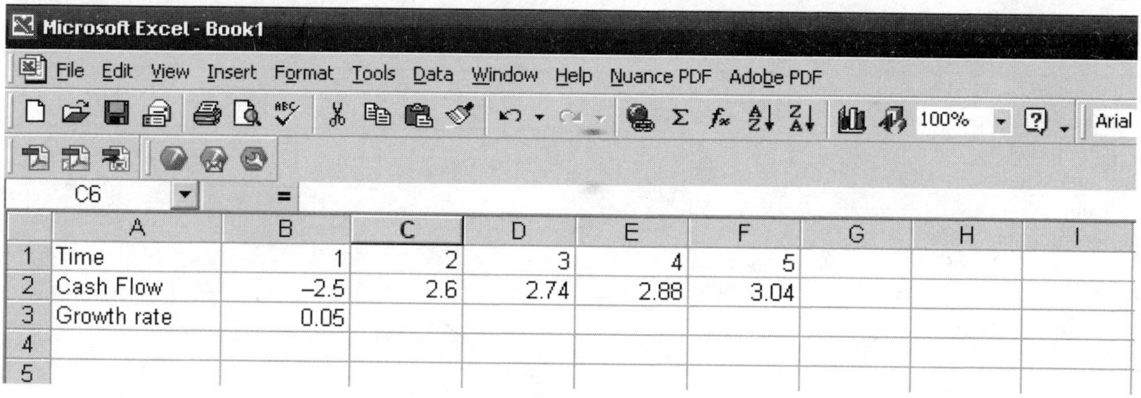

	A	B	C	D	E	F	G	H	I
1	Time	1	2	3	4	5			
2	Cash Flow	–2.5	2.6	2.74	2.88	3.04			
3	Growth rate	0.05							
4									
5									

To find out the growth rate, the Excel function RATE can be used. The equation of this function in Excel format is RATE (nper, PMT, PV, FV, Type, Guess). The initial figure is entered as a negative figure as has been done in cell B2. In cell B3, the function is entered as =RATE((F1-B1),0,B2,F2,0). The 'guess' input is to be left blank. The result would be the growth rate.

4. To determine the current values of debentures, the present value Tables A-3 and A-4 can be of immense use. The cash flow from a debenture consists of two parts: first, interest inflows at periodic intervals, say, semi-annually or annually and, second, the repayment of the principal on maturity. Since the interest payments on a debenture are made periodically throughout its life, it is easy to calculate the present value of this annuity type interest inflow by consulting Table A-4 and the present value of the face value of the debentures can be ascertained by discounting it at the market rate of interest by consulting Table A-3. The sum of the two values so obtained will be current worth of a debenture. If the interest is paid after six months, the factors are obtained for one-half of the discount rate and the number of years is doubled. Consider Example 2.14.

***Example* 2.14**

Suppose a particular debenture pays interest at 8 per cent per annum. The debenture is to be paid after 10 years at a premium of 5 per cent. The face value of the debenture is ₹1,000. Interest is paid after every six months. What is the current worth of the debenture, assuming the appropriate market discount rate on debentures of similar risk and maturity is equal to the debenture's coupon rate, that is, 8 per cent?

Solution

Since the interest is compounded semi-annually over 10 years, the relevant compounding period equals to 20 and the discount rate will be one-half (4 per cent) of the yearly interest of 8 per cent. In other words, the investor will have an annuity of ₹40 (4 per cent of ₹1,000) for a compounding period of 20 years. The present value factor for 20 years and 4 per cent from Table A-4 is 13.59 which, when multiplied by ₹40, gives us a present value for the interest cash flows of ₹543.60. The present value of a maturity value of ₹1,050 (as the debenture is to be redeemed at 5 per cent premium) will be found by multiplying ₹1,050 by the factor for the present value of ₹1 to be received 20 years from now at 4 per cent. The relevant present value factor from Table A-3 is 0.456. Multiplied by ₹1,050 maturity value, it gives us a present sum of ₹478.8. The total value of the debentures would be equal to the total of these two values, that is, ₹543.60 + ₹478.8 = ₹1,022.4.

Spreadsheet Solution 2.12

Microsoft Excel - Book10

S33

	A	B	C	D	E	F	G	H
1	Interest rate per period	0.04						
2	Number of payments	20						
3	Face Value	1,000						
4	Coupon	40						
5	Redemption Value	1,050.00						
6	PV of coupons	543.61						
7	PV of Redemption Value	479.21						
8	Current Price	1,022.82						
9								

Enter the interest rate per period in cell B1. Since the yearly rate of interest is 8 per cent and is payable half-yearly, the interest rate per period will be 4 per cent. Over a period of 10 years, 20 coupon payments will be received. Therefore, 20 will be entered in cell B2. The face value of the debenture is entered in cell B3. Coupon per period is calculated in cell B4 using the formula =B1*B3. In cell B5, the redemption value of the debenture will be entered. Cell B6 calculates the present value of coupon payments using the Excel function PV. The present value of the redemption value is calculated in cell B7 using the formula =B5/(1+B1)^B2. The current price is the sum of cells B6 and B7 and this is calculated in cell B8 using the formula =SUM(B6:B7).

APPENDIX 2-A

This Appendix further develops some aspects of application of compounding and discounting techniques. Those not interested in the detailed treatment of these aspects may skip over the Appendix.

Effective Rates of Interest and Discount

The effective rate of discount is used in computing the present values of certain types of annuities. Assuming i as the rate of interest per annum, an investor who deposits ₹1 at the beginning of the year would receive ₹(1 + i) at the end of the year. If he demands the interest payment in the beginning of the period, as money has time value, he would obviously get an amount less than i (assumed to be d). He would effectively lend ₹(1 – d) at the beginning of the year and get back ₹1 after one year. The relationship between i and d is called the effective rate of discount per annum. Symbolically,

$$d = \frac{i}{(1+i)} \qquad \textbf{(2-A.1)}$$

***Example* 2-A.1**

Given that PVIF (i, 1) = 0.95 find the value of i and d.

Solution

PVIF (i, 1) = 0.95

or $$\frac{1}{(1+i)} = 0.95 \qquad i = 0.0526$$

$$d = \frac{i}{(1+i)} = \frac{0.0526}{1.0526} = 0.05 = 5 \text{ per cent}$$

Nominal Rates of Interest and Discount

When compounding/discounting has to be done at intervals less than a year, a distinction should be made between (i) nominal and (iii) effective rates of interest. The coupon rate of interest is called the *nominal rate of interest.* The nominal rate of interest differs from the effective rate of interest due to the frequency of compounding (e.g. annual, half-yearly, quarterly, monthly) with the nominal rate. With annual compounding/conversion, the nominal rate and the effective rate would be the same. The effective rate of interest is higher and increases with an increase in the frequency of compounding. Consider Example 2-A.2.

***Example* 2-A.2**

The Premier Bank Ltd (PBL) offers 10 per cent interest on a deposit of one year. Assuming (i) annual, (ii) half-yearly and (iii) quarterly frequency of interest payments, compute the effective rates of interests in the three alternatives.

Solution

Assuming a deposit of ₹1,000, the computation of the effective rates of interest is shown below.

	Frequency of compounding		
	Annual	*Half-yearly*	*Quarterly*
Beginning amount	₹1,000.00	₹1,000.00	₹1,000.00
Interest	100.00	102.50	103.82
Effective rate of interest	0.10*	0.1025**	0.1038***

*(₹100 ÷ ₹1,000) **(₹102.50 ÷ ₹1,000) ***(₹103.82 ÷ ₹1,000)

We can determine the effective rate given the nominal rate and *vice-versa.* Denoting the nominal rate of interest compounded/convertible PTHLY (where P represents the frequency of payments during the year such as 12 for monthly payment, 4 for quarterly payment and two for half-yearly payment) as $i^{(p)}$ and the corresponding effective rate of interest as i, symbolically

$$i = \left[1+\frac{i^{(p)}}{p}\right] - 1 \quad \textbf{(2-A.2)}$$

or

$$i = \left[1+\frac{i^{(P)}}{P}\right] - 1 \quad \textbf{(2-A-3)}$$

Example **2-A.3**

Assuming (a) $i = 0.0125$ and (b) $i^{(2)} = 0.1025$, find the values of (1) $i^{(4)}$ and (2) $i^{(12)}$.

Solution

(a) $i^{(4)} = [(1.1025)^{1/4} - 1]\ 4$

$= 0.0988 = 9.88$ per cent

(b) $i = \left[1+\dfrac{0.1025}{2}\right]^2 - 1 = 0.0151 = 10.51$ per cent

$i^{(12)} = [(1.051)^{1/12} - 1]\ 12 = 0.1004 = 10.04$ per cent

Similar to the relationship between the nominal and effective rates of interest, the mathematical relationship between effective and nominal rates of discount is given by Equations 2-A.4 and 2-A.5. The nominal rates of interest and discount rate employed in computing the present value of annuities payable P-thly.

$$d = 1 - \left[1-\frac{d^{(p)}}{p}\right]^p \quad \textbf{(2-A.4)}$$

and

$$d^{(p)} = [1 - (1 - d)^{1/p}\ ]p \quad \textbf{(2-A-5)}$$

where

$$d = \frac{i}{1+i} \quad \textbf{(2-A.1)}$$

Example **2-A.4**

Assuming $d^{(12)} = 0.12$ and $(i)^2 = 0.12$ find the value of (a) d and (b) $d^{(4)}$

Solution

(a) $d = \left[1-\left(1-\dfrac{0.12}{12}\right)^{12}\right] = 0.1136 = 11.36$ per cent

(b) $(i)^2 = 0.12$

$i = \{(1.06)^2 - 1] = 0.1236$

$$d = \frac{0.1236}{1.1236} = 0.1100 = 11 \text{ per cent}$$

$$d^{(4)} = [1 - (1 - 0.11)^{1/4}]\ 4 = 0.1148 = 11.48 \text{ per cent}$$

Alternatively, $d^{(1)} = \left[1 - \left(1 + \frac{i^{(p)}}{p}\right)^{-p}\right]$

Therefore $d^{(4)} = \left[1 - \left(1 + \frac{0.12}{2}\right)^{-2/4}\right]$

$$= [1 - (1.06)^{-1/2}]\ 4 = 0.1148 = 11.48 \text{ per cent}$$

The relationship between various nominal and effective rates of interest and discount is given in Table A.5.

Present Value of an Annuity Payable PTHLY

An annuity payable PTHLY refers to equated/level payments to be made in advance (beginning)/ arrears (end) at intervals less than one year where p denotes the frequency of payment (e.g. 12 for monthly payment, 4 for quarterly payment and 2 for half-yearly payment). The present values of an annuity payable PTHLY in (a) arrears and (b) advance respectively are computed using Equations 2-A-6 and 2-A.7.

$$\text{PVIFA}\ (i,\ n) = \frac{i}{i^{(p)}}\ \text{PVIFA}\ (i,\ n) \tag{2-A.6}$$

$$\text{PVIF}\overline{\text{A}}_{\text{p}}\ (i,\ n) = \frac{i}{d^{(p)}}\ \text{PVIFA}\ (i,\ n) \tag{2-A.7}$$

The value of $\frac{i}{i^{(p)}}$ and $\frac{i}{d^{(p)}}$ are given in Table A-5.

***Example* 2-A.5**

The current lease rates quoted by the First Leasing Ltd (FLL) on its lease contracts are: (i) ₹18/₹1,000/month and (ii) ₹12.5/₹1,000/month for 3-year and 5-year terms respectively. While the monthly lease rentals on the 3-year contract are payable in arrears, those for the 5-year contract are payable in advance. Assuming 10 per cent marginal cost of debt to the lessee, calculate the present values of the lease payments.

Solution

(a) Present value of lease payments on the 3-year contract (in arrears)

$= (₹18 \times 12) \times \text{PVIFA}_{12}\ (10,3)$

$= ₹216 \times \frac{i}{i^{(12)}} \times \text{PVIFA}\ (i,\ 3)$ where $i = 0.10$ (10%)

$= ₹216 \times 1.045$ (Table A.5) $\times 2.487$ (Table A-4) $= ₹561$

(b) Present value of lease payments on the 5-year contract (in advance)

$= (₹12.5 \times 12) \times \text{PVIF}\overline{\text{A}}_{12}\ (10,3)$

$= ₹150 \times \frac{i}{d^{(p)}} \times \text{PVIF}\overline{\text{A}}\ (i,\ 5)$ where $i = 0.10$

$= ₹150 \times 1.0534$ (Table A-5) $\times 3.791$ (Table A-4) $= ₹599$

Loan Repayment Schedule for Annuities

Each instalment of an annuity payable PTHLY has two components: **(i)** the capital (repayment of principal) and **(ii)** the interest component. To identify these two components, a loan repayment schedule is to be developed. We illustrate below loan repayment schedule with reference to annuities payable (a) once a year and (b) PTHLY.

***Example* 2-A.6**

The lease rentals for a 5-year contract are ₹300/₹1,000 payable annually in arrears. Assuming no salvage value, compute the rate of interest implied by the contract and develop a lease amortisation schedule.

Solution

The implied rate of interest, i, = ₹300 × PVIFA (i, 5) = ₹1,000

PVIFA (i, 5) = 3.333 (The PVIFA closet to 3.333 is 3.52 at 15 per cent)

PVIFA (15, 5) (Table A-4) = 3.352

Therefore, i = 0.15 = 15 per cent.

Lease Amortisation Schedule

Year	*Outstanding amount at the beginning*	*Instalment*	*Interest content (0.15)*	*Capital content*
1	₹1,000	₹300	₹150	₹150
2	850	300	128	172
3	678	300	102	198
4	480	300	72	228
5	252	300	38	262

***Example* 2-A.7**

A hire-purchase plan requires a hirer to pay ₹91.68 per thousand per month (ptpm) in arrear over a 12-month period. Assuming a cash purchase price of ₹1,000 and no salvage value (a) compute the effective rate of interest implied by the plan, (b) develop the repayment schedule from the viewpoint of the hirer and (c) calculate the effective and the nominal rates of interest per annum.

Solution

(a) The implied effective rate of interest, i_m

₹91.68 × PVIFA (i_m, 12) = ₹1,000

PVIFA (i_m,12) = 10.9075

PVIFA (1,12) = 11.255 (Table A-4) and PVIFA (2,12) = 10.5753 (Table A-4)

By interpolation,

$$i_m = 0.01 + \left[0.01 \times \left\{\frac{10.9075 - 11.2551}{10.5753 - 11.251}\right\}\right]$$

$$= 0.01 + \left[0.01 \times \left(\frac{0.3476}{0.6798}\right)\right] = 0.015 = 1.5 \text{ per cent}$$

(b) **Loan Repayment Schedule**

Month	*Beginning amount*	*Instalment*	*Interest content (1.5)*	*Capital content*
1	₹1,000	₹91.68	₹15.00	₹76.68
2	923.32	91.68	13.85	77.83
3	845.49	91.68	12.68	79.00
4	768.49	91.68	11.50	80.18

(Contd)

(Contd)

5	686.31	91.68	10.29	81.38
6	604.93	91.68	9.07	82.61
7	522.32	91.68	7.83	83.85
8	438.47	91.68	6.58	85.10
9	353.37	91.68	5.30	86.38
10	266.99	91.68	4.00	87.67
11	179.32	91.68	2.69	88.99
12	90.33	91.68	1.35	90.33

(c) Effective rate of interest and nominal rate of interest per annum
Effective rate of interest = $(1.015)^{12} - 1 = 0.1956$ = 19.56 per cent
Nominal rate of interest per annum = $0.015 \times 12 = 0.18$ = 18 per cent

Example 2-A.8

A lease contract involves payment of ₹27 pm at the end of every month over a 5-year period. Develop a annual repayment schedule inherent in the contract.

Solution

Annual rate of interest (i) = (₹27 × 12) × $PVIFA_{12}$ (i, 5) = ₹1,000

$PVIFA_{12}$ (i, 5) = 3.086 [₹1,000 ÷ ₹324 (₹27 × 12)]

or $\frac{i}{i^{(12)}} \times PVIFA\ (i, 5) = 3.086$

PVIFA (22,5) = 3.142 (Table A-4) and PVIFA (24,5) = 3.035 (Table A-4) are the closest values to 3.086
By interpolation,

$$i = 0.22 + \left[0.02 \times \left(\frac{3.086 - 3.142}{3.035 - 3.142}\right)\right] = 0.2305 = 23.05 \text{ per cent}$$

$$i^{(12)} = [(1.2305^{1/12} - 1] \times 12 = 0.2092 = 20.92 \text{ per cent}$$

Equivalent annual interest instalment

$$= ₹27 \times 12 \times \frac{0.2305}{0.2305^{(12)}} = ₹357$$

Repayment Schedule Based on Equivalent Annual Instalments

Year	*Outstanding amount at the beginning*	*Equivalent annual instalment*	*Interest content (0.2305)*	*Capital content*
1	₹1,000.0	₹357	₹230.5	₹126.5
2	873.5	357	201.3	155.7
3	717.8	357	165.5	191.5
4	526.3	357	121.3	235.7
5	290.6	357	67.0	290.6

The required repayment schedule can be obtained by deducting the interest on interest of ₹33 [i.e. ₹357 – (₹27 ÷ 12)] from the interest and instalment amount of the repayment schedule based on equivalent annual instalments.

Required Repayment Schedule

Year	Outstanding amount at the beginning	Equivalent annual instalment	Interest content (0.2305)	Capital content
1	₹1,000.0	₹324	₹197.5	₹126.5
2	873.5	324	168.3	155.7
3	717.8	324	132.5	191.5
4	526.3	324	88.3	235.7
5	290.6	324	34.0	290.6

Effective and Flat Rates of Interest

As shown above in the loan repayment/amortisation schedule, effective rate of interest (also called annual percentage rate, APR) is applied to the diminishing balances of the loan amount to determine the interest content of each instalment. When the rate of interest is applied to the original amount of the loan to determine the interest component, the interest rate is called as the **flat rate**. The computation of the flat rate of interest and the APR/effective rate of interest is illustrated below.

***Example* 2-A.9**

(Flat Rate and APR) From the undermentioned facts, develop the repayment schedule for the three consumer financing schemes (A), (B) and (C) using the flat rate of interest. Also, compute the effective rate of interest (APR) using both long and short-cut approaches.

- Loan amount, ₹2,40,000
- Repayment period, 3 years
- Rate of interest (flat), 6 per cent
- Repayment pattern: Scheme (A), loan to be repaid in three equal instalments; Scheme (B), loan with interest to be repaid in three equated annual instalments; and Scheme (C), loan with interest to be repaid in three equal instalments.

Solution

Repayment Schedule for Scheme A

Year	Capital content	Interest content	Instalment amount	Loans outstanding after repayment
(1)	(2)	(3)	(4)	(5)
1	₹80,000	₹14,400	₹94,400	₹1,60,000
2	80,000	14,400	89,600	80,000
3	80,000	14,400	84,800	—

Repayment Schedule for Scheme B

Year	Instalment@@ amount	Interest content	Capital content	Loans outstanding after repayment
(1)	(2)	(3)	(4)	(5)
1	₹89,787	₹14,400	₹75,387	₹1,64,613
2	89,787	9,877	79,910	84,703
3	89,787	5,082	84,705	—

@@₹2,40,000 ÷ 2.673 [i.e. PVIFA (6,3)] = ₹89,787

Repayment Schedule for Scheme C

Year	*Instalment** amount*	*Interest content*	*Capital content*	*Loans outstanding after repayment*
(1)	*(2)*	*(3)*	*(4)*	*(5)*
1	₹94,400	₹14,400	₹80,000	₹1,60,000
2	94,400	14,400	80,000	80,000
3	94,400	14,400	80,000	—

**Annual instalment = (Loan amount + Interest for 3 years) ÷ 3 = [₹2,40,000 + ₹43,200 (₹2,40,000 × 0.06 × 3)] = ₹2,83,200 ÷ 3 = ₹94,400

Computation of APR/Effective Rate of Interest, *i*:

₹94,400 × PVIFA (i, 3) = ₹2,40,000

or PVIFA (i, 3) = ₹2,40,000 ÷ ₹94,400 = 2.542

At i = 0.08 = PVIFA = 2.577 (Table A-4)

i = 0.09 = PVIFA = 2.531 (Table A-4)

By Interpolation, i = 9 per cent

Computation of APR, using short-cut approach:

$$i = 2F\left[\frac{n}{n+1}\right] \qquad \textbf{(2-A.8)}$$

or

$$i = \frac{2F}{\dfrac{n+1}{n} + F\left(\dfrac{n-3m+2}{3m}\right)} \qquad \textbf{(2-A.9)}$$

where i = APR

F = flat rate

n = total number of repayments

m = number of repayments per unit of time

Substitution the values, the APR = 9.7 per cent.

SUMMARY

LO 2.1 Money has time value. A rupee today is more valuable than a rupee a year hence. A rupee a year hence has less value than a rupee today. Money has, thus, a future value and a present value. Although alternatives can be assessed by either compounding to find future value or discounting to find present value, financial managers rely primarily on present value techniques as they are at zero time (t = 0) when making decisions.

LO 2.2 Future value relies on compound interest to measure the value of future amounts. When interest is compounded, the initial principal/deposit in one period, along with the interest earned on it, becomes the beginning principal of the following period and so on. Interest can be compounded annually, semi-annually (half-yearly), quarterly, monthly and so on. The more frequently interest is compounded, the larger the future amount that would be accumulated and the higher the effective interest rate. The interest rate formula and the basic equation for the future value of a single amount are given below:

(i) Basic formula of compounding: $A = P(1 + i)^n$

(ii) Compounding more than once a year: $P[1 + i/n]^{mn} = A$

(iii) Compounded sum of an annuity: $Sn = CVIFA \times A$

LO 2.3

Present value represents an opposite of future value. The present value of a future amount is the amount of money today equivalent to the given future amount on the basis of a certain return on the current amount. The interest factor formula and the basic equation of the present value are given below:

(i) Basic formula: $A[1/(1 + i)^n]$

(ii) Present value of a series of cash flows: $= \sum_{t=1}^{N} \frac{C_t}{(1+i)^t} = \sum_{t=1}^{n} C_t (IF_t)$

(iii) Present value of an annuity: $C\left[\sum_{t=1}^{N} \frac{1}{(1+i)^t}\right]$

The annual deposit to accumulate a given future sum can be found by solving the equation for the future value of an annuity for the annual payment. A loan can be amortised into equal payments by solving the equation for the present value of an equity for the annual payment. Interest or growth rates can be estimated by finding the unknown interest in the equation for the present value of either a single amount or an annuity.

The effective rate of discount (d) is used in computing the present values of certain types of annuities. Symbolically, $d = \frac{i}{1+i}$

The coupon rate of interest is called nominal rate of interest. With more frequent compounding, effective rate of interest is different from the nominal rate of interest. Symbolically,

$$i = \left[1 + \frac{i^{(p)}}{p}\right]^p - 1 \quad \text{or} \quad i = [(1 + i)^{1/p} - 1]p$$

LO 2.4

A typical lease/hire-purchase contract calls for equated (level) payments to be made either in advance or in arrears at intervals less than one year. Such payments are annuity payable PTHY, where P denotes the frequency of payment such as half-yearly, quarterly and so on. Symbolically, the present value of a level annuity payable PTHLY in arrear and advance are:

$$PVIFA_p\,(i, n) = \frac{i}{i^{(p)}}\;PVIFA\,(i, n)$$

$$PVIF\bar{A}_p\,(i, n) = \frac{i}{d^{(p)}} PVIF\,(i, n)$$

If the rate of interest is applied to the original amount of the loan, to determine the interest of each loan, we refer to the rate as the flat rate. When the rate of interest is applied to the diminishing balances of the loan amount to determine the interest content of each instalment, it is called the effective rate of interest. Symbolically, effective rate of interest/annual percentage rate (APR) is given by the following equation:

$$i = 2F\left[\frac{n}{n+1}\right] \text{ or } i = \frac{2F}{\frac{n+1}{n} + F\left(\frac{n-3m+2}{3m}\right)}$$

SOLVED PROBLEMS

P.2.1 An investor deposits ₹100 in a bank account for 5 years at 8 per cent interest. Find out the amount which he will have in his account if interest is compounded (a) annually (b) semi-annually (6-monthly), (c) quarterly and (d) continuously. LO 2.2 LOD E

Solution $F_n = P(1 + i/m)n \times m = P \times \text{FVIF}_{i/m,\, n \times m}$

(a) Annual compounding (m = 1): F_5 = ₹100 $(1 + 0.08/1)^5$ = ₹100 (1.4693) = ₹146.93

(b) Semi-annual compounding (m = 2): F_5 = ₹100 $(1 + 0.08/2)^{5 \times 2} = P \times \text{FVIF}_{4,10}$ = ₹100(1.4802) = ₹148.02

(c) Quarterly compounding (m = 4): F_5 = ₹100 $(1 + 0.08/4)^{5 \times 4} = P \times \text{FVIF}_{2,20}$ = ₹100(1.4859) = ₹148.59

(d) Continuous compounding: $F_n = P \times e^{i \times n} = F_5$ = ₹100 $(2.71828)^{0.08 \times 5}$ = ₹100 $(2.71828)^{0.4}$ = ₹100 (1.4918) = ₹149.18

P.2.2 If the discount/required rate is 10 per cent, compute the present value of the cashflow streams detailed below: (a) ₹100 at the end of year 1; (b) ₹100 at the end of year 4; (c) ₹100 at the end of (i) year 3 and (ii) year 5 and (d) ₹100 for the next 10 years (for years 1 through 10). LO 2.3 LOD M

Solution $P = F_n[1/(1+i)^n] = F_n \times \text{PVIF}_{i,\,n}$

(a) ₹100 at the end of year 1 = ₹100$[1/(1.10)^1]$ = ₹100 × $\text{PVIF}_{10,1}$ = ₹100 × 0.9091 = ₹90.91.

(b) ₹100 at the end of year 4 = ₹100$[1/(1.10)^4]$ = ₹100 × $\text{PVIF}_{10,4}$ = ₹100 × 0.683 = ₹68.3

(c) ₹100 at the end of (i) year 3 and (ii) year 5 = ₹100$[1/(1.10)^3]$ + ₹100$[1/(1.10)^5]$ = (₹100 × $\text{PVIF}_{10,3}$) + (₹100 × $\text{PVIF}_{10,5}$) = (₹100 × 0.7513) + (₹100 × 0.6209) = ₹75.13 + ₹62.09 = ₹137.22.

(d) ₹100 for the next 10 years (annuity)
$P_n = A \times \text{PVIFA}_{i,\,n}$ = ₹100 × $\text{PVIFA}_{10,\,10}$ = ₹100(6.1446) = ₹614.46.

P.2.3 Compute the present/discounted value of the following future cash inflows, assuming a required rate of 10 per cent: (a) ₹100 a year for years 5 through 10 and (b) ₹100 a year for years 1 through 3, nil in years 4 through 5 and ₹100 a year for years 6 through 10. LO 2.3 LOD M

Solution

(a) P = ₹100($\text{PVIFA}_{10,10}$) – ₹100($\text{PVIFA}_{10,4}$) = ₹100(6.1446) – ₹100(3.1699) = ₹614.46 – ₹316.99 = ₹297.47.

(b) P = ₹100($\text{PVIFA}_{10,3}$) + [₹100($\text{PVIFA}_{10,10}$) – ₹100($\text{PVIFA}_{10,5}$)] = (₹100 × 2.4869) + [(₹100 × 6.1446) – (₹100 × 3.7908)] = ₹248.69 + (₹614.46 – ₹379.08) = ₹248.69 + ₹235.38 = ₹484.07.

P.2.4 An executive is about to retire at the age of 60. His employer has offered him two post-retirement options: (a) ₹20,00,000 lump sum, (b) ₹2,50,000 for 10 years. Assuming 10 per cent interest, which is a better option? LO 2.4 LOD M

Solution $P_n = A \times \text{PVIFA}_{i,\,n} = P_{10}$ = ₹2,50,000($\text{PVIFA}_{10,10}$) = ₹2,50,000(6.1446) = ₹15,36,150. Since the lumpsum of ₹20,00,000 is worth more now, the executive should opt for it.

P.2.5 Compute the present value of a perpetuity of ₹100 year if the discount rate is 10 per cent. LO 2.3 LOD E

Solution Present value of a perpetuity = A/i = ₹100/0.10 = ₹1,000.

P.2.6 ABC Ltd has ₹10 crore bonds outstanding. Bank deposits earn 10 per cent per annum. The bonds will be redeemed after 15 years for which purpose ABC Ltd wishes to create a sinking fund. How much amount should be deposited to the sinking fund each year so that ABC Ltd would have in the sinking fund ₹10 crore to retire its entire issue of bonds? LO 2.4 LOD M

Solution $A = S_n/\text{FVIFA}_{i,\,n} = S_{15}$ = ₹10 crore/$\text{FVIFA}_{10,15}$ = ₹10 crore/31.772 = ₹3,14,742.54.

P.2.7 ABC Ltd has borrowed ₹30,00,000 from Canbank Home Finance Ltd to finance the purchase of a house for 15 years. The rate of interest on such loans is 24 per cent per annum. Compute the amount of annual payment/instalment.

LO 2.4 LOD M

Solution $P_n = A \times \text{PVIFA}_{i,\,n}$

$A = P_n/\text{PVIFA}_{i,\,n} = \text{P}_{15}$ = ₹30,00,000/$\text{PVIFA}_{24,15}$ = ₹30,00,000/4.0013 = ₹7,49,756.32.

P.2.8 XYZ Ltd has borrowed ₹5,00,000 to be repaid in fival equal annual payments (interest and principal both). The rate of interest is 16 per cent. Compute the amount of each payment.

LO 2.4 LOD M

Solution $A = P_n/\text{PVIFA}_{i,\,n} = P_5/\text{PVIFA}_{16,5}$ = ₹5,00,000/3.2743 = ₹1,52,704.39

P.2.9 Assume the rate of interest is 12 per cent. Compute the annual percentage/effective rate (AP/ER) if interest is paid (a) annually, (b) semi-annually, (c) quarterly and (d) monthly. What are the implications of more frequent payments of interest?

LO 2.4 LOD D

Solution AP/ER = $(1 + r/m)^m - 1.0$

(a) Interest paid at the end of the year (m = 1):
AP/ER = $(1 + 0.12/1)^1 - 1.0 = 1.12 - 1.0 = 0.12$ = 12 per cent

(b) Interest paid at the end of each 6-month period (m = 2):
AP/ER = $(1 + 0.12/2)^2 - 1.0 = (1.06)^2 - 1.0 = 1.1236 - 1.0 = 0.1236$ = 12.36 per cent.

(c) Interest paid at the end of each quarter (m = 4):
AP/ER = $(1 + 0.12/42^4 - 1.0 = (1.03)^4 - 1.0 = 1.1255 - 1.0 = 0.1255$ = 12.55 per cent.

(d) Interest paid at the end of each month (m = 12):
AP/ER = $(1 + 0.12/12)^{12} - 1.0 = (1.01)^{12} - 1.0 = 1.1268 - 1.0 = 0.1268$ = 12.68 per cent.

Implications: More frequent payments increase the effective annual cost (AP/ER) paid by the borrower-company.

P.2.10 The earnings of Fairgrowth Ltd were ₹3 per share in year 1. They increased over a 10-year period to ₹4.02. Compute the rate of growth or compound annual rate of growth of the earnings per share.

LO 2.4 LOD D

Solution

$F_n = P \times \text{FVIF}_{i,n}$

$\text{FVIF}_{i,n} = F_n/P$

$\text{FVIF}_{i,10}$ = ₹4.02/₹3 = 1.340

According to Table-1 (Appendix), an FVIF of 1.340 at 10 years is at 3 per cent interest. The compound annual rate of growth in earnings per share is, therefore, 3 per cent.

P.2.11 Mr *X* has ₹1,00,000 to deposit in a bank account for 3 years. Assuming (i) annual compounding, (ii) semi-annual compounding and (iii) quarterly compounding at a stated annual interest rate of 4 per cent, compute (a) the amount he would have at the end of the third year, leaving all interest paid on deposits in the bank, (b) the effective rate of interest he would earn on each alternative, and (c) which plan should he choose?

LO 2.4 LOD D

Solution

(a) (i) Compound/future value (FV_3) = ₹1,00,000 × FVIFA (4,3)
= ₹1,00,000 × 1.125 = ₹1,12,500

(a) (ii) FV_3 = ₹1,00,000 × FVIFA (4/2, 2 × 3) = ₹1,00,000 × FVIFA (2,6)
= ₹1,00,000 × 1.126 = ₹1,12,600

(a) (iii) FV_3 = ₹1,00,000 × FVIFA (4/4,3) = ₹1,00,000 × PVIFA (1,12)
= ₹1,00,000 × 1.127 = ₹1,12,700

(b) (i) Effective rate of interest = $(1 + 4\%1)^1 - 1 = (1.04)^1 - 1$
= 1.04 – 1 = 0.04 = 4 per cent

(b) (ii) = $(1 + 4\%/2)^2 - 1 = (1.02)^2 - 1 = 1.0404 - 1$
= 0.0404 = 4.04 per cent

(b) (iii) = $(1 + 4\%/4)^4 - 1 = (1 + 0.01)^4 - 1 = 1.0406 - 1 = 0.0406$ = 4.06 per cent.

(c) Mr. *X* should choose alternative (iii). The quarterly compounding of interest has resulted in the highest future value as a result of the corresponding highest effective rate of interest.

REVIEW QUESTIONS

LOD: Easy

RQ.2.1 (a) Indicate whether the following statements are True or False. [LO 2.2, 3, 4]

(i) Time value of money signifies that the value of a unit of money remains unchanged during different time periods.

(ii) Time value of a unit of money is different over different periods on account of the reinvestment opportunities with the firms.

(iii) Cash flows accruing to the firms at different time periods are directly comparable.

(iv) Either compounding or discounting technique can be used, to make heterogeneous cash flows comparable.

(v) Effective and nominal rate of interest remain the same irrespective of the frequency of compounding.

(vi) Effective rate of interest is positively correlated with frequency of compounding.

(vii) To arrive at the present value of cash flows, discounting is done at the rate which represents opportunity cost of funds.

(viii) Present value tables for annuity can be directly applied to mixed stream of cash flows.

(ix) To facilitate comparison of cash flows that are occurring at different time periods, the technique of either compounding all cash flows to the terminal year or discounting all cash flows to the time zero period can be adopted.

[Answers: (i) False (ii) True (iii) False (iv) True (v) False (vi) True (vii) True (viii) False (ix) True]

(b) In the following multiple choice questions select the correct answers.

(i) Time value of money explains that

(a) a unit of money received today is worth more than a unit received in future

(b) a unit of money received today is worth less than a unit received in future

(c) a unit of money received today and at some other time in future is equal

(d) none of them.

(ii) Time value of money facilitates comparison of cash flows occurring at different time periods by

(a) compounding all cash flows to a common point of time

(b) discounting all cash flows to a common point of time

(c) using either (a) or (b)

(d) Neither (a) nor (b).

(iii) If the nominal rate of interest is 10 per cent per annum and frequency of compounding is 4 i.e. quarterly compounding, the effective rate of interest will be

(a) 10.25% per annum **(b)** 10.38% per annum

(c) 10% per annum **(d)** none of them.

(iv) Relationship between annual effective rate of interest and annual nominal rate of interest is, if frequency of compounding is more than 1,

(a) Effective Rate < Nominal rate **(b)** Effective Rate > Nominal rate

(c) Effective Rate = Nominal rate **(d)** None of these.

(v) If annual effective rate of interest is 10.25 % per annum and nominal rate of return is 10 per cent per annum what is the frequency of compounding

(a) 1 **(b)** 3 **(c)** 2 **(d)** None of these.

(vi) A student takes a loan of ₹50,000 from SBI. The rate of interest being charged by SBI is 10 per cent per annum. What would be the amount of equal annual instalment if he wishes to pay it back in five instalments and first instalment he will pay at the end of year 5?
(a) ₹11,000 **(b)** ₹19,310 **(c)** ₹15,000 **(d)** None of these.

(vii) How much amount should an investor invest now in order to receive five annuities starting from the end of this year of ₹10,000 if the rate of interest offered by bank is 10% per annum?
(a) ₹40,000 **(b)** ₹45,000 **(c)** ₹37,910 **(d)** none.

(viii) If, in case of question (vii), he wishes to receive ₹10,000 forever, investment amount required is
(a) ₹75000 **(b)** cannot be determined **(c)** ₹1,00,000 **(d)** none.

(ix) A company wants to retire a loan of ₹5,00,000, 10 years from today. What amount should it invest each year for 10 years if the funds can earn 8 per cent per annum. The first investment will be made at the beginning of this year.
(a) ₹50,000 **(b)** ₹31,950 **(c)** ₹40,000 **(d)** None of these.

[Answers: (i) a (ii) c (iii) b (iv) b (v) c (vi) b (vii) c (viii) c and (ix) b]

RQ.2.2 Briefly explain and illustrate the concept of 'time value of money'. [LO 2.1]

RQ.2.3 What is the difference between the future value and present value? [LO 2.2]

RQ.2.4 A person would need ₹100, 5 years from now. How much amount should he deposit each year in his bank account, if the yearly interest rate is 10 per cent? [LO 2.4]

LOD: Medium

RQ.2.5 What is annuity? Explain how can future value of an annuity be determined? [LO 2.2]

RQ.2.6 How is the present value of a mixed stream of cash flows calculated? [LO 2.3]

RQ.2.7 What is perpetuity? How may the present value for such stream of cash flows be determined? [LO 2.3]

RQ.2.8 What is a loan amoritsation schedule? Describe the procedure used to amortise a loan into a series of equal payments. [LO 2.4]

RQ.2.9 Compute the future values of (1) an initial ₹100 compounded annually for 10 years at 10 per cent and (2) an annuity of ₹100 for 10 years at 10 per cent. [LO 2.4]

RQ.2.10 An investor has two options to choose from: (a) ₹6,000 after 1 year; (b) ₹9,000 after 4 years. Assuming a discount rate of (i) 10 per cent and (ii) 20 per cent, which alternative should he opt for? [LO 2.4]

RQ.2.11 An investor is 50 years of age today. He will retire at the age of 60. In order to receive ₹2,00,000 annually for 10 years after retirement, how much amount should he invest at the time of retirement? Assume the required rate of return is 10 per cent. [LO 2.4]

RQ.2.12 ABC Ltd has borrowed ₹1,000 to be repaid in equal instalments at the end of each of the next 3 years. The interest rate is 15 per cent. Prepare a amortisation schedule. [LO 2.4]

LOD: Difficult

RQ.2.13 Explain briefly the effective rate of discount. [LO 2.4]

RQ.2.14 Distinguish between nominal rates of interest and effective rate of interest. [LO 2.4]

RQ.2.15 Explain the effective rates of interest and flat rates of interest. [LO 2.4]

RQ.2.16 *X* has taken a 20-month car loan of ₹6,00,000. The rate of interest is 12 per cent per annum. What will be the amount of monthly loan amortisation? [LO 2.4]

RQ.2.17 ABC Ltd has borrowed ₹1,000 to be repaid in 12 monthly instalments of ₹94.56. Compute the annual interest rate. [LO 2.4]

ANSWERS

2.4 ₹16.38

2.9 **(1)** Future value ₹259.4; **(2)** ₹1,593.7

2.10 **(i) (a)** ₹5,454.6
(i) (b) ₹6,147; ₹9,000 after 4 years
(ii) (a) ₹4,999.8
(ii) (b) ₹4,340.7; ₹6,000 after 1 year
At 10 per cent required rate, the investor should choose ₹9,000 after 4 years
At 20 per cent required rate, the investor should choose ₹6,000 after 1 year

2.11 ₹12,28,920

2.12 Equal instalment ₹437.98

2.16 ₹33,249.11

2.17 Annual interest rate 24 per cent

Scan the QR Code to access comprehensive solutions to all numerical review questions and additional material.

TABLE A-5 Relationship Between Nominal and Effective Rates of Interest and Discount

Effective / *Interest rate*	$i^{(2)}$	$i^{(4)}$	$i^{(12)}$	d	$d^{(2)}$	$d^{(4)}$	$d^{(12)}$
0.01	0.0100	0.0100	0.0100	0.0099	0.0099	0.0099	0.0099
0.02	0.0199	0.0199	0.0198	0.0196	0.0197	0.0198	0.0198
0.03	0.0298	0.0297	0.0296	0.0291	0.0293	0.0294	0.0295
0.04	0.0396	0.0394	0.0393	0.0385	0.0388	0.0390	0.0392
0.05	0.0494	0.0491	0.0489	0.0476	0.0482	0.0485	0.0487
0.06	0.0591	0.0587	0.0584	0.0566	0.0574	0.0578	0.0581
0.07	0.0688	0.0682	0.0678	0.0654	0.0665	0.0671	0.0675
0.08	0.0785	0.0777	0.0772	0.0741	0.0755	0.0762	0.0767
0.09	0.0881	0.0871	0.0865	0.0826	0.0843	0.0853	0.0859
0.10	0.0976	0.0965	0.0957	0.0909	0.0931	0.0942	0.0949
0.11	0.1071	0.1057	0.1048	0.0991	0.1017	0.1030	0.1039
0.12	0.1166	0.1149	0.1139	0.1071	0.1102	0.1117	0.1128
0.13	0.1260	0.1241	0.1228	0.1150	0.1186	0.1204	0.1216
0.14	0.1354	0.1332	0.1317	0.1228	0.1268	0.1289	0.1303
0.15	0.1448	0.1422	0.1406	0.1304	0.1350	0.1373	0.1390
0.16	0.1541	0.1512	0.1493	0.1379	0.1430	0.1457	0.1475
0.17	0.1633	0.1601	0.1580	0.1453	0.1510	0.1540	0.1560
0.18	0.1726	0.1690	0.1667	0.1525	0.1589	0.1621	0.1644
0.19	0.1817	0.1778	0.1752	0.1597	0.1666	0.1702	0.1727
0.20	0.1909	0.1865	0.1837	0.1667	0.1743	0.1782	0.1809
0.21	0.2000	0.1952	0.1921	0.1736	0.1818	0.1861	0.1891
0.22	0.2091	0.2039	0.2005	0.1803	0.1893	0.1940	0.1972
0.23	0.2181	0.2125	0.2088	0.1870	0.1967	0.2017	0.2052
0.24	0.2271	0.2210	0.2171	0.1935	0.2039	0.2094	0.2132
0.26	0.2450	0.2379	0.2334	0.2063	0.2183	0.2246	0.2289
0.28	0.2627	0.2546	0.2494	0.2188	0.2322	0.2394	0.2443
0.30	0.2804	0.2712	0.2653	0.2308	0.2459	0.2539	0.2595
0.32	0.2978	0.2875	0.2809	0.2424	0.2592	0.2682	0.2744
0.34	0.3152	0.3036	0.2963	0.2537	0.2723	0.2822	0.2891
0.36	0.3324	0.3196	0.3115	0.2647	0.2850	0.2960	0.3036
0.38	0.3495	0.3354	0.3264	0.2754	0.2975	0.3095	0.3178
0.40	0.3664	0.3510	0.3412	0.2857	0.3097	0.3227	0.3318

TABLE A-5 Relationship Between Nominal and Effective Rates of Interest and Discount

Interest \ i/effective rate	$i/i^{(2)}$	$i/i^{(4)}$	$i/i^{(12)}$	$i/d^{(2)}$	$i/d^{(4)}$	$i/d^{(12)}$
0.01	1.0025	1.0037	1.0046	1.0075	1.0062	1.0054
0.02	1.0050	1.0075	1.0091	1.0150	1.0125	1.0108
0.03	1.0074	1.0112	1.0137	1.0224	1.0187	1.0162
0.04	1.0099	1.0149	1.0182	1.0299	1.0249	1.0215
0.05	1.0123	1.0816	1.0227	1.0373	1.0311	1.0269
0.06	1.0148	1.0222	1.0272	1.0448	1.0372	1.0322
0.07	1.0172	1.0259	1.0317	1.0522	1.0434	1.0375
0.08	1.0196	1.0295	1.0362	1.0596	1.0495	1.0428
0.09	1.0220	1.0331	1.0406	1.0670	1.0556	1.0481
0.10	1.0244	1.0368	1.0450	1.0744	1.0618	1.0534
0.11	1.0268	1.0404	1.0495	1.0818	1.0679	1.0586
0.12	1.0292	1.0439	1.0539	1.0892	1.0739	1.0639
0.13	1.0315	1.0475	1.0583	1.0965	1.0800	1.0691
0.14	1.0339	1.0511	1.0626	1.1039	1.0861	1.0743
0.15	1.0362	1.0546	1.0670	1.1112	1.0921	1.0795
0.16	1.0385	1.0581	1.0714	1.1185	1.0981	1.0847
0.17	1.0408	1.0617	1.0757	1.1258	1.1042	1.0899
0.18	1.0431	1.0652	1.0800	1.1331	1.1102	1.0950
0.19	1.0454	1.0687	1.0843	1.1404	1.1162	1.1002
0.20	1.0477	1.0722	1.0887	1.1477	1.1222	1.1053
0.21	1.0500	1.0756	1.0929	1.1550	1.1281	1.1104
0.22	1.0523	1.0791	1.0972	1.1623	1.1341	1.1155
0.23	1.0545	1.0825	1.1015	1.1695	1.1400	1.1206
0.24	1.0568	1.0860	1.1057	1.1768	1.1460	1.1257
0.26	1.0612	1.0928	1.1142	1.1912	1.1578	1.1359
0.28	1.0657	1.0996	1.1226	1.2057	1.1696	1.1460
0.30	1.0701	1.1064	1.1310	1.2201	1.1814	1.1560
0.32	1.0745	1.1131	1.1393	1.2345	1.1931	1.1660
0.34	1.0788	1.1197	1.1476	1.2488	1.2047	1.1759
0.36	1.0831	1.1264	1.1559	1.2631	1.2164	1.1859
0.38	1.0874	1.1330	1.1641	1.2774	1.2280	1.1957
0.40	1.0916	1.1395	1.1722	1.2916	1.2395	1.2055

CHAPTER

3 Risk and Return

LEARNING OBJECTIVES

LO 3.1	Understand the fundamentals of risk and return
LO 3.2	Describe procedure for assessing and measuring the risk of a single asset
LO 3.3	Review the procedure to assess and measure the risk-return of a portfolio
LO 3.4	Discuss the selection of the optimal portfolio based on the Markowitz model
LO 3.5	Explain the capital asset pricing model (CAPM) as a framework for basic risk-return trade-off
LO 3.6	Examine the factors having a bearing on extended CAPM
LO 3.7	Describe the arbitrage pricing theory (APT) as a model of security/asset pricing as an alternative to CAPM

INTRODUCTION

The two key determinants of share/security prices are expected risk and expected return. The financial managers must understand these concepts as they have a bearing on the share prices as well as the valuation of the firm. This Chapter presents a framework for an explicit and quantitative understanding of these concepts and the nature of relationship between them.

The return and risk related to a single security/asset are examined first. The portfolio risk and return is covered subsequently. The selection of optimum portfolio is also explained. The theories/models, namely, Capital Asset Pricing Model (CAPM), extended CAPM, and the Arbitrage Pricing Theory (APT) explaining the relationship between the expected return and risk are also examined in subsequent discussions. The major points are also summarised by way of recapitulation.

LO 3.1 RISK AND RETURN

Return is the actual income received plus any change in market price of an asset/ investment.

The (rate of) **return** on an asset/investment for a given period, say a year, is the annual income received *plus* any change in market price, usually expressed as a per cent of the opening market price. Symbolically, the one-period actual (expected) return, R

$$= \frac{D_t + (P_t - P_{t-1})}{P_{t-1}} \tag{3.1}$$

where D_t = annual income/cash dividend at the end of time period, t

P_t = security price at time period, t (closing/ending security price)

P_{t-1} = security price at time period, $t - 1$ (opening/beginning security price)

Risk is the variability of actual return from the expected return associated with a given asset.

***Example* 3.1**

If the price of a share on April 1 (current year) is ₹25, the annual dividend received at the end of the year is ₹1 and the year-end price on March 31 is ₹30, the rate of return = [₹1 + (₹30 – ₹25)]/₹25 = 0.24 = 24 per cent. The rate of return of 24 per cent has two components: (i) ***Current yield***, i.e. annual income ÷ beginning price = ₹1/₹25 = 0.04 or 4 per cent and (ii) ***Capital gains/loss*** = (ending price – beginning price) ÷ beginning price = (₹30 – ₹25)/ 25 = 0.20 = 20 per cent.

The variability of the actual return from the expected returns associated with a given asset/investment is defined as **risk**. The greater the variability, the riskier the security (e.g. shares) is said to be. The more certain the return from an asset (e.g. T-bills), the less the variability and, therefore, the less the risk.

LO 3.2 RISK AND RETURN OF A SINGLE ASSET

Sensitivity analysis is a behavioural approach to assess risk using a number of possible return estimates to obtain a sense of the variability among outcomes.

The risk associated with a single asset is assessed from both a ***behavioural*** and a ***quantitative/statistical* point** of view. The behavioural view of risk can be obtained by using (i) sensitivity analysis and (ii) probability (distribution). The statistical measures of risk of an asset/security are (1) standard deviation and (2) coefficient of variation.

Sensitivity Analysis

Range is a measure of risk which is found by subtracting the pessimistic (worst) outcome from the optimistic (best) outcome.

Sensitivity Analysis takes into account a number of possible outcomes/returns estimates while evaluating an asset/assessing risk. In order to have a sense of the variability among return estimates, a possible approach is to estimate the worst (pessimistic), the expected (most likely) and the best (optimistic) return associated with the asset. Alternatively, the level of outcomes may be related to the state of the economy, namely, recession, normal and boom conditions. The difference between the optimistic and the pessimistic outcomes is the **range** which, according to the sensitivity analysis, is the basic measure of risk. The greater the range, the more variability (risk) the asset is said to have. Consider the facts in Table 3.1.

TABLE 3.1 Sensitivity Analysis (*Amount in ₹crore*)

Particulars	*Asset X*	*Asset Y*
Initial outlay (t = 0)	50	50
Annual return (per cent):		
Pessimistic	14	8
Most likely	16	16
Optimistic	18	24
Range (optimistic-pessimistic)	4	16

On the basis of the range of annual returns, asset Y is more risky.

The sensitivity analysis provides more than one estimate of return (range) to assess the risk involved, but it is a crude/rough basis of risk assessment.

Probability Distribution

Probability distribution is a model that relates probabilities to the associated outcome.

The risk associated with an asset can be assessed more accurately by the use of **probability distribution** than sensitivity analysis. The probability of an event represents the likelihood/percentage chance of its occurrence. For instance, if the expectation is that a given outcome (return) will occur seven out of ten times, it can be said to have a seventy per cent (0.70) chance of happening; if it is certain to happen, the **probability** of happening is 100 per cent (1). An outcome which has a probability of zero will never occur.

Probability is the chance that a given outcome will occur.

Based on the probabilities assigned (probability distribution of) to the rate of return, the **expected value** of the return can be computed. The expected rate of return is the weighted average of all possible returns multiplied by their respective probabilities. Thus, probabilities of the various outcomes are used as weights. The expected return, $\bar{R}$

$$= \sum_{i=1}^{n} R_i \times Pr_i \tag{3.2}$$

where R_i = return for the ith possible outcome

Pr_i = probability associated with its return

n = number of outcomes considered

The expected rate of return calculation using the returns for assets X and Y are presented in Table 3.2.

TABLE 3.2 Expected Rates of Returns (Probability Distribution)

Possible outcomes *(1)*	*Probability* *(2)*	*Returns (per cent)* *(3)*	*Expected returns [(2) × (3)]* *(4)*
Asset X			
Pessimistic (recession)	0.20	14	2.8
Most likely (normal)	0.60	16	9.6
Optimistic (boom)	0.20	18	3.6
	1.00		16.0

(*Contd*)

(Contd.)

Asset Y			
Pessimistic (recession)	0.20	8	1.6
Most likely (normal)	0.60	16	9.6
Optimistic (boom)	0.20	24	4.8
	1.00		16.0

Standard Deviation of Return

Standard deviation meaures the dispersion around the expected value.

Risk refers to the dispersion of returns around an expected value. The most common statistical measure of risk of an asset is the **standard deviation** from the mean/expected value of return. It represents the square root of the average squared deviations of the individual returns from the **expected returns**. Symbolically, the standard deviation, σ

$$= \sqrt{\sum_{i=1}^{n} (R_i - \overline{R})^2 \times Pr_i} \quad (3.3)$$

Expected value of a return is the most likely return on a given asset/security.

Table 3.3 presents the calculation of the standard deviation for the return of asset *X* and asset *Y*.

TABLE 3.3 Standard Deviation of Returns

i	R_i	$\overline{R}$	$R_i - \overline{R}$	$(R_i - \overline{R})^2$	Pr_i	$(R_i - \overline{R})^2 \times Pr_i$
			Asset X			
1	14%	16%	(–2)%	4%	0.20	0.80%
2	16	16	0	0	0.60	0
3	18	16	2	4	0.20	0.80
						1.6

$\sigma r_x = \sqrt{\sum_{i=1}^{3} (R_i - \overline{R})^2 \times Pr_i} = \sqrt{1.6} = 1.26$ per cent

i	R_i	$\overline{R}$	$R_i - \overline{R}$	$(R_i - \overline{R})^2$	Pr_i	$(R_i - \overline{R})^2 \times Pr_i$
			Asset Y			
1	8	16	(–8)	64	0.20	12.8
2	16	16	0	0	0.60	0
3	24	16	8	64	0.20	12.8
						25.6

$\sigma r_y = \sqrt{25.6} = 5.06$ per cent

The greater the standard deviation of returns, the greater the variability/dispersion of returns and the greater the risk of the asset/investment. However, standard deviation is an absolute measure of dispersion and does not consider variability of return in relation to the expected value. It may be misleading in comparing the risk surrounding alternative assets if they differ in size of expected returns.

Spreadsheet Solution 3.1

Alternatively, the calculation of risk can be carried out using Microsoft Excel (Spreadsheet). For the purpose, relevant data have been entered in the spreadsheet.

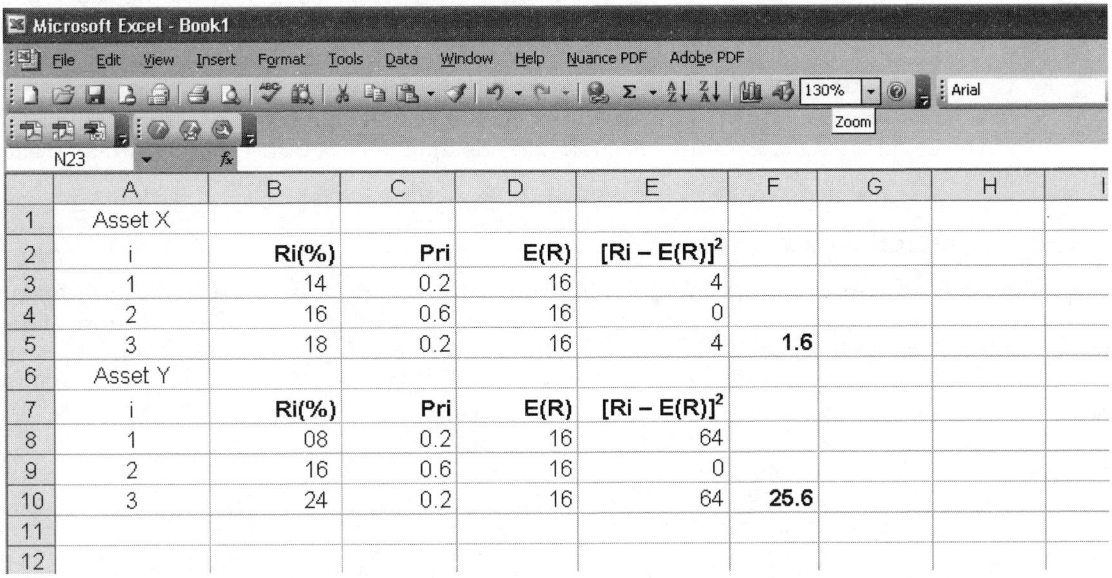

	A	B	C	D	E	F	G	H
1	Asset X							
2	i	**Ri(%)**	**Pri**	**E(R)**	**[Ri – E(R)]^2**			
3	1	14	0.2	16	4			
4	2	16	0.6	16	0			
5	3	18	0.2	16	4	**1.6**		
6	Asset Y							
7	i	**Ri(%)**	**Pri**	**E(R)**	**[Ri – E(R)]^2**			
8	1	08	0.2	16	64			
9	2	16	0.6	16	0			
10	3	24	0.2	16	64	**25.6**		
11								
12								

The data on returns for asset X has been entered in the cells B3 to B5. The associated probabilities have been entered in cells C3 to C5 and expected returns have been entered in cells D3 to D5. The squared deviation for the cell E3 has been calculated by using the formula =(B3-D3)^2. The calculation has been extended to the other two cells D4 and D5 by copying/ dragging the formula to these cells. Finally, the variance has been calculated using the formula =SUMPRODUCT(C3:C5,E3:E5) in cell F5. We can see that answer is the same as found in Table 3.3. The same steps have been repeated to get the variance for Asset Y.

Coefficient of Variation

Coefficient of Variation is a measure of *relative dispersion* (risk) or a measure of **risk per unit of expected return**. It converts standard deviation of expected values into relative values to enable comparison of risks associated with assets having different expected values. The **coefficient of variation** (*CV*) is computed by dividing the standard deviation, σ_r, for an asset by its expected value, $\bar{R}$. Symbolically,

Coefficient of variation is a measure of relative dispersion used in comparing the risk of assets with differing expected returns.

$$CV = \frac{\sigma_r}{\bar{R}} \quad (3.4)$$

The coefficient of variations for assets *X* and *Y* are respectively, 0.079 (1.26% ÷ 16%) and 0.316 (5.06% ÷ 16%).

The larger the *CV*, the larger the relative risk of the asset. As a rule, the use of the coefficient of variation for comparing asset risk is the best since it considers the relative size (expected value) of assets.

LO 3.3 RISK AND RETURN OF PORTFOLIO

A **portfolio** means a combination of two or more securities (assets). A large number of portfolios can be formed from a given set of assets. Each portfolio has risk-return characteristics of its own. Portfolio theory, originally developed by Harry Markowitz, shows that portfolio risk, unlike portfolio return, is more than a simple aggregation of the risks of individual assets. This depends on the interplay between the returns on assets comprising the portfolio. As investors construct a portfolio of investment rather than invest in a single asset, this Section extends the analysis of risk and return associated with portfolio investments.

Portfolio is a collection/ combination/group of assets/securities.

Portfolio Expected Return

The expected rate of return on a portfolio is the weighted average of the expected rates of return on assets comprising the portfolio. The weights, which add up to 1, reflect the fraction of total portfolio invested in each asset. Thus, there are two determinants of portfolio return: expected rate of return on each asset and the relative share of each asset in the portfolio. Symbolically, the expected return for a n-asset portfolio is defined by Equation 3.5.

$$E(r_p) = \Sigma w_i \, E(r_i) \tag{3.5}$$

where $E(r_p)$ = Expected return from portfolio
w_i = Proportion invested in asset i
$E(r_i)$ = Expected return for asset i
n = Number of assets in portfolio

***Example* 3.2**

Suppose the expected return on two assets, *L* (low-risk low-return) and *H* (high-risk high-return), are 12 and 16 per cents respectively. If the corresponding weights are 0.65 and 0.35, the expected portfolio return is = [0.65 × 0.12 + 0.35 × 0.16] = 0.134 or 13.4 per cent.

Portfolio Risk (Two-Asset Portfolio)

Total risk is measured in terms of variance (σ^2, pronounced sigma square) or standard deviation (σ, pronounced sigma) of returns. Unlike portfolio expected return, portfolio variance (or standard deviation) is *not* the weighted average of variance (or standard deviation) of returns on individual assets (securities) in the portfolio. The overall risk of the portfolio includes the interactive risk of an asset relative to the others, measured by the covariance of returns. The covariance, in turn, depends on the **correlation** between returns on assets in the portfolio. The total risk of a portfolio made up of two assets is defined by the Equation 3.6.

Correlation is a statistical measure of the relationship between series of numbers representing data of any kind.

$$\sigma^2_p = w^2_1 \, \sigma^2_1 + w^2_2 \, \sigma^2_2 + 2w_1 \, w_2 \, (\sigma_{12}) \tag{3.6}$$

Alternatively,

$$\sigma^2_p = (w_1 \, \sigma_1)^2 + (w_2 \, \sigma_2)^2 + 2w_1 w_2 \, (\rho_{12} \, \sigma_1 \, \sigma_2) \tag{3.7}$$

where σ^2_p = Var (r_p) or variance of returns of the portfolio
w_1 = Fraction of total portfolio invested in asset 1
w_2 = Fraction of total portfolio invested in asset 2
σ^2_1 = Variance of asset 1
σ_1 = Standard deviation of asset 1

σ^2_2 = Variance of asset 2
σ_2 = Standard deviation of asset 2
σ_{12} = Covariance between returns of two assets (= $\rho_{12}\ \sigma_1\ \sigma_2$)
ρ_{12} = Coefficient of correlation (pronounced *Rho*) between the returns of two assets.

Example **3.3**

Let us assume that standard deviations of assets *L* and *H*, of our Example 3.2 are 16 and 20 per cents respectively. If the coefficient of correlation between their returns is 0.6 and the two assets are combined in the ratio of 3:1, the expected return of the portfolio is determined as follows:

$$E(r_{\text{portfolio}}) = w_L E(r_L) + w_H E(r_H)$$
$$= (0.75 \times 12\%) + (0.25 \times 16\%) = 9.0\% + 4.0\% = 13 \text{ per cent}$$

The variance of the portfolio is given by:

$$\sigma^2_p = (w_1\ \sigma_1)^2 + (w_2\ \sigma_2)^2 + 2\ w_1\ w_2\ (\rho_{12}\ \sigma_1\ \sigma_2)$$
$$= (0.75 \times 16)^2 + (0.25 \times 20)^2 + 2\ (0.75)\ (0.25)\ [(0.6)\ (16 \times 20)]$$
$$= 144 + 25 + (0.375)(192) = 144 + 25 + 72 = 241$$

Thus, $\sigma_p = 15.52$ per cent $\left[\sqrt{241}\right]$

The above discussion shows that the portfolio risk depends on three factors: (a) Variance (or standard deviation) of each asset in the portfolio; (b) Relative importance or weight of each asset in the portfolio; (c) Interplay between returns on two assets or interactive risk of an asset relative to other, measured by the covariance of returns. Among these only weights can be controlled by the investor/portfolio manager. Thus, the primary task of a portfolio manager is to decide the proportion of each security in the portfolio.

The portfolio's expected rate of return and standard deviation (risk), for various combinations of assets *L* and *H*, with different degrees of correlation between their returns, are summarised in Table 3.4.

TABLE 3.4 Portfolio Return and Risk for Different Weights and Correlation Coefficients

(Figures are in per cent)

Weights		*Portfolio return*	*Portfolio risk (s_p) when correlation coefficient is*				
L	*H*	*$E(R_p)$*	*ρ =1.0*	*ρ = 0.5*	*ρ = 0*	*ρ = –0.5*	*ρ = –1.0*
100	0	12.0	16.00	16.00	16.00	16.00	16.00
90	10	12.4	16.40	15.50	14.54	13.51	12.40
80	**20**	**12.8**	**16.80**	**15.20**	**13.41**	**11.34**	**8.80**
70	30	13.2	17.20	15.12	12.71	9.71	5.20
60	40	13.6	17.60	15.26	12.50	8.91	1.60
50	50	14.0	18.00	15.62	12.81	9.17	2.00
40	60	14.4	18.40	16.18	13.60	10.40	5.60
30	70	14.8	18.80	16.92	14.80	12.32	9.20
20	80	15.2	19.20	17.82	16.32	14.66	12.80
10	90	15.6	19.60	18.85	18.07	17.26	16.40
0	100	16.0	20.00	20.00	20.00	20.00	20.00

A perusal of the Table 3.4 leads to the following notable inferences:

(i) Two assets/securities can be combined in such a way that the portfolio risk is less than the risk of individual assets comprising the portfolio. For example, portfolio standard deviation is 15.20 per cent when **correlation coefficient** (ρ) is 0.5 and *L* and *H* are combined in the ratio of 80:20. This is lower than the standard deviation of *L* (16 per cent) and *H* (20 per cent).

Correlation coefficient is a measure of the degree of correlation between two series.

(ii) For given weights, portfolio standard deviation declines as correlation coefficient moves from + 1.0 to – 1.0. For example, when *L* and *H* are combined in the ratio of 80:20, the range of portfolio standard deviation is 16.80 per cent for perfect positive correlation (ρ = +1.0) to 8.80 per cent for perfect negative correlation (ρ = –1.0).

(iii) When returns have less than perfect positive correlation, some combinations are more efficient than others; they do not involve risk-return trade-off. For correlation coefficient 0.5, increase in the weight of *H* from 0 per cent to 30 per cent raises the expected return from 12 per cent to 13.2 per cent, but standard deviation (risk) declines from 16 per cent to 15.12 per cent.

(iv) For given correlation coefficient, there is a **minimum variance** or **minimum risk portfolio**. The minimum variance portfolio has a standard deviation smaller than that of either of the individual component assets (securities). The optimal weights (w^*) that produce the minimum variance may be obtained from Equation (3.8) and Equation (3.9):

$$w^*_1 = [\sigma^2_2 - (\rho_{12}\ \sigma_1\ \sigma_2)\ ]/[\sigma^2_1 + \sigma^2_1 - 2(\rho_{12}\ \sigma_1\ \sigma_2)] \quad \textbf{(3.8)}$$

$$w^*_2 = 1 - w^*_1 \quad \textbf{(3.9)}$$

where w^*_1 = Optimal weight of asset 1

w^*_2 = Optimal weight of asset 2

σ^2_1 = Variance of asset 1

σ^2_2 = Variance of asset 2

$\rho_{12}\ \sigma_1\ \sigma_2$ = Covariance of returns

ρ_{12} = Coefficient of correlation between the returns of two assets

***Example* 3.4**

Determine optimal weights, at zero correlation, for the data provided in Example 3.3.

Solution

Optimal weights are:

$$w^*_L = [(20)^2 - (0)\ (16)\ (20))]/[(16)^2_1 + (20)^2 - 2\ (0)\ (16)\ (20)]$$
$$= (400)/(256 + 400) = (400)/(656) = 0.61 = 61 \text{ per cent}$$
$$w^*_H = 1 - 0.61 = 0.39 = 39 \text{ per cent}$$

The portfolio standard deviation with these weights is smaller than the standard deviations of assets included in the portfolio. This may be verified using Equation 3.7.

$$\sigma^2_p = (0.61 \times 16)^2 + (0.39 \times 20)^2 + 2\ (0.61)(0.39)\ [(0)(16 \times 20)]$$
$$= 95.26 + 60.84 = 156.1$$
$$\sigma_p = 12.5 \text{ per cent}$$

Spreadsheet Solution 3.2

The calculation of portfolio return and risk for different portfolio weights and different levels of correlations can be performed using a spreadsheet as well (**see Spreadsheet on next page 3.9**).

The data on risk and return for the assets L and H has been entered in the cells B2 through C3. The weights for asset L have been entered in the cells A5 to A15. The weight for the asset H in cell B5 has been calculated using the formula =100-A5; the formula has been copied to the cells B6 to B15 for calculating the rest of the weights. The portfolio return for the first combination of weights has been calculated using the formula =A5*B$2+B5*B$3. The formula has been copied to cells C6 through C15 to determine returns for the rest of the combinations of the two assets. Finally, the portfolio risks have been calculated. The different levels of association between the two assets have been entered in cells D4 to H4. To start with, the portfolio risk for the first combination of weights and ρ =1.0 has been determined using the formula =SQRT((($A5*$C$2)^2

+($B5*$C$3)^2)+2*$A5*$B5*$C$2*$C$3*D$4). For calculating the portfolio risks for the other combinations the formula has been copied to the rest of the cells.

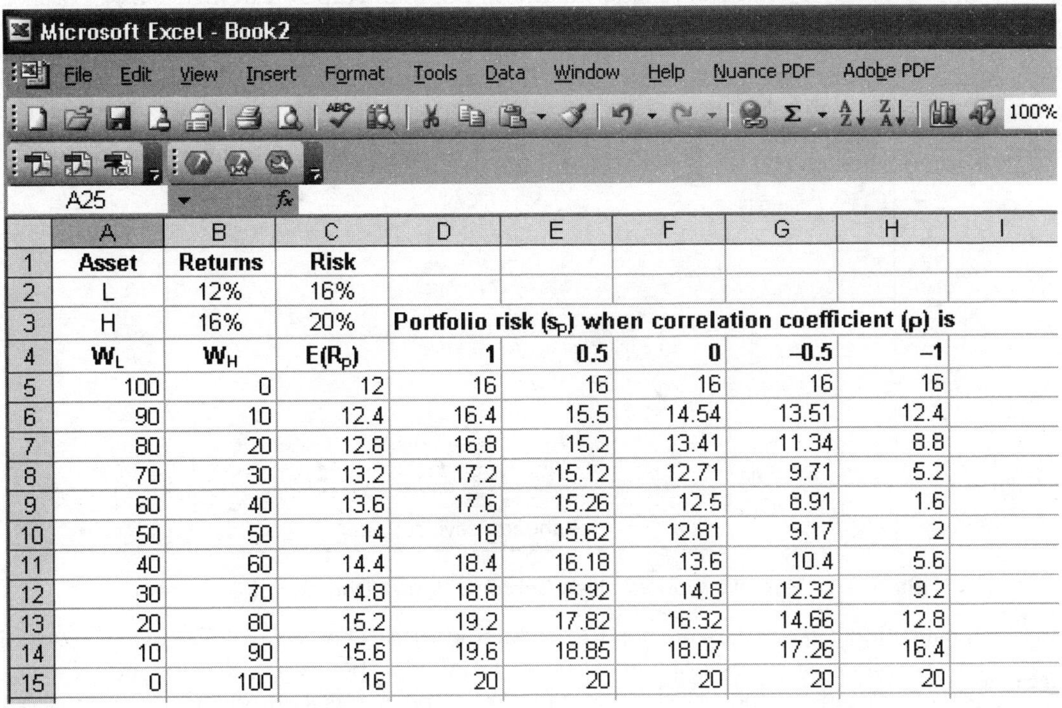

	A	B	C	D	E	F	G	H
1	**Asset**	**Returns**	**Risk**					
2	L	12%	16%					
3	H	16%	20%	**Portfolio risk (s_p) when correlation coefficient (ρ) is**				
4	**W_L**	**W_H**	**$E(R_p)$**	**1**	**0.5**	**0**	**–0.5**	**–1**
5	100	0	12	16	16	16	16	16
6	90	10	12.4	16.4	15.5	14.54	13.51	12.4
7	80	20	12.8	16.8	15.2	13.41	11.34	8.8
8	70	30	13.2	17.2	15.12	12.71	9.71	5.2
9	60	40	13.6	17.6	15.26	12.5	8.91	1.6
10	50	50	14	18	15.62	12.81	9.17	2
11	40	60	14.4	18.4	16.18	13.6	10.4	5.6
12	30	70	14.8	18.8	16.92	14.8	12.32	9.2
13	20	80	15.2	19.2	17.82	16.32	14.66	12.8
14	10	90	15.6	19.6	18.85	18.07	17.26	16.4
15	0	100	16	20	20	20	20	20

Portfolio Risk and Correlation

The effect of interaction (covariance and correlation) between returns on assets and portfolio risk is at the heart of modern portfolio theory. The degree and direction of correlation between asset returns have far-reaching effects on the reduction of portfolio risk through diversification. The correlation coefficient takes values between positive unity (perfect positive correlation) and negative unity (perfect negative correlation). The more negative (or less positive) is the correlation between asset returns, the greater is the risk-reducing benefits of diversification. Thus, for better understanding of the effect of correlation between asset returns on portfolio risk, we shall examine three special cases: (i) perfect positive correlation, (ii) perfect negative correlation and (iii) zero correlation.

Perfect Positive Correlation (ρ = +1.0) In this case, portfolio standard deviation is the weighted average of the standard deviation of returns on individual assets. Portfolio variance is given by the Equation 3.10.

$$\sigma^2_p = (w_1 \sigma_1 + w_2 \sigma_2)^2 \tag{3.10}$$

Thus, standard deviation becomes:

$$\sigma_p = w_1 \sigma_1 + w_2 \sigma_2 \tag{3.11}$$

Portfolio standard deviation when L (σ = 16) and H (σ = 20) are combined in equal proportions is:

$$\sigma_p = (0.5)\ (16) + (0.5)\ (20) = 8 + 10 = 18 \text{ per cent}$$

Perfect positive correlation between asset returns yields a direct and linear relationship between risk and return of portfolio (Figure 3.1). This implies a risk-return trade-off. As the proportion of high return and high risk asset is increased, higher return on portfolio comes with higher risk. For instance, for every 1 per cent increase in return, portfolio risk also goes up by 1 per cent (Table 3.4).

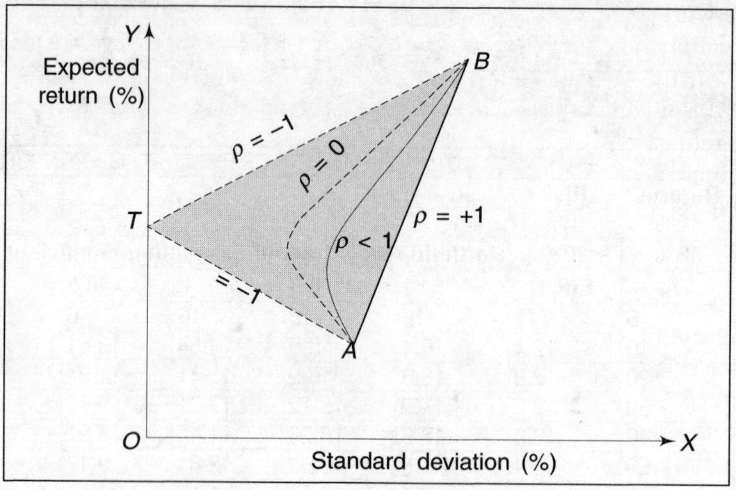

FIGURE 3.1 Portfolio Opportunities Set for Different Degrees of Correlation

Thus, diversification *per se* does not lead to reduction of risk for given level of return. Besides, diversification does not lower the portfolio risk below the risk of individual assets comprising the portfolio. For example, if the assets comprising the portfolio have equal risk, say, standard deviation of 10 per cent, the portfolio standard deviation is also 10 per cent (= $w_1 \times 10 + w_2 \times 10$; where $w_1 + w_2 = 1$).

Perfect negative correlation describes two negatively correlated series that have a correlation coefficient of –1.

Perfect Negative Correlation (σ = –1.0) In this case, portfolio standard deviation is the difference (non-negative value) caused by the standard deviation of returns on individual assets weighted by their respective shares in the portfolio. Portfolio variance is given by the Equation (3.12):

$$\sigma^2_p = (w_1\, \sigma_1 - w_2\, \sigma_2)^2 \tag{3.12}$$

Thus, standard deviation becomes:

$$\sigma_p = w_1\, \sigma_1 - w_2\, \sigma_2 \tag{3.13}$$

This equation shows that when the correlation coefficient between asset returns is negative unity, it is possible to combine them in a manner that will eliminate all risk. The portfolio contains two risky assets, but the portfolio risk (standard deviation) can be reduced to zero. The weights for such a minimum variance portfolio can be directly obtained from Equation (3.14):

$$w^*_1 = \sigma_2/(\sigma_1 + \sigma_2) \tag{3.14}$$

The calculation of optimal weights, for **perfect negative correlation** in Example 3.3, is illustrated below.

$$w^*_L = [(20)^2 - (-1.0)\,(16)\,(20))\,]/[(16)^2_1 + (20)^2 - 2\,(-1.0)\,(16)\,(20)]$$
$$= (400 + 320)/(256 + 400 + 640) = (720)/(1296) = 0.5556$$
$$= 55.56 \text{ per cent}$$
$$w^*_H = 1 - 0.5556 = 0.4444 = 44.44 \text{ per cent}$$

The portfolio variance and, hence, standard deviation with these weights are zero. This may be verified using Equation 3.4.

$$\sigma^2_p = (0.5556 \times 16)^2 + (0.4444 \times 20)^2 + 2\,(0.5556)(0.4444)\,[(-1.0)(16 \times 20)]$$
$$= 79.02 + 79.00 + (0.4938)\,(-320) = 158.02 - 158.02 = 0$$

When two assets with perfect negative correlation between their returns are combined in different proportions, the relationship between risk and return of these portfolios forms a V-shaped image with its tip resting on the axis of return (Figure 3.1). The clockwise movement of the risk-return relationship along this image implies that with gradual increase in the weight of an asset with high-risk and high-return, and with simultaneous decrease in the overall risk, the expected return from the portfolio increases. The process continues till the risk is completely eliminated (point T). After that, higher expected returns, with increase in the weight of the riskier asset, come with higher portfolio risk only.

When the risk-return relationship for various combinations of two assets under the assumption of perfect positive correlation is combined with the corresponding relationship for perfect negative correlation, a triangle ATB is formed (Figure 3.1). Points A and B, which are common to the two cases, represent pure or undiversified portfolio. Since the correlation coefficient takes values between positive unity to negative unity, this triangle specifies the limits for diversification. All portfolios represented by the three line segments are feasible but some are more efficient than others. The risk-return relationship for all other values of correlation coefficient will lie in this space only.

Zero Correlation ($\rho = 0$) When the returns on two assets are uncorrelated, their correlation and, hence, covariance terms become zero. In this case, portfolio variance is the sum of the square of standard deviation of each asset weighted by its proportion in the portfolio. Thus,

> **Zero correlation** describes two series that lack any relationship and have correlation coefficient close to zero.

$$\sigma^2_p = w^2_1\,\sigma^2_1 + w^2_2\,\sigma^2_2 \qquad \textbf{(3.15)}$$

Alternatively,

$$\sigma^2_p = (w_1\,\sigma_1)^2 + (w_2\,\sigma_2)^2 \qquad \textbf{(3.16)}$$

Thus,

$$\sigma_p = (w^2_1\,\sigma^2_1 + w^2_2\,\sigma^2_2)^{1/2} \qquad \textbf{(3.17)}$$

We extend Example 3.3 and assume that assets L (σ = 16) and H (σ = 20) are combined in equal parts. The portfolio standard deviation in this case is:

$$\sigma_p = [(0.5 \times 16)^{2} + (0.5 \times 20)^{2}]^{1/2}$$
$$= (64 + 100)^{1/2} = 12.81 \text{ per cent}$$

Again, diversification has helped in reducing the risk. The risk of the portfolio is less than the risk of either of the two assets in the portfolio.

In brief, the risk of an asset in the portfolio is the contribution it makes to overall risk. The true risk of an asset may be judged at the level of a portfolio only. A highly risky asset may act as portfolio risk stabiliser when returns on it bear low or negative correlation with returns on other assets in the portfolio.

Limit of Diversification Gains

We have seen that when two assets with less than perfectly correlated returns are combined in a portfolio, the variability of return can be reduced without compromising on the level of return. However, investors invariably hold more than two assets. How does the addition of the third asset to the portfolio affect the portfolio risk (standard deviation)? How far can diversification gains be achieved through successive addition of more assets to the portfolio? Is it possible to reduce portfolio risk to zero level just by increasing the number of assets in the portfolio? The answer to these questions depends on the nature of diversification—naïve versus Markowitz.

Naïve Diversification **Naïve diversification** means a portfolio consisting of stocks chosen at random. This is the familiar 'do not put all your eggs in one basket' approach. Intuitively, as the number of stocks in the portfolio increases, individual fluctuations in asset returns are cancelled out. Thus, the variance of returns on a portfolio should vary inversely with the number of securities in the portfolio. However, it is not possible to reduce portfolio risk to zero by increasing the number of assets in the portfolio. Equation 3.18 shows that when there are just two securities there are an equal number of variance and covariance terms. As the number of securities increases, the number of covariance terms increases much faster. In a portfolio of N securities, there are N variance terms, but $N^2 - N$ covariance terms. If the securities in the portfolio have equal weights, the portfolio variance is given by Equation 3.18.

Naïve diversification means a portfolio consisting of stock chosen at random.

$$\text{Portfolio variance} = 1/N \times \text{average variance} + (1 - 1/N)\ \text{average covariance} \quad \textbf{(3.18)}$$

As N increases, the portfolio variance steadily approaches to average covariance. This is the limit—the level of systematic risk—below which portfolio risk cannot be reduced through naïve diversification. **Systematic risk** refers to the overall market risk that affects all securities and cannot be diversified away. Empirical studies have shown that this limit is reached at a relatively low level of diversification; say 10 to 15 securities can eliminate most of the **non-systematic risk** of the portfolio.[1] Non-systematic risk is firm or specific and can be avoided by diversification.

Systematic risk implies the overall market risk that affects all securities and cannot be diversified away.

Markowitz Diversification In Markowitz diversification, the emphasis shifts from the number of securities to the covariance among them. In a portfolio of assets/securities that have strong negative covariance, it is possible to reduce the portfolio risk below the level of systematic risk. In fact, it can completely eliminate the portfolio risk, that is, reduce it to zero level in a portfolio of only two assets with perfect negative correlation between their return. As most securities have positive covariance, an important conclusion emerging from Markowitz diversification is that with an increase in the number of securities in the portfolio, the portfolio risk approaches the level of systematic risk.

Non-systematic risk is firm specific and can be avoided by diversification.

LO 3.4 PORTFOLIO SELECTION

The selection of the optimal portfolio based on the mean variance model developed by Harry Markowitz is discussed below. The model/procedure has two parts: (i) Technical—determination of the set of efficient portfolios from the available feasible set. (ii) Personal—choosing the best risk-return opportunity from the efficient set, which is consistent with the investor's attitude towards risk.

Depending upon the treatment of the technical part, there are two broad approaches to explain the portfolio theory, namely, one-step optimisation and two-step optimisation.

One-Step Optimisation This approach begins with the delimitation of efficient portfolios having one or more risky assets (securities) and culminates with the capital market line (CML). The CML is a straight line that represents the efficient portfolios that can be formed by combining a risky asset (portfolio of securities and/ or other assets) with risk-free lending (investment in risk-free asset) and borrowing opportunities.

Two-Step Optimisation This is also termed as the 'top-down' approach. It is more structured and preferred by institutional investors. This approach identifies three distinct stages in the selection of an optimal portfolio. The process of portfolio construction begins with the **capital allocation decision,** that is, apportionment of the total investible funds between a risk-free asset and the optimal portfolio of risky assets. The second stage, called the **asset allocation decision**, involves the construction of the optimal risky portfolio, referred to at the capital allocation decision stage. This consists of the distribution of the risky investment across broad asset classes—shares (stocks), debt instruments (bonds), real assets and so on. The final stage is the security selection decision, that is, choice of securities within each asset class.

It is called the two-step or **top-down optimisation** approach as the focus of the top management is on independent optimisation of risky portfolios, namely, the asset-class portfolios and security portfolios within each asset-class. Hence, the investment manager cannot benefit from low covariance between securities belonging to different asset classes. This deficiency is overcome by concentrating on covariance between various classes of assets. The weights of a risky portfolio vis-à-vis a risk-free asset, or various asset portfolios, are frequently adjusted to take advantage of forecasted changes in market conditions—an activity termed as the **market timing**.

The one-step optimisation is elaborated below.

Efficient Portfolios

As noted above, the first step or the 'technical' aspect of optimal portfolio selection is to determine the risk-return opportunities available to an investor. This is also referred to as the determination of the **feasible set of portfolios** or the **portfolio opportunity set** or the **minimum-variance portfolio opportunity set** (not to be confused with minimum-variance portfolio of two risky assets, as discussed earlier). Graphically, these are summarised by the minimum-variance frontier of risky assets (Figure 3.2). Each point along the minimum-variance frontier represents the lowest possible variance that can be attained for a given portfolio's expected return. The point to the extreme left on the minimum-variance frontier represents the **global minimum variance portfolio**. Similarly, the highest point represents the **global maximum return portfolio**. The line segment between the global minimum variance portfolio and global maximum return portfolio constitutes the efficient frontier. It represents efficient portfolios, that is, portfolios having maximum return at each level of risk (standard deviation). Efficient portfolios dominate all other portfolios and individual assets, which lie below the efficient frontier. By definition, dominant portfolios offer maximum return for the given level of risk or, conversely, the minimum risk for the selected rate of return.

It may be noted that the efficient frontier is convex towards the vertical axis (axis of expected return) as all assets have a correlation between positive unity and negative unity. It may be recalled from the discussion on portfolio diversification that assets with perfect positive correlation can only generate a linear combination of risk and return. The efficient frontier can never be concave to the vertical axis.

Delineation of the efficient frontier through the Markowitz portfolio analysis discussed above rests on four basic assumptions about asset selection behaviour of investors.[2]

(a) The rate of return from an investment is the most important outcome. Investors conceptualise the possible rates of return from an investment as a probability distribution of rates of return either consciously or subconsciously.

(b) Investors are averse to risks. They seek the highest level of return for a given risk class.

(c) Investors estimate risk in terms of the variability of expected returns.

(d) Investors base their decisions solely on two decision parameters—expected return and variance (or its square root standard deviation).

Investors who conform to the preceding assumptions are termed Markowitz diversifiers. They prefer efficient frontier portfolios.

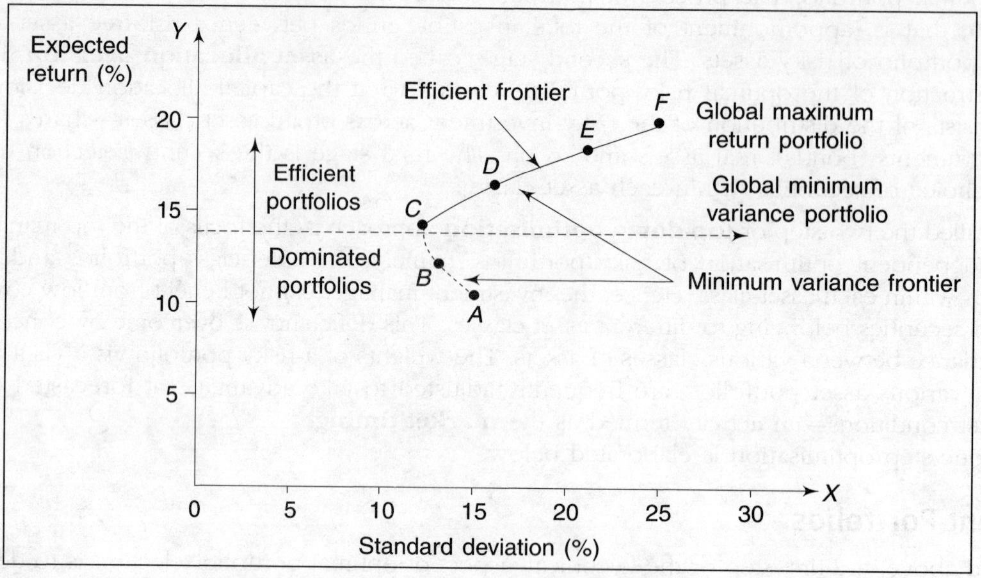

FIGURE 3.2 Minimum Variance Frontier of Risky Assets

***Example* 3.5**

To illustrate the concepts of dominance and efficient frontier, let us take a simple example with two assets *X* (expected return 10 per cent, standard deviation 15 per cent) and *Y* (expected return 20 per cent, standard deviation 26 per cent). Low positive correlation between their returns permits diversification gains. A large number of portfolios can be formed by blending these assets in different proportions. Table 3.5 presents six such portfolios with their expected returns and risk. Figure 3.2 shows a graph of these portfolios in risk-return space. Line segment AF depicts the minimum-variance portfolio opportunity set or the minimum-variance frontier of risky assets. Points A and F represent pure holdings (100 per cent) of assets *X* and *Y* respectively. There is an inflection at point C. This is the point to the extreme left on the minimum-variance frontier. Thus, it represents the global minimum variance portfolio. Point F represents global maximum return portfolio. All portfolios along line segment CF are more efficient than portfolios along line segment AC. Thus, it is the efficient frontier. Portfolios A and B are inefficient or dominated portfolios.

TABLE 3.5 Dominated and Efficient Portfolios

Portfolio	*Expected return (%)*	*Risk, σ (%)*	*Dominated or not*	*Efficient or not*
A	10	15	Yes, by B, C	No
B	12	13	Yes, by C	No
C	13	12	No	Yes
D	15	16	No	Yes
E	18	22	No	Yes
F	20	26	No	Yes

Short sales is the selling of a borrowed asset/ security.

Efficient Frontier with Margined Short Sales A **short sale** occurs when a person sells a second person an asset (security) borrowed from a third person (broker). A short seller seeks to profit from the expected fall in price, which may or may not take place. The **margin** here means the specified percentage of the market value of the transaction that the short seller (borrower of security), deposits with the lender (broker), effecting the transaction.

Edward A Dyl[3] has pointed out that when margined short sales are feasible, it is possible to construct portfolios that offer the same expected return with lower variance, that is, the efficient frontier with margined short sales dominates the efficient frontier without such sales (Figure 3.3).

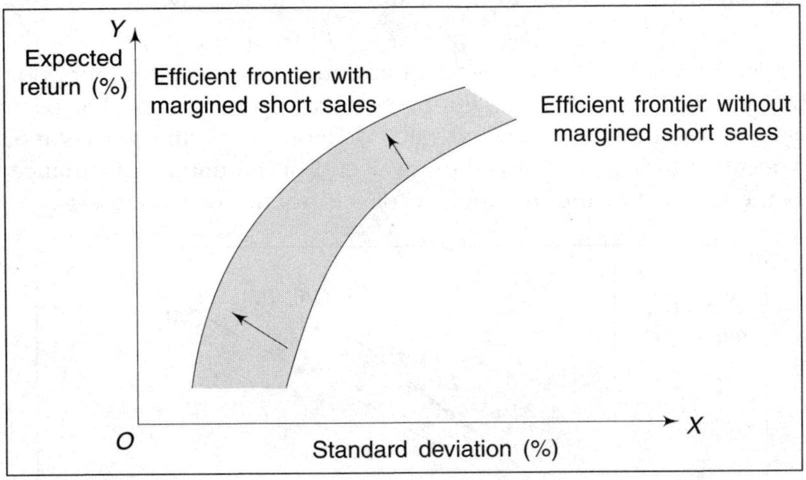

FIGURE 3.3 Effect of Margined Short Sales on Efficient Frontier

Efficient Frontier with One Risk-free Asset A **risk-free security** is one that has zero variance and, hence, standard deviation (square root of variance). James Tobin[4] has pointed out that: (a) Portfolios made up of risky assets and one risk-free asset generate investment opportunities (portfolio opportunity set) with linear relationship between expected return and risk; (b) One such portfolio opportunity set will dominate the portfolios formed by mixing only risky assets (securities and/or portfolios of securities/other assets).

Risk free security has zero variance.

To facilitate further discussion, let us denote a risk-free portfolio by F, a risky portfolio by M, and a complete portfolio formed by combining them as C. Further, w is the fraction of the overall portfolio invested in M, and the remaining (= 1 – w) in F. The expected return of the complete portfolio may be calculated by using Equation 3.19

$$E(r_c) = r_f + w[E(r_m) - r_f] \quad (3.19)$$

where $E(r_c)$ = Expected rate of return on complete portfolio
r_f = Risk-free rate of return
w = Fraction of complete portfolio, C, invested in risky asset M
$E(r_m)$ = Expected return for risky asset M
$E(r_m) - r_f$ = Risk premium of the risky portfolio

The standard deviation of the complete portfolio is given by:

$$\sigma_c = w\sigma_m \quad (3.20)$$

where σ_c = Standard deviation of complete portfolio C
w = Fraction of complete portfolio, C, invested in risky asset M
σ_m = Standard deviation of risky portfolio M

Solving the two equations for w and setting them as equal, we get the precise relationship between expected return and standard deviation:

$$E(r_c) = r_f + (\sigma_c/\sigma_m)\,[E(r_m) - r_f] \quad (3.21)$$

Rearranging the terms, we get

$$E(r_c) = r_f + \sigma_c \{[E(r_m) - r_f]/\sigma_m\} \quad \textbf{(3.22)}$$

This is the equation of portfolio opportunity set or portfolio possibility lines with one risk-free asset. It is termed as the **capital allocation line** (CAL). The slope of the CAL shows reward to variability ratio, that is, increase in the expected return of the portfolio per unit of additional standard deviation (variability). Symbolically,

Capital allocation line shows the reward to variability ratio in terms of additional beta.

$$\text{Slope} = [E(r_c) - r_f]/\sigma_m \quad \textbf{(3.23)}$$

Figure 3.4 shows three capital allocation lines originating from point *F* and passing through *A*, *M* and *Z*. Point *F* represents a pure portfolio (100 per cent holding) of risk-free assets, with expected rate of return $E(r_f)$ and zero standard deviation of expected returns. Point *A* is the lower end of the minimum variance frontier of risky assets. Point *Z* is the top end of the minimum variance frontier of risky assets.

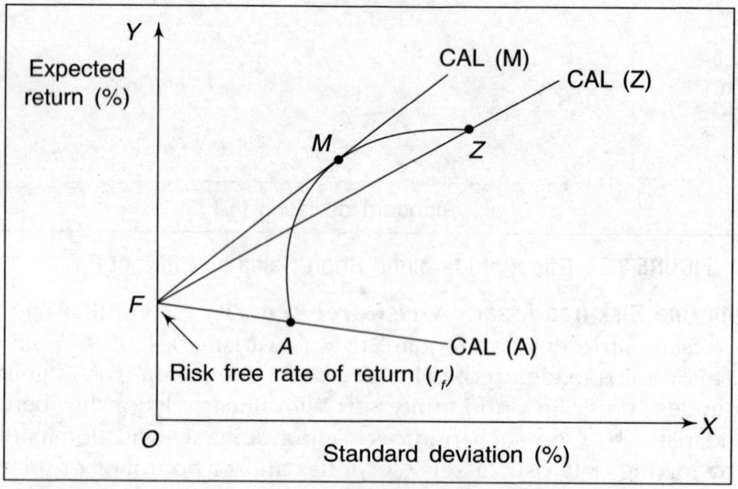

FIGURE 3.4 Portfolio Opportunities Set Risk-free Asset (CAL)

It is obvious from the figure that the highest CAL supported by the efficient frontier of the risky assets is tangential at point *M*. In other words, combinations of portfolio *M* with risk-free asset *F* offer the best risk-return trade-off. Point *M* represents the pure portfolio (100 per cent holding) of a risky asset, with expected return $E(r_m)$ and standard deviation σ_m. The investor can obtain any combination of risk and return on line segment *FM* by combining the risk-free asset *F* with a portfolio of risky assets, namely, *M*. Thus, portfolio *M* is the best risky portfolio to be combined with a risk-free asset. Portfolios represented by line segment *FM* are known as lending portfolios.

Efficient Frontier with Borrowing So far, portfolios have been constructed from owned funds. With owned funds, the efficient frontier of a portfolio with one risk-free asset ends at point *M*. Extending *FM* beyond *M* shows further opportunities for higher return. Are these opportunities real or hypothetical? What should an investor do to exploit these opportunities?

These are real opportunities, which the investor can avail of by borrowing funds at a risk-free rate, R_f, and investing the same in the risky asset, *M*. This is known as creating a **leveraged**, **margined** or **borrowing portfolio**. With borrowings, the weight of the risky asset in the portfolio exceeds one. Negative weight for risk-free asset ensures that the sum of weights equals unity. Negative weight for risk-free assets shows that the investor has created a leveraged portfolio by borrowing funds. For example, an investor has ₹2,00,000. He borrows an additional sum of ₹1,00,000 and invests it in the risky asset. The weight of the risky asset in the overall portfolio is 1.5 (= ₹3,00,000/₹2,00,000). The weight of the risk-free asset becomes –0.5 (= 1.5 – 1.), which means borrowings are 50 per cent of the owned funds.

It may be noted that the steepest CAL with borrowing and lending portfolios completely dominates the efficient frontier of risky assets (Figure 3.5). Thus, CAL tangential to the efficient frontier of risky assets constitutes the new efficient frontier with one risk-free asset. A very significant conclusion of the model is the **identical optimal risky portfolio** (M) for all investors, irrespective of their risk preference. The investor's risk aversion simply determines the exact point along the CAL. A risk-averse investor assigns greater weight to the risk-free asset in his portfolio than an investor with greater risk tolerance. However, both use identical sets of two assets—one risk-free and another risky. This result is called the **separation theorem**.[5]

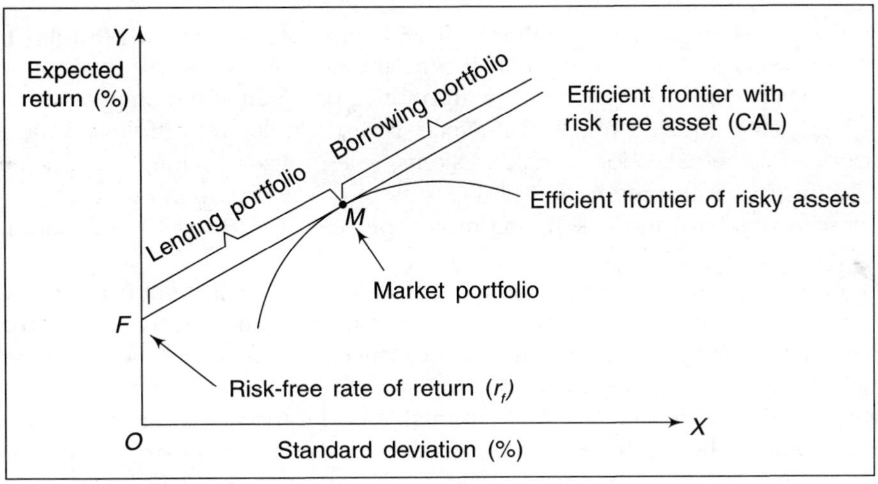

FIGURE 3.5 Efficient Frontier with One Risk-free Asset

Market Portfolio In the preceding discussion on the CAL, portfolio M was identified as the universally desirable portfolio of risky assets. It has the property of maximising return per unit of risk (standard deviation) as the steepest CAL passes through it. What is the nature of this portfolio M? How is it constructed?

Portfolio **M** refers to the **market portfolio**—a theoretical construct credited to Prof. Eugene Fama.[6] When we add up the portfolios of all individual investors, borrowing and lending cancel out each other, and the value of an aggregate risky portfolio is the entire wealth of the economy. Thus, market portfolio is a huge portfolio that includes all traded assets in exactly the same proportion in which they are supplied in equilibrium. The return on the market portfolio is the weighted average of return on all capital assets.

For simplicity, a portfolio containing all securities is used as a proxy for the market portfolio. Since all investors hold the same risky portfolio, (a) no security from it will be left out and (b) the proportion of each security in the market portfolio equals the market value of the security divided by the total market value of all securities. If these conditions are not fulfilled, prices adjust until the value of the security becomes consistent with its proportion in portfolio M. The concept of the capital market line in the capital asset pricing model rests on the notion of the market portfolio.

Capital Market Line The capital market line (CML) is a capital allocation line (CAL) provided by one-month T-bills as a risk-free asset and a market-index portfolio like Dow Jones, Standard and Poor's and NYSE, as the risky asset.[7] It is one of the two elements of the CAPM, the other being the security market line (SML). All investors end up somewhere along the CML. The CML indicates:

(i) The locus of all efficient portfolios (those plotting along CML). Not all securities and portfolios lie along the CML.

(ii) Risk-return relationship and measure of risk for efficient portfolios.

(iii) The appropriate measure of risk for the portfolio is standard deviation of returns on portfolios.

(iv) The relationship between risk (standard deviation) and expected return for efficient portfolios is linear.

Investor's Risk Preference

Rational investors invest in efficient portfolios. The choice of an optimal portfolio from efficient portfolios depends on the risk-return tradeoff for the investor. A risk-averse investor seeks risk-free opportunities or considers risky opportunities with positive risk premium (compensation for additional risk). Other things being equal, a highly risk-averse investor holds a portfolio on the lower end of the efficient frontier. As the aversion to risk weakens, one moves up along the efficient frontier. In Example 3.5, an investor who prefers portfolio C is more risk-averse than one who prefers portfolio E. Between these two points, the risk premium is 5 per cent (= 18% – 13%) for additional risk of 10 per cent (22% – 12%).

Is the risk-return tradeoff available and implicit in the slope of the efficient frontier (CML) adequate? Are all investors satisfied by it? Determination of the risk premium that the investor can expect in well functioning capital markets is one of the prime concerns of financial theory. However, the risk premium sought by an investor depends on his risk preference/tolerance.

Utility functions, or indifference curves, are normally used to portray an investor's attitude towards risk. Figure 3.6 portrays the indifference map for a hypothetical investor. All portfolios along an indifference curve are equally satisfactory to the concerned investor. The higher is the curve, the higher is the satisfaction. Many systems have been developed to measure the satisfaction or utility score of a portfolio. The investor is administered risk questionnaires containing questions on the investing experience of the person, financial security and tendency to make risky or conservative choices. The scores obtained are converted into a risk aversion index. The approach followed by the Association of Investment Management and Research (AIMR) combines the investor's risk aversion with the expected return and variance of returns to assign a utility score. The utility score (U) for a portfolio is defined as:[8]

$$U = E(r) - 0.005A\sigma^2 \qquad \textbf{(3.24)}$$

Where $E(r)$ = Expected return

A = Index of the investor's risk aversion

σ^2 = Variance of returns

0.005 = Scaling factor that allows expected return and standard deviation in the equation as percentages

Table 3.6 presents expected return, standard deviation of returns and utility scores for some portfolios that yield the same satisfaction to an investor, given his risk aversion index; this value is assumed as equal to 2. All portfolios lie along the same indifference curve with a utility score of 4. It is obvious that utility scores vary directly with expected return and inversely with variance (risk). The higher the utility score, the more attractive is the risk-return profile of a portfolio.

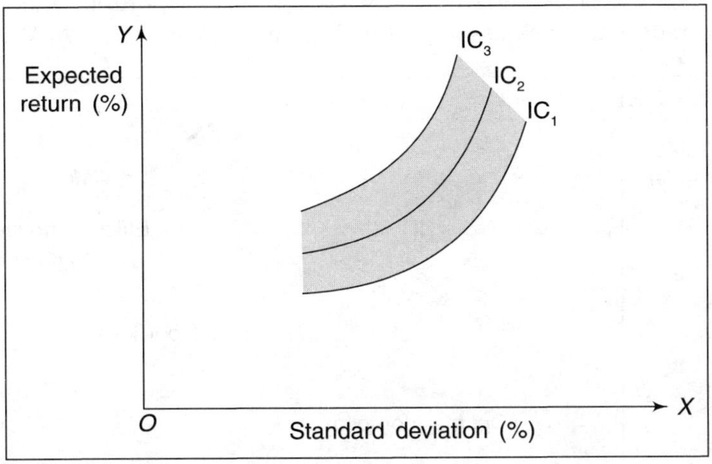

FIGURE 3.6 Risk-return Indifference Curves for a Hyopthetical Investor

TABLE 3.6 Portfolios on the Same Indifference Curve

Expected return, E(r) (%)	*Standard deviation, σ (%)*	*Utility = E(r) – 0.005Aσ²*
5	10.0	4 = 5 – 0.005 × 2 × 100
10	24.5	4 = 10 – 0.005 × 2 × 600
15	33.2	4 = 15 – 0.005 × 2 × 1102
20	40.0	4 = 20 – 0.005 × 2 × 1600
25	45.8	4 = 25 – 0.005 × 2 × 2098

Optimal Portfolio

Indifference curve maps an investor's utility with respect to expected return and risk.

Efficient portfolio maximises returns for a given level of risk or minimises risk for a given level of return.

A rational investor seeks an **efficient portfolio** tangent to the highest attainable indifference curve. It may be noted that the shape of the **indifference curve** may be linear or curvilinear. The point of tangency between the efficient frontier and risk-return indifference curve corresponds to the optimal portfolio for the concerned investor. In Figure 3.7 **(p.3.20)**, indifference curve IC_2 is tangent to the efficient frontier at point P, which represents the optimal portfolio.

CAPM is an equilibrium model of the trade-off between expected portfolio return and unavoidable (systematic) risk; the basic theory that links together risk and return of all assets.

LO 3.5 CAPITAL ASSET PRICING MODEL (CAPM)

The capital asset pricing model **(CAPM)**, as the name suggests, is a theory that explains how asset prices are formed in the market place. It is a logical and major extension of the portfolio theory of Markowitz by William Sharpe (1964),[9] John Lintner (1965)[10] and Jan Mossin (1967).[11]

The capital asset pricing model provides the framework for determining the equilibrium expected return for risky assets. It uses the results of capital market theory to derive the relationship between expected return and systematic risk of individual assets/securities and portfolios. Capital market theories, also referred to as asset pricing theories, deal with how asset prices are determined if investors behaved the way Markowitz's portfolio theory suggests. A price reflects the expected return and risk associated with an asset. Thus, the CAPM has implications for:

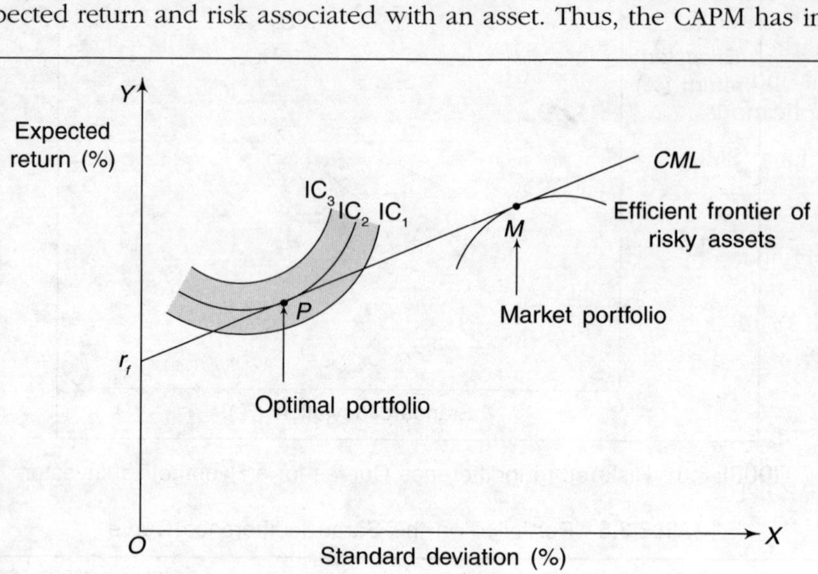

FIGURE 3.7 Determination of Optimal Portfolio with One Risk-free Asset

(a) Risk-return relationship for an efficient portfolio
(b) Risk-return relationship for an individual asset/security
(c) Identification of under- and over-valued assets traded in the market
(d) Pricing of assets not yet traded in the market
(e) Effect of leverage on cost of equity (rate of return required by equity shareholders)
(f) Capital budgeting decisions and cost of capital
(g) Risk of the firm through diversification of project portfolio

Assumptions

To grapple with the complexities of the real world, the CAPM makes certain simplifying assumptions. Some of these may be relaxed later.

1. All investors are price-takers. Their number is so large that no single investor can affect prices.
2. All investors use the mean-variance portfolio selection model of Markowitz.
3. Assets/securities are perfectly divisible.
4. All investors plan for one identical holding period.
5. Homogeneity of expectation for all investors results in identical efficient frontier and optimal portfolio.
6. Investors can lend or borrow at an identical risk-free rate.
7. There are no transaction costs and income taxes.

Elements of the Model

Capital market line depicts the risk-return relationship for efficient portfolios.

The capital asset pricing model consists of two elements: the capital market line (CML) and the security market line (SML). The **capital market line**, as discussed before, represents the efficient frontier formed by combining one-month T-bills with a broad index of common stocks. Its serves two functions. *First,* it depicts the risk-return relationship for efficient portfolios available to investors. *Second*, it shows that the appropriate measure of risk for an efficient portfolio is the standard deviation of return on the portfolio. The security market line, on the other hand, pertains to all portfolios (which plot on and below CML) as well as individual securities. This makes CML a special case of SML. We explore below SML and its implications in detail.

Security Market Line (SML) We know that risk averse investors seek risk premium to assume the risk embedded in risky assets. The risk is variability in return. The total risk consists of two components: **systematic risk** and **unsystematic risk**. In a portfolio of risky assets, the investor can eliminate unsystematic risk through diversification, as suggested by Markowitz. Systematic risk is unavoidable; this is the contribution of an individual asset to the risk of market portfolio.

Security market line is a graphic depiction of CAPM and describes the market price of risk in capital markets.

According to the capital market theory, the market compensates or rewards for systematic risk only. The level of systematic risk in an asset is measured by the beta coefficient (β). The CAPM links beta to the level of required return. Graphic depiction of the CAPM—the expected return-beta relationship—is referred to as the **Security Market Line** (SML). This is illustrated in Figure 3.8. SML is a linear relationship defined by Equation 3.25.

$$E(r_i) = r_f + \beta\,[E(r_m) - r_f] \quad \textbf{(3.25)}$$

Expected return = Risk-free return + (Beta × Risk premium of market) **(3.26)**

on security i = Intercept + (Beta × Slope of SML) **(3.27)**

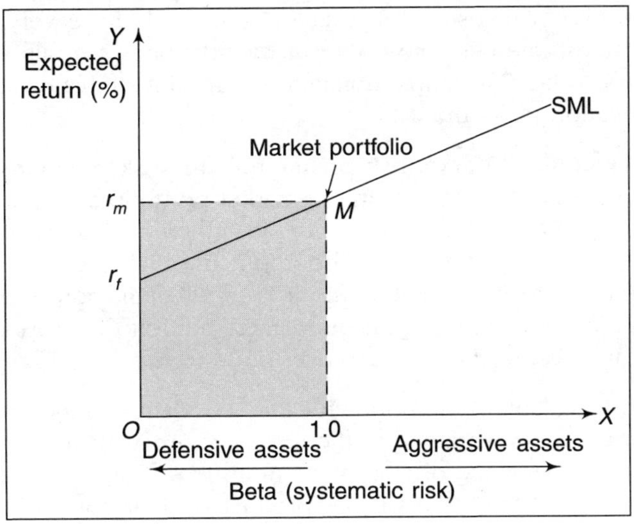

FIGURE 3.8 Security Market Line (SML)

The more familiar form of the SML:

$$E(r_i) - r_f = \beta\,[E(r_m) - r_f] \quad \textbf{(3.28)}$$

Risk premium on security i = Beta × Risk premium of market **(3.29)**

where $E(r_i)$ = Expected or required rate of return on asset i

r_f = Risk-free rate of return, vertical axis intercept

β = Systematic risk of the asset, beta

$E(r_m)$ = Expected return on market portfolio

Example 3.6 illustrates the application of CAPM.

***Example* 3.6**

There are three assets—Defensive, Moderate, and Aggressive—with beta values of 0.5, 1.0 and 1.5, respectively. The risk-free rate is assumed to be 5 per cent and the market return is expected to be 15 per cent. The expected return of 3 securities may be worked out as shown below:

$$E(r_i) = r_f + \beta \times E(r_m) - r_f$$
$$E(r_D) = 5 + 0.5 \times (15–5) = 5 + 5 = 10 \text{ per cent}$$
$$E(r_M) = 5 + 1.0 \times (15–5) = 5 + 10 = 15 \text{ per cent}$$
$$E(r_A) = 5 + 1.5 \times (15–5) = 5 + 15 = 20 \text{ per cent}$$

Expected return in a CAPM context is the risk-free rate plus a premium for systematic risk based on beta.

Risk-return Relationship In the CAPM, the **expected return** on an asset varies directly with its systematic risk (β) and the risk premium of the market portfolio. In other words, the risk premium for an asset or portfolio is a function of its beta. The risk premium added to the risk-free rate is directly proportional to beta. The risk premium of a market portfolio, also referred to as **reward**, depends on the level of risk-free return and return on the market portfolio. In short, information related to the following three aspects are needed to apply the CAPM: risk-free rate, risk premium on market portfolio and beta.

Risk-Free Rate The rate of return available on assets like T-bills, money market funds or bank deposits is taken as the proxy for risk-free rate. The maturity period of T-bills and bank deposits is taken to be less than one year, usually 364 days. Such assets have very low or virtually negligible default risk and interest rate risk. However, under inflationary conditions, they are risk-less in nominal terms only. In fact, the real return (nominal return minus inflation rate) may become zero, even negative, when inflation picks up.

Risk-Premium on Market Portfolio Market risk premium or the risk premium on market portfolio is the difference between the expected return on the market portfolio and the risk-free rate of return. The CAPM holds that in equilibrium, the market portfolio is the unanimously desirable risky portfolio. It contains all securities in exactly the same proportion in which they are supplied, that is, each security is held in proportion to its market value. It is an efficient portfolio, which entails neither lending nor borrowing. The risk premium on the market portfolio is proportional to its risk (σ^2_M) and the degree of risk aversion of the average investor.

Beta measures the risk (volatility) of an individual asset relative to market portfolio.

Beta It measures the risk (volatility) of an individual asset relative to the market portfolio. Accordingly, **beta** is the covariance of the asset's return with the market portfolio's return, divided by the variance of market portfolio ($\beta = Cov_{im}/\sigma^2_m$). It may be recalled that the covariance of two assets is the product of their correlation coefficient (ρ_{im}) and respective standard deviations ($Cov_{im} = \rho_{im}\ \sigma_i\ \sigma_m$). The covariance of the market portfolio with itself is the variance of the portfolio. Thus, the beta of the market portfolio is one. This classifies all others portfolios and assets in two risk classes. Assets with beta less than one are called **defensive assets**. Assets with beta greater than one are called **aggressive assets**. Risk-free assets have a beta equal to zero.

It may be noted that the beta of a portfolio is the weighted average of the betas of assets included in the portfolio. The weights are the relative share of assets in the portfolio. The concept is illustrated in Example 3.7.

***Example* 3.7**

Two assets with beta values of 0.8 and 1.2 have been combined in the proportion 3:1. The beta of the resultant portfolio will be 0.9 (= 0.8 × 0.75 + 1.2 × 0.25). If the standard deviation of market portfolio is 30 per cent, the standard deviation of the portfolio would be 27 per cent (= 0.9 × 30). This shows portfolio risk (standard deviation) is driven by security betas.

Unlevering and Relevering Beta It may be recalled that the beta of a portfolio formed by combining two assets is the weighted average of their betas. If we view all the assets of a firm as a portfolio of debt and equity (the two sides of the balance sheet of the firm), the market value of the firm (V) equals the asset value as well as the sum total of the market values of debt (D) and equity (E). Therefore, the weighted average of debt and equity betas should be equal to the assets beta.

$$\beta_{assets} = \beta_{portfolio} = (D/V)\,\beta_{debt} + (E/V)\,\beta_{equity} \quad \textbf{(3.30)}$$

It is evident from the above equation that in an all-equity or unlevered firm, the value of equity beta is equal to the assets beta. This is referred to as the *unlevered beta.* Determination of assets beta from observed securities betas is termed as *unlevering of beta. Relevering of beta* involves determination of equity beta, with given assets beta, for the proposed financing structure, using equation 3.31 (similar to the determination of K_e under net operating income (NOI) approach).

$$\beta_{equity} = \beta_{assets} + (\beta_{assets} - \beta_{debt})\,D/E \quad \textbf{(3.31)}$$

These concepts are relevant in the context of the determination of (i) the required rate of return for a new project/firm and (ii) the required rate of return on equity shares (cost of equity) with change in the financing structure. When the new project does not entail any change in business and financial risks of the firm, the beta of the existing assets of the firm may be used as a proxy for the project beta. Similarly, the required rate of return on the initial public offer (IPO) of a company may be determined based on the observed betas of a comparable firm (consider Example 3.8).

***Example* 3.8**

To illustrate this point, let us assume equity beta of Rely India Ltd. is 1.5 and debt beta is zero. Its present debt-equity is 1:2. A new firm, Progress India Ltd., which is similar in size and risk of operations, plans to issue equity shares for the first time. However, Progress India's financing structure has debt and equity in equal proportions. The equity beta of Progress India may be obtained by unlevering the equity beta of Rely India and then relevering for the proposed financing structure of Progress India, as explained below.

The unlevered or assets beta is obtained as

$$\beta_{assets} = (1/3) \times 0 + (2/3) \times 1.5 = 0.0 + 1.0 = 1.0$$

For the proposed debt-equity ratio of 1:1, the equity beta is

$$\beta_{equity} = 1.0 + (1.0 - 0.0)\,(1/1) = 1.0 + 1.0 = 2.0$$

Now the CAPM (SML) equation may be used to determine the expected rates of return for relevered beta values.

Under- and Over-valued Assets

If individual assets/securities and portfolios are priced correctly, they lie exactly on the SML. Assets plotting off the SML indicate mispricing of assets by the market. Assets that plot above the SML are undervalued. They offer higher expected return than assets of a similar risk class. Hence, they are attractive. The buying pressure for such assets will push up their price and lower the return, until they are correctly priced. Similarly, assets that plot below are unattractive because they are overpriced.

In a well functioning market, an investor can obtain the 'fair return' predicted by the SML for a given risk by mixing the risk-free asset and the market portfolio in the right proportions. Suppose, an investor expects that stock *X* with beta 0.5 would yield return of 6 per cent. If the risk-free rate is 5 per cent and the market risk premium is 6 per cent, the required rate of return is 8 per cent (5 + 0.5 × 6 = 5 + 3). Clearly, the stock is overpriced. The investor can obtain the SML indicated return of 8 per cent by mixing the risk-free asset and the market portfolio in equal proportions to create a portfolio that has beta of 0.5. Why a mixture of risk-free asset and the market portfolio? The reason is that, these opportunities are available to all investors. The only way to create beta 0.5 is to mix the two securities in equal proportions, that is, (0.5 × 0 + 0.5 × 1 = 0.5). As the expected return on the market portfolio is 11 per cent (= 5 + 1 × 6), the expected return on the new portfolio would be 8 per cent (= 0.5 × 5 + 0.5 × 11).

Let us take another example, the investor expects 15 per cent return on stock *Y*, which has a beta of 2. This time the SML determined required rate is 17 per cent. Again, the stock is overvalued. The investor can still earn 17 per cent by creating a leveraged portfolio with a beta of 2. For this, the investor needs to borrow funds equal to his owned funds and invest the entire amount in the market portfolio. The beta of this portfolio is 2 (= –1 × 0 + 2 × 1). The expected return is 17 per cent (= –1 × 5 + 2 × 11). Thus, when defensive stock is overvalued, the investor should combine market portfolio with lending (risk-free asset). When aggressive stock is overvalued, he should combine market portfolio with borrowing.

The vertical distance between the fair return predicted by the SML and return actually expected by an investor is called the *alpha* (α) of the asset. Thus, undervalued assets have a positive alpha, and overvalued assets have a negative alpha. For example, if the risk-free rate is 5 per cent and market return is expected to be 15 per cent, fair return, stipulated by the CAPM, on a security with beta of 1.2 will be 23 per cent (= 5 + 1.2 × 15). If a person expects the return to be 25 per cent, the implied alpha is 2 per cent. The security is undervalued and attractive. If the security is expected to return 20 per cent, the alpha is negative at 3 per cent, the security is mispriced and overvalued. The essence of security analysis is to search for securities with positive alpha.

In practice, minor deviations on both sides of the SML indicate the effect of transaction costs and taxes. Besides, due to imperfect information, investors fail to notice these opportunities and prices hover around their equilibrium level. Thus, SML is more of a band than a precise relationship between beta and the expected rate of return.

Validity of the CAPM

CAPM
Despite challenges the CAPM is widely used because it is a practical equilibrium model.

The capital asset pricing model is a rigorously derived equilibrium model. Like any other economic model, it is an abstraction and simplification of reality. It has been widely used and hailed. Its popularity may be ascribed to a set of four factors. *First*, the risk-return trade-off—the direct proportional relationship between the two—has a distinct intuitive appeal. *Second*, transition from the capital market line (CML) to the security market line (SML) shows that the undiversifiable nature of the systematic risk makes it the relevant risk for pricing of securities and portfolios. *Third*, beta, the measure of systematic risk, is easy to compute and use. *Finally*, the model shows that investors are content to put their money in a limited number of portfolios, namely, a risk-free asset like Treasury bills and a risky asset like a market index fund.

However, CAPM is beset with a number of problems. One of these relates to the maturity of the risk-free asset, namely, interest rate on a short-term government security like a T-bill or a long-term rate like that on a treasury bond or an intermediate term-rate like that on a 3 year treasury securities. The second problem relates to whether the market premium should be the expected or historical. Yet another problem relates to the use of an appropriate market index. The faulty use of a market index in likely to result in faulty measurement of security measurement. Finally, there is the question if beta is the appropriate risk measure. To provide a solution to these challenges, an extended CAPM and alternative models have emerged. These models incorporate multiple variables and factors. They are briefly discussed in the next Section.

LO 3.6 EXTENDED CAPM

The CAPM is essentially a single-factor model in that the security's expected return depends on a single factor, namely, beta. But there may be other factors, apart from beta, which may affect required returns. Therefore, the inclusion of these factors in the CAPM equation would provide better explanation of the variables impacting security returns. The major factors are: **(i)** taxes, **(ii)** inflation, **(iii)** liquidity, **(iv)** market capitalisation size and **(v)** price-earnings and market-to-book value ratios. These factors (showing extensions to the CAPM) are briefly explained in this Section.

Extended CAPM adds variables additional to beta to the model.

Taxes

The investor receives return on security in the form of dividend income and capital gains or losses. Accordingly, the tax liability of the investors is of two types: **(i)** tax on dividend income and **(ii)** tax on capital gains. In cases when both the types of income are either free-of-tax or they are taxed at the same rates, the CAPM results hold true whether company pays more or less dividends. However, in practice, capital gains are normally taxed at lower rates than dividend income.* Moreover, capital gain tax is payable only when securities are actually sold; the tax on capital gains is deferred till the actual sale of the securities. The different tax treatment of dividend and capital gains means that with less dividend (and more capital appreciation), the investor's tax liability would be lower—an attribute unrecognised by the CAPM.

***Example* 3.9**

Suppose the investor is expected to have return of 15 per cent (consisting of a dividend yield of 10 per cent and a 5 per cent capital gain on initial value) by holding securities in Company X. Company Y is expected to provide dividend yield of 11 per cent and capital appreciation of 3.5 per cent (total return of 14.5 per cent). Assume further that dividend income is taxed at 30 per cent and capital gain at 20 per cent. Though the before-tax return from company X's securities higher at 15 per cent, the after-tax return (effective/real return) is higher in the case of company Y at 11.25 per cent (Table 3.7)

TABLE 3.7 After-tax Return from Securities of Companies X and Y

	Return from Company X			*Return from Company Y*		
Particulars	*Before-tax*	*Tax rate*	*After-tax*	*Before-tax*	*Tax rate*	*After-tax*
Dividend yield	10%	30%	7%	3.5%	30%	2.45
Capital gain	5	20	4	11	20	8.80
Expected return	15%		11%	14.5%		11.25%

It is apparent from Table 3.7 that in spite of the lower expected return before taxes (14.5%) of company Y, its expected after-tax return is higher on account of the fact that a higher proportion of income/return consists of capital gains. Evidently, the tax-paying investor prefers securities of

*Dividend income from domestic companies and mutual funds in India is exempt from tax in the hands of the shareholders and investors.

company Y to those of company X; in contrast, the tax-exempt investor will have a preference for company X, all other things being the same.

As a logical corollary of the above follows that high dividend paying securities may be required to provide higher expected returns before taxes *vis-à-vis* the low dividend paying securities to offset the tax effect.

In view of the above, the CAPM equation for determining expected return is to be modified to include dividend yield and tax effect, as shown in Equation 3.32.

$$K_j = R_f + bB_j + t(D_j - R_f) \quad \textbf{(3.32)}$$

Where R_f = Required rate of return on security, j
b = Coefficient showing the relative importance of beta
B_j = Beta of security, j
t = Coefficient showing the relative importance of the tax effect.
D_j = Dividend yield on security, j

It is apparent from equation 3.32 that the higher is the dividend yield, the higher is the expected before-tax return the security may be expected to provide. In other words, if there is a systematic bias in the market in favour of capital gains, the expected return on a security is affected by beta as well as its dividend yield. Clearly, taxes, *albeit* indirectly, affect the required return from a security.

Inflation

In the event of the economy being subject to inflation, the realised *real return* for a security tends to be lower. In case inflation is highly predictable, the expected return is equal to the real required return plus inflation premium. However, in practice, this prediction of inflation may not be easy task. In other words, inflation is unpredictable or it is uncertain. Obviously, in such a situation investor will have a preference for securities which provide **hedge** against inflation. (The term 'hedge' implies that the return on the security increases with *unanticipated* increase in inflation). This desirable property of providing protection against inflation reduces the systematic risk of the security in *real* terms and, hence, the investor's expected return on such securities may be lower.

Covariance with unexpected inflation is desirable from the standpoint of the investor.

In statistical terms, the greater is the **covariance** (positive) of the return of a security with unanticipated changes in inflation, the lower is the expected nominal return the market requires on such a security or *vice-versa.* In other words, the expected nominal return of a security is a positive function of its beta and a negative function of its covariance with unanticipated inflation. Evidently, positive covariance with inflation is a desirable property and may reduce the required return on the part of the investor; in contrast, the securities with negative covariance (between return and inflation) are likely to raise the investor's nominal required return from such securities.

Liquidity

Liquidity refers to the ability to transform a security readily into cash without loss or at negligible loss (if any). The spread between the buying (bid) price and the selling (ask) price of a security may be regarded as a useful measure of its liquidity. In general, the lower is the spread between the two prices, the higher is the liquidity and *vice-versa.* Unforeseen events in future may require early redemption/conversion of securities into cash. Investors, presumably, therefore prefer more liquid securities. If this is so, the investors required return on liquid securities may be relatively lower *vis-à-vis* non-liquid securities, other things being equal. The factor of liquidity again causes distortion in CAPM.

Market Capitalisation Size

Market capitalisation is the product of the number of shares outstanding and the market price of the share. In general, the higher the market capitalisation of a corporate firm, the more secured the investor feels in investing in securities of such a company. Presumably, the higher the market capitalisation size of a corporate firm, the safer is considered the investments. Therefore, to offset the additional risk, the investors normally may require higher return from the securities belonging to 'small' corporate firms. In other words, the investors place premium on the securities of large-sized firms and may require lower returns on investments in such securities, other things being equal.

Price-Earnings and Market-to-Book Value Ratios

Van Horne states that the price/earnings (P/E) ratio effect has been observed in realised returns from securities/equity shares. Holding constant beta, observed returns tend to be higher for low P/E ratio shares and lower for high P/E ratio shares. In simple words, shares with low P/E ratio earn higher returns that predicted by CAPM and shares with high P/E ratio earn less returns that what the CAPM would predict. The modified CAPM equation with inclusion of the P/E ratio is 3.33.

$$K_j = R_f + bB_j - p\,(P/E_j - P/E_m) \qquad \textbf{(3.33)}$$

Where p = Coefficient showing the relative importance of a security's price/earnings ratio

P/E_j = Price-earnings ratio of the security under consideration.

P/E_m = Weighted average price/earnings ratio for the market portfolio.

The equation 3.33 points out two facts: (i) the required return increases with beta and decreases with the P/E ratio and (ii) beta does not capture all the risk associated with holding a security; inclusion of P/E ratio adds explanatory power to the CAPM.

Closely related to the P/E ratio is the market-to-book (M/B) value ratio which has been employed to explain security return. The M/B ratio is obtained dividing the market value of all claims on a corporate firm by the book value of its assets. Van Horne mentions that observed returns tend to be higher for low M/B ratio securities/shares than for high M/B ratio securities, holding beta constant. It may be noted that the results are similar to those observed in the relationship between returns on a security and the P/E ratio. It is perhaps for this reason that either P/E ratio or M/B ratio is used to explain security returns.

It is worth noting that among all the variables used to extend CAPM, market capitalisation size and the P/E ratio or the M/B ratio (not both) have been observed to be the most consistent and significant in their effect. For multiple variables, required rate of return is given by equation 3.34.

$$K_j = R_f + bB_j + c\ (\text{factor } 2) + d\ (\text{factor } 3) + e\ (\text{factor } 4) + \ldots + m\ (\text{factor } n) \qquad \textbf{(3.34)}$$

Where b, c, d, e and m are coefficients reflecting the relative importance of the factors involved. When these factors are added along with beta, a better explanation of security's total return (in the case of some securities) is obtained.

The extensions to the CAPM approach made in this section should not undermine the importance of the CAPM framework to explain the security return as beta continues to be the major determinant of the security returns. The merit of the CAPM extension exercise is that it provides a better insight into the market equilibrium process as well as more precise (comprehensive) measurement of the expected return from a specific share/security; it is supplementing in nature.

LO 3.7 ARBITRAGE PRICING THEORY

Although CAPM approach has been widely accepted as a determinant of required return of a security (asset), it is beset with a number of restrictive assumptions, affecting its application in practice. For instance, the CAPM framework assumes that there exists a market portfolio consisting of all risky assets. Apart from the unobservable aspect of such a portfolio, the portfolio itself may provide different results. For instance, portfolio in India (the rate of return earned on which is used as proxy of Rm in CAPM) may consist of the RBI's share price index, the Economic Times share price index, the Financial Express share price index, Sensex of BSE and the NIFTY of NSE. Obviously, the rates of return of these portfolios are not likely to be equal; the required return of the security will vary.

The **Arbitrage Pricing Theory** (APT) is an alternative model of asset/security pricing which has received considerable attention in the financial literature in recent year as it is devoid of the CAPM assumptions. The APT model was developed in the 1970s by Ross. As the name implies, the APT is based on the concept of arbitrage. In the context of pricing of (return from) securities, arbitrage implies finding/availability of two securities which are essentially the same (having different prices/returns). In such a situation, it will be profitable for the investor to sell the expensive one. The theory is based on the premise that security prices adjust as investors form portfolios in search of arbitrage profits. When such opportunities of earning arbitrage profits are completely exhausted, the prices of securities are said to be in equilibrium. This leads to the state of capital market efficiency, free of arbitrage opportunities. In other words, arbitrage will ensure that riskless assets (or securities) provide the same expected return in competitive financial markets[17].

> **Arbitrage pricing theory** has markets equilibrating across securities through arbitrage driving out mispricing.

Multifactor Linear Model

Another useful way of explaining the APT is that it relates the returns of security within a multivariate framework in which the return relationships are linear. Multivariate framework implies that there are a variety of different factors which influence security returns. However, the theory does not specify these factors on the basis of conceptual argument. The argument presumably is that factors may not be the same for all securities. Therefore, the factors to be used in APT model are to be identified empirically; the factor analysis, a statistical method, has been suggested to identify relevant factors.

The factors in the context of APT can be classified into two broad groups, namely, macroeconomic factors having a pervasive influence and micro (firm specific) factors. Viewed from this perspective, the APT model (as shown in equation 3.35) is akin to an extended CAPM model.

$$\text{Return} = R_f + \beta_{j1}(\overline{r}_{f1} - r_f) + \beta_{j2} + (\overline{r}_{f2} - r_f) + \ldots + \beta_{jk}(r_{jk} - r_f) \quad \textbf{(3.35)}$$

Where K = Number of factors that affect an asset (security) return

$\overline{r}_{f1}, \overline{r}_{f2}, \ldots \overline{r}_{jk}$ = Expected returns to factors 1,2, ...K

$\beta_{j1}, \beta_{j2}, \ldots \beta_{jk}$ = Sensitivities of an asset (security) to factors 1,2,...K.

Factors It may be emphasised here that the APT framework normally includes the market risk premium (return on the market portfolio minus risk free rate) as one of the factors; it may be recapitulated that market risk premium is the sole factor used in the CAPM. The other factors included are macroeconomic and firm specific, while the major macroeconomic factors are inflation, interest rates, growth rate in gross domestic product, GDP/general economic conditions, the firm specific factors include strikes, availability or otherwise or raw materials, competition, unique government regulations (say increase in the custom duty on the raw materials imported), and so on.

***Example* 3.10**

Suppose the riskless return is 5 per cent and the market portfolio's expected return (r_m) is 11 per cent. Assume further that beta coefficients for security *j* are β_1 = 1.3 (in relation to market portfolio, β_2 = 0.3 (in relation to growth rate of GDP) and β_3 = 0.2 (in relation to inflation). The expected growth rate in GDP is 8 per cent and inflation is 3 per cent/ Determine the expected return of security j.

$$\text{Return} = 5\% + 1.3\ (r_m - 5\%) + 0.3\ (r_{gdp} - 5\%) + 0.2\ (r_j - 5\%)$$
$$= 5\% + 1.3\ (11\% - 5\%) + 0.3\ (8\% - 5\%) + 0.2\ (3\% - 5\%)$$
$$= 5\% + 7.8\% + 0.9\% - 0.4\% = 13.3\%$$

Though the APT is intutively appealing, it is difficult to be applied in practice. For instance, the identification of the relevant factors (not specified in the APT model) itself is the formidable task. Moreover, the relative importance of the factors (identified) may change over time. Because of these difficulties, the researchers have found difficulties in testing the APT. As a result, there is a lack of practical acceptance of APT. In other words, the superiority of the APT to the CAPM has not been conclusively established or *vice-versa*. Both models involve expectations of risks and of returns which need to be estimated and these estimates are subject to wide error[18].

SUMMARY

LO 3.1

Risk refers to the variability of expected returns associated with a given security or asset.

The absolute return on an investment for a given period of time, say a year, consists of annual income plus change in the market price of the investment (capital appreciation or loss); total annual income (loss) in terms of the rate of return is expressed as a percentage of the opening market value of the investment.

LO 3.2

The two major concerns of an investor, while choosing a security (asset) as an investment, are the expected return from holding the security and the risk that the realised return may fall short of the expected return. Two commonly used approaches to assess risk from a behavioural point of view are sensitivity analysis and probability distribution. To obtain a more concrete measure of risk, two statistical measures of variability of return, namely, standard deviation and coefficient of variation, can be used.

LO 3.3

The term, portfolio refers to the collection of securities/assets held by an investor for investment purposes. The risk of a portfolio is measured in much the same way as the risk of a single asset. However, in the context of a portfolio, the risk of any single proposed investment in a security/asset is not to be viewed independent of other assets/securities already held; additional investments are considered in the light of their effect on the risk and return of the portfolios as a whole. The correlation among assets in portfolio affects the overall risk of the portfolio. The assets (or securities) whose returns are negatively correlated provides the best combination to minimise overall risk. In a way, the concept of correlation constitutes an integral part of the process of diversification that is used to develop an efficient portfolio of assets/securities. An efficient portfolio is a maximum return portfolio, at a given level of risk.

LO 3.4

Diversification through a combination of securities that are not perfectly positively correlated helps to reduce the overall risk of a portfolio. Total portfolio risk has two components: (i) systematic/ non-diversifiable/unavoidable risk and (ii) unsystematic/diversifiable/avoidable risk. The systematic risk is caused by factors that affect all the securities/overall market. Therefore, even an investor who holds a well-diversified portfolio is exposed to this type of risk. In contrast, the unsystematic risk is unique to a particular company/industry/security. This kind of risk can be reduced by diversification and can be eliminated even completely through efficient diversification.

LO 3.5	The non-diversifiable risk is the only relevant risk for which the investors are to be compensated. The higher is such a risk, the higher is the required/expected return of the investor. This risk-return trade-off is the theme of the capital asset pricing model (CAPM). The non-diversifiable risk is measured by beta coefficient. The CAPM uses beta to relate a security's risk relative to the market to determine the security's/asset's required rate of return.
LO 3.6	The CAPM is essentially a single factor model, based on beta. It may be extended to include other variables affecting security's expected return. The major factors in this regard are: (i) taxes, (ii) inflation, (iii) liquidity, (iv) market capitalisation size and (v) price-earnings and market-to-book value ratios.
	The differential tax treatment of dividend and capital gains may affect the effective return expected from the security. Since the investors are concerned with inflation, they may require the lower return on securities which provide hedge against inflation. Likewise, the liquid securities and the securities of companies having high market capitalisation size are preferred and may require a lower return on the part of investors. Finally, it has been observed that returns tend to be higher for low price-earning (P/E) ratio securities as well as for low market-to book (M/B) ratio securities. Of these multiple variables, market capitalisation size and either the P/E ratio or M/B ratio have been observed to be the most significant in their effect on security returns.
LO 3.7	The Arbitrage Pricing Theory (APT) is an alternative model of asset/security pricing. The APT is based on the concept of arbitrage. By eliminating arbitrage opportunities, the arbitragers help in developing the state of capital market efficiency in which all riskless securities yield the same expected return. This apart, the theory attempts to relate the return of a security within a multivariate framework in which the return relationships are linear.

REFERENCES

1. Evans, J L and S H Archer, "Diversification and the Reduction of dispersion: An Empirical Analysis," *Journal of Finance* (December 1968): pp 761– 69.
2. Francis, Jack Clark, *Investments: Analysis and Management*, McGraw-Hill, Inc. New York: 1991, p 623.
3. Edward A Dyl, "Negative Betas: The Attractions of Short Selling," *Journal of Portfolio Management*, (Spring 1975): pp 74–76.
4. James Tobin, " Liquidity Preference as Behaviour Towards Risk," *The Review of Economic Studies*, 26 no. 1 (Feb. 1958): pp 65–86.
5. *Ibid.*
6. Eugene, Fama, "Risk Return and Equilibrium: Some Clarifying Comments," *Journal of Finance* (March 1968): pp 32–33.
7. Bodie, Zvi et al, *Investments,* Tata McGraw-Hill Publishing Company Limited New Delhi: 2002, p 197.
8. This discussion is based on Bodie, *op. cit.* p 157.
9. William F. Sharpe, "Capital Asset Prices: A Theory of Market Equilibrium under Considerations of Risk," *Journal of Finance* 19 no. 3: pp 425–42.
10. John Lintner, "Security Prices, Risk, and Maximal Gains from Diversification," *Journal of Finance*, 1965, 20 no. 12: 587–615.
11. Jan Mossin, " Equilibrium in a Capital Asset Market," *Econometrica* 34 (4), (October 1966).
12. Van Horne, James, C. *Financial Management and Policy*, Prentice Hall of India, New Delhi, 2000, p 87.
13. Van Horne, James, C., *op. cit.*, p 88.
14. Van Horne, James, C., *op. cit.*, p 89.
15. Van Horne, James, C., *op. cit.*, p 90.
16. Ross, Stephen. A, "The Arbitrage Theory of Capital Asset Pricing," *Journal of Economic Theory,* Vol. 13, (December, 1976), pp 341-60.
17. Van Horne, James C, *op. cit.*, p 93.
18. Van Horne, James C, *op. cit.*, p 96.

SOLVED PROBLEMS

P.3.1 Hilt share is quoted at ₹60. Nitin expects the company to pay a dividend of ₹3 per share, one year from now. The expected price one year from now is ₹78.50. LO 3.1 LOD M

(a) What is the expected dividend yield, rate of price change and holding period yield (HPY)?

(b) If the beta of the share is 1.5, the risk-free rate is 6 per cent and the market risk premium is 10 per cent, what is the required rate of return?

(c) What is the intrinsic value of the share? How does it compare with the current market price?

Solution

(a) Dividend yield = ₹3/₹60 = 5 per cent

Rate of capital appreciation = (₹78.50 – ₹60)/₹60 = 30.83 per cent

Holding period yield = Dividend yield + Rate of capital appreciation
= 5 + 30.83 = 35.83 per cent

(b) Required return = Risk-free rate + β (Risk premium)
= 6% + 1.5 (10%) = 6% + 15% = 21 per cent

(c) Intrinsic value = (Dividend + Future price)/ (1 + Required rate)
= (₹3 + ₹78.50)/(1 + 0.21) = ₹81.50/1.21 = ₹67.36

The share is being traded at a price higher than its intrinsic value. It is a selling signal.

P.3.2 From the following information, isolate efficient portfolios from dominated ones. LO 3.4 LOD D

Portfolio	*A*	*B*	*C*	*D*	*E*	*F*	*G*
Expected return (%)	10	15	20	13	16	18	13
Standard deviation (%)	15	10	25	15	15	20	25

Solution Table showing dominated and efficient portfolios

Portfolio	*Expected return (%)*	*Risk, σ (%)*	*Dominated?*	*Efficient?*
A	10	15	Yes, by B, D, E	No
B	15	10	No	Yes
C	20	25	No	Yes
D	13	15	Yes, by B, E	No
E	16	15	No	Yes
F	18	20	No	Yes
G	13	25	Yes, by B, D	No

P.3.3 An investor with risk aversion coefficient A = 3 desires utility level (u) of 5 per cent. If standard deviation of returns for a portfolio is 10 per cent, what is the required rate of return? LO 3.4 LOD M

Solution

$$U = E(r) - 0.005A\sigma^2$$

$$\therefore \quad E(r) = U + 0.005A\sigma^2$$

$$E(r) = 5 + 0.005 \times 3 \times (10)^2 = 5 + 1.5 = 6.5 \text{ per cent.}$$

P.3.4 Mr Brij Bhushan has two investment options before him. Portfolio M offers risk-free expected return of 8 per cent. Portfolio N, which offers an expected return of 24 per cent has standard deviation of 25 per cent. His risk aversion index is 4. Given these parameters what is the rational choice for him? What is the maximum level of risk aversion for which he will continue to prefer the risky portfolio? LO 3.4 LOD M

Solution The utility score for a portfolio is given by the following equation:

$$U = E(r) - 0.005A\sigma^2$$

$$U(M) = 8 - 0.005 \times 4 \times (0)^2 = 8 - 0 = 8 \text{ per cent}$$

$$U(N) = 24 - 0.005 \times 4\ (25)^2 = 24 - 12.5 = 11.5 \text{ per cent}$$

Since the utility score for N is higher, he will derive greater satisfaction from the risky portfolio. The portfolio will continue to be more attractive so long as its utility score for the given risk level exceeds 8 per cent. Thus, the maximum level of risk aversion for which the risky asset will continue to be attractive can be obtained by solving U(N) = 8 as a function of A.

$$8 = 24 - 0.005 \times (25)^2 \times A$$

$$A = (8 - 24)/[-0.005 \times (25)^2] = (-16)/(-3.125) = 5.12$$

The risk-free portfolio M will be more attractive than N, when Brij Bhushan's risk aversion index exceeds 5.12.

P.3.5 Suppose the required rate of return on a portfolio with beta of 1.2 is 18 per cent and the risk-free rate is 6 per cent. According to the CAPM: **LO 3.5** LOD M

(a) What is the expected rate of return on the market portfolio?
(b) What is the expected return of a zero beta security?
(c) Suppose you choose to buy a stock *Z* for ₹50. The stock is expected to pay ₹2 as dividend next year and is hoped to sell at ₹53. The stock has been evaluated at $\beta = -0.5$. Is the stock fairly priced? What is the implication of including stock *Z* in the portfolio?
(d) A stock Delta, with beta of 1.5, sells for ₹50. One year from now, it is expected to yield a dividend income of ₹6. What price do investors expect after one year?

Solution

(a) $E(r_p) = r_f + \beta(r_m - r_f)$

$18\% = 6\% + 1.2\ (r_m - 6\%)$

$r_m = 6\% + (18\% - 6\%)/\ (1.2) = 6\% + 10\% = 16$ per cent

(b) The expected rate of return on zero beta security is the risk-free rate, that is 6 per cent.

(c) Total income = Dividend +/–Price change = ₹2 + (₹53 – ₹50) = ₹5

Expected return = Total income/ Initial price = ₹5/50 = 10 per cent

Required return = $E(r_Z) = 6\% + -0.5\ (16\% - 6\%) = 6\% - 5\% = 1$ per cent

The expected rate of return (10%) is ten times the required rate of return (1%). Clearly the stock is highly undervalued. Inclusion of stock in the portfolio will reduce the portfolio beta and the required return.

(d) $E(r_{\text{Delta}}) = 6\% + 1.5\ (16\% - 6\%) = 6\% + 15\% = 21$ per cent

For 21 per cent return, the total income from Delta should be ₹50 × 21% = ₹10.5. Out of this, the dividend component is ₹6. The expected price appreciation over ₹50 is ₹4.5. Thus, the expected price is ₹54.5.

P.3.6 An investment manager has chanced upon a couple of securities with identical variance of 25 per cent, but zero covariance between their returns. **LO 3.3** LOD D

(a) Calculate portfolio risk when any two securities are combined in equal proportions.
(b) Calculate portfolio risk when any three securities are combined in equal proportions.
(c) Generalise your results for the n-security case and examine its implications for an insurance company.

Solution

(a) $\sigma^2_p = w^2_a\sigma^2_a + w^2_b\sigma^2_b + 2\rho_{ab}w_a\sigma_a\, w_b\sigma_b$

Since covariance ($\sigma_{12} = \rho_{12}w_1\sigma_1\ w_2\sigma_2$) between securities is zero

$\sigma^2_p = w^2_a\sigma^2_a + w^2_b\sigma^2_b = (0.5)^2 \times (25) + (0.5)^2 \times (25) = 6.25 + 6.25$

$= 12.5$ per cent

(b) $\sigma^2_p = w^2_a\sigma^2_a + w^2_b\sigma^2_b + w^2_c\sigma^2_c + 2\rho_{ab}w_a\sigma_a w_b\sigma_b + 2\rho_{ac}w_a\sigma_a w_c\sigma_c + 2\rho_{bc}w_b\sigma_b w_c\sigma_c$

For zero covariance term

$$\sigma^2_p = w^2_a\sigma^2_a + w^2_b\sigma^2_b + w^2_c\sigma^2_c = (1/3)^2 \times (25) + (1/3)^2 \times (25) + (1/3)^2 \times (25)$$
$$= 2.78 + 2.78 + 2.78 = 8.34 \text{ per cent}$$

(c) The generalisation involves three conditions: (i) identical variance (σ^2), (ii) zero covariance and (iii) weight is equal to $1/n$.

$$\text{Portfolio variance} = \sigma^2_p = (w\sigma)^2 + (w\sigma)^2 + \ldots. \; n\text{-times}$$
$$= n\,(1/n)^2\,\sigma^2 = \sigma^2/n = 25/n$$

It is obvious that as the number of assets increases, the portfolio risk approaches zero. Based on this result, one is tempted to conclude that the insurance companies can reduce risk to zero level by increasing the number of policies sold. However, it is not so. As more assets with uncorrelated returns are entered into the portfolio, portfolio risk approaches zero, provided the size of wealth (portfolio) remains fixed. As insurance companies sell more policies, the size of portfolio increases. In this case, it is more appropriate to determine mean and standard deviation in value (rupee) terms rather than rates. Insurance companies pool risk (accumulate independent risky projects) by selling policies, which does not eliminate the risk of the insurance company.

P.3.7 Consider the following information. LO 3.3 LOD M

	Share Moon		*Share Mars*
Expected return (%)	15		20
Standard deviation (%)	10		15
Covariance (%)		120	

(a) What is the correlation between the two shares?

(b) What is the expected return and risk of a portfolio in which Moon and Mars have been combined in equal proportions?

Solution

(a) Correlation (ρ) $= \text{Covariance of Moon and Mars}/\sigma_{\text{Moon}}\,\sigma_{\text{Mars}}$
$$= 120/\,(10 \times 15) = 0.8$$

(b) Expected return $= \text{w}_{\text{Moon}} \times \text{return}_{\text{Moon}} + \text{w}_{\text{Mars}} \times \text{return}_{\text{Mars}}$
$$= 0.5 \times 20\% + 0.5 \times 15\% = 17.5 \text{ per cent}$$

$$\text{Risk } (\sigma) = (w^2_{\text{Moon}}\sigma^2_{\text{Moon}} + w^2_{\text{Mars}}\sigma^2_{\text{Mars}} + 2\rho_{\text{Moon, Mars}}\, w_{\text{Moon}}\sigma_{\text{Moon,}}\text{w}_{\text{Mars}}\,\sigma_{\text{Mars}})^{1/2}$$
$$= [(0.5 \times 15\%)^2 + (0.5 \times 20\%)^2 + 2 \times 120\%]^{1/2} = (56.25 + 100 + 240)^{1/2}$$
$$= (369.25\%)^{1/2} = 19.9 \text{ per cent}$$

P.3.8 Ajay held equity shares of Xenon Ltd. (expected return = 14%, standard deviation = 18%). Vijay has gifted him shares of identical market value of Year Ltd. (expected return = 20%, standard deviation = 24%). Determine the risk and return of the securities portfolio held by Ajay, if the correlation between the returns on the two securities is 0.8. LO 3.3 LOD M

Solution

$$E(r_p) = w_a\, r_a + w_b\, r_b$$
$$= 0.5 \times 14\% + 0.5 \times 20\% = 7\% + 10\% = 17 \text{ per cent}$$
$$\sigma^2_p = (w_a\,\sigma_a)^2 + (\text{w}_b\,\sigma_b)^2 + 2\,\rho_{ab}\,\text{wa}\,\sigma_a\,w_b\,\sigma_b$$
$$= (0.5 \times 18\%)^2 + (0.5 \times 24\%)^2 + 2\,(0.8)\,(0.5 \times 18\%)\,(0.5 \times 24\%)$$
$$= 81\% + 144\,\% + 172.8\% = 397.8\%$$
$$\sigma_p = 19.95 \text{ per cent}$$

P.3.9 Mr. Azad holds the following portfolio LO 3.3 LOD M

Share	Beta	Investment
Alpha	0.6	₹3,00,000
Beta	1.0	1,80,000
Carrot	1.2	1,20,000

What is the expected rate of return on his portfolio, if the risk-free rate is 6 per cent and the expected return on market portfolio is 15 per cent?

Solution For given beta (β), the required rate of return is obtained as

$$E(r_p) = r_f + \beta\,(r_m - r_f)$$
$$= 0.06 + \beta\,(0.15 - 0.06) = 0.06 + 0.09\beta$$

Share	Beta	$E(r) = r_f + \beta\,(r_m - r_f)$	Investment	Weight	Weighted return
Alpha	0.6	0.114	₹3,00,000	0.5	0.0570
Beta	1.0	0.150	1,80,000	0.3	0.0450
Carrot	1.2	0.168	1,20,000	0.2	0.0336
Portfolio	0.84	0.1356	6,00,000	1.0	0.1356

Portfolio beta is the simple weighted average of the betas of three shares.

$$\beta_{portfolio} = 0.6 \times 0.5 + 1 \times 0.3 + 1.2 \times 0.2 = 0.3 + 0.3 + 0.24 = 0.84$$

P.3.10 Determine the given beta values. **LO 3.3** LOD E

(a) Standard deviation of stock of Sunshine Ltd. (σ_s) = 10 per cent
Standard deviation of market portfolio (σ_m) = 8 per cent
Correlation of share with the market (r_{sm}) = +0.7

(b) Standard deviation of the portfolio (σ_p) = 3 per cent
Standard deviation of market portfolio (σ_m) = 2.5 per cent
Correlation of portfolio with the market (r_{pm}) = + 0.9

Solution

(a) Beta of Sunshine Ltd. share is obtained as

$$\beta_s = (\sigma_s \sigma_m r_{sm})/\sigma^2_m = (10 \times 8 \times 0.07)/(8)^2 = 0.875$$

(b) Beta of Sunshine Ltd. share is obtained as

$$\beta_s = (\sigma_p \sigma_m r_{pm})/\sigma^2_m = (3 \times 2.5 \times 0.9)/(2.5)^2 = 1.08$$

P.3.11 Risk-return features of two securities *X* and *Y* are given below **LO 3.4** LOD D

Portfolio	E (r)	σ	W
X (%)	12	16	0.5
Y (%)	20	24	0.5

(a) If the desired portfolio standard deviation is 20 per cent, determine the correlation coefficient that would yield the desired level of risk.

(b) Find the portfolio standard deviation if X and Y are mixed in the ratio of 3:1. Comment on the results.

(c) What should the correlation be, if the desired portfolio standard deviation of 18 per cent and assets are combined in equal proportion?

(d) What should the correlation be, if the desired portfolio standard deviation is 12 per cent and assets are combined in equal proportion?

Solution

(a)
$$\sigma^2_p = (w_x\,\sigma_x)^2 + (w_x\,\sigma_y)^2 + 2\,\sigma_x\,w_x\,\sigma_y\,w_y\,\rho$$
$$(20)^2 = (0.5 \times 16)^2 + (0.5 \times 24)^2 + 2\,(0.5)\,(0.5)\,(16 \times 24 \times \rho)$$

$$400 = 64 + 144 + 192\ \rho$$
$$192\rho = 400 - 208$$
$$\rho = 192/192 = 1.$$

There should be perfect positive correlation between *X* and *Y*.

(b) $\sigma^2_p = (0.75 \times 16)^2 + (0.25 \times 24)^2 + 2\ (1.0 \times 16 \times 24)\ (0.75 \times 0.25)$
$= 144 + 36 + 144 = 324$ per cent
$\sigma_p = 18$ per cent.

(c) For perfect positive correlation between *X* and *Y*, the portfolio standard deviation ranges between σx and σy.

$$\sigma^2_p = (18)^2 = (0.5 \times 16)^2 + (0.5 \times 24)^2 + 2\ (0.5 \times 0.5)\ (16 \times 24)\ \rho$$
$$324 = 64 + 144 + 192\ \rho$$
$$\rho = 324 - 64 - 144 = 0.604$$

(d)
$$(12)2 = 64 + 144 + 192\rho$$
$$192\rho = 144 - 208 = -64$$
$$\rho = -64/192 = -0.33$$

P.3.12 GTE Ltd is a renowned company in telecommunication industry. The company has a consistent profitability record for the last five years. Mr Satnam wishes to invest in this company, however, he wants to know how this company is expected to fare vis-à-vis the overall market. He has been advised by a financial expert to use beta for understanding the movement of any share vis-à-vis the market. The following data is available with Mr Satnam for analysis. LO 3.3 LOD M

σ GTE Ltd – 25 per cent
σ Nifty – 15 per cent

Correlation coefficient between returns in GTE Ltd. and Nifty index – 0.92.

As an advisor to Mr Satnam, calculate the beta and interpret the results.

Solution

$$\text{Beta GTE Ltd} = \frac{\sigma\text{GTE Ltd } \sigma\text{Nifty Correlation (GTE Ltd Nifty)}}{\sigma\text{Nifty}^2}$$
$$= 25 \times 15 \times 0.92/15 \times 15 = 1.53$$

The beta of GTE Ltd is 1.53, which indicates that GTE Ltd has a more risky share vis-à-vis the market portfolio, represented by the Nifty index. In case the Nifty index rises by 10 per cent, the return on this share is expected to rise by around 15.3 per cent and vice-versa.

P.3.13 Ranbaxy Ltd is a well-known company in the pharmaceutical industry. Based on the monthly data for the last 4 years from 1 January, 1999 to December 31, 2002, its beta appears equal to 1.75. During this period, the company has deployed an average debt-equity ratio of around 40 per cent in its capital structure. Looking at the challenges being posed by the new patent regime, the company has realised the need for making more investment in research and development activities. For meeting its funding requirement, the company is planning to raise additional funds from the market. The chief finance manager, CFO of the company, is exploring the option of raising the debt level to 60 per cent. However, he is concerned that a rising additional debt may increase the risk proposition of the company, as measured by beta. LO 3.5 LOD D

Calculate the beta of the firm at 50 per cent and 60 per cent debt level and comment upon the increase in the risk level.

Solution The increase in debt causes an increase in the equity beta in view of the increased financial risk resulting from the increase in the obligated payments on debt.

Let us first of calculate the beta for Ranbaxy Ltd as an unlevered firm:

β Unlevered = Current Beta/[1 + Debt/Equity] = 1.75/[1 + 0.40] = 1.75/1.40 = 1.25

β Levered = β Unlevered [1+ Debt/Equity]
β Levered (at D/E ratio of 50 per cent) = 1.25 (1 + 0.5) = 1.875.
β Levered (at D/E ratio of 60 per cent) = 1.25 (1 + 0.6) = 2.0.

With increase in the debt level in Ranbaxy Ltd, the beta would increase from 1.75 (current) to 1.875 (for 50 per cent debt-equity ratio) and 2.0 (for 60 per cent debt-equity ratio). Risk of the company is independent of the financing decision. Only the risk of equityholders increases with the use of debt.

P.3.14 RR Ltd is a diversified conglomerate that has major interests in agro based business, food processing and cement. Currently, the beta of this company, based on past two year weekly market price, is 1.45. The company is currently planning to hive off its cement division and get out of this business. Based on the trends prevailing in the industry, a comparable cement company would have a beta of around 1.86 with an average debt-equity ratio of 30 per cent.

LO 3.5,6 LOD **D**

What would the beta be for the cement division of RR Ltd, which employs, a debt-equity ratio of 70 per cent?

Solution First of all, let us calculate the unlevered beta for the comparable company, as follows:

β Unlevered Equity = Current Equity β/(1 + Debt/Equity) = 1.86/[1 + 0.30] = 1.86/1.30 = 1.43.

Based on the unlevered beta of the comparable, the beta for cement division of RR Ltd can be calculated as:

β Levered Equity = β Unlevered Equity (1+ Debt/Equity)
= 1.43 (1 + 0.70) = 1.43 × 1.70 = 2.43

MINI CASES

3.C.1 Mr. Alok Dixit is interested in investing in equity shares of Wipro and Dabur. Being conservative in nature, he wants to determine the risk associated with investments. In specific terms, he wants to seek data related to both levered and unlevered beta of these companies. He approaches Ankit Shah, a financial consultant to do the needful. Ankit has collected the relevant information detailed below.

(i) Monthly returns on equity shares of Wipro and Dabur for a period of 2 years (w.e.f. October 200X to September 200Y) along with portfolio of S&P CNX NIFTY.

Number (MONTHS)	*WIPRO**	*DABUR**	*S&P CNX NIFTY***
1	0.1455	0.0432	0.0654
2	0.1291	0.307	0.1536
3	–0.1036	–0.0498	–0.0749
4	–0.0643	–0.0369	0.0473
5	–0.0673	–0.0272	–0.0178
6	0.1361	0.0286	–0.0291
7	–0.0111	–0.1088	–0.1465
8	0.0452	–0.1338	0.0194
9	0.0277	0.0913	0.0663
10	0.0581	0.011	–0.0022
11	0.0313	0.0581	0.0854
12	0.1021	0.1043	0.0127
13	0.1652	0.0876	0.0914
14	–0.0237	0.0617	0.0604
15	–0.0581	0.0877	–0.0099
16	–0.0077	0.14	0.0119

(Contd)

(Contd)

17	–0.0401	–0.0369	–0.008
18	–0.0589	0.0473	–0.0605
19	0.1335	0.1054	0.0746
20	0.0693	0.0249	0.0596
21	–0.0391	0.1082	0.048
22	–0.0086	0.048	0.0378
23	0.0196	0.068	0.0813

*Based on CMIE database
**Based on NSE website

(ii) Return on 364-days treasury bills issued by Government of India for the period 2004-05 is 5.15 per cent per annum and 0.419 per month. This rate is to be used as a proxy for risk-free rate of return.
(iii) Debt-equity ratio (based on the average of 2001 to 2005) is 1.6 per cent for Wipro and 31.4 per cent for Dabur.
(iv) Corporate tax is 35 per cent.

Required Compute the beta and interpret it for Alok.

Solution Determination of Beta

It is based on bi-variate regression analysis using SPSS, statistical package.

Wipro

- Beta calculations for Wipro Ltd.

Model Summary

Model	*R*	*R Square*	*Adjusted R Square*	*Std. Error of the Estimate*
1	.500	.250	.214	.070662541

a Predictors: (Constant), Returns on index

Coefficients

Model	*Unstandardized Coefficients Beta*	*Std. Error*	*Standardized Coefficients Beta*	*t*	*Sig.*	*95% Confidence Interval for B Lower Bound*	*Upper Bound*
1 (Constant)	1.006E-02	.016		.637	.531	–.023	.043
Returns on index	*.616*	.233	.500	2.646	.015	.132	1.100

a Dependent Variable: Returns on Wipro Ltd

Since Wipro is a firm using both equity and debt in its capital structure, the beta reflects business as well as financial risk. By calculating unlevered beta, the financial risk can be separated and beta value can be viewed in light of business risk only. The calculations are as under:

Here β_L= 0.616, and β_U for Wipro can be calculated (assuming tax rate =35%)

$$\beta_L = \beta_U\,[1 + (1 - t)^*(D/E)]$$

$$0.616 = \beta_U[1 + (1 - 0.35)^*(.016)]$$

β_U = **0.6096,** which represents business risk component of Wipro Limited.

Interpretations: (i) The beta (levered) value of 0.616 implies that equity shares of Wipro is defensive in nature in that the returns on Wipro shares would change by 0.616 per cent with 1 per cent change in the returns on market portfolio (represented by S&P CNX NIFTY).

(ii) The R-square value of 0.25 or 25 per cent implies that only one-forth of total risk is systematic/market risk and three-forth of total risk is firm specific risk.

Dabur

- Beta calculations for Dabur Ltd.

Model Summary

Model	*R*	*R Square*	*Adjusted R Square*	*Std. Error of the Estimate*
1	.650	.422	.395	.070506822

a Predictors: (Constant), Returns on index

Coefficients

Model	*Unstandardized Coefficients Beta*	*Std. Error*	*Standardized Coefficients Beta*	*t*	*Sig.*	*95% Confidence Interval for B Lower Bound*	*Upper Bound*
1 (Constant)	2.232E-02	.016		1.415	.172	–.010	.055
Returns on index	*.910*	.232	.650	3.916	.001	.427	1.393

a Dependent Variable: Returns on Dabur Ltd

Since Dabur is also a firm using both equity and debt in its capital structure, the beta reflects both business and financial risk. By calculating unlevered beta, the financial risk can be separated and beta value can be viewed in light of business risk only. The calculations are as under:

Here $\beta_L = 0.91$, and β_U for Dabur can be calculated (assuming tax rate = 35%)

$$\beta_L = \beta_U\,[1 + (1 - t)^*(D/E)]$$

$$0.9 = \beta_U[1 + (1 - 0.35)^*(.314)]$$

β_U **= 0.7558,** which represents business risk component of Dabur India Ltd.

Interpretation: (i) The beta (levered) value is 0.91. It means that the equity share of Dabur is less defensive vis-à-vis that of Wipro as its value is close to one. One per cent change in the market portfolio will cause 0.91 per cent change in returns of Dabur's equity shares.

(ii) The R-square value of 0.422 or 42.2 per cent signifies that 42.2 per cent of total risk is systematic/ market risk and 57.8 per cent of total risk is unsystematic/diversifiable risk.

3.C.2 (Risk/Beta Analysis) The month-wise data of the S&P CNX Nifty and stock values of the HDFC Bank Ltd and the ICICI Bank Ltd for the past one are year presented below.

Date	*S&P CNX Nifty*	*ICICI Bank Ltd*	*HDFC Bank Ltd*
11/3/200X	2,755.10	327.69	878.36
12/1/200X	2,959.15	414.33	953.93
1/1/200Y	2,874.80	384.39	883.15
2/2/200Y	2,763.65	308.25	851.63
3/2/200Y	3,020.95	308.99	937.74
4/1/200Y	3,473.95	444.25	1,058.43
5/4/200Y	4,448.95	681.30	1,387.32
6/1/200Y	4,291.10	725.60	1,501.00
7/1/200Y	4,636.45	759.95	1,498.00
8/3/200Y	4,662.10	751.60	1,471.05
9/1/200Y	5,083.95	904.95	1,655.00
10/1/200Y	4,711.70	793.00	1,625.00

Required An investor seeks your advice as a financial consultant about the relative riskiness of the investments in the shares of the HDFC Ltd and the ICICI Ltd. What advice would you give him and why?

Solution

The relative risks would be reflected in the respective betas of the shares of the HDFC Bank Ltd and ICICI Bank Ltd.

Beta Calculation of HDFC Bank Ltd

Date	*S&P CNX Nifty*	*HDFC*	*X*[@]	*Y*[@@]	*XY*	X^2
11/3/200X	2,755.10	878.36				
12/1/200X	2,959.15	953.93	7.4063	8.6035	63.7200	54.8528
1/1/200Y	2,874.80	883.15	–2.8505	–7.4198	21.1501	8.1252
2/2/200Y	2,763.65	851.63	–3.8664	–3.5690	13.7992	14.9487
3/2/200Y	3,020.95	937.74	9.3102	10.1112	94.1368	86.6789
4/1/200Y	3,473.95	1,058.43	14.9953	12.8703	192.9939	224.8585
5/4/200Y	4,448.95	1,387.32	28.0660	31.0734	872.1066	787.7023
6/1/200Y	4,291.10	1,501.00	(–3.5480)	8.1942	(–29.0733)	12.5885
7/1/200Y	4,636.45	1,498.00	8.0481	(–0.1999)	(–1.6085)	64.7712
8/3/200Y	4,662.10	1,471.05	0.5532	(–1.7991)	(–0.9953)	0.3061
9/1/200Y	5,083.95	1,655.00	9.0485	12.5047	113.1485	81.8753
10/1/200Y	4,711.70	1,625.00	(–7.3221)	–1.8127	13.2726	5.6126
Sum			59.84058	68.55681	1,352.6510	1,390.3200
Count 10 Average			5.440053	6.232438	122.9682	125.3927

[@]Percentage change in S&P CNX Nifty. [@@]Percentage change in HDFC Stock Value

Beta = [n(Σ X Y) – ΣX ΣY] ÷ [(n ΣX)^2 – (ΣX)^2]

= 10(1,352.651) – (59.84 × 68.55) ÷ (10 × 1,390.32) – (59.84)^2

= (13,526.51 – 4,102.03) ÷ (13,903.2 – 3,580.83) = 9,424.48 ÷ 10,322.37 = 0.91

Beta Calculation of ICICI Bank Ltd

Date	*S&P CNX Nifty*	*ICICI*	*X*[@]	*Y*[@@]	*XY*	X^2
11/3/200X	2,755.10	327.69				
12/1/200X	2,959.15	414.33	7.4063	26.4396	195.8188	54.8528
1/1/200Y	2,874.80	384.39	(–2.8505)	(–7.2261)	20.5979	8.1252
2/2/200Y	2,763.65	308.25	(–3.8664)	(–19.8080)	76.5848	14.9487
3/2/200Y	3,020.95	308.99	9.3102	0.2401	2.2350	86.6789
4/1/200Y	3,473.95	444.25	14.9953	44.0985	661.2697	224.8585
5/4/200Y	4,448.95	681.30	28.0660	53.0152	1487.9253	787.7023
6/1/200Y	4,291.10	725.60	(–3.5480)	6.5023	(–23.0703)	12.5885
7/1/200Y	4,636.45	759.95	8.0481	4.7340	38.0996	64.7712
8/3/200Y	4,662.10	751.60	0.5532	(–1.0988)	(–0.6079)	0.3061
9/1/200Y	5,083.95	904.95	9.0485	20.4031	184.6178	81.8753
10/1/200Y	4,711.70	793.00	(–7.3221)	(–12.3708)	90.5801	53.6126
Sum			59.84058	114.9291	2,734.0510	1,390.3200
Count 10 Average			5.440053	10.4481	248.5501	126.3927

[@]Percentage change in S&P CNX Nifty. [@@]Percentage change in ICICI Stock Value

Beta = 10(2,734.05) – (5,44 × 10.448) ÷ (10 × 1,390.32) – (5.44)^2 = 1.97

Advice: The investor would be well advised to acquire the shares of the HDFC Bank, the reason being that the risk as reflected in its low beta (0.91) compared to the ICICI's (1.97) is much lower.

REVIEW QUESTIONS

LOD: Easy

RQ.3.1 (a) Indicate whether the following statements are True or False. [LO 3.1,2,3,4,5]

(i) Return on any financial asset consists of current yield and capital yield.

(ii) Risk of an individual financial asset refers to variability of its returns around its mean returns.

(iii) Return of a portfolio is simply weighted average of returns on individual securities in the portfolio multiplied by their corresponding proportions (weights) in the portfolio.

(iv) For a given correlation coefficient, a minimum variance portfolio can be created, for which risk of portfolio will be less than the risk of any security in the portfolio.

(v) Correlation among the securities in the portfolio has nothing to do with the risk of portfolio.

(vi) If a portfolio consists of two securities, which are perfectly positively correlated, the risk of portfolio will simply be the weighted average of the standard deviations of individual securities.

(vii) A portfolio consisting of two risky securities can be made riskless, if the securities are perfectly negatively correlated.

(viii) Efficient frontier consists of those portfolios which offer maximum risk for a given level of expected returns.

(ix) In CAPM, Beta represents total risk, i.e., systematic and unsystematic risk.

(x) The point of tangency between the efficient frontier and risk-return indifference curve provides optimal portfolio for the investor concerned.

(xi) Security market line (SML) and Capital market line (CML) are the same.

[Answers: (i) True (ii) True (iii) True (iv) True (v) False (vi) True (vii) True (viii) False (ix) False (x) True (xi) False]

(b) In the following multiple choice questions select the correct answers.

(i) Risk of two securities having different expected return can be compared with
(a) standard deviation of securities **(b)** variance of securities **(c)** coefficient of variation **(d)** None of these.

(ii) A portfolio consists of two securities and the expected return on two securities is 12 per cent and 16 per cent respectively. Calculate return of portfolio if first security accounts for 40 per cent of portfolio.
(a) 14 per cent **(b)** 14.4 per cent **(c)** 16 per cent **(d)** 12 per cent.

(iii) Calculate risk for the above portfolio (ii), given σ_1 = 10%, σ_2 = 12% and σ12 = 75
(a) 11 per cent **(b)** 15.62 per cent **(c)** 12.17 per cent **(d)** None.

(iv) What is the risk of a portfolio consisting of two securities which are perfectly positively correlated?
(a) $(\sigma_1^2 - \sigma_2^{\ 2})$ **(b)** $(w_1\sigma_1 + w_2\sigma_2)^2$ **(c)** $w_1\sigma_1^{\ 2} + w_2\sigma^2$ **(d)** None.

(v) What is the risk of portfolio in situation (iv) if two securities are perfectly negatively correlated
(a) $(\sigma_1^{\ 2} - \sigma_2^{\ 2})$ **(b)** $(w_1\sigma_1 + w_2\sigma_2)^2$ **(c)** $w_1\sigma_1^{\ 2} + w_2\sigma^2$ **(d)** None.

(vi) To create a minimum variance portfolio, in what proportion should the two securities be mixed if the following information is given σ_1 = 10%, σ_2 = 12%, P_{12} = 0.6?
(a) .72 and .28 **(b)** .70 and .30 **(c)** .60 and .40 **(d)** none of the above.

(vii) A portfolio consisting of two risky securities can be made risk less i.e., σ_p = 0, if
(a) the securities are perfectly positively correlated **(b)** the securities are perfectly negatively correlated **(c)** if the correlation ranges between 0 to 1 **(d)** none of the above.

(viii) Efficient portfolios are those portfolios, which offer (for a given level of risk)
(a) maximum return **(b)** minimum return **(c)** average return **(d)** none.

(ix) Efficient frontier consists of
(a) Efficient portfolios **(b)** Both efficient and inefficient portfolios **(c)** Portfolios that are positively correlated securities **(d)** Portfolios that are negatively correlated securities.

(x) Capital market line is
(a) capital allocation line of a risk free asset **(b)** capital allocation line of a market portfolio **(c)** capital allocation line of risk-free asset and market portfolio both **(d)** none.

(xi) The point of tangency between efficient frontier and risk-return indifferences curve depicts
(a) sub-optimal portfolio **(b)** optimal portfolio **(c)** efficient portfolio **(d)** none of them.

(xii) CAPM accounts for
(a) systematic risk **(b)** unsystematic risk **(c)** both **(d)** none.

[Answers: (i) c (ii) b (iii) c (iv) b (v) b (vi) a (vii) b (viii) a (ix) a (x) c (xi) b (xii) a]

RQ.3.2 Suppose two securities have a correlation of +1.0. Can a portfolio of these securities reduce risk? Explain. [LO 3.3]

RQ.3.3 "The Markowitz type of diversification stresses not the number of securities but the right kind of securities." Elaborate. [LO 3.4]

RQ.3.4 Outline the relationship between the size of standard deviation and the degree of asset risk. Explain in brief the reason for superiority of the coefficient of variation to standard deviation as a measure of comparing risk associated with different securities/assets. [LO 3.2]

RQ.3.5 Why is the correlation between securities returns in a portfolio important? [LO 3.2]

RQ.3.6 What would be the impact of the following changes on the required return for a given level of risk? (i) an increase in inflationary expectations, (ii) investors become less risk-averse and (iii) investors become more risk-averse. [LO 3.5,6]

RQ.3.7 Assume the following facts: [LO 3.5]
— Risk-free return, r_f, 7.75 per cent
— Beta, 2
— Expected return of investors, r, 16 per cent
Applying CAPM, compute the expected market return (r_m). [LO 3.5]

RQ.3.8 The following facts are available:
— $r_m = 0.14$
— $r_f = 0.0825$
— $r = 0.18$
Compute the beta coefficient (b).

LOD: Medium

RQ.3.9 Distinguish (a) Realised and expected return (b) Diversifiable and non-diversifiable risk (c) Capital market and security market line. [LO 3.4,5]

RQ.3.10 "Diversification of risk in the asset selection process allows the investor to combine risky assets in a way that risk of a portfolio is less than the risk of the individual assets." Elaborate the statement with appropriate example. [LO 3.3]

RQ.3.11 Why is the non-diversifiable risk only relevant risk? How is such a risk measured? [LO 3.5]

RQ.3.12 Explain with example the process of determining the expected return on a portfolio. [LO 3.4]

RQ.3.13 What is the CAPM? What are the components of CAPM equation? Explain the meaning of each component. What does it tell us about the required return on a risky investment? [LO 3.5]

RQ.3.14 How could an investor identify the best of a set of efficient portfolios of equity shares? Assume the investor can borrow or lend at the risk-free interest rate. [LO 3.3,4]

RQ.3.15 Describe in brief the Arbitrage Pricing Theory (APT). What is its major contribution and limitation? [LO 3.7]

RQ.3.16 The following facts are available: [LO 3.2,3]

- Risk-free rate, 9 per cent
- Required rate of return on market portfolio, 18 per cent
- Beta coefficient of the shares of ABC Ltd, 1.5
- Expected dividend during the next year, ₹3
- Growth rate in dividends/earnings, 8 per cent

Compute the price at which the shares of ABC Ltd should sell.

RQ.3.17 The probability distribution of expected future returns is as follows: [LO 3.2]

Probability	*Return on shares (percentage)*	
	X	Y
0.1	(16)	(18)
0.2	2	12
0.4	8	18
0.2	12	32
0.1	20	40

Compute the (a) standard deviation of expected returns of each share, (b) coefficient of variation. Which share is more risky? Why?

RQ.3.18 The rate on T-bill (risk-free return, r_f) is currently 7.75 per cent, while the expected market return (r_m) is 14.25 per cent. Compute the required rate of return of each security listed below: [LO 3.2,3]

Security	*Beta*
X_1	1.5
X_2	1.2
X_3	1.00
X_4	0.90

LOD: Difficult

RQ.3.19 An efficient market means identical returns on all securities. Do you agree? Explain. [LO 3.4]

RQ.3.20 "Beta is not the sole factor affecting security required rate of return." Elucidate the statement and also state the other factors which should be considered for determining required returns. [LO 3.6,7]

RQ.3.21 The total market value of the equity share of ORE Company is ₹60,00,000 and the total value of the debt is ₹40,00,000. The treasurer estimates that the beta of the stock is currently 1.5 and that the expected risk premium on the market is 10 per cent. The treasury bill rate is 8 per cent. [LO 3.3]

Required: **(i)** What is the beta of the company's existing portfolio of assets? **(ii)** Estimate the company's cost of capital and the discount rate for an expansion of the company's present business.

RQ.3.22 The expected return ($\overline{r}$) and standard deviation (σ) of shares of X Ltd and Y Ltd are: [LO 3.3]

	$\overline{r}$	σ
X Ltd	0.14	0.20
Y Ltd	0.09	0.30

Required: If the expected correlation between the two shares (p_{xy}) is (a) 0.1, (b) -1, compute the return and risk for each of the following portfolios: (i) *X*, 100 per cent, (ii) *Y*, 100 per cent, (iii) *X*, 50 per cent and *Y*, 50 per cent.

RQ.3.23 The aggregate average r_f and r_m for a 3-year period are 10 per cent and 18 per cent respectively.

The results for four portfolios during the same period are summarised as follows: [LO 3.5]

Portfolio	*Average return (per cent)*	*Beta*
X_1	18	0.90
X_2	18	1.12
X_3	24	1.50
X_4	16	0.95

Using the CAPM, compute the expected return for each portfolio and compare the actual and expected returns. Which portfolio has performed the best?

ANSWERS

3.7 r_m 11.87 per cent

3.8 b 1.7

3.16 Expected price ₹20.7

3.17 **(a)** Standard deviation X 8.94%
Y 14.98%

(b) Coefficient of variation X 1.4
Y 0.82

Share X is more risky.

3.18 X_1 17.50 per cent
X_2 15.55 per cent
X_3 14.25 per cent
X_4 13.60 per cent

3.21 **(i)** Beta 0.9
(ii) Cost of debt 8%; cost of capital 17%

3.22 **(a)** **(i)** 1.43
(ii) 3.33
(iii) $\bar{r}_p$ 11.5 per cent
σ_p 18.84 per cent

(b) **(i)** and **(ii)** same as in (a)(i) and (ii)
(iii) $\bar{r}_p$ 11.5 per cent
σ_p 5 per cent

3.23 X_1 17.2 per cent; 18 per cent
X_2 19.0 per cent; 18 per cent
X_3 22.0 per cent; 24 per cent
X_4 17.6 per cent; 16 per cent
X_3 has shown the best performance.

Scan the QR Code to access comprehensive solutions to all numerical review questions and additional material.

CHAPTER

4

Valuation of Bonds and Shares

LEARNING OBJECTIVES

LO 4.1	Explain the basic valuation model to value bonds/debentures, preference shares and equity shares
LO 4.2	Apply the basic valuation model to bonds/debentures to evaluate the relationship between both required return and time to maturity and bond values
LO 4.3	Discuss the valuation of perpetual and redeemable preference shares applying the basic valuation model
LO 4.4	Understand basic share valuation under each of three cases—zero growth, constant growth and variable growth
LO 4.5	Discuss three other approaches—book value, liquidation value and price-earnings/ multiple—that are used to estimate shares values
LO 4.6	Review the relationship between the impact of financial decisions on both expected return and risk and their combined effect on the value of a firm
LO 4.7	Describe equity returns in India

INTRODUCTION

Valuation is the process that links risk and return to determine the worth of an asset. It can be applied to expected benefits from real/physical as well as financial assets/securities to determine their worth at a given point of time. This Chapter focusses on valuation of two financial assets, namely, bonds/debentures and shares, ordinary as well as preference. To value them, we have to use the time value techniques (discussed in Chapter 2) and the risk and return framework (discussed in Chapter 3). The key inputs to the valuation process are **(i)** expected returns in terms of cash flows together with their timing and **(ii)** risk in terms of the required return. The value of an asset depends on the return (cash flow) it is expected to provide over the holding/ownership period. The cash flow stream can be **(1)** annual, **(2)** intermittent and **(3)** even one-time. In addition to the total cash flow estimates, their timing/pattern (e.g. amount year-wise) is also required to identify the return expected from

Valuation is the process that links risk and return to determine the worth of an asset.

the bond/share. The required return is used in the valuation process to incorporate risk into the analysis/exercise. Risk denotes the chance that an expected outcome (return/cashflow) would not be realised (Chapter 3). The level of risk associated with a given cash flow/return has a significant bearing on its value, that is, the greater the risk, the lower the value and *vice versa.* Higher risk can be incorporated into the valuation analysis by using a higher required/capitalisation/ discount rate (Chapter 2) to determine the present value. With CAPM (Chapter 3), the greater the Beta, β, the higher the required return. It is against this background that the present chapter dwells on the valuation of bonds/debentures and shares. We first describe the basic valuation model. It can be used in valuing bonds, preference shares, and ordinary/equity shares. Valuation of bonds is illustrated later. Valuation of preference shares and ordinary shares is discussed subsequently. In addition to the basic stock valuation equation (dividend valuation model), there are other approaches to the valuation of shares. They are briefly covered. The relationship among financial decisions, returns, risk and share value are examined. Finally, the main points are summarised.

LO 4.1 BASIC VALUATION MODEL

The value of an asset/security is the present/discounted value of all future cash flows (returns) associated with it over the relevant/specified period. The expected returns (cash inflows) are discounted, using the required return commensurate with the risk of the asset as the appropriate discount rate. Symbolically,

$$V = \frac{A_1}{(1+k)^1} + \frac{A_2}{(1+k)^2} + \ldots + \frac{A_n}{(1+k)^n} \tag{4.1}$$

where V = value of the asset/security at time zero (t = 0)

A_t = cash flow streams expected at the end of year t

k = appropriate required/capitalisation/discount rate

Alternatively, if the expected cash flow is a mixed stream

$$V = [(A_1 \times PVIF_{k,1}) + (A_2 \times PVIF_{k,2}) + \ldots\ldots + (A_n \times PVIF_{k,n})] \tag{4.2}$$

where

$PVIF_1$, $PVIF_2$ and $PVIF_n$ = present value interest factor in different periods at discount rate k.

If the expected cash flow is an annuity,

$$V = A \times PVIFA_{(k,n)} \tag{4.2.1}$$

***Example* 4.1**

Assuming a discount rate of 10 per cent, and the associated cash flows detailed below, compute the value of the assets X and Y.

Year	*Cash flows (expected returns)*	
	X	*Y*
1	₹10,000	₹5,000
2	10,000	10,000
3	10,000	15,000

Solution

Value of asset X: = ₹10,000 × $PVIFA_{(10,3)}$ = ₹10,000 × 2.487 = ₹24,870

Value of asset Y: = [(₹5,000 × $PVIF_{(10,1)}$] + (₹10,000 × $PVIF_{(10,2)}$) + (₹15,000 × $PVIF_{(10,3)}$)]

= [(₹5,000 × 0.909) + (₹10,000 × 0.826) + (₹15,000 × 0.751)]

= ₹4,545 + ₹8,260 + ₹11,265 = ₹24,070.

LO 4.2 VALUATION OF BONDS/DEBENTURES

A bond/debenture is a long-term debt instrument used by the government/government agency (ies) and business enterprises to raise a large sum of money. A detailed account of the main attributes of bonds is given in Chapter 23. Most bonds, particularly corporate bonds (i) pay interest half-yearly (semi-annually) at a stated coupon interest rate, (ii) have an initial maturity of 10-years and (iii) have a par/face value of ₹1,000 that must be repaid at maturity. **Par value** is the value on the face of the bond. It represents the amount the entity borrows and promises to repay at the time of maturity. **Coupon rate** is the specified interest rate. The interest payable to the bondholder is equal to par value × coupon rate. **Maturity period** refers to the number of years after which the par value is payable to the bondholder. To illustrate, a firm has issued a 10 per cent coupon interest rate, 10-year bond with a ₹1,000 par value that pays interest semi-annually. A bondholder would have the contractual right to (1) ₹100 annual interest (0.10, coupon rate interest × ₹1,000, par value) paid as ₹50 (½ × ₹100) at the end of every 6 months and (2) ₹1,000 par value at the end of the 10th year. We illustrate in this Section the valuation of bonds with reference to (i) basic bond valuation, (ii) yield to maturity, and (iii) semi-annual interest and bond values.

Par value is value on the face of the bond.

Coupon rate is the specified interest rate

Maturity period is the number of years after which the par/specified value is payable to the bondholders.

Basic Bond Valuation

The value of a bond is the present value of the contractual payments its issuer (corporate) is obliged to make from the beginning till maturity. The appropriate discount rate would be the required return commensurate with risk and the prevailing interest rate. Symbolically,

$$B = I\left[\sum_{t=1}^{n} \frac{1}{(1+k_d)^t}\right] + M \times \left[\frac{1}{(1+k_d)^n}\right] \tag{4.3}$$

$$= I \times (PVIFA_{k_d,n}) + M \times (PVIF_{k_d,n}) \tag{4.3-A}$$

where

B = value of the bond at $t = 0$

I = annual interest paid

n = number of years to maturity (term of the bond)

M = par/maturity value

k_d = required return on the bond

***Example* 4.2**

For the data given above and assuming interest is paid annually, compute the value of the bond.

Solution

$$B_0 = [₹100 \times (PVIFA_{10,10}) + ₹1{,}000\ (PVIF_{10,10})]$$
$$= (₹100 \times 6.145) + (₹1{,}000 \times 0.386)$$
$$= ₹614.5 + ₹386 = ₹1{,}000$$

The bond value is equal to the par value. As a general proposition, **when the required return is equal to the coupon rate, the bond value equals the par value**. However, the market value of the bond is rarely equal to its par value. Several external factors over which bondholders or issuers have no control tend to affect bond values. We discuss below the impact of two factors on bond values, namely, **(i)** required return and **(ii)** time to maturity.[1]

Impact of Required Return on Bond Values When the required return on a bond differs from its coupon rate, the value of a bond would differ from its par/face value. The reason for the differences in the required return and the coupon interest rate may be (i) change in the basic cost of long-term funds or (ii) change in the basic risk of the firm. When the required return (RR) is more than the coupon rate of interest (CR), the bond value would be less than its par value, that is, the bond would sell at a **discount** equal to (M – B). Conversely, in case the RR is less than CR, the bond value would be more than the par value, that is, the bond would sell at a **premium** equal to (B – M). Consider Example 4.3.

Discount is the amount by which a bond sells below its par/face value.

Premium is the amount by which a bond sells at a value higher than its par/face value.

***Example* 4.3**

Assuming for the facts in Example 4.2 the required return is (i) 12 per cent and (ii) 8 per cent, find the value of the bond.

Solution

(i) $B = [₹100 \times (PVIFA_{12,10}) + ₹1,000 \times (PVIF_{12,10})]$

$= [(₹100 \times 5.650) + (₹1,000 \times 0.322)$

$= ₹565 + ₹322 = ₹887$

The bond would sell at a discount of ₹113 (₹887 – ₹1,000)

(ii) $B = [₹100 \times (PVIFA_{8,10}) + ₹1,000 \times (PVIF_{8,10})]$

$= [(₹100 \times 6.710) + (₹1,000 \times 463)$

$= ₹671 + ₹463 = ₹1,134$

The bond would sell at a premium of ₹134 (₹1,134 – ₹1,000).

Impact of Maturity on Bond Value When the required return (RR) is different from the coupon rate of interest (CR), the time to maturity would affect value of bonds even though the RR remains constant till maturity. The relationship among **(i)** time to maturity, **(ii)** the RR and **(iii)** the bond value are related to **(a)** constant RR and **(b)** changing RR.

Constant Required Returns In such a situation the value of the bond would approach its par value as the passage of time moves the value of the bond closer to maturity.

Changing Required Returns The shorter the time period until a bond's maturity, the less responsive is its market value to a given change in the required return. In other words, short maturities have less "interest rate risk" than do long maturities when all other features, namely, CR, par value and frequency of interest payment, are the same.[2]

To illustrate, the results relating to the bonds values for various required returns of the computations in Examples 4.2 and 4.3 are summarised in Table 4.1 and graphically depicted in Figure 4.1.

Figure 4.2 depicts the behaviour of these bond values. Each of the three required returns (i.e. 12, 10, and 8) is assumed to remain constant over the 10 years to its maturity. In each case, the value ultimately equals the par value of ₹1,000 at its maturity. At the 12 per cent RR, its discount declines with the passage of time as its value increases from ₹887 to ₹1,000. When the 10 per cent RR equals the CR, its value remains unchanged at ₹1,000. Finally, at the 8 per cent RR, its premium will decline as its value drops from ₹1,134 to ₹1,000.

TABLE 4.1 Bond Values for Various Required Returns

Required returns (k_d)	*Bond value (B)*	*Status*
12	₹887	Discount
10	1,000	At par
8	1,134	Premium

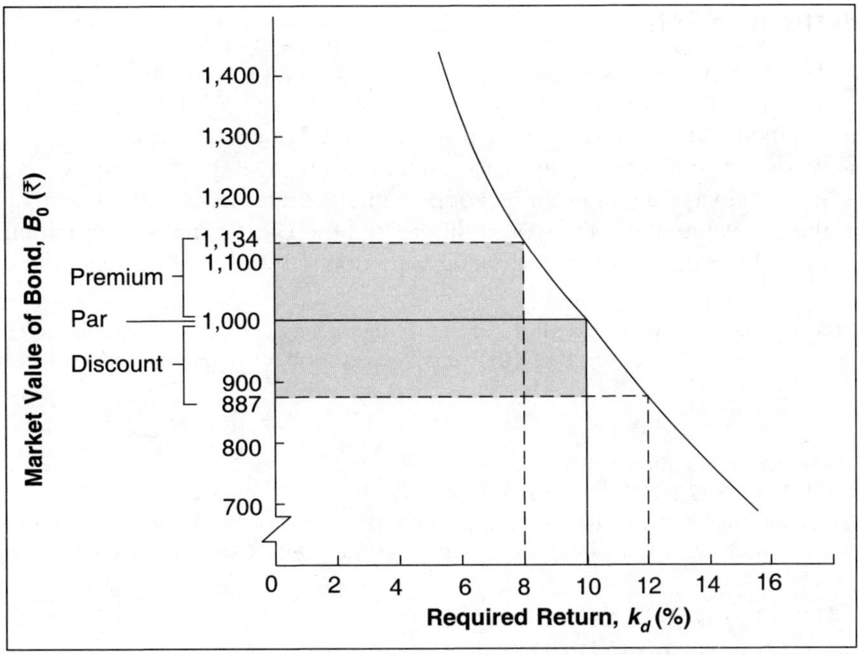

FIGURE 4.1 Bond Values and Required Returns

Thus, the value of a bond approaches ₹1,000 par/maturity value as the time to maturity declines.

The effect of changing RRs on bonds of differing maturities is also depicted in Fig 4.2, denoted by the dotted line.

The main conclusion is that **the shorter the time to maturity, the smaller the impact on bond value caused by a given change in the required return**.

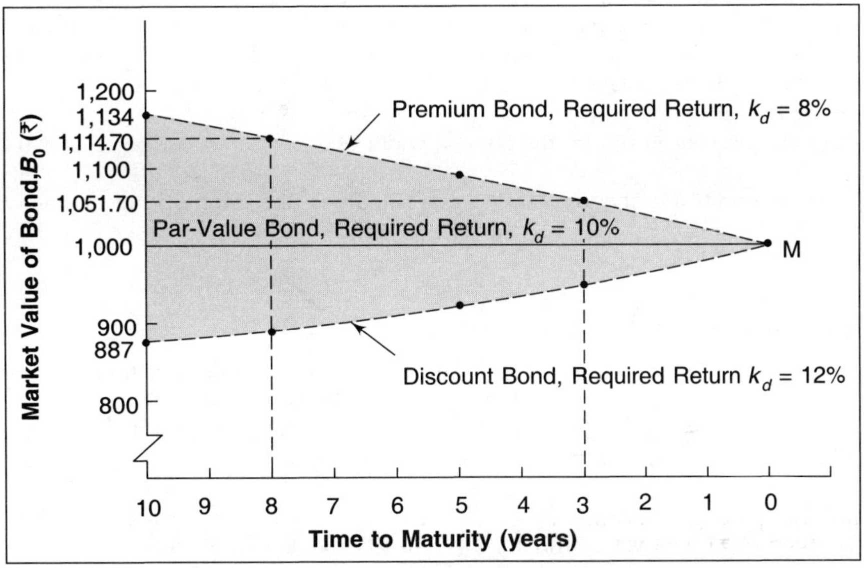

FIGURE 4.2 Time to Maturity and Bonds

Yield to Maturity (YTM)

Yield to maturity (YTM) is the rate of return an investor earns on a bond held till maturity.

The **YTM** is the rate of return that investors earn if they buy a bond at a specific price and hold it until maturity. It assumes that the issuer of the bond makes all due interest payments and repayments of principal as contracted/promised. The YTM on a bond whose current price equals its par/face value (i.e. purchase price = maturity value) would always be equal to its coupon interest rate. In case the bond value differs from the par value, the YTM would differ from the CR. Assuming annual interest payments, the YTM can be computed using Equation 4.3-A. Consider Example 4.4.

***Example* 4.4**

The bonds of the Premier Company Ltd (PCL) are currently selling for ₹10,800. Assuming **(i)** coupon rate of interest, 10 per cent, **(ii)** par value, ₹10,000, **(iii)** years to maturity, 10 years and **(iv)** annual interest payment, compute the YTM.

Solution

Substituting the values in Equation 4.3-A.

$$₹10{,}800 = [₹1{,}000 \times (PVIFAk_{d,10}) + ₹10{,}000 \times (PVIFAk_{d,10})]$$

If k_d = 10 per cent, that is, equal to the coupon rate, the value of the bond would be ₹10,000. Since the value of the bond is ₹10,800, the k_d must be less than 10 per cent. Using 9 per cent discount rate (k_d), we get

$$₹1{,}000 \times (PVIFA_{9,10}) + ₹10{,}000\ (PVIF_{9,10})$$
$$= (₹1{,}000 \times 6.418) + (₹10{,}000 \times 0.422)$$
$$= ₹6{,}418 + ₹4{,}220 = ₹10{,}638$$

Since the value of the bond (₹10,638) at k_d = 9 per cent is less than ₹10,800 (current market price), we try a lower rate of discount (k_d). Using 8 per cent, we get

$$(₹1{,}000 \times 6.710) + (₹10{,}000 \times 0.463)$$
$$= ₹6{,}710 + ₹4{,}630 = ₹11{,}340$$

Since the bond value (₹11,340) is higher than the current price of ₹10,800, the k_d (*YTM*) must be between 8 and 9 per cent. The exact value can be found by interpolation, as discussed below.

(i) Difference between the bond values at 8 and 9 per cent = ₹702 (₹11,340 – ₹10,638)

(ii) Difference between desired value (₹10,800) and the value with the lower, k_d = ₹540 (₹11,340 – ₹10,800)

(iii) Percent of the difference/distance across the discount rate range, 8-9 per cent, that is, divide the value from step (i) by the value found in step (ii) = 0.77 (₹540 ÷ ₹702)

(iv) Multiplying the per cent in (iii) by the interval width of 1 per cent (9-8) per cent = 0.77 per cent (0.77 × 1%)

(v) Adding the value in (iv) to the interest rate associated with the lower end of the interval/interest rate = 8.77 per cent (8 + 0.77).

Thus, the *YTM* = 8.77 per cent

Spreadsheet Solution 4.1

Alternatively, the Yield-to-Maturity (YTM) can be calculated using the yield function of the MS-Excel. To use the yield function, you need to click on the function tab in MS Excel, a window will appear; select Financial from the category of the functions, a list of financial functions will appear; scroll the list down and click on the function YIELD, a window listing the inputs required will appear.

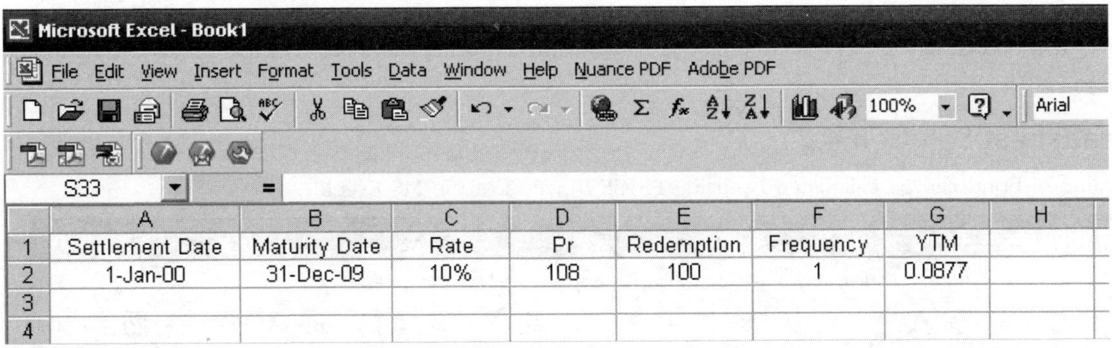

Else, you can directly enter the formula in the formula bar as =YIELD (settlement, maturity, rate, pr, redemption, frequency, [basis]). To solve the above example, relevant data has been entered in the spreadsheet. Since the excel function requires settlement and maturity dates instead of time period to maturity. We have chosen two dates representing the period of 10 years, i.e., bonds time left to maturity. The settlement and maturity dates have been entered in cells A2 and B2 respectively. Interest rate has been entered in cell C2. Notably, the other two inputs (Pr and redemption) need to be written per 100 rupees. Therefore, the current price has been written as 108 instead of 10800 and the redemption value has been written as 100 instead of 10000. The last input frequency denotes the frequency of coupon payment in the year, e.g., annual, semiannually etc. The input needed is 1 for annual payment, 2 for semiannual payments and so on. Finally, we have calculated the YTM by using the excel function in cell G2. The answer we get is the same as determined by the manual calculations, i.e., 0.0877 or 8.77%.

Semiannual Interest and Bond Values

The procedure to value bonds paying interest semiannually (half-yearly) is similar to that illustrated in Chapter 2 for compounding interest more frequently than annually. However, here we have to find out the present value. The following steps are involved in computing the value of a bond when interest is paid semiannually:

- Convert annual interest, I, to semiannual interest by dividing it by 2.
- Convert the number of years to maturity, n, to the number of 6-month periods to maturity by multiplying n by 2.
- Convert the required stated return for similar-risk bonds that also pay half-yearly interest from an annual rate, K_d, to a semiannual rate by dividing it by 2.

Symbolically,

$$B = \frac{I}{2} \times [PVIFAk_{d/2,2n}] + M \times [PVIFk_{d/2,\ 2n}] \qquad \textbf{(4.4)}$$

***Example* 4.5**

For facts in Example 4.4, assume (i) the bonds of the firm pay interest semiannually, (ii) the required stated return is 14 per cent for similar-risk bonds that also pays half-yearly interest. Compute the value of the bond.

Solution

Substituting the values in Equation 4.4, we get

$$\begin{aligned} B &= (₹1{,}000 \div 2) \times [PVIFA_{14/2 \times 2;10}] + ₹10{,}000 \times [PVIF_{14/2,\ 2 \times 10}] \\ &= (₹1{,}000/2) \times (PVIFA_{7,20}) + ₹1{,}000 \times (PVIF_{7,20}) \\ &= (₹500 \times 10.594) + (₹1{,}000 \times 0.258) \\ &= ₹5{,}297 + ₹2{,}580 = ₹7{,}877 \end{aligned}$$

The value of a bond selling at a discount is lower when semiannual interest is used compared to annual interest. For bonds selling at a premium, the value with semiannual interest is greater than with annual interest.

Spreadsheet Solution 4.2

The value of bond can be calculated by using PRICE function of the MS Excel.

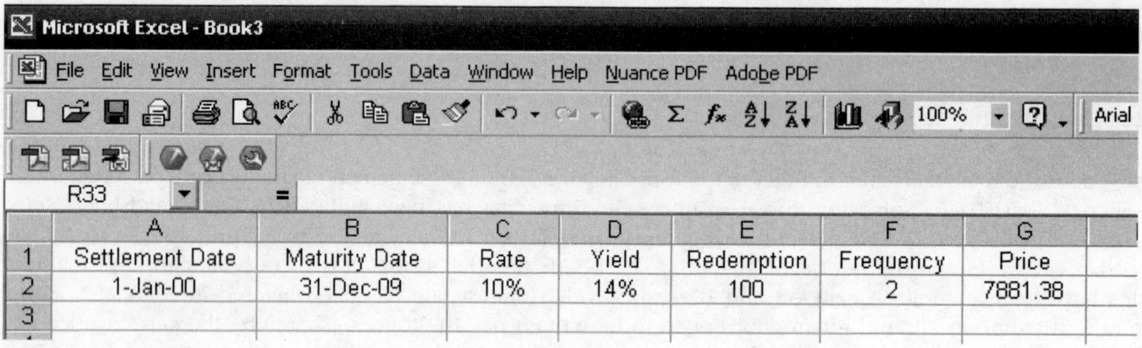

	A	B	C	D	E	F	G
1	Settlement Date	Maturity Date	Rate	Yield	Redemption	Frequency	Price
2	1-Jan-00	31-Dec-09	10%	14%	100	2	7881.38
3							

The function PRICE is similar to the function YIELD as the inputs needed are nearly the same. This function requires YTM (Yld) instead of current price of the bond. The required return on the other bond in the same risk class can be treated as YTM. It is important to note that the function requires redemption value per 100 rupees, the price generated is also per 100 rupees of face value. The price of the bond has been determined in cell G2 using the formula =PRICE (settlement, maturity, rate, yld, redemption, frequency, [basis]). The price per 10,000 rupees of face value can be determined by multiplying the price with 100. The difference in the prices is because of approximations in the manual calculations.

LO 4.3 VALUATION OF PREFERENCE SHARES

Preference shares, like debentures, are usually subject to fixed rate of return/dividend. In the case of no stated maturity, their valuation is similar to perpetual bonds. Symbolically,

$$V = \sum_{t=1}^{n} \frac{D_p}{(1+(k_p)^t} \text{ or } \frac{D_p}{k_p} \quad (4.5)$$

The valuation of redeemable preference shares is given by Equations 4.6 and 4.7.

$$V = \sum_{t=1}^{n} \frac{D_p}{(1+(k_p)^t} + \frac{MV}{(1+k_p)^n} \quad (4.6)$$

$$= D_p(PVIFAk_{p,n}) + MV(PVIF_{pv,n}) \quad (4.7)$$

Expected return is the return that is expected to be earned on a given security over an infinite time horizon.

LO 4.4 VALUATION OF ORDINARY SHARES

The ordinary/equity shareholders buy/hold shares in expectation of periodic cash dividends and an increasing share value. They would buy a share when it is under-valued (i.e. its true value is more than its market price) and sell it when its market price is more than its true value (i.e. it is overvalued). The value of a share is equal to the present value of all future dividends it is expected to provide over an infinite time horizon. symbolically,

$$P = \frac{D_1}{(1+K_e)^1} + \frac{D_2}{(1+K_e)^2} + \ldots + \frac{D_\infty}{(1+K_e)^\infty} \quad \textbf{(4.8)}$$

where P = value of shares
D_t = per share dividend expected at the end of year, t
K_e = required return on share

The equation is designed to compute the value of shares with reference to the expected growth pattern of future dividends and the appropriate discount rate. We illustrate below the computation of value of shares with reference to (i) zero growth, (ii) constant growth and (iii) variable growth.

Zero growth model is an approach to dividend valuation that assumes a constant, non-growing dividend stream.

Zero Growth Model

This approach to dividend valuation assumes a constant non-growing dividend stream. With zero growth in dividends, the value of share would equal the present value of a perpetuity of dividends (D_1) discounted at K_e. Symbolically,

$$P = D_1 \times \sum_{t=1}^{\infty} \frac{1}{(1+K_e)^t} = D_1(PVIFA_{Ke,\infty}) = D_1 \times \frac{1}{K_e} = \frac{D_1}{K_e} \quad \textbf{(4.9)}$$

Constant growth model assumes that dividend will grow at a constant rate that is less than the required rate.

where D_1 = constant dividend per share
K_e = required return of investors

Example **4.6**

The per share dividend of Premier Instruments Ltd (PIL) remains constant indefinitely at ₹10. Assuming a required rate of return of 16 per cent, compute the value of the PIL's shares.

Gordon model is the common name for the constant growth modal widely cited in dividend valuation.

Solution

$$P = \frac{D_1}{K_e} = \frac{₹10}{0.16} = ₹62.5$$

Constant Growth Model/Gordon Model

Required rate/return is a specified return required by investors for a given level of risk.

According to this approach, dividends are assumed to grow at a constant rate which is less than the required rate. This model is primarily known as the Gordon Model. The value of a share is given by Equation (4.10).

$$P = \frac{D_0 \times (1+g)^1}{(1+K_e)^1} + \frac{D_0 \times (1+g)^2}{(1+K_e)^2} + \ldots + \frac{D_0 \times (1+g)^\infty}{(1+K_e)^\infty} \quad \textbf{(4.10)}$$

or

$$P = \frac{D_1}{K_e - g} \quad \textbf{(4.11)}$$

Where P = value of share K_e = required rate g = growth rate in dividend
This is illustrated in Example 4.7

Example **4.7**

The Premier Instruments Ltd (PIL) had paid the following dividends per share.

Year	Dividend per share	Year	Dividend per share
6	₹2.80	3	2.24
5	2.58	2	2.10
4	2.40	1	2.00

Assuming a 16 per cent required return, and ₹3 per share dividend in year 7 (D_1) compute the value of the shares of PIL.

Solution

$$P = \frac{D_1}{K_e - g}$$

The expected constant rate of dividend growth, *g*, would be equal to the annual growth rate of dividends.

$$g = D_6 = D_1 \times (1 + g)^5$$

$$\frac{D_1}{D_6} = \frac{1}{(1+g)^5} = PVIF_{g,5}$$

$$PVIF = \frac{₹2}{₹2.80} = 0.714$$

Number of years of growth: year 6 – year 1 = 5

The *PVIF* closest to 0.714 (Table A-3) = 0.713 (at 7 per cent). Therefore, *g* = 7 per cent

$$P = \frac{₹3}{(0.16 - 0.07)} = \frac{₹3}{0.09} = ₹33.3 \text{ per share}$$

Variable Growth Model

Variable growth model is a dividend valuation approach that allows for a change in the dividend growth rate.

As a dividend valuation approach, this model incorporates a change in the dividend growth rate. Assuming g_1 = initial growth rate and g_2 = the subsequent growth rate occurs at the end of year *N*, the value of the shares can be determined as follows:[3]

Step 1: Compute the value of cash dividends at the end of each year (D_t) during the initial growth period (years 1 – *N*). Symbolically,

$$D_t = D_0 \times (1 + g_1)^t = D_0 \times PVIFg_{1,t}$$

Step 2: Compute the present value of the dividends expected during the initial growth period. Symbolically,

$$\sum_{t=1}^{N} \frac{D_0 \times (1+g)^t}{(1+K_e)^t} = \sum_{t=1}^{N} \frac{D_t}{(1+K_e)^t} = \sum_{t=1}^{N} (D_t \times PVIFk_{e,t})$$

Step 3: Find the value of the share at the end of the initial growth year, $P_N = (D_N + 1) \div (K_e - g_2)$. This is the present value of all dividends expected from year *N* + 1 onwards assuming a constant dividend growth rate, g_2. The present value of P_N would represent the value today of all dividends expected to be received from year *N* + 1 to infinity. Symbolically,

$$\frac{1}{(1+K_e)^N} \times \frac{D_N + 1}{K_e - g_2} = PVIFk_{e,N} \times P_N$$

Step 4: Add the present value components found in Step 2 and 3 to find the value of share, *P* given in Equation 4.9.

$$P = \underbrace{\sum_{t=1}^{N} \frac{D_0 \times (1+g_1)^t}{(1+K_e)^t}}_{\text{Present value of dividends during initial growth period}} + \underbrace{\left[\frac{1}{(1+K_e)^N} \times \frac{D_N+1}{K_e - g_2}\right]}_{\text{Present value of price of share at the end of initial growth period}} \quad \textbf{(4.12)}$$

We illustrate (Example 4.8) the computation of the value of shares with only one growth rate change.

***Example* 4.8**

The most recent (year zero, Y_0) annual dividend paid by the Premier Instruments Ltd (PIL) is ₹3 per share. An annual increase of 10 per cent (g_1) is expected over the next three years ($Y_1 - 3$). At the end of 3 years (Y_3), the dividend growth rate would slow down to 5 per cent for ever (g_2). Assuming 15 per cent required rate of return, compute the current value of the shares of the PIL.

Solution

Step 1: Present value of cash dividends, $Y_1 - 3$

Year-end (t)	$D_0 = D_{Y0}$	$PVIF_{10,t}$	D_t [(1) × (2)]	$PVIF_{15,t}$	Present value of dividends [(3) × (4)]
	(1)	*(2)*	*(3)*	*(4)*	*(5)*
Y_1	₹3	1.100	₹3.30	0.870	₹2.87
Y_2	3	1.210	3.63	0.756	2.75
Y_3	3	1.331	4.00	0.658	2.63
					8.25

Step 2: Sum of present value of dividends $= \sum_{t=1}^{3} \frac{D_0 \times (1+g_1)^t}{(1+K_e)^t} = ₹8.25$

Step 3: Value of shares at the end of the initial growth period ($N = Y_3$)

$$D_{N+1} = D_{Y4}$$

$$D_{Y4} = D_{Y3} \times (1 + 0.05) = ₹4 \times 1.05 = ₹4.2$$

By using $D_{Y4} = ₹4.2$, $K_e = 0.15$ and $g_2 = 0.05$, the value of shares at end - Y_3, P_{Y3}

$$= \frac{D_{Y4}}{K_e - g_2} = \frac{₹4.2}{0.15 - 0.05} = \frac{₹4.2}{0.10} = ₹42$$

Conversion of present value of ₹42 at the end of Y_3 to current value (Y_0) $= PVIF_{Ke,N} \times P_N$

$= PVIF_{15,3} \times P_{Y3} = 0.658 \times ₹42$

$= ₹27.64$

Step 4: Current (end-Y_0) value of shares of PIL:

$= ₹8.25 + ₹27.64 = ₹35.89$

Thus, the share is currently worth ₹35.89 per share.

Spreadsheet Solution 4.3

The value of a share can be calculated by using MS Excel as well.

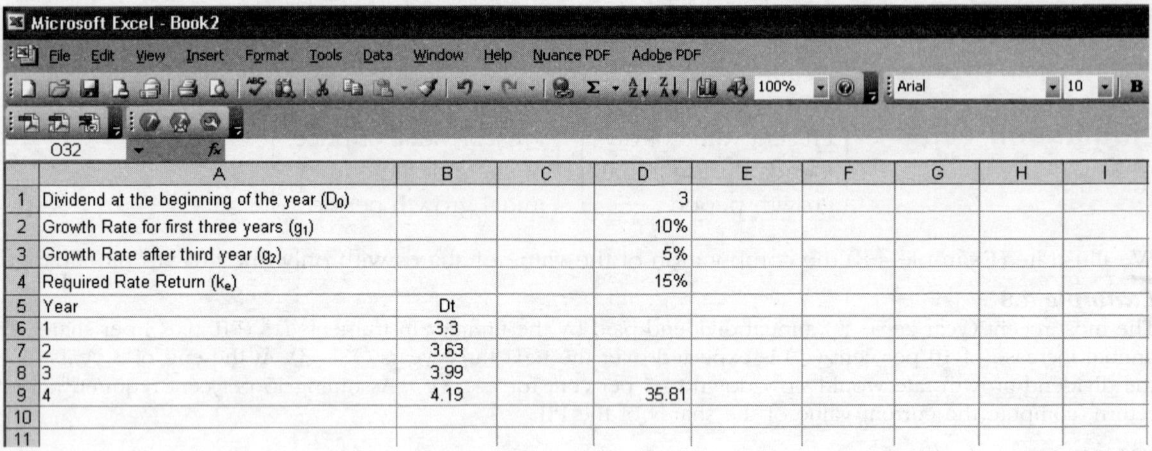

	A	B	C	D	E	F	G	H	I
1	Dividend at the beginning of the year (D_0)			3					
2	Growth Rate for first three years (g_1)			10%					
3	Growth Rate after third year (g_2)			5%					
4	Required Rate Return (k_e)			15%					
5	Year	Dt							
6	1	3.3							
7	2	3.63							
8	3	3.99							
9	4	4.19		35.81					
10									
11									

The data related to the initial dividend, initial growth rate, continuing growth rate and required rate of return has been entered in cells D1 to D4 respectively. The dividend at the end of year 1 has been calculated in cell B6 by using formula =D$1*(1+D$2)^A6. This formula has been copied to cells D7 and D8 for the dividends at the end of years 2 and 3 respectively. Since the growth rate for the year 4 and subsequent years has changed, the dividend for year 4 has been calculated by using the formula =B8*(1+D3). Finally, the value of a share has been determined using the formula =NPV(D4,B6:B8)+((B9/(D4-D3))/(1+D4)^3). The formula can be decomposed into two components. The first component represents the value of share based on the dividends for the first three years growing at 10%. This has been determined using NPV formula. The other component of the share value represents the continuing value based on the dividends fourth year onwards growing at 5%. This has been determined by using valuation formula and has been discounted to the time zero period or beginning of the year 1.

LO 4.5 OTHER APPROACHES TO VALUATION OF SHARES

In addition to the dividend valuation approach discussed in the preceding section, there are other approaches to valuation of shares. We discuss below three of these: (i) book value, (ii) liquidation value and (iii) price-earning multiples.

Book Value Approach

Book value per share is the amount per share on the sale of assets of the company at their exact book (accounting) value minus all liabilities including preference shares.

This approach uses the **book value per share (BVPS)** as the basis of valuation of shares. The **BVPS** is the *networth (i.e. equity capital plus reserves and surplus) divided by the number of outstanding equity shares.* Alternatively, the BVPS is the *amount per share on the sale of the assets of the company at their exact book (accounting) value minus all liabilities including preference shares.* Assuming total assets of Alert Ltd ₹60 crore, total liabilities including preference shares of ₹45 crore and 10,00,000 shares, its BVPS = (₹60 crore – ₹45 crore) ÷ 10,00,000 = ₹150. Alternatively, assuming a networth of ₹15 crore (i.e. capital ₹10 crore and reserves ₹5 crore), the BVPS of Alert Ltd

$$= \frac{₹15 \text{ crore}}{10,00,000} = ₹150$$

However, the BVPS is not a good proxy for true investment value. For one thing, this approach relies on historical balance sheet data. Moreover, it ignores the expected earning potential. Similarly, the BVPS has no true relationship to the market value of the firm.

Liquidation Value

This approach to valuation of shares is based on the **liquidation value per share (LVPS)**.

$$\text{LVPS} = \frac{\begin{bmatrix}\text{Value realised from} \\ \text{liquidating all assets}\end{bmatrix} - \begin{bmatrix}\text{Amount to be paid to all creditors} \\ \text{and preference shareholders}\end{bmatrix}}{\text{Number of outstanding shares}}$$

Liquidation value per share is the actual amount per share if all assets are sold, liabilities including preference shares paid and any remaining money is divided among the ordinary shareholders.

If the total assets of Alert Ltd can be liquidated for ₹52.5 crore, its LVPS = (₹52.5 crore – ₹45 crore) ÷ 10,00,000 = ₹75. The minimum value of the firm would be ₹75 per share. The LVPS is a more realistic measure than book value. But it ignores the earnings power of the assets of the firm. Moreover, it is difficult to estimate the liquidation value of a going concern. For these reasons, the LVPS is also not a true proxy of the true investment value.

Price/Earnings (P/E) Multiples/Ratio

Price/earnings multiple approach is a technique to compute value of shares multiplying expected earnings per share by the average price/earnings ratio for the industry.

The ***P/E* ratio/multiple** reflects the amount investors are willing to pay for each rupee of earnings. Based on the P/E multiple, market price of a share (MPS) can be determined as per equation 4.13

$$\text{MPS} = \text{EPS} \times \text{P/E ratio} \tag{4.13}$$

The earnings per share (EPS) of the firm are multiplied by the average P/E ratio for the industry to estimate the value of the firm on the assumption that the investors value the earnings of a given firm in the same manner as they do the "average" firm in the industry. Assuming on the basis of an analysis of historical earnings trends and expected economic and industry conditions, the Alert Ltd would earn ₹15 per share next year, and average *P/E* ratio for the firms in the industry is 10, value of its share = ₹15 × 10 = ₹150.

LO 4.6 RELATIONSHIP AMONG FINANCIAL DECISIONS, RETURN, RISK AND SHARE VALUES

Any action of the financial manger that **(i)** increases the level of expected return (D_1,g) without changing risk (k_e) should increase share value, **(ii)** reduces the level of expected return without changing risk should reduce share values. Likewise, any action that increases/reduces risk (required return) will reduce/increase share value. Since financial decisions affect both return and risk, an assessment of their effect on value must form part of the decision making process. We illustrate below their impact on share values.

Changes in Expected Return

Any management action that would increase the level of expected return without changing risk (required return) would have a positive effect on share values/owners wealth and should, accordingly, be undertaken. Consider Example 4.9.

***Example* 4.9**

For the facts in Example 4.7, assuming that the expected rate of growth would increase from 7 to 9 per cent due to proposal to upgrade technology, compute the value of the share.

Solution

$$P_0 = \frac{D_1}{K_e - g}$$

$$= \frac{₹3}{(0.16 - 0.09)} = \frac{₹3}{0.07} = ₹42.9$$

Thus, value of shares has increased from ₹33.3 to ₹42.9. The increase is caused by the higher expected future return/dividends as reflected in the increase in the growth rate.

Changes in Risk

Any action by the financial manager that increases risk will also increase the required return. It will result in reduction in value. Any action that decreases risk would contribute to an increase in value. Consider Example 4.10.

***Example* 4.10**

Assume for the facts in Example 4.7 that reflecting an increase in risk, the required rate increases to 17 per cent. Compute the value of the shares.

Solution

$$P_0 = \frac{D_1}{K_e - g}$$

$$= \frac{₹3}{(0.17 - 0.07)} = \frac{₹3}{(0.10)} = ₹30$$

Thus, the value of shares has declined from ₹33.3 to ₹30 due to increase in the required return (K_e) without any corresponding increase in the expected return.

Combined Effect

A financial decision typically affects both return and risk. Depending on the magnitude of change in these variables, the net effect on value can be assessed. This is shown in Example 4.11.

***Example* 4.11**

To illustrate the combined effect of the changes in the expected return and the required return in Examples 4.9 and 4.10, compute the value of the shares.

Solution

$$P_o = \frac{D_1}{K_e - g}$$

$$= \frac{₹3}{(0.17 - 0.09)} = \frac{₹3}{0.08} = ₹37.5$$

The net effect of the management decision which increased return (i.e. g from 7 to 9 per cent) as well as risk (i.e. K_e from 16 to 17 per cent) is positive resulting in increase value of shares from ₹33.3 to ₹37.5. As it increases the owners value, the decision seems to be in the interest of the shareholders.

LO 4.7 EQUITY RETURNS IN INDIA

Equity returns in India (from NSE 500 index companies) earned during 1994-2014 are summarized below:

- The Indian equity markets provide adequate returns to the technical (short-term) investors and also allow returns over the long-run to the fundamental (long-term) investors. However, in view of volatility in the short-run which increases the risk, it would be wiser to invest in the long-run in the Indian stock market. Such a strategy should result in relatively less risky and stable returns vis-à-vis the short-run returns.
- The average return on equity funds (ROEF) has been19.10 per cent. Even though there was a drop in the ROEF, post-recession, the sample companies were still able to record the return of 16.86 per cent. The adequate returns can be construed as good news/signal for further growth of equity markets in years to come. The companies are in a comfortable position to meet cost of equity.
- The average cost of equity has been nearly 14 per cent, assuming the average risk free rate to be 7.75 per cent.
- Market returns on equity substantially surpass the other relatively less risky investment avenues (debt) available in India. The average returns for the equity portfolios of 15-years, 10-years and 5-years durations were 18.41 per cent, 19.62 per cent and 17.33 per cent respectively.
  Further, the after-tax computation of equity returns would be greater than the after-tax computation of interest income (assuming the highest tax slab rate of 30 per cent). The other advantage that accrues to equity investment is the liquidity (in terms of transaction and the entry/exit into/from the market).
- There appears to be a negative correlation between age and returns. The 'young' companies with mean returns of 43.33 per cent fare far better than their 'middle-aged' and 'old' counterparts with mean returns of 33.72 and 31.09 per cent respectively.
- In terms of size, the 'small' and 'medium' size companies fare better (40 per cent retun) than their 'large' counterparts by 10 percentage points. Volatility remains evident in these segments as well.

Source: Singh, Shveta, Jain, P. K. and Yadav, Surendra S. (2016), "Equity Market in India: Returns, Risk and Price Multiples" India Studies in Business and Economics Series, Springer.

SUMMARY

LO 4.1

Valuation is the process that links risk and return to determine the worth of an asset/security. The key inputs in the valuation process are expected returns (cash flows), their timing/pattern and the risk (required return).

The value of a security is the present/discounted value of all future cashflows associated with it over the relevant/specified period. Symbolically,

$$V = \frac{A_1}{(1+k)^1} + \frac{A_2}{(1+k)^2} + \ldots + \frac{A_n}{(1+k)^n}$$

$$= [(A_1 \times PVIF_{k,1}) + (A_2 \times PVIF_{k,2}) + \ldots\ldots + (A_n \times PVIF_{k,n})] \text{ or } = A \times PVIFA_{(k,n)}$$

LO 4.2	The value of a bond is the present value of the contractual payments by its issuer from the beginning till maturity. Symbolically, $$B = I\left[\sum_{t=1}^{n}\frac{1}{(1+k_d)^d}\right] + M\times\left[\frac{1}{(1+k_d)^d}\right]$$ $$= I\times(PVIFAk_{d,n}) + M\times(PVIFk_{d,n})$$
LO 4.3	The valuation of redeemable prererence shares is equal to the sum of present value of all future dividends till maturity and redeemed value at maturity. Symbolically, $$V = \sum_{t=1}^{n}\frac{D_p}{(1+k_p)^t} + \frac{MV}{(1+k_p)}$$
LO 4.4	The value of a share is equal to the present value of all future dividends over an indefinite period of time. Symbolically, $$P = \frac{D_1}{(1+K_e)^1} + \frac{D_2}{(1+K_e)^2} + \ldots + \frac{D_\infty}{(1+K_e)^\infty}$$
	With zero growth in dividends, $P = \frac{D_1}{K_e}$
	With constant growth in dividends, $P = \frac{D_1}{K_e - g}$
	With variable growth in dividends $$P = \sum_{t=1}^{n}\frac{D_0\times(1+g)^t}{(1+K_e)^t} + \left[\frac{1}{(1-K_e)^n}\times\frac{D_N+1}{K_e-g_2}\right]$$
LO 4.5	In addition to the dividend approach, there are other approaches to value ordinary, shares, namely, book value, liquidation value and P/E multiples/ratio. The P/E multiple approach is the most popular in practice because, unlike the book value and liquidation value, this approach views the firm as a going concern whose value lies in its earning power rather than its asset values.
LO 4.6	Any action of a financial manager that increases the level of expected return without changing risk would increase share value and any action that reduces the level of expected returns without changing risk would reduce share values. Similarly, an action that increases risk will reduce value of shares and any action that reduces risk will increase share values. As most financial decisions affect both return and risk, an assessment of their combined effect on value must be part of the financial decision process.

REFERENCES

1. Gitman, L J, *Principles of Management Finance*, Addison-Wasley, (New York, 1997), p 284.
2. *Ibid*, p 286.
3. *Ibid*, p 296.

SOLVED PROBLEMS

P.4.1 The face value of a 10-year, 10 per cent bond (with 10 per cent coupon rate) is ₹1,000. The interest is payable semi-annually. Assuming 12 per cent required rate of return of investors, compute the value of the bond. What price would an investor be willing to pay, if the interest is payable annually. **LO 4.2** LOD E

Solution Interest paid semi-annually:

$V = I(PVIFA_{r,n}) + M(PVIF_{r,n})$

$= ₹50(PVIFA_{6,20}) + ₹1{,}000(PVIF_{6,20}) = (₹50 \times 11.4699) + (₹1{,}000 \times 0.3118) = ₹885.3$

Note: $I = ₹100/2 = ₹50$; $n = 10$ years × 2 = 20; $r = 12$ per cent/2 = 6 per cent.

Interest paid annually:

$V = ₹100(PVIFA_{12,10}) + ₹1{,}000(PVIF_{12,10}) = (₹100 \times 5.6502) + (₹1{,}000 \times 0.3220) = ₹887.02$

The investor would be willing to pay ₹887.02 for the bond.

P.4.2 ABC Ltd paid a dividend of ₹4 per share at the end of the year. It is expected to grow by 8 per cent each year for the next 4 years. The market price of the shares is expected to be ₹60 at the end of 4 years. Assuming 12 per cent required rate of return of investors, at what price should the shares of ABC Ltd sell? **LO 4.4** LOD M

Solution Expected price $(P_0) = \sum_{t=1}^{4} \frac{D_t}{(1+r)^t} + \frac{P_4}{(1+r)^4}$

$= D_1/(1.12) + D_2(1.12)^2 + D_3/(1.12)^3 + D_4(1.12)^4 + ₹60/(1.12)^4$

$= ₹4.32(0.893) + ₹4.67(0.797) + ₹5.04(0.712) + ₹5.44(0.567)$

$= ₹3.86 + ₹3.72 + ₹3.59 + ₹3.09 + ₹34.02 = ₹48.28.$

The shares of ABC Ltd should sell for ₹48.28.

Working Notes Dividends: Present $(D_0) = ₹4$

$D_1 = ₹4(1.08) = ₹4.32$ $\qquad D_3 = ₹4(1.08)^3 = ₹5.04$

$D_2 = ₹4(1.08)^2 = ₹4.67$ $\qquad D_4 = ₹4(1.08)^4 = ₹5.44$

P.4.3 The required rate of return of investors is 14 per cent. Assume the D_1 (next expected dividend) is ₹2.50. Compute the price at which the shares will sell if the investors expect the earnings/dividends to grow, (i) at 12 per cent, (ii) 14 per cent and (iii) at 16 per cent. **LO 4.4** LOD M

Solution $P_0 = D_1/(r - g)$

(i) Growth in dividends, 12 per cent: $P_0 = ₹2.5/(0.14 - 0.12) = ₹125.$

(ii) Growth in dividends, 14 per cent: $P_0 = ₹2.5/(0.14 - 0.14)$ = (the formula is invalid since a necessary condition is $r > g$).

(iii) Growth in dividends, 16 per cent: $P_0 = ₹2.5/(0.14 - 0.16)$ = undefined.

P.4.4 The following facts are available: **LO 4.4** LOD M

— Risk-free rate, 9 per cent
— Required rate of return, 18 per cent
— Beta coefficient of the shares of ABC Ltd, 1.5
— Expected dividend during the next year, ₹3
— Growth rate in dividends/earnings, 8 per cent

Compute the price at which the shares of ABC Ltd should sell?

Solution $P_0 = D_1/(r - g) = ₹3/(0.225 - 0.08) = ₹3/.0.145 = ₹20.7$

Working Notes $r = r_f + b(r_m - r_f) = 0.09 + 1.5(0.18 - 0.09) = 0.225$

P.4.5 The required rate of return of investors is 15 per cent. ABC Ltd declared and paid annual dividend of ₹4 per share. It is expected to grow @20 per cent for the next 2 years and at 10 per cent thereafter. Compute the price at which the shares should sell? **LO 4.4** LOD M

Solution $P_0 = [D_1(1 + r) + D_2/(1 + r)^2] + [D_3/(r - g)]/(1 + r)^2$

(a) Present value of dividends for the first 2 years: $(₹4.8 \times PVIF_{15,1}) + (₹5.76 \times PVIF_{15,2})$

$= (₹4.8 \times 0.8696) + ₹5.76 \times 0.7561) = ₹4.17 + ₹4.355 = ₹8.53.$

(b) Present value of price after 2 years (P_2) = ($D_3/r - g$) × (PVIF$_{15,2}$) = ₹6.34/(0.15 = 0.10)
= ₹106.8 × 0.7561 = ₹80.75
P_0= ₹8.53 + ₹80.75 = ₹89.28.

Working Notes Dividends: D_0 (present) = ₹4
D_1 = ₹4(1.2)^1 = ₹4.8
D_2 = ₹4(1.2)^2 = ₹5.76
D_3 = ₹5.76(1.10) = ₹6.34

P.4.6 A bond has 3 years remaining until maturity. It has a par value of ₹1,000. The coupon interest rate on the bond is 10 per cent. Compute the yield to maturity at current market price of (i) ₹1,100 (ii) ₹1,000 and (iii) ₹900, assuming interest is paid annually. **LO 4.2** LOD **M**

Solution

(i) Market price (above par or at premium) ₹1,100:
Yield to maturity = [(I + (M – V)/n]/(M + V)/2 = [₹100 + (₹1,000 – ₹1,100)/3]/(₹1,000 + ₹1,100)/2 = ₹66.67/₹1,050 = 0.063 = 6.3 per cent

(ii) Market price (at par), ₹1,000:
Yield to maturity = [₹100 + (₹1,000 – ₹1,000/3]/ (₹1,000 + ₹1,000)/2 = ₹100/₹1,000 = 0.10 = 10 per cent.

(iii) Market price (below par or at discount), ₹900:
Yield to maturity = [₹100 + (₹1,000 – ₹900/3]/ (₹1,000 + ₹900)/2 = ₹133.33/₹950 = 0.1403 = 14.03 per cent.

P.4.7 A note (secured premium note) is available for ₹1,400. It offers, including one immediate payment, 10 annual payments of ₹210. Compute the rate of return (yield) on the note. **LO 4.2** LOD **M**

Solution $$V = \sum_{t=1}^{n} \frac{C_t}{(1+r)^t}$$

= ₹1,400 = ₹210(1 + $PVIFA_{r,9}$)
(1 + $PVIFA_{r,9}$) = ₹1,400/₹210 = 6.67
$PVIFA_{r,9}$ = 6.67 – 1 = 5.67

From Table A-4 (Appendix), the closet values are 5.7590 (0.10) and 5.3282 (0.11). By interpolation, r = 10.2 per cent.

P.4.8 A share is selling for ₹50 on which a dividend of ₹3 per share is expected at the end of the year. The expected market price after the dividend declaration is to be ₹60. Compute (i) the return on investment (r) in shares, (ii) dividend yield and (iii) capital gain yield. **LO 4.3, 4** LOD **D**

Solution

(i) r = [D_1 + (P_1 – P_0)]/P_0 = [₹3 + (₹60 – ₹50)]/ ₹50 = 0.26 = 26 per cent.
Alternatively, ₹50 = ₹3/(1 + r) + ₹60/(1 + r)
r = 50(1 + r) = ₹3 + ₹60
1 + r = (₹3 + ₹60)/₹50
r = [(₹3 + ₹60)/₹50] – 1 = 1.26 – 1 = 0.26 = 26 per cent.

(ii) Dividend yield = D_1/P_0 = ₹3/₹50 = 0.06 = 6 per cent

(iii) Capital gain yield = (P_1 = P_0)/P_0 = ₹10/₹50 = 0.20 = 20 per cent.

P.4.9 Assume (i) ₹100 par value, (ii) 8 per cent coupon rate of interest and (iii) 10 years remaining to maturity date. **LO 4.2** LOD **D**

- If interest is paid annually, find the value of the bond when the required rate of return is (a) 7 per cent, (b) 8 per cent and (c) 10 per cent. Indicate for each case whether the bond is selling at a discount, at a premium or at its par value.
- Using 10 per cent required return, what would be the value of the bond if interest is paid semiannually?

Solution Value of bond, when interest is paid annually:

$B = I \times (PVIFA_{Kd,n}) + M \times (PVIF_{Kd,n})$

(a) $K_d = 7$ per cent

$B = (₹8 \times 7.024) + (₹100 \times 0.508)$

$= ₹56.19 + ₹50.8 = ₹106.99$ (sells at a premium)

(b) $K_d = 8$ per cent

$B = (₹8 \times 6.710) + (₹100 \times 0.463)$

$= ₹53.6 + ₹46.3 = ₹99.9$ (sells at par value)

(c) $K_d = 10$ per cent

$B = (₹8 \times 6.145) + (₹100 \times 0.386)$

$= ₹49.16 + ₹38.6 = ₹87.76$ (sells at a discount)

Value of bond when interest is paid semiannually:

$B = 1/2 \times (PVIFAk_{d/2,2n}) + M \times (PVIFk_{d/2,n})$

$= ₹8/2 \times (PVIFA_{10/2,2\times10}) + ₹100\ (PVIF_{10/2,2\times10})$

$= ₹4 \times (PVIFA_{5,20}) + ₹100(PVIF_{5,20})$

$= (₹4 \times 12.462) + (₹100 \times 0.377)$ or $= ₹49.85 + ₹37.7 = ₹87.55$

P.4.10 The bonds of Alert Ltd currently sell at ₹115. They have a 11 per cent coupon rate of interest and ₹100 par value. The interest is paid annually and the bonds have 18 years to maturity. Compute the yield to maturity (YTM) of the bond. Compare the computed YTM with the coupon interest rate. How do you explain the difference between the current price and the par value of the bond.

LO 4.2 LOD M

Solution $B = ₹115$

$I = ₹100 \times 0.11 = ₹11$

$M = ₹100$

$n = 18$

$₹115 = 11 \times (PVIFA_{Kd,18}) + ₹100 \times (PVIF_{Kd,18})$

If $K_d = 11$ per cent, $B = ₹100 = M$. So let us try a lower rate (say, 10 per cent)

$B = ₹11 \times (PVIFA_{10,18}) + ₹100\ (PVIF_{10.18})$

$= (₹11 \times 8.201) + (₹100 \times 0.180)$

$= ₹90.21 + ₹18 = ₹108.21$

As ₹108.21 < ₹115, let us try a lower rate (say, 9 per cent)

$B = ₹11\ (PVIFA_{9,18}) + ₹100\ (PVIF_{9,18})$

$= (₹11 \times 8.756) + (₹100 \times 0.212)$

$= ₹96.32 + ₹21.2 = ₹117.52$

Therefore, the YTM of the bond is between 9-10 per cent. By interpolation, YTM = 9.27 per cent).

The YTM (9.27%) is below the coupon interest rate (11%) of the bond as its market value (₹115) is above its par value (₹100). When the market value of a bond is above its par value (i.e. it sells at a premium), its YTM would be below its coupon rate of interest; when a bond sells at par, the YTM = its coupon rate of interest; when the bond sells at a discount (i.e. market value < par value), the YTM would be greater than its coupon rate of interest.

P.4.11 The Alert Ltd currently pays ₹3 per share as annual dividend. Assuming 10 per cent required rate of return on shares (K_e), compute the value of shares under each of the following dividend growth rate assumptions:

LO 4.4 LOD D

- Annual rate of growth, zero (0) per cent indefinitely.
- Annual constant rate of growth, 5 per cent to infinity.
- Annual rate of growth, 5 per cent for each of the next 3 years, followed by a constant annual rate of growth of 4 per cent in years 4 to infinity.

Solution Value of shares, zero growth:

$$P = \frac{D_1}{K_e} = \frac{D_1 = D_0 = ₹3}{0.10} = ₹30$$

Value of shares, constant growth, g = 5 per cent:

$$D_1 = D_0 \times (1 + g) = ₹3 \times (1 + 0.05) = ₹3.15$$

$$P = \frac{D_1}{K_e - g} = \frac{₹3.15}{(0.10 - 0.05)} = \frac{₹3.15}{0.05} = ₹63$$

Value of shares, with variable growth in dividends, $N = 3$,

g_1 = 5 per cent and g_2 = 4 per cent:

$$D_1 = D_0 \times (1 + g_1)^1 = ₹\ 3 \times (1 + 0.05)^1 = ₹3.15$$

$$D_2 = D_0 \times (1 + g_1)^2 = ₹\ 3 \times (1 + 0.05)^2 = ₹3.31$$

$$D_3 = D_0 \times (1 + g_1)^3 = ₹\ 3 \times (1 + 0.05)^3 = ₹3.47$$

$$D_4 = D_3 \times (1 + g_2) = ₹\ 3.47 \times (1 + 0.04) = ₹3.61$$

$$P = \sum_{t=1}^{N} \frac{D_0 \times (1+g)^t}{(1+K_e)^t} + \left[\frac{1}{(1+K_e)^N} \times \frac{D_N + 1}{K_e - g_2}\right]$$

$$= \sum_{t=1}^{n} \frac{D_0 \times (1+g)^t}{(1+K_e)^t} + \frac{₹3.15}{(1+0.10)^1} + \frac{₹3.31}{(1+0.10)^2} + \frac{₹3.47}{(1+0.10)^3}$$

$$= [₹3.15 \times (PVIF_{10,1})] + [₹3.31 \times (PVIF_{10,2})] + [₹3.47 \times (PVIF_{10,3})]$$

$$= [(₹3.15 \times 0.909) + (₹3.31 \times 0.826) + (₹3.47 \times 0.751)$$

$$= ₹2.86 + ₹2.73 + ₹2.61 = ₹8.2$$

$$\left[\frac{1}{(1+K_e)^N} \times \frac{D_N + 1}{K_e - g_2}\right] = \left[\frac{1}{(1+0.10)^3} \times \frac{D_4 = ₹3.61}{(0.10 - 0.04)}\right]$$

$$= (PVIF_{10,3}) \times \frac{₹3.61}{0.06}$$

$$= 0.751 \times ₹160.17 = ₹45.19$$

$$P = \sum_{t=1}^{N} \frac{D_0 \times (1+g)^t}{(1+K_e)^t} + \left[\frac{1}{(1+K_e)^N} \times \frac{D_N + 1}{K_e - g_2}\right] = ₹8.2 + ₹45.19$$

$$= ₹53.39 \text{ per share}$$

MINI CASES

4.C.1 (Gordon Growth Model) The BSES Rajdhani Ltd supplies power to homes and businesses in the New Delhi and the South Delhi areas. Its pricing is regulated by the Delhi Electricity Regulatory Commission (DERC). The BSES's average annual free cash flows available to the equity holders (FCFE) during the 5-year period 2006-10 were ₹551 crore and the average annual dividends during the same period amounted to ₹506 crore. The earnings per share (EPS) and the dividends per share (DPS) in 2009 were ₹3.13 and ₹2.19 respectively, the dividend pay-out ratio being 70 per cent. The return on equity averaged 11.63 per cent.

The management of the BSES has appointed Richa Singh as a financial consultant to compute the value of its shares. Richa Singh estimates that the beta for power distributors like BSES is 0.90. Similarly, the risk free rate and the market risk premium rate are 5.4 per cent and 4 per cent respectively. What is the per share value of the BSES Ltd?

Solution

Given that the BSES, based on size and area, has stable growth and that its pricing is regulated by the DERC, Richa Singh uses the Gordon Growth Model to value its shares:

The value of shares = DPS/(K_{e-g})

Where DPS = Expected dividend next year

K_e = Required rate of return on equity

g = Growth in dividends

1. Cost of equity capital = 0.54 (risk free return) + [0.90 (beta) × 0.40 (risk premium)] = 0.09 (9 per cent).
2. Expected growth in dividends = (1 – dividend pay-out ratio) × return on equity = (1 – 0.70) × (0.1163) = 0.0349 (3.49 per cent)
3. Value of shares = (₹2.19 × 1.0349) ÷ (0.09 – 0.0349) = ₹41.15.

4.C.2 (Valuation of Shares) Financial Technologies Ltd (FTL) creates leading-edge technologies for fast-growing markets. Its reported earnings and dividends per share were ₹11.50 and ₹2.40 respectively in 2009. For the next five years, the projected earnings growth is 30.1 per cent. It is expected to decline linearly to 8 per cent after five years. The (dividend) pay-out ratio is likely to remain stable during 2009-14. It would rise linearly after that and reach 21 per cent in 2019-20. The shares of FTL are expected to have a beta of 1.18 in the next five years but it is likely to decline linearly over the following five years to reach 1 by the time the FTL reaches its steady level of growth (8 per cent) in 2019-20. The risk free rate is currently 8 per cent and may be assumed to remain constant in the foreseeable future. The market risk premium may be assumed to be 4 per cent.

Required As a financial consultant, compute the value of the FTL's shares.

Solution

Using dividend valuation (discount) model, the value of the shares is shown in Table 1.

TABLE 1 Valuation of Shares (Dividend Growth Model)

	Year	*2009*	*2010*	*2011*	*2012*	*2013*	*2014*	*2015*	*2016*	*2017*	*2018*	*2019*	*2020*	*Total*
1	Earnings growth (%)	-	30.10	30.10	30.10	30.10	30.10	25.68	21.26	16.84	12.42	8.00	8.00	
2	Earnings (₹)	11.50	14.96	19.46	25.32	32.94	42.86	53.87	65.32	76.32	85.80	92.67	100.08	
3	Pay-out ratio (%)	0.209	0.209	0.209	0.209	0.209	0.209	0.291	0.292	0.294	0.297	0.21	0.21	
4	Dividend (₹)	2.40	3.12	4.06	5.28	6.88	8.95	11.26	13.67	15.99	18.00	19.46	21.02	
5	Beta	1.18	1.18	1.18	1.18	1.18	1.18	1.14	1.11	1.07	1.04	1.00	1.00	
6	Return on equity (%)	12.72@	12.72	12.72	12.72	12.72	12.72	12.58	12.43	12.29	12.14	12.00@@	-	
7	Compounded return (%)	12.72	12.72	12.72	12.72	12.72	12.72	12.70	12.66	12.61	12.56	12.50	-	
8	Present value factor at compound rate	1.00	0.89	0.79	0.70	0.62	0.55	0.49	0.43	0.39	0.34	0.31	-	
9	Present value of dividend payments (a)	-	2.77	2.40	3.69	4.26	4.92	5.49	5.93	6.18	6.20	5.99	-	47.84 (a)
10	Share price at end-2019 (Dividend)t+1 ÷ (Required return – Growth rate) = ₹21.02/(12% – 8%)											525.50		
11	Present value of share price at end – 2009 (₹525.50 × 0.31)													162.91(b)
12	Share value at end-2009 (a + b)													210.75

@Tax free return + (Beta × risk premium)

@@ Tax free return + (Beta × risk premium)

REVIEW QUESTIONS

LOD: Easy

RQ 4.1 **(a)** Indicate whether the following statements are True or False. [LO 4.2, 3, 4]

(i) Value of a bond is dependent solely on the interest payments it provides.
(ii) If coupon rate = Required rate, the value of the bond would be equal to its par value.
(iii) Bond value will differ from its par value, even though yield to maturity = coupon rate.
(iv) For a bond, yield to maturity (YTM) is always equal to coupon rate.
(v) Value of a bond with semi-annual interest rate, is greater than the value of bond providing interest on annual basis.
(vi) Constant/variable growth model, for the valuation of equity share, is applicable for the growth rate $g \geq k_e$.
(vii) In a variable growth model, the dividend is assumed to grow at a constant rate forever after a initial growth period.
(viii) Any action by finance manager that increase the risk will reduce the value.

[Answers: (i) False (ii) True (iii) False (iv) False (v) True (vi) False (vii) True (viii) True]

(b) In the following multiple choice questions select the correct answers.

(i) The value of a bond/debenture is
(a) present value of contractual payments it receives till maturity **(b)** present value of interest payments it receives **(c)** present value of its redemption amount/value **(d)** none of these.
(ii) When the required rate of return is greater than coupon rate, the bond will be valued at
(a) discount **(b)** premium **(c)** par value **(d)** none of these.
(iii) Given the coupon rate to be constant, the value of bond, as it approaches to maturity, will converge to
(a) its par value **(b)** redemption value **(c)** issued value **(d)** none.
(iv) A bond can be issued at premium if
(a) Coupon rate > Required returns **(b)** Coupon rate < Required returns **(c)** Coupon rate = Required returns **(d)** none.

[Answers: (i) a (ii) a (iii) b (iv) a]

RQ 4.2 Define and specify the general equation for the value of any asset/security. [LO 4.1]

RQ 4.3 Describe the basic procedure used to value a bond that pays interest (i) annually, (ii) semiannually. [LO 4.2]

RQ.4.4 An investor is considering the purchase of a share of ABC Ltd at the beginning of the year. If his required rate of return is 10 per cent, the year-end expected dividend is ₹4 and year-end price is expected to be ₹26, compute the value of the share. [LO 4.4]

RQ.4.5 An investor has invested in the shares of ABC Ltd which expects no (zero) growth in dividends. ABC Ltd has paid a dividend of ₹3 per share. If the required rate of return is 14 per cent, what would be the value of the share? [LO 4.4]

LOD: Medium

RQ 4.6 Explain the relationship between the required return and coupon interest rate that would cause a bond to sell at (i) a discount, (ii) premium, (iii) par. [LO 4.2]

RQ 4.7 Explain and illustrate the yield to maturity (YTM) on a bond. [LO 4.2]

RQ 4.8 Describe, illustrate, compare and contrast each of the following share valuation models: [LO 4.4]

- Zero growth
- Constant growth
- Variable growth

RQ 4.9 Explain the following other approaches to the valuation of shares: [LO 4.5]

- Book value
- Liquidation value
- P/E multiples

RQ.4.10 The Premier Instruments Ltd's (PIL's) bonds have the following attributes: (i) par value, ₹100; (ii) coupon interest rate, 10 per cent; (iii) interest payment, annually; (iv) years remaining to its maturity date, 12. [LO 4.2]

- Find the current sale value of the PIL's bonds if bonds of similar risk are currently earning 8 per cent rate of return.
- Why is a similar risk bond earning a return (8%) below the coupon interest rate (10%)?
- What would be the current value of PIL's bonds if the required return was 10 per cent and not 8 per cent?

RQ.4.11 The shares of ABC Ltd are currently selling for ₹100 on which the expected dividend is ₹4. Compute the total return on the shares if the earnings or dividends are likely to grow at **(a)** 5 per cent **(b)** 10 per cent and **(c)** 0 (zero) per cent (no growth). [LO 4.4]

RQ.4.12 ABC Ltd paid a dividend of ₹2 per share last year (D_0), which is expected to grow at 10 per cent. If the current market price is ₹40 and the required rate of return is 18 per cent, compute the expected dividend yield and capital gains yield next year. [LO 4.4]

LOD: Difficult

RQ 4.13 If the required return on a bond differs from its coupon interest rate and is assumed to be constant until maturity, describe the behaviour of the bond value over a period of time as the bond moves towards maturity. [LO 4.2]

RQ.4.14 The closing price of the shares of ABC Ltd on December 31, previous year, was ₹25. It paid a year-end dividend as detailed below: [LO 4.4]

Year	Dividend	Year	Dividend
1	₹2	4	₹2.50
2	₹2	5	₹2.50
3	₹2.20		

At what price should an investor sell his shares at the end of year 5 to earn a compound rate of return of 15 per cent on the initial investment (of ₹25)? Ignore commission and taxes.

ANSWERS

RQ.4.4 ₹27.28
RQ.4.5 ₹21.43
RQ.4.10 ₹115.06 (current sale value); ₹100 (current value of PIL bond)
RQ.4.11 **(a)** 9 per cent, **(b)** 14 per cent, **(c)** 4 per cent.
RQ.4.12 Dividend yield 5.5 per cent; capital gain yield 12.5 per cent
RQ.4.14 ₹35.46

Scan the QR Code to access comprehensive solutions to all numerical review questions and additional material.

PART 2

FINANCIAL ANALYSIS, PROFIT PLANNING AND CONTROL

Chapter 5
STATEMENT OF CASH FLOWS

Chapter 6
FINANCIAL STATEMENTS ANALYSIS

Chapter 7
VOLUME-COST-PROFIT ANALYSIS

Chapter 8
BUDGETING AND PROFIT PLANNING

Part Two of the book is devoted to the discussion of the use of financial statements and profit planning and control. The preparation and use of cash flow statement is covered in Chapter 5. Chapter 6 discusses the techniques to analyse the balance sheet and statement of profit and loss.

Cost data are an important input in internal managerial planning. The most widely- used profit planning techniques are also illustrated in this part. The volume-cost-profit analysis, as a tool of profit planning, is covered in Chapter 7. Budgeting, as a systematic approach to profit planning and control is elaborated in Chapter 8.

CHAPTER

5

Statement of Cash Flows

LEARNING OBJECTIVES

LO 5.1	Explain the concept of statement of cash flows
LO 5.2	Determine cash inflows and cash outflows transactions
LO 5.3	Understand the usefulness of statement of cash flows
LO 5.4	Illustrate preparation of statement of cash flows
LO 5.5	Discuss cash flow statement as per AS-7

The balance sheet and statement of profit and loss are the two major financial statements of a business/corporate firm. A balance sheet shows the financial position of the a firm as at the last day of the accounting period. An income statement focuses on financial performance (profit or loss) due to the operating activities of a firm during the period. Revenues recorded in income statement do not reflect cash inflows as the debtors may pay later. Likewise, some of the expenses shown in income statement may be non-cash expenses (depreciation, amortisation etc.) and some may not be paid in full (goods purchased on credit, salaries payable etc). Thus, the period's profit or loss does not bear direct relationship to the cash flows associated with the period's operations. It does not evidently provide information about the investing and financing activities of the firm during the accounting period.

This chapter describes the third financial statement a company is required to prepare, namely, the statement of cash flows. The objective of the cash-flow statement is to provide information about the cash flows associated with operating, investing and financing activities of the firm during the accounting period. The information is significant to the stakeholders of a company. Dividends payable to the shareholders obviously are dependent on cash flows; interest payment and debt repayment to the lenders require the availability of cash; payment to the employees, suppliers and taxes in time is contingent upon the company's ability to generate adequate cash flows to meet these financial obligations.[1] For these reasons, statement of cash flows/cash flow statement (CFS) is the third major financial statement of a company. The meaning, sources and uses of cash, and usefulness of the CFS are outlined first. The preparation of CFS is also covered. Its preparation in conformity with Ind AS-7 is illustrated subsequently. Annexure I contains the actual cash flow statement of the Reliance Industries Ltd. The main points are summarised by way of recapitulation.

LO 5.1 MEANING

Cash flow statement is a statement which indicates sources of cash inflows and transactions of cash outflows of a firm during an accounting period. The activities/transactions which generate cash inflows are known as sources of cash and activities which cause cash outflows are known as uses of cash. It is appropriately termed as *"**Where Got Where Gone Statement**"*.

It may be emphasised that the information contained in the CFS are objective and, hence, more credible and reliable *vis-à-vis* the other financial statements. The reason is that ***cash is cash*** and the amounts of cash flows are not affected by the subjective judgments and estimates that are normally made in revenues, expenses and other accruals.[2] The CFS is a financial document as it leaves no scope for any maneuvering on the amounts of cash inflows and cash outflows.

LO 5.2 SOURCES AND USES OF CASH

Exhibit 5.1 shows major items of cash inflows and cash outflows.

EXHIBIT 5.1 Statement of Cash Flows of Hypothetical Limited

Particulars	*Amounts*
(I) Sources of Cash Inflows:	
(1) Business operations/operating activities	
(2) Non-business/operating activities (interest/dividend received)	
(3) Sale of long-term assets (plant, building and equipment)	
(4) Issue of additional long-term securities (equity, preference shares and debentures)	
(5) Additional long-term borrowings (banks and financial institutions)	
(6) Others sources (specify them)	
(II) Sources of Cash Outflows:	
(1) Purchase of long-term assets (plant and machinery, land and building, office equipments and furniture)	
(2) Redemption of preference shares and debentures	
(3) Repurchase of equity shares	
(4) Repayment of long-term borrowings	
(5) Cash dividends paid to shareholders (preference and equity)	
(6) Others items (specify)	
Net Increase (Decrease) in Cash **[I – II]**	

LO 5.3 USEFULNESS OF STATEMENT OF CASH FLOWS

The cash flow statement helps to provide answers to users to some of the important questions related to the company such as the following:

- How much cash has been generated from normal business operating activities/operations of a company?
- What have been the other premier financing activities of the firm through which cash has been raised? What has happened to cash so obtained?
- How much cash has been spent on investment activities, say, on purchase of new plant and

equipments?

- How was the redemption of preference shares and debentures accomplished?
- Have long-term sources of cash (internally generated plus raised externally) adequate to finance purchase of new long-term/fixed assets?
- What has been the proportion of debt and equity for cash raised from outside?
- Why are dividends not larger?
- Is the company borrowing to pay cash dividends?
- Has the liquidity position of the company improved?

Thus, the CFS enables the management to see whether the long-term funds are adequate to finance major fixed assets expansion. A situation in which short-term sources (bank overdraft, temporary loans, etc.) constitute the bulk of sources for long-term purposes may not be desirable. Such a pattern of financing is likely to cause problems for the firm to meet its current liabilities in future. Besides, the CFS also indicates the extent of reliance on external resources *vis-a-vis* the internal sources. Thus, the CFS clearly highlights the firm's financing and investment activities.

The CFS, when prepared on a projected basis, has immense potential/utility as a tool of financial planning. It shows the effect of various financing and investment decisions on future cashflows. If the implementation of the decision results in excessive or inadequate cash, steps may be taken to improve the situation or review the decisions. For instance, if the cash position is expected to deteriorate, funds may be raised by borrowing or issuing new equity shares. If the required amount is not feasible to be raised, plans for acquisition of assets may be postponed or alternative operative plans can be developed to ensure that the desired future level of business operations, expansion, and so on, are achieved. Thus, the CFS enables the management to revise/review its investments, operations and financing activities so as to conform to the desired financial inflow and outflow of resources. Above all, the long-term lenders can use the statement as a means of estimating the firm's ability to service their debts.

LO 5.4 PREPARATION OF STATEMENT OF CASH FLOWS

You will remember that the balance sheet and income statement are prepared from the ledger account balances of a company. In contrast, the cash flow statement is derived from these two financial statements. The CFS explains factors which have caused changes in assets, liabilities and shareholders' funds between the opening and closing dates of the accounting period. Therefore, the CFS can be prepared by (i) finding the difference in amounts among the various items (say, changes in long-term liabilities, long-term assets) between the comparative balance sheets and then (ii) analysing the causes of difference. The analysis, in some cases, is facilitated by the use of 'T' accounts. The preparation of CFS is illustrated in Example 5.1.

***Example* 5.1**

Given below are the balance sheets as on March 31, previous year and current year, and a statement of income and reconciliation of earnings for the current year of Electronics Ltd (EL). The only item in the plant and machinery account sold during the year was a specialised machine that originally cost ₹15,00,000. The accumulated depreciation on this machine at the time of sale was ₹8,00,000. The machine was sold for ₹6,00,000 and full payment was received in cash. Electronics Ltd. purchased patents for ₹16,00,000 during the year. Besides cash purchases of plant and equipment, the assets of another company were also purchased for ₹1,00,00,000 payable in fully paid-up shares, issued at par; the assets purchased being goodwill, ₹30,00,000 and plant, ₹70,00,000.

Comparative Balance Sheets

Particulars	*March 31 Previous Year (₹ lakh)*	*March 31 Current Year (₹ lakh)*
Cash	74	37
Sundry debtors	54	47
Inventories	312	277
Prepaid expenses	6	4
Land	60	60
Patents	55	65
Plant and machinery	420	550
Less: Accumulated depreciation	(105)	(120)
Goodwill	–	30
Total Assets	876	950
Sundry creditors	86	102
Provision for income tax	89	17
Debentures	220	60
Equity capital	250	560
Retained earnings	231	211
Total Liabilities	876	950

Statement of Income and Reconciliation of Earnings for Current Year

Particulars		*Amount (₹ lakh)*
Net sales		1,977
Less: Cost of goods sold		1,480
Gross profit		497
Less: Operating expenses (includes depreciation on plant and machinery and amortisation of patents)		486
Less: Interest on debentures		14
Net loss from operations		(3)
Add: Retained earnings (previous year)		231
		228
Less: Dividend paid	16	
Less: Loss on sale of assets	1	17
Retained earnings (March 31, current year)		211

From the foregoing information, prepare a statement of cash-flows for Electronics Ltd.

Solution

Statement of Cash Flows of Electronics Limited the current year

Particulars		*Amount (in ₹ lakh)*
(A) Sources of cash inflows		
Business operations		
Cash from customers/debtors (1)*	₹1,984	
Less payment to creditors (2)*	(1,429)	
Less operating expenses (5)*	(455)	
Less interest on debentures	14	
Less taxes paid (₹89-₹17)	72	
Sale of machine		14
Issue of equity share capital (8)*		6
		210
		230

(*Contd.*)

(*Contd.*)

(B) Cash outflows	
Purchase of long-term assets	
Plant and machinery (6)*	75
Patents	16
Redemption of debentures (7)*	160
Dividends paid to equity shareholders	16
	267
(C) Net decrease in cash (B-A)	37
Cash at beginning of year	37
Cash at year-end	74

Note: Figures in brackets refer to working note number.

Working Notes

(A) Determination of cash from business operation requires recasting of income statement from accrual basis to cash basis. Exclusion of non-cash items, namely, depreciation and amortisation is obvious. The less obvious is the computation of cash inflows from debtors/customers and cash payments to creditors for goods purchased and expenses. The following working notes provide these required inputs.

(1) Cash Receipts from Debtors:

Sundry Debtors Account

(Amount in ₹ lakh)

Particulars	*Amount*	*Particulars*	*Amount*
To Balance b/f (opening balance)	54	By Cash (receipts from debtors, balancing figure)	1,984
To Net sales (assumed credit sales)	1,977	By Balance c/d	47
	2,031		2,031

Alternatively

(in ₹ lakh)

Net sales	1,977
Add debtors due at the beginning of current year	54
Total amount receivable from debtors	2,031
Less debtors due at the end of current year	(47)
Cash receipts from debtors during current year	1,984

(2) Cash Payment to Creditors

Sundry Creditors Account

(Amount in ₹ lakh)

Particulars	*Amount*	*Particulars*	*Amount*
To Cash (payments to creditors, balancing figure)	1,429	By Balance b/f (opening balance)	86
To Balance c/d	102	By purchases* (assumed credit)	1,445
	1,531		1,531

*Cost of goods sold = Opening stock + Purchases – Closing stock
= ₹1,480 = ₹312 + Purchases – ₹277
= ₹1,480 – ₹312 + ₹277 = ₹1,445 (Purchases)

Alternatively

(in ₹ lakh)

Credit purchases	1,445
Add sundry creditors at the beginning of year	86
Total amount due/payable to creditors	1,531
Less sundry creditors at the year-end	(102)
Cash payment to creditors during the year	1,429

(3) Determination of Depreciation Charges

(a) T-Account Approach

Accumulated Depreciation Account

(Amount in ₹ lakh)

Particulars	*Amount*	*Particulars*	*Amount*
To Machine (accumulated depreciation written off on machine sold)	8	By Balance b/f	105
To Balance c/d	120	By P&L A/c (depreciation amount charged during the year, balancing figure)	23
	128		128

(b) Statement Approach

(Amount in ₹ lakh)

Opening balance at the beginning of year	105
Less depreciation written off on plant sold during current year	(8)
	97
Closing balance	120
Difference represents current year depreciation	23

(4) Determination of Amortisation Charges

Patent Account

(Amount in ₹ lakh)

Particulars	*Amount*	*Particulars*	*Amount*
To Balance b/f	55	By Amortisation (balancing figures)	6
To Cash (purchases)	16	By Balance c/d	65
	71		71

(5) Determination Cash Operating Expenses

(Amount in ₹ lakh)

Total operating expenses	486
Less depreciation (as it does not cause current cash outflow)	(23)
Less amortisation (non-cash expense)	(6)
Operating expenses (other than depreciation and amortisation)	457
Less prepaid expenses (already paid in previous year)	(6)
Add expenses paid in advance in current year	4
Operating expenses paid in cash	455

(B) Likewise, changes in *long term assets*, in particular, plant and machinery require a more careful analysis to ascertain cash obtained from their sales and cash used in their acquisition because the straight difference of the two years values do not indicate either purchase or sale. Such assets are subject to depreciation. Therefore, depreciation amount should be adjusted to ascertain the amount of such assets purchased/sold.

(6) Purchase of Plant and Machinery

(a) T-Account Approach

Plant and Machinery Account (Gross Basis)

(Amount in ₹ lakh)

Particulars	*Amount*	*Particulars*	*Amount*
To Balance b/f	420	By Cash (sale value)	6
To Equity share capital	70	By Loss (P&L A/c)	1
To Cash (purchases, balancing figure)	75	By Accumulated depreciation (on plant sold)	8
		By Balance c/d	550
	565		565

(b) Statement Approach

(Amount in ₹ lakh)

Opening balance of plant and machinery	420
Less original purchase price of plant sold (₹6 + 1 + 8)	15
	405
Closing balance	550
Difference represents purchases	145
Less purchases against issue of share capital	70
Cash purchases of plant	75

(c) Equation Approach

Opening balance of plant and machinery (PM) + Purchases of PM during the year – *Initial* acquisition cost of PM sold during the year = Closing balance of PM (5.1)

₹420 + Purchases – ₹15 = ₹550

Purchases = ₹550 – ₹420 + ₹15 = ₹145

Cash purchases = Total purchases ₹145 – Purchases through issue of equity share capital ₹75 = ₹70

OR

(a) T-Account Approach

Plant and Machinery (Net Basis) *(Amount in ₹ lakh)*

Particulars	*Amount*	*Particulars*	*Amount*
To Balance b/f (₹420 – ₹105)	315	By Depreciation(charged during current year)	23
To Equtiy share capital	70	By Cash	6
To Cash (purchases, balancing figure	75	By P&L A/c (loss on sale of machine)	1
		By Balance c/d (₹550 – ₹120)	430
	460		460

(b) Statement Approach *(Amount in ₹ lakh)*

Opening balance of plant and machinery	₹315
Less book value of plant sold	7
Less depreciation charged during the year	23
	285

(Contd.)

(*Contd.*)

Closing balance	430
Difference represents purchases	145
Less purchases against issue of share capital	70
Cash purchase of plant	75

(c) Equation Approach

Opening balance of PM + Purchases of PM during the year – Book value of PM sold during the year – Depreciation charges during the year = Closing balance of PM (5.2)

₹315 + Purchases – ₹7 – ₹23 = ₹430

Purchases = ₹430 – ₹315 + ₹7 + ₹23 = ₹145

Cash purchases = Total purchases ₹145 = Purchases through issue of equity share capital ₹75 = ₹70

(C) Treatment of changes in long-term liabilities are the easiest to deal. They relate to (i) fresh issue of shares and debentures or their redemption and (ii) additional long-term borrowings or their repayment. The increase is indicative of additional issue of securities or additional borrowings and, hence, is a source of cash.

The decrease represents repayment and, therefore, is use of cash, that is, cash outflow. However, if the increase in securities, say, in equity capital is caused due to issue of bonus shares, it is not a source of cash. Likewise, if increase in shares is an outcome of **(i)** payment for purchase of plant and machinery, land and building or any other asset and **(ii)** conversion of debentures into shares, such transactions do not affect cash inflow and are excluded.

(7) Redemption of Debentures *(Amount in ₹ lakh)*

Opening balance (at the year beginning)	220
Closing balance (at year-end)	60
Decrease in balance represents redemption of debentures	160

(8) Issue of Equity Share Capital for Cash *(Amount in ₹ lakh)*

Closing balance at current year-end	560
Less opening balance	250
Increase in balance represents additional issue	310
Less payment for goodwill (₹30) and for plant (₹70) by equity capital	100
Difference indicates additional cash raised through equity capital	210

It is emphasised that the amount of cash from business operations (in preparation of the CFS of Electronics Limited) has been determined using 'T' accounts extensively. Alternatively, cash from business operation can be computed by another approach. This approach uses less of 'T' account and involves two steps: **(i)** to determine working capital from business operations by excluding depreciation, amortisation, loss/gain on sale of long-term assets, non-operating incomes and **(ii)** to adjust the working capital from business operations by changes in current liabilities and current assets (except cash).

The rules for relating the changes in current assets and current liabilities to the profit and loss account in the computation of a flow of cash from operations are summarised below.

1. **All the increases in current assets excluding cash and decreases in current liabilities which increase working capital decrease cash**. The decrease in current liabilities takes place when they are paid in cash. For instance, decrease in creditors, bank overdrafts, bills payable and dividends payable will occur due to their payment. A word of explanation is necessary to show the negative impact of increase in current assets on cash. For instance, an

increase in sundry debtors takes place when credit sales are greater than cash collections from them; inventories increase when the cost of goods purchased is more than the cost of goods sold. Increase in prepaid expenses involves payment of more cash than is required for their current services. Evidently, increase in current assets decreases cash.

2. **From the first follows the second rule—all decreases in current assets other than cash and increases in current liabilities which cause a decrease in working capital increase cash.** Debtors would decrease when cash collections are more than current credit sales. Inventories would decrease because cost of goods sold is more than cost of goods purchased; decrease in prepaid expenses reflects that the firm has paid less for services than are currently used. Exhibits 5.2 and 5.3 show the procedure for determining cash from business operations.

EXHIBIT 5.2 Cash from Business Operations (Direct Method)

(A) Sales revenues
(B) *Less:* Expenses using working capital
Cost of raw materials used (or cost of goods sold)
Wages and salary expenses
Others manufacturing expenses (excluding depreciation)
Office expenses
Selling and distribution expenses
Interest
Income tax
(C) Working capital from business operations
(D) Adjustment to convert to cash basis
(i) *Add*: Decrease in WC (–CA or +CL)
Decrease in current assets other than cash (item-wise)
Increase in current liabilities (item-wise)
(ii) *Less*: Increase in WC (+CA or –CL)
Increase in current assets other than cash (item-wise)
Decrease in current liabilities (item-wise)
(E) Cash flow from business operations

EXHIBIT 5.3 Cash from Business Operation (Indirect Method)

(A) Net income (or loss) as shown by profit and loss account
(B) *Add:* Depreciation expenses;
Amortisation of goodwill, patents and other intangible assets;
Amortisation of discount on debentures or share issue expenses;
Amortisation of extraordinary losses occurred in previous years;
Loss on sale of non-current assets;
(C) *Less:* Amortisation of premium received on debentures;
Profit on sale of equipment (already included under sources)
Profit on revaluation of non-current assets (does not contribute to working capital)
Dividends and interest received on investments (reported separately).
(A + B – C) = Working capital from business operations.
(D) Adjustment to convert to cash basis:
(i) *Add*: Decrease in WC (–CA or +CL)
Decrease in current assets other than cash (item wise)
Increase in current liabilities (item-wise)
(ii) *Less*: Increase in WC (+CA or –CL)
Increase in current assets other than cash (item-wise)
Decrease in current liabilities (item-wise)
(E) Cash flow from business operations

Cash from business operations has been computed in Exhibits 5.4 and 5.5 for Electronics Limited using Exhibits 5.2 and 5.3 respectively.

EXHIBIT 5.4 Cash from Business Operation [Based on Exhibit 5.2] *(Amount in ₹ lakh)*

Net sales		1,977
Less cost of goods sold	1,480	
Less operating expenses (other than depreciation and amortisation)	457	
Less interest on debentures	14	1,951
Working capital from business operations		26
Add (Decrease in WC i.e. - CA or + CL):		
Debtors	7	
Inventories	35	
Prepaid expenses	2	
Creditors	16	60
Less (increase in WC i.e. - CA or – CL)		
Provision for income-taxes		(72)
Cash from business operation		14

EXHIBIT 5.5 Cash from Business Operations [Based on Exhibit 5.3]

Net loss as per income statement		(3)
Add depreciation on plant and machinery		23
Add amortisation on patents		6
Working capital from business operations		26
Add (Decrease in WC i.e. – CA or + CL)		
Debtors	7	
Inventories	35	
Prepaid expenses	2	
Creditors	16	60
Less (increase in WC i.e. – CA or – CL)		
Provision for income-taxes		(72)
Cash from business operations		14

***Example* 5.2**

From the following information furnished to you relating to plant and equipment account of Hypothetical Ltd., determine cash obtained from sale of old plant and equipment.

Particulars	*Previous year (₹ thousand)*	*Current year (₹ thousand)*
Plant and equipment (gross)	100	125
Accumulated depreciation	20	30
Additional information:		
(i) Loss on sale of plant and equipment		1
(ii) Depreciation charged during the year on plant and equipment		14
(iii) Purchase of new plant during the year		35

Solution

Equations 5.1 and 5.3 can be used to determine the required information to ascertain the sale proceeds from old plant and equipment (*PE*).

(i) Opening balance of *PE* (+) Purchases of *PE* during the year (–) Initial acquisition cost of *PE* sold during the year = Closing balance of *PE* (5.1)

= ₹1,00,000 + ₹35,000 – x = ₹1,25,000

= x = ₹1,35,000 – ₹1,25,000 = ₹10,000 (Purchase price of *PE* sold)

(ii) Opening balance of accumulated depreciation, *AD* + Depreciation charged during the year – *AD* written off on the *PE* sold during the year = Closing balance of *AD* (5.3)

= ₹20,000 + ₹14,000 – x = ₹30,000

= x = ₹34,000 – ₹30,000 = ₹4,000 (*AD* on *PE* sold)

The following information relating to the plant and equipment that has been sold is, thus, available:

Gross book value (purchase cost)	₹10,000
Accumulated depreciation	4,000
Net book value (₹10,000 – ₹4,000)	6,000
Therefore, sale proceeds of plant (₹6,000 – ₹1,000 loss)	5,000

The preceding information can also be obtained by preparing ledger accounts.

Plant and Equipment Account

Particulars	*Amount (₹ thousand)*	*Particulars*	*Amount (₹ thousand)*
Opening balance	100	Acquisition cost of sold plant (balancing figure)	10
Cash purchase of new plant	35	Closing balance	125
	135		135

Accumulated Depreciation Account

Total depreciation on sold plant (balancing figure)	4	Opening balance	20
Closing balance	30	Depreciation expenses charged during the year	14
	34		34

LO 5.5 AS-7: STATEMENT OF CASH FLOWS

The preparation and presentation of cash flow statement was prescribed by Accounting Standard-3 (AS3) issued by the Institute of Chartered Accountants of India (ICAI). As a part of the process of convergence of Indian Accounting Standards with International Financial Reporting Standards (IFRS), ICAI has issued a new accounting standard Ind AS-7 that deals with the statement of cash flows.

All listed and unlisted companies having net worth above ₹500 crore are to follow the new accounting standard from April 1, 2016. The deadline is also applicable for other entities having net worth of ₹500 crore or more. It would also apply to holding, subsidiary, joint venture or associate companies of these two classes of entities.

From April 1, 2017, Ind AS-7 has become mandatory for (i) Companies—whose equity and/or debt securities are listed or are in the process of being listed within India or outside — having a net worth of less than ₹500 crore. (ii) Other companies, that are unlisted having a net worth of ₹250 crore or more but less than ₹500 crore. Holding, subsidiary, joint venture or associate companies of these entities would have to comply with this deadline.

Companies whose securities are listed or in the process of listing on SME exchanges would not be required to apply Ind AS. Such companies would continue to comply with the existing accounting standard unless they choose otherwise.

We explain and illustrate below the CFS mandated by the Ind AS-7. **Annexure-5.I illustrates the CFS of the Reliance Industries Limited.**

Objectives

Information about the cash flows of an enterprise is useful in providing users of financial statements with a basis to assess the ability of the enterprise to generate cash and cash-equivalents and the needs of the enterprise to utilise those cash flows. The economic decisions that are taken by users require an evaluation of the ability of an enterprise to generate cash and cash-equivalents and the timing and certainty of their generation.

The CFS deals with the provision of information about the historical changes in cash and cash-equivalents of an enterprise by means of a cash flow statement which classifies cash flows during the period among **(i)** operating, **(ii)** investing and **(iii)** financing activities.

Statement of Cash flows provides a summary of operating, investment and financing cashflows and reconciles them with changes in its cash and cash-equivalents (marketable securities) during the period.

Benefits of Cash Flow Operation

A cash flow statement, when used in conjunction with the other financial statements, provides information that enables users to evaluate the changes in net assets of an enterprise, its financial structure (including its liquidity and solvency), and its ability to affect the amounts and timing of cash flows in order to adapt to changing circumstances and opportunities. Cash flow information is useful in assessing the ability of the enterprise to generate cash and cash-equivalents and enables users to develop models to assess and compare the present value of the future cash flows of different enterprises. It also enhances the comparability of the reporting of operating performance by different enterprises because it eliminates the effects of using different accounting treatments for the same transactions and events.

Definitions Associated with Cash Flow

Cash It consists of cash in hand and demand deposits with banks.

Cash Equivalents These are short-term highly liquid investments that are readily convertible into known amounts of changes in value. They have short maturity, say, of three months or less from the date of acquisition, for example, treasury bills.

Cash management includes the investment of excess cash in cash equivalents. Bank overdrafts (which are repayable on demand) are to be included as a component of cash and cash equivalents; the reason is that the bank balance often fluctuates from being positive to overdrawn.

Operating cashflows are directly related to production and sale of the firm's products/ services.

Cash Flows These are inflows and outflows of cash and cash-equivalents.

Operating Activities Cash inflows from operating activities primarily accrue from the major revenue producing activities (i.e., sale of goods and rendering of services) of the enterprise. Therefore, they generally result from the transactions and other events that enter into the determination of net profit or loss. Examples of cash flows from operating activities are as follows:

- Cash receipts from the sale of goods and the rendering of services
- Cash receipts from royalties, fees, commissions, and other revenues
- Cash payments to suppliers for goods and services
- Cash payments to and on behalf of employees
- Cash receipts and cash payments of an insurance enterprise for premiums and claims, annuities and other policy benefits
- Cash payments or refunds of income taxes unless they can be specifically identified with financing and investing activities
- Cash receipts and payments from contracts held for dealing or trading purposes.

Since the focus is on determining cash flows due to business/operating activities, non-operating expenses as well as non-operating incomes are excluded. In other words, both interest/dividend receipts and interest/dividend payments are excluded.

Investing Activities The investing activities relate to the acquisition and disposal of long-term assets and other investments not included in cash-equivalents. Their separate disclosure is important as they represent the extent to which expenditures have been made for resources intended to generate future income and cash flows. The principal items covered under this category of activities are as follows:

> **Investment flows** are cashflows associated with purchase/sale of both fixed assets and business interests.

- Cash payments to acquire property, plant and equipment, intangible and other long-term assets: fixed assets (including intangibles). These payments include those relating to capitalised research and development costs and self-constructed property, plant and equipment.
- Cash receipts from disposal of property, plant and equipment, intangible and other long-term assets.
- Cash payments to acquire shares, warrants or debt instruments of other enterprises and interests in joint ventures
- Cash receipts from disposal of shares, warrants, or debt instruments of other enterprises and interests in joint ventures
- Cash advances and loans made to third parties
- Cash receipts from the repayment of advances and loans made to third parties
- Cash payments for futures contracts, forward contracts, option contracts and swap contracts.
- Cash recently from futures contracts forward contracts, option contracts and swap contracts.

Financing Activities The financing activities report the changes in the size and composition of the share/owner's capital and debt of the enterprise. Their separate disclosure is useful in predicting claims on future cash flows by providers of funds (both capital and borrowings) to the enterprise. Examples of cash flows arising from financing activities are as follows:

> **Financing flows** are cash flows that result from debt/ equity financing transactions and include incurrence and repayment of debt cashflows from the sale of shares and cash outflows to purchase shares or pay dividend.

- Cash proceeds from issue of shares or other equity instruments
- Cash proceeds from issue of debentures, loans, notes, bonds, mortgages and other short-term or long-term borrowings
- Cash repayments of amounts borrowed
- Dividend/interest paid
- Cash payments to owners to acquire or redeem the entity's shares i.e., buy back of shares and redemption of preference shares.
- Cash payments by a lessee for the reduction of the outstanding liability relating to a finance lease.

Reporting Cash Flows

From Operating Activities An enterprise is required to report cash flows from operating activities using either direct method or indirect method.

Direct Method Under this method, gross cash receipts and gross cash payments for the major items are disclosed, such as cash receipts from customers and cash paid to suppliers.

Indirect Method Under the indirect method, profit and loss account is adjusted for **(i)** the effects of transactions of non-cash nature such as depreciation, amortisation, deferred taxes, loss on sale of fixed assets and unrealised foreign exchange gains and losses, **(ii)** changes during the period in inventories and operating receivables and payables, and **(iii)** for all other items for which the cash effects are shown either in financing or investing activities.

From Investing and Financing Activities An enterprise is required to report separately major classes of gross cash receipts and gross cash payments arising from investing and financing activities. The cash flows from operating, financing and investing activities are to be reported on a *net* basis.

Treatment of Some Major Items

While most of the items (to be included in the CFS) are self-explanatory in nature, some transactions/ items merit more explanation. These relate to **(i)** foreign currency, **(ii)** interest, **(iii)** dividends, **(iv)** taxes on income, **(v)** deferred taxes, **(vi)** investments in subsidiaries, associates and joint ventures, **(vii)** Changes in ownership interests in subsidiaries and other business units, **(viii)** non-cash transactions and **(ix)** other disclosures.

Foreign Currency Cash Flows Cash flows arising from transactions in a foreign currency should be recorded in an enterprise's functional currency by applying to the foreign currency amount the exchange rate between the functional currency and the foreign currency at the date of the cash flow. A rate that approximates the actual rate may be used if the result is substantially the same as would arise if the rates at the dates of the cash flows were used.

The effect of changes in exchange rates on cash and cash-equivalents held in a foreign currency are to be reported as a separate part of the reconciliation of the changes in cash and cash-equivalents during the period.

Evidently, unrealised gains and losses arising from changes in foreign exchange rates are not cash flows.

Interest In general, cash flows arising from interest paid should be classified as cash flows from financing activities, say interest on loans/debts; interest paid on working capital loan and any other loan taken to finance operating activities are to be shown as a part of operating activities. Unless stated otherwise, interest paid is to be reported with financing activities. The reason is that they are cost of obtaining financial resources.

Interest received from short-term investments (classified as cash equivalents) are to be reckoned as cash inflows from operating activities.

Cash flows arising from interest paid and interest received in the case of a financial enterprises should be classified as cash flows from operating activities. The reason that is borrowing and lending are the normal business activities for such enterprises.

Dividends While dividends paid are classified as financing activities as they are cost of obtaining financial resources, dividends received on investments constitute a part of investment activities. The reason is that they are the returns on investments.

For the financial enterprises, dividends received form a part of operating activities and dividends paid as a part of financing activities.

Taxes on Income Taxes paid on income as well as tax refunds are usually classified as cash flows from operating activities. In the event of their specific identification with investment or financing activities, the tax cash flow is classified as an investing or financing activity as appropriate.

Deferred Taxes There can be differences in the amount of taxes payable, determined on the basis of financial accounting *vis-à-vis* tax accounting. One such item which can cause this distortion relates to the treatment of depreciation. For instance, for income-tax reporting, the machine may be subject to higher rate of depreciation compared to financial accounting. This lowers the taxes payable in the early years of machine purchased and increases the taxes payable in the latter years. **Deferred taxes are to be treated just like other expenses on accrual basis.** Deferring tax liabilities to the future years is referred to as deferred taxes. As a result, increase in deferred tax liabilities are considered as cash inflows and decrease as cash outflows.

Investments in Subsidiaries, Associates and Joint Ventures Enterprises having investments in subsidiaries, associates and joint ventures are required to report in the CFS the cash flows between themselves and the investee/joint venture, for example, cash flows relating to dividends and advances.

Changes in Ownership Interests in Subsidiaries and Other Business Units The aggregate cash flows arising from obtaining or losing control of subsidiaries or other business units should be presented separately and classified as investing activities.

An enterprise should disclose, in aggregate, in respect of both obtaining and losing control of subsidiaries or other business units during the period, each of the following: **(i)** the total purchase or disposal consideration paid or received; and **(ii)** the portion of the purchase consideration discharged by means of cash and cash-equivalents.

Non-Cash Transactions Investing and financing transactions that do not require the use of cash or cash-equivalents should be excluded from a cash flow statement. Such transactions should be disclosed elsewhere in the financial statements in a way that provides all the relevant information about these investing and financing activities. Examples of non-cash transactions are: **(i)** the acquisition of assets/an enterprise by means of issue of shares and/or debentures, **(ii)** conversion of debt into equity and **(iii)** issue of bonus shares.

Other Disclosures An enterprise should disclose, together with a commentary by management, the amount of significant cash and cash-equivalent balances held by the enterprise that are not available for use by it. Examples include cash and cash-equivalent balances held by a branch of the enterprise that operates in a country where exchange controls or other legal restrictions apply as a result of which the balances are not available for use by the enterprise.

Exhibits 5.6 to 5.8 show the procedure of the preparation of the cash flow statement as per AS-3 (revised).

EXHIBIT 5.6 Direct Method Statement of Cash Flows

Cashflow From Operating Activities
- Cash receipts from customers
- Cash paid to suppliers and employees
- Cash generated from operations
- Income tax

Net cash from operating activities

Cashflow From Investing Activities
- Purchase of fixed assets
- Proceeds from sale of equipments
- Interest received
- Dividends received

Net cash from investing activities

Cashflow From Financing Activities
- Proceeds from issuance of share capital
- Proceeds from long-term borrowings
- Repayments of long-term borrowings
- Interest paid
- Dividends paid

Net cash used in financing activities

Net Increase in Cash and Cash-equivalents*
- Cash and cash-equivalents at the beginning of a period
- Cash and cash-equivalents at the end of a period

*Consists of cash on hand and balance with banks, investment in money market (short-term) investments and effect of exchange rate changes.

EXHIBIT 5.7 Indirect Method Statement of Cash Flows

Cashflow From Operating Activities
- Net profit before taxation, and extraordinary items
- Adjustment for
  - Depreciation
  - Foreign exchange loss
  - Interest income
  - Dividend income
  - Interest expense
- Operating profit before working capital changes
- Decrease/(increase) in sundry debtors
- Decrease/(increase) in inventories
- Increase/(decrease) in sundry creditors
- Cash generated from operations
- Income tax paid

Net cash from operating activities

Cashflow From Investing Activities
- Purchase of fixed assets
- Proceeds from sale of equipment
- Interest received
- Dividends received

Net cash from investing activities

Cashflow From Financing Activities
- Proceeds from issuance of share capital
- Proceeds from long-term borrowings
- Repayment of long-term borrowings
- Interest paid
- Dividends paid

Net cash used in financing activities

Net Increases in Cash and Cash-equivalents
- Cash and cash-equivalents at the beginning of a period
- Cash and cash-equivalents at the end of a period

EXHIBIT 5.8 Statement of Cash Flows of a Financial Enterprise

Cashflows From Operating Activities
- Interest and commission receipts
- Interest payment
- Recoveries on loans previously written off
- Cash payments to employees and suppliers
- Operating profit before changes in operating assets
- Decrease (or increase) in operating assets:
  - Short-term funds
  - Deposit held for regulatory or monetary control purposes
  - Funds advanced to customers
  - Net increase in credit card receivables
  - Other short-term securities

Decrease (or increase) in operating liabilities
- Deposits from customers
- Certificates of deposit
- Net cash from operating activities before income tax
- Income taxes paid

(Contd.)

(*Contd.*)

Net cash from operating activities
Cashflows From Investing Activities
Dividends received
Interest received
Proceeds from sale of permanent investments
Purchase of permanent investments
Purchase of fixed assets
Net cash from investing activities
Cashflows From Financing Activities
Issue of shares
Repayment of long-term borrowings
Net decrease in other borrowings
Dividends paid
Net cash used in financing activities

For the Electronics Ltd. in Example 5.1, the cash flow statement as per AS-3 is shown in Exhibits 5.9 and 5.10.

EXHIBIT 5.9 Statement of Cash Flows of Electronics Limited for the Current Year (Direct Method)

(Amount in ₹ lakh)

Particulars		*Amount*
Cash Flows From Operating Activities		
Cash receipts from customers	1,984[1]	
Cash paid to suppliers and employees	1,884[2]	
Cash generated from operations	100	
Income taxes paid	(72)	
Net cash from operating activities		28*
Cash Flows From Investing Activities		
Purchase of plant and machinery	(75)	
Purchase of patents	(16)	
Proceeds from sale of plant	6	
Net cash used in investing activities		(85)
Cash Flows From Financing Activities		
Proceeds from issuance of equity share capital	210	
Repayment of debentures (₹220 – 60)	(160)	
Interest paid to debenture-holders	(14)	
Dividends paid	(16)	20
Net decrease in cash balance (₹85 – 48)		(37)
Less		
Cash and cash equivalents at beginning of the year		74
Cash and cash equivalents at end of the year		37

* It may be recalled that cash from operating activities (shown in Section II) was ₹14; the difference of ₹14 (₹28 as per AS3 and ₹14 as per CFS) is due to exclusion of interest payment on debentures (₹14); this interest payment is shown under financing activities.

Working Notes

(Amount in ₹ lakh)

(1) Cash receipts from debtors and customers:	
Debtors at the beginning of the year	54

(*Contd.*)

(*Contd.*)

Add: Net sales during the year	1,977
Total sum receivable	2,031
Less: Debtors at the end of the year	47
Total	1,984
(2) Cash paid to suppliers and employees:	
Cost of goods sold	1,480
Add: Operating expenses excluding depreciation and amortisation (₹486 – 23 – 6)	457
Add: Current year prepaid expenses	4
Less Previous year prepaid expenses	(6)
	455
Add: Creditors at the beginning of the year	86
Add: Inventories at the end of the year	277
Less: Creditors at the end of the year	(102)
Less: Inventories at the beginning of the year	(312)
Total	1,884

EXHIBIT 5.10 Statement of Cash Flows of Electronics Limited for the Current Year (Indirect Method)

(Amount in ₹ lakh)

Particulars		*Amount*
Cash flows From Operating Activities		
Net loss before taxation and extra-ordinary items	(4)	
Adjustments for:		
Depreciation	23	
Amortisation of patent	6	
Interest expenses	14	
Loss on sale of assets	1	
Operating profit before working capital changes	40	
Add: Decrease in debtors	7	
Add: Decrease in inventories	35	
Add: Prepaid expenses	2	
Add: Increase in creditors	16	
Cash generated from operations	100	
Less: Income-tax paid	72	
Net cash from operating activities		28
Cash flows From Investing Activities		
Purchase of plant and machinery	(75)	
Purchase of patents	(16)	
Proceeds from sale of plant	6	
Net cash used in investing activities		(85)
Cash flows From Financing Activities		
Proceeds from issuance of equity share capital	210	
Repayment of debentures (220 – 60)	(160)	
Interest paid to debentureholders	(14)	
Dividends paid	(16)	20
Net decrease in cash balance (78 – 41)		(37)
Cash and cash equivalents at beginning of the year		74
Cash and cash equivalents at end of the year		37

The statement highlights that the firm does not have enough funds from its operating activities (₹28 lakh) and financing activities (₹20 lakh) to cater to investment requirement of ₹85 lakh, causing decline in cash (₹37 lakh).

ANNEXURE 5.1

Cash Flow Statement of Reliance Industries Limited for the Year 2015–16

(₹ in crore)

Particulars		*2015-16*		*2014-15*
A: CASH FLOW FROM OPERATING ACTIVITES				
Net Profit Before Tax as per Profit and Loss Statement		35,701		29,468
Adjusted for:				
Write off of Investment [₹ Nil (Previous Year ₹26,96,800)]	—		—	
Loss on Sale/Discard of Assets (Net)	20		31	
Depreciation/Amortisation and Depletion Expenses	9,566		8,488	
Effect of Exchange Rate Change	(2,911)		1,408	
Net Gain on Sale of Investments	(2,781)		(3,046)	
Dividend Income	(691)		(250)	
Interest Income	(3,936)		(5,414)	
Finance costs	2,454		2,367	
		1,721		3,584
Operating Profit before Working Capital Changes		**37,422**		**33,052**
Adjusted for:				
Trade and Other Receivables	146		5,462	
Inventories	8,517		6,381	
Trade and Other Payables	6,126		(3,528)	
		14,789		8,315
Cash Generated from Operations		**52,211**		**41,367**
Taxes Paid (Net)		(8,129)		(6,082)
Net Cash from Operating Activities		**44,082**		**35,285**
B: CASH FLOW FROM INVESTING ACTIVITIES				
Purchase of Fixed Assets		(21,322)		(42,720)
Sale of Fixed Assets		293		86
Purchase of Investments in Subsidiaries/ Trusts		(25,255)		(11,506)
Redemption of Investment in Subsidiaries		444		169
Purchase of other Investments		(668,990)		(655,591)
Sale/ Redemption of other Investments		6,68,877		6,43,525
Movement in Loans and Advances		(917)		(133)
Maturity of Fixed Assets		—		3,400
Interest Income		3,850		6,584
Dividend Income from Subsidiary and Associates		47		5
Dividend Income from Others		644		183
Net Cash (Used in) Investing Activities		**(42,329)**		**(55,998)**
C: CASH FLOW FROM FINANCING ACTIVITIES				
Proceeds from Issue of Share Capital		283		226
Share Application Money		8		17
Proceeds from Long Term Borrowings		7,552		20,310
Repayment of Long Term Borrowings		(4,591)		(4,555)
Short Term Borrowings (net)		1,843		(10,302)
Dividends Paid (Including Dividend Distribution Tax)		(7,259)		(3,268)
Interest Paid		(4,268)		(3,368)
Net Cash (used in)/From Financing Activities		**(6,432)**		**(940)**
Net (Decrease) in Cash and Cash Equivalents		(4,679)		(21,653)
Opening Balance of Cash and Cash Equivalents		11,571		33,224
Closing Balance of Cash and Cash Equivalents		**6,892**		**11,571**

SUMMARY

LO 5.1	Cash flow statement indicates sources of cash inflows and transactions of cash outflows of a firm during a period. It is also called "Where-Got Where-Gone" statement. The statement provides answers to many important questions related to financial position of an enterprise.
LO 5.2	The major sources of cash inflows are cash from: **(i)** business operations, **(ii)** non-business operations (like interest, dividend etc), **(iii)** sale proceeds of long-term assets, **(iv)** raising additional share capital and **(v)** long-term borrowings. The principal uses of cash are: **(i)** purchase of long-term assets, **(ii)** redemption of preference shares/debentures, **(iii)** repayment of long-term borrowings and **(iv)** payment of dividends.
LO 5.3	Cash flow statement (CFS) is an important tool of financial analysis. It clearly highlights the firm's operating, financing and investment activities. It enables the management to assess whether the firm has adequate long-term funds to finance major fixed assets expansion.
LO 5.4	Preparation of cash flow statement is mandatory for all the listed companies as well as for all enterprises which have net worth of ₹500 crore or more.
	The CFS shows the sources and uses of cash and cash equivalents in terms of three components: **(i)** operating, **(ii)** financing and **(iii)** investing activities. The cash flows from each of these categories are to be reported on net basis.
	Cash flows from operating activities result from the major revenue producing activities of a firm. Accordingly, the income statement constitutes the main source of data. The major operating items are **(i)** cash receipts from customers, **(ii)** cash paid to suppliers and employees and **(iii)** income-tax.
	The items included in financing activities are: **(i)** proceeds from issue of share capital, **(ii)** proceeds from long-term borrowings, **(iii)** redemption of preference shares/debentures, **(iv)** repayment of long-term borrowings and **(v)** payment of interest and dividend to debenture-holders/lenders and shareholders respectively.
	Cash flows representing investment activities relate to capital expenditures incurred with intent to generate future earnings as cash flows and includes: **(i)** purchase of new fixed assets, **(ii)** proceeds from sale of existing fixed assets and **(iii)** interest and dividend received on investments made.

REFERENCES

1. Anthony, R. N. et al., *Accounting: Text and Cases,* (Tata McGraw-Hill, New Delhi), 2003, p.339.
2. *Ibid.*, p. 339.

SOLVED PROBLEMS

P.5.1 Answer the following: **LO 5.4** LOD E

(a) A company sold building for cash at ₹100 lakh. The profit and loss account has shown ₹40 lakh profit on sale of building. How will you report it in cash flow statement (based on Ind AS-7)?

(b) From the following information, determine cash received from debtors during current year:

Debtors in the beginning of current year	₹100 lakh
Total sales	2,000
Cash sales	500
Debtors at the end of current year	300

(c) Determine cash paid to suppliers/creditors from the following data during current year:

Cost of goods sold	₹480 lakh
Opening stock	30
Closing stock	50
Creditors at the beginning of year	60
Creditors at the end of the year	90
Cash purchases	40

(d) From the following **(i)** determine the gross amount of plant and machinery purchased and **(ii)** depreciation charged during the current year.

- Plant assets (net of depreciation) at year-end ₹285 lakh and at the year-beginning ₹127 lakh.
- Gross plant assets increased by ₹186 lakh even through machine costing initially ₹58 lakh with book value of ₹38 lakh was sold at loss of ₹25 lakh.

(e) Account balances relating to equipment during 2015–16 are as follows:

Particulars	*April 1, 2015*	*March 31, 2016*
Equipment	₹2,00,000	₹4,00,000
Less: Accumulated depreciation	50,000	70,000

Equipment with an original cost of ₹40,000, having an accumulated depreciation of ₹20,000, were sold at a gain of ₹5,000. Determine: **(i)** Cash provided by the sale of equipment; **(ii)** Cash used to acquire equipment; **(iii)** Depreciation expense on equipment during 2015–16.

(f) Would your answer for **(e) (i), (ii) and (iii)** be different if the equipment were sold at a loss of ₹5,000?

Solution

(a) Cashflows from Investing Activities:
Proceeds from sale of building ₹100 lakh.

(b) Cash Receipts from Debtors:

Debtors at the beginning of current year	₹100 lakh
Plus credit sales (₹2,000 lakh – ₹500 lakh)	1,500
Total sum receivable from debtors	1,600
Less debtors at the end of current year	300
Cash received from debtors	1,300

(c) **(i)** Determination of Credit Purchases:

- Cost of goods sold = Opening stock + Purchases (x) – Closing stock
  ₹480 lakh = ₹30 lakh + x – ₹50 lakh
  x = ₹480 lakh – ₹30 lakh + ₹50 lakh = ₹500 lakh
- Credit purchases = ₹500 lakh – ₹40 lakh = ₹460 lakh

(ii) Determination of Payment to Creditors:

Creditors at the beginning of year	₹60 lakh
Plus credit purchases	460
Total sum payable	520
Less creditors at the year-end	90
Payment to creditors	430

(d) (i) Plant and Machinery Purchased:

Net increase in gross value	₹186 lakh
Add initial cost of plant sold	58
	244

(ii) Depreciation Charges:

Plant assets (net) at year beginning	₹127 lakh
Plus purchase cost of new plant	244
Less book value of plant sold	(38)
	333
Closing balance	285
Difference represents depreciation	48

(e) (i) Cash From the Sale of Equipment

Original cost of the sold equipment	₹40,000
Less: Accumulated depreciation on the sold equipment	(20,000)
Net book value	20,000
Plus: Gain on the sold equipment	5,000
Cash proceeds from sale of equipment	25,000

(ii) Cash Spent on Purchase of Equipment

Balance of equipment on April 1, 2015 (gross)	₹2,00,000
Less: Gross book value of the sold equipment	(40,000)
Balance of equipment on March 31, 2016 (without purchases)	1,60,000
Actual balance as on March 31, 2016 of equipment	4,00,000
Difference representing purchases made during 2015–16	2,40,000

(iii) Determination of Depreciation Amount Charged to the P&L A/c During 2015–16:

Balance of accumulated depreciation (1.4.2015)	₹50,000
Less: Depreciation written-off on sold equipment during 2015–16	(20,000)
Balance of accumulated depreciation without additional depreciation during 2015–16	30,000
Actual balance as on March 31, 2016 of accumulated depreciation	70,000
Difference representing depreciation amount charged during 2015–16	40,000

(f) Answers for parts **(e)(ii)** and **(e)(iii)** would remain unchanged. However, cash provided by the sale of equipment would be reduced by ₹10,000. The relevant calculations would be as follows:

Net book value	₹20,000
Less loss on sale of equipment	(5,000)
	15,000

P.5.2 Compute cash generated from operations during the year 2015-16, from the following data: **LO 5.4** LOD M

Particulars	*April 1, 2015*	*March 31, 2016*
Sundry debtors	₹30,000	₹40,000
Sundry creditors	48,000	30,000
Outstanding expenses	3,000	6,000
Outstanding income	1,000	1,000
Stock in trade	55,000	60,000
Prepaid expenses	3,000	2,000
Accumulated depreciation (no retirements during the year)	50,000	60,000
Provision for doubtful accounts	1,500	2,000
Dividends payable	—	3,000
Bills receivable	10,000	12,000
Bills payable	8,000	6,000
Net income before taxes (as per profit and loss account)	—	80,000

Solution

Determination of Cash From Operations:

Net income as per P&L A/c		₹80,000
Add Depreciation		10,000
Working capital from business operations		90,000
Less: Transactions other than cash, increasing working capital:		
(i) Increase in current assets:		
Sundry debtors	₹10,000	
Outstanding income	500	
Stock-in-trade	5,000	
Bills receivable	2,000	(17,500)
(ii) Decrease in current liabilities:		
Sundry creditors	18,000	
Bills payable	2,000	(20,000)
Add: Transactions other than cash, decreasing working capital:		
(i) Decrease in current assets:	1,000	1,000
Prepaid expenses		
(ii) Increase in current liabilities:		
Outstanding expenses	3,000	
Provision for doubtful accounts	500	
Dividends payable	3,000	6,500
Cash from operations		60,000

P.5.3 From the following summary cash account of Y Ltd., prepare statement of cash flows for the current year ended March 31 in accordance with AS-7 using the direct method. The company does not have any cash equivalents. **LO 5.5** LOD M

Summary Cash Account

for the Current Year Ended March 31

Cash inflows	*₹ ('000)*	*Cash outflows*	*₹ ('000)*
Opening balance	50	Payment to suppliers	2,000
Issue of equity shares	300	Purchase of fixed assets	200
Receipts from customers	2800	Overhead expenses	200
Sale of fixed assets	100	Wages and salaries	100
		Taxation	250
		Dividend	50
		Repayment of bank loan	300
		Closing balance	150
	3,250		3,250

Solution

Statement of Cash Flows Y Ltd.

as per AS-3 for the Current Year ended March 31

		Amount
Cash flows from operating activities:		
Cash receipts from customers	₹28,00,000	
Cash paid to suppliers	(20,00,000)	
Wages and salaries	(1,00,000)	
Overhead expenses	(2,00,000)	
Cash generated from operations	5,00,000	
Income tax paid	2,50,000	
Net cash from operating activities		₹2,50,000
Cash flows from investing activities:		
Purchase of fixed assets	(2,00,000)	
Sale of fixed assets	1,00,000	
Net cash used in investing activities		(1,00,000)
Cash flows from financing activities:		
Issue of equity shares	3,00,000	
Repayment of bank loan	(3,00,000)	
Dividend	(50,000)	
Net cash used in financing activities		(50,000)
Net increase in cash and cash-equivalent		1,00,000
Cash and cash equivalent at beginning of year		50,000
Cash and cash equivalent at the end of year		1,50,000

P.5.4 Charatlal, the president and majority shareholder, was a superb operating executive. He was an imaginative, aggressive marketing man and an ingenious, creative production man. But he had little patience with financial matters. After examining the most recent balance sheet and income statement, he muttered, "We have enjoyed ten years of steady growth, this year was our most profitable year. Despite this, we are in the worst cash position in our history. Just look those current liabilities in relation to our available cash! This whole picture of the more you make, the poorer you get, just does not make sense. These statements must be cockeyed."

LO 5.5 LOD M

The balance sheets (in lakh of rupees) of Charat Engineering Ltd. are given below:

	March 31			*March 31*	
Assets	*Current Year*	*Previous year*	*Liabilities*	*Current year*	*Previous year*
Cash	2	10	Current liabilities	105	30
Receivables (net)	60	30	Long-term debt	150	—
Inventories	100	50	Stockholder's equity	207	160
Plan assets (net of accumulated depreciation)	300	100			
Total assets	462	190	Total equities	462	190

Net income before taxes, ₹81 lakh. Taxes paid are ₹27 lakh. Net income was ₹54 lakh. Cash dividend paid were ₹7 lakh. Depreciation was ₹20 lakh. Fixed assets were purchase for ₹220 lakh, ₹150 lakh of which was financed via the issuance of long-term debt outright for cash.

Using cash flow statement (based on AS-7), write a short memorandum to Mr Charatlal, explaining why there is such squeeze for cash. Show working.

Solution

Statement of Cash Flows of Charat Engineering Ltd. (Indirect Method)

Particulars		*Amount in ₹ lakh*
Cashflow from operating activities:		
Net profit before taxation	₹81	
Adjustment for		
Depreciation	20	
Operating profit before working capital changes	101	
Increase in receivables (net)	(30)	
Increase in inventories	(50)	
Increase in current liabilities	75	
Cash generated from operations	96	
Income tax paid	27	
Net cash from operating activities		69
Cashflow from investing activities:		
Purchase of fixed assets	(220)	(220)
Net cash used for investing activities		
Cashflow from financing activities:		
Issuance of long-term debt	150	
Dividends paid	(7)	
Net cash from financing activities		143
Net decrease in cash		(8)
Cash at the beginning of current year		10
Cash at the end of the year		2

Memorandum: The squeeze for cash has resulted from major fixed assets expansion programme. The cash flow statement highlights that the company does not have enough funds from operating activities (₹69 lakh) and financing activities (₹143 lakh) to cater to investment requirements of ₹220 lakh, causing decline in cash of ₹8 lakh.

P.5.5 Prepare a statement from the following financial information of ABC company, to explain the causes of increase in cash despite the firm incurring losses. LO 5.5 LOD M

Income statement *(Amount in ₹ lakh)*

Sales		₹600.0
Dividends from investment in another company		3.6
		603.6
Expenses		
Cost of goods sold	₹400	
Depreciation	50	
Other operating expenditure	175	
Interest	1.6	
Loss on sale of plant (sale value, ₹7.2)	3.0	629.6
Net loss		(26)

Retained earnings *(Amount in ₹ lakh)*

Beginning balance	₹50
Net loss	(26)
Dividends	(16)
Ending balance	8

Position statement *(Amount in ₹ lakh)*

	Previous year	*Current year*
Cash	₹19.2	₹43.2
Sundry debtors	28.6	16.8
Inventory	33.0	22.0
Prepayments	2.2	1.8
Investments	18.0	18.0
Land	15.0	15.0
Plant and machinery	119.8	110.4
Accumulated depreciation	(75.2)	(78.4)
Total assets	160.6	148.8
Accounts payable	18.2	10.2
Accrued liabilities	1.2	2.4
Dividends payable	1.2	2.2
Debentures	12.0	16.0
Equity capital	50.0	60.0
Preference share capital	28.0	50.0
Retained earnings	50.0	8.0
Total liabilities	160.6	148.8

Solution

Cash Flow Statement of ABC Company (Indirect Method)

Particulars		*Amount (in ₹ lakh)*
Casflow from operating activities:		
Net loss before extraordinary items	(₹26)	
Adjustment for		
Depreciation	50	
Interest expenses	1.6	
Loss on sale of plant	3.0	
Dividend income	(3.6)	
Operating profit before working capital changes	25.0	
Decrease in sundry debtors	11.8	
Decrease in inventories	11.0	
Decrease in prepayments	0.4	
Decrease in accounts payable	(8.0)	
Increase in accrued liabilities	1.2	
Net cash from operating activities		41.4
Cash flow from investing activities:		
Purchase of plant and machinery	(47.6)	
Sale of plant	7.2	
Dividends received	3.6	
Net cash used in investing activities		(36.8)
Cash from financing activities:		
Proceeds from issuance of equity share capital	10	
Proceeds from issuance of preference share capital	22	
Proceeds from debentures	4	
Dividends paid to shareholders	(15)	
Interest paid on debentures	(1.6)	
Net cash from financing activities		19.4
Increase in cash		24.0
Cash at the beginning of current year		19.2
Cash at the end of current year		43.2

Working Notes:

(i) *Accumulated depreciation account*

To Plant (accumulated deprecation on plant sold) (balancing figure)	₹46.8	By Balance b/d	₹75.2
To Balance c/d	78.4	By P&L A/c (depreciation of the current year)	50.0
	125.2		125.2

(ii) *Gross value of plant sold*

Cash A/c	Dr	₹7.2	
P&L A/c (Loss)	Dr	3.0	
Accumulated depreciation A/c	Dr	46.8	
To plant			₹57.0

(iii) *Purchase of plant* — *Plant account*

To Balance b/f	₹119.8	By Cash	₹7.2
To Plant purchased (balancing figure)	47.6	By P&L A/c	3.0
		By Accumulated depreciation A/c	46.8
		By Balance c/d	110.4
	167.4		167.4

(iv) *Dividends paid* = ₹1.2 payable of previous year + ₹16 of current year – ₹2.2 dividends payable at current year-end = ₹15

P.5.6 Nandini Ltd. provides the following data: **LO 5.5** LOD M

Comparative trial balance *(Amount in ₹ lakh)*

Particulars	March 31, year 2	March 31, year 1	Increase (decrease)
Debit balance			
Cash	15	5	10
Working capital (other than cash)	₹185	₹95	₹90
Investments (long-term)	100	150	(50)
Building and equipment	500	400	100
Land	40	50	(10)
	840	700	140
Credit balance			
Accumulated depreciation	200	160	40
Bonds	100	50	50
Reserves	340	340	—
Equity shares	200	150	50
	840	700	140

Income Statement
for the period ending March 31, year 2 *(Amount in ₹ lakh)*

Sales		₹1000
Cost of goods sold		500
Selling expenses	₹50	
Administrative expenses	50	100
Operating income		400
Other charges and credits:		
Gain on sale of building and equipment	₹5	
Loss on sale of investments	(10)	
Interest	(6)	
Taxes	(189)	(200)
Net income after taxes		200

Notes: (a) The depreciation charged for the year was ₹60 lakh.

(b) The book value of the building and equipment disposed off was ₹10 lakh.

Prepare a cash flow statement (based on AS-7).

Solution

Statement of Cash Flows of Nandini Limited (Indirect Method)

Particulars		*Amount in ₹ lakh*
Cashflow from operating activities:		
Net profit before taxation	₹389	
Adjustment for		
Depreciation	60	
Gain on sale of building and equipment	(5)	
Interest expense	6	
Loss on sale of investments	10	
Operating profit before working capital changes	460	
Increase in working capital	(90)	
Cash generated from operations	370	
Income tax paid	189	
Net cash from operating activities		181
Cashflow from investing activities:		
Proceeds from sale of long-term investments (1)	40	
Proceeds from sale of land	10	
Proceeds from sale of building and equipment (₹10 lakh + ₹5 lakh gain)	15	
Purchase of building and equipment (2)	(130)	
Net cash used in investing activities		(65)
Cashflow from financing activities:		
Proceeds from issuance of bonds (₹100 – ₹50)	50	
Proceeds from issuance of equity shares (₹200 – ₹150)	50	
Interest on debentures	(6)	
Dividend to equity shareholders (3)	(200)	
Net cash used in financing activities		(106)
Net increase in cash		10
Cash at the beginning of year 2		5
Cash at the end of year 2		15

Working Notes

(1) Proceeds from sale of long-term investments:

Investments at beginning of year -2	₹150 lakh
Less investment of year-end 2	100
Book value of investments sold	50
Less loss on sale of investments	(10)
Sale proceeds	40

(2) Purchase of building and equipment

Original cost of buildings and equipment at the beginning of year 2	₹400 lakh
Less original cost of building and equipment sold during year-2 (book value ₹10 lakh Plus accumulated depreciation ₹20 lakh*)	(30)
	370
Original cost of building and equipment at year-end 2	500
Difference represents purchases of building and equipment	130

*Accumulated Depreciation Account (in ₹ lakh)

Particular	*Amount*	*Particular*	*Amount*
To Building and equipment (accumulated depreciation on sale, balancing figure)	20	By Balance b/f	160
To Balance c/d	200	By P&L A/c (depreciation of current year)	60
	220		220

(3) Since there is no increase in reserves (₹340 lakh), the entire net income after taxes of ₹200 lakh represents payment of dividend to equity shareholders.

P.5.7 The manager of a small plastic manufacturing company has reviewed the annual financial statements for the current year and is unable to determine from a reading of the balance sheet the reasons for the changes in cash during the year. He asks you for assistance and presents the following balance sheets of the Hypothetical Ltd. **LO 5.5** LOD D

Particulars	*Previous year March 31*	*Current year March 31*	*Increase (Decreases)*
Assets:			
Goodwill	₹1,00,000	(Nil)	₹(1,00,000)
Buildings	2,80,000	₹4,05,000	1,25,000
Land	75,000	70,000	(5,000)
Machinery	1,00,000	1,65,000	65,000
Tools	35,000	20,000	(15,000)
Trade investments	7,500	9,000	1,500
Inventories	1,09,000	1,05,000	(4,000)
Sundry debtors	46,000	90,000	44,000
Bills receivable	13,500	10,500	(3,000)
Cash in hand	4,500	1,000	(3,500)
Unexpired insurance	700	600	(100)
Unamortised discount on debentures	1,250	1,050	(200)
	7,72,450	8,77,150	1,04,700
Liabilities:			
Equity share capital	2,00,000	3,50,000	1,50,000
Debentures	50,000	75,000	25,000
Sundry creditors	26,000	29,000	3,000
Bank overdraft	—	4,000	4,000
Bills payable	5,000	4,500	(500)
Bank loans (short-term)	3,400	750	(2,650)
Accrued taxes	1,500	2,500	1,000
Accrued interest	3,000	5,000	2,000
Allowance for doubtful accounts	1,150	2,250	1,100
Accumulated depreciation	90,500	1,35,600	45,100
Retained earnings	3,91,900	2,68,550	(1,23,350)
	7,72,450	8,77,150	1,04,700

Additional Information:

(i) There were no purchases or sales of tools.

(ii) Equity shares were issued at a discount of 10 per cent.

(iii) Old machinery that cost ₹2,250 was scrapped and written off the books. Accumulated depreciation on such equipment was ₹1,650.

(iv) The income statement for the current year is:

Sales (net)	₹6,25,000
Less: Expenses:	
Operating charges:	
Materials and supplies	1,25,000
Direct labour	1,05,000
Manufacturing overhead	90,750
Depreciation	61,750
Selling expenses	1,22,500
General expenses	1,15,000
Interest expenses	3,750
Unusual items:	
Writing off of goodwill	1,00,000
Writing off of land	5,000
Loss on machinery	600
Discount on issue of equity shares 15,000	7,44,350
Net loss	(1,19,350)

You are required to prepare cash flow statement based on Ind AS-7.

Solution

Statement of Cash Flows of Plastic Manufacturing Company
for the Current Year (Indirect method)

Particulars		*Amount*
Cash flow from operating activities:		
Net loss	₹(1,19,350)	
Adjusted for		
Depreciation	61,750	
Interest expenses	3,750	
Writing off of goodwill	1,00,000	
Writing off of land	5,000	
Loss on machinery	600	
Discount on issue of shares	15,000	
Amortisation of discount on debentures	200	
Operating profit before working capital changes	66,950	
Adjusted for changes in working capital:		
Decrease in inventories	4,000	
Increase in sundry debtors	(44,000)	
Decrease in bills receivable	3,000	
Decrease in unexpired insurance	100	
Increase in creditors	3,000	
Increase in bank overdraft	4,000	
Decrease in bills payable	(500)	
Decrease in bank loans (short-term)	(2,650)	
Increase in accrued taxes	1,000	
Allowance for doubtful debts	1,100	
Net cash from operating activities		₹36,000
Cash flow from investing activities:		
Purchase of machine (1)	(67,250)	
Purchase of building	(1,25,000)	
Purchase of trade investments	1,500	
Net cash used in investing activities		1,93,750
Cash flow from financing activities:		
Proceeds from issue of equity shares	1,35,000	
Proceeds from issue of debentures	25,000	
Interest paid (2)	(1,750)	
Dividend paid (3)	(4,000)	
Net cash from financing activities		1,54,250
Net decrease in cash and cash-equivalents		(3,500)
Cash and cash equivalents at the beginning of current year		4,500
Cash and cash equivalents at the end of current year		1,000

Working Notes

1. Purchase of Machine

Machinery at beginning of the year	₹1,00,000
Less scrap value of machine	2,250
	97,750
Closing balance of machine	1,65,000
Difference represents purchase of machine*	67,250

2. Interest paid

Accrued interest at the beginning of year	3,000
Interest due during the year	3,750*
	6,750
Less accrued interest at the end of the year	5,000
Interest paid	1,750

*Interest expenses are (₹1,750 paid + Payable, ₹2,000). In operating activities, ₹3,750 has been adjusted in determining figure of operating profit before working capital changes. Increase in accrued interest of ₹2,000 (₹5,000 – ₹3,000) is not adjusted subsequently as it would have added more to cash flow by ₹2,000. (to avoid double counting).

3. Determination of dividend amount:

Balance of retained earnings 31st March, previous year	₹3,91,900
Less: Net loss of current year	1,19,350
	2,72,550

However, the balance of retained earnings as on December 31, current year is ₹2,68,550, that is, ₹4,000 less. In the absence of any other information, this amount is assumed to have been paid as dividends to equityholders.

P.5.8 The following are the summarised balance sheets of Sound Ltd. as on March 31 for the two consecutive years 1 and 2: **LO 5.5** LOD D

(*₹ in thousand*)

Particulars	*Year 2*	*Year 1*
Assets:		
Plant and machinery	1,980	1,010
Land and buildings	1,000	1,000
Long-term investments	550	550
Short-term investments	470	85
Sundry debtors	2,195	2,500
Inventories	1,400	1,300
Interest receivable	100	65
Cash in hand	300	500
Cash in bank	405	300
	8,400	7,310
Liabilities:		
Share capital	2,600	2,150
Reserve and surplus	1,460	900
15% debentures	2,000	1,800
Sundry creditors	440	650
Wages outstanding	40	20
Income-tax payable	400	450
Accumulated depreciation:		
Plant and machinery	910	840
Land and buildings	550	500
	8,400	7,310

Income Statement

for the period ending March 31, year 2 (₹ *in thousand)*

Sales revenue	45,300
Less: Cost of sales	39,000
Gross profit	6,300
Less: Depreciation	(540)
Selling and administration expenses	(2,960)
Interest paid	(300)
Add: Interest income	65
Dividend income (gross)	95
Net profit before extraordinary items	2,660
Add: Insurance settlement received	10
	2,670
Less: Provision for income-taxes	550
Net profit after taxes	2,120

Additional information (₹ *in thousand*):

(1) 15% Debentures of ₹300 was redeemed during year 2.

(2) Tax deducted at source on dividends received (included in provision for taxes) amounts to ₹15.

(3) A plant costing ₹500, having accumulated depreciation of ₹420 was sold for ₹80.

(4) During year 2, interim dividend of ₹760 was paid; final dividend paid was ₹800.

(5) All sales and purchases are made on credit basis.

You are required to prepare a statement of cash flows as per Ind AS-7 (revised).

Solution

Direct Method Cash Flow Statement (₹ *in thousand)*

Cash flows from operating activities:		
Cash receipts from customers	45,605	
Cash paid to suppliers and employees	(42,250)	
Cash generated from operations	3,355	
Income tax paid	(585)	
Cash flow before extraordinary item	2,770	
Proceeds from insurance settlement	10	
Net cash from operating activities		2,780
Cash flows from investing activities:		
Purchases of plant and machinery	(1,470)	
Proceeds from sale of plant and machinery	80	
Interest received	30	
Dividends received (₹95 – 15)	80	
Net cash used in investing activities		(1,280)
Cash flows from financing activities:		
Proceeds from issuance of share capital	450	
Proceeds from issue of 15% debentures	500	
Redemption of 15% debentures	(300)	
Interest paid	(300)	
Dividends paid (interim + final)	(1,560)	
Net cash used in financing activities		(1,210)
Net increase in cash and cash-equivalent		290
Cash and cash-equivalent at beginning of year 2		885
Cash and cash-equivalents at the end of year 2		1,175

Working Notes

(figures in ₹ '000)

1. Cash receipts from customers:	
Sales	45,300
Add: Sundry debtors at the beginning of year 2	2,500
	47,800
Less: Sundry debtors at the end of year 2	(2,195)
	45,605
2. Cash paid to suppliers and employees:	
Cost of sales	39,000
Add: Administrative and selling expenses	2,960
Sundry creditors at the beginning of year 2	650
Wages outstanding at the beginning of year 2	20
Inventories at the end of year 2	1,400
	44,030
Less: Sundry creditors at the end of year 2	(440)
Wages outstanding at the end of the year 2	(40)
Inventories at the end of year 1	(1,300)
	42,250
3. Income tax paid (including tax deducted at source from dividends received)	
Income tax for year 2 (including tax deducted at source from dividends received)	550
Add: Income tax liability at the beginning of year 2	450
Less: Income tax liability at the end of year 2	(400)
	600

Out of ₹600, tax deducted at source on dividend received (amounting to ₹15) is included in cash flows from investing activities and the balance of ₹585 is included in cash flows from operating activities.

4. Interest received:	
Interest income for year 2	65
Add: Interest receivable in the beginning of year 2	65
Less: Amount receivable at the end of year 2	(100)
	30
5. Machinery purchased:	
Balance at the end of year 2	1,980
Add: Book value of machine sold	500
Less: Balance at the beginning of year 2	(1,010)
	1,470

Statement of Cash Flows Indirect Method *(Amount in '000 ₹)*

Cash flows from operating activities:	
Net profit before taxation	2,660
Adjustment for:	
Depreciation	540
Interest income	(65)
Dividend income	(95)
Interest expenses	300
Operating profit before working capital changes	3,740
Decrease in sundry debtors	305
Increase in wages outstanding	20

(Contd.)

(*Contd.*)

Increase in inventories	(100)	
Decrease in creditors	(210)	
Cash generated from operations	3,355	
Income taxes paid	(585)	
Cash flow before extraordinary item	2,770	
Add: Insurance settlement	10	
Net cash from operating activities		2,780
Cash flows from investing activities:		
Purchase of plant and machinery	(1,470)	
Proceeds from sale of plant and machinery	80	
Interest received	30	
Dividends received (95 – 15)	80	
Net cash used in investing activities		(1,280)
Cash flows from financial activities:		
Proceeds from issuance of share capital	450	
Proceeds from issue of 15% debentures	500	
Redemption of 15% debentures	(300)	
Interest paid	(300)	
Dividends paid (interim + final)	(1,560)	
Net cash used in financing activities		(1,210)
Net increase in cash and cash-equivalent		290
Cash and cash-equivalents at beginning of year 2		885
Cash and cash-equivalents at the end of year 2		1,175

Cash and Cash-equivalents *(Figures in '000 ₹)*

Particulars	*Year 2*	*Year 1*
Cash in hand	300	500
Cash at bank	405	300
Short-term investments	470	85
	1,175	885

P.5.9 The following are the summarised balance sheets of Hypothetical Ltd. as at March 31 for the two consecutive years 1 and 2. Prepare CFS as per Ind AS-7. **LO 5.5** LOD D

(₹ in thousand)

Particulars		*Year 2*		*Year 1*
Assets				
Cash on hand and balances with banks		200		25
Short-term investments		670		135
Sundry debtors		1,700		1,200
Interest receivable		100		—
Inventories		900		1,950
Long-term investments		2,500		2,500
Fixed assets at cost	2,180		1,910	
Accumulated depreciation	(1,450)		(1,060)	
Fixed assets (net)		730		850
Total assets		6,800		6,660
Liabilities				
Sundry creditors		150		1,890
Interest payable		230		100
Income taxes payable		400		1,000
Long-term debt		1,110		1,040
Total liabilities		1,890		4,030

(*Contd.*)

(*Contd.*)

Shareholders' Funds		
Share capital	1,500	1,250
Reserves	3,410	1,380
Total shareholders' funds	4,910	2,630
Total liabilities and shareholders' funds	6,800	6,660

Statement of Profit and Loss

for the year 2 ended March 31 (*₹ '000*)

Sales	30,650
Cost of sales	(26,000)
Gross profit	4,650
Depreciation	(450)
Administrative and selling expenses	(910)
Interest expense	(400)
Interest income	300
Dividend income	200
Foreign exchange loss	(40)
Net profit before taxation and extraordinary item	3,350
Extraordinary item-Insurance proceeds from earthquake disaster settlement	180
Net profit after extraordinary item	3,530
Income-tax	(300)
Net profit	3,230

Additional information (*₹ in thousand)*

(i) An amount of 250 was raised from the issue of share capital and a further 250 was raised from long-term borrowings.

(ii) Interest expense was 400 of which 170 was paid during the period. 100 relating to interest expense of the prior period was also paid during the period.

(iii) Dividends paid were 1,200.

(iv) Tax deducted at source on dividends received (included in the tax expense of 300 for the year) amounted to 40.

(v) During the period, the enterprise acquired fixed assets for 350. The payment was made in cash.

(vi) Plant with original cost of 80 and accumulated depreciation of 60 was sold for 20.

(vii) Foreign exchange loss of 40 represents the reduction in the carrying amount of a short-term investment in foreign-currency designated bonds arising out of a change in exchange rate between the date of acquisition of the investment and the balance sheet date.

(viii) Sundry debtors and sundry creditors include amounts relating to credit sales and credit purchases only.

Solution

Statement of Cash Flows Direct Method (*₹ '000*)

Cash flows from operating activities		
Cash receipts from customers	30,150	
Cash paid to suppliers and employees	(27,600)	
Cash generated from operations	2,550	
Income taxes paid	(860)	
Cash flow before extraordinary item	1,690	
Proceeds from earthquake disaster settlement	180	
Net cash from operating activities		1,870
Cash flows from investing activities		
Purchase of fixed assets	(350)	

(*Contd.*)

(*Contd.*)

Proceeds from sale of equipment	20	
Interest received	200	
Dividends received	160	
Net cash from investing activities		30
Cash flows from financing activities		
Proceeds from issuance of share capital	250	
Proceeds from long-term borrowings	250	
Repayment of long-term borrowings	(180)	
Interest paid	(270)	
Dividends paid	(1,200)	
Net cash used in financing activities		(1,150)
Net increase in cash and cash equivalents		750
Cash and cash equivalents at beginning of period (*see Note 1*)		160
Cash and cash equivalents at the end of period (*see Note 1*)		910

Statement of Cash Flows Indirect Method (₹ '000)

Cash flows from operating activities		
Net profit before taxation	3,350	
Adjustments for:		
Depreciation	450	
Foreign exchange loss	40	
Interest income	(300)	
Dividend income	(200)	
Interest expense	400	
Operating profit before working capital changes	3,740	
Increase in sundry debtors	(500)	
Decrease in inventories	1,050	
Decrease in sundry creditors	(1,740)	
Cash generated from operations	2,550	
Income taxes paid	(860)	
Cash flow before extraordinary item	1,690	
Proceeds from earthquake disaster settlement	180	
Net cash from operating activities		1,870
Cash flows from investing activities:		
Purchase of fixed assets	(350)	
Proceeds from sale of equipment	20	
Interest received	200	
Dividends received	160	
Net cash from investing activities		30
Cash flows from financing activities	250	
Proceeds from issuance of share capital	250	
Proceeds from long-term borrowings	(180)	
Repayment of long-term borrowings	(270)	
Interest paid	(1,200)	
Dividends paid		(1,150)
Net cash used in financing activities		750
Net increase in cash and cash equivalents		750
Cash and cash equivalents at beginning of period (*see Note 1*)		160
Cash and cash equivalents at end of period (*see Note 1*)		910

Notes to the cash flow statement (direct method and indirect method)

1. Cash and cash-equivalents
   Cash and cash equivalents consist of cash on hand and balances with banks, and investments in money-market instruments. Cash and cash-equivalents included in the cash flow statement comprise the following balance sheet amounts.

	Year 2	Year 1
Cash on hand and balances with banks	₹200	₹25
Short-term investments	670	135
Cash and cash-equivalents	870	160
Effect of exchange rate changes	40	—
Cash and cash equivalents as restated	910	160

   Cash and cash-equivalents at the end of the period include deposits with banks of 100 held by a branch which are not freely remissible to the company because of currency exchange restrictions.
   The company has undrawn borrowing facilities of 2,000 of which 700 may be used only for future expansion.
2. Total tax paid during the year (including tax deducted at source on dividends received) amounted to 900.
   Alternative Presentation (indirect method):
   As an alternative, in an indirect method cash flow statement, operating profit before working capital changes is sometimes presented as follows:

Revenues excluding investment income	₹30,650
Operating expense excluding depreciation	(26,910)
Operating profit before working capital changes	₹3,740

Working Notes

(Figures in ₹ '000)

1. Cash receipts from customers		
Sales		30,650
Add: Sundry debtors at the end of the year		1,200
		31,850
Less: Sundry debtors at the end of the year		1,700
		30,150
2. Cash paid to suppliers and employees		
Cost of sales		26,000
Administrative and selling expenses		910
		26,910
Add: Sundry creditors at the beginning of the year	1,890	
Inventories at the end of the year	900	2,790
Less: Sundry creditors at the end of the year	150	29,700
Inventories at the beginning of the year	1,950	2,100
		27,600
3. Income taxes paid (including tax deducted at source from dividends received)		
Income tax expense for the year (including tax deducted at source from dividends received)		300
Add: Income tax liability at the beginning of the year		1,000
		1,300
Less: Income tax liability at the end of the year		400
		900

Out of 900, tax deducted at source on dividends received (amounting to 40) is included in cash flows from investing activities and the balance of 860 is included in cash flows from operating activities.

4. Repayment of long-term borrowings

Long-term debt at the beginning of the year	1,040
Add: Long-term borrowing made during the year	250
	1,290
Less: Long-term borrowings at the end of the year	1,110
	180

5. Interest paid

Interest expense for the year	400
Add: Interest payable at the beginning of the year	100
	500
Less: Interest payable at the end of the year	230
	270

REVIEW QUESTIONS

LOD: Easy

RQ.5.1 Indicate whether the following statements are True or False. **[LO 5.4,5]**

(i) Cash from business operations can be determined from income statement.
(ii) Working capital from business operations can be determined from profit and loss account.
(iii) Sources of cash should always be more than uses of cash, in the context of cash flows statement.
(iv) Interest paid on debentures is a part of operating activities.
(v) Interest received on two-months deposits in bank is shown under investing activities.
(vi) Sources of cash and uses of cash are to be equal.
(vii) Cash flows are inflows and outflows of cash and cash-equivalents.
(viii) Revaluation of building affects cashflows.
(ix) Sale proceeds from machinery, being a source of finance, form part of financing activities.
(x) Cash flow statement is mandatory for all business firms.
(xi) In normal circumstances a firm has positive cash from operations and negative cash flow from investing activities.

[Answers: (i) False, (ii) True, (iii) False, (iv) False, (v) False, (vi) False, (vii) True, (viii) False, (ix) False, (x) False, and (xi) True]

RQ.5.2 Fill in the following blanks with right answer: **[LO 5.4,5]**

(i) Cash flow statement (based on AS-7) indicates change in ____________ (cash/bank/cash and cash-equivalents).
(ii) Decrease in creditors ____________ (Decreases/Increases) cash.
(iii) Interest received on long-term investments is shown under ____________ (Operating/Financing/Investing activities).
(iv) Decrease in inventory ____________ (Decreases/Increases) cash.
(v) Increase in pre-paid expenses ____________ (Decreases/Increases) cash.
(vi) Cash payments to suppliers for goods and services are shown under ____________ (Operating/Financing/Investing activities).
(vii) Cash-flow statement (based on AS-7) of listed companies should be presented as per the ____________ (Indirect/Direct) method.
(viii) Cash payments to acquire long-term assets form part of ____________ (Financing/Investing activities).
(ix) Buy back of shares is shown under (Financing/Investing activities).
(x) Dividends paid to shareholders are classified as ____________ (Financing/Investing activities).

[Answers: (i) cash and cash-equivalents, (ii) decreases, (iii) investing activities, (iv) increases, (v) decreases, (vi) operating, (vii) indirect, (viii) investing, (ix) financing and (x) financing]

RQ.5.3 "The analysis of cash flow statement in any organisation can be very useful to the management." Elucidate the statement. [LO 5.3]

RQ.5.4 The cash flow statement is as useful to shareholders and lenders as to management.Explain. [LO 5.3]

RQ.5.5 Name three activities in which cash flows are classified as per Accounting Standard 7. Also give three examples of transactions covered in these activities. [LO 5.5]

RQ.5.6 Describe in brief the procedure of determining cash flow from operating activities as per indirect method of AS-7. Take an appropriate example to illustrate your answer. [LO 5.5]

RQ.5.7 The directors of Precision Tools Ltd. are worried at the deteriorating financial position of the company. The company has utilised full overdraft facility from the bank and is still not able to pay its creditors on due dates, although the profits earned are satisfactory. [LO 5.5]

The following are the balance sheets as on March 31 for the recent 2 years.

		Previous year		*Current year*
Share capital: shares of ₹10 each fully paid		₹10,00,000		₹10,00,000
P & L appropriation A/c		60,000		80,000
Overdraft from bank		1,60,000		6,00,000
Sundry creditors		2,00,000		6,00,000
		14,20,000		22,80,000
Land and buildings		3,00,000		5,00,000
Plant and machinery	₹5,00,000		₹6,00,000	
Less depreciation	1,20,000	3,80,000	1,80,000	4,20,000
Vehicles	1,16,000		1,24,000	
Less depreciation	56,000	60,000	84,000	40,000
Stock		2,20,000		7,20,000
Debtors		4,60,000		6,00,000
		14,20,000		22,80,000

During the year, a dividend of 10 per cent was distributed to the shareholders. On April 1 of the current year, a motor car, which originally costed ₹20,000, and showed a book value of ₹10,000, was sold for ₹16,000.

You are required to prepare a statement of cash flows based on Ind AS-7.

LOD: Medium

RQ.5.8 From the following financial information, select non-cash investing, financing and operating activities: [LO 5.4, 5]

- Redemption of debentures by converting into equity shares
- Buy back of equity shares
- Purchase of fixed assets in exchange of preference shares
- Depreciation on fixed assets
- Increase in debtors
- Loss on sale of plant
- Decrease in inventories
- Amortisation of patents
- Issuance of equity share for cash
- Bonus shares

**[Answer: (Non-cash activities)
Investing: Purchase of fixed assets in exchange of preference shares.
Financing: (i) Redemption of debentures by converting into equity shares,
(ii) Issue of preference shares for purchase of fixed assets,
(iii) Bonus shares Operating: (i) Depreciation on fixed
assets, (ii) Amortisation of patents, (iii) Loss on sale of plant]**

RQ.5.9 Explain with example the two methods of determining cash provided by operating activities. [LO 5.5]

RQ.5.10 Explain why decrease in current liabilities decrease cash and decrease in current assets increase cash. [LO 5.4]

RQ.5.11 "Depreciation is a non-cash expense. Still it is an integral part of cash flows". Explain. [LO 5.4]

RQ.5.12 Write short notes on the following [LO 5.5]

(i) Cash-equivalents

(ii) Treatment of interest and dividends received in cash flow statement (based on AS-7).

(iii) Major non-cash items.

RQ.5.13 Given the following data (₹ thousands), prepare a statement of cash flows based on Ind AS-7. [LO 5.5]

	Year 2	*Year 1*
Liabilities		
Equity share capital	₹3,600	₹3,600
Reserves	2,545	2,100
Total shareholder's equity	6,145	5,700
Debentures	16,000	16,000
Current liabilities		
Bills payable	3,900	2,800
Creditors	4,800	4,100
Provision for taxation	155	400
Total liabilities	31,000	29,000
Assets		
Fixed assets		
Land	300	300
Buildings, plant and machinery (net)	7,000	5,800
Total fixed assets	7,300	6,100
Current assets		
Bank	2,600	2,200
Inventories at cost	14,600	14,400
Investments	600	600
Debtors	5,300	5,100
Advances	600	600
Total current assets	23,700	22,900
Total assets	31,000	29,000

Statement of Income and Reconciliation of Retained Profits
for the year-end 2

(₹ thousands)

Sales		₹55,000
Cost of goods sold		40,000
Gross profit on sales		15,000
Other operating expenses		
Selling expenses	₹8,900	

(Contd.)

(*Contd.*)

Administrative	2,000	
Depreciation	1,000	11,900
Operating profit		3,100
Interest charged		800
Profit before tax		2,300
Provision for taxation (0.35)		805
Profit after taxation		1,495
Dividends		1,050
Net profit retained		445
Add reserves (beginning)		2,100
Reserves (closing)		2,545

RQ.5.14 From the information contained in income statement and balance sheet of 'A' Ltd., prepare cash flow statement (based on AS-7): **[LO 5.5]**

Income statement for the year ended March 31, 2016

Net sales	(A)	₹2,52,00,000
Less:		
Cash cost of sales		1,98,00,000
Depreciation		6,00,000
Salaries and wages		24,00,000
Operating expenses		8,00,000
Provision for taxation		8,80,000
	(B)	2,44,80,000
Net operating profit (*A* – *B*)		7,20,000
Non-recurring income – Profits on sale of equipment		1,20,000
		8,40,000
Retained earnings and profits brought forward		15,18,000
		23,58,000
Dividends declared and paid during the year		7,20,000
Profit and Loss Account balance as on March 31, 2016		16,38,000

Balance sheet as on

Assets	*March 31, 2015*	*March 31, 2016*
Fixed Assets:		
Land	₹4,80,000	₹9,60,000
Building and equipment	36,00,000	57,60,000
Current assets:		
Cash	6,00,000	7,20,000
Debtors	16,80,000	18,60,000
Stock	26,40,000	9,60,000
Advances	78,000	90,000
	90,78,000	1,03,50,000
Liabilities and Equity	March 31, 2015	March 31, 2016
Share capital	₹36,00,000	₹44,40,000
Surplus in profit and loss account	15,18,000	16,38,000
Sundry creditors	24,00,000	23,40,000
Outstanding expenses	2,40,000	4,80,000
Income-tax payable	1,20,000	1,32,000
Accumulated depreciation on buildings and equipments	12,00,000	13,20,000
	90,78,000	1,03,50,000

The original cost of equipment sold during the year 2015-16 was ₹7,20,000.

LOD: Difficult

RQ.5.15 The Balance Sheet of Royal Limited as on 31st March, 2015 and 31st March, 2016 are given below: [LO 5.5]

Balance Sheet as on *(Amount in ₹ thousands)*

Liabilities	*31.03.15*	*31.03.16*	*Assets*	*31.03.15*	*31.03.16*
Share capital	1,440	1,920	Fixed assets	3,840	4,560
Capital reserve	—	48	*Less:* Depreciation	1,104	1,392
General reserve	816	960		2,736	3,168
Profit and loss account	288	360	Investment	480	384
9% Debenture	960	672	Cash	210	312
Current liabilities	576	624	Other current assets		
Proposed dividend	144	174	(including stock)	1,134	1,272
Provision for tax	432	408	Preliminary expenses	96	48
Unpaid dividend	—	18			
	4,656	5,184		4,656	5,184

Additional Informations:

(i) During the year 2015–2016, Fixed Assets costing ₹2,40,000 (accumulated depreciation ₹84,000) was sold for ₹1,20,000.

(ii) Provided ₹4,20,000 as depreciation.

(iii) Some investments are sold at a profit of ₹48,000 and Profit was credited to capital reserve.

(iv) It decided that stocks be valued at cost, whereas previously the practice was to value stock at cost less 10 per cent. The stock was ₹2,59,200 as on 31.03.15. The stock as on 31.03.16 was correctly valued at ₹3,60,000.

(v) It decided to write off fixed assets costing ₹60,000 on which depreciation amounting to ₹48,000 has been provided.

(vi) Debentures are redeemed at ₹105.

Required:

Prepare a Cash Flow Statement (based on Accounting Standard-7).

ANSWERS

RQ.5.7 Cash from operating activities, ₹4,12,000; Cash from investing activities, (₹3,12,000); Cash from financing activities, (₹1,00,000).

RQ.5.13 Cash from operating activities, ₹4,450; Cash from investing activities, (₹2,200); Cash from financing activities, (₹1,850).

RQ.5.14 Cash from operating activities, ₹30 lakh; Cash from investing activities, (₹30 lakh); Cash from financing activities, ₹1.2 lakh.

RQ.5.15 Cash from operating activities, ₹8,06,400; Cash from investing activities, (₹7,56,000); Cash from financing activities, ₹51,600.

Scan the QR Code to access comprehensive solutions to all numerical review questions and additional material.

CHAPTER 6

Financial Statements Analysis

LEARNING OBJECTIVES

LO 6.1	Know the meaning and rationale of ratio analysis
LO 6.2	Understand liquidity ratios
LO 6.3	Explain capital structure ratios
LO 6.4	Describe profitability ratios
LO 6.5	Interpret activity/efficiency ratios
LO 6.6	Discuss integrated analysis of ratios/Du Pont chart
LO 6.7	Review the common size statements
LO 6.8	Illustrate the importance of ratio analysis
LO 6.9	Outline the limitations of ratio analysis

INTRODUCTION

A basic limitation of the traditional financial statements comprising the balance sheet and the statement of profit and loss is that they do not give all the information related to the financial operations of a firm. Nevertheless, they provide some extremely useful information to the extent that the balance sheet mirrors the financial position on a particular date in terms of the structure of assets, liabilities and owners' equity, and so on and the statement of profit and loss shows the results of operations during a certain period of time in terms of the revenues obtained and the cost incurred during the year. Thus, the financial statements provide a summarised view of the financial position and operations of a firm. Therefore, much can be learnt about a firm from a careful examination of its financial statements as invaluable documents/performance reports. The analysis of financial statements is, thus, an important aid to financial analysis.

The focus of financial analysis is on key figures in the financial statements and the significant relationship that exists between them. The analysis of financial statements is a process of evaluating the relationship between component parts of financial statements to obtain a better understanding of the firm's position and performance.[1] The first task of the financial analyst is to select the information relevant to the decision under consideration from the total information contained in the financial statements. The second step is to arrange the information in a way to highlight significant relationships. The final step is interpretation and drawing of inferences and conclusions. *In brief, financial analysis is the process of selection, relation and evaluation.*[2]

The present chapter is devoted to an in-depth analysis of financial statements and its use for decision making by various external and internal parties interested in them. The focus of the Chapter is on ratio analysis as the most widely used technique of financial statement analysis. The Chapter also discusses common-size statements as method of analysis of financial statements. The importance of ratio analysis and its limitations are similarly briefly outlined. The major points are summarised by way of recapitulation.

LO 6.1 RATIO ANALYSIS—MEANING AND RATIONALE

Ratio Analysis is a widely-used tool of financial analysis. It can be used to compare the risk and return relationships of firms of different sizes. It is defined as the systematic use of ratio to interpret the financial statements so that the strengths and weaknesses of a firm as well as its historical performance and current financial condition can be determined. The term ratio refers to the numerical or quantitative relationship between two items/variables. This relationship can be expressed as **(i)** percentages, say, net profits are 25 per cent of sales (assuming net profits of ₹25 lakh and sales of ₹100 lakh, **(ii)** fraction (net profit is one-fourth of sales) and **(iii)** proportion of numbers (the relationship between net profits and sales is 1:4). These alternative methods of expressing items which are related to each other are, for purposes of financial analysis, referred to as ratio analysis. It should be noted that computing the ratios does not add any information not already inherent in the above figures of profits and sales. What the ratios do is that they reveal the relationship in a more meaningful way so as to enable equity investors, management and lenders make better investment and credit decisions.

Rationale

The rationale of ratio analysis lies in the fact that it makes related information comparable. A single figure by itself has no meaning but when expressed in terms of a related figure, it yields significant inferences. For instance, the fact that the net profits of a firm amount to, say, ₹10 lakh throws no light on its adequacy or otherwise. The figure of net profit has to be considered in relation to other variables. How does it stand in relation to sales? What does it represent by way of return on total assets used or total capital employed? If, therefore, net profits are shown in terms of their relationship with items such as sales, assets, capital employed, equity capital and so on, meaningful conclusions can be drawn regarding their adequacy. To carry the above example further, assuming the capital employed to be ₹50 lakh and ₹100 lakh, the net profits are 20 per cent and 10 per cent respectively. Ratio analysis, thus, as a quantitative tool, enables analysts to draw quantitative answers to questions such as: Are the net profits adequate? Are the assets being used efficiently? Is the firm solvent? Can the firm meet its current obligations and so on?

Basis of Comparison

Ratios, as shown above, are relative figures reflecting the relationship between variables. They enable analysts to draw conclusions regarding financial operations. The use of ratios, as a tool of financial analysis, involves their comparison, for a single ratio, like absolute figures, fails to reveal the true position. For example, if in the case of a firm, the return on capital employed is 15 per cent in a particular year, what does it indicate? Only if the figure is related to the fact that in the preceding year the relevant return was 12 per cent or 18 per cent, it can be inferred whether the profitability of the firm has declined or improved. Alternatively, if we know that the return for the industry as a whole is 10 per cent or 20 per cent, the profitability of the firm in question can be evaluated. Comparison with related facts is, therefore, the basis of ratio analysis. Four types of comparisons are involved: **(i)** trend ratios, **(ii)** interfirm comparison, **(iii)** comparison of items within a single year's financial statement of a firm, and **(iv)** comparison with standards or plans.

Trend ratios involve a comparison of the ratios of a firm over time, that is, present ratios are compared with past ratios for the same firm. The comparison of the profitability of a firm, say, year 1 through 5 is an illustration of a trend ratio. Trend ratios indicate the direction of change in the performance–improvement, deterioration or constancy–over the years.

Trend ratios involve evaluation of financial performance over a period of time using finanical ratio analysis.

The **inter-firm comparison** involving comparison of the ratios of a firm with those of others in the same line of business or for the industry as a whole reflects its performance in relation to its competitors.

Inter-firm comparison involves comparison of different firms' financial ratios at the same point of time; involves comparison of a firm's ratios to those of others in its industry or to industry average.

Other types of comparison may relate to comparison of items within a single year's financial statement of a firm and comparison with standards or plans.

Types of Ratios

Ratios can be classified into 5 broad groups: (i) Liquidity ratios, (ii) Capital structure/leverage ratios, (iii) Profitability ratios, (iv) Activity/Efficiency ratios and (v) Integrated analysis of ratios. **A checklist of financial ratios of Reliance Industries Limited (based on data for 2012 is provided in Annexure 6.1.**

LO 6.2 LIQUIDITY RATIOS

The importance of adequate liquidity in the sense of the ability of a firm to meet current/short-term obligations when they become due for payment can hardly be overstressed. In fact, liquidity is a prerequisite for the very survival of a firm. The short-term creditors of the firm are interested in the short-term solvency or liquidity of a firm. But liquidity implies, from the viewpoint of utilisation of the funds of the firm, that funds are idle or they earn very little. A proper balance between the two contradictory requirements, that is, liquidity and profitability, is required for efficient financial management. The liquidity ratios measure the ability of a firm to meet its short-term obligations and reflect the short-term financial strength/solvency of a firm. The ratios which indicate the liquidity of a firm are: **(i)** net working capital, **(ii)** current ratios, **(iii)** acid test/quick ratios, **(iv)** super quick ratios, **(v)** turnover ratios, **(vi)** defensive-interval ratios and **(vii)** cash flow from operations ratio.

Net Working Capital

Net working capital (NWC) represents the excess of current assets over current liabilities. The term current assets refers to assets which in the normal course of business get converted into cash without dimunition in value over a short period, usually not exceeding one year or length of operating/cash cycle whichever is more. Current liabilities are those liabilities which at the inception are required to be paid in short period, normally a year. Although NWC is really not a ratio, it is frequently employed as a measure of a company's liquidity position. An enterprise should have sufficient NWC in order to be able to meet the claims of the creditors and the

Net working capital is a measure of liquidity calculated by subtracting current liabilities from current assets.

day-to-day needs of business. The greater is the amount of NWC, the greater is the liquidity of the firm. Accordingly, NWC is a measure of liquidity. Inadequate working capital is the first sign of financial problems for a firm.

There is, however, no predetermined criterion as to what constitutes adequate NWC. Moreover, the size of the NWC is not an appropriate measure of the liquidity position of a firm as shown in Table 6.1:

TABLE 6.1 Net Working Capital

Particulars	*Company A (₹ lakh)*	*Company B (₹ lakh)*
Total current assets	180	30
Total current liabilities	120	10
NWC	60	20

If the size of NWC is a measure of liquidity, Company A must be three times as liquid as Company B. However, a deeper probe would show that this is not so. A comparison of current liabilities and current assets of both the firms shows that for each rupee of current liability, B has ₹3 of current assets, while A has only ₹1.50. Thus, while A has three times the NWC of B, the current assets of the former are only 1.5 times its current liabilities as compared to 3 times in case of the latter. Obviously, from the viewpoint of the ability to meet its current obligations, firm B is in a better position than firm A. Another limitation of NWC, as a measure of liquidity, is that a change in NWC does not necessarily reflect a change in the liquidity position of a firm. Witness Table 6.2.

TABLE 6.2 Change in Net Working Capital

Particulars	*End-year 1 (₹ lakh)*	*End-year 2 (₹ lakh)*
Current assets	150	300
Current liabilities	75	200
NWC	75	100

Although the NWC has gone up for the firm in Table 6.2 from ₹75 lakh to ₹100 lakh, that is, by ₹25 lakh or 33.3 per cent between two points of time, there is, in reality, a deterioration in the liquidity position. In the first year, the firm had ₹2 of current assets for each rupee of current liabilities; but by the end of the second year the amount of current assets for each rupee of current liabilities declined to ₹1.5 only, that is, by 25 per cent. For these reasons, NWC is not a satisfactory measure of the liquidity of a firm for inter-firm comparison or for trend analysis.[3] A better indicator is the current ratio.

Current Ratio

The **current ratio** is the ratio of total current assets to total current liabilities. It is calculated by dividing current assets by current liabilities:

Current ratio is a measure of liquidity calculated dividing the current assets by the current liabilities.

$$\text{Current ratio} = \frac{\text{Current assets}}{\text{Current liabilities}} \tag{6.1}$$

The current assets of a firm, as already stated, represent those assets which can be, in the ordinary course of business, converted into cash within a short period of time, normally not exceeding one year and include cash and bank balances, marketable securities, inventory of raw materials, semi-finished (work-in-progress) and finished goods, debtors net of provision for bad and doubtful debts, bills receivable and prepaid expenses. The current liabilities defined as liabilities which are short-term maturing obligations to be met, as originally contemplated, within a year, consist of trade creditors, bills payable, bank credit, provision for taxation, dividends payable and outstanding expenses. The current ratio for firms A and B of Table 6.1 are shown in Table 6.3.

TABLE 6.3 Current Ratio

Particulars	*Firm A (₹ lakh)*	*Firm B (₹ lakh)*
$\frac{\text{Current assets}}{\text{Current liabilities}}$	$= \frac{180}{120}$	$= \frac{30}{10}$
	= 3 : 2 (1.5 : 1)	3 : 1

Rationale The current ratio of a firm measures its short-term solvency, that is, its ability to meet short-term obligations. As a measure of short-term/current financial liquidity, it indicates the rupees of current assets (cash balance and its potential source of cash) available for each rupee of current liability/obligation payable. *The higher the current ratio, the larger is the amount of rupees available per rupee of current liability, the more is the firm's ability to meet current obligations and the greater is the safety of funds of short-term creditors.* Thus, current ratio, in a way, is a measure of margin of safety to the creditors.

The need for safety margin arises from the inevitable unevenness in the flow of funds through the current assets and liabilities account. If the flows were absolutely smooth and uniform each day so that inflows exactly equalled absolutely maturing obligations, the requirement of a safety margin would be small. The fact that a firm can rarely count on such an even flow requires that the size of the current assets should be sufficiently larger than current liabilities so that the firm would be assured of being able to pay its current maturing debt as and when it becomes due. Moreover, the current liabilities can be settled only by making payment whereas the current assets available to liquidate them are subject to shrinkage for various reasons, such as bad debts, inventories becoming obsolete or unsaleable and occurrence of unexpected losses in marketable securities and so on. The current ratio measures the size of the short-term liquidity 'buffer'. A satisfactory current ratio would enable a firm to meet its obligations even when the value of the current assets declines.

Interpretation In the case of company A in the above example, the current ratio is 1.5 : 1. It implies that for every one rupee of current liabilities, current assets of one-and-half rupees are available to meet them. In other words, the current assets are one-and-half times the current liabilities. The current ratio of 3 : 1 for company B signifies that current assets are three-fold its short-term obligations. The liquidity position, as measured by the current ratio, is better in the case of B as compared to A. This is because the safety margin in the former (200 per cent) is substantially higher than in the latter (50 per cent). A slight decline in the value of current assets will adversely affect the ability of firm A to meet its obligations and, therefore, from the viewpoint of creditors, it is a more risky venture. In contrast, there is a sufficient cushion in firm B and even with two-thirds shrinkage in the value of its assets, it will be able to meet its obligations in full. For the creditors the firm is less risky. The interpretation is: *in interfirm comparison, the firm with the higher current ratio has better liquidity/short-term solvency.*

It is important to note that a very high ratio of current assets to current liabilities may be indicative of slack management practices, as it might signal excessive inventories for the current requirements and poor credit management in terms of overextended accounts receivable. At the same time, the firm may not be making full use of its current borrowing capacity.[5] Therefore, a firm should have a reasonable current ratio.

Although there is no hard and fast rule, conventionally, a current ratio of 2 : 1 (current assets twice current liabilities) is considered satisfactory. The logic underlying the conventional rule is that even with a drop-out of 50 per cent (half) in the value of current assets, a firm can meet its obligations, that is, a 50 per cent margin of safety is assumed to be sufficient to wardoff the worst of situations.

The firm A of our example, having a current ratio of 1.5 : 1, can be interpreted, on the basis of the conventional rule, to be inadequately liquid from the point of view of its ability to always satisfy the claims of short-term creditors. The firm B, of course, is sufficiently liquid as its current ratio is 3 : 1. The rule of thumb (a current ratio of 2 : 1) cannot, however, be applied mechanically. What is a satisfactory ratio will differ depending on the development of the capital market and the availability of long-term funds to finance current assets, the nature of industry and so on.

In capital-rich countries, where long-term funds from the capital market are available in abundance, firms depend on current liabilities for financing a relatively small part of their current asset requirements and it is not unusual for a firm to finance two-thirds to three-quarters of its current assets by long-term sources.[6] This policy of relying to a limited extent on short-term credit (current liabilities) is probably to avoid the difficulty in which the firms may be put by the creditors in times of temporary adversity. In underdeveloped countries, there is no alternative to relying heavily on short-term financing. Yet, in view of the risk which such a practice entails, the firms would be well advised to keep the current liabilities within reasonable limits and finance a certain minimum part of the current assets by long-term sources.

Another factor which has a bearing on the current ratio is the nature of the industry. For in-stance, public utility companies generally have a very low current ratio, as normally such companies have very little need for current assets. The wholesale dealers, on the other hand, purchasing goods on cash basis or on credit basis for a very short period but selling to retailers on credit basis, require a higher current ratio. If, in our above example, firm A is a public utility, its liquidity position can be interpreted to be satisfactory even though its current ratio is less than the conventional norm. Thus, the standard norm of current ratio (2 : 1) may vary from industry to industry. However, a ratio of less than 1 : 1 would certainly be undesirable in any industry as at least some safety margin is required to protect the interest of the creditors and to provide cushion to the firm in adverse circumstances.

The current ratio, though superior to NWC in measuring short-term financial solvency, is a rather crude measure of the liquidity of a firm. The limitation of current ratio arises from the fact that it is a *quantitative* rather than a *qualitative* index of liquidity. The term quantitative refers to the fact that it takes into account the total current assets without making any distinction between various types of current assets such as cash, inventories and so on. A qualitative measure takes into account the proportion of various types of current assets to the total current assets. A satisfactory measure of liquidity should consider the liquidity of the various current assets *per se.* As already mentioned, while current liabilities are fixed in the sense that they have to be paid in full in all circumstances, the current assets are subject to shrinkage in value, for example, possibility of bad debts, unsaleability of inventory and so on. Moreover, some of the current assets are more liquid than others: cash is the most liquid of all; receivables are more liquid than inventories, the last being the least liquid as they have to be sold before they are converted into receivables and, then, into cash. A firm with a higher percentage of its current assets in the form of cash would be more liquid, in the sense of being able to meet obligations as and when they become due, than one with a higher percentage of slow moving and unsaleable inventory and/or slow paying receivables even though both have the same current ratio. In fact, the latter type of firm may encounter serious difficulties in paying its bills even though it may have a current ratio of 2 : 1, whereas the former may do well with a ratio lower than the conventional norm. Thus, the current ratio is not a conclusive index of the real liquidity of a firm. It fails to answer questions, such as, how liquid are the receivables and the inventory? What effect does the omission of inventory and prepaid expenses have on the liquidity of a firm? To answer these and related questions, an additional analysis of the quality of current assets is required. This is done in acid-test or quick ratio.

Acid-Test/Quick Ratio

As observed above, one weakness of the current ratio is that it fails to convey any information on the composition of the current assets of a firm. A rupee of cash is considered equivalent to a rupee of inventory or receivables. But it is not so. A rupee of cash is more readily available (i.e. more liquid) to meet current obligations than a rupee of, say, inventory. This impairs the usefulness of the current ratio. The acid-test ratio is a measure of liquidity designed to overcome this shortcoming of the current ratio. It is often referred to as quick ratio because it is a measurement of a firm's ability to convert its current assets quickly into cash in order to meet its current liabilities. Thus, it is a measure of quick or acid liquidity.

Acid-test ratio (quick ratio) is a measure of liquidity calculated dividing current assets minus inventory and prepaid expenses by current liabilities.

The **acid-test ratio** is the ratio between quick current assets and current liabilities and is calculated by dividing the quick assets by the current liabilities:

$$\text{Acid-test ratio} = \frac{\text{Quick assets}}{\text{Current liabilities}} \qquad (6.2)$$

The term **quick assets** refers to current assets which can be converted into cash immediately or at a short notice without diminution of value. Included in this category of current assets are (i) cash and bank balances; (ii) short-term marketable securities and (iii) debtors/receivables. Thus, the current assets which are excluded are: prepaid expenses and inventory. The exclusion of inventory is based on the reasoning that it is not easily and readily convertible into cash. Prepaid expenses by their very nature are not available to pay off current debts. They merely reduce the amount of cash required in one period because of payment in a prior period.[8] The acid-test ratio is calculated in Table 6.4.

TABLE 6.4 Acid-Test Ratio

Cash	₹20 lakh
Debtors	20
Inventory	120
Total current assets	160
Total current liabilities	80
(i) Current ratio	2 : 1
(ii) Acid-test ratio	0.5 : 1

Interpretation The acid-test ratio is a rigorous measure of a firm's ability to service short-term liabilities. The usefulness of the ratio lies in the fact that it is widely accepted as the best available test of the liquidity position of a firm. That the acid-test ratio is superior to the current ratio is evident from Table 6.4. The current ratio of the hypothetical firm is 2 : 1 and can certainly be considered satisfactory. This interpretation of the liquidity position of the firm needs modification in the light of the quick ratio. Generally, an acid-test ratio of 1:1 is considered satisfactory as a firm can easily meet all current claims. In the case of the hypothetical firm the quick ratio (0.5 : 1) is less than the standard/norm, the satisfactory current ratio notwithstanding. The interpretation that can be placed on the current ratio (2 : 1) and acid-test (0.5 : 1) is that a large part of the current assets of the firm is tied up in slow moving and unsaleable inventories and slow paying debts. The firm would find it difficult to pay its current liabilities. The acid-test ratio provides, in a sense, a check on the liquidity position of a firm as shown by its current ratio. The quick ratio is a more rigorous and penetrating test of the liquidity position of a firm. Yet, it is not a conclusive test. Both the current and quick ratios should be considered in relation to the industry average to infer whether the firm's short-term financial position is satisfactory or not.

A variation of this ratio,[9] may be super-quick/cash ratio. This ratio is calculated by dividing the super-quick assets by the current liabilities of a firm. The super-quick current assets are cash and marketable securities. This ratio is the most rigorous and conservative test of a firm's liquidity position. Further, it is suggested that it would be useful, for the management, if the liquidity measure also takes into account 'reserve borrowing power' as the firm's real debt paying ability depends not only on cash resources available with it but also on its capacity to borrow from the market at short notice.

Turnover Ratio The liquidity ratios discussed so far relate to the liquidity of a firm as a whole. Another way of examining the liquidity is to determine how quickly certain current assets are converted into cash. The ratios to measure these are referred to as **turnover ratios.** These are, as activity ratios, covered in detail later in this chapter. In fact, liquidity ratios are not independent of activity ratios. Poor debtor or inventory turnover ratios limit the usefulness of the current and acid-test ratios. Both obsolete/unsaleable inventory and uncollectible debtors are unlikely to be sources of cash. Therefore, the liquidity ratios should be examined in conjunction with relevant turnover ratios affecting liquidity. The three relevant turnover ratios are **(i)** inventory turnover ratio; **(ii)** debtors turnover ratio; and **(iii)** creditors turnover ratio.

Inventory Turnover Ratio It is computed by dividing the cost of goods sold by the average inventory. Thus,

$$\text{Inventory turnover ratio} = \frac{\text{Cost of goods sold}}{\text{Average inventory}} \qquad \textbf{(6.3)}$$

The cost of goods sold means sales minus gross profit. The average inventory refers to the simple average of the opening and closing inventory. The ratio indicates how fast inventory is sold. A high ratio is good from the viewpoint of liquidity and *vice versa.* A low ratio would signify that inventory does not sell fast and stays on the shelf or in the warehouse for a long time. This is illustrated in Example 6.1.

***Example* 6.1**

A firm has sold goods worth ₹300 lakh with a gross profit margin of 20 per cent. The stock at the beginning and the end of the year was ₹35 lakh and ₹45 lakh respectively. What is the inventory turnover ratio?

Solution

$$\text{Inventory turnover ratio} = \frac{(₹300 \text{ lakh} - ₹60 \text{ lakh})}{(₹35 \text{ lakh} + ₹45 \text{ lakh}) \div 2} = 6 \text{ (times per year)}$$

$$\text{Inventory holding period} = \frac{12 \text{ months}}{\text{Inventory turnover ratio, } (6)} = 2 \text{ months}$$

Debtors Turnover Ratio It is determined by dividing the net credit sales by average debtors outstanding during the year. Thus,

$$\text{Debtors turnover ratio} = \frac{\text{Net credit sales}}{\text{Average debtors}} \qquad \textbf{(6.4)}$$

Net credit sales consist of gross credit sales minus returns, if any, from customers. Average debtors is the simple average of debtors (including bills receivable) at the beginning and at the end of year.

The analysis of the debtors turnover ratio supplements the information regarding the liquidity of one item of current assets of the firm. The ratio measures how rapidly receivables are collected. A high ratio is indicative of shorter time-lag between credit sales and cash collection. A low ratio shows that debts are not being collected rapidly. This is shown in Example 6.2.

***Example* 6.2**

A firm has made credit sales of ₹240 lakh during the year. The outstanding amount of debtors at the beginning and at the end of the year respectively was ₹27.5 lakh and ₹32.5 lakh. Determine the debtors turnover ratio.

Solution

$$\text{Debtors turnover ratio} = \frac{₹240 \text{ lakh}}{(₹27.5 \text{ lakh} + ₹32.5 \text{ lakh}) \div 2} = 8 \text{ (times per year)}$$

$$\text{Debtors collection period} = \frac{12 \text{ months}}{\text{Debtors turnover ratio (8)}} = 1.5 \text{ month}$$

Creditors Turnover Ratio It is a ratio between net credit purchases and the average amount of creditors outstanding during the year. It is calculated as follows:

$$\text{Creditors turnover ratio} = \frac{\text{Net credit purchases}}{\text{Average creditors}} \qquad \textbf{(6.5)}$$

Net credit purchases = Gross credit purchases *less* returns to suppliers

Average creditors = Average of creditors (including bills payable) outstanding at the beginning and at the end of the year

A low turnover ratio reflects liberal credit terms granted by suppliers, while a high ratio shows that accounts are to be settled rapidly. The creditors turnover ratio is an important tool of analysis as a firm can reduce its requirement of current assets by relying on supplier's credit. The extent to which trade creditors are willing to wait for payment can be approximated by the creditors turnover ratio. Consider Example 6.3.

***Example* 6.3**

The firm of Examples 6.1 and 6.2 has made credit purchases of ₹180 lakh. The amount payable to the creditors at the beginning and at the end of the year is ₹42.5 lakh and ₹47.5 lakh respectively. Find out the creditors turnover ratio.

Solution

$$\text{Creditors turnover ratio} = \frac{(₹180 \text{ lakh})}{(₹42.5 \text{ lakh} + ₹47.5 \text{ lakh}) \div 2} = 4 \text{ (times per year)}$$

$$\text{Creditor's payment period} = \frac{12 \text{ months}}{\text{Creditors turnover ratio (4)}} = 3 \text{ months}$$

The summing up of the three turnover ratios (known as a cash cycle) has a bearing on the liquidity of a firm. The cash cycle captures the interrelationship of sales, collections from debtors and payment to credi-tors. The combined effect of the three turnover ratios is summarised below:

Inventory holding period	2 months
Add: Debtor's collection period	+ 1.5 months
Less: Creditor's payment period	– 3 months
	0.5 months

As a rule, the shorter is the cash cycle, the better are the liquidity ratios as measured above and *vice versa.*

Defensive-Interval Ratio

Defensive interval ratio is the ratio between quick assets and projected daily cash requirement.

The liquidity ratios of a firm outlined in the preceding discussions throw light on the ability of a firm to pay its current liabilities. Apart from paying current liabilities, the liquidity position of a firm should also be examined in relation to its ability to meet projected daily expenditure from operations. The **defensive-interval ratio** provides such a measure of liquidity. It is a ratio between the quick/liquid assets and the projected daily cash requirements and is calculated according to Equation 6.6.

$$\text{Defensive-interval ratio} = \frac{\text{Liquid assets}}{\text{Projected daily cash requirement}} \tag{6.6}$$

where

$$\text{Projected daily cash requirement} = \frac{\text{Projected cash operating expenditure}}{\text{Number of days in a year (365)}}$$

The projected cash operating expenditure is based on past expenditures and future plans. It is equivalent to the cost of goods sold excluding depreciation, plus selling and administrative expenditure and other ordinary cash expenses. Alternatively, a very rough estimate of cash oper-ating expenses can be obtained by subtracting the non-cash expenses like depreciation and amortisation from total expenses. Liquid assets, as already stated, include current assets excluding inventory and prepaid expenses.

The defensive-interval ratio measures the timespan a firm can operate on present liquid assets (comprising cash, marketable securities and debtors) without resorting to next year's income. Consider Example 6.4.

***Example* 6.4**

The projected cash operating expenditure of a firm from the next year is ₹182.5 lakh. It has liquid current assets amounting to ₹40 lakh. Determine the defensive-interval ratio.

Solution

$$\text{Projected daily cash requirement} = \frac{₹182.5 \text{ lakh}}{365} = ₹50{,}000$$

$$\text{Defensive-interval ratio} = \frac{₹40 \text{ lakh}}{₹50{,}000} = 80 \text{ days}$$

The figure of 80 days indicates that the firm has liquid assets which can meet the operating cash requirements of business for 80 days without resorting to future revenues. A higher ratio would be favourable as it would reflect the ability of a firm to meet cash requirements for a longer period of time. It provides a safety margin to the firm in determining its ability to meet basic operational costs. A higher ratio would provide the firm with a relatively higher degree of protection and tends to offset the weakness indicated by low current and acid-test ratios.[9] Sorter and Benston[10] have also suggested a ratio of liquid assets to daily cash operating expenditure as a measure of short-term solvency.

Cash-Flow From Operations Ratio

This ratio measures liquidity of a firm by comparing actual cash flows from operations (in lieu of current and potential cash inflows from CAs such as inventory and debtors) with current liability. It is calculated as per Equation 6.7

$$\text{Cash-flow from operations ratio} = \frac{\text{Cash flow from operations}}{\text{Current liabilities}} \tag{6.7}$$

Being a cash measure, the ratio does not encounter the problems of actual convertibility of current assets (such as debtors and inventory) and the need for maintaining minimum levels of these assets. In general, the higher the ratio, the better is a firm from the point of view of liquidity.

To conclude the discussion of liquidity ratios, the short-term solvency of a firm can be judged not merely in terms of the traditional liquidity ratios such as current and acid-tests, but the analysis should also be extended towards examining the quality of turnover of the items of current assets on which such ratios are based. These qualitative considerations (turnover ratios) coupled with the defensive-interval and cash flow from operation ratios would reveal the true liquidity position of the firm.

The liquidity ratios are, no doubt, primarily relevant from the viewpoint of the creditors of the firm. In theory, therefore, the higher the liquidity ratios, the better is the firm. But high ratios have serious implications from the firm's point of view. High current and acid-test ratios would imply that funds have unnecessarily accumulated and are not being profitably utilised. Similarly, an unusually high rate of inventory turnover may indicate that a firm is losing business by failing to maintain an adequate level of inventory to serve the customer's needs. A rapid turnover of debtors may reflect strict credit policies that hold revenue below levels that could be obtained by granting more liberal credit terms.

Finally, while interpreting the short-term position of the firm by the creditors, it should be recognised that the management may be tempted to indulge in 'window-dressing' just before the financial statements are prepared so as to make the current financial position appear better than what it actually is. For instance, by postponing purchases, allowing inventories to fall below the normal levels, using all available cash to pay off current liabilities and pressing collection on debtors, the current and acid-test ratios, and debtors turnover ratios may be artificially improved. Even when no deliberate attempt has been made to present a good picture, the current financial position shown by the year-end financial statements is probably more favourable than at any other time of the year. This is particularly true when a firm adopts a natural business year that ends during an ebb in the seasonal swing of business activity. At the time of peak activity, debtors, inventories and current liabilities tend to be at higher levels. In such cases, an analysis of current financial position based solely on year-end data will tend to over-state a firm's average liquidity position.[12]

LO 6.3 LEVERAGE/CAPITAL STRUCTURE RATIOS

The second category of financial ratios is leverage or capital structure ratios. The long-term lenders/creditors would judge the soundness of a firm on the basis of the long-term financial strength measured in terms of its ability to pay the interest regularly as well as repay the instalment of the principal on due dates or in one lump sum at the time of maturity. The long-term solvency of a firm can be examined by using leverage or capital structure ratios. The leverage or capital structure ratios may be defined as financial ratios which throw light on the long-term solvency of a firm as reflected in its ability to assure the long-term lenders with regard to **(i)** periodic payment of interest during the period of the loan and **(ii)** repayment of principal on maturity or in predetermined instalments at due dates.

There are, thus, two aspects of the long-term solvency of a firm: **(i)** ability to repay the principal when due, and **(ii)** regular payment of the interest. Accordingly, there are two different, but mutually dependent and interrelated, types of leverage ratios. First, ratios which are based on the relationship between borrowed funds and owner's capital. These ratios are computed from the balance sheet and have many variations such as **(a)** debt-equity ratio, **(b)** debt-assets ratio, **(c)** equity-assets ratio, and so on. The second type of capital structure ratios, popularly called coverage ratios, are calculated from the profit and loss account. Included in this category are **(a)** interest coverage ratio, **(b)** dividend coverage ratio, **(c)** total fixed charges coverage ratio, **(d)** cash flow coverage ratio, and **(e)** debt services coverage ratio.

Debt-Equity Ratios

Debt-equity ratio measures the ratio of long-term or total debt to shareholders equity.

The relationship between borrowed funds and owner's capital is a popular measure of the long-term financial solvency of a firm. This relationship is shown by the debt-equity ratios. This ratio reflects the relative claims of creditors and shareholders against the assets of the firm. Alternatively, this ratio indicates the relative proportions of debt and equity in financing the assets of a firm. The relationship between outsiders' claims and owner's capital can be shown in different ways and, accordingly, there are many variants of the debt-equity (D/E) ratio.

One approach is to express the D/E ratios in terms of the relative proportion of long-term debt and shareholders' equity. Thus,

$$\text{D/E ratio} = \frac{\text{Long-term debt}}{\text{Shareholders' equity}} \tag{6.8}$$

The debt considered here is exclusive of current liabilities. The shareholders' equity includes **(i)** equity and preference share capital, **(ii)** past accumulated profits but excludes fictitious assets like past accumulated losses, **(iii)** discount on issue of shares and so on.

Another approach to the calculation of the debt-equity ratio is to relate the total debt (not merely long-term debt) to the shareholders' equity. That is,

$$\text{D/E ratio} = \frac{\text{Total debt}}{\text{Shareholders' equity}} \tag{6.9}$$

The D/E ratio is, thus, the ratio of total outside liabilities to owners' total funds. In other words, it is the ratio of the amount invested by outsiders to the amount invested by the owners of business.

The difference between this and the first approach is essentially in respect of the treatment of current liabilities. While the former excludes them, the latter includes them in the numerator (debt). Should current liabilities be included in the amount of debt to calculate the D/E ratio? While there is no doubt that current liabilities are short-term and the ability of a firm to meet such obligations is reflected in the liquidity ratios, their amount fluctuates widely during a year and interest payments on them are not large, they should form part of the total outside liabilities to determine the ability of a firm to meet its long-term obligations for a number of reasons. For one thing, individual items of current liabilities are certainly short-term and may fluctuate widely, but, as a whole, a fixed amount of them is always in use so that they are available more or less on a long-term footing. Moreover, some current liabilities like bank credit, which are ostensibly short-term, are renewed year after year and remain by and large permanently in the business. Also, current liabilities have, like the long-term creditors, a prior right on the assets of the business and are paid along with long-term lenders at the time of liquidation of the firm. Finally, the short-term creditors exercise as much, if not more, pressure on management. The omission of current liabilities in calculating the D/E ratio would lead to misleading results.

How should preference share capital be treated? Should it be included in the debt or equity? The exact treatment will depend upon the purpose for which the D/E ratio is being computed. If the object is to examine the financial solvency of a firm in terms of its ability to avoid financial risk, preference capital should be clubbed with equity capital. If, however, the D/E ratio is calculated to show the effect of the use of fixed-interest/dividend sources of funds on the earnings available to the ordinary shareholders, preference capital should be clubbed with debt.

Interpretation The D/E ratio is an important tool of financial analysis to appraise the financial structure of a firm. It has important implications from the view-point of the creditors, owners and the firm itself. The ratio reflects the relative contribution of creditors and owners of business in its financing. A high ratio shows a large share of financing by the creditors of the firm; a low ratio implies a smaller claim of creditors. The D/E ratio indicates the margin of safety to the creditors. If, for instance, the D/E ratio is 1 : 2, it implies that for every rupee of outside liability, the firm has two rupees of owner's capital or the stake of the creditors is one-half of the owners. There is, therefore, a safety margin of 66.67 per cent available to the creditors of the firm. The firm would be able to meet the creditors claims even if the value of the assets declines by 66.67 per cent. Conversely, if the D/E ratio is 2 : 1, it implies low safety margin (one-third) for the creditors.

If the D/E ratio is high, the owners are putting up relatively less money of their own. It is danger signal for the creditors. If the project should fail financially, the creditors would lose heavily. Moreover, with a small financial stake in the firm, the owners may behave irresponsibly and indulge in speculative activity. If they are heavily involved financially, they will strain every nerve to make the enterprise a success. In brief, the greater the D/E ratio, the greater is the risk to the creditors.

A high debt-equity ratio has equally serious implications from the firm's point of view also. A high proportion of debt in the capital structure would lead to inflexibility in the operations of the firm as creditors would exercise pressure and interfere in management. Secondly, such a firm would be able to borrow only under very restrictive terms and conditions. Further, it would have to face a heavy burden of interest payments, particularly in adverse circumstances when profits decline. Finally, the firm will have to encounter serious difficulties in raising funds in future.

The shareholders of the firm would, however, stand to gain in two ways: **(i)** with a limited stake, they would be able to retain control of the firm and **(ii)** the return to them would be magnified. With a larger proportion of debt in the financial structure, the earnings available to the owners would increase more than proportionately with an increase in the operating profits of the firm. This is because the debt carries a fixed rate of return and if the firm is able to earn on the borrowed funds a rate higher than the fixed-charge on loans, the benefit will go to the shareholders. This is illustrated in Table 6.5. Technically, this is referred to as **leverage** or **trading on equity**. The expression 'trading on equity' describes the practice of using borrowed funds carrying a fixed-charge in the expectation of obtaining a higher return to the equity-holders. The leverage can, of course, work in the opposite direction also, if the return on borrowed funds is less than the fixed charge.[13]

Trading on equity (leverage) is the use of borrowed funds in expectation of higher return to equity-holders.

A low D/E ratio has just the opposite implications. To the creditors, a relatively high stake of the owners implies sufficient safety margin and substantial protection against shrinkage in assets. For the company also, the servicing of debt is less burdensome and consequently its credit standing is not adversely affected, its operational flexibility is not jeopardised and it will be able to raise additional funds. The shareholders of the firm are deprived of the benefits of trading on equity or leverage.

TABLE 6.5 Trading on Equity *(Amount in ₹ thousand)*

Particular	*A*	*B*	*C*	*D*
(a) Total assets	1,000	1,000	1,000	1,000
Financing pattern:				
Equity capital	1,000	800	600	200
15% Debt	—	200	400	800
(b) Operating profit (EBIT)	300	300	300	300
Less: Interest	—	30	60	120
Earnings before taxes	300	270	240	180
Less: Taxes (0.35)	105	94.5	84	63
Earnings after taxes	195	175.5	156	117
Return on equity (per cent)	19.5	21.9	26	58.5

The preceding discussion should leave no doubt that both high and low D/E ratios are not desirable. What is needed is a ratio which strikes a proper balance between debt and equity. What is the reasonable relationship between debt and equity? There cannot be a rigid rule. It will de-pend upon the circumstances, prevailing practices and so on. The general proposition is: *other's money should be in reasonable proportion to the owner's capital and the owners should have sufficient stake in the fortunes of the enterprise.* For instance, in a capital-rich country, the practice is to use as little debt as possible. A D/E ratio of 1 : 3 is regarded as indicative of a fairly heavy debt; a ratio of 1 : 1 would indicate an extremely heavy and unsatisfactory debt situation.[14] In underdeveloped countries such standards cannot be expected. It was not unusual to find firms having a D/E ratio of 2 : 1 or even 3 : 1 in the case of joint stock enterprises in India. One reason for such heavy dose of debt was to be found in the fact that enterprises had to depend, by and large, on public financial institutions (PFIs) which provided most of the funds in the form of loans. This had made the financial structure of companies lopsided and, on canons of sound financing practices, highly imprudent. The borrowers were finding it extremely difficult to service the debt burden and the overdues of the financial institutions rose unabated.[15] With the shift in the post-1991 period of dependence of the corporates on the capital market, their dependence on loans/debt has significantly declined.

Secondly, the D/E ratio cannot be applied mechanically without regard to the circumstances of each case, such as type and size of business, the nature of the industry and the degree of risk involved. For example, firms having a stable income such as an electricity company, can afford to have a higher D/E ratio. Similarly, capital intensive industries and firms producing a basic product, like cement, tend to use a larger proportion of debt. The tolerable D/E ratio of a new company would be much lower than for an established one.

Finally, there is an important issue whether to use book or market values to compute leverage ratio. Valuation models in finance are generally based on the market value of debt and equity. Therefore, the use of market values can make the D/E ratio a more useful analytical tool. For instance, if the market value of equity is higher than its book value, the market value based D/E ratio will be lower than the one using book value. This would imply that the firm can raise funds at attractive financial costs. The financial costs would be higher if the market value of equity is lower than its book value as equity capital can be issued at a discount to book value.

Debt to Total Capital Ratio

The relationship between creditors' funds and owner's capital can also be expressed in terms of another leverage ratio. This is the debt to total capital ratio. Here, the outside liabilities are related to the total capitalisation of the firm and not merely to the shareholder's equity. Essentially, this type of capital structure ratio is a variant of the D/E ratio described above. It can be calculated in different ways.

One approach is to relate the long-term debt to the permanent capital of the firm. Included in the permanent capital are shareholders' equity as well as long-term debt. Thus,

$$\text{Debt to total capital ratio} = \frac{\text{Long-term debt}}{\text{Permanent capital}} \quad \textbf{(6.10)}$$

Another approach to calculating the debt to capital ratio is to relate the total debt to the total assets of the firm. The total debt of the firm comprises long-term debt plus current liabilities. The total assets consist of permanent capital plus current liabilities. Thus,

$$\text{Debt to total assets/capital ratio} = \frac{\text{Total debt}}{\text{Total assets}} \quad \textbf{(6.11)}$$

Proprietary ratio indicates the extent to which assets are financed by owners funds.

Still another variant of the D/E ratio is to relate the owner's/proprietor's funds with total assets. This is called the **proprietary ratio**. The ratio indicates the proportion of total assets financed by owners. Symbolically, it is equal to:

$$\frac{\text{Proprietor's funds}}{\text{Total assets}} \times 100 \quad \textbf{(6.12)}$$

Finally, it may also be of some interest to know the relationship between equity funds (also referred to as net worth) and fixed-income bearing funds (preference shares, debentures and other borrowed funds). This ratio, called the **capital gearing ratio**, is useful when the objective is to show the effect of the use of fixed-interest/dividend source of funds on the earnings available to the equity shareholders.

Interpretation

As the ratio is like the D/E ratio, it gives results similar to the D/E ratio in respect of capital structure of a firm. The first of these (Equation 6.10), indicates what proportion of the permanent capital of a firm consists of long-term debt. If the ratio for a firm is 1 : 2, it implies that one-third of the total permanent capital of the firm is in the form of long-term debts. Although no hard and fast rules exist, conventionally a ratio of 1 : 2 is considered to be satisfactory.

The second ratio (Equation 6.11) measures the share of the total assets financed by outside funds. The third variant (Equation 6.12) shows what portion of the total assets are financed by the owner's capital. A low ratio of debt to total assets is desirable from the point of the creditors/ lenders as there is sufficient margin of safety available to them. But its implications for the shareholders are that debt is not being exploited to make available to them the benefit of trading on equity. A firm with a very high ratio would expose the creditors to higher risk. The implications of the ratio of equity capital of total assets are exactly opposite to that of the debt to total assets. A firm should have neither a very high ratio nor a very low ratio.

Coverage ratios measure the firm's ability to pay certain fixed charges.

Coverage Ratios

The second category of leverage ratios are **coverage ratios**. These ratios are computed from information available in the profit and loss account. For a normal firm, in the ordinary course of business, the claims of creditors are not met out of the sale proceeds of the permanent assets of the firm. The obligations of a firm are normally met out of the earnings or operating profits. These claims consist of **(i)** interest on loans, **(ii)** preference dividend, and **(iii)** amortisation of principal or repayment of the instalment of loans or redemption of preference capital on maturity. The soundness of a firm, from the view-point of long-term creditors, lies in its ability to service their claims. This ability is indicated by the coverage ratios. The coverage ratios measure the relationship between what is normally available from operations of the firms and the claims of the outsiders. The important coverage ratios are: **(i)** interest coverage, **(ii)** dividend coverage, **(iii)** total coverage, **(iv)** total cashflow coverage, and **(v)** debt service coverage ratio.

Interest coverage (time-interest-earned) ratio measures the firm's ability to make contractual interest payments.

Interest Coverage Ratio It is also known as **'time-interest-earned ratio'**. This ratio measures the debt servicing capacity of a firm insofar as fixed interest on long-term loan is concerned. It is determined by dividing the operating profits or earnings before interest and taxes (EBIT) by the fixed interest charges on loans. Thus,

$$\text{Interest coverage} = \frac{\text{EBIT}}{\text{Interest}} \tag{6.13}$$

It should be noted that this ratio uses the concept of net profits before taxes because interest is tax-deductible so that tax is calculated after paying interest on long-term loan. This ratio, as the name suggests, indicates the extent to which a fall in EBIT is tolerable in that the ability of the firm to service its interest payments would not be adversely affected. For instance, an interest coverage of 10 times would imply that even if the firm's EBIT were to decline to one-tenth of the present level, the operating profits available for servicing the interest on loan would still be equivalent to the claims of the lenders. On the other hand, a coverage of five times would indicate that a fall in operating earnings only to upto one-fifth level can be tolerated. From the point of view of the lenders, the larger the coverage, the greater is the ability of the firm to handle fixed-charge liabilities and the more assured is the payment of interest to them. However, too high a ratio may imply unused debt capacity. In contrast, a low ratio is a danger signal that the firm is using excessive debt and does not have the ability to offer assured payment of interest to the lenders.

Dividend Coverage Ratio It measures the ability of a firm to pay dividend on preference shares which carry a stated rate of return. This ratio is the ratio (expressed as x number of times) of net earnings after taxes (EAT) and the amount of preference dividend. Thus,

$$\text{Dividend coverage} = \frac{\text{EAT}}{\text{Preference dividend}} \tag{6.14}$$

It can be seen that although preference dividend is a fixed obligation, the earnings taken into account are after taxes. This is because, unlike debt on which interest is a charge on the profits of the firm, the preference dividend is treated as an appropriation of profit. The ratio, like the interest coverage ratio, reveals the safety margin available to the preference shareholders. As a rule, the higher the coverage, the better it is from their point of view.

Total fixed charge coverage ratios measure the firm's ability to meet all fixed payment obligations.

Total Fixed Charge Coverage Ratio While the interest coverage and preference dividend coverage ratios consider the fixed obligations of a firm to the respective suppliers of funds, that is, creditors and preference shareholders, the total coverage ratio has a wider scope and takes into account all the committed fixed obligations of a firm, that is, **(i)** interest on loan, **(ii)** preference dividend, **(iii)** lease payments, and **(iv)** repayment of principal. Symbolically,

$$\text{Total fixed charge coverage} = \frac{\text{EBIT + Lease payment}}{\text{Interest + Lease payments + (Preference dividend + Instalment of principal)}/(1-t)} \quad \textbf{(6.15)}$$

Total Cashflow Coverage Ratio However, coverage ratios mentioned above, suffer from one major limitation, that is, they relate the firm's ability to meet its various financial obligations to its earnings. In fact, these payments are met out of cash available with the firm. Accordingly, it would be more appropriate to relate cash resources of a firm to its various fixed financial obligations. The ratio, so determined, is referred to as ***total cash flow coverage ratio***. Symbolically,

$$\text{Total cash flow coverage} = \frac{\text{EBIT + Lease Payments + Depreciation + Non-cash expenses}}{\text{Lease payment + Interest} + \dfrac{\text{(Principal repayment)}}{(1-t)} + \dfrac{\text{(Preference dividend)}}{(1-t)}}$$

(6.16)

The overall ability of a firm to service outside liabilities is truly reflected in the total cash flow coverage ratio: the higher the coverage, the better is the ability.

Internally generated cash from operating activities (CFO) are required for investment as well as debt servicing. A typical firm requires funds both for growth, apart from replacement of existing fixed assets (in particular, plant and machinery) and servicing of debt. Accordingly, a firm's long-term solvency is a function of its ability **(i)** to finance the expansion and replacements needs of the business and **(ii)** to generate cash for servicing of debt.

Capital Expenditure Ratio measures the relationship between the firm's ability to generate CFO and its capital expenditure requirements. It is determined dividing CFO by capital expenditure. The higher the ratio, the better it is. The ratio greater than one indicates that the firm has cash to service debt as well as to make payment of dividends.

Debt service capacity is the ability of a firm to make the contractual payments required on a scheduled basis over the life of the debt.

Debt-Service Coverage Ratio (DSCR) is considered a more comprehensive and apt measure to compute **debt service capacity** of a business firm. It provides the value in terms of the number of times the total debt service obligations consisting of interest and repayment of principal in instalments are covered by the total operating funds available after the payment of taxes: Earnings after taxes, EAT + Interest + Depreciation + Other non-cash expenditures like amortisation (OA). Symbolically,

$$\text{DSCR} = \frac{\sum_{t=1}^{n} \text{EAT}_t + \text{Interest}_t + \text{Depreciation}_t + OA_t}{\sum_{t=1}^{n} \text{Instalment}_t} \quad \textbf{(6.17)}$$

The higher the ratio, the better it is. A ratio of less than one may be taken as a sign of long-term solvency problem as it indicates that the firm does not generate enough cash internally to service debt. In general, lending financial institutions consider 2:1 as satisfactory ratio. Consider Example 6.5.

***Example* 6.5**

Agro Industries Ltd has submitted the following projections. You are required to work out yearly debt service coverage ratio (DSCR) and the average DSCR: (Figures in ₹ lakh)

Year	Net profit for the year	Interest on term loan during the year	Repayment of term loan in the year
1	21.67	19.14	10.70
2	34.77	17.64	18.00
3	36.01	15.12	18.00
4	19.20	12.60	18.00
5	18.61	10.08	18.00
6	18.40	7.56	18.00
7	18.33	5.04	18.00
8	16.41	Nil	18.00

The net profit has been arrived after charging depreciation of ₹17.68 lakh every year.

Solution

TABLE 6.6 Determination of Debt Service Coverage Ratio *(Amount in lakh of rupees)*

Year	*Net profit*	*Depre- ciation*	*Interest*	*Cash available (col. 2+3+4)*	*Principal instalment*	*Debt obligation (col. 4+col. 6)*	*DSCR [col. 5 ÷ col. 7 (No. of times)]*
1	*2*	*3*	*4*	*5*	*6*	*7*	*8*
1	21.67	17.68	19.14	58.49	10.70	29.84	1.96
2	34.77	17.68	17.64	70.09	18.00	35.64	1.97
3	36.01	17.68	15.12	68.81	18.00	33.12	2.08
4	19.20	17.68	12.60	49.48	18.00	30.60	1.62
5	18.61	17.68	10.08	46.37	18.00	28.08	1.65
6	18.40	17.68	7.56	43.64	18.00	25.56	1.71
7	18.33	17.68	5.04	41.05	18.00	23.04	1.78
8	16.41	17.68	Nil	34.09	18.00	18.00	1.89
Average DSCR (DSCR ÷ 8)							1.83

LO 6.4 PROFITABILITY RATIOS

Apart from the creditors, both short-term and long-term, also interested in the financial soundness of a firm are the owners and management or the company itself. The management of the firm is naturally eager to measure its operating efficiency. Similarly, the owners invest their funds in the expectation of reasonable returns. The operating efficiency of a firm and its ability to ensure adequate returns to its shareholders/owners depends ultimately on the profits earned by it. The profitability of a firm can be measured by its profitability ratios. In other words, the profitability ratios are designed to provide answers to questions such as **(i)** is the profit earned by the firm adequate? **(ii)** what rate of return does it represent? **(iii)** what is the rate of profit for various divisions and segments of the firm? **(iv)** what are the earnings per share? **(v)** what was the amount paid in dividends? **(vi)** what is the rate of return to equity-holders? and so on.

Profitability ratios can be determined on the basis of either sales or investments. The profitability ratios in relation to sales are **(a)** profit margin (gross and net) and **(b)** expenses ratio. Profitability in relation to investments is measured by **(a)** return on assets, **(b)** return on capital employed, and **(c)** return on shareholders' equity.

Profitability Ratios Related to Sales

These ratios are based on the premise that a firm should earn sufficient profit on each rupee of sales. If adequate profits are not earned on sales, there will be difficulty in meeting the operating expenses and no returns will be available to the owners. These ratios consist of **(i)** profit margin, and **(ii)** expenses ratios.

Profit Margin The profit margin measures the relationship between profit and sales. As the profits may be gross or net, there are two types of profit margins: Gross profit margin and Net profit margin.

Gross Profit Margin is also known as gross margin. It is calculated by dividing gross profit by sales. Thus,

> **Gross profit margin** measures the percentage of each sales rupee remaining after the firm has paid for its goods.

$$\text{Gross profit margin} = \frac{\text{Gross profit}}{\text{Sales}} \times 100 \quad (6.18)$$

If the sales of a firm amount to ₹40,00,000 and its gross profit is ₹10,00,000, the gross margin would be 25 per cent (₹10,00,000 ÷ ₹40,00,000). If the gross margin (25 per cent) is deducted from 100, the result (75 per cent) is the ratio of cost of goods sold to sales. The former measures profits in relation to sales, while the latter reveals the relationship between cost of production and sale price.

Gross profit is the result of the relationship between prices, sales volume and costs. A change in the gross margin can be brought about by changes in any of these factors. The gross margin represents the limit beyond which fall in sales prices are outside the tolerance limit. Further, the gross profit ratio/margin can also be used in determining the extent of loss caused by theft, spoilage, damage, and so on in the case of those firms which follow the policy of fixed gross profit margin in pricing their products.

A high ratio of gross profit to sales is a sign of good management as it implies that the cost of production of the firm is relatively low. It may also be indicative of a higher sales price without a corresponding increase in the cost of goods sold. It is also likely that cost of sales might have declined without a corresponding decline in sales price. Nevertheless, a very high and rising gross margin may also be the result of unsatisfactory basis of valuation of stock, that is, overvaluation of closing stock and/or undervaluation of opening stock.

A relatively low gross margin is definitely a danger signal, warranting a careful and detailed analysis of the factors responsible for it. The important contributory factors may be **(i)** a high cost of production reflecting acquisition of raw materials and other inputs on unfavourable terms, inefficient utilisation of current as well as fixed assets, and so on; and **(ii)** a low selling price resulting from severe competition, inferior quality of the product, lack of demand, and so on. A thorough investigation of the factors having a bearing on the low gross margin is called for.

A firm should have a reasonable gross margin to ensure adequate coverage for operating ex-penses of the firm and sufficient return to the owners of the business, which is reflected in the net profit margin.

Net Profit Margin is also known as net margin. This measures the relationship between net profits and sales of a firm. Depending on the concept of net profit employed, this ratio can be computed in three ways:

> **Net profit margin** measures the percentage of each sales rupee remaining after all costs and expenses including interest and taxes have been deducted.

1. $$\text{Operating profit ratio} = \frac{\text{Earnings before interest and taxes (EBIT)}}{\text{Net sales}} \quad (6.19)$$

2. $$\text{Pre-tax profit ratio} = \frac{\text{Earnings before taxes (EBT)}}{\text{Net sales}} \quad (6.20)$$

3. Net profit ratio $= \dfrac{\text{Earnings after interest and taxes (EAT)}}{\text{Net sales}}$ **(6.21)**

The net profit margin is indicative of *management's ability to operate the business with sufficient success not only to recover from revenues of the period, the cost of merchandise or services, the expenses of operating the business (including depreciation) and the cost of the borrowed funds, but also to leave a margin of reasonable compensation to the owners for providing their capital at risk. The ratio of net profit (after interest and taxes) to sales essentially expresses the cost price effectiveness of the operation.*[16]

A high net profit margin would ensure adequate return to the owners as well as enable a firm to withstand adverse economic conditions when selling price is declining, cost of production is rising and demand for the product is falling.

A low net profit margin has the opposite implications. However, a firm with a low profit margin, can earn a high rate of return on investments if it has a higher inventory turnover. This aspect is covered in detail in the subsequent discussion. The profit margin should, therefore, be evaluated in relation to the turnover ratio. In other words, the overall rate of return is the product of the net profit margin and the investment turnover ratio. Similarly, the gross profit margin and the net profit margin should be jointly evaluated. The need for joint analysis arises because the two ratios may show different trends. For example, the gross margin may show a substantial increase over a period of time but the net profit margin may **(i)** have remained constant, or **(ii)** may not have increased as fast as the gross margin, or **(iii)** may actually have declined. It may be due to the fact that the increase in the operating expenses individually may behave abnormally. On the other hand, if either as a whole or individual items of operating expenses decline substantially, a decrease in gross margin may be associated with an improvement in the net profit margin.

Expenses Ratio Another profitability ratio related to sales is the **expenses ratio**. It is computed by dividing expenses by sales. The term 'expenses' includes **(i)** cost of goods sold, **(ii)** administrative expenses, **(iii)** selling and distribution expenses, **(iv)** financial expenses but excludes taxes, dividends and extraordinary losses due to theft of goods, good destroyed by fire and so on.

There are different variants of expenses ratios. That is,

1. Cost of goods sold ratio $= \dfrac{\text{Cost of goods sold}}{\text{Net sales}} \times 100$ **(6.22)**

2. Operating expenses ratio $= \dfrac{\text{Adminsitrative expenses + Selling expenses}}{\text{Net sales}} \times 100$ **(6.23)**

3. Administrative expenses ratio $= \dfrac{\text{Adminsitrative expenses}}{\text{Net sales}} \times 100$ **(6.24)**

4. Selling expenses ratio $= \dfrac{\text{Selling expenses}}{\text{Net sales}} \times 100$ **(6.25)**

5. Operating ratio $= \dfrac{\text{Cost of goods sold + Operating expenses}}{\text{Net sales}} \times 100$ **(6.26)**

6. Financial expenses ratio $= \dfrac{\text{Financial expenses}}{\text{Net sales}} \times 100$ **(6.27)**

Interpretation

The expenses ratio is closely related to the profit margin, gross as well as net. For instance, if the operating profit margin is deducted from 100 per cent, the resultant is the operating ratio. Alternatively, when the operating ratio is subtracted from 100 per cent, we get the operating profit margin. If the sales and total non-financial expenses of a firm are ₹40,00,000 and ₹32,00,000 respectively, the *operating ratio* would be 80 per cent. It implies that total operating expenses including cost of goods sold consume 80 per cent of the sales revenues of the firm and 20 per cent is left for meeting interest, tax and dividends obligations as also retaining profits for future expansion. *The cost of goods sold ratio* shows what percentage share of sales is consumed by cost of goods sold and, conversely, what proportion is available for meeting expenses such as selling and general distribution expenses as well as financial expenses consisting of taxes, interest and dividends, and so on.

The expenses ratio is, therefore, very important for analysing the profitability of a firm. It should be compared over a period of time with the industry average as well as firms of similar type. As a working proposition, a low ratio is favourable, while a high one is unfavourable. The implication of a high expenses ratio is that only a relatively small percentage share of sales is available for meeting financial liabilities like interest, tax and dividends, and so on. An analysis of the factors responsible for a low ratio may reveal changes in the selling price or the operating expenses. It is likely that individual items may behave differently. While some operating expenses may show a rising trend, others may record a fall. The specific expenses ratio for each of the items of operating cost may be calculated. These ratios would identify the specific cause. To illustrate, an increase in selling expenses, may be due to a number of reasons: **(i)** general rise in selling expenses, **(ii)** inefficiency of the marketing department leading to uncontrolled promotional and other expenses, **(iii)** growing competition, **(iv)** ineffective advertising, **(v)** inefficient utilisation of resources, and the like.

A low operating ratio is by and large a test of operational efficiency. In case of firms whose major source of income and expenses are non-operating, the operating ratio, however, cannot be used as a yardstick of profitability.

To conclude, the profitability ratios based on sales are an important indicator of the operational efficiency of a manufacturing enterprise. However, they suffer from a serious limitation in that they are not useful from the viewpoint of the owners of the firm. Consider Example 6.6.

***Example* 6.6**

From the following information of a firm, determine **(i)** gross profit margin and **(ii)** net profit margin.

1. Sales	₹200 lakh
2. Cost of goods sold	100 lakh
3. Other operating expenses	50 lakh

Solution

(i) Gross profit margin $= \dfrac{(₹200 \text{ lakh} - ₹100 \text{ lakh} = ₹100 \text{ lakh})}{₹200 \text{ lakh}} = 50$ per cent

(ii) Net profit margin (before taxes) $= \dfrac{(₹100 \text{ lakh} - ₹50 \text{ lakh} = ₹50 \text{ lakh})}{₹200 \text{ lakh}} = 25$ per cent

The operating efficiency of the firm is fairly good. Assume, however, that the investments are ₹1,000 lakh. The return on investments works out to be 5 per cent only. From the owner's point of view, rate of return on investments is a better measure of testing the profitability of a firm.

Profitability Ratios Related to Investments

Return on investments (ROI) measures the overall effectiveness of management in generating profits with its available assets.

As already observed, the profitability ratios can also be computed by relating the profits of a firm to its investments. Such ratios are popularly termed as return on investments (ROI). There are three different concepts of investments in vogue in financial literature: assets, capital employed and shareholders' equity. Based on each of them, there are three broad categories of ROIs. They are **(i)** return on assets, **(ii)** return on capital employed and **(iii)** return on shareholders' equity.

Return on Assets (ROA) Here, the profitability ratio is measured in terms of the relationship between net profits and assets. The ROA may also be called profit-to-asset ratio. There are various possible approaches to define net profits and assets, according to the purpose and intent of the calculation of the ratio. Depending upon how these two terms are defined, many variations of ROA are possible.

The concept of net profit may be **(i)** net profits after taxes, **(ii)** net profits after taxes plus interest, and **(iii)** net profits after taxes plus interest minus tax savings.[17] Assets may be defined as **(i)** total assets, **(ii)** fixed assets, and **(iii)** tangible assets. Accordingly, the different variants of the RAO are:

1. $$\text{Return on assets (ROA)} = \frac{\text{Net profit after taxes}}{\text{Average total assets}} \times 100 \qquad \textbf{(6.28)}$$

The ROA based on this ratio would be an underestimate as the interest paid to the lenders is excluded from the net profits. In point of fact, the real return on the total assets is the net earnings available to owners (EAT) and interest to lenders as assets are financed by owners as well as creditors. A more reliable indicator of the true return on assets, therefore, is the net profits inclusive of interest. It reports the total return accruing to all providers of capital (debt and equity).

2. $$\text{ROA} = \frac{\text{Net profit after taxes + Interest}}{\text{Average total assets}} \times 100 \qquad \textbf{(6.29)}$$

3. $$\text{ROA} = \frac{\text{Net profit after taxes + Interest}}{\text{Average tangible assets}} \times 100 \qquad \textbf{(6.30)}$$

4. $$\text{ROA} = \frac{\text{Net profit after taxes + Interest}}{\text{Average fixed assets}} \times 100 \qquad \textbf{(6.31)}$$

These measures, however, may not provide correct results for inter-firm comparisons particularly when these firms have markedly varying *capital structures* as interest payment on debt qualifies for tax deduction in determining net taxable income. Therefore the effective cash outflows is less than the actual payment of interest by the amount of tax shield on interest payment. As a measure of *operating performance*, therefore, Equations 6.29 to 6.31 should be substituted by the following.

$$\text{ROA} = \frac{\text{EAT + (Interest − Tax advantage on interest) or After tax interest cost}}{\text{Average total assets/Tangible assets/Fixed assets}} \qquad \textbf{(6.32)}$$

This equation correctly reports the operating efficiency of firms as if they are all equity-financed.

The ROA measures the profitability of the total funds/ investments of a firm. It, however, throws no light on the profitability of the different sources of funds which finance the total assets. These aspects are covered by other ROIs.

Return on Capital Employed (ROCE) The ROCE is the second type of ROI. It is similar to the ROA except in one respect. Here the profits are related to the total capital employed. The term capital employed refers to long-term funds supplied by the lenders and owners of the firm. It can be computed in two ways. First, it is equal to non-current liabilities (long-term liabilities) plus owners' equity. Alternatively, it is equivalent to net working capital plus long-term assets. Second, it is equal to long-term funds minus investments made outside the firm. Thus, the capital employed basis provides a test of profitability related to the sources of long-term funds. A comparison of this ratio with similar firms, with the industry average and over time would provide sufficient insight into how efficiently the long-term funds of owners and lenders are being used. The higher the ratio, the more efficient is the use of capital employed.

The ROCE can be computed in different ways, using different concepts of profits and capital employed. Thus,

1. $$\text{ROCE} = \frac{\text{EBIT}}{\text{Average total capital employed}} \times 100 \quad \textbf{(6.33)}$$

2. $$\text{ROCE} = \frac{\text{Net profit after taxes + Interest – Tax advantage on interest}}{\text{Average total capital employed}} \times 100 \quad \textbf{(6.34)}$$

3. $$\text{ROCE} = \frac{\begin{array}{c}\text{Net profit after taxes + Interest – Tax advantage on interest –}\\ \text{(Interest and/or Dividends received – Taxes paid)}\end{array}}{\text{Average total capital employed – Investments (long-term) made}} \times 100 \quad \textbf{(6.35)}$$

Return on Shareholders' Equity This profitability ratio carries the relationship of return to the sources of funds yet another step further. While the ROCE expresses the profitability of a firm in relation to the funds supplied by the lenders and owners taken together, the return on shareholders' equity measures exclusively the return on the owners' funds.

> **Return on shareholders equity** measures the return on the owners (both preference and equity shareholders) investment in the firm.

The shareholders of a firm fall into two broad groups: preference shareholders and equity shareholders. The holders of preference shares enjoy a preference over equity shareholders in respect of receiving dividends. In other words, from the net profits available to the shareholders, the preference dividend is paid first and whatever remains belongs to the ordinary shareholders. The profitability ratios based on shareholders' equity are termed as *return on shareholders' equity*. There are several measures to calculate the return on shareholders equity: **(i)** Rate of return on **(a)** total shareholders' equity and **(b)** equity of ordinary shareholders; **(ii)** earnings per share; **(iii)** dividends per share; **(iv)** dividend–pay-out ratio; **(v)** dividend and earnings yield; and **(vi)** price-earnings ratio.

Return on Total Shareholders' Equity According to this ratio, profitability is measured by dividing the net profits after taxes (but before preference dividend) by the average total shareholders' equity. The term shareholders' equity includes **(i)** preference share capital; **(ii)** ordinary shareholders' equity consisting of **(a)** equity share capital, **(b)** share premium, and **(c)** reserves and surplus less accumulated losses. The ordinary shareholders' equity is also referred to as net worth. Thus,

$$\text{Return on total shareholders' equity} = \frac{\text{Net profit after taxes}}{\text{Average total shareholders' equity}} \times 100 \quad \textbf{(6.36)}$$

The ratio reveals how profitably the owners' funds have been utilised by the firm. A comparison of this ratio with that of similar firms as also with the industry average will throw light on the relative performance and strength of the firm.

Return on Ordinary Shareholders' Equity (Net Worth) While there is no doubt that the preference shareholders are also owners of a firm, the real owners are the ordinary shareholders who bear all the risk, participate in management and are entitled to all the profits remaining after all outside claims including preference dividends are met in full. The profitability of a firm from the owners' point of view should, therefore, in the fitness of things be assessed in terms of the return to the ordinary shareholders. The ratio under reference serves this purpose.

Return on ordinary shareholders' equity measures the return on the total equity funds of ordinary shareholders.

It is calculated by dividing the profits after taxes and preference dividend by the average equity of the ordinary shareholders.

Thus,

$$\text{Return on equity funds} = \frac{\text{Net profit after taxes} - \text{Preference dividend}}{\text{Average ordinary shareholders' equity or net worth}} \times 100 \quad \textbf{(6.37)}$$

This is probably the single most important ratio to judge whether the firm has earned a satisfactory return for its equity-holders or not. Its adequacy can be judged by **(i)** comparing it with the past record of the same firm, **(ii)** inter-firm comparison, and **(iii)** comparisons with the overall industry average. The rate of return on ordinary shareholders' equity is of crucial significance in ratio analysis vis-a-vis from the point of the owners of the firm.

Earnings Per Share (EPS) measures the profit available to the equity shareholders on a per share basis, that is, the amount that they can get on every share held. It is calculated by dividing the profits available to the equity shareholders by the number of the outstanding shares. The profits available to the ordinary shareholders are represented by net profits after taxes and preference dividend. Thus,

$$\text{EPS} = \frac{\text{Net profit available to equity-holders}}{\text{Number of ordinary shares outstanding}} \quad \textbf{(6.38)}$$

Earnings Per Share (EPS) is a widely used ratio. Yet, EPS as a measure of profitability of a firm from the owner's point of view, should be used cautiously as it does not recognise the effect of increase in equity capital as a result of retention of earnings. In other words, if EPS has increased over the years, it does not necessarily follow that the firm's profitability has improved because the increased profits to the owners may be the effect of an enlarged equity capital as a result of profit retentions, though the number of ordinary shares outstanding still remains constant. Another limitation of EPS is that it does not reveal how much is paid to the owners as dividend, nor how much of the earnings are retained in the business. It only shows how much earnings *theoretically* belong to the ordinary shareholders (per share basis).

As a profitability ratio, the EPS can be used to draw inferences on the basis of **(i)** its trends over a period of time, **(ii)** comparison with the EPS of other firms, and **(iii)** comparison with the industry average.

Cash Earnings Per Share is computed using cash flows from business operations as the numerator. This value is determined by adding non-cash expenses, such as depreciation and amortisation to net profits available to equity owners. Thus,

$$\text{Cash EPS} = \frac{\text{Net profit available to equity–owners + Depreciation + Amortisation + Non-cash expenses}}{\text{Number of equity shares outstanding}} \quad \textbf{(6.39)}$$

The ratio indicates the cash generating ability (per equity share) of the firm. Like EPS, cash EPS should be used with caution. It is beset with all the limitations associated with EPS measure.

Book Value Per Share represents the equity/claim of the equity shareholder on a per share basis. It is computed dividing net worth (equity share capital + reserves and surplus – accumulated losses) by the number of equity shares outstanding (at balance sheet date), as shown in Equation 6.40)

$$\text{Book value per share} = \frac{\text{Net worth}}{\text{Number of equity shares outstanding}} \quad \textbf{(6.40)}$$

This ratio is sometimes used as a benchmark for comparisons with the market price per share. However, the book value per share has a serious limitation as a valuation tool as it is based on the historical costs of the assets of a firm. There may be a significant difference between the market value of assets from the book value of assets (as per balance sheet). Besides, there may be hidden assets or other intangible assets of uncertain value.

Price-to-Book Value Ratio Also known as price to book (P/B) ratio, measures the relationship between the market price of an equity share (MPS) with book value (net worth) per share (BPS). Thus,

$$\text{P/B ratio} = \frac{\text{MPS}}{\text{BPS}} \quad \textbf{(6.41)}$$

The P/B ratio is significant in predicting future stock returns. For instance, Fama and French observed that the P/B ratio (along with size) was the best predictor of future stock returns[18]. Firms with low P/B ratios had consistently higher returns compared to the firms with high P/B ratios.

Dividend Per Share (DPS) is the dividends paid to the equity shareholders on a per share basis. In other words, DPS is the net distributed profit belonging to the ordinary shareholders divided by the number of ordinary shares outstanding. That is,

$$\text{DPS} = \frac{\text{Dividend paid to ordinary shareholders}}{\text{Number of ordinary shares outstanding}} \quad \textbf{(6.42)}$$

The DPS would be a better indicator than EPS as the former shows what exactly is received by the owners. Like the EPS, the DPS also should not be taken at its face value as the increased DPS may not be a reliable measure of profitability as the equity base may have increased due to increased retention without any change in the number of outstanding shares.

> **Dividend payout (D/P) ratio** measures the proportion of dividends paid to earning available to shareholders.

Dividend Pay-out (D/P) Ratio is also known as pay-out ratio. It measures the relationship between the earnings belonging to the ordinary shareholders and the dividend paid to them. In other words, the D/P ratio shows what percentage share of the net profits after taxes and preference dividend is paid out as dividend to the equity-holders. It can be calculated by dividing the total dividend paid to the owners by the total profits/earnings available to them. Alternatively, it can be found out by dividing the DPS by the EPS. Thus,

1. $$\text{D/P ratio} = \frac{\text{Total dividend (cash dividend) to equityholders}}{\text{Total net profit belonging to equityholders}} \times 100 \quad \textbf{(6.43)}$$

2. $$\text{D/P} = \frac{\text{Dividend per ordinary share (DPS)}}{\text{Earnings per share (EPS)}} \times 100 \quad \textbf{(6.44)}$$

If the D/P ratio is subtracted from 100, retention ratio is obtained. The ratio indicates what percentage share of the net profits are retained in the business. To illustrate, if the net earnings after taxes and preference dividends are ₹50 lakh and the dividend paid to the ordinary shareholders amount to ₹30 lakh, the D/P = 60 per cent. This implies that 40 per cent of the profits of the firm are retained (retention ratio) and 60 per cent distributed as dividends. Similarly, if the DPS is ₹2 and EPS ₹5, the D/P is 60 per cent. While 60 per cent profits are used to pay dividends, 40 per cent are ploughed back.

The D/P ratio is an important and widely-used ratio. The pay-out ratio can be compared with the trend over the years or an inter-firm and intra-industry comparison would throw light on its adequacy.

Earnings and Dividend Yield is closely related to the EPS and DPS. While the EPS and DPS are based on the book value per share, the yield is expressed in terms of the market value per share. The earnings yield may be defined as the ratio of earnings per share to the market value per ordinary share. Similarly, the dividend yield is computed by dividing the cash dividends per share by the market value per share. That is,

1. Earnings yield $= \dfrac{\text{EPS}}{\text{Market value per share}} \times 100$ **(6.45)**

2. Dividend yield $= \dfrac{\text{DPS}}{\text{Market value per share}} \times 100$ **(6.46)**

The earnings yield is also called the earning-price ratio.

Price/Earnings (P/E) ratio measures the amount investors are willing to pay for each rupee of earnings; the higher the ratio, the larger the investors confidence in the firm's future.

Price Earnings (P/E) Ratio is closely related to the earnings yield/earnings price ratio. It is actually the reciprocal of the latter. This ratio is computed dividing the market price of the shares by the EPS. Thus,

$$P/E \text{ ratio} = \frac{\text{Market price of share}}{\text{EPS}} \quad \textbf{(6.47)}$$

The *P/E* ratio reflects the price currently being paid by the market for each rupee of currently reported EPS. In other words, the P/E ratio measures investors' expectations and the market appraisal of the performance of a firm. In estimating the earnings, therefore, only normally sustainable earnings associated with the assets are taken into account. That is, the earnings are adjusted for income from, say, discontinued operations and extraordinary items as well as many other items not expected to occur. This ratio is popularly used by security analysts to assess a firm's performance as expected by the investors.

LO 6.5 ACTIVITY/EFFICIENCY RATIOS

Activity ratios are concerned with measuring the efficiency in asset management. These ratios are also called **efficiency ratios** or **assets utilisation ratios.** The efficiency with which the assets are used would be reflected in the speed and rapidity with which assets are converted into sales. The greater is the rate of turnover or conversion, the more efficient is the utilisation of assets, other things being equal. For this reason, such ratios are also designated as turnover ratios. Turnover is the primary mode for measuring the extent of efficient employment of assets by relating the assets to sales. An activity ratio may, therefore, be defined as a test of the relationship between sales (more appropriately with cost of sales) and the various assets of a firm. Depending upon the various types of assets, there are various types of activity ratios.

Activity ratios measure the speed with which various accounts/assets are converted into sales or cash.

Inventory (or Stock) Turnover Ratio

This ratio indicates the number of times inventory is replaced during the year. It measures the relationship between the cost of goods sold and the inventory level. The ratio can be computed in two ways.

Inventory (stock) turnover measures the activity/liquidity of inventory of a firm; the speed with which inventory is sold.

First, it is calculated dividing the cost of goods sold by the average inventory. Symbolically,

$$\text{Inventory turnover} = \frac{\text{Cost of goods sold}}{\text{Average inventory}} \quad \textbf{(6.48)}$$

The average inventory figure may be of two types. In the first place, it may be the monthly inventory (stock) average. The monthly average can be found by adding the opening inventory of each month from, in case of the accounting year being a calendar year, January through January and dividing the total by thirteen. If the firm's accounting year is other than a calendar year, say a financial year, (April to March), the average level of inventory can be computed by adding the opening inventory of each month from April through April and dividing the total by thirteen.[19] This approach has the advantage of being free from bias as it smoothens out the fluctuations in inventory level at different periods. This is particularly true of firms in seasonal industries. However, a serious limitation of this approach is that detailed month-wise information may present practical problems of collection for the analyst. Therefore, average inventory may be obtained by using another basis, namely, the average of the opening inventory and the closing inventory.

Not only are there difficulties in getting detailed information regarding inventory level, but data may also not be readily available to an analyst in respect of the cost of goods sold. To solve the problem arising out of non-availability of the required data, the second approach to the computation of inventory turnover ratio is based on the relationship between sales and closing inventory. Thus, alternatively,

$$\text{Inventory turnover} = \frac{\text{Sales}}{\text{Closing inventory}} \quad \textbf{(6.49)}$$

In theory, this approach is not a satisfactory basis as it is not logical. For one thing, the numerator (sales) and the denominator (inventory) are not strictly comparable as the former is expressed in terms of market price, the latter is based on cost. Secondly, the closing inventory figures are likely to be underestimates as firms traditionally have lower inventory at the end of the year. The net effect will be that the ratio given by this approach will be higher than the one given by the first approach. Thus the ratio has built-in bias to show better utilisation of inventory.

In brief, of the two approaches to calculating the inventory turnover ratio, the first which relates the cost of goods sold to the average inventory is theoretically superior as it is logically consistent. The merit of the second approach is that it is free from practical problems of computation.

Interpretation The inventory/stock turnover ratio measures how quickly inventory is sold. It is a test of efficient inventory management. To judge whether the ratio of a firm is satisfactory or not, it should be compared over a period of time on the basis of trend analysis. It can also be compared with the level of other firms in that line of business as well as with industry average.

In general, a high inventory turnover ratio is better than a low ratio. A high ratio implies good inventory management. Yet,a very high ratio calls for a careful analysis. It may be indicative of underinvestment in, or very low level of, inventory. A very low level of inventory has serious implications. It will adversely affect the ability to meet customer demand as it may not cope with its requirements. That is, there is a danger of the firm being out of stock and incurring high 'stock out cost'. It is also likely that the firm may be following a policy of replenishing its stock in too many small sizes. Apart from being costly, this policy may retard the production process as sufficient stock of materials may not be available.

Similarly, a very low inventory turnover ratio is dangerous. It signifies excessive inventory or overinvestment in inventory. Carrying excessive inventory involves cost in terms of interest on funds locked up, rental of space, possible deterioration and so on. A low ratio may be the result of inferior quality goods, overvaluation of closing inventory, stock of unsaleable/obsolete goods and deliberate excessive purchases in anticipation of future increase in their prices and so on.

Thus, a firm should have neither too high nor too low inventory turnover. To avoid both 'stock out costs' associated with a high ratio and the costs of carrying excessive inventory with a low ratio, what is suggested is a reasonable level of this ratio. The firm would be well advised to maintain a close watch on the trend of the ratio and significant deviations on either side should be thoroughly investigated to locate the factors responsible for it. The computation of the turnover for the individual components of the inventory may be useful in this context. Such ratios can be computed in respect of raw materials and work-in-progress. Thus,

$$\text{Raw materials turnover} = \frac{\text{Cost of raw materials used}}{\text{Average raw material inventory}} \quad \textbf{(6.50)}$$

$$\text{Work-in-progress turnover} = \frac{\text{Cost of goods manufactured}}{\text{Average work-in-progress inventory}} \quad \textbf{(6.51)}$$

Receivables (Debtors) Turnover Ratio and Average Collection Period

Average collection period is the average amount of time needed to collect accounts receivable.

The second major activity ratio is the **receivables or debtors turnover ratio**. Allied and closely related to this is the average collection period. It shows how quickly receivables or debtors are converted into cash. In other words, the debtors turnover ratio is a test of the liquidity of the debtors of a firm.

The liquidity of a firm's receivables can be examined in two ways: **(i)** debtors/receivables turnover; **(ii)** average collection period.

The debtors turnover shows the relationship between credit sales and debtors of a firm. It can be calculated in two ways:

1. $$\text{Debtor turnover} = \frac{\text{Credit sales}}{\text{Average debtors + Average bills receivable (B/R)}} \quad \textbf{(6.52)}$$

This approach requires two types of data. First, credit sales, which may not be readily available to the analyst. Similarly, the computation of the figure of average debtors and bills receivable involves practical difficulties. In theory, these figures should be measured, as in the case of average inventory, on the basis of the monthly average. Since this type of information is not likely to be available to the analyst, the alternative is to use the average of the opening and closing balances of debtors and bills receivable.

To avoid the difficulty arising out of the non-availability of information in respect of credit sales and average debtors and bills receivable, the alternative method is to calculate the debtors turnover in terms of the relationship between total sales and closing balance of debtors. Thus,

2. $$\text{Debtors turnover}^{20} = \frac{\text{Total sales}}{\text{Debtors + Bills receivable}} \quad \textbf{(6.53)}$$

The first approach to the computation of the debtors turnover is superior in that the question of the speed of conversion of sales into cash arises only in the case of credit sales. The effect of adopting the second approach would be to inflate the receivables turnover ratio and deflate the collection period.

The second type of ratio for measuring the liquidity of a firm's debtors is the average collection period. This is, in fact, interrelated with, and dependent upon, the receivables turnover ratio. It is calculated dividing the days in a year by the debtors turnover. Thus,

$$\text{Average collection period} = \frac{\text{Months (days) in a year}}{\text{Debtors turnover}} \tag{6.54}$$

$$\text{Alternatively} = \frac{\text{Months (days) in a year } (\times) \text{ (Average Debtors + Average B/R)}}{\text{Total credit sales}} \tag{6.55}$$

***Example* 6.7**

The credit sales of a firm in a year amount to ₹120 lakh. The outstanding amount of debtors at the beginning and end of the year were ₹14 lakh and ₹16 lakh respectively. Determine the debtor turnover ratio and the average collection period.

Solution

1. Debtor turnover ratio $= \dfrac{₹120 \text{ lakh}}{(₹14 \text{ lakh} + ₹16 \text{ lakh})/2} = 8$ (times per year)

2. (i) Average debt collection period $= \dfrac{12 \text{ months}}{8} = 1.5$ months

(ii) (12 months × ₹15 lakh)/₹120 lakh = 1.5 months.

We can get the debtor turnover dividing the months (days) in the year by the average collection period (i.e. 12 ÷ 1.5 = 8). Likewise, if we divide the months (days) in the year by the debtor turnover ratio, we get the average collection period (12 ÷ 8 = 1.5).

Interpretation This ratio indicates the speed with which debtors/accounts receivable are being collected. A turnover ratio of 8 signifies that debtors get converted into cash 8 times in a year. The collection period of 1.5 months or 45 days implies that debtors on an average are collected in 45 days. Thus, it is indicative of the efficiency of trade credit management. The higher the turnover ratio and the shorter the average collection period, the better is the trade credit management and the better is the liquidity of debtors, as short collection period and high turnover ratio imply prompt payment on the part of debtors. On the other hand, low turnover ratio and long collection period reflect delayed payments by debtors. In general, therefore, short collection period (high turnover ratio) is preferable.

It is not, however, very prudent for a firm to have either a very short collection period or a very long one. A very long collection period would imply either poor credit selection or an inadequate collection effort. The delay in the collection of receivables would mean that, apart from the interest cost involved in maintaining a higher level of debtors, the liquidity position of the firm would be adversely affected. Moreover, there is the likelihood of a large number of accounts receivable becoming bad debts. Similarly, too short a period of average collection or too high a turnover ratio is not necessarily good. While it is true that it avoids the risk of receivables being bad debt as well as the burden of high interest on outstanding debtors, it may have an adverse effect on the volume of sales of the firm. Sales may be confined to only such customers as make prompt payments. The credit and collection policy of the firm may be very restrictive. Without reasonable credit, sales will be severely curtailed. Thus, a firm should have neither a very low nor a very high receivables turnover ratio; it should maintain it at a reasonable level. The reasonableness of the collection period can be judged in either of the following two ways.

First, the collection period of a firm can be compared with the industry practices of trade credit. Any notable deviation may result from **(i)** a more or less liberal policy of extending trade credit, or **(ii)** better/poor quality of receivables. A liberal trade credit policy may be aimed at augmenting sales.

Second, it may be more appropriately examined in relation to the credit terms and policy of the firm itself. In our example, the average collection period is 45 days or 1.5 months. This should be compared with the credit terms/period normally allowed by the firm. If the normal credit period, let us assume, as extended by the firm is 40-45 days, it means the firm is able to collect its receivables well within the due dates. If, however, the credit period normally allowed is 1 month or 30 days, it means that the debtors are outstanding for a period longer than warranted by the firm's credit policy. This may be a reflection on the efficiency of the credit collection department: it has made either poor credit selection or inadequate collection effort. The management should investigate the reasons for the difficulties in the collection of receivables.

Ageing schedule enables analysts to identify slow paying debtors.

A related aspect of the average collection period is the **ageing schedule**. While the former is concerned with the liquidity of debtors/receivables as a whole, the latter analyses them in a disaggregative manner by dividing the outstanding debtors on the basis of the duration during which they have been outstanding. The usefulness of the ageing schedule lies in the fact that it enables the analyst to identify the slow paying debtors in respect of whom the firm may have to encounter a serious collection problem. A hypothetical ageing schedule for the firm of our example, with an average collection period of 1.5 months is given in Table 6.7.

TABLE 6.7 Ageing Schedule

Outstanding period of debtors (1)	*Amount outstanding* (2)	*Percentage of total* (3)
Up to 30 days (1 month)	₹2,00,000	12.5
31-45 days (1.5 months)	4,00,000	25.0
46-60 days (2 months)	8,00,000	50.0
Above 60 days (more than two months)	2,00,000	12.5
	16,00,000	100

It can be seen from Table 6.7 that more than 60 per cent of the receivables are overdue as they remain outstanding beyond the average collection period of 45 days. Moreover, more than one-tenth of the outstanding debtors remain uncollected for more than 60 days. The ageing schedule, thus, supplements the collection period by showing how long the debtors are outstanding.

Assets turnover indicates the efficiency with which firm uses all its assets to generate sales.

Assets Turnover Ratio

This ratio is also known as the investment turnover ratio. It is based on the relationship between the cost of goods sold[21] and assets/investments of a firm. A reference to this was made while working out the overall profitability of a firm as reflected in its earning power. Depending upon the different concepts of assets employed, there are many variants of this ratio.

Thus,

1. Total assets turnover $= \dfrac{\text{Cost of goods sold}}{\text{Average total assets}}$ **(6.56)**

2. Fixed assets turnover $= \dfrac{\text{Cost of goods sold}}{\text{Average fixed assets}}$ **(6.57)**

3. $\text{Capital turnover} = \dfrac{\text{Cost of goods sold}}{\text{Average capital employed}}$ **(6.58)**

4. $\text{Current assets turnover} = \dfrac{\text{Cost of goods sold}}{\text{Average current assets}}$ **(6.59)**

5. $\text{Working capital turnover ratio} = \dfrac{\text{Cost of goods sold}}{\text{Net working capital}}$ **(6.60)**

Here, the total assets and fixed assets are net of depreciation and the assets are exclusive of fictitious assets like debit balance of profit and loss account and deferred expenditures and so on.

The assets turnover ratio, howsoever defined, measures the efficiency of a firm in managing and utilising its assets. The higher the turnover ratio, the more efficient is the management and utilisation of the assets while low turnover ratios are indicative of underutilisation of available resources and presence of idle capacity. In operational terms, it implies that the firm can expand its activity level (in terms of production and sales) without requiring additional capital investments. In the case of high ratios, the firm would normally be required, other things being equal, to make additional capital investments to operate at higher level of activity. To determine the efficiency of the ratio, it should be compared across time as well as with the industry average. In using the assets turnover ratios one point must be carefully kept in mind. The concept of assets/fixed assets is net of depreciation. As a result, the ratio is likely to be higher in the case of an old and established company as compared to a new one, other things being equal. The turnover ratio is in such cases likely to give a misleading impression regarding the relative efficiency with which assets are being used. It should, therefore, be cautiously used.

LO 6.6 INTEGRATED ANALYSIS OF RATIOS

The ratios discussed so far measure a firm's liquidity, solvency, efficiency of operations and profitability independent of one another. However, there exists interrelationship among these ratios. This aspect is brought out by integrated analysis of ratios. The disaggregation of ratios can reveal certain major economic and financial aspects, which otherwise would have been ignored. For instance, significant changes in profitability measured in terms of return on assets (ROA) and return on equity (ROE) are understood better through an analysis of its components.

The various profitability ratios discussed earlier throw light on the profitability of a firm from the viewpoint of **(i)** the owners of the firm, and **(ii)** the operating efficiency of the firm. The ratios covered under the rate of return to the equity-holders fall under the first category. The operating efficiency of a firm in terms of the efficient utilisation of the resources is reflected in net profit margin. It has been observed that although a high profit margin is a test of better performance, a low margin does not necessarily imply a lower rate of return on investments if a firm has higher investments/assets turnover. Therefore, the overall operating efficiency of a firm can be assessed on the basis of a combination of the two. The combined profitability is referred to as earning power/return on assets (ROA) ratio. The **earning power** of a firm may be defined as the overall profitability of an enterprise. This ratio has two elements: **(i)** profitability on sales as reflected in the net profit margin, and **(ii)** profitability of assets which is revealed by the assets/investment turnover. The earning power (ROA ratio) of a firm can be computed by multiplying the net profit margin and the assets turnover. Thus,

> **Earning power** is the overall profitability of a firm; is computed by multiplying net profit margin and assets turnover.

$$\text{Earning power} = \text{Net profit margin} \times \text{Assets turnover} \quad \textbf{(6.61)}$$

where, Net profit margin = Earning after taxes/Sales

Asset turnover = Sales/Total assets

$$\text{Earning power} = \frac{\text{Earnings after taxes}}{\text{Sales}} \times \frac{\text{Sales}}{\text{Total assets}} = \frac{\text{EAT}}{\text{Total assets}} \quad \textbf{(6.62)}$$

The basic elements of the earning power of a firm are portrayed in Figure 6.1. This chart is known as the Du Pont Chart.

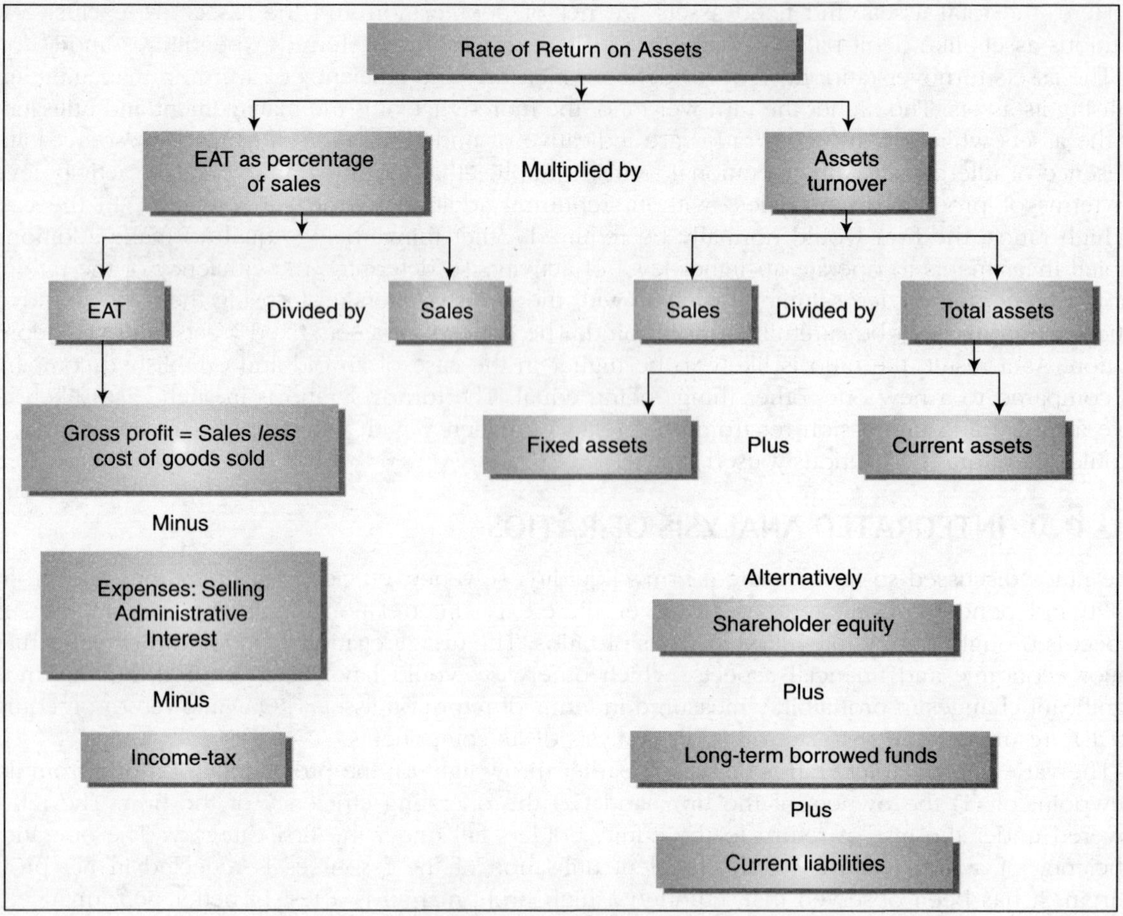

FIGURE 6.1 Du Pont Chart

The ROA ratio is a central measure of the overall profitability and operational efficiency of a firm. It shows the interaction of profitability and activity ratios. It implies that the performance of a firm can be improved either by generating more sales volume per rupee of investment or by increasing the profit margin per rupee of sales. Consider Example 6.8.

***Example* 6.8**

Assume that there are two firms, A and B, each having total assets amounting to ₹4,00,000, and average net profits after taxes of 10 per cent, that is, ₹40,000, each. Firm A has sales of ₹4,00,000, whereas the sales of firm B aggregate ₹40,00,000. Determine the ROA of firms A and B.

Table 6.8 shows the ROA based on two components.

Solution

TABLE 6.8 Return on Assets (ROA) of Firms A and B

Particulars	*Firm A*	*Firm B*
1. Net sales	₹4,00,000	₹40,00,000
2. Net profit	40,000	40,000
3. Total assets	4,00,000	4,00,000
4. Profit margin (2 ÷ 1) (per cent)	10	1
5. Assets turnover (1 ÷ 3) (times)	1	10
6. ROA ratio (4 × 5) (per cent)	10	10

Thus, the ROA of firms A and B is identical. While firm A has higher profit margin, B firm has higher assets turnover. Thus, the earning power is affected by two variables, namely, profit margin and assets turnover. Assets turnover ratio can further be segregated into inventory turnover, debtors turnover and fixed assets turnover ratios. Likewise, profit margin can be decomposed into gross profit, operating profit, profit before taxes and so on.

The usefulness of the integrated analysis lies in the fact that it presents the overall picture of the performance of a firm as also enables the management to identify the factors which have a bearing on profitability. In Example 6.8, if firm B could improve its profit margin even marginally, say, from 1 per cent to 2 per cent, its earning power (ROA) will be doubled, assuming sales are not affected. Similarly, firm A can double its earning power simply by a marginal increase in its investment turnover, as it indicates that the assets are used more efficiently, that is, more sales per rupee of investments. The two components of this ratio, namely, the profit margin and the investment turnover ratio, individually do not give an overall view as the former ignores the profitability of investments, while the latter fails to consider the profitability on sales.

The profitability analysis based on ROA can be extended further for a detailed examination of the return on equity (ROE). It is the most important measure of financial performance from the point of view of equityholders. The ROE can be decomposed into three following principal components:

$$\frac{\text{Earnings after taxes, EAT}}{\text{Sales}} \times \frac{\text{Sales}}{\text{Assets}} \times \frac{\text{Assets}}{\text{Equity}} \qquad \textbf{(6.63)}$$

The three components in the ROE are indicative of net profit margin (profitability), assets turnover (efficiency in operations) and financial leverage (indicating the extent to which assets are financed by owners funds). Thus, the ROE is the product of the following three ratios:

$$\text{Net profit ratio } (\times) \text{ Assets turnover } (\times) \text{ Financial leverage/Equity multiplier} \qquad \textbf{(6.64)}$$

The equation indicates that the management of the firm has three levers through which it can control ROE: **(i)** the net profit margin per rupee of sales, **(ii)** the sales generated per rupee of assets employed and **(iii)** the amount of equity used to finance the assets. While profit margin summarises profit performance as reflected in the income statement of a firm, assets turnover and financial leverage measure its performance with respect to assets and liabilities side of its balance sheet respectively. Thus, these three levers capture the major elements of financial performance of a firm.[22]

Suppose in Example 6.7, Firm A uses equity capital of ₹2 lakh and B of ₹2.5 lakh in fin-ancing total assets of ₹4 lakh. The financial leverage of A is 2 (₹4 lakh assets/₹2 lakh equity) and of B is 1.6 (₹4 lakh/₹2.5 lakh). The ROE for A and B can be computed using Equation 6.65.

$$\text{Net profit ratio} \times \text{Assets turnover} \times \text{Financial leverage} \qquad \textbf{(6.65)}$$

$$10\% \times 1 \times 2 = 20\% \text{ (A)}$$

$$1\% \times 10 \times 1.6 = 16\% \text{ (B)}$$

Though the ROA for both firms is the same (10%), A has higher ROE (20%) than B (16%). The higher ROE of A primarily can be attributed to its higher financial leverage. The management of B can explore the possibility of increasing its financial leverage and thereby enhance the ROE of its equity owners. It will be profitable for B to employ more debt if the ROA is higher than the cost of debt. The relationship between ROA and ROE may be expressed as per Equation 6.66.

$$\text{ROE} = (\text{ROA} - \text{Interest cost} \div \text{Assets}) \times \text{Assets} \div \text{equity} \qquad \textbf{(6.66)}$$

The three-component model of ROE (Equation 6.65) can be broadened further to consider the effect of interest and tax payments. The net profit ratio is to be disaggregated in the following three elements (the assets turnover and financial leverage ratios remaining unchanged).

$$\frac{\text{EAT}}{\text{Earnings before taxes (EBT)}} \times \frac{\text{EBT}}{\text{EBIT}} \times \frac{\text{EBIT}}{\text{Sales}} = \frac{\text{Net profit}}{\text{Sales}} \qquad \textbf{(6.67)}$$

As a result of three sub-parts of net profit ratio, the ROE is composed of the following 5 components.

$$\frac{\text{EAT}}{\text{EBT}} \times \frac{\text{EBT}}{\text{EBIT}} \times \frac{\text{EBIT}}{\text{Sales}} \times \frac{\text{Sales}}{\text{Assets}} \times \frac{\text{Assets}}{\text{Equity}} \qquad \textbf{(6.68)}$$

A 5-way break-up of ROE enables the management of a firm to analyse the effect of interest payments and tax payments separately from operating profitability.[23] To illustrate further assume 8 per cent interest rate, 35 per cent tax rate and other operating expense of ₹3,22,462 (Firm A) and ₹39,26,462 (Firm B) for the facts contained in Example 6.8. Table 6.9 shows the ROE (based on the 5 components) of Firms A and B.

TABLE 6.9 ROE (Five-way Basis) of Firms A and B

Particulars	*Firm A*	*Firm B*
Net sales	₹4,00,000	₹40,00,000
Less: Operating expenses	3,22,462	39,26,462
Earnings before interest and taxes (EBIT)	77,538	73,538
Less: Interest (8%)	16,000	12,000
Earnings before taxes (EBT)	61,538	61,538
Less: Taxes (35%)	21,538	21,538
Earnings after taxes (EAT)	40,000	40,000
Total assets	4,00,000	4,00,000
Debt	2,00,000	2,50,000
Equity	2,00,000	1,50,000
EAT/EBT (times)	0.65	0.65
EBT/EBIT (times)	0.79	0.84
EBIT/Sales (per cent)	19.4	1.84
Sales/Assets (times)	1	10
Assets/Equity (times)	2	1.6
ROE (per cent)	20	16

Table 6.9 shows that there is little impact of taxes and interest payment on the difference in the ROE of the two firms (as reflected in the EAT/EBT as well as EBT/EBIT ratios). The financial leverage ratio, as pointed out earlier, is a major explanatory factor for higher ROE of Firm A *vis-à-vis* Firm B.

ANNEXURE 6.I

Checklist of Financial Ratios of Reliance Industries Limited (For the Year 2012) (Amount is in ₹ Crore)

1. Liquidity Ratios

$$\text{Current Ratio} = \frac{\text{Current assets}}{\text{Current liabilities}} = \frac{₹1,28,175}{₹68,888} = 1.86:1$$

Total current assets = Cash and bank + Inventories + Trade receivables + Other current assets + Loans and advances (Note 16) + Current investments

= ₹39,598 + ₹35,955 + ₹18,424 + ₹249 + (11,089 – 4,169[@]) ₹6920 + ₹27,029

= ₹1,28,175

@ Not usually available to pay current liabilities.

Total current liabilities = Short-term borrowings + Trade payables + Short-term provisions + Other current liabilities

= ₹10,593 + ₹40,324 + ₹13,713 + ₹4,258 = ₹68,888

2. $$\text{Acid-test ratio} = \frac{\text{Liquid assets}}{\text{Current liabilities}} = \frac{₹85,300}{₹68,888} = 1.24:1$$

Liquid assets = Total current assets – Inventories –Advances

= ₹1,28,175 – ₹35,955 – ₹6,920 = ₹85,300

3. (a) $$\text{Inventory turnover ratio (Finished goods)} = \frac{\text{Cost of goods sold}}{\text{Average finished goods inventory}}$$

$$= \frac{₹2,97,023}{₹7,660} = 38.78 \text{ times}$$

Average finished goods inventory = (₹7,944 + ₹7,376)/2 = ₹7,660

(b) Inventory holding period = 365 Days/38.78 = 9.41 days

Cost of goods sold* = Opening stock of finished goods + Production cost – Closing stock of finished goods

= ₹7,376 + ₹2,97,591 – ₹7,944 = ₹2,97,023

Production cost = Opening stock in process + Raw materials consumed + Cash manufacturing expenses + Depreciation and amortisation (on net basis) + Other purchases (as per P/L Account) – Closing stock-in-process

= ₹4,909 + ₹2,74,814 + ₹10,307 + ₹11,394 + ₹1,441 – ₹5,274

= ₹2,97,591

*Source: Notes 13 and 25.

4. (a) Debtors turnover ratio (assuming all sales on credit basis)

$$= \frac{\text{Net credit sales}}{\text{Average debtors}} = \frac{₹3,39,792}{₹17,933} = 18.95 \text{ times}$$

(b) Debtors collection period = 365 Days/18.95 = 19.26 Days

Average debtors = (₹17,442 + ₹18,424)/2 = ₹17,933

(Ratio is based on gross turnover as the amount of taxes is also to be received)

5. (a) Creditors turnover ratio (assuming all purchases on credit basis)

$$= \frac{\text{Total credit purchases}^{@}}{\text{Average creditors}} = \frac{₹2{,}81{,}029}{₹37{,}584} = 7.47 \text{ times}$$

(b) Creditors payment period = 365 Days/7.47 = 48.86 Days

*Total credit purchases = Purchase of raw materials + Other purchases
= ₹2,79,588 + ₹1,441 = 2,81,029

Purchases of raw materials = Raw materials consumed + Closing stock of raw materials – Opening stock of raw materials
= ₹2,74,814 + ₹19,350 – ₹14,576 = ₹2,79,588

Average creditors = (₹34,844 + ₹40,324)/2 = 37,584

6. Cash flow from operations ratio* $= \frac{\text{Cash flow from operations}}{\text{Current liabilities}} = \frac{₹26{,}974}{₹68{,}888} = 0.39 : 1$

*(Source: Cash flow statement of Reliance Industries Ltd.)

II. Solvency Ratios

7. (a) Long-term debt to equity ratio $= \frac{\text{Long-term debt}}{\text{Shareholders' equity}} = \frac{₹60{,}156}{₹1{,}66{,}096} = 0.36 : 1$

Long-term debt = Long-term borrowings + Deferred tax liability (net)
= ₹48,034 + ₹12,122 = 60,156

(b) Total external obligations to equity ratio $= \frac{\text{Total external obligations}}{\text{Shareholders' equity}} = \frac{₹1{,}29{,}044}{₹1{,}66{,}096} = 0.78 : 1$

Total external obligations= Long-term borrowings + Short-term borrowings + Trade payables + Other current liabilities + Short-term provisions + Deferred tax liability (net)
= ₹48,034 + ₹10,593 + ₹40,324 + ₹13,713 + ₹4,258 + ₹12,122 = ₹1,29,044

(c) Total debt to equity Ratio $= \frac{\text{Total debt}}{\text{Shareholders' equity}} = \frac{₹70{,}749}{₹1{,}66{,}096} = 0.43 : 1$

(Gross D/E ratio)

Total debt= Long-term borrowings + Short-term borrowings + Deferred tax liability (net)
= ₹70,749

8. Total debt to assets ratio $= \frac{\text{Total debt}}{\text{Total assets}} = \frac{₹70{,}749}{₹2{,}95{,}140} = 0.24 : 1$

9. Long-term debt to assets ratio $= \frac{\text{Long-term debt}}{\text{Total assets}} = \frac{₹60{,}156}{₹2{,}95{,}140} = 0.20 : 1$

10. Total external obligations to assets ratio $= \frac{\text{Total external obligations}}{\text{Total assets}} = \frac{₹1{,}29.044}{₹2{,}95{,}140} = 0.44 : 1$

11. Proprietory ratio $= \frac{\text{Proprietor's funds/Shareholder's funds}}{\text{Total assets}} = \frac{₹1{,}66{,}096}{₹2{,}95{,}140} = 0.56 : 1$

12. Interest coverage ratio $= \frac{\text{EBIT}}{\text{Interest}} = \frac{₹27{,}716}{₹1{,}966} = 14.09 \text{ times}$

EBIT = EBT + Interest = ₹25,750 + ₹1,966 (see note 23) = ₹27,716

13. Total fixed charge coverage ratio = $\frac{\text{EBIT}}{\text{Finance Costs}} = \frac{₹27,716}{₹2,667}$ = 10.39 times

14. Total cash flow coverage ratio = $\frac{\text{EBIT + Depreciation and amortisation}}{\text{Interest}}$

$$= \frac{₹27,716 + ₹11,394}{₹1,966} = 19.89 \text{ times}$$

III. Profitability Ratios

15. Gross profit margin = $\frac{\text{Gross profit} \times 100}{\text{Net sales}} = \frac{₹32,881}{₹3,29,904} \times 100 = 9.97\%$

Gross profit = Revenue from operations – Cost of goods sold
= ₹3,29,904 – ₹2,97,023 = ₹32,881

16. Operating profit ratio = $\frac{\text{EBIT} - \text{Other incomes}}{\text{Net sales}} \times 100 = \frac{₹27,716 - ₹6,192}{₹3,29,904} \times 100 = 6.52\%$

17. Pre-tax profit ratio = $\frac{\text{EBT}}{\text{Net sales}} \times 100 = \frac{₹25,750}{₹3,29,904} \times 100 = 7.8\%$

18. Net profit ratio = $\frac{\text{EAT}}{\text{Net sales}} \times 100 = \frac{₹20,040}{₹3,29,904} \times 100 = 6.07\%$

19. Cost of goods sold ratio = $\frac{\text{Cost of goods sold}}{\text{Net sales}} \times 100 = \frac{₹2,97,023}{₹3,29,904} \times 100 = 90.03\%$

20. Operating expenses ratio = $\frac{\text{Operating expenses}}{\text{Net sales}} \times 100 = \frac{₹10,595}{₹3,29,904} \times 100 = 3.21\%$

Operating expenses = Employee benefit expenses + Selling and distribution expenses + Establishment expenses
= ₹2,862 + ₹5,393 + ₹2,340 = ₹10,595

21. Administrative expenses ratio = $\frac{\text{Administrative expenses}}{\text{Net sales}} \times 100$

$$= \frac{₹5,202}{₹3,29,904} \times 100 = 1.58\%$$

Administrative expenses = Employees benefits expenses + Establishment expenses
= ₹2,862 + ₹2,340 = ₹5,202

22. Selling expenses ratio = $\frac{\text{Selling expenses}}{\text{Net sales}} \times 100 = \frac{₹5,393}{₹3,29,904} \times 100 = 1.63\%$

23. Operating ratio= $\frac{\text{Cost of goods sold + Operating expenses}}{\text{Net sales}} \times 100$

$$= \frac{₹2,97,023 + ₹10,595}{₹3,29,904} = 93.24\%$$

24. (a) Return on assets (ROA) = $\frac{\text{Net profit after taxes}}{\text{Average total assets}} \times 100 = \frac{₹20,040}{₹2,89,930} \times 100 = 6.9\%$

Average total assets = (2,95,140 + ₹2,84,719)/2 = ₹2,89,930

(b) ROA = $\frac{\text{Net profit after taxes + Interest}}{\text{Average total assets}} \times 100 = \frac{₹20,040 + ₹1,966}{₹2,89,930} \times 100 = 7.6\%$

(c) ROA = $\frac{\text{EAT + Interest – Tax advantage on interest}}{\text{Average total assets}} \times 100$

$= \frac{₹20,040 + ₹1,966 - (₹1,966 \times 0.339)}{₹2,89,930} \times 100$

$= \frac{₹21,353.29}{₹3,89,930} \times 100 = 7.36\%$

Corporate Tax Rate = 30% + 7.5% (Surcharge) + 3% (Education cess on taxes payable)
= 33.2%

25. (a) ROCE = $\frac{\text{EBIT – Other income}}{\text{Average long-term (fixed) assets used + Net working capital}}$

(Excluding capital work-in-progress as it does not contribute to operating income)

$= \frac{₹27,716 - ₹6,192}{₹1,28,219 + ₹59,287} \times 100 = 11.48\%$

Average long-term asset used = (₹1,13,723 + ₹1,42,707)/2 = ₹1,28,219
Net working capital = Current assets – Current liabilities
= ₹1,28,175 – ₹68,888 = ₹59,287

(b) ROCE = $\frac{\text{Net profit after tax + Interest – Tax advantage on interest – (other income attributed primarily from interest/dividends received from investments made outside-taxes paid)}}{\text{Average long-term assets used + Net working capital}} \times 100$

$= \frac{₹20,040 + ₹1,966 - ₹652.71 - (₹6,192 - ₹6,192 \times 0.332)}{₹1,87,506} \times 100 = 9.18\%$

26. Return on total shareholders' equity = $\frac{\text{Net profit after taxes}}{\text{Average shareholders' equity}} \times 100$

$= \frac{₹20,040}{₹1,58.818} \times 100 = 12.62\%$

Average shareholders' equity (₹1,66,096 + ₹1,51,540)/2 = ₹1,58.818

27. Return on equity funds = $\frac{\text{Net profit after taxes – Preference dividend*}}{\text{Average ordinary shareholders' equity}}$

*(Preference dividend is zero in this case)

$= \frac{₹20,040}{₹1,58,818} \times 100 = 12.62\%$

28. Earnings Per Share (EPS) = $\frac{\text{Net profit available to equity holders}}{\text{Number of ordinary shares outstanding}} = \frac{₹20,040}{327.10} = 61.27$ per share

29. Cash EPS = $\frac{₹20,040 + ₹11,394}{327.10} = ₹96.10$ per share

30. Book value per share $= \dfrac{\text{Net worth/Equity funds}}{\text{Number of equity shares outstanding}} = \dfrac{₹1,66,096}{327.10} = ₹507.78$ per share

31. (a). Dividend per share $= \dfrac{\text{Dividend paid to ordinary shareholders*}}{\text{No. of ordinary shares outstanding}}$

$= \dfrac{₹2,531}{327.10} = ₹7.74$ per share

*Excluding tax on dividend

(b) Dividend payout ratio $= \dfrac{\text{Total dividend paid to equity holders}}{\text{Total net profit}}$

$= \dfrac{₹2,941}{₹20,040} \times 100 = 14.68\%$

*Including tax on dividend

(c) Earnings yield $= \dfrac{\text{EPS}}{\text{Market price per share*}} \times 100 = \dfrac{₹61.27}{₹810.38} \times 100 = 7.56\%$

*Market price per share = ₹810.35 (as on March 31, 2012 at NSE)

(d) Dividend yield $= \dfrac{\text{DPS}}{\text{MPS}} = \dfrac{₹7.74}{₹810.35} \times 100 = 0.96\%$

(e) P/E ratio $= \dfrac{\text{MPS}}{\text{EPS}} = \dfrac{₹810.35}{₹61.27} = 13.22$ times

IV. Efficiency Ratios

32. (a) Raw materials turnover $= \dfrac{\text{Cost of raw materials used}}{\text{Average raw materials inventory}} = \dfrac{₹2,74.814}{₹16,963} = 16.20$ times

Average raw materials inventory = (₹14,576 + 19,350)/2 = ₹16,963

(b) Raw material holding period = 365 Days/16.20 = 22.53 Days

33. Stock-in-process turnover ratio $= \dfrac{\text{Cost of goods manufactured}}{\text{Average stock in process inventory}} = \dfrac{₹2,97,591}{₹5,089} = 58.48$ times

Cost of goods manufactured = Cost of goods sold + Closing stock of finished goods – Opening stock of finished goods

= ₹2,97,023 + ₹7,944 – ₹7,376 = ₹2,97,591

Average stock-in-process = (₹4,904 + ₹5,274)/2 = ₹5,089

34. (a) Total assets turnover ratio $= \dfrac{\text{Cost of goods sold}}{\text{Average total assets}} = \dfrac{₹2,97,023}{₹2,89,930} = 1.02$ times

(b) Total assets turnover ratio (Based on sales) $= \dfrac{\text{Net sales}}{\text{Average total assets}} = \dfrac{₹3,29,904}{₹2,89,930} = 1.14$ times

35. (a) Fixed assets turnover ratio $= \dfrac{\text{Cost of goods sold}}{\text{Average fixed assets}} = \dfrac{₹2,97,023}{₹1,28,219} = 2.32$ times

(b) Total assets turnover ratio (Based on sales) $= \dfrac{\text{Net sales}}{\text{Average fixed assets}} = \dfrac{₹3,29,904}{₹1,28,219} = 2.57$ times

36. Capital turnover ratio = $\frac{\text{Cost of goods sold}}{\text{Average capital employed}} = \frac{₹2,97,023}{₹1,87,506}$ = 1.58 times

37. Current assets turnover Ratio = $\frac{\text{Cost of goods sold}}{\text{Average current assets}} = \frac{₹2,97,023}{₹1,14.111}$ = 2.60 times

(b) Total assets turnover ratio = $\frac{\text{Net sales}}{\text{Average current assets}} = \frac{₹3,29,904}{₹1,14,111}$ = 2.89 times

Average current assets = (₹1,32,344 + ₹95,877)/2 = ₹1,14,111

38. Working capital turnover ratio = $\frac{\text{Net sales}}{\text{Net working capital}} = \frac{₹3,29,904}{₹59,287}$ = 5.56 times

Net working capital = (₹1,28,175 – ₹68,888)

V. Integrated Ratios

39. (a) Earning power = Net profit margin × Assets turnover

Net profit margin = $\frac{\text{EAT}}{\text{Sales}} \times 100 = \frac{₹20,040}{₹3,29,904} \times 100$ = 6.07%

Assets turnover = $\frac{\text{Sales}}{\text{Total assets}} = \frac{₹3,29,904}{₹2,95,140}$ = 1.12 times

Earning power = 6.07% × 1.12 = 6.80%

(b) Return on Equity = $\frac{\text{EAT}}{\text{Sales}} \times \frac{\text{Sales}}{\text{Assets}} \times \frac{\text{Assets}}{\text{Equity}}$

$$= \frac{₹20,040}{₹3,29,904} \times \frac{₹3,29,904}{₹2,95,140} \times \frac{₹2,95,140}{₹1,66,096} = 11.96\%$$

or (c) ROE = $\frac{\text{EAT}}{\text{EBT}} \times \frac{\text{EBT}}{\text{EBIT}} \times \frac{\text{EBIT}}{\text{Sales}} \times \frac{\text{Sales}}{\text{Assets}} \times \frac{\text{Assets}}{\text{Equity}}$

$$= \left(\frac{₹20,040}{₹25,750} \times \frac{₹25,750}{₹27,716} \times \frac{₹27,716}{₹3,29,904} \times \frac{₹3,29,904}{₹2,95,140} \times \frac{₹2,95,140}{₹1,66,096}\right) \times 100 = 11.96\%$$

LO 6.7 COMMON SIZE STATEMENTS

Ratio analysis apart, another useful way of analysing financial statements is to convert them into common size statements by expressing absolute rupee amounts into percentages. When this method is pursued, the income statement exhibits each expense item or group of expense items as a percentage of net sales, and net sales are taken at 100 per cent. Similarly, each individual asset and liability classification is shown as a percentage of total assets and liabilities respectively. Statements prepared in this way are referred to as **common-size statements.**

Common-size comparative statements prepared for one firm over the years would highlight the relative changes in each group of expenses, assets and liabilities. These statements can be equally useful for inter-firm comparisons, given the fact that absolute figures of two firms of the same industry are not comparable. Financial statements and common-size statements of the Hypothetical Ltd are presented in Example 6.9.

***Example* 6.9**

The accompanying balance sheet and profit and loss account relate to Hypothetical Ltd. Convert these into common-size statements.

Balance Sheet as at March 31 *(Amount in lakh of rupees)*

Particulars	*Previous Year*	*Current Year*
Liabilities		
Equity share capital (of ₹10 each)	240	240.0
General reserves	96	182.0
Long-term loans	182	169.5
Creditors	67	52.0
Outstanding expenses	6	—
Other current liabilities	9	6.5
	600	650.0
Assets		
Plant [net of accumulated depreciation]	402	390
Cash	54	78
Debtors	60	65
Inventories	84	117
	600	650

Income Statement for the Year Ended March 31

(Amount in lakh of rupees)

Particulars	*Previous year*	*Current year*
Gross sales	370	480
Less: Returns	20	30
Net sales	350	450
Less: Cost of goods sold	190	215
Gross profit	160	235
Less: Selling, general and administrative cost	50	72
Operating profit	110	163
Less: Interest expenses	20	17
Earning before taxes	90	146
Less: Taxes	31.5	51.5
Earning after taxes	58.5	94.9

Solution

Income Statement (Common-size) for the Years Ended March 31 *(Percentages)*

Particulars	*Previous year*	*Current year*
Net sales	100.0	100.0
Cost of goods sold	54.3	47.8
Gross profit	45.7	52.2
Selling, general and administrative expenses	14.3	16.0
Operating profit	31.4	36.2
Interest	5.7	3.8
Earnings before taxes	25.7	32.4
Taxes	9.0	11.4
Earnings after taxes (EAT)	16.7	21.0

Balance Sheets (Common-size as at March 31) *(Percentages)*

Particulars	Previous year	Current year
Owners' equity:		
Equity share capital	40.0	36.9
General reserves	16.0	28.0
	56.0	64.9
Long-term borrowings:		
Loan	30.3	26.1
Current liabilities:		
Creditors	11.2	8.0
Outstanding expenses	1.0	
Other liabilities	1.5	1.0
	13.7	9.0
Total liabilities	100.0	100.0
Fixed assets:		
Plant (net of accumulated depreciation)	67.0	60.0
Current assets:		
Cash	9.0	12.0
Debtors	10.0	10.0
Inventories	14.0	18.0
	33.0	40.0
Total assets	100.0	100.0

These percentage figures bring out clearly the relative significance of each group of items in the aggregative position of the firm. For instance, in the current year the EAT of Hypothetical Ltd has increased to 21 per cent from 16.7 per cent in the previous year. This improvement in profitability can mainly be traced to the decrease of 6.5 per cent in the cost of goods sold, reflecting im-provement in efficiency of manufacturing operations. The decrease in financial overheads (interest) by 1.9 per cent during the current year can be traced to the repayment of a part of long-term loans. Further analysis indicates that profitability would have been more but for an increase in operating expenses ratio by 1.7 per cent.

The common-size balance sheets show that current assets as a percentage of total assets have increased by 7 per cent over previous year. This increase was shared by inventories (4 per cent) and cash (3 per cent); the share of debtors remained unchanged at 10 per cent. The proportion of current liabilities (mainly due to creditors) was also lower at 9 per cent in the current year compared to 13.7 per cent in the previous year. These facts signal overall increase in the liquidity position of the firm. Further, the share of long-term debt has also declined and owners' equity has gone up from 56 per cent in the previous year to 64.9 per cent in the current year.

LO 6.8 IMPORTANCE OF RATIO ANALYSIS

As a tool of financial management, ratios are of crucial significance. The importance of ratio analysis lies in the fact that it presents facts on a comparative basis and enables the drawing of inferences regarding the performance of a firm. Ratio analysis is relevant in assessing the performance of a firm in respect of the following aspects: (i) liquidity position, (ii) long-term solvency, (iii) operating efficiency, (iv) overall profitability, (v) inter-firm comparison, and (vi) trend analysis.

Liquidity Position

With the help of ratio analysis conclusions can be drawn regarding the liquidity position of a firm. The liquidity position of a firm would be satisfactory if it is able to meet its current obligations when they become due. A firm can be said to have the ability to meet its short-term liabilities if it has sufficient liquid funds to pay the interest on its short-maturing debt usually within a year as well as to repay the principal. This ability is reflected in the liquidity ratios of a firm. The liquidity ratios are particularly useful in credit analysis by banks and other suppliers of short-term loans.

Long-term Solvency

Ratio analysis is equally useful for assessing the long-term financial viability of a firm. This aspect of the financial position of a borrower is of concern to the long-term creditors, security analysts and the present and potential owners of a business. The long-term solvency is measured by the leverage/capital structure and profitability ratios which focus on earning power and operating efficiency. Ratio analysis reveals the strengths and weaknesses of a firm in this respect. The leverage ratios, for instance, will indicate whether a firm has a reasonable proportion of various sources of finance or if it is heavily loaded with debt in which case its solvency is exposed to serious strain. Similarly, the various profitability ratios would reveal whether or not the firm is able to offer adequate return to its owners consistent with the risk involved.

Operating Efficiency

Yet another dimension of the usefulness of the ratio analysis, relevant from the viewpoint of management, is that it throws light on the degree of efficiency in the management and utilisation of its assets. The various activity ratios measure this kind of operational efficiency. In fact, the solvency of a firm is, in the ultimate analysis, dependent upon the sales revenues generated by the use of its assets–total as well as its components.

Overall Profitability

Unlike the outside parties which are interested in one aspect of the financial position of a firm, the management is constantly concerned about the overall profitability of the enterprise. That is, they are concerned about the ability of the firm to meet its short-term as well as long-term obligations to its creditors, to ensure a reasonable return to its owners and secure optimum utilisation of the assets of the firm. This is possible if an integrated view is taken and all the ratios are considered together.

Inter-firm Comparison

Ratio analysis not only throws light on the financial position of a firm but also serves as a stepping stone to remedial measures. This is made possible due to interfirm comparison and comparison with industry averages. A single figure of a particular ratio is meaningless unless it is related to some standard or norm. One of the popular techniques is to compare the ratios of a firm with the industry average. It should be reasonably expected that the performance of a firm should be in broad conformity with that of the industry to which it belongs. An interfirm comparison would demonstrate the firm's position *vis-a-vis* its competitors. If the results are at variance either with the industry average or with those of the competitors, the firm can seek to identify the probable reasons and, in that light, take remedial measures.

Trend Analysis

Finally, ratio analysis enables a firm to take the time dimension into account. In other words, whether the financial position of a firm is improving or deteriorating over the years. This is made possible by the use of trend analysis. The significance of a trend analysis of ratios lies in the fact that the analysts can know the direction of movement, that is, whether the movement is favourable or unfavourable. For example, the ratio may be low as compared to the norm but the trend may be upward. On the other hand, though the present level may be satisfactory but the trend may be a declining one.

LO 6.9 LIMITATIONS OF RATIO ANALYSIS

Ratio analysis is a widely used tool of financial analysis. Yet, it suffers from various limitations. The operational implication of this is that while using ratios, the conclusions should not be taken on their face value. Some of the limitations which characterise ratio analysis are **(i)** difficulty in comparison, **(ii)** impact of inflation, and **(iii)** conceptual diversity.

Difficulty in Comparison

One serious limitation of ratio analysis arises out of the difficulty associated with their comparability. One technique that is employed is interfirm comparison. But such comparisons are vitiated by different procedures adopted by various firms. The differences may relate to:

- Differences in the basis of inventory valuation (e.g. last in first out, first in first out, average cost and cost);
- Different depreciation methods (i.e. straight line vs written down basis);
- Estimated working life of assets, particularly of plant and equipment;
- Amortisation of intangible assets like goodwill, patents and so on;
- Amortisation of deferred revenue expenditure such as preliminary expenditure and discount on issue of shares;
- Capitalisation of lease;
- Treatment of extraordinary items of income and expenditure; and so on.

Secondly, apart from different accounting procedures, companies may have different accounting periods, implying differences in the composition of the assets, particularly current assets. For these reasons, the ratios of two firms may not be strictly comparable.

Another basis of comparison is the industry average. This presupposes the availability, on a comprehensive scale, of various ratios for each industry group over a period of time. If, however, as is likely, such information is not compiled and available, the utility of ratio analysis would be limited.

Impact of Inflation

The second major limitation of the ratio analysis as a tool of financial analysis is associated with price level changes. This, in fact, is a weakness of the traditional financial statements which are based on historical costs. An implication of this feature of the financial statements as regards ratio analysis is that assets acquired at different periods are, in effect, shown at different prices in the balance sheet, as they are not adjusted for changes in the price level. As a result, ratio analysis will not yield strictly comparable and, therefore, dependable results. To illustrate, there are two firms which have identical rates of returns on investments, say 15 per cent. But one of these had acquired its fixed assets when prices were relatively low, while the other one had purchased them when prices were high. As a result, the book value of the fixed assets of the former type of firm would be lower, while that of the latter higher. From the point of view of profitability, the return on the investment of the firm with a lower book value would be overstated. Obviously, identical rates of returns on investment are not indicative of equal profitability of the two firms. This is a limitation of ratios.

Conceptual Diversity

Yet another factor which influences the usefulness of ratios is that there is difference of opinion regarding the various concepts used to compute the ratios. There is always room for diversity of opinion as to what constitutes shareholders' equity, debt, assets, profit and so on. Different firms may use these terms in different senses or the same firm may use them to mean different things at different times.

Reliance on a single ratio for a particular purpose may not be a conclusive indicator. For instance, the current ratio alone is not a adequate measure of short-term financial strength; it should be supplemented by the acid-test ratio, debtors turnover ratio and inventory turnover ratio to have a real insight into the liquidity aspect.

Finally, ratios are only a post-mortem analysis of what has happened between two balance sheet dates. For one thing, the position in the interim period is not revealed by ratio analysis. Moreover, they give no clue about the future.

In brief, ratio analysis suffers from some serious limitations. The analyst should not be carried away by its oversimplified nature, easy computation with a high degree of precision. The reliability and significance attached to ratios will largely depend upon the quality of data on which they are based. They are as good as the data itself. Nevertheless, they are an important tool of financial analysis.

SUMMARY

LO 6.1

Ratio analysis is a widely used tool of financial analysis. It is defined as the systematic use of ratio to interpret the financial statements so that the strengths and weaknesses of a firm, as well as its historical performance and current financial condition, can be determined.

Ratios make the related information comparable. A single figure by itself has no meaning, but when expressed in terms of a related figure, it yields significant inferences. Thus, ratios are *relative figures* reflecting the relationship between related variables. Their use as tools of financial analysis involves their comparison as single ratios, like absolute figures, are not of much use. Three types of comparisons are generally involved: namely, **(i)** trend analysis, **(ii)** inter firm comparison, and **(iii)** comparison with standards or industry average.

Trend analysis involves comparison of a firm over a period of time, that is, present ratios are compared with past ratios for the same firm. The comparison of the profitability ratios of a firm, say, year 1 to year 5, is an illustration of a trend analysis. It indicates the direction of change in the performance – improvement, deterioration or constancy – over the years.

Interfirm comparison involves comparing the ratios of a firm with those of others in the same lines of business or for the industry as a whole. It reflects the firm's performance in relation to its competitors. Other types of comparisons may relate to the comparison of items within a single year's financial statement of firm and comparison with standards or plans.

Ratios can broadly be classified into five groups: **(i)** liquidity, **(ii)** capital structure or leverage, **(iii)** profit-ability, **(iv)** activity/efficiency and **(v)** integrated.

LO 6.2

Liquidity ratios measure the ability of a firm to meet its short-term obligations and reflect its short-term financial strength or solvency. The important liquidity ratios are **(a)** current ratio, and **(b)** quick or acid test ratio.

Current ratio is the ratio of total current assets (CAs) to total current liabilities (CLs). A satisfactory current ratio would enable a firm to meet its obligations, even if the value of its CAs decline. It is, however, a quantitative index of liquidity as it does not differentiate among the components of CAs, such as cash and inventory which are not equally liquid.

LO 6.2

The quick or acid test ratio takes into consideration the differences in the liquidity of the components of CAs. It represents the ratio between quick CAs and the total CLs. It is a rigorous measure and superior to the current ratio. However, both these ratios should be used as complementary to each other to analyse the liquidity position of a firm.

The main liquidity ratios are computed as follows: **(i)** Current ratio = Current assets/Current liabilities. **(ii)** Acid test ratio = (Current assets – Stock – Pre-paid expenses)/Current liabilities. **(iii)** Super-quick ratio = (Cash + Marketable securities)/Current liabilities.

LO 6.3

The capital structure or leverage ratios throw light on the long-term solvency of a firm. This is reflected in its ability to assure the long-term creditors with regard to periodic payment of interest and the repayment of loan on maturity, or in pre-determined instalments at due dates. There are two types of such ratios: **(a)** debt-equity or debt-assets, and **(b)** coverage.

The first type is computed from the balance sheet and reflects the relative contribution or stake of owners and creditors in financing the assets of the firm. In other words, such ratios reflect the safety margin to the long-term creditors.

The second category of such ratios is based on the income statement, which shows the number of times the fixed obligations are covered by earnings before interest and taxes or cash inflows. In other words, they indicate the extent to which a fall in operating profit or cash inflows is tolerable, in that the ability to repay would not be adversely affected.

The important leverage ratios are: **(i)** Debt/equity ratios = Total debt (long-term debt + current liabilities)/Shareholders' funds. **(ii)** Debt to total capital ratio = Total debt/Permanent capital (shareholder's funds + long-term debt). **(iii)** Debt to total assets ratio = Total debt/Total assets. **(iv)** Proprietary ratio = Owner's funds/Total assets. **(v)** Capital gearing ratio = (Preference share capital + Debentures + Other borrowed funds)/Equity funds (net worth). **(vi)** Interest coverage ratio (times-interest earned) = Earnings before interest and taxes (EBIT/Interest. **(vii)** Dividend coverage ratio = Earnings after taxes (EAT)/Preference dividend (D_p).

(viii) Total coverage ratio = $$\frac{\text{EBIT} + \text{Lease payment}}{\text{Interest lease payment} + \left(\dfrac{D_p}{1-t}\right) + \dfrac{\text{Instalment of principal}}{(1-t)}}.$$

(ix) Cash flow coverage ratio = $$\frac{\text{EBIT} + \text{Lease payment} + \text{Depreciation}}{\text{Interest Lease payment} + \left(\dfrac{D_p}{1-t}\right) + \dfrac{\text{Instalment of principal}}{(1-t)}}.$$

(x) Debt service coverage ratio = $$\frac{\sum_{t=1}^{n} \text{EAT}_t + \text{Depreciation}_t + \text{Interest}_t + \text{Other non}-\text{cash expenses}_t}{\sum_{t=1}^{n} \text{Principal}_t + \text{Interest}_t}$$

LO 6.4

The profitability of a firm can be measured by the profitability ratios. Such ratios can be computed either from sales or investment.

The profitability ratios based on sales are **(a)** profit margin (gross and net), and **(b)** expenses or operating ratios. They indicate the proportion of sales consumed by operating costs and the proportion available to other expenses.

The profitability ratios related to investments include **(i)** return on assets, **(ii)** return on capital employed, and **(iii)** return on shareholders' equity, including earnings per share, dividend per share, dividend-payout ratio, earning and dividend yield.

LO 6.4	The procedure of calculating profitability ratios based on sales are: **(i)** Gross profit ratio/margin = Gross profit (sales – cost of goods sold)/Net sales. **(ii)** Operating profit ratio/margin = EBIT/Net sales. **(iii)** Net profit ratio/margin = Earnings after taxes (EAT)/Net sales. **(iv)** Cost of goods sold ratio = Cost of goods sold/Net sales. **(v)** Operating expenses ratio = (Administrative expenses + Selling expenses)/Net sales. **(vi)** Administrative expenses ratio = Administrative expenses/Net sales. **(vii)** Selling expenses ratio = Selling expenses/Net sales. **(viii)** Operating ratio = (Cost of goods sold + Operating expenses)/Net sales.
	Ratios related to total investment are calculated as follows: **(i)** Return on total assets = (*EAT* + Interest – Tax advantage on interest)/Average total assets. **(ii)** Return on capital employed = (EAT + Interest – Tax advantage on interest)/Average total capital employed. **(iii)** Return on shareholders' equity = EAT/Average total shareholders' equity. **(iv)** Return on equity funds = (EAT – Preference dividend)/Average ordinary shareholders' equity (net worth). **(v)** Earnings per share (EPS) = Net profit available to equity shareholders' (EAT – D_p)/Number of equity shares outstanding (*N*) **(vi)** Dividends per share (DPS) = Dividend paid to ordinary shareholders/Number of ordinary shares outstanding (*N*). **(vii)** Earnings yield = EPS/Market price per share. **(viii)** DPS/Market price per share. **(ix)** Dividend payment/payout (D/P) ratio = DPS/EPS. **(x)** Price-earnings (P/E) ratio = Market price of a share/EPS. **(xi)** Book value per share = Ordinary shareholders' equity/Number of equity shares outstanding.
LO 6.5	The activity ratios (also known as efficiency or turnover ratios) are concerned with measuring the efficiency in asset management. The efficiency with which assets are managed/used is reflected in the speed and rapidity with which they are converted into sales. Thus, the activity ratios are a test of relationship between sales/cost of goods sold and assets. Depending upon the type of assets, activity ratios may be **(a)** inventory/stock turnover, **(b)** receivables/debtors turnover, and **(c)** total assets turnover.
	The first of these indicates the number of times inventory is replaced during the year or how quickly the goods are sold. It is a test of efficient inventory management.
	The second category of turnover ratios indicates the efficiency of receivables management and shows how quickly trade credit is collected.
	The total assets turnover represents the ratio of total assets to sales/cost of goods sold. It reveals the efficiency in managing and utilizing the total assets.
	The computation procedure of these ratios is as follows: **(i)** Raw material turnover = Cost of raw materials used/Average raw materials inventory. **(ii)** Work-in-process turnover = Cost of goods manufactured/Average work-in-process inventory. **(iii)** Finished goods inventory turnover = Cost of goods sold/Average finished goods inventory. **(iv)** Debtors turnover ratio = Total credit sales/(Average debtors + Averages bills receivable). **(v)** Average collection period = Months (days) in year/Debtors turnover ratio. **(vi)** Total assets turnover = Cost of goods sold/Average total assets. **(vii)** Fixed assets turnover = Cost of goods sold/Average fixed assets. **(viii)** Current assets turnover = Cost of goods sold/Average current assets. **(ix)** Working capital turnover ratio = Cost of goods sold/Average net working capital. If data about cost of goods sold are not available, sales figures are used in the numerator.
LO 6.6	Integrated ratios provide better insight about financial and economic analysis of a firm. For instance of the rate of return on assets (ROA) can be decomposed in to net profit margin (EAT/Sales) and assets turnover (Sales/Total assets). Likewise, the ROE can be decomposed in the following two ways: **(i)** (EAT/Sales) × (Sales/Assets) × (Assets/Equity) and **(ii)** (EAT/EBT) × (EBT/EBIT) × (EBIT/Sales) × (Sales/Assets) × (Assets/Equity).
LO 6.7	Preparation of common-size financial statements is an extension of ratio analysis. These statements convert absolute sums into more easily understood percentages of some base amount. It is sales in the case of income statement and totals of assets and liabilities in the case of the balance sheet.
LO 6.8	As a tool of financial analysis, ratios are of crucial significance. The importance of ratio analysis lies in the fact that it enables to assess the performance of a firm in respect of: (i) liquidity position, (ii) long-term solvency, (iii) operating efficiency and (iv) overall profitability. Apart from facilitating inter-firm comparison, it also enables the firm to assess its performance over the years.

LO 6.9

Ratio analysis in view of its several limitations should be considered only as a tool for analysis rather than as an end in itself. The reliability and significance attached to ratios will largely hinge upon the quality of data on which they are based. They are as good or as bad as the data itself. Nevertheless, they are an important tool of financial analysis.

REFERENCES

1. Metcalf, R W and P L Titard, *Principles of Accounting*, W B Saunders, (Philadelphia) 1976, p 157.
2. Meigs, W B and others, *Intermediate Accounting*, McGraw-Hill, New York, 1978, p 1049.
3. It is, of course, useful in certain situations. In brief, NWC, as a measure of liquidity, is useful for purposes of internal control.
4. White, Gerald I, et. al. The Analysis and use of Financial Statements (John Wiley & Sons, New York), 1998, p 160.
5. Spiller, E A, *Financial Accounting*, Richard D Irwin, Homewood, Ill. 1977, p 644.
6. Bryce, M D, *Industrial Development*, McGraw-Hill, New York, 1960, p 256.
7. Metcalf, R W and P L Titard, *op. cit.*, p 170.
8. Davidson, S, and R L, Weil, *Handbook of Modern Accounting*, McGraw-Hill, (New York), 1977, pp 4-8.
9. Kieso, D E and J J Weygandt, *Intermediate Accounting*, John Wiley, (New York), 1969, pp 1023-1024.
10. Quoted in Davidson and Weil, *op. cit.*, pp 4-9.
11. White Gerald I, et. al, *op. cit.*, p 160.
12. Meig, W B and Others, *op. cit.*, p 1069.
13. This aspect has been discussed in great detail in Chapter 15.
14. Bryce, M D, *op. cit.*, p 254.
15. For a detailed account please refer to Khan, M Y, *Indian Financial System*, TMH, New Delhi, 2003.
16. Helfert, E A, *Techniques of Financial Analysis*, Richard D Irwin, Homewood Ill. 1972, p 53, Used with the permission of Rich ard D Irwin, USA.
17. Suggested by Spiller, E A, *op. cit.*, pp 653-54. This figure of profit represents what might have been earned if all assets had been financed by equity capital.
18. Fama, E and K R French, "The Cros-section of Expected Stock Returns, *Journal of Finance* (June, 1992), pp 427-66.
19. Metcalf and Titard, *op. cit.*, p 174.
20. Deduction should not be made in respect of provision for bad and doubtful depts.
21. If the information regarding the cost of goods sold is not available, the figure of sales can be used.
22. Higgins, R.C., *Analysis for Financial Managment*, Irwin McGraw-Hill, Boston, 2001, pp 34-5.
23. White, G. I et al, *The Analysis and Use of Financial Statments* (John Wiley & Sons, New York), 1998, p 186.
24. There are varying practices regarding its treatment. Assuming going concern concept and RIL to be profitable in future, it is treated as liability.

SOLVED PROBLEMS

P.6.1 B Raj Ltd sells goods on cash as well as credit. The following particulars are extracted from their books of accounts for the current year-end. LO 6.2 LOD E

Particulars	*Amount (in lakh of rupees)*
Total gross sales	100
Cash sales (included in above)	20
Sales returns	7
Total debtors at the end	9
Bills receivable	2
Provision for doubtful debts at the end of the year	1
Total creditors at the end	10

Calculate the average collection period.

Solution

Total net credit sales = Gross sales – Cash sales – Sales returns = ₹100 lakh – ₹20 lakh – ₹7 lakh = ₹73 lakh

$$\text{Debtors turnover} = \frac{\text{Credit sales}}{\text{Debtors + Bills receivable}} = \frac{₹73 \text{ lakh}}{₹11 \text{ lakh}} = \frac{73}{11}$$

$$\text{Average collection period} = \frac{365 \text{ days}}{\text{Debtors turnover } (73/11)} = 55 \text{ days}$$

P.6.2 The following are the ratios relating to the activities of National Traders Ltd: LO 6.3 LOD D

Debtors velocity (months)	3
Stock velocity (months)	8
Creditors velocity (months)	2
Gross profit ratio (%)	25

Gross profit for the current year ended December 31 amounts to ₹4,00,000. Closing stock of the year is ₹10,000 above the opening stock. Bills receivable amount to ₹25,000 and bills payable to ₹10,000. Find out: **(a)** Sales, **(b)** Sundry debtors, **(c)** Closing stock, and **(d)** Sundry creditors.

Solution

(a) Determination of sales: $\text{Sales} = \frac{₹4,00,000}{25} \times 100 = ₹16,00,000$

(b) Determination of sundry debtors: Debtors velocity is 3 months. In other words, debtors' collection period is 3 months, or debtors' turnover ratio is 4. Assuming all sales to be credit sales and debtors turnover ratio being calculated on the basis of year-end figures,

$$\text{Debtors turnover ratio} = \frac{\text{Credit sales}}{\text{Closing debtors + Bills receivable}}$$

or

$$\text{Closing debtors + Bills receivable} = \frac{\text{Credit sales}}{\text{Debtors turnover ratio}} = \frac{₹16,00,000}{4} = ₹4,00,000$$

$$\text{Closing debtors} = ₹4,00,000 - ₹25,000 = ₹3,75,000$$

(c) Determination of closing stock: Stock velocity of 8 months signifies that the inventory holding period is 8 months, stock turnover ratio is 1.5 = (12 months ÷ 8).

$$\text{Stock turnover} = \frac{\text{Cost of goods sold (Sales – Gross profit)}}{\text{Average stock}}$$

$$1.5 = \frac{₹12,00,000}{\text{Average stock}}$$

$$\text{Average stock} = \frac{₹12,00,000}{1.5} = ₹8,00,000$$

$$\text{Closing stock} - \text{Opening stock} = ₹10,000 \quad (1)$$

$$\frac{\text{Closing stock + Opening stock}}{2} = ₹8,00,000 \quad (2)$$

$$\text{Closing stock + Opening stock} = ₹16,00,000 \quad (3)$$

or

Subtracting (1) from (3) we have,

$$2 \text{ Opening stock} = ₹15,90,000$$

$$\text{Opening stock} = ₹7,95,000$$

Therefore, $\text{Closing stock} = ₹8,05,000$

(d) Determination of sundry creditors: Creditors velocity of 2 months signifies that the credit payment period is 2 months. In other words, creditors' turnover ratio is 6 (12 months ÷ 2). Assuming all purchases to be credit purchases and creditors turnover is based on year-end figures,

$$\text{Creditors turnover ratio} = \frac{\text{Credit purchases}}{\text{Creditors + Bills payable}}$$

$$6 = \frac{₹12,10,000}{\text{Creditors} + ₹10,000}$$

$$\text{Creditors} + ₹10,000 = \frac{₹12,10,000}{6} = ₹2,01,667$$

$$\text{Creditors} = ₹2,01,667 - ₹10,000 = ₹1,91,667$$

Credit purchases are calculated as follows:

Cost of goods sold = Opening stock + Purchases – Closing stock
₹12,00,000 = ₹7,95,000 + Purchases – ₹8,05,000
₹12,00,000 + ₹10,000 = Purchases
₹12,10,000 = Purchases (credit).

P.6.3 The Avon Ltd has a capital of ₹10,00,000; its turnover is 3 times the capital and the net profit margin on sales is 6 per cent. What is the return on investment? LO 6.4 LOD E

Solution

Rate of return on investment = Margin of profit × Capital/Investment turnover

$$= \frac{\text{Net profit}}{\text{Sales}} \times \frac{\text{Sales}}{\text{Capital}} = 0.06 \times 3 = 18 \text{ per cent}$$

P.6.4 The capital of E. Ltd. is as follows: LO 6.4 LOD M

9% Preference shares, ₹10 each	₹3,00,000
Equity shares of ₹10 each	8,00,000
	11,00,000

Additional information: Profit (after tax at 35 per cent), ₹2,70,000; Depreciation, ₹60,000; Equity dividend paid, 20 per cent; Market price of equity shares, ₹40.

You are required to compute the following, showing the necessary workings:

(a) Dividend yield on the equity shares.
(b) Cover for the preference and equity dividends.
(c) Earnings per shares.
(d) Price-earnings ratio.

Solution

(a) Dividend yield on the equity shares: $= \frac{\text{Dividend per share}}{\text{Market price per share}} \times 100$

$$= \frac{₹2\ (0.20 \times ₹10)}{₹40} \times 100 = 5 \text{ per cent}$$

(b) Dividend coverage ratio:

(i) Preference

$$= \frac{\text{Profit after taxes}}{\text{Dividend payable to preference shareholders}} = \frac{₹2,70,000}{₹27,000\ (0.09 \times ₹3,00,000)} = 10 \text{ times}$$

(ii) Equity $= \frac{\text{Profit after taxes – Preference share dividend}}{\text{Dividend payable to equity shareholders at current rate of ₹2 per share}}$

$$= \frac{₹2,70,000 - ₹27,000}{₹1,60,000\ (80,000 \text{ shares} \times ₹2)} = 1.52 \text{ times}$$

(c) Earnings per equity share $= \dfrac{\text{Earnings available to equity shareholders}}{\text{Number of equity shares outstanding}} = \dfrac{₹2,43,00}{80,000} = ₹3.04$ per share

(d) Price-earning (P/E) ratio $= \dfrac{\text{Market price per share}}{\text{Earnings pe share}} = \dfrac{₹40}{₹3.04} = 13.2$ time

P.6.5 Z Ltd purchased a retail store and commenced business on April 1. From the following information, you are required to prepare in as much details as possible, a trading and profit and loss account for the current year ended March 31 and a balance sheet as at the date. **LO 6.1,4,5** LOD **E**

Capital introduced on April 1	₹47,000
Drawings during the year	5,000
Working capital (current assets less current liabilities) at March 31	23,000
Depreciation of fixed assets during the year, based on a rate of 20 per cent per annum on cost	3,000
Ratio of annual sales to year-end values of fixed assets plus working capital	2:1
Ratio of current assets to current liabilities at the year-end	2:1
Ratio of liquid assets (cash plus debtors) to current liabilities on March 31	5:4
Debtors at the year-end as per cent of annual sales	12
General expenses (excluding depreciation) as per cent of annual sales	20

The current assets consist of stocks (which are unchanged throughout the year), debtors and cash. Stocks are turned over four times during the year. The current liabilities consist only of creditors.

Solution

Trading A/c of Z Ltd for the Current Year ended March 31

To Cost of sales	₹69,000	By Sales	₹1,00,000
To Gross profit c/f to P&L A/c	31,000		
	1,00,000		1,00,000

Profit and Loss A/c for the Current Year ended March 31

To General Expenses	₹20,000	By Gross profit b/f from trading A/c	₹31,000
To Depreciation	3,000		
To Net profit c/f to capital A/c	8,000		
	31,000		31,000

Balance Sheet as at March 31, Current Year

Liabilities		*Amount*	*Assets*		*Amount*
Capital	₹47,000		Fixed assets	₹30,000	
Add: Net profit	8,000		*Less:* Depreciation	3,000	₹27,000
	55,000				
Less: Drawings	5,000	₹50,000	Current assets		
			Cash	16,750	
Creditors		23,000	Debtors	12,000	
			Stock	17,250	46,000
		73,000			73,000

Working Notes

1. Determination of current assets and current liabilities:

$$CA - CL = ₹23{,}000 \quad (1)$$

$$0.5\ CA - CL = 0 \quad (2)$$

Subtracting equation (2) from equation (1)

$$0.5\ CA = ₹23{,}000$$

$$CA = ₹46{,}000$$

CL = ₹23,000 = Creditors as there are no other current liabilities.

2. Determination of fixed assets: Depreciation rate, 10 per cent = ₹3,000

$$\text{Cost of fixed assets} = ₹3{,}000 \times \frac{100}{10} = ₹30{,}000$$

3. Determination of sales $= \dfrac{\text{Sales}}{\text{Fixed assets + Working capital}} = 2$

$$\frac{\text{Sales}}{₹27{,}000 + ₹23{,}000} = 2$$

$$\text{Sales} = ₹1{,}00{,}000$$

4. Determination of liquid assets: liquid ratio $= \dfrac{\text{Liquid assets}}{\text{Current liabilities}}$, $1.25 = \dfrac{\text{Liquid assets}}{₹23{,}000}$

$$₹28{,}750 = \text{Liquid assets (cash + debtors)}$$

(a) Debtors are 12 per cent of annual sales = ₹12,000 (0.12 × ₹1,00,000)

(b) Cash = ₹28,750 – ₹12,000 = ₹16,750

5. Determination of stock: Current assets – Liquid assets

₹46,000 – ₹28,750 = ₹17,250

6. Determination of cost of sales: Stock turnover ratio $= \dfrac{\text{Cost of sales}}{\text{Average stock}}$

$$4 = \frac{\text{Cost of sales}}{₹17{,}250}$$

$$₹69{,}000 = \text{Cost of sales.}$$

P.6.6 Using the following information, complete the balance sheet given below: **LO 6.2,3,4,5** LOD D

Total debt to net worth: 0.5 to 1.

Turnover of total assets (based on year-end sales figures): 2.

Gross profit: 30 per cent

Average collection period (based on 360-day-year): 40 days

Inventory turnover (based on cost of goods sold and year-end inventory): 3 times.

Acid test ratio: 0.75:1.

Balance sheet

Cash		Notes and accounts payable	
Accounts receivable		Common stock	₹2,00,000
Inventory		Retained earnings	3,00,000
Plant and equipment			
Total		Total	

Solution

Balance sheet

Cash	₹20,833	Notes and accounts payable	₹2,50,000
Accounts receivable	1,66,667	Common stock	2,00,000
Inventory	3,50,000	Retained earnings	3,00,000
Plant and equipment	2,12,500		
Total	7,50,000	Total	7,50,000

Working notes

1. Debt to net worth ratio $= \dfrac{\text{Total debt}}{\text{Net worth (Common stock + Retained earnings)}}$

$$0.5 = \frac{\text{Total debt}}{₹5{,}00{,}000}$$

$$₹2{,}50{,}000 = \text{Total debt (notes and accounts payable)}$$

2. Substituting the value of 'notes and accounts payable' on the liabilities side, we have ₹7,50,000 as the total sum of liabilities and so the total assets will be ₹7,50,000.

$$\text{Total assets turnover} = \frac{\text{Sales}}{\text{Total assets}}$$

$$2 = \frac{\text{Sales}}{₹7{,}50{,}000}$$

or $₹15{,}00{,}000 = \text{Sales}$

3. Gross profit ratio $= \dfrac{\text{Gross profit}}{\text{Sales}} \times 100$

$$30 = \frac{\text{Gross profit}}{₹15{,}00{,}000} \times 100$$

$$₹4{,}50{,}000 = \text{Gross profit}$$

Cost of goods sold = Sales – Gross profit = ₹15,00,000 – ₹4,50,000 = ₹10,50,000

4. Assuming all sales to be credit sales, the figure of accounts receivable would be determined as follows:

$$\text{Accounts receivable turnover ratio} = \frac{360 \text{ days}}{\text{Average collection period}} = \frac{360 \text{ days}}{40 \text{ days}} = 9$$

$$\text{Accounts receivable turnover ratio} = \frac{\text{Credit sales}}{\text{Average debtors}}$$

$$9 = \frac{₹15{,}00{,}000}{\text{Average debtors}}$$

$$\text{Average debtors} = \frac{₹15{,}00{,}000}{9} = ₹1{,}66{,}667$$

In the absence of any figure of the opening debtors and closing debtors, it is assumed that accounts receivable ratio is calculated on the basis of year-end figures. Accordingly, the amount of ₹1,66,667 represents the balance of accounts receivable at the end of the year.

5. Inventory turnover ratio $= \dfrac{\text{Cost of goods sold}}{\text{Closing inventory}}$

$$3 = \frac{₹10{,}50{,}000}{\text{Closing inventory}}$$

or ₹3,50,000 = Closing inventory

6. Acid test ratio $= \dfrac{\text{Liquid assets}}{\text{Current liabilities}}$

$$0.75 = \frac{\text{Liquid assets}}{₹2{,}50{,}000}$$

₹1,87,500 = Liquid assets

₹1,87,500 = Cash + Accounts receivable

₹1,87,500 – ₹1,66,667 = ₹20,833 = Cash

P.6.7 As the manager of a financial services company, you have received a proposal seeking a term loan of ₹300 lakh, from a firm planning an investment in fixed assets of ₹500 lakh in a new project. The loan is indicated to be repayable in three annual instalments commencing from the end of the second year. The following information concerning the project is available: (₹ in lakhs)

LO 6.3 LOD M

Particulars	*Year*			
	1	*2*	*3*	*4*
Gross profit (before depreciation)	75	100	150	150
Depreciation	50	45	40	35
Interest on term loan	25	45	30	15
Working capital borrowing (interest)	10	15	20	20
Provision for tax	—	—	10	30

Assuming other *techno-economic* criteria to be satisfactory, you are required to:

(a) compute appropriate financial ratio which, in your opinion, would guide the financing decision, and

(b) interpret briefly the ratio so computed and give your views on the proposal.

Solution

(a) Debt service coverage ratio is the most appropriate ratio for the lending company as it indicates relationship between the total cash funds available with the borrowing firm to service debt/instalment (consisting of principal repayment and interest).

Debt-Service Coverage Ratio (DSCR): (Amount in lakhs of rupees)

Particulars	*Year*			
	1	*2*	*3*	*4*
Gross profit (before depreciation)	75	100	150	150
Less interest on working capital borrowing	10	15	20	20
Less provision for tax	—	—	10	30
(i) Cash available to service term loan	65	85	120	100
Debt service obligations:				
Interest on term loan	25	45	30	15
Instalment payment	—	100	100	100
(ii) Total debt service obligations	25	145	130	115
(iii) DSCR (i ÷ ii) (Number of times)	2.6	0.59	0.92	0.87

(b) COMMENT: The DSCR is very unsatisfactory as it is less than one for all the three years in which instalmetns are to be paid. The firm will not have enough cash to service instalment and is likely to commit default. The proposal is not financially viable and term loan should not be sanctioned by the financial services company.

P.6.8 The information below is taken from the records of two companies in the same industry. The companies are X Ltd and Y Ltd; and the data is as follows: LO 6.2,3,4 LOD M

Particulars	*X Ltd*	*Y Ltd*
Cash	₹2,10,000	₹3,20,000
Debtors (net)	3,30,000	6,30,000
Stock	12,30,000	9,50,000
Plant and equipment	16,95,000	24,00,000
Total assets	34,65,000	43,00,000
Sundry creditors	9,00,000	10,50,000
8% Debentures	5,00,000	10,00,000
Equity share capital	11,00,000	17,50,000
Retained earnings	9,65,000	5,00,000
Total liabilities	34,65,000	43,00,000
Sales	56,00,000	82,00,000
Cost of goods sold	40,00,000	64,80,000
Other operating expenses	8,00,000	8,60,000
Interest expenses	40,000	80,000
Income taxes	2,66,000	2,73,000
Dividends	1,00,000	1,80,000

Answer each of the following questions by making a comparison of one, or more, relevant ratios.

(i) Which company is using the equity shareholders' money more profitably?
(ii) Which company is better able to meet its current debts?
(iii) If you were to purchase the debentures of one company, which company's debentures would you buy?
(iv) Which company collects its receivables faster, assuming all sales to be credit sales?
(v) Which company is extended credit for a longer period by the creditors, assuming all purchases (equivalent to cost of goods sold) to be credit purchases?
(vi) How long does it take each company to convert an investment in stock to cash?
(vii) Which company retains the larger proportion of income in the business?

Solution

(i) *Rate of return (ROR) on shareholders' funds*
= (₹4,94,000*/₹20,65,000**) × 100 = 23.9 per cent (X Ltd)
= (₹5,07,000**/₹22,50,000) × 100 = 22.5 per cent (Y Ltd)
X Ltd is using the shareholders' money more profitably.

(ii) (a) *Current ratio* = ₹17,70,000/₹9,00,000 = 1.97 (X), ₹19,00,000/ ₹10,50,000 = 1.81 (Y)
(b) *Acid test ratio* = ₹5,40,000/₹9,00,000 = 0.6 (X), ₹9,50,000/ ₹10,50,000 = 0.9 (Y)
Y Ltd is better able to meet its current debts.

(iii) (a) *Debt-equity ratio* = ₹14,00,000/₹20,65,000 = 0.68 (X), ₹20,50,000/ ₹22,50,000 = 0.91 (Y)
(b) *Interest coverage ratio* = ₹8,00,000/₹40,000 = 20 times (X), ₹8,60,000/ ₹80,000 = 10.75 times (Y)
The debentures of X Ltd should be bought.

(iv) *Debtors collection period* = (360 × ₹3,30,000)/₹56,00,000 = 21 days (X Ltd), (360 × ₹6,30,000)/₹82,00,000 = 28 days (Y Ltd)
X Ltd collects its receivables faster.

(v) *Creditors payment period* = (360 × ₹9,00,000)/₹40,00,000 = 81 days (X Ltd), (360 × ₹10,50,000)/₹64,80,000 = 58 days (Y Ltd)
X Ltd is extended credit for a longer period by the creditors.

(vi) *Stock turnover ratio* = ₹40,00,000/₹12,30,000 = 3.25 times (X), ₹64,80,000/₹9,50,000 = 6.82 times (Y)
= 360 days/3.25 = 111 days (X), 360 days/6.82 = 53 days (Y)
Length of time required for conversion of investment in stock to cash:
111 days + 21 days (debtors collection period)= 132 days (X)
53 days + 28 days (debtors collection period) = 81 days (Y)

(vii) *Dividend payout ratio* = ₹1,00,000/₹4,94,000 = 20.2 per cent (X), ₹1,80,000/₹5,07,000 = 35.5 per cent (Y)
Retention ratio = 100 – 20.2 = 79.8 per cent (X), 100 – 35.5 = 64.5 per cent (Y)

X Ltd retains the larger proportion of its income in the business

* ₹56,00,000 – ₹51,06,000
** ₹82,00,000 – ₹76,93,000

P.6.9 The following information was taken from the financial statements of XYZ Ltd *(amount in thousand of rupees)* **LO 6.5** LOD M

Particulars	*Year 1*	*Year 2*	*Year 3*
Total assets	750	850	860
Credit sales	420	520	550
Cost of goods sold	450	595	645
Cash	50	60	55
Debtors	150	165	180
Inventory	130	160	170
Net fixed assets	120	260	250
Creditors	75	85	100
Short-term debt	125	175	170
Long-term debt	125	185	175
Equity	125	200	210

Calculate those ratios which indicate the efficient use of assets and discuss potential sources of trouble.

Solution

The efficient use of assets is indicated by the following key ratios: **(a)** Current assets turnover, **(b)** Debtors' turnover, **(c)** Inventory turnover, **(d)** Fixed assets turnover, and **(e)** Total assets turnover.

Computation or ratios

Particulars	*Year 1*	*Year 2*	*Year 3*
(a) Current assets turnover ratio (cost of goods sold ÷ total current assets)	1.36	1.55	1.59
(b) Debtors' turnover (credit sales ÷ average debtors)	2.8*	3.30	3.19
(c) Inventory turnover (cost of goods sold ÷ average inventory)	3.46*	4.10	3.91
(d) Fixed assets turnover (cost of goods sold ÷ fixed assets)	3.75	2.29	2.58
(e) Total assets turnover (cost of goods sold ÷ total assets)	1.00	0.92	0.98

*Based on debtors and inventory at the end, as their opening balances are not available.

COMMENTS: The first three ratios indicate the efficiency of current assets usage, and the latter two, namely, fixed assets turnover and total assets turnover ratio, show the efficacy of utilisation of these. Current assets utilisation appears to be very satisfactory as reflected in the first three types of ratios. No major change is noticeable in their values over a period of time, which is presumably indicative of consistency in debtors collection period and inventory turnover. There does not seem to be any significant problem regarding utilisation of current assets.

However, it appears that fixed assets are not being fully utilised. Investments in fixed assets have more than doubled during years 2 and 3. The fixed assets turnover ratio has sharply fallen to 2.58 in year 3 from 3.75 in year 1. Thus, investments in fixed assets are either excessive, or the capacity of the additional plant is under-utilised. This is corroborated by the fact that sales in the latter 2 years have increased by around 15 per cent. Therefore, the remedy lies in utilising the plant capacity by increasing production and sales.

P.6.10 From the ratios and other data set forth below for the Auto Accessories Ltd, indicate your interpretation of the company's financial condition: **LO 6.2,4,5** LOD M

Particulars	*Year 3*	*Year 2*	*Year 1*
Current ratio (per cent)	302	278	265
Acid-test ratio	99	110	155
Working capital turnover (times)	3.25	3.00	2.75
Receivable turnover (times)	7.2	8.41	9.83
Collection period (days)	50	43	37
Inventory to working capital (per cent)	110	100	95
Inventory turnover (times)	5.41	6.01	6.11
Income per equity share (₹)	2.5	4.05	5.10
Net income to net worth (per cent)	7	8.5	11.07
Operating expenses to net sales (per cent)	25	23	22
Sales increase during the year (per cent)	23	16	10
Cost of goods sold to net sales (per cent)	73	71	70
Dividend per share (₹)	3	3	3
Fixed assets to net worth (per cent)	22.7	18.0	16.4
Net profit on net sales (per cent)	2.0	5.09	7.03

Solution

The interpretation of the financial condition of Auto Accessories Ltd, as revealed by the ratios and other data, yields the following inferences:

(i) Declining profitability is evident from the following:

(a) Decrease in gross profit ratio from 30 in year 1 to 27 per cent in year 3, **(b)** decrease in net profit ratio from 7 in year 1 to 2 in year 3 and **(c)** decrease in rate of return on net worth from 11.1 per cent in year 1 to 7 per cent in year 3. This is in spite of increase in sales from 10 per cent in year 1 to 23 per cent in year 3.

In interpreting the profitability of the company, another relevant factor is the expenses ratios. The ratio of cost of goods sold to net sales has gone up from 70 to 73 per cent during the period. Likewise, there has been an increase in operating expenses ratio from 22 to 25 per cent. The high inventories as reflected in lower inventory turnover ratio of 5.41 in year 3 as compared to 6.11 in year 1 have also adversely affected the profit margin.

As a consequence, the EPS has declined by more than 50 per cent during year 1-3 from ₹5.1 in year 1 to ₹2.5 in year 3.

(ii) The emerging liquidity position of the company appears to be highly satisfactory. The current ratio has increased from 2.65 in year 1 to 3.02 in year 3. Though, the acid-test ratio has declined from 1.55 1 to 0.99, it meets the standard. The company is unlikely to encounter any serious difficulty in paying the short-term obligations as and when they become due for payment.

However, the management should realise that the policy relating to collection of debt is not sound as reflected in the declining trend of receivables turnover from 9.83 in year 1 to 7.2 in year 3. In other words, the average debt collection period has increased from 37 days to 50 days. There is carelessness either (i) in collecting the payments from debtors, or (ii) in extending credit sales to customers leading to an increase in bad debts and thereby an increase in the expenses ratio. Further, the inventory holding period requires investigation as the consistent increase in the current ratio and the consistent decrease in the acid-test ratio result from large accumulation of inventories. The excessive investment in current assets seem to be affecting the rate of return.

The investment in fixed assets appears excessive as shown by a consistent increase in the ratio of fixed assets to net worth. However, the overinvestment in fixed assets is not as clear as the overinvestment in working capital.

The stable dividend policy of the company is commendable and is likely to have a salutary effect on the market price of its shares.

In conclusion, the firm's financial position has not become so bad that it cannot be cured. What is required is a thorough probe into overinvestment in working capital, particularly inventories and fixed assets.

P.6.11 Below is given the balance sheet of Best Ltd, as on March 31, of the current year: **LO 6.2,3,4,5** LOD M

Equity and Liabilities	*Amount*	*Assets*	*Amount*
Equity share capital	₹20,00,000	Fixed assets (cost)	₹50,00,000
7.5% Preference share capital	10,00,000	Depreciation written-off	16,00,000
General reserve	4,00,000		34,00,000
6% Debentures	6,00,000	Stock	6,00,000
Sundry creditors	10,00,000	Sundry debtors	8,00,000
		Cash	2,00,000
	50,00,000		50,00,000

The following additional information is available:

(1) Fixed assets costing ₹10,00,000 to be installed on April 1, and would become operative on that date, payment to be made on March 31 of next year.

(2) The fixed assets turnover ratio (on the cost of the fixed assets) would be 1.5.

(3) The stock turnover ratio would be 14.4 (calculated on the basis of the average of the opening and closing stocks).

(4) The break-up of cost and profit would be as follows (percentages):

Materials	40
Labour	25
Manufacturing expenses	10
Office and selling expenses	10
Depreciation	5
Profit	10
Sales	100

The profit is subject to debenture interest and taxation @ 35 per cent.

(5) Debtors would be 1/9 of turnover.

(6) Creditors would be 1/5 of materials consumed.

(7) In March next year a dividend of 10 per cent on equity capital would be paid.

(8) ₹5,00,000, 6% debentures would be issued on April 1, next year.

You are required to prepare the forecast balance sheet as on March 31, next year and calculate the resultant:

(a) Current ratio;
(b) Fixed Assets/Net worth ratio; and
(c) Debt-equity ratio
(The turnover above refers to the value of sales).

Solution

Forecast Balance Sheet of Best Ltd as on March 31, Next Year

Equity and Liabilities	*Amount*	*Assets*		*Amount*
Equity share capital	₹20,00,000	Fixed assets:		
13.5% Preference share capital	10,00,000	Cost	₹60,00,000	
General reserves	6,67,100	*Less:* Depreciation	20,50,000	₹39,50,000
15% Debentures	11,00,000	Sundry debtors		10,00,000
Sundry creditors	7,20,000	Stock		6,50,000
Provision for taxation	2,91,900	Cash		1,79,000
	57,79,000			57,79,000

Resultant ratio:

Ratio	*Formula*	*Computation*
(i) Current ratio	$\frac{\text{Current assets}}{\text{Current liabilities}}$	$\frac{₹18,29,00}{₹11,37,000} = 1.61$
(ii) Fixed assets to net worth	$\frac{\text{Fixed assets}}{\text{Net worth}}$	$\frac{₹39,50,000}{₹35,42\ 000} = 1.12$
(iii) Debt-equity ratio	(a) $\frac{\text{External dept}}{\text{Internal equity}}$	$\frac{₹22,37,00}{₹35,42,000} = 0.63$
	(b) $\frac{\text{Long term debt}}{\text{Internal equity}}$	$\frac{₹11,00,000}{₹35,42,000} = 0.31$

Working notes

1. Determination of sales:

$$\text{Fixed assets turnover ratio} = \frac{\text{Sales}}{\text{Fixed assets}}$$

Or $$1.5 = \frac{\text{Sales}}{₹60,00,000}$$

Or $$₹90,00,000 = \text{Sales}$$

2. Determination of actual expenses

Particulars	*Percentage of sales*	*Amount*
Materials	40	₹36,00,000
Manufacturing expenses	10	9,00,000
Labour	25	22,50,000
Office & selling expenses	10	9,00,000
Depreciation	5	4,50,000
Profit	10	9,00,000
	100	90,00,000

3. Determination of net fixed assets:

Opening balance		₹50,00,000
Add: Purchases		10,00,000
		60,00,000
Less: Depreciation:		
Accumulated	₹16,00,000	
Additional	4,50,000	20,50,000
Closing balance		39,50,000

4. Determination of closing stock:

$$\text{Average stock} = \frac{\text{Sales}}{\text{Stock turnover ratio}}$$

$$= \frac{₹90,00,000}{14.4} = ₹6,25,000$$

$$\text{Average stock} = \frac{\text{Opening stock + closing stock}}{2}$$

$$₹12,50,000 = ₹6,00,000 + \text{Closing stock}$$

$$₹\ 6,50,000 = \text{Closing stock}$$

5. Determination of debtors:

$$\text{Debtors} = \frac{\text{Sales}}{9} = \frac{₹90,00,000}{9} = ₹10,00,000$$

6. Determination of creditors:

$$\text{Creditors} = \frac{\text{Materials consumed}}{5} = \frac{₹36,00,000}{5} = ₹7,20,000$$

7. Determination of interest and provision for taxation:

Net profit	₹9,00,000
Less: Interest (0.06 × ₹11,00,000)	66,000
	8,34,000
Less: Taxes (0.35 × ₹8,34,000)	2,91,900
Net-profit after taxes	5,42,100

8. Determination of amount to be transferred to general reserves:

Opening balance of general reserve		₹4,00,000
Transfer from the current year:		
Net profit	₹5,42,100	
Less: Preference dividend	(75,000)	
Less: Equity dividend	(2,00,000)	2,67,100
Closing balance		6,67,100

9. Determination of cash:

Cash flow statement

Sources of cash:	
Cash from operations:	
Profit after tax	₹5,42,100
Add: Depreciation	4,50,000
	9,52,100
Add: Increase in current liabilities (provision for taxation):	2,91,900
Less: Increase in current assets	
and decrease in current liabilities:	

(Contd.)

(Contd.)

Stock	₹50,000		
Debtors	2,00,000		
Creditors	2,80,000	(5,30,000)	₹ 7,54,000
Issue of debentures			5,00,000
Total cash (sources) (A)			12,54,000
Uses of cash:			
Purchase of fixed assets			10,00,000
Payment of dividend:			
Preference		75,000	
Equity		2,00,000	2,75,000
Total cash (uses) (B)			12,75,000
Net decrease in cash (B – A)		(21,000)	
Opening balance of cash		2,00,000	
Less: Decrease in cash		21,000	1,79,000
Closing balance of cash			

P.6.12 You have been supplied data for the Supreme Plastic Company Ltd, and its industry averages: **LO 6.2,3,4,5** LOD M

1. Determine the indicated ratios for the Supreme Plastic Company.
2. Indicate the company's strengths and weaknesses as shown by your analysis.

Balance sheet as at March 31

Equity and Liabilities	*Amount*	*Assets*	*Amount*
Equity share capital	₹12,00,000	Net fixed assets	₹6,05,000
10% Debentures	2,30,000	Cash	2,20,000
Sundry creditors	1,65,000	Sundry debtors	2,75,000
Bills payable	2,20,000	Stock	8,25,000
Other current liabilities	1,10,000		
	19,25,000		19,25,000

Statement of profit for the year ending March 31, current year

Sales	₹27,50,000	
Less: Cost of goods sold:		
Materials	₹10,45,000	
Wages	6,60,000	
Factory overheads	3,24,500	20,29,500
Gross profit		7,20,500
Less: Selling and distribution expenses		2,75,000
Less: Administrative and general expenses		3,07,000
Earnings before interest and taxes		1,38,500
Less: Interest		23,000
Earnings before taxes		1,15,500
Less: Income taxes (0.35)		40,425
Net profit		75,075

Ratios

Ratios	*Industry*	*Supreme Plastic*
Current assets/current liabilities	2.4	
Sales/debtors	8.0	
Sales/stock	9.8	
Sales/total assets	2.0	
Net profit/sales (per cent)	3.3	
Net profit/total assets (per cent)	6.6	
Net profit/net worth (per cent)	12.7	
Total debt/total assets (per cent)	63.5	

Solution

(1) Determination of Ratios

Ratios	*Computation*	*Indicated result*	*Industry*
Current assets / Current liabilities	₹12,20,000 / ₹4,95,000	2.7	2.4
Sales / Debtors	27,50,000 / 2,75,000	10.0	8.0
Sales / Stock	27,50,000 / 8,25,000	3.3	9.8
Sales / Total assets	27,50,000 / 19,25,000	1.4	2.0
Net profit / Sales (per cent)	75,075 / 27,50,000	2.7	3.3
Net profit / Total assets (per cent)	75,075 / 19,25,000	3.9	6.6
Net profit / Equity share capital	75,075 / 12,00,000	6.3	12.7
Total debt / Total assets	7,25,000 / 19,25,000	37.7	63.5

2. The level of stock maintained by Supreme Plastics is alarmingly high in that it is almost three times the industry average. The other turnover ratios are in conformity with that of the industry. In fact, current ratios and debtors turnover reflecting debt collection period of the company are better than those of the industry.

The greatest weakness of the company is the high level of inventories. It has caused a steep decline in the total assets turnover. The cost of carrying stocks is likely to adversely affect the profit margin. As a result of its low turnover and profit margin, the company's rate of return on net worth is less than one-half of the industry. The rate of return on equity capital of the company is also low because the company is using relatively less debt, i.e. 37.7 per cent as against the industry average of 63.5 per cent.

P.6.13 From the following particulars, prepare the balance sheet of Shri Mohan Ram and Co. Ltd as at March 31, current year. **LO 6.2,3,4,5** LOD **D**

Current ratio, 2
Working capital, ₹4,00,000
Capital block to current asset, 3:2

(Contd.)

(Contd.)
Fixed asset to turnover, 1:3
Sales cash/credit, 1:2
Debentures/share capital, 1:2
Stock velocity, 2 months
Creditors velocity, 2 months
Debtors velocity, 2 months
Gross profit ratio, 25 per cent (to sales)
Capital block:
Net profit, 10 per cent of turnover
Reserve, 2.5 per cent of turnover

Solution

Balance Sheet as at March 31

Liabilities	*Amount*	*Assets*	*Amount*
Share capital	₹6,00,000	Fixed assets (net)	₹8,00,000
Reserves	60,000	Current assets:	
Profit and loss A/c	2,40,000	Stock	3,00,000
Debentures	3,00,000	Debtors	2,66,667
Creditors	3,50,000	Other current assets	2,33,333
Other current liabilities	50,000		
	16,00,000		16,00,000

Working Notes

1. Current ratio of 2 implies that CA_s = twice CL, i.e., CA – 2CL = 0
   Further, CA - CL = ₹4,00,000 or, CL = ₹4,00,000 and CA = ₹8,00,000.
2. Capital block to current assets ratio of 3:2 implies that long-term capital funds (equity funds + debentures) are 1.5 times current assets, i.e., ₹8,00,000 × 1.5 = ₹12,00,000.
3. Total assets = Total liabilities = ₹16,00,000 (₹12,00,000 long-term funds + ₹4,00,000 CL).
4. Fixed assets = ₹16,00,000, Total assets – ₹8,00,000, CA = ₹8,00,000.
5. FA/Turnover (sales) = 1/3 or Sales = ₹8,00,000 × 3 = ₹24,00,000.
6. Proportion of cash sales to credit sales is 1:2 or cash sales are one-third of total sales, i.e. 1/3 × ₹24,00,000 = ₹8,00,000; credit sales = ₹16,00,000.
7. Gross profit = 0.25 × ₹24,00,000 = ₹6,00,000; cost of goods sold = ₹18,00,000.
8. Debtors = ₹16,00,000/6 (Debtors turnover ratio, 12 ÷ 2) = ₹2,66,667.
9. Stock = ₹18,00,000/6 (Stock turnover ratio, 12 ÷ 2) = ₹3,00,000.
10. Other CAs = ₹8,00,000 – (₹2,66,667 + ₹3,00,00) = ₹2,33,333.
11. Reserves = 0.025 × ₹24,00,000 = ₹60,000.
12. Credit purchases = Cost of goods sold + Closing stock = ₹18,00,000 + ₹3,00,000 = ₹21,00,000.
13. Creditors = ₹21,00,000 ÷ 6 (creditors turnover ratio, 12 ÷ 2) = ₹3,50,000.
14. Other CLs = Total CL – Creditors, i.e. ₹4,00,000 – ₹3,50,000 = ₹50,000.
15. Debentures to share capital ratio of 1:2 implies that debentures in value are equal to one-half of share capital (2 Debentures = Share capital). Further, capital block (as per working note 3) is ₹12,00,000.
    ₹12,00,000 = Debentures + Share capital + Net profit + Reserves
    ₹12,00,000 = 3 Debentures + ₹2,40,000 (10 per cent of sales) + ₹60,000
    ₹3,00,000 = Debentures; Share capital = ₹6,00,000

P.6.14 The following items appear in the accounts of XYZ Ltd as at March 31, current year: LO 6.4 LOD M

Cash	₹4,860	Bank overdraft	₹5,200
Land and building	80,000	Equity shares (₹10 each)	1,00,000
Deposits and payments in advance	6,200	Profit and loss A/c (Cr.)	21,700
Stock	37,280	Proposed equity dividend for current year	8,625
Trade creditors	40,575	Trade investments	2,000
General reserve	10,000	Provision for taxation	12,400
Debtors	52,300	Dividend reserve	14,000
Bills receivable	2,260	Bills payable	1,800
Plant and machinery	54,400	Net sales for current year	2,18,240
12% Debentures (secured)	25,000	Net profit for current year before taxation and dividend	32,783

Note:

The values of all fixed assets reflect current price levels after provision of depreciation.

You are required to arrange the above items in the form of financial statement and find out the rate of return on capital employed (by using different ways).

Solution

Financial Statement of XYZ Ltd as at March 31

Particulars			*Amount*
Shareholders' funds:			
Equity share capital			₹1,00,000
General reserve			10,000
Profit and loss account (credit)			21,700
Dividend reserve			14,000
			1,45,700
Add: 12% Debentures (secured)			25,000
Long-term funds (capital employed)			1,70,700
Investment of funds in:			
Fixed assets:			
Land and building		₹80,000	
Trade investments		2,000	
Plant and machinery		54,400	1,36,400
Working capital (net)			
Current assets:			
Cash	₹4,860		
Deposit and payments in advance	6,200		
Stock	37,280		
Debtors	52,300		
Bills receivable	2,260	1,02,900	
Less: Current liabilities:			
Trade creditors	40,575		
Bank overdraft	5,200		
Provision for taxation	12,400		
Bills payable	1,800		
Proposed equity dividends	8,625	(68,600)	34,300
			1,70,700

Rate of return on capital employed (ROCE)

(i) $\frac{\text{EBIT}}{\text{Capital employed}} \times 100 = \frac{₹32,783 + ₹3,00^{@}}{₹1,70,700} \times 100 = 21\%$ per cent

@Interest on 12% Debentures is ₹25,000 × 0.12 = ₹3,000

(ii) $\frac{\text{EAT + Interest}}{\text{Capital emploted}} \times 100 = \frac{₹32,783 - ₹12,400 + ₹3,000}{₹1,70,700} \times 100 = 13.7\%$ per cent

(iii) $\frac{\text{EAT + Interest − tax advantage on interest}^{@@}}{\text{Capital employed}} \times 100 = \frac{₹20,383 + \text{Rs } 3,000 - ₹1,134}{₹1,70,700} \times 100 = 13\%$ per cent

@@(Effective tax rate = ₹12,400/₹32,783 = 37.8 per cent)

P.6.15 Towards the end of previous year, the directors of *A* Ltd decided to expand the business. The annual accounts of the company for the previous year and current year are summarised as given: LO 6.4,5 LOD M

Particulars	*Previous year*		*Current year*	
Sales: Cash	₹30,000		₹32,000	
Credit	2,70,000	₹3,00,000	3,42,000	₹3,74,000
Cost of goods sold		2,36,000		2,98,000
Gross margin		64,000		76,000
Expenses:				
Warehousing		13,000		14,000
Transport		6,000		10,000
Administration		19,000		19,000
Selling		11,000		14,000
Debenture interest		—		2,000
		49,000		59,000
Net profit		15,000		17,000
Fixed assets (*less* depreciation)		30,000		40,000
Current assets:				
Stock	60,000		94,000	
Debtors	50,000		82,000	
Cash	10,000	1,20,000	7,000	1,83,000
Less: Current liabilities (trade creditors)		50,000		76,000
Net current assets		70,000		1,07,000
		1,00,000		1,47,000
Share capital		75,000		75,000
Reserves and undistributed profit		25,000		42,000
Debentures		—		30,000
		1,00,000		1,47,000

You are informed that, **(a)** all sales were from stocks in the company's warehouse, **(b)** the range of merchandise was not changed and buying prices remained steady throughout the 2 years, **(c)** the stocks as on April 1 previous year was ₹40,000 and **(d)** the debenture loan was received on April 1 current year and fixed assets were purchased on that date.

You are required to work out the following accounting ratios for both the years.

(i) Gross profit ratio

(ii) Operating expenses to sales
(iii) Operating profit ratio
(iv) Capital turnover ratio
(v) Stock turnover ratio
(vi) Net profit to capital employed ratio and
(vii) Debtors collection period (in days).

Your answer should give the figures calculated to one decimal place, together with possible reasons for changes in the ratios for 2 years. Ratios relating to capital employed should be based on the capital at the end of the year. Ignore taxation.

Solution

(i) Gross profit ratio (gross profit/sales) × 100

Previous year (₹64,000/₹3,00,000) × 100 = 21.3 per cent

Current year (₹76,000/₹3,74,000) × 100 = 20.3 per cent

The gross profit ratio has declined by 1 per cent. The possible reasons may be **(i)** decrease in unit selling price, **(ii)** increase in direct expenses other than purchases and value of stock and/or **(iii)** any combination of **(i)** and **(ii)**.

(ii) Operating expenses to sales (OES) ratio

Previous year (₹49,000/₹3,00,000) × 100 = 16.3 per cent

Current year (₹57,000/₹3,74,000) × 100 = 15.2 per cent

Operating expenses may not change *pari passu* with sales as such expenses are partly fixed in nature. As a result, the OES ratio has fallen in current year in spite of increase in sales. For instance, administration expenses remained unchanged (at ₹19,000) resulting in a decline in administration expenses ratio from 6.3 to 5.1 per cent. The warehousing expenses have similarly fallen from 4.3 to 3.7 per cent. These cost savings have been partly offset by increase in transport expenses ratio (from 2 per cent to 2.7 per cent and selling expenses ratio from 3.7 to 3.8 per cent) presumably caused by additional transport expenses and selling expenses due to market expansion and tapping of more distant customers.

(iii) Operating profit ratio (EBIT/sales) × 100

Previous year (₹15,000/₹3,00,000) × 100 = 5 per cent

Current year (₹19,000/₹3,74,000) × 100 = 5.1 per cent

The increase in operating profit ratio by 0.1 per cent is the result of (i) decrease in operating expenses ratio by 1.1 per cent (increase in profits) and (ii) decrease in gross profit ratio by 1 per cent. It implies that there is virtually no gain to the company from increased sales.

(iv) Capital turnover ratio (sales/capital employed)

Previous year (₹3,00,000/₹1,00,000) = 3 times

Current year (₹3,74,000/₹1,47,000) = 2.5 times

The reduction in capital turnover ratio signifies that the company is unable to employ the additional funds as profitably as the existing funds. The expected increase in sales does not seem to have materialised.

(v) Stock turnover ratio (cost of goods sold/average stock)

Previous year (₹2,36,000/₹50,000) = 4.7 times

Current year (₹2,98,000/₹77,000) = 3.9 times

The increase in sales was less than proportionate increase in stock.

(vi) Net profit to capital employed ratio [(net profit + interest)/capital employed] × 100

Previous year (₹15,000/₹1,00,000) × 100 = 15 per cent

Current year (₹19,000/₹1,47,000) × 100 = 12.9 per cent

The company seems to have failed to maintain the earning rate on the funds employed.

(vii) Debtors' collection period (debtors/average credit sales per day)

Previous year (₹50,000/₹739.7) = 68 days

Current year (₹82,000/₹937) = 88 days

The increase in debtors' collection period implies relaxation in credit terms to promote sales, in particular, to penetrate new market/customers.

To sum up, the expansion of the business does not seem to have yielded the anticipated benefits.

P.6.16 Hypothetical Industries Ltd (HIL) has submitted the following projections. (₹lakh) You are required to determine yearly debt service coverage ratio (DSCR) and the average DSCR and comment.

LO 6.3 LOD M

Year	*EAT*	*Interest on loan*	*Repayment of term loan*
1	20	19	11
2	35	17	18
3	40	15	18
4	20	12	18
5	18	10	18
6	18	7	8
7	16	5	8
8	16	2	8

The net profit (EAT) has been arrived at after charging depreciation of ₹20 lakh every year.

Solution

Determination of Debt Service Coverage Ratio (amount in lakh of rupees)

Year	*EAT*	*Depreciation*	*Interest*	*Cash available (Col. 2 + 3 + 4)*	*Principal instalment*	*Debt obligations*	*DSCR (Col. 5 ÷ Col. 7)*
1	2	3	4	5	6	7	8
1	20	20	19	59	11	30	1.97
2	35	20	17	72	18	35	2.06
3	40	20	15	75	18	33	2.27
4	20	20	12	52	18	30	1.73
5	18	20	10	48	18	28	1.71
6	18	20	7	45	8	15	3.00
7	16	20	5	41	8	13	3.15
8	16	20	2	38	8	10	3.80
Average DSCR (ODSCR/8) = 19.69/8 =							2.46

COMMENT: The DSCR of HIL is very satisfactory.

P.6.17 The financial statement of Excel AMP Graphics Limited are as under:

LO 6.6 LOD D

Balance sheet as at 31st March, 2013 (₹ *in crore)*

Sources of funds:	*2013*		*2012*
Shareholders' funds			
Share capital	₹1,121		₹931
Reserves and surplus	8,950	₹10,071	7,999
			8,930
Loan funds:			
Secured loans	—		259
Finance lease obligations	74		—
Unsecured loans	171	245	115
			374
		10,316	9,304
Application of funds:			
Fixed assets			
Gross block	6,667		5,747
Less: Depreciation	3,150		2,561
Net block	3,517		3,186
Capital work-in-progress	27	3,544	28
			3,214
Investments		288	222
Current assets, loans and advances:			
Inventories	2,709		2,540
Sundry debtors	9,468		9,428
Cash and bank balances	3,206		662
Loans and advances	2,043		1,712
	17,426		14,342
Less: Current liabilities and provisions:			
Current liabilities	10,109		7,902
Provisions	513		572
	10,622		8,474
Net current assets		6,804	5,868
Net deferred tax liability		(320)	—
		10,316	9,304

Profit and loss account for the year ended 31 March, 2013 (₹ *in crore)*

Particulars		*2013*		*2012*
Income:				
Sales and services		23,436		17,849
Other income		320		306
		23,756		18,155
Expenditure:				
Cost of materials		15,179		10,996
Personnel expenses		2,543		2,293
Other expenses		3,546		2,815
Depreciation	419		383	
Less: Transfer from revaluation reserve	7	412	6	377
Interest		164		88
			21,844	16,569
Profit before tax			1,912	1,586
Provision for tax:				
Current tax			450	371
Deferred tax			(6)	—
Profit after tax			1,468	1,215

Required:

(i) Compute and analyse the return on capital employed (ROCE) in a Du-Pont control chart framework.
(ii) Compute and analyse the average inventory holding period and average collection period.
(iii) Compute and analyse the return on equity (ROE) by bringing out clearly the impact of financial leverage.

Solution

(i) *Determination of Return on Capital Employed (ROCE) as per Du-Pont chart* *(Amount in ₹ crore)*

Particulars	2013	2012
(a) Determination of EBIT:		
Profit before tax	₹1,912	₹1,586
Add back interest	164	88
Less other incomes	(320)	(306)
Earnings before interest and taxes (EBIT)	1,756	1,368
(b) Determination of capital employed		
Shareholders funds	10,071	8,930
Add loan funds	245	374
Less capital work-in-progress	(27)	(28)
Less investments	(288)	(222)
Less loans and advances	(2,043)	(1,712)
Capital employed in business	7,958	7,342
(c) Sales and services (operating revenues)	23,436	17,849
(d) EBIT/sales (%)	7.49	7.66
(e) Sales/capital employed (times)	2.945	2.431
(f) ROC/= (d × e) (%)	22.06	18.62

(ii) *Computation of average inventory holding period and average collection period*

(Amount in ₹ crore)

Particulars	2013	2012
Cost of materials used during the year	₹15,179	₹10,996
Inventories at year-end	2,709	2,540
Average inventory holding period (365 days × Closing inventory)/ Cost of materials used (days)	65	84
Sales and services (assumed to be on credit)	23,436	17,849
Debtors at year-end	9,468	9,428
Average collection period (365 days × Closing debtors)/ Credit sales (days)	147	193

ANALYSIS: It is a matter of satisfaction for the firm that there has been a decrease in inventory holding period as well as debtors collection period in year 2001 *vis-à-vis* year 2000. There seems to be potentials of further reduction in debtors collection period. Debtors collection period of nearly 5 months (in 2001) *per-se* is high still.

(iii) *Return on Equity and Impact of Financial Leverage* *(Amount in ₹ crore)*

Particulars	2013	2012
(a) Return on equity:		
Profit after tax (EAT)	₹1,468	₹1,215
Shareholders funds (SHF)	10,071	8,930
ROR on equity (EAT/SHF) × 100 (%)	14.58	13.61

(*Contd.*)

(*Contd.*)

(b)	Return on capital employed (post-tax basis) (%)		
	ROCE (before tax)	22.06	18.62
	Tax rate	35	35
	ROCE	14.34	12.1
(c)	Debt funds to total funds:		
	Loan funds	245	374
	Total funds	10,316	9,304
	Share of loan funds to total funds (%)	2.37	4.02

ANALYSIS: The return on equity is marginally higher than the return on total assets/capital employed. The reason is loan funds constitute a meager portion of total funds. In other words, the impact of financial leverage (use of debt to magnify the ROE) is negligible.

P.6.18 The financial statistics pertaining to profitability of Asian Paints (India) Limited for years 1–6 are tabulated below: **LO 6.6** LOD D

(Amount is in ₹ crore)

Particulars	*Year, March 31*					
	1	*2*	*3*	*4*	*5*	*6*
EBIT	107.06	120.77	125.82	163.47	177.20	194.99
Interest	21.68	19.58	22.33	20.29	22.12	14.59
EBT	85.38	100.19	103.49	143.18	155.08	180.40
Tax provisions	30.00	33.00	24.00	45.75	49.50	66.09
EAT	55.38	67.19	79.49	97.43	105.58	114.31
Sales	938.11	1,046.80	1,158.38	1,383.55	1,526.01	1,659.72
Total assets	534.49	647.66	685.84	771.09	882.20	893.52
Average total assets (ATA)	—	591.07	666.75	728.46	826.64	887.86
Equity funds	226.41	260.50	304.51	357.41	411.20	410.56
Average equity funds (AEF)	—	243.45	282.50	330.96	384.30	410.88
Net fixed assets	194.28	256.68	306.87	333.29	382.95	375.76
Inventory (Finished goods)	72.66	81.60	86.58	106.50	114.50	88.26
Sundry debtors	66.92	80.74	79.95	86.67	121.65	118.96
Average fixed assets	—	225.48	281.77	320.08	358.12	379.35
Average inventory	—	77.13	84.09	96.54	110.50	101.38
Average debtors	—	73.83	80.34	83.31	104.16	120.30

From the above financial information, you are required to prepare a disaggregative analysis related to ROA and ROE (both on pre-tax and post-tax basis) and interpret the results.

Solution

Disaggregation of Pretax ROA and ROE of Asian Paints (India) Ltd

	(I) Return on Assets (TA)					*(II) Return on Equity (EF)*	
	Operating profit margin ×	*Assets turnover*	= *Pre-interest and tax ROA*	– *Interest on Assets*	*Post-interest ROA*	× *Leverage*	= *Pretax ROE*
	EBIT/sales ×	*Sales/ATA** =	*EBIT/ATA*	– *I/ATA*	*EBT/ATA*	× *ATA/AEF*	*EBT/AEF*
Year	*(%)*	*(times)*	*(%)*	*(%)*	*(%)*	*(times)*	*(%)*
2	11.54	1.77	20.43	3.31	17.12	2.43	41.6
3	10.86	1.74	18.90	3.35	15.55	2.36	36.70
4	11.82	1.90	22.46	2.79	19.67	2.20	43.27
5	11.61	1.85	21.48	2.68	18.80	2.15	40.42
6	11.75	1.87	21.97	1.64	20.33	2.16	43.91
Average	11.521.83	21.08	2.75	18.33	2.26	41.18	

*Average total assets.

Component Disaggregation of Return on Equity (After-tax) of Asian Paints

Year	Profitability (×) (EAT/Sales) (×) (%)	Assets turnover Sales/ATA = (times)	EAT/ATA (×) (%)	(×) Solvency = ATA/AEF = (times)	ROE EAT/AEF (%)
2	6.42	1.77	11.36	2.43	27.60
3	6.86	1.74	11.94	2.36	28.18
4	7.04	1.90	13.38	2.20	29.44
5	6.92	1.85	12.80	2.15	27.52
6	6.89	1.87	12.88	2.16	27.82
Average	6.83	1.83	12.50	2.26	28.11

Five-component Disaggregation of ROE (After-tax) of Asian Paints

Effects of: Year	Profitability (×) Taxes EAT/EBT (×) (times)	Turnover Financing EBT/EBIT (×) (times)	Operations EBIT/Sales (=) (%)	EAT/Sales (×) (%)	Sales/ATA = (times)	EAT/ATA (%)	(x) Solvency = ATA/AEF (times)	ROE EAT/AEF (%)
2	0.67	0.83	11.54	6.42	1.77	11.36	2.43	27.60
3	0.77	0.82	10.86	6.86	1.74	11.94	2.36	28.18
4	0.68	0.88	11.82	7.04	1.90	13.38	2.20	29.44
5	0.68	0.88	11.61	6.92	1.85	12.80	2.15	27.52
6	0.63	0.93	11.75	6.89	1.87	12.88	2.16	27.82
Average	0.69	0.87	11.52	6.83	1.83	12.50	2.26	28.11

INTERPRETATION: There has been no significant change in ROA (based on EBIT) of Asian Paints during year 2–6 (and in particular 4–6). The two components of ROA, namely, operating profit margin and assets turnover also do not show any noticeable change during the period. Except during year 3, the EBIT/sales ratio varied in a narrow range of 11.54 per cent and 11.82 per cent. Minor change is also observed in respect of assets turnover, the range being 1.74 – 1.90. Between the two components, the change in the operating profit margin largely accounted for the change in ROA.

MINI CASES

6.C.1 The financial statistics pertaining to profitability of Asian Paints (India) Limited for years 1–6 are tabulated below:

(Amount is in ₹ crore)

Particulars	Year, March 31					
	1	2	3	4	5	6
EBIT	107.06	120.77	125.82	163.47	177.20	194.99
Interest	21.68	19.58	22.33	20.29	22.12	14.59
EBT	85.38	100.19	103.49	143.18	155.08	180.40
Tax provisions	30.00	33.00	24.00	45.75	49.50	66.09
EAT	55.38	67.19	79.49	97.43	105.58	114.31
Sales	938.11	1,046.80	1,158.38	1,383.55	1,526.01	1,659.72
Total assets	534.49	647.66	685.84	771.09	882.20	893.52
Average total assets (ATA)	—	591.07	666.75	728.46	826.64	887.86
Equity funds	226.41	260.50	304.51	357.41	411.20	410.56

(Contd.)

Average equity funds (AEF)	—	243.45	282.50	330.96	384.30	410.88
Net fixed assets	194.28	256.68	306.87	333.29	382.95	375.76
Inventory (Finished goods)	72.66	81.60	86.58	106.50	114.50	88.26
Sundry debtors	66.92	80.74	79.95	86.67	121.65	118.96
Average fixed assets	—	225.48	281.77	320.08	358.12	379.35
Average inventory	—	77.13	84.09	96.54	110.50	101.38
Average debtors	—	73.83	80.34	83.31	104.16	120.30

From the above financial information, you are required to prepare a disaggregative analysis related to ROA and ROE (both on pre-tax and post-tax basis) and intrepret the results.

Solution

Disaggregation of Pretax ROA and ROE of Asian Paints (India) Ltd

	(I) Return on Assets (TA)				*(II) Return on Equity (EF)*		
	Operating profit margin ×	*Assets turnover* =	*Pre-interest and tax ROA* −	*Interest on Assets*	*Post-interest ROA* ×	*Leverage* =	*Pretax ROE*
Year	*EBIT/sales (%)* ×	*Sales/ATA* (times)* =	*EBIT/ATA (%)* −	*I/ATA (%)*	*EBT/ATA (%)* ×	*ATA/AEF (times)*	*EBT/AEF (%)*
2	11.54	1.77	20.43	3.31	17.12	2.43	41.6
3	10.86	1.74	18.90	3.35	15.55	2.36	36.70
4	11.82	1.90	22.46	2.79	19.67	2.20	43.27
5	11.61	1.85	21.48	2.68	18.80	2.15	40.42
6	11.75	1.87	21.97	1.64	20.33	2.16	43.91
Average	11.521.83	21.08	2.75	18.33	2.26	41.18	

*Average total assets.

Component Disaggregation of Return on Equity (After-tax) of Asian Paints

	Profitability (×)	*Assets turnover*		*(×) Solvency =*	*ROE*
Year	*(EAT/Sales) (×) (%)*	*Sales/ATA = (times)*	*EAT/ATA (×) (%)*	*ATA/AEF = (times)*	*EAT/AEF (%)*
2	6.42	1.77	11.36	2.43	27.60
3	6.86	1.74	11.94	2.36	28.18
4	7.04	1.90	13.38	2.20	29.44
5	6.92	1.85	12.80	2.15	27.52
6	6.89	1.87	12.88	2.16	27.82
Average	6.83	1.83	12.50	2.26	28.11

Five-component Disaggregation of ROE (After-tax) of Asian Paints

	Profitability (×) Turnover						*(×) Solvency = ROE*	
Effects of:	*Taxes*	*Financing*	*Operations*					
Year	*EAT/EBT (×) (times)*	*EBT/EBIT (×) (times)*	*EBIT/Sales (=) (%)*	*EAT/Sales (×) (%)*	*Sales/ATA = (times)*	*EAT/ATA (%)*	*ATA/ AEF (times)*	*EAT/ AEF (%)*
2	0.67	0.83	11.54	6.42	1.77	11.36	2.43	27.60
3	0.77	0.82	10.86	6.86	1.74	11.94	2.36	28.18
4	0.68	0.88	11.82	7.04	1.90	13.38	2.20	29.44
5	0.68	0.88	11.61	6.92	1.85	12.80	2.15	27.52
6	0.63	0.93.	11.75	6.89	1.87	12.88	2.16	27.82
Average	0.69	0.87	11.52	6.83	1.83	12.50	2.26	28.11

INTERPRETATION: There has been no significant change in ROA (based on EBIT) of Asian Paints during year 2–6 (and in particular 4–6). The two components of ROA, namely, operating profit margin and assets turnover also do not show any noticeable change during the period. Except during year 3, the EBIT/sales ratio varied in a narrow range of 11.54 per cent and 11.82 per cent. Minor change is also observed in respect of assets turnover, the range being 1.74 – 1.90. Between the two components, the change in the operating profit margin largely accounted for the change in ROA.

C.6.2 From the following selected financials of RIL for the period 2004-5 to 2015-16, appraise its financial health from the point of view of liquidity, solvency, profitability and efficiency.

Selected financial data and ratios (Amount in ₹ crore)

Description	2005	2006	2007	2008	2009	2010	2011	2012	2013	2014	2015	2016
(I) Related to Liquidity Analysis												
CURRENT ASSETS	24,258.04	22,062.33	25,908.92	40,133.24	53,051.10	67,870.64	93,814	1,28,175.00	1,40,302.00	130,967	109,389.00	85,591.00
Inventory	7,412.88	10,119.82	12,136.51	14,247.54	14,836.72	26,981.62	29,825	35,955	42,729	42,932	36,551.00	28,034.00
Debtors	3,927.81	4,163.62	3,732.42	6,227.58	4,571.38	11,660.21	17,442	18,424	11,880	10,664	4,661.00	3,495.00
Loans & Advances	3,711.64	3,609.84	6,024.56	12,019.68	8,545.04	7,247.20	9,851	6,920	7,300	6,911	5,544.00	6,965.00
Current Investments	3,509.26	1,997.83	2,177.01	3,285.85	2,873.57	8,427.56	9,361	27,029	28,366	33,370	50,515.00	39,429.00
Cash and bank balance	3,608.79	2,146.16	1,835.35	4,280.05	22,176.53	13,462.65	27,135	39,598	49,547	36,624	11,571.00	6,892.00
Other current assets	2,087.66	25.06	3.07	72.54	47.86	91.4	199	249	480	466	547.00	776.00
CURRENT LIABILITIES	20,572.23	21,804.33	26,741.53	32,560.59	41,928.87	45,650.70	66,525	68,888	83,286	95,566	91,301.00	125,022.00
Short-term bank borrowings	3,440.71	5,349.85	8,163.13	8,522.50	6,226.97	5,950.29	12,304	10,593	11,511	22,770	12,914.00	14,490.00
Trade Payables	13,209.76	12,166.87	16,467.24	20,590.45	31,579.09	36,055.60	48,846	40,324	45,787	57,862	54,470.00	54,521.00
Other current liabilities	449.96	396.63	398.29	455.02	1,111.91	79.38	811	13,713	21,640	10,767	19,063.00	54,841.00
Short-term provisions	3,471.80	3,890.98	1,712.87	2,992.62	3,010.90	3,565.43	4,563	4,258	4,348	4,167	4,854.00	1,170.00
Net working capital	3,685.81	258	−832.61	7,572.65	11,122.23	22,219.94	27,289	59,287	57,016	35,401	18,088.00	−39,431.00
Credit sales	73,164.10	89,124.16	1,18,353.71	1,39,269.46	1,46,328.07	2,00,399.79	2,58,651.20	3,39,721	3,71,021	4,01,200	340,727.00	251,100.00
Cost of goods sold	52,939.81	63,325.00	87,830.79	1,07,100.52	1,19,021.00	1,64,818.70	2,13,307.60	2,97,023	3,25,405	3,55,773	293,312.00	188,056.00
Cost of raw material used	43,575.32	55,826.18	76,871.66	90,303.85	1,04,805.05	1,47,919.20	1,93,233.90	2,74,814	3,06,127	3,29,313	255,998.00	152,769.00
Credit purchases	45,771.35	58,763.24	78,988.52	1,00,240.39	1,04,729.50	1,59,825.60	1,94,251.30	2,81,029	3,08,981	3,31,589	258,652.00	152,321.00
Average debtors	3,558.87	4,045.71	3,948.02	4,980.00	5,399.48	8,115.80	14,551	17,933	15,152	11,272	7,662.00	5,106.00
Average creditors	11,515.68	12,688.32	14,317.06	18,528.85	26,084.77	33,817.35	42,451	44,585	43,056	51,825	56,166.00	54,495.00
Current ratio	1.18	1.01	0.97	1.23	1.27	1.49	1.41	1.86	1.68	1.37	1.20	0.68
Acid test ratio	0.64	0.38	0.29	0.43	0.71	0.74	0.81	1.24	1.08	0.85	0.74	0.40
Debtors turnover	20.56	22.03	29.98	27.97	27.1	24.69	17.78	18.94	24.49	35.59	44.47	49.18
Creditors turnover	3.97	4.63	5.52	5.41	4.01	4.73	4.58	6.3	7.18	6.4	4.61	2.80
Debtors cycle (days)	17.8	16.61	12.21	13.09	13.51	14.82	20.59	19.32	14.91	10.25	8.20	7.42

Creditors cycle (days)	92.08	79.03	66.34	67.65	91.16	77.44	79.98	58.07	50.86	57.05	79.34	130.59
(II) Related to Solvency Analysis												
Share Capital	1,393.09	1,393.17	1,393.21	1,453.39	1,573.53	3,270.37	3,273.37	3,271.00	3,229.00	3,232	3,236.00	3,240.00
Equity Share Suspense	0	0	60.14	0	69.25	0	0	0	0	0	0.00	0.00
Equity Share Warrants	0	0	0	1,682.40	0	0	0	0	0	0	0.00	0.00
Reserves and surplus	39,010.23	48,411.09	62,513.78	78,312.81	1,24,730.19	1,33,900.24	1,48,266.95	1,62,825.00	1,76,766.00	1,93,842.00	212,923.00	236,936.00
Shareholders' fund	**40,403.32**	**49,804.26**	**63,967.13**	**81,448.60**	**1,26,372.97**	**1,37,170.61**	**1,51,540.32**	**1,66,096.00**	**1,79,995.00**	**1,97,074.00**	**216,159.00**	**240,176.00**
Long-term borrowings	15,343.88	16,515.76	19,662.60	27,957.18	67,677.51	56,544.40	55,092.34	48,034.00	43,012.00	62,711	76,227.00	77,866.00
Short-term bank borrowings	3,440.71	5,349.85	8,163.13	8,522.50	6,226.97	5,950.29	12,304.34	10,593.00	11,511.00	22,770	12,914.00	14,490.00
Deferred Tax Liability	4,266.82	4,970.82	6,982.02	7,872.54	9,726.30	10,926.30	11,561.80	12,122.00	12,193.00	12,215	12,677.00	13,159.00
Total debt	**23,051.41**	**26,836.43**	**34,807.75**	**44,352.22**	**83,630.78**	**73,420.99**	**78,958.48**	**70,749.00**	**66,716.00**	**97,696**	**101,818.00**	**105,515.00**
Long term debt	19,610.70	21,486.58	26,644.62	35,829.72	77,403.81	67,470.70	66,654.14	60,156.00	55,205.00	74,926	90,308.00	92,514.00
Total External obligations	40,182.93	43,290.91	53,386.15	68,390.31	1,19,332.68	1,13,121.40	1,33,179.08	1,29,044.00	1,38,491.00	1,70,492.00	180,205.00	216,047.00
EBT	9,068.68	10,704.06	14,520.47	23,010.14	18,433.23	20,547.44	25,242.24	25,750.00	26,284.00	27,818	29,468.00	35,701.00
Interest	1,468.66	877.04	1,188.89	1,077.36	1,745.23	1,997.21	2,327.62	1,966.00	2,574.00	1,867	1,540.00	1,527.00
EBIT	10,537.34	11,581.10	15,709.36	24,087.50	20,178.46	22,544.65	27,569.86	27,716.00	28,858.00	29,685	31,008.00	37,228.00
Total Assets	**80,586.25**	**93,095.17**	**1,17,353.28**	**1,49,838.91**	**2,45,705.65**	**2,50,292.01**	**2,84,719.40**	**2,95,140.00**	**3,18,486.00**	**3,67,566.00**	**397,785.00**	**457,720.00**
Total debt-equity ratio	0.57	0.54	0.54	0.54	0.66	0.54	0.52	0.43	0.37	0.5	0.47	0.44
Long-term debt-equity ratio	0.49	0.43	0.42	0.44	0.61	0.49	0.44	0.36	0.31	0.38	0.42	0.39
Interest coverage ratio	7.17	13.2	13.21	22.36	11.56	11.29	11.84	14.1	11.21	15.9	20.14	24.38
total debt asset ratio	0.29	0.29	0.3	0.3	0.34	0.29	0.28	0.24	0.21	0.27	0.26	0.23
Long term debt asset ratio	0.24	0.23	0.23	0.24	0.32	0.27	0.23	0.2	0.17	0.2	0.23	0.20
Total External obligations to asset ratio	0.5	0.47	0.45	0.46	0.49	0.45	0.47	0.44	0.43	0.46	0.45	0.47
(III) Related to Profitability Analysis												
Revenue from operations	66,051.30	81,211.33	1,11,692.72	1,33,443.00	1,41,847.47	1,92,461.02	2,48,170.00	3,29,904.00	3,97,062.00	3,90,117.00	329,076.00	233,158.00
Cost of goods sold	53,345.03	65,535.84	83,015.64	1,02,253.38	1,19,021.00	1,64,818.70	2,13,307.60	2,97,023.00	3,25,405.00	3,55,773.00	293,312.00	188,056.00
Gross Profit	12,706.27	15,675.49	28,677.08	31,189.62	22,826.47	27,642.32	34,862.40	32,881.00	71,657.00	34,344.00	35,764.00	45,102.00
EBIT	10,537.34	11,581.10	15,709.36	24,087.50	20,178.46	22,544.65	27,569.86	27,716.00	28,858.00	29,685.00	31,008.00	37,228.00
Other Incomes	1,449.81	682.92	478.28	5,628.79	2,059.88	2,460.47	3,051.71	6,192.00	7,867.00	8,936.00	8,721.00	7,582.00

Operating profit	9,087.53	10,898.18	15,231.08	18,458.71	18,118.58	20,084.18	24,518.15	21,524.00	20,991.00	20,749.00	22,287.00	29,646.00
EAT	7,571.68	9,069.34	11,943.40	19,458.29	15,309.32	16,235.67	20,286.30	20,040.00	21,003.00	21,984.00	22,719.00	27,417.00
Average total capital employed	52,978.70	61,033.61	74,974.88	96,517.76	1,51,728.13	1,93,882.75	2,00,173.84	2,10,381.33	2,18,568.50	2,41,396.00	276,084.00	305,214.00
Average total assets	76,206.70	86,840.71	1,05,224.23	1,33,596.10	1,97,772.28	2,47,998.83	2,67,505.71	2,89,929.70	3,06,813.00	3,43,026.00	382,684.00	427,753.00
Average equity funds	37,427.89	45,103.79	56,885.70	72,707.87	1,03,910.79	1,31,771.79	1,44,355.47	1,58,818.16	1,73,045.50	1,88,535.00	206,616.00	228,168.00
Gross profit %	19.24	19.3	25.67	23.37	16.09	14.36	14.05	9.97	18.05	8.8	10.87	19.34
Operating profit ratio %	13.76	13.42	13.64	13.83	12.77	10.44	9.88	6.52	5.29	5.32	6.77	12.71
Net profit ratio %	11.46	11.17	10.69	14.58	10.79	8.44	8.17	6.07	5.29	5.64	6.90	11.76
Cost of goods sold ratio%	80.76	80.7	74.33	76.63	83.91	85.64	85.95	90.03	81.95	91.2	89.13	80.66
ROR (Equity funds)	20.23	20.11	21	26.76	14.73	12.32	14.05	12.62	13.62	12.65	11.00	12.02
ROR on capital employed (ROCE)1	17.06	16.3	17.52	21.28	11.24	9.4	11.3	10.46	10.79	9.88	8.23	8.98
ROR (Total assets)2	11.86	11.45	12.48	15.37	8.62	7.35	8.45	7.59	7.68	6.95	5.94	6.41
(IV) Related to Efficiency Analysis												
Cost of raw materials used	43,575.32	55,826.18	76,871.66	90,303.85	1,04,805.05	1,47,919.20	1,93,233.90	2,74,814.00	3,06,127.00	3,29,313.00	255,998.00	152,769.00
Average raw materials inventory	3,315.10	3,958.83	4,317.08	6,429.29	7,253.28	10,568.13	14,800.00	16,963.00	20,526.00	22,578.00	21,214.00	16,629.00
Cost of goods manufactured	52,196.39	64,688.04	89,214.01	1,05,598.14	1,18,778.63	1,68,081.63	2,14,520.40	2,97,591.00	3,28,230.00	3,55,025.00	292,650.00	186,242.00
Average stock in process	861.92	1,355.53	1,814.17	1,706.35	1,858.93	2,536.37	3,893.98	5,089.00	5,817.50	6,453.50	5,877.00	4,040.00
Cost of goods sold	52,939.81	63,325.00	87,830.79	1,07,100.52	1,19,021.00	1,64,818.70	2,13,307.60	2,97,023.00	3,25,405.00	3,55,773.00	293,312.00	188,056.00
Average total assets	76,206.70	86,840.71	1,05,224.23	1,33,596.10	1,97,772.28	2,47,998.83	2,67,505.71	2,89,929.70	3,06,813.00	3,43,026.00	382,684.00	427,753.00
Average fixed assets	31,021.08	42,984.87	59,688.61	62,772.05	81,113.35	1,26,801.47	1,47,983.18	1,28,215.00	1,11,735.50	1,09,577.00	111,985.00	122,986.00
Average capital employed	52,978.70	61,033.61	74,974.88	96,517.76	1,51,728.13	1,93,882.75	2,00,173.84	2,10,381.33	2,18,568.50	2,41,396.00	276,084.00	305,214.00
Average current assets	20,055.98	23,160.19	23,985.63	33,021.08	46,592.17	60,460.87	80,842.20	1,14,111.00	1,34,238.50	1,35,634.50	120,178.00	97,490.00
Net working capital	3,685.81	258	–832.61	7,572.65	11,122.23	22,219.94	27,288.81	59,287.00	57,016.00	35,401.00	18,088.00	(39,431.00)
Net sales	66,051.30	81,211.33	1,11,692.72	1,33,443.00	1,41,847.47	1,92,461.02	2,48,170.00	3,29,904.00	3,97,062.00	3,90,117.00	329,076.00	233,158.00
Raw materials turnover ratio	13.14	14.1	17.81	14.05	14.45	14	13.06	16.2	14.91	14.59	12.07	9.19

Raw materials holding period (in days)	27.77	25.88	20.5	25.99	25.26	26.08	27.96	22.53	24.47	25.02	30.27	39.76
Stock in process turnover ratio	60.56	47.72	49.18	61.89	63.9	66.27	55.09	58.48	56.42	55.01	49.80	46.10
Stock in process cycle (in days)	6.03	7.65	7.42	5.9	5.71	5.51	6.63	6.24	6.47	6.63	7.33	7.92
Total assets turnover ratio (Based on COGS)	0.69	0.73	0.83	0.8	0.6	0.66	0.8	1.02	1.06	1.04	0.77	0.44
Total assets turnover ratio (Based on sales)	0.87	0.94	1.06	1	0.72	0.78	0.93	1.14	1.29	1.14	0.86	0.55
Fixed assets turnover ratio(Based on COGS)	1.71	1.47	1.47	1.71	1.47	1.3	1.44	2.32	2.91	3.25	2.62	1.53
Fixed assets turnover ratio (Based on sales)	2.13	1.89	1.87	2.13	1.75	1.52	1.68	2.57	3.55	3.56	2.94	1.90
Capital turnover ratio	1.25	1.33	1.49	1.38	0.93	0.99	1.24	1.57	1.82	1.62	1.06	0.62
Current assets turnover ratio (Based on COGS)	2.64	2.73	3.66	3.24	2.55	2.73	2.64	2.6	2.42	2.62	2.44	1.93
Current assets turnover ratio (Based on sales)	3.29	3.51	4.66	4.04	3.04	3.18	3.07	2.89	2.96	2.88	2.74	2.39
Working capital turnover ratio	17.92	314.77	–134.15	17.62	12.75	8.66	9.09	5.56	6.96	11.02	18.19	–5.91

Notes:

1. Liquid assets = Total current assets – Inventories – Advances
2. Cost of goods sold = Opening stock of finished goods + Production cost* – Closing stock of finished goods
3. Production cost* = Opening stock in process + Raw material consumed + Cash manufacturing expenses + Depreciation + Other purchases (as per profit and loss account) – Closing stock in process
4. Total credit purchases = Purchases of raw materials* + Other purchases
5. Purchases of raw material* = Raw material consumed + Closing stock of raw materials – Opening stock of raw materials
6. Total assets = Shareholders' funds + Long term borrowings + Deferred tax liability + Current liability & provisions
7. Total external obligations = Long term borrowings + Current liabilities & provisions + Deferred tax liability
8. Average total capital employed = Average long term assets used (excluding capital work-in-progress as it does not contribute to operating income) + Net working capital
9. EBIT = EBT + Interest
10. ROCE = (EAT + Interest) / Average capital employed
11. ROR (Total assets) = (EAT + Interest) / Average assets
12. Cost of goods manufactured = Cost of goods sold + Closing stock of finished goods – Opening stock of finished goods

Solution

The appraisal of financial health of RIL is presented below.

I. Liquidity Analysis: The liquidity position of RIL during the period of 2005-16 has shown both upward and downward trends. For instance, in the initial years, the current ratio was alarmingly low (1.01 in 2006 and less than one, i.e., 0.97 in 2007). Then, it steadily improved through the years 2008 to 2013 and increased from 1.23 to 1.68. However, in the subsequent years, from 2014, the current ratio witnessed a downward trend again. It decreased to 1.37 in 2014 to 1.20 in 2015 and finally was at alarmingly low level of less than one, in 2016. This sharp decrease in current ratio is a matter of concern. The closer analysis indicates that from 2015 to 2016, there has been a reduction in inventory, debtors, cash and bank balances and current investment; further, there has been a significant increase in 'other current liabilities', which has been the main driver for pulling the current ratio below 1.

We observe a similar pattern for the acid test ratio. A very low ratio in the initial years (0.38 in 2006 and 0.27 in 2007), has steadily improved from 2008 to 2012. In fact, in 2012 and 2013, the ratio was very satisfactory at 1.24 and 1.08 respectively (Conventionally, the ratio of 1:1 is considered satisfactory). However, from 2014 onwards acid test ratio started declining. It reached an alarmingly low level of 0.40 in 2016. Following the trend of current ratio, we find that significant increase in 'other current liabilities' along with decrease in debtors, cash and bank balances and current investment have contributed to such low/ unsatisfactory levels of acid test ratio.

The other notable observation is that RIL seems to be banking on bank borrowings (may be in the form of cash credit, enabling it to operate at lower liquidity ratios) to finance its working capital requirements as reflected in a substantial increase in such borrowing over the years. From ₹3,440.71 crore (in 2005), the amount steadily increased to ₹8,522.50 crore (by 2008) and to ₹10,593 crore by 2012 and finally touching ₹14,490 crore by 2016 (registering more than 4 times increase in 2016 compared to 2005).

The net working capital position has shown both an upward and downward trend during the period 2005-16. During the period 2008-2013, the net working capital position showed commendable improvement. From the negative sum of ₹832.61 crore in 2007, the amount has consistently increased over the years, the relevant figures being ₹27,288.81 crore and 59,287 crore in 2011 and 2012 respectively. From 2014, the net working capital has started to decline from ₹35,401 crore in 2014 to ₹18,088 crore in 2015 and has become negative ₹39,431 crore in 2016.

The other notable observation is that RIL has the advantage of much higher creditors payment period compared to debtors collection period. The debtors collection period (varying from 17 days in 2005 to around 20 days in 2012) has shown a further improvement in that the collection period has decreased to 10 days in 2014 and 7 days in 2016. Evidently, the debtors collection period is at a very satisfactory level.

In marked contrast, the creditors payment period is very high. It varied in the range of 66 days to 92 days till 2015. However; in 2016, it saw a sharp rise to 130 days. In 2016, the creditors payment period is 18 times the debtors collection period. This favourable gap provides some leverage to RIL to operate at relatively low liquidity ratios. However, a point of caution must not be ignored here. RIL has witnessed decreasing revenues from 2014 to 2016. A very low debtors turnover ratio could be responsible for the same and requires thorough investigation.

To conclude, the liquidity position of RIL at present does not appear to be satisfactory; it needs improvement.

II. Solvency Ratios: The solvency position of RIL is sound for two reasons: First, it has a satisfactory level of interest coverage ratio during all these years, being in the impressive range of 7.17 and 24.38. It is not likely to commit default in payment of interest to its lenders as its operating profits (EBIT) have incredible margins to meet its interest obligations.

Secondly, its various capital structure ratios have shown a substantial decrease (improvement) over the years. For instance, its total debt to equity ratio has shown a notable decrease from 0.57 in 2005 to 0.44 by 2016. Likewise, long-term debt to equity ratio has registered a substantial decrease from 0.49 in 2005 to 0.39 by 2016. Similarly, total external obligations to assets ratio has recorded a decrease (albeit small) over the years. In view of this commendable financial statistics, it can be concluded that solvency position of RIL is sound. As a result, it enjoys a very high credit rating among international credit rating agencies as well as domestic ones.

III. Profitability Ratios: The profit margins (gross, operating and net) of the RIL over the years had increased in the initial years (2005-08). After that (from 2009-12), the gross, operating and net profit margins have declined significantly. For instance, gross profit margins have declined to 9.97%, operating profit margins declined to 6.52% and net profit margins to 6.07% in the year 2012. Then, in the year 2013, gross profit margin hit a high of 18%, but subsequently dropped to 8% and 10% in 2014 and 2015 respectively. It has again shown a sharp rise in 2016, by jumping straight up to 19%.

The operating profit ratio and net margin ratio remained relatively stable at around 6% from 2012 to 2015. But, in 2016, they also jumped to 12% and 11% respectively.

This trend in operating profit margins has had an impact on the ROR on capital employed which has come down from 21.28% in 2008 to 10.46% in 2012 and is now at 8.98% in 2016.

It is also significant to note that there has been a significant decline in other rates of return too. For instance, the ROR on total assets has come down to 7.35% in 2010 from 15.37% in 2008. It has been consistently decreasing since 2009 and touched 5.94% in 2015. However, it showed improvement in 2016 by increasing to 6.41%.

Likewise, a notable decrease has been observed in ROR on equity funds. From 26.76 percent in 2008, it has decreased to 12.62% in 2012. Since then, it has been relatively stable in the range of 11 percent to 12% till 2016.

All this decline is primarily (perhaps) attributable to increase in the cost of goods sold ratio which touched a peak level of 90% in 2012 from 76 percent in 2008. Even when the cost of goods sold ratio declined considerably from 90% in 2012 to 80% in 2016, considerable improvement in ROR has not been noticed.

In conclusion, the profitability position of Reliance is less satisfactory and declining profits is a matter of concern and requires investigation.

IV. Efficiency: In terms of inventory turnover, raw materials holding period has varied in the range of 20 to 30 days during the period 2005-11. This period, *prima-facie*, appears to be satisfactory. However, it showed a sharp increase to 39 days in 2016. Such high inventory holding period merits a close examination.

In terms of debtors, debtors collection period of 20 to 28 days till 2012 appears to be satisfactory. However, its subsequent decrease to 7 days in 2016 compared to 13 days in 2013 though *prima-facie*, is a sign of notable improvement in the efficiency of debtors collection department, it needs to be carefully evaluated as the lower credit period offered to debtors may or could be the cause of lower sales (and hence of unsatisfactory profits) of RIL.

The Current assets turnover ratio during the period under study has been in the range of 2.89 to 4.66.

The fixed assets turnover ratio varied from 1.30 in 2010 to 2.62 in 2015. However, it has shown a sharp decrease in 2016 to 1.53.

RIL, being a capital intensive industry, the ratio of more than 2 (in most of the year, 2010-2016) seems to be indicative of the fact that long-term assets, by and large, operate at their higher levels of capacity.

To summarise its financial position, RIL has a sound solvency position. However, its liquidity position at present (2016) does not appear to be satisfactory. It needs improvement. Although its business operations are profitable, its margins of profits (on sales) as well as rates of return (on total assets, on capital employed and equity funds) have witnessed decline during 2012-16. Finally, it goes to the credit of RIL that it manages its assets/resources (by and large) well (as indicated by efficiency ratios).

C.6.3 From the following selected financials of ITC for the period 2011-12 to 2015-16, appraise its financial health from the point of view of liquidity, solvency, profitability and efficiency.

(Figures in ₹ crore)

Particulars	*2011-12*	*2012-13*	*2013-14*	*2014-15*	*2015-16*
(I) Related to Liquidity Analysis					
CURRENT ASSETS	14443.57	17591.47	20928.73	23955.03	24134.74
Current Investment	4363.31	5059.43	6311.26	5963.82	6461.34
Inventory	5637.83	6600.20	7359.54	7836.76	8519.82
Trade receivables	986.02	1163.34	2165.36	1722.40	1686.35
Cash and bank balances	2818.93	3615.00	3289.37	7588.61	6563.95
Short-term loans and advances	500.59	512.14	783.51	549.89	501.84
Other current assets	136.89	641.36	1019.69	293.55	401.44
CURRENT LIABILITIES	9101.83	10330.73	11504.32	11681.91	14587.86
Short-term bank borrowings	1.77	0.00	0.14	0.02	3.60
Trade payables	1424.84	1668.98	1987.59	1904.62	2265.59
Other current liabilities	3371.27	3528.62	3631.88	3671.18	4000.08
Short-term provisions	4303.95	5133.13	5884.71	6106.09	8318.59
Credit sales	34871.86	41809.82	46712.62	49964.82	51582.45
Cost of goods sold	12631.09	14747.90	17213.41	18219.98	17380.36
Cost of raw materials used	7660.91	8936.21	10263.28	10987.83	11054.75
Credit purchases	9698.12	12312.13	13284.75	14886.49	13644.83
Average debtors	935.56	1072.86	1664.35	1943.88	1704.38
Average creditors	1410.08	1559.10	1828.29	1946.11	2085.11
Current ratio	1.59	1.70	1.82	2.05	1.65
Acid test ratio	0.97	1.06	1.18	1.38	1.07
Net working capital	5341.74	7260.74	9424.41	12273.12	9546.88
Debtors turnover ratio	37.27	38.97	28.07	25.70	30.26
Creditors turnover ratio	6.88	7.90	7.27	7.65	6.54
Debtors cycle(days)	9.79	9.37	13.00	14.20	12.06
Creditors cycle(days)	53.07	46.22	50.23	47.72	55.78
(II) Related to Solvency Analysis					
Share Capital	781.84	790.18	795.32	801.55	804.72
Reserves and Surplus	18010.05	21497.67	25466.70	29934.14	32124.28
Shareholder's Funds	**18791.89**	**22287.85**	**26262.02**	**30735.69**	**32929.00**
Long Term Borrowings	77.32	66.40	51.00	38.69	25.83
Short Term Borrowings	1.70	0.00	0.14	0.02	3.60
Deferred Tax liabilities	872.72	1203.72	1296.96	1631.60	1848.42

Total Debt	**951.74**	**1270.12**	**1348.10**	**1670.31**	**1877.85**
Long Term Debt	950.04	1270.12	1347.96	1670.29	1874.25
Total External Borrowings	10174.51	11729.58	12967.37	13459.97	16589.43
EBT	8897.53	10684.18	12659.11	13997.52	14958.39
Interest	66.98	65.97	2.95	35.41	49.13
EBIT	8964.51	10750.15	12662.06	14032.93	15007.52
Total Assets	**28966.40**	**34017.43**	**39299.39**	**44195.66**	**49518.43**
Total debt-equity ratio	0.05	0.06	0.05	0.05	0.06
Long term debt-equity ratio	0.05	0.06	0.05	0.05	0.06
Interest coverage Ratio	133.84	162.96	4292.22	396.30	305.47
Total debt to asset Ratio	0.03	0.04	0.03	0.04	0.04
Long term debt to assets Ratio	0.03	0.04	0.03	0.04	0.04
Total external obligations to assets Ratio	0.35	0.34	0.33	0.30	0.34
(III) Related to Profitability					
Revenue from operations	25173.82	29901.27	33238.6	36507.4	36837.39
Cost of goods sold	12631.09	14747.90	17213.41	18219.98	17380.36
Gross profit	12542.73	15153.37	16025.19	18287.42	19457.03
EBIT	8964.51	10750.15	12662.06	14032.93	15007.52
Other income	825.34	938.7	1107.14	1543.13	1803.74
Operating profit	8139.17	9811.45	11554.92	12489.80	13203.78
EAT	6162.37	7418.39	8785.21	9607.73	9844.71
Average net block	8722.15	10154.27	11611.04	13095.62	14191.51
Average total capital employed	17587.82	22198.91	25429.34	30399.61	32429.74
Average total assets	27200.11	31502.82	36623.41	41712.53	46857.05
Average equity funds	17372.58	20539.87	24274.94	28498.86	31832.35
Gross profit ratio	50%	51%	48%	50%	53%
Operating profit ratio	32%	33%	35%	34%	36%
Net profit ratio	24%	25%	26%	26%	27%
Cost of goods sold ratio	50%	49%	52%	50%	47%
ROR on capital employed	51%	48%	50%	46%	46%
ROR on total assets	33%	34%	35%	34%	32%
ROR on equity funds	35%	36%	36%	34%	31%
(IV) Related to Efficiency Analysis					
Cost of materials used	7660.91	8936.21	10263.28	10987.83	11054.75
Cost of goods sold	12631.09	14747.90	17213.41	18219.98	17380.36
Average total assets	27200.11	31502.82	36623.41	41712.53	46857.05

Average fixed assets	8722.15	10154.27	11611.04	13095.62	14191.51
Average capital employed	17587.82	22198.91	25429.34	30399.61	32429.74
Average current assets	13744.56	16027.26	19260.10	22441.88	24044.89
Net working capital	5341.74	7260.74	9424.41	12273.12	9546.88
Net sales	25173.82	29901.27	33238.60	36507.40	36837.39
Total assets turnover ratio (based on COGS)	0.46	0.47	0.47	0.44	0.37
Total assets turnover ratio (based on Sales)	0.93	0.95	0.91	0.88	0.79
Fixed assets turnover ratio (based on COGS)	1.45	1.45	1.48	1.39	1.22
Fixed assets turnover ratio (based on Sales)	2.89	2.94	2.86	2.79	2.60
Capital turnover ratio	0.72	0.66	0.68	0.60	0.54
Current assets turnover ratio (based on COGS)	0.92	0.92	0.89	0.81	0.72
Current assets turnover ratio (based on Sales)	1.83	1.87	1.73	1.63	1.53
Working Capital Turnover ratio	2.36	2.03	1.83	1.48	1.82

Solution

The appraisal of the financial health of ITC is presented below:

I. Liquidity Analysis: The liquidity ratios of ITC appears to be satisfactory. In 2011, the current ratio was around 1.59 and it increased to 2.05 in 2014-15. Conventionally, a ratio of 2:1 is considered satisfactory. However, in 2015-16, the current ratio took a sharp decrease to 1.65. Closer analysis shows that there has been a substantial increase in current liabilities, contributing to the decrease in current ratio.

Similar trends are observed for the acid test ratio. A ratio of 0.97 in 2011-12, got stronger over the years and touched a high of 1.38 in 2014-15. However, it decreased in 2015-16 and reached 1.07 by the end of the 2016. A quick ratio of 1:1 is considered ideal, which ITC has maintained throughout.

Another observation is that net working capital of ITC has consistently increased during the period under reference. But, it has improved from ₹5,341 crores in 2011-12 to ₹12,273 crores in 2014-15. There has been a decline in net working capital in 2016 to ₹9,546 crores; in spite of this decrease, the liquidity position of ITC can be considered as satisfactory.

We also observe that ITC is enjoying a much higher creditors payment period as compared to the debtors collection period. The debtors collection period varied in the range of 9-12 days during 2012-16. In contrast, the creditors payment period was in the range of 53-55 days during the same period. This favourable gap provides leverage for the company and ensures better liquidity position of ITC to meet its short-term maturing obligations in time.

II. Solvency Analysis: The solvency position of ITC appears robust. Firstly, the interest coverage ratio is exorbitantly high. It was already very high i.e. 133 in 2011, and this further increased to become 305 in 2016. With such high ratio, the company is not likely to face any problem paying in interest to its lenders.

The various leverage ratios have been relatively stable and shows ITC does not heavily depend on debt for its financing. The total debt to assets ratio has been around 0.03 to 0.04 during the period under study. Similarly, the long-term debt to assets ratio has also been in the same range. Total debt to equity and long term debt to equity ratio has been stable around 0.05 to 0.06.

Evidently, the solvency position of the company is very sound.

III. Profitability Analysis: The profitability analysis is equally impressive. Over the years, there has been stability in its profitability ratios. For instance, the gross profit ratio has been in the range of 48% to 53%. Its net profit ratio also is stable in the range of 24% to 27%.

The rates of return on capital employed as well as total assets are also notable. For instance, ROR on capital employed has been as high as 51% and ROR on total assets touched a high of 35% in 2013-14. The ROR on equity funds is also lucrative at 31% to 35% during the five year period of the study.

IV. Efficiency Ratios: Analysing the performance with respect to utilisation of assets, we find it is unsatisfactory. The fixed assets turnover ratio has substantially declined from 2.89 in 2011-12 to 2.60 in 2015-16. The Current assets turnover ratio has also declined from 1.83 in 2011-12 to 1.53 in 2015-16. Better utilisation of assets can further augment its profitability.

To conclude, the financial health of ITC is sound given its liquidity, solvency and profitability ratios. However, the efficiency ratios have potential for further improvement.

C.6.4 From the following selected financials of Tata Motors for the period 2011-12 to 2015-16, appraise its financial health from the point of view of liquidity, solvency, profitability and efficiency.

(Amount in ₹ crore)

Particulars	*2011-12*	*2012-13*	*2013-14*	*2014-15*	*2015-16*
(I) Related to Liquidity Analysis					
CURRENT ASSETS	13633.39	10027.16	6700.55	8506.83	10616.45
Current Investment	2590.26	1762.68	100.85	20.22	1736.00
Inventory	4588.23	4455.03	3862.53	4802.08	4902.20
Trade receivables	2708.32	1818.04	1216.70	1114.48	1568.46
Cash and bank balances	1840.96	462.86	226.15	944.75	452.08
Short-term loans and advances	1792.21	1424.29	1185.26	1508.27	1704.86
Other current assets	113.41	104.26	109.06	117.03	252.85
CURRENT LIABILITIES	22138.17	21104.61	18797.53	20370.63	17751.06
Short-term bank borrowings	3007.13	6216.91	4769.08	7762.01	3351.74
Trade payables	8705.53	8455.02	9672.36	8852.65	8916.60
Other current liabilities	7470.95	4923.10	2463.18	3142.88	4267.23
Short term provisions	2954.56	1509.58	1892.91	613.09	1215.49
Credit sales	58650.42	48665.28	37101.74	38829.49	45879.45
Cost of goods sold	44303.71	36932.75	29152.13	33236.85	35816.47
Cost of raw materials used	33894.82	27244.28	20492.87	22155.23	24313.08
Credit purchases	40328.77	33108.73	25542.69	27920.47	29572.35
Average debtors	2655.56	2263.18	1517.37	1165.59	1341.47
Average creditors	8781.05	8580.28	9063.69	9262.51	8884.63

Current ratio	0.62	0.48	0.36	0.42	0.60
Acid test ratio	0.41	0.26	0.15	0.18	0.32
Net working capital	–8504.78	–11077.45	–12096.98	–11863.80	–7134.61
Debtors turnover ratio	22.09	21.50	24.45	33.31	34.20
Creditors turnover ratio	4.59	3.86	2.82	3.01	3.33
Debtors cycle (days)	16.53	16.97	14.93	10.96	10.67
Creditors cycle (days)	79.47	94.59	129.52	121.09	109.66
(II) Related to Solvency Analysis					
Share Capital	634.75	638.07	643.78	643.78	679.18
Reserves and Surplus	18732.91	18496.77	18532.87	14218.81	21688.90
Shareholder's Funds	**19367.66**	**19134.84**	**19176.65**	**14862.59**	**22368.08**
Long-term Borrowings	8004.50	8051.78	9746.45	12318.96	10687.94
Short-term Borrowings	3007.13	6216.91	4769.08	7762.01	3351.74
Deferred Tax liabilities	98.80	–126.88	–1360.32	764.23	–83.84
Total Debt	**11110.43**	**14141.81**	**13155.21**	**20845.20**	**13955.84**
Long Term Debt	8103.30	7924.90	8386.13	13083.19	10604.10
Total External Borrowings	34893.27	33049.93	30557.77	35080.58	30058.17
EBT	1926.27	600.80	–485.94	–3570.97	513.60
Interest	849.44	1051.45	1008.62	1151.07	1108.24
EBIT	2775.71	1652.25	522.68	–2419.90	1621.84
Total Assets	**13712.92**	**10134.96**	**6739.06**	**8572.97**	**10705.91**
Total debt-equity ratio	0.57	0.74	0.69	1.40	0.62
Long term debt-equity ratio	0.42	0.41	0.44	0.88	0.47
Interest coverage ratio	3.27	1.57	0.52	–2.10	1.46
Total debt to asset Ratio	0.81	1.40	1.95	2.43	1.30
Long term debt to assets Ratio	0.59	0.78	1.24	1.53	0.99
Total external obligations to assets Ratio	2.54	3.26	4.53	4.09	2.81
(III) Related to Profitability					
Revenue from operations	54306.56	44765.72	34288.11	36294.74	42369.82
Cost of goods sold	44303.71	36932.75	29152.13	33236.85	35816.47
Gross profit	10002.85	7832.97	5135.98	3057.89	6553.35
EBIT	2775.71	1652.25	522.68	–2419.90	1621.84
Other Income	574.08	2088.20	3833.03	1881.41	2132.92
Operating profit	2201.63	–435.95	–3310.35	–4301.31	–511.08

EAT	1242.23	301.81	334.52	–4738.95	234.23
Average net block	14218.30	15237.63	15348.16	15511.90	15773.60
Average total capital employed	28006.56	26219.56	24543.31	23465.61	28104.84
Average total assets	54354.87	53222.85	50959.59	49838.80	51184.71
Average equity funds	19819.65	19251.25	19155.75	17019.62	18615.34
Gross profit ratio	18%	17%	15%	8%	15%
Operating profit ratio	4%	–1%	–10%	–12%	–1%
Net profit ratio	2%	1%	1%	–13%	1%
Cost of goods sold ratio	82%	83%	85%	92%	85%
ROR on capital employed	10%	6%	2%	–10%	6%
ROR on total assets	5%	3%	1%	–5%	3%
ROR on equity funds	6%	2%	2%	–28%	1%
(IV) Related to Efficiency Analysis					
Cost of materials used	33894.82	27244.28	20492.87	22155.23	24313.08
Cost of goods sold	44303.71	36932.75	29152.13	33236.85	35816.47
Average total assets	54354.87	53222.85	50959.59	49838.80	51184.71
Average fixed assets	14218.30	15237.63	15348.16	15511.90	15773.60
Average capital employed	28006.56	26219.56	24543.31	23465.61	28104.84
Average current assets	12342.29	11923.94	8437.01	7656.02	9639.44
Net working capital	–8504.78	–11077.45	–12096.98	–11863.80	–7134.61
Net sales	54306.56	44765.72	34288.11	36294.74	42369.82
Total assets turnover ratio (based on COGS)	0.82	0.69	0.57	0.67	0.70
Total assets turnover ratio (based on Sales)	1.00	0.84	0.67	0.73	0.83
Fixed assets turnover ratio (based on COGS)	3.12	2.42	1.90	2.14	2.27
Fixed assets turnover ratio (based on Sales)	3.82	2.94	2.23	2.34	2.69
Capital turnover ratio	1.58	1.41	1.19	1.42	1.27
Current assets turnover ratio (based on COGS)	3.59	3.10	3.46	4.34	3.72
Current assets turnover ratio (based on sales)	4.40	3.75	4.06	4.74	4.40
Working capital turnover ratio	–5.21	–3.33	–2.41	–2.80	–5.02

Solution

The appraisal of the financial health of Tata Motors is presented below:

I. Liquidity Analysis: The liquidity ratios of Tata Motors do not portray its satisfactory position. In 2011, the current ratio was around 0.62 and it substantially reduced to an alarmingly low level of 0.36 in 2013-14. Although, since then the ratio improved to 0.60 (close to what it was in 2011), still it is at an unsatisfactory level. Conventionally, a ratio of 2:1 is considered satisfactory and Tata Motors is way below that level. Similar trends are observed for the acid test ratio. A weak ratio of 0.42 in 2011, got weaker over the years and touched a low of 0.15 in 2013. In spite of the fact that it has shown improvement and reached 0.32 by the end of the 2016, it remains at unsatisfactory level. There has been a substantial decrease in cash and bank balances since 2012-13, and this appears to be a significant contributor to the decreased levels of current ratio and acid test ratio.

Another observation is that the net working capital of Tata Motors has consistently been negative during the period. But, it has improved from ₹8,500 crores in 2011-12 to ₹7,100 crores in 2015-16. The decline in the sales revenue during the years could also be a factor for the reduced working capital needs.

We also observe that Tata Motors is enjoying a much higher creditors payment period as compared to the debtors collection period. The debtors collection period was about 17 days in 2011 and further dipped to 10 days in 2015. In contrast, the creditors payment period was 80 days in 2011 and increased to 109 days by the end of the period under study. This favourable gap provides some leverage/solace for the company to operate at such low liquidity ratios. However, a point of caution is the decreasing debtors collection period. A low credit period of 10 days could be the reason of declining sales and requires thorough investigation.

II. Solvency Analysis: The solvency position of Tata Motors also appears to be unsatisfactory. Firstly, the interest coverage ratio is inadequate. It was somewhat at a satisfactory level of 3.27 in 2011, it decreased to become -2 in 2014 (when the company suffered losses and had a negative EBIT). However, since then this ratio improved to 1.46. Even though the ratio is positive now, it is not satisfactory and may pose problems for the company to service its interest payments to lenders.

The total debt to assets ratio has increased from 0.81 in 2011-12 to 2.43 in 2014-15 and then decreased to 1.30 in 2015-16. Similarly, the long-term debt to assets ratio has increased from 0.59 in 2011-12 to 1.53 in 2014-15 and then decreased to 0.99 in 2015-16. Although there has been a decrease in total external obligations/debt to assets ratio as well as long term debt to assets ratio in 2016, given its very low interest coverage ratio, the level of debt of the firm seems to be on the higher side and needs to be reduced.

III. Profitability Analysis: The profitability analysis looks disturbing. Over the years, there has been a dip in its profitability ratios. For instance, the gross profit ratio decreased from 18% in 2011-12 to 15% in 2015-16. Its net profit ratio also decreased from 2% in 2011-12 to become negative in 2015 and finally to 1% in 2015-16. Consequently, the rates of return on capital employed as well as total assets declined during the period. ROR on capital employed declined from 10% to 6% and ROR on total assets declined from 5% to 3%. The ROR on equity funds presents a dismal picture as it turns negative in 2014-15. However, this ratio did improve in the subsequent year.

Overall, the profitability of Tata Motors is a matter of serious concern.

IV. Efficiency Ratios: Analysing the performance with respect to utilisation of assets, we find it is unsatisfactory. The total assets turnover ratio has declined from 0.82 in 2011-12 to 0.07 in 2015-16.

Also, the fixed assets turnover ratio has substantially declined from 3.12 in 2011-12 to 2.27 in 2015-16. For an automobile manufacturer, fixed assets form an important part in the total assets, and a decline in this ratio implies unutilised capacity.

The current assets turnover ratio has been stable varying from 3.59 in 2011-12 to 3.72 in 2015-16. This could be due to the inadequate amount of current assets with the company.

Conclusion: We can thus conclude, that the financial health of Tata Motors is not sound given its unsatisfactory liquidity, solvency, profitability and efficiency ratios.

REVIEW QUESTIONS

LOD: Easy

RQ.6.1 Indicate whether the following statements are true or false: [LO 6.2,3,4,5]

- **(i)** Current ratio and acid-test ratio of a business firm are virtually the same; this implies that the firm has low investment in inventory.
- **(ii)** A company's current ratio is 2.0. If it uses cash to pay creditors, this transaction would cause a decrease in current ratio.
- **(iii)** Solvency ratios measure the firm's ability to cater to the obligations arising out of long-term debt.
- **(iv)** Equity funds are greater than equity capital in a loss-incurring firm.
- **(v)** In general, low turnover ratios are desirable.
- **(vi)** Earnings yield is determined dividing EPS by acquisition price per equity share.
- **(vii)** Return on equity funds is determined by dividing EAT by average net worth.
- **(viii)** Internal growth rate is the maximum rate at which the firm can grow without external financing of any kind.
- **(ix)** It is conceptually correct to determine stock turnover ratio (finished goods) by dividing cost of goods sold by average stock.

[Answers: (i) True, (ii) False, (iii) True, (iv) False, (v) False, (vi) False, (vii) False, (viii) True, (ix) True.]

RQ.6.2 Fill in the blanks with the correct answer (out of the choices provided). [LO 6.2,3,4,5.6]

- **(i)** An analyst applied the DuPont System to the following data of a company: (a) equity turnover 4.2, (b) net profit margin 5.5%, (c) total assets turnover 2.0 and (d) dividend payout ratio 30%; the company's rate of return on equity is ____________ (11%/23.1%).
- **(ii)** Four-times stock turnover ratio implies ____________ months inventory holding period (3/4).
- **(iii)** The following information is given about a company: (a) current assets ₹900 lakh and current liabilities ₹450 lakh in current year and (b) current assets ₹1,100 lakh and current liabilities ₹530 in previous year. The approximate percentage decrease in current ratio is ____________ (0.04%/4.0%).
- **(iv)** Presently, current assets and current liabilities of a company are ₹16 lakh and ₹8 lakh respectively. The current ratio will ____________ (increase/decrease) on purchase of new machinery of ₹6 lakh.
- **(v)** Purchase of treasury bills will (weaken/not affect) acid-test ratio.
- **(vi)** Assume that the company's existing debt-equity ratio is 2:1, the ploughing back of profits by a company will ____________ (increase/decrease) it.
- **(vii)** A two-months debtor collection period implies that debtors turnover ratio is ____________ (6 times/2 times).
- **(viii)** ____________ is a more rigorous test of the solvency position of a business firm. (Interest coverage ratio/Debt service coverage ratio).
- **(ix)** ROR on shareholders' equity is computed dividing EAT by ____________ (share capital/shareholders' funds).
- **(x)** Issue of 12% preference shares will ____________ debt-equity ratio of a corporate enterprise. (decrease/increase)

[Answers: (i) 23.1%, (ii) 3, (iii) 4.0%, (iv) decrease, (v) not affect, (vi) decrease, (vii) 6 times, (viii) debt service coverage ratio, (ix) shareholders' funds, (x) decrease.]

RQ.6.3 What is the importance of ratio analysis? Briefly discuss the importance of the following accounting ratios: **[LO 6.2,3,4,5]**

(a) Liquidity ratio, **(b)** Debt-equity ratio, **(c)** Stock-turnover rate, and **(d)** Ratio of debtors to turnover.

RQ.6.4 What procedure would you adopt to study the liquidity of a business firm? **[LO 6.2,3,4]**

RQ.6.5 What is indicated when the average age of accounts receivable for a firm is 45 days, but credit terms require customers to pay accounts within 30 days? **[LO 6.5]**

RQ.6.6 What are the limitations of financial ratios as a technique for appraising the financial position of a company? **[LO 6.5]**

LOD: Medium

RQ.6.7 How would you analyse the financial position of a company from the point of view of **(a)** an investor, **(b)** a creditor, and **(c)** a long-term lender? **[LO 6.8]**

RQ.6.8 Discuss the importance of ratio analysis for interfirm and intrafirm comparisons, including circumstances responsible for its limitations. If any. **[LO 6.8]**

RQ.6.9 Distinguish between percentage analysis and ratio analysis relating to the interpretation of financial statements. What is the value of these two types of analysis? **[LO 6.1,7,8]**

RQ.6.10 How does the acid-test ratio differ from the current ratio? How are they similar? What is the usefulness of the defensive interval ratio? **[LO 6.2]**

RQ.6.11 What is the relationship of the assets turnover rate to the rate of return on total assets? **[LO 6.6]**

RQ.6.12 Discuss some inherent limitations of single-year financial statements for purposes of analysis and interpretation. To what extent are these limitations overcome by the use of the common size statements? **[LO 6.1,7]**

RQ.6.13 You have been furnished with the financial information of Aditya Mills Ltd. for the current year.

Balance sheet, March 31, current year

Liabilities	*Amount (₹ thousand)*	*Assets*		*Amount (₹ thousand)*
Equity share capital (₹100 each)	1,000	Plant and equipment		640
Retained earnings	368	Land and buildings		80
Sundry creditors	104	Cash		160
Bills payable	200	Sundry debtors	360	
Other current liabilities	20	*Less:* Allowances	40	320
	Stock		480	
		Prepaid insurance		12
	1,692			1,692

Statement of profit, year ended March 31, current year

Particulars	*(₹ thousand)*
Sales	4,000
Less: Cost of goods sold	3,080
Gross profit on sales	920
Less: Operating expenses	680
Net profit	240
Less: Taxes (0.35)	84
Net profit after taxes	156

Sundry debtors and stock at the beginning of the year were ₹3,00,000 and ₹4,00,000 respectively.

(a) Determine the following ratios of the Aditya Mills Ltd: **(i)** Current ratio, **(ii)** Acid-test ratio, **(iii)** Stock turnover, **(iv)** Debtors turnover, **(v)** Gross profit ratio, **(vi)** Net profit ratio, **(vii)** Operating ratio, **(viii)** Earnings per share, **(ix)** Rate of return on equity capital, and **(x)** Market value of the shares if P/E ratio is 10 times, [LO 6.2,3,4,5]

(b) Indicate for each of the following transactions whether the transaction would improve, weaken or have an effect on the current ratio of the Aditya Mills Ltd: **(i)** Sell additional equity shares, **(ii)** Sell 10% debentures, **(iii)** Pay bills payable, **(iv)** Collect sundry debtors, **(v)** Purchase additional plant, **(vi)** Issuing bills payable to creditors, **(vii)** Collecting bills receivable from debtors, **(viii)** Purchase of treasury bills, and **(ix)** Writing off bad debt. [LO 6.2]

RQ.6.14 The XYZ Ltd's financial statement contains the following information: [LO 6.2,3,4,5]

Balance sheet as at March 31, current year

Particulars	*Previous year (₹ thousand)*	*Current year (₹ thousand)*
Cash	200	160
Sundry debtors	320	400
Temporary investments	200	320
Stock	1,840	2,160
Prepaid expenses	28	12
Total current assets	2,588	3,052
Total assets	5,600	6,400
Current liabilities	640	800
15% Debentures	1,600	1,600
Equity share capital	2,000	2,000
Retained earnings	468	904

Statement of profits year ended March 31, current year

Particulars	*(₹ thousand)*
Sales	4,000
Less: Cost of goods sold	2,800
Less: Interest	160
Net profit for current year	1,040
Less: Taxes	364
Earnings after taxes	676
Dividend declared on equity shares	220

From the above, appraise the financial position of the company from the points of view of **(a)** liquidity, **(b)** solvency, **(c)** profitability, and **(d)** activity.

RQ.6.15 You have been supplied data for Royal Plastic Ltd. and its industry averages. [LO 6.2,3,4,5]

(a) Determine the indicated ratios for the Royal Plastic Ltd.

(b) Indicate the company's strengths and weaknesses in terms of liquidity, solvency and profitability, as revealed by your analysis.

Balance sheet, March 31, current year

Liabilities		Assets	
Equity share capital	₹1,00,000	Plant and equipment	₹1,51,000
10% Preference share capital	40,000	Cash	12,300
Retained earnings	27,400	Debtors	36,000
Long-term debt	34,000	Stock	60,800
Sundry creditors	31,500		
Outstanding expenses	1,200		
Other current liabilities	26,000		
	2,60,100		2,60,100

Statement of profit, year ended March 31, current year

Sales—net		₹2,25,000
Less: Cost of goods sold	₹1,52,500	
Selling expenses	29,500	
Administrative expenses	14,800	
Research and development expenses	6,500	
Interest	2,900	2,06,200
Earnings before taxes		18,800
Less: Income taxes (0.35)		6,580
Net income		12,220
Dividends paid to equity holders		5,000

Financial ratios of industry

1. Current ratio	2.2 : 1
2. Stock turnover (times)	2.8
3. Collection period (days)	56
4. Total debt/shareholders' equity (percentage)	45
5. Interest coverage ratio (times)	10
6. Turnover of assets (times)	1.35
7. Income before tax/sales (percentage)	11.9
8. Rate of return on shareholders' equity (percentage)	10.9

RQ.6.16 Below are selected ratios for two companies in the same industry, along with industry average: **[LO 6.2,3,4,5]**

Ratios	*A*	*B*	*Industry*
Current ratio	221	561	241
Acid-test ratio	121	301	131
Debt-asset ratio	36	5	35
Operating expenses ratio	18	17.5	20
Number of times interest earned	6	12	5
Stock turnover	8.5	6.5	7.0
Debtors turnover	11.0	15.0	11.4
Rate of return on total assets	17	10	13.5

Can we say on the basis of above ratios and information that company B is better than company A because its ratios are better in six out of eight areas (all except stock turnover and rate of return on total assets)? The company B is better than the industry average in the same six categories.

RQ.6.17 The following data are extracted from the published accounts of two companies, ABC Ltd. and XYZ Ltd., in an industry. [LO 6.2,3,4,5]

Particulars	*ABC Ltd.*	*XYZ Ltd.*
Sales	₹32,00,000	₹30,00,000
Net profit after tax	1,23,000	1,58,000
Equity capital (₹10 per share fully paid)	10,00,000	8,00,000
General reserves	2,32,000	6,42,000
Long-term debt	8,00,000	5,60,000
Creditors	3,82,000	5,49,000
Bank credit (short-term)	60,000	2,00,000
Fixed assets	15,99,000	15,90,000
Inventories	3,31,000	8,09,000
Other current assets	5,44,000	4,52,000

Prepare a statement of comparative ratios showing liquidity, profitability, activity and financial position of the two companies.

RQ.6.18 Hypothetical Industries Ltd. (HIL) has submitted the following projections (₹ lakh). You are required to determine yearly debt service coverage ratio (DSCR) and the average DSCR and comment. [LO 6.3]

Year	*EAT*	*Interest on loan*	*Repayment of term loan*
1	20	19	11
2	35	17	18
3	40	15	18
4	20	12	18
5	18	10	18
6	18	7	8
7	16	5	8
8	16	2	8

The net profit (EAT) has been arrived at after charging depreciation of ₹20 lakh every year.

LOD: Difficult

RQ.6.19 There are four groups of financial ratios; liquidity, leverage, activity, and profitability. Financial analysis is conducted by four types of analysts: management, equity investors, long-term creditors and short-term creditors. You are required to **(a)** explain each type of ratio, **(b)** explain the emphasis of each type of analyst, **(c)** state if the same basic approach to financial analysis should be taken by each group of analysts. [LO 6.2,3,4,5]

RQ.6.20 Two companies have the same amount of working capital. The paying ability of short-term maturing obligations one company is much weaker than that of the other. Explain how this could occur. [LO 6.2]

RQ.6.21 'A uniform system of accounts, including identical forms for balance sheets and income statements is a prerequisite of inter firm comparisons.' Elucidate. [LO 6.1,7]

RQ.6.22 A partial list of trend and common-size percentage for ABC Ltd. for years 1 and 2 is given below: [LO 6.7]

Particulars	Year 2	Year 1
Trend percentages:		
Sales (net)	120	100
Cost of goods sold	?	100
Gross profit on sales	?	100
Operating expenses and income taxes	?	100
Net income	?	100
Common size percentages:		
Sales (net)	100	100
Cost of goods sold	?	?
Gross profit on sales	40	?
Operating expenses and income taxes	20	25
Net income	20	10
		= (₹20,000)

(a) Determine the missing trend and common-size percentages.
(b) Compute the net income for year 2.

RQ.6.23 Presented below is the financial information of two companies—A and B, belonging to the same industry: [LO 6.3]

Particulars	A	B
Current ratio	3.2:1	2.0:1
Acid-test ratio	1.7:1	1.1:1
Debt-equity ratio (percentage)	30	40
Number of times interest earned	6	5

Assume you are loan officer of a bank and both the companies have requested a loan of equal amount to be repaid over the next two years. Based on the information above,

(a) If you could grant a loan to only one company, which would it be? Explain.
(b) If you could grant a loan to both the companies, would you be willing to do so? Explain.

RQ.6.24 Below are selected ratios for three years ending March 31 for the Worst Company Ltd: [LO 6.2,3,4,5]

Ratios	Year 1	Year 2	Year 3
Current ratio	200	500	150
Acid-test ratio	110	320	80
Debt-asset ratio	15	40	55
Operating expenses ratio	24	25	32
Number of times interest earned	6	6	(–1)
Stock turnover	5	4	3
Debtors turnover	12	10	6
Rate of return on total assets	15	10	5

Outline possible explanations for the drastic changes in some of the ratios during these years.

RQ.6.25 From the following details, prepare a statement of proprietary funds with as many details as possible: [LO 6.2,4,5]

(a) Stock velocity = 6
(b) Capital turnover = 2
(c) Fixed assets turnover ratio = 4
(d) Gross profit turnover ratio = 20
(e) Debtors velocity = 2 months
(f) Creditors velocity = 73 days

The gross profit was ₹60,000; Reserves and surplus amounted to ₹20,000; Closing stock was ₹5,000 in excess of opening stock.

RQ.6.26 From the following information of a textile company complete the proforma balance sheet if its sales are ₹32,00,000. [LO 6.2,3,4,5]

Sales to net worth (times)	2.3
Current debt to net worth (ratio)	42
Total debt to net worth (ratio)	75
Current ratio (times)	2.9
Net sales to inventory (times)	4.7
Average collection period (days)	64
Fixed assets to net worth (ratio)	53.2

ANSWERS

RQ.6.13 **(a)** **(i)** 3:1, **(ii)** 1.48:1, **(iii)** 7 times, **(iv)** 12.12 times, **(v)** 23 per cent, **(vi)** 3.9 per cent, **(vii)** 94 per cent, **(viii)** ₹15.6 **(ix)** 11.4 per cent, **(x)** ₹156,

(b) **(i)** Improve, **(ii)** Improve, **(iii)** Improve, **(iv)** No effect, **(v)** Weaken, **(vi)** No effect, **(vii)** No effect, **(viii)** No effect, **(ix)** Weaken.

RQ.6.14 The company's position is sound from the points of view of **(a)** liquidity, **(b)** profitability but its activity ratios do not seem to be adequate.

RQ.6.15 **(a)** **(1)** 1.86, **(2)** 2.51 times, **(3)** 58 days, **(4)** 55 per cent, **(5)** 7.48 times, **(6)** 0.58 times, **(7)** 8.36 per cent, **(8)** 5.45 per cent. **(b)** Company's position both in terms of profitability and solvency is weaker than that of industry.

RQ.6.16 Not necessarily.

RQ.6.17 ABC Limited is better placed than XYZ Ltd. in respect of liquidity, activity and solvency ratios; XYZ Limited has an edge over ABC Limited in respect of profitability ratio.

RQ.6.18 Average DSCR is 2.46; it is very satisfactory.

RQ.6.22 **(a)** Trend percentages: Cost of goods sold 110.8 per cent, Gross profit on sales 137.14 per cent, Operating expenses and income taxes 96.00 per cent, Net income 240 per cnet; Common-size percentages: Cost of goods sold 60 per cent year 2 and 65 per cent year 1, Gross profit on sales 35 per cent year 1 **(b)** Net income ₹48,000.

RQ.6.23 **(a)** Loan would be granted to company A on account of its lower debt-equity ratio and higher interest coverage ratio. **(b)** Yes. Company B's debt-equity ratio of 40 per cent and interest coverage ratio of 5 times are fairly satisfactory solvency ratios.

RQ.6.24 The reasons for the drastic changes may be conceived in terms of the **(a)** high operating expenses ratio not matched by increase in sales price, **(b)** excessive interest cost due to large amount of borrowings, **(c)** higher inventory cost, and **(d)** liberal grant of credit causing bad debts.

RQ.6.25 Proprietary funds, ₹1,20,000, Fixed assets, ₹60,000, Stock, ₹42,500, Debtors, ₹50,000, Cash, ₹16,500 and Creditors, ₹49,000.

RQ.6.26 Net worth ₹13,91,304, Long term debt ₹4,59,130, Current debt ₹5,84,348, Fixed assets ₹7,40,173, Cash ₹4,44,869, Stock ₹6,80,851 and S. debtors ₹5,68,889. Total of balance sheet ₹24,34,782.

Scan the QR Code to access comprehensive solutions to all numerical review questions and additional material.

CHAPTER 7

Volume-Cost-Profit Analysis

LEARNING OBJECTIVES

LO 7.1	Explain break-even point as well as algebraic and graphical methods through which it is determined
LO 7.2	Discuss break-even analysis applications in profit planning
LO 7.3	Understand cash break-even point and its applications

INTRODUCTION

Profit planning is a function of the selling price of a unit of product, the variable cost of making and selling the product, the volume of product units sold, and, in the case of multi-product companies, sales-mix and, finally, the total fixed costs. The **volume-cost-profit (VCP) analysis** is a management accounting tool to show the relationship between these ingredients of profit planning. The entire gamut of profit planning is associated with VCP inter-relationships. A widely-used technique to study VCP relationships is break-even analysis.

Volume-cost-profit analysis shows the relationship among the various ingredients of profit planning, namely, unit sale price, variable cost, sales volume, sales mix and fixed cost.

A break-even analysis is concerned with the study of revenues and costs in relation to sales volume and, particularly, the determination of that volume of sales at which the firm's revenues and total costs will be exactly equal. Thus, the break-even point (**BEP**) may be defined as a point at which the firm's total revenues are exactly equal to total costs, yielding zero income. The "no-profit, no-loss" point is a break-even point or a point at which losses cease and profits begin.

Break-even analysis, as a technique, seeks to provide answers to the following questions:

1. What sales volume is necessary to produce an *X* amount of operating profit?
2. What will the operating profit or loss at *X* sales volume be?
3. What profit will result from an *X* per cent increase in sales volume?

4. What is the additional sales volume required to make good an *X* per cent reduction in selling prices so as to maintain the current profit level?
5. What will the effect on operating profit be if the company's fixed costs have increased?
6. What will the effect on income be if the firm achieves a reduction in variable costs (say, material or direct labour)?
7. What is the required sales volume to cover the additional fixed charges from the proposed new project?
8. What will the effect on operating profit of the firm be if the sales mix is changed?
9. What will the effect on income be if there is an increase in fixed costs by an *X* amount due to new plant but will decrease the labour costs by *Y* amount per unit?
10. What sales volume is needed to achieve the budgeted profit?

LO 7.1 BREAK-EVEN ANALYSIS

A break-even analysis shows the relationship between the costs and profits with sales volume. The sales volume which equates total revenue with related costs and results in neither profit nor loss is called the **break-even volume or point (BEP)**. If all costs are assumed to be variable with sales volume, the BEP would be at zero sales. If all costs were fixed, profits would vary disproportionately with sales and the BEP would be at a point where total sales revenue equalled fixed costs. However, both are purely hypothetical situations. In actual practice, costs consist of both fixed and variable elements.

The BEP can be determined by two methods:

1. Algebraic methods: **(a)** Contribution margin approach and **(b)** Equation technique, and
2. Graphic presentation: Break-even chart/Volume-cost-profit chart.

Algebraic Methods

Contribution Margin Approach The logic underlying the determination of the BEP under this approach can be stated by answering the following question:

Contribution margin is the excess of unit sale price over unit variable cost.

"How many ice-creams, having a unit cost of ₹20 and a selling price of ₹30, must a vendor sell in a fair to recover the ₹8,000 fees paid by him for getting a selling stall and additional cost of ₹4,000 to install the stall?" The answer can be determined dividing the fixed cost by the difference between the selling price (₹30) and cost price (₹20). Thus,

$$\text{BEP (units)} = \frac{\text{Fixed cost (Entry fees + Stall expenses)}}{\text{(Sales price – Unit variable cost)}} \quad \textbf{(7.1)}$$

(₹8,000 + ₹4,000)/(₹30 – ₹20) = 1,200 units

Or,

$$\text{BEP (units)} = \frac{\text{Fixed costs}}{\text{Contribution margin } (CM) \text{ per unit}} \quad \textbf{(7.2)}$$

Or,

BEP (amount)/BEP (Sales revenue)/*BESR* = BEP (units) × Selling price (*SP*) per unit

= 1,200 × ₹30 = ₹36,000 **(7.3)**

Or,

$$\text{BEP (amount)} = \frac{\text{Fixed costs}}{\text{Profit volume ratio (P/V ratio)}} \quad \textbf{(7.4)}$$

$$\text{P/V ratio}^1 = \frac{\text{Contribution margin per unit}}{\text{Selling price per unit}} \quad \textbf{(7.5)}$$

$$\frac{₹1}{₹3} = \text{or} \quad 33.33 \text{ per cent}$$

$$\text{BEP (amount)} = ₹12{,}000 \div 0.3333 = ₹36{,}000$$

From the P/V ratio, the variable cost to volume ratio (*V/V* ratio) can be easily derived:

$$V/V \text{ ratio} = 1 - \text{P/V ratio} \quad \textbf{(7.6)}$$

In the vendor's case, it is = 1–1/3 = 2/3 = 66.67 per cent

The *V/V* ratio, as the name suggests, establishes the relationship between variable costs (VC) and sales volume in amount. The direct method of its computation is:

$$\frac{\text{Variable cost}}{\text{Sales revenue}} = ₹20 \div ₹30 = 66.67 \text{ per cent} \quad \textbf{(7.7)}$$

Thus, P/V ratio + *V/V* ratio = 1 or 100 per cent

$$(1/3 + 2/3) = 1 \text{ (33.33 per cent + 66.67 per cent)} = 100 \text{ per cent} \quad \textbf{(7.8)}$$

Margin of Safety The excess of the actual sales revenue (ASR) over the break-even sales revenue (*BESR*) is known as the **margin of safety**. Symbolically, margin of safety = (ASR – BESR) **(7.9)**

When the margin of safety (amount) is divided by the actual sales (amount), the margin of safety ratio (*M/S* ratio) is obtained. Symbolically,

Margin of safety is the excess of actual sales revenue over the break-even sales revenue.

$$M/S \text{ ratio} = \frac{\text{(ASR – BESR)}}{\text{ASR}} \quad \textbf{(7.10)}$$

The *M/S* ratio indicates the percentage by which the actual sales may be reduced before they fall below the break-even sales volume. It is important that there should be a reasonable margin of safety, lest a reduced level of activity should prove disastrous. The higher the margin of safety ratio, the better it is from the point of view of the company as it indicates that a "sizeable" sales volume can fall before the BEP is reached. This measure acquires special significance in depression/recession.

Assume in the vendor's case that sales is 2,000 units (₹60,000); margin of safety (₹60,000 – ₹36,000) = ₹24,000; and the *M/S* ratio is ₹24,000 ÷ ₹60,000 = 40 per cent.

The amount of profit can be directly determined with reference to the margin of safety and P/V ratio. Symbolically,

$$\text{Profit} = [\text{Margin of safety (amount)}] \times \text{P/V ratio} \quad \textbf{(7.11)}$$

$$\text{Or Profit} = [\text{Margin of safety (units)} \times CM \text{ per unit}] \quad \textbf{(7.12)}$$

In the vendor's case, profit = ₹24,000 × 0.3333 (33.33 per cent) = ₹8,000 or 800 × ₹10 = ₹8,000.

[1] A better term would be contribution to revenue ratio (*C/V*) as the numerator is the contribution margin (difference between the selling price and variable costs) and not profit. The *P/V* ratio in a strict sense of the term represents the relationship between profit and selling price only after the BEP, that is, when fixed costs have been recovered. Therefore, the *C/V* ratio is more appropriate term. In the text, both the terms have been used.

The reason is that once the total amount of fixed costs has been recovered, profits will increase by the difference of sales revenue and variable costs.

Equation Technique This is the most general form of analysis, which can be applied to any cost-volume-profit situation. It is based on an income equation: Sales revenue-Total costs = Net profit

Breaking up total costs into fixed and variable, Sales revenue – Fixed costs – Variable costs = Net profit. Or Sales revenue = Fixed costs + Variable costs + Net profit.

If *S* be the number of units required for break-even and sales revenue (*SP*) and variable costs (VC) are on per unit basis, the above equation can be written as follows:

$$SP\,(S) = \text{FC} + \text{VC}\,(S) + NI \qquad \textbf{(7.13)}$$

Where *SP* = Selling price per unit
S = Number of units required to be sold to break-even
FC = Total fixed costs
VC = Variable costs per unit
NI = Net income (zero)

$$SP\,(S) = \text{FC} + \text{VC}\,(S) + \text{zero}$$

$$SP\,(S) - \text{VC}\,(S) = \text{FC}$$

or

$$S\,(SP - \text{VC}) = \text{FC}$$

$$S = \frac{\text{FC}}{SP - \text{VC}} \qquad \textbf{(7.14)}$$

It can be seen that Eq. 7.14 is identical to Eq. 7.2 (contribution margin approach). Yet, it is *specially useful in situations in which unit price and unit variable costs are not clearly identifiable.*

Example **7.1**

SV Ltd, a multi-product company, furnishes you the following data relating to the current year:

Particulars	*First half of the year*	*Second half of the year*
Sales	₹45,000	₹50,000
Total costs	40,000	43,000

Assuming that there is no change in prices and variable costs and that the fixed expenses are incurred equally in the two half-year periods, calculate for the year: (i) The profit-volume ratio, (ii) Fixed expenses, (iii) Break-even sales, and (iv) Percentage margin of safety.

Solution

Sales revenue – Total costs = Net profit
₹45,000 – ₹40,000 = ₹5,000 (first half)
₹50,000 – ₹43,000 = ₹7,000 (second half)

On a differential basis: Δ Sales revenue, ₹5,000 – Δ Total costs, ₹3,000 = Δ Total profit, ₹2,000

We know that only VC changes with a change in sales volume and, hence, change in total costs are equivalent to VC (₹3,000). Accordingly, the additional sales of ₹5,000 has earned a contribution margin of ₹2,000 [₹5,000 (*S*) – ₹3,000 (VC)].

P/V ratio = ₹2,000 ÷ ₹5,000 = 40 per cent
V/V ratio = 100 per cent – 40 per cent = 60 per cent

Accordingly, 60 per cent of the total costs are made up of variable costs and the balance represents the total fixed costs (FC).

Sales revenue = Fixed costs + Variable costs + Net profit
₹95,000 = FC + 0.60 × (₹95,000) + ₹12,000

$$₹95{,}000 = FC + ₹57{,}000 + ₹12{,}000$$
$$₹95{,}000 - ₹69{,}000 = FC \text{ or } ₹26{,}000 = FC$$
$$\text{BEP (amount)} = ₹26{,}000 \div 0.40 = ₹65{,}000$$

TABLE 7.1 Verification

Particulars	*Amount*	*Per cent*
Break-even sales	₹65,000	100
Variable costs	39,000	60
Contribution	26,000	40
Fixed costs	26,000	40
Net income	Nil	Nil

$$M/S \text{ ratio} = \frac{(₹95{,}000 - ₹65{,}000)}{₹95{,}000} = 31.58 \text{ per cent}$$

LO 7.2 BREAK-EVEN ANALYSIS APPLICATIONS

The break-even applications in profit planning are illustrated below.

Sales Volume Required to Produce Desired Operating Profit

One application of a BE analysis is to determine the required sales volume to generate a budgeted amount of profit. The required sales are given by Eq. 7.15.

$$(\text{Fixed expenses} + \text{Desired operating profit}) \div \text{P/V ratio} \quad \textbf{(7.15)}$$

In Example 7.1, if the desired operating profit of *SV* Ltd is ₹13,000, required sales volume = (₹26,000 + ₹13,000)/0.40 = ₹97,500

A variant of the above approach is that the management may be interested in knowing the required sales volume to produce the desired profit after taxes. In this case, the analysis must be expanded slightly. Assume that *SV* Ltd wants a net income after taxes of ₹13,000 and that its current tax rate is 35 per cent, the net income after taxes is 65 per cent of the net income before taxes.

$$\text{Required sales volume} = \frac{\text{Fixed costs} + \left[\dfrac{\text{Desired income after taxes}}{1 - \text{tax rate}}\right]}{P/V \text{ ratio}} \quad \textbf{(7.16)}$$

$$= \frac{₹\,26{,}000 + \left[\dfrac{₹\,13{,}000}{1 - 0.35}\right]}{0.40} = ₹\,1{,}15{,}000$$

TABLE 7.2 Verification

Sales volume	₹1,15,000
Less: Variable costs (0.60)	69,000
Contribution	46,000
Less: Fixed costs	26,000
Profits before taxes	20,000
Less: Taxes (0.35)	7,000
Profit after taxes	13,000

Operating Profit at a Given Level of Sales Volume

[Actual Sales Revenue (ASR) – Break-even Sales Revenue (BESR)] × P/V ratio **(7.17)**

Effect on Operating Profit of a Given Increase in Sales Volume

[Budgeted Sales Revenue(*BSR*) – BESR] × P/V ratio **(7.18)**

Suppose that *SV* Ltd forecasts 10 per cent increase in sales next year, the projected profit will be:

(₹1,04,500 – ₹65,000) × 0.40 = ₹15,800

Additional Sales Volume Required to Offset a Reduction in Selling Price

The sales manager on the basis of a market research/survey may report to the management that due to increased competition in the market and the liberal import policy of the government, the present price is relatively higher. He may advise reduction in prices to stay in competition.

Suppose that *SV* Ltd reduces its selling price from ₹10 a unit to ₹9. The sales volume needed to offset reduced selling price/maintain a present operating profit of ₹12,000 would be:

$$= \frac{\text{Desired profit } (P) + \text{Fixed expenses } (FC)}{\text{Revised } P/V \text{ ratio } (₹3/₹9)} = ₹(12{,}000 + 26{,}000) \div 0.3333 = ₹1{,}14{,}000$$

The required sales volume of ₹1,14,000 represents an increase of about 20 per cent over the present level. The management should explore new avenues of sales potential to maintain the existing amount of profit.

On the other hand, if the firm has the opportunity to increase the unit selling price of the product, the impact of increased sales price would be that the BEP will be reached sooner because an increase in the selling price will raise the contribution margin, assuming no change in the variable costs. An increased contribution margin will decrease the sales volume necessary to reach a desired goals.

Assume that the management of *SV* Ltd increases the selling price of its product from ₹10 to ₹12, the desired sales volume would be: $\frac{FC + P}{\text{Revised } P/V \text{ ratio}}$ = ₹38,000 ÷ 0.50 (₹6 ÷ ₹12) = ₹76,000

Effect of Changes in Fixed Costs

A firm may be confronted with the situation of increasing fixed costs. An increase in the total budgeted fixed costs of a firm may be necessitated either by external factors, such as, an increase in property taxes, insurance rates, factory rent, and so on, or by a managerial decision of an increase in salaries of executives. More important than this in the latter category are expansion of the present plant capacity so as to cope with additional demand. The increase in the requirements of fixed costs would imply the computation of the following:

(a) Relative break-even points
(b) Required sales volume to earn the present profits
(c) Required sales volume to earn the same rate of profit on the proposed expansion programme as on the existing ones.

The effect of the increased FC*s* will be to raise the BEP of the firm. Assume the management of *SV* Ltd decides a major expansion programme of its existing production capacity. It is estimated that it will result in extra fixed costs of ₹8,000 on advertisement to boost sales volume and another ₹16,000 on account of new plant facility.

(a) *The relative BEPs will be:*

Present facilities = Fixed costs ÷ P/V ratio = ₹26,000/0.40 = ₹65,000

Proposed facilities = (Present FC*s* + Additional FC*s*) ÷ *P/V* ratio **(7.19)**

= (₹26,000 + ₹24,000)/0.40 = ₹1,25,000

It may be noted that increase in FC*s* (from ₹26,000 to ₹50,000) has caused disproportionate increase in the BEP (from ₹65,000 to ₹1,25,000).

(b) *The required sales volume to earn the present profit:*

[Present FC*s* + Additional FC*s* + Present profit (*NI*)] ÷ *P/V* ratio **(7.20)**

= [₹26,000 + ₹24,000 + ₹12,000] ÷ 0.40 = ₹1,55,000

(c) *The required sales volume to earn the present rate of profit on investment:*

(Present FC*s* + Additional FC*s* + Present return on investment + Return on new investment) *P/V*ratio **(7.21)**

Let us assume that the present investment is ₹1,00,000 and the new investment will involve an additional financial outlay of ₹60,000. The required sales volume will be (₹26,000 + ₹24,000 + ₹12,000+ ₹7,200 (0.12 × ₹60,000)/0.40 = ₹1,73,000

These computations may be reported in a summary form to the management as follows (Table 7.3).

TABLE 7.3 Effect of Changes in Fixed Costs

Particulars	*Present facilities*	*Prospective facilities*	*Increase*
Fixed costs	₹26,000	₹50,000	₹24,000
BEP sales volume	65,000	1,25,000	60,000
BEP sales volume (units)	6,500	12,500	6,000
Sales volume to earn existing profit	95,000	1,55,000	60,000
Sales volume in units to earn existing profit	9,500	15,500	6,000
Sales volume to earn existing ROI	95,000	1,73,000	78,000
Sales volume to earn existing ROI (in units)	9,500	17,300	7,800

Effect of Changes in Variable Costs

Assuming an increase of VC by ₹1 a unit for *SV* Ltd, the new contribution margin will be: ₹3 (₹10 – ₹7) and the revised P/V ratio 0.30 that is, (₹3 ÷ ₹10).

Revised BEP = (₹26,000)/0.30 = ₹86,667

Desired sales volume to earn existing profit = ₹38,000/0.30 = ₹1,26,667

Assuming that variable costs of *SV* Ltd decline by ₹1 per unit, revised BEP = ₹26,000/0.50 = ₹52,000. Desired sales volume to maintain existing profit = ₹38,000/0.50 = ₹76,000.

Effects of Multiple Changes

So far we have assumed that a change takes place in one of the three variable affecting profits—cost, price and sales volume. In cases where more than one factor is affected, the BEP *analysis* can be applied as shown below:

$$\frac{FC + FC\text{ (new)} + \left[\dfrac{\text{Desired } EAT}{1 - \text{tax rate}}\right]}{[\text{Contribution margin per unit (New } SP - \text{New } VC)] \div \text{New selling price (New } SP)]} \quad \textbf{(7.22)}$$

Assuming the following set of new Figures for *SV* Ltd:

Particulars	*Existing data*	*New data*
Selling price per unit	₹10	₹11
Fixed costs	26,000	40,000
Variable cost per unit	6	5.50
Contribution margin per unit	4	5.50
Desired earnings after taxes (to maintain the existing ROI)	12,000	25,000
Tax rate	35 per cent	

Solution

Desired sales volume (on the basis of new data) [₹26,000 + ₹14,000 + (₹25,000 ÷ 0.65)] ÷ 0.50, that is (₹5.5 ÷ ₹11) = (₹78,461.5) ÷ 0.50 = ₹1,56,923

Desired sales volume on the basis of existing data = [₹26,000 + (₹12,000 ÷ 0.65)] ÷ 0.40 (₹4 ÷ ₹10) = ₹44,462 ÷ 0.40 = ₹1,11,154.

VCP Analysis and a Segment of the Business

The fundamental approach of applying the VCP analysis to a segment of the business is the same as applying it to the business as a whole. The VCP approach "may be applied to problems relative to individual product lines, territories, methods of sale, channels of distribution or any particular segment of the business which is under scrutiny"[2]. In all these decisions, fixed costs and P/V ratio are the required inputs. Where fixed costs are inclusive of allocated costs also, in additional to direct costs, two BEPs may be determined.

Example **7.2**

SV Ltd has four sales divisions. The relevant data for its northern division is reproduced below:
Direct fixed costs, ₹10,000
P/V ratio, 0.40
Allocated fixed costs from head office, ₹5,000

The sales volume required to cover direct expenses would be: Direct fixed costs/ P/V ratio

$$= ₹10{,}000/0.40 = ₹25{,}000 \quad \textbf{(7.23)}$$

The total sales volume required to cover all fixed costs would be higher as shown by equation 7.24:

$$\frac{\text{Direct FC}s + \text{Allocated FCs}}{\text{P/V ratio}} \quad \textbf{(7.24)}$$

$$= (₹10{,}000 + ₹5{,}000) \div 0.40 = ₹37{,}500$$

Multi-product Firms (Sales-mix)

So far, we have confined our discussion to a one-product company. However, many manufacturers make more than one type of product. The relative proportion of each product sold in the aggregate sales is known as the sales-mix. A change in the mix of products sold usually affects the weighted average P/V ratio and, hence, the BEP. Thus, when the products have different P/V ratios, changes in the sales-mix/product-mix will affect the BEP and the results from operation.

Example **7.3**

The Garware Paints Ltd presents to you the following income statement in a condensed form for the first quarter ending March 31:

Particulars	Product X	Product Y	Product Z	Total
Sales	₹1,00,000	₹60,000	₹40,000	₹2,00,000
Variable costs	80,000	42,000	24,000	1,46,000
Contribution	20,000	18,000	16,000	54,000
Fixed costs				27,000
Net income				27,000
P/V ratio	0.20	0.30	0.40	0.27
Break-even sales				1,00,000
Sales-mix (per cent)	0.50	0.30	0.20	100

If ₹40,000 of the sales shown for Product *X* could be shifted equally to products *Y* and *Z*, the profit and the BEP would change as shown in Table 7.4.

TABLE 7.4 Break-even Point

Particulars	Product X	Product Y	Product Z	Total
Sales	₹60,000	₹80,000	₹60,000	₹2,00,000
Less: Variable costs	48,000	56,000	36,000	1,40,000
Contribution	12,000	24,000	24,000	60,000
Less: Fixed costs				27,000
Net income				33,000
P/V ratio	0.20	0.30	0.40	0.30
BE sales				90,000
Sales-mix (per cent)	0.30	0.40	0.30	100

Example 7.3 shows that by increasing the mix of high P/V products (*Y* from 30 to 40 per cent, *Z* from 20 to 30 per cent) and decreasing the mix of a low P/V product (*X* from 50 to 30 per cent), the company can increase its overall profitability. In fact, it can further augment its total profits, if it can make, and the market can absorb, more quantities of *Y* and *Z*, say ₹1 lakh each (Table 7.5).

TABLE 7.5

Particulars	Product Y	Product Z	Total
Sales	₹1,00,000	₹1,00,000	₹2,00,000
Less: Variable costs	70,000	60,000	1,30,000
Contribution	30,000	40,000	70,000
Less: Fixed costs			27,000
Net income			43,000
P/V ratio	0.30	0.40	0.35
BE sales			77,143
Sales-mix (per cent)	0.50	0.50	100

From the above, it can be generalised that, other things being equal, management should stress products with higher contribution margins. For individual product line income statements, fixed costs should not be allocated or apportioned.

Finally, it may be stressed that there is a need for a closer study of cost structures of individual product line/department within the same firm or of two different companies. It may be possible that the two departments/companies may have the same profits but very different cost structures. For instance, observe the Figures in Table 7.6 of two departments of *SV* Ltd.

TABLE 7.6

Particulars	Department X Amount	Department X Per cent	Department Y Amount	Department Y Per cent
Sales revenue	₹1,00,000	(100)	₹1,00,000	(100)
Less: Variable costs	70,000	(70)	20,000	(20)
Contribution / P/V ratio	30,000	(30)	80,000	(80)
Less: Fixed costs	20,000		70,000	
Profit	10,000		10,000	
BEP (amount)	66,667		87,500	
Margin of safety (MS)	33,333		12,500	
Margin of safety ratio	0.3333		0.125	

Department *Y* is operating closer to the BEP than Department *X*. Department *Y* has a narrower margin of safety (12.5 per cent) compared to 33.33 per cent of *X*. The margin of safety ratio signifies that if the sales of *Y* decreases by more than 12.5 per cent, it will operate at a loss. In other words, the margin/cushion of safety is relatively smaller. *X* will not operate at a loss unless its sales volume drops by more than 33.33 per cent.

This type of profit analysis for two different companies is of special significance from the point of view of outside investor who want to invest in one of the two companies. Assuming companies *X* and *Y* in place of the departments *X* and *Y* in the above tabulation, Company *X* is certainly less risky than Company *Y*.

Graphic Presentation

Under the algebraic technique of break-even analysis, separate computations were needed to arrive at the above set of figures. The utility of the graphical technique is that such a set of figures can be determined without involving any separate calculations.

Break-Even Chart/Volume Cost Profit (VCP) Graph The **break even chart** is a graphic relationship between volume, costs and profits. It shows not only the BEP but also the effects of costs and revenue at varying levels of sales. The break-even chart can, therefore, be more appropriately called the volume-cost-profit graph (VCP graph).

Assumptions Regarding the VCP Graph are

1. Costs can be bifurcated into variable and fixed components.
2. Fixed costs will remain constant during the relevant volume range of graph.
3. Variable cost per unit will remain constant during the relevant volume range of graph.
4. Selling price per unit will remain constant irrespective of the quantity sold within the relevant range of the graph.
5. In the case of multi-product companies, in addition to the above four assumptions, it is assumed that the sales-mix remains constant.
6. Finally, production and sales volumes are equal.

The VCP graph may be prepared in a simple or elaborate manner. Figure 7.1 is an example of a simple and traditional form. In Figure 7.1, sales are shown on the horizontal axis; the vertical axis measures costs and revenues corresponding to varying volume of sales. Sales are expressed in terms of units, rupees and percentage level of activity. The VCP relationships portrayed in such a graph are valid only within the relevant range that underlies the construction of the graph. The importance of a relevant range should be recognised because in practice most firms will progressively reduce fixed costs as the volume tends to decrease towards zero activity. Similarly, fixed costs are to be increased beyond a certain volume. Accordingly, in Figure 7.1 the lower limit and upper limit of the VCP have been drawn.

The BEP lies at the point of intersection of the sales line and the total cost line. The vertical distance between the sales revenue and the total cost line measures the estimated net income (after the BEP) and the estimated net loss (before the BEP) at the related sales volume. The fixed cost line is parallel to the horizontal axis. The variable cost line is superimposed on the fixed cost line and moves upward uniformly with sales volume at the variable cost to volume ratio. This is the total cost line. The sales revenue line starts from the point of origin and moves upward uniformly with volume. The meeting point of the total cost line and sales line is the BEP. At this point, an angle is formed known as the angle of incidence. The management objective should be to have an angle of as large a size as possible because a high angle is a sign of a high rate of profit after the fixed costs have been covered; the narrower angle will signify that profits after the fixed costs have been covered; the narrower angle will signify that profits will increase at a lower rate after the BEP, showing that variable costs form a large part of cost of sales. Figure 7.1 is based on the following data relating to Hypothetical Ltd (Example 7.4).

Example **7.4**

Selling price per unit		₹10
Fixed costs		60,000
Variable costs per unit		5
Relevant range (units) : Lower limit		6,000
: Upper limit		20,000
Break-up of variable costs per unit:		
Direct material	₹2	
Direct labour	1.50	
Direct expenses	1	
Selling expenses	0.50	
Actual sales, 18,000 units (₹1,80,000)		
Plant capacity, 20,000 units (₹2,00,000)		
Tax rate, 50 per cent		

Figure 7.1 has been drawn by using a sales line and a total cost line (including both fixed and variable costs). The steps involved in drawing the VCP graph are enumerated as follows:

1. Select an appropriate scale for sales volume on the horizontal axis, say, 2,000 units (₹20,000) per square, and plot the point for total sales revenues at relevant volume: 6,000 units × ₹10 = ₹60,000. Draw the sales line from the origin to ₹2,00,000 (the upper limit of the relevant range). Ensure that *all the points*, 0, ₹60,000 and ₹2,00,000 *fall in the same line.* This should be ensured for the total cost line also.
2. Select an appropriate scale for costs and sales revenues on the vertical axis, say, ₹10,000 per square. Draw the line showing ₹60,000 fixed cost parallel to the horizontal axis.
3. Determine the variable portion of costs at two volumes of scales (beginning and ending): 6,000 units × ₹5 = ₹30,000; 20,000 units × ₹5 = ₹1,00,000.
4. Variable costs are to be added to fixed costs (₹30,000 + ₹60,000 = ₹90,000). Plot the point at 6,000 units sales volume and ₹1,00,000 + ₹60,000 = ₹1,60,000. Point is to be plotted at 20,000 units sales volume. This obviously is the total cost line.
5. The point of intersection of the total cost line and sales line is the BEP. To the right of BEP, there is a profit area and to the left of it, there is a loss area.
6. *Verification*: FC ÷ *CM* per unit = ₹60,000 ÷ ₹5 per unit = 12,000 units or ₹1,20,000

Figure 7.1 has been drawn using different scales for the horizontal and vertical axis. Figure 7.2 has been drawn on a uniform scale for both axes. Since the scales are the same, the 45° *line will always be the proxy of the sales line.* Any amount of sales revenue on the horizontal axis will correspond to costs and revenue on the vertical axis. Let us illustrate taking two sales levels.

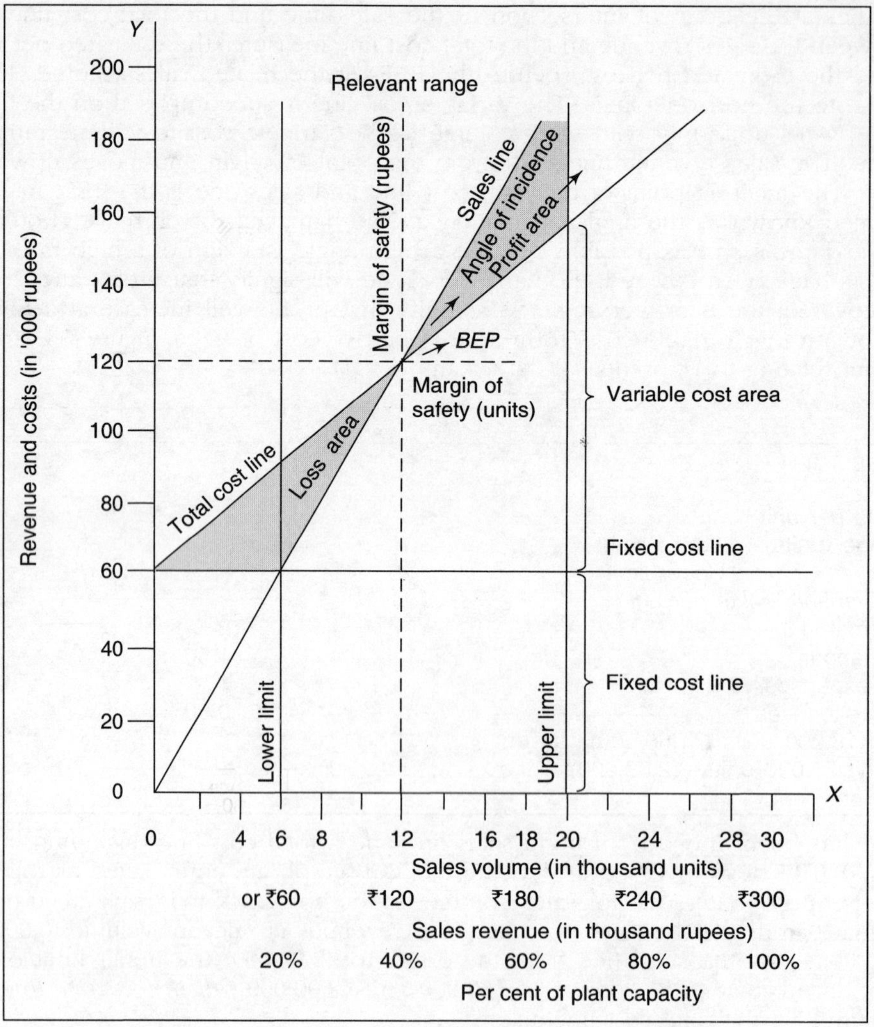

FIGURE 7.1 *Volume-Cost-Profit Graph, Different Scale*

1. ₹*60,000:* FC = ₹60,000
VC = 30,000 (50 per cent variable cost to volume ratio)
TC = 90,000
Loss = 30,000 (*TC*, ₹90,000 – ₹30,000, sales revenue)

Thus, ₹60,000 = ₹60,000 (FC) + ₹30,000 (VC)– ₹30,000 (Loss). Point A in Figure 7.2 clearly shows these three relevant figures at the sales volume of ₹60,000.

2. ₹*1,80,000:* FC = ₹ 60,000
VC = 90,000
TC = 1,50,000
Profit = 30,000

Thus, ₹1,80,000 = ₹60,000 (FC) + ₹90,000 (VC) + ₹30,000 (Profit). Point *B* in Figure 7.2 portrays these three relevant figures at the sales volume of ₹1,80,000.

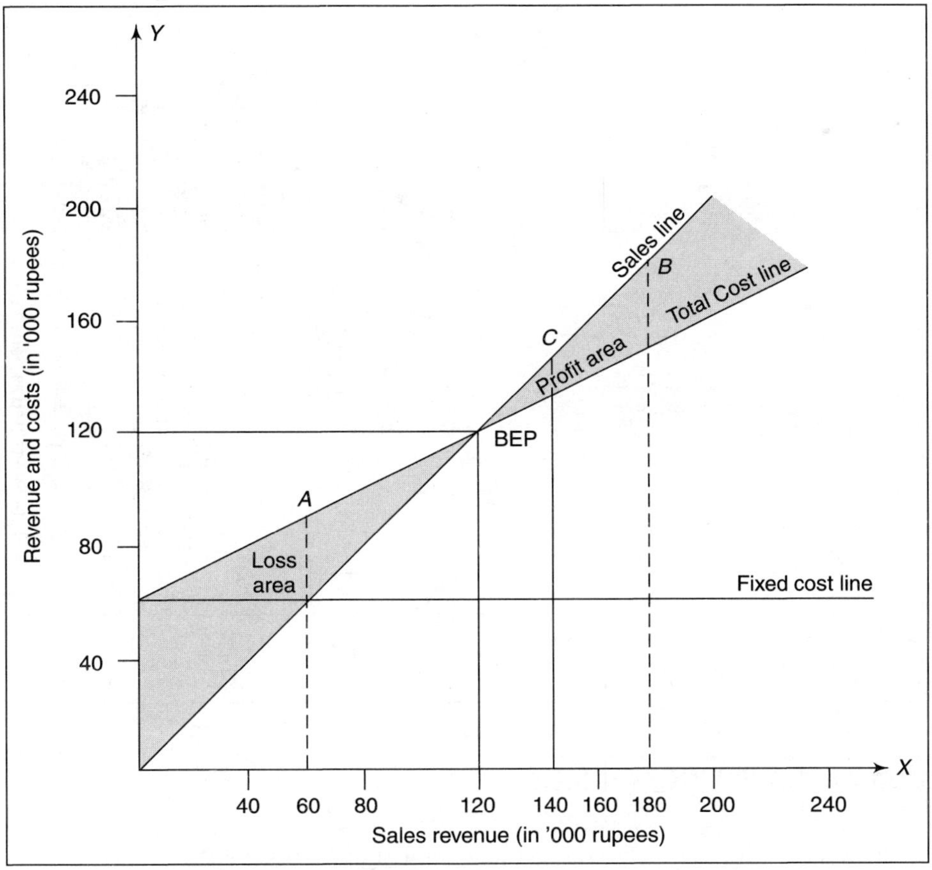

FIGURE 7.2 Volume-Cost-Profit Graph, Same Scale

The VCP graph in Figure 7.3 is drawn with the details of the individual segment of variable cost and is more informative. The steps involved in drawing the graph include an additional step of adding variable costs to the fixed cost. This is to be repeated four times for four different components: material, labour, direct expenses and selling expenses. In fact, fixed costs can also be further split-up into parts. Such a comprehensive graph provides a bird's-eye view of the entire cost structure to the management. By drawing a line perpendicular from any volume (horizontal axis), the corresponding cost and profit variables can be ascertained on the vertical axis. For instance, at 20,000 unit level, following are the various cost figures, as shown by the VCP graph (line *A*).

Fixed costs	₹60,000
Variable costs:	
Material	40,000
Labour	30,000
Direct expenses	20,000
Selling expenses	10,000
Profit before taxes	40,000

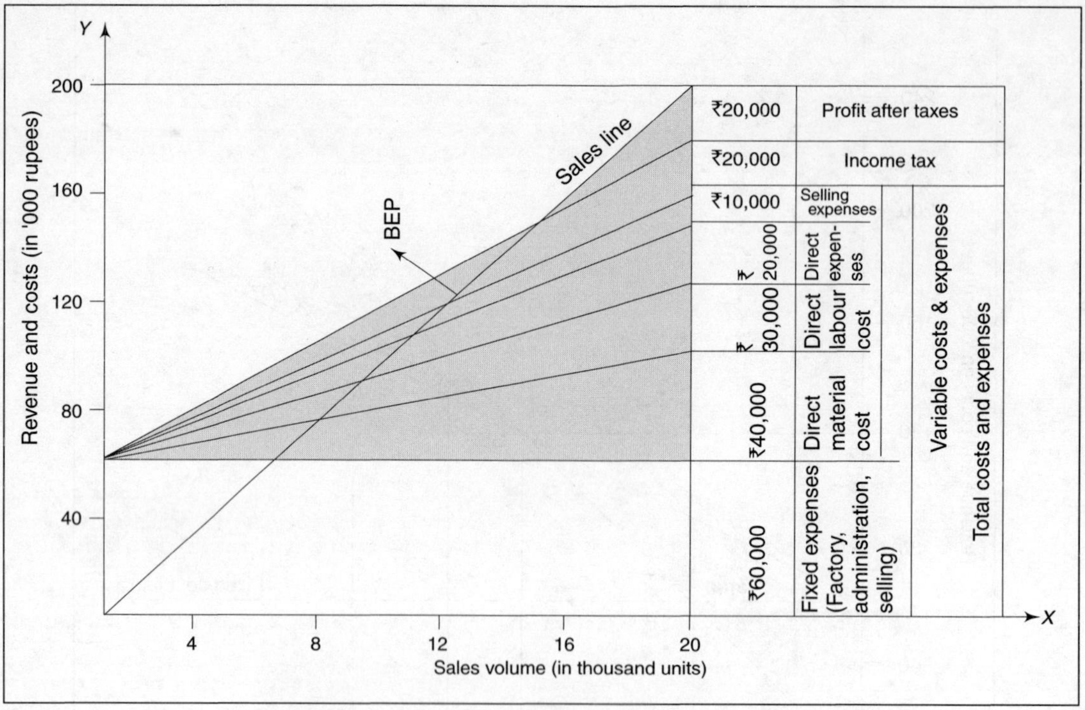

FIGURE 7.3 Volume-Cost-Profit Graph, Cost-Wise

Application of the P/V/(C/V) Ratio

1. Determination of BEP = FC ÷ P/V ratio
2. Determination of profit at given/budgeted sales volume = (Actual sales – *BE* sales) × *P/V* ratio.
3. Determination of sales volume to earn budgeted profit = (FC + *DP*) ÷ P/V ratio
4. Determination of change in sales volume to maintain the current level of profit if there is (a) a change in sales price, (b) change in variable cost = (FC + *DP*) ÷ Revised P/V ratio.
5. Determination of the percentage of net profit with the help of margin of safety ratio = (P/V ratio × *MS* ratio) **(7.25)**

LO 7.3 CASH BREAK-EVEN POINT

The VCP relationship can also be used to show the liquidity position of the firm. This is done through the computation of **cash break-even point** or cash break-even sales revenue (CBEP/CBESR). Algebraically:

$$CBEP = \frac{\text{Total cash fixed cost } (CFC)}{\text{Contribution margin per unit}} \quad \textbf{(7.26)}$$

$$CBESR = \frac{\text{Total cash fixed cost}}{P/V \text{ ratio}} \quad \textbf{(7.27)}$$

> **Cash break-even point** is total cash fixed cost divided by contribution margin per unit.

Graphically, the CBEP is determined at the point of intersection of total cash cost line and total sales line. The area to the left of the curve signifies cash losses and the area on the right side is indicative of cash profits.

Assuming for Example 7.4, the cash fixed cost to be ₹15,000, the CBESR using Equation 7.27 would be ₹30,000 = ₹15,000 ÷ 0.50

Figure 7.4 portrays the graphic presentation of the cash break-even sales revenue.

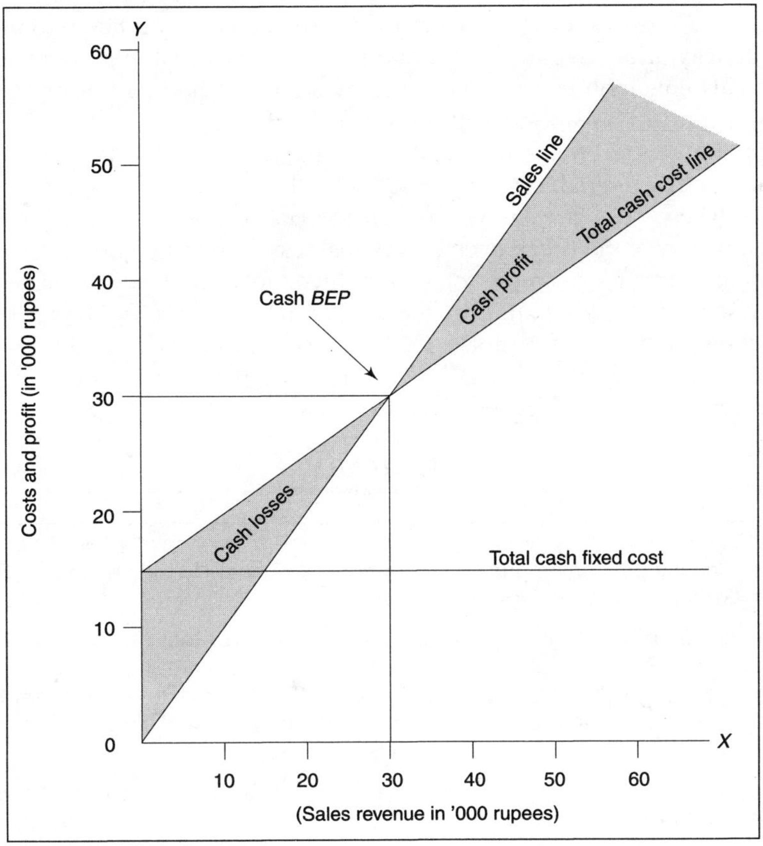

FIGURE 7.4 Cash Break-even Point

To conclude, the uses of break-even analysis, as a technique for profit planning, have been discussed in detail in this chapter. In brief, break-even analysis shows the interplay of profit factors, that is, cost, revenue and volume in a way, which assists management in choosing the best feasible alternative now and in the future. "The break-even system is at once an *X*-ray, exploratory and planning tool intended for frequent use and a proper cost-volume-profit analysis supported by the break-even chart can eliminate many of the time-consuming reports now being prepared at the company."[3]

The graphs can be used to analyse the impact of various alternative proposals under consideration on the profit structure. Thus, the break-even system provides more readily understandable facts than conventional accounting or statistical data regarding the profit structure of the company.

However, it is important to recognise its limitations which originate from the given assumptions. The greater the deviation of actual facts from the given assumptions, the more imperfect, incorrect and invalid are the break-even calculations. These limitations limit the usefulness of the break-even chart and must be borne in mind by those who prepare or interpret the break-even chart. These limitations suggest that the validity of the break-even chart is in proportion to the validity of the assumptions. One of the assumptions of the break-even analysis is that an enterprise's cost are either perfectly variable or absolutely fixed over all ranges of operating volume. In other words, variable cost is a linear function of volume: fixed costs are assumed not to be affected by volume at all. In practice, these assumptions are not likely to be valid over all ranges of volume. Even within the relevant range of volume, there is a likelihood of some degree of imprecision and to that extent validity of the results is affected. For instance, variable costs are likely to increase as the firm approaches full capacity. The reason may be due to less efficient labour or costly overtime having been resorted to. This limitation can be overcome by studying the relationship between total costs and volume, non-linear, to correspond with economic reality.

Another assumption of the break-even analysis is that it is possible to classify total costs of an enterprise as either fixed or variable. Many costs defy clear division because they are partly fixed and partly variable. These costs are known as **semi-variable costs**.

Yet another assumption of the break-even analysis is that selling price per unit remains unchanged, irrespective of volume. In other words, total sales revenue is perfectly variable with its physical sales volume. For some firms, operating in the seller's market, this assumption may be perfectly valid. For most others, however, it is not a realistic assumption because price reductions may be necessary to increase the sales volume. Once again, this limitation can be remedied by studying the relationship between total sales revenue and costs.

SUMMARY

LO 7.1

- The volume-cost-profit (*VCP*) analysis is a tool to show the relationship between various ingredients of profit planning, namely, unit sales price (*SP*), unit variable cost (*VC*), fixed costs (*FC*), sales volume, and sales-mix (in the case of multi-product firms).
- The *VCP* analysis shows the relationship between costs and profit, and sales volume. The crucial step in this analysis is the determination of break-even point (*BEP*), which is defined as the sales level at which the total revenues equal total costs. It is the level at which losses cease and beyond which profit starts. The break-even technique has many applications for purposes of the *VCP* analysis.
- *BEP* can be determined by the following two methods; (1) *Algebraic*, comprising (a) Contribution margin approach and (b) Equation technique. (2) *Graphic presentation*, comprising Break-even chart.
- In the *contribution margin approach, BEP* is computed on the basis of the relationship between the fixed costs and the contribution margin (*CM)*. The *CM* represents the difference between the sales revenue and the variable costs.
- The *equation technique* is particularly useful in situations where unit price and unit variable costs are not clearly defined. The excess of actual sales over the *BE* sales is the margin of safety. When margin of safety is divided by the actual sales, we get margin of safety ratio which indicates the percentage by which actual sales may decline without causing any loss to the firm.. The break-even analysis is summarised below:

Contribution Margin Approach

(1) $$BEP \text{ (units)} = \frac{\text{Fixed costs } (FC)}{\text{Unit sale price (SP)} - \text{Unit variable cost } (VC)}$$

(2) $$= \frac{\text{Total fixed costs}}{\text{Unit contribution margin } (CM)}$$

LO 7.1

(3) BEP (amount)/$BESR$ = BEP (units) × SP

(4) $$= \frac{\text{Total fixed costs}}{\text{Contribution/Profit volume ratio } (C/V \text{ or } P/V \text{ ratio})}$$

(5) $$C/V\ (P/V) \text{ ratio} = \frac{CM}{SP} \times 100$$

(6) $$= \frac{\text{Total contribution } (TC)}{\text{Total sales revenue } (TSR)} \times 100$$

(7) Variable cost to volume (V/V) ratio $= \dfrac{VC}{SP} \times 100$

(8) $$= \frac{\text{Total variable costs } (TVC)}{TSR} \times 100$$

(9) $= 1 - C/V\ (P/V)$ ratio

(10) In brief, $C/V(P/V)$ ratio + V/V ratio = 1 (100%)

(11) $$BESR \text{ (multi-product firm)} = \frac{FC}{\text{Weighted } C/V \text{ ratio}} \times 100$$

(12) $$\text{Weighted } C/V \text{ ratio} = \frac{TC \text{ from all products}}{TSR \text{ from all products}} \times 100$$

(13) Margin of safety (MS) = $TSR - BESR$

(14) $$\text{MS ratio} = \frac{TSR - BESR}{TSR} \times 100$$

(15) Profit = MS (rupees) × $C/V(P/V)$ ratio

(16) = MS (units) × CM

Equation Technique

(17) $BESR = TFC + TVC$ + zero profit

LO 7.2

The break-even applications are summarised below:

1. (a) *Sales revenue required to earn desired operating profits (EBIT)*

$$= \frac{FC + \text{desired EBIT}}{P/V \text{ ratio}}$$

(b) *Sales revenue required to earn desired profits/earnings after taxes (EAT)*

$$= \frac{FC + (EAT/1 - \text{tax rate}, t)}{P/V \text{ ratio}}$$

2. *Operating profit at a given sales volume*

$= (TSR - BESR) \times P/V$ ratio

3. *Sales revenue to off-set reduction in sales price to maintain existing operating profits*

$$= \frac{FC + EBIT}{\text{Revised } P/V \text{ ratio}}$$

4. *Effect of changes in fixed costs*

(a) *The required sales revenue to maintain present operating profit*

$$= \frac{\text{Present } FC + \text{Additional } FC + \text{Present } EBIT}{P/V \text{ ratio}}$$

LO 7.2

(b) *The required sales revenue to earn the present rate of return on investment*
Present F C + Additional FC + Present return on investment + Return on new investment

$$= \frac{\text{Present } FC + \text{Additional } FC + \text{Present return on investment} + \text{Return on new investment}}{P/V \text{ ratio}}$$

5. *Effect of changes in variable costs*
The required sales revenue to maintain existing operating profit

$$= \frac{FC + EBIT \text{ (Existing)}}{\text{Revised } P/V \text{ ratio}}$$

6. *Effect of multiple changes*
The required sales revenue to earn desired *EAT*

$$= \frac{FC + \text{Additional } FC + [\text{Desired } EAT/(1-t)]}{\text{Revised } P/V \text{ ratio}}$$

7. *Effect of change in sales-mix*
The desired sales revenue to maintain existing *EBIT*

$$= \frac{FC + EBIT}{\text{Revised Weighted } P/V \text{ ratio}}$$

$$\text{Revised weighted P/V ratio} = \frac{\text{Total contribution at revised mix}}{\text{Total sales revenue at revised mix}} \times 100$$

The break-even chart is a graphic presentation of the relationship between costs, profits, and sales. It shows not only the break-even sales but also the estimated costs and profit at various levels of the sales revenue. It is, therefore, also referred to as volume-cost-profit (*VCP*) graph/chart.
The volume-profit graph shows a direct relationship between sales revenue and profits.

LO 7.3

The VCP relationship is also useful to assess the liquidity position of the firm. For the purpose, cash break-even point (CBEP) or cash break-even sales revenue is computed.

1. $\text{Cash BEP (in units)} = \frac{\text{Total cash Fixed cost}}{\text{Contribution margin per unit}}$

2. $\text{Cash BESR (in amount)} = \frac{\text{Total cash Fixed cost}}{P/V \text{ ratio}}$

REFERENCES

1. Wilson, J.D., "Practical Application of Cost-Volume-Profit Analysis" quoted by Anderson, D.L and D.L. Raun, *Information Analysis in Management Accounting* (John Wiley, New York, 1978), p 162.
2. Tuckker, S.A., *Break-Even System: A Tool for Profit Planning,* (Prentice Hall, Englewood Cliffs, N.J. 1963).

SOLVED PROBLEMS

P.7.1 From the following data, calculate the: LO 7.1,2 LOD E
1. Break-even point expressed in terms of sale amount/revenue.
2. Number of units that must be sold to earn a profit of ₹60,000 per year.

Sales price (per unit)	₹20
Variable manufacturing cost per unit	11
Variable selling cost per unit	3
Fixed factory overheads (per year)	5,40,000
Fixed selling costs (per year)	2,52,000

Solution

1. BEP *(amount)* = (Fixed factory overheads + Fixed selling costs)/P/V ratio (Sales price – Variable manufacturing cost – Variable selling cost) ÷ Sales price = (₹5,40,000 + ₹2,52,000)/0.30 (₹6 ÷ ₹20) = ₹26,40,000
2. *Desired sales volume (in units) to earn a profit of* ₹60,000 = (₹7,92,000 + ₹60,000)/ ₹6 (CM per unit) = ₹1,42,000 units

P.7.2 Two businesses, *AB* Ltd and *CD* Ltd, sell the same type of product in the same type of market. Their budgeted profit and loss accounts for the current year ending March 31, are as follows: LO 7.1 LOD E

Particulars		*AB Ltd*		*CD Ltd*
Sales		₹150,000		₹1,50,000
Less: Variable costs	₹1,20,000		₹1,00,000	
Fixed costs	15,000	1,35,000	35,000	1,35,000
Net budgeted profit		15,000		15,000

You are required to:

1. Calculate the break-even points of each business; and
2. State which business is likely to earn greater profits in conditions of: (a) heavy demand for the product, (b) low demand for the product.

Solution

1. BEP (amount) = Fixed cost/ P/V ratio; P/V ratio = Contribution/Sales revenue
   BEP (AB Ltd) = ₹15,000/0.20 = ₹75,000
   P/V ratio = ₹30,000/ ₹1,50,000 = 20 per cent
   BEP (CD Ltd) = ₹35,000/0.3333 = ₹1,05,000
   P/V ratio = ₹50,000/ ₹1,50,000 = 33.33 per cent
2. Projected profit (heavy demand for the products):
   (a) CD Ltd is likely to earn larger profits in conditions of heavy demand of the product because its P/V ratio is higher than that of AB Ltd.
   (b) AB Ltd is likely to earn larger profits in condition of low demand of the product because its burden of fixed costs is much smaller than that of CD Ltd.

P.7.3 The Soft-Flow Ink Ltd's income statement for the preceding year is presented below. Except as noted, the cost/revenue relationship for the coming year is expected to follow the same pattern as in the preceding year. Income statement for the year ending March 31 is as follows: LO 7.2 LOD M

Sales (2,00,000 bottles @ ₹2.5 each)		₹5,00,000
Variable costs	₹3,00,000	
Fixed costs	1,00,000	4,00,000
Pre-tax profit		1,00,000
Less: Taxes		35,000
Profit after tax		65,000

1. What is the break-even point in amount and units?
2. Suppose that a plant expansion will add ₹50,000 to fixed costs and increase capacity by 60 per cent. How many bottles would have to be sold after the addition to break-even?
3. At what level of sales will the company be able to maintain its present pre-tax profit position even after expansion?

4. The company's management feels that it should earn at least ₹10,000 (pre- tax per annum) on the new investment. What sales volume is required to enable the company to maintain existing profits and earn the minimum required return on new investments?
5. Suppose the plant operates at full capacity after the expansion, what profit will be earned?

Solution

1. BEP (amount) = ₹1,00,000/0.40 (₹2,00,000 ÷ ₹5,00,000) = ₹2,50,000
BEP (units) = ₹1,00,000/₹1.0 = 1,00,000 units

2. BEP (increase in FC) = [₹1,00,000 + ₹50,000 (Additional FC)] ÷ ₹1.0 per unit = 1,50,000 units

3. Desired sales volume to maintain a pre- tax profit of ₹1,00,000 = [₹1,50,000 (FC) + ₹1,00,000]/0.40 = ₹6,25,000 (or 2,50,000 bottles)

4. Desired sales volume to earn a profit of ₹1,10,000 (₹1,00,000 +₹10,000) = [₹1,50,000 + ₹1,10,000]/0.40 = ₹6,50,000 (or 2,60,000 bottles)

5. Present capacity (assumed operating at 100 per cent capacity) (bottles) 2,00,000
Add: Additional capacity (60 per cent) 1,20,000
Total capacity (bottles) 3,20,000

Statement of income (3,20,000 units)

Sales (3,20,000 bottles @ ₹2.5)	₹8,00,000
Less: Variable costs, 0.60	4,80,000
Contribution	3,20,000
Less: Fixed costs	1,50,000
Pre-tax profits	1,70,000
Less: Income tax	59,500
Profits after income tax	1,10,500

P.7.4 The following data are obtained from the records of a factory: LO 7.2 LOD M

Sales (4,000 units @ ₹25 each)		₹1,00,000
Variable costs:		
Materials consumed	₹40,000	
Labour charges	20,000	
Variable overheads	10,000	
Fixed overheads	18,000	88,000
Net profit		12,000

Calculate:

1. Number of units by selling which the company will break-even.
2. Sales needed to earn a profit of 20 per cent on sales.
3. Extra units, which should be sold to obtain the present profit if it is proposed to reduce the selling price by 20 per cent and 25 per cent.
4. Selling price to be fixed to bring down its break-even point to 600 units under present conditions.

Solution

1. BEP (units), Fixed overheads = ₹18,000/CM per unit, ₹7.50 = 2,400 units

Determination of CM per unit

Sales revenue (4,000 units)		₹1,00,000
Less: Variable costs		
Materials consumed	₹40,000	
Labour charges	20,000	
Variable overheads	10,000	70,000
Contribution (4,000 units)		30,000
CM per unit (₹30,000 ÷ 4,000)		7.5

2. (a) Sales revenue (SR) is a sum of total costs (TC) and total profits (TP) or (SR = TC + TP).
(b) TC can be split into FC and VC.
(c) VC will vary in direct proportion to SR.
(d) Accordingly, SR = FC + VC (SR) + TP (SR). Let us suppose, SR = 100 per cent; TC = 80 per cent; TP = 20 per cent; VC = 70 per cent (₹70,000/₹1,00,000); FC = ₹18,000

Substituting the values, we have,

100% SR = ₹18,000 + 0.70 SR + 0.20 SR
0.10 SR = ₹18,000
SR = ₹18,000/0.10 = ₹1,80,000

Verification

Sales revenue		₹1,80,000
Less: Variable cost (0.70)	₹1,26,000	
Less: Fixed overheads	18,000	1,44,000
Net profit		36,000
Net profit as percentage of sales revenue		20

3. Revised contribution margin per unit and additional units required to maintain profit of ₹12,000

Particulars	*Selling price reduced by*	
	20 per cent	*25 per cent*
Revised selling price	₹20.00	₹18.75
Less: Variable cost (0.70 × ₹25, original sales price)	17.50	17.50
Contribution	2.50	1.25
Desired sales volume (FC + NP) ÷ CM	30,000/2.50	30,000/1.25
Number of units required	12,000	24,000
Less: Existing number of units sold	4,000	4,000
Extra units to be sold to maintain a profit of ₹12,000	8,000	20,000

4. BEP = FC/CM per unit
CM per unit = FC/BEP = ₹18,000/600 units = ₹30
Sales price (per unit) = CM per unit + Variable cost per unit = ₹30 + ₹17.50 = ₹47.5

P.7.5 *ABC* Ltd manufactures and sells four types of products under the brand names of *A*, *B*, *C* and *D*. The sales-mix in value comprises 33.33, 41.67, 16.67 and 8.33 per cents for products *A*, *B*, *C* and *D* respectively. The total budgeted sales (100 per cent) are ₹60,000 per month. Operating costs are: **LO 7.1** LOD D

Variable costs as per cent of selling price: Product *A*, 60, *B*, 68, *C*, 80, and *D* 40. Fixed costs, ₹14,700 per month.

Calculate the break-even point for the products on an over-all basis.

Solution

Determination of weighted PV ratio

Product	Sales revenue	(%)	Variable costs	(%)	Contribution	P/V ratio (%)
A	₹20,000	(33.33)	₹12,000	(60)	₹8,000	40
B	25,000	(41.67)	17,000	(68)	8,000	32
C	10,000	(16.67)	8,000	(80)	2,000	20
D	5,000	(8.33)	2,000	(40)	3,000	60
Total	60,000	(100)	39,000	(65)	21,000	35

BEP = Fixed costs/ Weighted P/V ratio = ₹14,700/0.35 = ₹42,000

Confirmation

Variable costs (0.65 × ₹42,000)	₹27,300
Fixed costs	14,700
Total costs	42,000
Total sales revenue	42,000

MINI CASES

7.C.1 (Break-even Point) Sybergrid Solutions is a Web Publishing firm involved in the design and hosting of websites for corporates and business houses. As the initial investment required to start web publishing is low, several new entrants have entered/are planning to enter this business. There are also some established players who are willing to operate at low margins. Website publishing is highly competitive coupled with low market demand.

A website consists of a number of web pages. On average, any website would be made up of 50 web pages. The costs, revenues and time are calculated on the basis of production of one web page, that is 1 unit = 1 web page (selling as ₹1,000).

Besides, Biplab Saha, the owner of Sybergrid Solutions, there are three permanent employees—a visualiser who does the conceptualising and designing the graphics, a DTP operator to enter data and make the design on the computer and an office boy. One contract programmer is also hired as and when Sybegrid gets an order for developing a website. The total hours available in a month are (7.5 × 25 × 3) 564 hours. The annual capacity is (564 × 12) 6,768 hours. The total man-hours per web page to make 1 web page are 8 hours consisting of 3 hours each taken by visualiser and owner/entrepreneur and 2 hours by the DTP operator.

The monthly man-power expenses are as follows: (i) Owner/entrepreneur, ₹12,000 (ii) Visualiser, ₹5,000, (iii) DTP operator, ₹4,000 and (iv) Office boy, ₹1,500.

The investments and operational expenses are summarised below:

Capital cost:		
Computers (2)	₹80,000	
Printer (1)	12,000	
Scanner (1)	35,000	
Internet connection per annum	15,000	₹1,42,500
Fixed cost per month:		
Rent	3,000	
Telephone	600	
Electricity	1,000	
Floppy disk, stationery and office expenses	500	
Books	250	
Magazines/newspapers	150	
Conveyance	1,000	6,500

The variable costs are given below:

Cost	*Rate*	*Time taken per web page*
Additional labour	₹30/hr	1 hour
Telephone	1.5/minute	10 minutes
Electricity	₹20 per web page	

These costs are classified into fixed and variable in Exhibit 1.

EXHIBIT 1 Fixed and Variable Costs

Cost element	*Fixed cost (annual)*	*Variable cost per 100 web page*		
		Direct labour	*Direct expenses*	*Selling expenses*
Labour:		₹3,000		
Owner/entrepreneur	₹1,44,000			
Visualiser	60,000			
DTP operator	48,000			
Office boy	18,000			
	2,70,000			
Rent	36,000			
Telephone	7,200		₹1,500	
Electricity	12,000		2,000	
Internet connection	15,000			
Floppy disks, stationery and office expenses	6,000		1,000	₹200
Depreciation (10%)*	12,700			
Interest (13%)**	16,500			
Conveyance	12,000			500
Magazine/newspapers	1,800			
Books	3,000			
Total	3,92,000	3,000	4,500	700

*₹1,27,000 (₹80,000 + ₹12,000 + ₹35,000) × 0.10

**₹1,27,000 × 0.13 (This is the opportunity cost of interest lost on owners funds used to buy computer, scanner and printer).

Required

(a) Compute break-even sales revenue to establish viability of business.
(b) Compute number of orders to make operating profit of ₹15,000 per month.
(c) Determine sales volume required to offset reduction in sale price from ₹1,000 to ₹700 to maintain operating profit of ₹15,000 per month.
(d) Determine selling price at which Sybergrid would not suffer cash losses.

Solution

(a) Viability of business:

- Breakeven point (amount): Fixed cost ÷ CV ratio = ₹3,92,000 ÷ 0.918[@] = ₹4,27,015
  [@]Sales price, ₹1,000 – ₹82, variable cost per unit (₹8,200 ÷ 100) = ₹918 ÷ ₹1,000 = 91.8% = 0.981
- Break-even point (units) = ₹4,27,015 ÷ ₹1,000 = 427 pages
  Number of orders for website to break-even in one year = 427 pages ÷ 50 pages for an order on website = 8.54 (9) orders.

Man-hours required = 398 × 8 = 3,184

Total capacity = 6,278 man-hours

Capacity utilisation = 6,278 ÷ 3,184 = 50%

(b) Number of orders to get a desired profit of ₹15,000 per month (₹1,80,000 annual)

= [Fixed expenses + Desired profit] ÷ C/V ratio

= (₹3,92,000 + ₹1,80,000] ÷ 0.918 = ₹6,23,094 ÷ ₹1,000 = 623 pages

Number of website sale to make classified profit = 623 pages ÷ 50 pages = 12.46(13) orders per year to get the desired profit of ₹15,000 per month

(c) Additional sales volume required to offset a reduction in selling price from ₹1,000 to ₹700

Contribution (₹700 – ₹82) = ₹618 (revised)

C/V ratio = 88.29%

Sales volume to offset reduced selling price = [Desired profit + Fixed expenses] ÷ Revised C/V ratio

= ₹5,72,000 ÷ 0.8829 = ₹6,47,865 ÷ 100 = 648 web pages to be sold

Number of orders per year = 648 pages ÷ 50 pages = 13 orders

(d) Lowest selling price at which Sybergrid would not suffer cash losses.

Cash fixed cost = ₹3,92,000 – ₹12,700 Depreciation = ₹3,79,300

Desired Contribution per page = ₹3,79,300/427 BEP = ₹888.29

Desired selling price per page = Desired contribution (₹888.29) per page + Variable cost (₹82) per page = ₹970.29

Thus, the minimum price per web page should be ₹970.29 to avoid any cash losses.

Scan the QR Code given at the end of chapter to access comprehensive cases.

REVIEW QUESTIONS

LOD: Easy

RQ.7.1 In the following multiple choice questions, select the correct answers. [LO 7.1,2,]

(i) The margin of safety for a firm in a very volatile market is 5 per cent. Which of the following is true?

(a) The margin of safety is probably too high, (b) The margin of safety is probably too low, (c) The margin of safety is adequate, (d) We can't tell.

(ii) Contribution per unit is ₹100. Fixed costs are ₹6,00,000. Production and sales are 8,000 units. When sales rise

(a) total contribution rises by an amount greater than profit, (b) total contribution rises by an amount smaller than profit, (c) total contribution and profit rise by the same amount, (d) contribution margin drops.

(iii) Contribution per unit is ₹100. Fixed costs are ₹6,00,000. Production and sales are 8,000 units. Total contribution is

(a) ₹6,00,000, (b) ₹4,00,000, (c) ₹8,00,000, (d) None of the above.

(iv) Contribution per unit is ₹100. Fixed costs are ₹6,00,000. Production and sales are 8,000 units. Profit is

(a) ₹2,00,000, (b) ₹6,00,000, (c) ₹6,00,000, (d) None of the above.

(v) Break-even is not affected with changes in

(a) sales price per unit, (b) variable cost per unit, (c) total fixed costs, (d) number of units sold.

(vi) Contribution margin ratio (C/V ratio) is 25%. The fixed costs are ₹30,00,000. The break even point is

(a) ₹1,20,00,000, (b) ₹60,00,000, (c) ₹30,00,000, (d) ₹15,00,000.

(vii) Variable cost is ₹400 per unit, fixed costs are ₹80,00,000, selling price per unit is ₹900, sales are 5,000 units. If selling price increases by ₹100, contribution increases by
(a) ₹10,000, (b) ₹100, (c) ₹5,00,000, (d) ₹80,00,000.

(viii) Variable cost is ₹400 per unit, fixed costs are ₹80,00,000, selling price per unit is ₹900, sales are 5,000 units. If fixed costs increase by ₹10,00,000, contribution
(a) increases by ₹10,00,000, (b) decreases by ₹10,00,000, (c) remains unchanged, (d) can't say.

(ix) Variable cost is ₹400 per unit, fixed costs are ₹80,00,000, selling price per unit is ₹900, sales are 5,000 units. If sales decrease by 2,000 units, contribution margin
(a) increases by ₹10,00,000, (b) decreases by ₹10,00,000, (c) remains unchanged, (d) can't say.

(x) Variable cost is ₹400 per unit, fixed costs are ₹80,00,000, selling price per unit is ₹900, sales are 5,000 units. The target profit is ₹1,00,00,000. What must the sales revenue be?
(a) ₹3,24,00,000, (b) ₹2,00,00,000, (c) ₹1,60,00,000, (d) ₹3,53,00,000.

(xi) Company B sells two products:
Product A: [Contribution margin ratio = 20%, Sales = ₹100,000]
Product B: [Contribution margin ratio = 40%, Sales = ₹200,000]
If actual sales were (A) ₹200,000 and (B) ₹100,000, total contribution would:
(a) increase by ₹20,000, (b) decrease by ₹20,000, (c) increase by ₹40,000, (d) decrease by ₹40,000

(xii) Company B sells two products:
Product A: [Contribution margin ratio = 20%, Sales = ₹100,000]
Product B: [Contribution margin ratio = 40%, Sales = ₹200,000]
If actual sales were (A) ₹200,000 and (B) ₹100,000, fixed costs are ₹50,000. The break-even point in sales revenue would be
(a) ₹175,000, (b) ₹200,000, (c) ₹150,000, (d) ₹187,970.

(xiii) One of the following is not an assumption that underlies CVP analysis.
(a) Fixed costs per unit will remain the same throughout the relevant range. (b) Variable cost per unit will increase as sales increases. (c) Variable costs have a linear relationship with sales. (d) Selling price is constant throughout the relevant range.

(xiv) Which is the correct equation that calculates P (profit before tax)
Assume, Selling Price per unit = ₹S, Variable Cost per unit = ₹V, Number of units sold = U units and Total Fixed costs = ₹F.
(a) $P = SV - F$, (b) $P = U(S - V) - F$, (c) $P = FS - V$, (d) $P = S(V - S)$.

(xv) The break-even point is 10,000 units, sales are 12,000 units. The margin of safety expressed in percentage is:
(a) 16.67%, (b) 80%, (c) 120%, (d) 20%.

[Answer: (i) b (ii) c (iii) c (iv) a (v) d (vi) a (vii) c (viii) c (ix) b (x) a (xi) b (xii) d (xiii) b (xiv) b (xv) a.]

RQ.7.2 Define break-even analysis and outline its uses and applications. [LO 7.2,]

RQ.7.3 (a) Discus the importance of the following in relation to break-even analysis: [LO 7.1,2,]
(1) Break-even point (2) Margin of safety (3) Contribution (4) Profit volume ratio.
(b) Write a short note on the angle of incidence in a break-even chart.

RQ.7.4 Explain the limitations of a break-even analysis. [LO 7.2,]

RQ.7.5 What is cash break-even point? Draw a cash break-even chart with hypothetical figures. [LO 7.3]

RQ.7.6 Asian Industries Ltd. specialises in the manufacture of small capacity motors. The cost structure of a motor is as under: Material, ₹50; Labour, ₹80; Variable overheads, 75 per cent of labour cost. Fixed overheads of the company amount to ₹2.40 lakh per annum. The sale price of the motor is ₹230 each. [LO 7.3]

(a) Determine the number of motors that have to be manufactured and sold in a year in order to break-even.

(b) How many motors have to be made and sold to make a profit of ₹1 lakh per year?
(c) If the sale price is reduced by ₹15 each, how many motors have to be sold to break-even?

LOD: Medium

RQ.7.7 Explain the significance and objective of a break-even chart and state the factors which would cause the break-even point to change. [LO 7.2]

RQ.7.8 A "break-even chart must be used with intelligent discrimination, with an adequate grasp of assumptions underlying the technique surrounding its practical application." Elucidate the statement giving illustrations. [LO 7.2]

RQ.7.9 (a) What is the significance to financial management, of increase in output, fixed costs, variable cost and selling price? [LO 7.2]
(b) Draw a break-even chart with a few illustrative figures. Explain the VCP relationship. How would a change in selling price affect the above? [LO 7.2]

RQ.7.10 The "volume-cost-profit relationships provide management with a simplified framework for organising its thinking on a number of problems." Discuss. [LO 7.2]

RQ.7.11 The per cycle price structure of a cycle made by the Cycle Company Ltd. is as follows: [LO 7.2]

Material	₹60
Labour	20
Variable overheads	20
	100
Fixed overheads	50
Profit	50
Selling price	200

This is based on the manufacture of 1 lakh cycles per annum.

The company expects that due to competition, they will have to reduce selling price, but they want to keep the total profit intact. What level of production will have to be reached, that is, how many cycles will have to be made to get the same amount of profits, if: (a) the selling price is reduced by 10 per cent, (b) the selling price is reduced by 20 per cent?

RQ.7.12 A company is considering expansion. Fixed costs amount to ₹4,20,000 and are expected to increase by 1,25,000 when plant expansion is completed. The present plant capacity is 80,000 units a year. Capacity will increase by 50 per cent with expansion. Variable costs are currently ₹6.80 per unit and are expected to go down by ₹0.40 per unit with the expansion. The current selling price is ₹16 per unit and is expected to remain the same under each alternative. What are the break-even points under each alternative? Which alternative is better, and why? [LO 7.2]

LOD: Difficult

RQ.7.13 "The effect of a price increase is always to increase the P/V ratio, to bring down the break-even point and to widen the margin of safety." Discuss. [LO 7.2]

RQ.7.14 A, B, and C are three similar plants under the same management; it wants to merge them for better operation. The details are as under: [LO 7.2]

Plant	*A*	*B*	*C*
Capacity operated (%)	100	70	50
Turnover (₹ lakh)	300	280	150
Variable costs	200	210	75
Fixed costs	70	50	62

You are to find out: (i) the capacity of the merged plant for breaking even, (ii) the profit at 75 per cent capacity of the merged plant, and (iii) the turnover from the merged plant to give a profit of ₹28 lakh.

RQ.7.15 The sales of Forma Ltd. in the first half of the current year amounted to ₹2,70,000 and profit earned was ₹7,200. The sales in the second half year registered an increase and amounted to ₹3,42,000. The profit earned was ₹20,700 in that half year. Assuming no change in fixed cost, calculate (i) the *P/V* ratio, (ii) the amount of profit when sales are ₹2,16,000, and (iii) the amount of sales required to earn a profit of ₹36,000. [LO 7.2]

ANSWERS

7.6 **(a)** 6,000 **(b)** 8,500 **(c)** 9,600
7.11 **(a)** 1,25,000 **(b)** 1,66,667
7.12 BEP Pre-expansion 45,653;
Post-expansion 56,771; The alternative of expansion appears to be better one.
7.14 **(i)** 52 per cent **(ii)** ₹80.5 lakh **(iii)** ₹600 lakh
7.15 **(i)** 18.75 per cent **(ii)** (₹2,925), 6 months; (₹46,350), 12 months **(iii)** ₹6,55,200

Scan the QR Code to access comprehensive solutions to all numerical review questions and additional material.

CHAPTER

8

Budgeting and Profit Planning

LEARNING OBJECTIVES

LO 8.1	Understand the planning process
LO 8.2	Explain the definition, meaning and purpose of a budget
LO 8.3	Discuss types of budgets and illustrate their preparation

INTRODUCTION

Budgets are an important tool of profit planning. The purpose of this chapter is to present a general view of budgeting as a device of planning and illustrate the preparation of various types of budgets. The chapter provides a brief account of the planning process *vis-à-vis* budgeting. It also elaborates on the meaning of a budget and the purpose of budgeting. The important types of budgets are discussed and illustrated subsequently. The major points are summarised by way of recapitulation.

LO 8.1 PLANNING PROCESS

Budgeting, as a tool of planning, is closely related to the broader system of planning in an organistion. **Planning** involves the specification of the basic objectives that the organisation will pursue and the fundamental policies that will guide it. In operational terms, it involves four stages: (i) Objectives (ii) Goals (iii) Strategies, and (iv) Plans/Budgets.

Planning involves specifications of basic objectives and fundamental policies.

Objectives

The first stage in the planning and control system is setting the **objectives** which are defined as the *broad and long-range desired state or position in the future.* They are motivational or directional in nature and are expressed in qualitative terms.

Objectives are broad and long-range desired state or position in future.

Examples of fundamental objectives are identification of the line of business, customer satisfaction, employee welfare, and so on. Thus, they are the basic policies.

Goals

Goals are quantitative targets to be achieved in specified period.

The second stage in the planning process is specifying the **goals**. The term goal, as an element in planning, represents targets, specific in quantitative terms, to be achieved in a specific period of time. The timing of introducing new products, purchase of new plant and machinery and expected rate of return are examples of time and quantity-oriented goals.

Strategies

Strategies represent specific course of action to achieve goals.

The next step involves laying down the strategies. **Strategies** denote specific methods/courses of action to achieve the goals, for instance, promotion of sales through price reduction or aggressive advertisement, financial alternatives, and so on.

Plans/Budgets

The final step is the preparation of budgets/profit plans. Basically, budgeting is the periodic planning to implement the alternatives during a particular fiscal period, usually one year. It converts, in other words, goals and strategies into annual operating plans.

LO 8.2 BUDGET—DEFINITION, MEANING AND PURPOSE

A budget is defined as a 'comprehensive and coordinated plan, expressed in financial terms, for the operations and resources of an enterprise for some specified period in the future.'[1] According to this definition, the essential elements of a budget are: (i) Plan, (ii) Operations and resources, (iii) Financial terms, (iv) Specified future period, (v) Comprehensiveness, and (vi) Coordination.

Plan

The first ingredient of a budget is its plan. The term 'plan' with reference to budgeting has a *specific connotation.* It includes two aspects which have a bearing on the operations of an enterprise. One set of factors, which determine a firm's future operations are wholly external and beyond its control. Included in this category of factors are general business conditions, government policy and size and composition of population. The second set of factors affecting future activities are within the firm's control and discretion, that is, they are internal. The promotional programmes and manufacturing processes are illustration of these factors. Budgeting, as a plan, covers both these aspects. In other words, budgeting not only suggests what should happen but should also make things happen.[2] In brief, a budget (plan) is an expression partly of what the management expects to happen and partly of what the management intends to happen.

Operations and Resources

A budget is a mechanism to plan for the firm's operations and resources. The operations are reflected in revenues and expenses. This means that a budget should quantify the revenues to be realised from products/services and the expenses to be incurred on goods/services used in generating revenues.

The plan also covers the resources of the firm. The planning of resources means the planning of the various assets and the sources of capital to finance these assets. The assets could be fixed assets as well as current assets.

Financial Terms

Budgets are prepared in financial terms, that is, in terms of monetary value such as the rupee, dollar, and so on. The reason is that the monetary unit is a common denominator. The various activities and operations are expressed in different units, for example, material in terms of weight, labour in terms of number/man-hours, sales in terms of territories, advertisement in terms of magazine space, and so on. If they have to be integrated in a plan, they must be expressed in comparable units of measurement. Monetary units provide such a measure.

Specified Future Period

A budget relates to a specified period of time, usually one year. If it is not related to a time horizon, it will be meaningless. Planning merely for a given amount of, say, sales/profits will not constitute a budget unless a time dimension is added, that is, the budget sales/profit is planned to be achieved in a predetermined time framework.

Comprehensiveness

A budget is comprehensive in that all the activities and operations of an organisation are included in it. It covers the organisation as a whole and not only some segments. The *modus operandi* is that budgets are prepared for each segment/facet/activity/division of an organisation. These are integrated into an overall budget for the entire organisation. The overall budget is referred to as the **master budget**.

Master budget is the overall budget for the entire organisation.

Coordination

Budgets are prepared for the different components/segments/divisions/facets/activities of an organisation so as to take care of the situations and problems of each component. The budgets for each of the components are prepared in harmony with each another. This is called coordination.

Budgets—Purpose

As a tool, budgets serve as a guide to the conduct of operations and a basis for evaluating actual results. The main objectives of budgeting are: (i) Explicit statement of expectations, (ii) Communication, (iii) Coordination, and (iv) Expectations as a framework for judging performance.[3]

Explicit Statement of Expectations One purpose of budgeting is to state expectations in formal terms so that most of the underlying assumptions may be identified. A firm has the basic objective of optimising long-run profit. Its long-range goals also include survival, consumer satisfaction, employee welfare, personal power and prestige, and so on. These long-range objectives can be achieved in successive phases over a period of time. In other words, long-range objectives have to be split into short-term operational plans. Thus, a budget can be said to be a device to express goals which are sought to be achieved in a short period of time. In other words, it is a means to establish congruence between short-term goals and the long-term objectives of the firm. Therefore, budgets formulate targets of expected performance. The advantage is that by laying down targets, budgets contain an explicit statement of expectations. These targets help direct their operations, identify problems, help motivate lower-level employees and clarify the relationship between current activities and future policies.[4] Another implication is that budgets explicitly state the underlying assumptions and goal and/or the means of attaining it. To illustrate, if the sales target (projected sales) for any given period is ₹5,00,000, the budget will not only indicate this figure but will also give details about the assumed prices, quantity, sales efforts, and so on. This explicit statement of assumption is one of the most important contributions of budgeting for managerial planning and control.

However, a budget does not lay down a statement of expectations in rigid terms. Budgets, as observed earlier, are based on factors which are either uncertain or are beyond the control of management. Some of these are economic, social and business conditions; supply and demand; competition; consumer taste; technological innovations; and so on. A budget should be modified when necessary in the light of the changes in the factors/assumptions on which the original estimates were based.

Communication Another purpose of budgeting is to communicate or inform others of the goals and methods selected by top management. Since budgeting deals with fundamental policies and objectives, it is prepared by top management. A formal budget by itself will not ensure that a firm's operations will be automatically geared to the achievement of the goals set in the budget. For this to happen, the managers and lower-level employees have to understand the goals and support them and coordinate their efforts to attain them. In other words, the employees should be aware well in advance of the level of performance expected of them. It is for this reason that a budget is viewed as a means of communicating to the employees the level of performance expected of them so that the goals set out in the budget can be accomplished.

Coordination Yet another purpose of budgeting is coordination. The term 'coordination' refers to the operation of all departments of an organisation in such a way that there is no bottleneck or imbalance. In other words, coordination implies a harmonious relationship between various departments to ensure smooth and uninterrupted operation of each of them. If an organisation is to achieve its long-run goals, coordination in the activities of all its departments is necessary. If there is no coordination, imbalances will be created which will hinder smooth operation and stand in the way of the accomplishment of the goals of the budgets.

To illustrate, one type of imbalance may be between the manufacturing/production and sales departments. The manufacturing department may be producing goods, which the sales department may not be able to sell. Conversely, the sales department may like the production department to produce goods which the production department is incapable of producing. Another example of lack of coordination is the purchasing-manufacturing imbalance when the production schedule is not related to the raw material purchases. Further, the production schedule may not be based on the capability of employees and capacity of plant and machinery.

In view of the above, coordination is a major function of budgeting. Budgets should be drafted in such a way that the operations of the various departments are related to each other for the achievement of the overall goal. Apart from the interdepartmental reconciliation, budgets also provide for flexibility to accommodate plans and operations to unexpected situations.

Expectations as a Framework for Judging Performance Finally, a budget establishes expectations as a framework for judging employee performance. A budget, as observed earlier, defines the goals, the means of implementing them and the level of performance by the employees. The extent to which employees have succeeded in the task assigned to them, can be judged on the basis of a comparison of the actual performance/achievement with the budget. If the actual performance equals or exceeds the budgeted level, it may be termed satisfactory, otherwise not. Thus, a budget can serve as a yardstick to judge employee performance or as a control device.

To conclude, budgeting, as a tool of planning and control, serves as a guide to conduct operations and a basis for evaluating actual results. Actual results can be judged satisfactory or unsatisfactory in the light of the relevant budgeted data and also in the light of changes in conditions. However, a budget should not be regarded as a rigid requirement of performance. Many of the factors upon which a budget is based are beyond the control of management and all of them are uncertain. The budget should, therefore, be regarded as a plan, not an immutable commitment of performance; it is a means of control, but not a straitjacket on operations.[5] In view of its significance as a managerial tool, the preparation of a budget is illustrated in the pages that follows.

LO 8.3 PREPARATION/TYPES OF BUDGETS

It may be recalled that a budget with reference to planning and control refers to a comprehensive and coordinated budget generally known as master budget. In operational terms, a comprehensive or overall budget has several components. A master budget normally consists of three types of budgets: **(i)** Operating budgets, **(ii)** Financial budgets, and **(iii)** Special decision budgets. Another classification of a master budget is: **(i)** Fixed/static budget and **(ii)** Flexible/variable/sliding budget. In the discussions that follow we illustrate the preparation of the various components of a master budget, namely, operating and financial budgets. The mechanics of the preparation of a flexible budget is also discussed.

Operating Budgets

Operating budgets relate to physical activities/operations such as sales, production, and so on.

Operating budgets relate to the physical activities/operations of a firm such as sales, production, purchasing, debtors collection and creditors payment schedules. In specific terms, an **operating budget** has the following components:

1. Sales budget,
2. Production budget,
3. Purchase budget,
4. Direct labour budget,
5. Manufacturing expenses budget, and
6. Administrative and selling expenses budget, and so on.

Financial Budgets

Financial budgets are concerned with expected cash flows, financial position and result of operations.

Financial budgets are concerned with expected cash receipts/disbursements, financial position and results of operations. In other words, a financial budget has the following components:

1. Budgeted income statement,
2. Budgeted statement of retained earnings,
3. Cash budget, and
4. Budgeted balance sheet.

Cash Budget* The principal aim of the cash budget, as a tool of planning, is to ascertain whether, at any time, there is likely to be an excess or shortage of cash. The preparation of a cash budget involves various steps.

The *first* element of a cash budget is the selection of the period of time to be covered by the budget. Alternatively, it is referred to as the 'planning horizon'. The planning horizon means the *time span* and the sub-periods within that time span over which the cash flows are to be projected. There is no hard and fast rule. The period coverage of a cash budget will differ from firm to firm depending upon its nature and the degree of accuracy with which the estimates can be made. As a general rule, the period selected should be neither too long nor too short. If it is too long, it is likely that the estimates will be upset as we cannot visualise them at the time of the preparation

* Discussed separately in detail in Chapter 14.

of the budget. If on the other hand, the time span is too small, the disadvantage are: **(i)** Failure to take into account important events which lie just beyond the period covered by the budget; **(ii)** Heavy workload in preparation; and **(iii)** Abnormal factors that may be operative.

The planning horizon of a cash budget should be determined in the light of the circumstances and requirements of a particular case. For instance, if the flows are expected to be stable and dependable, such a firm may prepare a cash budget covering a long period, say, a year and divide it into quarterly intervals. In the case of a firm whose flows are uncertain, a quarterly budget divided into monthly intervals may be appropriate. Where flows are affected by seasonal variations, monthly sub-divided into weekly or even daily budgets may be necessary. If the flows are subject to extreme fluctuations, a daily budget may be called for. The idea behind sub-dividing the budget period into smaller intervals is to highlight the movement of cash from one sub-period to another. The sub-division will provide information on the fluctuations in the cash reservoir level during the time span covered by the budget.

The *second* element of the cash budget is the factors that have a bearing on cash flows. The items included in the cash budget are the cash items only, non-cash items such as *depreciation* are excluded.[6] The factors that generate cash flow are generally divided, for purposes of constructing a cash budget, into two broad categories: **(a)** Operating and **(b)** Financial. This two-fold classification of cash budget items is based on their 'nature'. While the former category includes cash flows generated by the operations of the firms and are known as the 'operating cash flows,' the latter consist of the 'financial cash flows.' The major components of the two types of cash flows are outlined below.

Operating Cash Flows The main operating factors/items which generate cash outlfows and inflows over the time span of a cash budget are tabulated in Exhibit 8.1.

EXHIBIT 8.1 Operating Cash Flow Items

Cash inflows/Receipts	*Cash outflows/Disbursements*
1. Cash sales	1. Accounts payable/Payable payments
2. Collection of accounts receivable	2. Purchase of raw materials
3. Disposal of fixed assets	3. Wages and salary (pay roll)
	4. Factory expenses
	5. Administrative and selling expenses
	6. Maintenance expenses
	7. Purchase of fixed assets

Among the operating factors affecting cash flows, the collection of accounts receivable (inflows) and accounts payable (outflows) are the most important. The terms of credit and the speed with which the customers pay would determine the lag between the creation of the accounts receivable and their collection. Also, discounts and allowances for early payments, return from customers and bad debts affect the cash inflows. Similarly, accounts payable relating to credit purchases are affected by the purchase terms.

Financial Cash Flows The major financial factors/items affecting generation of cash flows are depicted in Exhibit 8.2.

EXHIBIT 8.2 Financial Cash Flow Items

Cash inflows/Receipts	*Cash outflows/Payments*
1. Loans/borrowings	1. Income tax/tax payments
2. Sale of securities	2. Redemption of loan
3. Interest received	3. Re-purchase of shares
4. Dividend received	4. Interest paid
5. Rent received	5. Dividends paid
6. Refund of tax	
7. Issues of new shares and securities	

After the time span of the cash budget has been decided upon and pertinent operating and financial factors have been identified, the final step is the construction of the cash budget.

The preparation of the master budget is illustrated in Example 8.1.

***Example* 8.1**

The following data relate to Hypothetical Limited:

Balance Sheet as at March 31, Current Year

Liabilities	*Amount*	*Assets*		*Amount*
Accounts payable (all for March purchases)	₹40,000	Cash		₹3,00,000
Taxes payable (all for March income)	25,000	Accounts receivable (all from March sales)		2,50,000
Share capital	11,00,000	Inventories:		
Retained earnings	10,26,800	Raw materials (9,600 kgs × ₹3)		28,800
		Finished goods (1,800 units × ₹35)		63,000
		Fixed assets:		
		Cost	₹20,00,000	
		Less: Accumulated depreciation	(4,50,000)	15,50,000
	21,91,800			21,91,800

2. *Sales forecasts:* Assume the marketing department has developed the following sales forecast for the first quarter of the next year and the selling price of ₹50 per unit.

Month	*Units sales*
April	9,000
May	12,000
June	16,000

3. The management desires closing inventory to equal 20 per cent of the following month's sales.
4. The manufacturing costs are as follows:

Direct materials: (5 kgs × ₹3) (per unit)	₹15
Direct labour	5
Variable overheads	9
Total fixed overheads (per annum)	7,20,000

5. Normal capacity is 1,20,000 units per annum. Assume absorption costing basis.
6. Each unit of final product requires 5 kgs of raw materials. Assume management desires closing raw material inventory to equal 20 per cent of the following month's requirements of production.
7. Assume fixed selling and administrative expenses are ₹20,000 per month and variable selling and administrative expenses are ₹5 per unit sold.
8. All sales are on account. Payment received within 10 days from the date of sale are subject to a 2 per cent cash discount. In the past, 60 per cent of the sales were collected during the month of sale and 40 per cent are collected during the following month. Of collections during the month of sale, 50 per cent are collected during the discount period. Accounts receivable are recorded at the gross amount and cash discounts are treated as a reduction in arriving at net sales during the month they are taken.
9. Tax rate is 35 per cent.

10. Additional information:

(a) All purchases are on account. Two-thirds are paid for in the month of purchase and one-third, in the following month.

(b) Fixed manufacturing costs include depreciation of ₹20,000 per month.

(c) Taxes are paid in the following month.

(d) All other costs and/or expenses are paid during the month in which incurred.

From the foregoing information prepare a master budget for the month of April only.

Solution

1. Production Budget

Particulars	*April*	*May*
Sales (units)	9,000	12,000
Add: Desired closing inventory (0.20 × next month's sales)	2,400	3,200
Total finished goods requirement	11,400	15,200
Less: Opening inventory	(1,800)	(2,400)
Required production (units)	9,600	12,800

2. Manufacturing Cost Budget

Particulars	*April*
Required production (units)	9,600
Direct material cost (5 kgs × ₹3 per kg)	× ₹15
Total direct material cost	₹1,44,000
Total direct labour cost (₹5 per unit)	48,000
Total variable overhead cost (₹9 per unit)	86,400
Total variable manufacturing costs	2,78,400
All fixed manufacturing overheads (₹7,20,000 ÷ 12 months)	60,000
Total manufacturing cost	3,38,400

3. Purchase Budget (Raw Materials)

Particulars	*April*	*May*
Production requirement (units)	9,600	12,800
Raw material required for production @ 5 kgs per unit (kgs)	48,000	64,000
Add: Desired closing inventory (0.20 × May requirements)	12,800	
Total requirements	60,800	
Less: Opening inventory	(9,600)	
Purchase requirement	51,200	
Purchase requirement (amount @ ₹3 per kg)	₹1,53,600	

4. Selling and Administrative Expenses Budget

Particulars	*April*
Units sales	9,000
Variable costs @ ₹5 per unit	₹45,000
Fixed costs	20,000
Total selling and administrative expenses	65,000

5. Cost of Goods Sold Budget

Particulars	*April*
Units sold	9,000

(Contd.)

(*Contd.*)

Cost per unit		
Variable	₹29	
Fixed (₹60,000 ÷ 10,000 units)	6	× ₹35
Total cost		3,15,000

6. Budgeted Income Statement for the Month of April

Gross sales (9,000 × ₹50)	₹4,50,000
Less: Cash discount (₹4,50,000 × 0.6 × 0.5 × 0.02)	2,700
Net sales	4,47,300
Less: Cost of goods sold	3,15,000
Gross margin (unadjusted)	1,32,300
Less: Capacity variance unfavourable (400 units × ₹6)	2,400
Gross margin (adjusted)	1,29,900
Less: Selling and administrative expenses	65,000
Earnings before taxes	64,900
Less: Taxes (0.35)	22,715
Earning after taxes	42,185

7. Budgeted Statement of Retained Earnings

Opening balance	₹10,26,800
Add: Earnings after taxes	42,185
Closing balance	10,68,985

8. Cash Budget (April)

Opening balance			₹3,00,000	
Cash inflows:				
Collection from debtors:				
March sales		₹2,50,000		
April sales (gross) (₹4,50,000 × 0.60)	₹2,70,000			
Less: Cash discount (₹2,70,000 × 0.5 × 0.02)	2,700	2,67,300	5,17,300	₹8,17,300
Cash outflows:				
Payment to creditors:				
For March purchases		40,000		
For April purchases (₹1,53,600 × 2/3)		1,02,400	1,42,400	
Direct labour			48,000	
Variable manufacturing overhead			86,400	
Fixed manufacturing overhead		60,000		
Less: Depreciation		(20,000)	40,000	
Variable selling and administrative overheads			45,000	
Fixed selling and administrative overheads			20,000	
Taxes			25,000	4,06,800
Closing balance				4,10,500

9. Proforma Balance Sheet as at March 31, Next Year

Liabilities	*Amount*	*Assets*	*Amount*
Accounts payable (₹40,000 + ₹1,53,600 – ₹1,42,400)	₹51,200	Cash	₹4,10,500
		Accounts receivable (₹4,50,000 × 0.40)	1,80,000

(*Contd.*)

(*Contd.*)

Taxes payable (₹25,000 + ₹22,715 – ₹25,000)	22,715	Inventories:		
		Raw material (12,800 × ₹3)	₹38,400	
Share capital	11,00,000			
Retained earnings	10,68,985	Finished goods (2,400 × ₹35)	84,000	1,22,400
		Fixed assets:		
		Cost	20,00,000	
		Less: Accumulated depreciation	(4,70,000)	15,30,000
	22,42,900			22,42,900

Special Decision Budgets

The third category of budgets are special decision budgets. They relate to inventory levels, break-even analysis, and so on. These are discussed comprehensively in other chapters of this volume.[7] The long-term capital budgets are covered in detail in Chapters 9 and 10.

Flexible Budgets

Flexible budget estimates costs at several levels of activity.

The discussion of the **master budget** and its components in the preceding section was based on the assumption of fixed level of activity. In other words, the budgets were related to a specific level of operation implying thereby that a firm can accurately and precisely forecast the level of its behaviour/operations in a given period of time. If the business environment is capable of accurate prediction, this approach to budgeting is likely to yield dependable results. If, however, changes take place during the budget period, the budget will serve no useful purpose. Such a budget is technically referred to as a fixed/static budget. In other words, budgets prepared at a single level of activity, with no prospect of modification in the light of the changed circumstances, are fixed or static budgets. The alternative to fixed budgets are **flexible/variable/sliding budgets**. The term 'flexible' is the most apt description of the essential features/characteristics of these budgets and is used here to refer to such budgets.

A **flexible budget** estimates costs at several levels of activity. The merit of a flexible budget is that instead of one estimate it contains several estimates/plans in different assumed circumstances. Since business activities cannot be accurately predicted as the business conditions/environment are uncertain, it is a useful tool in real business situations, that is, an unpredictable environment. In view of its significance as a more realistic basis of budgeting, the setting up of a flexible budget is demonstrated in the discussions that follow.

It may at the outset be noted that the construction of a flexible budget is similar to that of a fixed budget except in one respect. While the fixed budget is based on costs and other business operations/activities at one level, the flexible budget considers several alternatives/levels/volumes of activity. The term 'volume/level' of activity refers to the usage of capacity. In other words, volume/level of activity signifies the percentage use of capacity. The term 'capacity' means the *installed capacity* of plant and personnel, that is, the fixed amount invested in these. For instance, if a plant when fully operated can produce 5,000 units, its capacity is 5,000 units of production. Assuming 2,500 units of production in a given period, the volume/level of activity is 50 per cent.

Thus, the essence of a flexible budget is the presentation of estimated cost data in a manner that permits their determination at various levels of volume. This means that all costs must be identified as to how they behave with a change in volume—whether they vary or remain fixed.

The conceptual framework of flexible budgeting, therefore, relates to: **(i)** Measure of volume and **(ii)** Cost behaviour identified with change in volume.

Measure of Volume The volume measure selected for any given department/firm should be that quantity which displays the greatest degree of correlation with those costs that vary with the level of operating activity. Different departments may use different measures of volume. In the first place, the measure of volume may be expressed in terms of the activity or factor that causes costs to vary, for example, labour costs vary on the basis of number of hours worked, material costs vary due to quantity of materials consumed. Secondly, the volume measure should be related to factors controllable by management, that is, number of hours worked, the quantity of materials consumed and number of machine hours operated. Further, the activity chosen as a unit of measure should be one that is not greatly affected by factors other than volume, that is, quantity more useful than cost as indicator of volume. In brief, volume should be expressed in terms of some unit of input, such as direct labour hours, direct labour cost or machine hours. The measure applied in any particular case will depend on the peculiarities. For instance, in the light machinery department, direct labour hours may be an appropriate measure. But for the heavy machinery department, machine hours may be the best indicator of cost behaviour.

Cost Behaviour with Change in Volume Three different types of cost behaviour can be visualised with changes in volume/level of activity: **(i)** Fixed costs, **(ii)** Variable costs, and **(iii)** Mixed costs.

Fixed Costs The fixed costs are associated with inputs that do not fluctuate in response to changes in the total activity or output of the firm, within relevant range for a given budget period. They may also be called *non-variable costs.* They are normally fixed for a relevant range of volume but fluctuate beyond that range. Moreover, fixed costs are to be analysed in relation to a given period of time; they are subject to change over a period of time.

> **Fixed costs** are fixed for a relevant range of volume for a given budget period.

Fixed costs may be: **(i)** Committed and **(ii)** Discretionary. Fixed costs that are associated with the acquisition of capacity-producing assets are known as the committed fixed costs. The identifying characteristic of a committed cost is that its occurrence as well as amount are predetermined and can be altered only by another major decision to reverse or amend the earlier commitment. Also known as *managed costs,* discretionary costs result from management decisions. They are incurred as well as reduced at the discretion of the management.

Each of the two types of fixed costs has a different implication for the budgetary process. Committed fixed costs can be budgeted on the basis of past commitment. Discretionary fixed cost, on the other hand, can be budgeted on the basis of inquiry from the decision-makers/management.

Variable Costs The variable costs are costs that are assumed to fluctuate in direct proportion to production activity/sales activity/some other measure of volume within relevant range for a given budget period. The level of variable costs at any volume can be estimated easily if the relationship between costs and volume is shown.

> **Variable costs** fluctuate in direct proportion to activity/volume within relevant range for a given budget period.

Mixed Costs The mixed costs are composed of both fixed and variable elements. The fixed part of mixed costs often represents a cost of capacity, while the variable element is influenced by changed in activity. For budgeting purposes, mixed costs must be broken down into their fixed and variable components/segments. Once this is done, the amount of fixed costs and the rate at which total variable costs change in proportion to total changes in output/volume can be worked out. That is, the fixed costs remain constant regardless of activity, but the variable portion is assumed to

> **Mixed costs** are composed of both fixed and variable elements.

change in direct proportion to change in labour hours, labour costs, machine hours, material costs/ material quantity, and so on.

The main elements in the construction of a flexible budget have been outlined above. To summarise, a flexible budget, in a sense, is a series of fixed budgets and an increase or decrease (any change) in the level/volume of activity must be reflected in it. Each expense in each department/ segment is to be categorised into fixed, variable and mixed components. A budget may be first prepared at the expected level of activity, say, 100 per cent of capacity. Additional columns may then be added for costs below and above 100 per cent, say, 90 per cent and 110 per cent.

Hypothetical flexible budgets corresponding to the procedure described above for two departments of a firm: Maintenance and Manufacture, are illustrated in Tables 8.1 and 8.2.

TABLE 8.1 Hypothetical Ltd—Flexible Budget (Maintenance Department)

Volume (labour-hours)	*400*	*450*	*500*	*550*	*600*
Variable costs:					
Labour	₹6,000	₹6,750	₹7,500	₹8,250	₹9,000
Material	2,400	2,700	3,000	3,300	3,600
Others	800	900	1,000	1,100	1,200
Mixed costs:					
Labour	2,300	2,400	2,500	2,600	2,700
Maintenance	1,400	1,450	1,500	1,550	1,600
Other supplies	2,500	2,750	3,000	3,250	3,500
Discretionary fixed costs:					
Training	1,500	2,000	2,000	2,000	2,500
Experimental methods	3,500	4,000	4,000	4,000	4,500
Committed fixed costs:					
Depreciation	5,000	5,000	5,000	5,000	5,000
Rent, lease cost	3,500	3,500	3,500	3,500	3,500
Total	28,900	31,450	33,000	34,550	37,100

TABLE 8.2 Hypothetical Ltd—Flexible Budget (Manufacturing Department)

Volume(machine-hours)	*50*	*60*	*70*	*80*	*90*
Variable costs:					
Power	₹500	₹600	₹700	₹800	₹900
Helpers	250	300	350	400	450
Discretionary fixed costs:					
Training	800	900	900	900	1,000
Tools	200	200	200	300	300
Committed fixed costs:					
Depreciation	1,200	1,200	1,200	1,200	1,200
Rent	1,000	1,000	1,000	1,000	1,000
Total	3,950	4,200	4,350	4,600	4,850

Modified Flexible Budgets From the preceding discussion it should be clear that flexible budgets, as a tool of planning and control, are superior to fixed budgets. The major weaknesses of static budgets are their inability to: **(i)** Disclose the potential variability of various estimates used in preparing the budget and **(ii)** Indicate the range within which costs can be expected to fall. They are not useful, therefore, in an uncertain and unpredictable environment. Flexible budgets are better in that they present estimates of costs at different level/volume of activity. But their one limitation is that they do not explicitly consider the relative probability that any particular volume or cost will be achieved.[8] This limitation can be overcome by using a modified flexible budget, which will include columns for different levels of estimates—most likely, optimistic and pessimistic. The hypothetical modified flexible budget is shown in Table 8.3.

TABLE 8.3 Hypothetical Ltd—Modified Flexible Budget (Manufacturing Department)

	Pessimistic	*Most likely*	*Optimistic*
Volume (labour-hours)	*425*	*500*	*585*
Variable costs:			
Labour	₹6,375	₹7,500	₹8,775
Materials	2,650	3,000	3,510
Others	850	1,000	1,170
Mixed costs:			
Labour	2,350	2,500	3,425
Maintenance	1,425	1,500	1,585
Other supplies	2,625	3,000	2,670
Discretionary fixed costs:			
Training	1,750	2,000	2,250
Experimental methods	3,750	4,000	4,250
Committed fixed costs:			
Depreciation	5,000	5,000	5,000
Rent, etc.	3,500	3,500	3,500
Total	30,275	33,000	36,135

SUMMARY

LO 8.1

Budgeting is a tool of planning. Planning involves specification of the basic objectives that the organisation will pursue and the fundamental policies that will guide it. In operational terms, it involves four steps: **(i)** Objectives defined as the broad and long-range desired state/position of the firm, **(ii)** Specified goals-targets in quantitative terms to be achieved in a specified period of time, **(iii)** Strategies or specific methods/course of action to achieve these goals, and **(iv)** Budgets to convert goals and strategies into annual operating plans.

LO 8.2

A budget is defined as a comprehensive and coordinated plan, expressed in financial terms, for the operations and resources of an enterprise for some specified period in the future. The essential elements of a budget are: **(i)** Plan, **(ii)** Financial terms, **(iii)** Operations and resources, **(iv)** Specific future period, **(v)** Comprehensive coverage, and **(vi)** Coordination. As a tool, a budget serves as a guide to conduct operations and a basis for evaluating actual results. The main objectives of budgeting are: **(i)** Explicit statement of expectations, **(ii)** Communication, **(iii)** Coordination, and **(iv)** Expectations as a framework for judging performance.

The overall budget is known as the master budget. It has the following components: **(i)** Sales budget, **(ii)** Production budget, **(iii)** Purchase budget, **(iv)** Direct labour budget, **(v)** Manufacturing expenses budget, **(vi)** Administrative and selling expenses budget, **(vii)** Budgeted income statement, **(viii)** Cash budget, and **(ix)** Budgeted balance sheet.

The cash budget is a device to help a firm to plan for and control the use of cash. It is a statement showing the estimated cash inflows and cash outflows over the planning period. The principal aim of the cash budget, as a tool to predict cash flows over a period of time, is to ascertain whether there is likely to be excess/shortage of cash at any time.

LO 8.3

The preparation of a cash budget involves several steps. The first element of a cash budget is the selection of the period of the budget, that is, the planning horizon. The planning horizon of a cash budget should be determined in the light of the circumstances and requirements of a particular case. The second element of the cash budget is the selection/identification of the factors that have a bearing on cash flows. The factors that generate cash are generally divided into two broad categories: **(i)** Operating and **(ii)** Financial. The first category includes cash flows from the operations of the firm, for example, sales, collections of receivables and so on. The second category of cash flows comprise collections and payment of financial nature, for example, borrowings, dividends paid, taxes paid and so on.

Budgets prepared at a single level of activity, with no prospect of modification in the light of changed circumstances, are referred to as fixed budgets.

The alternative to fixed budgets are flexible/variable/sliding budgets. The term 'flexible' is an apt description of the essential features of these budgets. A flexible budget estimates costs at several levels of activity. Its merit is that instead of one estimate, it contains several estimates/plans in different assumed circumstances. It is a useful tool in real world situations, that is, unpredictable environment. A flexible budget, in a sense, is a series of fixed budgets and any increase/decrease in the level/volume of activity must be reflected in it. The conceptual framework of flexible budgeting relates to: **(i)** Measure of volume and **(ii)** Cost behaviour with change in volume. Each expense in each department/segment is to be categorised into fixed, variable and mixed components. A budget may first be prepared at the expected level of activity, say, 100 per cent capacity. Additional columns may then be added for costs below and above, 90 per cent and 110 per cent capacity and so on.

Flexible budgets, as a tool of planning and control, are superior to fixed budgets. The major weaknesses of fixed budgets are their inability to: **(i)** Show the potential variability of various estimates used in the preparation of the budget, and **(ii)** Indicate the range within which costs may be expected to vary. They are, therefore, not useful in an uncertain and unpredictable environment. Flexible budgets present estimates at different levels of activity, and are more useful.

Flexible budgets suffer from one limitation in that they do not explicitly consider the relative probability of a particular volume/cost being achieved. This limitation can be overcome by using a modified flexible budget which will include columns for different levels of estimates: most likely, optimistic and pessimistic.

REFERENCES

1. J M Fremgen, *Accounting for Managerial Analysis,* (Richard D. Irwin, Homewood, Illinois, 1976), p 150.
2. *Ibid.,* p. 151.
3. R M Copeland and P E Dascher, *Managerial Accounting,* (John Wiley and Sons, New York, 1978), p. 35.
4. *Ibid.,* p. 34.
5. Fremgen, *op cit.,* p. 153.
6. It should, however, be noted that depreciation will be relevant to the computation of taxes.
7. Break-even analysis is discussed in Chapter 7 and inventory in Chapter 16.
8. Copeland and Dascher, *op cit.,* p. 86.

SOLVED PROBLEMS

P.8.1 Your company manufacturers two products, A and B. A forecast of the units to be sold in the first seven months of the year is given below: LO 8.3 LOD E

Month	*Product A*	*Product B*
January	1,000	2,800
February	1,200	2,800
March	1,600	2,400
April	2,000	2,000
May	2,400	1,600
June	2,400	1,600
July	2,000	1,800

It is anticipated that (a) there will be no work-in-process at the end of any month, and (b) finished units equal to half the sale for the next month will be in stock at the end of each month (including the previous December).

Budgeted production and production costs for the whole year are as follows:

Particulars	*Product A*	*Product B*
Product (units)	22,000	24,000
Per unit direct material	₹12.50	₹19.00
Per unit direct labour	4.50	7.00
Total factory overhead (apportioned)	66,000	96,000

Prepare for the six months period ending June 30 (i) (a) production budget for each month, and (ii) a summarised production cost budget.

Solution

(i) Production budget of products A and B (units) for six months (January to June)

Month	*Sales*		*Planned inventory*				*Budget production*	
			closing		*opening*		*(Col. 2 + 4 – 6)*	*(Col. 3 + 5 – 7)*
	A	*B*	*A*	*B*	*A*	*B*	*A*	*B*
1	*2*	*3*	*4*	*5*	*6*	*7*	*8*	*9*
January	1,000	2,800	600	1,400	500	1,400	1,100	2,800
February	1,200	2,800	800	1,200	600	1,400	1,400	2,600
March	1,600	2,400	1,000	1,000	800	1,200	1,800	2,200
April	2,000	2,000	1,200	800	1,000	1,000	2,200	1,800
May	2,400	1,600	1,200	800	1,200	800	2,400	1,600
June	2,400	1,600	1,000	900	1,200	800	2,200	1,700

(ii) Cost of production budget for six months from January to June of products A and B

Particulars	Product A: Cost per unit	Product A: Number of units produced	Product A: Total cost	Product B: Cost per unit	Product B: Number of units produced	Product B: Total	Total cost (A + B)
Variable costs:							
Direct material	₹12.50	11,100	₹1,38,750	₹19	12,700	₹2,41,300	₹3,80,050
Direct labour	4.50	11,100	49,950	7	12,700	88,900	1,38,850
Fixed costs:							
Factory overheads apportioned at the rate of ₹3 (A) and ₹4 (B)	3.00	11,100	33,300	4	12,700	50,800	84,100
	20.00	11,100	2,22,000	30	12,700	3,81,000	6,03,000

P.8.2 The following data relate to the working of a factory at Wardha for the current year: LO 8.3 LOD M

Capacity worked, 50 per cent		
Fixed costs:		
Salaries	₹84,000	
Rent and rates	56,000	
Depreciation	70,000	
Other administrative expenses	80,000	₹2,90,000
Variable costs:		
Materials	2,40,000	
Labour	2,56,000	
Other expenses	38,000	5,34,000

Possible sales at various levels of working are:

Capacity (per cent)	Sales
60	₹9,50,000
75	11,50,000
90	13,75,000
100	15,25,000

Prepare a flexible budget and show the forecast of profit at 60, 75, 90, and 100 per cent capacity operations.

Solution

Flexible budget

Percentage of capacity worked	*60*	*75*	*90*	*100*
Sales revenue	₹9,50,000	₹11,50,000	₹13,75,000	₹15,25,000
Less: Costs:				
Variable costs:				
Materials	2,88,000	3,60,000	4,32,000	4,80,000
Labour	3,07,200	3,84,000	4,60,800	5,12,000
Other expenses	45,600	57,000	68,400	76,000
(A) Total variable cost	6,40,800	8,01,000	9,61,200	10,68,000
Fixed costs:				
Salaries	84,000	84,000	84,000	84,000
Rent and rates	56,000	56,000	56,000	56,000
Depreciation	70,000	70,000	70,000	70,000
Other administrative expenses	80,000	80,000	80,000	80,000
(B) Total fixed cost	2,90,000	2,90,000	2,90,000	2,90,000
Total cost (**A** + **B**)	9,30,800	10,91,000	12,51,200	13,58,000
Forecast profits	19,200	59,000	1,23,800	1,67,000

P.8.3 The operating results of a manufacturing company for the current years are summarised below: LO 8.3 LOD D

(₹ *in lakh*)

Sales (40,000 units)	₹48.00
Less: Trade discount	2.40
Net sales	45.60
Cost of sales	
Direct material	14.40
Direct labour	12.60
Factory overheads	6.30
Administration expenses	3.60
Selling and distribution expenses	4.50

The following changes are anticipated during the next year:

(a) Units to be sold to increase by 25 per cent
(b) Material price to increase by 15 per cent
(c) Direct wages to increase by 12 per cent
(d) Overheads—Factory overheads will be limited to ₹6.56 lakh; administration and selling and distribution expenses are estimated to increase by 8 per cent and 14 per cent respectively
(e) Inventory—No change in opening and closing inventories in quantity. The change in value may be ignored.
(f) Trade discount—No change in the rate
(g) Profit target for the year—₹6 lakh.

Calculate the unit selling price and present the budgeted operating results for the next year.

Solution

Budgeted operating income statement of a manufacturing company (₹ in lakh)

Particulars		*Amount*
Sales (50,000 units)		60.00
Less: Trade discount (5 per cent)		3.00
Net sales	57.00	
Less: Variable costs		
Direct material @ ₹41.40 per unit (₹36 + 15%)	20.70	
Direct labour @ ₹35.28 per unit (₹31.50 + 12%)	17.64	38.34
	18.66	
Contribution		
Less: Fixed overheads		
Factory	6.560	
Administration (₹3.60 lakh + 8%)	3.888	
Selling and distribution (₹4.50 lakh + 14%)	5.130	15.578
Net income (indicated)		3.082
Net income (desired)		6.000
Additional income needed		2.918
Contribution required (₹18.66 lakh + ₹2.918 lakh)		21.578
Add: Variable costs		38.340
Net sales		59.918
Add: Trade discount		3.154
Gross sales(50,000 units)[(₹59.918/95) × 100]		63.072
Sales price per unit		126.144

Scan the QR Code given at the end of chapter to access comprehensive cases.

REVIEW QUESTIONS

LOD: Easy

RQ.8.1 Fill in the following blanks: [LO 8.1,2,3]

(i) Overall budget is also known as __________.

(ii) Budgets prepared at the single level of activity are referred to as __________.

(iii) __________ estimates costs at several levels of activity.

(iv) For most of the business firms, __________ is key budget.

(v) Budgets are an important tool of __________.

(vi) Minimum desired cash balance concept is useful in the preparation of __________ budget.

(vii) Cash budget is a tool of __________ financial planning.

(viii) Factors generating cash are categorized into two broad categories, namely, __________.

(ix) The primary objective of cash budget is to ascertain whether there is likely to be __________ of cash at any time.

(x) Sales and production budgets are __________ budgets.

[Answers: (i) master budget, (ii) fixed budgets, (iii) flexible budget, (iv) sales budget, (v) profit planning, (vi) cash budget, (vii) short-term, (viii) operating and financial, (ix) excess/shortage, (x) operating.]

RQ.8.2 Are you in agreement with the view that budgeting should better be called 'profit planning and control'? [LO 8.1,2]

RQ.8.3 In what respects does the production budget contribute to managerial (I) planning, (ii) coordination, and (iii) control. [LO 8.2,3]

RQ.8.4 Write a note on the advantages and limitations of budgeting. [LO 8.2]

RQ.8.5 Define budgetary control and discuss the objectives of introducing a budgetary control system in a business organisation. [LO 8.1,2]

RQ.8.6 What do you understand by the terms budget and budgetary control? What are the advantages of budgetary control? [LO 8.2]

LOD: Medium

RQ.8.7 'If sales forecast is subject to error, then, there is no purpose of budgeting.' Do you agree? Also explain how a flexible budget can be used by management to help control costs. [LO 8.3]

RQ.8.8 Why do responsible people in an organisation tend to accept budgetary control in theory but resist in practice? Explain. [LO 8.1,2]

RQ.8.9 A manufacturing company operating a system of budgetary control finds that their production capacity during the year varies between 75 per cent and 90 per cent as against the budgeted capacity of 80 per cent for the year. It has been suggested that a system of flexible budgets should be introduced to effectively control costs. Outline the steps you would take to implement this suggestion keeping in mind that the management would still require periodic comparison with their overall budget during the year. [LO 8.3]

RQ.8.10 Readymade Textiles Ltd. makes and sells baby suits. It has brisk sales in the October-December period as shown by the following sales budget (in units): [LO 8.3]

July	5,000	October	8,000
August	5,000	November	10,000
September	5,500	December	12,500

The firm's normal inventory policy has been to have a two months' supply of finished product on hand. The production manager has criticised the policy because it requires wide swings in production, which adds to costs. He estimates that unit-variable manufacturing cost is ₹2 higher than normal for each unit produced in excess of 9,000 units per month. The finance manager also supports the production manager on this. He estimates that it costs the firm ₹1 per unit in ending inventory, consisting of insurance, financing, and handling costs. He stresses that these costs are variable.

All the managers agree that the firm should have 22,500 units on hand by the end of October. The production manager wants to spread the required production equally over the four months.

(i) Prepare a production budget for July-October following the firm's current policy. Inventory on July 1 is 10,000 units.

(ii) Prepare a production budget using the production manager's preference.

(iii) Determine which budget gives lower costs.

RQ.8.11 Lookahead Ltd. produces and sells a single product. Sales budget for the current calendar year by quarter is as under: [LO 8.3]

Quarter	*Units to be sold*
I	12,000
II	15,000
III	16,500
IV	18,000

The year is expected to open with an inventory of 4,000 units of finished product and close with an inventory of 6,500 units. Production is customarily scheduled to provide for two-thirds of the current quarter's sales demand plus one-third of the following quarter's demand. The standard cost details for one unit of the product is as follows:

Direct material, 10 lbs @ 50 paise per lb

Direct labour, 1 hour 30 minutes @ ₹4 per hour

Variable overheads, 1 hour 30 minutes @ ₹1 per hour

Fixed overheads, 1 hour 30 minutes @ ₹2 per hour based on a budgeted production volume of 90,000 direct labour-hours for the year.

(i) Prepare a production budget, by quarters, showing the number of units to be produced and the total costs of direct material, direct labour, variable overheads and fixed overheads.

(ii) If the budgeted selling price per unit is ₹17, what would be the budgeted profit for the year as a whole?

(iii) In which quarter of the year is the company expected to break-even?

RQ.8.12 The demand for output of a certain company is very elastic and a modern plant recently installed is capable of greatly increased production. Output at present is 80,000 units per year, and 5 lakh units are estimated to be within the capacity of the new plant. The present selling price per unit is ₹15.

The need for flexible budgeting is recognised and six alternative levels of output, in addition to the present level, are contemplated. Six equal increments in annual output level, up to a maximum of 5,00,000 units, would involve corresponding reductions of ₹1 each in unit price to ₹9 per unit at the maximum output. [LO 8.3]

The present variable costs amount to ₹4,00,000. Fixed costs which at present amount to ₹2,00,000 are not expected to increase for any of the six alternative output levels contemplated. Semi-fixed cost are expected to vary from the present annual figure of ₹2,30,000 to ₹3,20,000, the upward steps being to ₹2,60,000 at 2,20,000 units, ₹2,80,000 at 3,60,000 units, and ₹3,20,000 at 5,00,000 units. The costs classified as variable at the six projected levels of output are calculated to be as follows:

₹7,50,000	₹11,00,000	₹15,00,000
17,50,000	20,50,000	25,00,000

Prepare the flexible budget and identify the volume which should be set for the budgeted output.

RQ.8.13 Prepare a flexible budget from the following data made available in respect of a half-yearly period and forecast the working results at 70, 85, and 100 per cents of capacity when the respective sales are ₹50 lakh, ₹60 lakh, and ₹85 lakh. While fixed expenses remain constant, semi-variable expenses are constant between 55 and 75 per cent of capacity, increasing by 10 per cent between 75 and 90 per cent of capacity and by 20 per cent between 90 and 100 per cent of capacity. The expenses at 60 per cent capacity are as follows: *(Amount in lakh of rupees)* [LO 8.3]

Semi-variable:	Maintenance and repairs	1.25
	Indirect labour	5.00
	Sales department expenses	1.50
	Sundry overheads	1.25
Variable:	Material	12.00
	Labour	13.00
	Other expenses	2.00
Fixed:	Wages and salaries	4.20
	Rent, rates and taxes	2.80
	Depreciation	3.50
	Sundry overheads	4.50
		51.00

LOD: Difficult

RQ.8.14 Budgeting is profit planning. Elaborate this statement. What accounting devices would you use where output varies? [LO 8.2]

ANSWERS

RQ.8.10 **(i)** Product budget: July 5,500 units, August 8,000 units, September 10,000 units, October 12,500 units.
(ii) Monthly production 9,000 units.
(iii) Current budget provides lower costs (of ₹2,500).

RQ.8.11 **(i)** Production budget : Quarter I (13,000 units), Quarter II (15,500 units), Quarter III (17,000), Quarter IV (18,500 units)
Total cost: Quarter I (₹2,07,500) Quarter II (₹2,38,750),
Quarter III (₹2,57,500) Quarter IV (₹2,76,250)
(ii) Budgeted profit ₹96,750.
(iii) Quarter III (BEP = 40,000 units)

RQ.8.12 4,30,000 units; Budgeted profit is ₹17,70,000.

RQ.8.13 Budgeted loss at ₹5.5 lakh (at 70%), loss ₹3.15 lakh (at 85%), profit ₹14.20 lakh (at 100%).

Scan the QR Code to access comprehensive solutions to all numerical review questions and additional material.

PART 3

LONG-TERM INVESTMENT DECISION

Chapter 9
CAPITAL BUDGETING I: PRINCIPLES AND TECHNIQUES

Chapter 10
CAPITAL BUDGETING II: ADDITIONAL ASPECTS

Chapter 11
CONCEPT AND MEASUREMENT OF COST OF CAPITAL

Chapter 12
ANALYSIS OF RISK AND UNCERTAINTY

It has been argued in Chapter 1 that financial management focuses not only on the procurement of funds but also on their efficient use with the objective of maximising the owner's wealth. The allocation of funds is, therefore, an important function of financial management. The allocation of funds involves the commitment of funds to assets and activities. It is also referred to as the investment decision, that is, making a choice regarding the assets in which funds will be invested. These assets fall into two broad categories: (i) short-term or current assets, and (ii) long-term or fixed assets. Accordingly, there are two types of investment decisions. The first is the short-term investment decision. It is also known as management of current assets or working capital management. The second type of decision is the long-term investment decision. This is widely known as capital budgeting or the capital expenditure decision. The various dimensions of working capital management are covered in detail in Part IV of this volume. This part is devoted to an in-depth and comprehensive discussion of capital budgeting/ capital expenditure management decisions. Chapter 9 is concerned with the general principles of capital budgeting and evaluation techniques. Additional aspects of capital budgeting, namely, comparison of NPV and IRR, projects with unequal lives, capital rationing and inflation are described in Chapter 10. Cost of capital and the analysis of risk and uncertainty are examined subsequently in Chapters 11 and 12.

CHAPTER 9

Capital Budgeting I: Principles and Techniques

LEARNING OBJECTIVES

LO 9.1	Discuss the nature of capital budgeting
LO 9.2	Explain the relevant data requirement for capital budgeting decisions
LO 9.3	Describe, evaluate and interpret the traditional and time-adjusted capital budgeting evaluation techniques
LO 9.4	Summarise capital budget practices by Corporates in India

INTRODUCTION

This Chapter is devoted to a discussion of the principles and techniques of capital budgeting. The nature of capital budgeting in terms of meaning, importance, difficulties, rationale and types is discussed first. The identification of relevant data for capital budgeting decisions is explained subsequently. The chapter also examines the evaluation techniques. It also outlines the capital budgeting practices in India. The main points are summarised by way of recapitulation.

LO 9.1 NATURE OF CAPITAL BUDGETING

Meaning

Capital budgeting is the process of evaluating and selecting long-term investments that are consistent with the goal of shareholders (owners) wealth maximisation.

Capital expenditure is an outlay of funds that is expected to produce benefits over a period of time exceeding one year.

Capital budgeting decisions pertain to fixed/long-term assets which by definition refer to assets which are in operation, and yield a return, over a period of time, usually, exceeding one year. They, therefore, involve a current outlay or series of outlays of cash resources in return for an anticipated flow of future benefits.[1] In other words, the system of capital budgeting is employed to evaluate expenditure decisions which involve current outlays but are likely to produce benefits over a period of time longer than one year. These benefits may be either in the form of increased revenues or reduced costs. **Capital expenditure** management, therefore, includes addition, disposition, modification and replacement of fixed assets. From the preceding discussion may be deduced the following basic features of capital budgeting[2]: **(i)** potentially large anticipated benefits; **(ii)** a relatively high degree of risk; and **(iii)** a relatively long time period between the initial outlay and the anticipated returns. The term capital budgeting is used interchangeably with capital expenditure decision, capital expenditure management, long-term investment decision, management of fixed assets and so on.

Importance

Capital budgeting decisions are of paramount importance in financial decision making. In the first place, such decisions affect the profitability of a firm. They also have a bearing on the competitive position of the enterprise mainly because of the fact that they relate to fixed assets. The fixed assets represent, in a sense, the true earning assets of the firm. They enable the firm to generate finished goods that can ultimately be sold for profit. The current assets are not generally earning assets. Rather, they provide a buffer that allows the firms to make sales and extend credit. True, current assets are important to operations, but without fixed assets to generate finished products that can be converted into current assets, the firm would not be able to operate. Further, they are 'strategic' investment decisions as against 'tactical'—which involve a relatively small amount of funds. Therefore, such capital investment decisions may result in a major departure from what the company has been doing in the past. Acceptance of a strategic investment will involve a significant change in the company's expected profits and in the risks to which these profits will be subject. These changes are likely to lead stockholders and creditors to revise their evaluation of the company.[3] Thus, capital budgeting decisions determine the future destiny of the company. An opportune investment decision can yield spectacular returns. On the other hand, an ill-advised and incorrect decision can endanger the very survival even of the large firms. A few wrong decisions and the firm may be forced into bankruptcy.

Secondly, a capital expenditure decision has its effect over a long time span and inevitably affects the company's future cost structure. To illustrate, if a particular plant has been purchased by a company to start a new product, the company commits itself to a sizable amount of fixed costs, in terms of labour, supervisors' salary, insurance, rent of building, and so on. If the investment turns out to be unsuccessful in future or yields less profit than anticipated, the firm will have to bear the burden of fixed costs unless it writes off the investment completely. In short, future costs, break-even point, sales and profits will all be determined by the selection of assets.

Thirdly, capital investment decisions, once made, are not easily reversible without much financial loss to the firm because there may be no market for second-hand plant and equipment and their conversion to other uses may not be financially viable.

Finally, capital investment involves costs and the majority of the firms have scarce capital resources. This underlines the need for thoughtful, wise and correct investment decisions, as an incorrect decision would not only result in losses but also prevent the firm from earning profits from other investments which could not be undertaken for want of funds.

Difficulties

Capital expenditure decisions are of considerable significance as the future success and growth of the firm depends heavily on them. But, they are beset with a number of difficulties.

Firstly, the benefits from investments are received in some future period. The future is uncertain. Therefore, an element of risk is involved. For instance, a decision to acquire an asset that is going to last for 15 years requires a 15-year forecast. A failure to forecast correctly will lead to serious errors which can be corrected only at a considerable expense. Future revenue involves estimating the size of the market for a product and the expected share of the firm in that. These estimates depend on a variety of factors, including price, advertising and promotion, and sales effort and so on. Adding to the uncertainties are the possibilities of shifts in consumer preferences, the actions of competitors, technological developments and changes in the economic or political environment.

Secondly, costs incurred and benefits received from the capital budgeting decisions occur in different time periods. They are not logically comparable because of the time value of money.

Thirdly, it is not often possible to calculate in strict quantitative terms all the benefits or the costs relating to a particular investment decision.

Rationale

The rationale underlying the capital budgeting decision is efficiency. Thus, a firm must replace worn and obsolete plants and machinery, acquire fixed assets for current and new products and make strategic investment decisions. This will enable the firm to achieve its objective of maximising profits either by way of increased revenues or cost reductions. The quality of these decisions is improved by capital budgeting. Capital budgeting decision can be of two types: (i) those which expand revenues, and (ii) those which reduce costs.

Investment Decisions Affecting Revenues Such investment decisions are expected to bring in additional revenue, thereby raising the size of the firm's total revenue. They can be the result of either expansion of present operations or the development of new product lines. Both types of investment decisions involve acquisition of new fixed assets and are income-expansionary in nature in the case of manufacturing firms.

Investment Decisions Reducing Costs Such decisions, by reducing costs, add to the total earnings of the firm. A classic example of such investment decisions are the replacement proposals when an asset wears out or becomes outdated. The firm must decide whether to continue with the existing assets or replace them. The firm evaluates the benefits from the new machine in terms of lower operating cost and the outlay that would be needed to replace the machine. An expenditure on a new machine may be quite justifiable in the light of the total cost savings that result.

A fundamental difference between the above two categories of investment decision lies in the fact that cost-reduction investment decisions are subject to less uncertainty in comparison to the revenue-affecting investment decisions. This is so because the firm has a better 'feel' for potential cost savings as it can examine past production and cost data. However, it is difficult to precisely estimate the revenues and costs resulting from a new product line, particularly when the firm knows relatively little about the same.

> **Capital budgeting process** includes four distinct but interrelated steps used to evaluate and select long-term proposals: proposal generation, evaluation, selection and follow up.

Kinds

Capital budgeting process refers to the total process of generating, evaluating, selecting and following up on capital expenditure alternatives.[4] The firm allocates or budgets financial resources to new investment proposals. Basically, the firm may be confronted with three types of capital budgeting decisions: **(i)** the accept-reject decision; **(ii)** the mutually exclusive choice decision; and **(iii)** the capital rationing decision.

Accept reject decision is the evaluation of capital expenditure proposal to determine whether they meet the minimum acceptance criterion.

Accept-reject Decision This is a fundamental decision in capital budgeting. If the project is accepted, the firm would invest in it; if the proposal is rejected, the firm does not invest in it. In general, all those proposals which yield a rate of return greater than a certain required rate of return or cost of capital are accepted and the rest are rejecte d. By applying this criterion, all **independent projects** are accepted. Independent projects are projects that do not compete with one another in such a way that the acceptance of one precludes the possibility of acceptance of another. Under the accept-reject decision, all independent projects that satisfy the minimum investment criterion should be implemented.

Independent projects are projects whose cash flows are unrelated/ independent of one another; the acceptance of one does not eliminate the others from further consideration.

Mutually exclusive projects (decisions) are projects that compete with one another; the acceptance of one eliminates the others from further consideration.

Mutually Exclusive Project Decisions **Mutually exclusive projects** are those which compete with other projects in such a way that the acceptance of one will exclude the acceptance of the other projects. The alternatives are mutually exclusive and only one may be chosen. Suppose, a company is intending to buy a new folding machine. There are three competing brands, each with a different initial investment and operating costs. The three machines represent mutually exclusive alternatives, as only one of these can be selected. It may be noted here that the mutually exclusive project decisions are not independent of the accept-reject decisions. The project(s) should also be acceptable under the latter decision. In brief, in our example, if all the machines are rejected under the accept-reject decision, the firm should not buy a new machine. Mutually exclusive investment decisions acquire significance when more than one proposal is acceptable under the accept-reject decision. Then, some technique has to be used to determine the 'best' one. The acceptance of this 'best' alternative automatically eliminates the other alternatives.

Capital rationing is the financial situation in which a firm has only fixed amount to allocate among competing capital expenditures.

Unlimited funds is the financial situation in which a firm is able to accept all independent projects that provide an acceptable return.

Capital Rationing Decision In a situation where the firm has **unlimited funds**, all independent investment proposals yielding return greater than some predetermined level are accepted. However, this situation does not prevail in most of the business firms in actual practice. They have a fixed capital budget. A large number of investment proposals compete for these limited funds. The firm must, therefore, ration them. The firm allocates funds to projects in a manner that it maximises long-run returns. Thus, **capital rationing** refers to a situation in which a firm has more acceptable investments than it can finance. It is concerned with the selection of a group of investment proposals out of many investment proposals acceptable under the accept-reject decision. Capital rationing employs ranking of the acceptable investment projects. The projects can be ranked on the basis of a predetermined criterion such as the rate of return. The projects are ranked in the descending order of the rate of return. This aspect has been developed further in Chapter 10.

LO 9.2 DATA REQUIREMENT: IDENTIFYING RELEVANT CASH FLOWS

Cash Flows Vs Accounting Profit

Capital budgeting is concerned with investment decisions which yield return over a period of time in future. The foremost requirement for evaluation of any capital investment proposal is to estimate the future benefits accruing from the investment proposal. Theoretically, two alternative criteria are available to quantify the benefits: **(i)** accounting profit, and **(ii)** cash flows. The basic difference between them is primarily due to the inclusion of certain non-cash expenses in the profit and loss account, for instance, depreciation. Therefore, the accounting profit is to be adjusted for non-cash expenditures to determine the actual cash inflow. The cash flow approach of measuring future benefits of a project is superior to the accounting approach as cash flows are theoretically better measures of the net economic benefits of costs associated with a proposed project.

In the first place, while considering an investment proposal, a firm is interested in estimating its economic value. This economic value is determined by the economic outflows (costs) and inflows (benefits) related with the investment project. Only cash flows represent the cash transactions. The firm must pay for the purchase of an asset with cash. This cash outlay represents a foregone opportunity to use cash in some other productive alternatives. Consequently, the firm should measure the future net benefits in cash terms. On the other hand, under the accounting practices, the cost of the investment is allocated over its economic useful life in the nature of depreciation rather than at the time when costs are actually incurred. The accounting treatment clearly does not reflect the original need for cash at the time of inflows and outflows in later years. Only cash flows reflect the actual cash transactions associated with the project. Since investment analysis is concerned with finding out whether future economic inflows are sufficiently large to warrant the initial investment, only the cash flow method is appropriate for investment decision analysis.[5]

Secondly, the use of cash flows avoids accounting ambiguities. There are various ways to value inventory, allocate costs, calculate depreciation and amortise various other expenses. Obviously, different net incomes will be arrived at under different accounting procedures. But there is only one set of cash flows associated with the project. Clearly, the cash flow approach to project evaluation is better than the net income flow approach (accounting approach).

Thirdly, the cash flow approach takes cognisance of the time value of money whereas the accounting approach ignores it. Under the usual accounting practice, revenue is recognised as being generated when the product is sold, not when the cash is collected from the sale; revenue may remain a paper figure for months or years before payment of the invoice is received. Expenditure, too, is recognised as being made when incurred and not when the actual payment is made. Depreciation is deducted from the gross revenues to determine the before-tax earnings. Such a procedure ignores the increased flow of funds potentially available for other uses. In other words, accounting profits which are quite useful as performance measures often are less useful as decision criteria. Therefore, from the viewpoint of capital expenditure management, the cash flow approach can be said to be the basis of estimating future benefits from investment proposals. The data required for the purpose would be cash revenues and cash expenses. The difference between the cash flow approach and the accounting profit approach is depicted in Table 9.1.

TABLE 9.1 A Comparison of Cash Flow and Accounting Profit Approaches

Accounting Approach Towards 'Benefits'			*Cash Flow Approach Towards 'Benefits'*	
Revenues		₹1,000		₹1,000
Less: Expenses:				
Cash expenses	₹500		₹500	
Depreciation	300	800		
Earnings before tax		200		
Taxes (0.35)		70	70	570
Net earnings after taxes/Cash flow		130		430

Table 9.1 shows that the accounting profits amounting to ₹130 are less than the cash flow (₹430). This difference can be attributed to the depreciation charge of ₹300. The cash available with the firm is ₹430. This can be utilised for further investment. The accounting approach indicates that only ₹130 is available and hence gives only a partial picture of the tangible benefits available. Clearly, such an approach does not bring out the total benefits of the project available for reinvesting. Therefore, in place of earnings, the cash flow information is employed in evaluating capital expenditure alternatives.

Incremental Cash Flow

Relevant cash flow is the incremental after-tax cash outflow (investment) and resulting subsequent inflows associated with a proposed capital expenditure.

The second aspect of the data required for capital budgeting relates to the basis on which the **relevant cash outflows** and inflows associated with proposed capital expenditure are to be estimated. The widely prevalent practice is to adopt incremental analysis. According to incremental analysis, only differences due to the decision need be considered. Other factors may be important but not to the decision at hand.[6] For purposes of estimating cash flows in the analysis of investments, **incremental cash flows**, that is, those cash flows (and only those cash flows) which are directly attributable to the investment project are taken into account. It is for this reason that fixed overhead costs, which remain the same whether the proposal is accepted or rejected, are not considered. However, if there is an increase in them due to the new proposal, they must be considered.

Incremental cash flows are the additional cash flows (outflows as well as inflows) expected to result from a proposed capital expenditure.

Project may be referred to as a kind of **"mini firm"** with its own future revenues and costs, its own assets, it own earnings and its own cash flows[7].

Effect of Taxes

Finally, the incremental cash flows are adjusted for tax liability. In other words, taxes paid are deducted from the cash flows to estimate the benefits arising out of the investment decision.

To conclude the above discussion relating to the data required for the capital budgeting decision, the expenses/costs to be considered are 'incremental after-tax cash flows'. Table 9.2 summarises the relevant and irrelevant information in relation to asset selection decisions.

TABLE 9.2 Relevant and Irrelevant Outflows

Relevant Cash Outflows	*Irrelevant Cash Outflows*
1. Variable labour expenses	1. Fixed overhead expense (existing)
2. Variable material expenses	2. **Sunk costs**
3. Additional fixed overhead expenses	
4. Cost of the investment	
5. Marginal taxes	

Sunk costs are cash outflows that have already been made (i.e., past outlays) and therefore have no effect on the cash flows relevant to a current decision.

Cash Flow Pattern

Cash flow pattern associated with capital investment projects can be classified as conventional or non-conventional.

Conventional cash flow pattern is an initial outflow followed by only a series of inflows.

Conventional Cash Flows They consist of an initial cash outlay followed by a series of cash inflows. Most of the capital expenditure decisions display this pattern of cash flow. To illustrate, the firm may spend ₹1,500 in time period zero and as a result may expect to receive a ₹300 cash inflow at the end of each year for the next 8 years. The conventional cash flow pattern is diagrammed in Fig. 9.1.

Non-Conventional Cash Flows They refer to the cash flow pattern in which an initial cash outlay is not followed by a series of inflows. Alternating inflows and outflows and an inflow followed by outflows are examples of non-conventional cash flow patterns. A classic example of such cash flow patterns is that of the purchase of an asset that generates cash inflows for a period of years, is overhauled, and again generates a stream of cash inflows for a number of years. To illustrate, a machine purchased for ₹1,000 generates cash inflows of ₹250 each for five years. In the sixth year, an outlay of ₹400 is required to overhaul the machine, after which it generates cash inflows of ₹250 for four years. Such a non-conventional pattern of cash flows is shown in Fig. 9.2.

Non-conventional cash flow pattern is a pattern in which an initial outflow is not followed by only a series of inflows.

		₹	*300*	*300*	*300*	*300*	*300*	*300*	*300*	*300*
Cash inflows	0		1	2	3	4	5	6	7	8
Cash outflows			*	*	*	*	*	*	*	*
	₹1,500				Years					

FIGURE 9.1 Conventional Cash Flow Pattern

Cash Flow Estimates

For capital budgeting cash flows have to be estimated. There are certain ingredients of cash flow streams.

	₹	250	250	250	250	250	250	250	250	250
Cash inflows	0	1	2	3	4	5	6	7	8	9
Cash outflows	0						6			
	₹1,000			Years			₹400			

FIGURE 9.2 Non-conventional Cash Flow Pattern

Tax Effect It has been already observed that cash flows to be considered for purposes of capital budgeting are net of taxes. Special consideration needs to be given to tax effects on cash flows if the firm is incurring losses and, therefore, paying no taxes. The tax laws permit carrying losses forward to be set off against future income. In such cases, therefore, the benefits of tax savings would accrue in future years.

Effect on Other Projects Cash flow effects of the project under consideration, if it is not economically independent, on other existing projects of the firm must be taken into consideration. For instance, if a company is considering the production of a new product which competes with the existing products in the product line, it is likely that as a result of the new proposal, the cash flows related to the old product will be affected. Assume that there is a decline of ₹5,000 in the actual flow from the existing product. This should be taken into consideration while estimating the cash streams from the new proposal. In operational terms, the cash flow from the new product should be reduced by ₹5,000. This is in conformity with the general rule of the incremental cash flows which involves identifying changes in cash flows as a result of undertaking the project being evaluated. Clearly, the cash flow effects of the project should not be evaluated in isolation, if it affects other project(s) in any way.

Effect of Indirect Expenses Another factor which merits special consideration in estimating cash flows is the effect of overheads. The indirect expenses/overheads are allocated to the different products on the basis of wages paid, materials used, floor space occupied or some other similar common factor. The question that arises is: should such allocation of overheads be taken into account in the cash flows? The answer hinges upon whether the amount of overheads will change as a result of the investment decision. If yes, it should be taken into account. If, however, overheads will not change as a result of the investment decision, they are not relevant.

A company allocates overheads on the basis of the floor space used. Assume it intends to replace an old machine by a new one. Further assume that the new machine would occupy less space so that there would be a reduction in the overhead charged to it. Since there is no effect on cash flows, a change in the overhead is not relevant to the cash flow streams of the machine being acquired. But if the surplus space is used for an alternative use, and if any cash flow is generated, it will be relevant to the calculations. Thus, the deciding factor is whether there is any alternative use. The alternative use rule is a corollary of the incremental cash flow rule.[8]

Effect of Depreciation **Depreciation**, although a non-cash item of cost, is deductible expenditure in determining taxable income. Depreciation provisions are prescribed by the Companies Act for accounting purposes and by the Income Tax Act for taxation purposes.

The purpose of the provisions of depreciation contained in the Companies Act is the computation of managerial remuneration, dividend payment and disclosure in financial statements. Since companies in India are regulated by the Companies Act, they should provide depreciation in the books of accounts in accordance with Schedule XIV of the Act which prescribes the rate of depreciation for various types of depreciable assets on written down value (WDV) basis as well as straight line basis. It also permits companies to charge depreciation on any other basis provided it has the effect of writing off 95 per cent of the original cost of the asset on the expiry of the specified period and has the approval of the government. In actual practice, however, companies follow the provisions of the Income Tax Act with the basic objectives of its tax deductibility.

Depreciation is a non-cash expense that affects the taxes paid in cash.

The provisions of Income Tax Act relating to depreciation are contained in Section 32. The section envisages three important conditions for following depreciation, namely, **(i)** the asset is owned by the assessee, **(ii)** the asset is used by the assessee for the purpose of business and **(iii)** the asset is in the form of buildings, furniture, machinery and plants including ships, vehicles, books, scientific apparatus, surgical equipments and so on.

The amount of annual depreciation on an asset is determined by **(a)** the actual cost of the asset and **(b)** its classification in the relevant block of assets. The actual cost means the cost of acquisition of the asset and the expenses incidental thereto which are necessary to put the asset in a usable state, for instance, freight and carriage inwards, installation charges and expenses incurred to facilitate the use of the asset like expenses on the training of the operator or on essential construction work.

Block of assets are assets which fall in the same class and in respect of which the same depreciation rate is applicable irrespective of their nature.

Depreciation is charged, with a view to simplify computation, not on an individual asset but on a block of assets. A **block of assets** defined as a group of assets falling within a class of assets, being building, machinery, plant or furniture in respect of which the same rate of depreciation is prescribed. Thus, assets which fall within the same class of assets and in respect of which the same percentage/rate of depreciation has been prescribed irrespective of their nature form one block of assets. For example, all assets under the category of plant and machinery which qualify for depreciation at 15 per cent will form one block and depreciation is computed with reference to the actual cost of the block. Similarly, assets depreciable at 40 per cent will constitute another block; a third block consists of assets depreciable at 50 per cent, and the fourth block comprises assets subject to a 100 per cent write-off.

Depreciation is computed at block-wise rates on the basis of written down value (WDV) method only. Presently, the block-wise rates for plant and machinery are at 15 per cent, 20 per cent, 30 per cent, 40 per cent, 50 per cent, 60 per cent, 80 per cent and 100 per cent. The depreciation allowance on office buildings and furniture and fittings is 10 per cent. If an asset acquired during a year has been used for a period of less than 180 days during the year, depreciation on such assets is allowed only at 50 per cent of the computed depreciation according to the relevant rate.

Apart from the simplification of the computation of the amount of depreciation, a significant implication of categorising assets into blocks is that if an asset falling in a block is sold out, there is no capital gain or terminal depreciation or balancing charge. The sale proceeds of the asset are reduced from the WDV of the block. Capital gain/loss can arise in these situations:

(i) When the sale proceeds exceeds the WDV of the whole block;
(ii) When the entire block is sold out; and
(iii) In case of 100 per cent depreciable assets.

The terminal loss is not allowed in the relevant assessment year but is spread over a number of years to be allowed by way of depreciation.

In case of insufficiency/absence of profit, unabsorbed depreciation can be set off against income under any head against business income as in the case of unabsorbed loss.

The mechanics of computation of depreciation is illustrated in Example 9.1.

Example 9.1

Assume the following facts relating to Avon Ltd (AL):

Block of Assets	*Depreciation Rate (percentage)*	*WDV as on 1.4.20X7 (₹ lakh)*	*Addition During 20X7–8 (₹ lakh)*
A	25	500	250
B	40	300	150

Assets sold during 20X7–8 amounted to ₹35 lakh (Block A) and ₹50 lakh (Block B). It is expected that fresh investments in assets during 20X8–9 will be: Block A (₹160 lakh) and Block B (₹80 lakh). It is also projected by the AL that disinvestment proceeds from the assets will amount to ₹45 lakh in case of Block A and ₹25 lakh in case of Block B. Assume that about 50 per cent of additional investment during 20X8–9 will be made after September 20X8.

Compute the relevant depreciation charge for 20X7–8 and the projected depreciation charge for 20X8–9.

Solution

The relevant depreciation charge for 20X7–8 and the projected depreciation charge for 20X8–9 is calculated in Tables 9.3 and 9.4 respectively.

TABLE 9.3 Computation of Depreciation Charge During 20X7–8

(₹ *lakh*)

Particulars	*Blocks*	
	A	*B*
1. WDV as on 1.4.20 X7	500	300
2. *Add:* Cost of assets acquired during 20 X7 – 8	250	150
	750	450
3. *Less:* Sales during 20 X7 – 8	35	50
4. WDV (for depreciation)	715	400
5. Depreciation allowance	179	160
6. WDV as on 1.4. 20 X8	536	240

TABLE 9.4 Computation of Depreciation Charge During 20X8–9

(₹ lakh)

Particulars	Blocks A	Blocks B
1. WDV as on 1.4.20X8	536	240
2. *Add:* Cost of assets acquired during 20X8–9	160	80
	696	320
3. *Less:* Expected proceeds of sales during 20X8–9	45	25
4. WDV (for depreciation)	651	295
5. Depreciation allowance@	153	110
6. WDV as on 1.4. 20X9	498	185

	A	B
@Normal depreciation allowance	163	118
Less: Depreciation allowance inadmissible in respect of assets acquired after 30.9.20X8	10	8
	(80 × 0.25 × 0.5)	(40 × 0.4 × 0.5)
	153	110

Note: If the entire block of assets is sold during a year for an amount exceeding (1 + 2) or the sale proceeds of the block sold is higher than (1 + 2), the difference represents short-term capital gains subject to tax. Where the sale proceeds are lower than (1 + 2), the difference is short-term capital loss and the AL is entitled to tax shield.

In case block consists of a single asset (e.g. plant and machinery), **no depreciation is to be charged in the terminal year in which it is sold**. The difference between the written down value (WDV) of the machine at the beginning of the year and its sale proceeds represents short-term capital gain (when sale proceeds exceeds written down value/book vale of the machine) and short-term capital loss (in case the book value exceeds sale proceeds/salvage value). Such short-term capital gains (STCG) and losses (STCL) have been accorded **special tax treatment**. The STCL can be set off only against STCG or long-term capital gains. In case of inadequate/no profits, the STCL can be carried forward upto eight assessment years.

To illustrate the implication of the tax provisions for capital budgeting, let us assume, a company buys a new machine for ₹10 lakh (forming a separate block). The machine is subject to 20 per cent depreciation on WDV basis. It is expected to have economic useful life of 5 years at the end of which its expected salvage value is ₹1 lakh.

The depreciation in the first four years would be ₹2 lakh, ₹1.6 lakh, ₹1.28 lakh and ₹1.024 lakh respectively. The accumulated depreciation would be ₹5.90 lakh. As a result, the WDV/book value of the machine at the beginning of year-5 would be ₹4.10 lakh. With no depreciation charged in year-5 and sale proceeds of ₹1 lakh, there would be short-term capital loss of ₹3.10 lakh. This loss, in turn, would yield tax shield. Assuming 30 per cent tax rate and adequate STCG in year 5, the tax shield is (₹3.10 lakh × 0.30) ₹92,880. This amount would be reckoned as **cash inflow in year 5**.

The tax shield would be ₹92,880 in financial accounting also. It would consist of two components: (i) depreciation in year 5, ₹81,920 (0.20 × ₹4,09,600) and (ii) loss on sale of machine ₹2,27,680 (₹4,09,600 – ₹1,00,000 – ₹81,920). The tax advantage on depreciation would be ₹24,576 (0.30 × ₹81,920) and on loss ₹68,304 (0.30 × ₹2,27,680). The total (₹24,576 + ₹68,304) is ₹92,880. Thus, the firm does not suffer any loss by not charging depreciation in the terminal year (as per income-tax requirement).

In case block consists of several assets (plants/machinery/equipments), depreciation is charged in the terminal year in which the machine is sold on its **closing balance** (written down value at the beginning of year of sales – sale value). The terminal loss is allowed to be carried forward to be charged as depreciation in subsequent years (though the asset does not exist). This tax provision implies that the terminal loss would provide tax shield in the subsequent years.

To illustrate, continuing with the present example, assuming the machine purchased for ₹10 lakh is one of several machines, depreciation charged in year 5 would be on ₹3,09,600 (₹4,09,600 – ₹1,00,000, sale value) at 20 per cent, that is, ₹61,920. The terminal loss due to sale of machine is (₹3,09,600 – ₹61,920) ₹2,47,680. This loss in terms of unabsorbed depreciation would provide tax advantage in future years.

In practice, as the block is likely to consist of several machines for manufacturing firms, the tax provision puts business firms at disadvantage as the tax advantage on terminal loss is available in a number of years and not in single year.

Working Capital Effect Working capital constitutes another important ingredient of the cash flow stream which is directly related to an investment proposal. The term **working capital** is used here in net sense, that is, current assets minus current liabilities (**net working capital**). If an investment is expected to increase sales, it is likely that there will be an increase in current assets in the form of accounts receivable, inventory and cash. But part of this increase in current assets will be offset by an increase in current liabilities in the form of increased accounts and notes payable. Obviously, the sum equivalent to the difference between these additional current assets and current liabilities will be needed to carry out the investment proposal. Sometimes, it may constitute a significant part of the total investment in a project. The increased working capital forms part of the initial cash outlay. The additional net working capital will, however, be returned to the firm at the end of the project's life. Therefore, the recovery of working capital becomes part of the cash inflow stream in the terminal year. The initial investment in, and the subsequent recovery of, working capital do not balance out each other due to the time value of money.

Net working capital change is the difference between change in current assets and change in current liabilities.

The increase in the working capital may not only be in the zero time period, that is, at the time of initial investment. There can be continuous increase in the working capital as sales increase in later years. This increase in working capital should be considered as cash outflow of the year in which additional working capital is required.

Suppose, there is a project that requires an initial investment of ₹20,000 and has a useful life of 5 years. The requirements of working capital are detailed in Table 9.5.

TABLE 9.5 Working Capital Requirements

Particulars	*Year*					
	0	*1*	*2*	*3*	*4*	*5*
(a) Initial investment	₹20,000					
Sales		₹5,000	₹10,000	₹20,000	₹15,000	₹0
Expenses		1,000	2,000	5,000	4,000	500
(b) Changes in inventory (decrease)		1,000	2,000	6,000	(4,000)	(5,000)
(c) Changes in receivables		1,000	2,000	4,000	(2,000)	(5,000)
(d) Changes in payables		1,500	2,000	5,000	(3,500)	(5,500)
(e) Change in net working capital (*b* + *c* – *d*)		500	2,000	5,000	(2,500)	(4,500)

The changes in the net working capital are given in the last row of Table 9.5. The net working capital has increased in years 1, 2 and 3 representing cash outflows, while it has decreased in years 4 and 5 showing cash inflows as working capital is recovered.

Almost all revenue-expansion capital investment proposals require additional working capital. Likewise, almost all cost-reduction capital investment projects release the existing amount of working capital. Such projects enhance the firm's efficiency in such a way that the amount of inventory on hand or accounts receivable can be reduced. Improved inventory control systems or improved billing and collection systems are some classic examples. From the point of view of evaluating an investment project, the amount of working capital so released should be seen as a cash inflow in the zero time period (when the investment proposal is being considered), reducing the net cash investment required for the project. In the terminating year of the project, it should be treated as a cash outflow and adjusted against the cash inflow of that year.

Conventionally, the amount invested in net working capital at the time of starting the project as well as in subsequent years is assumed to have been recovered fully by the terminal year. In reality, the firm would most probably recover less than 100 per cent primarily because of bad debts and inventory loss. Therefore, the working capital recovered would be less than 100 per cent (say, 95 per cent). Accordingly, the cash inflow due to recovery of working capital in terminal year should be taken at less than 100 per cent amount.[9] Moreover, **for convenience**, it is assumed that net working capital is recovered instantaneously on termination of the project. In practice, however, it may take several months of the following year to recover it.[10]

Finally, tax considerations would not be involved when the net working capital recovered is less than 100 per cent[11] because bad debt loss due to some uncollectible debtors and loss due to obsolete inventory are already reckoned in operating costs.

Determination of Relevant Cashflows

The data requirement for capital budgeting are cash flows, that is, outflows and inflows. Their computation depends on the nature of the proposal. Capital projects can be categorised into: (i) single proposal, (ii) replacement situations and (iii) mutually exclusive.

Single Proposal The cash outflows, comprising cash outlays required to carry out the proposed capital expenditure are depicted in Format 9.1, while the computation of the cash inflows after taxes (CFAT) is shown in Format 9.2. The computation is illustrated in Example 9.2 and Example 9.3.

FORMAT 9.1 Cash Outflows of New Project [Beginning of the Period at Zero Time (t = 0)]

(1) Cost of new project

(2) + Installation cost of plant and equipments

(3) ± Working capital requirements

FORMAT 9.2 Determination of Cash Inflows: Single Investment Proposal (t = 1 – N)

Particulars	*Years*					
	1	*2*	*3*	*4*	....	*N*
Cash sales revenues						
Less: Cash operating cost						
Cash inflows before taxes (CFBT)						
Less: Depreciation						
Taxable income						
Less: Tax						
Earning after taxes						
Plus: Depreciation						
Cash inflows after tax (CFAT)						
Plus: Salvage value (in *n*th year)						
Plus: Recovery of working capital (in *n*th year)						

***Example* 9.2**

An iron ore company is considering investing in a new processing facility. The company extracts ore from an open pit mine. During a year, 1,00,000 tonnes of ore is extracted. If the output from the extraction process is sold immediately upon removal of dirt, rocks and other impurities, a price of ₹1,000 per ton of ore can be obtained. The company has estimated that its extraction costs amount to 70 per cent of the net realisable value of the ore.

As an alternative to selling all the ore at ₹1,000 per tonne, it is possible to process further 25 per cent of the output. The additional cash cost of further processing would be ₹100 per ton. The proposed ore would yield 80 per cent final output, and can be sold at ₹1,600 per ton.

For additional processing, the company would have to instal equipment costing ₹100 lakh. The equipment is subject to 20 per cent depreciation per annum on reducing balance (WDV) basis/method. It is expected to have useful life of 5 years. Additional working capital requirement is estimated at ₹10 lakh. The company's cut-off rate for such investments is 15 per cent. Corporate tax rate is 35 per cent.

Assuming there is no other plant and machinery subject to 20 per cent depreciation, should the company instal the equipment if (a) the expected salvage is ₹10 lakh, (b) there would be no salvage value at the end of year 5 and (c) for tax purposes, the firm would have sufficient short-term capital gains in year 5.

Solution

Financial Evaluation Whether to Instal Equipment for Further Processing of Iron Ore

(A) Cash Outflows

Cost of equipment	₹ 1,00,00,000
Plus: Additional working capital	10,00,000
	1,10,00,000

(B) Cash Inflows (CFAT)

Particulars	*Year*				
	1	*2*	*3*	*4*	*5*
Revenue from processing [(₹1,600 × 20,000) – ₹1,000 × 25,000)]	₹70,00,000	₹70,00,000	₹70,00,000	₹70,00,000	₹70,00,000

(*Contd*)

(*Contd*)

Less: Processing costs: Cash costs (₹100 × 25,000 tons)	25,00,000	25,00,000	25,00,000	25,00,000	25,00,000
Depreciation (*working note* 1)	20,00,000	16,00,000	12,80,000	10,24,000	—
Earnings before taxes	25,00,000	29,00,000	32,20,000	34,76,000	45,00,000
Less: Taxes (0.35)	8,75,000	10,15,000	11,27,000	12,16,600	15,75,000
Earnings after taxes (EAT)	16,25,000	18,85,000	20,93,000	22,59,400	29,25,000
Add: Depreciation	20,00,000	16,00,000	12,80,000	10,24,000	
CFAT	36,25,000	34,85,000	33,73,000	32,83,400	29,25,000

Working Notes

1 Depreciation Schedule

Year	*Depreciation base of equipment*	*Depreciation @ 20% on WDV*
1	₹ 1,00,00,000	₹ 20,00,000
2	80,00,000	16,00,000
3	64,00,000	12,80,000
4	51,20,000	10,24,000
5	40,96,000	Nil@

@As the block consists of a single asset, no depreciation is to be charged in the terminal year of the project.

(C) (a) Determination of NPV (Salvage Value = ₹10 lakh)

Year	*CFAT*	*PV factor (0.15)*	*Total PV*
1	₹ 36,25,000	0.870	₹ 31,53,750
2	34,85,000	0.756	26,34,660
3	33,73,000	0.658	22,19,434
4	32,83,400	0.572	18,78,105
5	29,25,000	0.497	14,53,725
Salvage value	10,00,000	0.497	4,97,000
Tax benefit on short-term capital loss	10,83,600 b	0.497	5,38,549
Recovery of working capital	10,00,000	0.497	4,97,000
Gross present value			1,28,72,223
Less: Cash outflows			1,10,00,000
Net present value (NPV)			18,72,223

(b) 0.35 × (₹40,96,000 – ₹10,00,000) = ₹10,83,600.

Recommendation The company is advised to instal the equipment as it promises a positive NPV.

(D) Determination of NPV (Salvage Value = Zero)

PV of operating CFAT (1 – 5 years)	₹ 1,13,39,674
Add: PV of tax benefit on short term capital loss (₹40,96,000 × 0.35 = ₹14,33,600 × 0.497, PV factor)	7,12,499
Add: PV of recovery of working capital	4,97,000
Total present value	1,25,49,173
Less: Cash outflows	1,10,00,000
NPV	15,49,173

Since the NPV is still positive, the company is advised to instal the equipment.

SPREADSHEET SOLUTION 9.1

Evaluation Whether to Install Equipment for Further Processing of Iron Ore (When salvage value is ₹10 lakh)

	A	B	C	D	E	F	G	H
1	Year	0	1	2	3	4	5	
2	Cost of Equipment (Rs)	10,000,000						
3	Working Capital (Rs)	1,000,000						
4	Expected output without further processing (tons)	25,000						
5	Expected realization per ton without futher processing (Rs)	1,000						
6	Expected output with further processing (%)	0.8						
7	Expected realisation per ton with further processing (Rs)	1,600						
8	Processing cost per ton (Rs)	100						
9	Corporate tax rate (%)	0.35						
10	Depreciation rate (%)	0.2						
11	Salvage Value (Rs)	1,000,000						
12	Discount rate (%)	0.15						
13								
14	Cost of Equipment	–10,000,000						
15	Working Capital	–1,000,000						
16	Total initial cost	–11,000,000						
17	Revenue from processing		7,000,000	7,000,000	7,000,000	7,000,000	7,000,000	
18	Processing cost		2,500,000	2,500,000	2,500,000	2,500,000	2,500,000	
19	Depreciation		2,000,000	1,600,000	1,280,000	1,024,000	0	
20	Earning before taxes		2,500,000	2,900,000	3,220,000	3,476,000	4,500,000	
21	Taxes		8,75,000	1,015,000	1,127,000	1,216,600	1,575,000	
22	Earning after taxes		1,625,000	1,885,000	2,093,000	2,259,400	2,925,000	
23	Operating CFAT		3,625,000	3,485,000	3,373,000	3,283,400	2,925,000	
24	Salvage value						1,000,000	
25	Tax benefit on short-term capital loss						1,083,600	
26	Release of Working Capital						1,000,000	
27	CFAT		3,625,000	3,485,000	3,373,000	3,283,400	6,008,600	
28	NPV	1,869,767.58						
29								
30								
31	Workings							
32	Depreciation Schedule							
33	Depreciation base of equipment		10,000,000	8,000,000	6,400,000	5,120,000	4,096,000	
34	Depreciation		2,000,000	1,600,000	1,280,000	1,024,000		
35								
36	Tax Benefit on Short-term capital loss							
37	Book Value of equipment						4,096,000	
38	Salvage Value						1,000,000	
39	Short-term capital loss						3,096,000	
42	Tax Benefit on short-term capital loss						1,083,600	
43								

Enter the years in cells B1 to G1 starting with year 0. Enter the input in cells B2 to B12.

Enter =–B2 in cell B14, =–B3 in cell B15 for investment in equipment and working capital respectively. Enter =SUM(B14:B15) in cell B16 to calculate the total initial investment.

Enter the formula =($B4*$B6*$B7)–($B4*$B5) in cell C17 and copy the formula in cells D17 to G17 to calculate revenue for all years. Enter the formula =$B4*$B8 in cell C18 and copy the formula to cells D18 to G18 to calculate the processing cost.

Depreciation is worked out in cells C33 to G34. For calculating depreciation enter =B2 in cell C33. Enter the formula =C33*$B10 in cell C34. Enter =C33–C34 in cell D33 and copy it to cells E33 to G33. Also copy the formula in cell C34 to cells D34 to G34. The Depreciation figures are carried to cells C19 to G19. This is done by entering =C34 in cell C19 and it is copied in cells D19 to G19.

To calculate earnings before taxes, enter =C17-C18-C19 in cell C20 and copy the formula to cells D20 to G20.

To calculate taxes, enter = C20*B9 in cell C21 and copy to cells D21 to G21.

To calculate earnings after taxes, enter =C20-C21 in cell C22 and copy to cells D22 to G22.

To calculate operating CFAT, enter =C22+C19 in cell C23 and copy to cells D23 to G23.

Salvage value is entered in cells G24 by entering =B11

Tax benefit on short-term capital loss is worked out in cells G37 to G40. Enter =G33 in cell G37 and =B11 in cell G38. Short-term capital loss is calculated in cell G39 by entering =G37-G38. Tax benefit on short-term capital loss is calculated in cell G40 by entering =G39*B9. This benefit is carried to cell G25 by entering =G40 in cell G25.

Working capital released is entered in cell G26 by providing reference to cell B15 by entering =B15 in cell G26.

Year-wise CFAT are calculated in row 27 by entering =sum(C23:C26) in cell C27 and copying it to cells D27 to G27.

NPV is calculated in cell B28 by entering =NPV(B12, C27:G27)+B16. **(The difference in NPV is due to approximations)**.

When Salvage Value is Zero

In case, the salvage value of the equipment is zero, only one change is required in spreadsheet. Enter 0 in cell B11 instead of 1,000,000. The spreadsheet will calculate the new NPV.

***Example* 9.3**

For the company in Example 9.2, assume there are other plants and machinery subject to 20 per cent depreciation (i.e. in the same block of assets). What course of action should the company choose?

Solution

(a) Cash outflows would remain unchanged.

(b) The annual depreciation will also remain the same for the first 4 yeas: In year 5, the depreciation = ₹30,96,000 (opening WDV of equipment, ₹40,96,000 – ₹10,00,000, salvage value) × 0.20 = ₹6,19,200.

(c) The CFAT (operating) for years, 1-4 will not change. In year 5, it will be shown as below:

Particulars	*CFAT (t = 5)*
Revenue from processing	₹70,00,000
Less: Processing costs:	
Cash costs	25,00,000
Depreciation	6,19,200
Earning before taxes	38,80,800
Less: Taxes (0.35)	13,58,280
EAT	25,22,520
CFAT	31,41,720

Determination of NPV (Salvage Value = ₹10 lakh)

Year	CFAT	PV factor	Total PV
1	₹36,25,000	0.870	₹31,53,750
2	34,85,000	0.756	26,34,660
3	33,73,000	0.658	22,19,434
4	32,83,400	0.572	18,78,105
5	31,41,720	0.497	15,61,435
Salvage value	10,00,000	0.497	4,97,000
Recovery of working capital	10,00,000	0.497	4,97,000
Gross present value			1,24,41,384
Less: Cash outflows			1,10,00,000
Net present value (NPV)			14,41,384@

@In fact, the NPV of the equipment is likely to be higher as tax advantage will accrue on the eligible depreciation of ₹24,76,800, i.e. (₹30,96,000 – ₹6,19,200) in future years.

Recommendation The company should instal the equipment.

Determination of NPV (Salvage Value = 0)

(i) For the first 4 years, depreciation amount will remain unchanged. In the fifth year, depreciation = ₹40,96,000 (₹40,96,000, opening WDV less zero salvage value) × 0.20 = ₹8,19,200.

(ii) Operating CFAT for years 1 – 4 will remain unchanged. The CFAT for 5th year would be ₹32,11,720 as shown below:

Revenues from processing	₹70,00,000
Less: Processing costs (₹25,00,000 + ₹8,19,200)	33,19,200
EBIT	36,80,800
Less: Taxes (0.35)	12,88,280
EAT	23,92,520
Add: Depreciation	8,19,200
CFAT	32,11,720

(iii) PV of operating CFAT (1 – 4 years)	98,85,949
Add: PV of operating CFAT (5th year) (₹32,11,720 × 0.497)	15,96,225
Add: PV of recovery of working capital	4,97,000
Total PV	1,19,79,174
Less: Cash outflows	1,10,00,000@
NPV	9,79,174

@In effect, NPV would be higher as tax advantage will accrue on depreciation of ₹32,76,800 in future years.

Recommendation ***The decision does not change, as NPV is positive.***

Replacement Situation In the case of replacement of an existing machine (asset) by a new one, the relevant cash outflows are after-tax incremental cash flows. If a new machine is intended to replace an existing machine, the proceeds so obtained from its sale reduce cash outflows required to purchase the new machine and, hence, part of relevant cash flows. The calculation of after-tax incremental cash outflows is illustrated in Format 9.3 and Format 9.4 which provide depreciation base in the case of replacement situations.

FORMAT 9.3 Cash Outflows in a Replacement Situation

1. Cost of the new machine
2. + Installation Cost
3. ± Working Capital
4. – Sale proceeds of existing machine

FORMAT 9.4 Depreciation Base of New Machine in a Replacement Situation

1. WDV of the existing machine
2. + Cost of the acquisition of new machine (including installation costs)
3. – Sale proceeds of existing machine

The computation is illustrated in Example 9.4.

***Example* 9.4**

Royal Industries Ltd is considering the replacement of one of its moulding machines. The existing machine is in good operating condition, but is smaller than required if the firm is to expand its operations. It is 4 years old, has a current salvage value of ₹2,00,000 and a remaining life of 6 years. The machine was initially purchased for ₹10 lakh and is being depreciated at 20 per cent on the basis of written down value method.

The new machine will cost ₹15 lakh and will be subject to the same method as well as the same rate of depreciation. It is expected to have a useful life of 6 years, salvage value of ₹1,50,000 at the sixth year end. The management anticipates that with the expanded operations, there will be a need of an additional net working capital of ₹1 lakh. The new machine will allow the firm to expand current operations and thereby increase annual revenues by ₹5,00,000; variable cost to volume ratio is 30 per cent. Fixed costs (excluding depreciation) are likely to remain unchanged.

The corporte tax rate is 35 per cent. Its cost of capital is 10 per cent. The company has several machines in the block of 20 per cent depreciation.

Should the company replace its existing machine? What course of action would you suggest, if there is no salvage value?

Solution

Financial Evaluation Whether to Replace Existing Machine

(A) Cash Outflows (Incremental)

Cost of the new machine	₹15,00,000
Add: Additional working captial	1,00,000
Less: Sale value of existing machine	2,00,000
	14,00,000

(B) Determination of Incremental CFAT (Operating)

Year	*Incremental contribution*[a]	*Incremental depreciation*[b]	*Taxable income*	*Taxes (0.35)*	*EAT [Col.4 – Col.5]*	*CFAT [Col.6 + Col.3]*
1	*2*	*3*	*4*	*5*	*6*	*7*
1	₹3,50,000	₹2,60,000	₹90,000	₹31,500	₹58,500	₹3,18,500
2	3,50,000	2,08,000	1,42,000	49,700	92,300	3,00,300
3	3,50,000	1,66,400	1,83,600	64,260	1,19,340	2,85,740
4	3,50,000	1,33,120	2,16,880	75,908	1,40,972	2,74,092
5	3,50,000	1,06,496	2,43,504	85,226	1,58,278	2,64,774
6	3,50,000	55,197	2,94,803	1,03,181	1,91,622	2,46,819

[a]₹5,00,000 – [₹5,00,000 × 0.30, variable cost to value (V/V) ratio] = ₹3,50,000

[b](Working note)

Working Notes

1. Incremental Depreciation (t = 1 – 6)

Year	Incremental asset cost base	Depreciation (20% on WDV)
1	₹13,00,000	₹2,60,000
2	10,40,000	2,08,000
3	8,32,000	1,66,400
4	6,65,600	1,33,120
5	5,32,480	1,06,496
6	4,25,984	55,197[c]

[c]0.20 × (₹4,25,984 – ₹1,50,000, salvage value) = ₹55,197

2. (i) Written Down Value (WDV) of Existng Machine at the Beginning of the Year 5

Initial cost of machine	₹10,00,000
Less: Depreciation @ 20% in year 1	2,00,000
WDV at beginning of year 2	8,00,000
Less: Depreicaiton @ 20% on WDV	1,60,000
WDV at beginning of year 3	6,40,000
Less: Depreciation @ 20% on WDV	1,28,000
WDV at beginning of year 4	5,12,000
Less: Depreciation @ 20% on WDV	1,02,400
WDV at beginning of year 5	4,09,600

(ii) Depreciation Base of New Machine

WDV of existing machine	4,09,600
Add: Cost of the new machine	15,00,000
Less: Sale proceeds of existing machine	2,00,000
	17,09,600

(iii) Base for Incremental Depreciation

Depreciation base of a new machine	17,09,600
Less: Depreciation base of an existing machine	4,09,600
	13,00,000

(C) Determination of NPV (Salvage Value = ₹1.50 lakh)

Year	CFAT	PV factor (0.10)	Total PV
1	₹3,18,500	0.909	₹2,89,517
2	3,00,300	0.826	2,48,048
3	2,85,740	0.751	2,14,591
4	2,74,092	0.683	1,87,205
5	2,64,774	0.621	1,64,424
6	2,46,819	0.564	1,39,206
6 Salvage value	1,50,000	0.564	84,600
6 Recovery of working capital	1,00,000	0.564	56,400
Gross present value			13,83,991
Less: Cash outflows			14,00,000
Net present value			(16,009)

Recommendation Since the NPV is negative, the company should not replace the existing machine. However, in effect, the NPV is likely to be positive as tax advantage will accrue on the eligible depreciation of ₹2,19,803 (₹4,25,984 – ₹1,50,000 – ₹55,197) in the future years.

Determination of NPV (Salvage Value = Zero)

(i) For the first 5 years, depreciation will remain unchanged. In the sixth year, it will be = ₹4,25,984 × 0.20 = ₹85,197.

(ii) Operating CFAT for years 1–5 will remain unchanged.

CFAT for year 6 would be:	
Incremental contribution	₹3,50,000
Less: Incremental depreciation	85,197
Taxable income	2,64,803
Less: Taxes (0.35)	92,681
EAT	1,72,122
Add: Depreciation	85,197
CFAT	2,57,319
(iii) PV of operating CFAT (1 – 5 years)	11,03,785
Add: PV of operating CFAT (6th year) (₹2,57,319 × 0.564)	1,45,128
Add: PV of working capital	56,400
Total present value	13,05,313
Less: Cash outflows	14,00,000
NPV	(94,687)

Recommendation Since the NPV is negative, the existing machine should not be replaced.

SPREADSHEET SOLUTION

(See the excel sheet screen shot on next page)
Enter the inputs in cells B1 to B11
Enter the years in row 16, starting with year 0.

Enter =–B1 in cell B17, =–B6 in cell B18 and =B3 in cell B19 for investment in equipment, working capital and salvage value of existing equipment respectively. Enter =SUM(B17:B19) in cell B20 to calculate the total initial investment.

Enter the formula =$B7 in cell C21 and copy the formula in cells D21 to H21 to calculate incremental revenue for all years. Enter the formula =C21*$B8 in cell C22 and copy the formula to cells D22 to H22 to calculate the incremental variable cost.

Depreciation is worked out in cells B38 to H42. For calculating depreciation, enter =B2*(1–B9)^B4 in cell B38. Enter the formula =B18+B1–B3 in cell B39. Enter =B39–B38 in cell B40 and copy it to cell C40. Enter =C40*$B9 in cell C41 and copy the formula in cells D41 to H41. Enter =C40–C41 in cell C42 and copy the formula in cell D42 to H42. The depreciation figures are carried to cells C23 to H23. This is done by entering =C41 in cell C23 and it is copied in cell D23 to H23.

To calculate taxable income, enter =C21–C22–C23 in cell C24 and copy the formula to cells D24 to H24.

To calculate taxes, enter =C24*$B11 in cell C25 and copy to cells D25 to H25.

To calculate earnings after taxes, enter =C24–C25 in cell C26 and copy to cells D26 to H26.

To calculate operating CFAT, enter =C26+C23 in cell C28 and copy to cells D28 to H28.

Salvage value is entered in cell H29 by entering =B5

Working capital released is entered in cell H28 by providing reference to cell B6 by entering =B6 in cell H28

Year-wise CFAT are calculated in row 30 by entering =SUM(C27:C29) in cell C30 and copying it to cells D30 to H30.

NPV is calculated in cell B31 by entering =NPV(B10, C30:H30)+B20. **(The difference in NPV is due to approximations)**.

SPREADSHEET SOLUTION 9.2

Financial Evaluation Whether to Replace Existing Machine (when salvage value is ₹1,50,000)

Microsoft Excel - ExcelSheet9-2

	A	B	C	D	E	F	G	H
1	Cost of new machine (Rs)	1,500,000						
2	Original cost of existing machine (Rs)	1,000,000						
3	Sale value of existing machine (Rs)	200,000						
4	Age of existing machine (years)	4						
5	Salvage value of new machine (Rs)	150,000						
6	Additional working capital (Rs)	100,000						
7	Incremental revenue per year (Rs)	500,000						
8	Variable cost as percentage of revenue	0.3						
9	Depreciation rate	0.2						
10	Cost of capital	0.1						
11	Corporate tax rate	0.35						
12								
13								
14								
15								
16	Year	0	1	2	3	4	5	6
17	Cost of new equipment	–1,500,000						
18	Working capital	–100,000						
19	Sale value of existing machine	200,000						
20	Initial investment	–1,400,000						
21	Investmental revenue		500,000	500,000	500,000	500,000	500,000	500,000
22	Variable cost		150,000	150,000	150,000	150,000	150,000	150,000
23	Depreciation		2,60,000	2,08,000	1,66,400	1,33,120	1,06,496	55,197
24	Taxable income		90,000	142,000	183,600	216,880	243,504	294,803
25	Taxes		31,500	49,700	64,260	75,908	85,226.40	103,181.10
26	Earnings after tax		58,500	92,300	119,340	140,972	158,278	191,622
27	Operating CFAT		318,500	300,300	285,740	274,092	264,774	246,819
28	Release of working capital							100,000
29	Salvage value							150,000
30	CFAT		318,500	300,300	285,740	274,092	264,774	496,819
31	NPV	–15,538.63						
32								
33								
34								
35								
36	Workings							
37	Depreciation							
38	Book value of existing machine	409,600						
39	New asset base	1,709,600						
40	Incremental asset base cost	1,300,000	1,300,000	1,040,000	832,000	665,600	532,480	275,984
41	Depreciation		260,000	208,000	166,400	133,120	106,496	55,196.80
42	Written down value		1,040,000	832,000	665,600	532,480	425,984	220,787
43								

Sheet1 / Sheet2 / Sheet3

Ready

When Salvage Value is Zero

In case, the salvage value of the equipment is zero, only one change is required in the spreadsheet. Enter 0 in cell B5 instead of ₹150,000. The spreadsheet will calculate the new NPV.

Mutually Exclusive Situations In the case of mutually exclusive proposals, the selection of one proposal precludes the choice of other(s). The calculation of the cash outflows and inflows are on lines similar to the replacement situations. This is illustrated in Example 9.5.

***Example* 9.5**

A company is considering two mutually exclusive proposals, X and Y. Proposal X will require the purchase of machine X, for ₹1,50,000 with no salvage value but an increase in the level of working capital to the tune of ₹50,000 over its life. The project will generate additional sales of ₹1,30,000 and require cash expenses of ₹30,000 in each of the 5 years of its life. Proposal Y will require the purchase of machine Y for ₹2,50,000 with no salvage value and additional working capital of ₹70,000. The project is expected to generate additional sales of ₹2,00,000 with cash expenses aggregating ₹50,000.

Both the machines are subject to written down value method of depreciation at the rate of 20 per cent. Assuming the company does not have any other asset in the block of 20 per cent; has 12 per cent cost of capital, would have sufficient STCG in year 5 and is subject to 35 per cent tax, advise which machine it should purchase? What course of action would you suggest if Machine X and Machine Y have salvage values of ₹10,000 and ₹25,000 respectively?

Solution

Financial Evaluation of Proposals, X and Y

Proposal X

Cash outflows	
Cost price of machine	₹1,50,000
Additional working capital	50,000
Initial investment	2,00,000
CFAT and NPV	
(i) Incremental sales revenue	1,30,000
Less: Cash expenses	30,000
Incremental cash profit before taxes	1,00,000
Less: Taxes (0.35)	35,000
CFAT (t = 1 – 5)	65,000
(×) PV factor of annuity for 5 years (0.12)	× 3.605
Present value	2,34,325

(ii) **PV of Tax Savings Due to Depreciation**

Year	*Depreciation*	*Tax savings*	*PVF*	*Present value*	
1	₹30,000	₹10,500	0.893	₹9,377	
2	24,000	8,400	0.797	6,695	
3	19,200	6,720	0.712	4,785	
4	15,360	5,376	0.636	3,419	24,276

(iii) PV of tax savings on short-term capital loss (STCL): (₹61,440 STCL × 0.35 × 0.567)	12,193
(iv) Release of working capital (₹50,000 × 0.567)	28,350
Total present value	2,99,144
Less: Cash outflows	2,00,000
NPV	99,144

Proposal Y

Cash outflows	
Cost price of machine	2,50,000
Additional working capital	70,000
Initial investment	3,20,000
CFAT and NPV	
(i) Incremental sales revenue	2,00,000
Less: Cash expenses	50,000
Incremental cash profits before taxes	1,50,000
Less: Taxes (0.35)	52,500
CFAT (t = 1 – 5)	97,500
(×) PV factor of annuity for 5 years (0.12)	× 3.605
Present value	3,51,488

(ii) PV of Tax Savings Due to Depreciation

Year	Depreciation	Tax savings	PVF	Present value	
1	₹50,000	₹17,500	0.893	₹15,628	
2	40,000	14,000	0.797	11,158	
3	32,000	11,200	0.712	7,974	
4	25,600	8,960	0.636	5,699	40,459

(iii) PV of tax savings on short-term capital loss (₹1,02,400 × 0.35 × 0.567)	20,321
(iv) Release of working capital (₹70,000 × 0.567)	39,690
Total present value	4,51,958
Less: Cash outflows	3,20,000
NPV	1,31,958

Advice: Proposal Y is recommended in view of its higher NPV.

Alternatively (Incremental Cashflow Approach)

Incremental Cash Outflows	
Investment required in Proposal **Y**	₹3,20,000
Less: Investment required in Proposal **X**	2,00,000
	1,20,000
Incremental CFAT and NPV	
(i) Incremental sales revenue (**Y** – **X**)	70,000
Less: Incremental cash expenses (**Y** – **X**)	20,000
Incremental cash profit before taxes	50,000
Less: Taxes (0.35)	17,500
Incremental CFAT (t = 1 – 5)	32,500
(×) PV of annuity for 5 years (0.12)	×3.605
Incremental present value	1,17,162

(ii) PV of Tax Savings Due to Incremental Depreciation

Year	Incremental depreciation	Tax savings	PVF	Present value	
1	₹ 20,000	₹ 7,000	0.893	₹6,251	
2	16,000	5,600	0.797	4,463	
3	12,800	4,480	0.712	3,190	
4	10,240	3,584	0.636	2,279	16,183

(iii) PV of tax savings on incremental (**Y** – **X**) short term capital loss (STCL): (₹1,02,400 – ₹61,440) × 0.35 × 0.567	8,129
(iv) Incremental (**Y** – **X**) *working capital* (₹70,000 – ₹50,000) × 0.567	11,340
Incremental present value	1,52,814
Less: Incremental cash outflows	1,20,000
Incremental NPV	32,814

Recommendation ***Proposal Y is better.***

Financial Evaluation of Proposals, Assuming Salvage Value of Machines X and Y (Incremental Approach)

(a) Sum of PV of items (i), (ii) and (iv) (₹1,17,162 + ₹16,183 + ₹11,340)@	₹1,44,685
(b) PV of incremental salvage value (₹15,000 × 0.567)	8,505
(c) PV of tax savings on incremental STCL@@ (₹77,400 – ₹54,440) × 0.35 × 0.567	5,152
Incremental present value	1,58,342
Less: Incremental cash outflows	1,20,000
Incremental NPV	38,342

Decision: Decision (superiority of proposal Y) remains unchanged.

@Items **(i)**, **(ii)** and **(iv)** when there is no salvage will not change due to salvage value.

@@As a result of salvage value, the amount of short-term capital loss (STCL) will change.

LO 9.3 EVALUATION TECHNIQUES

We discuss below the important evaluation techniques for capital budgeting. Included in the methods of appraising an investment proposal are those which are objective, quantified and based on economic costs and benefits.

The methods of appraising capital expenditure proposals can be classified into two broad categories: **(i)** traditional, and **(ii)** time-adjusted. The latter are more popularly known as discounted cash flow (DCF) techniques as they take the time factor into account. The first category includes **(i)** average rate of return method and **(ii)** pay back period method. The second category includes **(i)** net present value method, **(ii)** internal rate of return method, **(iii)** net terminal value method, and **(iv)** profitability index.

Traditional Techniques

Average Rate of Return

Computation The average rate of return (ARR) method of evaluating proposed capital expenditure is also known as the accounting rate of return method. It is based upon accounting information rather than cash flows. There is no unanimity regarding the definition of the rate of return. There are a number of alternative methods for calculating the ARR. The most common usage of the average rate of return (ARR) expresses it as follows:

$$\text{ARR} = \frac{\text{Average annual profits after taxes}}{\text{Average investment over the life of the project}} \times 100 \qquad \textbf{(9.1)}$$

The average profits after taxes are determined by adding up the after-tax profits expected for each year of the project's life and dividing the result by the number of years. In the case of annuity, the average after-tax profits are equal to any year's profits.

The average investment is determined by dividing the net investment by two. This averaging process assumes that the firm is using straight line depreciation, in which case the book value of the asset declines at a constant rate from its purchase price to zero at the end of its depreciable life. This means that, on the average, firms will have one-half of their initial purchase price in the books.[12] Consequently, if the machine has salvage value, then only the depreciable cost (cost-salvage value) of the machine should be divided by two in order to ascertain the average net investment, as the salvage money will be recovered only at the end of the life of the project. Therefore, an amount equivalent to the salvage value remains tied up in the project throughout its life time. Hence, no adjustment is required to the sum of salvage value to determine the average investment.[13] Likewise, if any additional net working capital is required in the initial year which is likely to be released only at the end of the project's life, the full amount of working capital should be taken in determining relevant investment for the purpose of calculating ARR. Thus,

$$\text{Average investment} = \text{Net working capital} + \text{Salvage value} + 1/2\,(\text{Initial cost of machine} - \text{Salvage value}) \qquad \textbf{(9.2)}$$

For instance, given the information: initial investment (purchase of machine), ₹11,000, salvage value, ₹1,000, working capital, ₹2,000, service life (years) 5 and that the straight line method of depreciation is adopted, the average investment is: ₹1,000 + ₹2,000 + 1/2 (₹11,000 – ₹1,000) = ₹8,000.

Example **9.6**

Determine the average rate of return from the following data of two machines, A and B.

Particulars		Machine A	Machine B
Cost		₹56,125	₹56,125
Annual estimated income after depreciation and income tax:			
Year	1	3,375	11,375
	2	5,375	9,375
	3	7,375	7,375
	4	9,375	5,375
	5	11,375	3,375
		36,875	36,875
Estimated life (years)		5	5
Estimated salvage value		3,000	3,000

Depreciation has been charged on straight line basis.

Solution ARR = (Average income/Average investment) × 100

Average income of Machines A and B = (₹36,875/5) = ₹7,375

Average investment = Salvage value + 1/2(Cost of machine – Salvage value)

= ₹3,000 + 1/2 (₹56,125 – ₹3,000) = ₹29,562.50

ARR (for machines A and B) = (₹7,375/₹29563.50) = 24.9 per cent

In addition to the above, there are other approaches to calculate the average rate of return (ARR). One approach, which is a variation of the above, involves using original rather than the average cost of the project. In the case of this alternative approach, the ARR for both the machines would be 13.1 per cent (₹7,375 ÷ ₹56,125).

Accept-reject Rule With the help of the ARR, the financial decision maker can decide whether to accept or reject the investment proposal. As an accept-reject criterion, the actual ARR would be compared with a predetermined or a minimum required rate of return or cut-off rate. A project would qualify to be accepted if the actual ARR is higher than the minimum desired ARR. Otherwise, it is liable to be rejected. Alternatively, the ranking method can be used to select or reject proposals. Thus, the alternative proposals under consideration may be arranged in the descending order of magnitude, starting with the proposal with the highest ARR and ending with the proposal having the lowest ARR. Obviously, projects having higher ARR would be preferred to projects with lower ARR.

Evaluation of ARR In evaluating the ARR, as a criterion to select/reject investment projects, its merits and drawbacks need to be considered. The most favourable attribute of the ARR method is its easy calculation. What is required is only the figure of accounting profits after taxes which should be easily obtainable. Moreover, it is simple to understand and use. In contrast to this, the discounted flow techniques involve tedious calculations and are difficult to understand. Finally, the total benefits associated with the project are taken into account while calculating the ARR. Some methods, pay back for instance, do not use the entire stream of incomes.

However, this method of evaluating investment proposals suffers from serious deficiencies. The principal shortcoming of the ARR approach aries from the use of accounting income instead of cash flows. The cash flow approach is markedly superior to accounting earnings for project evaluation. The earnings calculations ignore the reinvestment potential of a project's benefits while the cash flow takes into account this potential and, hence, the total benefits of the project.

The second principal shortcoming of ARR is that it does not take into account the time value of money. The timing of cash inflows and outflows is a major decision variable in financial decision making. Accordingly, benefits in the earlier years and later years cannot be valued at par. To the extent the ARR method treats these benefits at par and fails to take account of the differences in the time value of money, it suffers from a serious deficiency. Thus, in Example 9.6, the ARR in case of both machines, A and B is the same, although machine B should be preferred since its returns in the early years of its life are greater. Clearly, the ARR method of evaluating investment proposals fails to consider this.

Thirdly, the ARR criterion of measuring the worth of investment does not differentiate between the size of the investment required for each project. Competing investment proposals may have the same ARR, but may require different average investments, as shown in Table 9.6. The ARR method, in such a situation, will leave the firm in an indeterminate position.

TABLE 9.6

Machines	*Average Annual Earnings*	*Average Investment*	*ARR (per cent)*
1	*2*	*3*	*4*
A	₹6,000	₹30,000	20
B	2,000	10,000	20
C	4,000	20,000	20

Finally, this method does not take into consideration any benefits which can accrue to the firm from the sale or abandonment of equipment which is replaced by the new investment. The 'new' investment, from the point of view of correct financial decision making, should be measured in terms of incremental cash outflows due to new investments, that is, new investment minus sale proceeds of the existing equipment ± tax adjustment. But the ARR method does not make any adjustment in this regard to determine the level of average investments. Investments in fixed assets are determined at their acquisition cost.

For these reason, the ARR leaves much to be desired as a method for project selection.

Pay Back Method

Payback (period) method is the exact amount of time required for a firm to recover its initial investment in a project as calculated from cash inflows.

Computation The **pay back method** (PB) is the second traditional method of capital budgeting. It is the simplest and, perhaps, the most widely employed, quantitative method for appraising capital expenditure decisions. This method answers the question: How many years will it take for the cash benefits to pay the original cost of an investment, normally disregarding salvage value? Cash benefits here represent CFAT ignoring interest payment. Thus, the pay back method (PB) measures the number of years required for the CFAT to pay back the **original outlay** required in an investment proposal.

Original/initial investment (outlay) is the relevant cash outflow for a proposed project at time zero (t = 0).

There are two ways of calculating the PB period. The first method can be applied when the cash flow stream is in the nature of **annuity** for each year of the project's life, that is, CFAT are uniform. In such a situation, the initial cost of the investment is divided by the constant annual cash flow:

Annuity is a stream of equal cash inflows.

$$PB = \frac{\text{Investment}}{\text{Constant annual cash flow}} \tag{9.3}$$

For example, an investment of ₹40,000 in a machine is expected to produce CFAT of ₹8,000 for 10 years,

PB = ₹40,000/₹8,000 = 5 years

Mixed stream is a series of cash inflows exhibiting any pattern other than that of an annuity.

The second method is used when a project's cash flows are not uniform **(mixed stream)** but vary from year to year. In such a situation, PB is calculated by the process of cumulating cash flows till the time when cumulative cash flows become equal to the original investment outlay. Table 9.7 presents the calculations of pay back period for Example 9.6.

TABLE 9.7 Calculation of Payback Period

Year	*Annual CFAT*		*Cumulative CFAT*	
	A	*B*	*A*	*B*
1	₹14,000	₹22,000	₹14,000	₹22,000
2	16,000	20,000	30,000	42,000
3	18,000	18,000	48,000	60,000
4	20,000	16,000	68,000	76,000
5	25,000 *	17,000 *	93,000	93,000

* CFAT in the fifth year includes ₹3,000 salvage value also.

The initial investment of ₹56,125 on machine A will be recovered between years 3 and 4.

The pay back period would be a fraction more than 3 years. The sum of ₹48,000 is recovered by the end of the third year. The balance ₹8,125 is needed to be recovered in the fourth year. In the fourth year CFAT is ₹20,000. The pay back fraction is, therefore, 0.406 (₹8,125/₹20,000). The pay back period for machine A is 3.406 years. Similarly, for machine B the pay back period would be 2 years and a fraction of a year. As ₹42,000 is recovered by the end of the second year, the balance of ₹14,125 needs to be recovered in the third year. In the third year CFAT is ₹18,000. The pay back fraction is 0.785 (₹14,125/₹18,000). Thus, the PB period for machine B is 2.785 years.

Accept-Reject Criterion The pay back period can be used as a decision criterion to accept or reject investment proposals. One application of this technique is to compare the actual pay back with a predetermined pay back, that is, the pay back set up by the management in terms of the maximum period during which the initial investment must be recovered. If the actual pay back period is less than the predetermined pay back, the project would be accepted; if not, it would be rejected. Alternatively, the pay back can be used as a ranking method. When mutually exclusive projects are under consideration, they may be ranked according to the length of the pay back period. Thus, the project having the shortest pay back may be assigned rank one, followed in that order so that the project with the longest pay back would be ranked last. Obviously, projects with shorter pay back period will be selected.

Evaluation The pay back method has certain merits. It is easy to calculate and simple to understand. Moreover, the pay back method is an improvement over the ARR approach. Its superiority arises due to the fact that it is based on cash flow analysis. The results of Example 9.6 illustrated in Table 9.10

can be cited in support of this. Thus, though the average cash flows for both the machines under the ARR method were the same, the pay back method shows that the pay back period for machine B is shorter than for machine A. The pay back period approach shows that machine B should be preferred as it refunds the capital outlay earlier than machine A.

The pay back approach, however, suffers from serious limitations. Its major shortcomings are as follows:

The first major shortcoming of the pay back method is that it completely ignores all cash inflows after the pay back period. This can be very misleading in capital budgeting evaluations. Table 9.8 reveals alternative projects with the same pay back period (3 years).

TABLE 9.8

Particulars	*Project X*	*Project Y*
Total cost of the project	₹ 15,000	₹ 15,000
Cash inflows (CFAT)		
Year 1	5,000	4,000
2	6,000	5,000
3	4,000	6,000
4	0	6,000
5	0	3,000
6	0	3,000
Pay back period (years)	3	3

In fact, the projects differs widely in respect of cash inflows generated after the pay back period. The cash flow for project X stops at the end of the third year, while that of Y continues up to the sixth year. Obviously, the firm would prefer project Y because it makes available to the firm cash inflows of ₹12,000, in years 4 through 6, whereas project X does not yield any cash inflow after the third year. Under the pay back method, however, both the projects would be given equal ranking, which is apparently incorrect. Therefore, it cannot be regarded as a measure of profitability. Its failure lies in the fact that it does not consider the total benefits accruing from the project.

Another deficiency of the pay back method is that it does not measure correctly even the cash flows expected to be received within the pay back period as it does not differentiate between projects in terms of the timing or the magnitude of cash flows. It considers only the recovery period as a whole. This happens because it does not discount the future cash inflows but rather treats a rupee received in the second or third year as valuable as a rupee received in the first year. In other words, to the extent the pay back method fails to consider the pattern of cash inflows, it ignores the time value of money.

Table 9.9 shows that both the projects A and B have **(i)** the same cash outlays in the zero time period; **(ii)** the same total cash inflows of ₹15,000; and **(iii)** the same pay back period of 3 years. But project A would be acceptable to the firm because it returns cash earlier than project B, enabling A to repay a loan or reinvest it and earn a return. A possible solution to this problem is provided by determining the pay back period of discounted cash flows. This is illustrated in the subsequent section of this chapter.

The discounted payback method still has significant drawbacks. The major one is that the cut-off period is still arbitrarily set. As a result, there is a possibility that a project with positive NPV may be rejected because the cutoff is too short. Also, it does not ensure that a project accepted under shorter discounted payback period has necessarily the maximum NPV.[14]

TABLE 9.9 Cashflows of Projects

Particulars	*Project A*	*Project B*
Total cost of the project	₹15,000	₹15,000
Cash inflows (CFAT)		
Year 1	10,000	1,000
2	4,000	4,000
3	1,000	10,000

Another flaw of the pay back method is that it does not take into consideration the entire life of the project during which cash flows are generated. As a result, projects with large cash inflows in the latter part of their lives may be rejected in favour of less profitable projects which happen to generate a larger proportion of their cash inflows in the earlier part of their lives. Table 9.10 presents the comparison of two such projects. On the basis of the pay back criterion, project A will be adjudged superior to project B.

TABLE 9.10

Particulars	*Project A*	*Project B*
Total cost of the project	₹40,000	₹40,000
Cash inflows (CFAT)		
Year 1	14,000	10,000
2	16,000	10,000
3	10,000	10,000
4	4,000	10,000
5	2,000	12,000
6	1,000	16,000
7	Nil	17,000
Pay back period (years)	3	4

It is quite evident just from a casual inspection that project B is more profitable than project A, since the cash inflows of the former amount to ₹45,000 after the expiry of the pay back period and the cash flows of the latter beyond the pay back period are only ₹7,000.

The above weaknesses notwithstanding, the pay back method can be gainfully employed under certain circumstances.[15] In the first place, where the long-term outlook, say in excess of three years, is extremely hazy, the pay back method may be useful. In a politically unstable country, for instance, a quick return to recover the investment is the primary goal, and subsequent profits are almost unexpected surprises. Likewise, this method may be very appropriate for firms suffering from liquidity crisis. A firm with limited liquid assets and no ability to raise additional funds, which nevertheless wishes to undertake capital projects in the hope of easing the crisis, might use pay back as a selection criterion because it emphasises quick recovery of the firm's original outlay and little impairment of the already critical liquidity situation. Thirdly, the pay back method may also be beneficial in taking capital budgeting decisions for firms which lay more emphasis on short-run earning performance rather than its long-term growth. The pay back period is a measure of liquidity of investments rather than their profitability. Thus, the pay back period should more appropriately be treated as a constraint to be satisfied than as a profitability measure to be maximised.[16] In spite of the weakness of the payback period method, the method can be used in conjunction with other more sophisticated methods. It can be used to screen potential projects to the few that merit more careful scrutiny with more sophisticated methods such as DCFs.[17] Finally, the pay back period is useful, apart from measuring liquidity, in making calculations in certain situations. For instance, the internal rate of return can be computed easily from the pay back period. The pay back method is a good approximation of the internal rate of return which otherwise requires a trial and error approach.

To conclude the discussion of the traditional methods of appraising capital investment decisions, there are two major drawbacks of these techniques. They do not consider the total benefits in terms of **(i)** the magnitude and **(ii)** the timing of cash flows. For these reasons, the traditional methods are unsatisfactory as capital budgeting decision criteria. The two essential ingredients of a theoretically sound appraisal method, therefore, are that **(i)** it should be based on a consideration of the total cash stream, and **(ii)** it should consider the time value of money as reflected in both the magnitude and the timing of expected cash flows in each period of a project's life. The time-adjusted (also known as discounted cash flow) techniques satisfy these requirements and, to that extent, provide a more objective basis for selecting and evaluating investment projects.

Discounted Cashflow (DCF)/Time-Adjusted (TA) Techniques

The distinguishing characteristics of the DCF capital budgeting techniques is that they take into consideration the time value of money while evaluating the costs and benefits of a project. In one form or another, all these methods require cash flows to be discounted at a certain rate, that is, the cost of capital. The cost of capital (K) is the minimum discount rate earned on a project that leaves the market value unchanged.

The second commendable feature of these techniques is that they take into account all benefits and costs occurring during the entire life of the project.

In the discussions that follow, we have attempted to discuss the DCF evaluation methods. First, we have explained the general procedure behind DCF. This is followed by a discussion of the first DCF technique, namely, net present value (NPV). We have then covered the internal rate of return (IRR) method. The two variations of the NPV method, that is, terminal value and profitability index (PI) or benefit-cost ratio are also discussed. An attempt has also been made to compare the NPV method with IRR and the PI.

Present Value (PV)/Discounted Cash Flow (DCF)

General Procedure The present value or the discounted cash flow procedure recognises that cash flow streams at different time periods differ in value and can be compared only when they are expressed in terms of a common denominator, that is, present values. It, thus, takes into account the time value of money. In this method, all cash flows are expressed in terms of their present values. The procedure to determine present value is comprehensively covered in Chapter 2.

The present value of the cash flows in Example 9.6 are illustrated in Table 9.11.

TABLE 9.11 Calculations of Present Value of CFAT

	Machine A			*Machine B*		
Year	*CFAT*	*PV factor (0.10)*	*Present value*	*CFAT*	*PV factor (0.10)*	*Present value*
1	2	3	4	5	6	7
1	₹14,000	0.909	₹12,726	₹22,000	0.909	₹19,998
2	16,000	0.826	13,216	20,000	0.826	16,520
3	18,000	0.751	13,518	18,000	0.751	13,518
4	20,000	0.683	14,660	16,000	0.683	10,928
5	25,000*	0.621	15,525	17,000*	0.621	10,557
			69,645			71,521

*includes salvage value.

The PV so determined is compared with the PV of cash outflows. The present values of cash inflows of both the machines are higher than cash outflows, and, therefore both are acceptable.

The PV of CFAT (Col. 4 and Col. 7 of Table 9.11) now can be used to determine the 'discounted' pay back period. It is determined on the basis of discounted present value of CFAT vis-a-vis unadjusted cash flows (Col .2 and Col .5 of Table 9.11) used in the 'simple' pay back method. The relevant values of the 'discounted' pay back period are 4.2 and 3.66 years for Machines A and B respectively in Example 9.6.

Net present value (NPV is found by subtracting a projects initial investment from the present value of its cash inflows discounted at the firm's cost of capital.

Net Present Value (NPV) Method The first DCF/PV technique is the NPV. **NPV** may be described as the summation of the present values of cash proceeds (CFAT) in each year minus the summation of present values of the net cash outflows in each year. Symbolically, the NPV for projects having conventional cash flows would be:

$$NPV = \sum_{t=1}^{n} \frac{CF_t}{(1+K)^t} + \frac{S_n + W_n}{(1+K)^n} - CO_0 \quad \textbf{(9.4)}$$

If cash outflow is also expected to occur at some time other than at initial investment (non-conventional cash flows) the formula would be:

$$NPV = \sum_{t=1}^{n} \frac{CF_t}{(1+K)^t} + \frac{S_n + W_n}{(1+K)^n} - \sum_{t=0}^{n} \frac{CO_t}{(1+K)^t} \quad \textbf{(9.5)}$$

The decision rule for a project under NPV is to accept the project if the NPV is positive and reject if it is negative. Symbolically,

(i) NPV > zero, accept, (ii) NPV < zero, reject **(9.6)**

Zero NPV implies that the firm is indifferent to accepting or rejecting the project. However, in practice it is rare if ever such a project will be accepted, as such a situation simply implies that only the original investment has been recovered[18].

In Example 9.6 we would accept the proposals of purchasing machines A and B as their net present values are positive. The positive NPV of machine A is ₹13,520 (R 69,645 – ₹56,125) and that of B is ₹15,396 (₹71,521 – ₹56,125).

In Example 9.6, if we incorporate cash outflows of ₹25,000 at the end of the third year in respect of overhauling of the machine, we shall find the proposals to purchase either of the machines are unacceptable as their net present values are negative. The negative NPV of machine A is ₹6,255 (₹68,645 – ₹74,900) and of machine B is ₹3,379 (₹71,521 – ₹74,900).

As a decision criterion, this method can also be used to make a choice between mutually exclusive projects. On the basis of the NPV method, the various proposals would be ranked in order of the net present values. The project with the highest NPV would be assigned the first rank, followed by others in the descending order. If, in our example, a choice is to be made between machine A and machine B on the basis of the NPV method, machine B having larger NPV (₹15,396) would be preferred to machine A (NPV being ₹12,520).

Evaluation The present value method including the NPV variation possesses several merits. The first, and probably the most significant, advantage is that it explicitly recognises the time value of money. In Example 9.6, for instance (Table 9.11), the total cash inflows (CFAT) pertaining to the two machines (A and B) are equal. But the present value as well as the NPV is different. As can be seen from Table 9.11, this is primarily because of the differences in the pattern of the cash streams. The magnitude of CFAT in the case of machine A is lower in the earlier years as compared to the machine B while it is greater in the latter years. Because of larger inflows in the first two years, the NPV of machine B is larger than that of machine A. The need for recognising the time value of money is, thus, satisfied by this method.

Secondly, it also fulfills the second attribute of a sound method of appraisal in that it considers the total benefits arising out of the proposal over its lifetime.

Thirdly, a changing discount rate can be built into the NPV calculations by altering the denominator. This feature becomes important as this rate normally changes because the longer the time span, the lower is the value of money and the higher is the discount rate.

Fourthly, this method is particularly useful for the selection of mutually exclusive projects. This aspect will be discussed in detail in the latter part of the chapter, where it is shown that for mutually exclusive choice problems, the NPV method is the best decision-criterion.

Finally, this method of asset selection is instrumental in achieving the objective of financial management which is the maximisation of the shareholders' wealth. The rationale behind this contention is the effect on the market price of shares as a result of the acceptance of a proposal having present value exceeding the initial outlay or, as a variation having NPV greater than zero. The market price of the shares will be affected by the relative force of what the investors expect and what actual return is earned on the funds. The discount rate that is used to convert benefits into present values is the minimum rate or the rate of interest is that when the present values of cash inflows is equal to the initial outlay or when the NPV = 0, the return on investment just equals the expected or required rate by investors. There would, therefore, be no change in the market price of shares. When the present value exceeds the outlay or the NPV > 0, the return would be higher than expected by the investors. It would, therefore, lead to an increase in share prices. The present value method is, thus, logically consistent with the goal of maximising shareholders' wealth in terms of maximising the market price of the shares.

In brief, the present value method is a theoretically correct technique for the selection of investment projects. Nevertheless, it has certain limitations also.

In the first place, it is difficult to calculate as well as understand and use in comparison with the pay back method or even the ARR method. This, of course, is a minor flaw.

The second, and a more serious problem associated with the present value method, involves the calculation of the required rate of return to discount the cash flows. The discount rate is the most important element used in the calculation of the present values because different discount rates will give different present values. The relative desirability of a proposal will change with a change in the discount rate. For instance, for a proposal involving an initial outlay of ₹9,000, having annuity of ₹2,800 for 5 years, the net present values for different required rates of return are given in Table 9.12.

TABLE 9.12 Net Present Value with Different Discount Rates

Discount rate (per cent)	*Net present value*
Zero	₹5,000.00
4	3,465.00
8	2,179.50
10	1,614.00
12	1,093.50
16	168.00
20	(626.50)

The importance of the discount rate is, thus, obvious. But the calculation of the required rate of return presents serious problems. The cost of capital is generally the basis of the discount rate. The calculation of the cost of capital is very complicated. In fact, there is a difference of opinion even regarding the exact method of calculating it.

Another shortcoming of the present value method is that it is an absolute measure. Prima facie between two projects, this method will favour the project which has higher present value (or NPV). But it is likely that this project may also involve a larger initial outlay. Thus, in case of projects involving different outlays, the present value method may not give dependable results.

Finally, the present value method may also not give satisfactory results in the case of two projects having different effective lives. In general, the project with a shorter economic life would be preferable, other things being equal. A project which has a higher present value may also have a larger economic life so that the funds will remain invested for a longer period, while the alternative proposal may have shorter life but smaller present value. In such situations, the present value method may not reflect the true worth of the alternative proposals.

Internal Rate of Return (IRR) Method The second discounted cash flow (DCF) or time-adjusted method for appraising capital investment decisions is the internal rate of return (IRR) method. This technique is also known as yield on investment, marginal efficiency of capital, marginal productivity of capital, rate of return, time-adjusted rate of return and so on. Like the present value method, the IRR method also considers the time value of money by discounting the cash streams. The basis of the discount factor, however, is different in both cases. In the case of the net present value method, the discount rate is the required rate of return and being a predetermined rate, usually the cost of capital, its determinants are external to the proposal under consideration. The IRR, on the other hand, is based on facts which are internal to the proposal. In other words, while arriving at the required rate of return for finding out present values the cash flows—inflows as well as outflows—are not considered. But the IRR depends entirely on the initial outlay and the cash proceeds of the project which is being evaluated for acceptance or rejection. It is, therefore, appropriately referred to as internal rate of return.

Internal rate of return (IRR) is the discount rate that equates the present values of cash inflows with the initial investment associated with a project, thereby causing NPV = 0.

The **internal rate of return** is usually the rate of return that a project earns. It is defined as the discount rate (r) which equates the aggregate present value of the net cash inflows (CFAT) with the aggregate present value of cash outflows of a project. In other words, it is that rate which gives the project NPV of zero.

Assuming conventional cash flows, mathematically, the IRR is represented by the rate, *r*, such that

$$CO_0 = \sum_{t=1}^{n} \frac{CF_t}{(1+r)^t} + \frac{S_n + W_n}{(1+r)^n} \quad \textbf{(9.7)}$$

$$\text{Zero} = \sum_{t=1}^{n} \frac{CF_t}{(1+r)^t} + \frac{S_n + W_n}{(1+r)^n} - CO_0 \quad \textbf{(9.8)}$$

For unconventional cash flows, the equation would be:

$$= \sum_{t=0}^{n} \frac{CF_t}{(1+r)^t} + \frac{S_n + W_n}{(1+r)^n} - \sum_{t=1}^{n} \frac{CO_0}{(1+r)^t} \quad \textbf{(9.9)}$$

$$= \sum_{t=1}^{n} \frac{CF_t}{(1+r)^t} + \frac{S_n + W_n}{(1+r)^n} - \sum_{t=0}^{n} \frac{CO_t}{(1+r)^t} = \text{Zero} \qquad \textbf{(9.10)}$$

where r = The internal rate of return,
CF_t = Cash inflows at different time periods,
S_n = Salvage value,
W_n = Working capital adjustments and
CO_t = Cash outlay at different time periods

Accept-Reject Decision The use of the IRR, as a criterion to accept capital investment decisions, involves a comparison of the actual IRR with the required rate of return also known as the cut-off rate or hurdle rate. The project would qualify to be accepted if the IRR (r) exceeds the cut-off rate (k). If the IRR and the required rate of return are equal, the firm is indifferent as to whether to accept or reject the project.

Computation Unlike the NPV method, calculating the value of IRR is more difficult. The procedure will depend on whether the cash flows are annuity or mixed stream.

Annuities The following steps are taken in determining IRR for an annuity:

- Determine the pay back period of the proposed investment.
- In Table A-4 (present value of an annuity) look for the pay back period that is equal to or closest to the life of the project.
- In the year row, find two PV values or discount factor (DF_r) closest to PB period but one bigger and other smaller than it.
- From the top row of the table, note interest rate (r) corresponding to these PV values (DF_r).
- Determine actual IRR by interpolation. This can be done either directly using Equation 9.11 or indirectly by finding present values of annuity (Equation 9.12).

$$\text{IRR} = r - \left(\frac{\text{PB} - \text{DF}_r}{\text{DF}_{rL} - \text{DF}_{rH}} \right) \qquad \textbf{(9.11)}$$

where PB = Pay back period,
DF_r = Discount factor for interest rate r,
DF_{rL} = Discount factor for lower interest rate,
DF_{rH} = Discount factor for higher interest rate and
r = Either of the two interest rates used in the formula

Alternatively,

$$\text{IRR} = r - \left(\frac{\text{PV}_{\text{CO}} - \text{PV}_{\text{CFAT}}}{\Delta\,\text{PV}} \right) \times \Delta r \qquad \textbf{(9.12)}$$

where PV_{CO} = Present value of cash outlay,
PV_{CFAT} = Present value of cash inflows (DF_r x annuity),
r = Either of the two interest rates used in the formula,
Δr = Difference in interest rates and
ΔPV = Difference in calculated present values of inflows

The computations are shown in Example 9.7.

***Example* 9.7**

A project costs ₹36,000 and is expected to generate cash inflows of ₹11,200 annually for 5 years. Calculate the IRR of the project.

Solution

(1) The pay back period is 3.214 (₹36,000/₹11,200)

(2) According to Table A-4, discount factors closest to 3.214 for 5 years are 3.274 (16 per cent rate of interest) and 3.199 (17 per cent rate of interest). The actual value of IRR which lies between 16 per cent and 17 per cent can, now, be determined using Equations 9.11 and 9.12.

Substituting the values in Equation 9.11 we get: $$\text{IRR} = 16 + \left(\frac{3.274 - 3.214}{3.274 - 3.199}\right) = 16.8 \text{ per cent}$$

Alternatively (starting with the higher rate), $$\text{IRR} = 17 - \left(\frac{3.214 - 3.199}{3.274 - 3.199}\right) = 16.8 \text{ per cent}$$

Instead of using the direct method, we may find the actual IRR by applying the interpolation formula to the present values of cash inflows and outflows (Equation 9.12). Here, again, it is immaterial whether we start with the lower or the higher rate.

$$PV_{CFAT}\ (0.16) = ₹11{,}200 \times 3.274 = ₹36{,}668.8$$
$$PV_{CFAT}\ (0.17) = ₹11{,}200 \times 3.199 = ₹35{,}828.8$$

$$\text{IRR} = 16 + \left(\frac{36{,}668.8 - 36{,}000}{36{,}668.8 - 35{,}828.8}\right) \times 1 = 16.8 \text{ per cent}$$

Alternatively (starting with the higher rate), $$\text{IRR} = r - \frac{(PV_{CO} - PV_{CFAT})}{\Delta PV} \times \Delta r$$

$$\text{IRR} = 17 - \left(\frac{36{,}000 - 35{,}828.8}{840}\right) \times 1 = 16.8 \text{ per cent}$$

For a Mixed Stream of Cash Flows Calculating the IRR for a mixed stream of cash flows is more tedious. In a mixed stream of cash flows, the inflows in various years are uneven or unequal. One way to simplify the process is to use 'fake annuity' as a starting point.[19] The following procedure is a useful guide to calculating IRR:

1. Calculate the average annual cash inflow to get a 'fake annuity'.
2. Determine 'fake pay back period' dividing the initial outlay by the average annual CFAT determined in step 1.
3. Look for the factor, in Table A-4, closest to the fake pay back value in the same manner as in the case of annuity. The result will be a rough approximation of the IRR, based on the assumption that the mixed stream is an annuity (fake annuity).
4. Adjust subjectively the IRR obtained in step 3 by comparing the pattern of average annual cash inflows (as per step 1) to the actual mixed stream of cash flows. If the actual cash flows stream happens to be higher in the initial years of the project's life than the average stream, adjust the IRR a few percentage points upward. The reason is obvious as the greater recovery of funds in the earlier years is likely to give a higher yield rate (IRR). Conversely, if in the early years the actual cash inflows are below the average, adjust the IRR a few percentage

points downward. If the average cash flows pattern seems fairly close to the actual pattern, no adjustment is to be made.

5. Find out the present value (using Table A-3) of the mixed cash flows, taking the IRR as the discount rate as estimated in step 4.
6. Calculate the PV, using the discount rate. If the PV of CFAT equals the initial outlay, that is, NPV is zero, it is the IRR. Otherwise, repeat step 5. Stop, once two consecutive discount rates that cause the NPV to be positive and negative, respectively have been calculated. Whichever of these two rates causes the NPV to be closest to zero is the IRR to the nearest 1 per cent.
7. The actual value can be ascertained by the method of interpolation as in the case of an annuity.

***Example* 9.8**

Let us apply this procedure for determining the IRR of Example 9.6 of a mixed stream of CFAT for machines A and B. The cash flows associated with the machines are given in Table 9.7.

Solution

1. The sum of cash inflows of both the machines is ₹93,000 which when divided by the economic life of the machine (5 years), results in a 'fake annuity' of ₹18,600.
2. Dividing the initial outlay of ₹56,125 by ₹18,600, we have 'fake average pay back period' of 3.017 years.
3. In Table A-4, the factor closest to 3.017 for 5 years is 2.991 for a rate of 20 per cent.
4. Since the actual cash flows in the earlier years are greater than the average cash flows of ₹18,600 in machine B, a subjective increase of, say, 1 per cent is made. This makes an estimated rate of IRR 21 per cent for machine B. In the case of machine A, since cash inflows in the initial years are smaller than the average cash flows, a subjective decrease of, say, 2 per cent is made. This makes the estimated IRR rate 18 per cent for machine A.
5. Using the PV factors for 21 per cent (Machine B) and 18 per cent (Machine A) from Table A-3 for years 1-5, the PVs are calculated in Table 9.13.

TABLE 9.13 Computation of Present Value (PV)

Year	Machine A			Machine B		
	CFAT	PV factor (0.18)	Total PV	CFAT	PV factor (0.21)	Total PV
1	₹14,000	0.847	₹11,858	₹22,000	0.826	₹18,172
2	16,000	0.718	11,488	20,000	0.683	13,660
3	18,000	0.609	10,962	18,000	0.564	10,152
4	20,000	0.516	10,320	16,000	0.467	7,472
5	25,000	0.437	10,925	17,000	0.386	6,562
Total present value			55,553			56,018
Less: Initial investment		56,125			56,125	
NPV			(572)			(107)

6. Since the NPV is negative for both the machines, the discount rate should be subsequently lowered. In the case of machine A the difference is of ₹572 whereas in machine B the difference is ₹107. Therefore, in the former case the discount rate is lowered by 1 per cent in both the cases. As a result, the new discount rate would be 17 per cent for A and 20 per cent for B.

The calculations given in Table 9.14 shows that the NPV at discount rate of 17 per cent is ₹853 (machine A) and ₹1,049 for machine B at 20 per cent discount.

TABLE 9.14 Computation of Present Value (PV)

Year	Machine A			Machine B		
	CFAT	PV factor (0.17)	Total PV	CFAT	PV factor (0.20)	Total PV
1	₹14,000	0.855	₹11,970	₹22,000	0.833	₹18,326
2	16,000	0.731	11,696	20,000	0.694	13,880
3	18,000	0.624	10,232	18,000	0.579	10,422
4	20,000	0.534	10,680	16,000	0.484	7,712
5	25,000	0.456	11,400	17,000	0.442	6,834
PV of cash inflows			56,978			57,174
Less: Initial outlay			56,125			56,125
Net present value			853			1,049

(a) For machine A: Since 17 per cent and 18 per cent are consecutive discount rates that give positive and negative net present values, interpolation method can be applied to find the actual IRR which will be between 17 and 18 per cent.

$$\text{IRR} = 17 + \left[\frac{₹56{,}978 - ₹56{,}125}{₹56{,}978 - ₹55{,}553}\right] \times 1 = 17.6 \text{ per cent}$$

(b) For machine B: $\text{IRR} = 20 + \left[\frac{₹57{,}174 - ₹56\ 125}{₹57{,}174 - ₹56{,}018}\right] \times 1 = 20.9 \text{ per cent}$

Evaluation of IRR The IRR method is a theoretically correct technique to evaluate capital expenditure decisions. It has the advantages which are offered by the NPV criterion such as: (i) it considers the time value of money, and (ii) it takes into account the total cash inflows and outflows.

In addition, the IRR is easier to understand. Business executives and non-technical people understand the concept of IRR much more readily than they understand the concept of NPV. They may not be following the definition of IRR in terms of the equation but they are well aware of its usual meaning in terms of the rate of return on investment. For instance, business executives will understand the investment proposal in a better way if told that IRR of machine B is 21 per cent and k is 10 per cent instead of saying that the NPV of machine B is ₹15,396.

Another merit of IRR is that it does not use the concept of the required rate of return/the cost of capital. It itself provides a rate of return which is indicative of the profitability of the proposal. The cost of capital, of course, enters the calculations later on.

Finally, it is consistent with the overall objective of maximising shareholders' wealth. According to IRR, as a decision-criterion, the acceptance or otherwise of a project is based on a comparison of the IRR with the required rate of return. The required rate of return is, by definition, the minimum rate which investors expect on their investment. In other words, if the actual IRR of an investment proposal is equal to the rate expected by the investors, the share prices will remain unchanged. Since, with IRR, only such projects are accepted as have IRR > required rate, the share prices will tend to rise. This will naturally lead to the maximisation of shareholders' wealth.

Its theoretical soundness notwithstanding, the IRR suffers from serious limitations.

First, it involves tedious calculations. As shown above, it generally involves complicated computational problems. Secondly, it produces multiple rates which can be confusing. This aspect is further developed later in this chapter. Thirdly, in evaluating mutually exclusive proposals, the project with the highest IRR would be picked up to the exclusion of all others. However, in practice, it may not turn out to be the one which is the most profitable and consistent with the objectives of the firm, that is, maximisation of the shareholders' wealth. This aspect also has been discussed in detail later in this chapter. Finally, under the IRR method, it is assumed that all intermediate cash flows are reinvested at the IRR. In our example, the IRR rates for machines A and B are 17.6 per cent and 20.9 per cent respectively. In operational terms, 17.6 per cent IRR signifies that all cash inflows of machine A can be reinvested at 17.6 per cent whereas that of B at 20.9 per cent. It is rather ridiculous to think that the same firm has the ability to reinvest the cash flows at different rates.

There is no difference in the 'quality of cash' received either from project A or B. The reinvestment rate assumption under the IRR method is, therefore, very unrealistic. Moreover, it is not safe to assume always that intermediate cash flows from the project will be reinvested at all. A portion of cash inflows may be paid out as dividends. Likewise, a portion of it may be tied up in current assets such as stocks, debtors or cash. Clearly, the firm will get a wrong picture of the capital project if it assumes that it invests the entire intermediate cash proceeds. Further, it is not safe to assume, as is often done, that they will be reinvested at the same rate of return as the company is currently earning on its capital (IRR) or at the current cost of capital, k. In order to have correct and reliable results it is obvious, therefore, that they should be based on realistic estimates of the interest rate (if any) at which income will be reinvested. Terminal value takes care of this aspect.

Terminal Value Method The terminal value approach (TV) even more distinctly separates the timing of the cash inflows and outflows. The assumption behind the TV approach is that each cash inflow is reinvested in another asset at a certain rate of return from the moment it is received until the termination of the project. Consider Example 9.9.

***Example* 9.9**

Original outlay, ₹10,000; Life of the project, 5 years; Cash inflows, ₹4,000 each for 5 years; and Cost of capital (*k*), 10 per cent.

Expected interest rates at which cash inflows will be reinvested:

Year-end	*Per cent*
1	6
2	6
3	8
4	8
5	8

Solution

We would reinvest ₹4,000 received at the end of the year 1 for 4 years at the rate of 6 per cent. The cash inflows in year 2 will be re-invested for 3 years at 6 per cent, the cash inflows of year 3 for 2 years and so on.

There will be no reinvestment of cash inflows received at the end of the fifth year. The total sum of these compounded cash inflows is then discounted back for 5 years at 10 per cent and compared with the present value of the cash outlays, that is, ₹10,000 (in this case).

The PV of the terminal sum is given in Table 9.15.

TABLE 9.15 Computation of Terminal Value

Year	*Cash inflows*	*Rate of interest*	*Years for investment*	*Compounding factor*	*Total compounded sum*
1	*2*	*3*	*4*	*5*	*6*
1	₹4,000	6	4	1.262	₹5,048
2	4,000	6	3	1.191	4,764
3	4,000	8	2	1.166	4,664
4	4,000	8	1	1.080	4,320
5	4,000	8	0	1.000	4,000
					22,796

Now, we have to find out the present value of ₹22,796. The discount rate would be the cost of capital, k (0.10). The sum of ₹22,796 would be received at the end of year 5. Its present value = ₹22,796 × 0.621 = ₹14,156.3.

Accept-reject Rule The decision rule is that if the present value of the sum total of the compounded reinvested cash inflows (PVTS) is greater than the present value of the outflows (PVO), the proposed project is accepted otherwise not. Symbolically,

$$\begin{aligned} &PVTS > PVO \text{ accept} \\ &PVTS < PVO \text{ reject} \end{aligned} \quad \textbf{(9.13)}$$

The firm would be indifferent if both the values are equal. Thus, since the PVTS of ₹14,156.31 exceeds the original outlay of ₹10,000, we would accept the assumed project under the TV criterion.

A variation of the terminal value method (TV) is the net terminal value (NTV). Symbolically it can be represented as NTV = (PVTS – PVO). If the NTV is positive, accept the project, if the NTV is negative, reject the project. In the above example, the NTV is positive. Its value is ₹4,156.31. Therefore, the project is acceptable.

The NTV method is similar to NPV method, with the difference that while in the former, values are compounded, in the latter, they are discounted. Both the methods will give the same results provided of course the same figures have been discounted as have been compounded and the same interest rate (rates) is used for both discounting and compounding.

Evaluation The NTV (or TV) method has a number of advantages.

Firstly, these methods explicitly incorporate the assumption about how the cash inflows are reinvested once they are received and avoid any influence of the cost of capital on the cash inflow stream itself. Secondly, it is mathematically easier, making simple the process of evaluating the investment worth of alternative capital projects. Thirdly, this method would be easier to understand for business executives who are not trained in accountancy or economics than NPV for IRR, as the 'compounding technique', appeals more than 'discounting'. Fourthly, it is better suited to cash budgeting requirements. The NPV computation in spite of being a cash flow approach does not explicitly show all the cash inflows. It does not take into account cash inflows in respect of interest earnings.

The major practical problem of this method lies in projecting the future rates of interest at which the intermediate cash inflows received will be reinvested.

Profitability Index (PI) or Benefit-Cost Ratio (B/C Ratio) Yet another time-adjusted capital budgeting technique is profitability index/present value index (PI) or benefit-cost ratio (B/C). It is similar to the NPV approach. The **profitability index** approach measures the present value of returns per rupee invested, while the NPV is based on the difference between the present value of future cash inflows and the present value of cash outlays. A major shortcoming of the NPV method is that, being an absolute measure, it is not a reliable method to evaluate projects requiring different initial investments. The PI method provides a solution to this kind of problem. It is, in other words, a relative measure. It may be defined as the ratio which is obtained dividing the present value of future cash inflows by the present value of cash outlays. Symbolically,

> **Profitability index** measures the present value of returns per rupee invested.

$$PI = \frac{\text{Present value cash inflows}}{\text{Present value of cash outflows}} \quad \textbf{(9.14)}$$

This method is also known as the B/C ratio because the numerator measures benefits and the denominator costs. A more appropriate description would be present value index.

Accept-Reject Rule Using the B/C ratio or the PI, a project will qualify for acceptance if its PI exceeds one. When PI equals 1, the firm is indifferent to the project.

When PI is greater than, equal to or less than 1, the net present value is greater than, equal to or less than zero respectively. In other words, the NPV will be positive when the PI is greater than 1; will be negative when the PI is less than one. Thus, the NPV and PI approaches give the same results regarding the investment proposals.

The selection of projects with the PI method can also be done on the basis of ranking. The highest rank will be given to the project with the highest PI, followed by others in the same order.

In Example 9.6 (Table 9.15) of machine A and B, the PI would be 1.22 for machine A and 1.27 for machine B:

PI (Machine A) = ₹68,645/₹56,125) = 1.22

PI (Machine B) = (₹71,521/₹56125) = 1.27

Since the PI for both the machines is greater than 1, both the machines are acceptable.

Though it is common to define PI as the ratio of the PV of the cash inflows divided by the PV of cash outflows, the PI may also be measured on the basis of the net benefits of a project against its current cash outlay rather than measure its gross benefits against its total cost over the life of the project. This aspect becomes very important in situations of capital rationing.[19] In such a situation, the decision rule would be to accept the project if the PI is positive and reject the project it it is negative.

Evaluation Like the other discounted cash flow techniques, the PI satisfies almost all the requirements of a sound investment criterion. It considers all the elements of capital budgeting, such as the time value of money, totality of benefits and so on. Conceptually, it is a sound method of capital budgeting. Although based on the NPV, it is a better evaluation technique than NPV in a situation of capital rationing. For instance, two projects may have the same NPV of ₹10,000 but project A requires an initial investment of ₹50,000 whereas B only of ₹25,000. Project B should be preferred as will be suggested by the PI method. The NPV method, however, will give identical rankings of both the projects. Thus, the PI method is superior to the NPV method as the former evaluates the worth of projects in terms of their relative rather than absolute magnitudes. However, in some problems of a mutually exclusive nature, the NPV method would be superior to the PI method. The comparison of PI and NPV is further explored in Chapter 10.

This method is, however, more difficult to understand. Also, it involves more computation than the traditional methods but less than IRR.

LO 9.4 CAPITAL BUDGETING PRACTICES IN INDIA

The capital budgeting practices by corporate enterprises in India are summarised below.

- The discounted cash flow (DCF) tools/techniques/methodology are more popular now.
- The corporates firms use multiple criteria in their projected selection decisions. Vast majority of the sample corporates use a combination of traditional as well as DCF techniques.
- The IRR is the most frequently used (85 per cent) capital budgeting technique.
- The NPV technique is also used widely (65 per cent). The IRR method is preferred over the NPV method.
- The pay back period is equally popular method of project selection (68 per cent)
- Large firms more frequently use NPV while pay back period is more widely used by small firms. Similarly, high growth firms use IRR more frequently than small firms.
- PI technique is used more by public sector units than private sector firms.
- The survey (2011–2012) reveals that paucity of funds is not a major hurdle for exploring profitable capital budgeting decisions for a large majority of the sample companies.

- Capital budgeting decisions are undertaken at the top management level/central (Head) office and are planned in advance. The corporates follow mostly top-down approach in this regard.
- However, in several corporates (two-third of the sample corporates) investment proposals originate at plant/divisional levels as well.
- Highly competitive and volatile conditions seem to have restricted the planning horizon to the next five years only.
- The corporates are not guided by ad-hoc approach and they follow systematic approach to capital budgeting.
- Very high fixed-cost components of capital projects and the irregularities in prediction of future cash flows due to increased competition seem to be the major factors leading to failures of capital budgeting decisions for the sample companies.

Source: (i) Anand, Manoj, "Corporate Finance Practices in India: A Survey", *Vikalpa*, Vol. 27, No. 4, Oct-Dec. 2002, pps 29-56, (ii) Jain, P.K. and Surendra S. Yadav, "Financial Management Practices in India, Singapore and Thailand—A Comparison". *Management & Accounting Research*, Vol. 3, No. 4, April-June 2002, pp 55-103 and (iii) Singh, S., P. K. Jain and Surendra S. Yadav, "Capital Budgeting Decisions: Evidence from India" *Journal of Advances in Management Research*, Vol. 9, No. 1, 2012, pp 96-112.

SUMMARY

LO 9.1

Capital budgeting decisions relate to long-term assets which are in operation and yield a return over a period of time. They, therefore. involve current outlays in return for series of anticipated flow of future benefits.

Such decisions are of paramount importance as they affect the profitability of a firm, and are the major determinants of its efficiency and competing power. While an opportune investment decision can yield spectacular returns, an ill-advised/incorrect decision can endanger the very survival of a firm. A few wrong decisions and the firm may be forced into bankruptcy.

Capital expenditure decisions are beset with a number of difficulties. The two major difficulties are: (i) The benefits from long-term investments are received in some future period which is uncertain. Therefore, an element of risk is involved in forecasting future sales revenues as well as the associated costs of production and sales; (ii) It is not often possible to calculate in strict quantitative terms all the benefits or the costs relating to a specific investment decision.

Such decisions are of two types, namely, revenue expanding investment decisions and cost reducing investment decisions. The latter types of decisions are subject to less risk as the potential cash saving can be estimated better from the past production and cost data. It is more difficult to estimate revenues and costs of a new product line.

The capital outlays and revenue benefits associated with such decisions are measured in terms of cash flows after taxes. The cash flow approach for measuring benefits is theoretically superior to the accounting profit approach as it (i) avoids the ambiguities of the accounting profits concept, (ii) measures the total benefits and (iii) takes into account the time value of money.

The major difference between the cash flow and the accounting profit approaches relates to the treatment of depreciation. While the accounting approach considers depreciation in cost computation, it is recognised, on the contrary, as a source of cash to the extent of tax advantage in the cash flow approach.

For taxation purposes, depreciation is charged (on the basis of written down value method) on a block of assets and not on an individual asset. A block of assets is a group of assets (say, of plant and machinery) in respect of which the same rate of depreciation is prescribed by the Income-Tax Act. Depreciation is charged on the year-end balance of the block which is equal to the opening balance plus purchases made during the year (in the block considered) minus sale proceeds of the assets during the year.

LO 9.1

In case the entire block of assets is sold during the year (the block ceases to exist at year-end), no depreciation is charged at the year-end. If the sale proceeds of the block sold is higher than the opening balance, the difference represents short-term capital gain which is subject to tax. Where the sale proceeds are less than the opening balance, the firm is entitled to tax shield on short-term capital loss. The adjustment related to the payment of taxes/tax shield is made in terminal cash inflows of the project.

LO 9.2

The data requirement for capital budgeting are after tax cash outflows and cash inflows. Besides, they should be incremental in that they are directly attributable to the proposed investment project. The existing fixed costs, therefore, are ignored. In brief, incremental after-tax cash flows are the only relevant cash flows in the analysis of new investment projects.

The investment in new capital projects can be categorised into (i) a single proposal, (ii) a re-placement proposal and (iii) mutually exclusive proposals.

In the case of single/independent investment proposal, cash outflows primarily consist of (i) purchase cost of the new plant and machinery, (ii) its installation costs and (iii) working capital requirement to support production and sales (in the case of revenue expanding proposals/release of working capital in cost reduction proposals.

The cash inflows after taxes (CFAT) are computed by adding depreciation (D) to the projected earnings after taxes (EAT) from the proposal. In the terminal year of the project, apart from operating CFAT, the cash inflows include salvage value (if any, net of removal costs), recovery of working capital and tax advantage\taxes paid on short-term capital loss\gain on sale of machine (if the block ceases to exist).

In the case of replacement situation, the sale proceeds from the existing machine reduce the cash outflows required to purchase the new machine. The relevant CFAT are *incremental* after-tax cash inflows.

In the case of mutually exclusive proposals, the selection of one proposal precludes the selection of the other(s). The computation of the cash outflows and cash inflows are on lines similar to the replacement situation.

LO 9.3

The capital budgeting evaluation techniques are: (i) traditional, comprising (a) average/accounting rate of return (ARR) and (b) pay back (PB) period; (ii) discounted cash flow (DCF), primarily consisting of (a) net present value (NPV), (b) internal rate of return (IRR) and (iii) profitability/present value index (PI).

The ARR is obtained dividing annual average profits after taxes by average investments. Average investment = 1/2 (Initial cost of machine – Salvage value) + Salvage value + net working capital. Annual average profits after taxes = Total expected after tax profits/Number of years

The ARR is unsatisfactory method as it is based on accounting profits and ignores time value of money.

The pay back method measures the number of years required for the CFAT to pay back the initial capital investment outlay, ignoring interest payment. It is determined as follows:

(i) In the case of annuity CFAT: Initial investment/Annual CFAT.

(ii) In the case of mixed CFAT: It is obtained by cumulating CFAT till the cumulative CFAT equal the initial investment.

Although the pay back method is superior to the ARR method in that it is based on cash flows, it also ignores time value of money and disregards the total benefits associated with the investment proposal.

The DCF methods satisfy all the attributes of a good measure of appraisal as they consider the total benefits (CFAT) as well as the timing of benefits.

LO 9.3

The NPV may be described as the summation of the present values of (i) operating CFAT (CF) in each year and (ii) salvages value(S) and working capital(W) in the terminal year(n) minus the summation of present values of the cash outflows(CO) in each year. The present value is computed using cost of capital (k) as a discount rate. Symbolically,

$$\text{NPV} = \sum_{t=1}^{n} \frac{CF_t}{(1+k)^t} + \frac{S_n + W_n}{(1+k)^n} - \sum_{t=0}^{n} \frac{CO_t}{(1+k)^t}$$

The project will be accepted in case the NPV is positive.

The IRR is defined as the discount rate (r) which equates the aggregate present value of the operating CFTA received each year and terminal cash flows (working capital recovery and salvage value) with aggregate present value of cash outflows of an investment proposal. Symbolically,

$$\text{IRR} = \sum_{t=1}^{n} \frac{CF_t}{(1+r)^t} + \frac{S_n + W_n}{(1+r)^n} - \sum_{t=1}^{n} \frac{CO_t}{(1+r)^t}$$

The project will be accepted when IRR exceeds the required rate of return.

The profitability index/present value index measures the present value of returns per rupee invested. It is obtained dividing the present value of future cash inflows (bot operating CFAT and terminal) by the present value of capital cash outflows. The proposal will be worth accepting if the PI exceeds one.

REFERENCES

1. Quirin, G D, The Capital Expenditure Decision, Richard D. Irwin, Homewood Ill., 1967, p 2.
2. Osteryoung, J, *Capital Budgeting: Long-term Asset Selection*, Grid, Columbus, Ohio, 1992, p 4.
3. Bierman, H., and S. Smidt, *The Capital Budgeting Decision*, Macmillan, New York, 1974, p 4. Reprinted by permission from Macmillan Publishing Co. Inc. New York, USA.
4. Gitman, Lawrence, J, *Principles of Managerial Finance*, Harper and Row, New York, 1997, p 239.
5. Joy, O M, *Introduction to Financial Management*, Richard Irwin, Homewood, Ill, 1991, p 126.
6. Solomn, Ezra and J J Pringle. *An Introduction to Financial Management,* Goodyear Publishing Company, Santa Monica Calif. 1977, p 282.
7. Ross, S.A. *et al*., *Fundamentals of Corporate Finance*, Tata McGraw-Hill, Now Delhi, 2008, p. 303.
8. For further details, refer to Solomon, and J J Pringle, *op cit*., pp 282-92.
9. Ross, Stephen A. *et al*., *Fundamental of Corporate Finance*, Tata McGraw-Hill, New Delhi, 2008, p.308.
10. Gitman, L J, *Principles of Managerial Finance*, Pearson, New York, 2006, p.396.
11. Gitman, L J, *Ibid*, p.396.
12. Gitman, L J, *op cit*., 1997, p 287.
13. Osteryoung, *op cit*., p 55.
14. Ross, Stephen A. *et al*., *op. cit*, pp.273-74.
15. Bolten, S E, *Managerial Finance-Principles and Practices*, Houghton Mifflin Company, Boston, 1976, p 162.
16. Weingartner, H M, 'Some new views on the pay back period and capital budgeting decisions', *Management Science*, August 1969, pp 594-607.
17. Gitman, L.J., *op. cit*, 2006, p.421.
18. It may be noted that (i) NPV value is based on the assumption that cash inflows (CFAT) accrue at year end. However, in practice, CFAT accrue through out the period. Therefore, the actual NPV is likely to be higher than the estimated value. It also implies that determination of NPV is conservative in nature. (ii) As a corollary of (i) at implies that the project may be worth accepting even at zero NPV.
19. Gitman, L J, *op cit*., 1997, pp 295-96.
20. Osteryoung, J S, *op cit*., p 114.

SOLVED PROBLEMS

P.9.1 A company is considering an investment proposal to instal new milling controls at a cost of ₹50,000. The facility has a life expectancy of 5 years and no salvage value. The tax rate is 35 per cent. Assume the firm uses straight line depreciation and the same is allowed for tax purposes. The estimated cash flows before depreciation and tax (CFBT) from the investment proposal are as follows:

LO 9.3 LOD E

Year	CFBT
1	₹10,000
2	10,692
3	12,769
4	13,462
5	20,385

Compute the following:

(i) Pay back period, (ii) Average rate of return, (iii) Internal rate of return, (iv) Net present value at 10 per cent discount rate, (v) Profitability index at 10 per cent discount rate.

Solution

Determination of cashflows after taxes (CFAT)

Year	*CFBT*	*Depreciation (₹50,000/5)*	*Profits before tax (Col.2 – Col.3)*	*Taxes (0.35)*	*EAT (Col.4 – Col.5)*	*CFAT (Col.6+Col.3)*
1	*2*	*3*	*4*	*5*	*6*	*7*
1	₹10,000	₹10,000	Nil	Nil	Nil	₹10,000
2	10,692	10,000	₹692	₹242	₹450	10,450
3	12,769	10,000	2,769	969	1,800	11,800
4	13,462	10,000	3,462	1,212	2,250	12,250
5	20,385	10,000	10,385	3,635	6,750	16,750
					11,250	61,250

(i) Pay back (PB) period

Year	*CFAT*	*Cumulative CFAT*
1	₹10,000	₹10,000
2	10,450	20,450
3	11,800	32,250
4	12,250	44,500
5	16,750	61,250

The recovery of the investment falls between the fourth and fifth years. Therefore, the PB is 4 years plus a fraction of the fifth year. The fractional value = ₹5,500 ÷ ₹16,750 = 0.328. Thus, the PB is 4.328 years.

(ii) Average rate of return (ARR) $= \dfrac{\text{Average income}}{\text{Average investment}} \times 100 = \dfrac{₹2,250\ (₹11,250 \div 5)}{₹25,000\ (₹50,000 \div 2)} \times 100 = 9$ per cent

(iii) Internal rate of return (IRR) $₹50,000 = \dfrac{₹10,000}{(1+r)^1} + \dfrac{₹10,450}{(1+r)^2} + \dfrac{₹11,800}{(1+r)^3} + \dfrac{₹12,250}{(1+r)^4} + \dfrac{₹16,750}{(1+r)^5}$

The fake pay back period = 4.0816 (₹50,000/₹12,250). From Table A-4, the value closest to the fake pay back period of 4.0816 against 5 years is 4.100 against 7 per cent. Since the actual cash flow stream is the initial years is slightly below the average cash flow stream, the IRR is likely to be lower than 7 per cent. Let us try with 6 per cent.

Year	CFAT	PV factor (0.06)	PV factor (0.07)	Total PV (0.06)	Total PV (0.07)
1	₹10,000	0.943	0.935	₹9,430	₹9,350
2	10,450	0.890	0.873	9,300	9,123
3	11,800	0.840	0.816	9,912	9,629
4	12,250	0.792	0.763	9,702	9,347
5	16,750	0.747	0.713	12,512	11,942
Total PV				50,856	49,391
Less: Initial outlay				50,000	50,000
NPV				856	(609)

The IRR is between 6 and 7 per cent. By interpolation, IRR = 6.6 per cent.

(iv) Net present value (NPV)

Year	CFAT	PV factor (0.10)	Total PV
1	₹10,000	0.909	₹9,090
2	10,450	0.826	8,632
3	11,800	0.751	8,862
4	12,250	0.683	8,367
5	16,750	0.621	10,401
Total PV			45,352
Less: Initial outlay			50,000
NPV			(4,648)

(v) Profitability index (PI) $\text{PI} = \dfrac{\text{PV of cash inflows}}{\text{PV of cash outflows}} = \dfrac{₹45,352}{₹50,000} = 0.907$

P.9.2 A project costing ₹5,60,000 is expected to produce annual net cash benefits (CFAT) of ₹80,000 over a period of 15 years. Estimate the internal rate of return (IRR). Also, find the pay back period and obtain the IRR from it. How do you compare this IRR with the one directly estimated? **LO 9.3** LOD **E**

Solution PB value $= \dfrac{₹5,60,000}{₹80,000} = 7.000$

The factors closet to 7.000 are 7.191 at 11 per cent rate of discount and 6.811 at 12 per cent rate of discount against 15 years (Table A-4). The actual IRR would be between 11 and 12 per cent.

Using interpolation, the IRR would be 0.11 + 0.005 (0.19 ÷ 0.38) = 11.5 per cent.

IRR determination through PB period: The reciprocal of the PB period is a good approximation of the IRR if, (i) the life of the project is at least twice the PB period, and (ii) the project generates annuity cash inflows. Accordingly, IRR would be the reciprocal of the PB period, i.e. 1/7 = 0.1428 = 14.28 per cent.

Comparison: The two IRRs are different. But the IRR which is directly estimated is correct as at this rate of discount, NPV of cash flow stream of the project would be zero. The NPV cannot be zero at 14.28 per cent. The IRR through the PB period is only an approximate measure.

P.9.3 Modern Enterprises Ltd is considering the purchase of a new computer system for its research and development division, which would cost ₹35 lakh. The operation and maintenance costs (excluding depreciation) are expected to be ₹7 lakh per annum. It is estimated that the useful life of the system would be 6 years, at the end of which the disposal value is expected to be ₹1 lakh. **LO 9.3** LOD **M**

The tangible benefits expected from the system in the form of reduction in design and draftmanship costs would be ₹12 lakh per annum. The disposal of used drawing office equipment and furniture initially is anticipated to net ₹9 lakh.

As capital expenditure in research and development, the proposal would attract a 100 per cent write-off for tax purposes. The gains arising from disposal of used assets may be considered tax free. The effective tax rate is 35 per cent. The average cost of capital of the company is 12 per cent.

After appropriate analysis of cash flows, advise the company of the financial viability of the proposal. Ignore tax on salvage value.

Solution

Assessment of financial viability of proposal *(Amount in lakh of rupees)*

Incremental cash outflows	
Cost of new computer system	35
Less: Sale proceeds from drawing office equipment and furniture	9
	26
Incremental CFAT and NPV:	
(a) Cost savings (years 1–6)	
Reduction in design and draftmanship costs	12
Less: Operation and maintenance costs	7
Cost savings (earnings) before taxes	5
Less: Taxes (0.35)	1.75
Earnings after taxes (CFAT)	3.25
(×) PV factor of annuity for 6 years (0.12)	× 4.111
Total PV of cost savings	13.36
(b) Tax savings on account of depreciation	
Cost of new computer system (₹35 lakhs × 0.35)	12.25
(×) PV factor for year 1	× 0.892
Total PV	9.93
(c) Terminal salvage value at the end of year, 6 (₹1 lakh × 0.507)	0.507
(d) Gross PV of CFAT [(a) + (b) + (c)]	24.797
Less: Cash outflows	26.000
NPV	(1.203)

Recommendation Since NPV is negative, the proposal is not financially viable.

P.9.4 SCL Limited is engaged in the manufacture of power intensive products. As part of its diversification plans, the company proposes to put up a windmill to generate electricity. The details of the scheme are as follows: **LO 9.3** LOD M

1. Cost of the windmill, ₹300 lakhs
2. Cost of land, ₹15 lakhs
3. Subsidy from state government to be received at the end of first year of installation, ₹15 lakh.
4. Cost of electricity will be ₹2.25 per unit in year 1. This will increase by ₹0.25 per unit every year till year 7. After that, it will increase every year by ₹0.50 per year till year 10.
5. Maintenance cost will be ₹4 lakh in year 1 and the same will increase by ₹2 lakh every year.
6. Estimated life, 10 years.
7. Cost of capital, 15 per cent.
8. Residual value, nil. However, land value will go up to ₹60 lakh, at the end of year 10.
9. Depreciation will be 100 per cent of the cost of the windmill in year 1 and the same will be allowed for tax purposes.

10. As windmills are expected to work based on wind velocity, the efficiency is expected to be on an average 30 per cent. Gross electricity generated at this level will be 25 lakh units per annum; 4 per cent of which will be committed to the state electricity board as per the agreement.
11. Tax rate, 35 per cent.

From the above information, you are required to calculate the net present value. Ignore tax on capital profits. Use present value up to two digits.

Solution

Determination of NPV of windmill

(Amount in lakh of rupees)

Incremental cash outflows	
Cost of land	15
Cost of the windmill	300
Less: Subsidy from state government (₹15 lakh × 0.87)	13
	302

Incremental CFAT and NPV

Year	Gross savings on 24 lakh units	Maintenance costs	Net savings	Taxes	CFAT	PVF (0.15)	Total PV
1	54	4	50	(87.5)*	137.5	0.87	119.62
2	60	6	54	18.9	35.1	0.76	26.68
3	66	8	58	20.3	37.7	0.66	24.88
4	72	10	62	21.7	40.3	0.57	22.97
5	78	12	66	23.1	42.9	0.50	21.45
6	84	14	70	24.5	45.5	0.43	19.56
7	90	16	74	25.9	48.1	0.38	18.28
8	102	18	84	29.4	54.6	0.33	18.02
9	114	20	94	32.9	61.1	0.28	17.11
10	126	22	104	36.4	67.6	0.25	16.90
10	Land				60.0	0.25	15.00
Total present value							320.47
Less: Incremental cash outflows							302.00
NPV							18.47

*Assuming taxable income from other sources, there will be tax savings of ₹87.5 lakhs on negative EAT of ₹250 lakh (₹300 lakhs, depreciation – ₹50 lakh, net savings).

P.9.5 Techtronics Ltd is considering a new project for manufacture of pocket video games involving a capital expenditure of ₹600 lakh and working capital of ₹150 lakh. The capacity of the plant is for an annual production of 12 lakh units and capacity utilisation during the 6 year working life of the project is expected to be as indicated below:

LO 9.3 LOD M

Year	Capacity utilisation (per cent)
1	33.33
2	66.67
3	90
4-6	100

The average price per unit of the product is expected to be ₹200 netting a contribution of 40 per cent. The annual fixed costs, excluding depreciation, are estimated to be ₹480 lakh per annum from the third year onwards; for the first and second year, it would be ₹240 lakh and ₹360 lakh respectively. The average rate of depreciation for tax purposes is 33.33 per cent on the capital assets. The rate of income tax may be taken at 35 per cent. Cost of capital is 15 per cent.

At the end of the third year, an additional investment of ₹100 lakh would be required for working capital.

Terminal value for the fixed assets may be taken at 10 per cent and for the current assets at 100 per cent. For the purpose of your calculations, the recent amendments to tax laws with regard to balancing charge may be ignored.

Solution

Cash outflows	*(Amount in lakh of rupees)*
Cost of capital expenditure	600.00
Add: Working capital required:	
At the beginning of the project life	150.00
At the end of year 3, (₹100 × 0.658)	65.80
	815.80 = 816

Cash inflows (CFAT) and NPV

Particulars	*Year*						
	1	*2*	*3*	*4*	*5*	*6*	
Sales revenue	800	1,600	2,160	2,400	2,400	2,400	
Less: Variable costs	480	960	1,296	1,440	1,440	1,440	
Less: Fixed costs	240	360	480	480	480	480	
Less: Depreciation (D) (working note 1)	200	133	89	59	40	26	
Earnings before taxes	(120)	147	295	421	440	454	
Less: Taxes (0.35)	(42)	51	103	147	154	159	
EAT	(78)	96	192	274	286	295	
CFAT (EAT + D)	122@	229	281	333	326	321	
Add: Recovery of working capital						250	
Add: Effective sale proceeds of fixed assets (*working note 2*)						58	
						629	
Multiplied by PV factor	0.87	0.756	0.657	0.571	0.497	0.432	
Total PV (t = 1 – 6)	106	173	185	190	162	272	1,089
Less: PV of outflows							816
NPV							273

Recommendation Since the NPV is positive, the project should be accepted.

@ There will be tax savings of ₹42 lakh on the loss of ₹120 lakh. Therefore CFAT would be = ₹80 Lakh + ₹42 lakh = ₹122 lakh.

Working Notes

(1) Determination of depreciation as per written down value method

Year	*Cost/Written down value (₹lakh)*	*Depreciation (₹lakh)*
1	600	200
2	400	133
3	267	89
4	178	59
5	119	40
6	79	26

(2) Sales proceeds of fixed assets	60
Less: Written down value (₹79 – ₹26)	53
Profit on sale of fixed assets	7
Less: Taxes on profit (7 × 0.35)	2.45
Effective sale proceeds (60 – 2.45)	57.55

P.9.6 A plastic manufacturer has under consideration the proposal of production of high quality plastic glasses. The necessary equipment to manufacture the glasses would cost ₹1 lakh and would last 5 years. The tax relevant rate of depreciation is 20 per cent on written down value. There is no other asset in this block. The expected salvage value is ₹10,000. The glasses can be sold at ₹4 each. Regardless of the level of production, the manufacturer will incur cash cost of ₹25,000 each year if the project is undertaken. The overhead costs allocated to this new line would be ₹5,000. The variable costs are estimated at ₹2 per glass. The manufacturer estimates it will sell about 75,000 glasses per year; the tax rate is 35 per cent. Should the proposed equipment be purchased? Assume 20 per cent cost of capital and additional working requirement, ₹50,000. Also assume that the firm would have sufficient short-term capital gains in year-5.

LO 9.3 LOD M

Solution Cash outflows

Cost of production equipment	₹1,00,000
Additional working capital requirement	50,000
	1,50,000

Determination of CFAT and NPV

Particulars	*Years*				
	1	*2*	*3*	*4*	*5*
Sales revenue (75,000 × 4)	₹3,00,000	₹3,00,000	₹3,00,000	₹3,00,000	₹3,00,000
Less: Costs:					
Variable costs (75,000 × 2)	1,50,000	1,50,000	1,50,000	1,50,000	1,50,000
Additional fixed costs	25,000	25,000	25,000	25,000	25,000
Depreciation (D)	20,000	16,000	12,800	10,240	Nil@
Earnings before taxes	1,05,000	1,09,000	1,12,200	1,14,760	1,25,000
Less: Taxes	36,750	38,150	39,270	40,166	43,750
Earnings after taxes (EAT)	68,250	70,850	72,930	74,594	81,250
CFAT (EAT + D)	88,250	86,850	85,730	84,834	81,250
Add: Recovery of WC					50,000
Add: Salvage value (SV)					10,000
Add: Tax benefit on short term capital loss@@					10,836
					1,52,086
Multiplied by PV factor 0.20	0.833	0.694	0.579	0.482	0.402
PV (CFAT × PV factor)	73,512	60,274	49,638	40,890	61,139
Total PV (t = 1 – 5)					2,85,453
Less: Cash outflows					1,50,000
NPV					1,35,453

@As the block consists of single asset, no depreciation is to be charged in the terminating year as the asset has been sold in the year.

@@(₹1,00,000 – ₹59,040 accumulated depreciation – ₹10,000, SV) × 0.35 = ₹10,836.

Recommendation The company is advised to buy the proposed equipment.

P.9.7 The Domanhill Colliery, an underground mine, owned by the public sector Coal India Ltd has been producing coal through manual operations for the last eight years. The past and projected revenues and cost data are summarised below. LO 9.3 LOD D

Past and projected revenue and cost data (₹ crore)

Year	Sales revenue	Direct labour cost	Administrative and selling expenses	Fixed expenses (excluding depreciation)	Variable expenses
Past Data:					
1	70	14	12	15	23
2	81	16	14	17	25
3	101	21	17	22	30
4	123	30	22	25	39
5	162	34	25	31	45
6	201	41	33	49	64
7	245	48	40	51	77
8	302	61	53	68	94
Projected Data:					
9	309	62	52	68	89
10	342	69	58	75	97
11	375	76	63	83	106
12	408	82	69	91	115
13	441	88	75	98	124

With the liberalisation and opening up the coal sector to private firms, the Board of Directors of Coal India Ltd have decided to undertake a feasibility study for semi-mechanisation of Domanhill Colliery by introducing side dump and load (SDL) machine. With the introduction of the SDL machine, the following changes in the operating parameters are forecast:

- Increase in projected sales revenue by 25 per cent due to faster speed of work;
- Decrease in direct labour cost by 5 per cent resulting from ban on new recruitments;
- Fifteen per cent increase in administrative and selling expenses to support increased semi-mechanised production and sale;
- 10 per cent increase in fixed cost on account of setting up of additional maintenance facility;
- Increase in variable expenses, 50 per cent, as a result of additional electricity consumption;
- Loss in terms of disturbance charge due to opposition, strike and lockout: year 9, ₹2 crore, year 10 ₹0.80 crore and year 11, ₹0.30 crore;
- The semi-mechanisation would require acquisition of 20 machines at a cost of ₹1 crore each. An additional ₹2 crore would have to be spent on creation of additional facility like transformer, special cables and installation of the machines. The machines including the additional facility created would be depreciated over a five year period on the basis of written down value method @ 20 per cent. At the end of year 5, they are expected to be sold at ₹2 crore. The colliery does not have other machines in the block of 20 per cent. Also assume that the firm would have sufficient short-term capital gains in year 5.

Assuming tax-adjusted effective cost of capital of 8 per cent on World Bank loan to finance the project and 35 per cent tax, present a financial analysis of the feasibility of semi-automation of the Domanhill Colliery. As a financial consultant, what recommendation would you make to the Board of Directors of Coal India Ltd?

Solution Financial analysis for semi-mechanisation of Domanhill Colliery (using NPV method)

Incremental cash outflows *(Amount in crore of rupees)*

Cost of new machine (SDL) (20 × ₹1 crore)	20
Additional cost of semi-mechanisation	2
	22

Incremental CFAT and NPV

Particulars	*Year*				
	1	*2*	*3*	*4*	*5*
Incremental sales revenue (0.25 × projected sales revenue)	77.25	85.5	93.75	102	110.25
Add: Savings in direct labour cost (0.05 × DLC)	3.10	3.45	3.8	4.1	4.4
Less: Incremental administrative and selling expenses (0.15 × ASE)	7.8	8.70	9.45	10.35	11.25
Less: Incremental fixed costs (0.10 × FC)	6.8	7.5	8.3	9.1	9.8
Less: Increase in variable costs (0.50 × VC)	44.5	48.5	53	57.5	62
Less: Disruption charges	2.0	0.8	0.3	—	—
Less: Depreciation	4.4	3.52	2.82	2.25	Nil.@
Earnings before taxes	14.85	19.93	23.68	26.9	31.6
Less: Taxes	5.20	6.98	8.29	9.42	11.1
Earnings after taxes	9.65	12.95	15.39	17.48	20.5
CFAT (operating)	14.05	16.47	18.21	19.73	20.5
Salvage value					2.0
Tax benefit on short-term capital loss (0.35 × ₹7.01)					2.45
(x) PV factor (0.08)	0.926	0.857	0.794	0.735	0.681
Present value	13.01	14.11	14.46	14.50	16.99
Total present value (t = 1 – 5)					73.07
Less: Cash outflows					22.00
Net present value					51.07

@ No depreciation is charged in terminal year, as block ceases to exist.

Recommendation Since the NPV is positive, the proposal is financially viable.

P.9.8 The Projects Consultants (P) Ltd is a consultancy firm. Its main business is conducting market studies, surveys and techno-economic feasibility and industry reviews. Its final product is in the form of a printed report. The normal procedure is to produce handwritten drafts of the report and get it printed through an independent word processing service agency. Three copies of each report are prepared for submission to the clients.

LO 9.3 | LOD D

On an average 35 studies are completed every year. The average size of the report is 100 pages. In addition, about 50 proposals are sent in duplicate to various companies every year, the average size of these being 20 pages. The reports as well as the proposals are in laser print on bond paper. The handwritten drafts (printed 3 times for reports and 2 times for proposals) are on ordinary paper.

The external word processing is done at a rate of ₹10 per page with one draft free of cost. The variable overheads are 2 telephone calls a day to the word processing agency for 300 days @ ₹1 per call.

Recently, the firm has been offered a computer system with software and laser printer for ₹1,20,000. The system would have no salvage value at the end of 5 years. The maintenance cost of the system would include ₹5,000 on account of annual maintenance contract and ₹15,000 for spares. The annual insurance of the system is likely to be 1 per cent of the cost. The other associated annual costs are expected to be as follows:

- Cost of bond paper, ₹0.35 per sheet; cost of ordinary paper @ ₹0.18 per sheet. The experience has been that there is 10 per cent wastage of both bond and ordinary paper sheets;
- Laser toner, ₹0.10 per sheet;
- Draft print at ₹0.05 per sheet;
- Power charges, ₹3,000;
- Telephone charges, ₹100;
- Manpower charges, ₹3,000 per month as salary of a part-time computer operator;
- Additional working capital requirement, ₹25,000.

The firm is in the 35 per cent tax bracket. Assuming it would use written down value method of depreciation at the rate of 20 per cent and its required rate of return is 10 per cent, should the Projects Consultants (P) Ltd install its own computer system as an alternative to hiring word processing service from an outside agency? Assume further that the company does not have any other asset in the 20 per cent block and would have sufficient short-term capital gains in year 5.

Solution Financial analysis to purchase computer system

Cash outflows

Cost of computer system	₹1,20,000
Increased working capital required	25,000
Initial investment required	1,45,000

Incremental CFAT and NPV

Particulars	*Year*				
	1	2	3	4	5
Savings in word processing cost:					
— Reports (35 × 3 × 100 × ₹10)	₹1,25,000	₹1,25,000	₹1,25,000	₹1,25,000	₹1,25,000
— Proposals (50 × 20 × 2 × ₹10)					
Savings in telephone costs	500	500	500	500	500
Less: Incremental costs:					
Insurance (0.01 × ₹1,20,000)	1,200	1,200	1,200	1,200	1,200
Maintenance costs	20,000	20,000	20,000	20,000	20,000
Paper costs:					
— Bond paper (12,500 × ₹0.35 × 1.1)	7,288	7,288	7,288	7,288	7,288
— Ordinary paper (12,500 × ₹018 × 1.1)	1,375	1,375	1,375	1,375	1,375
Toner cost (Laser) (12,500 × 0.1 × 1.1)	688	688	688	688	688
Toner cost (Draft) (12,500 × 0.05 × 1.1)	3,000	3,000	3,000	3,000	3,000
Power charges					
Manpower charges	36,000	36,000	36,000	36,000	36,000
Depreciation	24,000	19,200	15,360	12,288	Nil
Earnings before taxes	31,949	36,749	40,589	43,661	55,949
Less: Taxes	11,182	12,862	14,206	15,281	19,582
Earnings after taxes	20,767	23,887	26,383	28,380	36,367
CFAT	44,767	43,087	41,743	40,668	36,367
Tax benefit on short-term capital loss (₹49,152 × 0.35)					17,203
Working capital recovery					25,000
(x)PV factor (0.10)	0.909	0.826	0.751	0.683	0.621
Present value	40,693	35,590	31,349	27,776	48,792
Total present value (t = 1 – 5)					1,84,200
Less: Cash outflows					1,45,000
NPV					39,200

Recommendation Since the net present value for this proposal is positive, the proposal is financially viable and the firm should use the option to install the computer system.

P.9.9 BS Electronics is considering a proposal to replace one of its machines. In this connection, the following information is available.

LO 9.3 LOD M

The existing machine was bought 3 years ago for ₹10 lakh. It was depreciated at 20 per cent per annum on reducing balance basis. It has remaining useful life of 5 years, but its annual maintenance cost is expected to increase by ₹50,000 from the sixth year of its installation. Its present realisable value is ₹6 lakh. The company has several machines, having 20 per cent depreciation.

The new machine costs ₹15 lakh and is subject to the same rate of depreciation. On sale after 5 years, it is expected to net ₹9 lakh. With the new machine, the annual operating costs (excluding depreciation) are expected to decrease by ₹1 lakh. In addition, the new machine would increase productivity on account of which net revenues would increase by ₹1.5 lakh annually.

The tax rate applicable to the firm is 35 per cent and the cost of capital is 10 per cent.

Is the proposal financially viable? Advise the firm on the basis of NPV of the proposal.

Solution

Financial evaluation whether to replace an existing machine (using NPV method)

(A) Incremental cash outflows	
Cost of new machine	₹15,00,000
Less: Sale value of existing machine	6,00,000
	9,00,000

(B) Determination of CFAT (operating)

Year	*Incremental cash profits before taxes*	*Incremental depreciation*	*Taxable income (col. 2 – col. 3)*	*Taxes (0.35)*	*EAT (col. 4 – col. 5)*	*CFAT (col. 6 + col. 3)*
1	*2*	*3*	*4*	*5*	*6*	*7*
1	₹2,50,000	₹1,80,000	₹70,000	₹24,500	₹45,500	₹2,25,500
2	2,50,000	1,44,000	1,06,000	37,100	68,900	2,12,900
3	3,00,000	1,15,200	1,84,800	64,680	1,20,120	2,35,320
4	3,00,000	92,160	2,07,840	72,740	1,35,096	2,27,256
5	3,00,000	73,728	2,26,272	79,195	1,47,077	2,20,805

(C) Determination of net present value

Year	*CFAT*	*PV factor (0.10)*	*Total present value*
1	₹2,25,500	0.909	₹2,04,980
2	2,12,900	0.826	1,83,010
3	2,35,320	0.751	1,75,855
4	2,27,256	0.683	1,55,216
5	2,20,805	0.620	1,36,899
5	9,00,000 (Net salvage value)*	0.620	5,58,000
Total present value			14,13,960
Less: Incremental cash outflows			9,00,000
Net present value			5,13,960

*at the beginning of year 6.

It is important to note that machine is sold after 5 years and not at the end of year 5.

Recommendation Since NPV is positive, the company is advised to replace the existing machine.

Working Notes

(i) WDV of existing machine in the beginning of year 4

Initial cost of machine	₹10,00,000
Less: Depreciation @ 20% in year 1	2,00,000
WDV at beginning of year 2	8,00,000

Less: Depreciation @ 20% on WDV	1,60,000
WDV at beginning of year 3	6,40,000
Less: Depreciation @ 20% on WDV	1,28,000
WDV at beginning of year 4	5,12,000
(ii) Depreciation base of new machine	
WDV of existing machine	5,12,000
Plus: Cost of the new machine	15,00,000
Less: Sale proceeds of existing machine	(6,00,000)
	14,12,000
(iii) Base for incremental depreciation	
Depreciation base of new machine	14,12,000
Less: Depreciation base of existing machine	(5,12,000)
	9,00,000

(iv) Incremental depreciation ($T = 1 - 5$)

Year	*Incremental asset cost base*	*Depreciation @ 20% on WDV*
1	₹9,00,000	₹1,80,000
2	7,20,000	1,44,000
3	5,76,000	1,15,200
4	4,60,800	92,160
5	3,68,640	73,728

(v) Incremental cash profits before taxes (in terms of decrease in operating costs and increase in revenues) owing to the new machine

Year	*Savings in operating costs*	*Increase in revenue*	*Incremental cash profit before taxes*
1	₹1,00,000	₹1,50,000	₹2,50,000
2	1,00,000	1,50,000	2,50,000
3	1,50,000 @	1,50,000	3,00,000
4	1,50,000	1,50,000	3,00,000
5	1,50,000	1,50,000	3,00,000

@Maintenance expenses of existing machine are expected to increase by ₹50,000 from sixth year of installation.

P.9.10 Seshasayee Industries Ltd is considering replacing a hand-operated weaving machine with a new fully automated machine. Given the following information, advise the management whether the machine should be replaced or not. Assume the company has only this machine in 20 per cent block of assets and the block will cease to exist after the useful life of the automated machine. Also assume that the firm would have sufficient short-term capital gains in year 5. **LO 9.3** LOD M

Existing situation:
- One full-time operator's salary, ₹36,000
- Variable overtime, ₹3,000
- Fringe benefits, ₹3,000
- Cost of defects, ₹3,000
- Original price of hand-operated machine, ₹60,000
- Expected life, (years), 10
- Age, (years) 5
- Depreciation method, written down value
- Current salvage value of old machine, ₹36,000
- Marginal tax rate, 35
- Required rate of return, 15

Proposed situation:
- Fully-automated operation, No operator is necessary
- Cost of machine, ₹1,80,000
- Transportation charges, ₹3,000
- Installation costs, ₹15,000
- Expected economic life (years), 5
- Depreciation method, written down value
- Annual maintenance, ₹3,000
- Cost of defects, ₹3,000
- Salvage value at year-end 5, ₹20,000.

Solution

Incremental cash outflows

Cost of machine	₹1,80,000
Add: Transportation charges	3,000
Add: Installation costs	15,000
Less: Cash inflow from the sale of old machine	36,000
	1,62,000

Determination of CFAT and NPV

Particulars	Years 1	2	3	4	5
Cost savings	₹39,000	₹39,000	₹39,000	₹39,000	₹39,000
Less: Incremental depreciation	32,400	25,920	20,736	16,589	—
Earnings before taxes	6,600	13,080	18,264	22,411	39,000
Less: Taxes (0.35)	2,310	4,578	6,392	7,844	13,650
Earnings after taxes	4,290	8,502	11,872	14,567	25,350
CFAT (EAT + D)	36,690	34,422	32,608	31,156	25,350
Add: Salvage value					20,000
Add: Tax advantage@					16,224
(×) PV factor (0.15)	0.870	0.756	0.656	0.572	0.497
Present value	31,920	26,023	21,391	17,821	30,602
Total PV (t = 1 – 5)					1,27,757
Less: Cash outflows					1,62,000
Net present value					(34,243)

@ on short-term capital loss (₹66,355 – ₹20,000) × 0.35 = ₹16,224.

Recommendation Since the NPV is negative, the machine is not recommended for purchase.

Working Notes

(i) Incremental depreciation (if machine is purchased)

(a) WDV of existing machine in the beginning of year 6:

Initial cost of machine		₹60,000
Less: Depreciation charges (year 1 to 5)		
Year 1 (₹60,000 × 0.20)	₹12,000	
2 (48,000 × 0.20)	9,600	
3 (38,400 × 0.20)	7,680	
4 (30,720 × 0.20)	6,144	
5 (24,576 × 0.20)	4,915	40,339
		19,661

(b) Depreciation base of new machine:

WDV of existing machine	19,661
Add: Cost of new machine (₹1,80,000 + ₹3,000 + ₹15,000)	1,98,000
Less: Sale of existing machine	(36,000)
	1,81,661

(c) Base of incremental depreciation (₹1,81,661 – ₹19,661) 1,62,000

(d) Incremental depreciation (t = 1 – 5)

Year	Incremental WDV base	Depreciation
1	₹1,62,000	₹32,400
2	1,29,600	25,920
3	1,03,680	20,736
4	82,944	16,589
5	66,355	Nil (as machine is sold)

(ii) Cost savings (if machine is purchased)

	Existing situation	Proposed situation	Differential cost savings
Salary	₹36,000	—	₹36,000
Variable overtime	3,000	—	3,000
Fringe benefits	3,000	—	3,000
Cost of defects	3,000	₹ 3,000	Nil
Annual maintenance	—	3,000	(3,000)
	45,000	6,000	39,000

P.9.11 An existing company has a machine which has been in operation for 2 years; its estimated remaining useful life is 4 years with no salvage value in the end. Its current market value is ₹25,000. The management is considering a proposal to purchase an improvement model of the machine which gives increased output. The relevant particulars are as follows:

LO 9.3 LOD M

Particulars	Existing machine	New machine
Purchase price (₹)	60,000	1,07,500
Estimated life (years)	6	4
Salvage value	0	0
Annual operating hours	1,000	1,000
Selling price per unit (₹)	3	3
Material per unit (₹)	0.40	0.40
Output per hour (units)	15	30
Labour cost per hour (₹)	11	16
Consumable stores per year (₹)	2,000	1,000
Repairs and maintenance per year (₹)	3,000	2,000
Working capital (₹)	10,000	20,000
Income-tax rate	35	35

Should the existing machine be replaced? Assume that (i) required rate of return is 10 per cent, and (ii) the company uses written down value method of depreciation @ 20 per cent and it has several machines in the 20 per cent block.

Solution

Incremental cash outflows

Purchase price of new machine	₹1,07,500
Add: Additional working capital	10,000
Less: Sale value of old machine	25,000
	92,500

Determination of CFAT and NPV

Particulars	Years			
	1	2	3	4
Incremental revenues	₹36,000	₹36,000	₹36,000	₹36,000
Less: Incremental depreciation	16,500	13,200	10,560	8,448

(*Contd*)

(*Contd*)

Earnings before taxes	19,500	22,800	25,440	27,552
Less: Taxes (0.35)	6,825	7,980	8,904	9,643
Earnings after taxes	12,675	14,820	16,536	17,909
CFAT (EAT + D)	29,175	28,020	27,096	26,357
Add: Recovery of working capital				10,000
(x) PV factor (0.10)	0.909	0.826	0.751	0.683
Present value	26,520	23,145	20,349	24,832
Total present value (t = 1 – 4)				94,846
Less: Incremental cash outflows				92,500
NPV				2,346

Recommendation Since NPV is positive, the company is advised to replace the existing machine.

Working Notes

(i) Incremental revenues

Particulars	*Existing machine* (1)	*New machine* (2)	*Differential* (1) – (2) (3)
1. Annual operating hours	1,000	1,000	—
2. Output per hour (units)	15	30	15
3. Total output (units)	15,000	30,000	15,000
4. Selling price per unit (₹)	3	3	3
5. Total sales revenue (3 × 4)	₹45,000	₹90,000	₹45,000
6. *Less:* Expenses:			
Material	6,000	12,000	6,000
Labour	11,000	16,000	5,000
Consumable stores	2,000	1,000	1,000
Repairs and maintenance	3,000	2,000	1,000
Incremental revenues	23,000	59,000	36,000

(ii) Incremental depreciation (if machine is purchased)

(a) WDV of existing machine in the beginning of year 3		
Initial cost of machine		₹60,000
Less: Depreciation charges (years 1 and 2):		
Year 1 (₹60,000 × 0.20)	₹12,000	
2 (₹48,000 × 0.20)	9,600	21,600
		38,400
(b) Depreciation base of new machine:		
WDV of existing machine		38,400
Add: Cost of new machine		1,07,500
Less: Sale value of existing machine		(25,000)
		1,20,900
(c) Base for incremental depreciation: (₹1,20,900 – ₹38,400)		82,500

(d) Incremental depreciation (t = 1 – 4)

Year	*WDV*	*Depreciation*
1	₹82,500	₹16,500
2	66,000	13,200
3	52,800	10,560
4	42,240	8,448

Note: There will be an additional tax advantage on depreciation of ₹33,792 (₹42,240 – ₹8,448) in the future years.

P.9.12 XYZ Company manufactures several different products. One of the principal products sells for ₹20 per unit. The sales manager of XYZ has stated repeatedly that he could sell more units of this product if they were available. To substantiate his claim, he conducted a market research study last year at a cost of ₹35,000. The study indicated that XYZ could sell 18,000 units of this product annually for the next five years.

LO 9.3 LOD D

The equipment currently in use has the capacity to produce 11,000 units annually. The variable production costs are ₹9 per unit. The equipment has a value of ₹60,000 for tax purposes and a remaining useful life of five years. The salvage value of the equipment is negligible now and will be zero in five years.

A maximum of 20,000 units could be produced annually on the new machinery which can be purchased. The new equipment costs ₹2,50,000 and has an estimated useful life of five years with no salvage value. The production manager estimates that the new equipment would provide increased production efficiencies that would reduce the variable production costs to ₹7 per unit.

XYZ Company uses written down value method of depreciation on all of its equipments. The firm is subject to a 35 per cent tax and its after-tax cost of capital is 15 per cent.

The sales manager felt so strongly about the need for additional capacity that he attempted to prepare an economic justification for the equipment although this was not one of his responsibilities. His analysis, presented below, disappointed him because it did not justify acquiring the equipment.

Purchase price of new equipment		₹2,50,000
Disposal of existing equipment:		
Loss on disposal	₹60,000	
Less: Tax benefit (0.35)	(21,000)	39,000
Cost of market research study		35,000
Total investment		3,24,000
Contribution margin from product:		
Using the new equipment [18,000 × (₹20 – 7)]		2,34,000
Using the existing equipment [11,000 × (₹20 – 9)]		1,21,000
Increase in contribution		1,13,000
Less: Depreciation		50,000
Increase in before-tax income		63,000
Income tax (0.35)		22,050
Increase in income		40,950
Less: Cost of capital on the additional investment required (0.15 × ₹3,24,000)48,600		
Net annual return of proposed investment in new equipment		(7,650)

The controller of XYZ Company plans to prepare a discounted cash flow analysis for this investment proposal. He has asked you to prepare corrected calculations of: **(a)** the required investment in new equipment, and **(b)** the recurring annual cash flows. Give your recommendation on the basis of above information and assuming 25 per cent depreciation on the block of assets to which the machine belongs.

Solution

Financial evaluation whether to replace existing equipment

(a) Required investment in new equipment:	
Purchase price of new equipment	₹2,50,000
(b) Recurring annual cash flows:	
(i) Depreciation base of new machine:	
Book value of existing machine	60,000
Add: Cost of new machine	2,50,000
	3,10,000
(ii) Base for incremental depreciation:	
Depreciation base of new machine	3,10,000
Less: Book value of existing machine	60,000
	2,50,000

(iii) Incremental depreciation (t = 1 – 5):

Year	*Incremental WDV base*	*Depreciation*
1	₹2,50,000	₹62,500
2	1,87,500	46,875
3	1,40,625	35,156
4	1,05,469	26,367
5	79,102	19,775

Note: Unabsorbed depreciation is ₹59,327 (₹79,102 – 19,775); tax advantage on this will be available in future years.

(c) Determination of CFAT and NPV

Particulars	*Years* 1	2	3	4	5
Incremental contribution	₹1,13,000	₹1,13,000	₹1,13,000	₹1,13,000	₹1,13,000
Less: Incremental depreciation	62,500	46,875	35,156	26,367	19,775
Incremental taxable income	50,500	66,125	77,844	86,633	93,225
Less: Taxes	17,675	23,144	27,245	30,322	32,629
Earnings after taxes	32,825	42,981	50,599	56,311	60,596
CFAT (EAT + Depreciation)	95,325	89,856	85,755	82,678	80,371
(x) PV factor (0.15)	0.870	0.756	0.658	0.572	0.497
Present value	82,933	67,931	56,427	47,292	39,944
Total present value (t = 1 – 5)					2,94,527
Less: Purchase price of new equipment					2,50,000
Net present value					44,527

Recommendation The company is advised to replace the existing equipment.

P.9.13 A company has spent ₹2,00,000 on research in developing a new product. It wants to launch this product in the market. For the purpose of financial analysis, the following information has been collected: LO 9.3 LOD D

1. The estimated life of the product is 3 years.
2. Projected sales are as follows:

Year	*Sales revenue*
1	₹15,00,000
2	20,00,000
3	6,00,000

On account of new machine, it is expected that it would result in additional sales of existing products, yielding additional contribution of ₹25,000 each year for next three years.

3. Variable cost to manufacture and sell the product are estimated at 60 per cent of the selling price.
4. Each year, the present cash fixed costs will increase by ₹35,000 to cover insurance, and maintenance of new equipment, and allocated fixed costs would be ₹30,000.
5. Advertising of the new product will total ₹1,25,000 in the first year, and ₹75,000 and ₹60,000 in the years 2 and 3 respectively.
6. New machinery will be purchased at an estimated cost of ₹7,50,000. The machinery will be depreciated at the rate of 20 per cent on the basis of written down value method of depreciation. The salvage value at the year-end 3 is estimated at ₹50,000. There are no other machines in the block of assets.

7. The working capital required is ₹2 lakh in year 1. Additional working capital of ₹1 lakh would be required at beginning of year 2. Total working capital required in the beginning of the year 3 is ₹80,000.
8. The new product will be stored in a company owned warehouse in a portion that is on rent of ₹15,000 per year at present.
9. The firm pays 30 per cent tax on its income.
10. Cost of capital of the firm is 15 per cent
11. The firm would have sufficient short-term capital gains in year 3.

Should the proposal be accepted? You may state your assumptions, if any.

Solution

Incremental cash outflows

Cost of new machine	₹7,50,000
Working capital (WC) requirement	2,00,000
	9,50,000

Incremental CFAT and NPV

Particulars	*Year*		
	1	*2*	*3*
Sales revenue	₹15,00,000	₹20,00,000	₹6,00,000
Add: Incremental contribution of existing products	25,000	25,000	25,000
Less: Costs:			
Variable costs	9,00,000	12,00,000	3,60,000
Additional fixed cost	35,000	35,000	35,000
Advertising cost	1,25,000	75,000	60,000
Depreciation	1,50,000	1,20,000	Nil@
Opportunity cost of Rented portion	15,000	15,000	15,000
Earnings before tax	3,00,000	5,80,000	1,55,000
Less: Taxes (30%)	90,000	1,74,000	46,500
Earnings after tax	2,10,000	4,06,000	1,08,500
CFAT (EAT + D)	3,60,000	5,26,000	1,08,500
Less: Additional WC	1,00,000		
Add: Recovery of WC		2,20,000	80,000
Add: Salvage value			50,000
Add: Tax benefit on short term capital loss@@			1,29,000
	2,60,000	7,46,000	3,67,500
Multiplied by PV factor @15%	0.870	0.756	0.658
PV(CFAT × PV factor)	2,26,200	5,63,976	2,41,815
Total PV			10,31,991
Less: Cash outflows			9,50,000
NPV			81,991

@ As, the block consists of single asset, no depreciation will be charged in the terminating year as the asset has been sold in that year.

@@(₹7,50,000 – ₹2,70,000 accumulated depreciation – ₹50,000,SV) × 0.30 = ₹1,29,000.

Recommendation Since the NPV is positive, the company is advised to purchase the new machine for new product.

MINI CASES

9.C.1 (Net Present Value) The Hotel Seawind is one of the premier four-star hotels in Goa. Since its inception in 1990, it has been the favourite choice of the visitors to the city. It boasts of facilities such as swimming pools, a gymnasium, boutiques, a discotheque, 24 × 7 coffee shop and multi-cuisine restaurant. It has rooms which are classified into three types, as shown below:

Class	*Number of rooms*	*Daily tariff*
Economy	200	₹2,500
Executive	100	4,000
Deluxe	25	6,000

The current financial details of Seawind are summaried below:

(i) Staff salaries

Grade	*Number*	*Amount per annum per person*	*Total*
(1)	*(2)*	*(3)*	*(4)*
A	1	₹20,00,000	₹20,00,000
B	25	8,00,000	2,00,00,000
C	70	3,00,000	2,10,00,000
D	200	1,50,000	3,00,00,000
Total			7,30,00,000

(ii) Profit from restaurant: ₹1,00,00,000

(iii) Profits from the coffee shop: ₹30,00,000

(iv) Profit from the boutique and discotheque: ₹25,00,000

(v) Room tariffs:

• Economy class: 200 × ₹2,500 × 350 days × 0.40 (occupancy)	₹7,00,00,000
• Executive class: 100 × ₹4,000 × 350 × 0.40	5,60,00,000
• Deluxe class: 25 × ₹6,000 × 350 × 0.40	2,10,00,000
	14,70,00,000

(vi) Annual maintenance cost (electricity charges, land tax, water tax, office stationery and other miscellaneous expenses): ₹5,00,00,000

(vii) Profits before tax (PAT/EBT): Total revenues – Total cost

Total revenues		
• Room tariffs	₹14,70,00,000	
• Profit from restaurant	1,00,00,000	
• Profit from coffee shop	30,00,000	
• Profit from boutique/discotheque	25,00,000	₹16,25,00,000
Total costs		
• Salary	7,30,00,000	
• Maintenance cost	5,00,00,000	12,30,00,000
		3,95,00,000

(viii) Profit after tax (PAT)

• Tax	1,38,25,000
	2,56,75,000

In the past few years, the occupancy in Seawind has declined from 55 per cent to 40 per cent which has dented its profits attributed to **(i)** stiff competition from new four-star hotels that have come up recently and (ii) its inability to offer value-added services to its customers.

In order to check the decline in profits and to plan out the future strategy to maximise its revenues, Rahul Singh, the CEO of Seawind, has hired the Trump Consultants.

The Trump Consultants have suggested two proposals for the consideration of the CEO of Hotel Seawind as detailed below:

Proposal I: The first proposal is to increase its rating from four-star to five-star. Due to this, the occupancy rate of new rooms would be 50 per cent; however, the occupancy rate of existing rooms would remain unchanged. The upgradation would involve the following:

- Increase in the number of rooms: economy class, 100; executive class, 80; and deluxe class, 25.
- Build a casino and a ball room.
- Increase in staff: B grade, 40; C grade, 100; and D grade, 300.

The upgradation plan would require additional expenses detailed below:

1. Cost of building of casino and ball room: ₹4,00,00,000
2. Cost of building extra rooms in the hotel;
   - Economy class, ₹8,00,000 per room
   - Executive class, ₹12,00,000 per room
   - Deluxe class, ₹20,00,000 per room

The additional maintenance cost would amount to ₹1,40,00,000.

As a result, incremental profit from casino would be ₹50 lakh and coffee shop would be ₹24 lakh.

Proposal II: The details of the second proposal of the consultants are given below:

(i) Creation of casino and entertainment centre at a cost of ₹4,00,00,000.
(ii) Creation of an *ayurveda* spa at a cost of ₹50,00,000
(iii) Creation of a helipad at a cost of ₹20,00,000
(iv) Increase in staff: B grade, 2; C grade, 10; and D grade, 30.

The incremental profit generated from the proposal would be as shown below:

- From casino, spa helipad and the entertainment centre, ₹2,50,00,000
- From restaurant, coffee shop and discotheque, ₹50,00,000
- Increase in occupancy rate to 45 per cent

The additional maintenance cost would be ₹1,00,00,000.

Required Which proposal of Trump Consultant should Rahul Singh accept? Why? Ignore depreciation for tax purposes. Assume cost of capital as 13%. Assume both proposals would provide incremental profits/room tariffs for next 4 years only. Assume national sale value of capital assets built in proposal I as ₹15 crore at year-end 4.

Solution

Evaluation of Proposal I (Upgradation to 5-star Level)

(A) Incremental Cash Outflows (t-0)	
(1) Expenditure on building extra rooms1	₹22,60,00,000
(2) Expenditure on building casino and ball room	4,00,00,000
	26,60,00,000
(B) Incremental Cash Inflows After Taxes (t = 1 – 4)	
(1) Incremental revenue from hotel rooms3	12,60,00,000
(2) Incremental profit from casino	50,00,000
(3) Incremental profit from coffee shop and discotheque	24,00,000
(4) Additional staff and maintenance cost	5,00,00,000
Total incremental earnings before taxes	8,34,00,000
(5) Less taxes (0.35)	2,91,90,000
Total incremental earnings after taxes (t = 1 – 4) [CFAT]	5,42,10,000

© Determination of NPV:

Year	*CFAT*	*PVIF (0.13)*	*Total PV*
1–4	₹5,42,10,000	2.974	₹16,12,20,540
4	15,00,00,000	0.613	9,19,50,000
Less incremental cash outflows			26,60,00,000
NPV			(–1,28,29,560)

1	Economy class: 100 rooms × ₹8,00,000	=	₹8,00,00,000
	Executive class: 80 rooms × ₹12,00,000	=	9,60,00,000
	Deluxe class: 25 rooms × ₹20,00,000	=	5,00,00,000
			22,60,00,000
2	Grade B staff: 15 × ₹8,00,000	=	1,20,00,000
	C : 30 × 3,00,000	=	90,00,000
	D : 100 × 1,50,000	=	1,50,00,000
			3,60,00,000
	Plus additional maintenance cost		1,40,00,000
			5,00,00,000
3	Economy class: 100 rooms × ₹2,500 × 350 × 0.50		₹4,37,50,000
	Executive class: 80 rooms × 4,000 × 350 × 0.50		5,60,00,000
	Deluxe class: 25 rooms × 6,000 × 350 × 0.50		2,62,50,000
			12,60,00,000

Evaluation of Proposal II (Creation of Casino, Entertainment Centre and Helipad)

Incremental Cash outflows: (t = 0)	
Expenditure on casino and entertainment centre	₹4,00,00,000
Expenditure on *ayurveda* spa	50,00,000
Expenditure on helipad	20,00,000
	4,70,00,000
Increment Cash Inflows: (t = 1 – 4)	
Revenue from rooms (increase in occupancy)[2]	1,83,75,000
Profit from casino, spa and helipad	2,50,00,000
Profit from restaurant, coffee shop and discotheque	50,00,000
Additional staff and maintenance costs	(1,91,00,000)
Total incremental before tax	2,92,75,000
Less taxes (0.35)	1,02,46,250
Incremental CFAT (t = 1 – 4)	1,90,28,750

Determination of NPV

Year	*CFAT*	*PVIF (0.13)*	*Total PV*
1–4	₹1,90,28,750	2.974	₹5,65,91,502
Less incremental cash outflows			4,70,00,000
NPV			95,91,502

1	B Grade : 2 × ₹80,000	=	₹16,00,000
	C Grade: 10 × ₹3,00,000	=	30,00,000
	D Grade: 30 × ₹1,50,000		45,00,000
	Additional maintenance cost		1,00,00,000
	Total		1,91,00,000

2 Room tariffs: (at 45% occupancy)	
Economy class: 200 × ₹2,500 × 350 × 0.45	₹7,87,50,000
Executive class: 100 × ₹4,000 × 350 × 0.45	6,30,00,000
Deluxe class: 25 × ₹6,000 × 350 × 0.45	2,36,25,000
	16,53,75,000
Less existing (at 40% occupancy)	14,70,00,000
	1,83,75,000

Decision: Proposal II, that is creation of casino and entertainment centre, an *ayurvedic* spa and a helipad should be accepted as it has a positive NPV.

9.C.2 (Hiring Vs Buying) Tel Samrat is a large Indian conglomerate with interest in petroleum, petroleum products, textiles, telecom and life sciences. It has a refinery in Ankleshwar in Gujarat. The refinery has a peak capacity for producing 27 lakh tons of finished petroleum products. Ankaleshwar is a major oil terminal with sophisticated state of art facility for docking of very large crude carrier (VLCC) and ultra large crude carrier (VLCC). Tel Samrat imports crude oil from the Middle East for its refinery operations and has its own fleet of oil tankers for this purpose.

Tel Samrat has been availing of the services of rented oil barges from the British Company, MAR-OIL for loading fuel oil for running its tankers in Ankaleshwar. MAR-OIL has an Indian subsidy—MAR OIL INDIA (MOI) which provides the barge services in India. Tel Samrat pays MOI for its services at the rate of ₹40,000 per hour to cover running and maintenance costs. On an average, Tel Samrat has been hiring barges for 90 hours per month for its fleet of 15 tankers. However, the contract with MOI stipulates payment for at least 100 hours.

An alternative to hiring the barges from MOI is to acquire oil barges. A Japanese firm Ichikawa Harima Heavy Industries (IHI) is offering two oil barges for 40 million Yen with a service life of 10 years. The barges would have a salvage value of 4 million Yens. [Exchange rate: Current, ₹2.5/Yen; After 10 years, ₹5/Yen).

The insurance cost for the barges would be 1 per cent per year for 1–5 years and 2 per cent for years 6–10 as per the Loyd Registrar of Shipping (LRS) regulations. The running and maintenance costs for the two barges would be ₹20,00,000 per year for the first 5 years and ₹40,00,000 annually for the next 5 years.

The yearly employee/staff/crew cost for the first 5 years would be as given below:

Rank	*Number*	*Monthly salary*
Captain	1	₹80,000
Chief Engineer	1	80,000
Chief Officer	1	60,000
Duty Engineer	1	60,000
Oil man	1	15,000
Seaman	1	15,000
Shore staff	2	14,000
		3,24,000

After 5 years, the salary of employees/crew/staff would increase by 10 per cent.

Required Should Tel Smart acquire the two barges from IHI? Or should it continue availing of the services of MOI? Assume 12 per cent required rate of return.

Solution

Financial Evaluation of Hiring Vs Buying of Barges

	Years	
Incremental Cash Outflows:	*1–5*	*6–10*
Present scenario (Hiring of barges)	₹4,80,00,000	₹4,80,00,000
Proposed scenario (Buying of barges)	1,48,80,000[1]	1,82,80,000[1]
Cost savings (EBT)	3,31,20,000	2,97,20,000
Less tax (0.375)	1,24,20,000	1,11,45,000
EAT	2,07,00,000	1,85,75,000
Add back depreciation	80,00,000	80,00,000
Savings in Cost (CFAT)	2,87,00,000	2,65,75,000

Determination of NPV:

Year	*CFAT*	*PV factor (0.12)*	*Total PV*
1–5	₹2,87,00,000	3.605	₹10,34,63,500
6–10	2,65,75,000	2.045@	5,43,45,875
10 salvage value	(–20,00,000) (4 million Yen × ₹5)	0.322	(–6,44,000)
Total			15,71,65,375
Less cash outflow (cost of barges) (40 million Yen × ₹2.5)			10,00,00,000
NPV			5,71,65,375

@PV annuity for 6–0 years = PV for annuity for 10 years – PV of annuity for 5 years = 5.65 – 3.605 = 2.045 1

Cost estimates

	Year 1–5	*Year 6–10*
Running and maintenance cost	₹20,00,000	₹40,00,000
Employee cost (₹3,24,000 × 12)	38,80,000	42,80,000*
Insurance cost	10,00,000	20,00,000
Depreciation (₹10,00,00,000 ÷ 20,00,000) ÷10	80,00,000	80,00,000
Total	1,48,80,000	1,82,80,000

*(₹3,24,000 × 1.10 × 12)

Decision: Since the NPV is positive (₹5,71,65,375), Tel Samrat should buy the two barges from IHI. It should stop hiring them from MOI.

9.C.3 (Net Present Value) Choolah Chimney Ltd (CCL) is a leading manufacturer of items used in kitchens such as gas stoves, electric chimneys, ovens and so on. It has grown significantly under the CEO Vivek Razdan's dynamic leadership. In line with his belief to enhance competitiveness by using research and development for launching innovative products in the market, the CCL has recently developed a zero Maintenance Electric Chimney (known as Zimney) which is ideally suited for Indian cooking. The research and development cost of Zimney amounts to ₹20,00,000.

To gauge the market prospects for Zimney, a market survey was conducted by Bazar Gyani, the V.P., Marketing, at an estimated cost of ₹5,00,000. The results of the survey were very positive showing a significant demand for Zimney. The survey report also indicated that Zimney could capture 8 per cent of the current market size of 1,00,000 units of gas electric chimney. Considering the growth of satellite towns/cities and residential colonies, the market is expected to grow at 2 per cent annually. The VP, Marketing suggested to the CEO that a market penetration pricing strategy would be most suitable and Zimney should be priced at ₹5,000 per unit in the initial year of the launch. The price could be raised in subsequent years by 5 per cent annually. The marketing and administrative costs are expected to be ₹4,00,000 per year.

The CCL is presently using 6 machines acquired 3 years ago at a cost of ₹10,00,000 each, having a useful life of 7 years, with no salvage value. These machines are currently being used for manufacturing other types of chimneys. They could be sold for ₹2,00,000 per machine with a removal cost of ₹30,000 for each.

The machine to manufacture Zimney is available in that market for ₹1,00,00,000 with a useful life of 4 years and salvage value of ₹10,00,000. It can produce other types of chimneys also.

The new machine, being state of the art technology would improve the productivity of the workers as well reduce the unit variable cost of manufacture to ₹600, which would increase by 5 per cent annually. Exhibit 1 summarises the labour cost with the existing machine and the new equipment.

Category	*Existing*		*New Machine/Equipment*	
	Number	*Monthly salary*	*Number*	*Monthly salary*
Skilled labour	20	₹4,000	15	₹4,000
Maintenance men	2	6,000	1	6,000
Floor managers	3	8,000	2	8,000

The maintenance costs currently amount to 1,00,000 per year (existing machine). They would total ₹70,000 with the new equipment. The net working capital required to start production of Zimney would be ₹60,00,000.

The policy of CCL is to pay five months salary as compensation in case of lay-off of employees.

Required

Should the CCL launch the Zimney. Assume the following: (i) Tax, 35 per cent (ii) Required rate of return, 14 per cent and (iii) Straight line depreciation for the tax purposes.

Solution

Financial Evaluation of Proposal to launch Zimney

(A) Incremental Cash Outflow (t = 0):	
1. Cost of new machine	₹1,00,00,000
2. Less sale proceeds of existing machines[a]	(10,20,000)
3. Less tax benefits on loss of sale of existing machines[b]	(8,42,999)
4. Cost of laying-off workers[c]	1,70,000
5. Additional working capital	60,00,000
	1,43,07,001

[a]Sale proceeds of existing machines [(6 × ₹2,00,000, sale price – (6 × ₹30,000, removal cost)] = ₹10,20,000

[b]Tax benefits on loss of existing machine

1. Book value of existing machine [(6 × ₹10,00,000) – (3 × ₹8,57142, annual depreciation i.e. ₹60,00,000 ÷ 7)] = ₹60,00,000 – ₹25,71,428 = ₹34,28,571.
2. Loss on sale of existing machine [book value, ₹34,28,571 – ₹10,20,000, sale proceeds] = ₹24,08,571.
3. Tax benefit (₹24,08,571 × 0.35) = ₹8,42,999.

[c]Cost of lay-off:

1. Skilled labour 5 × ₹4,000 × 5 (months)	=	₹1,00,000
2. Floor manager = 1 × ₹8,000 × 5	=	40,000
3. Maintenance person = 1 × ₹6,000 × 5	=	30,000
		1,70,000

(B) Incremental Cash Inflows: (t = 1 – 4):

Particulars	Year 1	2	3	4
1. Sales revenue[a]	₹4,00,00,000	₹4,28,40,000	₹4,58,81,640	₹4,91,34,408
2. Add savings in maintenance cost[b]	30,000	30,000	30,000	30,000
3. Add savings in labour cost[c]	4,08,000	4,08,000	4,08,000	4,08,000
4. Less variable cost[d]	(52,00,000)	(55,40,800)	(59,05,796)	(62,96,663)
5. Less incremental depreciation[e]	(13,92,858)	(13,92,858)	(13,92,858)	(13,92,858)
6. EBT	3,38,45142	3,63,44,342	3,90,20,986	4,18,82,887
7. Less tax (0.35)	(1,18,45,799)	(1,27,20,519)	(1,36,57,346)	(1,46,59,010)
8. EAT	2,19,99,342	2,36,23,822	2,53,63,640	2,72,23,876
9. Add incremental depreciation	13,92,858	13,92,858	13,92,858	13,92,858
10. CFAT	2,33,92,200	2,50,16,680	2,67,56,498	2,86,16,734
11. Release of working capital	—	—	—	60,00,000
12. Total	2,33,92,200	2,50,16,680	2,67,56,498	3,46,16,734

[a]Sales revenue : Year 1 (0.08 × 1,00,000 × ₹5,000) = ₹4,00,00,000
2 (0.08 × 1,02,000 × ₹5,250) = 4,28,40,000
3 (0.08 × 1,04,040 × ₹5,512) = 4,58,81,640
4 (0.08 × 1,06,120 × ₹5,787) = 4,91,34,408

[b]Savings in maintenance cost (₹1,00,000, existing – ₹70,000 proposed) = ₹30,000

[c]Savings in labour cost:

1	Existing:	Skilled labour (20 × ₹4,000 × 12 months)	₹9,60,000	
		Floor manager (3 × ₹8,000 × 12)	2,88,000	
		Maintenance (2 × ₹6,000 × 12)	1,44,000	₹13,92,000
2	New:	Skilled labour (15 × ₹4,000 × 12)	7,20,000	
		Floor manager (2 × ₹8,000 × 12)	1,92,000	
		Maintenance (1 × ₹6,000 × 12)	72,000	9,84,000
				4,08,000

[d]Variable cost and general administrative costs:

Year 1 [(0.08 × 1,00,000 × ₹600) + ₹4,00,000] = ₹52,00,000
2 [(0.08 × 1,02,000 × ₹630) + ₹4,00,000] = 55,40,000
3 [(0.08 × 1,04,040 × ₹661) + ₹4,00,000] = 59,05,796
4 [(0.08 × 1,06,120 × ₹694) + ₹4,00,000] = 62,96,663

[e]Incremental depreciation:

1. New equipment (₹1,00,00,000 – ₹10,00,000) ÷ 4 ₹22,50,000
2. Existing (Book value, ₹34,28,571 – 0) ÷ 4 8,57,142

13,92,858

(C) Computation of NPV

Year	Incremental cash inflows	PV factor (0.14)	Total PV
1	₹2,33,92,200	0.877	₹2,05,14,959
2	2,50,16,680	0.769	1,92,37,826
3	2,67,56,498	0.675	1,80,60,636
4	3,46,16,734	0.592	2,04,93,106
Total			7,83,06,527
Less Incremental cash outflow			1,43,07,001
NPV			6,39,99,526

Decision: The Chola Chimney should launch the Zimney

Note:

The research and development cost of Zimney (₹20,00,000) and expenses incurred on market survey (₹5,00,000) are sunk cost and, therefore, irrelevant for analysis.

9.C.4 (Buying Vs Hiring) The Continental Construction Ltd (CCL) has recently got a contract for construction of National Highway-8 near Gurgaon. The Continental would require vehicles to be used by its engineers for inspection of the sites.

One option before the Continental is to hire the inspection vehicle from Convenient Tours and Travels Ltd (CTL). Hiring charges would be ₹900 per day for 80 kms/eight hours and ₹7/km beyond 80 kms. The overtime rate for drivers would be ₹25/hour beyond 8 hours. It is estimated that, on an average, the inspection vehicle would be required for 10 hours/day and 100 kms/day. The hiring charges would be increased by 10 per cent every year.

The Chief Engineer, Himanshu Pandey, has submitted an alternative proposal to the CEO, Neeraj Bodra, to buy a Mahindra Bolero costing ₹7 lakh; Mahindra and Mahindra has an arrangement to buy back its vehicles after 5 years for ₹2,00,000. The associated operating costs are estimated as follows:

- Drivers' salary, ₹8000 per month; annual increments, 3 per cent
- Drivers' overtime beyond 8 hours, ₹30/hour
- Insurance of the vehicle, 1 per cent of depreciated value
- Annual maintenance cost, years 3 – 5, ₹15,000
- Fuel charges: year 1 – 2, ₹3/km; year 3, ₹3.5/km; and years, 4 – 5, ₹4/km
- Annual depreciation, 20 per cent (₹1,00,000)

Required The CEO seeks the opinion of the CFO, Vishnu Rawat, on the two alternative proposals for the required inspection vehicle. What advice should Rawat give? Why? Assume 35 per cent tax and 15 per cent required rate of return for the Continental.

Solution

Savings in Costs

		Year				
		1	*2*	*3*	*4*	*5*
1	Hiring charges (Working note 1)	₹3,92,400	₹4,31,640	₹4,74,804	₹5,22,284	₹5,74,513
2	Buying Charges (note 2)	3,32,600	3,34,480	3,69,446	3,89,502	3,91,649
3	Savings before taxes	59,800	97,160	1,05,358	1,32,782	1,82,864
4	Taxes (0.35)	20,930	34,006	36,875	46,474	64,002
5	Savings after taxes	38,870	63,154	68,483	86,308	1,18,862
6	Add depreciation	1,00,000	1,00,000	1,00,000	1,00,000	1,00,000
7	Net savings in costs	1,38,870	1,63,154	1,68,483	1,86,308	2,18,862
8	Salvage value	—	—	—	—	2,00,000
						4,18,862
9	PVIF (0.15)	0.870	0.756	0.658	0.572	0.497
10	Present values	1,20,817	1,23,344	1,10,862	1,06,568	2,08,174
11	Total (t = 1 – 5)		₹6,69,765			
12	Cash outflow (cost of Bolero)		(7,00,000)			
13	NPV		(30,235)			

Advice: Since the NPV of the net savings in cost is negative, the proposal to buy the Bolero from Mahindra and Mahindra is not financially viable and the Continental would be well advised to hire the inspection vehicle from the Convenient Tours and Travels Ltd.

Working Notes

1 Annual hiring charges

Year 1 = ₹900 (daily charges) + ₹140 (₹7 × 20 kms) extra charges + ₹50 (₹25 × 2 hours) extra charges
= ₹1,090 × 30 (days) × 12 (months) = ₹3,92,400

Year 2 = 3,92,400 × 1.10 = ₹4,31,640
3 = 4,31,650 × 1.10 = 4,74,804
4 = 4,74,804 × 1.10 = 5,22,284
5 = 5,22,284 × 1.10 = 5,74,513

2. Operating costs associated with the inspection vehicles

		Year				
		1	*2*	*3*	*4*	*5*
1	Salary of driver@	₹96,000	₹98,880	₹1,01,846	₹1,04,902	₹1,08,049
2	Overtime payment@@	21,600	21,600	21,600	21,600	21,600
3	Insurance (0.01)	7,000	6,000	5,000	4,000	3,000
4	Maintenance cost	–	–	15,000	15,000	15,000
5	Fuel@@@	1,08,000	1,08,000	1,26,000	1,44,000	1,44,000
6	Depreciation@@@@	1,00,000	1,00,000	1,00,000	1,00,000	1,00,000
	Total	3,32,600	3,34,480	3,69,446	3,89,502	3,91,649

@₹8,000 per month + 3 per cent annual increment

@@₹30 × 720 [60 hours (2 hours daily × 30 days) × 12 months]

@@@Year 1-2 36,000 kms × ₹3
3 36,000 kms × ₹3.5
4-5 36,000 × ₹4

@@@@₹(7,00,000 – ₹2,00,000) ÷ 5

9.C.5 AMR Paints (NPV) AMR Paints Ltd (APL) is a large paint company in India with a 32 per cent market share. The demand for decorative paints is expected to increase due to robust growth in the housing and the real estate sector. The current installed capacity of the APL is 3,54,000 **tpa**. It envisages a huge demand for premium emulsions in the decorative paints segment and plans to launch new products to cater to this rising demand and lay the foundation for its future growth.

The APL is planning to set up a greenfield plant at Kurukshetra in Haryana with an installed capacity of 1,50,000 **kl** on 130 acres of land. The initial cost of setting up the project is ₹407.25 crore to be financed from internal sources. The APL has purchased plant and machinery for ₹170 crore (salvage value after 10 years being ₹5 crore) and acquired land for ₹150 crore. Pre-construction clearing and development of land would cost ₹9 crore. A further ₹7 crore would be required for factory building and other civil construction. The machinery is subject to 20 per cent block depreciation. There is no other machine in this block.

The APL's expected percentage capacity utilisation of the Kurukhsetra plant is as follows: Year 1, 50; Year 2, 55; Year 3, 65; Year 4, 70, Year 5, 75; Year 6-7, 80; and Years 8-10, 85. The working capital requirements of APL during the 10-year period are projected at ₹71.25 crore. The paint could be sold at a mark-up of ₹5 per litre on the industry average price of ₹90/L. The projected operating expenses per rupee of sales are as shown below: (a) Material cost 0.5; Employee cost, 0.05; Manufacturing/selling distribution expenses, 0.059 (Total, 0.609).

The AMR Paints Ltd is listed on the NSE Ltd and the Nifty index has given an average of 19 per cent return over the last 10 years. The current yield on Government of India securities is 7.29 per cent. The APL's beta is 0.40. Its current balance sheet (as at March 31, Year 1) is given below.

Liabilities	*Amount (₹crore)*	*Assets*	*Amount (₹crore)*
Shareholders funds:		Fixed assets	727.33
■ Capital	95.92	Investments	234.77
■ Reserves and surplus	1100.00	Current assets, loans and advances	1,228.11
Loans[@]	138.00		
Current liabilities and provisions	856.29		
	2,190.21		2,190.21

[@]Annual interest, ₹16 crore.

Required The CEO of the APL, Mustafa Hakimuddin, is examining the feasibility of setting up of the new plant. He seeks the advice of the CFO, Rishi Singhal, in the matter. What advice should he give and why?

Solution

Computation of NPV (₹ crore)

(a) Cash outflows (t = 0):

Cost of plant and machinery	170.00
Cost of land and buildings	150.00
Land and site development	9.00
Building and other civil construction	7.00
Working capital requirement	71.25
	407.25

(b) Cash inflow

(₹ in crore)

		Year (capacity utilisation)									
		1 (0.50)	*2(0.55)*	*3(0.65)*	*4(0.70)*	*5(0.75)*	*6(0.80)*	*7(0.80)*	*8(0.85)*	*9(0.85)*	*10(0.85)*
1	Sales:										
	(i) Litres sold (lakh)	750	825	975	1,050	1,125	1,200	1,200	1,275	1,275	1,275
	(ii) Price per litre (₹)	95	95	95	95	95	95	95	95	95	95
		712.50	783.75	926.25	997.50	1,068.75	1,140.00	1,140.00	1,211.25	1,211.25	1211.25
2	Operating expenses (Working note 1)	433.91	477.30	564.09	607.48	650.87	694.26	694.26	737.65	737.65	737.65
3	Profit before depreciation	278.59	306.45	362.16	390.02	417.88	445.74	445.74	473.60	473.60	473.60
4	Depreciation (Working note 2)	34.00	27.20	21.76	17.41	13.93	11.14	8.91	7.13	5.70	4.56
5	Profits before tax	244.59	279.25	340.40	372.61	403.95	434.60	436.83	466.47	467.90	469.04
6	Tax (0.35)	85.61	97.74	119.14	130.41	141.38	152.11	152.89	163.26	163.76	164.16
7	Profit after tax	158.98	181.51	221.26	242.20	262.57	282.49	283.94	303.21	304.14	304.88
8	Depreciation	34.00	27.20	21.76	17.41	13.93	11.14	8.91	7.13	5.70	4.56
9	CFAT (operating)	192.98	208.71	243.02	259.61	276.50	293.63	292.85	310.34	309.84	309.44
10	Working capital release	–	–	–	–	–	–	–	–	–	71.25
11	Salvage value										5.00
12	Tax advantage on short term capital loss [(18.26 – 5) x 0.35]										4.64
	CFAT (total)	192.98	208.71	243.02	259.61	276.50	293.63	292.85	310.34	309.84	390.33

(c) Computation of NPV

Year	*CFAT (₹ crore)*	*PVIF*	*Present value (₹ crore)*
1	192.98	0.9034	174.34
2	208.71	0.8162	170.35
3	243.02	0.7373	179.18
4	259.61	0.6661	172.93
5	276.50	0.6018	166.40
6	293.63	0.5437	159.65
7	292.85	0.4912	143.85
8	310.34	0.4437	137.70
9	309.84	0.4009	124.22
10	390.33	0.3622	141.38
			1,570
Cash outflows			407.25
NPV			1,162.75

Advice: My advice is to set up the proposed plant as it would have a positive present value and add to value to the AMR Paints.

Working Notes

1. Depreciation schedule (₹ crore)

Year	*1*	*2*	*3*	*4*	*5*	*6*	*7*	*8*	*9*	*10*
Written down value (WDV) [beginning]	170.0	136.0	108.8	87.04	69.63	55.71	44.56	35.65	28.52	22.82
Depreciation (0.20)	34.0	27.2	21.76	17.41	13.93	11.14	8.91	7.13	5.70	4.56
WDV (at year-end 10)										18.26

2. Weighted average cost of capital

Source	*Amount (₹crore)*	*Weight*	*Cost (%)*	*Weighted cost*
Equity@	95.92	0.072	0.1197	0.0086
Debt@@	138.00	0.103	0.754	0.0078
Retained earnings@@@	1,100.00	0.825	0.1097	0.0905
Total	1,333.92			0.1069

@Using CAPM, Ke = Rf + b (Rm – Rf) = 0.729 + [0.40 × (0.19 – 0.0729) = 0.1197

@@ Kd = Interest (₹16 crore) – tax [₹5.6 crore (₹16 crore × 0.35, tax rate)]
= ₹10.4 ÷ ₹138 = 0.754

@@@ Assumed lower than Ke (by 1 per cent).

3. Operating expenses per rupee of sales = Raw material (0.50) + Wages (0.05) + Manufacturing, administration, selling and distribution expenses (0.059) = 0.609

Scan the QR Code given at the end of chapter to access comprehensive cases.

REVIEW QUESTIONS

LOD: Easy

RQ. 9.1(a) Indicate whether the following statements are true or false. [LO 9.2,3]

(i) Two mutually exclusive projects (A and B) have been evaluated. Project A has an NPV of ₹8 lakh and an IRR of 16 per cent; Project B has NPV of ₹7 lakh but has IRR or 18 per cent. Since Project B has higher IRR, it should be selected.

(ii) The cost of capital for new projects is 15 per cent. Two competing projects (X and Y) respectively have IRRs of 14 per cent and 12 per cent respectively; since IRR of project X is higher, it should be selected.

(iii) Two competing projects have the following NPVs: Project X, + ₹5 lakh (with initial outlay of ₹25 lakh) and Project Y, + ₹4,20,000 (with initial outlay of ₹20,00,000). The company should opt for project X as it has higher NPV.

(iv) A project requires an initial investment of ₹10,00,000. The estimated cash inflows from the project are as follows: ₹3 lakh (year 1), ₹1 lakh (year 2), ₹3 lakh (year 3), ₹6 lakh (Year 4) and ₹4 lakh (year 5). The pay back of the project is 4 years.

(v) A project requires an investment of ₹20 lakh. The estimated profit after tax for years 1-5 are: ₹3 lakh, ₹3 lakh, ₹3 lakh, ₹6 lakh and ₹8 lakh. The accounting rate of return is 21 per cent

(vi) In the case of independent investment projects, if the NPV of the project is zero, IRR is equal to cost of capital.

(vii) A company has evaluated 3 investment proposals under IRR method, yielding different rates of return. Though the IRR values are varying, reinvestment rate of intermediate cash inflows is assumed to be the same for all these 3 proposals.

(viii) Since IRR is expressed in percentage figure, it is the best method for evaluating capital budgeting projects.

(ix) The more distant the CFAT, the higher is the present value of such cash flows.

(x) NPV is the best method of evaluating long-term investment proposals.

(b) Fill in the following blanks:

(xi) ____________ present value tables can be used only when cashflows are uniform to determine NPV.

(xii) In the case of mixed stream of cash flows, ____________ present value tables are used to determine NPV.

(xiii) ____________ determines the number of years required to recover initial investment outlay.

(xiv) In the case of ____________ investment proposals, IRR and NPV method provides the same result.

(xv) In the case of conflict in ranking. ____________ method provides better result than ____________ method.

[Answers: (i) False (ii) False (iii) True (iv) False (v) False (vi) True (vii) False (viii) False (ix) False (x) True (xi) Annuity (xii) simple (xiii) Payback method (xiv) independent (xv) NPV, IRR

RQ. 9.2 Why is it important to evaluate capital budgeting projects on the basis of after-tax cash incremental flows? Why not use accounting data instead of cash flow? [LO 9.2]

RQ. 9.3 What are the components of net cash outlay in the capital budgeting decision? At what time is such an outlay incurred in the case of conventional cash flows? [LO 9.2]

RQ. 9.4 What is pay back period? Also, discuss the utility of the pay back period in determining the internal rate of return. [LO 9.3]

RQ. 9.5 What does the profitability index signify? What is the criterion for judging the worth of investments in the capital budgeting technique based on the profitability index? [LO 9.3]

RQ. 9.6 Arvind Mills Ltd is considering two mutually exclusive investment proposals for its expansion programme. Proposal A requires an initial investment of ₹7,50,000 and yearly cash operating costs of ₹50,000. Proposal B requires an initial investment of ₹5,00,000 and yearly cash operating costs of ₹1,00,000. The life of the equipment used in both the investment proposals will be 12 years, with no salvage value; depreciation is on the straight line basis for tax purposes. The anticipated increase in revenues is ₹1,50,000 per year in both the investment proposals. The firm's tax rate is 35 per cent and its cost of capital is 15 per cent. Which investment proposal should be undertaken by the company? [LO 9.3]

LOD: Medium

RQ. 9.7 How should working capital and sunk costs be treated in analysing investment opportunities? Explain with suitable examples. [LO 9.2]

RQ. 9.8 Explain clearly the concept of block of assets *vis-a-vis* depreciation in the context of replacement situations of capital budgeting. [LO 9.2]

RQ. 9.9 It is said that only cash costs are relevant for capital budgeting decision. However, depreciation which is a non-cash cost is a prominent part of cash flow analysis for such an investment decision. How do you explain this paradox? [LO 9.2]

RQ. 9.10 What are the critical factors to be observed while making replacement investment decision? [LO 9.3]

RQ. 9.11 Do the profitability index and the NPV criterion of evaluating investment proposals lead to the same acceptance-rejection and ranking decisions? [LO 9.3]

RQ. 9.12 One project of XYZ Ltd is doing poorly and is being considered for replacement. Three mutually exclusive projects A, B and C have been proposed. The projects are expected to require ₹2,00,000 each, and have an estimated life of 5 years, 4 years and 3 years, respectively, and have no salvage value. The company's required rate of return is 10 per cent. The anticipated cash inflows after taxes (CFAT) for the three projects are as follows: [LO 9.3]

Year	*CFAT*		
	A	B	C
1	₹50,000	₹80,000	₹1,00,000
2	50,000	80,000	1,00,000
3	50,000	80,000	10,000
4	50,000	30,000	—
5	1,90,000	—	—

(i) Rank each project applying the methods of PB, NPV, IRR and profitability index.
(ii) What would the profitability index be if the IRR equalled the required return on investment? What is the significance of a profitability index less than one?
(iii) Recommend the project to be adopted and give reasons.

RQ. 9.13 Royal Industries Ltd is considering the replacement of one of its moulding machines. The existing machine is in good operating condition, but is smaller than required if the firm is to expand its operations. The old machine is 5 years old, has a current salvage value of ₹30,000 and a remaining depreciable life of 10 years. The machine was originally purchased for ₹75,000 and is being depreciated at ₹5,000 per year for tax purposes. [LO 9.3]

The new machine will cost ₹1,50,000 and will be depreciated on a straight line basis over 10 years, with no salvage value. The management anticipates that, with the expanded operations, there will be need of an additional net working capital of ₹30,000. The new machine will allow the firm to expand current operations, and thereby increase annual revenues of ₹40,000, and variable operating costs from ₹2,00,000 to ₹2,10,000. The company's tax rate is 35 per cent and its cost of capital is 10 per cent.

Should the company replace its existing machine? Assume that the loss on sale of existing machine can be claimed as short-term capital loss in the current year itself.

LOD: Difficult

RQ. 9.14 A toy manufacturing company is considering replacing an existing piece of equipment with one of the two new, more sophisticated machines. The old machine was purchased 3 years ago at a cost of ₹70,000. The machine originally had a projected life of 7 years and was to be depreciated straight line to zero salvage value. The two new pieces of equipment being considered are machine X and machine Y. [LO 9.3]

Machine X would cost ₹80,000 to purchase, and ₹20,000 to install. Due to expansion in operation, the management estimates the net working capital requirement of machine X at ₹10,000. It has a 4-year life with no salvage value. It will be depreciated straight line.

Machine Y would cost ₹1,15,000 and ₹25,000 to install. It also has 4-year life with no salvage value. This machine would require a net working capital of ₹20,000.

The old machine can be sold for ₹25,000 on 1 year credit. The firm is taxed at 35 per cent. Assuming the cost of capital to be 10 per cent, which machine, if either, should the company acquire? The projected profits before depreciation and taxes currently and with each of the new machines are as follows:

Year	*With present Machine*	*With Machine X*	*With Machine Y*
1	₹25,000	₹50,000	₹90,000
2	25,000	50,000	90,000
3	25,000	50,000	90,000
4	25,000	50,000	90,000

What would be your answer, if the company has under consideration only the proposal to purchase machine X?

RQ. 9.15 Suppose a firm is considering replacing an old machine with a new one. The firm does not anticipate that any new revenues will be created by the replacement since demand for the product generation by both the machines is the same. However, in the CFAT work sheet used in evaluating the proposal, the analyst shows positive CFBT in the operating cash flow section. What creates operating CFBT in this situation? [LO 9.2,3]

ANSWERS

9.6 Proposal B should be accepted, since NPV is negative.

9.12 **(i)** PB: C, B, A; NPV: A, B; IRR: A, B

(ii) The profitability index would be 1. The significance of a PI less than 1 is that NPV is negative and the project should not be undertaken.

(iii) Project A, because its NPV is the highest.

9.13 NPV ₹9,915. The company should replace the existing machine.

9.14 The company should acquire machine Y, with NPV ₹1,05,912.

If the company has the proposal to buy machine X only, then it should continue with the existing machine because NPV of existing machine ₹62,607 is more than NPV from X which is ₹55,567.

Scan the QR Code to access comprehensive solutions to all numerical review questions and additional material.

CHAPTER 10

Capital Budgeting II: Additional Aspects

LEARNING OBJECTIVES	
LO 10.1	Use present value profiles to compare and evaluate NPV, IRR and PI techniques in context of conflicting rankings
LO 10.2	Describe project selection under capital rationing
LO 10.3	Explain the procedure to incorporate impact of inflation on capital budgeting decisions

INTRODUCTION

The simple accept-reject investment decisions with primarily conventional cash flows were discussed in the preceding Chapter. A firm generally faces complex investment situations and has to choose among alternatives. The evaluation techniques discussed earlier can be extended to handle such decisions. The focus of this Chapter is on extension of these techniques to complex investment situations. The chapter is devoted to a comparison of the DCF methods, namely, NPV, IRR and PI. It also outlines the conceptual framework of evaluating projects with unequal lives. Project selection under capital rationing is explained subsequently. The impact of inflation on capital budgeting decisions is also analysed. The major points are summarised by way of recapitulation.

LO 10.1 NPV, IRR, PROFITABILITY INDEX METHODS — A COMPARISON

NPV Vs. IRR Methods

The NPV and IRR methods would in certain situations give the same accept-reject decision. But they may also differ in the sense that the choice of an asset under certain circumstances may be mutually contradictory. The comparison of these methods, therefore, involves a discussion of **(i)** the similarities between them, and **(ii)** their differences, as also the factors which are likely to cause such differences.

NPV and IRR: Similarities The two methods-IRR and NPV- would give consistent results in terms of acceptance or rejection of investment proposals in certain situations. That is, if a project is sound, it will be indicated by both the methods. If, however, it does not qualify for acceptance, both the methods will indicate that it should be rejected.

Conventional investment projects are projects which cash outflows are confined to the initial period.

The situations in which the two methods will give a concurrent accept-reject decision will be in respect of conventional and independent projects. A **conventional investment** is one in which the cash flow pattern is such that an initial investment (outlay or cash outflow) is followed by a series of cash inflows. Thus, in the case of such investments, cash outflows are confined to the initial period. The **independent proposals** refer to investments the acceptance of which does not preclude the acceptance of others so that all profitable proposals can be accepted and there are no constraints in accepting all profitable projects. The reason why both the methods are equivalent and support or reject a proposal is simple. The decision-criterion with these methods may be recalled here. According to the NPV method, the decision rule is that a project will be accepted if it has a positive NPV, that is, NPV exceeds zero. The IRR method would support projects in whose case the IRR is more than the required rate of return (*r* exceeds *k*). When the NPV = zero or the IRR = *k*, the project may be accepted or rejected. The projects which have positive net present values will also have an IRR higher than the required rate of return.

Independent projects are all profitable projects that can be accepted.

Thus, Fig. 10.1 portrays NPV as (i) positive; (ii) zero; and (iii) negative corresponding to three situations (a) IRR > *K*; (b) IRR = *K*; (c) IRR < *K*.

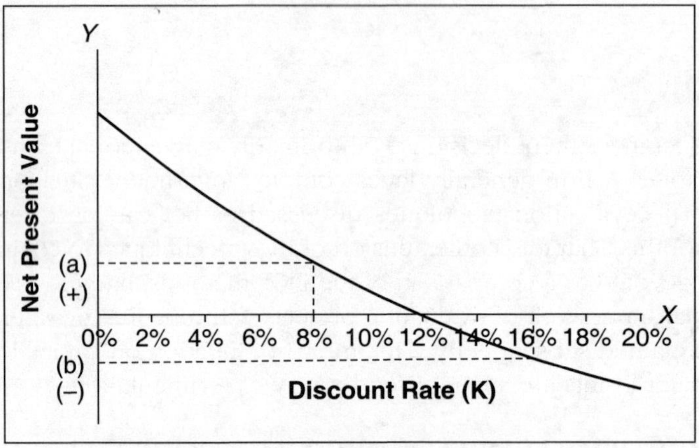

FIGURE 10.1 NPV and Discount Rate

Figure 10.1 shows the relationship between the NPV of a project and the discount rate. If there is no *K*, or discount rate is zero (a very unreal situation), NPV is maximum. As the value of *K* increases, the NPV starts declining. At 12 per cent rate of discount, the NPV is zero. This is the IRR also because by definition it is that rate of discount which reduces the NPV to zero. Assuming cost of capital to be 8 per cent, we find that NPV is positive by amount (a) and the project is acceptable and so is it under IRR as its value is > *K* (0.12 > 0.08). If we assume *K* to be 16 per cent, the project is unacceptable as the NPV is negative by amount (b) and so is it under IRR as IRR < *K* (0.12 < 0.16). The two approaches lead to identical results with regard to the accept-reject decision.

NPV and IRR Methods: Differences Thus, in the case of independent conventional investments, the NPV and IRR methods will give concurrent results. However, in certain situations they will give contradictory results such that if the NPV method finds one proposal acceptable, IRR favours another. This is so in the case of mutually exclusive investment projects. If there are alternative courses of action, only one can be accepted. Such alternatives are mutually exclusive. The mutual exclusiveness of the investment projects may be of two types: **(i)** technical, and **(ii)** financial. The term **technical exclusiveness** refers to alternatives having different profitabilities and the selection of that alternative which is the most profitable. Thus, in the case of a purchase or lease decision the more profitable out of the two will be selected. The mutual exclusiveness may also be financial. If there are resource constraints, a firm will be forced to select that project which is the most profitable rather than accept all projects which exceed a minimum acceptable level (say, k). The exclusiveness due to limited funds is popularly known as **capital rationing**.

Conflicting ranking is conflict in the ranking of a given project by NPV or IRR resulting from differences in magnitude or timing of cashflows.

The **different ranking** given by the NPV and IRR methods can be illustrated under the following heads:

1. Size-disparity problem;
2. Time-disparity problem; and
3. Unequal expected lives.

Size-disparity Problem This arises when the initial investment in projects under consideration, that is, mutually exclusive projects, is different. The cash outlay of some projects is larger than that of others. In such a situation, the NPV and IRR will give a different ranking. Consider Example 10.1.

Size-disparity arises when the initial investment in mutually exclusive projects is different.

***Example* 10.1**

A and *B* are two mutually exclusive investments involving different outlays. The details are:

Particulars	*Project A*		*Project B*	*Project B-A*
Cash outlays	(₹5,000)		(₹7,500)	(₹2,500)
Cash inflows at the end of year, 1	6,250		9,150	2,900
IRR (%)	25		22	16
Cost of capital, k_o (%)		10		
NPV	681.25		817.35	

Thus, the two methods rank the projects differently. Project A has a higher IRR (0.25) than project B (0.22) but the NPV of project B (₹817.35) is more than that of A (₹681.25). The important question is which method, in such a situation, gives better results? The answer should be related to the effect of the decision on the maximisation of the shareholders' wealth. The IRR method is not compatible with the goal of wealth maximisation. It is concerned with the rate of return on investment or yield rather than the total yield on the investment. In the above example, assuming 10 per cent to be the required rate of return, the firm would be left with ₹750 [₹6,250 – (₹5,000 + 0.10 × ₹5,000)] after one year in case project A is accepted and ₹900 [₹9,150 – (₹7,500) + 0.10 × ₹7,500] in case project B is accepted. The NPV method suggests that project B is better. This recommendation is consistent with the goal of the firm of maximising shareholders' wealth. When faced with mutually exclusive projects, each having a positive NPV, the one with the largest NPV will have the most beneficial effect on shareholders wealth. Since the selection criterion under the NPV method is to pick up the project with the largest NPV, the NPV is the best operational criterion. As long as the firm accepts the mutually exclusive investment proposal with the largest NPV, it will be acting consistently with the goal of maximising shareholders' wealth. This is because the project with the largest NPV will cause the share price and shareholders' wealth to increase more than will be possible with any of the other projects.[1]

Incremental Approach The conflict between the NPV and IRR in the above situation can be resolved by modifying the IRR so that it is based on incremental analysis. According to the incremental approach, when the IRR of two mutually exclusive projects whose initial outlays are different exceeds the required rate of return, the IRR of the incremental outlay of the project requiring a bigger initial investment should be calculated. This involves the following steps:

Incremental analysis involves computation of IRR of the incremental outlay of the project requiring bigger initial investment.

1. Find out the differential cash flows between the two proposals.
2. Calculate the IRR of the incremental cash flows.
3. If the IRR of the differential cash flows exceeds the required rate of return, the project having greater investment outlays should be selected, otherwise it should be rejected.

The logic behind the incremental approach is that the firm would get the profits promised by the project involving smaller outlay plus a profit on the incremental outlay. In general, projects requiring larger outlay would be more profitable if IRR on differential cash outlays exceeds the required rate or return. The modified IRR for mutually exclusive proposals involving size-disparity problem would provide an accept-reject decision identical to that given by the NPV method.

In Example 10.1, the IRR of the differential cash outlay of Project B is 16 per cent. The required rate of return is 10 per cent. Thus, project B is better than project A in spite of the fact that IRR in the latter is lower because it offers the benefits offered by project A plus a return in excess of the required return on ₹2,500, that is, differential cash outlays.

Time-disparity arises when the cash flow pattern of mutually exclusive projects is different.

To summarise the above discussion, the NPV method is superior to the IRR because the former supports projects which are compatible with the goal of maximisation of shareholders' wealth while the latter does not. On modifying the IRR method by adopting the incremental approach, IRR would give results identical to the NPV method. The modified IRR method has other merits also. It is easier to interpret and apply than the NPV measure. However, it requires additional computation, whereas the NPV method provides the correct answer in the first instance itself.

Time-disparity Problem The mutually-exclusive proposals may differ on the basis of the pattern of cash flows generated, although their initial investments may be the same. This may be called the time-disparity problem. The time-disparity problem may be defined as the conflict in ranking of proposals by the NPV and IRR methods which have different patterns of cash inflows. In such a situation, like the size-disparity problem, the NPV method would give results superior to the IRR method. This is illustrated in Example 10.2.

Example **10.2**

Year	*Cashflows*	
	Project A	*Project B*
0	₹1,05,000	₹1,05,000
1	60,000	15,000
2	45,000	30,000

(Contd.)

(Contd.)

3	30,000	45,000
4	15,000	75,000
IRR (%)	20	16
NPV (0.08)	23,970	25,455

We find on the basis of a comparison of the internal rate of returns that project A is better, but the NPV method suggests that project B is better. Since the cost of capital is 8 per cent, given the objective of the firm to maximise wealth, project B is definitely better.

Under the time-disparity problem it is the cost of capital which will determine the ranking of projects. If we take $k = 0.10$, we shall find project A is better as its net present value would be ₹19,185 compared to ₹18,435 of B. Its IRR is also more than that of B. Both the methods give identical prescription. But it does not imply that the IRR is superior to the NPV method, as the NPV is giving the same ranking as the IRR. In the event of conflicting rankings, the firm should rely on the rankings given by the NPV method.

Projects with Unequal Lives Another situation in which the IRR and NPV methods would give a conflicting ranking to mutually exclusive projects is when the projects have different expected lives. This is shown in Example 10.3.

Example 10.3

There are two projects A and B. A has a service life of one year, while B's useful life is five years. The initial cash outlay for both the projects may be assumed to be ₹20,000 each. The cash proceeds from project A (at the end of the first year) amount to ₹24,000. The cash generated by project B at the end of the fifth year is likely to be ₹40,200. Assume that the required rate of return is 10 per cent. Compute the NPV and the IRR of the two projects.

Solution

IRR and NPV of Projects A and B

Project	*IRR (per cent)*	*NPV*
A	20	₹1,816
B	15	4,900

Obviously, the ranking given by the IRR and NPV methods is different. According to the IRR method, the recommendation would favour project A while the NPV method would support project B. The conflict in the ranking by the two methods in such cases may be resolved by adopting a modified procedure. There are two approaches to do this: (i) **common time horizon approach** and (ii) **equivalent annual value/cost approach.**

Common time horizon approach makes a comparison between projects that extends over multiples of the lives of each.

According to the first appraoch, in order to have valid comparisons between the projects, they must be compared over the same period of time. The comparison may, thus, extend over multiples of the lives of each. Thus, if the service life of one project is 3 years and of another 4 years, the comparison must be over a 12 year period with replacements occurring for each.[2] Consider Example 10.4.

Example 10.4

Particulars	*Project A*	*Project B*
Initial outlay	₹10,000	₹20,000
Cash inflows after taxes		
Year-end 1	8,000	8,000
2	7,000	9,000

(Contd.)

(*Contd.*)

3	Nil		7,000
4	Nil		6,000
Service life (years)	2		4
Required rate of return		0.10	

Solution

Project A

Year	Cash flows	PV factor	Total present value
0	₹10,000	1.000	(₹10,000)
1	8,000	0.909	7,272
2	7,000	0.826	5,782
3	(10,000) [a]	0.826	(8,260)
3	8,000	0.751	6,008
4	7,000	0.683	4,781
NPV			5,583

[a] Machine replaced at the end of year 2.

Project B

Year	Cash flows	PV factor	Total present value
0	(₹20,000)	1.000	(₹20,000)
1	8,000	0.909	7,272
2	9,000	0.826	7,434
3	7,000	0.751	5,257
4	6,000	0.683	4,098
Net present value			4,061

Decision Project A should be preferred to project B because of its larger NPV. If we had compared the two projects without incorporating the consequences of replacing the machine at the end of year 2, the decision would have been the reverse, because the net present value of project A then would be ₹3,054 [₹7,272 + ₹5,782 – ₹10,000].

The implicit assumption of this approach is that the investment which is being replaced will produce cash flows of a similar pattern in future as it has done in the past.

We have taken a very simple situation where the project's life was only 2 years. But in actual practice, the competing alternatives may have much longer lives, say 15 years and 20 years. In such circumstances, it would probably not be possible to apply strictly the criterion mentioned above, that is, replacing the investment of the shorter-period project 4 times and longer-period project 3 times, in all having a 60 year life. It will obviously not be possible to make correct estimates for these projects for such a distant future.

Equal annual net present value (EANPV) approach evaluates unequal-lived projects that converts the net present value of unequal-lived mutually exclusive projects into an equivalent (in NPV terms) annual amount.

The application of the *common time horizon approach* encounters operational difficulty in terms of assumptions of the same technology, price of the capital asset, and operating costs and revenues.

The *equivalent annual value/cost* method obviates these difficulties. According to this method, equivalent annual value/cost of all mutually exclusive investment projects under consideration is determined. The **equivalent annual net present value** (EANPV) is determined dividing the NPV of cash flows of the project by the annuity factor corresponding to the life of the project at the given cost of capital. The decision-criterion, in the case of revenue-expanding proposals, is the maximisation of EANPV and minimisation of **equivalent annual cost** (EAC) in the case of cost-reduction proposals. For analysis purposes, it is assumed that the firm would need the equipment more or less indefinitely. Therefore, it would be replaced when it wears out.[3] The assumption is consistent with the going concern accounting principle. This is illustrated in Examples 10.5 and 10.6.

Equal annual cost (EAC) converts the present value of costs of unequal-lived mutually exclusive projects into an equivalent annual amount/ cost.

***Example* 10.5 (Revenue-expanding Investment Proposal)**

A firm is considering to buy one of the following two mutually exclusive investment projects:

Project A: Buy a machine that requires an initial investment outlay of ₹1,00,000 and will generate the CFAT of ₹30,000 per year for 5 years.

Project B: Buy a machine that requires an initial investment outlay of ₹1,25,000 and will generate the CFAT of ₹27,000 per year for 8 years.

Which project should be undertaken by the firm? Assume 10 per cent as cost of capital.

Solution

(i) Determination of NPV of Projects A and B

Project	*Years*	*CFAT*	*PV factor (0.10)*	*Total PV*	*NPV*
A	1-5	₹30,000	3.791	₹1,13,730	₹13,730
B	1-8	27,000	5.335	1,44,045	19,045

(ii) Determination of EANPV:

$$\text{EANPV} = \frac{\text{Net present value of the project}}{\text{PV of annuity corresponding to life of the project at given cost of capital}} \quad \textbf{(10.1)}$$

EANPV (A) = ₹13,730/3.791 = ₹3,621.74

EANPV (B) = ₹19,045/5.335 = ₹3,569.82

On the basis of NPV criterion, Project B is preferred. However, on the basis of EANPV, project A becomes more desirable, with higher EANPV. In fact, acceptance of project A would be a right decision.

***Example* 10.6**

(Cost-reduction Investment Proposal) A firm is considering to instal a large stamping machine. Two machines currently being marketed will do the job satisfactorily. Machine A costs ₹50,000 and will require cash running expenses of ₹15,000 per year. It has a useful life of 6 years and is expected to yield ₹2,000 salvage value at the end of its useful life. Machine B costs ₹65,000 but cash running expenses are expected to be ₹12,000. This machine is expected to have a useful life of 10 years with salvage value of ₹5,000. Assume both the machines would be depreciated on straight line basis for tax purposes.

If the corporate tax rate is 35 per cent and cost of capital is 10 per cent, which machine should be bought by the company?

Solution

Equivalent Annual Costs of Machines A and B

Particulars	*Costs*		*PV factor (0.10)*	*Adjusted PV*	
	Machine A	*Machine B*		*Machine A*	*Machine B*
0 (Initial cost)	₹50,000	₹65,000	1.000	₹50,000	₹65,000
(Operating cost):					
1-6 years (A)	6,950		4.355	30,267.25	
1-10 years (B)	—	5,700	6.145		35,026.50
				80,267.25	1,00,026.50

(Contd.)

(Contd.)

Less: Salvage value:					
6th year (A)	2,000		0.564	1,128.00	—
10th year (B)		5,000	0.386	—	1,930
Present value of total costs				79,139.25	98,096.50
Divided by annuity PV factor for 10 per cent corresponding to the life of the project (capital recovery factor)				4.355	6.145
Equivalent annual cost (EAC)				18,172	15,963.63

Recommendation Since Machine B has a lower equivalent annual cost, it is preferred investment.

Working Notes

Determination of Operating Costs

Particulars	*Machine A*	*Machine B*
Cash running cost	₹15,000	₹12,000
Less: Tax shield @35 per cent (assuming profitable operations)	5,250	4,200
Less: Tax advantage on depreciation charged every year:		
Machine A (₹8000 × 0.35)	2,800	—
Machine B (₹6,000 × 0.35)	—	2,100
Effective operating cash outflows	6,950	5,700

Reinvestment Rate Assumption The preceding discussions have revealed that in the case of mutually exclusive projects, the NPV and IRR methods would rank projects differently where **(a)** the projects have different cash outlays initially, **(b)** the pattern of cash inflows is different, and **(c)** the service lives of the projects are unequal. It has also been found that the ranking given by the NPV method in such cases is theoretically more correct. The conflict between these two methods is mainly due to different assumptions with regard to the reinvestment rate on funds released from the proposal. The assumption underlying the IRR method seems to be incorrect and deficient. The IRR criterion implicitly assumes that the cash flow generated by the projects will be reinvested at the internal rate of return, that is, the same rate as the proposal itself offers. With the NPV method, the assumption is that the funds released can be reinvested at a rate equal to the cost of capital, that is, the required rate of return. The crucial factor is which assumption is correct? The assumption of the NPV method is considered to be superior theoretically because it has the virtue of having a rate which can consistently be applied to all investment proposals. Moreover, the rate of return (k) represents an opportunity rate of investment. In contrast to the NPV method, the IRR method assumes a high reinvestment rate for investment proposals having a high IRR and a low investment rate for investment proposals having a low IRR. The **implicit reinvestment rate** will differ depending upon the cash flow stream for each investment proposal. Obviously, under the IRR method, there can be as many rates of reinvestment as there are investment proposals to be evaluated unless some investment proposals turn out to have an IRR which is equal to that of some other project(s).

Implicit investment rate is the rate at which interim cash flows can be invested.

The superficiality of the reinvestment rate under the IRR method can be demonstrated by comparing the following two investment projects.[4]

Project	Initial investment	Cash inflows	
		Year 1	Year 2
A	₹100	₹200	0
B	100	0	₹400

Under the IRR method, both projects have a rate of return of 100 per cent. If ₹100 were invested for one year at 100 per cent, it would grow to ₹200, and if invested for two years, to ₹400. Since both the projects have the same IRR, the firm should be indifferent regarding their acceptability, if only one of two projects is to be picked up as both the projects are equally profitable. For this to be true, it is necessary that ₹200 received at the end of year 1 in case of project A should be equal to ₹400 at the end of year 2. In order to achieve this, it necessarily follows that the firm must be able to reinvest the first year's earnings at 100 per cent. If not, it would be unable to transform ₹200 at the end of the first year into ₹400 at the end of the second. And if it cannot transform ₹200 into ₹400 in a year's time, the two projects *A* and *B* cannot be ranked equal. There is no reason to believe that a firm can find other investment opportunities at precisely the required rate.

In contrast, the present value method does not pose any problem. Let us calculate the present value of Example 10.7, assuming cost of capital (k) as 10 per cent.

***Example* 10.7**

Year	Project A			Project B		
	Cashflows	PV factor	Total PV	Cashflows	PV factor	Total PV
1	₹200	0.909	₹181.80	0	—	—
2	0	—		₹400	0.826	₹330.40
			181.80			330.40
Less: Initial outlay			100.00			100.00
Net present value			81.80			230.40

The PV method indicates that project B is preferable to project A as its net present value is greater. The reinvestment rate in the PV method seems more realistic and reasonable. It assumes that earnings are reinvested at the same rate as the market cost of capital.

However, the IRR can be modified assuming the cost of capital to be the reinvestment rate. The **intermediate cash inflows** will be compounded by using the cost of capital. The compounded sum so arrived at and the initial cost outflows can be used as the basis of determining the IRR. The limitation of IRR arising out of the inconsistency in the reinvestment rate assumption can be obviated through the modified approach.

> **Intermediate cash flows** are cash inflows received prior to the termination of the project.

Modified IRR Method Since investment at the cost of capital is generally more realistic, the modified IRR (MIRR) is a better indicator of a project's true profitability. The MIRR also solves the problem of multiple IRRs.[5]

The MIRR can be computed by using Equation 10.2

$$CO_0 = \frac{\text{Compounded sum}_n}{(1 + \text{MIRR})^n} \tag{10.2}$$

For facts contained in Example 9.6, the MIRR of Machine A is 14.57 per cent as shown below:

Year	*CFAT*	*Compounded factor at 10% for n – 1years*	*Compounded sum*
1	₹14,000	1.464 (for 4 years)	₹20,496
2	16,000	1.331 (for 3 years)	21,296
3	18,000	1.210 (for 2 years)	21,780
4	20,000	1.110 (for 1 year)	22,200
5	25,000	No compounding	25,000
Total compounded sum at year-end 5			1,10,772

Note: Cost of capital is 10 per cent (Compounded factors are as per Table A-1.)

$$₹56{,}125 = \frac{₹1{,}10{,}772}{(1 + \text{MIRR})^5}$$

1. Dividing the compound sum/terminal value (₹1,10,772) by the initial outlay (₹56,125), we have growth factor (1.9737).
2. In Table A-1, the factors closet to 1.9737 for 5 years are 1.925 (at 14%) and 2.011 (at 15%).
3. The MIRR would be between 14% and 15% as shown below.

₹56,125 compounds at 15% for 5 years =	₹1,12,867
₹56,125 compounds at 14% for 5 years =	1,08,041
Difference of 1 per cent	4,826

Based on interpolation:

$$\text{MIRR} = 14\% + \left(\frac{₹1{,}10{,}772 - ₹1{,}08{,}041 = ₹2{,}731}{₹4{,}826}\right) \times 1 = 14.57 \text{ per cent.}$$

(It may be noted that IRR for Machine A was 17.6 per cent).

The MIRR method, *prima-facie*, appears to be better than the standard IRR. But its superiority is open to question.[6] In the first place, the MIRR may look like a rate of return, but it is not a rate of return on the project's annual cash flows; instead, it is a rate of return on a modified set of cash flows. Secondly, therefore, in view of observation 1, it cannot be reckoned as a true 'internal' rate of return which depends only on cash flows generated from the investment project and, finally, the value of a project does not depend on what the firm does with the cash flows accruing from the project.

Thus, the assumption regarding the reinvestment rate of the cash inflows generated at the intermediate stage is theoretically more correct in the case of NPV as compared to the IRR. This is mainly because the rate is a consistent figure for the NPV but it can widely vary for the IRR according to the cash flow patterns.

Computational Problems Apart from inconsistency in the application of the reinvestment rate, the IRR method also suffers from computational problems. These may be discussed with reference to two aspects.

Computation in Conventional Cash Flows It has been shown while computing the IRR that the calculation of the IRR involves a trial-and-error procedure as a result of which complicated computation has to be done. In conventional proposals having a constant cash inflow stream (i.e. annuity) the computation, is not so tedious. But when the cash inflows are unequal over the years, laborious calculations are involved. The calculations of the NPV, on the other hand, is relatively simple and presents no special problems.

Computation in Non-conventional Flows The problem of computation of IRR gets accentuated when cash flow patterns are non-conventional. The complications in such cases are (a) that the IRR is indeterminate, and (b) there may be multiple IRRs.

Indeterminate IRR For the following pattern of cash flows of an investment proposal, the IRR cannot be determined.[7]

***Example* 10.8**

CO_0 = ₹1
$CFAT_1$ = 2
CO_2 = 2

Where subscripts 0, 1, 2 refer to respective time periods, CFAT = cash inflows, CO = cash outflows

The required equation to solve the IRR is:

$$1+\frac{2}{(1+r)^2}=\frac{2}{(1+r)}, \quad \text{which leads to } r^2 = -1$$

Clearly, the value of IRR is intermediate. On the other hand, the NPV of this project, given k as 10 per cent, can be easily ascertained. This would be negative (₹–0.834), as shown below:

Year	*Cash flows*	*PV factor*	*Total present value*
0	₹(1)	1.000	₹1.000
1	+2	0.909	1.818
2	(2)	0.826	(1.652)
			(0.834)

Multiple Rates of IRR Another serious computational deficiency of IRR method is that it can yield multiple internal rates of return. This is illustrated in Example 10.9.[8]

***Example* 10.9**

Initial cost	Year 0	(₹20,000)
Net cash flow	1	90,000
Net cash flow	2	(80,000)

The required equation is: $₹20{,}000 = \frac{₹\,90{,}000}{(1+r)} - \left(\frac{₹\,80{,}000}{(1+r)^2}\right)$

Let (1 + r) be = X and divide both sides of equation by ₹10,000, $2 = \frac{9}{X} - \frac{8}{X^2} = 0$

Multiplying by X^2, we can transform the equation into the quadratic form,

$$2X^2 - 9X + 8 = 0$$

Such an equation with a variable to the second power has 2 roots which can be identified as:

$$X = \frac{-b \pm \sqrt{b^2 - 4ac}}{2a} \qquad \textbf{(10.2)}$$

where a = coefficient of the variable raised to the second power
b = coefficient of the variable raised to the first power
c = constant or coefficient of the variable raised to the zero power

Substituting the values for a, b, and c into the quadratic formula produces value for X of 1.21. Since X = (1 + r), the internal rates for this project are 21.9 and 228 per cent.

Thus, the project yields a dual IRR. This kind of problem does not arise when the NPV method is used. The problem with the IRR is that if two rates of return make the present value of the project zero, (21.9 and 228 per cent respectively in our example), which rate should be used for decision-making purposes?

To conclude the discussion relating to the comparison of NPV and IRR methods, the two methods would give similar accept-reject decisions in the case of independent conventional investments. They would, however, rank mutually exclusive projects differently in the case of the (i) size-disparity problem, (ii) time-disparity problem, and (iii) unequal service life of projects. The ranking by the NPV decision criterion would be theoretically correct as it is consistent with the goal of maximisation of shareholders' wealth. Further, the reinvestment rate of funds released by the project is based on assumptions which can be consistently applied. The IRR can, of course, be modified by adopting the incremental approach to resolve the conflict in ranking. But it involves additional computation. Another deficiency of the IRR is that it may be indeterminate and give multiple rates in the case of a non-conventional cash flow pattern. In sum, therefore, the NPV emerges as a superior evaluation technique.

Net Present Value Vs. Profitability Index

In most situations, the NPV and PI, as investment criteria, provide the same accept and reject decision, because both the methods are closely related to each other. Under the PI method, the investment proposal will be acceptable if the PI is greater than one; it will be greater than one only when the proposal has a positive net present value. Likewise, PI will be less than one when the investment proposal has negative net present value under the NPV method. However, while evaluating mutually exclusive investment proposals, these methods may give different rankings. Example 10.10 presents such a case.

Example **10.10**

Year	*Project A*	*Project B*
0	(₹50,000)	(₹35,000)
1	40,000	30,000
2	40,000	30,000
Present value of cash inflow (0.10)	69,440	52,080
NPV	19,440	17,080
PI	69,440/50,000 = 1.39	52,080/35,000 = 1.49

Thus, project A is acceptable under the NPV method, while project B under the PI method. Which project should the firm accept? The NPV technique is superior and so project A should be accepted. The reasons for the superiority of NPV method are the same as given in comparing NPV and IRR techniques. The best project is the one which adds the most, among available alternatives, to the shareholders' wealth. The NPV method, by its very definition, will always select such projects. Therefore, the NPV method gives a better mutually exclusive choice than PI. The NPV method guarantees the choice of the best alternative.

LO 10.2 PROJECT SELECTION UNDER CAPITAL RATIONING

The **capital rationing situation** refers to the choice of investment proposals under financial constraints in terms of a given size of capital expenditure budget. The objective to select the combination of projects would be the maximisation of the total NPV. The project selection under capital rationing involves two stages: (i) identification of the acceptable projects. (ii) selection of the combination of projects. The acceptability of projects can be based either on profitability index or IRR.

Capital rationing implies the choice of investment proposals under financial constraints of capital expenditure budget.

Capital rationing can be of two types, namely, **soft rationing** and **hard rationing**. While hard rationing refers to the situation when a business firm cannot raise required finances to execute all potential available profitable investment projects, the soft rationing is internal to the firms in that different divisions/units of a firm are allocated a fixed amount of capital budget each year.[9]

Soft rationing is primarily used, as a means of control on the capital spending of divisional managers. It does not imply that the firm, as a whole, has paucity of funds. In other words, the firm can raise required funds, if it so desires.

The fallout of soft rationing is that the firm eventually is deprived of the profitable investment projects (in case divisions happen to have such projects). As a result, the imposition of soft rationing is in conflict with the basic goal of the firm of maximisation of the wealth/value.

Indivisible project is a project which can be accepted/ rejected in its entirety.

The method of selecting investment projects under capital rationing situation will depend upon whether the projects are **indivisible** or **divisible**. In case the project is to be accepted/rejected in its entirety, it is called an indivisible project; a divisible project, on the other hand, can be accepted/rejected in part. These are illustrated in Examples 10.11 and 10.12 respectively.

Divisible project is a project which can be accepted in parts.

***Example* 10.11 (Divisible Project)**

A company has ₹7 crore available for investment. It has evaluated its options and has found that only 4 investment projects given below have positive NPV. All these investments are divisible. Advise the management which investment(s)/projects it should select.

Project	*Initial investment (₹ crore)*	*NPV (₹ crore)*	*PI*
X	3.00	0.60	1.20
Y	2.00	0.50	1.25
Z	2.50	1.50	1.60
W	6.00	1.80	1.30

Solution

Ranking of the Projects in Descending Order of Profitability Index

Project and (rank)	*Investment outlay (₹ crore)*	*Profitability index*	*NPV (₹ crore)*
Z (1)	2.50	1.60	1.50
W (2)	6.00	1.30	1.80
Y (3)	2.00	1.25	0.50
X (4)	3.00	1.20	0.60

Accept Project Z in *full* and W in part (₹4,50,000) as it will maximise the NPV.

***Example* 10.12 (Indivisible Project)**

A company working against a self-imposed capital budgeting constraint of ₹70 crore is trying to decide which of the following investment proposals should be undertaken by it. All these investment proposals are indivisible as well as independent. The list of investments along with the investment required and the NPV of the projected cash flows are given as below:

Project	*Initial investment (₹ crore)*	*NPV (₹ crore)*
A	10	6
B	24	18
C	32	20
D	22	30
E	18	20

Which investment should be acquired by the company?

Solution

NPV from investments D, E and B is ₹68 crore with ₹64 crore utilised leaving ₹6 crore to be invested in some other investment outlet. No other investment package would yield an NPV higher than this amount. The company is advised to invest in D, E and B projects.

Trial and error process is an integral part of selecting optimal investment packages/set in capital rationing situation. Consider Example 10.13.

***Example* 10.13**

Sound Limited has a financial resource constraint of a maximum of ₹65 lakh in the current year. It has evaluated a large number of investment projects but has discarded all except those listed below. All the listed investment proposals are independent. The selected list of investments provide investment outlays, gross present value, NPV and present value index.

Project	*Investment outlay*	*NPV*	*Gross present value*	*Present value index*
A	₹21,85,000	₹15,07,500	₹36,92,500	1.69
B	19,10,000	10,70,000	29,80,000	1.56
C	15,50,000	2,15,000	17,65,000	1.14
D	13,00,000	2,75,000	15,75,000	1.21
E	11,45,000	15,80,000	27,25,000	2.38
F	9,40,000	4,25,000	13,65,000	1.45
G	6,75,000	6,20,000	12,95,000	1.92
H	5,35,000	3,90,000	9,25,000	1.73
I	4,65,000	6,10,000	10,75,000	2.31
J	4,30,000	4,77,500	9,07,500	2.11
K	4,10,000	2,95,000	7,05,000	1.72
L	3,50,000	3,05,000	6,55,000	1.87
M	2,75,000	1,07,500	3,82,500	1.39
N	2,45,000	2,05,000	4,50,000	1.84
O	1,90,000	3,00,000	4,90,000	2.58
	1,26,05,000	83,82,500	2,09,87,500	

Which investments should be acquired by Sound Limited?

Solution First, we should arrange the investment projects in descending order of present value (PI) index. The optimal investment portfolio/set will be one which yields the maximum NPV. The investment projects are accordingly listed below.

Project	*PI*	*Investment outlays of*		*NPV of*	
		Project	*Cumulative*	*Project*	*Cumulative*
O	2.58	₹1,90,000	₹1,90,000	₹3,00,000	₹3,00,000
E	2.38	11,45,000	13,35,000	15,80,000	18,80,000
I	2.31	4,65,000	18,00,000	6,10,000	24,90,000
J	2.11	4,30,000	22,30,000	4,77,500	29,67,500
G	1.92	6,75,000	29,05,000	6,20,000	35,87,500
L	1.87	3,50,000	32,55,000	3,05,000	38,92,500
N	1.84	2,45,000	35,00,000	2,05,000	40,97,500
H	1.73	5,35,000	40,35,000	3,90,000	44,87,500
K	1.72	4,10,000	44,45,000	2,95,000	47,82,500
A	1.69	21,85,000	66,30,000[1]	15,07,500	—
B	1.56	19,10,000	63,55,000	10,70,000	58,52,500[2]
F	1.45	9,40,000		4,25,000	
M	1.39	2,75,000		1,07,500	
D	1.21	13,00,000		2,75,000	
C	1.14	15,50,000		2,15,000	

[1]Not feasible at this stage; cumulative investment outlays exceed ₹65 lakh.

[2]Investment outlay as well as NPV consist of projects (from O to H) plus project B.

In case the company is guided simply by the PI index, then it selects the first nine projects (numbered from O through K) plus project B. This investment package yields an NPV of ₹58,52,500.

However, this is not the optimal investment package as it does not provide the highest possible NPV. By dropping Project K (₹4,10,000) and B (₹19,10,000) from the proposed investment package and substituting projects A (₹21,85,000) and M (₹2,75,000), the firm generates a higher NPV of ₹61,02,500, as shown below.

Project	*Investment outlays of*		*NPV of*	
	Project (s)	*Cumulative*	*Project (s)*	*Cumulative*
O to H	—	₹40,35,000	—	₹44,87,500
A	₹21,85,000	62,20,000	₹15,07,500	59,95,000
M	2,75,000	64,95,000	1,07,500	61,02,500

Such a substitution exercise involves a trial and error approach. Thus, the optimal investment package consists of 10 projects (O, E, I, J, G, L, N, H, A and M) requiring a total investment outlay of ₹64.95 lakh, yielding a total NPV of ₹61,02,500.

Fallout of Capital Rationing

Capital rationing limits the amount to be spent on capital expenditure decisions. The firm may impose such a limit primarily for two reasons: **(i)** there may be a paucity of funds and **(ii)** corporate managers/owners may be conservative and may not like to invest more than a specified/stated sum in capital projects at one point of time; they may like to accept projects with a greater margin of safety, measured by NPV.

Whatever might be the reasons for capital rationing, it usually results in an investment policy that is *less than optimal.* The reason is that capital rationing does not allow the business firm to accept all profitable investment projects which could add to net present value and, thus, add to the wealth of shareholders. In other words, capital rationing inflicts opportunity cost to the extent of NPV foregone on account of non-acceptance of otherwise acceptable (profitable) investment projects.

Another notable consequence is that capital rationing may lead to the acceptance of several small investment projects (promising higher return per rupee of investment) rather than a few large investment projects. Acceptance of such a package of investment projects is likely to have a bearing on the risk complexion of the business firm (perhaps it may decrease).

Finally, selection criterion of investment projects under capital rationing (based on one-period analysis) does not reckon intermediate cash inflows expected to be provided by an investment project. However, some investment projects may yield relatively higher CFAT in the initial/early years compared to other projects. Obviously, availability of such funds in the early years tends to reduce capital budgeting constraints of the early/future years as they can be used to finance profitable investment projects. For this reason, the management should consider more than one period in the allocation of limited capital for investment projects[10].

LO 10.3 INFLATION AND CAPITAL BUDGETING

The capital budgeting results would be unrealistic if the impact of inflation is not correctly factored in the analysis. The cash flow estimates will not reflect the real purchasing power. In other words, cash flows would be shown at inflated sums and, to that extent, cause distortion in capital budgeting decisions. Therefore, cash flows should be adjusted to accommodate the inflation factor so that the capital budgeting decisions reflect the 'true' picture. The discussion that follows on the procedure for adjusting data for inflation. Consider Example 10.14.

***Example* 10.14**

Proposal X requires an initial capital outlay of ₹2,00,000, with no salvage value, and will be depreciated on a straight line basis for tax purposes. The earnings before depreciation and taxes (EBDT) during its 5 year life are:

Year	*1*	*2*	*3*	*4*	*5*
EBDT	₹70,000	₹76,000	₹80,000	₹60,000	₹52,000

The corporate tax rate is 35 per cent and the company evaluates its capital budgeting projects at 12 per cent cost of capital. Advise the company whether the project should be accepted. (i) when there is no inflation and (ii) when there is inflation at the rate of 15 per cent per annum, and the stated gross earnings are also expected to grow at this rate of inflation.

Solution

Determination of NPV (When There is No Inflation)

(Amount in thousand rupees)

Year	*EBDT*	*Depreciation (200 ÷ 5)*	*Taxable income*	*EAT (Col. 4 × 0.65)*	*CFAT (Col. 5 + 3) (Col. 2 – 3)*	*PV factor*	*Total PV (Col. 6 × 7)*
1	*2*	*3*	*4*	*5*	*6*	*7*	*8*
1	70	40	30	19.5	59.5	0.893	53.13
2	76	40	36	23.4	63.4	0.797	50.53
3	80	40	40	26.0	66.0	0.712	46.99
4	60	40	20	13.0	53.0	0.636	33.71
5	52	40	12	7.8	47.8	0.567	27.10
Gross present value							211.46
Less: Cash outflows							200.00
Net present value							11.46

Since the net present value is positive, the project is worth accepting in a non-inflationary scenario.

In an inflationary situation, EBDT are expected to grow at 15 per cent. As per Table A-1 (showing compound sum of one rupee), EBDT can be determined (reflecting 15 per cent compound rate of growth). As amount of depreciation remains unchanged, taxable profits as well as taxes would go up as exhibited below:

Determination of CFAT in Inflationary Situation

(Amount in thousand rupees)

Year	*EBDT*	*Compound factor at 0.15*	*Revised EBDT (Col. 2 × 3)*	*Depreciation*	*Taxable income (Col. 4 – 5)*	*EAT (Col. 6 × 0.65)*	*CFAT (Col. 7 + 5)*
1	*2*	*3*	*4*	*5*	*6*	*7*	*8*
1	70	1.150	80.50	40	40.50	26.32	66.32
2	76	1.322	100.47	40	60.47	39.31	79.31
3	80	1.521	121.68	40	81.68	53.09	93.09
4	60	1.749	104.94	40	64.94	42.21	82.21
5	52	2.011	104.57	40	64.57	41.97	81.97

Since CFAT are inflated sums, they are to be deflated at the rate of inflation (15 per cent) to determine real cash flows. The relevant calculations are as follows:

Determination of Real Cash Flows

(Amount in thousand rupees)

Year	*CFAT*	*Discount/deflated factor at 0.15 as per Table A – 3*	*Real cash inflows (CFAT) (Col. 2 × 3)*
1	*2*	*3*	*4*
1	66.32	1/1.15 = 0.870	57.70
2	79.31	$1/(1.15)^2 = 0.756$	59.96
3	93.09	$1/(1.15)^3 = 0.658$	61.25
4	82.21	$1/(1.15)^4 = 0.572$	47.02
5	81.97	$1/(1.15)^5 = 0.497$	40.74

The **real cash flows** are substantially lower than nominal cash flows. This is due to the fact that increased income (as depreciation charges do not change) is subject to higher amount of taxes. The corporate tax rate is more than twice (35 per cent) the inflation rate (15 per cent). The NPV and real cash inflows are shown in the following tables.

Real cash flows are cash flows discounted/deflated to reflect effect of inflation on nominal cash flows.

NPV of Real CFAT

(Amount in ₹ thousands)

Year	*Real CFAT*	*PV factor at 12%*	*Total PV (Col. 2 × 3)*
1	*2*	*3*	*4*
1	57.70	0.893	51.53
2	59.96	0.797	47.79
3	61.25	0.712	43.61
4	47.02	0.636	29.90
5	40.74	0.567	23.10
Gross present value			195.93
Less: Cash outflows			200.00
Net present value			(4.07)

IRR of Real CFAT

(Amount in ₹ thousands)

Year	*Real CFAT*	*PV factor at 11%*	*Total PV (Col. 2 × 3)*
1	*2*	*3*	*4*
1	57.70	0.901	51.99
2	59.96	0.812	48.69
3	61.25	0.731	44.77
4	47.02	0.659	30.99
5	40.74	0.593	24.16
Gross present value			200.60
IRR (%)			11.00

Since the NPV is negative under inflationary situations, the investment proposal is not acceptable. Similar conclusions follow based on the internal rate of return method. The IRR based on real CFAT is 11 per cent—lower than the cost of capital (12 per cent).

Thus, inflation results both in lower cash flows and lower real rates of return. Example 10.14 highlights that firms (conscious of protecting the real purchasing power of their owners) may go for unprofitable investment projects, affecting the shareholders wealth adversely. It underlines the significance of incorporating the inflation factor in evaluating capital budgeting decisions, in particular for business firms interested in real returns.

Consistency warrants that the **real cost of capital** should be used to discount real cash inflows after taxes and the nominal cost of capital should be employed for nominal CFAT. This point is illustrated in Example 10.15.

Real cost of capital is cost of capital adjusted for inflation effect.

***Example* 10.15**

The investment data of Prudent Company Ltd launching a new product and with 12 per cent cost of capital, is as follows:

Particulars			*Amount*
Investment			₹7,00,000
CFAT:	Year	1	5,00,000
		2	4,00,000
		3	2,00,000
		4	1,00,000
		5	1,00,000

Assuming an inflation rate of 5 per cent, determine NPV of the project by using both the nominal rate of discount and the real rate of discount.

Solution

NPV Using Nominal Rate of Discount

Year	*CFAT*	*PV factor at 0.12*	*Total PV*
1	₹5,00,000	0.893	₹4,46,500
2	4,00,000	0.797	3,18,800
3	2,00,000	0.712	1,42,400
4	1,00,000	0.636	63,600
5	1,00,000	0.567	56,700
Total present value			10,28,000
Less: Cash outflows			7,00,000
Net present value			3,28,000

The nominal rate of discount (n) is obtained by compounding the real rate (r) and inflation rate (i).[11] In equations terms, it is

$$(1 + n) = (1 + r)\ (1 + i) \qquad \textbf{(10.3)}$$

or

$$(1 + r) = (1 + n)/(1 + i). \qquad \textbf{(10.4)}$$

Substituting the values,

$$(1 + r) = 1.12/1.05 = 1.0667$$

or

$$r = 0.0667 \quad \text{or} \quad 6.67 \text{ per cent.}$$

Since the discount rate now to be used is the real discount rate, the CFAT should also be adjusted for inflation so that they too are expressed in real terms. In operational terms, CFAT will be deflated by the inflation rate (5 per cent). While Table 10.1 shows real/deflated CFAT, NPV of real CFAT is provided in Table 10.2.

TABLE 10.1 Real Cash Flows

Year	*CFAT*	*Deflation factor at 0.05*	*Real CFAT*
1	₹5,00,000	$1/(1.05) = 0.952$	₹4,76,000
2	4,00,000	$1/(1.05)^2 = 0.907$	3,62,800
3	2,00,000	$1/(1.05)^3 = 0.864$	1,72,800
4	1,00,000	$1/(1.05)^4 = 0.823$	82,300
5	1,00,000	$1/(1.05)^5 = 0.784$	78,400

TABLE 10.2 NPV Using Real Rate of Discount

Year	*Real CFAT*	*PV factor at 6.67%*[a]	*Total PV*
1	₹4,76,000	0.938	₹4,46,488
2	3,62,800	0.879	3,18,901
3	1,72,800	0.824	1,42,387
4	82,300	0.772	63,536
5	78,400	0.724	56,761
Total present value			10,28,073
Less: Cash outflows			7,00,000
Net present value			3,28,073[b]

a Based on interpolation as per Table A – 3.

b Difference in NPV of ₹73 (₹3,28,073 – ₹3,28,000) between the two discount rates (nominal and real) is on account of rounding off the values. Both the approaches provide the same answer.

It is important to note that 'real' cash flows discounted at the 'real' discount rate yield an identical amount of NPV that is obtained by discounting 'nominal' cash flows by the 'nominal' discount rate. When estimates of CFAT and cost of capital include inflation, they are said to be expressed in nominal terms; when such estimates exclude the impact of inflation, they are said to be shown in real terms. For correct analysis, these estimates should either be stated in nominal or real terms. It implies that capital budgeting decisions should either reckon the inflation factor in CFAT, as well as the cost of capital, or exclude it completely.

SUMMARY

LO 10.1

- In case of independent investment proposals, all the discounted cash flow (DCF) methods provide consistent results in terms of acceptance or rejection of capital budgeting proposal(s). The independent proposals refer to investment projects, the acceptance of which does not preclude the acceptance of other profitable proposal (s).
  The reason is that all the DCF methods are based on cash flows and take into account total benefits as well as time value of money. The data inputs in terms of cash outflows, CFAT, cost of capital and so on is the same for all these methods. As a result, the investment projects which have positive NPV will also have (i) an IRR> required rate of return, (k) and (ii) a present value index >one
- In the case of mutually exclusive proposals, the DCF methods may provide conflicting rankings. The reason is while the NPV method is based on the *total* yield/earnings/NPV, the other two methods (IRR and PI) are concerned with the *rate* of return/earnings on investment.
- While IRR and PI methods are not compatible with the objective of financial decision making of the firm, that is, maximising shareholders' wealth, the recommendation of NPV method is consistent with the goal of the firm of maximising shareholders' wealth.
- The IRR and PI methods can be modified (by adopting the incremental approach) to give results identical to the NPV method. The logic behind the incremental approach is that the firm would get the profits promised by the smaller outlay investment project plus the profit on the incremental investments required in the project involving larger outlay.
- The conflict between the NPV and IRR methods is mainly ascribed to the different reinvestment rate assumptions of intermediate cash inflows accruing from projects. The IRR method implicitly assumes that the cash flows generated from the projects are subject to reinvestment at IRR. In contrast, the reinvestment rate assumption under the NPV method is the cost of capital. The assumption of the NPV method is conceptually superior to that of the IRR as the former has the virtue of having a uniform rate which can consistently be applied to all investment proposals.

LO 10.1	The IRR can be modified (to overcome the deficiency of the reinvestment rate assumption) assuming the cost of capital to be the reinvestment rate.
	The IRR method is beset with computational and other operational difficulties. In the case of mixed-stream of cash flows, it involves a trial-and-error procedure. When cash flows are non-conventional, its value is either indeterminate or it has multiple values. In contrast, the NPV calculations do not present any such problems.
	The NPV method continues to be the best alternative under capital rationing situations. For these reasons, therefore, the NPV emerges as a theoretically correct and better technique for evaluation of capital projects.
	There are two approaches to deal with investment projects of unequal/varying lives: (i) common time horizon approach and (ii) equivalent annual value, (EANPV)/cost approach (EAC). The first approach requires that the projects must be compared over the same period of time (by taking the LCM of the lives of the capital projects). The implicit assumption of this approach is that the investment which is being replaced will produce cash flows of a similar pattern in future as it has done in the past. Therefore, the approach lacks realism and presents operational difficulties to be used in the real business world.
	The EANPV/EAC is a better approach. The EANPV is determined dividing the NPV of cash flows of the project by the annuity factor corresponding to the life of the project at the given cost of capital. The EAC is obtained dividing the total PV of cash outflows by the relevant annuity factor. While the maximisation of EANPV is the decision-criterion in the case of revenue-expanding proposals, the minimisation of EAC is the guiding criterion for cost reduction proposals.
LO 10.2	Capital rationing involves the choice of combination of available projects maximise the total NPV, given the capital budget constraints. The ranking of investment projects can be done either on the basis of present value index or the IRR. The procedure to select the package of investment projects will relate to whether the project is divisible or indivisible, the objective being the maximisation of total NPV by exhausting the capital budget as far as possible.
LO 10.3	Cash flows of the project should be adjusted for the inflation factor so that they reflect the real purchasing power. The nominal CFAT should be deflated at the rate of inflation. The deflated CFAT are real cash flows. The real CFAT are then discounted at the real rate of discount.
	The nominal rate of discount (n) is obtained by compounding the real rate (r) and inflation rate (i). In equation terms, $(1 + n) = (1 + r)/(1 + i)$. From this equation the following real rate of discount (r) can be obtained: $(1 + r) = (1 + n)/(1 + i)$. The decision criterion is to accept the investment project if it has positive NPV of the real CFAT, discounted at the real rate.
	Alternatively, the nominal CFAT (not adjusted for inflation), are to be discounted at the nominal rate of discount. Both these approaches provide an identical amount of NPV. Therefore, the capital budgeting decisions should either reckon the inflation factor in CFAT as well as cost of capital or exclude it completely.

REFERENCES

1. Joy, O M, *op. cit.*, pp 161-62.
2. Murdick, R G and D D Deming, *The Management of Capital Expenditure*, McGraw-Hill, New York, 1968, p 71.
3. Ross, Stephen A, *op. cit,* p. 325.
4. This hypothetical example has been taken from Pottack, G A, 'The Capital budgeting controversy: present value v. discounted cash flow method', (Nov. 1961), quoted in Murdick, R G and D D Deming, *op. cit.*, p 242.
5. Brigham, E F and J F Houston, *Fundamentals of Financial Management*, South-Western/Cengage Learning India, New Delhi, 2004, p. 409. Also refer to Ross, S A et al. *op. cit*, p. 286.
6. For details, refer to Ross, S A et al, *op. cit*, p. 187.

7. This example is given in Portefield, J T S, *Investment Decisions and Capital Costs*, Prentice Hall, Englewood Cliffs, N J, 1965, p 25.
8. The hypothetical example has been taken from Osteryoung, J, *op. cit.*, pp 73-74.
9. Ross, S A, et al., *op. cit*, pp. 358-9.
10. van Horne, J C, *Financial Management & Policy,* Singapore Pearson Education Pvt. Ltd., 2000, p 149.
11. Emery, D R and J D Finnerty, *Corporate Financial Management,* Prentice–Hall International, London, 1997, p 378.

SOLVED PROBLEMS

P.10.1 Northern Chemicals Ltd owns a machine with the following characteristics:

Book value	₹1,10,000
Current market value	80,000
Expected salvage value at the end of 5 years remaining useful life	Nil
Annual cash operating costs	36,000

LO 10.1 LOD M

The firm's cost of capital is 15 per cent; its tax rate is 35 per cent. The company follows the straight line method of depreciation and the same is accepted for tax purposes.

The management of the company is considering selling the machine. If it does so, the total cash operating costs to perform the work now done by the machine will increase by ₹40,000 per year to ₹76,000 per year. Advise whether the machine should be sold.

Solution

Cash inflows (if machine is sold)

Selling price of the old machine	₹80,000
Add tax savings (0.35 × ₹30,000, short-term capital loss)	10,500
	90,500

Present value of cash outflows saved if machine is not sold (PV of keeping machine)

Particulars	*Amount before tax*	*Amount after tax*
Annual cash operating costs saved (₹76,000 – ₹36,000)	₹40,000	₹26,000
Plus: Tax savings on depreciation (₹1,10,000 ÷ 5)	22,000	14,300
Net annual cash flows		40,300
(x) $PVIFA_{15,5}$		(×) 3.352
PV of keeping machine		1,35,086
PV of selling machine		90,500
Difference favouring keeping the machine		44,586

Recommendation The machine should not be sold.

P.10.2 Avon Ltd is investigating the feasibility of manufacturing one of the components needed for its finished product rather than purchasing it from an outside supplier. Its present supplier has just announced that he intends to increase the price from ₹100 to ₹125 per unit.

LO 10.1 LOD D

The equipment needed to make this product can be purchased for ₹10 lakh, and is expected to have salvage value of ₹2,00,000 after the expiry of the fifth year. Additional fixed costs (excluding depreciation) are estimated to increase by ₹1,00,000 per year. The variable costs of manufacturing each component will be ₹30 per unit. The company is subject to a 35 per cent tax rate and 15 per cent is the appropriate cost of capital for this project. The company projects annual needs at 7,500 units per year for the 6-year period. The tax relevant rate of depreciation is 25 per cent and there are no other assets in the 25 per cent block.

Advise the company whether it should continue buying from outside suppliers, or start manufacturing on its own. Will your answer be different if the requirement of the company is only 6,000 units per year? Assume the firm would have sufficient short-term capital gains in year 6.

Solution *Cash outflows:*

Cost of equipment ₹10,00,000

(i) Cash inflows (CFAT)

Particulars	*7,500 units*	*6,000 units*
Buy costs @ ₹125 per unit	₹9,37,500	₹7,50,000
Less: Manufacturing costs:		
Variable cost @ ₹30 per unit	2,25,000	1,80,000
Fixed cost	1,00,000	1,00,000
Cost saving (profit) before taxes	6,12,500	4,70,000
Less: Taxes	2,14,375	1,64,500
Cash flows after taxes	3,98,125	3,05,500
(×) PV factor of annuity for 5 years	(×) 3.352	(×) 3.352
Total PV	13,34,515	10,24,036

(ii) Present value of tax shield due to depreciation

Year	*Depreciation*	*Tax shield*	*PV factor*	*Total PV*
1	₹2,50,000	₹87,500	0.870	₹76,125
2	1,87,500	65,625	0.756	49,612
3	1,40,625	49,219	0.658	32,386
4	1,05,469	36,914	0.572	21,115
5	79,101	27,685	0.497	13,752
				1,92,997

(iii) Present value of salvage value *(₹2,00,000 × 0.497) = ₹99,400.*

(iv) PV of tax shield on short-term captial loss: [0.35 × (₹2,37,305 – ₹2,00,000 salvage value) × 0.497] = ₹6,489.

(v) Determination of NPV

Particulars	*7,500 units*	*6,000 units*
PV of cash savings	₹13,34,515	₹10,24,036
PV of tax shield (depreciation)	1,92,997	1,92,997
PV of salvage value	99,400	99,400
PV of short-term capital loss	6,489	6,489
Total PV	16,33,401	13,22,922
Less: Cash outflows	10,00,000	10,00,000
NPV	6,33,401	3,22,922

Recommendation The company is advised to start manufacturing on its own, irrespective of the fact whether the required units are 7,500 or 6,000 as the NPV is positive in both the situations.

P.10.3 Avon Chemical Company Ltd is presently paying an outside firm ₹1 per gallon to dispose of the waste material resulting from its manufacturing operations. At normal operating capacity the waste is about 40,000 gallons per year.

LO 10.1 LOD M

After spending ₹40,000 on research, the company discovered that the waste could be sold for ₹15 per gallon if it was processed further. Additional processing would, however, require an investment of ₹6,00,000 in new equipment, which would have an estimated life of 5 years and no salvage value. Depreciation would be computed by the reducing balance method @ 25 per cent. There are no other assets in the 25 per cent block.

Except for the costs incurred in advertising ₹20,000 per year, no change in the present selling and administrative expenses is expected if the new product is sold. The details of additional processing costs are as follows: variable—₹5 per gallon of waste put into process; fixed (excluding depreciation)—₹30,000 per year.

In costing the new product, general factory overheads will be allocated at the rate of ₹1 per gallon.

There will be no losses in processing, and it is assumed that all of the waste processed in a given year will be sold in that very year. Waste that is not processed further will have to be disposed off at the present rate of ₹1 per gallon. Estimates indicate that 30,000 gallons of the new product could be sold each year.

The management, confronted with the choice of disposing off the waste, or processing it further and selling it, seeks your advice. Which alternative would you recommend? Assume that the firm's cost of capital is 15 per cent and it pays, on an average, 35 per cent tax on its income. Assume the firm would have sufficient short-term, capital gains in year 5.

Solution *Cash outflows:*

Cost of additional investment ₹6,00,000

(i) Present value of cash inflows (excluding depreciation), $t = 1 - 5$

Particulars		*Amount*
Increase in sales revenue (30,000 × ₹15)		₹4,50,000
Cost saving: reduction in disposal costs (30,000 × ₹1)		30,000
Less: Incremental costs:		4,80,000
Variable (30,000 × ₹5)	₹1,50,000	
Fixed, manufacturing or processing	30,000	
Advertising	20,000	2,00,000
Earnings before taxes		2,80,000
Less: Taxes		98,000
CFAT		1,82,000
× PVIFA		(×)3.352
Total present value		6,10,064

(ii) PV of tax shield due to depreciation

Year	*Depreciation*	*Tax advantage*	*PV factor*	*Total PV*
1	₹1,50,000	₹52,500	0.870	₹45,675
2	1,12,500	39,375	0.756	29,767
3	84,375	29,531	0.658	19,431
4	63,281	22,148	0.572	12,669
				1,07,542

(iii) PV of tax advantage due to short-term capital loss: [0.35 × (₹1,89,844) × 0.497] = ₹33,023.

(iv) Determination of NPV

Gross present value [(i) + (ii) + (iii)]	₹7,50,629
Less: Cost of additional investment	6,00,000
NPV	1,50,629

Note: ₹40,000 spent on research is irrelevant cost and so is the allocated share of factory overheads.

Recommendation Since the NPV is positive, the company is advised to purchase new equipment.

P.10.4 The North South Airlines (NSA) is considering two proposals to expand its current operations in a big way. At present, it has a fleet of two Boeing 737-200 jets and four Dornier aircrafts. The B-737s were leased from Wright Airways Inc. of USA. The profits of NSA on a revenue of ₹92 crore are ₹21 crore. **LO 10.1** LOD **D**

The Director (Operations) of NSA favours the induction of two additional latest model B737-400 aircrafts. With four jets, the NSA would get the airlines status while its present status is that of Air Taxi Operator (ATO). As a result of achieving the airlines status, the NSA would have to fly on unprofitable routes also. It is suggested that the existing B737-200 models would serve the unprofitable routes. Moreover, Fly-By-Wire Airways (FBWA) is ready to buy one Dornier aircraft for ₹12 crore whose book value is ₹10 crore with remaining useful life of 8 years.

According to an alternative proposal, NSA should acquire an one Airbus-320 (A-320) which has a capacity of 180 passengers compared to 120 of the B737. The NSA would not be required to fly on uneconomical routes with a total fleet of three aircrafts.

On a reference from the managing director of the NSA, the finance manager has worked out the financial parameters as detailed below.

(Amount in ₹ crore)

Particulars	*Option 1 (Buy 737-400 and sell Dornier)*	*Option 2 (Buy A-320)*
Cost of aircraft	150	120
Staff training	2	—
Recurring costs:		
Fuel (5 per cent annual increase)	20	12
Maintenance	10	8
Salary/wages	5	3
Insurance premium	5	6
Overheads (airport charges)	5	3
Sale of Dornier	12	—
Recurring revenues:		
Profitable routes (10 per cent annual increase)	70	55
Unprofitable routes (constant)	5	—
Salvage value (after 8 years)	30	40

The fuel costs are expected to increase 5 per cent annually, while the likely annual increase in salary, wages and overheads would be 10 per cent. The projected recurring revenues are based on the assumption of average occupancy of 70 per cent on profitable routes and 20 per cent on uneconomical routes.

Assuming 35 per cent tax rate, 10 per cent required rate of return and straight line method of depreciation for tax purposes, how do you evaluate the financial viability of the two proposals? Which one would you recommend and why? Ignore tax shield on staff training costs.

Solution

Financial evaluation of options I and II

Option I (to sell 1 Dornier and buy B-737) (amount in crore of rupees):
Cash outflows:

Cost of aircraft	150
Add: Cost of staff training	2
Less: Cale proceeds of Dornier	(12)
Add: Tax payment on sale of Dornier (₹12 crore − ₹10 crore) × 0.35	0.7
	140.7

Determination of CFAT and NPV (amount in crore of rupees)

Year	*Net cash inflow**	*Incremental depreciation***	*EBT*	*EAT (EBT × 0.65)*	*CFAT*	*PV factor (at 0.10)*	*Total PV*
1	30	13.75	16.25	10.56	24.31	0.909	22.10
2	35	13.75	21.25	13.81	27.56	0.826	22.76
3	40.55	13.75	26.80	17.42	31.17	0.751	23.41
4	46.72	13.75	32.97	21.43	35.18	0.683	24.03
5	53.54	13.75	39.79	25.86	39.61	0.621	24.60
6	61.11	13.75	47.36	30.78	44.53	0.564	25.11
7	69.49	13.75	55.74	36.23	49.98	0.513	25.64
8	78.79	13.75	65.04	42.28	56.03	0.467	26.17
8 Salvage value					30.00	0.467	14.01
Less: Cash outflows							(140.7)
NPV							67.13

*Working note 1

**Working note 2

Working Notes

1. Determination of net cash inflows (amount in crore of rupees)

	Gross revenues			Costs						Net cash
Year	PR	UR	Total	Fuel	Maintenance	Salary and wages	IP	OH	Total	inflows
1	70	5	75	20	10	5	5	5	45	30
2	77	5	82	21	10	5.5	5	5.5	47	35
3	84.7	5	89.7	22.05	10	6.05	5	6.05	49.15	40.55
4	93.17	5	98.17	23.15	10	6.65	5	6.65	51.45	46.72
5	102.49	5	107.49	24.31	10	7.32	5	7.32	53.95	53.54
6	112.74	5	117.74	25.53	10	8.05	5	8.05	56.63	61.11
7	124.01	5	129.01	26.80	10	8.86	5	8.86	59.52	69.49
8	136.41	5	141.41	28.14	10	9.74	5	9.74	62.62	78.79

PR = Profitable routes, UR = Unprofitable routes, IP = Insurance premium, OH = Overhead and airport charges

2. Incremental depreciation (₹ crore)

Depreciation (new base) (₹150 crore – ₹30 crore)/8 years	₹15
Less: Depreciation (Dornier) ₹10 crore/8 years	1.25
Incremental depreciation	13.75

Option II (buy A-320):
Cash outflows:

Cost of aircraft ₹120 crore

Determination of CFAT and NPV (amount in crore of rupees)

Year	Net cash inflow*	Depreciation**	EBT	EAT#	CFAT	PV factor	Total PV
1	23	10	13	8.45	18.45	0.909	16.77
2	27.3	10	17.3	11.24	21.24	0.826	17.54
3	32.06	10	22.06	14.34	24.34	0.751	18.28
4	37.34	10	27.34	17.77	27.77	0.683	18.97
5	43.16	10	33.16	21.55	31.55	0.621	19.59
6	49.60	10	39.60	25.74	35.74	0.564	20.16
7	56.74	10	46.74	30.38	40.38	0.513	20.71
8	64.61	10	54.61	35.50	45.50	0.467	21.25
8 Salvage value					40.00	0.467	18.68
Less: Cash outflows							(120.00)
NPV							51.95

* Working note 3

** (₹120 crore – ₹40 crore)/8 years = ₹10 crore

\# (EBT × 0.65)

Recommendation Option I is recommended for NSA as it has higher NPV.

Working Notes

3. Determination of net cash inflows (amount in crore of rupees)

Year	Revenues	Costs						Net cash inflows
		Fuel	Maintenance	Salary and wages	IP	OH	Total	
1	55	12	8	3	6	3	32	23
2	60.5	12.6	8	3.3	6	3.3	33.2	27.3
3	66.55	13.23	8	3.63	6	3.63	34.49	32.06
4	73.21	13.89	8	3.99	6	3.99	35.87	37.34
5	80.53	14.59	8	4.39	6	4.39	37.37	43.16
6	88.58	15.32	8	4.83	6	4.83	38.98	49.60
7	97.44	16.08	8	5.31	6	5.31	40.70	56.74
8	107.18	16.89	8	5.84	6	5.84	42.57	64.61

P.10.5 XYZ Ltd is considering a proposal to replace an existing piece of equipment by a new one. The new equipment is operationally efficient and will result in savings in operating costs estimated at ₹1,50,000 annually.

LO 10.1 LOD M

It will cost ₹3,00,000 and will be purchased at the beginning of the year. The equipment dealer states that most companies use a 4-year life while depreciating equipment with no salvage value. As the equipment will be operational during the second quarter of the year, only 60 per cent of the estimated annual savings would be obtained in the first year. The company will incur a one-time expense of ₹30,000 in transferring production activities from the old equipment to the new one.

The equipment currently being used has a book value of ₹20,000. A review of its condition reveals that it can be used for an additional 4 years. The firm would receive ₹5,000 net of removal costs if it is disposed off now. However, it will have no salvage value after 4 years.

The company uses the declining balance method of depreciation. The equipment is subject to 25 per cent depreciation together with other assets in the block. Assuming that the full year's depreciation is taken into account in the first year, and the corporate tax rate and required rate of return are 35 per cent and 15 per cent respectively, what action should XYZ Ltd's management take? Assume further that shifting expreses are allowed as a deductible item of expense for tax purposes in the year in which they are incurred.

Solution

Cash outflows

Cost of new equipment		₹3,00,000
Add: Shifting expenses	₹30,000	
Less: Tax benefit	10,500	19,500
Less: Sale proceeds of sold equipment		(5,000)
Incremental cash outflows		3,14,500

Determination of CFAT and NPV

Particualrs	Year 1	Year 2	Year 3	Year 4
Cash operating savings	₹90,000	₹1,50,000	₹1,50,000	₹1,50,000
Less: Incremental depreciation	73,750	55,312	41,484	31,113
Taxable earnings (incremental)	16,250	94,688	1,08,516	1,18,887
Less: Taxes (0.35)	5,687	33,141	37,981	41,610
Earnings after taxes (EAT)	10,563	61,547	70,535	77,277
CFAT (EAT + Depreciation)	84,313	1,16,859	1,12,019	1,08,390
× PVIF (0.15)	0.870	0.756	0.658	0.572
PV	73,352	88,345	73,709	61,999
Total present value				2,97,405
Less: Cash outflows				3,14,500
NPV			(17,095)	

Recommendation The company should reject the proposal as the NPV is negative.

Working Notes

Depreciation base of new equipment:

WDV of existing equipment	₹20,000
Add: Cost of new equipment	3,00,000
Less: Sale proceeds of existing equipment	5,000
Amount of equipment on which depreciation will be charged	3,15,000
Less: WDV of existing equipment	20,000
Base of incremental depreciation	2,95,000

P.10.6 Batch & Company Ltd is producing product 'A' and is presently commanding a market share of 15 per cent. The cost and profit margin for one unit of product 'A' is as under: LO 10.1 LOD M

Sale price		₹100
Variable costs:		
Material	₹40	
Labour	20	
Overhead	10	70
Contribution		30
Less: Fixed cost		20
Profit		10

The sale of the product is 15,000 units at 15 per cent market share in the current year.

It has now been estimated that the market share can be increased up to 25 per cent from next year if the following promotional expenses are incurred in the previous year:

For year 1	₹1,00,000
2	75,000
3	50,000

There will also be an increase in fixed cost by ₹30,000, if production has to be increased from present level.

The company wants to achieve a 15 per cent return and would apply DCF rate.

You are required to find out the effect when (i) Market share is increased to 25 per cent, (ii) Market share is increased to 20, and (iii) Market share is increased to 19 and also recommend action to be taken by the company. Ignore taxes.

Solution

Present value of promotional expenses incurred

Year	*Promotional expenses*	*PV factor*	*Total PV*
1	₹1,00,000	1.000	₹1,00,000
2	75,000	0.870	65,250
3	50,000	0.756	37,800
			2,03,050

NPV of increased market share (25, 20 and 19 per cent)

Particulars	*Increased market shares (Years 1 - 3)*		
	25 per cent	*20 per cent*	*19 per cent*
Incremental sales revenue	₹10,00,000	₹5,00,000	₹4,00,000
Less: Variable costs (0.70)	7,00,000	3,50,000	2,80,000
Less: Incremental fixed costs	30,000	30,000	30,000

(Contd.)

(*Contd.*)

Incremental profit	2,70,000	1,20,000	90,000
(×) PV factor annuity (0.15) for 3 years	2.283	2.283	2.283
PV of incremental profit	6,16,410	2,73,960	2,05,470
Less: PV of cash outflows	2,03,050	2,03,050	2,03,050
NPV	4,13,360	70,910	2,420

Recommendation It will be worthwhile to incur promotional expenses even if it is expected that market share will increase to 19 per cent.

P.10.7 An educational institute is planning to install air conditioners for its new computer centre. It has received proposals from 2 manufacturers. The first proposal is for the installation of 6 window air conditioners @ ₹25,000 each. The other is for the installation of split air conditioners of an equal capacity costing ₹2,00,000. The useful life of window air conditioners is 6 years and that of split air conditioners is 10 years. The cash operating costs associated with each proposal are given below: **LO 10.1** LOD E

Year	*Proposal 1*	*Proposal 2*
1	₹20,000	₹18,000
2	20,000	18,000
3	20,000	18,000
4	25,000	22,000
5	25,000	22,000
6	25,000	22,000
7		26,000
8		26,000
9		26,000
10		26,000

The salvage value of the window air conditioners at the end of 6 years is expected to be ₹10,000 and that of the split air conditioners ₹15,000. Advise the educational institute which proposal should be selected by it if its opportunity cost of funds is 10 per cent.

Solution Equivalent Annual Cost

Proposal 1

Particulars	*Year*	*Cost*	*PV factor (at 10%)*	*PV*
Purchase cost	0	₹1,50,000	1.000	₹1,50,000
Operating costs	1	20,000	0.909	18,180
	2	20,000	0.826	16,520
	3	20,000	0.751	15,020
	4	25,000	0.683	17,075
	5	25,000	0.621	15,525
	6	25,000	0.564	14,100
Salvage value	6	(10,000)	0.564	(5,640)
Total PV				₹2,40,780

Equivalent Annual Cost (EAC)

$$= \frac{\text{Total present value of the project}}{\text{PV of annuity corresponding to the life of the project at the given cost of capital}}$$

₹2,40,780/4.355 = ₹55,288.17

Proposal 2

Particulars	*Year*	*Cost*	*PV factor (at 10%)*	*PV*
Purchase cost	0	₹2,00,000	1.000	₹2,00,000
Operating costs	1	18,000	0.909	16,362
	2	18,000	0.826	14,868
	3	18,000	0.751	13,518
	4	22,000	0.683	15,026
	5	22,000	0.621	13,662
	6	22,000	0.564	12,408
	7	26,000	0.513	13,338
	8	26,000	0.467	12,142
	9	26,000	0.424	11,024
	10	26,000	0.386	10,036
Salvage Value	10	(15,000)	0.386	(5,790)
Total PV				₹3,38,174

Equivalent Annual Cost (EAC) = ₹3,32,384/6.145 = ₹55,032.38

Recommendation The educational institution should go for split air conditioners as their equivalent annual cost is lower.

P.10.8 A large profit making company is considering the installation of a machine to process the waste produced by one of its existing manufacturing process and convert it into a marketable product. At present, the waste is being removed, for disposal by a contractor against payment of ₹50 lakh per annum. This arrangement will continue for the next four years. The contract can be terminated upon installation of the aforesaid machine, on payment of a compensation of ₹30 lakh before the processing operation starts. This compensation is not allowed as deduction for tax purposes.

LO 10.1 LOD D

The machine required for carrying out the processing, costing ₹200 lakh will be financed by a loan repayable in 4 equal installments, commencing from the end of year 1. The interest rate is 16 per cent per annum. At the end of the 4th year, the machine can be sold for ₹20 lakh and the cost of dismantling and removal will be ₹15 lakh.

Sales and direct costs of the product emerging from waste processing, for 4 years, are estimated as under:

[₹ (lakh)]

Year	*1*	*2*	*3*	*4*
Sales	322	322	418	418
Material consumption	30	40	85	85
Wages	75	75	85	100
Other expenses	40	45	54	70
Factory overheads	55	60	110	145
Depreciation (as per income-tax rules)	50	38	28	21

Initial stock of materials required before commencement of the processing operations is ₹20 lakh at the start of year 1. The stock levels of materials to be maintained at the end of year 1, 2 and 3 will be ₹55 lakh and the stocks at the end of year 4 will be nil. The storage of materials will utilize space which would otherwise have been rented out at ₹10 lakh per annum. Labour costs include wages of 40 workers, whose transfer to this process will reduce idle time payments of ₹15 lakh in year 1 and ₹10 lakh in year 2. Factory overheads include apportionment of general factory overheads, except to the extent of insurance charges of ₹30 lacs per annum, payable on this venture. The company's tax rate is 50 per cent.

Present value factors for 4 years are as under:

Year	1	2	3	4
Present value factors at 15%	0.870	0.756	0.658	0.572

Advise the management on the desirability of installing the machine for processing the waste. All calculations should form part of the answer.

Solution

Determination of cash outflows (*Amount in ₹ lakh*)

Particulars	Time	
	Year 0	1
Cost of new machine	200	—
Compensation for cancellation of contract	30	—
Working capital required (in terms of carrying stock of materials)	20	35
	250	35
Multiply by PVIF at 15 per cent	1.000	0.870
PV of cash outflows	250.00	30.45
Total cash outflows at t = 0	280.45	

Determination of CFAT and NPV (*Amount in ₹ lakh*)

Particulars	Year 1	2	3	4
Sales	322	322	418	418
Add: Cost savings (reduction in waste disposal costs)	50	50	50	50
	372	372	468	468
Less: Incremental costs:				
Material consumption	30	40	85	85
Wages (net of idle time)	60	65	85	100
Other expenses	40	45	54	70
Insurance charges	30	30	30	30
Loss of rent	10	10	10	10
Depreciation	50	38	28	21
	220	228	292	316
Earnings before taxes	152	144	176	152
Less: Taxes	76	72	88	76
Earnings after taxes	76	72	88	76
CFAT 126	110	116	97	
Salvage value (net of removal costs)	—	—	—	5
Release of working capital				55
PV factor at 15%	0.870	0.756	0.658	0.572
Present value	109.62	83.16	76.33	89.80
Total present value				358.91
Less: Present value of cash outflows				280.45
Net present value				78.46

Notes:

(i) Interest has not been treated as expenses as CFAT are to be discounted at cost of capital (which includes after-tax cost of debt).

(ii) Since the cost of machine has been shown as cash outflow at t = 0, repayment of instalment has not been shown as cash outflow.

(iii) As the question has specifically stated depreciation as per income-tax rules, no tax treatment has been made in terminating year 4 due to unabsorbed depreciation.

Recommendation The company is advised to buy the machine for processing waste (since NPV is positive).

P.10.9 XYZ Ltd, an infrastructure company, is evaluating a proposal to build, operate and transfer a section of 35 kms of road at a project cost of ₹200 crore, to be financed as follows:

LO 10.1 LOD D

Equity share capital ₹50 crore, ₹150 crore loan at the rate of interest of 15 per cent per annum from financial institutions. The project, after completion will be opened to traffic and a toll will be collected, from the vehicles using the road, for a period of 15 years. The company is also required to maintain the road during the 15 years and after the completion of that period, it will be handed over to the highway authorities at zero value. It is estimated that the toll revenue will be ₹50 crore per annum and the annual toll collection expenses including maintenance of the roads will amount to 5 per cent of the project cost. The company considers to write off the total cost of the project in 15 years on a straight-line basis. For corporate income tax purposes the company is allowed to take depreciation @ 10 per cent on WDV basis. Financial institutions are agreeable to the repayment of the loan in 15 equal annual installments—consisting of principal and interest.

Calculate project IRR and equity IRR. Ignore corporate taxation.

Solution

(i) Determination of project IRR

	(₹ crore)
Cash outflow/project cost:	₹200
Cash inflows (t = 1 – 15 years):	
Toll revenue	50
Less: Toll collection expenses, maintenance of the roads, etc (₹200 crore × 0.05)	10
Net cash inflows	40

$$CO_0 = \sum_{t=1}^{15} \frac{CI_t}{(1+r)^t}; \text{₹}\,200 \text{ crore} = \frac{\text{₹}\,40 \text{ crore}}{(1+r)^{15}}$$

To determine IRR, payback is determined i.e., 5 years (₹200 crore/₹40 crore). Then PV table of annuity is referred to, to look for a PV factor which is equal to or closest to the payback period, corresponding to the life of the project (15 years). As per the PV table, the two closest figures are 5.092 (at 18 per cent) and 4.876 (at 19 per cent); evidently, the IRR is likely to be between the range of 18–19 per cent. Its value is 18% + (0.092 ÷ 0.216) = 18.43 per cent.

(ii) Determination of Equity IRR: It may be defined as a rate of discount which discounts future cash inflows available to equityholders in such a way that the PV of these cash inflows is equal to the equity owners' investment. Accordingly, the relevant values are:

(a) Equity share capital is ₹50 crore and (b) cash inflows available to equity holders are ₹14.35 crore as shown below

	(₹ crore)
Net cash inflow of the project	₹40
Less: Equated instalment of the project (₹150 crore / PVIF at 15% for 15 years i.e., 5.847)	25.65
Cash inflows for equityholders	14.35

$$\text{₹}50 \text{ crore} = \frac{\text{₹}\,14.35 \text{ crore}}{(1+r)^{15}}$$

Payback period is ₹50 crore/₹14.35 crore = 3.484

The PV factor closest to 3.484 (as per PV annuity table corresponding to 15 years) is 3.483, at 28 per cent rate of discount. In other words, 28 per cent is equity IRR.

Note: Depreciation is considered in capital budgeting decisions as it yields tax savings (depreciation per se does not cause cash outflows). Since taxes are to be ignored in the present question, therefore, depreciation is also not taken into account.

P.10.10 The capital budgeting department of a company has suggested 3 investment proposals. The after-tax cash flows for each are tabulated below. If the cost of capital is 12 per cent, rank them on the basis of the profitability index. LO 10.2 LOD E

Year	After-tax cash flows		
	Project A	*Project B*	*Project C*
0	₹20,000	₹60,000	₹36,000
1	5,600	12,000	13,000
2	6,000	20,000	13,000
3	8,000	24,000	13,000
4	8,000	32,000	13,000

Solution

Determination of present value

Year	*CFAT*			*PV factor*	*Total PV*		
	A	*B*	*C*		*A*	*B*	*C*
1	₹5,600	₹12,000	₹13,000	0.893	₹5,001	₹10,716	₹11,609
2	6,000	20,000	13,000	0.797	4,782	15,940	10,361
3	8,000	24,000	13,000	0.712	5,696	17,088	9,256
4	8,000	32,000	13,000	0.636	5,088	20,352	8,268
					20,567	64,096	39,494

Profitability index = PV of cash inflows/PV of cash outflows

$PI_{(A)}$ = ₹20,567/₹20,000 = 1.028

$PI_{(B)}$ = ₹64,096/₹60,000 = 1.068

$PI_{(C)}$ = ₹39,494/₹36,000 = 1.097

The projects in descending order of profitability are: C, B and A.

P.10.11 A textile company has ₹20 lakh available for investment. It has evaluated its options and found that only four investments (W, X, Y and Z) have positive net present values. All these investments are entirely independent of one other. However, they have an equal life period of 5 years. The risk-free interest rate is 5 per cent per annum. The cost of capital to the company is 10 per cent. The relevant data for the selected investments are: LO 10.2 LOD E

Investment	*Initial outlay*	*Present value of future cash inflows from the investment*
W	₹8,00,000	₹10,00,000
X	6,00,000	10,00,000
Y	7,00,000	11,40,000
Z	6,00,000	12,00,000

Which investment(s) should the firm adopt? Would your answer be different if the present value of future cash flows of project W were ₹12,50,000 instead of ₹10,00,000?

Solution

NPVs of investment projects

Investment	*Initial outlay*	*PV of future cash flows*	*NPV*
W	₹8,00,000	₹10,00,000	₹2,00,000
X	6,00,000	10,00,000	4,00,000
Y	7,00,000	11,40,000	4,40,000
Z	6,00,000	12,00,000	6,00,000

(i) NPV from investments Z, X and W = ₹12,00,000 (with full capital budget amount utilised).

(ii) NPV from investments X, Y and Z = ₹14,40,000 (with ₹19,00,000 utilised, leaving ₹1,00,000 to be invested elsewhere). ₹1,00,000 can be invested for a period of 5 years at 5 per cent. The compound sum of ₹1,00,000 would be ₹1,27,600 [₹1,00,000 × 1.276 (the sum of rupee one at 5 per cent in 5 years as per Table A-1)].

The NPV of ₹1,27,600 received at the end of the fifth year would be ₹79,240 [(₹1,27,600 × 0.621, that is, the present value of rupee one at 10 per cent rate of discount to be received in 5 years from now as per Table A-3)]. Thus, the total NPV is ₹14,40,000 + ₹79,240 = ₹15,19,240.

Therefore, the firm should adopt X, Y, and Z investment proposals.

(b) No. It is because the NPV from investments Z, X and W would still be lower than the package of investments as outlined in (a) (ii). The new NPV from investments Z, X and W would be ₹14,50,000, while from X, Y and Z, it is ₹15,19,240.

P.10.12 Alpha Limited is considering 5 capital projects for the years 1 and 2. The company is financed by equity entirely and its cost of capital is 12 per cent. The expected cash flows of the projects are as detailed below: LO 10.2 LOD M

(₹ '000)

Project	*Year and cashflows*			
	1	*2*	*3*	*4*
A	(70)	35	35	20
B	(40)	(30)	45	55
C	(50)	(60)	70	80
D	—	(90)	55	65
E	(60)	20	40	50

(Figures in brackets represent cash outflows.)

All projects are divisible, that is, size of investment can be reduced, if necessary, in relation to availability of funds. None of the projects can be delayed or undertaken more than once.

Calculate which project should Alpha Ltd undertake if the capital available for investment is limited to ₹1,10,000 in year 1 and with no limitation in subsequent years. For your analysis use the following present value factors:

Year	*1*	*2*	*3*	*4*
Factor	1.00	0.89	0.80	0.71

Solution

Determination of gross present value, NPV and PI of projects A to E

(Amount in ₹ '000)

Year	*Projects*				
	A	*B*	*C*	*D*	*E*
1	(70)	(40)	(50)	—	(60)
2	(35 × 0.89) = 31.15	(30 × 0.89) = 26.7	(60 × 0.89) = 53.4	(90 × 0.89) = 80.1	20 × 0.89 = 17.8
3	(35 × 0.80) = 28	(45 × 0.8) = 36	(70 × 0.8) = 56	(55 × 0.8) = 44	(40 × 0.8) = 32
4	(20 × 0.71) = 14.2	(55 × 0.71) = 39.05	(80 × 0.71) = 56.8	(65 × 0.71) = 46.15	(50 × 0.71) = 35.5
Gross present value	73.35	75.05	112.8	90.15	85.3
NPV	3.35	8.35	9.4	10.05	25.3
Profitability index (PI)	1.048	1.125	1.091	1.125	1.422
Ranking (on the basis of PI)	5	3	4	2	1

Recommendation Since project D is not subject to capital rationing (as it is to be undertaken in year 2) and it promises positive NPV, the project is worth accepting. For other projects (A, B, C and E), the requirement ia ₹2,20,000 against the available sum of ₹1,10,000. Based on ranking (descending order of PI), projects E and B will be accepted in full and a part of project C as shown below:

Project and rank	*Amount of investment*
E(1)	₹60,000
B(3)	40,000
C(4) (limited to)	10,000

P.10.13 A company (profile summarised below) with a 12 per cent cost of funds and limited investment funds of ₹4,00,000 is evaluating the desirability of several investment proposals. **LO 10.2** LOD M

Project	*Initial investment*	*Life (in years)*	*Year-end cash inflow*
A	₹3,00,000	2	₹1,87,600
B	2,00,000	5	66,000
C	2,00,000	3	1,00,000
D	1,00,000	9	20,000
E	3,00,000	10	66,000

(i) Rank the projects according to the profitability index, and NPV methods.
(ii) Determine the optimal investment package.
(iii) Which projects should be selected, if the company has ₹5,00,000 as the size of its capital budget?
(iv) Determine the optimal investment package in the above situations, assuming that the projects are divisible.

Solution

(i) Determination of NPV and PI for all projects

Project	Life in years	Year-end CFAT	PV factor at 0.12 correspon-ding to life of the project	Total PV of CFAT	Initial investment	NPV	PI	Ranking 1 to 5 in order of preference NPV	PI
A	2	₹1,87,600	1.690	₹3,17,044	₹3,00,000	₹17,044	1.057	4	5
B	5	66,000	3.605	2,37,930	2,00,000	37,930	1.189	3	3
C	3	1,00,000	2.402	2,40,200	2,00,000	40,200	1.200	2	2
D	9	20,000	5.328	1,06,560	1,00,000	6,560	1.066	5	4
E	10	66,000	5.650	3,72,900	3,00,000	72,900	1.243	1	1

(ii) Optimal investment package when capital budget is ₹4,00,000

Project	Investment	NPV
E	₹3,00,000	₹72,900
D	1,00,000	6,560
		79,460

(iii) Capital budget is ₹5,00,000

E	3,00,000	72,900
C	2,00,000	40,200
		1,13,100

(iv) (a) Capital budget is ₹4,00,000

Project	Investment	PI	NPV
E	₹3,00,000	1.243	72,900
C (0.50)	1,00,000 (0.50 × ₹2,00,000)	1.200	20,100
			93,000

(b) Capital budget is ₹5,00,000

E	3,00,000	1.243	72,900
C	2,00,000	1.200	40,200
			1,13,100

P.10.14 S Ltd has ₹10,00,000 allocated for capital budgeting purposes. The following proposals and associated profitability indexes have been determined: LO 10.2 LOD M

Project	Amount	Profitability Index
1	₹3,00,000	1.22
2	1,50,000	0.95
3	3,50,000	1.20
4	4,50,000	1.18
5	2,00,000	1.20
6	4,00,000	1.05

Which of the above investments should be undertaken? Assume that the projects are indivisible and there is no alternative use of the money allocated for capital budgeting.

Solution

Statement showing ranking of projects (in descending order of profitability index) and their NPV

Projects	*Initial investment*	*Profitability index*	*Gross present value (Col. 2 × Col. 3)*	*Net present value (Col. 4 – Col. 2)*
1	*2*	*3*	*4*	*5*
1	₹3,00,000	1.22	₹3,66,000	₹66,000
3	3,50,000	1.20	4,20,000	70,000
5	2,00,000	1.20	2,40,000	40,000
4	4,50,000	1.18	5,31,000	81,000
6	4,00,000	1.05	4,20,000	20,000

Notes: (i) Project 2 has been excluded in view of its profitability index being less than one, implying negative NPV. (ii) Since project 3 has a higher profitability index, it has been assigned a higher rank than project 5.

S Ltd. is advised to undertake projects 4, 3 and 5 as this package holds potentials of yielding the maximum NPV of ₹1,91,000 (₹81,000 + ₹70,000 + ₹40,000).

P.10.15 Owing to the ongoing recession in the world market, Strong company's bottom line suffered yet it managed to have just ₹65 lakh remaining for investment after paying off the dividends to the shareholders. The company is not willing to raise additional funds either through debt or equity, given the present state of business scenario. The finance department lists the following profitable projects (along with other necessary details like NPV, PVI, etc.) where the funds can be invested. You are required to evaluate these projects to help the company make the best investment decision possible under the current scenario. Assume all given investment proposals are independent and divisible. **LO 10.2** LOD **D**

Project	*Investment outlay*	*NPV*	*Gross present value*	*Present value index*
P1	₹21,85,000	₹10,92,500	₹32,77,500	1.50
P2	20,80,000	10,19,200	30,99,200	1.49
P3	2,25,000	92,250	3,17,250	1.41
P4	2,40,000	1,00,800	3,40,800	1.42
P5	11,50,000	15,41,000	26,91,000	2.34
P6	9,40,000	4,25,000	13,65,000	1.45
P7	8,55,000	7,95,150	16,50,150	1.93
P8	4,95,000	3,41,550	8,36,550	1.69
P9	6,05,250	7,38,405	13,43,655	2.22
P10	3,90,000	4,48,500	8,38,500	2.15
P11	4,00,000	2,08,000	6,08,000	1.52
P12	3,15,000	2,83,500	5,98,500	1.90
P13	1,55,000	73,800	2,28,800	1.48
P14	3,70,500	2,92,695	6,63,195	1.79
P15	280,500	4,80,968	7,61,468	2.71
Total	1,06,86,250	79,33,318	1,86,19,568	

Solution

First, arrange all the investment projects in descending order of present value index (PI). The optimal investment portfolio/ set will be one that yields the maximum NPV. The investment projects are accordingly listed below.

Project	PI	Investment outlays		NPV	
		Project	Cumulative	Project	Cumulative
P15	2.71	₹2,80,500	₹2,80,500	₹4,80,968	₹4,80,968
P5	2.34	11,50,000	14,30,500	15,41,000	20,21,968
P9	2.22	6,05,250	20,35,750	7,38,405	27,60,373
P10	2.15	3,90,000	24,25,750	4,48,500	32,08,873
P7	1.93	8,55,000	32,80,750	7,95,150	40,04,023
P12	1.90	3,15,000	35,95,750	2,83,500	42,87,523
P14	1.79	3,70,500	39,66,250	2,92,695	45,80,218
P8	1.69	4,95,000	44,61,250	3,41,550	49,21,768
P11	1.52	4,00,000	48,61,250	2,08,000	51,29,768
P1	1.50	21,85,000	70,46,250[a]	10,92,500	62,22,268
P1	1.50	16,38,750	65,00,000	8,19,375[b]	59,49,143

[a]Not feasible as cumulative investment outlays exceed ₹65 lakh.
[b]Project P1 can be undertaken to the extent of 75 per cent (₹16,38,750 amount short of ₹65,00,000/₹21,85,000, cost of project 1). Accordingly, NPV accruing from truncated project would be 0.75 × ₹10,92,500 = ₹8,19,375.

Recommendation Strong company is advised to select projects P15 to P11 (shown in solution table) in their entirety and 75 per cent of P1, utilising all available funds (₹65 lakh) and yielding a (maximum possible) NPV of ₹59,49,143.

P.10.16 A corporate firm's management policy is to earn a real rate of return (r) of 10 per cent on new projects. It is expected that the inflation rate (i) during the proposed project's life is 6 per cent per year. Determine the nominal discount rate (n) which should be used by the firm to the determine the present value of the project. **LO 10.3** LOD E

Solution

Nominal rate (n) = $(1 + r)(1 + i) - 1$
$= (1 + 0.10)(1 + 0.06) - 1$
$= (1.1)(1.06) - 1 = 1.166 - 1 = 0.166 = 16.6$ per cent

P.10.17 Sagar Industries employs 15 per cent as nominal required rate of return to evaluate its new investment projects. In the recent meeting of its board of directors, it has been decided to protect the interest of shareholders against purchasing power loss due to inflation. The expected inflation rate in the economy is 6 per cent. Determine the real discount rate to be employed now by Sagar Industries. **LO 10.3** LOD E

Solution

Real rate (r) = $(1 + n)/(1 + i) - 1$
$= (1 + 0.15)/(1 + 0.06) - 1$
$= (1.15/1.06) - 1 = 1.0849 - 1 = 0.0849 = 8.49$ per cent

P.10.18 A new machine is expected to generate the following set of incremental CFAT during its 5 year economic useful life: **LO 10.3** LOD M

Year	CFAT
1	₹10,00,000
2	12,00,000
3	15,00,000
4	8,00,000
5	5,00,000

The rate of inflation during the period is expected to be 8 per cent and the project's cost of capital in real terms would be 10 per cent. Should the machine be purchased if it costs ₹25 lakh?

Solution

Determination of real CFAT

Year	*CFAT*	*Deflation factor at 0.08**	*Real CFAT*
1	₹10,00,000	1/(1.08) = 0.926	₹9,26,000
2	12,00,000	1/(1.08)2 = 0.857	10,28,400
3	15,00,000	1/(1.08)3 = 0.794	11,91,000
4	8,00,000	1/(1.08)4 = 0.735	5,88,000
5	5,00,000	1/(1.08)5 = 0.681	3,40,500

*As per Table A-3.

Determination of NPV using real rate of discount

Year	*Real CFAT*	*Discount factor at 0.10*	*Total PV*
1	₹9,26,000	0.909	₹8,41,734
2	10,28,400	0.826	8,49,458
3	11,91,000	0.751	8,94,441
4	5,88,000	0.683	4,01,604
5	3,40,500	0.621	2,11,450
Total present value			31,98,687
Less: Cash outflows			25,00,000
Net present value			6,98,687

Recommendation The machine should be purchased as the NPV is positive.

P.10.19 Assume the data given in **P10.18** remains unchanged. Determine the NPV of machine in nominal terms. Does your answer change?

LO 10.3 LOD M

Solution

Nominal rate (n) = $(1 + r)(1 + i) - 1$

$= (1 + 0.10)(1 + 0.08) - 1$

$= (1.1)(1.08) - 1 = 1.188 - 1 = 0.188 = 18.8$ per cent

Determination of NPV in nominal terms requires discounting nominal CFAT by nominal rate of discount (18.8 %).

Determination of NPV using nominal rate of discount

Year	*CFAT*	*PV factor at 18.8%**	*Total PV*
1	₹10,00,000	0.841	₹8,41,000
2	12,00,000	0.709	8,50,800
3	15,00,000	0.596	8,94,000
4	8,00,000	0.502	4,01,600
5	5,00,000	0.423	2,11,500
Total present value			31,98,900
Less: Cash outflows			25,00,000
Net present value			6,98,900

* Based on interpolation as per Table A-3.

Recommendation The machine should be purchased, the answer does not change. The reason is that nominal CFAT are discounted at nominal discount rate; earlier real CFAT were discounted at real discount rate. Consistency is critical for a consistent answer.

P.10.20 Royal Industries is contemplating on buying a new moulding machine at ₹50 lakh, with an additional working capital requirement of ₹10 lakh. The machine is expected to have an economic useful life of 5 years, with no salvage value. The firm follows the straight-line method of depreciation and the same is accepted for tax purposes. The machine is expected to generate an incremental increase in the before tax cash operating income of ₹20 lakh (in real terms) per year for a period of 5 years. The relevant tax rate is 35 per cent. Inflation is expected to be 6 per cent per year and the firm's cost of capital in real terms is 10 per cent. Advise the company whether the machine should be purchased. Show your NPV calculation in real terms. Assume the working capital requirement will remain unchanged throughout the period, in spite of inflation.

LO 10.3 LOD M

Solution

(i) Cash outflows

Cost of moulding machine	₹50,00,000
Additional working capital	10,00,000
	60,00,000

(ii) CFAT and present value

(a) Incremental cash operating income	20,00,000
Less: Taxes (0.35)	7,00,000
CFAT (t = 1 – 5)	13,00,000
(X) PV factor of annuity for 5 years (0.10)	(×) 3.791
Present value	49,28,300
(b) Tax savings due to depreciation	
Depreciation (₹50 lakh/5 years) per year	10,00,000
(X) Tax rate (0.35)	(×) 0.35
Tax savings per year for 5 years	3,50,000

(c) Present value of tax shield due to depreciation

Year	*Tax savings (Nominal CFAT)*	*Discount/Deflated at 0.06 rate of inflation**	*CFAT (Real)*	*PVF at 0.10*	*Total PV*
1	₹3,50,000	0.943	₹3,30,050	0.909	₹3,00,015
2	3,50,000	0.890	3,11,500	0.826	2,57,299
3	3,50,000	0.840	2,94,000	0.751	2,20,794
4	3,50,000	0.792	2,77,200	0.683	1,89,328
5	3,50,000	0.747	2,61,450	0.621	1,62,360
Present value					11,29,796

*As per Table A-3

(d) Release of working capital (at year-end 5)	₹10,00,000
(X) Discount factor at 0.06 (at year-end 5)	(×) 0.747
Cash inflows (real)	7,47,000
(X) Discount factor at 0.10 (at year-end 5)	(×) 0.621
Present value	4,63,887
(iii) Total present value	
(a) ₹49,28,300 + (c) ₹11,29,796 + (d) ₹4,63,887	65,21,983
(iv) Net present value (₹65,21,983 – ₹60,00,000)	5,21,983

Recommendation The company should purchase the machine as the NPV of real cash flows is positive.

P.10.21 Assume everything to be the same as contained in P10.20, except that the firm follows written down value method of depreciation at the rate of 25 per cent. Assume further that the company does not have any other asset in the block of 25 per cent and the machine is expected to have salvage value of ₹5 lakh at year-end 5. Does your answer change? You are to compute NPV in real terms. Also assume that the firm would have sufficient short-term capital gains in year 5. **LO 10.3** LOD M

Solution There will be a change in PV of tax savings due to depreciation in view of change in the method of depreciation; there will be tax savings due to short-term capital loss at year-end 5 also.

Tax savings (CFAT) in nominal and real terms due to depreciation

Year	*Depreciation*	*Tax savings/Nominal CFAT, (Depreciation × 0.35)*	*Discount factor at 0.06*	*CFAT, (real)*
1	₹12,50,000	₹4,37,500	0.943	₹4,12,562
2	9,37,500	3,28,125	0.890	2,92,031
3	7,03,125	2,46,094	0.840	2,06,719
4*	5,27,344	1,84,570	0.792	1,46,179

* Since the block ceases to exist in the 5th year, no depreciation is charged in year 5.

Present value of tax shield, salvage value and short-term capital loss

Year	*Real CFAT*	*PV factor 0.10*	*Total PV*
1	₹4,12,562	0.909	₹3,75,019
2	2,92,031	0.826	2,41,218
3	2,06,719	0.751	1,55,246
4	1,46,179	0.683	99,840
(i) Present value of tax shield due to depreciation			8,71,323
Salvage value (at year-end 5)			
Salvage value			5,00,000
(X) Deflated/discount factor at 0.06 (at year-end 5)			(×) 0.747
Real Cash inflows			3,73,500
(X) Discount factor (at year-end 5) at 0.10			(×) 0.621
(ii) Present value of salvage value			2,31,943
Short-term capital loss (at year-end 5)			
Cost of machine			50,00,000
Less: Accumulated depreciation in 4 years			34,17,969
Book value of machine in year 5			15,82,031
Less: Sale value			5,00,000
Short-term capital loss (STCL)			10,82,031
Tax savings (₹10,82,031 × 0.35) on STCL/CFAT, nominal			3,78,711
(X) Deflation factor at 0.06 (at year-end 5)			(×) 0.747
Real CFAT			2,82,897
(X) Discount factor (at year-end 5) at 0.10			(×) 0.621
(iii) Present value of STCL			1,75,679
Total present value (₹8,71,323 + ₹2,31,943 + ₹1,75,679)			12,78,945

NPV of machine

Present value of operating CFAT	₹49,28,300
Present value of release of working capital	4,63,887
Present value of tax shield due to depreciation, salvage value and short-term capital loss	12,78,945
Total present value	66,71,132
Less: Present value of cash outflows	60,00,000
Net present value	6,71,132

Recommendation Since NPV is positive, the firm should accept the project. The answer regarding acceptance of the project remains unchanged.

P.10.22 XYZ Ltd wants to purchase a plant for its expanding operations. The desired plant is available at ₹10 lakh. The expected earnings before depreciation and taxes (EBDT) during its 5 years economic useful life are as shown in table. **LO 10.3** LOD D

Year	*EBDT*
1	₹3,50,000
2	3,80,000
3	4,00,000
4	3,25,000
5	2,50,000

The rate of inflation during the period is expected to be 8 per cent and the stated EBDT are also expected to grow at this rate of inflation. The management policy of the firm is to evaluate its capital budgeting proposal by using cost of capital in real terms at 10 per cent.

The firm follows the written down value method of depreciation at the rate of 25 per cent on this machine. There are several machines in this block. The machine is expected to a yield salvage value of ₹1,00,000 at year-end 5. The relevant tax rate is 35 per cent.

Advise the company whether the proposed machine should be purchased. Show your calculations in real terms.

Solution

Determination of CFAT in inflationary situation

Year	*EBDT*	*Compound factor at 0.08 as per Table A-1*	*Revised EBDT (Col. 2 × 3)*	*Depreciation @ 0.25 on WDV*	*Taxable income (Col. 4 – 5)*	*EAT (Col. 6 × 0.65)*	*CFAT (Col. 7 + 5)*
1	*2*	*3*	*4*	*5*	*6*	*7*	*8*
1	₹3,50,000	1.080	₹3,78,000	₹2,50,000	₹1,28,000	₹83,200	₹3,33,200
2	3,80,000	1.166	4,43,080	1,87,500	2,55,580	1,66,127	3,53,627
3	4,00,000	1.260	5,04,000	1,40,625	3,63,375	2,36,194	3,76,819
4	3,25,000	1.360	4,42,000	1,05,469	3,36,531	2,18,745	3,24,214
5	2,50,000	1.469	3,67,250	54,101*	3,13,149	2,03,547	2,57,648

*(₹2,16,406 × 0.25)

Determination of real CFAT and NPV

Year	*CFAT*	*Deflated factor at 0.08 as per Table A-3*	*Real CFAT*	*PV factor at 0.10*	*Total PV*
1	₹3,33,200	0.926	₹3,08,543	0.909	₹2,80,466
2	3,53,627	0.857	3,03,058	0.826	2,50,326
3	3,76,819	0.794	2,99,194	0.751	2,24,695
4	3,24,214	0.735	2,38,297	0.683	1,62,757
5	2,57,648	0.681	1,75,458	0.621	1,08,960
5	1,00,000**	0.681	68,100	0.621	42,290
Total present value					10,69,494
Less: Cash outflows					10,00,000
Net present value					69,494

** Salvage value

Recommendation Since NPV is positive, the company is advised to buy the plant.

MINI CASES

10.C.1 In-house Vs Outsourcing Computea Ltd is an IT Company based in Delhi. It is into outsourcing IT consulting and systems integration. Setup as a startup company three years ago by five entrepreneurs, the headcount of the company is presently 100, with an annual turnover of ₹80 lakh. As an employee-friendly organisation and to ensure good working environment, Computea Ltd arranges tea/coffee to each of its employees thrice a day. About half of the employees prefer tea and the remaining half prefer coffee.

Tea and coffee are presently supplied by a vendor who is paid on a monthly basis. The cost of a cup of tea is ₹3. The cost of coffee is ₹5 per cup. Labour charges amount to ₹500 per month.

The HR manager, K V Prasad, has proposed to the CEO, Vineet Barnwal, to install a coffee/tea vending machine in the premises of Computea Ltd. A vending machine is available from Good Serve Ltd for ₹2,00,000, having a useful life of five years with no salvage value. The machine would require an annual maintenance cost of ₹30,000 (i.e. ₹2,500 per month) in addition to spare parts amounting to ₹10,000. The operation of the vending machine would consume electricity at ₹500 per month. The other associated operating costs would be as estimated below:

- 2 packets of coffee beans per day at ₹30 per packet
- 2 packets of 1 kg tea powder per day at ₹20 per packet
- 7,500 plastic cups per month at ₹0.25 per cup
- 200 litres of milk per month (A litre of milk costs ₹14).
- 60 kgs of sugar per month (The price of sugar is ₹15 per kg).
- Labour charges would amount to ₹1,500 per month
- Electricity charges, ₹500 per month

The number of working days in month is 23. Computea Ltd would use straight-line method of depreciation and its cost of capital is 10 per cent. As a financial consultant, would you advise the CEO of Computea Ltd to install the vending machine? Why?

Solution

Financial Analysis to Instal Vending Machine

Savings in cost per annum			
(i) Cost of tea and coffee from the vendor:			
Tea (3 × ₹3 × 50 × 23 days × 12)	₹1,24,200		
Coffee (3 × ₹5 × 50 × 23 days × 12)	2,07,000	₹3,31,200	
Labour charges (₹500 × 12)		6,000	₹3,37,200
(ii) Vending machine costs:			
Annual maintenance cost (₹2,500 × 12)	30,000		
Spares	10,000		
Coffee beans packets (₹30 × 2 × 23 × 12)	16,560		
Plastic cups (₹0.25 × 7,500 × 12)	22,500		
Milk (₹14 × 200 × 12)	33,600		
Sugar (₹15 × 60 × 12)	10,800		
Tea powder (₹20 × 2 × 23 × 12)	11,040		
Labour charges (₹1,500 × 12)	18,000		
Electricity charges (₹500 × 12)	6,000		
Depreciation (₹2,00,000 ÷ 5)	40,000		1,98,500
Less taxes (0.35)			1,38,700
Earnings after taxes			48,545
			90,155
Add depreciation			40,000
CFAT			1,30,155
$PVIFA_{5,10}$			3.791
Total PV			4,93,418
Less cash outflows			2,00,000
NPV			2,93,418

Recommendation The proposal is viable. Computea Ltd should buy the vending machine.

10.C.2 Replacement Situation Gurgaon Chemicals supplies chemicals and dyes to various units in and around NCR Delhi. The onsite delivery of chemicals and dyes every month is 2,000 units. The unit sale price is ₹100. The cost per unit is ₹50. It is using a tempo which can carry a maximum of 80 units. The total distance covered in one trip is 400 kms. The cost of diesel in the NCR Delhi is ₹25.5 per litre. The average consumption of diesel is 8 kms per litre.

Due to increase in demand for dyes for industrial use, Gurgaon Chemicals has an opportunity to make and deliver 2,500 units per month. To cater to the increased demand, the company is contemplating buying a mini truck with a capacity to carry 165 units. The required mini truck is available from Eicher for ₹14,00,000. The tempo being currently used has a book value of ₹6,00,000. It can be sold for ₹4,00,000. The annual salary of the tempo driver is ₹6,000 per month. If the mini truck is acquired, Grugaon Chemicals would have to increase his monthly salary to ₹8,000. The consumption of diesel by the truck would average 5 kms per litre. The annual maintenance cost of the mini truck would be ₹8,500 compared to ₹6,200 maintenance cost of the tempo. Gurgaon Chemical uses straightline method of depreciation for tax purposes. The tempo has a remaining useful life of 5 years. The mini could truck serve the need of the Gurgaon Chemicals for the next 5 years. The applicable tax rate is 35 per cent. Assume that loss on sale of existing machine can be claimed as short-term capital loss in the current year itself.

Nitin Jain, the CEO of Gurgaon Chemicals, has asked the CFO, Rahul Joshi, to examine the financial viability of the proposal to replace the tempo by the mini truck and make appropriate recommendation in this regard. Assume a required rate of return of 14 per cent.

Solution

Financial Analysis of Replacement of Tempo by Mini Truck

(A) Incremental cashoutflow (t = 0)			
Cost of mini truck		₹14,00,000	
Less sale value of tempo		(4,00,000)	
Less tax advantage on loss on sale of tempo:			
• Current book value	₹6,00,000		
• Sale value	4,00,000		
• Loss on sale	2,00,000		
• Tax advantage	× 0.35	(70,000)	₹9,30,000
(B) Incremental cash inflows (t = 1 – 5)			
Incremental revenue[1] (500 units × 12 months × ₹100)		6,00,000	
Less incremental costs:			
• Cost of additional units[2]	3,00,000		
• Diesel charges[3]	(15,300)		
• Maintenance cost[4]	2,300		
• Driver's salary[5]	24,000		
• Depreciation[6]	1,60,000	4,71,000	
Earnings before taxes		1,29,000	
Less taxes (0.35)		45,150	
EAT		83,850	
Add depreciation		1,60,000	
CFAT (t = 1 – 5 years)		2,43,850	
$PVIFA_{5,14}$		× 3.433	
Total PV			8,37,137
NPV (B – A)			(92,863)

[1] [500 units (2,500 units – 2,000 units) × 12 months × ₹100]

[2] (500 units × 12 × ₹50)

[3] Diesel charges

(*Contd.*)

(*Contd.*)

		Truck	Tempo
Mileage km/lit		5	8
Kms per trip		400	400
Trips/month (2,500 units ÷ 165 units per trip)		15	—
(2,000 units ÷ 80 units per trip)		—	25
Kms annually (12 months × 15 × 400)		72,000	—
(12 months × 25 × 400)		—	1,20,000
Diesel consumed (72,000 ÷ 5)		14,400	—
(1,20,000 ÷ 8)		—	15,000
Total cost (14,400 × ₹25.5)		₹3,67,700	—
(15,000 × ₹25.5)		—	₹3,82,000
Savings in diesel cost (₹3,82,500 – ₹3,67,200) =		(₹15,300)	
[4] Maintenance cost (₹8,500 – ₹6,200)			
[5] Drivers salary [(₹8,000 – ₹6,000) × 12 months)			
[6] Depreciation (incremental):			
Depreciation on truck (₹14,00,000 ÷ 5)	₹2,80,000		
Depreciation on tempo (₹6,00,000 ÷ 5)	1,20,000		
	1,60,000		

Recommendation The proposal to acquire the mini truck and dispose off the tempo is not financially viable. The CEO may not approve it.

10.C.3 Equivalent Annual Value (EAV) The Iridium Jewellery Company produces and sells jewellery in its showrooms in the country. Iridium's Jewellery is always in much demand due to fine workmanship, reasonable prices and helpful and polite behaviour of its sales persons.

Iridium has recently entered into an arrangement with the Sale Well Gems of England for distribution of its products in the United Kingdom. Iridium expects yearly additional revenue to the tune of ₹75 lakh from its sales to Sale Well Gems. To meet the increased demand, it would have to replace its existing machine. The book value of the machine being currently used is ₹30 lakh with remaining usefulness of 6 years and salvage value of ₹6 lakh. It can be sold for ₹15 lakh. The choice of the machinery is between an imported Finesse machine from Amsterdam and a Work Horse machine available locally.

The cost of Finesse is ₹50 lakh. The freight and insurance costs associated with its import would amount to 40 per cent of the cost of the machine. The expected salvage value at the end of its 5-year life is ₹15 lakh. The enlarged operation would require ₹10 lakh as additional working capital. Iridium's cost of capital may be assumed to be 15 per cent.

Work Horse locally available would cost ₹35 lakh with no salvage value after 7 years of its useful life. The additional working capital requirement would be ₹5 lakh. The required rate of return for the 7-year period would be 16 per cent.

Finesse machine is technologically advanced and automated. Work Horse would require supervision for usage and would cost ₹3 lakh in training.

The operation of the new machine(s) would involve additional fixed costs and variable costs amounting to ₹2 lakh and ₹8 lakh respectively.

The CEO of Iridium, Anupam Saha, seeks your advice, as a financial consultant, on the course of action. Would you advise him to import Finesse or acquire Work Horse? You may assume 35 per cent tax, straightline method of depreciation for tax purposes, and the existing machine constitutes a separate block for depreciation purposes. Also assume that the firm would have sufficient short-term capital gains in year 5.

Solution

Financial Analysis of Imported Machine *vs* Local Machinery

(A) Import of finesse machine:		
Cost of machine		₹50,00,000
+ Freight and insurance cost (0.40 × ₹50 lakh)		20,00,000
+ Additional working capital		10,00,000
- Sale value of existing machine		(15,00,000)
- Tax advantage on short-term capital loss on sale of existing machine		
• Current book value	₹30,00,000	
• Less sale value	(15,00,000)	
• Loss	15,00,000	
• Tax advantage (0.35 × ₹15,00,000)		(5,25,000)
(a) Net cash outflows		59,75,000
Additional sales		75,00,000
Less: Additional fixed costs		(2,00,000)
Less: Additional variable costs		(8,00,000)
Incremental depreciation:		
• Depreciation on new machine (₹70 lakh – ₹15 lakh) ÷ 5	₹11,00,000	
• Depreciation on existing machine(₹30 lakh – ₹6 lakh) ÷ 6	4,00,000	(7,00,000)
Earnings before taxes		58,00,000
Less taxes (0.35)		20,30,000
Earnings after taxes		37,70,000
Add incremental depreciation		7,00,000
(b) CFAT (t = 1 – 4)		44,70,000
CFAT (t = 5) [₹44,70,000 + ₹10,00,000, WC + ₹15,00,000, SV]		69,70,000
(c) *Net present value*		
t = 1 – 4 ₹44,70,000 × 2.855 ($PVIFA_{4,15}$)		1,27,61,850
t = 5 69,70,000 × 0.497 ($PVIF_{5,15}$)		34,64,090
Total PV		1,62,25,940
Less cash outflow		(59,75,000)
NPV		1,02,49,060
EAV ($PVIFA_{5,15}$)		÷ 3.353
		30,56,684
(B) Purchase of Work Horse:		
Cost of machine		₹35,00,000
– Sale value of machine		(15,00,000)
+ Working capital		5,00,000
+ Training costs		3,00,000
– Tax advantage on short term capital loss on sale of existing machine as in (A) above		(5,25,000)
(a) Net cash outflows		22,75,000
Incremental sales		75,00,000
Less : Additional fixed costs		(2,00,000)
: Additional variable costs		(8,00,000)
: Incremental depreciation:		
Depreciation on new machine [₹35 lakh ÷ 7)	₹5,00,000	
Depreciation on existing machine [₹30 lakh – ₹6 lakh) ÷ 6	4,00,000)	(1,00,000)
Earnings before taxes		64,00,000
Less taxes (0.35)		22,40,000
Earnings after taxes		41,60,000
Add incremental depreciation		1,00,000
(b) CFAT (t = 1 – 6)		42,60,000
CFAT (t = 7) (₹42,60,000 + ₹5,00,000, WC)		47,60,000

(*Contd.*)

(Contd.)

(c) Net present value	
t = 1 – 6 ₹42,60,000 × 3.685 ($PVFIA_{6,16}$)	1,56,98,100
7 47,60,000 × 0.354 ($PVIFA_{7,16}$)	16,85,040
Total PV	1,73,83,140
Less cash outflow	22,75,000
NPV	1,51,08,140
EAV (Equivalent annual value) ($PVIFA_{7,16}$)	÷ 4.039
	37,40,564

Recommendation Based on EAV, I would recommend to the CEO of Iridium to buy the Work Horse.

10.C.4 Gas Pipeline Extension A proposal to extend the ABC Gas Company Ltd's gas distribution network to the NOIDA industrial cluster, about 40 kms east of Delhi, at a distance of about 20 kms from the ABC's existing transmission line, is under the consideration of its CEO, Prerna Goyal. The NOIDA industrial cluster is dominated by the textile industry including texturising, weaving, spinning and yarn units with over 2,500 small and medium-sized units. The potential of gas consumption in these industries is mainly on account of captive power. Power constitutes 40 – 65 per cent of the production costs in the key target sectors for gas supply. The units in the cluster have been considering reduction of power costs by moving away from the expensive grid supply to captive power generation. The total estimated potential of captive power presently is 45 MW which corresponds to 0.30 million standard cubic meters per day (MSCMD) of gas. The proposed project is essentially an extension of the distribution network in the existing Delhi distribution zone.

A market survey of potential customers to assess the gas demand potential in the region has identified over 40 customers with a combined gas demand of 0.25 MSCMD for captive power. Negotiations for gas supply have also been initiated with them. ABC Gas Ltd has received expression of interest for over 0.075 MSCMD. However, timing of gas supply is the key since alternative fuel options such as solid and liquid fuels and wind energy are available. The expression of interest would fall through if gas is not supplied by mid-2008.

Amit Kumar, an engineering consultant, is hired by Prerna Goyal to identify the most feasible and economical route for laying down the gas pipeline. A preliminary site survey is followed by reconnaisance survey by Amit. After conducting Quantified Risk Assessment and evaluating several pipeline options, the consultant has proposed a 12 inch, 150 class low pressure (19 bar) pipeline for a total length of 30 kms from the ABC's transmission pipeline. The capacity of the proposed pipeline will be 0.75 MSCMD.

The base investment/capital expenditure is estimated to be ₹24 crore consisting of the following heads: (i) engineering, ₹0.50 crore (ii) project clearance, ₹1.2 crore (iii) material costs, ₹13.2 crore (iv) contracts, ₹7.7 crore, (v) commissioning ₹0.10 crore and (vi) contingency and insurance, ₹1.3 crore. The pipeline is expected to have a life of 10 years.

The other parameters of the projects have been identified by the consultant as listed below:

1. Volumes build up (in MSCMD)

Year	*Volume*	*Year*	*Volume*
1	0.075	6	0.121
2	0.083	7	0.133
3	0.091	8	0.146
4	0.100	9	0.161
5	0.110	10	0.177

2. Sales price of gas, ₹8.90 per standard cubic meter (SCM) with an increase of 3 per cent every year.

3. Purchase price of gas, ₹7 per standard cubic meter with an increase of 3 per cent every year.

4. Variable costs are assumed to be constant throughout the 10-year life of the pipeline at ₹28 lakh per annum (consisting of pigging of pipeline, ₹20 lakh; cathodic protection of pipeline, ₹2 lakh supervision cost, ₹3 lakh; pipeline surveys, ₹2 lakh; and electricity charges, ₹1 lakh).

Assuming straight-line method of depreciation of material cost of initial capital investment for tax purposes and 12 per cent required rate of return, analyse, as a financial consultant, the financial viability of the proposal and make a recommendation to the CEO of the ABC Gas Ltd.

Solution

Financial Analysis of Extension of Gas Pipeline by ABC Gas Ltd (₹crore)

Year	*CFAT*@@	*PV Factor(0.12)*	*Present value*
2008	4.04	0.893	₹3.61
2009	4.51	0.797	3.59
2010	5.01	0.712	3.57
2011	5.58	0.636	3.55
2012	6.23	0.567	3.53
2013	6.99	0.507	3.54
2014	7.82	0.452	3.53
2015	8.75	0.404	3.53
2016	9.85	0.361	3.56
2017	11.07	0.322	3.56
Total			35.57
Less cash outflows			24.00
Net present value			11.57

@@Exhibit 10.1.

The proposal is financially viable. As a financial consultant, I would recommend to the CEO of ABC Gas Ltd to undertake the extension of gas pipeline to the NOIDA cluster.

EXHIBIT 10.1 Computation of Cash Inflows (2008-2017)

Particulars	*2008*	*2009*	*2010*	*2011*	*2012*	*2013*	*2014*	*2015*	*2016*	*2017*
1 Gas sold (MSCMD)	0.075	0.083	0.091	0.100	0.110	0.121	0.133	0.146	0.161	0.177
2 Annual sales (1 x 365 days)	27.375	30.295	33.215	36.500	40.150	44.165	48.545	53.290	58.765	64.605
3 Sales price (₹/SCM)	8.900	9.167	9.442	9.725	10.017	10.318	10.627	10.946	11.274	11.612
4 Cost price (₹/SCM)	7.000	7.210	7.426	7.649	7.879	8.115	8.358	8.609	8.867	9.133
5 Sales revenue [(₹crore (2 × 3)]	24.364	27.771	31.362	35.496	40.218	45.569	51.588	58.331	66.252	75.019
6 Cost of gas sold [₹crore (2 × 4)]	19.162	21.843	24.665	27.919	31.634	35.84	40.574	45.877	52.107	59.004
7 Variable cost (₹crore)	0.28	0.28	0.28	0.28	0.28	0.28	0.28	0.28	0.28	0.28
8 Depreciation@ (₹crore)	2.4	2.4	2.4	2.4	2.4	2.4	2.4	2.4	2.4	2.4
9 Earnings before taxes (₹crore) [5 – 6 – 7 – 8]	2.522	3.248	4.017	4.897	5.904	7.049	8.334	9.774	11.465	13.335
10 Less taxes (0.35)	0.883	1.137	1.406	1.714	2.066	2.467	2.917	3.421	4.013	4.667
11 Earnings after taxes (₹crore) [9 – 10]	1.639	2.111	2.611	3.183	3.838	4.582	5.417	6.353	7.452	8.668
12 Depreciation (₹crore)@	2.4	2.4	2.4	2.4	2.4	2.4	2.4	2.4	2.4	2.4
13 CFAT (₹crore) [11 + 12)]	4.039	4.511	5.011	5.583	6.238	6.982	7.817	8.753	9.852	11.068

@₹24 crore ÷ 10 = ₹2.4 crore

10.C.5 Unabsorbed Depreciation The Cements India Limited, a private sector company established in 1985, is a leading producer of cement in India. It has grown into the most trusted cement company in India. It presently has four manufacturing plants in India located at Raipur, Paradeep, Guntur and Amravati.

The company has observed that its existing production capacity is likely to fall short to meet the increased demand for cement. Therefore, Mr. Divyansh, CEO of Cements India Limited, decides to increase the capacity of its Raipur plant to meet the anticipated rise in demand for cement. The company decides to replace the grinder machine at Raipur plant, which was installed in 2013 (and at present is 5 years old) at a cost of ₹25,00,000. The machine has a current salvage value of ₹3,00,000 and has economic useful life of 7 more years. The machine is a part of a block of assets which is being depreciated at a rate of 20% using written down value approach.

The new machine is an integrated unit, which will lead to increase in sales of cement by ₹15,90,000. The fixed cost will remain unchanged and variable cost to volume ratio for the integrated unit is 30%. The machine will cost ₹41,00,000 and has an expected salvage value of ₹1,45,000 at the end of its economic useful life of 7 years. The new machine too is a part of the same block of assets as the existing machine is. The new machine will require additional working capital of ₹4,00,000 for uninterrupted operations throughout the period. The corporate tax rate is 30%.

Mr. Divyansh has asked the CFO of the company to assess the financial feasibility of replacement of old machine and make relevant recommendations in this regard. Assume a minimum required rate of return to be 14%.

Solution:

The CFO carries out the assigned task as per the following aspects:

I. Written Down Value of the existing machine in the beginning of 2018 (Year 6)

Initial Cost of grinder machine in 2013	₹25,00,000
Less: Depreciation @ 20% in Year 1	₹5,00,000
WDV at the beginning of 2014 (Year 2)	₹20,00,000
Less: Depreciation @ 20% in Year 2	₹4,00,000
WDV at the beginning of 2015 (Year 3)	₹16,00,000
Less: Depreciation @ 20% in Year 3	₹3,20,000
WDV at the beginning of 2016 (Year 4)	₹12,80,000
Less: Depreciation @ 20% in Year 4	₹2,56,000
WDV at the beginning of 2017 (Year 5)	₹10,24,000
Less: Depreciation @ 20% in Year 5	₹2,04,800
WDV at the beginning of 2018 (Year 6)	₹8,19,200

II. Depreciation base with new integrated machine

Written down value of grinder machine	₹8,19,200
Add: purchase price of the integrated unit	41,00,000
Less: salvage value of grinding machine	(3,00,000)
Depreciation Base	₹46,19,200

III. Base for incremental depreciation

Depreciation base of new integrated unit	₹46,19,200
Less: depreciation base of grinding machine	₹8,19,200
Base for incremental depreciation	₹38,00,000

IV. Incremental depreciation from 2018 to 2024 (Years 1-7)

Year	*Incremental Base*	*Depreciation @ 20% on Written Down Value*
1	₹38,00,000	₹7,60,000
2	₹30,40,000	₹6,08,000
3	₹24,32,000	₹4,86,400
4	₹19,45,600	₹3,89,120
5	₹15,56,480	₹3,11,296
6	₹12,45,184	₹2,49,037
7	₹9,96,147	₹1,70,230[@]

[@] 0.20 (₹9,96,147 – ₹1,45,000 salvage value)

V. Incremental cash outflows

Cost of integrated unit	₹41,00,000
Additional working capital requirement	₹4,00,000
Less: salvage value of grinding machine	₹(3,00,000)
Incremental cash outflows	₹42,00,000

VI. Incremental cash inflows after taxes

The new machine is expected to increase sales of cement by ₹15,90,000. Since the fixed costs remain unchanged and variable costs to volume ratio is 30%:

Net incremental contribution = Incremental Sales – Variable Cost

= ₹15,90,000 – (0.3 × ₹15,90,000) = ₹11,13,000

Determination of CFAT for years (2018-2024)

Year	*Incremental Contribution (a)*	*Incremental Depreciation Base (b)*	*Taxable Income (a)-(b) = (c)*	*Tax @ 30% (c)*0.3 = (d)*	*EAT (c)-(d) = (e)*	*CFAT (b) + (e)*
2018	₹11,13,000	₹7,60,000	₹3,53,000	₹1,05,900	₹2,47,100	₹10,07,100
2019	11,13,000	6,08,000	5,05,000	1,51,500	3,53,500	9,61,500
2020	11,13,000	4,86,400	6,26,600	1,87,980	4,38,620	9,25,020
2021	11,13,000	3,89,120	7,23,880	2,17,164	5,06,716	8,95,836
2022	11,13,000	3,11,296	8,01,704	2,40,511	5,61,193	8,72,489
2023	11,13,000	2,49,037	8,63,963	2,59,189	6,04,774	8,53,811
2024	11,13,000	1,70,230	9,42,770	2,82,831	6,59,939	8,30,169

VII. Calculation of NPV

Year	*CFAT (in ₹)*	*PV factor @ 14%*	*Present value (in ₹)*
2018	10,07,100	0.877	8,83,227
2019	9,61,500	0.769	7,39,394
2020	9,25,020	0.675	6,24,389

2021	8,95,836	0.592	5,30,335
2022	8,72,489	0.519	4,52,822
2023	8,53,811	0.456	3,89,338
2024	8,30,169	0.400	3,32,068
2024 - Salvage Value	1,45,000	0.400	58,000
2024 - Recovery of WC	4,00,000	0.400	1,60,000
Gross Present Value			41,69,571
Less: cash outflow			(42,00,000)
Net Present Value			**(30,429)**

Therefore, the CFO suggests non-acceptance of the replacement proposal. This makes the CEO sad. He has started exploring the ways by which the project can become profitable. During the process, he recapitulates the concept of unabsorbed depreciation. He immediately calls the CFO. He discusses the concept with him; the CFO realizes his mistake and recalls that the tax advantage is available on unabsorbed depreciation even after the sale of machine. Accordingly, he carries out the following two steps to complete the analysis:

VIII. The unabsorbed depreciation of the machine

Depreciation base in terminal year (2024) – depreciation in 2024 – salvage value of integrated unit

Unabsorbed depreciation = (₹9,96,147 – ₹1,70,230 – ₹1,45,000) = ₹6,80,917

The company will get tax advantage on unabsorbed depreciation of the machine.

IX. Calculation of tax advantage on unabsorbed depreciation for years (2025 -2031) after sale of machine

Year	*Unabsorbed Depreciation (in ₹)*	*Depreciation @20% (in ₹)*	*Tax advantage @30% (in ₹)*	*PVF @14%*	*Total PV (in ₹)*
2025	6,80,917	1,36,183	40,855	0.351	14,340
2026	5,44,734	1,08,947	32,684	0.308	10,067
2027	4,35,787	87,157	26,147	0.27	7,060
2028	3,48,630	69,726	20,918	0.237	4,958
2029	2,78,904	55,781	16,734	0.208	3,481
2030	2,23,123	44,625	13,387		2,437
2031	1,78,498	35,700	10,710		1,714
Total					**44,055***

Recommendation NPV is positive (₹44,055 – ₹30,429 = ₹ 3,626) after reckoning tax advantage on unabsorbed depreciation. Therefore, it is recommended that the existing machine should be replaced.

*The amount would be higher as tax advantage would be available on ₹1,42,798 (₹1,78,498 – ₹35,700) in subsequent years.

Scan the QR Code given at the end of chapter to access comprehensive cases.

REVIEW QUESTIONS

LOD: Easy

RQ. 10.1 Fill in the following blanks: [LO 10.1,2,3]

(i) ____________ method is the most appropriate measure for cost reduction investment projects with unequal lives.

(ii) ____________ is an appropriate method for revenue-expanding investment proposals with unequal lives.

(iii) Intermediate cash inflows are assumed to have been reinvested at the rate of ____________ under IRR method.

(iv) Intermediate cash inflows are assumed to be reinvested at ____________under NPV method.

(v) ____________ method is an appropriate measure in projects selection (when they are divisible) under capital rationing.

(vi) ____________ cash flows are substantially lower than ____________ cashflows, when adjusted for inflation factor.

(vii) ____________ should be used to discount real cashflows in selecting investment projects requiring adjustment for inflation.

(viii) Capital budgeting decisions should either reckon the inflation factor in ____________ as well as in cost of capital or exclude it completely.

(ix) Real cost of capital is obtained dividing nominal cost of capital by ____________.

(x) CFAT will be deflated by ____________ to determine real CFAT.

Answers: (i) Equivalent annual cost (ii) Equivalent annual NPV (iii) IRR (iv) Cost of capital (v) Present value index (vi) Real, nominal (vii) Real cost of capital (viii) cash inflows after taxes (ix) (1 + Inflation rate) (x) inflation rate.

RQ. 10.2 What is the criterion for judging the worth of investments in the capital budgeting technique based on the profitability index? What is its value, when its NPV is (a) zero, (b) negative and (c) positive? Also indicate the relationship between IRR and cost of capital in these situations. [LO 10.1,2]

RQ. 10.3 ABC Ltd is considering to install a machine, either *X* or *Y* which are mutually exclusive. The details of their purchase price and operating costs are: [LO 10.1]

Particulars	*Year*	*Machine X*	*Machine Y*
Purchase cost	0	₹10,000	₹8,000
Operating costs	1	2,000	2,500
	2	2,000	2,500
	3	2,000	2,500
	4	2,500	3,800
	5	2,500	3,800
	6	2,500	3,800
	7	3,000	
	8	3,000	
	9	3,000	
	10	3,000	

Machine X will recover a salvage value of ₹1,500 in the year 10 while machine *Y* will recover ₹1,000 in the year 6. Determine which is cheaper at the 10 per cent cost of capital, assuming that both the machines operate at the same efficiency?

LOD: Medium

RQ. 10.4 Contrast the IRR and the NPV methods. Under what circumstance may they lead to (a) comparable recommendations, and (b) give conflicting recommendations? In circumstances in which they give contradictory results, which criteria should be used to select the project and why? [LO 10.1]

RQ. 10.5 What are the critical factors to be observed while making capital budgeting decisions under capital rationing? [LO 10.2]

RQ. 10.6 Discuss the problems of ranking projects with varying economic lives, sizes and patterns of cash outflows and inflows. [LO 10.1]

RQ. 10.7 What is the relationship between the desired real rate of return, inflation rate and the rate used to discount project cash flows under conditions of inflation. [LO 10.3]

RQ. 10.8 The nominal cost of capital is not equivalent to the sum of the real cost of capital and the expected inflation rate. Elucidate with an appropriate example. [LO 10.3]

RQ. 10.9 Company X is forced to choose between two machines A and B. The two machines are designed differently, but have identical capacity and do exactly the same job. Machine A costs ₹1,50,000 and will last for 3 years. It costs ₹40,000 per year to run. Machine B is an 'economy' model costing only ₹1,00,000, but will last only for 2 years, and cost ₹60,000 per year to run. These are real cash flows. The costs are forecasted in rupees of constant purchasing power. Ignore tax. Opportunity cost of capital is 10 per cent. Which machine company X should buy? [LO 10.1]

RQ. 10.10 A machine purchased four years ago has been depreciated to its current book value of ₹50,000. The machine originally had a projected life of 10 years and zero salvage value.

A new machine will cost ₹80,000. Its installation cost estimated by the technician is ₹20,000. The technician also estimates that the installation of the new machine will result in a reduced operating cost of ₹30,000 per year for the next 6 years. The old machine would be sold for ₹20,000. The new machine will have a 6-year life with no salvage value. The company's income is taxed at 35. Assuming the cost of capital at 10 per cent, determine whether the existing machine should be replaced. Make your own assumption regarding depreciation of the machine. [LO 10.1]

RQ. 10.11 A company working against a self-imposed capital budgeting constraints of ₹3,50,000, is trying to decide which investment proposals should be undertaken by it. All the investments are mutually independent (do not affect one another's cash flows). The list of investments along with the investment required and the net present value of the projected cash flows are as follows:

Investments	*Outlays*	*NPV*
A	₹50,000	₹30,000
B	1,20,000	90,000
C	1,60,000	1,00,000
D	1,60,000	1,50,000
E	90,000	1,00,000

Which investments should be acquired by the company? [LO 10.2]

RQ. 10.12 Strong Company wants to launch a new product, suggested by its marketing department. For this purpose a new machine is to be purchased. The relevant data processed in this regard is as follows: [LO 10.3]

Cost of new machine		₹20,00,000
CFAT: year	1	6,00,000
	2	7,00,000
	3	8,00,000
	4	5,00,000
	5	4,00,000

The company uses 13 per cent as required cost of capital (nominal) to evaluate new projects. The rate of inflation during the period is expected to be 6 per cent. Determine NPV of the machine using both the nominal as well as real rate of discount, and comment on the results.

LOD: Difficult

RQ. 10.13 'For most investment decisions that the firm faces, net present value is either a superior decision criterion, or is at least as good as the competing techniques.' In what investment situation is the profitability index better than the net present value? **[LO 10.1,2]**

RQ. 10.14 Royal Industries is considering to buy a moulding machine. The machine (having capital cost of ₹20 lakh) is expected to have 4 years economic useful life with no salvage value; the company follows the straight line method of depreciation and the same is accepted for tax purposes. The expected CFAT (with corporate tax rate of 35 per cent) during its 4 years economic useful life are as follows: **[LO 10.3]**

Year 1	*2*	*3*	*4*
CFAT ₹8 lakh	₹10 lakh	₹7 lakh	₹5 lakh

Inflation is expected to be 8 per cent per year and the machine's cost of capital in real terms would be 10 per cent. Compute the NPV of purchasing this machine.

ANSWERS

10.3 Machine X is cheaper due to lower EAC (₹3,976.50). EAC of Y is ₹4,764.20.
10.9 Company X should buy Machine A due to its lower EAC of ₹1,00,297.55. EAC of Machine B is 1,17,569.12.
10.10 NPV is ₹25,698. Machine should be replaced.
10.11 D, E and B.
10.12 Real discount rate 6.6 per cent. NPV is ₹1,57,092.
10.14 Nominal rate of discount: 18.8 per cent. NPV: ₹50,800.

Scan the QR Code to access comprehensive solutions to all numerical review questions and additional material.

CHAPTER

11

Concept and Measurement of Cost of Capital

LEARNING OBJECTIVES

LO 11.1	Understand importance, the basic assumptions, relationships, concepts and specific sources of capital underlying the cost of capital
LO 11.2	Determine the cost of long-term debt using calculations and an approximation (short-cut) technique
LO 11.3	Compute the cost of preference shares
LO 11.4	Calculate the cost of equity shares using **(i)** dividend valuation approach, **(ii)** capital asset pricing model (CAPM) approach and **(iii)** debt-yield plus risk premium approach
LO 11.5	Determine the cost of retained earnings
LO 11.6	Find the weighted average/overall cost of capital and discuss the alternative weighting schemes—historical (book values as well as market values) and marginal
LO 11.7	Outline cost of capital practices followed by corporates in India

INTRODUCTION

The discussions in Chapters 9 and 10 relating to capital budgeting have shown the relevance of a certain required rate of return as a decision criterion. Such a rate is the cost of capital of a firm. Apart from its usefulness as an operational criterion to accept/reject an investment proposal, cost of capital is also an important factor in designing capital structure. The relationship of cost of capital and capital structure of the firm is explored in part four. This Chapter is devoted to a discussion of the concept and measurement of cost of capital. It first covers the importance of, and elaborates on the concept of, cost of capital. The measurement of the specific cost of capital is examined subsequently. The measurement of overall cost of capital and the related issues of determining the relative weights are also examined. While the corporate practices followed in India are outlined, the major points are summarised by way of recapitulation.

LO 11.1 IMPORTANCE AND CONCEPT

Importance

As mentioned above, the cost of capital is an important element, as a basic input information, in capital investment decisions. In the present value method of discounted cash flow technique, the cost of capital is used as the discount rate to calculate the NPV. The profitability index or benefit-cost ratio method similarly employs it to determine the present value of future cash inflows. When the internal rate of return method is used, the computed IRR is compared with the cost of capital. The cost of capital, thus, constitutes an integral part of investment decisions. It provides a yardstick to measure the worth of investment proposal and, thus, performs the role of accept-reject criterion. This underlines the crucial significance of cost of capital. It is also referred to as *cut-off rate, target rate, hurdle rate, minimum required rate of return, standard return* and so on.

The cost of capital, as an operational criterion, is related to the firms' objective of wealth maximisation. The accept-reject rules require that a firm should avail of only such investment opportunities as promise a rate of return higher than the cost of capital. Conversely, the firm would be well advised to reject proposals whose rates of return are less than the cost of capital. If the firm accepts a proposal having a rate of return higher than the cost of capital, it implies that the proposal yields returns higher than the minimum required by the investors and the prices of shares will increase and, thus, the shareholders' wealth. By virtue of the same logic, the shareholders' wealth will decline on the acceptance of a proposal in which the actual return is less than the cost of capital. The cost of capital, thus, provides a rational mechanism for making optimum investment decisions. In brief, *the cost of capital is important because of its practical utility as an acceptance-rejection decision criterion.*

The considerable significance of cost of capital in terms of its practical utility notwithstanding, it is probably the most controversial topic in financial management. There are varying opinions as to how this can be computed. In view of the crucial operational significance of this concept, our focus is on the general framework for the computation of cost of capital. We first define the term cost of capital in general terms. This is followed by a detailed account of the measurement of cost of capital—both specific as well as overall—of different sources of financing.

Definition

In operational terms, **cost of capital** refers to the discount rate that is used in determining the present value of the estimated future cash proceeds and eventually deciding whether the project is worth undertaking or not. In this sense, it is defined as the *minimum rate of return that a firm must earn on its investment for the market value of the firm to remain unchanged.*

> **Cost of capital** is the rate of return that a firm must earn on its project/investments to maintain its market value and attract funds.

The cost of capital is visualised as being composed of several elements. These elements are the cost of each component of capital. The term 'component' means the different sources from which funds are raised by a firm. Obviously, each source of funds or each component of capital has its cost. For example, equity capital has a cost, so also preference share capital and so on. The cost of each source or component is called **specific cost** of capital. When these specific costs are combined to arrive at overall cost of capital, it is referred to as the **weighted cost of capital**. The terms, *cost of capital, weighted cost of capital, composite cost of capital and combined cost of capital* are used interchangeably in this book. In other words, the term, cost of capital, as the acceptance criterion for investment proposals, is used in the sense of the combined cost of all sources of financing. This is mainly because our focus is on the valuation of the firm as a whole.[1]

Assumptions

The theory of cost of capital is based on certain assumptions. A basic assumption of traditional cost of capital analysis is that the firm's business and financial risks are unaffected by the acceptance and financing of projects.[2] **Business risk** measures the variability in operating profits [earnings before interest and taxes (EBIT)] due to change in sales. If a firm accepts a project that is considerably more risky than the average, the suppliers of the funds are quite likely to increase the cost of funds as there is an increased probability of committing default on the part of the firm in making payments of their money. A debenture-holder will charge a higher rate of interest to compensate for increased risk. There is similarly an increased uncertainty from the point of equity holders of getting dividend from the firm. Therefore, they will also require a higher return as a compensation for the increased risk. In analysing the cost of capital in this chapter, we assume that there would be no change whatsoever in the business risk complexion of the firm as a result of acceptance of new investment proposals.

Business risk is the risk to the firm of being unable to cover fixed operating costs.

The capital budgeting decision determines the business risk complexion of the firm. The financing decision determines its **financial risk**. In general, the greater the proportion of long-term debt in the capital structure of the firm, the greater is the financial risk because there is a need for a larger amount of periodic interest payment and principal repayment at the time of maturity. In such a situation, obviously, the firm requires higher operating profits to cover these charges. If it fails to earn adequate operating profits to cover such financial charges, it may be forced into cash insolvency. Thus, with the increase in the proportion of debt commitments and preference shares in its capital structure, fixed charges increase. All other things being the same, the probability that the firm will be unable to meet these fixed charges also increases. As the firm continues to lever itself, the probability of cash insolvency, which may lead to legal bankruptcy, increases.[3] Clearly, therefore, as a firm's financial structure shifts towards a more highly levered position, the increased financial risk associated with the firm is recognised by the suppliers of funds. They compensate for this increased risk by charging higher rates of interest or requiring greater returns. In short, they react in much the same way as they would in the case of increasing business risks.[4] In the analysis of the cost of capital in this Chapter, however, the firm's financial structure is assumed to remain fixed. In the absence of such an assumption, it would be quite difficult to find its cost of capital, as the selection of a particular source of financing would change the cost of other sources of financing. In operational terms, the assumption of a constant capital structure implies that the additional funds required to finance the new project are to be raised in the same proportion as the firm's existing financing.

Financial risk is the risk of being unable to cover required financial obligations such as interest and preference dividends.

For the purpose of capital budgeting decisions, benefits from undertaking a proposed project are evaluated on an after-tax basis. In fact, only the cost of debt requires tax adjustment as interest paid on debt is deductible expense from the point of view of determining taxable income whereas dividends paid either to preference shareholders or to equity-holders are not eligible items as a source of deduction to determine taxable income.

To sum up, it may be said that cost of capital (k) consists of the following three components:

(i) the riskless cost of the particular type of financing, r_j;

(ii) the business risk premium, b; and

(iii) the financial risk premium, f

Or $k = r_j + b + f$

Since the business and financial risks are assumed to be constant, the changing cost of each type of capital, *j*, over time should be affected by the change in the supply of, and demand for, each type of funds.

Explicit and Implicit Costs

The cost of capital can be either **explicit or implicit**. The distinction between explicit and implicit costs is important from the point of view of the computation of the cost of capital.

> The explicit cost of any source of capital is the discount rate that equates the present value of the cash inflows that are incremental to the taking of the financing opportunity with the present value of its incremental cash outflows.[5]

When firms raise funds from different sources, there is a series of cash flows. Initially, there is cash inflow to the extent of the amount raised. This is followed by a series of cash outflows in respect of interest payments, repayment of principal, or payment of dividends. For example, a firm raises ₹5,00,000 through the sale of 10 per cent perpetual debentures. There will be a cash inflow of ₹5,00,000 followed by an annual cash outflow of ₹50,000. The rate of return that equates the present value of cash inflows (₹5,00,000) with the present value of cash outflows (₹50,000) would be the explicit cost.

The determination of the explicit cost of capital is similar to the determination of the IRR, with one difference. While in the computation of the IRR, the cash outflows (assuming conventional flows) are involved in the beginning, followed by cash inflows subsequently, it is exactly opposite with the explicit cost of capital. Here, as shown above, the cash flows take place only once and there is a series of cash outflows subsequently.

The general formula for the explicit cost of capital of any source of raising finance would be as follows:

$$CI_0 = \sum_{t=1}^{n} \frac{CO_t}{(1+C)^t} \tag{11.1}$$

Where CI_0 = initial cash inflow, that is, net cash proceeds received by the firm from the capital source at time O, $CO_1 + CO_2 ... + CO_{n-1}$ = cash outflows at times 1, 2 ... $n-1$, that is, cash payment from the firm to the capital source. If CI_0 is received in instalments, then, CI_0

$$CI_0 + \frac{CI_1}{(1+C)^1} + \frac{CI_2}{(1+C)^2} + \frac{CI_3}{(1+C)^3} + ... + \frac{CI_{n-1}}{(1+C)^n}$$

$$= \frac{CO_1}{(1+C)^1} + \frac{CO_2}{(1+C)^2} + \frac{CO}{(1+C)^3} + ... + \frac{CO}{(1+C)} \tag{11.2}$$

It is evident from the above mathematical formulation that the **explicit cost** of capital is the '*rate of return of the cash flows of the financing opportunity.*'[6] In other words, it is the internal rate of return that the firm pays to procure financing. On the basis of the above formula, we can easily find out that the explicit cost of an interest-free loan is zero per cent because the discount rate that equates the present value of a future sum with an equivalent sum received today is zero. The explicit cost of capital of a loan bearing interest is that discount rate which equates the present value of the future cash outflows with

Explicit cost is the rate that the firm pays to procure financing.

the net amount of funds initially provided by the loan. The explicit cost of capital of a gift is minus 100 per cent. The explicit cost of capital derived from the sale of an asset is a discount rate that equates the present value of the future cash flows foregone by the asset's sale with the net proceeds to the firm resulting from its liquidation. The explicit cost of funds supplied by increases in certain liabilities such as accounts payable and accrued taxes is zero per cent unless, of course, penalties are incurred or discounts lost owing to the increase in these liabilities.[7]

The explicit cost of capital is concerned with the incremental cash flows that result directly from raising funds. Retained earnings used in the firm involve no future cash flows to, or from, the firm. Therefore, the explicit cost of retained earnings is minus 100 per cent. There are no future interest or principal payments imposed by the retention of earnings. There are no additional shares created and sold to outsiders on which dividends will be paid. From this, it should, however, not be concluded that retained earnings have no cost. (In fact, they also have costs like other sources of raising finance have). The retained earnings are undistributed profits of the company belonging to the shareholders. Given the ultimate objective of the firm to maximise the wealth of shareholders, the cost of retained earning would be equivalent to the **opportunity cost** of earning by investing elsewhere by the shareholders themselves or by the company itself. **Opportunity costs** are technically referred to as **implicit cost of capital**. The **implicit cost of capital** of funds raised and invested by the firm may, therefore, be defined as 'the rate of return associated with the best investment opportunity for the firm and its shareholders that would be foregone, if the projects presently under consideration by the firm were accepted.'[8] The cost of retained earnings is an opportunity cost or implicit capital cost, in the sense that it is the rate of return at which the shareholders could have invested these funds had they been distributed to them.[9] However, other forms of financing also have implicit cost once they are invested. The explicit cost arises when funds are *raised*, whereas the implicit costs arise when funds are *used*. Viewed in this perspective, implicit costs are ubiquitous. They arise whenever funds are used no matter what the source.

Implicit cost is the rate of return associated with the best investment opportunity foregone.

The term cost of capital, as a decision criterion, is the overall cost. This is the combined cost of the specific costs associated with specific sources of financing. The cost of the different sources of financing represents the components of the combined cost. The computation of the cost of capital, therefore, involves two steps: **(i)** the computation of the different elements of the cost in terms of the cost of the different sources of finance (specific costs), and **(ii)** the calculation of the overall cost by combining the specific costs into a composite cost.

The first step in the measurement of the cost of capital of the firm is the calculation of the cost of individual sources of raising funds. Apart from its relevance to the measurement of the combined cost, the specific cost will also indicate the relative cost of pursuing one line of financing rather than another. From the viewpoint of capital budgeting decision, the long-term sources of funds are relevant as they constitute the major sources of financing of fixed assets. In calculating the cost of capital, therefore, the focus is on long-term funds. In other words, the specific costs have to be calculated for **(i)** long-term debt (including debentures); **(ii)** preference shares; **(iii)** equity capital; and **(iv)** retained earnings.

LO 11.2 COST OF DEBT

The calculation of the **cost of debt** is relatively easy. The cost of funds raised through debt in the form of debentures or loan from financial institutions can be determined from Eq. 11.1. To apply the formulation of explicit cost of debt, we need data

Cost of debt is the after tax cost of long-term funds through borrowing.

regarding: **(i)** the **net cash proceeds**/inflows (the issue price of debentures/amount of loan minus all **floatation costs**) from specific source of debt, and **(ii)** the net cash outflows in terms of the amount of periodic interest payment and repayment of principal in instalments or in lump sum on maturity. The interest payments made by the firm on debt issues qualify for tax deduction in determining net taxable income. Therefore, the effective cash outflows is less than the actual payment of interest made by the firm to the debt holders by the amount of tax shield on interest payment.[10] The debt can be either perpetual/irredeemable or redeemable.

Net cash proceeds are the funds actually received from the sale of security.

Cost of Perpetual Debt The measurement of the cost of perpetual debt is conceptually relatively easy. It is the rate of return which the lenders expect. The debt carries a certain rate of interest. The coupon interest rate or the market yield on debt can be said to represent an approximation of the cost of debt. The nominal/coupon rate of interest on debt is the before-tax cost of debt. Since the effective cost of debt is the tax-adjusted rate of interest, the before-tax cost of debt should be adjusted for the tax effect. Finally, the bonds and debentures (debt) can be issued at (i) par, (ii) discount, and (iii) premium. The coupon rate of interest will require adjustment to find out the true cost of debt. Symbolically,

Floatation cost is the total cost of issuing and selling securities.

$$k_i = \frac{I}{SV} \quad \textbf{(11.3)}$$

$$k_d = \frac{I}{SV}(1-t) \quad \textbf{(11.4)}$$

k_i = Before-tax cost of debt
k_d = Tax-adjusted cost of debt
I = Annual interest payment
SV = Sale proceeds of the bond/debenture
t = Tax rate

The calculation is illustrated in Example 11.1.

***Example* 11.1**

A company has 10 per cent perpetual debt of ₹1,00,000. The tax rate is 35 per cent. Determine the cost of capital (before tax as well as after tax) assuming the debt is issued at (i) par, (ii) 10 per cent discount, and (iii) 10 per cent premium.

Solution

(i) Debt issued at par

Before-tax cost, $k_i = ₹\frac{10,000}{1,00,000}$ = 10 per cent

After-tax cost, $k_d = k_i(1 - t)$ = 10% (1 – 0.35) = 6.5 per cent

(ii) Issued at discount

Before-tax cost, $k_i = ₹\frac{10,000}{90,000}$ = 11.11 per cent

After-tax cost, k_d = 11.11% (1 – 0.35) = 7.22 per cent

(iii) Issued at premium

Before-tax cost, $k_i = ₹\frac{10,000}{1,10,000}$ = 9.09 per cent

After-tax cost, k_d = 9.09% (1 – 0.35) = 5.91 per cent

Cost of Redeemable Debt In the case of calculation of cost of redeemable debt, account has to be taken, in addition to interest payments, of the repayment of the principal. When the amount of principal is repaid in one lump sum at the time of maturity, the cost of debt would be given by solving Eq. 11.5. If, however, the repayments are in a number of instalments, the cost of debt can be calculated on the basis of Eq. 11.6.

$$CI_0 = \sum_{t=1}^{n} \frac{COI_t}{(1+k_d)^t} + \frac{COP_n}{(1+k_d)^n} \quad (11.5)$$

where CI_0 = Net cash proceeds from issue of debentures or from raising debt

$COI_1 + COI_2 + ... + COI_n$ = Cash outflow on interest payments in time period 1,2 and so on up to the year of maturity *after adjusting tax savings on interest payment.*

COP_n = Principal repayment in the year of maturity

k_d = Cost of debt.

If the repayment of debt is in a number of instalments instead of one lump sum payment, the equation would be:

$$CI_0 = \sum_{t=1}^{n} \frac{COI_t + COP_t}{(1+k_d)^t} \quad (11.6)$$

***Example* 11.2**

A company issues a new 10 per cent debentures of ₹1,000 face value to be redeemed after 10 years The debenture is expected to be sold at 5 per cent discount. It will also involve floatation costs of 5 per cent of face value. The company's tax rate is 35 per cent. What would the cost of debt be? Illustrate the computations using (i) trial and error approach and (ii) shortcut method.

Solution

(i) Trial and Error/Long Approach

Cash Flow Pattern of the Debentures

Years	*Cash flow*
0	+ ₹900 (₹1,000 – ₹100, that is, par value *less* flotation cost less discount)
1 – 10	– ₹100 (interest outgo)
10	– ₹1,000 (repayment of principal at maturity).

We are to determine the value of k_d in the following equation:

$$₹900 = \sum_{t=1}^{10} \frac{₹65}{(1+k_d)^t} + \frac{₹1,000}{(1+k_d)^{10}}$$

The value of k_d for this equation would be the cost of debt. The value of k_d can be obtained, as in the case of IRR, by trial and error.

Determination of PV at 7% and 8% Rates of Interest

Year(s)	*Cash outflows*	*PV factor at* 7%	*PV factor at* 8%	*Total PV at* 7%	*Total PV at* 8%
1-10	₹65	7.024	6.710 (Table A-4)	₹456.56	₹436.15
10	1,000	0.508	0.463 (Table A-3)	508.00	463.00
				964.56	899.15

The value of k_d would be 8 per cent.

(ii) Shortcut Method: The formula for approximating the effective cost of debt can, as a shortcut, be shown in the Equation (11.7):

$$k_d = \frac{I(1-t)+(f+d+pr-pi)/N_m}{(RV+SV)/2} \quad \textbf{(11.7)}$$

where I = Annual interest payment

RV = Redeemable value of debentures/debt

SV = Net sales proceeds from the issue of debenture/debt (face value of debt minus issue expenses)

N_m = Term of debt

f = Flotation cost

d = Discount on issue of debentures

pi = Premium on issue of debentures

pr = Premium on redemption of debentures

t = Tax rate

$$k_d = \frac{₹100\,(1-0.35)+(₹50+₹50)/10}{(₹900+₹1{,}000)/2} = 7.9 \text{ per cent}$$

***Example* 11.3**

A company issues 11 per cent debentures of ₹100 for an amount aggregating ₹1,00,000 at 10 per cent premium, redeemable at par after five years. The company's tax rate is 35 per cent. Determine the cost of debt, using the shortcut method.

Solution

$$k_i = \frac{[₹11(1-0.35)-₹(10/5)]}{(₹110+₹100)/2} = 4.9 \text{ per cent}$$

The shortcut, however, cannot be applied when the principal is repaid in a number of instalments in lieu of one lump sum repayment. We can compute the value of k_d with the help of Eq. 11.6.

***Example* 11.4**

A company has issued 10 per cent debentures aggregating ₹1,00,000. The flotation cost is 4 per cent. The company has agreed to repay the debentures at par in 5 equal annual instalments starting at the end of year 1. The company's rate of tax is 35 per cent. Find the cost of debt.

Solution

Net proceeds from the sale of debenture = ₹96,000.

Since the cash outflows are higher in the initial years than the average (₹24,500), let us try to determine PV at 7 per cent and 8 per cent.

Cash outflows	*PV factor at*		*Total PV at*	
	7%	*8%*	*7%*	*8%*
26,500 @	0.935	0.926	₹24,777	₹24,539
25,200	0.873	0.857	22,000	21,596
23,900	0.816	0.794	19,502	18,977
22,600	0.763	0.735	17,244	16,611
21,300	0.713	0.681	15,187	14,505
			98,710	96,228

@₹20,000 principal + ₹10,000 interest (1 – 0.35)

The value of k_d = 8 per cent.

To conclude, conceptually speaking, the calculation of the cost of debt is relatively easy. Moreover, debt is the cheapest source of long-term funds from the point of view of the company. In the first place, it is the safest form of investment from the point of view of the creditors because they are the first claimants on the company's assets at the time of its liquidation. Likewise, they are the first to be paid their interest before any dividend is paid to preference and equity shareholders. In fact, they are to be paid the interest even if the company incurs losses. Therefore, the suppliers' required rate of return on debt instruments is lower *vis-a-vis* other financial instruments, and, hence, lower cost of debt to the firm. Another, and more important, reason for debt having the lowest cost is the tax-deductibility of interest payments. The tax benefit would, however, be available only when the firm is profitable and pay taxes. A firm which suffers losses would not be required to pay any tax and its cost of debt would be before-tax cost (k_i) and not after-tax cost (k_d).

In practice, the corporates are normally likely to have multiple debt issues most likely subject to different interest rates. To determine the overall cost of debt, cost of each debt issue is to be separately computed. The weighted average of costs of all debt issues would be the cost of debt of the firm as a whole.

LO 11.3 COST OF PREFERENCE SHARES

The computation of the cost of preference shares is conceptually difficult as compared to the cost of debt. In the case of debt, as shown above, the interest rate is the basis of calculating cost, as payment of a specific amount of interest is legal commitment on the part of the firm. There is no such obligation in regard to preference dividend. It is true that a fixed dividend rate is stipulated on preference shares. It is also true that holders of such shares have a preferential right as regards payments of dividend as well as return of principal, as compared to the ordinary shareholders. But, unlike debt, there is no risk of legal bankruptcy if the firm does not pay the dividends due to the holders of such shares. Nevertheless, firms can be expected to pay the stipulated dividend, if there are sufficient profits, for a number of reasons. First, the preference shareholders, as already observed, carry a prior right to receive dividends over the equity shareholders. Unless, therefore, the firm pays out the dividend to its preference shareholders, it will not be able to pay anything to its ordinary shareholders. Moreover, the preference shares are usually cumulative which means that preference dividend will get accumulated till it is paid. As long as it remains in arrears, nothing can be paid to the equity holders. Further, non-payment of preference dividend may entitle their holders to participate in the management of the firm as voting rights are conferred on them in such cases. Above all, the firm may encounter difficulty in raising further equity capital mainly because the non-payment of preference dividend adversely affects the prospects of ordinary shareholders. Therefore, the stipulated dividend on preference shares, like the interest on debt, constitutes the basis for the calculation of the cost of preference shares. The **cost of preference capital** may be defined as the dividend expected by the preference shareholders.

> **Cost of preference share capital** is the annual preference share dividend divided by the net proceeds from the sale of preference shares.

However, unlike interest payments on debt, dividend payable on preference shares is not tax-deducible because preference dividend is not a charge on earnings or an item of expenditure; it is an appropriation of earnings. In other words, they are paid out of after-tax earnings of the company. Therefore, no adjustment is required for taxes while computing the cost of preference capital.

There are two types of preference shares: **(i) irredeemable**, and **(ii) redeemable**. The first category is a kind of perpetual security in that the principal is not to be returned for a long time or is likely to be available till the life of the company. The redeemable preference shares are issued with a maturity date so that the principal will be repaid at some future date. Accordingly, the cost of preference is calculated separately for these situations.

Perpetual Security The cost of preference shares which has no specific maturity date is given by Eq. (11.8) and Eq. (11.8A):

$$k_p = \frac{D_p}{P_0(1-f)} \tag{11.8}$$

$$k_p = \frac{D_p(1+D_t)}{P_0(1-f)} \tag{11.8A}$$

where k_p = Cost of preference capital
D_p = Constant annual dividend payment
P_0 = Expected sales price of preference shares
f = Flotation costs as a percentage of sales price
D_t = Tax on preference dividend

***Example* 11.5**

A company issues 11 per cent irredeemable preference shares of the face value of ₹100 each. Flotation costs are estimated at 5 per cent of the expected sale price. (a) What is the k_p, if preference shares are issued at (i) par value, (ii) 10 per cent premium, and (iii) 5 per cent discount? (b) Also, compute k_p in these situations assuming 13.125 per cent dividend tax.

Solution

(a) (i) Issued at par

$$k_p = \frac{₹11}{₹100(1-0.05)} = 11.6 \text{ per cent}$$

(ii) Issued at premium

$$k_p = \frac{₹11}{₹110(1-0.05)} = 10.5 \text{ per cent}$$

(iii) Issued at discount

$$k_p = \frac{₹11}{₹95(1-0.05)} = 12.2 \text{ per cent}$$

(b) (i) Issued at par

$$k_p = \frac{₹11(1.13125) = ₹12.44}{₹95} = 13.1 \text{ per cent}$$

(ii) Issued at premium

$$k_p = \frac{₹12.44}{₹104.5} = 11.9 \text{ per cent}$$

(iii) Issued at discount

$$k_p = \frac{₹12.44}{₹90.25} = 13.8 \text{ per cent}$$

Cost of Redeemable Preference Capital The explicit cost of preference shares in such a situation is the discount rate that equates the net proceeds of the sale of preference shares with the present value of the future dividends and principal repayments. The appropriate formula to calculate cost is given by Eq. (11.9).

$$P_0(1-f) = \frac{D_{p_1}}{(1+k_p)^1} + \frac{D_{p_2}}{(1+k_p)^2} + \ldots + \frac{D_{p_n}}{(1+k_p)^n} + \frac{P_n}{(1+k_p)^n}$$

$$P_0(1-f) = \sum_{t=1}^{n} \frac{D_{p_t}}{(1+k_p)^t} + \frac{P_n}{(1+k_p)^n} \tag{11.9}$$

where P_0 = Expected sale price of preference shares
f = Floatation cost as percentage of P_0
D_p = Dividends paid on preference shares
P_n = Repayment of preference capital amount

***Example* 11.6**

ABC Ltd has issued 11 per cent preference shares of the face value of ₹100 each to be redeemed after 10 years. Flotation cost is expected to be 5 per cent. Determine the cost of preference shares (k_p).

Solution

$$₹95 = \sum_{t=1}^{10} \frac{₹11}{(1+k_p)^t} + \frac{₹100}{(1+k_p)^{10}}$$

The value of k_p is likley to be between 11 and 12 per cent as the rate of dividend is 11 per cent.

Determination of the PV at 11 Per Cent and 12 Per Cent

Year	*Cash outflows*	*PV factor at*		*Total PV at*	
		11%	*12%*	*11%*	*12%*
1-10	₹11	5.889	5.65	₹64.78	₹62.15
10	100	0.352	0.322	35.15	32.20
				99.93	94.35

k_p = 11.9 per cent

LO 11.4 COST OF EQUITY CAPITAL

The cost of equity capital is by far, conceptually speaking, the most difficult and controversial cost to measure. It has been shown in the preceding discussions that the coupon rate of interest which forms the basis of calculation of cost of debt can be estimated with a high degree of accuracy since interest payments as well as the return of the principal are contractual obligations. The return on preference shares, although not a contractual obligation, can also be estimated fairly accurately as they are fixed in terms of the stipulations governing the issue of such shares. In contrast, the return to the equity-holders solely depends upon the discretion of the company management. Apart from the absence of any definite commitment to receive dividend, the equity shareholders rank at the bottom as claimants on the assets of the company at the time of its liquidation. It may, therefore, *prima facie*, appear that equity capital does not carry any cost. But this is not true. Equity capital, like other sources of funds, does certainly involve a cost to the firm. It may be recalled that the objective of financial management is to maximise shareholders' wealth and the maximisation of market price of shares is the operational substitute for wealth maximisation. When equity-holders invest their funds they also expect returns in the form of dividends. The market value of shares is a function of the return that the shareholders expect and get. If the company does not meet the requirements of its shareholders and pay dividends, it will have an adverse effect on the market price of shares. A policy of not paying dividends by a firm would be in conflict, in other words, with its basic objective, namely, net present value maximisation. The equity shares, thus, implicitly involve a return in terms of the dividend expected by the investors and, therefore, carry a cost. In fact, the cost of equity capital is relatively the highest among all the sources of funds. The investors purchase the shares, as already mentioned, in the expectation of a certain rate of return. The quantum of the rate of return, depends, *inter-alia*, on the business risk and financial risk of a company. The equity shares involve the highest degree of financial risk since they are entitled to receive dividend and return of principal after all other obligations of the firm are met. As a compensation to the higher risk exposure, holders of such securities expect a higher return and, therefore, higher cost is associated with them.

Cost of equity capital is the rate at which investors discount the expected dividends of the firm to determine its share value.

Therefore, one simple approach suggested to determine cost of equity is to add a judgmental risk premium of 3 to 5 percentage points to the interest rate paid by the firm on its own long-term debt. Such a method may be referred to as **debt-yield plus risk premium approach**.[11] Although this method does not ensure a precise cost of equity, it gets us into the right ballpark.[12] There is no direct basis of knowing the return the firm's equity investors require on their investments. Therefore, it is to be estimated.[13]

Conceptually, the **cost of equity capital**, k_e, may be defined as *the minimum rate of return that a firm must earn on the equity-financed portion of an investment project in order to leave unchanged the market price of the shares.*[14] To illustrate, suppose the required rate of return on equity (ordinary) shares of a firm is 12 per cent and the cost of debt is 8 per cent. Further assume that the policy of the firm is to use equity and debt respectively in the proportion of 75 : 25. The required rate of return for the project as a whole would be 11 per cent:

$$\begin{aligned} 0.75 \times 0.12 &= 9 \text{ per cent} \\ 0.25 \times 0.08 &= 2 \\ & \quad 11 \end{aligned}$$

In other words, if the firm accepts an investment project involving an outlay of ₹1,000 that was expected to continuously earn ₹110 per year, the project would provide a return just sufficient to leave unchanged the market price of its shares. With the assumption of no taxes, the rate of return on the equity-financed portion would be:

Total return	₹110.00
Less: Interest on debt (0.08 × ₹250)	20.00
Amount available to equity holders	90.00
Rate of return on equity (₹90 ÷ ₹750) 12 per cent	

Thus, the expected rate of return on equity shares is just equal to the required rate of return of investors. If the project earns less than ₹110 yearly, it would give a return on the equity-financed portion less than that required by the investors so that the market price of shares would decline. This rate of return is the cost of equity capital in theory.[15]

The measurement of the above required rate of return is the measurement of the cost of equity capital. There are two possible approaches that can be employed to calculate the cost of equity capital: (i) dividend approach, and (ii) capital asset pricing model approach.

Dividend Approach One approach to calculate the cost of equity capital is based on the **dividend valuation model**. According to this approach, the cost of equity capital is calculated on the basis of a required rate of return in terms of the future dividends to be paid on the shares. The cost of equity capital, k_e, is, accordingly, defined as *the discount rate that equates the present value of all expected future dividends per share with the net proceeds of the sale (or the current market price) of a share.*

Dividend valuation model assumes that the value of a share equals the present value of all future dividends that it is expected to provide over an indefinite period.

The process of determining k_e is similar to that used in calculating the explicit before-tax cost of debt (k_d) and cost of preference capital (k_p). The two elements of the calculation of k_e on the basis of the dividend approach are (i) net proceeds from the sale of a share/current market price of a share, and (ii) dividends and capital gains expected on the share. In arriving at the first, that is, the sale proceeds/current price, adjustments for flotation cost and discount/premium are necessary. In the case of dividends, the investors expect a rate of dividend which will not be constant over the years but will grow. The growth in expected dividends in future may be either at a uniform normal rate perpetually or it may vary so that for a few years it may be at level higher than in subsequent years after which it will increase at a normal rate. While calculating the cost of equity capital, therefore, the dividend approach takes into account expected dividends under different growth assumptions.

The cost of equity capital can be measured with the following equations:

(A) When dividends are expected to grow at a uniform rate perpetually:

$$P_0(1-f) = \frac{D_0(1+g)^1}{(1+k_e)^1} + \frac{D_0(1+g)^2}{(1+k_e)^2} + \ldots + \frac{D_0(1+g)^n}{(1+k_e)^n} = \sum_{t=1}^{n} \frac{D_0(1+g)^{t-1}}{(1+k_e)^t} \quad \textbf{(11.10)}$$

k_e in Eq. 11.10 is the rate of return (discount rate) which equates the two sides of the equation.

Simplifying Eq. 11.10, we get

$$P_0 = \frac{D_1}{k_e - g} \quad \textbf{(11.11)}$$

$$k_e = \frac{D_1}{P_0} + g \quad \textbf{(11.12)}$$

where D_1 = Expected dividend per share
P_0 = Net proceeds per share/current market price
g = Growth in expected dividends

The calculation of k_e on the basis of Eq. 11.12 is based on certain assumptions with respect to the behaviour of investors and their ability to forecast future values:

- the market value of shares depends upon the expected dividends;
- investors can formulate subjective probability distribution of dividends per share expected to be paid in various future periods;
- the initial dividend, D_0, is greater than zero ($D_0 > 0$);
- the dividend pay-out ratio is constant;
- investors can accurately measure the riskiness of the firm so as to agree on the rate at which to discount the dividends.

Note: Under the provisions of Section 115(O), of the Income Tax Act, 1961, a domestic company is liable to pay tax at a flat rate of 15 per cent (plus surcharge) on dividends declared/distributed/paid on/after April 1, 2010. With effect from April 1, 2018, the effective dividend distribution tax (including surcharge and cess) has been increased to 20.36 per cent. The payment of the dividend tax will reduce the growth (g) in dividends:

$g = b.r$, where b = retention rate, r = rate of return.

$$b = 1 - \left[\frac{DPS\,(1 + Dt)}{EPS}\right] = \left[\frac{EPS - DPS\,(1 + Dt)}{EPS}\right]$$

where Dt = Dividend distribution tax
$r = EPS/P_0$

$$\therefore \quad g = b \cdot r = \frac{EPS}{P_0} \times \frac{EPS - [DPS\,(1 + Dt)]}{EPS} = \left[\frac{EPS - DPS\,(1 + Dt)}{P_0}\right] \quad \textbf{(11.12A)}$$

Obviously, g without Dt would be higher.

(B) Under different growth assumptions of dividends over the years:

Equation 11.12 will have to be modified to take into account two (or more, if necessary) growth rates. The solution in the following Equation (11.13) for k_e would give the cost of equity capital:

$$P_0 = \sum_{t=1}^{n} \frac{D_0\,(1 + g_b)^{t-1}}{(1 + k_e)^t} + \sum_{t=n+1}^{\infty} \frac{D_n\,(1 + g_c)^{t-1}}{(1 + k_e)^t} \quad \textbf{(11.13)}$$

where g_b = Rate of growth in earlier years
g_c = Constant growth in later years

***Example* 11.7**

Suppose that dividend per share of a firm is expected to be ₹1 per share next year and is expected to grow at 6 per cent per year perpetually. Determine the cost of equity capital, assuming the market price per share is ₹25.

Solution

This is a case of constant growth of expected dividends. The k_e can be calculated by using Equation 11.12. Thus,

$$k_e = \frac{D_1}{P_0} + g = \frac{₹1}{₹25} + 0.06 = 10 \text{ per cent}$$

The dividend approach can be used to determine the expected market value of a share in different years. The expected value of a share of the hypothetical firm in Example 11.7 at the end of years 1 and 2 would be as follows, applying Eq. 11.12.

(i) Price at the end of the first year (P_1) $= \frac{D_2}{k_e - g} = \frac{₹1.06}{0.10 - 0.06} = ₹26.50$

(ii) $P_2 = \frac{D_3}{k_e - g} = \frac{₹1.124}{0.10 - 0.06} = ₹28$

In case company's past growth rate has been abnormally high or low, either due to its own unique situation or due to general economic fluctuations, historic growth rates **(g)** may not be reliable. In such situations, dividend growth forecasts should be based on factors such as projected sales, profit margins and competitive factors.[16] Accordingly, k_e would be as follows:

$$k_e = \frac{D_1}{P_0} + \text{Growth rate as projected} \quad \textbf{(11.13-A)}$$

Another method for estimating **g** can be conceived in terms of the company's projected retention rate and its expected future rate of return on equity. More profitable firms retain a large proportion of their earnings for reinvestment and will, therefore, tend to have higher growth rate compared to less profitable firms which distribute a large proportion of their earnings as dividends.[17]

In brief, careful analysis and sound judgments are essential and play more important role in determining the k_e *vis-à-vis* the k_d and the k_p.

However, the dividend growth model approach is beset with a number of practical problems and drawbacks. The major ones are: **(1)** It is applicable only to those corporates which pay dividends. Its results are really applicable to cases where a reasonably steady growth is likely to occur; **(2)** Cost of equity is very sensitive to the estimated growth. As explained earlier, it is not easy to estimate its value; **(3)** The approach does not explicitly reckon risk factor. There is no allowance for the degree of risk associated with the estimated growth rate for dividends.[18]

***Example* 11.8**

From the undermentioned facts determine the cost of equity shares of company X:

(i) Current market price of a share = ₹150.

(ii) Cost of floatation per share on new shares, ₹3.

(iii) Dividend paid on the outstanding shares over the past five years:

Year	*Dividend per share*
1	₹10.50
2	11.02
3	11.58
4	12.16
5	12.76
6	13.40

(iv) Assume a fixed dividend pay out ratio.

(v) Expected dividend on the new shares at the end of the current year is ₹14.10 per share.

Solution

As a first step, we have to estimate the growth rate in dividends. Using the compound interest table (Table A-1), the annual growth rate of dividends would be approximately 5 per cent. (During the five years the dividends have increased from ₹10.50 to ₹13.40, giving a compound factor of 1.276, that is, ₹13.40/₹10.50. The sum of ₹1 would accumulate to ₹1.276 in five years @ 5 per cent interest).

$$k_e = \frac{₹14.10}{₹147\,(₹150 - ₹3)} + 5\% = 14.6 \text{ per cent}$$

***Example* 11.9**

Z Ltd is foreseeing a growth rate of 12 per cent per annum in the next 2 years. The growth rate is likely to fall to 10 per cent for the third year and the fourth year. After that, the growth rate is expected to stabilise at 8 per cent per annum. If the last dividend was ₹1.50 per share and the investors' required rate of return is 16 per cent, find out the intrinsic value per share of Z Ltd as of date.

Solution

Intrinsic value of *Z* Ltd = the sum of: (i) *PV* of dividends payments during 1-4 years and (ii) *PV* of expected market price at the end of the fourth year based on a constant growth of 8 per cent.

Present value of dividends, year 1-4

Years	*Dividend*	*PVIF (0.16)*	*Total PV*
1	₹1.68	0.862	₹1.45
2	1.88	0.743	1.40
3	2.07	0.641	1.33
4	2.28	0.552	1.26
			5.44

$$P_4 = D_5/(k_e - g) = \frac{₹2.28\,(1.08)}{16\% - 8\%} = ₹30.78$$

PV of ₹30.78 = ₹30.78 × 0.552 = ₹16.99

Intrinsic value of share = ₹5.44 + ₹16.99 = ₹22.43

Capital Asset Pricing Model Approach Another technique that can be used to estimate the cost of equity is the capital asset pricing model (CAPM) approach. We first discuss the CAPM.[19] As an approach to measure the cost of equity capital, it is described subsequently.

Diversifiable/unsystematic risk is the portion of a security's risk that is attributable to firm-specific random causes; can be eliminated through diversification.

The CAPM explains the behaviour of security prices and provides a mechanism whereby investors could assess the impact of proposed security investment on their overall portfolio risk and return. In other words, it formally describes the risk-return trade-off for securities. It is based on certain assumptions. The basic assumptions of CAPM are related to **(a)** the efficiency of the security markets and **(b)** investor preferences.

The efficient market assumption implies that **(i)** all investors have common (homogeneous) expectations regarding the expected returns, variances and correlation of returns among all securities; **(ii)** all investors have the same information about securities; **(iii)** there are no restrictions on investments; **(iv)** there are no taxes; **(v)** there are no transaction costs; and **(vi)** no single investor can affect market price significantly.

Non-diversifiable risk is the relevant portion of a security's risk that is attributable to market factors that affect all firms; cannot be eliminated through diversification.

The implication of investors' preference assumption is that all investors prefer the security that provides the highest return for a given level of risk or the lowest amount of risk for a given level of return, that is, the investors are risk averse.

The risk to which security investment is exposed falls into two groups: **(i) diversifiable**/unsystematic, and **(ii)** non-diversifiable/systematic. The first represents that portion of the total risk of an investment that can be eliminated/minimised through diversification. The events/factors that cause such risks vary from firm to firm. The sources of such risks include management capabilities and decisions, strikes, unique government regulations, availability or otherwise of raw materials, competition, level of operating and financial leverage of the firm, and so on.

The systematic/**non-diversifiable risk** is attributable to factors that affect all firms. Illustrative sources of such risks are interest rate changes, inflation or purchasing power change, changes in investor expectations about the overall performance of the economy and political changes, and so on. As unsystematic risk can be eliminated by an investor through diversification, the systematic risk is the only relevant risk. Therefore, an investor (firm) should be concerned, according to CAPM, solely with the non-diversifiable (systematic) risk.

Capital asset pricing model (CAPM) describes the relationship between the required return or cost of equity capital and the non-diversifiable risk of a firm measured by beta coefficient, *b*.

Systematic risk can be measured in relation to the risk of a diversified portfolio which is commonly referred to as the **market portfolio** or **the market**. According to CAPM, the non-diversifiable risk of an investment/security/ asset is assessed in terms of the *beta* coefficient. *Beta* is a measure of the volatility of a security's return relative to the returns of a broad-based market portfolio. Alternatively, it is an index of the degree of responsiveness or *co-movement* of return on an investment with the market return. The beta for the market portfolio as measured by the broad-based market index equals one. Beta coefficient of 1 would imply that the risk of the specified security is equal to the market; the interpretation of zero coefficient is that there is no market-related risk to the investment. A negative coefficient would indicate a relationship in the opposite direction. The 'going' required rate of return in the market for a given amount of systematic risk is called the Security Market Line (SML).

With reference to the cost of capital perspective, the **CAPM** describes the relationship between the required rate of return, or the cost of equity capital, and the non-diversifiable or relevant risk, of the firm as reflected in its index of non-diversifiable risk, that is, beta. Symbolically,

$$K_e = R_f + b\,(K_m - R_f) \qquad \textbf{(11.14)}$$

Where
K_e = cost of equity capital
R_f = the rate of return required on a risk-free asset/security/investment
K_m = the required rate of return on the market portfolio of assets that can be viewed as the average rate of return on all assets.
b = the beta coefficient

The computation of the cost of equity capital using the CAPM approach is shown in Example 11.10.

***Example* 11.10**

The Hypothetical Ltd wishes to calculate its cost of equity capital using the capital asset pricing model approach. From the information provided to the firm by its investment advisors along with the firms' own analysis, it is found that the risk-free rate of return equals 10 per cent; the firm's beta equals 1.50 and the return on the market portfolio equals 12.5 per cent. Compute the cost of equity capital.

Solution

Substituting the values in Eq. 11.14

$$K_e = 10\% + [1.5 \times (12.5\% - 10\%)] = 13.75 \text{ per cent}$$

***Example* 11.11**

As an investment manager you are given the following information

Investment in equity shares of	*Initial price*	*Dividends*	*Year-end market price*	*Beta risk factor*
A Cement Ltd	₹25	₹2	₹50	0.80
Steel Ltd	35	2	60	0.70
Liquor Ltd	45	2	135	0.50
B Government of India Bonds	1,000	140	1,005	0.99
Risk-free return, 8 per cent				

You are required to calculate (i) expected rate of returns of market portfolio, and (ii) expected return in each security, using capital asset pricing model.

Solution

(i) Expected Returns on Market Portfolio

Security	Return: Dividends	Return: Capital appreciation	Return: Total	Investment
A Cement Ltd	₹2	₹25	₹27	₹25
Steel Ltd	2	25	27	35
Liquor Ltd	2	90	92	45
B Government of India Bonds	140	5	145	1,000
	146	145	291	1,105

Rate of return (expected) on market portfolio = ₹291/₹1,105 = 26.33 per cent

(ii) Expected Returns on Individual Security (in per cent)

$k_e = R_f + b(km - R_f)$	
Cement Ltd = 8% + 0.8 (26.33% – 8%)	22.66
Steel Ltd = 8% + 0.7 (26.33% – 8%)	20.83
Liquor Ltd = 8% + 0.5 (26.33% – 8%)	17.16
Government of India Bonds = 8% + 0.99 (26.33% – 8%)	26.15

The capital assets pricing model (CAPM) approach to calculate the cost of equity capital is different from the dividend valuation approach in some respects. In the first place, the CAPM approach directly considers the risk as reflected in beta in order to determine the K_e. The valuation model does not consider the risk; it rather uses the market price as a reflection of the expected risk-return preference of investors in the market. Secondly, the dividend model can be adjusted for flotation cost to estimate the cost of the new equity shares. The CAPM approach is incapable of such adjustment as the model does not include the market price which has to be adjusted. However, its big virtue is that it can be used to determine cost of equity for corporates which either do not pay dividends or are not subject to steady growth rate.

Both the dividend and CAPM approaches are theoretically sound. But major problems are encountered in the practical application of the CAPM approach in collecting data—which may not be readily available or in a country like India may be altogether absent—regarding expected future returns, the most appropriate estimate of the risk-free rate and the best estimates of the security's *beta*. Moreover, beta measure of risk considers only the systematic risk. Poorly diversified investors may be more interested in total risk rather than in systematic risk only. In such cases the CAPM may tend to underestimate the required rate of such investor. For these reasons, the use of the dividend approach would appear to be more appropriate to measure the cost of equity capital.

In brief, various methods of estimating k_e are most likely to provide different amounts because each method relies on different assumptions. There are two ways to deal with the situation: **(1)** Each estimate of k_e should be looked at to ascertain that its value is neither too high nor too low. It should intuitively appear to be reasonable; **(2)** Average the various estimates of k_e (as suggested by Ross, et al).[20]

LO 11.5 COST OF RETAINED EARNINGS

Retained earnings, as a source of finance for investment proposals, differ from other sources like debt, preference shares and equities. The use of debt is associated with a contractual obligation to pay a fixed rate of interest to the suppliers of funds and, often, repayment of principal at some predetermined date. An almost similar kind of stipulation applies to the use of preference shares also. In the case of ordinary shares, although there is no provision for any predetermined payment to the shareholders, yet a certain expected rate of dividend provides a starting point for the computation of cost of equity capital. That retained earnings do not involve any formal arrangement to become a source of funds is obvious. In other words, there is no obligation, formal or implied, on a firm to pay a return on retained earnings. Apparently, retained earnings may appear to carry no cost since they represent funds which have not been raised from outside. The contention that retained earnings are free of cost, however, is not correct. On the contrary, they do involve cost like any other source.

It is true that a firm is not obliged to pay a return (dividend or interest) on retained earnings. But retention of earnings does have implications for the shareholders of the firm. If earnings were not retained, they would have been paid out to the ordinary shareholders as dividends. In other words, retention of earnings implies withholding of dividends from holders of ordinary shares. When earnings are, thus, retained, shareholders are forced to forego dividends. The dividends foregone by the equity-holders are, in fact, an opportunity cost. Thus, retained earnings involve opportunity cost. In other words, the firm is implicitly required to earn on the retained earnings at least equal to the rate that would have been earned by the shareholders if they were distributed to them. This is the cost of retained earnings. Therefore, the cost of retained earnings may be defined as *opportunity cost in terms of dividends foregone by/withheld from the equity shareholders.*

The alternative use of retained earnings is based on 'external-yield criterion'.[21] According to this approach, the alternative to retained earnings is external investment of funds by the firm itself. In other words the opportunity cost of retention of earnings is the rate of return that could be earned by investing the funds in another enterprise by the firm instead of what would be obtained by the shareholders on other investments. The firm should estimate the yield it can earn from external investment opportunities by investing its retained earnings there. While doing so, the firm should bear in mind that it selects such investment opportunities as have the same degree of risk as that of the firm itself. The rate of return that could be thus earned constitutes the opportunity cost of retained earnings. Such a return would give the cost of retained earnings, k_r. The k_r under the assumption of external-yield criterion would be approximately k_e. The merits of this approach are obvious. The k_r here is simply the return on direct investment by the firm itself. Since the investments of funds are assumed to be made by the firm itself, the return would not be affected by the tax brackets in which the various shareholders of the firm are. The approach, in other words, can be consistently applied. The external-yield criterion, therefore, represents an economically justifiable opportunity cost.

Cost of retained earnings is the same as the cost of an equivalent fully subscribed issue of additional shares, which is measured by the cost of equity capital.

In brief, the **cost of retained earnings** represents an opportunity cost in terms of the return on their investment in another enterprise by the firm whose cost of retained earnings is being considered. The opportunity cost given by the external-yield criterion which can be consistently applied can be said to measure the k_r, which is likely to be equal to the k_e. Therefore, k_e should be used as k_r but the latter would be lower than the former due to differences in flotation cost and due to dividend payment tax.

Weighted average cost of capital is the expected average future cost of funds over the long run found by weighting the cost of each specific type of capital by its proportion in the firm's capital structure.

LO 11.6 COMPUTATION OF OVERALL COST OF CAPITAL

The calculations of the cost of specific sources, namely, debt, preference shares, equity shares and retained earnings have been shown in the preceding discussions. In this section we propose to dwell on the computation of the overall cost of capital. The term cost of capital means the overall composite cost of capital defined *as* **weighted average** *of the cost of each specific type of fund.* The use of *weighted* average and not the *simple* average is warranted by the fact that the proportions of various sources of funds in the capital structure of a firm are different. To be representative, therefore, the overall cost of capital should take into account the relative proportions of different sources and hence the *weighted* average.

The computation of the overall cost of capital (represented symbolically by k_o) involves the following steps:

1. Assigning weights to specific costs.
2. Multiplying the cost of each of the sources by the appropriate weights.
3. Dividing the total weighted cost by the total weights.

The crucial part of the exercise is the decision regarding appropriate weights and the related aspects. We first illustrate the relevant aspects of the choice of the weights. This is followed by the mechanics of computation of k_0 which is relatively simple.

Assignment of Weights

The aspects relevant to the selection of appropriate weights are (i) Historical weights versus Marginal weights; (ii) Historical weights can be—(a) Book value weights or (b) Market value weights.

Historical versus Marginal Weights The first aspect of the decision regarding the selection of appropriate weights for computing the overall cost of capital is: which system of weighting—marginal or historical—is preferable? The critical assumption in any weighting system is that *the firm will raise capital in the specified proportions.*

Marginal Weights The use of **marginal weights** involves weighting the specific costs by the proportion of each type of fund to the total funds to be raised. The marginal weights represent the percentage share of different financing sources the firm intends to raise/employ. The basis of assigning relative weights is, therefore, new/additional/incremental issue of funds and, hence, marginal weights.

Marginal weights use proportion of each type of capital to the total capital to be raised.

In using marginal weights, we are concerned with the actual amounts of each type of financing used in raising additional funds to finance new projects by the company. In fact, the use of marginal weights is more attuned to the actual process of financing projects. Another merit of marginal weights is that their use also reflects the fact that the firm does not have a great deal of control over the amount of financing obtained through retained earnings or other sources which are influenced by several factors, such as, temper of the market, investors' preference and so on.

What is the relative suitability of marginal weights to compute the overall cost of capital? The composite cost of capital is computed, it would be recalled, to be used as an investment criterion. The capital budgeting decision is concerned with the selection of new investment proposals. As already mentioned, the cost of capital, conceptually speaking, which is relevant is the cost of the new capital to be raised to finance the current capital expenditure decision, that is, marginal cost. It is, therefore, argued that the weights must correspond to the proportions of financing inputs the firm intends to employ, that is, the combined cost of capital should be calculated by employing marginal weights. If marginal weights are not used, the implication is that new capital is raised in proportions other than those used to calculate this cost. As a result,[22] the real overall cost of capital will be different from that calculated and used for asset-selection decision. There is obviously a bias in the exercise. If the real cost is more than the calculated one, certain investment proposals will be accepted that will have the effect of leaving the investor worse off than before because the potential profitability has been overestimated. On the other hand, if the real cost is less than the measured cost, projects that could increase the shareholders' wealth would be rejected. Finally, the problem of choosing between book-value weights and market value weights does not arise in the case of marginal weights.

However, the marginal weighting system suffers from serious limitations. One major criticism[23] of the use of marginal weights is that this approach does not consider the long-term implications of the firm's current financing. Since capital expenditure decisions are long-term investments of the firm, attention should be given to the long-term implications of any financing strategy. Using cheaper sources of funds to finance a given project may place the firm in a position where more expensive equity financing will have to be raised to finance a future project. For example, a firm may be able to sell debt at an after-tax cost of 9 per cent. If the best investment project has currently available returns of 10 per cent and the weighted average cost of capital based on marginal weights is used as a decision criterion, the project will be accepted. If next year, the firm must raise equity at a cost of 16 per cent, it will have to reject a project, returning 15 per cent. Thus, **the fact that today's financing affects tomorrow's cost is not considered in using marginal weights**.[24] In other words, the interrelationship among the various methods of financing is ignored if marginal weights are used to calculate the cost of capital.

Historic weights are based on actual capital structure proportion to calculate weights.

Historical Weights The alternative to the use of marginal weights is to use **historical weights**. Here, the relative proportions of various sources to the existing capital structure are used to assign weights. In other words, the basis of the weighting system is the funds already employed by the firm. The use of the historical weights is based on the assumption that the firm's existing capital structure is optimal and, therefore, should be maintained in the future. That is, the firm should raise additional funds for financing investments in the same proportion as they are in the existing capital structure. In other words, the existing proportion of various sources of long-term funds will be followed whenever the firm raises additional long-term funds to finance new investment projects. For instance, if the present capital structure of firm has 30 per cent debts, 20 per cent preference shares, 40 per cent equity capital and 10 per cent retained earnings, the company will be assumed to raise incremental funds in the same proportion as it has done in the past. Assume further, that the firm requires additional funds amounting to ₹1,00,000 to finance a new project. It should be expected, according to the historical weighting system, to raise this sum from different sources in the proportion of 30 per cent (debt), 20 per cent (preference shares), 40 per cent (ordinary shares) and 10 per cent (retained earnings). The break-up of the amount source-wise would be: debt, ₹30,000; preference capital, ₹20,000; equity capital, ₹40,000 and retained earnings, ₹10,000.

The problem with historical weighting is that the validity of the assumptions on which it is based is open to question. That firms should raise additional funds from different sources in the same proportion in which they are in the existing capital structure implies that there are no constraints on raising funds from these sources. This is not correct. For instance, the amount of retained earnings may actually fall short of its required share in financing new projects because firms cannot have control over the retained earnings. Similarly, raising funds from the capital market depends on several factors such as the state of the economy, requirements of investors, temper of the market and so on, over which the firms have obviously no control. There are, thus, practical difficulties in applying historical weights. Yet another problem with the application of the historical weights is that a choice has to be made between the book value weights and market value weights.

As against the above limitations, the system of assigning weights on the basis of the existing capital structure has one outstanding merit. As a decision criterion, the weighted cost of capital based on historical weights takes into account a long-term view. If the cost thus calculated is 12 per cent, using it as a decision-criterion for capital budgeting decision, a project returning 13 per cent next year will be accepted. While it is true that firms actually raise funds in lump sum amounts from one or two sources at a time instead of all the available sources, the use of historical weights to calculate the overall weighted average cost of capital is more consistent with the firm's long-term goal of maximising the owner's wealth. Therefore, the use of historical weights is much more likely to lead to an optimal selection of capital investment projects in the long run.[25] It is probably for this reason that historical weights are commonly used to calculate the weighted cost of capital, and are treated as superior to marginal weights, which, as already indicated, ignore the long-term implications of the firm's current financing.

Book Value and Market Value Weights The second aspect of assigning weights to various sources of finance in calculating the composite cost of capital relates to the choice between book value weights and market value weights. This problem will arise only in the case of historical weights.

Both these methods have their own merits. In theory, the use of **market value weights** for calculating the cost of capital is more appealing than the use of book value weights because: (i) market values of securities closely approximate the actual amount to be received from their sale; (ii) the costs of the specific sources of finance which constitute the capital structure of the firm are calculated using prevailing market prices. However, there are practical difficulties in its use as calculating the market value of securities may present difficulties, particularly the market values of retained earnings. Moreover, weights based on market values are likely to fluctuate widely.

Market value weights use market values to measure the proportion of each type of capital to calculate weighted average cost of capital.

On the other hand, the merits of **book value weights** are operational in nature. For one thing, book values are readily available from the published records of the firm. Also, firms set their capital structure targets in terms of book values rather than market values. Finally, the analysis of capital structure in terms of debt-equity ratio is based on book value.

In brief, the alternatives—book values and market values of securities—have their own commendable features. While the book value is operationally convenient, the market value basis is theoretically consistent and sound, and therefore a better indicator of a firm's true capital structure.

Book value weights use accounting (book) values to measure the proportion of each type of capital to calculate the weighted average cost of capital.

Mechanics of Computation

***Example* 11.12 (Book Value Weights)**

We now illustrate the mechanics of computation of the weighted average cost of capital.

(a) A firm's after-tax cost of capital of the specific sources is as follows:

Cost of debt	8	per cent
Cost of preference shares (including dividend tax)	14	
Cost of equity funds	17	

(b) The following is the capital structure:

Source	*Amount*
Debt	₹3,00,000
Preference capital	2,00,000
Equity capital	5,00,000
	10,00,000

(c) Calculate the weighted average cost of capital, k_0, using book value weights.

Solution

TABLE 11.1 Computation of Weighted Average Cost of Capital (Book Value Weights)

Source of funds	*Amount*	*Proportion*	*Cost (%)*	*Weighted cost (3 × 4)*
(1)	*(2)*	*(3)*	*(4)*	*(5)*
Debt	₹3,00,000	0.3 (30)	0.08	0.024
Preference capital	2,00,000	0.2 (20)	0.14	0.028
Equity capital	5,00,000	0.5 (50)	0.17	0.085
	10,00,000	1.00 (100)		0.137
Weighted average cost of capital = 13.7 per cent				

An alternative method of determining the k_0 is to compute, as shown in Table 11.2, the total cost of capital and then divide this figure by the total capital. This procedure obviously avoids fractional calculations.

TABLE 11.2 Computation of Weighted Average Cost of Capital (Alternative Method)

Sources	Amount	Cost (%)	Total cost (2 × 3)
(1)	(2)	(3)	(4)
Debt	₹3,00,000	8	₹24,000
Preference capital	2,00,000	14	28,000
Equity capital	5,00,000	17	85,000
Total	10,00,000		1,37,000

Weighted average cost of capital = $\frac{₹1,37,000}{₹10,00,000} \times 100 = 13.7$ per cent

***Example* 11.13 (Market Value Weights)**

From the information contained in Example 11.12, calculate the weighted average cost of capital, assuming that the market values of different sources of funds are as follows:

Source	Market value
Debt	₹2,70,000
Preference shares	2,30,000
Equity and retained earnings	7,50,000
Total	12,50,000

Solution

(1) The determination of the market value of retained earnings presents operational difficulties. The market value of retained earnings can be indirectly estimated. A possible criterion has been suggested by Gitman,[26] according to which, since retained earnings are treated as equity capital for purpose of calculation of cost of specific source of funds, the market value of the ordinary shares may be taken to represent the combined market value of equity shares and retained earnings. The separate market values of retained earnings and ordinary shares may be found by allocating to each of these a percentage of the total market value equal to their percentage share of the total based on book values.

On the basis of the foregoing criterion, the sum of ₹7,50,000 in Example 11.13 is allocated between equity capital and retained earnings as follows:

Source of funds	Book value	Per cent of book value	Market value
(1)	(2)	(3)	(4)
Equity shares	₹4,00,000	80	₹6,00,000*
Retained earnings	1,00,000	20	1,50,000**

*(0.8 × ₹7,50,000)
**(0.20 × ₹7,50,000)

(2) After the determination of market value, k_0 is calculated as shown in Table 11.3.

TABLE 11.3 Computation of Weighted Average Cost of Capital (Market Value Weights)

Sources	Market value	Cost (per cent)	Total cost (3 × 2)
(1)	(2)	(3)	(4)
Debt	₹2,70,000	8	₹21,600
Preference shares	2,30,000	14	32,200
Equity capital	6,00,000	17	1,02,000
Retained earnings	1,50,000	17	25,500
Total	12,50,000		1,81,300

k_0 = (₹1,81,300/₹12,50,000) × 100 = 14.5 per cent

One notable point that emerges from the computation of the weighted average cost of capital based respectively on book value weights and market value weights is that the k_0 with market value weights is higher. This is mainly due to the fact that equity shares have market values considerably greater than their book values. Since these sources of long-term funds have higher specific costs, the overall cost increases.

In operational terms, if book value weighted average cost of capital is used, some projects would be accepted that would not be acceptable based on the market value approach. The results given by the market value based weights are obviously better as a decision criterion.

***Example* 11.14 (Marginal Weights)**

The firm of Example 11.12 wishes to raise ₹5,00,000 for expansion of its plant. It estimates that ₹1,00,000 will be available as retained earnings and the balance of the additional funds will be raised as follows:

Long-term debt	₹3,00,000
Preference shares	1,00,000

Using marginal weights, compute the weighted average cost of capital.

Solution ***The computation is illustrated in Table 11.4.***

TABLE 11.4 Weighted Average Cost of Capital (Marginal Weights)

Sources of funds	*Amount*	*Proportion*	*Cost (%)*	*Total cost (2 × 4)*
(1)	(2)	(3)	(4)	(5)
Debt	₹3,00,000	0.60 (60)	8	₹24,000
Preference shares	1,00,000	0.20 (20)	14	14,000
Retained earnings	1,00,000	0.20 (20)	17	17,000
	5,00,000	1.00 (100)		55,000
Weighted average cost of capital = (₹55,000/₹5,00,000) × 100 = 11 per cent				

This cost is substantially lower than the weighted cost calculated using either book values or market values of historical weights. This is because debt finance has been used in large amount. Since only a limited amount of debt financing can be raised for a given equity base, it is quite likely that the firm will have to use primarily expensive equity financing for future projects. Obviously, this is not a happy situation because a project which gives a return of, say, 12 per cent this year will be accepted as the k_0 is only 11 per cent but next year another project which may give a higher return might have to be rejected because equity financing will imply/entail a higher k_0. The use of historical market value weights in calculating k_0 is much more likely to lead to an optimal selection of capital investment projects in the long run and, therefore, it should be preferred as the basis of assigning weights to calculate the composite cost of capital.

LO 11.7 COST OF CAPITAL PRACTICES IN INDIA

The main features of the cost of capital practices followed by the corporates in India are as follows:

- The most frequently used (67 per cent of cases) discount rate (i.e., minimum acceptable/required rate of return) to evaluate capital budgeting decision is based on the overall cost (WACC) of the corporate. There is a preference for the use of market weights over book value weights by a vast majority of the sample companies.

- Depending on the risk characteristics of the project, multiple risk-adjusted discount rates are used by about one-fifth of the corporate enterprises.
- The specific cost of capital used to finance the project (i.e. if the discount rate for a project that will be financed entirely with retained earnings is the cost of retained funds) is used by one-fourth of the sample corporates.
- The CAPM is the most popular method of estimating the cost of equity capital (54 per cent). The Gordon's dividend model is equally popular method to compute the cost of equity capital (52 per cent). The earnings yield approach is used by one-third of the sample corporates to estimate the cost of equity capital. The use of the multi-factor model is used by very few corporates (7 per cent).
- A significant feature of the methods used to estimate the cost of equity capital is that while the CAPM is significantly used by the large corporates, the Gordon's discount model is more popular with small firms. Moreover, the highly profitable corporate (based on ROCE and EAV) give significantly low importance to dividend yield and earnings yield to compute the cost of equity capital than the less profitable corporates.
- The Government of India (GOI) 10-year bonds are the most widely used risk-free rate to compute the cost of capital using the CAPM approach. The industry average beta is the most popular measure of the systematic risk used by the corporates. Each of the published sources of beta and the self-calculated beta are also used by about one-fifth of the corporates respectively.
- The self-calculated beta is more popularly used by the large and/highly profitable corporates. The small and low profitable corporates rely more on the published sources of beta.
- The majority of corporates (two-thirds) considers the last 5-year monthly share price data to estimate the equity beta. The highly profitable firms use weekly share price data for the purpose.
- The average market risk premium (9-10 per cent) is the most widely used measure by the corporates. The average of historical return and the implied return on the market portfolio are also fairly popular as an input while using the CAPM.
- As regards the cost of debt, the most widely used method is the interest tax shield (i.e., tax advantage of interest on debt).
- While the majority of the corporates revise their estimates of cost of capital annually, some of the sample corporates continuously revise it with every investment.
- Apart from project choice criterion, the cost of capital is also used widely for (a) divisional performance measurement, (b) EVA computation and (c) CVA computations.
- Majority of the sample companies adopt theoretically sound and conceptually correct basis of determining the cost of capital, namely, the weighted average cost of long-term sources of finance. However, there is no systematic procedure followed to compute it. It is more likely to be subjective in nature. The Indian corporates use mix of the WACC, marginal cost of capital of additional funds and management judgment in this regard.
- There is wide divergence in the corporate practices as regards the computation of the cost of equity capital. About one-tenth of the corporates do not attach any cost to equity capital. Another one-tenth treat the cost of equity capital as equivalent to primary rate of return available on securities of balanced mutual funds and debentures issued by blue chip companies.
- However, the vast majority of companies (two-thirds of the sample) follow the conceptually sound methods (i.e. primary rate of return plus risk premium, dividend valuation model and CAPM) of determining the cost of equity capital.
- About one-fifth of the sample corporates consider retained earnings as a cost-free source of finance. However, a sizeable proportion of the sample companies (75 per cent) regard cost of retained earnings either as equivalent to opportunity cost of using these funds by the corporate/equity-holders or equal to the cost of equity capital.

Sources: (i) Anand, M., *op. cit.*, pp 29–56, (ii) Jain, P. K. and Yadav, S. S., *op. cit.*, pp 55–103.

SUMMARY

LO 11.1

The cost of capital is an integral part of investment decisions as it is used to measure the worth of investment proposal. It is used as a discount rate in determining the present value of future cash flows associated with capital projects. Conceptually, it is the minimum rate of return that a firm must earn on its investments so as to leave market price of its shares unchanged. It is also referred to as cut-off rate, target rate, hurdle rate, required rate of return and so on.

In operational terms, it is defined as the weighted average cost of capital (k_0) of all long-term sources of finance. The major long-term sources of funds are (i) debt, (ii) preference shares, (iii) equity capital, and (iv) retained earnings. Thus, it comprises of several components in terms of specific cost of each source of finance. When these specific costs are combined, it results in the weighted average cost of capital.

The cost of capital can be explicit or implicit. The explicit cost of capital is associated with the raising of funds (from debt, preference shares and equity). The explicit cost of any source of capital (C) is the discount rate that equates the present value of the cash inflows (CI_o) that are incremental to the taking of financing opportunity with the present value of its incremental cash outflows (CO_t). Symbolically, $CI_o = \sum_{t=1}^{n} \frac{CO_t}{(1+C)^t}$

Its determination is similar to the determination of the internal rate of return (IRR). It is the internal rate of return that the firm pays to procure financing.

Retained earnings involve no future cash flows to, or from, the firm. Therefore, the retained earnings do not have explicit cost. However, they carry implicit cost in terms of the opportunity cost of the foregone alternative (*s*) in terms of the rate of return at which the shareholders could have invested these funds had they been distributed to them/or not retained by the firm.

There are four types of specific costs, namely, cost of debt (k_d), cost of preference shares (k_p), cost of equity capital (k_e) and cost of retained earnings (k_r).

LO 11.2

The debt carries a certain rate of interest. Interest qualifies for tax deduction in determining tax liability. Therefore, the effective cost of debt is less than the actual interest payment made by the firm by the amount of tax shield it provides. The debt can be either perpetual or redeemable.

In the case of perpetual debt, it is computed dividing effective interest payment, i.e., $I(1 - t)$ by the amount of debt/sale proceeds of debentures or bonds (SV). Symbolically, $K_d = \frac{I(1-t)}{SV}$

In the case of redeemable debt, the repayment of debt principal (COP) either in instalments or in lump sum (besides interest, COI) is also taken into account. k_d is computed based on the following equations:

$$CI_0 = \sum_{t=1}^{n} \frac{COI_t}{(1+k_d)^t}(1-t) + \frac{COP_n}{(1+k_d)^n} \quad \text{(When principal is paid in lump sum)}$$

$$\text{Alternatively, } K_d = \frac{I(1-t) + (\text{Redeemable value}, RV - SV/N)}{(RV+SV)/2}$$

$$CI_0 = \sum_{t=1}^{n} \frac{COI_t}{(1+k_d)^t}(1-t) + \frac{COP_t}{(1+k_d)^t} \quad \text{(When debt is paid in instalments)}$$

The cost of debt is generally the lowest among all sources partly because the risk involved is low but mainly because interest paid on debt is tax deductible.

LO 11.3

The cost of preference share (k_p) is akin to k_d. However, unlike interest payment on debt, dividend payable on preference shares is not tax deductible from the point of view assessing tax liability. On the contrary, tax (Dt) may be required to be paid on the payment of preference dividend.

The k_p in the case of irredeemable preference shares is based on dividends payable on them and the sale proceeds obtained by issuing such preference shares, P_0 (1 – f). In terms of equation:

$$K_p = \frac{D_p(1+Dt)}{P_0(1-f)}$$

The k_p for redeemable preference shares requiring lump sum repayment (P) is determined on the basis of the following equation:

$$P_0(1-f) = \sum_{t=1}^{n}\frac{D_p(1+Dt)}{(1+k_p)^t} + \frac{P_n}{(1+k_p)^n}$$

In the case of repayment required in instalments:

$$P_0(1-f) = \sum_{t=1}^{n}\frac{D_p(1+Dt)}{(1+k_p)^t} + \frac{P_t}{(1+k_p)^t}$$

Cost of preference shares would be higher due to dividend distribution tax (with effect from April 1, 2018, the rate is 20.36 per cent).

LO 11.4

The computation of cost of equity capital (k_e) is conceptually more difficult as the return to the equity-holders solely depends upon the discretion of the company management. It is defined as the minimum rate of return that a corporate must earn on the equity-financed portion of an investment project in order to leave unchanged the market price of the shares.

There are three approaches to measure k_e: (i) the dividend valuation model approach, (ii) capital asset pricing model (CAPM) approach and (iii) debt-yield plus risk premium approach.

As per the dividend approach, k_e is defined as the discount rate that equates the present value of all expected future dividends per share with the net proceeds of the sale (or the current market price) of a share. In equation terms,

$$P_0(1-f) = \sum_{t=1}^{n}\frac{D_1(1+g)^{t-1}}{(1+k_e)^t} \quad \text{Or,} \quad k_e = \frac{D_1}{P_0(1-f)} + g$$

The CAPM describes the relationship between the required rate of return or the cost of equity capital and the non-diversifiable or relevant risk of the firm as reflected in its index of non-diversifiable risk, that is, beta. Symbolically,

$$K_e = R_f + b(K_m - R_f),$$

R_f = Required rate of return on risk-free investment

b = Beta coefficient**, and

K_m = Required rate of return on market portfolio, that is, the average rate or return on all assets

$$** = \frac{\Sigma MJ - N\overline{M}\,\overline{J}}{\Sigma M^2 - N\overline{M}^2}, \text{where}$$

M = Excess in market return over risk-free rate,

J = Excess in security returns over risk-free rate,

MJ = Cross product of M and J and

N = Number of years

As per debt-yield plus risk premium approach, cost of equity is equal to judgemental risk premium of 3 to 5 percentage points + interest rate paid by the firm on its own long-term debt.

LO 11.5	The cost of retained earning (k_r) is equally difficult to calculate in theoretical terms. Since retained earnings essentially involves use of funds, it is associated with an opportunity/implicit cost. The alternative to retained earnings is the investment of the funds by the firm itself in a homogeneous outside investment. Therefore, k_r is equal to k_e. However, it might be slightly lower than k_e in the case of new equity issue due to flotation costs.
LO 11.6	The measurement of the weighted average/overall cost of capital (k_0) involves the choice of appropriate weights. The two systems of assigning weights, namely, historical and marginal, have their own suitability but historical weights appear to be superior to marginal weights as the former take into account the long-term implications of the firm's current financing. With historical weights, a choice is to be made between book value and market value weights. While the book value weights are operationally convenient, the market value basis is theoretically consistent and sound, and therefore, a better indicator of firm's capital structure.
	The k_0 is computed based on the following equation: $K_0 = K_dW_d + K_pW_p + K_eW_e + K_rW_r$ W_d = Percentage of debt to total capital, W_p = Percentage of preference shares to total capital, W_e = Percentage of external equity to total capital and W_r = Percentage of retained earnings to total capital

REFERENCES

1. Van Horne, J, *Financial Management and Policy*, Prentice-Hall, New Delhi 1998, p 91.
2. Gitman, L J, *Principles of Managerial Finance*, Harper & Row, New York 1997, p 33.
3. Van Horne, J C, *op. cit.*, p 220.
4. Gitman, L J, *op. cit.*, p 339.
5. Porterfield, J T S, *op. cit.*, p 45.
6. *Ibid.* p 46.
7. *Ibid.* p 46-51.
8. *Ibid.* p 61.
9. *Ibid.*
10. This apart, there may be additional tax advantage on account of amortisation of flotation costs. For instance, Sec. 35D of the Indian Income Tax Act provides that the aggregate amount of qualifying expenditure under the head of preliminary expenses (of which flotation cost is only one part) is available for amortisation in 10 equal instalments over a period of 10 years, subject to the limit 2.5 per cent of the cost of the project or capital employed. To keep the discussion simple, we have ignored these adjustments. However, in practice, cost of capital should be calculated after providing for the tax benefits accruing out of amortisation of flotation costs.
11. Brigham, E F and J F Houston, *op. cit*, p. 365.
12. Brigham, E F and J F Houston, *Ibid*, p. 365.
13. Ross, S A, *op cit*, p. 481.
14. Van Horne, *op. cit.*, p 93.
15. *Ibid*, p 93.
16. Brigham, E F and J F Houston, *op. cit*, p. 366.
17. Brigham, E F and J F Houston, *Ibid*, pp. 366-7.
18. Ross, S A et al., *op. cit.*, p. 483.
19. For a comprehensive account reference may be made to Moyer, R C, et al., Contemporary Financial Management, West Publishing Co., New York, 1984, pp 123-28.
20. For details refer to Ross, S.A., et al., *op. cit*, pp. 490-91.
21. Suggested by Solomon, E, *op. cit.*, pp. 53-55.
22. Van Horne, *op. cit.*, p 115.

23. Gitman, L J *op. cit.*, p 354.
24. *Ibid.*
25. *Ibid.*
26. *Ibid.* p 353.

SOLVED PROBLEMS

P.11.1 Calculate the explicit cost of debt for each of the following situations: **LO 11.2** LOD M

(a) Debentures are sold at par and flotation costs are 5 per cent.

(b) Debentures are sold at premium of 10 per cent and flotation costs are 5 per cent of issue price.

(c) Debentures are sold at discount of 5 per cent and flotation costs are 5 per cent of issue price.

Assume: (i) coupon rate of interest on debentures is 10 per cent; (ii) face value of debentures is ₹100; (iii) maturity period is 10 years; and (iv) tax rate is 35 per cent.

Solution

(a) $$k_d = \frac{I(1-t)+(RV-SV)/N}{(RV+SV)/2} = \frac{₹10(1-0.35)+(₹100-₹95)/10}{(₹100+95)/2} = 7.18 \text{ per cent}$$

Alternatively, $$CI_o = \sum_{t=1}^{n} \frac{COI_t}{(1+k_d)^t} + \frac{COP_n}{(1+k_d)^n}$$

$$₹95 = \sum_{t=1}^{10} \frac{₹10\,(1-0.35)}{(1+k_d)^t} + \frac{₹100}{(1+k_d)^{10}}$$

Year	*CO*	*PVIFA at*		*Total PV at*	
		7%	*8%*	*7%*	*8%*
1-10	₹6.5	7.024	6.710	₹45.66	₹43.61
10	100	0.508	0.463	50.80	46.30
				96.46	89.91

By interpolation, k_d = 7% + (₹1.46/6.55 = 0.22) = 7.22 per cent

(b) $$k_d = \frac{₹6.5+(₹100-₹104.50)/10}{(₹100+104.50)/2} = 5.92 \text{ per cent}$$

Alternatively, $$₹104.50 = \sum_{t=1}^{n} \frac{₹6.5}{(1+k_d)^t} + \frac{₹100}{(1+k_d)^{10}}$$

Year	*CO*	*PVIFA at*		*Total PV at*	
		5%	*6%*	*5%*	*6%*
1-10	₹6.5	7.722	7.360	₹50.19	₹47.84
10	100	0.614	0.558	61.40	55.80
				111.59	103.64

By interpolation, k_d = 6% – (₹0.86/7.95 = 0.11) = 5.89 per cent

(c) $$k_d = \frac{₹6.5+(₹100-₹90.25)/10}{(₹100+90.25)/2} = 7.86 \text{ per cent}$$

Alternatively, $$₹90.25 = \sum_{t=1}^{10} \frac{₹6.5}{(1+k_d)^t} + \frac{₹100}{(1+k_d)^{10}}$$

Year	CO	PVIFA at		Total PV at	
		7%	8%	7%	8%
1-10	₹6.5	7.024	6.710	₹45.66	₹43.61
10	100	0.508	0.463	50.80	46.30
				96.46	89.91

k_d = 8% – (₹0.34/6.55 = 0.05) = 7.95 per cent

P.11.2 Assume everything to be the same in P.11.1 (a) and (b) except that debentures are to be repaid in 10 equal annual instalments commencing from the year-end 1. Determine the cost of debt. LO 11.2 LOD M

Solution

(i) $₹95 = \sum_{t=1}^{10} \frac{COI_t + COP_t}{(1 + k_d)^t}$

Year	Cash outflows	PVIFA at		Total PV at	
		7%	8%	7%	8%
1	₹16.5[@]	0.935	0.926	₹15.43	₹15.28
2	15.85[@@]	0.873	0.857	13.84	13.58
3	15.20	0.816	0.794	12.40	12.07
4	14.55	0.763	0.735	11.10	10.69
5	13.90	0.713	0.681	9.91	9.47
6	13.25	0.666	0.630	8.82	8.35
7	12.60	0.623	0.583	7.85	7.35
8	11.95	0.582	0.540	6.95	6.45
9	11.30	0.544	0.500	6.15	5.65
10	10.65	0.508	0.463	5.41	4.93
				97.86	93.82

Cost of debt = 7% + (₹2.86/4.04 = 0.71) = 7.71 per cent

[@]₹100 ÷ 10 years = ₹10 + ₹10 interest (1 – 0.35) on ₹100 = ₹16.5

[@@]₹10 + ₹9 interest (1 – 0.35) on ₹90 = ₹15.85

(ii) $₹104.50 = \sum_{t=1}^{10} \frac{COI_t + COP_t}{(1 + k_d)^t}$

Year	Cash outflows	PVIFA at		Total PV at	
		5%	6%	5%	6%
1	₹16.50	0.952	0.943	₹15.71	₹15.56
2	15.85	0.907	0.890	14.38	14.11
3	15.20	0.864	0.840	13.13	12.77
4	14.55	0.823	0.792	11.97	11.52
5	13.90	0.784	0.747	10.89	10.38
6	13.25	0.746	0.705	9.88	9.34
7	12.60	0.711	0.665	8.38	8.38
8	11.95	0.677	0.627	8.09	7.49
9	11.30	0.645	0.592	7.29	6.69
10	10.65	0.614	0.558	6.54	5.94
				106.26	102.18

k_d = 5% + (₹1.76/4.08 = 0.43) = 5.43 per cent

P.11.3 (a) A company's debentures of the face value of ₹100 bear an 8 per cent coupon rate. Debentures of this type currently yield 10 per cent. What is the market price of debentures of the company? LO 11.2 LOD M

(b) What would happen to the market price of the debentures if interest rises to (i) 16 per cent, and (ii) drops to 12 per cent?

(c) What would be the market price of the debentures in situation (a) if it is assumed that debentures were originally having a 15 year maturity period and the maturity period is 4 years away from now?

(d) Would you pay ₹90 to purchase debentures specified in situation (c)? Explain.

Solution

(a) The market price of the debenture, $V_d = \dfrac{\text{Interest on debentures } (I)}{\text{Current interest rate } (k_i)} = \dfrac{₹8}{0.10} = ₹80.$

(b) (i) $V_d = \dfrac{₹8}{0.16} = ₹50$, (ii) $V_d = \dfrac{₹8}{0.12} = ₹66.67$

(c) Determine the PV of (i) interest to be received on these debentures for a period of 4 years and (ii) principal repayment of ₹100 at the end of the fourth year using the current interest rate, that is, 10 per cent as discount rate.

Year	*Cash outflows before taxes*	*PV factor at 10%*	*Total PV*
1-4	₹8	3.170 (Table A-4)	₹25.36
4	100	0.683 (Table A-3)	68.30
			93.66

The market price of the debentures = ₹93.66.

(d) Yes, we would pay ₹90 for the purchase of debentures because its current worth (₹93.66) is more than the purchase price.

P.11.4 The Elu Ltd is contemplating a debenture issue on the following terms: LO 11.2 LOD D

Face value : ₹100 per debenture
Term of maturity : 7 years
Yearly coupon rate of interest
Years 1 - 2 : 9 per cent
3 - 4 : 10
5 - 7 : 11

The current market rate on similar debentures is 11 per cent per annum. The company proposes to price the issue so as to yield a (compounded) return of 12 per cent per annum to the investors. Determine the issue price. Assume redemption at a premium of 5 per cent on face value.

Solution

The issue price of debenture will be the sum of (i) *PV* of interest payments during 1-7 years and (ii) PV of maturity value of debenture in the seventh year:

Year	*Cash outflows*	*PVIF at 12%*	*Total PV*
1	₹9	0.893	₹8.037
2	9	0.797	7.173
3	10	0.712	7.120
4	10	0.636	6.360
5	11	0.567	6.237
6	11	0.507	5.577
7	116*	0.452	52.432
			92.936

*Inclusive of ₹105 maturity value of debentures.

Issue price of debenture should be ₹93.

P.11.5 A company is considering raising ₹100 lakh by one of the two alternative methods, viz. 14 per cent institutional term loan and 13 per cent non-convertible debentures. The term loan option would attract no major incidental cost. The debentures would have to be issued at a discount of 2.5 per cent and would involve ₹1 lakh as cost of issue. LO 11.2 LOD E

Advise the company as to the better option based on the effective cost of capital in each case. Assume a tax rate of 35 per cent.

Solution

(i) Cost of 14 per cent institutional term loan: ₹14 lakh (1 – 0.35)/₹100 lakh = 9.1 per cent

(ii) Cost of 13 per cent non-convertible debentures: ₹13 lakh (1 – 0.35)/₹96.50 lakh* = 8.76 per cent

(*₹100 lakhs – ₹2.5 lakh discount – ₹1 lakh cost of issue).

Recommendation Raising of funds through non-convertible debentures is a better option.

P.11.6 ABC Ltd. has issued 14% Preference shares of face value of ₹100 each at a premium of 10% to be redeemed after 6 years at a premium of 3 per cent. Flotation cost is expected to be ₹1 per share. Determine cost of preference shares by both the methods. Out of the two costs, which do you consider more precise? Ignore dividend payment tax. LO 11.3 LOD M

Solution

(i) $$K_p = \frac{D_p + [RV - (SV - f)]/N}{[RV + (SV - f)]/2}$$

$$= \frac{₹14 + [₹103 - (₹110 - ₹1)]/6}{[₹103 + (110 - 1)]/2} = \frac{₹14 - ₹21}{₹106} = 12.26\%$$

Cost of preference share is 12.26 per cent.

(ii) $$k_p = \sum_{t=1}^{6} \frac{COD_t}{(1+k_p)^t} + \frac{COP_6}{(1+k_p)^6}$$

$$₹109 = \sum_{t=1}^{6} \frac{₹14_t}{(1+k_p)^t} + \frac{₹103}{(1+k_p)^6}$$

Year	COAT	PVIFA at		Total PV at	
		12%	13%	12%	13%
1-6	₹14	4.111	3.998	57.55	55.97
6	103	0.507	0.480	52.22	49.44
				109.77	105.41

k_p = 12% + (0.77/109.77-105.41 = 4.36) = 12% + 0.18% = 12.18%

Cost of preference share at 12.18 per cent is more precise/accurate.

P.11.7 XYZ company is planning for an issue of 13% Preference shares of ₹100 each redeemable at 8 per cent premium after 8 years. They are expected to be sold at premium of 2 per cent. The likely flotation cost is ₹2 per share. Determine cost of preference share capital assuming dividend payment tax of 17 per cent, using both the methods. LO 11.3 LOD M

Solution

(i) $$k_p = \frac{D_p(1 + DPt) + [RV - (SV - f)]/N}{[RV + (SV - f)]/2}$$

$$= \frac{₹13(1.17) + [₹108 - (₹102 - ₹2)]/8}{(₹108 + ₹100)/2}$$

$$\frac{₹15.21 + ₹1}{104} = \frac{₹16.21}{104} = 15.58 \text{ per cent}$$

(ii) $k_p = \sum_{t=1}^{8} \frac{COD_t}{(1 + k_p)^t} + \frac{COP_8}{(1 + k_p)^8}$

$$₹100 = \sum_{t=1}^{8} \frac{₹115.21_t}{(1 + k_p)^t} + \frac{₹108}{(1 + k_p)^8}$$

Year	COAT	PVIFA at		Total PV at	
		15%	16%	15%	16%
1-8	₹15.21	4.487	4.344	₹68.25	₹66.07
8	108	0.327	0.305	35.32	32.94
				103.57	99.01

k_p = 15% + (3.57 / 103.57 – 99.01 = 4.56) = 15% + 0.78% =15.78%

P.11.8 From the following information, determine the cost of equity capital using the CAPM approach. **LO 11.4** LOD E

(a) Required rate of return on risk-free security, 8 per cent.

(b) Required rate of return on market portfolio of investment is 13 per cent.

(c) The firm's beta is 1.6.

Solution $k_e = R_f + b(K_m - R_f)$

$= 0.08 + 1.6(0.13 - 0.08) = 16.0$ per cent

P.11.9 The beta coefficient of Target Ltd is 1.4. The company has been maintaining 8 per cent rate of growth in dividends and earnings. The last dividend paid was ₹4 per share. The return on government securities is 10 per cent while the return on market portfolio is 15 per cent. The current market price of one share of Target Ltd. is ₹36. **LO 11.4** LOD M

(a) What will be the equilibrium price per share of Target Ltd?

(b) Would you advise purchasing the share?

Solution

(a) The required rate of return (k_e) = $R_f + b(k_m - R_f)$ = 10% + 1.4(15% – 10%) = 17 per cent

Equilibrium price per share (P_o) $= \frac{D_1}{k_e - g} = \frac{₹4\ (1.08)}{17\% - 8\%} = ₹48$

(b) The share of Target Ltd is worth buying as it is undervalued.

P.11.10 Consider the following figures pertainig to risk free rate, market rate and return rate of a security of A Ltd during the last 6 years. **LO 11.4** LOD M

Year	Risk-free rate (R_f)	Market rate (R_m)	Security return (R_j)
1	0.06	0.14	0.08
2	0.05	0.03	0.11
3	0.07	0.21	0.29
4	0.08	0.26	0.25
5	0.09	0.03	0.07
6	0.07	0.11	0.04

On the basis of the above information, you are required to determine the cost of equity capital in the context of CAPM. Past data may be taken as proxy for the future.

Solution

Determination of various required values under CAPM approach

Year	*Risk-free rate (R_f)*	*Market return (K_m)*	*Excess in market returns (M) [col.3 – col.2]*	*$(M)^2$*	*Security return (R_j)*	*Excess in security return (J) [col.6 – col.2]*	*Cross product (MJ) [col.4 × col.7]*
1	*2*	*3*	*4*	*5*	*6*	*7*	*8*
1	0.06	0.14	0.08	0.0064	0.08	0.02	0.0016
2	0.05	0.03	(0.02)	0.0004	0.11	0.06	(0.0012)
3	0.07	0.21	0.14	0.0196	0.29	0.22	0.0308
4	0.08	0.26	0.18	0.0324	0.25	0.17	0.0306
5	0.09	0.03	(0.06)	0.0036	0.07	(0.02)	0.0012
6	0.07	0.11	0.04	0.0016	0.04	(0.03)	(0.0012)
Total	0.42	0.78	0.36	0.0640		0.42	0.0618
Average return	0.07	0.13	0.06	—		0.07	—

Figures in brackets represent negative returns.

$$b = \frac{\Sigma MJ - N\bar{M}\bar{J}}{\Sigma M^2 - N\bar{M}^2} = \frac{0.0618 - 6(0.06 \times 0.07)}{0.0640 - 6 \times (0.06)^2} = \frac{0.0366}{0.0424} = 0.863$$

$$k_e = R_f + b(k_m - R_f) = 0.07 + 0.863\ (0.13 - 0.07) = 12.18 \text{ per cent}$$

P.11.11 Investors require a 12 per cent rate of return on equity shares of company Y. What would be the market price of the shares if the previous dividend (D_0) was ₹2 and investors expect dividends to grow at a constant rate of (a) 4% (b) 0% (c) –4% (d) 11% (e) 12% and (f) 14%? **LO 11.4** LOD M

Solution

(a) $P_0 = \dfrac{₹2.08}{12\% - 4\%} = ₹26$,

(b) $= \dfrac{₹2.00}{12\%} = 16.67$,

(c) $= \dfrac{₹1.92}{12\% - (-4\%)} = 12$,

(d) $= \dfrac{₹2.22}{12\% - 11\%} = 222$,

(e) $= \dfrac{₹2.24}{12\% - 12\%} =$ Undefined and

(f) $= \dfrac{₹2.28}{12\% - 14\%} = (114)$, which is ridiculous (price cannot be negative).

The results in situation (e) and (f) show that the formula does not make sense if k_e is less than or equal to the growth rate.

P.11.12 A mining company's iron ore reserves are being depleted, and its cost of recovering a declining quantity of iron ore are rising each year. As a consequence, the company's earnings and dividends are declining, at a rate of 8 per cent per year. If the previous year's dividend was ₹10 and the required rate of return is 15 per cent, what would be the current price of the equity share of the company? **LO 11.4** LOD E

Solution

$$P_0 = \frac{₹9.20}{15\% + 8\%} = ₹40$$

The current price of the equity shares of the mining company would be ₹40.

P.11.13 The Chemicals and Fertilisers Ltd. has been growing at a rate of 18 per cent per year in recent years. This abnormal growth rate is expected to continue for another 4 years; then it is likely to grow at the normal rate (g_n) of 6 per cent. The required rate of return on the shares by the investment **LO 11.4** LOD D community is 12 per cent, and the dividend paid per share last year was ₹3 (D_0 = ₹3). At what price, would you, as an investor, be ready to buy the shares of this company now (t = 0), and at the end of years 1, 2, 3 and 4, respectively? Will there be any extra advantage by buying at t = 0, or in any of the subsequent four years, assuming all other things remain unchanged?

Solution

Year	$D_0(1 + g)^1 = D_t$		PV factor (0.12)	Total PV
1	₹3(1 + 0.18)^1 =	₹3.54	0.893	₹3.161
2	3(1 + 0.18)^2 =	4.176	0.797	3.328
3	3(1 + 0.18)^3 =	4.929	0.712	3.509
4	3(1 + 0.18)^4 =	5.817	0.636	3.700
Total PV of dividends				13.7

$$P_4 = D_5/(K_e - g) = D_4(1 + g_n)/0.06 = ₹5.817(1.06)/0.06 = ₹102.76.$$

PV of ₹102.76 would be ₹102.76 × 0.636 (PV factor at 0.12 for four years) = ₹65.36

$$P_0 = ₹65.36 + ₹13.7 = ₹79$$

I, as an investor, would be prepared to buy the shares of this company at a price less than ₹79 at t = 0.

$$P_1 = \text{PVD}_2 + \text{PVD}_3 + \text{PVD}_4 + \text{PVP}_4$$

Year	Dividends		PV factor (0.12)	Total PV
2	D_2 =	₹4.176	0.893	₹3.729
3	D_3 =	4.929	0.797	3.928
4	D_4 =	5.817	0.712	4.142
Total PV of dividends				11.80

PV of share at the end of year 1 would be: ₹102.76 × 0.712 (PV factor for 3 years) = ₹73.17.

$$P_1 = ₹11.80 + ₹73.17 = ₹84.97$$

$$P_2 = \text{PVD}_3 + \text{PVD}_4 + \text{PVP}_4:$$

Year	Dividends		PV factor (0.12)	Total PV
3	D_3 =	₹4.929	0.893	₹4.402
4	D_4 =	5.817	0.797	4.636
Total PV of dividends				9.04

PV of share at the end of year 2 would be = ₹102.76 × 0.797 (*PV* factor for 2 years) = ₹81.90.

$$P_2 = ₹81.90 + ₹9.04 = 90.94$$

$$P_3 = \text{PVD}_4 + \text{PVP}_4:$$

Year	Cash flows		PV factor (0.12)	Total PV
3	D_4 =	₹5.817	0.893	₹5.195
4	P_4 =	102.76	0.893	91.764
	P_3 =			96.96
	P_4 =			102.76

There will be no extra advantage by buying shares in any of the subsequent 4 years.

P.11.14 The shares of a chemical company are selling at ₹20 per share. The firm had paid dividend @ ₹2 per share last year. The estimated growth of the company is approximately 5 per cent per year. **LO 11.4** LOD E

(a) Determine the cost of equity capital of the company.

(b) Determine the estimated market price of the equity shares if the anticipated growth rate of the firm (i) rises to 8 per cent, and (ii) falls to 3 per cent.

Solution (a) $k_e = (D_1/P_o) + g$ = (₹2.10/₹20) + 0.05 = 15.5 per cent

(b) (i) $P_0 = D/(k_e - g)$ = ₹2.16/0.075 = ₹28.80

(ii) P_0 = ₹1.94/0.185 = ₹10.49

P.11.15 An investor has invested in a company which is growing at an above average rate, translated to an annual increase in dividends of 20 per cent for 15 years. Thereafter, dividend growth returns to an average rate of 7 per cent. The capitalisation rate of the company is 9 per cent and the current dividend per equity share is ₹1 per share. Determine the value of the equity shares.

LO 11.4 LOD M

Solution The value of the equity shares will be the sum of: (i) *PV* of dividend payments during 1-15 years and (ii) *PV* of expected market price at the end of the fifteenth year, based on a constant growth of 7 per cent.

Present value of dividends, years 1-15

Years	*Dividend*	*PVIF (0.09)*	*Total PV*
1	₹1.20	0.917	₹1.100
2	1.44	0.842	1.212
3	1.728	0.772	1.334
4	2.074	0.708	1.468
5	2.488	0.650	1.617
6	2.986	0.596	1.780
7	3.583	0.547	1.960
8	4.300	0.502	2.159
9	5.160	0.460	2.374
10	6.192	0.422	2.613
11	7.430	0.388	2.883
12	8.916	0.356	3.174
13	10.700	0.326	3.488
14	12.839	0.299	3.839
15	15.407	0.275	4.237
			35.238

$$P_{15} = D_{16}/(k_e - g) = \frac{₹15.407\,(1.07)}{9\% - 7\%} = ₹824.25$$

PV of ₹824.25 at $t = 0$ = ₹824.25 × 0.275 = ₹226.67

Value of equity shares = ₹35.24 + ₹226.67 = ₹261.91.

P.11.16 Analyst X is looking for including common stock of ABC Ltd in his client portfolio. The current price of its common stock is ₹16. So he gathered the following information in order to calculate cost of equity of ABC Ltd.

LO 11.4 LOD D

Balance sheet as on 31st March 2014

Liabilities	*Amount(₹)*	*Assets*	*Amount(₹)*
Equity capital (₹15 per share)	15,00,000	Net fixed assets	22,00,000
10% Debt	6,00,000	Current assets	11,00,000
Retained earnings	10,00,000		
Current liabilities	2,00,000		
	33,00,000		33,00,000

In the current year, company sold 24,000 units each at a price of ₹50, which includes 10% variable cost. Total fixed costs incurred by company during the year is ₹6,80,000. Corporate tax rate is 35% and dividend payout ratio is 40%. He then gathered following figures pertaining to risk free rate and market return during the last six years.

Year	1	2	3	4	5	6
Risk free rate (R_f)	6%	5	7	8	7	9
Market rate (R_m)	14%	10	16	17	9	18

Debt yield on long term Government bond having maturity greater than 10 years is 7.5% and risk premium for such a company is 4%. Assuming β for this company is 0.85, calculate cost of equity for ABC Ltd using various approaches. Determine K_e based on the average of all approaches.

Solution

Income Statement for the Current Year Ending March, 2014

Sales (24,000 × ₹50)	₹12,00,000
Less Variable cost(10% of sales)	1,20,000
Less Fixed Cost	6,80,000
EBIT	4,00,000
Less interest (10% of ₹6,00,000)	60,000
EBT	3,40,000
Less Taxes (35%)	1,19,000
EAT	2,21,000
Number of equity shares	1,00,000
EPS	₹2.21
Dividend Per Share (0.40 × EPS)	0.88
ROE (EAT/Total Equity) × 100	8.84%

Business Risk (Br) = Degree of operating leverage = (Sales – VC)/(Sales – VC – FC)
= (₹12,00,000 – 1,20,000)/(₹12,00,000 – ₹1,20,000 – ₹6,80,000) = 2.7

Financial Risk (Fr) = Degree of Financial leverage = EBIT/(EBIT – I) = ₹4,00,000/(₹4,00,000 – ₹60,000) = 1.76

Determination of cost of equity (K_e)

1. Calculating K_e using first approach
   $K_e = R_f + Br + Fr$ (Risk Free Rate + Business risk premium equivalent to DOL + Financial risk premium equivalent to DFL)
   = 7% + 2.7% + 1.18 = 10.88%
2. Calculating K_e using second approach
   K_e = Debt yield on long-term bonds + Risk premium
   = 7.5% + 4% = 11.5%
3. Calculating K_e using third approach (CAPM)

Year	1	2	3	4	5	6	Average
Risk free rate (R_f)	6%	5	7	8	7	9	7
Market rate (R_m)	14%	10	16	17	9	18	14

$$K_e = R_f + \beta(R_m - R_f)$$
$$= 7\% + 0.85\% \ (14\% - 7\%) = 12.95\%$$

4. Calculating K_e using fourth approach (Dividend discount model)

$$K_e = \frac{D_1}{P_0} + g$$

g = RR × ROE

RR = 1 – Dividend payout ratio
= 1 – 0.4 = 0.6

ROE = 8.84%

$$g = 0.6 \times 0.0884 = 5.30\%$$

$$D_1 = 0.88 \times (1 + 0.053) = 0.92$$

$$K_e = \frac{0.92}{16} + 0.053 = 11.05\%$$

K_e based on average of K_e of all 4 approaches

$$K_e = (10.88\% + 11.5\% + 12.95\% + 11.05\%)/4 = 11.60\%$$

P.11.17 A company has on its books the following amounts and specific costs of each type of capital.

Type of capital	*Book value*	*Market value*	*Specific costs (%)*
Debt	₹4,00,000	₹3,80,000	5
Preference	1,00,000	1,10,000	8
Equity	6,00,000		15
Retained earnings	2,00,000	12,00,000	13
	13,00,000	16,90,000	

Determine the weighted average cost of capital using (a) Book value weights and, (b) Market value weights. How are they different? Can you think of a situation where the weighted average cost of capital would be the same using either of the weights?

Solution

(a) Determination of weighted average cost of capital using book value weights:

Source of capital	*Amount of book value (BV)*	*Specific cost (%) (k)*	*Total costs BV (×) k*
Debt	₹4,00,000	5	₹20,000
Preference	1,00,000	8	8,000
Equity	6,00,000	15	90,000
Retained earnings	2,00,000	13	26,000
	13,00,000		1,44,000

$$k_0 = \frac{\text{Total cost (₹1,44,000)}}{\text{Total amount of capital (₹13,00,000)}} \times 100 = 11.1 \text{ per cent}$$

(b) Determination of weighted average cost of capital using market value weights

Source of capital	*Market value (MV)*	*Specific cost (%) (k)*	*Total costs MV (×) k*
Debt	₹3,80,000	5	₹19,000
Preference	1,10,000	8	8,800
Equity	9,00,000[a]	15	1,35,000
Retained earnings	3,00,000[a]	13	39,000
	16,90,000		2,01,800

$$k_0 = \frac{₹\,2,01,800}{₹\,16,90,000} \times 100 = 11.9 \text{ per cent}$$

[a] The total market value of equity shares and retained earnings is apportioned three-fourths and one-four respectively on the basis of their book values.

The k_0 based upon market value is greater than k_0 based upon book value because the market value of equity funds is considerably larger than their book value and since these sources of long-term funds have higher specific costs, the overall cost of capital increases.

The weighted average cost of capital would be the same with both the book value weights and market value weights when there is no difference between the book value and the market value of securities used in raising the capital.

P.11.18 Aries Limited wishes to raise additional finance of ₹10 lakh for meeting its investment plans. It has ₹2,10,000 in the form of retained earnings available for investment purposes. The following are the further details:

LO 11.5 LOD D

1. Debt-equity mix, 30:70
2. Cost of debt: Upto ₹1,80,000, 10 per cent (before tax); Beyond ₹1,80,000, 12 per cent (before tax)
3. Earnings per share, ₹4
4. Dividend payout, 50 per cent of earnings
5. Expected growth rate in dividend, 10 per cent
6. Current market price per share, ₹44
7. Tax rate, 35 per cent

You are required:

(a) To determine the pattern for raising the additional finance, assuming the firm intends to maintain existing debt/equity mix.
(b) To determine the post-tax average cost of additional debt.
(c) To determine the cost of retained earnings and cost of equity.
(d) Compute the overall weighted average after tax cost of additional finance.

Solution

(a) Pattern for raising additional finance:
Debt = 0.30 × ₹10 lakh = ₹3 lakh,
Equity Funds = 0.70 × ₹10 lakh = ₹7 lakh

Retained earnings	₹2,10,000	
Equity share capital (additional)	4,90,000	₹7,00,000
Debt funds (₹3,00,000)		
10% Debt	1,80,000	
12% Debt	1,20,000	3,00,000
		10,00,000

(b) k_d = Total interest $(1 - t)$/₹3,00,000 = ₹18,000 + ₹14,400 = ₹32,400 (1 – 0.35)/₹3,00,000 = 7.02 per cent

(c) (i) $k_e = \frac{D_t}{P_0} + g, \frac{₹4(50\%) + 10\%}{₹44}$ + 10% = 15 per cent

(ii) $k_r = k_e$ = 15 per cent

(d) Overall cost of capital (k_0) of additional finance

Source	*Amount*	*After-tax cost*	*Total cost*
Equity share capital	₹4,90,000	0.15	₹73,500
Retained earnings	2,10,000	0.15	31,500
Debt	3,00,000	0.0702	21,060
			1,26,060

k_0 = ₹1,26,060/₹10,00,000 = 12.61 per cent

P.11.19 Three companies A, B and C are in the same business and hence have similar operating risks. However, the capital structure of each of them is different. The following are the details: LO 11.4 LOD M

	A	B	C
Equity share capital (₹) (Face value ₹10 per share)	4,00,000	2,50,000	5,00,000
Market value per share (₹)	15	20	12
Dividend per share (₹)	2.70	4	2.88
Debentures (₹)	Nil	1,00,000	2,50,000
Market value (MV) per debenture (₹)		125	80
Interest rate		10	8

Assume the current levels of dividends are generally expected to continue indefinitely and the income-tax rate is 35 per cent. You are required to compute the weighted average cost of capital (k_0) of each company.

Solution

Cost of debentures:	*A*	*B*	*C*
$I(1-t)/MV$ of debentures (%)	—	₹6.5/₹125 = 5.2	₹5.2/₹80 = 6.5
Cost of equity:			
D_t/P_0 (%)	₹2.7/₹15 = 18	₹4/₹20 = 20	₹2.88/₹12 = 24

Weighted average cost of capital (k_0)

Source	*Amount*	*After-tax cost (%)*	*Total cost*
Company A:			
Equity	₹6,00,000	18	₹1,08,000
Debentures	Nil	—	—
	6,00,000	18	1,08,000
Company B:			
Equity	5,00,000	20	1,00,000
Debentures (1,000 × ₹125)	1,25,000	5.2	6,500
	6,25,000	17.04	1,06,500
Company C:			
Equity	6,00,000	24	1,44,000
Debentures (2,500 × ₹80)	2,00,000	6.5	13,000
	8,00,000	19.625	1,57,000

Overall cost of capital: 0.18 (A), 0.17 (B) and 0.196 (C).

P.11.20 As a financial analyst of a large electronics company, you are required to determine the weighted average cost of capital of the company using (a) book value weights and (b) market value weights. The following information is available for your perusal. LO 11.6 LOD M

The company's present book value capital structure is:

Debentures (₹100 per debenture)	₹8,00,000
Preference shares (₹100 per share)	2,00,000
Equity shares (₹10 per share)	10,00,000
Retained earnings	8,00,000
	28,00,000

All these securities are traded in the capital markets. Recent prices are:

Debentures, ₹110 per debenture, Preference shares, ₹120 per share, and Equity shares, ₹22.5 per share

Anticipated external financing opportunities are:

(i) ₹100 per debenture redeemable at par; 10 year maturity, 11 per cent coupon rate, 4 per cent flotation costs, sale price, ₹100.

(ii) ₹100 preference share redeemable at par; 10 year maturity, 12 per cent dividend rate, 5 per cent flotation costs, sale price, ₹100.

(iii) Equity shares: ₹0.5 per share flotation costs, sale price = ₹22.5.

In addition, the dividend expected on the equity share at the end of the year is ₹2.20 per share; the anticipated growth rate in dividends is 7 per cent and the firm has the practice of paying all its earnings in the form of dividends. The corporate tax rate is 35 per cent. Cost of retained earnings is 15 per cent.

Solution

Determination of specific costs:

(i) Cost of debt, $(k_d) = \dfrac{I(1-t)+(f \div N_m)}{(RV+SV)\div 2} = \dfrac{₹11\,(0.35)+(₹4 \div 10)}{(₹100+₹96)\div 2} \times 100 = 7.7$ per cent

(ii) Cost of preference shares $(k_p) = \dfrac{D+(f \div N_m)}{(RV+SV)\div 2} = \dfrac{₹12+(₹5 \div 10)}{(₹100+₹95)\div 2} \times 100 = 12.8$ per cent

(iii) Cost of equity shares $(k_e) = \dfrac{D_1}{P_0\,(1-f)} + g = \dfrac{₹2.20}{₹22} + 0.07 = 17$ per cent

Using these specific costs we can calculate the book value and market value weights as follows:

(a) k_0 based on book value weights

Source of capital	*Book value (BV)*	*Specific cost (k) (%)*	*Total costs [BV (×) k]*
Debentures	₹8,00,000	7.7	₹61,600
Preference shares	2,00,000	12.8	25,600
Equity shares	10,00,000	17.0	1,70,000
Retained earnings	8,00,000	15.0	1,20,000
	28,00,000		3,77,200

k_0 = ₹3,77,200/₹28,00,000 = 13.47 per cent

(b) k_0 based on market value weights

Source of capital	*Market value (MV)*	*Specific cost (k) (%)*	*Total costs [MV (×) k]*
Debentures	₹8,80,000	7.7	₹67,760
Preference shares	2,40,000	12.8	30,720
Equity shares	12,50,000*	17.0	2,12,500
Retained earnings	10,00,000**	15.0	1,50,000
Total capital	33,70,000		4,60,980

k_0 = ₹4,60,980/₹33,70,000 = 13.68 per cent

*Market value of equity shares (₹22,50,000 × 10/18) = ₹12,50,000.

**Market value of retained earnings (₹22,50,000 × 8/18) = ₹10,00,000.

P.11.21 From the following capital structure of XYZ Ltd. determine appropriate weighted average cost of capital. **LO 11.6** LOD M

Equity shares (1,00,000)	₹38,00,000
Preference shares	8,00,000
Debentures	50,00,000
Bank loan (long-term)	18,00,000
Bank loan (short-term)	14,00,000
Trade creditors	6,00,000

Additional information:

(i) Equity shares include the existing 60,000 shares having current market value of ₹40 per share and the balance is net proceeds from the new issue in the current year (issue price of the share, ₹40; flotation cost per share, ₹5). The projected EPS and DPS for the current year are ₹8 and ₹5 respectively.
(ii) Dividend indicated on preference shares is 12 per cent
(iii) Pre-tax cost of debentures—11 per cent
(iv) Interest on bank loan—12 per cent (long-term) and 11.5 per cent (short-term).
(v) Corporate tax: 35 per cent. Dividend tax: 10 per cent
(vi) Market value of preference shares is ₹8,50,000.

Solution

Determination of cost of specific sources:

(i) Equity existing; g = [EPS – DPS (1 + t)]/P_0 = [₹8 – ₹5(1 + 0.1)]/₹40 = 6.25 per cent
$k_e = (D_1/P_0) + g$ = (₹5/40) + 0.0625 = 18.75 per cent
Equity (new issue) = (₹5/35) + 0.0625 = 20.54 per cent

(ii) Cost of debentures = 0.11 (1 – 0.35) = 7.15 per cent

(iii) Cost of bank loan = 0.12 (1 – 0.35) = 7.8 per cent

(iv) Cost of preference shares = (Total dividends on preference shares + Dividend tax) ÷ Market value of preference shares = (₹96,000 + ₹10,000)/₹8,50,000 = 12.47 per cent

Determination of overall cost of capital (based on market value, MV weights)

Sources of capital	*MV (1)*	*Cost (per cent) (2)*	*Total cost [1 × 2] (3)*
Equity capital (existing)	₹24,00,000	0.1875	₹4,50,000
Equity capital (new)	14,00,000	0.2054	2,87,560
Preference shares	8,50,000	0.1247	1,05,995
Debentures	50,00,000	0.715	3,57,500
Long-term bank loan	18,00,000	0.078	1,40,400
	1,14,50,000		13,41,455

K_0 = ₹13,41,455/1,14,50,000 = 11.72 per cent.

P.11.22(a) XYZ Ltd., has the following book value capital structure: *(₹ crore)*

Equity capital (in shares of ₹10 each, fully paid up—at par)	₹15
12% Preference capital (in shares of ₹100 each, fully paid up—at par)	1
Retained earnings	20
11.5% Debentures (of ₹100 each)	10
11% Term loans	12.5

LO 11.6 LOD M

The next expected dividend on equity shares per share is ₹3.60; the dividend per share is expected to grow at the rate of 7 per cent. The market price per share is ₹40.
Preference stock, redeemable after ten years, is currently selling at ₹75 per share.
Debentures, redeemable after six years, are selling at ₹80 per debenture.
The Income- tax rate for the company is 40 per cent.

(i) Required:
Calculate the weighted average cost of capital using:
(a) Book value proportions; and
(b) Market value proportions.

Solution

(a) Statement showing determination of K_o (using book value proportions)

Source of finance	Amount	Proportion	After-tax cost (%)	Total cost (%)
Equity capital	₹15,00,00,000	0.256	16[1]	4.096
12% Preference capital	1,00,00,000	0.017	16.57[2]	0.282
Retained earnings	20,00,00,000	0.342	16[3]	5.472
11.5% Debentures	10,00,00,000	0.171	11.37[4]	1.944
11% Term loans	12,50,00,000	0.214	6.6[5]	1.412
	58,50,00,000			13.206

Overall cost of capital is 13.21 per cent approximately

[1] k_e = (₹3.60/₹40) + 7% = 16 per cent

[2] $k_p = \left(D_p + \dfrac{RV - MV}{N}\right) \Big/ (RV + MV) \div 2 = \left(₹12 + \dfrac{₹100 - 75}{10 \text{ years}}\right) \Big/$ ₹87.5 = 16.57 per cent

[3] Cost of retained earnings is equial to K_e

[4] $K_d = \left(I(1-t) + \dfrac{RV - MV}{N}\right) \Big/ (RV + MV) \div 2$

$= \left(₹11.5(1 - 0.4) + \dfrac{₹20}{6}\right) \Big/$ ₹90 = (₹6.9 + ₹3.33)/₹90 = 11.37 per cent

[5] Cost of term loan = 11% (1 – 0.4) = 6.6 per cent

(b) Statement showing determination of K_0 (using market value proportions)

(amount in ₹ crore)

Source of finance	Amount	Proportion	After-tax cost (%)	Total cost (%)
Equity capital	₹25.71	0.316	16	5.056
12% Preference capital	0.75	0.009	16.57	0.149
Retained earnings	34.29	0.422	16.0	6.752
11.5% Debentures	8.00	0.098	11.37	1.114
11% Term loans	12.50	0.154	6.6	1.016
	81.25			14.087

Overall cost of capital is 14.09 per cent approximately

Note: The total market value of equity shares ₹60 crore (1.5 crore shares × ₹40) is apportioned between equity capital and retained earnings in the ratio of 15 : 20 based on their book values.

P11.22(b) Determine the weighted marginal cost of capital schedule for the above company, if it raises ₹10 crore next year, given the following information: **LO 11.6** LOD D

(a) The amount will be raised by equity and debt in equal proportions;

(b) The company expects to retain ₹1.5 crore earnings next year;

(c) The additional issue of equity shares will result in the net price per share being fixed at ₹32;

(d) The debt capital raised by way of term loans will cost 12 per cent for the first ₹2.5 crore and 13 per cent for the next ₹2.5 crore.

Solution

Statement showing weighted marginal cost of capital of ₹10 crore funds

Source of finance	*Weight*	*After-tax cost (%)*	*Total cost (%)*
Equity:			
Retained earnings	0.15[1]	16.0[2]	2.4
Equity share capital	0.35[3]	18.25[4]	6.39
Debt:			
12% Loan	0.25	7.2[5]	1.80
13% Loan	0.25	7.8[6]	1.95
			12.54

Weighted marginal cost of capital = 12.54 per cent

1. ₹1.5 crore/₹10 crore = 0.15
2. Cost of retained earnings is equivalent to existing cost of equity.
3. ₹3.5 crore external equity share capital to be raised/₹10 crore total funds = 0.35
4. K_e = (₹3.60/₹32) + 7% = 18.25 per cent
5. Cost of 12% Loan = 12%(1 – 0.4) = 7.2 per ccent
6. Cost of 13% Loan = 13% (1 – 0.4) = 7.8 per cent

P.11.23 Malaysian Paints (India) Limited has paid a dividend of 30 per cent on its shares of ₹10 each in the current financial year. In the opinion of Choksi, finance director, the dividend is expected to grow @ 5 per cent annum. The required rate of return of the company is 15 per cent. **LO 11.4** LOD D

Malaysian Paints is facing tough competition in the market because a large number of multinational companies have started their operations in India in the same line of business. Therefore, the management of the company is seriously thinking of diversifying the activities of the company. In a quarterly meeting of the Board, a special executive committee consisting of finance director, marketing director and production director was formed. The special committee was chaired by the CMD of the company.

The special executive committee had a brain-storming session and a series of meetings. It suggested the following alternative courses of action for the consideration of the Board:

(i) To increase the dividend growth rate to 6 per cent, and lower the required rate of return to 14 per cent.
(ii) To increase the dividend growth rate to 7 per cent and raise the required rate of return to 17 per cent.
(iii) To raise the required rate of return to 16 per cent and reduce the growth rate of dividend to 4 per cent.
(iv) To increase the dividend growth rate to 8 per cent and increase the required rate of return to 17 per cent.

You are the finance manager of the company. The Board of Directors has confidence in your abilities because, in the past, you have helped the Board in making such decisions. The Board has requested you to suggest, with calculations, the most suitable course of action for the company (assuming the firm has an objective of maximising its shareholders wealth). State your assumptions if any.

Solution As a finance manage, I will prefer a course of action which maximises the price of shares as the pursuance of such a policy is consistent with the objective of optimal financial decision making. Keeping this perspective in mind, the five courses of action (emerged in brain-storming session) are analysed.

$$\text{(i)}\quad P_0 = \frac{D_t}{K_{e-g}} = \frac{₹3.15}{15\% - 5\%} = \frac{₹3.15}{10\%} = ₹31.50$$

$$\text{(ii)}\quad P_0 = \frac{₹3.18}{14\% - 6\%} = \frac{₹3.18}{8\%} = ₹39.75$$

$$\text{(iii)}\quad P_0 = \frac{₹3.21}{17\% - 7\%} = \frac{₹3.21}{10\%} = ₹32.10$$

(iv) $P_0 = \frac{₹3.12}{16\% - 4\%} = \frac{₹3.12}{12\%} = ₹26$

(v) $P_0 = \frac{₹3.24}{17\% - 8\%} = \frac{₹3.24}{9\%} = ₹36$

Recommendation Alternative second to increase the dividend growth rate to six per cent and lower the required rate of return to 14 per cent is the most suitable course of action as such an action is likely to fetch the maximum price of equity shares.

MINI CASES

11.C.1 Mr Aggarwal recently attended an investor's meet in Mumbai wherein he came across some brokers who advised him to measure the systematic risk of shares using beta before finally investing money in the same. Mr. Aggarwal picked the old financial newspapers and prepared the following table containing the data of equity share prices of Infotech Limited, Cantaxy Limited and S&P CNX Nifty, collected on the last trading day of the month for the last thirteen months.

Date	*Share price of Infotech Ltd*	*Share price of Cantaxy Ltd*	*S&P CNX Nifty*
February 28	₹115	₹28	976
March 29	125	26	985
April 30	140	21	991
May 31	167	20	1035
June 28	189	20	1049
July 31	177	15	989
August 30	142	19	977
September 30	121	21	965
October 31	102	32	956
November 29	94	29	951
December 31	102	31	957
January 31	126	28	962
February 28	149	39	975

Calculate beta for Infotech Limited and Cantaxy Limited. Use S&P CNX Nifty data as a proxy for market portfolio and comment.

Solution

$$\text{BETA} = \frac{N\,\Sigma XY - (\Sigma X)(\Sigma Y)}{N\,\Sigma X^2 - (\Sigma X)^2}$$

Y = Return on security

X = Return on market portfolio (index)

N = Total number of observations

X = (Market index level on last trading day of 't' month – Market index level on last trading day of 't – 1' month) × 100]/Market index level on last trading day of 't – 1' month.

Y = Price of share on last trading day of 't' month – Price of share on last trading day of 't – 1' month) × 100)/Price of share on last trading day of 't – 1' month.

Determination of beta in respect of equity shares of Infotech Limited

Date	*Infotech limited*	*S&P CNX Nifty*	*Return on Infotech limited Y*	*X*	*Return on Nifty index X × Y*	*X²*
February 28	115	976				
March 29	125	985	8.70	0.92	8.02	0.85
April 30	140	991	12.00	0.61	7.31	0.37
May 31	167	1035	19.29	4.44	85.63	19.71
June 28	189	1049	13.17	1.35	17.82	1.83
July 31	177	989	–6.35	–5.72	36.32	32.72
August 30	142	977	–19.77	–1.21	23.99	1.47
September 30	121	965	–14.79	–1.23	18.16	1.51
October 31	102	956	–15.70	–0.93	14.64	0.87
November 29	94	951	–7.84	–0.52	4.10	0.27
December 31	102	957	8.51	0.63	5.37	0.40
January 31	126	962	23.53	0.52	12.29	0.27
February 28	149	975	18.25	1.35	24.67	1.83
Sum			38.99	0.21	258.33	62.10
Average			3.25	0.02		
Observations (N)			12			

BETA = 12 × 258.33 – (0.21 × 38.99)/12 × 62.10 – (0.21 × 0.21) = 4.15

Determination of beta in respect of equity shares of Cantaxy Limited

Date	*Cantaxy limited*	*S&P CNX Nifty*	*Return on Infotech limited Y*	*X*	*Return on Nifty index X × Y*	*X²*
February 28	28	976				
March 29	26	985	–7.14	0.92	–6.59	0.85
April 30	21	991	–19.23	0.61	–11.71	0.37
May 31	20	1035	–4.76	4.44	–21.14	19.71
June 28	20	1049	–0.00	1.35	0.00	1.83
July 31	15	989	–25.00	–5.72	142.99	32.72
August 30	19	977	26.67	–1.21	–32.36	1.47
September 30	21	965	10.53	–1.23	–12.93	1.51
October 31	32	956	52.38	–0.93	–48.85	0.87
November 29	29	951	–9.38	–0.52	4.90	0.27
December 31	31	957	6.90	0.63	4.35	0.40
January 31	28	962	–9.68	0.52	–5.06	0.27
February 28	39	975	39.29	1.35	53.09	1.83
Sum			60.57	0.21	66.70	62.10
Average			5.05	0.02		
Observations (N)			12			

BETA = 12 × 66.70 – (0.21 × 60.57)/12 × 62.10 – (0.21 × 0.21) = 1.06

Comment: Since the beta of Infotech Limited is substantially higher (4.15) than that of Cantaxy Limited (1.06), the equity shares of Infotech Limited are evidently more risky compared to those of Cantaxy Limited.

11.C.2 NTPC, India's largest power company, was set up in 1975 with a vision "A world class integrated power major, powering India's growth, with increasing global presence" to accelerate power development in India. It has emerged as an Integrated Power Major, with a significant presence in the entire value chain of power generation business.

NTPC ranked 317th in the 2011, Forbes Global 2000 ranking of the World's biggest companies. With a current generating capacity of above 34,000 MW, NTPC has embarked on plans to become a 75,000 MW company by 2017. (For details refer to websitewww.ntpcindia.com).

The company intends to determine its weighted average cost of capital for year 2012.

Solution

Calculation of cost of capital:

Weighted average cost of capital has been calculated as on 31st March 2012 using the data inputs from its annual reports for the financial years ended March 31, 2011 and 2012.

Calculation of cost of equity:

Using CAPM approach: $K_e = R_f + \beta e \times (R_m - R_f)$

Where: R_f= Risk-free Return (Obtained from 10 year G- sec benchmark)

R_m = Average market return

βe = Systematic risk factor (Equity Beta)

Calculation of equity beta of NTPC:

The beta has been calculated using daily returns of NTPC Stock prices and NIFTY returns for five years 2006-2011; by using regression approach.

RNTPC = $a + \beta e \times$ RNIFTY

Where: RNTPC = Returns given by NTPC stock.

RNIFTY = Returns given by Nifty.

The output for the regression analysis is

Regression Statistics

Multiple R	0.668
R Square	0.446
Adjusted R Square	0.444
Standard Error	0.032
Observations	257

ANOVA

	df	*SS*	*MS*	*F*	*Significance F*
Regression	1	0.213	0.213	205.082	0.000
Residual	255	0.265	0.001		
Total	256	0.478			

	Coefficients	*Standard error*	*t Stat*	*P-value*	*Lower 95%*	*Upper 95%*	*Lower 95%*	*Upper 95%*
Intercept	0.002	0.002	0.771	0.441	0.002	0.006	0.002	0.006
X Variable	0.700	0.049	14.321	0.000	0.604	0.796	0.604	0.796

$\beta e = 0.7$

The value of beta is 0.700. This implies that NTPC stock is low risk stock. The coefficient of correlation of 0.668 between NIFTY returns and NTPC returns shows moderate positive relationship. This implies the movement in NTPC follows the movement of NIFTY.

Calculation of risk-free rate of return:

The 10 year Govt.- sec. benchmark rate has been taken as the risk-free rate of return. The Govt.-Sec. rate is 8.79%. Therefore, risk-free rate of return is taken as 8.79%. (Source: http://www.fimmda.org)

$$R_f = 8.79\%$$

Calculation of market risk premium:

It is the excess of market return over the risk-free return. The market return has been computed using NIFTY returns for 5 years 2006-11. The market return is 20.48%. (Source: http://www.nseindia.com).

$$R_m = 20.48\% \text{ (Market Nifty Return)}$$

Calculation of cost of equity:

$$K_e = R_f + \beta e \times (R_m - R_f)$$
$$K_e = 8.79 + 0.7 \times (20.48 - 8.79) = 16.97\%$$

Calculation of cost of debt:

$$K_d = \text{(Interest on loan funds during the year / Long Term Loans)} \times 100$$
$$K_i = (₹28507 \text{ million}/₹404926 \text{ million}) \times 100 = 7.04\%$$ (before tax; based on average long-term loans)
$$K_d = 7.04\% (1 - 0.33) = 4.72\%$$

Calculation of cost of retained earnings:

Assuming flotation cost of 5%, cost of retained earnings (k_r) would be:

$K_r = 16.97\% (1 - 0.05) = 16.12\%$. The main difference between the cost of equity and cost of retained earnings is the flotation costs.

Calculation of weighted average cost of capital:

Source of funds	*Cost of funds*	*Capital (in ₹ million)*	*Total cost (in ₹ million)*
Debt	4.72%	₹404926	₹19,112.51
Share capital	16.97	82455	13,992.61
Retained earnings	16.12	573415	92,434.50
Total		1060796	1,25,539.61

$K_o = (₹125539.61 \text{ million}/₹1060796 \text{ million}) \times 100 = 11.84$ per cent

11.C.3 ITC is one of India's foremost private sector companies with a market capitalization of US $ 35 billion and a turnover of US $ 7 billion. It has a diversified presence in FMCG, Hotels, Paperboards and Specialty Papers, Packaging, Agri-Business, and Information Technology. While ITC is an outstanding market leader in its traditional businesses of Cigarettes, Hotels, Paperboards, Packaging and Agri-Exports, it is rapidly gaining market share even in its nascent businesses of Packaged Foods and Confectionery, Branded Apparel, Personal Care and Stationery.

Estimate the cost of equity capital for ITC Ltd using the following methods:

1. Dividend approach
2. Capital asset pricing model approach
3. Debt-yield plus risk premium approach

4. Risk free rate plus risk premium approach
5. Average approach (as per Ross et. al)

1. Dividend approach

$$k_e = \frac{D_1}{P_0} + g$$

The dividend history (2004 – 2013) of ITC Ltd is as follows:

Year	*2004*	*2005*	*2006*	*2007*	*2008*	*2009*	*2010*	*2011*	*2012*	*2013*
Ordinary dividend per share	₹5.25	4.50	2.80	2.25	1.84	1.74	1.54	1.31	1.02	0.66

Source: http://www.itcportal.com/about-itc/shareholder-value/annual-reports/itc-annual-report-2013/pdf/ITC-Ten-years-at-glance.pdf

Based on the ten-year dividend history, the dividend growth rate can be estimated as:

$$g = \left(\frac{5.25}{0.66}\right)^{\frac{1}{10}} - 1 = 23.04 \text{ per cent per annum}$$

and the expected dividend per share for next year (2014) would be ₹5.25 × (1 + 23.04%) = ₹6.46 per share. Further, the market price per share as on 31 March 2013 was: ₹309.1

k_e = (₹6.46/₹309.1) + 23.04% = 25.13%

Therefore, the cost of equity as per dividend approach is 25.13 per cent.

2. Capital asset pricing model approach

$$k_e = R_f + \beta \cdot (k_m - R_f)$$

The risk-free rate of return was computed based on the yield to maturity on government securities for a period of 30 years (Reserve Bank of India Bulletin). This value was found to be 8.5 per cent (http://www.rbi.org.in/scripts/BS_ViewBulletin.aspx?Id=13790).

The market portfolio was chosen as the BSE Sensex. BSE SENSEX is a widely reported/accepted index in both domestic and international markets.
Base value of index in 1979: 100
Value of index in March 2013: 18835.77
Number of years: 34

$$\text{Market rate of return} = \left(\frac{18835.77}{100}\right)^{\frac{1}{34}} - 1 = 16.66\%$$

The beta value was obtained as

$$\beta = \frac{Co\,\text{var}(r_a, r_m)}{\text{Var}(r_m)}$$

Through regression of the monthly data, the beta value was calculated as follows:

$$\beta = \frac{Co\,\text{var}(r_{ITC}, r_m)}{Var(r_m)} = \frac{0.002313411}{0.005739118} = 0.403$$

(For details refer to www.mhhe.com/khanjainfm8e)

$k_e = R_f + \beta \cdot (k_m - R_f)$

k_e = 8.5% + 0.403 · (16.66% – 8.5%)

k_e = 11.79%

Therefore, the cost of equity through the CAPM approach is estimated to be 11.79 per cent.

3. Debt-yield plus risk premium approach

The debt-yield approach determines cost of equity by adding a judgmental risk premium of 3 to 5 percentage points to the interest paid by the firm on its long-term debt.

ITC Ltd has a very low debt-equity ratio. Long-term borrowings form only 0.2% of the total liabilities of the company. As per the annual report for FY 2012-13, term loans from banks are repayable in equated periodic instalments up to a 5 year period from the date of respective loan. These are repayable by 2014-15 and carry an interest of 11.25 per cent p.a.

(***Source:*** http://www.itcportal.com/about-itc/shareholder-value/annual-reports/itc-annual-report-2013/pdf/ITC-Notes-Financial-Statements.pdf Page 92).

ITC Ltd is a well-established company and is well-positioned in the market.

Hence, we can estimate the cost of equity using the debt-yield plus risk premium of 3 per cent.

$$k_e = 11.25\% + 3\% = 14.25\%.$$

4. Risk free rate plus risk premium approach

In this approach

$$k_e = R_f + b_r + f_r$$

The degree of operating leverage is calculated as follows:

$$DOL = \frac{SR - VC}{SR - VC - FC}$$

In the absence of data about variable costs and fixed costs of the company, it is difficult to estimate the degree of operating leverage.

$$DFL = \frac{\text{EBIT}}{\text{EBIT} - I}$$

As per the data in Annual Report for FY 2012-13:

(*Source:*http://www.itcportal.com/about-itc/shareholder-value/annual-reports/itc-annual-report-2013/pdf/ITC-Profit-Loss.pdf)

$$DFL = \frac{10790.09}{10790.09 - 105.91} = 1.0099$$

The degree of financial leverage is very close to one and hence the financial risk is virtually negligible, warranting no/insignificant premium.

However, since the company is working in the areas of FMCG, Hotels, Paperboards & Specialty Papers, Packaging, Agri-Business, and Information Technology, it is reasonable to assume that the operating fixed costs would constitute a significant component of the cost structure and hence the company is likely to have a significant business risk. 4 per cent business risk premium has been assumed/considered adequate to compensate for such a substantial business risk.

Therefore, $k_e = 8.5\% + 4\% = 12.5\%$

Cost of equity is computed using the average of k_e determined by 4 approaches (as suggested by Ross et.al).

Approach	*Cost of equity*
Dividend approach	25.13%
Capital asset pricing model approach	11.79
Debt-yield plus risk premium approach	14.25
Risk free rate plus risk premium approach	12.50
Average from four approaches (63.67%/4)	15.92

Cost of equity of ITC has been estimated as 15.92 per cent.

Scan the QR Code given at the end of chapter to access comprehensive cases.

REVIEW QUESTIONS

LOD: Easy

RQ. 11.1 Indicate whether the following statements are true or false. **[LO 11.2, 3, 4, 5, 6]**

(i) Cost of capital is cost of borrowing funds.

(ii) Equity capital does not carry any cost as a company is under no legal obligation to pay dividends.

(iii) Like equity capital, retained earnings also do not cause any cost to the company.

(iv) Weighted average cost of capital takes into consideration cost of long-term sources of finance.

(v) Retained earnings do not have explicit cost. They carry implicit cost.

(vi) Overall cost of capital decreases on payment of entire long-term debt.

(vii) Cost of retained earning is less then cost of equity.

(viii) Beta is a measure of unsystematic risk.

(ix) Cost of additional equity share capital is the same as that of existing equity share capital.

(x) The higher is the corporate tax rate, the higher is the cost of debt.

(xi) Beta is a measure of systematic risk.

(xii) Cost of debt is higher than cost of equity.

(xiii) Cost of preference share capital is higher than cost of debt.

(xiv) Cost of preference share capital is higher that cost of equity share capital.

(xv) Among all long-term sources of finance, equity capital carries maximum cost.

[Answers: (i) False (ii) False (iii) False (iv) True (v) True (vi) False (vii) True (viii) False (ix) False (x) False (xi) True (xii) False (xiii) True (xiv) False (xv) True]

RQ. 11.2 Discuss how the cost of capital enters into the process of evaluating capital budgeting proposals? Particularly, how is it related to the various discounted cash flow techniques for determining a project's acceptability? **[LO 11.1]**

LOD: Medium

RQ. 11.3 What is financial risk? Is it necessary to assume that firm's financial structure remains unchanged when evaluating the firm's cost of capital? Why is this assumption impractical? **[LO 11.1]**

RQ. 11.4 Explain why: **[LO 11.2,3,4,5]**

(a) Debt is usually considered the cheapest source of financing available to the firm.

(b) The cost of preference shares is less than the cost of equity.

(c) The cost of retained earnings is less than the cost of new equity.

(d) The cost of equity and retained earnings is not zero.

(e) The cost of capital is dependent only on the cost of long-term funds.

(f) The cost of capital is a hurdle for new investment projects.

(g) The cost of capital is most appropriately measured on an after-tax basis.

RQ. 11.5 Explain the problems faced in determining the cost of capital. How is the cost of capital relevant in capital budgeting decisions? **[LO 11.1,4]**

RQ. 11.6 Examine critically the different approaches to the calculation of cost of equity capital. **[LO 11.4]**

RQ. 11.7 Explain the CAPM approach for computing the cost of equity. Discuss the merits and demerits of the approach. **[LO 11.4]**

RQ. 11.8 State briefly the assumptions on which the Gordon (valuation) Model for the cost of equity is based. What does each component of the equation represent? **[LO 11.4]**

RQ. 11.9 Discuss the approach to determine the cost of retained earnings. Also explain the rationale behind treating retained earnings as a fully subscribed issue of equity shares. **[LO 11.5]**

RQ. 11.10 Other things being equal, explain how the following events would affect the company's weighted average cost of capital: [LO 11.6]

(a) The corporate income tax rate is increased/ decreased.

(b) The company has started making substantial new investments in assets that are considerably riskier than the company's presently owned assets.

(c) The company begins to make use of substantial amounts of debt to finance its new projects.

(d) The company has repaid its long-term debts.

(e) Flotation costs of issuing new securities increase/decrease.

RQ. 11.11 What is the weighted average cost of capital? Examine the rationale behind the use of weighted average cost of capital. [LO 11.6]

RQ. 11.12 The weighted average cost of capital (k_0) may be determined using 'book' or 'market' weights. Compare the pros and cons of using market value weights rather than book value weights in calculating the value of k_0. [LO 11.6]

RQ. 11.13 ABC company sold ₹1,000, 6 per cent debentures carrying no maturity date to the public a decade earlier. Interest rates since have risen so that debentures of the quality represented by this company are now selling at 9 per cent yield basis. [LO 11.2]

(a) Determine the current indicated market price of the debentures. Would you buy the debentures for ₹700? Explain your answer.

(b) Assuming that debentures of the company are selling at ₹850, and if the debentures have 8 years to run to maturity, compute the approximate effective yield an investor would earn on his investment?

RQ. 11.14 Assuming a corporate tax rate of 35 per cent, compute the after-tax cost of the capital in the following situations: [LO 11.2,3,4]

(a) A perpetual 15 per cent debentures of ₹1,000, sold at the premium of 10 per cent with no flotation costs.

(b) A ten year 14 per cent debenture of ₹2,000, redeemable at par, with 5 per cent flotation costs.

(c) A ten year 14 per cent preference share of ₹100, redeemable at premium of 5 per cent, with 5 per cent flotation costs.

(d) An equity share selling at ₹50 and paying a dividend of ₹6 per share, which is expected to be continued indefinitely.

(e) The same equity share (that is, described in situation (d), if dividends are expected to grow at the rate of 5 per cent.

(f) An equity share, selling at ₹120 per share, of a company that engages only in equity financing. The earning per share is ₹20 of which 50 per cent is paid in dividends. The shareholders expect the company to earn a constant after-tax rate of 10 per cent on its investment of retained earnings.

RQ. 11.15 From the following information supplied to you, determine the appropriate weighted average cost of capital, relevant for evaluating long-term investment projects of the company: [LO 11.2,4,6]

Cost of equity	12 per cent
After-tax cost of long-term debt	7
After-tax cost of short-term loans	4

Source of capital	*Book value*	*Market value*
Equity	₹5,00,000	₹7,50,000
Long-term debt	4,00,000	3,75,000
Short-term debt	1,00,000	1,00,000
	10,00,000	12,25,000

LOD: Difficult

RQ. 11.16 The determination of any explicit cost of capital requires two things: (i) the net proceeds the firm will receive from the particular capital source and (ii) the expected future payments the firm will make to the investors. In spite of the similarity of estimation problems, it is recognised that the cost of equity (both internal and external) is the most difficult cost to estimate. Briefly explain why this is so. [LO 11.1,4,5]

RQ. 11.17 Compare the advantages and disadvantages of using marginal as opposed to historical weights for calculating the weighted average cost of capital. Which of the weights are more consistent with the company's goal of wealth maximisation? [LO 11.6]

RQ. 11.18 The shares of a textile company are selling at ₹20 per share. The firm had paid ₹2 per share dividend last year. The estimated growth of the company is approximately 5 per cent per year. [LO 11.4]

(a) Determine the cost of equity capital of the company.

(b) Determine the estimated market price of the equity shares if the anticipated growth rate of the firm (i) rises to 8 per cent (ii) falls to 3 per cent.

(c) Determine the market price of the company assuming a growth rate of 20 per cent. Are you satisfied with your calculations?

RQ. 11.19 A paper company has the following specific cost of capital along with the indicated book and market value weights. [LO 11.2,3,4,5,6]

Type of capital	*Cost (%)*	*Book value weights (%)*	*Market value weights (%)*
Long-term debt	5	30	25
Preference shares	10	20	17
Equity shares	12	40	46
Retained earnings	12	10	12
		100	100

(a) Calculate the weighted average cost of capital using book value and market value weights. Which of them do you consider better and why?

(b) Calculate the weighted average cost of capital using material weights if the company intends to raise the needed funds using 50 per cent long-term debt, 35 per cent preference shares and 15 per cent retained earnings.

ANSWERS

11.13 (a) ₹666.67. No. Its current worth is only ₹666.67; (b) 8.69%.
11.14 (a) 8.86%, **(b)** 9.85%, **(c)** 15%, **(d)** 12%, **(e)** 17%, **(f)** 13.33%
11.15 10.33%.
11.18 (a) Cost of equity, 15.5%, **(b) (i)** ₹28.8, **(ii)** ₹15.43, **(c)** (₹53.33) (ridiculous). The reason is $k_e > g$.
11.19 (a) k_0 based on book value weights 9.5%, k_0 based on market value weights 9.9% **(b)** 7.8%.

Scan the QR Code to access comprehensive solutions to all numerical review questions and additional material.

CHAPTER

12

Analysis of Risk and Uncertainty

LEARNING OBJECTIVES

LO 12.1	Discuss the basic risk concept and its precise expression—sensitivity analysis, scenario analysis and simulation
LO 12.2	Describe two precise measures of risk measurement—standard deviation as an absolute measure and coefficient of variation as a relative measure of risk
LO 12.3	Explain and illustrate the main risk evaluation approaches, namely, risk adjusted discount rate (RADR), certainty-equivalent (CE), Probability distribution and Decision tree
LO 12.4	Discuss risk and real options and their types
LO 12.5	Outline the features relating to the methodology followed by Indian corporates to assess project risk and the relative significance assigned to different risk assessment techniques

INTRODUCTION

This Chapter discusses the risk and uncertainty associated with capital budgeting. The importance of the risk dimension in capital budgeting can hardly be overstressed. In fact, profitability and risk are closely related. It is very likely that a project which is potentially very profitable may also increase the perceived risk of the firm. This trade-off between risk and profitability would have a bearing on the investors' perception of the firm before and after the acceptance of a specific proposal. If the acceptance of a proposal, for instance, makes a firm more risky, the investors would not look to it with favour. This may have an adverse implication for the market price of shares, total valuation of the firm and its goal. It is, therefore, necessary to incorporate the risk factor in the analysis of capital budgeting. The present Chapter is concerned with methods for doing this. The effect on the risk of the firm as a whole has not been covered here; the focus is on the project risk. The Chapter explores first the basic risk concepts. The discussion of the various methods for incorporating the risk factor into the capital budgeting decisions for an individual investment proposal is the theme of the subsequent discussions. The chapter also examines risk and real options. The main points are summarised by way of recapitulation.

LO 12.1 DESCRIPTION AND MEASUREMENT OF RISK

Definition of Risk

As already observed, risk analysis should be incorporated in the capital budgeting exercise. In general, other things being equal, a firm would be well advised to accept a project which is less risky and reject those that involve more risk. This recommendation is consistent with the assumption that the management is averse to risk.

The capital budgeting decision is based on the benefits derived from the project. These benefits are measured in terms of cash flows. As shown in Chapter 9, these cash flows are estimates. The estimation of future returns is done on the basis of various assumptions. The actual returns in terms of cash inflows depend, in other words, on a variety of factors such as price, sales volume, effectiveness of the advertising campaign, competition, cost of raw materials, manufacturing costs and so on. Each of these, in turn, depends on other variables like the state of economy, the rate of inflation, and so on. The accuracy of the estimates of future returns and, therefore, the reliability of the investment decision would largely depend upon the precision with which these factors are forecast.

Risk is the variability in the actual returns in relation to the estimated returns.

There are strong reasons to believe that howsoever carefully the factors having a bearing on future returns emanating from the project are forecast, the actual returns will not precisely correspond to the estimate. In other words, the actual returns will vary from the estimate. This is technically referred to as risk. The term **risk** with reference to capital budgeting/investment decision may, therefore, be defined as the variability in the actual returns emanating from a project over its working life, in relation to the estimated return as forecast at the time of the initial capital budgeting decision.

The decision situations with reference to risk analysis in capital budgeting decisions can be bro-ken up into three types[1]: **(i)** uncertainty, **(ii)** risk, and **(iii)** certainty. The risk situation is one in which the probabilities of occurrence of a particular event are known. These probabilities are not known under the uncertainty situation. The difference between risk and uncertainty, therefore, lies in the fact that variability is less in risk than in uncertainty. In other words, in a strict mathematical sense, there is a distinction between the two:

> Risk refers to a set of unique outcomes for a given event which can be assigned probabilities, while uncertainty refers to the outcomes of a given event which are too unsure to be assigned probabilities.[2]

That is, risk exists when the decision maker is in a position to assign probabilities to various outcomes (i.e. probability distribution is known to him). This happens when the decision maker has some historical data on the basis of which he assigns probabilities to other projects of the same type. Uncertainty exists when the decision maker has no historical data from which to develop a probability distribution, and must make intelligent guesses in order to develop a subjective probability distribution. For example, if the proposed project is completely new to the firm, the decision maker, through research and consultation with others, may be able to subjectively assign probabilities to various outcomes.[3] Throughout this chapter, however, the terms **risk** and **uncertainty** will be used interchangeably to refer to an uncertain decision making situation.

It is, then, obvious that if the future returns are certain, that is, if they could be forecast accurately, there would be no risk involved in such situations. The less accurately they are forecast, the more likely would be the risk involved in the investment decision. The variability of returns and, hence, risk would vary with the type of project. For instance, lease–purchase capital budgeting will, according to this criterion, have no risk since no variability is associated with the returns. This is because the firm purchases the asset to give it on lease for a specified number of annual lease payments. The return, in other words, is absolutely certain. Another example of risk-free investment is the various types of government and government-guaranteed securities. Excepting these few cases, the investment decision is faced with the problem of uncertain returns, which vary widely depending on the nature and purpose of the decision. Thus, the capital budgeting decision for starting a new product will have more uncertain returns than the one involving expansion of an existing one. Further, the estimates of returns from cost-reduction type of capital budgeting will be subject to a lower degree of risk, than the revenue-expanding capital budgeting project.

In brief, risk, with reference to capital budgeting, results from the variation between the estimated and the actual returns. The greater the variability between the two, the more risky is the project. In the discussions that follow, we will discuss the measures to quantify risk in more precise terms.

Sensitivity Analysis

Sensitivity analysis is a behavioural approach that uses a number of possible values for a given variable to assess its impact on a firm's returns.

One measure which expresses risk in more precise terms is **sensitivity analysis**. It provides information as to how sensitive the estimated project parameters, namely, the expected cash flow, the discount rate and the project life are to estimation errors. The analysis on these lines is important as the future is always uncertain and there will always be estimation errors. Sensitivity analysis takes care of estimation errors by using a number of possible outcomes in evaluating a project. The method adopted under sensitivity analysis is to evaluate a project using a number of estimated cash flows to provide to the decision maker an insight into the variability of the outcomes.

Sensitivity analysis provides different cash flow estimates under three assumptions: (i) the worst (i.e. the most pessimistic), (ii) the expected (i.e. the most likely), and (iii) the best (i.e. the most optimistic) outcomes associated with the project. This is illustrated in Example 12.1.

***Example* 12.1**

From the undermentioned facts, compute the net present values (NPVs) of the two projects for each of the possible cash flows, using sensitivity analysis.

Particulars	*Project X ('000)*	*Project Y ('000)*
Initial cash outlays (t = 0)	₹40	₹40
Cash inflow estimates (t = 1 – 15)		
Worst	6	0
Most-likely	8	8
Best	10	16
Required rate of return	0.10	0.10
Economic life (years)	15	15

Solution

The NPV of each project, assuming a 10 per cent required rate of return, can be calculated for each of the possible cash flows. Table A-4 indicates that the present value interest factor annuity (PVIFA) of ₹1 for 15 years at 10 per cent discount is 7.606. Multiplying each possible cash flow by PVIFA, we get, (Table 12.1):

TABLE 12.1 Determination of NPV

	Project X		*Project Y*	
Expected cash inflows	*PV*	*NPV*	*PV*	*NPV*
Worst	₹45,636	₹5,636	Nil	(₹40,000)
Most likely	60,848	20,848	₹60,848	20,848
Best	76,060	36,060	1,21,696	81,696

Table 12.1 demonstrates that sensitivity analysis can produce some very useful information about projects that appear equally desirable on the basis of the most likely estimates of their cash flows. Project X is less risky than Project Y. The actual selection of the project (assuming that the projects are mutually exclusive) will depend on the decision maker's attitude towards risk. If the decision maker is conservative, he will select Project X as there is no possibility of suffering losses. On the other hand, if he is willing to take risks, he will choose Project Y as it has the possibility of paying a very high return as compared to project X. Sensitivity analysis, in spite of being crude, does provide the decision maker with more than one estimate of the project's outcome and, thus, an insight into the variability of the returns.

Assigning Probability It has been shown above that sensitivity analysis provides more than one estimate of the future return of a project. It is, therefore, superior to single-figure forecast as it gives a more precise idea regarding the variability of the returns. But it has a limitation in that it does not disclose the chances of occurrence of these variations. To remedy this shortcoming of sensitivity analysis so as to provide a more accurate forecast, the probability of the occurring variations should also be given. Probability assignment to expected cash flows, therefore, would provide a more precise measure of the variability of cashflows. The concept of probability is helpful as it indicates the percentage chance of occurrence of each possible cash flow. For instance, if some expected cash flow has 0.6 probability of occurrence, it means that the given cash flow is likely to be obtained in 6 out of 10 times (i.e. 60 per cent). Likewise, if a cash flow has a probability of 1, it is certain to occur (as in the case of purchase–lease capital budgeting decision that is, the chances of its occurrence are 100 per cent). With zero probability, the cash flow estimate will never materialise. Thus, probability of obtaining particular cash flow estimates would be between zero and one.

The quantification of variability of returns involves two steps. First, depending on the chance of occurrence of a particular cash flow estimate, probabilities are assigned. The assignment of probabilities can be *objective* or *subjective*. Objective probability refers to the assignment of a probability which is based on a large number of observations, under independent and identical situations, on the basis of the experience of happening or not happening of the event. However, objective probability is not of much use in capital budgeting situations because they do not satisfy the requirement of independent observations repeated over time. They are rather based on single event. Probability assignments which are not based on objective evidence of a large number of trials of identical events are called subjective or personal probability assignments. The assignment of probabilities to cash flow estimates is subjective.

The second step is to estimate the expected return on the project. The returns are expressed in terms of expected monetary values. The expected value of a project is a weighted average return, where the weights are the probabilities assigned to the various expected events, that is, the expected monetary values of the estimated cash flows multiplied by the probabilities.

The procedure for assigning probabilities and determining the expected value is illustrated in Table 12.2 by using the NPVs for projects X and Y of Example 12.1.

TABLE 12.2 Calculation of Expected Values

Possible NPV	*Probability of the NPV occurrence*		*NPV (×) Probability*
Project X			
₹5,636	0.25		₹1,409
20,848	0.50		10,424
36,060	0.25		9,015
	1.00	Expected NPV	20,848
Project Y			
(40,000)	0.25		(10,000)
20,848	0.50		10,424
81,696	0.25		20,424
	1.00	Expected NPV	20,848

The mechanism for calculating the expected monetary value and the NPV of these estimates is further illustrated in Example 12.2.

***Example* 12.2**

The following information is available regarding the expected cash flows generated, and their probability for company X. What is the expected return on the project? Assuming 10 per cent as the discount rate, find out the present values of the expected monetary values.

Year 1		*Year 2*		*Year 3*	
Cash flows	*Probability*	*Cash flows*	*Probability*	*Cash flows*	*Probability*
₹3,000	0.25	₹3,000	0.50	₹3,000	0.25
6,000	0.50	6,000	0.25	6,000	0.25
8,000	0.25	8,000	0.25	8,000	0.50

Solution

TABLE 12.3 (i) Calculation of Expected Monetary Values

Year 1			*Year 2*			*Year 3*		
Cash flows	*Probability*	*Monetary values*	*Cash flows*	*Probability*	*Monetary values*	*Cash flows*	*Probability*	*Monetary values*
₹3,000	0.25	₹750	₹3,000	0.50	₹1,500	₹3,000	0.25	₹750
6,000	0.50	3,000	6,000	0.25	1,500	6,000	0.25	1,500
8,000	0.25	2,000	8,000	0.25	2,000	8,000	0.50	4,000
Total		5,750			5,000			6,250

(ii) Calculation of Present Values

Year 1	₹5,750 × 0.909	= ₹5,226.75
Year 2	5,000 × 0.826	4,130.00
Year 3	6,250 × 0.751	4,693.75
Total		14,050.50

Sensitivity analysis can also be used to ascertain how change in key variables (say, sales volume, sales price, variable costs, operating fixed costs, cost of capital and so on) affect the expected outcome (measured in terms of NPV) of the proposed investment project. For the purpose of analysis, only one variable is considered, holding the effect of other variables constant, at a point of time.

Assume a manufacturing company determines a positive NPV of ₹5 lakh for a new investment project requiring a cash outlay of ₹25 lakh. Its management may find it useful to know the impact of change in sales price (±5 per cent) on the NPV of the project. Assume further that the sensitivity analysis indicating a drop in selling price by 5 per cent will cause NPV to be negative. Evidently, it signals that the project is highly risky. On the contrary, if it is found that the NPV continues to be positive even with 25 per cent drop in sales, the project can be viewed as one which has low risk.

Likewise, the management may carry out sensitivity exercises in relation to increase in variable costs. Assuming that 5 per cent increase in variable costs converts the status of positive NPV to negative NPV, the project will be designated as a risky one. In this way, sensitivity analysis can be carried out with respect to identified critical variables to the base NPV. The project is said to be highly sensitive if the small change brings out a magnified change in NPV. These examples eloquently demonstrate the usefulness of sensitivity analysis as a technique of assessing the risks associated with the proposed project.

It will be equally useful to have a graphic presentation to assess the impact of change in key variables on the NPV; the more steep the curve is, the more sensitive/risky the project is, a flatter curve is the manifestation of the low risk.

Thus, the primary objective of sensitivity analysis is to determine how sensitive the NPV is to changes in any of the key variables and to identify which variable has the most significant impact on the NPV. Clearly, sensitivity analysis brings a good insight/feel to the decision maker about the riskiness of the project.

Scenario Analysis

Scenario analysis is akin to sensitivity analysis but is broader in scope. Unlike sensitivity analysis which analyses the impact of only one variable at a time, the scenario analysis evaluates the impact on the project's profitability of simultaneous changes in more than one variable at a time, such as cash inflows, cash outflows and cost of capital.[4] The decision-maker begins with the base case (most likely scenario). Then, he asks operating managers (production sales, personnel and so on) to specify the worst-case (most pessimistic) scenario in terms of high fixed costs, high variable costs, low selling price, low sales volume, higher cost of capital, and so on and the best-case (most optimistic) scenario (in terms of high sales price, higher sales volume, low variable costs, low fixed costs, lower cost of capital, and so on.)[5] Each scenario will affect the firm's cash inflows, cash outflows, cost of capital and NPV. The values of NPV can be used by the decision-maker to assess the risk involved in the project.

In reality, there is an incredibly remote possibility of either of the two scenarios (the best and the worst) to take place. However, their computation is useful. For instance, in the worst scenario, if NPV remains positive, it indicates that the project has very low risk and is worth accepting. In contrast, if the project shows moderate NPV in the best scenario, the project may be considered highly risky and may not be worth accepting.

Thus, the scenario analysis provides a useful insight into the risk complexion of the proposed project. However, its usefulness is limited in that it considers only a few discreet outcomes (e.g., NPVs). In practice, there are infinite number of other possibilities. Simulation analysis (**discussed below**) is a more comprehensive method of assessing the project's risk. The excel application has greatly enhanced the use of these techniques in project risk assessment.

Simulation

Simulation is a statistically based behavioural approach used in capital budgeting to get a feel for risk by applying predetermined probability distributions and random numbers to estimate risky outcomes.

Simulation is a statistical technique employed to have an insight into risk in a capital budgeting decisions. This technique applies predetermined probability distributions and random numbers to estimate risky outcomes.

A simulation model is akin to sensitivity analysis as it attempts to answer 'what if' questions. However, the advantage of simulation is that it is a more comprehensive than sensitivity analysis. Instead of showing the impact on the NPV for change in one key variable (say, change in sales price or cost of capital) at one point of time in sensitivity analysis, simulation enables the distribution of probable values (of NPV), for change in all the key variables, in one iteration/run only. Being so, it provides more information and better understanding about the risk associated with investment decisions to the finance manager.

To be effective, simulation requires a sophisticated computing package as it then enables to try out a large number of outcomes with much ease.

The first step in any simulation exercise is to develop the precise model of the investment project to be used by the computer. Once the model is developed, the computer calculates a random value of project returns (say, in terms of NPV) for each variable identified for the model. From each set/iteration/run of random values (consisting of all the variables listed in the model), a new series of cash flows (cash inflows and cash outflows) is generated and so also of NPV. The important variables in any typical capital budgeting project (most often used in the model) are market size and its growth rate, market share the proposed project is likely to capture, sales price, unit variable cost, total fixed costs, salvage value of the asset, economic useful life span of the project, cost of capital, working capital requirement, tax rate and so on.

This process of generating a random set of values is repeated numerous times (perhaps as many as a thousand times or even more for very large and complex investment projects). This iteration exercise enables the decision maker to develop a probability distribution of the net present value of the proposed investment project; this probability distribution is then used to compute the project's expected mean value of NPV and its standard deviation. The value of standard deviation 'then' can be used to assess the level of risk associated with the project.

It is evident from the above that the probability distribution so developed (through the simulation process) is not only more credible, but it also enables the decision maker/finance manager to view a **continuum of possible outcomes** rather than a single point estimate.[6]

Given the complex nature of a full simulation exercise, it is beyond the scope of the present volume. We have taken a simple example to illustrate the *modus-operandi* of the simulation exercise.

***Example* 12.3**

Let us assume that the marketing department of Hypothetical Ltd has developed the following two tables (one for sale price and another for sales volume) for its new product, containing probability and assigned random numbers.

TABLE 12.4 Probability assessment and Assigned random numbers at various sale prices

Sale price	*Probability*	*Random numbers*
₹10	0.04	1–10
11	0.06	11–20
12	0.07	21–30
13	0.08	31–40
14	0.10	41–50
15	0.15	51–60
16	0.18	61–70
17	0.17	71–80
18	0.09	81–90
19	0.06	91–100

TABLE 12.5 Probability Assessment and Assigned random numbers at various sales Volumes

Sale volume (units)	*Probability*	*Random numbers*
10,000	0.04	1–6
15,000	0.05	7–15
20,000	0.06	16–28
25,000	0.09	29–40
30,000	0.11	41–50
35,000	0.23	51–64
40,000	0.22	65–80
45,000	0.12	81–88
50,000	0.05	89–96
60,000	0.03	97–100

On the first run of a model, the computer will generate two numbers—one for sale price and another for sales volume. Suppose, the random numbers generated are ₹15 (price) and 30,000 (volume). Based on these two numbers, the total sales value for the model will be ₹4,50,000 (₹15 × 30,000 units). This value is to be placed with all other key variables (say, unit variable cost and fixed costs) to generate the first set of NPV. The data for all the other key variables will be also in the form of a table containing probability assessment and assigned random numbers. As stated earlier, this process will be repeated many times to develop probability distribution of expected NPVs. From the distribution so generated, mean and standard deviation values can be determined.

Evidently, the simulation exercise is more comprehensive. It enables the decision maker to have a deeper and thorough understanding of the proposed investment project; he has a better feel of its risk dimension. Besides, the simulation exercise can cope with both independence and dependence among variables.[7]

However, simulation suffers from certain limitations that render this technique inappropriate/infeasible to be used to assess risk profile of a capital budgeting proposal in real life situations. In fact, the model often becomes so complex (and so quickely) that the decision maker loses interest and finds it difficult to go along with the model.

The other problem associated with using simulation is that probability assessments of the key variables (required for model) are most often subjective and difficult to estimate in practice (for example probability values assigned to sale price and sales volume are subjective in nature). Finally, the simulation exercise is both costly and time consuming. Therefore, this exercise has restricted application in that it is likely to be used only in analysing very complex and large investment projects, involving substantial funds.

LO 12.2 PRECISE MEASURES OF RISK: STANDARD DEVIATION AND COEFFICIENT OF VARIATION

Assigning probabilities to cash flow estimates, as a measure of variability of future returns, represents a further improvement over sensitivity analysis, which, as already mentioned, was itself superior to the method which involved the estimation of future cash flows in the form of a single figure. The assignment of probabilities and the calculation of expected values, without doubt, takes into account the risk in terms of variability in explicit terms in investment decisions. But it suffers from a limitation to the extent that it does not provide the decision maker with a concrete value indicative of variability and, therefore, of risk. In other words, for a more meaningful incorporation of risk into the capital budgeting analysis, a more precise statistical measure is called for. The standard deviation (σ) and the coefficient of variation (V) are two such measures which tell us about the variability associated with the expected cash flow in terms of degree of risk. Standard deviation is an absolute measure which can be applied when the projects involve the same outlay. If the projects to be compared involve different outlays, the coefficient of variation is the correct choice, being a relative measure.

Standard Deviation: Absolute Measure of Risk In statistical terms, **standard deviation** is defined as the square root of the mean of the squared deviation, where deviation is the difference between an outcome and the expected mean value of all outcomes. Further, to calculate the value of standard deviation, we provide weights to the square of each deviation by its probability of occurrence.

> **Standard deviation** is the square root of the mean of the squared deviation; the deviation being the difference between an outcome and the expected mean value of all outcomes.

Assume there are n possible levels of cash flows which are signified as CF_1, CF_2 ... CF_n. The mean of these cash flows equals $\overline{CF}$. The probability of any CF_i is signified as P_i, for example, the probability of CF_4 is signified as P_4 and so on. The formula to calculate the standard deviation (σ) is as follows:

$$\sigma = \sqrt{P_1(CF_1 - \overline{CF})^2 + P_2(CF_2 - \overline{CF})^2 + ... + P_n(CF_n - \overline{CF})^2}$$

$$\sigma = \sqrt{\sum_{i=1}^{n} P_i(CF_i - \overline{CF})^2} \quad \textbf{(12.1)}$$

The greater the standard deviation of a probability distribution, the greater is the dispersion of outcomes around the expected value. Standard deviation is a measure that indicates the degree of uncertainty (or dispersion) of cash flow and is one precise measure of risk.

If two projects have the same expected value (mean), then one which has a greater σ will be said to have higher degree of uncertainty or risk. Table 12.6 presents the calculations of the standard deviation for Projects X and Y based on the data presented in our Example 12.1 (Table 12.1).

TABLE 12.6 Calculation of Standard Deviation

CF_i	$\overline{CF}$	$(CF_i - \overline{CF})$	$(CF_i - \overline{CF})^2$	P_i	$(CF_i - \overline{CF})^2 P_i$
Project X					
₹5,636	₹20,848	₹(15,212)	₹23,14,04,944	0.25	₹5,78,51,236
20,848	20,848	Nil	Nil	0.50	Nil
36,060	20,848	15,212	23,14,04,944	0.25	5,78,51,236
				$\Sigma (CF_i - \overline{CF})^2 P_i$	= 11,57,02,472
Project Y					
(40,000)	20,848	(60,848)	3,70,24,79,104	0.25	92,56,19,776
20,848	20,848	Nil	Nil	0.50	Nil
81,696	20,848	60,848	3,70,24,79,104	0.25	92,56,19,776
				$\Sigma(CF_i - \overline{CF})^2 P_i =$	1,85,12,39,552
			$\sigma X = \sqrt{11,57,02,472}$ =		10,756.4
			$\sigma Y = \sqrt{1,85,12,39,552}$ =		43,026

The standard deviation of project X is smaller than that of project Y. Therefore, it can be concluded that project X is less risky than project Y.

The conclusion regarding the superiority of project X over project Y would hold because both the projects have an equal outlay. However, if the sizes of the projects' outlay differ, the decision maker should make use of the coefficient of variation to judge the riskiness of the projects.

Coefficient of Variation: A Relative Measure of Risk Standard deviation can be misleading in comparing the uncertainty of alternative projects, if they differ in size. The coefficient of variation (V) is a correct technique in such cases. It is calculated as follows:

$$V = \frac{\text{Standard deviation}}{\text{Expected cash flow}} \quad \text{or} \quad \frac{\sigma}{\overline{CF}} \tag{12.2}$$

The coefficient of variation for projects X and Y are 0.516 (₹10,756.4 ÷ ₹20,848) and 2.06 (₹43,026 ÷ ₹20,848). The higher the coefficient, the more risky is the project. Project Y, therefore, is more risky than project X. Thus, we find that V is not providing any additional information. However, the real utility of V is apparent when we compare the projects having differing expected values. The following example (Example 12.4) demonstrates the point further.

***Example* 12.4**

A company is considering selecting one of the two mutually exclusive projects, A and B. The relevant information required to evaluate the riskiness of the project is given below:

Data pertaining to NPV	*Project A*	*Project B*
(A) Expected value ($\overline{CF}$)	₹36,000	₹50,000
(B) Standard deviation (σ)	27,000	32,000
(C) Coefficient of variation (V)	0.75	0.64

On the basis of standard deviation alone, project B would be labelled as a more risky project than A since B has larger standard deviation (32,000) than A (27,000). But on the basis of V, project B would be considered less risky than project A since it has V lower than that of A (0.64 vs 0.75).

We can, therefore, conclude that the coefficient of variation is a better measure of the uncertainty of cash flow returns than the standard deviation. This is because the coefficient of variation adjusts for the size of the cash flow, whereas the standard deviation does not.

LO 12.3 RISK EVALUATION APPROACHES

Once the nature of risk is understood and its quantum estimated, it is to be incorporated within the decision-making framework. This section examines the popular techniques to handle risk. They are:

1. Risk-adjusted Discount Rate Approach
2. Certainty-Equivalent Approach
3. Probability Distribution Approach
4. Decision-tree Approach.

Risk-adjusted Discount Rate Approach

Risk adjusted discount rate is a method to incorporate risk in the discount rate employed in computing the present values.

The Risk-adjusted Discount Rate (RAD) Approach is one of the simplest and the most widely used methods for incorporating risk into the capital budgeting decision. Under this method, the amount of risk inherent in a project is incorporated in the discount rate employed in the present value calculations. Relatively risky projects would have relatively high discount rates and relatively safer projects would have relatively lower discount rates. For example, we would use a very low RAD if we intend to purchase a risk-free asset such as treasury bills. On the other hand, a much higher RAD would be used if we intend to invest in a new project which introduces a new product into an untried market. In fact, in practice, the companies may be using different RADs for different types of projects. For instance, RAD may be, say, 10 per cent for projects involving expansion programmes, 15 per cent for new projects and a still higher rate, say, 20 per cent if the project is concerned with introducing a new product to new types of customers.

The risk-adjusted discount rates presumably represent the differential risk in different classes of investments. The rationale for using different RADs for different projects is as follows. The rate of discount or the cost of capital (k) is the minimum acceptable required rate of return. It is the rate which the investors demand in providing capital to the firm for an investment having a specified risk since such rate is available elsewhere in the economy on assets of similar risk. Therefore, if the project earns less than the rates earned in the economy for that risk, the shareholders will be earning less than the prevailing rate for that risk level, and the market value of the company's shares will fall. The cost of capital, therefore, represents the investors' time preference for money for a typical investment project. Thus, the cost of capital is equivalent to the prevailing rate in the market on that risk class of investment. A well-accepted economic premise is that the required rate of return should increase as risk increases. Therefore, the greater the riskiness of the project, the greater should be the discount rate and *vice versa*. The risk-adjusted discount rate is the discount rate which combines time as well as risk preference of investors.

The use of a single rate of discount without considering the differing risk of various projects would be logically inconsistent with the firm's goal of shareholders' wealth maximisation. Figure 12.1 portrays the relationship between the amount of risk and the required k. It indicates that cash flows of project X with no risk will be discounted at the lowest rate (6 per cent). But as the risk (measured in terms of coefficient of variation) increases, the cash flows of other Projects (Y, Z and W) have to be discounted at progressively higher rates, viz. 10 per cent, 14 per cent and 18 per cents respectively.

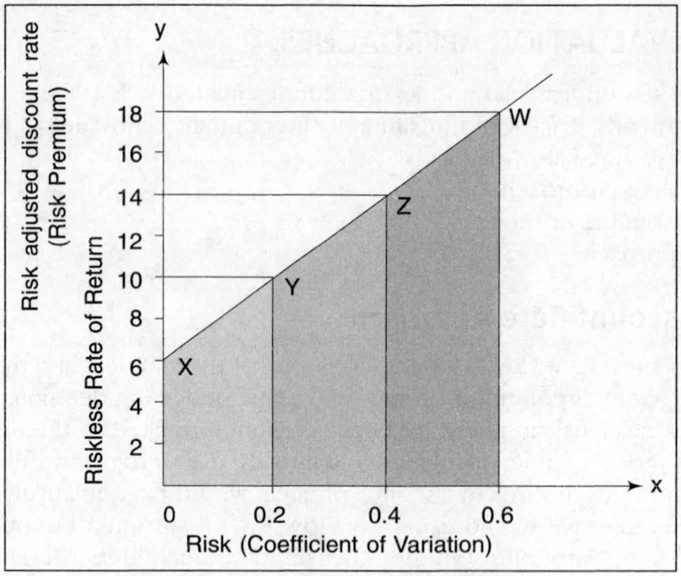

FIGURE 12.1 Risk and Required Return

Accept-reject Decision The Risk-adjusted Discount Rate Approach can be used with both the NPV and the IRR. If the NPV method is used to evaluate capital expenditure decision, NPV would be calculated using the risk-adjusted rate. If the NPV is positive, the proposal would qualify for acceptance. A negative NPV would signify that the project should be rejected. In case of the *IRR* as a decision criterion, the internal rate of return (*r*) would be compared with the risk-adjusted required rate of return. If the *r* exceeds the risk-adjusted rate, the proposal would be accepted, otherwise not.

The risk associated with future returns has two dimensions. First, as already mentioned, the degree of risk of different projects may be different at a particular point of time because of the nature of the proposals such as expansion or new products and so on. The risk may also be different in the case of the same project over time. That is to say, the return at the end of the second year may be more risky than that at the end of the first year and so on. We have illustrated below the calculations of the NPV in both types of situations.

We shall be using the following equation for the purpose of determining NPV under the RAD method.

$$NPV = \sum_{t=1}^{n} \frac{CFAT_t}{(1+K_r)^t} - CO \qquad \textbf{(12.3)}$$

where $CFAT_t$ = expected *CFAT* in year *t*, K_r = risk-adjusted discount rate, *CO* = cash outflows

Thus, projects are evaluated on the basis of future cash flow projections and an appropriate discount rate. Example 12.5 clarifies how the K_r can be used to evaluate capital budgeting projects.

***Example* 12.5**

		(₹1,00,000)
Cash outlays		(₹1,00,000)
CFAT	Year 1	50,000
	Year 2	60,000
	Year 3	40,000

Riskless rate of return = 6 per cent

Risk-adjusted rate of return for the current project = 20 per cent

Solution

$$NPV = (₹1,00,000) + \frac{₹50,000}{(1+.20)} + \frac{₹60,000}{(1+.20)^2} + \frac{₹40,000}{(1+.20)^3} = (₹1,00,000) +$$

$$[₹50,000\ (0.833)] + [₹60,000\ (0.694)] + [₹40,000\ (0.579)] = ₹6,410$$

Given the expected cash flows and estimated risk-adjusted discount rate (K_r), the project's expected NPV is positive and the project should be accepted.

If the risk-adjusted discount rate is 28 per cent, the NPV will be negative (₹5,550). Then, the project will have to be rejected. If the riskiness of the return from the same project differs for future periods, different rates of discount for different future periods can be used. Thus, in Example 12.5, if it is felt that the cash flow is riskier for the second and the third year compared to the first year, a higher discount rate would be used for the return in the second year than that for the first year and so on. Let the rate of discount be 20 per cent, 22 per cent and 25 per cent for the returns for the years 1, 2 and 3 respectively. Then NPV = (₹1,00,000) + ₹50,000 (0.833) + ₹60,000 (0.672) + ₹40,000 (0.512) = ₹2,450.

Evaluation The Risk-adjusted Discount Rate Approach to incorporate risk in the capital budgeting analysis has certain virtues. First, it is simple to calculate and easy to understand. Moreover, companies in actual practice apply different standards of cost of capital for different projects. It has, therefore, the merit of operational feasibility.

However, it is beset with certain operational and conceptual difficulties. The principal operational difficulty of this approach to the incorporation of risk relates to the determination of the risk-adjusted discount rate. While it is logical to assume that projects which involve more risk should be discounted at a higher rate and *vice-versa*, the difficulty encountered is how to precisely express a higher risk in terms of a higher discount rate. In other words, determining an appropriate discount rate in consonance with differing degrees of risks of various projects or, over the years for the same project, is bound to be arbitrary and, therefore, inconsistent in application. It is doubtful if the exercise would give objective results.

The second criticism of this approach is that it does not make direct use of the information available from the probability distribution of expected future cash.[8] Moreover, conceptually, this approach adjusts the wrong element. It is the future cash flow of a project which is subject to risk. What is needed is that the cash flow should be adjusted and not the required rate of return.

Finally, the process of adding the risk premium to the discount rate leads to a compounding of risk over time. This is not a theoretically desirable practice. It is because the discounting process should only take into account time value considerations and not risk considerations. In other words, this method implies that risk necessarily increases with time and, therefore, proposals in which risk does not necessarily increase with time may not be properly evaluated by this method.

In brief, this approach can at best be described as a crude method of incorporating risk into capital budgeting analysis.

Certainty equivalents are risk adjusted factors that represent the per cent of estimated cash inflow that investors would be satisfied to receive for certain rather than the cash inflows that are possible/uncertain for each year.

Certainty-Equivalent Approach

The certainty-equivalent approach (CEA), as an alternative to the risk-adjusted rate method, overcomes some of the weaknesses of the latter method. Under the former approach, the riskiness of the project is taken into consideration by adjusting the expected cash flows and not the discount rate. This method eliminates the problem arising out of the inclusion of risk premium in the discounting process.

Steps Involved The incorporation of risk in the investment decision on the basis of the certainty-equivalent approach involves the following steps.

Comparable Riskless Flow As already observed, the incorporation of risk in capital budgeting analysis is done, according to this approach, by modifying the expected cash inflows. The first step, therefore, involves the determination of the basis for modifying the cash flows to adjust for risk. The risk adjustment factor is expressed in terms of a certainty-equivalent coefficient. The certainty-equivalent coefficient represents the relationship between certain (riskless) cash flows and uncertain (risky) cash flows. Thus, the coefficient is equal to:

$$\frac{\text{Riskless cash flow}}{\text{Risky cash flow}} \tag{12.4}$$

Investment decisions are associated with risk as the future returns are uncertain in the sense that the actual returns are likely to vary from the estimates. If the returns could be made certain, there would be no element of risk. It can reasonably be expected that investors would prefer a relatively smaller but certain cash flows rather than an uncertain, though slightly larger cash flow. How much less they would accept would depend on their perception or utility preference with respect to risk. Therefore, depending on the perception, the first step in the use of the certainty-equivalent approach is to ascertain riskless cash flows comparable to the expected cash flows streams from the project.

Suppose a project is expected to generate a cash flow amounting to ₹20,000. Since this involves risk, a smaller but certain cash flow would be as acceptable to the firm as this one. Let us assume that, on the basis of the utility preference of the management with respect to risk, the firm would rank a certain cash flow of ₹12,000 as equal to an uncertain cash flow of ₹20,000. In other words, the certainty-equivalent of ₹20,000 is ₹12,000. Or, the comparable risky flow for the riskless flow of ₹12,000 is ₹20,000. Thus, the certainty equivalent coefficient is 0.60(₹12,000 ÷ ₹20,000). This coefficient, when multiplied by the risky cash flow, would generate the riskless cash flows, that is, 0.6 × ₹20,000 = ₹12,000.

The coefficient is a fractional amount which can assume a value between 0 and 1. There is an inverse relationship between the degree of risk and the value of the coefficient; the higher the risk associated with the projected cash flow, the lower is the coefficient.

Present Value Calculations After the expected cash flows have been converted into certainty-equivalents, the second step under this approach is to calculate their present values. The rate of discount used for the purpose is the *risk-free rate* or the rate which appropriately reflects the time value of money. It is the same discount rate which is used for computing the present values in the normal course of evaluating capital expenditure. This rate differs from the rate used in the risk-adjusted discount method in that the latter is a modified version of the former.

Accept-Reject Rule The decision-criterion here can either be the NPV method or the IRR method. Using the NPV method, the proposal would be accepted if the NPV of the certainty-equivalent cash flow is positive, otherwise it would be rejected. If the IRR method is employed, the internal rate of return (r), that equates the present value of certainty-equivalent cash inflows with the present value of the cash outflows, would be compared with the risk-free discount rate. As is the practice with this method, if r exceeds the risk-free rate, the investment project would be accepted. If not, it would be rejected.

The mathematical formulation to give the NPV would be:

$$\text{NPV} = \frac{a_1 CFAT_1}{(1+i)^1} + \frac{a_2 CFAT_2}{(1+i)^2} + \frac{a_3 CFAT_3}{(1+i)^3} + \ldots + \frac{a_n CFAT_n}{(1+i)^n} - CO$$

$$= \sum_{t=1}^{n} \frac{a_t CFAT_t}{(1+i)^t} - CO \qquad \textbf{(12.5)}$$

where a_t = certainty-equivalent coefficient for year t, i = riskless interest rate, CO = Cash outflow

We illustrate below the certainty-equivalent approach to adjust risk to capital budgeting analysis on the basis of Example 12.5.

Let us further assume that the certainty-equivalent coefficients for future cash inflows in different years are:

Year	*Coefficient*
1	0.90
2	0.70
3	0.60

The certainty-equivalent cash inflows would be as follows:

Year 1 = ₹45,000 (coefficient 0.9 × ₹50,000, the expected cash inflows)
Year 2 = ₹42,000 (0.70 × ₹60,000)
Year 3 = ₹24,000 (0.60 × ₹40,000)

This would be discounted by the riskless rate of return, which is, 6 per cent. Substituting the value in Equation (12.5), $\text{NPV} = \frac{₹45{,}000}{(1+0.06)^1} + \frac{₹42{,}000}{(1+0.06)^2} + \frac{₹24{,}000}{(1+0.06)^3} - ₹1{,}00{,}000$

$= ₹45{,}000\ (0.943) + ₹42{,}000\ (0.890) + ₹24{,}000\ (0.840) - ₹1{,}00{,}000 = (₹25)$

Since the NPV is negative, the project should be rejected. This decision is in conflict with the decision using the risk-adjusted discount rate where K = 20 per cent. Thus, both these methods may not yield identical results.

Evaluation The certainty-equivalent approach has the merit of being simple to calculate. Another merit of this approach is that it incorporates risk by modifying the cash flows which are subject to risk. It is, therefore, conceptually superior to the time-adjusted discount rate approach.

Its weaknesses arise out of the practical problems of implementation. The crucial element in the application of this approach is the certainty-equivalent coefficient. It depends upon the utility preferences of the management and the perception of the investors. Being a subjective estimate, it cannot be objective, precise and consistent. The conclusions based on such an estimate would be open to question. Another weakness of this method is that it does not directly use the probability distribution of possible cash flows. Moreover, it is not as intuitively appealing as the risk-adjusted discount rate approach and is more difficult to calculate as well as understand.

However, despite these shortcomings, the certainty-equivalent approach is theoretically superior to the risk-adjusted discount rate approach.[9] The reasons, in brief, are as follows.[10] The risk-adjusted discount rate method implies increasing risk over time when the discount rate, K, is constant. It may well be the case that this assumption is appropriate. However, management is unable to consider increasing risk explicitly with this approach and make serious errors in measuring risk over time. For many projects, risk does increase with the length of time in future. As a result, the assumption implicit in the risk-adjusted discount rate approach may well be valid. However, all projects do not necessarily conform to this pattern. For example, an investment proposal may be more risky in the initial years, but when established it may not be that risky, for instance, a tree plantation. In such circumstances, the assumption of risk increasing with the length of time is not valid. This project would be penalised by the risk-adjusted discount rate approach. With the certainty-equivalent approach, management is able to specify directly the degree of risk for a particular future period and then discount the cash flow back to the present value, employing the time value of money. For this reason, the certainty-equivalent approach is superior to the risk-adjusted discounted rate method.

We have discussed so far two common techniques of handling risk in capital budgeting. They are at best crude attempts to incorporate risk. Their major shortcoming is that specifying the ap-propriate degree of risk for an investment project is beset with serious operational problems. Another common weakness of both these methods is that they cannot be consistently applied to various projects and over time. A method to incorporate risk in the capital budgeting analysis should possess two attributes: (a) it should be able to specify in precise terms the appropriate degree of risk, and (b) these specifications should be consistently applied. **The methods that satisfy these two requirements of a satisfactory approach are: (i) Probability Distribution Approach and (ii) Decision-tree Approach.**

Probability Distribution Approach

Dependent cash flows are cash flows in a period which depend upon the cash flows in the preceding periods.

Independent cash flows are cash flows not affected by cash flows in the preceding or following years.

In the earlier part of this chapter dealing with basic risk concepts, we had introduced the use of the concept of probability for incorporating risk in evaluating capital budgeting proposals. As already observed, the probability distribution of cash flows over time provides valuable information about the expected value of return and the dispersion of the probability distribution of possible returns. On the basis of this information an accept-reject decision can be taken. We discuss the application of probability theory to capital budgeting in this section.

The application of this theory in analysing risk in capital budgeting depends upon the behaviour of the cash flows, from the point of view of behavioural cash flows being **(i)** independent, or **(ii)** dependent. The assumption that cash flows are independent over time signifies that future cash flows are not affected by the cash flows in the preceding or following years. Thus, cash flows in year 3 are not dependent on cash flows in year 2 and so on. When cash flows in one period depend upon the cash flows in previous periods, they are referred to as dependent cash flows.

Independent Cash Flows Over Time The mathematical formulation to determine the expected values of the probability distribution of NPV for any project is:

$$NPV = \sum_{t=1}^{n} \frac{\overline{CF_t}}{(1+i)^t} - CO \tag{12.6}$$

where $\overline{CF_t}$ is the expected value of net CFAT in period t and i is the riskless rate of interest. The standard deviation of the probability distribution of NPV is equal to

$$\sigma\ (NPV) = \sqrt{\sum_{t=1}^{n} \frac{\sigma_t^2}{(1+i)^{2t}}} \tag{12.7}$$

where σ_t is the standard deviation of the probability distribution of expected cash flows for period t, σ_t would be calculated as follows:

$$\sigma_t = \sqrt{\sum_{J=1}^{m} (CF_{jt} - \overline{CF_t})^2 \cdot P_{jt}} \qquad \textbf{(12.8)}$$

The above calculations of the standard deviation and the *NPV* will produce significant volume of information for evaluating the risk of the investment proposal. The calculations are illustrated in Example 12.6.

***Example* 12.6**

Suppose there is a project which involves initial cost of ₹20,000 (cost at $t = 0$). It is expected to generate net cash flows during the first 3 years with the probability as shown in Table 12.7. Risk free rate of return is 10 per cent.

TABLE 12.7 Expected Cash Flows

Year 1		*Year 2*		*Year 3*	
Probability	*Net cash flows*	*Probability*	*Net cash flows*	*Probability*	*Net cash flows*
0.10	₹6,000	0.10	₹4,000	0.10	₹2,000
0.25	8,000	0.25	6,000	0.25	4,000
0.30	10,000	0.30	8,000	0.30	6,000
0.25	12,000	0.25	10,000	0.25	8,000
0.10	14,000	0.10	12,000	0.10	10,000

Solution

(i) Expected Values: For the calculation of standard deviation for different periods, the expected values are to be calculated first. These are calculated in Table 12.8.

(ii) The standard deviation of possible net cash flows is:

$$\sigma_t = \sqrt{\sum_{j=1}^{m} \left(CF_{jt} - \overline{CF_t}\right)^2 \cdot P_{jt}}$$

Thus, the standard deviation for period 1 is:

$$\sigma_1 = \sqrt{\begin{array}{l}[0.10(6{,}000 - 10{,}000)^2 + 0.25\,(8{,}000 - 10{,}000)^2 + 0.30\,(10{,}000 - 10{,}000)^2 \\ + 0.25\,(12{,}000 - 10{,}000)^2 + 0.10\,(14{,}000 - 10{,}000)^2\,]\end{array}} = ₹\,2{,}280$$

When calculated on similar lines the standard deviations for periods 2 and 3 (σ_2 and σ_3) also work out to ₹2,280.

(iii) NPV= ₹10,000 (0.909) + ₹8,000 (0.826) + ₹6,000 (0.751) – ₹20,000 = ₹204.

TABLE 12.8 Calculation of Expected Values of Each Period

Time period	*Probability* (1)	*Net cash flow* (2)	*Expected value (1 × 2)* (3)
	0.10	₹6,000	₹600
	0.25	8,000	2,000
Year 1	0.30	10,000	3,000
	0.25	12,000	3,000
	0.10	14,000	1,400
			$\overline{CF_1}$ = 10,000

(Contd.)

(Contd.)

	0.10	4,000	400
	0.25	6,000	1,500
Year 2	0.30	8,000	2,400
	0.25	10,000	2,500
	0.10	12,000	1,200
		$\overline{CF}_2$ =	8,000
	0.10	2,000	200
	0.25	4,000	1,000
Year 3	0.30	6,000	1,800
	0.25	8,000	2,000
	0.10	10,000	1,000
		$\overline{CF}_3$ =	6,000

(iv) The standard deviation under the assumption of independence of cash flows over time:

$$\sigma = \sqrt{\sum_{t=1}^{n} \frac{\sigma_t^2}{(1+i)^{2t}}} = \sqrt{\frac{₹(2{,}280)^2}{(1.10)^2} + \frac{₹(2{,}280)^2}{(1.10)^4} + \frac{₹(2{,}280)^2}{(1.10)^6}} = ₹3{,}283$$

Normal Probability Distribution We can make use of the normal probability distribution to further analyse the element of risk in capital budgeting. The use of the normal probability distribution will enable the decision maker to have an idea of the probability of different expected values of NPV, that is, the probability of NPV having the value of zero or less; greater than zero and within the range of two values, say, ₹1,000 and ₹1,500 and so on. If the probability of having NPV of zero or less is considerably low, say, .01, it implies that the risk in the project is negligible. Thus, the normal probability distribution is an important statistical technique in the hands of decision makers for evaluating the riskiness of a project.

The normal probability distribution as shown in Fig. 12.2 has a number of useful properties.

The area under the normal curve, representing the normal probability distribution, is equal to 1 (0.5 on either side of the mean). The curve has its maximum height at its expected value (mean). The distribution (curve) theoretically runs from minus infinity to plus infinity. The probability of occurrence beyond $3\sigma_s$ is very near zero (0.26 per cent).

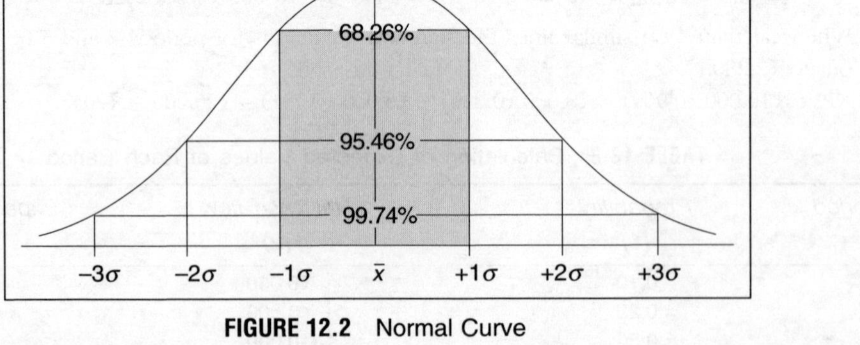

FIGURE 12.2 Normal Curve

For any normal distribution, the probability of an outcome falling within plus or minus 1σ from the mean is 0.6826 or 68.26 per cent. If we take the range within $2\sigma_s$ (X ± 2σ), the probability of an occurrence within this range is 95.46 and 99.74 per cent of all outcomes and lie within $3\sigma_s$ of the $\overline{X}$.

Example **12.7**

Assume that a project has a mean of ₹40 and standard deviation of ₹20. The management wants to determine the probability of the NPV under the following ranges: (i) Zero or less, (ii) Greater than zero, (iii) Between the range of ₹25 and ₹45, (iv) Between the range of ₹15 and ₹30.

Solution

(i) Zero or less: The first step is to determine the difference between the expected outcome X and the expected net present value $\overline{X}$. The second step is to standardise the difference (as obtained in the first step) by the standard deviation of the possible net present values. Then, the resultant quotient is to be seen in statistical tables of the area under the normal curve. Such a table (Table Z) is given at the end of the book. The table contains values for various standard normal distribution functions. Z is the value which we obtain through the first two steps, that is:

$$Z = \frac{0 - ₹\,40}{₹\,20} = -2.0$$

This is also illustrated in Fig. 12.3.

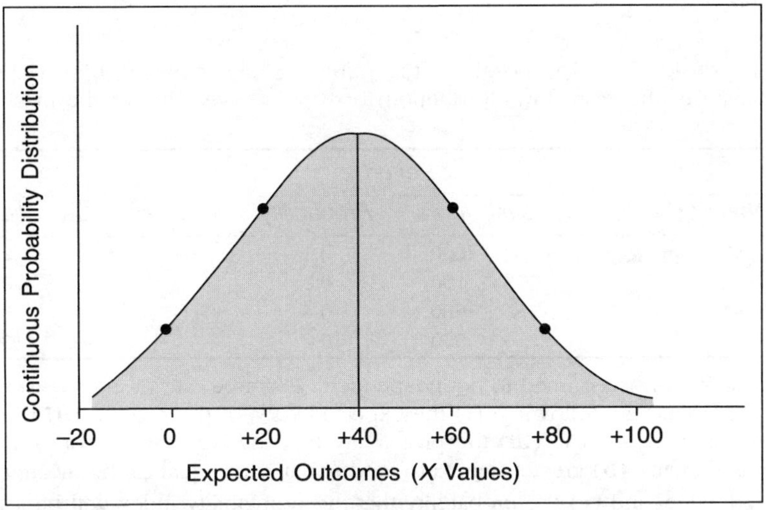

FIGURE 12.3

The figure of –2 indicates that a NPV of 0 lies 2 standard deviation to the left of the expected value of the probability distribution of possible NPV. Table Z indicates that the probability of the value within the range of 0 to 40 is 0.4772. Since the area of the left-hand side of the normal curve is equal to 0.5, the probability of NPV being zero or less would be 0.0228, that is, 0.5 – 0.4772. It means that there is 2.28 per cent probability that the NPV of the project will be zero or less.

(ii) Greater than zero: The probability for the NPV being greater than zero would be equal to 97.72 per cent, that is, 100 – 2.28 per cent probability of NPV being zero or less.

(iii) Between the range of ₹25 and ₹45: The first step is to calculate the value of Z for two ranges: (a) between ₹25 and ₹40, and (b) between ₹40 and ₹45. The second and the last step is to sum up the probabilities obtained for these values of Z:

$$Z_1 = \frac{₹25 - ₹40}{₹20} = -0.75$$

$$Z_2 = \frac{₹45 - ₹40}{₹20} = +0.25$$

The area as per Table Z for the respective values of –0.75 and 0.25 is 0.2734 and 0.0987 respectively. Summing up, we have 0.3721. In other words, there is 37.21 per cent probability of NPV being within the range of ₹25 and ₹45. (It maybe noted that the negative signs for the value of Z in any way does not affect the way Table Z is to be consulted. It simply reflects that the value lies to the left of the mean value).

(iv) Between the range of ₹15 and ₹30:

$$Z_1 = \frac{₹15 - ₹40}{₹20} = -1.25 \qquad Z_2 = \frac{₹30 - ₹40}{₹20} = -0.50$$

According to Table Z, the area for respective values –1.25 and –0.5 is 0.3944 and 0.1915. The probability of having value between ₹15 and 40 is 39.44 per cent, while the probability of having value between ₹30 and 40 = 19.15 per cent. Therefore, the probability of having value between ₹15 and ₹30 would be 20.29 per cent = (39.44 per cent – 19.15 per cent).

The application of the probability distribution approach in evaluating risky projects is comprehensively illustrated in Example 12.8.

***Example* 12.8**

The Cautious Ltd is considering a proposal for the purchase of a new machine requiring an outlay of ₹1,500 lakh. Its estimate of the cash flow distribution for the three-year life of the machine is given below (amount in ₹lakh):

Period 1		*Period 2*		*Period 3*	
Cash flows	*Probability*	*Cash flows*	*Probability*	*Cash flows*	*Probability*
₹800	0.1	₹800	0.1	₹1,200	0.2
600	0.2	700	0.3	900	0.5
400	0.4	600	0.4	600	0.2
200	0.3	500	0.2	300	0.1

The probability distribution is assumed to be independent. Risk-free rate of interest is 5 per cent. From the above information, determine the following: **(i)** the expected NPV of the project; **(ii)** the standard deviation of the probability distribution of NPV; **(iii)** the probability that the NPV will be **(a)** zero or less (assuming that the distribution is normal); **(b)** greater than zero; and **(c)** at least equal to the mean; **(iv)** the profitability index of the expected value; and **(v)** the probability that the profitability index will be less than 1.

Solution

TABLE 12.9 (i) Determination of Expected NPV

(₹ lakh)

Period 1			*Period 2*			*Period 3*		
CF	P_j	*Cash flow* ($CF \times P_j$)	*CF*	P_j	*Cash flow* ($CF \times P_j$)	*CF*	P_j	*Cash flow* ($CF \times P_j$)
800	0.1	80	800	0.1	80	1,200	0.2	240
600	0.2	120	700	0.3	210	900	0.5	450
400	0.4	160	600	0.4	240	600	0.2	120
200	0.3	60	500	0.2	100	300	0.1	30
	Mean ($\overline{CF_1}$)	420		Mean ($\overline{CF_2}$)	630		Mean ($\overline{CF_3}$)	840

NPV = ₹420 (0.952) + ₹630 (0.907) + ₹840 (0.864) – ₹1,500 = ₹197 lakh.

(ii) Standard Deviation of Expected Cash Flow for Period, *t*

Period 1

$(CF_{j1} - \overline{CF_1})^2 \ (\times) P_{j1} = (CF_{j1} - \overline{CF_1})^2 P_{j1}$

₹1,44,400 × 0.1 = ₹14,440

32,400 × 0.2 = 6,480

400 × 0.4 = 160

48,400 × 0.3 = 14,520

$\Sigma(CF_{j1} - \overline{CF_1})^2 P_{j1} = 35{,}600 \qquad \sigma_1 = \sqrt{35{,}600} = 188$

Period 2

$(CF_{j2} - \overline{CF_2})^2 \ (\times) P_{j2} = (CF_{j2} - \overline{CF_2})^2 P_{j2}$

₹28,900 × 0.1 = ₹2,890

4,900 × 0.3 = 1,470

900 × 16,900 × 0.2 = 3,380

$\Sigma(CF_{j2} - \overline{CF_2})^2 P_{j2} = 8{,}100 \qquad \sigma_2 = \sqrt{8{,}100} = 90$

Period 3

$(CF_{j3} - \overline{CF_3})^2 \ (\times) P_{j3} = (CF_{j3} - \overline{CF_3})^2 P_{j3}$

₹1,29,600 × 0.2 = ₹25,920

3,600 × 0.5 = 1,800

57,600 × 0.2 = 11,520

2,91,600 × 0.1 = 29,160

$\Sigma(CF_{j3} - \overline{CF_3})^2 P_{j3} = ₹68{,}400 \qquad \sigma_3 = \sqrt{68{,}400} = 262$

Calculation of standard deviation about NPV:

$$\sigma(NPV) = \sqrt{\sum_{t=1}^{n} \frac{\sigma_t^2}{(1+i)^{2t}}} = \sqrt{\frac{₹(188)^2}{(1+0.05)^2} + \frac{₹(90)^2}{(1+0.05)^4} + \frac{₹(262)^2}{(1+0.05)^6}}$$

$$= \sqrt{\frac{₹35{,}520}{1.102} + \frac{₹8{,}100}{1.216} + \frac{₹68{,}400}{1.340}} = ₹300$$

(iii) (a) Calculation of Probability of the NPV Being Zero or Less: $Z = \frac{0 - 197}{300} = -.6567$

According to Table *Z*, the probability of the NPV being zero is = 0.2454, that is, 24.54 per cent. Therefore, the probability of the NPV being zero or less would be 0.5 – 0.2454 = 0.2546 or 25.46 per cent.

(b) The probability of the NPV being greater than zero would be 1 – 0.2546 = 0.7454 or 74.54 per cent

(c) At least equal to mean: $Z = \frac{197 - 197}{300} = 0$

Reading from the normal distribution table, we get the probability corresponding to 0 as 0. Therefore, the probability of having NPV at least equal to mean would be equivalent to the area to the right of the curve, that is, 0.5 = 50 per cent.

(iv) Profitability Index: $= \frac{PV \text{ of cash inflows}}{PV \text{ of cash outflows}} = \frac{₹197 + ₹1{,}500}{₹1{,}500} = 1.13$

(v) The probability of the index being less than 1: For the index to be 1 or less, the NPV would have to be zero or negative. Thus, the probability would be equal to 25.46 per cent as calculated in part (iii) (a) of the answer.

Decision-tree Approach

The Decision-tree Approach (DT) is another useful alternative for evaluating risky investment proposals. The outstanding feature of this method is that it takes into account the impact of all probabilistic estimates of potential outcomes. In other words, every possible outcome is weighed in probabilistic terms and then evaluated. The DT approach is especially useful for situations in which decisions at one point of time also affect the decisions of the firm at some later date. Another useful application of the DT approach is for projects which require decisions to be made in sequential parts.

Decision tree is a pictorial representation in tree form which indicates the magnitude, probability and inter-relationships of all possible outcomes.

A **decision tree** is a pictorial representation in tree form which indicates the magnitude, probability and inter-relationship of all possible outcomes.[11] The format of the exercise of the investment decision has an appearance of a tree with branches and, therefore, this method is referred to as the decision-tree method. A decision tree shows the sequential cash flows and the NPV of the proposed project under different circumstances. In Example 12.9 we illustrate the application of this method to a particular investment decision problem.

***Example* 12.9**

Suppose a firm has an investment proposal, requiring an outlay of ₹2,00,000 at present ($t = 0$). The investment proposal is expected to have 2 years' economic life with no salvage value. In year 1, there is a 0.3 probability (30 per cent chance) that CFAT will be ₹80,000; a 0.4 probability (40 per cent chance) that CFAT will be ₹1,10,000 and a 0.3 probability (30 per cent chance) that CFAT will be ₹1,50,000. In year 2, the CFAT possibilities depend on the CFAT that occurs in year 1. That is, the CFAT for the year 2 are conditional on CFAT for the year 1. Accordingly, the probabilities assigned with the CFAT of the year 2 are conditional probabilities. The estimated conditional CFAT and their associated conditional probabilities are as follows:

If $CFAT_1$ = ₹80,000		If $CFAT_1$ = ₹1,10,000		If $CFAT_1$ = ₹1,50,000	
$CFAT_2$	Probability	$CFAT_2$	Probability	$CFAT_2$	Probability
₹40,000	0.2	₹1,30,000	0.3	₹1,60,000	0.1
1,00,000	0.6	1,50,000	0.4	2,00,000	0.8
1,50,000	0.2	1,60,000	0.3	2,40,000	0.1

Solution

The estimated values have been portrayed in Fig. 12.4.

It may be noted that the DT figure covers all the dimensions of the problem: (i) the timing of the CFAT, (ii) the possible CFAT outcomes in each year (including the conditional nature of the CFAT outcomes in year 2), and the probabilities associated with these outcomes. The DT shows 9 distinct possibilities, the project could assume if accepted. For example, one possibility is that the CFAT for the year one may amount to ₹80,000 and for the year 2 ₹40,000. A close perusal of Fig. 12.4 would also indicate that this is the worst event that could happen. Assuming a 8 per cent risk free/discount rate for the project, the NPV would be negative. Likewise, the best outcome that could occur is $CFAT_1$ = ₹1,50,000 and $CFAT_2$ = ₹2,40,000. The NPV would be the highest among all the 9 possible combinations. Figure 12.4 shows the NPV at 8 per cent discount rate of each of the estimated CFATs.

The expected NPV ($\overline{NPV}$) of the project is given by the following mathematical formulation:

$$\overline{NPV} = \sum_{j=1}^{m} P_j NPV_j \tag{12.9}$$

Time: 0	Year 1 Probabilities	Year 1 CFAT	Year 2 Probabilities	Year 2 CFAT	Path	Expected NPV at 8% rate of discount*	Joint Probability (P_j)**	Expected NPV NPV (×) P_j
Cash Outlays ₹2,00,000	0.3	₹80,000	0.2	₹40,000	1	₹(– 91,640)	0.06	₹(– 5,498.4)
			0.6	1,00,000	2	(–40,220)	0.18	(–7,239.6)
			0.2	1,50,000	3	(–2,630)	0.06	(–157.8)
	0.4	1,10,000	0.3	1,30,000	4	13,270	0.12	1,592.4
			0.4	1,50,000	5	30,410	0.16	4,865.6
			0.3	1,60,000	6	38,980	0.12	4,677.6
	0.3	1,50,000	0.1	1,60,000	7	76,020	0.03	2,280.6
			0.8	2,00,000	8	1,10,300	0.24	26,472.0
			0.1	2,40,000	9	1,44,580	0.03	4,337.4
							1.00	31,329.8

* *PV* factors for years 1 and 2 at 8% discount rate as per Table A-3 are 0.926 and 0.857 respectively. Multiply $CFAT_1$ by 0.926 and $CFAT_2$ by 0.857; summing up, we get total *PV* for individual possible *CFAT*; subtracting ₹2,00,000 (CO), we get the *NPV*.

** Product of probabilities of *CFAT* for years 1 and 2.

FIGURE 12.4 Decision Tree

where P_j = The probability of the *j*th path occurring which is equal to the joint probability along the path;

NPV_j = NPV of the *j*th path occurring.

In our example, the joint probability, P_j for the worst path is 0.06 (0.3 × 0.2) and for the best path is 0.03 (0.3 × 0.1). The sum of all these joint probabilities must be equal to 1. The last column shows the expected NPV ($\overline{NPV}$), which is obtained by summing up the product of NPV of *j*th path and the corresponding probability of *j*th path ($EP_j \times NPV_j$). The sum of these weighted NPVs is positive and, therefore, the project should be accepted.

This approach has the advantage of exhibiting a bird's eye view of all the possibilities associated with the proposed project. It also makes the management aware well in advance of the adverse possibilities (when the NPV is negative). The conditional nature of CFAT associated with the project is clearly shown. The primary limitation of the method is that the decision tree format may itself become very unwieldy, complex and difficult to understand and construct if the number of years of the expected life of the project and the number of possible outcomes for each year are large. For instance, if we have a 3 year project, there will be 27 paths and, 60,000 paths if the project life is 10 years, assuming only 3 possible outcomes.

LO 12.4 RISK AND REAL OPTOINS

As discussed earlier, a capital budgeting project is accepted if it promises positive NPV and is rejected in case the NPV is negative. This traditional capital budgeting procedure has yielded good decisions for a considerable period. A more strategic approach for recognising **real options** in investment projects has emerged in recent years.[12]

Real options are opportunities to respond to changing market conditions and influence the outcomes of a project.

It may be recalled that the traditional capital budgeting theory, by and large, is silent about actions that can be taken after the project has been accepted and placed in operation which might cause cash flows to change.[13] However, this may not hold true in practice. Managers can (and often do) make changes that affect future cash flows and/or the life of the project. The traditional DCF methods often ignores these options and the future managerial flexibility that accompanies them. The **flexibility** relates to changes in the old decisions when conditions change.[14] Professional managers can most often respond to changing market conditions and the actions of competitors. Opportunities to respond to changing circumstances and as a result influence the outcome of a project are called **managerial strategic options**.[15] They are more popularly known as **real options** as they are associated with real assets.

Real options have value. There may be a negative NPV of a project but it may have the potential to provide the opportunity to make follow-on investments that could be extremely profitable. In operational terms, a project having negative NPV may turn out eventually worth accepting, keeping in mind the option such as those a project creates in terms of opportunities to expand in future. The real options have value and enhance the worth of an investment project. The value of an investment project would be the sum of the NPV of the project (determined in the usual way) and the value of the option(s). Symbolically, its value is given by Equation 12.10

$$\text{Project worth} = [\text{NPV (traditional)} + \text{Option value}] \quad \textbf{(12.10)}$$

The option value will depend on the number of options available; the greater is the number of options, the greater is the option value and the greater is the project's worth.

Types of Option

There are four major types of options: **(1)** Growth option **(2)** Abandonment option **(3)** Timing option and **(4)** Flexibility option.

Growth Option It is an option to expand production/markets if the sales demand for a product were to exceed expectations (i.e., the project turns out to be highly successful). Such an option has the potential to develop follow-on projects. If an investment project under consideration has the potentials to open new doors, if successful, then recognition of cash flows from such opportunities should be included to judge the worth of an investment project, at its initiation stage itself. Clearly, growth opportunities embedded in a capital budgeting project (not reckoned in the traditional capital budgeting procedure) often contribute in enhancing the project's NPV.[16]

Growth option is an option to expand production/markets if sales exceed expectation.

Abandonment option is an option to abandon/shut-down/terminate a project prior to its expected useful life.

Abandonment Option This is an option to abandon/terminate/shut-down an investment project prior to its expected economic useful life. Such an embedded option enables the management to minimise a firm's losses, if the project turns out to be bad/unsuccessful. In other words, the projects having abandonment value, in many cases, can lower the project's risk by limiting downside losses and enhancing its expected profitability (NPV). For instance, if sales demand were significantly lower than expectations, it might be possible for the firm to sell off some capacity or put it to another use. Another possibility is to improve or redesign the product or service.

A variant of abandonment option is an option to suspend or contract operations. The option to suspend operations temporarily is particularly valuable in natural resource extractions (mines).[17] If there is significant fall in the market price of mineral (say, iron ore) and its extraction costs are higher than the selling price, operations might be **temporarily suspended** and can be resumed when the prices increase sufficiently to cover costs and generate surplus. Likewise, the quantity of production can be scaled down when there is excess supply of products in the market. Higher production level can be resumed when excess supply is exhausted.

The difference between the expected NPV with and without the abandonment represents the value of abandonment options.

Timing Option Also known as **investment timing options**, it is an option to begin an investment at an optimal time. In effect, it is an option to postpone an investment project for one or more periods to accelerate or slow the process of implementing a project in response to new information.[18] Put differently, investment timing option emphasises upon the need for comparing the NPV of an investment project if it is undertaken now (time = 0) or later (at time 1 or 2). There is no guarantee that the project undertaken earlier necessarily generates higher NPV. For example, there are projects in which there is an option to wait. For instance, selling real estate in an adjoining metropolitan city in a future period may more often be more profitable than to sell now. The option to wait in such situations can be valuable.

Timing option is an option to postpone/accelerate/slow down a project in response to new information.

There is yet another advantage of timing option. A project having negative NPV today does not mean that it should never be re-considered. The scenario may change in future and the project may turn out to be profitable.

The investment timing option is in sharp contrast to the traditional NPV analysis which provides decision criterion either to accept the project now or never. The timing option can cause decisive impact on the project's projected profitability and risk. In general, the greater is the uncertainty about the future market conditions, the more attractive it becomes to wait. But this advantage of risk reduction should be more to offset the loss of the 'first-move advantage'.[19]

Flexibility Option Flexibility option is an option to incorporate flexibility into the firm's operations, particularly production. It includes, among others, the opportunity to design the production process to accept multiple inputs and use versatile plant/technology to produce a variety of products by reconfiguring the same plant and equipment.[20] *Prima-facie*, there may be an increase in the capital spendings of an investment project which enables the firm to have the desired valuable flexibility options. More often, such projects may have higher NPV.

Flexibility option is an option to redesign the production process by reconfiguring the plant/equipment.

The above discussion underlines the importance of incorporating the value of real options in determining true worth of an investment project. Their non-recognition runs the risk for management to reject investment projects which are acceptable. Given their importance and usefulness in capital budgeting decisions, the use of real options is likely to become more common in years to come.

LO 12.5 ASSESSMENT OF PROJECT RISK PRACTICES IN INDIA

The major features relating to the methodology followed by the Indian corporates to assess the project risk and the relative significance assigned to different risk assessment techniques are summarised below.10

- The respondent firms use, as can be expected, more than one technique out of the available techniques, namely, sensitivity analysis, scenario analysis, risk adjusted discounted rate, decision-tree analysis and Monte Carlo simulation.
- The sensitivity analysis is used overwhelmingly (91 per cent). It is used more significantly by public sector units and private sector firms having chartered accounts (CAs) as chief financial officers (CFOs).
- The scenario analysis is also used widely (62 per cent) more frequently by large firms than small firms.
- The risk adjusted discount rate is used by around one-third of the corporates.
- The decision tree analysis as well as Monte Carlo simulation to analyse project risk is not popular among corporates to any significant extent.
- Sensitivity analysis is the most popular approach for quantifying risk. It is followed by shorter pay back period and higher cut-off rate.
- Diversification of corporate investment is also used by the sample corporates (53 per cent) for risk reduction.
- The survey (undertaken in 2011–2012) indicates the emergence of new techniques of real options and abandonment options as a part of practice by the sample companies in evaluating capital budgeting proposals.

Sources: (1) Anand, Manoj, "Corporate Financial Practices in India: A Survey", Vikalpa, Vol. 27, No. 4, Oct.-Dec. 2002, pp. 29–56 and
(2) Jain, P.K. and Surendra S. Yadav, "Financial Management Practices in India, Singapore and Thailand: A Comparison", Management and Accounting Research, Vol. 3, No. 4, 2002, pp. 55–103.
(3) Jain, P.K., Shveta Singh and Surendra S. Yadav, "*Financial Management Practices: An Empirical Study of Indian Corporates*", Springer, New Delhi, 2013, pp. 61–62.

SUMMARY

LO 12.1

Risk refers to the variability in the actual returns *vis-à-vis* the estimated returns, in terms of cash flows.

Risk involved in capital budgeting can be measured in absolute as well as relative terms. The absolute measures of risk include sensitivity analysis, simulation and standard deviation. The coefficient of variation is a relative measure of risk.

Sensitivity analysis provides information as to how sensitive the various estimated project parameters, namely, cash flows, cost of capital and project's economic life are to estimation errors. The estimates are normally made under three assumptions: (i) the most pessimistic, (ii) the most likely and (iii) the most optimistic.

Scenario analysis evaluates the impact of simultaneous changes in more than one variable at a time on the project's profitability. The analysis normally is carried out on three sets of scenarios: (1) most likely (2) worst-case and (3) best-case. The values of NPV can be used to assess project risk. In case the project promises positive NPV even in the worst case scenario, it is considered to have low risk. The project is considered highly risky if it generates moderate NPV even in the best-case.

Simulation technique employs predetermined probability distributions and random numbers to estimate risky outcomes. It shows impact of changes in all the key variables on the distribution of probable values of NPV, in one iteration only.

LO 12.2	Standard deviation measures the variability of cash flows around the expected value. Symbolically, the expected value ($\overline{CF}$) is $\sum_{t=1}^{n} CF_i\, P_i$. The formula to calculate standard deviation (σ) is $\sqrt{\sum_{t=1}^{n} P_i\,(CF_i - \overline{CF})^2}$. The greater is the value of (σ), the higher is the degree of risk associated with the pro-posed investment project.
	Coefficient of variation (V) is an appropriate technique of measuring risk of alternative projects involving different investment outlays. It is $\sigma/\overline{CF}$.
LO 12.3	There are four important methods of incorporating risk: (1) Risk adjusted discount rate (RAD) approach, (2) Certainty equivalent (CE) approach, (3) Probability distribution (PD) approach and (4) Decision-tree (DT) approach.
	According to the RAD approach, the element of risk is incorporated by adjusting the required rate of return, using higher discount rates for more risky projects and lower discount rates for less risky projects. The $NPV = \sum_{t=1}^{n} \frac{CFAT_t}{(1+k_r)^t} - CO$.
	The CE approach adjusts the risk through the cash flows associated with the projects with the help of certainty-equivalent coefficient. The CE coefficient (a) indicates the relationship bet-ween riskless cash flows and risky cash flows. The $NPV = \sum_{t=1}^{n} \frac{a_t\, CFAT_1}{(1+i)^t} - CO.$
	The PD approach illustrates the analysis of risk through the application of probability distribution, assuming independence of cash flows over time. The steps involved are: (i) Determination of expected NPV, (ii) computation of standard deviation of expected cash flows and (iii) calculation of probability of different value of NPV based on Z value. The value of $Z = (X_t - \overline{X})/\sigma$.
	The DT approach takes into account the impact of all probable estimates of potential out-comes. Every possible outcome is weighed in probability terms and then evaluated, assuming dependence of cash flows. The expected NPV ($\overline{NPV}$) $= \sum_{j=1}^{m} P_j\, NPV_j$.
LO 12.4	Real options are associated with real assets. They have value in that they provide opportunities to the management to respond to the changing circumstances likely to have positive impact on the eventual outcome of an investment project. As a result, the project's worth is higher by the value of the option.
	There are four major types of options: (1) growth option, (2) abandonment option, (3) timing option and (4) flexibility option.
	Growth option is an option to expand production in case the sales demand for a product exceeds expectation. It has also the potential to develop follow-on projects.
	Abandonment option is an option to abandon the investment project prior to the completion of its expected economic useful life. A variant to abandonment option is an option to suspend or contract business operations temporarily.
	Investment timing option is an option to undertake an investment project at an appropriate time. This option emphasises upon the value to wait; an investment/project started early need not necessarily yield the maximum NPV.
	Flexibility option is an option to incorporate flexibility into the firm's operations. In particular, it focuses on the need to design a production process to accept multiple inputs and use a versatile plant to produce a variety of products by reconfiguring the same plant and equipment.

REFERENCES

1. Luce, R D and H Raiffa, *Games and Decision,* 1957, p 13.
2. Osteryoung, J S Capital Budgeting: *Long-Term Asset Selection,* Grid, (Columbus, Ohio), 1979, p 155.
3. Gitman, L J, Principles of Managerial Finance, Harper and Row, New York, 1997, p 310.
4. Gitman, L J, *op. cit,* p.455.
5. Brigham, E F and J F Houston, *op. cit,* p. 439.
6. McMenamin, Jim, *Financial Management—An Introduction,* New Delhi: Oxford University Press, 2000, p 402.
7. McMenamin, Jim, *op. cit.,* p 409.
8. Osteryoung, J S, *op. cit.,* p 161.
9. For an illustration of this superiority, refer to Robichek, A and S C Myers, *Optional Financing Decision,* Prentice-Hall, Englewood Cliffs, 1965, pp 82-86. See also Van Horne *op. cit.,* pp 128-30.
10. Van Horne, *op. cit.,* p 129.
11. Osteryoung, *op. cit.,* p 162.
12. Gitman, L J, *op. cit,* 2006 p.470
13. Brighman, E F and J F Houston, *op. cit,* p. 456.
14. Van Horne, J C, *Financial Management & Policy,* Prentice Hall, New Delhi, 2002, p.195.
15. Brighman, E F and J F Houston, *op. cit,* p.457.
16. Gitman, L J, *op. cit.,* 2006 p.471.
17. Ross, S A, *op. cit.,* p. 463.
18. Gitman, L J, *op. cit.,* 2006 p. 471.
19. Brighman, E F and J F Houston, *op. cit,* p. 462.
20. Gitman, L J, *op. cit.,* 2006 p. 471.

SOLVED PROBLEMS

P.12.1 A textile company is considering two mutually exclusive investment proposals. Their expected cash flow streams (CFAT) are given as follows: **LO 12.3** LOD E

Year	*Proposal X (₹ thousand)*	*Proposal Y (₹ thousand)*
0	(500)	(700)
1	145	100
2	145	110
3	145	130
4	145	150
5	145	160
6	145	150
7		120
8		120
9		110
10		100

The company employs the risk-adjusted method of evaluating risky projects and selects the appropriate required rate of return as follows:

Project pay back	*Required rate of return (percentage)*
Less than 1 year	8
1 to 5 years	10
5 to 10 years	12
Over 10 years	15

Which proposal should be acceptable to the company?

Solution

(i) Pay back period (PB) for Proposal X:

= ₹5,00,000/₹1,45,000 = 3.448 years.

The appropriate risk adjusted rate of return for pay back period of 3.448 years is 0.10.

(ii) Pay back period for proposal Y:

Year	*Cash flows (₹ thousand)*	*Cumulative cash flows (₹ thousand)*
1	100	100
2	110	210
3	130	340
4	150	490
5	160	650
6	150	800

The pay back period for Proposal Y is 5 years and 4 months and the appropriate risk adjusted rate of return is 0.12.

(iii) Net present value of proposal X:

Years	*CFAT*	*PV factor (at 0.10)*	*Total PV*
1-6	₹1,45,000	4.355	₹6,31,475
Less: Cash outflows			5,00,000
NPV			1,31,475

(iv) Net present value of proposal Y:

Year	*CFAT (₹ thousand)*	*PV factor (at 0.12)*	*Total PV*
1	100	0.893	₹89,300
2	110	0.797	87,670
3	130	0.712	92,560
4	150	0.636	95,400
5	160	0.567	90,720
6	150	0.507	76,050
7	120	0.452	54,240
8	120	0.404	48,480
9	110	0.361	39,710
10	100	0.322	32,200
Total PV			7,06,330
Less: Cash outflows			7,00,000
NPV			6,330

Proposal X should be acceptable to the company as its NPV is higher than that of Proposal Y.

P.12.2 A company employs certainty-equivalent approach in the evaluation of risky investments. The capital budgeting department of the company has developed the following information regarding a new project:

LO 12.3 LOD E

Year	*Expected CFAT (₹ thousand)*	*Certainty-equivalent quotient*
0	(200)	1.0
1	160	0.8
2	140	0.7
3	130	0.6
4	120	0.4
5	80	0.3

The firm's cost of equity capital is 18 per cent; its cost of debt is 9 per cent and the riskless rate of interest in the market on the government securities is 6 per cent. Should the project be accepted?

Solution

Determination of NPV

Year	*Expected CFAT (₹ thousand)*	*Certainty-equivalent (CE)*	*Adjusted CFAT (CFAT × CE) (₹ thousand)*	*PV factor (at 0.06)*	*Total PV*
0	(200)	1.0	(200)	1.000	₹(2,00,000)
1	160	0.8	128	0.943	1,20,704
2	140	0.7	98	0.890	87,220
3	130	0.6	78	0.840	65,520
4	120	0.4	48	0.792	38,016
5	80	0.3	24	0.747	17,928
NPV					1,29,388

The project should be accepted.

P.12.3 The Delta Corporation is considering an investment in one of the two mutually exclusive proposals: Project A which involves an initial outlay of ₹1,70,000 and Project B which has an outlay of ₹1,50,000. The Certainty-Equivalent Approach is employed in evaluating risky investments. The current yield on treasury bills is 0.05 and the company uses this as the riskless rate. The expected values of net cash flows with their respective certainty-equivalents are:

LO 12.3 LOD M

Year	*Project A*		*Project B*	
	Cash flow (₹ thousand)	*Certainty-equivalent*	*Cash flows (₹ thousand)*	*Certainty-equivalent*
1	90	0.8	90	0.9
2	100	0.7	90	0.8
3	110	0.5	100	0.6

(i) Which project should be acceptable to the company?
(ii) Which project is riskier? How do you know?
(iii) If the company was to use the risk-adjusted discount rate method, which project would be analysed with higher rate?

Solution

(i) Determination of NPV of project A

Year	CFAT (₹ thousand)	CE	Adjusted CFAT (CFAT × CE) (₹ thousand)	PV factor (at 0.05)	Total PV
1	90	0.8	72	0.952	₹68,544
2	100	0.7	70	0.907	63,490
3	110	0.5	55	0.864	47,520
Total PV					1,79,554
Less: Initial outlay					1,70,000
NPV					9,554

(ii) Determination of NPV of project B:

Year	CFAT (₹ thousand)	CE	Adjusted CFAT (CFAT × CE) (₹ thousand)	PV factor (at 0.05)	Total PV
1	90	0.9	81	0.952	₹77,112
2	90	0.8	72	0.907	65,304
3	100	0.6	60	0.864	51,840
Total PV					1,94,256
Less: Initial outlay					1,50,000
NPV					44,256

The NPV being greater, Project B should be acceptable to the company.

(ii) Project A is riskier. It is because certainty-equivalent associated with expected CFAT of Project A is lower.

(iii) Project A being more risky would be analysed using a higher discount rate, if the company was to use risk-adjusted discount rate method.

P.12.4 A company is considering two mutually exclusive projects. The company uses the risk adjusted discount rate method. Certain CFAT and certainty equivalents for projects (X and Y) are as follows: **LO 12.3** LOD D

Year	Project X		Project Y	
	Certain CFAT	Certainty equivalents	Certain CFAT	Certainty equivalents
0	(₹40,00,000)	1.00	(₹45,00,000)	1.00
1	14,25,000	0.95	22,50,000	0.90
2	15,30,000	0.85	16,00,000	0.80
3	14,00,000	0.70	17,50,000	0.70
4	13,00,000	0.65	10,80,000	0.60

Which project should be accepted, if risk free rate of return of the firm is 9 %, cost of capital is 13%, and the risk-adjusted discount rate (for projects X and Y) is 16%?

Solution

Determination of NPV of Projects X and Y

Year	Certain CFAT	Certainty equivalent (CE)	Estimated CFAT (Certain CFAT/CE)	PV factor at 16%	Total PV
Project X:					
1	₹14,25,000	0.95	₹15,00,000	0.862	₹12,93,000
2	15,30,000	0.85	18,00,000	0.743	13,37,400
3	14,00,000	0.70	20,00,000	0.641	12,82,000
4	13,00,000	0.65	20,00,000	0.552	11,04,000
Total present value					50,16,400
Less cost of machine					(40,00,000)
NPV					10,16,400
Project Y:					
1	₹22,50,000	0.90	₹25,00,000	0.862	₹21,55,000
2	16,00,000	0.80	20,00,000	0.743	14,86,000
3	17,50,000	0.70	25,00,000	0.641	16,02,500
4	10,80,000	0.60	18,00,000	0.552	9,93,600
Total present value					62,37,100
Less cost of machine					(45,00,000)
NPV					17,37,100

Recommendation Since NPV of Project Y is higher than Project X, project Y should be accepted.

P.12.5 A company has under consideration two mutually exclusive projects for increasing its plant capacity. The management has developed pessimistic, most likely and optimistic estimates of the annual cash flows associated with each project. The estimates are as follows: **LO 12.1** LOD E

	Project A	Project B
Net investment	₹30,000	₹30,000
CFAT estimates:		
Pessimistic	1,200	3,700
Most likely	4,000	4.000
Optimistic	7,000	4,500

(a) Determine the NPV associated with each estimate given for both the projects. The projects have 20 year life each and the firm's cost of capital, 10 per cent.

(b) Which project do you consider should be selected by the company and why?

Solution

(a) Determination of NPV of project A

Expected cash flow	CFAT (t = 1 – 20)	PV factor at 0.10	Total PV	NPV (PV–₹30,000)
Pessimistic	₹1,200	8.514	₹10,217	(₹19,783)
Most likely	4,000	8.514	34,056	4,056
Optimistic	7,000	8.514	59,598	29,598

Determination of NPV of project B

Expected cash flow	CFAT (t = 1 – 20)	PV factor at 0.10	Total PV	NPV (PV–₹30,000)
Pessimistic	3,700	8.514	31,501	1,501
Most likely	4,000	8.514	34,056	4,056
Optimistic	4,500	8.514	38,313	8,313

(b) The calculations suggest that the projects are equally desirable on the basis of the most likely estimates of their cash flows. However, Project A is riskier than Project B because the NPV can be negative by an amount as high as ₹19,783. On the other hand, in the case of Project B, there is no possibility of the firm incurring losses as the values of NPV are positive under all expected cash flow situations. Since the projects are mutually exclusive, the actual selection will depend on the decision maker's attitude towards risk. If he is willing to take risk, he will select Project A, because it has also the possibility of yielding a much higher amount of NPV as compared to Project B; if he is risk-averse, he will obviously select Project B.

P.12.6 The initial investment outlay for a capital investment project consists of ₹100 lakh for plant and machinery and ₹40 lakh for working capital. Other details are summarised below: LO 12.1 LOD D

Sales (lakh units per annum for years 1 to 5)	1
Selling price (per unit)	120
Variable cost (per unit)	60
Fixed overheads (excluding depreciation) (lakh per annum for years 1 to 5)	15
Rate of depreciation on plant and machinery (per cent on WDV)	25
Salvage value of plant and machinery (Equal to the WDV at the end of year 5)	
Applicable tax rate (per cent)	40
Time horizon (years)	5
Post-tax cut off rate (per cent)	12

Required:

(i) Indicate the financial viability of the project by calculating the net present value.

(ii) Determine the sensitivity of the project's NPV under each of the following conditions:

(a) Decrease in selling price by 10 per cent.

(b) Increase in variable cost by 10 per cent.

(c) Increase in variable cost by 5 per cent and increase in selling price by 5 per cent.

Solution

(i) Financial viability of capital investment decision (*₹ lakh*)

Cash outflows	
Cost of plant and machinery	100
Add working capital	40
Total cash outflows	140

Determination of CFAT and NPV (*Amount in lakh of rupees*)

Particulars	*Years*				
	1	*2*	*3*	*4*	*5*
Sales	120	120	120	120	120
Less: Variable cost	60	60	60	60	60
Less: Fixed cost	15	15	15	15	15
EBDT	45	45	45	45	45
Less: Depreciation*	25	18.75	14.06	10.55	7.91
EBT	20	26.25	30.94	34.45	37.09
Less: Taxes @ 40%	8	10.5	12.38	13.78	14.84
EAT	12	15.75	18.56	20.67	22.25
CFAT (EAT + Depreciation)	37	34.5	32.62	31.22	30.16

(*Contd.*)

(Contd.)

Salvage value					23.73
Recovery of working capital					40.00
					93.89
(X) PV Factor (0.12)	0.893	0.797	0.712	0.636	0.567
PV of cash inflows	33.04	27.50	23.22	19.86	53.23
Total present value of cash inflows					156.85
Less: Cash outflows					140
NPV					16.85

Working Notes

* Determination of depreciation

(Amount in ₹ lakh)

Year	*Value of the machine at beginning of the year*	*Depreciation*
1	100	25
2	75	18.75
3	56.25	14.06
4	42.19	10.55
5	31.64	7.91

Recommendation Since the NPV of project is positive, the project is financially viable.

(a) Decrease in selling price by 10 per cent

Determination of CFAT and NPV *(Amount in lakh of rupees)*

Particulars	*Years*				
	1	*2*	*3*	*4*	*5*
Sales	108	108	108	108	108
Less: Variable cost	60	60	60	60	60
Less: Fixed cost	15	15	15	15	15
EBDT	33	33	33	33	33
Less: Depreciation	25	18.75	14.06	10.55	7.91
EBT	8	14.25	18.94	22.45	25.09
Less: Taxes @ 40%	3.2	5.7	7.58	8.98	10.04
EAT	4.8	8.55	11.36	13.47	15.05
CFAT (EAT + Depreciation)	29.8	27.3	25.42	24.02	22.96
Salvage value					23.73
Recovery of working capital					40
					86.69
(X) PV Factor (0.12)	0.893	0.797	0.712	0.636	0.567
PV of cash inflows	26.61	21.75	18.10	15.27	49.15
Total present value of cash inflows					130.88
Less: Cash outflows					140
NPV					(9.12)

(b) Increase in selling price by 10 per cent

Determination of CFAT and NPV (*Amount in lakh of rupees*)

Particulars	*Years*				
	1	*2*	*3*	*4*	*5*
Sales	120	120	120	120	120
Less: Variable cost	66	66	66	66	66
Less: Fixed cost	15	15	15	15	15
EBDT	39	39	39	39	39
Less: Depreciation	25	18.75	14.06	10.55	7.91
EBT	14	20.25	24.94	28.45	31.09
Less: Taxes @ 40%	5.6	8.1	9.98	11.38	12.44
EAT	8.4	12.15	14.96	17.07	18.65
CFAT	33.4	30.9	29.02	27.62	26.56
Salvage value					23.73
Recovery of working capital					40
					90.29
(×) PV Factor (0.12)	0.893	0.797	0.712	0.636	0.567
PV of CFAT	29.83	24.63	20.66	17.56	51.20
Total present value of CFAT					143.88
Less: Cash outflows					140
NPV					3.88

(ii) Increase in variable cost by 5 per cent and increase in selling price by 5 per cent.

Determination of CFAT and NPV (*Amount in lakh of rupees*)

Particulars	*Years*				
	1	*2*	*3*	*4*	*5*
Sales	126	126	126	126	126
Less: Variable cost	63	63	63	63	63
Less: Fixed cost	15	15	15	15	15
EBDT	48	48	48	48	48
Less: Depreciation	25	18.75	14.06	10.55	7.91
EBT	23	29.25	33.94	37.45	40.09
Less: Taxes @ 40%	9.2	11.7	13.58	14.98	16.04
EAT	13.8	17.55	20.36	22.47	24.05
CFAT	38.8	36.3	34.42	33.02	31.96
Salvage value					23.73
Recovery of working capital					40.00
					95.69
(×) PV Factor (0.12)	0.893	0.797	0.712	0.636	0.567
PV of cash flows	34.64	28.93	24.50	21	54.26
Total present value of cash inflows					163.33
Less: Cash outflows					140
NPV					23.33

Determination of financial viability of the project under various scenarios *(₹ lakh)*

Particulars	*NPV*	*Change in NPV*	
Base case	₹16.851		
Sensitivity			
(i) Decrease in selling price by 10 per cent	(–9.12)	₹(–25.971)	(–154.1%)
(ii) Increase in variable cost by 10 per cent	3.88	12.971	(–76.9%)
(iii) Increase in variable cost by 5 per cent and increase in selling price by 5 per cent	23.33	6.48	(38.5%)

It can be observed from the above

1. The project becomes profitably unviable (as the NPV becomes negative) if the selling price declines by 10 per cent.
2. The project remains viable (thought he NPV decreases) if the variable cost increases by 10 per cent.
3. The project viability improves (as NPV increases) if the selling price and variable cost increases by 5 per cent.

SPREADSHEET SOLUTION

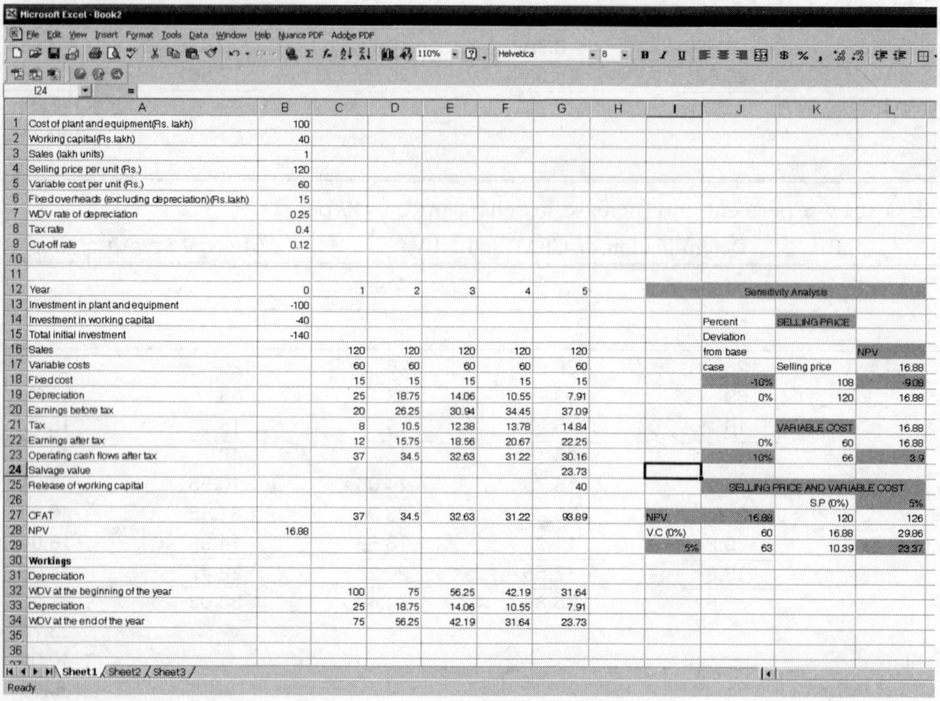

	A	B	C	D	E	F	G	H	I	J	K	L
1	Cost of plant and equipment(Rs. lakh)	100										
2	Working capital(Rs.lakh)	40										
3	Sales (lakh units)	1										
4	Selling price per unit (Rs.)	120										
5	Variable cost per unit (Rs.)	60										
6	Fixed overheads (excluding depreciation)(Rs.lakh)	15										
7	WDV rate of depreciation	0.25										
8	Tax rate	0.4										
9	Cut-off rate	0.12										
10												
11												
12	Year	0	1	2	3	4	5		Sensitivity Analysis			
13	Investment in plant and equipment	-100										
14	Investment in working capital	-40								Percent	SELLING PRICE	
15	Total initial investment	-140								Deviation		
16	Sales		120	120	120	120	120			from base		NPV
17	Variable costs		60	60	60	60	60			case	Selling price	16.88
18	Fixed cost		15	15	15	15	15			-10%	108	-9.08
19	Depreciation		25	18.75	14.06	10.55	7.91			0%	120	16.88
20	Earnings before tax		20	26.25	30.94	34.45	37.09					
21	Tax		8	10.5	12.38	13.78	14.84				VARIABLE COST	16.88
22	Earnings after tax		12	15.75	18.56	20.67	22.25			0%	60	16.88
23	Operating cash flows after tax		37	34.5	32.63	31.22	30.16			10%	66	3.9
24	Salvage value						23.73					
25	Release of working capital						40			SELLING PRICE AND VARIABLE COST		
26											S.P (0%)	5%
27	CFAT		37	34.5	32.63	31.22	93.89		NPV	16.88	120	126
28	NPV	16.88							V.C (0%)	60	16.88	29.86
29									5%	63	10.39	23.37
30	**Workings**											
31	Depreciation											
32	WDV at the beginning of the year		100	75	56.25	42.19	31.64					
33	Depreciation		25	18.75	14.06	10.55	7.91					
34	WDV at the end of the year		75	56.25	42.19	31.64	23.73					
35												
36												

Financial Viability of Capital Investment Decision

Enter the inputs in cells B1 to B9

Enter =- B1 in cell B13, =- B2 in cell B14 for investment in equipment and working capital respectively. Enter =SUM(B13:B14) in cell B15 to calculate the total initial investment.

Enter the formula =($B3*$B4) in cell C16 and copy the formula in cells D16 to G16 to determine sales for all the years. Enter the formula =$B3*$B5 in cell C17and copy the formula to cells D17 to G17 to show the variable cost.

Enter =$B6 in cell c18 and copy it to cells D18 to G18 to show the fixed cost.

Depreciation is worked out in cells C32 to G34. For calculating depreciation enter =b1in cell C32. Enter the formula =C32*$B7 in cell C33. Enter =C32-C33 in cell c34 and copy it to cells D34 to G34. Also copy the formula in cell C33 to cells D33 to G33. Enter =C34 in cell D32 and copy it to cells E32 to G32. The Depreciation figures are carried to Cells C19 to G19. This is done by entering =C33 in cell C19 and it is copied in cells D19 to G19.

To calculate earnings before taxes, enter =C16-(SUM(C17:C19)) in cell C20 and copy the formula to cells D20 to G20.

To calculate taxes, enter =C20*$B.$8 in cell C21 and copy to cells D21to G21.

To calculate earnings after taxes, enter =C20-C21 in cell C22 and copy to cells D22 to G22.

To calculate operating CFAT, enter =C22+C19 in cell C23 and copy to cells D23 to G23.

Salvage value is entered in cell G24 by entering =G34.

Working capital released is entered in cell G25 by providing reference to cell B2 by entering =B2 in cell G25.

Year wise CFATs are calculated by entering =SUM(C23:C25) in cell C27 and copying it to cells D27 to G27.

NPV is calculated in cell B28 by entering =NPV(B9, C27:G27)+B15.

Sensitivity Analysis for Change in Selling Price

First of all, enter =B28 in cell L17. Enter -10% in cell J18 and 0% in cell J19. Enter 120 in cell K19 and formula = K19*(1+J18) in cell K18.

Select cells K17 to L19. Choose Data/What if Analysis/ Data Table from the main menu. A table dialogue box pops up. Enter the address B4 in column input cell and click on OK. The new NPV will be displayed in cell L18.

Sensitivity Analysis for Change in Variable Cost

Enter 0% in cell J22 and 10% in cell J23. Enter 60 in cell K22 and formula = K22*(1+J23) in cell K23.

Select cells K21 to L23. Choose Data/What if Analysis/ Data Table from the main menu. A table dialogue box pops up. Enter the address B5 in column input cell and click on OK. The new NPV will be displayed in cell L23.

Sensitivity Analysis for Changes in Selling Price and Variable Cost

Enter =B28 in cell J27. Enter SP(0%) in cell I28 and VC(0%) in cell K26.Enter 5% in cell I29 and in cell L26. Enter 120 in cell K27 and the formula =K27*(1+L26) in cell L27. Enter 60 in cell J28 and formula =J28*(1+I29) in cell J29.

Select cells J27 to L29. Choose Data/What if Analysis/ Data Table from the main menu. A table dialogue box pops up. Enter the address B4 in the row input cell and B5 in the column input cell and click on OK. The new NPV will be displayed in cell L29.

P.12.7 A company is considering an investment in a project that requires an initial net investment of ₹3,000 with an expected cash flow (CFAT) generated over three years as follows: LO 12.3 LOD M

CFAT	*Probability*	*CFAT*	*Probability*	*CFAT*	*Probability*
₹800	0.1	₹800	0.1	₹800	0.2
1,000	0.2	1,000	0.3	1,000	0.5
1,500	0.4	1,500	0.4	1,500	0.2
2,000	0.3	2,000	0.2	2,000	0.1

(a) What is the expected NPV of this project? (Assume that the probability distributions are independent and the risk-free rate of interest in the market is 0.05).

(b) Calculate the standard deviation about the expected value.

(c) Find the probability that the NPV will be less than zero (Assume that the distribution is normal and continuous).

(d) What is the probability that the NPV will be greater than zero?

(e) What is the probability that NPV will be (i) between the range of ₹500 and ₹750, (ii) between the range of ₹400 and ₹600, (iii) at least ₹300 and (iv) at least ₹1,000.

Solution

(a) Determination of expected NPV

Period 1			Period 2			Period 3		
CF	P_j	*Cash flow* $(CF \times P_j)$	*CF*	P_j	*Cash flow* $(CF \times P_j)$	*CF*	P_j	*Cash flow* $(CF \times P_j)$
₹800	0.1	₹80	₹800	0.1	₹80	₹800	0.2	₹160
1,000	0.2	200	1,000	0.3	300	1,000	0.5	500
1,500	0.4	600	1,500	0.4	600	1,500	0.2	300
2,000	0.3	600	2,000	0.2	400	2,000	0.1	200
	Mean $(\overline{CF_1})$	1,480		$(\overline{CF_2})$	1,380		$(\overline{CF_3})$	1,160

Determination of NPV

CF	*PV factor (0.05)*	*Total PV*
₹1,480	0.952	₹1,409
1,380	0.907	1,252
1,160	0.864	1,002
Total PV		3,663
Less: Cash outflows		3,000
NPV		663

(b) Determination of standard deviation for each period

Period 1

$(CF_{j1} - \overline{CF_1})^2$	(×)	P_{j1}	$(CF_{j1} - \overline{CF_1})^2 P_{j1}$
₹4,62,400	×	0.1	₹46,240
2,30,400	×	0.2	46,080
400	×	0.4	160
2,70,400	×	0.3	81,120
			1,73,600

$$\sigma_1 = \sqrt{1,73,600} = 417$$

Period 2

$(CF_{j2} - \overline{CF_2})^2$	(×)	P_{j2}	$(CF_{j2} - \overline{CF_2})^2 P_{j2}$
₹3,36,400	×	0.1	₹33,640
1,44,400	×	0.3	43,320
14,400	×	0.4	5,760
3,84,400	×	0.2	76,880
			1,59,600

$$\sigma_2 = \sqrt{1,59,600} = 400$$

(Contd.)

(Contd.)

Period 3

$(CF_{j3} - \overline{CF}_3)^2$	(×)	P_{j3}	$(CF_{j3} - \overline{CF}_3)^2 P_{j3}$
₹1,29,600	×	0.2	₹25,920
25,600	×	0.5	12,800
1,15,600	×	0.2	23,120
7,05,600	×	0.1	70,560
			1,32,400
			$\sigma_3 = \sqrt{1,32,400} = 364$

Standard deviation about the expected value:

$$\sigma = \sqrt{\frac{417^2}{(1+0.05)^2} + \frac{400^2}{(1+0.05)^4} + \frac{364^2}{(1+0.05)^6}}$$

$$= \sqrt{3,87,588} = 622$$

(c) The probability that the NPV will be zero or less:

$$Z = \frac{0 - NPV}{\sigma} = \frac{0 - 663}{622} = -1.0659 = -1.07$$

According to Table Z, the probability of the NPV being zero is 0.3577; therefore, the probability of the NPV being less than zero would be 0.5 – 0.3577 = 0.1423 = 14.23 per cent.

(d) The probability of the NPV being greater than zero would be:

1 – 0.1423 = 0.8577 = 85.77 per cent

(e) (i) The probability of the NPV being within the range of ₹500 and ₹750:

$$Z_1 = \frac{₹500 - ₹663}{₹622} = (0.262) \qquad Z_2 = \frac{₹750 - ₹663}{₹622} = (0.141)$$

According to Table Z, the probability corresponding to the respective values of Z_1 and Z_2 is 0.1026 and 0.0557. Summing up the values, we have, 0.1583, that is 15.83 per cent.

(ii) Between the range of ₹400 and ₹600

$$Z_1 = \frac{₹400 - ₹663}{₹622} = (0.42) \qquad Z_2 = \frac{₹600 - ₹663}{₹622} = (0.10)$$

According to Table Z, the probability corresponding to the respective values of Z are 0.1628 and 0.0398 respectively.

To put it explicitly: The probability of NPV having a value between ₹400 and ₹663 = 0.1628. The probability of it having a value between ₹600 and ₹663 = 0.0398. Therefore, the probability of having its value between ₹400 and ₹600 would be = 0.1628 – 0.0398 = – 0.1230 = 12.3 per cent.

(iii) At least ₹300

$$Z = \frac{₹300 - ₹663}{₹622} = (0.5836)$$

According to Table Z, probability of the NPV being 300 = 0.2190. The probability of having NPV at least equal to ₹300 would be more by 0.50 (area to the right side of mean), that is, 0.7190 or 71.9 per cent.

(iv) At least ₹1,000

$$Z = \frac{₹1,000 - ₹663}{₹622} = 0.5418$$

According to Table Z the probability of having the NPV value ₹1,000 is 0.254. The probability of having NPV ₹1,000 or more would be 0.5 – 0.2054 = 0.2946 = 29.46.

P.12.8 Tiny limited is considering a proposal to purchase a new machine. The machine has an initial cost of ₹50,000. The company has developed the following data based on probability distribution approach for cashflows generated by the machine during its economic useful life of 3 years. **LO 12.3** LOD D

Gross present value for (t = 1 – 3)	₹73,206
Standard deviation for (t = 1 – 3):	
Year 1	4,500
2	3,208
3	9,000

(I) Assuming that the probability distribution of cash flows for future periods are independent, determine the expected NPV.

(II) Determine the standard deviation about the expected value; the firm's risk free rate of return is 5 per cent.

(III) Assuming normal distribution, (a) what is the probability of the NPV being less than zero, (b) greater than zero, (c) at least equal to mean and (d) 10 per cent below mean?

Solution

(i) Determination of expected NPV

Gross present value	₹73,206
Less cost of new machine	50,000
Net present value	23,206

(ii) Standard deviation about the expected value

$$\sqrt{\frac{4{,}500^2}{(1+0.05)^2}+\frac{3{,}208^2}{(1+0.05)^4}+\frac{9{,}000}{(1+0.05)^6}}$$

$$\sqrt{\frac{2{,}02{,}50{,}000}{1.102}+\frac{1{,}02{,}91{,}264}{1.216}+\frac{8{,}10{,}00{,}000}{1.340}}$$

$$\sigma = \sqrt{1{,}83{,}75{,}681 + 84{,}63{,}211 + 6{,}04{,}47{,}761} = \sqrt{8{,}72{,}86{,}653} = 9{,}343$$

(iii) (a) Probability of NPV less than zero

$$Z = \frac{0 - \text{NPV}}{\sigma} = \frac{0 - 23{,}206}{9{,}343} = -2.484$$

According to Table Z, probability of NPV being zero is 0.4934. Therefore, the probability of less than zero would be 0.5 – 0.4934 = 0.0066 or 0.66 per cent.

(b) Probability of NPV greater than zero

1 – 0.0066 = 0.9934 or 99.34 per cent.

(c) Probability of NPV atleast equal to mean

Z = (23,206 – 23,206)/9,343 = 0

According to table Z, probability corresponding to 0.0 is 0. Therefore, the probability of having NPV at least equal to mean would be equivalent to the area to the right of curve, that is, 0.5 = 50 per cent.

(d) Probability of NPV 10 per cent below mean

Z = (0.9 × 23,206 = 20,885.4 – 23,206) /9,343 = 0.2483

The area as per Table Z, corresponding to 0.2483 (= 0.25) is 0.0987. In other words, there is 9.87 per cent probability of NPV being less than 10 per cent of the value of mean.

P.12.9 Toy Enterprises Ltd designs and manufactures toys. Past experience indicates that the product life of a toy is 3 years. Promotional advertising produces an increase in sales in the early years, but there is a substantial sales decline in the final year of a toy's life. LO 12.3 LOD D

Consumer demand for new toys placed on the market tends to fall into three classes. About 30 per cent of the new toys sell well above expectations, 60 per cent sell as anticipated, and 10 per cent have poor consumer acceptance.

A new toy has been developed. The following sales projections were made by carefully evaluating the consumer demand.

Consumer demand for a new toy	*Probability of occurrence*	*Estimated sales in year (₹ in lakh)*		
		1	*2*	*3*
Above average	0.30	12	25	6
Average	0.60	7	17	4
Below average	0.10	2	9	1.5

Variable costs are estimated at 30 per cent of the selling price. Special machinery must be purchased at a cost of ₹8,60,000 which will be installed in an unused portion of the factory. The company has been trying unsuccessfully for several years to rent out the vacant portion at ₹50,000 per year. Fixed expenses (excluding depreciation) are estimated at ₹50,000 per year. The new machinery will be depreciated by the written down value method @ 20 per cent with an estimated value of ₹1,10,000 at the year-end 3. Assume this is the only asset in the block. Advertising and promotional expenses will be incurred uniformly, and will total ₹1,00,000 in the first year, ₹1,50,000 in the second year, and ₹50,000 in the third year.

The company is subject to a corporate tax rate of 35 per cent. Its cost of capital is 10 per cent.

(i) Prepare a schedule computing the probable sales of this new toy in each of the three years. Also, determine the NPV of the proposal.

(ii) Assuming that cash flows occur uniformly throughout each year, determine the NPV of the proposal. The present value of ₹1 earned uniformly throughout the year discounted at 10 per cent is as follows:

Year	*Discount factor*
1	0.95
2	0.86
3	0.78

(iii) Assume that the firm would have sufficient short-term capital gains in year 3.

(iv) Give your recommendations in both the situations.

Solution

(i) Schedule showing probable sales of the new toy, years 1–3 *(₹ in lakh)*

Consumer demand for new toy	*Probability of occurrence (P_j)*	*Years (estimated sales)*			*Probable sales per year*		
		1	*2*	*3*	*1*	*2*	*3*
Above average	0.30	12	25	6	3.6	7.5	1.80
Average	0.60	7	17	4	4.2	10.2	2.40
Below average	0.10	2	9	1.5	0.2	0.9	0.15
					8.0	18.6	4.35

Determination of CFAT

Particulars	*Years*		
	1	*2*	*3*
Probable sales revenue	₹8,00,000	₹18,60,000	₹4,35,000
Less: Variable costs (0.30)	2,40,000	5,58,000	1,30,500
Less: Depreciation	1,72,000	1,37,600	Nil*

(Contd.)

(*Contd.*)

Cash fixed costs	50,000	50,000	50,000
Advertising expenses	1,00,000	1,50,000	50,000
EBT	2,38,000	9,64,400	2,04,500
Less: Taxes (0.35)	83,300	3,37,540	71,575
EAT	1,54,700	6,26,860	1,32,925
CFAT (EAT + Depreciation)	3,26,700	7,64,460	1,32,925
Add: Salvage value	—	—	1,10,000
Add: Tax savings on short-term capital loss**	—	—	1,54,140
	3,26,700	7,64,460	3,97,065

* No depreciation in terminal year.

** (₹4,40,400 x 0.35)

Determination of NPV

Year	*CFAT*	*PV factor (0.10)*	*Total PV*
1	₹3,26,700	0.909	₹2,96,970
2	7,64,460	0.826	6,31,444
3	3,97,065	0.751	2,98,196
Total present value			12,26,610
Less: Cash outflows			8,60,000
NPV			3,66,610

(ii) Determination of NPV assuming CFAT occurs uniformly throughout the year

Year	*CFAT*	*PV factor (0.10)*	*Total PV*
1	₹3,26,700	0.95	₹3,10,365
2	7,64,460	0.86	6,57,436
3	3,97,065	0.78	3,09,711
3	1,10,000 (salvage value)	0.751	82,610
3	1,54,140 (tax savings on short-term capital loss)	0.751	1,15,759
Total present value			14,75,880
Less: Cash outflows			8,60,000
NPV			6,15,880

(iii) *Recommendation* The project should be accepted in both the situations.

P.12.10 A company has spent ₹75,000 on research in developing a new product. The product will be marketed if it promises a risk-adjusted rate of return (applicable to such projects) of at least 25 per cent after taxes. For the purposes of financial analysis, the following information has been collected. **LO 12.3** LOD **D**

1. The estimated life of the product is 3 years
2. Projected sales are as follows:

Year	*Sales revenue*
1	₹15,00,000
2	25,00,000
3	6,00,000

3. Variable costs to manufacture and sell the product are estimated at 60 per cent of the selling price.
4. The present cash fixed costs will be increased by ₹10,000 to cover insurance, and maintenance of new equipment.
5. Advertising of the new product will be incurred uniformly, and will total ₹1,25,000 in the first year, and ₹75,000 and ₹60,000 in years 2 and 3, respectively.

6. New machinery will have to be purchased at an estimated cost of ₹9,60,000. The machinery will be depreciated at the rate of 33.33 per cent on the basis of written down value method of depreciation. The salvage value at the expiry of 3 years is estimated at ₹1,00,000. There are several other machines in this block of assets.
7. The new machinery will be installed in a factory area now occupied by equipment that can be no longer be used, that is, scrap equipment. The company has already arranged for removal of the old equipment at a cost of ₹10,000.
8. The new product will be stored in a company owned warehouse in a portion that is vacant now. The company has been trying unsuccessfully to rent this space at ₹25,000 per year. Several offers have been rejected, the highest rent offer being ₹15,000 per year, payable uniformly over the year under a 3-year lease.
9. The firm pays 35 per cent tax on its income. It is assumed that these taxes will be paid uniformly as income is earned.
10. PV of ₹1 at a 25 per cent discount rate are as follows:

Year	*₹1 received at the end of year*	*₹1 received uniformly over the year*
1	0.80	0.88
2	0.64	0.69
3	0.51	0.54

Evaluate the financial implications of the proposal, assuming that the operating cash flows occur uniformly throughout the period of the project's life.

Solution

Determination of CFAT

Particulars	*Year 1*	*Year 2*	*Year 3*
Sales revenue	₹15,00,000	₹25,00,000	₹6,00,000
Less: Costs:			
Variable costs (0.60)	9,00,000	15,00,000	3,60,000
Incremental fixed costs	10,000	10,000	10,000
Advertising costs	1,25,000	75,000	60,000
Depreciation (0.333)	3,20,000	2,13,333	1,42,222
Rent (opportunity cost of the space used)	15,000	15,000	15,000
Total costs	13,70,000	18,13,333	5,87,222
EBT	1,30,000	6,86,667	12,778
Less: Taxes paid (0.35)	45,500	2,40,333	4,472
EAT	84,500	4,46,334	8,306
CFAT (EAT + Depreciation)	4,04,500	6,59,667	1,50,528

Determination of NPV assuming CFAT are received uniformly throughout the year

Year	*CFAT*	*PV factor (0.25)*	*Total PV*
1	₹4,04,500	0.88	₹3,55,960
2	6,59,667	0.69	4,55,170
3	1,50,528	0.54	81,285
4	1,00,000 (salvage value)*	0.51	51,000
Total present value			9,43,415
Less: Cash outflows			9,60,000
NPV			(16,585)

*At the beginning of year 4.

Recommendation The proposal is not financially viable.

P.12.11 A company is trying to decide whether to invest in a new project. Two mutually exclusive projects are available, each requiring an investment of ₹3,00,000. Project A is expected to generate cash inflows of ₹2,00,000 per year in the next 2 years. It is estimated that the cash inflows associated with project B would either be ₹1,80,000, or ₹2,20,000 (each with 0.5 probability of occurrence) next year. If ₹1,80,000 is received in the first year, the cash inflow for the second year is likely to be ₹1,50,000 (probability of 0.3), ₹1,80,000 (probability of 0.4) and ₹2,00,000 (probability of 0.3). In case the first year's cash inflow is ₹2,20,000, the second year's likely cash inflow would be ₹1,80,000 and ₹2,70,000 (each with 0.3 probability), and ₹2,20,000 (probability 0.4). **LO 12.3** LOD M

The firm uses a 14 per cent minimum required rate of return for deciding whether to invest in projects comparable in risk to the ones under consideration.

(i) Calculate the risk adjusted expected NPV for projects A and B.

(ii) Identify the best and the worst possible outcomes for B.

(iii) Which of the projects, if any, would you recommend? Why?

Solution

(i) Determination of expected NPV of project A

Year	*CFAT*	*PV factor (0.14)*	*Total PV*
1	₹2,00,000	0.877	₹1,75,400
2	2,00,000	0.769	1,53,800
Total present value			3,29,200
Less: PV of cash outflows			3,00,000
NPV			29,200

Decision Tree

Determination of expected NPV of project B

Time 0	*1*		*CFAT$_2$*	*NPV at 14%*	*Joint probability*	*Expected NPV*
Cost of the project (₹3,00,000)	0.5 CFAT ₹1,80,000	0.3	₹1,50,000	(₹26,790)	0.15	(₹4,019)
		0.4	1,80,000	(3,720)	0.20	(744)
		0.3	2,00,000	11,660	0.16	1,749
	0.5 CFAT ₹2,20,000	0.3	1,80,000	31,360	0.15	4,704
		0.4	2,20,000	62,120	0.20	12,424
		0.3	2,70,000	1,00,570	0.15	15,085
						29,199

(ii) The worst possible outcome is a CFAT of ₹1,80,000 (year 1) and ₹1,50,000 (year 2) with the maximum negative NPV as ₹26,790.

The best possible outcome is when NPV is maximum, ₹1,00,570. It results when CFAT in year 1 is ₹2,20,000, followed by ₹2,70,000 in year 2.

(iii) The expected NPVs are the same for both projects. However, from the point of view of risk, project A should be chosen as there is no variability of possible events.

P.12.12 A company has the following estimates of the present values of the future cash flows after taxes associated with the investment proposal, concerned with expanding the plant capacity. It intends to use a decision-tree approach to get a clear picture of the possible outcomes of this investment. The plant expansion is expected to cost ₹3,00,000. The respective PVs of future CFAT and probabilities are as follows: **LO 12.3** LOD M

PV of future CFAT

With expansion	*Without expansion*	*Probabilities*
₹3,00,000	₹2,00,000	0.2
5,00,000	2,00,000	0.4
9,00,000	3,50,000	0.4

Advise the company regarding the financial feasibility of the project.

Solution

The relevant computations are depicted below.

Decision Tree

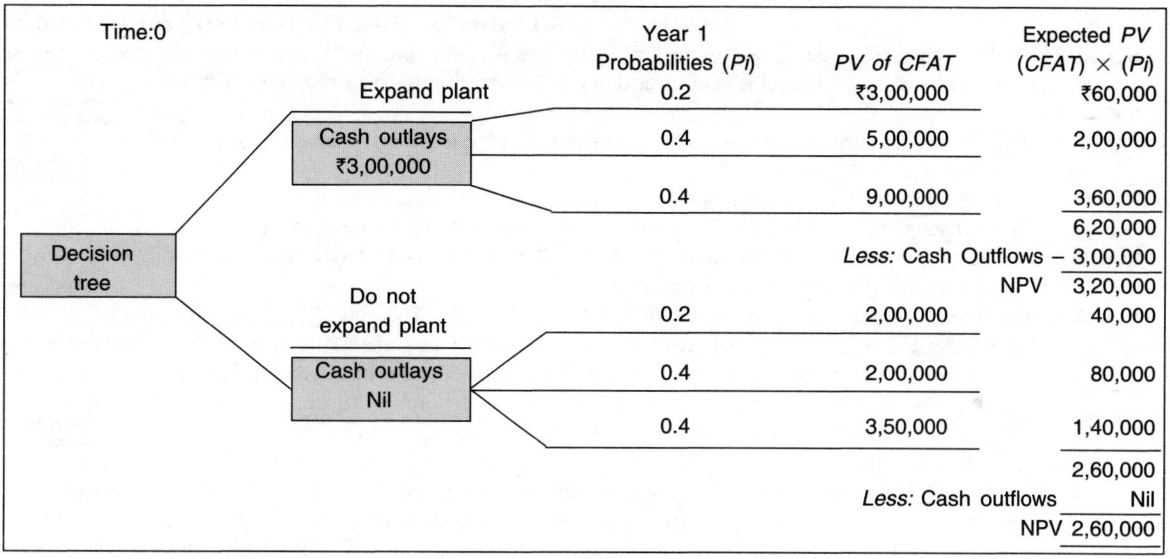

The expected NPV with plant expansion and without expansion is ₹3,20,000 and ₹2,60,000 respectively. Therefore, the company is advised to expand the plant capacity.

Scan the QR Code given at the end of chapter to access comprehensive cases.

REVIEW QUESTIONS

LOD: Easy

RQ.12.1 Indicate whether the following statements are true or false. **[LO 12.1,2,3]**

(i) Coefficient of variation is an absolute measure of risk.

(ii) Sensitivity analysis is an absolute measure of risk.

(iii) The estimates under sensitivity analysis are normally made under two categories.

(iv) The higher the value of the coefficient of variation, the lower is the degree of the risk associated with the proposed investment project.

(v) Simulation technique shows the impact of changes in all the variables on the distribution of probable values of NPV, in one iteration only.

(vi) The higher is the risk, the higher is the certainty equivalent coefficient.

(vii) Conceptually the terms risk and uncertainty can be used interchangeably.

(viii) Projects involving expansions programmes of existing products employ the same risk adjusted discount rate as those required to be used for new products meant for the new types of customers.

(ix) Risk-adjusted discount rate approach is conceptually superior to certainty-equivalent approach to incorporate risk factor in evaluating investment projects.

(x) Risk-free rate of return is employed as a discount rate to evaluate investment projects using certainty equivalent approach.

(xi) The probability distribution approach determines probability of different values of NPV based on Z value.

(xii) The decision-tree approach shows the select/important probable outcomes along with their probabilities.

[Answers: (i) False (ii) True (iii) False (iv) False (v) False (vi) False (vii) False (viii) False (ix) False (x) True (xi) True (xii) False]

RQ.12.2 Why are cash flow estimates for distant years usually less reliable than for more immediate years? How can this time factor be accommodated when evaluating the riskiness of a project? **[LO 12.1,2,3]**

RQ.12.3 **(a)** What similarities are there between the risk-adjusted discount rate method and the certainty-equivalent Method? **[LO 12.3]**

(b) Enumerate the fundamental conceptual differences between the two methods.

(c) Discuss the comparative advantages and disadvantages of each.

RQ 12.4 Describe how **(a)** sensitivity analysis **(b)** scenario analysis and **(c)** simulation approach can be used to assess risk of investment projects. **[LO 12.1]**

RQ.12.5 ABC Ltd is considering a proposal to buy a machine for ₹30,000. The expected cash flows after taxes from the machine for a period of 3 consecutive years are ₹20,000 each. After the expiry of the useful life of the machine, the seller has guaranteed its repurchase at ₹2,000. The firm's cost of capital is 10 per cent and the risk adjusted discount rate is 18 per cent. Should the company accept the proposal of purchasing the machine? **[LO 12.3]**

RQ.12.6 The Premier Ltd is considering a proposal to buy one of the two machines to manufacture a new product. Each of these machines requires an investment of ₹50,000, and is expected to provide benefits over a period of 12 years. The firm has made pessimistic, most likely, and optimistic estimates of the returns associated with each of these alternatives. These estimates are as follows:

	Machine A	*Machine B*
Cost	₹50,000	₹50,000
Cash flow estimates:		
Pessimistic	8,000	0
Most likely	12,000	10,000
Optimistic	16,000	20,000

Assuming 14 per cent cost of capital, which project do you consider more risky, and why? **[LO 12.1]**

LOD: Medium

RQ.12.7 What is the sensitivity approach for dealing with project risk? What is one of the most common methods used to evaluate projects using sensitivity analysis? **[LO 12.1]**

RQ.12.8 Why may the use of standard deviation as a measure of risk lead to a wrong decision? What modifications can be made to obtain an improved measure? **[LO 12.2]**

RQ.12.9 How is risk assessed for a particular investment by using a probability distribution? Take a simple example to illustrate the method. [LO 12.3]

RQ.12.10 When would the use of tree diagrams be beneficial? When would it be impossible to use them? [LO 12.3]

RQ 12.11 What are real options? State the major types of real options. [LO 12.4]

RQ 12.12 What are the options to expand, abandon and suspend operations? [LO 12.4]

RQ.12.13 The Hypothetical Ltd is examining two mutually exclusive proposals. The management of the company uses certainty equivalents (CE) approach to evaluate new investment proposals. From the following information pertaining to these projects, advise the company as to which project should be taken up by it. [LO 12.3]

	Proposal A		*Proposal B*	
Year	*CFAT*	*CE*	*CFAT*	*CE*
0	₹(25,000)	1.0	₹(25,000)	1.0
1	15,000	0.8	9,000	0.9
2	15,000	0.7	18,000	0.8
3	15,000	0.6	12,000	0.7
4	15,000	0.5	16,000	0.4

The firm's cost of capital is 12 per cent, and risk-free borrowing rate is 6 per cent.

RQ.12.14 ABC Ltd is considering a proposal to purchase a new machine. The machine has an initial cost of ₹50,000. The capital budgeting department has developed the following discrete probability distribution for cash flows generated by the project during its useful life of 3 years. [LO 12.3]

Period 1		*Period 2*		*Period 3*	
CFAT	*Probability*	*CFAT*	*Probability*	*CFAT*	*Probability*
₹15,000	0.2	₹20,000	0.5	₹25,000	0.1
20,000	0.4	23,000	0.1	30,000	0.3
25,000	0.3	25,000	0.2	35,000	0.3
30,000	0.1	28,000	0.2	50,000	0.3

(i) Assuming that the probability distribution of cash flows for future periods are independent, the firm's cost of capital is 10 per cent, and the firm can invest in 5 per cent treasury bills, determine the expected NPV.

(ii) Determine the standard deviation about the expected value.

(iii) If the total distribution is approximately normal, and assumed continuous, (a) what is the probability of the NPV being zero or less, (b) greater than zero, (c) profitability index being 1 or less, (d) at least equal to mean, (e) 10 per cent below mean, and (f) 10 per cent above mean?

LOD: Difficult

RQ.12.15 What makes risk important in the selection of projects? Explain briefly the various methods of evaluating risky projects? Can you think of a capital budgeting project that would have perfectly certain returns? [LO 12.1]

RQ.12.16 A company has made the following estimates of the CFAT associated with an investment proposal. The company intends to use a decision tree to get a clearer picture of the project's cash inflows. The project has an expected life of 2 years. [LO 12.3]

CFAT (t = 1)	*Probability*
₹25,000	0.4
30,000	0.6
CFAT (t = 2)	
If $CFAT_1$ = ₹25,000 ... ₹12,000	0.2
16,000	0.3
22,000	0.5
If $CFAT_2$ = ₹30,000 ... 20,000	0.4
25,000	0.5
30,000	0.1

The equipment costs ₹40,000 and the company uses a 10 per cent discount rate for this type of investment.

(i) Construct a decision tree for the proposed investment project.
(ii) What NPV will the project yield if the worst outcome is realised? What is the probability of occurrence of this NPV?
(iii) What will be the NPV if the best outcome occurs? What is its probability?
(iv) Will the project be accepted?

ANSWERS

12.5 Yes, the company should accept the proposal with positive NPV ₹14,982

12.6 Project B is more risky because the NPV can be negative as high as ₹50,000 while in Project A, the NPV can be negative only by ₹4,720.

12.13 NPV Project A ₹9,161
NPV Project B ₹7,579
The company should take up Project A.

12.14 **(i)** NPV (expected) ₹23,206
(ii) Period 1 ₹4,500; Period 2 ₹3,208;
Period 3 ₹9,000; Standard deviation of expected value ₹9,343.
(iii) **(a)** 0.66 per cent
(b) 99.34 per cent
(c) 0.66 per cent
(d) 50 per cent
(e) 9.87 per cent
(f) 9.87 per cent

12.16 **(i)** NPV ₹3,111.88
(ii) If the worst outcome is realized, the NPV (₹7,363)
(iii) Best outcome NPV ₹12,050 with 6 per cent probability.
(iv) Yes, the project, should be accepted, because NPV ₹3,111.88

Scan the QR Code to access comprehensive solutions to all numerical review questions and additional material.

TABLE A-5 Z-Table Values of the Standard Normal Distribution Function

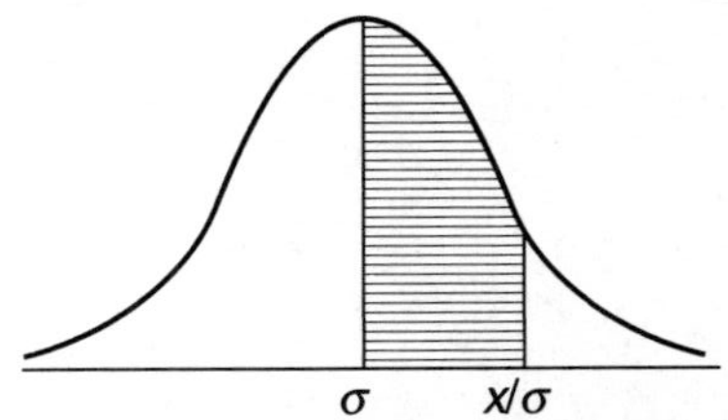

x/σ	.00	.01	.02	.03	.04	.05	.06	.07	.08	.09
0.0	.0000	.0040	.0080	.0120	.0160	.0199	.0239	.0279	.0319	.0359
0.1	.0398	.0438	.0478	.0517	.0557	.0596	.0636	.0675	.0714	.0753
0.2	.0793	.0832	.0871	.0910	.0948	.0987	.1020	.1064	.1103	.1133
0.3	.1179	.1217	.1255	.1293	.1331	.1363	.1406	.1443	.1480	.1515
0.4	.1554	.1591	.1628	.1664	.1700	.1736	.1772	.1808	.1844	.1570
0.5	.1915	.1950	.1935	.2019	.2054	.2088	.2123	.2157	.2190	.2324
0.6	.2257	.2291	.2324	.2357	.2389	.2422	.2454	.2486	.2518	.2549
0.7	.2580	.2612	.2642	.2673	.2704	.2734	.2764	.2794	.2823	.2892
0.8	.2881	.2910	.2939	.2967	.2995	.3023	.3051	.3078	.3106	.3185
0.9	.3159	.3186	.3212	.3238	.3264	.3289	.3315	.3340	.3365	.3389
1.0	.3413	.3438	.3461	.3485	.3508	.3531	.3554	.3577	.3599	.3621
1.1	.3648	.3665	.3686	.3708	.3729	.3749	.3770	.3790	.3810	.3830
1.2	.3849	.3869	.3888	.3907	.3925	.3944	.3962	.3980	.3997	.4015
1.3	.4032	.4049	.4066	.4082	.4099	.4115	.4131	.4147	.4162	.4177
1.4	.4192	.4207	.4222	.4236	.4251	.4265	.4279	.4292	.4305	.4319
1.5	.4332	.4345	.4357	.4370	.4382	.4394	.4406	.4418	.4429	.4441
1.6	.4452	.4463	.4474	.4484	.4495	.4505	.4515	.4525	.4535	.4545
1.7	.4554	.4564	.4573	.4582	.4591	.4599	.4608	.4616	.4625	.4633
1.8	.4641	.4649	.4656	.4664	.4671	.4678	.4686	.4693	.4699	.4706
1.9	.4713	.4719	.4726	.4732	.4738	.4744	.4750	.4750	.4761	.4767
2.0	.4772	.4778	.4783	.4788	.4793	.4798	.4803	.4803	.4812	.4817
2.1	.4821	.4826	.4830	.4834	.4838	.4842	.4846	.4850	.4854	.4857
2.2	.4861	.4864	.4868	.4871	.4875	.4878	.4881	.4884	.4887	.4890
2.3	.4893	.4896	.4898	.4901	.4904	.4906	.4909	.4911	.4913	.4916
2.4	.4918	.4920	.4922	.4925	.4927	.4929	.4931	.4932	.4934	.4936
2.5	.4938	.4940	.4941	.4943	.4945	.4946	.4948	.4949	.4951	.4952
2.6	.4953	.4955	.4956	.4957	.4959	.4960	.4961	.4962	.4963	.4964

(*Contd.*)

TABLE A-5 Z-Table Values of the Standard Normal Distribution Function *(Contd.)*

x/σ	.00	.01	.02	.03	.04	.05	.06	.07	.08	.09
2.7	.4965	.4966	.4967	.4968	.4969	.4970	.4971	.4972	.4973	.4974
2.8	.4974	.4975	.4976	.4977	.4977	.4978	.4979	.4979	.4980	.4981
2.9	.4981	.4982	.4982	.4983	.4984	.4984	.4985	.4985	.4986	.4986
3.0	.49865	.4987	.4987	.4988	.4988	.4989	.4989	.4889	.4990	.4990
3.1	.49903	.4991	.4991	.4991	.4992	.4992	.4992	.4992	.4993	.4993
3.2	.4993129	.4993	.4994	.4994	.4994	.4994	.4994	.4995	.4995	.4995
3.3	.4995166	.4995	.4996	.4996	.4996	.4996	.4996	.4996	.4996	.4997
3.4	.4996631	.4997	.4997	.4997	.4997	.4997	.4997	.4997	.4998	.4998
3.5	.4997674	.4998	.4998	.4998	.4998	.4998	.4998	.4998	.4998	.4998
3.6	.4998409	.4998	.4999	.4999	.4999	.4999	.4999	.4999	.4999	.4999
3.7	.4998922	.4999	.4999	.4999	.4999	.4999	.4999	.4999	.4999	.4999
3.8	.4999277	.4999	.4999	.4999	.4999	.4999	.4999	.5000	.5000	.5000
3.9	.4999519	.5000	.5000	.5000	.5000	.5000	.5000	.5000	.5000	.5000
4.0	.4999683									
4.5	.4999966									
5.0	.4999997133									

PART 4

CURRENT ASSETS MANAGEMENT

Chapter 13
WORKING CAPITAL MANAGEMENT: AN OVERVIEW

Chapter 14
MANAGEMENT OF CASH AND MARKETABLE SECURITIES

Chapter 15
RECEIVABLES MANAGEMENT

Chapter 16
INVENTORY MANAGEMENT

Chapter 17
WORKING CAPITAL FINANCING

Our discussion in Part III of this book related to the management of the fixed assets which yield returns over a period of time. In practice, a firm has also to employ short-term assets and short-run resources of financing. The management of such assets, described as working capital management or current assets management, (short-term financial management) is one of the most important aspects of the overall financial management. Technically, working capital management is an integral part of the overall financial management. To that extent, it is similar to the long-term decision making process because both entail an analysis of the effect of risk and profitability.

The problems involved in the management of working capital differ from those in the management of fixed assets. In the first place, fixed assets are acquired to be retained in the business over a period of time and yield returns over the life of the assets. Probably, the most notable feature of such assets, from the view point of financial analysis, is the time dimension. The operational implication is that discounting and compounding techniques to adjust the value of benefits accruing from such assets over time play a fairly significant role in financial management. In contrast, the stock-in-trade of working capital management, by definition, is short-term assets which loses its identity fairly quickly, usually within an operating cycle not exceeding a year. In the management of working capital, therefore, the time factor is not at all crucial as a decision variable.

Yet another notable feature of short-term assets is the question of profitability versus liquidity and the related aspect of risk. If the size of such assets is large, the liquidity position would improve, but profitability would be adversely affected as funds will remain idle. conversely, if the holdings of such assets are relatively small, the overall profitability will no doubt increase, but it will have an adverse effect on the liquidity position and make the firm more risk–prone. Working capital management should, therefore, aim at striking a balance such that there is an optimum amount of short-term assets. The purpose of this part is to provide an insight into the problems of managing working capital. There are two issues involved: first, the overview of working capital management in terms of the basic concepts, basic relationships between different kinds of short-term assets and liabilities, their financing and so on. Chapter 13 presents an in-depth discussion of the theory of working capital management. The basic concepts/strategies/policies are covered in the Chapter. Chapter also deals with the planning of working capital and its determinants. Secondly, the components of working capital, the individual assets, are covered in the subsequent chapters of this Part. The chapters 14 through 16 respectively analyse the management of cash, receivables and inventory. Finally, some important aspects of the financing of working capital in India are covered in Chapter 17.

CHAPTER 13

Working Capital Management: An Overview

LEARNING OBJECTIVES

LO 13.1	Understand the nature of working capital in terms of basic concepts, strategies, policies and financing strategies
LO 13.2	Analyse the planning of working capital requirements in terms of need, determinants and its computation
LO 13.3	Outline the main elements of management of working capital in India

INTRODUCTION

This chapter presents an overview of working capital management. It explains the nature of working capital and the determination of financing mix. It is also concerned with the planning of working capital requirements. The main points are summarised by way of recapitulation.

LO 13.1 NATURE OF WORKING CAPITAL

We explain below the nature of working capital in terms of the basic concepts, strategies and policies of working capital management. It also illustrates the determination of financing mix.

Working capital management is concerned with the problems that arise in attempting to manage the current assets, the current liabilities and the interrelationship that exists between them. The term *current assets* refer to those assets which in the ordinary course of business can be, or will be, converted into cash within one year without undergoing a diminution in value and without disrupting the operations of the firm. The major current assets are cash, marketable securities, accounts receivable and inventory. Current liabilities are those liabilities which are intended, at their inception, to be paid in the ordinary course of business, within a year, out of the current assets or earnings of the concern. The basic current liabilities are accounts payable, bills payable, bank overdraft, and outstanding expenses. *The goal of working capital management is to manage the firm's current assets and liabilities in such a way that a satisfactory level of working capital is maintained.* This is so because if the firm cannot maintain a satisfactory level of working capital, it is likely to become insolvent and may even be forced into bankruptcy. The current assets should be large enough to cover its current liabilities in order to ensure a reasonable margin of safety. Each of the current assets must be managed efficiently in order to maintain the liquidity of the firm while not keeping too high a level of any one of them. Each of the short-term sources of financing must be continuously managed to ensure that they are obtained and used in the best possible way. *The interaction between current assets and current liabilities is, therefore, the main theme of the theory of working management.*

Concepts and Definitions of Working Capital

There are two concepts of working capital: gross and net.

The term **gross working capital**, also referred to as working capital, means the total current assets.

The term **net working capital** can be defined in two ways: (i) the most common definition of net working capital (NWC) is the difference between current assets and current liabilities; and (ii) alternate definition of NWC is that portion of current assets which is financed with long-term funds.[1]

Gross working capital means the current assets which represent the proportion of investment that circulates from one form to another in the ordinary conduct of business.

The task of the financial manager in managing working capital efficiently is to ensure sufficient liquidity in the operations of the enterprise. The liquidity of a business firm is measured by its ability to satisfy short-term obligations as they become due. The three basic measures of a firm's overall liquidity are **(i)** the current ratio, **(ii)** the acid-test ratio, and **(iii)** the net working capital. The suitability of the first two measures has already been discussed in detail in Chapter 6. In brief, they are very useful in interfirm comparisons of liquidity. Net working capital (NWC), as a measure of liquidity, is not very useful for comparing the performance of different firms, but it is quite useful for internal control. The NWC helps in comparing the liquidity of the same firm over time. *For purpose of working capital management, therefore, NWC can be said to measure the liquidity of the firm. In other words, the goal of working capital management is to manage the current assets and liabilities in such a way that an acceptable level of NWC is maintained.*

Net working capital is the difference between current assets and current liabilities or alternatively the portion of current assets financed with long-term funds.

The Common Definition of NWC and its Implications *NWC is commonly defined as the difference between current assets and current liabilities.* Efficient working capital management requires that firms should operate with some amount of NWC, the exact amount varying from firm to firm and depending, among other things, on the nature of industry. The theoretical justification for the use of NWC to measure liquidity is based on the premise that the greater the margin by which the current assets cover the short-term obligations, the more is the ability to pay obligations when they become due for payment. The NWC is necessary because the cash outflows and inflows do not coincide. In other words, it is the *non-synchronous* nature of cash flows that makes NWC necessary. In general, the cash outflows resulting from payment of current liabilities are relatively predictable. The cash inflows are, however, difficult to predict. The more predictable the cash inflows are, the less NWC will be required. A firm, say an electricity generation company, with almost certain and predictable cash inflows can operate with little or no NWC. But where cash inflows are uncertain, it will be necessary to maintain current assets at a level adequate to cover current liabilities, that is, there must be NWC.

Alternative Definition of NWC *NWC can alternatively be defined as that part of the current assets which are financed with long-term funds.* Since current liabilities represent sources of short-term funds, as long as current assets exceed the current liabilities, the excess must be financed with long-term funds.

Concept of Zero Working Capital[2] The zero working capital (ZWC) concept of net working capital differs from the commonly used concept of working capital (CA – CL). The ZWC = Inventories (+) Receivables (-) Payables. The rationale is that inventories and receivables are the major constituents of current assets which affect sales. Further, suppliers finance inventories through account payable.

> **Zero working Capital** is inventory plus receivables minus payables.

There are financial benefits of reducing the working capital. First, it results in a one-time release of cash flow. Second, the release of cash flow enhances the firm's earnings. Put differently, permanent reduction in working capital funds results in less financial costs (saving in capital costs). The zero working capital concept forces the corporates to produce and deliver faster. This, in turn, may help to gain new business. With low inventories, storage cost as well as loss due to obsolete inventories are also minimised, leading to another set of savings in operating costs. Just-in-time method of inventory control (**discussed in Chapter 16**) facilitate carrying relatively low level of raw-material inventories. Efficient production system (production in tune with sales) can further help in reducing work-in-process and finished goods inventories.

In reality, however, it may not be possible for most firms to operate at zero working capital. Yet, the concept is important as it focuses that the firms should strive for carrying minimum safety stock of inventories, pursuing good credit collection policies leading to minimum investment in debtors and bargaining for maximum credit payment period from suppliers. These measures would result in financial and production economies, leading to higher return on investments.

Policies Related to Current Assets Investment

There are three alternative policies related to the total amount of investments made in current assets: (1) Relaxed, (2) Aggressive and (3) Moderate. These policies differ in respect of the total amount of current assets carried to support any given level of sales.[3] As a result, these policies have an impact on current assets turnover ratio.

Relaxed Current Assets Investment Policy This refers to the policy where the firms carry relatively large amounts of cash and cash-equivalents, inventories and receivables. They use liberal credit policy implying relatively longer time-span of credit period extended to debtors, as a means of promoting sales (**explained in Chapter 15**). In view of the relatively higher amount of investment in current assets, the current assets turnover ratio of such firms tend to be relatively low.

> **Relaxed policy** involves large amounts of cash/ cash-equivalents, receivables and inventory.

Aggressive Current Assets Investment Policy This refers to the policy where the firm's holdings of cash and cash-equivalents, inventories and receivables are minimised. Since there is relatively lower amount of current assets to support given level of sales, the current assets turnover ratio tends to be high.

Under such a policy, the firm would hold minimum level of safety stocks of cash and inventories, and would pursue a tight/strict credit policy for credit sales (though at times, it runs the risk of losing sales). An aggressive/restricted/lean-and-mean current

> **Aggressive policy** implies minimum cash/cash equivalents, receivables and inventory.

assets investment policy generally provides the highest expected return on investment. At the same time, it entails the greatest risk[4] The reverse is true for a relaxed policy.

Moderate Current Assets Investment Policy This falls between the above two extreme policies in terms of current assets carried as well as expected return and risk.

Determining Financing Mix

One of the most important decisions, involved in the management of working capital is how current assets will be financed. There are, broadly speaking, two sources from which funds can be raised for current asset financing; **(i)** short-term sources (current liabilities), and **(ii)** long-term sources, such as share capital, long-term borrowings, internally generated resources like retained earnings and so on. What proportion of current assets should be financed by current liabilities and how much by long-term resources? *Decisions on such questions will determine the financing mix.*

There are three basic approaches to determine an appropriate **financing mix**: **(a)** Hedging approach, also called the Matching approach; **(b)** Conservative approach,and **(c)** Trade-off between these two.

Financing mix is the choice of sources of financing of current assets.

Hedging Approach The term 'hedging' is often used in the sense of a risk-reducing investment strategy involving transactions of a simultaneous but opposing nature so that the effect of one is likely to counterbalance the effect of the other. With reference to an appropriate financing-mix, the term hedging can be said to refer to the process of matching maturities of debt with the maturities of financial needs.[5] This approach to the financing decision to determine an appropriate financing mix is, therefore, also called as **Matching approach**.

Matching approach to financing is the process of matching maturities of debt with the maturities of the financial needs.

According to this approach, the maturity of the source of funds should match the nature of the assets to be financed. For the purpose of analysis, the current assets can be broadly classified into two classes:

1. those which are required in a certain amount for a given level of operation and, hence, do not vary over time.

2. those which fluctuate over time.

The hedging approach suggests that long-term funds should be used to finance the fixed portion of current assets requirements as spelt out in (1) above, in a manner similar to the financing of fixed assets. The purely temporary requirements, that is, the seasonal variations over and above the permanent financing needs should be appropriately financed with short-term funds (current liabilities). This approach, therefore, divides the requirements of total funds into permanent and seasonal components, each being financed by a different source. This has been illustrated in Table 13.1.

TABLE 13.1 Estimated Total Funds Requirements of Hypothetical Ltd *(Amount in ₹ lakh)*

Month	*Total funds required*	*Permanent requirements*	*Seasonal requirements*
(1)	*(2)*	*(3)*	*(4)*
January	₹8,500	₹6,900	₹1,600
February	8,000	6,900	1,100
March	7,500	6,900	600
April	7,000	6,900	100

(Contd.)

(*Contd.*)

May	6,900	6,900	0
June	7,150	6,900	250
July	8,000	6,900	1,100
August	8,350	6,900	1,450
September	8,500	6,900	1,600
October	9,000	6,900	2,100
November	8,000	6,900	1,100
December	7,500	6,900	600
			11,600

According to the hedging approach, the **permanent portion** of funds required (Col.3) should be financed with long-term funds and the **seasonal portion** (Col.4) with short-term funds. With this approach, the short-term financing requirements (current assets) would be just equal to the short-term financing available (current liabilities).

Permanent needs implies financing needs for fixed assets plus the permanent portion of current assets which remain unchanged over the year.

Conservative Approach This approach suggests that the estimated requirement of total funds should be met from long-term sources; the use of short-term funds should be restricted to only emergency situations or when there is an unexpected outflow of funds. In the case of the Hypothetical Ltd in Table 13.1, the total requirements, including the entire ₹9,000 needed in October, will be financed by long-run sources. The short-term funds will be used only to meet contingencies. The amounts given in column 4 of Table 13.1 represent the extent to which short-term financial needs are being financed by long-term funds, that is, the NWC. The NWC reaches the highest level (₹2,100) in October (₹9,000 – ₹6,900). Any long-term financing in excess of ₹6,900 in permanent financing the needs of the company represents NWC.

Seasonal portion implies the financing requirements for temporary current assets which vary over the year.

Comparison of Hedging Approach with Conservative Approach A comparison of the two approaches can be made on the basis of **(i)** cost considerations, and **(ii)** risk considerations.

Conservative financing approach is a strategy by which the firm finances all funds requirement, with long-term funds for emergencies or unexpected outflows.

Cost Considerations The cost of these financing plans has a bearing on the profitability of the enterprise. We assume that the cost of short-term funds and long-term funds is 3 per cent and 8 per cent respectively.

Hedging Plan The cost of financing under the hedging plan can be estimated as follows:

(i) Cost of short-term funds: The cost of short-term funds = average annual short-term loan x interest rate.

Average annual short-term loan = total of monthly seasonal requirements (Col.4) divided by the number of months.

Average annual short-term loan = ₹11,600 lakh ÷ 12 = ₹966.67 lakh.

Short-term cost = ₹966.67 lakh × 0.03 = ₹29 lakh.

(ii) Cost of long-term funds = (Average annual long-term fund requirement) × (annual interest rate) = ₹6,900 lakh × 0.08 = ₹552 lakh.

(iii) Total cost under hedging plan = total of (i) + (ii) = ₹29 lakh + ₹552 lakh = ₹581 lakh

Conservative Plan The cost of financing under the conservative plan is equal to the cost of the long-term funds, that is, annual average loan, multiplied by the long-term rate of interest = ₹9,000 lakh × 0.08 = ₹720 lakh.

Thus, the cost of financing under the conservative approach (₹720 lakh) is higher than the cost using the hedging approach (₹581 lakh). The conservative plan for financing is more expensive because the available funds are not fully utilised during certain periods; moreover, interest has to be paid for funds which are not actually needed (i.e. the period when there is NWC).

Risk Considerations The two approaches can also be contrasted on the basis of the risk involved.

Hedging Approach The hedging approach is more risky in comparison to the conservative approach. There are two reasons for this. First, there is, as already observed, no NWC with the hedging approach because no long-term funds are used to finance short-term seasonal needs, that is, current assets are just equal to current liabilities. On the other hand, the conservative approach has a fairly high level of NWC. Secondly, the hedging plan is risky because it involves almost full utilisation of the capacity to use short-term funds and in emergency situations it may be difficult to satisfy the short-term needs.

Conservative Approach With the conservative approach, in contrast, the company does not use any of its short-term borrowings. Therefore, the firm has sufficient short-term borrowing capacity to cover unexpected financial needs and avoid technical insolvency.

To summarise, the hedging approach is a high profit (low cost)-high risk (no NWC) approach to determine an appropriate financing-mix. In contrast, the conservative approach is low profit (high cost)-low risk (high NWC). The contrast between these approaches is indicative of the need for trade-off between profitability and risk.

A Trade-off between the Hedging and Conservative Approaches It has been shown that the hedging approach is associated with high profits as well as high risk, while the conservative approach provides low profits and low risk. Obviously, neither approach by itself would serve the purpose of efficient working capital management. A trade-off between these two extremes would give an **acceptable financing strategy**. The third approach–trade-off between the two approaches–strikes a balance and provides a financing plan that lies between these two extremes.

Acceptable financing strategy is a trade-off between matching and conservative financing strategies.

The exact trade-off between risk and profitability will differ from case to case depending on risk perception of the decision makers. One possible trade-off could be assumed to be equal to the average of the minimum and maximum monthly requirements of funds during a given period of time. This level of requirement of funds may be financed through long-run sources and for any additional financing need, short-term funds may be used. The breakdown of the requirement of funds of the Hypothetical Ltd between long-term and short-term sources under the trade-off plans is shown in Table 13.2.

TABLE 13.2 Trade-off between Hedging and Conservative Approaches

(Amount in ₹ lakh)

Month	*Total funds required*	*Permanent requirements*	*Seasonal requirements*
(1)	*(2)*	*(3)*	*(4)*
January	₹8,500	₹7,950	₹550
February	8,000	7,950	50
March	7,500	7,950	0
April	7,000	7,950	0

(Contd.)

(Contd.)

May	6,900	7,950	0
June	7,150	7,950	0
July	8,000	7,950	50
August	8,350	7,950	400
September	8,500	7,950	550
October	9,000	7,950	1,050
November	8,000	7,950	50
December	7,500	7,950	0
			2,700

The figures in Table 13.2 reveal that the maximum fund required is ₹9,000 lakh (October) and the minimum is ₹6,900 lakh (May). The average $\left(\frac{₹9{,}000 \text{ lakh} + ₹6{,}900 \text{ lakh}}{2}\right)$ = ₹7,950 lakh. In other words, the company should use ₹7,950 lakh each month (Col.3) in the form of long-term funds and raise additional funds, if needed, through short-term resources (current liabilities). It is clear from the table that no short-term funds are required during 5 months, namely, March, April, May, June and December, because long-term funds available exceed the total requirements for funds. In the remaining 7 months, the company will have to use short-term funds totalling ₹2,700 lakh (Col. 4).

Cost of the Financing Plan under the Trade-off Approach

(i) Cost of short-term funds: = (Average annual short-term funds required) × (Rate of short-term interest) = ₹2,700 lakh/12 = ₹225 lakh × 0.03 = ₹6.75 lakh

(ii) Cost of long-term funds = (Average long-term funds required) × (Rate of interest on long-term funds) = ₹7,950 lakh × 0.08 = ₹636 lakh

(iii) Total cost of the trade-off plan = ₹6.75 lakh + ₹636 lakh = ₹642.75 lakh

Risk Consideration The NWC under this plan would be ₹1,050 lakh (₹7,950 lakh – ₹6,900 lakh).

Comparison of the Trade-off Plan with the Hedging and Conservative Approaches For a comparison of the three approaches to determine an appropriate financing-mix, the summary of the results of these approaches on profitability and risk is given in Table 13.3.

TABLE 13.3 Comparison of Trade-off Plan *(Amount in ₹ lakh)*

Financing Plan	*Maximum NWC**	*Degree of risk*	*Total cost of financing*	*Level of profits*
(1)	*(2)*	*(3)*	*(4)*	*(5)*
Hedging	0	Highest	₹581.00	Highest
Trade-off	₹1,050	Intermediate	642.75	Intermediate
Conservative	2,100	Lowest	720.00	Lowest

*The minimum level would be zero in each case.

Interpretation From the summary of results in Table 13.3, it can be seen clearly that the hedging approach is the most risky while the conservative approach is the least risky. The trade-off plan stands midway; less risky than the hedging approach but more risky than the conservative approach. The measure of risk is the level of NWC. From the point of view of profitability (as reflected in the level of total cost of financing plan) a similar kind of relationship is found to exist, the trade-off plan lying between the other two approaches. The preceding analysis, thus, established the trade-off between profitability and risk. In this connection two generalisations are warranted: **(i)** the lower the NWC, the higher is the risk present, and **(ii)** the higher the risk of insolvency, the higher is the expected profits.

LO 13.2 PLANNING OF WORKING CAPITAL

The main aspects covered here are the need for working capital, the determinants of working capital and its computation.

Need for Working Capital

Operating cycle implies the continuing flow from cash to suppliers, to inventory to accounts receivable and back into cash.

The need for working capital (gross) or current assets cannot be overemphasized. Given the objective of financial decision making to maximsie the shareholders' wealth, it is necessary to generate sufficient profits. The extent to which profits can be earned will naturally depend, among other things, upon the magnitude of the sales. A successful sales programme is, in other words, necessary for earning profits by any business enterprise. However, sales do not convert into cash instantly; there is invariably a time-lag between the sale of goods and the receipt of cash. There is, therefore, a need for working capital in the form of current assets to deal with the problem arising out of the lack of immediate realisation of cash against goods sold. Therefore, sufficient working capital is necessary to sustain sales activity. Technically, this is referred to as the **operating** *or cash cycle.* The operating cycle can be said to be at the heart of the need for working capital. 'The continuing flow from cash to suppliers, to inventory, to accounts receivable and back into cash is what is called the operating cycle'.[6] In other words, the term cash cycle refers to the length of time necessary to complete the following cycle of events:

1. Conversion of cash into inventory;
2. Conversion of inventory into receivables;
3. Conversion of receivables into cash.

The operating cycle, which is a continuous process, is shown in Fig. 13.1.

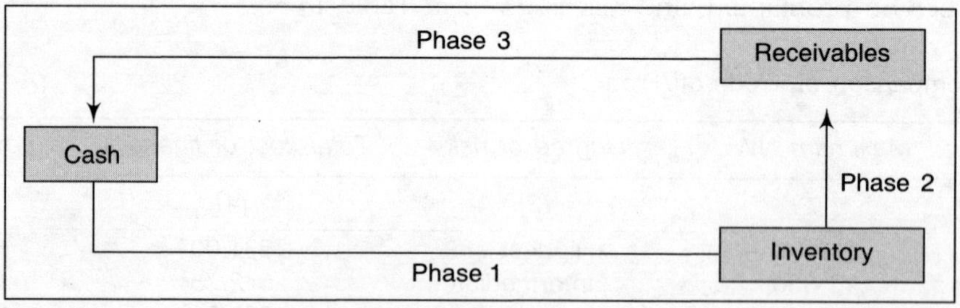

FIGURE 13.1 *Operating Cycle*

If it were possible to complete the sequences instantaneously, there would be no need for current assets (working capital). But since it is not possible, the firm is forced to have current assets. Since cash inflows and outflows do not match, firms have to necessarily keep cash or invest in short-term liquid securities so that they will be in a position to meet obligations when they become due.

Similarly, firms must have adequate inventory to guard against the possibility of not being able to meet demand for their products. Adequate inventory, therefore, provides a cushion against being out of stock. If firms have to be competitive, they must sell goods to their customers on credit which necessitates the holding of accounts receivable. It is in these ways that an adequate level of working capital is absolutely necessary for smooth sales activity which, in turn, enhances the owner's wealth.

The operating cycle consists of three phases. In phase 1, cash gets converted into inventory. This includes purchase of raw materials, conversion of raw materials into work-in-progress, finished goods and finally the transfer of goods to stock at the end of the manufacturing process. In the case of trading organisations, this phase is shorter as there would be no manufacturing activity and cash is directly converted into inventory. The phase is, of course, totally absent in the case of service organisations.

In phase II of the cycle, the inventory is converted into receivables as credit sales are made to customers. Firms which do not sell on credit obviously not have phase II of the operating cycle.

The last phase, phase III, represents the stage when receivables are collected. This phase completes the operating cycle. Thus, the firm has moved from cash to inventory, to receivables and to cash again.

Permanent and Temporary Working Capital The operating cycle, thus, creates the need for current assets (working capital). However, the need does not come to an end after the cycle is completed. It continues to exist. To explain this continuing need of current assets, a distinction should be drawn between *permanent* and *temporary* working capital.

Business activity does not come to an end after the realisation of cash from customers. For a company, the process is continuous and, hence, the need for a regular supply of working capital. However, the magnitude of working capital required is not constant, but fluctuating. To carry on business, a certain minimum level of working capital is necessary on a continuous and uninterrupted basis. For all practical purposes, this requirement has to be met permanently as with other fixed assets. This requirement is referred to as **permanent or fixed working capital**.

> **Permanent (fixed) working capital** is a certain minimum level of working capital on a continuous and uninterrupted basis.

Any amount over and above the permanent level of working capital is **temporary, fluctuating or variable working capital**.[7] The position of the required working capital is needed to meet fluctuations in demand consequent upon changes in production and sales as a result of seasonal changes. The basic distinction between permanent and temporary working capital is illustrated in Fig. 13.2.

> **Temporary (fluctuating/ variable) working capital** is the working capital needed to meet seasonal as well as unforeseen requirements.

Figure 13.2 shows that the permanent level is fairly constant, while temporary working capital is fluctuating–increasing and decreasing in accordance with seasonal demands. In the case of an expanding firm, the permanent working capital line may not be horizontal. This is because the demand for permanent current assets might be increasing (or decreasing) to support a rising level of activity. In that case the line would be a rising one as shown in Fig. 13.3.

Both kinds of working capital are necessary to facilitate the sales process through the operating cycle. Temporary working capital is created to meet liquidity requirements that are of a purely transient nature.

Changes in Working Capital The changes in the level of working capital occur for the following three basic reasons: **(i)** changes in the level of sales and/or operating expenses, **(ii)** policy changes, and **(iii)** changes in technology.

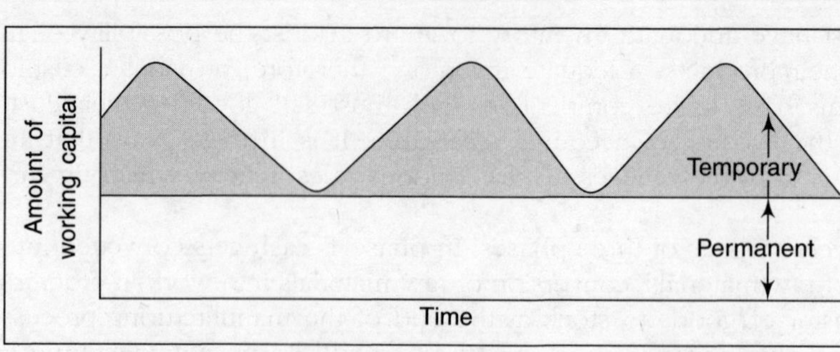

FIGURE 13.2 *Permanent and Temporary Working Capital*

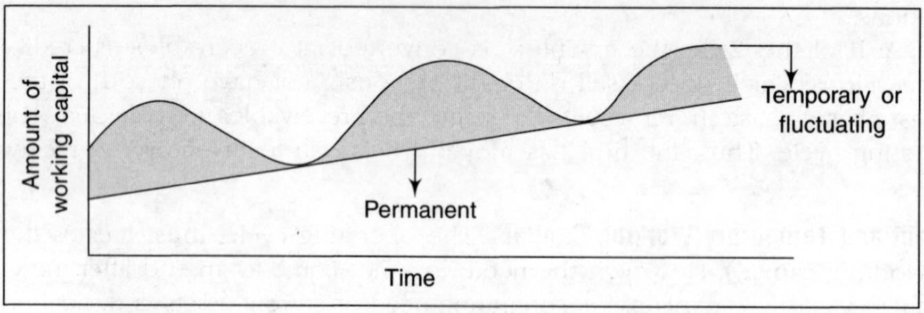

FIGURE 13.3 *Permanent and Temporary Working Capital*

Changes in Sales and Operating Expenses The first factor causing a change in the working capital requirement is a change in the sales and operating expenses. The changes in this factor may be due to three reasons: First, there may be a *long-run* trend of change. For instance, the price of a raw material, say oil, may constantly rise, necessitating the holding of a large inventory. The *secular* trends would mainly affect the need for permanent current assets. In the second place, *cyclical* changes in the economy leading to ups and downs in business activity influence the level of working capital, both permanent and temporary. The third source of change is seasonality in sales activity. Seasonality–peaks and troughs–can be said to be the main source of variation in the level of temporary working capital.

The change in sales and operating expenses may be either in the form of an increase or decrease. An increase in the volume of sales is bound to be accompanied by higher levels of cash, inventory and receivables. The decline in sales has exactly the opposite effect–a decline in the need for working capital. A change in the operating expenses–rise or fall–has a similar effect on the levels of working capital.

Current assets policy is the relationship between current assets and sales volume.

Policy Changes The second major cause of changes in the level of working capital is because of policy changes initiated by the management. There is a wide choice in the matter of **current assets policy**. The term current asset policy may be defined as the relationship between current assets and sales volume. A firm following a conservative policy in this respect having a very high level of current assets in relation to sales may deliberately opt for a less conservative policy and *vice versa.* These conscious managerial decisions certainly have an impact on the level of working capital.

Technological Changes Finally, technological changes can cause significant changes in the level of working capital. If a new process emerges as a result of technological developments, which shortens the operating cycle, it reduces the need for working capital and *vice versa*.

Determinants of Working Capital

A firm should plan its operations in such a way that it should have neither too much nor too little working capital. The total working capital requirement is determined by a wide variety of factors. These factors, however, affect different enterprises differently. They also vary from time to time. In general, the following factors are involved in a proper assessment of the quantum of working capital required.

General Nature of Business The working capital requirements of an enterprise are basically related to the conduct of business. Enterprises fall into some broad categories depending on the nature of their business. For instance, public utilities have certain features which have a bearing on their working capital needs. The two relevant features are: **(i)** the cash nature of business, that is, cash sale, and **(ii)** sale of services rather than commodities. In view of these features, they do not maintain big inventories and have, therefore, probably the least requirement of working capital. At the other extreme are trading and financial enterprises. The nature of their business is such that they have to maintain a sufficient amount of cash, inventories and book debts. They have necessarily to invest proportionately large amounts in working capital. The manufacturing enterprises fall, in a sense, between these two extremes. The industrial concerns require fairly large amounts of working capital though it varies from industry to industry depending on their asset structure. The proportion of current assets to total assets measures the relative requirements of working capital of various industries. Available data in respect of companies in India confirm the wide variations in the use of working capital by different enterprises. The percentage of current assets to total assets was found to be the lowest in hotels, restaurants and eating houses (10-20 per cent range), while in electricity generation and supply it was in the range of 20-30 per cent. The enterprises in the tobacco, construction and trading groups had, as is to be expected, the highest component of working capital (80-90 per cent range). The other industrial groups fall between these limits though there are very wide inter-industry variations.[8]

Production Cycle Another factor which has a bearing on the quantum of working capital is the production cycle. The term 'production or manufacturing cycle' refers to the time involved in the manufacture of goods. It covers the time-span between the procurement of raw materials and the completion of the manufacturing process leading to the production of finished goods. Funds have to be necessarily tied up during the process of manufacture, necessitating *enhanced* working capital. In other words, there is some time gap before raw materials become finished goods. To sustain such activities the need for working capital is obvious. The longer the time-span (i.e. the production cycle), the larger will be the tied-up funds and, therefore, the larger is the working capital needed and *vice versa.* There are enterprises which, due to the nature of business, have a short operating cycle. A distillery, which has an ageing process, has generally to make a relatively heavy investment in inventory. The other extreme is provided by a bakery. The bakeries sell their products at short intervals and have a very high inventory turnover. The investment in inventory and, consequently, working capital is not very large.

Further, even within the same group of industries, the operating cycle may be different due to technological considerations. For economy in working capital, that process should be selected which has a shorter manufacturing process. Having selected a particular process of manufacture, steps should be taken to ensure that the cycle is completed in the expected time. This underlines the need for effective organisation and coordination at all levels of the enterprise. Appropriate policies concerning terms of credit for raw materials and other supplies can help in reducing working capital requirements. Often, companies manufacturing heavy machinery and equipment minimise the investment in inventory or working capital by requiring advance payment from customers as work proceeds against orders. Thus, a part of the financial burden relating to the manufacturing cycle time is passed on to others.

Business Cycle The working capital requirements are also determined by the nature of the business cycle. Business fluctuations lead to cyclical and seasonal changes which, in turn, cause a shift in the working capital position, particularly for temporary working capital requirements. The variations in business conditions may be in two directions: **(i)** *upward phase* when boom conditions prevail, and **(ii)** *downswing phase* when economic activity is marked by a decline. During the upswing of business activity, the need for working capital is likely to grow to cover the lag between increased sales and receipt of cash as well as to finance purchases of additional material to cater to the expansion of the level of activity. Additional funds may be required to invest in plant and machinery to meet the increased demand. The downswing phase of the business cycle has exactly an opposite effect on the level of working capital requirement. The decline in the economy is associated with a fall in the volume of sales which, in turn, leads to a fall in the level of inventories and book debts. The need for working capital in recessionary conditions is bound to decline. In brief, business fluctuations influence the size of working capital mainly through the effect on inventories. The response of inventory to business cycles is mild or violent according to nature of the business cycle.

Production Policy The quantum of working capital is also determined by production policy. In the case of certain lines of business, the demand for products is seasonal, that is, they are purchased during certain months of the year. What kind of production policy should be followed in such cases? There are two options open to such enterprises: either they confine their production only to periods when goods are purchased or they follow a steady production policy throughout the year and produce goods at a level to meet the peak demand. In the former case, there are serious production problems. During the slack season, the firms have to maintain their working force and physical facilities without adequate production and sale. When the peak period arrives, the firms have to operate at full capacity to meet the demand. This kind of arrangement would not only be expensive but also inconvenient. Thus, serious difficulties will be encountered in trying to match production to the ebb and flow of the seasonal demand pattern. A better alternative is a steady production policy independent of shifts in demand for the finished goods. This means a large accumulation of finished goods (inventories) during the off-season and their abrupt sale during the peak season. The progressive accumulation of stock naturally requires an increasing amount of working capital which remains tied up for some months. Working capital planning has to incorporate this pattern of requirement of funds when production and seasonal sales are steady. This strategy (steady production policy) is, however, not necessarily adopted by everyone. It may be possible, for instance, for some to follow a policy of diversification which enables them to engage the working force and the physical facilities in some other activity. If this is possible, there will be no major working capital problem. Moreover, the nature of some products may be such that accumulation of inventories may create special risk and cost problems. For them, a production policy in tune with the changing demands may be preferable. Therefore, production policies have to be formulated on the basis of the individual setting of each enterprise and the magnitude and dimension of the working capital problems will accordingly vary.

Credit Policy The credit policy relating to sales and purchases also affects the working capital. The credit policy influences the requirement of working capital in two ways: **(i)** through credit terms granted by the firm to its customers/buyers of goods; **(ii)** credit terms available to the firm from its creditors.

The credit terms granted to customers have a bearing on the magnitude of working capital by determining the level of book debts. The credit sales result in higher book debts (receivables). Higher book debts mean more working capital. On the other hand, if liberal credit terms are available from the suppliers of goods (trade creditors), the need for working capital is less. The working capital requirements of a business are, thus, affected by the terms of purchase and sale, and the role given to credit by a company in its dealings with creditors and debtors.

Credit terms fixed by an enterprise are affected by the prevailing trade practices as well as changing economic conditions. If, for example, competition is keen, there would be pressure to grant generous credit terms. Nevertheless, there is wide scope for managerial discretion in working out a suitable credit policy relevant to each customer based on the merits of each case. For instance, liberal credit facilities can be extended on the basis of credit rating. This will avoid the problem of having excess working capital. Similarly, the collection procedure can be so framed that funds, which would otherwise be available for meeting operating needs[9] are not locked up. Thus, adoption of rationalised credit policies would be a significant factor in determining the working capital needs of an enterprise.

Such discretion may, however, not be available to a company which operates in a highly competitive market. To win and retain customers, it may be forced, among other things, to offer generous credit terms to them. The investment in book debts will consequently be of a higher order, necessitating large working capital in another way. To be able to enjoy consumer patronage on a continuous basis, a firm will have to offer a variety of products quite unlike a firm which has a hold on the market and, hence, does not need special efforts to satisfy customer requirements. The consequence of a higher level of inventories would be an additional need for working capital. The degree of competition is, therefore, an important factor influencing working capital requirements.

Growth and Expansion As a company grows, it is logical to expect that a larger amount of working capital is required. It is, of course, difficult to determine precisely the relationship between the growth in the volume of business of a company and the increase in its working capital. The composition of working capital in a growing company also shifts with economic circumstances and corporate practices. Other things being equal, growth industries require more working capital than those that are static. 'The critical fact, however, is that the need for increased working capital funds does not follow the growth in business activities but precedes it.'[10] Advance planning of working capital is, therefore, a continuing necessity for a growing concern. Or else, the company may have substantial earnings but little cash.

Vagaries in the Availability of Raw Material The availability or otherwise of certain raw materials on a continuous basis without interruption would sometimes affect the requirement of working capital. There may be some materials which cannot be procured easily either because of their sources are few or they are irregular. To sustain smooth production, therefore, the firm might be compelled to purchase and stock them far in excess of genuine production needs. This will result in an excessive inventory of such materials. The procurement of some essential raw materials is difficult because of their sporadic supply. This happens very often with raw materials which are in short supply and are controlled to ensure equitable distribution. The buyer has in such cases very limited options as to the quantum and timing of procurement. It may so happen that a bulk consignment may be available but the firm may be short of funds, while when surplus funds are available the commodities may be in short supply. This element of uncertainty would lead to a relatively high level of working capital. Finally, some raw materials may be available only during certain seasons. They would have to be necessarily obtained, when available, to provide for a period when supplies are lean. This will cause seasonal fluctuations in working capital requirements.

Profit Level The level of profits earned differ from enterprise to enterprise. In general, the nature of the product, hold on the market, quality of management and monopoly power would by and large determine the profit earned by a firm. *A priori*, it can be generalised that a firm dealing in a high quality product, having a good marketing arrangement and enjoying monopoly power in the market, is likely to earn high profits and vice versa. Higher profit margin would improve the prospects of generating more internal funds thereby contributing to the working capital pool. *The net profit is a source of working capital to the extent that it has been earned in cash*. The cash profit can be found by adjusting non-cash items such as depreciation, outstanding expenses and losses written off, in the net profit. But, in practice, the net cash inflows from operations cannot be considered as cash available for use at the end of cash cycle. Even as the company's operations are in progress, cash is used for augmenting stock, book debts and fixed assets.[11] It must, therefore, be seen that cash generation has been used for furthering the interest of the enterprise. It is in this context that elaborate planning and projections of expected activities and the resulting cash inflows on a day-to-day, week-to-week and month-to-month basis assume importance because steps can then be taken to deal with surplus and deficit cash.

The availability of internal funds for working capital requirements is determined not merely by the profit margin but also by the manner of appropriating profits. The availability of such funds would depend upon the profit appropriations for taxation, dividend, reserves and depreciations.

Level of Taxes The first appropriation out of profits is payment or provision for tax. The amount of taxes to be paid is determined by the prevailing tax regulations. The management has no discretion in this respect. Very often, taxes have to be paid in advance on the basis of the profit of the preceding year. Tax liability is, in a sense, short-term liability payable in cash. An adequate provision for tax payments is, therefore, an important aspect of working capital planning. If tax liability increases, it leads to an increase in the requirement of working capital and vice versa. Management has no discretion in regard to the payment of taxes; in some cases non-payment may invite penal action. There is, however, wide scope to reduce the tax liability through proper tax planning. The service of tax experts can be availed of to take advantage of the various concessions and incentives through avoidance as opposed to evasion of taxes. Tax planning can, therefore, be said to be an integral part of working capital planning.

Dividend Policy Another appropriation of profits which has a bearing on working capital is dividend payment. The payment of dividend consumes cash resources and, thereby, affects working capital to that extent. Conversely, if the firm does not pay dividend but retains the profits, working capital increases. In planning working capital requirements, therefore, a basic question to be decided is whether profits will be retained or paid out to shareholders. In theory, a firm should retain profits to preserve cash resources and, at the same time, it must pay dividends to satisfy the expectations of investors. When profits are relatively small, the choice is between retention and payment. The choice must be made after taking into account all the relevant factors.

There are wide variations in industry practices as regards the interrelationship between working capital requirements and dividend payment. In some cases, shortage of working capital has been a powerful reason for reducing or even skipping dividends in cash. There are occasions, on the other hand, when dividend payments are continued in spite of inadequate earnings in a particular year because of sound liquidity. Sometimes, the dilemma is resolved by the payment of bonus shares. This enables the payment of dividend without draining away the cash resources and, thus, without reducing working capital. Dividend policy, is thus, a significant element in determining the level of working capital in an organisation.

Depreciation Policy Depreciation policy also exerts an influence on the quantum of working capital. Depreciation charges do not involve any cash outflows. The effect of depreciation policy on working capital is, therefore, indirect. In the first place, depreciation affects the tax liability and retention of profits. Depreciation is allowable expenditure in calculating net profits. Enhanced rates of depreciation lower the profits and, therefore, the tax liability and, thus, more cash profits. Higher depreciation also means lower disposable profits and, therefore, a smaller dividend payment. Thus, cash is preserved. In the second place, the selection of the method of depreciation has important financial implications. If current capital expenditure falls short of the depreciation provision, the working capital position is strengthened and there may be no need for short-term borrowing. If, on the other hand, the current capital expenditure exceeds the depreciation provision, either outside borrowing will have to be resorted to or a restriction on dividend payment coupled with retention of profits will have to be adopted to prevent the working capital position from being adversely affected. It is in these ways that depreciation policy is relevant to the planning of working capital.

Price Level Changes Changes in the price level also affect the requirements of working capital. Rising prices necessitate the use of more funds for maintaining an existing level of activity. For the same level of current assets, higher cash outlays are required. The effect of rising prices is that a higher amount of working capital is needed. However, in the case of companies which can raise their prices proportionately, there is no serious problem regarding working capital. Moreover, the price rise does not have a uniform effect on all commodities. It is likely that some firms may not be affected at all. In brief, the implications of changing price levels on working capital position vary from company to company depending on the nature of its operations, its standing in the market and other relevant considerations.

Operating Efficiency The operating efficiency of the management is also an important determinant of the level of working capital. The management can contribute to a sound working capital position through operating efficiency. Although the management cannot control the rise in prices, it can ensure the efficient utilisation of resources by eliminating waste, improving coordination, and a fuller utilisation of existing resources, and so on. Efficiency of operations accelerates the pace of cash cycle and improves the working capital turnover. It releases the pressure on working capital by improving profitability and improving the internal generation of funds.

To conclude, the level of working capital is determined by a wide variety of factors which are partly internal to the firm and partly external (environmental) to it. Efficient working capital management requires efficient planning and a constant review of the needs for an appropriate working capital strategy.

Computation of Working Capital

The two components of working capital (WC) are current assets (CA) and current liabilities (CL). They have a bearing on the cash operating cycle. In order to calculate the working capital needs, what is required is the holding period of various types of inventories, the credit collection period and the credit payment period. Working capital also depends on the budgeted level of activity in terms of production/sales. The calculation of WC is based on the assumption that the production/sales is carried on evenly throughout the year and all costs accrue similarly. As the working capital requirements are related to the cost excluding depreciation and not to the sale price, WC is computed with reference to cash cost. The cash cost approach is comprehensive and superior to the operating cycle approach based on holding period of debtors and inventories and payment period of creditors. Some problems have been solved, however, using the operating cycle approach also.

The steps involved in estimating the different items of CA and CL are as follows:

Estimation of Current Assets: *Raw Materials Inventory* The investment in raw materials inventory is estimated on the basis of Eq. 13.1.

$$\frac{\begin{matrix}\text{Budgeted} \\ \text{production} \\ \text{(in units)}\end{matrix} \times \begin{matrix}\text{Cost of raw} \\ \text{material(s)} \\ \text{per unit}\end{matrix} \times \begin{matrix}\text{Average inventory} \\ \text{holding period} \\ \text{(months/days)}\end{matrix}}{\text{12 months/365 days}} \qquad \textbf{(13.1)}$$

Work-in-Process (W/P) Inventory The relevant costs to determine work-in-process inventory are the proportionate share of cost of raw materials and conversion costs (labour and manufacturing overhead costs excluding depreciation).[12] In case, full unit of raw material is required in the beginning, the unit cost of work-in-process would be higher, that is, cost of full unit + 50 per cent of conversion cost, compared to the raw material requirement throughout the production cycle; W/P is normally equivalent to 50 per cent of total cost of production. Symbolically,

$$\frac{\text{Budgeted production (in units)} \times \text{Estimated work-in-process cost per unit} \times \text{Average time span of work-in-progress inventory (months/days)}}{\text{12 months/365 days}} \quad \textbf{(13.2)}$$

Finished Goods Inventory Working capital required to finance the inished goods inventory is given by factors summed up in Eq. 13.3.

$$\frac{\text{Budgeted production (in units)} \times \text{Cost of goods produced per unit (excluding depreciation)} \times \text{Finished goods holding period (months/days)}}{\text{12 months/365 days}} \quad \textbf{(13.3)}$$

Debtors The WC tied up in debtors should be estimated in relation to total cost price (excluding depreciation) Symbolically,

$$\frac{\text{Budgeted credit sales (in units)} \times \text{Cost of sales per unit excluding depreciation} \times \text{Average debt collection period (months/days)}}{\text{12 months/365 days}} \quad \textbf{(13.4)}$$

Cash and Bank Balances Apart from WC needs for financing inventories and debtors, firms also find it useful to have some minimum cash balances with them. It is difficult to lay down the exact procedure of determining such an amount. This would primarily be based on the motives for holding cash balances[13] of the business firm, attitude of management toward risk, the access to the borrowing sources in times of need and past experience, and so on.

Estimation of Current Liabilities The working capital needs of business firms are lower to the that extent such needs are met through the current liabilities (other than bank credit[14]) arising in the ordinary course of business. The important current liabilities (CL), in this context are, trade-creditors, wages and overheads:

Trade Creditors

$$\frac{\text{Budgeted yearly production (in units)} \times \text{Raw material cost per unit} \times \text{Credit period allowed by creditors (months/days)}}{\text{12 months/365 days}} \quad \textbf{(13.5)}$$

Note: Proportional adjustment should be made to cash purchases of raw materials.

Direct Wages

$$\frac{\text{Budgeted yearly production (in units)} \times \text{Direct labour cost per unit} \times \text{Average time-lag in payment of wages (months/days)}}{\text{12 months/365 days}} \quad \textbf{(13.6)}$$

The average credit period for the payment of wages approximates to a half-a-month in the case of monthly wage payment: The first days' monthly wages are paid on the 30th day of the month, extending credit for 29 days, the second day's wages are, again, paid on the 30th, extending credit for 28 days, and so on. Average credit period approximates to half-a-month.

Overheads (Other than Depreciation and Amortisation)

$$\frac{\text{Budgeted yearly production (in units)} \times \text{Overhead cost per unit} \times \text{Average time-lag in payment of overheads (months/days)}}{\text{12 months/365 days}} \quad (13.7)$$

Goods and Services Tax (GST)

$$\text{Budgeted yearly sales (in units)} \times \text{GST per unit} \times \text{Average time-lag in payment of GST (weeks/days)} \quad (13.8)$$

The amount of overheads may be separately calculated for different types of overheads. In the case of selling overheads, the relevant item would be sales volume instead of production volume. Since cash cost approach is the basis of determining NWC, the sums due to provision for taxes are excluded as they are payable only when the firm has profits; likewise, it is equally important to note the rationale of excluding short-term bank loan and bank overdraft; the rationale is computation of working capital should indicate the required amount of NWC and not the source of financing it. Obviously, the inclusion of source would distort the NWC required.

The computation of working capital is summarised in format 13.1.

FORMAT 13.1 *Determination of Working Capital*

	Amount
(I) *Estimation of Current Asset*:	
(a) Minimum desired cash and bank balances	
(b) Inventories	
Raw material	
Work-in-process	
Finished Goods	
(c) Debtors*	
Total Current Assets	
(II) *Estimation of Current Liabilities*:	
(a) Creditors**	
(b) Wages	
(c) Overheads	
(d) Goods and Services Tax (GST)	
Total Current Liabilities	
(III) *Net Working Capital (I – II)*	
Add margin for contingency	
(IV) Net Working Capital Required	

*If payment is received in advance, the item would be listed in CL.

**If advance payment is to be made to creditors, the item would appear under CA. The same would be the treatment for advance payment of wages and overheads.

LO 13.3 MANAGEMENT OF WORKING CAPITAL IN INDIA

- Indian corporates seem to have adequate and satisfactory level of working capital as reflected in their liquidity ratios. The foreign controlled companies are placed in a better position relative to the domestic companies.
- There are wide inter-industry variations in the liquidity ratios of the corporate enterprises. With the exception of sugar, all other industry groups have safe and satisfactory liquidity position.
- The majority of Indian companies maintains relatively lower cash/bank balances. Marketable securities have emerged as a popular means of cash management. The excess cash is also deployed to retire short-term debt/in short-term bank deposits. Bank overdraft/cash credit has been cited as the major source of dealing with cash deficit situations by the vast majority of the sample companies. Discounting bill receivables and having special arrangement with some lending agency are less frequently used techniques by them to meet such situations.
- In spite of the notable decline over the years, inventory constitutes a sizeable part of the total current assets of the Indian corporates. The most important objective of inventory management in India is 'avoid loss of production/sales'. The popular control techniques are ABC, FSN and SDE and inventory turnover ratio and comparison with competitors are widely used to assess the performance of inventory management. The low average value of inventory holding periods of raw materials and space parts, work-in-process and finished goods for eleven years (2001-2011) period is indicative of efficient inventory management of the sample companies.
- Debtors/receivables also constitute a significant component of current assets. 'growth in sales' is the most important objective of credit policy and the 'open credit with approval if exceeds a specified limit' is the most favoured policy. It is common practice to prepare 'ageing schedule' of debtors' to assess the financial health of the customers before granting credit and monitoring purposes. To speed up collections, the corporates offer cash discount. The majority of the companies also charge penal interest. The vast majority of sample companies do not reckon 'offering credit terms better than those of competitors' as the primary objective of the credit policy.
- Accounts payable and short-term loans/advances are the major components of current liabilities.
- The 'length of the operating cycle' is the most widely use method to determine working capital need. The working capital financing policy is based on the matching approach. The majority of the companies have occasionally experienced working capital shortage due mainly to excess inventory accumulation and poor debt collection.
- The sample companies have increasingly become more aggressive in managing their working capital with more than one-fourth companies operating at a zero working capital in 2011 compared to 14.8 per cent in 2001.

Source: Jain, P.K. and Yadav, S.S, *op. cit,* pp 81-102. Also Singh, Shveta, P. K. Jain and Surendra S. Yadav, "Working Capital Management: Empirical Evidence From Indian Corporates". *The Management Accountant*, Vol. 48, No. 6, 2013, pp. 691-706.

SUMMARY

LO 13.1

Working capital management is concerned with the problems that arise in managing the current assets (CA), current liabilities (CL) and the interrelationships between them. Its operational goal is to manage the CA and CL in such a way that a satisfactory/acceptable level of net working capital (NWC) is maintained.

There are three concepts of working capital (WC): gross, net and zero. The gross WC means the total CA. The NWC is the difference between the CA and CL. Zero WC = inventories plus receivables minus payables.

LO 13.1	The NWC is necessary due to non-synchronous nature of expected cash inflows and required cash outflows. The more predictable the cash inflows are, the less NWC will be required and *vice-versa.* The NWC represents the liquidity position of a firm.
	The NWC has a bearing on liquidity, profitability and risk of becoming technically insolvent. In general, the greater is the NWC, the higher is the liquidity, the lower is the risk and the profitability, and *vice-versa.* The trade-off between profitability and risk is an important element in the evaluation of the level of NWC of a firm.
	Determination of financing mix is another important constituent of WC management. The financing mix refers to the proportion of CA to be financed by short-term sources (CL) and long-term sources (such as share capital and long-term borrowings). It is concerned with determination of relative share of these two broad sources in financing CA.
	There are three approaches to determine an appropriate financing mix: (i) hedging/matching approach, (ii) conservative approach and (iii) trade-off between these two.
	According to hedging approach, long-term funds should be used to finance the permanent/core part of the CA and the purely temporary and seasonal requirements (over and above the permanent needs) should be met out of short-term funds. This approach is a high profit-high risk financing mix.
	According to the conservative approach, the estimated total requirements of the CA should be financed from long-term sources. The short-term sources of finance should be used only in emergency situations. The firm has NWC equal to the excess of long-term financing over the permanent requirement. This approach is a low-profit, low-risk combination.
	Neither the hedging approach nor the conservative approach is suitable for determining an appropriate financing mix. A trade-off between these two extreme approaches would give an acceptable financing strategy.
LO 13.2	The need for working capital (WC) arises from the cash/operating cycle of a firm. It refers to the length of time required to complete the following sequence of events: conversion of cash into inventory, inventory into receivables and receivables into cash. The operating cycle creates the need for working capital and its length in terms of time-span required to complete the cycle is the major determinant of the firm's working capital needs.
	Working capital can be (i) permanent and (ii) temporary. While the permanent component reflects the need for a certain irreducible level of current assets on a continuous and uninterrupted basis, the temporary portion is needed to meet seasonal and other temporary requirements. While permanent working capital requirements should be financed from long-term sources, short-term funds should be used to finance temporary working capital needs of a firm.
	Working capital requirements are determined by a variety of factors. These factors, however, affect different enterprises differently. In general, the factors relevant for proper assessment of the quantum of working capital required are: general nature of business, production cycle, business cycle, production policy, credit policy, growth and expansion, availability of raw materials, profit-level, level of taxes, dividend policy, depreciation policy, price level changes and operating efficiency.
	Manufacturing and trading enterprises require fairly large amounts of working capital to maintain a sufficient amount of cash, inventories and book debts to support their production (purchases) and sales activity. Service enterprises (like public utilities) and hotels, restaurants and eating houses need to carry less WC.
	The longer is the production cycle, the larger is the WC needed or *vice-versa.*
	While during boom conditions, reflecting upswing in business activity, the need for WC is likely to grow to cater to the increased level of activity, the need for working capital in the downswing phase/recessionary conditions tend to be low due to fall in the volume of sales and production.
	While the liberal credit policy offered to customers would necessitate more working capital, tight credit terms would reduce its requirement. The liberal credit terms available from creditors/suppliers of materials would be an offsetting factor.

LO 13.2
Growth industries and firms require more working capital.
To meet vagaries in the unavailability, a firm should have excess inventory of raw materials to sustain smooth production. Such a firm would tend to have high level of WC.
Cash profit, *per-se*, should not be viewed as a source of financing WC. The actual availability of such funds would depend upon the firm's requirement for payment of dividend, payment of loan instalment, creation of sinking fund, purchase of fixed assets, and so on. In case these requirements are substantial, cash profit is not likely to be available to meet the needs of a firm. Alternatively, only adjusted cash profits after provisioning for these requirements should be reckoned for WC financing.
The payment of dividend consumes cash resources and, therefore, decreases WC of a firm. Conversely, the non-payment of dividend increases WC.
Higher depreciation (enhanced rates of depreciations) has a positive impact on WC for two reasons: (i) lower tax liability and, hence, more cash profits and (ii) lower disposable profits and, therefore, a smaller dividend payment. They imply more cash with a corporate.
Rising prices in input costs (without corresponding increase or less than a proportionate increase in selling prices of products) necessitates more WC to sustain an existing level of activity.
Efficiency of operations accelerates the pace of cash cycle and improves the WC turnover resulting in reduced requirement of WC.
A firm should have adequate WC to support its budgeted level of activity in terms of production/sales. It should have neither more nor less WC than required. While the excessive WC adversely affects its profits, the inadequate WC interrupts its smooth operations. Therefore, its correct computation is an important constituent of efficient WC management.
There are two components of WC, namely, CA and CL. Each component is to be separately estimated to determine the correct amount of WC. The relevant factors are the holding periods of the various types of inventories, debtors collection period, creditors payment period, budgeted yearly production/sales, cost of goods produced, cost of sales, average time-lag in payment of wages and other overheads, average time-lag in payment of goods and services tax (GST), minimum cash balances and so on.
Working capital requirements are to be computed with reference to cash costs (excluding depreciation) and not the sale price as depreciation is a non-cash cost and, hence, does not need WC. The investment required to finance debtors are at cost price. The 'cash cost approach' is appropriate to determine WC requirement of a firm.

REFERENCES

13.1 Gitman, L J, *Principles of Managerial Finance*, Harper and Row, New York, 1997, p. 150.

13.2 For details, refer to Brigham, E F and J F Houston, *op. cit.*, p. 570-71.

13.3 Brigham, E F and J F Houston, *op. cit.*, p. 572.

13.4 Brigham, E F and J F Houston, *Ibid.*, p. 573.

13.5 *Ibid.*, p. 157.

13.6 Joy, O M, *Introduction to Financial Management*, Richard D Irwin, Homewood, Ill. 1977, p. 406.

13.7 *Ibid.*, p. 407.

13.8 Ramamoorthy, V E, *Working Capital Management*, Institute of Financial Management and Research Madras, 1976, p. 54.

13.9 These aspects are covered in detail in Chapter 15.

13.10 Ramamoorthy, V E, *op. cit.*, p. 58.

13.11 *Ibid.*, p. 60.

13.12 Administrative overheads are normally ignored for valuation of work-in-process. Depreciation is excluded as it does not involve any cash expenditure.

13.13 Please refer to Chapter 14.

13.14 Bank credit is excluded as it is a source of finance of WC.

SOLVED PROBLEMS

P.13.1 X & Y Ltd is desirous to purchase a business and has consulted you, and one point on which you are asked to advise them, is the average amount of working capital which will be required in the first year's working. LO 13.2 LOD M

You are given the following estimates and are instructed to add 10 per cent to your computed figure to allow for contingencies.

Particulars	*Amount for the year*
(i) Average amount backed up for stocks:	
Stocks of finished product	₹5,000
Stocks of stores and materials	8,000
(ii) Average credit given:	
Inland sales, 6 weeks' credit	3,12,000
Export sales, 1.5 weeks' credit	78,000
(iii) Average time lag in payment of wages and other outgoings:	
Wages, 1.5 weeks	2,60,000
Stocks and materials, 1.5 months	48,000
Rent and royalties, 6 months	10,000
Clerical staff, 0.5 month	62,400
Manager, 0.5 month	4,800
Miscellaneous expenses, 1.5 months	48,000
(iv) Payment in advance:	
Sundry expenses (paid quarterly in advance)	8,000
Undrawn profits on an average throughout the year	11,000

Set up your calculations for the average amount of working capital required.

Solution

Statement to determine net working capital for X & Y Ltd

(a) Current assets:	
(i) Stock of finished product	₹5,000
(ii) Stock of stores and materials	8,000
(iii) Debtors:	
Inland sales (₹3,12,000 × 6/52)	36,000
Export sales, (₹78,000 × 3/104)	2,250
(iv) Advance payment of sundry expenses (₹8,000 × 1/4)	2,000
Total investment in current assets	53,250
(b) Current liabilities:	
(i) Wages (₹2,60,000 × 3/104)	7,500
(ii) Stocks/materials, (₹48,000 × 3/24)	6,000
(iii) Rent, royalties, (₹10,000 × 6/12)	5,000
(iv) Clerical staff (₹62,400 × 1/24)	2,600
(v) Manager (₹4,800 × 1/24)	200
(vi) Miscellaneous expenses (₹48,000 × 3/24)	6,000
Total estimate of current liabilities	27,300
(c) Net working capital:	
(i) Current assets – Current liabilities (*A* – *B*)	25,950
(ii) *Add* 10 per cent contingency allowance	2,595
Average amount of working capital required	28,545

Assumptions:

(i) A time period of 52 weeks/12 months has been assumed in year.

(ii) Undrawn profit has been ignored in the working capital computation for the following reasons:

(a) For the purpose of determining working capital provided by net profit, it is necessary to adjust the net profit for income tax and dividends/drawings, and so on.

(b) Profit need not always be a source of financing working capital. It may be used for other purposes like purchase of fixed assets, repayment of long-term loans, and so on. Since the firm does not seem to have such uses, ₹11,000 may be treated as source of working capital. But the NWC will not change.

(iii) Actual working capital requirement would be more than what is estimated here as the cash component of current assets is not known.

P.13.2 While preparing a project report on behalf of a client you have collected the following facts. Estimate the net working capital required for that project. Add 10 per cent to your computed figure to allow contingencies: LO 13.2 LOD E

Particulars	*Amount per unit*
Estimated cost per unit of production:	
Raw material	₹80
Direct labour	30
Overheads (exclusive of depreciation, ₹10 per unit)	60
Total cash cost	170

Additional information:

Selling price, ₹200 per unit. The product is subject to GST of 18 per cent.
Level of activity, 1,04,000 units of production per annum
Raw materials in stock, average 4 weeks
Work in progress (assume 50 per cent completion stage in respect of conversion costs and 100 per cent completion in respect of materials), average 2 weeks
Finished goods in stock, average 4 weeks
Credit allowed by suppliers, average 4 weeks
Credit allowed to debtors, average 8 weeks
Lag in payment of wages, average 1.5 weeks
Lag in payment of GST, average 4 weeks
Cash at bank is expected to be, ₹25,000.

You may assume that production is carried on evenly throughout the year (52 weeks) and wages and overheads accrue similarly. All sales are on credit basis only.

Solution

Net working capital estimate of a project

(A) Current assets:	
(i) Raw materials in stock, (1,04,000 × ₹80 × 4/52)	₹6,40,000
(ii) Work-in-progress	
(a) Raw material (1,04,000 × ₹80 × 2/52)	3,20,000
(b) Direct Labour (1,04,000 × ₹15 × 2/52)	60,000
(c) Overheads (1,04,000 × ₹30 × 2/52)	1,20,000
(iii) Finished goods stock: (1,04,000 × ₹170 × 4/52)	13,60,000
(iv) Debtors: (1,04,000 × ₹206 × 8/52)	32,96,000
(v) Cash at bank	25,000
Total investment in current assets	58,21,000

(Contd.)

(*Contd.*)

(B) Current liabilities:	
(i) Creditors, average 4 weeks: (1,04,000 × ₹80 × 4/52)	6,40,000
(ii) Lag in payment of wages (1,04,000 × ₹30 × 1.5/52)	90,000
(iii) Lag in payment of GST (1,04,000 × ₹36 × 4/52)	2,88,000
Total current liabilities	10,18,000
(C) Net working capital: Current assets – Current liabilities	48,03,000
Add: 10 per cent contingencies	4,80,300
Net working capital required	52,83,300

Working Notes:

1. A full unit of raw material is required at the beginning of the manufacturing process and, therefore, total cost of the material, that is, ₹80 per unit has been taken into consideration, while in the case of expenses, viz. direct labour and overheads, the unit has been finished only to the extent of 50 per cent. Accordingly, ₹15 and ₹30 have been charged for direct labour and overheads respectively in valuing work-in-process.
2. Debtors: ₹170 + (18% GST × ₹200 = ₹36) = ₹206

P.13.3 A newly formed company has applied for a loan to a commercial bank for financing its working capital requirements. You are requested by the bank to prepare an estimate of the requirements of the working capital for the company. Add 10 per cent to your estimated figure to cover unforeseen contingencies. The information about the projected profit and loss account of this company is as under:

LO 13.2 LOD D

Sales		₹21,00,000
Cost of goods sold		15,30,000
Gross profit		5,70,000
Administrative expenses	₹1,40,000	
Selling expenses	1,30,000	
		2,70,000
Profit before tax		3,00,000
Provision for tax		1,00,000

Note: Cost of goods sold has been derived as follows:

Materials used	8,40,000
Wages and manufacturing expenses	6,25,000
Depreciation	2,35,000
	17,00,000
Less: Stock of finished goods (10 per cent not yet sold)	1,70,000
	15,30,000

The figures given above relate only to the goods that have been finished and not to work in progress; goods equal to 15 per cent of the year's production (in terms of physical units) are in progress on an average, requiring full materials but only 40 per cent of other expenses. The company believes in keeping two months consumption of material in stock; Desired cash balance, ₹40,000.

Average time-lag in payment of all expenses is 1 month; suppliers of materials extend 1.5 months credit; sales are 20 per cent cash; rest are at two months credit; 70 per cent of the income tax has to be paid in advance in quarterly instalments.

You can make such other assumptions as you deem necessary for estimating working capital requirements.

Solution

Net working capital estimate of a company

(A) Current assets:		
(i) Raw material in stock = (₹8,40,000 × 2/12)		₹1,40,000
(ii) Work-in-progress:		
(a) Raw material (₹8,40,000 × 15/100)		1,26,000
(b) Wages and manufacturing expenses = (₹6,25,000 × 0.4 × 15/100)		37,500
(iii) Stock of finished goods: [₹1,70,000 – ₹23,500 (0.10 × ₹2,35,000, depreciation)]		1,46,500
(iv) Debtors		
(a) Cost of goods sold	₹15,30,000	
Less: Depreciation (₹2,35,000 × 0.9)	2,11,500	
	13,18,500	
(b) Administrative expenses	1,40,000	
(c) Selling expenses	1,30,000	
Total	15,88,500	
Credit sales (4/5 of ₹15,88,500) = ₹12,70,800 (12,70,800 × 2/12)		2,11,800
(v) Cash required		40,000
Total investment in current assets		7,01,800
(B) Current liabilities:		
(i) Average time-lag in payment of expenses:		
(a) Wages and manufacturing expenses	6,25,000	
(b) Administrative expenses	1,40,000	
(c) Selling expenses	1,30,000	
	8,95,000/12	74,583
(ii) Creditors (₹8,40,000 × 3/24)		1,05,000
Total current liabilities		1,79,583
(C) Net working capital: Current assets – Current liabilities (*A* – *B*)		5,22,217
Add: 10 per cent contingencies		52,222
Net working capital required		5,74,439

Assumption and Working Notes

(i) Depreciation is not a cash expense and, therefore, excluded from cost of goods sold for the purpose of determining work-in-progress, finished goods and investment in debtors.

(ii) Since profit is not taken into consideration in our calculation as a source of working capital, income tax has been excluded as it is to be paid out of profits.

P.13.4 From the following projections of XYZ & Ltd for the next year, you are required to determine the working capital required by the company. **LO 13.2** LOD D

Annual sales, ₹14,40,000

Cost of production (including depreciation of ₹1,20,000), ₹12,00,000

Raw material purchases, ₹7,05,000

Monthly expenditure, ₹30,000

Estimated opening stock of raw materials, ₹140,000

Estimated closing stock of raw materials, ₹1,25,000

Inventory norms:

Raw materials, 2 months, Work-in-process, 1/2 month, and Finished goods, 1 month

The firm enjoys a credit of half-a-month on its purchases and allows one month credit on its supplies. On sales orders, the company receives an advance of ₹15,000. You may assume that production is carried out evenly throughout the year and minimum cash balance desired to be maintained is ₹35,000.

Solution Statement showing determination of net working capital

(A) Current assets:			
Cash balance			₹35,000
Inventories:			
Raw materials:	Opening stock	₹1,40,000	
	Add: Purchases	7,05,000	
	Less: Closing stock	1,25,000	
	Annual consumption	7,20,000	
	Two months requirement: (₹7,20,000 × 2/12)		1,20,000
Work-in-process: (₹10,80,000 × 1/24)			45,000
Finished goods: (₹10,80,000 × 1/12)			90,000
Debtors: (₹10,80,000 × 1/12)			90,000@
Total current assets			3,80,000
(B) Current liabilities:			
Trade creditors: (₹7,05,000 × 1/24)			29,375
Advance received from debtors			15,000
Total current liabilities			44,375
(C) Net working capital (*A* – *B*)			3,35,625

@It is assumed that there is neither opening nor closing stock of finished stock and, therefore, cost of sales is ₹10,80,000 excluding depreciation.

Monthly expenditure is excluded as the cost of production includes it (₹7.2 lakh, raw materials + ₹3.6 lakh, other expenses @ ₹30,000 per month).

P.13.5 From the following data, compute the duration of the operating cycle for each of the two years and comment on the increase/decrease: **LO 13.2** LOD E

Particulars	*Year 1*	*Year 2*
Stocks:		
Raw materials	₹20,000	₹27,000
Work-in-process	14,000	18,000
Finished goods	21,000	24,000
Purchase of raw materials	96,000	1,35,000
Cost of goods sold	1,40,000	1,80,000
Sales	1,60,000	2,00,000
Debtors	32,000	50,000
Creditors	16,000	18,000

Assume 360 days per year for computations purposes.

Solution Determination of operating cycle

Particulars	*Year 1 (Days)*	*Year 2 (Days)*
(i) Raw materials holding period:		
$\frac{\text{360 days} \times \text{Stock of raw meteriasls}}{\text{Cost of raw material consumed}}$	$\left(\frac{360 \times ₹20{,}000}{₹96{,}000}\right) = 75$	$\left(\frac{360 \times ₹27{,}000}{₹1{,}35{,}000}\right) = 72$
(assumed to be equivalent to purchases)		
(ii) *Less:* Creditors payment period:		
$\frac{\text{360 days} \times \text{Creditors}}{\text{Purchases}}$	$\left(\frac{360 \times ₹16{,}000}{₹96{,}000}\right) = (60)$	$\left(\frac{360 \times ₹18{,}000}{₹1{,}35{,}000}\right) = (48)$

(Contd.)

(*Contd.*)

	Year 1	Year 2
(iii) Work-in-process holding period:		
$\frac{\text{360 days} \times \text{Stock of WIP}}{\text{Cost of goods manufactured}}$	$\left(\frac{360 \times ₹14{,}000}{₹1{,}40{,}000}\right) = 36$	$\left(\frac{360 \times ₹18{,}000}{₹1{,}80{,}000}\right) = 36$
(assumed equal to cost of goods sold)		
(iv) Finished goods holding period:		
$\frac{\text{360 days} \times \text{Stock of finished goods}}{\text{Cost of goods sold}}$	$\left(\frac{360 \times ₹21{,}000}{₹1{,}40{,}000}\right) = 54$	$\left(\frac{360 \times ₹24{,}000}{₹1{,}80{,}000}\right) = 48$
(v) Debtors collection period:		
$\frac{\text{360 days} \times \text{Debtors}}{\text{Credit sales}}$	$\left(\frac{360 \times ₹32{,}000}{₹1{,}60{,}000}\right) = 72$	$\left(\frac{360 \times ₹50{,}000}{₹2{,}00{,}000}\right) = 90$
(assumed equal to total sales)		
Duration of operating cycle [sum of (i) to (v)]	= 177	= 198

The duration of the operating cycle has increased by 21 days in year 2 compared to year 1. It will necessitate more working capital in year 2. This increase has been primarily caused by an increase in debtors collection period and decrease in creditors payment period (as shown below):

Increase in debtors collection period	18 days
Decrease in creditors payment period	12
Less: Decrease in raw material holding period	(3)
Less: Decrease in finished goods holding period	(6)
Net increase in operating cycle	21

P.13.6 *X* Ltd sells goods at a gross profit of 20 per cent. It includes depreciation as a part of cost of production. The following figures for the 12 month-period ending March 31, current year are given to enable you to ascertain the requirements of working capital of the company on a cash cost basis. **LO 13.2** LOD M

In your working, you are required to assume that:

(i) A safety margin of 15 per cent will be maintained;

(ii) Cash is to be held to the extent of 50 per cent of current liabilities;

(iii) There will be no work-in-progress;

(iv) Tax is to be ignored;

(v) Finished goods are to be valued at manufacturing costs. Stocks of raw materials and finished goods are kept at one month's requirements.

Sales at 2 month's credit, ₹27,00,000

Materials consumed (suppliers' credit is for 2 months), ₹6,75,000

Wages (paid on the last day of the month), ₹5,40,000

Manufacturing expenses outstanding at the end of the year (cash expenses are paid one month in arrear), ₹60,000

Total administrative expenses (paid as above), ₹180,000

Sales promotion expenses (paid quarterly in advance), ₹90,000

Solution Statement showing determination of working capital

(A) Current assets:	
(i) Raw materials (₹6,75,000/12)	₹56,250
(ii) Finished goods (₹19,35,000/12)	1,61,250

(*Contd.*)

(*Contd.*)

(iii) Debtors (₹22,05,000 × 2/12)	3,67,500
(iv) Sales promotion expenses (₹90,000 × 3/12)	22,500
(v) Cash in hand (₹2,10,000 × 0.50)	1,05,000
Total current assets	7,12,500
(B) Current liabilities:	
(i) Creditors (₹6,75,000 × 2/12)	1,12,500
(ii) Manufacturing expenses	60,000
(iii) Administrative expenses (₹1,80,000/12)	15,000
(iv) Wages (₹5,40,000 × 1/24)	22,500
Total current liabilities	2,10,000
(C) Net working capital (A – B)	5,02,500
Add: Safety margin (0.15 × ₹5,02,500)	75,375
Working capital required on cash cost basis	5,77,875

Working Notes

(i) Determination of manufacturing expenses		
Sales		₹27,00,000
Less: Gross profit margin (₹27 lakh × 0.20)		5,40,000
Total manufacturing costs		21,60,000
Less: Cost of materials consumed	₹6,75,000	
Less: Wages	5,40,000	12,15,000
Manufacturing expenses (balancing figure)		9,45,000
(ii) Cash manufacturing expenses (₹60,000 × 12)		7,20,000
(iii) Depreciation (₹9,45,000 – ₹7,20,000)		2,25,000
(iv) Cash manufacturing costs (₹21,60,000 – ₹2,25,000)		19,35,000
(v) Cash cost of sales (₹19,35,000 + ₹1,80,000 + ₹90,000)		22,05,000

P.13.7 Marks Limited is launching a new project for the manufacture of a unique component. At full capacity of 24,000 units, the cost per unit will be as follows: **LO 13.2** LOD D

Material	₹80
Labour and variable expenses	40
Fixed manufacturing and administrative expenses	20
Depreciation	10
	150

The selling price per unit is expected at ₹200 and the selling expenses per unit will be ₹10, 80 per cent being variable.

In the first two years, production and sales are expected to be as follows:

Year	*Production units*	*Sales units*
1	15,000	14,000
2	20,000	18,000

To assess working capital requirement, the following additional information is given:

(a) Stock of raw material - 3 month's average consumption.
(b) Work-in-process - Nil
(c) Debtors - 1 month average cost of sales. Ignore GST.
(d) Creditors for supply of materials - 2 months average purchases of the year.
(e) Creditors for expenses - 1 month average of all expenses during the year.
(f) Minimum desired cash balance - ₹20,000
(g) Stock of finished goods is taken at average cost.

You are required to prepare a projected statement of working capital requirements for two years.

Solution

Projected statement to determine net working capital of Marks Limited for Year 1 and 2

Particulars			*Year 1*	*Year 2*
(A) Current assets:				
(i) Stock of raw materials:				
(15,000 units × ₹80 × 3/12) for year, 1			₹3,00,000	
(20,000 units × ₹80 × 3/12) for year, 2				₹4,00,000
(ii) Finished goods:				
			1,52,000*	4,33,143**
Cash cost of production	*Year 1*	*Year 2*		
Materials @ ₹80 per unit	₹12,00,000	₹16,00,000		
Labour and variable expenses @ ₹40 per unit	6,00,000	8,00,000		
Total fixed and administrative expenses (24,000 units × ₹20)	4,80,000	4,80,000		
Current cost (cash)	22,80,000	28,80,000		
Add: Opening stock at average cost ((₹22,80,000 × 1000)/15,000) for year 2	—	1,52,000*		
Less: Closing stock at average cost ((₹30,32,000 × 3,000)/21,000)	1,52,000	4,33,143**		
Cost of goods sold (cash)	21,28,000	25,98,857		
(iii) Debtors: (₹22,88,000/12; ₹27,90,857/12)			1,90,667	2,32,571
Cost of goods sold (cash)	21,28,000	25,98,857		
Add: Variable expenses @ ₹8	1,12,000	1,44,000		
Add: Total fixed selling expenses (24,000 × ₹2)	48,000	48,000		
Cost of sales (cash)	22,88,000	27,90,857		
(iv) Minimum desired cash			20,000	20,000
Total investments in current assets			6,62,667	10,85,714
(B) Current liabilities:				
(i) Creditors for supply of materials: (₹15,00,000 × 2/12; ₹17,00,000 × 2/12)			2,50,000	2,83,333
Materials consumed	12,00,000	16,00,000		
Add: Closing stock (equivalent to 3 month's average consumption)	3,00,000	4,00,000		
Less: Opening stock	—	(3,00,000)		
Purchases	15,00,000	17,00,000		
(ii) Creditors for expenses: (₹12,40,000 × 1/12; ₹14,72,000 × 1/12)			1,03,333	1,22,667
Labour and variable	6,00,000	8,00,000		
Fixed manufacturing and administrative	4,80,000	4,80,000		
Selling (fixed & variable)	1,60,000	1,92,000		
Total expenses	12,40,000	14,72,000		
Total current liabilities			3,53,333	4,06,000
Working capital (net)			3,09,334	6,79,714

Note: Working capital is required in respect of the full amount of fixed overheads.

MINI CASES

13.C.1 Strong Cement Company Ltd has an installed capacity of producing 1.25 lakh tonnes of cement per annum; its present capacity utilisation is 80 per cent. The major raw material to manufacture cement is limestone which is obtained from the company's own mechanised mine located near the plant. The company produces cement in 200 kgs bags. From the information given below, determine the net working capital (NWC) requirement of the company for the current year.

Cost structure per bag of cement (estimated)

Gypsum	₹25
Limestone	15
Coal	30
Packing material	10
Direct labour	50
Factory overheads (including depreciation of ₹10)	30
Administrative overheads	20
Selling overheads	25
Total cost	205
Selling price	250
Add: GST (18 per cent of selling price)	45
Invoice price to consumers	295

Additional information:

(i) Desired holding period of raw materials: Gypsum, 3 months, Limestone, 1 month, Coal, 2.5 months, and Packing material, 1.5 months

(ii) The product is in process for a period of 0.5 month (assume full units of materials, namely gypsum limestone and coal are required in the beginning; other conversion costs are to be taken at 50 per cent).

(iii) Finished goods are in stock for a period of 1 month before they are sold.

(iv) Debtors are extended credit for a period 3 months.

(v) Average time lag in payment of wages is approximately 0.5 month and of overheads, 1 month.

(vi) Average time lag in payment of GST is 1 month.

(vii) The credit period extended by various suppliers are:
Gypsum, 2 months, Coal, 1 month, and Packing material, 0.5 month.

(viii) Minimum desired cash balance is ₹25 lakh.

You may state your assumptions, if any.

Solution

TABLE 13.C.1 Statement showing determination of net working capital of Strong Cement Company Ltd

Current assets:	
Minimum desired cash balance	₹25,00,000
Raw materials:	
Gypsum (5 lakh bags[1] × ₹25 × 3/12)	31,25,000
Limestone (5 lakh bags × ₹15 × 1/12)	6,25,000
Coal (5 lakh bags × ₹30 × 2.5/12)	31,25,000
Packing material (5 lakh bags × ₹10 × 1.5/12)	6,25,000

(*Contd.*)

(*Contd.*)

Work-in-process: (5 lakh bags × ₹115 × 1/24)		23,95,833
— Raw material cost 100 per cent (₹25 + ₹15 + ₹30)	₹70	
— Other conversion costs (₹50 + ₹20 cash factory overheads + ₹20) × 0.5	45	
	115	
Finished goods (5 lakh bags × ₹170** × 1/12)		70,83,333
Debtors (5 lakh bags × ₹240*** × 3/12)		3,00,00,000
Total		4,94,79,166
Current liabilities:		
Creditors:		
Gypsum (5 lakh bags × ₹25 × 2/12)		20,83,333
Coal (5 lakh bags × ₹30 × 1/12)		12,50,000
Packing material (5 lakh bags × ₹10 × 1/24)		2,08,333
Wages (5 lakh bags × ₹50 × 1/24)		10,41,667
Overheads (5 lakh bags × ₹65 × 1/12)		27,08,333
GST (5 lakh bags × ₹45 × 1/12)		18,75,000
Total		91,66,666
NWC		4,03,12,500

*1.25 lakh tons × 0.8 = 1 lakh ton/200 kgs = 5,00,000 bags

**(Total cost, ₹205 – Depreciation, ₹10 – selling overheads, ₹25)

***(Cash cost, ₹195 + GST, ₹45)

13.C.2 Crimson Industries Ltd is desirious of assessing its working capital requirements for the next year. The finance manager has collected the following information for the purpose.

Estimated cost per unit of finished product

Raw materials	₹90
Direct labour	50
Manufacturing and administrative overhead (excluding depreciation)	40
Depreciation	20
Selling overheads	30
Total cost	230

The product is sold at ₹300 per unit. GST applicable is 18 per cent.

Additional information:

(i) Budgeted level of activity is 1,20,000 units of output for the next year.

(ii) Raw material cost consists of the following:
Pig iron ₹65 per unit, Ferro alloys 15 per unit, and Cast iron borings 10 per unit

(iii) Raw materials are purchased from different suppliers, extending different credit period:
Pig iron, 2 months, Ferro alloys, 1/2 month, and Cast iron borings, 1 month.

(iv) Product is in process for a period of 1/2 month. Production process requires full unit (100 per cent) of pig iron and ferro alloys in the beginning of production; cast iron boring is required only to the extent of 50 per cent in the beginning and the remaining is needed at a uniform rate during the process. Direct labour and other overheads accrue similarly at a uniform rate throughout production process.

(v) Past trends indicate that the pig iron is required to be stored for 2 months and other materials for 1 month.

(vi) Finished goods are in stock for a period of 1 month.

(vii) It is estimated that one-fourth of total sales are on cash basis and the remaining sales are on credit. The past experience of the firm has been to collect the credit sales in 2 months.

(viii) Average time-lag in payment of all overheads is 1 month and 0.5 month in the case of direct labour.

(ix) Average time-lag in payment of GST is 1 month.

(x) Desired cash balance is to be maintained at ₹10 lakh.

You are required to determine the amount of net working capital of the firm. State your assumpitions, if any.

Solution

TABLE 13.C.2 Determination of net working capital of Crimson Industries Ltd

Current assets:	
Minimum desired cash balance	₹10,00,000
Raw materials:	
Pig iron (1,20,000 × ₹65 × 2/12)	13,00,000
Ferro alloys (1,20,000 × ₹15 × 1/12)	1,50,000
Cast iron borings (1,20,000 × ₹10 × 1/12)	1,00,000
Work-in-process (1,20,000 × ₹132.5[1] × 1/24)	6,62,500
Finished goods (1,20,000 × ₹180 × 1/12)	18,00,000
Debtors (1,20,000 × 0.75 × ₹264[2] × 2/12)	39,60,000
Total	89,72,500
Current liabilities:	
Creditors:	
Pig iron (1,20,000 × ₹65 × 2/12)	13,00,000
Ferro alloys (1,20,000 × ₹15 × 1/24)	75,000
Cast iron borings (1,20,000 × ₹10 × 1/12)	1,00,000
Wages (1,20,000 × ₹50 × 1/24)	2,50,000
Total overheads (1,20,000 × ₹70 × 1/12)	7,00,000
GST (1,20,000 × ₹54 × 1/12)	5,40,000
Total	29,65,000
NWC	60,07,500

Working Notes

(1) *Determination of work-in-process*

Pig iron		₹65
Ferro alloys		15
Cast iron boring (0.50 × ₹10)		5
Other costs:		
Cast iron borings (0.50 × ₹5)	₹2.5	
Direct labour (0.5 × ₹50)	25	
Manufacturing and administrative overhead (0.50 × ₹40)	20	47.5
		132.5

(2) *Debtors*

Raw material	90
Direct labour	50
Manufacturing and administraive overheads	40
Selling overheads	30
GST (0.18 × ₹300)	54
	264

13.C.3 (Working Capital) Powerful CD Ltd manufactures high-tech CDs. After two years of operation, it is planning to expand its operations to meet the increased demand for CDs. The current level of production is 5,00,000 packs of 50 CDs. The budgeted level of production after expansion is 7,00,000 packs annually. The CEO of Powerful CD Ltd, Priti Chopra, wants the CFO, Bhavna Upadhyay, to submit a report relating to the projected working capital requirement after expansion. The cost and price data for the budgeted level of production are summarized in Exhibit 1.

EXHIBIT 1 Post-expansion Cost and Price Data of one CD Pack of 50 CDs

Raw materials:			
Optical storage media (₹2 × 50)		₹100	
Packing material		5	₹105
Direct labour			55
Overheads:			
Manufacturing (excluding depreciation)			
Fixed	₹40		
Variable	70	110	
Selling and Distribution			
Fixed	30		
Variable	50	80	
Depreciation		60	250
Total cost per CD pack			410
Selling price			500
GST (18% of selling price)			90
Invoice price to customers			590

Additional information:

- Budgeted level of production, 7,00,000 packs annually
- Raw materials for optical storage media are purchased on 2 months credit from suppliers.
- Packing materials are purchased on 1 month credit
- Average time-lag in payment of overheads, 1 month
- Average time-lag in payment of wages, half a month
- Average time-lag in payment of GST is 1 month
- Production process on an average, half a month. Full unit of raw materials is required in the beginning of manufacturing process.
- Sales on 3 months credit
- Stock of raw materials and finished goods equal half a month requirements
- Safety margin, 10 per cent
- Minimum desired cash balance, ₹50,00,000

Solution

Assessment of Working Capital Requirement (Post-expansion)

(a) Current Assets:		
Raw materials (7,00,000 units × ₹105 × 1/24)		₹30,62,500
Work-in-process:		
Raw materials* (7,00,000 × ₹100 × 1/24)	₹29,16,667	
Direct labour (7,00,000 × ₹55 × 1/24) × 0.5	8,02,083	
Overheads (7,00,000 × ₹110 × 1/24) × 0.5	16,04,167	53,22,917
Stock of finished goods (7,00,000 × ₹270 × 1/24)		78,75,000
Debtors:		
Cost of goods sold (7,00,000 × ₹330 × 3/12)	5,77,50,000	
Less: depreciation (7,00,000 × ₹60 × 3/12)	(1,05,00,000)	
Selling and distribution expenses (7,00,000 × ₹80 × 3/12)	1,40,00,000	
GST (7,00,000 × ₹90 × 3/12)	1.57,50,000	7,70,00,000

Cash balance		50,00,000
Total		9,82,60,417
(b) Current Liabilities:		
Creditors for materials (7,00,000 × ₹100 × 2/12)		1,16,66,667
Creditors for packing material (7,00,000 × ₹5 × 1/12)		2,91,667
Expenses:		
Wages (7,00,000 × ₹55 × 1/24)	16,04,167	
Overheads (7,00,000 × ₹190 × 1/12)	1,10,83,333	
GST (7,00,000 × ₹90 × 1/12)	52,50,000	1,79,37,500
Total		2,98,95,834
Networking capital (a – b)		6,83,64,583
Working capital required (NWC × 1.10)		7,52,01,041

*Excluding packing material

Working capital required after expansion is ₹7,52,01,041.

Scan the QR Code given at the end of chapter to access comprehensive cases.

REVIEW QUESTIONS

LOD: Easy

RQ.13.1 Indicate whether the following statements are true or false. [LO 13.1,2]

(i) Working capital is primarily required due to non-synchronous nature of the expected cash inflows and required cash outflows.

(ii) Higher net working capital leads to higher liquidity and higher profitability.

(iii) Conservative approach warrants that long-term funds should be used to finance the permanent part of the current assets and the temporary/seasonal requirements should be financed by short-term funds.

(iv) According to hedging approach, current assets should be financed from long-term sources.

(v) Trade-off plan, in general, is considered an appropriate financing strategy for working capital.

(vi) There is an inverse relationship between the length of operating cycle of a firm and its working capital requirements.

(vii) In general, manufacturing enterprises require higher working capital than trading firms.

(viii) The longer the production cycle, the higher is the working capital needed or *vice- versa.*

(ix) There is a positive correlation between level of business activity and working capital needs of a business firm.

(x) Efficiency of operation accelerates the pace of cash cycle of a firm but it does not affect its working capital requirements.

(xi) A firm should carry higher working capital than required to execute smoothly its planned level of business activity.

(xii) The entire sum of net profit earned by a corporate can, *per-se,* be considered a source of financing working capital.

(xiii) Cash cost approach is an appropriate basis of computing working capital requirements of a business firm.

(xiv) Working capital tied up with debtors should be estimated in relation to the selling price.

(xv) From the perspective of determining net working capital, all current liabilities including short-term sources of finance are considered.

[Answers: (i) True (ii) False (iii) False (iv) False (v) True (vi) False (vii) True (viii) True (ix) True (x) False (xi) False (xii) False (xiii) True (xiv) False (xv) False]

RQ.13.2 How are net working capital, liquidity, technical insolvency, and risk related? **[LO 13.1]**

RQ.13.3 Hypothetical Ltd has forecast its total fund requirements for the coming year as follows:

Month	*Amount (₹ in lakh)*	*Month*	*Amount (₹ in lakh)*
January	30	July	200
February	30	August	180
March	40	September	110
April	60	October	70
May	100	November	40
June	150	December	20

The firm's cost of short-term and long-term financing is expected to be 4 per cent and 10 per cent respectively. **[LO 13.1]**

(i) Calculate the cost of financing, using the hedging approach.

(ii) Calculate the cost of financing, using the conservative approach.

(iii) Discuss the basic profitability risk trade-off associated with each of these plans.

LOD: Medium

RQ.13.4 What is the basic premise of the hedging approach for meeting funds requirements? What are the effects of this approach on the profitability and risk? **[LO 13.1]**

RQ.13.5 What is the conservative approach to financing funds requirements? What kind of profitability-risk trade-off is involved? **[LO 13.1]**

RQ.13.6 Length of operating cycle is a major determinant of working capital needs of a business firm. Explain. **[LO 13.2]**

RQ.13.7 Distinguish between: (a) Gross working capital and Net working capital, (b) Permanent and Temporary working capital (c) Production and operating cycle. **[LO 13.1,2]**

RQ.13.8 The board of directors of Nanak Engineering Company Private Ltd requests you to prepare a statement showing the working capital requirements for a level of activity at 1,56,000 units of production. The following information is available for your calculation: **[LO 13.2]**

		Per unit
(A)	Raw materials	₹90
	Direct labour	40
	Overheads (excluding depreciation of ₹10)	75
	Total	205
	Selling price	250
	GST (18 per cent)	45
	Invoice price to debtors	295

(B) **(i)** Raw materials are in stock, on average, for 1 month.

(ii) Materials are in process, (50 per cent complete) on average for 4 weeks.

(iii) Finished goods are in stock on average for 1 month

(iv) Credit allowed by suppliers is 1 month.

(v) Time lag in payment from debtors is 2 months.
(vi) Average lag in payment of wages is 1.5 weeks.
(vii) Average lag in payment of overheads is 1 month.
(viii) Average time-lag in payment of GST is 1 month.
(ix) 20 per cent of the output is sold against cash. Desired minimum cash in hand and in bank, ₹60,000. It is to be assumed that production is carried on evenly throughout the year; wages and overheads accrue similarly, and a time period of 4 weeks is equivalent to a month.

RQ.13.9 POR Ltd sells goods in domestic market on a gross profit of 25 per cent, not counting depreciation as a part of the 'cost of goods sold'. Its estimates for next year are as follows: [LO 13.2]

Particulars	*Amount (₹ in lakh)*
Sales – Home at 1 month's credit	1,200
Exports at 3 months' credit, selling price 10 per cent below home price	540
Materials used (suppliers extend 2 months' credit)	450
Wages paid, 1/2 month in arrears	360
Manufacturing expenses (cash) paid, 1 month in arrears	540
Depreciation on fixed assets	60
Administrative expenses, paid 1 month in arrears	120
Sales promotion expenses (payable quarterly—in advance)	60
Income–tax payable in 4 instalments of which one falls in the next financial year	150

The company keeps 1 month's stock of each of raw materials and finished goods and believes in keeping ₹20 lakh as cash. Assuming a 15 per cent safety margin, ascertain the estimated working capital requirement of the company (ignore work-in-process as well as GST).

LOD: Difficult

RQ.13.10 If a firm has constant funds requirement throughout the year, which, if any, of the three financing plans is preferable? Why? [LO 13.1]

RQ.13.11 Hypothetical Ltd estimates its requirements of funds for the coming year to be constant at a level of ₹1,00,000. If the cost of both current liabilities and long-term financing are 8 per cent, calculate the cost, using the hedging and conservative approaches, and discuss your preference with respect to applying either of them to finance the firm. [LO 13.1]

RQ.13.12 MA Ltd is commencing a new project to manufacture a plastic component. The following cost information has been ascertained for annual production of 12,000 units which is the full capacity.

Materials	₹40	per unit
Direct labour and variable expenses	20	
Fixed manufacturing expenses	6	
Depreciation	10	
Fixed administration expenses	4	
	80	

The selling price per unit is expected to be ₹96 and the selling expenses ₹5 per unit, 80 per cent of which is variable. In the first 2 years of operations, production and sales are expected to be as follows: [LO 13.2]

Year	*Production*	*Sales*
1	6,000 units	5,000 units
2	9,000 units	8,500 units

To assess the working capital requirements, the following additional information is available:

(a) Stock of materials, 2.25 months average consumption.

(b) Work-in-process, Nil.

(c) Debtors, 1 month's average cost of sales.

(d) Cash balance, ₹10,000.

(e) Creditors for materials, 1 month's average purchases during the year.

(f) Creditors for expenses, 1 month's average of all expenses during the year.

You are required to prepare a projected statement of working capital requirements for 2 years. Assume that there is no GST applicable on the product.

ANSWERS

13.3 **(i)** ₹4.63 lakh
(ii) ₹20 lakh
(iii) ₹11.67 lakh

13.8 Current assets ₹1,04,27,500
Current liabilities ₹29,25,000
NWC ₹75,02,500

13.9 NWC ₹237.50 lakh

13.11 The cost would be the same under both the plans. Preference should be given to a plan involving long-term financing. The cost is ₹8,000

13.12 NWC ₹1,24,583 (Year 1)
₹1,84,042 (Year 2)

Scan the QR Code to access comprehensive solutions to all numerical review questions and additional material.

CHAPTER

14 Management of Cash and Marketable Securities

LEARNING OBJECTIVES

LO 14.1	Discuss the motives for holding cash and marketable securities
LO 14.2	Understand the objectives of cash management
LO 14.3	Describe the factors that determine the required cash balances
LO 14.4	Illustrate the two approaches to derive optional cash balance, namely, analytical models of cash management as a normative framework and cash budget as a cash management tool
LO 14.5	Demonstrate, using the operating and cash conversion cycles, the three basic strategies for the efficient management of cash to minimise financing/cash balance needs
LO 14.6	Explain popular techniques for speeding up collections (concentration banking and lock-box system) and slowing disbursements (centralised disbursements, float, etc.)
LO 14.7	Understand the basic characteristics of marketable securities and the key features of the popular types of Government and non-Government issues
LO 14.8	Outline cash management practices in India

INTRODUCTION

Cash management is one of the key areas of working capital management. Apart from the fact that it is the most liquid current asset, cash is the common denominator to which all current assets can be reduced because the other major liquid assets, that is, receivables and inventory get eventually converted into cash. This underlines the significance of cash management.

The present Chapter gives a detailed account of the problems involved in managing cash. It outlines the motives for holding cash followed by the objectives of cash management. A discussion of the factors determining cash needs follows. The approaches to derive optimal cash balances, namely, cash management models and cash budgets are also examined in-depth. The basic strategies for efficient management of cash are the subject-matter of the subsequent discussions. We have explained specific techniques to manage cash subsequently. The remainder of the chapter is devoted to the discussion of marketable securities and Indian practices. It concludes with a summary of the major points by way of recapitulation.

LO 14.1 MOTIVES FOR HOLDING CASH

Cash is the ready currency to which all liquid assets can be reduced.

Near cash implies marketable securities viewed the same way as cash because of their high liquidity.

Marketable securities are short-term interest earning money market instruments used by firms to obtain a return on temporarily idle funds.

The term **'cash'** with reference to cash management is used in two senses. In a narrow sense, it is used broadly to cover currency and generally accepted equivalents of cash, such as cheques, drafts and demand deposits in banks. The broad view of cash also includes **near-cash** assets, such as **marketable securities** and time deposits in banks. The main characteristics of these is that they can be readily sold and converted into cash. They serve as a reserve pool of liquidity that provides cash quickly when needed. They also provide a short-term investment outlet for excess cash and are also useful for meeting planned outflow of funds. Here, the term *cash management* is employ-ed in the broader sense. Irrespective of the form in which it is held, a distinguishing feature of cash, as an asset, is that it has no earning power. If cash does not earn any return, why is it held? There are four primary motives for maintaining cash balances: **(i)** Transaction motive; **(ii)** Precautionary motive; **(iii)** Speculative motive; and **(iv)** Compensating motive.

Transaction Motive

Transaction motive is a motive for holding cash/near cash to meet routine cash requirements to finance transaction in the normal couse of business.

An important reason for maintaining cash balances is the **transaction motive**. This refers to the holding of cash to meet routine cash requirements to finance the transactions which a firm carries on in the ordinary course of business. A firm enters into a variety of transactions to accomplish its objectives which have to be paid for in the form of cash. For example, cash payments have to be made for purchases, wages, operating expenses, financial charges like interest, taxes, dividends, and so on. Similarly, there is a regular inflow of cash to the firm from sales operations, returns on outside investments, and so on. These receipts and payments constitute a continuous two-way flow of cash. But the inflows (receipts), and outflows (disbursements) do not perfectly coincide or synchronise. At times, receipts exceed outflows while, at other times, payments exceed inflows. To ensure that the firm can meet its obligations when payments become due in a situation in which disbursements are in excess of the current receipts, it must have an adequate cash balance. The requirement of cash balances to meet routine cash needs is known as the **transaction motive** and such motive refers to the holding of cash to meet anticipated obligations whose timing is not perfectly synchronised with cash receipts. If the receipts of cash and its disbursements could exactly coincide in the normal course of operations, a firm would not need cash for transaction purposes. Although a major part of transaction balances are held in cash, a part may also be in such marketable securities whose maturity conforms to the timing of the anticipated payments, such as payment of taxes, dividends, and so on.

Precautionary Motive

Precautionary motive is a motive for holding cash/near-cash as a cushion to meet unexpected contingencies/demand for cash.

In addition to the non-synchronisation of anticipated cash inflows and outflows in the ordinary course of business, a firm may have to pay cash for purposes which cannot be predicted or anticipated. The unexpected cash needs at short notice may be the result of:

- Floods, strikes and failure of important customers;
- Bills may be presented for settlement earlier than expected;

- Unexpected slow down in collection of accounts receivable;
- Cancellation of some order for goods as the customer is not satisfied; and
- Sharp increase in cost of raw materials.

The cash balances held in reserve for such random and unforeseen fluctuations in cash flows are called as **precautionary balances**. In other words, precautionary motive of holding cash implies the need to hold cash to meet unpredictable obligations. Thus, precautionary cash balance serves to provide **a cushion to meet unexpected contingencies**. The more unpredictable are the cash flows, the larger is the need for such balances.

Another factor which has a bearing on the level of such cash balances is the availability of short-term credit. If a firm can borrow at short notice to pay for unforeseen obligations, it will need to maintain a relatively small balance and *vice versa*.

Such cash balances are usually held in the form of marketable securities so that they earn a return.

Speculative Motive

It refers to the desire of a firm to take advantage of opportunities which present themselves at unexpected moments and which are typically outside the normal course of business. While the precautionary motive is defensive in nature in that firms must make provisions to tide over un-expected contingencies, the **speculative motive** represents a positive and aggressive approach. Firms aim to exploit profitable opportunities and keep cash in reserve to do so. The speculative motive helps to take advantage of:

- An opportunity to purchase raw materials at a reduced price on payment of immediate cash;
- A chance to speculate on interest rate movements by buying securities when interest rates are expected to decline;
- Delay purchases of raw materials on the anticipation of decline in prices; and
- Make purchase at favourable prices.

Speculative motive is a motive for holding cash/near-cash to quickly take advantage of opportunities typically outside the normal course of business.

Compensating Motive

Yet another motive to hold cash balances is to compensate banks for providing certain services and loans.

Banks provide a variety of services to business firms, such as clearance of cheque, supply of credit information, transfer of funds, and so on. While for some of these services banks charge a commission or fee, for others they seek indirect compensation. Usually clients are required to maintain a minimum balance of cash at the bank. Since this balance cannot be utilised by the firms for transaction purposes, the banks themselves can use the amount to earn a return. Such balances are **compensating balances**.

Compensating motive is a motive for holding cash/near-cash to compensate banks for providing certain services or loans.

Compensating balances are also required by some loan agreements between a bank and its customers. During periods when the supply of credit is restricted and interest rates are rising, banks require a borrower to maintain a minimum balance in his account as a condition precedent to the grant of loan. This is presumably to 'compensate' the bank for a rise in the interest rate during the period when the loan will be pending.

The compensating cash balances can take either of two forms: **(i)** an absolute minimum, say, ₹5 lakh, below which the actual bank balance will never fall; **(ii)** a minimum average balance, say, ₹5 lakh over the month. The first alternative is more restrictive as the average amount of cash held during the month must be above ₹5 lakh by the amount of the transaction balance. From the firm's viewpoint, this is obviously dead money. Under the second alternative, the balance could fall to zero one day provided it was ₹10 lakh some other day with the average working to ₹5 lakh.

Of the four primary motives of holding cash balances, the two most important are the transactions motive and the compensation motive. Business firms normally do not speculate and need not have speculative balances. The requirement of precautionary balances can be met out of short-term borrowings.

LO 14.2 OBJECTIVES OF CASH MANAGEMENT

The basic objectives of cash management are two-fold: **(a)** to meet the cash disbursement needs (payment schedule); and **(b)** to minimise funds committed to cash balances. These are conflicting and mutually contradictory and the task of cash management is to reconcile them.

Meeting Payments Schedule

In the normal course of business, firms have to make payments of cash on a continuous and regular basis to suppliers of goods, employees and so on. At the same time, there is a constant inflow of cash through collections from debtors. Cash is, therefore, aptly described as the 'oil to lubricate the ever-turning wheels of business: without it the process grinds to a stop'.[1] A basic objective of cash management is to meet the payment schedule, that is, to have sufficient cash to meet the cash disbursement needs of a firm.

The importance of sufficient cash to meet the payment schedule can hardly be overemphasised. The advantages of adequate cash are: **(i)** it prevents insolvency or bankruptcy arising out of the inability of a firm to meet its obligations; **(ii)** the relationship with the bank is not strained; **(iii)** it helps in fostering good relations with trade creditors and suppliers of raw materials, as prompt payment may help their own cash management; **(iv)** a cash discount can be availed of if payment is made within the due date. For example, a firm is entitled to a 2 per cent discount for a payment made within 10 days when the entire payment is to be made within 30 days. Since the net amount is due in 30 days, failure to take the discount means paying an extra 2 per cent for using the money for an additional 20 days. If a firm were to pay 2 per cent for every 20-day period over a year, there would be 18 such periods (360 days ÷ 20 days). This represents an annual interest rate of 36 per cent;[2] **(v)** it leads to a strong credit rating which enables the firm to purchase goods on favourable terms and to maintain its line of credit with banks and other sources of credit; **(vi)** to take advantage of favourable business opportunities that may be available periodically; and finally, **(vii)** the firm can meet unanticipated cash expenditure with a minimum of strain during emergencies, such as strikes, fires or a new marketing campaign by competitors. Keeping large cash balances, however, implies a high cost. The advantage of prompt payment of cash can well be realised by **sufficient** and not **excessive** cash.

Minimising Funds Committed to Cash Balances

The second objective of cash management is to minimise cash balances. In minimising the cash balances, two conflicting aspects have to be reconciled. A high level of cash balances will, as shown above, ensure prompt payment together with all the advantages. But it also implies that large funds will remain idle, as cash is a non-earning asset and the firm will have to forego profits. A low level of cash balances, on the other hand, may mean failure to meet the payment schedule. The aim of cash management, therefore, should be to have an optimal amount of cash balances.

Keeping in view these conflicting aspects of cash management, we propose to discuss the planning/determination of the need for cash balances. There are two aspects involved in cash planning: first, an examination of those factors which have a bearing on the firm's required cash balances; second, a review of the approaches to achieve optimum cash balances.

LO 14.3 FACTORS DETERMINING CASH BALANCES

The factors that determine the required cash balances are: **(i)** synchronisation of cash flows, **(ii)** short costs, **(iii)** excess cash balance, **(iv)** procurement and management, and **(v)** uncertainty.

Synchronisation of Cash Flows

The need for maintaining cash balances arises from the non-synchronisation of the inflows and outflows of cash: if the receipts and payments of cash perfectly coincide or balance each other, there would be no need for cash balances. The first consideration in determining the cash need is, therefore, the extent of non-synchronisation of cash receipts and disbursements. For this purpose, the inflows and outflows have to be forecast over a period of time, depending upon the planning horizon which is typically a one-year period with each of the 12 months being a subperiod. The technique adopted is a cash budget. The preparation of a cash budget is discussed in the next section of this chapter. A properly prepared budget will pinpoint the months/periods when the firm will have an excess or a shortage of cash.

Short Costs

Another general factor to be considered in determining cash needs is the cost associated with a shortfall in the cash needs. The cash forecast presented in the cash budget would reveal periods of cash shortages. In addition, there may be some unexpected shortfall. Every shortage of cash—whether expected or unexpected—involves a cost 'depending upon the severity, duration and frequency of the shortfall and how the shortage is covered. Expenses incurred as a result of shortfall are called **short costs**'.[3] Included in the short costs are the following:

- **(i) Transaction costs** associated with raising cash to tide over the shortage. This is usually the *brokerage* incurred in relation to the sale of some short-term near-cash assets such as marketable securities.
- **(ii) Borrowing costs** associated with borrowing to cover the shortage. These include items such as interest on loan, commitment charges and other expenses relating to the loan.
- **(iii) Loss of cash-discount,** that is, a substantial loss because of a temporary shortage of cash.
- **(iv) Cost associated with deterioration of the credit rating** which is reflected in higher bank charges on loans, stoppage of supplies, demands for cash payment, refusal to sell, loss of image and the attendant decline in sales and profits.
- **(v) Penalty rates** by banks to meet a shortfall in compensating balances.

Excess Cash Balance Costs

The cost of having excessively large cash balances is known as the *excess cash balance cost.* If large funds are idle, the implication is that the firm has missed opportunities to invest those funds and has thereby lost interest which it would otherwise have earned. This loss of interest is primarily the excess cost.

Procurement and Management

These are the costs associated with establishing and operating cash management staff and activities. They are generally fixed and are mainly accounted for by salary, storage, handling of securities, and so on.

Uncertainty and Cash Management

Finally, the impact of uncertainty on cash management strategy is also relevant as cash flows cannot be predicted with complete accuracy. The first requirement is a precautionary cushion to cope with irregularities in cash flows, unexpected delays in collections and disbursements, defaults and unexpected cash needs.

The impact of uncertainty on cash management can, however, be mitigated through **(i)** improved forecasting of tax payments, capital expenditure, dividends, and so on; and **(ii)** increased ability to borrow through overdraft facility.

LO 14.4 DETERMINING CASH NEED

After the examination of the pertinent considerations and cost that determine cash needs, the next aspect relates to the determination of cash needs.

There are two approaches to derive an optimal cash balance, namely, **(a)** minimising cost cash models and **(b)** cash budget.

Cash Management/Conversion Models

While it is true that financial managers need not necessarily follow cash management models exactly but a familiarity with them provides an insight into the normative framework as to how cash management should be conducted. This section, therefore, attempts to outline the following analytical models for cash management: **(i)** Baumol Model, **(ii)** Miller-Orr Model and **(iii)** Orgler's Model. The Control Theory Model Approach is highly mathematical and outside the scope of this book.[4]

Baumol Model[5] The purpose of this model is to determine the minimum cost amount of cash that a financial manager can obtain by converting securities to cash, considering the cost of conversion and the counter-balancing cost of keeping idle cash balances which otherwise could have been invested in marketable securities. The total cost associated with cash management, according to this model, has two elements: **(i)** cost of converting marketable securities into cash and **(ii)** the lost opportunity cost.

Baumol Model is a model that provides for cost-efficient transactional balances and assumes that the demand for cash can be predicted with certainty and determines the optimal conversion size/lot.

The *conversion costs* are incurred each time marketable securities are converted into cash. Symbolically,

$$\text{Total conversion cost per period} = \frac{Tb}{C} \qquad \textbf{(14.1)}$$

Where b = cost per conversion assumed to be independent of the size of the transaction,

T = total transaction cash needs for the period,

C = value of marketable securities sold at each conversion.

The *opportunity cost* is derived from the lost/forfeited interest rate (i) that could have been earned on the investment of cash balances. The total opportunity cost is the interest rate times the average cash balance kept by the firm. The model assumes a constant and a certain pattern of cash outflows. At the beginning of each period, the firm starts with a cash balance which it gradually spends until at the end of the period it has a zero cash balance and must replenish its each supply to the level of cash balance in the beginning. Symbolically, the average lost opportunity cost.

$$i\left(\frac{C}{2}\right) \tag{14.2}$$

Where i = interest rate that could have been earned.

$C/2$ = the average cash balance that is, the beginning cash (C) plus the ending cash balance of the period (zero) divided by 2.

The total cost associated with cash management comprising total conversion cost plus opportunity cost of not investing cash until needed in interest-bearing instruments can be symbolically expressed as:

$$i\left(\frac{C}{2}\right) + \left(\frac{Tb}{C}\right) \tag{14.3}$$

Optimal conversion size/amount is the cost of minimising quantity in which to convert marketable securities to cash or cash to marketable securities.

To minimise the cost, therefore, the model attempts to determine the **optimal conversion amount**, that is, the cash withdrawal which costs the least. The reason is that a firm should not keep the total beginning cash balance during the entire period as it is not needed at the beginning of the period. For example, if the period were one thirty day month, only one-thirtieth of the opening cash balance each day will be required. This means if only one-thirtieth of the entire amount is withdrawn, the rest could be left invested in interest-earning marketable securities. As a result, on the one-thirtieth of the cash not needed to the last day of the month, twenty-nine day's interest could be earned by the firm and so on. Symbolically, the optimal conversion amount (C),

$$C = \sqrt{\frac{2bt}{i}} \tag{14.4}$$

The model in terms of Eq. 14.4 has important implications. First, as the total cash needs for transaction rises because of expansion/diversification, the optimal withdrawal increases less than proportionately. This is the result of economy of scale in cash management. Each project does not need its own additional cash balances. It only needs enough additions to the general cash balance of the firm to facilitate expanded operations. Secondly, as the opportunity interest rate (i) increases, the optimal cash withdrawal decreases. This is so because as (i) increases it is more costly to forfeit the investment opportunity and financial managers want to keep as much cash invested in securities for as long as possible. They can afford to do this at the higher interest rates because at those higher rates any shortfall costs caused by a lower withdrawal are offset.

In sum, the Baumol Model of cash management is very simplistic. Further, its assumptions of certainty and regularity of withdrawal of cash do not realistically reflect the actual situation in any firm. Also, the model is concerned only with transaction balances and not with precautionary balances. In addition, the assumed fixed nature of the cash withdrawals is also not realistic.

Nevertheless, the model does clearly and concisely demonstrate the economies of scale and the counteracting nature of the conversion and opportunity costs which are undoubtedly major considerations in any financial manager's cash management strategy.

***Example* 14.1**

The ABC Ltd requires ₹30 lakh in cash to meet its transaction needs during the next three-month cash planning period. It holds marketable securities of an equal amount. The annual yield on these marketable securities is 20 per cent. The conversion of these securities into cash entails a fixed cost of ₹3,000 per transaction. Using

Baumol model, compute the amount of marketable securities converted into cash per order. Assuming ABC Ltd can sell its marketable securities in any of the five lot sizes: ₹1,50,000, 3,00,000, 6,00,000, 7,50,000 and 15,00,000, prepare a table indicating the economic lot size using numerical analysis.

Solution

$C = \sqrt{\frac{2bT}{i}}$, where C = optimal conversion amount/amount of marketable securities converted into cash per order; b = cost of conversion into cash per lot/transaction; T = projected cash requirement during the planning period; i = interest rate earned per planning period on investment in marketable securities.

$$= \sqrt{\frac{2 \times ₹3{,}000 \times ₹30{,}00{,}000}{0.05^{@}}} = ₹6{,}00{,}000$$ @Annual yield 20 per cent/4 = 5 per cent.

TABLE 14.1 Optimal Cash Conversion Size/Lot

1. Total cash requirement (*₹ lakh*)	30	30	30	30	30
2. Lot size (*₹ lakh*)	1.5	3	6	7.5	15
3. Number of lots (1 ÷ 2)	20	10	5	4	2
4. Conversion cost per lot (*₹ thousand*)	3	3	3	3	3
5. Total conversion cost (3 × 4) (*₹ thousand*)	60	30	15	12	6
6. Average lot size (*₹ lakh*)	0.75	1.5	3	3.75	7.5
7. Interest cost (6 × 0.05) (*₹*)	3,750	7,500	15,000	18,750	37,500
8. Total cost (5 + 7) (*₹*)	63,750	37,500	30,000	30,750	42,500

The optimal cash conversion size is ₹6 lakh.

Working Notes

1. Number of conversion during the planning period = $\frac{\text{Total cash requirement (₹30 lakh)}}{\text{Cash conversion lot/size}}$
2. Average cash balance = Cash conversion size/2.
3. Interest income foregone = Average cash balance × interest rate for the cash planning period; interest rate = annual yield/4.
4. Cost of cash conversion = Number of conversions × cost per conversion.
5. Total cost of converting and holding cash = Interest income foregone + Cost of cash conversion.

***Example* 14.2**

The management of Popular Traders anticipates ₹15 lakh in cash outlays (demand) during the next year. The recent experience has been that it costs ₹30 to convert marketable securities to cash and *vice versa.* The marketable securities currently earns 8 per cent annual return. Find the total cost of managing cash according to Banmol model.

Miller-Orr model is a model that provides for cost-efficient transactional balances and assumes uncertain cash flows and determines an upper limit and return point for cash balances.

Solution

Economic/optimal conversion size/lot = $\frac{\sqrt{2 \times ₹30 \times ₹15{,}00{,}000}}{0.08}$ = ₹33,541

Number of conversions = ₹15,00,000 ÷ ₹33,541 = 45
Average cash balance = ₹16,770.50 (₹33,541 ÷ 2)
Total cost = (₹30 × 45) + (0.08 × ₹16,770.50) = ₹2,692

Miller-Orr Model[6] The objective of cash management, according to Miller-Orr (MO), is to determine the optimum cash balance level which minimises the cost of cash management. Symbolically,

$$C = \frac{bE\,(N)}{t} + iE\,(M) \qquad \textbf{(14.5)}$$

where b = the fixed cost per conversion, $E(M)$ = the expected average daily cash balance, $E(N)$ = the expected number of conversions, t = the number of days in the period, i = the lost opportunity costs, and C = total cash management costs

The MO Model is, in fact, an attempt to make the Baumol Model more realistic as regards the pattern of cash flows. As against the assumption of uniform and certain levels of cash balances in the Baumol Model, the MO Model assumes that *cash balances randomly* fluctuate between an upper bound (h) and a lower bound (O). When the cash balances hit the upper bound, the firm has too much cash and should buy enough marketable securities to bring the cash balances back to the optimal bound (z). When the cash balances hit zero, the financial manager must return them to the optimum bound (z) by selling/converting securities into cash. According to the MO Model, as in Baumol model, the optimal cash balance (z) can be expressed symbolically as

$$z = \sqrt{\frac{3br^2}{4i}} \qquad \textbf{(14.6)}$$

where r^2 = the variance of the daily changes in cash balances.

Thus, as in Baumol Model, there are economies of scale in cash management and the two basic costs of conversion and lost interest that have to be minimised.

MO Model also specifies the optimum upper boundary (h) as three times the optimal cash balance level such that

$$h = 3z \qquad \textbf{(14.7)}$$

Further, the financial manager could consider the use of less liquid, potentially more profitable securities as investments for the cash balances in excess of h.

***Example* 14.3**

Assuming for Popular Traders in Example 14.2 that variance of daily net cash flows is estimated to be ₹27,000, show the cash balances as per Miller-Orr model.

Solution

$$\text{Return point} = \frac{\sqrt{3 \times ₹\,30 \times ₹\,27{,}000}}{4 \times 0.000222^{@}} = ₹1{,}399$$

@daily portfolio return = (8% ÷ 360 days)

upper limit = 3 × ₹1,399 = ₹4,197

The cash balance of Popular Traders would be allowed to vary between ₹0 (zero) and ₹4,197. When the upper limit is reached, ₹2,798 (₹4,197 – ₹1,399) is converted from cash to marketable securities that will earn interest. When the cash balance falls to zero, ₹1,399 (₹1,399 – ₹0) is converted from marketable securities into cash.

Orgler's Model[7] According to this model, an optimal cash management strategy can be determined through the use of a multiple linear programming model. The construction of the model comprises three sections: **(1)** selection of the appropriate planning horizon, **(2)** selection of the appropriate decision variables and **(3)** formulation of the cash management strategy itself. The advantage of linear programming model is that it enables coordination of the optimal cash management strategy with the other operations of the firm such as production and with less restrictions on working capital balances.

Orgler's model is a model that provides for integration of cash management with production and other aspects of the firm.

The model basically uses one year *planning horizon* with twelve monthly periods because of its simplicity. It has four basic sets of *decisions variables* which influence cash management of a firm and which must be incorporated into the linear programming model of the firm. These are: **(i)** payment schedule, **(ii)** short-term financing, **(iii)** purchase and sale of marketable securities and **(iv)** cash balance itself.

The formulation of the model requires that the financial managers first specify an objective function and then specify a set of constraints.

Orgler's objective function is to 'minimise the horizon value of the net revenues from the cash budget over the entire planning period'. Using the assumption that all revenues generated are immediately re-invested and that any cost is immediately financed, the objective function represents the value of the net income from the cash budget at the horizon 'by adding the net returns over the planning period'. Thus, the objective function recognises each operation of the firm that generates cash inflows or cash outflows as adding or subtracting profit opportunities for the firm from its cash management operations. In the objective function, decision variables which cause inflows, such as payments on receivables, have positive co-efficient, while decision variables which generate cash outflows, such as interest on short-term borrowings have negative co-efficients. The purchase of marketable securities would, for example, produce revenue and thus have a positive co-efficient while the sale of those securities would incur conversion costs and have a negative co-efficient.

The constraints of the model could be **(i)** institutional or **(ii)** policy-constraints. The institutional constraints are those imposed by external factors, that is, bank-required compensating balance. Policy constraints are imposed on cash management by the firm itself. For instance, the financial manager may be prohibited from selling securities before maturity. Either constraint can occur in the model during one monthly period or over several or all the months in the one year planning horizon.

An example of the linear programming model is as follows:

Objective function:

$$\text{Maximise profit} = a_1x_1 + a_2x_2 \qquad \textbf{(14.8)}$$

Subject to:

$$b_1x_1 \leq \text{production}$$

$$b_2x_2 \leq \text{constraints} \qquad \textbf{(14.9)}$$

$$C_1x_1 + C_2x_2 \leq \text{Cash available constraint} \qquad \textbf{(14.10)}$$

$$a_1x_1 + a_2x_2 > \text{Current assets requirement constraint} \qquad \textbf{(14.11)}$$

$$x_i \geq O_i = 1,\ n \text{ non-negativity constraint} \qquad \textbf{(14.12)}$$

A very important feature of the model is that it allows the financial managers to integrate cash management with production and other aspects of the firm.

Cash Budget: Management Tool

Cash budget is a statement of the inflows and outflows of cash that is used to estimate its short-term requirements.

A firm is well advised to hold adequate cash balances but should avoid *excessive* balances. The firm has, therefore, to assess its need for cash properly. The cash budget is probably the most important tool in cash management. It is a device to help a firm to plan and control the use of cash. It is a statement showing the estimated cash inflows and cash outflows over the planning horizon. In other words, the net cash position (surplus or deficiency) of a firm as it moves from one budgeting subperiod to another is highlighted by the cash budget.

The various purposes of cash budgets are: **(i)** to coordinate the timings of cash needs. It identifies the period(s) when there might either be a shortage of cash or an abnormally large cash requirement; **(ii)** it pinpoints the period(s) when there is likely to be excess cash; **(iii)** it enables a firm which has sufficient cash to take advantage of cash discounts on its accounts payable, to pay obligations when due, to formulate dividend policy, to plan financing of capital expansion and to help unify the production schedule during the year so that the firm can smooth out costly seasonal fluctuations;[8] finally, **(iv)** it helps to arrange needed funds on the most favourable terms and prevents the accumulation of excess funds. With adequate time to study his needs, the finance manager can select the best alternative. In contrast, a firm which does not budget its cash requirements, may suddenly find itself short of funds. With pressing needs and little time to explore alternative avenues of financing, the management would be forced to accept the best terms offered in a difficult situation. 'These terms will not be as favourable, since the lack of planning indicates to the lender, that there is an organisational deficiency. The firm, therefore, represents a higher risk.'[9]

Elements/Preparation of Cash Budget Thus, the principal aim of the cash budget, as a tool to predict cash flows over a given period of time, is to ascertain whether at any point of time there is likely to be an excess or shortage of cash. The preparation of a cash budget involves various steps. These may be described as the elements of the cash budgeting system.

The *first* element of a cash budget is the selection of the period of time to be covered by the budget. It is referred to as the **planning horizon**. The planning horizon means the *time span* and the sub-periods within that time span over which the cash flows are to be projected. There is no fixed rule. The coverage of a cash budget will differ from firm to firm depending upon its nature and the degree of accuracy with which the estimates can be made. As a general rule, the period selected should be neither too long nor too short. If it is too long, it is likely that the estimates will be inaccurate. If, on the other hand, the time span is too small, many important events which lie just beyond the period cannot be accounted for and the work associated with the preparation of the budget becomes excessive.

The planning horizon of a cash budget should be determined in the light of the circumstances and requirements of a particular case. For instance, if the flows are expected to be stable and dependable, such a firm may prepare a cash budget covering a long period, say, a year and divide it into quarterly intervals. In the case of a firm whose flows are uncertain, a quarterly budget, divided into monthly intervals, may be appropriate. Where flows are affected by seasonal variations, monthly budgets, sub-divided on a weekly or even a daily basis, may be necessary. If the flows are subject to extreme fluctuations, even a daily budget may be called for. The idea behind subdividing the budgeting period into smaller intervals is to highlight the movement of cash from one subperiod to another. The sub-division will provide information on the fluctuations in the cash reservoir level during the time span covered by the budget.

Operating cashflows are cashflows generated by the operations of the firm.

The *second* element of the cash budget is the selection of the factors that have a bearing on cash flows. The items included in the cash budget are only cash items; non-cash items such as depreciation and amortisation are excluded.[10] The factors that generate cash flows are generally divided, for purposes of the construction of cash budget, into two broad categories: **(a)** operating, and **(b)** financial. This two-fold classification of cash budget items is based on their *nature*. While the former category includes cash flows generated by the operations of the firms and are known as **operating cash flows**, the latter consists of **financial cash flows**.

Financial cashflows are cashflows generated by the financial activties of the firm.

Operating Cash Flows The main operating factors/items which generate cash outflows and inflows over the time span of a cash budget are tabulated in Exhibit 14.1.

EXHIBIT 14.1 Operating Cash Flow Items

Inflows/Cash Receipts	*Outflows/Disbursements*
1. Cash sales	1. Accounts payable/Payable payments
2. Collection of accounts receivable	2. Purchase of raw materials
3. Disposal of fixed assets	3. Wages and salary (payroll)
	4. Factory expenses
	5. Administrative and selling expenses
	6. Maintenance expenses
	7. Purchase of fixed assets

Cash receipts implies all cash inflows in a given financial period.

Cash disbursements implies all cash outflows during a given financial period.

Among the operating factors affecting cash flows, are the collection of accounts receivable (inflow) and accounts payable (outflows). The terms of credit and the speed with which the customers pay would determine the lag between the creation of the accounts receivable and their collection. Also, discounts and allowances for early payments, returns from customers and bad debts affect cash inflows. Similarly, in the case of accounts payable relating to credit purchase, cash outflows are affected by the purchase terms.

The calculation of the collection on credit sales and payments on credit purchases, is generally done in the form of a statement known as the *worksheet.*[11] The results are subsequently incorporated in the cash budget. We illustrate in Example 14.4 how the credit policy of a firm and the purchase terms affect cash flows.

***Example* 14.4**

A firm sells goods on credit and allows a cash discount for payments made within 20 days. If the discount is not availed of, the buyer must pay the full amount in 40 days. However, the firm finds that some of its customers delay payments up to 90 days. The experience has been that on 20 per cent of sales, payment is made during the month in which the sale is made, on 70 per cent of the sales payment is made during the second month after sale and on 10 per cent of sales payment is made during the third month.

The raw materials and other supplies required for production amount to 70 per cent of sales and are bought in the month before the firm expects to sell its finished products. Its purchase terms allow the firm to delay payment on its purchases for one month.

The credit sales of the firm are: *(₹ lakh)*

May	10	August	30	November	20
June	10	September	40	December	10
July	20	October	20	January	10

Prepare a worksheet, showing the anticipated cash inflows on account of collection of receivables and disbursement of payables.

Solution

The expected cash inflows through collection of receivables and the anticipated outflows on account of accounts payable are presented in Table 14.2 in the form of a worksheet.

TABLE 14.2 Worksheet

(₹ lakh)

	May	June	July	Aug.	Sept.	Oct.	Nov.	Dec.	Jan.
1. Credit sales	10	10	20	30	40	20	20	10	10
2. Collections:									
During month of sale (20%)	2	2	4	6	8	4	4	2	2
During the first month after sale (70%)	—	7	7	14	21	28	14	14	7
During second month after sale (10%)	—	—	1	1	2	3	4	2	2
Total collections	2	9	12	21	31	35	22	18	11
3. Credit purchases (70% of next month's sale)	7	14	21	28	14	14	7	7	7
Payment (one month lag)	—	7	14	21	28	14	14	7	7
Total payments	—	7	14	21	28	14	14	7	7

Financial Cash Flows The major financial factors/items affecting the generation of cash flows are depicted in Exhibit 14.2.

EXHIBIT 14.2 Financial Cash Flow Items

Cash Inflows/Receipts	*Cash Outflows/Payments*
1. Loans/Borrowings	1. Income-tax/Tax payments
2. Sales of securities	2. Redemption of loan
3. Interest received	3. Repurchase of shares
4. Dividend received	4. Interest paid
5. Rent received	5. Dividends paid
6. Refund of tax	
7. Issue of new shares and securities	

Preparation of Cash Budget After the time span of the cash budget has been decided and pertinent operating and financial factors have been identified, the final step is the construction of the cash budget. The preparation of a cash budget is illustrated in Examples 14.5 and 14.6.

***Example* 14.5**

A firm adopts a six-monthly time span, subdivided into monthly intervals for its cash budget.

(A) The following information is available in respect of its operations: (₹ lakh)

Particulars	*Months*					
	1	*2*	*3*	*4*	*5*	*6*
1. Sales	40	50	60	60	60	60
2. Purchases	1	1.50	2	2	2	1
3. Direct labour	6	7	8	8	8	6
4. Manufacturing overheads	13	13.50	14	14	14	13
5. Administrative expenses	2	2	2	2	2	2
6. Distribution expenses	2	3	4	4	4	2
7. Raw materials (30 days credit)	14	15	16	16	16	15

(B) Assume the following financial flows during the period:

(a) *Inflows*:
1. Interest received in month 1 and month 6, ₹1 lakh each;
2. Dividend received during months 3 and 6, ₹2 lakh each;
3. Sales of shares in month 6, ₹160 lakh.

(b) *Outflows*:
1. Interest paid during month 1, ₹0.4 lakh;
2. Dividends paid during months 1 and 4, ₹2 lakh each;
3. Instalment payment on machine in month 6, ₹20 lakh;
4. Repayment of loan in month 6, ₹80 lakhs.

(c) Assume that 10 per cent of each month's sales are for cash; the balance 90 per cent are on credit. The terms and credit experience of the firm are:
1. No cash discount;
2. 1 per cent of credit sales is returned by the customers;
3. 1 per cent of total accounts receivable is bad debt;
4. 50 per cent of all accounts that are going to pay, do so within 30 days;
5. 100 per cent of all accounts that are going to pay, do so within 60 days.

Using the above information prepare a cash budget.

Solution The cash budget is constructed in Table 14.3.

TABLE 14.3 Cash Budget for Six Months

(₹ lakh)

Particulars	*Months*					
	1	*2*	*3*	*4*	*5*	*6*
(A) Cash inflows:						
1. Cash sales (10% of total)	4.00	5.00	6.00	6.00	6.00	6.00
2. Receivables collection	—	17.64	39.68	48.50	52.92	52.92
3. Interest received	1.00	—	—	—	—	1.00
4. Dividends received	—	—	2.00	—	—	2.00
5. Sale of shares	—	—	—	—	—	160.00
Total (A)	5.00	22.64	47.68	54.50	58.92	221.92
(B) Cash outflows:						
1. Purchases	1.00	1.50	2.00	2.00	2.00	1.00
2. Labour	6.00	7.00	8.00	8.00	8.00	6.00
3. Manufacturing overheads	13.00	13.50	14.00	14.00	14.00	13.00
4. Administrative expenses	2.00	2.00	2.00	2.00	2.00	2.00
5. Distribution charges	2.00	3.00	4.00	4.00	4.00	2.00
6. Raw materials (30 days credit)	—	14.00	15.00	16.00	16.00	16.00
7. Interest paid	0.40	—	—	—	—	—
8. Dividend paid	2.00	—	—	2.00	—	—
9. Instalment of machine	—	—	—	—	—	20.00
10. Repayment of loan	—	—	—	—	—	80.00
Total (B)	26.40	41.00	45.00	48.00	46.00	140.00
(C) Net Receipt or (Payment) (*A* – *B*)	(21.40)	(18.36)	2.68	6.50	12.92	81.92

It can be seen from Table 14.3 that the cash budget helps to reconcile the need for cash with the financing arrangement. For instance, in the first two months, the cash receipts fall below the disbursements and the firm obviously needs temporary financing which it will be able to pay in the subsequent months. In month 6, it has, in fact, excess cash for which temporary investment will have to be made until the funds can be employed in business.

***Example* 14.6**

The following information is available in respect of a firm:

(A) **Balance Sheet as on March 31**

Liabilities	*Amount*	*Assets*		*Amount*
Accrued salaries	₹500	Cash		₹3,000
Other liabilities	2,500	Inventory*		8,000
Capital	65,000	Other assets	₹70,000	
		Less: Depreciation	13,000	57,000
	68,000			68,000

*Consists of ₹2,000 minimum inventory plus ₹6,000 of inventory scheduled to be sold next month.

(B) **Sales Forecast**

April	₹10,000	July	₹50,000
May	20,000	August	40,000
June	30,000	September	20,000
		October	5,000

(C) **Salary Expenses Budget**

April	₹1,500	July	₹4,000
May	2,000	August	3,000
June	2,500	September	2,000

(D) The firm is expected to operate on the following lines:

- Other expenses approximate 12 per cent of sales (paid in the same month).
- Sales will be 80 per cent cash and 20 per cent credit. The all credit sales will be collected in the following month and no bad debts are expected.
- All inventory purchases will be paid for during the month in which they are made.
- A basic inventory of ₹2,000 (at cost) will be maintained. The firm will follow a policy of purchasing additional inventory each month to cover the following month's sale.
- A minimum cash balance of ₹3,000 will be maintained.
- New orders for equipment amounting to ₹20,000 scheduled for May 1 delivery and ₹10,000 for June 1 delivery have been made. Payment will be made at the time of delivery.
- Accrued salaries and other liabilities will remain unchanged.
- Gross profit margin is 40 per cent of sales.

Prepare a cash budget for 6 months (April to September). Borrowings are made in thousands of rupees. Ignore interest.

Solution

TABLE 14.4 Cash Budget (Amount in '000 rupees)

Particulars	*April*	*May*	*June*	*July*	*Aug.*	*Sept.*
(A) Cash inflows:						
1. Cash sales (0.80)	8	16	24	40	32	16
2. Accounts receivable collections (0.2)	—	2	4	6	10	8
Total	8	18	28	46	42	24

(*Contd.*)

(*Contd.*)

(B) Cash outflows:						
1. Inventory	12	18	30	24	12	3
2. Salary	1.5	2	2.5	4	3	2
3. Expenses	1.2	2.4	3.6	6	4.8	2.4
4. Equipment	—	20	10	—	—	—
Total	14.7	42.4	46.1	34	19.8	7.4
(C) Net monthly cash gain or loss by end of month (*A* – *B*)	(6.7)	(24.4)	(18.1)	12	22.2	16.6
Cumulative cash gain or loss by end of month	(6.7)	(31.1)	(49.2)	(37.2)	(15)	1.6
Cumulative borrowing (month-end)	7	32	50	38	15	—

LO 14.5 CASH MANAGEMENT: BASIC STRATEGIES

Cash cycle is the amount of time cash is tied up between payment for production inputs and receipt of payment from the sale of the resulting finished product; calculated as average age of inventory plus average collection period minus average accounts payable period.

Cash turnover is the number of times cash is used during the year; calculated by dividing number of days in a year by the cash cycle.

The cash budget, as a cash management tool, would throw light on the net cash position of a firm. After knowing the cash position, the management should work out the basic strategies to be employed to manage its cash. The discussion that follows and attempts to outline the basic strategies of cash management.

The broad cash management strategies are essentially related to the cash turnover process, that is, the cash cycle together with the cash turnover. The **cash cycle** refers[12] to the process by which cash is used to purchase materials from which are produced goods, which are then sold to customers, who later pay the bills. The firm receives cash from customers and the cycle repeats itself. The **cash turnover** means the number of times cash is used during each year.[13] The cash cycle involves several steps along the way as funds flow from the firm's accounts, as shown in Exhibit 14.3.

EXHIBIT 14.3 Details of Cash Cycle

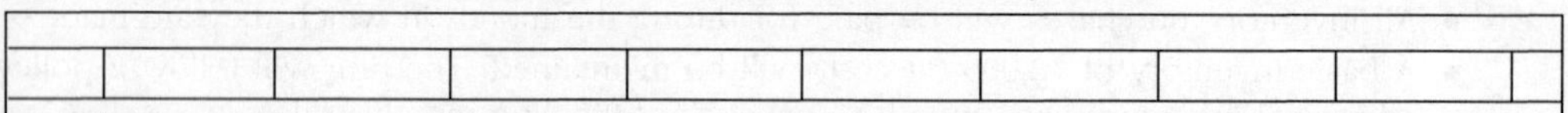

A = Materials ordered; B = Materials received;
C = Payments; D = Cheque clearance; E = Goods sold;
F = Customer mails payments; G = Payment received;
H = Cheques deposited; I = Funds collected

In addressing the issue of cash management strategies, we are concerned with the time periods involved in stages B, C, D, and F, G, H, I. A firm has no control over the time involved between stages A and B. The lag between D and E is determined by the production process and inventory policy. The time period between stages E and F is determined by credit terms and the payments policy of customers.

The cash cycle and cash turnover are illustrated in Example 14.7.

Example **14.7**

A firm which purchases raw materials on credit is required by the credit terms to make payments within 30 days. On its side, the firm allows its credit buyers to pay within 60 days. Its experience has been that it takes, on an average, 35 days to pay its accounts payable and 70 days to collect its accounts receivable. Moreover, 85 days elapse between the purchase of raw materials and the sale of finished goods, that is to say, the average age of inventory is 85 days. What is the firm's cash cycle? Also, estimate the cash turnover.

Solution

The cash cycle of the firm can be calculated by finding the average number of days that elapse between the cash outflows associated with paying accounts payable and the cash inflows associated with collecting accounts receivable:

(i) Cash cycle = 85 days + 70 days – 35 days = 120 days

(ii) Cash turnover = the assumed number of days in a year divided by the cash cycle = 365/120 = 3

Minimum Operating Cash

The higher the cash turnover, the less is the cash a firm requires. A firm should, therefore, try to maximise the cash turnover. But it must maintain a **minimum amount of operating cash balance** so that it does not run out of cash. The minimum level of operating cash is determined by dividing the total operating annual outlays by the cash turnover rate. If, for example, the total operating annual outlay of a firm is ₹240 lakh, its minimum cash requirement is ₹80 lakh (i.e. ₹240 lakh ÷ 3). The operational implication of the minimum operating cash requirement is that if the firm has opening cash balance of ₹80 lakh, it would be able to meet its obligations when they become due. In other words, it would not have to borrow anything. But the minimum operating cash involves a cost in terms of the earnings foregone from investing it temporarily, that is to say, there is an opportunity cost. Assuming 10 per cent return on a riskless investment (or retirement of a debt carrying 10 per cent interest), the cost of the minimum cash balance of ₹80 lakh works out to ₹8 lakh.

Minimum operating cash is the level of opening cash balance at which a firm would meet all obligations and is computed by dividing total annual outlays by the cash turnover.

Cash management strategies are intended to minimise the operating cash balance requirement. The basic strategies that can be employed to do the needful are as follows:[14]

(a) Stretching Accounts Payable,
(b) Efficient Inventory-Production Management,
(c) Speedy Collection of Accounts Receivable, and
(d) Combined Cash Management Strategies.

We spell out the implications of these strategies to the minimum cash balance and the associated cost with the underlying assumption that a firm should adopt such cash management strate-gies as will lead to the minimising of the operating cash requirement. In other words, efficient cash management implies minimum cash balances consistent with the need to pay bills when they become due.

Stretching Accounts Payable

One basic strategy of efficient cash management is to stretch the accounts payable. In other words, a firm should pay its accounts payable as late as possible without damaging its credit standing. It should, however, take advantage of the cash discount available on prompt payment.

If the firm, in our Example 14.7, can stretch its accounts payable from the current level of 35 days to 45 days, its cash cycle will be 110 days (i.e. reduced by 10 days from the original 120 days). The reduction in the cash cycle by 10 days as a result of the stretching of the accounts payable by 10 days will increase the cash turnover from 3 (initially) to 3.27 (360 ÷ 110). This will lead to a decrease in the minimum cash requirement from ₹80 lakh to ₹73.40 lakh (₹240 lakh ÷ 3.27). That is, the requirement has been reduced by ₹6.60 lakh. Assuming a 10 per cent rate of interest, there will be a saving in cost to the firm to the extent of ₹0.66 lakh.

Efficient Inventory-Production Management

Another strategy is to increase the inventory turnover, avoiding stock-outs, that is, shortage of stock. This can be done in the following ways:

1. *Increasing the raw materials turnover* by using more efficient inventory control techniques.
2. *Decreasing the production cycle* through better production planning, scheduling and control techniques; it will lead to an increase in the work-in-progress inventory turnover.
3. *Increasing the finished goods turnover* through better forecasting of demand and a better planning of production.

Assume that the firm in Example 14.7 is able to reduce the average age of its inventory from 85 to 70, that is, by 15 days. As a result, the cash cycle will decline by 15 days from 120 days to 105 days. The cash turnover will increase to 3.43 (360 ÷ 105) from the original level of 3. The effect of an increase in the cash turnover will be to reduce the minimum cash requirement from ₹80 lakh to ₹70 lakh (₹240 lakh ÷ 3.43). The saving in cost on ₹10 lakh will ₹1 lakh (₹10 lakh × 0.10). Thus, efficient inventory and production management causes a decline in the operating cash requirement and, hence, a saving in cash operating cost.

Speeding Collection of Accounts Receivable

Yet another strategy for efficient cash management is to collect accounts receivable as quickly as possible without losing future sales because of high-pressure collection techniques. The average collection period of receivables can be reduced by changes in **(i)** credit terms, **(ii)** credit standards, and **(iii)** collection policies. These are elaborated in the next chapter. In brief, **credit standards** represent the criteria for determining to whom credit should be extended. The collection policies determine the effort put forth to collect accounts receivable promptly.

If the firm in our Example 14.7 manages to reduce the average age of its accounts receivable from the current level of 70 days to 50 days, the cash cycle will be reduced to 100 days from 120 days (decline by 20 days). The cash turnover will increase in consequence to 3.60 (360 ÷ 100) from the original level of 3. The operating cash requirement will fall from ₹80 lakh to approximately ₹66.67 lakh (₹240 ÷ 3.60). The reduction in cash balance of about ₹13.33 lakh will lead to a saving in cost amounting to ₹1.33 lakh (0.10 × ₹13.33 lakh). Thus, a reduction in the average collection period by 20 days, releases funds equivalent to ₹13.33 lakh and leads to a saving in cash operating cost of ₹1.33 lakh.

Combined Cash Management Strategies

We have shown the effect of individual strategies on the efficiency of cash management. Each one of them has a favourable effect on the operating cash requirement. We now illustrate their combined effect, as firms will be well advised to use a combination of these strategies.

Assume the firm in Example 14.7 simultaneously **(i)** increases the average accounts payable by 10 days; **(ii)** reduces the average age of inventory by 15 days; **(iii)** speeds up the collection of accounts receivable by 20 days. Now, the cash cycle will be 75 days (120 days–10 days–15 days–20 days); the cash turnover will increase to 4.8 (360 ÷ 75); the minimum operating cash requirement will go down to ₹50 lakh, that is, a reduction of ₹30 lakh; assuming a 10 per cent rate of interest, the saving in cash operating cost will be ₹3 lakh.

The foregoing discussion clearly shows that the three basic strategies of cash management, related to (1) accounts payable, (2) inventory, and (3) accounts receivable, lead to a reduction in the cash balance. But, they imply certain problems for the management. *First,* if the accounts payable are postponed too long, the credit standing of the firm may be adversely affected. *Secondly,* a low level of inventory may lead to a stoppage of production as sufficient raw materials may not be available for uninterrupted production, or the firm may be short of enough stock to meet the demand for its product, that is, '**stock-out**'. *Finally,* restrictive credit standards, credit terms and collection policies may jeopardise sales. These implications should be constantly kept in view while working out cash management strategies.

Stock-out implies shortage of enough stock to meet the demand for the product.

LO 14.6 CASH MANAGEMENT TECHNIQUES/PROCESSES

The basic strategies of cash management have been outlined in the preceding section. It has been shown that the strategic aspects of efficient cash management are: **(i)** efficient inventory management, **(ii)** speedy collection of accounts receivable, and **(iii)** delaying payments on accounts payable. The main elements of an efficient management of inventory are discussed in some detail in Chapter 31. There are some specific techniques and processes for speedy collection of receivables from customers and slowing disbursements. We discuss them below.

Speedy Cash Collections

In managing cash efficiently, the cash inflow process can be accelerated through systematic planning and refined techniques. There are two broad approaches to do this. In the first place, the customers should be encouraged to pay as quickly as possible. Secondly, the payment from customers should be converted into cash without any delay.

Prompt Payment by Customers One way to ensure prompt payment by customers is *prompt billing.* What the customer has to pay and the period of payment should be notified accurately and in advance. The use of mechanical devices for billing along with the enclosure of a self-addressed return envelope will speed up payment by customers. Another, and more important, technique to encourage prompt payment by customers, is the practice of offering cash discounts. The availability of discount implies considerable saving to the customers. To avail of the facility, the customers would be eager to make payment early.

Early Conversion of Payments into Cash Once the customer makes the payment by writing a cheque in favour of the firm, the collection can be expedited by prompt encashment of the cheque. There is a lag between the time a cheque is prepared and mailed by the customer and the time the funds are included in the cash reservoir of the firm. This is represented by stages F to I in Exhibit 14.3. Within this time interval three steps are involved: **(a)** transit or mailing time, that is, the time taken by the post offices to transfer the cheque from the customers to the firm. This delay or lag is referred to as **postal float; (b)** time taken in processing the cheques within the firm before they are deposited in the banks, termed as **lethargy;** and **(c)** collection time within the bank, that is, the time taken by the bank in collecting the payment from the customer's bank. This is called **bank float.** The early conversion of payment into cash, as a technique to speed up collection of accounts receivable, is done to reduce the time lag between posting of the cheque by the customer and the realisation

Postal float is delay between the time when a payer mails a payment and the time when the payee receives it.

Lethargy/ processing float is the delay between the receipt of a cheque by the payee and its deposit in the account.

of money by the firm. The postal float, lethargy and bank float are collectively referred to as **deposit float**. The term deposit float is defined as *the sum of cheques written by customers that are not yet usable by the firm.*[15]

Bank/clearing float is the delay between the deposit of a cheque by the payee and the actual availability of funds.

The collection of accounts receivable can be considerably accelerated, by reducing transit, processing and collection time. An important cash management technique is reduction in deposit float. This is possible if a firm adopts a policy of **decentralised collections**. We discuss below some of the important processes that ensure decentralised collection so as to reduce **(i)** the amount of time that elapses between the mailing of a payment by a customer, and **(ii)** the point the funds become available to the firm for use. The principal methods of establishing a decentralised collection network are **(a)** Concentration Banking, and **(b)** Lock-box System.

Deposit float is the funds despatched by a payer that are not yet in a form that can be spent/used by the payee.

Concentration banking is a collection procedure in which payments are made to regionally dispersed collection centres, then deposited in local banks for quick clearing; reduces float by shortening the postal and bank float.

Concentration Banking In this system of decentralised collection of accounts receivable, large firms which have a large number of branches at different places, select some of the strategically located branches as collection centres for receiving payment from customers. Instead of all the payments being collected at the head office of the firm, the cheques for a certain geographical area are collected at a specified local collection centre. Under this arrangement, the customers are required to send their payments (cheques) to the collection centre covering the area in which they live and these are deposited in the local account of the concerned collection centre, after meeting local expenses, if any. Funds beyond a predetermined minimum are transferred daily to a *central* or *disbursing* or *concentration* bank or account. A concentration bank is one with which the firm has a major account–usually a disbursement account.[16] Hence, this arrangement is referred to as concentration banking.

Concentration banking, as a system of decentralised billing and multiple collection points, is a useful technique to expedite the collection of accounts receivable. It reduces the time needed in the collection process by reducing the *mailing* time. Since the collection centres are near the customers, the time involved in sending the bill to the customer is reduced. Moreover, the time-lag between the despatch of the cheque by the customer and its receipt by the firm is also reduced. Mailing time is saved both in respect of sending the bill to the customers as well as in the receipt of payment. The second reason why deposit float is reduced by concentration banking is that the banks of the firm as well as the customers may be in close proximity. Thus, the arrangement of multiple collection centres with concentration banking results in a saving of time in both mailing and clearance of customer payments and leads to a reduction in the operating cash requirements. Another advantage is that *concentration* permits the firm to 'store' its cash more efficiently.[17] This is so mainly because by pooling funds for disbursement in a single account, the aggregate requirement for cash balance is lower than it would be if balances are maintained at each branch office.

Lock-Box System The concentration banking arrangement is instrumental in reducing the time involved in mailing and collection. But with this system of collection of accounts receivable, *processing* for purpose of internal accounting is involved, that is, some time elapses before a cheque is deposited by the local collection centre in its account. The lock-box system takes care of this kind of problem, apart from effecting economy in mailing and clearance times. Under this arrangement, firms hire a post office lock-box at important collection centres. The customers are required to remit payments to the post office lock-box. The local banks of the firm, at the respective places, are authorised to open the box and pick up the remittances (cheques) received from the customers. Usually, the authorised banks pick up the cheques several times a day and deposit them in the firm's accounts. After crediting the account of the firm, the banks send a deposit slip alongwith the list of payments and other enclosures, if any, to the firm by way of proof and record of the collection.

Lock-box system is a collection procedure in which payers send their payments/cheques to a nearby post box that is emptied by the firm's bank several times and the bank deposits the cheque in the firm's account; reduces float by shortening the lethargy as well as postal and bank floats.

Thus, the **lock-box system** is like concentration banking in that the collection is decentralised and is done at the branch level. But they differ in one very important respect. While the customer sends the cheques, under the concentration banking arrangement, to the collection centres, he sends them to a post office box under the lock-box system. The cheques are directly received by the bank which empties the box and not from the firm or its local branch.

In a way, the lock-box arrangement is an improvement over the concentration banking system. Its superiority arises from the fact that one step in the collection process is eliminated with the use of lock-box: the receipt and deposit of cheques by the firm. In other words, the processing time within the firm before depositing a cheque in the bank is eliminated. Also, some extra saving in mailing timing is provided by the lock-box system as the cheques received in the post office box are not delivered either by the post office or the firm itself to the bank; rather, the bank itself picks them up at the post office.

Thus, the lock-box system, as a method of collection of receivables, has a two-fold advantage: **(i)** the bank performs the clerical task of handling the remittances prior to deposits, services which the bank may be able to perform at lower cost; **(ii)** the process of collection through the banking system begins immediately upon the receipt of the cheque/remittance and does not have to wait until the firm completes its processing for internal accounting purposes. In terms of the steps involved in the cash cycle, as shown in Exhibit 14.3, GH and HI would take place simultaneously. As a result, the time-lag between payment by a customer and the availability of funds to the firm for use would be reduced and, thereby, the collection of receivables would be accelerated.

Although the use of concentration banking and lock-box systems accelerate the collection of receivables, they involve a cost. While in the case of the former, the cost is in terms of the maintenance of multiple collection centres, compensation to the bank for services represents the cost associated with the latter. The justification for the use or otherwise of these special cash management techniques would be based on a comparison of the cost with the return generated on the released funds.[18] If the income exceeds the cost, the system is profitable and should be used; otherwise, not. For this reason, these techniques can be pressed into service only by large firms which receive a large number of cheques from a wide geographical area.

***Example* 14.8**

A firm uses a continuous billing system that results in an average daily receipt of ₹40,00,000. It is contemplating the institution of concentration banking, instead of the current system of centralised billing and collection. It is estimated that such a system would reduce the collection period of accounts receivable by 2 days.

Concentration banking would cost ₹75,000 annually and 8 per cent can be earned by the firm on its investments. It is also found that a lock-box system could reduce its overall collection time by four days and could cost annually ₹1,20,000.

(i) How much cash would be released with the concentration banking system?

(ii) How much money can be saved due to reduction in the collection period by 2 days? Should the firm institute the concentration banking system?

(iii) How much cash would be freed by lock-box system?

(iv) Between concentration banking and lock-box system, which is better?

Solution

(i) Cash released by the concentration banking system = ₹40,00,000 × 2 days = ₹80,00,000

(ii) Saving = 0.08 × ₹80,00,000 = ₹6,40,000.

The firm should institute the concentration banking system. It costs only ₹75,000 while the savings expected are ₹6,40,000.

(iii) Cash released by the lock-box system = ₹40,00,000 × 4 days = ₹1,60,00,000

(iv) Saving in lock-box system: 0.08 × ₹1,60,00,000 = ₹12,80,000

Lock-box system is better. Its net savings ₹11,60,000 (₹12,80,000 – ₹1,20,000) are higher than that of concentration banking.

Slowing Disbursements

Apart from speedy collection of accounts receivable, the operating cash requirement can be redu-ced by slow disbursements of accounts payable. In fact, slow disbursements represent a source of funds requiring no interest payments. There are several techniques to delay payment of accounts payable, namely, **(i)** avoidance of early payments; **(ii)** centralised disbursements; **(iii)** floats; and **(iv)** accruals.

Avoidance of Early Payments One way to delay payments is to avoid early payments. According to the terms of credit, a firm is required to make a payment within a stipulated period. It entitles a firm to cash discounts. If, however, payments are delayed beyond the due date, the credit standing may be adversely affected so that the firms would find it difficult to secure trade credit later. But if the firm pays its accounts payable before the due date it has no special advantage. Thus, a firm would be well advised not to make payments early, that is, before the due date.

Centralised Disbursements Another method to slow down disbursements is to have centralised disbursements. All the payments should be made by the head office from a centralised disbursement account. Such an arrangement would enable a firm to delay payments and conserve cash for several reasons. Firstly, it involves increase in the *transit* time. The remittance from the head office to the customers in distant places would involve more mailing time than a decentralised payment by the local branch. The second reason for reduction in operating cash requirement is that since the firm has a centralised bank account, a relatively smaller total cash balance will be needed. In the case of a decentralised arrangement, a minimum cash balance will have to be maintained at each branch which will add to a large operating cash balance. Finally, schedules can be tightly controlled and disbursements made exactly on the right day.

Float A very important technique of slow disbursements is float. The term float refers to the amount of money tied up in cheques that have been written, but have yet to be collected and encashed. Alternatively, float represents the difference between the bank balance and book balance of cash of a firm. The difference between the balance as shown by the firm's record and the actual bank balance is due to *transit* and processing delays. There is a time-lag between the issue of a cheque by the firm and its presentation to its bank by the customer's bank for payment. The implication is that although the cheque has been issued, cash would be required later when the cheque is presented for encashment. Therefore, a firm can send remittances although it does not have cash in its bank at the time of issuance of the cheque. Meanwhile, funds can be arranged to make payment when the cheque is presented for collection after a few days. Float used in this sense is called as **cheque kiting**.[19] There are two ways of doing it: (a) paying from a distant bank, (b) scientific cheque-cashing analysis.

Cheque-kiting is a method of consciously anticipating the resulting float or delay associated with the payment process using it to keep funds in an interest-earning form for as long as possible.

Paying From a Distant Bank The firm may issue a cheque on banks away from the creditor's bank. This would involve relatively longer transit time for the creditor's bank to get payment and, thus, enable the firm to use its funds longer.

Cheque-encashment Analysis Another way to make use of float is to analyse, on the basis of past experience, the time-lag in the issue of cheques and their encashment. For instance, cheques issued to pay wages and salary may not be encashed immediately; it may be spread over a few days, say, 25 per cent on one day, 50 per cent on the second day and the balance on the third day. It would mean that the firm should keep in the bank not the entire amount of a payroll but only a fraction represented by the actual withdrawal each day. This strategy would enable the firm to save operating cash.

Cheque encashment analysis is a way to play the float by depositing a certain proportion of a payroll payment in the firm's account on several successive days following the actual issue of cheques.

Accruals Finally, a potential tool for stretching accounts payable is accruals which are defined as current liabilities that represent a service or goods received by a firm but not yet paid for. For instance, payroll, that is, remuneration to employees who render service in advance and receive payment later. In a way, they extend credit to the firm for a period at the end of which they are paid, say, a week or a month. The longer the period after which payment is made, the greater is the amount of free financing consequently and the smaller is the amount of cash balances required. Thus, less frequent payrolls, that is, weekly as compared to monthly, are an important source of accrual. They can be manipulated to slow down disbursements. Other examples of accrual are rent to lessors and taxes to government. But these can be utilised only to a limited extent as there are legal constraints beyond which such payments cannot be extended.

LO 14.7 MARKETABLE SECURITIES

We present below a brief description of the marketable securities. Attention is focussed on the meaning and characteristics of marketable securities, the general selection criterion and the basic types of such securities.

Meaning and Characteristics

Breadth of market is a characteristic of a ready market determined by the number of participants (buyers) in the market.

Once the optimum level of cash balance of a firm has been determined, the residual of its liquid assets is invested in marketable securities. Such securities are short-term investment instruments to obtain a return on temporarily idle funds. In other words, they are securities which can be converted into cash in a short period of time, typically a few days. The basic characteristics of marketable securities affect the degree of their marketability/liquidity. To be liquid, a security must have two basic characteristics: a ready market and safety of principal. Ready marketability minimises the amount of time required to convert a security into cash. A ready market should have both **breadth** in the sense of a large number of participants scattered over a wide geographical area as well as **depth** as determined by its ability to absorb the purchase/sale of large amounts of securities.

Depth of market is a characteristic of a ready market, determined by its ability to absorb the purchase/sale of a large amount of a particular securities.

The second determinant of liquidity is that there should be little or no loss in the value of a marketable security over time. Only those securities that can be easily converted into cash without any reduction in the principal amount qualify for short-term investments. A firm would be better off leaving the balances in cash if the alternative were to risk a significant reduction in principal.

Selection Criterion

A major decision confronting the financial managers involves the determination of the mix of cash and marketable securities. Some of the quantitative models for determining the optimum amounts of marketable securities to hold in certain circumstances have been outlined in an earlier section. In general, the choice of the mix is based on a trade-off between the opportunity to earn a return on idle funds (cash) during the holding period, and the brokerage costs associated with the purchase and sale of marketable securities. For example, take the case of a firm paying ₹350 as brokerage costs to purchase and sell ₹45,000 worth of marketable securities, yielding an annual return of 8 per cent and held for one month. The interest earned on the securities works out at ₹300 (1/12 × .08 × ₹45,000). Since this amount is less than the cost of the transaction (₹350), it is not advisable for the firm to make the investments. This trade-off between interest returns and brokerage costs is a key factor in determining what proportion of liquid assets should be held in the form of marketable securities.

There are three motives for maintaining liquidity (cash as well as marketable securities) and, therefore, for holding marketable securities: transaction motive, safety/precautionary motive and speculative motive. Each motive is based on the premise that a firm should attempt to earn a return on temporarily idle funds. The type of marketable security purchased will depend on the motive for the purchase. An assessment of certain criteria can provide the financial manager with a useful framework for selecting a proper marketable securities mix. These considerations include evaluation of **(i)** financial risk, **(ii)** interest rate risk, **(iii)** taxability, **(iv)** liquidity, and **(v)** yield among different financial assets.

Financial/Default Risk It refers to the uncertainty of expected returns from a security attributable to possible changes in the financial capacity of the *security-issuer* to make future payments to the *security-owner*. If the chance of default on the terms of the investment is high (low), then the financial risk is said to be high (low). As the marketable securities portfolio is designed to provide a return on funds that would be otherwise tied up in idle cash held for transaction or precautionary purposes, the financial manager will not usually be willing to assume such financial/default risk in the hope of greater return within the makeup of the portfolio.

> **Default risk** is the uncertainty of expected return attributable to possible change in financial capacity of issuer of security to make future payments.

Interest Rate Risk The uncertainty that is associated with the expected returns from a financial instrument attributable to changes in interest rate is known as **interest rate risk**. Of particular concern to the corporate financial manager is the price volatility associated with instruments that have long, as opposed to short, terms to maturity.

> **Interest rate risk** is the uncertainty associated with expected return attributable to change in interest rate.

If prevailing interest rates rise compared with the date of purchase, the market price of the securities will fall to bring their yield to maturity in line with what financial managers could obtain by buying a new issue of a given instrument, for instance, treasury bills. The longer the maturity of the instrument, the larger will be the fall in prices. To hedge against the price volatility caused by interest rate risk, the market securities portfolio will tend to be composed of instruments that mature over short periods.

Taxability Another factor affecting observed difference in market yields is the differential impact of taxes. Securities, income on which is tax-exempt, sell in the market at lower yields to maturity than other securities of the same maturity. A differential impact on yields arises also because interest income is taxed at the ordinary tax rate while capital gains are taxed at a lower rate. As a result, fixed-interest securities that sell at a discount because of low coupon rate in relation to the prevailing yields are attractive to taxable investors. The reason is that part of the yield to maturity is a capital gain. Owing to the desirability of discount on low-interest fixed-income securities, their yield to maturity tends to be lower than the yield on comparable securities with higher coupon rates. The greater the discount, the greater is the capital gains attraction and the lower is its yield relative to what it would be if the coupon rate were such that the security was sold at par.

Liquidity With reference to marketable securities portfolio, **liquidity** refers to the ability to transform a security into cash. Should an unforeseen event require that a significant amount of cash be immediately available, a sizeable portion of the portfolio might have to be sold. The financial manager will want the cash *quickly* and will not want to accept a large price reduction in order to convert the securities. Thus, in the formulation of preferences for the inclusion of particular instruments in the portfolio, consideration will be given to **(i)** the time period needed to sell the security and **(ii)** the likelihood that the security can be sold at or near its prevailing market price. The latter element, here, means that 'thin' markets, where relatively few transactions take place or where trades are accomplished only with large price changes between transaction, should be avoided.

Liquidity is the ability to transform a security into cash.

Yield The final selection criterion is the yields that are available on the different financial assets suitable for inclusion in the marketable/near-cash portfolio. All the four factors listed above, *financial risk, interest rate risk, liquidity* and *taxability*, influence the available yields on financial instruments. Therefore, the yield criterion involves a weighing of the risks and benefits inherent in these factors. If a given risk is assumed, such as lack of liquidity, then a higher yield may be expected on the instrument lacking the liquidity characteristics.

In brief, the finance manager must focus on the risk-return trade-offs associated with the four factors on yield through his analysis. Coming to grips with these trade-offs will enable the finance mananger to determine the proper marketable securities mix for his firm.

Marketable Security Alternatives

We describe below briefly the more prominent marketable/near-cash securities available for investment. Our concern is with money market instruments.

Treasury bills are Indian government obligations issued on auction basis having maturities of 91-days and 364-days and virtually no risk.

Treasury Bills These are obligations of the government. They are sold on a discount basis. The investor does not receive an actual interest payment. The return is the difference between the purchase price and the face (par) value of the bill.

The **treasury bills** are issued only in *bearer* form. They are purchased, therefore, without the investors' name upon them. This attribute makes them easily transferable from one investor to another. A very active secondary market exists for these bills. The secondary market for bills not only makes them highly liquid but also allows purchase of bills with very short maturities. As the bills have the full financial backing of the government, they are, for all practical purposes, risk-free. The negligible financial risk and the high degree of liquidity makes their yield lower than those on the other marketable securities. Due to their virtually risk-free nature and because of active secondary market for them, treasury bills are one of the most popular marketable securities even though the yield on them is lower.

Negotiable certificates of deposits are negotiable instruments representing specific cash deposits in banks having varying maturities and yields based on size, maturity and prevailing money market conditions.

Negotiable Certificates of Deposit (CDs) These are marketable receipts for funds that have been deposited in a bank for a fixed period of time. The deposited funds earn a fixed rate of interest. The denomination and maturities are tailored to the investors' need. The **CDs** are offered by banks on a basis different from treasury bills, that is, they are not sold at a discount. Rather, when the certificates mature, the owner receives the full amount deposited plus the earned interest. A secondary market exists for the CDs. While CDs may be issued in either registered or bearer form, the latter facilitates transactions in the secondary market and, thus, is the most common. The default risk is that of the bank failure, a possibility that is low in most cases.

Commercial Paper It refers to short-term unsecured promissory note sold by large business firms to raise cash. As they are unsecured, the issuing side of the market is dominated by large companies which typically maintain sound credit ratings. **Commercial papers** (CPs) can be sold either directly or through dealers. Companies with high credit rating can sell directly to investors. The denominations in which they can be bought vary over a wide range. They can be purchased similarly with varying maturities. These papers are *generally* sold on discount basis in bearer form although at times commercial papers can be issued carrying interest and made payable to the order of the investor. For all practical purposes, there is no active trading in secondary market for commercial paper although direct sellers of CPs often repurchase it on request. This feature distinguishes CPs from all of the previously discussed short-term investment vehicles. When, there-fore, a financial manager evaluates these for possible inclusion in marketable securities portfolio, he should plan to hold it to maturity. Owing to its lack of marketability, CPs provide a yield advantage over other near-cash assets of comparable maturity.

Commercial papers is a short-term, unsecured promissory note issued by a firm that has high credit rating/standing.

Bankers' Acceptances These are drafts (order to pay) drawn on a specific bank by an exporter in order to obtain payment for goods he has shipped to a customer who maintains an account with that specific bank. They can also be used in financing domestic trade. The draft guarantees payment by the accepting bank at a specific point of time. The seller who holds such acceptance may sell it at a discount to get immediate funds. Thus, the acceptance becomes a marketable security. Since acceptances are used to finance the acquisition of goods by one party, the document is not 'issued' in specialised denominations; its size/denomination is determined by the cost of goods being purchased. They serve a wide range of maturities and are sold on a discount basis, payable to the bearer. A secondary market for the acceptances of large banks does exist. Owing to their greater financial risk and lesser liquidity, acceptances provide investors a yield advantage over treasury bills of like maturity. In fact, the acceptances of major banks are a very safe investment, making the yield advantage over treasury bills worth looking for marketable securities portfolio.

Banker's acceptances are short-term, low-risk marketable securities arising from bank guarantees of business transactions.

Repurchase (Repo) Agreements These are legal contracts that involve the actual sale of securities by a borrower to the lender with a commitment on the part of the former to repurchase the securities at the current price plus a stated interest charge. The securities involved are government securities and other money market instruments. The borrower is either a financial institution or a security dealer.

There are two major reasons why a firm with excess cash prefers to buy **repurchase agreements** rather than a marketable security. First, the original maturities of the instrument being sold can, in effect, be adjusted to suit the particular needs of the investing firm. Therefore, funds available for a very short period, that is, one/two days can be employed to earn a return. Closely related to the first is the second reason, namely, since the contract price of the securities that make up the

Repurchase agreement is an agreement whereby a bank sells securities and agrees to buy them back at a specific price and time.

arrangement is fixed for the duration of the transaction, the firm buying the repurchase agreement is protected against market fluctuations throughout the contract period. This makes it a sound alternative investment for funds that are surplus for only short periods.

Units The units of mutual funds offer a reasonably convenient alternative avenue for investing surplus liquidity as **(i)** there is a very active secondary market for them, **(ii)** the income from units is tax-exempt up to a specified amount and, **(iii)** the units appreciate in a fairly predictable manner.

Intercorporate Deposits Intercorporate deposits, that is, short-term deposits with other companies is a fairly attractive form of investment of short-term funds in terms of rate of return which currently ranges between 12 and 15 per cent. However, apart from the fact that one month's time is required to convert them into cash, intercorporate deposits suffer from high degree of risk.

Bills Discounting Surplus funds may be deployed to purchase/discount bills. Bills of exchange are drawn by seller (drawer) on the buyer (drawee) for the value of goods delivered to him. During the pendency of the bill, if the seller is in need of funds, he may get it discounted. On maturity, the bill should be presented to the drawee for payment. A bill of exchange is a self-liquidating instrument. Bill discounting is superior to intercorporate deposits for investing surplus funds. While parking surplus funds in bills discounting, it should be ensured that the bills are trade bills arising out of genuine commercial transaction and, as far as possible, they should be backed by letter of credit/acceptance by banks to ensure absolute safety of funds.

Money market mutual funds are professionally managed portfolios of popular marketable securities having instant liquidity, competitive yield and low transaction costs.

Money Market Mutual Funds/Liquid Funds are professionally managed portfolios of marketable securities. They provide instant liquidity. Due to high liquidity, competitive yields and low transactions, these funds have achieved significant growth in size and popularity in recent years.

LO 14.8 CASH MANAGEMENT PRACTICES IN INDIA

Cash management in India presents a daunting task in light of the huge number of clearing houses (1,056) and bank branches (more than 75,000). The main features of cash management practices in India are: (i) collection methods, (ii) payment mechanisms, and (iii) electronic banking.

Collection Methods

Collection services provided by banks use their own branches and their correspondent bank's network as well as country-wide arrangements with couriers and coordinators. There are two broad categories of collection products offered by banks in India: local collection and upcountry collection/ outstation clearing.

Local collection is used for cheques deposited with the bank/its correspondent bank in the location on which it is drawn. Compared with outstation cheque collections, local collection funds are realised faster.

Outstation clearing is used when the location where the cheque is deposited with the bank is different from the location on which it is drawn. Banks offer two types of outstation cheque collection products: one for cheques drawn on a correspondent bank location and the other for cheques drawn on locations that are not covered by the correspondent bank. In the case of the former, the typical clearing period of the cheque is relatively faster, and the risk involved (loss of cheques in transit) is also much lower.

The collection proceeds can be made available to the customer on either a cleared funds or guaranteed basis (i.e. cheque-discounting) depending on the corporate's cashflow requirements. Value-added services such as cheque pick-ups, customised management information reporting, data-entry of deposit-slip information and so on are also provided.

Bulk Collection is offered by banks for processing high-volume collections such as cheque collection for initial public offerings (IPOs), utility bill collections for telephone, electricity, cellular service providers and so on through timely clearing of instruments together with strong reconciliation and reporting.

Post-dated Cheque (PDC) Management solutions are critical for non-banking finance companies that collect PDCs from their retail and auto-loan disbursement customers.

Electronic Clearing Service—Debit Scheme of the RBI enables corporates typically utility or insurance companies to collect the proceeds of small value large-volume payments from their customers.

Cheque Truncation removes the need for much of the physical handling and movement of paper-based payment instruments as only the electronic image of the instrument is transmitted through the clearing system.

Payment Mechanism

Currently payments are significantly paper-based through cash/cheques/demand drafts. The key mechanism available to customers in India are illustrated below:

Payment mechanism	*Features*
Cheque	Currently the most prevalent mode of payment. The customer's account is debited only when a cheque is presented in clearing by the beneficiary.
Cheque payable at par	A cheque that can be redeemed at par at any of the locations where the bank has a branch. The customer's account is debited only on clearing.
Customer's or pay order	A pre-funded payment instrument issued by a bank, i.e. the customer's account is debited up front, and is typically payable at all locations where the bank has branches.
Demand draft	A pre-funded out-station pay order, which is drawn on a location where the bank does not have its own branch, but has a tie-up with a correspondent bank. The customer's account is debited upfront.
Real-time gross settlement (RTGS)	A domestic electronic payment mechanism for funds transfer (credit-push). The beneficiary's bank is required to credit the proceeds of an inward RTGS transaction to the beneficiary's account, or return the funds, within two hours of receipt of the payment notification. Participation by banks in RTGS customer payments is currently voluntary.

(*Contd.*)

(Contd.)

Electronic Funds Transfer (EFT)	An electronic payment mode for same-day inter- and intra-city funds transfer (credit-push). It is mandatory for all bank branches, in 16 large metros in India, directly involved in clearing, to participate in RBI's EFT System for inward EFT.
Special Electronic Funds Transfer (SEFT)	An electronic payment mode for same-day inter- and intra-city funds transfer (credit-push). This is an extension of RBI's EFT system, but participation in SEFT is voluntary for banks, and only networked branches are allowed to participate. Thus, location coverage is wider than EFT, but not all banks participate in SEFT.
Electronic Clearing Service (ECS) – Credit	ECS (credit) is an electronic mode of payment which is designed for large-volume payments. The ECS scheme is operational in some 46 cities and all banks directly participating in clearing have to process inward ECS. The ECS settlement cycle is four days; much longer than for RTGS, EFT or SEFT.
Interest/Dividend warrants	These are paper-based payment instruments that are required to be pre-funded (based on applicable regulations) and are used for large-volume interest and dividend payments.

The migration from paper-based to electronic modes of payment has been relatively slow and gradual. Corporates are realising the potential of cost-savings in processing electronic payments as these are conducive to system-integration with the client's internal systems.

Payment Outsourcing Corporates and financial institutions are increasingly outsourcing payment-processing to banks. Payment outsourcing products eliminate manual processing and the overhead costs associated with preparing, verifying and signing/despatching individual cheques. Banks facilitate the interfacing of corporate's back-office payment system with the bank's electronic banking plateforms.

Electronic Banking

Banks offer sophisticated electronic banking delivery channels. They not only allow customers to access account-balance information in real-time but also enable them to initiate transactions for payments, inter-account transfers, deposit placements and so on. Corporates have access to extensive management information reports. The internet banking offerings also allow corporates to access their accounts with the banks from different countries.

SUMMARY

LO 14.1

Cash management is one of the key areas of working capital management. There are four motives for holding cash: (i) transaction motive, (ii) precautionary motive, (iii) speculative motive, and (iv) compensating motive. The transaction motive refers to the holding of cash to meet anticipated obligations whose time is not perfectly synchronised with cash receipts

LO 14.1	The cash balances held in reserve for random and unforeseen fluctuations in cash flows are called precautionary balances. The speculative motive indicates the desire of a firm to take advantage of opportunities which present themselves at unexpected moments and which are typically outside the normal course of business. The compensating motive means keeping the bank balance sufficient to earn a return equal to the cost of free services provided by the banks.
LO 14.2	The basic objectives of cash management are to reconcile two mutually contradictory and conflicting tasks: to meet the payment schedule and to minimise funds committed to cash balances.
LO 14.3	The factors that determine the required cash balances are: (i) synchronisation of cash flows, (ii) the cost associated with a shortfall in the firm's cash needs, (iii) excess cash balance cost, (iv) cost associated with establishing an operating cash management staff and activities, and (v) the impact of uncertainties on cash management strategy.
LO 14.4	There are two approaches to derive an optimal cash balance: (i) minimising cash cost models and (ii) cash budget. The important models are: (1) Baumol Model, (2) Miller-Orr Model and (3) Orgler's Model.
	The focus of Baumol model is to minimise the total cost associated with cash management comprising total conversion costs (that is, costs incurred each time marketable securities are converted into cash) and the opportunity cost of keeping idle cash balances which otherwise could have been invested in marketable securities.
	The objective of Miller-Orr Model is to determine the optimum cash balance level which minimises the cost of cash management.
	Orgler's model requires the use of multiple linear programming to determine an optimal cash management strategy. An important feature of this model is that it allows the financial managers to integrate cash management with production, current assets requirement and other aspects of the corporate.
	Cash budget is probably the most important tool in cash management. It is a device to help a firm to plan and control the use of cash. The cash position of a firm as it moves from one period to another period is highlighted by the cash budget. A cash budget has normally three parts, namely, cash collections, cash payments and cash balances. The major sources of cash receipts and payments are operating and financial. The operating sources are repetitive in nature, while the financial sources are non-recurring.
LO 14.5	The cash management strategies are intended to minimise the operating cash balance requirement. The basic strategies that can be employed are (i) stretching accounts payable without affecting the credit of the firm, (ii) efficient inventory management and (iii) speedy collections of accounts receivable. Some of the specific techniques and processes for speedy collection of receivables from customers are ensuring prompt payment for customers and early payment/conversion into cash. Concentration banking and lock-box system deserve specific mention as principal methods of establishing a decentralised collection network. The techniques to delay payments of accounts payable include avoidance of early payment, centralised disbursements and float.
LO 14.6	Concentration banking, as a system of decentralised billing and multiple collection points, is a useful technique to expedite the collection of accounts receivable by reducing the mailing time. The mailing time is saved both in respect of sending the bill to the customers as well as in the receipt of payment.
	Under the lock-box system, firms hire a post office lock-box at important collection centers where the customers remit payments. The local banks are authorized to open the box and pick up the remittances (cheques) received from the customers. As a result, there is some extra saving in mailing time compared to concentration banking.
	The financial evaluation of concentration banking and lock-box system would be based on the incremental analysis by comparing the cost of operations and benefits in terms of interest earnings on the early release of funds.

LO 14.7

Marketable securities are an outlet for surplus cash as liquid security/assets. To be liquid a security must have two basic characteristics, that is, a ready market and safety of principal.

The selection criteria for marketable securities include the evaluation of financial risk, interest-rate risk, liquidity, taxability and yield among different financial assets. The prominent marketable securities available for investment are: treasury bills, negotiable certificates of deposits, commercial paper, bankers' acceptance, units of mutual funds, intercorporate deposits, interbank call money, commercial bills under the bill market scheme and short-term deposits.

REFERENCES

1. Bolten, S E, *Managerial Finance*, Houghton Mifflin Co., Boston, 1976, p 388.
2. Weston, J F and E F Brigham, *Essentials of Managerial Finance*, Holt, Rinehart and Winston, New York, 1974, p 161.
3. Bolten, S E, *op. cit.*, p 390. Reprinted by permission of Houghton Mifflin Co., Boston, USA.
4. For an account of this model, please refer to Sethi, SP and Thompson, GL, 'An Application of Mathematical Control Theory to Finance: Modelling Simple Dynamic Cash Balance Problems', *Journal of Financial and Quantitative Analysis*, Dec. 1970, pp 381-394.
5. Baumol, W J, 'The Transaction Demand for Cash: An Inventory Theoretic Approach', *Quarterly Journal of Economics*, LXV November, 1952, pp 545-56.
6. Miller, M H and Orr, D, 'A Model of the Demand for Money in Firms', *Quarterly Journal of Economics*, LXX Aug., 1966, pp 413-435.
7. Orgler, Y E, *Cash Management: Methods and Models*, Wadsworth Publishing Company, Balmont, California, 1970.
8. *Ibid.* p 392.
9. Nemmers, E E and A E Gruenwald, *Basic Managerial Finance*, West Publishing Co., New York, 1975, p 109.
10. It should, however, be noted that depreciation will be relevant to the computation of taxes. This aspect has been elaborated in Chapter 10.
11. Brigham, E F *Financial Management* (Illinois), Drydon Press, 1977, p 221.B.
12. Solomon, E and J J Pringle, *Introduction to Financial Management*, Goodyear Publishing Co., Santa Monica, Calif. 1977, p 178.
13. Gitman, L J, *Principles of Managerial Finance*, Harper and Row, New York, 1997, p 170.
14. *Ibid.*, p 169.
15. Joy, O M, *Introduction to Financial Management*, irwin, Homewood, Ill., 1977, p 431.
16. Cf. Van Horne, *Financial Management and Policy*, Prentice-Hall, New Delhi, 1998, p 423.
17. Solomon, E and JJ Pringle, *op. cit.*, p 181.
18. Cf. Van Horne, *op. cit.*, p 425.
19. Cf. Gitman, *op. cit.*, p 180.

SOLVED PROBLEMS

P.14.1 The following information is available in respect of a trading firm:

LO 14.5 LOD M

(i) On an average, debtors are collected after 45 days; inventories have an average holding period of 75 days and creditors payment period on an average is 30 days.

(ii) The firm spends a total of ₹120 lakh annually at a constant rate.

(iii) It can earn 10 per cent on investments.

From the above information, compute: (a) the cash cycle and cash turnover, (b) minimum amounts of cash to be maintained to meet payments as they become due, (c) savings by reducing the average inventory holding period by 30 days.

Solution

(a) Cash cycle = 45 days + 75 days – 30 days = 90 days (3 months)
Cash turnover = 12 months (360 days)/3 months (90 days) = 4.

(b) Minimum operating cash = Total operating annual outlay/cash turnover, that is, ₹120 lakh/4 = ₹30 lakh.

(c) Cash cycle = 45 days + 45 days – 30 days = 60 days (2 months)
Cash turnover = 12 months (360 days)/2 months (60 days) = 6.
Minimum operating cash = ₹120 lakh/6 = ₹20 lakh
Reduction in investments = ₹30 lakh – ₹20 lakh = ₹10 lakh
Savings = 0.10 × ₹10 lakh = ₹1 lakh.

P.14.2 A firm has been offered a cash management service by a bank for ₹1,00,000 per year. It is estimated that such a service would not only eliminate 'excess' cash on deposits (₹8,00,000) but also reduce its administration and other costs to the tune of ₹5,000 per month. Assuming the cost of capital of 15 per cent, is it worthwhile for the firm to engage the cash management service?

LO 14.5 LOD E

Solution

Benefits (annual):	
Savings in interest (₹8,00,000 × 0.15)	₹1,20,000
Reduction in administration and other costs (₹5,000 × 12)	60,000
Total	1,80,000
Less: Cost (annual):	
Bank service charges	1,00,000
Net annual benefits	80,000

Recommendation It is worthwhile to engage the bank services.

P.14.3 Royal Industries feels a lock-box system can shorten its accounts receivable collection period by 3 days. Credit sales are estimated at ₹365 lakh per year, billed on a continuous basis. The firm's opportunity cost of funds is 15 per cent. The cost of lock box system is ₹50,000.

LO 14.6 LOD M

(a) Will you advise 'Royal' to go for lock-box system?
(b) Will your answer be different if accounts receivable collection period is reduced by 5 days?

Solution

(a) Cash released by lock-box system (₹365 lakh/365 days = ₹1 lakh × 3 days)	₹3,00,000
Savings (₹3 lakh × 0.15)	45,000
Less: Cost of lock-box system	50,000
Net loss	(5,000)

The firm is advised not to go for the lock-box system.

(b) Cash released: ₹1 lakh × 5 days	₹5,00,000
Savings (₹5 lakh × 0.15)	75,000
Less: Cost of lock-box system	50,000
Net savings	25,000

Recommendation The firm should go for the lock box system.

P.14.4 Sagar Industries sells its products through widely dispersed distributors in Northern India. It currently takes on an average 8 days for cash receipt cheques to become available to the firm from the day they are mailed. The firm is contemplating the institution of concentration banking to reduce this period. It is estimated that such a system would reduce the collection period of accounts receivable by 3 days. The daily cheque receipts currently average ₹10,00,000.

LO 14.6 LOD M

The concentration banking would cost ₹1,50,000 annually and the cost of funds is 15 per cent.

(a) Advise Sagar whether it should introduce concentration banking system.

(b) Will your answer be different, if it is estimated that a lock-box system can reduce the collection time by 4 days and its annual cost would be ₹2,00,000?

Solution

(a) Cash released by concentration banking system (₹10 lakh × 3 = ₹30 lakh)	
Savings (₹30 lakh × 0.15)	₹4,50,000
Less: Costs	1,50,000
Net savings	3,00,000

The firm should introduce concentration banking system.

(b) Cash released by lock-box system (₹10 lakh × 4 = ₹40 lakh)	
Savings (₹40 lakh × 0.15)	6,00,000
Less: Costs	2,00,000
Net savings	4,00,000

The lock box system is better.

P.14.5 The following results are expected by XYZ Ltd by quarters next year, in thousands of rupees.

Particulars	*Quarter*			
	1	*2*	*3*	*4*
Sales	7,500	10,500	18,000	10,500
Cash payments:				
Production costs	7,000	10,000	8,000	8,500
Selling, administrative and other costs	1,000	2,000	2,900	1,600
Purchases of plant and other fixed assets	100	1,100	2,100	2,100

LO 14.4 LOD M

The debtors at the end of a quarter are one-third of sales for the quarter. The opening balance of debtors is ₹30,00,000. Cash on hand at the beginning of the year is ₹6,50,000 and the desired minimum balance is ₹5,00,000. Borrowings are made at the beginning of quarters in which the need will occur in multiples of ₹10,000 and are repaid at the end of quarters. Interest charges may be ignored. You are required to prepare:

(a) a cash budget by quarters for the year; and

(b) state the amount of loan outstanding at the end of the year.

Solution

(a) Cash budget next year (quarter-wise) *(thousands of rupees)*

Particulars	*Quarter*				
	1	*2*	*3*	*4*	*Total*
(A) Cash inflows:					
Collection from debtors					
(i) From prior quarter (1/3 of sales)	3,000	2,500	3,500	6,000	15,000
(ii) From current quarter (2/3 of sales)	5,000	7,000	12,000	7,000	31,000
Total	8,000	9,500	15,500	13,000	46,000
(B) Cash outflows:					
Production costs	7,000	10,000	8,000	8,500	33,500
Selling, administrative and other costs	1,000	2,000	2,900	1,600	7,500
Plant and other fixed assets purchased	100	1,100	2,100	2,100	5,400
Total	8,100	13,100	13,000	12,200	46,400

(Contd.)

(*Contd.*)

(C) Surplus/(deficiency)	(100)	(3,600)	2,500	800	(400)
Beginning balance	650	550	500	500	650
Ending balance (indicated)	550	(3,050)	3,000	1,300	250
Borrowings required (deficiency + minimum cash required)		3,550			3,550
(Repayments) made (balance – minimum cash required)			(2,500)	(800)	(3,300)
Ending balance (actually now estimated)	550	500	500	500	500

(b) Loan outstanding = ₹35,50,000 – ₹33,00,000 = ₹2,50,000.

P.14.6 The following data pertain to a shop. The owner has made the following sales forecasts for the first 5 months of the coming year: LO 14.4 LOD D

January	₹40,000	April	60,000
February	45,000	May	50,000
March	55,000		

Other data are as follows:

(a) Debtors and creditors' balances at the beginning of the year are ₹30,000 and ₹14,000, respectively. The balances of other relevant assets and liabilities are:

Cash balance	₹7,500
Stock	51,000
Accrued sales commission	3,500

(b) 40 per cent sales are on cash basis. Credit sales are collected in the month following sale.
(c) Cost of goods sold is 60 per cent of sales.
(d) The only other variable cost is a 5 per cent commission to sales agents. The sales commission is paid in month after it is earned.
(e) Inventory (stock) is kept equal to sales requirements for the next two months' budgeted sales.
(f) Trade creditors are paid in the following month after purchases.
(g) Fixed costs are ₹5,000 per month, including ₹2,000 depreciation.

You are required to prepare a cash budget for each of the first three months of coming year.

Solution

Cash budget for 3 months (January-March)

Particulars	*Month*		
	January	*February*	*March*
(A) Cash inflows:			
Cash sales (40% of total sales)	₹16,000	₹18,000	₹22,000
Collection from debtors (one month after sales)	30,000	24,000	27,000
Total	46,000	42,000	49,000
(B) Cash outflows:			
Paid to trade creditors for purchases (see working note on purchase budget)	14,000	33,000	36,000
Sales commission (5 per cent of prior month's sales)	3,500	2,000	2,250
Fixed costs (₹5,000 – ₹2,000 depreciation)	3,000	3,000	3,000
Total	20,500	38,000	41,250
(C) Surplus/(deficiency) (*A*) – (*B*)	25,500	4,000	7,750
Beginning balance	7,500	33,000	37,000
Ending balance (indicated)	33,000	37,000	44,750

Working Notes

Purchase budget	January	February	March
Desired ending inventory (at cost price)	₹60,000	₹69,000	₹66,000
Plus cost of goods sold (current month)	24,000	27,000	33,000
Total requirements	84,000	96,000	99,000
Less: Beginning inventory	51,000	60,000	69,000
Purchases	33,000	36,000	30,000

LO 14.4 LOD M

P.14.7 Prepare the cash budget for July-December from the following information:

(i) The estimated sales, expenses, etc. are as follows: *(₹ lakh)*

	June	*July*	*August*	*September*	*October*	*November*	*December*
Sales	35	40	40	50	50	60	65
Purchases	14	16	17	20	20	25	28
Wages and salaries	12	14	14	18	18	20	22
Miscellaneous expenses	5	6	6	6	7	7	7
Interest received	2	—	—	2	—	—	2
Sale of shares	—	—	20	—	—	—	—

(ii) 20 per cent of the sales are on cash and the balance on credit.

(iii) 1 per cent of the credit sales are returned by the customers; 2 per cent debts are uncollectible; 50 per cent of the good accounts receivable are collected in the month of the sales and the rest during next month.

(iv) The time-lag in payment of miscellaneous expenses and purchase is one month. Wages and salaries are paid fortnightly with a time-lag of 15 days.

(v) The company keeps a minimum cash balance of ₹5 lakhs. Cash in excess of ₹7 lakh is invested in government securities in multiples of ₹1 lakh. Shortfalls in the minimum cash balance are made good by borrowings from the banks. Ignore interest received and paid.

Solution

Cash budget for the months of July-December *(Amount in lakh of rupees)*

Particulars	*July*	*August*	*September*	*October*	*November*	*December*
(a) Cash inflows						
Cash sales	8.00	8.00	10.00	10.00	12.00	13.00
Collection from debtors (see working notes)	14.10	31.05	34.93	38.81	42.69	48.51
Interest received	—	—	2.00	—	—	2.00
Sale of shares	—	20.00	—	—	—	—
Total	37.10	59.05	46.93	48.81	54.69	63.51
(b) Cash outflows						
Payment to suppliers (1 month time-lag)	14.00	16.00	17.00	20.00	20.00	25.00
Miscellaneous expenses (1 month time-lag)	5.00	6.00	6.00	6.00	7.00	7.00
Wages and salaries: (time-lag of 15 days)						
Δ Paid for the previous month (50%)	6.00	7.00	7.00	9.00	9.00	10.00
Δ Paid for the current month (50%)	7.00	7.00	9.00	9.00	10.00	11.00
Total	32.00	36.00	39.00	44.00	46.00	53.00
(c) Surplus/(deficiency) [(a) – (b)]	5.10	23.05	7.93	4.81	8.69	10.51
Beginning balance	5.00	7.10	7.15	7.08	7.89	7.58
Closing balance (indicated)	10.10	30.14	15.08	11.89	16.58	18.09
Investment in Government securities	3.00	23.00	8.00	4.00	9.00	11.00
Closing balance (now actually estimated)	7.10	7.15	7.08	7.89	7.58	7.09

Working Notes

(1) Collection from debtors *(amount in lakh of rupees)*

Particulars	*June*	*July*	*August*	*September*	*October*	*November*	*December*
Sales	35	40	40	50	50	60	65
Less: Cash sales (20%)	7	8	8	10	10	12	13
Credit sales	28	32	32	40	40	48	52
Less: Return (1%)	0.28	0.32	0.32	0.40	0.40	0.48	0.52
Net credit sales	27.72	31.68	31.68	39.60	39.60	47.52	51.48
Less: Bad debts (2%)	0.55	0.63	0.63	0.79	0.79	0.95	1.03
Good accounts receivable	27.17	31.05	31.05	38.81	38.81	46.57	50.45
Collections							
50% in the month of sale	13.59	15.52	15.52	19.40	19.40	23.28	25.22
50% in the next month	—	13.58	15.53	15.53	19.41	19.41	23.29
	13.59	29.10	31.05	34.93	38.81	42.69	48.51

P.14.8 JPL has two dates when it receives its cash inflows, that is, February 15, and August 15. On each of these dates, it expects to receive ₹15 crore. Cash expenditures are expected to be steady throughout the subsequent 6 month period. Presently, the ROI in marketable securities is 8 per cent per annum, and the cost of transfer from securities to cash is ₹125 each time a transfer occurs.

LO 14.4 LOD M

(i) What is the optimal transfer size using the EOQ model? What is the average cash balance?

(ii) What would be your answer to part (i), if the ROI were 12 per cent per annum and the transfer costs were ₹75? Why do they differ from those in part (i)?

Solution

(i) Optimal transfer size using the EOQ model

$$C = \sqrt{\frac{2bT}{i}}$$

Where, C = Optimal conversion amount of marketable securities converted into cash per order

T = Projected cash requirement during the planning period

b = Cost of conversion into cash per lost/transaction

i = Rate of interest earned on securities

Therefore, $C = \sqrt{\frac{2 \times ₹30 \text{ Crore} \times ₹125}{0.08}} = ₹9,68,245$

Average cash balance = $C/2$ = ₹9,68,245/2 = ₹4,84,123

(ii) Optimal transfer size using EOQ model

Given, $i = 0.12$

$b = ₹75$

$$C = \sqrt{\frac{2 \times ₹30 \text{ crore} \times ₹75}{0.12}} = ₹6,12,372$$

Average cash balance = $C/2$ = ₹6,12,372/2 = ₹3,06,186

(b) The major reasons for holding lower balances in the latter situations are: (i) higher opportunity cost for holding cash (the ROI is 12 per cent *vis-à-vis* 8 per cent in the former situation) and (ii) lower transaction costs favour frequent conversion of marketable securities into cash.

P.14.9 The annual cash requirement of A Ltd is ₹10 lakh. The company has marketable securities in lot sizes of ₹50,000, ₹1,00,00, ₹2,00,000, ₹2,50,000 and ₹5,00,000. Cost of conversion of marketable securities per lot is ₹1,000. The company can earn 5 per cent yield on its securities.

LO 14.4 LOD D

You are required to prepare a table indicating which lot size will have to be sold by the company. Also, show that economic lot size can be obtained by the Baumol Model.

Solution

(a) Table showing lot size of marketable securities

1. Total annual cash requirement	₹10,00,000	₹10,00,000	₹10,00,000	₹10,00,000	₹10,00,000
2. Lot size	50,000	1,00,000	2,00,000	2,50,000	5,00,000
3. Number of lots (1 ÷ 2)	20	10	5	4	2
4. Conversion cost per lot	1,000	1,000	1,000	1,000	1,000
5. Total conversion cost (3 × 4)	20,000	10,000	5,000	4,000	2,000
6. Average lot size	25,000	50,000	1,00,000	1,25,000	2,50,000
7. Interest cost (Average lot size × 0.05)	1,250	2,500	5,000	6,250	12,500
8. Total cost (5 + 7)	21,250	12,500	10,000	10,250	14,500

Economic lot size = ₹2,00,000 as at this size the total costs are minimum.

(b) Baumol Model = $\sqrt{\frac{2bt}{i}}$

where b = Cost per conversion
t = Total cash transaction needs for the period (year)
i = Interest rate that could be earned.

$$= \sqrt{\frac{2 \times ₹1{,}000 \times ₹10{,}00{,}000}{0.05}} = ₹2{,}00{,}000.$$

MINI CASES

14.C.1 Alcobex Metal Company (AMC) does business in three products P_1, P_2 and P_3. Products P_1 and P_2 are manufactured in the company, while product P_3 is procured from outside and resold as a combination with either product P_1 or P_2. The sales volume budgeted for the three products for the current year (April – March) are as under:

Product	*₹ in lakh*		
P_1	1,200		
P_2	500		
P_3	400	[Dec. to March previous year]	₹20.00 lakh per month
		[April to July current year]	25.00 lakh per month
		[August to November]	30.00 lakh per month
		[December to March]	45.00 lakh per month

Based on the budgeted sales value, the cash flow forecast for the company is prepared based on the following assumptions:

(1) Sales realisation is considered at:
50 per cent current month
25 per cent second month
25 per cent third month
(2) Production programme for each month is based on the sales value of the next month.
(3) Raw material consumption of the company is kept at 59 per cent of the month's production.
(4) 81 per cent of the raw materials consumed are components.

(5) Raw material and components to the extent, at 25 per cent are procured through import.

(6) The purchases budget is as follows:
   (i) Indigenous raw materials are purchased two months before the actual.
   (ii) Components are procured in the month of consumption.
   (iii) Imported raw materials and components are bought three months prior to the month of consumption.

(7) The company avails of the following credit terms from suppliers:
   (i) Raw materials are paid for in the month of purchases;
   (ii) Company gets one month's credit for its components;
   (iii) For imported raw material and components payments are made one month prior to the dates of purchases.

(8) Currently, the company has a cash credit facility of ₹140.88 lakh.

(9) Expenses are given below and are expected to be constant throughout the year (₹ lakh).

Wages and salaries	₹312
Administrative expenses	322
Selling and distribution expenses	53

(10) Dividend of ₹58.03 lakh is to be paid in October.

(11) Tax of ₹23.92 lakh will be paid in equal instalments in four-quarters: i.e., January, April, July and October.

(12) The term-loan of ₹237.32 lakh is repayable in two equal instalments half-yearly, i.e., June/December.

(13) Capital expenditure of ₹292.44 lakh for the year is expected to be spread equally during the 12 month period.

Your are required to prepare a cash flow statement (Cash budget) for the current year period of June to November.

Solution

Cash budget for the period June-November *(Amount in ₹ lakh)*

Particulars	*June*	*July*	*August*	*September*	*October*	*November*	*Total cash flow*
(A) Cash inflows							
Collection from customers[2]	166.67	166.67	169.17	170.42	171.67	171.67	1016.27
Total	166.67	166.67	169.17	170.42	171.67	171.67	1016.27
(B) Cash outflows							
Payment to suppliers	99.49	101.70	103.5	104.76	104.76	104.76	618.97
Wages & salaries	26	26	26	26	26	26	156
Administrative expenses	26.83	26.83	26.83	26.83	26.83	26.83	160.98
Selling and distribution	4.42	4.42	4.42	4.42	4.42	4.42	26.52
Dividend	—	—	—	—	58.03	—	58.03
Tax	—	5.98	—	—	5.98	—	11.96
Capital expenditure	24.37	24.37	24.37	24.37	24.37	24.37	146.22
Repayment of term loan	118.66	—	—	—	—	—	118.66
Total	299.77	189.30	185.12	186.38	250.39	186.38	1,297.34
Surplus/(Deficiency) A – B	(133.10)	(22.63)	(15.95)	(15.96)	(78.72)	(14.71)	(281.07)
Opening balance	(140.88)[1]	(273.98)	(296.61)	(312.56)	(328.52)	(407.24)	(140.88)
Closing balance	(273.98)	(296.61)	(312.56)	(328.52)	(407.24)	(421.95)	(421.95)

Working Notes

(1) In view of the fact that no information is provided about opening cash balance, it is assumed that it is equivalent to its credit facility i.e., ₹140.88 lakh.

(2) Schedule showing collection from debtors

Particulars	*April*	*May*	*June*	*July*	*August*	*September*	*October*	*November*
Credit sales:								
Product P_1 (₹1,200/12)	100	100	100	100	100	100	100	100
Product P_2 (₹500/12)	41.67	41.67	41.67	41.67	41.67	41.67	41.67	41.67
Product P_3	25	25	25	25	30	30	30	30
	166.67	166.67	166.67	166.67	171.67	171.67	171.67	171.67
Collections:								
Current month (50%)			83.33	83.33	85.83	85.83	85.83	85.83
Second month (25%)			41.67	41.67	41.67	42.92	42.92	42.92
Third month (25%)			41.67	41.67	41.67	41.67	42.92	42.92
			166.67	166.67	169.17	170.42	171.67	171.67

Assumption: There is a uniform sale per month of products P_1 and P_2.

(3) Production programme

Months	*Sales value*	*Total raw material consumption [59% of (2)]*	*Components [81% of (3)]*	*Other raw materials [(3 – 4)]*	*Imported raw materials & components [25% of (3)]*	*Indigenous raw materials and components [(3 – 6)]*	*Indigenous raw materials [75% of (5)]*	*Indigenous components [75% of (4)]*
1	*2*	*3*	*4*	*5*	*6*	*7*	*8*	*9*
April	166.67	98.33	79.65	18.68	24.58	73.75	14.01	59.74
May	166.67	98.33	79.65	18.68	24.58	73.75	14.01	59.74
June	166.67	98.33	79.65	18.68	24.58	73.75	14.01	59.74
July	171.67	101.28	82.04	19.24	25.32	75.96	14.43	61.53
August	171.67	101.28	82.04	19.24	25.32	75.96	14.43	61.53
September	171.67	101.28	82.04	19.24	25.32	75.96	14.43	61.53
October	171.67	101.28	82.04	19.24	25.32	75.96	14.43	61.53
November	186.67	110.13	89.21	20.93	27.53	82.60	15.69	66.91

(4) Purchase programme

Months	*Indigenous raw materials*	*Indigenous components*	*Imported raw materials and components*
1	*2*	*3*	*4*
May	14.43	59.74	25.32
June	14.43	59.74	25.32
July	14.43	59.74	25.32
August	14.43	61.53	27.53
September	15.69	61.53	27.53
October	15.69	61.53	27.53
November	15.69	66.91	27.53

(5) Payment to suppliers (₹ *in lakhs)*

Month	*Indigenous raw materials*	*Indigenous components (Previous month paid now)*	*Imported raw materials and components (Next month purchase – Advance payment)*	*Total payment*
May	14.43	59.74	25.32	99.49
June	14.43	59.74	25.32	99.49
July	14.43	59.74	27.53	101.70
August	14.43	61.53	27.53	103.50
September	15.69	61.53	27.53	104.76
October	15.69	61.53	27.53	104.76
November	15.69	61.53	27.53	104.76

14.C.2 The following is the balance sheet of Amar Industries Limited as on March 31 of the current year (amount in lakh of rupees)

Liabilities	*Amount*	*Assets*		*Amount*
Capital and reserves	1,650	Fixed assets at cost	1300	
12% Debentures	900	*Less:* Depreciation	(400)	900
Creditors for purchases	600	Sundry debtors		700
Creditors for expenses	70	Stocks and stores		1,200
Provision for bonus	30	Loans and advances		500
Provision for tax	100	Cash and bank balances		100
Proposed dividends	50			
	3,400			3,400

Projected P & L A/c for the first 4 months (April-July) of the next year shows the following

(₹ *in lakhs)*

Particulars	*April*	*May*	*June*	*July*
Sales	800	800	900	900
Excise duty recoveries	80	80	90	90
	880	880	990	990
Materials:				
Opening stock	1,200	1,200	1,260	1,320
Add: Purchases	600	660	720	720
Less: Closing stock	(1,200)	(1,260)	(1,320)	(1,320)
Cost of materials used	600	600	660	720
Expenses	180	180	200	200
Excise duty	80	84	88	92
	860	864	948	1,012
Profit (loss)	20	16	42	(22)

The following are the other relevant additional information:

(i) 10 per cent of sales are for cash and the balance on 30 days' credit.
(ii) Creditors for purchases are paid in 30 days.
(iii) Expenses include:
  (a) Interest payable at the end of each quarter;
  (b) Depreciation of ₹10 lakh per month.
  (c) Provision for bonus to workmen, ₹5 lakh per month, payable only in October.
  (d) One-half of rest of the expenses payable in the following month.
(iv) ₹200 lakh of debentures are redeemable on June 30.

(v) Provision for taxation includes ₹20 lakh of surplus provision carried forward from earlier year besides the balance for the current year payable before June 30.
(vi) Annual general meeting is to be held on May 31.
(vii) Overdraft is permissible; however, interest on overdraft may be ignored.

You are required to prepare cash budget for the months of April to July (on a monthly basis) for the next year.

Solution

Cash budget of Amar Industries Ltd from April to July

(Amount in lakh of rupees)

Particulars	*April*	*May*	*June*	*July*
Gross sales (including excise duty)	880	880	990	990
Credit sales (90 per cent)	792	792	891	891
Credit purchases	600	660	720	720
Cash inflows:				
Cash sales	88	88	99	99
Collection from debtors: in the month following sales	700	792	792	891
Total	788	880	891	990
Cash outflows:				
Payment to creditors (in the month following purchases)	600	600	660	720
Interest (0.12 × ₹900 lakh × 1/4)	—	—	27	—
Excise duty (assumed to be paid in the same month)	80	84	88	92
Expenses (working note 1)	148	156	166	177
Redemption of debentures	—	—	200	—
Tax (assumed to be paid in June)	—	—	80	—
Dividends (assumed to be paid in July)	—	—	—	50
Total	828	840	1,221	1,039
Surplus (deficiency)	(40)	40	(330)	(49)
Beginning balance	100	60	100	(230)
Closing balance (overdraft)	60	100	(230)	(279)

Working Notes

Payment for expenses *(Amount in lakh of rupees)*

	April	*May*	*June*	*July*
Total expenses	180	180	200	200
Less: Interest on debentures	9	9	9	7
Less: Depreciation	10	10	10	10
Less: Provision for bonus	5	5	5	5
Net expenses (for a month)	156	156	176	178
50 per cent payable in the same month	78	78	88	89
50 per cent of the previous month	70	78	78	88
	148	156	166	177

Scan the QR Code given at the end of chapter to access comprehensive cases.

REVIEW QUESTIONS

LOD: Easy

RQ.14.1 Indicate whether the following statements are true or false. [LO 14.1–7]

(i) Cash, in a narrow sense, implies currency and bank balances only.
(ii) Cash, in broad sense, includes marketable securities and time deposits in banks.
(iii) Transaction, precautionary and speculative are three motives for holding cash.
(iv) Speculative motive cash balance serves to provide a cushion to meet unexpected contingencies.
(v) To meet the payment schedule and to minimize funds committed to cash balance are two basic objectives of cash management.
(vi) Costs caused due to inadequate cash are referred to as short costs.
(vii) Baumol model takes into account all motives of holding cash.
(viii) Miller-Orr model assumes that cash balances randomly fluctuate between an upper bound and lower bound.
(ix) Orgler's model is based on the use of a simple linear programming model.
(x) Cash budget is based on operating cash flows.
(xi) The higher the period of cash cycle, the higher is cash turnover.
(xii) Time taken by the bank in collecting payment from the customer's bank is referred to as deposit float.
(xiii) Investment in marketable securities is intended to obtain a return on temporarily idle cash.

[Answers: (i) False (ii) True (iii) False (iv) False (v) True (vi) True (vii) False (viii) True (ix) False (x) False (xi) False (xii) False (xiii) True]

RQ.14.2 What are the principal motives for holding cash? [LO 14.1]

RQ.14.3 What are the objectives of cash management? [LO 14.2]

RQ.14.4 What is the significance of speedy receivables collection? In this context briefly explain concentration banking and lock-box system. [LO 14.6]

LOD: Medium

RQ.14.5 Briefly explain the factors that determine the cash needs of a firm. Give examples to illustrate the short, long and procurement costs. [LO 14.3]

RQ.14.6 Discuss the utility of cash budget as a tool of cash management. What are the steps involved in the construction of a cash budget. [LO 14.4]

RQ.14.7 What are the basic strategies of efficient cash management? Illustrate with suitable examples the effect of these on the operating cash requirements of a firm. [LO 14.5]

RQ.14.8 What specific strategies can be adopted to slow disbursements of accounts payable? [LO 14.6]

RQ.14.9 Explain and contrast deposit float and payment float. [LO 14.6]

RQ.14.10 The following information is available relating to the PQR Ltd.: [LO 14.4]

1 *Sales forecast*

May	₹75,000	September	₹3,00,000
June	75,000	October	1,50,000
July	1,50,000	November	1,50,000
August	2,25,000	December	1,37,500
		January	75,000

2 *Raw materials*

May	₹37,500	September	₹1,27,500
June	37,500	October	97,500
July	52,500	November	67,500
August	3,67,500	December	37,500

3 *Collection estimates*:
(1) Within the month of sale, 5 per cent
(2) During the month following sale, 80 per cent
(3) During the second month the following sale, 15 per cent.
4 *Payment for raw materials*:
During the month following the month in which purchase take place.
5 *Miscellaneous*:
(1) General and administrative salary, ₹11,250 per month.
(2) Monthly lease payment, ₹3,750.
(3) Monthly depreciation charges, ₹15,000.
(4) Monthly miscellaneous expenses, ₹1,150.
(5) Income tax, ₹26,250 each in September and December.
(6) Payment for research in October, ₹75,000.
(7) Opening balance of cash on July 1, ₹55,000.
(8) Minimum cash balance of ₹37,500 throughout the cash budget period.
Prepare:
(1) a monthly cash budget for 6 months — July to December
(2) an estimate of excess cash or shortage of cash for each month.

LOD: Difficult

RQ.14.11 What purpose do the following models serve? • Banmol model, • Miller-orr model, and • Orgler's model. **[LO 14.4]**

RQ.14.12 Breifly describe similarities and differences among cash management models. **[LO 14.4]**

RQ.14.13 Prepare a cash budget of XYZ Ltd for the 6 months, commencing April, on the basis of the following information: **[LO 14.4]**

(i) Costs and prices remain unchanged.
(ii) Cash sales are 25 per cent of the total sales and balance 75 per cent are credit sales.
(iii) 60 per cent of credit sales are collected in the month following the sales, balance 30 per cent and 10 per cent in the two following months, respectively. No bad debts are anticipated.
(iv) Sales forecast is as follows:

January	₹12,00,000	June	₹8,00,000
February	14,00,000	July	12,00,000
March	16,00,000	August	10,00,000
April	6,00,000	September	8,00,000
May	8,00,000	October	12,00,000

(v) Gross profit margin, 20 per cent.
(vi) Anticipated purchases:

April	₹6,40,000
May	6,40,000
June	9,60,000
July	8,00,000
August	6,40,000
September	9,60,000

(vii) Wages and salaries to be paid:

April	₹1,20,000
May	1,60,000
June	2,00,000
July	2,00,000
August	1,60,000
September	1,40,000

(viii) Interest @ 6 per cent on debentures of ₹20,00,000 is paid quarterly and is payable in June and September.

(ix) Excise duty due in July, ₹2,00,000.

(x) Capital expenditure for plant and machinery planned for September, ₹1,20,000.

(xi) Company has a cash balance of ₹4,00,000 as on March 31. This is the minimum desired cash balance per month.

(xii) The company can borrow on monthly basis. Ignore interest on borrowings.

(xiii) Rent is ₹8,000 per month.

RQ.14.14 The following information is available about a firm: **[LO 14.5]**

(a) On an average, accounts receivable are collected after 80 days; inventories have an average of 100 days and accounts payable are paid approximately 60 days after they arise.

(b) The firm spends a total of ₹1,81,20,000 annually at a constant rate.

(c) It can earn 8 per cent on investments.

Calculate: (i) the firm's cash cycle and cash turnover assuming a 360-days year; (ii) minimum amount of cash to be maintained to meet payments as they become due; (iii) savings by reducing the average age of inventories to 70 days.

RQ.14.15 Hypothetical Ltd uses a continuous billing system that results in an average daily receipt of ₹40,00,000. It is contemplating the institution of concentration banking, instead of the current system of centralised billing and collection. It is estimated that such a system would reduce the collection period of accounts receivable by 2 days. **[LO 14.6]**

Concentration banking would cost ₹75,000 annually, and 8 per cent can be earned by the firm on its investments. It is also found that a lock-box system could reduce it overall collection time by 4 days and would cost annually ₹1,20,000.

(i) How much would cash be released with the concentration banking system?

(ii) How much money can be saved due to reduction in the collection period by 2 days? Should the firm institute the concentration banking system?

(iii) How much would cash be freed by lock-box system?

(iv) How much can be saved with lock-box?

(v) Between concentration banking and lock-box system, which is better?

ANSWERS

14.10	**(i)**	July	₹80,100;	August	₹1,53,950;	September	₹37,500
		October	₹37,500;	November	₹45,500;	December	₹84,975
	(ii)	September	₹75,950;	Shortage			
		October	₹62,600;	Repayments			
		November	₹13,350;	Repayments			
14.13	**(i)**	April	₹907;	May	1,034;	June	₹651
		July	₹400;	August	550;	September	₹400
		(Figures are in thousands of rupees)					

14.14 **(i)** **(a)** 120 days **(b)** 3
(ii) ₹60,40,000
(iii) 110 days; 3.273; ₹55,36,713; ₹5,03,287; ₹40,263

14.15 **(i)** ₹80,00,000 **(ii)** ₹640,000
(iii) ₹1,60,00,000 **(iv)** ₹12,80,000
(v) ₹11,60,000

Scan the QR Code to access comprehensive solutions to all numerical review questions and additional material.

CHAPTER 15

Receivables Management

LEARNING OBJECTIVES

LO 15.1	Explain the objectives of receivables management with reference to the specific relevant costs and benefits
LO 15.2	Describe the key aspects of credit policies, namely, credit selection: obtaining credit information and analysing credit information
LO 15.3	Examine the three basic components of a firm's credit terms, the effects of changes in each of them on key variables and profits and the procedure for evaluating the quantitative effects of the proposed changes
LO 15.4	Explain the key features of collection policy, the basic tradeoffs and the popular collection techniques

INTRODUCTION

In the preceding Chapter, which was devoted to an in-depth examination of one of the most important components of current assets, that is, cash, it was observed that a basic strategy to reduce the operating cash requirement of a firm is to accelerate the collection of receivables so as to reduce the average collection period. The receivables represent an important component of the current assets of a firm. The purpose of the present Chapter is to analyse the important dimensions of the efficient management of receivables within the framework of a firm's objectives of value maximisation. This chapter discusses the objectives of receivables management. This is followed by an in-depth analysis of the three crucial aspects of management of receivables. The first aspect, that is, credit policies, have two dimensions: **(i)** credit standard defined as the criteria to determine to whom credit should be extended and **(ii)** credit analysis. The policies regarding both these aspects have been evaluated. The second major part of receivables management is 'credit terms' comprising **(i)** cash discount, **(ii)** cash discount period, and **(iii)** credit period. This is extensively spelt out later in the Chapter. The next discussion is concerned with the third major component of receivables management, collection policies, that is, the types and degree of effort made to collect receivables from customers. The main points are summarised by way of recapitulation.

LO 15.1 OBJECTIVES

The term receivables is defined as 'debt owed to the firm by customers arising from sale of goods or services in the ordinary course of business'.[1] When a firm makes an ordinary sale of goods or services and does not receive payment, the firm grants trade credit and creates accounts receivable which could be collected in the future. Receivables management is also called *trade credit management.* Thus, accounts receivable represent an extension of credit to customers, allowing them a reasonable period of time in which to pay for the goods received.

The sale of goods on credit is an essential part of the modern competitive economic systems. In fact, credit sales and, therefore, receivables, are treated as a marketing tool to aid the sale of goods. The credit sales are generally made on open account in the sense that there are no formal acknowledgements of debt obligations through a financial instrument. As a marketing tool, they are intended to promote sales and thereby profits. However, extension of credit involves risk and cost. Management should weigh the benefits as well as cost to determine the goal of receivables management. The objective of receivables management is 'to promote sales and profits *until* that point is reached where the return on investment in further funding receivables is less than the cost of funds raised to finance that additional credit (i.e. cost of capital)'.[2] The specific costs and benefits which are relevant to the determination of the objectives of receivables management are examined below.

Costs

The major categories of costs associated with the extension of credit and accounts receivable are: (i) collection cost, (ii) capital cost, (iii) delinquency cost, and (iv) default cost.

Collection Cost **Collection costs** are administrative costs incurred in collecting the receivables from the customers to whom credit sales have been made. Included in this category of costs are: **(a)** additional expenses on the creation and maintenance of a credit department with staff, accounting records, stationery, postage and other related items; **(b)** expenses involved in acquiring credit information either through outside specialist agencies or by the staff of the firm itself. These expenses would not be incurred if the firm does not sell on credit.

> **Collection cost** is the administrative cost incurred in collecting receivables.

Capital Cost The increased level of accounts receivable is an investment in assets. They have to be financed thereby involving a cost. There is a time-lag between the sale of goods to, and payment by, the customers. Meanwhile, the firm has to pay employees and suppliers of raw materials, thereby implying that the firm should arrange for additional funds to meet its own obligations while waiting for payment from its customers. The **cost on the use of additional capital** to support credit sales, which alternatively could be profitably employed elsewhere, is, therefore, a part of the cost of extending credit or receivables.

> **Capital cost** is the cost on the use of additional capital to support credit sales which alternatively could have been employed elsewhere.

Delinquency Cost This cost arises out of the failure of the customers to meet their obligations when payment on credit sales become due after the expiry of the credit period. Such costs are called **delinquency costs**. The important components of this cost are: **(i)** blocking-up of funds for an extended period, **(ii)** cost associated with steps that have to be initiated to collect the overdues, such as, reminders and other collection efforts, legal charges, where necessary, and so on.

> **Delinquency cost** is cost arising out of failure of customers to pay on due date.

Default Cost Finally, the firm may not be able to recover the overdues because of the inability of the customers. Such debts are treated as bad debts and have to be written off as they cannot be realised. Such costs are known as **default costs** associated with credit sales and accounts receivable.

Default costs are the over dues that cannot be recovered.

Benefits

Apart from the costs, another factor that has a bearing on accounts receivable management is the *benefit* emanating from credit sales. The *benefits* are *the increased sales* and *anticipated profits* because of a more liberal policy. When firms extend trade credit, that is, invest in receivables, they intend to increase the sales. The impact of a liberal trade credit policy is likely to take two forms. First, it is oriented to sales expansion. In other words, a firm may grant trade credit either to increase sales to existing customers or attract new customers. This motive for investment in receivables is growth-oriented. Secondly, the firm may extend credit to protect its current sales against emerging competition. Here, the motive is sales-retention. As a result of increased sales, the profits of the firm will increase.

From the above discussion, it is clear that investments in receivables involve both benefits and costs. The extension of trade credit has a major impact on sales, costs and profitability. Other things being equal, a relatively liberal policy and, therefore, higher investments in receivables, will produce larger sales. However, costs will be higher with liberal policies than with more stringent measures. Therefore, accounts receivable management should aim at a trade-off between profit (benefit) and risk (cost). That is to say, *the decision to commit funds to receivables (or the decision to grant credit) will be based on a comparison of the benefits and costs involved, while determining the optimum level of receivables.* **The costs and benefits to be compared are marginal costs and benefits**. The firm should only consider the incremental (additional) benefits and costs that result from a change in the receivables or trade credit policy.[3]

While it is true that general economic conditions and industry practices have a strong impact on the level of receivables, a firm's investments in this type of current assets is also greatly affected by its internal policy. A firm has little or no control over environmental factors, such as economic conditions and industry practices. But it can improve its profitability through a properly conceived trade credit policy or receivables management.

LO 15.2 CREDIT POLICIES

In the preceding discussions it has been clearly shown that the firm's objective with respect to receivables management is not merely to collect receivables quickly, but attention should also be given to the benefit-cost trade-off involved in the various areas of accounts receivable management. The first decision area is credit policies.

The **credit policy** of a firm provides the framework to determine **(a)** whether or not to extend credit to a customer and **(b)** how much credit to extend. The credit policy decision of a firm has two broad dimensions: **(i)** Credit standards and **(ii)** Credit analysis. A firm has to establish and use *standards* in making credit decisions, develop appropriate sources of credit information and methods of credit analysis. We illustrate below how these two aspects are relevant to the accounts receivable management of a firm.

Credit policy is the determination of credit standards and credit analysis.

Credit Standards

Credit standards are basic criteria/ minimum requirement for extending credit to a customer.

The term '**credit standards**' represents the basic criteria for the extension of credit to customers. The quantitative basis of establishing credit standards are factors such as credit ratings, credit references, average payments period and certain financial ratios.[4] Since we are interested in illustrating the trade-off between benefit and cost to the firm as a whole, we do not consider here these individual components of credit standards. To illustrate the effect, we have divided the overall standards into (a) tight or restrictive, and (b) liberal or non-restrictive. That is to say, *our aim is to show what happens to the trade-off when standards are relaxed or, alternatively, tightened.* The trade-off with reference to credit standards covers **(i)** the collection cost, **(ii)** the average collection period/cost of investment in accounts receivable, **(iii)** level of bad debt losses, and **(iv)** level of sales. These factors should be considered while deciding whether to relax creditstandards or not. If standards are relaxed, it means more credit will be extended while if standards are tightened, less credit will be extended. The implications of the four factors are elaborated below.

Collection Costs The implications of relaxed credit standards are **(i)** more credit, **(ii)** a large credit department to service accounts receivable and related matters, **(iii)** increase in collection costs. The effect of tightening of credit standards will be exactly the opposite. These costs are likely to be semi-variable. This is because up-to a certain point the existing staff will be able to carry on the increased workload, but beyond that, additional staff would be required. These are assumed to be included in the variable cost per unit and need not be separately identified.

Investments in Receivables or the Average Collection Period The investment in accounts receivable involves a capital cost as funds have to be arranged by the firm to finance them till customers make payments. Moreover, the higher the average accounts receivable, the higher is the capital or carrying cost. A change in the credit standards–relaxation or tightening–leads to a change in the level of accounts receivable either through a change in **(a)** sales, or **(b)** collections.

A relaxation in credit standards, as already stated, implies an increase in sales which, in turn, would lead to higher average accounts receivable. Further, relaxed standards would mean that credit is extended liberally so that it is available to even less *creditworthy* customers who will take a longer period to pay overdues. The extension of trade credit to slow-paying customers would result in a higher level of accounts receivable.

In contrast, a tightening of credit standards would signify **(i)** a decrease in sales and lower average accounts receivable, and **(ii)** an extension of credit limited to more creditworthy customers who can promptly pay their bills and, thus, a lower average level of accounts receivable.

Thus, a change in sales and change in collection period together with a relaxation in standards would produce a higher carrying costs, while changes in sales and collection period result in lower costs when credit standards are tightened. These basic reactions also occur when changes in credit terms or collection procedures are made. We have discussed these in the subsequent sections of this chapter.

Bad Debt Expenses Another factor which is expected to be affected by changes in the credit standards is bad debt (default) expenses. They can be expected to increase with relaxation in credit standards and decrease if credit standards become more restrictive.

Sales Volume Changing credit standards can also be expected to change the volume of sales. As standards are relaxed, sales are expected to increase; conversely, a tightening is expected to cause a decline in sales.

The basic changes and effects on profits arising from a relaxation of credit standards are summarised in Exhibit 15.1. If the credit standards are tightened, the opposite effects, as shown in the brackets, would follow.

EXHIBIT 15.1 Effect of Relaxation of Standards

Item	*Direction of Change (Increase = I Decrease = D)*	*Effect on Profits (Positive + Negative –)*
1. Sales Volume	I(D)	+(–)
2. Average Collection Period	I(D)	–(+)
3. Bad Debt	I(D)	–(+)

The effect of alternative credit standards is illustrated in Example 15.1.

***Example* 15.1**

A firm is currently selling a product @ ₹10 per unit. The most recent annual sales (all credit) were 30,000 units. The variable cost per unit is ₹.6 and the average cost per unit, given a sales volume of 30,000 units, is ₹8. The total fixed cost is ₹60,000. The average collection period may be assumed to be 30 days.

The firm is contemplating a relaxation of credit standards that is expected to result in a 15 per cent increase in units sales; the average collection period would increase to 45 days with no change in bad debt expenses. It is also expected that increased sales will result in additional net working capital to the extent of ₹10,000. The increase in collection expenses may be assumed to be negligible. The required return on investment is 15 per cent.

Should the firm relax the credit standard?

Solution

The decision to put the proposed relaxation in the credit standards into effect should be based on a comparison of **(i)** additional profits on sales and **(ii)** cost of the incremental investments in receivables. If the former exceeds the latter, the proposal should be implemented, otherwise not.

Profit on Incremental Sales This can be computed in two ways: **(i)** long approach, and **(ii)** short-cut-method.

Long Approach According to this approach, the costs and profits on both the present and the proposed sales level are calculated and the difference in profit at the two levels will be the incremental profit. This is shown in Table 15.1.

TABLE 15.1 Long Method to Calculate Marginal Profits

(A) Proposed Plan:		
1. Sales revenue (34,500 × units ₹10)		₹3,45,000
2. *Less:* Costs:		
(a) Variable (34,500 × ₹6)	₹2,07,000	
(b) Fixed	60,000	2,67,000
3. Profits from sales (I)		78,000
(B) Current Plan:		
1. Sales revenue (30,000 × units ₹10)		3,00,000
2. *Less:* Costs:		
(a) Variable (30,000 × ₹6)	1,80,000	
(b) Fixed	60,000	2,40,000
3. Profits from sales (II)		60,000
(C) Marginal profits with new plan (I – II):		18,000

Short-Cut Method The profits on sales will increase by an amount equal to the product of the additional units sold and additional profit per unit. Since the 30,000 units representing the current level of sales absorb all the fixed costs, any additional units sold will cost only the variable cost per unit. The marginal profit per unit will be equal to the difference between the sales price per unit (₹10) and the variable cost per unit (₹6). The marginal profit/contribution margin per unit would, therefore, be ₹4. The total additional (marginal) profits from incremental sales will be ₹18,000 (₹4,500 × ₹4).

Cost of Marginal/Incremental Investment in Receivables The second variable relevant to the decision to relax credit standards is the cost of marginal investment in accounts receivable. This cost can be computed by finding the difference between the cost of carrying receivables before and after the proposed relaxation in credit standards. It can be calculated as follows:

(i) Turnover of accounts receivable:

$$\text{Proposed plan} = \frac{\text{Number of days in the year}}{\text{Average collection period}} = \frac{360}{45} = 8$$

$$\text{Present plan} = \frac{360}{30} = 12$$

(ii) Total cost of sales:

Present plan = Number of units × cost per unit = 30,000 × ₹8 = ₹2,40,000

Proposed plan = (30,000 × ₹8) + (4,500 × ₹6) = ₹2,67,000

(iii) Average investment in accounts receivable:

Present plan = ₹2,40,000/12 = ₹20,000

Proposed plan = ₹2,67,000/8 = ₹33,375

(iv) The cost of marginal investments in accounts receivable: This is the difference between the average investments in accounts receivable under (i) the proposed plan and (ii) under the present plan. It is calculated as follows:

Average investments with proposed plan	₹33,375
Less average investment with present plan	20,000
Marginal investments	13,375

Marginal investments represent the amount of additional funds required to finance incremental accounts receivable if the proposal to relax the credit standards is implemented. The additional cost of ₹13,375 is the cost of marginal investment in accounts receivable.

$$\text{Given 15 per cent as required return on the investments, the cost} = \frac{₹13{,}375 \times 15}{100} = ₹2{,}006.25$$

This is an opportunity cost in that the firm would earn this amount from alternative uses if the funds are not tied up in additional accounts receivable.

(v) Cost of working capital: ₹10,000 × 0.15 = ₹1,500.

In the above illustration, since the additional profits on increased sales as a result of relaxed credit standards (₹18,000) is considerably more than the cost of incremental investments in accounts receivable (₹2,006.25) and working capital (₹1,500), the firm should relax its credit standards. Such an action would lead to an overall increase in the profits of the firm by ₹14,493.75 (₹18,000 – ₹2,006.25 – ₹1,500).

The effect of tightening credit standards would be just the opposite and can be illustrated on the above lines.

Credit Analysis

Besides establishing credit standards, a firm should develop procedures for evaluating credit applicants. The second aspect of credit policies of a firm is **credit analysis** and investigation. Two basic steps are involved in the credit investigation process: **(a)** obtaining credit information, and **(b)** analysis of credit information. It is on the basis of credit analysis that the decisions to grant credit to a customer as well as the quantum of credit would be taken.

Credit analysis involves obtaining credit information and evaluation of credit applicants.

Obtaining Credit Information The first step in credit analysis is obtaining credit information on which to base the evaluation of a customer. The sources of information, broadly speaking, are (i) internal, and (ii) external.

Internal Usually, firms require their customers to fill various forms and documents giving details about financial operations. They are also required to furnish trade references with whom the firms can have contacts to judge the suitability of the customer for credit. This type of information is obtained from internal sources of credit information. Another internal source of credit information is derived from the records of the firms contemplating an extension of credit. It is likely that a particular customer/applicant may have enjoyed credit facility in the past. In that case, the firm would have information on the behaviour of the applicant(s) in terms of the historical payment pattern. This type of information may not be adequate and may, therefore, have to be supplemented by information from other sources.

External The availability of information from external sources to assess the credit-worthiness of customers depends upon the development of institutional facilities and industry practices. In India, the external sources of credit information are not as developed as in the industrially advanced countries of the world. Depending upon the availability, the following external sources may be employed to collect information.

Financial Statements One external source of credit information is the published financial statements, that is, the balance sheet and the profit and loss account. The financial statements contain very useful information. They throw light on an applicant's financial viability, liquidity, profitability and debt capacity. Although the financial statements do not directly reveal the past payment record of the applicant, they are very helpful in assessing the overall financial position of a firm, which significantly determines its credit standing.

Bank References Another useful source of credit information is the bank of the firm which is contemplating the extension of credit. The *modus operandi* here is that the firm's banker collects the necessary information from the applicant's banks. Alternatively, the applicant may be required to ask his banker to provide the necessary information either directly to the firm or to its bank.

Trade References These refer to the collection of information from firms with whom the applicant has dealings and who on the basis of their experience would vouch for the applicant.

Credit Bureau Reports Finally, specialist *credit bureau* reports from organisations specialising in supplying credit information can also be utilised.

Analysis of Credit Information Once the credit information has been collected from different sources, it should be analysed to determine the credit worthiness of the applicant. Although there are no established procedures to analyse the information, the firm should devise one to suit its needs. The analysis should cover two aspects: **(i)** quantitative, and **(ii)** qualitative.

Quantitative The assessment of the quantitative aspects is based on the factual information available from the financial statements, the past records of the firm, and so on. The first step involved in this type of assessment is to prepare an *Aging Schedule* of the accounts payable of the applicant as well as calculate the average age of the accounts payable. This exercise will give an insight into the past payment pattern of the customer. Another step in analysing the credit information is through a ratio analysis of the liquidity, profitability and debt capacity of the applicant. These ratios should be compared with the industry average. Moreover, trend analysis over a period of time would reveal the financial strength of the customer.

Qualitative The quantitative assessment should be supplemented by a qualitative/subjective interpretation of the applicant's creditworthiness. The subjective judgement would cover aspects rela-ting to the quality of management. Here, the references from other suppliers, bank references and specialist bureau reports would form the basis for the conclusions to be drawn. In the ultimate analysis, therefore, the decision whether to extend credit to the applicant and what amount to extend will depend upon the subjective interpretation of his credit standing.

LO 15.3 CREDIT TERMS

The second decision area in accounts receivable management is the credit terms. After the credit standards have been established and the creditworthiness of the customers has been assessed, the management of a firm must determine the terms and conditions on which trade credit will be made available. The stipulations under which goods are sold on credit are referred to as **credit terms**. These relate to the repayment of the amount under the credit sale. Thus, credit terms specify the repayment terms of receivables.

Credit terms specify the repayment terms required of credit customers/ receivables.

Credit terms have three components: **(a) credit period**, in terms of the duration of time for which trade credit is extended–during this period the overdue amount must be paid by the customer; **(b) cash discount**, if any, which the customer can take advantage of, that is, the overdue amount will be reduced by this amount; and **(c) cash discount period**, which refers to the duration during which the discount can be availed of. These terms are usually written in abbreviations, for instance, '2/10 net 30'. The three numerals are explained below:

Credit period is the time for which trade credit is extended to customer in the case of credit sales.

- 2 signifies the rate of cash discount (2 per cent), which will be available to the customers if they pay the overdue within the stipulated time;
- 10 represents the time duration (10 days) within which a customer must pay to be entitled to the discount;
- 30 means the maximum period for which credit is available and the amount must be paid in any case before the expiry of 30 days.

Cash discount is the incentive to customer to make early payment of sum due.

In other words, the abbreviation 2/10 net 30 means that the customer is entitled to 2 per cent cash discount (discount rate) if he pays within 10 days (discount period) after the beginning of the credit period (30 days). If, however, he does not want to take advantage of the discount, he may pay within 30 days. If the payment is not made within a maximum period of 30 days, the customer would be deemed to have defaulted.

Cash discount period is the duration of the period during which discount can be availed of.

The credit terms, like the credit standards, affect the profitability as well as the cost of a firm. A firm should determine the credit terms on the basis of cost-benefit trade-off. We illustrate below how the three components of credit terms, namely, rate of discount, period of discount and the credit period, affect the trade-off. It should be noted *that our focus in analysing the credit terms is from the view point of suppliers of trade credit and not the recipients for whom it is a source of financing.*[5]

Cash Discount

The cash discount has implications for the sales volume, average collection period/average investment in receivables, bad debt expenses and profit per unit. In taking a decision regarding the grant of cash discount, the management has to see what happens to these factors if it initiates increase, or decrease in the discount rate. The changes in the discount rate would have both positive and negative effects. The implications of increasing or initiating cash discount are as follows:

1. The sales volume will increase. The grant of discount implies reduced prices. If the demand for the products is elastic, reduction in prices will result in higher sales volume.
2. Since the customers, to take advantage of the discount, would like to pay within the discount period, the average collection period would be reduced. The reduction in the collection period would lead to a reduction in the investment in receivables as also the cost. The decrease in the average collection period would also cause a fall in bad debt expenses. As a result, profits would increase.
3. The discount would have a negative effect on the profits. This is because the decrease in prices would affect the profit margin per unit of sale.

The effects of increase in the cash discount are summarised in Table 15.2. The effect of decrease in cash discount will be exactly opposite.

TABLE 15.2 Effects of Increase in Cash Discounts

Item	*Direction of Change (I = Increase D = Decrease)*	*Effect on Profits (Positive+ or Negative–)*
Sales Volume	I	+
Average Collection Period	D	+
Bad Debt Expenses	D	+
Profit Per Unit	D	–

The cash discount decision is illustrated in Example 15.2.

***Example* 15.2**

Assume that the firm in our Example 15.1 is contemplating to allow 2 per cent discount for payment within 10 days after a credit purchase. It is expected that if discounts are offered, sales will increase by 15 per cent and the average collection period will drop to 15 days. Assume bad debt expenses will not be affected; return on investment expected by the firm is 15 per cent; 60 per cent of the total sales will be on discount. Should the firm implement the proposal?

Solution

(i) Profit on sales: The profit on sale = sale of additional units multiplied by the difference between the sales price and the variable cost per unit = 4,500 (₹10 – ₹6) = 4,500 × ₹4 = ₹18,000

(ii) Saving on average collection period: This saving is what would have been earned on the reduced investments in accounts receivable as a result of the cash discount.

$$\text{Average investment in accounts receivable} = \frac{\text{Cost of sales}}{\text{Receivables turnover}}$$

(a) Present plan (without discount) $= \frac{(30{,}000 \times ₹8)}{12 \text{ (i.e. } 360/30)} = ₹20{,}000$

(b) Proposed plan (with discount) $= \frac{(30{,}000 \times ₹8) + (4{,}500 \times ₹6)}{24 \text{ (i.e. } 360/15)} = \frac{₹2{,}67{,}000}{24} = ₹11{,}125$

Thus, if cash discount is allowed, the average investments in receivables will decline by ₹8,875 (i.e. ₹20,000 – ₹11,125). Given a 15 per cent rate of return, the firm could earn ₹1,331.25 on ₹8,875. Thus, the saving resulting from a drop in the average collection period is ₹1,331.25.

(iii) The total benefits associated with the cash discount

Profit on additional sale	₹18,000.00
Saving in cost	1,331.25
Total	19,331.25

(iv) Cash discount: The cost involved in the cash discount on credit sales, that is, 2 per cent of credit sales = 0.02 × ₹2,07,000 (i.e. 0.60 × ₹3,45,000) = ₹4,140

Thus, against a cost of ₹4,140, the benefit from initiating cash discount is ₹19,331.25; that is, there is a net gain of ₹15,191.25 (₹19,331.25 – ₹4,140). The firm should, therefore, implement the proposal to allow 2 per cent cash discount for payment within 10 days of the credit purchase by the customers.

A similar type of analysis can be made to illustrate the effect of either reduction or elimination of cash discount.

Credit Period

The second component of credit terms is the credit period. The expected effect of an increase in the credit period is summarised in Table 15.3.

TABLE 15.3 Effect of Increase in Credit Period

Item	*Direction of Change (I = Increase D = Decrease)*	*Effect on Profits (Positive or Negative)*
Sales Volume	I	+
Average Collection Period	I	–
Bad Debt Expenses	I	–

A reduction in the credit period is likely to have an opposite effect. The credit period decision is illustrated in Example 15.3.

***Example* 15.3**

Suppose, a firm is contemplating an increase in the credit period from 30 to 60 days. The average collection period which is at present 45 days is expected to increase to 75 days. It is also likely that the bad debt expenses will increase from the current level of 1 per cent to 3 per cent of sales. Total credit sales are expected to increase from the level of 30,000 units to 34,500 units. The present average cost per unit is ₹8, the variable cost and sales per unit is ₹6 and ₹10 per unit respectively. Assume the firm expects a rate of return of 15 per cent.

Should the firm extend the credit period?

Solution

(i) Profit on additional sales: = (₹4 × 4,500) = ₹18,000

(ii) Cost of additional investments in receivables: = Average investments with the proposed credit period less average investments in receivables with the present credit period:

$$\text{Proposed plan} = \frac{\text{Cost of sales}}{\text{Turnover of receivables}} = \frac{(₹8 \times 30{,}000) + (₹6 \times 4{,}500)}{360 \div 75} = ₹55{,}625$$

$$\text{Present plan} = \frac{(₹8 \times 30{,}000)}{360 \div 45} = ₹30{,}000$$

Additional investment in accounts receivable = ₹55,625 – ₹30,000 = ₹25,625
Cost of additional investment at 15 per cent = 0.15 × ₹25,625 = ₹3,843.75.

(iii) Additional bad debt expenses: This is the difference between the bad debt expenses with the proposed and present credit periods.
Bad debt with proposed credit period = 0.03 × ₹3,45,000 = ₹10,350
Bad debt with present credit period = 0.01 × ₹3,00,000 = ₹3,000
Additional bad debt expense = (₹10,350 – ₹3,000) = ₹7,350

Thus, the incremental cost associated with the extension of the credit period is ₹11,193.75 (₹3,843.75 + ₹7,350). As against this, the benefits are ₹18,000. There is, therefore, a net gain of ₹6,806.25, that is, (₹18,000 – ₹11,193.75). The firm would be well-advised to extend the credit period from 30 to 60 days.

TABLE 15.4 Effect of Relaxation of Credit Period to Two Months

Particulars	*Amount*
Incremental sales revenue (4,500 × ₹10)	₹45,000
Less: incremental variable costs (4,500 × ₹6)	27,000
Incremental contribution	18,000
Less: incremental cost of additional investment in debtors	3,843.75
Less: increase in bad debts	7,350.00
Incremental profit	6,806.25

The effect of a decrease in the credit period can be similarly analysed.

Cost of Additional Investment in Debtors

There are two approaches to determine the cost of additional investment in debtors: **(1)** Total cost (FC + VC) and **(2)** Variable costs only. The rationale for the total cost is that the firm needs to finance total cost, whether it is fixed or variable as far as credit sales/investment in debtors is concerned. Its investments are not limited to VC only. The variable cost approach contends that the existing fixed costs are sunk costs and they are to be incurred by the corporate irrespective of the production/sales volume. Therefore, they are irrelevant costs as they are not additional out-of-pocket costs, as far as, additional investment in debtors is concerned. Therefore, the average investment in debtors in present as well as proposed plans should be computed dividing the total variable costs of sales by debtors turnover.[6]

The concept of additional investment in debtors, based on variable cost approach, is explained, based on the data contained in Example 15.3, below.

Average investment in debtors = Total VC/Debtors turnover
Present plan: (₹6 × 30,000 units = ₹1,80,000) ÷ 8 = ₹22,500
Proposed plan: (₹6 × 34,500 units = ₹2,07,000) ÷ 4.8 = ₹43,125
Additional investment: (₹43,125 – ₹22,500) = ₹20,625
Cost of additional investment (₹20,625 × 0.15) = ₹3,093.75
Incremental profit (₹3,843.75 – ₹3,093.75) = ₹750 (Total = ₹7,556.25)

The marginal/additional investment in debtors based on VC approach would obviously be lower than the total cost (TC) approach, leading to less financial cost. This, in turn, would result in higher incremental profits (or lower loss) in the VC approach compared to the total cost approach.

Cost of Additional Investment in Cash and Inventories (Net of Additional Creditors)

Liberal credit terms, in general, lead to additional sales which, in turn, would require higher level of production. To support this higher level of operations, the corporates would evidently require additional working capital in terms of higher level of safety stocks of cash and inventories of all types, besides increased investments in debtors (**explained earlier**). Assuming the requirement net of additional accounts payable is positive, this also needs to be financed. In operational terms, there is need to take into account financial cost of such additional investments to evaluate true profitability of the proposed relaxation in credit terms.

Continuing with Examples 15.3, assume additional net working capital (duly adjusted for increased creditors), besides debtors, is ₹4,000; the cost of ₹4,000 at 15 per cent is ₹600. As a result of this additional cost, profits would decrease by ₹600 to ₹6,206.26 (total cost approach) and to ₹6,956.25 (variable cost approach.)

LO 15.4 COLLECTION POLICIES

The third area involved in the accounts receivable management is collection policies. They refer to the procedures followed to collect accounts receivable when, after the expiry of the credit period, they become due. These policies cover two aspects:
(i) degree of effort to collect the overdues, and **(ii)** type of collection efforts.

Collection policy involves procedures for collecting accounts receivables when they are due.

Degree of Collection Effort

To illustrate the effect of the collection effort, the credit policies of a firm may be categorised into **(i)** strict/light, and **(ii)** lenient. The collection policy would be tight if very rigorous procedures are followed. A tight collection policy has implications which involve benefits as well costs. The management has to consider a trade-off between them. Likewise, a lenient collection effort also affects the cost-benefit trade-off. The effect of tightening the collection is discussed below.

In the first place, the bad debt expenses (default cost) would decline. Moreover, the average collection period will be reduced. As a result of these two effects, the firm will benefit and its profits will increase. But, there would be a negative effects also. A very rigorous collection strategy would involve increased collection costs. Yet another negative effect may be in the form of a decline in the volume of sales. This may be because some customers may not like the pressure and intense efforts initiated by the firm, and may switch to other firms. These effects are tabulated in Table 15.5.

TABLE 15.5 Basic Trade-off from Tight Collection Effort

Item	*Direction of Change (I = Increase D = Decrease)*	*Effect on Profits [Positive (+) or Negative (–)]*
Bad Debt Expenses	D	+
Average Collection Period	D	+
Sales Volume	D	–
Collection Expenditure	I	–

The effect of the lenient policy will be just the opposite. We illustrate the basic trade-off in Example 15.4.

Example 15.4

A firm is contemplating stricter collection policies. The following details are available:

1. At present, the firm is selling 36,000 units on credit at a price of ₹32 each; the variable cost per unit is ₹25 while the average cost per unit is ₹29; average collection period is 58 days; and collection expenses amount to ₹10,000; bad debts are 3 per cent.
2. If the collection procedures are tightened, additional collection charges amounting to ₹20,000 would be required, bad debts will be 1 per cent; the collection period will be 40 days; sales volume is likely to decline by 500 units.

Assuming a 20 per cent rate of return on investments, what would be your recommendation? Should the firm implement the decision?

Solution

(i) Bad debt expenses:

Present plan: (0.03 × ₹11,52,000)	₹34,560
Proposed plan: (0.01 × ₹11,36,000)	11,360
Savings in bad debt expenses	23,200

(ii) Average collection period/average investment in receivables:

$$\text{Present plan} = \frac{36{,}000 \times ₹\,29}{360 \div 58} \qquad 1{,}68{,}200 \text{ (a)}$$

$$\text{Proposed plan} = \frac{(36{,}000 \times ₹\,29) - (500 \times ₹\,25)}{360 \div 40} \qquad 1{,}14{,}611 \text{ (b)}$$

Savings in average investments (a – b) 53,589

Assuming a 20 per cent return, the firm will be able to earn ₹10,718 on this saving.

(iii) Sales volume: Since the sales volume will decline by 500 units, there would be a loss of ₹3,500 (500 × ₹7).

(iv) Additional collection charges = ₹20,000.

Thus, the total benefits from a tightening of the collection policy will be ₹33,918 (₹23,200 + ₹10,718) and the total cost will be ₹23,500 (₹3,500 + ₹20,000). Therefore, there would be a net gain of ₹10,418 (₹33,918 – ₹23,500). The firm should, therefore, implement the proposed strategy.

Example 15.5

Super Sports, dealing in sports goods, has an annual sale of ₹50 lakh and currently extending 30 days' credit to the dealers. It is felt that sales can pick up considerably if the dealers are willing to carry increased stocks, but the dealers have difficulty in financing their inventory. The firm is, therefore, considering shifts in credit policy. The following information is available:

The average collection period now is 30 days.
Variable costs, 80 per cent of sales.
Fixed costs, ₹6 lakh per annum
Required (pre-tax) return on investment: 20 per cent

Credit policy	Average collection period (days)	Annual sales (₹ lakh)
A	45	56
B	60	60
C	75	62
D	90	63

Determine which policy the company should adopt.

Solution

Evaluation of Proposed Credit Policies *(Amount in ₹ lakh)*

Particulars	Present	Proposed (number of days)			
	(30)	A(45)	B(60)	C(75)	D(90)
(a) Sales revenue	50	56	60	62	63
Less: Variable costs (80% of sales)	40	44.8	48	49.6	50.4
Total contribution	10	11.2	12	12.4	12.6
Less: Fixed costs	6	6	6	6	6
Profit	4	5.2	6	6.4	6.6
Increase in profits due to increase in total contribution (20% of sales) compared to present profits	—	1.2	2	2.4	2.6
(b) Investment in debtors:					
Total cost (VC + FC)	46	50.8	54	55.6	56.4
Debtors turnover (DT) (360 days collection period)	12	8	6	4.8	4
Average investment (total cost ÷ DT)	3.83	6.35	9	11.58	14.10
Additional investment compared to present level	—	2.52	5.17	7.75	10.27
Cost of additional investment	—	0.50	1.03	1.55	2.05
(c) Incremental profit (a – b)	—	0.70	0.97	0.85	0.55

Policy B (average collection period 60 days) should be adopted as it yields maximum profit.

Example 15.6

XYZ Corporation is considering relaxing its present credit policy and is in the process of evaluating two alternative policies. Currently, the firm has annual credit sales of ₹50 lakh and accounts receivable turnover ratio of 4 times a year. The current level of loss due to bad debts is ₹1,50,000. The firm is required to give a return of 25 per cent on the investment in new accounts receivable. The company's variable costs are 70 per cent of the selling price. Given the following information, which is a better option?

Particulars	Present policy	Policy option I	Policy option II
Annual credit sales	₹50,00,000	₹60,00,000	₹67,50,000
Accounts receivable turnover ratio	4	3	2.4
Bad debt losses	1,50,000	3,00,000	4,50,000

Solution

Relative Suitability of Policy Options

Particulars	Present policy	Policy option I	Policy option II
Sales revenue	₹50,00,000	₹60,00,000	₹67,50,000
Less: Variable cost (70%)	35,00,000	42,00,000	47,25,000
Contribution margin (manufacturing)	15,00,000	18,00,000	20,25,000
Less: Other relevant costs:			
Bad debt losses	1,50,000	3,00,000	4,50,000
Investment cost (see working notes)	2,18,750	3,50,000	4,92,187.50
Contribution margin (final)	11,31,250	11,50,000	10,82,812.50

Recommendation The firm is advised to adopt policy option I (extend credit terms to 4 months).

Working Notes

Strictly speaking, investment in accounts receivable should be determined with reference to total cost of goods sold on credit. However, fixed costs are not given. It is assumed that there are no fixed costs and investment in debtors/receivables is determined with reference to variable costs only.

$$\text{Present policy: } \frac{₹35{,}00{,}000}{4} = ₹8{,}75{,}000 \times 0.25 = ₹2{,}18{,}750$$

$$\text{Policy option I: } \frac{₹42{,}00{,}000}{3} = ₹14{,}00{,}000 \times 0.25 = ₹3{,}50{,}000$$

$$\text{Policy option II: } \frac{₹47{,}25{,}000}{2.4} = ₹19{,}68{,}750 \times 0.25 = ₹4{,}92{,}187.5$$

Type of Collection Efforts

The second aspect of collection policies relates to the steps that should be taken to collect overdues from the customers. A well-established collection policy should have clear-cut guidelines as to the sequence of collection efforts. After the credit period is over and payment remains due, the firm should initiate measures to collect them. The effort should in the beginning be polite, but, with the passage of time, it should gradually become strict. The steps usually taken are **(i)** letters, including reminders, to expedite payment; **(ii)** telephone calls for personal contact; **(iii)** personal visits; **(iv)** help of collection agencies; and finally, **(v)** legal action. The firm should take recourse to very stringent measures, like legal action, only after all other avenues have been fully exhausted. They not only involve a cost but also affect the relationship with the customers. The aim should be to collect as early as possible; genuine difficulties of the customers should be given due consideration.

SUMMARY

LO 15.1	When a firm sells goods and services on credit, it creates accounts receivable/debtors which would be collected in future. Accounts receivable, repesent an extension of credit to customers, allowing them a reasonable period of time, in which to pay for the goods/services purchased by them. In fact, credit sales and, therefore, receivables are considered as a marketing tool to promote sales and thereby profits.
	The extension of credit involves risk and cost. The objective of receivables management, therefore, is to have a trade-off between the benefits and costs associated with the extension of credit. The benefits are increased sales and anticipated increased profits/incremental contribution. The major costs are collection costs, capital costs, delinquency costs and default costs. The firm should consider only the incremental benefits and costs that result from a change in the receivables or trade credit policy.
	The management of receivables involves crucial decision in three areas: (i) credit policies, (ii) credit terms and (iii) collection policies.
LO 15.2	The credit policy of a firm provides the framework to determine whether or not to extend credit to a customer and how much credit to extend. The two broad dimensions of credit policy decision of a firm are credit standards and credit analysis.
	Credit standards represent the basic criterion for the extension of credit to customers. These can be either tight/restrictive or liberal/non-restrictive. The trade-off with reference to credit standards cover: (i) collection cost, (ii) cost of investment in debtors, (iii) bad debts and (iv) level of sales profit/contribution. The credit analysis component of credit policies includes obtaining credit information from different sources and its analysis.

LO 15.2	In case, the standards are relaxed, it implies credit for a longer period will be extended. More credit results in increase in sales. The benefits of incremental sales are to be weighed against incremental collection costs, interest costs due to additional investment in debtors, delinquency cost and bad debts.
	When standards are tightened, it implies less period of credit extended to customers. It would result in decrease in sales. The contribution foregone due to decrease in sales is to be compared with savings due to the lower collection costs, interest costs and bad debt losses.
LO 15.3	Credit terms specify the repayment terms. The credit terms have three components: (i) credit period, (ii) cash discount and (iii) cash discount period. The credit terms should be determined on the basis of cost-benefit trade-off in these three components.
LO 15.4	Collection policies refer to the procedure followed to collect the receipts when they become due. The collection policies may be classified into (i) strict and (ii) liberal. The effects of tightening the collection policy would be: (i) decline in debts, (ii) decline in collection period resulting lower interest costs, (iii) increase in collection costs and (iv) decline in sales. The effects of a lenient policy would be exactly the opposite.
	The framework of analysis of all the three decision areas in receivables management is to secure a trade-off between the costs and benefits of the measurable effects on the sales vol-ume, capital cost due to change in investment in debtors, collection costs, bad debts and so on. The firm should select an alternative which has potentials of more benefits than the cost.

REFERENCES

1. Joy, O M, *Introduction to Financial Management,* Irwin, Homewood Ill., 1992, p 456.
2. Bolten, S E, *Managerial Finance,* Houghton, Mifflin Co., Boston, 1991, p 446.
3. Cf. Joy, *op. cit.*, p 458.
4. *Ibid.*, pp 462-64.
5. For a penetrating description of the implications of credit terms from the point of recipients (accounts payable) refer to Gitman, L J, *Principles of Managerial Finance,* Harper and Row, New York, 1993, Chapter 17; also Joy, O M, *op. cit.*, Chapter 19; and Bolten, SE, *Managerial Finance,* Houghton Mifflin Co., Boston, 1991, Chapter 15.
6. Gitman, L J, *op. cit.*, 2006, p. 643. Also refer to Van Horne, J C, *op. cit.*, 2002, p. 470. There are merits each approach.

SOLVED PROBLEMS

P.15.1 H Ltd has at present annual sales level of ₹10,000 units at ₹300 per unit. The variable cost is ₹200 per unit and fixed cost amount to ₹3,00,000 per annum. The present credit period allowed by the company is 1 month. The company is considering a proposal to increase the credit period to 2 months and 3 months and has made the following estimates:

LO 15.2,4 | LOD E

	Existing		*Proposed*
Credit period (month)	1	2	3
Increase in sales (per cent)	—	15	30
Bad debts (per cent)	1	3	5

There will be increase in fixed cost by ₹50,000 on account of increase in sales beyond 25 per cent of present level. The company plans a pre-tax return of 20 per cent on investment in receivables.

You are required to calculate the most paying credit policy for the company.

Solution

Decision-making (liberalisation of credit period to 2 months or 3 months)

Particulars	*1 month*	*2 months*	*3 months*
Sales (units)	10,000	11,500	13,000
Sale revenue	₹30,00,000	₹34,50,000	₹39,00,000
Less: Variable costs	20,00,000	23,00,000	26,00,000
Total contribution	10,00,000	11,50,000	13,00,000
Less: Other costs:			
Fixed costs	3,00,000	3,00,000	3,50,000
Bad debts	30,000	1,03,500	1,95,000
Investment cost (*see working notes*)	38,333	86,667	1,47,500
Profit	6,31,667	6,59,833	6,07,500

Recommendation The firm is advised to adopt policy of extending credit of 2 months as it yields maximum profit.

Working Note

	Existing	*2 months*	*3 months*
Investment in debtors (VC + FC)/Debtors turnover	(₹23,00,000) / 12	(₹26,00,000) / 6	(₹29,50,000) / 4
	= ₹1,91,667	= ₹4,33,333	= ₹7,37,500
Cost of investment (Investment in debtors × 0.20)	38,333	86,667	1,47,500

P.15.2 Golden Syntex has annual sales of ₹24,00,000. The selling price per unit is ₹10 and the variable cost is 70 per cent of the selling price. The required rate of return on investment is 20 per cent, average cost, ₹9 per unit; annual collection expenditure, ₹50,000 and percentage of default, 3 per cent; credit terms, 2 months. Golden Syntex is considering the change in credit policy by following Programme A or Programme B.

LO 15.2,4 LOD M

	Programme	
	A	*B*
Average collection period (months)	1.5	1
Annual collection expenditure (₹)	75,000	1,50,000
Percentage of default (%)	2	1

Determine which collection programme should Golden Syntex follow?

Solution

Financial evaluation of proposed programmes (A or B) relating to credit policy

Particulars	*Existing*	*Programme A*	*Programme B*
Cost of operation:			
Annual collection expenditure	₹50,000	₹75,000	₹1,50,000
Losses due to default/bad debts (on sales of ₹24,00,000)	72,000	48,000	24,000
Cost of investment in debtors (see working note 1)	72,000	54,000	36,000
Total	1,94,000	1,77,000	2,10,000

Recommendation Golden Syntex is advised to adopt Programme A as its entails minimum cost of operation.

Working Note

Cost of investment in debtors

Particulars	Existing	Programme A	Programme B
(a) Investment in debtors			
[(2,40,000 units × ₹7) + (2,40,000 × ₹2)]	(₹21.6 lakh) / 6	(₹21.6 lakh) / 8	(₹21.6 lakh) / 12
	= ₹3,60,000	= ₹2,70,000	= ₹1,80,000
(b) Required rate of return (%)	20	20	20
(c) Cost of investment in debtors (a × b)	72,000	54,000	36,000

P.15.3 Sagar company currently makes all sales on credit and offers no cash discount. It is considering a 2 per cent cash discount for payment within 10 days. The firm's current average collection period is 60 days, sales are 2,00,000 units, selling price is ₹30 per unit, variable cost per unit is ₹20 and average cost per unit is ₹25 at the current sales volume. **LO 15.3,4** LOD M

It is expected that the change in credit terms will result in increase in sales to 2,25,000 units and the average collection period will fall to 45 days. However, due to increased sales, increased working capital required will be ₹1,00,000 (it does not take into account the effect on debtors). Assuming that 50 per cent of the total sales will be on cash discount and 20 per cent is the required return on investment, should the proposed discount be offered?

Solution

Effect of extending cash discount to customers

Particulars	Amount
Increased sales revenue (25,000 × ₹30)	₹7,50,000
Less: Variable costs (25,000 × ₹20)	5,00,000
Incremental contribution	2,50,000
Add: Savings in cost due to decrease in investment in debtors (see working note 1)	29,167
Less: Cost of additional working capital required (₹1,00,000 × 0.20)	(20,000)
Less: Cost involved in cash discount (0.02 × 2,25,000 units × ₹30 × 0.5)	(67,500)
Profit	1,91,667

It is advised that the firm should offer cash discount to its customers.

Working Note

1. Savings due to decrease in average collection period:

$$\text{Present investment in debtors (without cash discount)} = \frac{2,00,000 \times ₹25}{6\ (360\ \text{days}/60)} = ₹8,33,333$$

$$\text{Expected investment in debtors (with cash discount)} = \frac{2,00,000 \times ₹25 + 25,000 \times ₹20}{8\ (360\ \text{days}/45)} = ₹6,87,500$$

Decrease in investment in debtors = ₹8,33,333 – ₹6,87,500 = ₹1,45,833
Savings in cost = ₹1,45,833 × 0.20 = ₹29,167

P.15.4 Easy Limited specialises in the manufacture of a computer component. The component is currently sold for ₹1,000 and its variable cost is ₹800. For the current year ended December 31, the company sold on an average 400 components per month. **LO 15.3,4** LOD M

At present, the company grants one month's credit to its customers. It is thinking of extending the same to two months on account of which the following are expected:

Increase in sales, 25 per cent
Increase in stock, ₹2,00,000
Increase in creditors, ₹1,00,000

You are required to advise the company on whether or not to extend credit terms if (a) all customers avail of the extended credit period of two months and (b) existing customers do not avail of the credit terms but only the new customers avail of the same. Assume the entire increase in sales is attributable to the new customers.

The company expects a minimum return of 40 per cent on the investments.

Solution

(a) Effect of relaxation of credit period to two months

Particulars	*Amount*
Incremental sales revenue (100 components × 12 × ₹1,000)	₹12,00,000
Less: Increased variable costs (₹12,00,000 × 0.80)	9,60,000
Incremental contribution	2,40,000
Less: Cost of additional working capital required (see working note 1)	2,32,000
Incremental profit	8,000

Working Note 1

(i) Present investment in debtors: $\frac{400 \times 12 \times ₹800}{12 \text{ (Debtors turnover ratio)}}$	₹3,20,000
(ii) Proposed investment in debtors: $\frac{500 \times 12 \times ₹800}{6 \text{ (Debtors turnover ratio)}}$	8,00,000
(iii) Additional investment in debtors	4,80,000
Add: Increase in stock	2,00,000
Less: Increase in creditors	1,00,000
Additional working capital required	5,80,000
(iv) Minimum return expected on additional working capital (₹5,80,000 × 0.40)	2,32,000

(b) Effect of relaxation of credit period to two months

Particulars	*Amount*
Incremental contribution (as per (a) above	₹2,40,000
Less: Cost of additional working capital (see working note 2)	1,04,000
Incremental profit	1,36,000

Working Note 2

(i) Additional investment in debtors (100 × 12 × ₹800/6)	₹1,60,000
Add: Increase in stock	2,00,000
Less: Increase in creditors	1,00,000
Additional working capital required	2,60,000
(ii) Minimum return expected on additional working capital (₹2,60,000 × 0.40)	1,04,000

P.15.5 Star Limited, manufacturers of colour TV sets, are considering the liberalisation of existing credit terms to three of their large customers. The credit period and likely quantity of TV sets that will be lifted by the customers are as follows: **LO 15.3,4** LOD D

Credit period (days)	Quantity lifted		
	A	B	C
0	1,000	1,000	—
30	1,000	1,500	—
60	1,000	2,000	1,000
90	1,000	2,500	1,500

The selling price per TV set is ₹9,000. The expected contribution is 20 per cent of the selling price. The cost of carrying debtors averages 20 per cent per annum.

You are required:

(a) To determine the credit period to be allowed to each customer (assume 360 days in a year for calculation purposes).

(b) What other problems the company might face in allowing the credit period as determined in (a) above?

Solution

(a) In case of customer A, liberalisation of credit period does not affect sales. No credit should be allowed to him.

Effect of extending credit period to customer B and C *(Amount in lakhs of rupees)*

Particulars	Customer B (days)				Customer C (days)	
	0	30	60	90	60	90
Sales	90	135	180	225	90	135
Less: Variable costs (0.80)	72	108	144	180	72	108
Contribution (0.20)	18	27	36	45	18	27
Less: Cost of investments in debtors (at VC)	—	1.8	4.8	9.0	2.4	5.4
$\left(\frac{\text{Total VC}}{\text{Debtors turnover}}\right) \times 0.20$	—	$\left(\frac{108}{360/30}\right)$	$\left(\frac{144}{360/60}\right)$	$\left(\frac{180}{360/90}\right)$	$\left(\frac{72}{360/60}\right)$	$\left(\frac{108}{360/90}\right)$
Profit	18	25.2	31.2	36	15.6	21.6

Profits are maximum when credit period is 90 days to both customers.

(b) When customer A comes to know of 90 days credit extended to customer B and C, he will either seek similar credit period or press for cash discount.

Customer B will seek either higher credit period or trade discount for buying more than Customer C.

P.15.6 Radiance garments Ltd. manufactures readymade garments and sells them on credit basis through a network of dealers. Its present sale is ₹60 lakh per annum with 20 days credit period. The company is contemplating an increase in the credit period with a view to increasing sales. Present variable costs are 70 per cent of sales and the total fixed costs ₹8 lakh per annum. The company expects pre-tax return on investment @ 25 per cent. Some other details are given as under:

LO 15.2,4 LOD M

Proposed credit policy	Average collection period (days)	Expected annual sales (₹ lakh)
I	30	65
II	40	70
III	50	74
IV	60	75

Required: Which credit policy should the company adopt? Present your answer in a tabular form. Assume 360-day a year. Calculations should be made upto two digits after decimal.

Solution

Evaluation of proposed credit policies *(Amount in ₹ lakh)*

Particulars	*Present*	*Proposed (number of days)*			
	(20)	*I (30)*	*II (40)*	*III (50)*	*IV (60)*
(a) Sales revenue	60	65	70	74	75
Less: Variable costs (VC)	42	45.5	49	51.8	52.5
Total contribution	18	19.5	21	22.2	22.5
Less: Fixed costs (FC)	8	8	8	8	8
Profit	10	11.5	13	14.2	14.5
Increase in profit due to increase in total contribution compared to present profit	—	1.5	3	4.2	4.5
(b) Investment in debtors/receivables:					
Total costs (VC + FC)	50	53.5	57	59.8	60.5
Debtors turnover ratio (DT) (360 ÷ Average collection period)	18	12	9	7.2	6
Average investment in debtors (Total cost ÷ DT)	2.78	4.46	6.33	8.3	10.08
Additional investment compared to present level	—	1.68	3.55	5.52	7.30
Cost of additional investment @ 25%	—	0.42	0.89	1.38	1.83
(c) Incremental profit [(a) – (b)]	—	1.08	2.11	2.82	2.67

Recommendation Policy III (average collection period 60 days) is recommended as it yields maximum profit.

P.15.7 A company is currently engaged in the business of manufacturing computer component. The computer component is currently sold for ₹1,000 and its variable cost is ₹800. For the current year ended March 31, the company sold on an average 500 components per month.

LO 15.2,4 LOD D

Presently the company grants one month credit to its customers. The company is thinking of extending the credit to two months on account of which the following is expected

Increase in sales	25 per cent
Increase in stock	₹2,00,000
Increase in creditors	₹1,00,000

You are required to advise the company on whether or not to extend the credit terms if:

(a) All customers avail the credit period of two months and (b) the new credit policy is given to only new customers. Assume that the entire increase in sales is attributable to the new customers. The company expects a minimum return of 40 per cent on investment.

Solution

Incremental analysis whether to extend credit period of two months to all customers or the new customers only

Particulars	*All customers*	*New customers only*
Incremental sales:		
Sales at proposed 2 months credit period (500 units × 12 months × ₹1,000 per unit) × 1.25	₹75,00,000	₹75,00,000
Less sales at existing 1 month credit period (500 units × 12 months × ₹1,000 per unit)	60,00,000	60,00,000
Increase in sales	15,00,000	15,00,000

(*Contd.*)

(*Contd.*)

Less increased variable costs (@80% of sales)	12,00,000	12,00,000
Incremental contribution	3,00,000	3,00,000
Less cost of additional working capital required (see working note 1)	2,80,000	1,20,000
Incremental profit	20,000	1,80,000

Recommendation The company is advised to extend the credit terms only for new customers as it yields higher incremental profit.

Working Note 1

(i) Existing investment in debtors at variable cost with credit period of 1 month (₹60,00,000 × 0.8)/Debtors turnover ratio 12 = ₹4,00,000

(ii) (a) Investment in debtors with incremental sales due to 2 months credit period. When all customers are extended 2 months credit period:
(₹75,00,000 × 0.8)/Debtors turnover ratio 6 = ₹10,00,000).
(b) When credit period is extended to new customers only: (₹15,00,000 × 0.8)/Debtors turnover ratio 6 = ₹2,00,000.

(iii) Additional investment in working capital required and its cost:

Particulars	*All customers*	*New customers only*
Incremental investment in debtors	₹6,00,000*	2,00,000
Increase in stock	2,00,000	2,00,000
Less increase in creditors	(1,00,000)	(1,00,000)
Increase in working capital	7,00,000	3,00,000
Cost of additional working capital @ 40%	2,80,000	1,20,000

(*₹10,00,000 – ₹4,00,000)

P.15.8 A company deals with consumer durables, having an annual turnover of ₹80 lakh, 75 per cent of which are credit sales effected through a large number of dealers while the balance sales are made through show rooms on cash basis. Normal credit allowed is 30 days. **LO 15.2,4** LOD M

The company proposes to expand its business substantially and there is good demand as well. However, the marketing manager finds that the dealers have difficulty in holding more stocks due to financial problems. He therefore proposes a change in the credit policy as follows:

(*₹ in lakh*)

Proposal	*Credit period*	*Anticipated credit sales*
A	60 days	70
B	90 days	75

The products yield an average contribution of 25 per cent on sales.

Fixed costs amount to ₹5 lakh per annum. The company expects a pre-tax return of 20 per cent on capital employed.

The finance manager after a review of the proposal has recommended increasing the provision for bad debts from the current 0.5 per cent to 1 per cent for proposal A and to 1.5 per cent for proposal B.

Evaluate the merits of the new proposals and recommend the best policy.

Solution

Evaluation of Proposed Credit Policies

Particulars	*Present*	*Proposal A*	*Proposal B*
Sales revenue	₹60,00,000	₹70,00,000	₹75,00,000
Less variable costs (0.75)	45,00,000	52,50,000	56,25,000
Less fixed cost	5,00,000	5,00,000	5,00,000
Less bad debts	30,000	70,000	1,12,500
Less cost of investment in debtors*	83,333	1,91,667	3,06,250
Profit	8,86,667	9,88,333	9,56,250

Recommendation Proposal A is recommended as it yields maximum profit.

Working Note

Cost of Investment in Debtors

Particulars	*Present*	*Proposal A*	*Proposal B*
(i) Total investment in debtors (Total VC + Total FC)	₹50,00,000	₹57,50,000	₹61,25,000
(ii) Debtors turnover ratio (360 days/Average collection period)	12 (360/30)	6 (360/60)	4 (360/90)
(iii) Average investment in debtors (i/ii)	4,16,667	9,58,333	15,31,250
(iv) Cost of average investment in debtors (iii) × 0.20	83,333	1,91,667	3,06,250

P.15.9 Exxon Ltd. has current sales of ₹6,00,000 per annum. To push up sales, Exxon is considering a more liberal credit policy as one of the strategies. The current average collection period of the company is 30 days. Proposed increases in collection period and their impact on sales and default rate (on total sales) are given below:

LO 15.2,4 LOD M

Credit Policy	*Increase in collection period*	*Increase in sales*	*Default rate*
I	15 days	₹25,000	0.5%
II	30 days	60,000	1.0%
III	40 days	70,000	2.0%

Exxon is selling its product at ₹10 each. Average cost per unit at the current level is ₹8 and variable cost per unit is ₹6. If Exxon requires a rate of return of 20 per cent on its investment, which credit policy do you recommend and why? Assume 360 days a year.

Solution

Evaluation of Proposed Credit Policies

Particulars	*Present*	*Proposed (number of days)*		
	30 days	*I (45)*	*II (60)*	*III (70)*
Sales (in units)	60,000	62,500	66,000	67,000
Sales revenue	₹6,00,000	₹6,25,000	₹6,60,000	₹6,70,000
Less variables costs @ ₹6 per unit	3,60,000	3,75,000	3,96,000	4,02,000
Less total fixed costs	1,20,000	1,20,000	1,20,000	1,20,000
(60,000 units × ₹2)	—	3,125	6,600	13,400
Less bad debts	8,000	12,375	17,200	20,311
Less cost of investment in debtors*	1,12,000	1,14,500	1,20,200	1,14,289
Profit				

Recommendation Policy II (of increasing credit period by 30 days) is recommended as it yields maximum profit.

*Cost of Investment in Debtors

Particulars	Present	Proposed I	II	III
(i) Total investment in debtors (Total VC + Total FC)	₹4,80,000	₹4,95,000	₹5,16,000	₹5,22,000
(ii) Debtors turnover ratio 360/Average collection period	12	8	6	5.14
(iii) Average investment in debtors (i)/(ii)	40,000	61,875	86,000	1,01,556
(iv) Cost of investment in debtors (iii) × 0.20	8,000	12,375	17,200	20,311

P.15.10 The credit manager of XYZ Ltd. is reappraising the company's credit policy. The company sells its products on terms of net 30. Cost of goods sold is 85 per cent of sales and fixed costs are further 5 per cent of sales. XYZ classifies its customers on a scale of 1 to 4. During the past five years, the experience was as under:

LO 15.2,4 LOD M

Classification	Default as a percentage of sales	Average collection period-in days for non-defaulting accounts
1	0	45
2	2	42
3	10	40
4	20	80

The average rate of interest is 15 per cent. What conclusions do you draw about the company's credit policy? What other factors should be taken into account before changing the present policy? Discuss.

Solution

Statement showing evaluation of credit policy

Classification	Gross profit @ 15%	Fixed costs @ 5%	Bad debts	Interest cost[1]	Total costs (3 + 4 + 5)	Net profit (2 – 6)
1	2	3	4	5	6	7
1	₹15	₹5	Nil	₹1.66	₹6.66	₹8.34
2	15	5	₹2	1.55	8.55	6.45
3	15	5	10	1.48	16.48	(1.48)
4	15	5	20	2.96	27.96	(12.96)

Note: Assuming ₹100 as the amount of revenue generated from each type of customer.

Working Notes

(1) Computation of interest costs

Particulars	1 (45)	2 (42)	3 (40)	4 (80)
Investment in debtors (Total cost, TC)	90	90	90	90
Debtors turnover (DT) (365 ÷ average collection period)	8.11	8.69	9.125	4.5625
Average investment (TC ÷ DT)	11.096	10.36	9.86	19.73
Interest @ 15 per cent	1.66	1.55	1.48	2.96

The analysis indicates that there seems to be laxity on the part of credit collection department in that the average collection period is higher (40-80 days) than the period allowed (30 days) for all categories of customers. Given the low profit margin of the firm (say 10 per cent as 90 per cent virtually are incremental costs to sales revenue), the firm cannot afford such a policy. In fact, the firm is actually suffering loss on sales made to the two categories of customers (namely, classified as 3 and 4). Losses in these categories are primarily due to substantial amount of bad debts.

To promote sales, firm can afford liberal credit policy as the interest cost constitutes a small percentage of total costs. What is required is that the credit collection department of the firm should make more rigorous efforts to judge credit-worthiness of its customers; this, in turn, will reduce bad debts.

MINI CASES

15.C.1 (Credit Policy) Khoobsurat Industries Ltd is a major player in the soap and detergent business. It has a market share of 25 per cent which is almost twice as much as that of the next competitor. The current sales of Khoobsurat amount to ₹1,400 crore. Its bad debts are in the range of 1 per cent. The company has a P/V ratio of 45 per cent. The policy of Khoobsurat is to extend to all its customers a credit of 30 days. The existing fixed costs are ₹120 crore which are unaffected by changes in sales.

Khoobsurat Industries is facing severe competition both from multinational and regional players. The CEO of the company, Sushant Sachdeva, has asked Amit Gupta, the chief marketing manager, to submit proposals to meet the challenge from the competitors. Amit Gupta has, after a detailed survey and discussion, proposed three options for the consideration of the CEO:

Option 1: Increase the credit period to 60 days. In that case, the sales are likely to increase by 20 per cent. But bad debts would go up to 2 per cent and an additional investment of ₹20 crore will be required in working capital (without taking into account the effect of debtors).

Option 2: Offer a credit term, 2/10 net 30. In this case, sales are expected to increase by 10 per cent. Fifty per cent of the debtors are likely to avail of the discount. There would be no change in bad debts.

Option 3: Offer both extended credit to 60 days and cash discount of 2 per cent (2/10 net 30). An increase of 25 per cent in sales could be expected and cash discount could be availed of by 30 per cent of the customers. But bad debts will increase to 2 per cent and the additional investment in working capital of ₹20 crore will be required (without taking into account the effect of debtors).

The CEO of Khoobsurat Industries desires the CFO to carry out a financial evaluation of the above alternative proposals and suggest the course of action to be taken. The required rate of return of Khoobsurat is 20 per cent.

Solution

Financial Evaluation of Credit Proposal (₹ crore)

		Option 1		*Option 2*		*Option 3*
Incremental sales	(₹1,400 × .20)	280	(1,400 × 0.10)	140	(1,400 × 0.25)	350
Less incremental variable cost	(280 × 0.55)	154	(140 × 0.55)	77	(350 × 0.55)	192.5
Incremental contribution	(280 × 0.45)	126	(140 × 0.45)	63	(350 × 0.45)	157.5
Less other relevant costs:						
Bad debts		19.6[a]		1.4[c]		21[d]
Cost of investment in working capital (20 × 0.20)		4		—		4
Cost of investment in debtors		19.97[b]		—		12.2[e]
Cash discount		—		15.4		10.5
Add savings on account of reduction in debtors		—		4.1[f]		
Incremental profit		82.43		50.3		109.8

[a](₹1,680 crore × 0.02) – (₹1,400 crore × 0.01) = ₹19.6 crore

[b] Proposed investment in debtors [(₹1,680 crore × 0.55) + ₹120 crore] ÷ 6

(Debtors turnover, 360 days ÷ 60 days = 6 days)	= ₹174 crore
Present investment in debtors [(₹1,400 crore × 0.55) + ₹120 crore] ÷ 12 (360 ÷ 30)	74.2 crore
Incremental investment in debtors	99.8
Cost of incremental investment in debtors (₹99.8 crore × 0.20)	19.97

[c] (₹1,540 crore × 0.01) – (₹1,400 crore × 0.01) = 1.4 crore

[d] (₹1,750 × 0.20) – (₹1,400 crore × 0.01) = 21 crore

[e] Proposed investment in debtors [(₹1,750 crore × 0.55) × ₹120 crore)

÷ 8 (360 days ÷ 45 days)	135.3
Present investment in debtors	74.2
Incremental investment in debtors	61.1
Cost of incremental investment in debtors (₹61.1 crore × 0.20)	12.2

[f]Debtors turnover = 360 days/[(0.5 × 10 days) + (0.5 × 30 days) = 20 days] = 18
Proposed investment in debtors [(₹1,540 crore × 0.55) + ₹120 crore) ÷ 18 = ₹53.7 crore
Decrease in investment in debtors (₹74.2 crore – ₹53.7 crore) = ₹20.5 crore
Savings on account of reduction in debtors (₹20.5 crore × 0.2) = ₹4.1 crore

Recommendation Option 3 which combines extended credit period and cash discount would result in the maximum incremental profit. The CEO may consider the proposed policy change due to its beneficial effect.

15.C.2 (Credit Period Policy) Addidas India Ltd is one of the leading global sports goods and apparel company, having a large presence in India. The region-wise break-up of Addidas' most recent sales are: (i) Western region—₹290 crore, Eastern region—₹105 crore, Northern region—₹285 crore and Southern region—₹265 crore. The market share of Addidas in this category are: West—30 per cent, East—5 per cent, North—25 per cent and South—26 per cent. Ashish Dhakde is the general manager incharge of the Western region. He was instrumental in generating the huge sales in the region which resulted in capturing an extra 6 per cent market share in the last one year only. Priyadarshi Sarkar, the CEO of Addidas India, is highly impressed with Ashish's performance and has promoted him as regional diretor of the Eastern region.

Ashish's immediate plan involves using the existing distribution channels, dealers and retailers to strengthen the Addidas brand in the Eastern region. He has identified that the Kolkatta area provides the largest share of revenue in the region amounting to ₹92 crore. In a brain-storming session with his managers, he came to the conclusion that strengthening the performance of at least three other centres as major revenue-earning areas is his topmost priority. The three identified areas are: (i) Bhubneshwar (existing sales, ₹6 crore) (ii) Jamshedpur (existing sale, ₹1.6 crore) and (iii) Guwahati (existing sale, ₹1.4 crore). After using ISM (Interpretation Structured Modelling), Ashish has identified the Bhubneshar area as the first priority.

The most influential dealer for Bhubneshar area is Soshit and Sons. During the first personal visit to the dealer, Dhakde met Soshit to discuss the possibilities of increasing the business in Bhubneshwar region. Soshit has assured Ashish of buying an extra 50 per cent over the current purchase of ₹5 crore if Addidas India relaxes its credit policies for him.

As per the current policy, Addidas India offers 27.5 per cent commission on MRP on cash purchases and 27 per cent commission on 30-day credit purchases. Soshit and Sons purchases on 30-day credit only as the cash purchase gives him only 0.5 per cent extra margin. The policy proposed by Soshit to Ashish is as follows:

- Cash purchase – 30 per cent commission on MRP
- 30-day credit purchase – 28 per cent commission on MRP
- 60-day credit purchase – 27 per cent commission on MRP

Soshit and Sons would be ready to buy (i) 50 per cent on cash basis (ii) 25 per cent on 30-day credit and (iii) 25 per cent on 60-day credit if Addidas India approves the policy proposed by Soshit.

Ashish is personally inclined to accept the proposal in principle. To figure out the benefits of the revised policy, he asks a financial consultant to carry out a financial analysis and prepare a report for the consideration of the CEO of Addidas India. The variable cost of Addidas India's products is 40 per cent of the MRP.

Solution

Financial Analysis of Proposed Credit Policy

Expected sales revenue [₹5,00,00,000 + (0.50 × ₹5,00,00,000)]	₹7,50,00,000
Less current sales	5,00,00,000
Incremental sales revenue	2,50,00,000

(*Contd.*)

(*Contd.*)

Incremental effective sales revenue to Addidas (₹2,50,00,00 × 0.73 net of dealers margin)		1,82,50,000
Less incremental cost:		
Ø Variable costs (₹2,50,00,000 × 0.40)	₹1,00,00,000	
Ø Cash discount (₹7,50,00,000 × 0.5 × 0.03)	11,25,000	
Ø Extra commission on 30-day credit (₹7,50,00,000 × 0.25 × 0.01)	1,87,500	
Ø Cost of incremental investments in debtors@ (₹2,08,333 × 0.20)	41,667	1,13,54,167
Incremental profit		68,95,833

@ Proposed investment in debtors (₹7,50,00,000 × 0.50 × 0.40) ÷ 8	₹18,75,000
Current investment in debtors (₹5,00,00,000 × 0.40) ÷ 12	16,66,667
Incremental investment in debtors	2,08,333

*Average collection period = [(30 days × 0.50) + (60 days × 0.50) = 45 days

Debtors turnover (360/45) = 8

Recommendation The proposal seems to be financially sound as it has potentials of incremental profit.

15.C.3 (Receivables Management Policy) Auto-Comp Ltd manufactures auto components for some of the major car manufacturing companies in India. With several foreign car manufacturing firms set to establish their manufacturing facilities in India, Auto-Comp is looking ahead at a bright future. However, the company management feels that it first needs to consolidate its position among the domestic auto players before it can capture the business of the foreign auto manufacturers. As a first step in this direction, it appoints Arpita Sharma as its new financial controller with extensive experience in the auto sector, having worked with some of the leading auto firms in the country. Immediately after her appointment, Arpita immediately examines the working capital management policy of the company, particularly the receivables management. Upon examining the receivables management policy, Arpita comes across the following facts:

The current sales of Auto-Comp amount to ₹20,000 crore. Its bad debts are to the tune of 2 per cent. The company has a Contribution to Volume (C/V) ratio of 45 per cent. The existing fixed cost are ₹3,000 crore, which will remain unchanged in the coming period. The current cash discount of 1.5/10, net 50, is being currently availed by 50 per cent of its customers. The cost of capital for Auto-Comp is 20 per cent.

Aprita with her significant expertise in the auto sector, decides that she must talk to the customers directly to find out what they want. After a small survey, she comes up with the following three options for the consideration of the CEO of Auto-Comp.

Option 1: Increase the credit period to 60 days. This is expected to increase sales by 20 per cent and bad debts to 3 per cent. An incremental investment of ₹600 crore will be required in working capital (without taking into account the effect of debtors).

Option 2: Offer a cash discount, the terms of which are 2/10, net 30. This is expected to increase sales by 5 per cent. It is estimated that 50 per cent of the customers will avail of the cash discount. This will result in a decrease in bad debts to 1.5 per cent.

Option 3: Offer both extended credit of 60 days as well as cash discount, terms of which are 1.5/10, net 60. The estimated incremental sales would be 20 per cent. It is estimated that 40 per cent of the customers would avail of the cash discount. Due to more lenient credit terms, bad debts are expected to increase to 3 per cent. The incremental investment in working capital (without taking into account the effect of debtors) is ₹600 crore.

Required The CEO of Auto-Comp appoints a financial consultant to carry out an objective analysis and recommend which policy would be the most beneficial for the company. As a financial consultant, what advice would you give? Why?

Solution

Financial Analysis of Proposed Credit Policies to Determine The Optimal Credit Policy for Auto-Comp Ltd (₹ crore)

Options	*Existing position*	*Option 1*	*Option 2*	*Option 3*
Sales revenue	20,000	24,000	21,000	24,000
Variable costs	11,000	13,200	11,550	13,200
Fixed costs	3,000	3,000	3,000	3,000
Incremental revenues	6,000	7,800	6,450	7,800
Bad debts	400	720	315	720
Cash discounts	150	0	210	144
Financial cost of Incremental working capital excluding debtors	0	120	0	120
Financial cost of Investment in debtors	233.33	540	161.67	360
Profit	5,216.67	6,420	5,763.33	6,456

Recommendation Auto-Comp is advised to adopt the policy of extending credit of 60 days (option 3) and a cash discount at 1.5/10, net 60 as it yields the maximum profit.

Working Notes

Debtors turnover period:

Existing (0.5 × 10 days) + (0.5 × 50 days) = 30 days

Option 2: (0.50 × 10 days) + (0.50 × 30 days) = 20 days

Option 3: (0.40 × 10 days) + (0.60 × 60 days) = 40 days

Investment in debtors:

Existing: 0.20 × [(0.55 × ₹20,000 + ₹3,000) ÷ (360 days/30 days)] = ₹233.33 crore

Option 1: 0.20 × [(0.55 × ₹24,000 + ₹3,000) ÷ (360 days/60 days)] = ₹540 crore

Option 2: 0.20 × [(0.55 × ₹21,000 + ₹3,000) ÷ (360 days/20 days)] = ₹161.67 crore

Option 3: 0.20 × [(0.55 × ₹24,000 + ₹3,000) ÷ (360 days/40 days)] = ₹360 crore

Scan the QR Code given at the end of chapter to access comprehensive cases.

REVIEW QUESTIONS

LOD: Easy

RQ.15.1 Indicate whether the following statements are true or false. **[LO 15.1,2,3,4]**

(i) Default costs are caused due to failure of customers to pay on time.

(ii) Financial costs to support credit-sales are referred to as collection costs.

(iii) Credit standards represent minimum requirements for extending credit to a customer.

(iv) Financial costs of investment in debtors are determined with reference to selling price at which credit sales are made.

(v) It is always in the interest of a business firm to pursue tight credit standards as they yield lower collection costs and bad debts.

(vi) Business firms should not opt for relaxation of credit standards as they cause increase in collection costs, amount of bad debts and financial costs.

(vii) The credit term '3/10 net 30' implies that the debtor would be entitled for cash discount of 3 per cent if payment is made within 10 days, 2 per cent if it is made within 20 days and 1 per cent if it is made in 30 days.

(viii) The credit term '2/10 net 30' implies that the customer is entitled to 2 per cent cash discount only when he pays within 10 days after the beginning of credit period.

(ix) Financial costs of investment in debtors are determined with reference to cash cost of sales.

(x) The financial framework of analysis of various decision areas in receivable management should factor all measurable costs and benefits.

[Answers: (i) False (ii) False (iii) True (iv) False (v) False (vi) False (vii) False (viii) True (ix) True (x) True]

RQ.15.2 What is meant by credit terms? What are the expected effects of (a) a decrease in the cash discount, and (b) a decrease in the credit period? [LO 15.3]

RQ.15.3 Explain the objectives of receivables management. [LO 15.1]

RQ.15.4 Hypothetical Ltd has currently an annual credit sales of ₹8,00,000. Its average age of accounts receivable is 60 days. It is contemplating a change in its credit policy that is expected to increase sales to ₹10,00,000, and increase the average age of accounts receivable to 72 days. [LO 15.2]

Its sale price is ₹25 per unit, the variable cost per unit is ₹12 and the average cost per unit is ₹8,00,000 sales volume is ₹17. Assuming a 360-days year, calculate the following:

(i) What is the average accounts receivable with both the present and the proposed plans?

(ii) What is the average cost per unit with the proposed plan?

(iii) What are the marginal investments in accounts receivable resulting from the proposed change?

(iv) What is the cost of marginal investment, if the assumed rate of return is 15 per cent?

LOD: Medium

RQ.15.5 What are credit standards? What key variables should be considered in evaluating possible changes in credit standards? [LO 15.2]

RQ.15.6 What are collection policies? How can they be evaluated? [LO 15.4]

RQ.15.7 XYZ Ltd has credit sales amounting to ₹32,00,000. The sale price per unit is ₹40, the variable cost is ₹25 per unit while the average cost per unit is ₹32. The average age of accounts receivable of the firm is 72 days. [LO 15.4]

The firm is considering to tighten the credit standards. It will result in a fall in sales to ₹28,00,000, and the average age of accounts receivable to 45 days.

Assume 20 per cent rate of return. Is the proposal under consideration feasible?

RQ.15.8 Hypothetical Ltd is examining the question of relaxing its credit policy. It sells at present 20,000 units at a price of ₹100 per unit, the variable cost per unit is ₹88 and average cost per unit at the current sales volume is ₹92. All the sales are on credit, the average collection period being 36 days.

A relaxed credit policy is expected to increase sales by 10 per cent and the average age of receivables to 60 days. Assuming 15 per cent return, should the firm relax its credit policy?

[LO 15.4]

RQ.15.9 A firm has a current sales of ₹2,56,48,750. The firm has unutilized capacity. In order to boost its sales, it is considering the relaxation in its credit policy. The proposed terms of credit will be 60 days credit against the present policy of 45 days. As a result, the bad debts will increase from 1.5 per cent to 2 per cent of sales. The firm's sales are expected to increase by 10 per cent. The variable operating costs are 72 per cent of the sales. The firm's corporate tax rate is 35 per cent, and it requires an after-tax return of 15 per cent on its investment. Should the firm change its credit period?

[LO 15.2,4]

ANSWERS

15.4 **(i)** ₹90,667 (Present); ₹1,28,000 (Proposed)
(ii) ₹16
(iii) ₹37,333
(iv) ₹5,600

15.7 The firm should not adopt more strict credit collection policy, as it will decrease profits by ₹1,05,350.

15.8 The firm should relax its credit policy as it increases profit by ₹1,200.

15.9 The firm is advised to relax its credit terms as the expected rate of return on additional investment in debtors is 32.5 per cent vis-à-vis required after-tax return of 15 per cent on investments.

Scan the QR Code to access comprehensive solutions to all numerical review questions and additional material.

CHAPTER 16

Inventory Management

LEARNING OBJECTIVES

LO 16.1	Discuss the tradeoffs between costs and benefits associated with the level of inventory
LO 16.2	Describe the common techniques for managing inventory—ABC system, the basic economic order quantity (EOQ) model, the recorder point and the safety stock
LO 16.3	Discuss just-in time inventory/production

INTRODUCTION

The preceding two Chapters have discussed the basic strategies and considerations in managing two individual current assets, namely, cash and receivables. The third major current asset is inventory. The term inventory refers to the stockpile of the products a firm is offering for sale and the components that make up the product.[1] In other words, inventory is composed of assets that will be sold in future in the normal course of business operations. The assets which firms store as inventory in anticipation of need are **(i)** raw materials, **(ii)** work-in-process (semi-finished goods) and **(iii)** finished goods. The raw material inventory contains items that are purchased by the firm from others and are converted into finished goods through the manufacturing (production) process. They are an important input of the final product. The work-in-process inventory consists of items currently being used in the production process. They are normally semi-finished goods that are at various stages of production in a multi-stage production process. Finished goods represent final or completed products which are available for sale. The inventory of such goods consists of items that have been produced but are yet to be sold.

Inventory, as a current asset, differs from other current assets because only financial managers are not involved. Rather, all the functional areas, finance, marketing, production, and purchasing, are involved. *The views concerning the appropriate level of inventory would differ among the different functional areas.[2] The job of the financial manager is to reconcile the conflicting viewpoints of the various functional areas regarding the appropriate inventory levels in order to fulfil the overall objective of maximising the owner's wealth*. Thus, inventory management, like the management of other current assets, should be related to the overall objective of the firm. It is in this context that the present chapter is devoted to the main elements of inventory management from the viewpoint of financial managers. The objectives of inventory management are explained in some detail. The chapter also focuses on inventory management techniques. Attention is given here to basic concepts relevant to the management and control of inventory. The aspects covered are: **(i)** determination of the type of control required, **(ii)** the basic economic order quantity, **(iii)** the reorder point and **(iv)** safety stocks. As a matter of fact, the inventory management techniques are a part of production management. But a familiarity with them is of great help to the financial managers in planning and budgeting inventory, hence, they are explained here. The just-in time inventory/production is also described. The chapter concludes with the main points.

LO 16.1 OBJECTIVES

The basic responsibility of the financial manager is to make sure the firm's cash flows are managed efficiently. Efficient management of inventory should ultimately result in the maximisation of the owner's wealth. It was indicated in Chapter 29 that in order to minimise cash requirements, inventory should be turned over as quickly as possible, avoiding stock-outs that might result in closing down the production line or lead to a loss of sales. It implies that while the management should try to pursue the financial objective of turning inventory as quickly as possible, it should at the same time ensure sufficient inventories to satisfy production and sales demands. In other words, the financial manager has to reconcile these two conflicting requirements. Stated differently, the objective of inventory management consists of two counter-balancing parts: **(i)** to minimise investments in inventory, and **(ii)** to meet a demand for the product by efficiently organising the production and sales operations. These two conflicting objectives of inventory management can also be expressed in terms of cost and benefit associated with inventory. That the firm should minimise investment in inventory implies that maintaining inventory involves costs, such that the smaller the inventory, the lower is the cost to the firm. But inventories also provide benefits to the extent that they facilitate the smooth functioning of the firm: the larger the inventory, the better it is from this viewpoint. Obviously, the financial managers should aim at a level of inventory which will reconcile these conflicting elements. That is to say, an optimum level of inventory should be determined on the basis of the trade-off between costs and benefits associated with the levels of inventory.

Costs of Holding Inventory

One operating objective of inventory management is to minimise cost. Excluding the cost of merchandise, the costs associated with inventory fall into two basic categories: **(i)** ordering or acquisition or set-up costs, and **(ii)** carrying costs. These costs are an important element of the optimum level of inventory decisions.

Ordering Costs This category of costs is associated with the acquisition or ordering of inventory. Firms have to place orders with suppliers to replenish inventory of raw materials. The expenses involved are referred to as **ordering costs**. Apart from placing orders outside, the various production departments have to acquire materials from the stores. Any expenditure involved here is also a part of the ordering cost. Included in the ordering costs are costs involved in **(i)** preparing a purchase order or requisition form and **(ii)** receiving, inspecting, and recording the goods received to ensure both quantity and quality. The cost of acquiring materials consists of clerical costs and costs of stationery. It is, therefore, called a *set-up cost.* These costs are generally fixed *per order placed*, irrespective of

Ordering cost is the fixed cost of placing and receiving an inventory order.

the amount of the order. The larger the orders placed, or the more frequent the acquisition of inventory made, the higher are such costs. From a different perspective, the larger the inventory, the fewer are the acquisitions and the smaller/lower are the order costs. The acquisition costs are inversely related to the size of inventory: they decline with the level of inventory. Thus, such costs can be minimised by placing fewer orders for a larger amount. But acquisition of a large quantity would increase the cost associated with the maintenance of inventory, that is, carrying costs.

Carrying costs are the variable costs per unit of holding an item in inventory for a specified time period.

Carrying Costs The second broad category of costs associated with inventory are the **carrying costs**. They are involved in maintaining or carrying inventory. The cost of holding inventory may be divided into two categories:

1. Those that Arise Due to the Storing of Inventory The main components of this category of carrying costs are **(i)** storage cost, that is, tax, depreciation, insurance, maintenance of the building, utilities and janitorial services; **(ii)** insurance of inventory against fire and theft; **(iii)** deterioration in inventory because of pilferage, fire, technical obsolescence, style obsolescence and price decline; **(iv)** serving costs, such as, labour for handling inventory, clerical and accounting costs.

2. The Opportunity Cost of Funds This consists of expenses in raising funds (interest on capital) to finance the acquisition of inventory. If funds were not locked up in inventory, they would have earned a return. This is the opportunity cost of funds or the financial cost component of the cost.

The carrying costs and the inventory size are positively related and move in the same direction. If the level of inventory increases, the carrying costs also increase and *vice-versa.*

The sum of the order and carrying costs represents the **total cost** of inventory. This is compared with the benefits arising out of inventory to determine the optimum level of inventory.

Total cost is the sum of the ordering costs and carrying costs of inventory.

Benefits of Holding Inventory

The second element in the optimum inventory decision deals with the benefits associated with holding inventory. The major benefits of holding inventory are the basic functions of inventory. In other words, inventories perform certain basic functions which are of crucial importance in the firm's production and marketing strategies.

The basic function of inventories is to act as a buffer to decouple or uncouple the various activities of a firm so that all do not have to be pursued at exactly the same rate[3]. The key activities are **(1)** purchasing, **(2)** production, and **(3)** selling. The term *uncoupling* means that these interrelated activities of a firm can be carried on independently. Without inventories, purchasing and production would be completely controlled by the sales schedules. If the sales of a firm increases, these two would also increase and *vice-versa.* In other words, purchase and production functions would depend upon the level of sales. It is, of course, true that in the long run, the purchasing and production activities are and, in fact, should be tied to the sales activity of a firm. But, if in the short term they are rigidly related, the three key activities cannot be carried out efficiently. Inventories permit short-term relaxation so that each activity may be pursued efficiently. Stated differently, *inventories enable firms in the short run to produce at a rate greater than purchase of raw materials and vice-versa, or to sell at a rate greater than production and vice-versa.*

Since inventory enables uncoupling of the key activities of a firm, each of them can be operated at the most efficient rate. This has several beneficial effects on the firm's operations. In other words, three types of inventory, raw materials, work-in-process and finished goods, perform certain useful functions. Alternatively, rigid tying (coupling) of purchase and production to sales schedules is undesirable in the short run as it will deprive the firms of certain benefits. The effect of uncoupling (maintaining inventory) are as follows.

Benefits in Purchasing If the purchasing of raw materials and other goods is not tied to production/sales, that is, a firm can purchase independently to ensure the most efficient purchase, several advantages would become available. In the first place, a firm can purchase larger quantities than is warranted by usage in production or the sales level. This will enable it to avail of discounts that are available on bulk purchases. Moreover, it will lower the ordering cost as fewer acquisitions would be made. There will, thus, be a significant saving in the costs. Second, firms can purchase goods before anticipated or announced price increases. This will lead to a decline in the cost of production. Inventory, thus, serves as a hedge against price increases as well as shortages of raw materials. This is a highly desirable inventory strategy.

Benefits in Production Finished goods inventory serves to uncouple production and sale. This enables production at a rate different from that of sales. That is, production can be carried on at a rate higher or lower than the sales rate. This would be of special advantage to firms with seasonal sales pattern. In their case, the sales rate will be higher than the production rate during a part of the year (peak season) and lower during the off-season. The choice before the firm is either to produce at a level to meet the actual demand, that is, higher production during peak season and lower (or nil) production during off-season, or, produce continuously throughout the year and build up inventory which will be sold during the period of seasonal demand. The former involves discontinuity in the production schedule while the latter ensures level production. The level production is more economical as it allows the firm to reduce the cost of discontinuities in the production process. This is possible because excess production is kept as inventory to meet future demands. Thus, inventory helps a firm to coordinate its production scheduling so as to avoid disruptions and the accompanying expenses.[4] In brief, since inventory permits *least cost* production scheduling, production can be carried on more efficiently.

Benefits in Work-in-Process The inventory of work-in-process performs two functions. In the first place, it is necessary because production processes are not instantaneous. The amount of such inventory depends upon technology and the efficiency of production. The larger the steps involved in the production process, the larger the work-in-process inventory and *vice-versa.* By shortening the production time, efficiency of the production process can be improved and the size of this type of inventory reduced. In a multi-stage production process, the work-in-process inventory serves a second purpose also. It uncouples the various stages of production so that all of them do not have to be performed at the same rate. The stages involving higher set-up costs may be most efficiently performed in batches with a work-in-process inventory accumulated during a production run.[5]

Benefits in Sales The maintenance of inventory also helps a firm to enhance its sales efforts. For one thing, if there are no inventories of finished goods, the level of sales will depend upon the level of current production. A firm will not be able to meet demand instantaneously. There will be a lag depending upon the production process. If the firm has inventory, actual sales will not have to depend on lengthy manufacturing processes. Thus, inventory serves to bridge the gap between current production and actual sales. A related aspect is that inventory serves as a competitive marketing tool to meet customer demands. A basic requirement in a firm's competitive position is its ability *vis-a-vis* its competitors to supply goods rapidly. If it is not able to do so, the customers are likely to switch to suppliers who can supply goods at short notice. Inventory, thus, ensures a continued patronage of customers. Moreover, in the case of firms having a seasonal pattern of sales, there should be a substantial finished goods inventory prior to the peak sales season. Failure to do so may mean loss of sales during the peak season.

To summarise the preceding discussion relating to the objective of inventory management, the two main aspects pertain to the minimisation of investment in inventory, on the one hand, and the need to ensure that there is enough inventory to meet demand such that production and sales operations are smooth. They are often in conflict with each other. By holding less inventory, cost can be minimised, but there is a risk that the operations will be disturbed as the emerging demands cannot be met. On the other hand, by holding a large inventory, the chances of disruption of operations are reduced, but, the cost will increase. The appropriate level of inventory should be determined in terms of a trade-off between the benefits and costs associated with maintaining inventory.

LO 16.2 TECHNIQUES

In the preceding discussion the objectives of inventory management have been outlined. The financial managers should aim at an optimum level of inventory on the basis of the trade-off between cost and benefit to maximise the owner's wealth. Many sophisticated mathematical techniques are available to handle inventory management problems. But they are more appropriately a part of production management and lie outside the scope of this book. Nevertheless, they involve in-built financial costs. The financial managers should, therefore, be familiar with them. We have discussed below some simple production-oriented methods of inventory control to indicate a broad framework for managing inventories efficiently in conformity with the goal of wealth-maximisation. The major problem—areas that comprise the heart of inventory control[5] are **(i)** the *classification problem* to determine the type of control required, **(ii)** the *order quantity problem*, **(iii)** *the order point problem*, and **(iv)** *safety stocks*.

Classification Problem: A B C System

A B C system is an inventory management technique that divides inventory into three categories of descending importance based on the rupee investment in each.

The first step in the inventory control process is classification of different types of inventories to determine the type and degree of control required for each. The **A B C** system is a widely-used classification technique to identify various items of inventory for purposes of inventory control. This technique is based on the assumption that a firm should not exercise the same degree of control on all items of inventory. It should rather keep a more rigorous control on items that are **(i)** the most costly, and/or **(ii)** the slowest-turning, while items that are less expensive should be given less control effort.

On the basis of the cost involved, the various inventory items are, according to this system, categorised into three classes: **(i)** A **(ii)** B and **(iii)** C. The items included in group A involve the largest investment. Therefore, inventory control should be the most rigorous and intensive and the most sophisticated inventory control techniques should be applied to these items. The C group consists of items of inventory which involve relatively small investments although the number of items is fairly large. These items deserve minimum attention. The B group stands midway. It deserves less attention than A but more than C. It can be controlled by employing less sophisticated techniques.

The task of inventory management is to properly classify all the inventory items into one of these three groups/categories. The typical breakdown of inventory items is as shown in Table 16.1[7].

TABLE 16.1 Inventory Breakdown between Number of Items and Inventory Value

Group	*Number of items (per cent)*	*Inventory value (per cent)*
A	15	70
B	30	20
C	55	10
Total	100	100

Some points stand out from Table 16.1. While group A is the least important in terms of the number of items, it is by far the most important in terms of the investments involved. With only 15 per cent of the number, it accounts for as much as 70 per cent of the total value of inventory. The firm should direct most of its inventory control efforts to the items included in this group. The items comprising B group account for 20 per cent of the investments in inventory. They deserve less attention than A, but more than C, which involves only 10 per cent of the total value although number-wise its share is as high as 55 per cent. The A B C analysis is illustrated in Example 16.1.

***Example* 16.1**

A firm has 7 different items in its inventory. The average number of each of these items held, alongwith their units costs, is listed below. The firm wishes to introduce an A B C inventory system. Suggest a breakdown of the items into A, B, and C classifications.

Item number	*Average number of units in inventory*	*Average cost per unit*
1	20,000	₹60.80
2	10,000	102.40
3	32,000	11.00
4	28,000	10.28
5	60,000	3.40
6	30,000	3.00
7	20,000	1.3

Solution

The A B C analysis is presented in Table 16.2.

TABLE 16.2 ABC Analysis

Item (1)	*Units* (2)	*Per cent of total* (3)		*Unit cost* (4)	*Total cost* (5)	*Per cent of total* (6)	
1	20,000	10	15	₹60.80	₹12,16,000	38.00	70
2	10,000	5		102.40	10,24,000	32.00	
3	32,000	16	30	11.00	3,52,000	11.00	20
4	28,000	14		10.28	2,88,000	9.00	
5	60,000	30	55	3.40	2,04,000	6.38	10
6	30,000	15		3.00	90,000	2.80	
7	20,000	10		1.30	26,000	0.82	
Total	2,00,000	100			32,00,000	100.00	

The A B C system of classification should, however, be used with caution. For example, an item of inventory may be very inexpensive. Under the A B C system it would be classified into C category. But it may be very critical to the production process and may not be easily available. It deserves the special attention of management. But in terms of the A B C framework, it would be included in the category which requires the least attention. This is a limitation of the A B C analysis.

Order Quantity Problem: Economic Order Quantity (EOQ) Model

After various inventory items are classified on the basis of the A B C analysis, the management becomes aware of the type of control that would be appropriate for each of the three categories of the inventory items. The A group of items warrants the maximum attention and the most rigorous control. A key inventory problem particularly in respect of the Group A items relates to the determination of the size or quantity in which inventory will be acquired. In other words, while purchasing raw materials or finished goods, the questions to be addressed are[8]: *How much inventory should be bought in one lot under one order on each replenishment? Should the quantity to be purchased be large or small? Or, should the requirement of materials during a given period of time (say, six months or one year) be acquired in one lot or should it be acquired in instalments or in several small lots?* Such inventory problems are called order quantity problems.

The determination of the appropriate quantity to be purchased in each lot to replenish stock as a solution to the order quantity problem necessitates resolution of conflicting goals. Buying in large quantities implies a higher average inventory level which will assure **(i)** smooth production/sale operations, and **(ii)** lower ordering or set-up costs. But it will involve higher carrying costs. On the other hand, small orders would reduce the carrying cost of inventory by reducing the average inventory level but the ordering costs would increase as there is a likelihood of interruption in the operations due to stock-outs. A firm should place neither too large nor too small orders. On the basis of a trade-off between benefits derived from the availability of inventory and the cost of carrying that level of inventory, the appropriate or optimum level of the order to be placed should be determined. The optimum level of inventory is popularly referred to as the **economic order quantity** (EOQ). It is also known as the *economic lot size.* The economic order quantity may be defined as *that level of inventory order that minimises the total cost associated with inventory management.* As explained in the earlier section dealing with the objectives of inventory management, the costs associated with inventories are **(i)** ordering costs, and **(ii)** carrying costs. Stated with reference to cost perspectives, EOQ refers to *the level of inventory at which the total cost of inventory comprising acquisition/ ordering/set-up costs and carrying cost is minimal.*

> **Economic order quantity (EOQ) model** is the inventory management technique for determining optimum order quantity which is the one that minimises the total of its order and carrying costs; it balances fixed ordering costs against variable ordering costs.

For analysing the EOQ, as an inventory management technique, several sophisticated mathematical models are available.[9] These are, however, outside the scope of this book. We illustrate here the analysis of EOQ on the basis of simple non-mathematical approach. Nevertheless, the main ele-ments of the order quantity problem are covered by the analytical method followed here.

Assumptions The EOQ model, as the technique to determine the economic order quantity, illustrated by us, is based on three restrictive assumptions:

1. The firm knows with certainty the annual usage (consumption) of a particular item of inventory.
2. The rate at which the firm uses inventory is steady over time.
3. The orders placed to replenish inventory stocks are received at exactly that point in time when inventories reach zero.

In addition, it may also be assumed that ordering and carrying costs are constant over the range of possible inventory levels being considered.

Approaches The EOQ model can be illustrated by **(i)** the long analytical approach or trial and error approach, and **(ii)** the short cut or simple mathematical approach.

Trial and Error (Analytical) Approach Given the total requirements of inventory during a given period of time depending upon the inventory planning horizon, a firm has different alternatives to purchase its inventories. For instance, it can buy its entire requirements in one single lot at the beginning of the inventory planning period. Alternatively, the inventories may be procured in small lots periodically, say, weekly, monthly, quarterly, six-monthly and so on. If the purchases are made in one lot, the average inventory holdings would be relatively large whereas it would be relatively small when the acquisition of inventory is in small lots: the smaller the lot, the lower is the average inventory and *vice-versa.* High average inventory would involve high carrying costs. On the other hand, low inventory holdings are associated with high ordering cost. The trial and error or long analytical approach for the determination of EOQ uses different permutations and combinations of lots of inventory purchases so as to find out the least ordering and carrying cost combination. In other words, according to this approach, the carrying and acquisition costs for different sizes of orders to purchase inventories are computed and the order size with the lowest total cost (ordering plus carrying) of inventory is the economic order quantity. The mechanics of the computation of EOQ with the analytical approach is illustrated in Example 16.2.

***Example* 16.2**

A firm's inventory planning period is one year. Its inventory requirement for this period is 1,600 units. Assume that its acquisition costs are ₹50 per order. The carrying costs are expected to be ₹1 per unit per year for an item.

The firm can procure inventories in various lots as follows: **(i)** 1,600 units, **(ii)** 800 units, **(iii)** 400 units, **(iv)** 200 units, and **(v)** 100 units. Which of these order quantities is the economic order quantity?

Solution

The calculations of the inventory costs for different order quantities are shown in Table 16.3.

TABLE 16.3 Inventory Cost for Different Order Quantities

1. Size of order (units)	1,600	800	400	200	100
2. Number of orders	1	2	4	8	16
3. Cost per order (₹)	50	50	50	50	50
4. Total ordering cost (2 × 3) (₹)	50	100	200	400	800
5. Carrying cost per unit (₹)	1	1	1	1	1
6. Average inventory (units)	800	400	200	100	50
7. Total carrying cost (5 × 6) (₹)	800	400	200	100	50
8. Total cost (4 + 7) (₹)	850	500	400	500	850

It can be seen from Table 16.3 that the carrying and ordering costs taken together are the lowest for the order size of 400 units. This, therefore, is the economic order quantity.

Working Notes

(i) Number of orders = Total inventory requirement/order size

(ii) Average inventory = Order size/2

The calculation of EOQ is further developed in Example 16.3.

***Example* 16.3**

The following details are available in respect of a firm:

1. Inventory requirement per year, 6,000 units

2. Cost per unit (other than carrying and ordering costs), ₹5
3. Carrying costs per item for one year, ₹1
4. Cost of placing each order, ₹60
5. Alternative order sizes: (units) 6,000, 3,000, 2,000, 1,200, 1,000, 600 and 200.

Determine the economic order quantity.

Solution

The EOQ is determined in Table 16.4.

TABLE 16.4 Determination of Economic Order Quantity

1. Cost of items purchased each year (₹)	30,000	30,000	30,000	30,000	30,000	30,000	30,000
2. Order size (*units*)	6,000	3,000	2,000	1,200	1,000	600	200
3. Number of orders	1	2	3	5	6	10	30
4. Average inventory (*units*)	3,000	1,500	1,000	600	500	300	100
5. Total carrying costs (₹)	3,000	1,500	1,000	600	500	300	100
6. Total ordering costs (₹)	60	120	180	300	360	600	1,800
7. Total cost (carrying plus ordering cost) (₹)	3,060	1,620	1,180	900	860	900	1,900
8. Total cost (₹)	33,060	31,620	31,180	30,900	30,860	30,900	31,900

Clearly, the EOQ is 1,000 units.

Working Notes

(i) Number of orders = Demand per year/order size
(ii) Average inventory = Order size/2
(iii) Total carrying cost = Average inventory × Carrying cost per unit
(iv) Total ordering cost = Number of orders × Cost per order
(v) Total cost = Cost of items purchased + Total carrying and ordering costs

Mathematical (Short cut) Approach The economic order quantity can, using a short-cut method, be calculated by the following equation:

$$EOQ = \sqrt{\frac{2AB}{C}} \qquad \textbf{(16.1)}$$

where A = Annual usage of inventory (units),
B = Buying cost per order, and
C = Carrying cost per unit

Example **16.4**

Using the facts in Example 16.2, find out the EOQ by applying the short-cut mathematical approach.

Solution

$$EOQ = \sqrt{\frac{2 \times 1{,}600 \times 50}{1}} = 400 \text{ units}$$

Limitations While using the EOQ model, it should be noted that it suffers from shortcomings which are mainly due to the restrictive nature of the assumptions on which it is based. The important limitations are explained below.

The assumption of a constant consumption/usage and the instantaneous replenishment of inventories are of doubtful validity. As discussed subsequently, deliveries from suppliers may be slower than expected for reasons beyond control. It is also possible that there may be an unusual and unexpected demand for stocks. To meet such contingencies, firms have to keep additional inventories which are known as *safety* stocks.

Another weakness of the EOQ model is that the assumption of a *known annual demand* for inventories is open to question. There is likelihood of a discrepancy between the actual and the expected demand, leading to a wrong estimate of the economic order quantity.

In addition, there are some computational problems involved. For instance, Equation 16.1 may give the EOQ in fractions, say, 232.5 units. A more difficult situation may occur when the number of orders to be placed may turn out to be a fraction.

Order Point Problem

The EOQ technique determines the size of an order to acquire inventory so as to minimise the carrying as well as the ordering costs. In other words, the EOQ provides an answer to the question: how much inventory should be ordered in one lot? Another important question pertaining to efficient inventory management is: when should the order to procure inventory be placed? This aspect of inventory management is covered under the reorder point problem.

Reorder point is the point at which to order inventory expressed equationally as: lead time in days × daily usage.

The reorder point is stated in terms of the level of inventory at which an order should be placed for replenishing the current stock of inventory. In other words, **reorder point** may be defined as the level of inventory when fresh order should be placed with the suppliers for procuring additional inventory equal to the economic order quantity. Although some sophisticated reorder point formula are available, they are outside the scope of this book. We have, therefore, used a simple formula to calculate the reorder point. It is based on the following assumptions: **(i)** constant daily usage of inventory, and **(ii)** fixed lead time. In other words, the formula assumes conditions of certainty.

$$\text{The reorder point} = \text{Lead time in days} \times \text{average daily usage of inventory} \quad \textbf{(16.2)}$$

Lead time is time normally taken in receiving delivery after placing orders with suppliers.

The term **lead time** refers to the time normally taken in receiving the delivery after placing orders with the suppliers. It covers the time-span from the point when a decision to place the order for the procurement of inventory is made to the actual receipt of the inventory by the firm. Another way of saying it is that the lead time consists of the number of days required by the suppliers to receive and process the order as well as the number of days during which the goods will be in transit from the supplier. The lead time may also be called as the procurement time of inventory.

The average usage means the quantity of inventory consumed daily. *We can, therefore, define reorder point as the inventory level which should be equal to the consumption during the lead time.*

The average consumption (daily usage) of inventory of a firm is 5,000 units. The number of days required to receive the delivery of inventory after placing order (lead i.e. processing and transit time) is 15 days. The reorder point = 5,000 units × 15 days = 75,000 units. The implication is that the firm should place an order for replenishing the stock of inventory as soon as the level reaches 75,000 units. The size of the order would obviously be equal to the EOQ.

Safety Stock

The economic order quantity and the reorder point, as inventory management techniques, have been explained, to keep the discussion simple, on the assumption of *certainty conditions.* That is to say, we had assumed **(i)** constant/fixed usage/requirement of inventory, and **(ii)** instantaneous replenishment of inventory. The assumptions are, however, of questionable validity in actual situations, that is, under conditions of uncertainty. For instance, the demand for inventory is likely to fluctuate from time to time. In particular, at certain points of time the demand may exceed the anticipated level. In other words, a discrepancy between the assumed (anticipated/expected) and actual usage rate of inventory is likely to occur in practice. Similarly, the receipt of inventory from the suppliers may be delayed beyond the expected lead time. The delay may arise from strikes, floods, transportation and other bottlenecks. Thus, a firm would come across situations in which the actual usage of inventory is higher than the anticipated level and/or the delivery of the inventory from the suppliers is delayed.

The effect of increased and/or slower delivery would be a shortage of inventory. That is, the firm would face a stock-out situation. This, in turn, as explained in detail below, would disrupt the production schedule and alienate the customers. The firm would, therefore, be well-advised to keep a sufficient safety margin by having additional inventory to guard against stock-out situations. Such stocks are called **safety stocks**. This would act as a buffer or cushion against a possible shortage of inventory caused either by increased usage or delayed delivery of inventory. The safety stock may, then, be defined as the *minimum additional inventory to serve as a safety margin or buffer or cushion to meet an unanticipated increase in usage resulting from an unusually high demand and or an uncontrollable late receipt of incoming inventory.*

Safety stock implies extra inventories that can be drawn down when actual lead time and/or usage rates are greater than expected.

How can a financial manager determine the safety stock? What is his responsibility? The safety stock involves two types of costs: **(i)** stock-out, and **(ii)** carrying costs. The job of the financial manager is to determine the appropriate level of safety stock on the basis of a trade-off between these two types of conflicting costs.

The term *stock-out costs* refers to the cost associated with the shortage (stock-out) of inventory. It is, in fact, an opportunity cost in the sense that due to the shortage of inventory the firm would be deprived of certain benefits. The denial of those benefits which would otherwise be available to the firm are the stock-out costs. The first, and the most obvious, of these cots is the loss of profit which the firm could have earned from increased sales if there was no shortage of inventory. Another category of stock-out costs is the damage to the relationship with the customers.[10] Owing to shortage of inventory, the firm would not be able to meet the customer's requirements and the latter may turn to the firm's competitors. It should, of course, be clearly understood that this type of cost cannot be easily and precisely quantified. Last, the shortage of inventory may disrupt the production schedule of the firm. The production process would grind to a halt involving idle time.

The carrying costs, as already explained in the earlier part of this chapter, are the costs associated with the maintenance of inventory. Since the firm is required to maintain additional inventory, in excess of the normal usage, additional carrying costs are involved.

The stock-out and the carrying costs are counterbalancing. The larger the safety stock, the larger would be the carrying costs and *vice-versa.* Conversely, the larger is the safety stock, the smaller would be the stock-out costs. In other words, if the firm minimises the carrying costs, the stock-out costs are likely to rise; on the other hand, an attempt to minimise the stock-out costs implies increased carrying costs. The object of the financial managers should be to have the lowest total cost (i.e. carrying cost plus stock-out cost). The safety stock with the minimum carrying and stock-out costs is the economic (appropriate) level which financial managers should aim at. In brief, the appropriate level of safety stock is determined by the trade-off between the stock-out and the carrying costs. We illustrate in Example 16.5, using a simple method,[11] the determination of the optimum (least-cost) safety stock.

***Example* 16.5**

The experience of a firm being out of stock is summarised below:

(a) *Stock-out (number of units)*	*Number of times*
500	1 (1)
400	2 (2)
250	3 (3)
100	4 (4)
50	10 (10)
0	80 (80)
Total	100 (100)

Figures in brackets represents percentage of time the firm has been out of stock.

(b) Assume that the stock-out costs are ₹40 per unit.

(c) The carrying cost of inventory per unit is ₹20.

Determine the optimum level of stock-out inventory.

Solution

TABLE 16.5 Computation of Expected Stock-out Costs

Safety stock level (units)	*Stock-out (units)*	*Stock-out costs (₹40 per unit)*	*Probability of stock-out*	*Expected stock-out cost at this level*	*Total expected stock-out cost*
(1)	(2)	(3)	(4)	(5)	(6)
500	0	0	0	0	0
400	100	₹4,000	0.01	₹40	₹40
250	250	10,000	0.01	100	
	150	6,000	0.02	120	220
100	400	16,000	0.01	160	
	300	12,000	0.02	240	
	150	6,000	0.03	180	580
50	450	18,000	0.01	180	
	350	14,000	0.02	280	
	200	8,000	0.03	240	
	50	2,000	0.04	80	780
0	500	20,000	0.01	200	
	400	16,000	0.02	320	
	250	10,000	0.03	300	
	100	4,000	0.04	160	
	50	2,000	0.10	200	1,180

Working Notes

(i) The determination of the optimum safety stock involves dealing with *uncertain* demand. The first step, therefore, is to estimate the probability of being out of stock as well as the size of stock-out in terms of the shortage of inventory at different levels of safety stock.

Size of stock-out (units) The shortage of inventory at different levels of safety stock can be computed as follows:

(a) The firm's experience has been that it has been short of inventory by 500 units only once in 100 times. If, therefore, the level of safety stock is 500 units, it will never be short of inventory. It means that with 500 units of safety stock, the size of stock-out would be zero.

(b) When the firm has a safety stock of 400 units, it could be short by 100 units.

(c) Further, with 250 units of safety stock, the firm could be short by 250 units if the actual demand turns out to be 500 units greater than expected; 150 units short if the demand turn out to be 400 units greater than expected. Thus, the size of stock-out could be 250 units or 150 units depending upon the level of actual demand.

(d) It should be obvious that the size of stock-out increases with a decrease in the level of safety stock. The size of the stock-out for safety stock levels of 100 units, 50 units and 0 units can be computed on the lines of step (c).

The stock-out size at different safety stock levels is computed in column (2) of Table 16.5.

Probability of Stock-out The probability of stock-out at different levels of safety stock can be computed as follows:

(a) If the safety stock of the firm is 500 units, there is no chance of the firm being out of stock. The probability of stock-out is, therefore, zero.

(b) When the safety stock is 400 units, there is 1 per cent chance that the firm will be short of inventory. The probability of stock-out is, therefore, 0.01.

(c) The probability of stock-out for other levels of safety stock is similarly computed in column (4) of Table 16.5.

(ii) After the determination of the size and probability of stock-out, the next step is the calculation of the stock-out cost. The expected stock-out cost can be found out by multiplying the stock-out cost and the probability of stock-out.

When the stock-out is expected to be 100 units (safety stock being 400 units), the stock-out cost would be 100 × ₹40 = ₹4,000. But the probability of stock-out of this size is only 0.01. Therefore, the expected cost stock-out would be ₹4,000 × 0.01 = ₹40. For other levels of safety stock, the expected stock-out cost can be similarly computed (column 5 of Table 16.5).

(iii) The next step is to compute the total expected stock-out costs (column 6 of Table 16.5).

(iv) Then, the carrying costs should be calculated. The carrying costs are equal to the safety stock multiplied by the carrying costs per unit. (Table 16.6 column 3).

TABLE 16.6 Computation of Total Safety Stock Costs

Safety stock level (units) (1)	*Expected stock-out costs* (2)*	*Carrying costs (₹20 per unit) (3)*	*Total safety stock cost (4) (2 + 3)*
0	₹1,180	0	₹1,180
50	780	₹1,000	1,780
100	580	2,000	2,580
250	220	5,000	5,220
400	40	8,000	8,040
500	0	10,000	10,000

*from Table 16.5 column 6.

(v) Finally, the carrying costs and the expected stock-out costs at each safety stock level should be added (Table 16.6, column 4). The optimum safety stock would be that level of inventory at which total of these two costs is the lowest.

Thus, the optimum safety stock is zero units.

LO 16.3 JUST-IN TIME INVENTORY/PRODUCTION

The level of inventories by retailers are influenced by the demand patterns of their customers and supply relationship with their distributors and manufacturers, the suppliers to their manufacturers and so on. Supply chain describes the flow of goods/services/information from the initial source of materials and services to the delivery of products to consumers regardless of whether those activities occur in the same organisation or in other organisations. There are significant gains to companies in the supply chain from coordinating their activities and sharing information. There would be **(a)** fewer stock-outs at the retail level, **(b)** reduced manufacture of goods not immediately needed by retailers, **(c)** fewer manufacturing orders that have to be "rushed" or "expedited" and **(d)** lower inventories held by each company in the supply chain. Of the numerous systems developed by manufacturing companies to plan and implement production and inventory activities within their plants, just-in-time (JIT) production/inventory is a widely used system.

Just-in-time refers to acquiring materials and manufacturing goods only as needed to fill customer orders.

Concept

The JIT is an innovative manufacturing system. It refers to acquiring materials and manufacturing goods only as needed to fill customer orders. The JIT production, also called *lean production,* is a **demand-pull**[12] manufacturing system because each component in a production line is produced as soon as and only when needed by the next step in the production line. Demand triggers each step of the production process, starting with customer demand for a finished product at the end of the process and working all the way back to the demand for direct materials at the beginning of the process. In this way, demand pulls an order through the production line. The JIT production systems aim to simultaneously **(i)** meet customer demand in a timely way, **(ii)** with high quality products and **(iii)** at the lowest possible total cost.[13]

Non-value added activities refers to those functions that do not directly increase the worth of a product to a coustomer.

As a demand-pull manufacturing system, JIT contrasts with more traditional *supply push* system in which manufacturers simply produce as many goods as possible. The JIT system is characterised by extremely small/non-existent inventories of material, work-in-process, and finished goods. Materials are scheduled to arrive only as needed, and products flow quickly from one production process to the next without having to move into temporary storage facilities. Finished goods in excess of existing customer orders are not produced.

Value added activities do increase the value of a product to the customers.

The JIT is, however, more than an approach to inventory management. It is a philosophy of eliminating *non-value-added activities* and increasing product quality throughout the manufacturing process. Non-value-added activities refer to those functions that do not directly increase the worth of a product to a customer. Examples of such activities are: storing direct materials, setting up machinery and time during which machinery/employees stand idle. Cost savings through the reduction/elimination of such activities usually do not influence customer satisfaction. In contrast, value-added-activities do increase the value of the product to the customers. Included in such activities are product design, all manufacturing processes, manufacturing to customer specifications and convenient channels of distribution.

Financial Benefits of JIT and Relevant Costs

In computing the relevant benefits and costs of reducing inventories in JIT production systems, account should be taken of all benefits. In addition to lower carrying costs of inventory, other benefits of lower inventory are[14]: **(i)** greater transparency of the production process, **(ii)** heightened emphasis on eliminating the specific causes of rework, scrap and waste, and **(iii)** lower manufacturing to lead times.

***Example* 16.6**

To illustrate, Hindustan Tools Corporation (HTC), manufacturer of brass fittings, is considering implementing a JIT production system. The HTC would have to incur ₹10,00,000 in annual tooling costs to reduce setup times. It is expected that JIT will reduce average inventory by ₹50,00,000. The relevant costs of insurance, storage, materials handling and setup are likely to decline by ₹3,00,000. The HTC's required rate of return on inventory investment is 10 per cent.

The other benefits associated with low inventories in JIT production system of HTC are: **(i)** improved quality and reduced rework on 500 units each year would result in a saving of ₹500 per unit; and **(ii)** better quality and faster delivery will enable HTC to charge ₹20 more per unit on the 20,000 units that it sells every year.

Based on the cost savings in carrying costs of inventory only, HTC would not find the implementation of JIT system feasible as the additional tooling cost (₹10,00,000) exceeds the annual cost savings in carrying costs of ₹8,00,000 [(0.10 × ₹50,00,000) + ₹3,00,000]. However, on the basis of the total benefits in terms of cost savings in carrying costs plus the annual relevant quality and delivery benefits, HTC would be well advised to implement the JIT systems as the total benefits exceed the annual implementation costs of ₹10,00,000 as shown below.

1. Cost savings in carrying cost of inventory	₹8,00,000	
2. Plus quality and delivery benefits:		
• Rework savings (₹500 × 500 units)	₹2,50,000	
• Additional contribution margin (₹20 × 20,000)	4,00,000	₹6,50,000
		14,50,000

Performance Measure

The measures that managers can use to evaluate and control JIT production are discussed below.

Personal Observation The production layout in a JIT plant is streamlined and operations are not obscured by piles of inventory/rework. For this reason, personal observation is more effective in JIT plants compared to traditional plants.

Financial Performance Measure The financial measure that is widely used is inventory turnover ratio, that is, cost of goods sold ÷ inventory. This ratio would increase in a JIT system.

Non-financial Performance Measures Included in this category of measures are:

- Decrease in manufacturing lead time
- Increase in units produced per hour
- Decrease in number of days inventory on hand
- Decrease in total setup time for machines ÷ total manufacturing time
- Decrease in number of units requiring rework or scrap ÷ total number of units started and completed.

Effect on Costing System

The JIT system has effect on the costing systems. In the first place, by reducing material handling, warehousing and inspection, it reduces overhead costs. Second, it facilitates direct tracing of some costs usually classified as indirect, for example, material handling, and machine operating costs. Finally, the use of multi-skilled workers allows the costs of setup, maintenance and quality inspection to be traced as direct costs.

SUMMARY

LO	Summary
LO 16.1	Inventory refers to the stockpile of the products a firm would sell in future in the normal course of business operations and the components that make up the product. The firm stores three types of inventories, namely, raw materials, work-in-process/semi-finished goods and finished good.
	The management of inventory is different from the management of other current assets in that virtually all the functional areas are involved. The job of the finance manager is to reconcile the conflicting viewpoints of the various functional areas regarding the appropriate inventory levels.
	The objectives of inventory management consists of two counterbalancing parts: (i) to minimise investments in inventory and (ii) to meet the demand for products by efficiently organising the production and sales operations. In operational terms, the goal of inventory management is to have a trade-off between these two conflicting objectives which can be expressed in terms of costs and benefits associated with different levels of inventory.
	The costs of holding inventory are ordering costs and carrying costs. While ordering costs are associated with the acquisition or ordering of inventory, carrying costs arise due to the storing of inventory. The major benefits of holding inventory are in the area of purchasing, production and sales. The total cost of inventory are to be compared with the total benefits arising out of inventory to determine its optimum level.
LO 16.2	There are four decision areas in inventory management: (i) classification problem, (ii) order quantity problem, (iii) order point problem and (iv) safety stock.
	The ABC system is a widely-used classification technique to identify various items of inventory for purposes of inventory control. On the basis of the cost involved, the various items are classified into three categories: (i) A, consisting of items with the large investment, (ii) C, with relatively small investments but fairly large number of items and (iii) B, which stands mid-way between category A and C. Category A needs the most rigorous control, C requires minimum attention and B deserves less attention than A but more than C.
	The order quantity problem relates to the determination of the quantity of inventory which should be ordered. The economic order quantity (EOQ) is that level of inventory order which minimises the total cost associated with inventory management. Symbolically, EOQ = $\sqrt{2AB/C}$.
	The re-order point is that level of inventory when a fresh order should be placed with suppliers to procure additional inventory equal to the EOQ. It is that inventory level which is equal to the consumption during the lead time plus safety stock.
	Safety stocks are the minimum additional inventory which serve as a safety margin to meet an unanticipated increase in usage resulting from an unusually high demand and/or an uncontrollable late receipt of incoming inventory.
LO 16.3	JIT, as an innovative manufacturing system, refers to acquiring materials and manufacturing goods only as needed to fill customer orders. Also called lean production system, it is a demand-pull manufacturing system because each component in a production line is produced as soon as and only when needed by the next step in the production line.
	However, it is more than an approach to inventory management. It is a philosophy of eliminating non-value-added activities.
	The benefits of JIT are in addition to lower carrying cost of inventory, improved quality, reduced rework, faster delivery and so on.
	The measures of performance that managers use to evaluate and control JIT are personal observations, financial, and non-financial measures.
	The effects of JIT on costing system are reduced overheads and direct tracing of some indirect costs.

REFERENCES

1. Bolten, S E, *Managerial Finance*, Houghton Mifflin Co., Boston, 1976, p 426.
2. For a comprehensive discussion of the viewpoints of marketing, production and purchasing areas refer to Gitman, L J, *principles of Managerial Finance*, Harper and Row, New York, 1976, 216-19.
3. Johonson, R W, *Financial Management*, Allyn and Bacon, Boston, 1977, p 136.
4. Bolten, S E, *op. cit.*, p 441.
5. Solomon E and J J Pringle, *Introduction to Financial Management*, Goodyear Publishing Co., Santa Monica, Calif., 1977, p 211.
6. Joy, O M, *Introduction to Financial Management*, Irwin, Homewood III., 1977, p 469.
7. Based on studies by Synder, A., 'Principles of inventory management, *Financial Executive*, April 1964, pp 13-21.
8. A similar kind of problem will arise in the case of deciding the best production quantity. Since our focus is on control of inventory, we will not consider the production aspect.
9. For a detailed development and discussion of such models refer to Lewin, R I and C A Kirkpatrick, *Quantitative Approaches to Management*, McGraw-Hill, New York, 1975.
10. Bolten, S E, *op. cit.*, p 437.
11. For a more comprehensive and sophisticated treatment please refer to Findlay, M C and E E Williams, *An Integrated Analysis for Managerial Finance*, (Englewood Cliffs), Prentice-Hall, 1970, p 87.
12. Williams, J R, *Financial and Management Accounting*, TMH, 2004, p. 788.
13. Horngren, C T, *Cost Accounting*, Pearson, 2004, p. 697.
14. *Op. cit.*, pp. 697-698.

SOLVED PROBLEMS

P.16.1 Economic Enterprises require 90,000 units of certain items annually. The cost per unit is ₹3. The cost per purchase order is ₹300 and the inventory carrying cost is ₹6 per unit per year.

LO 16.2 LOD M

(a) What is the EOQ?

(b) What should the firm do if the suppliers offer discounts as detailed below:

Order quantity	*Discount*
4,500 – 5,999	2 per cent
6,000 and above	3

Solution

(a) EOQ $= \sqrt{\dfrac{2AB}{C}} = \sqrt{\dfrac{2 \times 90{,}000 \times ₹300}{₹6}} = 3{,}000$ units

(b) Determination of optimal order quantity

1. Order size (units)	3,000	4,500	6,000
2. Average inventory (units)	1,500	2,250	3,000
3. Annual requirements (units)	90,000	90,000	90,000
4. Number of orders	30	20	15
5. Price per unit (₹)	3	2.94[a]	2.91[b]
6. Cost of purchase (₹)	2,70,000	2,64,600	2,61,900
7. Carrying cost @ ₹6 per unit (₹)	9,000	13,500	18,000
8. Total ordering cost (₹)	9,000	6,000	4,500
9. Total cost (6 + 7 + 8)	2,88,000	2,84,100	2,84,400

[a][(3) – (2%)]

[b][(3) – (3%)]

The total cost is minimum at the order size of 4,500 units and, therefore, the firm should place order for 4,500 units.

P.16.2 Two components, A and B are, used as follows:

LO 16.2 LOD M

Normal usage	:	50 units each per week
Minimum usage	:	25 units each per week
Maximum usage	:	75 units each per week
Re-order quantity	:	A: 300 units; B: 500 units
Re-order period	:	A: 4 to 6 weeks; B: 2 to 4 weeks

Calculate for each component:

(a) Reorder level, **(b)** Minimum level, **(c)** Maximum level, and **(d)** Average stock level.

Solution

(a) Reorder level = (maximum usage × maximum delivery time)
A = 75 × 6 weeks = 450 units
B = 75 × 4 weeks = 300 units

(b) Minimum level = Reorder level – (normal usage × average delivery time in weeks)
A = 450 units – (50 units × 5 weeks) = 200 units
B = 300 units – (50 units × 3 weeks) = 150 units

(c) Maximum level = Reorder level – (minimum usage × minimum delivery time) + reorder quantity
A = 450 units – (25 × 4) + 300 units = 650 units
B = 300 units – (25 × 2) + 500 units = 750 units

(d) Average stock level = minimum level + (Reorder quantity/2)
A = 200 + 300/2 = 350 units
B = 150 + 500/2 = 400 units

P.16.3 The Peekay Company has been buying a given item in lots of 1.200 units which is a six months' supply, the cost per units is ₹12, order cost is ₹8 per order, and carrying cost is 25 per cent. You are required to calculate the savings per year by buying in economical lot quantities.

LO 16.2 LOD M

Solution

$$EOQ = \sqrt{\frac{2AB}{C}} = \sqrt{\frac{2 \times 2,400 \times 8}{3}} = 114 \text{ units}$$

$$\text{Total carrying cost} = \frac{2,400 \times ₹12 \times 25}{100} = ₹7,200$$

$$\text{Carrying cost per unit (C)} = ₹7,200 \div 2,400 \text{ units} = ₹3$$

Savings due to EOQ

Particulars	*Present*	*With EOQ*
1. Size of order (units)	1,200	114
2. Number of orders	2	22
3. Cost per order (₹)	8	8
4. Total ordering cost (2 × 3) (₹)	16	176
5. Carrying cost per unit (₹)	3	3
6. Average inventory (units)	600	57
7. Total carrying cost (5 × 6) (₹)	1,800	171
8. Total cost (4 + 7) (₹)	1,816	347
Differential costs (savings) (₹)	1,469	

P.16.4 The Ganges Pump Company uses about 75,000 valves per year and the usage is fairly constant at 6,250 per month. The valve costs ₹1.50 per unit when bought in quantities and the carrying cost is estimated to be 20 per cent of average inventory investment on an annual basis. The cost to place an order and process the delivery is ₹18. It takes 45 days to receive delivery from the date of an order and a safety stock of 3,250 valves is desired.

LO 16.2 LOD M

You are required to determine:

(a) The most economical order quantity and frequency of orders.

(b) The order point.

(c) The most economical order quantity if the valves cost ₹4.50 each instead of ₹1.50 each.

Solution

(a) $\text{EOQ} = \sqrt{\dfrac{2AB}{C}} = \sqrt{\dfrac{2 \times 75{,}000 \times 18}{0.3}} = 3{,}000 \text{ units}$

Working Notes

(a) (i) Total carrying cost $= \dfrac{75{,}000 \times ₹1.50 \times 20}{100} = ₹22{,}500$

(ii) Carrying cost per unit = ₹22,500/75,000 = 0.30

(b) Order point = (Lead Time × Normal usage during lead time) + Safety stock (1.5 months × 6,250 units per month) + 3,250 units = 12,625 units.

(c) EOQ when cost per valve is ₹4.50:

$$\text{EOQ} = \sqrt{\frac{2AB}{C}} = \sqrt{\frac{2 \times 75{,}000 \times 18}{0.90}} = 1{,}733 \text{ units}$$

$$\text{Total carrying cost} = \frac{75{,}000 \times ₹4.50 \times 20}{100} = ₹67{,}500$$

Carrying cost per unit = ₹67,500/75000

P.16.5 Royal Industries manufactures plastic lunch boxes in a moulding process. On an annual basis, the industry manufactures 1,000 plastic lunch boxes at a cost of ₹4 per unit. The industry's differential costs of carrying the item in the finished goods inventory are 20 per cent of the inventory value per year and the set-up costs per production run is ₹200. What is the optimum production-run? LO 16.2 LOD E

Solution The optimum production run is $= \sqrt{\dfrac{2AB}{C}}$, B = set-up costs per production run

$$= \sqrt{\frac{2 \times 1{,}000 \times 200}{₹0.80}} = 707 \text{ units.}$$

P.16.6 M/s Tubes Ltd are the manufacturers of picture tubes for T.V. The following are the details of the operations during the current year. LO 16.2 LOD E

Average monthly market demand (tubes)	2,000
Ordering cost (per order)	₹100
Inventory carrying cost (per cent per annum)	20
Cost of tubes (per tube)	500
Normal usage (tubes per week)	100
Minimum usage (tubes per week)	50
Maximum usage (tubes per week)	200
Lead time to supply (weeks)	6-8

Compute from the above:

1. Economic order quantity. If the supplier is willing to supply quarterly 1,500 units at a discount of 5 per cent, is it worth accepting?
2. Maximum level of stock
3. Minimum level of stock
4. Reorder level

Solution

1. Economic order quantity

Annual demand (A) = Normal usage per week × 52 weeks = 100 tubes × 52 = 5,200 tubes. Ordering cost per order (B) = ₹100 per order

Inventory carrying cost per unit per annum (C) = ₹500 × 0.20 = ₹100 per unit per annum

$$\text{EOQ} = \sqrt{2\ \text{AB/C}} = \sqrt{(2 \times 5{,}200 \text{ units} \times ₹100) \div ₹100} = 102 \text{ tubes}$$

If supplier is willing to supply 1,500 units at a discount of 5 per cent:

Total cost (When order size is 1,500 units) = Cost of 5,200 units + Ordering cost + Carrying cost

$$= [5{,}200 \times (500 \times 0.95)] + \left[(5{,}200/1{,}500) \times ₹100) + \left(\frac{1}{2} \times 1{,}500 \times 0.20 \times 475 \right) \right]$$

= ₹24,70,000 + ₹346.67 + ₹71,250 = ₹25,41,596.67

Total cost (when order size is 102 units) = (5,200 × 500) + (5,200/102 × ₹100) + (1/2 × 102 × 0.20 × 500)

= ₹26,00,000 + ₹5,098.03 + ₹5,100 = ₹26,10,198.03

Since the total cost under quarterly supply of 1,500 units with 5 per cent discount is lower than when order size is 102 units, the offer should be accepted. While accepting this offer, consideration of capital blocked on order size of 1,500 units per quarter has been ignored.

2. Maximum level of stock = Reorder level + Reorder quantity – (Minimum usage × Minimum reorder period)

= 1,600 units + 102 units – (50 units × 6 weeks) = 1,402 units

3. Minimum level of stock = Reorder level – (Normal usage × Average reorder period)

= 1,600 units – (100 units × 7 weeks) = 900 units

4. Reorder level = Maximum consumption × Maximum reorder period = 200 units × 8 weeks = 1,600 units.

P.16.7 The purchase department of an organisation has received an offer of quantity discounts on its order of materials as under: **LO 16.2** LOD D

Price per tonne	*Tonnes*
₹1,400	Less than 500
1,380	500 and less than 1,000
1,360	1,000 and less than 2,000
1,340	2,000 and less than 3,000
1,320	3,000 and above

The annual requirement of the material is 5,000 tonnes. The delivery cost per order is ₹1,200 and the annual stock holding cost is estimated at 20 per cent of the average inventory.

The purchase department wants you to consider the following purchase options and advise which among them will be the most economical order quantity, presenting the information in a tabular form:

The purchase quantity options to be considered are: 400 tonnes, 500 tonnes, 1,000 tonnes, 2,000 tonnes, and 3,000 tonnes

Solution

Determination of economic order quantity (EOQ)

1. Annual requirements (tonnes)	5,000	5,000	5,000	5,000	5,000
2. Order size (tonnes)	400	500	1,000	2,000	3,000
3. Number of orders (1 Π 2)*	12.5	10	5	2.5	1.67
4. Price per tonne (₹)	1,400	1,380	1,360	1,340	1,320
5. Cost of inventory (1 × 4) ₹lakh	70	69	68	67	66
6. Ordering cost (₹) (No. of orders × ₹1,200)	15,000	12,000	6,000	3,000	2,004
7. Average inventory (tonnes)	200	250	500	1,000	1,500
8. Average inventory (₹ lakh)	2.8	3.45	6.8	13.4	19.8
9. Carrying cost (0.20 × Average inventory) (₹ lakh)	0.56	0.69	1.36	2.68	3.96
10. Total cost (5 + 6 + 9) (₹ lakh)	70.71	69.81	69.42	69.71	69.98

*Number of orders can be in fraction figure as per going concern concept.

Recommendation The purchase department is advised to have order size of 1,000 tonnes as at this order size total cost is minimum.

P.16.8 G. Ltd. produces a product which has a monthly demand of 4,000 units. The product requires a component X which is purchased at ₹20. For every finished product, one unit of component is required. The ordering cost is ₹120 per order and the holding cost is 10 per cent per annum. **LO 16.2** LOD **D**

You are required to calculate:

(i) Economic order quantity.

(ii) If the minimum lot size to be supplied is 4,000 units, what is the extra cost, the company has to incur?

(iii) What is the minimum carrying cost, the company has to incur?

Solution

(i) Determination of EOQ

$$\text{EOQ} = \sqrt{\frac{2\,\text{AB}}{\text{C}}} = \sqrt{\frac{2 \times 48{,}000 \text{ units} \times ₹120}{₹2}} = 2{,}400 \text{ units}$$

A = 4,000 units per month × 12 months = 48,000 units
C = ₹20 cost per unit × 0.10 = ₹2 per unit per annum

(ii) Determination of extra cost when lot size is 4,000 units

Particulars	*Cost when lot size is*	
	4,000 units	*2,400 units*
1. Annual usage (units)	48,000	48,000
2. Size of order	4,000	2,400
3. Number of orders (1 ÷ 2)	12	20
4. Cost per order	₹120	₹120
5. Total ordering costs (3 × 4)	1,440	2,400
6. Carrying cost per unit per annum	2	2
7. Average inventory (size of order/2)	2,000	1,200
8. Total carrying cost (6 × 7)	4,000	2,400
9. Total costs (5 + 8)	5,400	4,800

Extra costs to be incurred is ₹640 (₹5,440 – ₹4,800), when the order size is 4,000 units.

(iii) There is a positive relationship between the total carrying cost the firm incurs and the size of the average inventory it carries; this average size of inventory, in turn, is positively related to the size of order. In view of these facts, the minimum carrying costs the firm is to incur is ₹2,400 (corresponding to EOQ of 2,400 units and the average inventory level of 1,200 units)

P.16.9 A company manufactures a product from a raw material, which is purchased at ₹60 per kg. The company incurs a handling cost of ₹360 plus freight of ₹390 per order. The incremental carrying cost of inventory of raw material is ₹0.50 per kg per month. In addition, the cost of working capital finance on the investment in inventory of raw material is ₹9 per kg per annum. The annual production of the product is 1,00,000 units and 2.5 units are obtained from one kg of raw material. **LO 16.2** LOD D

Required:

(i) Calculate the economic order quantity of raw materials.
(ii) Advise, how frequently should orders for procurement be placed.
(iii) If the company proposes to rationalise placement of orders on quarterly basis, what percentage of discount in the price of raw materials should be negotiated?

Solution

(i) $\text{EOQ} = \sqrt{\frac{2\text{AB}}{\text{C}}} = \sqrt{\frac{2 \times 40{,}000 \text{ kgs} \times ₹750}{₹15}} = 2{,}000 \text{ kgs}$

Annual usage in kgs (A) = 1,00,000 units/2.5 units = 40,000 kgs
Ordering cost per order (B) = ₹360 + ₹390 = ₹750
Carrying cost per kg per annum (C) = (₹0.50 per kg per month × 12 months) + ₹9 per kg cost of working capital finance per annum = ₹15

(ii) Frequency of placing an order in a year

Annual usage (in kgs)	40,000
EOQ (in kgs)	2,000
Number of orders placed in a year (40,000 kgs/2,000 kgs)	20*

*Frequency of placing an order is 18 days (360 days/20)

(iii) (a) Incremental total cost to be incurred when orders are placed on quarterly basis i.e. 10,000 kgs (40,000 annual usage/4 quarters)

Particulars	*On EOQ Basis*	*On Quarterly Basis*
1. Annual usage (kgs)	40,000	40,000
2. Size of orders	2,000	10,000
3. Number of order (1 ÷ 2)	20	4
4. Cost per order	₹750	₹750
5. Total ordering costs (3 × 4)	15,000	3,000
6. Carrying cost per unit	15	15
7. Average inventory (size of order/2) (kgs)	1,000	5,000
8. Total carrying cost (6 × 7)	15,000	75,000
9. Total cost (5 + 8)	30,000	78,000
Incremental costs (₹78,000 – ₹30,000) per year = ₹48,000		

(b) The firm should be able to earn discount of ₹48,000 on its total annual purchases of 40,000 kgs (40,000 kgs × ₹60 per kg = ₹24,00,000). The negotiated discount sum will be: (₹48,000/₹24,00,000) × 100 = 2 per cent

P.16.10 A Company has the option to procure a particular material from two sources: Source I assures that defectives will not be more than 2 per cent of supplied quantity. Source II does not give any assurance, but on the basis of past experience of supplies received from it, it is observed that defective percentage is 2.8 per cent.

LO 16.2 LOD M

The material is supplied in lots of 1,000 units. Source II supplies the lot at a price, which is lower by ₹100 as compared to source 1. The defective units of material can be rectified for use at a cost of ₹5 per unit.

You are required to find out which of the two sources is more economical.

Solution

Statement showing comparative costs associated with two sources of material supplies

Particulars	Material source I	Material source II
1. Material supplied (in units)	1,000	1,000
2. Defective units (in percentage)	2	2.8
3. Total defective units (1 × 2)	20	28
4. Rectification cost per unit	₹5	₹5
5. Total rectification (3 × 4)	100	140
6. Additional price paid in Source I	100	—
7. Total additional costs (5 + 6)	200	140

Material Source II is more economical as it entails lower cost. The company is advised to buy materials from Source II.

P.16.11 A factory uses 4,000 varieties of inventory. In terms of inventory holding and inventory usage, the following information is compiled.

LO 16.2 LOD M

Number of varieties of inventory	Percentage	% value of inventory holding (average)	% of inventory usage (in end-product)
3,875	96.875	20	5
110	2.750	30	10
15	0.375	50	85
4,000	100.00	100	100

Classify the items of inventory as per ABC analysis with reasons.

Solution

(i) 15 number of varieties of inventory items should be classified as 'A' category (as per ABC analysis) as, while they constitute less than one per cent (0.375 per cent) of total number of inventory items handled by the store, their value is 50 per cent. Besides, these varieties (15) account for 85 per cent of total inventory usage (in end-product). Thus, this group is the most important.

(ii) 3,875 number of inventory items should be classified as 'C' category as they constitute 96.875 per cent of total varieties of inventory items handled by the store; such inventories account for only for 20 per cent of total value and 5 per cent of total inventory usage (in-end product). Thus, this group is the least important.

(iii) 10 number of inventory items should be classified as 'B' category as they occupy intermediate position between A category (15 items) and C category (3,875 items). These items (110) require more attention than C category items but less attention than A category items as per ABC analysis. In financial terms also, these items require 30 per cent investment (less than A category but more than C category) with 2.75 per cent of total number of varieties of inventory handled by store; such number is much higher for C category (96.875 per cent) and lower for A category (0.375 per cent).

REVIEW QUESTIONS

LOD: Easy

RQ.16.1 Fill in the following blanks: [LO 16.1,2]

(i) Finance manager is to ______________ of the various functional areas regarding the appropriate inventory levels.

(ii) ______________ is fixed cost of placing and receiving an order for acquisition of inventory.

(iii) Costs of holding inventory are referred to as ______________.

(iv) ______________ is a widely-used classification technique to identify various items of inventory for purposes of inventory control.

(v) While category ______________ items warrant the most rigorous control, category ______________ items minimum attention.

(vi) ______________ is the level of inventory at which total cost of inventory consisting of acquisition/ordering and carrying cost is minimal.

(vii) ______________ is the level of inventory at which fresh order for procuring additional inventory is placed.

(viii) ______________ refers to the time normally taken in receiving the inventory supplies after placing orders with suppliers.

(ix) ______________ is the amount of inventory that needs to be maintained to meet unforeseen situations, say, unanticipated increase in daily usage and increase in lead time.

(x) In EOQ, average inventory is determined dividing ______________.

[Answers: (i) Reconcile the conflicting consideration/viewpoints (ii) Ordering costs (iii) Carrying costs (iv) ABC system (v) A, C, (vi) Economic order quantity (vii) Reorder point (viii) Lead time (ix) Safety stock (x) order size/2]

RQ.16.2 What is inventory? Why do firms maintain inventory? What are the objectives of inventory management? [LO 16.1]

RQ.16.3 What purpose doe safety stock serve? What are the benefits and costs associated with safety stock? [LO 16.2]

RQ.16.4 What is the financial manager's role in management of inventory? [LO 16.1,2]

RQ.16.5 From the following data, determine the EOQ. [LO 16.2]

(i) Annual requirement, 12,00,000 units

(ii) Purchase price, ₹3 per unit

(iii) Ordering cost, ₹50 per order

(iv) Carrying cost of inventory, 10 per cent of cost

LOD: Medium

RQ.16.6 What is meant by the ABC inventory control system? On what key premise is this system based? What are its limitations? [LO 16.2]

RQ.16.7 Define economic order quantity (EOQ). How can it be computed? What are the limitations of the EOQ model? [LO 16.2]

RQ.16.8 (a) What is inventory reorder point? How is it determined? [LO 16.3]

(b) Define JIT. What are its benefits? What measures can managers take to control and evaluate JIT?

RQ.16.9 The following information is available relating to the stock-out of a firm: [LO 16.2]

Stock-out (units)	*Number of months*
800	2
600	3
400	5
200	10
0	30
	50

The selling price of each unit is ₹200. The carrying costs are ₹19 per unit. The stock-out costs are ₹50 per unit.

(i) If the firm wishes to never miss a sale, what should be its safety stock? What is the total cost associated with this level of safety stock? What are the associated costs with safety stock of 300, 200, 100 and 20 units, respectively?

(ii) What is the optimal safety stock level?

RQ.16.10 [LO 16.2]

(i) From the following data, determine the EOQ.

(a) List price of product X is ₹800 per gross.

(b) 40 per cent trade discount is allowed on list price on purchases in gross lots.

(c) Freight cost is ₹20 per gross from the transport company to the factory premises.

(d) Annual usage or product X: 36 gross per year.

(e) Cost of placing an order is ₹10, the cost of receiving an order is ₹20.

(f) Carrying cost is 20 per cent of the effective purchase price of goods per year.

(g) Insurance and taxes are approximately 12 per cent of the net delivered cost of inventory.

(ii) Determine the total annual cost of inventory based on uniform order lot sizes of 1, 2, 3, 4, 5 and 6 gross of product X.

(iii) Determine the minimum stock re-order point of product X, given the following: (a) Working days: 240; (b) Normal delivery time to receive an order: 20 working days from the date of purchase request is initiated; (c) Safety stock: 1 gross.

LOD: Difficult

RQ.16.11 ABC Ltd has several items of inventory. The average number of each of these as well as their unit costs is listed below: [LO 16.2]

Item	*Average inventory (units)*	*Average cost per unit*	*Item*	*Average inventory (units)*	*Average cost per unit*
1	4,000	₹1.96	11	1,800	₹25
2	200	10	12	130	2.70
3	440	2.40	13	4,400	9.50
4	2,000	16.80	14	3,200	2.60
5	20	165	15	1,920	2
6	800	6	16	800	1.20
7	160	76	17	3,400	2.20
8	3,000	3	18	2,400	10
9	1,200	1.90	19	120	21
10	6,000	0.50	20	320	4

The company wishes to adopt an ABC inventory system. How should the items be classified into A, B and C?

ANSWERS

16.5 20,000 units

16.9 **(i)** 800 units safety stock; ₹15,200 total cost
(ii) 200 units

16.10 **(i)** 4.4
(ii) 1,080; 540; 360; 270; 240; 180 (for size of gross order 1 to 6 respectively)
(iii) 4 Gross

16.11 A : 68.24; B : 21.17; C : 10.46

Scan the QR Code to access comprehensive solutions to all numerical review questions and additional material.

CHAPTER

17

Working Capital Financing

LEARNING OBJECTIVES

LO 17.1	Review the key features and characteristics of, and the costs associated with, trade credit as a source of working capital financing
LO 17.2	Describe the various forms of bank credit and the modes of security and outline a rating and scoring model used by banks to assess borrowers for lending
LO 17.3	Explain the key features of commercial papers (CPs) as sources of working capital financing
LO 17.4	Discuss the main features of Certificate of Deposits (CDs) as a source of working capital financing
LO 17.5	Analyse the key features of factoring and evaluate its role in working capital financing

INTRODUCTION

After determining the level of working capital, as illustrated in Chapter 13, a firm is to decide how it is to be financed. The need for financing arises mainly because the investment in working capital/current assets, that is, raw materials, work/stock-in-process, finished goods and receivables typically fluctuates during the year. The present chapter discusses the main sources of finance for working capital. Although long-term funds partly finance current assets and provide the margin money for working capital, such assets/working capital are also, to a marked extent, supported by short-term sources; this is true, in particular, for seasonal industries. The main sources of working capital financing, namely, trade credit, bank credit, commercial papers, certificate of deposits and factoring are covered in this chapter. The major points are summarised by way of recapitulation.

LO 17.1 TRADE CREDIT

Features

Trade credit is the credit extended by suppliers of goods and services in the normal course of business.

Trade credit refers to the credit extended by the supplier of goods and services in the normal course of transaction/business/sale of the firm. According to trade practices, cash is not paid immediately for purchases but after an agreed period of time. Thus, deferral of payment (trade credit) represents a source of finance for credit purchases.

There is, however, no formal/specific negotiation for trade credit. It is an informal arrangement between the buyer and the seller. There are no legal instruments/acknowledgements of debt which are granted on an open account basis. Such credit appears in the records of the buyer of goods as sundry creditors/accounts payable.

A variant of accounts payable is bills/notes payable. Unlike the open account nature of accounts payable, bills/notes payable represent documentary evidence of credit purchases and a formal acknowledgement of obligation to pay for credit purchases on a specified (maturity) date failing which legal/penal action for recovery will follow. A notable feature of bills/notes payable is that they can be rediscounted and the seller does not necessarily have to hold it till maturity to receive payment. However, it creates a legally enforceable obligation on the buyer of goods to pay on maturity whereas the accounts payable have more flexible payment obligations. Although most of the trade credit is on open account as accounts payable, the suppliers of goods do not extend credit indiscriminately. Their decision whether or not to extend the trade credit as well as the quantum is based on a consideration of factors such as earnings record over a period of time, liquidity position of the firm and past record of payment.

Advantages

Trade credit, as a source of short-term/working capital finance, has certain advantages. It is easily, almost automatically, available. Moreover, it is a flexible and spontaneous source of finance. The availability and magnitude of trade credit is related to the size of operations of the firm in terms of sales/purchases. For instance, assume the requirement of credit purchases to support the existing sales is ₹5 lakh per day. If the purchases are made on a credit of 30 days, the average outstanding accounts payable/trade credit (finance) will amount to ₹1.5 crore (₹5 lakh × 30 days). The increase in purchases of goods to support higher sales level to ₹6 lakh will imply a trade credit finance of ₹1.8 crore (₹6 lakh × 30 days). If the credit purchases of goods decline, the availability of trade credit will correspondingly decline. Trade credit is also *an informal, spontaneous source of finance.* Not requiring negotiation and formal agreement, trade credit is free from the restrictions associated with formal/negotiated source of finance/credit.

Costs

Cash discount implies a percentage deduction from the purchase price if the buyer pays within a specified time that is shorter than the credit period.

Trade credit does not involve any explicit interest charge. However, there is an implicit cost of trade credit. It depends on the credit terms offered by the supplier of goods. If the terms of the credit are, say, 45 days net, the payable amount to the supplier of goods is the same whether paid on the date of purchase or on the 45th day and, therefore, trade credit has no cost, that is, it is cost-free. But if the credit terms are, say, 2/15, net 45, that is, there is **cash discount** for prompt payment, the trade **credit period** beyond the **cash discount period** has a cost = [(Discount/1 – Discount) × (360 days/Credit period – Discount period)]. The implicit interest rate/cost = [(0.02/1 – 0.02) × (360/45 – 15)] = 24.5 per cent. Alternatively, the credit terms, 2/15, net 45, imply that the firm (buyer) is entitled to 2 per cent discount for payment made within 15 days when the entire payment is to be made within 45 days. Since the net amount is due in 45 days, failure to take the discount means paying an extra 2 per cent for using the money for an additional 30 days. If a firm were

Cash discount period implies the number of days after the beginning of the credit period during which the discount is available.

Trade credit period is the number of days until full payment of an account payable is required.

to pay 2 per cent for every 30 days period over a year, there would be 12 such periods (360 days ÷ 30 days). This represents an annual interest rate/cost of 24 per cent. If the terms of credit are 2/10, net 30, the cost of credit works out to 36.4 per cent. *The smaller the difference between the payment day and the end of the discount period, the larger is the annual interest/cost of trade credit.*

To sum up, as the **cost of trade credit** is generally very high beyond the discount period, firms should avail of the discount on prompt payment. If, however, they are unable to avail of discount, the payment of trade credit should be delayed till the last day of the credit (net) period and beyond without impairing their credit-worthiness. But a precondition for obtaining trade credit particularly by a new company is cultivating good relationship with suppliers of goods and obtaining their confidence by honouring commitments.

Cost of trade credit is the implicit cost of not availing cash discount.

LO 17.2 BANK CREDIT

Bank credit is the primary institutional source of working capital finance in India. In fact, it represents the most important source for financing of current assets.

Forms of Credit

Working capital finance is provided by banks in five ways: **(i)** cash credits/overdrafts, **(ii)** loans, **(iii)** purchase/discount bills, **(iv)** letter of credit and **(v)** working capital term loans. Proposal form for obtaining working capital funds from Punjab National Bank is given in *Appendix 17.A* on website: **www.mhhe.com/khanjainfm8e.**

A rating and scoring model used by an Indian bank to assess working capital requirements of clients is also given.

Cash credit/Overdrafts Under cash credit/overdraft form/arrangement of bank finance, the bank specifies a predetermined borrowing/credit limit. The borrower can draw/borrow up to the stipulated credit/overdraft limit. Within the specified limit/**line of credit**, any number of drawals/drawings are possible to the extent of his requirements periodically. Similarly, repayments can be made whenever desired during the period. The interest is determined on the basis of the running balance/amount actually utilised by the borrower and not on the sanctioned limit. However, a minimum (commitment) charge may be payable on the unutilised balance irrespective of the level of borrowing for availing of the facility. This form of bank financing of working capital is highly attractive to the borrowers because, firstly, it is flexible in that although borrowed funds are repayable on demand, banks usually do not recall cash advances/roll them over and, secondly, the borrower has the freedom to draw the amount in advance as and when required while the interest liability is only on the amount actually outstanding. However, cash credit/overdraft is inconvenient to the banks and hampers credit planning.

Line of credit is an agreement between a bank and a firm specifying the amount of short-term borrowing the bank would make available to the firm over a given period of time.

Loans Under this arrangement, the entire amount of borrowing is credited to the current account of the borrower or released in cash. The borrower has to pay interest on the total amount. The loans are repayable on demand or in periodic instalments. They can also be renewed from time to time. As a form of financing, loans imply a financial discipline on the part of the borrowers.

Bills Purchased/Discounted This arrangement is of relatively recent origin in India. With the introduction of the New Bill Market Scheme in 1970 by the Reserve Bank of India (RBI), bank credit is being made available through discounting of *usance bills* by banks. The RBI envisaged the progressive use of bills as an instrument of credit as against the prevailing practice of using the widely-prevalent cash credit arrangement for financing working capital. The cash credit arrangement gave rise to unhealthy practices. As the availability of bank credit was unrelated to production needs, borrowers enjoyed facilities in excess of their legitimate needs. Moreover, it led to double financing. This was possible because credit was taken from different agencies for financing the same activity. This was done, for example, by buying goods on credit from suppliers and raising cash credit by hypothecating the same goods. The bill financing is intended to link credit with the sale and purchase of goods and, thus, eliminate the scope for misuse or diversion of credit to other purposes.

The amount made available under this arrangement is covered by the cash credit and overdraft limit. Before discounting the bill, the bank satisfies itself about the credit-worthiness of the drawer and the genuineness of the bill. To popularise the scheme, the discount rates are fixed at lower rates than those of cash credit, the difference being about 1-1.5 per cent. The discounting banker asks the drawer of the bill (i.e. seller of goods) to have his bill accepted by the drawee (buyers) bank before discounting it. The latter grants acceptance against the cash credit limit, earlier fixed by it, on the basis of the borrowing value of stocks. Therefore, the buyer who buys goods on credit cannot use the same goods as a source of obtaining additional bank credit.

The *modus operandi* of bill finance as a source of working capital financing is that a bill arises out of a trade sale-purchase transaction on credit. The seller of goods draws the bill on the purchaser of goods, payable on demand or after a usance period not exceeding 90 days. On acceptance of the bill by the purchaser, the seller offers it to the bank for discount/purchase. On discounting the bill, the bank releases the funds to the seller. The bill is presented by the bank to the purchaser/acceptor of the bill on due date for payment. The bills can also be rediscounted with the other banks/RBI. However, this form of financing is not popular in the country.

Term Loans for Working Capital Under this arrangement, banks advance loans for 3-7 years repayable in yearly or half-yearly instalments.

Letter of Credit While the other forms of bank credit are direct forms of financing in which banks provide funds as well as bear risk, letter of credit is an indirect form of working capital financing and banks assume only the risk, the credit being provided by the supplier himself.

> **Letter of credit** is a letter written by a bank stating that the bank guarantees payment of an invoiced amount if all the underlying agreements are met.

The purchaser of goods on credit obtains a **letter of credit** from a bank. The bank undertakes the responsibility to make payment to the supplier in case the buyer fails to meet his obligations. Thus, the *modus operandi* of letter of credit is that the supplier sells goods on credit/extends credit (finance) to the purchaser, the bank gives a guarantee and bears risk only in case of default by the purchaser.

Mode of Security

Banks provide credit on the basis of the following modes of security:

Hypothecation Under this mode of security, the banks provide credit to borrowers against the security of movable property, usually inventory of goods. The goods hypothecated, however, continue to be in the possession of the owner of these goods (i.e., the borrower). The rights of the lending bank (hypothecatee) depend upon the terms of the contract between the borrower and the lender. Although the bank does not have physical possession of the goods, it has the legal right to sell the goods to realise the outstanding loan. Hypothecation facility is normally not available to new borrowers.

> **Hypothecation** is the use of inventory as a security/collateral to obtain a short-term loan.

Pledge **Pledge**, as a mode of security, is different from hypothecation in that in the former, unlike in the latter, the goods which are offered as security are transferred to the physical possession of the lender. An essential prerequisite of pledge, therefore, is that the goods are in the custody of the bank. The borrower who offers the security is, called a 'pawnor' (pledgor), while the bank is called the 'pawnee' (pledgee). The lodging of the goods by the pledgor to the pledgee is a kind of bailment. Therefore, pledge creates some liabilities for the bank. It must take reasonable care of goods pledged with it. The term '*reasonable care*' means care which a prudent person would take to protect his property. He would be responsible for any loss or damage if he uses the pledged goods for his own purposes. In case of non-payment of the loans, the bank enjoys the right to sell the goods.

> **Pledge** is the use of goods as security/collateral to obtain a short-term loan.

Lien The term '**lien**' refers to the right of a party to retain goods belonging to another party until a debt due to him is paid. Lien can be of two types: **(i)** particular lien, and **(ii)** general lien. Particular lien is a right to retain goods until a claim pertaining to these goods is fully paid. On the other hand, general lien can be applied till all dues of the claimant are paid. Banks usually enjoy general lien.

> **Lien** is a publicly disclosed legal claim on collateral.

Mortgage It is the transfer of a legal/equitable interest in specific immovable property for securing the payment of debt. The person who parts with the interest in the property is called 'mortgagor' and the bank in whose favour the transfer takes place is the 'mortgagee'. The instrument of transfer is called the 'mortgage deed'. **Mortgage** is, thus, conveyance of interest in the mortgaged property. The mortgage interest in the property is terminated as soon as the debt is paid. Mortgages are taken as an additional security for working capital credit by banks.

> **Mortgage** is the additional security of immovable property to obtain short-term loan.

Charge Where immovable property of one person is, by the act of parties or by the operation of law, made security for the payment of money to another and the transaction does not amount to mortgage, the latter person is said to have a charge on the property and all the provisions of simple mortgage will apply to such a charge. The provision are as follows:

- A charge is not the transfer of interest in the property though it is security for payment. But mortgage is a transfer of interest in the property.
- A charge may be created by the act of parties or by the operation of law. But a mortgage can be created only by the act of parties.
- A charge need not be made in writing but a mortgage deed must be attested.
- Generally, a charge cannot be enforced against the transferee for consideration without notice. In a mortgage, the transferee of the mortgaged property can acquire the remaining interest in the property, if any is left.

Scoring and Rating Model of X Bank

The RBI has prescribed a comprehensive risk rating and scoring framework to serve as a single point indicator of the diverse risk factors of the borrowers to help in taking a credit decision in a consistant manner. We outline below a scoring and rating model of an Indian bank.

Rating of Borrowers Based on Percentage of Score as Given Below

% Score obtained	*Credit rating*
80% and above	AAA
79%–65%	AA
64%–50%	A
49%–35%	B
Below 35%	BB

Scoring and Rating Parameters:

A. Financial Risk (Based on Latest Balance Sheet)

Current Ratio	Ratio value	1.33 and above	1.32 – >1.25	1.24 – 1.10	<1.0
	Score	5	3	2	0
Debt Equity Ratio	Ratio value	> 2.0	2.0 – 3.0	3.01 – 4.0	>4.0
	Score	6	4	2	0
Profit After Tax/Net Sales	%age Value	5% and above	4 – 5%	3 – 4%	2 – 3% < 2.0%
	Score	5	3	2	1 0
Interest Service Coverage Ratio	Ratio	> 3.0	3.0 – 2.0	1.99 – 1.50	< 1.50
	Score	6	4	2	0

B. Financial Risk: Moving Average (Based on Last 3 Years Balance Sheet)

1. Current Ratio	Value	1.33 and more with increasing trend	1.33 and more with uneven and decreasing trend	Between 1.33–1.1 with increasing trend	Between 1.33–1.1 with decreasing trend	All others
	Score	5	3	2	1	0
2. Debt-Equity Ratio	Value	3.0 and more with decreasing trend	3.0 and less with uneven or increasing trend 4	More than 3.0 but < 4 with decreasing trend	> 3.0 but < 4.0 with uneven or increasing trend	All others
	Score	6	3.0 and	2	1	0
3. Interest Coverage Ratio	Value	3.0 and more with increasing trend	more with uneven or decreasing trend	Between 3 to 2 with increasing trend	Between 3 to 2 with uneven or decreasing trend	All Others
	Score	6	4	2	1	0
4. Net Sales	Value	Increasing trend and last year achievement of >90% of projections	Uneven or decreasing trend and last year's achievement of >90% of projections	Increasing trend and last year achievement of >75% of projection but < 90%	Decreasing or uneven trend and last year achievement >75% projection but <90%	Others
	Score	5	3	2	1	0

C. Market Risk

<table>
<tr><td rowspan="2">1. Competition and threat from imports</td><td>Value</td><td>Monopoly highest market share</td><td>Increasing market share</td><td>Supply exceeding the demand</td><td>Insignificant market share/ high threat from imports</td></tr>
<tr><td>Score</td><td>4</td><td>3</td><td>2</td><td>0</td></tr>
<tr><td rowspan="2">2. Industry cycle</td><td>Value</td><td colspan="2">Fairly stable industry cycle with long term prospects</td><td colspan="2">Unfavourable changes in the market/idustry cycles</td></tr>
<tr><td>Score</td><td colspan="2">3</td><td colspan="2">0</td></tr>
<tr><td rowspan="2">3. Regulatory risk</td><td>Value</td><td>Not affected by regulatory framework</td><td colspan="2">Regulatory/legislative issues can affect company but it has the capacity to withstand them</td><td>Regulatory changes are likely to threaten the viability</td></tr>
<tr><td>Score</td><td>4</td><td colspan="2">2</td><td>0</td></tr>
<tr><td rowspan="2">4. Technology</td><td>Value</td><td>Proven technology</td><td colspan="2">Technology likely to undergo changes but company can survive</td><td>Outside obsolete technology</td></tr>
<tr><td>Score</td><td>3</td><td colspan="2">1</td><td>0</td></tr>
</table>

D. Managerial Risk

<table>
<tr><td rowspan="2">Expertise</td><td>Value</td><td colspan="2">Promoters/owners are highly qualified professionals or employing qualified professionals</td><td>Owners managed with professionals but by persons with experience</td><td>Owner-managed with no professionals new company/ firm</td></tr>
<tr><td>Score</td><td colspan="2">5</td><td>3</td><td>0</td></tr>
<tr><td rowspan="2">Track value record</td><td>Value</td><td>Accounts regular, financially disciplined, committed honouring commitments</td><td>Accounts regular, but repayments are slightly delayed. Group companies are not doing well.</td><td>Repayments are delayed but accounts continued to be standard. Overall performance of group companies is average</td><td>No financial discipline—poor adherence to terms of sanction. Accounts are frequently irregular</td></tr>
<tr><td>Score</td><td>6</td><td>4</td><td>2</td><td>0</td></tr>
</table>

E. Security Value

<table>
<tr><td colspan="2">Securities (including collaterals offered) %age coverage of loan amount</td><td>% coverage</td><td>> 175</td><td>> 150 but < 175</td><td>> 100 but < 150</td><td>< 100</td></tr>
<tr><td colspan="2"></td><td>Score</td><td>4</td><td>3</td><td>2</td><td>0</td></tr>
<tr><td>Guarantees type</td><td colspan="2">Central Government/reputed Fis/Scheduled banks</td><td colspan="2">Promoters/Directos/ third party</td><td colspan="2">No guarantee</td></tr>
<tr><td>Score</td><td colspan="2">3</td><td colspan="2">2</td><td colspan="2">0</td></tr>
</table>

F. Capital Market Perception

Dividend payment	Track record	Continuously 3 years	Continuously 2 years	Less than 2 years	No dividend paid
	Score	4	3	2	0
Price earning Ratio (P/E ratio)	Value	Above sector/industry average	Equal to sector/industry average	Less than sector/industry average	
	Score	3	2	0	

G. Contingent Plan

Balance sheet practices	Qualifications	No qualifications for last 3 years	No qualification for last 2 years	Other cases
	Score	2	1	0
Contingent liabilities (%age to TNW and only such liabilities which may affect borrowers net worth/profit)	Percentage	< 10	> 10 – < 30	> 30
	Score	2	1	0
Reliability/accuracy of data including QIS (quarterly information statement)	Value	No deviation/moderate deviation		Deviations are of considerable extent
	Score	2		0

H. Compliance

Submission of stock statement, monitoring data etc.	Value	Timely submission	Delayed/irregular submission upto maximum 30 days	Non/delayed submission beyond 30 days
	Score	2	1	0
Submission of audited balance sheet & profit/loss accounts/financial data/CMA formats for timely renewal of accounts	Value	Timely submission	Delayed/irregular submission (within 2 months from due date)	Non/delayed submission beyond 2 months
	Score	3	2	0
Over limit business	Value	No drawals beyond limits without prior approval/no returning of cheques	Sometimes drawals are beyond limits but accounts are regularised	Frequent withdrawals
	Score	3	2	0
Compliance with terms/conditions of sanction	Value	Terms/conditions complied with/no deviations	Import terms/creation of securities complied	Important terms pending/non-complied
	Score	3	2	0

LO 17.3 COMMERCIAL PAPERS

Features

The CP is a short-term unsecured negotiable instrument consisting of usance primary notes with a fixed maturity, thus, indicating the short-term obligation of an issuer. It is generally issued by companies as a means of raising short-term debt and, by a process of securitisation, intermediation of the bank is eliminated. The PDs and all-India financial institutions can also issue CPs. It is issued on a discount to face value basis but it can also be issued in interest-bearing form. The issuer promises the buyer a fixed amount at a future date but pledges no assets. His liquidity and earning power are the only guarantee. In other words, the CP is not tied to any specific self liquidating trade transaction in contrast to the commercial bills that arise out of specific trade/ commercial transaction. A CP can be issued by a company directly to the investor or through bank/merchant banks (dealers). When the companies directly deal with the investors, rather than use a securities dealer as an intermediary, the CP is called a *direct paper*. Such companies/borrowers announce the current rates of CPs of various maturities. Investors can then select those maturities that closely approximate their holding period and acquire the security/paper directly from the issuer. When CPs are issued by security dealer/ dealers on behalf of their corporate customers, they are called *dealer papers*. They buy at a price less the commission and sell at the highest possible level. It is generally backed by a revolving underwriting facility from banks to ensure continuous availability of funds on each roll-over of the CP. Moreover, unlike commercial bills, maturities, within the range can be tailored to specific requirements.

Commerical paper is a form of financing consisting of short-term insecured promissory notes issued by a firm with high credit rating.

Advantages

A CP, as a short-term financial instrument, has several advantages both to the issuers and the investors. It is a simple instrument and hardly involves any documentation between the issuer and the investor. It is additionally flexible in terms of maturities of the underlying promissory note, which can be tailored to match the cash flow of the issuer. Further, a well rated company can diversify its sources of finance from banks to the short-term money market at a cheaper cost. This is particularly relevant in a system, such as in India, in which reserve requirements on banks are in vogue in the form of SLR and CRR, which raise the effective cost *of* bank lending. Also, the CP provides investors with returns higher than what they obtain from the banking system. In addition, companies that are able to raise funds through CPs become better known in the financial world and are thereby placed in a more favourable position for raising long-term capital. Thus, there is an in-built incentive for companies *to* remain financially strong. Unlike bank credit which is secured by a first charge on the current assets, CP is unsecured. There are no limitations on the end-use *of* funds raised through CPs, and as negotiable/transferable instruments, they are highly liquid. Finally, in the Indian context, the creation *of* a commercial paper market has resulted in a part *of* the inter-corporate funds flowing into this market, which is under the control *of* the monetary authorities.

Framework of Indian CP Market

Commercial paper (CP) is an unsecured money market instrument issued in the form of a promissory note. As a privately placed instrument, CP was introduced in India in 1990 with a view to enabling highly rated corporate borrowers to diversify their sources of short-term borrowings and to provide additional instrument to investors. Subsequently, primary/satellite dealers and all-India financial institutions (FIs) were also permitted to issue CP to enable them to meet their short-term funding requirements for their operations. The issue of CP is governed by the directions/guidelines issued by the RBI from time to time. These guidelines provide the broad framework of the CPs market in India. The main elements of the present framework of the Indian CP market, prescribed by the RBI, are outlined below.

Eligibility for Issue of CP Companies, primary dealers (PDs) and financial institutions (FIs) that have been permitted to raise short-term resources under the umbrella limit fixed by the RBI are eligible to issue CP. A company would be eligible to issue CP provided: **(a)** the tangible net worth of the company, as per the latest audited balance sheet, is not less than ₹4 crore; **(b)** company has been sanctioned working capital limit by bank(s) or FIs; and **(c)** the borrowal account of the company is classified as a standard asset by the financing bank(s)/institution(s). **Working capital** limit means the aggregate limits including those by way of purchase/discount of bills sanctioned by banks/FIs for meeting the working capital requirements.

Rating Requirements All eligible participants/issuers should obtain the credit rating for issuance of the CP from any one of the SEBI-registered credit rating agencies. The minimum credit rating should be **A-3** as per the standardised rating symbols/definitions provided by the SEBI. The issuers should ensure at the time of issuance of the CP that the rating obtained is current and has not fallen due for review.

Tenor A CP can be issued for maturities between a minimum of 7 days and a maximum up to one year from the date of issue. The maturity date of the CP should not go beyond the date up to which the credit rating of the issuer is valid.

Issue of CP: Credit Enhancement Limits A CP can be issued as a "stand alone" product. It would not be obligatory for banks/FIs to provide stand-by facility. Banks/FIs may, based on their commercial judgement, subject to the prudential norms applicable to them, with the specific approval of their respective Board of Directors, choose to provide stand-by assistance/credit, backstop facility by way of credit enhancement for a CP issue. Non-bank entities (including corporates) may provide unconditional/irrevocable guarantee for credit enhancement for CP issue provided: (i) the issuer fulfils the eligibility criteria for issuance of CP, **(ii)** the guarantor has a credit rating at least one notch higher than the issuer by an approved agency, and **(iii)** the offer document properly discloses the networth of the guarantor company, the names of companies to which the guarantor has issued similar guarantees, the extent of guarantee offered and the condition under which the guarantee would be invoked. The aggregate amount of a CP from an issuer should be within the limit as approved by its Board of Directors or the quantum indicated by the credit rating agency for the specified rating, whichever is lower. Banks and FIs will, however, have the flexibility to fix working capital limits duly taking into account the resource pattern of companies' financing including CPs. An FI can issue a CP within the overall umbrella limit fixed by the RBI.

The total amount of CP proposed to be issued should be raised within a period of two weeks from the date on which the issuer opens the issue for subscription. The CP may be issued on a single date or in parts on different dates provided that in the latter case, each CP should have the same maturity date. Every issue of CP, including renewal, should be treated as a fresh issue.

Investment in CP Individuals, banks, other corporate bodies registered or incorporated in India and unincorporated bodies, NRIs and FIIs would be eligible to invest in CP. However, FPIs would be eligible to invest subject to **(i)** conditions set by the SEBI, and **(ii)** compliance with the provisions of the FEMA/Foreign Exchange Deposit Regulations and Foreign Exchange Management (Transfer/ Issue of Security by a Person Resident Outside) Regulations.

Mode of Issuance The CP can be issued either in the form of a promissory note or in a dematerialised form through any depository approved by and registered with the SEBI. However, RBI-regulated entities are required to make fresh investments and hold CPs only in dematerialised form. The CPs should be issued in denominations of ₹5 lakh and multiples. The amount invested by a single investor should not be less than ₹5 lakh (face value). It will be issued at a discount to face value as may be determined by the issuer. No issuer should have the issue of a CP underwritten or co-accepted. Options (call/put) are not permitted on CPs.

Investment/Redemption The investor in CP (primary subscriber) should pay the discounted value of the CP to the account of the issuer through the IPA. When CP is held in demat form, the holder of the CP will have to get it redeemed and receive payment from the IPA.

Procedure for Issuance Every issuer must appoint an IPA for issuance of a CP. He should disclose to the potential investors its financial position as per the standard market practice. After the exchange of deal confirmation between the investor and the issuer, the issuer should arrange for crediting the CP to the investor's account with a depository through the IPA. The investors should be given a copy of the IPA certificate to the effect that the issuer has a valid agreement with the IPA and documents are in order.

Trading and Settlement All OTC trades in CP should be reported within 15 minutes of the trade to the Financial Markets Trade Reporting and Confirmation Platform (F-TRAC) of Clearcorp Dealing System (India) Ltd (CDSL). The requirement of exchange of physical confirmation of trades matched on F-TRAC is waived subject to the participants **(i)** entering into one-time bilateral agreement for eliminating the exchange of confirmation or multilateral agreement drafted by the FIMMDA, **(ii)** adhering to the applicable laws such as stamp duty and **(iii)** ensuring adherence to a sound risk management framework and complying with all the regulatory/legal requirements/practices in this regard. They should be settled through the clearing house of the NSE/BSE. The settlement cycle for OTC trades in CPs should be T+0/T+1.

Buyback of CP Issuers may with the approval of their Board of Directors, buy-back CPs from the investors before maturity through the secondary market at prevailing market price. The buy-back cannot be before a minimum period of seven days from the issue date and the issuer should intimate the IPA of the buy-back undertaken.

Duties/Obligations The duties/obligations of the issuer, the issuing and the paying agent (IPA) and credit rating agency (CRA) are set out below:

(a) Issuer They should ensure that the guidelines and procedures laid down for the CP issuance are strictly adhered to.

(b) Issuing and Paying Agent (IPA) The IPA should ensure that the issuer has the minimum credit rating as stipulated by the RBI and the amount mobilised through issuance of CP is within the quantum indicated by the CRA for the specified rating or as approved by its Board of Directors, whichever is lower. It has to verify all the documents submitted by the issuer, namely, copy of the Board resolution, signatures of authorised executants (when CP in physical form) and issue a certificate that the documents are in order. It should also certify that it has a valid agreement with the issuer. The certified copies of original documents verified by the IPA should be held in its custody. All banks acting as IPAs should report the details of issuance of CPs on the Online Returns Filing System (ORFS) module of the RBI within two days from the date of issuance. They should immediately report, on occurrence, full particulars of default in repayment of CP in the prescribed format to the RBI. They should similarly report all instances of buy-back undertaken by the issuers.

(c) Credit Rating Agency (CRA) The code of conduct prescribed by the SEBI for CRAs for undertaking rating of capital market instruments would be applicable to them for rating a CP. Further, the CRA would have the discretion to determine the validity period of the rating depending upon its perception about the strength of the issuer. Accordingly, the CRA should at the time of rating, clearly indicate the date when the rating is due for review. They would have to closely monitor the rating assigned to the issuers vis-à-vis their track record at regular intervals and make their revision in the ratings public through their publications and website.

Documentation Procedure Standardised procedures/documentation for CPs are prescribed by the Fixed Income Money Market and Derivatives Association of India (FIMMDA) in consonance with international best practices. Issuers/IPAs should follow the guidelines issued by the FIMMDA with the RBI's approval.

Non-applicability of Certain Other Directions Nothing contained in the RBI NBFCs Directions, would apply to any NBFC insofar as it relates to the acceptance of deposits by issuance of CP, in accordance with these guidelines.

Effective Cost/Interest Yield As CPs are issued at discount and redeemed at their face value, their effective pre-tax interest yield

$$= \left(\frac{\text{Face value} - \text{Net amount realised}}{\text{Net amount realised}}\right) \times \left(\frac{360}{\text{Maturity period}}\right)$$

where net amount realised = face value – discount – issuing and paying agent (IPA) charges, that is, stamp duty, rating charges, dealing bank fee and fee for stand by facility.

Assuming face value of a CP to be ₹5,00,000, maturity period to be 90 days, net amount realised = ₹4,80,000, discount and other charges associated with the issue of CP = 1.5 per cent, the pre-tax

$$\text{effective cost of CP} = \left(\frac{₹5{,}00{,}000 - (₹4{,}80{,}000 - ₹7{,}500)}{(₹4{,}80{,}00 - ₹7{,}500)}\right) \times \left(\frac{360}{90}\right) = 23.3 \text{ per cent}$$

The participants in the market are corporatre bodies, banks, mutual funds, the UTI, LIC, GIC and so on, which have surplus funds and are on a lookout for opportunities for short-term investments. The PDs also operate both in the primary and secondary markets for CPs by quoting its bid and offering prices.

Although the CP market has become fairly popular now, a secondary market is yet to develop and when fully developed, it would impart strength and vitality to the money market. Investors, with temporary surplus, would be able to get attractive yields for their short-term funds and borrowers would be able to raise resources at market-related rates. The development of a secondary market with the active participation of the PDs will improve the liquidity of CPs.

LO 17.4 CERTIFICATE OF DEPOSITS (CDs)

A CD is a document of title to a time deposit and can be distinguished from a conventional time deposit in respect of its free negotiability and, hence, marketability. In other words, CDs are a marketable receipt of funds deposited in a bank for a fixed period at a specified rate of interest. They are bearer documents/instruments and are readily negotiable. They are attractive both to the bankers and the investors in the sense that/he former is not required to encash the deposit prematurely, while the latter can sell the CDs in the secondary market before its maturity and thereby the instrument has liquidity/ready marketability.

Certificate of deposit is a marketable receipt of funds deposited in a bank for a fixed period at a specified rate of interest.

RBI Guidelines

A CD is a negotiable money market instrument, issued in a demat form or a usance promissory note for funds deposited at a bank/other eligible financial institutions (FIs) for a specified time period.

Eligibility The CDs can be issued by (i) commercial banks [excluding the RRBs/Local Area Banks (LABs)] and **(ii)** select all-India FIs permitted by the RBI to raise resources by way of term money/ deposits, certificate of deposits, CPs and inter-corporate deposits within the umbrella limit fixed by it.

Aggregate Amount Banks have freedom to issue CDs depending on their funding requirements. An FI may issue CDs within the overall umbrella limit fixed by the RBI, time to time.

Minimum Size of Issue and Denominations The minimum amount of a CD should be ₹1 lakh, that is, the minimum deposit that could be accepted from a single subscriber should not be less than ₹1 lakh and in multiples of ₹1 lakh.

Investors The CDs can be issued to individuals/corporations/companies/(including banks/PDs) trusts/funds/associations and so on. The NRIs may also subscribe to CDs on a non-repatriable basis only. They cannot be endorsed to another NRI in the secondary market.

Maturity The maturity period of a CD issued by a bank should be between 7 days (minimum) and one year (maximum). The FIs can issue CDs with maturity of 1-3 years.

Discount/Coupon Rate The CDs may be issued at a discount on face value. They can also be issued on floating rate basis provided the methodology of the compiling the floating rate is objective, transparent and market-based. The issuer is free to determine the discount/coupon rate. The interest rate on the floating rate CDs should be set periodically according to the predetermined formula that indicates the spread over a transparent benchmark. The investors should be clearly informed of the same.

Reserve Requirements Banks have to maintain the appropriate SLR and CRR on the issue price of the CDs.

Transferability The physical CDs can be freely transferred by endorsement and delivery. The demated CDs can be transferred as per the procedure applicable to other demat securities. There is no lock-in period for the CDs.

Trade in CDs The trading procedure applicable to the CPs **(discussed earlier)** is also applicable to the CDs.

Settlement All OTC traders in CDs must be cleared and settled through the authorised clearing houses of the stock exchanges, that is, NSCCL/ICCL/CCL.

Loans/Buy-backs Loans against CDs and buy-back of CDs by the issuers before maturity are not permitted.

Format The CDs should be issued only in demat form. Issuance of CDs in physical form, if any, on the insistence of the investors should be separately reported to the RBI. The issuance of CD would attract stamp duty. There would be no grace period for repayment.

Security Since physical CDs are freely transferable by endorsement and delivery, they should be printed on good quality security paper and necessary precautions should be taken to guard against tampering with the document. They should be signed by two/more authorised signatories.

Payment of Certificate Since CDs are transferable, the physical certificate may be presented for payment to the last holder. Since the question of liability on account of any defect in the chain of endorsements may arise, banks should be cautious and make payments only by a crossed cheque. The holders of the dematted CD should approach their respective Depository Participants (DPs) and give transfer/delivery instructions to transfer the demat security represented by informational securities identification number (ISIN) to the CD Redemption Account maintained by the issuer. The holder should also communicate to the issuer by a letter/fax a copy of the delivery instruction given to the DP and intimate the place at which the payment is requested to facilitate prompt payment. Upon receipt of the demat credit of CDs in the CD Redemption Account, the issuer on maturity date would arrange to pay to the holder/transferor by way of bankers cheque/high value cheque.

Duplicate Certificate Duplicate certificates can be issued in case of loss of physical certificates only in physical form after compliance with the following: **(i)** a notice in at least one local newspaper of loss of CD certificate, **(ii)** lapse of 15 days from the date of notice and **(iii)** execution of an indemnity bond by the investor tot he satisfaction of the issuer of the CD. The duplicate certificates should be only in physical form and fresh stamping would not be required.

LO 17.5 FACTORING

Factoring involves the outright sale of receivables at a discount to a factor to obtain funds.

Factoring provides resources to finance receivables as well as facilitates the collection of receivables. Although such services constitute a critical segment of the financial services scenario in the developed countries, they appeared in the Indian financial scene only in the early nineties as a result of RBI initiatives. There are two bank-sponsored organisations which provide such services: **(i)** SBI Factors and Commercial Services Ltd, and **(ii)** Canbank Factors Ltd. The first private sector factoring company, Foremost Factors Ltd, started operations since the beginning of 1997.

Definition and Mechanism

Definition Factoring can broadly be defined as an agreement in which receivables arising out of sale of goods/services are sold by a firm (client) to the 'factor' (a financial intermediary) as a result of which the title of the goods/services represented by the said receivables passes on to the factor. Henceforth, the factor becomes responsible for all credit control, sales accounting and debt collection from the buyer(s). In a full service factoring concept (without recourse facility), if any of the debtors fails to pay the dues as a result of his financial inability/insolvency/bankruptcy, the factor has to absorb the losses.

Mechanism Credit sales generate the factoring business in the ordinary course of business dealings. Realisation of credit sales is the main function of factoring services. Once a sale transaction is completed, the factor steps in to realise the sales. Thus, the factor works between the seller and the buyer and sometimes with the seller's banks together.

Functions of a Factor

Depending on the type/form of factoring, the main functions of a **factor**, in general terms, can be classified into five categories:

- Financing facility/trade debts;
- Maintenance/administration of sales ledger;
- Collection facility/of accounts receivable;
- Assumption of credit risk/credit control and credit restriction; and
- Provision of advisory services.

Factor is a financial institution that specialises in purchasing accounts receivables from business firms.

Financing Trade Debts The unique feature of factoring is that a factor purchases the book debts of his client at a price and the debts are assigned in favour of the factor who is usually willing to grant advances to the extent of, say, 80 per cent of the assigned debts. Where the debts are factored **with recourse**, the finance provided would become refundable by the client in case of non-payment of the buyer. However, where the debts are factored **without recourse**, the factor's obligation to the seller becomes absolute on the due date of the invoice whether or not the buyer makes the payment.

With recourse is the basis on which receivables are sold to the factor with the understanding that all credit risks would be borne by the firm.

Administration of Sales Ledger The factor maintains the clients' sales ledgers. On transacting a sales deal, an invoice is sent by the client to the customer and a copy of the same is sent to the factor. The ledger is generally maintained under the **open-item method** in which each receipt is matched against the specific invoice. The customer's account clearly reflects the various open invoices outstanding on any given date. The factor also gives periodic (fortnightly/weekly depending on the volume of transactions) reports to the client on the current status of his receivables, receipts of payments from the customers and other useful information. In addition, the factor also maintains a customer-wise record of payments spread over a period of time so that any change in the payment pattern can be easily identified.

Without recourse is the basis on which accounts receivables are sold to a factor with the understanding that the factor accepts all credit risks on the purchased accounts.

Provision of Collection Facility The factor undertakes to collect the receivables on behalf of the client relieving him of the problems involved in collection, and enables him to concentrate on other important functional areas of the business. This also enables the client to reduce the cost of collection by way of savings in manpower, time and efforts. The use of trained manpower with sophisticated infrastructural back-up enables a factor to systematically follow up and make timely demands on the debtors to make payments. Also, the debtors are more responsible to the demands from a factor being a credit institution.

Collection of receivables can be considered as the most important function of a factor. He is generally not required to consult the client with regard to the collection procedure. But he may consult the client if legal action has to be initiated in case of non-payment and so on.

Credit Control and Credit Restriction Assumption of credit risk is one of the important functions of a factor. This service is provided where debts are factored without recourse. The factor in consultation with the client fixes credit limits for approved customers. Within these limits, the factor undertakes to purchase all trade debts of the customer without recourse. In other words, the factor assumes the risk of default in payment by the customer. Arising from this function of the factor, there are two important incidental benefits accruing to the client: firstly, factoring relieves the client of the collection work; secondly, with access to extensive information available on the financial standing and credit rating of individual customers and their track record of payments, the factor is able to advise the client on the credit worthiness of potential customers leading to better credit control.

Operationally, the line of credit/credit limit up to which the client can sell to the customer depends on his financial position, his past payment record and the value of the goods sold by the client to the customer. One approach followed by the factors is to define the monthly sales turnover for each customer which will be automatically covered by the approved credit limit. If, for instance, the approved limit for a customer is ₹5 lakh and the average collection period is 60 days, sales up to ₹2.5 lakh [(5 × 30)/60] per month will be automatically covered. Alternatively, some factors provide periodic reports to the clients on customer-credit utilisation before any major sale is made. The credit-worthiness of customers is assessed by the factors on the basis of information from a number of sources such as credit rating reports, if available; bank reports and trade references; analysis of financial statements on the basis of current ratio, quick ratio, net profit margin and return on investment (ROI); prior collection experience; and customer visits.

Advisory Services These services are a *spin-off* of the close relationship between a factor and a client. By virtue of their specialised knowledge and experience in finance and credit dealings and access to extensive credit information, factors can provide a variety of incidental advisory services to their clients:

- Customer's perception of the client's products, changes in the marketing strategies, emerging trends and so on;
- Audit of the procedures followed for invoicing, delivery and dealing with sales returns;
- Introduction to the credit department of a bank/subsidiaries of banks engaged in leasing, hire-purchase and merchant banking.

Cost of Services The factors provide various services at a charge. The charge for collection and sales ledger administration is in the form of a commission expressed as a per cent of debt purchased. It is collected up-front/in advance. The commission for short-term financing as advance part-payment is in the form of interest charge for the period between the date of advance payment and the date of collection/guaranteed payment date. It is also known as **discount charge**.

Discount charge is the interest charge for short-term financing by the factor for the period between the date of advance payment and date of guaranteed payment/collection.

Advantages and Evaluation

Advantages Factoring has several positive features from the point of view of the firm (client of the factor). Some of these advantages are briefly discussed as follows:

Impact on the Balance Sheet The impact of factoring on the balance sheet of the client and its implications are illustrated in Tables 17.1 and 17.2.

TABLE 17.1 Balance Sheet: Pre-Factoring Scenario

(₹ lakh)

Current liabilities			*Current assets*	
Bank borrowings:			Inventory	100
Cash credit against inventory	70		Receivables	80
Cash credit against receivables	40	110	Other current assets	20
Other current liabilities (OCL)		40		
Net working capital (NWC)		50		
Total current liabilities + NWC		200	Total current assets	200

Current ratio = 1.33:1

The requirement of NWC is ₹50 lakh (current assets minus current liabilities). As the borrower carries other current liabilities to the extent of ₹40 lakh, he is eligible for a maximum permissible bank finance (MPBF)/ working capital limit of ₹110 lakh. This is bifurcated into cash credit limits of ₹70 lakh against inventory and ₹40 lakh against receivables, taking into account the stipulated margins for inventory and receivables and also the proportion of individual levels of inventory of ₹100 lakh and receivables of ₹80 lakh.

On the basis of the above configuration, the borrower is eligible for working capital limits aggregating ₹110 lakh under the second method of lending.

Assume the borrower decides to factor his debts. The factoring transaction is as follows: Receivables aggregating ₹80 lakh are purchased by a factor who makes prepayment of 80 per cent, that is, ₹64 lakh. He retains ₹16 lakh (factor reserve) which will be repaid on payment by the customer. The impact on the balance sheet is shown in Table 17.2.

TABLE 17.2 Balance Sheet: Post-Factoring Scenario

(₹ lakh)

Current liabilities			*Current assets*	
Bank borrowings:			Inventory	100
Cash credit against inventory	70		Receivables	16
Cash credit against receivables	—	70	Other current assets	20
Other current liabilities (OCL)		16		
Net working capital (NWC)		50		
Total current liabilities + NWC		136	Total current assets	136

Current ratio = 1.58:1

The impact of factoring on the balance sheet as revealed by Tables 17.1 and 17.2 is three fold:

Off-balance Sheet Financing As the client's debts are purchased by the factor, the finance provided by him is off the balance sheet and appears in the balance sheet only as a contingent liability in the case of recourse factoring. In case of non-recourse factoring, it does not appear anywhere in the financial statements of the borrower. The prepayment of ₹64 lakh made by the factor goes off the balance sheet getting converted into cash, leaving the balance of ₹16 lakh in the balance sheet as due from the factor.

Reduction of Current Liabilities From the factoring proceeds of ₹64 lakh, the bank borrowings are liquidated to the extent of ₹40 lakh. The balance of ₹24 lakh can be used by the client for paying off other current liabilities comprising of trade creditors for goods and services, creditors for expenses, loan instalments payable, statutory liabilities and provisions. The client may meet any of these obligations with the balance of ₹24 lakh. The net effect is to reduce current liabilities by ₹64 lakh.

Improvement in Current Ratio As the factoring transaction is off the balance sheet, it removes from the asset side the receivables factored to the extent of the prepayment made and on the liabilities side, the current liabilities are also reduced. The result is a desirable improvement in the current ratio, from 1.33:1 to 1.58:1.

In brief, the effect of factoring is to improve the financial discipline of the firm.

Higher Credit Standing There are several reasons why factoring should improve a client's standing. With cash flow accelerated by factoring, the client is able to meet his liabilities promptly as and when they arise. The factor's acceptance of the client's receivables itself speaks highly of the quality of the receivables. In the case of non-recourse factoring, the factor's assumption of credit risk relieves the client, to a significant extent, from the problem of bad debts. This enables him to minimise his bad debts reserve.

Improved Efficiency In order to accelerate cash flow, it is essential to ensure the flow of critical information for decision making and follow-up and eliminate delays and wastage of man-hours. This requires sophisticated infrastructure for high level specialisation in credit control and sales ledger administration. Small and medium-sized units are likely to face a resource constraint in this area. Factoring is designed to place such units on the same level of efficiency in the areas of credit control and sales ledger administration as that of the more sophisticated large companies.

More Time for Planning and Production In any business concern, it is inevitable that a certain proportion of management time has to be diverted to credit control. Large companies can afford to have special departments for the purpose. However, smaller units cannot afford it. The factor undertakes the responsibility for credit control, sales ledger administration and debt collection problems. Thus, the client can concentrate on functional areas of the business line planning, purchase, production, marketing and finance.

Reduction of Cost and Expenses Since the client need not have a special administrative set-up to look after credit control, he can have the benefit of reduced overheads by way of savings on manpower, time and efforts. With the steady and reliable cash flow facilitated by factoring, the clients have many opportunities to cut costs and expenses like taking supplier's prompt payment and quantity discounts, ordering for materials at the right time and at the right place, avoidance of disruption in the production schedule, and so on.

Additional Source The supplier gets an additional source of funding the receivables which eliminates the uncertainty associated with the collection cycle. More importantly, funds from a factor is an additional source of finance for the client outside the purview of bank credit.

Evaluation Framework The distinct advantages of factoring notwithstanding, it does involve costs. The evaluation framework should be on a consideration of the relative costs and benefits associated with the two alternatives to receivables management. They are: **(i)** in-house management by the firm itself, **(ii)** factoring service, either recourse or non-recourse. The relevant costs and benefits associated with these are listed below.

Cost Associated with In-house Management **(i)** cash discount, **(ii)** cost of funds invested in receivables, **(iii)** bad debts, **(iv)** lost contribution on foregone sales and **(v)** avoidable costs of sales ledger administration and credit monitoring.

Costs Associated with Recourse and Non-recourse Factoring **(i)** factoring commission, **(ii)**, discount charge and **(iii)** cost of long-term funds invested in receivables.

Benefits Associated with Recourse Factoring They are in terms of the costs associated with the in-house management alternative with the exception of item **(iii)**, namely, bad debt loss.

Benefit Associated with Non-Recourse Factoring The above plus the bad debt losses relevant to in-house management of receivables.

The evaluation framework of factoring is elaborated in Example 17.1.

Example 17.1

The Reliance Industries Ltd (RIL) is presently managing its accounts receivable internally by the sales and credit department. Its credit terms for sales are 2/10 net, 30. The past experience of RIL has been that on an average 30 per cent of the customers avail of the discount, while the balance of the receivables is collected on an average 60 days after the invoice date. Further, 2 per cent of the sales turnover results in bad debts.

The firm is financing its investments in receivables through a mix of bank finance and long-term finance (own funds) in the ratio of 2:1. The effective rate of interest on bank finance is 12 per cent and the cost of own funds is 15 per cent.

The projected sales for the next year is ₹500 lakh. The credit and collection department spends on an average one-fourth of its time on collection of receivables.

A proposal to avail of factoring service from Fairgrowth Factors Ltd (FFL) as an alternative to in-house management of receivables collection and credit monitoring is under the consideration of the Board of Directors of the RIL. If the proposal, details of which are given as follows, is accepted, it is expected that the projected sales for the next year can increase by ₹50 lakh as a result of the diversion of the time of the executives of the sales, credit and collection department to sales promotion. For the type of product the RIL is producing, the gross margin on sales in the past has been 20 per cent. Moreover, there would be a saving in administrative overheads amounting to ₹2.5 lakh due to discontinuance of sales ledger administration and credit monitoring.

According to the factoring proposal, the FFL offers a guaranteed payment of 30 days. The other details are listed as follows:

The FFL would advance 80 per cent and 85 per cent in case of recourse and non-recourse factoring deals respectively, the balance would be retained as factor reserve. The discount charge in advance (up-front) would be 13 per cent of recourse type and 14 per cent for non-recourse type of service. The FFL would also charge a commission @ 2 per cent (recourse) and 4 per cent (non-recourse). The commission is payable up-front.

Before taking a decision on the proposal, the Board seeks your advice as a financial consultant, on the course of action. What advice would you give? Why?

Solution

Relevant Costs: In-House Management Alternative

	Relevant costs	*Amount (₹ lakh)*	
1.	Cash discount	3.0	(₹500 × 0.02 × 0.30)
2.	Cost of funds in receivables	8.125	(Working note 1)
3.	Bad debt losses	10.0	(₹500 × 0.02)
4.	Lost contribution on foregone sales	9.0	₹50 × (0.20 – 0.02 Bad debts)
5.	Avoidable administrative overheads	2.50	
	Total	32.625	

Working Note (1)

Cost of funds invested in receivables:

Average collection period = (10 days × 0.3) + (60 days × 0.70) = 45 days

Cost of bank finance = ₹500 lakh × 2/3 × 45/360 × 0.12 = ₹5.0 lakh

Cost of own funds = ₹500 lakh × 1/3 × 45/360 × 0.15 = 3.125 lakh

Total = ₹8.125 lakh

Relevant Costs: Recourse Factoring Alternative

Relevant costs	Amount (₹ lakh)	
6. Factoring commission	11.0	(₹550 × 0.02)
7. Discount charge	4.671	(Working note 2)
8. Cost of long-term funds invested in receivables	1.485	[(₹550 – ₹431.2) × 0.15 × 30/360)]
Total	17.156	

Working Note (2)

Eligible amount of advance = 0.80 × (₹550 – ₹11) = ₹431.2 lakh

Discount charge = ₹431.2 × 0.13 × 30/360 = ₹4.671 lakh

Relevant Costs: Non-recourse Factoring Alternative

Relevant costs	Amount (₹ lakh)	
9. Factoring commission	22.0	(₹550 × 0.04)
10. Discount charge	5.236	(Working note 3)
11. Cost of long-term funds invested in receivables	1.265	[(₹550 – ₹448.8) × 0.15 × 30/360)]
Total	28.501	

Working Note (3)

Eligible amount of advance = 0.85 × (₹550 – ₹22) = ₹448.8 lakh

Discount charge = ₹448.8 × 0.14 × 30/360 = ₹5.236 lakh

Decision Analysis: Recourse Factoring (₹ lakh)

Benefits (₹32.625 – ₹10.00 Bad debts yet to be met by RIL)	22.625
Costs	17.156
Net benefits	5.469

Decision Analysis: Non-Recourse Factoring (₹ lakh)

Benefits (₹32.625 + ₹1.00 Bad debts loss to be borne by factor)	33.625
Costs	28.501
Net benefits	5.124

Alternatively, incremental analysis approach can be used for the decision.

(i) Incremental Analysis to Decide whether the Company should go for Recourse Factoring or not.

Particulars		Amount (₹ lakh)
Incremental Benefits		
1. Incremental contribution on additional sales (₹50 × 0.18)	₹9.00	
2. Savings in cost of investment in receivables (₹8.125 – 1.485)	6.64	
3. Savings in avoidable administrative overheads	2.50	
4. Savings in cash discount	3.00	21.14
Incremental Costs		
5. Factoring commission	11.00	
6. Discount charge	4.671	15.671
Net benefits		5.469

(ii) Incremental Analysis to decide whether the Company should go for Non-Recourse Factoring or Not

Particulars		Amount (₹ lakh)
Incremental Benefits		
1. Incremental profit on additional sales (₹50 × 0.20)	₹10.00	
2. Savings in cost of investment in receivables (₹8.125 – 1.265)	6.86	
3. Savings in avoidable administrative overheads	2.50	
4. Savings in cash discount	3.00	
5. Savings in existing bad debts (₹500 lakh × .02)	10.00	32.36
Incremental costs		
6. Factoring commission	22.00	
7. Discount charge	5.236	27.236
Net benefits		5.124

As a financial consultant, my advice to the Board of RIL would be to choose recourse factoring due to higher net benefits.

Factoring in India

Factoring service is of recent origin in India. There was no codified legal framework to regulate factoring in India. The legal relationship between the factor and the client was governed by the provisions of the factoring contract. In recognition of the importance of the factoring services in the emerging financial services scenario in the country, the legal framework relating to them has been codified recently. The three elements of the framework are: **(i)** Factoring Regulation Act (FRA) 2011, **(ii)** Registration of Assignment of Receivables (Government) Rules, 2012, and **(iii)** RBI's Non-Banking Financial Company – Factor Directions, 2012. The main elements of the Factoring Act are discussed below.

The object of the **FRA** is to provide for and regulate **(i)** assignment of receivables through registration and **(ii)** rights and obligations of partners to the contract for assignment of receivables. **Assignment** means transfer by agreement of individual interest of any assignor in any receivable due from any debtors in favour of a factor in India or abroad. However, individual interest would not include creation of rights in receivables as security for loans/advances/other obligations by a bank/financial institution. **Debtor** means any person liable to the assignor to pay any receivables/discharge any obligation in respect of the receivables. The main provisions of the FRA are: **(i)** registration of factors,**(ii)** assignment of receivables, **(iii)** rights and obligations of parties to the contract for assignment of receivables, **(iv)** registration of assignments, **(v)** offences and penalties and **(vi)** miscellaneous.

> **Assignment** means transfer by agreement of individual interest of any assignor in any receivable due from any debtors in favour of a factor in India or abroad.

> **Debtor** means any person liable to the assignor to pay any receivables/ discharge any obligation in respect of the receivables.

Registration of Factors To commence/carry on factoring business by a factor, a certificate of registration from the RBI is necessary excepting a bank/Government company/company under the Companies Act. **Factoring business** means the business of acquisition of receivables of assignor (i.e. the owner of any receivables) by accepting or financing their assignment by way of loans/advances or otherwise against the security interest over any receivables but excludes **(i)** credit facilities by banks in the ordinary course of business against the security of receivables, and **(ii)** any activity **(a)** as commission agent or otherwise for sale of agricultural produce/

> **Factoring business** means the business of acquisition of receivables of **assignor** (i.e. the owner of any receivables) by accepting or financing their assignment by way of loans/advances or otherwise against the security interest over any receivables.

goods of any kind, **(b)** relating to production, storage, supply, distribution, acquisition or control of such produce/goods or provision of any services. **Factor** means a RBI-registered NBFC, a body corporate, a bank, a company engaged in factoring business.

An existing NBFC engaged in factoring business would be granted registration by the RBI only if factoring is its **principal business** in terms of at least 50 per cent of its **(i)** assets are financial assets and **(ii)** gross income from factoring business. The provisions of the RBI Act relating to the registration of NBFCs would *mutatis mutandis* apply to factors also. (**These are discussed in Chapter 1**). All factors would be governed by RBI Act/rules/directions/guidelines. All provisions of Chapter III-B of the RBI Act relating to the NBFCs would apply *mutatis mutandis* to a factor. The RBI may at any time by general/special order direct a factor to furnish statements/ information/ particulars relating to its business in the specified form/intervals/time. It may also issue directions in the interest of **(a)** business enterprise (i.e. enterprise/medium/micro/small enterprise in terms of Micro, Small and Medium Enterprise Development Act) availing of factoring services, **(b)** factors, **(c)** other stakeholders in respect of any matters relating to/connected with their factoring business.

Assignment of Receivables Any assignor (i.e. owner of the receivables) may by a written agreement assign any receivables due/payable to him by any debtor in favour of a factor as an **assignee** for a mutually agreed consideration. The assignor should disclose to the assignee any defences/rights of set-off available to the debtor. All the rights/remedies and any security interest created over any property exclusively to secure the due payment of the receivables would vest in the assignee who will have an absolute right to recover it and exercise all the rights/remedies of the assignor. **Property** means **(i)** movable/immovable property, **(ii)** any secured/unsecured debt/right to receive payment of money, **(iii)** receivables, and **(iv)** intangible assets (i.e. know-how, patent, copyright, design, trade mark, licence, franchise or another similar business/ commercial right). **Receivables** mean all/part of, or individual interest in, any existing/ future/accruing/conditional/contingent right of any person under a contract including international contract to payment of toll or any other monetary sum, by whatever name called, for the use of any infrastructure facility/services. The assignee/factor would pay to a bank/creditor the consideration for assignment of receivables constituting security for repayment of any loan in case the assignor/owner of the receivables has given notice of the encumbrance.

Property means **(i)** movable/ immovable property, **(ii)** any secured/unsecured debt/right to receive payment of money, **(iii)** receivables, and **(iv)** intangible assets.

Receivables mean all/part of, or individual interest in, any existing/ future/accruing/ conditional/ contingent right of any person under a contract including international contract to payment of toll or any other monetary sum for the use of any infrastructure facility/services.

A notice of assignment should be given to the debtor by the assignor/assignee with express authority in favour of the assignor to demand/receive payment from the debtor. Payment made to the assignee would fully discharge the debtor from corresponding liability in respect of such payment. Where such a notice is not given, any payment by the debtor to the assignor would be held in trust for the benefit of the assignee and paid forth to him/duly authorised agent.

Rights and Obligations of Parties to Contract for Assignment of Receivables The rights/obligations of the respective parties relate to: **(i)** notice of assignment, **(ii)** liability of debtors, **(iii)** assignors to be trustees of assignee, **(iv)** principle of debtor protection, **(v)** liability of debtor in case of micro/small enterprises, **(vi)** defences and rights of set-off of debtors, **(vii)** modification of original contract and **(viii)** breach of contract.

Notice of Assignment The debtor would have the right to notice of assignment to make payment to the assignee failing which he would be entitled to make payments to the assignor(s) in accordance with the original contract in full discharge of his corresponding liability under the original contract.

Liability of Debtors In case of the notice of assignment, the debtor would be **(i)** **(a)** obliged to intimate the assignee the details of deposits/advances/payments on account already made to the assignor, **(b)** provide any other information sought by the assignor; **(ii)** entitled to a valid discharge of his liability only by making payment to the assignee.

Assignor to be Trustee of Assignee A payment due on an assigned receivables by a debtor to an assignor would be deemed to be for the benefit of the assignee and as a trustee the assignor should pay the amount to the assignee.

Liability of Debtor in Case of Micro/Small Enterprises In the event of delay in payment of receivables of a micro/small enterprise by a debtor, the assignee would be entitled to interest for the delayed period under the provisions of the Micro/Small and Medium Enterprises Development Act and he should take necessary steps to recover the interest on behalf of the assignor.

Principles of Debtor Protection The rights/obligations of a debtor including the terms/conditions of the contract can be changed only with his written consent. Consequent upon the assignment of receivables, however, no changes can be made in the payment instruction between the debtor and the assignor in regard to the original: **(i)** amount of debt, **(ii)** place of payment, and **(iii)** date of payment/other terms relating to payment.

Defences and Rights of Set-off of Debtor In any claim of payment by any assignee, the debtor may raise all defences/rights of set-off arising from the original contract which he could avail of as if the assignment had not been made and the claim was made by the assignor and not the assignee. The assignee would be entitled to recover from the assignor any loss suffered resulting from the defences/rights of set-off. The debtor may also raise against the assignee any other right of set-off if it was available to it at the time the notice of assignment from the assignor/assignee was received by him.

Modification of Original Contract Any modification in the original contract before notice of assignment of receivables between the assignor and the debtor would be binding on the assignee and he will acquire the modified rights in the assigned receivables. However, any modification made after the notice of agreement adversely affecting the rights of the assignee would be effective against him only with his consent as a reasonable assignee.

Breach of Contract If the assignor commits any breach of the original contract, the debtor would not be entitled to recover from the assignee any sum paid to the assignor/assignee pursuant to the factoring transaction. He would, however, have the right to claim from the assignor any loss/damages caused to him by the breach.

Registration of Assignments For purposes of registration, factors should file the particulars of every transaction of assignment of receivables in his favour with the Central Registry set up under the provisions of the Securitisation and Reconstruction of Financial Assets and Enforcement of Security Interest (SRFAESI) Act within 30 days from the date of assignment in the prescribed manner and on payment of the specified fee. The receivables may be described specifically/generally with reference to the debtor/period to which they relate/other identifiable general description. The central registry would maintain a central register to enter the particulars of the transaction(s) in favour of factor(s). The provisions for registration of transactions contained in the SRFAESI Act/rules would, *mutatis* *mutandis*, apply to the record of assignment of receivables in favour of a factor in the Central Register with the Central Registry.[1]

The particulars of transactions of assignment of receivables entered in the Central Register would be open for inspection by any person on payment of the prescribed fee. The provisions for maintenance of Central Register and its public inspection contained in the SRFAESI Act/rule would, *mutatis mutandis* apply.[1]

Offences and Penalties ***Penalties*** **(i)** Default in filing penalties of any transaction with the Central Registry would be punishable with fine upto five thousand rupees for every day of default; **(ii)** Penalty for non-compliance of any direction of the RBI may extend upto five lakh rupees payable within 14 days and upto ten thousand rupees for every day of continuing default. Failure to pay within the specified period would be punishable with a levy/sum specified by the principal civil court/having jurisdiction in the area where the registered office/principal business of the factor is located. The levy would be enforceable in the same manner as if it were a decree made by the court in a civil suit.

Offences Contravention/attempt to contravention/abetment to contravention of the provisions of the Factoring Regulation Act/rules, for which no penalty has been provided, would be punishable with imprisonment upto one year or with fine or with both.

In case of an offence by a factor, the factor as well as every person who was in charge of/ responsible to the factor for the conduct of business would be deemed to be guilty of offence and punished accordingly, unless it is proved that the offence was committed without his knowledge and he exercised due diligence to prevent commission of the offence.

Miscellaneous Some other provisions of the **FRA**, namely, confidentiality of information, inapplicability of provisions and stamp duty exemption, are discussed below:

Confidentiality of Information A factor should maintain confidentiality and not disclose to any person information obtained by it from any **(i)** assignor, **(ii)** present/future customers, **(iii)** its commercial/ business activities and **(iv)** the term of sale between the assignor and any debtor and other details about the assignor except when required by order of a court/tribunal/other statutory authority.

SUMMARY

LO 17.1	Typically, working capital requirements/current assets are financed by a combination of long-term and short-term sources. The important traditional short-term sources of current assets financing are trade credit and bank credit. Two newly emerging sources of working capital finance are factoring and commercial papers.
	Trade credit represents credit extended by suppliers of goods and services in the normal course of transactions of the firm. As cash is not paid immediately for purchase but after an agreed period of time, the deferral of payment (trade credit) represents a source of finance for credit purchases (current assets). It does not involve any explicit interest charge/cost. The implicit cost of trade credit depends on the terms offered by the supplier of goods. When the terms include cash discount for prompt payment, the cost of trade credit is generally very high beyond the discount period.
LO 17.2	Bank credit is the single most important institutional source of working capital finance. It is provided mainly in three forms (i) cash credit/overdraft, **(ii)** loans, and **(iii)** purchase/discount of bills. Of these, loans contribute the most important component. The security for working capital advances by banks is in the form of hypothetication or pledge.

[1]For details refer to Khan, M Y, *Indian Financial System*, McGraw Hill Education (India), 2018, Chapter 11.

LO 17.3

Commercial papers which are unsecured promissory notes issued by firms which enjoy high credit rating are emerging as an innovative short-term source of current assets financing.

LO 17.4

Certificates of deposit is negotiable instrument issued in demat form or as usance promissory note for funds deposited at banks/FIs for a specified time period. It is a marketable receipt of funds. The framework of CD market is prescribed by the RBI.

LO 17.5

Factoring means the sale of receivables (book debts) by a firm (client) to a financial intermediary (factor) who pays when they are collected or in a guaranteed payment date. It basically involves transfer of collection of receivables and the related maintenance of records from the client to the factor. In essence, factoring is a source of financing of receivables and facilitates the process of their collection

- Depending on the type of factoring, the main functions of a factor, in general terms, are five-fold: **(i)** maintenance of sales ledger, **(ii)** collection of receivables, **(iii)** financing of trade debts, **(iv)** assumption of credit risk/control/protection and **(v)** provision of advisory services. For providing these services, the factors levy two types of charges. The charge for collection of receivables and sales ledger administration in the form of a commission/fee payable in advance expressed as a flat percentage of the value of the debt purchased. The charge for short-term financing in the form of advance part-payment is an interest charge/discount charge for the period between date of advance payment and the date of collection/guaranteed payment date.
- On the basis of the features built into the factoring deal to cater to the varying needs of the trade/ clients, there are different types of factoring. The main classification of factoring arrangements are: (a) Recourse and non-recourse based on the assumption of credit risk associated with the collection of the receivables, (b) Advance, maturing and participation factoring related to the time of payment on account of receivables by the factor to the client, (c) Full factoring, (d) Disclosed and undisclosed factoring on the basis of the disclosure/non-disclosure of the name of the factor in the invoice, (e) Domestic and export/cross-border/international factoring based on the domicile of the parties involved.
- There is no codified legal framework to regulate factoring in India. The legal relationship between the factor and the client is governed by the provisions of the factoring contract.
- Domestic factoring, as a fund-based service, differs from bills discounting and export factoring from forfaiting which finances deferred credit transactions related to exports.
- Factoring offers several advantages to a client including (1) off-balance sheet financing, (2) reduction in current liabilities, (3) improvement in current ratio, (4) higher credit standing, (5) improved efficiency, (6) reduction of costs (7) additional sources and of funds so on. However it involves a cost in terms of fee and discount charge and evaluation of factoring should be done as a cost-benefit analysis before resorting to factoring.
- Factoring offers several advantages to a client including (1) off-balance sheet financing, (2) reduction in current liabilities, (3) improvement in current ratio, (4) higher credit standing, (5) improved efficiency, (6) reduction of costs (7) additional sources and of funds so on. However it involves a cost in terms of fee and discount charge and evaluation of factoring should be done as a cost-benefit analysis before resorting to factoring.
- There was no codified legal framework to regulate factoring in India. The legal relationship between the factor and the client was governed by the provisions of the factoring contract. In recognition of the importance of the factoring services in the emerging financial services scenario in the country, the legal framework relating to them has been codified recently. The three elements of the framework are: **(i)** Factoring Regulation Act (FRA) 2011, **(ii)** Registration of Assignment of Receivables (Government) Rules, 2012, and **(iii)** RBI's Non-Banking Financial Company – Factor Directions, 2012.

LO 17.5

- The object of the **FRA** is to provide for and regulate **(i)** assignment of receivables through registration and **(ii)** rights and obligations of partners to the contract for assignment of receivables. **Assignment** means transfer by agreement of individual interest of any assignor in any receivable due from any debtors in favour of a factor in India or abroad. Debtor means any person liable to the assignor to pay any receivables/discharge any obligation in respect of the receivables. The main provisions of the FRA are: **(i)** registration of factors, **(ii)** assignment of receivables, **(iii)** rights and obligations of parties to the contract for assignment of receivables, **(iv)** registration of assignments, **(v)** offences and penalties and **(vi)** miscellaneous.
- To commence/carry on factoring business by a factor, a certificate of registration from the RBI is necessary excepting a bank/Government company/company under the Companies Act. **Factoring business** means the business of acquisition of receivables of assignor (i.e. the owner of any receivables) by accepting or financing their assignment by way of loans/advances or otherwise against the security interest over any receivables. Factor means a RBI-registered NBFC, a body corporate, a bank, a company engaged in factoring business.
- All factors would be governed by RBI Act/rules/directions/guidelines. All provisions of Chapter III-B of the RBI Act relating to the NBFCs would apply mutatis mutandis to a factor.
- Any assignor (i.e. owner of the receivables) may by a written agreement assign any receivables due/payable to him by any debtor in favour of a factor as an **assignee** for a mutually agreed consideration. All the rights/remedies and any security interest created over any property exclusively to secure the due payment of the receivables would vest in the assignee who will have an absolute right to recover it and exercise all the rights/remedies of the assignor. **Receivables** mean all/part of, or individual interest in, any existing/future/accruing/conditional/contingent right of any person under a contract including international contract to payment of toll or any other monetary sum, by whatever name called, for the use of any infrastructure facility/services.
- The rights/obligations of the respective parties relate to: **(i)** notice of assignment, **(ii)** liability of debtors, **(iii)** assignors to be trustees of assignee, **(iv)** principle of debtor protection, **(v)** liability of debtor in case of micro/small enterprises, **(vi)** defences and rights of set-off of debtors, **(vii)** modification of original contract and **(viii)** breach of contract.
- The debtor would have the right to notice of assignment to make payment to the assignee.
- In case of the notice of assignment, the debtor would be entitled to a valid discharge of his liability only by making payment to the assignee.
- A payment due on an assigned receivables by a debtor to an assignor would be deemed to be for the benefit of the assignee.
- In the event of delay in payment of receivables of a micro/small enterprise by a debtor, the assignee would be entitled to interest for the delayed period under.
- Consequent upon the assignment of receivables, however, no changes can be made in the payment instruction between the debtor and the assignor in regard to the original: **(i)** amount of debt, **(ii)** place of payment, and **(iii)** date of payment/other terms relating to payment.
- If the assignor commits any breach of the original contract, the debtor would not be entitled to recover from the assignee any sum paid to the assignor/assignee pursuant to the factoring transaction.
- For purposes of registration, factors should file the particulars of every transaction of assignment of receivables in his favour with the Central Registry set up under the provisions of the Securitisation and Reconstruction of Financial Assets and Enforcement of Security Interest (SRFAESI) Act within 30 days from the date of assignment in the prescribed manner and on payment of the specified fee.
- Default in filing details of any transaction with the Central Registry would be punishable with fine upto five thousand rupees for every day of default; **(ii)** Penalty for non-compliance of any direction of the RBI may extend upto five lakh rupees payable within 14 days and upto ten thousand rupees for every day of continuing default. Failure to pay within the specified period would be punishable with a levy/sum specified by the principal civil.
- Contravention/attempt to contravention/abetment to contravention of the provisions of the Factoring Regulation Act/rules, for which no penalty has been provided, would be punishable with imprisonment upto one year or with fine or with both.

SOLVED PROBLEMS

P.17.1 The turnover of R Ltd is ₹60 lakh of which 80 per cent is on credit. Debtors are allowed one month to clear off the dues. A factor is willing to advance 90 per cent of the bills raised on credit for a fee of 2 per cent a month plus a commission of 4 per cent on the total amount of debts. R. Ltd as a result of this arrangement is likely to save ₹21,600 annually in management costs and avoid bad debts at 1 per cent on the credit sales. LO 17.5 LOD M

A bank has come forward to make an advance equal to 90 per cent of the debts at an annual interest rate of 18 per cent. However, its processing fee will be at 2 per cent on the debts. Would you accept factoring or the offer from the bank?

Solution

Cost of factoring:		
Fee (0.02 × 0.90 × ₹4,00,000)[@]		₹7,200
Commission (0.04 × ₹4,00,000)		16,000
		23,200
Less: Savings in cost:		
Management costs (₹21,600 ÷ 12)	₹1,800	
Savings in bad debts (0.01 × ₹4,00,000)	4,000	5,800
Net cost of factoring		17,400
Cost of bank advance:		
Interest (0.18 × 1/12 × 0.90 × ₹4,00,000)		5,400
Processing fee (0.02 × ₹4,00,000)		8,000
Bad debts (0.01 × ₹4,00,000)		4,000
		17,400

[@](Annual credit sales ₹48 lakh ÷ 12 months)

Note: It is assumed that R Ltd will continue to incur management costs.

Since the costs of both the alternatives are equal, R Ltd is likely to be indifferent between factoring and bank advance.

P.17.2 The Udar Ltd sells goods on credit. Its current annual credit sales amount to ₹900 lakh. The variable cost ratio is 80 per cent. The credit terms are 2/10, net 30. On the current level of sales, the bad debts are 0.75 per cent. The past experience has been that 50 per cent of the customers avail of the cash discount, the remaining customers pay on an average 50 days after the date of sale. LO 17.5 LOD D

The book debts (receivables) of the firm are presently being financed in the ratio of 2:1 by a mix of bank borrowings and owned funds which cost per annum 25 per cent and 28 per cent respectively.

As an alternative to the in-house management of receivables, Udar Ltd is contemplating use of full advance non-recourse factoring deal with the Indbank Factors Ltd. The main elements of such a deal structured by the factor are (i) factor reserve, 15 per cent; **(ii)** guaranteed payment date, 24 days after the date of purchase; **(iii)** discount charge, 22 per cent and (iv) commission for other services (payable up-front), 4 per cent of the value of receivables.

The finance manager of Udar Ltd seeks your advice, as a consultant, on the cost-benefit of the factoring arrangement. What advice would you give? You can make your own assumptions, where necessary.

Solution

Relevant Costs: In-House Management Alternative

Relevant costs		*Amount (₹ lakh)*
Cash discount	9.00	(₹900 × 0.02 × 0.5)
Cost of funds in receivables	19.50	(*working note 1*)
Bad debt losses	6.75	(₹900 × 0.0075)
Total	35.25	

Working Note

1. Cost of funds invested in receivables:

Average collection period = (10 days × 0.5) + (50 days × 0.5) = 30 days

Average investment in debtors = ₹900 lakh/12 = ₹75 lakh

Cost of bank funds = (₹75 lakh × 2/3 × 0.25) = ₹12.5 lakh

Cost of owned funds = ₹75 lakh × 1/3 × 0.28) = ₹7 lakh

Total cost = ₹12.5 lakh + ₹7 lakh = ₹19.5 lakh

Decision Analysis: Non-recourse Factoring Alternative

Relevant costs		*Amount (₹ lakh)*
Factoring commission	36.00	(₹900 × 0.04)
Discount charge	10.77	(working note 2)
Cost of owned funds invested in receivables	3.09	(₹900 lakh – ₹734.4 lakh) × 0.28 × 24/360
Total	49.86	

Working Note

2. Eligible amount of advance = 0.85 × (₹900 lakh – ₹36 lakh) = ₹734.4 lakh

Discount charge = (₹734.4 lakh × 0.22 × 24/360) = ₹10.77 lakh

Decision Analysis: Cost Benefit of Non-recourse Factoring

	Amount (₹ lakh)
Benefits (savings of cost as per in-house management alternative)	35.25
Cost (of non-recourse factoring alternative)	49.86
Net loss	(14.61)

Recommendation Udar Limited should not go for the factoring alternative.

MINI CASES

17.C.1 (Factoring) Sunlight Industries Ltd manages its accounts receivables internally by its sales and credit department. The cost of sales ledger administration stands at ₹9 crore annually. It supplies chemicals to heavy industries. These chemicals are used as raw material for further use or are directly sold to industrial units for consumption. There is good demand for both the types of uses. For the direct consumers, the company has a credit policy of 2/10, net 30. Past experience of the company has been that on average 40 per cent of the customers avail of the discount while the balance of the receivables are collected on average 75 days after the invoice date. Sunlight Industries also has small dealer networks that sell the chemicals. Bad debts of the company are currently 1.5 per cent of total sales.

Sunlight Industries finances its investment in debtors through a mix of bank credit and own long-term funds in the ratio of 60:40. The current cost of bank credit and long-term funds are 12 per cent and 15 per cent respectively.

There has been a consistent rise in the sales of the company due to its proactive measures in cost reduction and maintaining good relations with dealers and customers. The projected sales for the next year are ₹800 crore, up 15 per cent from last year. Gross profits have been maintained at a healthy 22 per cent over the years and are expected to continue in future.

With escalating cost associated with the in-house management of debtors coupled with the need to unburden the management with the task so as to focus on sales promotion, the CEO of Sunlight Industries is examining the possibility of outsourcing its factoring service for managing its receivables. He assigns the responsibility to Anita Guha, the CFO of Sunlight. Two proposals, the details of which are given below, are available for Anita's consideration.

Proposal from Canbank Factors Ltd: The main elements of the proposal are: (i) Guaranteed payment within 30 days (i) Advance, 88 per cent and 84 per cent for the resource and non-recourse arrangements respectively **(iii)** Discount charge in advance, 21 per cent for with recourse and 22 per cent without recourse (iv) Commission, 4.5 per cent without recourse and 2.5 per cent with recourse.

Proposal from Indbank Factors: (i) Guaranteed payment within 30 days **(ii)** Advance, 84 per cent with recourse and 80 per cent without recourse **(iii)** Discount charge upfront, without recourse 21 per cent and with recourse, 20 per cent and (iv) Commission upfront, without recourse 3.6 per cent and with recourse 1.8 per cent.

The opinion of the Chief Marketing Manager is that in the context of the factoring arrangement, his staff would be able to exclusively focus on sales promotion which would result in additional sales of ₹75 crore.

Required The CFO of Sunlight Industries seeks your advice as a financial consultant on the alternative proposals. What advice would you give? Why? Calculations can be upto one digit only.

Solution

Financial Analysis of Receivables Management Alternatives (₹ crore)

(A) In-house Management:

Cash discount (₹800 crore × 0.40 × 0.02)	₹6.4
Bad debts (₹800 crore × 0.015)	12.0
Opportunity cost (Foregone contribution on lost sales) [₹75 crore × 0.205 net of bad debts]	15.4
Avoidable administrative and selling expenses	9.0
Cost of investment in receivables@	14.4
Total cost	57.2

@ Average collection period (0.40 × 10 days) + (.60 × 75 days) = 49 days

Investment in debtors = ₹800 crore × 49/360 = ₹108.9 crore

Cost of investment in debtors: (₹108.9 × 0.60 × 0.12) + (₹108.9 × 0.40 × 0.15) = ₹14.4 crore

(B) Canbank Factors Proposal:

	With recourse	Without recourse
Factoring commission (₹875 crore × 0.025)	21.9	—
(₹875 crore × 0.045)	—	39.4
Discount charge (₹750.7* crore × 0.21 × 30/360)	13.1	-
(₹701.9** × 0.22 × 30/360)	—	12.9
Cost of long-term funds invested in debtors:		
[(₹875 crore – ₹750.7 crore) × 0.15 × 30/360]	1.6	—
[(₹875 – ₹701.9 crore) × 0.15 × 30/360]	—	2.2
	36.6	54.5

* Amount of advance = 0.88 × (₹875 crore – ₹21.9 crore) = ₹750.7 crore

** Amount of advance = 0.84 × (₹875 crore – ₹39.4 crore) = ₹701.9 crore

(C) Indbank Factors Proposal:

	With recourse	Without recourse
Factoring commission (₹875 crore × 0.018)	15.7	—
(₹875 crore × 0.036)	—	31.5
Discount charge (₹721.8£ crore × 0.20 × 30/360)	12.0	—
(₹674.8££ crore × 0.21 × 30/360)	—	11.8
Cost of long-term funds invested in debtors:		
[(₹875 crore – ₹721.8 crore) × 0.15 × 30/360]	1.9	—
[(₹875 – ₹674.8 crore) × 0.15 × 30/360]	—	2.5
	29.6	45.8

£ Amount of advance = (₹875 crore – ₹15.7 crore) × 0.84 = ₹721.8 crore

££ Amount of advance = (₹875 crore – ₹31.5 crore) × 0.80 = ₹674.8 crore

Decision Analysis: Recourse Factoring (₹ *crore*)

Particulars	*Can bank*	*Ind bank*
Benefits (₹57.2 – ₹12 Bad debts to be borne by company)	45.2	45.2
Costs	36.6	29.6
Net benefits	8.6	15.6

Decision Analysis: Non-Recourse Factoring (₹ *crore*)

Particulars	*Can bank*	*Ind bank*
Benefits (₹57.2 + ₹1.1 Bad debts loss to be borne by factor)	58.3	58.3
Costs	54.5	45.8
Net benefits	3.8	12.5

Advice My advice to the CFO of Sunlight Industries would be to accept the proposal of Indbank Factors for recourse factoring.

Scan the QR Code given at the end of chapter to access comprehensive cases.

REVIEW QUESTIONS

LOD: Easy

RQ.17.1 Indicate whether the following statements are true or false. **[LO 17.1,2,3,4,5]**

(i) Trade credit is a spontaneous source of finance.

(ii) There are neither explicit nor implicit financial (interest) costs of trade credit.

(iii) Cash credits and working capital term loans are two ways by which working capital finance is obtained by banks in India.

(iv) Like cash credit, letter of credit is also a direct form of working capital finance provided by banks.

(v) Under hypothecation mode of security, banks provide credit to borrowers against the security of movable property, say, inventory of goods.

(vi) Under hypothecation mode of security, goods hypothecated continue to be in the possession of the borrower.

(vii) Like hypothecation, under pledge mode of security, goods continue to be in possession of the borrower.

(viii) While a mortgage can be created only by the act of parties, a charge may be created by the operation of law also.

(ix) Commercial paper is a short-term secured negotiable instrument of a fixed maturity.

(x) Commercial papers are regulated by the SEBI.

(xi) All public limited companies whose securities are listed on the stock exchange are entitled to raise funds by issuing commercial papers.

(xii) Factoring involves the outright sale of receivables at a discount to a factor to obtain funds.

(xiii) Since factoring involves the outright sale of receivables, bad-debts losses are to be borne by the factor.

(xiv) Rate of commission charged by a factor is the same whether the debts are factored with recourse or without recourse.

(xv) Factoring without resource facilitates off-balance sheet financing.

[Answers: (i) True (ii) False (iii) False (iv) False (v) True (vi) True (vii) False (viii) True (ix) False (x) False (xi) False (xii) True (xiii) False (xiv) False (xv) True]

RQ. 17.2 What are the features of trade credit as a short-term source of working capital finance? How can the cost of trade credit be calculated? [LO 17.1]

LOD: Medium

RQ. 17.3 Discuss the main forms of working capital advance by banks. What is the kind of security required by them? [LO 17.2]

RQ. 17.4 Briefly outline the main elements of the emerging system of bank financing of industry. [LO 17.2,3]

RQ. 17.5 Discuss the main features of certificates of deposits (CDs) as a source of working capital financing. [LO 17.4]

RQ. 17.6 Discuss briefly commercial papers as source of working capital finance. How would you compute the cost of commercial papers? [LO 17.3]

RQ. 17.7 What is factoring? Give a brief account of the major functions of a factor. [LO 17.5]

LOD: Difficult

RQ. 17.8 Show, with illustration, the impact of factoring on the balance sheet of the client. [LO 17.5]

RQ. 17.9 Explain and illustrate the framework of evaluation of a factoring deal. [LO 17.5]

RQ.17.10 Discuss the main elements of the Factoring Act. [LO 17.5]

RQ.17.11 The Udar Ltd sells goods on credit. Its current annual credit sales (turnover) amount to ₹810 lakh. The credit terms of Udar Ltd are 2/10, net 30. On the current level of sales, the bad debts are 1 per cent. The past experience has been that 50 per cent of the customers avail of the cash discount; the remaining customers pay on an average 70 days after the date of sale. [LO 17.5]

The book debts (receivables) of Udar Ltd are at present being financed on a 67:33 basis by a mix of bank borrowings and owned funds which cost per annum 25 per cent and 28 per cent respectively.

As an alternative to the in-house management of receivables, Udar Ltd is contemplating the use of full advance non-recourse factoring deal with the Fairgrowth Factors Ltd. The main elements of such a deal structured by the factor are (i) factor reserve, 15 per cent; **(ii)** guaranteed payment date, 24 days after the date of purchase; **(iii)** discount charge, 22 per cent and (iv) commission for other services, 4 per cent of the value of receivables.

The finance manager of Udar Ltd seeks your advice, as a consultant, on the cost-benefit of the factoring arrangement. What advise would you give? You can make your own assumptions, where necessary.

RQ.17.12 The following facts relate to the Avon Industries Ltd (AIL): [LO 17.5]

- Annual credit turnover in the current financial year, ₹1,200 lakh;
- Average collection period, 75 days;
- Cost of funds, 0.21 per annum;
- Annual credit and collection expenditure, ₹20 lakh of which three-fourths is avoidable;
- Bad debts, 1 per cent of sales

The Foremost Factors Ltd offers a factoring deal to the AIL. It proposes to charge a commission as percentage of the value of book debts of 2 per cent for recourse factoring and 3.5 per cent for non-recourse factoring. In addition, it would charge 22 per cent per annum as discount/interest for pre-payment (advance against uncollected and not due receivables) to the extent of 80 per cent of the value of the receivables. The guaranteed payment/collection date is 60 days.

Making your own assumption where necessary, what advice would you give to AIL, to continue with the in-house management of receivables or accept the factoring arrangement?

ANSWERS

17.11 Cost of non-recourse factoring alternative, ₹44.87 lakh; Cost of In-house management alternative, ₹39.59 lakh; Factoring alternative is not recommended.

17.12 Factoring alternative is not recommended; Non-recourse factoring, net loss (6.05 lakh); Recourse factoring, net loss (0.07 lakh).

Scan the QR Code to access comprehensive solutions to all numerical review questions and additional material.

PART 5

FINANCING DECISION

Chapter 18
OPERATING, FINANCIAL AND COMBINED LEVERAGE

Chapter 19
CAPITAL STRUCTURE, COST OF CAPITAL AND VALUATION

Chapter 20
DESIGNING CAPITAL STRUCTURE

The second major area in financial management is the financing/capital structure decision. The financing decision involves the choice of an appropriate mix of different sources of financing, namely, owners' funds and outsider/lenders' funds. The selection of the capital structure will obviously depend on the bearing that it has on the firm's objective of maximisation of shareholders' wealth. A financing mix which will lead to maximisation of shareholders' wealth as reflected in the market price of shares is termed as an optimum capital structure. This Part of the book is devoted to a comprehensive discussion of the important dimensions of the financing decision of a firm. Chapter 18 discusses operating, financial and combined leverage as a setting to the in-depth analysis of the relationship between the composition of the source of financing and the value of the firm. The theoretical relationship between capital structure and the valuation of a firm is examined in Chapter 19. The appropriateness of a capital structure will vary from firm to firm and, therefore, an optimum capital structure should be designed in the light of facts and circumstances of each firm. The factors having a bearing on designing a suitable capital structure are outlined in Chapter 20.

CHAPTER

18 Operating, Financial and Combined Leverage

LEARNING OBJECTIVES

LO 18.1	Understand the concept, measurement and behaviour of operating
LO 18.2	Discuss the financial leverage, financial BEP, indifference point and the EBIT-EPS approach to compare alternative capital structures using both algebraic determination and graphic presentation
LO 18.3	Explain the relationship between total/combined leverage and total risk of a firm

INTRODUCTION

The purpose of this Chapter is to set forth a framework for the financing decision of a firm. It discusses the principles and types of leverage. As mentioned earlier, a firm can make use of different sources of financing whose costs are different. These sources may be, for purposes of exposition, classified into those which carry a fixed rate of return and those on which the returns vary. The fixed returns on some sources of finance have implications for those who are entitled to a variable return. Thus, since debt involves the payment of a stated rate of interest, the return to the ordinary shareholders is affected by the magnitude of debt in the capital structure of a firm.

The employment of an asset or source of funds for which the firm has to pay a fixed cost or fixed return may be termed as **leverage**. Consequently, the earnings available to the shareholders as also the risk are affected. If earnings less the variable costs exceed the fixed cost, or earnings before interest and taxes exceed the fixed return requirement, the leverage is called favourable. When they do not, the result is unfavourable leverage.

Leverage is the employment of an asset/source of finance for which firm pays fixed cost/fixed return.

There are two types of leverage—'operating' and 'financial'. The leverage associated with investment (asset acquisition) activities is referred to as **operating leverage**, while leverage associated with financing activities is called **financial leverage**.[1] While we are basically concerned with financial leverage for purposes of the financing decision of a firm, the discussion of operating leverage is to serve as a background to the understanding of financial leverage because the two types of leverage are closely related.

Operating leverage is determined by the relationship between the firm's sales revenues and its earnings before interest and taxes (EBIT). The earnings before interest and taxes (albeit includes non-operating incomes) are also generally called as **operating profits**. Financial leverage represents the relationship between the firm's earnings before interest and taxes (operating profits) and the earnings available for ordinary shareholders. The operating profits (EBIT) are, thus, used as the pivotal point in defining operating and financial leverage. In a way, operating and financial leverage represent two stages in the process of determining the earnings available to the equity shareholders and, hence, their discussion in this chapter. Apart from the elaboration of the return-risk implications, their combined effect has also been discussed. The major points are also summarised by way of recapitulation.

LO 18.1 OPERATING LEVERAGE

Operating leverage results from the existence of fixed operating expenses in the firm's income stream. The operating costs of a firm fall into three categories: **(i)** fixed costs which may be defined as those which do not vary with sales volume; they are a function of time and are typically contractual; they must be paid regardless of the amount of revenues available; **(ii)** variable costs which vary directly with the sales volume; and **(iii)** semi-variable or semi-fixed costs are those which are partly fixed and partly variable. They are fixed over a certain range of sales volume and increase to higher levels for higher sales volumes. Since the last category of costs can be broken down into fixed and variable components, the costs of a firm, in operational terms, can be divided into **(a)** fixed, and **(b)** variable.

Operating leverage is caused due to fixed operating expenses in a firm.

The operating leverage may be defined as the *firm's ability to use fixed operating costs to magnify the effects of changes in sales on its earnings before interest and taxes.* Operating leverage occurs any time a firm has fixed costs that must be met regardless of volume. We employ assets with fixed cost in the hope that volume will produce revenues more than sufficient to cover all fixed and variable costs. In other words, with fixed costs, the percentage change in profits accompanying a change in volume is greater than the percentage change in volume. This occurrence is known as operating leverage. Consider Example 18.1.

***Example* 18.1**

A firm sells products for ₹100 per unit, has variable operating costs of ₹50 per unit and fixed operating costs of ₹50,000 per year. Show the various levels of EBIT that would result from sale of (i) 1,000 units (ii) 2,000 units and (iii) 3,000 units.

Solution

If sales level of 2,000 units are used as a base for comparison, the operating leverage is illustrated in Table 18.1

TABLE 18.1 EBIT for Various Sales Levels

	Case 2	*Base*	*Case 1*
	–50%		*+50%*
1. Sales in units	1,000	2,000	3,000
2. Sales revenue	₹1,00,000	₹2,00,000	₹3,00,000
3. *Less:* Variable operating cost	50,000	1,00,000	1,50,000
4. Contribution	50,000	1,00,000	1,50,000
5. *Less:* Fixed operating cost	50,000	50,000	50,000
6. EBIT	Zero	50,000	1,00,000
	–100%		+100%

From the results contained in Table 18.1, certain generalisations follow:

(i) Case 1: A 50 per cent increase in sales (from 2,000 to 3,000 units) results in a 100 per cent increase in EBIT (from ₹50,000 to ₹1,00,000).

(ii) Case 2: A 50 per cent decrease in sales (from 2,000 to 1,000 units) results in a 100 per cent decrease in EBIT (from ₹50,000 to zero).

***Example* 18.2**

A firm sells its products for ₹50 per unit, has variable operating costs of ₹30 per unit and fixed operating costs of ₹5,000 per year. Its current level of sales is 300 units. Determine the degree of operating leverage. What will happen to EBIT if sales change: (a) rise to 350 units, and (b) decrease to 250 units?

Solution

The EBIT for various sales levels is computed in Table 18.2.

TABLE 18.2 EBIT at Various Sales Levels

	Case 2 *–16.7%*	*Base*	*Case 1* *+16.7%*
1. Sales in units	250	300	350
2. Sales revenue	₹12,500	₹15,000	₹17,500
3. *Less:* Variable cost	7,500	9,000	10,500
4. Contribution	5,000	6,000	7,000
5. *Less:* Fixed operating cost	5,000	5,000	5,000
6. EBIT	Zero	1,000	2,000
	–100%		+100%

Interpretation In case 2, 16.7 per cent decrease in sales volume (from 300 units to 250 units) leads to 100 per cent decline in the EBIT (from ₹1,000 to zero). On the other hand, a 16.7 per cent increase in the sales level in case 1 (from 300 units to 350 units) results in 100 per cent increase in EBIT (from ₹1,000 to ₹2,000).

The two illustrations (Tables 18.1 and 18.2) clearly show that when a firm has fixed operating costs, an increase in sales volume results in a more than proportionate increase in EBIT. Similarly, a decrease in the level of sales has an exactly opposite effect. This is operating leverage; the former being favourable leverage, while the latter is unfavourable. Leverage, thus, works in both directions.

Alternative Definition of Operating Leverage

Operating leverage can also be defined and illustrated in another way. This is a more precise measurement in terms of degree of operating leverage (DOL). The DOL measures in quantitative terms the extent or degree of operating leverage.

When proportionate change in EBIT as a result of a given change in sales is more than the proportionate change in sales, operating leverage exists. The greater the DOL, the higher is the operating leverage. Symbolically,

$$\text{DOL} = \frac{\text{Percentage change in EBIT}}{\text{Percentage change in sales}} > 1 \qquad \textbf{(18.1)}$$

$$\text{Alternatively, DOL} = \frac{\Delta\,\text{EBIT} \div \text{EBIT}}{\Delta Q \div Q}$$

$$EBIT = Q(S - V) - F, \Delta\ EBIT = \Delta\ Q(S - V)$$

Where Q = Sales quantity in units,
S = Selling price per unit,
V = Variable cost per unit, and
F = Total fixed costs.

$$DOL = \frac{\Delta Q(S-V)}{Q(S-V)-F} \times \frac{Q}{\Delta Q} = \frac{Q(S-V)}{Q(S-V)-F} = \frac{\text{Total Contribution (at base level)}}{\text{EBIT (at base level)}} \quad \textbf{(18.2)}$$

Applying Equations 18.1 and 18.2 to Example 18.1 we get,

$$DOL = \frac{+100\%}{+50\%} = 2 \text{ (Case 1)}, \quad \frac{-100\%}{-50\%} = 2 \text{ (Case 2)}$$

or $\quad = ₹1,00,000/₹50,000 = 2$

Similarly, in Example 18.2,

$$DOL = \frac{+100\%}{+16.7\%} = 6 \text{ (Case 1)}, \quad \frac{-100\%}{-16.7\%} = 6 \text{ (Case 2)}$$

or $\quad = ₹6,000/₹1,000 = 6$

Since the DOL exceeds 1 in both the illustrations, operating leverage exists. However, the degree of operating leverage is higher (3 times) in the case of the firm in Example 18.2 as compared to the firm in Example 18.1, the respective quotients being 6 and 2. The quotients mean that for every 1 per cent change in sales, there will be 6 per cent (Examples 18.2) and 2 per cent (Example 18.1) change in EBIT in the direction the sales change.

However, operating leverage exists only when there are fixed operating costs. If there are no fixed operating costs, there will be no operating leverage. Consider Example 18.3.

***Example* 18.3**

Particulars	*Base Level*	*New Level*
1. Units sold	1,000	1,100
2. Sales price per unit	₹10	₹10
3. Variable cost per unit	6	6
4. Fixed operating cost	Nil	Nil

Solution

The relevant computations are given in Table 18.3.

TABLE 18.3 EBIT for Various Sales Volume

Particulars	*Base Level*	*New Level*
1. Sales revenues	₹10,000	₹11,000
2. *Less:* Variable costs	6,000	6,600
3. *Less:* Fixed costs	—	—
4. EBIT	4,000	4,400

Applying Equation 18.1, DOL = 1. Since the quotient is 1, there is no operating leverage.

Since operating leverage (magnifying the effects of a change in sales) can be favourable or unfavourable, higher levels of risk are attached to higher degrees of leverage. Since DOL depends on fixed operating costs, it logically follows that the larger the fixed operating cost, the higher is the firm's operating leverage and its operating risk. High operating leverage is good when revenues are rising and bad when they are falling. **Operating risk** is the risk of the firm not being able to cover its fixed operating costs. The larger the magnitude, the larger the volume of sales required to cover all fixed costs.

Operating risk is risk of not being able to cover fixed operating costs.

LO 18.2 FINANCIAL LEVERAGE

As already indicated, financial leverage relates to the financing activities of a firm. The sources from which funds can be raised by a firm, from the point of view of the cost/charges, can be categorised into **(i)** those which carry a fixed financial charge, and **(ii)** those which do not involve any fixed charge. The sources of funds in the first category consist of various types of long-term debt, including bonds, debentures, and preference shares. Long-term debts carry a fixed rate of interest which is a contractual obligation for the firm. Although the dividend on preference shares is not a contractual obligation, it is a fixed charge and must be paid before anything is paid to the ordinary shareholders. The equity shareholders are entitled to the remainder of the operating profits of the firm after all the prior obligations are met. We assume in the subsequent discussions that all preference dividends are paid in order to ascertain the operating profits available for distribution to ordinary shareholders.

Financial leverage results from the presence of fixed financial charges in the firm's income stream. These fixed charges do not vary with the earnings before interest and taxes (EBIT) or operating profits. They are to be paid regardless of the amount of EBIT available to pay them. After paying them, the operating profits (EBIT) belong to the ordinary shareholders. Financial leverage is concerned with the effects of changes in EBIT on the earnings available to equityholders. It is defined as the **ability of a firm to use fixed financial charges to magnify the effects of changes in EBIT on the earnings per share**[2]. In other words, financial leverage involves the use of funds obtained at a fixed cost in the hope of increasing the return to the shareholders.

Financial leverage is caused due to fixed financial costs (interest).

Favourable or positive leverage occurs when the firm earns more on the assets purchased with the funds, than the fixed cost of their use. Unfavourable or negative leverage occurs when the firm does not earn as much as the funds cost. Thus, financial leverage is based on the assumption that the firm is to earn more on the assets that are acquired by the use of funds on which a fixed rate of interest/dividend is to be paid. The difference between the earnings from the assets and the fixed cost on the use of the funds goes to the equity holders. In a way, therefore, use of fixed-interest sources of funds provides increased return on equity investment without additional requirement of funds from the shareholders. Financial leverage is also, therefore, called as 'trading on equity'. However, in periods of persisting adversity when earnings are not adequate, the presence of fixed charges will imply that the shareholders will have to bear the burden. Thus, the leverage/trading on equity will operate in the opposite direction such that the earnings per share, instead of increasing, will actually fall as a result of the use of funds carrying fixed cost.

The financial leverage is illustrated in Example 18.4.

***Example* 18.4**

The financial manager of the Hypothetical Ltd expects that its earnings before interest and taxes (EBIT) in the current year would amount to ₹10,000. The firm has 5 per cent bonds aggregating ₹40,000, while the 10 per cent preference shares amount to ₹20,000. What would be the earnings per share (EPS)? Assuming the EBIT being (i) ₹6,000, and (ii) ₹14,000, how would the EPS be affected? The firm can be assumed to be in the 35 per cent tax bracket. The number of outstanding ordinary shares is 1,000.

Solution

TABLE 18.4 EPS for Various EBIT Levels

	Case 2 *–40%*	*Base*	*Case 1* *+40%*
EBIT	₹6,000	₹10,000	₹14,000
Less: Interest on bonds	2,000	2,000	2,000
Earnings before taxes (EBT)	4,000	8,000	12,000
Less: Taxes (35%)	1,400	2,800	4,200
Earning after taxes (EAT)	2,600	5,200	7,800
Less: Preference dividend	2,000	2,000	2,000
Earnings available for ordinary shareholders	600	3,200	5,800
Earnings per share (EPS)	0.6	3.2	5.8
	–81.25%		+81.25%

The interpretation of Table 18.4 is as follows:

Case 1: A 40 per cent increase in EBIT (from ₹10,000 to ₹14,000) results in 81.25 per cent increase in EPS (from ₹3.2 to ₹5.8).

Case 2: A 40 per cent decrease in EBIT (from ₹10,000 to ₹6,000) leads to 81.25 per cent decrease in EPS (from ₹3.2 to ₹0.6).

***Example* 18.5**

A company has ₹1,00,000, 10% debentures and 5,000 equity shares outstanding. It is in the 35 per cent tax-bracket. Assuming three levels of EBIT (i) ₹50,000, (ii) ₹30,000, and (iii) ₹70,000, calculate the change in EPS (base level of EBIT = ₹50,000).

Solution

TABLE 18.5 EPS at Various EBIT Levels

	Case 2 *–40%*	*Base*	*Case 1* *+40%*
EBIT	₹30,000	₹50,000	₹70,000
Less: interest	10,000	10,000	10,000
Earnings before taxes	20,000	40,000	60,000
Less: Taxes	7,000	14,000	21,000
Earning after taxes	13,000	26,000	39,000
Earnings per share (EPS)	2.6	5.2	7.8
	–50%		+50%

Thus, a 40 per cent increase in EBIT in case 2 from the base level of EBIT has led to 50 per cent increase in EPS. And a decrease of 40 per cent in EBIT has decreased the EPS by 50 per cent.

The preceding examples show that the presence of fixed-interest sources funds leads to a more than proportionate change in EPS as a result of change in EBIT level. Whenever a firm has fixed cost in its capital structure, financial leverage is present. The greater the amount of fixed-interest sources of funds (and, therefore, the larger is the fixed-financial cost), the higher is the financial leverage. For instance, in Example 18.4, the amount of fixed financial cost is higher than in Example 18.5 owing to the preference dividend. As a result of this difference, the proportionate change in EPS was much higher (± 81.25 per cent) for Example 18.4 as compared to Example 18.5 (± 50 per cent) although the changes in EBIT in both cases are the same (± 40 per cent).

Alternative Definition of Financial Leverage

The procedure outlined above is merely indicative of the presence or absence of financial leverage. Financial leverage can be more precisely expressed in terms of the degree of financial leverage (DFL). The DFL can be calculated by Eq. (18.3)

$$\text{DFL} = \frac{\text{Percentage change in EPS}}{\text{Percentage change in EBIT}} > 1 \tag{18.3}$$

Alternatively, $\text{DFL} = \dfrac{\Delta\,\text{EPS} \div \text{EPS}}{\Delta\,\text{EBIT} \div \text{EBIT}}$

$$\text{EPS} = \frac{[(\text{EBIT} - I)(1-t) - D_P}{N}$$

$$= \frac{[Q(S-V) - F - I](1-t) - D_P}{N}$$

Since, F, I and D_p are constants,

$$\Delta\text{EPS} = [\Delta\ Q(S - V)]\ (1 - t)]/N$$

$$\frac{\Delta\text{EPS}}{\text{EPS}} = \frac{[\Delta\ Q(S-V)](1-t)}{[Q(S-V)-F-I](1-t)-D_P}$$

Dividing numerator and denominator by $(1 - t)$

$$\frac{\Delta Q(S-V)}{[Q(S-V)-F-I]-D_P/(1-t)}$$

$$\text{DFL} = \frac{\Delta Q(S-V)}{[Q(S-V)-F-I]-D_P/(1-t)} \times \frac{Q(S-V)-F}{\Delta Q(S-V)}$$

$$= \frac{Q(S-V)-F}{[Q(S-V)-F-1]-D_P/(1-t)} = \frac{\text{EBIT}}{\text{EBIT} - I - D_P/(1-t)} \tag{18.4}$$

Applying Equations 18.3 to Case 1 and Case 2 in Examples 18.4 and 18.5,

(i) For Example 18.4: *Case 1* $= \dfrac{+81.25\%}{+40\%} = 2.03$, *Case 2* $= \dfrac{-81.25\%}{-40\%} = 2.03$

$$= \frac{₹10{,}000}{₹10{,}000 - ₹2{,}000 - [₹2{,}000/(1-0.35)]} = 2.03$$

(ii) Example 18.5: *Case 1* $= \dfrac{+50\%}{+40\%} = 1.25$, *Case 2* $= \dfrac{-50\%}{-40\%} = 1.25$

$$= \frac{₹50{,}000}{₹50{,}000 - ₹10{,}000} = 1.25$$

As a rule, when a percentage change in EPS resulting from a given percentage change in EBIT is greater than the percentage change in EBIT, financial leverage exists. In other words, financial leverage occurs when the quotient in Equation 18.3 is more than one.

In both the examples, the relevant quotient is larger than one. Therefore, financial leverage exists. But the degree of financial leverage is higher in Example 18.4 (2.03) than in Example 18.5 (1.25). The higher the quotient of percentage change in EPS due to percentage change in EBIT, the greater is the degree of financial leverage. The quotient of 2.03 implies that 1 per cent change in EBIT will cause 2.03 per cent change in EPS in the same direction (± increase/decrease) in which the EBIT changes. With 1.25 quotient the proportionate change in EPS as a result of 1 per cent change in EBIT will be comparatively less, that is, 1.25 per cent in either direction.

There will be, however, no financial leverage, if there is no fixed-charged financing. (Table 18.6).

TABLE 18.6 EPS at Various EBIT Levels

	Case 2 *–40%*	*Base*	*Case 1* *+40%*
EBIT	₹30,000	₹50,000	₹70,000
Less: Taxes (0.35)	10,500	17,500	24,500
Earnings available for equity-holders	19,500	32,500	45,500
Number of shares	10,000	10,000	10,000
EPS	1.95	3.25	4.55
	–40%		+40%

Degree of financial leverage (DFL): Applying Eq. (18.3)

(i) Case 1 = $\frac{+40\%}{+40\%} = 1$ **(ii)** Case 2 = $\frac{-40\%}{-40\%} = 1$

Thus, the quotient is 1. Its implication is that 1 per cent change in EBIT will result in 1 per cent change in EPS, that is, proportionate. There is, therefore, no magnification in the EPS.

Like operating leverage, higher levels of risks are attached to higher degrees of financial leverage also. High fixed financial costs increase the financial leverage and, thus, financial risk. The **financial risk** refers to the risk of the firm not being able to cover its fixed financial costs. With the increase in financial charges, the firm is also required to raise the level of EBIT necessary to meet financial charges. If the firm cannot cover these financial payments, it can be technically forced into liquidation. Therefore, the very existence of the business is at stake. Obviously, the financial manager should take into consideration all such factors while formulating the firm's financing plan in terms of the mix of various sources of long-term funds, viz. long-term debts, preference shares, equity funds including retained earnings. One of the objectives of planning an appropriate capital structure is to provide a high income for the equity owners, that is, to increase the EPS. To devise an appropriate capital structure or financing plan, the amount of EBIT under various financing plans should be related to EPS. Thus, one widely used means of examining the effect of leverage is to analyse the relationship between EBIT and EPS.

Financial risk is the risk of not being able to cover fixed financial costs by a firm.

EBIT-EPS analysis involves comparison of alternative methods of financing at various levels of EBIT.

EBIT-EPS Analysis

The **EBIT-EPS analysis**, as a method to study the effect of leverage, essentially involves the comparison of alternative methods of financing under various *assumptions* of EBIT. A firm has the choice to raise funds for financing its investment proposals from different sources in different proportions. For instance, it can

(i) exclusively use equity capital **(ii)** exclusively use debt, **(iii)** exclusively use preference capital, **(iv)** use a combination of **(i)** and **(ii)** in different proportions; **(v)** a combination of **(i)**, **(ii)** and **(iii)** in different proportions, **(vi)** a combination of **(i)** and **(iii)** in different proportions, and so on. The choice of the combination of the various sources would be one which, *given the level of earnings before interest and taxes*, would ensure the largest EPS. Consider Example 18.6.

***Example* 18.6**

Suppose a firm has a capital structure exclusively comprising of ordinary shares amounting to ₹10,00,000. The firm now wishes to raise additional ₹10,00,000 for expansion. The firm has four alternative financial plans:

(A) It can raise the entire amount in the form of equity capital.

(B) It can raise 50 per cent as equity capital and 50 per cent as 5% debentures.

(C) It can raise the entire amount as 6% debentures.

(D) It can raise 50 per cent as equity capital and 50 per cent as 5% preference capital.

Further assume that the existing EBIT are ₹1,20,000, the tax rate is 35 per cent, outstanding ordinary shares 10,000 and the market price per share is ₹100 under all the four alternatives.

Which financing plan should the firm select?

Solution

TABLE 18.7 EPS Under Various Financial Plans

Particulars	*Financing plans*			
	A	*B*	*C*	*D*
EBIT	₹1,20,000	₹1,20,000	₹1,20,000	₹1,20,000
Less: Interest	—	25,000	60,000	—
Earnings before taxes	1,20,000	95,000	60,000	1,20,000
Taxes	42,000	33,250	21,000	42,000
Earnings after taxes	78,000	61,750	39,000	78,000
Less: Preference dividend	—	—	—	25,000
Earnings available to ordinary shareholders	78,000	61,750	39,000	53,000
Number of shares	20,000	15,000	10,000	15,000
Earnings per share (EPS)	3.9	4.1	3.9	3.5

The calculations in Table 18.7 reveal that given a level of EBIT of ₹1,20,000, the financing alternative B, which involves 50 per cent ordinary shares and 50 per cent debt, is the most favourable with respect to EPS. Another disclosure of the table is that although the proportion of ordinary shares in the total capitalisation under the financing plan D is also 50 per cent, that is, equal to plan B, EPS is considerably different (lowest). The difference in the plans B and D is due to the fact that interest on debt is tax-deductible while the dividend on preference shares is not. With 35 per cent income tax, the explicit cost of preference shares would be higher than the cost of debt.

Table 18.7 also indicates that the annual before-tax costs of the various financing plans are:

1. Financing Plan B	₹25,000
2. Financing Plan C	60,000
3. Financing Plan D (₹25000/1 – 0.35)	38,462

Financing plan A involves no cost as there is no fixed financial charge. That the financing plan involves a specific amount of cost, is another way of saying that an equal amount of earnings before interest and taxes is necessary to cover the fixed financial charges. Since preference dividend is not tax-deductible, we must divide the total dividends by one, minus the tax rate, in order to obtain the EBIT necessary to cover these dividends as a financial charge. Assuming a 35 per cent tax rate, preference dividend of ₹25,000 can be paid on EBIT of ₹38,462. The fixed financial charge would, therefore, be higher. Earnings per share would be zero for plans B, C and D for the EBIT level of ₹25,000, ₹60,000 and ₹38,462 respectively. This level of EBIT may be termed as **financial break even (BEP)** level of earnings before interest and taxes because it represents the level of EBIT necessary for the firm to break even on its fixed financial charge. In other words, it is the level of EBIT at which the firm can satisfy all fixed financial charges (i.e. interest and preference dividend). EBIT less than this level will result in negative EPS. The financial break-even point can be determined by Eq. (18.5).

Financial BEP is the level of EBIT which is equal to firm's fixed financial costs.

$$\text{Financial break-even point} = I + \frac{D_P}{1-t} \quad \textbf{(18.5)}$$

where I = Annual interest charges,
D_P = Preference dividend, and
t = Tax rate

Equation 18.5 gives before-tax earnings necessary to cover the firm's fixed financial obligations. As fixed financial charges are added, the break-even point for zero EPS is increased by the amount of the additional fixed cost. Beyond the financial break-even point, increase in EPS is more than the proportionate increase in EBIT. This is illustrated in Table 18.8, which presents the EBIT-EPS relationship for the data in Example 18.6 under the various EBIT assumptions given in the box:

(i) ₹80,000 (4 per cent return on total assets)
(ii) 1,00,000 (5 per cent return on total assets)
(iii) 1,30,000 (6.5 per cent return on total assets)
(iv) 1,60,000 (8 per cent return on total assets)
(v) 2,00,000 (10 per cent return on total assets)

TABLE 18.8 EBIT-EPS Analysis under Various EBIT Assumptions for the Four Financing Plans of Example 18.6

(i) EBIT = ₹80,000 (4 per cent return on investments)

Particulars	*Financing Plans*			
	A	B	C	D
EBIT	80,000	80,000	80,000	80,000
Less: Interest	—	25,000	60,000	—
EBT	80,000	55,000	20,000	80,000
Less: Taxes	28,000	19,250	7,000	28,000
EAT	52,000	35,750	13,000	52,000
Less: Preference dividend	—	—	—	25,000
EAT for equity-holders	52,000	35,750	13,000	27,000
EPS	2.6	2.38	1.3	1.8

(Contd.)

(*Contd.*)

(ii) EBIT = ₹1,00,000 (5 per cent return)

EBIT	1,00,000	1,00,000	1,00,000	1,00,000
Less: Interest	—	25,000	60,000	—
EBT	1,00,000	75,000	40,000	1,00,000
Less: Taxes	35,000	26,250	14,000	35,000
EAT	65,000	48,750	26,000	65,000
Less: Preference dividend	—	—	—	25,000
EAT for equity-holders	65,000	48,750	26,000	40,000
EPS	3.25	3.25	2.6	2.67

(iii) EBIT = ₹1,30,000 (6.5 per cent return)

EBIT	1,30,000	1,30,000	1,30,000	1,30,000
Less: Interest	—	25,000	60,000	—
EBT	1,30,000	1,05,000	70,000	1,30,000
Less: Taxes	45,500	36,750	24,500	45,500
EAT	84,500	68,250	45,500	84,500
Less: Preference dividend	—	—	—	25,000
EAT for equity-holders	84,500	68,250	45,500	59,500
EPS	4.22	4.55	4.55	3.97

(iv) EBIT = ₹1,60,000 (8 per cent return)

EBIT	1,60,000	1,60,000	1,60,000	1,60,000
Less: Interest	—	25,000	60,000	—
EBT	1,60,000	1,35,000	1,00,000	1,60,000
Less: Taxes	56,000	47,250	35,000	56,000
EAT	1,04,000	87,750	65,000	1,04,000
Less: Preference dividend	—	—	—	25,000
EAT for equity-holders	1,04,000	87,750	65,000	79,000
EPS	5.2	5.8	6.5	5.3

(v) EBIT = ₹2,00,000 (10 per cent return)

EBIT	2,00,000	2,00,000	2,00,000	2,00,000
Less: Interest	—	25,000	60,000	—
EBT	2,00,000	1,75,000	1,40,000	2,00,000
Less: Taxes	70,000	61,250	49,000	70,000
EAT	1,30,000	1,13,750	91,000	1,30,000
Less: Preference dividend	—	—	—	25,000
EAT for equity-holders	1,30,000	1,13,750	91,000	1,05,000
EPS	6.5	7.6	9.1	7

It can be seen from Table 18.8 that when the EBIT level exceeds the financial break-even level (₹25,000, ₹60,000 and ₹38,462 for financing alternatives, *B*, *C* and *D* respectively) EPS increases. The percentage increase in EPS is the greatest when EBIT is nearest the break-even point. Thus, in Plan *C*, an increase of 25 per cent in EBIT (from ₹80,000 to ₹1,00,000) results in a 100 per cent increase in EPS (from ₹1.3 to ₹2.6), whereas the percentage increase in EPS is only 40 per cent (from ₹6.5 to ₹9.1) as a result of the change in EBIT at higher levels from ₹1,60,000 to ₹2,00,000 (i.e. 25 per cent increase).

We can also see from Tables 18.7 and 18.8 that the EPS for different financing plans at a given level of EBIT is equal. At EBIT levels above or below the given level, the EPS is higher or lower. Thus, for alternatives *A* and *C* at the EBIT level of ₹1,20,000 (Table 18.7) the EPS is the same, that is, ₹3.9. If EBIT is below this level, alternative *A* (ordinary shares) will provide higher EPS; above this level, the debt alternative (*C*) is better from the viewpoint of EPS.

Between preference share (*D*) and ordinary share (*A*) alternatives, the EPS is equal (₹5.2) at ₹1,60,000 EBIT level. Above this level, alternative *D* will give better EPS; while below it, alternative *A* would provide higher EPS.

The earnings per share (EPS) in alternatives *A* and *B* are the same at EBIT level of ₹1,00,000. Above this, *B* plan would lead to higher EPS; at levels lower than this, financing plan *A* would provide higher EPS.

The debt alternative (*B*) gives higher EPS for all levels of EBIT as compared to the preference share alternative (*D*).

Indifference Point

The EBIT level at which the EPS is the same for two alternative financial plans is referred to as the **indifference point/level**. The indifference point may be defined as the *level of* EBIT *beyond which the benefits of financial leverage begin to operate with respect to earnings per share* (EPS). In operational terms, if the expected level is to exceed the indifference level of EBIT, the use of fixed-charge source of funds (debt) would be advantageous from the viewpoint of EPS, that is, financial leverage will be favourable and lead to an increase in the EPS available to the shareholders. The capital structure should include debt. If, however, the expected level of the EBIT is less than the indifference point, the advantage of EPS would be available from the use of equity capital.

Indifference point is the EBIT level beyond which benefits of financial leverage accrue with respect to EPS.

The indifference point between two methods of financing can be obtained mathematically (algebraic approach) as well as graphically.

Algebraic Approach Mathematically, the indifference point can be obtained by using the following symbols:

X = earnings before interest and taxes (EBIT) at the indifference point
N_1 = number of equity shares outstanding if only equity shares are issued
N_2 = number of equity shares outstanding if both debentures and equity shares are issued
N_3 = number of equity shares outstanding if both preference and equity shares are issued
N_4 = number of equity shares outstanding if both preference shares and debentures are issued
I = the amount of interest on debentures
D_P = the amount of dividend on preference shares
t = corporate income tax rate
Dt = tax on preferance dividend

For a New Company The indifference point can be determined by using the following equations:

(i) Equity shares versus Debentures/Debt:

$$\frac{X(1-t)}{N_1} = \frac{(X-I)(1-t)}{N_2} \quad (18.6)$$

(ii) (a) Equity shares versus Preference shares:

$$\frac{X(1-t)}{N_1} = \frac{X(1-t)-D_P}{N_3} \quad (18.7)$$

(ii) (b) Equity shares versus Preference shares with tax on Preference dividend:

$$\frac{X(1-t)}{N_1} = \frac{X(1-t) - D_P\,(1+Dt)}{N_3} \qquad \textbf{(18.7A)}$$

(iii) Equity shares versus Preference shares and Debentures/Debt:

$$\frac{X(1-t)}{N_1} \quad \frac{(X-I)(1-t)-D}{N_4} \qquad \textbf{(18.8)}$$

For an Existing Company If the debentures are already outstanding, let us assume I_1 = interest paid on existing debt, and I_2 = interest payable on additional debt, then the indifference point would be determined by Equation (18.9).

$$\frac{(X-I_1)(1-t)}{N_1} = \frac{(X-I_1-I_2)(1-t)}{N_2} \qquad \textbf{(18.9)}$$

***Example* 18.7**

The financial manager of a company has formulated various financial plans to finance ₹30,00,000 required to implement various capital budgeting projects:

(i) Either equity capital of ₹30,00,000 or ₹15,00,000 10% debentures and ₹15,00,000 equity;

(ii) Either equity capital of ₹30,00,000 or 13% preference shares of ₹10,00,000 and ₹20,00,000 equity;

(iii) Either equity capital of ₹30,00,000 or 13% preference capital of ₹10,00,000, (subject to dividend tax of 10 per cent), ₹10,00,000 10% debentures and ₹10,00,000 equity; and

(iv) Either equity share capital of ₹20,00,000 and 10% debentures of ₹10,00,000 or 13% preference capital of ₹10,00,000, 10% debentures of ₹8,00,000 and ₹12,00,000 equity.

You are required to determine the indifference point for each financial plan, assuming 35 per cent corporate tax rate and the face value of equity shares as ₹100.

Solution

TABLE 18.9 Determination of Indifference Point

(i) $$\frac{X(1-t)}{N_1} = \frac{(X-I)(1-t)}{N_2}$$

Or $$\frac{X(1-0.35)}{30{,}000} = \frac{(X-₹1{,}50{,}000)(1-0.35)}{15{,}000}$$

Or $$\frac{0.65X}{30{,}000} = \frac{0.65X-₹97{,}500}{15{,}000}$$

Or $0.65X = 1.3X - ₹1{,}95{,}000$

Or $-0.65X = -\ ₹1{,}95{,}000$

$X = ₹1{,}95{,}000/0.65 = ₹3{,}00{,}000$

Confirmation Table

Particulars	*Equity financing*	*Equity + debt financing*
EBIT	₹3,00,000	₹3,00,000
Less: Interest	—	1,50,000
Earning before taxes	3,00,000	1,50,000
Less: Taxes	1,05,000	52,500
Earnings for equity-holders	1,95,000	97,500
Number of equity shares	30,000	15,000
EPS	6.5	6.5

(ii) $\dfrac{X(1-t)}{N_1} = \dfrac{X(1-t)-D_P}{N_3}$

Or $\dfrac{X(1-0.35)}{30,000} = \dfrac{X(1-0.35)-₹1,30,000}{20,000}$

Or $\dfrac{0.65X}{30,000} = \dfrac{0.65X-₹1,30,000}{20,000}$

$X = ₹6,00,000$

Confirmation Table

Particulars	*Equity financing*	*Equity + Preference financing*
EBIT	₹6,00,000	₹6,00,000
Less: Taxes	2,10,000	2,10,000
Earning after taxes	3,90,000	3,90,000
Less: Dividends on preference shares	—	1,30,000
Earnings for equity-holders	3,90,000	2,60,000
Number of equity shares	30,000	20,000
EPS	13	13

(iii) $\dfrac{X(1-t)}{N_1} = \dfrac{(X-I)(1-t)-D_P\,(1+Dt)}{N_4}$

Or $\dfrac{X(1-0.35)}{30,000} = \dfrac{(X-₹1,00,000)(1-0.35)-₹1,30,000\,(1+0.1)}{10,000}$

Or $\dfrac{0.65X}{30,000} = \dfrac{0.65X-₹65,000-₹1,43,000}{10,000}$

Or $X = ₹4,80,000$

Confirmation Table

Particulars	*Equity financing*	*Equity + Preference + Debentures financing*
EBIT	₹4,80,000	₹4,80,000
Less: Interest	—	1,00,000
Earnings after interest	4,80,000	3,80,000
Less: Taxes	1,68,000	1,33,000
Earning after taxes	3,12,000	2,47,000
Less: Dividends including dividend tax on preference shares	—	1,43,000
Earnings available for equity holders	3,12,000	1,04,000
Number of equity shares	30,000	10,000
EPS	18.4	18.4

(iv) $\dfrac{(X-I)(1-t)}{N_2} = \dfrac{(X-I)(1-t)-D_P}{N_4}$

Or $\dfrac{(X-1,00,000)(1-0.35)}{20,000} = \dfrac{(X-80,000)(1-0.35)-1,30,000}{12,000}$

$X = ₹5,50,000$

Confirmation Table

Particulars	*Equity financing*	*Equity + Debt + Preference financing*
EBIT	₹5,50,000	₹5,50,000
Less: Interest	1,00,000	80,000
Earnings before taxes	4,50,000	4,70,000
Less: Taxes	1,57,500	1,64,500
Earning after taxes	2,92,500	3,05,500
Less: Dividends on preference shares	—	1,30,000
Earnings for equity-holders	2,92,500	1,75,500
Number of equity shares	20,000	12,000
EPS	14.625	14.625

Graphic Approach The indifference point can also be determined graphically. Figures 18.1 and 18.2 portray the graphic representation of financial plans **(i)** and **(ii)** of Example 18.7. The horizontal X-axis represents EBIT while EPS is represented on the Y-axis.

In order to graph the financial plan, two sets of EBIT-EPS coordinates are required. The EPS values associated with EBIT values of ₹2,00,000 and ₹6,00,000 are calculated and plotted on the graph paper under each financial plan in case of Figure 18.1. It may be noted that 100 per cent equity financing plan starts from origin (O) because EPS would be zero if EBIT is zero. However, EBIT required to have the value of the EPS as zero is ₹1,50,000, that is, the interest charges payable on 10% debentures of ₹15,00,000. Therefore, the starting point of 50 per cent equity financing plan is away from the point of the origin (i.e. it starts from ₹1.5 lakh). The point at which the two lines intersect is the **indifference point (IP)**. When we draw a perpendicular to the X-axis from the point of intersection, we have EBIT required for the IP. A line drawn from the point of intersection and joined with the Y-axis determines the EPS at the indifference point of EBIT.

An important point to be remembered in relation to the drawing of 13 per cent preference share financial plan (Fig. 18.2), is that EPS would not be zero if the firm's EBIT is ₹1,30,000, because dividend payable on preference share is not tax-deductible. The firm must earn so much more than

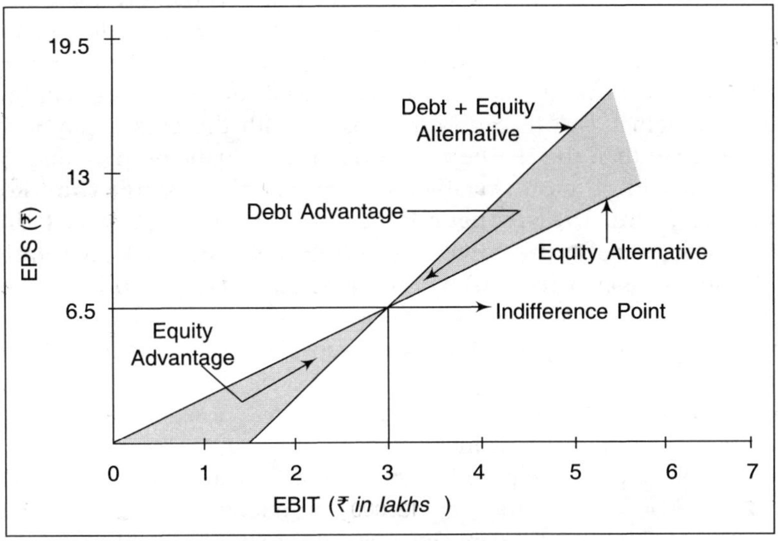

FIGURE 18.1 EBIT-EPS Analysis

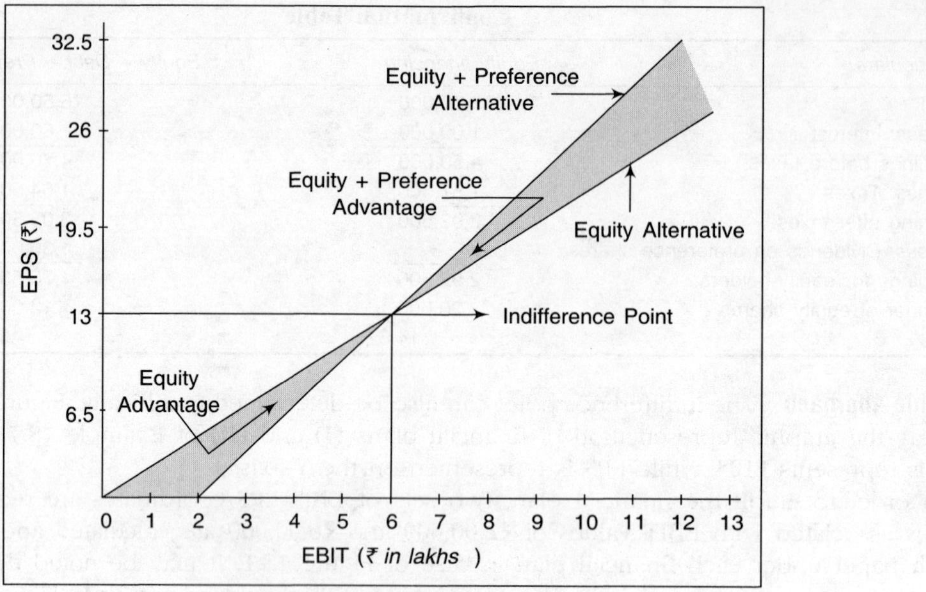

FIGURE 18.2 EBIT-EPS Analysis

₹1,30,000 that it is left with ₹1,30,000 after paying taxes. This amount can be calculated dividing ₹1,30,000 by (1 – *t*). The required amount is ₹2,00,000 [₹1,30,000) ÷ (1 – 0.35)]. Thus, the starting point of preference share financial plan would be ₹2 lakh.

The indifference points of Figs. 18.1 and 18.2 correspond to what we have determined through the algebraic approach. But the utility of the EBIT-EPS chart lies in its being more informative regarding the EBIT-EPS relationship. It gives a bird's eye view of EPS at various levels of EBIT. The EPS value at the estimated level of EBIT can be promptly ascertained. Moreover, it more easily explains why an equity financing plan is better than other plans requiring debenture and/or preference shares for the EBIT level below the IP. For instance, Fig. 18.2 indicates that for all EBIT levels below ₹6 lakh, the EPS under equity alternative is greater than 13 per cent preference share financing plan and for all EBIT levels above ₹6 lakh, the EPS is greater under 13 per cent financing plan than 100 per cent equity financing. The IP can be compared with the most likely level of EBIT. If the likely level of EBIT is more than the IP, the use of fixed cost financing plan may be recommended, otherwise equity plan would be more suitable. To sum up, **the greater the likely level of EBIT than the indifference point, the stronger is the case for using levered financial plans to maximise the EPS. Conversely, the lower the likely level of EBIT in relation to the indifference point, the more useful the unlevered financial plan would be** from the view point of EPS. In other words, financial leverage will be favourable and shareholders will get higher EPS if the return on total investment is more than the fixed cost (interest and preference dividend). If the return is less than the fixed financial charge, the EPS will decline with the use of debt and the leverage will be unfavourable. The financial leverage will have no effect on EPS in case the return on investment is exactly equal to the fixed financial costs.

The indifference point may be computed in another way using market value as the basis. Since the operational objective of financial management is the maximisation of share prices, the market price of shares of a firm with two different financial plans should be identical. Thus, on the basis of level of EBIT which ensures identical market price for alternative financial plans, the indifference point can be symbolically computed by Equation 18.10.

$$P/E_1\left[\frac{X(1-t)}{N_1}\right] = P/E_2\left[\frac{(X-I)(1-t)-D_P}{N_2}\right] \quad \textbf{(18.10)}$$

where PE_1 = P/E ratio of unlevered plan and P/E_2 = P/E ratio of levered plan.

***Example* 18.8**

Determine the indifference point at which market price of equity shares of a corporate firm will be the same from the following data:

1. Funds required, ₹50,000.
2. Existing number of equity shares outstanding, 5,000 @ ₹10 per share.
3. Existing 10% debt, ₹20,000
4. Funds required can be raised either by (a) issue of 2,000 equity shares, netting ₹25 per share or (b) new 15 per cent debt.
5. The P/E ratio will be 7 times in equity alternative and 6 times in debt alternative.
6. Corporate tax rate, 35 per cent.

Solution

$$P/E_1\left[\frac{(x-I_1)(1-t)}{N_1}\right] = P/E_2\left[\frac{(x-I_1-I_2)(1-t)}{N_2}\right]$$

or $$7\left[\frac{(x-₹2{,}000)\,0.65}{7{,}000}\right] = 6\left[\frac{(x-₹9{,}500)\,0.65}{5{,}000}\right]$$

or $$\frac{0.65\,x-₹1{,}300}{7{,}000} = \frac{0.65\,x-₹6{,}175}{5{,}000}$$

or $$5(4.55x-₹9{,}100) = 7(3.9x \times ₹37{,}050)$$

or $$4.55x = ₹2{,}13{,}850, \text{ i.e. } x = ₹47{,}000$$

Confirmation Table

Particulars	*15% Debt issue*	*Equity issue*
EBIT	₹47,000	₹47,000
Less: Interest	9,500	2,000
Earning before taxes	37,500	45,000
Less: Taxes	13,125	15,750
Earning after taxes	24,375	29,250
Number of equity shares	5,000	7,000
Earnings per share	4.875	4.18
P/E ratio (times)	6	7
Market price of the share	29.25	29.25

Measures of Financial Leverages

Financial leverage measures the degree of the use of debt and other fixed-cost sources of fund to finance the assets the firm has acquired. As shown above, the use of debt has a magnifying effect on the earnings per share. It can be said that the higher the proportion of debt in the capital structure, the higher is the financial leverage and *vice-versa*. Broadly speaking, financial leverage can be measured in two ways: **(i)** stock terms, and **(ii)** flow terms.

Stock Terms It can be measured either by **(a)** a simple ratio of debt to equity, or **(b)** by the ratio of long-term debt plus preference share to total capitalisation. Each of these measures indicates the relative proportion of the funds to the total funds of the firm on which it is to pay fixed financial charges.

Flow Terms The financial leverage can be measured either by (a) the ratio of EBIT to interest payments or (b) the ratio of cash flows to interest payment, popularly called the **debt service capacity/coverage**. These coverage ratios are useful to the suppliers of the funds as they assess the degree of risk associated with lending to the firm.

In general, the higher the 'stock' ratios and the lower the 'flow' ratios, the greater is the risk and *vice-versa*.

LO 18.3 COMBINED LEVERAGE: TOTAL RISK

The operating leverage has its effects on operating risk and is measured by the percentage change in EBIT due to percentage change in sales. The financial leverage has its effects on financial risk and is measured by the percentage change in EPS due to percentage change in EBIT. Since both these leverages are closely concerned with ascertaining the ability to cover fixed charges (fixed-operating costs in the case of operating leverage and fixed-financial costs in the case of financial leverage), if they are combined, the result is total leverage and the risk associated with **combined leverage** is known as **total risk**. Symbolically, Degree of combined leverage (DCL)

Combined leverage is the product of operating leverage and financial leverage.

$$DCL = DOL \times DFL \tag{18.11}$$

Substituting the values of DOL and DFL, we have:

Total risk is the risk associated with combined leverage.

$$DCL = \frac{\%\text{ change in EBIT}}{\%\text{ change in sales}} \times \frac{\%\text{ change in EPS}}{\%\text{ change in EBIT}} = \frac{\%\text{ change in EPS}}{\%\text{ change in sales}} \tag{18.12}$$

or

$$DCL = \frac{\text{Contribution}}{\text{EBIT}} \times \frac{\text{EBIT}}{\text{EBIT} - I} = \frac{\text{Contribution}}{\text{EBIT} - I} \tag{18.13}$$

Thus, the DCL measures the percentage change in EPS due to percentage change in sales. If the degree of operating leverage of a firm is 6 and its financial leverage is 2.5, the combined leverage of this firm would be 15(6 x 2.5). That is, 1 per cent change in sales would bring about 15 per cent change in EPS in the direction of the change in sales. The combined leverage can work in either direction. It will be favourable if sales increase and unfavourable when sales decrease because changes in sales will result in more than proportionate returns in the form of EPS.

The usefulness of DCL lies in the fact that it indicates the effect that sales changes will have on EPS. Its potential is also great in the area of choosing financial plans for new investments. If, for example, a firm begins to invest heavily in more risky assets than usual, the operating leverage will obviously increase. If it does not change its financing policy, that is, the capital structure remains constant, there would be no change in its financial leverage. As a result, the combined leverages would increase causing an increase in its total risk. The firm, in order to keep its risk constant, may like to lower its financial leverage. This could be done if the new investments are financed with more equity than the firm has used in the past. This would lower the financial leverage and compensate for the increased operating leverage caused by investment in more risky investments. If the operating leverage has decreased due to low fixed costs, the firm can afford to have a more levered financial plan to keep the total risk constant at the same time having the same prospects of magnifying effects on EPS due to change in sales.

The degree of operating leverage (DOL), financial leverage (DFL) and combined leverage (DCL) of the Reliance Industries Ltd (RIL) in summarised in Exhibit 18.1.

EXHIBIT 18.1 DOL, DFL and DCL of RIL, 2005-2017

Years	*DOL*	*DFL*	*DCL*
2017	1.09	0.96	1.05
2016	–0.68	1.02	–0.69
2015	–0.28	0.72	–0.20
2014	0.52	1.13	0.59
2013	0.28	2.28	0.64
2012	0.02	1.16	0.02
2011	0.77	1.08	0.83
2010	0.33	1.08	0.36
2009	–2.58	1.05	–2.70
2008	2.74	1.09	3.00
2007	0.95	1.10	1.04
2006	0.43	1.09	0.47
2005	1.32	1.08	1.42
Mean 2005-2008	1.36	1.09	1.48
Mean 2009-2012	0.37	1.09	0.40
Mean 2013-2017	0.63	1.22	0.77

Note: Negative values are excluded for calculating mean values.

SUMMARY

LO 18.1

Leverage refers to the use of an asset or source of funds which involves fixed costs or fixed returns. As a result, the earnings available to the shareholders/owners are affected as also their risk. There are three types of leverage, namely, operating, financial and combined.

Leverage associated with asset acquisition or investment activities is referred to as the operating leverage. It refers to the firm's ability to use fixed operating costs to magnify the effect of changes in sales on its operating profits (EBIT) and results in more than a proportionate change (±) in EBIT with change in the sales revenue.

Degree of operating leverage (DOL) is computed in two ways: (i) Percentage change in EBIT/Percentage change in sales and (ii) (Sales – Variable costs)/EBIT.

The operating leverage is favourable when increase in sales volume has a positive magnifying effect on EBIT. It is unfavourable when a decrease in sales volume has a negative magnifying effect on EBIT. Therefore, high DOL is good when sales revenues are rising and bad when they are falling.

The DOL is a measure of the business/operating risk of the firm. Operating risk is the risk of the firm not being able to cover its fixed operating costs. The larger is the magnitude of such costs, the larger is the volume of sales required to recover them. Thus, the DOL depends on fixed operating costs.

LO 18.2

Financial leverage is related to the financing activities of a firm. It results from the presence of fixed financial charges (such as interest on debt and dividend on preference shares). Since such financial expenses do not vary with the operating profits, financial leverage is concerned with the effect of changes in EBIT on the earnings available to equity-holders. It is defined as the ability of a firm to use fixed financial charges to magnify the effect of changes in EBIT on the earnings per share (EPS).

LO 18.2

The degree of financial leverage (DFL) can be computed in the following ways:

(i) DFL = Percentage change in EPS/Percentage change in EBIT.

(ii) DFL = EBIT/(EBIT – I), when debt is used.

(iii) DFL = EBIT/[EBIT – I – D_p/(1 – t)], when debt as well as preference capital is used.

(iv) DFL = EBIT/[EBIT – I – (D_p + D_t)/(1 – t)], when dividends paid on preference share capital are subject to dividend tax.

Financial leverage involves the use of funds obtained at a fixed cost in the hope of increasing the return to the equity-holders. When a firm earns more on the assets purchased with the funds than the fixed cost of their use, the financial leverage is favourable. Unfavourable leverage occurs when the firm does not earn as much as the funds cost.

High fixed financial costs increase the financial leverage and, thus, financial risk. The financial risk refers to the risk of the firm not being able to cover its fixed financial costs. In case of default, the firm can be technically forced into liquidation. The larger is the amount of fixed financial costs, the larger is EBIT required to recover them. Thus, the DFL depends on fixed financial costs.

To devise an appropriate capital structure, the amount of EBIT under various financing plans should be related to EPS. The EBIT-EPS analysis is a widely-used method of examining the effect of financial leverage/use of debt. A financial alternative that ensures the largest EPS is preferred, given the level of EBIT.

Financial break-even point (BEP) represents a point at which before-tax earnings are equal to the firm's fixed financial obligations. Symbolically, it is computed as follows: [I + D_p + D_t)/(1 – t)]. In other words, at financial BEP, EPS is zero.

The EBIT level at which the EPS is the same for two alternative financial plans is known as the indifference point/level. Beyond the indifference level of EBIT, the benefits of financial leverage begin to operate with respect to EPS.

The indifference point (IP) can be determined by using the following equations:

(a) For a new company

(i) $$\frac{X(1-t)}{N_1}=\frac{(X-I)(1-t)}{N_2}$$ (Equity versus Debentures/Debt)

(ii) $$\frac{X(1-t)}{N_1}=\frac{X(1-t)-D_p(1+D_t)}{N_3}$$ (Equity versus Preference shares)

(iii) $$\frac{X(1-t)}{N_1}=\frac{(X-I)(1-t)-D_p(1+D_t)}{N_4}$$ (Equity versus Preference shares and Debentures/Debt)

(b) For an existing company (having existing debentures/debt)

$$\frac{(X-I_1)(1-t)}{N_1}=\frac{(X-I_1-I_2)(1-t)-D_p(1+D_t)}{N_4}$$ (Equity versus Preference shares and Debentures/Debt)

The indifference point can also be determined graphically. In order to graph the financial plan, two sets of EBIT-EPS coordinates are required for each financial plan. The point at which the two lines intersect is the IP.

The greater is the likely level of EBIT than the IP, the stronger is the case for using levered plan (debt) to maximise the EPS. Conversely, the lower is the likely level of EBIT in relation to IP, the unlevered (equity) plan would be more useful from the perspective of EPS.

LO 18.2	The IP can be computed using market value (instead of EPS) as the basis. Under this method, the IP is that level of EBIT at which market price of the share (MPS) is the same for two alternative financial plans. Symbolically, $P/E_1\left[\frac{X(1-t)}{N_1}\right]=P/E_2\left[\frac{(X-I)(1-t)-D_p\,(1+D_t)}{N_4}\right]$ (Equity versus preference shares and debentures)
LO 18.3	Combined leverage (DCL) is the product of operating and financial leverage. It indicates the effect that changes in sales will have on EPS. Symbolically, it can be computed by the following methods: (i) DCL = DOL × DFL (ii) DCL = Percentage change in EPS/Percentage change in sales (iii) DCL = (Sales – Variable costs)/(EBIT – *I*)
	Combined leverage is a measure of the total risk of the firm. To keep the risk within manageable limits, a firm which has high degree of operating leverage should have low financial leverage and *vice-versa*.

REFERENCES

1. Joy, P M, *Introduction to Financial Management,* Irwin Homewood Ill., p 226.
2. Gitman, L J, *Principles of Managerial Finance,* Harper & Row, New York, 1997, p 84.

SOLVED PROBLEMS

P.18.1 Calculate the operating leverage for each of the four firms, A, B, C and D from the following price and cost data. What conclusions can you draw with respect to levels of fixed cost and the degree of operating leverage result? Explain. Assume number of units sold is 5,000. LO 18.1 LOD E

	Firms			
	A	*B*	*C*	*D*
Sale price per unit	₹20	₹32	₹50	₹70
Variable cost per unit	6	16	20	50
Fixed operating cost	80,000	40,000	2,00,000	Nil

Solution

	Firms			
	A	*B*	*C*	*D*
Sales (units)	5,000	5,000	5,000	5,000
Sales revenue (Units × price)	₹1,00,000	₹1,60,000	₹2,50,000	₹3,50,000
Less: Variable cost (Units × VC per unit)	30,000	80,000	1,00,000	2,50,000
Less: Fixed operating costs	80,000	40,000	2,00,000	Nil
EBIT	(10,000)	40,000	(50,000)	1,00,000

$$\text{DOL} = \frac{\text{Current sales (S)} - \text{Variable costs (VC)}}{\text{Current EBIT}}$$

$$\text{DOL}_{(A)} = \frac{₹1,00,000 - ₹30,000}{₹10,000} = 7 \qquad \text{DOL}_{(B)} = \frac{₹1,60,000 - ₹80,000}{₹40,000} = 2$$

$$\text{DOL}_{(C)} = \frac{₹2,50,000 - ₹1,00,000}{₹50,000} = 3 \qquad \text{DOL}_{(D)} = \frac{₹3,50,000 - ₹2,50,000}{₹1,00,000} = 1$$

The operating leverage exists only when there are fixed costs. In the case of firm D, there is no magnified effect on the EBIT due to change in sales. A 20 per cent increase in sales has resulted in a 20 per cent increase in EBIT. In the case of other firms, operating leverage exists. It is maximum in firm A, followed by firm C and minimum in firm B. The interpretation of DOL of 7 is that 1 per cent change in sales results in 7 per cent change in EBIT level in the direction of the change of sales level of firm A.

P.18.2 A firm's sales, variable costs and fixed cost amount to ₹75,00,000, ₹42,00,000 and ₹6,00,000 respectively. It has borrowed ₹45,00,000 at 9 per cent and its equity capital totals ₹55,00,000.

LO 18.1,2,3 LOD M

(a) What is the firm's ROI?
(b) Does it have favourable financial leverage?
(c) If the firm belongs to an industry whose asset turnover is 3, does it have a high or low asset leverage?
(d) What are the operating, financial and combined leverages of the firm?
(e) If the sales drop to ₹50,00,000, what will the new EBIT be?
(f) At what level will the EBT of the firm equal to zero?

Solution

(a) ROI = EBIT/Investment

EBIT = Sales – VC – FC = ₹75 lakh – ₹45 lakh – ₹6 lakh = ₹27 lakh.

ROI = ₹27 lakh/₹100 lakh = 27 per cent.

(b) Yes, the firm has favourable financial leverage as its ROI is higher than the interest on debt.

(c) Asset turnover = Sales/Total assets or Total investments. = ₹75 lakh/₹100 lakh = 0.75 It is lower than the industry average.

(d) $$\text{Operating leveage} = \frac{\text{Sales} - \text{Variable costs}}{\text{EBIT}} = \frac{₹75 \text{ lakh} - ₹42 \text{ lakh}}{₹27 \text{ lakh}} = 1.22$$

$$\text{Financial leverage} = \frac{\text{EBIT}}{\text{EBIT} - \text{Interest}} = \frac{₹27 \text{ lakh}}{(₹27 \text{ lakh} - ₹4.05 \text{ lakh})} = 1.18$$

$$\text{Combined leverage} = \frac{\text{Sales} - \text{VC}}{\text{EBIT} - \text{Interest}} = \frac{₹33 \text{ lakhs}}{₹22,95,000} = 1.44$$

Alternatively = OL × FL = 1.22 × 1.18 = 1.44

(e) EBIT at sales level of ₹50 lakh

Sales revenue	₹50,00,000
Less: Variable costs (50 lakh × 0.56)	28,00,000
Less: Fixed costs	6,00,000
EBIT	16,00,000

(f) Zero EBT implies break-even sales (BESR) = FC/CV ratio, CV ratio = ₹33 lakhs/₹75 lakhs = 44 per cent

BESR = (₹6 lakh + ₹4.05 lakh)/0.44 = ₹22,84,091.

Confirmation table

Sales revenue	₹22,84,091
Less: VC (0.56)	12,79,091
Less: FC (operating)	6,00,000
Less: Interest (additional fixed cost)	4,05,000
EBT	ZERO

P.18.3 The selected financial data for A, B and C companies for the current year ended March 31 are as follows:

LO 18.1,2,3 LOD D

Particulars	*A*	*B*	*C*
Variable expenses as a percentage of sales	66.67	75	50
Interest expenses (₹)	200	300	1,000
Degree of operating leverage	5	6	2
Degree of financial leverage	3	4	2
Income-tax rate	0.35	0.35	0.35

(a) Prepare income statements for A, B, and C companies.
(b) Comment on the financial position and structure of these companies.

Solution

(a) Income statement of companies A, B and C for the current year, ended March 31

Particulars	*A*	*B*	*C*
Sales	₹4,500	₹9,600	₹24,000
Less: Variable costs	3,000	7,200	12,000
Less: Fixed costs (Sales – VC – EBIT)	1,200	2,000	10,000
EBIT	300	400	2,000
Less: Interest	200	300	1,000
Earnings before taxes	100	100	1,000
Less: Taxes	35	35	350
EAT (Net income)	65	65	650

Working Notes

(a) The preparation of the income statement requires data for **(i)** sales revenue, **(ii)** variable costs and **(iii)** fixed costs.

$$\text{DFL} = 3,\ \text{DFL} = \frac{\text{EBIT}}{\text{EBIT} - I}$$

Company A:

$$3 = \frac{\text{EBIT}}{\text{EBIT} - ₹\,200}$$

$$\text{EBIT} = ₹300$$

$$\text{DOL} = \frac{\text{Sales} - \text{Variable costs (V)}}{\text{EBIT}}$$

$$5 = \frac{S - 0.667\,S}{₹\,300}$$

where S = sales = ₹4,500

VC = 0.667 × ₹4,500 = ₹3,000

Company B:

$$4 = \frac{\text{EBIT}}{\text{EBIT} - ₹\,300}$$

$$\text{EBIT} = ₹400$$

$$6 = \frac{S - 0.75\,S}{₹\,400} = ₹\,9{,}600$$

VC = 0.75 × ₹9,600 = ₹7,200

Company C:

$$2 = \frac{\text{EBIT}}{\text{EBIT} - ₹\,1{,}000}$$

$$\text{EBIT} = ₹2{,}000$$

$$6 = \frac{S - 0.50\,S}{₹\,2{,}000} = ₹\,24{,}000$$

VC = 0.50 – ₹24,000 = ₹12,000

(b) The financial position of company *C* can be regarded better than other companies: **(i)** It has the least financial risk as it is has minimum degree of financial leverage. It is true that there will be a more magnified impact on EPS of *A* and *B* due to change in EBIT, but, their EBIT level due to low sales is very low. **(ii)** From the point of view of DCL, company *C* is better placed. The degree of combined leverage is maximum in company *B* (24); for company *A* (15) and for company *C* it is 4. The total risk (business plus financial) of company *C* is the lowest. **(iii)** The ability of the company *C* to meet interest liability is better. The EBIT/interest ratios for the three companies are:

C, 2.0 (₹2,000 ÷ ₹1,000)
B, 1.5 (₹300 ÷ ₹200)
A, 1.33 (₹400 ÷ ₹300)

P.18.4 Calculate operating leverage and financial leverage under situations *A*, *B* and *C* and financial plans 1, 2 and 3 respectively from the following information relating to the operation and capital structure of *X, Y, Z* Ltd. Also find out the combinations of operating and financial leverage which give the highest value and the least value. **LO 18.1,2** LOD M

Installed capacity (units)		1,200
Actual production and sales (units)		800
Selling price per unit (₹)		15
Variable cost per unit (₹)		10
Fixed costs (₹):	*Situation A*	1,000
	Situation B	2,000
	Situation C	3,000

Capital Structure:

Particulars	*Financial plan*		
	1	*2*	*3*
Equity	₹5,000	₹7,500	₹2,500
Debt	5,000	2,500	7,500
Cost of debt (for all plans) (%)		12	

Solution

Determination of operating leverage

Particulars	*Situations*		
	A	*B*	*C*
Sales level (units)	800	800	800
Sales revenue	₹12,000	₹12,000	₹12,000
Less: Variable costs	8,000	8,000	8,000
Less: Fixed cost	1,000	2,000	3,000
Operating profits (EBIT)	3,000	2,000	1,000
DOL $= \dfrac{S - VC}{EBIT}$	1.33	2	4

Determination of financial leverage

	Financial plan		
	1	*2*	*3*
Situation A:			
EBIT	₹3,000	₹3,000	₹3,000
Less: Interest	600	300	900
Earnings after interest	2,400	2,700	2,100
Financial leverage (EBIT/EBIT – I)	1.25	1.11	1.43
Situation B:			
EBIT	2,000	2,000	2,000
Less: Interest	600	300	900
Earnings after interest	1,400	1,700	1,100
Financial leverage	1.43	1.18	1.82
Situation C:			
EBIT	1,000	1,000	1,000
Less: Interest	600	300	900
Earnings after interest	400	700	100
Financial leverage	2.5	1.43	10

Determination of the highest and the lowest value of combined leverage (combined leverage = DOL × DFL)

Situations	*Financial plan*		
	1	*2*	*3*
A	1.66	1.48	1.90
B	2.86	2.36	3.64
C	10.00	5.72	40.00

The above calculations suggest that the highest value is in situation C financed by plan 3 and the lowest value is in situation A financed by plan 2.

P.18.5 Consider the following information about *X* Ltd. **LO 18.1,2,3** LOD M

EBIT	₹12,00,000
EBT	3,00,000
Operating fixed cost	24,00,000
Preference dividend	60,000
Tax rate (%)	40

Calculate the degree of operating, financial and combined leverage. By what percentage, the operating profits would increase, if sales increase by 10%?

Solution

Statement showing computation of DOL, DFL and DCL

Particulars	*Amount*
Total contribution (EBIT + Operating fixed cost)	₹36,00,000
Less fixed cost	24,00,000
EBIT	12,00,000
Less interest (EBIT – EBT ₹3,00,000)	9,00,000
EBT	3,00,000
Less taxes (40%)	1,20,000
EAT	1,80,000
Less dividend paid to preference shareholders	60,000
Earnings available to equityholders (EAEHs)	1,20,000
DOL = Total contribution/EBIT": ₹36 lakh/₹12 lakh	3
DFL = EBIT/[EBIT – *I* – Dp(1 – *t*):	
= ₹12 lakh/[₹12 lakh – ₹9 lakh – ₹60,000/0.6] = ₹2 lakh	6
DCL = DOL × DFL : 3 × 6	18

DOL = Percentage change in EBIT/Percentage change in sales

3 × 10% = 30% increase in EBIT. Operating profits would increase by 30% when sales increases by 10%.

P.18.6 From the following data, calculate: **(i)** Operating, financial and combined leverage, **(ii)** Financial break-even point, and **(iii)** Percentage drop in sales to make the earnings per share zero. **LO 18.1,2,3** LOD D

Earnings before Interest and Taxes (EBIT)	₹20,00,000
Profit after tax (PAT)	9,60,000
Operating fixed cost	15,00,000
Tax rate (%)	40
Preference dividend	2,40,000

Solution

(i) and **(ii)** Statement showing computation of DOL, DFL, DCL and FBEP

Particulars	*Amount*
Contribution (EBIT + operating fixed costs)	₹35,00,000
Less operating fixed costs	15,00,000
EBIT	20,00,000
Less interest (EBIT – EBT)	4,00,000
EBT = (EAT/1 – *t*): (₹9,60,000/0.6)	16,00,000
Less taxes (₹16,00,000 × 0.40)	6,40,000
EAT/PAT	9,60,000
Less preference dividend (Dp)	2,40,000
Earnings available for equityholders (EAEH)	7,20,000
DOL = Contribution/EBIT: (₹35,00,000/₹20,00,000)	1.75
DFL = EBIT/(EBIT – *I* – Dp/1 – *t*)	
[₹20,00,000/(₹20,00,000 – ₹4,00,000 – ₹2,40,000/0.6)]	1.67
DCL = DOL 3 DFL: (1.75 × 1.67)	2.92
Financial BEP = *I* + Dp/(1 – *t*): (₹4,00,000 + ₹4,00,000)	₹8,00,000

(iii) In order to make EPS zero, EAEH should be zero. It would be sum of the following:

Operating fixed cost	₹15,00,000
Interest payment	4,00,000
Preference dividend (adjusted for taxes)	4,00,000
Required contribution	23,00,000

Desired reduction in contribution:

Present contribution	₹35,00,000
Less required contribution	23,00,000
Reduction in contribution (desired)	12,00,000
Desired drop in sales would be equal to desired drop in contribution to make EPS zero: (₹12 lakh/₹35 lakh) (%)	34.29

P.18.7 A firm has sales of ₹75,00,000, variable cost of ₹42,00,000 and fixed cost of ₹6,00,000. It has a debt of ₹45,00,000 at 9% and equity of ₹55,00,000. **(i)** What is the firm's ROI?, **(ii)** Calculate OL, FL and CL. Are leverages favourable or unfavourable?, and **(iii)** At what level of EBIT and sales, EPS will be equal to zero? **LO 18.1,2,3** LOD M

Solution

Statement showing determination of ROI, DOL, DFL and DCL.

Particulars	*Amount*
Sales	₹ 75,00,000
Less variable cost (56%)	42,00,000
Total contribution (c/v ratio 44%)	33,00,000
Less fixed cost	6,00,000
EBIT	27,00,000
Less interest	4,05,000

(Contd.)

(*Contd.*)

EBT	22,95,000
ROI = EBIT/Total capital employed	
(₹ 45 lakh debt + ₹ 55 lakh equity): ₹ 27 lakh/₹ 100 lakh (%)	27
DOL = Contribution/EBIT: ₹ 33 lakh/₹ 27 lakh	11/9
DFL = –EBIT/EBT: ₹ 27 lakh/₹ 22.95 lakh	20/17
DCL = DOL × DFL: 11/9 × 20/17	1.44

Leverages are favourable as ROI is higher than rate of interest (9%).

(iii) BESR (comprehensive) at which total operating fixed cost and fixed interest costs are fully recovered would indicate sales at which EPS will be zero and EBIT = interest. BESR (comprehensive) = (₹ 6,00,000 + ₹ 4,05,000)/0.44 = ₹ 22,84,091

Income statement showing EPS at sales of ₹ 22,84,091

Sales	₹ 22,84,091
Less variable costs (56%)	12,79,091
Less fixed cost	6,00,000
EBIT	4,05,000
Less interest	4,05,000
EBT	0
Less taxes	0
EAT	0
EPS	0

P.18.8 Compute the operating leverage, financial leverage and combined leverage from the following data: **LO 18.1,2,3** LOD M

Net worth	₹25,00,000
Debt/equity ratio	3:1
Interest rate	12 per cent
EBIT	₹20,00,000
Operating fixed costs	10,00,000

Solution

Determination of DOL, DFL and DCL

Contribution (EBIT + Operating fixed costs)	₹30,00,000
Less fixed costs (Operating)	10,00,000
EBIT	20,00,000
Less interest (₹75,00,000 × 12%)	9,00,000@
EBT	11,00,000
DOL = (Contribution/EBIT)	1.5
DFL= (EBIT/EBT)	1.82
DCL = (DOLXDFL)	2.73

@ Interest on debt = (₹25,00,000 Net worth × 3 D/E ratio = ₹75,00,000) × 0.12 = ₹9,00,000

P.18.9 Exel Limited is considering three financing plans. The key information is as follows: **LO 18.2** LOD M

(a) Total funds to be raised, ₹2,00,000.

(b) Financing plans

Plans	Equity (%)	Debt (%)	Preference (%)
A	100	—	—
B	50	50	—
C	50	—	50

(c) Cost of debt 8 per cent; cost of preference shares 8 per cent
(d) Tax rate, 35 per cent
(e) Equity shares of the face value of ₹10 each will be issued at a premium of ₹10 per share.
(f) Expected EBIT, ₹80,000.

Determine for each plan:

(i) earnings per share (EPS) and financial break-even point.
(ii) indicate if any of the plans dominate, and compute the EBIT range among the plans for indifference.

Solution

(i) Determination of EPS under plans A, B and C

EBIT	₹80,000	₹80,000	₹80,000
Less: Interest	—	8,000	—
EBT	80,000	72,000	80,000
Less: Taxes (0.35)	28,000	25,200	28,000
EAT	52,000	46,800	52,000
Less: Dividend on preference shares	—	—	8,000
Earnings for equity-holders	52,000	46,800	44,000
÷ number of shares	10,000	5,000	5,000
EPS	5.2	9.36	8.8

Financial BEP for plans, *A*, *B* and *C*

Plan A	= Zero
Plan B	= ₹8,000 (₹1,00,000 × 0.08)
Plan C $= \dfrac{D_P}{(1-t)} = \dfrac{₹8,000}{0.65}$	= ₹12,308

(ii) Indifference point among financial plans

(a) A and B:

$$\frac{X(1-t)}{N_1} = \frac{(X-I)(1-t)}{N_2};\ \frac{0.65X}{10,000} = \frac{(X-₹8,000)\,0.65}{5,000}$$

X = ₹10,400/0.65 = ₹16,000.

(b) B and C:

$$\frac{(X-I)(1-t)}{N_1} = \frac{X(1-t)-D_P}{N_2};\ \frac{0.65(X-₹8,000)}{5,000} = \frac{0.65X-₹8,000}{5,000}$$

or $0.65X$ – ₹5,200 = $0.65X$ – ₹8,000
or $0.65X - 0.65X$ = ₹5,200 – ₹8,000

Thus, indifference point between plans B and C is indeterminate.

(c) A and C:

$$\frac{X(1-t)}{N_1}=\frac{X(1-t)-D_P}{N_2};\ \frac{0.65X}{10{,}000}=\frac{0.65X-₹8{,}000}{5{,}000}$$

or $0.65X = 13X - ₹16{,}000$ or $X = ₹16{,}000/0.65$ i.e. ₹24,615

Domination of plan: Plan *B* dominates plan *C* as the financial BEP of plan *B* is lower.

P.18.10 The XYZ Company plans to expand assets by 50 per cent. To finance the expansion it is choosing between a straight 6 per cent debt issue and equity issue. Its current balance sheet and income statement are shown below: **LO 18.2** LOD M

Balance sheet of XYZ company as on March 31

5% Debt	₹4,00,000	Total assets	₹20,00,000
Equity shares (₹10 per share)	10,00,000		
Earned surplus	6,00,000		
	20,00,000		20,00,000

Income statement for the year ended March 31

Sales	₹60,00,000
Total costs (excluding interest)	53,80,000
EBIT	6,20,000
Less: Interest on debt	20,000
EBT	6,00,000
Less: Taxes	2,10,000
Net income	3,90,000

If company finances the proposed expansion with debt, the rate on the incremental debt will be 6 per cent and the price/earning ratio of the equity shares will be 10. If expansion is financed by equity, the new shares can be sold at ₹33.33 and the price/earnings ratio of all the outstanding equity shares will remain 12.

(a) Assuming that net income before interest on debt and taxes (EBIT) is 10 per cent on sales, calculate EPS at assumed sales of ₹20 lakh, ₹40 lakh, ₹80 lakh and ₹100 lakh under the alternative forms of financing the expansion programme (assume no fixed costs).

(b) Using the price/earnings ratio indicated, calculate the market value for equity share for each sales level for both debt and equity methods of financing.

(c) If the firm follows the policy of seeking to maximise the price of its shares, which form of financing should be employed?

Solution

(a) and **(b)** Determination of EPS and MPS under alternative financial plans

	Sales levels							
	₹20 lakh		*₹40 lakh*		*₹80 lakh*		*₹100 lakh*	
	Debt	*Equity*	*Debt*	*Equity*	*Debt*	*Equity*	*Debt*	*Equity*
EBIT	₹2,00,000	₹2,00,000	₹4,00,000	₹4,00,000	₹8,00,000	₹8,00,000	₹10,00,000	₹10,00,000
Less: Interest	80,000	20,000	80,000	20,000	80,000	20,000	80,000	20,000
Earnings before taxes	1,20,000	1,80,000	3,20,000	3,80,000	7,20,000	7,80,000	9,20,000	9,80,000
Less: Taxes (0.35)	42,000	63,000	1,12,000	1,33,000	2,52,000	2,73,000	3,22,000	3,43,000
EAT	78,000	1,17,000	2,08,000	2,47,000	4,68,000	5,07,000	5,98,000	6,37,000

(Contd.)

(Contd.)

Number of equity shares	1,00,000	1,30,000	1,00,000	1,30,000	1,00,000	1,30,000	1,00,000	1,30,000
EPS	0.78	0.90	2.08	1.90	4.68	3.9	5.98	4.9
P/E ratio	10	12	10	12	10	12	10	12
Market price of a share	7.8	10.80	20.8	22.80	46.80	46.80	59.80	58.80

Working Note

In debt financing, the number of equity shares outstanding = 1,00,000 (₹10,00,000 ÷ ₹10 per share). In the case of equity financing the total number of outstanding shares = 30,000 additional shares (total = 1,30,000 shares).

(c) The answer will depend on the expected level of sales. If the sales level is at ₹40 lakh, equity form of financing should be employed. At the sales level of ₹80 lakh, the company is indifferent. If the sales level is likely to be at ₹100 lakh, the debt form of financing should be employed.

P.18.11 The ABC Ltd has the following balance sheet and income statement information: LO 18.1,2,3 LOD M

Balance sheet as on March 31

Liabilities		*Assets*	
Equity capital (₹10 per share)	₹8,00,000	Net fixed assets	₹10,00,000
10% Debt	6,00,000	Current assets	9,00,000
Retained earnings	3,50,000		
Current liabilities	1,50,000		
	19,00,000		19,00,000

Income statement for the year ending March

Sales	₹3,40,000
Operating expenses (including ₹60,000 depreciation)	1,20,000
EBIT	2,20,000
Less: Interest	60,000
Earning before tax	1,60,000
Less: Taxes	56,000
Net earnings (EAT)	1,04,000

(a) Determine the degree of operating, financial and combined leverages at the current sales level, if all operating expenses, other than depreciation, are variable costs.

(b) If total assets remain at the same level, but sales (i) increase by 20 per cent and (ii) decrease by 20 per cent, what will be the earnings per share in the new situation?

Solution

(a) $$\text{DOL} = \frac{₹3,40,000 - ₹60,000}{₹2,20,000} = 1.27 \qquad \text{DFL} = \frac{₹2,20,000}{₹1,60,000} = 1.37$$

$$\text{DCL} = \text{DOL} \times \text{DFL} = 1.27 \times 1.37 = 1.75$$

(b) Earnings per share at the new sales level

Sales level	₹4,08,000	₹2,72,000
Less: Variable expenses	72,000	48,000
Less: Fixed cost	60,000	60,000
Earnings before interest and taxes	2,76,000	1,64,000

(Contd.)

(*Contd.*)

Less: Interest	60,000	60,000
Earnings before taxes	2,16,000	1,04,000
Less: Taxes	75,600	36,400
Earnings after taxes (EAT)	1,40,400	67,600
Number of equity shares (N)	80,000	80,000
EPS	1.75	0.84

Working Notes

(i) Variable costs = ₹60,000 (total cost – depreciation).

(ii) Variable costs = (a) at sales level, ₹4,08,000 = ₹72,000, (b) at the sales level, ₹2,72,000 = 48,000

P.18.12 The Well Established Company's most recent balance sheet is as follows: **LO 18.1,2,3** LOD M

Liabilities	*Amount*	*Assets*	*Amount*
Equity capital (₹10 per share)	₹60,000	Net fixed assets	₹1,50,000
10% Long-term debt	80,000	Current assets	50,000
Retained earnings	20,000		
Current liabilities	40,000		
	2,00,000		2,00,000

The company's total assets turnover ratio is 3, its fixed operating costs are ₹1,00,000 and the variable operating costs ratio is 40 per cent. The income tax rate is 35 per cent.

(a) Calculate all the three types of leverages.

(b) Determine the likely level of EBIT if EPS is **(i)** ₹1, **(ii)** ₹3, and **(iii)** Zero.

Solution

Income statement

Sales	₹6,00,000
Less: Variable costs	2,40,000
Less: Fixed costs	1,00,000
EBIT	2,60,000
Less: Interest	8,000
Earnings before interest	2,52,000
Less: Taxes	88,200
Earnings after taxes	1,63,800

(a) $$\text{DOL} = \frac{₹\,6{,}00{,}000 - 2{,}40{,}000}{₹\,2{,}60{,}000} = 1.38$$

DFL = ₹2,60,000/₹2,52,000 = 1.03

DCL = 1.38 × 1.03 = 1.42

(b) (i) $$\text{EPS} = \frac{(\text{EBIT} - I)(1 - t)}{N}$$

$$₹1 = \frac{(\text{EBIT} - ₹\,8{,}000)\,(1 - 0.35)}{6{,}000}$$

₹6,000 = 0.65 EBIT – ₹5,200

EBIT = ₹17,231

(ii) $$₹3 = \frac{(\text{EBIT} - ₹\,8{,}000) \times 0.65}{6{,}000}$$

EBIT = ₹35,692

(iii) $$0(\text{Zero}) = \frac{(\text{EBIT} - ₹\,8{,}000) \times 0.65}{6{,}000}$$

EBIT = ₹8,000

Confirmation table

EBIT	₹8,000	₹17,231	₹35,692
Less: Interest	8,000	8,000	8,000
Earnings after interest	Nil	9,231	27,692
Less: Taxes	Nil	3,231	9,692
Net income (NI)	Nil	6,000	18,000
Number of shares (N)	6,000	6,000	6,000
EPS (NI ÷ N)	Zero	1	3

Working Notes

Total assets turnover ratio, 3 = Sales/₹2,00,000 or Sales = ₹6,00,000

P.18.13 A company has 20,000 equity shares of ₹50 each outstanding. The following is the income statement relating to the previous year as well as four proforma statements reflecting different assumptions regarding a new project. The new project is expected to cost ₹5,00,000 in each case. **LO 18.2** LOD M

Proforma

	Actual (previous year)	*Sell 10,000 equity shares*		*Sell 10% debentures*	
		Optimistic	*Pessimistic*	*Optimistic*	*Pessimistic*
		₹12,00,000	*₹9,00,000*	*₹12,00,000*	*₹9,00,000*
Sales	₹8,00,000				
Variable expenses	2,40,000				
	5,60,000				
Fixed costs	3,00,000				
EBIT	2,60,000				
Interest	Nil				
Earning after interest	2,60,000				
Taxes	91,000				
EAT	1,69,000				
EPS	8.45				

Assuming variable cost as per cent of sales remains constant and additional fixed cost with new project is likely to be ₹1,00,000, complete the tabulation. Which plan would you recommend to finance the new project?

Solution

Completion of table *(Amount in ₹ thousand)*

Particulars	*Actual (Previous year)*	*Proforma*			
		Sell 10,000 equity shares		*Sell 10% debentures*	
		Optimistic	*Pessimistic*	*Optimistic*	*Pessimistic*
Sales	800	1,200	900	1,200	900
Variable costs	240	360	270	360	270
	560	840	630	840	630
Fixed costs	300	400	400	400	400
EBIT	260	440	230	440	230
Interest	Nil	Nil	Nil	50	50
Earnings after interest	260	440	230	390	180
Taxes	91	154	80.5	136.5	63
EAT	169	286	149.5	253.5	117
EPS (₹)	8.45	9.53	4.98	12.67	5.85

The debt form of financing would be recommended to finance the new project as the EPS is more under debt form of financing than equity, in both optimistic and pessimistic situations.

Assumption: The company can sell its equity shares at ₹50 each without incurring any floatation costs.

P.18.14 A plastic manufacturing company is planning to expand its assets by 50 per cent. All financing for this expansion will come from external sources. The expansion will generate additional sales of ₹3 lakh with a return of 25 per cent on sales before interest and taxes. The finance department of the company has submitted the following plans for the consideration of the Board. LO 18.2 LOD M

Plan 1: Issue of 10% debentures.

Plan 2: Issue of 10% debentures for half the required amount and balance in equity shares to be issued at 25 per cent premium.

Plan 3: Issue equity shares at 25 per cent premium.

Balance sheet of the company as on March 31

Liabilities	*Amount*	*Assets*	*Amount*
Equity capital (₹10 per share)	₹4,00,000	Total assets	₹12,00,000
8% Debentures	3,00,000		
Retained earnings	2,00,000		
Current liabilities	3,00,000		
	12,00,000		12,00,000

Income statement for the year ending March 31

Sales	₹19,00,000
Operating costs	16,00,000
EBIT	3,00,000
Interest	24,000
Earning after interests	2,76,000
Taxes	96,600
EAT	1,79,400
EPS	4.48

(a) Determine the number of equity shares that will be issued if financial plan 3 is adopted.

(b) Determine indifference point between (i) plans 1 and 2, (ii) plans 1 and 3, and (iii) plans 2 and 3.

(c) Assume that the price earnings ratio is expected to remain unchanged at 8 if plan 3 is adopted, but is likely to drop to 6 if either plan 1 or 2 is used to finance the expansion. Determine the expected market price of the shares in each of the situations.

Solution

(a) Number of shares issued $= 48{,}000 = \dfrac{₹6{,}00{,}000}{₹12.5}$

(b) (i) $$\frac{(X - I_1 - I_2)(1-t)}{N_1} = \frac{(X - I_1 - I_2)(1-t)}{N_2}$$

or $$\frac{(X - ₹24{,}000 - ₹60{,}000)\times 0.65}{40{,}000} = \frac{(X - ₹24{,}000 - ₹30{,}000)(0.65)}{64{,}000}$$

$$X = ₹1{,}34{,}000$$

(ii) $$\frac{(X - I_1 - I_2)(1-t)}{N_1} = \frac{(X - I_1)(1-t)}{N_2}$$

$$\frac{(X - ₹84{,}000)\times(0.65)}{40{,}000} = \frac{(X - ₹24{,}000)\times 0.65}{88{,}000}$$

$$X = ₹1{,}34{,}000$$

(iii) $$\frac{(X - I_1 - I_2)}{N_1} = \frac{(X - I_2)(1 - t)}{N_2}$$

$$\frac{(X - ₹54{,}000) \times 0.65}{40{,}000} = \frac{(X - ₹24{,}000) \times 0.65}{88{,}000}$$

$$X = ₹1{,}34{,}000$$

Verification table

Particulars	*Plans*		
	1	*2*	*3*
EBS	₹1,34,000	₹1,34,000	₹1,34,000
Less: Interest	84,000	54,000	24,000
Earnings before taxes	50,000	80,000	1,10,000
Less: Taxes	17,500	28,000	38,500
EAT	32,500	52,000	71,500
Number of equity shares (N)	40,000	64,000	88,000
EPS	0.812	0.812	0.812

(c) Determination of market price per share under various alternative financial plans:

Particulars	*Plans*		
	1	*2*	*3*
EBIT	₹3,75,000	₹3,75,000	₹3,75,000
Less: Interest	84,000	54,000	24,000
Earnings before taxes	2,91,000	3,21,000	3,51,000
Less: Taxes	1,01,850	1,12,350	1,22,850
EAT	1,89,150	2,08,650	2,28,150
N	40,000	64,000	88,000
EPS	4.73	3.26	2.59
P/E ratio	6	6	8
Market price	28.38	19.56	20.72

P.18.15. Arvind Textile Mill currently has 10,00,000 shares of equity outstanding with a market price of ₹50 per share. It has also ₹4 crore in 12% bonds. The company is considering a ₹5 crore expansion programme that it can finance through: **(1)** All equity shares at ₹40 per share or **(2)** Straight bonds at 15% interest or **(3)** Half equity shares at ₹40 per share and half 15% bonds. You are required to do the following:
(i) Assume EBIT level of ₹2,50,00,000 after the expansion programme, calculate the earnings per share for each of the alternative modes of financing. Assume a corporate tax rate of 50%; **(ii)** What are the indifference points between alternatives? **(iii)** What is your interpretation of the results?

LO 18.2 LOD **D**

Solution

(i) Determination of EPS under 3 financing options

Particulars	*Financial options*		
	1 (E)	*2 (D)*	*3 (E + D)*
EBIT	₹2,50,00,000	₹2,50,00,000	₹2,50,00,000
Less interest (existing)	48,00,000	48,00,000	48,00,000
Less interest (additional)	—	75,00,000	37,50,000
EBT	2,02,00,000	1,27,00,000	1,64,50,000
Less taxes (50%)	1,01,00,000	63,50,000	82,25,000

(Contd.)

(*Contd.*)

EAT/Earnings for equity holders, EAEH	1,01,00,000	63,50,000	82,25,000
Number (N) of existing equity shares	10,00,000	10,00,000	10,00,000
Number of additional equity shares	12,50,000	—	6,25,000
EPS (EAEH/N)	₹4.49	₹6.35	₹5.06

(ii) Indifference point between plans 1 and 2

$$= \frac{(X - I_1)}{N_1} = \frac{(X - I_1 - I_2)(1 - t)}{N_2}$$

where, X = EBIT, I_1, and I_2 = existing and additional interest respectively.

$$= \frac{(X - ₹48,00,000)0.5}{22,50,000} = \frac{(X - ₹1,23,00,000)0.5}{10,00,000}$$

Multiplying left equation by 4 and right by 9.

4 (0.5X – ₹24,00,000) = 9 (0.5X – ₹61,50,000)

2X – ₹96,00,000 = 4.5X – ₹5,53,50,000

2.5X = ₹4,57,50,000 or X = ₹4,57,50,000/2.5 = ₹1,83,00,000 (EBIT)

(iii) Indifference point between plans 1 and 3

$$= \frac{(X - I_1)(1 - t)}{N_1} = \frac{(X - I_1 - I_3)(1 - t)}{N_3}$$

$$= \frac{(X - ₹48,00,000)0.5}{22,50,000} = \frac{(X - ₹85,50,000)0.5}{16,25,000}$$

Multiplying left equation by 13 and right by 18

13(0.5X – ₹24,00,000) = 18(0.5X – ₹42,75,000)

6.5X – ₹3,12,00,000 = 9X – ₹7,69,50,000

2.5X = ₹4,57,50,000 or X = ₹4,57,50,000/2.5 = ₹1,83,00,000 (EBIT)

(iv) Indifference point between plans 2 and 3

$$= \frac{(X - I_1 - I_2)}{N_1} = \frac{(X - I_1 - I_3)(1 - t)}{N_2}$$

$$= \frac{(X - ₹1,23,00,000)0.5}{10,00,000} = \frac{(X - ₹85,50,000)(0.5)}{16,25,000}$$

Multiplying left equation by 13 and right by 8

13(0.5X – ₹61,50,000) = 8(0.5X – ₹42,75,000)

6.5X – ₹7,99,50,000 = 4X – ₹3,42,00,000

2.5X = ₹7,99,50,000 – ₹3,42,00,000/2.5 = ₹4,57,50,000

X = ₹4,57,50,000/2.5 = ₹1,83,00,000

Interpretation: Indifference points are the same in all the options. Since EPS is maximum under option 2, the company is advised to raise funds through debt.

P.18.16. TeleTalk Ltd is a leading telecommunications service provider in India. It has recently launched its DTH (Direct To Home) services called "DigiTV". TeleTalk has decided to set up a small plant to manufacture the DTH devices within the country. The cost of required machine is ₹80 lakh and the working capital required is ₹20 lakh. With the new machine it is expected to have higher sales level of ₹70 lakh and the total operating (fixed and variable) costs of ₹20 lakh. The corporate tax rate is 35%.

LO 18.2 LOD M

The existing capital structure of TeleTalk Ltd. includes 10% Debentures of ₹50 lakh, 2 lakh equity shares (₹50 per share) and retained earnings of ₹20 lakh. The company is considering the two proposed financial plans to meet the required financing needs. Their details along with P/E ratios are as follows:

Plan 1

1.4 lakh Equity Shares (₹50 per share)	=	₹70 lakh
11% Debt	=	30 lakh
P/E ratio	=	10 times

Plan 2

1 lakh Equity Shares (₹50 per share)	=	₹50 lakh
12.5% Debt	=	50 lakh
P/E ratio	=	9 times

Required: (a) Which of the two financing alternatives should the company choose? Assume company wants to maximise market price per share. (b) Determine indifference point with respect to EPS and MPS.

Solution: **Determination of MPS under two proposed financial plans**

Particulars	*Plan1*	*Plan2*
Sales	₹70,00,000	₹70,00,000
Less : Total operating costs	20,00,000	20,00,000
EBIT	50,00,000	50,00,000
Less: Interest on existing debt	5,00,000	5,00,000
Less: Interest on additional debt	3,30,000	6,25,000
EBT	41,70,000	38,75,000
Less: Taxes (at 35%)	14,59,500	13,56,250
EAT	27,10,500	25,18,750
Total No. of Shares (existing + new)	3,40,000	3,00,000
EPS	7.97	8.40
P/E Ratio (times)	10	9
MPS	₹79.70	₹75.60

Recommendation: The Company should choose plan 2 as it has higher MPS.

Determination of indifference point with reference to EPS

(a) $$\frac{(X - I_e - I_1)(1-t)}{(N_e + N_1)} = \frac{(X - I_e - I_2)(1-t)}{(N_e + N_2)}$$

$$\frac{(X - ₹5,00,000 - ₹3,30,000)(1-0.35)}{(2,00,000+1,40,000)} = \frac{(X - ₹5,00,000 - ₹6,25,000)(1-0.35)}{(2,00,000+1,00,000)}$$

X = ₹33,37,500

Determination of indifference point with reference to EPS

(b) $$\left[\frac{(X - I_e - I_1)(1-t)}{(N_e + N_1)}\right] \times \left[\frac{P}{E}\right] = \left[\frac{(X - I_e - I_2)(1-t)}{(N_e + N_2)}\right] \times \left[\frac{P}{E}\right]$$

$$\left[\frac{(X - ₹5,00,000 - ₹3,30,000)(1-0.35)}{(2,00,000+1,40,000)}\right] \times 10 = \left[\frac{(X - ₹5,00,000 - ₹6,25,000)(1-0.35)}{(2,00,000+1,00,000)}\right] \times 9$$

X = ₹1,58,75,000

P.18.17 Mr Marker is an entrepreneur and has recently set up manufacturing unit of Pens. He currently sells 1 million pens a year at ₹5 each. His variable cost to produce the pen is ₹3 per pen and he has ₹15 lakh in fixed costs. His sales to assets ratio is 5 times, and 40 per cent of his assets are financed with 8% debt, with the balance being financed by ordinary shares of ₹10 per share. The tax rate is 35 per cent.

LO 18.1,2,3 LOD **D**

His newly appointed finance manager, Mr Impression, feels that Mr Marker is doing it all wrong. By reducing his price to ₹4.50 per pen, he could increase his sales volume of pens by 40 per cent. Fixed costs would remain constant, and variable costs would remain ₹3 per unit. His sales to asset ratio would be 6.3 times. Furthermore, he could increase his debt to assets ratio to 50 per cent, with the balance in shares. It is assumed that the interest rate would go up 1 per cent and that the price of shares would remain constant.

(a) Compute the EPS under the Marker and Impression plans. Is Mr Impression's perception right?

(b) Mr Marker's partner does not think that fixed costs would remain constant under the Impression plan but they would go up by 15 per cent. If this is the case, should Mr Marker shift to the Impression plan, based on earnings per share.

(c) What is the effect on the total risk of the firm on switching from one plan to another?

Solution

(a) and (b) Computation of EPS under Marker and Impression Plans

Marker Plan:	
Sales revenue (1 million × ₹5)	₹50,00,000
Less: Variable cost (1 million × ₹3)	30,00,000
Contribution	20,00,000
Less: Fixed costs	15,00,000
EBIT	5,00,000
Less: Interest (*Working note 1*)	32,000
EBT	4,68,000
Less: Tax (0.35)	1,63,800
EAT	3,04,200
N (Number of shares)	60,000
EPS	5.07
Impression Plan:	
Sales revenue (1 million × 1.4 × ₹4.5)	63,00,000
Less: Variable cost (1 million × 1.4 × ₹3)	42,00,000
Contribution	21,00,000
Less: Fixed costs	15,00,000
EBIT	6,00,000
Less: Interest (*Working note 2*)	45,000
EBT	5,55,000
Less: Tax (0.35)	1,94,250
EAT	3,60,750
N (Number of shares)	50,000
EPS	7.72

Working Note 1

Sales/Assets = 5

₹50 lakh/Assets = 5 or Assets = ₹10 lakh

40% of assets financed by 8% debt = ₹4 lakh.

Interest (0.08 × ₹4 lakh) = ₹32,000.
Number of shares (₹6 lakh ÷ ₹10 each share) = 60,000.

Working Note 2

Total assets = ₹10 lakh
Debt/Assets = 50%
∴ Debt = ₹5 lakh at 8% + 1% = 9%
Interest = 0.09 × ₹5 lakh = ₹45,000
Number of shares (₹5 lakh ÷ ₹10) = 50,000.

Yes, Mr Impression is right in his perceptions. Following his plan would increase the EPS to ₹7.22 from ₹5.07.

(c) Computation of EPS

The total risk is determined by the combined leverage which in turn is evaluated by combining operating and financial leverage. (Amount in rupees lakh, *L*)

Marker Plan:

$$\text{DOL} = \frac{\text{Contribution}}{\text{EBIT}} = \frac{20\,L}{5L} = 4 \quad \text{DFL} = \frac{\text{EBIT}}{\text{EBIT} - I} = \frac{5\,L}{5\,L - 0.32\,L} = 1.068$$

$$\text{DCL} = \text{DOL} \times \text{DFL} = 4.27$$

Impression Plan:

$$\text{DOL} = ₹21\ L/₹6\ L = 3.5$$

$$\text{DFL} = \frac{6\ L}{6\ L - 0.45\ L} = 1.08$$

$$\text{DCL} = \text{DOL} \times \text{DFL} = 3.78$$

There is a decrease in the degree of combined leverage, reflecting a decline in the total risk of the company. With a lower degree of risk, the market price of its shares is likely to go up.

P.18.18 The current capital structure of RSS Ltd. as on 31st March 2018 is as follows: LO 18.2 LOD D

Equity share capital (5 lakh shares @ ₹100 per share)	₹5,00,00,000
Reserves and surplus	1,00,00,000
10% Preference share capital (20 lakh shares @ ₹10 per share)	2,00,00,000
8% Debt	4,00,00,000
	12,00,00,000

Annual sales of the company for the year 2018 was at ₹30 crore and its EBIT was ₹3 crore.

The company wants to undertake a huge expansion plan for which an additional capital of ₹8 crore is required. The management of the company has two following financial plans for consideration of the Board:
Plan 1: Issue 1,25,000 equity shares of ₹100 each at ₹60 premium and raise a debt for the balance. However, the new debt will be available @ 9.5% interest rate per annum.
Plan 2: Raise the entire requirement by issuing equity shares of ₹100 each at ₹60 premium.

After the expansion, the sales level is estimated at ₹50 crore and EBIT is expected at 8% of sales.
The Board is having conflict of opinion. Some members of the Board opine that the company should go for Plan 1 as it would result in higher EPS (earnings per share); while others are in favour of Plan 2 as it would yield higher MPS (market price per share).
Which plan is better in your opinion? The P/E ratio is estimated to be 7 under Plan 1 and 10 under Plan 2. Corporate tax rate is 35%.

Solution

Determination of EPS

EBIT	₹3,00,00,000
Less: Interest (₹4,00,00,000 × 8%)	32,00,000
EBT	2,68,00,000
Less: Taxes (@35%)	93,80,000
EAT	1,74,20,000
Less: Preference dividend (₹2,00,00,000 × 10%)	20,00,000
EAEH (Earnings available for equity-holders, EAEH)	1,54,20,000
Number of equity shares (N)	5,00,000
EPS (₹1,54,20,000/5,00,000)	₹30.84

Two proposed financial plans:

Plan 1: 1,25,000 Equity shares @ ₹(100 + 60)	₹2,00,00,000
Debt (balancing figure)	6,00,00,000
	8,00,00,000
Plan 2: Equity shares @ ₹(100 + 60)	
Number of shares = (₹8,00,00,000/₹160)	5,00,000 shares

Calculation of indifference point based on EPS (without considering P/E ratio):

$$\frac{(X - I_e - I_a)(1 - t) - D_p}{N_e + N_{a1}} = \frac{(X - I_e)(1 - t) - D_p}{N_e + N_{a2}}$$

Where:

N_e = Number of existing equity shares

N_{a1} = Number of additional equity shares issued under Plan 1

N_{a2} = Number of additional equity shares issued under Plan 2

$$\frac{[(X - ₹32{,}00{,}000 - ₹57{,}00{,}000)(1 - 0.35)] - ₹20{,}00{,}000}{5{,}00{,}000 + 1{,}25{,}000} = \frac{[(X - ₹32{,}00{,}000)(1 - 0.35)] - ₹20{,}00{,}000}{5{,}00{,}000 + 5{,}00{,}000}$$

X = ₹2,14,76,923.08

Verification Table

Particulars	*Plan I*	*Plan II*
EBIT	₹2,14,76,923.08	₹2,14,76,923.08
less: Interest		
Existing	32,00,000.00	32,00,000.00
Additional	57,00,000.00	0.00
EBT	1,25,76,923.08	1,82,76,923.08
less: Taxes	44,01,923.08	63,96,923.08
EAT	81,75,000.00	1,18,80,000.00
less: Preference dividend	20,00,000.00	20,00,000.00
EAEH	61,75,000.00	98,80,000.00
Number of equity shares	6,25,000	10,00,000
EPS	₹9.88	₹9.88

Since the estimated EBIT (₹4 crore) is sufficiently higher than required EBIT, it will be beneficial for the company to opt for a more levered plan 1, as it results in higher EPS (shown below):

Particulars	*Plan 1*	*Plan 2*
EBIT (10% of ₹50,00,00,000)	₹5,00,00,000	₹5,00,00,000
Less: Interest		
Existing: ₹4,00,00,000 × 8%	32,00,000	32,00,000
Additional: ₹6,00,00,000 × 9.5%	57,00,000	—
EBT	4,11,00,000	4,68,00,000
Less: Taxes (@35%)	1,43,85,000	1,63,80,000
EAT	2,67,15,000	3,04,20,000
Less: Preference dividend (₹2,00,00,000 × 10%)	20,00,000	20,00,000
EAEH	2,47,15,000	2,84,20,000
Number of equity shares	(5,00,000 + 1,25,000)	(5,00,000 + 5,00,000)
EPS (EAEH/Number of equity shares)	₹39.54	₹28.42

Thus, from EPS perspective, Plan 1 is better.

However, P/E ratio is not equal under the two Plans. Therefore, the P/E multiple for each plan should also be considered to have sound decision making. In other words, there is a need to compute real indifference point based on MPS.

Calculation of indifference point based on MPS (real indifference point):

$$\left[\frac{(X - I_e - I_a)(1-t) - D_p}{N_e + N_{a1}}\right] \times \text{P/E}_1 = \left[\frac{(X - I_e)(1-t) - D_p}{N_e + N_{a2}}\right] \times \text{P/E}_2$$

$$\left[\frac{[(X - ₹32{,}00{,}000 - ₹57{,}00{,}000)(1 - .35)] - ₹20{,}00{,}000}{5{,}00{,}000 + 1{,}25{,}000}\right]^7 = \left[\frac{[(X - ₹32{,}00{,}000)(1 - .35)] - ₹20{,}00{,}000}{5{,}00{,}000 + 5{,}00{,}000}\right]^{10}$$

X = ₹5,94,76,923.08

Verification Table:

Particulars	*Alternative I*	*Alternative II*
EBIT	₹5,94,76,923.08	₹5,94,76,923.08
less: Interest		
Existing	32,00,000.00	32,00,000.00
Additional	57,00,000.00	0.00
EBT	5,05,76,923.08	5,62,76,923.08
less: Taxes	1,77,01,923.08	1,96,96,923.08
EAT	3,28,75,000.00	3,65,80,000.00
less: Preference dividend	20,00,000.00	20,00,000.00
EAEH	3,08,75,000.00	3,45,80,000.00
Number of equity shares	6,25,000	10,00,000
EPS	49.40	34.58
P/E ratio	7	10
MPS	₹345.80	₹345.80

It may be noted that required EBIT at real indifference level is higher than estimated EBIT. Therefore, a less levered Plan 2 (in spite of lower EPS) would be more profitable for the company.

Particulars	Alternative 1	Alternative 2
EPS (already calculated)	₹39.54	₹28.42
P/E ratio	7	10
MPS (EPS × P/E)	₹276.8	₹284.2

Given the fact that maximisation of shareholders' wealth is the primary objective of financial decision making of any company, and it gets reflected in market price of shares, the company should opt for Plan 2 (as it results in higher market price).

MINI CASES

18.C.1 *G* Manufacturing company is an important producer of lawn furniture and decorative objectives for the patio and garden. The last year's income statement and balance sheet are as follows:

Income statement

Sales	₹75,00,000
Variable costs	46,90,000
Contribution	28,10,000
Fixed costs	14,00,000
Earnings before interest and tax (EBIT)	14,10,000
Interest	2,00,000
Earnings before tax (EBT)	12,10,000
Taxation	6,05,000
Net Income after tax	6,05,000

Balance sheet

Liabilities	Amount	Assets	Amount
Equity capital	₹10,00,000	Fixed assets	₹60,00,000
Reserves and surplus	42,00,000	Inventory	6,00,000
Long-term debt (10%)	20,00,000	Receivables	7,00,000
Current liabilities	5,00,000	Cash	4,00,000
	77,00,000		77,00,000

Figures for industry comparison:
Normal asset turnover 1.2 : 1. Normal profit margin 20 per cent

For the current year, the forecasted sales are ₹80,00,000 and it is likely that variable costs will remain at approximately the same percentage of sales as was in the last year. (Figures could be rounded off). Fixed costs will rise by 10 per cent.

G has short-listed the following two product lines to be sold through its existing distribution channels:

(1) Production and sale of metal table and chair unit that will be sold for issue around swimming pools. This will require an investment of ₹20,00,000, which would involve installation of manufacturing and packaging machinery. Sales forecast are ₹15,00,000 per annum, variable costs account for 2/3rd of sales value, fixed costs are ₹2,00,000 and no additional working capital is needed.

(2) Hardwood planter with three separate components, will be appropriate for medium sized shrubs. This will require an investment of ₹30,00,000 with forecasted sales per annum of ₹25,00,000, variable costs 64 per cent of sales value and fixed costs of ₹5,00,000.

Two financial plans are available:

(a) It could borrow on a 10 years note at 9 per cent for either or both of the projects of an amount not to exceed ₹60,00,000.

(b) Cumulative preference shares with a 10 per cent dividend upto an amount of ₹30,00,000. Financing through the issue of equity shares would not be possible at the present time.

Required

(1) Without the new proposals, what would be the company's operating, fixed charges and combined leverages next year? Would the company have favourable financial leverage?

(2) How does the acceptance of each project affect the differing leverages including asset leverages?

(3) With each financing alternatives, do the company's future earnings per share increase or decrease, why?

Solution

(1) Income statement at projected sales of ₹80 lakh in current year

Sales revenue	₹80,00,000
Less: Variable costs (₹80 lakh × 62.5% V/V ratio)	50,00,000
Contribution	30,00,000
Less: Fixed costs (₹14 lakh + 10%)	15,40,000
EBIT	14,60,000
Less: Interest	2,00,000
Earnings before taxes (EBT)	12,60,000
Less: Taxes (0.50)	6,30,000
Earnings after taxes	6,30,000

Determination of leverages (without the new proposals)

DOL = Contribution/EBIT (₹30,00,000/₹14,60,000)	2.0548
DFL = EBIT/EBT (₹14,60,000/₹12,60,000)	1.1587
DCL = Contribution/EBT (₹30,00,000/₹12,60,000) Or 2.0548 × 1.1587	2.3809

The company is said to have favourable financial leverage if it earns more on the assets purchased (with debt funds) than the interest it pays on debt. For the purpose, ROR on capital employed is computed. It is (₹14,60,000/₹72,00,000) = 20.28 per cent. This return is higher than 10 per cent interest payable on long-term debt. Evidently, the firm is having positive financial leverage.

(2) Income statement showing earnings of two projects, DOL and assets leverage

Particulars	Projects	
	Metal table and chair unit	Hardwood planter
Sales revenue	₹15,00,000	₹25,00,000
Less: Variable costs	10,00,000	16,00,000
Contribution	5,00,000	9,00,000
Less: Fixed costs	2,00,000	5,00,000
EBIT	3,00,000	4,00,000
DOL (Contribution/EBIT)	1.667	2.25
Assets leverage (Sales/Total assets)	0.75	0.83

To determine other leverages, it will be useful to extend income statement to include the impact of financing costs.

Income statement showing other leverages (DFL and DCL) and other ratios

Particulars	*Projects*	
	Metal table and chair unit (Investments ₹20 lakh)	*Hardwood planter (Investments ₹30 lakh)*
(i) Financed through debt plan:		
EBIT	₹3,00,000	₹4,00,000
Less: Interest	1,80,000	2,70,000
Earnings before taxes (EBT)	1,20,000	1,30,000
Less: Taxes (0.50)	60,000	65,000
Earnings after taxes	60,000	65,000
DFL (EBIT/EBT)	2.5	2.0
DCL (DOL × DFL)	4.1675	4.5
Rate of return on capital employed (%)	15	13.33
(ii) Financed through cumulative preference share (₹30 lakh) + ₹20 lakh debt for two combined projects EBIT		7,00,000
Less: Interest (₹20 lakh × 9%)		1,80,000
Earnings before taxes		5,20,000
Less: Taxes (0.50)		2,60,000
Earnings after taxes		2,60,000
Less: Dividends to preference share holders (₹30 lakh × 10%)		3,00,000
EAT		(40,000) *

*Since EAT is negative, this financial plan is worth rejecting and hence warrants no more calculations for other leverages.

It is apparent that acceptance of the Hardwood Planter project will adversely affect risk level (reflected in higher DOL, DFL and DCL). While the acceptance of Metal Table project decreases operating risk (lower DOL), it increases total risk (as DCL is 4.15). The asset leverages are also very low.

Though the ROR on capital employed is higher for both the projects than the interest rate paid, the acceptance of these projects will decrease the firm's overall rate of return on capital employed (the existing ROR on capital employed is 20, 28 per cent).

(3) The impact of financing alternatives on company's future EPS:

Financial plan (a): Since the rate of return on capital employed is higher (for both the projects) than the rate of interest (9 per cent) payable on funds borrowed, the projects will increase EPS.

Financing plan (b): Under this plan, funds are to be raised by the issue of ₹30 lakh cumulative 10 per cent Preference shares, the EPS will decrease as payment of 10 per cent preference dividend requires 20 per cent pre-tax return on ₹30 lakh; the projected pre-tax return is 17.33 per cent (₹5,20,000/₹30,00,000). In fact, taking two projects in a combined manner, the firm has negative returns for equity-holders. As a result, this financial plan will have depressing effect on the EPS and is not desirable.

In sum, the firm should go for both projects only when debt financing is possible for both such projects.

18.C.2 AMR Paints (Operating, Financial and Combined Leverage) AMR Paints Ltd is a leading manufacturer of decorative and industrial paints in India. The income statement (Exhibit 1) and the balance sheet (Exhibit 2) for the current year are given. Its sales next year are estimated to be 25 per cent higher on account of increase in demand for paints from the housing and commercial real estate sectors. The variable costs as percentage to sale are likely to remain constant. An increase of 12.5 per cent is estimated in fixed costs.

AMR Paints is planning to launch two new brands of luxury emulsions—Supercoat and Luxurycoat. The Supercoat paint would generate an additional ₹600 crore sales and require an extra ₹400 crore investment involving installation of manufacturing and packaging machinery. While the additional fixed costs requirement would be ₹150 crore, variable cost to sales ratio would not change. For manufacturing the Luxurycoat paint the additional investment requirement and sales generated would amount to ₹600 crore and ₹800 crore respectively. The variable cost ratio would remain constant but the fixed cost are expected to increase by ₹240 crore. The AMR has four alternative financing plans to choose from (Exhibit 3). Its current debt-equity ratio is 5:1.

AMR Paints has hired Mustafa Hakimuddin as a financial consultant to carry out the following tasks:

(1) What would its operating, financial and total leverages be next year without the new proposal?
(2) Assuming that the AMR paints finances the projects using financing plan (A), determine the three leverages for the two projects individually. Which new brand is better?
(3) Which financing option should AMR choose to if only Supercoat is to be manufactured?
(4) Calculate the financial breakeven points of each plan.

EXHIBIT 1 Income Statement, Current Year and Market Data (₹ crore)

Sales	₹5,000
Variable costs (0.50)	2,500
Contribution	2,500
Fixed costs	1,000
EBIT	1,500
Interest	500
EBT	1,000
Tax (0.35)	350
EAT	650
Shares outstanding	10
EPS (₹)	65
P/E ratio	20
Market price per share (MPS) (₹)	1,300

EXHIBIT 2 Balance Sheet As at March 31, Current Year (₹ crore)

Liabilities		*Assets*		
Equity capital	₹100	Fixed assets		₹5,850
Reserve and Surpluses	900	Current assets:		
10% Debt	5,000	Inventory	₹550	
Current liabilities	950	Receivables	300	
		Cash	250	1,100
	6,950			6,950

EXHIBIT 3 Financing Options/Plans (₹ crore)

Plans	*Debentures*		*Equity Shares*		*Preference Shares*		*P/E*
	Coupon rate	*Amount*	*Number (Crore)*	*Face value*	*Rate*	*Amount*	
(1)	*(2)*	*(3)*	*(4)*	*(5)*	*(6)*	*(7)*	*(8)*
A	0.12	₹1,000	—	—	—	—	14
B	—	—	100	₹10	—	—	30
C	0.11	400	60	10	—	—	20
D	—	—	70	10	0.11	₹300	28

Solution

(1) Determination of Leverage (Without New Proposal)

Degree of operating leverage (DOL) = $\left[\dfrac{\text{Sales} - \text{VC}}{\text{EBIT}}\right]$	= 1.56
Degree of financial leverage (DFL) = EBIT/(EBIT – I)	= 1.33
Degree of combined leverage (DCL) = [DOL × DFL]	= 2.07

Working Note

Income statement (₹ crore)

Project sales (₹5,000 + 0.25)	₹6,250
Variable costs (50%)	3,125
Contribution	3,125
Fixed costs (₹1,000 + 0.125)	1,125
EBIT	2,000
Interest	500
EBT	1,500
Taxes (0.35)	525
EAT	975
EPS	97.5
P/E	20
MPS	1,950

(2) Determination of Leverage

	Supercoat	*Luxurycoat*
DOL	2	2.5
DFL	1.47	1.82
DCL	2.94	4.55
ROCE (Return on capital employed)	0.375	0.267

Comment: Supercoat is a superior alternative as its leverages are lower and the ROCE is higher.

Working Note

Income Statement (₹ crore)

	Supercoat	*Luxurycoat*
Sales	₹600	₹800
Variable costs (0.50)	300	400
Contribution	300	400
Fixed costs	150	240
EBIT	150	160
Interest	48	72
EBT	102	88
Tax	35.7	30.8
EAT	66.3	57.2

(3) Determination of Leverages

Particulars	*Financing Plans*			
	A	*B*	*C*	*D*
DOL	1.59	1.59	1.59	1.59
DFL	1.34	1.30	1.32	1.32
DCL	2.13	2.07	2.10	2.10
Outstanding shares (crore)	10.00	50.00	34.00	38.00
EPS (₹)	104.13	21.45	31.21	27.88
P/E ratio	14	30	20	28
MPS (₹)	1,457.82	643.50	624.22	780.64

Comment: Plan A is preferable as it has the highest MPS.

Working Notes

Income Statement (₹ crore)

Particulars	*Plans*			
	A	*B*	*C*	*D*
Projected sales	₹6,850	₹6,850	₹6,850	₹6,850
Variable costs	3,425	3,425	3,425	3,425
Contribution	3,425	3,425	3,425	3,425
Fixed costs	1,275	1,275	1,275	1,275
EBIT	2,150	2,150	2,150	2,150
Interest	548	500	517.6	500
EBT	1,602	1,650	1,632.4	1,650
Tax	560.7	577.5	571.4	577.5
EAT	1,041.3	1,072.5	1,061.0	1,072.5
Preference dividend	—	—	—	13.2
Earning available for shareholders	1,041.3	1,072.5	1,061.0	1,059.3

(4) Financial Break-even Point

= (I + D/PD) ÷ (1 – t)

Plan A = ₹548.0 crore (Interest)

B 500.0 (Interest)

C 517.6 (Interest)

D 520.30 [₹500 + (₹13.2/0.65)]

REVIEW QUESTIONS

LOD: Easy

RQ.18.1 Indicate whether the following statements are true or false. [LO 18.1,2,3]

(i) The degree of operating leverage is a measure of financial risk.

(ii) The degree of financial leverage is a measure of business risk.

(iii) The EBIT level at which the EPS is the same for two alternative financial plans is known as the financial break-even point.

(iv) At financial break-even point, EPS is zero.

(v) The greater the projected level of EBIT than the indifference point, the stronger is the case for the use of equity.

(vi) The combined leverage is the summation of the degree of operating leverage and financial leverage.
(vii) The combined leverage is a measure of total risk of the firm.
(viii) High fixed operating costs increase the financial leverage.
(ix) The larger the amount of fixed financial costs, the larger is the EBIT required to recover them.
(x) There exists inverse relationship between fixed costs and leverage.
(xi) Financial BEP is a summation of interest payable on debt and dividend on preference shares.

[Answers: (i) False (ii) False (iii) False (iv) True (v) False (vi) False (vii) True (viii) False (ix) True (x) False (xi) False]

RQ.18.2 What is the 'indifference point' and why is it so called? What is its usefulness? [LO 18.2]

RQ.18.3 How would you compute indifference point? [LO 18.2]

RQ.18.4 Royal Industries Ltd, a well-established firm in plastics, is considering the purchase of one of the two manufacturing companies. The financial manager of the company has developed the following information about the two companies. Both companies have total assets of ₹15,00,000. [LO 18.1]

Operating statement

Particulars	*X Ltd*	*Y Ltd*
Sales revenue	₹30,00,000	₹30,00,000
Less: cost of goods sold	22,50,000	22,50,000
selling expenses	2,40,000	2,40,000
administrative expenses	90,000	1,50,000
depreciation	1,20,000	90,000
EBIT	3,00,000	2,70,000
Cost break-ups		
Variable costs:		
Cost of goods sold	9,00,000	18,00,000
Selling expenses	1,50,000	1,50,000
Total	10,50,000	19,50,000

(i) Prepare operating statements for both the companies, assuming that sales increase by 20 per cent. The total fixed costs are likely to remain unchanged and the variable costs are a linear function of sales.
(ii) Calculate the degree of operating leverage.
(iii) If Royal Industries Ltd wishes to buy a company which has a lower degree of business risk, which company would be purchased by it?

LOD: Medium

RQ.18.5 What is meant by the term 'leverage'? What are its types? With what type of risk is each leverage generally associated? Why is increasing leverage also indicative of increasing risk? State the situation when there is neither a financial risk nor business risk. [LO 18.1,2,3]

RQ.18.6 Why must the finance manager keep in mind the degree of financial leverage in evaluating various financing plans? When does financial leverage become favourable? [LO 18.2]

RQ.18.7 Premier Ltd's capital structure consists of the following: [LO 18.2]

Particulars	*Amount (in ₹ lakh)*
Equity shares of ₹100 each	20
Retained earnings	10
9% Preference shares	12
7% Debentures	8
	50

The company's EBIT is at the rate of 12 per cent on its capital employed which is likely to remain unchanged after expansion. The expansion involves additional finances aggregating ₹25 lakh for which the following alternatives are available to it:

(i) Issue of 20,000 equity shares at a premium of ₹25 per share.
(ii) Issue of 10% Preference shares.
(iii) Issue of 8% Debentures.

It is estimated that the P/E ratio in case of equity shares, preference shares and debentures financing would be 15, 12, and 10 respectively.

Which of the financing alternatives would you recommend and why? The corporate tax rate is 35 per cent.

RQ.18.8 Hypothetical Ltd is in need of ₹1,00,000 to finance its increased net working capital requirements. The finance manager of the company believes that its various financial costs and share price will be unaffected by the selection of a particular plan, since a small sum is involved. Debentures will cost 10 per cent, preference shares 11 per cent, and equity shares can be sold for ₹25 per share. The tax rate is 35 per cent. **[LO 18.2]**

Sources of funds	*Financial plans (per cent)*		
	1	*2*	*3*
Equity shares	100	30	50
Preference shares	0	10	20
Debentures	0	60	30

(i) Determine the financial break even point.
(ii) Which plan has grater risk? Assume EBIT level of ₹50,000.

LOD: Difficult

RQ.18.9 A financial analyst is interested in ascertaining business risk of two similar firms. If all operating data for the two firms were the same, save the following differences, which firm would have greater amount of business risk in each instance? **[LO 18.1]**

(a) Firm X has a higher sales level than Firm Y, **(b)** Firm X has a higher EBIT level, and **(c)** Firm Y has a lower variable cost ratio.

RQ.18.10 What is combined leverage? What does it measure? What would be the changes in the degree of combined leverage, assuming other things being equal, in each of the following situations?

(a) The fixed costs increase, **(b)** The EBIT level increases, **(c)** The sale price decreases, and **(d)** The variable cost decreases. **[LO 18.3]**

RQ.18.11 Explain the significance of operating and financial leverage analysis for a financial executive in corporate profit and financial structure planning. **[LO 18.1,2]**

RQ.18.12 Key information pertaining to the proposed new financing plans of Hypothetical Ltd is given below: **[LO 18.2]**

Sources of funds	*Financing plans*	
	1	*2*
Equity	15,000 shares of ₹100 each	30,000 shares of ₹100 each
Preference shares	12%, 25,000 shares of ₹100 each	—
Debentures	₹5,00,000 at a coupon rate of 0.10	15,00,000, coupon rate of 0.11

Assuming 35 per cent tax rate,

(i) Determine the two EBIT - EPS coordinates for each financial plan.
(ii) Determine the (a) indifference point, and (b) financial break-even point for each financing plan.
(iii) Which plan has more financial risk and why?

(iv) Indicate over what EBIT range, if any, one plan is better than the other.
(v) If the firm is fairly certain that its EBIT will be ₹12,50,000, which plan would you recommend, and why?

RQ.18.13 The operating and cost data of ABC Ltd are: [LO 18.1,2,3]

Sales	₹20,00,000
Variable costs	14,00,000
Fixed costs	4,00,000 (including 15 per cent interest on ₹10,00,000)

Calculate its operating, financial and combined leverage.

ANSWERS

18.4 **(i)** EBIT ₹6,90,000 (X); ₹4,80,000 (Y)
(ii) DOL (X) 6.5
DOL (Y) 3.88
(iii) Royal Industries Ltd should purchase Y Ltd.

18.7 Issuing equity shares is the best alternative as it maximizes the MPS (₹165.30).

18.8 **(i)** ₹6,385
(ii) DFL of Financial Plan 1: 1
Plan 2 : 1.18
Plan 3 : 1.15
Financial Plan 2 has higher financial risk.

18.12 **(i)** **(a)** EBIT : ₹5,11,538; ₹1,65,000
(b) EPS : ₹32; ₹23.51
(ii) **(a)** ₹8,58,077
(b) ₹5,11,538 (Plan 1); ₹1,65,000 (Plan 2)
(iii) Financial risk is measured by DFL. Plan 1 has more financial risk as its DFL is likely to be higher.
(iv) Financial Plan 2 is better for EBIT level of less than ₹8,58,077; Plan 1 is better for EBIT ranges beyond that level.
(v) Plan 1, as EPS will be higher.

18.13 DOL 1.71
DFL 1.75
DCL 2.99

Scan the QR Code to access comprehensive solutions to all numerical review questions and additional material.

CHAPTER 19

Capital Structure, Cost of Capital and Valuation

LEARNING OBJECTIVES

LO 19.1	Review the assumptions, definitions and symbols relating to capital structure theories
LO 19.2	Explain the major capital structure theories—Net Income Approach, Net Operating Income Approach, Modigliani and Miller (MM) Approach and Traditional Approach—and evaluate them to explore the relationship between leverage and cost of capital from the standpoint of valuation

INTRODUCTION

The discussions in the preceding Chapter have shown that financial leverage has a magnifying effect on EPS, such that, for a given level of change in EBIT, there will be a more than proportionate change in the same direction in the EPS. But financial leverage also increases the financial risk, defined as the risk of possible insolvency arising out of inadequacy of available cash as well as the variability in the earnings available to the ordinary shareholders. Given the objective of the firm to maximise the value of the equity shares, the firm should select a financing-mix/capital structure/ financial leverage which will help in achieving the objective of financial management. As a corollary, the **capital structure** should be examined from the viewpoint of its impact on the *value* of the firm. It can be legitimately expected that if the capital structure decision affects the total value of the firm, a firm should select such a financing-mix as will maximise the shareholders' wealth. Such a capital structure is referred to as the optimum capital structure. The **optimum capital structure** may be defined as the *capital structure or combination of debt and equity that leads to the maximum value of the firm.*

Capital structure is the proportion of debt and preference and equity shares on a firm's balance sheet.

Optimum capital structure is the capital structure at which the weighted average cost of capital is minimum and thereby maximum value of the firm.

The importance of an appropriate capital structure is, thus, obvious. There is a viewpoint that strongly supports the close relationship between leverage and value of a firm. There is an equally strong body of opinion which believes that financing-mix or the combination of debt and equity has no impact on the shareholders' wealth and the decision on financial structure is irrelevant. In other words, there is nothing such as optimum capital structure.

In theory, capital structure can affect the value of a company by affecting either its expected earnings or the cost of capital, or both. While it is true that financing-mix cannot affect the total operating earnings of a firm, as they are determined by the investment decisions, it can affect the share of earnings belonging to the ordinary shareholders. The capital structure decision can influence the value of the firm through the earnings available to the shareholders. But the leverage can largely influence the value of the firm through the cost of capital. In exploring the relationship between leverage and value of a firm in this chapter, we are concerned with the relationship between leverage and cost of capital from the standpoint of valuation. We discuss the assumptions, definitions and symbols relating to capital structure theories first. The next four major capital structure theories, namely: **(i)** Net Income Approach, **(ii)** Net Operating Income Approach, **(iii)** Modigliani-Miller (MM) Approach, and **(iv)** Traditional Approach are explained and evaluated from the starpoint of valuation. The main points are summarised by way of recapitulation.

LO 19.1 ASSUMPTIONS, DEFINITIONS AND SYMBOLS

Assumptions

1. There are only two sources of funds used by a firm: *perpetual riskless* debt and *ordinary* shares.
2. There are no corporate taxes. This assumption is removed later.
3. The dividend-payout ratio is 100. That is, the total earnings are paid out as dividend to the shareholders and there are no retained earnings.
4. The total assets are given and do not change. The investment decisions are, in other words, assumed to be constant.
5. The total financing remains constant. The firm can change its degree of leverage (capital structure) either by selling shares and use the proceeds to retire debentures or by raising more debt and reduce the equity capital.
6. The operating profits (EBIT) are not expected to grow.
7. All investors are assumed to have the same subjective probability distribution of the future expected EBIT for a given firm.
8. Business risk is constant over time and is assumed to be independent of its capital structure and financial risk.
9. Perpetual life of the firm.

Definitions and Symbols

In addition to the above assumptions, we shall make use of some symbols in our analysis of capital structure theories:

S = total market value of equity
B = total market value of debt
I = total interest payments
V = total market value of the firm ($V = S + B$)
NI = net income available to equity-holders.

We shall also make use of some basic definitions:

(1) Cost of debt $(k_i) = \frac{I}{B}$ **(19.1)**

$$\text{Value of debt } (B) = \frac{I}{k_i} \tag{19.2}$$

(2) Cost of equity capital (k_e) $= \dfrac{D_1}{P_0} + g$ **(19.3)**

where D_1 = net dividend; P_0 = current market price of shares and g is the expected growth rate. According to assumption (3), the percentage of retained earnings is zero. Since $g = br$, where r is the rate of return on equity shares and b is the retention rate, $g = 0$, the growth rate is zero. This is consistent with assumption (6). In operational terms $D_1 = E_1$, $g = 0$. Therefore,

$$k_e = \frac{E_1}{P_0} + g = \frac{E_1}{P_0} + 0 = \frac{E_1}{P_0} \tag{19.4}$$

where E_1 = earnings per share. Equation 19.4 is on a per share basis. Multiplying both the numerator and the denominator by the number of shares outstanding (N) and assuming there are no income taxes, we have

$$K_e = \frac{E_1 (\times) N}{P_0 (\times) N} = \frac{\text{EBIT} - I \text{ or } NI}{S}$$

Or

$$= \frac{\text{Net income available to equity holders}}{\text{Total market value of equity shares}} \tag{19.5}$$

Thus, k_e may be defined on either per share or total basis.

From Eqs. 19.4 and 19.5 follow the equations of determining the value of equity shares on per share basis and total basis.

(i) *Per share basis,* $P_0 = \dfrac{E_1}{k_e}$ **(19.6)**

(ii) *Total basis,* $S = P_0 N = \dfrac{\text{EBIT} - I}{k_e}$ **(19.7)**

(iii) *Overall cost of capital or weighted average cost of capital:*

$K_0 = W_1 k_i + W_2 k_e$ (where W_1 and W_2 are relative weights)

$$= (B/V)k_i + (S/V)k_e = \left[\frac{B}{B+S}\right]k_i + \left[\frac{S}{B+S}\right]k_e \tag{19.8}$$

or

$$k_0 = \frac{I + NI}{V} = \frac{\text{EBIT}}{V} \tag{19.9}$$

From Eq. 19.9 follows the equation of total value of the firm. Thus,

$$V = \frac{\text{EBIT}}{k_0} \tag{19.10}$$

Alternatively:

$$V = \frac{I}{k_i} + \frac{\text{EBIT} - I}{k_e} \tag{19.11}$$

Another useful way of measuring the cost of equity capital is described below:

We know k_0 is the weighted average of the cost of equity and the cost of debt. Symbolically,

$$k_0 = \left[\frac{B}{B+S}\right]k_i + \left[\frac{S}{B+S}\right]k_e \tag{19.8}$$

$$= k_i\left(\frac{B}{V}\right) + k_e\left(\frac{S}{V}\right) \tag{19.8.1}$$

$$k_e = \frac{k_0 - k_i\,(B/V)}{S/V} \tag{19.8.2}$$

We know that $V = B + S$. Therefore, equity ratio, S/V can be expressed as:

$$\frac{S}{V} = \frac{S}{B+S} = 1 - \frac{B}{B+S} \tag{19.8.3}$$

Substituting the value of Eq. 19.8.3 in Eq. 19.8.2, we have

$$k_e = k_0 - k_i\left[\frac{B}{B+S}\right]\bigg/ 1 - \frac{B}{B+S}$$

$$= \frac{k_0\,(B+S) - k_i B}{B+S}\bigg/\frac{B+S-B}{B+S} \tag{19.8.4}$$

Or

$$= \frac{k_0 B + k_0 S - k_i B}{B+S}\bigg/\frac{S}{B+S} \tag{19.8.5}$$

Simplifying Eq. 19.8.5, we have

$$k_e = \frac{k_0 B + k_0 S - k_i B}{S} \tag{19.8.6}$$

$$k_e = k_0 + (k_0 - k_i)\,B/S \tag{19.12}$$

While exploring the relationship between capital structure and value of the firm, our concern is with the cost of equity capital (k_e), cost of debt (k_i) and overall cost of capital (k_0) when the capital structure/leverage changes, as measured by the change in the relationship between total value of debt and debt to total of ordinary shares (B/S).

LO 19.2 CAPITAL STRUCTURE THEORIES

The capital structure theories explain the relationship between leverage and cost of capital from the standpoint of valuation. The major capital structure theories explored here are Net income, Net operating income, MM and Traditional approaches.

Net Income Approach

According to the Net Income (NI) Approach, suggested by the Durand[1], the capital structure decision is relevant to the valuation of the firm. In other words, a change in the financial leverage will lead to a corresponding change in the overall cost of capital as well as the total value of the firm. If, therefore, the degree of financial leverage as measured by the ratio of debt to equity is increased, the weighted average cost of capital will decline, while the value of the firm as well as the market price of ordinary shares will increase. Conversely, a decrease in the leverage will cause an increase in the overall cost of capital and a decline both in the value of the firm as well as the market price of equity shares.

The NI Approach to valuation is based on three assumptions: first, there are no taxes; second, that the cost of debt is less than the equity-capitalisation rate or the cost of equity; third, that the use of debt does not change the risk perception of investors. That the financial risk perception of the investors does not change with the introduction of debt or change in leverage implies that due to change in leverage, there is no change in either the cost of debt or the cost of equity. The implication of the three assumptions underlying the NI Approach is that as the degree of leverage increases, the proportion of a cheaper source of funds, that is, debt in the capital structure increases. As a result, the weighted average cost of capital tends to decline, leading to an increase in the total value of the firm. Thus, with the cost of debt and cost of equity being constant, the increased use of debt (increase in leverage), will magnify the shareholder's earnings and, thereby, the market value of the ordinary shares.

The financial leverage is, according to the NI Approach, an important variable to the capital structure of a firm. With a judicious mixture of debt and equity, a firm can evolve an optimum capital structure which will be the one at which value of the firm is the highest and the overall cost of capital is the lowest. At that structure, the market price per share would be maximum.

If the firm uses no debt or if the financial leverage is zero, the overall cost of capital will be equal to the equity-capitalisation rate. The weighted average cost of capital will decline and will approach the cost of debt as the degree of leverage reaches one.

The NI Approach is illustrated in Example 19.1.

***Example* 19.1**

A company's expected annual net operating income (EBIT) is ₹50,000. The company has ₹2,00,000, 10% debentures. The equity capitalisation rate (k_e) of the company is 12.5 per cent.

Solution

With no taxes, the value of the firm, according to the Net Income Approach is depicted in Table 19.1.

TABLE 19.1 Value of the Firm (Net Income Approach)

Net operating income (EBIT)	₹50,000
Less: Interest on debentures (I)	20,000
Earnings available to equity holders (NI)	30,000
Equity capitalisation rate (k_e)	0.125
Market value of equity (S) = NI/k_e	2,40,000
Market value of debt (B)	2,00,000
Total value of the firm ($S + B$) = V	4,40,000
Overall cost of capital = k_0 = EBIT/V (%)	11.36
Alternatively: $k_0 = k_i\,(B/V) + k_e(S/V)$ where k_i and k_e are cost of debt and	
cost of equity respectively, $= 0.10\left(\dfrac{₹2,00,000}{₹4,40,000}\right) + 0.125\left(\dfrac{₹2,40,000}{₹4,40,000}\right)$ (%)	11.36

Increase in Value

In order to examine the effect of a change in financing-mix on the firm's overall (weighted average) cost of capital and its total value, let us suppose that the firm has decided to raise the amount of debenture by ₹1,00,000 and use the proceeds to retire the equity shares. The k_i and k_e would remain unaffected as per the assumptions of the NI Approach. In the new situation, the value of the firm is shown in Table 19.2.

TABLE 19.2 Value of the Firm (Net Income Approach)

Net operating income (EBIT)	₹50,000
Less: Interest on debentures (*I*)	30,000
Earnings available to equity holders (*NI*)	20,000
Equity capitalisation rate (k_e)	0.125
Market value of equity (*S*) = NI/k_e	1,60,000
Market value of debt (*B*)	3,00,000
Total value of the firm (*S* + *B*) = *V*	4,60,000
$k_0 = \left[\dfrac{₹50{,}000}{₹4{,}60{,}000}\right]$ Or $0.10\left[\dfrac{₹3{,}00{,}000}{₹4{,}60{,}000}\right] + 0.125\left[\dfrac{₹1{,}60{,}000}{₹4{,}60{,}000}\right]$	10.9 per cent

Thus, the use of additional debt has caused the total value of the firm to increase and the overall cost of capital to decrease.

Decrease in Value

If we decrease the amount of debentures in Example 19.1, the total value of the firm, according to the NI Approach, will decrease and the overall cost of capital will increase. Let us suppose that the amount of debt has been reduced by ₹1,00,000 to ₹1,00,000 and a fresh issue of equity shares is made to retire the debentures. Assuming other facts as given in Example 19.1, the value of the firm and the weighted average cost of capital are shown in Table 19.3.

TABLE 19.3 Value of the Firm (Net Income Approach)

Net operating income (EBIT)	₹50,000
Less: Interest on debentures (*I*)	10,000
Earnings available to equity holders (*NI*)	40,000
Equity capitalisation rate (k_e)	0.125
Market value of equity (*S*) = NI/k_e	3,20,000
Market value of debt (*B*)	1,00,000
Total value of the firm (*S* + *B*) = *V*	4,20,000
$k_0 = \dfrac{₹50{,}000}{₹4{,}20{,}000}$ Or $0.10\left[\dfrac{₹1{,}00{,}000}{₹4{,}20{,}000}\right] + 0.125\left[\dfrac{₹3{,}20{,}000}{₹4{,}20{,}000}\right]$ (%)	11.9

Thus, we find that the decrease in leverage has increased the overall cost of capital and has reduced the value of firm.

Market Price

Thus, according to the NI Approach, the firm can increase/decrease its total value (*V*) and lower/increase its overall cost of capital (k_0) as it increases/decreases the degree of leverage. As a result, the market price per share is affected. To illustrate, assume in Example 19.1 that the firm with ₹2,00,000 debt has 2,400 equity shares outstanding. The market price per share works out to ₹100 (₹2,40,000 ÷ 2,400). The firm issues ₹1,00,000 additional debt and uses the proceeds of the debt to repurchase/retire ₹1,00,000 worth of equity shares or 1,000 shares. It, then, has 1,400 shares outstanding. We have observed in Example 19.1 that the total market value of the equity after the change in the capital structure is ₹1,60,000 (Table 19.2). Therefore, the market price per share is ₹114.28 (₹1,60,000 ÷ 1,400), as compared to the original price of ₹100 per share.

Likewise, when the firm employs less amount of debt, the market value per share declines. To continue with Example 19.1, the firm raises ₹1,00,000 additional equity capital by issuing 1,000 equity shares of ₹100 each and uses the proceeds to retire the debenture amounting to ₹1,00,000. It would then have 3,400 shares (2,400 old + 1,000 new) outstanding. With this capital structure, we have seen in Example 19.1 that the total market value of equity shares is ₹3,20,000 (Table 19.3). Therefore, the market price per share has declined to ₹94.12 (₹3,20,000 ÷ 3,400) from ₹100 before a change in the leverage.

We can graph the relationship between the various factors (k_e, k_i, k_0) with the degree of leverage (Fig. 19.1).

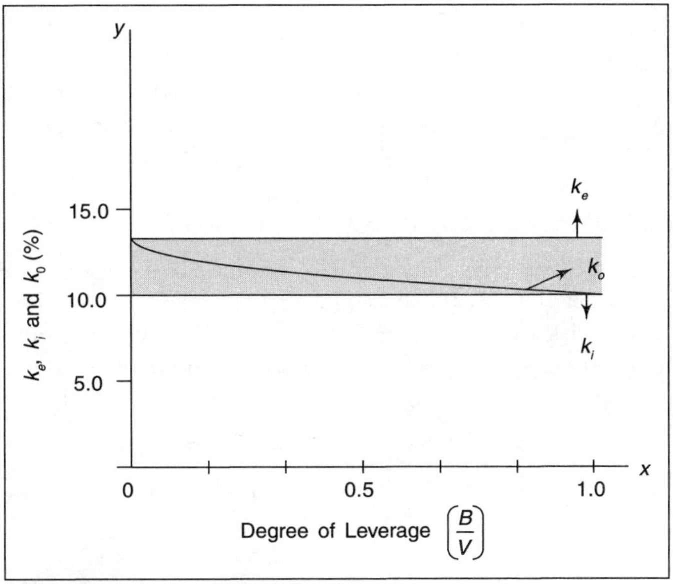

FIGURE 19.1 Leverage and Cost of Capital (NI Approach)

The degree of leverage (B/V) is plotted along the X-axis, while the percentage rates of k_i, k_e and k_0 are on the Y-axis. This graph is based on Example 19.1. Due to the assumptions that k_e and k_i remain unchanged as the degree of leverage changes, we find that both the curves are parallel to the X-axis. But as the degree of leverage increases, k_0 decreases and approaches the cost of debt when leverage is 1.0, that is, ($k_0 = k_i$). It will obviously be so owing to the fact that there is no equity capital in the capital structure. At this point, the firm's overall cost of capital would be minimum. The significant conclusion, therefore, of the NI Approach is that the firm can employ almost 100 per cent debt to maximise its value.

Net Operating Income (NOI) Approach

Another theory of capital structure, suggested by Durand[2], is the Net Operating Income (NOI) Approach. This Approach is diametrically opposite to the NI Approach. The essence of this Approach is that the capital structure decision of a firm is irrelevant. Any change in leverage will not lead to any change in the total value of the firm and the market price of shares as well as the overall cost of capital is independent of the degree of leverage.

The NOI Approach is based on the following propositions.

Overall Cost of Capital/Capitalisation Rate (k_0) is Constant

The NOI Approach to valuation argues that the overall capitalisation rate of the firm remains constant, for all degrees of leverage. The value of the firm, given the level of EBIT, is determined by Eq. 19.13.

$$V = \frac{\text{EBIT}}{k_0} \tag{19.13}$$

In other words, the market evaluates the firm as a whole. The split of the capitalisation between debt and equity is, therefore, not significant.

Residual Value of Equity

The value of equity is a residual value which is determined by deducting the total value of debt (B) from the total value of the firm (V). Symbolcially, Total market value of equity capital (S) = $V - B$.

Changes in Cost of Equity Capital

The equity-capitalisation rate/cost of equity capital (k_e) increases with the degree of leverage. The increase in the proportion of debt in the capital structure relative to equity shares would lead to an increase in the financial risk to the ordinary shareholders. To compensate for the increased risk, the shareholders would expect a higher rate of return on their investments. The increase in the equity-capitalisation rate (or the lowering of the price-earnings ratio, that is, P/E ratio) would match the increase in the debt-equity ratio. The k_e would be $= k_0 + (k_0 - k_i)\left[\frac{B}{S}\right]$

Cost of Debt

Explicit cost is the rate of interest paid on debt.

Implicit cost is the increase in cost of equity due to increase in debt.

The cost of debt (k_i) has two parts: (a) **Explicit cost** which is represented by the rate of interest. Irrespective of the degree of leverage, the firm is assumed to be able to borrow at a given rate of interest. *This implies that the increasing proportion of debt in the financial structure does not affect the financial risk of the lenders* and they do not penalise the firm by charging higher interest; (b) **Implicit** *or* '**hidden**' *cost.* As shown in the assumption relating to the changes in k_e, increase in the degree of leverage or the proportion of debt to equity causes an increase in the cost of equity capital. This increase in k_e, being attributable to the increase in debt, is the implicit part of k_i.

Thus, the advantage associated with the use of debt, supposed to be a 'cheaper' source of funds in terms of the explicit cost, is exactly neutralised by the implicit cost represented by the increase in k_e. As a result, **the real cost of debt and the real cost of equity**, according to the NOI Approach, **are the same and equal k_0.**

Optimum Capital Structure

The total value of the firm is unaffected by its capital structure. No matter what the degree of leverage is, the total value of the firm will remain constant. The market price of shares will also not change with the change in the debt-equity ratio. There is nothing such as an *optimum capital structure.* Any capital structure is optimum, according to the NOI Approach.

The effect of NOI Approach on value of the firm, k_e, and the market price per share is illustrated in Example 19.2.

***Example* 19.2**

Assume the figures given in Example 19.1: operating income ₹50,000; cost of debt, 10 per cent; and outstanding debt, ₹2,00,000. If the overall capitalisation rate (overall cost of capital) is 12.5 per cent, what would be the total value of the firm and the equity-capitalisation rate?

Solution

The computation is depicted in Table 19.4.

TABLE 19.4 Total Value of the Firm (Net Operating Income Approach)

Net operating income (EBIT)	₹50,000
Overall capitalisation rate (k_0)	0.125
Total market value of the firm (V) = EBIT/k_0	4,00,000
Total value of debt (B)	2,00,000
Total market value of equity (S) = (V – B)	2,00,000
Equity-capitalisation rate, $k_e = \frac{\text{EBIT} - \text{I}}{V - B} = \frac{\text{Earnings available to equityholders}}{\text{Total market value of equity shares}}$	
$= \frac{₹50,000 - ₹20,000}{₹2,00,000}$	0.15
Alternatively, $k_e = k_0 + (k_0 - k_i)B/S$: $0.125 + (0.125 - 0.10)\left[\frac{₹2,00,000}{₹2,00,000}\right]$	0.15
The weighted average cost of capital to verify the validity of the NOI Approach:	
$k_0 = k_i(B/V) + k_e(S/V) = 0.10\left[\frac{₹2,00,000}{₹4,00,000}\right] + 0.15\left[\frac{₹2,00,000}{₹4,00,000}\right]$	0.125

Thus, we find that the overall cost of capital is 12.5 per cent as per the requirement of the NOI Approach.

In order to examine the effect of leverage, let us assume that the firm increases the amount of debt from ₹2,00,000 to ₹3,00,000 and uses the proceeds of the debt to repurchase equity shares. The value of the firm would remain unchanged at ₹4,00,000, but the equity-capitalisation rate would go up to 20 per cent as shown in Table 19.5.

TABLE 19.5 Value of the Firm (NOI Approach)

Net operating income (EBIT)	₹50,000
Overall capitalisation rate (k_0)	0.125
Total market value of the firm (V) = EBIT/k_0	4,00,000
Total value of debt (B)	3,00,000
Total market value of equity (S) = (V – B)	1,00,000
$k_e = \frac{₹50,000 - ₹30,000}{₹1,00,000}$	0.20

(Contd.)

(Contd.)

Alternatively: $k_e = 0.125 + (0.125 - 0.10)\left[\dfrac{₹3{,}00{,}000}{₹1{,}00{,}000}\right]$	0.20
$k_0 = 0.10\left[\dfrac{₹3{,}00{,}000}{₹4{,}00{,}000}\right] + 0.20\left[\dfrac{₹1{,}00{,}000}{₹4{,}00{,}000}\right]$	0.125

Let us further suppose that the firm retires debt by ₹1,00,000 by issuing fresh equity shares of the same amount. The value of the firm would remain unchanged at ₹4,00,000 and the equity-capitalisation rate would come down to 13.33 per cent as manifested in the calculations in Table 19.6.

TABLE 19.6 Total Value of the Firm (NOI Approach)

Net operating income (EBIT)	₹50,000
Overall capitalisation rate (k_0)	0.125
Total market value of the firm (V) = EBIT/k_0	4,00,000
Total value of debt (B)	1,00,000
Total market value of equity (S) = (V – B)	3,00,000
$k_e = \dfrac{₹50{,}000 - ₹10{,}000}{₹3{,}00{,}000}$	0.133
Alternatively: $k_e = 0.125 + (0.125 - 0.10)\left[\dfrac{₹1{,}00{,}000}{₹3{,}00{,}000}\right]$	0.133
$k_0 = 0.10\left[\dfrac{₹1{,}00{,}000}{₹4{,}00{,}000}\right] + 0.133\left[\dfrac{₹3{,}00{,}000}{₹4{,}00{,}000}\right]$	0.125

The significant feature is that the equity-capitalisation rate, k_e, increases with the increase in the degree of leverage. It has gone up from 15 per cent to 20 per cent with the increase in leverage from 0.50 to 0.75. The equity capitalisation rate decreases with the decrease in the degree of leverage. It has come down from 15 per cent to 13.33 per cent with the decrease in leverage from 0.50 to 0.25.

Market Price of Shares

In Example 19.2, let us suppose the firm with ₹2 lakh debt has 2,000 equity shares (of ₹100 each) outstanding. The firm has issued additional debt of ₹1,00,000 to repurchase its shares amounting to ₹1,00,000; it has to repurchase 1,000 shares of ₹100 each from the market. It, then, has 1,000 equity shares outstanding, having total market value of ₹1,00,000. The market price per share, therefore, is ₹100 (₹1,00,000 ÷ 1,000) as before.

In the second situation the firm issues, 1,000 equity shares of ₹100 each to retire debt aggregating ₹1,00,000. It will have 3,000 equity shares outstanding, having total market value of ₹3,00,000, thus, giving a market price of ₹100 per share.

Thus, we note that there is no change in the market price per share due to change in leverage.

We have portrayed the relationship between the leverage and the various costs, viz. k_i, k_e and k_0 in Fig. 19.2.

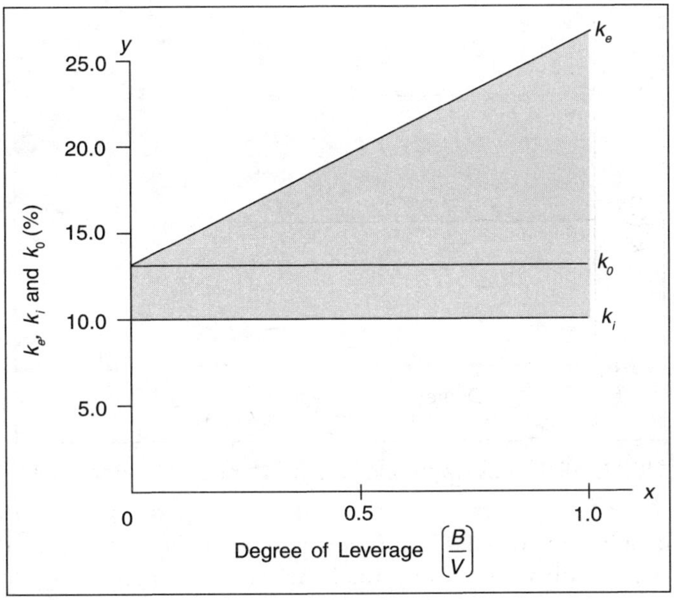

FIGURE 19.2 Leverage and Cost of Capital (NOI Approach)

The graph is based on Example 19.2. Due to the assumption that k_0 and k_i remain unchanged as the degree of leverage changes, we find that both the curves are parallel to the X-axis. But as the degree of leverage increases, the k_e increases continuously.

Modigliani-Miller (MM) Approach

The Modigliani-Miller Thesis[3] relating to the relationship between the capital structure, cost of capital and valuation is akin to the NOI Approach. The NOI Approach, as explained above, is definitional or conceptual and lacks behavioural significance.[4] The NOI Approach, in other words, does not provide operational justification for the irrelevance of the capital structure. The MM proposition supports the NOI Approach relating to the independence of the cost of capital of the degree of leverage at any level of debt-equity ratio. The significance of their hypothesis lies in the fact that it provides behavioural justification for constant overall cost of capital and, therefore, total value of the firm. In other words, the MM Approach maintains that the weighted average (overall) cost of capital does not change, as shown in Fig. 19.3, with a change in the proportion of debt to equity in the capital structure (or degree of leverage). They offer operational justification for this and are not content with merely stating the proposition.

Basic Propositions

There are three basic propositions of the MM Approach:

I The overall cost of capital (k_0) and the value of the firm (V) are independent of its capital structure. The k_0 and V are constant for all degrees of leverage. The total value is given by capitalising the expected stream of operating earnings at a discount rate appropriate for its risk class.

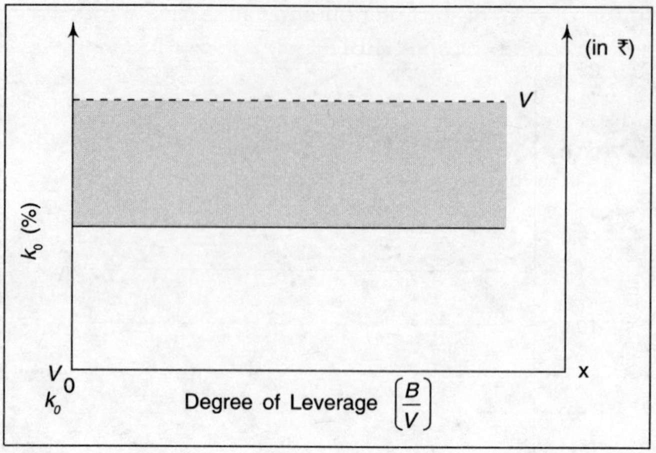

FIGURE 19.3 Leverage and Cost of Capital (MM Approach)

II The second proposition of the MM Approach is that the k_e is equal to the capitalisation rate of a pure equity stream plus a premium for financial risk equal to the difference between the pure equity-capitalisation rate (k_e) and k_i times the ratio of debt to equity. In other words, k_e increases in a manner to offset exactly the use of a less expensive source of funds represented by debt. MM proposition II states that the corporate's cost of equity (k_e) consists of two elements: **(i)** k_o, the required, rate of return on the total assets of the firm whose value depends on the business risk; and **(ii)** $(k_o - k_i)$ B/S which is determined by the company's capital structure.[5] For a zero-debt company, this component is zero. As the company starts using debt, the k_e increases **and the equity-investor is to be compensated for it**. The higher the employment of debt in financing company's assets, the higher is the financial risk as well as the financial risk premium.

Debt financing increases financial risk. The cost of equity depends on business risk and financial risk. Business risk is affected by the business operations of the firm and is independent of its financing pattern. Financial risk is determined exclusively by the financing pattern/capital structure.

Thus, MM proposition II is in conformity with the NOI approach (**already explained**).

III The cut-off rate for investment purposes is completely independent of the way in which an investment is financed.

We are interested mainly in exploring the relationship between leverage and valuation. Our focus, therefore, is on proposition(1).

Assumptions

The proposition that the weighted average cost of capital is constant irrespective of the type of capital structure is based on the following assumptions:

(a) *Perfect capital markets*: The implication of a perfect capital market is that (i) securities are infinitely divisible; (ii) investors are free to buy/sell securities; (iii) investors can borrow without restrictions on the same terms and conditions as firms can; (iv) there are no transaction costs; (v) information is perfect, that is, each investor has the same information which is readily available to him without cost; and (vi) investors are rational and behave accordingly.

(b) Given the assumption of perfect information and rationality, all investors have the same expectation of firm's net operating income (EBIT) with which to evaluate the value of a firm.

(c) Business risk is equal among all firms within similar operating environment. That means, all firms can be divided into 'equivalent risk class' or 'homogeneous risk class'. The term equivalent/homogeneous risk class means that the expected earnings have identical risk characteristics. Firms within an industry are assumed to have the same risk characteristics. The categorisation of firms into equivalent risk class is on the basis of the industry group to which the firm belongs.

(d) The dividend payout ratio is 100 per cent.

(e) There are no taxes. This assumption is removed later.

Proposition I The basic premise of the MM Approach (proposition I) is that, given the above assumptions, the total value of a firm must be constant irrespective of the degree of leverage (debt-equity ratio). Similarly, the cost of capital as well as the market price of shares must be the same regardless of the financing-mix.

> **Arbitrage** implies buying a security in a market where price is low and selling where it is high.

The operational justification for the MM hypothesis is the **arbitrage process**. The term 'arbitrage' refers to an act of buying an asset/security in one market (at lower prices) and selling it in another (at higher price). As a result, equilibrium is restored in the market price of a security in different markets. The essence of the arbitrage process is the purchase of securities/assets whose prices are lower (undervalued securities) and, sale of securities whose prices are higher, in related markets which are temporarily out of equilibrium. The arbitrage process is essentially a balancing operation. It implies that a security cannot sell at different prices. The MM Approach illustrates the arbitrage process with reference to valuation in terms of two firms which are exactly similar in all respects except leverage so that one of them has debt in its capital structure while the other does not. Such homogeneous firms are, according to Modigliani and Miller, perfect substitutes. The total value of the homogeneous firms which differ only in respect of leverage cannot be different because of the operation of arbitrage. The investors of the firm whose value is higher will sell their shares and instead buy the shares of the firm whose value is lower. Investors will be able to earn the same return at lower outlay with the same perceived risk or lower risk. They would, therefore, be better off. The behaviour of the investors will have the effect of **(i)** increasing the share prices (value) of the firm whose shares are being purchased; and **(ii)** lowering the share prices (value) of the firm whose shares are being sold. This will continue till the market prices of the two identical firms become identical. Thus, the switching operation (arbitrage) drives the total value of two homogeneous firms in all respects, except the debt-equity ratio, together. The arbitrage process, as already indicated, ensures to the investor the same return at lower outlay as he was getting by investing in the firm whose total value was higher and yet, his risk is not increased. This is so because the investors would borrow in the proportion of the degree of leverage present in the firm. The use of debt by the investor for arbitrage is called as 'home-made' or 'personal' leverage. The essence of the arbitrage argument of Modigliani and Miller is that the investors (arbitragers) are able to substitute personal leverage or home-made leverage for corporate leverage, that is, the use of debt by the firm itself.

> **Homemade leverage** can replicate the firm's capital structure, thereby causing investers to be indifferent to it.

The operation of the arbitrage process is illustrated in Example 19.3.

***Example* 19.3**

Assume there are two firms, L and U, which are identical in all respects except that firm L has 10 per cent, ₹5,00,000 debentures. The earnings before interest and taxes (EBIT) of both the firms are equal, that is, ₹1,00,000. The equity-capitalisation rate (k_e) of firm L is higher (16 per cent) than that of firm U (12.5 per cent).

Solution

The total market values of firms L and U are computed in Table 19.7.

TABLE 19.7 Total Value of Firms L and U

Particulars	*Firms*	
	L	*U*
EBIT	₹1,00,000	₹1,00,000
Less: Interest	50,000	—
Earnings available to equity-holders	50,000	1,00,000
Equity-capitalisation rate (k_e)	0.16	0.125
Total market value of equity (*S*)	3,12,500	8,00,000
Total market value of debt (*B*)	5,00,000	—
Total market value (*V*)	8,12,500	8,00,000
Implied overall capitalisation rate/cost of capital (k_0) = EBIT/*V*	0.123	0.125
Debt-equity ratio = *B*/*S*	1.6	—

Thus, the total market value of the firm which employs debt in the capital structure (L) is more than that of the unlevered firm (U). According to the MM hypothesis, this situation cannot continue as the arbitrage process, based on the substitutability of personal leverage for corporate leverage, will operate and the values of the two firms will be brought to an identical level.

Arbitrage Process The *modus operandi* of the arbitrage process is as follows:

Suppose an investor, Mr X, holds 10 per cent of the outstanding shares of the levered firm (L). His holdings amount to ₹31,250 (i.e. 0.10 × ₹3,12,500) and his share in the earnings that belong to the equity shareholders would be ₹5,000 (0.10 × ₹50,000).

He will sell his holdings in firm L and invest in the unlevered firm (U). Since firm U has no debt in its capital structure, the financial risk to Mr X would be less than in firm L. To reach the level of financial risk of firm L, he will borrow additional funds equal to his proportionate share in the levered firm's debt on his personal account. That is, he will substitute personal leverage (or home-made leverage) for corporate leverage. In other words, instead of the firm using debt, Mr X will borrow money. The effect, in essence, of this is that he is able to introduce leverage in the capital structure of the the unlevered firm by borrowing on his personal account. Mr X in our example will borrow ₹50,000 at 10 per cent rate of interest. His proportionate holding (10 per cent) in the unlevered firm will amount to ₹80,000 on which he will receive a dividend income of ₹10,000. Out of the income of ₹10,000 from the unlevered firm (U), Mr X will pay ₹5,000 as interest on his personal borrowings. He will be left with ₹5,000 that is, the same amount as he was getting from the levered firm (L). But his investment outlay in firm U is less (₹30,000) as compared with that in firm L (₹31,250). At the same time, his risk is identical in both the situations. The effect of the arbitrage process is summarised in Table 19.8.

TABLE 19.8 Effect of Arbitrage

(A) Mr X's position in firm L (levered) with 10 per cent equity-holding	
(i) Investment outlay	₹31,250
(ii) Dividend Income	5,000

(Contd.)

(*Contd.*)

(B) Mr X's position in firm U (unlevered) with 10 per cent equity holding		
(i) Total funds available (own funds, ₹31,250 + borrowed funds, ₹50,000)		81,250
(ii) Investment outlay (own funds, ₹30,000 + borrowed funds, ₹50,000)80,000		
(iii) Dividend Income:		
Total Income (0.10 × ₹1,00,000)	₹10,000	
Less: Interest payable on borrowed funds	5,000	5,000
(C) Mr X's position in firm U if he invests the total funds available		
(i) Investment costs		81,250.00
(ii) Total income		10,156.25
(iii) Dividend income (net) (₹10,156.25 – ₹5,000)		5,156.25

It is, thus, clear that Mr X will be better off by selling his securities in the levered firm and buying the shares of the unlevered firm. With identical risk characteristics of the two firms, he gets the same income with lower investment outlay in the unlevered firm. He will obviously prefer switching from the levered to the unlevered firm. Other investors will also, given the assumption of rational investors, enter into the arbitrage process. The consequent increasing demand for the securities of the unlevered firm will lead to an increase in the market price of its shares. At the same time, the price of the shares of the levered firm will decline. This will continue till it is possible to reduce the investment outlays and get the same return. Beyond this point, switching from firm L to firm U or arbitrage will not be identical. This is the point of equilibrium. At this point, the total value of the two firms would be identical. The cost of capital of the two firms would also be the same. Thus, it is unimportant what the capital structure of firm L is. The weighted cost of capital (k_0) after the investors exercise their home-made leverage is constant because investors exactly offset the firm's leverage with their own.[6]

Arbitrage Process: Reverse Direction According to the MM hypothesis, since debt financing has no advantage, it has no disadvantage either. In other words, just as the total value of a levered firm cannot be more than that of an unlevered firm, the value of an unlevered firm cannot be greater than the value of a levered firm. This is because the arbitrage process will set in and depress the value of the unlevered firm and increase the market price and, thereby, the total value of the levered firm. The arbitrage would, thus, operate in the opposite direction. Here, the investors will dispose of their holdings in the unlevered firm and obtain the same return by acquiring proportionate share in the equity capital and the debt of the levered firm at a lower outlay without any increase in the risk. This is illustrated in Example 19.4.

Example 19.4

Assume that in Example 19.3, the equity-capitalisation rate (k_e) is 20 per cent in the case of the levered firm (L), instead of the assumed 16 per cent. The total values of the two firms are given in Table 19.9.

TABLE 19.9 Total Value of Firms L and U

Particulars	*L*	*U*
EBIT	₹1,00,000	₹1,00,000
Less: Interest	50,000	—
Income to equity holders	50,000	1,00,000
Equity-capitalisation rate (k_e)	0.20	0.125
Market value of equity	2,50,000	8,00,000
Market value of debt	5,00,000	—
Total value (V)	7,50,000	8,00,000
(k_0)	0.133	0.125
B/S	2	0

Since both firms are similar, except for financing-mix, a situation in which their total values are different, cannot continue, as arbitrage will drive the two values together.

Suppose, Mr Y has 10 per cent shareholdings of firm U. He earns ₹10,000 (0.10 × ₹1,00,000). He will sell his securities in firm U and invest in the undervalued levered firm, L. He can purchase 10 per cent of firm L's debt at a cost of ₹50,000 which will provide ₹5,000 interest and 10 per cent of L's equity at a cost of ₹25,000 with an expected dividend of ₹5,000 (0.10 × ₹50,000). The purchase of a 10 per cent claim against the levered firm's income costs Mr Y only ₹75,000, yielding the same expected income of ₹10,000 from the equity shares of the unlevered firm. He would prefer the levered firm's securities as the outlay is lower. Table 19.10 portrays the reverse arbitrage process.

TABLE 19.10 Effect of Reverse Arbitrage Process

(A) Mr Y's current position in firm U		
Investment outlay		₹80,000
Dividend income		10,000
(B) Mr Y sells his holdings in firm U and purchases 10 per cent of the levered firm's equity and debentures		
	Investment	*Income*
Debt	₹50,000	₹5,000
Equity	25,000	5,000
Total	75,000	10,000
Y would prefer alternative B to A, as he is able to earn the same income with a smaller outlay.		
(C) He invests the entire sum of ₹80,000 in firm L		
	Investment	*Income*
Debt	₹53,333.00	₹5,333.30
Equity	26,667.00	5,333.40
Total	80,000,00	10,666.70
He augments his income by ₹666.70.		

The above illustrations establish that the arbitrage process will make the values of both the firms identical. Thus, Modigliani and Miller show that the value of a levered firm can neither be greater nor smaller than that of an unlevered firm; the two must be equal. There is neither an advantage nor a disadvantage in using debt in the firm's capital structure. The principle involved is simply that investors are able to reconstitute their former position by off-setting changes in corporate leverage with personal leverage. As a result the investment opportunities available to them are not altered by changes in the capital structure of the firm.[7]

Limitations

Does the MM hypothesis provide a valid framework to explain the relationship between capital structure, cost of capital and total value of a firm? The most crucial element in the MM Approach is the *arbitrage process* which forms the behavioural foundation of, and provides operational justification to, the MM hypothesis. The arbitrage process, in turn, is based on the crucial assumption of perfect substitutability of personal/home-made leverage with corporate leverage. The validity of the MM hypothesis depends on whether the arbitrage process is effective in the sense that personal leverage is a perfect substitute for corporate leverage. The arbitrage process is, however, not realistic and the exercise based upon it is purely theoretical and has no practical relevance.

Risk Perception In the first place, the risk perceptions of personal and corporate leverage are different. If home-made and corporate leverages are perfect substitutes, as the MM Approach assumes, the risk to which an investor is exposed, must be identical irrespective of whether the firm has borrowed (corporate leverage) or the investor himself borrows proportionate to his share in the firm's debt. If not, they cannot be perfect substitutes and consequently the arbitrage process will not be effective. The risk exposure to the investor is greater with personal leverage than with corporate leverage. The liability of an investor is limited in corporate enterprises in the sense that he is liable to the extent of his proportionate shareholdings in case the company is forced to go into liquidation. The risk to which he is exposed, therefore, is limited to his relative holding. The liability of an individual borrower is, on the other hand, unlimited as even his personal property is liable to be used for payment to the creditors. The risk to the investor with personal borrowing is higher. In Example 19.3, for instance, Mr X's liability (risk), when the firm has borrowed (levered firm), is ₹31,250, that is, his 10 per cent share in firm L. If he were to borrow equal to his proportionate share in the firm's debt (₹50,000), his total liability will be ₹80,000. Thus, investments in a levered firm (corporate leverage) and in an unlevered firm (personal leverage) are not on an equal footing from the viewpoint of risks to the investors. Since investors can reasonably be expected to prefer an arrangement which, while giving the same return, ensures lower risk, the personal and corporate leverages cannot be perfect substitutes.

Convenience Apart from higher *risk exposure*, the investors would find the personal leverage *inconvenient*. This is so because with corporate leverage the formalities and procedures involved in borrowing are to be observed by the firms while these will be the responsibility of the investor-borrower in case of personal leverage. That corporate borrowing is more convenient to the investor means, in other words, that investors would prefer them rather than to do the job themselves. The perfect substitutability of the two types of leverage is, thus, open to question.

Cost Another constraint on the perfect substitutability of personal and corporate leverage and, hence, the effectiveness of the arbitrage process is the relatively *high cost of borrowing* with personal leverage. If the two types of leverage are to be perfect substitutes, the cost of borrowing ought to be identical for both: borrowing by the firm and borrowing by the investor-borrower. If the borrowing costs vary so that they are higher/lower depending on whether the borrowing is done by a firm or an individual, the borrowing arrangement with lower cost will be preferred by the investors. That lending costs are not uniform for all categories of borrowers is, as an economic proposition, well recognised. As a general rule, large borrowers with high credit-standing can borrow at a lower rate of interest compared to borrowers who are small and do not enjoy high credit-standing. For this reason, it is reasonable to assume that a firm can obtain a loan at a cost lower than what the individual investor would have to pay. As a result of higher interest charges, the advantage of personal leverage would largely disappear and the MM assumption of personal and corporate leverages being perfect substitutes would be of doubtful validity. In fact, borrowing by a firm has definite superiority over a personal loan from the viewpoint of the cost of borrowing. Investors can be expected to definitely prefer corporate borrowing as they would not be in the same position by borrowing on personal account.

Institutional Restrictions Yet another problem with the MM hypothesis is that *institutional restrictions* stand in the way of a smooth operation of the arbitrage process. Several institutional investors such as insurance companies, mutual funds, commercial banks and so on are not allowed to engage in personal leverage. Thus, switching the option from the unlevered to the levered firm may not apply to all investors and, to that extent, personal leverage is an imperfect substitute for corporate leverage.

Double Leverage A related dimension is that in certain situations, the arbitrage process (substituting corporate leverage by personal leverage) may not actually work. For instance, when an investor has already borrowed funds while investing in shares of an unlevered firm. If the value of the firm is more than that of the levered firm, the arbitrage process would require selling the securities of the overvalued (unlevered) firm and purchasing the securities of the levered firm. Thus, an investor would have *double leverage* both in personal portfolio as well as in the firm's portfolio. The MM assumption would not hold true in such a situation.

Double leverage includes leverage both in personal portfolio as well as in the firm's portfolio.

Transaction Costs Transaction costs would affect the arbitrage process. The effect of transaction/flotation cost is that the investor would receive net proceeds from the sale of securities which will be lower than his investment holding in the levered/unlevered firm, to the extent of the brokerage fee and other costs. He would, therefore, have to invest a larger amount in the shares of the unlevered/levered firm, than his present investment, to earn the same return.

Personal leverage and corporate leverage are, therefore, not perfect substitutes. This implies that the arbitrage process will be hampered and will not be effective. To put it differently, the basic postulate of the MM Approach is not valid. Therefore, a firm may increase its total value and lower its weighted cost of capital with an appropriate degree of leverage. Thus, the capital structure of the firm is not irrelevant to its valuation and the overall cost of capital. In brief, imperfections in the capital market retard perfect functioning of the arbitrage. As a consequence, the MM Approach does not appear to provide a valid framework for the theoretical relationship between capital structure, cost of capital and valuation of a firm.

Taxes Finally, if corporate taxes are taken into account, the MM Approach will fail to explain the relationship between financing decision and value of the firm. Modigliani and Miller themselves, as shown below, are aware of it and have, in fact, recognised it.

Corporate Taxes

As already mentioned, MM agree[8] that the value of the firm will increase and cost of capital will decline with leverage, if corporate taxes are introduced in the exercise. Since interest on debt is tax-deductible, the effective cost of borrowing is less than the contractual rate of interest. Debt, thus, provides a benefit to the firm because of the *tax-deductibility* of interest payments. Therefore, a levered firm would have greater market value than an unlevered firm. Specifically, MM state that the value of the levered firm would exceed that of the unlevered firm by an amount equal to the levered firm's debt multiplied by the tax rate. Symbolically,

$$V_l = V_u + Bt \tag{19.14}$$

where V_l = value of levered firm,
V_u = value of unlevered firm,
B = amount of debt and
t = tax rate

Since the value of the levered firm is more than that of the unlevered firm, it is implied that the overall cost of capital of the former would be lower than that of the latter.

Equation 19.14 also implies that the market value of a levered firm (V_l) is equal to the market value of an unlevered firm (V_u) in the same risk class plus the discounted present value of the tax saving resulting from tax-deductibility of interest payments.[9]

***Example* 19.5**

The earnings before interest and taxes are ₹10 lakh for companies L and U. They are alike in all respects except that Firm L uses 15 per cent debt of ₹20 lakh; Firm U does not use debt. Given the tax rate of 35 per cent, the stakeholders of the two firms will receive different amounts as shown in Table 19.11.

TABLE 19.11 Effect of Leverage on Shareholders

Particulars	*Company L*	*Company U*
EBIT	₹10,00,000	₹10,00,000
Less: Interest	3,00,000	—
Earnings before taxes	7,00,000	10,00,000
Less: Taxes	2,45,000	3,50,000
Income available for equity-holders	4,55,000	6,50,000
Income available for debt-holders and equity-holders	7,55,000	6,50,000

The total income to both debt holders and equity holders of levered Company L is higher. The reason is that while debt-holders receive interest without tax-deduction at the corporate level, equity-holders of Company L have their incomes after tax-deduction. As a result, total income to both types of investors increases by the interest payment times the rate, that is, ₹3,00,000 × 0.35 = ₹1,05,000.

Assuming further that the debt employed by Company L is permanent, the advantage to the firm is equivalent to the present value of the tax shield, that is, ₹7 lakh (₹1,05,000/0.15). Alternatively, it can be determined with reference to Equation 19.15.

$$\frac{Brt}{r} = Bt \qquad \textbf{(19.15)}$$

where t = Corporate tax,

r = Rate of interest on debt and

Bt = Amount of debt = 0.35 × ₹20 lakh = ₹7 lakh.

It may be noted that value of levered firm (as shown by equation 19.14) reckons this tax shield due to debt.

The implication of MM analysis in this case is that the value of the firm is maximised when its capital structure contains only debt. In other words, a firm can lower its cost of capital continually with increased leverage. However, the extensive use of debt financing would expose business to high probabilities of default; it would find it difficult to meet the promised payments of interest and principal. Moreover, the firm is likely to incur costs and suffer penalties if it fails to make payments of interest and principal when they become due. Legal expenses, disruption of operations, and loss of potentially profitable investment opportunities may result. As the amount of debt in the capital structure increases, so does the probability of incurring these costs. Consequently, there are disadvantages of debt; and excessive use of debt may cause a rise in the cost of capital owing to the increased financial risk and may reduce the value of the firm.[10] Again, we find that MM's proposition is unjustified when leverage is extreme, that is, when the firm uses virtually 100 per cent debt and no equity. Clearly, the optimal capital structure is not one which has the maximum amount of debt, but, one which has the desired amount of debt, determined at a point and/or range where the overall cost of capital is minimum. Modigliani and Miller also recognise that extreme leverage increases financial risk as also the cost of capital. They suggest that firms should adopt '*target debt ratio*' so as not to violate limits of leverage imposed by the creditors. This suggestion indirectly admits that there is a safe limit for the use of debt and firms should not use debt beyond that limit/point. It implies that the cost of capital rises beyond a certain level on the use of debt. There is, therefore, an optimal capital structure.

Bankruptcy Costs

Bankruptcy costs imply high probability of default.

MM assume that there are no bankruptcy costs. However, in practice, excessive use of debt would involve such costs. These costs expose businesses to high probabilities of default. A firm would find it difficult to meet the obligations relating to payments of interest and repayment of principal. This, in turn, may lead to liquidation of the firm. Bankruptcy costs can be classified into two categories: **(1)** direct bankruptcy costs and **(2)** indirect bankruptcy costs.

Direct bankruptcy costs are legal and administrative costs associated with bankruptcy proceedings and dismantling/removal costs of undersold assets.

Direct Bankruptcy Costs These are the legal and administrative costs associated with the bankruptcy proceedings of the firm. They also include the costs of selling assets at a price lower than their worth/book value. In fact, it is very hard to find buyers for the expensive assets like plant and equipment as they are configured to a company's specific needs and it is not easy to dismantle and move them.[11] The firm may incur heavy dismantling and removal costs.

Direct bankruptcy costs can be staggering and may be a disincentive to debt financing. Such costs are referred to as **bankruptcy tax**.[12] There is a tax shield on debt/borrowings, but it has potential dangers/threats in that the more a company borrows, the more likely it is that it will become bankrupt and pay the bankruptcy tax. Therefore, a company faces a trade-off between advantages and disadvantages of debt financing.

Indirect bankruptcy costs are costs of the threat of bankruptcy in terms of disruption of normal business and adverse effect on sales.

Indirect Bankruptcy Costs These are the costs of avoiding a bankruptcy filing by a financially distressed firm.[13] What happens in such firms is that valuable employees leave, suppliers do not grant credit, customers seek more reliable suppliers and lenders demand higher interest rates and impose more restrictive/protective covenants in loan agreements. In brief, normal business operations are disrupted and sales are adversely affected. Customers avoid buying from such firms as they fear that the company might not honour the warranty and it might be difficult to purchase/replaced parts. All these costs are the costs of the threat of bankruptcy and not bankruptcy *per se*. Therefore, prohibitive bankruptcy costs discourage corporates to use excessive levels of debts. Debt should, therefore, be used in safe limits. Figure 19.4 is modified to incorporate the impact of bankruptcy cots on k_e.

Figure 19.4 portrays the cost components of k_e (Risk-free rate of return R_f, Business risk premium, B_p, Financial risk premium, F_p) and the impact of bankruptcy costs on it. Business risk premium is a constant amount as it is not affected by debt financing. Therefore, the line representing it is parallel to the '*X*' axis. Financial risk premium increases with the increased debt-equity ratio. Bankruptcy costs result when debt is used beyond some point and such costs increase with higher debt-equity ratio entailing increasing probability of bankruptcy. As leverage increases, so does the penalty. For extreme leverage, the penalty becomes very substantial indeed.[14]

Thus, the value of a levered firm would be lower due to bankruptcy costs. As a result, the value of a levered firm would be less than the value shown as per equation 19.14 by the amount of bankruptcy costs (BC). Symbolically,

$$V_l = V_u + Bt - BC \quad \textbf{(19.16)}$$

Figure 19.5 shows the impact of MM approach on weighted average cost of capital, WACC (k_o) in three specific cases. The Case I shows k_o remains constant at varying debt-equity ratios (in a world of no taxes). The advantage of debt as a cheaper source of finance is exactly offset by the increased equity capitalisation rate. In a situation of taxes (Case II), there is always an advantage in

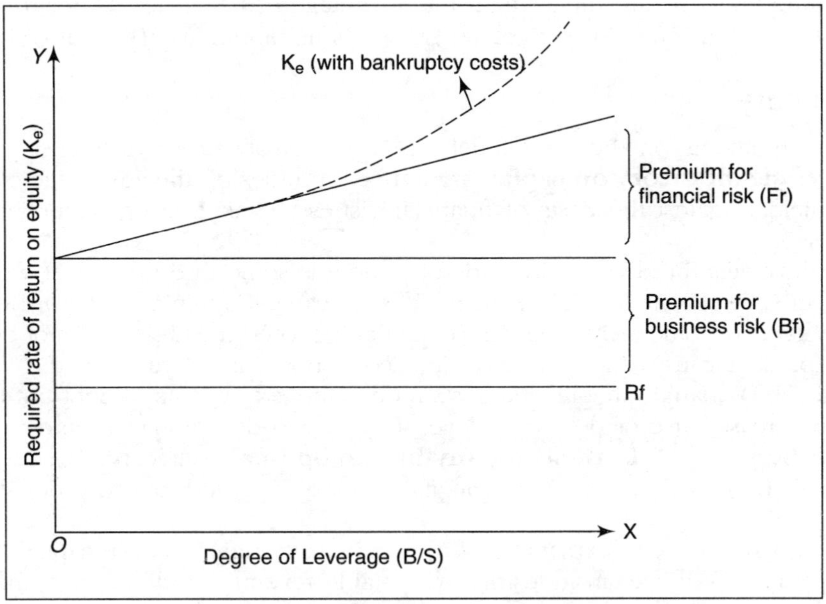

FIGURE 19.4 Cost of Equity, k_e and Bankruptcy Costs
source: Pearson Education, "Cost of Equity, k_e and Bankruptcy Costs", Financial Management and Policy

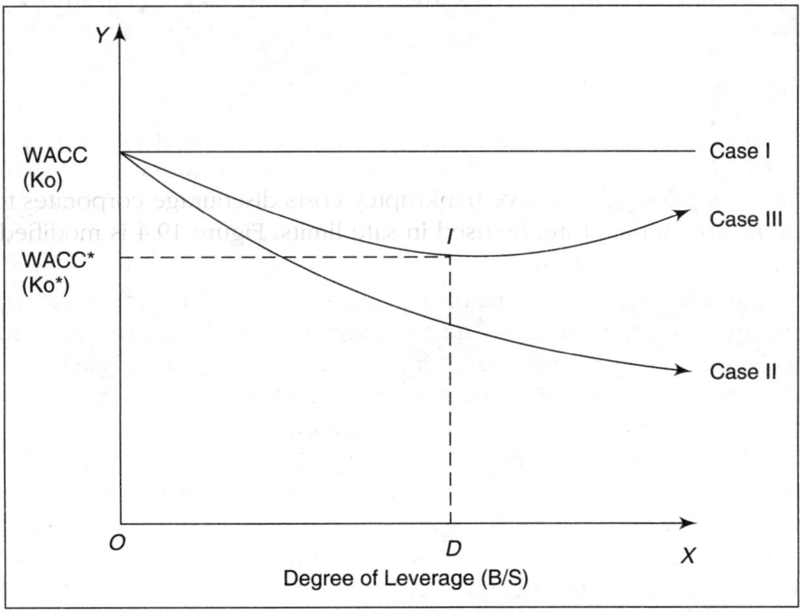

FIGURE 19.5 Degree of Leverage (*B/S*) and WACC
source: McGraw Hill Education, "Degree of Leverage (B/S) and WACC", Fundamentals of Corporate Finance

using debt according to MM. Therefore, k_o consistently decreases with the increased leverage. Case III recognises the presence of bankruptcy costs due to excessive use of debt. As a result, beyond point, '**D**', bankruptcy costs are higher than the advantage of using debt. Prior to point '**D**', there is a net advantage of leverage. Therefore, $WACC^*/k_o^*$ is minimum at **OD** point of leverage.

Trade-off Theory

The preceding arguments on the use of debt as a means of corporate finance have led to the genesis of **the trade-off theory on capital structure**. It trades off the advantage of debt financing (interest tax shields) against the costs of financial distress (consisting of higher interest rates and bankruptcy costs).

Figure 19.5 illustrates the debt-equity trade-off. There is some threshold level of debt (indicated by labeled '**D**' in Case III), at which the overall cost of capital is minimum (k_o^*). Beyond level '**D**', the bankruptcy costs become increasingly important and exceed the tax benefits of debt. As a result, increased use of debt causes increase in k_o and corresponding decrease in the valuation of the firm. Prior to level '**D**', bankruptcy-related costs reduce the tax benefits of debt but not completely. Therefore, the increased use of debt upto level 'D' leads to decrease in k_o and increase in value of the firm. **At the point of 'D' the company has an optimal structure.** The level of '*d*' (debt) would vary from firm to firm depending on its business risk (indicated by degree of operating leverage) and bankruptcy costs.

The theory provides a useful explanation for inter-industry differences in capital structure. While debt ratios are relatively higher in industries with stable revenues and earnings, they are lower in more risky industries with volatile revenues and earnings.

The traditional theory (**explained subsequently in this chapter**) does not make a reference to bankruptcy-related costs and interest tax shield. Yet, it explicitly recognises the pros and cons of debt financing. **Its conclusion that debt should be used within safe limits converges with the trade-off theory.**

Signalling Theory

Asymmetric information is a situation in which managers have more information about operations/ prospects of a firm than its investors.

MM assume that there is an information symmetry about the firm's prospects between management and investors/shareholders (i.e., **symmetric information)**. Symmetric information refers to the situation in which shareholders and managers have identical information about a firm's prospects.[15] In reality, this is not true. Managers, in general, have more information about business operations and future prospects of a firm than its investors. This situation is technically called **asymmetric information**. The empirical evidence suggests that the greater the asymmetry in information between the inside managers and outside investors, the greater is the likely share price reaction to a financing announcement.[16] In operational terms, asymmetric information has an important impact on the capital structure decisions.

Let us assume that the management of a firm (through its Research and Development) has discovered a new product, leading to a very profitable investment opportunity. Its execution needs additional financing. In case the corporate decides to sell equity shares when profits start accruing from the new product, their prices would rise sharply and the new subscribers would be as much benefited as the current shareholders. Evidently, the existing shareholders would have benefited more, if the additional financing would not have been through the equity. The issue of equity shares has created a situation in which the existing shareholders have to share the benefits from increased earnings of a new product with the new subscribers. In other words, it would be more beneficial to the existing shareholders if the management uses debt instead of equity to raise the required funds. The decision of issuing debt in such a favourable situation is consistent with the basic objective of financial management to maximise the wealth of the existing shareholders.

In view of the above, it is expected that a corporate with very favourable prospects would avoid selling shares. The required funds should be raised through other means, including debt even beyond the normal target capital structure.[17] The operational implication is that debt financing is a positive signal suggesting that the management believes that the share prices are under-valued.

In contrast, the management may apprehend poor outlook of the firm in the future. The reason may be that a competitor has come out with a better quality product due to installation of a new technology. Obviously, the management of the firm has no option but to buy new technology even to maintain its existing sales. As a result, there would be an adverse impact on its profitability. The firm would be required to raise additional funds. It would like to raise funds through issue of equity shares as the price of its shares would decline when the market comes to know of its depressed rates of return/.lower profitability. Issuing of shares enables the existing shareholders to have the new subscribers to share the losses. Hence, the theory that the unfavourable business prospects warrant the equity issue so that the loss of the existing shareholders is minimised.

In view of the above, shareholders more often interpret the announcement of a share issue as a **negative signal** that the firm's prospects (as perceived by the management) are not bright and as a result share prices decline.[18]

In brief, as per the signalling theory, debt issues are considered as "**good news**" and share issues as "**bad news**", the underlying principle being that the management would prefer to issue overvalued security. The theory suggests that since share issue sends a negative signal, which in turn, causes decline in share prices even when future prospects are bright, the firm should maintain some **reserve borrowing capacity** by keeping relatively low levels of debt than suggested by the trade-off theory. This debt reserve can be used to avail of good investment opportunities in future without causing an adverse impact on the share price as the required finances would be raised through debt.

Pecking-Order Theory

Pecking-order theory enumerates the preferred order of raising finance normally followed by corporates.

The pecking-order theory enumerates the **preferred** order of financing normally followed by most of the corporates in practice. The firms prefer internal financing/ retained earnings to external financing. The key principle of pecking-order theory is in conformity with the, signalling theory, the presence of asymmetric information and the need to incur flotation costs for new issues. The rationale for the preference for retained earnings is that selling securities to raise funds externally involves flotation costs and which the corporates would like to avoid. The most profitable companies within an industry tend to have the least amount of debt/leverage.[19] In view of their large earnings, more often than not, they never need external financing.

Retentions are justifiable from the view point of equity-owners. As such companies can earn more on retained earnings than what the shareholders themselves could have earned, if the earnings were distributed among them as dividends. The payment of lower dividend is more than offset by the enhanced market price of their shares.

Continuing with the argument of very profitable investment opportunities with such firms and now assuming that the retained earnings falling short of investment requirements, the management would prefer, as per asymmetric information and signalling theory, debt to raise the residual required funds. It may not be out of place to mention here that the flotation costs of raising debt are lower *vis-à-vis* share issue. It is for these reasons that the pecking-order theory aptly suggests the first preference for debt, among the external sources of finance, followed by preference shares and hybrid securities like convertible debentures. The issue of new equity shares is the last resort.[20]

In a nutshell, the financing choices in order of preferences are: **(1)** retained earnings, **(2)** non-convertible debt, **(3)** preference shares, **(4)** hybrid securities like convertible debentures, and **(5)** equity.

Implications of the Pecking-Order[21] The significant implications of the pecking-order theory are as follows:

(1) No Target-Capital Structure Finance theory strongly advocates for target and sound capital structure which minimises the overall cost of capital and maximises the value of a firm. In contrast, the pecking-order choice virtually ignores the concept of target or optimal debt-equity mix. In fact, a firm's capital structure is dictated essentially with reference to the availability of current retained earnings, *vis-à-vis* its current investment requirement. In case of a deficiency, debt is to be raised, disregarding the requirement of target/optimal capital structure.

(2) Relatively Less Use of Debt by Profitable Firms Profitable firms, in view of large internal cash accruals at their disposal to meet their investment requirements, tend to use less amount of debt as external financing requirement not because they have low target debt-ratios, but because of preference for internally-generated funds. This again flouts sound tenets of finance theory. Such firms, due to favourable financial leverage, can magnify their **RoR** (rate of return) for their equity owners by employing higher debt.

(3) Need to Build-up Cash Reserves Corporates would need to have reserves in the form of cash and marketable securities so that they are readily available to finance investment projects.

(4) Tax-shield on Interest is Secondary In the pecking-order theory, the tax-shield on interest is regarded as the secondary consideration and relegated to the second place in designing capital structure.

In brief, the capital structure decisions under pecking-order theory are essentially a by-product of the corporate's financial requirements and internally generated cash surplus retained after meeting the dividend requirements (**explained in Chapter 30**).

PECKING ORDER THEORY IN INDIA

Findings related to pecking order adherence among Indian corporates are summarized below:

- The survey (2013-14) reveals that Indian firms prefer internal funds first and banks form the second important source, indicating adherence to pecking order theory.
- Indian corporates prefer debt (long-term debt) to equity in both deficit and surplus situations. The major reasons for debt preference are its being cheaper than equity, flexibility and easier to raise.
- The regression results indicate that corporate firms frequently issue debt to fill up their deficiency requirements (coefficient value of 1.13). Most of these new proceeds are used to finance investments or other operational needs.
- In marked contrast, surplus firms occasionally redeem debt (coefficient value of 0.39) to reduce their existing debt levels. They retain funds for future expansion and other operational needs.
- Surplus firms prefer to deposit their surpluses with banks for a short-period.
- During deficiency, large firms use more debt compared to other firms. Small and medium firms have large deficiencies but low-debt capacities that are quickly exhausted. Therefore, a significant portion of funds for these firms is obtained through equity issues.
- Across surplus groups, firms across varying sizes do not make large debt redemptions.

- During surplus situation, industries affiliated to chemicals, Information technology, communication seem to redeem more debt. In deficit situations, most of the industries raise debt to finance their deficit requirements.

Source: (i) Bhama, V., Jain P.K. and Yadav, S.S. (2017). Pecking Order among Select Industries from India and China. ***Vision – The Journal of Business Perspective,*** Vol. 21 (1), pp. 1-13. (ii) Bhama.V., Jain P.K. and Yadav, S.S. (2016). Testing the Pecking Order Theory of Deficit and Surplus Firms: Indian Evidence. ***International Journal of Managerial Finance,*** Vol. 12 (3), pp. 335-350. and (iii) Bhama.V., Jain P.K. and Yadav, S.S. (2015). Does Firms' Pecking Order vary during Large Deficits and Surpluses? An Empirical Study on Emerging Economies. ***Procedia Economics and Finance***, Vol. 30, pp. 155-163.

Traditional Approach

The preceding discussions clearly show that the Net Income Approach (NI) as well as Net Operating Income Approach (NOI) represent two extremes as regards the theoretical relationship between financing decisions as determined by the capital structure, the weighted average cost of capital and total value of the firm. While the NI Approach takes the position that the use of debt in the capital structure will *always* affect the overall cost of capital and the total valuation, the NOI Approach argues that capital structure is totally irrelevant. The MM Approach supports the NOI Approach. But the assumptions of MM hypothesis are of doubtful validity. The Traditional Approach is midway between the NI and NOI Approaches. It partakes of some features of both these Approaches. It is also known as the **Intermediate** Approach. It resembles the NI Approach in arguing that cost of capital and total value of the firm are not independent of the capital structure. But it does not subscribe to the view (of NI Approach) that value of a firm will necessarily increase for all degrees of leverage. In one respect it shares a feature with the NOI Approach that beyond a certain degree of leverage, the overall cost increases leading to a decrease in the total value of the firm. But it differs from the NOI Approach in that it does not argue that the weighted average cost of capital is constant for all degrees of leverage.

The crux of the traditional view relating to leverage and valuation is that through **judicious** use of debt-equity proportions, a firm can increase its total value and thereby reduce its overall cost of capital. The rationale behind this view is that debt is a relatively cheaper source of funds as compared to ordinary shares. With a change in the leverage, that is, using more debt in place of equity, a relatively cheaper source of funds replaces a source of funds which involves a relatively higher cost. This obviously causes a decline in the overall cost of capital. If the debt-equity ratio is raised further, the firm would become financially more risky to the investors who would penalise the firm by demanding a higher equity-capitalisation rate (k_e). But the increase in k_e may not be so high as to neutralise the benefit of using cheaper debt. In other words, the advantages arising out of the use of debt is so large that, even after allowing for higher k_e, the benefit of the use of the cheaper source of funds is still available. If, however, the amount of debt is increased further, two things are likely to happen: **(i)** owing to increased financial risk, k_e will record a substantial rise; **(ii)** the firm would become very risky to the creditors who also would like to be compensated by a higher return such that k_i will rise. The use of debt beyond a certain point will, therefore, have the effect of raising the weighted average cost of capital and conversely the total value of the firm. Thus, up to a point/degree of leverage, the use of debt will favourably affect the value of a firm; beyond that point, use of debt will adversely affect it. At that level of debt-equity ratio, the capital structure is an optimal capital structure. **At the optimum capital structure, the marginal real cost of debt, defined to include both implicit and explicit, will be equal to the real cost of equity. For a debt-equity ratio before that level, the marginal real cost of debt would be less than that of equity capital, while beyond that level of leverage, the marginal real cost of debt would exceed that of equity.**

There are, of course, variations to the Traditional Approach. According to one of these, the equity-capitalisation rate (k_e) rises only after a certain level of leverage and not before, so that the use of debt does not necessarily increase the k_e. This happens only after a certain degree of leverage. The implication is *that a firm can reduce its cost of capital significantly with the initial use of leverage.*

Another variant of the Traditional Approach suggests that there is no one single capital structure, but, there is a range of capital structures in which the cost of capital (k_0) is the minimum and the value of the firm is the maximum. In this range, changes in leverage have very little effect on the value of the firm.

The *modus operandi* of the Traditional Approach is illustrated in Example 19.6.

***Example* 19.6**

Let us suppose that a firm has 20 per cent debt and 80 per cent equity in its capital structure. The cost of debt and the cost of equity are assumed to be 10 per cent and 15 per cent respectively. What is the overall cost of capital, according to the traditional Approach?

Solution

The overall cost of capital (k_0) $= k_i$ i.e. $0.10\left[\dfrac{20}{100}\right] + k_e$ i.e. $0.15\left[\dfrac{80}{100}\right] = 14$ per cent

Further, suppose, the firm wants to increase the percentage of debt to 50. Due to the increased financial risk, the k_i and k_e will presumably rise. Assuming, they are 11 per cent (k_i) and 16 per cent (k_e), the cost of capital (k_0) would be: $= 0.11\left[\dfrac{50}{100}\right] + 0.16\left[\dfrac{50}{100}\right] = 13.5$ per cent

It can, thus, be seen that with a rise in the debt-equity ratio, k_e and k_i increase, but, k_0 has declined presumably because these increases have not fully offset the advantages of the cheapness of debt.

Assume further, the level of debt is raised to 70 per cent of the capital structure of the firm. There would consequently be a sharp rise in risk to the investors as well as creditors. The k_e would be, say, 20 per cent and the k_i 14 per cent. The k_0 $= 0.14\left[\dfrac{70}{100}\right] + 0.20\left[\dfrac{30}{100}\right] = 15.8$ per cent

The overall cost of capital has actually risen when the firm tries to employ more of what appeared, at the previous debt-equity ratio, to be the least costly source of funds, that is, debt. Therefore, the firm should take into account the consequences of raising the percentage of debt to 70 per cent on the cost of both equity and debt.

The above illustration eloquently demonstrates that the increasing use of debt does not always lower k_0. In fact, excessive use of debt greatly increases financial risk and completely offsets the advantage of using the lower-cost debt. Therefore, the firm should consider the two off-setting effects of increasing the proportion of debt in the capital structure: the rise in k_i and k_e and the decrease or increase in k_0 and total value (V), generated by using a greater proportion of debt. The traditional Approach is illustrated in Example 19.7.

***Example* 19.7**

Assume a firm has EBIT of ₹40,000. The firm has 10 per cent debentures of ₹1,00,000 and its current equity capitalisation rate is 16 per cent. The current value of the firm (V) and its overall cost of capital would be, as shown in Table 19.12.

TABLE 19.12 Total Value and Cost of Capital (Traditional Approach)

Net operating income (EBIT)	₹40,000
Less: Interest (I)	10,000
Earnings available to equityholders (NI)	30,000
Equity capitalisation rate (k_e)	0.16
Total Market value of equity (S) = NI/k_e	1,87,500
Total Market value of debt (B)	1,00,000
Total value of the firm (V) = $S + B$	2,87,500
Overall cost of capital, k_0 = EBIT/V	0.139
Debt-equity ratio (B/S) = (₹1,00,000 ÷ ₹1,87,500)	0.53

The firm is considering increasing its leverage by issuing additional ₹50,000 debentures and using the proceeds to retire that amount of equity. If, however, as the firm increases the proportion of debt, k_i would rise to 11 per cent and k_e to 17 per cent, the total value of the firm would increase and k_0 would decline as shown in Table 19.13.

TABLE 19.13 Total Value and Cost of Capital (Traditional Approach)

Net operating income (EBIT)	₹40,000
Less: Interest (I)	16,500
Earnings available to equityholders (NI)	23,500
Equity capitalisation rate (k_e)	0.17
Total Market value of equity (S) = NI/k_e	1,38,235
Total Market value of debt (B)	1,50,000
Total value of the firm (V) = $S + B$	2,88,235
Overall cost of capital, k_0 = EBIT/V	0.138
Debt-equity ratio (B/S)	1.08

Let us further suppose that the firm issues additional ₹1,00,000 debentures instead of ₹50,000 (that is, having ₹2,00,000 debentures) and uses the proceeds to retire that amount of equity. Due to increased financial risk, k_i would rise to 12.5 per cent and k_e to 20 per cent, the total value of the firm would decrease and k_0 would rise as is clear from Table 19.14.

TABLE 19.14 Total Value and Cost of Capital (Traditional Approach)

Net operating income (EBIT)	₹40,000
Less: Interest (I)	25,000
Earnings available to equityholders (NI)	15,000
Equity capitalisation rate (k_e)	0.20
Total Market value of equity (S) = NI/k_e	75,000
Total Market value of debt	2,00,000
Total value of the firm (V) = $S + B$	2,75,000
Overall cost of capital, k_0 = EBIT/V	0.145
Debt-equity ratio (B/S) (₹2,00,000 ÷ ₹75,000)	2.67

In Example 19.7, it is clear that the optimal debt-equity ratio must be less than 2.67 since at this ratio, the value of the firm is ₹2,75,000, while at a debt-equity ratio of 1.08 it is ₹2,88,235.

The traditional Approach suggests that:

> Other things being equal, the market value of a company's securities will rise as the amount of leverage (L) in its financial structure is increased from zero to some point determined by the capital market's evaluation of the level of business uncertainty involved. Beyond this point and up to a second point, changes in leverage have very little effect, that is, within this range of leverage the total market value of the company is unchanged as leverage changes. Beyond this range of 'acceptable' leverage, the total market value of securities will decline with further increase in L.[22]

The effect of increase in leverage from zero, on cost of capital and valuation of the firm, can be thought to involve three distinct phase.[23]

Increased Valuation and Decreased Overall Cost of Capital

During the first phase, increasing leverage increases the total valuation of the firm and lowers the overall cost of capital. As the proportion of debt in the capital structure increases, the cost of equity (k_e) begins to rise as a reflection of the increased financial risk. But it does not rise fast enough to offset the advantage of using the cheaper source of debt capital. Likewise, for most of the range of this phase, the cost of debt (k_i) either remains constant or rises to a very small extent because the proportion of debt by the lender is considered to be within safe limits. Therefore, they are prepared to lend to the firm at almost the same rate of interest. Since debt is typically a cheaper source of capital than equity, the combined effect is that the overall cost of capital begins to fall with the increasing use of debt. Example 19.7 has shown that an increase in leverage (B/S) from 0.53 to 1.08 has had the effect of increasing the total market value from ₹2,87,500 to ₹2,88,235 and decreasing the overall capitalisation rate from 13.9 to 13.8 per cent.

Constant Valuation and Constant Overall Cost of Capital

After a certain degree of leverage is reached, further moderate increases in leverage have little or no effect on total market value. During the middle range, the changes brought in equity-capitalisation rate and debt-capitalisation rate balance each other. As a result, the values of (V) and (k_0) remain almost constant.

Decreased Valuation and Increased Overall Cost of Capital

Beyond a certain critical point, further increases in debt proportions are not considered desirable. They increase financial risks so much that both k_e and k_i start rising rapidly causing (k_0) to rise and (V) to fall. In Example 19.7, the effect of an increase in B/S ratio from 1.08 to 2.67 is to increase (k_0) from 13.8 to 14.5 per cent and to decrease (V) from ₹2,88,235 to ₹2,75,000.

A numerical illustration, given in Table 19.15[24] and its graphic presentation in Fig. 19.4[25] further help to clarify the relationship between leverage and cost of capital. They present hypothetical changes similar to those envisaged by the traditional approach and examine the effect of leverage on the individual variables. We have assumed, in addition to other assumptions already stated at the beginning of the chapter, that given capital market conditions, the company can repurchase its own shares. The face value of a share is ₹10 and that of debentures ₹100 each. The symbols used in Table 19.15 have the same meaning as explained at the beginning of the chapter.

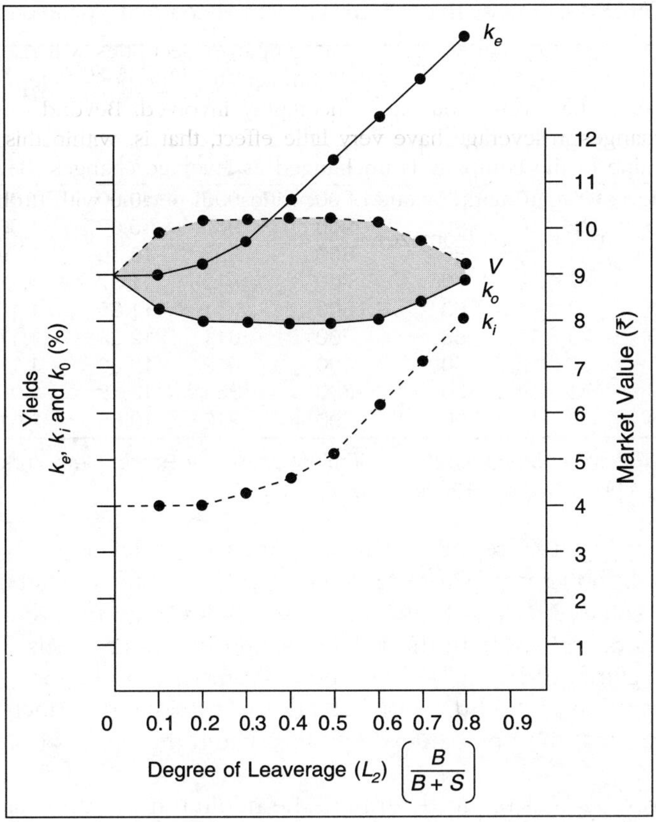

FIGURE 19.6 Leverage and Cost of Capital (Traditional Approach)

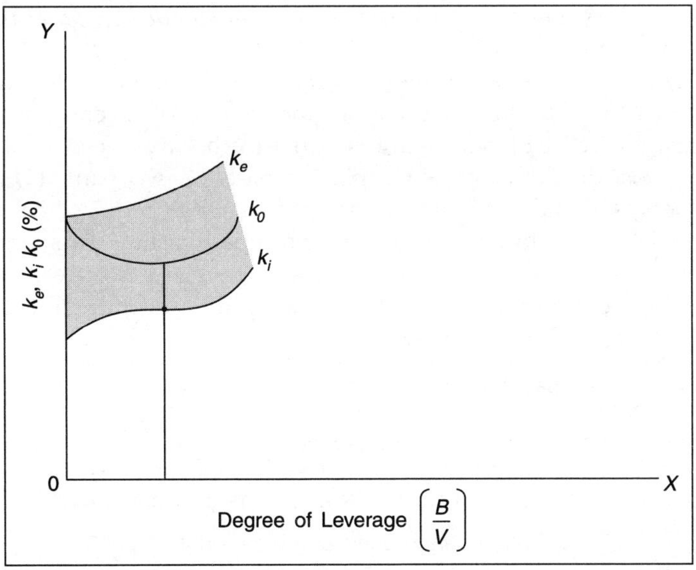

FIGURE 19.7 Leverage and Cost of Capital (Traditional Approach)

TABLE 19.15 Leverage, Capitalisation Rates and Valuation[a]

B	k_i (%)	*EBIT*	*I*	*NI* (*EBIT-I*)	k_e (%)	*Number of shares*	*Amount of shares (book value)*	*S* ($NI \div k_e$)	*Market value per share*	*V* (*B + S*)	k_0 %	L_1 (*B/S*)	L_2 (*B/V*)
1	*2*	*3*	*4*	*5*	*6*	*7*	*8*	*9*	*10*	*11*	*12*	*13*	*14*
0	4.0	₹100	₹Nil	₹100	10.0	100	₹1,000	₹1,000	₹10.00	₹1,000	10.2	0	0
100	4.0	100	4.0	96	10.0	90	900	960	10.67	1,060	9.4	0.10	0.09
200	4.0	100	8.0	92	10.3	80	800	893	10.16	1,093	9.1	0.22	0.18
300	4.2	100	12.6	87.4	10.8	70	700	810	11.57	1,111	9.0	0.33	0.27
400	4.5	100	18.0	82	11.5	60	600	711	11.85	1,111	9.0	0.56	0.36
500	5.0	100	25.0	75	12.3	50	500	611	12.22	1,111	9.0	0.82	0.45
600	5.5	100	33.0	67	13.1	40	400	512	12.80	1,111	9.0	1.17	0.54
700	7.0	100	49.0	51	14.0	30	300	364	12.13	1,064	9.4	1.92	0.65
800	8.5	100	68.0	32	15.0	20	200	213	10.65	1,013	9.9	3.76	0.79

[a] Solomon, E., *Theory of Financial Management*, Columbia University Press, New York, 1969, p. 95. Reprinted with permission from Columbia University Press, New York, USA.

Table 19.15 as well as Fig. 19.6 reveal that with an increase in leverage (B/V) from zero to 0.27, the market value of the firm increases (from ₹1,000 to ₹1,111) and the overall cost of capital declines from 10 to 9 per cent (Phase I). With further increases in leverage from 0.27 up to 0.54, there is no change either in (*V*) or in (k_0); both the values remain constant, that is, ₹1,111 and 9 per cent respectively (Phase 2). During Phase 3, with an increase in the ratio beyond 0.54 up to 0.79, there is a decrease in market value of the firm (from ₹1,111 to ₹1,013) and an increase in (k_0) (from 9 to 9.4 per cent), suggesting that the optimal leverage lies within the range of 0.27 to 0.54 debt-equity ratio.

In practice, it may not be possible to determine the minimum overall cost of capital. Therefore, a diagrammatic presentation is useful as it depicts a range over which the cost of capital is minimised. The (k_0) curve developed in Fig. 19.6 is a fairly shallow saucer with a horizontal section over the middle ranges of leverage (0.27 to 0.54). *The firm should not go to the left or to the right of the saucer* part of the curve.

The traditional view on leverage is commonly referred to as one of **'U' shaped cost of capital curve** (as shown in Fig. 19.7). In such a situation, the degree of leverage is optimum at a point at which the rising marginal cost of borrowing is equal to the average overall cost of capital. For this purpose, marginal cost of a unit of debt capital consists of two parts: **(i)** the increase in total interest payable on debt; **(ii)** the amount of extra net earnings required to restore the value of equity component to what it would have been under the pre-existing capitalisation rate before the debt is increased.

Thus, in Table 19.15, the marginal cost of borrowing the seventh to ₹100 units of funds is ₹19 or 19 per cent. It is determined as follows:

(i)	Increase in total interest payable (*I*) ₹49 (when B is ₹700) – ₹33 (when B is 600)	₹16
Plus: (ii)	Increase in net income required for shareholders (When the value of a share is ₹12.13, the required earnings are ₹51. Therefore, to maintain the value of share at ₹12.80, the earnings are ₹54 i.e. $\left[\frac{₹12.80}{₹12.13}\right] \times$ ₹51; thus, the increased earnings required is ₹3).	3

Since the marginal cost of debt is 19 per cent, while the over all cost of capital is 9 per cent, the use of more debt at this stage is imprudent. In other words, *a mix of debt of ₹600 with equity capital of ₹400 provides the optimum combination of debt and equity and optimum capital structure.*

Thus, according to the traditional approach, the cost of capital of a firm as also its valuation is dependent upon the capital structure of the firm and there is an optimum capital structure in which the firm's k_0 is minimum and its (V) the maximum.

SUMMARY

LO 19.2

Capital structure refers to the mix or proportion of different sources of finance (debt and equity) to total capitalisation. A firm should select such a financing-mix which maximises its value/the shareholders' wealth (or minimises its overall cost of capital). Such a capital structure is referred to as the optimum capital structure.

Capital structure theories explain the theoretical relationship between capital structure, overall cost of capital (k_0) and valuation (V). The four important theories are: (i) Net income (NI) approach, (ii) Net operating income (NOI) approach, (iii) Modigliani and Miller (MM) approach and (iv) Traditional approach.

According to the NI approach, capital structure is relevant as it affects the k_0 and V of the firm. The core of this approach is that as the ratio of less expensive source of funds (i.e., debt) increases in the capital structure, the k_0 decreases and V of the firm increases. With a judicious mixture of debt and equity, a firm can evolve an optimum capital structure at which the k_0 would be the lowest, the V of the firm the highest and the market price per share the maximum.

The NOI approach is diametrically opposite to the NI approach. The essence of this approach is that capital structure decision of a corporate does not affect its cost of capital and valuation, and, hence, irrelevant.

The main argument of NOI is that an increase in the proportion of debt in the capital structure would lead to an increase in the financial risk of the equityholders. To compensate for the increased risk, they would require a higher rate of return (k_e) on their investment. As a result, the advantage of the lower cost of debt would exactly be neturalised by the increase in the cost of equity.

The cost of debt has two components: (i) explicit, represented by rate of interest, and (ii) implicit, represented by the increase in the cost of equity capital. Therefore, the real cost of debt and equity would be the same and there is nothing like an optimum capital structure.

Modigliani and Miller (MM) concur with NOI and provide a behavioural justification for the irrelevance of capital structure. They maintain that the cost of capital and the value of the firm do not change with a change in leverage.

They contend that the total value of homogeneous firms that differ only in respect of leverage cannot be different because of the operations of arbitrage. The arbitrage refers to the switching over operations, that is, the investors switch over from the over-valued firm (levered firm) to the under-valued firms (unlevered). The essence of arbitrage is that the investors (arbitragers) are able to substitute personal or home-made leverage for corporate leverage. The switching operation drives the total value of the two homogeneous firms equal.

The basic premises of the MM approach, in practice, are of doubtful validity. As a result, the arbitrage process is impeded. To the extent, the arbitrage process is imperfect, it implies that the capital structure matters.

MM contend that with corporate taxes, debt has a definite advantage as interest paid on debt is tax-deductible and leverage will lower the overall cost of capital. The value of the levered firm (V_1) would exceed the value of the unlevered firm (V_u) by an amount equal to levered firm's debt multiplied by tax rate.

LO 19.2

Bankruptcy costs arise due to a firm's inability to meet the promised payments of interest and principal. These costs, sometimes, may lead to its liquidation.

Bankruptcy costs are of two types: direct and indirect. Direct bankruptcy costs are the legal and administrative costs associated with the bankruptcy proceedings of the firm. Indirect bankruptcy costs are the costs of avoiding a threat to bankruptcy which, in turn, causes valuable employees to leave, suppliers shy of granting credit, customers seeking more reliable suppliers and lenders demanding higher interest rates. As a result, normal business operations are disrupted and sales are adversely affected.

Bankruptcy costs can be exorbitant and a disincentive to use excessive levels of debt. Primarily due to these costs, the use of debt beyond safe limits offsets the tax advantage of using debt.

Bankruptcy costs depress the value of levered firm (V_l). MM suggest $V_l = V_u + B_t$. The $V_l = V_u + B_t -$ Bankruptcy Costs.

Trade-off theory on capital structure trades off the advantages of debt financing (interest tax shield) against the costs of financial distress (consisting of higher interest rates and bankruptcy costs). It warns against the excessive use of debt.

While symmetric information refers to a situation in which inside managers and outside investors have identical information about business operations and future prospects of a firm, asymmetric information implies a situation in which managers have more information than the investors do.

Signalling theory is based on the premise of asymmetric information. The theory suggests that a corporate with favourable prospects would avoid selling shares as future increase in profits would tend to increase share prices. The advantage of increase in share prices would be shared with the new equity shareholders, if equity shares have been used as a source of financing. Debt financing is a positive signal to the market for upward trend of share price. Equity shares should be used to finance the projects if prospects of a firm are not good. It enables existing shareholders to have new subscribers to share the losses.

According to signalling theory, debt issues are considered as good news and share issues as bad news. Since issue of shares causes a decline in share prices, the corporates should maintain reserve borrowing capacity by keeping relatively low levels of debt to finance profitable investment projects in the future.

The pecking-order theory enumerates the preferred order of raising finances normally followed by the corporates in practice. These choices in order of preference are: (1) retained earnings, (2) non-convertible debt/straight debentures, (3) preference shares, (4) hybrid securities like convertible bonds and (5) equity.

The suggestions of pecking-order theory are in conformity with the signalling theory and the presence of asymmetric information. The rationale for the first preference for retained earnings is that corporates would like to avoid flotation costs associated with raising funds externally.

The major implications of pecking order theory are: (1) It, by and large, disregards target/optimal capital structure concept (2) Profitable firms depend more on retained earnings to finance investment projects and (3) Tax shield on debt is of secondary importance.

The traditional approach is mid-way between the two extreme (the NI and NOI) approaches. The crux of this approach is that through a judicious combination of debt and equity, a firm can increase its value (V) and reduce its cost of capital (k_0) upto a point. However, beyond that point, the use of additional debt will increase the financial risk of the investors as well as of the lenders and as a result will cause a rise in the k_0. At such a point, the capital structure is optimum. In other words, at the optimum capital structure the marginal real cost of debt (both implicit and explicit) will be equal to the real cost of equity.

REFERENCES

1 Durand, D, 'The cost of debt and equity funds for business', Solomon, E. (Ed.), *Management of Corporate Capital*, The Free Press, New York, 1959, pp. 91-116.
2 *Ibid.*, pp. 91-116.
3 Modigliani, F and M H Miller, 'The cost of capital, corporation finance and the theory of investments', *American Economic Review*, XLVIII, June 1958.
4 Van Horne, J C, *op. cit.* p. 228.
5 Ross, S A, *op. cit.*, pp. 561-62.
6 Bolten, S E, *Managerial Finance*, Houghton Mifflin Co., Boston, 1976, p. 358.
7 Van Horne, *op. cit.* p. 235.
8 Modigliani and Miller, "Corporate income taxes and the cost of capital: A correction", *American Economic Review*, June 1963, pp. 433-44.
9 Lewellen, W G, *The Cost of Capital* Kendal/Hung Publishing Company, Dubuque, Iowa, 1969, p. 41.
10 Schall, L D and C W Haley, *Introduction to Financial Management*, McGraw-Hill, New York 1977, p. 373.
11 Brigham, E F and J F Houston, *op. cit.*, p. 500.
12 Ross, S A *et al.*, *op. cit.*, p. 568.
13 Ross, S.A. *et al.*, *Ibid.*, p. 568.
14 Van Horne, James C., *op. cit.*, p. 287.
15 Brighman, E F and J F Houston, *op. cit.*, p. 502.
16 Van Horne, J C, *op. cit.*, 2002, p. 296.
17 Brigham, E F and J F Houston, *op. cit.*, p. 502.
18 Gitman, L J, *op. cit.*, 2006, p. 562.
19 Van Horne, J C, *op. cit.*, 2002, p. 317.
20 For details, refer to Brealey, R A, *et al*, *op. cit.*, pp. 492-95.
21 Ross, S A, *et al.*, *op. cit.*, p. 576.
22 Solomon, E, *op. cit.* p. 93. Reprinted with permission from Columbia University Press, New York, USA.
23 *Ibid.* p. 94.
24 Based on Solomon, E *op. cit.* p. 95.
25 *Ibid.* p. 96.

SOLVED PROBLEMS

P.19.1 Assuming no taxes and given the earnings before interest and taxes (EBIT), interest (*I*) at 10 per cent and equity capitalisation rate (k_e) below, calculate the total market value of each firm. **LO 19.2** LOD E

Firms	*EBIT*	*I*	k_e *(per cent)*
X	₹2,00,000	₹20,000	12
Y	3,00,000	60,000	16
Z	5,00,000	2,00,000	15
W	6,00,000	2,40,000	18

Also, determine the weighted average cost of capital for each firm.

Solution

Determination of K_0 and V of firms X, Y, Z and W

Particulars	*X*	*Y*	*Z*	*W*
EBIT	₹2,00,000	₹3,00,000	₹5,00,000	₹6,00,000
Less: Interest	20,000	60,000	2,00,000	2,40,000
Net income for equity-holders	1,80,000	2,40,000	3,00,000	3,60,000
Equity capitalisation rate (k_e)	0.12	0.16	0.15	0.18
Market value of equity (S))	15,00,000	15,00,000	20,00,000	20,00,000
Market value of debt (B) = I/0.10	2,00,000	6,00,000	20,00,000	24,00,000
Total value of firm (V)	17,00,000	21,00,000	40,00,000	44,00,000
Weighted average cost of capital (k_0) = EBIT/V (%)	11.76	14.29	12.5	13.64

P.19.2 Company X and Company Y are in the same risk class, and are identical in every respect except that company X uses debt, while company Y does not. The levered firm has ₹9,00,000 debentures, carrying 10 per cent rate of interest. Both the firms earn 20 per cent operating profit on their total assets of ₹15 lakhs. Assume perfect capital markets, rational investors and so on; a tax rate of 35 per cent and capitalisation rate of 15 per cent for an all-equity company. **LO 19.2** LOD D

(a) Compute the value of firms X and Y using the Net Income (NI) Approach.
(b) Compute the value of each firm using the Net Operating Income (NOI) Approach.
(c) Using the NOI Approach, calculate the overall cost of capital (k_0) for firms X and Y.
(d) Which of these two firms has an optimal capital structure according to the NOI Approach? Why?

Solution

(a) Valuation under NI approach

Particulars	*Firm X*	*Firm Y*
EBIT	₹3,00,000	₹3,00,000
Less: Interest	90,000	—
Taxable income	2,10,000	3,00,000
Less: Taxes	73,500	1,05,000
Earnings for equity holders	1,36,500	1,95,000
Equity capitalisation rate (k_e)	0.15	0.15
Market value of equity (S)	9,10,000	13,00,000
Market value of debt (B)	9,00,000	—
Total value of firm (V)	18,10,000	13,00,000

(b) Valuation under NOI Approach

$$V_Y = \frac{₹3,00,000\ (1 - 0.35)}{0.15} = ₹13,00,000$$

$$V_X = ₹13,00,000 + ₹9,00,000\ (0.35) = ₹16,15,000$$

(c) $$K_{o_x} = k_d\ (.065)\left[\frac{₹9,00,000}{₹16,15,000}\right] + k_e\ (0.191)\left[\frac{₹7,15,000}{₹16,15,000}\right] = 12.1 \text{ per cent}$$

Similarly, K_{oy} = 15 per cent

Working Notes

EBIT	₹3,00,000
Less: Interest	90,000
Taxable income	2,10,000
Less: Taxes	73,500
NI	1,36,500
V as determined in (ii)	16,15,000
B	9,00,000
S (*V* – *B*)	7,15,000

$$k_e = \frac{₹1,36,500}{₹7,15,000} = 19.1 \text{ per cent}$$

$$k_d = 0.10\ (1–0.35) = 6.5 \text{ per cent}$$

(d) Neither firm has an optimum capital structure according to the NOI Approach. Under the MM assumptions, the optimum capital structure requires 100 per cent debt.

P.19.3 Companies U and L are identical in every respect, except that U is unlevered while L is levered. Company L has ₹20 lakh of 8 per cent debentures outstanding. Assume (1) that all the MM assumptions are met, (2) that the tax rate is 35 per cent, (3) that EBIT is ₹6 lakh and that equity-capitalisation rate for company U is 10 per cent. **LO 19.2** LOD M

(a) What would be the value for each firm according to the MM's Approach?

(b) Suppose V_u = ₹25,00,000 and V_l = ₹35,00,000. According to MM do they represent equilibrium values? If not, explain the process by which equilibrium will be restored.

Solution

(a) $V_u = \dfrac{\text{EBIT}\ (1-t)}{k_e} = \dfrac{₹6,00,000\ (1-0.35)}{0.10} = ₹39,00,000$

$V_l = V_u + Bt$ = ₹39,00,000 + ₹20,00,000 (0.35) = ₹46,00,000

(b) Firm U is undervalued and firm L is overvalued. Investors will be better off by investing in the undervalued firm as they will require lower investment cost to earn the same income as they earn in the overvalued firm. Therefore, they will sell their holdings of the overvalued firm (L) and buy shares of the undervalued firm (U). As a result, the price of shares of company L will come down while that of company U will rise. This process will continue until equilibrium in the values is restored.

P.19.4 In considering the most desirable capital structure of a company, the following estimates of the cost of debt and equity capital (after tax) have been made at various levels of debt-equity mix: **LO 19.2** LOD M

Debt as percentage of total capital employed	*Cost of debt (per cent)*	*Cost of equity (per cent)*
0	5.0	12.0
10	5.0	12.0
20	5.0	12.5
30	5.5	13.0
40	6.0	14.0
50	6.5	16.0
60	7.0	20.0

You are required to determine the optimal debt-equity mix for the company by calculating the composite cost of capital.

Solution

Solution table

k_d(%)	k_e(%)	W_1 (B/V)	W_2 S/V = (1 – B/V)	$k_d(W_1)+K_e(W_2)= k_0$(%)
5.0	12.0	0.0	1.0	12.00
5.0	12.0	0.1	0.9	11.30
5.0	12.5	0.2	0.8	11.00
5.5	13.0	0.3	0.7	10.75
6.0	14.0	0.4	0.6	10.80
6.5	16.0	0.5	0.5	11.25
7.0	20.0	0.6	0.4	12.20

Optimal debt-equity mix for the company is at a point where the composite cost of capital is minimum. When debt is 30 per cent of the total capital employed, the k_0 is minimum. Therefore, 30 per cent debt and 70 per cent equity mix would be an optimal debt-equity mix for the company.

P.19.5 A company wishes to determine the optimal capital structure. From the following selected information supplied to you, determine the optimal capital structure of the company. LO 19.2 LOD M

Situation	Debt	Equity	After tax cost of debt (%)	k_e (%)
1	₹4,00,000	₹1,00,000	9	10
2	2,50,000	2,50,000	6	11
3	1,00,000	4,00,000	5	14

Solution

Situation	k_d (%)	k_e (%)	W_1 (B/V)	W_2 (S/V)	$k_d(W_1) + k_e(W_2) = k_0$ (%)
1	9	10	0.8	0.2	9.2
2	6	11	0.5	0.5	8.5
3	5	14	0.2	0.8	12.2

The optimal capital structure for the company is in situation 2, when it uses 50 per cent debt and 50 per cent equity, as its cost of capital at this level of debt is minimum.

P.19.6 Compute the equilibrium values and capitalisation rates of equity (*K*) of the companies A and B on the basis of the following data. Assume that (i) there is no income tax, and (ii) the equilibrium value of average cost of capital (P) is 8.5 per cent. LO 19.2 LOD M

Particulars	Initial disequilibrium	
	Company A	Company B
Total market value	₹250	₹300
Debt (*L*)	0	150
Equity (*S*)	250	150
Expected net operating income (*X*)	25	25
Interest (*K.L*)	0	9
Net income (*X* – *K.L*)	25	16
Cost of equity (k_e)	0.10	0.107
Leverage (*L/V*)	0	0.5
Average cost of capital (*P*)	0.10	0.833

Solution

(i) The equilibrium values $(V_e) = \frac{X}{P} = \frac{₹25}{₹0.085} = ₹294.12$

(ii) Equity-capitalisation rates for companies A and B

Particulars	Company A	Company B
Expected net operating income (X)	₹25	₹25
Less: Interest $(K.L)$	—	9
NI available for equity $(X - K.L)$	25	16
Equilibrium cost of capital (P)	0.085	0.085
Total value of company (X/P)	294.12	294.12
Market value of debt (L)	—	150.00
Market value of equity (S)	294.12	144.12
Cost of equity, $\frac{(X - K.L)}{S}$	0.085	0.111

Alternatively, k_e for the levered company B can be determined as follows:

$$k_e = k_0 + (k_0 - k_i)\ \frac{B}{S},\ k_i = 0.06\ (₹9 \text{ interest on } ₹150 \text{ debt})$$

$$= 0.085 + (0.085 - 0.06) \times \left[\frac{₹150}{₹144.12}\right]\ 0.1111$$

For the unlevered company (A) $K_e = k_0$, as there is no k_i.

P.19.7 The values of two firms X and Y in accordance with the traditional theory are given below: LO 19.2 LOD M

Particulars	X	Y
Expected operating income $(\bar{X})$	₹50,000	₹50,000
Total cost of debt $(k_d.D = R)$	0	10,000
Net income $(\bar{X} - R)$	50,000	40,000
Cost of equity (k_e)	0.10	0.1111
Market value of shares (S)	5,00,000	3,60,000
Market value of debt (D)	0	2,00,000
Total value of firm $(V = S + D)$	5,00,000	5,60,000
Average cost of capital (k_0)	0.10	0.09
Debt equity ratio	0	0.556

Compute the values of firms X and Y as per the MM thesis. Assume that (i) corporate income taxes do not exist, and (ii) the equilibrium values of k_0 is 12.5 per cent.

Solution

Valuation of firms X and Y

Particulars	Company X	Company Y
Expected operating income $(\bar{X})$	₹50,000	₹50,000
Total cost of debt $(kd.D = R)$	0	10,000
Net income for equity, $\bar{X} - R$	50,000	40,000
Equilibrium cost of capital (k_0)	0.125	0.125
Total value of company $= \bar{X}/k_0$	4,00,000	4,00,000
Market value of debt (D)	—	2,00,000
Market value of equity $(V - D)$	4,00,000	2,00,000
Cost of equity $(k_e) = \frac{\bar{X} - R}{S}$	0.125	0.20

P.19.8 Given **(i)** the EBIT of ₹2,00,000, **(ii)** the corporate tax rate of 35 per cent, and **(iii)** the following data, determine the amount of debt that should be used by the firm in its capital structure to maximise the value of the firm. LO 19.2 LOD D

Debt	k_i *(before tax) (%)*	k_e*(%)*
Nil	Nil	12.0
₹1,00,000	10.0	12.0
2,00,000	10.5	12.6
3,00,000	11.0	13.0
4,00,000	12.0	13.6
5,00,000	14.0	15.6
6,00,000	17.0	20.0

Solution

Valuation of firm at varying amount of debt

EBIT	*I*	*NI*	*Taxes (t)*	*EAT (NI – t)*	K_d *(%)*	K_e *(%)*	*B*	*S*	*V*
₹2,00,000	—	₹2,00,000	₹70,000	₹1,30,000	—	12.0	—	₹10,83,333	₹10,83,333
2,00,000	₹10,000	1,90,000	66,500	1,23,500	6.5	12.0	₹1,00,000	10,29,167	11,29,167
2,00,000	21,000	1,79,000	62,650	1,16,350	6.8	12.6	2,00,000	9,23,413	11,23,413
2,00,000	33,000	1,67,000	58,450	1,08,550	7.1	13.0	3,00,000	8,35,000	11,35,000
2,00,000	48,000	1,52,000	53,200	98,800	7.8	13.6	4,00,000	7,26,471	11,26,471
2,00,000	70,000	1,30,000	45,500	84,500	9.1	15.6	5,00,000	5,41,667	10,41,667
2,00,000	1,02,000	98,000	34,300	63,700	11.0	20.0	6,00,000	3,18,500	9,18,500

The firm should use ₹3,00,000 debt to maximise the value of the firm.

P.19.9 A company's current operating income is ₹4 lakh. The firm has ₹10 lakh of 10 per cent debt outstanding. Its cost of equity capital is estimated to be 15 per cent. LO 19.2 LOD D

(a) Determine the current value of the firm, using traditional valuation approach.

(b) Calculate the overall capitalisation rate as well as both types of leverage ratio: (a) *B*/*S* (b) *B*/*V*.

(c) The firm is considering increasing its leverage by raising an additional ₹5,00,000 debt and using the proceeds to retire that amount of equity. As a result of increased financial risk, k_i is likely to go up to 12 per cent and k_e to 18 per cent. Would you recommend the plan?

Solution

(a) and **(b)** Valuation of firm and overall capitalisation rate

EBIT	₹4,00,000
Less: Interest	1,00,000
Earnings for equityholders (*NI*)	03,00,000
Equity-capitalisation rate (k_e)	0.15
Market value of equity (*S*)	20,00,000
Market value of debt (*B*)	10,00,000
Total market value of firm (*S* + *B*)	30,00,000
Overall capitalisation rate = EBIT/*V*	0.1333
(a) Debt/equity ratio (*B*/*S*)	0.5
(b) Debt/value ratio (B/*V*)	0.33

Alternatively, $k_0 = k_i(B/V) + k_e(S/V) = 0.10\left[\frac{₹10,00,000}{₹30,00,000}\right] + 0.15\left[\frac{₹20,00,000}{₹30,00,000}\right] = 0.1333$

(c) Valuation of firm at higher level of debt

EBIT	₹4,00,000
Less: Interest	1,80,000
Earnings for equity-holders (*NI*)	2,20,000
Equity-capitalisation rate (k_e)	0.18
Market value of equity (*S*)	12,22,222
Market value of debt (*B*)	15,00,000
Total market value of firm (*S* + *B*) = *V*	27,22,222

No, we shall not recommend the plan, as the increased proportion of debt would lower the value of the firm from ₹30,00,000 to ₹27,22,222.

P.19.10 The two companies, U and L, belong to an equivalent risk class. These two firms are identical in every respect except that U company is unlevered while Company L has 10 per cent debentures of ₹30 lakh. The other relevant information regarding their valuation and capitalisation rates are as follows: LO 19.2 LOD E

Particulars	*Firm U*	*Firm L*
Net operating income (EBIT)	₹7,50,000	₹7,50,000
Interest on debt (*I*)	—	3,00,000
Earnings to equityholders (*NI*)	7,50,000	4,50,000
Equity-capitalisation rate (k_e)	0.15	0.20
Market value of equity (*S*)	50,00,000	22,50,000
Market value of debt (*B*)	—	30,00,000
Total value of firm (*S* + *B*) = *V*	50,00,000	52,50,000
Implied overall capitalisation rate (k_0)	0.15	0.143
Debt-equity ratio (*B*/*S*)	0	1.33

(a) An investor owns 10 per cent equity shares of company L. Show the arbitrage process and the amount by which he could reduce his outlay through the use of leverage.

(b) According to Modigliani and Miller, when will this arbitrage process come to an end?

Solution

(a) Arbitrage process

(i) Investor's current position (in firm L)	
Dividend income	₹45,000
Investment cost	2,25,000
(ii) He sells his holdings of firm L for ₹2,25,000 and creates a personal leverage by borrowing ₹3,00,000 (0.10 × ₹30,00,000 debt of firm L).	
The total amount with him is ₹5,25,000. Income required to break even would be:	
Dividend income (L firm)	45,000
Interest on personal borrowing (0.10 × ₹3,00,000)	30,000
	75,000
(iii) He purchases 10 per cent equity holdings of the firm U for ₹5,00,000.	
Dividend income (U firm) (0.10 × ₹7,50,000)	75,000
Amount of investment	5,00,000

He will reduce his outlay by ₹25,000 through the use of leverage.

(b) According to Modigliani and Miller, this arbitrage process will come to an end when the values of both the firms are identical.

P.19.11 The two companies X and Y belong to the same risk class. They have everything in common except that firm Y has 10% debentures of ₹5 lakh. The valuation of the two firms is assumed to be as follows: LO 19.2 LOD M

Particulars	*X*	*Y*
Net operating income (EBIT)	₹7,50,000	₹7,50,000
Interest on debt (*I*)	Nil	50,000
Earnings to equityholders (*NI*)	7,50,000	7,00,000
Equity-capitalisation rate (k_e)	0.125	0.14
Market value of equity (*S*)	60,00,000	50,00,000
Market value of debt (*B*)	—	5,00,000
Total market value of the firm (*V*)	60,00,000	55,00,000
Implied overall capitalisation rate (k_0)	0.125	0.1363
Debt-equity ratio (*B*/*S*)	0	0.1

An investor owns 10 per cent of the equity shares of the overvalued firm. Determine his investment cost of earnings the same income so that he is at a break-even point? Will he gain by investing in the undervalued firm?

Solution

Arbitrage process

(a) Investor's position in over valued firm X		
Investment cost (0.10 × ₹60,00,000)		₹6,00,000
Dividend income (0.10 × ₹7,50,000)		75,000
(b) He sells his holdings in firm X and purchases 10 per cent equity shares and 10 per cent of debentures of under valued firm Y to earn ₹75,000.		
	Investment	Income
Shares	₹5,00,000	₹70,000
Debentures	50,000	5,000
	5,50,000	75,000

The investment of ₹5,50,000 earns the same amount of income which he was earning on an investment of ₹6,00,000 in the overvalued firm. Clearly, he will gain by investing in the under valued firm Y.

P.19.12 The following is the data regarding two companies 'X' and 'Y' belonging to the same risk class: **LO 19.2** LOD M

Particulars	*Company X*	*Company Y*
Number of ordinary shares	90,000	1,50,000
Market price per share	₹1.20	1.00
6% Debentures	60,000	—
Profit before interest	18,000	18,000

All profits after debentures interest are distributed as dividends.

Explain how under Modigliani and Miller Approach an investor holding 10 per cent of shares in Company X will be better off in switching his holdings to Company Y.

Solution

Arbitrage process

(a) Investor's current position in Firm X with 10 per cent equity holdings:	
(i) Investments (9,000 shares × ₹1.20)	₹10,800
(ii) Dividend income 0.10 × (₹18,000 – ₹3,600)	1,440
(b) Investor sells his holdings of Firm X for ₹10,800 and creates a personal leverage by borrowing ₹6,000 (0.10 × ₹60,000). Thus, the total amount available with him is ₹16,800.	

(Contd.)

(*Contd.*)

(c) He purchases 10 per cent equity holdings of Company Y for ₹15,000 (15,000 shares × ₹1); his dividend income is ₹1,800 (₹18,000 × 0.10).

(d) Gross income	1,800
Less: Interest on personal borrowings (0.06 × ₹6,000)	360
Net income	1,440

He breaks-even by investing in Firm Y. But in the process he reduces his investment outlay by ₹1,800. Therefore, he is better off by investing in Firm Y.

Alternatively, by investing ₹16,800, he could augment his income to ₹1,656:

Dividend income from Firm Y ₹18,000 $\left(\frac{₹16,800}{₹1,50,000}\right)$	₹2,016
Less: Interest on personal borrowings	360
Net income	1,656

MINI CASES

19.C.1 In considering the most appropriate capital structure for the NOID Manufacturers Ltd (NML), its finance department has made estimates of the interest rate on debt and the cost of equity capital at various levels of debt-equity mix summarised below:

Debt-equity mix (leverage)	*Coupon rate (%)*	*Cost of equity (%)*
0	8	12.0
10	8	12.0
20	9	12.5
30	9	13.5
40	10	14.5
50	13	16.0
60	15	20.0
70	18	25.0

The debt is in the form of 10-year redeemable at par ₹1,000 debentures with coupon rates varying with the equity-debt ratio and 5 per cent flotation cost. As a matter of policy, NML always keeps 10 per cent of its finances in the form of preference shares carrying 2 per cent extra return compared to the debenture coupon rates. The duration and the flotation costs are similar to debentures.

Required Assuming (i) 17.5 per cent dividend distribution tax and (ii) corporate tax rate, 35 per cent, determine the optimal capital structure (debt-equity mix) for the NML.

Solution

Determination of Optimum Capital Structure

Degree of leverage	*Coupon rate (%) (I)*	*Preference dividend (%) (D_p)*	*Cost of equity (ke)*	K_d@	*Kp*@@	*Ko*@@@
0	8.0	10.0	12.0	0.0585	0.1256	0.1206
10	8.0	10.0	12.0	0.0585	0.1256	0.1144
20	9.0	11.0	12.5	0.0651	0.1377	0.1143
30	9.0	11.0	13.5	0.0651	0.1377	0.1143
40	10.0	12.0	14.5	0.0718	0.1497	0.1162
50	13.0	15.0	16.0	0.0918	0.1859	0.1285
60	15.0	17.0	20.0	0.1051	0.2100	0.1441
70	18.0	20.0	25.0	0.1251	0.2462	0.1622

Conclusion: The optimum capital structure lies between 20 and 30 per cent of leverage.

Working Notes

@ k_d = [I (1 – t) + Flotation costs/N] ÷ (RV + SV)/2

@ @ k_p = [D_p (1 + D_t) + Flotation costs/N] ÷ (RV + SV)/2

where I = Interest, D_p = dividend on preference shares, t = tax rate, RV = redemption value, SV = sale value (face value – flotation cost), n = maturity period, D_t = dividend payment tax

@ @ @ k_o = (W_d x K_d) + (W_p x K_p) + (W_e + K_e). It may be noted that 10% debt-equity mix implies, 90% shareholders equity (consisting 10 % of preference shares and 80% of ordinary shares].

19.C.2 Royal Hotels Ltd. is a luxury hotel with following financials.

Income Statement of Royal Hotels Ltd for the year ending on March 31, 2014 *(Amount in ₹ crore)*

Particulars	*Amount*
Sales revenue	650
Operating costs	450
Operating profit	200
Financing costs	10
Earnings before tax	190
Taxes (30.9%)	58.71
Earnings after tax	131.29
Preference dividend	6.50
Preference dividend tax @16.995%	1.10
Earnings available to equity shareholders	123.68

Balance Sheet of Royal Hotels Ltd as at March 31, 2014 *(Amount in ₹ crore)*

Particulars		*Amount*
Shareholders' funds:		
Share capital:		
Equity	₹250	
13% Preference shares	50	₹300
Reserves and surplus:		
General reserve	90	
Long-term assets replacement reserve	10	100
Non-current liabilities:		
Secured loans: 10% Debentures		100
Current liabilities		100
		600
Application of funds:		
Long-term assets:		
Land and buildings (net)	200	
Furniture and fittings	200	400
Current assets		200
		600

Due to growing concept of 3Ps (Planet, People and Profit) and the desire to emerge as socially responsible organisation, the Board of Directors of Royal Hotels, comes up with the novel idea of "Green Hotel". A green hotel is to be environment friendly (in terms of reduced CFC emissions, reduced power usage, etc.) and economically sustainable. Building on this concept, various studies conducted have concluded that the project is likely to be technically feasible, economically viable, commercially profitable and financially sound. The Board also proposes to rename the hotel as Royal Greens Ltd. Projected Income statement of Royal Greens is as follows:

(Amount in ₹ crore)

Particulars	*Amount*
Total revenue	850
Operating costs	550
EBIT	300

To execute the investment proposal, the management is faced with the daunting task of raising the required finances of ₹100 crore. The CEO uses this opportunity to evaluate two Finance Managers, Mr. Rohan and Mr. Sohan, who are due for promotion. He asks each of them to suggest the soundest way of financing this expansion project.

Proposal of Mr. Rohan

He recommends raising ₹100 crore through 2 crore equity shares of face value of ₹10 each, issued at a premium of ₹40 each: Reasons to justify this proposal are: **(1)** Equity does not involve any fixed commitments, its cost is zero; **(2)** Payment of interest on debt and eventual redemption of debt will reduce available cash; **(3)** The benefit from increased revenues should go to equity-holders only; **(4)** Raising debt will increase financial risk of the firm; **(5)** Firm will be able to have a favourable debt equity ratio; and **(6)** Such favourable debt equity ratio and no risk of default of non- payment to financiers may increase the firm's overall rating.

Proposal of Mr. Sohan

He recommends raising ₹100 crore through issue of 11% debentures. The reasons for his proposal are:

1. EPS under debt plan is likely to be higher compared to equity plan as shown by lower indifference point (shown below) *vis-à-vis* projected EBIT.

$$\frac{(X - I_1)(1-t) - PD(1+PD_T)}{N_1} = \frac{(X - I_2)(1-t) - PD(1+PD_T)}{N_2}$$

$$\frac{(X - ₹10\text{ crore})(1-0.309) - ₹6.5\text{ crore}(1.16995)}{27\text{ crore}} = \frac{X - ₹21\text{crore})(1-0.309) - ₹6.5\text{ crore}(1.16995)}{25\text{ crore}}$$

   X (EBIT) = ₹169 crore

   Since expected EBIT ₹300 crore is more than required EBIT ₹169 crore (for indifference point), EPS (based on EBIT-EPS analysis) is higher under debt plan.
2. Interest on debt is tax deductible; it leads to cash inflow to the extent of tax saving on interest.
3. Equity is more costly *vis-à-vis* debt as a source of finance.
4. As per signaling Theory, issue of debt is a good signal, and leads to increase in market price of shares.
5. Even after raising debt, the firm will still have better debt equity ratio than industry average.
6. Above all, equityholders are in pensive mood due to uncertain and volatile conditions prevailing in Indian stock market; raising funds through equity is most likely to be difficult proposition.

Perplexed by the contradicting recommendations of his two prodigies, the CEO refers this complex task to consultant, Ms. Shivaani who is considered to be a financial wizard. She states that equity capital carries a higher cost due to higher risk compared to debt; leveraging up to a point reduces overall cost of capital (*as enunciated in Traditional approach of capital structure*) and equity-shareholders are benefitted by a higher EPS. Thus, an optimum mix of debt and equity is a prerequisite of sound capital structure. She submits the following report to CEO of Royal Greens.

Evaluation of proposed financing mix on the basis of desirable attributes of sound financing mix:

S. No.	*Attributes*	*Debt*	*Equity*	*Debt + Equity*	*Refer Note*
1.	EBIT-EPS analysis	✓	×	✓	1
2.	Compliance of covenants	×	✓	✓	2
3.	Wealth maximisation	✓	×	✓	1,4
4.	Avoidance of bankruptcy costs	×	✓	×	3
5.	Flexibility	×	×	✓	3
6.	Capital structure ratios	×	✓	✓	5,6,
7.	Tolerable financial leverage	✓	✓	✓	7
8.	Signaling theory	✓	×	✓	8
9.	Tax saving on interest	✓	×	✓	9
10.	Absence of agency cost	×	✓	✓	10
11.	Security rating	✓	✓	✓	11
12.	Timing	✓	✓	✓	12

Based on the above attributes, Shivaani recommends a mix of debt and equity to raise required funds of ₹100 crore. Due to a covenant in working capital loan agreement, it is advised to *raise debt and equity in ratio of 50:50* (refer Note 2), that is, ₹50 crore through issue of 50,00,000 11 per cent debentures of face value ₹100 and balance ₹50 crore through 1 crore equity shares of face value ₹10, issued at a premium of ₹40 per share.

Notes:

1. The basic objective of financial management is maximisation of shareholders wealth, (MPS is a proxy for the same) and, therefore, *real* indifference point (instead of indifference point based on EPS) would be rational guide in determining the source of finance.

$$\frac{P/E_1 X[(X - I_1)(1-t) - PD(1+PD_T)]}{N_1} = \frac{P/E_2 X[(X - I_2)(1-t) - PD(1+PD_T)]}{N_2}$$

$$\frac{10[(X - ₹10\text{ crore})(1-0.309) - ₹6.5\text{ crore}(1.16995)]}{27\text{ crore}}$$

$$= \frac{9.75[(X - ₹21\text{ crore})(1-0.309) - ₹6.5\text{ crore}(1.16995)]}{25\text{ crore}}$$

$$X = ₹239.5\text{ crore}$$

Since the projected EBIT at ₹300 crore is more than ₹239.5 crore, firm can finance through debt.

2. In WC loan agreement, a restrictive covenant has been found stating that, the long-term debt/equity ratio cannot be more than 40 per cent at any given point of time.
So, maximum debt that can be raised = (100 + *x*) = .4[400 + (100 – *x*)]
This implies firm can raise only ₹71.4 crore through debt.
3. Since raising debt can lead to bankruptcy costs, a schedule of bankruptcy cost at varying levels of debt is presented below.

Level of debt	₹100 crore	110	120	130	140	150	160	170
Bankruptcy costs	Zero	₹50 lakh	1 crore	2	4	7	11	16

In case the maximum possible debt, that is, ₹70 crore is raised, the total debt would amount to ₹170 crore, and accordingly bankruptcy costs are likely to be ₹16 crore. Also, exhausting the complete debt source reduces the flexibility to raise funds in future. Keeping this in mind, raising ₹50 crore through debt and the balance ₹50 crore through equity seems reasonable. This way total debt would amount to ₹150 crore, thereby leading to a saving of ₹9 crore towards bankruptcy costs. Therefore, a 50:50 debt-equity mix is proposed.

4. Statement showing determination of market price per share under various financing plans:

Figures in ₹ (crore)

Particulars	*Existing*	*Proposed mix*	*Only debt*	*Only equity*
Sales revenue	650	850	850	850
Operating costs	450	550	550	550
EBIT	200	300	300	300
Interest	10	15.50	21	10
EBT	190	284.50	279	290
Taxes @30.9%	58.71	87.91	86.21	89.61
EAT	131.29	196.58	192.78	200.39
Preference dividend	7.60	7.60	7.60	7.60
Earnings available to equity-holders	123.68	188.98	185.18	192.78
Number of equity shares	25	26	25	27
EPS (₹)	4.95	7.26	7.40	7.14
Expected P/E multiple*		9.95	9.5	10
MPS (₹)		72.32	70.37	71.40

*In view of high profitability, less financial risk, favourable ratios and lower fixed obligation, there is no significant difference in P/E ratio under varying financial alternative.

5. If the funds are raised in proposed ratio:
Long-term debt/ Equity ratio is likely to be:
₹150 crore/₹450 crore = 3 times or debt is 33.3 per cent of equity, hence, the covenant can be said to be complied with.

6. To ensure that the firm does not default on interest payment, interest coverage ratio has been calculated as follows:
EBIT ₹300 crore/ Interest ₹15.5 crore = 19.35 times
It means that even if EBIT falls by whopping 90 per cent, firm will be still able to meet its interest obligations. In operational terms, the firm is not likely to commit default in meeting its interest obligations.

7. To further assure that the proposed mix does not increase financial risk of the firm, degree of financial leverage is calculated as follows:

$$\frac{\text{EBIT}}{\dfrac{\text{EBT} - \text{Preference dividend}\,(1 + \text{dividend payment tax})}{(1 - \text{Tax rate})}}$$

$$\frac{₹\,300 \text{ crore}}{\dfrac{₹\,284.5 \text{ crore} - ₹\,6.5 \text{ crore}\,(1.16995)}{(1 - .309)}} = 1.0968$$

The degree of financial leverage is close to 1. It represents almost negligible chance of default in meeting commitments towards fixed charges.

8. Signaling theory states that investors see issue of debt as a good news.
9. Since interest on debentures is allowed to be deducted while calculating taxable income, interest × tax rate is a tax saving.
10. Usually issue of debt leads to emergence of agency costs; in the present context, debt is just one-third of equity, therefore, it is believed agency costs are not likely to arise.
11. Given sound capital structure ratios, firm's security rating is not expected to deteriorate (subsequent to raising of debt).
12. Given firm's credentials and market conditions, issuance of either or both of debt and equity are likely to succeed.

REVIEW QUESTIONS

LOD: Easy

RQ.19.1 Provide the appropriate answers to the following: [LO 19.2,]

(i) According to NI approach capital structure decision is ________ to the valuation of the firm. (relevant/irrelevant)

(ii) Market price per share ________ if more debt is used in NI approach. (increases/decreases/remains unchanged)

(iii) According to NOI approach, cost of equity is ________.

(iv) ________ implies buying securities in a market where price is low and selling where it is high.

(v) In the traditional approach, the cost of equity is independent of amount of debt. (True/False)

(vi) In practice, equity financing allows firm to go for cheaper sources of finance in future. (True/False)

(vii) What is the value of a levered firm L if it has the same EBIT as an unlevered firm U, (with value of ₹700 lakh), has a debt of ₹200 lakh, tax rate is 35 per cent under MM approach?

(a) ₹770 lakh **(b)** ₹500 lakh **(c)** ₹630 lakh **(d)** ₹900 lakh

(viii) What is the value of an unlevered firm U if it has the same EBIT as a levered firm L, (with value of ₹700 lakh), has a debt of ₹200 lakh, tax rate of 35 per cent under MM approach?

(a) ₹770 lakh **(b)** ₹500 lakh **(c)** ₹630 lakh **(d)** ₹900 lakh

(ix) According to the traditional approach, what is the effect of increase in degree of leverage on the valuation of the firm?

(a) Increases **(b)** Decreases

(c) Remains Unaffected **(d)** Increases first and then decreases

(x) According to NOI approach, with increase in debt/equity ratio the financial risk of equityholders ________

(a) decreases **(b)** increases

(c) no Change **(d)** depends on degree of leverage

[Answers: (i) Relevant (ii) Increases (iii) Residual (iv) Arbitrage process (v) False (vi) True (vii) ₹770 lakh (viii) ₹630 lakh (ix) Increase first then decreases and (x) Increases]

RQ.19.2 What is meant by the concept 'financial risk'? What is the relationship between leverage and the cost of capital? Explain. [LO 19.2,]

RQ.19.3 State the order in which firms will obtain financing under the pecking-order theory. Also state, in brief, the rationale for the order. [LO 19.2,]

RQ.19.4 Companies U and L are identical in every respect except that the former does not use debt in its capital structure, while the latter employs ₹6 lakh of 15 per cent debt. Assuming that, (a) all the MM assumptions are met, (b) the corporate tax rate is 35 per cent, (c) the EBIT is ₹2,00,000, and (d) the equity capitalisation of the unlevered company is 20 per cent, what will be the value of the firms, U and L? Also, determine the weighted average cost of capital for both the firms. [LO 19.2,]

LOD: Medium

RQ.19.5 Give a critical appraisal of the (a) traditional Approach and (b) the Modigliani-Miller Approach to the theory of capital structure. [LO 19.2,]

RQ.19.6 Explain briefly the view of traditional writers on the relationship between capital structure and the value of a firm. [LO 19.2,]

RQ.19.7 'The total value of a firm remains unchanged regardless of variations in its financing mix'. Discuss this statement and point out the role of arbitraging and homemade leverage. [LO 19.2,]

RQ.19.8 Is the MM thesis realistic with respect to capital structure and the value of a firm? If not, what are its main weaknesses? [LO 19.2,]

RQ.19.9 Write notes on: **(a)** Home made leverage, **(b)** Arbitrage process, **(c)** NI and NOI Approaches, **(d)** Reverse leverage, and (e) MM's thesis with corporate taxes. [LO 19.2,]

RQ.19.10 How would you determine the following? [LO 19.1,2,]

(a) The cost of equity in the NOI Approach,

(b) The value of equity, given the equity capitalisation rate, EBIT and interest,

(c) The overall capitalisation rate, given the EBIT, value of equity and value of debentures,

(d) The value of levered firm under MM's thesis with taxes, and

(e) The overall capitalisation rate, given k_e, k_d, S and B.

RQ.19.11 Enumerate the direct and indirect bankruptcy costs. How do such costs affect the valuation of levered firm, in a world of taxes? [LO 19.2,]

RQ.19.12 Briefly describe the trade-off theory of capital structure. How does it differ from MM proposition with taxes? [LO 19.2,]

RQ.19.13 Determine the optimal capital structure of a company from the following information supplied to you, assuming 35 per cent tax rate: [LO 19.2,]

Cost of debt, K_i (per cent)	*Cost of equity, K_e (per cent)*	*Debt/(Equity + Debt) (B/V)*
11	13	0
11	13	0.1
11.6	14	0.2
12	15	0.3
13	16	0.4
15	18	0.5
18	20	0.6

RQ.19.14 From the following selected data, determine the value of the firms, P and Q belonging to the homogeneous risk class under (a) NI approach, and (b) the NOI approach. [LO 19.2,]

	Firm P		*Firm Q*
EBIT	₹2,25,000		₹2,25,000
Interest (0.15)	75,000		
Equity capitalisation rate (K_e)		0.20	
Tax rate		0.35	

Which of the two firms has an optimal capital structure?

RQ.19.15 Two companies, X and Y belong to equivalent risk group. The two companies are identical in every respect except that company Y is levered, while X is unlevered. The outstanding amount of debt of the levered company is ₹6,00,000 in 10 per cent debentures. The other information for the two companies is as follows: [LO 19.2,]

	X	*Y*
NOI (net operating income)	₹1,50,000	₹1,50,000
Interest on debt	—	−60,000
Earnings to equityholders	1,50,000	90,000
Equity capitalisation rate	0.15	0.20
Market value of equity	10,00,000	4,50,000
Market value of debt	—	6,00,000
Total value of firm	10,00,000	10,50,000
Overall capitalisation rate	0.15	0.143
Debt/equity ratio	0	1.33

An investor owns 5 per cent equity shares of company Y. Show the process and the amount by which he could reduce his outlay through use of the arbitrage process. Are there any limits to the 'process'?

RQ.19.16 "The value of a firm is independent of the proportion of debt to total capitalisation. The arbitrage process will establish a market equilibrium in which the total value of the firm will depend only on investor's estimate of the firm's business risk, and its expected future income." Explain the above mentioned statement (assume 10 per cent holding) with the help of the following data regarding two companies, A and B with the same expected annual income and same risk class. **[LO 19.2,]**

Variables	*Company A*	*Company B*
Expected annual income (*Y*)	₹30,000	₹30,000
Market value of debt (*L*)	—	1,20,000
Rate of interest on debt (*i*)	—	0.125
Required rate of return on equity (*K*)	0.15	0.16
Market value of equity (*E*)	2,00,000	93,750
Market value of company (*V*), where *V* = *L* + *E*	2,00,000	2,13,750

LOD: Difficult

RQ.19.17 How will a firm go about determining its 'optimal capital structure'? **[LO 19.2,]**

RQ.19.18 Explain how 'asymmetric information' and "signals" affect corporate's capital structure decisions. How do the firm's financing decisions give investors signals that reflect the management's view of share value. **[LO 19.2,]**

ANSWERS

19.4 Value of unlevered firm ₹6,50,000
Value of levered firm ₹8,60,000
Ko of unlevered firm 0.20
Ko of levered firm 0.1511

19.13 Capital structure, having a debt of 10 per cent, is optimal.

19.14 Firm P has better capital structure (compared to firm Q) under both the NI and NOI approaches.

19.15 The investor can reduce his outlay by ₹2,500 through the use of leverage.
Yes, there are limits to the arbitrage process; this process will come to an end when the values of both firm become identical.

19.16 Mr X is earning the same amount of income as in company B. But his investment outlay in company A is less by ₹1,375.

Scan the QR Code to access comprehensive solutions to all numerical review questions and additional material.

CHAPTER

20

Designing Capital Structure

LEARNING OBJECTIVES

LO 20.1	Review the key factors having a bearing on the choice of an appropriate capital structure
LO 20.2	Illustrate EBIT-EPS analysis and coverage ratio as an approach to design capital structure
LO 20.3	Explain cash flow analysis as an approach to set debt policy for a firm
LO 20.4	Examine the other factors having a bearing on planning the sources of funds
LO 20.5	Analyse financing alternatives from the viewpoint of tax planning
LO 20.6	Outline capital structure practices by corporates in India

INTRODUCTION

The preceding chapter, focusing on the theoretical relationship between capital structure, cost of capital and valuation, has shown that although the empirical evidence is not conclusive, theoretically a judicious combination of debt and equity does affect the cost of capital as also the total value of the firm. There is, in other words, an optimum capital structure. The capital structure is said to be optimum when the marginal real cost (explicit as well as implicit) of each available source of financing is identical. With an optimum debt and equity mix, the cost of capital is minimum and the market price per share (or total value of the firm) is maximum. The use of debt in capital structure or financial leverage has both benefits as well as costs. While the principal attraction of debt is the tax benefit, its cost is *financial distress* and reduced commercial profitability. The term **financial distress**[1] includes a broad spectrum of problems ranging from relatively minor liquidity shortages to bankruptcy. The problem of financial distress will magnify with an increase in financial leverage. Beyond a certain point, the expected cost of financial distress will outweigh the tax benefit. A firm is, thus, concerned with a trade-off between risk and return emanating from the use of debt. A proper balance between the two is, therefore, called for.

Financial distress includes a broad spectrum of problems ranging from minor liquidity shortages to bankruptcy.

Given the objective of maximisation of shareholders' wealth, the need for an optimal capital structure cannot, therefore, be overemphasised. In operational terms, every firm should try to design such a capital structure. But the determination of an optimum capital structure is a formidable task. It should be clearly understood that identifying the *precise percentage* of debt that will maximise price per share is almost impossible. It is possible, however, to determine the *approximate proportion* of debt to use in the financial plan in conformity with the objective of maximising share prices.

In theory, one can speak of an **optimum** capital structure, but, in practice, it is very difficult to design one. There are significant variations among industries as also among individual companies within the same industry in respect of capital structure. This is so because there are a host of factors, both quantitative and qualitative, including subjective judgement of financial managers which determine the capital structure of a firm. These factors are highly complex and cannot fit entirely into a theoretical framework. From the operational standpoint, therefore, what should be attempted is an **appropriate** capital structure, given the facts of a particular case.

The present chapter which focuses on determining the *appropriate* mix of debt to be used along with equity in the capital structure discusses the important factors which have a bearing on designing capital structure of a firm. The terms **designing capital structure, capital structure decision, factors determining capital structure and capital structure planning** are used interchangeably here.

LO 20.1 KEY FACTORS

There are certain common, and often, conflicting considerations involved in determining the methods of financing assets because the position of each company is different. Accordingly, the weight given to various factors also varies widely, according to conditions in the economy, the industry and the company itself. Above all, the freedom of management to adjust the mix of debt and equity in accordance with these criteria is limited by the availability of the various types of debt to have an appropriate capital structure, but the debt may not be available to the company because the suppliers of the funds may think that it will involve too much financial risk for them. Consequently, the plans that management ultimately makes in the light of these considerations often involve a compromise between the desires and conditions imposed by the suppliers of funds. Moreover, none of the factors by itself is completely satisfactory. But, collectively, they provide sufficient information for taking rational decisions. The key factors governing the capital structure decisions are **(i)** profitability aspect, **(ii)** liquidity aspect, **(iii)** control, **(iv)** leverage ratios in industry, **(v)** nature of industry, **(vi)** consultation with investment banks/lenders, **(vii)** commercial strategy, **(viii)** timing, **(ix)** company characteristics and **(x)** tax planning.

LO 20.2 PROFITABILITY ASPECT: EARNINGS BEFORE INTEREST AND TAX (EBIT) - EARNINGS PER SHARE (EPS) ANALYSIS

EBIT-EPS analysis/ approach is an approach for selecting capital structure that maximises earnings per share (EPS) over the expected range of earnings before interest and taxes.

Keeping in view the primary objective of financial management of maximising the market value of the firm, the **EBIT-EPS analysis** should be considered logically as the first step in the direction of designing a firm's capital structure. As discussed in detail in Chapter 18, the EBIT-EPS analysis shows the impact of various financing alternatives on EPS at various levels of EBIT. This analysis is useful for two reasons: **(i)** the EPS is a measure of a firm's performance—given the P/E ratio, the larger the EPS, the larger would be the value of a firm's shares; and **(ii)** given the importance of EPS and the function of the EBIT-EPS analysis to show the value of EPS under various financial alternatives at different levels of EBIT, the EBIT-EPS analysis information can be extremely useful to the finance manager in arriving at an appropriate financing decision. The EBIT-EPS analysis is illustrated in Chapter 18. From Fig. 18.5, [based on Example 18.8 (i)], we see that the EPS is ₹6.5 per share at the point of intersection of two financial alternatives: **(i)** 100 per cent equity financing, and **(ii)** 50 per cent equity financing and 50 per cent debt financing. At that point, EPS is equal under both the plans. At the point of intersection, the EBIT level is ₹3 lakh. Beyond the point of intersection, the EPS is higher under alternative **(ii)** which uses 50 per cent debt than alternative **(i)**. Below the point of intersection, the EPS is higher under alternative **(i)** which exclusively uses equity rather than the half debt-mixed alternative (ii) which financial plan should be adopted, is to be determined with reference to the likely level of EBIT. If the company's likely level of EBIT is ₹4.5 lakh, the debt-mixed alternative should be preferred as the EPS is ₹13 under this alternative while it is ₹9.75 under the equity alternative. Thus, the finance manager can compare the point of intersection with the most likely level of EBIT and can decide the financing mix. The manager should determine the probability of 'critical' levels of EBIT. If the probability of EBIT going below ₹3 lakh is negligible or very low, the debt-mix alternative should be recommended by the finance manager. On the other hand, if the probability of EBIT falling below the indifference point is high, the equity-alternative should be preferred. In general, the higher the level of EBIT and the lower the probability of downward fluctuation, the greater is the amount of debt that can be employed. While taking a decision in this respect, it should be remembered that P/E ratio is less for a levered financial plan due to increased financial risk. Therefore, increase in EPS should be greater so that its advantage is not completely offset or more than offset by using debt in the capital structure. Moreover, if the debt alternative entails a provision for creating a sinking fund, the finance manager should keep in mind that earnings available for payment of dividends and reinvestment to further expand facilities would be reduced by the amount of the sinking fund payment. The indifference point would then be computed using Eq. 20.1.

$$\frac{\text{UEPS-Debt Plan}}{\dfrac{(\text{EBIT} - I)(1-t) - SF}{N_1}} = \frac{\text{UEPS-Equity Plan}}{\dfrac{(\text{EBIT})(1-t)}{N_2}} \quad \textbf{(20.1)}$$

where UEPS = uncommitted earnings per share

SF = sinking fund payment per annum

I = interest payments

Let us suppose in our example 14.8, the sinking fund payment is ₹1,40,000 for 8 years. The indifference point would have to be escalated to ₹5,00,000. The earlier decision of going for debt at the most likely level of EBIT of ₹4.5 lakh will be reversed. Likewise, in calculating the indifference level of EBIT, he should take cognizance of fixed interest or sinking fund liability on the other debts already outstanding. If preference shares are outstanding, its dividend (and sinking fund, if any, in the case of redeemable preference shares) requirements should also be provided for.

Coverage Ratio

Coverage ratio measures the size of interest payments relative to the EBIT and the adequacy of EBIT to meet payment obligations.

Apart from the EBIT-EPS/EBIT-MPS analysis, the ability of a firm to use debt, from the profitability point of view, can also be judged in terms of a coverage ratio, namely,

$$\text{EBIT}/I \quad \textbf{(20.2)}$$

Or

$$\frac{\text{EBIT}}{I + \left[\dfrac{SF}{1-t}\right]} \quad \textbf{(20.3)}$$

The ratio measures the size of the interest payments relative to the EBIT. The reciprocal of this ratio (I/EBIT) measures the proportion of EBIT devoted to interest payments. The higher the coverage ratio, the greater is the certainty that the firm would be in a position to meet its obligations of interest payment.

The coverage ratio can be calculated, like the EPS, for various levels of EBIT. This would provide a better picture of the firm's most likely EBIT to meet out specific commitments. It will throw light on the adequacy of EBIT to meet the firm's annual burden of payments connected with interest on loan, preference dividend, contribution to sinking fund (if any) and other repayments of principal.

LO 20.3 LIQUIDITY ASPECT: CASH FLOW ANALYSIS

EBIT-EPS analysis and coverage ratios are very useful in making explicit the impact of leverage on EPS and on the firm's ability to meet its commitments at various levels of EBIT. But the EBIT/interest ratio is less than a perfect measure to analyse the firm's ability to service fixed charges because the firm's ability to do so depends on the total payments required, that is, interest and principal, in relation to the cash flow available to meet them. Therefore, the analysis of the cash flow ability of the firm to service fixed charges is an important exercise to be carried out in capital structure planning in addition to profitability analysis. The exercise is of overwhelming significance in the context of the risk of bankruptcy. If the firm borrows more than its debt capacity and, therfore, fails to meet its obligations in future, the lenders may seize the assets of the company to satisfy their claims. Thus, the basic existence of the company would be endangered.

It may be possible that the company's EBIT is adequate to cover its specific commitments, arising out of debt obligations; but, the firm may not have sufficient cash to pay as its income is blocked within the firm in the form of higher inventory, receivables and/or sometimes purchases of fixed assets, particularly, when the company is a growing one. In the absence of cash flow analysis, a company, which is otherwise profitably sound, would, in case of default, run into great difficulties. Thus, cash flow analysis is an essential ingredient of any sound capital structure decision.

Cash flow analysis yields a number of distinct advantages in the crucial task of setting debt policy: **(i)** it focuses on the *solvency* of the firm during adverse circumstances in contrast to EBIT-EPS analysis which is concerned with the effects of leverage under normal circumstances; **(ii)** it takes into consideration the balance sheet changes and other cash flows that do not appear in the profit and loss account; **(iii)** it gives an insight into the **inventory of financial resources** available in the event of recession; and **(iv)** finally, it views the problem in a dynamic context over time whereas EBIT/EPS and coverage analysis normally consider only a single year. From all these points, it can be concluded that the cash flow analysis evaluates the risk of financial distress and should be recognised as a good supporting supplement to the EBIT/EPS analysis in framing the firm's capital structure.

Cash flow analysis evaluates the risk of financial distress.

In assessing the liquidity position of a firm in terms of its **cash flow analysis**, various measures can be employed. One such measure[2] is the *ratio of fixed charges to net cash inflows.* This ratio measures the coverage of fixed financial charges (interest plus repayment of principal, if any) to net cash inflows. In other words, it indicates the number of times the fixed financial requirements are covered by the net cash inflows. The greater the coverage ratio, the greater is the amount of debt (and other sources of funds carrying a fixed rate of interest/dividend) that a firm can use.

Another measure[3] to analyse the cash flow ability of a firm to service fixed charges in determining an appropriate capital structure is to prepare a cash budget to determine whether the expected cash flows are sufficient to cover the fixed obligations.[4] The purpose of preparing the cash budget is to find out possible deviations in actual cash flows from those that are expected. Therefore, cash budgets should be prepared for a range of possible cash inflows with a probability attached to each of them. This information can be used to evaluate the ability of the firm to meet its fixed obligations. Since the probability of various cash flow patterns is known, the firm can work out the amount of fixed charges as well as the debt that the firm can employ and still remain within an **insolvency limit tolerable to the management**.[5]

Suppose, the firm is of the view that 5 per cent is the maximum probability of not having cash to meet charges that can be tolerated (i.e. it will not cause insolvency). Further, suppose that the actual probability of being out of cash on the basis of the cash budget prepared under adverse circumstances is also 5 per cent. In such a situation, according to Van Horne, debt can be employed up to a point where the cash balance is just sufficient to cover the fixed charges. That is to say, debt can be increased up to the point at which the additional cash drain would cause the probability of cash insolvency to equal the risk tolerance specified by management. It is, of course, not necessary that the debt would be increased to that point. This method of analysis suggested by Van Horne provides a means for assessing the effect of increase in debt on the risk of cash insolvency. On the basis of the information available from this analysis, the firm would determine the most appropriate level of debt.

A similar type of analysis has been suggested by Gordon Donaldson.[6] It is argued that a firm will normally be able to meet its fixed obligations in terms of interest as well as repayment of principal. It is only during adverse circumstances that firms will not be able to maintain their ability to meet contractual obligations and would be exposed to the *risk of bankruptcy* or the extreme form of **risk of financial distress**. Donaldson terms these as **recession** conditions. To examine the impact of alternative debt policies on the risk of bankruptcy, therefore, what is required is a careful analysis of how a firm's cash flows would be affected by recession conditions. We illustrate below the effect of alternative debt policies on the risk of bankruptcy so as to determine debt capacity or optimum amount of debt appropriate to a particular firm.[7]

Debt capacity relates to how much debt can be comfortably serviced.

Cashflow Analysis in Recession The alternative debt policies in recession are illustrated in Example 20.1.

***Example* 20.1** A firm, Hypothetical Ltd, is planning its financial structure. At present the debt-equity ratio is 1:4, that is, debt is 20 per cent of the total. The firm has to choose an appropriate amount of debt. The question at issue is whether the Hypothetical Ltd should **(i)** continue with the present level of debt, **(ii)** use more debt or **(iii)** use less debt.

The Hypothetical Ltd manufactures a wide variety of industrial products. Its sales are moderately affected by the business cycle. Its sales and cash flow data for four years are given in Table 20.1.[8]

TABLE 20.1 Actual Sales and Cash Flows

(₹ lakh)

Particulars	Year 1	Year 2	Year 3	Year 4
Sales	116.6	121.1	112.0	126.5
Profits after taxes	5.8	7.7	6.7	6.5
Sources of funds:				
Operations	21.1	23.1	22.4	22.4
Working capital	3.0	(0.6)	3.1	(1.2)
Total	24.2	22.5	25.5	21.2
Uses of funds:				
Plant and equipment	(6.8)	(8.2)	(13.2)	(14.5)
Taxes	(3.8)	(3.7)	(3.4)	(3.2)
Lease payments	(1.9)	(2.0)	(2.1)	(2.1)
Interest	(2.0)	(1.8)	(1.7)	(1.6)
Repayment of debt	(1.4)	(1.4)	(1.4)	(1.4)
Dividend	(2.8)	(2.8)	(2.8)	(3.0)
Miscellaneous	(0.1)	(0.2)	(0.7)	(0.3)
Total	(18.8)	(20.1)	(25.3)	(26.1)
Changes in cash balance	5.4	2.4	0.2	(4.9)

The firm expects that in the subsequent years there will be recession. On the basis of past experience, the assumed pattern of sales during the recession is as given in Table 20.2.

TABLE 20.2 Assumed Patterns of Sales during Recession (Percentages)

Year prior to recession	*Year of recession*			
0	*1*	*2*	*3*	*4*
100	90	80	80	100

The implication of this pattern of sales is that the decline in sales during the recession period ranges between 10 and 20 per cent. Also, assume that the prices would decline by 3 per cent but would recover in the fourth year to the level of the year prior to the recession.

Prepare cash forecasts under recession conditions to determine the debt capacity of the Hypothetical Ltd.

Solution To prepare forecasts of cash flows under recession conditions, cash flows are divided into three categories: **(i)** operating; **(ii)** non-operating; and **(iii)** financial flows.

Operating Cash Flows cover sales revenues and cash operating expenses. Using the above information/assumptions regarding sales volume and price, the operating cash flows of the Hypothetical Ltd over the recession period are computed in Table 20.3.

TABLE 20.3 Operating Cash Flows Under Recession Conditions for Hypothetical Ltd (₹ lakh)

Particulars	Year prior to recession	Recession years			
	0	1	2	3	4
1. Sales at stable prices	126.5	113.9	101.2	101.2	126.5
2. As % of sales for year 4 (year prior to recession)	100	90	80	80	100
3. Sales at 3% price decline	126.5	110.5	98.2	98.2	126.5
4. Cash operating expenses	101.6	90.7	84.4	82.6	101.6
5. Net operating cash flows (3 – 4)	24.9	19.8	13.8	15.6	24.9

Non-operating Cash Flows include capital outlays and changes in working capital. The non-operating financial flows of the Hypothetical Ltd are given in Table 20.4.

TABLE 20.4 Non-operating Cash Flows Under Recession Conditions for Hypothetical Ltd (₹ in lakh)

Particulars	Year prior to recession	Recession years			
	0	1	2	3	4
1. Plant and equipment	(10.0)	(10.0)	(5.0)	(3.0)	(7.0)
2. Expenditure for working capital:					
Cash	(0.2)	0.3	—	—	(0.4)
Marketable securities	—	0.4	—	—	—
Accounts receivable	(1.2)	(1.6)	2.4	(1.1)	(3.6)
Inventory	(1.7)	2.6	0.4	(1.2)	(3.4)
Accounts payable	1.6	(2.1)	(2.0)	0.8	1.0
Total	(1.5)	(0.4)	0.8	(1.5)	(6.4)
3. Net operating cash outflow (1 + 2)	(11.5)	(10.4)	(4.2)	(4.5)	(13.4)

Financial Flows cover lease payments, interest on debt, repayment of principal, taxes and dividends. The financial flows of the Hypothetical Ltd under the present capital structure are shown in Table 20.5.

TABLE 20.5 Projected Financial Flows Under the Existing Capital Structure (₹ in lakh)

Particulars	Year prior to recession	Recession years			
	0	1	2	3	4
1. Lease payments	(2.1)	(2.1)	(2.1)	(2.1)	(2.1)
2. Interest on debt*	(1.5)	(1.4)	(1.3)	(1.2)	(1.0)
3. Repayment of debt	(1.4)	(1.4)	(1.4)	(1.4)	(1.4)
4. Dividend[a]	(3.0)	(3.0)	(3.0)	(3.0)	(3.0)
5. Taxes	(3.2)	(2.6)	(2.1)	(2.6)	(3.2)
Total	(11.2)	(10.5)	(9.9)	(10.3)	(10.7)

* Principal due at the beginning of year. 0 = ₹18.6 lakh. Rate of interest 8 per cent. Interest shown for year 0 is that due in year, 0. Sinking fund payments are ₹1.4 lakh per year.

[a] Dividend is ₹2 per share on 1.5 lakh outstanding shares.

Alternative Debt Policies We now show cash flows for three debt policies: (i) for the current capital structure with 20 per cent debt; (ii) for Alternative A with 35 per cent debt; and (iii) for 50 per cent debt which may be referred to as Alternative B. While total financial flows for proposed alternative debt policies are presented in Table 20.6, Table 20.7 contains the relevant cash flows for the three alternative debt policies for the Hypothetical Ltd.

TABLE 20.6 Projected Total Financial Flows Under Proposed Debt Policies

Debt policies	*Year prior to recession (0)*	*Recession year (1)*	*(2)*	*(3)*	*(4)*
35% Debt	(12.3)	(11.5)	(10.8)	(11.1)	(11.5)
50% Debt	(13.3)	(12.4)	(11.6)	(11.8)	(12.1)

TABLE 20.7 Alternative Debt Policies for Hypothetical Ltd[aa] (₹ *lakh*)

Particulars	*Year prior to recession* 0	*Recession years* 1	2	3	4
Current Capital Structure:					
1. Non-financial flows, net (Tables 20.3 & 20.4)	13.4	9.4	9.6	11.1	11.5
2. Financial flows (Table 20.5)	(11.2)	(10.5)	(9.9)	(10.3)	(10.7)
3. Change in cash balance (1 – 2)	2.2	(1.1)	(0.3)	0.8	0.8
4. Cumulative change	2.2	1.1	0.8	1.6	2.4
5. Change in cash with dividend eliminated in year 1[a] (Item 3+₹3 lakh)	2.2	1.9	2.7	3.8	3.8
6. Cumulative change	2.2	4.1	6.8	10.6	14.4
Alternative A: 35% debt:					
7. Financial flows	(12.3)	(11.5)	(10.8)	(11.1)	(11.5)
8. Change in cash balance (1-7)	1.1	(2.1)	(1.2)	—	—
9. Cumulative change	1.1	(1.0)	(2.2)	(2.2)	(2.2)
10. Change in cash with dividend eliminated in year[b] (Item 8 + ₹2.4 lakh)	1.1	0.3	1.2	2.4	2.4
11. Cumulative change	1.1	1.4	2.6	5.0	7.4
Alternative B: 50% debt:					
12. Financial flows	(13.3)	(12.4)	(11.6)	(11.8)	(12.1)
13. Change in cash balance (1 - 12)	0.1	(3.0)	(2.0)	(0.7)	(0.6)
14. Cumulative change	0.1	(2.9)	(4.9)	(5.6)	(6.2)
15. Change in cash with dividend eliminated in year 1[c] (Item 13 + ₹1.9 lakh)	0.1	(1.1)	(0.1)	1.2	1.3
16. Cumulative change	0.1	(1.0)	(1.1)	0.1	1.4

[aa]Solomon, E and J J Pringle, *op. cit.* p. 486. Reprinted by permission from Goodyear Publishing Company, Santa Monica, USA.

[a] Dividend of ₹3.0 lakh per year. Item 5 assumes that dividend is eliminated completely in year 1 and no dividend at all is paid in years 1-4.

[b] Dividend of ₹2.4 lakh per year with less equity and more debt in capital structure. Same assumptions regarding elimination in year 1.

[c] Dividend of ₹1.9 lakh per year, with same assumptions regarding elimination.

Interpretation of Cash Flow Analysis in Recession It can be seen from Table 20.7 that interest on incremental debt is 8 per cent a year, that is, the same in all alternatives. However, dividends, repayment of principal and tax payments change as a result of change in the amount of debt under various alternatives.

The conclusions that emerge from the cash flow analysis in Table 20.7 are:

1. Under the current financing plan, with 20 per cent debt, there is a cash deficit in years 1 and 2, assuming there is no cut in divided (Item 3). These deficits are financed by the surplus in the year prior to the onset of recession (0 year). On a cumulative basis (Item 4), the firm could survive the recession without cutting the divided to the shareholders.
2. Under Alternative A, with 35 per cent debt, the cash deficit is somewhat larger in years 1 and 2 (Item 8). The surplus (₹1.1 lakh) in year 0 is not sufficient to finance the subsequent deficits. To eliminate cash deficit, dividends are to be cut. It implies that the firm can survive the recession only if it cuts the dividends to the shareholders.
3. Finally, when the debt is increased to 50 per cent (Alternative B), there is cash deficit in all the years of recession (Item 13). Even after eliminating dividends, there is cash deficit in years 1 and 2, even on a cumulative basis (Items 15 and 16). Thus, Alternative B cannot be sustained during a recession even after no dividends are paid.

Given the above facts, it may be concluded that the Hypothetical Ltd can use 30-35 per cent debt and avoid financial bankruptcy during recession.

The approach illustrated above to analyse cash flows to determine debt capacity can be refined by introducing probabilities. Probability distributions would be required for revenues and other uncertain cash flows. Probability distributions then could be estimated for the changes in cash balance shown in Table 20.7. A complete analysis would yield a probability distribution for each cash balance figure in each year. Such a procedure is very difficult and complex. We have, therefore, excluded this aspect.[9] Thus, cash flow analysis under recession conditions provides information on the effects of alternative financing plans on the risk of insolvency. This information is extremely useful in taking capital structure decisions.

LO 20.4 OTHER FACTORS

Control

Another consideration in planning the types of funds to use is the attitude of the management towards control. Lenders have no direct voice in the management of a company. They may, of course, place certain restrictions in the loan agreement on the management's activities. So long as there is no default in the payment of interest or the repayment of the principal, there is little that they can do legally against the company. For all practical purposes, they have very little say in the policy-decisions of the company or in the selection of the board of directors. Likewise, preference shareholders do not have the right to vote for the appointment of the board of directors. However, if the financial affairs of the company have deteriorated to such an extent that dividends on preference shares have not been paid for a certain number of years (2-year period in India), they are given the right to attend the meetings and participate in the voting. In most of the cases, they, like the creditors, do not have any say in the selection of the management. The power to choose the management in most cases rests with the equity-holders. Accordingly, if the main object of the management is to maintain control, they will like to have a greater weightage for debt and preference shares in additional capital requirements, since by obtaining funds through them the management sacrifices little or no control. However, it should be remembered that if the company borrows more than what it can service or repay, the creditors may seize the assets of the company to satisfy their claims. In that situation, the management would lose all control. It might be better to sacrifice a measure of control by some additional equity financing rather than run the risk of losing all control to creditors by employing too much debt.[10] The same holds true for preference shares. In such a situation, equity would be a better source of financing. However, if the firm has the ability, as determined by profitability and solvency considerations discussed above, and the management wants to maintain control in its own hands, the issue of senior securities will be recommended as the issue of additional equity shares would involve the risk of losing control. This will be all the more true if the company is *closely held.* The management of widely-held companies runs little risk of losing continuation of control. The shares of such companies are widely distributed. Most of the shareholders are interested simply in the return and have neither the time nor the inclination to participate in management. If they are not satisfied, they will switch over to other companies.

Leverage Ratios For Other Firms in the Industry

Yet another approach to the capital structure decisions is to make a comparison with the debt-equity ratios of companies belonging to the same industry, having a similar business risk. The rationale of the use of industry standards is that debt-equity ratios appropriate for other firms in a similar line of business should be appropriate for the company as well. Industry standards provide a useful benchmark. If the firm is out of line, it is conspicuous in the market place. This does not necessarily imply that the firm's capital structure planning is inappropriate. It may well be possible that other firms may not be using appropriate debt-equity ratios. They may be more conservative or more aggressive risk-takers than desired. However, comparison is helpful as it acts as a red signal to the management that there may be something wrong with the debt-equity mix of the company. In other words, what it suggests is that if a firm is out of line, it should know the reasons why and be satisfied that there are good reasons for it.[11]

Nature of Industry

The nature of industry is one of the most important elements in determining the degree of financial leverage a firm can carry safely without any risk of bankruptcy. If an industry's sales are subject to wide fluctuations, over a business cycle, the firm should have a low degree of financial leverage. Such firms will already have a high operating leverage. In case both are high, the total risk of the firm as determined by the combined leverage (the product of operating leverage and financial leverage) would become unduly high.[12] The firms with high debt ratios belonging to industries such as refrigeration, televisions, machine tools and capital equipment manufacturing, run the risk of not being able to meet the required payments in lean years which would cause financial distress. Clearly, such firms should have a more conservative capital structure and rely less on debt. On the other hand, industries dealing with non-durable consumer goods (food) or with inexpensive items (paper clips, match boxes) or with items in habitual use (cigarettes) or all those products which have an inelastic demand are not likely to be subject to wide fluctuations in sales. Such industries can afford to have higher debt proportions in capital structure as in lean years they do not run the risk of being unable to meet their commitments.

Judging industry by its competitive nature, it may be inferred that those industries which have keen competition among themselves should have a relatively greater proportion of equity than debt.

For example, in the garment industry much of the competition is based on style. The styles being unpredictable and transitory the profits also fluctuate accordingly. Therefore, such firms should emphasise equity over debt because of the excessive risk of not being able to meet payments on borrowed funds. At the other extreme, there are public utility undertakings involved in the production of electricity, gas, water, transportation services or telephone services, which are relatively free from intra-industry competition. Their sales are more stable and predictable. Therefore, such companies can afford to use more debt.

The stage of the life cycle of the industry has also a crucial bearing in assigning relative weightage to various sources of raising finance. If the industry is in its infancy, the probability of the rate of mortality would be high. Therefore, more emphasis needs to be placed on equity capital. The firm would do well to avoid seeking funds from senior securities which require fixed payments. At such a stage, risk outweighs the attractions of financial leverage. When the industry has reached maturity and is passing through the period of rapid growth, the firm should pay special attention to manoeuverability to assure that as it grows it obtains funds when needed and under acceptable terms. If the outlook is for a long-term decline in business, the firm should build such a plan which allows for easy contraction in the sources of the funds used.[13] For this purpose, the firm can have 'call' provision in the case of senior securities.

Consultation with Investment Bankers and Lenders

Another useful approach in deciding the proportion of various securities in a firm's structure is to seek the opinion of investment analysts, institutional investors, investment bankers and lenders. These analysts, having been in business for a considerable period of time, acquire expertise and have access to information regarding securities of a large number of companies and know how the market evaluates them. They are, therefore, in a better position to assess a particular financial plan.

Similarly, the opinions of prospective lenders and investors are likely to be very useful to the firm; it is they who will ultimately provide funds to the firm. Therefore, the type of securities which they will prefer to buy is very significant information for the financial manager and helps him in taking a decision regarding the form of securities to be issued. It is imperative that if a financial decision is to contribute to the valuation of the firm, the finance manager must think in a way similar to that of the investors.

Maintaining Manoeuverability for Commercial Strategy

Manoeuverability refers to a firm's ability to adjust its sources of funds in either direction–increase or decrease–in response to changes in the need for funds. That is, the finance manager must keep himself in a situation where he can change positions. Therefore, while designing the capital structure, he should not lose sight of the future impact on the present financial plan. For instance, the firm may adopt an aggressive debt policy as it looks good at one point but if in future the firm is in need of additional funds, it may be forced to issue equity shares on unfavourable terms as the firm has a too heavy debt and is, therefore, unable to obtain funds in this form. Due to increased financial risk, the cost of equity would be higher. Clearly, the opportunity cost of an unwise debt-policy could turn out to be very high. Therefore, in order to preserve operating flexibility, a firm is well advised to have unused debt capacity for future needs, that is, it should operate below the maximum safe debt level. The preservation of unused debt capacity can be an

> **Manoeuverability** implies the ability to adjust source of funds in response to change in the need for funds.

important consideration for the company whose funds requirements are sudden and unpredictable. It gives the company financial manoeuverability by virtue of leaving the options open.[14]

There should be room for **flexibility** not only in obtaining funds but also in refunding them. To provide the desired flexibility, the firm might incorporate a call provision as one of the covenants of the agreement with the suppliers of funds. The call provision implies that the firm with an adequate notice can repay their principal sum.

Flexibility as to financing is important when future external financing will be necessary.

Flexibility, however, can be obtained only at a cost. When a finance manager achieves flexibility, it means that the party at the other end of the transaction is foregoing something and for doing this would like to be compensated. *Callable* preference shares and options for advance payment of long-term debt are devices for maintaining flexibility. But, they will require higher yield to be paid than *non-callable* preference shares and long-term debts for a definite number of years. Therefore, the finance manager faces the task of risk/return trade-off. He is to assure himself that he is *not buying flexibility at a higher cost than is warranted by gains achieved through flexibility.*

Timing of Issue

Closely related to flexibility in deciding the types of funds to be used, is the question of timing. Frequently very substantial savings may be obtained by proper timing of security issues. Thus, the timing of the public offerings is also an important consideration in capital structure decisions of a firm. Public offering should be made at a time when the state of the economy as well as the capital market is ideal to provide the funds. The monetary and fiscal policies that are pursued by the government are also important in this regard. *The government follows a cheap money policy to boost the economy during a recession and a dear money policy during inflationary periods.* The type of policy pursued by the government reflects itself in prices as well as yields on senior securities and equity. High debentures yields are associated with relative scarcity of debt money and low P/E ratios on shares are an indication of the relative scarcity of equity funds. Frequently, therefore, the company has to decide whether to finance initially with an equity issue and later with a debt issue, or *vice-versa.* Consequently, it is forced to evaluate the alternative methods of financing in the light of general market conditions and expectations for the company itself. If the management feels that borrowed funds will become costly or scarce, the firm may like to use the benefit of financial leverage immediately. An expected decline in interest rates may encourage the firms to postpone borrowings, and remain in a flexible position which helps to take advantage of lower interest rates in the future.

At times, funds will be needed and must be obtained if they are relatively costly. This aspect of our discussion is related to the internal rate of return (IRR). If the project materialises just when demand for the product involved is strong, the early return to flow of funds is higher; the IRR is higher and perhaps a somewhat higher cost of capital can be profitably tolerated. The differential increase in the rate of return, at this time, is more than the differential in the cost of money. It is foolhardy for a finance manager to chase the lowest cost of money only to find that he has procured the funds at bargain rates when the time for their usefulness has passed.[15]

However, it should be borne in mind, that timing is not the only consideration. The timing analysis may suggest, for instance, use of debt. But the company cannot go in for debt if its existing capital structure is already top-heavy with debt. Agreements with the existing lenders of the funds may impose certain other restrictions. Thus, timing in obtaining funds is exercised within limits imposed by the timing of needs for funds, the extent of flexibility, and existing explicit agreements, sometimes an implicit understanding, with lenders and owners.

Characteristics of the Company

The characteristics of a company in terms of size and credit standing, among others, also play a vital role in determining the share of senior securities and equity in its capital structure.

The management's freedom of choice is extremely limited in the case of small and very large companies. Companies that are very small must rely, to a considerable degree, upon the owner's funds for their financing; they find it very difficult to obtain long-term debts. In the minds of investors, generally, small firms are considered to be more risky than large firms. Therefore, such firms do not have ready access to different types of funds from various sources. They are generally in a weak bargaining position in obtaining funds. Since their sources of raising funds are limited, they can assign larger weights to the factor of flexibility. In contrast, very large companies are compelled to make use of different sources of raising funds as no single source can cater to their total requirements of funds.

Firms enjoying a high credit standing among investors/lenders in the capital market are in a better position to get funds from the sources of their choice. If the credit standing is poor, the firm's choice of obtaining funds is rather limited.

LO 20.5 TAX PLANNING

Tax planning is likely to have a significant bearing on capital structure decisions. Under the Income Tax Act, 1961, while interest on borrowed funds is allowed as a deduction under Section 36(1)(iii), dividend on shares is not deductible from the operating profits of a company. With effect from April 1, 2003, distributed profits are subject to an extra 10 per cent tax under Sections 115O. Secondly, cost of raising finance through borrowings is deductible in the year of incurrence. If, however, it is incurred during pre-commencement of business period, it has to be capitalised. The cost of issue of shares is allowed as a deduction in 10 years under Section 35 D. As a result, corporate taxation is an important determinant of the choice between different sources of financing. For a widely-held company with expansion involving ₹100 lakh, the implication on taxes on the rate of return on equity capital with reference to the alternative capital structures are depicted in Table 20.8: (1) Alternative I, ₹100 lakh equity capital; (2) Alternative II, equity capital, ₹40 lakh + debentures, ₹40 lakh + institutional loans, ₹20 lakh, and (3) Alternative III, equity capital, ₹20 lakh + debentures, ₹30 lakh + loans from financial institutions, ₹50 lakh. The before-tax expected rate of return = 25 per cent. The rate of dividend is 20 per cent.

TABLE 20.8 Effect of Taxes on Capital Structure Decision *(₹ thousand)*

Particulars	*Alternative I*	*Alternative II*	*Alternative III*
Return (₹100 lakh × 0.25)	₹2,500	₹2,500	₹2,500
Less: Interest on debentures (0.14)	—	560	420
Less: Interest on loan (0.18)	—	360	900
Taxable profit	2,500	1,580	1,180
Tax (0.35)	875	553	413
Return on equity capital	1,625	1,027	767
Rate of return on equity capital (before dividend tax)	16.25	25.68	38.35

The alternative III is obviously the best.

The effect of corporate taxation on capital structure decision is further illustrated in Example 20.2.

***Example* 20.2**

The paid-up capital of a company is ₹100 lakh. It has been declaring 20 per cent dividend for the last 5 years.

It has under consideration an expansion programme involving an investment of ₹100 lakh and its board of directors desires to raise the dividend to 25 per cent. The expansion programme can be financed by four alternatives: A, 100 per cent equity; B, 18 per cent institutional loan (debt) and equity 50:50. C, equity and debt, 70:30; and D, 100 per cent debt. Income tax and dividend tax are 35 per cent and 10 per cent respectively.

Assuming rate of return of X, analyse the various financing alternatives from the point of view of taxes.

Solution The computation are shown in Table 20.9.

TABLE 20.9 Effect of Taxes on Financing Alternatives (*₹ lakh*)

Particulars	*A*	*B*	*C*	*D*
1. Return on ₹100 lakh	100X	100X	100X	100X
2. *Less:* Interest (0.18)	—	9	5.4	18
3. Balance	100X	100X – 9	100X – 5.4	100X – 18
4. *Less:* Tax (0.35)	35X	35X – 3.16	35X – 1.9	35X – 6.30
5. Balance	65X	65X – 5.86	65X – 3.52	65X – 11.70
6. *Add:* Distributable profit before expansion (0.20×₹100 lakh)	20	20	20	20
7. Total profits available for distribution (a)	20+65X	14.14 + 65X	16.48 + 65X	8.30 + 65X
8. Expected rate of dividend (%)	25	25	25	25
9. Expected dividend (0.25 × [₹100 lakh + new capital]	50	37.50	42.50	25
10. Dividend tax (0.10)	5	3.76	4.26	2.5
11. Total of dividend and dividend tax (b) [9 + 10]	55	41.26	46.76	27.5
12. Rate of return (value of X) to pay dividend and dividend tax [value of X if (a) = (b)] (%)	54@	42	47	30

@ 20 + 65 X = 55 or X = 35/65 = 54 per cent; other values are also determind like this.

Thus, the company will be able to raise dividend on shares to 25 per cent only if the return on the new project under the four alternatives are 54(A), 42(B), 47(C) and 30(D).

The choice of an appropriate debt policy involves a trade-off between tax benefits and the cost of financial distress. The greater the operating risk, the less is the debt the firm can use. Moreover, the management should consider the implicit cost of the tax subsidy in using debt. 'The tax subsidy is valuable, but, to go too far in exploiting it can be costly. The use of debt in lieu of equity represents essentially a gamble in which the firm sets a part of its future to obtain the tax benefit today. Such sets should be placed with caution.'[16]

Above all, it should be remembered that 'financial theory has not developed to the point where data relative to these considerations are fed at one end of a computer and an ideal financial structure pops out of the other. Consequently, human judgement must be used to resolve the many conflicting forces in laying plans for the types of funds to be sought.'[17]

LO 20.6 CAPITAL STRUCTURE PRACTICES IN INDIA

- Indian corporates employ substantial amount of debt in their capital structure in terms of the debt-equity ratio as well as total debt to total assets ratio. Nonetheless, the foreign controlled companies in India use less debt than the domestic companies. The dependence of the Indian corporate sector on debt as a source of finance has over the years declined particularly since the mid-nineties.
- The study (for the period (2001-11) indicates that debt is steadily being replaced by equity for the majority of the sample companies in India. This gets support from many aspects of the survey: (i) retained earnings have been cited as the most preferred source by the sample companies; (ii) the majority of the sample companies state that debt should not be used to the maximum extent; and (iii) higher equity enables the firm to face bad periods better than firms with high debt-equity ratios.
- The corporate enterprises in India seem to prefer long-term borrowings over short-term borrowings. Over the years, they seem to have substituted short-term debt for long-term debt. The foreign controlled companies use more long-term loans relatively to the domestic companies.
- However, as per the study of 2001-11, there is a significant portion of short-term debt (primarily from banks) in total debt.
- As a result of debt-dominated capital structure, the Indian corporates are exposed to a very high degree of total risk as reflected in high degree of operating leverage and financial leverage and, consequently, are subject to a high cost of financial distress which includes a broad spectrum of problems ranging from relatively minor liquidity shortages to extreme cases of bankruptcy. The foreign controlled companies, however, are exposed to lower overall risk as well as financial risk.
- The debt service capacity of the a sizeable segment of the corporate borrowers as measured by (i) interest coverage ratio and (ii) debt service coverage ratio is inadequate and unsatisfactory.
- Retained earnings are the most favoured source of finance. There is significant difference in the use of internally generated funds by the highly profitable corporates relative to the low profitable firms. The low profitable firms use different form of debt funds more than the highly profitable firms.
- Loan from financial institutions and private placement of debt are the next most widely used source of finance. The large firms are more likely to issue bonds in the market than small corporates.
- The hybrid securities are the least popular sources of finance amongst corporate India. They are more likely to be used by low growth firms. Preference shares are used more by public sectors units and low growth corporates.
- Banks have been the major providers of debt requirements of the sample companies. The declining role of financial institutions in corporate financing in India is very evident.
- The sample companies show non-adherence to the pecking order hypothesis.
- There is a low component of secured loans to total borrowings.

Source: (i) Jain, P K and Yadav, S S, *op. cit*, pp. 55-104.
(ii) Jain P K, Shveta Singh and Surendra S Yadav, "Financial Management Practices: An Empirical Study of Indian Corporates", Springer, New Delhi, 2013, Chapter 3.

SUMMARY

LO 20.1

A host of factors, both quantitative and qualitative, including subjective judgment of financial managers, have a bearing on the determination of an optional capital structure of a firm. They are not only highly complex but also conflicting in nature and, therefore, cannot fit entirely into a theoretical framework. Moreover, the weights assigned to various factors also vary widely, according to conditions in the economy, the industry and the company itself. Therefore, a corporate should attempt to evolve an appropriate capital structure, given the facts of a particular case.

The key factors relevant to designing an appropriate capital structure are: (i) profitability, (ii) liquidity, (iii) control, (iv) leverage ratios in industry, (v) nature of industry, (vi) consultation with investment banks/lenders, (vii) commercial strategy, (viii) timing, (ix) company characteristics and (x) tax planning.

LO 20.2	Given the objective of financial management to maximise the shareholders wealth, a corporate should carry out profitability analysis in terms of determining the amount of EBIT (indifference point) at which its MPS is identical under two proposed financial plans. In general, the higher the level of EBIT than the indifference point and the lower the probability of its downward fluctuation, the greater is the amount of debt that can be employed by a corporate. Coverage ratio can also be used to judge the adequacy of EBIT to meet the firm's obligations to pay financial charges, interest on loan, preference dividend and repayment of principal. A higher ratio implies that the firm can go for larger proportion of debt in its capital structure.
LO 20.3	Liquidity position of a firm is analysed by cash flow analysis. One measure relates the ratio of fixed financial charges to net cash inflows. A firm can afford higher debt if the ratio is high. Another measure to determine the adequacy of cash flows to meet the fixed obligations in cash budget. A cash budget should be prepared for a range of possible cash inflows with a probability attached to each of them. Since the probability of various cash flow pattern is known, the firm can determine the level of debt it can employ and still remain within an insolvency limit tolerable to the management. The impact of alternative debt policies should also be examined under adverse circumstances/recession conditions.
LO 20.4	To retain control over management, a firm would prefer use of debt to equity.
	The debt-equity ratio of a firm should be similar to those of other companies in the industry.
	In case sales are subject to wide fluctuations, a firm should employ less debt. Firms subject to keen competition should prefer a greater proportion of equity. The corporates in industry groups which are at their infancy should rely more on equity capital.
	Investment analysts/bankers/institutional investors understand the capital market better as well as requirements of investors/lenders. Their opinion is also useful in designing capital structure.
	An appropriate capital structure should provide room for flexibility not only in obtaining funds but also in refunding them.
	Public issue of share as well as debt capital should be made at a time when the state of the economy as well as the capital market is ideal to provide the funds. For instance, it will be useful to postpone borrowings if decline in interest rates is expected in the future.
	The characteristics of company, *inter-alia,* in terms of size and credit standing are decisive in determining its capital structure. While large firms enjoying a high credit standing among investors are in a better position to obtain funds from the sources of their choice, the relatively small firms, new firms and firms having poor credit standing have limited option in this regard.
LO 20.5	The choice of an appropriate debt policy involves a trade-off between tax benefits and the cost of financial distress. Moreover, the management should consider the implicit cost of the tax subsidy in using debt.

REFERENCES

1. Solomon, E and J J Pringle, *Introduction to Financial Mangement,* Goodyear Publishing Co., Santa Monica, California 1977, p 471.
2. Johnson, R L, *Financial Decision Makving,* Goodyear Publishing Co., California, 1973, p 216.
3. Van Horne, *op. cit.* p 232.
4. The preparation of cash budget is discussed in detail in Chapter 18.
5. Van Horne, *op. cit.* p 233.
6. Donaldson, G, *Corporate Debt Capacity,* Harvard University Press, Boston, 1961; also 'Strategy for Financial Emergencies', *Harvard Business Review,* December 1969, pp 67-79.
7. Solomon, E and J J Pringle, *op. cit.* pp 479-90.

8. From Solomon, E and J J Pringle, *op. cit.* p 482. Reprinted by permission of Goodyear Publishing Company, Santa Monica, USA.
9. For such analysis, refer to Donaldson, *op. cit.* pp 67-79. Also Van Horne, *op. cit.* pp 234-36.
10. Johnson, R W, *Financial Management*, 1971, Allyn and Bacon, Boston, p 227.
11. Solomon, E and J J Pringle, *op. cit.* p 478.
12. For a discussion of 'operating and financial leverage' refer to Chapter 10.
13. Johnson, R W, *op. cit.* p 233.
14. Van Horne, *op. cit.* p 259.
15. Nemmers, E F and A Grunewald, *Basic Managerial Finance*, West Publishing Co., New York, 1975, p 556.
16. Solomon, E and J J Pringle, *op. cit.* p 491.
17. Johnson, R W, *op. cit.* p 234.

SOLVED PROBLEMS

P.20.1 The Hardware Company Ltd has to make a choice between debt issue and equity issue for its expansion programme. Its current position is as follows: LO 20.2 LOD E

5% Debt	₹20,000
Equity capital (₹10 per share)	50,000
Surpluses	30,000
Total capitalisation	1,00,000
Sales	3,00,000
Total costs	2,69,000
Income before interest and taxes	31,000
Interest	1,000
Earnings before taxes	30,000
Income tax	10,500
Income after taxes	19,500

The expansion programme is estimated to cost ₹50,000. If this is financed through debt, the rate of interest on new debt will be 7 per cent and the price-earnings ratio will be 6. If the expansion programme is financed through equity, new shares can be sold netting ₹25 per share; and the price-earnings ratio will be 7. The expansion will generate additional sales of ₹1,50,000 with a return of 10 per cent on sales before interest and taxes.

If the company is to follow a policy of maximising the market value of its shares, which form of financing should it choose?

Solution

Determination of market value of a share under different financing alternatives

Particulars	*Financial plan*	
	7% debt issue	*Equity issue*
EBIT	₹46,000	₹46,000
Less: Interest	4,500	1,000
Earnings after interest	41,500	45,000
Less: Taxes	14,525	15,750
EAT	26,975	29,250
EPS (EAT/Number of shares)	5.395	4.18
Price earning ratio	6	7
Market value per share	32.37	29.25

Recommendation The company should choose debt form of financing to maximise the market value of its shares.

Working Notes

(i) Present EBIT ₹31,000
Plus expected EBIT (0.10 × ₹1,50,000) 15,000
Total EBIT 46,000

(ii) Number of equity shares: With debt financing, the number of ordinary shares = 5,000 (₹50,000 ÷ ₹10). In case of equity financing = additional 2,000 (₹50,000 ÷ ₹25) new equity shares.

P.20.2 AB Limited provides you with the following information: LO 20.2 LOD M

Profit	₹3,00,000
Less: Interest on debentures (0.12)	60,000
Earnings before taxes	2,40,000
Less: Taxes (0.35)	84,000
Earnings after taxes	1,56,000
Number of equity shares (₹10 each)	40,000
Earnings per share	3.9
Ruling market price	39
P/E ratio (Price/EPS) (times)	10

The company has undistributed reserves, ₹6,00,000. It needs ₹2,00,000 for expansion which will earn the same rate as funds already employed.

You are informed that a debt-equity ratio (debt/debt-equity) higher than 35 per cent will push the P/E ratio down to 8 and raise the interest rate on additional amount borrowed to 14 per cent.

You are required to ascertain the probable price of the equity share:

(a) If the additional funds are raised as debt; and

(b) If the amount is raised by rising equity shares (at current market price).

Solution

Probable price of equity share of AB Ltd under different alternatives

Particulars	*14% Debt*	*Equity shares*
EBIT at 20%* on capital employed@	₹3,40,000	₹3,40,000
Less: Debenture interest	60,000	60,000
Less: Interest on borrowings	28,000	—
Earnings before taxes	2,52,000	2,80,000
Less: Taxes	88,200	98,000
Earnings after taxes	1,63,800	1,82,000
Number of equity shares	40,000	45,128
EPS	4.095	4.033
X P/E ratio (times)	8	10
MPS	32.76	40.33

@₹17,00,000 [₹4,00,000 equity + ₹6,00,000 reserves + ₹5,00,000 (₹60,000/0.12 debentures) + ₹2,00,000 proposed to be raised).
* ₹3,00,000/₹15,00,000 = 0.20

P.20.3 The Evergreen Company has the choice of raising an additional sum of ₹50 lakh either by the sale of 10 per cent debentures or by issue of additional equity shares of ₹50 per share. The current capital structure of the company consists of 10 lakh ordinary shares. LO 20.2 LOD D

At what level of earnings before interest and tax (EBIT) after the new capital is required, would earnings per share (EPS) be the same whether new funds are raised by issuing ordinary shares or by issuing debentures? Also, determine the level of EBIT at which uncommitted earnings per share (UEPS) would be the same if sinking fund obligations amount to ₹5 lakhs per year. Assume a 35 per cent tax rate. Discuss the relevance of the calculation.

Solution

(i) Determination of indifference point

Debt alternative	=	*Equity alternative*
$\frac{(X - I)(1 - t)}{N_1}$	=	$\frac{(X)(1 - t)}{N_2}$
$\frac{(X - ₹5{,}00{,}000)(1 - 0.35)}{10{,}00{,}000}$	=	$\frac{x(1 - 0.35)}{11{,}00{,}000}$
X	=	₹55,00,000

Verification table

Particulars	*10% Debt alternative*	*Equity alternative*
EBIT	₹55,00,000	₹55,00,000
Less: Interest	5,00,000	Nil
Earnings after interest	50,00,000	55,00,000
Less: Taxes	17,50,000	19,25,000
EAT	32,50,000	35,75,000
N	10,00,000	11,00,000
EPS	3.25	3.25

(ii) Determination of indifference point with sinking funds

Debt alternative	=	*Equity alternative*
$\frac{(X - I)(1 - t) - S}{N_1}$	=	$\frac{(X)(1 - t)}{N_2}$
$\frac{(X - ₹5{,}00{,}000) \times (0.65) - (₹5{,}00{,}000)}{10{,}00{,}000}$	=	$\frac{0.65X}{11{,}00{,}000}$
X	=	₹1,39,61,538

Verification table

Particulars	*10% Debt*	*Equity*
EBIT	₹1,39,61,538	₹1,39,61,538
Less: Interest	5,00,000	Nil
EBT	1,34,61,538	1,39,61,538
Less: Taxes	47,11,538	48,86,538
Earnings after taxes	87,50,000	90,75,000
Less: Sinking fund payment	5,00,000	Nil
Earnings for equityholders	82,50,000	90,75,000
N	10,00,000	11,00,000
EPS	8.25	8.25

The relevance of indifference level of EBIT is that it enables the management to take better financial decisions. It is a point beyond which the leverage (use of debt) becomes favourable in that the use of debt could be employed to enhance the EPS. Therefore, if the estimated EBIT is more than the indifference level, debt alternative to raise finance should be used, otherwise the equity alternative would be preferred.

The uncommitted EPS approach is useful to the conservative decision makers, who look to debt not only in terms of interest payment but also in terms of its repayment. Therefore, they want to get an idea of earnings which, could meet both the payments. However, this approach is of short-term significance only as after the redemption of debentures, the sinking fund balance is transferred to general reserves and thus forms a part of the equity holders' funds.

P.20.4 The balance sheet of Smart Ltd as on March 31, current year is as follows (*Figures in lakhs of rupees*): **LO 20.2,3** LOD D

Liabilities	*Amount*	*Assets*	*Amount*
Share capital	200	Fixed assets	500
Reserves	140	Inventories	300
Long-term loans	360	Receivables	240
Short-term loans	200	Cash and bank	60
Payables	120		
Provisions	80		
	1,100		1,100

Sales for the current year were ₹600 lakh. For the next year ending on March 31, they are expected to increase by 20 per cent. The net profit margin after taxes and dividend payout are expected to be 4 and 50 per cent respectively.

You are required to:

(a) Quantify the amount of external funds required.

(b) Determine the mode of raising the funds given the following parameters.

(i) current ratio should be 1.33.

(ii) Ratio of fixed assets to long-term loans should be 1.5.

(iii) Long-term debt to equity ratio should not exceed 1.06.

(iv) The funds are to be raised in the order of (1) short-term bank borrowings, (2) long-term loans and (3) equities.

Solution Assuming, assets will increase *pari passu* with sales, the level of projected assets will be ₹1,100 lakh × 1.2 = ₹1,320 lakh. The incremental assets required are ₹1,320 lakhs – ₹1,100 lakh = ₹220 lakh.

Assuming that payables and other provisions (CL) are also likely to move with sales, the projected payables and provisions will be ₹200 lakh × 1.2 = ₹240 lakh.

Expected retained earnings = (Expected EAT – Divdiend paid) = (0.04 × ₹720 lakh = ₹28.8 lakh – ₹14.4 lakh Dividend paid) = ₹14.4 lakh.

(a) External funds needed: *(₹ lakh)*

Projected level of assets	₹1,320
Less: Payable and provisions	240
Less: Retained earnings	14.4
Less: Existing funds used (₹200 lakh + ₹140 lakh + ₹360 lakh + ₹200 lakh)	900
External funds required	165.6

(b) Mode of raising funds:

(i) Short-term borrowings (additional)

$$1.33 = \text{CA/CL} = \frac{\text{Existing CA, ₹600 lakh} \times 1.2}{(\text{Existing payable + Provision}) \times 1.2 + \text{Short-term loan (STL)}}$$

1.33 = ₹720 lakh/₹240 lakh + STL

1.33 (240 lakh+ STL) = ₹720 lakh or 1.33 STL = ₹400.8 or STL = ₹400.8/1.33 = ₹301.35 lakh.

Additional STL = ₹301.35 lakh – ₹200.00 = ₹101.35 lakh.

(ii) Long-term loan (additional)

Desired ratio of fixed assets (FA) to long-term loan (LTL) = 1.5

$$1.5 = \frac{\text{FA (₹500 lakh} \times 1.2)}{\text{LTL}} = 1.5 \text{ LTL} = ₹600 \text{ lakh or LTL} = ₹400 \text{ lakh}$$

Additional LTL = ₹400 lakh – ₹360 lakh = ₹40 lakh

(iii) Equity funds (additional): (₹lakh)

Total external funds required	₹165.6
Less: Additional short-term bank borrowings	101.35
Less: Additional long-term loan	40.00
Equity capital to be issued	24.25

$$\frac{\text{New level of debt (long-term)}}{\text{Equity funds (ESC + Reserves)}} = ₹400 \text{ lakh}/(₹224.25 \text{ lakh} + ₹154.5 \text{ lakh}) = 1.056^*$$

*Requirement of LTD/equity ratio of not more than 1.06 is satisfied.

Funds required to be raised: (₹lakh)

Short-term bank borrowings	₹101.35
Long-term loans	40.00
Equity share capital	24.25
	165.60

P.20.5 The Heavy Metal Tools Company Ltd is embarking on an expansion plan requiring an outlay of ₹500 million. The management of the firm is confident that it can raise the entire amount by perpetual debt finance at the following rates: (i) 20% for the first ₹200 million, (ii) 22% for the next ₹200 million, and (iii) 25% for the balance ₹100 million. However, there is some apprehension about the firm's ability to meet interest burden during a recessionary year. The management feels that in a recessionary year, the net cash inflows of the company, not taking into account the interest burden on the new debt, would have an expected value of ₹180 million with a standard deviation of ₹80 million.

LO 20.2 LOD D

(a) If the management is prepared to accept only a 5 per cent chance of cash inadequacy, what proportion of the ₹500 million requirement should be raised as debt finance?

(b) What is the probability of cash inadequacy during a recessionary year if the entire ₹500 million are raised as debt finance?

Solution

(a) Assuming the cash flows to be normally distributed with a mean of ₹180 million and standard deviation = ₹80 million for a 5 per cent chance of cash inadequacy, we have to find out the *Z*-value, the area to whose left is 0.05. From the normal distribution table (A-5) the *Z*-value is –1.645. Corresponding to this value, the cash inflow (*C*) is given by the equation (C-180/80 = –1.645).

Given C = ₹48.4 million, the probability of the cash flow being less than ₹48.4 million is only 5 per cent which meets the management criterion. The interest on ₹200 million @ 20% = ₹40 million. The remaining amount of (₹48.4 million – ₹40 million) ₹8.4 million can service an amount of debt = (8.4/0.22) = ₹38.2 million. Thus, the cash flow of ₹48.4 million can service a maximum amount of debt = ₹200 million + ₹38.2 = ₹238.2 million, **OR** (238.2/500) × 100 = 47.64 per cent of the total requirement. Thus, the firm should not finance more than 47.64 per cent of its total requirement through debt. In practice, it should restrict itself to somewhere around 40 per cent to keep some margin of safety.

(b) Interest burden each year on account of debt of ₹500 million = (0.20 × 200) + (0.22 × 200) + (0.25 × 100) = ₹109 million. Thus, the minimum cash flow required to service the debt = ₹109 million. Assuming the cash flows to be normally distributed with a mean of ₹180 million and standard deviation = 80 million, the *Z*-value corresponding to ₹109 million is: $Z = (109 - 180)/80 = -0.8875$ or –0.89.

From the normal distribution table, the probability of the cash inflow being less than ₹109 million (or Z being less than –0.89) is 0.1867, that is, there is a 18.67 per cent chance of cash inadequacy during a recessionary year.

MINI CASES

20.C.1 A company is evaluating a new venture that will cost ₹10 crore. The venture will have a return on investment of 20 per cent and the firm forecasts a 12 per cent growth in earnings from the project. The treasurer has identified the following sources for financing the project:

(a) Equity shares to be sold at ₹400 per share.

(b) Convertible debentures with a 6 per cent coupon to net ₹980 (face value ₹1,000), and convertible at ₹500 per share after 2002.

(c) Debentures with warrants with a 6 per cent coupon to net ₹980 (face value ₹1000), and with each bond having one warrant entitling the holder to buy one equity share at ₹500 after 2002.

The financing decision is being made in the fourth quarter of 2000. Over the past ten years, A company has been growing at a 10 per cent rate of sales and earnings.

The treasurer expects the company to continue to grow at 10 per cent even though the firm has traditionally paid 40 per cent of its earnings as dividends. The treasurer expects A's equity shares to continue to rise in price. Using the price trend over the past 5 years, he has projected probable market price ranges for the next three years. The historical data and the projections of the treasurer are given below:

Year	*Historical market price*	*Year*	*Forecasted*	
			Probability (%)	*Market price*
2002	₹220	2008	20	₹450
2003	250		60	500
2004	330		20	600
2005	270	2009	20	480
2006	380		60	550
Current 2007	450		20	620
		2010	20	500
			60	600
			20	700

The proforma balance sheet and income statement prepared by the treasurer for the year 2007 is shown as below:

Proforma balance sheet (December 31, 2007) (₹ '000)

Liabilities	*2007*	*2006*	*Assets*	*2007*	*2006*
Equity shares (₹10 each)	₹10,000	₹10,000	Plant and equipment	₹2,25,000	₹2,31,000
Shares premium	40,000	40,000	(*Less:* Accumulated	(62,000)	(59,000)
Retained earnings	1,36,000	1,27,000	depreciation)	1,90,000	1,72,000
Bonds (7%)	90,000	52,000	Inventories	64,000	62,000
Mortgage (6%)	30,000	55,000	Receivables	44,000	45,000
Accounts payable	7,000	6,000	Cash and bank balance	22,000	18,000
Other current liabilities	11,000	10,000	Other current assets	4,000	3,000
	3,24,000	3,00,000		3,24,000	3,00,000

Proforma income statement (₹ '000)

	Sales	EBIT	Interest*	EBT	NIAT	EPS
2007	4,20,000	71,500	8,000	63,500	31,750	31.75
2006	3,80,000	65,000	7,000	58,000	29,000	29.00

*Rounded off.

The management of A Ltd was initially impressed by the fact that the new venture will increase sales by ₹12 crore. Management is also interested in the expected 12 per cent growth rate of the venture. As per company's financial policy, the firm's debt-asset ratio should not be above 40 per cent.

With the above information and detailed analysis for next 3 years, what will be the long-term sources of financing for the new proposal?

Make suitable assumptions in your answer, wherever necessary figures could be rounded off. Income-tax rate applicable to the company is to be taken at 50 per cent.

Solution

Statement showing EPS in 2007 (end) under various financing options (*Amount in ₹ lakh*)

Particulars	*With existing business*	*With new business financed by*		
		Equity shares	*Convertible debt*	*Debt (+) Warrant*
EBIT[1]	₹786.50	₹986.50	₹986.50	₹986.50
Less: Interest on debt:				
Existing (₹9 crore × 0.07) + (₹3 crore × 0.06)	81.00	81.00	81.00	81.00
New debt (1,02,040[2] debentures × ₹60 per debenture)	—	—	61.22	61.22
Earnings before taxes	705.50	905.50	844.28	844.28
Less: Taxes (0.50)	352.75	452.75	422.14	422.14
Earnings after taxes	352.75	452.75	422.14	422.14
Number of shares (in lakh)	10.00	12.5[3]	10.00	10.00
EPS (₹)	35.275	36.22	42.214	42.214

Statement showing EPS in 2010 (end) under various financing options (*Amount in ₹ lakh*)

Particulars	*With existing business*	*With new business financed by*		
		Equity shares	*Convertible debt*	*Debt (+) Warrant*
EBIT	₹951.66[4]	₹1,202.54[5]	₹1,202.54	₹1,202.54
Add: Additional EBIT due to additional funds raised[6]	—	—	—	102.04[7]
Less: Interest on existing debt	81.00	81.00	81.00	81.00
Less: Interest on new debt (in the case of warrant option)	—	—	—	61.22
EBT	870.66	1,121.54	1,121.54	1,162.36
Less: Taxes (0.50)	435.33	560.77	560.77	581.18
EAT	435.33	560.77	560.77	581.18
Number of shares (lakh)	10.00	12.50	12.04[8]	11.02[8]
EPS (₹)	43.533	44.862	46.576	52.74

Statement showing debt (assumed to be long-term) to assets ratio in 2007 and 2010

(*Amount in ₹ lakh*)

Particulars	*With existing business*	*With new business financed by*		
		Equity shares	*Convertible debt*	*Debt (+) Warrant*
Year-end-2007				
Total assets	₹3,240	₹4,240	₹4,240	₹4,240
Existing debt	1,200	1,200	1,200	1,200
Additional debt	—	—	1,020	1,020
Total debt	1,200	1,200	2,220	2,220
Debt/Assets ratio (%)	37.03	28.3	52.36	52.36
Year-end 2010				
Total assets[9]	3,949.27	5,152.17	5,124.62	5,142.99
Existing debt	1,200	1,200	1,200	1,200
Net debt	—	—	—	1,020
Total debt	1,200	1,200	1,200	2,220
Debt/Assets ratio (%)	30.39	23.29	23.42	43.19

Recommendation Though EPS is the highest (at ₹52.74) under debt plus warrant plan, it cannot be implemented as debt/assets ratio exceed 40 per cent (43.19%). In view of this, the next best alternative is that the company should opt for convertible debt plan as under this plan potential EPS is the maximum (at ₹46.576 in 2010 and at ₹42.214 in 2007).

Working Notes

(₹ *lakh*)

1. (a) Without new venture		
EBIT (2000)	₹715	
Add: 10 per cent growth	71.50	₹786.50
(b) With new venture		
Expected EBIT without new venture		786.50
Add: 20 per cent growth on ₹10 crore new investment (₹10 crore × 0.20)		200.00
		986.50
2. *Number of new debentures to be issued* (Amount to be raised ₹10 crore/Net proceeds per debenture, ₹980)		1,02,040
3. *Number of new equity shares to be issued* (₹10 crore/sale price of equity shares, ₹400)		2,50,000
4. *EBIT in 2003* = Current EBIT, ₹715 lakh × Growth factor @ 10 per cent for 3 years i.e., 1.331		951.66
5. *EBIT in 2003 with new business:* ₹951.66 lakh + (₹10 crore × 20 per cent ROR × 12 per cent growth factor for 2 years i.e., 1.254 = 250.88 lakh)		1,202.54
6. Determination of expected market price in 2008 to 2010		

Years					
2008		*2009*		*2010*	
₹450 × 0.2 =	₹90	₹480 × 0.2 =	₹96	₹500 × 0.2 =	₹100
500 × 0.6 =	300	550 × 0.6 =	330	600 × 0.6 =	360
600 × 0.2 =	120	620 × 0.2 =	124	700 × 0.2 =	140
	510		550		600

Since expected market price is higher (at ₹550 in 2002 and at ₹600 in 2003) than the conversion price (i.e., ₹500 after 2002), it is reasonable to assume that debt-holders/warrant-holders will like to exercise their option, resulting in higher number of equity shares in 2003.

7. In the case of convertible debt, no additional funds will accrue. There will be additional funds in the case of warrant option equivalent to (1,02,040 warrants × ₹500 issue price of equity share) = ₹510.20 lakh.

As per the principle of conservatism, the ROR likely to be earned on these funds (₹510.20 lakh) is ROR promised by a new venture i.e., 20 per cent or existing ROR which-ever is lower. (Conventionally, ROR is computed on existing long-term funds employed in business at book value).

$$\text{ROR (on capital employed)} = \frac{\text{EBIT}}{\text{Equity funds + Long-term debt}}$$

$$= (₹715 \text{ lakh}/(1860 \text{ lakh} + 1200 \text{ lakh}) = 23.37 \text{ per cent}$$

Thus, expected additional EBIT with warrant option is = ₹510.20 lakh × 0.2 = 102.04 lakh

8. Number of new equity shares issued
   (i) Convertible debts = 1,02,040 debentures × 2 = 2,04,080
   (ii) Warrants = 1,02,040 × 1 = 1,02,040

9. Increase in retained earnings during 3 years under various options:
It is computed as per the following ratio:

$$\left[\frac{\text{EAT (year-end 2000) + EAT (year-end 2003)}}{2}\right] \times \text{Retention ratio} \times 3 \text{ years}$$

(i) No new venture $= \left[\frac{₹352.75 \text{ lakh} + ₹435.33 \text{ lakh}}{2}\right] \times 0.6 \times 3 \text{ years} = ₹709.27 \text{ lakh}$

(ii) Issue of equity shares $= \left[\frac{₹452.75 \text{ lakh} + ₹560.77 \text{ lakh}}{2}\right] \times 0.6 \times 3 \text{ years} = ₹912.17 \text{ lakh}$

(iii) Issue of convertible debentures $= \left[\frac{₹422.14 \text{ lakh} + ₹560.77 \text{ lakh}}{2}\right] \times 0.6 \times 3 \text{ years} = ₹884.62 \text{ lakh}$

(iv) Issue of debt + warrant $= \left[\frac{₹422.14 \text{ lakh} + ₹581.18 \text{ lakh}}{2}\right] \times 0.6 \times 3 \text{ years} = ₹902.99 \text{ lakh}$

It is assumed that the assets will increase by the amount of increase in retained earnings under various options.

20.C.2 Zip Zap Zoom Company is into manufacturing cars in the small car (800 cc) segment. Established 15 years back, it has since seen a phenomenal growth in both its market share and profitability. The financial statements (Statement of P&L and Balance Sheet) are shown in Exhibits 20.1 and 20.2 respectively.

The company enjoys the confidence of its shareholders who have been rewarded with growing dividends year after year. Last year too, the company had announced 20 per cent dividend, which was the highest in the automobile sector. The company has never defaulted on its loan payments and enjoys a favourable face with its lenders, which include financial institutions, commercial banks and other private debenture-holders.

The competition in the car industry has increased in the past few years and the company foresees further intensification of competition with the entry of several foreign car manufacturers; many of whom are market leaders in their respective countries. The small car segment especially, will witness entry of foreign majors in the near future, with latest technology being offered to the Indian customer. Zip Zap Zoom company's senior management realises the need for large scale investment in upgradation of technology and improvement of manufacturing facilities to preempt competition.

While on one hand, the competition in the car industry has been intensifying, on the other hand, there has been a slowdown in the Indian economy, which has not only reduced the demand for cars, but also led to adoption of price cutting strategies by various car manufacturers.

EXHIBIT 20.1 Balance sheet as at March 31 current year (*Amount in ₹ crore*)

Sources of funds		
Share capital	₹350	
Reserves and surplus	250	₹600
Loans		
Debentures (@14%)	50	
Institutional borrowing (@10%)	100	
Commercial loans (@12%)	250	400
Current liabilities		200
Total		1,200
Application of funds		
Fixed assets:		
Gross block	₹1000	
Less: Depreciation	(250)	
Net block	750	
Capital WIP	190	₹940
Current assets:		
Inventory	200	
Sundry debtors	40	
Cash and bank balance	10	
Other current assets	10	260
Total		1,200

EXHIBIT 20.2 Statement of Profit and Loss for the year ended March 31, Current year

(*Amount in ₹ crore*)

Sales volume	80,000	
(×) Selling price	₹250,000	
Sales revenue		₹2,000.0
Operating expenditure:		
Variable cost		
Raw material and manufacturing expenses[2]	₹1,300.0	
Variable overheads	100.0	1,400.0
Fixed cost:		
R&D	₹20.0	
Marketing and advertising	25.0	
Depreciation	250	
Personnel	70.0	365.0
Total operating expenditure		1,765.0
EBIT		235.0
Financial expenses:		
Interest on debentures	₹7.7	
Interest on institutional borrowings	11.0	
Interest on commercial loan	33.0	51.7
EBT		183.3

(*Contd*)

(*Contd*)	
Taxes (@ 35%)	64.2
EAT	119.1
Dividends	70.0
Debt redemption (Sinking fund obligation)3	40.0
Contribution to reserves and surplus	9.1

[2]Includes the cost of inventory and WIP which is dependant on demand (sales).
[3]The loans are to be retired in the next ten years and the firm redeems ₹40 crore every year.

The company is to decide how much to invest in upgradation of its plants and technology. Capital investment upto a maximum of ₹100 crore is required. The decision has three aspects:

- The company cannot forgo the capital investment as that could lead to reduction in its market share. Technological competence in this industry is a must. Customers would shift to manufacturers providing latest in car technology.
- The company does not want to issue new equity and its retained earnings are not enough for such a large investment. Thus, the only option is raising debt.
- The company wants to limit its additional debt to a figure that it can service without taking undue risks. With the looming recession and uncertain market conditions, the company perceives that additional fixed obligations could become a cause of financial distress, and, thus, wants to determine its additional debt capacity to meet the Investment requirements.

Mr. Shortsighted, the company's Finance Manager, is given the task of determining the additional debt that the firm can raise. He thinks that the firm can raise ₹100-crore debt and service it even in years of recession. The company can raise debt at 15% from a financial institution. While working out the debt capacity, Mr. Shortsighted takes the following assumptions for the recession years:

(a) A maximum of 10% reduction in sales volume will take place.
(b) A maximum of 6% reduction in sales price of cars will take place.

Mr. Shortsighted prepares the following income statement which is representative of the recession years. While doing so, he determines what he thinks are the "irreducible minimum" expenditures under recessionary conditions. For him, the risk of insolvency is the main concern while designing capital structure. To support his view, he presents the statement of profit and loss, as shown in Exhibit 20.3. He works on the assumptions (given after the Exhibit 20.3).

EXHIBIT 20.3 Statement of Projected Profit and Loss

(*Amount in ₹ crore*)

Sales volume	72,000	
(×) Selling price	(×) ₹235,000	
Sales revenue		₹1,692.0
Operating expenditure		
Variable cost:		
Raw material and manufacturing expenses	₹1,170.0	
Variable overheads	90.0	1,260.0
Fixed cost:		
R&D	—	
Marketing and advertising	₹15.0	
Depreciation	187.5	
Personnel	70.0	272.5
Total operating expenditure		1,532.5
EBIT		159.5

(*Contd*)

(*Contd*)

Financial expenses:		
Interest on existing debentures	₹7.0	
Interest on existing institutional borrowings	10.0	
Interest on existing commercial loan	30.0	
Interest on additional debt	15.0	62.0
EBT		97.5
Taxes (@ 35%)		34.1
EAT		63.4
Dividends		—
Debt redemption (Sinking fund obligation)*		50.0
Contribution to reserves and surplus		13.4

*(₹40 crore (existing debt) + ₹10 crore (additional debt).

Assumptions of Mr. Shortsighted

- R&D expenditures can be done away with till the economy picks-up.
- Marketing and advertising expenditure can be reduced by 40 per cent.
- Keeping in mind the investor confidence that the company enjoys, he feels that the company can forgo paying dividends in the recession period.

He goes with his worked-out statement to the Director (Finance) Mr. Arthashastra and advocates raising ₹100 crore worth of debt to finance the intended capital investments. Mr. Arthashastra does not feel comfortable with the statements and calls for the company's financial analyst Mr. Longsighted. Mr. Longsighted carefully analyses Mr. Shortsighted's assumptions and points out that insolvency should not be the sole criterion while determining the debt capacity of the firm. He also points out the following:

- "Apart from debt servicing, there are certain expenditures like that on R&D and marketing that need to be continued to ensure the long-term health of the firm".
- "Certain management policies like those relating to dividend pay-out, send out important signals to the investors. Zip Zap Zoom's management has been paying regular dividends and discontinuing this practice (even though just for the recession phase) could raise serious doubts in the investor's mind about the health of the firm. The firm should pay atleast 10 per cent dividend in the recession years".
- "Mr. Shortsighted has used the accounting profits to determine the amount available each year for servicing the debt obligations. This does not give the true picture. Net cash inflows should be used to determine the amount available for servicing the debt".
- "Net cash inflows are determined by interplay of many variables and such a simplistic view should not be taken while determining the cash flows in recession. It is not possible to accurately predict the fall in any of the factors such as sales volume, sales price, marketing expenditure etc.

  Probability distribution of variation of each of the factors that affect net cash inflow should be analysed (the net cash inflows follow a normal probability distribution). This will give a true picture of how the company's cash flows will behave in recession conditions."

The management recognises that the alternative suggested by Mr. Longsighted rests on data, which are complex and require expenditure of time and effort to obtain and interpret. Considering the importance of capital structure design, The Director (Finance) asks Mr. Longsighted to carry out his analysis. Information on the behaviour of cash flows during the recession periods is taken into account.

The methodology undertaken is as follows:

(a) Important factors that affect cash flows (especially contraction of cash flows), like sales volume, sales price, raw materials expenditure, etc., are identified and the analysis is carried out in terms of cash receipts and cash expenditures.

(b) Each factor's behaviour (variation behaviour) in adverse conditions in the past is studied and future expectations are combined with past data, to describe limits (maximum favourable, most probable and maximum adverse) for all the factors.

(c) Once this information is generated for all factors affecting cash flow, Mr. Longsighted comes up with a range of estimates of the cash flow in future recession periods based on all possible combinations of the several factors. He also estimates the probability of occurrence of each estimate of cash flow.

Assuming a normal distribution of the expected behaviour, the mean expected value of net cash inflow in adverse conditions came out be ₹220.27 crore with standard deviation of ₹110 crore.

Keeping in mind the looming recession and the uncertainty of the recession behaviour, Mr. Arthashastra feels that the firm should cater to a risk of cash inadequacy of 5 per cent even in the most adverse industry conditions. Thus, the firm should take up only that amount of additional debt that it can service 95 per cent of the times, while maintaining cash adequacy.

To maintain an annual dividend of 10 per cent, an additional ₹35 crore has to he kept aside. Hence, the expected available net cash inflow is ₹185.27 crore (subtracting ₹35 crore from ₹220.27 crore).

The following formula is used to calculate the additional cash available in recession conditions to service debt (catering for 5% risk tolerance):

$$\frac{X - \mu}{\sigma} = 1.64$$

X = is the additional cash available each year for servicing fixed obligations

μ = 185.27

σ = 110 crore

–1.64 is that value of Z which caters to 95% of the area of the standard normal curve.

Taking all the above into account, Mr. Longsighted works out the additional debt capacity as shown in Exhibit 20.4. The additional debt capacity as calculated by him is ₹73.15 crore.

EXHIBIT 20.4 Determination of Cash Flows *(Amount in ₹ crore)*

Cash available for dividends (EAT + Depreciation - SF Obligation)	₹259.15
Cash available at 15% contraction	220.27
Cash required for dividends	35.00
Average cash flow available for additional debt obligations	185.27
Determination of Debt Capacity	
Tolerance limit	5%
Standard deviation	120
Cash flow under most adverse conditions*	4.45
Existing cash reserve	10.00
Cash available	14.45
Debt obligation per ₹ crore of additional debt	
Interest (35 % less tax shield)	0.0975
Sinking fund obligation	0.1000
Total	0.1975
Debt capacity (₹14.45 crore/0.1975)	73.15

*Calculation of cash flow under most adverse conditions is based on the normal distribution (Z distribution):

$$Z \text{ value} = \frac{\text{Cash inflow} - \text{Mean value of cash inflow}}{\text{Std. Deviation}}$$

The Z value corresponding to tolerance limit is –1.64

Replacing the values in equation, obtained is the value of cash inflow ₹4.45 crore.

Mr. Arthashastra too is convinced that there is no need to assume risk of not having required cash to service debt, especially in the present economic scenario. Mr. Shortsighted agrees with observations of Mr. Arthashastra. Based on the analysis, it has been decided that the firm will raise an additional debt of only ₹73.15 crore at present and not take any undue risk, additional investments can be undertaken when the industry conditions revive.

Scan the QR Code given at the end of chapter to access comprehensive cases.

REVIEW QUESTIONS

LOD: Easy

RQ.20.1 Provide the appropriate answers for the following: [LO 20.1,2,3,4]

(i) Financial distress is exclusively related to the risk of bankruptcy. (True/False)

(ii) In case, the projected level of EBIT is substantially higher than the indifference point, the levered plan is likely to be beneficial for the firm. (True/False)

(iii) ____________ analysis is better than EBIT-EPS analysis (from the point of view of profitability) in evaluating proposed financial plans.

(iv) Indifference point which factors provision for sinking fund also provides ____________ earnings per share. (uncommitted/committed)

(v) Coverage ratio which considers sinking fund payments also is determined dividing EBIT by ____________.

(vi) To retain control over management, a firm would prefer use of ____________. (debt/equity)

(vii) In case sales are subject to wide fluctuations, a firm should employ more ____________. (debt/equity)

(viii) Firms at their infancy should rely more on (debt/equity).

(ix) The ____________ implies that the firm with an adequate notice can repay the suppliers of funds.

(x) Cost of debt relates only to the amount of interest payable on borrowings. (True/False)

[Answers: (i) False (ii) True (iii) EBIT-MPS (iv) Uncommitted (v) EBIT/I + [SF/(I-t)] (vi) Debt (vii) Equity (viii) Equity (ix) Call provision (x) False]

RQ.20.2 Write a note on the important determinants of the capital structure of a firm. [LO 20.2,3,4]

LOD: Medium

RQ.20.3 '......an analysis of the magnitude and stability of cash flows relative to fixed charges is extremely important in determining an appropriate capital structure.' Comment. [LO 20.3]

RQ.20.4 How can the effect of profitability on designing an appropriate capital structure be analysed? Illustrate your answer with the help of EBIT-EPS analysis. [LO 20.2]

RQ.20.5 A growing company is confronted with a choice between 15% Debt issue and equity issue to finance its new investments. Its pre-expansion income statement is as follows: [LO 20.2]

Sale (production capacity of ₹60,00,000 at current sales price)	₹45,00,000
Fixed cost	5,00,000
Variable cost (2/3 of sales)	30,00,000
EBIT	10,00,000
Interest at (0.125)	1,00,000
EBT	9,00,000
Income tax (0.35)	3,15,000
Net income	5,85,000
EPS	11.7

The expansion programme is estimated to cost ₹5,00,000. If this is financed through debt, the rate of interest will be 15 per cent and the P/E ratio will be 10. If expansion programme is financed through equity, new shares can be sold at ₹100 per share, and the P/E ratio will be 12. Expansion will generate additional sales of ₹12,75,000. No additional fixed costs would be needed to meet the expansion operation. If the company is to follow a policy of maximising the market value (MV) of its shares, which form of financing should be employed by the company?

RQ.20.6 The ZBB Ltd needs ₹5,00,000 for construction of a new plant. The following three financial plans are feasible: [LO 20.2]

(i) The company may issue 50,000 equity shares of ₹10 per share.

(ii) The company may issue 25,000 equity shares at ₹10 per share and 8 % debentures of ₹100 each.

(iii) The company may issue 25,000 equity shares of ₹10 per shere and 10 % preference shares of ₹100 per share.

If the company's EBIT are ₹40,000, ₹80,000 and ₹1,20,000, what are the EPS under each of the three financing plans? Which alternative would you recommend and why? Assume tax of 35 per cent and P/E ratio of 10 in equity plan, 9 in equity + preference plan and 8 in equity + debt plan.

RQ.20.7 The finance advisor of Aggarwal Industries Ltd is confronted with two alternative financing plans for raising ₹10 lakh that is needed for plant expansion and modernisation. One choice is 12% Debt issue. The other is to issue 8,000 equity shares at the current market price per of ₹125. [LO 20.2,3]

The modernisation and expansion programme is expected to increase the firm's operating profits (EBIT) by ₹2,00,000 annually. The firm's condensed financial statements for current year are given below:

Balance sheet as on March 31 current year

Liabilities	*Amount*	*Assets*	*Amount*
Current liabilities	₹5,00,000	Current assets	₹16,00,000
10% Long-term loan	15,00,000	Plant and equipment (net)	34,00,000
Reserves and surpluses	10,00,000		
Equity capital (shares of ₹100 each)	20,00,000		
	50,00,000		50,00,000

Income statement for the current year

Operating profits	₹8,00,000
Less interest expenses (0.10 × ₹15,00,000)	1,50,000
Income before taxes	6,50,000
Less taxes (0.35)	2,27,500
Net income	4,22,500
Earnings per share	21.12
Dividends per share	10.56

However, the finance advisor is concerned about the effect that issuing debt might have on the firm. The average debt ratio for firms in industry is 45 per cent. He believes that if this ratio is exceeded, the P/E ratio will be 7 because of the potentially greater risk. If the firm increases its equity capital, he expects the P/E ratio to increase to 8.5. He also wonders as to what will happen to the dividend yield under each plan. The firm follows the practice of paying dividends equal to 50 per cent of net income.

(i) Determine the debt ratio, under each financing plan, after the securities are issued.
(ii) Determine the expected net income in the next year, expected EPS and the expected market price of the equity shares.
(iii) Determine the dividend yield.
(iv) Which form of financing should be employed by the company, if the company is to follow a policy of maximising market value of its shares?

LOD: Difficult

RQ.20.8 ABC Ltd gives you the following information: **[LO 20.2,3]**

Profit (before interest and tax)		₹24,00,000
Less interest on debentures (0.125)	₹2,00,000	
Less interest on long-term loans (0.16)	2,00,000	4,00,000
EBT		20,00,000
Less income tax (0.35)		7,00,000
Profit after tax		13,00,000
Number of equity shares (of ₹10 each)		4,00,000
EPS		3.25
Ruling market price		20
P/E ratio		6.15

The company has undistributed reserves and profits of ₹81,50,000. The company needs to raise ₹36,00,000 for repayment of debentures and modernisation of its plants.

It seeks your opinion on the advisability of taking recourse to one of the following modes of raising the required funds, on the consideration of the probable price of the share to rule on implementation.

(a) Raising the entire amount by term loans from bank: Interest @ 16 per cent.
(b) Raising partly by issue of 1,00,000 equity shares: Estimated price ₹18 per share, and the rest by term loan from bank @ 16 per cent.

The company expects that the operating profit on funds employed will improve by 4 per cent because of modernisation and that, if the debt equity ratio (debt/debt plus shareholders' fund) exceeds 25 per cent, the P/E ratio will go down to 6.

ANSWERS

RQ.20.5 Equity financing should be adopted by the company, as it maximizes the MPS (₹187.92).
RQ.20.6 (i) Equity plan is preferred when EBIT is ₹40,000 **(ii)** In cases of EBIT levels of ₹80,000 and ₹1,20,000, equity + debt plan is preferred.
RQ.20.7 (i) 0.50; 0.333
(ii) ₹4,74,500; 23.72; ₹166.1
₹5,52,500; 19.73; ₹167.72
(iii) The company should use the equity financing plan to maximize market value of its shares.
RQ.20.8 Plan A (16% loan) is better as the MPS is higher under this plan.

Scan the QR Code to access comprehensive solutions to all numerical review questions and additional material.

PART 6

LONG-TERM FINANCING

Chapter 21
CAPITAL MARKETS

Chapter 22
EQUITY/ORDINARY SHARES

Chapter 23
TERM LOANS, DEBENTURES/BONDS AND SECURITISATION

Chapter 24
HYBRID FINANCING/INSTRUMENTS

Chapter 25
LEASE FINANCING AND HIRE-PURCHASE FINANCE

Chapter 26
VENTURE CAPITAL FINANCING

The long-term investment decisions of a firm involves the acquisition of long-term/fixed assets. They have to be financed with long-term sources of finance. The main sources of long-term finance fall into two broad groups: (i) Internal and (ii) External.

The internal sources of long-term funds of an existing company consist of depreciation charges and retained earnings. The depreciation charges are normally used to replace the concerned asset(s). In a way, therefore, the only internal source of financing expansion/growth/diversification for such companies are retained earnings. In fact, they are an important source of long-term finance for corporate enterprises in India.

As a source of long-term finance, retained earnings have some commendable features. They are readily available to the firm. Flotation/issue costs and losses on account of underpricing associated with external equity are avoided/eliminated. There is no dilution of control of the firm by the existing shareholders. However, the magnitude of financing through retained earnings may be limited and variable/unstable/fluctuating primarily as a result of the quantum and variability of profits after taxes. It has, moreover, high opportunity cost in terms of dividends foregone by the shareholders.

For the shareholders, retention of profits by a firm is a convenient way of reinvestment of their profits. But shareholders who want a current income would find it inconvenient to the extent that they will be constrained to sell some shares to convert them into income. Moreover, the easy availability of retained earnings coupled with the notion of low cost may result in investment in sub-marginal/unprofitable projects which would have serious implications for, and hurt the interest of, the shareholders.

Thus, retained earnings have both positive and negative attributes from the viewpoint of the firm as well as the shareholders/investors and should be employed with caution. They involve high cost and no risk and put no restraint on management freedom and do not dilute control. Retained earnings, as an internal source of finance, are significantly affected by the dividend policy of the firm. The focus of Part 6 of the book is, therefore, on the long-term external financing sources.

The external sources of long-term funds comprise of (i) equity capital, (ii) term loans, (iii) debentures/notes/bonds including innovative debt instruments, (iv) hybrid sources such as preference capital, convertibles, warrants and options, (v) leasing and hire-purchase finance and (vi) venture capital financing. The equity and preference capitals represent ownership securities/capital, while debentures and term loans are creditorship securities/loan capital. Firms that require long-term funds from external sources obtain them from the capital market. This part of the book describes the features of the various sources and evaluates them from the point of both the firm which uses them and the investors who provide them. It also briefly outlines the procedures involved in raising funds from these sources. A brief overview of the organisation/structure of the capital market is presented in Chapter 21. The main instruments of long-term financing are covered in Chapters 22-24: Chapter 22 (Equity shares/capital); Chapter 23 (Debt instruments/capital) and Chapter 24 (Hybrid instruments). Chapters 25 and 26 discuss lease and hire-purchase finance and venture capital financing respectively.

CHAPTER 21

Capital Markets

LEARNING OBJECTIVES

LO 21.1	Define 'financial system' and describe its three main components—financial assets/instruments, financial intermediaries/institutions and the two key financial markets, namely, capital and money markets
LO 21.2	Compare and contrast the two parts of the capital/securities markets—stock exchanges/secondary market and new issue/primary market
LO 21.3	Discuss the three vital functions of secondary markets—nexus between savings and investments, market place and continuous price formation
LO 21.4	Understand the triple-service-functions of primary market—origination, underwriting and distribution—and the methods by which issues are made in the primary market

LO 21.1 FINANCIAL SYSTEM

Capital markets are a sub-part of the **financial system**. Conceptually, the financial system includes a complex of institutions and mechanism which affects the generation of savings and their transfer to those who will invest. It may be said to be made of all those channels through which savings become available for investments. The main elements of the financial system are a variety of **(i)** financial instruments/assets/securities, **(ii)** financial intermediaries/institutions and **(iii)** financial markets.

> **Financial system** includes a complex of institutions and mechanism which affects generation of savings and their transfer to those who invest.

Financial Assets

A financial asset/instrument/security is a claim against another economic unit and is held as a store of value and for the return that is expected. While the value of a tangible/physical asset depends on its physical properties such as buildings, machines, furniture, vehicles and so on, a financial asset represents a claim to future cash flows in the form of interest, dividends and so on. They are a claim on a stream of income and/or particular assets. The entity/economic unit that offers the future cash flows is the 'issuer of the financial instrument' and the owner of the security is the 'investor'. Depending upon the nature of claim/return, an instrument may be

> **Financial asset/instrument/security** is a claim against another economic unit and held as a store of value and for the expected return.

(i) debt (security) such as bonds, debentures, term loans, **(ii)** equity (security) shares and **(iii)** hybrid security such as preference shares and convertibles. Based on the type of issuer, the security may be **(1)** direct **(2)** indirect and **(3)** derivative. The securities issued by manufacturing companies are direct assets (e.g. shares/debentures). Indirect assets are claims against financial intermediaries (e.g. units of mutual funds). The derivative instruments include options and futures. The prevalence of a variety of securities to suit the investment requirements of heterogeneous investors offers differentiated investment choice to them and is an important element in the maturity and sophistication of the financial system.

Financial Intermediaries

Financial intermediaries are institutions that channelise the savings of investors into investments/loans. As institutional source of finance, they act as a link between the savers and the investors which results in institutionalisation of personal savings. Their main function is to convert direct financial assets into indirect securities. The indirect securities offer to the individual investor better investment alternative than the direct/primary security by pooling which it is created, for example, units of mutual funds. The main consideration underlying the attractiveness of indirect securities is that the pooling of funds by the financial intermediary leads to a number of benefits to the investors. The services/benefits that tailor indirect financial assets to the requirements of the investors are **(i)** convenience, **(ii)** lower risk, **(iii)** expert management and **(iv)** lower cost.

Financial intermediaries convert direct financial assets into indirect securities.

Convenience Financial intermediaries convert direct/primary securities into a more convenient vehicle of investment. They divide primary securities of higher denomination into indirect securities of lower denomination. They also transform a primary security of a certain maturity into an indirect security of a different maturity. For instance, as a result of the redemption/repurchase facility available to unitholders of mutual funds, maturities on units would conform more with the desires of the investors than those on primary securities.

Lower Risk The lower risk associated with indirect securities results from the benefits of diversification of investments. In effect, the financial intermediaries transform the small investors in matters of diversification into large institutional investors as the former share proportionate beneficiary interest in the total portfolio of the latter.

Expert Management Indirect securities give to the investors the benefits of trained, experienced and specialised management together with continuous supervision. In effect, financial intermediaries place the individual investors in the same position in the matter of expert management as large institutional investors.

Low Cost The benefits of investment through financial intermediaries are available to the individual investors at relatively lower cost due to the economies of scale.

The major financial intermediaries are banks, insurance organisations, both life and non-life/general, mutual funds, non-banking financial companies and so on.

Financial markets provide a forum in which suppliers of funds and demanders of loans/investments can transact business directly.

Financial Markets

Financial markets perform a crucial function in the financial system as facilitating organisations. Unlike financial intermediaries, they are not a source of funds but are a link and provide a forum in which suppliers of funds and demanders of loans/investments can transact business directly. While the loans and investments of financial intermediaries are made without the direct knowledge of the suppliers of funds (i.e. investors), suppliers in the financial market know where their funds are being lent/invested. The two key financial markets are the money market and the capital market.

Money Market The **money market** is created by a financial relationship between suppliers and demanders of short-term funds which have maturities of one year or less. It exists because investors (i.e. individuals, business entities, government and financial institutions) have temporarily idle funds that they wish to place in some type of liquid asset or short-term interest-earning instrument. At the same time, other entities/organisations find themselves in need of seasonal/temporary financing. The money market brings together these suppliers and demanders of short-term liquid funds. The broad objectives of money market are three-fold:

Money market is created by a financial relationship between suppliers and demanders of short-term funds having maturities of one year or less.

- An equilibrating mechanism for evening out short-term surplus and deficiencies in the financial system;
- A focal point of intervention by the central bank (e.g. Reserve Bank of India) intervention for influencing liquidity in the economy; and
- A reasonable access to the users of short-term funds to meet their requirements at realistic/ reasonable cost and temporary deployment of funds for earning returns to the suppliers of funds.

Capital Market The **capital market** is a financial relationship created by a number of institutions and arrangements that allows suppliers and demanders of long-term funds (i.e. funds with maturities exceeding one year) to make transactions. It is a market for long-term funds. Included among long-term funds are securities issues of business and Government. The backbone of the capital market is formed by the various securities exchanges that provide a forum for equity (equity market) and debt (debt market) transactions. Mechanisms for efficiently offering and trading securities contribute to the functioning of capital markets which is important to the long-term growth of business. Thus, the capital market comprises of **(1)** stock/security exchanges/markets (secondary markets) and **(2)** new issue/primary market [initial public offering (IPO) market].

Capital market/ securities market is a financial relationship created by a number of institutions and arrangements that allows suppliers and demanders of long-term funds with maturities exceeding one year to make transactions.

This Chapter describes the functions, organisation and structure of the capital/ securities market. In section 1 we discuss the relationship between the two parts of the securities market, namely, primary market/new issue market (NIM) and secondary markets/stock exchanges. Section 2 describes the functions of the stock exchanges. The functions of the NIM and the issue mechanism/methods of flotation of new issues are outlined in Sections 3. The main points are summarised in the last Section.

LO 21.2 RELATIONSHIP BETWEEN NEW ISSUE MARKET AND STOCK EXCHANGE

The industrial securities market is divided into two parts, namely, NIM and stock market. The relationship between these parts of the market provides an insight into its organisation. One aspect of their relationship is that they differ from each other organisationally as well as in the nature of functions performed by them. They have some similarities also.

Differences

The differences between NIM and stock exchanges pertain to **(i)** Types of securities dealt, **(ii)** Nature of financing and **(iii)** Organisation.

New vs Old Securities The NIM deals with **new** securities, that is, securities which were not previously available and are, therefore, offered to the investing public for the first time. The market, therefore, derives its name from the fact that it makes available a new block of securities for public subscription. The stock market, on the other hand, is a market for **old** securities which may be defined as securities which have been issued already and granted stock exchange quotation. The stock exchanges, therefore, provide a regular and continuous market for buying and selling of securities. The usual procedure is that when an enterprise is in need of funds, it approaches the investing public, both individuals and institutions, to subscribe to its issue of capital. The securities thus floated are subsequently purchased and sold among the individual and institutional investors. There are, in other words, two stages involved in the purchase and sale of securities. In the first stage, the securities are acquired from the issuing companies themselves and these are, in the second stage, purchased and sold continuously among the investors without any involvement of the companies whose securities constitute the stock-in-trade except in the strictly limited sense of registering the transfer of ownership of the securities. The section of the industrial securities market dealing with the first stage is referred to as the NIM, while secondary market covers the second stage of the dealings in securities.

New securities are offered to the investing public for the first time.

Old securities are securities which have been issued already and listed on a stock exchange.

Nature of Financing Another aspect related to the separate functions of these two parts of the securities market is the nature of their contribution to industrial financing. Since the primary market is concerned with new securities, it provides additional funds to the issuing companies either for starting a new enterprise or for the expansion or diversification of the existing one and, therefore, its contribution to company financing is **direct**. In contrast, the secondary markets can in no circumstance supply additional funds since the company is not involved in the transaction. This, however, does not mean that the stock markets have no relevance in the process of transfer of resources from savers to investors. Their role regarding the supply of capital is **indirect**. The usual course in the development of industrial enterprise seems to be that those who bear the initial burden of financing a new enterprise pass it on to others when the enterprise becomes well-established. The existence of secondary markets which provide institutional facilities for the continuous purchase and sale of securities and, to that extent, lend liquidity and marketability, play an important part in the process.

Organisational Differences The two parts of the market have organisational differences also. The stock exchanges have, organisationally speaking, physical existence and are located in a particular geographical area. The NIM is not rooted in any particular spot and has no geographical existence. The NIM has neither any tangible form any administrative organisational set up like that of stock exchanges, nor is it subjected to any centralised control and administration for the consummation of its business. It is recognised only by the services that it renders to the lenders and borrowers of capital funds at the time of any particular operation. The precise nature of the specialised institutional facilities provided by the NIM is described in a subsequent section.

Similarities

Nevertheless, in spite of organisational and functional differences, the NIM and the stock exchanges are inseparably connected.

Stock Exchange Listing One aspect of this inseparable connection between them is that the securities issued in the NIM are invariably **listed** on a recognised stock exchange for dealings in them. In India, for instance, one of the conditions to which a prospectus is to conform is that it should contain a stipulation that the application has been made, or will be made in due course for admitting the securities to dealings on the stock exchange. The practice of **listing** of new issues on the stock market is of immense utility to the potential investors who can be sure that should they receive an allotment of new issues, they will subsequently be able to dispose them off any time. The absence of such facilities would act as some sort of psychological barrier to investments in new securities. The facilities provided by the secondary markets, therefore, encourage holdings of new securities and, thus, widen the initial/primary market for them.

Listing enables dealings in securities on a stock exchange.

Control The stock exchanges exercise considerable control over the organisation of new issues. In terms of regulatory framework related to dealings in securities, the new issues of securities which seek stock quotation/listing have to comply with statutory rules as well as regulations framed by the stock exchanges with the object of ensuring fair dealings in them. If the new issues do not conform to the prescribed stipulations, the stock exchanges would refuse listing facilities to them. This requirement obviously enables the stock exchange to exercise considerable control over the new issues market and is indicative of close relationship between the two.

Economic Interdependence The markets for new and old securities are, economically, an integral part of a single market—the industrial securities market. Their mutual interdependence from the economic point of view has two dimensions. One, the behaviour of the stock exchanges has a significant bearing on the level of activity in the NIM and, therefore, its responses to capital issues: **Activity in the new issues market and the movement in the prices of stock exchange securities are broadly related: new issues increase when share values are rising and vice versa.**[1] This is because the two parts of the industrial securities market are susceptible to common influences and they act and react upon each other. The stock exchanges are usually the first to feel a change in the economic outlook and the effect is quickly transmitted to the new issue section of the market.

The second dimension of the mutual interdependence of the two parts of the market is that the prices of new issues are influenced by the price movements on the stock market. The securities market represents an important case where the **stock-demand-and-supply curves**, as distinguished from **flow-demand-and-supply curves**, exert a dominant influence on price determination.[2] The quantitative predominance of old securities in the market usually ensures that it is these which set the tone of the market as a whole and govern the prices and acceptability of the new issues.[3] Thus, the flow of new savings into new securities is profoundly influenced by the conditions prevailing in the old securities market—the stock exchange.

LO 21.3 FUNCTIONS OF STOCK/SECONDARY MARKETS/ EXCHANGES

Stock exchanges discharge three vital functions in the orderly growth of capital formation: **(i)** Nexus between savings and investments, **(ii)** Market place and **(iii)** Continuous price formation.

Nexus between Savings and Investment

First and foremost, they are the nexus between the savings and the investments of the community. The savings of the community are mobilised and channelled by stock exchanges for investment into those sectors and units which are favoured by the community at large, on the basis of such criteria as good return, appreciation of capital, and so on. It is the preference of investors for individual units as well as industry groups, which is reflected in the share price, that decides the mode of investment. Stock exchanges render this service by arranging for the preliminary distribution of new issues of capital, offered through prospectus, as also offers for sale of existing securities, in an orderly and systematic manner. They themselves administer the same, by ensuring that the various requisites of listing (such as offering at least the prescribed minimum percentage of capital to the public, keeping the subscription list open for a minimum period of days, making provision for receiving applications at least at the prescribed centres, allotting the shares against applications on a fair and unconditional basis) are duly complied with. Members of stock exchanges also assist in the flotation of new issues by acting **(i)** as brokers, in which capacity they, *inter alia*, try to procure subscription from investors spread all over the country, and **(ii)** as underwriters. This quite often results in their being required to nurse new issues till a time when the new ventures start making profits and reward their shareholders by declaring reasonable dividends when their shares command premiums in the market. Stock companies also provide a forum for trading in rights shares of companies already listed, thereby enabling a new class of investors to take up a part of the rights in the place of existing shareholders who renounce their rights for monetary considerations.

Market Place

The second important function discharged by stock markets/exchanges is that they provide a market place for the purchase and sale of securities, thereby enabling their free transferability through several successive stages from the original subscriber to the neverending stream of buyers, who may be buying them today to sell them at a later date for a variety of considerations like meeting their own needs of liquidity, shuffling their investment portfolios to gear up for the everchanging market situations, and so on. Since the point of aggregate sale and purchase is centralised, with a multiplicity of buyers and sellers at any point of time, by and large, a seller has a ready purchaser and a purchaser has a ready seller at a price which can be said to be competitive. This guarantees saleability to one who has already invested and surety of purchase to the other who desires to invest.

Continuous Price Formation

The third major function, closely related to the second, discharged by the stock exchanges is the process of continuous price formation. The collective judgement of many people operating simultaneously in the market, resulting in the emergence of a large number of buyers and sellers at any point of time, has the effect of bringing about changes in the levels of security prices in small graduations, thereby evening out wide swings in prices. The everchanging demand and supply conditions result in a continuous revaluation of assets, with today's prices being yesterday's prices, altered, corrected, and adjusted, and tomorrows values being again today's values altered, corrected and adjusted. The process is an unending one. Stock exchanges thus act as a barometer of the state of health of the nations economy, by constantly measuring its progress or otherwise. An investor can always have his eyes turned towards the stock exchanges to know, at any point of time, the value of the investments and plan his personal needs accordingly.

LO 21.4 FUNCTIONS OF NEW ISSUES/PRIMARY MARKET

The main function of NIM is to facilitate the transfer of resources from savers to entrepreneurs seeking to establish new enterprise or to expand/diversify existing ones. Such facilities are of crucial importance in the context of the dichotonomy of funds available for capital uses from those in whose hands they accumulate, and those by whom they are applied to productive uses. Conceptually, the NIM should not, however, be conceived as exclusively serving the purpose of raising finance for new capital expenditure. In fact, the organisation and facilities of the market are also utilised for selling concerns to the public as going concerns through the conversion of existing proprietary enterprises or private companies into public companies. The NIM is a complex of institutions through which funds can be obtained directly or indirectly by those who require them from investors who have savings.

New issues can be classified in various ways. The first category of new issues are by new companies and old companies. This classification was first suggested by R.F. Henderson.[4] The distinction between *new* also called *initial* and *old* also known as *further*, does not bear any relation to the age of the company. The securities issued by companies for the first time either after the incorporation or conversion from private to public companies are designated as initial issues, while those issued by companies which already have stock exchange quotation, either by public issue or by *rights* to existing shareholders, are referred to as further or old.

The new issues by corporate enterprise can also be classified on the basis of companies seeking quotation, namely, new money issues and no *new money issues*. The term **new money issues** refers to the issues of capital involving newly created shares; **no new money issues** represent the sale of securities already in existence and sold by their holders. The *new money issues* provide funds to enterprises for additional capital investment. According to Merrett and others,[5] *new money* refers to the sum of money equivalent to the number of newly created shares multiplied by the price per share minus all the administrative cost associated with the issue. This money may not be used for additional capital investment; it may be used wholly or partly to repay debt. Henderson[6] uses the term in a rather limited sense so that it is the net of repayment of long-term debt and sums paid to vendors of existing securities. The differences in the approaches by Merrett and others, on the one hand, and Henderson, on the other, arise because of the fact that while the concern of the former is with both flow of funds into the market as well as flow of money money, Henderson was interested only in the latter.

However, two types of issues are excluded from the category of new issues. First, *bonus/capitalisation* issues which represent only book-keeping entries, and, second, *exchange* issues by which shares in one company are exchanged for securities of another.

The general function of the NIM, namely, the channelling of investible funds into industrial enterprises, can be split from the operational stand-point, into three services:[7] **(i) Origination**, **(ii)** *Underwriting*, and **(iii)** *Distribution*. The institutional set-up dealing with these can be said to constitute the NIM organisation. In other words, the NIM facilitates the transfer of resources by providing specialist institutional facilities to perform the **triple-service function**.

Origination

The term **origination** refers to the work of investigation and analysis and processing of new proposals. These two functions[8] are performed by the specialist agencies which act as the sponsors of issues. One aspect is the preliminary investigation which entails a careful study of technical, economic, financial, and legal aspects of the issuing companies. This is to ensure that it warrants the backing of the issue houses in the sense of lending their name to the company and, thus, give the issue the stamp of respectability, to satisfy themselves that the company is strongly-based, has good market prospects, is well-managed and is worthy of stock exchange quotation. In the process of origination the sponsoring institutions render, as a second function, some services of an advisory nature which go to improve the quality of capital issues. These services include advice on such aspects of capital issues as: **(i)** determination of the class of security to be issued and price of the issues in the light of market conditions, **(ii)** the timing and magnitude of issues, **(iii)** methods of flotation, and **(iv)** technique of selling, and so on. The importance of the specialised services provided by the NIM organisation in this respect can hardly be overstressed in view of its pivotal position in the process of flotation of capital in the NIM. On the thoroughness of investigation and soundness of judgement of the sponsoring institutions depends, to a large extent, the allocative efficiency of the market.

Origination is the work of investigation and analysis and processing of new issue proposals.

Underwriting

The origination howsoever thoroughly done, will not, by itself, guarantee the success of an issue. To ensure success of an issue, therefore, the second specialist service—**underwriting**—provided by the institutional setup of the NIM takes the form of a guarantee that the issues would be sold by eliminating the risk arising from uncertainty of public response. That adequate institutional arrangement for the provision of underwriting is of crucial significance both to the issuing companies as well as the investing public cannot be overstressed.[9]

Underwriting is a form of guarantee that the new issues would be sold by eliminating the risk arising from uncertainty of public response.

Distribution

Underwriting, however, is only a stop-gap arrangement to guarantee the success of an issue. The success of an issue, in the ultimate analysis, depends on the issues being acquired by the investing public. The sale of securities to the ultimate investors is referred to as **distribution**. It is a specialist job which can best be performed by brokers and dealers in securities, who maintain regular and direct contact with the ultimate investors.

Distribution is the sale of securities to the ultimate investors.

Thus, the NIM is a complex of institutions through which funds can be obtained by those who require them from investors who have savings. The ability of the NIM to cope with the growing requirements of the expanding corporate sector would depend on the presence of specialist agencies to perform the *triple-service-function* of origination, underwriting and distribution. While the nature of the services provided by an organised NIM is the same in all developed countries,[10] the degree of development and specialisation of market organisation, the type of institutions found and the actual procedures followed differ from country to country, as they are determined partly by history and partly by the particular legal, social, political, and economic environment.

Issue Mechanism

The success of an issue depends, partly, on the issue mechanism. The methods by which new issues are made are: **(i)** Public issue through prospectus, **(ii)** Tender/Book building, **(iii)** Offer for sale **(iv)** Placement and **(v)** Rights issue.

Public Issue through Prospectus A common method followed by corporate enterprises to raise capital through the issue of securities is by means of a prospectus inviting subscription from the investing public. Under this method, the issuing companies themselves offer directly to the general public a fixed number of shares at a stated price, which in the case of new companies is invariably the face value of the securities, and in the case of existing companies, it may sometimes include a premium amount, if any. Another feature of **public issue** method is that generally the issues are underwritten to ensure success arising out of unsatisfactory public response.

Public issue are securities that are offered to the general public directly at a stated price.

The foundation of the public issue method is a prospectus, the minimum contents of which are prescribed by the Companies Act, 1956. It also provides both civil and criminal liability for any misstatement in the prospectus. Additional disclosure requirements are also mandated by the SEBI. The contents of the prospectus, *inter alia*, include: **(i)** Name and registered office of the issuing company; **(ii)** Existing and proposed activities; **(iii)** Board of directors; **(iv)** Location of the industry; **(v)** Authorised, subscribed and proposed issue of capital to public; **(vi)** Dates of opening and closing of subscription list; **(vii)** Name of broker, underwriters, and others, from whom application forms along with copies of prospectus can be obtained; **(viii)** Minimum subscription; **(ix)** Names of underwriters, if any, along with a statement that in the opinion of the directors, the resources of the underwriters are sufficient to meet the underwriting obligations; and **(x)** A statement that the company will make an application to stock exchange(s) for the permission to deal in or for a quotation of its shares and so on. A detailed account of the regulatory framework relating to issues of capital is given in the next chapter.

The public issue method through prospectus has the advantage that the transaction is carried on in the full light of publicity coupled with approach to the entire investing public. Moreover, a fixed quantity of stock has to be allotted among applicants on a non-discriminatory basis. The issues are, thus, widely distributed and the danger of an artificial restriction on the quantity of shares available is avoided. It would ensure that the share ownership is widely-diffused, thereby contributing to the prevention of concentration of wealth and economic power.

A serious drawback of public issue, as a method to raise capital through the sale of securities, is that it is a highly expensive method. The cost of flotation involves underwriting expenses, brokerage, and other administrative expenses. The administrative cost includes printing charges of prospectus, advertisement/publicity charges, accountancy charges, legal charges, bank charges, stamp duty, listing fee, registration charges, travelling expenses, filling of document charges, mortgage deed registration fee and postage and so on.[11] In view of the high cost involved in raising capital, the public issue method is suitable for large issues and it cannot be availed of in case of small issues.

Tender/Book Building Method The essence of the **tender/book building** method is that the pricing of the issues is left to the investors. The issuing company incorporates all the details of the issue proposal in the offer document on the lines of the public issue method including the reserve/minimum price. The investors are required to quote the number of securities and the price at which they wish to acquire. **The detailed procedure followed in India is elaborated upon in the next chapter**.

Book building is a price discovery and investors response mechanism.

Offer for Sale Another method by which securities can be issued is by means of an **offer for sale**. Under this method, instead of the issuing company itself offering its shares directly to the public, it offers through the intermediary of issue houses/merchant banks/investment banks or firms of stockbrokers. The *modus operandi* of the offer of sale is akin to the public issue method in that the prospectus with strictly prescribed minimum contents which constitutes the foundation for the sale of securities, and a known quantity of shares are distributed to the applicants in a non-discriminatory manner. Moreover, the issues are underwritten to avoid the possibility of the issue being left largely in the hands of the issuing houses. But the mechanism adopted is different. The sale of securities with an offer for sale method is done in two stages.

Offer for sale is the sale of existing shares by promoters to the investing public.

In the first stage, the issuing company sells the securities *enbloc* to the issuing houses or stock-brokers at an agreed fixed price and the securities, thus acquired by the sponsoring institutions, are resold, in the second stage, by the issuing houses to the ultimate investors. The securities are offered to the public at a price higher than the price at which they were acquired from the company. The difference between the sale and the purchase price, technically called as *turn*, represents the remuneration of the issuing houses. In the case of public method, the issuing houses receive a fee based upon the size and the complications involved in supervision as they act as agents of the issuing companies. Although this is theoretically possible, but usually the issuing houses' remuneration in offer for sale is the turn' out of which they also meet subsidiary expenses such as underwriting commission, the cost of advertisement and prospectus, and so on, whereas these are borne by the companies themselves in the case of public issue method.

The offer for sale method shares the advantage available to public issue method. One additional advantage of this method is that the issuing company is saved from the cost and trouble of selling the shares to the public. Apart from being expensive, like the public issue method, it suffers from another serious shortcoming. The securities are sold to the investing public usually at a premium. The margin between the amount received by the company and the price paid by the public does not become additional funds, but it is pocketed by the issuing houses or the existing shareholders.

Placement Method Yet another method to float new issues of capital is the placing method defined by London Stock Exchange as *"sale by an issue house or broker to their own clients of securities which have been previously purchased or subscribed"*.[12] Under this method, securities are acquired by the issue houses, as in offer for sale method, but instead of being subsequently offered to the public, they are *placed* with the clients of the issue houses, both individual and institutional investors. Each issue house has a list of large private and institutional investors who are always prepared to subscribe to any securities which are issued in this manner. Thus, the flotation of the securities involves two stages: In the first stage, shares are acquired by the issuing houses and in the second stage, they are made available to their investor-clients. The issue houses usually place the securities at a higher price than the price they pay and the difference, that is, the *turn* is their remuneration. Alternatively, though rarely, they may arrange the placing in return for a fee and act merely as an agent and not principal.

Another feature of placing is that the placing letter and the other documents, when taken together, constitute a *prospectus/offer document* and the information concerning the issue has to be published. In this method, no formal underwriting of the issue is required as the placement itself amounts to underwriting since the issue houses agree to place the issue with their clients. They endeavour to ensure the success of the issue by carefully *vetting* the issuing company concerned and offering generous subscription terms.

Placing of securities that are unquoted is known as **private placing**. The securities are usually in small companies but these may occasionally be in large companies. When the securities to be placed are newly quoted, the method is officially known as stock exchange placing.[13]

> **Placement of securities** is the sale of unquoted securities.

The main advantage of placing, as a method of issuing new securities, is its relative cheapness. This is partly because many of the items of expenses in public issue and offer for sale methods like underwriting commission, expense relating to applications and allotment of shares, and so on are avoided. Moreover, the stock exchange requirements relating to contents of the prospectus and its advertisement are less onerous in the case of placing.[14]

Its weakness arises from the point of view of distribution of securities. As the securities are offered only to a select group of investors, it may lead to the concentration of shares into a few hands who may create artificial scarcity of scrips in times of hectic dealings in such shares in the market.

The placement method is advantageous to the issuing companies but it is not favourably received by the investing public. The method is suitable in case of small issues which cannot bear the high expenses entailed in a public issue, and also in such issues which are unlikely to arouse much interest among the general investing public. Thus, with the placement method, new issues can be floated by small companies which suffer from a financial disadvantage in the form of prohibitively high cost of capital in the case of other methods of flotation as well as at times when conditions in the market may not be favourable as it does not depend for its success on public response. This underscores the relevance of this method from the viewpoint of the market.

Rights Issue The methods discussed above can be used both by new companies as well as by established companies. In the case of companies whose shares are already listed and widely-held, shares can be offered to the existing shareholders. This is called **rights issue**. Under this method, the existing shareholders are offered the right to subscribe to new shares in proportion to the number of shares they already hold. This offer is made by circular to 'existing shareholders' only.

> **Rights issue** is the sale of securities to the existing shareholders.

In India, Section 81 of the Companies Act, 1956 provides that where a company increases its subscribed capital by the issue of new shares, either after two years of its formation or after one year of first issue of shares whichever is earlier, these have to be first offered to the existing shareholders with a right to renounce them in favour of a nominee. A company can, however, dispense with this requirement by passing a special resolution to the same effect.

Rights issues are not normally underwritten but to ensure full subscription and as a measure of abundant precaution, a few companies have resorted to underwriting of rights shares. The experience of these companies has been that underwriters were not called upon to take up shares in terms of their obligations. It is, therefore, observed that such underwriting serves little economically useful purpose in that "it represents insurance against a risk which is **(i)** readily avoidable and **(ii)** of extremely rare occurrence even where no special steps are taken to avoid it."[15] The chief merit of rights issue is that it is an inexpensive method. The usual expenses like underwriting commission, brokerage and other administrative expenses are either non-existent or are very small. Advertising expenses have to be incurred only for sending a letter of rights to shareholders. The management of applications and allotment is less cumbersome because the number is limited. As already mentioned, this method can be used only by existing companies and the general investing public has no opportunity to participate in the new companies. The pre-emptive right of existing shareholders may conflict with the broader objective of wider diffusion of share-ownership.

The above discussion shows that the available methods of flotation of new issues are suitable in different circumstances and for different types of enterprises. The issue mechanism would vary from market to market.

SUMMARY

LO 21.1

- The financial system consisting of a variety of financial instruments, financial intermediaries, and financial markets related in a systematic manner provides the principal mechanism by which savings are transformed into investments.
- A financial instrument/asset/security represents claims against the future income/wealth of an entity. The financial assets are: (i) direct (e.g. shares and debentures of manufacturing companies), (ii) indirect (e.g. units of mutual funds) and derivatives (e.g. futures and options).
- Financial intermediaries act as a link between savers and investors. Their main function is to convert a direct/primary security into an indirect security. In the process of conversion, they offer to the investors the benefits of convenience, low risk, expert management and lower risk. The indirect securities offer to the investors better investment alternative than the direct securities by pooling which they are created.
- Financial markets facilitate transfer of funds from savers to investors. They are a market for creation and exchange of financial assets. The two key financial markets are money market and capital/securities market.
- The money market is a market for short-term funds having maturities of one year or less. Short-term marketable securities are traded in the money market.

LO 21.2

- Capital market is the market for long-term funds. The backbone of the market is formed by the securities markets/exchanges comprising the new issue markets and the stock exchanges.
- The new issue/primary market and secondary market/stock market/exchange differ from each other organisationally as well as in the nature of functions performed by them. While the primary market deals in new securities, that is, securities which were not previously available and are offered to the investors for the first time, the stock market is a market for old securities defined as those already issued and granted stock exchange quotations/listing. Functionally, they also differ in that the new issue market supplies funds to corporate enterprise directly but the secondary markets play only an indirect role in industrial financing by providing liquidity to investments already made.
- The two parts of the securities market have organisational differences as well. The stock exchange has a physical existence and is located in a particular geographical area. The new issue market does not have any organisational set up in any particular place and is recognised only by the specialist institutional services that it renders to the lenders/borrowers of capital funds at the time of any particular operation.
- The new issue market and the stock exchanges are inseparably interconnected. The securities issued in the primary market are invariably listed on a recognised stock exchange for dealings in them. Moreover, the stock exchanges exercise considerable control over the organisation of new issues in terms of regulatory framework relating to the listing of securities. Further, economically, the behaviour of the stock exchange as reflected in the prices of listed securities has a significant bearing on the level of activity in the new issue market in terms of its response to issue of capital. Similarly, the price of new issues are greatly influenced by the price movements in the stock market.

LO 21.3

The stock markets, as an integral part of the industrial securities market, discharge three vital functions in the orderly growth of capital formation. First and foremost, they are a nexus between the savings and investments of the community. They also provide a market price for purchase/sale of securities. The process of continuous price formation is the third function discharged by the stock exchanges.

LO 21.4

The main function of the new issue market, namely, the channelling of investible funds into industrial enterprises, is divided, in operational terms, into three distinct services: (i) Origination, (ii) Underwriting and (iii) Distribution. The new issue market facilitates the transfer of resources of providing specialist institutional facilities to perform this *triple-service function.*

The origination functions cover the work of investigation and analysis and processing of new issue proposals. Apart from a careful study of technical, economic, financial and legal aspects of the issuing companies to ensure that it warrants the backing of the issue houses/merchant banks/originators, it also refers to advices relating to the important aspects of the issue proposal such as class of security to be issued, price of an issue, timing and magnitude of issue, methods of flotation and so on.

The underwriting service provided by the new issue market organisation is a form of a guarantee that the issue would be sold by eliminating the risk arising out of uncertainty of public response.

The distribution of securities is undertaken by brokers and dealers in securities who maintain regular and direct contact with the investors.

The issue mechanism consists of five methods of flotation of securities: (i) Public issue through prospectus, (ii) Offer for sale, (iii) Placement, (iv) Rights issues and (v) Tender/Book-building. Under the first method, issuing companies offer the securities directly to the general public at a stated price. The cost of raising capital through this method is high. It is suitable for large issues. The offer for sale and placement methods are indirect methods of sale of securities through financial/investment institutions to the investing public. They are suitable for small issues of capital. The rights issue is a method to sell securities to the existing shareholders of a company. The pricing of issues is left to the investors in book building method.

REFERENCES

1. Grant, A T K, *A Study of Capital Market in Post-war Britain*, London, 1937, p 135.
2. Kaldor, N, *Essays on Economic Stability and Growth* (London, 1961), p. 3, quoted in Gupta, L C, *op. cit.* p 120.
3. *Ibid.*, p 120.
4. Henderson, R F, *The New Issues Market and Finance for Industry*, 1951, p 24.
5. Merrett, Howe and Newbould, *Equity Issues and the London Capital Market*, London, 1967, p 4.
6. Henderson, R F, *op. cit.*, p 94.
7. Briston, R J, *op. cit.*, pp 75-78.
8. *Ibid.*
9. For a comprehensive account of the use of under-writing please refer to Finnie, D, *Capital Underwriting*, 1934, pp 11-14.
10. Gupta, L C, *op. cit.*, p 121.
11. For actual information regarding flotation in public issue method in India please refer to Khan, M Y, 'Cost of Capital—An Exploratory Analysis', *Indian Economic Journal*, Oct.-Dec., 1976, pp 161-70.
12. Committee of the Federation of Stock Exchange in Great Britain and Ireland, *London Stock Exchange: Admission of Securities to Quotation*, 1966.
13. Merrett and Others, *op. cit.*, p 8.

14. That the cost of raising capital in placement method is low even in small issues is empirically shown by Merrett and others, *ibid.*, p 126.
15. *Ibid.*, p 58.

REVIEW QUESTIONS

LOD: Easy

RQ.21.1 Fill in the following blanks by appropriate answers: [LO 21.1-4]

(i) Capital markets are a sub-part of the __________ system.

(ii) __________ intermediaries act as a link between savers and investors.

(iii) The primary function of financial intermediaries is to convert __________ securities into __________ securities.

(iv) The two key financial markets are __________.

(v) Money market is a market for __________ funds having maturity of __________.

(vi) The capital market consists of __________ and the stock exchanges.

(vii) While the primary market deals in __________ securities, the stock market is a market for __________ securities.

(viii) The price of new issues are influenced, to a marked extent, by the price movements in the __________ market.

(ix) Origination, underwriting and __________ are three services provided by the new issue market.

(x) __________ is a method to sell securities to the existing shareholders of a company.

(xi) Pricing of issues is left to the investors in __________.

[Answers: (i) financial (ii) financial (iii) direct, indirect (iv) money market and Capital market (v) short-term one year or less (vi) new issue markets (vii) new, old (viii) stock (ix) distribution (x) right issue and (xi) book building method]

RQ.21.2 Discuss the main elements of the financial system. [LO 21.1]

RQ.21.3 Explain briefly financial assets/instruments. [LO 21.1]

RQ.21.4 Explain briefly the two key financial markets. [LO 21.2]

RQ.21.5 Briefly discuss the functions of the NIM. [LO 21.4]

LOD: Medium

RQ.21.6 Describe briefly the functions of financial intermediaries. [LO 21.1]

RQ.21.7 Write a brief note on the differences between the new issue market and the stock exchanges. [LO 21.2]

RQ.21.8 What are the functions of the stock exchanges? [LO 21.3]

RQ.21.9 What are the different methods of flotation of issues in the primary market? [LO 21.4]

LOD: Difficult

RQ.21.10 What are the similarities between the NIM and the stock market? [LO 21.3]

CHAPTER 22

Equity/Ordinary Shares

LEARNING OBJECTIVES

LO 22.1	Discuss the general features of equity/ordinary shares, the important aspects of preemptive rights of shareholders and the merits and demerits of ordinary share financing
LO 22.2	Review the procedure relating to equity shares and securities convertible/exchangeable into equity shares in India in terms of common conditions for public/rights issues, provisions as to public issues, rights issues, preferential issues and qualified institutional placement

INTRODUCTION

Equity/ordinary share capital, as a long-term source of finance, represents ownership capital/securities and its owners—equity-holders/ordinary shareholders—share the reward and risk associated with the ownership of corporate enterprises. It is also called ordinary share capital in contrast with preference share capital which carries certain preferences/prior rights in regard to income and redemption. When a company is formed, it first issues equity shares to the promoters. As the need for financing increases, the company may issue ordinary shares to specific and small number privately to promoters' relatives, friends, business associates, employees, financial institutions, mutual funds, venture capital funds and so on. As the company grows further, it raises capital from the public. The first issue of equity shares to the public by an unlisted company is called the **initial public offering** (IPO). Subsequent offerings are called further issues/offerings. This chapter discusses the ordinary/equity shares. The chapter first describes their fundamentals in terms of **(1)** types, **(2)** features/attributes and **(3)** evaluation. The procedure involved in issuing them to the public is the focus of the subsequent discussion. The main points are summarised by way of recapitulation.

LO 22.1 FUNDAMENTALS OF EQUITY SHARES

This section focuses on the types, features and evaluation of equity/ordinary shares.

Types

Authorised equity/share capital represents the maximum amount which a company can raise from the ordinary share holders and can be changed in the prescribed manner. The portion of the authorised capital offered by the company to the investors is the **Issued** capital. **Subscribed** share capital is that part of the issued capital which has been accepted/subscribed by the investors. The actual amount paid by the shareholders is the *Paid-up capital.* The issued, subscribed and *paid-up* capitals are generally the same.

Authorised share capital is the number of ordinary shares capital that a firm can raise without further shareholder approval.

Ordinary shares have typically a **par/face value** in terms of the price for each share, the most popular denomination being ₹10. The price at which the equity shares are issued is the **Issue** price. The issue price for new companies is generally equal to the face value. It may be higher for existing companies, the difference/excess being *share premium.* The **book value** of ordinary shares refers to the paid-up capital plus reserves and surplus (net worth) divided by the number of outstanding shares. The price at which equity shares are traded in the stock market is their **market value**. However, the market value of unlisted/thinly traded shares is not available.

Subscribed share capital is the number of shares (capital) outstanding.

Par (face) value is a value arbitrarily placed on the shares.

Features

The ordinary shares have some special features in terms of the rights and claims of their holders.

Residual Claim to Income The equity shareholders have a residual claim to the income of the company. They are entitled to the remaining income/profits of the company after all outside claims are met. The earnings/income available to the shareholders (EAS) equals profit after tax (PAT) minus preference dividend; the PAT is equal to operating profits (EBIT) less taxes. However, the residual claim is only a theoretical entitlement as the amount actually received by the shareholders in the form of dividend will depend on the decision of the board of directors. The directors have the right to decide what portion of the EAS will be distributed to the shareholders as cash dividend and what portion will be ploughed back as retained earnings which the shareholders will receive later in the form of capital appreciation/bonus shares. In other words, the payment of dividends depends on the discretion of management and the shareholders have no legal right to receive/the company has no legal obligation to distribute, dividends out of EAS. This is in sharp contrast to the claims of debenture-holders which as a contractual obligation of the company must always be honoured irrespective of its financial position.

Residual Claim on Assets The ordinary shareholders' claim in the assets of the company is also residual in that their claim would rank after the claims of the creditors and preference shareholders in the event of liquidation. If the liquidation value of assets is insufficient, their claims may remain unpaid.

Right to Control As owners of the company, the equity-holders have the right to control the operations of/ participate in the management of, the company. Their control is, however, indirect. The major policies/decisions are approved by the Board of Directors and the Board-appointed management carries out the day-to-day operations. The shareholders have the legal right/power to elect the board of directors as well as vote on every resolution placed in various meetings of the company. Though, in theory, they have indirect right to control/participate in management, in actual practice, it is weak and ineffective partly because of the apathy and indifference of the majority of the shareholders who rarely bother to cast their votes and partly because scattered and by and large unorganised equity-holders are unable to exercise their collective power effectively.

Voting System The ordinary shareholders exercise their right to control through voting in the meetings of the company. According to the most commonly used system of voting in India, namely, **majority rule voting**, each share carries one vote and each director is elected individually. Therefore, a shareholder can cast the total number of shares held by him for the election of each director separately. As a result, shareholders/group holding more than 50 per cent of the outstanding equity shares would be able to elect all the directors of their choice. An alternative is **proportionate rule voting** under which the number of votes held by a shareholder/group equals the number of shares held by him multiplied by/times the number of directors to be elected. The total votes held may be cast/spread in any manner: all just for one candidate or spread over as many candidates as the shareholders wishes to vote for. The proportionate voting system may enable even minority shareholders some representation on the board while all the members of the board may be elected by the holders of the majority of ordinary shares.

Proportionate voting is the system under which each share is allotted a number of votes equal to the number of directors to be elected and votes can be given to any director.

Majority rule voting is the system where by in the election of directors, each shareholder is entitled to one vote for each share held and he can vote all shares for each director separately.

Pre-emptive right (rights) is a legal right of existing shareholders to be offered by the company in the first opportunity to purchase additional equity shares in proportion to their current holdings.

Pre-emptive Right The ordinary shareholders of a company enjoy **pre-emptive** rights in the sense that they have a legal right to be offered by the company the first opportunity to purchase additional issue of equity capital in proportion to/pro rata basis their existing/current holdings/ownership. A shareholder owning 2 per cent of the existing issued capital is entitled/has a pre-emptive right to acquire 2 per cent of additional shares to be issued by the company. The option to the shareholders to purchase a specified number of equity shares at a stated price during a given period is called **rights**. The shareholders can **(i)** exercise, **(ii)** sell in the market and **(iii)** renounce/forfeit their pre-emptive right partially or completely. The shares available as a result of non-exercise of right would be allotted on a *pro rata* basis to shareholders exercising the right. Any balance of shares can be offered to the public for subscription.

Dilution of control/financial interest occurs when a new share issue results in each existing shareholder having a claim in a smaller part of the firm's earnings than before.

While the pre-emptive rights ensure that management cannot issue additional shares to strengthen its control by selling them to persons/groups favourably inclined to it, on one hand, it protects the existing shareholders from **dilution of their financial interest** as a result of new equity issues, on the other.

Assume Avon Industries Ltd (AIL) has currently 30,00,000 shares outstanding. The market price is ₹65 per share. The AIL plans to issue 10,00,000 additional shares at a subscription/issue price of ₹40 per share. The number of rights to buy a new share = 30 lakh/10 lakh = 3. The market price of a share after right issue $= \frac{(30,00,000 \times ₹65) + (10,00,000 \times ₹40)}{(30,00,000 + 10,00,000)}$ = ₹58.75. A shareholder can buy one new share for ₹40 plus 3 rights. The total value of 3 rights = ₹58.75 – ₹40 = ₹18.75. The value of each right = ₹18.75/3 = ₹6.25. Thus, the *ex-right* price of a share drops by ₹6.25 from the *cum-right* (rights-on) price of ₹65 to the ex-rights price of ₹58.75. The existing shareholders do not gain/lose from rights issue. What he receives in the form of value of a right, he loses in the form of a decline in the share price. His financial interest remains unaffected when he exercises his right or sells his rights. In case he does not exercise his right, there will a dilution of his financial interest.

Assume further, Mr X owns 300 shares of AIL. His total wealth/financial interest is ₹19,500 (300 × ₹65). After the exercise of his right, his holdings will be 400 shares. His total wealth would be ₹23,500 (400 × ₹58.75). But he has spent ₹4,000 (₹40 × 100) to acquire additional shares. So his net financial interest = ₹23,500 – ₹4,000 = ₹19,500, that is, equal to before rights issue.

In case Mr X sells his right @ ₹6.25, his total financial position in AIL would be ₹19,500 [(₹58.75 × 300) + (₹6.25 × 300)]: the same as before the rights issue.

If he does not exercise his right to buy/sell, his financial interest will suffer a dilution as his total wealth = ₹17,625 (₹58.75 × 300), that is, a dilution of ₹1,875 (₹19,500 – ₹17,625).

In brief, **an investor suffers dilution of financial interest when he does not exercise his pre-emptive rights**.

Limited Liability Although the equity holders share the ownership risk, their liability is limited to the extent of their investment in the share capital of the company.

Evaluation

As the single most important source of long term funds, equity capital has merits as well demerits from the viewpoint of the company as well as the shareholders.

Merits The advantages of equity capital to a company are: first, it is a permanent source of funds without any repayment liability; second, it does not involve obligatory dividend payment and, thirdly, it forms the basis of further long-term financing in the form of borrowing related to the creditworthiness of the firm. The shareholders with limited liability exercise control and share other ownership rights in the income/assets of the firm.

Demerits The disadvantages of equity capital from the viewpoint of a company are: **(i)** High cost of funds reflecting the high required rate of return of investors as a compensation for higher risk as also the fact that equity dividends are not tax-deductible payments. They are paid out of post-tax profits; **(ii)** High flotation cost in terms of underwriting, brokerage and other issue expenses compared to other securities; **(iii)** Dilution of control of existing shareholders on sale of new shares to outsiders/public. The disadvantages associated with equity capital for the shareholders are: **(i)** The equity capital is in reality risk capital as it ranks the last as a claimant to income as well as the assets of the company. **(ii)** The scattered and unorganised shareholders are unable to exercise effective and real control over the company. **(iii)** The shareholders cannot claim dividend as a matter of right. **(iv)** There is a wide fluctuation in share prices with attendant risk for the investors.

In brief, equity capital is a high risk-high reward permanent source of long-term finance for corporate enterprises. The shareholders who desire to share the risk, return and control associated with ownership of companies would invest in corporate equity. **As a source of long-term fund, it has high cost, low/nil risk, does not dilute control and puts no restraint on managerial freedom**.

LO 22.2 ISSUE PROCEDURES

The procedural aspects of raising of equity shares and securities convertible/exchangeable into equity shares prescribed by the Securities and Exchange Board of India (SEBI) in terms of the following: **(i)** common conditions for public and rights issues, **(ii)** provisions as to public issues, **(iii)** rights issues, **(iv)** preferential issues, and **(v)** qualified institutional placement are discussed below.

Common Conditions for Public/Rights Issues

While public issue means an initial public offer (IPO) or a further public offer (FPO), a rights issue means an offer of equity shares and convertible securities by a listed issuer to its shareholders as on the record date. An **IPO** is an offer of shares/convertible securities by an unlisted issuer to the public for subscription including an offer for sale by existing holders in an unlisted issuer. A **FPO** is an offer of shares/convertible securities by a listed issuer including an offer for sale in a listed issuer. The common conditions for public/rights issues are: general conditions, appointment of intermediaries, filing of offer document, documents submitted before issue opening, draft offer documents made public, issue pricing, fast track issues, issue opening, desptach of material, underwriting, minimum subscription, oversubscription, monitoring agency, manner of calls, allotment/refund, restrictions on further issues, additional requirements for issue of convertible debt instruments (CDIs), rollover, conversion, issue of CDIs for financing and alteration of rights of holders of securities.

> **IPO** is an offer of shares/convertible securities by an unlisted issuer to the public for subscription including an offer for sale by existing holders in an unlisted issuer.

> **FPO** is an offer of shares/convertible securities by a listed issuer including an offer for sale in a listed issuer.

The general conditions to be satisfied by an issuer at the time of filing/registering the draft/final offer documents (in case of public issue) and letter of offer (in case of rights issue) with the SEBI/Register of Companies (RoCs)/Designated Stock Exchange (DSE) are: **(i)** The issuer/its promoters/promoter group/person(s) in control are not debarred from accessing the capital market, **(ii)** The issuer of CDIs is not in the list of RB1's willful defaulters/in default for more than six months, has made an application for listing on a RSE (recognised stock exchange) and has entered into an agreement with a depository for demat of securities **(iii)** All existing partly paid-up shares are fully paid up/forfeited, **(iv)** Firm arrangements for 75 per cent of the stated means of finance excluding the amount from the proposed issue/internal accruals have been made.

The issuer should appoint (lead) merchant banker(s)/intermediaries to carry out the issue-related obligations. It should also appoint syndicate members in book-built issues, bankers to an issue at all mandatory collection centres and registrars to an issue who have connectivity with all the depositories. Book building is the process to elicit demand/assess the price to determine quantum/ value of securities/IDRs.

An offer document together with the specified fee should be filed with the SEBI not less than 30 days before registering the prospectus/red herring prospectus/shelf prospectus with the ROCs or letter of offer with the DSE. Any changes/observations by the SEBI should be complied with before filing them with the ROCs/DSE/SEBI.

Issuers must obtain in-principle approval for listing of the securities from the concerned RSEs having nation-wide trading terminals.

The lead merchant banker should submit to the SEBI along with the offer document **(i)** copy of the agreement with the issuer **(ii)** *inter se* allocation of responsibilities of each merchant banker **(iii)** due diligence certificates from the concerned lead merchant banker/debenture trustees **(iv)** statements certifying all changes/observations by SEBI have been incorporated in the offer document/ certificate from a Chartered Accountant in respect of promoters contribution and Board of Directors resolution for allotment of securities to promoters. The issuer should submit PAN/ bank account/ passport number of its promoters.

The offer document should be hosted on the website of the SEBI/concerned RSEs/merchant bankers for public comment for not less than 21 days.

The above requirements relating to filing of offer documents, in-principle approval for listing and submission of documents before issue opening would not apply if the **(i)** issuers (fast track issue) shares have been listed for at least three years **(ii)** the average market capitalisation of its public shareholding is at least ₹10,000 crore **(iii)** the annualised turnover of its shares has been at least two per cent of weighted average number of shares listed during the last six months **(iv)** it has redressed at least 95 per cent of its investors grievances/complied with the equity listing agreement for at least three years **(v)** the impact of the auditor's qualification on its accounts does not exceed five per cent of its net profits/loss after tax, **(vi)** no show-cause notice has been issued/proceedings initiated by the SEBI pending against it/promoters/whole time directors and **(vii)** the entire promoters holding is in demat form.

An issue should open within **(a)** 12 months from the date of the SEBI's observations on the offer document **(b)** three months after 30 days in case of no observation from the SEBI.

The offer document/other issue material should be despatched to the DSE/syndicate members/ underwriters/banker to an issue/investors association/SCSBs (Self-Certified Syndicate Banks) in case of ASBA (Application Supported by Blocked Amount) in advance.

Issues can be underwritten only by SEBI-registered underwriters/book runners (syndicate members). But securities compulsorily allotted to QIBs (Qualified Institutional Buyers) cannot be underwritten. The lead merchant banker/book runner must undertake a minimum underwriting of the lower of the five per cent of the total commitment or ₹25 lakh.

The minimum subscription in an issue should be 90 per cent of the offer. In case of its non-receipt the entire application money received should be refunded within 15 days and seven days from the date of closure of the issue in non-underwritten and underwritten issues respectively.

For issue size exceeding ₹500 crore, a PFI (Public Financial Institution)/bank should be appointed to monitor the use of the issue proceeds. Where a monitoring agency is not appointed, the outstanding subscription must be called within 12 months of allotment. Shares with calls in arrear should be forfeited. Within 15 days of the failure of an issue, the application money must be refunded failing which the specified interest would have to be paid.

In addition to the other requirements, an issuer of CDIs should comply with the following conditions: **(i)** obtain credit rating **(ii)** appoint debenture trustees **(iii)** create debenture redemption fund **(iv)** assets on which charge is proposed are sufficient to discharge the liability and free from encumbrances. They should be redeemed in terms of the offer document.

The non-convertible portion of the partly CDIs can be rolled over without change in the interest rate if 75 per cent of the holders approve it, an auditor's certificate on its liquidity position has been sent to them, the holding of all holders who have not agreed would be redeemed, credit rating has been obtained and communicated to them before rollover.

Positive consent of the holders would be necessary for the optional conversion or CDIs into shares. The holders should be given the option not to convert them if the conversion price was not determined/disclosed to the investors at the time of the issue.

The terms of issue of securities adversely affecting the investors can be altered with the consent/ sanction in writing of at least 75 per cent/special resolution of the holders.

Public Issues

The provisions as to public issues are: eligibility requirements, pricing, promoters contribution, lock-in and minimum offer to public/reservations.

The eligibility conditions relate to IPOs and FPOs. An IPO can be made by an issuer who has **(i)** net tangible assets of at least ₹3 crore in the preceding three years not more than 50 per cent of which should be monetary assets, **(ii)** a track record of distributable profits for at least three out of immediately preceding five years; in case of a partnership converted into a company/company formed out of a diversion, their track record would be considered only if their financial statements of the respective years are revised to conform to the format prescribed by the Companies Act and certified by a chartered accountant to that effect, **(iii)** net worth of at least ₹1 crore in the preceding three years, **(iv)** the aggregate of all issues in one financial year does not exceed five times of its pre-issue net worth and **(v)** at least 50 per cent of the revenue of the preceding year has been earned from the activity indicated by the new name in case of change of its name within the last one year.

An issuer who does not satisfy any of the above five conditions can make an IPO if it alternatively satisfies the following two conditions: **(a)** it is through book building with at least 50 per cent of the net offer to the public allotted to QIBs or at least 15 per cent of the project cost is contributed by PFIs/banks of which a minimum 10 per cent is from appraisers and 10 per cent of the net offer to the public is allotted to QIBs, **(b)** its minimum post-issue face value of capital is ₹10 crore or there would be compulsorily market making for at least two years from the date of listing of the securities provided the minimum depth of securities for buy and sell quotes is 300, the bid-ask spread never exceeds 10 per cent and the inventory of the market is not less than five per cent of the issue.

An IPO of CDIs can be made without a prior issue/listing of shares. The minimum number of allottees in a public issue is 1,000. An IPO cannot be made if on the date of registration of the prospectus with the ROCs there are outstanding convertible securities/rights entitling a person the option to receive shares after the IPO. Shares held for at least one year prior to the filing of the draft offer document with the SEBI may be offered for sale. An IPO grading from a SEBI-registered rating agency is mandatory.

A FPO can be made if the issuer satisfies the two requirements of an IPO, namely, the aggregate of the issue size in one year (i.e. 5 times its pre-issue net worth) and the minimum revenue (i.e. 50 per cent) from the activity indicated by the new name in case of change within the last one year. If these two conditions are not satisfied, a FPO can be made in a manner similar to an IPO when the issuer does not satisfy the five conditions.

The price of specified securities/coupon rate/conversion price of CDIs should be determined by the issuer in consultation with the merchant banker(s) or through the book building process.

Book Building There are two alternative methods of book built issues. According to the **first method**, the lead merchant banker would act as the lead book runner and be primarily responsible for book building. Other merchant banker would act as co-book runners/syndicate members. The issue should be compulsorily underwritten by the book runner(s) and sub-underwritten by the syndicate members. The book runners/ syndicate members should appoint SEBI-registered brokers and the self certified syndicate banks in case of ASBA would act as bidding/collection centres.

> **Book building** is a process to elicit demand for securities and assess price for them.

If the issue size is disclosed, the red-herring prospectus may not contain the price/ number of securities, but the floor price/price band may be mentioned. In case of its non-disclosure, the price should be disclosed at least one/two working days before the bid opening in an IPO and FPO respectively. In case of opting price band by the issuer, the cap should not be more than 120 per cent of the floor. In case of revision of price, the bidding period should be extended by three days.

The minimum application value of an anchor investor should be ₹10 crore in a public issue. Upto 30 per cent available to QIBs may be allocated to them, one-third of which to mutual funds. The bidding for them should open one day before the issue opening date and they should pay at least 25 per cent margin on application and the balance within two days of the closure of the issue. The margin money from non-Q1B category should be uniform for each category.

The bidding should be through an electronically-linked transparent facility of a RSE. All non-ASBA investors can revise their bids and the QIBs cannot withdraw their bids after the closure of the bidding.

The issue price should be fixed on the basis of the bids received and the number of securities to be offered. All the successful bidders whose bids are above the final/cut-off price would be entitled for allotment. The retail individual investor may bid at the cut-off rate.

The allotments to categories except anchor investors should be made proportionately and the unsubscribed portion in any category should be allocated as per the disclosures in the red-herring prospectus.

The **alternative method of book-building** issue, available only in case of further public offer, differs from the first in respect of determination of prices and allocation to non-anchor-investors on proportionate basis.

A floor price should be disclosed in the red-herring prospectus or announced at least one day before bid opening. The QIBs should bid above the floor price. Allotment of shares should be on price priority basis to the QIBs and on proportionate basis to the RIIs (retail individual investors)/non-institutional investors and employees at the floor price. The issuer may place **(a)** cap in terms of **(i)** number of securities **(ii)** percentage of its issued capital that may be allotted to a single bidder and **(b)** decide whether a bidder be allowed **(i)** to revise the bid upwards/ downwards in terms of price/quantity **(ii)** single/ multiple bids.

The securities may be offered at differential prices **(i)** to retail individual investors/shareholders or employees and **(ii)** in a composite issue on public-cum-rights basis. A price/price band (in draft prospectus) and floor price/price band (in red-herring prospectus) may be mentioned and the (one) price/specific coupon rate on CDIs may be determined at a later stage. The cap on the price band/coupon rate can be upto 120 per cent of the floor price/rate. The floor/final price should not be less than the face value. The face value of shares should be between ₹10 and 1 and ₹10 per share in case of issue prices being ₹500 and above and below ₹500 respectively.

The minimum promoters contribution in a public issue should be at least 20 per cent of the post-issue capital (in IPO)/proposed issue size/post issue capital (in FPO) and composite issue excluding the rights component. It should be by way of shares/subscription to convertible securities. In case of an IPO of CDIs without a prior public issue, it should be 20 per cent of the project cost in the form of shares and at least 20 per cent of the issue size should be from their own funds. Any excess contribution should be at the higher of the price applicable to preferential issues (**discussed later**) and the issue price. The contribution should be brought in at least one day before the issue opening date.

The specified securities held by promoters and others are not transferable. The lock-in of securities held by promoters in a public issue would be three years from the date of commencement of commercial production and allotment in public issue whichever is earlier, in respect of minimum contribution and one year in case of excess contribution. In case of an IPO, the entire pre-issue capital held by other investors would be locked-in for one year. Securities lent to a stabilising agent under green shoe option would be subject to lock-in for the remaining period from the date of their return to the lender. The lock-in securities may be pledged by the promoters with a bank/PFI for loan for financing the object(s) of the issue. Promoters as well non-promoter holders of lock-in securities can transfer them respectively to another promoter/person. The lock-in will continue till the remaining period with the transferee till its expiry.

The minimum/net offer to public should be 10 and 25 per cent of the post-issue capital (in an IPO) and issue size (in FPO). Reservations on competitive/proportionate basis out of the issue size (excluding promoters contribution and net offer to public) can be made: **(a)** in a book-built issue, to employees, shareholders and persons associated with the issuer as depositors/bondholders/subscribers to its services upto five per cent of the issue size, **(b)** in a non-book-built issue to employees and shareholders and **(c)** in case of FPO (other than a composite issue) to retail individual shareholders. The unsubscribed portion in a reserved category may be added to the other and the unsubscribed portion after the *inter se* adjustment should be added to the net offer to the public category. The allocation to the net offer to the public would be: **(a)** in a book-built issue **(i)** retail individual investors, at least 35 per cent, **(ii)** non-institutional investors, at least 15 per cent, **(iii)** QIBs, not more than 50 per cent of which five per cent to mutual funds who would also be eligible for allocation under the balance available for QIBs; upto 35 per cent of the QIB share to an anchor investor making an application for at least ₹10 crore, **(iv)** issuer who does not satisfy the five eligibility conditions, at least 50 per cent to QIBs, **(v)** where the issuer is required to allocate 60 per cent to the QIBs, to retail individual investors, 30 per cent and non-institutional investors, 10 per cent; **(b)** in a non-book built issue, at least 50 per cent to retail individual investors, the balance to other individual/institutional investors. An issuer may provide a safety net to purchase upto a maximum of 1,000 securities at the issue price per allottee within six months from the date of dispatch of security certificates/credit of demat amount.

An issuer may provide **green shoe option** for stabilisation of the post-listing price of its securities by allotting excess shares. Upto 15 per cent of the issue size may be borrowed by the stabilising agent from the promoters/pre-issue shareholders holding more than 5 per cent of the securities. The stabilisation would be available upto 30 days from the date on which permission for trading is given by the RSE. The securities should be returned within two working days after the stabilisation period. If the stabilising agent is unable to buy the securities from the market to the extent of the overallotment, the issuer would allot securities at the issue price to the extent of the shortfall within five days of the stabilisation period. These would be returned to the promoters/pre-issue shareholders in lieu of those borrowed from them.

> **Green shoe option** is the option for stabilisation of the post-listing price of securities in a public issue by allotting excess shares.

Unless otherwise provided, a public issue should be open for a minimum of three and a maximum of 10 days. The pre-issue advertisement should be made in one English/Hindi national daily and one regional language newspaper. The minimum application value is in the range of ₹5,000 — ₹7,500. Applicants should be invited in multiples of this value. The minimum application should be 25 per cent of the issue price. The entire issue price in an offer for sale should be brought in as application money. The allotment of securities to non-anchor investors should be on proportionate basis within the specified categories.

Rights Issues

The main elements of the framework of rights issues are record date, restrictions, letter/abridged letter of offer, pricing and subscription period, pre-issue advertisement and utilisation of funds.

To determine the eligibility of the shareholders, a record date should be announced after which a rights issue cannot be withdrawn. Rights issue can be made only after reserving shares of the same class in favour of holders of outstanding fully/partly CDIs in proportion to the convertible part. The abridged letter of offer together with the application form should be sent to all the existing shareholders at least three days before the opening of the issue. Applications can also be made on plain paper. Such applicants cannot renounce their rights. Applications by shareholders on application form as well as on plain paper would be rejected. The issue price should be determined before the record date and the issue should be open for a minimum of 15 days and a maximum of 30 days. The pre-issue advertisement in one English/Hindi/regional newspaper should be made at least three days before the date of opening of the issue. The funds collected can be utilised after the finalisation of the basis of allotment.

Preferential Issues

Preferential issue is an issue of specified securities by a listed issuer to any select group/ group of persons on a private placement basis.

Preferential issue is an issue of specified securities by a listed issuer to any select group/group of persons on a private placement basis. The main elements of such issues are: conditions, disclosures, allotments, tenure of convertible securities, pricing of shares payment of consideration, lock-in and transferability of lock-in securities/ warrants.

The conditions for preferential issues are a special resolution by the shareholders, all shares held by the proposed allottees are in demat form and the issuer **(i)** is in compliance with the conditions for continuous listing and **(ii)** has obtained the PAN of the allottees.

In the explanatory statement to the notice for the special resolution the issuer should disclose **(i)** objects of the issue, **(ii)** shareholding pattern before/after issue, **(iii)** the time-frame for the issue, **(iv)** identity of the proposed allottees, and **(v)** undertaking relating to recomputation of prices of the securities and lock-in till the payment of the recomputed prices by the allottees. The resolution should specify the relevant date to calculate the share prices. A copy of the certificate of the statutory auditors should also be placed before the general body meeting. The valuation of the assets other than cash in consideration for which shares are being issued should be done by an independent qualified valuer.

The allotment should be completed within 15 days from the date of passing the resolution failing which a fresh special resolution would be necessary.

The tenure of convertible securities should not exceed 18 months from the date of their allotment.

If shares have been listed for six months and more, they should be allotted at a price higher of the average of the weekly high and low of the quoted closing prices of the related shares during the **(i)** six months, **(ii)** two weeks preceding the relevant date. If listed for less than six months, the shares should be allotted at a price higher than **(a)** the average of the weekly high and low of the closing prices during **(i)** the shares have been listed and **(ii)** two weeks preceding the relevant date and **(b)** the price at which they were issued in the IPO. On completion of the six months, the price should be recomputed with reference to the average of the weekly high and low of the closing prices during those months and the allottees would have to pay the difference between the recomputed price and the allotment price. Preferential issues to the QIBs should be made not below the average of the weekly high and low of the closing prices of the related shares during the two weeks preceding the relevant date.

Full price of the securities other than warrants should be paid by the allottees at the time of allotment. At least 25 per cent of the price should be paid against each warrant on the date of their allotment and the balance 75 per cent on allotment of shares pursuant to the exercise of option.

The allotted securities to promoters and others should be locked-in for three and one year(s) respectively. Partly-paid shares would be locked-in for one year of becoming fully paid-up. The entire pre-preferential allotment shareholding of allottees would be lock-in from the relevant date upto six months from the date of such allotment.

The lock-in securities held by promoters may be transferred among them or new promoters/ persons in control of the issuer. The lock-in would continue for the remaining period with the transferee.

Qualified Institutional Placement

The **qualified institutional placement (QIP)** is the allotment of shares/CDIs/warrants and other convertible securities by a listed issuer to QIBs on private placement basis. The main elements of QIP are: conditions, placement document, pricing, allotment restrictions, minimum number of allottees, validity of the special resolution, tenure and transferability.

> **QIP** is the allotment of shares/ CDIs/ warrants and other convertible securities by a listed issuer to QIBs on private placement basis.

The QIP should satisfy the following conditions: **(i)** a special shareholders' resolution, **(ii)** listing of shares of the same class on a stock exchange for at least one year and **(iii)** is in compliance with the requirement of minimum public shareholding. It should be made on the basis of a placement document containing all the specified material information.

The QIP should be made at a price not below the average of the quoted weekly high and low of the closing prices of shares of the same class during the two weeks preceding the relevant date. Partly paid-up eligible securities should not be allotted. Equity shares allotted on exercise of option attached to a warrant should be fully paid-up.

A minimum of 10 per cent of the eligible securities should be allotted to mutual funds. Direct/ indirect allotment cannot be made to a promoter-QIB/a person related to the promoter. Bids by applicants cannot be withdrawn after the closure of the issue.

The minimum number of allottees for each placement should be a least two for issue size upto ₹250 crore and five for more than ₹250 crore. No single allottee can be allotted more than 50 per cent of the issue size.

The allotment of securities should be completed within 12 months from the date of the resolution. There should be a gap of at least six months between each placement in case of multiple placements. The aggregate of the QIP together with all the QIPs in one financial year should not exceed five times the networth of the issuer. The maximum tenure of convertible/exchangeable securities would be five years. The allottees can sell the securities for one year only on a recognised stock exchange.

SUMMARY

LO 22.1	Equity/ordinary share capital represents ownership capital and its owners—equity-holders/ordinary shareholders—share the reward and risk associated with the ownership of corporate enterprises.
	The ordinary shares have some special features in terms of the rights and claims of their holders: (i) residual claim to income, (ii) residual claim on assets, (iii) right to control, (iv) pre-emptive rights and (v) limited liability.
	A shareholder can (1) exercise (2) sell in the market and (3) renounce/forfeit his pre-emptive right partially/completely. He does not gain/lose from rights issues. However, he would suffer dilution of financial interest if he does not exercise his pre-emptive right.
	Ordinary share capital is a high-risk-reward source of finance for corporates. The shareholders share the risk, return and control associated with ownership of companies.
LO 22.2	The common conditions for public/rights issues are: general conditions, appointment of intermediaries, filing of offer document, documents submitted before issue opening, draft offer documents made public, issue pricing, fast track issues, issue opening, despatch of material, underwriting, minimum subscription, oversubscription, monitoring agency, manner of calls, allotment/refund, restrictions on further issues, additional requirements for issue of convertible debt instruments (CDIs), rollover, conversion, issue of CDIs for financing and alteration of rights of holders of securities.

LO 22.2

The provisions as to public issues are: eligibility requirements, pricing, promoters contribution, lock-in and minimum offer to public/reservations.

The main elements of the framework of rights issues are record date, restrictions, letter/abridged letter of offer, pricing and subscription period, pre-issue advertisement and utilisation of funds.

Preferential issue is an issue of specified securities by a listed issuer to any select group/group of persons on a private placement basis. The main elements of such issues are: conditions, disclosures, allotments, tenure of convertible securities, pricing of shares payment of consideration, lock-in and transferability of lock-in securities/warrants.

The qualified institutional placement (QIP) is the allotment of shares/CDIs/warrants and other convertible securities by a listed issuer to QIBs on private placement basis. The main elements of QIP are: conditions, placement document, pricing, allotment restrictions, minimum number of allottees, validity of the special resolution, tenure and transferability.

SOLVED PROBLEMS

P.22.1 Delhi Manufacturers (DMs) intend to raise ₹40,00,000 of equity capital through a rights offering. It currently has 10,00,000 shares outstanding which have been most recently selling/trading for ₹50 and ₹56 per share. In consultation with the SEBI Caps, the DM has set the subscription price for the rights at ₹50 per share. LO 22.1 LOD M

Required

1. Determine the number of new shares DM should sell to raise the desired amount of capital.
2. Ascertain the number of shares each right would entitle a holder of one share to purchase. How many additional shares can an investor who holds 10,000 shares of DM purchase?
3. Compute the theoretical value of a right if the current market price is ₹54 **with rights** and the subscription price is ₹50 for both shares selling **with rights** and shares selling **ex-rights** (i.e. the value of the right is not included in the market price of shares).

Solution

1. Number of new shares = $\dfrac{₹40{,}00{,}000 \text{ (to be raised)}}{₹50 \text{ (subscription price)}}$ = 80,000 shares

2. Number of shares per right = $\dfrac{80{,}000 \text{ (new shares)}}{10{,}00{,}000 \text{ (shares outstanding)}}$ = 0.08 share

   Additional shares = 0.08 shares/right × 1 right/share × 10,000 shares = 800 shares

3. Theoretical value of right with rights, Rw:

$$R_w = \frac{M_w - S}{N + 1}$$

Where

R_w = theoretical value of a right when the share is selling with rights/cum rights

M_w = market value of the stock with rights/cum-rights

S = subscription price of the shares

N = number of rights needed to purchase one share

Substituting the values,

$$R_w = \frac{₹54 - ₹50}{12.5^{@} + 1} = \frac{₹4}{13.5} = ₹0.296$$

$^{@}N = \dfrac{1}{0.08}$ = 12.5 rights need to purchase one new share.

Theoretical value of right ex-right,

$$R_e = \frac{M_e - S}{N}$$

Where

R_e = theoretical value of a right when the share is trading **ex-right**
M_e = market value of shares trading ex-right.

Substituting the values,

$$\frac{₹53.704^{@@} - ₹50}{12.5} = \frac{₹3.704}{12.5} = ₹0.296$$

@@ $M_w - R_w$ = ₹54 – ₹0.296 = ₹53.704

The investor would receive at least the theoretical value of ₹0.296 per right × 10,000 shares = ₹2,960. If he expects the price of DMs shares to increase during the period the rights are exercisable, the market value of the rights would be more than their theoretical value.

P.22.2 The Standard Company (SC) wishes to raise ₹30,00,000 through a rights offering. It has currently 2,40,000 shares outstanding which have been most recently trading between ₹106 and ₹116 per share. On the advice of the SBI Caps, the SC has set the subscription price for the rights at ₹100 per share on the assumption that they will be fully subscribed. LO 22.1 LOD M

Required

(a) How many new shares should SC sell to raise the desired amount?
(b) How many shares will each right entitle a holder of one share to purchase?
(c) What is the theoretical value of a right if the current market price is ₹109 with rights and the subscription price is ₹100? Answer for both shares selling with rights and shares selling ex-rights?

Solution

(a) Number of new shares $= \frac{₹30,00,000}{₹100}$ = 30,000 shares

(b) Number of shares per right $= \frac{2,40,000}{30,000}$ = 8, that is, 8 shares rights are needed to purchase a new share at ₹100. Each right entitles its holder to purchase one- right of a share.

(c) Value of a right, with rights

$$= \frac{₹109 - ₹100}{8 + 1} = ₹1$$

Value of a right, ex-right

$$= \frac{₹108^{@} - ₹100}{8} = ₹1$$

@ ₹109 – ₹1

Thus, the theoretical value of the right when the share is selling with rights or ex-rights is the same.

REVIEW QUESTIONS

LOD: Easy

RQ.22.1 Fill in the following blanks with appropriate answers: [LO 22.1,2]

(i) An equity shareholder can renounce his ________ to subscribe to the additional issue partially/completely.

(ii) Ordinary share capital is a high-risk ____________ source of finance for investors.
(iii) Companies can freely ____________ their share issues.
(iv) ____________ is a process to elicit demand for, and price of, securities.
(v) The entire net offer should be compulsorily ____________ by the syndicate members/book runners(s).
(vi) The book runner(s) and the issuing company would determine the ____________ price on the ____________ received through the syndicate members.
(vii) A company making an IPO can avail of the ____________ option.
(viii) Under the green shoe option the amount of the shares to be over-allotted can be ____________ of the issue size out of the shares borrowed from the promoters.
(ix) A listed company can raise funds upto ____________ times of its networth through qualified institutional placement.
(x) A maximum of ____________ per cent of the issue size can be allotted to one single QIB/allottee.

[Answers: (i) pre-emptive right (ii) high-reward (iii) price (iv) Book-building (v) underwritten (vi) issue, bid (vii) green shoe (viii) upto 15 per cent (ix) five and (x) 50]

RQ.22.2 What are the different types of equity/ordinary share capital? [LO 22.1]
RQ.22.3 Explain briefly preferential issues of securities. [LO 22.2]

LOD: Medium

RQ.22.4 Discuss briefly the features of equity shares as sources of long-term finance. [LO 22.1]
RQ.22.5 Discuss the merits and demerits of equity shares. [LO 22.1]
RQ.22.6 Give a brief account of eligibility norms for **(i)** IPOs/offer for sale by unlisted companies and **(ii)** public issues by listed companies. [LO 22.2]
RQ.22.7 What are the requirements relating to **(i)** promoters' contribution and **(ii)** lock-in in public issues? [LO 22.2]
RQ.22.8 Explain the main features of the 75 per cent book-building process. [LO 22.2]
RQ.22.9 Discuss the offer to public through book-building process. [LO 22.2]
RQ.22.10 Explain the allocation/allotment in book-building mechanism. [LO 22.2]
RQ.22.11 Explain and illustrate green shoe option. [LO 22.2]
RQ.22.12 What is rights? Compare the value of rights when a share is selling with/cum-rights with its ex-rights value. [LO 22.1]
RQ.22.13 Hypothetical Ltd (HL) is interested in raising ₹18,00,000 of new equity capital through a rights issue/offering. Its current capital consists of 9,00,000 shares. It would set the subscription price at ₹50 and anticipates that the shares would sell for ₹58 with rights. [LO 22.1]

Required

1. Number of shares the HM should sell to raise the desired amount of funds.
2. Number of rights needed to purchase one share at the subscription price.
3. Additional shares an investor holding 96,000 shares of HL can purchase on exercising his rights.
4. Theoretical value of a right when the share sells (i) with/cum-rights and (ii) ex-rights.
5. Amount the investor holding 96,000 shares of HL would get for his rights immediately after the share goes **ex-rights**.

LOD: Difficult

RQ.22.14 Explain the pre-emptive rights of the ordinary shareholders. How is their financial interest affected by the issue of rights shares? [LO 22.1]
RQ.22.15 How can issues of securities be priced by the issuing companies? [LO 22.2]

RQ.22.16 Define book-building. What kind of options are available to companies for book-building mechanism? [LO 22.2]

ANSWERS

22.13
1. 36,000 shares
2. 25 shares @ ₹50
3. 3,840 shares
4. Cum-rights ₹0.31;
   Ex-rights ₹0.31
5. ₹29,760

Scan the QR Code to access comprehensive solutions to all numerical review questions and additional material.

CHAPTER

23 Term Loans, Debentures/Bonds and Securitisation

LEARNING OBJECTIVES

LO 23.1	Understand the characteristics of term-loans, positive and negative covenants in a loan agreement, loan amortisation and the procedure associated with a term-loan
LO 23.2	Describe the basic characteristics of corporate debentures/bonds/notes, general features of a debenture issue, bond refunding options, innovative debt instrument, the procedure of issuing debt instruments and rating of debt instruments
LO 23.3	Define securitisation, describe the general features of securitisation process, credit enhancement, parties to a securitisation transaction, asset characteristics and types of securitised assets

INTRODUCTION

Apart from owners share capital, corporate enterprises raise long-term funds from creditors in the form of term loans, debentures, bonds and so on. The bulk of term loans raised by the corporates was provided earlier by the financial institutions such as IDBI, ICICI and IFCI. Banks have entered term-lending business in the last few years, particularly in the infrastructure/core sector. Bonds/ debentures have emerged as substantial source of debt finance to corporates in India in the context of **(i)** absence of term loan support by financial institutions, **(ii)** freedom to corporates to design debt instruments, **(iii)** withdrawal of interest ceilings on debt instruments, **(iv)** credit rating of debt instruments, and **(v)** setting up of the wholesale debt market (WDM) segment by the NSE. Securitisation of loan portfolios is also emerging as a popular instrument in the corporate debt market in India. This Chapter focuses on term loans, debentures/bonds and securitisation. The main points are summarised by way of recapitulation.

LO 23.1 TERM LOANS

Term loans are also known as term/**project finance**. The primary source of such loans are financial institutions. Commercial banks also provide term finance in a limited way. The financial institutions provide project finance for new projects as also for expansion/diversification and modernisation whereas the bulk of term loans extended by banks is in the form of working capital term loan to finance the working capital gap. Though they are permitted to finance infrastructure projects on a long-term basis, the quantum of such financing is marginal.

> **Term (long-term) loan** is a loan made by a bank/financial institution to a business having an initial maturity of more than 1 year.

Features of Term Loans

> **Secured loan** is a loan that has specific assets pledged as collateral.

Maturity The maturity period of term loans is typically longer in case of sanctions by financial institutions in the range of 6-10 years in comparison to 3-5 years of bank advances. However, they are rescheduled to enable corporates/borrowers tide over temporary financial exigencies.

Negotiated The term loans are negotiated loans between the borrowers and the y are akin to private placement of debentures in contrast to their public offering to

> **Collateral (secondary)** involves the items used by a borrower to back up a loan; any asset against which a lender has a legal claim if the borrower defaults on some provisions of the loan agreement.

term loans are **secured**. While the assets financed by term loans serve as primary security, all the other present and future assets of the company provide **collateral/ secondary** security for the term loan. Generally, all the present as well as the future immovable properties of the borrower constitute a general mortgage/ first equitable mortgage/floating charges for the entire institutional loan including commitment charges, interest, liquidated damages and so on. They are additionally secured by hypothetication of all movable properties subject to prior charge in favour of banks in respect of working capital finance/advance.

> **Restrictive covenants** are contractual clauses in loan agreements that place certain operating and financial constraints on the borrower.

Covenants

Negative To protect their interest, the financial institutions reinforce the asset security stipulation with a number of restrictive terms and conditions. These are known as **covenants**. They are both positive/affirmative and negative in the sense of what the borrower should and should not do in the conduct of its operations and fall broadly into four sets as respectively related to assets, liabilities, cashflows and control. *Some negetive covenants are discussed as under:*

Asset-Related Covenants are intended to ensure the maintenance of a minimum asset base by the borrowers. Included in this set of covenants are:

- Maintenance of working capital position in terms of a minimum current ratio,
- Restriction on creation of further charge on asset,
- Ban on sale of fixed assets without the lenders concurrence/approval.

Liability-Related Covenants may, *inter alia*, include:

- Restrain on the incurrence of additional debt/repayment of existing loan, say, without the concurrence/prior approval of the lender/financial institution,
- Reduction in debt-equity ratio by issue of additional capital, and
- Prohibition on disposal of promoters shareholding.

Cashflow Related Covenants which are intended to restrain cash outflows of the borrowers may include:

- Restriction on new projects/expansion without prior approval of the financial institution,
- Limitation on dividend payment to a certain amount/rate and prior approval of the financial institutions for declaration of higher amount/rate,
- Arrangement to bring additional funds as unsecured loans/deposits to meet overrun/shortfall, and
- Ceiling on managerial salary and perks.

Control Related Covenants aim at ensuring competent management for the borrowers. This set of covenants may include

- Boroadbasing of board of directors and finalisation of management set-up in consultation with the financial institution,
- Effective organisational changes and appointment of suitable professional staff, and
- Appointment of nominee directors to represent the financial institutions and safeguard their interests.

Positive In addition to the foregoing negative covenants, certain positive/affirmative covenants stating what the borrowing firm should do during the term of a loan are also included in a loan agreement. They provide, *inter alia*, for **(i)** furnishing of periodical reports/financial statements to the lenders, **(ii)** maintenance of a minimum level of working capital, **(iii)** creation of sinking fund for redemption of debt and **(iv)** maintenance of certain net worth.

Repayment Schedule/Loan Amortisation The term loans have to be amortised according to predetermined schedule. The payment/repayment has two components: **(i)** interest and **(ii)** repayment of principal.

The interest component of loan amortisation is a legally enforceable contractual obligation. The borrowers have to pay a commitment charge on the unutilised amount. The interest on term loans by the financial institutions, subject to a minimum prime lending/floor rate (PLR), is risk-related and varies with the credit risk of the borrower. In case of default in respect of both the interest and principal components, liquidated damages/penal interest at a specified rate for the period of default on the default amount has to be paid.

Typically, the principal is repayable over 6-10 years period after an initial grace period of 1-2 years. Whereas the mode of repayment of term loans is equal semi-annual instalments in case of institutional borrowings, the term loans from banks are repayable in equal quarterly instalments. With this type of loan amortisation pattern, the total debt servicing burden declines over time, the interest burden declining and principal repayment remaining constant. In other words, the common practice in India to amortise loan is repayment of principal in equal instalments (semi-annual/annual) and payment of interest on the unpaid/outstanding loans. A loan amortisation schedule is illustrated in Table 23.1.

TABLE 23.1 Loan Amortisation Schedule (Equal Principal Repayment)

(₹ thousands)

Year	*Beginning loan*	*Principal repayment*	*Interest (0.14)*	*Loan payment*	*Ending loan*
(1)	*(2)*	*(3)*	*(4)*	*(5)*	*(6)*
1	60.00	7.50	8.40	15.90	52.50
2	52.50	7.50	7.35	14.85	45.00
3	45.00	7.50	6.30	13.80	37.50
4	37.50	7.50	5.25	12.75	30.00
5	30.00	7.50	4.20	11.70	22.50
6	22.50	7.50	3.15	10.65	15.00
7	15.00	7.50	2.10	9.60	7.50
8	7.60	7.50	1.05	8.55	0.00

The debt servicing/loan amortisation pattern involving equal instalment (interest + repayment of principal) is portrayed in Table 23.2.

TABLE 23.2 Loan Amortisation Schedule (Equal Instalment)

Year	*Beginning loan*	*Payment instalment*@	*Interest (0.14)*	*Principal repayment [3 – 4]*	*Ending loan [2 – 5]*
(1)	*(2)*	*(3)*	*(4)*	*(5)*	*(6)*
1	₹60,000	₹12,934	₹8,400	₹4,535	₹55,466
2	55,466	12,934	7,776	5,168	50,298
3	50,298	12,934	7,042	5,896	44,406
4	44,406	12,934	6,216	6,718	37,688
5	37,688	12,934	5,276	7,658	30,030
6	30,030	12,934	4,204	8,730	21,300
7	21,300	12,934	2,982	9,952	11,348
8	11,348	12,934	1,588	11,346	0

@ Payment instalment = (₹60,000/PVIFA 8,14) = (₹60,000/4.6389) = ₹12,934

Evaluation

Term loans have merits as well demerits both for the borrower and the lenders.

From the perspective of borrowers, term loan offer all the advantages and disadvantages associated with debenture financing. An additional demerit is that term loan contracts contain restrictive covenants restricting managerial freedom. The right of lenders to nominate directors on the board of the borrowing company may further restrict managerial discretion.

Similarly, the term loans provide all the advantages and disadvantages of debenture financing to the lending institutions together with the additional benefit of restrictive covenants to protect their interests. However, term loans are not represented by negotiable securities. Debt securitisation would go a long way in removing this limitation of term loans *vis-a-vis* debentures.

To conclude, *term loans carry low cost and involve high risk. There is no adverse effect on control but there is moderate restraint on managerial freedom.*

Obtaining a Term Loan

Term Loan Procedure The procedure associated with a term loan involves the following principal steps:

The borrower submits an application form which seeks comprehensive information about the project. The application form covers the following aspects: **(i)** promoters' background, **(ii)** particulars of the industrial concern, **(iii)** particulars of the project (capacity, process, technical arrangements, management, location, land and buildings, plant and machinery, raw materials, effluents, labour, housing, and schedule of implementation), **(iv)** cost of project, **(v)** means of financing, **(vi)** marketing and selling arrangements, **(vii)** profitability and cash flow, **(viii)** economic considerations, and **(ix)** Government consents.

When the application is received, an officer of the financial institution reviews it to ascertain whether it is complete for processing. If it is incomplete, the borrower is asked to provide the required additional information. When the application is considered complete, the financial institution prepares a 'Flash Report' which is essentially a summarisation of the loan application. On the basis of the 'Flash Report', it is decided whether the project justifies a detailed appraisal or not.

The detailed appraisal of the project covers the marketing, technical, financial, managerial, and economic aspects (discussed in detail later). The appraisal memorandum is normally prepared within two months after site inspection. Based on that, a decision is taken whether the project will be accepted or not.

If the project is accepted, a financial letter of sanction is issued to the borrower communicating the assistance sanctioned and the terms and conditions relating thereto.

On receiving the letter of sanction from the financial institution, the borrowing unit convenes its board meeting at which the terms and conditions associated with the letter of sanction are accepted and an appropriate resolution is passed to that effect. The acceptance of the terms and conditions has to be conveyed to the financial institution within a stipulated period.

The financial institution, after receiving the letter of acceptance from the borrower, sends the draft of the agreement to the borrower to be executed by authorised persons and properly stamped as per the Indian Stamp Act, 1899. The agreement, properly executed and stamped, along with other documents as required by the financial institution, must be returned to it. Once the financial institution also signs the agreement, it becomes ineffective.

Periodically, the borrower is required to submit information on the physical progress of the projects, financial status of the project, arrangements made for financing the project, contribution made by the promoters, projected funds flow statement, compliance with the various statutory requirements, and fulfilment of the predisbursement conditions. Based on the information provided by the borrower, the financial institution will determine the amount of term loan to be disbursed from time to time. Before the entire term loan is disbursed, the borrower must fully comply with all terms and conditions of the loan agreement.

The term loans are secured through the first mortgage, by way of deposit of title deeds, of immovable properties and hypothecation of movable properties. As the creation of mortgage, particularly in the case of land, tends to be a time consuming process, the institutions permit interim disbursements against alternate security (in the form of guarantees by the promoters). The mortgage, however, has to be created within a year from the date of the first disbursement. Otherwise, the borrower has to pay an additional charge of 1 per cent interest.

Monitoring of the project is done at the implementation stage as well as the operational stage. During the implementation stage, the project is monitored through: **(i)** regular reports, furnished by the promoters, which provide information about placement of orders, construction of buildings, procurement of plant, installation of plant and machinery, trial production, and so on, **(ii)** periodic site visits, **(iii)** discussion with promoters, bankers, suppliers, creditors, and other connected with the project, **(iv)** progress reports submitted by the nominee directors, and **(v)** audited accounts of the company.

During the operational stage, the project is monitored with the help of (i) quarterly progress report on the project, (ii) site inspection, (iii) reports of nominee directors, and (iv) comparison of performance with promise.

The most important aspect of monitoring, of course, is the recovery of dues represented by interest and principal repayment.

Project Appraisal Financial institutions appraise a project from the marketing, technical, financial, economic, and managerial angles. The principal issues considered and the criteria employed in such appraisal are discussed below.

Market Appraisal The importance of the potential market and the need to develop a suitable marketing strategy cannot be over-emphasised. Hence, efforts are made to **(i)** examine the reasonableness of the demand projections, **(ii)** assess the adequacy of the marketing infrastructure in terms of promotional effort, distribution network, transport facilities, stock levels and so on, and **(iii)** judge the knowledge, experience, and competence of the key marketing personnel.

Technical Appraisal The technical review done by the financial institutions focuses mainly on the following aspects: **(i)** product mix, **(ii)** capacity, **(iii)** process of manufacture, **(iv)** engineering know-how and technical collaboration, **(v)** raw materials and consumables, **(vi)** location and site, **(vii)** building, **(viii)** plant and equipment, **(ix)** manpower requirements, and **(x)** break-even point.

Financial Appraisal The financial appraisal seeks to assess the following:

Reasonableness of the Estimate of Capital Cost While assessing the capital cost estimates, efforts are made to ensure that **(i)** padding or under-estimation of costs is avoided, **(ii)** specification of machinery is proper, **(iii)** proper quotation are obtained from potential suppliers, **(iv)** contingencies are provided, and **(v)** inflation factors are considered.

Reasonableness of the Estimate of Working Results The estimate of working results is sought to be based on **(i)** a realistic market demand forecast, **(ii)** price computations for inputs and outputs that are based on current quotations and inflationary factors, **(iii)** an approximate time schedule for capacity utilisation, and **(iv)** cost projections that distinguish between fixed and variable costs.

Adequacy of Rate of Return The general norms for financial desirability are as follows: **(i)** internal rate of return, 15 per cent, **(ii)** return on investment, 20-25 per cent after tax, **(iii)** debt-service coverage ratio, 1.5 to 2. In applying these norms, however, a certain degree of flexibility is shown on the basis of the nature of the project, the risks inherent in the project, and the status of the promoter.

Appropriateness of the Financing Pattern The institutions consider the following in assessing the financial pattern: **(i)** a general debt-equity ratio norm of 1.5:1, **(ii)** a requirement that promoters should contribute a certain percentage of the project cost, **(iii)** stock exchange listing requirements, and **(iv)** the means of the promoter and his capacity to contribute a reasonable share of the project finance.

Managerial Appraisal In order to judge the managerial capability of the promoters, the following aspects are considered:

Resourcefulness This is judged in terms of the prior experience of the promoters, the progress achieved in organising various aspects of the project, and the skill with which the project is presented.

Understanding This is assessed in terms of the credibility of the project plan (including, *inter alia*, the organisation structure, the staffing plan, the estimated costs, the financing pattern, the assessment of various inputs, and the marketing programme) and the details furnished to the financial institutions.

Commitment This is gauged by the resources (financial, managerial, material, and other) applied to the project and the zeal with which the objectives of the project, short-term as well as long-term, are pursued. Managerial review also involves an assessment of the calibre of the key technical and managerial personnel working on the projects, the schedule for training them, and the remuneration structure for rewarding and motivating them.

LO 23.2 DEBENTURES/BONDS/NOTES

Debenture/bond is a debt instrument indicating that a company has borrowed certain sum of money and promises to repay it in future under clearly defined terms.

Akin to a promissory note, **debentures/bonds** represent creditorship securities and debenture-holders are long-term creditors of the company. As a secured instrument, it is a promise to pay interest and repay principal at stipulated times. In contrast to equity capital which is a variable income (dividend) security, the debentures/notes are fixed income (interest) security.

Attributes

As a long-term source of borrowing, debentures have some contrasting features compared to equities.

Trust (bond) indenture is a complex and lengthy legal document stating the conditions under which a bond has been issued.

Trust Indenture When a debenture is sold to investing public, a trustee is appointed through an **indenture/trust deed**. It is a legal agreement between the issuing company and the trustee who is usually a financial institution/bank/ insurance company/firm of attorneys. The trust deed provides the specific terms of agreement such as description of debentures, rights of debenture-holders, rights of the issuing company and responsibilities of the **trustee**. The trustee is responsible to ensure that the borrower/company fulfills all its contractual obligations.

Trustee is a bank/financial institution/ insurance company/ firm of attorneys that acts as the third party to a bond/debenture indenture to ensure that the issuer does not default on its contractual responsibilities to the bond/ debentureholders.

Interest The debentures carry a fixed (coupon) rate of interest, the payment of which is legally binding/enforceable. The debenture interest is tax-deductible and is payable annually/semi-annually/quarterly. Some public sector undertakings issue tax-free bonds the income from which is exempted from tax in the hands of the investors. A company is free to choose the coupon rate which may be fixed or floated, being determined in relation to some benchmark rate. It is also related to the credit rating of the debenture as an instrument.

Debenture redemption reserve is a requirement in a debenture indenture providing for the systematic retirement of debentures/bonds prior to their maturity.

Maturity It indicates the length of time for redemption of par value. A company can choose the maturity period, though the redemption period for non-convertible debentures is typically 7-10 years. The redemption of debentures can be accomplished in either of two ways: (i) debentures redemption reserve (sinking fund) and (ii) call and put (buy-back) provision.

Debenture Redemption Reserve (DRR) A **DRR** has to be created for the redemption of all debentures with a maturity period exceeding

18 months equivalent to at least 50 per cent of the amount of issue/redemption before commencement of redemption.

Call and Put Provision The call/buy-back provision provides an option to the issuing company to redeem the debentures at a specified price before maturity. The **call price** may be more than the par/face value by usually 5 per cent, the difference being **call premium**. The put option is a right to the debenture-holder to seek redemption at specified time at predetermined prices.

Call price is the stated price at which a bond may be repurchased by use of a call feature prior to maturity.

Call premium is the amount by which a bonds' call price exceeds its par value.

Security Debentures are generally secured by a charge on the present and future immovable assets of the company by way of an equitable mortgage.

Convertibility Apart from pure non-convertible debentures (NCDs), debentures can also be converted into equity shares at the option of the debenture-holders. The conversion ratio and the period during which conversion can be affected are specified at the time of the issue of the debenture itself. The convertible debentures may be fully convertible (FCDs) or partly convertible (PCDs). The FCDs carry interest rates lower than the normal rate on NCDs; they may even have a zero rate of interest. The PCDs have two parts: (a) convertible part, (b) non-convertible part. Typically, the convertible portion is converted into equity share at a specified premium after a specified date from the date of allotment, while the non-convertible portion is payable/redeemable in specified equal instalments on the expiry of specified years from the date of allotment.

Credit Rating To ensure timely payment of interest and redemption of principal by a borrower, all debentures must be compulsorily rated by one or more of the four credit rating agencies, namely, Crisil, Icra, Care and FITCH India.

Claim on Income and Assets The payment of interest and repayment of principal is a contractual obligation enforceable by law. Failure/default would lead to bankruptcy of the company. The claim of debenture-holders on income and assets ranks *pari passu* with other secured debt and higher than that of shareholders–preference as well as equity.

Evaluation

The merits and demerits of debentures as a source of long-term funds from the point of view of the company and investors/debenture-holders are as follows:

Advantages The advantages for company are **(i)** lower cost due to lower risk and tax-deductibility of interest payments, **(ii)** no dilution of control as debentures do not carry voting rights. For the investors, debentures offer stable return, have a fixed maturity, are protected by the debenture trust deed and enjoy preferential claim on the assets in relation to shareholders.

Disadvantages The disadvantages for the company are the restrictive covenants in the trust deed, legally enforceable contractual obligations in respect of interest payments and repayments, increased financial risk and the associated high cost of equity. The debenture-holders have no voting rights and debenture prices are vulnerable to change in interest rates.

To summarise, *debentures, as long-term source of funds, have low cost, do not dilute control, involve high risk and put some restraint on managerial freedom.*

Innovative Debt Instruments

In order to improve the attractiveness of bonds/debentures, some new features are added. As a result, a wide range of innovative debt instruments have emerged in India in recent years. Some of the important ones among these are discussed below.

Zero Interest Bonds/Debentures (ZIB/D) Also known as zero coupon bonds/debentures, ZIBs do not carry any explicit/coupon rate of interest. They are sold at a discount from their maturity value. The difference between the face value of the bond and the acquisition cost is the gain/return to the investors. The implicit rate of return/interest on such bonds can be computed by Equation 23.1.

$$\text{Acquisition price} = \text{Maturity (face) value}/(1 + i)^n \tag{23.1}$$

Where i = rate of interest, and n = maturity period (years)

Deep Discount Bond (DDB) A deep discount bond is a form of ZIB. It is issued at a deep/steep discount over its face value. It implies that the interest (coupon) rate is far less than the yield to maturity. The DDB appreciates to its face value over the maturity period.

The DDBs are being issued by the public financial institutions in India, namely, IDBI, SIDBI and so on. For instance, IBDI sold in 1992 a DDB of face value of ₹1 lakh at a deep discount price of ₹2,700 with a maturity period of 25 years. If the investor could hold the DDB for 25 years, the annualised rate of return would work out to 15.54 per cent. The investor had the option to withdraw (put option) at the end of every five years with a specified maturity/deemed face value ranging between ₹5,700 (after 5 years) and ₹50,000 (after 20 years), the implicit annual rate of interest being 16.12 and 15.71 per cent respectively. The investors could also sell the DDBs in the market. The IBDI had also the option to redeem them (call option) at the end of every 5 years presumably to take advantage of prevailing interest rates. A second series of DDBs was issued by the IDBI in 1996 with a face value of ₹2 lakh and a maturity period of 25 years, the deep discount issue price being ₹5,300.

The merit of DDBs/ZIDs is that they enable the issuing companies to conserve cash during their maturity. They protect the investors against the reinvestment risk to the extent the implicit interest on such bonds is automatically reinvested at a rate equal to its yield to maturity. However, they are exposed to high repayment risk as they entail a balloon payment on maturity.

Secured Premium Notes (SPNs) The SPN is a secured debenture redeemable at a premium over the face value/purchase price. It resembles a ZIB. There is a lock-in period for SPN during which no interest is paid. The holder has the option to sell back the SPN to the issuing company at par after the lock-in-period. The redemption is made in instalments. The SPN is a tradeable instrument. A typical example is the SPN issued by TISCO in 1992. Its salient features were:

- Each SPN had a face value of ₹300. No interest would accrue during the first year after allotment.
- During years 4-7, principal will be repaid in annual instalment of ₹75. In addition, ₹75 will be paid each year as interest and redemption premium. The investor could choose a mix of low interest/high premium or high interest/low premium from three options: (i) interest, ₹37.5, premium, ₹37.50; (ii) interest, ₹25 and premium, ₹50 and (iii) interest, ₹50 and premium, ₹25.
- A warrant was attached to the SPN entitling the holder to acquire one equity share for cash by payment of ₹100. The option could be exercised between first year and one-and-a-half year after allotment by which time the SPN will be fully paid up.
- The holder was given an option to sell back the SPN at the par value of ₹300.

Although the SPN is akin to a ZIB to the extent it has no coupon rate of interest, the interest payment and principal repayment are spread over a period of 4 years whereas in case of ZIBs the entire payment is made in lump sum on maturity.

The before tax rate of return on the SPN = 13.65 per cent, that is,

$$300 = \frac{0}{(1+r)} + \frac{0}{(1+r)^2} + \frac{0}{(1+r)^3} + \frac{150}{(1+r)^4} + \frac{150}{(1+r)^5} + \frac{150}{(1+r)^6} + \frac{150}{(1+r)^6}$$

Floating Rate Bonds (FRBs) The interest on such bonds is not fixed. It is floating and is linked to a benchmark rate such as interest on treasury bills, bank rate, maximum rate on term deposits. It is typically a certain percentage point higher than the benchmark rate. The prices of FRBs tend to be fairly stable and close to par value in comparison with fixed interest bonds. They provide a protection against inflation risk to investors, particularly banks and financial institutions.

Call provision is a provision/feature that gives the issuers the opportunity to repurchase bonds at a stated price prior to maturity.

Callable/Puttable Bonds/Debentures/Bond Refunding Beginning from 1992 when the Industrial Development Bank of India issued bonds with **call features**, several callable/puttable bonds have emerged in the country in recent years. The call provisions provide flexibility to the company to redeem them prematurely. Generally, firms issue bonds presumably at lower rate of interest when market conditions are favourable to redeem such bonds. In other words, the firm refunds its debt.

Evaluation The bond refunding decision can be analysed as a capital budgeting decision. **If the present value of the stream of net cash savings exceeds the initial cash outlay, the debt should be refunded**.

***Example* 23.1**

The 22 per cent outstanding bonds of the Bharat Industries Ltd (BIL) amount to ₹50 crores, with a remaining maturity of 5 years. It can now issue fresh bonds of 5 year maturity at a coupon rate of 20 per cent. The existing bonds can be refunded at a premium (call premium) of 5 per cent. The flotation costs (issue expenses + discount) on new bonds are expected to be 5 per cent. The unamortised portion of the issue expenses on existing bonds is 1.5 crore. They would be written off as soon as the existing bonds are called/refunded.

If the BIL is in 35 per cent tax bracket, would you advise it to call the bond?

Solution

(Amount in ₹ crore)

Annual net cash savings (Working note 2)	0.71
PVIFA (10,13) (Working note 3)	3.517
Present value of annual net cash savings	2.497
Less: Initial outlay ((Working note 1)	3.600
NPV (bond refunding)	(1.103)

It is not advisable to call the bond as the NPV is negative.

Working Notes

(1) (a) Cost of calling/refunding existing bonds			
Face value		50.0	
Plus: Call premium (5 per cent)		2.5	52.5
(b) Net proceeds of new bonds			
Gross proceeds		50.0	
Less: Flotation costs		2.5	47.5
(c) Tax savings on expenses			
Call premium	2.5		
Plus: Unamortised issue costs	1.5		
	4.0 × (0.35 tax)		1.40
Initial outlay [(1a) – (1b) – (1c)]			3.60

(2) (a) Annual net cash outflow on existing bonds		
Interest expenses	11.00	
Less: Tax savings on interest expenses and amortisation of issue costs : 0.35 [11.0 + (1.5/5)]	3.96	7.04
(b) Annual net cash outflow on new bonds		
Interest expenses	10.00	
Less: Tax savings on interest expenses and amortisation of issue costs : 0.35 [11.0 + (2.5/5)]	3.67	6.33
Annual net cash savings [(2a) – (2b)]		0.71

(3) Present value interest factor of 5 year annuity, using a 13 per cent after tax [0.20 (1 – 0.35)] cost of new bonds = 3.517

Rating of Debt Instruments

Credit rating is, essentially, the symbolic indicator of the current opinion of the rating agency on the relative ability and willingness of the issuer of a debt instrument to meet the debt service obligations as and when they arise. It provides a relative ranking of the credit quality of debt instruments or their grading according to investment qualities. In other words, credit rating provides a simple system of gradation by which the relative capacities of companies (borrowers) to make timely payment of interest and repayment of principal on a particular type of debt instrument can be noted.

Credit rating is a symbolic indicator of the relative ability of the issuer of the debt instruments to meet obligations when due.

Credit rating, however, is neither a general purpose evaluation of a corporate entity nor an overall assessment of the credit risk likely to be involved in all the debts instruments contracted or to be contracted by such issues. A rating is specific to a debt instrument and is intended to grade different and specific instruments in terms of the credit risk associated with the particular instruments. Although it is an opinion expressed by an independent professional organisation, on the basis of a detailed study of all the relevant factors, the rating does not amount to any recommendation to buy, hold or sell an instrument as it does not take into consideration factors such as market prices, personal risk preferences of an investor and such other considerations, which may influence an investment decision.

As a fee-based financial advisory service, credit rating is, obviously, extremely useful to investors, corporates (borrowers), banks, and financial institutions. For the investors, it is an indicator expressing the underlying credit quality of a (debt) issue programme. The investor is fully informed about the company as any effect of changes in business/economic conditions on the company is evaluated and published regularly by the rating agencies.

The corporate borrower can raise funds at a cheaper rate with a good rating. It minimises the role of 'name recognition' and lesser-known companies can also approach the market on the basis of their rating. The fund ratings are useful to the banks and other financial institutions when they decide on lending and investment strategies.

Although credit rating has been a long-established part of the financial mechanism abroad, it is of relatively recent origin in the country. The first raging agency, Credit Rating Information Services of India Ltd (CRISIL), was started in 1988. Initially, it played a rather subdued role presumably because the institutional investors did not require the wisdom of a rating agency. In a changed scenario where corporates are increasingly dependent on the public, the removal of restrictions on interest rates and the stipulation of a mandatory credit rating of a number of instruments since 1991 by the Government/SEBI, credit rating has emerged as a critical element in the functioning of the Indian debt/financial markets. In response to the ever-increasing role of credit rating, two more agencies were set up in 1990 (Information and Credit Rating Services (ICRA) Ltd and 1993 Credit Analysis and Research (CARE) Ltd respectively.

The first private sector credit rating institution was set up as a joint venture between the JM Financials, Alliance Group and the international rating agency Duffs and Phelps in 1995, known as Phelps Credit Rating India Ltd (DCR). It is now known as FITCH India Ltd.

Rating Methodology The rating methodology involves an analysis of the industry risk, the issuer's business and financial risks. A rating is assigned after assessing all the factors that could affect the credit worthiness of the entity. Typically, the industry risk assessment sets the stage for analysing more specific company risk factors and establishing the priority of these factors in the overall evaluation. For instance, if the industry is highly competitive, careful assessment of the issuer's market position is stressed. If the company has large capital requirements, the examination of cash flow adequacy assumes importance. The ratings are based on the current information provided by the issuer or facts obtained from reliable sources. Both qualitative and quantitative criteria are employed in evaluating and monitoring the ratings.

The main elements of the rating methodology for manufacturing companies are outlined below.

Business Risk Analysis The rating analysis begins with an assessment of the company's environment focusing on the strength of the industry prospects, pattern of business cycles as well as the competitive factors affecting the industry. The vulnerability of the industry to Government controls/regulations is assessed.

The nature of competition is different for different industries based on price, product quality, distribution capabilities, image, product differentiation, service and so on. The industries characterised by a steady growth in demand, ability to maintain margins without impairing future prospects, flexibility in the timing of capital outlays, and moderate capital intensity are in a stronger position.

When a company participates in more than one business, each segment is analysed separately. A truly diversified company does not have a single business segment that is dominant, and the company's ability to manage diverse operations is a significant factor. As part of the industry analysis, key rating factors are identified into keys to success and areas of vulnerability. The main industry and business factors assessed include:

Industry Risk Nature and basis of competition, key success factors, demand and supply position, structure of industry, cyclical/seasonal factors, government policies and so on.

Market Position of the Issuing Entity Within the Industry Market share, competitive advantages, selling and distribution arrangements, product and customer diversity and so on.

Operating Efficiency of the Borrowing Entity Locational advantages, labour relationships, cost structure, technological advantages and manufacturing efficiency as compared to competitors and so on.

Legal Position Terms of the issue document/prospectus, trustees and their responsibilities, systems for timely payment and for protection against fraud/forgery and so on.

While the CRAs do not have a minimum size criterion for any given rating level, the size of the company is a critical factor in the rating decision as smaller companies are more vulnerable to business cycle swings as compared to larger companies. In general, small companies are more concentrated in terms of product, number of customers and geography and, consequently, lack the benefits of diversification that can benefit larger firms.

If the company being rated is a subsidiary or an affiliate, that is controlled by/has strong links with a dominant parent company, then the rating also includes an analysis of the parent company's credit quality. The parent company's credit quality could have an impact on the issuer's own credit quality.

Financial Risk Analysis After evaluating the issuer's competitive position and operating environment, the analysts proceed to analyse the financial strength of the issuer. Financial risk is analysed largely through quantitative means, particularly by using financial ratios. While the past financial performance of the issuer is important, emphasis is placed on the ability of the issuer to maintain/improve its future financial performance.

As ratings rely on audited data (the rating process does not entail auditing a company's financial records), the analysis of the audited financial results begin with a review of accounting quality. The purpose is to determine whether ratios and statistics derived from financial statements can be used to accurately measure a company's performance and its position, relative to both its peer group and the larger universe of companies.

The profitability of a company is an important determinant of its ability to withstand business adversity as well as generate capital internally. The main measures of profitability studied include operating and net margins and return on capital employed. The absolute levels of these ratios, trends in movement of the ratios as well as comparison of the ratios with other competitors, is analysed. As a rating exercise is a forward-looking exercise, greater emphasis is laid on the future, rather than the past earning capability of the issuer.

Emphasis is also laid on an analysis of cash flow patterns, as it provides a better indictor of the issuer's debt servicing capability compared to reported earnings. A cash flow analysis reveals the usage of cash for different purposes, and, consequently, the extent of cash available for debt service.

The future debt claims on the issuer's as well as the issuer's ability to raise capital is also assessed in order to arrive at the level of the issuer's financial flexibility. The areas considered in financial analysis include:

Accounting Quality Overstatement/understatement of profits, auditors qualifications, method of income recognition, inventory valuation and depreciation policies, off Balance sheet liabilities and so on.

Earnings Protection Sources of future earnings growth, profitability ratios, earnings in relation to fixed income charges and so on.

Adequacy of Cash Flows In relation to debt and working capital needs, stability of cash flows, capital spending flexibility, working capital management and so on.

Financial Flexibility Alternative financing plans in times of stress, ability to raise funds, asset deployment potential and so on.

Interest and Tax Sensitivity Exposure to interest rate changes, tax law changes and hedging against interest rates and so on.

Management Risk A proper assessment of debt protection levels requires an evaluation of the management philosophies and its strategies. The analyst compares the company's business strategies and financial plans (over a period of time) to provide insights into a management's abilities with respect to forecasting and implementing of plans. Specific areas reviewed include: **(i)** Track record of the management: planning and control systems, depth of managerial talent, succession plans; **(ii)** Evaluation of capacity to overcome adverse situations; and **(iii)** Goals, philosophy and strategies.

Rating Symbols The **rating symbols** are symbolic expression of opinion/assessment of the credit rating agency/(agencies) (CRAs) regarding the investment/credit quality/grade of the debt/obligations/instrument. They group together similar, though not necessarily identical, entities in terms of their relative capacity of timely servicing of the obligations as per the terms of the contract.

Rating symbol is a symbolic expression of opinion of the rating agency regarding the investment/credit quality/grade of the debt instrument/ obligation.

The SEBI-registered CRAs have been using different rating symbols and definitions. There is need to have common rating symbols and definitions **(i)** for their easy understanding and meanings by the investors, and **(ii)** to achieve high standards of integrity and fairness in ratings. The standardised symbols and their definitions for **(a)** Long-term debt instruments; **(b)** Short-term debt instruments are listed in the annexure below

Annexure: Standardised Rating Symbols/Definitions

I. Rating Symbols and Definitions for Long-term Debt Instruments: *The instruments with original maturity exceeding one year*. The rating symbols should have CRA's first name as prefix

AAA Instruments with this rating are considered to have the highest degree of safety regarding timely servicing of financial obligations and carry lowest credit risk.

AA Instruments with this rating are considered to have high degree of safety regarding timely servicing of financial obligations and carry very low credit risk.

A Instruments with this rating are considered to have adequate degree of safety regarding timely servicing of financial obligations and carry low credit risk.

BBB Instruments with this rating are considered to have moderate degree of safety regarding timely servicing of financial obligations and carry moderate credit risk.

BB Instruments with this rating are considered to have moderate risk of default regarding timely servicing of financial obligations.

B Instruments with this rating are considered to have high risk of default regarding timely servicing of financial obligations.

C Instruments with this rating are considered to have very high risk of default regarding timely servicing of financial obligations.

D Instruments with this rating are in default or are expected to be in default soon.

Modifiers {"+" (plus) / "–"(minus)} can be used with the rating symbols for the categories AA to C. The modifiers reflect the comparative standing within the category.

II. Rating Symbols and Definitions for Short Term Debt instruments: *The instruments with original maturity of upto one year. Rating symbols should have CRA's first name as prefix*

A1 Instruments with this rating are considered to have very strong degree of safety regarding timely payment of financial obligations and carry lowest credit risk.

A2 Instruments with this rating are considered to have strong degree of safety regarding timely payment of financial obligations and carry low credit risk.

A3 Instruments with this rating are considered to have moderate degree of safety regarding timely payment of financial obligations and carry higher credit risk as compared to instruments rated in the two higher categories.

A4 Instruments with this rating are considered to have minimal degree of safety regarding timely payment of financial obligations and carry very high credit risk and are susceptible to default.

D Instruments with this rating are in default or expected to be in default on maturity.

Modifier {"+" (plus)} can be used with the rating symbols for the categories A1 to A4. The modifier reflects the comparative standing within the category.

Issue Procedure

Debt securities mean non-convertible securities, including bonds/debentures and other securities of a body corporate/any statutory body, which create/acknowledge indebtedness, but excluding bonds issued by Government/other bodies specified by the SEBI, security receipts and securitised debt instruments. **Private placement** is an offer to less than 50 persons, while public issue is an offer/invitation to public to subscribe to debt securities. The main element of the SEBI regulations relating to issue and listing of debt securities are: issue requirements, listing, conditions for continuous listing and trading, obligations of intermediaries/issuers, procedure for action for violation, and powers of the SEBI to issue general order.

Debt securities mean non-convertible securities, including bonds/debentures and other securities of a body corporate/any statutory body, which create/acknowledge indebtedness.

Any issuer who has been restrained/prohibited/debarred by the SEBI from accessing the securities market/dealing in securities cannot make public issue of debt securities. To make such an issue the conditions to be satisfied on the date of filing of draft/final offer document are in-principle approval for their listing, credit rating from at least one SEBI-registered rating agency and agreement with a SEBI-registered depository for their dematieralisation. The issuer should appoint merchant bankers/trustees and not issue such securities to provide loan to, acquisition of shares of, any person who is a part of the same group/under the same management. The issuer should advertise in a national daily with wide circulation on/before the issue opening date. Application forms should be accompanied by a copy of the abridged prospectus. The issue could be fixed-price or book-built. The minimum subscription and underwriting arrangement should be disclosed in the offer document and it should not contain any false/misleading statement. A trust deed must be executed and debenture redemption reserve should be created. The creation of security should be disclosed in the offer document.

Private placement is an offer to less than 50 persons.

The listing of debt securities is mandatory. The issuer should comply with the conditions of listing specified in the listing agreement.

The debt securities issued to public or on private placement basis should be traded/cleared/settled in a recognised stock exchange subject to conditions specified by the SEBI including conditions for reporting of all such trades.

The debenture trustees, issuers and merchants bankers should comply with their obligations specified by the SEBI.

In case of violation of any regulation(s), the SEBI may carry out inspection of books of accounts/records/documents of the issuers/intermediaries. It can issue such directions as it may deem fit. An aggrieved party may prefer an appeal with the SAT.

In addition to the other requirements, an issuer of CDIs (Convertible debt instruments) should comply with the following conditions: **(i)** obtain credit rating, **(ii)** appoint debenture trustees, **(iii)** create debenture redemption fund, **(iv)** assets on which charge is proposed are sufficient to discharge the liability and free from encumbrances. They should be redeemed in terms of the offer document.

The non-convertible portion of the partly CDIs can be rolled over without change in the interest rate if 75 per cent of the holders approve it; an auditors certificate on its liquidity position has been sent to them; the holding of all holders who have not agreed would be redeemed; credit rating has been obtained and communicated to them before rollover.

Positive consent of the holders would be necessary for conversion of optionally CDIs into shares. The holders should be given the option not to convert them if the conversion price was not determined/disclosed to the investors at the time of the issue.

The terms of issue of securities adversely affecting the investors can be altered with the consent/ sanction in writing of at least 75 per cent/special resolution of the holders.

LO 23.3 SECURITISATION

Concept

Securitisation is the process of pooling and repackaging of homogeneous illiquid financial assets into marketable securities that can be sold to investors. The process leads to the creation of financial instruments that represent ownership interest in, or are secured by a segregated income producing asset or pool, of assets. The pool of assets collateralises securities. These assets are generally secured by personal or real property such as automobiles, real estate, or equipment loans but in some cases are unsecured, for example, credit card debt and consumer loans.

Securitisation Process

> **Securitisation** is the process of pooling and repackaging of homogeneous illiquid financial assets, such as residential mortgage, into marketable securities that can be sold to investors.

1. Asset are originated through receivables, leases, housing loans or any other form of debt by a company and funded on its balance sheet. The company is normally referred to as the "originator".
2. Once a suitably large portfolio of assets has been originated, the assets are analysed as a portfolio and then sold or assigned to a third party, which is normally a special purpose vehicle company ('SPV') formed for the specific purpose of funding the assets. It issues debt and purchases receivables from the originator. The SPV is owned by a trust/the originator.
3. The administration of the asset is then subcontracted back to the originator by the SPV. It is responsible for collecting interest and principal payments on the loans in the underlying pool of assets and transfer to the SPV.
4. The SPV issues tradable securities to fund the purchase of assets. The performance of these securities is directly linked to the performance of the assets and there is no recourse (other than in the event of breach of contract) back to the originator.
5. The investors purchase the securities because they are satisfied that the securities would be paid in full and on time from the cash flows available in the asset pool. The proceeds from the sale of securities are used to pay the originator.

6. The SPV agrees to pay any surpluses which, may arise during its funding of the assets, back to the originator. Thus, the originator, for all practical purposes, retains its existing relationship with the borrowers and all of the economies of funding the assets.
7. As cash flow arise on the assets, these are used by the SPV to repay funds to the investors in the securities.

Credit Enhancement

Investors in securitised instruments take a direct exposure on the performance of the underlying collateral and have limited or no recourse to the originator. Hence, they seek additional comfort in the form of **credit enhancement**. It refers to the various means that attempt to buffer investors against losses on the asset collateralising their investment. These losses may vary in frequency, severity and timing, and depend on the asset characteristics, how they are originated and how they are administered. The credit enhancements are often essential to secure a high level of credit rating and for low cost funding. By shifting the credit risk from a less-known borrower to a well-known, strong, and larger credit enhancer, credit enhancements correct the imbalance of information between the lender(s) and the borrowers. They are either external (third party) or internal (structural or cash-flow-driven).

> **Credit enhancement** are the various means that attempt to buffer investors against losses on the asset collaterising their investment.

External Credit Enhancements They include insurance, third party guarantee and letter of credit.

Insurance Full insurance is provided against losses on the assets. This tantamounts to a 100 per cent guarantee of a transaction's principal and interest payments. The issuer of the insurance looks to an initial premium or other support to cover credit losses.

Third-Party Guarantee This method involves a limited/full guarantee by a third party to cover losses that may arise on the non-performance of the collateral.

Letter of Credit For structures with credit ratings below the level sought for the issue, a third party provides a letter of credit for a nominal amount. This may provide either full or partial cover of the issuer's obligation.

Internal Credit Enhancements Such form of credit enhancement comprise the following:

Credit Trenching (Senior/Subordinate Structure) The SPV issues two (or more) tranches of securities and establishes a predetermined priority in their servicing, whereby first losses are borne by the holders of the subordinate tranches (at times the originator itself). Apart from providing comfort to holders of senior debt, credit tranching also permits targeting investors with specific risk-return preferences.

Over-collateralisation The originator sets aside assets in excess of the collateral required to be assigned to the SPV. The cash flows from these assets must first meet any overdue payments in the main pool, before they can be routed back to the originator.

Cash Collateral This works in much the same way as the over-collateralisation. But since the quality of cash is self-evidently higher and more stable than the quality of assets yet to be turned into cash, the quantum of cash required to meet the desired rating would be lower than asset over-collateral to that extent.

Spread Account The difference between the yield on the assets and the yield to the investors from the securities is called **excess spread**. In its simplest form, a spread account traps the excess spread (net of all running costs of securitisation) within the SPV up to a specified amount sufficient to satisfy a given rating or credit equity requirement. Only realisations in excess of this specified amount are routed back to the originator. This amount is returned to the originator after the payment of principal and interest to the investors.

Triggered Amortisation This works only in structures that permit substitution (for example, rapidly revolving assets such as credit cards). When certain preset levels of collateral performance are breached, all further collections are applied to repay the funding. Once amortisation is triggered, substitution is stopped and the early repayment becomes an irreversible process. The triggered amortisation is typically applied in future flow securitisation.

Parties to a Securitisation Transaction

The parties to securitisation deal are **(i)** primary and **(ii)** others. There are three primary parties to a securitisation deal, namely, originators, special purpose vehicle (SPV) and investors. The other parties involved are obligors, rating agency, administrator/servicer, agent and trustee, and structurer.

Originator is the entity on whose books the assets to be securitised exist.

Originator This is the entity on whose books the assets to be securitised exist. It is the prime mover of the deal, that is, it sets up the necessary structures to execute the deal. It sells the assets on its books and receives the funds generated from such sale. In a true sale, the **originator** transfers both the legal and the beneficial interest in the assets to the SPV.

SPV (special purpose vehicle) is the entity which would typically buy the assets to be securitised from the originator.

SPV An issuer, also known as the **SPV**, is the entity, which would typically buy the assets to be securitised from the originator. An SPV is typically a low-capitalised entity with narrowly defined purposes and activities, and usually has independent trustees/ Directors. As one of the main objectives of securitisation is to remove the assets from the balance sheet of the originator, the SPV plays a very important role in as much as it holds the assets in its books and makes the upfront payment for them to the originator.

Investors The investors may be in the form of individuals or institutional investors like FIs, mutual funds, provident funds, pension funds, insurance companies and so on. They buy a participating interest in the total pool of receivables and receive their payment in the form of interest and principal as per agreed pattern.

Obligors are the borrowers of the original loan.

Obligor(s) The **obligors** are the originator debtors (borrowers of the original loan). The amount outstanding from an obligor is the asset that is transferred to an SPV. The credit standing of an obligor(s) is of paramount importance in a securitisation transaction.

Rating Agency Since the investors take on the risk of the asset pool rather than the originator, an external credit rating plays an important role. The rating process would assess the strength of the cash flow and the mechanism designed to ensure full and timely payment by the process of selection of loans of appropriate credit quality, the extent of credit and liquidity support provided and the strength of the legal framework.

Receiving and paying agent is one who collects the payment due from the obligors and passes it on to the SPV.

Administrator or Servicer It collects the payment due from the obligor(s) and passes it to the SPV, follows up with delinquent borrowers and pursues legal remedies available against the defaulting borrowers. Since it receives the instalments and pays it to the SPV, it is also called the **Receiving and Paying Agent (RPA)**.

Agent and Trustee It accepts the responsibility for overseeing that all the parties to the securitisation deal perform in accordance with the securitisation trust agreement. Basically, it is appointed to look after the interest of the investors.

Structurer Normally, an investment banker is responsible as structurer for bringing together the originator, the credit enhancer(s), the investors and other partners to a securitisation deal. It also works with the originator and helps in structuring deals.

The different parties to a securitisation deal have very different roles to play. In fact, firms specialise in those areas in which they enjoy competitive advantage. The entire process is broken up into separate parts with different parties specialising in origination of loans, raising funds from the capital markets, servicing of loans and so on. It is this kind of segmentation of market roles that introduces several efficiencies securitisation is so often credited with.

The securitisation process is depicted in Figure 23.1.

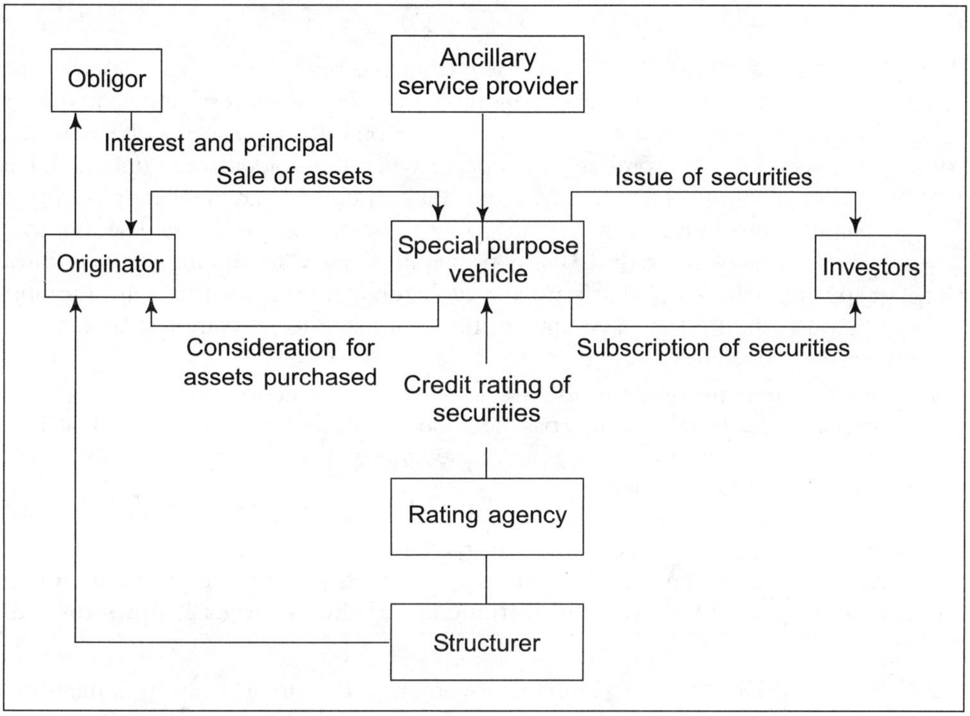

FIGURE 23.1 Securitisation Process

Asset Characteristics

The assets to be securities should have the following characteristics.

Cash Flow A principal part of the assets should be the right to receive from the debtor(s) on certain dates, that is, the asset can be analysed as a series of cash flows.

Security If the security available to collateralise the cash flows is valuable, then this security can be realised by a SPV.

Distributed Risk Assets either have to have a distributed risk characteristic or be backed by suitably-rated credit support.

Homogeneity Assets have to relatively homogenous, that is, there should not be wide variations in documentation, product type or origination methodology.

No Executory Clauses The contracts to be securitised must work even if the originator goes bankrupt.

Independence From the Originator The ongoing performance of the assets must be independent of the existence of the originator.

Instruments of Securitisation

Securitisation can be implemented by three kinds of instruments differing mainly in their maturity characteristics. They are: **(i)** Pass through certificates, **(ii)** Pay through securities, **(iii)** Stripped securities.

Pass Through Certificates (PTCs) The cash flows from the underlying collateral are passed through to the holders of the securities in the form of monthly payment of interest, principal and pre-payments. In other words, the cash flows are distributed on a *pro-rata* basis to the holders of the securities. The pre-payments occur when the holder of the underlying asset prepays the remaining principal before the final scheduled payment month. Any pre-payment is also proportionately passed on to the security-holders leading to the quicker retirement of their underlying principal. Critical to pricing of pass through are the specific features of that particular collateral. All the securities are terminated simultaneously as the last payment on the pool leads to its complete amortisation. Some of the main features of PTCs are:

Pass through certificate Is a conduit for sale of ownership in receivables (mortgages).

- They reflect ownership rights in the assets backing the securities.
- Pre-payment precisely reflects the payment on the underlying mortgage. If it is a home loan with monthly payments, the payments on securities would also be monthly but at a slightly less coupon rate than the loan.
- As underlying mortgage is self-amortising. Thus, by whatever amount it is amortised, it is passed on to the security-holders with re-payment.
- Pre-payment occurs when a debtor makes a payment, which exceeds the minimum scheduled amount. It shortens the life of the instrument and skews the cash flows towards the earlier years.

Pay Through Security (PTS) The PTS structure overcomes the single maturity limitations of the pass through certificates. Its structure permits the issuer to restructure receivables flow to offer a range of investment maturities to the investors associated with different yields and risks. The issuer of assets-backed debt are thus freed from the limitations imposed by the pass through structure which simply provides a conduit for sale of ownership interest in the receivables. By contrast, in a PTS structure, the issuer typically owns the receivables and simply sells the debt that is backed by the assets. As a result, the issuer of debt is free to restructure the cash flow from the receivable into payments on several debt tranches with varying maturities.

A key difference between PTC and PTS is the mechanics of principal repayment process. In PTC, each investor receives a pro-rata distribution of any principal and interest payment made by the borrower. Because these assets are self-amortising assets, a pass through, however, does not occur until the final asset in the pool is retired. This results in large difference between average life and final maturity as well as a great deal of uncertainty with regard to the timing of the return of the principal. The PTS structure, on the other hand, substitutes a sequential retirement of bonds for the pro-rata principal return process found in pass through. Cash flows generated by the underlying collateral is used to retire bonds. Only one class of bonds at a time receives principal. All principal payments go first to the fastest pay trance in the sequence then becomes the exclusive recipients of principal. This sequence continues till the last tranches of bonds is retired.

Stripped Securities Under this instrument, securities are classifies as Interest only (IO) or Principally only (PO) securities. The IO holders are paid back out of the interest income only while the PO holders are paid out of principal repayments only. However, these securities are highly volatile by nature and are least preferred by the investors. Normally, PO securities increase in value when interest rates go down because it becomes lucrative to prepay existing mortgagor and undertake fresh loans at lower interest rates. As a result of prepayment of mortgages, the maturity period of these securities goes down and investors are returned the money earlier than they anticipated. In contrast, IOs increase in value when interest rates go up because more interest is collected on underlying mortgages. However, in anticipation of a decline in the interest rates, prepayments of mortgages declines and maturities lengthen. These are normally traded by speculators who make money by speculating about interest rate changes.

Types of Securities

The securities fall into two groups:

Asset Backed Securities (ABS) The investors rely on the performance of the assets that collateralise the securities. They do not take an exposure either on the previous owner of the assets (the originator), or the entity issuing the securities (the SPV). Clearly, classifying securities as 'asset-backed' seeks to differentiate them from regular securities, which are the liabilities of the entity issuing them. An example of ABS is credit card receivables. Securitisation of credit card receivables is an innovation that has found wide acceptance. Although the average tenure of credit available to a credit card holder is generally very short, it is revolving by nature. The lacuna of short tenor of the receivables is, hence, overcome by 'substitution', whereby collections are used for fresh purchases of receivables. Thus, a securitisable asset of marketable tenure comes into being. The structure in the case is generally 'Pay Through', since it is impossible to match the payment made by the card-holder with the payment to the investor.

Mortgage Backed Securities (MBS) The securities are backed by the mortgage loans, that is, loans secured by specified real estate property, wherein the lender has the right to sell the property, if the borrower defaults.

Issue Procedure

The main elements of the SEBI regulations relating to public offers of securitised debt instruments **(SDIs)** and listing on a recognised stock exchange are: registration of trustees, constitution/management of special purpose distinct entities (SPDEs), schemes of SPDEs, public offer of SDIs, rights of investors, listing of SDIs, inspection and disciplinary proceedings, and action in case of default.

SDI means any certificate/ instrument issued to an investor by SPDE which possesses any debt/receivables including mortgage debt assigned to it and acknowledging beneficial interest of such investors.

Public offer and listing of SDIs can be made only by SPDEs if their trustees are registered with the SEBI and it complies with all the applicable provisions of these regulations and the Securities Contracts (Regulation) Act. However, SEBI-registered debenture trustees, RBI-registered securitisation/asset reconstruction companies, NHB and NABARD would not require registration to act as trustees. A **SDI** means any certificate/instrument issued to an investor by SPDE which possesses any debt/

receivables including mortgage debt assigned to it and acknowledging beneficial interest of such investors.

While considering registration, the SEBI would have regard to all relevant factors, including: **(i)** track record, professional competence and general reputation of the applicant, **(ii)** objectives of a body corporate applicant, **(iii)** adequacy of its infrastructure, **(iv)** compliance with the provisions of these regulations, **(v)** rejection by the SEBI of any previous application and **(vi)** the applicant/promoters/directors are fit and proper person.

The registration of the trustees would be subject to the following conditions: **(i)** prior approval of the SEBI to change its management/control, **(ii)** adequate steps for redressal of investors grievances, **(iii)** abide by the provisions of these regulations/Securities Contracts (Regulation) Act, **(iv)** forthwith inform the SEBI **(a)** if information/particulars previously submitted is false/misleading **(b)** of any material change in the information submitted and **(v)** abide by the specified code of conduct.

The SPDE should be constituted as a trust entitled to issue SDIs. The trust deed should contain the specified clauses.

A SPDE may raise funds by offering SDIs through a scheme. The scheme should consist of the following elements: **(i)** obligation to redeem the SDIs, **(ii)** credit enhancement and liquidity facilities, **(iii)** servicers, **(iv)** accounts, **(v)** audit, **(vi)** maintenance of records, **(vii)** holding of originator and **(viii)** winding up.

The stipulations relating to the public offer of the SDIs are: **(i)** offer to the public, **(ii)** submission of draft offer document and filing of final offer document, **(iii)** arrangement for dematerialisaion, **(iv)** mandatory listing, **(v)** credit rating, **(vi)** contents of the offer document, **(vii)** prohibition on misstatements in the offer document, **(viii)** underwriting of the issue, **(ix)** offer period, **(x)** minimum subscription, **(xi)** allotment and other obligations and **(xii)** post-issue obligations.

The rights of investors are two-folds: free transferability of the SDIs and their rights in the securities issued by the SPDE.

The provisions relating to the listing of the SDIs include: **(a)** application for listing, **(b)** minimum public offering for listing, **(c)** continuous listing conditions and **(d)** trading.

As regards inspection and disciplinary proceedings, the provisions relate to **(1)** power of the SEBI to call for information, **(2)** right of inspection by the SEBI, **(3)** obligations of the SPDE on inspection, **(4)** appointment of auditor/valuer and **(5)** submission of report to the SEBI.

Action in case of default would result in suspension/cancellation of registration of the SPDE. The SEBI may also issue the specified directions to the SPDE/trustees. An aggrieved party may prefer an appeal to the SAT.

SUMMARY

LO 23.1

Term loans/term/project finance are negotiated loans between the borrower and the lenders with a maturity of up to 10 years. They are employed to finance acquisition of fixed assets and working capital margin. All term loans are secured. The asset security stipulations are reinforced by a number of positive/affirmative and negative covenants. While negative covenants are (i) asset-related, (ii) liability-related, (iii) cashflow-related and (iv) control-related, the positive covenants relate to maintenance of (i) networth, (ii) level of working capital, (iii) creation of redemption funds and so on. The term loans have to be amortised according to the predetermined schedule. They carry low cost and involve high risk. They have no adverse effect on control but there is a moderate restraint on managerial freedom. Term loans are sanctioned and disbursed by the financial institutions banks/according to the prescribed procedure. Financial institutions appraise a term loan proposal/project from the marketing, technical, financial and managerial angles.

LO 23.2	Debentures represent creditorship securities and debenture-holders are long-term creditors of the company. As long-term source of finance, debentures have some contrasting features compared to equity shares. When they are sold to public, a trustee is appointed through a trust deed/indenture to ensure that the borrower fulfills all contractual obligations. The coupon rate of interest is legally enforceable as well as tax-deductible. A typical non-convertible debenture (NCD) has a maturity of 7-10 years. The redemption of debentures can be accomplished in either of the two ways: (i) debenture redemption reserves (sinking fund) and (ii) call and put (buy-back) provision. They are generally secured by way of an equitable mortgage. The convertible debentures can be partly/fully converted into equity shares. All debentures must be rated by a rating agency. As long-term source of funds, debentures (i) have low cost, (ii) do not dilute control, (iii) involve high risk and (iv) put some restraint on managerial freedom. To improve the attractiveness of debentures, a wide range of innovative instruments have emerged such as deep discount bonds, secured premium notes and floating rate bonds.
	A company offering convertible/non-convertible debt instruments has to comply with the requirements prescribed by the SEBI. These relate to (1) credit rating, (2) debenture trustees, (3) debenture redemption reserve, (4) distribution of dividends, (5) creation of charge, (6) letter of option, (7) rollover and so on.
	Credit rating of debentures by a rating agency is mandatory. It provides a simple system of gradation by which relative capacities of borrowers to make timely payment of payment and repayment of principal on a particular type of debt instrument can be noted. The main elements of the rating methodology are (1) business risk analysis in terms of industry risk, market position of the issuing entity within the industry, its operating efficiency, and legal position, (2) financial risk analysis as reflected in accounting quality, earnings protection, adequacy of cash flows, financial flexibility and interest and tax sensitivity and (3) management risk. The rating agencies in India are CRISIL, ICRA, CARE and Fitch India. The CRAs have to use the SEBI-prescribed standardised rating symbols for long/short-term debt instruments.
LO 23.3	Securitisation is the process of pooling and repackaging of homogeneous illiquid financial assets/loans into marketable securities that can be sold to investors. The parties to a securitisation transaction are (1) originator, (2) SPV, (3) investors, (4) obligor, (5) rating agency, (6) administrator/servicer, (7) agent/trustee and (8) structurer. Securitisation can be implemented by three kinds of instruments differing mainly in their maturity characteristics, namely, (i) PTCs, (ii) PTS and (iii) stripped securities. These securities fall into two groups: (a) ABS and (b) MBS.

SOLVED PROBLEMS

P.23.1 Hindustan Copper Industries (HCI) manufactures copper pipe. It is contemplating calling ₹3 crore of 30-year, ₹1,000 bonds (30,000 bonds) issued 5 years ago with a coupon interest rate of 14 per cent. The bonds have a call price of ₹1,140 and had initially collected proceeds of ₹2.91 crore due to a discount of ₹30 per bond. The initial flotation cost was ₹3,60,000. The HCI intends to sell ₹3 crore of 12 per cent coupon interest rate, 25-year bonds to raise funds for retiring the old bonds. It intends to sell the new bonds at their par value of ₹1,000. The estimated flotation costs are ₹4,40,000. The HCI is in 35 per cent tax bracket and its after cost of debt is 8 per cent. As the new bonds must first be sold and their proceeds then used to retire the old bonds, the HCI expects a 2-month period of overlapping interest during which interest must be paid on both the old and the new bonds. Analyse the feasibility of the bond refunding by the HCI. **LO 23.2** LOD M

Solution

Decision analysis for bond refunding decision

Present value of annual cashflow savings (*Refer working note 2*):		
₹3,81,460 × 10.675 ($PVIF_{8,25}$)		₹40,72,086
Less: Initial investment (*Refer working note 1*)		32,57,500
NPV		8,14,586

Decision The proposed refunding is recommended as it has a positive NPV.

Working Notes

1. Initial investment:

(a) Call premium:		
Before tax [(₹1,140 – ₹1,000) × 30,000 bonds]	₹42,00,000	
Less: Tax (0.35 × ₹42,00,000)	14,70,000	
After tax cost of call premium		₹27,30,000
(b) Flotation cost of new bond		4,40,000
(c) Overlapping interest:		
Before tax (0.14 × 2/12/ × ₹3 crore)	7,00,000	
Less: Tax (0.35 × 7,00,000)	2,45,000	4,55,000
(d) Tax savings from unamortised discount on old bond [25/30 × (₹3 crore – 2.91 crore) × 0.35]		(2,62,500)
(e) Tax savings from unamortised flotation cost of old bond (25/30 × ₹3,60,000 × 0.35)		(10,5,000)
		32,57,500

2. Annual cash flow savings

(a) Old bond			
(i) Interest cost:			
Before tax (0.14 × 3 crore)	₹42,00,000		
Less: Tax (0.35 × ₹42,00,000)	14,70,000	27,30,000	
(ii) Tax savings from amortisation of discount [(₹9,00,000[@] × 30) × 0.35]		(10,500)	
(iii) Tax savings from amortisation of flotation cost [(₹3,60,000 × 30) × 0.40)		(4,200)	
Annual after tax debt payment (a)			27,15,300
(b) New bond			
(i) Interest cost:			
Before tax (0.12 × 3 crore)	36,00,000		
Less: Taxes (0.35 × ₹36,00,000)	12,60,000		
After tax interest cost		23,40,000	
(ii) Tax savings from amortisation of flotation cost [₹4,40,000 × 25) × 0.35		(6,160)	
Annual after-tax debt payment (b)			23,33,840
Annual cash flow savings [(a) – (b)]			3,81,460

[@]Par value – net proceeds for sale.

P.23.2 Dua Manufacturing (DM) has under consideration refunding of ₹2 crore outstanding bonds at ₹1,000 par value as a result of recent decline in long-term interest rates. The bond-refunding plan involves issue of ₹2 crore of new bonds at the lower interest and the proceeds to call and retire the ₹2 crore outstanding bonds. The DM is in 35 per cent tax bracket. LO 23.2 LOD D

The details of the new bonds are: (i) sale at par value of ₹1,000 each, (ii) 11 per cent coupon rate, (iii) 20-year maturity, (iv) flotation costs, ₹4,00,000, and (iv) a 3-month period of overlapping interest.

DMs outstanding bonds were initially issued 10 years ago with a 30-year maturity and 13 per cent coupon rate of interest. They were sold at ₹12 par bond discount from par value with flotation costs amounting to ₹1,50,000 and their call at ₹1,130.

Assuming 7 per cent after-tax cost of debt, analyse the bond-refunding proposal. Would you recommend it? Why?

Solution

Decision analysis for bond refunding decision

Present value of annual cashflow savings (*Refer working note 2*):	
₹2,62,450 × 10.594 ($PVIF_{7,20}$)	₹27,80,395
Less: Initial investment (*Refer working note 1*)	24,21,500
Net present value of refunding	3,58,895

Decision ***As the NPV is positive, the proposed bond-refunding is recommended.***

Working Notes

1. Initial investment:

(a) Call premium:

Before tax [(₹1,130 – ₹1,000) × 20,000 bonds]	₹26,00,000	
Less: Tax (0.35 × ₹26,00,000)	9,10,000	
After-tax cost of call premium		₹16,90,000
(b) Flotation cost of new bond		4,00,000
(c) Overlapping interest:		
Before tax (0.13 × 3/12[@] × ₹2 crore)	6,50,000	
Less: Tax (0.35 × 6,50,000)	2,27,500	
After-tax cost of overlapping interest		4,22,500
(d) Tax savings from unamortised discount on old bond [25/30[@@] × (20,000 bonds × ₹12/bond discount) × 0.35]		(56,000)
(e) Tax savings from unamortised flotation cost of old bond (20/30[@@] × ₹1,50,000 × 0.35)		(35,000)
		24,21,500

[@]3 months ×12 months
[@@]20 years maturity × 30 years maturity

2. Annual cash flow savings

(a) Old bond

(i) Interest cost:

Before tax (0.13 × ₹2 crore)	₹26,00,000	
Less: Tax (0.35 × ₹26,00,000)	9,10,000	
After tax interest cost		16,90,000
(ii) Tax savings from amortisation of discount [(₹2,40,000* × 30) × 0.35]		(2,800)

(iii) Tax savings from amortisation of

flotation cost [(₹1,50,000 ÷ 30) × 0.35]		(1,750)	
Annual after-tax debt payment (a)			16,85,450
(b) New bond			
(i) Interest cost:			
Before tax (0.11 × 2,00,00,000)	22,00,000		
Less: Taxes (0.35 × ₹22,00,000)	7,70,000		
After tax interest cost		14,30,000	
(ii) Tax savings from amortisation of flotation cost [₹4,00,000 ÷ 20) × 0.35]		(7,000)	
Annual after tax debt payment (b)			14,23,000
*20,000 bonds × ₹12 per bond			
Annual cash flow savings [(a) – (b)]			2,62,450

REVIEW QUESTIONS

LOD: Easy

RQ.23.1 Give appropriate answers for the following: **[LO 23.1,2,3]**

(i) Term loans are akin to ____________ of debentures in contrast to their public offering to investors.

(ii) Term loans are secured while debentures are non-secured instruments. (True/False)

(iii) The creation of the Debenture Redemption is non-obligatory and depends on the discretion of the management for all debenture issues. (True/False)

(iv) Credit rating of all debenture issues is compulsory in India. (True/ False)

(v) ____________ is a secured debenture redeemable at a premium over the face value/purchase price.

(vi) Companies which have defaulted on the payment of interest to the debenture holders cannot distribute dividends without the permission of the debenture trustees and the lead institution, if any. (True/False)

(vii) A "AAA" rating given by CRISIL to a company guarantees timely payment of the interest and repayment of the principal by the issuing company. (True/False)

(viii) Only those assets which are secured by a collateral can be securitized. (True/False)

(ix) ____________ refers to the various means that attempt to buffer investors against losses on the asset collateralizing their investment.

(x) The sale of the securities by the SPV after the securitization of the assets is open to retail investors. (True/False)

(xi) ______________ are backed by loans secured by specified real estate property.

[Answers: (i) private placement (ii) False (iii) False (iv) True (v) Secured premium note (vi) True (vii) False (viii) False (ix) Credit enhancement (x) False, and (xi) Mortgage backed security]

RQ.23.2 Define credit rating. What is its function? **[LO 23.2]**

RQ.23.3 What are the main elements of the rating methodology? **[LO 23.2]**

RQ.23.4 Discuss the securitisation process. **[LO 23.3]**

RQ.23.5 What is credit enhancement? **[LO 23.3]**

RQ.23.6 Explain the parties to a securitisation process. **[LO 23.3]**

LOD: Medium

RQ.23.7 Describe briefly the features of term loans and term loan procedure. **[LO 23.1]**

RQ.23.8 What are the principal issues considered and the criteria employed in appraisal of a project/term loan/finance? [LO 23.1]

RQ.23.9 What are the main attributes of debentures/bonds? What are their merits and demerits? [LO 23.2]

RQ.23.10 Explain the innovative debt instruments. [LO 23.2]

RQ.23.11 What is bond refunding? How can bond refunding decision be analysed? [LO 23.2]

RQ.23.12 Discuss the main elements of the issue procedure for debt instruments. [LO 23.2]

RQ.23.13 What are the requirements for secondary market for corporate debt securities on a private placement basis? [LO 23.2]

RQ.23.14 Define rating symbol. [LO 23.2]

RQ.23.15 Explain briefly (i) instruments of securitisation and (ii) types of securitisation. [LO 23.3]

RQ.23.16 New Delhi Company (NDC) has under consideration offering a new ₹4 crore bond issue to replace outstanding ₹4 crore bond issue to take advantage of the decline in interest rate. The NDC is in 35 per cent tax bracket. The details of the old bond and new bond are as follows. [LO 23.2]

Old Bonds The outstanding have a ₹1,000 par value and 15 per cent coupon interest rate. They were issued 5 years ago with a 25-year maturity. They were initially sold at par value and the flotation costs were ₹3,30,000. They are callable at ₹1,140.

New Bonds They would have par value of ₹1,000 and 13 per cent coupon rate of interest. With a maturity of 20 years, they could be sold at par. The flotation costs would be ₹5,30,000. The NDC does not expect any overlapping interest.

Assuming 7 per cent after-tax cost of debt, analyse the bond refunding proposal. Would you recommend it?

LOD: Difficult

RQ.23.17 Discuss the symbols and their implications used by (i) CRISIL, (ii) ICRA, (iii) CARE and (iv) FITCH India for rating debentures. [LO 23.2]

RQ.23.18 Dua Company (DC) is contemplating replacing an outstanding ₹2 crore bond issue by a new ₹2 crore bond issue to take advantage of decline in interest rates that has occurred since the original issue. Assuming 35 per cent tax, 8 per cent after-tax cost of debt to evaluate low-risk decisions and the undermentioned details, find the NPV of the bond refunding decision. Is the bond-refunding worthwhile?

The new bonds would have (1) 15-year maturity, (2) a par value of ₹1,000 and (3) 12 per cent coupon rate. They can be sold at par at a flotation cost of ₹4,00,000. The DC expects a 2-month period of overlapping interest while it retires the old bonds.

The outstanding bonds have (1) ₹1,000 par value, and (2) 16 per cent coupon rate interest rate. They were issued 5 years ago with a maturity of 20 years. They were initially sold at ₹20 per-bond discount and ₹2,40,000 flotation cost was incurred. They are callable at ₹1,170.

ANSWERS

23.16 Yes, as NPV of refunding is positive at ₹14,80,595

23.18 NPV = ₹17,33,218. The bond refunding is worthwhile

Scan the QR Code to access comprehensive solutions to all numerical review questions and additional material.

CHAPTER 24

Hybrid Financing/Instruments

LEARNING OBJECTIVES

LO 24.1	Understand the basic rights of preference shareholders, the features of preferences shares and the advantages and disadvantages of preference share financing
LO 24.2	Describe the general features of convertible debentures and illustrate the procedure for determining the value of both optionally convertible debentures and compulsorily convertible debentures
LO 24.3	Explain the basic characteristics of warrants, the implied price of a warrant and the value of a warrant—theoretical, market and warrant premium
LO 24.4	Define option and explain call and put option

INTRODUCTION

As hybrid source of financing has characteristics of both straight debt and straight equity falling somewhere in between. The important hybrid instruments/sources of financing are: **(i)** preference shares/capital, **(ii)** convertible/exchangeable debentures/bonds, **(iii)** warrants and **(iv)** options. The focus in this chapter is on their features and valuation. The procedural aspects of raising hybrid securities is similar to raising equity capital (discussed in Chapter 22). The main points are summarised by way of recapitulation.

LO 24.1 PREFERENCE SHARE CAPITAL

Preference capital is a unique type of long-term financing in that it combines some of the features of equity as well as debentures. As a *hybrid* security/form of financing, it is similar to debenture insofar as: **(i)** it carries a fixed/stated rate of dividend, **(ii)** it ranks higher than equity as a claimant to the income/assets, **(iii)** it normally does not have voting rights and **(iv)** it does not have a share in residual earnings/assets. It also partakes some of the attributes of equity capital, namely, **(i)** dividend on preference capital is paid out of divisible/after tax profit, that is, it is not tax-deductible, **(ii)** payment of preference dividend depends on the discretion of management, that is, it is not an obligatory payment and non-payment does not force insolvency/liquidation and **(iii)** irredeemable type of preference shares have no fixed maturity date.

Features/Attributes

The main attributes of preference shares/capital are discussed below.

Cumulative (dividend) preference shares are preference shares for which all unpaid dividends in arrears must be paid along with the current dividend prior to the payment of dividends to ordinary shareholders.

Prior Claim on Income/Assets Preference capital has a prior claim/preference over equity capital both on the income and assets of the company. In other words, preference dividend must be paid in full before payment of any dividend on the equity capital and in the event of liquidation, the whole of preference capital must be paid before anything is paid to the equity capital. Thus, preference capital stands midway between debentures and equity as regards claim on income and assets of the company. It is also referred to as a *senior security*. Stated in terms of risk perspective, preference capital is less risky than ordinary shares but more risky than debentures.

Cumulative Dividends Preference capital is cumulative in the sense that all unpaid dividends are carried forward and payable before any ordinary dividend is paid.

Straight preference shares value/price is the price at which a preference share would sell without the redemption/call feature.

Redeemability Preference capital has a limited life/specified/fixed maturity after which it must be retired. However, there are no serious penalties for breach of redemption stipulation.

The preference shares have a stated call price which is above the original issue price and decreases over time. Like the call feature on bonds, the call feature on preference shares provides flexibility to the issuer company. Since the market price of **straight preference shares** tends to fluctuate with changes in interest rate, the value of the preference share call feature is determined by the same considerations as is the call feature for bonds (discussed in Chapter 23). The refund of preference share is illustrated in Example 24.1.

***Example* 24.1**

Delhi Manufacturing Company (DMC) is considering refunding its preference shares. They have a par value of ₹100 and a stated dividend of 12 per cent. The call price is ₹104 per share and 5,00,000 shares are outstanding. The DMC can issue new preference shares at 11 per cent. The new issue can be sold at par, the total par value being ₹5 crore. Flotation costs would be ₹13,60,000. Marginal tax rate is 35 per cent. A 90-day period of overlap is expected between the time the new preferences share are issued and the time the existing preference shares are retired. Should the DMC refund its preference shares?

Solution

Analysis of Preference Shares Refund Using Capital Budgeting Analysis

Net Cash Outflow:	
1 Cost of calling old preference shares (5,00,000 × ₹104)	₹5,20,00,000
2 Net proceeds of new issues (₹5 crore – ₹13,60,000)	4,86,40,000
3 Difference (1 – 2)	33,60,000
4 Preference share dividend on old preference shares during overlap (5,00,000 × ₹104 × 3/12)	15,60,000
5 Net cash outlay (3 + 4)	49,20,000
6 Annual net cash outflow on old preference shares:	
Preference share dividend	60,00,000
7 Annual net cash outflow on new preference share:	
Preference share dividend	55,00,000

(Contd.)

(Contd.)

8	Difference (6 – 7)	5,00,000
9	Present value (₹5,00,000 ÷ 0.11[@])	45,45,454
10	Net benefit (₹45,45,454 – ₹49,20,000)	(3,74,454)

[@]Discounted at 11 per cent for a perpetuity.

Decision The preference share issue should not be refunded as the benefit is negative.

Fixed Dividend Preference dividend is fixed and is expressed as a percentage of par value. Yet, it is not a legal obligation and failure to pay will not force bankruptcy. Preference capital is also called a *fixed income* security.

Conversion feature (convertibility) is a feature that allows preference shareholders to change each share in a stated number of ordinary shares.

Convertibility Preference share capital may sometimes be convertible partly/fully into equity shares/debentures at a certain ratio during a specified period. A variant in India is cumulative convertible preference shares which combine the cumulative and convertibility features. It has, however, been a non-starter so far.

Voting Rights Preference capital ordinarily does not carry voting rights. It is, however, entitled to vote on every resolution if (i) the preference dividend is in arrears for two years in respect of cumulative preference shares or (ii) the preference dividend has not been paid for a period of two/more consecutive preceding years or for an aggregate period of three/more years in the preceding six years ending with the expiry of the immediately preceding financial year.

Participation is a feature that provides for dividend payments based on certain formula allowing preference shareholders to participate with ordinary shareholders in the receipt of dividends beyond a specified amount.

Participation Features Preference capital may be participating, entitling **participation** in surplus profits, if any, that is, profits after payment of preference dividend and equity dividend at a certain specified rate. Similarly, it may be entitled to participate in the residual assets after the payment of their normal claim according to a specific formula in the event of liquidation of the company.

Evaluation

Preference capital, as a source of long-term financing, has merits and demerits from the point of view of the investors/ shareholders as well as the company.

Merits The advantages for the investors are: **(i)** stable dividend, **(ii)** the exemption to corporate investors on preference income to the extent of dividend paid out. The issuing companies enjoy several advantages, namely, **(i)** no legal obligation to pay preference dividend and skipping of dividend without facing legal action/bankruptcy, **(ii)** redemption can be delayed without significant penalties, **(iii)** as a part of net worth, it improves the credit-worthiness/ borrowing capacity and, **(iv)** no dilution of control.

Demerits The shareholders suffer serious disadvantages such as (a) vulnerability to arbitrary managerial action as they cannot enforce their right to dividend/right to payment in case of redemption, and (b) modest dividend in the context of the associated risk. For the company, the preference capital is an expensive source of finance due to non-tax deductibility of preference dividend.

In brief, preference capital ***(i)*** *involves high cost;* ***(ii)*** *does not dilute control,* ***(iii)*** *has negligible risk and* ***(iv)****, puts no restraint on managerial freedom.* The shareholders receive modest returns and are vulnerable to arbitrary managerial actions. It is not a popular source of long-term finance in India.

LO 24.2 CONVERTIBLE DEBENTURES/BONDS

Features

Convertible debentures give the holders the right (option) to change them into a stated number of shares.

Conversion ratio is the ratio at which a convertible debenture can be exchanged for shares.

Conversion price is the per share price that is effectively paid for the shares as the result of exchange of a convertible debenture.

Conversion time is the period from the date of allotment after which the option can be exercised.

Convertible debentures give the debenture-holders the right (option) to convert them into equity shares on certain terms. The holders are entitled to a fixed income till the conversion option is exercised and would share the benefits associated with equity shares after the conversion. The operational features of convertible debentures in India at present are as follows.

All the details about conversion terms, namely, conversion ratio, conversion premium/price and conversion timing are specified in the offer document/prospectus. The companies can issue fully convertible debentures (FCDs) or partly convertible debentures (PCDs). The number of ordinary shares for each convertible debenture is the **conversion ratio**. The **conversion price** is the price paid for the ordinary share at the time of conversion. Thus, conversion ratio equals par value of convertible debentures divided by the conversion price. The **conversion time** refers to the period from the date of allotment of convertible debentures after which the option to convert can be exercised. If the conversion is to take place between 18-36 months, the holder will have the option to exercise his rights in full or part. A conversion period exceeding 36 months is not permitted without put and call options. The call options give the issuer the right to redeem the debentures/bonds prematurely on stated terms. The investor has the right to prematurely sell them back to the issuer on specified terms. In addition, compulsory credit rating is necessary for fully convertible debentures.

Issue Procedure

The issue procedure of convertible debt instruments (CDIs) is summarised below:

In addition to the other requirements, an issuer making a public/rights issues of CDIs should comply with the following conditions: **(i)** Obtain credit rating(s); **(ii)** Appoint debenture trustee(s); **(iii)** Crate debenture redemption reserve (DRR); **(iv)** Ensure that assets on which charge/security is proposed to be created are **(a)** sufficient to discharge the principal amount at all times and **(b)** free from encumbrances. Moreover, the consent of financial institutions/banks and lessors for a second/*pari passu* charge should be obtained and submitted to the debenture trustees before the opening of the issue where security is already created on such assets/issue of CDIs is proposed to be secured by creation of security on a leasehold land respectively. The security/asset cover should be arrived at after deduction of the liabilities having a first charge in case the CDIs are secured by a second/subsequent charge. They should be redeemed in terms of the offer document.

The non-convertible portion of partly CDIs by a listed issuer amounting to more than ₹50 lakh may be rolled over without change in the rate of interest subject to compliance, in addition to the provisions of Section 121 of the Companies Act, with the following conditions: **(i)** 75 per cent of the holders have approved it through postal ballot, **(ii)** an auditors' certificate on the cash flow of the issuer and with comments on its liquidity position has been sent, along with the notice for passing the resolution, to all holders, **(iii)** the issuer has undertaken to redeem the CDIs of all holders who have not agreed to the resolution and **(iv)** credit rating from at least one SEBI-registered rating agency has been obtained and communicated to them before the rollover. If the existing trust deed/security document(s) provide for the continuance of the security till redemption, the creation of fresh security/ execution of fresh trust deed would not be mandatory.

Positive consent of the holders would be necessary for conversion of such CDIs into equity shares and non-receipt of reply to any notice by the issuer for this purpose would not be construed as consent for conversion. The holders of CDIs, where the value of the convertible portion of CDIs by a listed company exceeds ₹50 lakh and the conversion price has not been determined, should have the option not to convert them into shares. Such an option may not be given in case the upper limit on their price together with the justification was determined/disclosed to the investors at the time of the issue. If some holders who have been given the option do not exercise it, the issuer should redeem the concerned instruments within one month from the last date for exercise of option at a price not below its face value. This condition would not be applicable if redemption is in terms of the disclosures in the offer document.

Issue of CDIs for **(i)** financing replenishment of funds, **(ii)** providing loan to or for acquiring shares of any person in the same group [in terms of Section 2(ef) or 2(g) of the Monopolies and Restrictive Trade Practice Act] or under the same management [in terms of Section 370 (1-B) of the Companies Act] are prohibited. However, fully CDIs may be issued for these purposes with a conversion period of less than 18 months from the date of their issue.

Valuation

The convertible debentures presently in India can be of three types: **(i)** compulsorily convertible within 18 months, **(ii)** optionally convertible within 36 months and **(iii)** convertible after 36 months with *call* and *put* features. However, only the first two types are popular.

Compulsory Partly/Fully Convertible Debentures

Value The holders of PCDs receive interest at a specified rate over the term of the debenture plus equity share(s) on part conversion and repayment of unconverted part of principal. Symbolically,

$$V_0 = \sum_{t=1}^{n} \frac{I_t}{(1+k_d)^t} + \frac{aP_i}{(1+k_e)^i} + \sum_{j=m} \frac{F_j}{(1+k_d)^j} \qquad \textbf{(24.1)}$$

where V_0 = Value of the convertible debenture at the time of issue,

I_t = Interest receivable at the end of period, t,

n = Term of debentures,

a = Equity shares on part conversion at the end of period, i,

P_i = Expected pre-equity share price at the end of period, i,

F_j = Instalment of principal payment at the end of period, j,

k_d = Required rate of return on debt, and

k_e = Required rate of return on equity.

***Example* 24.2**

The Tata Iron & Steel Ltd (TISCO) had offered in June 1989, ₹30 lakh partly convertible debentures of ₹1,200 each at par. The conversion terms were: (i) compulsory conversion of ₹600 par value into an equity share of ₹100 at a premium of ₹500 within six months of the date of allotment, that is, on February 1, 1990. (ii) 12 per cent per annum interest payable half-yearly and (iii) redemption of non-convertible portion of the debentures at the end of 8 years.

It had also simultaneously issued 32, 54, 167, 12 per cent FCDs of ₹600 each at par on rights basis to the existing shareholders. Each debenture was fully convertible into one share of ₹600, that is, ₹100 par plus a premium of ₹500 within six months from the date of allotment of debentures.

Assuming 8 and 10 per cent as the half-yearly required rate of return on debt and equity respectively, find the value of a TISCO convertible debenture at the time of issue.

Solution

$$\text{Value of the PCD} = \left[\frac{₹72}{1.08}\right] + \sum_{t=2}^{16}\left[\frac{36}{(1.08)^t}\right] + \left[\frac{1 \times ₹1{,}200}{(1.10)^1}\right] + \left[\frac{₹600}{(1.08)^{16}}\right]$$

$$= ₹352.03 + ₹1{,}090.91 + ₹175.20 = ₹1{,}618.14$$

Cost The cost of partly convertible debenture (k_c) is given by Equation 24.2.

$$S_0 = \sum_{t=1}^{n} \frac{I_t(1-T)}{(1+k_c)^t} + \frac{aP_i b}{(1+k_c)^i} + \sum_{j=m}^{n} \frac{F_j}{(1+k_c)^j} \qquad \textbf{(24.2)}$$

S_0 = net subscription price of debentures at the time of issue,
I_t = interest payable at the end of period, t,
T = tax rate,
a = number of equity shares offered on the occurrence of conversion at the end of period, i,
P_i = per equity share price at the end of period i,
b = proportion of net realisable proportion of Pi on the equity share issues to the public,
F_j = principal repayment instalment at the end of period, j, and
k_c = cost of capital/discount rate.

For the TISCO convertible issue as detailed in Example 24.1, assuming further issue expenses, ₹80, 35 per cent tax rate and 75 per cent as the net realisable proportion of equity shares issued to public, the cost of capital (convertible debenture) on a semi-annual basis is the discount rate by solving the following equation:

$$1{,}120 = \frac{72(1-0.35)}{(1+k_c)} + \sum_{t=2}^{16} \frac{36(1-0.35)}{(1+k_c)^t} + \frac{1 \times 1{,}200 \times 0.75}{(1+k_c)} + \frac{600}{(1+k_c)^{16}} \quad \text{or} \quad k_c = 11.5 \text{ per cent}$$

Optionally Convertible Debentures The value of a debenture depends upon three factors: **(i)** straight debenture value, **(ii)** conversion value and **(iii)** option value.

Straight debenture value is the price at which a convertable bond would sell in the market without the conversion feature.

Straight Debenture Value (SDV) equals the discounted value of the receivable interest and principal repayment, if retained as a straight debt instrument. The discount factor would depend upon the credit rating of the debenture.

$$\text{Symbolically SDV} = \sum_{t=1}^{n} \frac{I}{(1+k_d)} + \frac{P}{(1+k_d)^{16}} = \sum_{t=1}^{8} \frac{12}{(1.16)^t} + \frac{100}{(1.16)^8} \qquad \textbf{(24.3)}$$

where,

Maturity period = 8 years, Discount factor = 0.16, Interest = 0.12 payable annually and Face value of debenture = ₹100.

Conversion Value (CV) if the holders opt for conversion, is equal to the share price multiplied by the conversion ratio, that is, the number of equity share offered for each debenture.

If the price of share is, ₹50 and one debenture is convertible into 5 shares (conversion ratio = 5), the CV = ₹250 (₹50 × 5).

Conversion value is the value of a convertible debenture measured in terms of the market price of shares into which it can be converted.

The value of a convertible debenture cannot be less than the SDV and CV which, in a sense, represent its two floor values. In other words, the value of convertible debenture would be the higher of the SDV and CV.

Option Value (OV) The investors have an option, that is, they may not exercise the right/exercise the right at a time of their choosing and select the most profitable alternative. Thus, the option has value in the sense that the value of debenture will be higher than the floor values. Therefore, the value of the convertible debentures = Max [SDV, CV] + OV.

Evaluation

Convertible debentures/bonds have emerged as fairly popular instruments of long-term finance in India in recent years. In the first place, they improve *cash flow matching* of firms. With the invariably lower initial interest burden, a growing/expanding firm would be in a better position to service the debt/debenture. Subsequently, when it would do well, it can afford the servicing of the financing instrument after conversion.

Secondly, they generate *financial synergy*. The assessment of risk characteristics of a new firm is costly and difficult. Convertible debentures provide a measure of protection against error of risk assessment. They have two components: straight debentures and call option. In case the firm turns out risky, the former will have a low value while the latter will have a high value and *vice versa* if the firm turns out to be relatively risk free. As a result, the required yield will not be very sensitive to default risk. In other words, firms with widely varying risks can issue convertible debentures on similar terms whereas the cost for straight debentures would be substantially different. Thus, convertible debentures offer a combination/financial synergy/risk synergy to companies to obtain capital on more favourable terms.

Finally, convertible debentures can mitigate agency problems associated with financing arising out of conflicting demand of equity-holders and debenture-holders/lenders. The focus of the latter is on minimising default risk whereas the former would like the firm to undertake high risk projects. This conflict can be resolved by the issue of convertible debentures/bonds. The debenture-holders would not impose highly restrictive covenants to protect the interest and firms cane undertake profitable investment opportunities.

LO 24.3 WARRANTS

A **warrant** entitles its holders to subscribe to the equity capital of a company during a specified period at a stated/particular/certain price. The holder acquires only the right (option) but he has no obligation to acquire the equity shares. Warrants are generally issued in conjunction with/tied to other instruments, for example, attached to (i) secured premium notes of TISCO in 1992, (ii) debentures of Deepak Fertilisers & Petrochemical Corporation Ltd in 1987, Ranbaxy and Reliance in 1995. They can be/are issued independently also.

Warrant is an instrument that gives its holder the right to purchase a certain number of shares at a specified price over a certain period of time.

Difference with Convertible Debentures

Warrants are akin to convertible debentures to the extent that both give the holder the option/right to buy ordinary shares but there are differences between the two. While the debenture and conversion option are inseparable, a warrant can be detached. Similarly, conversion option is tied to the debenture but warrants can be offered independently also. Warrant are typically exercisable for cash.

Features

The important features of warrants are as follows:

Exercise price is the price at which holders of warrant can purchase a specified number of shares.

Exercise Price It is the price at which the holder of a warrant is entitled to acquire the ordinary shares of the firm. Generally, it is set higher than the market price of the shares at the time of the issue.

Exercise Ratio It reflects the number of shares that can be acquired per warrant. Typically, the ratio is 1:1 which implies that one equity share can be purchased for each warrant.

Expiry Date It means the date after which the option to buy shares expires, that is, the life of the warrant. Usually, the life of warrants is 5-10 years although theoretically perpetual warrants can also be issued.

Types Warrants can be **(i)** detachable, and **(ii)** non-detachable. A detachable warrant can be sold separately in the sense that the holder can continue to retain the instrument to which the warrant was tied and at the same time sell it to take advantage of price increases. Separate sale independent of the instrument is not possible in case of non-detachable warrants. The detachable warrants are listed independently for stock exchange trading but non-detachable warrants are not.

Implied Price of an Attached Warrant

The **implied price of a warrant** is the price effectively paid for each warrant attached to a bond. It can be computed using Equation 24.4

Implied price of a warrant is the price effectively paid for each warrant attached to a bond.

$$\text{Implied price of all warrants} = \text{Price of bond with warrants attached} - \text{Straight bond/debenture value} \quad (24.4)$$

The straight debenture value can be computed using the method to value convertible debentures.

$$\text{The implied price of each warrant} = \frac{\text{Implied price of all warrants}}{\text{Number of warrants attached to each bond}}.$$

The procedure is illustrated in Example 24.3.

***Example* 24.3**

Delhi Traders (TD) has issued 10 per cent, ₹1,000 at par, 10-year bond paying annual interest and having 15 warrants attached for the purchase of its shares. The bonds were initially sold for their par value. Similar-risk straight bonds were selling to yield 12 per cent rate of return. Determine the implied price of an attached warrant.

Solution

Computation of Straight Bond Value

Years	Payments (1)	PVIF (0.12) (2)	Total present value (3) [(1) × (2)]
1 – 10	₹100	5.650	₹565
20	1,000	0.322	322
Straight bond value			887

Implied price of all warrants = ₹1,000 – ₹887 = ₹113

Implied price of each warrant = ₹113 ÷ 15 = ₹7.53

The implication is that an investor is effectively paying ₹7.53 each warrant while purchasing bonds with attached warrants for ₹1,000.

The implied price of each warrant would be useful to estimate the true market value of each warrant if compared with the specific features of each warrant such as **(i)** number of shares that can be purchased and **(ii)** the specified exercise price. If the implied price is more than the estimated market value, the price of the bond with attached warrants may be too high. The bond may be quite attractive in case estimated market value exceeds the implied price.

Value of Warrants

Warrant premium is the difference between the actual market value and theoretical value of a warrant.

Like convertible bonds, a warrant has a **(i)** market value and **(ii)** and a theoretical value. The difference between them is known as the warrant premium.

Theoretical Value of Warrant (TVW) The theoretical value of a warrant is the amount for which the warrant can be expected to be sold in the market. Symbolically, theoretical value of a warrant (TVW)

$$= (P_0 - E) \times N \qquad \textbf{(24.5)}$$

Where, P_0 = current market of a share, E = exercise price of the warrant, and N = number of shares obtainable with one warrant.

***Example* 24.4**

Avon Manufacturers (AM) has outstanding warrants that are exercisable at ₹100 per share. They entitle the holders to purchase 2 shares. The shares of AM are currently selling for ₹112.50 per share. What is the theoretical value of the warrants of AM?

Solution

Theoretical value of warrants = $(P_0 - E) \times N$

= [(₹11.250 – ₹100) × 2] = ₹25

The warrants should sell for ₹25 in the market.

Market Value of Warrant (MVW) The MVW is generally more than the TVW. The two values are close only when (i) the TVW is very high or (ii) the warrant is near its expiration date. The max-imum excess of MVW over the TVW generally is when the market price of shares is close to the exercise price of the warrant per share. The amount of time until expiration also effects the MVW. In general, the closer the warrant is to its expiration date, the more likely the MVW would equal the TVW.

Warrant Premium The warrant premium is the amount by which MVW exceeds the TVW. It results from a combination of (i) positive investor expectations and (ii) the ability of the investor to obtain larger potential return/risk by trading in warrants instead of the underlying shares (i.e. leverage opportunities). Consider Example 24.5.

***Example* 24.5**

An investor has ₹24,300 to invest in Avon Manufacturers (AM). Its shares are currently selling for ₹112.50 per share. The MVW is ₹45 per warrant. Each warrant entitles the holder to purchase 2 shares of AM at ₹100 per share. Compute the warrant premium for the investor.

Solution

The investor could invest his ₹24,300 in either of two ways. Assuming no transaction costs, he could purchase (i) 216 shares of AM at ₹112.50 per share or (ii) 540 warrants at ₹45 per warrant. Assuming the market price of shares of AM increase by ₹7.50 to ₹120. If the investor sells his shares, his gain (₹7.50 × 216) = ₹1,620. His total gain on the sale of warrants = ₹8,100 [(₹7.50 × 2 shares) × 540 warrants. Thus, warrant premium = ₹6,480 (₹18,100 – ₹1,620).

If the market price of shares decline by ₹7.50 per share, the loss to the investor would be: **(i)** on sale of shares, (₹7.50 × 216) = ₹1,620; **(ii)** on sale of warrants [(₹7.50 × 2) × 540) = ₹8,100. Thus, the use of warrants by the investor is more risky than trading the underlying shares of AM.

LO 24.4 OPTIONS

Option is an instrument that provides its holders with an opportunity to purchase/sell a specified asset at a stated price on or before a set expiration date.

Derivative security is a security that derives its value from an underlying asset that is often another security for example, equity shares.

Option is a **derivative security** and derives its value from an underlying security/asset. An option is an instrument that provides to its holders an opportunity to purchase/sell a specified security/asset at a stated price on/before a specified expiration date. The focus in options is on options related to shares. They are traded in India on the NSE and the BSE as securities. There are three basic forms of options: **(i)** rights, **(ii)** warrants, and **(iii)** calls and puts. While rights are discussed in Chapter 18, warrants are described and illustrated in the preceding section. This section explains the call and put option As an investment vehicle, however, they are not a source of financing. The options are issued by investors and not by firms. They are used to earn a return or to protect/lock-in returns already earned on securities by fund managers. But they do stabilise market prices of shares by increasing trading activity in them. Unlike shareholders, buyers of option have no voting rights. The finance managers do not deal with them as a part of fund-raising activities.

Striking price is the price at which the holder of a call option can buy (or the holder of a put option can sell) a specified amount of shares at any time prior to the expiration date.

Calls and Puts Option

Call option is an option to purchase a specified number of shares on or before a specified future date at a stated price.

A **call option** is an option to purchase a specified number of shares on/before a specified future date at stated/strike price. The **striking price** is the price at which the holder of the option can buy the shares at any time prior to the expiration date of the option. It is set at/near the prevailing market price of the shares at the time the option is issued.

Put option is an option to sell a given number of shares on or before a specified future date at a stated price.

A **put option** is an option to sell a given number of shares on/before a specified future date at a stated striking price. Like the call option, the striking price of the put is also set close to the market price of the underlying stock at the time of the deal.

Options transactions are done on futures and options (F&O) segment of the NSE/BSE. The call and put option contracts have one month, two months and three months expiry cycles. All contracts expire on the last Thursday of every month. Thus, a January expiration contract would expire on the last Thursday of January. On the Friday following the last Thursday, a new contract having a 3-month expiry would be introduced for trading. Thus, at any point of time, three contracts would be available for trading with the first contract expiring on the last Thursday of that month. The contract size is 100 or multiples thereof, minimum value being ₹2,00,000. The minimum tick size for a contract is ₹0.05. A single move in option trading would imply a resultant gain/loss of ₹10 (i.e. ₹0.05 × 200 units) on an open position of 200 units.

Call options are purchased in the expectation that the market price of the underlying shares will rise while put options are purchased in the expectation that the share price would decline over the life of the option. The logic underlying the purchase of a put is exactly the opposite of that underlying the use of call options.

***Example* 24.6**

Assume an investor pays ₹2,500 for a 3-month call option on Reliance Industries (RI) at a striking price of ₹500. By paying ₹2,500, the investor is entitled to purchase 100 shares of RI at ₹500 per share at any time during the next 3 months. It implies that the share price must rise to ₹525, that is, ₹5 per share (₹500 ÷ 100 shares) to cover the cost of option (₹2,500), assuming no transaction costs. Suppose the share prices of RI increase to ₹600 during the 3-month period, the net profit to the investor would be ₹7,500 [(100 shares × ₹600) – (₹500 × 100 shares) – ₹2,500]. Thus, option offers a very high return on in-vestment of ₹2,500. However, if the share prices do not rise above ₹500 per share, the investor would lose ₹2,500 as he would not exercise the option. If the share prices increase between ₹500 and ₹525, he would exercise the option to reduce loss to below ₹2,500.

***Example* 24.7**

Assume an investor pays ₹3,250 for a 3-month put option on Reliance Industries (RI) at a striking price of ₹400. The investor is sure that he can sell 100 shares at ₹400 at any time during the next 3 months by paying option money of ₹3,250. Assuming no transaction cost, the price of shares of RI must decline by (₹3,250 ÷ 100 shares) ₹32.5 to ₹367.5 per share to cover the cost of option (₹3,250) of the investor. In case the share prices drop to ₹300 during the 3-month period, the net profit to the investor would be [(100 shares × ₹400) – (100 shares × ₹300) – ₹3,250] ₹6,750. Thus, on an investment of ₹3,250, option offer a very high potential profit (₹6,750) to the investor. If the share price fall to between ₹367.5 and ₹400 per share, the investor should exercise the option to reduce his loss below ₹3,250. However, if the prices rise above ₹400, the investor would not exercise his option and lose ₹3,250.

SUMMARY

LO 24.1	A hybrid source of financing partakes some features of equity shares and some features of debt instruments. The important hybrid instruments are: preference shares, convertible debentures/bonds, warrants and options. The issue procedure for these instruments is similar to the raising of equity shares.
	The main attributes of preference shares (i) prior claim on income/assets, (ii) cumulative dividends, (iii) redeemability, (iv) voting rights when preference dividend is in arrears, (v) participation in surplus profits/excess assets and so on.
	Preference capital involves high cost, does not dilute owners control of the company, has negligible risk and puts no restraint on managerial freedom. The shareholders receive modest return and are vulnerable to arbitrary managerial actions. It is not a popular source of long-term finance in India.
LO 24.2	Convertible debentures (CDs) confer on their holders the right/option to convert them partly (PCDs)/ fully (FCDs) into equity at a later date on specified terms/conditions.
	Their operational features, namely, conversion ratio, conversion premium and conversion timing are specified in advance. The call option gives the issuer the right to redeem to redeem the debentures prematurely. The investor has also the right to prematurely sell them back.

LO 24.2	The value of a compulsorily/fully/partly CDs, $V_0 = \sum_{t=1}^{n} \frac{I_t}{(1+K_d)^t} + \frac{aP_i}{(1+K_e)^j} + \sum_{j=m} \frac{F_j}{(1+K_d)^j}$
	The cost of a PCDs, $Kc = S_0 = \sum_{t=1}^{n} \frac{I_t(1-T)}{(1+K_c)^t} + \frac{aP_i b}{(1+K_c)^j} + \sum_{j=m}^{n} \frac{F_j}{(1+K_c)^j}$
	The value of optionally CDs depends upon three factors: (i) straight debenture value, (ii) conversion value and (iii) option value.
	The reasons for the popularity of CDs are (1) cashflow matching of firms, (2) financial synergy and (3) mitigation of agency problem.
LO 24.3	A warrant entitles its holders to subscribe to the equity capital of a company during a specified period at a stated/particular/striking price. It differs from a CD in that while debenture and conversion option are irreparable a warrant can be detached. Unlike CDs, warrants can be offered independently also.
	The important features of warrants are (1) exercise, price, (2) exercise ratio and (3) expiry date.
	The implied price of an attached warrant is the price effectively paid for each warrant. It is equal to price of bond with attached warrants less straight debenture/warrant value.
	A warrant has a market value and a theoretical value. The difference between them is the warrant premium.
	The theoretical value of a warrant = $(P_0 - E) \times N$.
	A warrant premium results from a combination of (1) positive investor expectation and (ii) the ability of the investor to obtain larger potential return by trading in warrants instead of under-lying shares.
LO 24.4	Options are not a source of financing like shares, debentures, CDs and warrants. But they do stabilise prices of shares by increasing trading activity in them.
	An option is an instrument that provides to its holders an opportunity to purchase (call option)/sell (put option) specified security/asset at a stated striking price on/before a specified expiration date.

SOLVED PROBLEMS

P.24.1 Allied Manufacturers (AM) has an outstanding issue of convertible debentures with a ₹1,000 par value. They are convertible into 100 ordinary shares. They have 10 per cent annual coupon rate and 10-year maturity. The interest rate on straight bond of similar risk is 12 per cent. **LO 24.2** LOD M

Required

(a) Calculate the (i) straight debenture value of the debentures, (ii) conversion (or share) values of the debenture when the market price of the ordinary shares is ₹20, 25, 28, 35 and 50 per share.

(b) For each of the price given in (a) (ii), at what price would you expect the debenture to sell?

(c) What is the lowest price you would expect the debentures to sell for irrespective of the behaviour of the price of the ordinary shares?

Solution

(a) (i) Computation of straight debenture value

Years	*Payments (1)*	*PVIFA (0.12) (2)*	*Present value (3) [(1) × (2)]*
1 – 10	₹100*	5.650	₹565
10	1,000	0.322	322
			887

*(₹1,000 × 0.10)

(ii) Computation of conversion value of debentures

Market price of shares (1)	Conversion ratio (2)	Conversion value (3) [(1) × (2)]
₹8.0	100	₹800
10.0 (conversion price)	100	1,000 (par value)
11.2	100	1,120
14.0	100	1,400
20.0	100	2,000

(b) The debenture would be expected to sell at the higher of the conversion value and straight value. In no case it would sell for less than the straight value (i.e. ₹887). At a price of ₹8, the debenture would sell for its straight value of ₹887. At other prices, it would be expected to sell at the associated conversion values respectively [as calculated in (a) (ii)].

(c) The lowest price would be the straight debenture value (i.e. ₹887).

P.24.2 Delhi Manufacturing Company (DMC) is planning to issue ₹10 crore in 10 per cent convertible debentures. Currently, the market price of its shares is ₹40 per share. The DMC expects to obtain a conversion premium, that is, excess of issue price over conversion value, of 10 per cent. The call price of the debentures in the first 5 years is ₹1,050 per debenture, after which it drops to ₹1,020 in the next 5 years and to ₹1,000 in the last 5 years. To allow for fluctuation in market price of shares, DMC does not want to call the debentures until their conversion value is at least 12 per cent higher than the call price. Earnings per share are expected to grow at 6 per cent compound annual rate and DMC does not envisage any change in its P/E ratio.

LO 24.2 LOD D

Required

Determine the length of time when DMC would be in a position to force conversion.

Solution Expected length of time to force conversion

Conversion price = ₹40 × 1.10 = ₹44

Call price per share in the first 5 years = ₹44 × 1.05 = ₹46.2

Price to which the shares must increase when the DMC would be in a position to force conversion = ₹46.2 × 1.12 = ₹51.74.

Increase from present price = ₹51.74 ÷ ₹40 = 1.294.

At 6 per cent compound growth rate, EPS would grow to 1.262 in 4 years and 1.338 in 5 years (Table A-1). If the P/E ratio remains the same, it would take 4-5 years before the DMC can force conversion.

P.24.3 New Delhi Manufacturers has current earnings of ₹6 per shares with 5,00,000 shares outstanding. It is planning to issue 40,000 shares of 9 per cent, ₹100 par value convertible preference shares at par. The preference share is convertible into 2 ordinary shares for each preference share held. The current market price of ordinary shares is ₹42 per share.

LO 24.1 LOD M

Required

(a) Compute the conversion value of preference shares.

(b) Compute the conversion premium.

(c) Assuming total earnings remain the same, determine the effect of issue on basic earnings per share (i) before conversion (ii) on a fully diluted basis.

(d) If profits after taxes increases by ₹10 lakh, determine the basic earnings per share (i) before conversion and (ii) on a fully diluted basis.

Solution

(a) Conversion value = Conversion ratio × market price per share = 2 × ₹42 = ₹84.

(b) Conversion premium = (₹100 ÷ ₹84) – 1 = 19.05 per cent.

(c) Earnings per share effect

(i) Total after-tax earnings (₹6 × 5,00,000 shares)	₹30,00,000
Preference share dividend (0.09 × 40,000 × ₹100)	3,60,000
Earnings available to ordinary shareholders (NI)	26,40,000
Number of shares (N)	5,00,000
EPS (basic) (₹26,40,000 ÷ 5,00,000)	5.28
(ii) Total earnings	30,00,000
Number of shares (5,00,000 + 80,000)	5,80,000
EPS (diluted) (₹30,00,000 ÷ 5,80,000)	5.17

(d) Earnings per share effect with increase in profit

(i) Total after-tax earnings	₹40,00,000
Preference dividend	3,60,000
NI	36,40,000
N	5,00,000
EPS (NI ÷ N)	7.28
(ii) Total earnings (NI)	40,00,000
N (5,00,000 + 80,000)	5,80,000
EPS (NI ÷ N)	6.90

REVIEW QUESTIONS

LOD: Easy

RQ.24.1 Give appropriate answers for the following: [LO 24.1-4]

(i) Payment of preference share dividend is not obligatory and depends on the discretion of the management. (True/False)

(ii) Preference shares do not entail voting rights under all circumstances. (True/False)

(iii) Convertible debentures are also akin in nature to ______________

(a) Call options (b) Put options (c) Futures contract

(iv) Conversion ratio (in debentures) equals ______________ divided by the conversion price.

(v) ______________ is the price at which a convertible bond will sell in the market without the conversion feature.

(vi) Which of the following instruments is similar in nature to call options?

(a) Warrants (b) Redeemable preference shares (c) Debentures

(vii) For the same strike price and maturity, which of the following strategies is theoretically safer than the other?

(a) Selling a call option (b) Selling a put option

(viii) ______________ is an instrument that gives its holder the right to purchase a certain number of shares at a specified price over a certain period of time.

(ix) ______________ is the price at which holders of warrant can purchase a specified number of shares.

(x) The market value of a warrant is the amount at which the warrant is expected to be sold in the market (True / False).

[Answers: (i) True (ii) False (iii) Call options (iv) Par value of convertible debentures (v) Straight debenture value (vi) Warrants (vii) Selling a put option (viii) Warrant (ix) Exercise price and (x) False]

RQ.24.2 What is preference share? What are the key merits and demerits of preference shares as a source of long-term finance? [LO 24.1]

RQ.24.3 What is call/redeemable feature in a preference share? [LO 24.1]

RQ.24.4 What is conversion feature? What is conversion ratio? [LO 24.1,2]

LOD: Medium

RQ.24.5 Define straight bond value, conversion value, market value and market premium. [LO 24.2]

RQ.24.6 What is a warrant. How does it differ from convertible securities? [LO 24.3]

RQ.24.7 What is implied price of a warrant? How is it estimated? [LO 24.3]

RQ.24.8 What is an option? Define call and put option. Do they play any role in fund-raising activities of a firm? [LO 24.4]

RQ.24.9 How does option trading take place? [LO 24.4]

RQ24.10 The North Traders has an outstanding issue of convertible debentures with a par value of ₹1,000. They are convertible into 50 shares, have 10 per cent annual coupon rate and 10-year maturity. The interest on a straight bond of a similar risk is currently 11 per cent. [LO 24.2]

Required

1. Calculate the straight value of the debentures.
2. Calculate the conversion values of the debentures when the market price of shares is ₹15, 20, 23, 30 and 45 per share.
3. For each of the stock prices given in (2), at what price can the debentures be expected to sell?
4. What is the minimum price the debenture would be expected to sell at irrespective of the behaviour of share prices.

RQ24.11 The warrants of Dua Manufacturers allow the purchase of its 2 shares at ₹75 per share. The price per share and the market value of the warrants associated with the relevant share prices are given below. [LO 24.3]

Per share price	*Market value of warrant*
₹63	₹3
69	12
72	13.5
81	27
87	42
93	57
99	72

Required

Compute the theoretical warrant value for each of the share prices.

LOD: Difficult

RQ.24.12 Discuss the method for valuation of compulsorily convertible debentures into shares. [LO 24.2]

RQ.24.13 How is the value of an optionally convertible debenture affected by the straight debenture value, conversion value and option value. [LO 24.2]

RQ.24.14 Explain briefly (1) theoretical value of a warrant, (2) its market value, and (3) warrant premium. [LO 24.3]

RQ24.15 An investor wishes to ascertain if the ₹1,000 price of debentures of Southern Petrochemicals (SP) is fair in the light of the theoretical value of the attached warrants. The debentures (1) have a par value of ₹1,000 (2) pay 12 per cent coupon interest rate annually, (3) have a 10-year maturity and (4) have 10 warrants attached for purchase of shares. The theoretical value of each warrant (TVW) is ₹12.50. The interest on an equal risk striaght debenture is 14 per cent. [LO 24.2]

Required

(a) Compute the straight value of SP's debentures.
(b) What is the implied price of all warrants attached to SP's debentures?
(c) What is the implied price of each warrant?
(d) Compare the implied price computed in (c) to its theoretical value. On the basis of the comparison, is the price of SP's debentures fair? Why?

ANSWERS

24.10 **1.** ₹940.9
2. ₹750; ₹1,000; ₹1,150; ₹1,500; ₹2,250
3. The debenture would be expected to sell at the higher of conversion value and straight value. In no case, it would sell for less than the straight value (₹940.9). At a market price of ₹15, the debenture would sell for its straight value ₹940.9; at others prices, it would be expected to sell at respective conversion value.
4. Straight value ₹940.9

24.11 0*; 0*; 0*; ₹12; ₹24; ₹36; ₹48 (For price ranges from ₹63–₹99)
* The value of warrant cannot be negative. Its value is, therefore, taken as zero

24.15 **(a)** ₹895.92
(b) ₹104.08
(c) ₹10.41
(d) The implied price (₹10.41) is less than theoretical value (₹12.5).
Yes, price is fair. The debenture has been issued at ₹20.92 which is less than expected market value.

Scan the QR Code to access comprehensive solutions to all numerical review questions and additional material.

CHAPTER 25

Lease Financing and Hire-purchase Finance

LEARNING OBJECTIVES

LO 25.1	Define leasing, describe its main features and classification of leasing—finance lease, operating lease, sale and lease back, single investor and leveraged lease, domestic and international lease—and the significance and limitations of leasing
LO 25.2	Review and illustrate financial evaluation of leasing both from lessee's perspective and lessor's perspective
LO 25.3	Describe the general features of hire-purchase, comparison of hire-purchase with leasing and instalment payment, and financial evaluation of hire-purchase transaction from the viewpoint of the hirer as well the finance company

INTRODUCTION

This chapter dwells on two sources of long-term finance, namely, lease financing and hire-purchase financing. The main points are also summarised by way of recapitulation.

LO 25.1 LEASE FINANCING

We explain the theoretical framework of leasing in terms of concept and classification of leasing and its significance and limitation.

Leasing is the process by which a firm can obtain the use of a certain fixed asset for which it must make a series of contractual, periodic, tax-deductible payments (lease rentals).

Concept and Classification

Concept The conceptual aspect of leasing include its meaning and essential elements.

Meaning Conceptually, a **lease** may be defined as a contractual arrangement/transaction in which a party owning an asset/equipment (lessor) provides the asset for use to another/transfer the right to use the equipment to the user (lessee), over a certain/for an agreed period of time, for consideration in form of/in return for periodic payment (rentals), with or without a further payment (premium). At the end of the period of contract (lease period), the asset/equipment reverts back to the lessor unless there is a provision for the renewal of the contract. Leasing essentially involves the *divorce of ownership from the economic use of an asset/equipment.* It is a device of financing the cost of an asset. It is a contract in which a specific equipment required by the lessee is purchased by the lessor (financier) from a manufacturer/vendor selected by the lessee. The lessee has possession and use of the asset on payment of the specified rentals over a predetermined period of time. Lease financing is, thus, a device of financing/money lending. The position of a lessee is akin to that of a person who owns the same asset with borrowed money. The real function of a lessor is not renting of the asset but lending of funds/finance/credit, and lease financing is, in effect, a contract of lending money. The lessor (financier) is the nominal owner of the asset as the possession and economic use of the equipment vests in the lessee. The lessee is free to choose the asset according to his requirements and the lessor does not take recourse to the equipment as long as the rentals are regularly paid to him.

Essential Elements The essential elements of leasing are the following:

Parties to the Contract There are essentially two parties to a contract of lease financing, namely, the owner and the user, called the **lessor** and the **lessee**, respectively. Lessors as well as lessees, may be individuals, partnerships, joint stock companies, corporations or financial institutions. Sometimes there may be joint lessors or joint lessees, particularly where the properties or the amount of finance involved is enormous. Besides, there may be a lease broker who acts as an intermediary in arranging these deals. Merchant banking divisions of certain foreign banks in India, subsidiaries of some Indian banks and even some private merchant bankers are acting as lease brokers. They charge a certain percentage of fees for their services, ranging between 0.50 to 1 per cent. Besides, a lease contract may involve a *lease financier*, who refinances the lessor, either by providing term loans or by subscribing to equity or lending under a specific refinance scheme.

Lessor is the owner of the assets that are being leased.

Lessee is the receiver of the services of the assets under a lease contract.

Assets The assets, property or equipment to be leased is the subject matter of a lease financing contract. The asset may be an automobile, plant and machinery, equipment, land and building, factory, a running business, an aircraft and so on. The asset must, however, be of the lessee's choice, suitable for his business needs.

Ownership Separated from User The essence of a lease financing contract is that during the lease tenure, ownership of the asset vests with the lessor and its use is allowed to the lessee. On the expiry of the lease tenure, the asset reverts to the lessor.

Term of Lease The term of lease is the period for which the agreement of lease remains in operation. Every lease should have a definite period, otherwise it will be legally inoperative. The lease period may sometimes stretch over the entire economic life of the asset (i.e. financial lease) or a period shorter than the useful life of the asset (i.e. operating lease). The lease may be perpetual, that is, with an option at the end of lease period to renew the lease for the further specific period.

Lease Rentals The consideration that the lessee pays to the lessor for the lease transaction is the lease rental. Lease rentals are structured so as to compensate (in the form of depreciation) the lessor for the investment made in the asset, and for expenses like interest on the investment, repairs and servicing charges borne by the lessor over the lease period.

Modes of Terminating the Lease At the end of the lease period, the lease is terminated and various courses are possible, namely,

(a) The lease is renewed on a perpetual basis or for a definite period, or
(b) The asset reverts to the lessor, or
(c) The asset reverts to the lessor and the lessor sells it to a third party or
(d) The lessor sells the asset to the lessee.

The parties may mutually agree to and choose any of the aforesaid alternatives at the beginning of a lease term.

Classification An equipment lease transaction can differ on the basis of (i) the extent to which the risks and rewards of ownership are transferred, (ii) number of parties to the transactions, (iii) domiciles of the equipment manufacturer, the lessor, the lessee and so on. **Risk,** with reference to leasing, refers to the possibility of loss arising on account of under-utilisation or technological obsolescence of the equipment, while **reward** means the incremental net cash flows that are generated from the usage of the equipment over its economic life and the realisation of the anticipated residual value on expiry of the economic life. On the basis of these variations, leasing can be classified into the following types: **(a)** Finance lease and Operating lease, **(b)** Sales and lease back and Direct lease, **(c)** Single investor lease and Leveraged lease and **(d)** Domestic lease and International lease.

> **Risk** is the possibility of loss arising on account of under-utilisation or technological obsolescence of the equipment.

Finance Lease and Operating Lease: **Finance Lease** According to the International Accounting Standards (IAS-17), in a **finance lease** the lessor transfers, substantially all the risks and rewards incidental to the ownership of the asset to the lessee, whether or not the title is eventually transferred. It involves payment of rentals over an obligatory non-cancellable lease period, sufficient in total to amortise the capital outlay of the lessor and leave some profit. In such leases, the lessor is only a financier and is usually not interested in the assets. It is for this reason that such leases are also called **full payout leases**, as they enable a lessor to recover his investment in the lease and derive a profit. Types of assets included under such leases are ships, aircrafts, railway wagons, lands, buildings, heavy machinery, diesel generating sets and so on.

> **Finance (capital) leases** are for terms that approach the economic life of the asset; the total payments over the term of the lease are greater than the lessor's initial cost of the leased asset.

The IAS-17 stipulates that a substantial part of the ownership related risks and rewards in leasing are transferred when:

(i) The ownership of the equipment is transferred to the lessee by the end of the lease firm; or
(ii) The lessee has the option to purchase the asset at a price that is expected to be sufficiently lower than the fair market value at the date the option becomes exercisable and if at the inception of the lease it is reasonably certain that the option will be exercised; or
(iii) The lease term is for a major part of the useful life of the asset; the title may not eventually be transferred. The useful life of an asset refers to the minimum of its (i) *physical* life in terms of the period for which it can perform its function, (ii) *technological life* in the sense of the period in which it does not become obsolete and (iii) *product market life* defined as the period during which its product enjoys a satisfactory market. The criterion/cut-off point is that if the lease term exceeds 75 per cent of the useful life of the equipment, it is a finance lease or
(iv) The present value of the minimum lease payment is greater than, or substantially equal to, the fair market value of the asset at the inception of the lease (cost of equipment). The title may or may not be eventually transferred. The cut-off point is that the present value exceeds 90 per cent of the fair market value of the equipment. The present value should be computed

by using a discount rate equal to the rate implicit in the lease, in the case of the lessor, and the incremental rate in the case of the lessee.

According to the Accounting Standard (AS)-19: Lease issued by the Institute of Chartered Accountants of India (ICAI) in January 2001, the classification of leases is based on the extent to which risks and rewards incidental to ownership of a leased asset lie with the lessor or the lessee. Risks include the possibility of losses from the idle capacity or technological obsolescence and of variation in return due to changing economic conditions. Rewards may be represented by the expectation of profitable operation over the economic life of the asset and of gain from appreciation in the value of the residual value that has been realised.

A lease is classified as a *finance lease* if it transfers substantially all the risk and rewards incidental to ownership. Title may or may not eventually be transferred. A lease is classified as an *operating lease* if it does not transfer substantially all the risks and rewards incidental to ownership. Since the transaction between a lessor and lessee is based on a lease agreement common to both parties, it is appropriate to use consistent definitions. The application of these definitions to the differing circumstances of the two parties may sometimes result in the same lease being classified differently by the lessor and the lessee. Whether a lease is a finance lease or an operating lease depends on the substance of the transaction rather than its form. Examples of situations that would normally lead to a lease being classified as a finance lease are:

(a) The lease transfers ownership of the asset to the lessee by the end of the lease term;

(b) The lessee has the option to purchase the asset at a price that is expected to be sufficiently lower than the fair value at the date the option becomes exercisable such that, at the inception of the lease, it is reasonably certain that the option will be exercised;

(c) The lease term is for the major part of the economic life of the asset even if title is not transferred;

(d) At the inception of the lease, the present value of the minimum lease payments amounts to greater than or at least substantially equal to the fair value of the leased asset and

(e) The leased asset is of a specialised nature such that only the lessee can use it without major modifications being made.

Indicators of situations, that individually or in combination, could also lead to a lease being classified as a finance lease are:

(a) If the lessee can cancel the lease, the lessor's losses associated with the cancellation are borne by the lessee;

(b) Gains or losses from the fluctuation in the fair value of the residual fall to the lessee (for example in the form of a rent rebate equalling most of the sales proceeds at the end of the lease) and

(c) The lessee can continue the lease for a secondary period at a rent that is substantially lower than market rent.

Lease classification is made at the inception of the lease. If at any time, the lessee and the lessor agree to change the provisions of the lease, other than by renewing the lease, in a manner that would have resulted in a different classification of the lease under the criteria outlined above, or had the changed terms been in effect at the inception of the lease, the revised agreement is considered as a new agreement over its revised term. Changes in estimates (for example, changes in estimate of the economic life or of the residual value of the leased asset) or changes in circumstances (for example, default by the lessee), however, do not give rise to a new classification of a lease for accounting purposes. A finance lease is structured to include the following features:

(i) The lessee (the intending buyer) selects the equipment according to his requirements, from its manufacturer or distributor;

(ii) The lessee negotiates and settles with the manufacturer or distributor, the price, the delivery schedule, installation, terms of warranties, maintenance and payment and so on;

(iii) The lessor purchases the equipment either directly from the manufacturer or distributor (under straight forward leasing) or from the lessee, after the equipment is delivered (under sale and lease back);

(iv) The lessor then leases out the equipment to the lessee. The lessor retains the ownership while lessee is allowed to use the equipment;

(v) A finance lease may provide a right or option, to the lessee, to purchase the equipment at a future date. However, this practice is rarely found in India;

(iv) The lease period spreads over the expected economic life of the asset. The lease is originally for a non-cancellable period called the **primary lease period** during which the lessor seeks to recover his investment alongwith some profit. During this period, cancellation of lease is possible only at a very heavy cost. Thereafter, the lease is subject to renewal for the **secondary lease period**, during which rentals are substantially low;

(vii) The lessee is entitled to exclusive and peaceful use of the equipment during the entire lease period, provided he pays the rentals and complies with the terms of the lease;

(viii) As the equipment is chosen by the lessee, the responsibility of its suitability, the risk of obsolescence and the liability for repair, maintenance and insurance of the equipment rest with the lessee.

Operating Lease According to the IAS-17 and AS-19, an **operating lease** is one that is not a finance lease. In a operating lease, the lessor does not transfer all the risks and rewards incidental to the ownership of the asset and the cost of the asset is not fully amortised during the primary lease period. The lessor provides services (other than the financing of the purchase price) attached to the leased asset, such as maintenance, repair and technical advice. For this reason, an operating lease is also called a '**service lease**'. The lease rental is an operating lease that includes a cost for the 'services' provided, and the lessor does not depend on a single lessee for recovery of his cost. An operating lease is generally used for computers, office equipment, automobiles, trucks, other equipment, telephones and so on. An operating lease is structured with the following features:

> **Operating leases** are for a time shorter than the economic life of the asset; generally the payments over the term of the lease are less than the lessor's initial cost of the leased asset.

(i) An operating lease is generally for a period significantly shorter than the economic life of the leased asset. In some cases, it may be even on an hourly, daily, weekly or monthly basis. The lease is cancellable by either party during the lease period.

(ii) Since the lease periods are shorter than the expected life of the asset, the lease rentals are not sufficient to totally amortise the cost of assets.

(iii) The lessor does not rely on the single lessee for recovery of his investment. His ultimate interest is in the residual value of the asset. The lessor bears the risk of obsolescence, since the lessee is free to cancel the lease at any time;

(iv) Operating leases normally include a maintenance clause requiring the lessor to maintain the leased asset and provide services such as insurance, support staff, fuel and so on.

Examples of operating leases are:

(a) Providing mobile cranes with operators;

(b) Chartering of aircrafts and ships, including the provision of crew, fuel and support services;

(c) Hiring of computers with operators;

(d) Hiring a taxi for a particular travel, which includes service of the driver, provision for maintenance, fuel, immediate repairs and so on.

Sale and Lease Back and Direct Lease: Sale and Lease Back In a way, it is an indirect form of leasing. The owner of an equipment/asset sells it to a leasing company (lessor) that leases it back to the owner (lessee). A classic example of this type of leasing is the sale and lease back of safe deposit vaults by banks. Banks sell the vaults in their custody to a leasing company at a market price substantially higher than the book value and the leasing company in turn offers these lockers on a long-term basis to the bank. The bank sub-leases the lockers to its customers. The *lease back* arrangement in sale and lease back type of leasing can be in the form of a finance lease or an operating lease.

Sale-lease back is a lease under which the lessee sells an asset for cash to a prospective lessor and then leases back the same asset, making fixed periodic payments for its use.

Direct Lease In direct lease, the lessee, and the owner of the equipment are two different en-tities. A direct lease can be of two types: bipartite and tripartite lease.

Bipartite Lease There are two parties in this lease transaction, namely, **(i)** the equipment supplier-cum-lessor and **(ii)** the lessee. Such a lease is typically structured as an operating lease with inbuilt facilities like upgradation of the equipment (Upgrade lease), addition to the original equipment configuration and so on. The lessor maintains the asset and, if necessary, replaces it with a similar equipment that is in working condition (Swap lease).

Direct lease is a lease under which a lessor owns/acquires the assets that are leased to a given lessee.

Tripartite Lease Such a lease involves three different parties in the lease agreement: **(i)** the equipment supplier, **(ii)** the lessor and **(iii)** the lessee. An innovative variant of the tripartite lease is the sales-aid lease under which the equipment supplier arranges for lease finance in various forms by:

- Providing reference about the customer to the leasing company;
- Negotiating the terms of the lease with the customer and completing all the formalities on behalf of the leasing company;
- Writing the lease on his own account and discounting the lease receivables with the designated leasing company. The effect is that the leasing company owns the equipment and obtains an assignment of the lease rental.

The sales-aid lease is usually with recourse to the supplier in the event of default by the lessee, either in the form of an offer from the supplier to buy back the equipment from the lessor or a guarantee on behalf of the lessee.

Single Investor Lease and Leveraged Lease: **Single Investor Lease** There are only two parties to this lease transaction: the lessor and the lessee. The leasing company (lessor) funds the entire investment by an appropriate mix of debt and equity funds. The debt raised by the leasing company to finance the asset are without recourse to the lessee, that is, in the case of default in servicing the debt by the leasing company, the lender is not entitled to payment from the lessee.

Leveraged Lease There are three parties to the transaction: **(i)** the lessor (equity investor), **(ii)** the lender and **(iii)** the lessee. In such a lease, the leasing company (equity investor) buys the asset through substantial borrowing, with full recourse to the lessee and any recourse to it. The lender (loan participant) obtains an assignment of the lease and the rentals to be paid by the lessee as well as first mortgage assets on the leased asset. The transaction is routed through a trustee who looks after the interests of the lender and lessor. On receipt of the rentals from the lessee, the trustee remits the debt-service component of the rental to the loan participant and the balance to the lessor.

Leveraged lease is a lease under which the lessor acts as an equity participant supplying a fraction of the total cost of the asset while the lender supplies the major part (balance).

To illustrate, assume the Hypothetical Ltd (HLL) has structured a leveraged lease with an investment cost of ₹50 crore. The investment is to be financed by equity from the company and loan from the Hypothetical Bank Ltd (HBL) in the ratio of 1:5. The interest on loan may be assumed to be 20 per cent per annum, to be repaid in five equated annual instalments. If the required rate of return (gross yield) of the HLL is 24 per cent, calculate (i) the equated annual instalment and (ii) the annual lease rental.

(i) Equated Annual Instalment to HBL:

$$= \frac{\text{Loan amount}}{\text{PVIFA [at 20 per cent, after 5 years (20,5)]}}$$

$$= \frac{₹40 \text{ crore } (0.8 \times ₹50 \text{ crore})}{2.991} = ₹13.4 \text{ crore}$$

(ii) Annual Lease Rental (X):

Annual cash flow to HLL = (X – ₹13.4 crore)

Given HLL's required rate of return of 24 per cent, (X – ₹13.4 crore) × PVIFA (24,5) – ₹10 crore (equity) or 2.745 X – ₹36.783 crore (ie, 2.745 × ₹13.4 crore) = ₹10 crore

Or

$$2.745\ X = ₹46.783 \text{ crore}$$
$$X = ₹17.04 \text{ crore}$$

In terms of the standard quote, the lease rental works out to be ₹340/₹1,000 per annum $\left(₹17.04 \text{ core} \times \frac{₹1{,}000}{₹50 \text{ crore}}\right)$

Like other lease transactions, leverage lease entitles the lessor to claim tax shields on depreciation and other capital allowances on the entire investment cost, including the non-recourse debt. The return on equity (profit after tax divided by networth) is, therefore, high.

From the lessee's point of view, the effective rate of interest implicit in the lease arrangement is less than on a straight loan as the lessor passes on a portion of the tax benefits, in the form of lower rental payments, to the lessee. Leveraged lease packages are generally structured for leasing investment intensive assets like aircrafts, ships and so on.

Domestic Lease and International Lease: **Domestic Lease** A lease transaction is classified as domestic if all parties to the agreement, namely, equipment supplier, lessor and the lessee are domiciled in the same country.

Domestic lease is a lease transaction if all parties to the agreement are domiciled in the same country.

International Lease If the parties to the lease transaction are domiciled in different countries, it is known as an international lease. This type of lease is further sub-classified into **(1)** the import lease and **(2)** the cross-border lease.

Import Lease In an import lease, the lessor and the lessee are domiciled in the same country but the equipment supplier is located in a different country. The lessor imports the asset and leases it to the lessee.

International lease is a lease transaction if all parties to the agreement are domiciled in different countries.

Cross-Border Lease When the lessor and the lessee are domiciled in different countries, the lease is classified as cross-border lease. The domicile of the supplier is immaterial.

Operationally, the domestic and international leases are differentiated on the basis of risk. The latter type of lease transaction is affected by two additional risk factors, that is, country risk and currency risk. The country risk arises from the need to structure the lease transaction in the light of an understanding of the political and economic climate and a knowledge of the tax and regulatory environment governing them in the foreign countries concerned. As the payment to the supplier and the lease rentals are denominated in different currencies, any variation in the exchange rate will involve currency risk.

Significance and Limitations

The advantages and limitations of leasing are summarised below.

***Advantage of Leasing:* To the Lessee** Lease financing has the following advantages to the lessee:

Financing of Capital Goods Lease financing enables the lessee to avail of finance for huge investments in land, building, plant, machinery, heavy equipment, and so on, upto 100 per cent, without requiring any immediate down payment. Thus, the lessee is able to commence his business virtually without making any initial investment (of course, he may have to invest a minimal sum for working capital needs).

Additional Sources of Finance Leasing facilitates the acquisition of equipment, plant and machinery without the necessary capital outlay and, thus, has a competitive advantage of mobilising the scarce financial resources of a business enterprise. It enhances the working capital position and makes available the internal accruals for business operations.

Less Costly Leasing as a method of financing is less costly than other alternatives available.

Ownership Preserved Leasing provides finance without diluting the ownership or control of the promoters. As against it, other modes of long-term finance—for example, equity—normally dilute the ownership of the promoters.

Avoids Conditionalities Lease finance is considered preferable to institutional finance as in the former case there are no strings attached. Lease financing is beneficial since it is free from restrictive covenants and conditionalities, such as representation on the board, conversion of debt into equity, payment of dividend and so on, which usually accompany institutional finance and term loans from banks.

Flexibility in Structuring of Rentals Lease rentals can be structured to accommodate the cash flow situation of the lessee, making the payment of rentals convenient to him. Lease rentals are so tailor-made that the lessee is able to pay the rentals from the funds generated from operations. The lease period is also chosen so as to suit the lessee's capacity to pay rentals and considering the operating life-span of the asset. Some of the ways to structure lease rentals are illustrated below.

The following data relate to the Hypothetical Leasing Ltd:

(1) Investment outlay/cost, ₹100 lakh
(2) Pre-tax required rate of return, 20 per cent per annum
(3) Primary lease period, 5 years
(4) Residual value (after primary period), Nil
(5) Assumptions regarding alternative rental structures:
  (A) Equated/Level
  (B) Stepped (15 per cent increase per annum),
  (C) Ballooned (annual rental of ₹10 lakh for years, 1–4),
  (D) Deferred (deferment period of 2 years)

The annual lease rentals under the above four alternatives are computed below:

(A) Equated Annual Lease Rental (Y):

$$Y = Y \times \text{PVIFA [at 20 per cent for 5 years (20,5)} = ₹100 \text{ lakh}$$

$$= \frac{₹100 \text{ lakh}}{2.991} = ₹33.43 \text{ lakh}$$

(B) Stepped Lease Rental (assuming 15 per cent increase annually):

$$Y = Y \times \text{PVIF }(20,1) + (1.15)Y \times \text{PVIF }(20,2) + (1.15)^2 Y \times \text{PVIF }(20,3) + (1.5)^3 Y \times \text{PVIF }(20,4) + (1.5)^4 Y \times \text{PVIF }(20,5) = ₹100 \text{ lakh}$$

$$= 8.33Y + 0.798Y(0.694 \times 1.15Y) + 0.764Y(0.579 \times 1.32Y) + 0.733Y (0.482 \times 1.52Y) + 0.703Y(0.402 \times 1.75Y)$$

$$= (0.482 \times 1.52\ Y) + 0.703\ (0.402 \times 1.75\ Y) = 3.833Y = ₹100 \text{ lakh}$$

Y = ₹26.10 lakh, where Y denotes the annual rental in year 1.

The lease rentals in different years over the lease term will be: Year 2, ₹30.02 lakh; Year 3, ₹34.52 lakh; Year 4, ₹39.70 lakh; an Year 5, ₹45.65 lakh.

(C) Ballooned Leased Rental (₹10 lakh for years 1–4):

$$Y = [10 \times \text{PVIFA }(20,4) + Y \times \text{PVIF }(20,5)] = ₹100 \text{ lakh}$$

$$Y = ₹100 \text{ lakh} - ₹25.9 \text{ lakh}$$

or Y = (₹74.10 lakh ÷ 0.402) = ₹184.33 lakh, where Y denotes the ballooned payment in year 5.

(D) Deferred Lease Rental (deferment of 2 years):

Denoting Y as the equated annual rental to be charged between years 3-5,

$$Y = Y \times \text{PVIF }(20,3) + Y \times \text{PVIF }(20,4) + Y \times \text{PVIF }(20,5) = ₹100 \text{ lakh}$$

$$1.463\ Y = ₹100 \text{ lakh}$$

$$Y = ₹68.35 \text{ lakh}$$

This flexibility is not available in the debt servicing pattern of a conventional loan; institutional borrowings, for instance. Such loans have to be typically repaid over a specified number of instalments resulting in heavy debt servicing burden in the earlier years of a project, whereas the project may actually generate substantial cash flows in later years.

Simplicity A lease finance arrangement is simple to negotiate and free from cumbersome procedures with faster and simple documentation. As against it, institutional finance and term loans require compliance of covenants, formalities and a bulk of documentation, causing procedural delays.

Tax Benefits By suitable structuring of lease rentals, a lot of tax advantage can be derived. If the lessee is in a tax paying position, the rental may be increased to lower his taxable income. The cost of the asset is thus amortised more rapidly than in a case where the asset is owned by the lessee, since depreciation is allowable at the prescribed rates. If the lessor is in a tax paying position, the rentals may be lowered to pass on a part of the tax benefit to the lessee. Thus, rentals can be suitably adjusted for postponement of taxes.

Obsolescence Risk is Averted In a lease arrangement, the lessor, being the owner, bears the risk of obsolescence and the lessee is always free to replace the asset with the latest technology.

To the Lessor A lessor has the following advantages:

Full Security The lessor's interest is fully secured since he is always the owner of the leased asset and can take repossession of the asset if the lessee defaults. As against it, realising an asset secured against a loan is more difficult and cumbersome.

Tax Benefit The greatest advantage of the lessor is the tax relief by way of depreciation. If the lessor is in a high tax bracket, he can lease out assets with high depreciation rates and, thus, reduce his tax liability substantially. Besides, the rentals can be suitably structured to pass on some tax benefit to the assessee.

High Profitability The leasing business is highly profitable since the rate of return is more than what the lessor pays on his borrowings. Also, the rate of return is more than in case of lending finance directly.

Trading on Equity The lessor usually carry out his operations with greater financial leverage. That is, he has a very low equity capital and use a substantial amount of borrowed funds and deposits. Thus, the ultimate return on equity is very high.

High Growth Potential The leasing industry has a high growth potential. Lease financing enables the lessees to acquire equipment and machinery even during a period of depression, since they do not have to invest any capital. Leasing, thus, maintains the economic growth even during a recessionary period.

Limitations of Leasing Lease financing suffers from certain limitations too:

Restrictions on Use of Equipment A lease arrangement may impose certain restrictions on use of the equipment, acquiring compulsory insurance and so on. Besides, the lessee is not free to make additions or alterations to the leased asset to suit his requirement.

Limitations of Financial Lease A financial lease may entail a higher payout obligation if the equipment is not found to be useful and the lessee opts for premature termination of the lease agreement. Besides, the lessee is not entitled to the protection of express or implied warranties since he is not the owner of the asset.

Loss of Residual Value The lessee never becomes the owner of the leased asset. Thus, he is deprived of the residual value of the asset and is not even entitled to any improvements done by the lessee or caused by inflation or otherwise, such as appreciation in value of leasehold land.

Consequence of Default If the lessee defaults in complying with any terms and conditions of the lease contract, the lessor may terminate the lease and take over the possession of the leased asset. In case of finance lease, the lessee may be required to pay for damages and accelerated rental payments.

Understatement of Lessee's Asset Since the leased asset does not form part of the lessee's assets, there is an effective understatement of his assets, which may sometimes lead to gross underestimation of the lessee. However, there is now an accounting practice to disclose the leased assets by way of a footnote to the balance sheet.

LO 25.2 FINANCIAL EVALUATION OF LEASING

The process of financial appraisal in a lease transaction generally involves three steps: **(i)** appraisal of the client, in terms of his financial strength and credit worthiness; **(ii)** evaluation of the security/ collateral security offered and **(iii)** financial evaluation of the proposal. The most critical part of a leasing transaction, both to the lessor and the lessee, is the financial evaluation of the proposal. The analytical framework/technique to evaluate the financial terms of a leasing proposal is discussed below. The objective of the evaluation is to identify the cheaper source of finance to a lessee and better investment alternative to the lessor.

Lessee's Perspective

Finance lease effectively transfers the risk and rewards associated with the ownership of an equipment from the lessor to the lessee. A lease can be evaluated either as an investment decision or as a financing alternative. Given that an investment decision has already been made, a firm (lessee) has to evaluate whether it will purchase the asset/equipment or acquire it on lease basis. Since lease rental payments are similar to payments of interest on debt, leasing in essence is an alternative to borrowing. The lease evaluation from the lessee's point of view, thus, essentially involves a choice between debt financing versus lease financing. It is in this context that an evaluation of lease financing from the view point of the lessee is presented here. The decision criterion used is the Net Present Value of Leasing [NPV(L)]/Net Advantage of Leasing (NAL). The discount rate used is the marginal cost of capital for all cash flows other than lease payments and the pre-tax cost of debt for lease payments. The value of the interest tax shield is included as a foregone cash flow in the computation of NPV(L)/NAL

Equationally NPV(L)/NAL

= Investment cost

Less: Present value of lease payments (discounted by K_d)

Plus: Present value of tax shield on lease payments (discounted by K_c)

Less: Management fee

Plus: Present value of tax shield on management fee (discounted by K_c)

Minus: Present value of depreciation (tax) shield (discounted by K_c)

Minus: Present value of (tax) shield on interest (discounted by K_c)

Minus: Present value of residual/salvage value (discounted by K_c)

where K_c = Post-tax marginal cost of capital

K_d = Pre-tax cost of long-term debt

If the NAL/NPV(L) is positive, the leasing alternative should be used, otherwise the borrowing alternative would be preferable.

An alternative approach is to compare the leasing and buying/borrowing alternative. Given the fact that investment decision has already been taken, the lessee is to evaluate whether it should purchase an equipment through borrowing or acquire it on lease basis. Why borrowings only? Since lease rentals are similar to the payment of interest on debt, leasing, in essence, is an alternative to borrowing. The lease, as a source of finance, should be logically compared exclusively with debt as an alternative source of finance to purchase the required equipment/plant. The lessee, obviously, would opt for the cheaper source of finance. For the purpose of financial evaluation, the two methods in vogue are: **(1)** Present-value method and **(2)** Internal-rate of return method.

Present-Value Method The present value method involves a comparison of present value (PV) of cash outflows after taxes (COAT) under both the alternatives. An alternative with the lower PV would be a preferred choice. The steps involved are summarised below.

(1) Determine the cash outflows after taxes for each year under the lease alternative. This is arrived at multiplying the lease rental payments (L) by (1 – tax rate, t).

(2) Determine the cash outflows after taxes for each year under the buy/borrow alternative. The COAT is equal to the loan instalment (Gross cash outflows, GCO) less **(i)** tax advantage on interest (I) component of loan instalment (I × t) and **(ii)** tax shield due to depreciation allowance (D × t).

(3) Compare the PV of the cash outflows associated with leasing (Step 1) and buy/borrow alternative (Step 2) by employing after-tax cost of debt (k_d) as the discount rate. The focus of analysis, essentially, is to compare the two sources of finance, namely, leasing and debt. Therefore, the relevant required values are after-tax cost of **(i)** leasing and **(ii)** debt.

(4) Select the alternative with the lower PV of cash outflow after taxes.

(5) Decision criterion is:

(a) **In favour of buy/borrow alternative if** PV of COAT under lease alternative > PV of COAT under buy/borrow alternative

(b) **In favour of lease alternative in case** PV of COAT under lease alternative < PV of COAT under buy/borrow alternative.

Note: (A) In Step 2, cash inflows in the terminal year are expected from two more avenues: (i) Salvage value and (ii) Tax shield on short-term capital loss (as machine, more often than not, is sold at a price lower than its book value). In rare cases, when the sale yields profits, the tax due on short-term capital gains should be subtracted from the salvage value.

(B) Normally, taxes and maintenance expenses are borne by the lessee. Since such costs are common costs under both options, they might be ignored. However, if they are to be incurred by the lessor, after tax maintenance costs are incremental costs under buy/borrow alternative and should be taken into account.

Internal Rate Return (IRR) Under the IRR method/alternative, the after-tax cost of leasing is determined and is compared with the after-tax cost of debt. The alternative with the lower cost is selected. Both methods provide identical answers. The virtue of IRR method is that it is devoid of the problem of choosing an appropriate discount rate. The steps required to compute IRR (representing after tax cost of leasing) is summarised below.

(1) Capital cost of plant and machinery is saved due to lease option. The cost saved is equal to the present value of cash outflows after taxes (for the lease period) associated with lease alternative (determined as per Step 2). The rate which makes the two sides equal is the IRR.

(2) Cash outflows after taxes (COAT) under the lease alternative are equal to the lease payments (L) minus the tax advantage on the excess amount of lease payments over depreciation allowed on plant and machinery. Symbolically, it is [L – t (L – D)]. These net cash outflows are to be determined for each year. Alternatively, COAT = LRAT + Tax advantage on depreciation allowed on own plant and machinery foregone.

(3) In the terminal year, the salvage value (SV) as well as the tax advantage on short-term capital loss (TASTCL) are to be reckoned as opportunity costs of using the lease alternative. The sum of the two would constitute the cash outflows in terminal (nth) year.

(4) Symbolically, the IRR representing the cost of leasing would be:

$$\text{Cost of plant and machinery} = \sum_{t=1}^{n} \frac{\text{COAT(net)}_t}{(1+k_l)^t} + \frac{SV_n + TASTCL_n}{(1+k_l)^n}$$

(5) Decision criterion: If the after tax cost of leasing (k_l) < the after tax cost of debt (k_d), choose the leasing alternative and vice versa.

The mechanics of computation of **(i)** PV/IRR associated with the two alternatives—leasing and borrowing and **(ii)** NAL/RIPV(L) is illustrated now.

***Example* 25.1**

XYZ Ltd is in the business of manufacturing steel utensils. The firm is planning to diversify and add a new product line. The firm either can buy the required machinery or get it on lease.

The machine can be purchased for ₹15,00,000. It is expected to have a useful life of 5 years with a salvage value of ₹1,00,000 after the expiry of 5 years. The purchase can be financed by 20 per cent loan repayable in 5 equal annual instalments (inclusive of interest) becoming due at the end of each year. Alternatively, the machine can be taken on year-end lease rentals of ₹4,50,000 for 5 years. Advise the company on the option it should choose. For your exercise, you may assume the following:

(i) The machine will constitute a separate block for depreciation purposes. The company follows written down value method of depreciation, the rate of depreciation being 20 per cent.

(ii) Tax rate is 35 per cent and cost of capital is 20 per cent.

(iii) Lease rentals are to be paid at the end of the year.

(iv) Maintenance expenses estimated at ₹30,000 per year are to be borne by the lessee.

(v) Assume the firm would have sufficient short-term capital gains in year of sale of machine.

Solution

(A) Present Value Approach

PV of Cash Outflows Under Leasing Alternative

Year-end	*Lease rent after taxes [R(1 – t)]* [₹4,50,000 (1 – 0.35)]	*PVIFA at 13%* [20% (1 – 0.35)]	*Total PV*
1–5	₹2,92,500	3.517	₹10,28,723

Borrowing/Buying Option:

Equivalent annual loan instalment = ₹15,00,000/2.991 (PVIFA for 5 years at 20% i.e., 20,5) =₹5,01,505.

PV of Cash Outflows Under Buying Alternative

Year-end	*Loan intsalment*	*Tax advantage on*		*Net cash outflows*	*PVIF at*	*Total*
		Interest (I × 0.35)	*Depreciation (D × 0.35)*	*col. 2 – (col. 3 + 4)*	*13%*	*PV*
1	*2*	*3*	*4*	*5*	*6*	*7*
1	₹5,01,505	₹1,05,000	₹1,05,000	₹2,91,505	0.885	₹2,57,982
2	5,01,505	90,895	84,000	3,26,610	0.783	2,55,736
3	5,01,505	73,968	67,200	3,60,337	0.693	2,49,714
4	5,01,505	53,656	53,760	3,94,089	0.613	2,41,577
5	5,01,505	29,114	43,008	4,29,383	0.543	2,33,155
						12,38,164
Less: PV of salvage value (₹1,00,000 × 0.543)						54,300
Less: PV of tax savings on short-term capital loss (₹4,91,520 – ₹1,00,000) × 0.35 = (₹1,37,032 × 0.543)					74,408	
Total						11,09,456

Recommendation

The company is advised to go for leasing as the PV of cash outflows under the leasing option is lower than under the buy/borrowing alternative.

Working Notes

Schedule of Debt Payment

Year-end	*Loan intsalment*	*Loan at the beginning of the year*	*Payments*		*Loan outstanding at the end of the year*
			Interest (col. 3 × 0.20)	*Principal repayment*	*(col. 3 – col. 5)*
1	*2*	*3*	*4*	*5*	*6*
1	₹5,01,505	₹15,00,000	₹3,00,000	₹2,01,505	₹12,98,495
2	5,01,505	12,98,495	2,59,699	2,41,806	10,56,689
3	5,01,505	10,56,689	2,11,338	2,90,167	7,66,522
4	5,01,505	7,66,522	1,53,304	3,48,201	4,18,321
5	5,01,505	4,18,321	83,184*	4,18,321	—

*Difference between the loan instalment and loan outstanding.

Schedule of Depreciation

1	₹15,00,000 * 0.20 =	₹3,00,000
2	12,00,000 * 0.20 =	2,40,000
3	9,60,000 * 0.20 =	1,92,000
4	7,68,000 * 0.20 =	1,53,600
5	6,14,400 * 0.20 =	1,22,880

Example 25.1 Spreadsheet Solution

Microsoft Excel - Ex25-1

File Edit View Insert Format Tools Data Window Help Adobe PDF

85% Arial

A20 fx Cash Flows Under Buy/Borrow Alternative

	A	B	C	D	E	F	G	H
1	Invoice price	1500000				Summary		
2	Expected life of equipment	5		CASH FLOWS-LEASING			–1028790.14	
3	Salvage value	100000		CASH FLOWS-BUY/BORROW			–1109755.85	
4	Loan interest rate	0.2		RECOMMENDATION: GO FOR LEASING				
5	Length of loan	5						
6	Lease rental	450000						
7	Maintenance expenses	30000						
8	Depreciation rate	0.2						
9	Tax rate	0.35						
10	Cost of capital	0.2						
11	Loan interest rate after tax	0.13						
12								
13	**Cash Flows Under Leasing Alternative**							
14	Year	0	1	2	3	4	5	
15	Lease rental		–450000	–450000	–450000	–450000	–450000	
16	Tax saving on lease payment		157500	157500	157500	157500	157500	
17	Net cash flow from leasing		–292500	–292500	–292500	–292500	–292500	
18	PV of cash flows under leasing	–1028790.14						
19								
20	**Cash Flows Under Buy/Borrow Alternative**							
21	Loan Installment		–501569.55	–501569.55	–501569.55	–501569.55	–501569.55	
22	Tax advantage of interest		105000	90890.13	73958.29	53640.08	29258.22	
23	Tax advantage on depreciation		105000	84000	67200	53760	43008	
24	Salvage value						100000	
25	Tax saving on short-term capital loss						137032	
26	Net cash outflow		–291569.55	–326679.42	–360411.27	–394169.48	–192271.33	
27	PV of cash outflows under buy/borrow	–1109755.85						
28								
29	**Workings**							
30	**Loan Amortisation**							
31	Loan installment		501569.55	501569.55	501569.55	501569.55	501569.55	
32	Loan at the beginning of the year		1500000	1298430.45	1056546.98	766286.82	417974.63	
33	Interest payment		300000	259686.09	211309.396	153257.36	83594.93	
34	Principa1 payment		201569.55	241883.47	290260.16	348312.19	417974.63	
35								
36	**Depreciation**							
37	Book value of equipment at the beginning of the year		1500000	1200000	960000	768000	614400	
38	Depreciation for the year		300000	240000	192000	153600	122880	
39	Book value of equipment at the end of the year		1200000	960000	768000	614400	491520	
40								

Enter inputs in cells B1 to B10. Enter =B4*(1-B9) in cell B11 to calculate after tax interest cost.
Enter years in row 14 starting from year 0. Enter =-$B6 in cell C15 and copy to cells D15 to G15.
Enter = -C15*B9 in cell C16 and copy to cells D16 to G16. Enter = C15+C16 in cell C17 and copy to cells D17 to G17.
Enter =NPV(B11, C17:G17) in cell B18 to calculate PV of cash flows under leasing.
Enter = PMT(B4,B5,B1,0,0) in cell C21 to calculate loan installment and copy the formula to cells D21 to G21.
Enter =-C21 in cell C31 and copy to cells D31 to G31. Enter = B1 in cell C32; =C32*B4 in cell C33 and copy to cells D33 to G33.
Enter =C31-C33 in cell C34 and copy to cells D34 to G34. Enter =C32-C34 in cell D32 and copy to cells E32 to G32.
Enter =C33*B9 in cell C22 and copy to cells D22 to G22. Enter b1 in cell C37.
Enter =C37*B8 in cell C38 and copy to cells D38 to G38. Enter =C37-C38 in cell C39 and copy to cells D39 to G39.
Enter =c39 in cell D37 and copy to cells E37 to G37.
Enter =C38*B9 in cell C23 and copy to cells D23 to G23. Enter b3 in cell G24. Enter =(G39-B3)*B9 in cell G25.
Enter = SUM(C21:C25) in cell C26 and copy to cells D26 to G26.
Enter =NPV(B11, C26:G26) in cell B27 to calculate PV of cash flows under buy /borrow alternative.
Enter =B18 in cell G2 and =B27 in cell G3 to present summary results.
The final results in the spreadsheet differ marginally from those of the numerical solution due to approximations.

(B) IRR Approach

Determination of After-tax Cost of Lease Financing (IRR Approach)

Year-end	Cost of machine	Lease payments (L)	Depreciation of machine (D)	Incremental tax shield on leasing 0.35 × (L – D)	Net cash outflows under leasing [(3) – (5)]
(1)	(2)	(3)	(4)	(5)	(6)
0	₹15,00,000	—	—	—	₹15,00,000
1		₹4,50,000	₹3,00,000	₹52,500	(3,97,500)
2		4,50,000	2,40,000	73,500	(3,76,500)
3		4,50,000	1,92,000	90,300	(3,59,700)
4		4,50,000	1,53,600	1,03,740	(3,46,260)
5		4,50,000	1,22,880	1,14,492	(3,35,508)
5* Salvage value					(1,00,000)*
5* Tax savings on short-term capital loss					(1,37,032)/**

*Machine has been sold after the expiry of five years (that is, at the beginning of year 6). The PV of salvage value and tax savings can be computed with reference to year-end 5.
**Salvage value of machine foregone and short-term capital loss constitute the opportunity cost of lease financing and, therefore, cash outflows of lease financing.

Determination of IRR

Year	Net cash outflows under leasing	PV factor at		Total PV at	
		10%	11%	10%	11%
1	₹3,97,500	0.909	0.901	₹3,61,375	₹3,58,148
2	3,76,500	0.826	0.812	3,10,989	3,05,718
3	3,59,700	0.751	0.731	2,70,135	2,62,941
4	3,46,260	0.683	0.659	2,36,496	2,28,185
5	5,72,540@	0.621	0.593	3,55,547	3,39,516
				15,34,542	14,94,508

@[₹3,35,508 + ₹1,00,000, salvage value + ₹1,37,032, tax advantage on short-term capital loss]
IRR1 = 11% – (₹5,492/₹40,034 = 0.14) = 10.86 per cent.

Recommendation: The company is advised to go for leasing to take advantage of its lower cost relative to the cost of debt.

***Example* 25.2 (Annual Lease Rentals)**

The following details relate to an investment proposal of the Hypothetical Industries Ltd (HIL):

- Investment outlay, ₹180 lakh
- Useful life, 3 years
- Net salvage value after 3 years, ₹18 lakh
- Annual tax relevant rate of depreciation, 40 per cent

The HIL has two alternatives to choose from to finance the investment:

Alternative I: Borrow and buy the equipment. The cost of capital of the HIL, 0.12; marginal rate of tax, 0.35; cost of debt, 0.17 per annum.

Alternative II: Lease the equipment from the Hypothetical Leasing Ltd on a three year full payout basis @₹444/₹1,000, payable annually in arrears (year-end). The lease can be renewed for a further period of 3 years at a rental of ₹18/₹1,000, payable annually in arrears.

Which alternative should the HIL choose? Why?

Solution

Decision Analysis (*₹ lakh*)

1. Investment outlay	₹180.00
2. *Less:* Present value of lease rentals (working note 1)	176.61
3. *Plus:* present value of tax shield on lease rentals (2)	67.19
4. *Minus:* present value of tax shield on depreciation (3)	41.01
5. *Less:* Present value of interest shield on displaced debt (4)	18.29
6. *Less:* Present value of net salvage value (5)	12.81
NAL/NPV(L)	(1.53)

Since the NAL is negative, the lease is not economically viable. The HIL should opt for the alternative of borrowing and buying.

Working Notes

1. Present value of lease rentals: = ₹(180 lakh × 0.444) × PVIFA (17,3) = ₹79.92 lakh × 2.210 = ₹176.61 lakh

2. Present value of tax shield on lease rentals: = ₹(180 lakh × 0.444 × 0.35) × PVIFA (12,3) = ₹27.972 lakh × 2.402 = ₹67.19 lakh

3. Present value of tax shield on depreciation = [72 × PVIF (12,1) + 43.2 × PVIF (12,2) + 25.92 × PVIF (12,3)] × 0.35 = [(72 × 0.893) + (43.2 × 0.797) + (25.92 × 0.712)] × 0.35 = ₹41.01 lakh

4. Present value of interest tax shield on displaced debt: = [30.03 × PVIF (12,1) + 21.54 × PVIF (12,2) + 11.61 × PVIF (12,3)] × 0.35 = [(30.03 × 0.893) + (21.54 × 0.797) + (11.61 × 0.712) × 0.35] = ₹18.29 lakh.

(Displaced) Debt (Present Value of Lease Rentals) Amortisation Schedule (*₹ lakh*)

Year	*Loan outstanding at the beginning**	*Interest content (at 17%)*	*Capital content*	*Instalment amount (176.61 ÷ 2.210)*
1	176.61	30.03	49.89	79.92
2	126.72	21.54	58.38	79.92
3	68.34	11.61	68.34	79.92

*Equal to the present value of lease rentals

5. Present value of net salvage value = 18 × PVIF (12,3) = 18 × 0.712 = ₹12.81 lakh

***Example* 25.3 (Monthly Lease Rentals)**

In **Example 25.2**, assume a lease rental of ₹35/₹1,000 payable monthly, in advance. Compute the NAL/NPV(L). Should the HIL opt for lease financing?

Solution

Decision Analysis *(₹ lakh)*

1. Investment outlay	₹180.00
2. *Less:* Present value of lease rentals (working note **1**)	182.10
3. *Plus:* Present value of tax shield on lease rentals (**2**)	63.56
4. *Less:* Present value of tax shield on depreciation (**3**)	41.01
5. *Less:* Present value of interest shield on displaced debt (**4**)	13.12
6. *Less:* Present value of net salvage value (**5**)	12.81
NAL	(5.48)

As the NAL is negative, the lease is not financially advantageous and HIL should not opt for it.

Working Notes

1. Present value of lease rentals: = ₹(180 × 0.035 × 12) × PVIFA$_m$ (17,3) = 75.6 × $i/_d$(12) × PVIFA (I,3), where I = 0.17 = 75.6 × 1.09 (Table A-3) × 2.210 (Table A-2) = ₹182.10 lakh
2. Present value of tax shield on lease payments: = ₹[(180 × 0.035 × 12) × PVIFA (12,3) × 0.35] = 75.6 × 2.402 × 0.35 = ₹63.56 lakh
3. Present value of tax shield depreciation: No change from the annual payment (₹41.01 lakh)
4. Present value of interest tax shield on displaced debt: = [(24.15 × 0.893) + (15.39 × 0.797) + (5.16 × 0.712)] × 0.35 = ₹13.12 lakh

Debt Amortisation Schedule *(₹ lakh)*

Year	*Loan outstanding at the beginning**	*Interest content*	*Capital content*	*Instalment amount [182.10 ÷ 2.409 (1.09 × 2.210)]*
1	181.10	24.15	51.45	75.60
2	130.65	15.39	60.21	75.60
3	70.44	5.16	70.44	75.60

*Equal to the present value of lease rentals

5. Present value of net salvage value: No change from annual payment basis (₹12.81 lakh)

It can be seen that in the case of monthly lease payment, the component of the lease-related cash flow streams that will change are: **(1)** Lease rentals, **(2)** Tax shield on lease rentals and **(3)** Interest tax shield on displaced debt.

Break-Even Lease Rental The break-even lease rental (BELR) is the rental at which the lessee is indifferent to a choice between lease financing and borrowing/buying. Alternatively, BELR has a NAL of zero. It reflects the maximum level of rental that the lessee would be willing to pay. If the BELR exceeds the actual lease rental, the lease proposal would be accepted, otherwise it would be rejected. The computation of the BELR is shown in example 25.4.

***Example* 25.4**

For the HIL in Example 25.2, assume monthly lease payments in advance. Compute the break-even monthly lease rental. Can the HIL accept a lease quote of ₹35/₹1,000 per month, payable in advance?

Solution

The monthly break-even lease rental (B_L) can be obtained when NAL = zero. Thus, [180 – (12 B_L × 3.27 × 2.210) + (12 B_L × 0.35 × 2.402) – 58.59 – [(11.49 × 0.893) + (7.35 × 0.797) + (2.43 × 0.712)] × 0.35 B_L – 12.81 = 0. B_L = ₹2.78 lakh

Monthly lease rental payable by HIL = ₹180 lakh × 0.035 = ₹6.30 lakh
Since the B_L is less than the actual rental to be paid, the lease proposal cannot be accepted.

Working Notes

Required Amortisation Schedule *(₹ lakh)*

Year	*Loan outstanding at the beginning**	*Interest content*	*Capital content*	*Instalment amount*
1	86.73 B_L	24.51 B_L	11.49 B_L	12 B_L
2	66.22 B_L	28.65 B_L	7.35 B_L	12 B_L
3	33.57 B_L	33.57 B_L	2.43 B_L	12 B_L

Lessor's Viewpoint

The lease evaluation from the point of the lessor aims at ascertaining whether to accept a lessee proposal or to choose from alternative proposals. As in the case of an evaluation by a lessee, the appraisal method used is the discounted cash flow technique based on the lessor's cash flows. The lease related cash flow from his angle consists of **(a)** outflows in terms of the initial investment/ acquisition cost of the asset at the inception of the lease; income tax on lease payments, sales tax on lease transaction, if any; lease administration expenses such as rental collection charges, expenses on suits for recovery, other direct costs and so on; **(b)** inflows such as lease rentals, management fee, tax shield on depreciation, residual value and security deposit, if any, and so on. The lease evaluation from the point of view of a lessor is illustrated here and includes aspects such as break-even rental for the lessor, negotiation and fixing of lease rentals.

***Example* 25.5**

For the firm in our Example 25.1, assume further that; **(i)** the lessor's weighted average cost of capital is 14 per cent. **(ii)** The lessor would have sufficient short-term capital gain in year of sale of machine. Is it financially profitable for a leasing company to lease out the machine?

Solution

Determination of NPV of Cash Inflows

Particulars	*Year* 1	2	3	4	5
Lease rent	₹4,50,000	₹4,50,000	₹4,50,000	₹4,50,000	₹4,50,000
Less: Depreciation	3,00,000	2,40,000	1,92,000	1,53,600	1,22,880
Earnings before taxes	1,50,000	2,10,000	2,58,000	2,96,400	3,27,120
Less: Taxes (0.35)	52,500	73,500	90,300	1,03,740	1,14,492
Earnings after taxes	97,500	1,36,500	1,67,700	1,92,660	2,12,628
Cash inflows after Taxes	3,97,500	3,76,500	3,59,700	3,46,260	3,35,508
PV factor at (0.14)	0.877	0.769	0.675	0.592	0.519
Total	3,48,608	2,89,529	2,42,798	2,04,986	1,74,129
Total PV (operations)					12,60,050
Add: PV of salvage value of machine (1,00,000 × 0.519)					51,900
Add: PV of tax savings on short-term capital loss (₹1,37,032 × 0.519)					71,120
Gross PV					13,83,070
Less: Cost of machine					15,00,000
NPV					(1,16,930)

It is not financially profitable to let out the machine on lease by the leasing company, as NPV is negative.

Break-Even Lease Rental From the viewpoint of a lessor, the break-even lease rental represents the minimum (floor) lease rental that he can accept. The NAL/NPV(L) at this level of rental is zero. The discount rate to compute the NAL is the marginal overall cost of funds to the lessor. The application of the NAL approach to compute the break-even lease rental to a lessor is illustrated below.

***Example* 25.6**

For facts contained in Example 25.5, (a) determine the minimum lease rentals at which the lessor would break-even. Also, prepare a verification table. Determine the lease rentals if the lessor wants to earn an NPV of ₹1 lakh.

Solution

(a) **Break-even Lease Rental**

Cost of machine	₹15,00,000
Less: PV of salvage value to be received at the end of 5 years (₹1,00,000 × 0.519)	51,900
Less: PV of tax savings on short-term capital loss at the end of the 5th year (₹1,37,032 × 0.519)	71,120
Less: PV of tax shield on depreciation: (₹3,00,000 × 0.35 × 0.877) + (₹2,40,000 × 0.35 × 0.769) + (₹1,92,000 × 0.35 × 0.675) + (₹1,53,600 × 0.35 × 0.592) + (₹1,22,880 × 0.35 × 0.519)	2,56,188
Required total PV of after tax lease rent	11,20,792
Divided by PVIFA for 5 years at 0.14	÷3.433
After tax lease rentals	3,26,476
Break-even lease rentals (₹3,26,476/(1 – 0.35)	5,02,271

Verification Table

Particulars	Year 1	2	3	4	5
Lease rent	₹5,02,271	₹5,02,271	₹5,02,271	₹5,02,271	₹5,02,271
Less: Depreciation	3,00,000	2,40,000	1,92,000	1,53,600	1,22,880
Earnings before taxes	2,02,271	2,62,271	3,10,271	3,48,671	3,79,391
Less: Taxes (0.35)	70,795	91,795	1,08,595	1,22,035	1,32,787
Earnings after taxes	1,31,476	1,70,476	2,01,676	2,26,636	2,46,604
CFAT (EAT + Depreciation)	4,31,476	4,10,476	3,93,676	3,80,236	3,69,484
´PV factor at (0.14)	0.877	0.769	0.675	0.592	0.519
Total	3,78,404	3,15,656	2,65,731	2,25,100	1,91,762
PV of Lease rent					13,76,653
Add: PV of salvage value					51,900
Add: PV of tax savings on short-term capital loss					71,120
Total PV					14,99,673*

(b) **Lease-Rentals to be Charged to Earn NPV of ₹1,00,000**

Required total PV of after-tax lease rentals (₹11,20,792 for break-even + ₹1,00,000)	₹12,20,792
Divided by PVIFA for 5 years at 0.14	÷3.433
After-tax lease rentals	3,55,605
Lease rentals to be charged [₹3,55,605/(1 – 0.35)]	5,47,085

*Difference of ₹327 is due to rounding off the figures.

***Example* 25.7**

The under mentioned facts relate to a lease proposal before the Hypothetical Leasing Ltd (HLL):

The initial cost of equipment to be leased out is ₹300 lakh, on which 10 per cent sales tax would be levied. At the end of the lease term, after 5 years, the salvage value is estimated to be ₹33 lakh. The other costs associated with the lease proposal payable in advance (front-ended) are initial direct cost, ₹3 lakh and management fee, ₹5 lakh. The marginal cost of funds to the HIL is 14 per cent while the marginal rate of tax is 35 per cent.

What is the break-even rental for HLL if the tax relevant rate of depreciation is 25 per cent?

Solution

Computation of Break-even Lease Rental (L)

Particulars	*Amount (₹ lakh)*
1. Equipment cost (including ST)	3,30.000
2. Present value of lease rentals (working note 1)	3.433 L
3. Present value of tax on lease rentals (2)	1.202 L
4. Present value of tax shield on depreciation)	64.900
5. Present value of direct initial cost	3.000
6. Present value of management fee	5.000
7. Present value of tax shield on initial direct cost (4)	0.920
8. Present value of tax on management fee (5)	1.530
9. Present value of salvage value (6)	17.100

The break-even rental (L) can be derived from the equation:

3.433 L – 1.202 L + ₹64.90 lakh – ₹3 lakh + ₹5 lakh + ₹0.902 lakh – ₹1.53 lakh + ₹17.10 lakh – ₹330 lakh = 0

L = ₹123.30 lakh

Working Notes

1. Present value of lease rental = L [PVIFA (14,5)] = 3.433 L
2. Present value of tax on lease rental = 0.35 × L × PVIFA (14,5) = 1.202 L
3. Present value of tax shield on depreciation = [₹82.50 lakh × PVIF (14,1) + ₹61.90 lakh × PVIF (14,2) + ₹46.40 lakh × PVIF (14,3) + ₹34.80 lakh × PVIF (14,4) + ₹26.1 lakh × PVIF (14,5)] × 0.35 = [(₹82.50 × 0.877) + (₹61.90 × 0.769) + (₹46.40 × 0.675) + (₹34.80 × 0.592) + (₹26.1 × 0.519)] × 0.35 = ₹64.90 lakh
4. Present value of tax shield on initial direct costs = ₹3 lakh × 0.35 × PVIF (14,1) = ₹0.92 lakh
5. Present value of tax shield on management fee = 0.35 × ₹5 lakh × PVIF (14,1) = ₹1.53 lakh
6. Present value of salvage value = ₹33 lakh × PVIF (14,5) = ₹17.10 lakh

***Example* 25.8**

The Hypothetical Leasing Ltd (HLL) has a lease proposal under consideration. Its post-tax cost of funds is 14 per cent and it has to pay central sales tax (CST) @ 10 per cent of the basic price of the capital equipment on inter-state purchases. The marginal tax rate of the HLL is 35 per cent. The details of the proposed lease are given below:

- Primary lease period, 3 years
- Tax relevant depreciation, 40 per cent on written down basis (with other assets in the block)
- Residual value, 8 per cent of the original cost.

(a) If the monthly lease rentals are collected in advance, what is the minimum lease rental the HLL should charge for per ₹1,000 for the lease?

(b) What is the minimum monthly lease rental for a lease proposal costing ₹660 lakh (including CST at 10 per cent)?

Solution

(a) **Minimum Monthly Rental per ₹1,000**

1	Investment cost	₹1,000.00
2	Present value of lease rentals (working note 1)	29.93 L
3	Present value of tax shield on rentals (2)	9.75 L
4	Present value of tax shield on depreciation (3)	221.48
5	Present value of residumal value (4)	54.00

The break-even level of rental (L) can be derived from the equation (NAL = 0)

= ₹1,000 + 29.93 L – 9.75 L + ₹221.48 + ₹54 = 0

L = ₹35.90, that is, ₹35.90/₹1,000/month

(b) Minimum monthly lease rental for the proposal costing ₹660 lakh = ₹660 lakh × 0.03590 = ₹23.69 lakh

Working Notes

1. Present value of lease rentals = 12 L × $PVIFA_m$ (14,3) = 12L × 2.322 × 1.0743 = 29.93 L
2. Present value of tax shield on lease rentals = 12L × PVIFA (14,3) × 0.35 = 12L × 2.322 × 0.35 = 9.75 L
3. Present value of tax shield on depreciation = [₹400 × PVIF 914,1) + ₹240 × PVIF (14,2) + ₹144 × PVIF (14,3)] × 0.35 = (₹400 × 0.877) + (₹240 × 0.769) + (₹144 × 0.675) = ₹221.48
4. Present value of residual value = ₹1,000 (0.08) × PVIF (14,3) = ₹54.

LO 25.3 HIRE-PURCHASE FINANCE

We examine below the conceptual, taxation, accounting and evaluation framework of hire-purchase finance. Historically, hire purchase finance has been associated with financing of commercial vehicles for road transport operators. It has emerged, in recent years as a source of equipment financing and an alternative to lease financing. We first explain the salient features/basics of hire-purchase transactions. The evaluation framework of hire-purchase transactions, from the viewpoint of the hirer as well as the intermediary (finance company), is outlined subsequently.

Conceptual Framework

Hire-purchase agreement is a peculiar type of transaction in which goods are let on hire with an option to the hirer to purchase them.

Meaning and Characteristics Hire-purchase is a mode of financing the price of the goods to be sold on a future date. In a hire-purchase transaction, the goods are let on hire, the purchase price is to be paid in instalments and hirer is allowed an option to purchase the goods by paying all the instalments. A **hire-purchase agreement** is defined as peculiar kind of transaction in which the goods are let on hire with an option to the hirer to purchase them, with the following stipulations:

(a) Payment has to be made in instalments over a specified period;
(b) The possession is delivered to the hirer at the time of entering into the contract;
(c) The property in the goods passes to the hirer on payment of the last instalment;
(d) Each instalment is treated as hire charges so that if a default is made in payment of any instalment, the seller becomes entitled to take away the goods and
(e) The hire/purchaser is free to return the goods without being required to pay any further instalments falling due after the return.

Thus, a hire-purchase agreement has two aspects, firstly, an aspect of bailment of goods, subject to the hire purchase agreement, and secondly, an element of sale that fructifies when the option to purchase is exercised by the intending purchaser. Though the option to purchase is allowed in the very beginning, it can be exercised only at the end of the agreement. The property in the goods does not pass at the time of the agreement but remains with the intending seller, it only passes later when the option is exercised by the intending purchaser.

The *modus operandi* of a hire-purchase transaction is structured around the following features: The finance (hire purchase) company purchases the equipment from the equipment supplier and lets it on hire to the hirer who is required to make a down payment of 20 – 25 per cent of the cost and pay the balance with interest in Equated Monthly Instalments (EMI), in advance or arrears, spread over 36 – 48 months. Alternatively, in place of the margin in the down payment plan, under a deposit-linked plan, the hirer has to put in an equal amount as fixed deposit with the finance company, which provides the entire finance, on hire-purchase terms, repayable with interest in EMI's over 36 – 48 months. The deposit together with the accumulated interest is returned to the hirer after the payment of the last instalment. *The interest component of each hire purchase instalment is computed on the basis of a flat rate of interest and the effective rate of interest is applied to the declining balance of the original loan amount to determine the interest component of each instalment.* For a given flat rate of interest, the equivalent effective rate of interest is higher.

Hire-purchase Vs Instalment Payment

In an instalment sale, the contract of sale is entered into, the goods are delivered and the ownership is transferred to the buyer, but the price of the goods is paid in specified instalments over a definite period.

The first distinction between hire purchase and instalment purchase is based on the call option (to purchase the goods at any time during the term of the agreement) and the right of the hirer to terminate the agreement at any time before the payment of the last instalment (right of termination) in the former while in the latter the buyer is committed to pay the full price. Secondly, in instalment sale the ownership in the goods passes on to the purchaser simultaneously with the payment of the initial/first instalment, whereas in hire purchase the ownership is transferred to the hirer only when he exercises the option to purchase/or on payment of the last instalment.

Lease Financing Vs Hire-purchase Financing These two modes of financing differ in the following aspects:

Ownership The lessor (finance company) is the owner and the lessee (user/manufacturer) is entitled to the economic use of the leased asset/equipment only in case of lease financing. The ownership is never transferred to the user (lessee). In contrast, the ownership of the asset passes on to the user (hirer), in case of hire purchase finance, on payment of the last instalment; before the payment of the last instalment, the ownership of the asset vests in the finance company/intermediary (seller).

Depreciation The depreciation on the asset is charged in the books of the lessor in case of leasing while the hirer is entitled to the depreciation shield on assets hired by him.

Magnitude Both lease finance and hire-purchase are generally used to acquire capital goods. However, the magnitude of funds involved in the former is very large, for example, for the purchase of aircrafts, ships, machinery, air conditioning plants and so on. The cost of acquisition in hire purchase is relatively low, hence, automobiles, office equipments, generators and so on are generally hire purchased.

Extent Leasing financing is invariably 100 per cent financing. It requires no margin money or immediate cash down payment by the lessee. In a hire-purchase transaction typically a margin equal to 20-25 per cent of the cost of the equipment is required to be paid by the hirer. Alternatively, the hirer has to invest an equivalent amount on fixed deposits with the finance company, which is returned after the payment of the last instalment.

Maintenance The cost of maintenance of a hired asset is to be borne, typically, by the hirer himself. In case of finance lease only, the maintenance of the leased asset is the responsibility of the lessee. It is the lessor (seller) who has to bear the maintenance cost in an operating lease.

Tax Benefits The hirer is allowed the depreciation claim and finance charge and the seller may claim any interest on borrowed funds to acquire the asset for tax purposes. In case of leasing, the lessor is allowed to claim depreciation and the lessee is allowed to claim the rentals and maintenance cost against taxable income.

Parties to a Hire-purchase Contract Basically, there are two parties in a hire-purchase contract, namely, the intending seller and the intending purchaser or the hirer. Nowadays, however, hire-purchase contracts generally involve three parties, namely, the seller, the financier and the hirer. With the acknowledgement of the finance function as a separate business activity and the substantial growth of finance companies in the recent times, the sale element in a hire purchase contract has been divorced from the finance element. A dealer now normally arranges a hire purchase agreement through a finance company with the customer. It is, therefore, a tripartite deal. A tripartite hire-purchase contract is arranged with following modalities:

1. The dealer contracts a finance company to finance hire-purchase deals submitted by him. For this purpose, they enter into a contract drawing out the terms, warranties that the dealer gives with each transaction and so on.
2. The customer selects the goods and expresses his desire to acquire them on hire purchase. The dealer arranges for a full set of documents to be completed to make a hire-purchase agreement with a customer. The documents are generally printed by the finance company.
3. The customer then makes a cash down payment on completing the proposal form. The down payment is generally retained by the dealer as a payment on account of the price to be paid to him by the finance company.
4. The dealer then sends the documents to the finance company requesting him to purchase the goods and accept the hire purchase transactions.
5. The finance company, if it decides to accept the transactions, signs the agreement and sends a copy to the hirer, along with the instructions as to the payment of the instalments. The finance company also notifies the same to the dealer and asks him to deliver the goods, if they are not already delivered.
6. The dealer delivers the goods to the hirer against acknowledgements and the property in the goods passes on to the finance company.
7. The hirer makes payment of the hire instalment periodically.
8. On completion of the hire term, the hirer pays the last instalment and the property in the goods passes on to him on issue of a completion certificate by the finance company.

Financial Evaluation

The framework of financial evaluation of a hire purchase deal *vis-à-vis* a finance lease, discussed below, covers both the hirer's as well the finance company's viewpoint.

From the Point of View of the Hirer (Hire-Purchaser) The tax treatment given to hire-purchase is exactly the opposite of that given to lease financing. It may be recalled that in leasing financing, the lessor is entitled to claim depreciation and other deductions associated with the ownership of the equipment, including interest on the amount borrowed to purchase the asset, while the lessee enjoys full deduction of lease rentals. In sharp contrast, in a hire-purchase deal, the hirer is entitled to claim depreciation and the deduction for the finance charge (interest) component of the hire instalment. Thus, hire purchase and lease financing represent alternative modes of acquisition of assets. The evaluation of hire purchase transaction from the hirers' angle, therefore, has to be done in relation to the leasing alternative.

Decision Criterion The decision criterion from the point of view of a hirer is the cost of hire-purchase *vis-à-vis* the cost of leasing. If the cost of hire-purchase is less than the cost of leasing, the hirer (purchaser) should prefer the hire purchase alternative and vice versa.

Cost of Hire-purchase The cost of hire-purchase to the hirer (CHP) consists of the following:

1. Down payment
2. *Plus:* Service charges
3. *Plus:* Present value of hire purchase discounted by cost of debt (K_d)
4. *Minus:* Present value of depreciation tax shield discounted by cost of capital (K_c)
5. *Minus:* Present value of the net salvage value discounted by cost of capital (K_c)

Cost of Leasing The cost of leasing (COL) consists of the following elements:

1. Lease management fee
2. *Plus:* Present value of lease payments discounted by K_d
3. *Less:* Present value of tax shield on lease payments, and lease management fee discounted by K_c
4. *Plus:* Present value of interest tax shield on hire purchase discounted by K_c

The computation of the CHP and CL is shown in Example 25.9.

***Example* 25.9**

The Hypothetical Industries Ltd (HIL) has an investment plan amounting to ₹108 lakh. The tax relevant rate of depreciation of the HIL is 25 per cent, its marginal cost of capital and marginal cost of debt are 16 per cent and 20 per cent respectively and it is in 35 per cent tax bracket.

It is examining financing alternatives for its capital expenditure. A proposal from the Hypothetical Finance Ltd (HFL), with the following salient features, is under its active consideration:

Hire Purchase Plan: The (flat) rate of interest charged by the HFL is 16 per cent. Repayment of the amount is to be made, in advance, in 36 equated monthly instalments. The hirer/hire-purchaser is required to make a down payment of 20 per cent.

Leasing Alternative: Lease rentals are payable @ ₹28 ptpm, in advance. The primary lease period can be assumed to be 5 years.

Assume that the SOYD method is used to allocate the total charge for credit under the hire-purchase plan. The net salvage value of the equipment after 3 years can be assumed to be ₹33 lakh.

Which alternative—leasing or hire-purchase—should the HIL use? Why?

Solution

The choice will depend on the relative cost of hire purchase and leasing

Cost of Hire-Purchase (CHP) (₹ *lakh*)

1	Down payment (*working note 1*)	₹21.60
2	*Plus:* Present value of monthly hire-purchase instalment (*working note 2*)	99.19
3	*Minus:* present value of depreciation tax shield (*working note 3*)	20.44
4	*Minus:* present value of net salvage value	15.70
	Total	84.65

Working Notes

1. Down payment = ₹108 lakh × 0.20 = ₹21.6 lakh
2. Monthly hire-purchase instalment = [₹86.4 lakh (₹108 lakh less 20 per cent down payment) + (₹86.4 lakh × 0.16 × 3 years)] ÷ 36 = ₹3.552 lakh
   Present value of monthly hire purchase instalment

$$= ₹3.552 \text{ lakh} \times 12 \times \frac{I}{d^{(12)}} \times \text{PVIFA } (20,3) \text{ where I} = 0.20$$

$$= (₹3.553 \text{ lakh} \times 12) \times 1.105 \times 2.106 = ₹99.19 \text{ lakh}$$

3. Present value of depreciation tax shield:
   = [₹27 lakh × PVIF (16,1) + ₹20.25 lakh × PVIF (16,2) + ₹15.19 lakh × PVIF (16,3) + ₹11.39 lakh × PVIF (16,4) + ₹8.54 lakh × PVIF (16,5)] × 0.35
   = [(27 × 0.862) + (20.25 × 0.743) + (15.19 × 0.641) + (11.39 × 0.552) + (8.54 × 0.476)] × 0.35 = ₹20.44 lakh

Cost of Leasing (COL) (₹ *lakh*)

1	Present value of lease payments (working note 1)	₹119.93
2	Minus present value of tax shield on lease payment (2)	41.58
3	Plus present value of tax shield on charge of credit (3)	11.56
	Total	89.91

Working Notes

1. Present value of lease payments:

$$= [₹108 \text{ lakh} \times 0.028 \times 12) \times \frac{I}{d^{(12)}} \times \text{PVIFA } (20,5)], \text{ where I} = 0.20$$

   = ₹value of tax shield on lease payment = [₹108 lakh × 0.028 × 12 × PVIFA (16,5) × 35
   = (₹36.29 lakh × 3.274)] × 0.35 = ₹41.58 lakh
2. Present value of tax shield on charge for credit:
   Total charge for credit = ₹108 lakh × 0.80 × 0.16 × 3 = ₹41.47 lakh

Allocation of Total Charge for Credit; SOYD Method

Year	*SOYD factor*	*Annual charge (₹ lakh)*
1	$\frac{36+35+\ldots+25}{36+35+\ldots+1}=\frac{366}{666}$	22.79
2	$\frac{24+23+\ldots+13}{36+35+\ldots+1}=\frac{222}{666}$	13.82
3	$\frac{12+11+\ldots+1}{36+35+\ldots+1}=\frac{366}{666}$	4.86

Present value of tax shield = [(₹22.79 × 0.862) + (₹13.82 × 0.743) + (₹4.86 × 0.641)] × 0.35
= ₹11.56 lakh

Decision Since the cost of leasing exceeds the cost of hire purchase, the HIL should acquire the equipment from the HFL under the hire purchase plan.

From the Viewpoint of Finance Company (Hire Vendor) Hire-purchase and leasing represents two alternative investment decisions of a finance company/financial intermediary/hire vendor. The decision criterion, therefore, is based on a comparison of the net present values of the two alternatives, namely, hire-purchase and lease financing. The alternative with a higher net present value would be selected and the alternative having a lower net present value would be rejected.

Net Present Value of Hire Purchase Plan [NPV (HPP)] The NPV (HPP) consists of:

1. Present value of hire purchase instalments
2. *Plus:* Documentation and service fee
3. *Plus:* Present value of tax shield on initial direct cost
4. *Minus:* Loan amount
5. *Minus:* Initial cost
6. *Minus:* Present value of interest tax on the finance income
7. *Minus:* Present value of income tax on finance income (interest) netted for interest tax
8. *Minus:* Present value of income tax on documentation and service fee

Net Present Value of Lease Plan [NPV (LP)] The NPV (LP) consists of the following elements:

1. Present value of lease rentals
2. *Add:* Lease management fee
3. *Add:* Present value of tax shield on initial direct costs and depreciation
4. *Add:* Present value of net salvage value
5. *Less:* Initial investment
6. *Less:* Initial direct costs
7. *Less:* Present value of tax liability on lease rentals and lease management fee

The decision analysis is shown in Example 25.10.

Example 25.10

For the HFL in Example 25.9, assume the following:

- Front-end (advance) cost of structuring the deal: 0.5 (half) per cent of the amount financed
- Marginal cost of debt: 20 per cent
- Marginal cost of equity: 25 per cent
- Target long-term debt-equity ratio: 4:1
- Marginal tax rate: 35 per cent
- Residual value under lease plan: 10 per cent of the investment cost

Required Which plan—hire-purchase or lease—is financially more attractive to the HFL? Why?

Solution

A **(i) Net Present Value of Hire-Purchase Plan** (₹ *lakh)*

1	Present value of monthly hire-purchase instalment (working note 1)	104.46
2	*Plus* present value of tax shield on initial direct costs (working note 2)	0.13
3	*Less:* Amount financed (₹108 lakh – ₹21.60 lakh, down payment)	86.40
4	*Less:* Initial direct cost (0.5 per cent of ₹86.4 lakh)	0.43
5	*Less:* Present value of interest tax on hire purchase-related income (working note 3)	0.67
6	*Less:* Present value of income tax on net finance income (working note 4)	11.41
	Total	5.68

Working Notes

Marginal cost of capital [0.80 × 0.20 × 0.65] + [0.20 × 0.25] = (0.104 + 0.05) = 15.4 per cent

1. Monthly hire-purchase instalment = [(₹86.4 lakh + (₹86.4 lakh × 0.16 × 3)] ÷ 36 = ₹3.552 lakh
   Present value of monthly hire-purchase instalments:
   = ₹3.552 lakh × $PVIFA_m$ (15.4,3)
   = ₹3.552 lakh × 12 × 2.265 × 1.082 = ₹104.46 lakh
2. Present value of tax shield on initial direct cost:
   Initial direct cost (0.5 per cent of ₹86.4 lakh) = 0.432 lakh
   Present value = ₹0.432 lakh × 0.866 × 0.35 = ₹0.13 lakh

3. Present value of interest tax on hire purchase related income:
Unexpired finance income (total charge for credit) at inception = ₹86.4 lakh × 0.16 × 3
= ₹41.47 lakh

Allocation of Unexpired Finance Income, Based on the SODY Method (₹ *lakh*)

Year	*SOYD factor*	*Annual charge (₹ lakh)*
1	$\frac{36+35+...+25}{36+35+...+1}=\frac{366}{666}$ × ₹41.47 lakh	22.79
2	$\frac{24+23+...+13}{36+35+...+1}=\frac{222}{666}$ × ₹41.47 lakh	13.82
3	$\frac{12+11+...+1}{36+35+...+1}=\frac{78}{666}$ × ₹41.47 lakh	4.86

Interest Tax and Income Tax on Annual Finance Income (₹ *lakh*)

Year	*Gross Finance Income*	*Interest tax (2%)*	*Net finance income*	*Income tax (0.35)*
1	22.79	0.46	22.33	7.82
2	13.82	0.28	13.54	4.74
3	4.86	0.10	4.76	1.67

Present value = (₹0.46 lakh × 0.866) + (₹0.28 lakh × 0.751) + (₹0.10 lakh × 0.648)
= ₹0.67 lakh

4. Present value of income tax on net finance income:
= (₹7.82 lakh × 0.866) + (₹7.74 lakh × 0.751) + (₹1.67 lakh × 0.648) = ₹11.41 lakh

A **(ii) Net Present Value of Leasing** (₹ *lakh*)

1	Present value of lease rentals/receipts (working note 1)	130.08
2	*Plus:* Present value of depreciation tax shield (note 2)	20.62
3	*Plus:* Present value of tax shield on initial direct cost (note 3)	0.16
4	*Plus:* Present value of residual value (note 4)	5.21
5	*Less:* Initial investment	108.00
6	*Less:* Initial direct cost	0.54
7	*Less:* Present value of income tax on lease rentals (note 5)	42.09
	Total	5.44

Working Notes

1. Present value of lease rentals = ₹108 lakh × 0.028 × 12 × PVIFA (15.4, 5)
= ₹108 lakh × 0.028 × 12 × 1.082 × 3.313 = ₹130.08 lakh

2. Present value of depreciation tax shield = [₹27 lakh × PVIF (15.4,1) + ₹20.25 lakh × PVIF (15.4,2) + ₹15.19 lakh × PVIF (15.4,3) + ₹11.34 lakh × PVIF (15.4,4) + ₹8.55 lakh × PVIF (15.4,5)] × 0.35 = [₹27 lakh × 0.866) + (₹20.25 lakh × 0.751) + (₹15.19 lakh × 0.648) + (₹11.34 lakh × 0.562) + (₹8.55 lakh × 0.482)]
= ₹20.62 lakh

3. Present value of tax shield on initial direct cost:
= 0.54 lakh (0.5 per cent of ₹108 lakh) × PVIF (15.4,1) × 0.35 = ₹0.16 lakh

4. Present value of residual value = ₹10.80 lakh (0.10 × ₹108 lakh) × PVIF (15.4,5) = ₹5.21 lakh

5. Present value of income tax on lease rentals = ₹108 lakh × 0.028 × 12 × PVIFA (15.4,5) × 0.35
= (₹36.29 lakh × 3.314) × 0.35 = ₹42.09 lakh

As the present value of hire-purchase (₹5.68 lakh) exceeds the net present value of leasing (₹5.44 lakh), the hire purchase plan is financially more attractive to the HFL.

SUMMARY

LO 25.1

Lease is a contractual arrangement under which the owner of an asset (lessor) allows the use of the asset to the user (lessee) for an agreed period of time (lease period) in consideration for the periodic payment (lease rent). At the end of the lease period, the asset reverts back to the owner, unless there is a provision for the renewal of the lease contract.

Leasing can be classified into four categories: (i) sale and lease back, and direct lease, (ii) single investor lease and leveraged lease, (iii) domestic lease and international lease, and (iv) finance lease and operating lease.

Sale and lease back arrangement provides for the sale of the asset by the present owner to the lessor who leases it back to the owner (lessee). In contrast, the lessee and the owner of the asset are two different entities in direct lease.

While a single investor lease involves two parties to the lease transaction, namely, the single investor/ the leasing company (lessor) and the lessee, a leveraged lease involves, besides the lessor and the lessee, a third party (a lender) who ordinarily funds a major share of the asset's price.

In domestic lease, all parties of a lease transaction are domiciled in the same country. In international lease, parties to the lease transactions are domiciled in different countries.

Short-term or cancelable leases (at the option of the lessee) are referred to as operating leases while long-term or non-cancellable leases are known as financial leases. The distinction between the two is based on the extent to which the risks and rewards of ownership are transferred from the lessor to the lessee. If a lease transfers a substantial part of the risks and rewards, it is called finance lease; otherwise, it is operating lease.

The cut-off criterion in India is that if the lease term exceeds 75 per cent of the useful life of the asset or if the present value of the minimum lease rentals exceeds 90 per cent of the fair market value (cost) of the equipment at the inception of the lease, the lease is classified as finance lease.

Lease financing provides several advantages to the lessee such as hundred per cent financing, tax-based benefits, convenience, better utilisation of own funds, expeditious use of asset, flexibility in lease rentals, and so on.

Full security, tax benefit, high profitability, trading on equity and so on are the major advantages to the lessor.

LO 25.2

Finance lease can be evaluated from the point of view of both the lessee and the lessor. From the perspective of the lessee, leasing should be evaluated as a financing alternative to borrow and buy. The decision-criterion requires comparison of the present value (PV) of cash outflows after taxes under the leasing option *vis-á-vis* borrowing-buy alternative. The alternative with the lower PV should be selected.

The Net Advantage of Leasing (NAL) approach is the alternate approach to evaluate finance lease. The benefits from leasing are compared with cost of leasing. The benefits from leasing are: (i) Investment cost of asset (saved), (ii) Plus PV of tax shield on lease payment, discounted by k_c and (iii) Plus PV of tax shield on management fee, discounted by k_c.

The cost of leasing are: (i) Present value of lease rentals, discounted by k_d, (ii) Plus management fee, (iii) Plus PV of depreciation shield foregone, discounted by k_c, (iv) Plus PV of salvage value of asset, discounted by k_c and (v) Plus PV of interest shield, discounted by k_c.

In case NAL is positive (benefits > costs), leasing alternative is preferred.

For the lessor, lease decision is akin to a capital budgeting decision. The leasing is viable when the PV of cash inflows after taxes (CFAT) accruing to him exceeds the cost of asset. The CFAT are discounted at the weighted average cost of capital.

The NAL approach can also be used by the lessor to assess the financial viability of the lease decision. The NAL to a lessor = Present value of lease payment *plus* (i) Present value of management fee, (ii) Present value of depreciation tax shield, (iii) Present value of net salvage value, (iv) Present value of tax shield on initial direct costs, *minus,* (i) Initial investment, (ii) Present value of tax on lease payments, (iii) Present value of tax on management fee, and (iv) Present value of initial direct cost.

LO 25.2	The break-even lease rental is the rental at which the lessee is indifferent to the choice between the option of leasing and buying and borrowing. At this level, the NAL is zero. In a way, it represents the maximum lease rental which the lessee is willing to pay and constitutes an important input in the negotiation/determination of the lease rental.
	From the point of view of the lessor, the break-even lease rental is the minimum which he can accept in lieu of leasing the equipment. At this level of rental, the NAL/NPV(L) to the lessor is zero. The lease-related cash flow streams relevant to the computation of the NAL are initial investment and often direct costs, income tax on lease payments, management fee, lease payments, tax shield on depreciation and residual value.
	The lease rental is determined on the basis of the negotiation between the lessor and the lessee. The difference between the break-even lease rentals to the lessee and the lessor represents the spread/range for negotiation of lease rentals. A lease rental within the range ensures a positive NAL both to the lessor and the lessee.
LO 25.3	Hire-purchase is an agreement relating to a transaction in which goods are let on hire, the purchase price is to be paid in instalments and the hirer is allowed the option to purchase the goods, paying all the instalments. Though the option to purchase the goods is allowed in the very beginning, it can be exercised only at the end of the agreement. It implies ownership is transferred at the time of sale.
	The ownership of the goods passes on to the purchaser simultaneously with the payment of the initial/first instalment in instalment sale. The hire-purchase also differs from the instalment sale in terms of the call option and right of termination in the former but not in the latter.
	Hire-purchase and leasing as modes of financing are different in several respects such as ownership of the asset, its capitalisation, depreciation charge, extent of financing, tax treatment, and accounting and reporting.
	Hire-purchase contract, basically, requires two parties, namely, the intending seller and the intending buyer. When such a sales is executed through the involvement of finance companies, the hire-purchase contracts involve three parties: the financier, the seller and the buyer.
	The decision-criterion for evaluation of a hire-purchase deal from the point of view of hirer is the cost of hire-purchase *vis-á-vis* the cost the leasing. The cost of hire-purchase consists of: (i) Cash down payment, (ii) Plus service charges, (iii) Plus PV of hire-purchase payment (discounted by cost of debt), (iv) Minus PV of depreciation tax shield, discounted by cost of capital and (v) Minus PV of the net salvage value discounted by the cost of capital. The cost of leasing consists of: (i) Lease management fee, (ii) Plus PV of lease payments discounted by k_d, (iii) Less PV of tax shield on lease payments and lease management fee discounted by k_c and (iv) Plus PV of interest tax shield on hire-purchase discounted by k_c. The alternative with lower cost is preferred.
	The decision-criteria from the viewpoint of hire vendor/financing company is based on a comparison of the net present values of the hire-purchase and the leasing alternatives. The finance company would choose the financing plan with the higher NPV.

SOLVED PROBLEMS

P.25.1 XYZ Builders Ltd need to acquire the use of a crane for their construction business, and are considering buying or leasing a crane. The crane costs ₹10,00,000, and is subject to the straight line method of depreciation to a zero salvage value at the end of 5 years. In contrast, the lease rent is ₹2,20,000 per year to be paid in advance each year for 5 years. XYZ Builders Ltd can raise debt at 14 per cent payable in 5 equal annual instalments, each instalment due at the beginning of the year. The company is in the 50 per cent tax bracket. Should it lease or buy the crane?

LO 25.2 LOD M

Solution

PV of cash outflows under leasing alternative

Year	Lease payment	Tax shield (Lease sum x Tax rate: 0.50)	Cash outflows after taxes	PV factor at 0.07(K_d)	Total PV
0	₹2,20,000	—	₹2,20,000	1.000	₹2,20,000
1–4	2,20,000	₹1,10,000	1,10,000	3.387	3,72,570
5	—	1,10,000	(1,10,000)	0.713	(78,430)
					5,14,140

Determination of interest and principal components of loan instalment

Year	Loan instalment	Loan at the beginning of the year	Payment of Interest (Col 3 × 0.14)	Payment of Principal (Col 2 – Col 4)	Principal outstanding at the end of the year (Col 3 – Col 5)
1	2	3	4	5	6
0	₹2,55,493*	₹10,00,000	—	₹2,55,493	₹7,44,507
1	2,55,493	7,44,507	₹1,04,231	1,51,262	5,93,245
2	2,55,493	5,93,245	83,054	1,72,439	4,20,806
3	2,55,493	4,20,806	58,913	1,96,580	2,24,226
4	2,55,493	2,24,226	31,267	2,24,226	—

*Annual instalment of loan can be determined by solving the following equation:

$$₹10,00,000 = \sum_{t=0}^{4} \frac{\text{Loan instalment}}{3.914\ [2.914 + 1.0\ (\text{PV factor for making payment in } t = 0)]}$$

Loan instalment = ₹10,00,000/3.914 = ₹2,55,493

PV of cash outflows under buying alternative

Year	Loan instalment	Tax advantage on Interest ($I \times t$)	Tax advantage on Depreciation ($D \times t$)	Cash outflows after taxes [Col 2 – (Col 3 + Col 4)]	PV factor at 0.07	Total PV
1	2	3	4	5	6	7
0	₹2,55,493	—	—	₹2,55,493	1.000	₹2,55,493
1	2,55,493	₹52,115	1,00,000	1,03,378	0.935	96,658
2	2,55,493	41,527	1,00,000	1,13,966	0.873	99,492
3	2,55,493	29,456	1,00,000	1,26,037	0.816	1,02,846
4	2,55,493	15,633	1,00,000	1,39,860	0.763	1,06,713
5	—	—	1,00,000	(–1,00,000)	0.713	(–71,300)
						5,89,902

Recommendation The company is advised to opt for leasing as the total PV of cash outflows is lower (₹5,14,140) than that of the buying and borrowing option (₹5,89,902).

P.25.2 An industrial unit desires to acquire a diesel generating set costing ₹20 lakh which has an economic life of 10 years at the end of which the asset is not expected to have any residual value. The unit is considering the alternative choices of (a) taking the machinery on lease, or (b) purchasing the asset outright by raising a loan.

LO 25.2 LOD M

Lease payments (₹2,95,902) are to be made in advance and the lessor requires the asset to be completely amortised over its useful period.

The cost of debt is worked out at 16 per cent per annum. The lender requires the loan to be re-paid in 10 equal annual instalment becoming due at the beginning of the first year. Average rate of income tax is 50 per cent. It is expected that the operating costs would remain the same under either method. The firm follows straight line method of depreciation and the same is accepted for tax purposes. As a financial consultant, indicate what your advice will be.

Solution

PV of cash outflows under leasing alternative

Year end	*Lease payment*	*Tax shield*	*Cash outflows after taxes*	*PV factor [0.16 (1 – 0.5) = (0.08)]*	*Total present value*
0	₹2,95,902	—	₹2,95,902	1.000	₹2,95,902
1–9	2,95,902	₹1,47,951	1,47,951	6.247	9,24,250
10	—	1,47,951	(1,47,951)	0.463	(68,501)
					11,51,651

Schedule of debt payment

Year-end	*Loan instalment*	*Loan at the beginning of the year*	*Payments*		*Principal out-standing at the end of the year (Col 3 – Col 5)*
			Interest on loan (Col 3 × 0.16)	*Principal re-payment (Col 2 – Col 4)*	
1	*2*	*3*	*4*	*5*	*6*
0	₹3,56,697*	₹20,00,000	—	₹3,56,697	₹16,43,303
1	3,56,697	16,43,303	₹2,62,928	93,769	15,49,534
2	3,56,697	15,49,534	2,47,925	1,08,772	14,40,762
3	3,56,697	14,40,762	2,30,522	1,26,175	13,14,587
4	3,56,697	13,14,587	2,10,334	1,46,363	11,68,224
5	3,56,697	11,68,224	1,86,916	1,69,781	9,98,443
6	3,56,697	9,98,443	1,59,751	1,96,946	8,01,497
7	3,56,697	8,01,497	1,28,240	2,28,457	5,73,040
8	3,56,697	5,73,040	91,686	2,65,011	3,08,029
9	3,56,697	3,08,029	48,668	3,08,029	—

*Annual instalment of loan = ₹20,00,000/5.607, that is, 4.607 + 1.0 (the PV factor for making payment in 0 year) = ₹3,56,697.

PV of cash outflows under buying alternative

Year	*Loan instalment*	*Tax advantage*		*Net cash outflows (Col 2– Col 3 + 4)*	*PV factor at after tax cost of debt (0.08)*	*Total PV*
		On interest I(t = 0.5)	*On depreciation ₹2,00,000 (0.08) × (0.5)*			
1	*2*	*3*	*4*	*5*	*6*	*7*
0	₹3,56,697	—	—	₹3,56,697	1.000	₹3,56,697
1	3,56,697	₹1,31,464	₹1,00,000	1,25,233	0.926	1,15,966
2	3,56,697	1,23,962	1,00,000	1,32,735	0.857	1,13,754
3	3,56,697	1,15,261	1,00,000	1,41,436	0.794	1,12,300
4	3,56,697	1,05,167	1,00,000	1,51,530	0.735	1,11,375

(Contd.)

(Contd.)

5	3,56,697	93,458	1,00,000	1,63,239	0.681	1,11,166
6	3,56,697	79,875	1,00,000	1,76,822	0.630	1,11,398
7	3,56,697	64,120	1,00,000	1,92,557	0.583	1,12,272
8	3,56,697	45,843	1,00,000	2,10,854	0.540	1,13,861
9	3,56,697	24,334	1,00,000	2,32,363	0.500	1,16,181
10	—		1,00,000	(1,00,000)	0.463	(46,300)
						13,28,670

Recommendation The company is advised to go for leasing of diesel generating set as the PV of cash outflows under leasing alternative is lower than that under buying alternative.

P.25.3 Mr. X, the Finance Manager of ABC Ltd, had almost decided to finance the purchase of ₹20 lakh in new computer equipment with 15% long-term debt when he was contacted by First Leasing Company Ltd. The manager of the leasing company tried to convince Mr. X that leasing the equipment would be more beneficial to ABC Ltd. **LO 25.2** LOD M

If ABC borrowed, the firm would be required to pay 15 per cent interest on the borrowed funds plus an annual principal repayment of ₹4,00,000 (at each-year end for 5 years). The equipment has an expected life of 5 years, with an anticipated salvage value of ₹2,00,000 at the year-end. The company follows written down value method, the depreciation rate being 20 per cent. The company has no other assets in the assets block of 20 per cent. The company is in 40 per cent tax bracket and is to bear maintenance expenses of ₹2,00,000 per annum. Assume the firm would have sufficient short-term capital gains in year 5.

The leasing company is willing to lease the equipment for ₹6,00,000 per year (with no maintenance). Further, it was stressed that the lease payments were fully tax deductible, while debt repayment was not.

Mr. X seeks your advice before committing to lease the computer equipment. What advice would you, as a financial consultant, give to the finance manager of ABC Ltd.?

Solution

PV of cash outflow under leasing alternative

Year	*Lease rent*	*Lease rent after tax*	*PVF at 9%*	*Total PV*
1-5	₹6,00,000	₹3,60,000	3.890	₹14,00,400

Tax shield on depreciation

Year	*1*	*2*	*3*	*4*	*5*
Depreciation	₹4,00,000	₹3,20,000	₹2,56,000	₹2,04,000	—
Tax advantage	₹1,60,000	₹1,28,000	₹1,02,400	₹81,920	—

Tax shield on interest

At year end	*Principal outstanding*	*Interest*	*Tax advantage on interest*
1	₹20,00,000	₹3,00,000	₹1,20,000
2	16,00,000	2,40,000	96,000
3	12,00,000	1,80,000	72,000
4	8,00,000	1,20,000	48,000
5	4,00,000	60,000	24,000

PV of cash outflow under buying option

Year	*Gross cash outflow*	*Tax advantage on*		*Net COAT*	*PVF at 9%*	*Total PV*
		Depreciation	*Interest*			
1	₹7,00,000	₹1,60,000	₹1,20,000	₹4,20,000	0.917	₹3,85,140
2	6,40,000	1,28,000	96,000	4,16,000	0.842	3,50,272

(Contd.)

(*Contd.*)

3	5,80,000	1,02,400	72,000	4,05,600	0.772	3,13,123.20
4	5,20,000	81,920	48,000	3,90,080	0.708	2,76,176.64
5(a)	4,60,000	—	24,000	4,36,000	0.650	2,83,400.00
						16,08,111.84
5(b) Less PV of salvage value (₹2 lakh × 0.650)						(1,30,000)
5(c) Less PV of tax advantage on STCL (₹2,47,680@ × 0.650)						(1,60,992)
NPV						13,17,119.84

@(₹20,00,000- accumulated depreciation, ₹11,80,000 – ₹2,00,000, SV) × 0.40 = ₹2,47,680

Recommendation Borrow-buy option is better.

P.25.4 Alfa Ltd is thinking of installing a computer. Decide whether the computer is to be purchased outright (through 14 per cent borrowing) or to be acquired on lease rental basis. The company is in the 50 per cent tax bracket. The other data available are: **LO 25.2** LOD M

Purchase of computer:

Purchase price: ₹20,00,000

Annual maintenance, (to be paid in advance), ₹50,000 per year

Expected economic useful life, 6 years

Depreciation (for tax purposes), Straight line method

Salvage value: ₹2,00,000

Leasing of computer:

Lease charges (to be paid in advance): ₹4,50,000

Maintenance expense to be borne by lessor

Payment of Loan: 6 year-end equal instalments of ₹5,14,271

Solution

PV of cash outflows under leasing alternative

Year-end	*Lease payment (net)*	*Tax shield*	*Cash outflows after taxes*	*PV factor (0.07)*	*Total PV*
0	₹4,00,000*	—	₹4,00,000	1.000	₹4,00,000
1–5	4,00,000	₹2,00,000	2,00,000	4.100	8,20,000
6	—	2,00,000	(2,00,000)	0.666	(1,33,200)
					10,86,800

*(₹4,50,000, lease rent – ₹50,000 saving in maintenance expenses).

Schedule of debt payment

Year end	*Loan instalment*	*Loan at the beginning of the year*	*Payment*		*Principal out-standing at the end of the year*
			Interest on loan (Col 3 × 0.14)	*Principal re-payment (Col 2 – Col 4)*	*(Col 3 – Col 5)*
1	*2*	*3*	*4*	*5*	*6*
1	₹5,14,271	₹20,00,000	₹2,80,000	₹2,34,271	₹17,65,729
2	5,14,271	17,65,729	2,47,202	2,67,069	14,98,660
3	5,14,271	14,98,660	2,09,812	3,04,459	11,94,201
4	5,14,271	11,94,201	1,67,188	3,47,083	8,47,118
5	5,14,271	8,47,118	1,18,596	3,95,675	4,51,443
6	5,14,271	4,51,443	62,828	4,51,443	—

PV of after tax cash outflows under buying alternative

Year-end	Loan instalment	Tax advantage on interest	Tax advantage on depreciation	Net cash outflows (Col 2 – Col 3 + 4)	PV factor at after tax cost of debt (0.07)	Total PV
1	2	3	4	5	6	7
1	₹5,14,271	₹1,40,000	₹1,50,000	₹2,24,271	0.935	₹2,09,693
2	5,14,271	1,23,601	1,50,000	2,40,670	0.873	2,10,105
3	5,14,271	1,04,906	1,50,000	2,59,365	0.816	2,11,642
4	5,14,271	83,594	1,50,000	2,80,677	0.763	2,14,157
5	5,14,271	59,298	1,50,000	3,04,973	0.713	2,17,446
6	5,14,271	31,414	1,50,000	3,32,857	0.666	2,21,683
Present value of after-tax cash outflows						12,84,726
Less: PV of salvage value (₹2,00,000 × 0.666)						(1,33,200)
Net cash outflows under buying alternative						11,51,526

Recommendation Computer should be acquired on lease basis.

P.25.5 ABC Machine Tool Company Ltd is considering the acquisition of a large equipment to set up its factory in a backward region for ₹12,00,000. The equipment is expected to have an economic useful life of 8 years. The equipment can be financed either with an 8-year term loan at 14 per cent interest, repayable in equal instalments of ₹2,58,676 per year, or by an equivalent amount of lease rent per year. In both cases, payments are due at the end of the year. The equipment is subject to the straight line method of depreciation for tax purposes. Assuming no salvage value after the 8-year useful life and 50 per cent tax rate, which of the financing alternatives should it select?

LO 25.2 LOD E

Solution

PV of cash inflows under leasing alternative

Year end	Lease payment after taxes (L) (1 – 0.5)	PV factor at 0.07 (K_d)	Total PV
1–8	₹1,29,338	5.971	₹7,72,277

Determination of interest and principal components of loan instalment

Year end	Loan instalment	Loan at the beginning of the year	Payment of interest (Col 3 × 0.14)	Payment of principal (Col 2 – Col 4)	Principal outstanding at the end of the year (Col 3 – Col 5)
1	2	3	4	5	6
1	₹2,58,676	₹12,00,000	₹1,68,000	₹90,676	₹11,09,324
2	2,58,676	11,09,324	1,55,305	1,03,371	10,05,953
3	2,58,676	10,05,953	1,40,833	1,17,843	8,88,110
4	2,58,676	8,88,110	1,24,335	1,34,341	7,53,769
5	2,58,676	7,53,769	1,05,528	1,53,148	6,00,621
6	2,58,676	6,00,621	84,087	1,74,589	4,26,032
7	2,58,676	4,26,032	59,644	1,99,032	2,27,000
8	2,58,676	2,27,000	31,676	2,27,000	—

PV of cash outflows under buying alternative

Year	Loan instalment	Tax advantage on interest (I × t)	Tax advantage on depreciation (D × t)	Cash outflows after taxes [Col 2 – (Col 3 + Col 4)]	PV factor at 0.07	Total PV
1	2	3	4	5	6	7
1	₹2,58,676	₹84,000	₹75,000	₹99,676	0.935	₹93,197
2	2,58,676	77,652	75,000	1,06,024	0.873	92,559
3	2,58,676	70,416	75,000	1,13,260	0.816	92,420
4	2,58,676	62,167	75,000	1,21,509	0.763	92,711
5	2,58,676	52,764	75,000	1,30,912	0.713	93,340
6	2,58,676	42,043	75,000	1,41,633	0.666	94,328
7	2,58,676	29,822	75,000	1,53,854	0.623	95,851
8	2,58,676	15,838	75,000	1,67,838	0.582	97,682
						7,52,088

Recommendation The borrowing (buying) alternative of financing the purchase of the large equipment should be selected.

P.25.6 For P.25.5 compute the net advantage of leasing (NAL) to the lessee assuming (i) The company follows written down value method of depreciation, the deprecation rate being 25 per cent; (ii) The corporate tax is 35 per cent; (iii) Post-tax marginal cost of capital (K_c) is 12 per cent and (iv) The company has several assets in the asset block of 25 per cent. LO 25.2 LOD E

Solution

Computation of NAL to the lessee

Benefits from lease:	
Cost of the equipment (investment saved)	₹12,00,000
PV of tax shield on lease rentals (working note **2**)	4,49,786
Total	16,49,786
Cost of lease:	
PV of lease rental **(1)**	11,99,998
PV of tax shield foregone on depreciation **(3)**	2,72,333
PV of interest tax shield foregone on debt **(4)**	2,08,381
Total	16,80,712
NAL	(30,926)

Recommendation The lease is not financially viable.

Working Notes

(1) PV of lease rentals: Lease rentals × PVIFA (14,8) = ₹2,58,676 × 4.639 = ₹11,99,998.

(2) PV of tax shield on lease rentals: Lease rentals × tax rate × PVIFA (12,8) = ₹2,58,676 × 0.35 × 4.968 = ₹4,49,786

(3) PV of tax shield foregone on depreciation

Year	Depreciation	Tax shield	PV factor (at 0.12)	Total PV
1	₹3,00,000	₹1,05,000	0.893	₹93,765
2	2,25,000	78,750	0.797	62,764
3	1,68,750	59,062	0.712	42,052
4	1,26,562	44,297	0.636	28,173

(Contd.)

(*Contd.*)

5	94,922	33,223	0.567	18,837
6	71,191	24,917	0.507	12,633
7	53,393	18,688	0.452	8,447
8	40,045	14,016	0.404	5,662
				2,72,333

(4) PV of interest tax shield

Year	*Interest*	*Tax shield*	*PV factor (at 0.12)*	*Total PV*
1	₹1,68,000	₹58,800	0.893	₹52,508
2	1,55,305	54,357	0.797	43,322
3	1,40,833	49,292	0.712	35,096
4	1,24,335	43,517	0.636	27,677
5	1,05,528	36,935	0.567	20,942
6	84,087	29,430	0.507	14,921
7	59,644	20,875	0.452	9,436
8	31,676	11,087	0.404	4,479
				2,08,381

P.25.7 For facts in **P.25.6**, determine the break even lease rentals (BELR) for the lessee. LO 25.2 LOD M

Solution

Computation of BELR

Benefits from lease:		
Cost of the equipment	₹12,00,000	
PV of tax shield on lease rentals (working note 2)		1.62365L
Cost of lease:		
PV of lease rentals (note 1)		4.639L
PV of tax shield foregone on depreciation	2,72,333	
PV of interest tax shield foregone on debt	2,08,381	

BELR (L) = 4.639L + ₹4,80,714 = 1.62365L + ₹12,00,000

4.639*L* – 1.62365L = ₹12,00,000 – ₹4,80,714

L = ₹7,19,286/3.01535 = ₹2,38,541

Working Notes

(i) PV of lease rentals: L × PVIFA (14,8) = 4.639 × *L* = 4.639*L*

(ii) PV of tax shield on lease rentals: L × PVIFA (14,8) × tax rate = 4.639*L* × 0.35 = 1.62365*L*

P.25.8 The Hypothetical Manufacturers Ltd (HML) has under consideration investment in a project. The cost of the equipment estimated to be ₹936 lakh. The useful life of the equipment is 5 years, with a salvage value of 40 per cent of the book value after 5 years. The depreciation relevant for tax purposes is 25 per cent. The HML has other assets in this block of 25 per cent. The investment is likely to generate an incremental earnings before depreciation, interest and tax of ₹720 lakh per annum for the first 3 years and ₹480 lakh per annum for the last 2 years. LO 25.2 LOD D

The HML has two alternatives to choose from to finance the equipment:

Alternative I: Leasing of the equipment from the Hypothetical Leasing Ltd (HLL). The lease rental for a 5-year non-cancellable lease is ₹27 pmpt (per month per thousand) payable in arrears (at the end of the year). The purchase of the equipment by the HLL is subject to a CST of 10 per cent.

Alternative II: Borrow and buy the equipment at 20 per cent per annum. The debt is repayable in 5 equated annual instalment payable at the end of the year. The target debt-equity ratio of the HML is 2:1. Its cost of debt may be assumed to be 20 per cent while the cost of equity is 22 per cent. The marginal tax rate of HML is 35 per cent.

You are required to compute the BELR for the lessee (HML). Should it buy or lease the equipment?

Solution

Computation of BELR (L) for the lessee (₹ *lakh)*

Benefits of leasing:	
Investment cost (saved)	936
PV of tax shield on lease rentals (working note 2)	13.75*L*
Cost of leasing:	
PV of lease rentals (note 1)	39.66*L*
PV of tax shield foregone on depreciation (3)	177.18
PV of the interest tax shield foregone on debt	6.58*L*
PV of salvage value (5)	178.21
₹936 lakh + 13.75*L* = 39.66*L* + 6.58*L* + ₹177.18 lakh + 178.12 lakh	
Or 32.49*L* = ₹580.61 lakh or *L* = ₹580.61/32.49 = ₹17.87 lakh per month	

Working Notes

(1) PV of lease rentals: $= 12L \times i/d^{(12)} \times$ PVIFA(20,5) $= 12L \times 1.015 \times 2.991 = 39.66L$

(2) PV of tax shield on lease rentals: $= 12L \times$ PVIFA (16*,5) $\times 0.35 = 13.75L$

*0.16 = (cost of debt, 0.13 × 2/3) + (cost of equity, 0.22 × 1/3)

(3) PV of tax shield foregone on depreciation (₹ *lakh)*

Depreciation	*(Tax shield × PVf)*	*PV of tax shield*
234	(81.90 × 0.862)	70.6
175	(61.25 × 0.743)	45.51
132	(46.20 × 0.641)	29.61
99	(34.65 × 0.552)	19.13
74	(25.90 × 0.476)	12.33
		177.18

(4) PV of interest on tax shield:

(a) Equated annual instalment = Amount borrowed/PVIFA(20,5) = $39.66L/2.991$ = ₹$13.26L$

(b) Debt repayment schedule (₹ *lakh)*

Year	*Amount outstanding at the beginning*	*Interest content (at 0.20)*	*Capital content*	*Instalment*
1	39.66*L*	7.93*L*	5.33*L*	13.26*L*
2	34.33*L*	6.87*L*	6.39*L*	13.26*L*
3	27.94*L*	5.59*L*	7.67*L*	13.26*L*
4	20.27*L*	4.05*L*	9.21*L*	13.26*L*
5	11.06*L*	2.20*L*	11.06*L*	13.26*L*

(c) PV of interest tax shield: $[(7.93L \times 0.862) + (6.87L \times 0.743) + (5.59L \times 0.641) + (4.05L \times 0.552) + (2.20L \times 0.476)] \times 0.35 = (6.84L + 5.10L + 3.58L + 2.24L + 1.05L) \times 0.35 = 6.58L$

(5) PV of salvage value: ₹936 lakh × 0.4 × 0.476 = ₹178.21 lakh

P.25.9 For the Hypothetical Manufacturers Ltd (HIM) of **P.25.8** compute the NAL to the lessee. Is the lease economically viable?

LO 25.2 LOD D

Solution

Computation of NAL to the lessee *(in lakh of rupees)*

Benefits from leasing:	
Investment cost (saved)	936
PV of tax shield on lease rentals (2)	367.57
Total	1,303.57
Cost of leasing:	
PV of lease rentals (working note 1)	1,064.93
PV of tax shield foregone on depreciation	177.18
PV of the interest tax shield foregone on debt (3)	176.73
PV of salvage value	178.21
Total	1,597.05
NAL (₹1,303.57 – ₹1,597.05)	(293.48)

Since NAL is negative, the lease is economically not viable.

Working Notes

(1) PV of lease rentals: (₹990 lakh × 0.027 × 12 months) × i/d^{12} × PVIFA(20,5) = ₹320.76 lakh × 1.11 × 2.991 = ₹1,064.93 lakh

(2) PV of tax shield on lease rentals: (₹320.76 lakh × 0.35) × PVIFA(16,5) = ₹112.27 lakh × 3.274 = ₹367.57 lakh

(3) **(a)** Debt repayment schedule

Year	*Amount outstanding at the beginning*	*Interest content (at 0.20)*	*Capital content*	*Instalment**
1	1,064.93	212.99	143.05	356.04
2	921.88	184.38	171.66	356.04
3	750.22	150.04	206.00	356.04
4	544.22	108.84	247.20	356.04
5	297.02	59.02	297.02	356.04

*₹1,064.93/2.991 = ₹356.04

(3) (b) *PV of interest tax shield (in lakh of ₹)*

[(₹212.99 × 0.862) + (₹184.38 × 0.743) + (₹150.04 × 0.641) + (₹108.84 × 0.552) + (₹59.02 × 0.476)] × 0.35 = (₹183.60 + ₹137 + ₹96.18 + ₹60.08 + ₹28.09) × 0.35 = ₹176.73 lakh.

P.25.10 For the facts in **P.25.8** assume the lease rental is payable annually in arrear. What is the break even lease rental (BELR) from the point of view of the lessor? Which alternative would you suggest and why? Assume the marginal cost of funds to the HLL is 15 per cent. **LO 25.2** LOD **D**

Solution

Computation of BELR (L) for the lessor *(₹ in lakh)*

Benefits from leasing:	
PV of lease rentals (working note 1)	3.352*L*
PV of tax shield on depreciation (3)	190.56
PV of salvage proceeds (₹990 lakh × 0.4 × 0.476)	188.50
Cost of leasing:	
Cost of equipment (₹900 lakh + 10%)	990
PV of tax payment on lease rentals (2)	1.173*L*

3.352*L* + 190.56 lakh + ₹188.50 lakh – ₹990 lakh – 1.173*L* = 0

3.352*L* – 1.173L = ₹990 lakh – ₹190.56 – ₹188.50

2.179*L* = ₹610.94 lakh or *L* = ₹610.94/2.179 = ₹280.38 lakh

Working Notes

(1) PV of lease rentals: $L \times$ [PVIFA(15,5)] = 3.352L

(2) PV of tax payment on lease: 0.35 × 3.352L = 1.173L

(3) PV of tax shield on depreciation *(Amount in lakh of rupees)*

Depreciation	*Tax shield × PVf*	*PV of tax shield*
247	₹86.45 × 0.870	₹75.21
185	64.75 × 0.756	48.95
139	48.65 × 0.658	32.01
104	36.40 × 0.572	20.82
78	27.30 × 0.497	13.57
		190.56

P.25.11 The Hypothetical Manufacturers Ltd (HML) has taken a plant on lease, valued at ₹20 crore. The lease arrangement is in the form of a leveraged lease. The HLL is the equity participant and the Hypothetical Bank Ltd (HBL) is the loan participant. They fund the investment in the ratio of 2 : 8. The loan from HBL carries a fixed rate of interest of 19 per cent, payable in 6 equated annual instalments. The lease term is 6 years, with lease rental payable annually in arrear.

LO 25.1,2 LOD D

(a) Compute the equated annual instalment from the point of view of HBL.

(b) If the lease rate is unknown, and HBL's per-tax yield is 25 per cent, what is the minimum lease rate that must be quoted?

Solution

(a) Equated annual instalment to HBL: Loan amount, or ₹20 crore × 8/10 = ₹16 crore/PVIFA(19, 6), or 3.410 = ₹4.692 crore

(b) Annual lease rental (Y): Annual cash flow to HLL = (Y – ₹4.692 crore). Given the required rate of return to HLL of 25 per cent, Y would be, (Y – ₹4.692 crore) × PVIFA (25,6) = ₹4 crore equity or 2.951 (Y – ₹4.692 crore) = ₹4 crore, Y = 17.846 crore/2.951 = ₹6.05 crore.

P.25.12 The controller of General Electronics Corporation of India Ltd has been analysing the firm's policy regarding computers, which are now being leased on a yearly basis on rental amounting to ₹1,00,000 per year. The computers can be bought for ₹5,00,000. The purchase would be financed by 16 per cent loan repayable in 4 equal annual instalments.

LO 25.2 LOD D

On account of rapid technological progress in the computer industry, it is suggested that a 4-year economic life should be used, instead of the 10-year physical life. It is estimated that the computers would be sold for ₹2,00,000 at the end of 4 years.

The company uses the straight line method of depreciation. Corporate tax rate is 50 per cent.

(a) Comment on whether the equipment should be bought or leased?

(b) Analyse the financial viability from the point of view of the lessor, assuming 14 per cent cost of capital.

(c) Determine the minimum lease rent at which the lessor would break even.

(d) Determine the lease rent which will yield an IRR of 16 per cent to the lessor.

Solution

(a) PV of cash outflows under leasing alternative

Year	*Lease rent after taxes*	*PV factor (0.08)*	*Total PV*
1–4	₹50,000	3.312	₹1,65,600

Cash outflows under buying alternative

Year-end	*Loan at the beginning of the year*	*Loan instalment*	*Interest on loan (0.16)*	*Principal repayment*	*Principal outstanding at the end of year*
1	₹5,00,000	₹1,78,699*	₹80,000	₹98,699	₹4,01,301
2	4,01,301	1,78,699	64,208	1,14,491	2,86,810

(Contd.)

(*Contd.*)

3	2,86,810	1,78,699	45,890	1,32,809	1,54,001
4	1,54,001	1,78,699	24,698	1,54,001	—

*[₹5,00,000 ÷ 2.798 (PV factor of annuity of ₹1 at 16 per cent for 4 years)]

PV of cash outflows under buying alternatives

Year	*Loan instalment*	*Payment of*		*Net cash outflows*	*PV factor (0.08)*	*Total PV*
		Interest	*Depreciation*			
1	₹1,78,699	₹40,000	₹37,500	₹1,01,199	0.926	₹93,710
2	1,78,699	32,104	37,500	1,09,095	0.857	93,494
3	1,78,699	22,945	37,500	1,18,254	0.794	93,894
4	1,78,699	12,349	37,500	1,28,850	0.735	94,705
4	Salvage value			(2,00,000)	0.735	(1,47,000)
						2,28,803

Recommendation The leasing option is financially superior.

(b) Viability from the lessor's point of view

(i) Determination of CFAT

Lease rent received	₹1,00,000
Less: Depreciation	75,000
EBT	25,000
Less: Taxes (0.50)	12,500
EAT	12,500
Add: Depreciation	75,000
CFAT	87,500

(ii) Determination of NPV

Year	*CFAT*	*PV factor (at 0.14)*	*Total PV*
1–4	₹87,500	2.914	₹2,54,975
4	2,00,000	0.592	1,18,400
Total PV			3,73,375
Less: Cost of computer			5,00,000
NPV			(1,26,625)

The proposal is not financially viable to the lessor.

(c) Lease rent, at which lessor would break-even

Cost of computers	₹5,00,000
Less: PV of salvage price of computers	1,18,400
Net cost to be recovered	3,81,600
Divide by PV annuity factor (14,4)	÷ 2.914
CFAT (desired)	1,30,954
Less: Depreciation	75,000
EAT	55,954
Add: Taxes	55,954
EBT	1,11,908
Add: Depreciation	75,000
Lease rental (desired)	1,86,908

(d) Lease rent to yield 16 per cent IRR

CFAT (desired)	₹1,39,242
Less: Depreciation	75,000
EAT	64,242
Add: Tax (0.50)	64,242
EBT	1,28,484
Add: Depreciation	75,000
Lease rental (desired)	2,03,484

Working Notes

Desired CFAT: $₹5{,}00{,}000 \sum_{t=1}^{4} \frac{X}{(1+0.16)^t} + \frac{₹2{,}0{,}000}{(1+0.16)^4}$, where X = CFAT

$$₹5{,}00{,}000 - \left(\frac{₹2{,}00{,}000}{(1.16)^4}\right) = \sum_{t=1}^{n} \frac{x}{(1.16)^t}$$

Substituting (i) PV factor of annuity (16, 4) 2.798 and (ii) PV factor (16, 4), 0.552, ₹5,00,000 – (₹2,00,000 × 0.552) = X/2.798

3,89,600/2.798 = X, or X = ₹1,39,242.

P.25.13 NBT Ltd is thinking of installing a computer. It is to decide whether the computer should be acquired on lease, or be purchased through borrowings at a 12 per cent rate of interest payable at the end of the each year. Principal is due for repayment after 10 years. The following data has been collected for the purpose: **LO 25.2** LOD M

Purchase of computer:
- Purchase price, ₹40,00,000
- Annual maintenance, ₹50,000 (to be paid in advance every year)
- Life of the computer, 10 years
- Depreciation, 15 per cent per annum on written down value basis
- Salvage value, ₹4,00,000

Leasing of computer:
- Initial lease payment, ₹4,00,000
- Lease rent, ₹7,00,000 (payable in advance every year for 10 years)
- Maintenance expenses, to be borne by the lessor.

You are required to advise NBT Ltd as to whether it should purchase the computer or acquire its services on lease basis, assuming it does not pay tax.

Solution

PV of cash outflows under leasing alternative

Year	*Payment under lease contract*	*PV factor (at 0.12)*	*Total PV*
0	₹4,00,000	1.000	₹4,00,000
1–10	7,00,000	6.328*	44,29,600
			48,29,600

*6.328, that is, 5.328 (PV factor for 9 years) + 1.000 (PV factor for payment at the beginning of year 1).

PV of cash outflows under buying alternative

Particulars	*Year*	*Amount*	*PV factor (0.12)*	*Total PV*
Annual maintenance (advance)	1–10	₹50,000	6.328	₹3,16,400
Interest (end of the year)	1–10	4,80,000	5.650	27,12,000

(Contd.)

(*Contd.*)

Principal repayment	10	40,00,000	0.322	12,88,000
Salvage value	10	(4,00,000)	0.322	(1,28,800)
Total				41,87,600

Note: Depreciation is ignored as no tax advantage is accruing to the firm.

Recommendation NBT Ltd is advised to buy the computer under consideration, as it is economical compared to the leasing alternative.

P.25.14 HCL Ltd is considering acquiring an additional computer to supplement its time-share computer services to its clients. It has two options: **LO 25.2** LOD M

(i) To purchase the computer for ₹22,00,000.

(ii) To lease the computer for 3 years from a leasing company for ₹5,00,000 annual lease rent plus 10 per cent of gross time-share service revenue. The agreement also requires an additional payment of ₹6,00,000 at the end of the third year. Lease rent are payable at the year end, and the computer reverts to the lessor after the contract period.

The company estimates that the computer under review now will be worth ₹10 lakh at the end of the third year.

Forecast revenues are:

Year 1	₹22,50,000
2	25,00,000
3	27,50,000

Annual operating costs (excluding depreciation and lease rent of computer) are estimated at ₹9,00,000, with an additional ₹1,00,000 for start-up and training costs at the beginning of the first year.

HCL Ltd will borrow at 16 per cent interest to finance the acquisition of the computer; repayments are to be made according to the following schedule.

Year-end	*Principal*	*Interest*	*Total*
1	₹5,00,000	₹3,52,000	₹8,52,000
2	8,50,000	2,72,000	11,22,000
3	8,50,000	1,36,000	9,86,000

The company uses the straight line method to depreciate its assets and pays 50 per cent tax on its income. The management of HCL Ltd approaches you for advice. Which alternative would you recommend? Why?

Solution

PV of cash outflows under leasing alternative

Year	*Payment under lease contract*			*Tax shield @ 50% on lease payments*	*Net cash outflows*	*PV factor (0.08)*	*Total PV*
	Lease rent	*10% of gross revenue*	*Lumpsum payment*				
1	₹5,00,000	₹2,25,000	—	₹3,62,500	₹3,62,500	0.926	₹3,35,675
2	5,00,000	2,50,000	—	3,75,000	3,75,000	0.857	3,21,375
3	5,00,000	2,75,000	₹6,00,000	6,87,500	6,87,500	0.794	5,45,875
							12,02,925

PV of cash outflows under borrowing alternative

Year	Loan instalment	Tax advantage on (I × 0.50)	Tax advantage on (D × 0.50)	Net cash outflows	PV factor (0.08)	Total PV
1	₹8,52,000	₹1,76,000	₹2,00,000	₹4,76,000	0.926	₹4,40,776
2	11,22,000	1,36,000	2,00,000	7,86,000	0.857	6,73,602
3	9,86,000	68,000	2,00,000	7,18,000	0.794	5,70,092
	Salvage value			(10,00,000)	0.794	(7,94,000)
						8,90,470

Assumption The start-up and training costs are to be borne by the lessee even if the computer is acquired on lease basis.

Recommendation The management is advised to buy the computer.

P.25.15 Infotel Broadband Limited is in need to acquire towers for its 4G rollout. It is considering buying or leasing them. Towers can be acquired at ₹150 lakh and are expected to have economic useful life of 5 years. At year-end 5, these towers are expected to have salvage value of ₹6 lakh. In contrast, the towers can be taken at lease rent of ₹39 lakh. **LO 25.2** LOD **D**

Infotel Broadband can raise loan at 15 per cent payable in 5 equal instalments, each instalment is due at the end of year. For your exercise, you may assume the following:

(1) Towers will constitute a separate block for depreciation purposes. The company follows written down value method of depreciation, the rate of depreciation being 20 per cent, **(2)** Tax rate is 33 per cent, **(3)** Lease rents are to be for 5 years (and are to be paid at the end of the year), **(4)** Maintenance expenses are estimated at ₹10 lakh per year and are to be borne by the lessee, **(5)** Assume firm would have sufficient short-term capital gains in year 5.

Required: Should Infotel lease or buy towers? Use present value method as well as IRR method in support of your answer. Also analyse the financial viability from the point of view of the lessor, assuming 16 per cent cost of capital and tax rate of 33 per cent. Assume further the lessor would have sufficient short-term capital gains in year 5. Also, determine minimum lease rent acceptable to lessor.

Solution

Financial Analysis whether to have towers on a lease option basis or buying option basis (set up towers)

Determination of present value of cash outflows under leasing option

Year	Lease rent after taxes [R(1-T)] [₹39,00,000 (1 – 0.33)]	PVIFA factor at [15% (1 – 0.33)] 10%*	Total PV
1-5	₹26,13,000	3.791	₹99,05,883

*For calculation purposes, 10.05% has been taken as 10%.

Present value of cash outflow under buying option

Year-end	Loan instalment	Tax advantage on (I × 0.33)	Tax advantage on (D × 0.33)	Net cash outflow 2 – (3 + 4)	PVIF at 10%	Total PV 5 × 6
1	2	3	4	5	6	7
1	₹44,74,940	₹7,42,500	₹9,90,000	₹27,42,440	0.909	₹24,92,878
2	44,74,940	6,32,365	7,92,000	30,50,575	0.826	25,19,775

(*Contd.*)

(*Contd.*)

3	44,74,940	5,05,711	6,33,600	33,35,629	0.751	25,05,057
4	44,74,940	3,60,058	5,06,880	36,08,002	0.683	24,64,265
5	44,74,940	1,93,017	4,05,504	38,76,419	0.621	24,07,256
						1,23,89,238
Less: PV of salvage value (₹6,00,000 × 0.621)						3,72,600
Less: PV of tax savings on STCL						8,84,314
(₹49,15,200 – ₹6,00,000) × 0.33 = (₹14,24,016 × 0.621)						
Total						1,11,32,324

Working Notes

(i) Equivalent annual loan instalment = Price of towers/ PVF at 15% for 5 years
= ₹1,50,00,000/3.352 = ₹44,74,940

(ii) Schedule of debt payment

Year-end	*Loan instalment*	*Loan at the beginning of the year*	*Payments*		*Loan outstanding at the end of the year (col. 3 – col. 5)*
			Interest (col. 3 × 0.15)	*Principal repayment*	
1	*2*	*3*	*4*	*5*	*6*
1	₹44,74,940	₹1,50,00,000	₹22,50,000	₹22,24,940	₹1,27,75,060
2	44,74,940	1,27,75,060	19,16,259	25,58,681	1,02,16,379
3	44,74,940	1,02,16,379	15,32,457	29,42,483	72,73,896
4	44,74,940	72,73,896	10,91,084	33,83,856	38,90,040
5	44,74,940	38,90,040	5,84,900*	38,90,040	—

*Difference between the loan instalment and loan outstanding

Schedule of depreciation

Year	*1*	*2*	*3*	*4*	*5*
WDV	₹1,50,00,000	1,20,00,000	96,00,000	76,80,000	61,44,000
Depreciation	₹30,00,000	24,00,000	19,20,000	15,36,000	12,28,800

Cost of Leasing

Determination of after-tax cost of lease financing

Year-end	*Cost of towers*	*Lease payments (L)*	*Depreciation (D)*	*Incremental tax shield on leasing 0.33 × (L – D)*	*Net cash outflows under leasing (3 – 5)*
1	*2*	*3*	*4*	*5*	*6*
0	₹1,50,00,000	—	—	—	—
1		₹39,00,000	₹30,00,000	₹2,97,000	(₹36,03,000)
2		39,00,000	24,00,000	4,95,000	(34,05,000)
3		39,00,000	19,20,000	6,53,400	(32,46,600)
4		39,00,000	15,36,000	7,80,120	(31,19,880)
5 (a)		39,00,000	12,28,800	8,81,496	(30,18,504)
5 (b) Salvage value					(6,00,000)
5 (c) Tax saving on STCL					(14,24,016)
Total					1,84,17,000

Average cash outflow per year = ₹1,84,17,000/5 = ₹36,83,400
Pay Back Period = ₹1,50,00,000/₹36,83,400 = 4.07

Look for the PV factors closest to 4.07 in the present value of annuity table in year 5. The two closest factors are 4.100 (at 7%) and 3.993 (at 6%). Given the fact that net cash outflows in year 5 is substantially higher (at ₹50,42,520) compared to average cash outflows of ₹36,83,400, IRR has been attempted at 6 per cent and 7 per cent.

Determination of IRR

Year	*Net cash outflow under leasing*	*PV Factor at*		*Total PV at*	
		7%	*6%*	*7%*	*6%*
1	₹36,03,000	0.935	0.943	₹33,68,805	₹33,97,629
2	34,05,000	0.873	0.890	29,72,565	30,30,450
3	32,46,600	0.816	0.840	26,49,226	27,27,144
4	31,19,880	0.763	0.792	23,80,468	24,70,945
5	50,42,520*	0.713	0.747	35,95,317	35,95,317
				1,49,66,381	1,52,21,485

* [5(a) +5(b) +s(c) = ₹30,18,504 + ₹6,00,000 + ₹14,24,016]

$$\text{IRR (by interpolation)} = 7\% - \frac{[₹1{,}50{,}00{,}00 - ₹1{,}49{,}66{,}381]}{[₹1{,}52{,}21{,}485 - ₹1{,}49{,}66{,}381]}$$

$$= 7\% - \frac{₹33{,}619}{₹2{,}55{,}104} = 7\% - 0.13 = 6.83\ \%$$

Cost of leasing = 6.83 per cent; after tax cost of debt = 10 per cent

Recommendation Infotel Broadband is advised to go for leasing to take advantage of its lower cost relative to the cost of debt. Similar conclusion follows based on comparison of PV of cash outflows under lease option compared to borrow/buy option.

Financial Analysis whether to give towers by Reliance Infratel on lease rent or not using NPV method

Determination of NPV of cash inflows

Particulars	*Year* 1	2	3	4	5
Lease rent	₹39,00,000	₹39,00,000	₹39,00,000	₹39,00,000	₹39,00,000
Less: Depreciation	30,00,000	24,00,000	19,20,000	15,36,000	12,28,800
Earnings before taxes	9,00,000	15,00,000	19,80,000	23,64,000	26,71,200
Less: Taxes (0.33)	2,97,000	4,95,000	6,53,400	7,80,120	8,81,496
Earnings after taxes	6,03,000	10,05,000	13,26,600	15,83,880	17,89,704
CFAT (EAT + D)	36,03,000	34,05,000	32,46,600	31,19,880	30,18,504
PV factor at (0.16)	0.862	0.743	0.641	0.552	0.476
Total	31,57,786	25,29,915	20,81,071	17,22,174	14,36.808
Total PV of lease rent					1,08,75,754
Add: PV of salvage value (₹6,00,000 × 0.476)					2,85,600
Add: PV of tax savings on STCL (₹14,24,016 × 0.476)					6,77,832
Gross PV					1,18,39,186
Less: Cost of towers					1,50,00,000
NPV					(31,60,814)

Recommendation It is not financially profitable to let out towers on lease by Reliance Infratel, as NPV is negative.

Break-even lease rental—minimum lease rental Infratel can accept

Cost of Towers	₹1,50,00,000
Less: PV of Salvage value to be received at the end of year 5 (₹ 6,00,000 × 0.476)	2,85,600
Less: PV of tax saving on STCL at the end of 5th year (₹ 14,24,016 × 0.476)	6,77,832
Less: PV of tax shield on Depreciation: (₹30,00,000 × 0.33 × 0.862 + ₹24,00,000 × 0.33 × 0.743 + ₹19,20,000 × 0.33 × 0.641 + ₹15,36,000 × 0.33 × 0.552 + ₹12,28,800 × 0.33 × 0.476)	23,20,791
Total PV after tax lease rent	1,17,15,777
Divided by PVIFA for 5yrs at 0.16	÷3.274
After tax lease rentals	35,78,429
Break-even lease rentals [₹35,78,429/(1 – 0.33)]	₹53,40,939

Recommendation Thus, the minimum lease rental that Infratel should charge is ₹53,40,939.

Verification table—for Break-even lease rental

Particulars	*Year*				
	1	*2*	*3*	*4*	*5*
Lease rent	₹53,40,939	₹53,40,939	₹53,40,939	₹53,40,939	₹53,40,939
Less: Depreciation	30,00,000	24,00,000	19,20,000	15,36,000	12,28,800
Earnings before taxes	23,40,939	29,40,939	34,20,939	38,04,939	41,12,139
Less: Taxes (0.33)	7,72,510	9,70,510	11,28,910	12,55,630	13,57,006
Earnings after tax	15,68,429	19,70,429	22,92,029	25,49,309	27,55,133
CFAT (EAT + D)	45,68,429	43,70,429	42,12,029	40,85,309	39,83,933
PV Factor at (0.16)	0.862	0.743	0.641	0.552	0.476
Total	39,37,986	32,47,229	26,99,911	22,55,091	18,96,352
Total PV of lease rent					1,40,36,569
Add: PV of salvage value (₹6,00,000 × 0.476)					2,85,600
Add: PV of tax savings on STCL (₹14,24,016 × 0.476)					6,77,832
Total PV					₹1,50,00,000

P.25.16 A departmental store owns a large building and the land on which it is situated. Their respective book values are ₹20 crore and ₹8 crore. The building is being depreciated @ ₹1 crore per year over 20 years. **LO 25.1.2** LOD M

Canhome Finance Ltd has offered to buy the land and building at book value and to lease it back to the firm for 20 years at annual rental of ₹3 crore, payable at the end of each year. At the end of the 20th year, it is estimated that, after paying the costs of demolishing the building, the land could net ₹9 crore.

If the sale and lease back proposals were accepted, the departmental store would still be responsible for maintenance, insurance and so on, but would have no residual claims on the property at the end of the 20th year. The finance manager of the departmental store estimates the firm's after tax cost of capital is 12 per cent. The firm can borrow at 10.75 per cent. The corporate tax rate on ordinary income is likely to remain unchanged at the present level of 35 per cent and on capital gains at 20 per cent.

Advise the company on the relative suitability of the options.

Solution

PV of cash outflows under leasing alternative

Year	*Lease payment after taxes*	*PV factor (0.07)*	*Total PV*
1	₹1,95,00,000	10.594	₹20,65,83,000

PV of cash outflows under retaining the asset alternative

PV of land and building	₹28,00,00,000
Less: PV of tax shield on depreciation foregone [₹1,00,00,000 × 0.35 (*t*)] × 7.469 (PV factor of annuity for 20 years at 12%)	2,61,41,500
Less: Effective salvage value foregone [₹9 crore – ₹0.20 crore (capital gain tax on ₹1,00,00,000 × PV factor at 12% in 20th year, ie, 0.104]	91,52,000
	24,47,06,500

Advice It will be advantageous for the firm to sell, and then acquire the asset on lease basis.

MINI CASES

25.C.1 Leasing Vs. Buying—Borrowing Teddy Bear Ltd is in the business of making toys of different ranges. Presently, Teddy Bear has one manufacturing plant having production capacity of 30,00,000 toys annually. They are sold through registered dealers in India who take delivery of toys directly from the factory situated in NOIDA. Teddy Bear does not incur any transport cost.

The demand for toys has shown tremendous growth in recent years. The Vice President Marketing, Sanjay Khanna, has submitted a proposal to the CEO, Bikrant Kumar Singh, to expand the production capacity of Teddy Bear to 40,00,000 toys. The CEO directs the Vice President, Manufacturing, Virender Kumar Rathi, to put a proposal regarding the availability of the required equipment for the expansion of the plant. A survey shows that the machinery is available for ₹12.5 crore having a useful life of five years and no salvage. Assume straight line depreciation for tax purposes. It also shows that there are two alternatives to finance the proposal. The equipment can be bought and financed by borrowing from the Udharwala Financial Services Ltd at 10 per cent interest. The equipment can be alternatively taken on lease from the First Leasing Company of India Ltd at ₹3.5 crore annual lease rental. The First Leasing would bear the associated taxes, insurance and maintenance cost amounting to ₹60,00,000 annually.

Required Bikrant Singh engages you as a financial consultant to advise him on the choice of the funding alternatives. Should Teddy Bear buy the equipment through borrowing or acquire it on lease? What advice would you give and why? Assume 30 per cent corporate tax.

Solution

1. Present Value of Cash Outflows Under Leasing Alternative (₹ crore)

Year-end	*Lease rent after taxes* [₹3.50 (1 – 0.30)]	*PVIFA* [10% (1-0.30)]	*Total PV*
1 – 5	₹2.45	4.100	₹10.04

2. Present Value of Cash Outflows Under Buying-Borrowing Alternative (₹ crore)

	Year-end tax advantage					
	1	*2*	*3*	*4*	*5*	*Total*
Tax advantage:						
Interest on loan (Working note 10	₹1.25	₹1.04	₹0.82	₹0.57	₹0.30	3.98

(*Contd.*)

(*Contd.*)

Taxes/maintenance cost	0.60	0.60	0.60	0.60	0.60	3.00
Depreciation (₹12.50 crore ÷ 5 years)	2.50	2.50	2.50	2.50	2.50	12.50
	4.35	4.14	3.92	3.67	3.40	19.48
(A) Tax advantage (0.30)	1.30	1.24	1.18	1.10	1.02	5.84
(B) Payments:						
(a) Loan payment (Working note 1)	3.30	3.30	3.30	3.30	3.30	16.5
(b) Taxes/ maintenance costs	0.60	0.60	0.60	0.60	0.60	3.00
	3.90	3.90	3.90	3.90	3.90	19.50
(C) Net cash outflows (B-A)	2.60	2.66	2.72	2.80	2.88	13.66
(D) PVIF (0.07)	0.935	0.873	0.816	0.763	0.713	
(E) Total present value	2.43	2.31	2.22	2.14	2.05	11.15

Advice: As the present value of cash flow under the buying-borrowing alternative is higher, lease financing is a better alternative.

Working Note

1. Loan repayment schedule (₹ crore)

Year	*Total@*	*Interest*	*Principal*
1	3.30	1.25	2.05
2	3.30	1.04	2.26
3	3.30	0.82	2.48
4	3.30	0.57	2.73
5	3.30	0.30	3.00

@₹12.5 ÷ 3.791

25.C.2 Symphosis is planning to open a new office in Safdarjung Enclave, Delhi to expand its operations and to cater to the clients emerging as entrepreneurs in NCR area. For the purpose, it has acquired a complex spread in 2 acres. The complex has 30 rooms in total (spread across 4 floors). There are 20 corridors and 2 staircases that connect the floors on two sides. The company plans to employ a Security-cum- Surveillance system in the complex. The team has met with a consultancy firm (headed by Mr. Sukhvinder) and has decided upon the following requirements in the context of Surveillance system.

Equipment/product	*Quantity*	*Cost per unit/₹*	*Remarks*
IP cameras	50	13,000	0.5 lux
PTZ (pan till zoom) cameras	8	45,000	SMGH/PELCO
Video server	1	2,00,000	3 client access
POE server	1	32,000	—
LCD screen	1	55,000	With screens for all the camera feeds

Apart from the equipment, certain other costs are also to be incurred. Installation costs are ₹3.5 lakh and the civil construction costs are at real-time. The rate for the same is ₹150 per square feet of digging undertaken. Based on this exercise and after allowing for contingencies, total costs are ₹12,97,000. The annual maintenance costs can be covered through an AMC (with increase of 10 per cent per year). The AMC would cost ₹10 lakh in year 1. The useful life of such a system is 10 years. The company is thinking of financing its initiative by bank loan. The bank has agreed to finance ₹12.97 lakh and has agreed to charge interest at 14 per cent for the loan payable in 10 annual equal instalments of ₹2, 48,652.

As the agreement with the bank was about to be signed, the CFO received an email from his junior stating that Convenience Ltd. is a company that provides such equipment on lease and has been in the industry for 6 years and before that has been actively involved in providing security solutions across the globe for the past 15 years. The company is offering the equipment for 10 years financial lease (along with the AMC) for an annual lease rental of ₹14 lakh.The CFO now wants to evaluate the two options (borrow – buy and leasing).

You are also required to evaluate financial soundness of the proposal from the point of view of leasing company. The company can arrange the AMC for ₹7 lakh per annum (with increase of 10 per cent per year). The cost of capital for the lessor is 18 per cent. Also, suggest the minimum lease rent it can offer.

The depreciation rates are 15 per cent as CCTVs fall under plant and machinery category and not specifically under any block. Tax rate applicable for both the companies is 30 per cent. Assume that the block ceases to exist at the end of year 10 and the salvage value is ₹50,000 (for both the companies). Assume further both the companies would have sufficient short-term capital gains in year 10.

Solution

Evaluation from Lessee's perspective

Present value of Cash Outflows under Leasing Option

Year end	*Annual lease rent*	*Tax shield @ 30%*	*Lease rent after taxes*	*PVIFA@9.8% (K_d)*	*Total PV*
1-10	₹14,00,000	₹4,20,000	₹9,80,000	6.198	₹60,73,762

K_d has been calculated as follows. Given K_i = 14% (as leasing is compared with borrow-buy option) and t = 30%, $K_d = ki \times (1 - t)$ = 14% (1 – 0.3) = 9.8%. Since the present values are not given in the table for fractional rates, these have been calculated by using the following formula:

So PVIFA (9.8,10)= [{1/(1+*Kd*)} + {1/(1+*Kd*)}2 + {1/(1+*Kd*)}3 + ... + {1/ (1+*Kd*)}10]

Present value of Cash Outflows under Borrow-Buy Option (*Amount in ₹*)

Year end 1	*Loan instalment 2*	*Maintenance expenses 3*	*Tax shield on maintenance expenses 4 = 3 × t*	*Total interest on loan 5*	*Tax shield on interest 6 = 5 × t*	*Tax shield on depreciation 7*	*NCOAT 8 = (2 + 3 – 4 – 6 – 7)*	*PVIFA @9.8% (K_d) 9*	*Total PV 10 = 8 × 9*
1	248652.00	1000000.00	300000.00	181580.00	54474.00	58365.00	835813.00	0.911	761214.03
2	248652.00	1100000.00	330000.00	172189.92	51656.98	49610.25	917384.77	0.829	760933.75
3	248652.00	1210000.00	363000.00	161485.23	48445.57	42168.71	1005037.72	0.755	759233.46
4	248652.00	1331000.00	399300.00	149281.88	44784.56	35843.41	1099724.03	0.688	756613.97
5	248652.00	1464100.00	439230.00	135370.06	40611.02	30466.89	1202444.09	0.627	753447.84
6	248652.00	1610510.00	483153.00	119510.59	35853.18	25896.86	1314258.96	0.571	750009.75
7	248652.00	1771561.00	531468.30	101430.80	30429.24	22012.33	1436303.13	0.520	746499.85
8	248652.00	1948717.10	584615.13	80819.83	24245.95	18710.48	1569797.54	0.473	743061.78
9	248652.00	2143588.81	643076.64	57323.32	17197.00	15903.91	1716063.26	0.431	739796.43
10	248652.00	2357947.69	707384.31	30537.31	9161.19	0.00	1890054.19	0.393	742080.22

Present value of after tax cash outflows	₹75,12,891
Less PV of salvage value (₹50,000×0.393)	₹19,650
Less PV of tax advantage on STCL (₹75,122.1 × 0.393)	₹29,523
Net cash outflow	₹7,46,318

Tax advantage on short-term capital loss in year 3 = (₹3,00,407 – Salvage Value) × t

= (₹3,00,407 – ₹50,000) × t = ₹2,50,407 × 0.3 = ₹75,122.10

Working Notes

Depreciation Schedule

(Amount in ₹)

Year end	*Incremental asset cost base*	*Depreciation @ 15%*	*Tax shield @ 30%*
1	₹12,97,000	₹1,94,550	₹58,365
2	11,02,450	1,65,367.50	49,610.25
3	9,37,083	1,40,562.37	42,168.71
4	7,96,520	1,19,478.02	35,843.41
5	6,77,042	1,01,556.32	30,466.89
6	5,75,486	86,322.87	25,896.86
7	4,89,163	73,374.44	22,012.33
8	4,15,788	62,368.27	18,710.48
9	3,53,420	53,013.03	15,903.91
10	3,00,047	—	—

Recommendation Since the present value of cash outflows is less in leasing option than borrow–buy option, leasing is a better option.

Evaluation from Lessor's perspective

Determination of NPV

(Amount in ₹)

	Years									
Particulars	*1*	*2*	*3*	*4*	*5*	*6*	*7*	*8*	*9*	*10*
Annual lease rent	1400000	1400000	1400000	1400000	1400000	1400000	1400000	1400000	1400000	1400000
Less depreciation	194550	165367.5	140562.37	119478.01	101556.3	86322.87	73374.44	62368.27	53013.03	0
Less maintenance cost	700000	770000	847000	931700	1024870	1127357	1240093	1364102	1500512	1650563
EBT	505450	464632.5	412437.62	348821.98	273573.7	186320.1	86532.86	(–26470.2)	(–153525)	(–250563)
Less taxes (30%)	151635	139389.75	123731.28	104646.59	82072.11	55896.04	25959.86	(–7941.07@)	(–46057.6@)	(–75169@)
EAT	353815	325242.75	288706.33	244175.38	191501.60	130424.10	60573	(–18529.20)	(–107468)	(–175394)
	548365	490610.25	429268.71	363653.40	293057.9	216747	133947.4	43839.1	(–54454.6)	(–175394)
Add SV at the end of the third year			50000							
Add STCL										75122
	548365	490610.25	429268.71	363653.40	293057.9	216747	133947.4	43839.1	(–54454.6)	(–50272.3)
PV factor @18%	0.847	0.718	0.609	0.516	0.437	0.37	0.314	0.266	0.225	0.191
Total PV	464465.1	352258.15	261424.64	187645.15	128066.3	80196.38	42059.5	11661.2	(–12252.3)	(–9602)
Total PV of CFAT										1505922
Total CO										1297000
NPV										208922

@Assuming the firm has taxable income from other sources, it has tax advantage on losses accruing in years 8-10.

Recommendation Since NPV is positive, the leasing proposal is financially sound and profitable for Convenience Ltd.

Calculation of Break-Even Lease Rental

Cost of machine	₹12,97,000.00
Add PV of after tax cost of providing AMC per year	30,88,710.49
Less PV of SV after expiry of third year	9,550.00
Less PV of tax savings on STCL after expiry of third year	14,348.32
Less PV of tax shield on depreciation	1,67,594.40
Required total PV of after tax lease rent	41,94,217.77
Divided by PVIFA for 3 years at 18%	4.494
After tax lease rental	9,33,292.76
Break even lease rental (₹9,33,292.76/0.7)	13,33,275.30

25.C.3 XYZ Telecom Limited is a data telecom service and IT solutions provider. It offers innovative IP based infrastructural solutions and has been the front-runner in providing and managing multi-location wide-area networks for various industry verticals. XYZ Ltd. is a Bombay Stock Exchange (BSE) and National Stock Exchange (NSE) listed company with secure assets and loyal customer base that includes some of the biggest blue-chip companies in the world.

The company has number of customers in Delhi- Bombay corridor who require internet connection. However, presently, company is faced with a problem of bandwidth. Its financial manager suggests that it should build its own infrastructure, i.e., it should lay own optical fiber cable for communication given bulk demand from customers in present and future scenario) while the company technical manager feels that it is beneficial to take the bandwidth on lease from ABC Transmission Ltd.

ABC Transmission Ltd is discharging its responsibilities efficiently in construction, operation and maintenance of regional power grids. The company has achieved many milestones and established benchmarks in various areas of its business operations and is playing a strategic role in Indian power sector in establishing and maintaining transmission infrastructure.

Cost of building its own infrastructure (buying the fiber, digging and laying of cable, etc.) is estimated at ₹300 million. Optical fiber cable is expected to have a life of 10 year with salvage value of 5 per cent at year-end 10. The purchase can be financed at 15 per cent debt from a bank payable in 10 equal instalments (inclusive of interest) becoming due at the end of each year.

Alternatively, the financial manager of the XYZ Telecom Limited suggests that it should go for year-end lease rentals of ₹50 million.

Additional information:

(i) The fiber would constitute a separate block for depreciation purpose. For tax purposes, the company is to follow written down value method of depreciation with the rate of depreciation at 10 per cent.

(ii) Tax rate is 40 per cent.

(iii) Lease rentals are to be paid at the end of each year.

(iv) Maintenance and insurance expenses estimated ₹10 million per year is to be borne by ABC Transmission Ltd (lessor)

The question remains whether XYZ Telecom Limited should construct its own infrastructure for solving the problem of bandwidth (i.e. buying the optical fiber cable, digging, laying and taking permission for right of way etc.) or it should take it on lease from ABC Transmission Ltd. Assume the firm would have sufficient short-term capital gains in year 10.

Solution

Option-1: **Leasing Option**

PV of Cash Outflow Under Leasing Alternative

Year End	*Lease rent (LR)*	*Lease rent after tax LR × (1-0.4)*	*PVIF at 9 % [15% × (1-0.4)]*	*Total PV*
1-10	₹50,000,000	₹30,000,000	6.418	₹192,540,000

Option-2: **Borrow-buy** (Building his own infrastructure for communication):

Computation of loan installment

Loan Amount = ₹3,00,000,000

Present value of annuity of ₹1 for 10 years @15% = 5.019 (PVIF for 10 years at 15% i.e., 15, 10)

Loan instalment payable (i / ii) = ₹300,000,000/5.019 = ₹59,772,863

Computation of Interest and Principal Component of Loan Repayment

Year	*Loan instalment*	*Loan at beginning of the year*	*Payment*		*Loan outstanding at end of the year*
			Interest(I)	*Principal(P) repayment*	
(1)	*(2)*	*(3)*	*(4)*	*(5)*	*(6)*
1	₹59,772,863	₹300,000,000	₹45,000,000	₹14,772,863	₹285,227,137
2	59,772,863	285,227,137	42,784,071	16,988,792	268,238,345
3	59,772,863	268,238,345	40,235,752	19,537,111	248,701,233
4	59,772,863	248,701,233	37,305,185	22,467,678	226,233,555
5	59,772,863	226,233,555	33,935,033	25,837,830	200,395,725
6	59,772,863	200,395,725	30,059,359	29,713,504	170,682,221
7	59,772,863	170,682,221	25,602,333	34,170,530	136,511,692
8	59,772,863	136,511,692	20,476,754	39,296,109	97,215,582
9	59,772,863	97,215,582	14,582,337	45,190,526	52,025,057
10	59,772,863	52,025,057	7,747,806	52,025,057	

Computation of Depreciation

Year	*WDV at beginning of the Year*	*Depriciation@10%*	*WDV at end of the Year*
1	₹300,000,000	₹30,000,000	₹270,000,000
2	270,000,000	27,000,000	243,000,000
3	243,000,000	24,300,000	218,700,000
4	218,700,000	21,870,000	196,830,000
5	196,830,000	19,683,000	177,147,000
6	177,147,000	17,714,700	159,432,300
7	159,432,300	15,943,230	143,489,070
8	143,489,070	14,348,907	129,140,163
9	129,140,163	12,914,016	116,226,147
10	116,226,147	11,622,615	104,603,532

Computation of short-term capital loss

WDV at the end of 10 years = ₹104,603,532

Salvage Value = 0.05 × ₹300,000,000 = ₹15,000,000

Short-term capital loss = (i) – (ii) = ₹(104,603,532 – 15,000,000) = ₹89,603,532

PV of cash outflow under borrowing (building its own infrastructure for telecommunication) alternative

(Amount in ₹)

Year	Loan Instalment	Maintenance	Tax advantage on			Net Cash outflows	PVIF at 9 % [15%*(1-0.4)]	Total PV
			Interest	Depreciation	Maintenance			
(1)	(2)	(3)	(4)=I*0.4	(5)=D*0.4	(6)=(2)*0.4	(7)=(2)+(3)-(4)-(5)-(6)	(8)	(9)
1	59,772,863	10,000,000	18,000,000	12,000,000	4,000,000	35,772,863	0.917	32,819,140
2	59,772,863	10,000,000	17,113,628	10,800,000	4,000,000	37,859,235	0.842	31,865,360
3	59,772,863	10,000,000	16,094,301	9,720,000	4,000,000	39,958,562	0.772	30,855,342
4	59,772,863	10,000,000	14,922,074	8,748,000	4,000,000	42,102,789	0.708	29,826,677
5	59,772,863	10,000,000	13,574,013	7,873,200	4,000,000	44,325,650	0.650	28,808,631
6	59,772,863	10,000,000	12,023,744	7,085,880	4,000,000	46,663,239	0.596	27,823,765
7	59,772,863	10,000,000	10,240,933	6,377,292	4,000,000	49,154,638	0.547	26,889,270
8	59,772,863	10,000,000	8,190,701	5,739,563	4,000,000	51,842,599	0.502	26,018,052
9	59,772,863	10,000,000	5,832,935	5,165,607	4,000,000	54,774,322	0.460	25,219,619
10-a	59,772,863	10,000,000	3,099,123	4,649,046	4,000,000	58,024,695	0.422	24,510,258
10-b	Less PV of salvage value (₹1,50,00,000*0.422)							(6,336,162)
10-c	Less PV of tax saving on short term capital loss (₹89,603,532*0.422)							(37,849,500)
Total								240,450,453

Recommendation The company XYZ Telecom Limited is advised to go for leasing as present value of cash outflow under leasing option (₹19,25,40,000) is lower than buying option(i.e. laying his own optical fiber cable, digging and taking permission for right of way, etc., for Delhi-Bombay corridor) (₹24,04,50,453)

IRR based approach

Determination of After-tax-cost of Lease Financing

(Amount in ₹)

Year end	Cost of machine	Lease rent after tax	Tax advantage foregone on depreciation	After tax maintenance expenses to be borne by lessor	Effective COAT under leasing
0	300,000,000				300,000,000
1		30,000,000	12,000,000	(6,000,000)	36,000,000
2		30,000,000	10,800,000	(6,000,000)	34,800,000
3		30,000,000	9,720,000	(6,000,000)	33,720,000
4		30,000,000	8,748,000	(6,000,000)	32,748,000
5		30,000,000	7,873,200	(6,000,000)	31,873,200
6		30,000,000	7,085,880	(6,000,000)	31,085,880

(Contd.)

(Contd.)

7	30,000,000	6,377,292	(6,000,000)	30,377,292
8	30,000,000	5,739,563	(6,000,000)	29,739,563
9	30,000,000	5,165,607	(6,000,000)	29,165,607
10	30,000,000	4,649,046	(6,000,000)	28,649,046
10* Salvage value				15,000,000
10* Tax saving on short term capital loss				89,603,552

*Salvage value of machine foregone and short-term capital loss constitute the opportunity cost of lease financing and, therefore, cash outflows of lease financing.

Given the fact that lease option is better, the cost of leasing, that is, IRR is to be lower than after tax cost of debt of 9 per cent. Further, there is a substantial difference between present value of COAT under leasing compared to borrow-buy option, the IRR has been attempted at 5 per cent and 6 per cent.

Determination of IRR

Year	*Effective cash outflows under leasing*	*PV factor at*		*Total PV at*	
		5%	*6%*	*5%*	*6%*
1	₹36,000,000	0.952	0.943	₹34,272,000	₹33,948,000
2	34,800,000	0.907	0.890	31,563,600	30,972,000
3	33,720,000	0.864	0.840	29,134,080	28,324,800
4	32,748,000	0.823	0.792	26,951,604	25,936,416
5	31,873,200	0.784	0.747	24,988,589	23,809,280
6	31,085,880	0.746	0.705	23,190,066	21,915,545
7	30,377,292	0.711	0.665	21,598,255	20,200,899
8	29,739,563	0.677	0.627	20,133,684	18,646,706
9	29,165,607	0.645	0.592	1,881,1817	1,726,6039
10	133,252,598	0.614	0.558	81,817,095	74,354,950
Total				312,460,790	295,374,635

IRR = 5 + [(₹312,460,790 – ₹300,000,000)/(₹312,460,790 – ₹295,374,635)] × 1 = 5.73%

Scan the QR Code given at the end of chapter to access comprehensive cases.

REVIEW QUESTIONS

LOD: Easy

RQ.25.1 Provide appropriate answer for the following: **[LO 25.1,2,3]**

(i) While operating leases are ______________ (cancelable/non-cancelable) during lease period at the option of the lessee, financial leases are ______________ (cancelable/non-cancelable).

(ii) Lease rents are higher in case of ______________ (financial/operating) leases.

(iii) Lease period is higher for ______________ (operating/financial) leases.

(iv) Lease is classified as a ______________ if it transfers substantially all the risk and rewards incidental to ownership.

(v) Lease is classified as an ________________ if it does not transfer substantially all the risk and rewards incidental to ownership.

(vi) It is mandatory for the lessor to transfer ownership to the lessee in the case of Financial leases. (True/False)

(vii) Sale and lease back is ________________ (a direct/an indirect) form of leasing.

(viii) There are ________________ (two/three) parties in the leveraged lease.

(ix) ________________ lease is subject to renewal for the secondary lease period during which lease rents are substantially low.

(x) From the perspective of lessee, the lease is similar to ________________ (debt/equity) form of financing.

(xi) From the perspective of lessor, leasing is ________________ (capital budgeting/financing) decision.

(xii) In ________________ (hire-purchase/lease) agreement, the ownership is transferred on payment of last installment.

(xiii) In ________________ (hire-purchase/lease), it is customary to make cash down payment to the owner of the asset.

(xiv) In ________________ (installment/hire-puchase/lease) contract of sales is entered into, the goods are delivered and the ownership is transferred to the buyer.

(xv) Depreciation is charged in the books of the owner in leasing as well as hire-purchase. (True/False)

(xvi) The lessor uses ________________ (pre-tax cost of debt/cost of capital) as a discount rate to evaluate financial lease.

(xvii) The lessee will opt for the leasing decision if the NAL amount is ________________ (positive/negative).

[Answers: (i) cancelable, non-cancelable, (ii) operating, (iii) financial, (iv) financial, (v) operating, (vi) false, (vii) an indirect, (viii) three, (ix) financial, (x) debt, (xi) capital budgeting, (xii) hire-purchase, (xiii) hire-purchase, (xiv) installment, (xv) false, (xvi) cost of capital, (xvii) positive]

RQ.25.2 What is equipment lease? What are its essential elements? [LO 25.1]

RQ.25.3 Briefly discuss an operating lease. [LO 25.1]

RQ.25.4 Distinguish between import lease and cross-border lease. What are the advantages of the latter? [LO 25.1]

RQ.25.5 Discuss the advantages of leasing. What are its limitations? [LO 25.1]

LOD: Medium

RQ.25.6 List the criteria for classifying lease as finance lease. What are the features around which it is structured? [LO 25.1]

RQ.25.7 Distinguish between a single investor lease and a leveraged lease. [LO 25.1]

RQ.25.8 Compare and contrast sales and leasing and bipartite leasing. How can sales aid leasing be done? [LO 25.1]

RQ.25.9 Explain sale and lease back arrangement. [LO 25.1]

RQ.25.10 Briefly discuss the framework for lease evaluation from the point of view of a lessee under disounted cash flow methods. [LO 25.2]

RQ.25.11 Briefly discuss the framework for evaluation of lease from the viewpoint of a lessor. [LO 25.2]

RQ.25.12 Differentiate between (i) hire-purchase, (ii) instalment sale and (iii) leasing. [LO 25.2,3]

RQ.25.13 Briefly explain the framework of financial evaluation of a hire-purchase transaction from the view point of (a) hirer and (b) financing company. [LO 25.3]

RQ.25.14 What are the unique features of hire-purchase accounting? [LO 25.3]

RQ.25.15 The Hypothetical Equipments Ltd (HEL) has recently leased assets worth ₹2,500 lakh from the Hypothetical Leasing Ltd (HLL). The following facts are available: [LO 25.1]

(1) Lease period, 9 years, of which the first 6 years constitute the lease term

(2) Annual lease rates: First 6 years, ₹360/₹1,000; Next 3 years, ₹15/₹1,000

(3) Incremental borrowing rates for HEL, 22 per cent

(a) Assuming 14 years as the average economic life of the equipment, is the lease a finance lease or an operating lease"

(b) Assuming further (i) physical life of 14 years, (ii) technological life of 9 years and (iii) product-market life of 11 years, how will you classify the lease?

RQ.25.16 In RQ 25.15, assume the following: [LO 25.1,2]

(1) Monthly lease rentals payable in advance; first 6 years: ₹26/1,000; next 3 years, ₹1.50/1,000;

(2) Incremental borrowing rate of HEL, 23 per cent compounded monthly.

$$\left[\text{hint}: \frac{i(.23)}{(d)^{12}} = 1.121 \text{ (Table A} - 6)\right]$$

What will be your answer to RQ.25.17 (a) and (b)?

RQ.25.17 For RQ 25.15, assume (i) average economic life of the equipment, 10 years, (ii) salvage value, 10 per cent of the original cost, (iii) implicit rate of interest in lease, 25 per cent. Is it a finance lease? [LO 25.1]

RQ.25.18 Alfa Ltd is thinking of installing a computer. Decide whether the computer is to be purchased outright (through 14 per cent borrowing) or to be acquired on lease rental basis. The company is in the 50 per cent tax bracket. The other data available are: [LO 25.2]

Purchase of computer:

Purchase price: ₹20,00,000

Annual maintenance, (to be paid in advance), ₹50,000 per year

Expected economic useful life, 6 years

Depreciation (for tax purposes), Straight line method

Salvage value: ₹2,00,000

Leasing of computer:

Lease charges (to be paid in advance): ₹4,50,000

Maintenance expense to be borne by lessor

Payment of Loan: 6 year-end equal instalments of ₹5,14,271

RQ.25.19 Engineers Ltd. is in the business of manufacturing nut bolts. Some more product lines are being planned to be added to the existing system. The machinery required may be bought or may be taken on lease. The cost of machine is ₹20,00,000 having a useful life of 5 years with the salvage value of ₹4,00,000 (consider short term capital loss/gain for the income tax). The full purchase value of the machine can be financed by a bank loan at the rate of 20 per cent interest repayable in five equal instalments falling due at the end of each year. Alternatively, the machine can be procured on a 5 years' lease, year-end lease rentals being ₹6,00,000 per annum. The company follows the written down value method of depreciation at the rate of 25 pr cent. The company's tax rate is 35 per cent and cost of capital is 14 per cent. [LO 25.2]

(i) Advise the company which option it should choose - lease or borrow.

(ii) Assess the proposal from the lessor's point of view examining whether leasing the machine is financially viable at 14 per cent cost of capital.

(iii) Assume both the companies would have sufficient short-term capital gains in year 5.

Detailed working notes should be given.

RQ.25.20 Armada Leasing Company is considering a proposal to lease out a school bus. The bus can be purchased for ₹5,00,000 and, in turn, be leased out at ₹1,25,000 per year for 8 years with payments occurring at the end of each year: [LO 25.2]

(i) Estimate the internal rate of return for the company assuming tax is ignored.

(ii) What should be the yearly lease payment charged by the company in order to earn 20 per cent annual compounded rate of return before expenses and taxes?

(iii) Calculate the annual lease rent to be charged so as to amount to 20 per cent after tax annual compound rate of return, based on the following assumptions:

(i) Tax rate, 40 per cent

(ii) Straight line depreciation

(iii) Annual expenses, ₹50,000 and

(iv) Resale value, ₹1,00,000 after the turn.

LOD: Difficult

RQ.25.21 What is the debt displacement effect of leasing? [LO 25.2]

RQ.25.22 Leasing and buying cannot be considered as two mutually exclusive investment proposals for the purpose of financial evaluation. Comment. [LO 25.1,2]

RQ.25.23 Computeronics Ltd sells computer services to its clients. The company has recently completed a feasibility study and decided to acquire an additional computer the details of which are as follows: [LO 25.2]

1. The purchase price of the computer is ₹2,30,000; maintenance, property taxes and insurance will be ₹20,000 per year. The additional annual expenses to operate the computer are estimated at ₹80,000. If the computer is rented, the annual rent will be ₹85,000, plus 5 per cent of annual billings. The rent is due on the last day of each year.

2. Due to competitive conditions, the company feels it will be necessary to replace the computer after the expiry of 3 years with a more advanced model. The resale value is estimated at ₹1,10,000.

3. The appropriate income tax rate is 35 per cent. The relevant block-wise depreciation on the written down value basis is 25 per cent. There are no other assets in this block.

4. The estimated annual billing for the services of the new computer will be ₹2,20,000 during the first year, and ₹2,60,000 during the subsequent 2 years.

5. If the computer is purchased, the company will borrow to finance the purchase from a bank with interest at 20 per cent. The interest will be paid regularly, and the principal will be returned in one lumpsum at the end of year 3.

Should the company purchase the computer or lease it?

Assuming **(i)** cost of capital at 12 per cent, **(ii)** straight-line method of depreciation, **(iii)** Salvage Value of ₹1,10,000, **(iv)** the firm would have sufficient short-term capital gains in year of sale of computer, and **(v)** corporate tax rate of 35 per cent, you are also required to analyse the financial viability of the proposal from the view point of the leasing company.

RQ.25.24 Assume for the firm in RQ.25.23 the following: **(a)** the leasing company follows written down value method of depreciation, the depreciation rate being 30 per cent; there is no other asset in this block, **(b)** the expected salvage value after the expiry of 3 years of the computer is ₹1,00,000. **(c)** the corporate tax rate is 35 per cent. Assume the leasing company would have sufficient short-term capital gain in year of sale of machine. [LO 25.2]

Determine **(a)** NAL and **(b)** BELR for the lessor.

ANSWERS

25.15 **(a)** Finance lease as PV ₹2,873 lakh exceeds the cost of asset.
(b) Finance lease as term of lease is 9/9 = 100 per cent.

25.16 **(a)** Finance lease
(b) Finance lease

25.17 Yes, it is a finance lease.

25.18 Computer should be acquired on lease basis as PV of cash outflow ₹10,86,800 is less than PV of cash outflow in buying alternative ₹11,51,526.

25.19 Since the present value of cash outflows is lower under buy-borrow alternative, the company is advised to opt for purchase of machinery.
PV of cash outflows under leasing ₹13,71,630; and under buy-borrow alternative ₹13,67,084.

25.20 **(i)** IRR 18.63%;
(ii) ₹1,30,310.14;
(iii) ₹2,23,729.47

25.23 Computeronics Ltd should buy the computer; From the point of view of lessor, the proposal is financially sound with positive NPV (₹2,564).

25.24 **(a)** NAL ₹58,839;
(b) BLER ₹58,795

Scan the QR Code to access comprehensive solutions to all numerical review questions and additional material.

CHAPTER

26 Venture Capital Financing

LEARNING OBJECTIVES

LO 26.1	Discuss the basic features of venture capital: selection of investments, stages of financing, financial analysis, structuring the deal/financing instruments; investment monitoring/nurturing in terms of style, objectives of after care and techniques; portfolio valuation; structure and legal framework; and exit of investments
LO 26.2	Review of Indian venture capital scenario in terms of the SEBI regulations

INTRODUCTION

Venture capital institutions which emerged the world over to fill gaps in the conventional financial mechanism focused on new entrepreneurs, commercialisation of new technologies and support to small and medium enterprises in the manufacturing and the service sectors. Over the years, the concept of venture capital has undergone significant changes. The *modus operandi* has shifted from technology-oriented manufacturing organisations to being very close to "private equity class" for unlisted new companies in all sectors of the economy, irrespective of the nature of their projects. They also maintain a close rapport and a *hands-on* approach in nurturing investments during their association with the assisted/investee companies as active partners rather than as passive investors.

Although the development of the venture capital started in the US in the mid-fifties, venture capital institutions are of fairly recent origin in India. Before their emergence, the development finance institutions partially played the role of venture capitalists by providing assistance for direct equity participation to ventures in the pre-public issue stage and by selectively supporting new technologies. The initial steps for the institutionalisation of venture capital in India were taken by the Government in November, 1988, when guidelines were issued for setting up of venture capital funds/companies (VCFs/VCCs) for investing in unlisted companies and to avail of a concessional facility of capital gains tax.

The various facets of venture capital institutions/financing are discussed in this Chapter. The theoretical aspects of such organisations are examined first. A brief account of the venture capital scenario in India in terms of SEBI regulations is presented subsequently. The main points are summarised by way of recapitulation.

LO 26.1 THEORETICAL FRAMEWORK[1]

Venture capital financing is emerging as a new institutional mechanism post-1990 in the country. As a new technique of financing to inject long-term capital into the small and medium sectors, it has made notable contribution to growth in the developed countries, particularly in the US and the UK. The nascent venture capital industry in India can profitably draw upon their experiences. The theoretical aspects of the venture capital institutions, based largely on these experiences, are briefly described in this Section. The aspects covered below include features, selection of investments, investment monitoring/nurturing, portfolio valuation, structure and legal framework and existing form of investments.

Features

Venture capital has, somehow, come to acquire various connotations. It is defined as an equity/ equity-related investment in a growth-oriented small/medium business to enable investees to accomplish corporate objectives, in return for minority shareholding in the business or the irrevocable right to acquire it.

Venture capital is a way in which investors support entrepreneurial talent with finance and business skills to exploit market opportunities and, thus, to obtain long-term capital gains. It is the provision of risk-bearing capital, usually in the form of participation in equity, to companies with high-growth potential.

In addition, it provides some value addition in the form of management advice and contribution to over-all strategy. The relatively high risks are compensated by the possibility of high return, usually through substantial capital gains in the medium term.[2]

According to a very widely-accepted definition, venture capital is described as a separate asset class, often labelled as private equity. Private equity investment sits at the furthest end of the risk-reward spectrum from Government bonds and can broadly describe equity investment in private companies not quoted on the stock market.[3]

Based on the above description of venture capital, some of the distinguishing features of VC as against other capital investments can be identified as:

— Venture capital is basically equity finance in relatively new companies when it is too early to go to the capital market to raise funds. However, such investment is not exclusively equity investment. It can also be made in the form of loan finance/convertible debt to ensure a running yield on the portfolio of venture capitalists. Nonetheless, the basic objective of venture capital financing is to earn capital gain on equity investment at the time of exist and debt financing is only supplementary.

— It is a long-term investment in growth-oriented small/medium firms. The acquisition of outstanding shares from other shareholders cannot be considered venture capital investment. It is new, long-term capital that is injected to enable the business to grow rapidly.

— There is a substantial degree of active involvement of the venture capital institutions with the promoters of the venture capital undertakings. It means such finance also provides business skills to the investee firms which is termed as '**hands-on**' approach/management. However, venture capitalists do not seek/acquire a majority/controlling interest in the investees, though under special circumstances and for a limited period, they might have a controlling interest. But the objective is to provide business/managerial skill only and not interfere in management.

- Venture capital financing involves high risk-return spectrum. Some of the ventures yield very high returns to more than compensate for heavy losses on others which also may have had potential of profitable returns. The returns in such financing are essentially through capital gains at the time of exits from disinvestments in the capital market.
- Venture capital is not technology finance though technology finance may form a sub-set of venture capital financing. The concept of venture capital embraces much more than financing new, high technology-oriented companies. It essentially involves the financing of small and medium-sized firms through early stages of their development until they are established and are able to raise finance from the conventional, industrial finance market. The scope of venture capital activity is fairly wide.

In brief, a **venture capital institution** is a financial intermediary between investors looking for high potential returns and entrepreneurs who need institutional capital as they are yet not ready/able to go to the public.[4]

Venture capital institution (fund) is a financial intermediary between investors looking for high potential returns and entrepreneurs who need institutional capital as they are yet not ready to go to the public.

Selection of Investment

The first step in the venture capital financing decision is the selection of investment. The starting point of the evaluation process by the venture capital institution (VCI) is the business plan of the venture capital undertaking (promoter). The appraisal is akin to the feasibility studies of the development finance institutions for grant of term loans and other financial assistance.

In addition to the project history, if any, track record of the entrepreneur, market potential study and projections of future turnover, profitability and so on, it also covers a review of the likely threats from technological obsolescence/competing technologies and preliminary views on preferred exits.

The selection of the investment proposal includes, *inter alia*, stages of financing, methods to evaluate deals and the financial instruments to structure a deal.

Stages of Financing The selection of investment by a VCI is closely related to the stages and type of investment. From analytical angle, the different stages of investments are recognised and vary as regards the time-scale, risk perceptions and other related characteristics of the investment decision process of the VCIs. The stages of financing, as differentiated in the venture capital industry, broadly fall into two categories: **(a)** early stage, and **(b)** later stage.

Early Stage Financing This stage includes **(i)** seed capital/pre-start-up, **(ii)** start-up and **(iii)** second-round financing.

Seed Capital This stage is essentially an *applied research* phase where the concepts and ideas of the promoters constitute the basis of a pre-commercialisation research project usually expected to end in a prototype which may or may not lead to a business launch. This phase gradually moves towards the development phase leading to a prototype product testing and then to commercialisation. The evaluation of the project by the VCIs has to ensure that the technology skills of the entrepreneur matches with market opportunities.

The main risk at this stage is marketing related. The commercial acumen of the promoter to take advantage of the market opportunity, awareness of competition, the timing of launching the product and so on, are important elements of the appraisal. The risk perception of investment at this stage is extremely high. However, very few VCIs invest in this pre-commercialisation/seed stage of product development.

Start up is a stage when product/service is commercialised for the first time in association with venture capital institutions.

Start-Up This is the stage when commercial manufacturing has to commence. Venture capital financing here is provided for product development and initial marketing. The essence of this stage is that the product/service is being commercialised for the first time in association with the VCIs. It includes several types of new projects such as **(i)** greenfield based on a relatively new or high technology, **(ii)** new business in which the entrepreneur has good knowledge and working experience, **(iii)** new projects by established companies and **(iv)** a new company promoted by an existing company with limited finance to commercialise new technology.

At this stage, some indication of the potential market for the new product/service is available. Partly because of the equity dilution syndrome[5], in the sense of resistance from the promoters to the dilution of control of the business, and partly due to the unviability of the small amount of equity investment, the involvement of VCIs in start-up projects is generally and relatively low. The risk perception is very high.

Second Round Financing This represents the stage at which the product has already been launched in the market but the business has not yet become profitable enough for public offering to attract new investors. The promoter has invested his own funds but further infusion of funds by the VCIs is necessary. The time-scale for the investment is shorter than in the case of start-ups. The VCIs provide larger funds at this stage than at other early-stage financing. This financing is partly in the form of debt to also provide some income to them.

Later Stage Financing This stage of venture capital financing involves established businesses which require additional financial support but cannot take recourse to public issues of capital. It includes mezzanine/development capital, bridge/expansion, buyouts and turnarounds.

Mezzanine/Development Capital This is financing of established businesses which have overcome the extremely high-risk early stage, have recorded profits for a few years but are yet to reach a stage when they can go public and raise money from the capital market/conventional sources.

Buyouts implies transfer of management control.

Among the uses of such types of venture capital financing are purchase of new equipment/plant, expansion of marketing and distribution facilities, re-finance of existing debt, penetration into new regions, induction of new management and so on. The development finance stage has a time-frame of one to three years and falls in the medium risk category. It constitutes a significant part of the activities of many VCIs.

Bridge/Expansion This finance by VCIs involves low risk perception and a time-frame of one to three years. Venture capital undertakings use such finance to expand business by way of growth of their own productive asset or by the acquisition of other firms/assets of other firms. In a way, it represents the last round of financing before a planned exit.

Management buyouts are provisions of funds to enable existing management/investors to acquire an existing product.

Buyouts These refer to the transfer of management control. They fall into two categories: **(a)** management buyouts (MBOs), and **(b)** management buyins (MBIs).

Management Buyouts In **MBOs**, VCIs provide funds to enable the current operating management/investors to acquire an existing product line/business. They represent an important part of the activity of VCIs.

Management Buyins **MBIs** are funds provided to enable an outside group [of manager(s)] to buy an ongoing company. They usually bring three elements together: a management team, a target company and an investor (VCI). MBIs are less popular than MBOs. An MBI is inherently more risky because the management comes from outside and finds it difficult to assess the actual potential of the target company. Generally, MBIs are able to target only the weaker/underperforming companies.

Management buyins are funds provided to enable an outside group buy an ongoing venture/company.

Buyouts involve a time-frame from investment to public offering of one to three years with low risk perception.

Turnarounds These are a sub-set of buyouts and involve buying the control of a sick company. Two kinds of inputs are required in a turnaround—namely, money and management. The VCIs have to identify good management and operations leadership. Such form of venture capital financing involves medium to high risk and a time-frame of three to five years. It is gaining widespread acceptance and increasingly becoming the focus of attention of VCIs.

To conclude, venture capital firms finance both early and later stage investments to maintain a trade-off between risk and profitability. In early stage investment, particularly start-ups in high-technology industries, the technology is often untried at a commercial level of operation, market is undeveloped and potential competition is unknown as the product itself is new. Apart from the evaluation of the technology and the likely market, the most important factor to be considered by VCIs is the capability of the promoter/entrepreneur to implement the project with a reasonable chance of success.

In later stage investments, the technology has already been tried out commercially, the products have been introduced in the market and the business/entrepreneur has a track record which is closely examined by the VCIs.[7]

Financial Analysis[8] Venture capital investments are generally *idea-based* and *growth-based* in contrast to the conventional investments which are *asset-based.* While the latter type are generally valued on the basis of tangible assets/future earnings streams, the former have to be in the nature of things valued differently in order to decide the required venture capital percentage ownership of the VCIs in venture capital undertaking. Some of the valuation methods which illustrate the approach that VCIs can adopt are: **(i)** conventional venture capitalist valuation method, **(ii)** the first Chicago method and **(iii)** the revenue multiplier method.

Conventional Venture Capitalist Valuation Method This method of valuation of venture capital undertakings (VCUs)/investee companies (ICs) takes into account only two points of time in the life of the venture capital investment, namely, the starting time of investment and the exit time when the investments would be liquidated through sale to public/third party and so on. The sequence of steps in the valuation of the VCUs and the determination of the percentage share ownership of the VCIs in the ICs are:

Conventional method is a method of valuation of venture capital undertakings which takes into account only the starting time of investment and the exit time.

(i) To compute the annual revenue at the time of liquidation of the investments, the present annual revenue in the beginning is compounded by an expected annual growth rate for the holding period, say, seven years;

(ii) Compute the expected earnings level, that is equal to future earnings level multiplied by after tax margin percentage at the time of liquidation;

(iii) Compute the future market valuation of the VCU, that is equal to earnings levels multiplied by expected P/E ratio on the date of liquidation;

(iv) Obtain the present value of the ICs, using a suitable discount factor; and

(v) If the present value of the VCU is ₹50 lakh and the entrepreneur wants ₹20 lakh as the venture capital from the VCIs, the minimum percentage of ownership required is two-fifths (40 per cent).

The weakness of this method is that it ignores the stream of earnings (losses) during the entire period and over-emphasises the one exit date.

The First Chicago Method This method is an improvement over the conventional method of valuation to the extent it gives allowance to the nature of the path between the starting point and the exit point/date and considers the entire earnings stream. The steps involved in the valuation process are:

The first chicago method is a method of valuation that considers the entire earnings stream of the venture capital undertaking/ investor companies.

(i) Three alternative scenarios, are perceived/considered, namely, *success, sideways survival* and *failure*. Each one of these is assigned a probability rating;

(ii) Using a discount rate, the discounted present value of the VCU is computed. The discount rate is substantially higher to reflect risk dimension.

(iii) The discounted present value is multiplied by the respective probabilities. The expected present value of the VCU is equal to the total of these in the three alternative scenarios.

(iv) Assuming expected present value of the VCU at ₹5 crore and the fund requirement from the VCIs as ₹2.5 crore, the minimum ownership required is 50 per cent (half).

Revenue Multiplier Method A revenue multiplier is a factor that can be used to estimate the value of a VCU. By multiplying that factor the annual revenue of the company is estimated by VCIs. Symbolically,

$$M_t = \frac{V}{R} = \frac{(1+r)^n\,(a)\,(p)}{(1+d)^n}$$

Where, V = present value of the VCU,
R = annual revenue level,
r = expected annual rate of growth of revenue,
n = expected number of years from the starting date to the exit date (holding period),
a = expected after-tax profit margin percentage at the time of exit,
P = expected price/earnings (P/E) ratio at exit time, and
d = appropriate discount rate for a venture investment at this stage, risk and other relevant factors

This method can be used in the case of early stage/start-up venture capital investments when earnings, based on after-tax profits, may be low/negative in early years but there may be revenue/ sales income. However, the technique requires a wealth of data which may not be available in a country like India at this stage of the growth of VCFs. Where it is difficult to estimate the revenue multiplier, the Chicago method would give better results than the conventional valuation method.

Structuring the Deal/Financial Instruments The structuring of the deal refers to the financial instruments through which venture capital investment is made. The availability of a wide variety of financial instruments provides considerable flexibility in structuring a venture capital deal. From the point of view of nature, the financial instruments a VCI can choose from, can be broadly divided into equity and debt instruments.

Equity Instruments **(1)** Ordinary equity shares; **(2)** Non-voting equity shares which are entitled to a higher dividend but carry no voting rights; **(3)** Deferred ordinary shares on which the ordinary share rights are deferred for a specified period/until the happening of a certain event such as listing of shares on the stock exchange or the sale of the company; **(4)** Preferred ordinary shares. In addition to the voting rights, such shares also carry rights to a modest fixed dividend; **(5)** Equity warrants entitle investors in debentures/bonds to acquire ordinary shares at a future date; **(6)** Preference shares; **(7)** Cumulative convertible preference shares which are converted into equity shares after a specified time; **(8)** Participating preference shares which, in addition to the preference dividend, are entitled to an extra dividend after the payment of dividend to the equity shareholders; **(9)** Cumulative convertible participatory preferred ordinary shares combine the benefit of preferred dividend and cumulative as well as participative features and **(10)** Convertible cumulative redeemable preference shares have two elements, namely, convertibility into equity at specified point of time and redeemability on the expiry of a certain period. The redeemable part carries a fixed coupon rate by way of preference dividend. Of the types of equity-linked financial instruments, the equity warrants, non-voting equity shares and cumulative convertible participating preferred ordinary shares can be used to structure a flexible venture capital deal.

Debt Instruments To ensure that the entrepreneur retains managerial control and the VCI receives a running yield during the early years when the equity portion is unlikely to yield any return, debt instruments are also used by VCIs. They include, in addition to conventional loans, income notes, non-convertible debentures, partly convertible debentures, fully convertible debentures, zero interest bonds, secured premium notes and deep discount bonds.

Conditional Loan This is a form of loan finance without any pre-determined repayment schedule or interest rate. The suppliers of such loans recover a specified percentage of sales towards the recovery of the principal as well as revenue in a pre-determined ratio, usually 50:50. The charges on sales is known as **royalty**. The investor stands to gain/lose depending on whether the actual sales are higher/lower than the projected sales. Conditional loan, in a sense, is *quasi-equity* instrument.

Conditional loan is a quasi-equity instrument without any pre-determined repayment schedule or interest rate; the charge is a royalty on sales.

Conventional Loans These are modified to the requirements of venture capital financing. They carries lower interest initially which increases after commercial production commences. A small royalty is additionally charged to cover the interest foregone during the initial years. Although the repayment of the principal is based on a pre-stipulated schedule, VCIs usually do not insist upon mortgage/other security.

Income Notes These fall between the conventional and the conditional loans and carry a uniform low rate of interest plus a royalty on sales. The principal is repaid according to a stipulated schedule.

Income notes are instruments which carry a uniform low rate of interest plus a royalty on sales.

Non-convertible Debentures (NCDs) These carry a fixed/variable rate of interest, are redeemable at par/premium, are secured, and can be cumulative/non-cumulative.

Partly Convertible Debentures (PCDs) These have two components: **(i)** a convertible portion and **(ii)** a non-convertible portion. The convertible portion is converted into equity shares at par/premium. The non-convertible portion earns interest till redemption generally at par. Such instruments are best suited to second round venture capital financing.

Zero Interest/Coupon Bonds/Debentures These can be either convertible or non-convertible with zero/no interest rate. The non-convertible bonds are sold at a discount from their maturity value while the convertible ones are converted into equity shares at a stipulated price and time. They offer considerable flexibility and are an appropriate instrument for later stage venture capital financing.

Secured Premium Notes These are secured, redeemable at premium in lumpsum/instalments, have zero interest and carry a warrant against which equity shares can be acquired. This instrument is also useful for later stage financing.

Deep Discount Bonds These are issued at a large discount to their maturity value. As a long-term instrument, these are not suited to venture capital investment.

Investment Nurturing/Aftercare

Unlike the conventional financial institutions, which normally keep aloof from the management and operations of the assisted concerns, VCIs have an active, intimate and constant ongoing involvement during the entire life of the investment in VCUs. The enduring relationship between the VCIs and VCUs and the active role by the former in the management of the latter is termed as **investment nurturing/after care**. The main elements of after care are: **(i)** after the stage of investment decision, provision of continuing guidance and support to optimise the benefits of investment to both—VCIs and VCUs, **(ii)** building of joint relationship to tackle operational and other problems of business and **(iii)** protection of the investment/interest of the VCIs. Investment nurturing differs from the investment monitoring by the conventional financial institutions which collect and use specific information about the operations of the assisted project, whereas the former is wider in coverage to include the provision of guidance and skills for the management of the venture. The after care stage of venture capital financing relates, *inter alia*, to different styles of nurturing, its objectives and techniques.

Styles The styles of nurturing refers to the extent of participation by VCIs in the affairs of VCUs. The style depends upon a variety of factors such as the specialisation of the VCI, stage of investment, financing plan, the stage of the development of the venture capital industry itself and so on. It broadly falls into three categories: **(i)** hands-on, **(ii)** hands-off and **(iii)** hand-holding.

Hands-on nurturing is a continuous and constant involvement in the operations of the investee company by the venture capital institution which is institutionalised in the form of representation on the board of directors.

Hands-on Nurturing It refers to continuous and constant involvement in the operations of the investee company which is institutionalised in the form of representation on the board of directors. With wider exposure and experience, VCIs can provide useful guidance on aspects of long-term business planning, technology development, financial planning, marketing strategy and so on. The hands-on care style is useful/essential in early stage financing, i.e., seed capital and start-up investments. This type of care is provided either by the in-house expertise or by a core group of external advisors/experts in specific areas if the former is not available in all types of projects.

Hand-off nurturing is the passive role played by venture capital funds in formulating strategies/policy matters.

Hands-off Nurturing VCIs play a relatively passive role in the hands-off style. Although they usually reserve the right, they rarely have nominee directors on the board of the VCUs. Normally, they do not actively participate in formulating strategies/policy matters in spite of the right to do so. This type of nurturing style is appropriate in case of syndicated/joint/consortium venture financing in which some financiers may follow the hands-on approach while others may follow the hands-off approach. The hands-off style may also be appropriate after the initial plan of the venture is over and the business is running smoothly.

Hands-holding Nurturing This is mid-way between hands-on and hands-off styles. It is, essentially, a reactive approach. Like the hands-on style, the VCI has the right to have a nominee on the board of directors of the VCU, but actively participates in the decision making process only on being approached by the latter. If the VCU experiences any difficulty, the VCI provides either in-house assistance or assistance from outside experts.

Objectives of Aftercare[9] The objectives of nurturing by VCIs, *inter alia*, are:

(i) To ensure the proper utilisation of assistance provided. Any deviation from the programme/appraisal should be within the prior approval of the VCI;
(ii) To ensure the implementation of the project/venture within the time and costs envisaged;
(iii) In case of time and cost overruns beyond the control of the VCU, to assist in finding additional/supplementary finance;
(iv) To provide strategic inputs in technology production, finance, marketing, personnel and so on;
(v) To anticipate likely problems and advise preventive/remedial actions;
(vi) To ensure that the venture does not default in any statutory/other obligations;
(vii) To evaluate the performance of the project and suggest measures for improvement, if required;
(viii) To use the feedback received during the course of nurturing the investment for studying the problems and finding suitable solutions; and
(ix) To utilise the experience gained for a better appraisal of new ventures.

Techniques VCIs follow systematic techniques to achieve the foregoing objective. Some of the important techniques are briefly discussed below.

Personal Discussions One technique for obtaining information from a VCU is personal/informal discussion with the entrepreneur(s). Though the information, thus, collected does not have any formal sanctity, it provides the most comprehensive and effective insight into the working of the venture. This technique is especially useful when the venture is facing operational problems.

Plant Visits These refer to the collection of information from on the spot visit of the plant site. In the case of ventures at the implementation stage, the purpose of plant visit is to review the progress of the project, to see that adequate and well-qualified personnel have been appointed for its implementation, to ensure that the requisite sanctions are obtained for funds from other sources, if necessary, and to check if the venture has initiated action for obtaining working capital from banks. For projects which are complete and on which production has started, the plant visit technique examines, *inter alia*, the following aspects:

— The staffing pattern of the production, marketing, finance and personnel departments;
— Operational performance of the project;
— Marketing aspects with special reference to product acceptance, market penetration, distribution, pricing, product awareness, advertising, competition and so on;
— Management of accounts with special reference to overdues of receivables;
— Proper costing of products and efficient control of inventory;
— Position regarding statutory liabilities; and
— Labour relations.

Feedback Through Nominee Directors The nominee directors not only protect the interest of the VCIs, but they are also expected to effectively contribute to the management and provide requisite guidance. They should also ensure that the business is run on a sound basis. Moreover, they should be able to anticipate problems and suggest solutions. The nominee directors should, therefore, have a good exposure to industry, have adequate knowledge about technological development, changes in government policies, financial management, laws, regulations and so on.

Periodic Reports VCIs should receive periodic reports about the operations of projects. These should be properly analysed. The projected and actual performance should be compared and analysed and follow-up action initiated.

Commissioned Studies If VCUs are not performing well/experiencing difficulties which cannot be solved by VCIs themselves, special studies may be commissioned to identify problems and offer solutions so that preventive action may be taken.

Valuation of Portfolio[10]

The venture capital portfolio has to be valued from time to time to monitor and evaluate the performance of the venture capital investment, that is, whether there has been an appreciation in the value of the investment or otherwise. The portfolio valuation approaches/techniques depend on the type of investments, namely, equity and debt instruments. These, in turn, depend on the stage of investment: seed, start-up, early and later stages of the venture.

Equity Investments The valuation methods for equity instruments of VCUs are: **(i)** cost method, and **(ii)** market value-based methods.

Cost Method According to this method, the value of equity holding is computed/recorded at the historical cost of acquisition until it is disposed of. Although simple, objective, and easy to understand, it does not indicate a fair value of investment, does not reflect management performance and may result in two values for equity acquired at two different points in time. It does not provide a satisfactory basis of valuation of venture capital investments.

Market Value-based Methods Such methods can be divided into: **(i)** quoted market value, **(ii)** fair market value and **(iii)** others. They are conceptually superior to the cost method.

Quoted Market Value Method This is based on market quotations of securities. It is, therefore, relevant only to organisations listed on stock exchanges. Moreover, market values may not be available for infrequently traded shares. In addition, if the holdings of VCIs are substantially large, the realisable value on the market may be considerably lower than the quoted valued. In the foregoing situations, the market value may not reflect the real/true valuation. Therefore, an appropriate discount should be applied to the quoted price while valuing the portfolio. This approach is better than the cost-based approach for evaluation of a venture portfolio.

Fair value is the price to be agreed upon in an open and unrestricted market between parties and equationally expressed as: a representative level of earnings ¥ appropriate capitalisation rate.

Fair Market Value Method This considers the fair price as the basis of portfolio valuation and is used where the quoted market value does not reflect the correct value of the venture capital investment. The fair value refers to the price that would be agreed upon in an open and unrestricted market between fully informed, knowledgeable and willing parties at an arm's length without constraint. It is, thus, a subjective value.

This approach to valuation of venture capital investments is based on the assumption that *assets are worth what they can earn.* In operational terms, a representative level of earnings is selected and capitalised by an appropriate multiplicity/capitalisation rate which provides a reasonable return on the basis of the estimated future earnings and degree of risk.

Stages of Investments As pointed out earlier, the methods of portfolio valuation of shares depend on the stage of venture capital investments. From the viewpoint of stages of investments, the equity investments fall into three broad categories:

Unquoted Venture Investments Unquoted venture investments are defined as investments in immature companies, namely, seed, start-up and early stage, until the companies stabilise and grow. They should generally be valued at cost as their market value is not available. They may, however, have to be written up (valued at higher than cost) or written down in (assigned a lower value than cost) exceptional circumstances/cases.

The unquoted venture investments can be written up in cases where a third party with arm's length relationship with the VCU values it at a significantly higher value which may be taken to represent the value of the investment. They can also be valued at a price higher than the cost when the operating results are significantly higher than those projected originally. The investment should be valued using an appropriate P/E ratio and suitably adjusted/discounted to account for the unquoted nature of investments as well as the relatively short profit-earning record of the venture. However, care should be taken while upvaluing investment that the venture has started generating a reasonable turnover and independent third party transactions have taken place.

Investments should be written down if the venture is facing long-term problems, requires additional finance or the operating results are substantially below the original projections or a third party with an arm's length relationship values it at less than the original cost. However, undervaluation should be revalued as early as justified.

Unquoted Development Investments Unquoted development investments are investments in mature companies with a profit record and where an exit can be reasonably foreseen. They also do not have a market value. The basis of valuation should be somewhat similar to unquoted venture investments, based on a suitable P/E ratio applied to earnings of the venture, suitability discounted to take care of the limited marketability of the unquoted nature of the investment. The discount would depend upon the subjective judgement of the valuer but should generally vary between 20 and 25 per cent depending on various factors. The percentage of discounts would depend on the proximity to the exit point: *a lower discount when prospects of an exit are foreseen early and a higher discount if it is likely to be delayed.*

Quoted Investments Quoted investments in companies which have achieved a possible exit by floatation of issues. They are valued at market quotations. In case of restrictions/limitations on the sale of shares, a suitable discount should be applied to the market value of the shares. The rate of discount would depend on the size and depth of the market, the period of applicability of restrictions, the holdings of VCIs relative to public holdings, restrictions in any buy-back agreement with promoters and statutory restrictions.

Debt Instruments VCIs provide, in addition to equity capital, debt finance. From the point of view of their valuation as a part of the overall portfolio (fund), they are divided into **(i)** convertible, **(ii)** non-convertible and **(iii)** leveraged.

Convertible Debt Debt instruments are generally valued at cost. But convertible debts are converted into equity at a specified price and time. They should, therefore, be valued in the case of VCIs on the same basis as equity investments. There are two appropriate methods for valuing them, that is, market value method and fair value method.

Market Value Method This is appropriate for quoted convertible debt investments on the basis of the same principles as are applicable to quoted investments. A modified/refined version of this approach is the use of the moving average/weighted average of the market values of the investments at the end of a pre-determined number of periods as the basis of valuation of convertibles.

The merit of this modification is that it retains the benefit of market value method and, at the same time, the effects of temporary fluctuations are minimised as the average value represents the long-term value of investment. The market value method, however, underestimates the net realisable value in a growing VCU.

Fair Value Method This is appropriate, as in the case of unquoted equity investments, for unquoted convertible debt investments. As pointed out earlier, the valuation according to this method is based on the price agreed upon in an open and unrestricted market. This is a subjective method as the valuation is significantly influenced by judgement and experience.

Non-convertible Debt This debt supplied by VCIs can be of two types: fixed interest bearing such as bonds/debentures and mortgages and non-interest bearing such as zero interest bonds and secured premium notes.

Fixed Interest Non-convertible Debt This should be valued by relating the nominal yield of the investment to an appropriate current yield which depends upon a number of factors such as interest yield on the date of valuation, maturity date of the issue, safety of the principal, debt-service coverage, stability and growth of the earnings of the venture and so on.

Non-interest Non-convertible Debt A factor of critical importance in this case is the solvency of the venture. If it is doubtful, an appropriate discount rate may be used to the value computed according to the method used for valuating fixed interest non-convertible debt.

Highly Leveraged Investments These should, generally, be valued at cost.

Structural Aspects[11]

The structuring of VCIs is important from the viewpoint of the profitability of such organisations and their contributors and participants. While deciding upon a structure, the objectives generally sought are:

— Limited liability of investors;
— Simple operation of funds;
— Tax transparency of the fund in the sense that double taxation is avoided;
— Tax exemption of the **carried interest** defined as the extra incentive/profit to the managers over and above the share attributed to their capital contribution and the management fee;
— Maximum tax benefits to investors.

The alternative forms in which VCIs can be structured are: **(i)** limited partnership, **(ii)** investment company, **(iii)** investment trust, **(iv)** offshore funds and **(v)** small business investment company.

Limited partnership consists of two types of partners: (i) with unlimited liability and (ii) limited liability.

Limited Partnership Normally, the partnership form of organisation/structure has unlimited liability of partners. Limited partnership has evolved to cater to the needs of venture capital industry in the US as the most favoured method of their structuring but is, relatively, less popular in the UK. Limited partnership consists of two types of partners: general and limited. The general partner, whose liability is unlimited, invites other investors to become limited partners in the partnership with limited liability and invest but do not participate in the actual operations of the business.

The general partners can be individuals, a corporate body or a partnership. In other words, a venture capital organisation can be structured as a limited partnership and one more partnership acting as the general partner can be formed. As an alternative to the second partnership, the general partners as individuals may set up a service corporation to discharge the functions of the general partner on payment of fee. The main functions of the general partners/service corporations are: **(i)** business identification and development, **(ii)** investment appraisal and investigation of potential investment, **(iii)** negotiation and closing of deals, **(iv)** investment monitoring, advice and assistance to VCUs; **(v)** arrangement for sale of shares at the exit time and **(vi)** other fund management functions.

Mode of Compensation The general partner/service corporation as a fund manager is compensated in two ways: **(1)** annual management fee, **(2)** carried interest.

Annual Management Fee This covers the normal operating expenses such as salary and allowances of employees, administrative expenses and all expenses related to the selection of investments as well as disinvestments but excludes legal expenses and professional fee related to investment portfolio which are reimbursed separately. It is generally 2-3 per cent of the net asset value (NAV) or the capital of the fund, the latter being the more preferred basis.

Carried Interest The most popular approach is that the general partner contributes one per cent and the limited partners contribute 99 per cent of the capital of the fund. The general partner normally receives one-fifth of the net gains as carried interest while the remaining four-fifths is distributed among the limited partners.

Evaluation The benefit of limited partnership, as a form of structuring of VCIs, is its tax treatment. The profit of limited partnership is taxed only at the level of the partners. It is completely tax free if the partner is a tax free entity such as pension funds. The second advantage is operational in the sense that the fund managers are entitled to an incentive in the form of carried interest. However, a major drawback is the unlimited liability of the general partner. Moreover, he is liable to tax on gains on sale of investments, whether distributed or not. Nevertheless, on balance, the advantages outweigh the disadvantages and limited partnership emerges as a satisfactory form of venture capital organisation.

Investment Company This is organised as a limited company. Although it is the simplest structure for a VCI, a serious drawback is the double taxation of income. Both the investment company and its shareholders are liable to tax on their respective incomes.

Investment Trust This is a company and is, generally, not liable to tax on chargeable gains/dividends but most of the other income of the trust is taxable. The entitlement to tax concessions is subject to certain stipulations such as income should be derived wholly/mainly from investment in shares/securities, holding in any single company other than another investment trust should not exceed 15 per cent of the value of the investment, the shares are listed, it distributes at least 85 per cent of the income from shares/securities and so on.

Offshore Investment Company This is incorporated in a country other than the country in which the offshore company makes an investment. Its tax liability depends on the tax laws applicable to the resident status of the company.

Offshore Unit Trust This resembles an offshore investment company in organisation but enjoys tax concessions and has a very flexible structure.

Small Business Investment Company This provides an impetus to banks to participate in ventures in the form of equity and long term debt. It can, however, invest only in small concerns. It is prohibited from investing more than 20 per cent of its capital and reserves nor is it allowed to acquire controlling interest in a single company. The loans must be for more than five years. It has a very flexible structure of equity investments.

Exit

The last stage in venture capital financing is the exit to realise the investment so as to make a profit/ minimise losses. In fact, the potential exit in terms of the realisation horizon (exit timing) has to be planned at the time of the initial investment itself. The precise timing of exit depends on several factors such as nature of the venture, the extent and type of financial stake, the state of actual and potential competition, market conditions, the style of functioning as well as perception of VCIs and so on. For example, early stage financing typically takes a long-term view of eventual realisation/exit from five to seven years. In case of later stage financing, the realisation horizon could be shorter in the range of three to five years.

The important aspect of the exit stage of venture capital financing is the decision regarding the disinvestments/realisation alternatives which are related to the type of investment, namely, equity/ quasi-equity and debt instruments.

Disinvestments of Equity/Quasi-Equity Investments There are five disinvestment channels for realisation of such investments: **(i)** going public, **(ii)** sale of shares to entrepreneurs/employees, **(iii)** trade sales/sale to another company, **(iv)** selling to a new investor and **(v)** liquidation/receivership. The first four alternative routes are voluntary while the last one is involuntary.

Going Public/Initial Public Offering/Flotation The most common channel of disinvestment by a VCI is through public issue of capital of the VCU, including its own holdings. The merits of public issues are liquidity of investments through listing on stock exchanges, higher price of securities compared to private placement, better image and credibility with public, managers, customers, financial institution and so on. However, companies going public are subject to reporting requirements, stock exchange regulations and disclosure requirements; the cost of issue is higher; the accountability to shareholders' increases and so on.[12] On the whole, public issue method is the most popular exit route for VCIs.

Related to the public issues method is the OTCEI route. A VCI can exit by way of a boughtout deal to a member of the OTCEI who would offer the shares thus acquired to the public at a future date.

Earnout is the sale of shares/stake of venture capital institution to entrepreneurs/ investee companies themselves.

Sale of Shares to Entrepreneurs/Employees/Earnout The shares/stakes of VCIs may be sold to the entrepreneurs/companies themselves who are allowed to buy their own equity. Alternatively, the entrepreneurs can acquire the shares from VCIs through employees by forming an 'employees stock ownership trust'. The sources of the trust to acquire the shareholding of the VCIs are contribution by the employees/company and borrowing from financial institutions and banks.

A related alternative is *exit by puts and calls* when VCIs may have entered into a formal exit agreement at a price based on a pre-determined formula with the entrepreneurs. The **put option** is the right to sell while the **call option** is the right of the entrepreneurs to buy. This is a fairly popular exit route.

Important Put-and-call Formulae

Book Value Method This is used in mature companies that have achieved a healthy track record, that is they have achieved a reasonable degree of stability in operations.

P/E Ratio This is the most common method for exercising the put and call option. The price is equal to the earnings per share multiplied by the P/E ratio.

Percentage of Sales Method This is a modified P/E ratio. On the basis of the pre-tax earnings/profit before tax as a percentage of sales for the industry, the hypothetical/notional profit before tax for the investee company is determined as also the earnings per share. The value of the shares is obtained by multiplying the notional earnings per share with the industry P/E ratio. This method is suitable in the early stages when profits are lower but the sales have reached a reasonable level.

Multiple of Cash Flow Method In this, cash flow is used in place of the earnings or sales. The cash flow is multiplied by the industry multiplier to arrive at the value of the company/shares.

Independent Valuation This is valuation by outside experts on the basis of either earnings potential method/price-earnings ratio method or the liquidation method. On the assumption of liquidation a VCU, the net value is computed on the basis of the net/relisable value of all the assets less the liabilities.

Agreed Price This is the price between the VCIs and the entrepreneur agree on at the time of making the investment itself.

Trade Sales The entire company is sold to another company/third party. Highly popular method, at times the trade sales may be through a management buyin or buyout. The most appropriate method for such a sale would vary from one case to another, keeping in view taxation and other considerations. The alternative modalities for trade sales are:

(i) Cash sales of equity ownership of both the parties which would attract heavy tax burden.

(ii) Against issue of notes secured by the assets of the buyer company and receive cash in pre-determined instalments in order to ensure proper tax planning.

(iii) In consideration for the shares of the buying company with no tax liability.

Trade sales implies the sale of entire investee company to another company/third party.

Sales to a New Investor/Takeout The equity stake of VCIs can be sold to a new investor who may be a corporate body or even another venture capital organisation. The corporate investor may acquire the stake to develop a business relationship due to considerations of synergy of operations.

The purchase of the equity holdings of a VCI by another VCI may be related to the nature of the business objectives of the original VCI. For instance, he may have financed an early stage venture and may like to exit after its operations have stabilised. For second round financing, he may sell his equity to another VCI which is willing to provide financing to the venture.

Takeout is the sale of equity stake of a VCI to a new investor including another VCF.

Liquidation This is an involuntary exit forced on the VCI as a result of a totally failed investment. The VCIs can use this exit method when the venture is not performing well and has reached a stage beyond recovery due to stiff competition, technology failure/obsolescence of technology, poor management and so on.

Exit of Debt Instruments Exit in case of debt component of venture capital financing, in contrast with equity/quasi-equity component, has to normally follow the pre-determined route. In case of a normal loan, the exit is possible only at the end of the period of loan. If the loan agreement permits, whole or part can be converted into equity prior to that. For conditional loans, exit, earlier than projected at the time of initial investment, is possible on the basis of lumpsum repayment consistent with the expectations of the VCI of the likely return on the loan.

LO 26.2 INDIAN VENTURE CAPITAL SCENARIO

AIF means any fund established/incorporated in India in the form of a trust/company/limited liability partnership/body corporate which is (i) a privately pooled investment vehicle and collects funds from Indian/foreign investors for investing in accordance with a defined investment policy for the benefit of its investors, and (ii) not covered under the mutual fund/other regulations of the SEBI to regulate fund management activities.

The venture capital funds were regulated by the **(i)** SEBI Venture Capital Funds Regulation, 2000 and **(ii)** SEBI Foreign Venture Capital Investors Regulation Act, 2000. The SEBI Alternative Investment Fund Regulations, 2012 has replaced the SEBI VCF Regulations. The salient features of the regulatory framework in terms of these two SEBI regulations are discussed below.

SEBI Alternative Investment Funds Regulation, 2012

Alternative Investment Fund (AIF) means any fund established/incorporated in India in the form of a trust/company/limited liability partnership/body corporate which is **(i)** a privately pooled investment vehicle and collects funds from Indian/foreign investors for investing in accordance with a defined investment policy for the benefit of its investors, and **(ii)** not covered under the mutual fund/other regulations of the SEBI to regulate fund management activities. However, it excludes: **(i)** family trusts set up for the benefit of relatives, **(ii)** ESOP (employees stock option plans) trusts, **(iii)** employee welfare/gratuity trusts, **(iv)** holding companies, **(v)** other special purpose vehicles (SPVs) including securitisation trusts, **(vi)** funds managed by a securitisation/reconstruction company, and **(vii)** any such pool of funds directly regulated by another regulator in India. The main elements of the SEBI regulation relating to AIFs, namely, **(a)** registration, **(b)** investment conditions/restrictions, **(c)** general obligations and responsibilities and transparency, **(d)** inspection, and **(e)** procedure for action in case of default are discussed below.

Registration of Alternative Investment Funds (AIFs) To set-up an **AIF**, an entity/person has to obtain a certificate of registration from the SEBI. However, the funds registered as venture capital fund under SEBI Venture Capital Funds Regulations, would continue to be regulated by the respective regulations till the existing fund or scheme managed by the fund is wound up and such funds would not launch any new scheme. Moreover, the existing fund or scheme would not increase the targeted corpus of the fund or scheme. The venture capital funds may seek re-registration as AIFs subject to approval of two-thirds of their investors by value of their investment. The AIFs can seek registration in one of the three categories: **(i)** I, **(ii)** II, **(iii)** III.

Venture capital fund means an alternative investment fund which invests primarily in unlisted securities of start-ups, emerging/early-stage venture capital undertakings mainly involved in new products/services, technology/intellectual property right based activities/a new business model.

"**Category I AIF**" which invests in start-up or early stage ventures/social ventures/small and medium enterprises (SMEs)/infrastructure/other sectors or areas which the Government/regulators consider as socially/economically desirable and would include venture capital funds, SME funds, social venture funds, infrastructure funds and such other specified alternative investment funds. The **AIFs** which are generally perceived to have positive spillover effects on economy and for which the SEBI/Government of India/other regulators in India might consider providing incentives/concessions would be included and such funds which are formed as trusts/companies would be construed as "venture capital company/fund" as specified under the Income Tax Act. **Venture capital fund** means an alternative investment fund which invests primarily in unlisted securities of start-ups, emerging/early-stage venture capital undertakings mainly involved in new products/new services, technology/intellectual property right based activities/a new business model. **Venture capital undertaking** means a domestic company which is **(i)** not listed on a recognised stock exchange in India at the time of making investment; and **(ii)** engaged in the business for providing services, production/manufacture of article/things and does not include the following activities/sectors: **(1)** non-banking financial companies; **(2)** gold financing; **(3)** activities not permitted under industrial policy of Government of India; and **(4)** any other activity which may be specified by the SEBI in consultation with the Government of India from time to time. **SME fund** means an alternative investment fund which invests primarily in unlisted securities of investee companies which are SMEs or securities of those SMEs which are listed/proposed to be listed on a SME exchange/SME segment of an exchange.

SME fund means an alternative investment fund which invests primarily in unlisted securities of investee companies which are SMEs or securities of those SMEs which are listed/proposed to be listed on a SME exchange/ SME segment of an exchange.

Venture capital undertaking means a domestic company which is (i) not listed on a recognised stock exchange in India at the time of making investment; and (ii) engaged in the business for providing services, production/ manufacture of article/things.

Social venture means a trust/society/company/venture capital undertaking/limited liability partnership formed with the purpose of promoting social welfare/solving social problems/providing social benefits and includes: **(i)** public charitable trusts registered with the charity commissioner; **(ii)** societies registered for charitable purposes/promotion of science, literature/fine arts; **(iii)** company registered under Section 25 of the Companies Act; **(iv)** micro finance institutions. **Social venture fund** means an alternative investment fund which invests primarily in securities/units of social ventures and which satisfies social performance norms laid down by the fund and whose investors may agree to receive restricted or muted returns. **Infrastructure funds** invest primarily in unlisted securities/partnership interest/listed debt/securitised debt instruments of investee companies/SPVs engaged in or formed for the purpose of, operating/ developing/holding infrastructure.

Social venture means a trust/ society/company/ venture capital undertaking/ limited liability partnership formed with the purpose of promoting social welfare/solving social problems/ providing social benefits.

Social venture fund means an alternative investment fund which invests primarily in securities/units of social ventures and which satisfies social performance norms laid down by the fund and whose investors may agree to receive restricted or muted returns.

"Category II AIF" which does not fall in Category I and III and which does not undertake leverage or borrowing other than to meet day-today operational requirements. Funds such as private equity funds/debt funds for which no specific incentives or concessions are given by the Government or any other regulator would be included. **Private equity fund** means an **AIF** which invests primarily in equity/ equity linked instruments (i.e. instruments convertible into equity/ preference shares, share warrants, compulsorily/optionally convertible debentures) or partnership interests of investee companies (i.e. companies/SPVs/limited partnership/body corporate in which an AIF makes an investment) according to the stated objectives of the fund. **Debt fund** is an AIF which invests primarily in debt/debt securities of listed/unlisted investee companies according to its stated objectives.

Private equity fund means an **AIF** which invests primarily in equity/equity linked instruments (i.e. instruments convertible into equity/ preference shares, share warrants, compulsorily/ optionally convertible debentures) or partnership interests of investee companies (i.e. companies/SPVs/ limited partnership/ body corporate in which an AIF makes an investment) according to the stated objectives of the fund.

Infrastructure funds invest primarily in unlisted securities/ partnership interest/listed debt/securitised debt instruments of investee companies/ SPVs engaged in. or formed for the purpose of, operating/ developing/holding infrastructure.

"Category III AIF" which employs diverse or complex trading strategies and may employ leverage including through investment in listed or unlisted derivatives. Funds such as hedge funds or funds

Debt fund is an AIF which invests primarily in debt/debt securities of listed/unlisted investee companies according to its stated objectives.

Hedge funds employ diverse/complex trading strategies and invest in securities having diverse risks or complex products including listed/unlisted derivatives.

which trade with a view to make short-term returns or such other funds which are open-ended and for which no specific incentives or concessions are given by the Government or any other regulator would be included. **Hedge funds** employ diverse/complex trading strategies and invest in securities having diverse risks or complex products including listed/unlisted derivatives.

An application for grant of certificate should be made for any of these categories of ₹1,00,000. The certificate of registration would be valid till the alternative investment fund is wound up. The SEBI may, in the interest of the investors, issue directions with regard to the transfer of records, documents or securities or disposal of investments relating to its activities as an alternative investment fund. It may, in order to protect the interests of investors, also appoint any person to take charge of records, documents, securities on specified terms and conditions of such an appointment.

Eligibility Criteria The eligibility criteria for registration as AIF are:

(a) The memorandum of association/trust/partnership deed respectively in case of company/trust/limited liability partnership permits it to carry on the activity of an AIF;

(b) The applicant is prohibited by its memorandum and articles of association/trust/partnership deed from making an invitation to the public to subscribe to its securities;

(c) The instrument of trust in case of a trust-applicant is in the form of a deed and has been duly registered under the provisions of the Registration Act;

(d) The partnership in case of partnership-applicant is duly incorporated and the partnership deed has been duly filed with the Registrar under the provisions of the Limited Liability Partnership Act;

(e) A body corporate-applicant is set up/established under the laws of the central or state legislature and is permitted to carry on the activities of an AIF;

(f) The applicant, sponsor and manager are fit and proper persons based on the criteria specified in **SEBI Intermediaries Regulations**;[@@]

(g) The key investment team of the manager of the AIF has adequate experience, with at least one key personnel having not less than five years experience in advising/managing pools of capital or in fund/asset/wealth/portfolio management or in the business of buying, selling and dealing of securities/other financial assets and has relevant professional qualification;

(h) The manager/sponsor has the necessary infrastructure and manpower to effectively discharge its activities;

(i) The applicant has clearly described at the time of registration the investment objective, the targeted investors, proposed corpus, investment style/strategy and proposed tenure of the fund/scheme;

(j) Whether the applicant or any entity established by the sponsor/manager has earlier been refused registration by the SEBI.

Furnishing of Information The SEBI may require the applicant to furnish any such further information/clarification regarding the sponsor/manager or nature of the fund/fund management activities or any such matter connected thereto to consider the application for grant of a certificate or after registration. If required, the applicant/sponsor/manager would appear before the SEBI for personal representation.

[@@]**An account available in Khan, M.Y., *Indian Financial System*, MHE, India, 2018, Chapter 4.**

Procedure for Grant of Certificate The SEBI may grant certificate under any specific category of alternative investment fund, if it is satisfied that the applicant fulfills the specified requirements. It would, on receipt of the registration fee (₹5,00,000) grant a certificate of registration. The registration may be granted with such conditions as may be deemed appropriate by the SEBI.

Conditions of Certificate The certificate would, *inter-alia,* be subject to the following conditions. The AIF would **(a)** abide by the provisions of the SEBI Act/regulations; **(b)** not carry on any other activity other than the permitted activities; **(c)** forthwith inform the SEBI in writing, if any information or particulars previously submitted are found to be false or misleading in any material particular or if there is any material change in the information already submitted. Prior approval of the SEBI would be necessary to change category of registration.

Investment Conditions and Restrictions The investment conditions/restrictions relate to: **(i)** investment strategy, **(ii)** investment in AIF, **(iii)** placement memorandum, **(iv)** schemes, **(v)** tenure, **(vi)** listing, **(vii)** general investment conditions, **(viii)** conditions for category I AIF, **(ix)** conditions for category II AIF, **(x)** conditions for category III AIFs and **(xi)** other AIF.

Investment Strategy The AIF should state investment strategy, investment purpose and its investment methodology in its placement memorandum to the investors. Any material alteration to the fund strategy can be made with the consent of atleast two-thirds of unit holders by value of their investment.

Investment in AIF Investment in all categories of AIFs would be subject to the following conditions:

(a) The AIF may raise funds from any Indian, foreign or non-resident Indian investor by way of issue of **units** (i.e. a beneficial interest of the investors in the AIF/a scheme of the AIF including shares/partnership interests);

(b) Each scheme of the AIF would have **corpus** (i.e. total amount of funds committed by the investor in the AIF by way of a written contract/any such document as on a particular date) of atleast twenty crore rupees;

(c) The AIF would not accept an investment of value less than one crore rupees from an investor. In case of investors who are employees or directors of the AIF/manager, the minimum value of investment should be twenty five lakh rupees;

(d) The manager/sponsor would have a continuing interest in the AIF of not less than the lower of 2.5 percent of the corpus or five crore rupees in the form of investment in the AIF and such interest should not be through the waiver of management fees. For Category III AIF, the continuing interest should be not less than 5 percent of the corpus or ten crore rupees, whichever is lower;

(e) The manager/its sponsor should disclose their investment in the AIF to investors;

(f) No scheme of the AIF would have more than one thousand investors;

(g) The fund would not solicit/collect funds except by way of private placement.

> **Units** are beneficial interest of the investors in the AIF/a scheme of the AIF including shares/partnership interests.

> **Corpus** is total amount of funds committed by the investor in the AIF by way of a written contract/ any such document as on a particular date.

Placement Memorandum Funds would be raised by the AIFs through private placement by issue of information/placement memorandum containing all material information about the AIF and the manager, background of key investment team of the manager, targeted investors, fees and all other expenses proposed to be charged, tenure of the AIF/scheme, conditions/limits on redemption, investment strategy, risk management tools and parameters employed, key service providers, conflict of interest and procedures to identify and address them, disciplinary history, the terms and conditions on which the manager offers investment services, its affiliations with other intermediaries, manner of winding up of the AIF/scheme and such other information as may be necessary for the investor to take an informed decision on whether to invest in the AIF.

Schemes The placement memorandum should be filed with the SEBI atleast thirty days prior to launch of scheme along with the specified fees of ₹100,000. Payment of fees would not be required in case of launch of first scheme by the AIF. The SEBI may communicate its comments, if any, to the applicant who should incorporate them in placement memorandum prior to launch of scheme.

Tenure Category I and Category II AIF would be close-ended and the tenure of fund/scheme would be determined at the time of application subject to a minimum tenure of three years. Category III AIF may be open-ended or close-ended. Extension of the tenure of the close-ended AIF may be permitted up to two years subject to approval of two-thirds of the unit holders by value of their investment. In the absence of consent of unit holders, the AIF should fully liquidate within one year following expiration of the fund tenure/extended tenure.

Listing Units of close-ended AIF may be listed on stock exchange only after final close of the fund/scheme subject to a minimum tradable lot of one crore rupees and permitted.

General Investment Conditions Investments by all categories of AIFs would be subject to the following conditions:

(a) They may invest in securities of companies incorporated outside India subject to such conditions/guidelines that may be stipulated/issued by the RBI/SEBI;

(b) Co-investment in an investee company by a manager/sponsor would not be on terms more favourable than those offered to the AIF;

(c) Category I and II AIFs should invest not more than 25 percent and Category III 10 per cent of the corpus in one investee company;

(d) The AIFs should not invest in **associates** (i.e. a company/limited liability partnership/body corporate in which a director/trustee/partner/sponsor/manager of the AIF or director/partner of the manager/sponsor holds individually/collectively more than 15 per cent of its paid-up equity share capital/partnership interest) except with the approval of 75 percent of investors by value of their investment;

(e) The un-invested portion of the corpus may be invested in liquid mutual funds/bank deposits/other liquid assets of higher quality such as T-bills, CBLOs, CPs, CDs, till deployment of funds as per the investment objective;

(f) The AIFs may act as nominated investor as specified in SEBI Issue of Capital and Disclosure Requirements Regulations. **(discussed in Chapter 14).** The SEBI may specify additional requirements/criteria for AIF/for a specific category.

> **Associates** is a company/limited liability partnership/body corporate in which a director/trustee/partner/sponsor/manager of the AIF or director/partner of the manager/sponsor holds individually/collectively more than 15 per cent of its paid-up equity share capital/partnership interest.

Conditions for Category I AIF *(a)* The following investment conditions would apply to all Category I AIFs:

They should invest in investee companies/venture capital undertaking/special purpose vehicles/limited liability partnerships/units of other AIFs. They may invest in units of Category I AIFs of same sub-category subject to the condition that they would not invest in units of other fund of funds. The investment conditions applicable to the venture capital funds (**discussed later**) would not be applicable to investments by them. Such investment funds cannot borrow funds directly/indirectly/engage in any leverage except for meeting temporary funding requirements for not more than thirty days, on not more than four occasions in a year and not more than 10 percent of the corpus.

(b) Venture Capital Funds The following additional investment conditions would apply to venture capital funds:

(1) At least two-thirds of the corpus should be invested in unlisted equity shares/equity linked instruments of a venture capital undertaking/in companies listed/proposed to be listed on a SME exchange or SME segment of an exchange;

(2) Not more than one-third of the corpus should be invested in: **(i)** subscription to initial public offer of a venture capital undertaking whose shares are proposed to be listed; **(ii)** debt/debt instrument of a venture capital undertaking in which the fund has already made an investment by way of equity or contribution towards partnership interest; **(iii)** preferential allotment, including through qualified institutional placement, of equity shares or equity-linked instruments of a listed company subject to lock-in period of one year; **(iv)** the equity shares/equity-linked instruments of a **financially weak company**, (i.e. a company, which has at the end of the previous financial year accumulated losses, resulting in erosion of more than 50 per cent but less than 100 per cent of its net worth as at the beginning of the previous financial year) or a sick industrial company whose shares are listed, **(v)** special purpose vehicles which are created by the fund for the purpose of facilitating/promoting investment in accordance with these regulations. The above investment conditions/restrictions should be achieved by the fund by the end of its life cycle.

Financially weak company is a company, which has at the end of the previous financial year accumulated losses, resulting in erosion of more than 50 per cent but less than 100 per cent of its net worth as at the beginning of the previous financial year.

(3) Such funds may enter into an agreement with a merchant banker to **(i)** subscribe to the unsubscribed portion of the issue **(ii)** receive/deliver securities in the process of market making under SEBI Issue of Capital and Disclosure Requirements Regulations.

(4) They would be exempt from **SEBI Prohibition of Insider Trading Regulations**,[@@] in respect of investment in companies listed on SME exchange or SME segment of an exchange pursuant to due their diligence subject to the following conditions: **(i)** the fund would disclose within two working days of such acquisition/dealing to the stock exchanges where the investee company is listed; **(ii)** such investment would be locked -in for a period of one year from the date of investment.

(c) SME Funds The following additional conditions would apply to SME funds: Atleast 75 per cent of the corpus should be invested in unlisted securities/partnership interest of venture capital undertakings/investee companies which are SMEs or in companies listed/proposed to be listed on SME exchange/SME segment of an exchange. The conditions stipulated in **(b) (3)** and **(b) (4)** above in relation to venture capital fund would be applicable to the SME funds also.

(d) Social Venture Funds The following additional conditions would apply to social venture funds: **(1)** Atleast 75 percent of their corpus would be invested in unlisted securities/partnership interest of social ventures. **(2)** They may **(i)** accept grants, provided that utilisation of such grants would be restricted to investment specified in **(1)** above; **(ii)** give grants to social ventures, provided that appropriate disclosure is made in the placement memorandum; **(iii)** accept **muted returns** for their investors, that is, they may accept returns on their investments which may be lower than the prevailing returns for similar investments.

(e) Infrastructure Funds The following additional conditions would apply to infrastructure funds: Atleast 75 percent of the corpus should be invested in unlisted securities/units or partnership interest

[@@]An account available in Khan, MY, *Financial Services*, MHE, India, 2018, chapter 13.

of venture capital undertaking/investee companies/special purpose vehicles, which are engaged in, or formed for the purpose of, operating, developing or holding infrastructure projects. They may also invest in listed securitised debt instruments/debt securities of investee companies/special purpose vehicles, which are engaged in, or formed for the purpose of, operating, developing or holding infrastructure projects.

Conditions for Category II AIFs The applicable investment conditions are as follows. They should invest primarily in unlisted investee companies/units of other AIFs specified in the placement memorandum. They may also invest in units of Category I/II AIFs but not in units of other fund of funds. The restrictions on borrowing funds/leveraging applicable to Category I funds would also apply to them. They may engage in hedging, subject to SEBI guidelines, The conditions stipulated in **(b) (3)** and **(b) (4)** in relation to venture capital funds would also be applicable to such funds.

Conditions for Category III Alternative Investment Funds The applicable investment conditions are. They may invest in **(i)** securities of listed/unlisted investee companies/derivatives/complex/structured products, **(ii)** units of Category I/II AIFs. But they cannot invest in units of other fund of funds. They may engage in leverage or borrow subject to consent from the investors in the fund and subject to a SEBI-specified maximum limit. They should disclose information regarding the overall level of leverage employed, the level of leverage arising from borrowing of **(i)** cash, **(ii)** position held in derivatives/in any complex product and the **(iii)** main source of leverage in their fund to the investors and to the SEBI periodically. They would be regulated through issuance of SEBI-specified directions regarding areas such as operational standards, conduct of business rules, prudential requirements, restrictions on redemption and conflict of interest.

Other AIFs The SEBI may lay down framework for AIFs other than the Category I, II and III funds.

General Obligations and Responsibilities and Transparency Included in general obligations/responsibility and transparency of the AIFs are: **(i)** general obligations, **(ii)** conflict of interest, **(iii)** transparency, **(iv)** valuation, **(v)** obligation of manager, **(vi)** dispute resolution, **(vii)** power to call for information, **(viii)** maintenance of records, **(ix)** submission of reports to the SEBI, and **(x)** winding-up.

General Obligations The AIFs should review the policies and procedures, and their implementation, on a regular basis, or as a result of business developments to ensure their continued appropriateness. Their sponsor/manager should appoint a SEBI-registered custodian for safekeeping of securities if the corpus of the AIF is more than five hundred crore rupees. However, the sponsor/manager of a Category III AIF should appoint custodian irrespective of the size of corpus. The should inform the SEBI in case of any change in the sponsor/manager/designated partners/any other material change from the information provided by them at the time of application for registration. In case of change in **control** (i.e. change in control in terms of **SEBI Substantial Acquisition of Shares/ Takeovers**[@@] if its shares are listed and change in the controlling interest/legal form in other cases) of the AIF, sponsor/manager, prior approval from the SEBI should be taken by the AIF. Their books of accounts should be audited annually by a qualified auditor.

Conflict of Interest The sponsor/manager of the AIF should act in a fiduciary capacity towards its investors and disclose to them all conflicts of interests as and when they arise or seem likely to arise. The manager should establish and implement written policies and procedures to identify, monitor and appropriately mitigate conflicts of interest throughout the scope of business. They should abide by SEBI-specified high level principles on avoidance of conflicts of interest with associated persons.

[@@]An account available in Chapter 32.

Transparency All the AIFs should ensure transparency and periodical disclosure of information to investors on the following: **(a)** financial, risk management, operational/portfolio, and transactional information regarding fund investments; **(b)** any fees **(i)** ascribed to the manager /sponsor **(ii)** charged to the AIF/any investee company by an associate of the manager/sponsor; **(c)** any inquiries/ legal actions by legal/regulatory bodies in any jurisdiction, as and when occurred; **(d)** any material liability arising during the AIF's tenure as and when occurred; **(e)** any breach of a provision of the placement memorandum/agreement made with the investor or any other fund documents as and when occurred; **(f)** change in control of the sponsor/manager/investee company; **(g)** provide at least on an annual basis, within 180 days from the year-end, reports to investors including the following information, **(1)** financial information of investee companies, **(2)** material risks and how they are managed which may include: **(i)** concentration risk at fund level, **(ii)** foreign exchange risk at fund level, **(iii)** leverage risk at fund and investee company levels, **(iv)** realisation risk (i.e. change in exit environment) at fund and investee company levels, **(v)** strategy risk (i.e. change in or divergence from business strategy) at investee company level, **(vi)** reputation risk at investee company level, **(vii)** extra-financial risks, including environmental, social and corporate governance risks, at fund and investee company level. Category III fund should, however, provide quarterly reports to investors within 60 days of the end of the quarter, **(h)** any significant change in the key investment team; **(i)** When required by the SEBI, information for systemic risk purposes (including the identification, analysis and mitigation of systemic risks).

Valuation The AIF should provide to its investors, a description of its **(i)** valuation procedure and **(ii)** the methodology for valuing assets. The Category I and II funds should undertake valuation of their investments, atleast once in every six months, by an independent valuer. Such period may be enhanced to one year on approval of atleast 75 percent of the investors by value of their investment. Category III funds should ensure that calculation of the net asset value (NAV) is independent from the fund management function of the AIF and disclosed to the investors at intervals not longer than a quarter for close-ended funds and a month for open-ended funds.

Obligation of Manager The manager would be obliged to: **(a)** address all investor complaints; **(b)** provide to the SEBI any information sought; **(c)** maintain all specified records; **(d)** take all steps to address conflict of interest; and **(e)** ensure transparency and disclosure.

Dispute Resolution By itself or through the manager/sponsor, the AIF should lay down procedures for resolution of disputes between the investors, AIF, manager/sponsor through arbitration or any such mechanism as mutually decided between the investors and the AIF.

Power to Call for information The SEBI may at any time call for any information from an AIF, its manager/sponsor/trustee/investor with respect to any matter relating to its activity as an AIF or for the assessment of systemic risk or prevention of fraud. The information should be furnished within the specified time.

Maintenance of Records The manager/sponsor of the AIF should maintain for a period of five years after the winding up of the fund the following records describing: **(a)** the assets under the scheme/ fund; **(b)** valuation policies and practices; **(c)** investment strategies; **(d)** particulars of investors and their contribution; and **(e)** rationale for investments made.

Submission of Reports to the SEBI The SEBI may at any time call upon the AIF to file such reports, as it may desire, with respect to the activities carried on by the AIF.

Winding-up An AIF set up as a trust would be wound up: **(a)** when its tenure or all schemes launched by it, as mentioned in the placement memorandum, is over; **(b)** if it is the opinion of the trustees/trustee company, that it be wound-up in the interests of investors in the units; **(c)** if 75 percent of the investors by value of their investment pass a resolution at a meeting of unitholders that it be wound up; and **(d)** if the SEBI so directs in the interests of investors.

An AIF set up as a limited liability partnership should be wound up in accordance with the provisions of The Limited Liability Partnership Act: in terms of stipulations **(a), (c)** and **(d)** applicable to the winding up of trust-AIFs.

An AIF set up as a company should be wound up in accordance with the provisions of the Companies Act. An AIF set up as a body corporate should be wound up in accordance with the provisions of the statute under which it is constituted.

The trustees/trustee company/Board of Directors/designated partners of the AIF should intimate to the SEBI and investors of the circumstances leading to its winding up. On and from the date of intimation, no further investments should be made on behalf of the AIF. Within one year from the date of intimation, the assets should be liquidated, and the proceeds accruing to investors distributed to them after satisfying all liabilities. Upon winding up, the certificate of registration should be surrendered to the SEBI.

Inspection The SEBI may, *suo motu,* or upon receipt of information/complaint, appoint person(s) as inspecting authority to undertake inspection of the books of account, records and documents relating to an AIF for any of the following reasons: to **(a)** ensure that the books of account, records and documents are being maintained by the in the specified manner; **(b)** inspect complaints received from investors, clients or any other person, on any matter having a bearing on its activities; **(c)** ascertain whether the provisions of the SEBI Act/regulations are being complied with; **(d)** inspect *suo motu* its affairs in the interest of the securities market/investors. Before ordering an inspection, the SEBI should give not less than ten days notice to the AIF. However, where the SEBI is satisfied that in the interest of the investors no such notice should be given, it may by an order in writing direct that the inspection of the affairs of the AIF be taken up without such notice.

Obligations During the course of an inspection, the concerned AIF would be duty bound to discharge its obligations specified below. It would be the duty of every officer of the AIF and any other associated person who is in possession of relevant information pertaining to its conduct and affairs of including manager to produce such books, accounts and other documents in his custody or control and furnish him with such statements and information as the inspecting authority may require for the purposes of the inspection. It would also be their duty to give to the inspecting authority all such assistance and extend all such co-operation as may be required in connection with the inspection and furnish such information as sought in connection with the inspection. The inspecting authority would, have the power to examine on oath and record the statement of any employees/directors/person responsible for, or connected with, their activities of or any other associated person having relevant information pertaining to the fund. The inspecting authority would also have power to obtain authenticated copies of documents, books, accounts from any person having control over or custody of them. The inspecting authority would, as soon as possible, on completion of the inspection, submit an inspection report to the SEBI and if directed submit an interim report.

The SEBI may after consideration of the inspection report and giving reasonable opportunity of hearing to the AIF or its trustees/directors/manager issue such direction as it deems fit in the interest of securities market/investors including directions in the nature of: **(a)** requiring not to launch new schemes or raise money from investors for a particular period; **(b)** prohibiting the person concerned from disposing of any of the properties of the fund or scheme acquired in violation of these regulations; **(c)** requiring the person connected to dispose of the assets of the fund/scheme in a manner as may be specified in the directions; **(d)** requiring the person concerned to refund any money or the assets to the concerned investors along with the requisite interest or otherwise, collected under the scheme; and **(e)** prohibiting the person concerned from operating in the capital market or from accessing the capital market for a specified period.

Procedure for Action in Case of Default An AIF which: **(a)** contravenes any of the provisions of the SEBI Act/regulations, **(b)** fails to furnish any information relating to its activity, **(c)** furnishes information which is false or misleading in any material particular, **(d)** does not submit periodic returns or reports as required, **(e)** does not co-operate in any enquiry, inspection or investigation conducted, **(f)** fails to resolve the complaints of investors/give a satisfactory reply in this behalf, would be dealt with in the manner provided under the **SEBI Intermediaries Regulations**.[@@] The SEBI may also to issue directions or measures under the SEBI Act or under any other law for the time being in force.

SEBI Foreign Venture Capital Investors (FVCIs) Regulations, 2000

A foreign venture capital investor (FVCI) is an investor incorporated and established outside India and proposes to make investment in accordance with these regulations. The main elements of FVCIs are described below.

Registration A FVCI should be registered with SEBI to carry on business in India. To seek registration with SEBI, an applicant should apply in the prescribed form along with an application fee of US$ 2,500. The eligibility criteria for registration of an applicant include the following conditions: **(i)** its track record, professional competence, financial soundness, experience, general reputation of fairness and integrity; **(ii)** the RBI's approval for investing in India; **(iii)** it is an investment company/trust/partnership, pension/mutual/endowment fund, charitable institution or any other entity incorporated outside India; **(iv)** it is an asset/investment management company, investment manager or any other investment vehicle incorporated outside India; **(v)** it is authorised to invest in Venture Capital Funds (VCFs)/Alternative Investment Fund/carry on activity as a FVCI; **(vi)** it is regulated by an appropriate foreign regulatory authority or is an income tax payer or submits a certificate from its banker of its promoters' track record where it is neither a regulated entity nor an income tax payer; **(vii)** it has not been refused a certificate by SEBI and **(viii)** it is a fit and proper person. The provisions of the **SEBI Intermediaries Regulation, 2008** would apply to determine if the applicants are fit and proper persons. The applicant may be required by SEBI to furnish such further information as it may consider necessary. A VCF means a fund established in the form of a trust/company including a body corporate and registered under the SEBI VCF Regulations which **(i)** has dedicated pool of capital, **(ii)** raised in the manner specified under the regulations and **(iii)** invests in accordance with the regulations.

On being satisfied that the applicant is eligible and on receipt of the registration fee of US$ 10,000, SEBI would grant it a certificate of registration subject, *inter alia*, on the conditions that it would **(a)** abide by the *SEBI Act* and FVCIs regulation, **(b)** appoint a domestic custodian (i.e. a person registered under SEBI Custodian of Securities Regulations, 1996) for custody of securities **(c)** enter into an

[@@]An account available in Khan, M.Y., *Indian Financial System*, MHE, India, 2018, Chapter 4.

arrangement with a designated bank (i.e. any bank in India permitted by the RBI to act as a banker to the FVCI) for operating a special non-resident rupee/foreign currency account, and **(d)** forthwith inform SEBI, in writing, if any information/particulars previously submitted to it are found to be false/ misleading in any material particular or if there is any change in any information already submitted.

Investment Criteria The investments by FVCIs should conform to the norms prescribed by SEBI. First, they should disclose their investment strategy to SEBI. They can invest their total funds committed in one VCF/AIF. At least 66.67 per cent of the investible fund (i.e. the funds committed for investment in India net of expenditure for administration/management of the fund) should be invested in unlisted equity shares or equity linked instruments of venture capital undertakings (VCUs). Further, not more than 33.33 per cent of the investible funds may be invested by way: **(a)** subscription to the IPO (initial public offer) of VCUs whose shares are proposed to be listed, **(b)** debt/debt instruments of a VCU in which the FVCI has already made an investment by way of equity, **(c)** preferential allotment of equity shares of a listed company subject to lock-in period of one year, **(d)** it should disclose the duration of the life cycle of the fund, and **(e)** special purpose vehicles (SPVs) created to facilitate/promote investment according to share regulations.

Equity-linked instruments include instruments convertible into equity shares or share warrants, preference shares, debentures compulsorily/optionally convertible into equity. A VCU means a domestic company **(i)** whose shares are not listed on a recognised stock exchange in India, **(ii)** which is engaged in the business of providing services, production/manufacture of articles/things but excludes such activities/sectors which are specified in the negative list by the SEBI with approval of Government, namely, **(a)** non-banking financial services excluding the NBFCs registered with and categorised as asset finance companies by the RBI, **(b)** gold financing excluding companies engaged in gold financing for jewellery, **(c)** activities not permitted under the industrial policy of the Government of India, and **(d)** any other activity specified by the SEBI from time to time.

General Obligations and Responsibilities The FVCIs have to maintain, for a period of eight years, books of accounts/records/documents which would give a true and fair picture of their affairs and intimate to SEBI the place where they are being maintained. They may be called upon at any time by SEBI to furnish within a specified time any information with respect to any matter relating to their activities. Moreover, they/a global custodian acting on their behalf should enter into an agreement with the domestic custodian to act as a custodian of securities for them. They have also to ensure that the domestic custodian takes steps for **(i)** monitoring of their investments in India, **(ii)** furnishing of periodic reports to, and such information as may be called for by SEBI. A branch of a bank approved by the RBI should be appointed by the FVCIs the as designated bank for opening of foreign currency denominated accounts/special non-resident rupee account.

Inspection and Investigation The SEBI has the right to, *suo moto*, or upon receipt of information/ complaint, order an inspection/investigation in respect of conduct and affairs of any FVCI by an officer to **(i)** ensure that the books/accounts/documents are being maintained in the specified manner, **(ii)** inspect/investigate into complaints from investors/clients/any other person on any matter having a bearing on its activities, **(iii)** ascertain whether the provisions of the SEBI Act and FVCIs regulations are being complied with and **(iv)** inspect/investigate, *suo moto*, into its affairs in the interest of the securities market/investors. The FVCI/any other associated person, including asset management company/fund manager, in possession of information relevant to its conduct/affairs must **(1)** produce to the investigating/inspecting officer such books/accounts/other documents in his custody/control and furnish him such statements and information as he may acquire and **(2)** give to him all assistance and extend all cooperation, and furnish all information sought by him.

He would also have the power **(1)** to examine on oath and record the statement of any person responsible for or connected with the activities of the FVCI and **(2)** to get authenticated copies of documents/books/accounts of the FVCI from any person having control/custody over them. On the basis of the inspection/investigation report, SEBI has the right to require the FVCI to take such measures or issue such directions as it deems fit in the interest of the capital market and investors, including directions in the nature of **(a)** requiring the disposal of the securities or investment in a specified manner, **(b)** requiring not to further invest for a particular period and **(c)** prohibiting operation in the capital market in India for a specified period.

Procedure for Action in Case of Default In addition to the issue of appropriate directions specified above, SEBI can also suspend/cancel registration of the FVCI on the basis of the investigation report in terms of the **Intermediaries Regulation, 2008**.

Suspension of Registration The registration of a FVCI can be suspended by SEBI if it **(1)** contravenes any of the provisions of the SEBI Act or SEBI FVCI Regulations, **(2)** fails to furnish any information relating to its activities as required by SEBI, **(3)** furnish to it information which is false/misleading in any material particular, **(4)** does not submit periodic returns/reports as required by it and **(5)** does not cooperate in any enquiry/inspection conducted by it.

Cancellation of Registration The SEBI may cancel the registration of a FVCI when he **(1)** is guilty of fraud/has been convicted of an offence involving moral turpitude, **(2)** has been guilty of repeated defaults of the nature resulting in suspension of registration; **(3)** does not meet the eligibility criteria laid down in SEBI FVCIs Regulations and **(4)** contravenes any of the provisions of *SEBI Act*/these regulations.

The order of suspension/cancellation of registration may be published by SEBI in two newspapers. Action may also be initiated by SEBI for suspension/cancellation of registration of an intermediary who fails to exercise due diligence in the performance of its functions/comply with its obligations under these regulations. Any person aggrieved by an order of SEBI may prefer an appeal to Securities Appellate Tribunal (SAT).

SUMMARY

LO 26.1

Venture capital, as a fund-based financial service, has emerged the world over to fill gaps in the conventional financial mechanism, focusing on new entrepreneurs, commercialisation of new technologies and support to small/medium enterprises in the manufacturing and the service sectors. Over the years, the concept of venture capital has undergone significant changes. The nascent venture capital industry in India can profitably draw upon the experiences of the developed countries.

The characteristics features of venture capital differentiate it from other capital investments. It is basically equity finance in relation to new listed companies and debt financing is only supplementary to ensure running yield on the portfolio of the venture capitalists/capital institution (VCIs). It is long-term investment in growth-oriented small/medium firms. There is a substantial degree of active involvement of VCIs with the promoters of venture capital undertakings (VCUs) to provide, through a hands-on approach, managerial skills without interfering in the management. The venture capital financing involves high risk-return spectrum. It is not technology finance, though technology finance may form a sub-set of such financing. Its scope is much wider.

The first step in venture capital financing is the selection of the investment. It includes stages of financing, methods to evaluate deals and the financial instruments to structure a deal. The stages of

LO 26.1	financing as differentiated in venture capital industry are early stage and later stage. Included in early stage are seed capital/pre-start-up, start-up and second-round financing. The later stage of venture capital financing covers mezzanine/development capital, bridge/expansion, buyouts and turnarounds. The venture investments are generally **idea-based and growth-based**. Of the three methods of financial analysis/evaluation which VCIs can adopt, namely, conventional venture capital valuation method, the first Chicago method and the revenue multiplier method, the first Chicago method gives better results. The structuring of venture capital deals is a mix of the available financial instruments: equity and debt. The equity instruments include ordinary, non-voting, deferred ordinary, preference, warrants, cumulative convertible preference, participating preference and so on. The main types of debt instruments are conventional loan, conditional loan, income notes, NCDs, PCDs, zero interest bonds, secured premium notes and deep discount bonds.
	The after-care stage of venture capital financing relates to different styles of nurturing, its objectives and techniques. The style of nurturing which refers to the extent of participation by VCIs in the affairs of the venture, falls into three broad categories: hands on, hands off and hands holding. Some of the important techniques to achieve the objectives are personal discussion; plant visits, nominee directors, periodic reports and commissioned studies.
	The valuation of the venture capital portfolio to monitor and evaluate the performance of the equity investment is done by using cost method or market value-based methods consisting of quoted market value method and fair market value method. The methods of valuing debt instruments vary with the nature of such instruments.
	The alternative forms in which VCIs can be structured are: limited partnership, company, trust and small business investment company.
	The last stage in venture capital financing is the exit to realise the investment so as to maximise profit/minimise loss. The alternative routes for disinvestments of equity/quasi-equity instruments are market flotation, arnout, trade sales, takeout and liquidation.
LO 26.2	The venture capital industry in India is of relatively recent origin. Before its emergence, the DFIs had partially been playing the role of venture capitalists by providing assistance for direct equity participation to ventures in the pre-public stage and by selectively supporting new technologies. The concept of venture capital was institutionalised/operationalised in November 1988 when the CCI issued guidelines for setting up of VCFs for investing in unlisted companies and to avail of a concessional facility of capital gains tax. These guidelines, however, construed venture capital rather narrowly as a vehicle for equity-oriented finance for technological upgradation and commercialisation of technology promoted by relatively new entrepreneurs. These were repealed on July 25, 1995. Recognising the growing importance of venture capital, the Government announced a policy for governing the establishment of domestic VCFs. They were exempted from tax on income by way of dividends and long-term capital gains from equity investment in the specified manner and in conformity with stipulations in unlisted companies in the manufacturing sector, including software units, but excluding other service industries. To augment the availability of venture capital, guidelines were issued in September, 1995 for overseas venture capital investments in the country. After empowerment to register and regulate VCFs, SEBI issued VCF Regulations, 1996. They have now been replaced by the Alternative Investment Fund Regulations.
	Alternative investment fund (AIF) means any fund established/incorporated in India in the form of a trust/company/limited liability partnership/body corporate which is **(i)** a privately pooled investment vehicle and collects funds from Indian/foreign investors for investing in accordance with a defined investment policy for the benefit of its investors, and **(ii)** not covered under the mutual fund/other regulations of the SEBI to regulate fund management activities. The main elements of the SEBI regulation relating to AIFs, namely, **(a)** registration, **(b)** investment conditions/restrictions, **(c)** general obligations and responsibilities and transparency, **(d)** inspection, and **(e)** procedure for action in case of default are discussed in this Section.

LO 26.2

To set an **AIF**, an entity/person has to obtain a certificate of registration from the SEBI. The existing venture capital funds may seek re-registration as AIFs subject to approval of two-thirds of their investors by value of their investment. The AIFs can seek registration in one of the three categories: **(i)** I, **(ii)** II, **(iii)** III.

"Category I AIF" which invests in start-up or early stage ventures/social ventures/small and medium enterprises (SMEs)/infrastructure/other sectors or areas which the Government/regulators consider as socially/economically desirable and would include venture capital funds, SME funds, social venture funds, infrastructure funds and such other specified alternative investment funds. The **AIFs** which are generally perceived to have positive spillover effects on economy and for which the SEBI/Government of India/other regulators in India might consider providing incentives/concessions would be included and such funds which are formed as trusts/companies would be construed as "venture capital company"/ fund" as specified under the Income Tax Act. **Venture capital fund** means an alternative investment fund which invests primarily in unlisted securities of start-ups, emerging/early-stage venture capital undertakings mainly involved in new products/new services, technology/intellectual property right based activities/a new business model. **Venture capital undertaking** means a domestic company which is **(i)** not listed on a recognised stock exchange in India at the time of making investment; and **(ii)** engaged in the business for providing services, production/manufacture of article/things and does not include the following activities/sectors: **(1)** non-banking financial companies; **(2)** gold financing; **(3)** activities not permitted under industrial policy of Government of India; and **(4)** any other activity which may be specified by the SEBI in consultation with the Government of India from time to time. **SME fund** means an alternative investment fund which invests primarily in unlisted securities of investee companies which are SMEs or securities of those SMEs which are listed/proposed to be listed on a SME exchange/ SME segment of an exchange. **Social venture** means a trust/society/company/venture capital undertaking/limited liability partnership formed with the purpose of promoting social welfare/solving social problems/providing social benefits and includes: **(i)** public charitable trusts registered with the charity commissioner; **(ii)** societies registered for charitable purposes/promotion of science, literature/fine arts; **(iii)** company registered under Section 25 of the Companies Act; **(iv)** micro finance institutions. **Social venture fund** means an alternative investment fund which invests primarily in securities/units of social ventures and which satisfies social performance norms laid down by the fund and whose investors may agree to receive restricted or muted returns. **Infrastructure funds** invest primarily in unlisted securities/partnership or interest/listed debt/securitised debt instruments of investee companies/SPVs engaged in. or formed for the purpose of, operating/developing/holding infrastructure.

"Category II AIF" which does not fall in Category I and III and which does not undertake leverage or borrowing other than to meet day-today operational requirements. Funds such as private equity funds/ debt funds for which no specific incentives or concessions are given by the Government or any other regulator would be included. **Private equity fund** means an **AIF** which invests primarily in equity/ equity linked instruments (i.e. instruments convertible into equity/preference shares, share warrants, compulsorily/optionally convertible debentures) or partnership interests of investee companies (i.e. companies/SPVs/limited partnership/body corporate in which an AIF makes an investment) according to the stated objectives of the fund. **Debt fund** is an AIF which invests primarily in debt/debt securities of listed/unlisted investee companies according to its stated objectives.

LO 26.2

"Category III AIF" which employs diverse or complex trading strategies and may employ leverage including through investment in listed or unlisted derivatives. Funds such as hedge funds or funds which trade with a view to make short term returns or such other funds which are open-ended and for which no specific incentives or concessions are given by the Government or any other regulator would be included. **Hedge funds** employ diverse/complex trading strategies and invest in securities having diverse risks or complex products including listed/unlisted derivatives.

The eligibility criteria for registration as AIF are: **(a)** The memorandum of association/trust/partnership deed respectively in case of company/trust/limited liability partnership permits it to carry on the activity of an AIF; **(b)** The applicant is prohibited by its memorandum and articles of association/trust/partnership deed from making an invitation to the public to subscribe to its securities; **(c)** The instrument of trust in case of a trust-applicant is in the form of a deed and has been duly registered under the provisions of the Registration Act; **(d)** The partnership in case of partnership-applicant is duly incorporated and the partnership deed has been duly filed with the Registrar under the provisions of the Limited Liability Partnership Act; **(e)** A body corporate-applicant is set up/established under the laws of the central or state legislature and is permitted to carry on the activities of an AIF; **(f)** The applicant, sponsor and manager are fit and proper persons based on the criteria specified in SEBI Intermediaries Regulations; **(g)** The key investment team of the manager of the AIF has adequate experience, with at least one key personnel having not less than five years experience in advising/managing pools of capital or in fund/asset/wealth/portfolio management or in the business of buying, selling and dealing of securities/ other financial assets and has relevant professional qualification; **(h)** The manager/sponsor has the necessary infrastructure and manpower to effectively discharge its activities; **(i)** The applicant has clearly described at the time of registration the investment objective, the targeted investors, proposed corpus, investment style/strategy and proposed tenure of the fund/scheme; **(j)** Whether the applicant or any entity established by the sponsor/manager has earlier been refused registration by the SEBI.

The investment conditions/restrictions relate to: **(i)** investment strategy, **(ii)** investment in AIF, **(iii)** placement memorandum, **(iv)** schemes, **(v)** tenure, **(vi)** listing, **(vii)** general investment conditions, **(viii)** conditions for category I AIF, **(ix)** conditions for category II AIF, **(x)** conditions for category III AIFs and **(xi)** other AIF.

Investment in all categories of AIFs would be subject to the following conditions:- **(a)** The AIF may raise funds from any Indian, foreign or non-resident Indian investor by way of issue of **units** (i.e. a beneficial interest of the investors in the AIF/a scheme of the AIF including shares/partnership interests); **(b)** Each scheme of the AIF would have **corpus** (i.e. total amount of funds committed by the investor in the AIF by way of a written contract/any such document as on a particular date) of atleast twenty crore rupees; **(c)** The AIF would not accept an investment of value less than one crore rupees from an investor. In case of investors who are employees or directors of the AIF/manager, the minimum value of investment should be twenty five lakh rupees. **(d)** The manager/sponsor would have a continuing interest in the AIF of not less than the lower of 2.5 percent of the corpus or five crore rupees in the form of investment in the AIF and such interest should not be through the waiver of management fees. For Category III AIF, the continuing interest should be not less than 5 percent of the corpus or ten crore rupees, whichever is lower. **(e)** The manager/its sponsor should disclose their investment in the AIF to investors; **(f)** No scheme of the AIF would have more than one thousand investors; **(g)** The fund would not solicit/collect funds except by way of private placement.

LO 26.2

Category I and Category II AIF would be close-ended fund/scheme. Category III AIF may be open-ended or close-ended.

Units of close-ended AIF may be listed on stock exchange only after final close of the fund/scheme subject to a minimum tradable lot of one crore rupees and permitted.

Investments by all categories of AIFs would be subject to the following conditions: **(a)** They may invest in securities of companies incorporated outside India subject to such conditions/guidelines that may be stipulated/issued by the RBI/SEBI; **(b)** Co-investment in an investee company by a manager/ sponsor would not be on terms more favourable than those offered to the AIF; **(c)** Category I and II AIFs should invest not more than 25 percent and Category III 10 per cent of the corpus in one investee company; **(d)** The AIFs should not invest in **associates** (i.e. a company/limited liability partnership/ body corporate in which a director/trustee/partner/ sponsor/manager of the AIF or director/partner of the manager/sponsor holds individually/collectively more than 15 per cent of its paid-up equity share capital/partnership interest) except with the approval of 75 percent of investors by value of their investment; **(e)** The un-invested portion of the corpus may be invested in liquid mutual funds/ bank deposits/other liquid assets of higher quality such as T-bills, CBLOs, CPs, CDs, till deployment of funds as per the investment objective; **(f)** The AIFs may act as nominated investor as specified in SEBI Issue of Capital and Disclosure Requirements Regulations. **(discussed in Chapter 14).** The SEBI may specify additional requirements/criteria for AIF/for a specific category.

The following investment conditions would apply to all Category I AIFs: **(a)** They should invest in investee companies/venture capital undertaking/special purpose vehicles/limited liability partnerships/ units of other AIFs. They may invest in units of Category I AIFs of same sub-category subject to the condition that they would not invest in units of other fund of funds. The investment conditions applicable to the venture capital funds (**discussed later**) would not be applicable to investments by them. Such investment funds cannot borrow funds directly/indirectly/engage in any leverage except for meeting temporary funding requirements for not more than thirty days, on not more than four occasions in a year and not more than 10 percent of the corpus. **(b) Venture Capital Funds** The following additional investment conditions would apply to venture capital funds: **(1)** At least two-thirds of the corpus should be invested in unlisted equity shares/equity linked instruments of a venture capital undertaking/in companies listed/proposed to be listed on a SME exchange or SME segment of an exchange; **(2)** Not more than one-third of the corpus should be invested in: **(i)** subscription to initial public offer of a venture capital undertaking whose shares are proposed to be listed; **(ii)** debt/debt instrument of a venture capital undertaking in which the fund has already made an investment by way of equity or contribution towards partnership interest; **(iii)** preferential allotment, including through qualified institutional placement, of equity shares or equity-linked instruments of a listed company subject to lock-in period of one year; **(iv)** the equity shares/equity-linked instruments of a **financially weak company**, (i.e. a company, which has at the end of the previous financial year accumulated losses, resulting in erosion of more than 50 per cent but less than 100 per cent of its net worth as at the beginning of the previous financial year) or a sick industrial company whose shares are listed, **(v)** special purpose vehicles which are created by the fund for the purpose of facilitating/promoting investment in accordance with these regulations. The above investment conditions/restrictions should be achieved by the fund by the end of its life cycle. **(3)** Such funds may enter into an agreement with a merchant banker to **(i)** subscribe to the unsubscribed portion of the issue **(ii)** receive/deliver securities in the process of market making under SEBI Issue of Capital and Disclosure Requirements Regulations. **(4)** They would be exempt from SEBI Prohibition of Insider Trading Regulations, in respect of investment in companies listed on SME exchange or SME segment of an exchange pursuant to due their diligence subject to the following conditions: **(i)** the fund would disclose within two working days of such acquisition/dealing to the stock exchanges where the investee company is listed; **(ii)** such investment would be locked -in for a period of one year from the date of investment. **(c) SME Funds**

LO 26.2

The following additional conditions would apply to SME funds: **(1)** Atleast 75 per cent of the corpus should be invested in unlisted securities/partnership interest of venture capital undertakings/investee companies which are SMEs or in companies listed/proposed to be listed on SME exchange/SME segment of an exchange. The conditions stipulated in **(b) (3)** and **(b) (4)** above in relation to venture capital fund would be applicable to the SME funds also. **(d) Social Venture Funds** The following additional conditions would apply to social venture funds: **(1)** Atleast 75 percent of their corpus would be invested in unlisted securities/partnership interest of social ventures. **(2)** They may **(i)** accept grants, provided that utilisation of such grants would be restricted investment specified in **(1)** above; **(ii)** give grants to social ventures, provided that appropriate disclosure is made in the placement memorandum; **(iii)** accept muted returns for their investors, that is, they may accept returns on their investments which may be lower than the prevailing returns for similar investments. **(e) Infrastructure Funds** The following additional conditions would apply to infrastructure funds: Atleast 75 percent of the corpus should be invested in unlisted securities/units or partnership interest of venture capital undertaking/investee companies/special purpose vehicles, which are engaged in, or formed for the purpose of, operating, developing or holding infrastructure projects. They may also invest in listed securitised debt instruments/debt securities of investee companies/special purpose vehicles, which are engaged in, or formed for the purpose of, operating, developing or holding infrastructure projects.

The applicable investment conditions are as follows. They should invest primarily in unlisted investee companies/units of other AIFs specified in the placement memorandum. They may also invest in units of Category I/II AIFs but not in units of other fund of funds. The restrictions on borrowing funds/leveraging applicable to Category I funds would also apply to them. They may engage in hedging, subject to SEBI guidelines, The conditions stipulated in **(b) (3)** and **(b) (4)** in relation to venture capital funds would also be applicable to such funds.

The applicable investment conditions are. They may invest in **(i)** securities of listed/unlisted investee companies/derivatives/complex/structured products, **(ii)** units of Category I/II AIFs. But they cannot invest in units of other fund of funds. They may engage in leverage or borrow subject to consent from the investors in the fund and subject to a SEBI-specified maximum limit. They should disclose information regarding the overall level of leverage employed, the level of leverage arising from borrowing of **(i)** cash, **(ii)** position held in derivatives/in any complex product and the **(iii)** main source of leverage in their fund to the investors and to the SEBI periodically. They would be regulated through issuance of SEBI-specified directions regarding areas such as operational standards, conduct of business rules, prudential requirements, restrictions on redemption and conflict of interest.

The SEBI may lay down framework for AIFs other than the Category I, II and III funds.

Valuation The AIF should provide to its investors, a description of its **(i)** valuation procedure and **(ii)** the methodology for valuing assets. The Category I and II funds should undertake valuation of their investments, atleast once in every six months, by an independent valuer. Such period may be enhanced to one year on approval of atleast 75 percent of the investors by value of their investment. Category III funds should ensure that calculation of the net asset value (NAV) is independent from the fund management function of the AIF and disclosed to the investors at intervals not longer than a quarter for close-ended funds and a month for open-ended funds.

An AIF which: **(a)** contravenes any of the provisions of the SEBI Act/regulations, **(b)** fails to furnish any information relating to its activity, **(c)** furnishes information which is false or misleading in any material particular, **(d)** does not submit periodic returns or reports as required, **(e)** does not co-operate in any enquiry, inspection or investigation conducted, **(f)** fails to resolve the complaints of investors/give a satisfactory reply in this behalf, would be dealt with in the manner provided under the SEBI Intermediaries Regulations. The SEBI may also to issue directions or measures under the SEBI Act or under any other law for the time being in force.

REFERENCES

1. Ramesh, S and A Gupta, *Venture Capital and the Indian Financial Sector*, (Oxford University Press, New Delhi), 1995.
2. Bovaird, C, *Venture Capital Finance*, (Pitman, London), 1990, quoted in Ramesh and Gupta, *ibid.*, p 48.
3. Anson, G, 'Venture Capital in Europe', *Europe Venture Capital Association Year Book* (London), 1992, quoted in *ibid.*, p 49.
4. *Ibid.*, p 49.
5. *Ibid.*, p 69.
6. Lorenz, T, *Venture Capital Today* (Woodhead-Faulkner, London), 1989.
7. *Ibid.*, p 75.
8. *Report on Venture Capital Financial Analysis: Valuation, Pricing and Risk Management*, QED Research Incorporated, Polo Alto, California, 1987.
9. *Ibid.*, pp 97-98.
10. Canadian Institute of Chartered Accountants, '*Study on Accounting and Financial Reporting by Venture Capital *Organisations*', Toronto, 1987.
11. Lee, S J, *Venture Capital Manual*, (Warren Gorham and Lamont Inc., Boston), 1990.
12. For details please refer to Khan, M Y, *Indian Financial System* (TMH, New Delhi), 2013.

REVIEW QUESTIONS

LOD: Easy

RQ.26.1 (a) Indicate whether the following statements are true or false: [LO 26.1,2]

(i) Venture capital is a vehicle for equity-oriented finance for technological upgradation and commercialisation of technology promoted by relatively new entrepreneurs.

(ii) Before the emergence of venture capital financing in India, developmental financial institutions played the role of venture capitalists.

(iii) In management buyins, funds are provided to enable the current operating management to acquire an existing business.

(iv) Venture capital investments are generally idea-based and growth-based in contrast to conventional investments, which are asset-based.

(v) The First Chicago Method of valuing venture capital undertakings takes into account only two points of time in the life of the venture capital investment, namely, the starting time of investment and the exit time.

(vi) A conditional loan is a form of loan finance without any pre-determined repayment schedule or interest rate.

(vii) An offshore investment company is incorporated in the country in which it makes an investment.

(viii) Carried interest is defined as the extra incentive/profit to the managers over and above the share attributed to their capital contribution and the management fee.

(ix) Under the Venture Capital Funds (VCFs) Regulations,1996, any type of organisation can file an application for being registered as a VCF.

(x) A venture capital investor can be structured as a limited partnership.

[Answers: (i) False (ii) True (iii) False (iv) True (v) False (vi) True (vii) False (viii) True (ix) False (x) True]

(b) Fill in the blanks with the correct answer (out of the choices provided).

(i) In the First Chicago Method for valuation of venture capital undertakings ________ (two/three) alternative scenarios are perceived/considered.

(ii) Venture capital funds invest in equity that is ___________ (quoted/unquoted) on the stock market.

(iii) When the venture capital fund also provides business skills to the investee company, the approach is called ___________ (hands-on/hands-off) approach.

(iv) Venture capital funds finance small and medium sized firms in the ___________ (early/late) stages of their development.

(v) The minimum investment in a venture capital fund by an investor must be ₹ ___________ (5/10) lakh under the SEBI Venture Capital Funds Regulations, 1996.

(vi) Under the SEBI Venture Capital Funds Regulations, 1996, a venture capital fund must invest not less than ___________ (65/75) per cent of its investible funds in unlisted equity shares/equity linked instruments.

(vii) A venture capital fund, under the provisions of the SEBI Venture Capital Funds Regulations, 1996, is entitled to get its units listed on any recognised stock exchange after the expiry of ___________ (two/three) years from the date of issuance of its units.

(viii) Under the SEBI Foreign Venture Capital Investors (FVCIs) Regulations, 2000, a FVCI cannot invest more than ___________ (30/25) per cent of the funds committed for investment in India in one venture capital unit.

(ix) Under the provisions of the SEBI Venture Capital Funds Regulations, 1996, before a venture capital fund can start its operation, it must have a firm commitment of at least ___________ (₹7.5 crore/₹5 crore) from the investors for contribution.

(x) A venture capital fund can be wound up when ___________ (67/75) per cent of the investors in the scheme resolve in a meeting of the unit holders that the fund should be wound up.

[Answers: (i) Three (ii) Unquoted (iii) Hands-on (iv) Early (v) 5 (vi) 75 (vii) Three (viii) 25 (ix) ₹5 crore (x) 75]

RQ.26.2 Describe briefly the main features of venture capital. [LO 26.1]

LOD: Medium

RQ.26.3 What are the (1) early and (2) later stage of venture capital financing? [LO 26.1]

RQ.26.4 Give a brief account of the financial instruments through which venture capital investment is made. [LO 26.1]

RQ.26.5 Examine critically the alternative forms in which VCFs can be structured? [LO 26.1]

RQ.26.6 Explain briefly the main features of the SEBI VCF Regulations. [LO 26.2]

RQ.26.7 Discuss in brief the main features of the SEBI FVCIs Regulations. [LO 26.2]

LOD: Difficult

RQ.26.8 Explain briefly the following valuation approaches/methods for financial analysis of venture capital investments: (i) conventional, (ii) the First Chicago and (iii) revenue multiplier. [LO 26.1]

RQ.26.9 Discuss briefly the style of investment nurturing/aftercare by the venture capital funds. What are the objectives of aftercare? Also explain briefly the important techniques to achieve these. [LO 26.1]

RQ.26.10 What are the venture capital portfolio valuation approaches for (a) equity investments and (b) debt instruments? [LO 26.1]

RQ.26.11 "The important aspect of exit stage of VC financing is the decision regarding the realisation/disinvestment alternatives which are related to the type of investment". Elaborate. [LO 26.1]

PART 7

RISK MANAGEMENT

Chapter 27
OPTION VALUATION

Chapter 28
DERIVATIVES: MANAGING FINANCIAL RISK

The framework for an explicit understanding of risk and return and the nature of relationship between them was discussed in Chapter 3. This part explores further how financial managers can deal with various types of risks. Chapter 27 covers option valuation in terms of pay-off boundaries and the relevant factors. It also describes the Black-Scholes model of option valuation. The management of financial risk through derivatives—forwards, futures and options—is described in Chapter 28.

CHAPTER

27 Option Valuation

LEARNING OBJECTIVES

LO 27.1	Define option and describe the two types of options—call option and put option
LO 27.2	Discuss the call option payoffs and the put option payoff—returns and losses to the buyers and sellers of options
LO 27.3	Describe the range/boundaries of the value of call option
LO 27.4	Enumerate the factors—current share price, exercise price, risk-free rate, time to maturity and price volatility of shares—which determine the worth of a call option
LO 27.5	Explain and illustrate the Black-Scholes Option Pricing Model
LO 27.6	Provides option market practices in India

INTRODUCTION

"We should keep our options open" is the phrase preferred in our day-to-day life. The reason is option brings privileged position to its holder by providing him discretion to use it if he so desires. In finance, an option entitles its holder to buy or sell an asset at a specified (predetermined/fixed) price on or before a specified date. Although the concept is generic, option is more commonly used in the context of corporate securities. This Chapter, therefore, focuses on stock/share options only. It describes the concept of option and its types first. Option payoffs and option boundaries have been explained in the subsequent discussions. The factors influencing its valuations are also explained. The Black-Scholes model of option valuation has been described subsequently. The summary of the main points is provided by way of recapitulation.

LO 27.1 OPTION: CONCEPT AND TYPES

Concept

Option is a contract that confers to its holder/owner the right but not the obligation to buy/sell a specified security at a specified price on/before a given date.

An option belongs to the family of derivative securities. It is a contract that confers the right to its owner/holder but not the obligation to buy or sell a specified security at a specified price on or before a given date. **Options** are a special type of financial contracts in that the buyer of the option has the right to buy or sell the securities but is under no obligation to do so. The buyer of the option is placed in an advantageous/favourable situation as he will exercise his option only when it is profitable to do so. In other words, the seller of the option is in disadvantageous position as he is under obligation to buy or sell the securities in case the buyer exercises his option. In operational terms, the seller/writer of the option runs the risk of loss for assuming which he charges **option premium** from the buyer of the option.

Some options are European while others are American. **American options** are more flexible in nature in that they can be exercised at any time upto the expiration date. In contrast, **European options** can be exercised only on the expiration date. In view of greater flexibility, most exchange traded options are American.

Important Terms Associated with Options

Buyer of an Option is the one, who by paying the option premium buys the right to buy/sell securities but not the obligation to exercise his option on the seller/writer of the option.

Writer of an Option is the one who receives the option premium and is thereby obliged to sell/buy the securities if the buyer exercises the option on him.

Option Price/Premium is the price that the option buyer pays to the option seller. It is aptly referred to as the option premium.

Expiration Date is the date specified in the options contract by which the option can be exercised. It is also known as the exercise date, the strike date or the maturity date.

Strike Price The price specified in the options contract at which the buyer can exercise his right to buy or sell the securities is known as the strike price or the exercise price.

At-the-Money Option is an option that would lead to zero cash flow (no profit no loss) to the holder if it were exercised immediately.

In-the-Money Option is an option that would lead to a positive cashflow to the holder if it were exercised immediately.

Out-of-the-Money Option is an option that would lead to a negative cashflow to the holder if it were exercised immediately.

Types

Call option entitles the holder the right but not the obligation to buy securities.

American call option can be exercised at any time up to expiration.

Options are essentially of two types, namely, call options and put options.

Call Option An **American call option** is a contract that gives the holder the right but not the obligation to buy (i.e., to call in) specified securities at a specified price on or before a specified exercise date. For instance, if an investor buys one call option (normally consisting of 100 shares) on Reliance, he has the right to buy 100 equity shares of Reliance at a specified exercise price anytime between today and a specified date by paying option premium. The fact that the call holder is under no obligation to buy securities implies that he has limited liability. In case the price of the equity shares of Reliance falls at expiration date, he would prefer to walk away from the call contract. In other words, he would not exercise his right to buy equity shares of Reliance. In such a situation, his loss is equal/limited to the option premium paid by him at the time of contract. Should the price of Reliance shares increase, he would exercise his right to buy these shares and gain from the transaction. His gain is equal to the difference between the share price and exercise price minus the option premium.

In contrast, **European call options** can be exercised only on the maturity date. Since American options provide the owner an additional timing option (to exercise early), they cannot be less valuable than equivalent European options. Given the fact that European options are easier to analyse than American options, and properties of an American option are frequently deduced from those of its European counterpart, our discussion in this Chapter primarily focuses on European options.

European call option can be exercised only on maturity.

The call option buyers expect the price of securities to go up as it benefits them. They are bullish. The reverse holds true for the call writers; they expect/hope the price of securities to fall. They are bearish. In case of the decrease in price, the call buyer does not buy the securities (as the prevailing share price is less than the exercise price). In such a situation, the call writer gains equivalent to the option premium he has received at the time of selling the call option.

From the above discussion, it can be deduced that the value of call option is either zero (when the prevailing share price, S_1, on the date of maturity is equal to or less than the exercise price, E,) or positive (when $S_1 > E$). It cannot be negative as it implies that the call-holder buys the share at E price which is higher than the market price of the share, S_1. Obviously, no rational investor will act that way. The value of call option (C_1) on is expiration date is given by Equation 27.1.

$$C_1 = Max\,(S_1 - E,\, 0) \qquad \textbf{(27.1)}$$

Where Max implies the maximum value of $S_1 - E$ or Zero whichever is higher.

***Example* 27.1**

Suppose the market price of equity share of Reliance on the expiration date is ₹140 and the exercise price is ₹125. The value of call option is ₹15 (₹140 – ₹125). In case, the value of the share on expiration date turns out to be ₹120, the value of C_1 would not be negative ₹5 (₹120 – ₹125); it would be zero as the investor would not purchase shares at ₹125 which is available in the market and thereby incur a loss of ₹5 per share.

The value of call option (for the facts contained in Example 27.1) is shown in Fig. 27.1. The price of share is plotted on X-axis and the call option value on Y-axis. It may be noted that for market price of share less than exercise price, the value of the option is zero; for $S_1 > E$, the option has a positive value and increases in a linear manner, rupee for rupee, with the increase in the share price. For instance, when S_1 goes up from ₹140 to ₹150 (by ₹10), the value of call option also increases by ₹10 (from ₹15 to ₹25).

Gain or Loss Assuming no transaction costs, the purchase of call option primarily requires the payment of premium to the option writer. Assuming premium (P) paid is ₹5 per share, the gain (G) to the call-holder of Reliance (assuming S_1 = ₹140) will be reduced by the amount of P as shown by Equation 27.2.

$$G = \text{Max}\,(S_1 - E,\, 0) - P \qquad \textbf{(27.2)}$$
$$= (₹140 - ₹125) - ₹5 = ₹10$$

In case the value of the share is ₹120, the loss to the call-holder would be ₹5 (equivalent to the amount of the premium paid). His loss will not increase to ₹10 ($E - S_1$ = ₹125 – ₹120 = ₹5 + ₹5, premium paid) because the call-holder is under no obligation to buy the share. He will obviously not buy the share at ₹125 whose market price is ₹120. Therefore, it can be generalised that the loss is equal to the premium paid whenever $S_1 < E$. When $S_1 > E$, gain would be as shown by Equation 27.2. This is illustrated in Fig. 27.2. It may be noted from the Figure that the call-holder suffers a

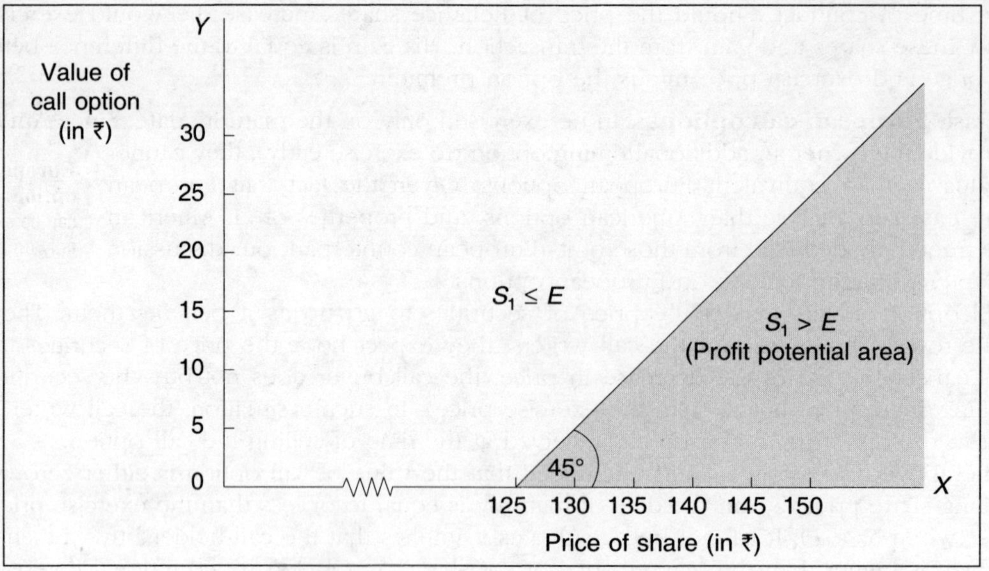

FIGURE 27.1 Value of Call Option to Buyer

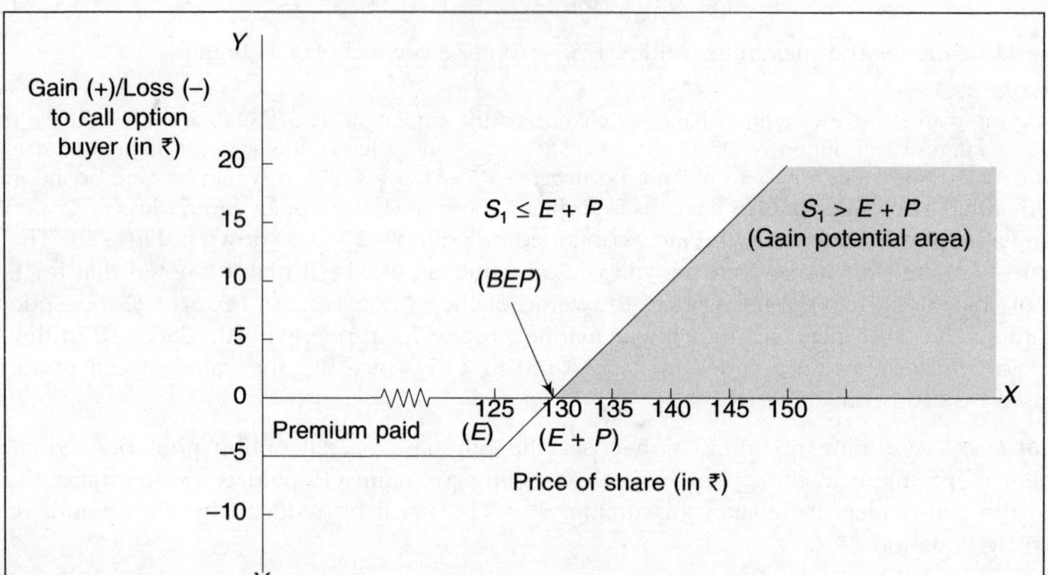

FIGURE 27.2 Gain/Loss to Call Option Buyer

loss until the S_1 rises to the point where it equals $E + P$. This point of equality can be referred to as break-even point (BEP), given by Equation 27.3.

$$BEP = S_1 - (E + P) = \text{zero} \tag{27.3}$$

Beyond the BEP, the call-holder would gain with rise in share prices.

In contrast, the writer of the call option gains as long as the price of the share (S_1) on the date of maturity is less than the sum of exercise price and premium received. Equation 27.4 indicates gain to the writer of the call option.

$$S_1 > (E + P) \text{ subject to } (S_1 - E) < P \qquad \textbf{(27.4)}$$

Continuing with Example 27.1, the call option writer gains if the price of the share on the date of expiration is less than ₹130, that is ₹125, E + ₹5, P. However, the maximum gain would be ₹5 only (equivalent to the option premium received) and this will accrue to him if $S_1 < E$ at the date of maturity. The profit margin would be lower if $S_1 > E$, but less than $E + P$. Assume Reliance share's market value is ₹128. The call-holder gains by exercising his right to buy Reliance share at ₹125. The call option writer's profit margin would be reduced by ₹3 as he would have to buy the share at ₹128 and sell at ₹125; his profit margin would be ₹2 (P, ₹5 – ₹3, $S_1 - E$).

Whereas the call writer's profits are limited to ₹5 per share, his losses can rise sharply with increase in the market price of the share. Suppose Reliance share's market price jumps to ₹200; his loss will be ₹70 per share ($S_1 - E + P$ = ₹200 – ₹125 + ₹5). Figure 27.3 shows the profit or loss position of the call option writer.

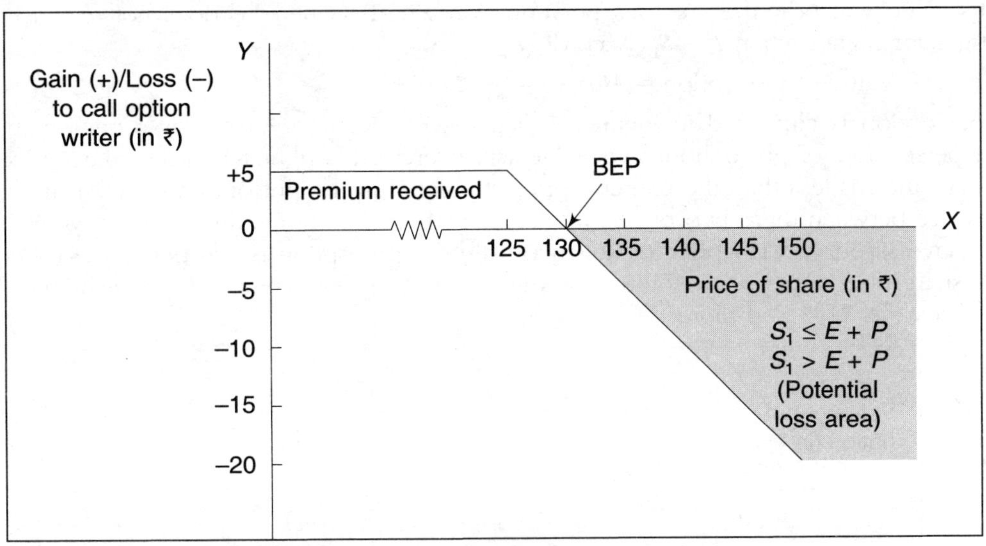

FIGURE 27.3 Gain/Loss to Call Option Writer

The call writer will be at the *BEP* when $S_1 = E + P$. In Example 27.1, he would be at break-even when share price is ₹130 = ₹125, E + ₹5, P.

> **Put option** entitles the holder the right but not the obligation to sell securities.

Put Option A put option is just the opposite of a call option. A put option gives the holder the right but not the obligation to sell securities (i.e. to put them) on or by a certain date at a fixed exercise price. In other words, the seller/writer of the put option has the obligation to buy securities in case the put owner decides to exercise his option. Since the put option writer is at the receiving end, he receives the **put premium** (as a compensation for risk assumed) from the put buyer.

> **Put premium** is the compensation received by the put option writer from the put option buyer.

The put option holder will exercise his right to sell the securities should the price of the securities fall below the exercise price (E) at the date of expiration. In case

$S_1 > E$, he will prefer to sell at a higher price in the market than to sell to the put option writer. Consider Example 27.2.

***Example* 27.2**

Suppose an investor wants the right to sell Reliance equity shares at ₹135 after 2 months. He is to buy a 2-month put option with a ₹135 exercise price. In case the market price of Reliance share increases to ₹150 ($S_1 > E$), the put option will expire worthless as it will be more profitable for an investor to sell in the open market (at ₹150) than to the put option writer (at ₹135).

Assuming the market price of the share falls below the strike price, say to ₹125, it will be profitable for the put option holder to excise his put option right as it fetches him ₹135 compared to ₹125 he can otherwise obtain from the market.

Equations 27.5-A and 27.5-B can be inferred from Example 27.2. The equation can serve as a benchmark/guide when to avail put option and when not to avail it.

$E > S_1$, avail put option **(27.5-A)**

$E < S_1$, do not avail put option **(27.5-B)**

Like call options, put options cannot have negative value as the put option owner will not sell securities at a lower price (compared to the higher price available in the market) to the put option writer. Its value will be either zero as per equation 27.5-B (when he does not exercise his put option right) or higher when $E > S_1$. Accordingly,

$$\text{Value of put option} = Max\ (E - S_1,\ 0) \tag{27.6}$$

The put option is illustrated in Figures 27.4 and 27.5. Figure 27.4 shows profit potential area from the perspective of put option owner. He will exercise his right when the share price on the date of expiration is less than the exercise price stipulated in the put option contract; the bigger is the difference between these two prices, the larger is the put option value to the buyer. The curve has a negative slope. At ₹115 price of Reliance, value of put option is ₹20 per share; it declines to ₹5 when share price increases to ₹130. The value of put option is zero when the market price of Reliance's share is ₹135 and more.

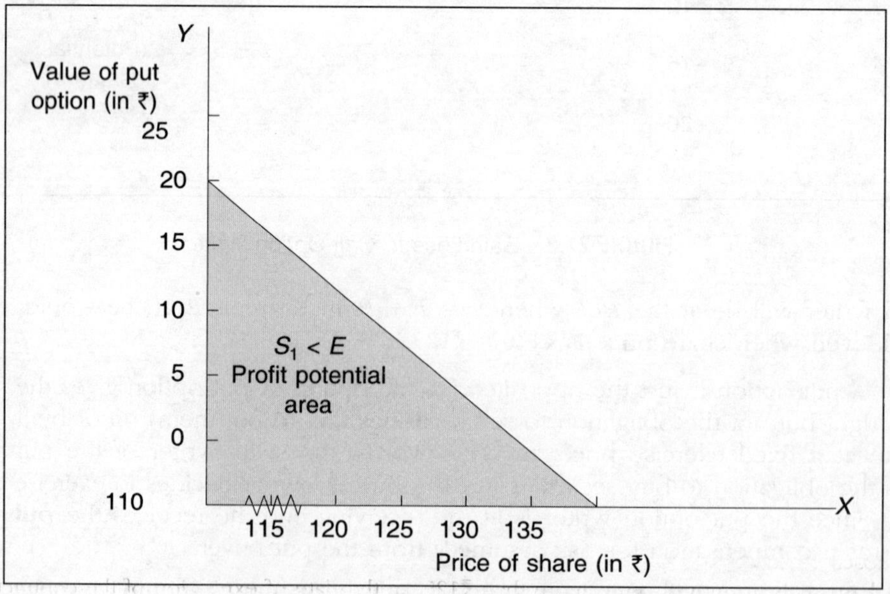

FIGURE 27.4 Value of Put Option to Buyer

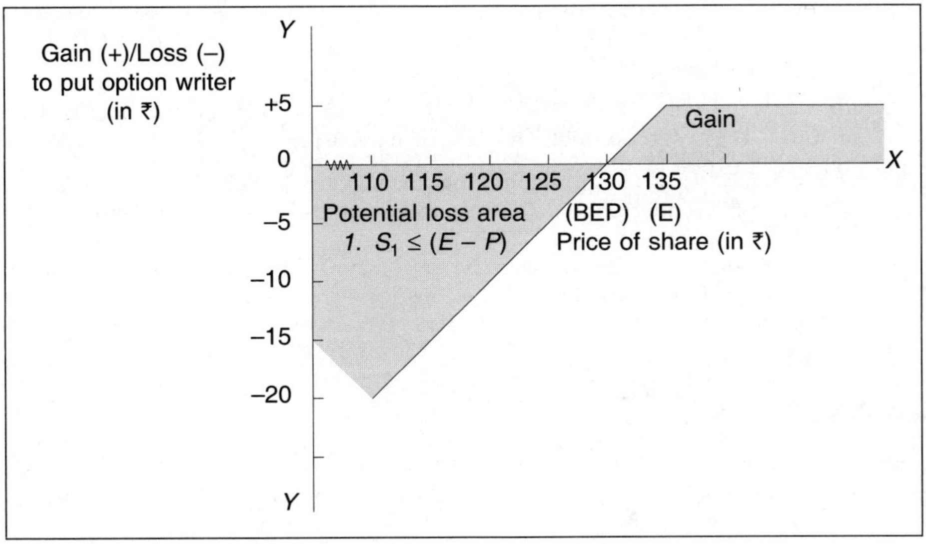

FIGURE 27.5 Gain/Loss to Put Option Writer

The financial impact of changes in market prices of shares on the put option writer is exactly the opposite of what it is to the put option buyer. The gain of the put option buyer is the loss of the put option seller. It is shown in Fig. 27.5. At S_1 of ₹130, the put option writer is at break-even; at prices lower than ₹130, he incurs loss and gains at price higher than ₹130. His maximum gain is ₹5 per share (equivalent to the premium received) at S_1 = ₹135 and above.

LO 27.2 OPTION PAYOFFS

The discussions that follow provide a comparative picture of financial returns (or losses) available to the option buyer *vis-à-vis* the buyer of securities. The gain to the option buyer is the loss to the option seller. Call option payoffs are discussed first, followed by put option payoffs.

Call Option Payoffs

The call option owner's loss is limited to the call **option premium**. The profit he can earn is not so limited. In case the market price of the share on the expiration date turns out to be substantially higher than the exercise price, his total profit from the call option contract would be substantial in relation to the investment (equivalent to the call option premium paid up-front) he has made. Consider Example 27.3.

> **Option premium** is the price the option buyer pays to the option seller.

***Example* 27.3**

Suppose an investor buys 3-month 100 call option contracts (one call contract consists of 100 equity shares) of Reliance with strike price of ₹125 and call option premium of ₹5 per share. The one call option contract involves cost/investment of ₹500 (i.e., 100 equity shares × ₹5). Therefore, the total sum invested is ₹50,000 (i.e. ₹500 per contract × 100 contracts).

After 3 months, if the market price of Reliance turns out to be ₹125 or less, the option is of no value and the investor loses ₹50,000.

In case Reliance's price moves up to more than ₹125 on the date of expiration of the contract, the investor would exercise his option as the share price exceeds the exercise price. Assume Reliance has risen to ₹150 per share. The investor gains ₹25 per share (i.e. ₹150, S_1 – ₹125, E). His gross profit would be ₹2,50,000 (i.e. ₹25 per share × 100 contracts × 100 share per contract). His net profit will be ₹2,00,000 (₹2,50,000 – ₹50,000 option premium paid). An investment of ₹50,000 would yield him a profit of ₹2,00,000.

To illustrate further, suppose investor purchases the shares of Reliance with ₹50,000 instead of buying call option. The total shares purchased (assuming Reliance share was selling at ₹125 on the date of call option contract) would be 400 (i.e., ₹50,000/₹125), yielding him profit of ₹10,000 only (i.e. 400 shares × ₹25 profit per share). To put it differently, the option position brings magnifying financial impact. This, in turn, is caused by large shares dealing possible under option. The respective figures of shares dealt in option and purchase are 10,000 and 400 (25 times larger in option).

In case the Reliance price ends up below the exercise price (say, at ₹115), the loss to the call option investor would be ₹50,000. In contrast, in the case of purchase, his loss would be restricted to ₹4,000 only (i.e. ₹10 per share × 400 shares). Therefore, the investor should also be conscious of comparatively larger losses under option contract.

Put Option Payoffs

The put option owner/investor is benefited when the share price prevailing on the date of maturity is less than the strike price at which he has acquired the right to sell the shares to the put option writer. This is illustrated in Example 27.4.

***Example* 27.4**

Assume an investor buys 3-month 200 put option contracts (each contract involving 100 shares) of Reliance with strike price of ₹200 and put option premium of ₹8 per share. On the date of maturity, Reliance is selling at ₹180.

Solution

- The investor will obviously exercise his option of selling 20,000 shares (200 contracts × 100) at strike price of ₹200 as the market price is lower at ₹180.
- His gross profit will be ₹4 lakh (i.e. 20,000 shares × ₹20 profit per share).
- His net profits will be ₹2.4 lakh (i.e. ₹4 lakh – put option premium of ₹1,60,000 on 20,000 shares @ ₹8 per share).
- Had he invested ₹1.6 lakh in Reliance, his shares purchases would have been ₹1,60,000/₹200 = 800.
- Instead of earning profits, he would have, in fact, suffered a loss of ₹16,000 (i.e. 800 shares × ₹20 per share) in case of purchase of shares.
- In case the market price of Reliance ends up with a price higher than strike price (say, ₹210), the put option has zero value as the investor can sell his shares in open market at a higher price.
- He would lose ₹1.6 lakh put option premium.
- He would have gained ₹8,000 by investing in shares (₹10 × 800 shares owned).
- Thus, the risk-return trade-off in put option is of more severe nature than in call option.

LO 27.3 CALL OPTION BOUNDARIES

Hitherto we have focussed on call option valuation on the date of its maturity. What will be its value before maturity? To explain the concept let us consider Example 27.3 where the option is to buy Reliance shares at ₹125. In case the ruling price on the exercise date is less than ₹125, the call option has zero value; if the share price turns out to be higher than ₹125, the option would have worth equivalent to the price of the share (S_1) minus the exercise price (E). This position was depicted in Fig. 27.1.

Even before maturity, the price of the call option can never remain below the heavy line in Fig. 27.6 (replicated from Fig. 27.1) as the value of option can never be negative and its worth will be positive at least equivalent to S_0 – E when the price of the share (before maturity) is higher than the exercise price. Otherwise, it will create/cause arbitrage opportunity. Continuing with our Example

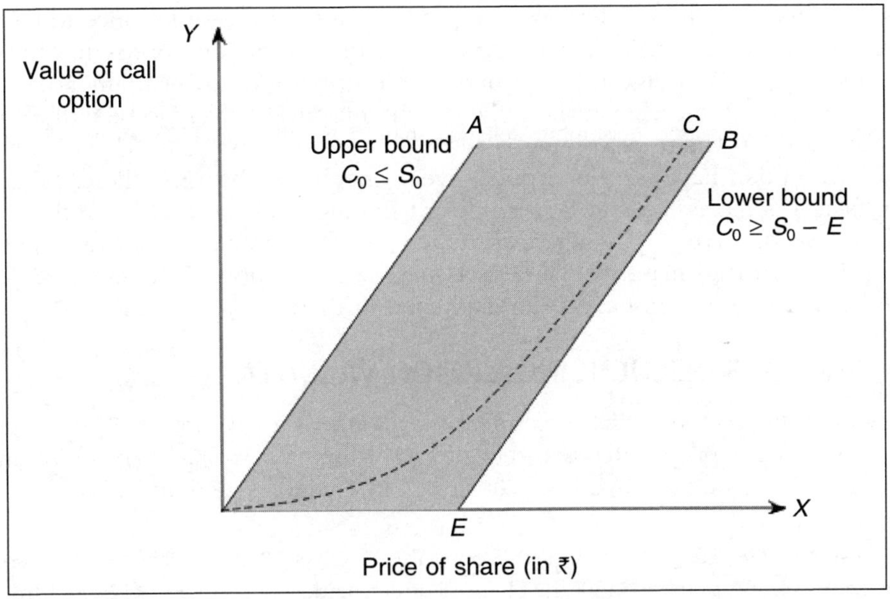

FIGURE 27.6 Upper and Lower Boundaries of Call Option Value

27.3, suppose Reliance share is selling at ₹133 (with strike price of ₹125 and call option premium of ₹5). Clearly, there are profit opportunities; the arbitrageur/investor can buy the call for ₹5 and immediately exercise it by buying shares at ₹125; his total cost/investment is ₹130 per share; by immediately selling it at ₹133, he earns *riskless profit* of ₹3 per share. What holds true for the hypothetical investor will also be applicable to other investors in the well-organised/**efficient markets**. As a result, there will be more demand for call option (at ₹5) till such time there is an upward revision of the option price (in this case to ₹8). Therefore, to prevent arbitrage, the value of the call today (C_0) must be either greater than or equal to the difference of the share price today (S_0) and the exercise price. In equation terms:

Efficient markets embrace all information and arbitrage opportunities do not exist.

$$C_0 \geq S_0 - E \tag{27.7}$$

From the above, it can be deduced that the call options which have still some time to run have their *lower bound* either zero or $S_0 - E$, whichever is higher. This has been depicted by point A in Figure 27.6.

The lower bound determines the **intrinsic value** of the call option. The intrinsic value of a call is the amount the option is *in the money (ITM)*, that is, the excess of share price over exercise price; if it is *out of the money (OTM)*, that is, the exercise price is higher than share price; its intrinsic value is zero. On the other hand, the *time value of an option* is the difference between the option premium and its intrinsic value. The longer the time to expiration, the greater is an option's time value, other things being equal. At expiration, an option would have no time value.

Intrinsic value of a call is the excess of share price over exercise price.

Time value of an option is the difference between the option premium and the intrinsic value.

The highest value of the call option *(the upper bound)* can never be more than the price of the share itself (shown as point B in Figure 27.6). This value can be reached only if the option has a very long time to expiration or is not likely to be exercised until far into the future. In these situations, the present value of the strike price to be paid in very distant future approaches zero. As a result, the value of the call option approaches the value of the share. Thus, lines A and B in Figure 27.6 represent the upper and lower boundaries.

However, in a realistic/practical situation, the call option price is likely to be in the shaded region (between lines A and B). The upper bound is more a theoretical possibility. This is so because if the share and the call option have the same price, every one will rush to sell the call option and buy the share. In fact, it is more likely to be an upward-sloping line (more close to the lower bound) shown by the dashed curve, *C*. In other words, curve *C* represents *typical* call option values at varied share prices, prior to maturity. The exact shape and position of the curve *C* depends on a number of factors. These factors have been explained in the following Section.

LO 27.4 FACTORS INFLUENCING OPTION VALUATION

We describe below the factors which determine the worth of a call option. These are: **(i)** current share price, **(ii)** exercise price, **(iii)** risk-free rate, **(iv)** time to expiration/maturity and **(v)** price volatility of share. These factors have been illustrated in Examples 27.5 and 27.6.

***Example* 27.5**

Suppose an investor is interested in buying a call option to purchase Reliance share to be exercised exactly after one year with exercise price of ₹130; the share's current market price (S_0) is ₹125 and the risk-free rate available on T-bills (R_f) is 7 per cent.

Assume further that the share price of Reliance will be either ₹140 or at ₹160 after one year. Since the exercise price is ₹130, the call option will either carry the value of ₹10 (i.e. ₹140 – ₹130) or of ₹30 (i.e. ₹160 – ₹130). In both the situations, the call option will be in the money to the investor.

Let us assume further that the investor wants to have the same value of investment/financial return (i) either from purchase of shares (ii) or from buying a call option. In case of the latter alternative, the investor is required to invest present value of the exercise price (₹130) in T-bills/risk-free securities to exercise call option at year-end 1. The requisite sum is provided by Equation 27.8.

$$E/(1 + R_f)^t \quad \textbf{(27.8)}$$

= ₹130/(1 + 0.07)

= ₹130 × 0.935 (PV of rupee one at year-end 1 discounted at 7 per cent as per Table A–1).

In both the situations the value of his investments (depending on the price of share at year-end) will be the same as shown in Table 27.1.

TABLE 27.1 Value of Investment at Year-end 1 (i) When Shares are Purchased and (ii) When Call Options are Purchased in Conjunction with Treasury Bills

Particulars	*Amount (year-end 1)*
(a) When call value is ₹10:	
(i) Compounded value of ₹121.55 invested at 7 per cent risk-free rate [₹121.55 (1 + 0.07)]	₹130
(ii) Plus call value	10
(iii) Equal to market price of share	140
(b) When call value is ₹30:	
(i) Compounded value of ₹121.55	130
(ii) Plus call value	30
(iii) Equal to market price of share	160

Since both the alternatives have the same financial returns, they must *a priori* have the same value today or it will cause arbitrage opportunity. Since the current price of the share is ₹125, the value of the call option today (C_0) is logically given by Equation 27.10.

$$S_0 = C_0 + E/(1 + R_f)^t \quad \textbf{(27.9)}$$

Or $$C_0 = S_0 - E/(1 + R_f)^t \quad \textbf{(27.10)}$$

$$= ₹125 - (₹130/1.07) = ₹125 - 121.55 = ₹3.45$$

The value of call option has to be ₹3.45 as shown in verification Table 27.2. The investment outlay under both the alternatives is the same.

TABLE 27.2 Value of Call Option

Particulars		*Amount*
(A) Investment in shares		₹125
(B) Investment in risk-free securities and call option		
Risk-free securities/T-bills	₹121.55	
Plus: Call option premium	3.45	125

From Equation 27.10, follows the generalisation that the value of a call option is the current market price of share less the present value of exercise price (discounted at risk-free rate of return). To put it differently, the value of call option is a function of **(i)** current share price, S_0, **(ii)** exercise price, *E*, **(iii)** risk-free rate of return, R_f and **(iv)** time to expiration, *t*. The impact of these factors on call option value is now explained.

Current Share Price

The current share price prevailing in the market has a positive impact on the call value. In other words, the higher is the current market price (S_0), the higher is the value of the call option. Other things being equal, assume in Example 27.5, the value of S_0 is ₹127 (instead of ₹125), the value of call option, C_0 increases by ₹2 [from ₹3.45 to ₹5.45 (i.e. ₹127 – ₹121.55)].

Exercise Price

The exercise price on the date of expiration has a negative influence on the value of a call option, that is, the value of C_0 is negatively related to *E*; the higher the value of *E*, the lower is the value of C_0 and *vice-versa*. Assuming other factors constant and the value of *E* increases to ₹132, the value of C_0 decreases to ₹1.68 (i.e. ₹125 – ₹123.42, *PV* of ₹132 × 0.935).

Risk-Free Rate

Risk-free rate (interest rate) has a positive relationship with the value of call option. The higher is the interest rate the higher is the C_0. This is so because the final payment for the purchase of shares is delayed till the time the option is exercised at some future date. The higher is the R_f, the lower is the *PV* of exercise price; since this price is to be subtracted from S_0 as per Equation 27.10, the value of call option increases. To put differently, the *PV* of exercise price will be less with higher discount rate causing higher value of C_0. Assuming 10 per cent discount rate (in place of 7 per cent), the value of C_0 increases to ₹6.83 (i.e. ₹125 – ₹118.17, *PV* of ₹130 × 0.909, *PV* factor at 10%), other factors remaining unchanged.

Time to Expiration/Maturity

It is very evident from the right part of Equation 27.10, $[E/(1 + r)^t]$ that the higher is the value of t, the lower will be the present value of exercise price (to be paid in future year, t). Since this amount is to be subtracted from S_0, to determine C_0, it obviously implies the higher value of call option, assuming other things remain constant. In Example 27.5, let us assume time to expiration of 2 years instead of one year. The value of call option enhances to ₹11.51 (i.e. ₹125 – ₹113.49, *PV* of ₹130 × 0.873, *PV* factor for two years at 7 per cent rate of discount).

The above four factors are the only relevant factors affecting the value of call option when an option is certain to finish in the money. However, in practice, the option may finish out of the money also. In the latter situation, the fifth factor related to price volatility of share becomes relevant. This is illustrated in Example 27.6.

***Example* 27.6**

For the facts in Example 27.5 assume that (i) the exercise price is ₹145 instead of ₹130 and (ii) current market price of the share is ₹135 and not ₹125. Determine the value of call option.

In case, the share price of year-end 1 ends up at ₹140, the value of call option will be zero as $S_1 < E$ (₹140 < ₹145). If the share price ends up at ₹160, the value of call option will be (₹160 – ₹145) = ₹15.

The basic approach of determining the value of the call option remains the same, that is, the payoffs to the investor should be identical whether he purchases shares or he goes for a combination of buying risk-free asset and call option.

To make the two alternatives comparable, **(i)** the investor will be required to invest the present value of the lower price of the share in a riskless asset and **(ii)** purchase the number of call options, determined by Equation 27.11.

$$\Delta S/\Delta C \tag{27.11}$$

Where ΔS = Difference in possible share prices, and ΔC = Difference in call option values. Accordingly,

(i) The investor will be required to invest ₹130.90 (i.e. ₹140 × 0.935, *PV* factor at 7 per cent for one year).

(ii) The number of call options purchased is 4/3, that is,

$$\frac{₹160 - ₹140}{₹15 - \text{zero}}$$

Thus, either buying 4/3 call options and investing ₹130.90 in a riskless security or making investment in shares fetch the identical financial returns to the investor (Table 27.3)

TABLE 27.3 Value of Investment at Year-end 1 (i) When Shares are Purchased and (ii) when Call Options are Purchased in Conjunction with Treasury Bills

Particulars	*Amount (year-end 1)*
(A) When call value is zero	
(i) Compounded sum of ₹130.90 (1 + 0.07)	₹140
(ii) Plus call value	0
(iii) Equal to market price of share	140
(B) When call value is ₹15	
(i) Compounded sum of ₹130.90	140
(ii) Plus call value (₹15 × 4/3)	20
(iii) Equal to market price of share	160

Since both the alternatives have exactly the same value in the *future*, they should have the same value *today;* otherwise, difference in value gives rise to arbitrage. The value of call option (C_0) should be:

$$S_0 = 4/3\ C_0 + (₹140/1 + R_f)$$
$$₹135 = 4/3\ C_0 + ₹130.90$$
$$4/3\ C_0 = ₹135 - ₹130.90 = ₹4.10$$
$$C_0 = (₹4.10 \times 3)/4 = ₹3.075$$

Each call option is worth ₹3.075. Table 27.4 contains its verification.

TABLE 27.4 Value of Call Option

(A) Investment in shares		₹135
(B) Investment in risk free security and call option:		
Purchase of Treasury Bills	₹130.90	
Add: Call option premium (₹3.075 × 4/3)	4.10	135

Thus, with the same investment outlay/cost (of ₹135) both the alternatives yield the same value to the investor.

Price Volatility of Share

Volatility in the share price significantly influences the call option value. In operational terms, the greater is the possibility of extreme outcomes, the greater is the call option value to its holder, all other things remaining the same. In statistical terms, the greater is the variance/standard deviation of the financial returns on the associated share, the more is the worth of the option to its owner. The reason is that a decrease in the lower possible share price, say, to ₹130 (from ₹140 in Example 27.6) does not cause loss to the call owner as the call option worth remains zero at both the levels of price. However, any possible increase in the upper share price (say, to ₹170 from ₹160) makes the option worth more as the call option is in the money.

To make things more explicit, the value of C_0 is determined with reference to new set of possible market prices of the underlying share for the facts contained in Example 27.6. The steps involved are as follows:

(i) The investor is required to invest in risk free security/treasury bills equivalent to the present value of the lower share price (₹130 in this case); the amount of investment is ₹121.55 (discount rate is 7 per cent). In addition, he is to buy 1.6 call options (explained in step ii). In case, the share price ends up at ₹130, the call option has no value as the exercise price is ₹145.

(ii) In case the share price turns out to be ₹170, the call option has worth of (₹170 – ₹145) ₹25. The investor would get ₹130 from his investments in risk-free asset. He would fall short of ₹40 to make his portfolio worth of ₹170 (equal to the share price). Since, one call is worth of ₹25, the required number of calls to be purchases is (₹40/₹25) 1.6.

(iii) Alternatively, the number of call options to be purchased to make it equal to the price of a share can be determined by Equation 27.11.

$$\frac{(₹170 - 130) = ₹40}{(₹25 - 0) = ₹25} = 1.6$$

Since the variance of the financial return associated with the security has increased (in view of greater span of plausible price range, now of ₹130 and ₹170 *vis-à-vis* ₹140 and 160 earlier) the call value has risen to ₹8.4 as shown below.

$$₹135 = 1.6\ C + ₹130/(1 + 0.07)$$
$$1.6\ C = ₹135 – ₹121.55 = ₹13.45$$
$$C_0 = ₹13.45/1.6 = ₹8.406$$

With increased volatility in share prices as reflected in the higher value of variance, the value of C_0 has more than doubled from ₹3.075 to ₹8.406.

Assigning Probabilities Hitherto volatility in share prices has been explained without assigning any probability. The induction of an element of probability would provide more insight into the matter. Consider Example 27.7.

***Example* 27.7**

An investor is considering call option on the two shares, X and Y. Details are as follows:

Particulars	*Probability*	*Share price*	*Expected share price*
Share X:	0.10	₹90	₹9
	0.25	108	27
	0.30	120	36
	0.25	132	33
	0.10	150	15
			120
Share Y:	0.10	60	6
	0.25	90	22.5
	0.30	120	36
	0.25	150	37.5
	0.10	180	18.0
			120.0

The expected value of share price at the end of the period is the same for both shares, X and Y: ₹120. There is a much larger dispersion of possible outcomes for share Y (the range being ₹60 – ₹180) *vis-à-vis* share X (the range of price variation is ₹90 – ₹150). Suppose the exercise prices of both the shares at year-end 1 is ₹115. Will these shares (having the same expected value of ₹120 and the exercise price of ₹115) have the same call value? Since the price volatility is comparatively more in share Y, its call option value is higher at ₹16.75 than that of share X of ₹9.25 (Table 27.5).

TABLE 27.5 Determination of Call Option Value

Particulars	*Expected share price*	*Exercise price*	*Call value*	*Probability*	*Expected call value*
Share X:	₹90	₹115	₹0	0.10	₹0
	108	115	0	0.25	0
	120	115	5	0.30	1.50
	132	115	17	0.25	4.25
	150	115	35	0.10	3.50
					9.25
Share Y:	60	115	0	0.10	0
	90	115	0	0.25	0
	120	115	5	0.30	1.50
	150	115	35	0.25	8.75
	180	115	65	0.10	6.50
					16.75

To conclude, the greater is the dispersion of the possible outcomes for share prices, the greater is the call option value. Thus, there are five factors which have a bearing on the value of call option*. Their impact on the value of call option in terms of their positive or negative relationship is shown in Exhibit 27.1.

EXHIBIT 27.1 Factors Affecting Call Value

Factor	*Impact*
Current share price	Positive (+)
Exercise price	Negative (–)
Risk-free rate of return/Interest-rate	Positive (+)
Time to expiration on the option	Positive (+)
Variance/Price-volatility of share	Positive (+)

Finally, the stock index options (say NIFTY Index) are valued in the same way as options related to ordinary/equity shares. The market lot size of stock index options for trading purposes in India is 200.

So far we have considered simple examples showing how to value a call option. In fact, the option value was applicable only for the given example. In the following section, a more comprehensive and precise option valuation framework known as the Black-Scholes option pricing mode l (associated with seminal work of Fischer Black and Myron Scholes) is discussed.

LO 27.5 THE BLACK-SCHOLES OPTION PRICING MODEL

Black and Scholes (BS) developed a precise model to arrive at the equilibrium value of an option. Before the BS model is discussed in detail, it will be useful to understand the concept of **option equivalent**. The concept involves the purchase of a certain number of equity shares (say Δ shares) through the partial sum raised by debt. This combination should be such that the payoffs from the levered investment in the share (or index) are identical to the payoffs from the call option. This is illustrated in Example 27.8.

Option equivalent involves purchase of equity shares partially through debt.

***Example* 27.8**

Suppose an investor can purchase one-year call option of Reliance with an exercise price of ₹150; its current market price is also ₹150. The interest rate is 10 per cent. It is assumed that in a year's time only two things are possible. Its price may fall by 10 per cent to ₹135 or increase by 20 per cent to ₹180. In case Reliance share price decreases to ₹135, the call option will be worthless and have zero value. However, if the price increases, the call option will be worth (₹180 – ₹150) ₹30. The possible payoffs from the call option are either zero or ₹30. The payoffs from the levered investment in shares must be identical to that of call option so that both the investments have the same value.

Black Scholes option pricing model is a precise model to arrive at the equilibrium value of an option.

To ascertain the number (or a fraction) of shares to be purchased, the amount to be borrowed and other aspects, the following steps are suggested.

(i) The inverse of the ratio $\Delta S \div \Delta C$ given by Equation 27.11 referred to as **hedge ratio** or **option delta** is useful here. Symbolically,

$$\text{Option delta} = \frac{\text{Spread of possible option prices, } \Delta C}{\text{Spread of possible share prices, } \Delta S} \quad \textbf{(27.12)}$$

$$= (₹30 - 0)/(₹180 - ₹135) = ₹30/₹45 = 2/3$$

(ii) The option delta of 2/3 implies that the investor will buy 2/3 of Reliance share and borrow ₹81.82. (explained in step iii).

(iii) Investor will borrow ₹81.82 at 10 per cent; the *modus-operandi* of determining ₹82.82 is explained in Table 27.6.

TABLE 27.6 Payoffs with Purchase of 2/3 Share with Borrowings

Particulars	*Possible share price at year-end 1*	
	₹135	*₹180*
2/3 market price of a share	90	120
Less: Payoffs (as under call option)	0	30
Repayment of loan along with interest	90	90
Borrowings at t = 0 [₹90/(1 + 0.1)] = ₹81.82		

(iv) Since both alternatives yield identical payoffs, both investments today must have the same value to avoid arbitrage (explained earlier).

C_0 = Value of 2/3 of a share – Borrowings
= ₹100 – ₹81.82 = ₹18.18.

The call option should sell at ₹18.18. The net cost of buying the *option equivalent* (Price of 2/3rd share, ₹100 – Borrowings, ₹81.82) is equal to the value of call option.

The BS Formula

Pricing of an option requires building a portfolio in shares and a loan in such a manner that its payoffs are equivalent to the payoffs from the option. We also know that there are five factors which influence the value of option: current share price, exercise price, risk free rate of interest, time to expiration on the option and price volatility of share (measured in terms of variance).

The BS model/formula makes, *inter-alia*, use of the above propositions and factors to determine the value of call option. The additional/redeeming feature of the BS model is that it takes into account the changes in the price of shares at shorter and shorter intervals, with each interval showing two possible changes in share; eventually, a situation is reached in which price of the share is changing continuously and generating a continuum of possible share prices, and, therefore, to replicate option investors must continuously adjust their holdings in the shares. Though in practice, it is not feasible, the BS formulas (explained below) performs remarkably well in the real world where shares trade only intermittently and prices jump from one level to another. In fact, it has become the standard model for valuing options and is used by dealers on the options exchange.

Assumptions[5] The BS model is based on the following assumptions.

(1) It considers only those options which can be exercised at their maturity, that is, European options.

(2) The market is efficient and there are no transaction costs and taxes. Options and shares are infinitely divisible. Information is available to all investors with no costs.

(3) The risk-free rate or interest rate are known and constant during the period of option contract. Investors can borrow as well as lend at this rate.

(4) No dividend is paid on the shares.

(5) Share prices behave in a manner consistent with a random walk in continuous time.

(6) The probability distribution of financial returns on the share is normal.

(7) The variance/standard deviation of the return is constant during the life of the option contract and is known to market participants/investors.

Given these assumptions, the Black-Scholes formulas for the prices of European calls and puts on a non-dividend paying stock are:

$$C = SN(d_1) - E_e^{-rt}\, N(d_2) \quad \textbf{(27.13)}$$

$$P = E_e^{-rt}\, N(-d_2) - SN(-d_1) \quad \textbf{(27.14)}$$

Where $d_1 = \dfrac{\ln S/E + (r + \sigma^2/2)t}{\sigma\sqrt{t}}$

$$d_2 = d_1 - \sigma\sqrt{t}$$

or $\dfrac{\ln(S/E) + \left[r - \frac{1}{2}\sigma^2\right]t}{\sigma\sqrt{t}}$

- The Black-Scholes equation is done in continuous time. This requires continuous compounding. The r is short-term annual interest rate compounded annually.
- $N(d)$ is the cumulative normal distribution. $N(d_1)$ is called the *delta of the option,* which is a measure of change in option price with respect to change in the price of the underlying asset.
- σ, *a measure of volatility,* is the annualised standard deviation of continuously compounded returns on the underlying stock. When daily sigma are given, they need to be converted into annulaised sigma.
- $\text{Sigma}_{\text{annual}} = \text{sigma}_{\text{daily}} \times \sqrt{\text{Number of trading days per year.}}$ On an average, there are 250 trading days in a year.
- E is the exercise price, S the spot price and t the time to expiration measured in years.
- e is 2.71828, the base of natural logarithms and ln is natural logarithm.

In Equation 27.13 $N(d_1)$ represents the option delta or hedge ratio (already explained). The ratio indicates number of shares required to be purchased for each option to maintain a fully hedged position. Further, the option holder is considered as a levered investor and, hence, is required to borrow an amount equal to the present value (*PV*) of exercise price at risk-free interest rate. The aspect of loan is represented on the right side of Equation 27.13; it indicates the *PV* of the exercise price times an adjustment factor of $N(d_2)$. In simple terms, Equation 27.13 shows the following value of call option,

$$C = (\text{Option delta} \times \text{Share price}) - \text{Loan adjusted} \quad \textbf{(27.15)}$$

Application of BS Model The solution of *BS* formula requires five variables. Out of these 5 variables, the four variables, namely, *E, R, T* and *S* are easily observable/known to market participants. The only unknown variable is the standard deviation of the share price; its value can be determined by referring to weekly observations of the share prices in the immediate preceding year; this value of standard deviation can, then, be used as a surrogate in the *BS* formula. The application of *BS* formula is illustrated in Example 27.9.

***Example* 27.9**

From the following information available to a market participant, determine the value of an European call option as per the BS formula.

Spot price of the share = ₹1,120

Exercise price of the call option = ₹1,100

Short-term risk-free interest rate (continuously compounded) = 10 per cent per annum

Time remaining for expiration = 1 month

Volatility of the share/standard deviation = 0.2

Solution

$$C = SN(d_1) - E_e^{-rt} N(d_2)$$

$$d_1 = \frac{\ln S/E + (r + \sigma^2/2)t}{\sigma\sqrt{t}}$$

$$= \frac{\ln(1{,}120/1{,}100) + (0.1 + (0.2)^2/2)(0.08)}{0.2\sqrt{0.08}}$$

$$= \frac{\ln(1.02)\,(\text{as per Table A-6}) + (0.1 + 0.02)(0.08)}{0.2 \times 0.28284}$$

$$d_1 = \frac{0.019803^* \text{ (As per Table A-6(website}^{**}\text{))} + (0.12)(0.08)}{0.2 \times 0.28284 = 0.056568} = 0.5197^*$$

$d_2 = 0.5197 - 0.2\sqrt{0.08}$

$= 0.5197 - 0.2\ (0.28284)$

$= 0.5197 - 0.056568 = 0.4631$

$E_e^{-rt} = 1100e^{-0.008}$

$1100e^{-0.01}$

1100[0.9901 As per Table A-7] (website**)

$= 1089.1$

$C = 1120\ N(0.5197) - 1089.1\ N(0.4631)$

= Values of $N(0.5917)$ and $N(0.4631)$ have been determined with reference to cumulative standardised normal probability distribution Table A-8 (website**)

$= 1120\ [N(0.51) + 0.97\ (N(0.52) - N(0.51))]$

$= 1089.1\ [N(0.46) + 0.31\ (N(0.47) - N(0.46))]$

$= 1120\ [0.6950 + 0.97\ (0.6985 - 0.6950)] - 1089.1\ [0.6772 + 0.31\ (0.6808 - 0.6772)]$

$= 1120\ [0.6950 + 0.003395] - 1089.1\ [0.6772 + 0.001116]$

$= 1120\ [0.698395] - 1089.1\ [0.678316]$

$= 782.20 - 738.75 = 43.45$

Thus, the value of the call option is ₹43.45.

From Example 27.9, it is evident that the application of the BS formula is straight forward, given the availability of statistical tables, computer package or specifically programmed calculators to determine the required inputs. The model has immense theoretical and practical significance to identify the over-valued and under-valued options in the market.

LO 27.6 OPTION MARKET IN INDIA

- The vast majority of participants have relatively a meagre share (upto 20 per cent) in the options compared with other derivative products in the portfolio.
- They have accorded relatively less weightage to options; their major interest being in future contracts.
- An overwhelming majority (95 per cent) of the respondents have been using the option market primarily for hedging; speculation has been the second most preferred objective (75 per cent); and arbitrage emerged as the least preferred objective.

- The respondents encounter more difficulty in valuation of options *vis-à-vis* futures.
- The Black-Scholers (BS) model (of valuing options) has been found to be the most popular amongst the respondents compared with the other two models, namely, Binomial-Tree (BT) and Hull and White (HW) models, the respective percentages being 49, 3 and zero.
- Respondents using BD and BT models (in pricing options) have not considered all the factors reckoned by these models in valuating options; out of six factors, two factors, namely, interest rate and dividend yield have generally not been used.
- A significant number of respondents do not have a proper understanding of the put-call-parity (PCP) relationship. The finding has serious implications for the pricing efficiency of options in India, as the PCP relationship helps to identify the pricing anomalies/arbitrage opportunities to the relative price of call and put options and, in turn, helps to restore equilibrium in the market.
- Majority of the respondents perceived that options in Indian securities market are not correctly priced, causing arbitrage opportunities to exist in the market.
- The vast majority of respondents strongly feel the need of enhanced investors' education on derivatives and recommend for a separate educational body with the public-private partnership (PPP) kind of ownership pattern.

Source: AMDISA, "Option Market in India", South Asian Journal of Management

SUMMARY

LO 27.1

Options are a special type of financial contracts under which the buyers of the options have the right to buy or sell the shares/stocks but do not have obligation to do so.

Essentially, options are of two types: call and put. A call option gives the holder the right, but not the obligation to buy specified stocks at a specified price (known as the exercise price) on or before a specified maturity date. A put option provides the holder the right, but not the obligation to sell securities on or by a certain date at a predetermined exercise price.

The buyer of an option (of call as well as put) is in a privileged position as he will exercise it when he finds it profitable. In other words, the seller/writer of the option is under obligation to buy or sell the securities in case the buyer decides to exercise his option. The writer of the option runs the risk of loss. For assuming such a risk, he is paid option premium by the option buyer; the higher is the risk, the higher is the option premium.

Options can either be an European or an American. While an European option can be exercised only on the expiration date, an American option is more flexible in nature and can be exercised at any time up to the expiration date.

Since the buyer of the option has the right to buy (in the case of call option) and sell (in the case of put option) the stock at a predetermined fixed exercise price, its value at a maturity/expiration date depends on the price of the associated stock on such a date. The value of the call option on the date of maturity is equal to the price of the stock on this date minus the exercise price. It cannot be a negative value as it implies that the call-holder buys the stock at an exercise price (E) which is higher than the market price of the share (S_1). The value of a call option (C_1) on its expiration date is either positive ($S_1 > E$) or zero.

As the call owner is to pay option premium (P), his profit would be $S_1 - (E + P)$. In case the price of a share is less than or equal to exercise price ($S_1 \leq E$), he incurs loss equivalent to the amount of call option premium paid up-front by him. He is at the break-even point (BEP) when $S_1 - (E + P) = $ zero.

LO 27.1	The put option holder will exercise his right to sell the securities if the price of securities fall below the exercise price at the date of expiration. Accordingly, the value of a put option (P_1) is equal to the difference between the exercise price and stock price ($E - S$). Like call options, put options cannot have negative value as the put-owner will obviously not sell at a price lower than the market price ($E < S_1$). In such a situation, his loss is equal to the put option premium. He is at the BEP when $E - (S_1 + P) =$ zero.
LO 27.2	The option - payoffs are very attractive because while the option owner's loss is limited (to the extent of option premium paid), his gains are not so limited. For instance, in the case of a call option, if the market price of the share turns out to be substantially higher than the exercise price, total profit accruing to him will be substantial, in relation to the investment (of option premium) he has made. In other words, options have magnifying financial impact. This, in turn, is caused by large scale dealing possible under option contracts *vis-à-vis* the investment in shares.
LO 27.3	The value of the option is to be in a certain range. While upper range/bound of a call option can never be more than the price of share, its lower bound/range is either zero or equal to the price of the share less exercise price ($C_0 \geq S_0 - E$) which ever is higher. However, in a real/practical market situation, the upper bound is more a theoretical possibility; it is more close to the lower bound. Its value depends on five factors: (i) current share price, S_0, (ii) exercise price, E, (iii) risk-free rate of return, R_f, (iv) time to expiration, t and (v) price-volatility of stock (measured in terms of variance/standard deviation).
LO 27.4	The value of call option (C_0) is $= S_0 - E/(1 + R_f)^t$. The value of C_0 is affected positively by increase in current share price, increase in the risk-free rate of return/interest rate and time to expiration of the option; exercise price has a negative relationship with its value. The greater is the price volatility of share, the greater is the value of the option, all other things remaining the same.
	In efficient markets, it is possible for the market participant (say, call-buyer) to establish a riskless hedged position. The payoffs to the investor would be identical whether he invests in shares or goes for a combination of buying risk-free security (say, invest in treasury bills) and call option from the same investment. This situation of identical payoffs enables us to determine the value of call option at the beginning of the period itself (C_0). Difference in payoffs give rise to riskless arbitrage opportunities to investors. In an efficient/well-organised market, significant arbitrages will, of course, be rare.
LO 27.5	The Black-Scholes option pricing model provides a precise formula to determine the value of call as well as put options. Given certain assumption, the BS formula requires input of five variables, namely, spot price of the share, exercise price, short-term risk-free interest rate (continuously compounded), time remaining for expiration and standard deviation. Out of these five variables, the first four are known to the market participants. The fifth variable related to standard deviation can be determined by referring to weekly observations of the share prices in the immediate preceding year. Given the availability of computer package or specifically programmed calculators, the application of BS formula, in practice, is straight forward and widely used by dealers for valuing options on the options exchange.

REFERENCES

1. Van Horne, James C, *op. cit.*, p. 106.
2. Brealey, R A and Myers, S C, *Principles of Corporate Finance,* (Tata McGraw-Hill, N. Delhi), 2002, p. 597.
3. The discussion is based on Ross, Stephen A et al, *Fundamentals of Corporate Finance* (Tata McGraw Hill, N. Delhi), 2002, pp. 461-467.
4. Brealey, R A and Myers, S C, *op. cit.*, pp. 606-7.
5. Van Horne, James C, *op. cit.*, p. 113.

SOLVED PROBLEMS

P.27.1 An investor has purchased a 4-month call option on the equity share of Birla company for ₹5. It has a present market price per share of ₹112, exercise price of ₹120. At the end of 4 months, the investor expects the price of share to be in the following range of ₹90 to 170 with varying probabilities.

LO 27.1,4 LOD M

Expected price	₹100	₹110	₹125	₹150	₹170
Probability	0.10	0.25	0.30	0.25	0.10

From the above, you are required to answer the following:

1. What is the expected value of share price 4-months hence? What is the value of call option at its expiration (C_1) if the expected value of share price prevails at the end of 4 months?
2. Determine the expected value of option price at maturity, assuming that the call option is held to this time. Why does it differ from the option value determined in part (*i*)?
3. What is the theoretical value of the option, at the beginning of 4-month period? Give comments on the market value of the call option in relation to its theoretical value.

Solution

(i) Expected value of share at the end of 4 months

Expected price	*Probability*	*Expected value of share price*
₹100	0.10	₹10.00
110	0.25	27.50
125	0.30	37.50
150	0.25	37.50
170	0.10	17.00
Expected value of share price		129.50

$C_1 = S_1 - E$

₹129.50 – ₹120 = ₹9.5

(ii) Expected Value of Call Option

Expected price	*Exercise price*	*Call value*	*Probability*	*Expected call value*
₹100	₹120	0	0.10	0
110	120	0	0.25	0
125	120	5	0.30	1.50
150	120	30	0.25	7.50
170	120	50	0.10	5.00
Expected call option value				14.00

Reason for difference: At share prices of less than ₹120, the call option has zero value (as the call option cannot have a negative value). This has enhanced the expected call option value (i.e. ₹14.00) *vis-à-vis* ₹9.5 in part (i). In part (i), calculation is based on negative call option values also as all the share prices have been considered (from ₹100 to 170).

(iii) Theoretical value of call option = *Max.* (S_0 – E, 0) = (₹112 – ₹120, 0) = 0. However, the call option has a positive value of ₹5. The reason is probability distribution of possible share prices (higher than exercise price) is relatively wide. This optimism of the market price of the share explains the positive call option price.

P.27.2 For facts given in **P.27.1**, answer the following:

LO 27.2 LOD M

(i) Determine the gain (loss) to the call option holder if the price of the share at the end of 4-month period ends up at ₹129.50.

(ii) Determine the price of share (on the expiry date of the call option contract) at which the call owner will be at the break-even.

(iii) Determine the maximum loss to the call owner.
(iv) Determine the maximum gain to the call option holder and what is its probability?
(v) What is the maximum gain to the call writer and when will it be possible?
(vi) Determine the price of share (at the end of 4 months) at which the call writer will be at break-even.
(vii) State the major assumption in computing values from (i) to (vi).

Solution

(i) Gain to the call-holder = $S_1 - (E + P)$ where P = Call option premium
= ₹129.50 – (₹120 + ₹5) = ₹4.50
Alternatively, Gain = Value of call option, ₹9.50 – Option premium, ₹5 = ₹4.50.
(ii) *BEP* = (Exercise price on maturity date of call option contract + Option premium paid) = ₹120 + ₹5 = ₹125.
(iii) Maximum loss to the call owner is limited to the call option premium of ₹5 per share.
(iv) The maximum gain to the call option holder = The maximum price of S_1 on the date of maturity, ₹170 – (Exercise price, ₹120 + Premium paid, ₹5) = ₹45. Its probability is 0.10.
(v) The maximum gain to the call writer is ₹5 (i.e., the call option premium received). It will be possible when the price of the share at the expiry date is equal to the exercise price of ₹120 or less.
(vi) *BEP* = Exercise price + Call option premium received = ₹120 + ₹5 = ₹125.
(vii) There are no transaction costs for both call option buyer and call option writer.

P.27.3 A call option at a strike price of ₹170 is selling at a premium of ₹15. At what share price on maturity will it break-even for the buyer of the option? Will the writer of the option also break-even at the same price?

LO 27.2 LOD E

Solution

(i) To recover the call option premium of ₹15, the share price on the date of expiration should rise to (₹15 + ₹170) = ₹185. The buyer of the call option would be at break-even if the share price (S_1) ends-up at ₹185.
(ii) The option writer will also break-even at ₹185. This price is equal to ₹170 exercise price received from the buyer plus ₹15 option premium already received up-front.

P.27.4 A stock currently sells at ₹120. The put option to sell the stock sells at ₹135 and costs ₹18. Determine the time value of the option.

LO 27.2 LOD E

Solution

Time value of option = (Option premium – Intrinsic value of the option, $S_1 - E$)
= ₹18 – (₹134 – ₹120) = ₹4.

P.27.5 An investor is bullish about Cipla which trades in the spot market at ₹1,025. He buys two one-month call option contracts (having a market lot of 100) on Cipla with a strike price of ₹1,050 at a premium of ₹10 per call. Three months later, Cipla is selling at ₹1,080. Compute his profit on the position.

LO 27.2 LOD E

Solution Investor's profits are = (₹1,080, S_1 – ₹1,050, E – ₹10, P) × 2 × 100 = ₹4,000.

P.27.6 Vijay is bullish about the index. Spot Nifty stands at ₹1,300. He decides to buy one three-month Nifty call option contract with a strike price of ₹1,350 at ₹50 a call. Three months later, the index closes at 1,340. Determine the amount of profit (or loss) to Vijay. Assume the market lot is of 200.

LO 27.2 LOD E

Solution Vijay loses as the Nifty index on the date of maturity is lower (at ₹1,340) than the exercise price (₹1,350). He loses the entire sum of call premium (₹50 × 200 units) = ₹10,000.

P.27.7 Akbar is bearish about the index. Spot Nifty stands at ₹1,250. He decides to buy two three-month Nifty put option contract (each contract has a market lot of 200) with a strike price of ₹1,275 at a premium of ₹40. Three months later, the index closes at ₹1,225. Compute his pay off on the position.

LO 27.2 LOD E

Solution Akbar earns on the put option contract as the closing index is lower than the strike price. His gain is (₹1,275, E – ₹1,225, S_1 – ₹40, P) × 400 = ₹4,000.

P.27.8 An investor buys one market lot of December ₹1,230 Nifty calls at ₹70 a call, and sells one market lot of December ₹1,300 Nifty calls for ₹34 a call. If the Nifty closes at ₹1,210 on the expiration date, what is the payoff from this spread position. LO 27.2 LOD M

Solution Since Nifty closes at ₹1,210 on the expiration date (lower than the exercise prices of ₹1,230 and ₹1,300), both the options are out-of-the-money. Therefore, neither the investor himself nor the call-buyer from him will exercise their call options. Therefore, the payoff from the spread is the amount he has paid on buying the call option and the amount he has received on selling the option. As the amount paid as premium is more than the amount received, he suffers loss of (₹70 – ₹34) × 200 = ₹7,200.

P.27.9 Maurti's share price is at present ₹120. After 6-months, its price will be either ₹150 with probability of 0.8 or ₹110 with probability of 0.20. An European call option exists with an exercise price of ₹130. Based on these facts, answer the following: LO 27.1,2 LOD M

(i) As a call option writer, if you intend to create a perfectly hedged position, what will you do?

(ii) What will be the value of your hedged position in each of these two possibilities?

(iii) What is the expected value of call option price at the maturity date?

Solution

(i) Hedge ratio = (Spread of possible call option prices, ΔC/Spread of possible share prices, ΔS)

ΔC = (₹20 – 0); ΔS = (₹150 – ₹110)

C_1 = Max (S_1 – E, 0) = ₹150 = ₹130 = ₹20 when share price is ₹150 and it is zero when share price is ₹110. Hedge ratio = ₹20/₹40 = 0.5

The hedge ratio of 0.5 implies that the call option writer is to purchase one share of Maruti in a long position for every 2 call options sold (short position).

(ii) Value of hedged position at two share prices

Particulars	*Amount*
(a) When the share price is ₹150/Call option value is ₹20	
Value of long position in shares (1 × ₹150)	₹150
Less: Loss on exercising call option right on 2 calls by call option buyer (2 × ₹20)	40
'Value of hedged position	110
(b) When share price is ₹10/Call option value is zero	
Value of long position in share (1 × ₹110)	110
Less: Value of call option	0
Value of hedged position	110

Thus, the value of the hedged position to the call option writer is the same irrespective of the share price of Maruti, six months hence.

(iii) Expected value of call option

Expected share price	*Exercise price*	*Call value*	*Probability*	*Expected call option value*
₹110	₹130	0	0.2	0
150	130	20	0.8	16
Expected value of call option				16

P.27.10 A patient investor is interested in buying a call option on TCS equity share to be exercised exactly after two years from now with exercise price of ₹200. The share's current market price is ₹180. He expects after two years, the price of TCS share will be either at ₹210 or ₹240. The risk-free rate of interest is 6 per cent. Based on the above information, answer the following: LO 27.1,2 LOD D

(i) What are the expected value of option prices at the end of two years?
(ii) As a call option buyer, what will you do to have the same payoffs from both alternatives, i.e., shares and call option?

Solution

(i) $C_1 = Max\,(S_1 - E, 0)$

(a) *When* S_1 = *₹210*

C_1 = ₹210 – ₹200 = ₹10

(b) *When* S_1 = *₹240*

C_1 = ₹240 – 200 = ₹40

(ii) (a) In the case of investment in shares of TCS, his investment value will be either ₹210 or ₹240 at year-end 2.

(b) In the case of the second alternative, the investor is to invest in risk-free securities (say, treasury bills). The amount is given by $E/(1 + R_f)^t$ = ₹200/(1 + 0.06)2

= ₹200 × 0.890 (PV of rupee one at year-end 2 discounted at 6 per cent) = ₹178.

Obviously, this sum will compound to ₹200 after 2 years at rate of interest of 6 per cent.

To this sum of ₹200, the value of call option is to be added which will be either ₹10 or ₹40. As a result, the investment value will be either ₹200 + ₹10 = ₹210 or ₹200 + ₹40 = ₹240.

Thus, the value of the investment at year-end 2 is the same irrespective of the price of the TCS share at the date of expiration.

P.27.11 If the daily volatility of the Nifty is 1.75 and 250 trading days in a year, compute the *sigma* figure used in the BS formula. LO 27.5 LOD E

Solution The Black-Scholes formula uses the annualised sigma. The daily sigma must be expressed in terms of the annualised sigma.

Sigma (annual) = Sigma (daily) × $\sqrt{\text{Number of trading days per year}}$

On an average, there are 250 trading days in a year.

Sigma (annual) = 1.75 × $\sqrt{250}$ = 1.75 × 15.81 = 27.67 per cent.

P.27.12 If the continuously compounded annual risk free rate is 0.095 per cent, compute the '*r*' used in the BS formula. LO 27.5 LOD E

Solution The BS equation is based on continuous compounding. The '*r*' that figures in this must be the continuously compounded rate. In this case, it is 0.095.

P.27.13 On March 1, a call option on the Nifty with a strike price of ₹1,300 is available for trading. Expiration date is 31st March. Compute '*t*' that is used in the BS formula. LO 27.5 LOD M

Solution The time to expiration is 31 days. The '*t*' used in the BS is time-to-expiration measured in years. Hence, the '*t*' used = 31/365 = 0.08.

P.27.14 A stock is currently trading for ₹28. The riskless interest rate is 6 per cent per annum continuously compounded. Estimate the value of European call option with a strike price of ₹30 and a time of expiration of 3 months. The standard deviation of the stock's annual return is 0.44. Apply BS model. LO 27.5 LOD M

Solution

Spot price of the share (*S*)	₹28
Exercise price of the call option (*E*)	30
Risk-free interest rate (*r*)	0.06
Time remaining for expiration (*t*) = 3 months = 3/12 (year)	0.25
Volatility of the stock (*σ*)	0.44

The value of European call option can be obtained by using Black-Scholes option pricing model. $C = S\,N(d_1) - E_e^{-rt}\,N(d_2)$

Computation of call option essentially requires calculation of three values, viz., d_1, d_2 and present value of the exercise price (E_e^{-rt}).

$$d_1 = \frac{\ln S/E + (r + \sigma^2/2)t}{\sigma\sqrt{t}}$$

Substituting values from the information given above we get

$$d_1 = \frac{\ln(28/30) + (0.06 + (0.44)^2/2)\,0.25}{0.44\sqrt{0.25}}$$

$$d_1 = \frac{\ln(0.9333) + (0.06 + 0.0968)\,0.25}{0.44(0.5)}$$

$$\ln(0.9333) = \text{Log}_{10}(0.9333) \times 2.3026$$
$$= (\bar{1}.9700) \times 2.3026$$
$$= (\bar{1} + 0.9700) \times 2.3026$$
$$= -2.3026 + 2.2335$$

$$\ln(0.9333) = -0.0691$$

$$d_1 = \frac{-0.0691 + 0.0392}{0.22} = -0.1359$$

$$d_2 = d_1 - \sigma\sqrt{t} = -0.1359 - (0.44)\sqrt{0.25}$$
$$d_2 = -0.3559$$

and $$E\,e^{-rt} = 30\,e^{-(0.06 \times 0.25)} = 30\,e^{-0.015}$$
$$= 30\,e^{-0.02}\ (e^{-0.02} = 0.9802 \text{ as per Table A – 7})$$
$$= 30\,(0.9802) = 29.406$$

The equation of call option looks like $C = 28\,N(-0.1359) - 29.406\,N(-0.3559)$

The next step is to look up the values of a cumulative standardised normal probability distribution at (– 0.1359) and (– 0.3559)

$$N(-0.1359) = N(-0.13) - 0.59\,[N(-0.13) - N(-0.14)]$$
$$= 0.4483 - 0.59\,[0.4483 - 0.4443]$$
$$= 0.4483 - 0.00236 = 0.4459$$
$$N(-0.3559) = N(-0.35) - 0.59\,[N(-0.35) - N(-0.36)]$$
$$= 0.3632 - 0.59\,[0.3632 - 0.3594]$$
$$= 0.3632 - 0.00224 = 0.3610$$
$$C = 28\,(0.4459) - 29.406\,(0.3610)$$
$$= 12.4852 - 10.6156 = ₹1.87$$

Thus, the value of European call option is ₹1.87.

REVIEW QUESTIONS

LOD: Easy

RQ.27.1 Indicate whether the following statements are true or false: [LO 27.1-5]

(i) An option is a contract that gives a right to its holder along with the responsibility to purchase/sell stipulated units of underlying asset at the predetermined rate on/up to a specified date.

(ii) An option writer is one who sells an option contract.

(iii) Expiration date is the date beyond which the option has no value.

(iv) Strike price is the price at which the holder of the option can buy/sell the underlying asset.

(v) American and European options are alike.

(vi) At a given point of time, spot rate > exercise price in the case of in-the-money option, either call or put.

(vii) A call/put option is a contract that gives the right but not the responsibility to its holder to purchase/sell the underlying asset at a stipulated price on/up to a specified date.

(viii) Writing a call option and a put option will result in the same course of action.

(ix) A holder of a call option can incur losses at the most upto the amount of premium he pays.

(x) A put option holder can earn profits at the most (theoretically) up to its strike price.

(xi) The intrinsic value of an out of the money option is negative.

[Answers: (i) False (ii) True (iii) True (iv) True (v) False (vi) False (vii) True (viii) False (ix) True (x) True (xi) False]

(b) Identify the correct answer out of the choices provided:

(i) Value of an out of the money option is
(a) Zero **(b)** Negative **(c)** $(S_0 - E)$ **(d)** $(E - S_0)$

(ii) The price of a call option contract should not be less than
(a) $(S_0 - E)$ **(b)** $(E - S_0)$ **(c)** S_0 **(d)** E

(iii) The maximum price of a call option contract should not be more than
(a) $(S_0 - E)$ **(b)** $(E - S_0)$ **(c)** S_0 **(d)** E

(iv) Time value of an option is
(a) Price of the option – Intrinsic value of the option
(b) Intrinsic value of the option – Price of the option
(c) $(S_0 - E)$ **(d)** $(E - S_0)$

(v) Fair value of an option represents
(a) Intrinsic value of the option **(b)** Time value of the option
(c) Both **(d)** None of the above

(vi) Which of the following factor(s) has/have a bearing on the option price
(a) Price of the underlying asset **(b)** Time to maturity
(c) Strike price **(d)** Volatility of underlying asset
(e) Risk-free rate of return **(f)** All of them

[Answers: (i) a (ii) a (iii) c (iv) a (v) c (vi) f]

RQ.27.2 What is a call option? State the situation when you will like to go for such an option. When will you not exercise it? [LO 27.1]

RQ.27.3 What is a put option? Specify whether put option owner expects the share price to rise or fall. [LO 27.1]

RQ.27.4 Mr. Kapoor is bullish about the index. Spot Nifty stands at ₹1,250. He decides to buy one three-month Nifty call option contract with a strike of ₹1,290, at ₹20 per call three months later, the index closes at ₹1,330. Assuming a market lot size of 200, compute his payoff on the position. [LO 27.2]

RQ.27.5 Assuming that the daily volatility of the Nifty is 1.75 and trading happens on 256 days in a year. Compute the sigma figure used in the Black-Scholes formula. [LO 27.4]

LOD: Medium

RQ.27.6 Do you subscribe to the view that the buyer of the call as well as the seller of the put have the identical expectations pertaining to the share prices? Explain your answer with appropriate example. [LO 27.1]

RQ.27.7 What is the value of a call option on maturity? When the call option owner is said to be at break-even? Can the value of call option be negative? [LO 27.1,2]

RQ.27.8 "Option investments have magnifying impact on financial gains and losses compared to share investments." Elucidate the statement with appropriate example. [LO 27.1,2]

RQ.27.9 Indicate the factors that influence call option's value. What is the effect of an increase in each of these factors on the value of a call option? [LO 27.4]

RQ.27.10 Describe in brief the Black-Scholes model of option pricing. State its major assumptions also. [LO 27.5]

RQ.27.11 Ramesh is bearish about the index. Spot Nifty stands at 1,250. He decides to buy one three-month Nifty put option contract (of 200) with a strike of ₹1,225 at ₹27 a put. Three months later the index closes at 1,260. What is his pay off on the position? [LO 27.2]

RQ.27.12 An investor has purchased a 3-month call option on Reliance share for ₹8 with exercise price of ₹132. Its current market price is ₹120. At the end of 3 months, the investor expects the price of share to be in the following range of ₹100 to 160 with varying probabilities. [LO 27.4]

Expected price	₹100	₹115	₹130	₹150	₹160
Probability	0.15	0.20	0.30	0.20	0.15

From the above, determine the expected value of option price at maturity, assuming that the call option is held to this time.

LOD: Difficult

RQ.27.13 What are the upper and lower boundaries on the value of a call option any time before maturity? Which limit do you expect to be more realistic? State reasons in support of your answer. [LO 27.3]

RQ.27.14 Do you agree that an option is always more risky than the associated share with it? How does the risk of an option change when the share price changes? [LO 27.1,2]

ANSWERS

27.4 Gain = ₹4,000
27.5 28 per cent
27.11 Loss = ₹5,400
27.12 Value of call option = ₹7.8

Scan the QR Code to access comprehensive solutions to all numerical review questions and additional material.

CHAPTER

28 Derivatives: Managing Financial Risk

LEARNING OBJECTIVES

LO 28.1	Discuss forward contracts and their usefulness in hedging and speculation, and limitations of forward contracts
LO 28.2	Explain the features of future contracts, the distinction between futures and forwards, payoffs for futures and pricing of futures—index futures and stock futures
LO 28.3	Examine the fundamental characteristics of option contracts, the distinction between futures and options and the option payoffs and pricing of options
LO 28.4	Summarise the structure of derivative market in India

INTRODUCTION

This Chapter describes derivatives. **Derivative** instruments are defined by the Securities Contracts (Regulation) Act to include **(1)** a security derived from a debt instrument, share, secured/unsecured loan, risk instrument or contract for differences, or any other form of security and **(2)** a contract that derives its value from the prices/index of prices of underlying securities. Derivative contracts have several variants. The most common variants are forwards, futures and options. Three broad categories of participants—*hedgers*, *speculators* and *arbitrageurs*—trade in the derivatives market. Hedgers face risk associated with the price of an asset. They use futures or options markets to reduce/eliminate this risk. Speculators wish to bet on future movements in the price of an asset. Futures and options contracts can give them an extra leverage, that is, they can increase both the potential gains and potential losses in a speculative venture. Arbitrageurs are in business to take advantage of a discrepancy between prices in two different markets. If, for example, they see the futures price of an asset getting out of line with the cash price, they will take offsetting positions in the two markets to lock-in a profit.

Derivatives are instruments which include (a) security derived from a debt instrument, share, loan, risk instrument or contract for differences or any other form of security and (b) a contract that derives its value from the price/index of prices of underlying securities.

The derivatives market performs a number of *economic functions*. First, prices in an organised derivatives market reflect the perception of the market participants about the future and lead the prices of underlying to the perceived future level. The prices of derivatives converge with the prices of the underlying at the expiration of the derivatives contract. Thus, derivatives help in the discovery of the future as well as current prices. Second, the derivatives market helps to transfer risks from those who have them but may not like them to those who have an appetite for them. Third, derivatives, due to their inherent nature, are linked to the underlying cash markets. With the introduction of derivatives, the underlying market witnesses higher trading volumes because of participation by more players who would not otherwise participate for lack of an arrangement to transfer risk. Fourth, speculative trades shift to a more controlled environment of derivatives market. In the absence of an organised derivatives market, speculators trade in the underlying cash markets. Margining, monitoring and surveillance of the activities of various participants become extremely difficult in these kind of mixed markets. Fifth, an important incidental benefit that flows from derivatives trading is that it acts as a catalyst for new entrepreneurial activity. Derivatives have a history of attracting many bright, creative, well educated people with an entrepreneurial attitude. They often energise others to create new businesses, new products and new employment opportunities, the benefit of which are immense. Finally, derivatives markets help increase savings and investment in the long-run. Transfer of risk enables market participants to expand their volume of activity. The chapter dwells on the three most commonly used derivative contracts, namely, forwards, futures and options. The main points are summarised by way of recapitulation.

LO 28.1 FORWARD CONTRACTS

> **Forward contract** is an agreement to buy (long position) or sell (short position) an asset/security on a specified date for a specified price; settlement happens at the end of the period.

A **forward contract** is an agreement to buy or sell an asset on a specified date for a specified price. One of the parties to the contract assumes a long position and agrees to buy the underlying asset on a certain specified future date, for a certain specified price. The other party assumes a short position and agrees to sell the asset on the same date for the same price. Other contract details like delivery date, price and quantity are negotiated bilaterally by the parties to the contract. Forward contracts are normally traded outside stock exchanges. They are popular on the Over the Counter (OTC) market. The *salient features* of forward contracts are as follows: **(i)** They are bilateral contracts and, hence, exposed to counterparty risk; **(ii)** Each contract is customer designed, and, hence, is unique in terms of contract size, expiration date and the asset type and quality; **(iii)** The contract price is generally not available in public domain; **(iv)** On the expiration date, the contract has to be settled by delivery of the asset and **(v)** If a party wishes to reverse the contract, it has to compulsorily go to the same counterparty, which often results in a high price being charged. However, forward contracts in certain markets have become very standardised, as in the case of foreign exchange, thereby reducing transaction costs and increasing transaction volume. This process of standardisation reaches its limit in the organised futures market.

Forward contracts are very useful in hedging and speculation. A classic hedging application would be that of an exporter who expects to receive payment in dollars, three months later. He is exposed to the risk of exchange rate fluctuations. By using the currency forward market to sell dollars forward, he can lock-on a rate today and reduce his certainty. Similarly, an importer who is required to make a payment in dollars two months hence can reduce his exposure to exchange rate fluctuations by buying dollars forward. If a speculator has information or analysis, which forecasts an upturn in a price, he can go along on the forward market instead of the cash market. The speculator would go long on the forward, wait for the price to rise and then take a reversing transaction to book profits. Speculators may well be required to deposit a margin up-front. However, this is generally a relatively small proportion of the value of the assets underlying the forward contract. The use of forward markets here supplies leverage to the speculator.

Limitations of Forward Contracts

Forward markets are afflicted by several problems: **(i)** Lack of centralisation of trading, **(ii)** Liquidity and **(iii)** Counterparty risk. The basic problem in the first two is that they have too much flexibility and generality. The forward market is like a real estate market in that any two consenting adults can form contracts against each other. This often makes them design terms of the deal that are very convenient in that specific situation, but makes the contracts non-tradable. **Counterparty risk** arises from the possibility of default by any one party to the transaction. When one of the two sides to the transaction declares bankruptcy, the other suffers. Even when forward markets trade standarised contracts and, hence, avoid the problem of illiquidity, the counterparty risk remains a very serious issue.

Counter party risk is the possibility of default by any one party to the transaction.

LO 28.2 FUTURES/FUTURE CONTRACTS

Futures markets are designed to solve the problems that exist in forward markets. A **futures contract** is an agreement between two parties to buy or sell an asset at a certain time in the future, at a certain price. But unlike forward contracts, futures contracts are standardised and stock ex-change traded. To facilitate liquidity in the futures contracts, the exchange specifies certain standard features for the contract. It is a standardised contract with a standard underlying instrument, a standard quantity and quality of the underlying instrument that can be delivered, (or which can be used for reference purposes in settlement) and a standard timing of such settlement. A futures contract may be offset prior to maturity by entering into an equal and opposite transaction. The standardised items in a futures contract are: **(i)** Quantity of the underlying, **(ii)** Quality of the underlying, **(iii)** The date/month of delivery, **(iv)** The units of price quotation and minimum price change and **(v)** Location of settlement. The distinction between forward and future contracts are listed in Table 28.1.

Future contract/ futures is an agreement between two parties to buy/sell an asset /security at a certain time in future; it follows daily settlement.

TABLE 28.1 Distinction Between Futures and Forwards

Futures	*Forwards*
1. Traded on an organised stock exchange	1. Over the Counter (OTC) in nature
2. Standardised contract terms, hence, more liquid	2. Customised contract terms, hence, less liquid
3. Requires margin payments	3. No margin payment
4. Follows daily settlement	4. Settlement happens at the end of the period

Thus, future contracts are a significant improvement over forward contracts as they eliminate counterparty risk and offer more liquidity. This section illustrates future contracts with reference to **(i)** Futures terminology, **(ii)** Payoff for futures, **(iii)** Pricing futures, **(iv)** Issuing index futures and **(v)** Using futures on individual securities (stock futures).

Futures Terminology

Important terms associated with futures contracts are as follows:

Spot Price The price at which an instrument/asset trades in the spot market.

Future Price The price at which the futures contract trade in the future market.

Contract Cycle The period over which a contract trades. For instance, the index futures contracts typically have one month, two months and three months expiry cycles that expire on the last Thursday of the month. Thus, a January expiration contract expires on the last Thursday of January and a February expiration contract ceases trading on the last Thursday of February. On the Friday following the last Thursday, a new contract having three month expiry is introduced for trading.

Expiry Date It is the date specified in the futures contract. This is the last day on which the contract will be traded, at the end of which it will cease to exist.

Contract Size The amount of asset that has to be delivered under one contract. For instance, the contract size of the NSE future market is 200 Nifties.

Basis Basis is defined as the futures price minus the spot price. There will be a different basis for each delivery month for each contract. In a normal market, basis will be positive. This reflects that futures prices normally exceed spot prices.

Cost of Carry The relationship between futures prices and spot prices can be summarised in terms of the cost of carry. This measures the storage cost plus the interest that is paid to finance the asset, less the income earned on the asset.

Initial Margin The amount that must be deposited in the margin account at the time a futures contract is first entered into is the initial margin.

Marking to Market In the futures market, at the end of each trading day, the margin account is adjusted to reflect the investor's gain or loss depending upon the futures closing price. This is called marking to market.

Maintenance Margin This is somewhat lower than the initial margin. This is set to ensure that the balance in the margin account never becomes negative. If the balance in the margin account falls below the maintenance margin, the investor receives a margin call and is expected to top up the margin account to the initial margin level before trading commences on the next day.

Payoff for Futures

Payoffs is the likely profit/loss that should accrue to the market participant with change in the price of the underlying asset.

A **payoff** is the likely profit/loss that would accrue to a market participant with change in the price of the underlying asset. Futures contracts have **linear payoffs**. In simple words, it means that the losses as well as profits, for the buyer and the seller of futures contracts, are unlimited. The pay off for futures, that is, for buyers (long futures) and sellers (short futures) is discussed below.

Linear payoff implies losses as well as profits for both the buyer and the seller of futures are unlimited.

Payoff for Buyer of Futures: Long Futures The pay offs for a person who buys a futures contract is similar to the pay off for a person who holds an asset. He has a potentially unlimited upside as well as downside. Take the case of a speculator who buys a two month Nifty index futures contract when the Nifty stands at 1220. The underlying asset in this case is the Nifty portfolio. When the index moves up, the long futures position starts making profits and when the index moves down it starts making losses.

Payoff for Seller of Futures: Short Futures The payoff for a person who sells a futures contract is similar to the payoff for a person who shorts an asset. He has a potentially unlimited upside as well as downside. Take the case of a speculator who sells a two month Nifty index futures contact when the Nifty stands at 1220. The underlying asset in this case is the Nifty portfolio. When the index moves down, the short futures position starts making profits and when the index moves up, it starts making losses. The payoff for futures is illustrated in Examples 28.1 to 28.4.

***Example* 28.1**

On January 15, X bought a January Nifty futures contract that cost him ₹5,38,000. For this he had to pay an initial margin of ₹43,040 to his broker. Each Nifty futures contract is for the delivery of 200 Nifties. On January 25, the index closed at 2,720. How much profit/loss did he make?

Solution

X bought one futures contract costing him ₹5,38,000. At a market lot of 200, this means he paid ₹2,690 per Nifty future. On the futures expiration day, the futures price converges to the spot price. If the index closed at 2,720 this must be the futures close price as well. Hence, he would have made of profit of (₹2,720 – ₹2,690) × 200 = ₹6,000.

***Example* 28.2**

X sold a January Nifty futures contract for ₹5,38,000, on January 15. For this he had to pay an initial margin of ₹43,040 to his broker. Each Nifty futures contract is for the delivery of 200 Nifties. On January 25, the index closed at 2,520. How much profit/loss did me make?

Solution

X sold one futures contract costing in ₹5,38,000. At a market lot of 200, this works out to be ₹2,690 per Nifty future. On the futures expiration day, the futures price converges to the spot price. If the index closed at 2,520 this must be the futures close price as well. Hence, he would have made profit of (₹2,690 – ₹2,520) × 200 = ₹34,000.

***Example* 28.3**

On January 15, X bought one January Nifty futures contract that cost him ₹2,69,000. For this he had to pay an initial margin of ₹21,520 to his broker. Each Nifty contract is for the delivery of 200 Nifties. On January 25, the index closed at 1,280. How much profit/loss did he make?

Solution

X bought one futures contract for ₹2,69,000. At a market lot of 200, this means he paid ₹1,345 per Nifty future. On the futures expiration day, the futures price converges to the spot price. If the index closed at 1,280, this must be the futures close price as well. Hence, he made of loss of (₹1,345 – ₹1,280) × 200 = ₹13,000.

***Example* 28.4**

X sold one January Nifty futures contract for ₹2,69,000, on January 15. For this he had to pay an initial margin of ₹21,520 to his broker. Each Nifty futures contract is for the delivery of 200 Nifties. On January 25, the index closed at 1,390. How much profit/loss did he make?

Solution

X sold one futures contract for ₹2,69,000. In a market lot of 200, this works out to be ₹1,345 per Nifty future. On the futures expiration day, the futures price converges to the spot price. If the index closed at 1,390, this must be the futures close price as well. Hence, he made of loss of (₹1,390 – ₹1,345) × 200 = ₹9,000.

Pricing Futures

The pricing of futures is illustrated below with reference to **(1)** The Cost-of-Carry Model, **(2)** Pricing equity index futures and **(3)** Pricing stock futures.

The Cost-of-Carry Model The cost-of-carry model explains the dynamics of pricing that constitute the estimation of the fair value of futures. The fair value calculation of futures is used to decide the no arbitrage limits on the price of a future contract. According to this model, using discrete compounding, where interest rates are compounded at discrete intervals, (for example, annually/semi-annually) the price of the contract is defined as:

Cost of carry model explains the dynamics of pricing that constitute the estimation of the fair value of futures.

$$F = S + C \quad \textbf{(28.1)}$$

where F = Futures price,
S = Spot price, and
C = Holdings costs or carry posts

This can also be expressed as:

$$F = S(1 + r)^T \quad \textbf{(28.1.1)}$$

where r = Cost of financing and T = Time till expiration

If $F < S(1 + r)^T$ or $F > S(1 + r)^T$, arbitrage opportunities would exist, that is, whenever the futures price moves away from the fair value, there would be chances for arbitrage. The components of holding cost vary with contracts on different assets. At times, the holding cost may even be negative. In the case of commodity futures, the holding cost is the cost of financing plus cost of storage and insurance purchased and so on. In the case of equity futures, the holding cost is the cost of financing minus the dividends returns.

Using continuous compounding, the Equation 28.1 would be expressed as

$$F = Se^{rT} \quad \textbf{(28.2)}$$

where r = Cost of financing (using continuously compounded interest rate),
T = Time till expiration, and
e = 2.71828

To illustrate cost of carry, let us take an example of a futures contract on a commodity and work out the cost of contract. The spot price January 1, Year 1, of silver is assumed to be ₹7,000/ kg. Assuming an annual cost of financing of 15 per cent and no storage cost, the fair value of the future price of 100 gms of silver one month hence (January 30, Year 1) would be as follows:

$$F = S(1 + r)^T + C = ₹700\ (₹7{,}000 \div 10)\ [1.15] \times 30/365 = ₹708$$

If the contract is for a three month period expiring on March 30, Year 1, the cost of financing would increase the future price, that is, F = ₹700 (1.15) × 90/365 = ₹724.5. If, however, the one month contract was for 10,000 kgs, it would involve storage cost and the price of the future contract would be ₹708 plus the cost of storage.

Pricing Index Futures A futures contract on the stock market gives its owner the right and obligation to buy or sell the portfolio of stocks characterised by the index. Stock index futures are cash settled; there is no delivery of the underlying stocks. The main differences between commodity and equity index futures are that: **(i)** There are no costs of storage involved in holding equity and **(ii)** Equity comes with a dividend stream, which is a negative cost if you are long the stock and a positive cost if you are short the stock. Therefore, cost of carry = financing cost – dividends. Thus, a crucial aspect of dealing with equity futures, as opposed to commodity futures, is an accurate forecasting of dividends. The better the forecast of dividend offered by a security, the better is the estimate of the futures price. The pricing of equity index futures is illustrated below with reference to **(i)** expected dividend amount and **(ii)** expected dividend yield.

Index futures is a future contract that gives the owner the right/obligation to buy/sell the portfolio of stocks characterised by the index.

Pricing Index Futures Given Expected Dividend Amount The pricing of index futures is also based on the cost-of-carry model, where the carrying cost is the cost of financing the purchase of the portfolio underlying the index, minus the present value of dividends obtained from the stocks in the index portfolio. Consider Example 28.5.

***Example* 28.5**

Nifty futures trades on a stock exchange (NSE) as one, two and three-month contracts. Money can be borrowed at a rate of 15 per cent per annum. Compute the price of a new two month futures contract on Nifty of X Ltd (XL).

Solution Let us assume that XL will be declaring a dividend of ₹10 per share after 15 days of purchasing the contract. The current value of Nifty is 1,200 and Nifty trades with a multiplier of 200. The value of the contract is 200 × ₹1200 = ₹2,40,000. If XL has a weight of 7 per cent in Nifty, its value in Nifty is ₹16,800 (₹2,40,000 × 0.07). If the market price of XL is ₹140, a traded unit of Nifty involves 120 shares (₹16,800/140). To calculate the futures price, we need to reduce the cost-of-carry to the extent of the dividend received. The amount of dividend received is ₹1,200 (120 × ₹10). The dividend is received 15 days later and, hence, compounded only for the reminder of the 45 days. To calculate the futures price we need to compute the amount of dividend received per unit of Nifty. Hence, we divide the compounded dividend figure by 200. Thus, the futures price is

$$F = 1{,}200\ (1.15)\ 60/365 - \frac{[120 \times 10\,(1.15) \times 45/365]}{200} = ₹1{,}221.80$$

Pricing Index Futures Given Expected Dividend Yield If the dividend flow throughout the year is generally uniform, that is, there are few historical cases of clustering of dividends in any particular month, it is useful to calculate the annual dividend yield.

$$F = S(1 + r - q)^T \qquad \textbf{(28.3)}$$

where F = futures price,
S = spot index value,
r = cost of financing,
q = expected dividend yield, and
T = holding period

***Example* 28.6**

A two month futures contract trades on the NSE. The cost of financing is 15 per cent and the dividend yield on Nifty is 2 per cent annualised. The spot value of Nifty is ₹1,200. What is the fair value of the futures contract?

Solution

Fair value = ₹1,200 (1 + 0.15 – 0.02) × 60.365 = ₹1,224.35

The cost-of-carry model explicitly defines the relationship between the futures price and the related spot price. The difference between the spot price and the futures price is called the **basis**. As the date of expiration comes near, the basis reduces: there is a *convergence* of the futures price towards the spot price. On the date of expiration, the basis is zero. If it is not, then there is an arbitrage opportunity. Arbitrage opportunities can also arise when the basis (difference between spot and futures price) or the spreads (difference between prices of two futures contracts) during the life of a contract are incorrect. How these arbitrage opportunities can be exploited is discussed subsequently. There is nothing but cost-of-carry related arbitrage that drives the behaviour of the futures price. Moreover, transactions costs are very important in the business of arbitrage. However, these pricing models give an approximate idea about the true future price. The price observed in the market is the outcome of the price discovery mechanism (demand-supply principle) and may differ from the so called true price.

Pricing Stock Futures A futures contract on a stock gives its owner the right and obligation to buy or sell the stocks. Like index futures, stock futures are also cash settled; there is no delivery of the underlying stocks. Just as in the case of index futures, the main difference between commodity and stock futures are that: **(i)** There are no costs of storage involved in holding stock, and **(ii)** Stocks come with a dividend stream, which is a negative cost if you are long) the stock and a positive cost if you are short the stock. Therefore, cost of carry = financing cost – dividends. Thus, a crucial aspect of dealing with stock futures, as opposed to commodity futures, is an accurate forecasting of dividends. The better the forecast of dividend offered by a security, the better is the estimate of the futures price. The pricing of stock futures is discussed below when **(i)** no dividend is expected, **(ii)** when dividend is expected.

Stock futures is a future contract that gives its owner the right/obligation to buy/sell the stocks (shares).

Pricing Stock Futures When No Dividend Expected The pricing of stock futures is also based on the cost-of-carry model, where the carrying cost is the cost of financing the purchase of the stock, minus the present value of dividends obtained from the stock. If no dividends are expected during the life of the contract, pricing futures on that stock is very simple. It simply involves multiplying the spot price by the cost of carry.

Example **28.7**

SBI futures trade on NSE as one, two and three-month contracts. Money can be borrowed at 15 per cent per annum. What will the price of a unit of new two month futures contract on the SBI be if no dividends are expected during the two month period, assuming spot price of the SBI is ₹228?

Solution

Futures price, F = ₹228 × (1.15) × 60/365 = ₹233.30

Pricing Stock Futures When Dividends Are Expected When dividends are expected during the life of the futures contract, pricing involves reducing the cost of carry to the extent of the dividends. The net carrying cost is the cost of financing the purchase of the stock, minus the present value of dividends obtained from the stock.

Example **28.8**

XL futures trade on NSE as one, two and three month contracts. What will the price of a unit of new two-month futures contract on XL be if dividends are expected during the two month period? Assume that XL will be declaring a dividend of ₹10 per share after 15 days of purchasing the contract. The market price of XL may be assumed as ₹140.

Solution

To calculate the futures price, we need to reduce the cost-of-carry to the extent of dividend received. The amount of dividend received is ₹10. The dividend is received 15 days later and, hence, compounded only for the remainder of 45 days. Thus, the futures price, F = ₹140 × (1.15) × 60/365 – [10 × (1.15) × 45/365] = ₹133.08.

LO 28.3 OPTIONS/OPTIONS CONTRACTS

Options are fundamentally different from forward and futures contracts. An **option** gives the holder of the option the right to do something. The holder does not have to necessarily exercise this right. In contrast, in a forward or futures contract, the two parties have committed themselves to doing something. Whereas it costs nothing (except margin requirements) to enter into a futures contract, the purchase of an option requires an up front payment. This section discusses and illustrates options as a derivative contract, with reference to **(i)** Option terminology, **(ii)** Comparison of options and futures, **(iii)** Option payoffs, **(iv)** Pricing options and **(v)** Using stock options.

Option/option contract is a contract that gives the holder the right but not the obligation to buy/sell an asset/security.

Option Terminology

Index Options These options have the index as the underlying. Some options are European while others are American. American options can be exercised at any time upto the expiration date. Most exchange traded options are American. European options can be exercised only on the expiration date itself. European options are easier to analyse than American options, and properties of an American option are frequently deduced from those of its European counterpart. Like index futures contracts, index options contracts are also cash settled.

Stock Options Stock options are options on individual stocks. A contract gives the holder the right to buy or sell shares at the specified price.

Buyer of an Option The buyer of an option is the one who by paying the option premium buys the right but not the obligation to exercise his option on the seller/writer.

Writer of an Option The writer of a call/put option is the one who receives the option premium and is thereby obliged to sell/buy the asset if the buyer exercises the option on him.

There are two basic types of options, call options and put options.

Call Option A call option gives the holder the right but not the obligation to buy an asset by a certain date for a certain price.

Put Option A put option gives the holder the right but not the obligation to sell an asset by a certain date for a certain price.

Option Price/Premium Option price is the price that the option buyer pays to the option seller. It is also referred to as the option premium.

Expiration Date The date specified in the options contract is known as the expiration date, the exercise date, the strike date or the maturity.

Strike Price The price specified in the options contract is known as the strike price or the exercise price.

In-the-Money Option An in-the-money (ITM) option is an option that would lead to a positive cashflow to the holder if it were exercised immediately. A call option on the index is said to be in-the-money when the current index stands at a level higher than the strike price (that is, spot price > strike price). If the index is much higher than the strike price, the call is said to be deep ITM. In the case of a put, the put is ITM if the index is below the strike price.

At-the-Money Option An at-the-money (ATM) option is an option that would lead to zero cashflow if it were exercised immediately. An option on the index is at-the-money when the current index equals the strike price (that is, spot price = strike price).

Out-of-the-Money Option An out-of-the-money (OTM) option is an option that would lead to a negative cashflow if it were exercised immediately. A call option on the index is out-of-the-money when the current index stands at a level that is less than the strike price (that is, spot price < strike price).

If the index is much lower than the strike price, the call is said to be deep OTM. In the case of a put, the put is OTM if the index is above the strike price.

Intrinsic Value of an Option The option premium can be broken down into two components (i) intrinsic value and (ii) time value. The intrinsic value of a call is the amount the option is ITM, if it is ITM. If the call is OTM, its intrinsic value is zero. Putting it another way, the intrinsic value of a call is Max[0,($S_t - K$)] which means the intrinsic value of a call is the greater of 0 or ($S_t - K$). Similarly, the intrinsic value of a put is Max[0, $K - S_t$], that is, the greater of 0 or ($K - S_t$). K is the strike price and S_t is the spot price.

Time Value of an Option The time value of an option is the difference between its premium and its intrinsic value. Both calls and puts have time value. An option that is OTM or ATM only has time value. Usually, the maximum time value exists when the option is ATM. The longer the time to expiration, the greater is an option's time value, other things being equal. At expiration, an option would have no time value.

Futures and Options

Options are different from futures in several respects. At a practical level, the option buyer pays for the option in full at the time it is purchased. After this, he only has an upside. There is no possibility of the options position generating any further loss to him (other than the funds already paid for the option). In contrast, futures are free to enter into but can generate very large losses. This characteristic makes options attractive to many occasional market participants who cannot put in the time to closely monitor their futures positions.

Buying put options is buying insurance. To buy a put option on the Nifty is to buy insurance that reimburses the full extent to which the Nifty drops below the strike price of the put option. This is attractive to many people and to mutual funds creating "guaranteed return products". The Nifty index fund industry will find it very useful to make a bundle of a Nifty index fund and a Nifty put option to create a new kind of Nifty index fund, which gives the investor protection against extreme drops in the Nifty. Selling put options is selling insurance. Anyone who feels like earning revenues by selling insurance can set himself up to do so on the index options market.

More generally, options offer "non-linear payoffs", whereas futures only have "linear payoffs". By combining futures and options, a wide variety of innovative and useful payoff structures can be created. The distinction between futures and option is summarised in Table 28.2.

TABLE 28.2 Distinction Between Futures and Options

Futures	*Options*
Exchange traded, with novation	Same as futures
Exchange defines the product	Same as futures
Price is zero, strike price moves	Strike price is fixed, price moves
Price is zero	Price is always positive
Linear payoff	Non linear payoff
Both long and short at risk	Only short at risk

Options Payoffs

A pay off for derivative contacts is the likely profit/loss that would accrue to the market participant with change in the price of the underlying asset. The optionality characteristic of options results in a **non-linear payoff** for options. In simple words, it means that the losses for the buyer of an option are limited. However, the profits are potentially unlimited. For a writer, the pay off is exactly the opposite. His profits are limited to the **option premium**. However, his losses are potentially unlimited. These non-linear payoffs are fascinating as they lend themselves to be used to generate various payoffs by using combinations of options and the underlying. We illustrate below six basic pay offs.

Non-linear payoff implies the losses for the buyer of the option are limited but profits are potentially unlimited; profits to the writer of the option are limited to the option premium but losses are potentially unlimited.

Payoff Profile of Buyer of Asset: Long Asset In this basic position, an investor buys the under-lying asset, the Nifty for instance, for 1,220 and sells it at a future date at an unknown price, S_t. Once it is purchased, the investor is aid to be "long" the asset. The investor would make profit if the index goes up. If the index falls he would lose.

Payoff Profile for Seller of Asset: Short Asset In this basic position, an investor shorts the underlying asset, the Nifty for instance, for 1,220 and buys it back at a future date at an unknown price, S_t. Once it is sold, the investor is said to be "short" the asset. The investor sold the index at 1,220. If the index falls, he profits. If the index rises, he loses.

Option premium is the price that the option buyer pays to the option seller.

Payoff Profile for Buyer of Call Options: Long Call A call option gives the buyer the right to pay the underlying asset at the strike price specified in the option. The profit/loss that the buyer makes on the option depends on the spot price of the underlying. If upon expiration, the spot price exceeds the strike price, he makes a profit. The higher the spot price, the more profit he makes. If the spot price of the underlying is less than the strike price, he lets his option expire unexercised. His loss in this case is the premium he paid for buying the option.

Payoff Profile for Writer to Call Options: Short Call A call option gives the buyer the right to buy the underlying asset at the strike price specified in the option. For selling the option, the writer of the option charges a premium. The profit/loss that the buyer makes on the option depends on the spot price of the underlying. Whatever is the buyer's profit is the seller's loss. If upon expiration, the spot price exceeds the strike price, the buyer will exercise the option on the writer. Hence, as the spot price increases, the writer of the option starts making losses. The higher the spot price, the more is the loss he makes. If upon expiration the spot price of the underlying is less than the strike price, the buyer lets his option expire unexercised and the writer gets to keep the premium.

Payoff Profile for Buyer of Put Options: Long Put A put option gives the buyer the right to sell the underlying asset at the strike price specified in the option. The profit/loss that the buyer makes on the option depends on the spot price of the underlying. If upon expiration the spot price is below the strike price, he makes a profit. The lower the spot price, the more is the profit he makes. If the spot price of the underlying is higher than the strike price, he lets his option expire unexercised. His loss in the case is the premium he paid for buying the option.

Payoff Profile for Writer of Put Options: Short Put A put option gives the buyer the right to sell the underlying asset at the strike price specified in the option. For selling the option, the writer of the option charges a premium. The profit/loss that the buyer makes on the option depends on the spot price of the underlying. The buyer's profit is the seller's loss. If upon expiration the spot price happens to be below the strike price, the buyer will exercise the option on the writer. If upon expiration the spot price of the underlying is more than the strike price, the buyer gets his option expire unexercised and the writer gets to keep the premium.

Pricing Options

An option buyer has the right but not the obligation to exercise on the seller. The worst that can happen to a buyer is the loss of the premium paid by him. His downside is limited to this premium, but his upside is potentially unlimited. This optionality has a value expressed in terms of the option price. Just like in other free markets, it is the supply and demand in the secondary market that drives the price of an option. There are various models that help us get close to the true price of an option. Most of these are variants of the celebrated Black-Scholes Model for pricing European options.

Black-Scholes Option Pricing Model/Formulae Black and Scholes start by specifying a simple and well known equation that models the way in which stock prices fluctuate. This equation, called **Geometric Brownian Motion**, implies that stock returns will have a lognormal distribution, meaning that the logarithm of the stock's return will follow the normal (bell shaped) distribution. They then propose that the option's price is determined by only two variables that are allowed to change: time and the underlying stock price. The other factors, namely, the volatility, the exercise price, and the risk free rate do affect the option's price but they are not allowed to change. By forming a portfolio consisting of a long position in stock and a short position in calls, the risk associated with the stock is eliminated. This hedged portfolio is obtained by setting the number of shares of stock equal to the approximate change in the call price for a change in the stock price. This mix of stock and calls must be revised continuously. This process is known as **delta hedging**. They then turn to a little known result in a specialised field of probability known as stochastic calculus. This result defines how the option price changes in terms of the change in the stock price and time to expiration. They then reason that this hedged combination of options and stock should grow in value at the risk free rate. The result then is a partial differential equation. The solution is found by forcing a condition called a *boundary condition* on the model that requires the option price to converge to the exercise value at expiration. The end result is the Black and Scholes Model.

The Black-Scholes formulas for the prices of European calls and puts on a non-dividend paying stock are:

$$C = SN(d_1) - Xe^{-rT} N(d_2) \quad \textbf{(28.4)}$$

$$P = Xe^{-rT} N(-d_2) - SN(-d_1)$$

where $d_1 = \dfrac{\ln \dfrac{S}{X} + (r + \sigma^2/2)T}{\sigma\sqrt{T}}$

and $d_2 = d_1 - \sigma\sqrt{T}$

- The Black-Scholes equation is done in continuous time. This requires continuous compounding. The r that figures in this is $1n(1 + r)$. Example, if the interest rate per annum is 12 per cent, you need to use $1n$ 1.12 or 0.1133, which is the continuously compounded equivalent of 12 per cent per annum.
- $N()$ is the cumulative normal distribution. $N(d_1)$ is called the *delta of the option*, which is a measure of change in option price with respect to change in the price of the underlying asset.
- σ a measure of volatility, is the annualised standard deviation of continuously compounded returns on the underlying. When daily *sigma* are given, they need to be converted into annualised *sigma*.

- $\text{Sigma}_{\text{annual}} = \text{sigma}_{\text{daily}} \times \sqrt{\text{Number of trading days per year}}$. On a average there are 250 trading days in a year.
- X is the exercise price, S the spot price and T the time to expiration measured in years.

Pricing Index Options Under the assumption of the Black-Scholes Options Pricing Model, index options should be valued in the same way as ordinary options on common stock, the assumption being that investors can purchase, without cost, the underlying stocks in the exact amount necessary to replicate the index, that is, stocks are infinitely divisible and the index follows a diffusion process such that the continuously compounded returns distribution of the index is normally distributed. To use the Black-Scholes formula for index options we must, however, make adjustments for the dividend payments, replacing the current index value S in the model with Se^{-qT} where q is the annual dividend yield and T is the time to expiration in years. Consider Example 28.9.

***Example* 28.9**

A three-month call option on the Nifty with a strike of 1,180 is available for trading. The Nifty stands at ₹1,150, and it has a volatility of 30 per cent per annum. The annual risk free rate is 12 per cent. We can calculate the price of the 1,180 option using the Black-Scholes option pricing formula. We take $T = 0.25$, $S = 1{,}150$, $X = 1{,}180$, $r = 1n(1.12)$, and $\sigma = 0.3$. Substituting these values in the formula, we get the call price as ₹70.15. The put price on an option with the same strike works out to be ₹67.19.

Pricing Stock Options Much of what was discussed about index options also applies to stock options. The factors that affect option prices are listed below.

The Stock Price The payoff from a call option will be the amount by which the stock prices exceeds the strike price. Call option, therefore, becomes more valuable as the stock price increases and less valuable as the stock prices decreases. The payoff from a put option will be the amount by which the strike price exceeds the stock price. Put options, therefore, become more valuable as the stock price decreases and less valuable as the stock price increases.

The Strike Price In the case of a call, as the strike price increases, the stock price has to make a larger upward move for the option to go in-the-money. Therefore, for a call option, as the strike price increases, options become less valuable and as the strike price decreases they become more valuable. Put options behave exactly in the opposite way to call options.

Time to Expiration Both put and call American options become more valuable as the time to expiration increases. Consider the case of two options that differ only as far as their expiration date is concerned. The owner of the long-life option has all the exercise opportunities open to the owner of the short-life option, and more. The long-life option must, therefore, always be worth at least as much as the short life option.

Volatility The volatility of a stock price is a measure of how uncertain we are about future stock price movements. As volatility increases, the chance that the stock will do very well or very poorly increases. The value of both calls and puts, therefore, increases as volatility increases.

Risk Free Interest Rate The affect of the risk free interest rate is less clear cut. It is found that the put option prices decline as the risk free rate increases, whereas the prices of calls always increase as the risk free interest rate increases.

Dividends Dividends have the effect of reducing the stock price on the ex-dividend date. This has a negative affect on the value of call options and a positive affect on the value of put options.

Application of Black-Scholes Option Pricing Formula to Stock Options The Black-Scholes option pricing formula, with some adjustment, can be used to price American calls and puts options on stocks. Pricing American options becomes a little difficult because unlike European options, American options can be exercised any time prior to expiration. However, it is never optimal to exercise a call option on a non-dividend paying stock before expiration. When no dividends are expected during the life of the option, the option can be valued simply by substituting the values of the stock price, strike price, stock volatility, risk free rate and time-to-expiration in the Black-Scholes formula. However, when dividends are expected during the life of the option, it is sometimes optimal to exercise the option just before the underlying stock goes ex-dividend. Hence, when valuing options on dividend paying stock, we should consider exercise possibilities at to times: **(i)** just before the underlying stock goes ex-dividend and **(ii)** at the expiration of the options contract.

Therefore, owning an option on a dividend paying stock today is like owning two options: one being a long maturity option with a time-to-maturity from the starting date till the expiration day, and the other being a short maturity option with a time-to-maturity from the starting date till just before the stock goes ex-dividend.

Some adjustment needs to be made before using the Black-Scholes formula. The first step is to value the option on the assumption that it will be exercised on expiry. Thus, the present value of the dividends is deducted from the stock price and the adjusted value, S_d, is used in the Black-Scholes Model. The second step is to assume that the option will be exercised just before the ex-dividend date. The unadjusted stock price is used. In addition, the time to expiry is shortened to be the period up to the ex-dividend date. Following these adjustments, the Black-Scholes model can be applied. The actual value of the option will be the highest of the two valuations. Consider Example 28.10.

***Example* 28.10**

Assume that the price of a stock is ₹50, the exercise price is ₹45, the risk free rate of interest is 6 per cent per annum and that the ex dividend adjustment of 2.5 will occur 0.1644 years hence. The volatility of the stock is 20 per cent. The discount rate on dividend is also taken to be 6 per cent. We have now two call options, a long maturity call option with a maturity of 0.25 years, which can be exercised on the expiration date, and a short maturity call option with a maturity of 0.166 years, which can be exercised just before the ex-dividend date. We will now value both these options.

- The details of the long option are: $T = 0.25$, $r = 0.06$, $D = 2.5$, $S =$ ₹50, $X =$ ₹45, and $S_d = [S - D/(1 = r)^T]$ = ₹47.52. The stock price to be used in the Black-Scholes option pricing formula is S_d, the adjusted price of the stock after deducing the present value of the dividends. Using these values, we get the price of the long option as ₹3.84.
- The details of the short option are: $T = 0.166$, $r = 0.06$, $D = 2.5$, $S =$ ₹50 and $X =$ ₹45. Since the option is exercised just before the stock goes ex-dividend, the unadjusted stock price of ₹50 is used. Using these values, we get the price of the short option as ₹5.56.

Thus, using the above approximation, the American option on the dividend paying stock would be valued at the higher of the two options, that is, at ₹5.58.

LO 28.4 STRUCTURE OF DERIVATIVE MARKET IN INDIA

- High networth individuals (HNIs) and proprietary traders contribute to the major proportion of trading volumes in the derivative segment. Foreign institutional investors and mutual funds are relatively small players in this segment and so also the corporate clients. Surprisingly, retail investors contributed to 25-30 per cent of the total trading turnover. The maximum trading was done in futures on individual shares. These contracts accounted for more than 50 per cent of the turnover. Shock index futures accounted for less than 25 per cent of the total turnover.

- Brokers attributed the high acceptability of futures on individual shares to the similarity of these contracts with **badla**. There is a need to popularise option instruments as they may be a useful medium for enhancing retail participation. Derivative securities have definitely penetrated into the Indian stock market and investors are using these securities for different purposes, namely, risk management, profit enhancement, speculation and arbitrage.
- As far as pricing of derivative securities is concerned, spot price are an important factor in the pricing of future contacts. Dividend yield and future outlook are the other factors. Only 54 per cent identified time to maturity as relevant for pricing. The other factors like interest rate, implied cost of carry, trading volume, and so on seemed to be not very relevant in pricing. The Black-Scholes Option Pricing Model figured among the most popularly used models.

Source: Srivastava, Sandeep, Surender S Yadav and P K Jain, "Derivative Trading in Indian Stock Market: Broker's Perception", *IIMB Management Review*, September, 2008, Vol. 20, No. 3, pp. 311-323.

SUMMARY

LO	
LO 28.1	Derivative instruments include (a) a security derived from a debt instrument, share, loan, risk instrument or contract for differences or any other form of security and (b) a contract that derives its value from the price/index of prices of underlying securities.
	The economic functions performed by the derivatives markets are: (i) they help in the discovery of the future as well as current prices, (ii) they transfer risk to those who have an appetite for them, (iii) the underlying cash markets witness high trading volumes, (iv) speculative trades shift to a more controlled environment, and (v) they help increase savings and investment in the long run.
	The most common variants of derivatives are forward, futures and options.
	A forward contract is an agreement to buy/sell an asset on a specified date for a specified price. It is very useful in hedging and speculations. A very serious limitation of forward contracts is counterparty risk arising from possibility of default of any one party to the transaction.
LO 28.2	A future contract is an agreement between two parties to buy/sell an asset at a certain time in future at a certain price. It may be offset prior to maturity by entering into an equal but opposite transaction. It eliminates counterparty risk and offers more liquidity.
	Future contracts have linear payoffs. It means that the losses as well as the profit, for the buyer and the seller are unlimited.
	Pricing of futures is done with reference to (1) the cost of carry model, (2) pricing equity index futures and pricing stock futures.
	According to the cost of carry method, the price of a future contract, $F = S + C$.
	Pricing of equity index futures given expected dividend, F = carrying cost/cost of financing the purchase of the portfolio less the present value of dividends.
	Pricing of equity index given expected dividend yield, $F = S(1 + r - q)^T$
	Price of stock futures when no dividend expected = Spot price × Cost of carry.
	Price of stock future when dividends are expected = Cost of financing the purchase of stock less present value of dividend received.
LO 28.3	An option gives the holder the right but not the obligation to do something.
	Options offer non-linear payoffs in that while the losses for the buyer of the option are limited, the profits are potentially unlimited. For a writer, the pay-off is exactly the opposite.
	The pricing of an option is based on the Black-Scholes Pricing formula: $P = X_e^{-rT} (N - d_2) - SN(-d_1)$

SOLVED PROBLEMS

P.28.1 Suppose the Nifty spot is at ₹1,000 and two month futures trade at ₹1,040. Suppose the transaction costs involved in placing an index trade are 0.25 per cent and the Nifty index dividends over two months are 0.10 per cent. What is the net rate of return? **LO 28.2** LOD E

Solution The return on the futures is ₹1,040/₹1,000 = 4 per cent. After adding 0.10 per cent dividends and deducting 0.25 per cent transaction cost, the total return over 2 months works out to be 3.85 per cent. Therefore, the net return per month works out to be 1.92 per cent.

P.28.2 What is the riskless profit that can be earned over two months if the Nifty spot is at 1,000 and the two month futures are at 1,010, suppose cash can be risklessly invested at 12 per cent per annum and there are no transaction costs. **LO 28.2** LOD M

Solution At a risk-free rate of 12 per cent, futures are underpriced. One can make an arbitrage profit by buying Nifty futures at 1,010, selling the Nifty spot and investing the 1,000 risklessly for two months. At the end of two months, this money would grow to be about ₹1,019, that is, a return of (1019 – 1010)/1000 = 0.09 per cent.

P.28.3 What is the fair value of one month futures if the spot value of Nifty is 1150? The money can be invested at 11 per cent per annum and Nifty gives a dividend yield of 1 per cent per annum. **LO 28.2** LOD M

Solution The fair value = ₹1,150 × [1 + (0.11 – 0.01)] × 1/12 = ₹1,159.

P.28.4 What is the fair value of one month future if the spot value of Nifty is 1,150? The money can be invested at 14 per cent per annum and Nifty gives a dividend yield of 4 per cent per annum. **LO 28.2** LOD M

Solution The fair value = 1,150 × [1 + (0.14 – 0.04)] × 1/12 = ₹1,159.

P.28.5 Nifty futures trade on NSE as one, two and three month contracts. Spot Nifty stands at 1,200. BASF which currently trades at ₹120 has a weight of 5 per cent in Nifty. It is expected to declare a dividend of ₹20 per share after 15 days of purchasing the contract. The cost of borrowing is 15 per cent per annum. What will the price of a new two-month futures contract on Nifty be? **LO 28.2** LOD D

Solution Since the Nifty stands at 1,200, the value of the contract = 200 – ₹1200 = ₹2,40,000. As the BASF has a weight of 5 per cent in Nifty, its value in Nifty = ₹12,000 (₹2,40,000 × 0.05). If the market price = ₹120, a traded unit of Nifty involves 100 shares. Thus, the futures price,

$$F = 1{,}200 \times (1.15) \times 60/365 - \left(\frac{100 \times 200 \times (1.15) \times 45/365}{200}\right) = ₹1{,}217.70$$

P.28.6 The Tata Tea trades on the spot market at ₹177. The cost of financing is 12 per cent per year. What is the fair value of one month futures on Tata Tea? **LO 28.2** LOD E

Solution The price of the futures contract = ₹177 × (1.12) × 30/365 = ₹178.65. This could also be computed as ₹177 × $((1.12)^{1/12})$ = ₹178.65.

P.28.7 The ITC trades on the spot market at ₹720. The cost of financing is 15 per cent per year. What is the fair value of two month futures on ITC? **LO 28.2** LOD E

Solution The price of the futures contract is = 720 × ((1.15) × 60/365) = ₹736.73.

P.28.8 If the annual risk free rate is 12 per cent, compute the '*r*' used in the Black-Scholes formula. **LO 28.3** LOD E

Solution The Black-Scholes equation is done in continuous time. This requires continuous compounding. The *r* that figures in this is 1*n*(1 + *r*). Therefore, if the interest rate is 12 per cent, we need to use 1n 1.12 or 0.1133.

P.28.9 On February 1, a call option on the Nifty with a strike of ₹1,280 is available for trading. Expiration date is February 22. Compute *T* that is used in the Black-Scholes formula. **LO 28.3** LOD E

Solution The time to expiration is 22 days. The *T* used in the Black-Scholes is time-to-expiration measured in years. Hence, the *T* used = 22/365 = 0.06.

P.28.10 On May 1, a two-month call option on the Nifty with a strike of ₹1,280 is available for trading. Compute the T that is used in the Black-Scholes formula. LO 28.3 LOD E

Solution The time to expiration is 2 months. The T used in the Black-Scholes is the time-to-expiration measured in years. Hence, the T used = 2/12 = 0.166.

P.28.11 A three-month call option on the Nifty with a strike of ₹1280 is available for trading. Nifty stands at 1,260 and has a volatility of 30 per cent per annum. If the annual risk free rate is 12 per cent, what is the price of the call? LO 28.3 LOD M

Solution Using the Black-Scholes option pricing formula with $T = 0.25$, $S = 1{,}260$, $X = 1{,}280$, $r = 1n(1.12)$, and $\sigma = 0.3$ and substituting these values in the formula, the price = ₹83.10.

P.28.12 A three-month put option on the Nifty with a strike of 1,280 is available for trading. The Nifty stands at 1,260 and has a volatility of 30 per cent per annum. If the annual risk free rate is 12 per cent, compute the price of the put. LO 28.3 LOD M

Solution Using the Black-Scholes option pricing formula with $T = 0.25$, $S = 1260$, $X = 1280$, $r = 1n(1.12)$, $\sigma = 0.3$ and substituting these values in the formula, the price of the put = ₹67.35.

P.28.13 A three-month put option on the Nifty with a strike of 1,280 is available for trading. Nifty stands at 1,260 and has a volatility of 30 per cent per annum. The continuous dividend yield on the Nifty is 5 per cent. If the annual risk free rate is 12 per cent, compute the price of the put. LO 28.3 LOD M

Solution Using the Black-Scholes option pricing formula with $T = 0.25$, $S = 1{,}260$, $X = 1{,}280$, $r = 1n(1.12)$, $\sigma = 0.3$, in this case where the annual dividend yield is known, replace the index value 1,260 with 1,244 ($1{,}260e^{-0.05 \times 0.25}$). Substituting these values in the formula, the price of the put = ₹74.60.

P.28.14 A three-month call option on a stock with a strike of ₹45 is available for trading. The spot price is ₹50. The risk free rate of interest is 6 per cent per annum and an ex-dividend adjustment of 2.5 will occur two months hence. The volatility of the stock is 20 per cent. The discount rate on dividend is also taken to be 6 per cent. Compute the maturity of the short maturity option. LO 28.3 LOD M

Solution The short maturity option has a maturity of 0.166 years since the ex-dividend date is two months later.

P.28.15 A three-month call option on a stock with a strike of ₹45 is available for trading. The spot price is ₹50. The risk free rate of interest is 6 per cent per annum and an ex-dividend adjustment of 2.5 will occur two months hence. The volatility of the stock is 20 per cent. The discount rate on dividends is also taken to be 6 per cent. Compute the maturity of the long maturity option. LO 28.3 LOD M

Solution The long maturity option has a maturity of 0.25 years since it is a three-month call option.

P.28.16 A three-month call option on a stock with a strike of ₹45 is available for trading. The spot price is ₹50. The risk free rate of interest is 6 per cent per annum and an ex-dividend adjustment of 5 will occur one month hence. The volatility of the stock is 20 per cent. The discount rate on dividends is also taken to be 8 per cent. Compute the stock price to be used for valuing the long maturity option. LO 28.3 LOD D

Solution The stock price to be used for valuing the long maturity option is S_d = ₹50 – $2.5/(1.08)^{0..083}$ = ₹45.03.

REVIEW QUESTIONS

LOD: Easy

RQ.28.1 **(a)** Indicate whether the following statements are true or false: [LO 28.1-3]

(i) Arbitrageurs participate in the derivatives market to take advantage of a discrepancy between prices in two different markets.

(ii) A futures contract is custom designed.
(iii) Stock index futures are cash settled, i.e., there is no delivery of the underlying stocks.
(iv) In a normal market, basis, i.e., the difference between the futures price and the spot price, is negative.
(v) Buying a put option is equivalent to buying insurance.
(vi) The payoff for a person who buys a futures contract is similar to the payoff for a person who shorts an asset.
(vii) The cost of carry includes cost of storage in case of stock index futures.
(viii) The difference between the spot price and the futures price is called the basis.
(ix) Delta of the option measures the change in the option price with respect to the change in the price of the underlying asset.
(x) An American option can be exercised only at its expiration date.

[Answers: (i) True (ii) False (iii) True (iv) False (v) True (vi) False (vii) False (viii) True (ix) True (x) False]

(b) Fill in the blanks with the correct answer (out of the choices provided)
(i) __________ (Hedgers/Speculators/Arbitrageurs) take advantage of leverage, i.e., the possibility of large potential gains and large potential losses in the derivatives market.
(ii) Standardisation and trading on stock exchanges are the features of a __________ (forward/futures) contract.
(iii) Futures contracts have __________ (linear/non-linear) pay-offs.
(iv) As the date of expiration of a futures contract comes near, the basis __________ (increases/reduces).
(v) If a call option is out-of- the- money, its intrinsic value is __________ (positive/zero).
(vi) The maximum time value of an option exists when it is __________ (in-the-money/at-the-money)
(vii) The downside risk of an option buyer is __________ (limited/unlimited).
(viii) A call option becomes more valuable as the stock price __________ (decreases/increases).
(ix) A put option becomes more valuable as the stock price __________ (decreases/increases).
(x) It is __________ (optimal/not optimal) to exercise a call option on a non-dividend paying stock before expiration.

[Answers: (i) Speculators (ii) Futures (iii) Linear (iv) Reduces (v) Zero (vi) At the money (vii) Limited (viii) Increases (ix) Decreases (x) Not optimal]

RQ.28.2 What are derivative instruments? What are the economic functions performed by the derivatives markets? [LO 28.1]

RQ.28.3 Explain briefly forward contracts. What are their limitations? [LO 28.1]

RQ.28.4 What are option contracts? [LO 28.3]

RQ.28.5 A call option at a strike price of ₹176 is selling at a premium of ₹18. At what price will it break even for the buyer of the option? [LO 28.3]

RQ.28.6 If the daily volatility of the Nifty is 1.92, compute the sigma figure used in the Black Scholes formula. [LO 28.3]

LOD: Medium

RQ.28.7 Define futures/futures contracts. How do they differ from forward contracts? [LO 28.1,2]

RQ.28.8 Explain and illustrate payoffs for future contracts. [LO 28.2]

RQ.28.9 How are future contracts priced? [LO 28.2]

RQ.28.10 Discuss the differences between options and futures. [LO 28.2,3]

RQ.28.11 Explain and illustrate option payoffs. [LO 28.3]

RQ.28.12 Spot value of S&P CNX Nifty is 1200. An investor bought one-month S&P CNX Nifty at 1,220 with a call option for a premium of ₹10. What type of option is it? [LO 28.3]

RQ.28.13 A stock currently sells for ₹120. The put option to sell the stock sells at ₹134 and costs ₹18. Compute the time value of option. [LO 28.3]

LOD: Difficult

RQ.28.14 How are options priced? [LO 28.3]

ANSWERS

28.5 The buyer of the call option with strike price of ₹176 and a premium of ₹18 will be able to break even; it would happen when the price of underlying security becomes ₹194 (₹176 + 18).

28.6 30.72 per cent

28.12 Out-of-the-money (OTM) call option because strike price > spot price.

28.13 ₹4

Scan the QR Code to access comprehensive solutions to all numerical review questions and additional material.

PART 8

DIVIDEND DECISION

Chapter 29
DIVIDEND AND VALUATION

Chapter 30
DETERMINANTS OF DIVIDEND POLICY

The third major decision area in financial management relates to dividend policy. The dividend policy decision involves the choice between distributing the profits belonging to the shareholders and their retention by the firm. The selection would be influenced by the effect on the objective of financial management of maximising shareholders' wealth. Given the net value maximisation objective, there are two aspects of dividend decision which are relevant. The first of these, that is, whether the dividend policy has a bearing on the value of the firm is discussed in Chapter 29. The focus of the chapter is primarily on the different theories/approaches to analyse the relationship between dividend policy and valuation of the firm. Chapter 30 describes the determinants of an appropriate dividend policy for a firm in the light of its facts and circumstances.

CHAPTER 29

Dividend and Valuation

LEARNING OBJECTIVES

LO 29.1	Describe the residual theory of dividends and Modigliani-Miller (MM) approach to the irrelevance of dividends and evaluate its validity
LO 29.2	Explain and illustrate the two models—Walter's and Gordon's—according to which dividends are relevant and affect the value of the firm

INTRODUCTION

Dividend refers to the corporate net profits distributed among shareholders.

Dividends refer to that portion of a firm's net earnings which are paid out to the shareholders. Our focus here is on dividends paid to the ordinary shareholders because holders of preference shares are entitled to a stipulated rate of dividend. Moreover, the discussion is relevant to widely-held public limited companies as the dividend issue does not pose a major problem for closely-held private limited companies. Since dividends are distributed out of the profits, the alternative to the payment of dividends is the retention of earnings/profits. The retained earnings constitute an easily accessible important source of financing the investment requirements of firms. There is, thus, a type of inverse relationship between retained earnings and cash dividends: *larger retentions, lesser dividends; smaller retentions, larger dividends*. Thus, the alternative uses of the net earnings–dividends and retained earnings–are competitive and conflicting.

A major decision of financial management is the dividend decision in the sense that the firm has to choose between distributing the profits to the shareholders and ploughing them back into the business. The choice would obviously hinge on the effect of the decision on the maximisation of shareholders' wealth. Given the objective of financial management of maximising present values, the firm should be guided by the consideration as to which alternative use is consistent with the goal of wealth maximisation. That is, the firm would be well advised to use the net profits for paying dividends to the shareholders if the payment will lead to the maximisation of wealth of the owners. If not, the firm should rather retain them to finance investment programmes. The relationship between dividends and value of the firm should, therefore, be the decision criterion.

There are, however, conflicting opinions regarding the impact of dividends on the valuation of a firm. According to one school of thought, dividends are irrelevant so that the amount of dividends paid has no effect on the valuation of a firm. On the other hand, certain theories consider the dividend decision as relevant to the value of the firm measured in terms of the market price of the shares.

The purpose of the present Chapter is, therefore, to present a critical analysis of some important theories representing these two schools of thought with a view to illustrating the relationship between dividend policy and the valuation of a firm. It focuses on the theory(ies) relating to the irrelevance of dividends to valuation as well as the theories which support the relevance hypothesis. The main points are summarised by the way of recapitulation.

LO 29.1 IRRELEVANCE OF DIVIDENDS

General

The crux of the argument supporting the irrelevance of dividends to valuation is that the dividend policy of a firm is a part of its financing decision. As a part of the financing decision, *the dividend policy of the firm is a* **residual decision** *and dividends are a passive residual.*[1]

Residual dividend policy pays out only excess cash.

If dividend policy is strictly a financing decision, whether dividends are paid out of profits, or earnings are retained, will depend upon the available investment opportunities. It implies that when a firm has sufficient investment opportunities, it will retain the earnings to finance them. Conversely, if acceptable investment opportunities are inadequate, the implication is that the earnings would be distributed to the shareholders. The test of adequate acceptable investment opportunities is the relationship between the return on the investments (r) and the cost of capital (k). As long as r exceeds k, a firm has acceptable investment opportunities. In other words, if a firm can earn a return (r) higher than its cost of capital (k),it will retain the earnings to finance investment projects. If the retained earnings fall short of the total funds required it will raise external funds–both equity and debt–to make up the shortfall. If, however, the retained earnings exceed the requirements of funds to finance acceptable investment opportunities, the excess earnings would be distributed to the shareholders in the form of cash dividends. The amount of dividend will fluctuate from year to year depending upon the availability of acceptable investment opportunities. With abundant opportunities, the dividend payout ratio (D/P ratio, that is, the ratio of dividends to net earnings) would be zero. When there are no profitable opportunities, the D/P ratio will be 100. For situations between these extremes, the D/P ratio will range between zero and 100.

That dividends are irrelevant, or are a passive residual, is based on the assumption that the investors are indifferent between dividends and capital gains. So long as the firm is able to earn more than the equity-capitalisation rate (k_e), the investors would be content with the firm retaining the earnings. In contrast, if the return is less than the k_e, investors would prefer to receive the earnings (i.e. dividends).

Residual Theory of Dividends

The residual theory of dividend suggests that the dividends paid by a corporate should be viewed as a **residual**, that is, the amount left over after meeting the financing requirements of all the acceptable/profitable investment projects.[2] Dividends can be paid only out of the left over amount after financing all new projects with positive NPV. If no amount is left, there will be no dividend payments. The treatment of dividend payments as a **passive residual** implies that the dividend decisions are **irrelevant**. The approach is guided not only by the availability of acceptable investment opportunities but is also concerned with maintaining a desirable/target capital structure in deciding about cash dividends. They are guided by the following four steps. The firm should:

(1) Prepare a **capital budget** indicating the capital expenditure requirements of all profitable investment projects.

(2) Determine the total equity funds requirements, based on the desired debt-equity ratio, to support the capital expenditure requirements in **Step 1**.

(3) Use the retained earnings to the maximum extent possible to meet the funds requirements as per **Step 2**. The retained earnings are preferred to the external equity as the cost of the former is lower than that of the latter due to flotation costs. This is consistent with the pecking order hypothesis and signalling theory (**explained in Chapter 19**). New equity shares should be issued only when retained earnings are insufficient to meet the funds requirements of the target capital structure.

(4) Pays cash dividend only if its available earnings are more than the required amount of equity funds in terms of the desired debt-equity ratio.

Example **29.1**

Assume a company has **(i)** earnings after taxes (available for equityholders) of ₹90 lakh, **(ii)** target debt-equity ratio of 1:2 and **(iii)** new profitable investment projects in the size range of (1) ₹150 lakh, (2) ₹120 lakh, (3) ₹75 lakh, (4) ₹60 lakh, and (5) zero. Determine the amount of dividends paid and dividend payout ratio at varying levels of investment requirements as per residual theory of dividends.

Solution

Table 29.1: Dividends Paid and Dividend Payout Ratio Under Residual Theory of Dividends (Amount in ₹ lakh).

Particulars	*Profitable investment projects*				
	Case 1	*2*	*3*	*4*	*5*
Capital budget	₹150	₹120	₹75	₹60	Nil
Earnings after taxes	90	90	90	90	90
Target D/E ratio	1:2	1:2	1:2	1:2	1:2
Equity funds needed	100	80	50	40	Nil
Retained earnings available to pay dividends/ Dividends paid	Nil	10	40	50	90
Dividend payout ratio (%)	Nil	11.11	44.44	55.55	100

Table 29.1 indicates that the amount of dividends fluctuates depending on the availability of profitable investment projects and earnings. With abundant investment opportunities (**Case 1**), the dividend payout (D/P) ratio is zero. In contrast, in **Case 5** when there are no profitable investment projects, the D/P ratio is 100. For cases between these two extremes (i.e., **Cases 2 to 4**), the D/P ratio varies in the range of 11.11 to 55.55. Thus, it has inverse relationship with the available investment opportunities.

Given the fact that the earnings of a firm as well as the profitable investment projects available to it are likely to vary from year to year, strict adherence to the residual theory of dividends would result in wide fluctuations in dividend payments/unstable dividend policy from period to period. Since investors prefer stable dividend policies (**explained in Chapter 30**), the residual dividend policy by a firm would require higher required rate of return for equity investors (k_e). This, in turn, would result in lower share prices. A firm should, therefore, attempt to stabilise its dividend over time. To achieve the same, it is suggested that[3] firms should **(1)** Estimate their net earnings after taxes and investment opportunities, on an average, for the next 5 years or so, **(2)** Use this forecasted information to determine the residual model payout ratio and absolute sum of dividend payments during the planning period and **(3)** Set a target dividend payout ratio on the basis of the projected data. A firm may smooth out actual dividend payments by saving some funds in surplus years, in anticipation of deficit/lean years.[4] Surplus funds may be invested temporarily in marketable securities.

The residual theory of dividends provides an explanation why mature industries (with few opportunities for growth) have large dividend payments and high dividend-payment ratios. They succeed in attracting equity investors–clientele who prefer high dividends. In contrast, high growth industries with abundant investment opportunities, prefer low dividend payments and attract equity investors who prefer capital gains.

In brief, the residual theory of dividends indicates that the dividend policy of a firm is a residual decision and not an active decision variable and dividends are a passive residual/irrelevant decision. Its strength is that a firm should retain its earnings when it has profitable investment projects and should favour its distribution when such opportunities are lacking. The rationale is sound as firms would retain profits when they can earn higher than what the equityholders can and prefer distribution of earnings when shareholders can earn higher. Its adverse impact in terms of unstable dividends can be minimised by creating **dividend equalisation reserve**. Funds can be transferred to this reserve in surplus years to be used in lean years.

Modigliani and Miller (MM) Hypothesis

Dividend irrelevance implies that the value of a firm is unaffected by the distribution of dividends and is determined solely by the earning power and risk of its assets.

The most comprehensive argument in support of the **irrelevance of dividends** is provided by the MM hypothesis.[5] Modigliani and Miller maintain that dividend policy has no effect on the share price of the firm and is, therefore, of no consequence. What matters, according to them, is the investment policy through which the firm can increase its earnings and thereby the value of the firm. Given the investment decision of the firm, the dividend decision—splitting the earnings into packages of retentions and dividends—is a matter of detail and does not matter. 'Under conditions of perfect capital markets, rational investors, absence of tax discrimination between dividend income and capital appreciation, given the firm's investment policy, its dividend policy may have no influence on the market price of shares.'[6]

Assumptions The MM hypothesis of irrelevance of dividends is based on the following critical assumptions:

1. Perfect capital markets in which all investors are rational. Information is available to all free of cost, there are no transactions costs; securities are infinitely divisible; no investor is large enough to influence the market price of securities; there are no flotation costs.
2. There are no taxes. Alternatively, there are no differences in tax rates applicable to capital gains and dividends.
3. A firm has a given investment policy which does not change. The operational implication of this assumption is that financing of new investments out of retained earnings will not change the business risk complexion of the firm and, therefore, there would be no change in the required rate of return.
4. There is a perfect certainty by every investor as to future investments and profits of the firm. In other words, investors are able to forecast future prices and dividends with certainty. This assumption is dropped by MM later.

Crux of the Argument The crux of the MM position on the irrelevance of dividend is the arbitrage argument. The arbitrage process involves a switching and balancing operation. In other words, arbitrage refers to entering simultaneously into two transactions which exactly balance or completely offset each other. The two transactions here are the acts of paying out dividends and raising external funds—either through the sale of new shares or raising additional loans—to finance investment programmes. Assume that a firm has some investment opportunity. Given its investment decision, the firm has two alternatives: **(i)** it can retain its earnings to finance the investment programme; **(ii)** or distribute the earnings to the shareholders as dividend and raise an equal amount externally through the sale of new shares/bonds for the purpose. If the firm selects the second alternative, **arbitrage process** is involved, in that payment of dividends is associated with raising funds through other means of financing. The effect of dividend payment on shareholders' wealth will be exactly offset by the effect of raising additional share capital.

Arbitrage implies the distribution of earnings to shareholders and raising an equal amount externally; the effect of dividend payment would be offset by the effect of raising additional funds.

When dividends are paid to the shareholders, the market price of the shares will decrease. What is gained by the investors as a result of increased dividends will be neutralised completely by the reduction in the market value of the shares. The terminal value before and after the payment of dividend would be identical. The investors, according to Modigliani and Miller, would, therefore, be indifferent between dividend and retention of earnings. Since the shareholders are indifferent, the wealth would not be affected by current and future dividend decisions of the firm. It would depend entirely upon the expected future earnings of the firm.

There would be no difference to the validity of the MM premise, if external funds are raised in the form of debt instead of equity capital. This is because of their indifference between debt and equity with respect to leverage. The cost of capital is independent of leverage and the real cost of debt is the same as the real cost of equity.[7]

That investors are indifferent between dividend and retained earnings implies that the dividend decision is irrelevant. The arbitrage process[8] also implies that the total market value plus current dividends of two firms which are alike in all respects except D/P ratio will be identical. The individual shareholder can retain and invest his own earnings as well as the firm would.

With dividends being irrelevant, a firm's cost of capital would be independent of its D/P ratio.

Finally, the arbitrage process will ensure that under conditions of *uncertainty* also the dividend policy would be irrelevant. When two firms are similar in respect of business risk, prospective future earnings and investment policies, the market price of their shares must be the same. This, MM argue, is because of the rational behaviour of investors who are assumed to prefer more wealth to less wealth. Differences in current and future dividend policies cannot affect the market value of the two firms as the present value of prospective dividends plus terminal value is the same.

Proof MM provide the proof in support of their argument in the following manner.

Step 1 The market price of a share in the beginning of the period is equal to the present value of dividends paid at the end of the period plus the market price of share at the end of the period. Symbolically,

$$P_0 = \frac{1}{(1+k_e)}(D_1 + P_1) \quad \textbf{(29.1)}$$

where P_0 = Prevailing market price of a share,
k_e = Cost of equity capital,
D_1 = Dividend to be received at the end of period 1, and
P_1 = Market price of a share at the end of period 1

Step 2 Assuming no external financing, the total capitalised value of the firm would be simply the number of shares (n) times the price of each share (P_0). Thus,

$$nP_0 = \frac{1}{(1+k_e)}(nD_1 + nP_1) \quad \textbf{(29.2)}$$

Step 3 If the firm's internal sources of financing its investment opportunities fall short of the funds required, and Δn is the number of new shares issued at the end of year 1 at price of P_1, Eq. 29.2 can be written as:

$$nP_0 = \frac{1}{(1+k_e)}[(nD_1 + (n+\Delta n)P_1 - \Delta nP_1)] \tag{29.3}$$

where n = Number of shares outstanding at the beginning of the period, and
Δn = Change in the number of shares outstanding during the period/Additional shares issued

Equation 29.3 implies that the total value of the firm is the capitalised value of the dividends to be received during the period plus the value of the number of shares outstanding at the end of the period, considering new shares, less the value of the new shares. Thus, in effect, Eq. 29.3 is equivalent to Eq. 29.2.

Step 4 If the firm were to finance all investment proposals, the total amount raised through new shares issued would be given in Eq. 29.4.

$$\Delta nP_1 = I - (E - nD_1)$$

or

$$\Delta nP_1 = I - E + nD_1 \tag{29.4}$$

where ΔnP_1 = Amount obtained from the sale of new shares of finance capital budget,
I = Total amount/requirement of capital budget,
E = Earnings of the firm during the period,
nD_1 = Total dividends paid, and
$(E - nD_1)$ = Retained earnings

According to Equation 29.4, whatever investment needs (I) are not financed by retained earnings, must be financed through the sale of additional equity shares.

Step 5 If we substitute Eq. 29.4 into Eq. 29.3 we derive Eq. 29.5.

$$nP_0 = \frac{1}{(1+k_e)}[nD_1 + (n+\Delta n)P_1 - (I - E + nD_1)] \tag{29.5}$$

Solving Eq. 29.5 we have

$$nP_0 = \frac{nD_1 + (n+\Delta n)P_1 - I + E - nD_1}{(1+k_e)}$$

There is a positive nD_1 and negative nD_1. Therefore, nD_1 cancels. We then have

$$nP_0 = \frac{(n+\Delta n)P_1 - I + E}{(1+k_e)} \tag{29.6}$$

Step 6 Conclusion Since dividends (D) are not found in Eq. 29.6, Modigliani and Miller conclude that dividends do not count and that dividend policy has no effect on the share price.

MM's approach to irrelevance of dividend to valuation is illustrated in Example 29.2.

Example 29.2

A company belongs to a risk class for which the approximate capitalisation rate is 10 per cent. It currently has outstanding 25,000 shares selling at ₹100 each. The firm is contemplating the declaration of a dividend of ₹5 per share at the end of the current financial year. It expects to have a net income of ₹2,50,000 and has a proposal for making new investments of ₹5,00,000. Show that under the MM assumptions, the payment of dividend does not affect the value of the firm.

Solution

(a) Value of the Firm, When Dividends Are Paid:

(i) Price per share at the end of year 1,

$$P_0 = \frac{1}{(1+k_e)}(D_1 + P_1)$$

$$₹100 = \frac{1}{1.10}(₹5 + P_1)$$

$$110 = ₹5 + P_1 \quad \text{or} \quad 105 = P_1$$

(ii) Amount required to be raised from the issue of new shares,

$$\Delta nP_1 = I - (E - nD_1)$$
$$= ₹5{,}00{,}000 - (₹2{,}50{,}000 - ₹1{,}25{,}000) = ₹3{,}75{,}000$$

(iii) Number of additional shares to be issued,

$$\Delta n = ₹3{,}75{,}000/₹105 = 75{,}000/21 \text{ shares}$$

(iv) Value of the firm,

$$nP_0 = \frac{(n+\Delta n)P_1 - I + E}{(1+k_e)} = \left[\frac{25{,}000}{1} + \frac{75{,}000}{21}\right](₹105) - ₹5{,}00{,}000$$
$$+ ₹2{,}50{,}000/1.1 = ₹27{,}50{,}000/1.1 = ₹25{,}00{,}000$$

(b) Value of the Firm When Dividends Are Not Paid:

(i) Price per share at the end of the year 1, $₹100 = \frac{P_1}{1.10}$, or $110 = P_1$

(ii) Amount required to be raised from the issue of new shares,

$$\Delta nP_1 = (₹5{,}00{,}000 - ₹2{,}50{,}000) = ₹2{,}50{,}000$$

(iii) Number of additional shares to be issued,

$$= ₹2{,}50{,}000/₹110 = 25{,}000/11 \text{ shares}$$

(iv) Value of the firm

$$= \left[\frac{25{,}000}{1} + \frac{25{,}000}{11}\right](₹110) - ₹5{,}00{,}000 + ₹2{,}50{,}000/1.1$$
$$= ₹27{,}50{,}000/1.1 = ₹25{,}00{,}000$$

Thus, whether dividends are paid or not, value of the firm remains the same.

The above example clearly demonstrates that the shareholders are indifferent between the retention of profits and the payment of dividend.

A Critique Modigliani and Miller argue that the dividend decision of the firm is irrelevant in the sense that the value of the firm is independent of it. The crux of their argument is that the investors are indifferent between dividend and retention of earnings. This is mainly because of the balancing nature of internal financing (retained earnings) and external financing (raising of funds externally) consequent upon distribution of earnings to finance investment programmes. Whether the MM hypothesis provides a satisfactory framework for the theoretical relationship between dividend decision and valuation will depend, in the ultimate analysis, on whether external and internal financing really balance each other. This, in turn, depends upon the critical assumptions stipulated by them. Their conclusions, it may be noted, under the restrictive assumptions, are logically consistent and intuitively appealing. But these assumptions are unrealistic and untenable in practice. As a result, the conclusion that dividend payments and other methods of financing exactly offset each other and, hence, the irrelevance of dividends, is not a practical proposition; it is merely of theoretical relevance. The validity of the MM Approach is open to question on two counts: **(i)** Imperfection of capital market, and **(ii)** Resolution of uncertainty.

Market Imperfection Modigliani and Miller assume that capital markets are perfect. This implies that there are no taxes; flotation costs do not exist and there is absence of transaction costs. These assumptions are untenable in actual situations.

Tax Effect An assumption of the MM hypothesis is that there are no taxes. It implies that *retention of earnings* (internal financing) and *payment of dividends* (external financing) are, from the viewpoint of tax treatment, on an equal footing. The investors would find both forms of financing equally desirable. The tax liability of the investors, broadly speaking, is of two types: **(i)** tax on dividend income, and **(ii)** capital gains. While the first type of tax is payable by the investors when the firm pays dividends, the capital gains tax is related to retention of earnings. From an operational viewpoint, capital gains tax is **(i)** lower than the tax on dividend income and **(ii)** it becomes payable only when shares are actually sold, that is, it is a deferred tax till the actual sale of the shares. The types of taxes, corresponding to the two forms of financing, are different, although the MM position would imply otherwise. The different tax treatment of dividend and capital gains means that with the retention of earnings the shareholders' tax liability would be lower or there would be tax saving for the shareholders. For example, a firm pays dividends to the shareholders out of the retained earnings. To finance its investment programmes, it issues rights shares. The shareholders would have to pay tax on the dividend income at rates appropriate to their income bracket. Subsequently, they would purchase the shares of the firm. Clearly, the tax could have been avoided if, instead of paying dividend, the earnings were retained. If, however, the investors required funds, they could sell a part of their investments, in which case they will pay tax (capital gains) at a lower rate. There is a definite advantage to the investors owing to the **tax differential** in dividend and capital gains tax and, therefore, they can be expected to prefer retention of earnings. This line of reasoning is also supported by empirical evidence. Elton and Gruber[9] have shown that investors in high income brackets have a preference for capital gains over dividends while those in low tax brackets favour dividends. In a more comprehensive study Brittain[10] found an inverse relationship between dividend payout ratios and the differential between tax rates on dividend income and capital gains. That is, *rising tax rates tend to depress dividends.* In brief, the investors are not, from the viewpoint of taxes, indifferent between dividends and retained earnings. The MM assumption is, therefore, untenable.

> **Tax differentials** are the different rates of taxes applicable to dividend and capital gains.

With effect from financial year 2003-4, dividend income from Indian corporate firms, and mutual funds is exempt from tax. However, the companies paying dividend are required to pay dividend distribution tax. Currently the effective dividend distribution tax rate in India works out at 16.61 per cent.

Flotation Costs Another assumption of a perfect capital market underlying the MM hypothesis of dividend irrelevance is the absence of flotation costs. The term '**flotation cost**' refers to the cost involved in raising capital from the market, for instance, underwriting commission, brokerage and other expenses. The presence of flotation costs affects the balancing nature of internal (retained earnings) and external (dividend payments) financing. The MM position, it may be recalled, argues that given the investment decision of the firm, external funds would have to be raised, equal to the amount of dividend, through the sale of new shares to finance the investment programme. The two methods of financing are not perfect substitutes because of flotation costs. The introduction of such costs implies that the net proceeds from the sale of new shares would be less than the face value of the shares, depending upon their size.[11] It means that to be able to make use of external funds, equivalent to

> **Flotation cost** is the cost involved in raising capital from the market.

the dividend payments, the firm would have to sell shares for an amount in excess of retained earnings. In other words, external financing through sale of shares would be costlier than internal financing *via* retained earnings. The smaller the size of the issue, the greater is the percentage flotation cost.[12] To illustrate, suppose the cost of flotation is 10 per cent and the retained earnings are ₹900. In case dividends are paid, the firm will have to sell shares worth ₹1,000 to raise funds equivalent to the retained earnings. That external financing is costlier is another way of saying that firms would prefer to retain earnings rather than pay dividends and then raise funds externally.

Transaction and Inconvenience Costs Yet another assumption which is open to question is that there are no transaction costs in the capital market. Transaction costs refer to costs associated with the sale of securities by the shareholder-investors. The *no-transaction costs postulate* implies that if dividends are not paid (or earnings are retained), the investors desirous of current income to meet consumption needs can sell a part of their holdings without incurring any cost, like brokerage and so on. This is obviously an unrealistic assumption. Since the sale of securities involves cost, to get current income equivalent to the dividend, if paid, the investors would have to sell securities in excess of the income that they will receive. Apart from the transaction cost, the sale of securities, as an alternative to current income, is inconvenient to the investors. Moreover, uncertainty is associated with the sale of securities. For all these reasons, an investor cannot be expected, as MM assume, to be indifferent between dividend and retained earnings. The investors interested in current income would certainly prefer dividend payment to ploughing back of profits by the firm.

> **Transaction costs** are costs involved in selling securities by the shareholders.

Institutional Restrictions The dividend alternative is also supported by legal restrictions as to the type of ordinary shares in which certain investors can invest. For instance, the life insurance companies are permitted in terms of section 27-A (1) of the Insurance Act, 1938, to invest in only such equity shares on which a dividend of not less than 4 per cent including bonus has been paid for 7 years or for atleast 7 out of 8 or 9 years immediately preceding. To be eligible for institutional investment, the companies should pay dividends. These legal impediments, therefore, favour dividends to retention of earnings. A variation of the legal requirement to pay dividends is to be found in the case of mutual funds. They are required in terms of the stipulations governing their operations, to distribute at least 90 per cent of its net income to investors. The point is that the eligible securities for investment by the mutual funds are assumed to be those that are on the dividend-paying list.

To conclude the discussion of market imperfections, there are four factors which dilute the indifference of investors between dividends and retained earnings. Of these, flotation costs seem to favour retention of earnings. On the other hand, the desire for current income and, the related transaction and inconvenience costs, legal restrictions as applicable to the eligible securities for institutional investment and tax exemption of dividend income imply a preference for payment of dividends. In sum, therefore, market imperfections imply that investors would like the company to retain earnings to finance investment programmes. The dividend policy is not irrelevant.

Resolution of Uncertainty Apart from the market imperfection, the validity of the MM hypothesis, insofar as it argues that dividends are irrelevant, is questionable under conditions of uncertainty. MM hold, it would be recalled, that dividend policy is as irrelevant under conditions of uncertainty as it is when perfect certainty is assumed. The MM hypothesis is, however, not tenable as investors cannot be indifferent between dividend and retained earnings under conditions of uncertainty. This can be illustrated with reference to four aspects: **(i)** near vs distant dividend; **(ii)** informational content of dividends; **(iii)** preference for current income; and **(iv)** sale of stock at uncertain price/ underpricing.

Near Vs Distant Dividend One aspect of the uncertainty situation is the payment of dividend now or at a later date. If the earnings are used to pay dividends to the investors, they get 'immediate' or 'near' dividend. If, however, the net earnings are retained, the shareholders would be entitled to receive a return after some time in the form of an increase in the price of shares (capital gains) or bonus shares and so on. The dividends may, then, be referred to as 'distant' or 'future' dividends. The crux of the problem is: are the investors indifferent between immediate and future dividends? Or would they prefer one over the other? According to Gordon[13], investors are not indifferent; rather, they would prefer near dividend to distant dividend. The payment of dividend is uncertain; how much dividend and when it would be paid by the firm to the investors cannot be precisely forecast. The longer the distance in future dividend payment, the higher is the uncertainty to the shareholders. The uncertainty increases the risk of the investors. The payment of dividend is not associated with any such uncertainty. In other words, payment of immediate dividend resolves uncertainty. The argument that near dividend implies resolution of uncertainty is referred to as the **'bird-in-hand' argument**. This argument is developed in some detail in the later part of this chapter. In brief, since current dividends are less risky than future/distant dividends, shareholders would favour dividends to retained earnings.

Bird-in-hand argument is the belief that current dividend payments reduce uncertainty and result in higher value of shares of a firm.

Informational Content of Dividends Another aspect of uncertainty, very closely related to the first (i.e. resolution of uncertainty or the 'bird-in-hand' argument) is the '**informational content of dividend**' argument. According to the latter argument, as the name suggests, the dividend contains some information vital to the investors. The payment of dividend conveys to the shareholders information relating to the profitability of the firm. If, for instance, a firm has been following a stable dividend policy in the sense of, say, ₹4 per share dividend, an increase in the amount to, say, ₹5 per share will signify that the firm expects its profitability to improve in future or *vice-versa*. The dividend policy is likely to cause a change in the market price of the shares. The significance of this aspect of current dividend payments is expressed by Ezra Solomon in these words:[14]

Informational content is the information provided by dividends of a firm with respect to future earnings which causes owners to bid up or down the price of shares.

> In an uncertain world in which verbal statements can be ignored or misinterpreted, dividend action does provide a clear-cut means of 'making a statement' that speaks louder than a thousand words.

Modigliani and Miller also concede the possibility of the effect of the informational content. But they still maintain that dividend policy is irrelevant as dividends do not determine the market price of shares. They contend that value is determined by the investment decision of the firm. All that the informational content of dividends implies is that dividends reflect the profitability of the firm. They cannot by themselves determine the market price of shares. The basic factor, therefore, is not dividend, but, **expectation of future profitability**.

The informational content argument finds support in some empirical evidence.[15] It is contended that changes in dividends convey more significant information than what earnings announcements do. Further, the market reacts to dividend changes—prices rise in response to a significant increase in dividends and fall when there is a significant decrease or omission.

Preference for Current Income The third aspect of the uncertainty question relating to dividends is based on the desire of investors for current income to meet consumption requirements. The MM hypothesis of irrelevance of dividends implies that in case dividends are not paid, investors who prefer current income can sell a part of their holdings in the firm for the purpose. But, under uncertainty conditions, the two alternatives are not on the same footing because **(i)** the prices of shares fluctuate so that the selling price is uncertain, and **(ii)** selling a small fraction of holdings periodically is inconvenient. That selling shares to obtain income, as an alternative to dividend, involves uncertain price and inconvenience, implies that investors are likely to prefer current dividend. The MM proposition would, therefore, not be valid because investors are not indifferent.

Underpricing Finally, the MM hypothesis would also not be valid when conditions are assumed to be uncertain because of the prices at which the firms can sell shares to raise funds to finance investment programmes consequent upon the distribution of earnings to the shareholders. The irrelevance argument would be valid provided the firm is able to sell shares to replace dividends at the current price. Since the shares would have to be offered to new investors, the firm can sell the shares only at a price below the prevailing price. It is rightly contended by Lintner[16] that the equilibrium price of shares will decline as the firm sells additional stock to replace dividends. The **underpricing** or sale of shares at prices lower than the current market price implies that the firm will have to sell more shares to replace the dividend. The firm would be better off by retaining the profits as opposed to paying dividends.

Underpricing implies sale of shares at prices lower than the current market price.

Under conditions of uncertainty, therefore, the MM doctrine of irrelevance does not hold good.

To recapitulate the preceding discussion, in the context of market imperfections and uncertainty situations, shareholders are not indifferent between retained earnings and current dividends. The considerations that support the proposition that investors have a systematic preference for current dividend relative to retained earnings are **(i)** desire for current income, **(ii)** resolution of uncertainty and the allied aspect of informational content of dividends, **(iii)** transaction and inconvenience costs, and **(iv)** underpricing of new shares. The more favourable tax treatment of dividend income relative to capital gains favours distribution of earnings. The empirical evidence regarding the effect of dividends on the market price of shares is only suggestive.[17] Yet, it is indicative of the fact that companies behave as if dividends are relevant. The MM hypothesis, therefore, is untenable.

LO 29.2 RELEVANCE OF DIVIDENDS

In sharp contrast to the MM position, there are some theories that consider dividend decisions to be an active variable in determining the value of a firm. The dividend decision is, therefore, relevant. We critically examine below two theories representing this notion: **(i)** Walter's Model and **(ii)** Gordon's Model.

Dividend relevance implies that shareholders prefer current dividends and there is no direct relationship between dividend policy and market value of a firm.

Walter's Model

Proposition Walter's model[18] supports the doctrine that dividends are relevant. The investment policy of a firm cannot be separated from its dividends policy and both are, according to Walter, interlinked. The choice of an appropriate dividend policy affects the value of an enterprise.

The key argument in support of the relevance proposition of Walter's model is the relationship between the return on a firm's investment or its internal rate of return (r) and its cost of capital or the required rate of return (k). The firm would have an optimum dividend policy which will be determined by the relationship of r and k. In other words, if the return on investments exceeds the cost of capital, the firm should retain the earnings, whereas it should distribute the earnings to the shareholders in case the required rate of return exceeds the expected return on the firm's investments. The rationale is that if $r > k$, the firm is able to earn more than what the shareholders could by reinvesting, if the earnings are paid to them. The implication of $r < k$ is that shareholders can earn a higher return by investing elsewhere.

Walter's model, thus, relates the distribution of dividends (retention of earnings) to available investment opportunities. If a firm has adequate profitable investment opportunities, it will be able to earn more than what the investors expect so that $r > k$. Such firms may be called *growth firms.* For growth firms, the optimum dividend policy would be given by a D/P ratio of zero. That is to say, the firm should plough back the entire earnings within the firm. The market value of the shares will be maximised as a result.

In contrast, if a firm does not have profitable investment opportunities (when $r < k$), the shareholders will be better off if earnings are paid out to them so as to enable them to earn a higher return by using the funds elsewhere. In such a case, the market price of shares will be maximised by the distribution of the entire earnings as dividends. A D/P ratio of 100 would give an optimum dividends policy.

Finally, when $r = k$ (normal firms), it is a matter of indifference whether earnings are retained or distributed. This is so because for all D/P ratios (ranging between zero and 100) the market price of shares will remain constant. For such firms, there is no optimum dividend policy (D/P ratio).

Assumptions The critical assumptions of Walter's Model are as follow:

1. All financing is done through retained earnings: external sources of funds like debt or new equity capital are not used.
2. With additional investments undertaken, the firm's business risk does not change. It implies that r and k are constant.
3. There is no change in the key variables, namely, beginning earnings per share, E, and dividends per share, D. The values of D and E may be changed in the model to determine results, but, any given value of E and D are assumed to remain constant in determining a given value.
4. The firm has perpetual (or very long) life.

Formula Walter has evolved a mathematical formula to arrive at the appropriate dividend decision. His formula is based on a share valuation model which states:

$$P = \frac{D}{k_e - g} \tag{29.7}$$

where P = Price of equity shares,
D = Initial dividend,
k_e = Cost of equity capital, and
g = Expected growth rate of earnings

To reflect earnings retentions, we have

$$P = \frac{D}{k_e - rb} \tag{29.8}$$

where r = Expected rate of return on firm's investments, and b = Retention rate $(E - D)/E$

Thus, rb measures growth rate in dividends, which is the product of the rate of profitability of retained earnings (r) and the earnings retention percentage (b).

From Eq. 29.7, we derive an equation for determining k_e

$$k_e = \frac{D}{P} + g \tag{29.9}$$

since $g = \frac{\Delta P}{P}$ we have,

$$k_e = \frac{D}{P} + \frac{\Delta P}{P}$$

and since $\Delta P = \frac{r}{k_e}(E - D)$,

substituting the value of ΔP, we have

$$k_e = \frac{D + \frac{r}{k_e}(E - D)}{P}$$

or $$P = \frac{D + \frac{r}{k_e}(E - D)}{k_e} \qquad \textbf{(29.10)}$$

where P = The prevailing market price of a share,
D = Dividend per share,
E = Earnings per share, and
r = The rate of return on the firm's investment

Equation 29.10 shows that the value of a share is the present value of all dividends plus the present value of all capital gains. Walter's model with reference to the effect of dividend/retention policy on the market value of shares under different assumptions of r (return on investments) is illustrated in Example 29.3.

***Example* 29.3**

The following information is available in respect of a firm:

Capitalisation rate (k_e) = 0.10
Earnings per share (E) = ₹10

Assumed rate of return on investments (r): (i) 15, (ii) 8, and (iii) 10.

Show the effect of dividend policy on the market price of shares, using Walter's model.

Solution

(i) *When r is 0.15, that is, $r > k_e$*: The effect of different D/P ratios depicted in Table 29.2.

(ii) *When r = 0.08 and 0.10, that is, $r < ke$ and $r = k_e$ respectively*: The effect of different D/P ratios on the value of shares is shown in Table 29.3.

TABLE 29.2 Dividend Policy and Value of Shares (Walter's Model)

(a) D/P ratio = 0 (Dividend per share = zero)

$$P = \frac{0 + \left[\frac{0.15}{0.10}\right](10 - 0)}{0.10} = ₹150$$

(b) D/P ratio = 25 (Dividend per share = ₹2.5)

$$P = \frac{2.5 + \left[\frac{0.15}{0.10}\right](10 - 2.5)}{0.10} = ₹137.50$$

(c) D/P ratio = 50 (Dividend per share = ₹5)

$$P = \frac{5 + \left[\frac{0.15}{0.10}\right](10 - 5)}{0.10} = ₹125$$

(d) D/P ratio = 75 (Dividend per share = ₹7.5)

$$P = \frac{7.5 + \left[\frac{0.15}{0.10}\right](10 - 7.5)}{0.10} = ₹112.50$$

(Contd.)

(Contd.)

(e) D/P ratio = 100 (Dividend per share = ₹10)

$$P = \frac{10 + \left[\frac{0.15}{0.10}\right](10 - 10)}{0.10} = ₹100$$

TABLE 29.3 Dividend Policy and Value of Shares (Walter's Model)

	(A) r = 0.8 (r < k_e)	*(B) r = 0.10 (r = k_e)*
(a) D/P ratio = Zero	$P = \frac{0 + \left[\frac{0.08}{0.10}\right](10 - 0)}{0.10} = ₹80$	$P = \frac{0 + \left[\frac{0.10}{0.10}\right](10 - 0)}{0.10} = ₹100$
(b) D/P Ratio = 25	$P = \frac{2.5 + \left[\frac{0.08}{0.10}\right](10 - 2.5)}{0.10} = ₹85$	$P = \frac{2.5 + \left[\frac{0.10}{0.10}\right](10 - 2.5)}{0.10} = ₹100$
(c) D/P Ratio = 50	$P = \frac{5 + \left[\frac{0.08}{0.10}\right](10 - 5)}{0.10} = ₹90$	$P = \frac{5 + \left[\frac{0.10}{0.10}\right](10 - 5)}{0.10} = ₹100$
(d) D/P Ratio = 75	$P = \frac{7.5 + \left[\frac{0.08}{0.10}\right](10 - 7.5)}{0.10} = ₹95$	$P = \frac{7.5 + \left[\frac{0.10}{0.10}\right](10 - 7.5)}{0.10}$ ₹100
(e) D/P Ratio = 100	$P = \frac{10 + \left[\frac{0.08}{0.10}\right](10 - 10)}{0.10} = ₹100$	$P = \frac{10 + \left[\frac{0.10}{0.10}\right](10 - 10)}{0.10} = ₹100$

Interpretation The calculations of the value of shares according to Walter's formula in Tables 29.2 and 29.3 yield the following conclusions:

1. When the firm is able to earn a return on investments exceeding the required rate of return that is, $r > K_e$, *the value of shares is inversely related to the D/P ratio: as the payout ratio increases, the market value of shares declines.* (Table 29.1). Its value is the highest when the D/P ratio is zero. If, therefore, the firm retains its entire earnings, it will maximise the market value of shares (₹150). When all earnings are distributed, its value is the lowest. In other words, the *optimum payout ratio (dividend policy) is zero.*
2. It is clear from Table 29.2 that when $r < k_e$ that is, when the firm does not have ample profitable investment opportunities, *the D/P ratio and the value of shares are positively correlated: as the payout ratio increases, the market price of the shares also increases. The dividend policy is optimum when the D/P ratio = 100 per cent.* In other words, when $r < k_e$, the firm would be well advised to distribute the entire earnings to the shareholders.

3. For a situation in which $r = k_e$, the market value of shares is constant irrespective of the D/P ratio (Table 29.2); there is *no optimum dividend policy (D/P)* ratio. In other words, the market price of shares in not affected by the *D/P ratio*. Whether the firm retains the profits or distributes dividends is a matter of indifference. *This is a hypothetical situation.* In actual practice, the two values (*r* and k_e) are different and Walter concludes that dividend policy does matter as a variable in maximising share prices.

Limitations The Walter's model, one of the earliest theoretical models, explains the relationship between dividend policy and value of the firm under certain simplified assumptions. Some of the assumptions do not stand critical evaluation. In the first place, the Walter's model assumes that the firm's investments are financed exclusively by retained earnings; no external financing is used. The model would be only applicable to all-equity firms. Secondly, the model assumes that *r* is constant. This is not a realistic assumption because when increased investments are made by the firm, *r* also changes. Finally, as regards the assumption of constant, k_e, the *risk complexion* of the firm has a direct bearing on it. By assuming a constant k_e, Walter's model ignores the effect of risk on the value of the firm.

Gordon's Model

Another theory which contends that dividends are relevant is Gordon's model.[19] This model, which opines that dividend policy of a firm affects its value, is based on the following assumptions:

1. The firm is an all-equity firm. No external financing is used and investment programmes are financed exclusively by retained earnings.
2. *r* is constant, k_e increases with retention rate.
3. The firm has perpetual life.
4. The retention ratio, once decided upon, is constant. Thus, the growth rate, ($g = br$) is also constant.
5. $k_e > br$.

Arguments It can be seen from the assumptions of Gordon's model that they are similar to those of Walter's model. As a result, Gordon's model, like Walter's, contends that dividend policy of the firm is relevant and that investors put a positive premium on current incomes/dividends. The crux of Gordon's arguments is a two-fold assumption: **(i)** investors are risk averse, and **(ii)** they put a premium on a *certain* return and discount/penalise *uncertain* returns.

As investors are rational, they want to avoid risk. The term risk refers to the possibility of not getting a return on investment. The payment of current dividends *ipso facto* completely removes any chance of risk. If, however, the firm retains the earnings (i.e. current dividends are withhled), the investors can expect to get a dividend in future. The future dividend is uncertain, both with respect to the amount as well as the timing. The rational investors can reasonably be expected to prefer current dividend. In other words, they would discount future dividends, that is, they would place less importance on it as compared to current dividend. The retained earnings are evaluated by the investors as a risky promise. In case the earnings are retained, therefore, the market price of the shares would be adversely affected.

The above argument underlying Gordon's model of dividend relevance is also described as a *bird-in-the-hand argument.*[20] That a bird in hand is better than two in the bush is based on the logic that *what is* available at present is preferable to *what may* be available in the future. Basing his model on this argument, Gordon argues that the future is uncertain and the more distant the future is, the more uncertain it is likely to be. If, therefore, current dividends are withheld to retain

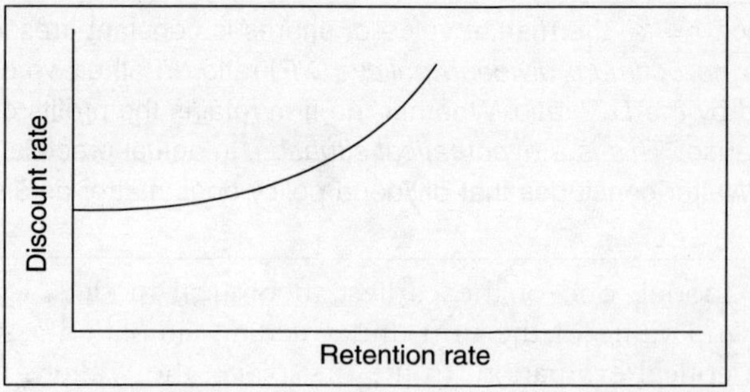

FIGURE 29.1 Retention Rate and Discount Rate

profits, whether the investors would at all receive them later is uncertain. Investors would naturally like to avoid uncertainty. In fact, they would be inclined to pay a higher price for shares on which current dividends are paid. Conversely, they would discount the value of shares of a firm which postpones dividends. The discount rate would vary, as shown in Figure 29.1, with the *retention rate* or level of retained earnings. The term retention ratio means the percentage of earnings retained. It is the inverse of D/P ratio. The omission of dividends, or payment of low dividends, would lower the value of the shares.

Dividend Capitalisation Model According to Gordon, the market value of a share is equal to the present value of future streams of dividends. A simplified version of Gordon's model can be symbolically[21] expressed as

$$P = \frac{E(1-b)}{k_e - br} \quad \textbf{(29.11)}$$

where P = Price of a share,
E = Earnings per share,
b = Retention ratio or percentage of earnings retained,
$1 - b$ = D/P ratio, i.e. percentage of earnings distributed as dividends,
k_e = Capitalisation rate/cost of capital, and
$br = g$ = Growth rate = rate of return on investment of an all-equity firm.

The implications of dividends policy according to Gordon's model are illustrated in Example 29.4.

***Example* 29.4**

The following information is available in respect of the rate of return on investment (r), the capitalisation rate (k_e) and earnings per share (E) of Hypothetical Ltd.

r = 12 per cent
E = ₹20

Determine the value of its shares, assuming the following:

	D/P ratio (1 – b)	*Retention ratio (b)*	*k_e (%)*
(a)	10	90	20
(b)	20	80	19
(c)	30	70	18
(d)	40	60	17
(e)	50	50	16
(f)	60	40	15
(g)	70	30	14

Solution

The value of shares of Hypothetical Ltd for different D/P and retention ratios is depicted in Table 29.4.

TABLE 29.4 Dividend Policy and Value of Shares of Hypothetical Ltd (Gordon's Model)

(a) D/P ratio 10 (Retention ratio 90)

$br(g) = 0.9 \times 0.12 = 0.108$

$$P = \frac{₹20\,(1-0.9)}{0.20-0.108} = \frac{₹2}{0.092} = ₹21.74$$

(b) D/P ratio 20 (Retention ratio 80)

$br = 0.8 \times 0.12 = 0.096$

$$P = \frac{₹20\,(1-0.8)}{0.19-0.096} = ₹42.55$$

(c) D/P ratio 30 (Retention ratio 70)

$br = 0.7 \times 0.12 = 0.084$

$$P = \frac{₹20\,(1-0.7)}{0.18-0.084} = ₹62.50$$

(d) D/P ratio 40 (Retention ratio 60)

$br = 0.6 \times 0.12 = 0.72$

$$P = \frac{₹20\,(1-0.6)}{0.17-0.072} = ₹81.63$$

(e) D/P ratio 50 (Retention ratio 50)

$br = 0.5 \times 0.12 = 0.060$

$$P = \frac{₹20\,(1-0.5)}{0.17-0.072} = ₹100$$

(f) D/P ratio 60 (Retention ratio 40)

$br = 0.4 \times 0.12 = 0.048$

$$P = \frac{₹20\,(1-0.4)}{0.15-0.048} = ₹117.65$$

(g) D/P ratio 70 (Retention ratio 30)

$br = 0.3 \times 0.12 = 0.036$

$$P = \frac{₹20\,(1-0.3)}{0.14-0.036} = ₹134.62$$

Gordon, thus, contends that the dividend decision has a bearing on the market price of the share. The market price of the share is favourably affected with more dividends. (Table 29.4).

SUMMARY

LO 29.1

There are divergent views regarding the impact of dividend policy (dividend payout, D/P ratio) on the market price of the share and the value of the firm.

The residual theory of dividends suggests that the dividends paid by a corporate should be viewed as a residual – the amount left over from corporate earnings after taxes after meeting the requirement of all profitable investment projects, while maintaining a target debt-equity ratio. Cash dividends can be paid only if its available earnings are more than the required amount of funds to meet the desired debt-equity ratio.

LO 29.1

It results in fluctuating dividend payments, as earnings of a firm as well as profitable investment opportunities available to it are likely to vary from year to year.

The dividend payment ratio may vary in the size range of zero to one-hundred depending on the size of earnings, capital expenditure requirements and the desired debt-equity ratio.

Since stable dividend policy is desirable, a firm may smooth out actual dividend payments by creating a dividend equalisation fund.

The other view, led by Modigliani and Miller (MM), takes a diametrically opposite position and contends that the dividend policy of a firm has no effect on its value.

MM's proof in support of their argument is depicted in the following equation:

$$nP_0 = \frac{nD_1 + (n + \Delta n)p_1 - I + E - nD_1}{(1 + k_e)}$$

Since nd_1 in numerator of the equation cancels nd_1 and dividends (D) are not found, MM conclude that dividends do not count and the dividend policy has no effect on the share price.

The arguments in support of MM do not stand the test of scrutiny under real world/business situations. Investors, in general, prefer current dividends to retained earnings. The major factors affecting the validity of MM model are: (i) tax effect, (ii) flotation cost, (iii) transaction and inconvenience costs, (iv) preference for current dividend and (v) resolution of uncertainty.

LO 29.2

According to yet another view represented by Walter, Gordon and others, the D/P ratio is relevant and it certainly affects the market price of shares.

The key argument in support of the relevance of Walter's model is the relationship between the return on a firm's investment(r) and its cost of capital/required rate of return (k). If $r > k$, the firm should retain the earnings (or D/P ratio should be zero) as it is able to earn higher than what the shareholders could by investing on their own. In case $r < k$, it implies that shareholders can earn a higher return by investing elsewhere. Therefore, the entire earnings (D/P ratio should be 100 per cent) should be distributed to them. By following such a policy, the market price of share is maximised.

According to Walter, the value of the firm, as measured by the market price per share (P) is given by the following equation:

$$P = \frac{D + \frac{r}{k}(E - D)}{k}$$

The value of P is maximum when D is zero (in situations of $r > k$); when $r < k$, the value of $E = D$ gives maximum P.

Gordon's proposition that dividend policy of the firm is relevant is based on two tenable assumptions: (i) investors are risk averse, and (ii) they put a positive premium on current incomes/dividends. The retained earnings are evaluated by the investors as a risky promise as the future dividend receipts are perceived by them as uncertain, both with respect to the amount as well as the timing.

According to Gordon, the market value of a share is equal to the present value of future streams of dividend. Symbolically,

$$P = \frac{E(1 - b)}{k_e - b_r}$$

The value of P increases with the increase in the D/P ratio, and is maximum when there are no retentions.

The available empirical evidence seems to support the view that dividend policy is relevant. A firm should try to follow an optimum dividend policy which maximises the shareholder's wealth in the long run.

REFERENCES

1. Solomon, E, *Theory of Financial Management,* Columbia University Press, New York, 1969, pp 139-40.
2. Gitman, L J, *op. cit.*, 2006, p. 594.
3. Brigham, E F and J F Houston, *op. cit.*, p. 534.
4. Van Horne, J C, *op. cit,* 2002, p. 328.
5. Miller, M H and Modigiliani, 'Dividend policy, growth and the valuation of shares', *Journal of Business,* October 1961, pp. 441-33.
6. Miller, M H and F Modigliani, 'Some estimates of the cost of capital to the electric utility industry, 1954-57', *American Economic Review,* June 1966, p. 345.
7. This aspect has been covered in detail in Chapter 15.
8. For illustration of the arbitrage process for the dividend decision, refer to Lewllen, W G, *The Cost of Capital,* Kandall/Hunt Publishing Company, Dubuque, Iowe, 1976, pp. 54-57. Also Walter, J E, *Dividend Policy and Enterprise Valuation,* Wadsworth, Belmont, Calif, 1967, pp. 106-110.
9. Eleton, E J and M J Gruber, 'Marginal stockholder tax rates and the clientele effect', *Review of Economics and Statistics,* February 1970, pp. 68-74.
10. Brittain, J A, *Corporate Dividend Policy,* The Brookings Institution, Washington, DC. 1966, Chapter IV.
11. Such costs in India during 1961-75 have ranged between 5-10%. See Khan, M Y, *New Issues and Finance for Industry in India,* Allied Publishers, New Delhi, 1978, Chapter VI.
12. *Ibid.*
13. Gordon, M J, 'Optimal investment and financing policy', *Review of Economics and Statistics,* February, 1962, pp 37-51.
14. Solomon, E, *op. cit.*, p 142.
15. Pettit, R R, 'Dividend announcements, security performance and capital market efficiency', *Journal of Finance,* December 1972, pp. 993-1007. Also Fama, E and others, 'The adjustment of stock prices to new information', *International Economic Review,* February 1969, pp. 1-26.
16. Lintner, J, 'Dividends, earnings, leverage, stock pries and the supply of capital to corporations', *Review of Economics and Statistics,* August 1962, pp. 243-69.
17. For instance, Van Horne, J C and J G McDonald, 'Dividend policy and the new equity financing', *Journal of Finance,* May 1971, pp. 507-19.
18. Walter, J E, 'Dividend Policy: Its influence on the value of the enterprise', *Journal of Finance,* May 1963, pp. 280-91.
19. Gordon, M J, *The Investment, Financing and Valuation of the Corporation,* 1962; also 'Optimum investment and financing policy', *Journal of Finance,* May 1963, pp. 264-72; 'The savings, investment and valuation of a corporation', *Review of Economics and Statistics,* February, 1962, pp. 37-51.
20. Krishman, J E, *Principles of Investment,* McGraw-Hill, New York, 1933, p. 737.
21. Bolten, S F, *op. cit.*, p. 383.

SOLVED PROBLEMS

P.29.1 (a) X company earns ₹5 per share, is capitalised at a rate of 10 per cent and has a rate of return on investment of 18 per cent. **LO 29.1,2** LOD M

According to Walter's model, what should be the price per share at 25 per cent dividend payout ratio? Is this the optimum payout ratio according to Walter?

(b) Omega company has a cost of equity capital of 10 per cent, the current market value of the firm (V) is ₹20,00,000 (@ ₹20 per share). Assume values for I (new investment), Y (earnings) and D (dividends) at the end of the year as I = ₹6,80,000, Y = ₹1,50,000 and D = ₹1 per share. Show that under the MM assumptions, the payment of dividend does not affect the value of the firm.

Solution

(a) $$P = \frac{D + \frac{r}{k_e}(E - D)}{k_e} = \frac{₹1.25 + \left[\frac{0.18}{0.10}\right](₹5.0 - ₹1.25)}{0.10} = ₹80$$

This is not the optimum dividend payout ratio because Walter suggests a zero per cent dividend payout ratio in situations where $r > k_e$ to maximise the value of the firm. At this ratio, the value of the share would be maximum, that is, ₹90.

(b) Value of the firm, when dividends are paid (MM assumptions):

(i) Market price of the share at the end of the year: $P_0 = \frac{1}{(1+k_e)}(P_1 + D_1)$

$$₹20 = \frac{(P_1 + ₹1)}{1.10} = ₹21 = P_1$$

(ii) Amount required for new financing: $I - (Y - nD_1)$ = ₹6,80,000 – (₹1,50,000 – ₹1,00,000) = ₹6,30,000

(iii) Number of shares to be issued: $= \frac{₹6,30,000}{₹21} = 30,000$ shares

(iv) Value of the firm: $= \frac{1}{(1+k_e)}[nD_1 + (n + \Delta n)P_1 - I + Y - nD1]$

$$\frac{₹1,00,000 + [(1,00,000 + 30,000) \times ₹21] - ₹6,80,000 + ₹1,50,000 - ₹1,00,000}{1.10} = 20,00,000$$

(c) Value of the firm when dividends are not paid:

(i) Market price of the share at the end of the year: $₹20 = \frac{P_1 + \text{Zero}}{1.10}$, $₹22 = P_1$

(ii) Amount required for new financing: $I - (Y - nD_1)$ = ₹6,80,000 – ₹1,50,000 = ₹5,30,000

(iii) Number of new shares to be issued $= \frac{₹5,30,000}{₹22}$ shares

(iv) Value of the firm: $= \frac{1}{1+k_e}[(n + \Delta n)P_1 - I + Y]$

$$= \frac{\left[1,00,000 + \frac{5,30,000}{22}\right]₹22 - ₹6,80,000 + ₹1,50,000}{1.10} = ₹20,00,000$$

Since the value of the firm is ₹20,00,000, in both the situations when dividends are paid and when dividends are not paid, dividend does not affect the value of the firm.

P.29.2 The Apex Company which earns ₹5 per share, is capitalised at 10 per cent and has a return on investment of 12 per cent. Using Walter's dividend policy model, determine optimum dividend pay out ratio and the price of the share at this pay out. It currently has 1,00,000 shares selling at ₹100 each. The firm is contemplating the declaration of ₹5 as dividend at the end of the current financial year, which has just begun. What will be the price of the share at the end of the year, if a dividend is not declared? What will it be if it is paid? Answer these on the basis of Modigliani and Miller model and assume no taxes.

LO 29.2 LOD E

Solution

(a) (i) According to Walter's formula, the optimum dividend payout ratio would be zero as $r > k_e$ because the value of the share of the firm would be maximum.

(ii) $$P = \frac{D + \frac{r}{k_e}(E - D)}{k_e} = \frac{(0.12/0.10)(₹5)}{0.10} = ₹60$$

(b) (i) Price of the share when dividends are declared (MM assumptions): $P = \frac{1}{(1 + k_e)}(D_1 + P_1)$

$$₹100 = \frac{1}{1.10}(₹5 + P_1),\ ₹105 = P_1$$

(ii) Price of share when dividends are not declared: $₹100 = \frac{(₹0 + P_1)}{1.10}$ or $P_1 = ₹110$

P.29.3 Expandent Ltd had 50,000 equity shares of ₹10 each outstanding on January 1. The shares are currently being quoted at par in the market. The company now intends to pay a dividend of ₹2 per share for the current calendar year. It belongs to a risk class whose appropriate capitalisation rate is 15 per cent. Using Modigliani-Miller model and assuming no taxes, ascertain the price of the company's share at it is likely to prevail at the end of the year (a) when dividend is declared, and (b) when no dividend is declared. (c) Also, find out the number of new equity shares that the company must issue to meet its investment needs of ₹2 lakh, assuming a net income of ₹1.1 lakh and also assuming that the dividend is paid.

LO 29.1 LOD E

Solution

(a) Price of the share, when dividends are paid: $P_0 = \frac{D_1 + P_1}{(1 + k_e)}$, $₹10 = \frac{₹2 + P_1}{1.15}$, $₹9.5 = P_1$

(b) Price of the share, when dividends are not paid: $₹10 = \frac{P_1}{1.15}$, $₹11.5 = P_1$

(c) Number of new equity shares to be issued:

$$\Delta n = \frac{I - (E - nD_1)}{P_1} = \frac{₹2{,}00{,}000 - (₹1{,}10{,}000 - 1{,}00{,}000)}{₹9.5} = 20{,}000 \text{ shares}$$

P.29.4 The Asbestos Company belongs to a risk class of which the appropriate capitalisation rate is 10 per cent. It currently has 1,00,000 shares selling at ₹100 each. The firm is contemplating the declaration of a ₹6 dividend at the end of the current fiscal year, which has just begun. Answer the following questions based on Modigliani and Miller model and the assumptions of no taxes.

LO 29.1 LOD E

(a) What will be the price of the shares at the end of the year, if a dividend is not declared? What will it be if it is declared?

(b) Assuming that the firm pays dividend, has a net income of ₹10,00,000 and makes new investments of ₹20,00,000 during the period, how many new shares must be issued?

Solution

(a) (i)Price of the share, when dividend is declared: $\frac{D_1 + P_1}{(1 + k_e)}$, $₹100 = \frac{P_1 + ₹6}{1.10}$, $₹104 = P_1$

(ii)Price of the share, when dividends are not paid: $₹100 = \frac{P_1 + 0}{1.10}$, $₹110 = P_1$

(b) Number of new shares to be issued: $= \frac{I - (E - nD_1)}{P_1}$

$$= \frac{₹20{,}00{,}000 - (₹10{,}00{,}000 - 6{,}00{,}000)}{₹104} = 15{,}385 \text{ shares}$$

P.29.5 From the following information supplied to you, determine the theoretical market value of equity shares of a company as per Walter's model:

LO 29.2 LOD M

Earnings of the company	₹5,00,000
Dividends paid	3,00,000
Number of shares outstanding	1,00,000
Price earning ratio	8
Rate of return on investment	0.15

Are you satisfied with the current dividend policy of the firm? If not, what should be the optimal dividend payout ratio in this case?

Solution

$$P = \frac{D + \frac{r}{k_e}(E - D)}{k_e} = \frac{₹3 + \left[\frac{0.15}{0.125}\right](₹5 - ₹3)}{0.125} = ₹43.20$$

No, we are not satisfied with the current dividend policy. The optimal dividend payout ratio, given the facts of the case ($r > k_e$), should be zero.

Working Notes

(i) k_e is the reciprocal of P/E ratio = 1/8 = 12.5 per cent
(ii) E = Total earnings ÷ Number of shares outstanding
(iii) D = Total dividends ÷ Number of shares outstanding

P.29.6 The earnings per share of a company is ₹8 and the rate of capitalisation applicable is 10 per cent. The company has before it, an option of adopting (i) 50, (ii) 75 and (iii) 100 per cent dividend pay out ratio. Compute the market price of the company's quoted shares as per Walter's Model if it can earn a return of (a) 15, (b) 10 and (c) 5 per cent on its retained earnings.

LO 29.2 LOD M

Solution

(i) D/P ratio = 0.50	(ii) D/P ratio = 0.75	(iii) D/P ratio = 1
(a) Price of shares if r = 0.15		
$P = \frac{₹4 + \frac{0.15}{0.10}(₹8 - ₹4)}{0.10}$ = ₹100	$P = \frac{₹6 + \frac{0.15}{0.10}(₹8 - ₹6)}{0.10}$ = ₹90	$P = \frac{₹8 + \frac{0.15}{0.10}(₹8 - ₹8)}{0.10}$ = ₹80
(b) Price of share if r = 0.10		
$P = \frac{₹4 + \frac{0.10}{0.10}(₹8 - ₹4)}{0.10}$ = ₹80	$P = \frac{₹6 + \frac{0.10}{0.10}(₹8 - ₹6)}{0.10}$ = ₹80	$P = \frac{₹8 + \frac{0.10}{0.10}(₹8 - ₹8)}{0.10}$ = ₹80
(c) Price of share if r = 0.05		
$P = \frac{₹4 + \frac{0.05}{0.10}(₹8 - ₹4)}{0.10}$ = ₹60	$P = \frac{₹6 + \frac{0.05}{0.10}(₹8 - ₹6)}{0.10}$ = ₹70	$P = \frac{₹8 + \frac{0.05}{0.10}(₹8 - ₹8)}{0.10}$ = ₹80

P.29.7 A closely-held plastic manufacturing company has been following a dividend policy which can maximise the market value of the firm as per Walter's model. Accordingly, each year at dividend time, the capital budget is reviewed in conjunction with the earnings for the period and alternative investment opportunities for the shareholders. In the current year, the firm reports net earnings of ₹5,00,000. It is estimated that the firm can earn ₹1,00,000 if the amounts are retained. The investors have alternative investment opportunities that will yield them 10 per cent. The firm has 50,000 shares outstanding. What should be the D/P ratio of the company if it wishes to maximise the wealth of the shareholders? Also state minimum MPS.

LO 29.2 LOD M

Solution D/P ratio of the company should be zero because at this ratio, market price of the share would be the maximum as shown by the following calculations:

$$P = \left[D + \left(\frac{r}{K_e}\right)(E - D)\right] / K_e = [0 + 0.20/0.10\ (₹10 - 0)]/0.10 = ₹20/0.10 = ₹200$$

Minimum MPS = [₹10 + 0.2/0.1 (₹10 – ₹10)]/10.1 = ₹10/0.1 = ₹100

Working Notes

r = (₹1,00,000/₹5,00,000) × 100 = 20 per cent

E = ₹5,00,000/50,000 = ₹10

P.29.8 (i) From the following information supplied to you, ascertain whether the firm's D/P ratio is optimal according to Walter. The firm was started a year ago with an equity capital of ₹20 lakh.

Earnings of the firm	₹2,00,000
Dividend paid	1,50,000
P/E ratio	12.5

Number of shares outstanding, 20,000 @ ₹100 each. The firm is expected to maintain its current rate of earnings on investment. **LO 29.2** LOD M

(ii) What should be the P/E ratio at which the dividend payout ratio will have no effect on the value of the share?

(iii) Will your decision change if the P/E ratio is 8, instead of 12.5?

Solution

(i) P = [₹7.5 + (0.10/0.08) × (₹10 – ₹7.5)]/0.08 = ₹10.625/0.08 = ₹132.81.

The firm's D/P ratio is not optimal. At 75 per cent D/P ratio, the price per share is ₹132.81. The zero per cent D/P ratio would be optimum, as at this ratio the value of the share would be maximum as shown in the following calculations:

P = [0 + (0.10/0.08) × (₹10 – 0)]/0.08 = ₹12.50/0.08 = ₹156.25.

Working Notes

(a) K_e is the reciprocal of P/E ratio = 1/0.125 = 8 per cent

(b) EPS = ₹2,00,000 ÷ 20,000 = ₹10

(c) ROI(r) = (₹2,00,000 ÷ ₹20,00,000) × 100 = 10 per cent

(ii) At P/E ratio of 10 times, D/P ratio would have no effect on the value of the share because at this rate $K_e = r$.

(iii) Yes, the decision would change if the P/E ratio is 8. This implies that K_e is 12.5 per cent. Since $K_e > r$, the 100 per cent dividend payout ratio would maximise the value of the share: P = [10 + (0.10/0.125) × (₹10 – ₹10)]/0.125 = ₹80. At all other D/P ratios, the value would be lower.

P.29.9 The following figures are collected from the current year annual report of XYZ Ltd: **LO 29.2** LOD D

Earnings of firm	₹18 lakh
Number of equity shares	3 lakh
Return on investment	22.5%
Cost of equity	15%

What should be dividend payout ratio so as to keep the share price at ₹42 by using Walter Model? Also, determine the optimum dividend payout ratio. Determine the market price of share at optimum D/P ratio. What will be the minimum and maximum price under this model? When D/P ratio will be irrelevant under Walter's proposition?

Solution

Earnings of the firm	18 lakh
Number of equity shares	3 lakh
EPS	₹6

$P = (D + r/k\,(E - D))/k$

For $P = ₹42$

$42 = x + 1.5\,(6 - x) = (x + 9 - 1.5x)/0.15 = (9 - 0.5\,x)\,/0.15$

$6.3 = 9 - 0.5x$

$X = ₹5.4\ (2.7/0.5)$

D/P ratio $= ₹5.4\,/6 = 0.9 = 90\%$

The company's D/P ratio is not optimal. The zero per cent D/P ratio would be optimum, as at this ratio the value of the share would be maximum as shown below:

$$P = [0 + (22.5\%/15\%)\ (₹6\text{-}0)]/15\% = ₹60$$

Minimum price under this model will be at 100% D/P ratio:

$$P = [6 + (22.5\%/15\%)\ (₹6 - ₹6)]/15\% = ₹40$$

Maximum price (₹60, already computed) under this model will be at zero per cent D/P ratio. D/P ratio would be irrelevant when $k_e = r$.

P.29.10 A textile company belongs to a risk-class for which the appropriate P/E ratio is 10. It currently has 50,000 outstanding shares selling at ₹100 each. The firm is contemplating the declaration of ₹8 dividend at the end of the current fiscal year which has just started. Given the assumption of MM, answer the following questions.

LO 29.1 LOD M

(i) What will the price of the share be at the end of the year: (a) if dividend is not declared, and (b) if it is declared?

(ii) Assuming that the firm pays the dividend, has a net income (y) of ₹5,00,000 and makes new investments of ₹10,00,000 during the period, how many new shares must be issued?

(iii) What will the value of the firm be: (a) if dividend is declared, and (b) if dividend is not declared?

Solution

(i) **(a)** Price, P_1, when dividend is not declared

$P_0 = (D_1 + P_1)/(1 + K_e)$ or $₹100 = 0 + P_1/(1 + 0.10) = ₹110 = P_1$

(b) When dividend is declared

Price, $P_0 = (D_1 + P_1)/(1 + K_e) = ₹100 = (₹8 + P_1)/0.10 = ₹102$

(ii) **(a)** Amount required for new financing

$= I - (Y - nD_1) = ₹10{,}00{,}000 - (₹5{,}00{,}000 - ₹4{,}00{,}000) = ₹9{,}00{,}000$

(b) New shares to be issued

$Dn = ₹9{,}00{,}000/102$

(iii) **(a)** Value of the firm (V) when dividend is declared

$V = [nD_1 + (n + n)P_1 - I + Y - nD_1]/(1 + K_e)$

$= [(₹4{,}00{,}000 + 102 \times (50{,}000 + (₹9{,}00{,}000/102)] - 10{,}00{,}000 + 5{,}00{,}000 - 4{,}00{,}000]/1.10$

$= ₹55{,}00{,}000/1.10 = ₹50{,}00{,}000.$

(b) Value, when dividend is not declared

$V = [(n + \Delta n)P_1 - I + Y]/(1 + K_e)$

$= [(50{,}000 + ₹5{,}00{,}000/100) \times 110 - ₹10{,}00{,}000 + ₹5{,}00{,}000]/1.1$

$= [₹60{,}00{,}000 - ₹10{,}00{,}000 + ₹5{,}00{,}000]/1.10 = ₹50{,}00{,}000.$

P.29.11 The following information is supplied to you, about a company:

LO 29.2 LOD M

Earnings of the company	₹15,00,000
Dividends paid	5,00,000
Number of issued shares	1,00,000
Price earnings ratio	10
Rate of return on investment (%)	15

(i) Determine the theoretical market price of the share.

(ii) Are you satisfied with the current dividend policy of the Firm? If not, what should be the optimal dividend payment ratio in this case?

Solution

(i) $P = \dfrac{[₹5 + (0.15/0.10)\,(15 - 5)]}{0.10} = \dfrac{₹5 + 1.5\,(10)}{0.10} = \dfrac{₹20}{0.10} = ₹200$

(ii) The Company's D/P ratio is not optimal. At 33.33 per cent D/P ratio, the price per share is ₹200. The zero per cent D/P ratio would be optimum, as at this ratio the value of the share would be maximum as shown below:

$$P = \frac{[0 + 0.15/0.10][₹15 - 0]}{0.10} = \frac{1.5[₹15]}{0.10} = ₹225$$

Working Notes

(a) K_e is the reciprocal of P/E ratio = 1/0.10 = 10 per cent.

(b) EPS = ₹15,00,000 ÷ 1,00,000 = ₹15.

(c) DPS = ₹5,00,000 ÷ 1,00,000 = ₹5.

P.29.12 *X* Limited just declared a dividend of ₹14 per share. Mr. B is planning to purchase the share of *X* Limited, anticipating increase in growth rate from 8% to 9%, which will continue for three years. He also expects the market price of this share to be ₹360 after three years. You are required to determine: **(i)** the maximum amount Mr. B should pay for shares, if he requires a rate of return of 13% per annum. **(ii)** the maximum price Mr. B will be willing to pay for share, if he is of the opinion that the 9% growth can be maintained indefinitely and 13% is his rate of return per annum, **(iii)** the price of share at the end of three years, if 9% growth rate is achieved and assuming other conditions remaining same as in **(i)** above. Calculate rupee amount up to two decimal points.

LO 29.2 LOD D

	Year-1	*Year-2*	*Year-3*
FVIF @ 9%	1.090	1.188	1.295
FVIF @ 13%	1.130	1.277	1.443
PVIF @ 13%	0.885	0.783	0.693

Solution

(i) Expected dividend for next 3 years.

Year 1 (D_1) ₹14.00 (1.09) = ₹15.26

Year 2 (D_2) ₹14.00 $(1.09)^2$ = ₹16.63

Year 3 (D_3) ₹14.00 $(1.09)^3$ = ₹18.13

Required rate of return = 13% (K_e)

Market price of share after 3 years = (P_3) = ₹360

The present value of share

$$P_0 = \frac{D_1}{(1+K_e)} + \frac{D_2}{(1+K_e)^2} + \frac{D_3}{(1+K_e)^3} + \frac{P_3}{(1+K_e)^3}$$

$$P_0 = \frac{15.26}{(1+0.13)} + \frac{16.63}{(1+0.13)^2} + \frac{18.13}{(1+0.13)^3} + \frac{360}{(1+0.13)^3}$$

P_0= 15.26(0.885) + 16.63(0.783) + 18.13(0.693) + 360(0.693) = ₹288.56

(ii) If 9% growth rate is achieved for indefinite period, then maximum price of share Mr. B should be willing to pay is:

$P_0 = D_1/(K_e\text{-}g)$= ₹15.26/0.13-0.09 = ₹381.50

(iii) Assuming that conditions mentioned above remain same, the price expected after 3 years will be:

$P_3 = D_4/K_e\text{-}g = D_3\ (1.09)/(0.13 - 0.09)$ = 18.13 × 1.09/0.04 =19.76/0.04 = ₹494

P.29.13 The following information is available in respect of Hypothetical Ltd: Dividend per share (D) at dividend payout ratio of 20% = ₹2. As per Gordon's model, equity capitalisation rate is 15% (at *D/P* ratio of 20%). Company earns ₹10 on every ₹100 invested. Determine the value of its shares (as per Gordon's approach).

LO 29.2 LOD M

Solution

Retention ratio (b) = 1 – 0.20 = 0.80 = 80%

EPS = DPS ÷ D/P ratio = ₹2/0.20 = ₹10

Rate of return (r) = ₹10/₹100 = 10%

As per Gordon model,

$$P = [E(1 - b)]/(k_e - br)$$
$$= [₹10\ (1 - 0.8)]/[0.15 - (0.8 \times 0.1)]$$
$$= ₹2/0.07 = ₹28.57$$

P.29.14 The following information is available for the Hypothetical Ltd: EPS = ₹5.00, D/P ratio = 40%, K_e at D/P ratio of 40% is 16%. Assuming that Gordon valuation model holds true, what rate of return should be earned on investments to ensure that that the market price per share is ₹50? **LO 29.2** LOD D

Solution

$$P = E(1 - b)/(k_e - br)$$
$$₹50 = ₹5(1 - 0.6)/(0.16 - 0.6r)$$
$$₹50 = ₹2/(0.16 - 0.6r)$$
$$₹50(0.16 - 0.6r) = ₹2$$
$$₹8 - 30r = ₹2$$
$$₹6 = 30r$$

Or $r = 6/30 = 0.2 = 20$ per cent

P.29.15 Assume the Hypothetical Ltd expects a potential earnings after taxes of ₹200 lakh next year. Its target debt ratio is 30 per cent. The capital budgeting department of the company projects the likely capital expenditure next year amounting to (i) ₹100 lakh (ii) ₹200 lakh and (iii) ₹400 lakh. Determine the cash dividends likely to be paid and dividend payout ratio at varying levels of investment requirement under the residual dividend policy. **LO 29.1** LOD D

Solution

Dividends Paid and Dividend Payout Ratio Under Residual Dividend Policy (Amount in ₹ lakh)

Particulars	*Size of Capital Budget*		
	(1)	*(2)*	*(3)*
Capital expenditure	₹100	₹200	₹400
Projected earnings after taxes	200	200	200
Target debt ratio (%)	30	30	30
Equity funds needed	70	140	280
Earnings available to pay dividends	130	60	Zero
Dividend payout ratio (%)	65	30	Zero

P.29.16 The existing debt/debt + equity ratio of company is 30%, with equity funds being ₹700 lakh. Based on this information and that provided in table, fill in the blanks.

Dividend and Dividend Payout Ratio Under Residual Dividend Policy

(Amount in ₹ lakh)

Particulars	*Size of capital budget*		
	(1)	*(2)*	*(3)*
Capital expenditure	200	300	400
Projected earnings after tax	400	400	400
Target debt/debt + equity ratio	40%	40%	40%
Equity funds needed	?	?	?
Earnings available to pay dividends	?	?	?
Dividend payout ratio	?	?	?

Solution

Dividend and Dividend Payout Ratio Under Residual Dividend Policy

(Amount in ₹ lakh)

Particulars	*Size of capital budget*		
	(1)	*(2)*	*(3)*
Capital expenditure	200	300	400
Projected earnings after tax	400	400	400
Target debt/debt + equity ratio	40%	40%	40%
Equity funds needed@	20	80	140
Earnings available to pay dividends	380	320	260
Dividend payout ratio	95%	80%	65%

@ Determination of equity funds needed

(Amount in ₹ lakh)

Particulars	*Size of capital budget*		
	(1)	*(2)*	*(3)*
Existing debt (0.3 × ₹1,000)	300	300	300
Debt (Target) allowed	(0.4 × 1200) 480	(0.4 × 1300) 520	(0.4 × 1400) 560
Debt to be raised	180	220	260
Equity funds needed	20	80	140

REVIEW QUESTIONS

LOD: Easy

RQ.29.1 Give appropriate answers for the following: [LO 29.1,2]

(i) Which of the following is not an assumption of the MM theory for irrelevance of dividends? (a) Irrational investors (b) No tax discrimination on capital gains and dividends (c) No transaction costs (d) No flotation costs

(ii) According to Walter's model, the value of the share is ___________ proportion to the D/P ratio
(a) in inverse (b) in direct (c) not related at all (d) in linear

(iii) The test of adequate acceptable opportunities for the firm while considering its dividend policy is the relation between ___________ and ___________

(iv) If the cost of capital of the firm (k) is higher than the rate of return (r), the firm will retain its earnings as it would lead to the reduction of its cost of capital. (True/False)

(v) MM theory of irrelevance of dividends is applicable only to firms which have a constant investment policy. (True/False)

(vi) According to MM theory, the market price of the share will remain unchanged even after the payment of dividends (True/False)

(vii) The arbitrage process implies that the market value plus current dividends of two firms which are alike in all respects except ___________ ratio will be identical.
(a) D/P (b) P/E (c) debt/equity

(viii) Investors can be expected to prefer ___________ to ___________ owing to the tax differential between the dividend and capital gains tax.

(ix) Under what condition is the Walter model similar to the MM hypothesis with regards to the payment of dividends?
(a) $r > k$ (b) $r = k$ (c) $r < k$

(x) Walter's model and Gordon's model are applicable to firms in which all financing is done through ____________ and with ____________ leverage.

(xi) According to the Gordon model, the discount rate used by the investors exhibits ____________ relationship with the retention rate.
(a) a directly proportional (b) an inversely proportional (c) no relationship at all

(xii) The market price of the share, according to Gordon model, is ____________ affected with the increasing payment of dividends.
(a) favourably **(b)** unfavourably **(c)** unaffected

[Answers: (i) Irrational investors (ii) Not related at all (iii) Return on investment and Cost of capital (iv) False (v) True (vi) True (vii) D/P Ratio (viii) Retention of earnings Payment of dividend (ix) r = k (x) Retained earnings, zero (xi) Directly proportional, and (xii) Favourably]

RQ.29.2 What is 'informational content' of dividend payments? Explain. [LO 29.2]

RQ.29.3 The cost of capital and the rate of return on investments of WM Ltd is 10 per cent and 15 per cent respectively. The company has 10 lakh equity shares of ₹10 each outstanding and its earnings per share is ₹5. [LO 29.2]

Calculate the value of the firm in the following situations using Walter's model: (i) 100 per cent retention; (ii) 50 per cent retention; and (iii) no retention. Comment on your result.

RQ.29.4 An engineering company has a cost of equity capital of 15 per cent. The current market value of the firm is ₹30,00,000 @ ₹30 per share. Assuming values for I (new investment), ₹9,00,000, E (earnings), ₹5,00,000, and D(total dividends), ₹3,00,000, show that under the MM assumptions, the payment of dividend does not affect the value of the firm. [LO 29.1]

RQ.29.5 X Ltd. has 8 lakh equity shares outstanding at the beginning of the current year. The current market price per share is ₹120. The Board of Directors of the company is contemplating ₹6.4 per share as dividend. The rate of capitalisation, appropriate to the risk-class to which the company belongs, is 9.6 per cent. [LO 29.1]

(i) Based on M-M approach, calculate the market price of the share of the company, when the dividend is – (a) declared; and (b) not declared.

(ii) How many new shares are to be issued by the company, if the company desires to fund an investment budget of ₹3.20 crore by the end of the year assuming net income for the year will be ₹1.60 crore?

LOD: Medium

RQ.29.6 In a world of no taxes and no transaction costs, a firm cannot be made more valuable by manipulating the dividend payout ratio. Examine the validity of the statement. [LO 29.1]

RQ.29.7 What are the assumptions and arguments used by Modigliani and Miller in support of the irrelevance of dividends? Are dividends really irrelevant? If not, what are the arguments for relevance of dividend policy? [LO 29.1,2]

RQ.29.8 Explain, giving suitable illustrations, the formula given by Walter for determining dividend policy. What are the merits and limitations of this formula in designing the dividend policy for a company? [LO 29.2]

RQ.29.9 How far do you agree with the proposition that dividends are irrelevant? [LO 29.1,2]

RQ.29.10 What is the rationale of the residual theory of dividends? What are the steps a corporate should take to implement it? [LO 29.1]

RQ.29.11 The EPS of a company is ₹16. The market capitalisation rate applicable to the company is 12.5 per cent. Retained earnings can be employed to yield a return of 10 per cent. The company is considering a pay-out of 25 per cent, 50 per cent and 75 per cent. Which of these would maximise the wealth of shareholders as per Walter's model. [LO 29.2]

RQ.29.12 Arvind Ltd belongs to a risk-class for which the appropriate capitalisation rate is 10 per cent. It currently has outstanding 25,000 shares selling at ₹100 each. The firm is contemplating the declaration of dividend of ₹5 per share at the end of the current financial year. The company expects to have a net income of ₹2.5 lakh and has a proposal for making new investments of ₹5 lakh.

Show that under the MM assumption, the payment of dividend does not affect the value of the firm. Is the MM model realistic with respect to valuation? What factors might mar its validity? **[LO 29.1,2]**

LOD: Difficult

RQ.29.13 In what way can the residual theory of dividend be used to establish a long-run target dividend payout ratio instead of dividend payments of each year? Explain with an appropriate example. **[LO 29.1]**

RQ.29.14 The following figures are collected from the annual report of *XYZ* Ltd.: **[LO 29.2]**

Net profit	₹30 lakh
Outstanding 12% preference shares	100 lakh
Number of equity shares	3 lakh
Return on investment	20%

What should be the approximate dividend pay-out ratio so as to keep the share price at ₹42 by using Walter Model?

ANSWERS

29.3 **(i)** ₹750 lakh;
(ii) ₹625 lakh;
(iii) ₹500 lakh

If the firm earn a higher return than the shareholders, a 100 per cent retention is suggested and *vice-versa.*

29.4 Since the value of the firm remains at ₹30 lakh in both the situations when dividends are paid and when dividends are not paid, it can be concluded that the payment of dividend does not affect the value of the firm.

29.5 **(i)** **(a)** ₹125.12; **(b)** ₹131.52
(ii) 1,68,798; 1,21,655

29.11 Value of P at 25% ₹108.8;
at 50% ₹115.2;
at 75% ₹121.6;

None of the above D/P ratio would maximize the wealth of shareholders. The wealth will be maximum (₹128) when D/P ratio is 100.

29.12 Since the value of the firm is ₹25 lakh, in both the situations when dividends are paid and when dividends are not paid, it can be concluded that the payment of dividend does not affect the value of the firm.

The major factors affecting the validity of MM's model are (i) Tax effect, (ii) Flotation cost, (iii) Transaction cost and inconvenience costs, (iv) Preference for current dividend by investors and resolution of uncertainty.

29.14 85 per cent

Scan the QR Code to access comprehensive solutions to all numerical review questions and additional material.

CHAPTER

30

Determinants of Dividend Policy

LEARNING OBJECTIVES

LO 30.1	Describe the general factors that affect dividend policy
LO 30.2	Contrast the basic features of bonus shares and share splits
LO 30.3	Explain share repurchase including the procedural aspects
LO 30.4	Understand the legal, procedural and tax aspects of dividend policy
LO 30.5	Summarise share split practices in India
LO 30.6	Outline bonus share practices in India
LO 30.7	Comprehend shares repurchase practices in India

INTRODUCTION

The previous Chapter has provided an overview of the relationship between the dividend decision of a firm and its total value. In the light of the conflicting and contradictory viewpoints as also the available empirical evidence, there appears to be a case for the proposition that dividend decisions are relevant in the sense that investors prefer them over retained earnings and they have a bearing on the firm's objective of maximising the shareholders' wealth. Given the relevance proposition of the dividend decision of the firm, the present Chapter is devoted to a discussion of the determinants of the dividend policy of a firm. Unlike the theoretical nature of the discussion in the previous Chapter, this aspect of dividend policy is more practical. The Chapter discusses the factors which determine the dividend policy of a firm. The issues of bonus shares (Stock dividends), share (stock) split and related issues are covered in the subsequent discussion. The legal, procedural and tax aspects of dividend payments are outlined subsequently. The main points are summarised by way of recapitulation.

LO 30.1 FACTORS AFFECTING DIVIDEND POLICY

The factors determining the dividend policy of a firm may, for purpose of exposition, be classified into: **(a)** Dividend payout (D/P) ratio, **(b)** Stability of dividends, **(c)** Legal, contractual and internal constraints and restrictions, **(d)** Owner's considerations, **(e)** Clientele effect, **(f)** Capital market considerations, and **(g)** Inflation.

Dividend Payout (D/P) Ratio

Dividend policy involves decision to pay out earnings or to retain them for re-investment.

D/P (dividend payout) ratio indicates the percentage earnings distributed to shareholders in cash, calculated dividing the cash dividend per share by its earnings per share.

A major aspect of the **dividend policy** of a firm is its dividend payout (D/P) ratio, that is, the percentage share of the net earnings distributed to the shareholders as dividends. The relevance of the **D/P ratio**, as a determinant of the dividend policy of a firm, has been examined at some length in the preceding chapter. It is briefly recapitulated here.

Dividend policy involves the decision to pay out earnings or to retain them for reinvestment in the firm. The retained earnings constitute a source of financing. The payment of dividends results in the reduction of cash and, therefore, in a depletion of total assets. In order to maintain the asset level, as well as to finance investment opportunities, the firm must obtain funds from the issue of additional equity or debt. If the firm is unable to raise external funds, its growth would be affected. Thus, dividends imply outflow of cash and lower future growth. In other words, the dividend policy of the firm affects both the shareholders' wealth and the long-term growth of the firm. The optimum dividend policy should strike the balance between current dividends and future growth which maximises the price of the firm's shares.[1] The D/P ratio of a firm should be determined with reference to two basic objectives—maximising the wealth of the firm's owners and providing sufficient funds to finance growth. These objectives are not mutually exclusive, but interrelated.

Given the objective of wealth maximisation, the firm's dividend policy (D/P ratio) should be one which can maximise the wealth of its owners in the 'long run'. In theory, it can be expected that the shareholders take into account the long-run effects of D/P ratio, that is, if the firm is paying low dividends and having high retentions, they recognise the element of growth in the level of future earnings of the firm. However, in practice, they have a clear cut preference for dividends because of uncertainty and imperfect capital markets. The payment of dividends can, therefore, be expected to affect the price of shares: a low D/P ratio may cause a decline in share prices, while a high ratio may lead to a rise in the market price of the shares.

Making a sufficient provision for financing growth can be considered a *secondary* objective of dividend policy. Without adequate funds to implement acceptable projects, the objective of wealth maximisation cannot be achieved. The firm must forecast its future needs for funds, and taking into account the external availability of funds and certain market considerations, determine *both the amount of retained earnings needed and the amount of retained earnings available after the minimum dividends have been paid.* Thus, dividend payments should not be viewed as a residual, but rather a required outlay after which any remaining funds can be reinvested in the firm.[2]

The D/P ratio of the Reliance Industries Ltd. (RIL) is summarised in Exhibit 30.1.

EXHIBIT 30.1 D/P Ratio of RIL, 2005-2017

Years	*DP ratio*
2017	11.53
2016	11.28
2015	12.95
2014	12.70
2013	12.51
2012	14.68

(Contd)

(Contd)

2011	13.66
2010	14.97
2009	14.50
2008	9.81
2007	13.75
2006	17.52
2005	15.79
Mean 2005-2017	13.51
Mean 2005-2008	14.22
Mean 2009-2017	13.20

Stability of Dividends

The second major aspect of the dividend policy of a firm is the stability of dividends. The investors favour a stable dividend as much as they favour the payment of dividends (D/P ratio).

Dividend stability refers to the payment of a certain minimum amount of dividend regularly.

The term **dividend stability** refers to the *consistency or lack of variability* in the stream of dividends. In more precise terms, it means that a *certain minimum amount of dividend* is paid out regularly. The *stability* of dividends can take any of the following three forms: (i) constant dividend per share, (ii) constant/stable D/P ratio, and (iii) constant dividend per share plus extra dividend.

Constant Dividend Per Share According to this form of stable dividend policy, a company follows a policy of paying a certain fixed amount per share as dividend. For instance, on a share of face value of ₹100, a firm may pay a fixed amount of, say ₹15 as dividend. This amount would be paid year after year, irrespective of the level of earnings. In other words, fluctuations in earnings would not affect the dividend payments. In fact, when a company follows such a dividend policy, it will pay dividends to the shareholder even when it suffers losses. A stable dividend policy in terms of a fixed amount of dividend per share does not, however, mean that the amount of dividend is fixed for all times to come. The dividends per share are increased over the years when the earnings of the firm increase and it is expected that the new level of earnings can

Constant dividend per share policy is a policy of paying a certain fixed amount per share as dividend.

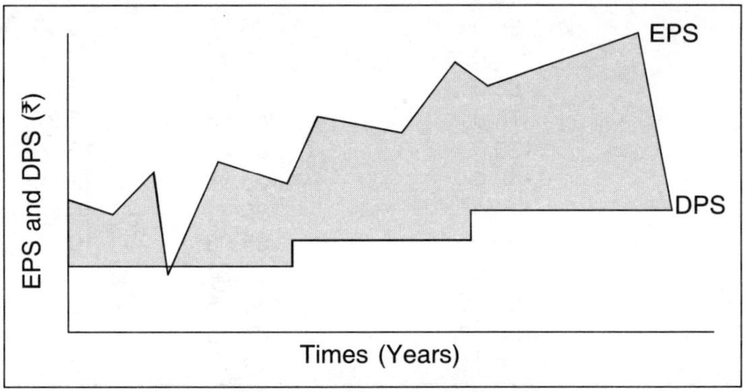

FIGURE 30.1 Stable Dividend Policy

be maintained. Of course, if the increase is expected to be temporary, the annual dividend remains at the existing level. The relationship between the earnings per share (EPS) and dividends per share (DPS) with a constant dividend policy per year is shown in Figure 30.1.

Constant/target payout ratio is a policy to pay a constant percentage of net earnings as dividend to shareholders in each dividend period.

It can, thus, be seen that while the earnings may fluctuate from year to year, the dividend per share is constant. To be able to pursue such a policy, a firm whose earnings are not stable would have to make provisions in years when earnings are higher for payment of dividends in lean years. Such firms usually create a '**reserve for dividends equalisation**'. The balance standing in this fund is normally invested in such assets as can be readily converted into cash.

Stable rupee plus extra dividend is a policy based on paying a fixed dividend to shareholders supplemented by an additional dividend when earnings warrant it.

Constant Payout Ratio With constant payout ratio, a firm pays a constant percentage of net earnings as dividend to the shareholders. In other words, a stable dividend payout ratio implies that the percentage of earnings paid out each year is fixed. Accordingly, dividends would fluctuate proportionately with earnings and are likely to be highly volatile in the wake of wide fluctuations in the earnings of the company. As a result, when the earnings of a firm decline substantially or there is a loss in a given period, the dividends, according to the target payout ratio, would be low or nil. To illustrate, if a firm has a policy of 50 per cent target payout ratios, its dividends will range between ₹5 and zero per share on the assumption that the earnings per share are ₹10 and zero respectively.

Stable Rupee Dividend Plus Extra Dividend Under this policy, a firm usually pays a fixed dividend to the shareholders and in years of marked prosperity additional or extra dividend is paid over and above the regular dividend. As soon as normal conditions return, the firm cuts the extra dividend and pays the normal dividend per share.

The EPS/DPS/RPS/equity dividend of RIL during 2005-17 are shown in Exhibit 30.2.

EXHIBIT 30.2 Equity Dividend, EPS, DPS, and Retention Per Share of RIL, 2005–2017

Years	*Equity dividend (%)*	*EPS*	*DPS*	*Retention per share*
2017	110.0	₹96.65	₹11.00	₹85.65
2016	105.0	84.61	10.50	74.11
2015	100.0	70.21	10.00	60.21
2014	95.0	84.61	9.50	58.52
2013	90.0	96.75	9.00	56.04
2012	85.0	61.27	7.74	53.53
2011	80.0	61.98	7.29	54.69
2010	70.0	49.65	6.37	43.27
2009	130.0	97.28	12.05	85.23
2008	130.0	133.86	11.22	122.64
2007	110.0	85.71	10.34	75.37
2006	100.0	65.08	10.00	55.08
2005	75.0	54.34	7.50	46.84
Mean 2005-2017	98.46	80.15	9.42	67.01
Mean 2005-2008	103.75	84.75	9.77	74.98
Mean 2009-2017	96.11	78.11	9.27	63.47

Evaluation An examination of the three variants of a stable dividend policy require addressing the following questions. What is their relative suitability? What are their implications to the shareholders and the firm? Which form would find favour with the investors?

The target payout ratio, as a form of stable dividend policy, commends itself insofar as it relates to the payment of actual dividend and to the ability of the firm to pay dividends: the higher the earnings, the higher is the dividend per share to the investors. It also implies that funds are automatically ploughed back to the extent of the retained earnings. It also guards against overpayment as well as underpayment of dividends[3] because management cannot pay dividends if there are no profits and it cannot withhold them when profits are earned. But from the shareholder's viewpoint, this method involves *uncertainty* and *irregularity* in regard to the expected dividends. The policy of paying sporadic dividends may not find favour with them.

The alternative to the combination of a small regular dividend and an extra dividend is suitable for companies whose earnings fluctuate widely. With this method, a firm can regularly pay a fixed, though small, amount of dividend so that there is no risk of not being able to pay dividend to the shareholders. At the same time, the investors can participate in the prosperity of the firm. By calling the amount by which the dividends exceed the normal payments as *extra,* the firm, in effect, cautions the investors–both existing as well as prospective—that they should not consider it as a permanent increase in dividends. It may, therefore, be noted that, from the investor's viewpoint, the extra dividend is of a sporadic nature.

What the investors expect is that they should get an assured fixed amount as dividends which should gradually and consistently increase over the years. The most commendable form of stable dividend policy is the constant dividend per share policy. There are several reasons why investors would prefer a stable dividend policy and pay a higher price for a firm's shares which observes stability in dividend payments.

Desire for Current Income A factor favouring a stable policy is the desire for current income by some investors. Investors such as retired persons and widows, for example, view dividends as a source of funds to meet their current living expenses. Such expenses are fairly constant from period to period. Therefore, a fall in dividend will necessitate selling shares to obtain funds to meet current expenses and, conversely, reinvestment of some of the dividend income if dividends rise significantly. For one thing, many of the income-conscious investors may not like to 'dip into their principal' for current consumption. Moreover, either of the alternatives involves, inconvenience apart, transaction costs in terms of brokerage, and other expenses. These costs are avoided if the dividend stream is stable and predictable. Obviously, such a group of investors may be willing to pay a higher share price to avoid the inconvenience of erratic dividend payments which disrupt their budgeting. They would place **positive utility on stable dividends**.

Informational Contents Another reason for pursuing a stable dividend policy is that investors are thought to use dividends and changes in dividends as a source of information about the firm's profitability. If investors know that the firm will change dividends only if the management foresees a permanent earnings change, then the level of dividends informs investors about the company's expected earnings. Accordingly, the market views the changes in the dividends of such a company as of a semi-permanent nature. A cut in dividend implies poor earnings expectation; no change, implies earnings stability; and a dividend increase, signifies the management's optimism about earnings. On the other hand, a company that pursues an erratic dividend payout policy does not provide any such information, thereby increasing the risk associated with the shares. Stability of dividends, where such dividends are based upon long-run earning power of the company, is, therefore, a means of reducing share-riskiness and consequently increasing share value to investors.[4]

Requirements of Institutional Investors A third factor encouraging stable dividend policy is the requirement of institutional investors like life insurance companies, general insurance companies, mutual funds and so on, to invest in companies which have a record of continuous and stable dividend. These financial institutions owing to the large size of their investible funds, represent a significant force in the financial markets and their demand for the company's securities can have an *enhancing effect* on its price and, thereby, on the shareholder's wealth. A stable dividend policy is a prerequisite to attract the investible funds of these institutions. One consequential impact of the purchase of shares by them is that there may be an increase in the general demand for the company's shares. Decreased **marketability risk**, coupled with decreased **financial risk**, will have a positive effect on the value of the firm's shares.

Apart from theoretical postulates for the desirability of stable dividends, there are also many empirical studies, classic among them being that of Lintner[5], to support the viewpoint that companies pursue a stable dividend policy. In other words, companies, while taking decisions on the payment of dividend, bear in mind the dividend amount paid in the previous years. There is a resistance on the part of companies to reduce dividends below the amount paid in previous years. Actually, most firms seem to favour a policy of establishing a non-decreasing *dividend per share stream* over time, but firms seem to be specially careful not to raise dividends per share above a level than cannot be safely sustained in the future. **This cautious *creep up* of dividends per share results in stable dividend per share pattern during fluctuating earnings per share periods, and a rising step-function pattern of dividends per share during increasing earning per share periods[6]**.

According to John Lintner's study, dividends are 'sticky' in the sense that they are slow to change and lag behind shifts in earnings by one or more periods. Most firms, in addition to maintaining a stable rupee amount of dividend, also have target payout ratios (long-run dividend payout ratio) which they aim at. The firms may plan a high or low long-run target payout ratio regardless of their policy towards period-to-period dividend stability. The desire to maintain the present dividend level may conflict with strict adherence to any particular target payout ratio especially when earnings per share drop off, even temporarily. To avoid the necessity of reducing the dividend because of a lean year and to maintain progress towards the target payout ratio, firms raise their dividends per share gradually, as the earnings per share rise. Thus, Lintner concludes that dividends represent the primary active decision variable in most situations. Savings or retained earnings in a given period generally are largely a by-product of dividends action, taken in terms of well-established practices and policies. Dividends are seldom the residual decision.

According to Lintner, *dividend is a function of earnings of that year, existing dividend rate, target payout ratio and speed of adjustment.* In symbolic terms,

$$D_t - D_{t-1} = a_0 + c(D_t^* - D_{t-1}) \tag{30.1}$$

where D_t = Dividend amount under consideration,

D_{t-1} = Dividend paid in the previous year,

a_0 = A constant which may have value of zero, but never negative and generally has a positive value to reflect the greater reluctance to reduce than to raise dividends,

c = Speed of adjustment,

D_t^* = Target payout ratio (r) multiplied by profit after taxes (p) = rp, and

$D_t - D_{t-1}$ = Change in dividend payout (ΔD)

The right hand side of Equation 30.1 can be rewritten as:

$$a_0 + c\,(rP_t - D_{t-1}) = a_0 + crP_t - cD_{t-1}$$

Adding D_{t-1} on both sides of Eq. 30.1

$$D_t = a_0 + crP_t - cD_{t-1} + D_{t-1} = a_0 + crP_t + D_{t-1}(1 - c)$$

Let cr be represented by b_1 (short-run propensity to pay dividends) and $(1 - c)$ be represented by b_2 (long-run propensity to pay dividends), we have:

$$D_t = a_0 + b_1P_t + b_2D_{t-1} \tag{30.2}$$

Thus, dividends paid by an individual company are a function of a_0 (constant), short-run propensity to pay (b_1) and long-run propensity to pay dividends (b_2).

Bolten[7] has also formulated a formula based on key variables suggested by Lintner:

$$D_{t+1} = D_t + a\left[P^* - \frac{D_t}{E_t}\right]E_t \tag{30.3}$$

where D_{t+1} = dividend amount under consideration,
D_t = prevailing dividend,
D_t/E_t = prevailing payout ratio,
P^* = target payout ratio,
E_t = latest earnings per share, and
a = adjustment cushion.

Equation 30.3 suggests that the increase in dividends would be less than the increase in earnings owing to the speed of adjustment.

Suppose the target payout ratio of a company is 50 per cent and the present dividend is ₹2 per share. The firm would not immediately pay a dividend of ₹3 share if the earnings per share rose from ₹5 per share to ₹6, since that would expose the firm to the necessity of reducing the dividend in the following year, if the earnings per share fell below ₹6. Rather, the firm might decide to gradually move toward the 50 per cent target payout by declaring a ₹2.50 per share dividend. With ₹2.50 dividend, the firm's earnings per share could drop to ₹5 in the following year and still be at the 50 per cent target ratio, avoiding the necessity of reducing the dividend. Thus,

$$D_{t+1} = ₹2 + 0.50\left[0.50 - \frac{₹2}{₹6}\right](₹6) = ₹2.50$$

In summing up, it can be commended that a company should seek a stable dividend policy which avoids occasional reduction of dividends. Investors favourably react to the price of shares of such companies and there is a **price enhancing effect** of such a policy as it resolves the uncertainty from the minds of the investors regarding the anticipated stream of dividends. Above all, it projects the image of a stable operating environment. An increase in the dividend communicates the feeling of a firm entering a new period of prosperity.

Legal, Contractual, and Internal Constraints and Restrictions

The dividend decision is also affected by certain legal, contractual, and internal requirements and constraints. The legal factors stem from certain statutory requirements, the contractual restrictions arise from certain loan covenants and the internal constraints are the result of the firm's liquidity position.

Legal Requirements Legal stipulations do not require a dividend declaration but they specify the conditions under which dividends must be paid. Such conditions pertain to **(i)** capital impairment, **(ii)** net profits and **(iii)** insolvency.

Capital Impairment Rules Legal enactments limit the amount of cash dividends that a firm may pay. A firm cannot pay dividends out of its paid-up capital, otherwise there would be a reduction in the capital adversely affecting the security of its lenders. The rationale of this rule lies in protecting the claims of preference shareholders and creditors on the firm's assets by providing a sufficient equity base since the creditors have originally relied upon such an equity base while extending credit. Any dividends that impair capital are illegal and the directors are personally held liable for the amount of illegal dividend. Therefore, the financial manager should keep in mind that payment of dividend is in order and does not violate capital impairment rules.

Net Profits The net profits requirement is essentially a corollary of the capital impairment requirement, in that it restricts the dividend to be paid out of the firm's current profits plus past accumulated retained earnings. Alternatively, a firm cannot pay cash dividends greater than the amount of current profits plus the accumulated balance of retained earnings. For instance, section 205 of the Indian Companies Act provides that dividends shall be paid only out of the current profits or past profits after providing for depreciation. The point to be recognised is that the company can count on the profits of previous years, if the current year's profits fall short of the required funds for maintaining a desired stable dividend policy. Likewise, if there are past accumulated losses, they should be first set off against current earnings before the payment of dividend.

Insolvency A firm is said to be insolvent in two situations: *first*, when its liabilities exceed the assets; and *second*, when it is unable to pay its bills. If the firm is currently insolvent in either sense, it is prohibited from paying dividends. Similarly, a firm would not pay dividends if such a payment leads to insolvency of either type. The rationale of the rule is to protect the creditors by prohibiting the liquidation of near-bankrupt firms through cash dividend payments to the equity owners.

Contractual Requirements Important restrictions on the payment of dividend may be accepted by a company when obtaining external capital either by a loan agreement, a debenture indenture, a preference share agreement, or a lease contract. Such restrictions may cause the firm to restrict the payment of cash dividends until a certain level of earnings has been achieved or limit the amount of dividends paid to a certain amount or percentage of earnings. Since the payment of dividend involves a cash outflow, firms are forced to reinvest the retained earnings within the firm. The restriction on dividends may take three forms. In the first place, firms may be prohibited from paying dividends in excess of a certain percentage, say, 12 per cent. Alternatively, a ceiling in terms of the maximum amount of profits that may be used for dividend payment may be laid down, say not more than 60 per cent of the net profits, or a given absolute amount of such profits can be paid as dividends. Finally, dividends may be restricted by insisting upon a minimum of earnings to be retained.[8] Reinvestment leads to a lower debt/equity ratio and, thus, enhances the margin of cushion (safety) for the lenders.

Therefore, contractual constraints on dividend payments are quite common. The payment of cash dividend in violation of a restriction would amount to default in the case of a loan and the entire principal would become due and payable. Keeping in view the severity of penalty, the financial manager must ensure that the amount of dividend is within the covenants already committed to lenders.

Internal Constraints Such factors are unique to a firm and include (i) liquid assets, (ii) growth prospects, (iii) financial requirements, (iv) availability of funds, (v) earnings stability and (iv) control.

Liquid Assets Once the payment of dividend is permissible on legal and contractual grounds, the next step is to ascertain whether the firm has sufficient cash funds to pay cash dividends. It may well be possible that the firm's earnings are substantial, but the firm may be short of funds. This situation is common for **(a)** growing companies; **(b)** companies which have to retire past loans as their maturity year has come; and **(c)** companies whose preference shares are to be redeemed. Such companies may not like to borrow at exorbitant rates because of the increased financial risk especially if their existing leverage ratio is already very high. Moreover, lenders may be reluctant to lend money for dividend payments since they produce no tangible or operating benefits that will help the firm to repay the loan. Thus, the firm's ability to pay cash dividends is largely restricted by the level of its liquid assets. On the other hand, if excess cash is available, the firm can have a more liberal dividend policy.

Growth Prospects Another set of factors that can influence dividend policy relates to the firm's growth prospects. The firm is required to make plans for financing its expansion programmes. In this context, the availability of external funds and its associated cost together with the need for investment funds would have a significant bearing on the firm's dividend policy.

Financial Requirements Financial requirements of a firm are directly related to its investment needs. The firm should formulate its dividends policy on the basis of its foreseeable investment needs. If a firm has abundant investment opportunities, it should prefer a low payout ratio, as it can usually reinvest earnings at a higher rate than the shareholders can. Such firms, designated as 'growth' companies, are constantly in need of funds. Their financial requirements may be charcterised as large and immediate. That retention of earnings is less costly than selling a new issue of equity needs no reiteration. Moreover, retention of earnings provides the base upon which the firm can borrow additional funds. Therefore, it provides flexibility in the company's capital structure, that is, it make room for **unused debt capacity**. The importance of creation of debt raising potentials for a growing firm is overwhelming.

On the other hand, if the firm has little or no growth opportunities, it will probably prefer low retention and relatively high dividend payouts. This is so for two vital reasons. First, the shareholders can reinvest earnings at a higher rate than the firm can do, and, secondly, such firms may need funds largely to replace or modernise assets. In many instances, these outlays may not be required immediately but after two or three years. Therefore, the need for funds is small and periodic *vis-a-vis* large and fast growing companies. The nature of the firm's needs, therefore, is an important factor in determining the destination of the firm's fund–retention or distribution.

Availability of Funds The dividend policy is also constrained by the availability of funds and the need for additional investment. In evaluating its financial position, the firm should consider not only its ability to raise funds but also the cost involved in it and the promptness with which financing can be obtained. In general, large, mature firms have greater access to new sources for raising funds than firms which are growing rapidly. For this reason alone, the availability of external funds to the growing firms may not be sufficient to finance a large number of acceptable investment projects. Obviously, such firms have to depend on their retained earnings so as to amount of maximum number of available profitable projects. Therefore, large retentions are necessary for such firms.

Earnings Stability The stability of earnings also has a significant bearing on the dividend decision of a firm. Generally, the more stable the income stream, the higher is the dividend payout ratio. Such firms are more confident of maintaining a higher payout ratio. Public utility companies are classic examples of firms that have relatively stable earnings pattern and high dividend payout ratio. Growing firms, characterised by stable earnings, can muster debt funds at a relatively lower cost because of a smaller total risk (business and financial). This is unlike the experience of other firms which, though growing, suffer from fluctuating earnings.

However, the financial manager should remember that dividends have information value. Withholding the payment of dividends will raise the required rate of return of the investors and, therefore, depress the market price of the shares. The increase in earnings should be such that it can offset the unfavourable effect of the increased cost of equity (k_e).

Control Dividend policy may also be strongly influenced by the shareholders' or the management's control objectives. That is to say, sometimes management employs dividend policy as an effective instrument to maintain its position of command and control. The management, in order to retain control of the company in its own hands, may be reluctant to pay substantial dividends and would prefer a smaller dividend payout ratio. This will particularly hold good for companies which require funds to finance profitable investment opportunities when an outside group is seeking to gain control of the firm. Added to this, if a controlling group of shareholders either cannot or does not wish to purchase new shares of equity, under such circumstances, by the issue of additional shares to finance investment opportunities, management may lose its existing control. Conversely, if management is securely in control, either through substantial holdings or because the shares are widely held, and the firm has a good image, it can afford to have a high dividend payout ratio. If it requires funds later, the firm can easily raise additional funds owing to its reputation.

Owner's Considerations

The dividend policy is also likely to be affected by the owner's considerations of **(a)** the tax status of the shareholders, **(b)** their opportunities of investment, and **(c)** the dilution of ownership. It is well-nigh impossible to establish a policy that will maximise each owner's wealth. The firm must aim at a dividend policy which has a beneficial effect on the wealth of the majority of the shareholders.

Taxes The dividend policy of a firm may be dictated by the income tax status of its shareholders. If a firm has a large percentage of owners who are in high tax brackets, its dividend policy should seek to have higher retentions. Such a policy will provide its owners with income in the form of capital gains as against dividends. Since capital gains are taxed at a lower rate than dividends, they are worth more, after taxes, to the individuals in a high tax bracket. On the other hand, if a firm has a majority of low income shareholders who are in a lower tax bracket, they would probably favour a higher payout of earnings because of the need for current income and the greater certainty associated with receiving the dividend now, instead of the less certain prospects of capital gains later. With effect from financial year 2003-4, dividend income from Indian corporate firms, mutual funds and Unit Trust of India is fully exempt from tax in the hands of the shareholders/investors/ unit-holders.

Opportunities The firm should not retain funds if the rate of return earned by it would be less than one which could have been earned by the investors themselves from external investments of funds. Such a policy would obviously be detrimental to the interests of shareholders. It is difficult to ascertain the alternative investment opportunities of each of its shareholders and, therefore, the alternative investment opportunity rate. However, the firm should evaluate the rate of return obtainable from external investments in firms belonging to the same risk class. If evaluation shows that the owners have better opportunities out side, the firm should opt for a higher D/P ratio. On the other hand, if the firm's investment opportunities yield a higher rate than that obtained from similar external investment, a low D/P is suggested. Therefore, in formulating dividend policy, the evaluation of the external investment opportunities of owners is very significant.

Dilution of Ownership The financial manager should recognise that a high D/P ratio may result in the dilution of both control and earnings for the existing equity holders. The control aspect has already been discussed. Dilution in earnings results because low retentions may necessitate the issue of new equity shares in the future, causing an increase in the number of equity shares outstanidng and ultimately lowering earnings per share and their price in the market. By retaining a high percentage of its earnings, the firm can minimise the possibility of dilution of earnings.

Thus, in framing the dividend policy of a firm, consideration must be given to the requirements of equity-holders.

> Although the ultimate dividend policy depends on numerous factors, the avoidance of shareholders' discontent is important. If the shareholders become dissatisfied with the existing dividend policy, they may sell their shares, increasing the possibility that control of the firm will be seized by some outside group. The 'takeover' of a firm by outsiders is more likely when owners are dissatisfied with its dividend policy. It is the 'financial manager's responsibility to keep in touch with the owner's general attitude toward dividends.[9]

Clientele Effect

It is a well established fact that all the groups of investors do not have identical preferences for dividend payout policies. For example, wealthy/young investors in their peak earning years have a marked preference for low or zero dividend payment. They have less need for current income from investments and would simply reinvest dividends received net of taxes. They would be put to disadvantage if the firm pursues a high dividend payout policy. Since they are '**savers**' and, '**not-spenders**' of dividends, they would be first paying taxes on dividends received and then reinvesting after-tax dividends, incurring in the process brokerage cost, besides inconvenience. Such investors prefer firms with low dividend payout policies. Profits are ploughed back in the business to yield higher share price in future, resulting in higher capital appreciation.

In sharp contrast, other groups like retired individuals, widows, pensioners, endowment funds related to colleges, Universities, hospitals, and so on generally have a marked preference for higher dividend payout. Such investors are more often in need of current incomes from their investment to support their current spendings. They do not prefer low dividend paying firms. The value of their equity shares might increase, but they would be in many situations forced to sell their shares incurring brokerage costs to obtain cash to cater to their current consumption needs. While individual investors have an option to liquidate their holdings, this option may not be available with many trustees of endowment funds. They may be legally prevented to do so as it amounts to reduction of '**funds**'. Therefore, such class of investors prefer shares of high dividend payout firms.

Evidently, companies with high dividend payouts would attract one class of investors and low dividend payout companies would attract another. These different groups are called **clienteles**. The **clientele effect** argument states that different groups of investors desire different levels of dividends. When a company chooses to pursue a particular dividend policy, it has chosen a policy to attract a particular clientele. If a firm changes its dividend policy, then it just attracts a different clientele.[10]

Clientele effect argues that different group of investors desire different levels of dividend payment.

The clientele effect indicates that one clientele is as good as another. The existence of a clientele effect does not necessarily imply that one dividend policy is better than another.[11] The clientele effect also helps to bring in the **supply and demand** argument pertaining to share prices of different categories. For example, if the equity shares of dividend-payment firms are in short supply, their prices would rise. If there is more demand for low dividend payout shares, that is, **growth shares**, their share prices would tend to rise. In other words, changes in share prices can be explained not only in terms of financial fundamental factors of earnings, growth, investment policy and so on, but also by demand and supply of shares at a point in time.

Capital Market Considerations

Yet another set of factors that can strongly affect dividend policy is the extent to which the firm has access to the capital markets. In case the firm has easy access to the capital market, either because it is financially strong or large in size, it can follow a liberal dividend policy. However, if the firm has only limited access to capital markets, it is likely to adopt low dividend payout ratios. Such firms are likely to rely more heavily on retained earnings as a source of financing their investments.

Firms which lean heavily on financial institutions for procuring funds, declare a minimum dividend so that they can remain on the 'eligible' list of these institutions. It is because, in general, most financial institutions are prohibited by their charter from buying shares in companies which pay no dividends. A company should be paying dividends at a certain minimum rate for at least some specified number of year (say, 5 years). Since such institutions are significant buyers of corporate securities, some firms that would otherwise have not paid any amount of dividend, would pay some dividend so that they remain on the eligible list.

Inflation

Finally, inflation is another factor which affects the firm's dividend decision. With rising prices, funds generated from depreciation may be inadequate to replace obsolete equipments. These firms have to rely upon retained earnings as a source of funds to make up the shortfall. This aspect becomes all the more important if the assets are to be replaced in the near future. Consequently, their dividend payout tends to be low during periods of inflation.

DIVIDEND POLICY IN INDIA

The main features of the corporate dividend policy in India are summarised below.

- Most of the corporates have a policy of long-run dividend pay-out ratio.
- Dividend changes follow shift in the long-term sustainable earnings.
- Dividend policy as a residual decision after meeting the desired investment needs is endorsed by about 50 per cent of the sample corporates. The corporates which are creating shareholders value (EVA) significantly rescind dividend increase in the event of growth opportunities available to them. Large firms are significantly less willing to rescind dividend increases.
- Dividend policy provides a signalling mechanism of the future prospects of the corporate and, to that extent, affects its market value.
- Investors have different relative risk perceptions of dividend income and capital gains and are not indifferent between receiving dividend income and capital gains. Management should be responsive to the shareholders preferences regarding dividend and the share buy back programme should not replace the dividend payments of the corporates.
- Dividend payments provide a bonding mechanism so as to encourage manager to act in the best interest of the shareholders.

- The corporate enterprises in India seem to have a tendency to pay relatively less dividends. In fact, a fairly large number of them hardly pay any dividend. The foreign controlled companies seem to follow a policy of larger distribution of profits relative to the domestic companies. Retained earnings are a significant source of corporate finance.
- The vast majority of the Indian corporates follows a stable dividend policy in the sense that they pay either constant dividend per share in the following year with fluctuating EPS or increased dividend with increase in EPS.
- An overwhelming majority of corporates have a long-run target D/P ratio. The dividend changes follow shift in long-run sustainable earnings. Their dividend policy is in agreement with the findings of Lintner's study on dividend policy.
- The empirical evidence from 11-year (2001-2011) period suggests that the sample firms have dividend payout ratio of much less than 25 per cent and these ratios have been gradually decreasing during the period of the study, indicating perhaps better growth opportunities for companies, necessitating more retentions.
- There are wide industry variations in the D/P ratios. For instance, the fast moving consumer goods (FMCG) and health care sectors had high D/P ratios whereas sectors like metals and diversified reported low D/P ratios during 2001-2011 period of the study.
- Firms which are creating shareholder value are significantly more willing to rescind dividend increase in the event of growth opportunities available to them. The larger firms are significantly less willing to rescind dividend increase than the small firms.
- Dividend policy provides a signalling mechanism of the future prospects of the firm and thus affects its market value. The investors are not indifferent between receiving dividend income and capital gains.
- The survey findings (undertaken in 2011-12) indicate that dividend policy is guided by the consideration of returns to shareholders in the case of two-fifths of the respondent companies. Cash flow constraints was the consideration affecting dividend policy for more than one-fourth companies.

Source: (i) Anand, Manoj, "Corporate Finance Practices in India, A Survey", *Viklapa*, Vol. 27, No. 4, Oct.–Dec. 2003, pp. 29–56 and Jain P K and Suvendra S Yadav, *op. cit.*, pp. 55–103, (ii) Jain, P K, Shveta Singh and Surendra S Yadav, *Financial Management Practices: An Empirical Study of Indian Corporates*, Springer, New Delhi, 2013, Chapter 4.

LO 30.2 BONUS SHARES (STOCK DIVIDEND) AND STOCK (SHARE) SPLITS

Bonus shares involve payment to existing owners of dividend in the form of shares.

Stock splits is a method commonly used to lower the market price of shares by increasing the number of shares belonging to each shareholder.

An integral part of dividend policy of a firm is the use of **bonus shares** and stock splits. Both involve issuing new shares on a *pro rata* basis to the current shareholders while the firm's assets, its earnings, the risk being assumed and the investors percentage ownership in the company remain unchanged. The only definite result from either a bonus share or share split is the increase in the number of shares outstanding. Table 30.1 illustrates their effect on the capitalisation of the firm. Part one of the table shows the equity of the balance sheet before the bonus issue and part two after the issue. The effect of **share splits** is shown in part three.

TABLE 30.1 Effect of Bonus Shares and Share Splits

(I) Equity portion before the bonus issue:	
Equity share capital (30,000 share of ₹100 each)	₹30,00,000
Share premium (@ ₹25 per share)	7,50,000
Retained earnings	62,50,000
Total equity	1,00,00,000
(II) Equity portion after the bonus issue (1 : 2 ratio):	
Equity share capital (45,000 shares of ₹100 each)	45,00,000
Share premium (45,000 shares × ₹25)	11,25,000
Retained earnings (₹62,50,000 – 15,000 shares × ₹125)	43,75,000
Total equity	1,00,00,000
(III) Equity portion after the share splits (10 : 1 ratio):	
Equity share capital (3,00,000 shares of ₹10 each)	30,00,000
Share premium	7,50,000
Retained earnings	62,50,000
Total equity	1,00,00,000

From Table 30.1 it is clear that a share split is similar to bonus issue from the economic point of view though there are some differences from the accounting point of view. In the equity portion of the firm, a bonus issue reduces the retained earnings and correspondingly increases paid-up equity and share premium, if any, whereas stock/share split has no such effect. The economic effect of both is to increase the number of equity shares outstanding.

Reverse Stock Splits

Reverse stock split reduces the number of outstanding shares.

Instead of increasing the number of shares outstanding, a company may like to reduce it through a reverse split. There is no impact of the reverse split on corporate earnings and shareholders' wealth. Reverse split reflects an aversion on the part of many companies to see the prices of their shares falling below a certain amount. Whatever be the reasons for decrease of price, it can be increased with a reverse split.[12]

In the case of **straight stock split**, the number of outstanding shares increases, but it decreases when the company chooses reverse split. The reverse split of 1:5 implies that for each five shares held by a shareholder, he would receive one share in exchange. The company L.G. Balakrishnan & Brothers Limited has gone for reserve split of 1:10 in March 2010.

Rationale

As pointed out earlier, no major economic benefit results from bonus shares and share splits. Yet, certain advantages are associated with them. In the first place, the issue of bonus shares/share splits would have the effect of bringing the market price of shares within more popular range as a result of larger number of shares outstanding. The larger number of outstanding shares will also promote more active trading in the shares due to availability of floating stock. Yet another advantage might relate to the *informational content of bonus/split* announcement. The announcement is perceived as favourable news by the investors in that with growing earnings, the company has bright prospects and the investors can reasonably look for increase in future dividends. Moreover, it enables the conservation of corporate cash. If the bonus share is an effort to conserve cash for profitable investment opportunities, the share prices will tend to rise and the shareholders benefit. However, if the move to conserve cash relates to financial difficulties within the firm, the market price will most likely react adversely. Finally, bonus/split announcements improve the prospect of raising additional funds particularly through the issue of convertible debentures.

As pointed out earlier, no major economic benefits result from bonus shares and share splits. For this reason, they are, by and large, considered as '**cosmetic**' corporate events. Yet, certain advantages are associated with them.

Various hypothesis have been put forward to explain the rationale for issuing bonus shares and share splits. These hypotheses are not mutually exclusive and are normally considered in an integrated manner. The major hypotheses are: **(1)** Signalling hypothesis, **(2)** Trading range hypothesis, **(3)** Liquidity hypothesis, **(4)** Tax-timing hypothesis, **(5)** Cash substitution hypothesis, and **(6)** Attention hypothesis.[13]

Signalling Hypothesis This hypothesis suggests that announcement of bonus shares conveys/signals about the optimistic future of the issuing firm to the market as there is information asymmetry between managers and investors. Managers, as company insiders, usually have better estimates about the future prospects of their company than the current and the prospective shareholders do. Therefore, bonus shares announcements convey positive signals about the company to the investors. The announcement is perceived as favourable news by the investors in that with growing earnings, the company has bright prospects and the investors can reasonably look for increase in future dividends.

Signalling hypothesis conveys/signals optimistic future prospects about the issuer.

Trading Range Hypothesis The hypothesis suggests that the issue of bonus shares and share splits would have the effect of bringing the market price of shares within a more popular range as a result of larger number of shares outstanding. This would enable more investors to trade in the share, thereby increasing liquidity.

Trading range hypothesis would bring market price of shares within optimum range.

Liquidity Hypothesis This hypothesis is a logical corollary of trading range hypothesis. The issue of bonus shares and stock splits brings the share price in an optimum trading range, making the stock more attractive to the new individual investors. This, in turn, enhances liquidity by increasing the volume of shares traded and decreasing the bid-ask spread.

Liquidity hypothesis suggests enhanced liquidity.

Tax-timing Hypothesis This hypothesis consider, the taxation aspect. The benefit of bonus shares is that the tax is deferred till such time the shareholders sell their shares. Thus, shareholders have an advantage of delaying taxes.

Cash Substitution Hypothesis This hypothesis suggest, that the issue of bonus shares enables the conservation of corporate cash. If the bonus share is an effort to conserve cash for profitable investment opportunities, the share prices will tend to rise and the shareholders benefit. However, if the move to conserve cash relates to financial difficulties, the market price will most likely react adversely.

Cash substitution hypothesis enables conservation of cash.

Attention Hypothesis This hypothesis suggest that managers use bonus shares to attract attention from the professional analysts to revalue their future cash flows. This, in turn, is likely to augment valuation of the firm in the market.

Tables 30.2 and 30.3 respectively list selected companies which have issued bonus shares and share splits during 1999–2018.

TABLE 30.2 Bonus Ratio of Select Companies, 1999-2018

Year	*Company Name*	*Bonus Ratio*
1999	Infosys Technologies Ltd	1:1
1999	Hindustan Petroleum Corporation Ltd	1:2
2000	Thomas Cook (India) Ltd	2:3
2000	Asian Paints Ltd	3:5
2001	DSP Merrill Lynch Ltd	1:1
2001	Polaris Software Labs Ltd	1:2
2002	Camlin Ltd	1:1
2002	Karnataka Bank Ltd	1:1
2003	Procter & Gamble Hygiene & Health Care Ltd	1:2
2003	Moser Baer India Ltd	1:1
2004	Wockhardt Ltd	1:2
2004	Kotak Mahindra Bank Ltd	1:1
2005	Mahindra & Mahindra Ltd	1:1
2005	Torrent Pharmaceuticals Ltd	1:1
2006	Tata Consultancy Services Ltd	1:1
2006	HCL Technologies Ltd	1:1
2007	NIIT Technologies Ltd	1:2
2007	Television Eighteen India Ltd	1:1
2008	Reliance Power Ltd	3:5
2008	GAIL (India) Ltd	1:2
2009	Jindal Steel and Power Ltd	5:1
2009	Reliance Industries Ltd	1:1
2010	Castrol India Ltd	1:1
2010	ITC Ltd	1:1
2011	Hindustan Zinc	1:1
2011	SVC Resources	1:3
2012	Oil India Ltd	3:2
2012	Castrol India Ltd	1:1
2013	Motherson Sumi	1:2
2013	Tata Teleservice	2:15
2014	Infosys	1:1
2014	Parshwanath	1:5
2015	Bharat Elec	2:1
2015	SVP Global	9:1
2016	Balmer Lawrie	3:1
2016	HPCL	2:1
2017	Wipro	1:1
2017	Oil India	1:3
2018	Excel Realty	2:1
2018	VKJ Infra	1:3

TABLE 30.3 Split Ratio of Select Companies, 1999-2018

Year	*Company Name*	*Split Ratio (Old Face Value to New Face Value)*
1999	ACC Ltd	100:10
1999	Wipro Ltd	100:10
2000	Hindustan Unilever Ltd	10:1
2000	Dabur India Ltd	10:1
2001	Hero Honda Motors Ltd	10:2
2001	Dr. Reddy's Laboratories Ltd	10:5
2002	Balaji Telefilms Ltd	10:2
2002	Panacea Biotec Ltd	10:1
2003	TVS Motors Ltd	10:1
2003	Jindal Steel and Power Ltd	10:5
2004	Ashok Leyland ltd	10:1
2004	Cipla Ltd	10:2
2005	Bharat Forge Ltd	10:2
2005	ITC Ltd	10:1
2006	Volats Ltd	10:1
2006	Unitech Ltd	10:2
2007	Marico Ltd	10:1
2007	Apollo Tyres Ltd	10:1
2008	Sesa Goa Ltd	10:1
2008	Provogue India Ltd	10:2
2009	Bharti Airtel Ltd	10:5
2009	Educomp Solutions Ltd	10:2
2010	HDFC Bank Ltd	10:2
2010	Bajaj Electricals Ltd	10:2
2011	Tata Power	10:1
2011	HDFC Bank	10:2
2012	Shalimar Paints	10:2
2012	Bombay Dyeing	10:2
2013	Asian Paints	10:1
2013	PI Industries	5:1
2014	Zen Tech	10:1
2014	Godfrey Philip	10:2
2015	Bata India	10:5
2015	Cadila Health	5:1
2016	Grasim	10:2
2016	Welspun India	10:1
2017	Borosil Glass	10:1
2017	Sunteck Realty	2:1
2018	Singer India	10:2
2018	Super Crop Safe	10:2

LO 30.3 SHARE REPURCHASE (SHARE BUYBACK)

Share repurchase implies that a company buys back its own shares. It is an alternative method to pay cash dividends. Share repurchases reduce the number of equity shares outstanding in the market. Given no change in corporate earnings and price-earning ratio, share repurchase would result in higher **(i)** EPS and **(ii)** market price of a share. Moreover, such repurchases not only convey a positive signal to shareholders that management believes that the share is under-valued but also helps in preventing decline in the firm's share prices.[14] Example 30.1 illustrates that share repurchases is similar to the payment of cash dividends.

***Example* 30.1**

Assume the earnings available to the equityholders of the Hypothetical Ltd is ₹50 lakh. Since there are not sufficient profitable investment projects available, the Hypothetical wants to utilise ₹40 lakh of these earnings either to pay cash dividends or to repurchase shares. There are 20 lakh shares (of face value of ₹10) outstanding and the current market price is ₹20 per share. The company can pay cash dividend of ₹2 per share or can repurchase shares at ₹22 per share through a tender offer. Show the impact of repurchase on the EPS and MPS (market price per share) of the remaining shares assuming no change in total earnings and price-earning ratio.

Solution

Table 30.4 shows the impact of share repurchases.

TABLE 30.4 Effect of Share Repurchase on EPS and MPS

(1)	Current EPS = ₹50 lakh ÷ 20 lakh shars = ₹2.5
(2)	Current P/E ratio [₹20, MPS ÷ ₹2.5, EPS] = 8 times
(3)	Number of shares repurchased [₹40 lakh ÷ ₹22] = 1,81,818 shares
(4)	EPS after repurchasing 1,81,818 shares = [₹50 lakh ÷ the shares left (20 lakh – 1,81,818 = 18,18,182)] = ₹2.75
(5)	Expected MPS after repurchase (EPS x P/E ratio) [₹2.75 x 8 times] = ₹22
(6)	Expected receipts per share to equity shareholder (a) When cash dividends are paid = MPS remains unchanged at ₹20 + ₹2, cash dividend = ₹22 (b) When shares are repurchased = MPS rises to ₹22 + zero dividend = ₹22
(7)	**Conclusion**: In both situations, the shareholder receives ₹22 per share

It may be noted that if shares are repurchased at less than ₹22, it would be advantageous to the holders of the remaining shares. Given the assumptions of no change in corporate earnings and P/E ratio, the price of the share would tend to exceed ₹22. They would suffer a loss, if the shares are repurchased at a price higher than ₹22 per share.

Equilibrium Formula Out of the various methods of repurchase of shares, fixed-price tender offer provides all shareholders equal treatment. Further, a company may also like to set repurchase price at a level which puts the remaining shareholders at the same level as the outgoing shareholders. This is referred to as equilibrium share repurchase price (P^*)[15]. It is determined as per Equation 30.4.

$$P^* = (N_c \times MPS_c) \div (N_c - RS) \quad \textbf{(30.4)}$$

Where

N_c = the number of equity shares outstanding prior to the repurchase operation
MPS_c = current market price per share prior to the repurchase activity
RS = the number of shares to be repurchased.

Applying Equation 30.4 to data in Example 30.1.

P^* = (20 lakh shares × ₹20) ÷ (20 lakh shares – 1,81,818 shares) = ₹22 per share.
This was the equilibrium price in Example 30.1.

Advantage of Share Repurchase[16] The major advantages of share repurchases are as follows:

(1) Signalling Effect Share repurchases may have a positive signalling effect on the investors. Since shares are repurchased, by and large, at a price higher than the market price prevailing at that point in time, it is indicative of the management's belief that the firm's shares are undervalued.

(2) Tax Advantage The market price enhancement resulting from a share repurchase is subject to capital gains tax. Dividends are taxed as ordinary income; capital gains are taxed at a lower rate compared to ordinary income. Due to favourable tax treatment, equity shareholders prefer share repurchase in lieu of cash dividend. Moreover, the shareholders have no choice whether or not to receive dividend. In other words, a shareholder is to receive dividends and pay taxes. Whereas, in the case of share repurchase, a shareholder pays taxes only when he actually sells his shares and has a capital gain on the sale. Thus, he can defer tax payments. Finally, there is an option to sell shares for those shareholders who want cash and for others who want to retain the shares. In a way, share repurchases provides 'win-win' situations for all the shareholders.

(3) Price-enhancing Effect Share repurchase results in the availability of lesser number of shares in the market. This, in turn, tends to increase the EPS. Assuming no change in price-earning ratio, the market price of the firm's shares increases (Example 30.1).

(4) Helps in Maintaining Stable Dividend Policy Firms following a stable dividend policy (**as per Lintner's approach**) are most often reluctant to reduce the dividends on decrease in their earnings. The reduction conveys a negative signal to the market. Therefore, in situations when excess cash earnings are perceived by management as temporary in nature, share repurchase mode of dividend distribution is preferred to the alternative increased cash dividend which is most unlikely to be maintained in future years.

(5) Flexibility in Dividend Payment Flexibility is the added virtue of share repurchase as a form of dividend payment. The reason is repurchases can be varied from year to year without conveying adverse signals to the investors. Therefore, corporates with wide variations in their corporate earnings, given their volatile level of sales, should resort to repurchase of shares.

(6) Facilitates Desired Debt-Equity Ratio Share repurchase facilitates firms with very low debt ratio to increase it so that either it conforms to the target or approaches towards the target level. The firms may be reluctant to increase borrowings to achieve the desired D/E ratio as it raises interest burden.

(7) Useful for Employee Stock Option Plan Companies, which follow stock option plan as an important means of employee compensation, can use repurchased shares when employees exercise their options. It is beneficial to the firm and its shareholders as it enables the firm to avoid the issuance of new shares, causing a dilution in EPS which, in turn, decreases MPS.

Disadvantage of Repurchases The two major disadvantages of share repurchases are:

(1) The shareholders selling their shares, may not be aware of the full implications of a repurchase. They may not have access to all the relevant information about the future prospects and outlook of the firm's operations and business activities. In the case of bright prospects, the share repurchase turns to be more profitable for the "**remaining**" shareholders who do not sell their shares than the '**outgoing**' shareholders. The reverse holds true when prospects turn out to be bleak. Therefore, there is an uneven share of prosperity and adversity between these two categories of shareholders. Cash dividend payments do not cause any such discrimination.

(2) The companies may repurchase shares at an unwarranted high premium to the disadvantage of the remaining shareholders. This again raises an ethical problem of fair play and equity. There is no issue of unfairness to any shareholders when dividends are paid in cash.

Considering all the pros and cons of share repurchases, there appears to be a net advantage of share repurchases mode of dividend distribution.

Issue Procedure

The procedure involved in bonus issues and buy-back of shares are outlined below.

Issue of Bonus Shares The main elements of the issue procedure of bonus issues in terms of the SEBI's Issue of Capital and Disclosure Requirements Regulation, 2009 are: conditions for issue, restrictions and completion of the issue.

Conditions Subject to the provisions of the Companies Act/any other applicable law, a listed company can issue bonus shares, if it **(i)** is authorised by its articles of association, **(ii)** has not defaulted in payment of interest/principal in respect of fixed deposits/debt securities issued by it, **(iii)** has sufficient reasons to believe that it has not defaulted in respect of the payment of statutory dues of the employees such as contribution to the provident fund/gratuity/bonus, and **(iv)** the outstanding partly paid shares are made fully paid up. The issuer would have to pass a resolution at its general body meeting for capitalisation of reserves if its articles of association do not have a provision in this respect.

Restrictions An issuer can issue bonus shares in case it has outstanding fully/partly convertible debt instruments (CDIs) only if reservation of (equity) shares of the same class is made in their favour in proportion to the convertible portion. These reserved shares should be issued at the time of the conversion of the CDIs on the same terms/proportions on which the bonus shares were issued.

Bonus shares can be issued by capitalising the **(i)** genuine profits and **(ii)** securities premium collected in cash only. Any reserves created by revaluation of fixed assets should not be capitalised for this purpose. Similarly, bonus shares should not be issued in lieu of dividends.

Completion The bonus issue should be completed/implemented within 15 days from the date of its approval by the Board of Directors of the issuer. It should be implemented within two months from the date of the meeting of the Board of Directors wherein the decision to announce the issue was taken subject to the shareholders' approval in case their approval for capitalisation of profits/reserves is required. Once the decision to issue bonus shares is announced, it cannot be withdrawn.

Buy-back of Securities (Stock Repurchase) The buy-back of securities by listed companies has to conform to **(i)** the provisions of the Companies Act and **(ii)** SEBI's buy-back regulations for listed companies.

Companies Act Requirement The Companies Act permits buy-back of shares/specified securities, from out of the reserves/securities premium account and the proceeds of an earlier issue other than a fresh issue made specifically for buy-back purposes. The stipulations for buy-back are: the articles of association must permit it, authorisation by a special resolution in a general meeting, ceiling of 25 per cent of paid-up capital and free reserves, ratio of debt to equity should not exceed 2:1, fully paid-up shares/specified securities and in conformity with SEBI regulations.

Companies are not allowed to buy-back securities **(i)** through subsidiary/investment companies and **(ii)** if default subsits in respect of repayment of deposits/term loans/redemption of debentures/ preference shares.

The buy-back may be from **(i)** the existing securityholders on a proportionate basis, **(ii)** open market, **(iii)** odd lots, and **(iv)** employees, pursuant to a scheme of stock option/sweat equity issued for considerations other than cash.

All listed companies have to file with the Registrar of Companies (ROCs)/SEBI, a declaration of solvency. The securities purchased under the buy-back arrangement should be extinguished and physically destroyed within seven days of the last date of completion of buy-back. Within 30 days of the completion of the buy-back, a return containing all the particulars must be filed with the ROCs/SEBI.

SEBI Regulations The main elements of the SEBI Buy-Back of Securities Regulations are: conditions of buy-back, buy-back through tender offer, buy-back from the open-market, general obligations and penalties.

Conditions To buy-back securities, a listed company should be authorised to do so by a special resolution in a general meeting of the shareholders or through a resolution by its Board of Directors. A copy of the special resolution should be filed with the SEBI/concerned stock exchange(s) within seven days from the date of passing the resolution. In the case of a Board resolution, public announcement should be preceded by a notice within two days, in at least one English national daily, one Hindi daily and a regional language daily. A copy of the resolution should be filed with the SEBI in case of a Board resolution and the explanatory statement annexed to the notice for general meeting in case of the special resolution would be the same.

Tender Offer A tender offer means an offer by a company to buy-back through a letter of offer, from the holders of shares or other specified securities, on a proportionate basis. The explanatory statement/public announcement should also discuss the maximum price at which the buy-back would be made and the quantum proposed to be tendered by the promoters, together with details of their transactions and holdings for the last six months, including information about the number of shares/securities acquired, and the price and the date of acquisition. The offer should remain open for a minimum of 15 days and a maximum of 30 days. The date of opening of the offer should not be earlier than seven days or later than 30 days from the specified date. The letter of offer should reach the securityholders before the opening of the offer. The company should deposit in an escrow account, 25 per cent on or before the opening of the offer. In case of non-fulfilment of obligations by the company, the escrow account may be forfeited by the SEBI. The company should pay the consideration within seven days of the time specified for accepted offers. The security certificates should be extinguished and destroyed within 15 days of acceptance of the shares/securities. A certificate of compliance should be furnished to the SEBI.

The provisions pertaining to buy-back through a tender offer are also applicable to odd-lot shares/ other specified securities.

Open Market A buy-back from the open market may be through a stock exchange and book-building process.

Stock Exchange The buy-back through a stock exchange can be made only on a stock exchange with nation-wide trading terminals and through the order matching mechanism. The maximum price at which the buy-back would be made should be specified. Information on a daily basis regarding purchases for the buy-back should be given to the stock exchange and published in a national daily on a fortnightly basis and every time an additional five per cent of the buy-back has been completed. The provisions pertaining to the extinguishment of certificates in the case of a tender offer are also applicable in this method.

Book Building The public announcement in case of buy-back through book building should contain a detailed methodology of the book building process, the manner of acceptance, the details of the bidding centres and so on. The offer should remain open for 15-30 days. The final (highest) buy-back price, based on the acceptances received, should be paid to all holders whose shares/ securities have been accepted for buy-back. The provisions pertaining to the verification of acceptances, opening of a special account, payment of consideration and extinguishment of certificates, applicable to a tender offer, are also applicable to this method.

Obligations The company and the merchant banker have to ensure compliance with the obligations prescribed by the SEBI. On a failure to comply with the obligations or to observe due diligence, the SEBI may initiate action against the merchant banker in terms of the relevant SEBI regulations. Similarly, it can initiate action against the registrar to the issue or the broker, in terms of the SEBI regulations applicable to them.

Panalties The SEBI may order an investigation in respect of the conduct of affairs of any person associated with the process of buy-back, to ascertain any contravention of the SEBI regulations. It can also issue directions as it deems fit. Any person guilty of insider trading or market manipulation would be dealt with according to the provisions of the SEBI Insider Trading Regulations and the Prohibition of Fraudulent and Unfair Trading Practices, relating to securities regulations.

Table 30.5 lists select companies which have gone for shares buyback during 2003-18.

TABLE 30.5 Shares Buyback of Select Companies, 2003-2018

Year	*Company name*	*Buyback Type*
2003	–	–
2003	–	–
2004	ADF Foods Ltd	Tender Offer
2004	India Motor Parts and Accessories Ltd	Tender Offer
2005	Reliance Industries Ltd	Tender Offer
2005	Glaxosmithkline Consumer Healthcare Ltd	Tender Offer
2006	Berger Paints	Tender Offer
2006	India Forge and Drop Stampings Ltd	Open Market Through Stock Exchange
2007	Revathi Equipment Ltd	Tender Offer
2007	Natco Pharma Ltd	Tender Offer
2008	Ace Software Ltd	Tender Offer

(Contd.)

(Contd.)

2008	Hindustan Unilever Ltd	Open Market Through Stock Exchange
2009	Eicher Motors Ltd	Tender Offer
2009	Zen Technologies Ltd	Open Market Through Stock Exchange
2010	Zensar Technologies Ltd	Tender Offer
2010	Mangalam Cement Ltd	Open Market Through Stock Exchange
2011	Piramal Health Care Ltd	Tender Offer
2011	FDC Ltd	Open Market Through Stock Exchange
2012	Amrutanjan Health Care Ltd	Tender Offer
2012	JK Lakshmi Cement Ltd	Open Market Through Stock Exchange
2013	Gavis Hospitality Ltd	Tender Offer
2013	Rain Commodities Ltd	Open Market Through Stock Exchange
2014	Jagran Prakashan Ltd	Tender Offer
2014	Aptech Ltd	Open Market Through Stock Exchange
2015	Spenta International ltd	Tender Offer
2015	OnMobile Global Ltd	Open Market Through Stock Exchange
2016	Tips Industries Ltd	Open Market Through Stock Exchange
2016	Clariant Chemicals (India) Ltd	Tender Offer
2017	Dr. Reddy's Laboratories Ltd	Open Market Through Stock Exchange
2017	Oil India Ltd	Tender Offer
2018	SJVN Ltd	Tender Offer
2018	The Ramco Cements Ltd	Open Market Through Stock Exchange

***Note:** '–' indicates no buybacks during this period*

LO 30.4 LEGAL, PROCEDURAL AND TAX ASPECTS

Legal Aspects

The amount of dividend that can be legally distributed is governed by company law, judicial pronouncements in leading cases, and contractual restrictions.[11] The important provisions of company law pertaining to dividends are described below.

1. Companies can pay only cash dividends (with the exception of bonus shares). Apart from cash, dividend may also be remitted by cheque or by warrant. The same may also be transmitted electronically to shareholders after obtaining their consent in this regard to the bank account number specified by them. The step has been proposed by the Department of Company Affairs to avoid delay in the remittance of dividend.
2. Dividends can be paid only out of the profits earned during the financial year after providing for depreciation and after transferring to reserves such percentage of profits as prescribed by law. The Companies (Transfer to Reserve) Rules, 1975, provide that before dividend delcaration, a percentage of profit as specified below should be transferred to the reserves of the company.
   (a) Where the dividend proposed is upto 10 per cent of the paid up capital, no amount of the current profits needs to be transferred.

(b) Where the dividend proposed exceeds 10 per cent but not 12.5 per cent of the paid-up capital, the amount to be transferred to the reserves should bot be less than 2.5 per cent of the current profits.

(c) Where the dividend proposed exceeds 12.5 per cent but not 15 per cent, the amount to be transferred to reserves should not be less than 5 per cent of the current profits.

(d) Where the dividend proposed exceeds 15 per cent but not 20 per cent, the amount to be transferred to reserves should not be less than 7.5 per cent of the current profits.

(e) Where the dividend proposed exceeds 20 per cent, the amount to be transferred to reserve should not be less 10 per cent.

(f) A company may voluntarily transfer a percentage higher than 10 per cent of the current profits to reserves in any financial year provided the following conditions are satisfied:

(i) It ensures that the dividend declared in that financial year is sufficient to maintain average rate of dividend declared by it over three years immediately preceding the financial year.

(ii) In case, it has issued bonus shares in the year in which dividend is declared or in the three years immediately preceding the financial year, it maintains the amount of dividend equal to the average amount of dividend declared over the three years immediately preceding the financial year.

However, maintenance of such minimum rate or quantum of dividend is not necessary if the net profits after tax in a financial years are lower by 20 per cent or more than the average profits after tax of the two immediately preceding financial years.

(g) A newly incorporated company is prohibited from transferring more than ten per cent of its profits to reserves. The 'current profit' for the purpose of transfer to reserves will be profits after providing for statutory transfer to the Development Rebate Reserve and arrears of depreciation if any.

3. Due to inadequacy or absence of profits in any year, dividend may be paid out of the accumulated profits of previous years. In this context, the following conditions, as stipulated by the Companies (Declaration of Dividend out of Reserves) Rules, 1975, have to be satisfied.

(a) The rate of the declared dividend should not exceed the average of the rates at which dividend was declared by the company in 5 years immediately preceding that year or 10 per cent of its paid-up capital, whichever is less.

(b) The total amount to be drawn from the accumulated profits earned in previous years and transferred to the reserves[18] should not exceed an amount equal to one-tenth of the sum of its paid-up capital and free reserves and the amount so drawn should first be utilised to set off the losses incurred in the financial year before any dividend in respect of preference or equity shares is declared.

(c) The balance of reserves after such *drawal* should not fall below 15 per cent of its paid-up capital.

4. Dividends cannot be declared for past years for which accounts have been adopted by the shareholders in the annual general meeting.

5. Dividend declared, interim or final, should be deposited in a separate bank account within 5 days from the date of declaration and dividend will be paid within 30 days from such a date.

6. Dividend including interim dividend once declared becomes a debt. While the payment of interim dividend cannot be revoked, the payment of final dividend can be revoked with the consent of the shareholders.

Procedural Aspects

The important events and dates in the dividend payment procedure are:

1. **Board Resoultion:** The dividend decision is the prerogative of the board of directors. Hence, the board of directors should in a formal meeting resolve to pay the dividend.
2. **Shareholder Approval:** The resolution of the board of directors to pay the dividend has to be approved by the shareholders in the annual general meeting. However, their approval is not required in the case of declaration of interim dividend. Further, it should be noted that the shareholders in the annual general meeting have neither the power to declare the dividends (if the Broad of Directors do not recommend it) nor to increase the amount of dividend. However, they can reduce the amount of the proposed dividend.
3. **Record Date:** The dividend is payable to shareholders whose names appear in the register of members as on the record date.
4. **Dividend Payment:** Once a dividend declaration has been made, dividend warrant must be posted within 30 days. Within a period of 7 days, after the expiry of 30 days, unpaid dividends must be transferred to a special account opened with a scheduled bank.

   In case the company fails to transfer the unpaid dividend to the 'unpaid dividend account' within 37 days of the declaration of dividend, an interest of 12 per cent per annum on the unpaid amount is to be paid by the company. The interest so accruing is to be paid to the shareholders in the proportion of the dividend amount remaining unpaid to them.

   The dividend will be paid to the registered shareholder or to his order or to his banker or in case a share warrant has been issued to the bearer of such a share warrant. In the case of joint-holders, the dividends should be paid to be first joint-holder.

   In the case of dividend payable to non-resident shareholders, authorised dealers are empowered to remit payment of dividend. For the purpose, they are empowered to devise their own documentation to comply with Section 10(5) of FEMA 1999.

   Further, as per the notification issued by the Department of Company Affairs, the payment of dividend to the shareholders involving the fraction of 50 paise and above be rounded off to the rupee and the fraction of less than 50 paise may be ignored.

   In the case of demateralised shares (i.e., the shares held in electronic form), the corporate firms are required to collect the list of members holding shares in the depository and pay them the dividend.
5. **Unpaid Dividend·** if the money transferred to the 'unpaid dividend account' in the scheduled bank remains unpaid/unclaimed for a period of 7 years from the date of such transfer, the company is required to transfer the same to the 'Investor. Education and Protection Fund' established for the purpose.

Record date is the specified future date set by the Directors on which all persons whose names are recorded as shareholders receive the declared dividend.

Tax Aspects

With effect from financial year 2003-4, dividend income from domestic companies and mutual funds is exempt from tax in the hands of the shareholders/investors/unit-holders. However, the domestic companies will be liable to pay dividend distribution tax at the effective rate of 16.995 per cent on dividends paid after April 1, 2007.

LO 30.5 SHARE SPLITS IN INDIA

- Managers view stock splits as a tool to enhance trading liquidity. At a time when share prices are high, the issue of stock splits brings the share price to a preferred trading range, making the share more attractive to the investors.
- Issue of stock splits prior to the public offer also improves the marketability of the shares.
- Lowering of the face value through stock splits decision prior to the public offer seems to be a common practice.
- High face value of the share results in high issue price leading to the reduced number of potential participants, especially retail investors, in the public offer.
- Managers prefer a wider distribution of shares as it increases the trading liquidity in the secondary market also, besides in the new issue market.
- While issuing the stock splits, the managers consider that the face value of the share and its market price should be comparable with other companies in the same industry.
- Stock splits do not provide any positive signals about the future prospects of a firm.

Source: *Based on the survey carried out by Dr Chhavi Mehta as a part of her doctoral dissertation at Department of Management Studies, IIT Delhi.*

LO 30.6 ISSUE OF BONUS SHARES IN INDIA

- Bonus shares attract the attention of the investors, send positive signal about the firm's future prospects and bring the share price in a popular trading range, making the stock more attractive to the investors.
- The primary motive for issuing bonus shares is to increase the total returns for the shareholders.
- The secondary motive is to improve liquidity.
- The tertiary motive for issuance of bonus shares is to attract more investors.
- Managers believe that even though the issue of bonus shares is only a cosmetic corporate event, it has a positive psychological impact on the shareholders, providing positive signal about the firm's future prospects.

Source: Mehta, Chhavi, P K Jain and S S Yadav, *op. cit.*, pp. 28-39.

LO 30.7 SHARES REPURCHASE PRACTICES IN INDIA

The shares repurchase practices by corporate enterprises in India are summarized below:

- The majority of the Indian firms undertaking repurchases are from the capital goods, chemical and petrochemical, consumer durables, oil and gas, healthcare and housing sectors.
- A substantial majority of the Indian finance managers believe that shares repurchases enable investors to express confidence in the firm and are an attractive means of obtaining a sound capital structure.
- Shares repurchase convey positive information possessed by management to the market, creates favorable effect on firm's stock price and signals that the stock is undervalued.
- Indian finance managers strongly support the undervaluation hypothesis. The primary motive in India for announcing shares repurchases is to signal the management's confidence in the future; the secondary motive is to signal undervaluation of shares and the tertiary motive is to return excess cash to the shareholders.

- Indian companies utilise available cash balances for the purpose of repurchases rather than raising externally by debt or other sources.
- Managers view open-market as the popular method of shares repurchase followed by the fixed price offer.
- Indian managers have expressed a sudden increase in stock prices as the primary reason for the companies not completing their shares repurchase programs. Since, the share prices have increased, the repurchases decision has served its purpose. This may, therefore, be the major reason for non-completion of the shares repurchase program in the case of some of the corporates.

Source: Based on the survey carried out by Dr. Sadaf Anwar as a part of her Doctoral Thesis (2018), Impact of Cash Dividend and Shares Repurchase Announcements on Returns, Liquidity and Risk: An Empirical Evidence from Indian Corporates, Department of Management Studies, IIT Delhi.

SUMMARY

LO 30.1

The determinants of the dividend policy of a firm are dividend payout (*D/P*) ratio, stability of dividends, legal, contractual and internal constraints and restrictions, owners' considerations, capital market considerations and inflation.

The *D/P* ratio indicates the percentage share of the net earnings distributed to the shareholders as dividends. Given the objective of wealth maximisation, the *D/P* ratio should be such as can maximise the wealth of its owners in the 'long-run'. In practice, investors, in general, have a clear cut preference for dividends because of uncertainty and imperfect capital markets. Therefore, a low *D/P* ratio may cause a decline in share prices, while a high ratio may lead to a rise in the market price of the shares.

A stable dividend policy refers to the consistency or lack of variability in the stream of dividends, that is, a certain minimum amount of dividend is paid out regularly. Of the three forms of stability of dividend, namely, constant dividend per share, constant *D/P* ratio and constant dividend per share plus extra dividend, the first one is the most appropriate. The investors prefer a stable dividend policy for a number of reasons, such as, desire for current income their, informational contents, institutional requirement, and so on.

There are many empirical studies, (e.g. Lintrer) to support the contention that companies pursue a stable dividend policy.

According to John Lintrer's study, dividends are 'sticky' in the sense that they are slow to change and lag behind shifts in earnings by one or more periods. This leads to the pattern of stable dividend per share during the periods of fluctuating earnings per share and a rising step-function pattern of dividends per share during increasing earnings per share periods.

A firm should seek a stable dividend policy which avoids occasional reductions in dividends. Investors favourably react to the price of shares of such companies and there is a price enhancing effect of such a policy.

The legal restrictions on payment of dividends stipulate conditions pertaining to capital impairment, net profits, insolvency and illegal accumulation of excess profits. The contractual restrictions on payment of dividends are imposed by loan agreements. The internal constraints impinging on the dividend restrictions relate to growth prospects, availability of funds, earnings stability and control. The dividend policy is also likely to be affected by the owners' consideration of (a) tax status of the shareholders, (b) their opportunities for investment and (c) dilution of ownership.

While a firm which has easy access to the capital market can follow a liberal dividend policy, a firm having only limited access to the capital markets is likely to adopt low dividend payout ratio as they are likely to rely, to a greater extent, on retained earnings as a source of financing their investments.

With rising prices, funds generated from depreciation may be inadequate to replace obsolete equipments. As a result, the *D/P* ratio tends to be low during periods of inflation.

LO 30.2	Apart from cash dividend, a firm can also reward its investors by paying bonus shares. The bonus shares/share splits do not have any economic impact on the firm in that its assets, earnings and investors' proportionate ownership remain unchanged. As a result, the number of shares outstanding increases. The increased number of shares outstanding tends to bring the market price of shares within more popular range and promote more active trading in shares. Moreover, bonus/split announcements have informational content to the investors. It will also enable the conservation of corporate cash and further enable a firm to raise additional funds particularly through the issue of convertible securities.
	With effect from financial year 2003-4, dividend income from domestic companies, mutual funds and UTI is exempt from tax in the hands of the shareholders/investors/unitholders. However, the domestic companies will be liable to pay dividend distribution tax.
	While the number of shares outstanding increases in the case of normal split, the reverse split decreases it. Like the normal split, there is no economic impact of the reverse split on (i) corporate earnings and (ii) shareholders' wealth.
LO 30.3	Share repurchase implies that a company buys its own shares. It is an alternative method to pay cash dividends. In India, the companies are allowed to buy back their shares. They are to conform to (i) the provisions of the Companies Act and (2) SEBI's buy-back regulations of listed companies.
	The major advantages of share repurchases are (1) Positive signaling effect, (2) Preferential tax treatment, (3) Price-enhancing effect on shares due to increased earnings per share, (4) Help in maintaining stable dividend policy, (5) Flexibility in dividend payment compared to the requirements of regular dividend policy, (6) Facilitates desired debt-equity ratio and (7) Useful for employee stock option plan. The only major drawback of the buyback is that it may sometimes cause discrimination between the shareholders who sell their shares and those who do not.

REFERENCES

1. Brigham, E F, *Readings in Managerial Finance,* Holt, Rinehart and Wiston, New York, 1971, p. 675.
2. Gitman, L J, *Principles of Managerial Finance,* Harper and Row, New York, 1976, p. 580.
3. Brandt, L K, *Analysis for Financial Management,* Prentice-Hall, Englewood Cliffs, 1972, p. 448.
4. Schall, L D, and C W Haley, *Introduction to Finance Management,* McGraw-Hill, New York, 1977, p. 382.
5. Lintner, K, 'Distribution of income of corporations among dividends, retained earnings and taxes', *American Economic Review,* May 1956, pp. 97-113.
6. Joy, O M, *Introduction to Financial Management,* Richard D Irwin, Homewood I11., 1977, p. 274.
7. Bolten, S E, *Managerial Finance,* Houghton Mifflin Co., Boston, 1976, pp. 368-69.
8. For dividend restrictions imposed by the financial institutions in India, refer to Industrial Finance Corporation of India, *Manual,* New Delhi, 1970.
9. Gitman, I J, *op. cit.,* p. 578.
10. Ross, S A, *op. cit.,* p. 603.
11. Brigham, E F and J F Houston, *op. cit.,* pp..528-9.
12. Van Horne, J C, *op. cit.,* 2002, p..346.
13. For details, refer to Mehta, C, P K Jain and S S Yadav, "Rationale of Stock Dividends/Bonus Shares: An Empirical Study of Private Sector Enterprises in India", *Journal of Financial Management and Analysis,* 22(1), 2009, pp. 28-39.
14. Gitman, L J, *op. cit.,* 2006, p. 607.
15. Van Horne, J C, *op. cit.,* 2002, p. 340.
16. For economics of repurchases, refer to Brigham, E F and J F Houston, *op. cit.,* pp. 549-51.
17. In addition, the provisions of the Income tax Act are also relevant, certain rebates and penalties depend on certain appropriations from profits and the amount of dividend.
18. Profits earned by a company in previous years and transferred to reserves mean the total amount of net profits after taxes, profits transferred to reserves as at the beginning of the year for which the dividend

is to be declared and in computing the said amount, and the appropriations out of the amount transferred from the Developments Rebate Reserve at the expiry of the period specified under the Income Tax Act, 1961 (43 of1961 should be included and all items of capital) reserves including reserves created by revaluation of assets shall be excluded.

SOLVED PROBLEMS

P.30.1 Royal Industries has for many years enjoyed a moderate but stable growth in sales and earnings. In recent years, it is facing a stiff competition in its plastic product line and, consequently, its sales have been declining. Apprehending further decline in its sales, its management is planning to move eventually out of plastic business altogether and develop new diversified product line in growth-oriented industries. To execute the proposed investment plan of this year, a capital outlay of ₹12 crore is necessary to purchase new facilities to start manufacturing a new product; the estimated rate of return on fresh investment is 20 per cent.

LO 30.1 LOD E

The company has been paying a dividend of ₹1.50 per share on 4 crore outstanding equity shares. The dividend policy has been to maintain a stable rupee dividend, raising it only when it appears that earnings have reached a new, permanently higher level. The directors may change such a policy if there are compelling reasons to do so. Total earnings of the current year are ₹10 crore. The current market price of the equity share is ₹15 and the firm's current leverage ratio (debt/assets) is 40 per cent. Current costs of various forms of financing are:

Debentures, 13 per cent
New equity shares sold at ₹15 to yield, ₹14.
Required rate of return on equity, 10 per cent

(a) What would be an appropriate dividend policy for Royal Industries?
(b) What assumptions, if any, do you make in your answer about investors' preference for dividends versus capital gains?

Solution **(a)** The management of Royal Industries should recognise that it will be in constant need of more funds owing to its intended policy of moving into new diversified product lines in growth-oriented industries. This could be done immediately by reducing the current dividend, or by, over time, maintaining the current dividends as earnings rise. To the extent the shareholders have strong expectations about maintenance of the current dividend, the current policy (of maintaining current dividend at ₹1.50 per share) might be appropriate.

The company through advertisement should make the investors aware of the new growth prospects and the greater investment opportunities ahead. Such an announcement would help to prevent the share prices from falling on reduction of the dividend paid, if the company adopts a policy of immediate dividend cut. A better policy, perhaps, would be to maintain the current dividend of ₹1.50 per share and not allow to increase until earnings are so much higher that ₹1.50 represents a lower percentage of earnings.

(b) As discussed in part (a), it might perhaps be appropriate for the management to reduce its dividend payout ratio. This would tend to decrease the dividend yield (D_1/P_0) component of the investors' required rate of return in relation to the growth component. This assumes that the shareholders are basically indifferent between returns earned by them either in the form of dividend or capital gains. However, the investors are not indifferent between payment of dividends or retentions; they have a preference for current dividends as dividends are totally exempt from tax; the equity capitalisation rate would go up if current dividends are reduced.

P.30.2 *X* Cement Ltd requires you, as their financial consultant, to advise them with respect to the dividend policy they have to follow for the current year. The cement industry has been through a very trying period in the last five years and the constraints on operations have been removed in the early part of the year. The company hopes to improve its position in the years to come and has plans to put up an additional plant in the neighbourhood of the present factory. The increased profits, due to expansion in capacity, are expected to be 25 per cent of the additional capital investment after meeting interest charges but before depreciation on the additional plant installed. The shares of X Cement Ltd are

LO 30.1 LOD D

widely held and there is a large majority of holdings in the hands of middle class investors whose average holdings do not exceed 500 shares. The following further data is also made available to you:

Particulars	*Last 5 years*					*Current year*
	1	*2*	*3*	*4*	*5*	*6*
Earnings per share (₹)	6.00	5.0	4.5	4.5	4.0	17.5
Cash availability per share (₹)	7.50	6.0	5.0	4.0	4.0	20.0
Dividend/share (₹)	3.00	3.0	3.0	2.0	Nil	?
Pay out ratio	50	60	67	45	—	?
Average market price (face value of ₹100)	80	70	70	70	60	140
P/E ratio	13.33:1	14:1	15.6:1	15.6:1	15:1	8:1

What recommendations would you make? Give reasons for your answers.

Solution The company appears to be following a stable dividend policy, that is, a policy of maintaining a stable rupee dividend, decreasing it only when it appears that earnings have reached a new, permanently low level or *vice-versa* in that although the EPS has declined from ₹6 in Year 1 to ₹4.50 in Year 3, no corresponding decrease was effected in the DPS. However, when the declining trend of earnings continued in subsequent years too, the dividends had been lowered inasmuch as no dividends were paid in year 5. Consequently, its share prices fell from ₹80 in Year 1 to ₹60 in Year 5. The decline in market prices is less pronounced in the context of much distressing profitability and dividend record of the company during the period as a whole. The rate of return of 6 per cent on equity capital in Year 1 was the maximum. Even this modest amount consistently declined to eventually a very low figure of 4 per cent by current year; the dividend yield was still smaller. The only off-setting factor was the stable dividend policy.

Given the improved record of earnings in the current year and the trend which is likely to continue in future years, coupled with favourable liquidity position, a rise in dividend is commended for the undermentioned reasons.

(a) The investors would receive dividend income free of tax, especially if this category of investors includes retired persons who need the current income for living expenses and do not wish to sell even a small portion of their shares either because of transaction costs involved or because they are reluctant to 'eating their own capital'.

(b) The investors must be expecting a substantial rise in dividend in the light of the current market price of ₹140 compared to ₹60 last year. Failure to pay dividend commensurate to the shareholder's expectation will have an adverse effect on share prices.

(c) Cement industry with stable sales and earnings can afford high leverage ratios. The company is not likely to encounter any major difficulty in raising funds to finance an additional plant due to bright future prospects.

(d) The payment of dividend resolves uncertainty; investors in general are risk averters; they prefer *current* dividends to larger *deferred* dividends.

The payment was 50 per cent in Year 1; the payment of 60 per cent is recommended this year, assuming that target dividend payout ratio is 75 per cent. Moreover, the company through advertisements should make the investors aware of the growth prospects and the investment opportunities ahead which would have a positive effect on share prices.

P.30.3 *X* and *Y* are two fast growing companies in the engineering industry. They are close competitors and their assets composition, capital structure, and profitability records have been very similar for several years. The primary difference between them from a financial management perspective is their dividend policy. The company *X* tries to maintain a non-decreasing dividend per share, while the company *Y* maintains a constant dividend payout ratio. Their recent earnings per share (EPS), dividend per share (DPS), and share price (P) history are as follows:

LO 30.1 LOD M

Year	Company X			Company Y		
	EPS	DPS	P (range)	EPS	DPS	P (range)
1	₹9.30	₹2	₹75-90	₹9.50	₹1.90	₹60-80
2	7.40	2	55-80	7.00	1.40	25-65
3	10.50	2	70-110	10.50	2.10	35-80
4	12.75	2.25	85-135	12.25	2.45	80-120
5	20.00	2.50	135-200	20.25	4.05	110-225
6	16.00	2.50	150-190	17.00	3.40	140-180
7	19.00	2.50	155-210	20.00	4.00	130-190

In all calculations below that require a share price, use the average of the two prices given in the share price range.

(a) Determine the dividend payout ratio (D/P) and price to earnings (P/E) ratio for both companies for all the years.

(b) Determine the average D/P and P/E for both the companies over the period 1 through 7.

(c) The management of Company *Y* is puzzled as to why their share prices are lower than those of Company *X*, in spite of the better profitability record particularly of the past three years. As a financial consultant, how would you explain the situation?

Solution

(a) and **(b)** D/P and P/E Ratios

Year	Company X					Company Y				
	EPS	DPS	D/P ratio (DPS÷EPS)	P	P/E ratio (P÷EPS) (Number of times)	EPS	DPS	D/P ratio	P	P/E ratio (P÷EPS) (Number of times)
1	₹9.30	₹2.00	21.5	₹82.50	8.87	₹9.50	₹1.90	20	₹70	7.37
2	7.40	2.00	27.0	67.50	9.12	7.00	1.40	20	45	6.43
3	10.50	2.00	19.0	90.00	8.57	10.50	2.10	20	57.50	5.48
4	12.75	2.25	17.6	110.00	8.63	12.25	2.45	20	100.00	8.16
5	20.00	2.50	12.5	167.50	8.37	20.25	4.05	20	167.50	8.27
6	16.00	2.50	15.6	170.00	10.62	17.00	3.40	20	160.00	9.41
7	19.00	2.50	13.2	182.50	9.6	20.00	4.00	20	160.00	8.00
	94.95	15.75	16.6	870.00	9.16	96.50	19.30	20	760.00	7.88

(c) Company X is following a stable dividend policy whereas company Y is following a stable dividend payout ratio. In the latter type of policy, sporadic dividend payments occur which make its owners very uncertain about the returns they can expect from their investment in the firm and, therefore, generally depress the share prices. It is probably for this reason that the company X's average price per share exhibited a consistent increase compared to company Y, volatile pattern of earnings of both companies (during the last three years) notwithstanding. Company Y is advised to follow a stable dividend policy.

P.30.4 The shareholders' funds of XYZ Ltd for the year ending March 31 are as follows: The earnings available for equity shareholders from this period's operations are ₹1,50,000, which have been included as part of the ₹3,00,000 retained earnings. LO 30.1 LOD M

(i) What is the maximum dividend per share (DPS) the firm can pay?

(ii) If the firm has ₹60,000 in cash, what is the largest DPS it can pay without borrowing?

(iii) Indicate what accounts, if any, will be affected if the firm pays the dividends indicated in (ii) above?

12% Preference share capital	₹1,00,000
Equity share capital (₹100 each)	4,00,000
Share premium	40,000
Retained earnings	3,00,000
	8,40,000

Solution

(i) Maximum DPS = Total distributable profits/Number of equity shares outstanding = ₹3,00,000/4,000 (₹4,00,000 ÷ 100) = ₹75

(ii) Maximum DPS (without borrowing) = Cash available/Number of equity shares outstanding = ₹60,000/4,000 = ₹15

(iii) Accounts relating to retained earnings and cash will be affected. Retained earnings balance will decline by ₹60,000, that is the amount of dividend paid. Cash will be reduced to zero.

Note: It is assumed that preference share dividends have been paid in full.

P.30.5 Following is the EPS record of AB Ltd over the past 10 years: LO 30.1 LOD M

Year	*EPS*	*Year*	*EPS*
10	₹20	5	₹12
9	19	4	6
8	16	3	9
7	15	2	(2)
6	16	1	1

(i) Determine the annual dividend paid each year in the following cases:

(a) If the firm's dividend policy is based on a constant dividend payout ratio of 50 per cent for all years.

(b) If the firm pays dividend at ₹8 per share, and increases it to ₹10 per share when earnings exceed ₹14 per share for the previous two consecutive years.

(c) If the firm pays dividend at ₹7 per share each year except when EPS exceeds ₹14 per share, when an extra dividend equal to 80 per cent of earnings beyond ₹14 would be paid.

(ii) Which type of dividend policy will you recommend to the company and why?

Solution

(i) (a) Dividend per share, DPS paid in years, 10 – 1

Year	*EPS*	*DPS*	*Year*	*EPS*	*DPS*
10	₹20	₹10	5	₹12	₹6
9	19	9.5	4	6	3
8	16	8	3	9	4.5
7	15	7.5	2	(2)	Nil
6	16	8	1	1	0.5

(b) Dividend per share, DPS, years 10 – 1

Year	*EPS*	*DPS*	*Year*	*EPS*	*DPS*
10	₹20	₹10	5	₹12	₹8
9	19	10	4	6	8
8	16	10	3	9	8
7	15	8	2	(2)	8*
6	16	8	1	1	8

* It is assumed that the company has past accumulated earnings which are not only enough to write-off current year's losses, but also can meet the dividend payment needs (number of equity shares outstanding × ₹8) of this year.

(c) Dividend per share, DPS, years 10 – 1

Years	EPS	DPS	Year	EPS	DPS
10	₹20	₹11.8	5	₹12	₹7
9	19	11	4	6	7
8	16	8.6	3	9	7
7	15	7.8	2	(2)	7
6	16	8.6	1	1	7

(ii) What the investors expect is that they should get an assured fixed amount as dividend which should gradually and consistently increase over the years, that is, a stable dividend.

Stable dividend policy [(i) (b) above] is commended. There are several reasons why investors would prefer a stable dividend, and pay a higher price for firm's shares which observes stability in dividend payments.

Dividend policy on pattern [(i) (a)] involves uncertainty and irregularity in regard to the expected dividends. The policy of paying sporadic dividends may not find favour with them.

Likewise, dividend policy on pattern [(i) (c)] has some element of uncertainty. By calling the amount by which the dividends exceed the normal payments as extra, the firm, in effect, cautions the investors, both existing as well as prospective, that they should not consider it as a permanent increase in dividends. Obviously, such increase in dividends will not have much price-enhancing effect.

In the light of these facts, the dividend policy [(i) (b)] is the most appropriate among all the alternatives.

P.30.6 From the following financial statistics of Infosys Ltd for the period 1993-94 to 2001-02 (along with Sensex), comment on its dividend policy. Are its shares overvalued? **LO 30.1** LOD M

Year	MPS	Networth (₹ lakh)	Equity dividend (₹ lakh)	EAT (₹ Lakh)	EPS	NWPS	D/P (%)	DPS	Sensex
1993-94	₹343	2,870	117	809	₹24.15	₹85.67	14.46	₹3.49	4,485
1994-95	607	6,247	231	1,332	19.88	93.24	17.34	3.45	4,385
1995-96	458	7,984	363	2,101	28.94	109.97	17.28	5.00	3,259
1996-97	731	11,284	399	3,698	50.94	155.43	10.79	5.50	3,440
1997-98	1,493	17,296	703	6,036	39.53	113.28	11.65	4.60	3,770
1998-99	2,597	57,443	1,211	13,526	84.43	358.57	8.95	7.56	3,286
1999-00*	6,891	83,330	2,976	29,352	91.64	260.16	10.14	9.29	4,543
2000-01	7,173	1,38,964	6,615	62,881	196.32	433.86	10.52	20.65	4,355
2001-02	3,606	2,08,031	13,236	80,796	244.32	629.06	16.38	40.02	3,336

* Company issued bonus shares in the ratio of 1:1.

Solution The Infosys Ltd appears to be following a stable dividend policy. The dividend per share (DPS) have consistently increased from ₹3.5 in 1993-94 to ₹7.56 in 1998-99 and, further, to ₹40.02 in 2001-02. Though the DPS has shown a significant increase over the years, the dividends paid are low in relation to the market price of its share (MPS). The dividend yield (DPS/MPS) is less than one per cent in most of the years. In 2001-02, when dividends paid were maximum, the dividend yield was 1.1 per cent only. The dividend payout (*D/P*) ratios is also a pointer towards the same, varying in the range of 8.95 per cent (1993-94) and 17.34 per cent (2001-02). The *D/P* ratios of less than 20 per cent, for a software/information technology company is below the mark.

The DPS are also not commensurate with the pronounced increase in the EAT as well as the EPS over the years particularly since 1998-99. For instance, while EPS was ₹196.32 and ₹244.32 in 2001 and 2002 respectively, the corresponding DPS in these years were ₹20.65 and ₹40.02 only. However, Infosys has virtually doubled the payment of DPS in 2002 over 2001. Given the improved record of earnings, particularly since 1998-99 and the trend which is likely to continue in future years in view of increased level of projects from the US, Infosys would be well advised to pay higher dividend.

All along the period under reference, the market price of its shares seem to be over-valued as reflected in the market price/book value (net worth) ratio (P/B ratio) as shown below:

Year	MPS	NWPS	P/B ratio
1993-94	₹343	₹85.67	4.00
1994-95	607	93.24	6.51
1995-96	458	109.97	4.16
1996-97	731	155.43	4.70
1997-98	1,493	113.28	13.18
1998-99	2,597	358.57	7.24
1999-00	6,891	260.16	26.49
2000-01	7,173	433.86	16.53
2001-02	3,606	629.06	5.73

The P/B ratio indicates that the MPS of Infosys' shares is substantially overvalued. It was maximum (26.49 times) in 1999-2000. The reason may be higher expected of growth of software industry by the investors in view of large number of project and service outsourcing done from India by the USA. However, the MPS is not warranted by the fundamental factors such as EPS, DPS, NWPS, P/B ratio and so on.

P 30.7 The following financial statistics is available in respect of a listed company: **LO 30.1,3** LOD D

Price-earnings (P/E) ratio	8 times
Number of equity shares	4 lakh
Earnings available to equity shareholders	₹40 lakh
Earnings per share	10
Market price per share	80

The company is currently considering whether it should use ₹20 lakh of its earnings to pay cash dividends or to repurchase shares at ₹85 per share.

Required:

(a) How many equity shares can be repurchased, using the funds that would have been disbursed to pay the cash dividend?

(b) Determine the EPS after the proposed share repurchase.

(c) Assuming no change in the current P/E ratio, compute the market price after share repurchase.

(d) Compare and contrast the shareholders' positions under the dividend and repurchase alternatives.

(e) Is ₹85 the equilibrium share repurchase price?

(f) In case share repurchase price is higher than ₹85, which category of shareholders—those who have sold their shares or those who have not—are financially better off?

Solution

(a) ₹20,00,000 ÷ ₹85 = 23,529 shares

(b) Shares outstanding after repurchase = 4,00,000 – 23, 529 = 3,76,471 shares.
EPS after proposed repurchase (₹40 lakh ÷ 3,76,471) = ₹10.625.

(c) MPS = ₹10.625 × 8 times = ₹85

(d) Under the dividend alternative, the shareholders receive ₹5 per share. Given the market price of ₹80, their total receipts per share are ₹85. Under the repurchase alternative, the MPS is ₹85. In both cases, the effective receipts per share are identical.

(e) Yes, ₹85 is the equilibrium share repurchase price as the effective receipts per share are identical under dividend and repurchase alternatives. It can be computed also:

$P^* = (N_c \times MPS_c) \div (N_c - RS)$ = (4,00,000 × ₹80) ÷ (4,00,000 – 23,529)
= ₹320 lakh ÷ 3,76,471 shares = ₹85 per share.

(f) The shareholders who have sold the shares are at an advantage because the expected MPS after repurchase is likely to be lower than the repurchase price.

MINI CASES

30.C.1 Short Circuit Electric Company (SCEC) is one of the market leaders in electric product manufacturing. Its market share in the same sector is more than 34 percent and is way ahead of its competitors. The performance of the SCEC has been eye catching for the past 15 years. Its earnings per share (EPS) have been impressive at more than ₹2 during the last ten years (given face value of the equity share as ₹10). The management had been satisfaction of paying adequate dividends to its shareholders which, in turn, has boosted the share prices and the market value of SCEC.

EPS, DPS and D/P ratio of SCEC, 2003–12

Particulars	*2003*	*2004*	*2005*	*2006*	*2007*	*2008*	*2009*	*2010*	*2011*	*2012*
EPS (₹)	2.62	3.11	3.20	3.30	3.42	3.52	2.86	2.48	2.32	2.1
DPS(₹)	1.8	1.8	2.0	2.0	2.0	2.2	2.2	2.2	2.2	2.2
D/P Ratio (%)	68.7	57.9	62.5	60.6	58.5	62.5	76.9	88.7	95.7	104.8

However, the past four years' (2009-12) have been the cause of concern to management due to a downward trend and sharp decline in EPS from ₹3.52 in 2008 to ₹2.2 by 2012. In spite of this decrease, SCEC maintained high DPS of ₹2.2 (increased in 2008) in years 2009-2012 and has adhered to a stable dividend policy. This policy, in turn, has arrested the decline in its MPS. However, the position had worsened during 2010-2012 inasmuch as dividend payments in 2012 were higher than EPS in 2012.

The CEO, Mr. Wireman, when analysed the situation with his Financial Manager, Mr. Cable, concluded that the reasons for such a downward trend were two-fold:

(i) Increasing competition in the electric product manufacturing market. Few small firms offered products at lower prices; which, in turn, has caused dent in its profit margins.

(ii) Decline in technological upgradation of its R&D unit, which has resulted in lagging behind of SCEC in developing newer and more advanced products in comparison with its competitors.

At this juncture, SCEC is confronted with a choice whether to cut down on the payment of dividends or to continue with the same dividend payment of ₹2.2 per share. The CEO also wants to evaluate the option of having stock repurchase concurrently with decrease in DPS.

In order to analyse the same, the CEO asked his Chief Financial Analyst, Mr. Switch, to give recommendations regarding his prospective action, taking into account all the pros and cons of the action and its impact.

Solution

First, Switch attempted to analyse the impact that the dividend decision may have on the market position of SCEC.

He observes that the company has been following a stable dividend policy. The investors immensely value DPS of ₹2.2 (at a face value of ₹10). He also notes that the sales of the company have shown an upward trend and the capital expenditures have shown reduction. Mr. Switch also believes that the shareholders are the owners of the firm, and good dividend payments induce shareholders to continue investing in the company rather than investing elsewhere in the market. The advantage of paying dividends is that, the adequate dividend payment signals the firm's financial stability and soundness. Dividends not only encourage current shareholders to retain their investment in the firm, but also increase the firm's attractiveness to potential investors.

However, on the other hand, cutting down on the dividend would allow SCEC to both reinvest a significant portion of its earnings in capital investment projects and R&D (which he finds has shown a decline). This helps meet the challenges of increased competition in the company's future and offer higher rates of dividend growth in subsequent years. Therefore, cutting down on dividend payment may help the same. However, cutting dividends would impact the shareholders who expected to receive at least the same dividend as last year (2012).

Maintaining the stable dividend policy would, therefore, require a trade-off between the need to reinvest earnings in order to expand and the need to satisfy shareholders who expect no decrease in DPS. The dividend payout decision must be consistent with the future goals of SCEC also.

In a meeting that Mr. Switch arranged with the Board of Directors of the company, he received varied opinions on the subject. Some of them were:

- The dividend payout ratio had been in the range of 58-69% from 2003-08, but it has gone up to more than 95% in the recent years (2011–2012).
- The firm has successfully followed stable dividend policy till date. Although many of the promoters believed that the firm should continue with the stable dividend policy, many of them favoured the share repurchase programme, saying that it might lead to greater EPS and market value of the share. The justifications given by them were:

(i) The negative signal sent by the action of cutting down on the dividends (if any) would be somewhat offset by the positive action of the share repurchase.
(ii) A repurchase programme provides flexibility in distributing capital to investors in case the earnings were not as high as expected.
(iii) Further, some board members also contended that the stable dividend policy has a price-enhancing effect and should continue.
(iv) Above all, many promoters were of the Modigliani and Miller school of thought and believed that dividend decisions were irrelevant and share prices are unaffected due to them.

On the basis of recommendations on the above analysis and the current market position of SCEC, Mr Switch summarised that cutting down on dividend payment for the year 2013 (say, to ₹1.1) and share repurchase will provide SCEC with the following advantages:

(i) Give a positive signalling effect offsetting the negative signalling effect of reduction dividend payment.
(ii) Provide SCEC with a tax advantage (as there is a dividend payment tax).
(iii) Keeping the *P/E* ratio constant, a change in EPS is likely to have a positive impact on market value of the share.
(iv) Provide SCEC with greater flexibility in terms of cash reserves.
(v) Insulate SCEC from the impact of lost earnings due to increased competition. This would also enable SCEC to carry out pending investment projects and invest in R&D.

In view of the above, Switch suggested that SCEC should go for a reduction in dividend payment and simultaneously go for share repurchase. The policy can be published in annual report and also highlighted in annual general meeting.

SCEC's dividend decision for the year 2013, based on Mr. Switch's recommendation was as follows:

- 50% reduction in dividend payment.
- Dividend payout targeted at 65-70%.
- Repurchase of 5 million shares over 2 years

Market Observations

- On April 3rd, 2013 SCEC suggested that it would be difficult to maintain the dividend.
- Then on May 9th, 2013 SCEC announced that the dividend cut with the stock repurchase programme and the stock price fell by ₹4.30, coming down to ₹27.50.
- Then on May 31st, 2013 SCEC's stock closed at ₹32.17, or about ₹0.30 higher than the pre-announcement price (₹31.87).
- By Dec'31st 2013, SCEC's stock price closed at ₹37.75, giving stockholders a return of 23.8%.
- Finally, on January 1, 2014 SCEC's stock was trading at ₹45.25, which provided stockholders with a post announcement return of 52.9%.

Explanation for volatility The volatility in market behaviour on SCEC"s dividend decision can have the following possible explanations:

(i) One explanation would be that, the market over-punished the shares of SCEC when it announced both a stock repurchase programme and a dividend cut. Then, once the market realised that the company made a strategic move, and signalled to the public that the company's basic earning power was still strong the share prices again rose.

(ii) The other explanation can be attributed to clientele effect. When the company reduced the dividend, the clientele of investors who desired a high dividend payout sold their shares and the share prices dropped. Soon after the old clientele left, a new clientele that desired a lower dividend payout (and have a preference for capital appreciation) replaced them, and as a result the share prices increased.

REVIEW QUESTIONS

LOD: Easy

RQ.30.1 Give appropriate answer for the following: [LO 30.1-4]

(i) In a stock split, the par value of the share is __________ (reduced/increased) and the number of shares is proportionately __________ (reduced/increased).

(ii) __________ involves payment to existing owners of dividend in the form of shares.

(iii) Dividends can only be paid out of the current years earnings (True/False)

(iv) A company is free to choose whatever dividends it must pay. It does not have restrictions from any of the stakeholders. (True/False)

(v) Stock repurchases increase during boom times when firms accumulate excess cash. (True/False)

(vi) The effective wealth of shareholders does not change with the issue of bonus shares. (True/False)

(vii) An optimum dividend policy should strike a balance between __________ and __________ in order to maximize the wealth of the shareholders.

(viii) A new firm can pay dividends to its shareholders out of its paid-up capital as it may not have enough profits to pay dividends but has strong growth prospects in the future. (True/False)

(ix) A firm cannot pay dividends out of its accumulated balance of retained earnings. (True/False)

(x) Firms with more stable income streams generally tend to retain a majority of their earnings so as not to impair the stability of their income (True/False)

(xi) Share splits tend to dilute the ownership of the firm as more shares are offered to shareholders. (True/False)

[Answers: (i) Reduced, Increased (ii) Bonus shares (iii) False (iv) False (v) False (vi) True (vii) Current dividends, Future growth (viii) False (ix) False (x) False (xi) False]

RQ.30.2 X Ltd and Y Ltd are two fast growing companies in the engineering industry. They are close competitors, and their asset composition, capital structure, and profitability records have been very similar for several years. The primary difference between the companies, from a financial management perspective, is their dividend policy. The X Ltd tries to maintain a non-decreasing dividend per share, while Y Ltd maintains a constant dividend pay-out ratio. Their recent EPS, DPS, and share price (P) history are as follows: [LO 30.1]

	X Ltd			*Y Ltd*		
Year	*EPS*	*DPS*	*P (range)*	*EPS*	*DPS*	*P (range)*
1	₹9.3	₹2	₹75–90	₹9.5	₹1.9	₹60-80
2	7.4	2	55–80	7	1.4	25–65
3	10.5	2	70–110	10.5	2.1	35–80
4	12.75	2.25	85–135	12.25	2.45	80–120
5	20	2.5	135–200	20.25	4.05	110–225
6	16	2.5	150–190	17	3.4	140–180
7	19	2.5	155–210	20	4	130–190

In all calculations below that require a share price, use the average of the two prices given in the share price range.

(i) Determine the dividend pay-out (D/P), and P/E ratios for both companies for all the years.
(ii) Determine the average D/P and P/E for both the companies over the period 1 through 7.
(iii) The management of Y Ltd is puzzled as to why their share prices are lower than those of X Ltd, in spite of the fact that its profitability record is slightly better (particularly of past 3 years). As a financial consultant, how would you explain the situation?

RQ.30.3 The structure of equity funds of Sound Technologies Limited is given below (₹ lakh): [LO 30.2]

Authorised equity share capital (50 lakh shares of ₹10 each)	₹500 lakh
Paid-up equity shares capital (20 lakh equity shares of ₹10 each)	200
Share premium (@ ₹15 each)	300
Retained earnings	650

The current market price of the company's share is ₹60. Show the impact on equity funds in the following situations:

(a) Issue of bonus shares in the ratio of 1:5. Shares would be issued at premium.
(b) Share split in the ratio of 5:1.

LOD: Medium

RQ.30.4 What are the determinants of the dividend policy of corporate enterprises? Also, explain the terms bonus shares and share splits. What is their rationale? [LO 30.1,2]

RQ.30.5 What are the factors that determine the dividend policy of a company? Do you believe it will be justifiable for a company to obtain a short-term loan from a bank to allow payment of a dividend? [LO 30.1]

RQ.30.6 What is stable dividend policy? Why should a firm follow such a policy? [LO 30.1]

RQ.30.7 What is the clientele effect/Explain how does it effect dividend policy? [LO 30.1]

RQ.30.8 What is the share repurchase? Enumerate its major advantages and disadvantages. [LO 30.3]

RQ.30.9 How is equilibrium share repurchase price determined? Explain your answer with an example. [LO 30.3]

RQ.30.10 From the following financial statistics of Hypothetical Ltd, compute the equilibrium share repurchase price: [LO 30.3]

Number of equity shares outstanding	50 lakh
Current market price of a share	₹40
Proposed number of shares to be repurchased	10 lakh

RQ.30.11 From the following financial statistics of Wipro Technologies for the period ending March 31, 2002 to March 31, 2008 (along with sensex), comment on its dividend policy. Are its shares overvalued? [LO 30.1]

Year (March -end)	*MPS*	*Net worth (in crore)*	*Equity dividend (in crore)*	*EAT (in crore)*	*EPS*	*NWPS*	*D/P (%)*	*DPS*	*Sensex*
2002	₹306	₹2,532.78	₹23.25	₹866.11	₹37.26	₹108.95	2.68	₹1.00	₹3,469
2003	227	3,330.33	23.26	813.23	34.97	143.20	2.86	1.00	3,048
2004	247	3,507.59	675.00	914.88	39.31	150.69	73.77	29.00	5,590
2005	360	4,893.65	351.79	1,494.82	21.25	69.55	23.53	5.00	6,492
2006	522	6,427.94	712.88	2,020.48	14.17	45.08	35.29	5.00	11,279
2007	556	9,320.40	873.70	2,842.10	19.48	63.88	30.74	6.00	13,072
2008	415	11,610.70	876.50	3,063.30	20.96	79.44	28.61	6.00	15,644

LOD: Difficult

RQ.30.12 To what extent are firms able to establish definite long-run dividend policies? What factors would affect these policies? To what extent might these policies affect market value of a firm's securities? Explain. [LO 30.1]

RQ.30.13 Explain how share repurchases can be of help in (1) changing capital structure and (2) employee stock option plan. [LO 30.3]

RQ.30.14 You are working as a finance manager with Avon Chemicals Limited. The earnings available for its equity shareholders are ₹50 lakh. It has 5 lakh equity shares outstanding. Its share are currently sold at ₹60 per share. The company is currently contemplating the payment of ₹5 per share in cash dividend. The Board of Avon has asked you to determine the following: [LO 30.1,3]

(a) The current EPS and the P/E ratio.

(b) If the firm can repurchase shares at ₹65 per share, how many equity shares can be repurchased instead of cash dividend payment?

(c) The EPS after the proposed share repurchase.

(d) Assuming no change in the current P/E ratio, compute the market price after share repurchase.

(e) Are the equity shareholders who have sold the shares better off than the shareholders who have not sold their shares?

RQ.30.15 Assuming everything to be the same as in RQ 30.14, state whether the shareholders who have not sold their shares are financially better off than those who have sold their shares when shares are repurchased at (a) ₹67, and (b) ₹62 per share. [LO 30.3]

ANSWERS

30.2 **(i)**

X Ltd :	D/P ratio:	21.5;	27;	19;	17.6;	12.5;	15.6;	13.2;
	P/E ratio:	8.87;	9.12;	8.57;	8.63;	8.37;	10.62;	9.6;
Y Ltd :	D/P ratio:	20;	20;	20;	20;	20;	20;	20;
	P/E ratio:	7.37;	6.43;	5.48;	8.16;	8.27;	9.41;	8.00;

(ii) X Ltd : average D/P 16.6 per cent
average P/E 9.16 per cent
Y Ltd : average D/P 20 per cent
average P/E 7.88

(iii) X Ltd is following a stable dividend policy, whereas Y Ltd is following constant D/P ratio policy. In the latter policy, sporadic dividend payments occur, which make its owners very uncertain about the returns they can expect from their investment in the firm and, therefore, generally depress the share prices. It is probably for this reason that X Ltd's average price per share exhibited a stable increasing behaviour *vis-à-vis* that of Y Ltd, volatile pattern of earnings of both companies (during the last three years), notwithstanding. Company Y is advised to follow a stable dividend policy

30.3 **(a)** Retained earnings would reduce to ₹550 lakh.

(b) Number of issued shares would increase to 100 lakh.

30.10 ₹50 per share.

30.11 Shares are over-valued.

30.14 **(a)** EPS ₹10, P/E ratio 6 times
(b) 38,462 shares
(c) ₹10.833
(d) ₹65
(e) No

30.15 **(a)** Outgoing shareholders are better off
(b) Shareholders who have not sold the shares are better off.

Scan the QR Code to access comprehensive solutions to all numerical review questions and additional material.

PART 9

VALUATION AND CORPORATE RESTRUCTURING

Chapter 31
BUSINESS VALUATION

Chapter 32
CORPORATE RESTRUCTURING

It is important for the finance managers, in particular, and other managers, in general, to understand the process and methods of valuing a business/firm. The term 'business' is more comprehensive than the assets deployed in it. The reason is that the valuation of business is to reckon all types of assets (tangible and intangible) as well as all liabilities (recorded and contingent). Irrespective of this difference in scope, the business valuation exercise is akin to the valuation of an asset/a security and is dependent on basic financial concepts of time value of money, risk and return and future cash flows. The subject of business valuation assumes special significance in the case of mergers and acquisitions with a view to, firstly, determining the price that the acquiring firm should be willing to pay for the acquisition of a business and, secondly, deciding 'fair' exchange ratio between the shareholders of the two companies. Part 9 focuses on business valuation (Chapter 31) and corporate restructuring (Chapter 32).

CHAPTER 31 Business Valuation

LEARNING OBJECTIVES

LO 31.1	Explain the basic valuation framework in terms of different concepts of value—book value, market value, intrinsic/economic value, liquidation value, replacement value, salvage value and fair value
LO 31.2	Describe the four major approaches to valuation of business—asset-based, earnings-based, market-value-based and fair value-based
LO 31.3	Discuss market value added (MVA) and economic value added (EVA) approaches to measure value with focus on shareholders

INTRODUCTION

This Chapter dwells on business valuation. It outlines the conceptual framework of valuation first. The various methods/approaches used/recommended for the purpose of business valuation are also delineated. The valuation techniques relevant to measure value accretion in share-holders wealth are covered subsequently. The main points are summarised by way of recapitulation.

LO 31.1 CONCEPTUAL FRAMEWORK OF VALUATION

The term 'valuation' implies the task of estimating the worth/value of an asset, a security or a business. The price an investor or a firm (buyer) is willing to pay to purchase a specific asset/security would be related to this value. Obviously, two different buyers may not have the same valuation for an asset/business as their perception regarding its worth/value may vary; one may perceive the asset/business to be of higher worth (for whatever reason) and hence may be willing to pay a higher price than the other. A seller would consider the negotiated selling price of the asset/business to be greater than the value of the asset/business he is selling.

Evidently, there are unavoidable subjective considerations involved in the task and process of valuation. *Inter-se*, the task of business valuation is more awesome than that of an asset or an individual security. In the case of business valuation, the valuation is required not only of tangible assets (such as plant and machinery, land and buildings, office equipments, and so on) but also of intangible assets (like, goodwill, brands, patents, trademark and so on) as well as human resources that run/manage the business. Likewise, there is an imperative need to take into consideration recorded liabilities as well as unrecorded/contingent liabilities so that the buyer is aware of the total sums payable, subsequent to the purchase of business. Thus, the valuation process is affected by subjective considerations. In order to reduce the element of subjectivity, to a marked extent, and help the finance manager to carry out a more credible valuation exercise in an objective manner, the following concepts of value are explained in this Section: **(i)** book value, **(ii)** market value, **(iii)** intrinsic value, **(iv)** liquidation value, **(v)** replacement value, **(vi)** salvage value, **(vii)** value of goodwill and **(viii)** fair value.

Book Value

Book value is the value at which assets are shown in balance sheet.

The **book value** of an asset refers to the amount at which an asset is shown in the balance sheet of a firm. Generally, the sum is equal to the initial acquisition cost of an asset less accumulated depreciation. Accordingly, this mode of valuation of assets is as per the going concern principle of accounting. In other words, book value of an asset shown in balance does not reflect its current sale value.

Book value of a business refers to total book value of all valuable assets (excluding fictitious assets, such as accumulated losses and deferred revenue expenditures, like advertisement, preliminary expenses, cost of issue of securities not written off) less all external liabilities (including preference share capital). It is also referred to as **net worth**.

Market Value

In contrast to book value, market value refers to the price at which an asset can be sold in the market. The market value can be applied with respect to tangible assets only; intangible assets (in isolation), more often than not, do not have any sale value. Market value of a business refers to the aggregate market value (as per stock market quotation) of all equity shares outstanding. The market value is relevant to listed companies only.

Intrinsic/Economic Value

Intrinsic (economic) value is the present value of incremental future cash inflows using an appropriate discount rate.

The **intrinsic value** of an asset is equal to the present value of incremental future cash inflows likely to accrue due to the acquisition of the asset, discounted at the appropriate required rate of return (applicable to the specific asset intended to be purchased). It represents the maximum price the buyer would be willing to pay for such an asset. The principle of valuation based on the dis-counted cash flow approach (economic value) is used in capital budgeting decisions.

In the case of business intended to be purchased, its valuation is equivalent to the present value of incremental future cash inflows after taxes, likely to accrue to the acquiring firm, discounted at the relevant risk adjusted discount rate, as applicable to the acquired business. The economic value indicates the maximum price at which the business can be acquired.

Liquidation Value

Liquidation value is the price at which an asset can be sold if the firm is liquidated.

As the name suggests, liquidation value represents the price at which each individual asset can be sold if business operations are discontinued in the wake of liquidation of the firm. In operational terms, the liquidation value of a business is equal to the sum of **(i)** realisable value of assets and **(ii)** cash and bank balances minus the payments required to discharge all external liabilities. In general, among all measures of value, the liquidation value of an asset/or business is likely to be the least.

Replacement Value

The replacement value is the cost of acquiring a new asset of equal utility and usefulness. It is normally useful in valuing tangible assets such as office equipment and furniture and fixtures, which do not contribute towards the revenue of the business firm.

Replacement value is the cost of acquisition of a new asset of equal utility.

Salvage Value

Salvage value represents realisable/scrap value on the disposal of assets after the expiry of their economic useful life. It may be employed to value assets such as plant and machinery. Salvage value should be considered net of removal costs.

Value of Goodwill

The valuation of goodwill is conceptually the most difficult. A business firm can be said to have 'real' goodwill in case it earns a rate of return (ROR) on invested funds higher than the ROR earned by similar firms (with the same level of risk). In operational terms, goodwill results when the firm earns excess ('super') profits. Defined in this way, the value of goodwill is equivalent to the present value of super profits (likely to accrue, say for 'n' number of years in future), the discount rate being the required rate of return applicable to such businessfirms.

The value of goodwill in terms of the present value of super profits method can serve as a useful benchmark in terms of the amount of goodwill the firm would be willing to pay for the acquired business. In the case of mergers and acquisition decisions, the value of goodwill paid is equal to the net difference between the purchase price paid for the acquired business and the value of assets acquired net of liabilities the acquiring firm has undertaken to pay for.

Fair Value

The concept of **'fair' value** draws heavily on the value concepts discussed above, in particular, book value, intrinsic value and market value. The fair value is hybrid in nature and often is the average of these three values. In India, the concept of fair value has evolved from case laws (and hence is more statutory in nature) and is applicable to certain specific transactions, like payment to minority shareholders.

Fair value is the average of book value, market value and intrinsic value.

It may be noted that most of the concepts related to value are 'stock' based in that they are guided by the worth of assets at a point of time and not the likely contribution they can make towards earnings/ cash flows of the business in the future. Ideally, business valuation should be related to the cash flow generating ability of acquired business. The intrinsic value reflects the firm's capacity to generate cash flows over the long-run and, hence, seems to be more aptly suited for business valuation.

In fact, in general, business firms are not acquired with the intent to sell their assets in the post-acquisition period. They are to be deployed primarily for generating more earnings. However, from the conservative point of view, it will be useful to know the realisable value, market value, liquidation value and other values, if the acquiring firm has to resort to liquidation. In brief, the finance manager will find it useful to know business valuation from different perspectives. For instance, the book value may be very relevant form accounting/tax purposes; the market value may be useful in determining share exchange ratio and liquidation value may provide an insight into the maximum loss, if the business is to be wound up.

LO 31.2 APPROACHES/METHODS OF VALUATION

The various approaches to valuation of business with focus on equity share valuation are examined below. These approaches should not be considered as competing alternatives to the dividend valuation model. Instead, they should be viewed as providing a range of values, catering to varied needs, depending on the circumstances. The major approaches, namely, the **(i)** asset based approach to valuation, **(ii)** earnings based approach to valuation, **(iii)** market value based approach to valuation and **(iv)** the fair value method to valuation are described below.

Asset-Based Approach to Valuation

Asset-based approach focuses on determining the value of *net assets* from the perspective of equity share valuation. What should the basis of assets valuation be, is the central issue of this approach.

It should be determined whether the assets should be valued at book, market, replacement or liquidation value. More often than not, they are (and should be) valued at *book value*, that is, original acquisition cost minus accumulated depreciation, as assets are normally acquired with the intent to be used in business and not for resale. Thus, the valuation of assets is based on the going concern concept. Some other value measure may be used depending on circumstances of the case. For instance, if the plant and machinery has outlived its economic useful life (earlier than its initial estimated period), and is not in use for production, it will be in order to value the machinery at liquidation value.

Apart from tangible assets, intangible assets, such as goodwill, patents, trademark, brands, know how, and so on, also need to be valued satisfactorily. It may be useful to adopt the super profit method to value some of these assets.

To arrive at the net assets value, total external liabilities (including preference share capital) payable are deducted from total assets (excluding fictitious assets). The company's net assets are computed as per Equation 31.1.

$$\text{Net assets} = \text{Total assets} - \text{Total external liabilities} \quad \textbf{(31.1)}$$

The value of net assets is also known as net worth or equity/ordinary shareholders funds. Assuming the figure of net assets to be positive, it implies the value available to equity shareholders after the payment of all external liabilities. Net assets per share can be obtained, dividing net assets by the number of equity shares issued and outstanding. Thus,

$$\text{Net assets per share} = \text{Net assets/Number of equity shares issued and outstanding} \quad \textbf{(31.2)}$$

The value of net assets is contingent upon the measure of value adopted for the purpose of valuation of assets and liabilities. In the case of book value, assets and liabilities are taken at their balance sheet values. In the market value measure, assets shown in the balance sheet are revalued at the current market prices. For the purpose of valuing assets and liabilities, it will be useful for a finance manager/valuer to accord special attention to the following points[1]:

(i) While valuing tangible assets, such as plant and machinery, he should consider aspects related to technological obsolescence and capital improvements made in the recent years. Depreciation adjustment may also be needed in case the company is following unsound depreciation policy in this regard.

(ii) Is the valuation of goodwill satisfactory, given the amount of profits, capital employed and average rate of return available on such businesses?

(iii) With respect to current assets, are additional provisions required for "unrealisability" of debtors? Likewise, are adjustments required for "unsaleable" stores and stock?

(iv) With respect to liabilities, there is a need for careful examination of 'contingent liabilities', in particular when there is mention of them in the auditor's report, with a view to assess what portion of such liabilities may fructify. Similarly, adjustments may be required on account of guarantees invoked, income tax, sales tax and other tax liabilities that may arise.

The net assets valuation based on book value is in tune with the going concern principle of accounting. In contrast, liquidation value measure is guided by the realisable value available on the winding up/liquidation of a corporate firm.

Liquidation value is the final net asset value (if any) per share available to the equity shareholder. The value is given as per Equation 31.3.

Net assets per share = (Liquidation value of assets – Liquidation expenses – Total external liabilities)/Number of equity shares issued and outstanding. **(31.3)**

In the case of liquidation, assets are likely to be sold through an auction. In general, they are likely to realise much less than their market values. This apart, sale proceeds from assets are further dependent on whether the company has been forced to go into liquidation or has voluntarily liquidated. In the case of the 'former' type of liquidation, the realisable value is likely to be still lower.

The net asset value (NAV) per share will be the lowest under the liquidation value measure (Example 31.1).

***Example* 31.1**

Following is the balance sheet of Hypothetical Company Limited as on March 31, current year:

(₹ lakh)

Liabilities	*Amount*	*Assets*		*Amount*
Share capital		Fixed assets	₹150	
40,000 11% Preference shares of		*Less:* Depreciation	30	120
₹100 each, fully paid-up	40	Current assets:		
1,20,000 Equity shares of		Stocks	100	
₹100 each, fully paid-up	120	Debtors	50	
Profit and loss account	23	Cash and bank	10	160
10% Debentures	20	Preliminary expenses		2
Trade creditors	71			
Provision for income tax	8			
	282			282

Additional Information:

(i) A firm of professional valuers has provided the following market estimates of its various assets: fixed assets ₹130 lakh, stocks ₹102 lakh, debtors ₹45 lakh. All other assets are to be taken at their balance sheet values.

(ii) The company is yet to declare and pay dividend on preference shares.

(iii) The valuers also estimate the current sale proceeds of the firm's assets, in the event of its liquidation: fixed assets ₹105 lakh, stock ₹90 lakh, debtors ₹40 lakh. Besides, the firm is to incur ₹15 lakh as liquidation costs.

You are required to compute the net asset value per share as per book value, market value and liquidation value bases.

Solution

Determination of Net Asset Value per Share (₹ *lakh*)

(i) Book value basis		
Fixed assets (net)		₹120
Current assets:		
Stock	₹100	
Debtors	50	
Cash and bank	10	160
Total assets		280
Less: External liabilities:		
10% Debentures	20	
Trade creditors	71	
Provision for taxation	8	
11% Preference share capital	40	
Dividend on preference shares (0.11 × ₹40 lakh)	4.4	143.4
Net assets available for equityholders		136.6
Divided by the number of equity shares (*in lakh*)		1.2
Net assets value per share (₹)		113.83
(ii) Market value basis		
Fixed assets (net)		130
Current assets:		
Stock	102	
Debtors	45	
Cash and bank	10	157
Total assets		287
Less: External liabilities (as per details given above):		143.4
Net assets available for equityholders		143.6
Divided by the number of equity shares (*in lakh*)		1.2
Net assets value per equity share (₹)		119.67
(iii) Liquidation value basis		
Fixed assets (net)		105
Current assets:		
Stock	90	
Debtors	40	
Cash and bank	10	140
Total assets		245
Less: External liabilities (listed above):		143.4
Less: Liquidation costs		15.0
Net assets available for equityholders		86.6
Divided by the number of equity shares (in lakh)		1.2
Net assets value per equity share (in ₹)		72.17

The asset based approach is intuitively appealing in that it indicates the net assets backing per equity share. However, the approach ignores the future earnings/cash flow generating ability of the company's assets. In fact, the assets acquisition by business firms are not an end in themselves; they are means to an end. The end is value maximisation and firms acquire assets for the purpose of creating value[2]. The earning based approach reckons this perspective.

Earnings Based Approach to Valuation

The earnings approach is essentially guided by the economic proposition that business valuation should be related to the firm's potential of future earnings or cash flow generating capacity. This approach overcomes the limitation of assets-based approach, which ignores the firm's prospects of future earnings and ability to generate cash in business valuation. Earnings can be expressed in the sense of accounting as well as financial management. Accordingly, there are two major variants of this approach: **(i)** earnings measure on accounting basis and **(ii)** earnings measure on cash flow (financial management) basis.

Earnings Measure Based on Accounting—Capitalisation Method As per this method, the earnings approach of business valuation is based on two major parameters, that is, the earnings of the firm and the capatilisation rate applicable to such earnings (given the level of risk) in the market. Earnings, in the context of this method, are the normal expected annual profits. Normally to smoothen out the fluctuations in earnings, the average of past earnings (say, of the last three to five years) is computed.

Apart from averaging, there is an explicit need for making adjustments, to the profits of the past years, in extraordinary items (which are not likely to occur in the future), with a view to arriving at credible **future maintainable profits**. The notable examples of extraordinary/non-recurring items include profits from the sale of land, losses due to sale of plant and machinery, abnormal loss due to major fire, theft or natural calamities, substantial expenditure incurred on the voluntary retirement scheme (not to be repeated) and abnormal results due to strikes and lock-outs of major competing firm(s). Obviously, their non-exclusion will cause distortion in determining sustainable future earnings.

Above all, it will be useful to understand the profile of the business, focussing on identifying the major growth and income drivers. Are such drivers likely to continue in future years? If not, projected profits need to be discounted. Finally, additional income expected in the coming years—say, due to launch of a new product—should also be considered. In brief, the valuer should try to familiarise himself or herself with all major factors/events that had affected the profits of the business in the past year(s) and are likely to affect them in the future years too.

Determination of appropriate capitalisation rate is another major requirement of this approach. Capitalisation rate, normally expressed in percentages, refers to the investment sum, that an investor is willing to make to earn a specified income. For instance, 12.5 per cent capitalisation rate implies that an investor is prepared to invest ₹100 to earn an income of ₹12.5 or an acquiring firm is prepared to invest ₹100 to buy the expected profits of ₹12.5 of another business.

Given the risk return framework of financial decision making, businesses that exhibit (or are exposed to) higher business and financial risks obviously warrant a higher capitalisation factor. Conversely, businesses carrying a low degree of risk are subject to lower capitalisation factor. There are a host of factors that affect the risk complexion including fluctuation in sales/earnings, degree of operating leverage, degree of financial leverage, nature of competition, availability of substitute products and their prices, pace of change in technology and the level of governmental regulations. Thus, there are a number of internal and external factors associated with a business that can influence the risk and, hence, the capitalisation factor.

The determination of the capitalisation factor is not an easy task in practice. A few guidelines/principles may, however, be helpful to the valuer in its quantification. First, the capitalisation factor for a business firm should be higher than that of a government security (normally considered riskless). Secondly, the capitalisation factor should match/hover around the one that is used for other firms operating in similar type of businesses. In case the valuer wants to apply different capitalisation rate, there should be weighty and convincing reasons to do so. For instance, firms having the potential and prospects of achieving abnormal growth rates (for reasons that are firm specific), *vis-à-vis* other firms in the industry, managed by a well known management team (having a good track record), may have low capitalisation factor and *vice versa*.

Having determined the two major inputs, Equation 31.4, can be used to compute the value of business, V_B, (from the perspective of share owners).

$$V_B = \text{Future maintainable profits} \div \text{Relevant capitalisation factor} \qquad \textbf{(31.4)}$$

***Example* 31.2**

In the current year, a firm has reported a profit of ₹65 lakh, after paying taxes @ 35 per cent. On close examination, the analyst ascertains that the current year's income includes: (i) extraordinary income of ₹10 lakh and (ii) extraordinary loss of ₹3 lakh. Apart from existing operations, which are normal in nature and are likely to continue in the future, the company expects to launch a new product in the coming year.

Revenue and cost estimates in respect of the new product are as follows: *(₹ lakh)*

Sales	₹60
Material cost	15
Labour cost (additional)	10
Allocated fixed costs	5
Additional fixed costs	8

From the given information, compute the value of the business, given that capitalisation rate applicable to such business in the market is 15 per cent.

Solution

TABLE 31.1 Valuation of Business

(₹ lakh)

Profit before tax (₹65 lakh/(1 – 0.35))			₹100
Less: Extraordinary income (not likely to accrue in future)			(10)
Add: Extraordinary loss (non-recurring in nature)			3
Add: Incremental income expected from the launch of the new product:			
Sales			₹60
Less: Incremental costs:			
Material costs	₹15		
Labour costs	10		
Fixed costs (additional)	8	33	27
Expected profits before taxes			120
Less: Taxes (0.35)			42
Future maintainable profits after taxes			78
Relevant capitalisation factor			0.15
Value of business (₹78 lakh/0.15)			520

Some useful insights into estimate of capitalisation rate can be made by referring to the *Price earnings (P/E) ratio*. The reciprocal of the P/E ratio is indicative of the capitalisation factor employed for the business by the market. In Example 31.2, the P/E ratio is approximately 6.67 (1/0.15). The product of future maintainable profits, after taxes, ₹78 lakh and the P/E multiple of 6.67 times, yield ₹520 lakh. Given the fact that P/E ratio is a widely used measure, it is elaborated below.

Price Earnings (P/E) Ratio The P/E ratio (also known as the P/E multiple) is the method most widely used by finance managers, investment analysts and equity shareholders to arrive at the market price of an equity share. The application of this method primarily requires the determination of earnings per equity share (EPS). The EPS is computed as per Equation 31.5.

EPS = Net earnings available to equity shareholders during the period/
Number of equity shares outstanding during the period. **(31.5)**

The net earnings/profits are after deducting taxes, preference dividend, and after adjusting for exceptional and extraordinary items (related to both incomes and expenses/losses) and minority interest. Likewise, appropriate adjustments should be made for new equity issues or buybacks of equity shares made during the period to determine the number of equity shares.

The EPS is to be multiplied by the P/E ratio to arrive at the market price of equity share (MPS).

MPS = EPS × P/E ratio **(31.6)**

A high P/E multiple is suggested when the investors are confident about the company's future performance/prospects and have high expectations of future returns; high P/E ratios reflect optimism. On the contrary, a low P/E multiple is suggested for shares of firms in which investors have low confidence as well as expectations of low returns in future years; low P/E ratios reflect pessimism.

The P/E ratio may be derived given the MPS and EPS.

P/E ratio = MPS/EPS **(31.7)**

The future maintainable earnings/projected future earnings should also be used to determine EPS. It makes economic sense in that investors have access to future earnings only. There is a financial and economic justification to compute forward or projected P/E ratios with reference to projected future earnings, apart from historic P/E ratios. This is all the more true of present businesses that operate in a highly turbulent business environment. Witness in this context, the following: "In a dynamic business world, a firm's past earnings record may not be an appropriate guide to its future earnings. For example, past earnings may have been exceptional due to a period of rapid growth. This may not be sustainable in the future…"[3]

The P/E ratios should, however, be used with caution as the published P/E multiples are normally based on the published financial statements of corporate enterprises. Obviously, earnings are not adjusted for extraordinary items and, therefore, to that extent, may be distorted. Besides, all financial fundamentals are often ignored in published data. Finally, they reflect market sentiments, moods and perceptions. For instance, if investors are upbeat about retail stocks, the P/E ratios of these stocks will be higher to reflect this optimism. This can be viewed as a weakness as well, in particular when markets make systematic errors in valuing entire sector. Assuming retail stocks have been overvalued, this error has to be built into the valuation also[4].

In spite of these limitations attributed to the P/E ratio, it is the most widely used measure of valuation. The major plausible reasons are: **(i)** It is intuitively appealing in that it relates price to earnings. **(ii)** It is simple to compute and is conveniently available in terms of published data. **(iii)** It can be a proxy for a number of other characteristics of the firm, including risk and growth.[5]

Example **31.3**

For facts in Example 31.2, determine the market price per equity share (based on future earnings). Assuming:

(i) The company has 1,00,000 11% Preference shares of ₹100 each, fully paid-up.

(iii) The company has 4,00,000 Equity shares of ₹100 each, fully paid-up.

(iii) P/E ratio is 8 times.

Solution

Determination of Market Price of Equity Share

Future maintainable profits after taxes	₹78,00,000
Less: Preference dividends (1,00,000 × ₹11)	11,00,000
Earnings available to equity-holders	67,00,000
Divided by number of equity shares	4,00,000
Earnings per share (₹67 lakh/4 lakh)	16.75
Multiplied by P/E ratio (times)	8
Market price per share (₹16.75 × 8)	134

To conclude, the P/E ratios should be used/interpreted with caution and care. In particular, the investors should focus on prospective/future P/E ratios, risk and growth attributes of business and comprehensive company analysis with a view to have more authentic and credible valuation.

Earnings Measure on Cash Flow Basis (DCF Approach) The P/E ratio approach, as a measure of valuation of equity shareholders wealth, is essentially based on accounting profits/earnings. Normally, such earnings are either of the current year or prospective earnings of the next year. The single year earnings can be camouflaged by either recording revenues earlier or by postponing expenses. Ideally, valuation should be based on the likely earnings of all the future years. The cash flow approach is superior to the accounting profit approach. The discounted cash flow method is also driven by the firm's cash flow generating ability in future years.

Discounted cash flow approach is used to evaluate capital expenditure proposals in terms of their potential for creating net present value for the firm. The DCF approach is applied to the entire business, which may consist of individual capital budgeting projects. Accordingly, the value of business/firm is equal to the present value of expected future cash flows (CF) to the firm, discounted at a rate that reflects the riskiness of the cash flows (k_0). In equation terms:

$$\text{Value of firm}_0 = \sum_{t=1}^{\infty} \frac{\text{CF to Firm}_t}{(1 + k_0)^t} \quad \textbf{(31.8)}$$

To use the DCF approach, accounting earnings (as shown by the firm's income statement) are to be converted to cash flow figures as shown in Format 31.1.

FORMAT 31.1 Computation of Cash Flows

After tax operating earnings*
Plus: Depreciation
Plus: Other non-cash items (say, amortisation of non-tangible asset, such as patents, trade marks, etc and loss on sale of long-term assets)

* The interest costs are included as a part of the discount rate (K_0).

However, analysts/valuers prefer to discount expected *future free cash flows* (FCFF) to operating cash flows (as per Format 31.1) for the purpose of firm valuation. The reason is that firms, in general, are required to make investments in long-term assets as well as in working capital to generate/earn future cash flows; hence, the need for adjusting operating cash flows to free cash flows.

Format 31.2 shows computation of operating free cash flows (OFCF) for the purpose of valuation of a business.

FORMAT 31.2 Determination of Operating Free Cash Flows to Firm (OFCFF)

After tax operating earnings*
Plus: Depreciation, amortisation and other non-cash items
Less: Investments in long-term assets
Less: Investments in operating net working capital**
Operating free cash flows to firm (OFCFF)

*Exclusive of income from (i) marketable securities and non-operating investments and (ii) extraordinary incomes or losses.
**Addition is to be made in the event of decrease of net working capital.

The free cash flow (FCFF) is the legitimate cash flow for the purpose of business valuation in that it reflects the cash flows generated by a company's operations for all the providers (debt and equity) of its 'capital'[6]. The FCFF is a more comprehensive term as it includes cash flows due to after tax non-operating income as well as adjustments for non-operating assets. Format 31.3 exhibits the procedure of determining FCFF.

FORMAT 31.3 Determination of Free Cash Flows to Firm (FCFF)

Operating free cash flows (as per Format 31.2)
Plus: After tax non-operating income/cash flows*
Plus: Decrease (minus increase) in non-operating
Assets, say marketable securities
Free cash flows to Firm (FCFF)

* Non-operating income (1 – tax rate)

Since the FCFFs are available to all the capital providers of a corporate enterprise, the discount rate to be applied to such cash flows should be indicative of the opportunity cost of the funds made available by them, weighted by their relative contribution to the total capital of a corporate enterprise. The opportunity cost is equivalent to the rate of return the investors expect to earn on other investments of equivalent risk. The cost to the firm equals the investors' cost less any tax benefits received by the company itself (say, tax advantage on the payment of interest)[7] plus any tax payments required to be made (say, dividend payment tax).

The value of the firm is given by Equation 31.9

$$\text{Value of firm}_0 = \sum_{t=1}^{\infty} \frac{\text{FCFF to all investors}_t}{(1+K_0)^t} \tag{31.9}$$

Thus, the value of a firm is the present value of FCFF through infinity. The equity valuation can be deduced by subtracting the total external liabilities (debtholders and preference shareholders) from the value of the firm. Alternatively, the value of equity can be obtained, straight way, by discounting future free cash flowsavailable to equity-holders, (FCFE), after meeting interest, preference dividends and principal payments, the discount rate being rate of return required by equity investors, that is, cost of equity (k_e)

$$\text{Valuation of equity}_0 = \sum_{t=1}^{\infty} \frac{\text{FCFE to equityholders}_t}{(1+k_e)^t} \tag{31.10}$$

Thus, there are varying connotations of FCFF to serve different needs. However, while the valuation of a firm and equity use different definitions of FCFF as well as of discount rates, they provide identical answers as long as the same set of assumptions is used in both the equations. Example 31.4 illustrates it.

***Example* 31.4**

Suppose a firm has employed a total capital of ₹1,000 lakh (provided equally by 10 per cent debt and 5 lakh equity shares of ₹100 each), its cost of equity is 14 per cent and it is subject to corporate tax rate of 40 per cent. The projected free cash flows to all investors of the firm for 5 years are give in the table:

(₹ *lakh*)

Year-end	1	₹300
	2	200
	3	500
	4	150
	5	600

Compute (i) valuation of firm and (ii) valuation from the perspective of equityholders. Assume 10 per cent debt is repayable at the year-end 5 and interest is paid at each year-end.

Solution

(i) Computation of Overall Cost of Capital

Source of capital	*After tax cost (%)*	*Weights*	*Total cost (%)*
Equity	14	0.5	7
Debt	6*	0.5	3
Weighted average cost of capital (k_0)			10

* 10% (1 – 0.4 tax rate) = 6 per cent

(ii) Valuation of Firm, Based on K_0 (₹ *lakh*)

Year-end	*FCFF*	*PV factor (0.10)*	*Total present value*
1	₹300	0.909	₹272.70
2	200	0.826	165.20
3	500	0.751	375.50
4	150	0.683	102.45
5	600	0.621	372.60
Total present value/Valuation of firm			1,288.45
Less: Value of debt			500.00
Value of equity			788.45

(iii) Valuation of Equity, Based on K_e (₹ *lakh*)

Year-end	*FCFF to all investors*	*After tax payment to debtholders*	*FCFE to equityholders*	*PV factor (0.14)*	*Total present value*
1	₹300	₹30*	₹270	0.877	₹236.79
2	200	30	170	0.769	130.73
3	500	30	470	0.675	317.25
4	150	30	120	0.592	71.04
5	600	530**	70	0.519	36.33
Total present value					792.14

* Interest on ₹500 lakh @ 10% = ₹50 lakh; ₹50 lakh (1 – 0.4) = ₹30 lakh

** Inclusive of debt repayment of ₹500 lakh at year-end 5.

Thus, the valuation of equity by both the methods is virtually the same (₹788.45 lakh and ₹792.14 lakh). The minor difference of ₹3.69 lakh can be attributed primarily to rounding-off the present value figures.

Total present value of the projected free cash flows to equityholder can be used to compute free cash flows per equity share FCFE as per Equation 31.11.

$$\text{FCFE per equity share} = \frac{\text{PV of FCFE to equityholders}}{\text{Number of equity shares outstanding}} \quad \textbf{(31.11)}$$

$$\text{In Example 31.4, FCFE per equity share is} = \frac{₹792.14 \text{ lakh}}{5 \text{ lakh}} = ₹158.428$$

In Example 31.4, for the sake of simplicity, we have assumed the life of the corporate firm as 5 years. In practice, firms have perpetual long-term existence/indefinite life. Evidently, the indefinite life of business/corporate firms, in general, is an additional aspect to be reckoned in a firm's valuation. Ideally, one approach is to forecast future FCFF for a very long period of time, say 30-40 years and ignore all subsequent year's FCFF. The reason is the discounted value of such FCFF in such distant years will be insignificant. However, there are genuine difficulties in explicitly forecasting decades of performance. In fact, it is virtually impossible to make reasonably accurate forecasts of profits/cash flows beyond a certain period (say 7–10 years) in most of the businesses.

To overcome the problem Copeland *et al*[8] suggest that the exercise related to valuation of business can be segregated into two periods, during and after an explicit forecast period. The value of a business/firm is:

Present value of cash flows during explicit forecast period + Present value of cash flows after explicit forecast period. **(31.12)**

What constitutes an ideal explicit forecast period? This question is not easy to answer. The following guidelines may be relevant and useful in selecting such a period. Whereas in cyclical businesses, the period can correspond to one full business cycle, in other businesses, the period can match with the number of years during which they are likely to perform well. In operational terms, the period should not be very short, say 2–3 years, and given the current turbulent dynamic business world, the period, in general, should not be very long also, say 10–15 years.

The explicit forecast period is the period in which the firm grows at a rapid pace; it is said to be at saturation point at the end of the explicit forecast period, so far as growth rate is concerned (the economic premise is that firms, in general cannot sustain abnormal rates of growth for an indefinite period). The firm is expected to have attained a steady rate (at the end of explicit forecast period) and starts growing at a stable growth rate, which is likely to continue in future years. The value determined after the explicit forecast period is referred to as the **continuing value**. According to Copeland *et al*,[9] the continuing value can be estimated as per Equation 31.13.

$$\text{Continuing value} = \frac{NOPLAT_{T+1}\,(1 - g/ROIC_I)}{k_0 - g} \quad \textbf{(31.13)}$$

Where $NOPLAT_{T+1}$ = The normalised level of net operating profits less adjusted taxes in the first year after the explicit forecast period.

g = The expected growth rate in $NOPLAT$ in perpetuity.

$ROIC_I$ = The expected rate of return on the net new investment.

The derivation of the formula as per Equation 31.13 to compute continuing value is as follows:

$$\text{Continuing value} = \frac{FCFF_{T+1}}{k_0 - g} \quad \textbf{(31.13.1)}$$

Where $FCFF_{T+1}$ refers to the normalised level of free cash flow in the first year after the explicit forecast period.

Free cash flows (FCFF) can be defined in terms of *NOPLAT* and investment rate, IR (that is, the percentage of *NOPLAT* reinvested in the business each year).

$$FCFF = NOPLAT\,(1 - IR) \quad \textbf{(31.13.2)}$$

We know, growth rate, g is the product of return on invested capital, $ROIC_I$ and IR, i.e.,

$$g = ROIC_I \times IR \quad \textbf{(31.13.3)}$$

or

$$IR = g/ROIC_I \quad \textbf{(31.13.4)}$$

Incorporating value of IR in $FCFF$ definition

$$FCFF = NOPLAT\,(1 - g/ROIC_I) \quad \textbf{(31.13.5)}$$

$$\text{Continuing value} = \frac{NOPLAT\,(1 - g/ROIC_I)}{k_0 - g}$$

Equation 31.13 is termed as a value driven formula. Since Equations 31.13 and 31.13.1 provide the same answer of continuing value, it is logistically more convenient to compute continuing value based on Equation 31.13.1.

The major simplifying *assumptions* made in determining continuing value are: **(i)** the firm earns a constant return on the existing invested capital; **(ii)** the firm's *NOPLAT* grows at a constant rate and it invests the same proportion of its gross cash flow in business each year and **(iii)** the firm earns a constant return on all new investments.

All the items in equation 31.13 are self explanatory, except the term *adjusted taxes.* Adjusted taxes is the increase in the estimated tax liability due to the exclusion of the tax shield provided by interest charges. This is illustrated in Example 31.5.

***Example* 31.5**

Following is the summarised income statement of Hypothetical Ltd: *(₹ lakh)*

Sales revenues	₹100
Less: Cost of goods sold	42
Less: Administrative expenses	8
Less: Selling and distribution expenses	20
Earnings before interest and taxes (EBIT)	30
Less: Interest	10
Earnings before taxes	20
Less: Taxes (0.40)	8
Earnings after taxes	12

Solution

Determination of NOPLAT *(₹ lakh)*

Net operating profit or EBIT	₹30
Less: Taxes as per income statement	8
Less: Adjusted taxes (interest, ₹10 lakh × 0.4, tax rate)	4
Net operating profit less adjusted taxes*	18
Alternatively, it can be determined as EBIT less taxes	
EBIT	30
Less: Taxes (0.40 × ₹30 lakh, EBIT)	12
NOPLAT	18

*Adjusted taxes = (Taxes as per income statement, ₹8 lakh + Tax shield on interest, i.e., ₹10 lakh × 0.4 = ₹4 lakh). The rationale for enhancing tax liability is that the weighted average cost of capital uses the after tax cost of debt. Advantage of tax savings on interest should not be counted twice.

According to Copeland, the firm's value is the aggregate of **(i)** the present value (PV) of FCFF during the explicit forecast period, **(ii)** PV of continuing value (of FCFF/NOPLAT) and **(iii)** value of non-operating assets (if any) at the end of explicit forecast period (say, marketable securities).

Among the various variants of the earnings approach, the DCF approach (that is, free cash flows) seems to be conceptually superior for business valuation as well as equity valuation. The computation of FCFF and continuing value is illustrated in Example 31.6.

***Example* 31.6**

Sagar Industries deals in production and sales of consumer durables. Its expected sales revenues for the next 8 years (in ₹ million) are given in the table:

Year	*Sales revenue*
1	₹ 80
2	100
3	150
4	220
5	300
6	260
7	230
8	200

Its condensed balance sheet as on March 31, current year is as follows: (*₹ million*)

Liabilities	*Amount*	*Assets*	*Amount*
Equity funds	120	Current assets	30
12% Debt	80	Long-term assets (net)	170
	200		200

Additional information:

(i) Its variable expenses will amount to 40 per cent of sales revenue. Fixed cash operating costs are estimated to be ₹16 million per year for the first 4 years and at ₹20 million for years 5 – 8. In addition, an extensive advertisement campaign will be launched, requiring annual outlays as follows:

(*₹ million*)

1	₹ 5
2 – 3	15
4 – 6	30
7 – 8	10

(ii) Long-term assets are subject to 15 per cent rate of depreciation on diminishing balance method.

(iii) The company has planned the following capital expenditure (assumed to have been incurred in the beginning of each year) for the next 8 years.

(*₹ million*)

Year 1	₹5
2	8
3	20
4	25
5	35
6	25
7	15
8	10

(iv) Working capital in terms of investment in current assets are estimated at 20 per cent of sales revenue.

(v) It is expected to have non-operating assets in terms of investments in marketable securities in the initial year. The expected after tax non-operating cash flow in year 1 = ₹0.5 million.

(vi) Given the tax benefits available to Sagar, the effective tax rate estimated is 30 per cent.

(vii) The corporate equity capital is estimated at 16 per cent.

(viii) The free cash flow of the firm are expected to grow at 5 per cent per annum, after 8 years.

Determine the discounted cash flow (DCF) value of the (i) firm and (ii) equity.

Solution

(i) **Determination of Weighted Average Cost of Capital**

Source of funds	Cost (%)	Weights	Total (%)
Equity	16	0.6*	9.60
12% Debt	8.4	0.4**	3.36
			12.96 = 13

* (₹120 million/₹200 million); ** (₹80 million/₹200 million)

(ii) **Determination of Depreciation (Years 1 – 8)** (₹ million)

Year	Long-term assets at beginning of year	Additions during the year	Total at the year-end	Depreciation @ 15%
1	₹170.00	₹5	₹175.00	₹26.25
2	148.75	8	156.75	23.51
3	133.24	20	153.24	22.99
4	130.25	25	155.25	23.29
5	131.96	35	166.96	25.04
6	141.92	25	166.92	25.04
7	141.88	15	156.88	23.53
8	133.35	10	143.35	21.50

(iii) **Determination of Investment [Capital Expenditure + Current Assets, (CA)] Required, Years 1 – 8** (₹ million)

Year	Investment required			Existing investments in CA	Additional investments required
	Capital expenditure	CA (Sales × 0.2)	Total		
1	₹5	₹16	₹21	30*	Nil
2	8	20	28	25**	3
3	20	30	50	20	30
4	25	44	69	30	39
5	35	60	95	44	51
6	25	52	77	60	17
7	15	46	61	52	9
8	10	40	50	46	4

*including marketable securities

**Balance of CA in year 1: ₹30 million – Capital expenditure incurred in year 1, ₹5 million

(iv) **Determination of Present Value for Explicit Period Projections (years 1 – 8)** (₹ million)

Particulars Years	1	2	3	4	5	6	7	8
A Sales revenue	₹80	₹100	₹150	₹220	₹300	₹260	₹230	₹200
B *Less:* Expenses								
Variable costs	32	40	60	88	120	104	92	80
Fixed cash operating costs	16	16	16	16	20	20	20	20
Advertisement	5	15	15	30	30	30	10	10
Depreciation	26.25	23.51	22.99	23.29	25.04	25.04	23.53	21.50
C EBIT (*A* – *B*)	0.75	5.49	36.01	62.71	104.96	80.96	84.47	68.50
D *Less:* Taxes (0.30)	0.22	1.65	10.80	18.81	31.49	24.29	25.34	20.55
E NOPAT	0.53	3.84	25.21	43.90	73.47	56.67	59.13	47.95

(*Contd.*)

(*Contd.*)

F Non-operating income	0.50	—	—	—	—	—	—	—
G Gross cash flow (*E* + *F* + Depreciation)	27.28	27.35	48.20	67.19	98.51	81.71	82.66	69.45
H *Less:* Investment in (capital expenditure plus current assets)	—	3	30	39	51	17	9	4
I Free cash flow (*G* – *H*)	27.28	24.35	18.20	28.19	47.51	64.71	73.66	65.45
J PV factor (0.13)	0.885	0.783	0.693	0.613	0.543	0.480	0.425	0.376
K Total PV (*I* × *J*)	24.14	19.07	12.61	17.28	25.80	31.06	31.31	24.61

Total present value = ₹185.88 million

(v) Determination of PV in Respect of Continuing Value (CV)

CV_8 = $FCF_9/(k_0 - g)$ = ₹65.45 million (1.05)/(13% – 5%) = 68.7225 million/8% = ₹68.7225/0.08
= ₹859.03 million

PV of CV_0 = ₹859.03 million/$(1.13)^8$ = ₹859.03 × 0.376 = ₹323 million

(vi) Total Value of the Firm, Based on the DCF Approach of Free Cash Flows:

	(₹ million)
PV of free cash flows during explicit period	₹185.88
PV of free cash flows after explicit period (known as CV)	323
Total value	508.88

(vii) Value of Equity:

	(₹ million)
Total value of firm	₹508.88
Less: Value of debt	80.00
Value of equity	428.88

Market Value Based Approach to Valuation

The market value, as reflected in the stock market quotations, is another method for estimating the value of a business. The market value of securities used for the purpose can be either **(i)** twelve months average of the stock exchange prices or **(ii)** the average of the high and low values of securities during a year. Alternatively, some other fair and equitable method of averaging (on the basis of the number of months/years) can be worked out. The justification of market value as an approximation of the true worth of a firm is derived from the fact that market quotations by and large indicate the consensus of investors as to the firm's earning potentials and the corresponding risk. The market value approach is one of the most widely-used in determining value, in particular of large listed firms.

The major problem with this method is that the market value of a firm is influenced not only by financial fundamentals but also by speculative factors. As a result, this value can change abruptly due to speculative influences, market sentiments and personal expectations. Market makers as well as other 'willing buyers or sellers' (interested in purchases or sales) can at times significantly influence these prices. Another limitation of this approach is that this approach cannot be applied if the shares are unlisted or are not actively traded.

Apart from the limited applicability of this method only to listed corporate enterprises, whose shares/securities are actively traded, the valuation of a business is not in tune with the going concern concept. Nevertheless, it may be/is of immense usefulness in deciding swap ratios of shares in merger decisions. In fact, the market prices of the two companies can be the objective of the decision. Alternatively, a certain percentage of premium, above the market price may be offered as an inducement to the shareholders of the acquired company to convince them to agree to sell their shares or to make them agree to the merger decisions.

Fair Value Method

The fair value method is not an independent method of share valuation like those discussed above. This method uses the average/weightage average or one or more of the above methods. Since this method uses the average concept, its virtue is that it helps in smoothening out wide variations in estimated valuations as per different methods. In other words, this approach provides, in a way, the 'balanced' figure of valuation.

In general, this method has limited application for business valuation. For instance, this method of valuation of shares had been used till the early 1990's, by the erstwhile Controller of Capital Issues (CCI) in India, for fixing the price of new equity issues. In case the equity shares were to be issued at a premium, the amount of premium was based as the CCI guidelines.

To sum up, no one method is appropriate for all circumstances/situations/requirements. Therefore, it is important to recognise that the different methods are based on different assumptions and depending on the circumstances, some methods may be more appropriate than others. For instance, where there is paucity of information about profits, say **(i)** in the case of new companies whose accounts do not serve as a guide to future profits, **(ii)** in the case of companies operating at a loss with no prospects of earning profits in the near future and **(iii)** in the case of companies having unreliable statistics of profits owing to factors such as disruption of business, the net asset method of valuation seems would be more appropriate. In normal situations, the DCF (based on free cash flows) method would be suitable. In the event of wide variations in the valuations as per these two methods, the fair value method may be used. In fact, it is useful for the finance manager/investor/valuer/analyst to know a range of values from various perspectives.

LO 31.3 OTHER APPROACHES TO VALUE MEASUREMENT

In recent years, a number of new approaches/techniques/methods to measure value (with focus on shareholders) have been developed and practised. The two major approaches are market value added (MVA) and economic value added (EVA). They are explained below.

Market Value Added Approach (MVA)

The **MVA** approach measures the change in the market value of the firm's equity vis-à-vis equity investment (consisting of equity share capital and retained profits). Accordingly,

MVA = Market value of firm's equity – Equity capital investment/funds **(31.14)**

Though the concept of MVA is normally used in the context of equity investment (and, hence, is of greater relevance for equity shareholders), it can also be adapted (like other previous approaches) to measure value from the perspective of providers of all invested funds (ie, including preference share capital and debt).

MVA = [Total market value of firm's securities – (Equity shareholders funds + Preference share capital + Debentures)] **(31.15)**

The MVA approach cannot be used for all types of firms. It is applicable to only firms whose market prices are available. In that sense, the method has limited application. Besides, the value provided by this approach may exhibit wide fluctuations, depending on the state of the capital market/stock market in the country.

***Example* 31.7**

Suppose, Supreme Industries has an equity market capitalisation of ₹3,400 crore in current year. Assume further that its equity share capital is ₹2,000 crore and its retained earnings are ₹600 crore. Determine the MVA and interpret it.

Solution

MVA = (₹3,400 core – ₹2,600 crore) = ₹800 crore.

The value of ₹800 crore implies that the management of Supreme Industries has created wealth/value to the extent of ₹800 crore for its equity shareholders.

Well managed companies (engaged in sunrise businesses), having good growth prospects, and perceived so by the investors, have positive MVA. Investors may be willing to pay more than the net worth. In contrast, companies relatively less known or engaged in businesses that do not hold future growth potentials may have negative MVA.

***Example* 31.8**

Suppose, Hypothetical Limited has equity market capitalisation of ₹900 crore in the current year. Its equity share capital and accumulated losses are of ₹1,200 crore and ₹200 crore respectively. Determine the MVA of the firm.

Solution

MVA = (₹900 crore – ₹1,000 crore) = (–₹100 crore).

The firm has negative MVA of ₹100 crore. The investors discount its value/worth, as it is loss incurring firm.

The market value added approach reflects market expectations and is essentially a future-oriented and forward looking approach. The investors, willing to pay a different price (other than one suggested by book value), are guided by the individual company's future prospects, future growth rates, risk complexion of the firm, industry to which the firm belongs, required rate of return and so on.

Economic Value Added (EVA)

Economic value added (EVA) implies the difference between operating profits after taxes and total cost of funds.

The EVA method is based on the past performance of the corporate enterprise. The underlying economic principle in this method is to determine whether the firm is earning a higher rate of return on the entire invested funds than the cost of such funds (measured in terms of the weighted average cost of capital, WACC). If the answer is positive, the firm's management is adding to the shareholders value by earning extra for them. On the contrary, if the WACC is higher than the corporate earning rate, the firm's operations have eroded the existing wealth of its equity shareholders. In operational terms, the method attempts to measure economic value added (or destroyed) for equity shareholders, by the firm's operations, in a given year.

Since WACC takes care of the financial costs of all sources of providers of invested funds in a corporate enterprise, it is imperative that *operating profits after taxes* (and not *net profits after taxes*) should be considered to measure EVA. The accounting profits after taxes, as reported by the income statement, need adjustments for interest costs. The profits should be the net operating profits after taxes and the cost of funds will be product of the total capital supplied (including retained earnings) and WACC.

$$\text{EVA} = [\text{Net operating profits after taxes} - (\text{Total capital} \times \text{WACC})] \quad \textbf{(31.16)}$$

or

$$\text{EVA} = \text{Earnings after taxes} - (\text{Cost of shareholders funds}) \quad \textbf{(31.17)}$$

The computation of EVA is illustrated in Example 31.9.

***Example* 31.9** Following is the condensed income statement of a firm for the current year: *(₹ lakh)*

Sales revenue	₹500
Less: Operating costs	300
Less: Interest costs	12
Earnings before taxes	188
Less: Taxes (0.40)	75.2
Earnings after taxes	112.8

The firm's existing capital consists of ₹150 lakh equity funds, having 15 per cent cost and of ₹100 lakh 12 per cent debt. Determine the economic value added during the year.

Solution

(i) Determination of Net Operating Profit After Taxes *(₹ lakh)*

Sales revenue	₹500
Less: Operating costs	300
Operating profit (EBIT)	200
Less: Taxes (0.40)	80
Net operating profit after taxes (NOPAT)*	120

*Alternatively, [EAT, ₹112.8 lakh + Interest ₹12 lakh – (Tax savings on interest, ₹12 lakh × 0.4 = ₹4.8 lakh)]

(ii) Determination of WACC

Equity (₹150 lakh × 15%)	=	₹22.5 lakh
12% Debt (₹100 lakh × 7.2%)*	=	7.2
Total cost		29.7
WACC (29.7 lakh/₹250 lakh)		11.88%

* Cost of debt = 12% (1 – 0.4 tax rate) = 7.2 per cent

(iii) Determination of EVA

EVA = NOPAT* – (Total capital × WACC)
₹120 lakh – (₹250 lakh × 11.88%)
₹120 lakh – ₹29.7 lakh = ₹90.3 lakh

or EVA = EAT - cost of shareholders funds
= ₹112.8 lakh – (₹150 lakh × 0.15 = 22.5) = ₹90.3 lakh

During the current year, the firm has added an economic value of ₹90.3 lakh to the existing wealth of the equity shareholders. Essentially, the EVA approach is a *modified* accounting approach to determine profits earned after meeting all financial costs of all the providers of capital. Its major advantage is that this approach reflects the *true profit* position of the firm. What may happen is that the firm may exhibit positive profits after taxes (as per the conventional income statement) ignoring costs of shareholders funds, giving an impression to the owners as well as outsiders that the firm's operations are profitable. The profit picture, in fact, may be illusory. Consider Example 31.10.

***Example* 31.10**

For Example 31.9, assuming sales revenues are ₹330 lakh, compute the earnings after taxes.

Solution

Income Statement (Conventional) *(₹ lakh)*

Sales revenue	₹330
Less: Operating costs	300
Less: Interest costs	12
Earnings before taxes	18
Less: Taxes (0.40)	7.2
Earnings after taxes	10.8

The firm has registered profits of ₹10.8 lakh during the current year on the equity funds of ₹150 lakh, which has financial costs of ₹22.5 lakh. Therefore, the firm has suffered a loss (of ₹11.7 lakh) as the opportunity costs of equity funds invested by equityholders is more than what has been earned by the firm for them. This point is brought to the fore by the EVA approach. It is for this reason that the EVA approach is getting more attention. It is superior to the conventional approach of determining profits.

Determination of EVA (₹ lakh)

(a)	Sales revenue	₹330
	Less: Operating costs	300
	Operating profits	30
	Less: Taxes (0.4)	12
	Net operating profits after taxes	18
(b)	EVA = ₹18 lakh – (₹29.7 lakh, already computed above) = – ₹11.7 lakh	

Example 31.10 demonstrates that there may be a substantial difference between profits determined as per accounting approach and the EVA approach. Profits shown as per the EVA approach are conceptually realistic than shown by traditional accounting approach. In no way, the firm can be said to have earned profits without meeting financial costs of all sources of finance. The EVA approach is in tune with the basic financial tenet of cost-benefit analysis; financial benefits have to be more than financial costs to have true profits.

Though the MVA and EVA are two different approaches, the MVA of the firm (in a technical sense) can be conceived in terms of the present value of all the EVA profits that the firm is expected to generate in the future[10].

SUMMARY

LO 31.1

The term 'valuation' implies the estimated worth of an asset or a security or a business. The alternative approaches to value a firm/an asset are: (i) book value, (ii) market value, (iii) intrinsic value, (iv) liquidation value, (v) replacement value, (vi) salvage value and (vii) fair value.

While book value refers to the amount at which an asset is shown in the balance sheet of a firm, market value is the price at which an asset can be sold in the market. Intrinsic value is equal to the present value of incremental future cash inflows likely to accrue due to the acquisition of an asset, discounted at an appropriate discount rate. The fair value is the average of the book value, market value and intrinsic value.

LO 31.2

There are 4 approaches to valuation of business (with focus on equity share valuation): (i) assets based, (ii) earnings based, (iii) market value based and (iv) the fair value method.

Assets-based method focuses on determining the value of net assets = (Total assets – Total external obligations).

Net assets per share can be obtained dividing total net assets by the number of equity shares outstanding. It indicates the net assets backing per equity share (also known as net worth per share).

Earnings based method relates the firm's value to its potential future earnings or cash flow generating capacity. Accordingly, there are two major variants of this approach (i) earnings measure on accounting basis and (ii) earnings measure on cash flow basis. As per the first method, the value of business = Future maintainable profits, excluding extraordinary items related to income and losses (÷) Relevant capitalisation factor.

The second method makes use of the discounted cash flow technique to value the business. According to the DCF approach, the value of business/firm is equal to the present value of expected future operating cash flows (CF) to the firm, discounted at a rate that reflects the riskiness of the cash flows (k_0), that is,

$$\text{Value of firm}_0 = \sum_{t=1}^{\infty} \frac{\text{CF to Firm}_t}{(1+k_0)^t}$$

LO 31.2

Another variant of cash flow approach is to discount estimated free cash flows to the firm (FCFF) instead of operating cash flows. The FCFFs are computed by deducting incremental investments in long-term assets as well as investment in working capital from operating cash flows. The value of firm is $= \sum_{t=1}^{\infty} \frac{FCFF_t}{(1+k_0)^t}$. The value of equity can be determined by subtracting the total external liabilities from the value of the firm.

Alternatively, the value of equity can be determined directly by discounting the free cash flows available to equityholders (FCFE) after meeting interest, preference dividends and principal payments, the discount rate being k_e, that is,

$$V_E = \sum_{t=1}^{\infty} \frac{\text{FCFE to equity-holders}_t}{(1+k_e)^t}$$

The value of the firm/business can be segregated into two sub-periods: (i) PV of cash flows during explicit forecast period and (ii) PV of cash flows after explicit forecast period.

In the context of cyclical businesses, the explicit forecast period can correspond to one full business cycle; in other businesses, the period can match with the number of years during which they are likely to perform well. The firm is said to have attained a steady state at the end of explicit period. Subsequent to this period, the firm grows at a steady rate (normal or less than normal) which is likely to continue in future years.

The value determined after the explicit forecast period ($T + 1$) is referred to as the continuing value. Its value can be determined as per the following equation:

$$\text{Continuing value} = \frac{FCFF_{T+1}}{k_0 - g}$$

The market value (reflected in the stock market quotations) is the most widely used approach to determine the value of a business, in particular of large listed firms. The market value indicates the price the investors are willing to pay for the firm's earning potentials and the corresponding risk. This method is particularly useful in deciding swap ratios in the case of merger decisions.

Fair value method is not an independent method of share valuation. The method uses the average/weighted average of two or more of the above methods. Therefore, such a method helps in smoothening out wide variations caused by different methods and indicates the 'balanced' figure of valuation.

LO 31.3

The market value added (MVA) approach measures the change in the value of the firm from the perspective of all the providers of funds (i.e., shareholders as well as debentureholders).

MVA = [Total market value of the firm's securities – (Equity shareholder funds + Preference share capital + Debentures)].

The MVA from the point of view of equity shareholders is = (Market value of firm's equity – Equity funds).

The EVA method measures economic value added (or destroyed) for equity-owners by the firm's operations in a given year. The underlying economic principle in this method is to determine whether the firm is earning a higher rate of return on the entire invested funds than the cost of such funds.

EVA = [Net operating profits after taxes – (Total invested funds × WACC)]

EVA = Earnings after taxes – (Cost of shareholders funds)

Thus, the EVA approach measures the true profit position of the firm.

Though the MVA and EVA are two different approaches, the MVA of the firm can be conceived as the present value of all the EVA profits that the firm is expected to generate in the future years.

REFERENCES

1. The points are just illustrative in nature and by no means exhaustive. For details, refer to Ramanujam, S, *Mergers et al,* Tata McGraw-Hill Publishing Co., N Delhi, 2000, pp. 354–55.
2. *Ibid,* p. 268.
3. *Ibid,* p. 272.
4. Damodaran, Aswath, *Investment Valuation,* John Wiley & Sons, New York: 1996, p. 291.
5. *Ibid,* p. 291.
6. Copeland, Tom, *et al, Valuation—Measuring and Managing the Value of Companies,* John Wiley & Sons, New York: 2000, p. 134.
7. *Ibid,* p. 134.
8. *Ibid,* p. 136.
9. Though the FCFF perpetuity formula and value driven formula, as per equation 31.13, are technically the same, Copeland *et al* explain the superiority of the value driven formula. Refer to *Ibid,* pp. 269–70.
10. Mc Menamin, Jim, *op. cit.,* p. 281.

SOLVED PROBLEMS

P.31.1 (a) The following particulars are available in respect of a corporate: LO 31.1 LOD E

(i) Capital employed, ₹500 million.

(ii) Operating profits, after taxes, for last three years are: ₹80 million, ₹100 million, ₹90 million; current year's operating profit, after taxes, is ₹105 million.

(iii) Riskless rate of return, 10 per cent.

(iv) Risk premium relevant to the business of corporate firm, 5 per cent.

You are required to compute the value of goodwill, based on the present value of the super profits method. Super profits are to be computed on the basis of the average profits of 4 years. It is expected that the firm is likely to earn super profits for the next 5 years only.

(b) Assume that super profits in years 1-5 would be (in million ₹) as ₹18.75, ₹15.00, ₹11.00, ₹6.00, ₹2.00. Determine the value of goodwill. Assume no change in data inputs shown in (a).

Solution

(a) Determination of goodwill, using super profit method *(₹ million)*

Average profits (₹80 million + ₹100 million + ₹90 million + ₹105 million = ₹375 million)/ 4 years	₹93.75
Less: Normal profits (₹500 million × 0.15)	75.00
Super profits	18.75
Multiplied by the PV of annuity for 5 years at 15 per cent	(×) 3.352
PV of super profits/Value of goodwill	62.85

(b) Determination of goodwill *(₹ million)*

Years	*Super profits*	*PV factor (0.15)*	*Total PV*
1	₹18.75	0.870	₹16.31
2	15.00	0.756	11.34
3	11.00	0.658	7.24
4	6.00	0.572	3.43
5	2.00	0.497	0.99
Total value of goodwill			39.31

P.31.2 The following is the balance sheet of a corporate firm as on March 31, current year. LO 31.2 LOD M

(₹ lakh)

Liabilities	*Amount*	*Assets*	*Amount*
Share capital (of ₹100 each fully paid-up)	₹100	Land and buildings	₹40
Reserves and surplus	40	Plant and machinery	80
Sundry creditors and other liabilities	30	Marketable securities	10
		Stock	20
		Debtors	15
		Cash and bank balances	5
	170		170

Profit before tax for current year-end amount to ₹64 lakh, including ₹4 lakh as extraordinary income. Besides, the firm has earned interest income of ₹1 lakh in the current year from investments in marketable securities. It is not usual for the firm to have excess cash and invest in marketable securities. However, an additional amount of ₹5 lakh per annum, in terms of advertisement and other expenses, will be required to be spent for the smooth running of the business in the years to come.

Market values of land and buildings, and plant and machinery are estimated at ₹90 lakh and ₹100 lakh respectively. In order to match the revalued figures of these fixed assets, additional depreciation of ₹6 lakh is required to be taken into consideration. Effective corporate tax rate may be taken at 30 per cent. The capitalisation rate applicable to businesses of such risks is 15 per cent.

From the above information, compute the value of business, value of equity and price per equity share, based on the capitalisation method.

Solution

Valuation of business, value of equity and price per equity share (capitalisation method) (₹ lakh)

Profit before tax	64
Less: Extraordinary income	4
Less; Interest on marketable securities (not likely to accrue in future)	1
Less: Additional expected recurring expenses	5
Less: Additional depreciation	6
Expected earnings before taxes	48
Less: Taxes (0.30)	14.40
Future maintainable profits after taxes	33.60
Divided by relevant capitalisation factor	0.15
Value of business (₹33.60 lakh/0.15)	224.00
Value of equity (₹224 lakh – ₹30 lakh external liabilities)	194.00
Price per equity share (₹194 lakh/ 1 lakh)	194

P.31.3 Assume every thing to be the same as contained in P.31.2. Determine the expected market price of the share, given the P/E multiple of (i) 8 times and (ii) 5 times, and interpret the result. LO 31.2 LOD M

Solution

Determination of market price per share (P/E basis) (₹ lakh)

Future maintainable profits after taxes (computed in P.31.2)	₹33.60
Divided by the number of equity shares issued and outstanding	1.00
Earnings per equity share, EPS, (₹33.60 lakh/1 lakh)	33.60
Multiplied by P/E ratio	8
(i) Market price per share (₹33.60 × 8 times)	268.8
Multiplied by P/E ratio	5
(ii) Market price per share (₹33.60 × 5 times)	168

Interpretation

(i) The P/E ratio of 8 times suggests that investors are confident about the company's future prospects; they have high expectations of future returns. It is for this reasons that they are prepared to pay a higher market price per equity share than warranted by the capitalisation method (ie, ₹194 per share). (ii) In contrast, the P/E multiple of 5 times suggests that investors are less optimistic about the company's future performance. They have low confidence as well as expectations of low returns in future years and therefore are willing to pay a lower price vis-à-vis the capitalised price.

P.31.4 For facts contained in **P.31.2**, determine the value of business as per the net assets method. Assets are to be valued at market value for this purpose. Value of goodwill is also to be considered to value assets. Its value is to be reckoned as an equivalent to the present value of super profits, which are likely to accrue for 4 years. For the purpose of determining super profits, normal profits are to be computed with reference to the year-end value of net assets/capital employed (excluding goodwill).

LO 31.2 LOD M

Also compute the market value of equity share as per this approach.

Solution

Determination of valuation of business and net asset value per share as per the net assets method (assets are valued at market price) *(₹ lakh)*

Land and buildings	₹90
Plant and machinery	100
Goodwill[1]	6
Marketable securities	10
Stock	20
Debtors	15
Cash and bank balances	5
Total assets	246
Less: External liabilities	30
Net assets available for equity to shareholders	216
Divided by the number of equity shares issued and outstanding	1
Net assets value per share (₹216 lakh/1 lakh)	216

[1]Valuation of goodwill

Future maintainable profits after taxes	₹33.60
Less: Normal profit (15% of capital employed, i.e., 0.15 × ₹210 lakh*)	31.50
Super profits	2.10
Multiplied by PV factor at 15% for annuity of 4 years	2.855
Value of goodwill (₹2.10 lakh × 2.855)	6.0

*(Market value of assets, excluding goodwill, ₹240 lakh – External liabilities, ₹30 lakh).

P.31.5 Assume everything to be the same as given in **P.31.2**. Determine the fair price of an equity share. The fair price of an equity share is to be taken as an average of prices estimated according to the capitalisation method and the net assets method.

LO 31.2 LOD M

Solution

Determination of a fair price of an equity share (fair value method)

Price per equity share (capitalisation method)	₹194
Net assets value per equity share (net assets method)	216
Fair value per equity share (₹194 + ₹216)/2	205

P.31.6 Determine the continuing value of the firm from the following information: *(₹ million)*

Cash flow from business operations at the end of explicit forecast period (Year 6)	₹56
Investment required in capital expenditure and current assets during year 6	12
Expected annual growth rate in free cash flows to the firm, after forecast period (%)	8
Weighted average cost of capital (WACC) (%)	12
Cost of equity capital (%)	15

LO 31.2 LOD E

Solution

Determination of PV with respect to continuing value (CV)

$$CV_6 = \frac{FCFF_7}{WACC - g} = \frac{₹44 \text{ million}^*(1.08)}{12\% - 8\%} = \frac{₹47.52 \text{ million}}{4\%}$$

CV_6 = ₹1,188 million

CV_0 = ₹1,188 million × Present value factor at 12% for 6 years

CV_0 = ₹1,188 million × 0.507 = ₹602.316 million

*(Gross cash flows ₹56 million – Investment required in capital expenditures and current assets ₹12 million = ₹44 million)

P.31.7 Hypothetical Limited is growing at an above average rate. It foresees a growth rate of 20 per cent per annum in free cash flows to equityholders in the next 4 years. It is likely to fall to 12 per cent in the next two years. After that, the growth rate is expected to stabilise at 5 per cent per annum. The amount of free cash flow (FCFE) per equity share at the beginning of current year is ₹10. Find out the maximum price at which an investor, follower of the free cash approach, will be prepared to buy the company's shares as on date, assuming an equity capitalisation rate of 14 per cent.

LO 31.2 LOD M

Solution Maximum price of the equity share will be the sum of (i) PV of FCFE during 1 – 6 years and (ii) PV of expected market price at the end of year 6, based on a constant growth rate of 5 per cent.

(i) Present value of FCFE (years 1 – 6)

Year	*FCFE per share*	*PV factor (0.14)*	*Total PV*
1	₹10 $(1 + 0.20)^1$ = ₹12	0.877	₹10.52
2	10 $(1 + 0.20)^2$ = 14.40	0.769	11.07
3	10 $(1 + 0.20)^3$ = 17.28	0.675	11.66
4	10 $(1 + 0.20)^4$ = 20.74	0.592	12.28
5	20.74 (1 + 0.12) = 23.23	0.519	12.06
6	23.23 (1 + 0.12) = 26.02	0.456	11.86
Total PV of FCFE			69.45

$$\text{Market price of share at year-end } 6 = \frac{FCFE_7}{k_e - g} = \frac{₹26.02\,(1.05)}{14\% - 5\%}$$

$$P_6 = \frac{₹27.321}{14\% - 5\%} = ₹303.57$$

(ii) PV of ₹303.57 = ₹303.57 × 0.456 = ₹138.43

Maximum price of share = ₹69.45 + ₹138.43 = ₹207.88

P.31.8 The Chemicals and Fertilizer Limited is a growing company. Its free cash flows for equityholders (FCFE) have been growing at a rate of 25 per cent in recent years. This abnormal growth rate is expected to continue for another 5 years; then these FCFE are likely to grow at the normal rate of 8 per cent. The required rate of return on these shares, by the investing community, is 15 per cent; the firm's weighted average cost of capital is 12 per cent. The amount of FCFE per share at the beginning of the current year is ₹30. Determine the maximum price an investor should be willing to pay now ($t = 0$), based on free cash flow approach. The issue price of share is ₹500.

LO 31.2 LOD M

Solution

(i) Present value of FCFE (years 1 – 5)

Year	*FCFE per share*			*PV factor (0.15)*	*Total PV*
1	₹30 $(1 + 0.25)^1$	=	₹37.50	₹0.870	₹32.62
2	30 $(1 + 0.25)^2$	=	46.86	0.756	35.43
3	30 $(1 + 0.25)^3$	=	58.59	0.658	38.55
4	30 $(1 + 0.25)^4$	=	73.23	0.572	41.89
5	30 $(1 + 0.25)^5$	=	91.56	0.497	45.51
Total PV of FCFE					194.00

$$\text{Market price of share at year-end } 5 = \frac{FCFE_6}{k_e - g} = \frac{₹91.56\,(1.08)}{15\% - 8\%} = ₹1{,}412.64$$

$$\text{PV at } t = 0 = ₹1{,}412.64 \times 0.497 = ₹702.08$$

Investor will be prepared to pay the maximum price at t = 0 = ₹194 + ₹702.08 = ₹896.08

P.31.9 The most recent accounts of a corporate firm engaged in manufacturing business are summarized below: **LO 31.2** LOD M

(₹ *million*)

Income statement for the current year ended March 31	*Amount*
Sales revenue	₹93.5
EBIT	18.0
Less: Interest on loan	1.8
Earnings before taxes	16.2
Less: Corporate taxes (0.35)	5.67
Earnings after taxes	10.53

Balance sheet as at March 31, current year (₹ *million*)

Liabilities	*Amount*	*Assets*	*Amount*
Equity share capital (1 lakh shares of ₹100 each)	₹10.0	Freehold land and buildings (net)	₹20.0
		Plant and machinery (net)	29.5
Reserves and surplus	32.5	Current assets:	
10% Loan	18.0	Stock	10.0
Creditors and other liabilities	18.0	Debtors	15.0
		Bank and cash balance	4.0
	78.5		78.5

Additional Information:

(i) The finance manager of the firm has estimated the future free cash flows of the company as follows:

(₹ *million*)

Year 1	₹22
2	23
3	24.5
4	26.0
5	30.0
6	32.0

Free cash flows in subsequent years, after year 6, are estimated to grow at 4 per cent. The company's weighted average cost of capital is 12 per cent.

(ii) The current resale value of the following assets has been assessed by the professional valuer as follows:

Freehold land and buildings	₹60 million
Plant and machinery	20
Stock	11

The current resale values of the remaining assets are as per their book values.

(iii) A similar sized company (which is listed on Bombay Stock Exchange) and is engaged in the same business has a P/E ratio of 7 times.

You are required to compute the value of the firm as well as value of an equity share on the basis of the following methods: (i) Net assets method (book value and market value), (ii) Price-earnings ratio method and (iii) Free cash flows to the firm.

Solution

Determination of value of firm and value of equity share (using various methods) (*₹ million*)

(i) (a) Net asset method—book value basis:		
Freehold land and buildings		₹20.0
Plant and machinery		29.5
Stock		10.0
Debtors		15.0
Bank and cash balances		4.0
Total assets		78.5
Less: External liabilities		
10% Loan	₹18	
Creditors and other liabilities	18	36.0
Net assets available to equityholders		42.5
Divided by number of equity shares outstanding (lakh)		1
Net assets backing per share (₹42.5 million/1 lakh) (₹)		425
(b) Market value basis:		
Freehold land and buildings		60
Plant and machinery		20
Stock		11
Debtors		15
Bank and cash balances		4
Total assets		110
Less: External liabilities		36
Net assets at market value		74
Net assets backing per share (₹74 million/1 lakh shares)		740
(ii) Price-earnings ratio approach:		
Earnings after taxes (assumed to be normal and expected to be maintained in future years; no adjustment is made as there are no extraordinary items)		10.53
Earnings per share (₹10.53 million/1 lakh shares)		105.30
Multiplied by P/E multiple		7
Market price of equity share (₹105.30 × 7 times)		737.10

(iii) Free cash flow basis:

(a) PV of FCFE during explicit forecast period:

(*₹ in million*)

Year	*FCFF*	*PV factor (0.12)*	*Total PV*
1	₹22	0.893	₹19.646
2	23	0.797	18.331
3	24.5	0.712	17.444
4	26.0	0.636	16.536
5	30.0	0.567	17.010
6	32.0	0.507	16.224
Total present value			105.191

(b) PV of FCFF subsequent to explicit forecast period

$$CV_6 = \frac{₹32\ (1.04)}{0.12 - 0.04} = \frac{₹33.28}{0.08} = ₹416$$

PV_0 = ₹416, continuing value × PV factor at 12% for 6 years
= ₹416 × 0.507 = ₹210.912

(c) Total PV of FCFF (₹105.191 + ₹210.912) =	316.103 million	316.103
Less: External liabilities	36.000	36.00
FCFE available to equityholders	280.103	280.103
MPS (₹280.103 million/ 1 lakh shares) =	₹2801.03	280.10

P.31.10 Assume everything to be the same as given in P.31.9, determine the economic value added during the current year. Assume the long-term funds shown in the balance sheet as the total capital employed in the business. **LO 31.3** LOD **E**

Solution

Determination of economic value added (EVA) (*₹ in million*)

Net operating profits before taxes	₹18
Less: Corporate taxes (0.35)	6.3*
Net operating profits after taxes	11.7
Less: Cost of capital employed (₹60.5 million** × 0.12 WACC)	7.26
Economic value added	4.44

*Alternatively, corporate taxes can be conceived as sum of (i) taxes as per income statement (₹5.67 million plus (ii) tax savings on interest (₹1.8 million × 0.35 = 0.63 million) = ₹6.3 million

**Equity share capital ₹10 million + Reserves and surplus ₹32.50 million + 10% loan ₹18 million = ₹60.5 million.

P.31.11 Determine EVA from the following data of a company: **LO 31.3** LOD **M**

EBIT	₹36 crore
Less interest on 12% Debt	6
Earnings before taxes	30
Less corporate taxes (30%)	9
Earnings after taxes	21
Less dividend on 13% Preference share capital (₹30 crore × 0.13)	3.9
Earnings for equity shareholders	17.1
Equity funds (having cost of 16%)	80.0

Also determine EVA as a percentage of total capital employed.

Solution

(i) Determination of EVA

Determination of weighted average cost of capital

(*Amount in ₹ crore*)

Particulars	*Amount*	*After- tax cost (%)*	*Total cost*
Equity funds	₹80	0.16	₹12.8
Preference share capital	30	0.13	3.9
Debt (₹6 crore/0.12)	50	0.84	4.2
Total	160		20.9

K_o = (₹20.9/₹160) × 100 = 13.06 per cent

Determination of NOPAT

EBIT	₹36 crore
Less taxes (0.3)	10.8
NOPAT	25.2

EVA = NOPAT – (WACC × Total capital employed)
= ₹25.2 crore – ₹20.9 crore = ₹4.3 crore

Alternatively,

(Amount in ₹ crore)

Earnings after taxes	₹21.00
Less cost of shareholders funds	
Equity funds	(12.80)
Preference share capital	(3.90)
EVA	4.30

(ii) EVA as a percentage of total capital employed (₹4.3 crore/₹160 crore) × 100 = 2.69 per cent

P.31.12 Assume every thing to be the same as given in P.31.9. Assume further that the equity shares of this company are currently quoted in the market at ₹500 per share. Determine the amount of market value added (MVA). **LO 31.3** LOD E

Solution

Determination of market value added

A. Market value per equity share	₹500
B. Multiplied by number of equity shares outstanding (lakh)	1
C. Total market value (A × B) (₹million)	50
D. Equity funds (₹10 million equity share capital plus ₹32.5 million reserves and surplus)	42.5
E. Market value added (₹50 million – ₹42.5 million)	7.5

MINI CASES

31.C.1 Economic Value Added Nova Chemicals Ltd manufactures a wide-range of high-quality and competitively-priced products including soda ash, sodium bicarbonate, salt, caustic soda and urea. Its products go into numerous end-use applications in a variety of industries such as glass, detergents, papers, textiles, agriculture, photography, pharmaceuticals, food tanning, ryon, pulp, paints, buildings and construction.

The most recent balance sheet of Nova Chemicals is summarised in Exhibit 31.C.1.

EXHIBIT 31.C.1 Balance Sheet of Nova Chemicals *(Amount ₹ Crore)*

Liabilities		*Amount*	*Assets*	*Amount*
Borrowings:			Fixed Assets:	
15% term loan from banks	₹91.19		Net block	₹1,741.45
14.5% loan from financial institutions	239.95		Investments	626.94
Debentures[@]	98.47		Net current assets	871.38
Others (short-term)	336.03	₹765.64	Miscellaneous	3.14
Shareholder's equity:				
Share capital	215.16			
Reserves	1,820.18	2,035.34		
Deferred tax liability		442.03		
		3,242.91		3,242.91

[@]Details of Debentures:

- 13% debentures nineteenth series (2007), face value of ₹50,00,000 each redeemable at par in three equal yearly instalments commencing September 1, 2007, ₹46.67 crore.
- 11.15% secured redeemable non-convertible debentures, face value ₹1,00,00,000 each redeemable at par in the ratio of 33:33:34 in three monthly instalments commencing from January 2010 or earlier at the option of the company, ₹6.80 crore.
- 7.18% secured redeemable non-convertible debentures, face value ₹2,50,00,000 each redeemable at par in the ratio of 40:20:40 on March 31 2008, 2009 and 2010, ₹45 crore.

The most recent profit and loss account of Nova Chemicals is summarised in Exhibit 31.C.2.

EXHIBIT 31.C.2 Profit and Loss Account of Nova Chemicals (Amount in ₹ crore)

Income:		
Sales and operating income	₹2,544.15	
Investment income	38.85	
Interest on refund of taxes	38.26	₹2,621.26
Expenditure:		
Raw materials, stores, wages and other expenses	2,084.36	
Depreciation	144.15	
Interest (net)	50.91	2,279.42

Required Compute the Economic Value Added for Nova Chemicals.

Solution Economic Value Added = Net operating profit after taxes (NOPAT) – (Weighted average cost of capital × Capital employed)

Weight Average Cost of Capital = Net payments ÷ Capital employed (amount outstanding)

Computation of Weighted Average Cost of Capital

Sources of Funds	*Outstanding amount (₹ crore)*	*Rate (%)*	*Amount paid (₹ crore)*	*Tax advantage on debt[@] (₹ crore)*	*Net amount paid*
(1)	*(2)*	*(3)*	*(4)*	*(5)*	*(6)*
Debt:					
13.25% Debentures	46.67	0.13	7.10*	2.485	4.615
11.15% redeemable debentures	6.80	0.1115	0.758	0.265	0.4927
7.18% Debentures	45.00	0.0718	3.23	1.1305	2.0995
15% term loans from banks	91.19	0.15	13.67	4.78	8.88
14.5% loan from financial institutions	239.95	0.145	34.79	12.18	22.61
Equity:	2,035.34	0.1885**	383.66	—	383.66
Total	2,464.95				413.47

Weighted average cost of capital = (₹413.47 ÷ ₹2,464.95) × 100 = 16.75%

EVA = –₹208.3 crore (₹413.47 crore – ₹205.17[@@] crore)

[@]Assumed tax rate, 35 per cent

[@@]Total operating profit (₹2,544.15 crore, operating income – ₹2,084.36, crore, cost of raw materials, stores, wages, other expenses – ₹144.15 crore, depreciation) = ₹315.64 crore

Net operating profit after taxes [₹315.64 crore – ₹110.47 crore taxes (₹315.64 crore × 0.35] = ₹205.17 crore

**Cost of Equity Capital:

Using CAPM approach and assuming the (i) yield on 10-year RBI bonds as the risk free rate of return of 7.32%, (ii) long term rate of return on BSE-500 Index of 18 per cent (iii) beta of Nova Chemicals from the NSE, 1.08

$$Ke = 0.0732 + 1.08\ (0.18 - 0.732)$$
$$= 0.188544 = 18.85 \text{ per cent}$$

*Interest paid:

$PVIFA_{2,13} = 2.107$

Single instalment = ₹46.67 ÷ 2.107 = ₹22.15 crore

Total amount payable = 3 × ₹22.15 = ₹66.45 crore

Interest paid for 5 months = (₹66.45 crore × 0.13 × 5) ÷ 12 = ₹3.56 crore

Interest paid for 7 months = (₹46.67 crore × 0.13 × 7) ÷ 12 = ₹3.54 crore

Total interest paid (₹3.65 crore + ₹3.54 crore) = ₹7.10 crore.

31.C.2 (EVA) The management of Infosys Technologies limited is desirous of determining economic value added (EVA) by its operations for its shareholders during 2001-05. Infosys has been a debt free company for the period –mentioned. The summarized income statement for the period under reference is as follows:

(a) Income Statement of Infosys Technologies Limited, 2001-05

(Amount in ₹ crore)

Particulars	*2005*	*2004*	*2003*	*2002*	*2001*
Income (Overseas and domestic)	6,859.66	4,760.89	3,622.69	2,603.59	1,900.56
Less: Expenses (Software development, selling, general, administrative)	4,534.55	3,177.24	2,350.65	1,565.96	1,135.72
Operating profit before interest,* depreciation and amortization	2,325.11	1,583.65	1,272.04	1037.63	764.84
Less: Depreciation and amortization	268.22	230.90	188.95	160.65	112.89
Net operating profit before taxes	2,056.89	1,352.75	1,083.09	876.98	651.95
Less: Taxes**	325.58	227.54	201	135.43	72.71
	(15.8%)	(16.8%)	(18.6%)	(15.5%)	(11.2%)
Net operating profit after taxes (NOPAT)	1,731.31	1,125.21	882.09	741.55	579.24

*(i) Interest charge is zero in view of debt-free capital structure.

**(ii) It pays taxes on its income in the range of 11 to 19 per cent. The reason is it enjoys 100 per cent tax rebate on income accruing from its operations in software Technology Parks (STPs). STPs constitute the major source of revenue. In view of the fact that Infosys has its operations in various parts of the globe and is to pay taxes in those countries, its exact tax rate could not be known.

(b) Data Related to Average Equity Funds and Cost of Equity, 2001-05

Particulars	*2005*	*2004*	*2003*	*2002*	*2001*
Average equity funds (in ₹ Crore)	4,330.95	3,124.82	2,493.4	1,734,97	1,111.47
Risk free cost (%)	7.0	6.75	7.5	8.0	8.0
Return on market Portfolio (%)	15.0	16.0	16.5	14.0	14.0
Beta	0.98	1.27	1.57	1.41	1.54
Cost of equity* (Ke) (%)	14.84	18.30	21.63	16.46	17.24

*Ke = *$R_f + b(R_m - R_f)$

Required The CEO of Infosys Technologies has approached Apeksha Jain, a financial consultant to compute EVA and report to him for inclusion in the annual report.

Solution The EVA computation by Apeksha Jain are given in **Exhibit 31.C.3.**

EXHIBIT 31.C.3 Determination of Economic Value Added of Infosys Technologies Limited

(*Amount in ₹ crore*)

Particulars	*2005*	*2004*	*2003*	*2002*	*2001*
(I) NOPAT	1,731.31	1,125.21	882.09	741.55	579.24
(II) Less: Cost of funds					
a. Average equity funds	4,330.95	3,124.82	2,493.4	1,734.97	1,111.47
b. cost of equity	14.84%	18.30%	21.63%	16.46%	17.24%
Total cost [(II)a* (II)b]	624.71	571.84	539.32	285.58	191.62
EVA [I – II]	1088.60	553.37	342.77	455.97	387.62

EVA = NOPAT – (Average capital employed × WACC).

In the case of Infosys it is = NOPAT – (Average equity funds × Ke) as it is debt-free company.

Conclusion Infosys has been successful in adding significant value to its shareholders wealth.

31.C.3 Chemicals and Pesticides Mangalore Ltd (Business Valuation) Chemicals and Pesticides Mangalore Ltd (CPML) has had a phenomenal growth in the recent years. Its current balance sheet is summarised below (amount in ₹ lakh).

Liabilities	*Amount*	*Assets*		*Amount*
Share capital:		Fixed assets:	₹150.0	
• 11% Preference shares (₹100 each)	₹40.0	Less Depreciation	30.0	120.0
		Current assets:		
• Equity shares (₹100 each)	120.0	Inventory	100.0	
10% Debentures	20.0	Debtors	50.0	
Profit and loss account	23.0	Cash and bank	10.0	160.0
Trade creditors	71.0	Preliminary expenses		2.0
Provisions for Tax	8.0			
	282.0			282.0

The CPML's free cashflows for equity holders (FCFEs) have been growing at a rate of 25 per cent in recent years. But it suffered a huge loss in the current year when the Centre for Science and Environment (CSE) published in one of its reports the harmful effect of the pesticide **Endosulfan** produced by the CPML. The report claimed that the studies done by the CSE have proved that the pesticides was responsible for serious health hazards in some of the districts in Kerala where the particular pesticides had been used extensively in the past. Acting on the report of the CSE, the Ministry of Environment and Forest imposed a ban on all the pesticides products of CPML. As a consequence of the CSE report and Government ban, the market sentiment for CPML suffered a serious setback. Owning moral responsibility, the CPML management has decided to pay due compensation to the victims for damage to their health. Meanwhile, it was also decided to sell the CPML. The CEO of CPML, Harpal Singh, hired Latha and Raveesh (LR) Associates as a financial consultant for valuation of its current business.

The market research team of LR Associates has estimated a projected growth rate of the CPML's FCFE of its chemicals business after the closure of the pesticides business for the next five years as listed below:

Year	*FCFE growth (%)*
1	15
2	12
3	10
4	9
5	7

After five years, the FCFE are likely to grow at the normal rate of six per cent. The CPML's weighted average cost of capital is 12 per cent. The current per share FCFE is ₹7. The investors required rate of return may be assumed to be 15 per cent.

Required What is the value of CPML using **(i)** net-asset based and **(ii)** FCFEs approaches?

Solution The values of the CPML using the two approaches are given in Annexures 1 and 2.

Annexure 1 Net Asset Based Valuation (₹ lakh)

Fixed asset (net)		₹120.0
Current assets:		
Inventory	₹100.0	
Debtors	50.0	
Cash and Bank	10.0	160.0
Total assets		280.0
Less external liabilities:		
11% Preference shares	40.0	
10% Debentures	20.0	
Trade creditors	71.0	
Provision for taxation	8.0	
Preference dividend	4.4	143.40
Net asset available for equity holders		136.60
÷ Number of equity shares (in lakh)		1.2
Net asset value per share (₹)		113.83

Annexure 2 Free Cash Flow-Based Valuation (₹ lakh)

Year	*Free cash flow (FCFE)*	*Growth in FCFE* $(1 + g)^n$	*FCFE per share (1 × 3)*	*PV factor (0.15)*	*Total present value (4 × 5)*
(1)	(2)	(3)	(4)	(5)	(6)
1	7.0	1.150	8.050	0.870	7.000
2	8.05	1.12	9.016	0.756	6.816
3	9.016	1.10	9.918	0.658	6.526
4	9.918	1.09	10.811	0.572	6.184
5	10.811	1.07	11.568	0.497	5.749
					32.275

Market price of share at year-end 5 = $FCFE_6 \div (K_e - g)$

= ₹11.568 (1.06) = ₹12.262 / 0.09 = ₹136.24

PV (t=0) = 136.24 × 0.497 = ₹67.11

Maximum price investors would be prepared to pay = ₹32.275 + ₹67.711 = ₹99.986 (₹100)

Comment: The valuation of CPML based on net asset is higher compared to the FCFE approach. The former ignores the future earnings/cash flow generating ability of the assets. Considering the present scenario of the CPML when the pesticide business faces serious threat with virtual prospect of no future return, the FCFE-based value per share is more realistic (conservative).

31.C.4 (Business Valuation) SGA Ltd was set-up as a start-up company by three first-time-entrepreneurs – Sunny Kapoor, Gaurav Joshi and Abhishek Luthra. After initial difficulties, the SGA has grown into a successful company. IBM Ltd, which operates in the same business has offered to acquire majority stake in the SGA. The acquisition is likely to add considerable value to the combined entity with expanded client base and enhanced economies of scale. The top management of the SGA is favourably inclined to accept IBM's proposal. The CEO, Sunny Kapoor, asks the CFO, Gaurav Joshi and the COO, Abhishek Luthra, to determine the value of the SGA to take a final view on the IBM's proposal.

Gaurav and Abhishek decide to compute the value of the SGA based on free cash flow method. The forecasted investment expenditure during 2010-2016 is summarised in Annexure 1.

Annexure 1 Forecast Investment

Year	*Gross investment in fixed assets (₹ crore)*	*Working capital requirement (₹ crore)*	*Total (2+3)*
(1)	(2)	(3)	(4)
2010	4.26	1.39	5.65
2011	10.50	0.60	11.10
2012	3.34	0.28	3.62
2013	3.65	0.42	4.07
2014	4.18	0.93	5.11
2015	5.37	1.57	6.94
2016	6.28	2.00	8.28
Total	37.58	7.19	44.77

The projected profits and dividends during the same period are summarised in Annexure 2.

Annnexure 2 Projected Profits/Dividends (₹ *crore*)

Year	*Cash flow*	*Depreciation*	*Profits before tax (2 – 3)*	*Tax (0.35)*	*Profit after tax (4 – 5)*	*Dividends*	*Retained profits (6 – 7)*
(1)	(2)	(3)	(4)	(5)	(6)	(7)	(8)
2010	10.48	2.40	8.08	2.83	5.25	2.00	3.25
2011	11.87	3.10	8.77	3.07	5.70	2.00	3.70
2012	7.74	3.12	4.62	1.62	3.00	2.50	0.50
2013	8.40	3.17	5.23	1.83	3.40	2.50	0.90
2014	9.95	3.26	6.69	2.34	4.35	2.50	1.85
2015	12.67	3.44	9.23	3.23	6.00	2.50	3.50
2016	15.37	3.68	11.69	4.09	7.60	3.00	4.60

@ Surplus operating cash flows

Gaurav and Abhishek project a 7.2 per cent growth rate after 2016. The cost of capital of SGA and IBM is 10 and 9 per cent respectively. The risk free rate of return is 6 per cent. The value of the SGA is determined in the Solution Table.

Solution Table (*Amount in* ₹ *crore*)

Year	*Profit after tax*	*Depreciation*	*Investments in fixed assets*	*Working capital investment*	*Free cashflows*	*Discounted cashflow*
(1)	(2)	(3)	(4)	(5)	(6) [2+3–4–5]	(7) [(6) × at 10% PVF]
2010	5.25	2.40	4.26	1.39	2.00	1.82
2011	5.70	3.10	10.50	0.60	(2.30)	(1.90)
2012	3.00	3.12	3.34	0.28	2.50	1.88
2013	3.40	3.17	3.65	0.42	2.50	1.71
2014	4.35	3.26	4.18	0.93	2.50	1.55
2015	6.00	3.44	5.37	1.57	2.50	1.41
2016	7.60	3.68	6.28	2.00	3.00	1.54

Total discounted values of free cashflow at end-2016	8.01(a)
Terminal value after 2016 = (3 × 1.072) ÷ (0.10 – 072) = 114.8571	
Present value of terminal value = 114.8571 × 0.513	58.92(b)
Value of business (a + b)	66.93

31.C.5 The e-retailing business is growing at a fast pace and as a result, more and more players are coming into this business. The penetration of e-commerce is high in India. India's e-commerce market which was at \$2.5 billion in 2011 rose to \$6.3 billion in 2013 and is expected to be at \$14 billion in 2015. This shows a huge potential of Indian market, since 10 per cent of India's population only (at present) is using internet services.

Big & Bang Company is a US based e-retail company. It is market leader in US and wants to enter in India. Growing organically will take considerable time because of factors like development of efficient distribution system, winning trust of people, etc. To overcome this, Big & Bang wants to acquire an already existing e-commerce company (Bazinga).

In such a scenario, credible business valuation becomes very important. Big & Bang has engaged services of Mr. Sanuj Mittal, a leading financial consultant, to suggest a price at which Bazinga is worth acquiring.

Mr. Mittal knows that there are various approaches of business valuation. It would be appropriate to determine value of Bazinga (based on each approach) and subsequently apply fair value method (based on weighted average instead of simple average) to asses the price (in terms of payment to equityholders) at which, the business of Bazinga would be worth acquiring. Accordingly, Sanuj collects relevant data. He has planned to use free cash flow approach, capitalisation method and net assets basis to value the target firm.

(i) Balance sheet as at March 31, 2013

(Amount in ₹ million)

Particulars	*Amount*	*Particulars*	*Amount*
Share capital (1 lakh @ ₹100 each)	10.0	Fixed assets	42.5
Reserves and surplus	28.5	Inventories	20.0
Long term borrowings	25.0	Trade receivables	15.0
Short term borrowings	5	Cash and cash equivalents	4.5
Trade payables	9		
Other current liabilities	4.5		
	82		82

(II) Income statement for the current year ended March 31, 2013

(Amount in ₹ million)

Particulars	
Revenue from operations	109.0
Expenses:	
Cost of material consumed	32.3
Purchases of stock in trade	2.4
Changes in inventories	2.7
Employee benefit expenses	42.3
Financing costs	2.1
Depreciation and ammortisation expenses	7.7
Other expenses	1.0

(Contd.)

(*Contd.*)

Total expenses	90.5
Profits before exceptional and extraordinary items	18.5
Exceptional items	0.0
Profits before extraordinary items and taxes	18.5
Extraordinary items	2.0
Profits before tax	20.5
Taxes (35%)	7.18
Profits for the period from continuing operations	13.32

(III) Contingent liabilities (in ₹ Million)

(i) Claims against company not acknowledged as debt (likely to be paid) 0.6

(ii) Guarantees (likely to be invoked) 0.4

(IV) Future estimated free cash flows of the company for years 2014-2020 (explicit period indicated as years 1 to 7)

Year	1	2	3	4	5	6	7
Amount in ₹ million	₹18	20	22.5	28	27	29.5	30

(V) After the 7th year, the cash flows are estimated to remain stable. The WACC for the company is 12 per cent.

(VI) Additional information:

(a) Market value of fixed assets of the company is estimated at ₹90 million.

(b) Additional amount of expenses of ₹3 million for advertisement will be required for smooth running of business in years to come.

(c) Value of goodwill is to be considered as equivalent to the present value of super profits likely to accrue till perpetuity.

(d) For the purpose of goodwill, super profits are to be computed on long term capital employed.

(e) Following weights will be given to each method:

- FCFF method 0.50
- Capitalisation method 0.20
- Assets based approach 0.30

(f) Weighted average cost of capital is 12 per cent

After collecting all the above relevant data, Mr. Mittal went on with the calculations with each method.

Solution

Method I: Free discounted cash flow (FCFF) approach

(a) PV of FCFF during explicit forecast period (*₹ in million*)

Year	*FCFF*	*PV factor (0.12)*	*Total PV*
1	18.0	0.893	16.074
2	20.0	0.797	15.940
3	22.5	0.712	16.020
4	28.0	0.636	17.808
5	27.0	0.567	15.309
6	29.5	0.507	14.956
7	30.0	0.452	13.560
Total			109.667

(b) PV of FCFF subsequent to explicit forecast period

CV_7 = ₹30 million/0.12 = ₹250 m

PV_0 = ₹250 million × PV factor at 12% for 7th year

= ₹250 million × 0.452 = ₹113 million

(c) Total PV of FCFF (₹109.667 million + ₹113 million)	₹222.67 million
Less External Liabilities (including contingent liabilities)	₹44.5 million
FCFE available to equity shareholders	₹178.17 million
MPS (₹178.17 m/1 lakh shares)	= ₹1781.7

Method II: Capitalisation method

Earnings before tax	₹20.50 million
Less extraordinary income	2.00
Recurring expenses	1.00
Expected earnings before tax	17.50
Less taxes	6.12
Future sustainable profits after taxes	11.38
Value of business (11.38/0.12)	₹94.83 m
Value of equity (less external liabilities and contingent liabilities) (94.83 m – 44.5 m)	₹50.33 m
Price per equity share (50.33 m/1 lakh)	₹503.30

Method III: Asset Based Approach

Fixed assets	₹90.0 million
Inventories	20.0
Trade receivables	15.0
Cash and cash equivalents	4.5
Goodwill	31.33
Total assets	160.83
Less External liabilities (including contingent liabilities)	44.5
Net assets at market value	116.33
Net assets backing per share (₹94.83 m /1 lakh)	**₹1163.3**

**Valuation of goodwill*	*₹million*
Future maintainable profits after taxes	11.38
Less normal profit (12% (ko) × 63.5** (Long term capital employed)	7.62
Super profits	3.76
Value of goodwill (₹3.76 million/12% (ko))	31.33

**Long term capital employed

₹10.0 + 28.5 + 25.0 million = ₹63.5 million

Final value calculations:

(*Amount in ₹ million*)

Method used	*Value*	*Weight factor*	*Weighted value*
Free cash flow	178.17	0.50	89.08
Capitalisation approach	50.33	0.20	10.07
Net assets based approach	116.33	0.30	34.90
Fair value approach			134.05

Conclusion: Mr. Sanuj observed that there were huge variations in the values calculated through different methods. By using fair value approach (based on weighted average), the impact of variations is minimised. He recommends the payment of ₹134.05 million to equityholders, apart from making payment to external liabilities and contingent liabilities of ₹44.5 million. In effect, the valuation of business is ₹178.55 million.

31.C.6 Herbal India Ltd is a renowned company that is emerging as an important growth engine in India's consumption market. It is the fourth largest FMCG company in India with revenue of over ₹6,146 crore, operating in various verticals like hair care, skin care, health care, home care and foods.

The cost of equity capital (calculated by capital asset pricing model) of the firm is 15.79 per cent, shown as follows:

$$K_e = R_f + b\,(R_m - R_f).$$

$$K_e = 9\% + 0.71(18.56\% - 9\%) = 15.79 \text{ per cent}$$

The before-tax cost of debt of the firm is 13.1% and after- tax cost of debt is 13.1 × (1 – 0.35) = 8.5% The cost of preference shares (including dividend payment tax) for the firm is 13%.

The company plans to expand its operations through the establishment of new vertical business units in rural areas. As a precautionary step, the CEO of the company, Mr. Gupta, suggested that the business be evaluated for the return being generated, before setting up the new vertical units. The CEO had learnt that the profit after taxes margin (PAT) had taken a downward trend from 14.8% for the year 2010 to 12.4% for the year 2013. But the sales showed a continuously increasing trend over the years, encouraging the business's further expansion into newer verticals. The CEO, Mr. Gupta, however, was not very confident with setting-up of the new vertical, and wanted a more detailed analysis of the trends. Hence, Mr. Gupta approached their firm's financial controller.

The Financial Controller of the firm, Mr. Manohar, then used the most popular yardstick of calculating the overall performance through 'Return on Investment' technique and came up with the following results:

TABLE 31.1 Calculation of Return on Investment (ROI) (₹ *in crore*)

Financial results	*FY 2008*	*FY 2009*	*FY 2010*	*FY 2011*	*FY 2012*	*FY 2013*
Net sales	2361	2805	3391	4077	5283	6146
Other income	34	47	48	59	80	124
EBITDA	443	517	667	833	948	1124
PBT (Profit before tax)	384	445	601	708	791	953
Taxes @ 35%	134.4	155.75	201.35	247.8	276.85	333.55
PAT (Profit after tax)	249.6	289.25	399.65	460.2	514.15	619.45
Add back interest	8.42	19.55	15.22	89.34	90.87	97.72
NOPAT (Net operating profit after tax)	258.02	308.8	414.87	549.54	605.02	717.17
Average capital employed	1841	2573	2912	5855	7102	8265
Return on investment (%)	14.1%	12.0%	14.24%	9.4%	8.52%	8.667%

The results suggest that the return on investment has dipped to less than 10 per cent during (2011-2013) compared to 12-14 per cent (during 2008-2010) alarming the entire business unit. However, the only respite is that, the return on investment is still adequate for the business to sustain in the market. At this point, he recollects Ms Revathi (MBA in finance) has joined; her colleagues are appreciative of her work. He discussed the problem with her and explored the best way of determining financial returns earned by the company. She suggests use of EVA for measuring true/ credible financial performance. The rationale of EVA is that it is based on profits earned after meeting cost of all sources of finance (and not debt alone). The CEO was convinced and entrusted her task of determining EVA for 2008-13.

Solution

$$\text{EVA} = \text{NOPAT} - \text{WACC} \times \text{Capital Employed}$$

$$\text{WACC} = K_e \times (\text{ESF / CE}) + K_d \times (\text{LTD / CE}) + K_p \times (\text{PSC/CE})$$

where K_e = Cost of equity,

ESF = Equity shareholders fund,

CE = Capital employed,

K_d = Cost of debt,

LTD = Long term debt,

K_p = Cost of preference share,

PSF = Preference share capital.

Based on the annual financial statements for the past 6 years (2008-13), the book value weights for cost of equity, cost of debt and cost of preferential shares were obtained as follows:

TABLE 31.2 WACC based on book value method, 2008-13

Particulars	*Proportions of equity, preference and debt for each year*					
	2008	*2009*	*2010*	*2011*	*2012*	*2013*
Cost of equity (15.79%)	0.770	0.72	0.778	0.531	0.580	0.615
Cost of preference shares (13%)	0.107	0.076	0.072	0.066	0.058	0.050
Cost of debt (8.5%)	0.123	0.202	0.149	0.401	0.361	0.334
Weighted average cost of capital	14.6%	14.07%	14.48%	12.65%	12.98%	13.20%

Based on the values of average capital employed, profit after taxes, interest (as obtained from Table 31.1) and WACC (as obtained from Table 31.2), the economic value added was calculated by Ms. Revathi (shown in Table 31.3).

TABLE 31.3 Computation of EVA, 2008-13 (*₹ in Crore*)

Particulars	*2008*	*2009*	*2010*	*2011*	*2012*	*2013*
Average capital employed	1,841	2,573	2,912	5,855	7,102	8,265
WACC	14.6%	14.07%	14.48%	12.65%	12.98%	13.20%
Cost of capital employed	268.79	362.02	421.66	740.66	921.84	1090.98
Profit after tax	249.6	289.25	399.65	460.2	514.15	619.45
Interest	8.42	19.55	15.22	89.34	90.87	97.72
NOPAT	258.02	308.8	414.87	549.54	605.02	717.17
EVA	(10.766)	(53.22)	(6.78)	(191.12)	(316.82)	(373.81)

Ms. Revathi then submitted the report to the CEO of Herbal India Ltd and he gets startled on seeing the report. While he was hoping to expand his business and establish new vertical units, he realises that the business itself is at a stake.

The EVA on capital employed (%), shown in Table 31.3, very clearly shows that the surplus over and above the cost of capital is in effect negative during the years 2008-2010. It is even more worrying for Mr. Gupta, to realise that in the years 2011-2013 the business was suffering huge losses.

TABLE 31.4 Return on investment and EVA, 2008-13

Financial Year	*2008*	*2009*	*2010*	*2011*	*2012*	*2013*
Return on Investment (ROI %)	14.10	12.00	14.24	9.40	8.52	8.67
EVA on capital employed (%)	(0.58)	(2.07)	(0.23)	(3.26)	(4.46)	(4.52)

Table 31.4 shows that, divergence exists between the performance results given by traditional measure (based on ROI) and percentage of EVA on capital employed. The return on investment (ROI) does not reflect the real value addition to shareholders' wealth, but EVA based performance measurement system provides more credible information about the shareholders' value addition or value destruction. The company has not been able to create value for its shareholders during the period of 2011-2013.

Recommendation Therefore, Ms. Revathi suggests the CEO that expansion of the business unit should be kept on hold for the time being until the business ceases to have negative EVA.

Scan the QR Code given at the end of chapter to access comprehensive cases.

REVIEW QUESTIONS

LOD: Easy

RQ.31.1 Provide the appropriate answers in the following: [LO 31.1.2,3]

(i) Book value is total value of all valuable assets including fictitious assets, less external liabilities. (True/False)

(ii) Discounted cash flow approach of valuation of business is superior to the P/E ratio approach if the future cash earnings are well predictable. (True/False)

(iii) Valuation of firm and valuation of equity in discounted cash flow approach provide identical results despite using different definitions of FCFF and discount rates. (True/False)

(iv) Unpaid dividends on preference shares are reckoned liability of the firm in asset based valuation. (True/False)

(v) For business valuation, adjustments are required for contingent liabilities that may fructify. (True/False)

(vi) Market value approach cannot be applied to ____________ firms. (listed/unlisted)

(vii) A positive net profit after taxes always implies that there is an economic value addition to the firm. (True/False)

(viii) Unrecorded assets should be accounted in asset based valuation. (True/False)

(ix) Goodwill is discounted present value of ____________ to be earned by the firm in future

(x) What is the value of a firm with cost of capital 20%, with profit after taxes ₹33.6 lakh, with extraordinary income of ₹6 lakh, tax rate is 40 per cent?

(a) ₹150 lakh, (b) ₹300 lakh, (c) ₹180 lakh, (d) ₹120 lakh

(xi) Determine the market price per share of a firm having equity capital of ₹100,000 (face value of ₹50 per share) the profit after taxes is ₹12,000 and P/E ratio is 5

(a) ₹30 (b) ₹60 (c) ₹50 (d) ₹20

(xii) Which is the best method among these for valuation of a firm where not much data about its profit is available and its shares are not actively traded?

(a) Market value (b) Discounted Cash Flow
(c) Net asset based approach (d) None of these

[Answers: (i) False (ii) True (iii) True (iv) True (v) True (vi) Unlisted firm (vii) False (viii) True (ix) Super profits (x) ₹150 lakh (xi) ₹30 per share and (xii) Net asset based approach]

RQ.31.2 Why is the business valuation exercise undertaken by corporate finance managers and investors? [LO 31.1]

RQ.31.3 What is continuing value? How is it determined? [LO 31.2]

RQ.31.4 From the following data, determine the value of goodwill of a firm: (i) Funds invested ₹100 crore (ii) Normal rate of return (expected) 10 per cent (iii) Profits after taxes (current year) ₹14 crore which are likely to continue for next 4 years only. [LO 31.1]

LOD: Medium

RQ.31.5 Explain the following concepts of value with the help of examples. (i) book value, (ii) market value, (iii) intrinsic value and (iv) liquidation value. [LO 31.1]

RQ.31.6 "The discounted cash flow (DCF) approach is conceptually the most ideal among various approaches for business valuation." Do you agree? Explain your answer. [LO 31.2]

RQ.31.7 "Earnings shown by income statement need to be adjusted for valuation" Elucidate the statement. Name the items that require to be adjusted. [LO 31.2]

RQ.31.8 Explain the term free cash flow to the firm. What are its components? [LO 31.2]

RQ.31.9 What is the major difference between the terms 'Free cash flow to the firm' and 'Free cash flow to equity'? Will these approaches provide identical answers of equity valuation? Explain. [LO 31.2]

RQ.31.10 What are the major factors that should be borne in mind while valuing a firm? [LO 31.2]

RQ.31.11 What is economic value added approach? In what respects it is considered superior to the accounting approach of determining profits? Explain with an appropriate example. [LO 31.3]

RQ.31.12 Distinguish between the following: [LO 31.1.2,3]

(i) Market value added and economic value added
(ii) Book value and market value
(iii) Operating free cash flow and non-operating cash flow
(iv) Weighted average cost of capital and cost of equity

RQ.31.13 The following particulars are available in respect of a corporate: **(i)** Profits after taxes (for the current year) ₹30 crore which include extraordinary gains of ₹8 crore. **(ii)** To maintain sales, the firm is to increase advertisement expenditure by ₹2 crore. **(iii)** Capitalisation rate applicable to business to which corporate belongs is 12 per cent. [LO 31.2]

From the above information, determine the value of business, value of equity (assume total external liabilities of ₹50 crore) and price per equity share (assume 1 crore equity shares of ₹100 each outstanding) based on the capitalisation method. Assume tax rate of 40 per cent.

RQ.31.14 Determine continuing value of a corporate from the following information: [LO 31.2]

	(₹ crore)
Cash flow from business operations at the end of the explicit forecast period (year 5)	₹20
Investment in current assets required in year 5	2
Expected annual growth rate in free cash flows after forecast period (%)	5
Weighted average cost of capital (%)	12
Cost of debt (%)	8

RQ.31.15 The finance manager of 'Mobile Fast' has estimated future free cash flows (FCFF) of the company for 6 years as follows: [LO 31.2]

	(₹ crore)
Year-end 1	400
2	800
3	1,050
4	1,400
5	950
6	600

The FCFF are expected to be constant at ₹600 crore after 6 years as the mobile scenario in the country is likely to be stabilised by then. You are required to compute the value of corporate as well as value of equity. Assume 13 per cent overall cost of capital and total external liabilities of ₹2,400 crore based on free cash-flow approach.

RQ.31.16 From the following condensed income statement of a corporate for the current year, determine the EVA added during the year. [LO 31.3]

		(₹ crore)
Sales revenue		100
Less: Cost of goods sold	₹40	
Administrative expenses	4	
Selling expenses	16	
Interest	10	70
Earnings before taxes		30
Less: Taxes (0.40)		12
Earnings after taxes		18

The firm's weighted average cost of total capital employed (consisting of equity and debt of ₹150 crore) is 12 per cent; its cost of equity capital is 15 per cent.

RQ.31.17 Calculate economic value added (EVA) with the help of the following information of Hypothetical Limited: [LO 31.3]

Financial leverage	1.4 times
Capital structure:	Equity capital, ₹170 lakh
	Reserves and surplus, ₹130 lakh
	10% Debentures, ₹400 lakh
Cost of equity	17.5%
Income tax rate	30%.

LOD: Difficult

RQ.31.18 What are the major weaknesses of P/E ratio as a technique of share valuation? In spite of such limitations, why is it so popular? What safeguards would you suggest to make them more credible? [LO 31.2]

RQ.31.19 Balance sheet of a corporate as on March 31, current year is as follows: [LO 31.2]

(Amount in ₹ crore)

Liabilities	*Amount*	*Assets*	*Amount*
Equity share capital (1 crore shares)	200	Plant and machinery	250
Reserves and surplus	180	Land and buildings	150
12% Debentures	150	Inventory	80
Total creditors	35	Receivables	60
Other current liabilities	15	Other current assets	40
	580		580

The market value of its assets as assessed by professional valuer is as follows: (₹ crore)

Plant and machinery	180
Land and building	300

The current resale value of the remaining assets are as per their book values.
You are required to compute the value of equity share on the basis of net assets method (book value and market value).

ANSWERS

31.4 Goodwill, ₹12.68 crore

31.13 Value of business, ₹200 crore
Value of equity, ₹150 crore
Price of equity share, ₹150

31.14 Continuing Value, ₹270 crore

31.15 Value of corporate, ₹5,585.48 crore
Value of equity, ₹3,185.48 crore

31.16 EVA, ₹6 crore

31.17 EVA, ₹17.5 lakh

31.19 Value of equity (book value), ₹380 crore
Value of equity (market value), ₹460 crore

Scan the QR Code to access comprehensive solutions to all numerical review questions and additional material.

CHAPTER

32 Corporate Restructuring

LEARNING OBJECTIVES

LO 32.1	Explain the conceptual framework of mergers/acquisitions in terms of the meaning, types, economics and limitations
LO 32.2	Describe and illustrate how to determine the firm's value, financing techniques in merger and the evaluation of merger as a capital budgeting decision
LO 32.3	Understand the relevant tax provisions applicable to mergers and demergers
LO 32.4	Describe the legal and procedural aspects of mergers/amalgamation/takeovers
LO 32.5	Discuss financial restructuring and demerger/divestiture as other forms of corporate restructuring
LO 32.6	Outline the motives and assessment of mergers and acquisitions practices in India

INTRODUCTION

Activities related to expansion or contraction of a firm's operations or changes in its assets or financial or ownership structure are referred to as **corporate restructuring**[1]. The most common forms of corporate restructuring are mergers/amalgamations and acquisitions/takeovers, financial restructuring, divestitures/demergers and buyouts. The focus of this chapter is on mergers and acquisitions. The different aspects of mergers and acquisitions, namely, conceptual framework, financial framework, taxation and legal and procedural compliances are covered first. Other forms of corporate restructuring, that is, financial restructuring, demerger and buyouts are discussed subsequently. The motives and financial assessment for corporate mergers in India are also outlined. The main points are summarised by way of recapitulation.

Corporate restructuring implies activities related to expansion/ contraction of a firm's operations or changes in its assets or financial or ownership structure.

LO 32.1 CONCEPTUAL FRAMEWORK

Profitable growth constitutes one of the prime objectives of most of the business firms. It can be achieved 'internally' either through the process of introducing/ developing new products or by expanding/enlarging the capacity of existing product(s). Alternatively, the growth process can be facilitated 'externally' by acquisitions of existing business firms. This acquisition may be in the form of *mergers, acquisitions, amalgamations, takeovers, absorption, consolidation,* and so on. Although the legal procedure involved in these are different, in view of the perspective of economic considerations (motives and effect) these terms are used interchangeably here.

There are strengths and weaknesses of both the processes of promoting growth. For instance, internal expansion apart from enabling the firm to retain control with itself also provides flexibility in terms of choosing equipment, mode of technology, location, and the like which are compatible with its existing operations. However, internal expansion usually involves a longer implementation period and also entails greater uncertainties particularly associated with developing new product(s). Above all, there may be sometimes an added problem of raising adequate funds to execute the required capital budgeting projects involving expansion. Acquisition/merger obviates, in most of the situations, financing problems as substantial/full payments are normally made in the form of shares of the purchasing company. Further, it also expedites the pace of growth as the acquired firm already has the facilities or products (acceptable to the market) and, therefore, obviously, saves the time otherwise required in building up the new facilities from scratch in the case of internal expansion programme.

A growing firm may, therefore, be in constant search for identifying potential firms which may be merged. The finance manager's job is to evaluate such merger decisions. These decisions, in a way, are analogous to capital budgeting decisions in that the cost of present investment (purchase consideration paid for acquisition of an enterprise either through issuance of shares and/or cash) is to be compared with expected future benefits accruing to the merging firm. The firm will opt for merger if it adds to the wealth of shareholders, otherwise merger will not be a financially viable proposition.

However, merger evaluations are relatively more difficult *vis-a-vis* capital budgeting decisions, the two chief reasons being: **(i)** all benefits from merger are not easily quantifiable and so also all costs, for instance, benefits of less competition and economies of scale (technical, managerial, financial) are not easily measurable attributes; and **(ii)** buying a company is more complicated than buying a new machine in that the firm is to address itself to many tax, legal and accounting issues.

We describe below the conceptual aspects of mergers, acquisitions, amalgamations, takeovers, absorption and so on, in terms of their types, economics and limitations. Although the terms mergers, amalgamations and acquisitions are different, their economic impact is the same as far as the business firms involved are concerned. **For this reason, these terms are used interchangeably. The differences in these terms are explained later in this chapter.**

Horizontal merger is a merger when two or more firms dealing in similar lines of activity combine together..

Types of Mergers

Notwithstanding terminological differences mergers can be usefully distinguished into the following three types: **(i)** horizontal, **(ii)** vertical and **(iii)** conglomerate.

Horizontal Merger Horizontal merger takes place when two or more corporate firms dealing in similar lines of activity combine together. Elimination or reduction in competition, putting an end to price-cutting, economies of scale in production, research and development, marketing and management are often motives underlying such mergers.

Vertical merger is a merger that involves two or more stages of production/distribution that are usually separate.

Vertical Merger Vertical merger occurs when a firm acquires firms 'upstream' from it and/or firms 'downstream' from it. In the case of an 'upstream' merger, it extends to the firms supplying raw materials and to those firms that sell eventually to the consumer in the event of a 'downstream' merger. Thus, the combination involves two or more stages of production or distribution that are usually separate[1]. Lower buying cost of materials, lower distribution costs, assured supplies and market, increasing or creating barriers to entry for potential competitors or placing them at a cost disadvantage are the chief gains accruing from such mergers.

Conglomerate Merger Conglomerate merger is a combination in which a firm established in one industry combines with a firm from an unrelated industry. In other words, firms engaged in two different/unrelated economic/business activities combine together. Diversification of risk constitutes the rationale for such mergers.

Corporate restructuring implies activities related to expansion/contraction of a firm's operations or changes in its assets or financial or ownership structure.

Economics of Mergers

The major economic advantages of a merger are: **(i)** economies of scale, **(ii)** synergy, **(iii)** fast growth, **(iv)** tax benefits and **(v)** diversification.

Economies of Scale The operating cost advantage in terms of economies of scale is considered to be the primary motive for mergers, in particular, for horizontal and vertical mergers. They result in lower average cost of production and sales due to a higher level of operations. For instance, overhead costs can be substantially reduced on account of sharing central services such as accounting and finance, office, executive and top level management, legal, sales promotion and advertisement and so on.

Koutsoyiannis classifies these economies into two groups, namely, real and pecuniary. **Real economies** arise from a reduction in the factor inputs per unit of output, while **pecuniary economies** are realised from paying lower prices for factor inputs due to bulk transactions.'[2]

In operational terms, real economies may arise from **(i)** the production activity of the firm, **(ii)** the research and development/technological activities, **(iii)** the synergy effects, **(iv)** marketing and distribution activities, **(v)** transport, storage, inventories, and **(vi)** managerial economies.

Cheaper finance is the most vital ingredient of pecuniary economies. A post-merger large firm is likely to raise finance at cheaper/lower rates either of the pre-merger units could have. The reason is that the larger the size of the firm, the more secured the investors consider their funds, resulting in lower risk of default/financial risk. Besides, the flotation cost (in making new issues) per unit decreases with the increase in the size of shares and debentures. Above all, the merger may bring about optimal debt capacity, in that, before the merger both firms may have had lopsided capital structures—one overextended and another underextended by debt. Both these firms will be under-valued firms.

Synergy Synergy results from complementary activities. For instance, one firm may have a substantial amount of financial resources while the other has profitable investment opportunities. Likewise, one firm may have a strong research and development (R & D) team whereas the other may have a very efficiently organised production department. Similarly, one firm may have well established brands of its products but lacks marketing organisation and another firm may have a very strong marketing organisation. The merged business unit in all these cases will be more efficient than the individual firms. And, hence, the combined value of the merged firms is likely to be greater than the sum of the individual entities (units). Symbolically,

Combined value = Stand alone value of acquiring firm, V_A + Stand alone value of acquired/target firm, V_T + Value of synergy, ΔV_{AT} **(32.1)**

Normally, the value of synergy is positive and this constitutes the rationale for the merger. In valuing synergy, costs attached with acquisitions should also be taken into account. These costs primarily consist of costs of integration and payment made for the acquisition of the target firm, in excess of its value, V_T. Therefore, the *net gain* from the merger is equal to the difference between the value of synergy and costs (Equation 33.2)

$$\text{Net gain} = \text{Value of synergy, } \Delta V_{AT} - \text{Costs} \tag{32.2}$$

Example **32.1**

Assume Firm A has a pre-merger value of ₹320 lakh and Firm T has a pre-merger value of ₹90 lakh. It is estimated that the merger would yield cost savings with a present value of ₹40 lakh. For acquisition of Firm T, Firm A will be required to make payment of ₹100 lakh (consisting of issue of shares worth ₹80 lakh and cash of ₹20 lakh). Besides, it is to incur acquisition costs of ₹5 lakh. Determine the value of gain, costs and net gain from merger.

Solution

Gain = Value of synergy (in terms of present value of cost savings), ΔV_{AT} = ₹40 lakh

Costs = Value of cash and shares paid + Other acquisition costs – Pre-merger value of Firm T

= ₹100 lakh + ₹5 lakh – ₹90 lakh = ₹15 lakh

Net gain = ΔV_{AT} – Costs = ₹40 lakh – ₹15 lakh = ₹25 lakh.

In practice, the value of synergy, in well thought out mergers, is likely to be of higher value than the costs involved, yielding net gain.

Fast Growth A merger often enables the amalgamating firm to grow at a rate faster than is possible under the internal expansion route, via its own capital budgeting proposals, because the acquiring company enters a new market quickly, avoiding the delay associated with building a new plant and establishing a new line of products. 'Internal growth is time consuming, requiring research and development, organisation of the product, market penetration and in general a smoothly working organisation[3]. Above all, there may sometimes be an added problem of raising adequate funds to execute the required/profitable capital budgeting projects. A merger obviates all these obstacles and, thus, steps up the pace of corporate growth.

Tax Benefits Under certain conditions, tax benefits may turn out to be the underlying motive for a merger. These conditions relate to the tax laws allowing set off and carry forward of losses. It may be beneficial to merge a firm saddled with large tax carry forward losses with a firm having sufficient current earnings. The argument is that this tax loss carry forward will reduce the taxable income of the newly merged firm, with its obvious impact on the reduction of tax liability. The merged firm is taxed as if the two firms (acquiring and target) had always been together. In operational terms, the losses of target firm will be allowed to be set off against the profits of the acquiring firm.

Example **32.2**

Firm A acquires Firm T. As of date Firm T has accumulated losses of ₹1,000 lakh. Firm A is a well managed company with a good profit record. The projected profits before taxes, of Firm A, for the next 3 years are given in the table:

Year		
	1	₹350
	2	500
	3	700

Assuming corporate tax rate of 35 per cent and discount rate of 12 per cent, determine the present value of tax gains likely to accrue on account of merger to A.

Solution

TABLE 32.1 Present Value (PV) of Tax Shield

(₹ lakh)

Particulars	*Years*		
	1	*2*	*3*
(a) Profit before tax	₹350	₹500	₹700
(b) *Less:* Adjustment against loss of firm T/Reduction in taxable income	350	500	150*
(c) Reduction in tax payments ($b \times 0.35$)	122.5	175	52.5
(d) Multiple by PV factor at 12%	0.893	0.797	0.712
(e) Total PV of tax shield is ₹286.24 lakh [(*c*) × PV factor)]	109.39	139.47	37.38

*(₹1,000 lakh accumulated loss of Firm T—₹350 lakh and ₹500 lakh adjusted in years 1 and 2 respectively).

Firm A gains ₹286.24 lakh in terms of tax savings on acquisition of Firm T.

Diversification Diversification is yet another major advantage, especially in a conglomerate merger. The argument is that a merger between two unrelated firms would tend to reduce business risk, which, in turn, reduces the discount rate/required rate of return (k_e) of the firm's earnings (as investors are risk averse) and, thus, increases the market value. In other words, such mergers help stabilise or smoothen overall corporate income, which would otherwise fluctuate due to seasonal or economic cycles. In operational terms, the greater the combination of statistically independent, or negatively correlated income streams of the merged companies, the higher will be the reduction in the business risk factor and the greater will be the benefit of diversification or *vice versa*.

However, such diversification can also be attained by individual shareholders on their own. Therefore, the financial managers should ensure that the merger should not be at a cost higher than the one at which shareholders would have attained the same risk reduction by diversifying their individual investment portfolios; corporate diversification should be less expensive than personal diversification.

Limitations

However, merger suffers from certain weaknesses. First, a merger may not turn out to be a financially profitable proposition in view of non-realisation of potential economies in terms of cost reduction. Second, the management of the two companies may not go along because of friction. Third, dissenting minority shareholders may cause problems. Finally, it may attract Government antitrust action in terms of the Competition Act.

LO 32.2 FINANCIAL FRAMEWORK

The financial framework of a merger decision covers three inter-related aspects: **(i)** determining the firm's value, **(ii)** financing techniques in merger and **(iii)** analysis of the merger as a capital budgeting decision.

Determining the Firm's Value

One of the first problems in analysing a potential merger involves determining the value of the acquired firm. The value of a firm depends not only upon its earnings but also upon the operating and financial characteristics of the acquiring firm. It is, therefore, not possible to place a single value for the acquired firm. Instead, a range of values is determined, which would be economically justifiable to the prospective acquirer. The final price within this range is negotiated by the two firms. To determine an acceptable price for a firm, a number of factors, quantitative as well as qualitative, are relevant. However, placing a value on qualitative factors, such as managerial talent, strong sales staff, excellent production department and so on, is difficult. Therefore, the focus of determining the firm's value is on several quantitative variables. The quantitative factors relate to **(i)** the value of the assets and **(ii)** the earnings of the firm. Based on the assets' values and earnings, these factors include book value, appraisal value, market value and earnings per share.

Book Value The book value of a firm is based on the balance sheet value of the owner's equity. It is determined dividing net worth by the number of equity shares outstanding. The book value, as the basis of determining a firm's value, suffers from a serious limitation as it is based on the historical costs of the assets of the firm. Historical costs do not bear a relationship either to the value of the firm or to its ability to generate earnings. Nevertheless, it is relevant to the determination of a firm's value for several reasons: **(i)** it can be used as a starting point to be compared and complemented by other analyses, **(ii)** in industries where the ability to generate earnings requires large investments in fixed assets, the book value could be a critical factor where especially plant and equipment are relatively new, **(iii)** a study of the firm's working capital is particularly appropriate and necessary in mergers involving businesses consisting primarily of liquid assets, for example, financial institutions.

> **Book value** is the value of owner's equity determined dividing net worth by the equity shares outstanding.

Appraisal Value Appraisal value is another measure of determining a firm's value. Such a value is acquired from an **independent appraisal agency**. This value is normally based on the replacement cost of assets. The appraisal value has several merits. In the first place, it is an important factor in special situations such as in financial companies, natural resource enterprises or organisations that have been operating at a loss. For instance, the assets of a financial company largely consist of securities. The value of the individual securities has a direct bearing on the firm's earning capacity. Similarly, a company operating at a loss may only be worth its liquidation value, which would approximate the appraisal value. Secondly, appraisal by independent appraisers may permit reduction in accounting goodwill by increasing the recognised worth of specific assets. Goodwill results when the purchase price of a firm exceeds the value of the individual assets. Third, appraisal by an independent agency provides a test of the reasonableness of result obtained through methods based upon the going-concern concept. Further, the appraiser may identify strengths and weaknesses that otherwise might not be recognised, such as in the valuation of patents and partially completed research and development expenditure. On the other hand, this method of analysis is not adequate by itself since the value of individual assets may have little relation to the firm's overall ability to generate earnings and, thus, the going-concern value of the firm. In brief, the appraisal value procedure is useful if carried out in conjunction with other evaluation processes. In specific cases, it is an important instrument for valuing a firm.

> **Appraisal value** is the value acquired from an independent appraisal agency.

Market Value The market value, as reflected in the stock market quotations, comprises yet another approach for estimating the value of a business. The justification of market value as an approximation of true worth of a firm is derived from the fact that market quotations by and large indicate the consensus of investors as to the firm's earning potentials and the corresponding risk. The market value approach is one of the most widely used in determining value, specially of large listed firms. The market value of a firm is determined by investment as well as speculative factors. This value can change abruptly as a result of change not only in analytical factors but also due to purely speculative influences and is subject to market sentiments and personal decisions. Nevertheless, the market value provides a close approximation of the true value of a firm. In actual practice, a certain percentage premium above the market price is often offered as an inducement for the current owners to sell their shares.

Earnings Per Share According to this approach, the value of a prospective acquisition is considered to be a function of the impact of the merger on the earnings per share (EPS). In other words, the analysis could focus on whether the acquisition will have a positive impact on the EPS after the merger or if it will have the effect of diluting the EPS. The future EPS will affect the firm's share prices, which is a function of price-earnings (P/E) ratio and EPS. The effect of acquisition on the EPS is illustrated in Example 32.3.

***Example* 32.3**

Company A is contemplating the purchase of Company B. Company A has 2,00,000 shares outstanding with ₹25 market value per share while Company B has 1,00,000 shares selling at ₹18.75. The EPS are ₹3.125 for Company A and ₹2.5 for Company B. Assuming that the two managements have agreed that the shareholders of Company B are to receive Company A's shares in exchange for their shares (i) in proportion to the relative earnings per share of the two firms or (ii) 0.9 share of Company A for one share of Company B (share exchange ratio of 0.9: 1), illustrate the impact of merger on the EPSc (earnings per share of the combined firm). Also, compute the EPS after merger on the assumption that the anticipated growth rate in earnings is 8 per cent for Company A and 14 per cent for Company B.

Solution

TABLE 32.2 Merger Effect on EPS (Exchange Ratio in Proportion to Relative Earnings Per Share, 0.8 that is ₹2.5/₹3.125)

Company	*Original number of shares*	*EPS*	*Total earnings after taxes Col. 2 × Col. 3*
1	*2*	*3*	*4*
A	2,00,000	₹3.125	₹6,25,000
B	1,00,000	2.50	2,50,000
Total post-merger earnings			8,75,000
Number of shares after the merger: 2,00,000 + 80,000 i.e. (1,00,000 × 0.8)			2,80,000
Earnings per share for Company A:			
1. Equivalent before the merger			3.125
2. After the merger (₹8,75,000/2,80,000)			3.125
Earnings per share for Company B:			
1. Before the merger			2.50
2. Equivalent EPS after the merger: (EPS after the merger × Share exchange ratio) i.e ₹3.125 × 0.8			2.50

TABLE 32.3 Merger Effect on EPS (Exchange ratio, 0.9 : 1)

(1) Total post-merger earnings (EPSc)	₹8,75,000
(2) Number of shares after the merger: (2,00,000 + 90,000 i.e (0.9 × 1,00,000)	2,90,000
(3) Earnings per share: (₹8,75,000 ÷ ₹2,90,000)	3.017
(4) Company A's shareholders	
EPS before the merger	3.125
EPS after the merger	3.017
Dilution in EPS	(0.108)
(5) Company B's shareholders	
EPS before the merger	2.50
Equivalent EPS after the merger (EPS after the merger × share exchange ratio), i.e (₹3.017 × 0.9)	2.715
Accretion in EPS	0.215

TABLE 32.4 Projections of Earnings Per Share

Year	*Post-merger earnings*			*Post-merger EPS*			*Accretion (Dilution) in EPS*	
	Company A (8% growth)	*Company B (14% growth)*	*Total earnings (A + B)*	*Combined EPS Col. 4 ÷ 2,90,000*[a]	*Company A Col.2 ÷ 2,00,000*	*Company B Col.3 ÷ 90,000*[b]	*Company A*	*Company B*
1	*2*	*3*	*4*	*5*	*6*	*7*	*8*	*9*
1	₹6,25,000	₹2,50,000	₹8,75,000	₹3.02	₹3.13	₹2.78	₹(0.11)	₹0.24
2	6,75,000	2,85,000	9,60,000	3.31	3.38	3.17	(0.01)	0.20
3	7,29,000	3,24,900	10,53,900	3.63	3.65	3.61	(0.02)	0.02
4	7,87,320	3,70,386	11,57,706	3.99	3.94	4.11	0.05	(0.12)
5	8,50,306	4,22,240	12,72,546	4.39	4.25	4.69	0.14	(0.30)
6	9,18,330	4,81,354	13,99,684	4.83	4.59	5.34	0.24	(0.51)

a. 2,00,000 shares of Company A + 90,000 of Company B i.e. (1,00,000 × 0.9, exchange ratio).
b. 0.9 × 1,00,000 shares of Company B = 90,000 equivalent shares in Company A.

To summarise the discussion relating to earnings per share approach to determine the value of a firm, when the share exchange ratio is in proportion to the EPS, there is no effect on the EPS of the acquiring/surviving firm as well as on the acquired firm (Table 32.2). When, however, the share exchange ratio is different, it may result in dilution in the EPS of the acquiring firm and accretion in the EPS of the acquired firm (Table 32.3). For management of a firm considering acquiring another firm, a merger that results in dilution in EPS should be avoided. However, the fact that the merger immediately dilutes a firm's current EPS need not necessarily make the transaction undesirable. Such a criterion places undue emphasis upon the immediate effect of the prospective merger on the EPS. In examining the consequences of the merger upon the surviving concern's EPS, the analysis should be extended into future periods and the effect of the expected future growth rate in earnings should also be included in the analysis (Table 32.4) The dilution in the EPS of company A is more than offset by accretion in the EPS, with effect from year 4.

Financing Techniques in Mergers

After the value of firm has been determined on the basis of the preceding analysis, the next step is the choice of the method of payment of the acquired firm. The choice of financial instruments and techniques of acquiring a firm usually have an effect on the purchasing agreement. The payment may take the form of either cash or securities, that is, ordinary shares, convertible securities, deferred payment plans and tender offers.

Ordinary Share Financing When a company is considering the use of common (ordinary) shares to finance a merger, the relative price-earnings (P/E) ratios of two firms are an important consideration. For instance, for a firm having a high P/E ratio, ordinary shares represent an ideal method for financing mergers and acquisitions. Similarly, ordinary shares are more advantageous for both companies when the firm to be acquired has a low P/E ratio. This fact is illustrated in Table 32.5.

TABLE 32.5 Effect of Merger on Firm A's EPS and MPS

(a) **Pre-merger Situation:**		
	Firm A	*Firm B*
Earnings after taxes (EAT) (₹)	5,00,000	2,50,000
Number of shares outstanding (N)	1,00,000	50,000
EPS (EAT/N) (₹)	5	5
Price-earnings (P/E) ratio (times)	10	4
Market price per share, MPS (EPS × P/E ratio) (₹)	50	20
Total market value of the firm (N × MPS) or (EAT × P/E ratio) (₹)	50,00,000	10,00,000
(b) **Post-merger Situation:**		
	Assuming share exchange ratio as	
	1: 2.5*	1:1
EATc of combined firm (₹)	7,50,000	7,50,000
Number of shares outstanding after additional shares issued	1,20,000	1,50,000
EPSc (EATc/N) (₹)	6.25	5
P/Ec ratio (times)	10	10
MPSc (₹)	62.50	50
Total market value (₹)	75,00,000	75,00,000

* Based on current market price per share

From a perusal of Table 32.5 certain facts stand out. The exchange ratio of 1:2.5 is based on the exchange of shares between the acquiring and acquired firm on their relative current market prices. This ratio implies that Firm A will issue 1 share for every 2.5 shares of Firm B. The EPS has increased from ₹5 (pre-merger) to ₹6.25 (post-merger). The post-merger market price of the share would be higher at ₹6.25 × 10 (P/E ratio) = ₹62.50.

When the exchange ratio is 1: 1 it implies that the shareholders of the Firm B demand a heavy premium per share ₹30 in this case i.e., (₹50 worth of share obtained in post-merger situation – ₹20 worth of equity share in pre-merger situation).

As shown in Table 32.6, at such an exchange ratio, the entire merger gain (of ₹15 lakh) accrues to the shareholders of Firm B. Evidently, this is the most favourable exchange ratio for shareholders of Firm B; the management of Firm A, in general, is not likely to agree to a more favourable exchange ratio (as it will cause decrease in shareholders' wealth of Firm A). This is the tolerable exchange ratio from the perspective of Firm A. Likewise, the management of Firm B is not likely to agree to a share exchange ratio that is detrimental to the wealth of its shareholders. Such an exchange ratio is 1: 3.25 (Table 32.7). At this ratio, the total gains accruing from the merger rests with the shareholders of Firm A. This is another set of tolerable exchange ratio from the viewpoint of Firm B. Thus, it may be generalised that *the maximum and the minimum exchange ratio should be between these two sets of tolerable exchange ratio.*

The exchange ratio eventually negotiated/agreed upon would determine the extent of merger gains to be shared between the shareholders of the two firms. This ratio would depend on the relative bargaining position of the two firms and the market reaction of the merger move.

TABLE 32.6 Apportionment of Merger Gains Between the Shareholders of Firms A and B

(1) Total market value of the merged firm		₹75,00,000
Less: Market value of the pre-merged firms:		
Firm A	₹50,00,000	
Firm B	10,00,000	60,00,000
Total merger gains		15,00,000
(2) (a) Apportionment of gains (assuming share exchange ratio of 2.5:1)		
Firm A:		
Post-merger market value (1,00,000 shares × ₹62.50)		62,50,000
Less: Pre-merger market value		50,00,000
Gains for shareholders of Firm A		12,50,000
Firm B:		
Post-merger market value (20,000 shares × ₹62.50)		12,50,000
Less: Pre-merger market value		10,00,000
Gains for shareholders of Firm B		2,50,000
(b) Assuming share exchange ratio of 1:1		
Firm A:		
Post-merger market value (1,00,000 shares × ₹50)		50,00,000
Less: Pre-merger market value		50,00,000
Gains for shareholders of Firm A		NIL
Firm B:		
Post-merger market value (50,000 shares × ₹50)		25,00,000
Less: Pre-merger market value		10,00,000
Gains for shareholders of Firm B		15,00,000

TABLE 32.7 Determination of Tolerable Share Exchange Ratio for shareholders of Firms, Based on Total Gain Accruing to Shareholders of Firm A

(a) Total market value of the merged firm (Combined earnings, ₹7,50,000 × P/E ratio, 10 times)	₹75,00,000
(b) *Less:* Pre-merger or minimum post-merger value acceptable to shareholders of Firm B	10,00,000
(c) Post-merger market value of Firm A (a – b)	65,00,000
(d) Divided by the Number of equity shares outstanding in Firm A	1,00,000
(e) Desired post-merger MPS (₹65 lakh/1 lakh shares)	₹65
(f) Number of equity issues required to be issued in Firm A to have MPS of ₹65 and to have post-merger value of ₹10 lakh of Firm B, that is, (₹10 lakh/₹65)	15,385
(g) Existing number of equity shares outstanding of Firm B	50,000
(h) Share exchange ratio (g)/(h) i.e. 50,000/15,385 For every 3.25 shares of Firm B, 1 share in Firm A will be issued	1 : 3.25

Note: Share exchange ratio of 1:1 (shown in Table 32.6) can also be determined on the basis of procedure shown in Table 32.7.

Debt and Preference Shares Financing From the foregoing discussion it is clear that financing of mergers and acquisitions with equity shares is advantageous both to the acquiring firm and the acquired firm when the P/E ratio is high. However, since some firms may have a relatively lower P/E ratio as also the requirement of some investors might be different, other types of securities, in conjunction with/in lieu of equity shares, may be used for the purpose.

In an attempt to tailor a security to the requirements of investors who seek dividend/ interest income in contrast to capital appreciation/growth, convertible debentures and preference shares might be used to finance mergers. The use of such sources of financing has several advantages.

(i) Potential earning dilution may be partially minimised by issuing a convertible security. For example, assume that the current market price of the shares of an acquiring company is ₹50 and the value of the acquired firm is ₹50,00,000. If the merger proposal is to be financed with equity, 1,00,000 additional shares will be required to be issued. Alternatively, convertible debentures of the face value of ₹100 with conversion ratio of 1.8, which would imply a conversion value of ₹90 (₹50 × 1.8), may be issued. To raise the required ₹50,00,000, 50,000 debentures convertible into 90,000 equity shares would be issued. Thus, the number of shares to be issued would be reduced by 10,000, thereby reducing the dilution in EPS, which could ultimately result, if convertible security was not resorted to in place of equity shares. **(ii)** A convertible issue might serve the income objectives of the shareholders of the target firm without changing the dividend policy of the acquiring firm. **(iii)** Convertible security represents a possible way of lowering the voting power of the target company. **(iv)** Convertible security may appear more attractive to the acquired firm as it combines the protection of fixed security with the growth potential of ordinary shares.

In brief, fixed income securities are compatible with the needs and purposes of mergers and acquisitions. The need for changing the financial leverage and the need for a variety of securities is partly resolved by the use of senior securities.

Deferred Payment Plan Under this method, the acquiring firm, besides making an initial payment, also undertakes to make additional payments in future years to the target firm in the event of the former being able to increase earnings consequent to the merger. Since the future payment is linked to the firm's earnings, this plan is also known as **earn-out plan**. Adopting such a plan ensures several advantages to the acquiring firm: **(i)** It emerges to be an appropriate outlet for adjusting the differences between the amount of shares the acquiring firm is willing to issue and the amount the target firm is agreeable to accept for the business; **(ii)** In view of the fact that fewer number of shares will be issued at the time of acquisition, the acquiring firm will be able to report higher EPS immediately; **(iii)** There is a built-in cushion/protection to the acquiring firm as the total payment is not made at the time of acquisition; it is contingent on the realisation of the projected earnings after merger.

Earn-out plan is a plan for payment to shareholders of target firm in merger that is linked to the earnings of the firm.

Notwithstanding the above benefits, there are certain problems in this mode of payment, the important ones being: **(i)** The target firm must be capable of being operated as an autonomous business entity so that its contribution to the total projects may be determined; **(ii)** There must be freedom of operation to the management of the newly acquired firm; **(iii)** On the part of the management of the acquiring firm, there must be willing cooperation to work towards the success and growth of the target firm, realising that only by this way the two firms can gain from the merger.

There could be various types of deferred payment plans. The arrangement eventually agreed upon would depend on the imagination of the management of the two firms involved. One of the often used plans, for this purpose is the **base-period earnout**. Under this plan, the shareholders of the target firm are to receive additional shares for a specified number of future years, if the firm is able to improve its earnings *vis-à-vis* the earnings of the base period (the earnings in the previous year before the acquisition). The amount becoming due for payment, in shares, in the future years will primarily be a function of excess earnings, price-earnings ratio and the market price of the shares of the acquiring firm. The basis for determining the required number of shares to be issued is as per Equation 32.3.

Base-period earnout is the payment to shareholders of target firm in shares related to increase in firm's earnings in future years over the base period earnings.

$$(\text{Excess earnings} \times P/E \text{ ratio})/\ \text{Share price of Acquiring firm} \quad \textbf{(32.3)}$$

Example **32.4**

Company A has purchased Company B in the current year. Company B had its base year earnings of ₹3,00,000. At the time of merger, its shareholders received an initial payment of 75,000 shares of Company A. The market value of the Company A's shares is ₹30 per share and the P/E ratio is 8. The projected post-merger earnings of Company B for the next three years are ₹3,30,000, ₹3,90,000 and ₹4,14,000. Assuming no changes in share prices and P/E ratio of Company A, determine the number of shares required to be issued to the shareholders of Company B during these three years. As per the agreement with Company B, they will receive shares for 3 years only.

$$\text{Year 1: } \frac{₹30{,}000 \times 8}{₹30} = 8{,}000 \text{ shares}$$

$$\text{Year 2: } \frac{₹90{,}000 \times 8}{₹30} = 24{,}000 \text{ shares}$$

$$\text{Year 3: } \frac{₹1{,}14{,}000 \times 8}{₹30} = 30{,}400 \text{ shares}$$

Thus, the shareholders of Company B will receive a total of 1,37,400 shares (75,000 initially + 62,400 in the subsequent three years). In financial terms, they have received Company A shares worth ₹41.22 lakh (1,37,400 shares × ₹30). This sum is higher than the shareholders would have received initially. Assuming the *P/E* ratio of Company B is 7 times (the assumption is reasonable in that the P/E ratio of Company A is 8 times; the *P/E* multiple of the acquiring firm is normally higher than that of the acquired firm), its valuation/purchase consideration would have been ₹21 lakh only (₹3 lakh × 7 times). Clearly, there is a substantial gain to the shareholders of Company B and this gain is not at the cost of the wealth of the shareholders of Company A. Evidently, the method is fair and equitable.

To conclude, the deferred plan technique provides a useful means by which the acquiring firm can eliminate part of the guesswork involved in purchasing a firm. In essence, it allows the merging management the privilege of hindsight.

> **Tender offer** is a method to acquire control in another firm through bidding.

Tender Offer An alternative approach to acquire another firm is the tender offer. A tender offer, as a method of acquiring a firm, involves a bid by the acquiring firm for controlling interest in the acquired firm. The essence of this approach is that the purchaser approaches the shareholders of the firm rather than the management to encourage them to sell their shares generally at a premium over the current market price. Since the tender offer is a direct appeal to the shareholders, prior approval of the management of the target firm is not required.

As a form of acquiring firms, the tender offer has certain advantages and disadvantages. The disadvantages are: **(i)** If the target firm's management attempts to block it, the cost of executing the offer may increase substantially and **(ii)** the purchasing company may fail to acquire a sufficient number of shares to meet the objective of controlling the firm.

The major advantages of acquisition through tender offer include: **(i)** If the offer is not blocked, say in 'friendly' takeover, it may be less expensive than the normal route of acquiring a company. This is so because it permits control by purchasing a smaller proportion of the firm's shares and **(ii)** The fairness of the purchase price is not questionable as each shareholder individually agrees to part with his shares at the negotiated price.

> **Free cash flows** are after-tax operating earnings from acquisition plus non-cash expenses applicable to the target firm less expected additional investments in long-term assets and working capital.

Merger as a Capital Budgeting Decision

As a normative financial framework, the merger should be evaluated as a capital budgeting decision. The target firm should be valued in terms of its potential to generate incremental future cash inflows. As explained in the previous chapter, such cash flows should be incremental *future free cash flows* likely to accrue due to the acquisition of the target firm. Free cash flows, in the context of a merger, are equal to after-tax operating earnings (expected from acquisition) plus non-cash expenses, such as depreciation and amortisation (applicable to the target firm), less additional investments expected to be made in the long-term assets and working capital of the acquired firm. These cash flows are then to be discounted at an appropriate rate that reflects the riskiness of target firm's business.

Like the capital budgeting decision, the present value of the expected benefits from the merger are to be compared with the cost of the acquisition of the target firm. Acquisition costs include the payment made to the target firm's shareholders and debenture-holders, the payment made to discharge the external liabilities, estimated value of the obligations assumed, liquidation expenses to be met by the acquiring firm and so on less cash proceeds expected to be realised by the acquiring firm from the sale of certain asset(s) of the target firm (not intended to be used in business subsequent to merger). The decision criterion is to 'go for the merger' if the net present value, NPV, is positive; the decision would be 'against the merger' in the event of the NPV being negative. Being a comprehensive measure of evaluation, it is not surprising to note that most of the merger decisions in America are evaluated in the capital budgeting framework[4].

The following are the steps used to evaluate merger decisions as per the capital budgeting approach.

(i) Determination of Incremental Projected Free Cash Flows to The Firm (FCFF) These FCFF should be attributable to the acquisition of the business of the target firm. Format 32.1 contains constituent items of such cash flows.

FORMAT 32.1 Determination of FCFF

After-tax operating earnings
Plus: Non-cash expenses, such as depreciation and amortisation
Less: Investment in long-term assets
Less: Investment in net working capital
Note: All the financial inputs should be on incremental basis.

(ii) Determination of Terminal Value The firm is normally acquired as a going concern. It is worth recapitulating from chapter 32 that the projected FCFF in such situations are made in two segments, namely, during the explicit forecast period and after the forecast period. Terminal value, TV (also referred to as continuing value as explained in chapter 32) is the present value of FCFF, after the forecast period. Its value can be determined as per Equations 33.3 to 33.5.

(a) When FCFF are likely to be *constant till infinity*:

$$TV = FCFF_{T+1}/K_0 \quad \textbf{(32.4)}$$

Where $FCFF_{T+1}$ refers to the expected FCFF in the first year after the explicit forecast period.

(b) When FCFF are likely to *grow (g)* at a constant rate:

$$TV = FCFF_T\ (1 + g)/\ (K_0 - g) \quad \textbf{(32.5)}$$

(c) When FCFF are likely to *decline* at a constant rate:

$$TV = FCFF_T\ (1 - g)/\ (K_0 + g) \quad \textbf{(32.6)}$$

(iii) Determination of Appropriate Discount Rate/Cost of Capital In the event of the risk complexion of the target firm matching with the acquired firm (say in the case of horizontal merger and firms having virtually identical debt-equity ratio), the acquiring firm can use its own weighted average cost of capital (k_0) as discount rate. In case the risk complexion of the acquired firm is different, the appropriate discount rate is to be computed reflecting the riskiness of the projected FCFF of the target firm.

(iv) Determination of Present Value of FCFF The present value of FCFF during the explicit forecast period [as per step **(i)**] and of terminal value [as per step **(ii)**] is determined by using appropriate discount rate [as per step **(iii)**].

(v) Determination of Cost of Acquisition The cost of acquisition is determined as per Format 33.2.

FORMAT 32.2 Cost of Acquisition

Payment to equity shareholders (Number of equity shares issued in acquiring company ¥ Market price of equity share)
Plus: Payment to preference shareholders
Plus: Payment to debenture-holders
Plus: Payment of other external liabilities (say creditors)
Plus: Obligations assumed to be paid in future
Plus: Dissolution expenses (to be paid by acquiring firm)
Plus: Unrecorded/contingent liability
Less: Cash proceeds from sale of assets of target firm (not to be used in business after acquisition)

Example 32.5 illustrates the application of capital budgeting approach to merger decision.

***Example* 32.5**

The Hypothetical Limited wants to acquire Target Ltd. The balance sheet of Target Ltd. as on March 31 (current year) has the following assets and liabilities:

(₹ lakh)

Liabilities	*Amount*	*Assets*	*Amount*
Equity share capital			
(4 lakh shares of ₹100 each)	₹400	Cash	₹10
Retained earnings	100	Debtors	65
10.50% Debentures	200	Inventories	135
Creditors and other liabilities	160	Plant and Equipment	650
	860		860

Additional information:

(i) The shareholders of Target Ltd. will get 1.5 share in Hypothetical Ltd. for every 2 shares; the shares of the Hypothetical Ltd. would be issued at its current market price of ₹180 per share. The debenture-holders will get 11% debentures of the same amount. The external liabilities are expected to be settled at ₹150 lakh. Dissolution expenses of ₹15 lakh are to be met by the acquiring company.

(ii) The following are projected incremental free cash flows (FCFF) expected from acquisition for 6 years (₹lakh):

Year-end 1	₹150
2	200
3	260
4	300
5	220
6	120

(iii) The free cash-flow of Target limited is expected to grow at 3 per cent per annum, after 6 years.
(iv) Given the risk complexion of Target limited, cost of capital relevant for Target limited cash flows has been decided at 13 per cent.
(v) There is unrecorded liability of ₹20 lakh.

Advise the company regarding financial feasibility of the acquisition.

Solution

TABLE 32.8 Financial Evaluation of Merger Decision

(i) Cost of Acquisition ($t = 0$) *(₹ lakh)*

Share capital (3,00,000 shares × ₹180)	₹540
11% Debentures	200
Settlement of external liabilities	150
Unrecorded liability	20
Dissolution expenses of Target firm	15
	925

(ii) PV of Free Cash Inflows (years = 1 – 6) *(₹ lakh)*

Year-end	*FCFF*	*PV factor (0.13)*	*Total PV*
1	₹150	0.885	₹132.75
2	200	0.783	156.60
3	260	0.693	180.18
4	300	0.613	183.90
5	220	0.543	119.46
6	120	0.480	57.60
			830.49

(iii) PV of FCFF After the Forecast Period (Referred to as Terminal Value, TV)

TV6 = $FCFF_6\ (1 + g)/(k_0 - g)$
= ₹120 lakh (1.03)/(0.13 – 0.03) = ₹123.6/0.1 = ₹1,236 lakh
PV of TV = ₹1,236 lakh × 0.480 = ₹593.28 lakh

(iv) Determination of Net Present Value

PV of Free cash flows (years 1 – 6)	₹830.49 lakh
PV of Free cash flows subsequent to year 6	593.28
Total PV of benefits/FCFF	1,423.77
Less: Cost of acquisition	925.00
Net present value	498.77

Recommendation As the NPV is positive, acquisition of Target limited is financially viable.

***Example* 32.6**

Would your decision for acquiring Target limited (in **Example 32.5**) change, if FCFF after the forecast period are assumed to be (a) constant and (b) decline by 10 per cent per annum after 6 years.

Solution

TABLE 32.9 Determination of NPV, When FCFF are Constant after year-6

	(₹ lakh)
PV of FCFF (years 1 – 6)	₹830.49
PV of FCFF (subsequent to year 6)	443.08*
Total PV of benefits	1,273.57
Less: Cost of acquisition	925.00
Net present value	348.57

* Determination of PV related to TV:

TV = $FCFF_6/k_0$ = ₹120 lakh/0.13 = ₹923.08 lakh

PV = ₹923.08 lakh × 0.480 = 443.08 lakh

TABLE 32.10 Determination of NPV when FCFF are Expected to Decline at 10 per cent after year 6

	(₹ lakh)
PV of FCFF (years 1 – 6)	₹830.49
PV of FCFF (subsequent to year 6)	225.39*
Total PV of benefits	1,055.88
Less: Cost of acquisition	925.00
Net present value	130.88

* Determination of PV related to TV:

TV = FCFF6(1 – g)/(k_0 + g) = ₹108 lakh/(0.13 + 0.10) = ₹469.57 lakh

PV = ₹469.57 lakh × 0.480 = ₹225.39

Recommendation Since the NPV is positive in both the situations, the merger proposal continues to be financially viable.

The finance manager can use *sensitivity analysis* to have a range of NPV values within which acquisition price may vary. Sensitivity analysis can be carried out by making changes in the target firm's key financial parameters such as growth rate in FCFF (during the explicit forecast period as well as in subsequent years), sales, profit margins, investment in plant and machinery, investment in working capital and the period of growth itself[5].

Adjusted Present Value (APV) Approach The APV approach is a variant of the DCF approach used to value the target firm. This approach is very appropriate for valuing companies with changing capital structures (such as leveraged buyout targets[6]) and for valuing target companies which are having capital structures substantially different from those of acquiring companies. The approach values FCFF of target firm in two components: **(i)** the value of the target company if it were entirely equity financed and **(ii)** value the impact of debt financing both in terms of the tax benefit and bankruptcy costs.

Adjusted present value a variant of DCF, is value of the target company if it were entirely financed by equity plus the value of the impact of debt financing in terms of the tax benefits as well as bankruptcy cost.

The APV based valuation has its genesis in the Modigliani-Miller (MM) propositions on capital structure, according to which in a world of no taxes, the valuation of the firm (the sum of equity and debt) is independent of capital structure (change in debt/equity proportion). In other words, the capital structure can affect the valuation only through taxes and other market imperfections and distortions[7].

The APV approach uses these concepts of MM to show the impact of debt financing in terms of tax shield on valuation. The approach, as stated earlier, first values the company as if it were wholly equity financed by discounting future FCFF at a discount rate referred to as *unlevered cost of equity*. Since interest is a deductible item of expense to determine taxable income, it provides tax savings (assuming the firm has taxable income). The value of these tax savings are then added. Finally, to have the full impact of debt financing reflected in the valuation of the Target, adjustment is required to be made for incremental bankruptcy costs; the adjustment value may be determined subjectively or may be based on some suitable financial surrogate. Consider Example 32.7.

***Example* 32.7**

For the facts in **Example 32.5**, compute the value of Target Limited based on the APV approach, given the cost of unlevered equity as 16 per cent, perpetual debentures and a corporate tax rate of 35 per cent. Ignore bankruptcy costs. Also estimate the NPV.

Solution

TABLE 32.11 (i) PV of FCFF, Discounted at Unlevered Cost of Equity (k_u) *(₹ lakh)*

Year-end	*FCFF*	*PV factor (0.16)*	*Total PV*
1	₹150	0.862	₹129.30
2	200	0.743	148.60
3	260	0.641	166.66
4	300	0.552	165.60
5	220	0.476	104.72
6	120	0.410	49.20
			764.08

(ii) PV of FCFF After the Forecast Period/Terminal Value *(₹ lakh)*

TV6 = FCFF6 $(1 + g)/(k_u - g)$

= ₹120 lakh (1.03)/(0.16 – 0.03) = ₹950.77 lakh

PV of TV = ₹950.77 lakh × 0.410 = ₹389.82 lakh

(iii) PV of Tax Savings Due to Interest *(₹ lakh)*

Amount of Debt (11% Debentures)	₹200
Amount of interest (₹200 lakh × 0.11)	22
Tax savings (₹22 lakh per year × 0.35 tax rate)	7.7
Present value of tax shield (₹7.7 lakh/0.11)	70.0

TABLE 32.12 (iv) Adjusted Present Value and NPV of Target Limited *(₹ lakh)*

(i) PV of FCFF (years 1 – 6)	₹764.08
(ii) PV of terminal value	389.82
(iii) PV of tax shield	70.00
Total adjusted present value	1223.90
Less: Cost of acquisition	925.00
Net present value	298.90

The acquisition of Target limited is financially profitable according to the APV approach. However, the approach brings to fore the fact that the tax advantage of debt may not be sizable, particularly when viewed along with bankruptcy costs.

In valuing the present value of a tax shield, the cost of debt is used as a discount rate. One argument for using the cost of debt as discount rate is that the tax benefits are likely to be realised and are, therefore, subject to low risk. Another argument is that uncertainty about company's ability to realise the tax shield is best measured by the rate at which the lenders are willing to lend to the company, that is, cost of debt[8].

However, there is a counter argument for using higher discount rates (say, weighted average cost of capital or unlevered cost of equity) to value the tax shield. Tax shields are not certain in nature; future tax shields are tied to the business operations in future, that is, future profits. In other words, there will be a high correlation between the profits and cash flows and the interest tax shield. Hence, the risk will be similar. With similar risk, the interest tax shields should also be discounted at the same rate as the operations of the target firm, that is, the unlevered cost of equity[9].

To sum up it may be said that the discount rate to value the tax shield will depend on the circumstances of each case. When the firm has a low target debt ratio and business prospects are very promising, there is a greater probability of realising tax shields in the future. Therefore, in such a situation, the cost of debt can be used as the discount rate. On the contrary, if the target debt ratio of the firm as well as its business risk is high, there is obviously a greater uncertainty in realising potential tax shields and, hence, they should be subject to a higher discount rate. Finally, the finance manager may also consider (say, in undecisive situations) a discount rate lying somewhere between the cost of debt and the weighted average cost of capital or unlevered cost of equity.

LO 32.3 TAX ASPECTS OF AMALGAMATION, MERGER AND DEMERGERS

The important and relevant tax provisions applicable to amalgamations, acquisitions, mergers and demergers are summarised below.

Tax Aspects Related to Amalgamation/Mergers

Amalgamation for the purposes of income tax is recognised only if the conditions given under Section 2 (1B) of the Income Tax Act, 1961 (ITA) are fulfilled. According to Section 2 (1B) 'amalgamation', in relation to companies, means the merger of one or more companies with another company or the merger of two or more companies to form one company (the company or companies that so merge are referred to as the amalgamating company or companies and the company with which they merge or which is formed as a result of the merger is the amalgamated company) in such a manner that:

(i) all the property/liabilities of the amalgamating company(ies) immediately before the amalgamation, becomes the property/liabilities of the amalgamated company by virtue of the amalgamation;

(ii) Shareholders holding not less than three-fourths (in value) of the shares in the amalgamating company(ies) (other than shares already held therein immediately before the amalgamation by the amalgamated company, its subsidiary or by a nominee of the said company) become shareholders of the amalgamated company by virtue of the amalgamation.

Tax Concessions to Amalgamated Company The following are the major tax benefits available to the amalgamated company.

1. Carry Forward and Set off of Business Losses and Unabsorbed Depreciation According to Section 72 A, the amalgamated company is entitled to carry forward accumulated losses as well as unabsorbed depreciation of the amalgamating company, provided the following conditions are fulfilled:

(i) The amalgamated company continuously holds, for a minimum period of 5 years, from the date of amalgamation at least three-fourths of the above value of fixed assets of the amalgamating company, acquired in the scheme of amalgamation.

(ii) The amalgamated company continues the business of the amalgamating company for a minimum period of 5 years from the date of amalgamation.

(iii) The amalgamated company fulfils such other conditions as may be prescribed to ensure the revival of the business of the amalgamating company or to ensure that the amalgamation is for genuine business purposes.

(iv) The amalgamation should be of a company owning an industrial undertaking or ship. Industrial undertaking, in this context, means an undertaking that is engaged in

- the manufacture or processing of goods; or
- the manufacture of computer software; or
- the business of generation or distribution of electricity or any other form of power; or
- the business of providing telecommunication services, whether basic or cellular, including radio paging, domestic satellite service, network of trunking, broadband network and internet services; or
- mining or
- the construction of ships, aircrafts or rail systems.

In case where any of the above conditions (i – iv) are not complied with, the set off of loss or allowance of depreciation made in any previous year in the books of the amalgamated company would be deemed to be the income of the amalgamated company and chargeable to tax for the year in which such conditions are not complied with.

2. Expenditure on Scientific Research Where an amalgamating company transfers any asset represented by capital expenditure on scientific research to the amalgamated Indian company, unabsorbed capital expenditure in the books of the amalgamating company would be eligible to be carried forward and set off in the hands of the amalgamated company.

3. Expenditure on Acquisition of Patent Rights or Copy Rights The expenditure on patents and copyrights not yet written off in the books of amalgamating company would be allowed to be written off by the amalgamated company in the same number of balance instalments.

Where such rights are later on sold by the amalgamated company, the profit/loss on such sales would be treated in the hands of the amalgamated company, in the same manner as it would have been allowed to be treated by the amalgamating company.

In case such expenditure has been incurred by the amalgamating company after March 31, 1998, such an expenditure would be eligible for depreciation, as intangible asset and provisions of depreciation would apply.

4. Expenditure on Know-how Regarding the expenditure incurred on know-how, the amalgamated company would be entitled to claim deduction with respect to the transferred undertaking, to the same extent and for the same residual period as otherwise would have been allowed to the amalgamating company, had such an amalgamation not taken place. Like patent rights, in case such an expenditure is incurred by the amalgamating company after March 31, 1998, such an expenditure will be eligible for depreciation as intangible asset and provisions of depreciation would apply.

5. Expenditure for Obtaining Licence to Operate Telecommunication Services When the amalgamating company transfers licence to the Indian amalgamated company, the expenditure on acquisition of licence, not yet written off, is allowed to the amalgamated company in the same number of balance instalments. When such licence is sold by the amalgamated company, the treatment of surplus/deficiency would be the same as would have been in the case of the amalgamating company.

6. Preliminary Expenses Deduction of preliminary expenses (to the extent not amortised) would be made in the books of the amalgamated company in the same manner as would have been allowed to the amalgamating company.

7. Expenditure on Prospecting of Certain Minerals Where an amalgamating company merges with the amalgamated company, the amount of expenditure on prospecting, etc, of certain minerals of the amalgamating company that are not yet written off, would be allowed as deduction to the amalgamated company in the same manner as would have been allowed to the amalgamating company.

8. Capital Expenditure on Family Planning The capital expenditure on family planning not yet written off would be allowed to the amalgamated company in the same number of balance instalments.

9. Bad Debts When the debts of amalgamating company have been taken over by the amalgamated company and subsequently such debt or part of debt becomes bad, they would be allowed as a deduction to the amalgamated company in the same manner as would have been allowed to the amalgamating company.

In brief, the Income tax Act for all types of business reorganisations/amalgamations/mergers has become **fully tax neutral**. Virtually all fiscal concessions/incentives/deductions (in respect of fixed assets, capital expenditures, intangible assets, deferred revenue expenditure and so on) that would otherwise have been available to the amalgamating company are made available to the amalgamated company as well. In other words, the unwritten off amount, with respect to all these items, is treated in the hands of the amalgamated company in the same manner as would have been treated by the amalgamating company. Thus, the amalgamated company is not put to any disadvantage as far as the income tax concessions and incentives are concerned. The present generous/favourable fiscal provisions are indicative/reflective of Government policy to facilitate, promote and create opportunities for more amalgamations and mergers.

Tax Concessions to Amalgamating Company The tax concessions to the amalgamating are summarised below.

(i) Free of Capital Gains Tax According to Section 47 (vi), where there is a transfer of any capital asset by an amalgamating company to any Indian amalgamated company, such transfer will not be considered as a transfer for the purpose of capital gain.

(ii) Free of Gift-Tax According to Section 45 (b) of the Gift Tax Act, where there is a transfer of any asset by an Indian amalgamating company, gift tax will not be attracted.

Tax Concessions to the Shareholders of an Amalgamating Company According to Section 47 (vii), where a shareholder of an Indian amalgamating company transfers his shares, such transaction will be disregarded for capital gain purposes, provided the transfer of shares is made in consideration of the allotment of any share to him or shares in the amalgamated company.

Further, for computing the period of holding of such shares, the period for which such shares were held in the amalgamating company would also be included so that the shareholders of the amalgamating company are not put to disadvantage.

Demerger is the transfer by a company one or more of its undertakings to another company.

Tax Aspects Related to Demergers

Meaning of Demerger Pursuant to a scheme of arrangement under Sections 391 to 394 of the Companies Act, a demerger means the transfer, by the demerged company, of one or more of its undertakings to any resulting company in such a manner that:

(i) all the property/liabilities of the undertaking, being transferred by the demerged company, immediately before the merger becomes the property/liabilities of the resulting company by virtue of the demerger;
(ii) the property and the liabilities of the undertaking(s) being transferred by the demerged company immediately before the demerger are transferred at values appearing in its books of account;
(iii) the resulting company issues, in consideration of the demerger, its shares on a proportionate basis to the shareholders of the demerged company;
(iv) shareholders holding not less than three-fourths in value of the shares in the demerged company (other than shares already held therein immediately before the demerger, or by a nominee for the resulting company or, its subsidiary) become shareholders of the resulting company or companies by virtue of the demerger;
(v) the transfer of the undertaking is on a going concern basis;
(vi) the demerger is in accordance with the conditions, if any, notified in this behalf under Section 72 A (5) by the Central Government.

The undertaking, in the present context, means any part of an undertaking or a unit or division of an undertaking or a business activity taken as a whole, but does not include individual assets or liabilities or any combination thereof not constituting a business activity.

Meaning of Demerged Company Demerged company means the company whose undertaking is transferred, pursuant to a demerger, to a resulting company.

Meaning of Resulting Company Resulting company means one or more companies (including a wholly owned subsidiary thereof) to which the undertaking of the demerged company is transferred in a demerger and the resulting company, in consideration of such transfer of undertaking, issues shares to the shareholders of the demerged company and may include any authority or body/local authority/public sector company/company established, constituted or formed as a result of demerger.

Tax Concessions to Resulting Company The resulting company is entitled virtually to all the tax concessions as are available to the amalgamated company. These are listed as follows.

(i) Carry Forward and Set off of Business Losses and Unabsorbed Depreciation of the Demerged Company The accumulated loss and unabsorbed depreciation 'in a demerger' should be allowed to be carried forward by the resulting company, if these are directly related to the undertaking proposed to be transferred. Where it is not plausible to relate these to the undertaking, such loss and depreciation would be apportioned between the demerged company and the resulting company in proportion of the assets coming to the share of each as a result of the demerger.

(ii) Expenditure on Acquisition of Patent Rights or Copyrights Where the patent or copyrights acquired by the demerged company is transferred to the resulting Indian company, the expenditure on patents or copyrights not written off would be allowed to be written off in the hands of the resulting company in the same number of balance instalments. On their subsequent sales, the treatment of deficiency/surplus in the resulting company would be the same as would have been in the case of the demerged company.

(iii) Expenditure on Know How

(iv) Expenditure for Obtaining Licence to Operate Telecommunication Services

(v) Expenditure on Prospecting, etc of Certain Minerals Where there is a transfer of items listed (iii to v) above by the demerged company to the resulting Indian company, the amount of expenditure not yet written off would be allowed to the resulting company in the same number of balance instalments. In the case of sales of any of these items, the treatment of the deficiency/surplus in the books of the resulting company would be the same as would have been in the case of a demerged company.

(vi) Preliminary Expenses Where the undertaking of an Indian company is transferred before the expiry of 10/5 years, to another company, the preliminary expenses of such an undertaking that are not yet written off would be allowed as deduction in the same manner as would have been allowed to the demerged company.

(vii) Bad Debts Where due to demerger, the debts of the demerged company have been taken over by the resulting company and subsequently such debt or part of debt becomes bad, such bad debts would be allowed as a deduction to the resulting company.

(viii) Expenditure Related to Demerger In the case of expenditures that are incurred after the April 1, 1999, wholly and exclusively for the purpose of the demerger of an undertaking, the resulting Indian company incurring such an expenditure would be allowed a deduction of an amount equal to one-fifth of such expenditure for five successive previous years beginning with the previous year in which the demerger takes place.

Tax Concessions for the Demerged Company The concessions for the demerged company are as follows.

(i) Free of Capital Gains Tax Where there is a transfer of any capital asset in a demerger, such transfer would not be regarded as a transfer for the purpose of capital gain.

(ii) Reserves for Shipping Business Where a ship acquired out of the reserve is transferred even within the period of eight years of acquisition, there would be no deemed profits to the demerged company.

Tax Concessions to the Shareholders

Any transfer or issue of shares by the resulting company to the shareholders of the demerged company would not be regarded as transfer if the transfer or issue is made in consideration of the demerger of the undertaking. In the case of demerger, the existing shareholders of the demerged company would hold shares in the resulting company as well as shares in the demerged company.

Further, for computing the period of holding of such shares in the resulting company, the period for which such shares were held in the demerged company would also be included.

LO 32.4 LEGAL AND PROCEDURAL ASPECTS OF MERGERS/ AMALGAMATIONS AND ACQUISITON/TAKEOVERS

Following the economic reforms in India in the post-1991 period, there is a discernible trend among promoters and established corporate groups towards consolidation of market share and diversification into new areas through acquisition/takeover of companies, and in a more pronounced manner through mergers/amalgamations. Although the financial evaluation and the economic considerations, in terms of motive and effect, of the above mentioned are similar, the legal procedures involved are different. The pre-entry scrutiny of mergers/combinations in India is presently carried out by the Competition Commission of India under the Competition Act 2002. The merger and amalgamation of corporates constitutes the subject matter of the Companies Act. The acquisition/takeover bids fall under the purview of the SEBI. We first cover the framework of pre-entry scrutiny and mergers/ amalgamations. The regulatory framework governing acquisition/takeovers is described subsequently.

Combination and Competition Act

Prior to 1991, pre-entry scrutiny of mergers/combinations in India was conducted by the Monopolies and Restrictive Practices (MRTP) Commission under the MRTP Act, 1969. Since 2003, the Competition Commission of India (CCI) is empowered under the Competition Act 2002 to scrutinise and clear combinations that may give rise to monopoly situations. The CCI is mandated, upon its own knowledge or information, to enquire within one year of its happening whether an acquisition/ acquisition of control/amalgamation or merger has caused/is likely to cause an appreciable adverse effect on competition in India. The main feature of the regulation of combination by the CCI are discussed below.

Regulation of Combination Any combination entered into by any **person** (i.e. individual/Hindu Undivided Family/company/firm/association of person(s) incorporated in India or abroad/corporation or Government company/body corporate/cooperative society/local authority/every other artificial judicial person) or **enterprise** which causes or is likely to cause an **appreciable adverse effect** on competition within the **relevant market** in India would be void. Whether a combination would have the effect of/is likely to have appreciable adverse effect on competition in the relevant market, the CCI would have due regard to all/any of the factors listed below:

- Actual/potential level of competition through imports in the market;
- Extent of barriers to entry to the market;
- Degree of countervailing power in the market;
- Likelihood of the combination resulting in the concerned parties being able to significantly and sustainably increase price/profit margin;
- Extent of effective competition likely to sustain the market;
- Extent to which substitutes are/likely to be available in the market;
- Market share in the relevant market of the concerned person/enterprise individually/jointly;
- Likelihood of the combination resulting in the removal of a vigorous/effective competitor(s) in the market;
- Nature/extent of vertical integration in the market;
- Possibility of a failing business;
- Nature/extent of innovation;
- Relative advantage by way of contribution to economic development by any combination having/likely to have appreciable adverse effect on competition;
- The benefits of combination outweigh the adverse impact of combination.

The term **enterprise** means a person/department of Government who/which is/has been engaged in any activity relating to production/storage/supply/distribute/acquisition/ control of articles/goods or the provision of any kind of services or **investment or in the business of acquiring/holding/ underwriting/dealing with shares/debentures/other securities of any other body corporate directly/indirectly through one of its units/divisions/subsidiaries**.

Relevant market means the market determined by the CCI with reference to the relevant **(i)** product, **(ii)** geographic market or both. While the geographic market refers to the area in which the conditions of competition are homogeneous distinct from the neighbouring area, product market comprises all interchangeable/ substitute products/services.

> **Relevant market** means the market determined by the CCI with reference to the relevant (i) product, (ii) geographic market or both.

Any person/enterprise proposing to enter into combination should give notice to the CCI containing the details of the proposal within 30 days of **(a)** approval of the mergers/amalgamation by the Board of Directors, (i.e. the individual himself/herself including sole proprietor, Karta in a HUF, Board of Directors of a company, body/person empowered in Government company/corporation, association of persons, body of individuals whether incorporated or not, body corporate incorporated in India/abroad, cooperative society, local authority, partners of a firm and person(s) competent to act in case of any other judicial person), **(b)** execution of any agreement/other documents for acquisition/acquiring control. The combination would be effective after 210 days from the date of the notice.

Combination The acquisition of an enterprise(s) by a person(s) or merger or amalgamation of enterprises would constitute their combination subject to the conditions **discussed later.** **Acquisition** means directly/indirectly acquiring/agreeing to acquire **(i)** share/voting rights/assets or **(ii)** control over management/assets of an enterprise. Included in **control** is controlling the affairs/management by an enterprise(s)/group(s) either jointly or singly over another enterprise/group. **Group** means two/more enterprises which directly/indirectly are in a position to **(i)** exercise at least 26 per cent of the voting rights or **(ii)** appoint more than 51 per cent of the Board of Directors or **(iii)** control the management/ affairs of the other enterprise. The value of assets would be determined on the basis of their audited book value less depreciation in the financial year immediately preceding the financial year in which the date of merger falls. Such value will include the brand value, value of goodwill/copyrights/patents/permitted use/collective work/ registered proprietor/trade mark/user/homogenous geographical indication/ geographical indication/design/layout design/similar other commercial rights and so on.

> **Combination** is the acquisition of an enterprise(s) by a person(s) or merger or amalgamation of enterprises.

> **Acquisition** means directly/ indirectly acquiring/ agreeing to acquire **(i)** share/voting rights/assets or **(ii)** control over management/assets of an enterprise.

The conditions for pre-combination scrutiny by the CCI pertain to the value of assets and turnover, that is, value of goods and services. **Goods** include **(i)** product manufactured/proceed/mined, **(ii)** debentures/stocks/shares after allotment and **(iii)** goods incorporated into India. **Service** means service of any description made available to potential users, including services in connection with business of any industrial/commercial matters such as banking/communication/education/financing/ insurance/chit funds/real estate/transport/ storage/material treatment/processing/supply of electrical or other energy/boarding, lodging, entertainment, amusement/ construction/ repair/conveying of news or information and advertising.

> **Group** means two/more enterprises which directly/indirectly are in a position to **(i)** exercise at least 26 per cent of the voting rights or **(ii)** appoint more than 51 per cent of the Board of Directors or **(iii)** control the management/ affairs of the other enterprise.

> **Control** is controlling the affairs/management by an enterprise(s)/ group(s) either jointly or singly over another enterprise/group.

Conditions To constitute combination, the following conditions must be satisfied in regard to **(i)** acquisition, **(ii)** acquiring control and **(iii)** merger/amalgamation:

The acquirer and the concerned enterprise jointly have in **(a)** India assets and turnover exceeding ₹1,000 crore and ₹3,000 crore, respectively, **(b)** India/outside India, the respective amounts are more than 500 million US dollars (including at least ₹500 crore in India), and 1,500 million US dollars (including at least ₹1,500 crore in India). The stipulations for the group to which the concerned enterprise belongs are that their joint holdings in India are/would be ₹4,000 crores (assets) and ₹12,000 crores (turnover). Such holdings in India/outside India should aggregate more than two billion US dollars (of which at least ₹500 crore in India) in terms of assets and six billion US dollars (including at least ₹1,500 crore in India) in terms of turnover.

Procedure for Investigation Where the CCI is of the *prima facie* opinion that a combination is likely to cause/has caused an appreciable adverse effect on competition within the relevant market in India or any person/enterprise has given a notice to the CCI proposing to enter into a combination, it would issue a show cause notice to the parties to the combination to respond within 30 days as to why an investigation should not be conducted. After receipt of their response, the CCI may call for a report from its Directors General within specified time. Within 7 days from the receipt of the response of the parties concerned or the report from the Director General whichever is later, the CCI would direct the parties to publish details of the combination within 10 days in a manner appropriate for bringing to the knowledge/information of the public/persons affected/likely to be affected by the combination. The CCI may invite any person/member of the public affected/likely to be affected to file written objections within 15 days of the publication of the details of the combination. Within 15 days of the expiry of the period for filing objection, additional/other information deemed fit by the CCI may be sought from the parties concerned to be furnished within the next 15 days. After receipt of all information, the CCI would proceed within 45 days to deal with the case in the manner specified below.

Orders of CCI On the basis of its assessment of the appreciable adverse effect of combination on competition, the CCI would **(i)** approve, **(ii)** disapprove, **(iii)** propose appropriate/suitable modification to eliminate the adverse effect within the specified period. In case of failure of parties who accept the suggested modification to carry it out, the combination would be deemed to have an appreciable adverse effect on competition and the CCI would deal with it according to the provisions of the Competition Act.

The parties concerned can within 30 days of the proposed modification submit an amendment to the modification and the CCI, if satisfied, would approve the combination. If, however, the CCI does not accept the amendment, the parties would have to accept the CCI-proposed modifications failing which the combination would be deemed to have an appreciable adverse effect on competition and deal with in accordance with the provisions of the Competition Act. The proposed acquisition/acquiring of control/merger or amalgamation by the parties concerned, without prejudice to the imposition of any penalty or initiation of any prosecution under the Competition Act, would not be given effect to after the CCI's direction/the combination being deemed to have an appreciable adverse effect or competition. The CCI can also frame a scheme to implement its order.

If, however, the CCI does not pass an order/issue direction on the expiry of the 210-day period from the date of the original notice by the parties, the combination would be deemed to have been approved by it. The limits of 210 days would not include the 60 days given to the parties to file an amendment to the modification proposed by the Commission (30 days) and accept the modification after rejection of their amendment (30 days). Similarly, any extension of time sought/granted by the parties/CCI would be deducted for reckoning the 210 day-period. Where a combination is ordered by the CCI to be void, the acquisition/acquiring of control/merger or amalgamation would be dealt with under any other law as if the combination had not taken place and the parties concerned dealt with accordingly.

Penalties The CCI may cause an inquiry into compliance of its orders/directions. Failure, without reasonable cause, to comply with its orders/directions would be punishable with a fine upto rupees one lakh for each day of non-compliance subject to a maximum of ₹10 crore. If any person fails to pay any monetary penalty imposed on him, the CCI would proceed to recover it in the specified manner, including under the Income Tax Act as assessee in default. Non-compliance with CCI's orders/directions or failure to pay the fine would be punishable with imprisonment up to 3 years or with fine up to ₹25 crore or with both. Any person can approach the Appellate Tribunal for recovery of compensation from any enterprise for any loss/damage suffered by him as a result of violation of CCI's directions or contravention without reasonable ground, of any decision/order of the CCI or any condition/restrictions subject to which any approval/sanction/direction/exemption in relation to any matter has been accorded/given/made/granted under the Competition Act or delay in carrying out such orders/directions of the CCI. Penalty for **(i)** failure to comply with directions of the CCI/Director General, fine up to Rupees one lakh for each day of failure subject to a maximum of ₹1 crore; **(ii)** non-furnishing of information on combination, up to 1 per cent of the highest of the total turnover or assets; **(iii)** making of false statements/omission to furnish material information, not less than ₹50 lakh and upto ₹1 crore, **(iv)** offences relating to furnishing of information, fine up to ₹1 crore and any other order deemed fit by the CCI. Included in these offences are **(1)** making of a statement/furnishing of a document knowing or having reasons to believe to be false in any material particular, **(2)** omission to state any material fact knowing it to be material, and **(3)** willfully altering/suppressing/destroying any document required to be furnished.

In case of contravention of provision(s) of the Competition Act/rules/regulations/order/direction by a company, the company as well as every person incharge of, and responsible for the conduct of its business would be deemed to be guilty of the contravention. In case of contravention with the consent/connivance of, or attributable to any neglect on the part of any director/manager/secretary/other officer, they would also be deemed to be guilty.

CCI Procedure in Regard to the Transactions of Business Relating to Combination of Regulations, 2011 According to the CCI's regulations 2011 in regard to the transaction of business relating to combination, an enterprise which proposes to enter into a combination should give/file a notice to the CCI in the specified format (ordinary Form I) together with the evidence of payment of fee of ₹50,000 by the concerned parties, including instances where:

- Parties are **(a)** not engaged **(i)** in the production/supply/distribution/storage, sale/trade or provisions of similar/identical/substitutable goods or services, **(ii)** at different stages/levels of the production chain in different markets in respect of production/supply/distribution/storage, sale/trade in goods or provision of services in which another party to the combination is engaged; **(b)** continues to be predominantly engaged in export of goods/services from India after the combination takes effect. At least 75 per cent of its turnover should be derived from export and the market share of the combined entity should be less than 15 per cent in the relevant market in India.

- Acquisition/acquiring of control over an enterprise **(a)** is by a liquidator/ administrator/receiver appointed through **(i)** court proceeding or **(ii)** any scheme approved under the Securitisation and Reconstruction of Financial Assets and Enforcement of Security Interest (SRFAESI) Act/Sick Industrial Companies Act/any other law; **(b)** results from gift/inheritance; **(c)** is of a trustee company/arises from a change of trustees of a mutual fund.
- Parties are engaged **(a)** in production/supply/distribution/storage, sale/trade or provision of similar/identical/substitutable goods or services and their combined market share after combination is below 15 per cent in the relevant market; **(b)** at different stages/levels of the production chain in different markets in respect of production/supply/distribution/storage in goods or provision of services with their individual/combined share being less than 25 per cent in the relevant market.

Since the categories of combination listed below are not likely to cause an appreciable adverse on a competition in India, the requisite notice need not normally be filed:

- An acquisition of shares/voting rights **(i)** solely as an investment/in the ordinary course of business up to 15 per cent of the shares/voting rights of the company concerned, **(ii)** where the acquirer already holds 50 per cent or more shares/voting rights except where the transaction results in transfer from joint to sole control, **(iii)** pursuant to bonus issue/stock splits/ consolidation of face value of shares or subscription to rights issue to the extent of entitled proportion not leading to acquisition of control, **(iv)** by a person acting as underwriter/stock broker on behalf of clients in the process of underwriting/in the ordinary course of business.
- An acquisition of assets not related to the business activity of the acquirer or made solely as an investment/in the ordinary course of business not leading to control except where the acquired assets represent substantial business operations in a particular location/for particular product/service irrespective of whether the assets are organised as a separate legal entity or not.
- An amended/renewed tender offer where a prior notice has been filed to CCI by the party concerned.
- An acquisition of stock-in-trade/raw materials/stores/spares/current assets in the ordinary course of business.
- An acquisition of control/shares/voting rights/assets by one person/enterprise of another person/enterprise within the same group.

However, parties to the combination may, at their option, annex additional supporting documents with **Form I** or file notice in **Form II**. During the course of the enquiry, the CCI may direct them to file any additional information. The time taken by the parties in filing the additional information would be excluded from the 210-day period after which the combination would be effective.

The CCI can direct the concerned parties to file the notice in Form II to form its *prima facie* opinion whether combination is likely to cause or has caused appreciable adverse effect on competition within the relevant market. The fee for filing the notice in Form II (₹10,00,000) would be reduced by the fee already paid while filing Form I (₹50,000). The additional time taken in filing the notice would also be excluded from the 210-day period.

The details of acquisition by a public financial institution/FII/bank/VCF should be filed without any fee in Form III.

Where the concerned parties fail to file the requisite notice, the CCI may upon its own knowledge/information inquire into whether a combination has caused/is likely to cause an appreciable adverse effect on competition within India. It may direct them to file notice in Form II along with the fee of ₹10,00,000 within 30 days of the communication/direction. In case of acquisition/acquiring of control of enterprises, the acquirer should file the notice in Form I/II. If the enterprise is being acquired without its consent, the acquirer should furnish the available information relating to the enterprise being acquired within 15 days of the notice. The CCI may direct the enterprise being acquired to furnish such information as it deems fit and the time taken by the acquirer/acquired enterprises would be excluded from the 210-day period. The parties should jointly file the notice in respect of merger/amalgamation.

The parties to the combination should inform the CCI of any change in the information provided in the notice at the earliest during the continuation of the proceedings. The CCI would assess the significance of information relating to that change and act accordingly.

The proceedings under the Competition Act relating to combination would be terminated upon **(i)** a notice from the parties filing the notice that the proposed combination would not take effect, **(ii)** passing of an order by the CCI to approve the combination or otherwise.

The CCI would form the *prima facie* opinion as to whether the combination is likely to cause/has already caused an appreciable adverse effect on competition within the relevant market in India within 30 days of the receipt of the notice. In forming *prima facie* opinion, it may require the parties to file additional information/accept modification. It may also call for information from any other enterprise. Within 4 days of the CCI's decision, its direction should be conveyed to the parties to publish the details of the combination within 10 days in all-India editions of four leading daily newspapers, including two business newspapers. The details should also be posted on the website of the CCI as well as the parties to the combination. The concerned parties should submit copies of the publications to the CCI within 15 days of the direction.

The CCI may propose appropriate modification to the combination to eliminate its adverse effect. The parties may proposed amendment to the modification. They should carry out within the specified time the modification as per the specified terms/conditions. If parties fail to accept the modification within the specified period/further period allowed, the combination would be deemed to have an appreciable effect on competition. The CCI would pass an order that it would not take effect. Any party aggrieved by any direction may prefer an appeal to the Competition Appellate Tribunal (CAT).

Combination and Companies Act

The provisions of the Companies Act, 2013 relating to combination contained in Sections 230–32 are summarised below.

(1) Merger can be by **(i)** absorption or **(ii)** formation of a new company. Merger by absorption involves the transfer of the undertaking, property and liabilities of the companies to another existing company. Their transfer to a new company is merger by formation of a new company. While absorption relates to the transferor and transferee companies, merger by formation of a new company is in relation to the transferor companies. Any proposal/scheme/arrangement for reconstruction of a company (or companies) involving merger/amalgamation under which the whole/part of the undertaking, property (includes assets/rights and interest of every description)/liabilities (includes debts and obligations of every description) of the transferor company are required to the transferred to the transferee company or are proposed to be divided among and transferred to two/more companies would require sanction by the National Company Law Tribunal (NCLT). On receipt of the application of the company, any creditor or member, the NCLT would order a meeting of the creditors/members to be called/held/ conducted in a manner directed by it. The notice for the meeting should be sent to all the creditors/members and debentureholders individually at their registered address accompanied by a statement disclosing, *inter-alia*, the details of the arrangement/scheme, a copy of the valuation report and explaining their effect on creditors, key managerial personnel, promoters/ non-promoter members, debentureholders and any material interest of the directors/debenture trustees. The notice and other documents should also be **(i)** placed on the website of the company, **(ii)** sent to the SEBI/concerned stock exchanges for placing on their websites, and **(iii)** published in newspapers in the prescribed manner. The notice for the meeting issued by way of an advertisement should indicate the time within which copies of the scheme would be made available to the concerned persons free of charge from the registered office of the company.

The notice should, moreover, provide that the person to whom it is sent may vote in the meeting either themselves or through proxies or by postal ballot to the adoption of the proposal within one month only. Persons **(i)** holding at least 10 per cent of the shareholding or **(ii)** having a minimum 5 per cent of the total outstanding debt can make objections to the scheme.

Further, the notice with all the documents in the prescribed form should also be sent to the **(i)** Central Government, **(ii)** Income Tax authorities, **(iii)** RBI, **(iv)** SEBI, **(v)** Registrar of Companies, **(vi)** Respective stock exchanges, **(vii)** Official liquidator, **(viii)** Competition Commission of India and **(ix)** other sectoral regulators/authorities likely to be affected by the arrangement. Any representation by them should be made within 30 days from the receipt of the notice failing which it would be presumed that they have no representations to make on the proposal.

The scheme approved by three-fourths in value of creditors/members and sanctioned by the NCLT would be binding on the company/all creditors/members.

(2) The merging companies would have to circulate in the meeting ordered by the NCLT the following: **(i)** Draft of the proposed terms of the scheme drawn up and adopted by its directors, **(ii)** Confirmation that a copy of the draft scheme has been filed with the Registrar of Companies, **(iii)** A report adopted by its directors explaining the effect on each class of shareholders, key managerial personnel, promoter/non-promoter shareholders, laying out in particular the share exchange ratio, specifying any special valuation difficulties, **(iv)** Expert valuation report and **(v)** A supplementary accounting of the last annual accounts of any merging company related to the financial year ending more than six months before the first meeting of the company summoned for approving the scheme.

(3) On being satisfied that the above procedures have been complied with, the NCLT would sanction the scheme /arrangement. It would also make provision for the matters specified below:

- **(a)** Transfer to the transferee company of the whole/any part of the undertaking, property/ liabilities of the transferor company from a date to be determined by the parties;
- **(b)** Allotment/appropriation by the transferee company of any shares/debentures, policies/other like instruments in the company which under the scheme are to be allotted/appropriated by the company to/or for any person. However, the transferee company cannot hold any

shares in its own name/in the name of any trust on its behalf/on behalf of any subsidiary/ associate companies and such shares should be cancelled/extinguished.

(c) Continuation by/against the transferee company of any legal proceedings pending by/ against transferor company on the date of the transfer;

(d) Dissolution, without winding up, of transferor company;

(e) Provision to be made for any person who dissents from the arrangement;

(f) Allotment of shares of the transferee company to a non-resident shareholder;

(g) Transfer of employees of the transferor to the transferee company;

(h) In case the transferor company is a listed company and the transferee company is an unlisted company, **(i)** the transferee company would remain an unlisted company until it becomes a listed one, **(ii)** provision for payment of the value of shares held by shareholders of the transferor company who decide to opt of the transferee company and their other benefits according to a pre-determined price formula or after a valuation. However, the amount can in no case be less than what has been specified by any SEBI regulation;

(i) Set-off any dissolution fee paid by the transferor company against any similar fee paid by the transferee company subsequent to the amalgamation; and

(j) Such incidental/consequential/supplemental matters as deemed necessary to secure that the merger/amalgamation is fully/effectively carried out. However, the NCLT would sanction any scheme only if the auditors certify that the accounting treatment proposed in the scheme is in conformity with the accounting standards prescribed by the Government.

(4) The property/liabilities of the transferor company would be by virtue of the sanction order of the NCLT transferred to the transferee company.

(5) Every concerned company should file a certified copy of the order with the Registrar of the Companies (ROCs) within 30 days of its receipt.

(6) The merger/amalgamation scheme should clearly indicate an appointed date from which it would be effective.

(7) The company concerned should, until the completion of the scheme, file a statement in the prescribed form/within prescribed time with the ROCs every year duly certified by a practicing Chartered/Cost Accountant /Company Secretary that the scheme is being complied with the orders of NCLT.

(8) Contravention of the above provisions by the transferor/transferee company would be punishable with a minimum fine of one lakh rupees which may extend to 25 lakh rupees. Every defaulting officer would be punishable with imprisonment upto one year or fine between 1-3 lakh rupees or with both.

Annexure 1 below contains the gist of the scheme of merger of Reliance Pertrochemicals Ltd with Reliance Industries Ltd. The demerger scheme of DCM Ltd is outlined in Annexure 2 below.

Annexure 1 Merger of Reliance Pertrochemicals Ltd (RPL) with Reliance Industries Ltd (RIL)

The merger of RPL with RIL in March 1992 was the biggest ever merger till date and resulted in the creation of the largest Indian corporate. RIL was engaged in the manufacture and sale of textiles, fibre and fibre intermediates and petrochemicals. In particular, it was engaged in the manufacture of polyester staple fibre (PSF), polyester filament yearn (PFY), purified teraphtalic acid (PTA), linear alkyl benzene (LAB) and other products. Its paid-up capital (₹157.94 crore) consisted of (i) equity capital, ₹152.14 crore

(15.21 crore shares of ₹10 each) (ii) 11 per cent cumulative redeemable preference shares of ₹100 each, ₹30 lakh; and 15 per cent cumulative redeemable preference shares of ₹100 each, ₹5.5 crore.

The RPL was incorporated in November 1988 with the main objective of manufacturing poly vinyl chloride (PVC), mono ethylene glycol (MEG) and high density poly ethylene (HDPE). Its paid-up equity capital stood at ₹749.30 crore consisting of 74.93 crore shares of ₹10 each.

In terms of a scheme of amalgamation approved by the shareholders of the two companies and Mumbai and Gujarat High Courts in July/August 1992, the RPL was merged with the RIL with effect from March 2, 1992. The merger was aimed to enhance shareholders' value by realising significant synergies of both the companies. Liberalization of government policy and the accompanying economic reforms created this opportunity for the RIL's shareholders.

As per the scheme of amalgamation, the expected benefits of merger to the amalgamated entity, *inter-alia,* were:

- Benefit from diversification as the risks involved in the operation of different units would be minimised
- Business synergy due to economies of scale and integrated operations
- Higher retailed earning leading to enhanced intrinsic values of shareholding to investors. The capital requirement would also be at manageable levels
- Strong fundamentals which would enhance its credit rating and resource raising ability in financial markets, both national and international

The exchange ratio was one equity share of ₹10 each in RIL for every 10 equity shares of RPL with a par value of ₹10 each. The exchange ratio was based on the expert valuation made by three reputed firms of chartered accountants, namely, S.B. Billimoria & Co, Choksi & Co and Heribhakthi & Co. Pursuant to the above, 7,49,26,428 equity shares of ₹10 each were issued as fully paid-up to the shareholders of RIL without payment being received in cash.

All the assets, liabilities and obligations of RPL were taken over by the merged entity—RIL. The excess of assets over liabilities takenover by RIL consequent on the amalgamation less the face value of the equity shares issued to the shareholders of the RPL represented amalgamation reserve. All the employees of RPL on the date immediately preceding the effective date became the employees of the RIL.

The post-merger scenario of the RIL is reflected in the increase in its capital, turnover, net profit and equity dividend. Compared to the pre-merger capital of ₹157.94 crore, the post-merger capital rose to ₹358.74 crore. The turnover increased from ₹2,298 crore in 1991–92 to ₹7,019 crore in 1994–95. Net profit of RIL stood at ₹10,651 crore in 1994–95 compared to ₹163 crore in 1991–92. The equity dividend rose phenomenally to 55 per cent (1994–95) from 30 per cent (1991–92). The RIL emerged post-merger as a mega corporation and became a global player. Its foreign exchange earnings in 1994–95 aggregated ₹174 crore.

Annexure 2 Demerger of DCM Ltd

DCM Ltd, promoted by Late Shri Ram in 1889, has become a conglomerate of 13 units with multifarious manufacturing activities in sugar, textile, chemicals, ryon tyre cord, fertilisers and so on. These units on their own being of the size of independent companies, the directors felt that greater focus on the operation of the various units of the company would result in substantial improvement in the results of their operations. The post-reorganisation slogan would be: "**The Trimmer We Are, The Faster We Are**".

On the basis of the various discussions, meetings, consultations between the members of the Board of Directors, financial institutions and consultants, it was decided to take appropriate steps to carry on the business of various units more effectively and efficiently in the larger interest of shareholders, debenture-holders, creditors, employees and in the general public interest. To achieve the objective of carrying the business of DCM Ltd more smoothly and profitably, DCM Ltd was reorganised by dividing its business among four companies having shareholders with the same interest *inter-se* in DCM but to be managed and operated independently (Exhibit 1).

EXHIBIT 1 Division of DCM Ltd.

1. **DCM Ltd** comprising DCM Mills (DCM Estate) DCM Engineering Products, DCM Data Products, Hissar Textiles Mills, Shri Ram Fibres Ltd, and DCM Toyota Ltd.
2. **DCM Shri Ram Industries Ltd** comprising Shri Ram Rayons, Daurala Sugar Works, and Hindon River Mills.
3. **DCM Shri Ram Consolidated Ltd** comprising Shri Ram Fertilises and Chemicals Industries Ltd, Shri Ram Cement Works Ltd, Swatantra Bharat Mills Ltd, and DCM Silk Mils Ltd.
4. **Shri Ram Industrial Enterprises Ltd** comprising Shri Ram Food and Fertilisers Ltd, and Mawana Sugar Works Ltd.

The division of DCM Ltd took place through the scheme of arrangement approved by the Delhi High Court on April 16, 1990 according to which three new companies were formed. The scheme of arrangement became effective from April 1, 1990. The four companies thereafter started operating independently, each with their respective Boards of Directors.

Some of the notable features of the scheme of reorganisation of the erstwhile DCM Ltd into four companies were:

- The total paid-up capital of ₹23 crore was divided equally.
- The allocation of various assets and liabilities among them was done as under:

	DCM Shri Ram Industries Ltd	*DCM Shri Ram Consolidated Ltd*	*Shri Ram Industrial Enterprises Ltd*	*DCM Ltd*
Fixed deposits	16%	33%	36%	15%
Debentures	16%	12%	36%	36%
Common assets/liabilities/ income/benefit	16.66%	16.66%	33.33%	33.33%
Expenses and cost of arrangement	16.66%	16.66%	33.33%	33.33%
Specific assets	(All at book value as on 1.4.1990 unit-wise)			

- Though the liability for debentures was divided, the debentures were physically retained in DCM Ltd. The mortgage of assets of various units already created with the trustees for debentureholders were modified to the effect that each group's assets would stand charged only for the liability allocated to it.
- For payment of interest and principal amount to debentureholders, Indian Bank, which was the debenture trustees was appointed a Registrar by all the four companies and they remitted their share of liabilities to the Registrar on due dates for onward payment to debentureholders. The cost of Registrar would be shared by all the companies.
- The fixed deposit receipts were split into four new receipts in the proportion in which the fixed deposits appeared in the books of account as on the effective date.

- Upon transfer of the undertakings to them, the new companies allotted one equity share each to the holders of four equity shares in DCM Ltd. The paid-up value of DCM equity share was thereupon reduced for ₹10 each to ₹2.5 each. Thereafter, the DCM equity shares were consolidated into equity shares of the face value of ₹10 each. Any fraction arising on allotment/consolidation of shares was disposed of and sales proceed distributed *pro rata* to the eligible shareholders.
- The equity shares of the four companies were subsequently listed in the stock exchange(s).
- Disputes with respect to the provisions of the scheme of arrangement were to be settled by two arbitrators and an umpire appointed by the arbitrators.

Thus, the demerger of DCM Ltd was completed with lots of innovation and practical solutions to the complex problem of reorganising a century-old company. After reorganisation, all the DCM Group companies have grown tremendously. From a non-dividend position prior to the demerger, all the companies have grown manifold adding value both to the shares as well as to the new entities.

Acquisition/Takeovers

Takeover implies acquisition of controlling interest in a company by another company. It does not lead to the dissolution of the company whose shares are being/have been acquired. It simply means a change of controlling interest in a company through the acquisition of its shares by another group. Takeovers can assume three forms: **(i)** negotiated/friendly, **(ii)** open market/hostile and **(iii)** bail out. The first type of takeover is organised by the incumbent management with a view to parting with the control of management to another group, through negotiation. The terms and conditions of the takeover are mutually settled by both the groups. Hostile takeovers are also referred to as raid on the company. In order to takeover the management of, or acquire controlling interest in, the target company, a person/group of persons acquire shares from the open market/financial institutions/mutual funds/willing shareholders at a price higher than the prevailing market price. Such takeovers are hostile to the existing management. When a profit earning company takes over a financially sick company to bail it out, it is known as **bail out takeover**. Normally, such takeovers are in pursuance of a scheme of rehabilitation approved by public financial institutions/scheduled banks. The takeover bids, in respect of purchase price, track record of the acquirer and his financial position, are evaluated by a leading financial institution. Corporate takeovers in the country are governed by the listing agreement with stock exchanges and the SEBI Substantial Acquisition of Shares and Takeover (SEBI Code) Code. The main elements of the regulatory framework for takeovers are briefly described below.

> **Takeover** implies acquisition of controlling interest in a company by another company/group.

> **Bail out takeover** is the takeover of a financially weak company by a profitable company.

Listing Agreement The takeover of companies listed on the stock exchanges is regulated by Clause 40-A and 40-B of the listing agreement. While Clause 40-A deals with minimum level of public shareholding, Clause 40-B contains the requirements to be met when a takeover offer is made.

Minimum Level of Public Shareholding In order to ensure availability of floating stock, every listed company should maintain, on a continuous basis, public shareholding of atleast 25 per cent of the total number of issued shares of a class/kind of its listed shares. Public shareholding exclude shares held by **(1)** promoters/promoter group and **(2)** custodians against which depository receipts are issued overseas. The minimum level of public shareholding in a company **(a)** which offers/

had offered in the past a particular class/kind of shares to the public under Rule 19**(2)(b)** of the Securities Contracts (Regulation) Rules or **(b)** which has atleast two crore shares outstanding with a market capatalisation of atleast ₹1,000 crore, should be 10 per cent of the total number of issued shares. Market capitalisation means the average capitalisation for the previous financial year. The average should be computed as the sum of the daily market capitalisation over one year divided by the number of trading days. The market capitalisation would be considered for the succeeding four quarters.

Takeover Offer The company also agrees that it is a condition for continuous listing that whenever the takeover offer is made or there is any change in the control of the management of the company, the person who secures the control and the company whose shares have been acquired would comply with the relevant provisions of the SEBI Takeover Code.

The SEBI Substantial Acquisition of Shares and Takeover Code (SEBI Takeover Code) A takeover bid is generally understood to imply the acquisition of shares carrying voting rights in a company, in a direct or indirect manner, with a view to gaining control over the management of the company. Such takeovers could take place through a process of friendly negotiation or in a hostile manner, in which the existing management resists the change in control. Both the substantial acquisition of shares and change in the control of a listed company are covered by takeover bids. The main elements of the SEBI Code are: **(i)** Substantial Acquisition of Shares, Voting Rights/Control, **(ii)** Open Offer Process, **(iii)** Other Obligations, **(iv)** Disclosures of Shareholding and Control, and **(v)** Miscellaneous. However, these regulations do not apply to direct/indirect acquisition of shares/voting rights in, or control over a company, listed on the institutional trading platform of a stock exchange.

Acquisition means directly/indirectly acquiring/agreeing to acquire shares/voting rights in, or control over, a target company..

Substantial Acquisition of Shares, Voting Rights or Control **Acquisition** means directly/indirectly acquire/agree to acquire shares voting rights in, or control over, a target company. **Control** includes the right to appoint majority of directors or to control the management or policy decisions exercisable by a person(s) acting individually or in concert, directly/indirectly, including by virtue of their shareholding/management rights/shareholders agreement/voting agreements or in any other manner. **Shares** means shares/security carrying voting rights including depository receipts carrying an entitlement to exercise voting rights. **Target company** means a company listed on a stock exchange. **Person acting in concert** means persons who, with a common objective/purpose of acquisition of shares/voting rights in, or exercising control, over a target company, pursuant to a formal/informal agreement/understanding, directly/indirectly co-operate for acquisition of shares/voting rights in, or exercise of control over, the target company. The persons falling within the following categories would be deemed to be persons acting in concert with other persons within the same category, unless the contrary is established: **(i)** a company, its holding company, subsidiary company and any company under the same management/control; **(ii)** a company, its directors, and any person entrusted with the management of the company; **(iii)** directors of companies referred to

Control includes the right to appoint majority of directors or to control the management or policy decisions exercisable by a person(s) acting individually or in concert, directly/indirectly, including by virtue of their shareholding/management rights/shareholders agreement/voting agreements or in any other manner.

Person(s) acting in concert means persons who, with a common objective/purpose of acquisition of shares/voting rights in, or exercising control, over a target company, pursuant to a formal/informal agreement/understanding, directly/indirectly co-operate for acquisition of shares/voting rights in, or exercise of control over, the target company.

above and associates of such directors. **Associate** of a person means **(a)** any immediate relative, **(b)** trust of which the person/immediate relative is a trustee, **(c)** firm in which he/immediate relative is a partner, and **(d)** member of a Hindu Undivided Family of which he is a coparcener. **Immediate relative** means his spouse including parents/brothers/ sisters/children or of the spouse; **(iv)** promoters and members of the promoter group; **(v)** immediate relatives; **(vi)** a mutual fund, its sponsor, trustee, trustee company, and asset management company; **(vii)** a collective investment scheme and its collective investment management company, trustees and trustee company; **(viii)** a venture capital fund and its sponsor, trustees, trustee company and asset management company; **(ix)** an alternate investment fund and its sponsor/trustee/manager; **(x)** a merchant banker and its client, who is an acquirer; **(xi)** a portfolio manager and its client, who is an acquirer; **(xii)** banks, financial advisors and stock brokers of the acquirer, or of the company which is a holding company or subsidiary of the acquirer, and where the acquirer is an individual, of the immediate relative of such individual. However, a bank whose sole role is that of providing normal commercial banking services or activities in relation to an open offer under these regulations would be excluded; **(xiii)** an investment company or fund and any person who has an interest in such investment company or fund as a shareholder or unitholder having not less than 10 per cent of the paid-up capital of the investment company or unit capital of the fund, and any other investment company or fund in which such person or his associate holds not less than 10 per cent of the paid-up capital of that investment company or unit capital of that fund. However, holding of units of mutual funds registered with the SEBI would be excluded.

> **Associate** means (a) any immediate relative, (b) trust of which the person/ immediate relative is a trustee, (c) firm in which he/ immediate relative is a partner, and (d) member of a Hindu Undivided Family of which he is a coparcener.

The main elements of the SEBI code relating to substantial acquisition of shares/voting rights/ control: **(i)** substantial acquisition of shares/voting rights, **(ii)** acquisition of control, **(iii)** indirect acquisition of shares/control, **(iv)** voluntary offer, **(v)** offer size, **(vi)** offer price, **(vii)** mode of payment, **(viii)** general exemptions, and **(ix)** exemptions by the SEBI.

Substantial Acquisition of Shares/Voting Rights To acquire shares/voting rights in a target company which together with shares/voting rights already held by him and by persons acting in concert with him entitle them to exercise 25 per cent./more of the voting rights in the target company, an **acquirer** (i.e. person who directly/indirectly acquire/agrees to acquire by himself/through or with person(s) acting in concert with him shares/voting rights in or control over a target company), would have to make a public announcement of an open offer for acquiring the shares. Similar announcement would be required by an acquirer, who has already acquired/holds shares/voting rights entitling him to exercise 25 per cent/more of the voting rights but less than the permissible non-public shareholding, to acquire within any financial year additional shares/voting rights entitling him to exercise more than 5 per cent of the voting rights, subject to a ceiling of the maximum permissible non-public shareholding under the Securities Contracts (Regulation) Rules, namely, 75 per cent. For determining the quantum of acquisition of additional voting rights, only gross acquisition would be taken into account. In case of acquisition by way of issue of new shares by the target company or where it has issued new shares in any financial year, the difference between the pro- and post-allotment percentage voting rights would be regarded as the additional acquisition.

> **Acquirer** is a person who directly/indirectly acquire/agrees to acquire by himself/ through or with person(s) acting in concert with him shares/voting rights in or control over a target company.

The acquisition of shares/voting rights of a company by the promoter/shareholders in control in terms of the SEBI ICDR regulations pertaining to conditions/manner of providing exit opportunity to dissenting shareholders should be exempt from these requirements.

Acquisition of Control Irrespective of acquisition/holding of shares/voting rights in a target company, no acquirer would directly/indirectly acquire, control over the target company unless he makes a public announcement of an open offer.

Indirect Acquisition of Shares/Voting Rights/Control Acquisition of shares/voting rights in/control over, any company/other entity, that would enable any person(s) acting in concert with him to exercise/direct the exercise of such percentage of voting rights in/control over, the acquisition of which would otherwise attract the obligation to make a public announcement of an open offer for acquiring shares, would be considered as an **indirect acquisition** of shares/voting rights in/control over the target company. In the case of an indirect acquisition where **(a)** the proportionate net asset value of the target company as a percentage of the consolidated net asset value of the entity or business being acquired, **(b)** the proportionate sales turnover of the target company as a percentage of the consolidated sales turnover of the entity or business being acquired, or **(c)** the proportionate market capitalisation of the target company as a percentage of the **enterprise value** for the entity or business being acquired, is in exercise of 80 per cent, on the basis of the most recent audited annual financial statements, such indirect acquisition would be regarded as a direct acquisition of the target company for all purposes including without limitation, the obligations relating to timing, pricing and other compliance requirements for the open offer. **Enterprise value** means market capitalisation of the company **plus** debt, minority interest and preference shares **minus** total cash and cash equivalents.

Indirect acquisition is acquisition by a person enabling him to exercise/direct the exercise of such percentage of voting rights the acquisition of which would otherwise attract the obligation to make public announcement.

Delisting Offer The acquirer who makes a public announcement of an open offer for acquiring shares of a target company can delist the company in terms of the SEBI delisting of shares regulations. He should declare upfront his intention to do so at the time of the detailed public statement. Failure to delist should be announced within two working days in all the concerned newspapers. Within five working days from the date of the announcement of failure, the acquirer through the manager of the open should offer file with the SEBI a draft of the letter of offer and comply with all other applicable provisions. Moreover, the offer price should be enhanced by 10 per cent per annum for the period between the scheduled date and the actual date of payment of consideration to the shareholders.

Enterprise value means market capitalistaion of the company plus debt, minority interest and preference shares minus total cash and cash equivalents.

In case of completing offer (**discussed** later), the acquirer would **(i)** not be entitled to delist the company, **(ii)** not be liable to pay interest to the shareholders on account of delay due to the competing offer and **(iii)** comply with all the applicable provisions and make an announcement within two working days from the date of public announcement regarding competing offer in all the newspapers in which the detailed public statement was made.

The shareholders who have tendered shares in acceptance of the unsuccessful offer can withdraw them within 10 working days from the date of its announcement. Those who have not tendered their shares would be entitled to tender their shares in acceptance of the offer made to them.

Voluntary Offer An acquirer, who holds shares or voting rights in a target company (**shares in brief**) entitling them to exercise 25 per cent or more but less than the maximum permissible non-public (75 per cent) shareholding, would be entitled to voluntarily make a public announcement of an open offer for acquiring shares subject to their aggregate shareholding after completion of the open offer not exceeding the maximum permissible non-public shareholding. However, where an acquirer has acquired shares of the target company in the preceding 52 weeks without attracting the obligation to make a public announcement, he would not be eligible to voluntarily make a public announcement of an open offer. Moreover, during the offer period he would not be entitled to acquire any shares otherwise than under the open offer.

An acquirer who has made a public announcement to acquire shares would not be entitled to acquire any shares of the target company for a period of six months after completion of the open offer except pursuant to another voluntary open offer. However, such restriction would not prohibit him from making a competing offer upon any other person making an open. Shares acquired through bonus issue or stock splits would not be considered for purposes of this dis-entitlement. A **willful defaulter** (i.e. a [person/director/promoter/partner categorised by a bank/financial institution/their consortium in accordance with the RBI guidelines) cannot make a public announcement of an offer for acquiring shares/ enter into any transaction that would attract the obligation to make an announcement of an open offer. He can make a competing offer.

Tendering period is the period within which shareholders may tender their shares in acceptance of an open offer.

Offer Size The open offer for acquiring shares to be made by the acquirer should be for at least 26 per cent of total shares of the target company, as of the tenth working day from the closure of the **tendering** period (i.e. period within which shareholders may tender their shares in acceptance of an open offer).

Offer period is period between the date of entering into a formal/ informal agreement to acquire shares/ voting right in, or control over, a target company requiring public announcement or the date of public announcement and the date on which the payment of consideration to shareholders who have accepted the open offer is made or the date on which open offer is withdrawn.

The total shares of the target company as of the tenth working day from the closure of the tendering period would take into account all potential increases in the number of outstanding shares during the **offer period** (i.e. period between the date of entering into a formal/informal agreement to acquire shares/voting right in, or control over, a target company requiring public announcement or the date of public announcement and the date on which the payment of consideration to shareholders who have accepted the open offer is made or the date on which open offer is withdrawn) contemplated as of the date of the public announcement. The offer size should also be proportionately increased in case of an increase in total number of shares, after the public announcement, which is not contemplated on the date of the public announcement.

The voluntary open offer should be for acquisition of at least such number of shares as would entitle their holder(s) to exercise an additional 10 per cent of the total shares of the target company, and would not exceed such number of shares as would result in the post-acquisition holding of the acquirer exceeding the maximum permissible non-public shareholding applicable to the target company. However, in the event of a competing offer, the acquirer who has voluntarily made a public announcement of an open offer would be entitled to increase the number of shares to such number as he deems fit. The increase in offer size be made within 15 working days from the public announcement, failing which the acquirer would not be entitled to increase the offer size. Upon an acquirer opting to increase the offer size, the such open offer would be deemed to be a voluntary offer. In the event of the shares accepted in the open offer were such that the shareholding of the acquirer(s) pursuant to completion of the open offer results in their shareholding exceeding the maximum permissible non-public shareholding, he would be required to bring down the non-public shareholding to the level specified and within the time permitted under Securities Contract (Regulation) Rules.[@@] The acquirer whose shareholding exceeds the maximum permissible non-public shareholding, pursuant to an open offer, would not be eligible to make a voluntary delisting offer under the SEBI Delisting of Equity Shares Regulations, within 12 months from the date of the completion of the offer period. Any open offer should be made to all shareholders of the target company, other than the acquirer and the parties to any underlying agreement for the sale of shares of the target company.

Offer Price The open offer for acquiring shares should be made at a price not lower than the price determined in the manner specified below:

1. Direct Acquisition In the case of direct acquisition and indirect **acquisition deemed to be direct acquisition** of shares, the offer price should be the highest of: **(a)** the highest negotiated price per share of the target company for any acquisition under the agreement attracting the obligation to make a public announcement of an open offer; **(b)** the **volume-weighted average price** (i.e. product of number of equity shares bought and price of each share divided by the number of shares bought) paid/payable for acquisitions, by the acquirer during the 52 two weeks immediately preceding the date of the public announcement; **(c)** the highest price paid/payable for any acquisition by the acquirer during the 26 weeks immediately preceding the date of the public announcement; **(d)** the **volume-weighted average market price** (i.e. product of number of shares traded on a stock exchange and price of each share divided by the total number of shares traded) of such shares for a period of 60 trading days immediately preceding the date of the public announcement as traded on the stock exchange where the maximum volume of trading in the shares of the target company are recorded during such period, provided such shares are **frequently traded**. Frequently traded shares mean shares in which the traded turnover on any stock exchange during 12-calendar months preceding the calendar month in which the public announcement is made is at least 10 per cent of the total shares of the target company; **(e)** where the shares are not frequently traded, the price determined by the acquirer and the manager to the open offer taking into account valuation parameters including, book value, comparable trading multiples, and such other parameters as are customary for valuation of shares of such companies; and **(f)** the per share value computed in case of indirect acquisition (**discussed later**).

> **Volume-weighted average price** is a product of number of equity shares bought and price of each share divided by the number of shares bought.
>
> **Volume-weighted average market price** is a product of number of shares traded on a stock exchange and price of each share divided by the total number of shares traded.

2. Indirect Acquisition Deemed Direct Acquisition In the case of an indirect acquisition of shares, the offer price would be the highest of: **(a)** the highest negotiated price per share of the target company for any acquisition under the agreement attracting the obligation to make a public announcement; **(b)** the volume-weighted average price paid/payable for any acquisition, during the 52 weeks immediately preceding the earlier of, the date on which the primary acquisition is contracted, and the date on which the intention or the decision to make the primary acquisition is announced in the public domain; **(c)** the highest price paid/payable for any acquisition by the acquirer during the 26 weeks immediately preceding the earlier of, the date on which the primary acquisition is contracted, and the date on which the intention or the decision to make the primary acquisition is announced in the public domain; **(d)** the highest price paid/payable for any acquisition between the earlier of, the date on which the primary acquisition is contracted, and the date on which the intention or the decision to make the primary acquisition is announced in the public

[@@]**For an account refer to Khan, M.Y., *Indian Financial System*, McGraw Hill Education (India), 2018, Chapter 4.**

domain, and the date of the public announcement of the open offer for shares of the target company; **(e)** the volume-weighted average market price of the shares for a period of 60 days earlier of, the date on which the primary acquisition is contracted, and the date on which the intention or the decision to make the primary acquisition is announced in the public domain, as traded on the stock exchange where the maximum volume of trading in the shares of the target company are recorded during such period, provided such shares are frequently traded; and **(f)** the per share value in case of indirect acquisition (**discussed later**).

3. In case the offer price is incapable of being determined under any of the parameters above, the offer price should be the fair price of shares of the target company to be determined by the acquire and the manager to the open offer taking into account valuation parameters including, book value, comparable trading multiples, and such other parameters as are customary for valuation of shares of such companies.

4. Indirect Acquisition In the case of an indirect acquisition and open offers, where the proportionate **(a)** net asset value of the target company as a percentage of the consolidated net asset value; **(b)** sales turnover of the target company as a percentage of the consolidated sales turnover; or **(c)** market capitalisation of the target company as a percentage of the enterprise value for the entity or business being acquired is in excess of 15 per cent, the acquirer would be required to compute and disclose, in the letter of offer, the per share value of the target company taken into account for the acquisition, along with a detailed description of the methodology adopted for such computation. The **market capitalisation** of the target company would be taken into account on the basis of the volume-weighted average market price of the shares on the stock exchange for a period of 60 trading days preceding the earlier of, the date on which the primary acquisition is contracted, and the date on which the intention or the decision to make the primary acquisition is announced in the public domain, as traded on the stock exchange where the maximum volume of trading in the shares of the target company are recorded during such period.

5. In respect of direct and indirect deemed direct acquisition, where the acquirer has any outstanding convertible instruments convertible into shares of the target company at a specific price, the price at which such instruments are to be converted into shares, would also be considered as a parameter. The price paid for shares of target company would include any price paid/agreed to be paid for the shares in the target company, in any form whatsoever, whether stated in the agreement for acquisition of shares or in any incidental, contemporaneous or collateral agreement, whether termed as control premium or as non-compete fees or otherwise.

6. Where the acquirer has acquired/agreed to acquire any shares in the target company during the **offer period** (i.e. period between the date of entering into formal/informal agreement to acquire shares/voting rights/control of a target company requiring public announcement and the date of public announcement and the date on which the payment of consideration to shareholders who have accepted the open offer is made or the date on which open offer is withdrawn) by subscription/ purchase, at a price higher than the offer price, the offer price would stand revised to the highest price for any acquisition. However, no acquisition would be made after the third working day prior to the commencement and until the expiry of the tendering period.

7. The price parameters outlined above may be adjusted by the acquirer in consultation with the manager to the offer, for corporate actions such as issuances pursuant to rights issue, bonus issue, stock consolidations, stock splits, payment of dividend, de-mergers and reduction of capital, where the record date for effecting such corporate actions falls prior to three working days before the commencement of the tendering period. However, adjustment should be made for dividend declared if the per share dividend is more than 50 per cent higher than the average paid during the three financial years preceding the date of the public announcement.

8. Where the acquirer acquires shares of the target company during the period of 26 weeks after the tendering period at a price higher than the offer price, he would pay the difference between the highest acquisition price and the offer price, to all the shareholders whose shares were accepted in the open offer, within 60 days from the date of such acquisition.

9. Where the open offer is subject to a minimum level of acceptances, the acquirer may indicate a lower price, but not be less than the price determined under this regulation, for acquiring all the acceptances despite the acceptance falling short of the indicated minimum level of acceptance, in the event the open offer does not receive the minimum acceptance.

10. In the case of any indirect acquisition, the offer price would stand enhanced by an amount equal to a sum determined at the rate of 10 per cent per annum for the period between the earlier of the date on which the primary acquisition is contracted or the date on which the intention or the decision to make the primary acquisition is announced in the public domain, and the date of the detailed public statement, provided such period is more than five working days.

11. The offer price for partly-paid-up shares should be computed as the difference between the offer price and the amount due towards calls-in-arrears including calls remaining unpaid with interest.

12. The offer price for equity shares carrying differential voting rights should be determined by the acquirer and the manager to the open offer with full disclosure of justification for the price so determined, being set out in the detailed public statement and the letter of offer. However, the price should not be lower than the amount determined by applying the percentage rate of premium that the offer price for the equity shares carrying full voting rights represents to the price parameter computed above to the volume-weighted average market price of the shares carrying differential voting rights in the aforesaid provisions, subject to shares carrying full voting rights and the shares carrying differential voting rights, both being frequently traded shares.

13. In the event of any of the price parameters not being available or denominated in Indian rupees, the conversion of such amount into Indian rupees would be effected at the exchange rate as prevailing on the date preceding the date of public announcement and the acquirer should set out the source of such exchange rate in the public announcement, the detailed public statement and the letter of offer.

14. The SEBI may, at the expense of the acquirer, require valuation of the shares by an independent merchant banker other than the manager to the open offer or an independent practicing chartered accountant having a minimum experience of 10 years.

Mode of Payment The offer price may be paid **(a)** in cash; **(b)** by issue/exchange/transfer of listed shares **(i)** shares, **(ii)** secured debt instruments with a rating not below investment grade as rated by a SEBI-registered agency, **(iii)** convertible debt securities; **(c)** a combination of the mode of payment of consideration stated in Clauses **(a)** and **(b)**. However, where any shares have been acquired/agreed to be acquired by the acquirer and persons acting in concert with him during the 52 weeks immediately preceding the date of public announcement constitute more than ten per cent of the voting rights in the target company and has been paid for in cash, the open offer would entail an option to the shareholders to require payment of the offer price in cash, and a shareholder who has not exercised an option in his acceptance would be deemed to have opted for receiving the offer price in cash. In case of revision in offer price, the mode of payment of consideration may be altered subject to the condition that the component of the offer to be paid in cash prior to such revision is not reduced.

The shares sought to be **(i)** issued/exchanged/transferred or **(ii)** upon conversion of other securities, towards payment of the offer price, should conform to the following requirements: **(a)** they are listed for at least two years on a stock exchange preceding the date of public announcement and frequently traded at the time of the public announcement; **(b)** the issuer has redressed at least 95 per cent of the complaints received from investors by the end of the calendar quarter immediately preceding the calendar month in which the public announcement is made; **(c)** the issuer has been in material compliance with the listing agreement for at least two years immediately preceding the date of the public announcement. In case where the SEBI is of the view that a company has not been materially compliant with the provisions of the listing agreement, the offer price should be paid in cash only; **(d)** the impact of auditors' qualifications on the audited accounts of the issuer for three immediately preceding financial years does not exceed 5 per cent of the net profit or loss after tax for the respective years; and **(e)** the SEBI has not issued any direction against the issuer to access the capital market/to issue fresh shares.

Where the shareholders have been provided with options to accept payment in cash or by way of securities, or a combination, the pricing for the open offer may be different for each option subject to compliance with minimum offer price requirements. The detailed public statement and the letter of offer should contain justification for such differential pricing.

In the event the offer price consists of consideration to be paid by issuance of securities, which requires compliance with any applicable law, the acquirer should ensure that compliance before the commencement of the tendering period failing which the entire consideration should be paid in cash.

Where listed securities are offered as consideration, their value should be the higher of: **(a)** the average of the weekly high and low of their closing prices quoted on the stock exchange during **(i)** the six months **(ii)** 2 weeks preceding the **relevant** date (i.e. 30th day prior to the date on which the meeting of shareholders is held to consider the proposed issues of shares); **(b)** the volume-weighted average market price for a period of 60 trading days preceding the date of the public announcement, on the stock exchange where the maximum volume of trading in the shares of the company are recorded during the six-month period prior to the relevant date and the ratio of exchange of shares should be duly certified by an independent merchant banker (other than the manager to the open offer)/chartered accountant having a minimum experience of ten years.

General Exemptions

(1) The following acquisitions would be exempt from the obligation to make an open offer:

(a) Acquisition pursuant to *inter se* transfer of shares amongst qualifying persons, being **(i)** immediate relatives; **(ii)** persons named as promoters in the shareholding pattern for at least three years prior to the proposed acquisition; **(iii)** a company, its subsidiaries/holding company/ their other subsidiaries of such holding company, persons holding not less than 50 per cent of the equity shares of the company, other companies in which such persons hold not less than 50 per cent of the equity shares, and their subsidiaries subject to control over such qualifying persons being exclusively held by the same persons; **(iv)** persons acting in concert for not less than three years prior to the proposed acquisition, and disclosed under the listing agreement; **(v)** shareholders of a target company who have been persons acting in concert for a period of not less than three years prior to the proposed acquisition and are disclosed under the listing agreement, and any company in which the entire equity share capital is owned by such shareholders in the same proportion as their holdings in the target company without any differential entitlement to exercise voting rights in such company. For purposes of availing of the exemption, **(i)** If the shares of the target company are frequently traded, the acquisition price per share should not be higher by more than 25 per cent of the volume-weighted average market price for a period of 60 trading days preceding the date of issuance of notice for the proposed *inter se* transfer on the stock exchange where the maximum volume of trading in these shares are recorded; and **(ii)** the transferor and the transferee should have complied with the applicable disclosure requirements (**discussed later in this Chapter**).

(b) Acquisition in the ordinary course of business by SEBI-registered **(i)** underwriter by way of allotment pursuant to an underwriting agreement of; **(ii)** stock broker on behalf of his client in exercise of lien over the shares purchased on behalf his client under the bye-laws of concerned the stock exchange; **(iii)** merchant banker/a nominated investor in the process of market making/subscription to the unsubscribed portion of an issue; **(iv)** any person acquiring shares pursuant to a scheme of safety net; **(v)** a merchant banker acting as a stabilising agent or by the promoter or pre-issue shareholder; **(vi)** by a market-maker of a stock exchange during the course of market making; **(vii)** a bank, acting as a escrow agent; and **(viii)** invocation of pledge by banks or public financial institution as a pledgee.

(c) Acquisition at subsequent stages, by an acquirer who has made a public announcement of an open offer for acquiring shares pursuant to an agreement of disinvestment provided: **(i)** both the acquirer and the seller are the same at all the stages of acquisition; and **(ii)** full disclosures of all the subsequent stages of acquisition have been made in the public announcement of the open offer/the letter of offer.

(d) Acquisition pursuant to a scheme: **(i)** made under the Sick Industrial Companies (Special Provisions) Act; **(ii)** of arrangement involving the target company as a transferor/a transferee company, or reconstruction of the target company, including amalgamation, merger/demerger, pursuant to an order of a court/competent authority under any law/regulation, Indian or foreign; or **(iii)** of arrangement not directly involving the target company as a transferor/transferee company, or reconstruction not involving the target company's undertaking, including amalgamation, merger/demerger, pursuant to an order of a court/competent authority under any law/regulation, Indian or foreign, subject to: **(1)** the component of cash and cash equivalents in the consideration paid being less than 25 per cent of the consideration paid under the scheme; and **(2)** where after implementation of the scheme of arrangement, persons directly/indirectly holding at least 33 per cent of the voting rights in the combined entity are the same as the persons who held the entire voting rights before the implementation of the scheme.

(e) Acquisition pursuant to the provisions of the Securitisation and Reconstruction of Financial Assets and Enforcement of Security Interest Act (SRFAESA);

(f) Acquisition pursuant to the provision of the SEBI Delisting of Equity Shares Regulations.

(g) Acquisition by way of transmission/succession/inheritance.

(h) Acquisition of voting rights/preference shares carrying voting rights arising out of the operation of Section 87(2) of the Companies Act.

(i) Acquisition of shares by the consortium of banks/financial institutions/other secured lenders on conversionof debt under strategic debt restructuring scheme in accordance with the RBI specified guidelines.

(j) Increase in voting rights/pursuant to forfeiture of shares by the target company in compliance with the provisions of the Companies Act.

(2) The acquisition of shares not involving a change of control over the target company, pursuant to a scheme of corporate debt restructuring authorised by the shareholders by way of special resolution passed by postal ballot.

(3) An increase in voting rights in a target company of any shareholder beyond the limit attracting an obligation to make an open offer pursuant to buy-back of shares by the target company provided he reduces his shareholding such that his voting rights fall below the threshold within 90 days from the date of the closure of the buy-back offer.

(4) The following acquisition would be exempt from the obligation to make an open offer:

(a) Acquisition of shares by any shareholder of a target company, up to his entitlement, pursuant to a rights issue;

(b) Acquisition of shares by any shareholder of a target company, beyond his entitlement, pursuant to a right issue, subject to the fulfilment of the following conditions the: **(i)** acquirer has not renounced any of his entitlement; and **(ii)** price at which the rights issue is made is not higher than the *ex-rights* price of the shares of the target company, being the sum of: **(1)** the volume weighted average market price of the shares of the target company during a period of 60 trading days ending on the day prior to the date of determination of the rights issue price, multiplied by the number of shares outstanding prior to the rights issue, divided by the total number of shares outstanding after allotment under the rights issue. The volume weighted average market price should be determined on the basis of trading on the stock exchange where the maximum volume of trading in the shares is recorded during the period; and **(2)** the price at which the shares are offered in the rights issue, multiplied by the number of shares offered in the rights issue divided by the total number of shares outstanding after allotment under the rights issue.

(c) Increase in voting rights in a target company of any shareholder pursuant to buy-back of shares provided that: **(i)** the shareholder has not voted in favour of the resolution authorising the buy-back; **(ii)** in the case of a shareholder resolution, voting is by way of postal ballot; **(iii)** where a resolution of shareholders is not required for the buy-back, the shareholder, in his capacity as a director, or any other interested director has not voted in favour of the resolution of the Board of Directors authorising the buy-back; and **(iv)** the increase in voting rights does not result in an acquisition of control by the shareholder over the target company. Where, however, the aforesaid conditions are not met, in case the shareholder reduces his shareholding such that his voting rights fall below the level at which the obligation to make an open offer would be attracted within 90 days from the date of closure of the buy-back offer by the target company, the shareholder would be exempt from the obligation to make an open offer;

(d) Acquisition of shares in a target company by any person in exchange for shares of another target company tendered pursuant to an open offer for acquiring shares;

(e) Acquisition of shares from State-level financial institutions/their subsidiaries/companies promoted by them, by promoters of the target company pursuant to an agreement between the transferors and the promoter;

(f) Acquisition of shares in a target company from a SEBI-registered venture capital fund/ category I alternative investment fund/foreign venture capital investor by promoters of the target company pursuant to an agreement between them.

(5) In respect of acquisition **(i)** pursuant to *inter se* transfer of shares among qualifying persons, **(ii)** from state-level financial institutions and venture capital funds/foreign venture capital investor, the acquirer should intimate the stock exchanges the details of the proposed acquisition in the specified form at least four working days prior to the proposed acquisition, and the stock exchange should forthwith disseminate the information to the public.

(6) In respect of any acquisition made pursuant to exemption under these regualtions, the acquirer should file a report with the stock exchanges where the shares of the target company are listed, in the specified form within four working days from the acquisition, and the stock exchange should forthwith disseminate such information to the public.

(7) In respect of any acquisition of or increase in voting rights pursuant to exemption pursuant to **(i)** *inter se* transfer, **(ii)** court order, **(iii)** operation of the Companies Act, **(iv)** corporate debt restructuring, **(v)** buy-back and **(vi)** rights issue, the acquirer should, within 21 working days of the date of the acquisition, submit a report in the specified form along with supporting documents to the SEBI giving all details in respect of acquisitions, along with a non-refundable fee of ₹1,50,000.

Exemption by the SEBI The SEBI may, for reasons recorded in writing, grant **(i)** exemption from the obligation to make an open offer for acquiring shares, **(ii)** relaxation from strict compliance with any procedural requirement relating to open offer process and other obligations (**discussed later**) deemed fit in the interests of investors in securities/securities market on being satisfied that: **(a)** the Central/State Government/other regulatory authority has superseded the Board of Directors of the target company and has appointed new directors if the **(i)** Board of Directors has formulated a plan which provides for transparent, open, and competitive process for acquisition of shares/voting rights in, or control over, the target company to secure its smooth and continued operation in the interests of all its stakeholders and the plan does not further the interests of any particular acquirer; **(ii)** conditions and requirements of the competitive process are reasonable and fair and; **(iii)** process provides for details including the time when the open offer for acquiring shares would be made/completed and the manner in which the change in control would be effected; and **(b)** the provisions relating to open offer process and other obligations are likely to act as impediment to the implementation of the plan of the target company and exemption from strict compliance with one/more such provisions is in **(1)** public interest, **(2)** the interests of investors in securities/securities market. For seeking exemption/relaxation, the acquirer/target company should apply to the SEBI together with the non-refundable fee of ₹3,00,000 supported by an affidavit detailing the proposed acquisition and the grounds for the exemption.

Open Offer Process The main elements of the open offer process are: **(i)** manager to the offer, **(ii)** timing, **(iii)** publication, **(iv)** contents, **(v)** filing of letter with SEBI, **(vi)** provision of escrow, **(vii)** other procedures, **(viii)** conditional offer, **(ix)** competing offer, **(x)** payment of consideration, **(xi)** completion of acquisition, and **(xii)** withdrawal of open offer.

Manager to the Open Offer Prior to making a public announcement, the acquirer should appoint a SEBI-registered merchant banker, other than an associate, as the manager to the open offer who should make the public announcement.

Timing The public announcement in terms of its publication and contents should be made on the date of agreeing to acquire shares/voting rights in, or control over the target company. It should be made: **(a)** in the case of market purchases, prior to the placement of the purchase order with the stock broker to acquire the shares, that would take the entitlement to voting rights beyond the stipulated thresholds; **(b)** upon conversion of convertible securities without a fixed date of conversion/depository receipts for the underlying shares of the target company on the same days as the date of exercise of the option to convert such securities into shares; **(c)** upon conversion of convertible securities with a fixed date of conversion on the second working day preceding the scheduled date of conversion of the securities into shares; **(d)** pursuant to a disinvestment on the same day as the date of executing the agreement for acquisition of shares/voting rights in, or control over the target company; **(e)** in the case of indirect acquisition of shares/voting rights in, or control over the target company at any time within four working days from the earlier of, the date on which the primary acquisition is contracted, and the date on which the intention or the decision to make the primary acquisition is announced in the public domain; **(f)** under preferential issue on the date on which the Board of Directors of the target company authorises the preferential issue; **(g)** the public announcement pursuant to an increase in voting rights consequential to a buy-back not qualifying for exemption not later than the ninetieth day from the date of closure of the buy-back offer by the target company; **(h)** pursuant to any acquisition of shares or voting rights in or control over the target company where the specific date on which the title to such shares, voting rights or control is acquired is beyond the control of the acquirer, not later than two working days from the date of receipt of intimation of having acquired the title.

The announcement should be made on the date of the first acquisition if the acquirer discloses in the public announcement the details of the proposed subsequent acquisitions.

The public announcement relating to voluntary offer should be made on the same day on which the acquirer takes the decision to voluntarily make a public announcement of an open offer. A detailed public statement should be published by the acquirer through the manager to the open offer, within five working days of the public announcement and in case of a public announcement relating to indirect acquisition within five working days of the completion of the primary acquisition. In the event the acquirer does not succeed in acquiring the ability to exercise or direct the exercise of voting rights in, or control over, the target company, a detailed public statement of an open offer for acquiring shares would not be required.

Publication The public announcement should be sent to all the concerned stock exchanges, who should forthwith disseminate the information to the public. A copy should be sent to the SEBI and the target company at its registered office within one working day of the date of the public announcement. The detailed public statement should also be published in all editions of any one English national daily with wide circulation, any one Hindi national daily with wide circulation, and any one regional language daily with wide circulation at the place where the registered office of the target company is situated and one regional language daily at the place of the stock exchange where the maximum volume of trading in the shares of the target company are recorded during the 60 trading days preceding the date of the public announcement. Simultaneously, with publication of such detailed public statement in the newspapers, a copy of the same should be sent to: **(i)** the SEBI through the manager to the open offer, **(ii)** all the stock exchange on which the shares of the target company are listed, who should forthwith disseminate the information to the public, and **(iii)** the target company at its registered office to be forthwith circulated to the members of its Board of Directors.

Contents The public announcement should contain the specified information including the following: **(a)** name and identity of the acquirer; **(b)** name and identity of the seller; **(c)** nature of the proposed acquisition such as purchase/allotment of shares, any other means of acquisition of shares/voting rights; **(d)** consideration for the proposed acquisition that attracted the obligation to make an open offer and the price per share; **(e)** the offer price, and mode of payment of consideration; and **(f)** offer size, and conditions as to minimum level of acceptance. The detailed public statement pursuant to public announcement should contain the specified information in order to enable shareholders to make an informed decision with reference to the open offer. The public announcement of the open offer, the detailed public statement, and any other statement, advertisement, circular, brochure, publicity material or letter of offer issued in relation to the acquisition of shares should not omit any relevant information, or contain any misleading information.

Filing of Letter of Offer with the SEBI Within five working days from the date of the detailed public statement, the acquirer should, through the manager to the open offer, file with the SEBI, a draft of the letter of offer, containing the specified information along with a non-refundable fee, as per the following scale:

Consideration payable under the open offer	*Amount*
Up to ten crore rupees	₹1,25,000
More than ten crore rupees, but less than or equal to one thousand crore rupees	₹1,25,000 *plus* 0.025 per cent of the portion of the offer size in excess of ten crore rupees
More than one thousand crore rupees, but less than or equal to five thousand crore rupees	₹1,25,00,000 *plus* 0.03125 per cent of the portion of the offer size in excess of one thousand crore rupees
More than five thousand crore rupees	₹2,50,00,000 *plus* 0.01 per cent of the portion of the offer size in excess of five thousand crore rupees subject to a maximum of three crore rupees

The consideration payable under the open offer should be calculated at the offer price, assuming full acceptance of the open offer, and in the event the open offer is subject to differential pricing, at the highest offer price, irrespective of mode of payment of the consideration. However, in the event of consideration being enhanced owing to a revision to the offer price/size, the payable fees would stand revised accordingly, and paid within five working days from the date of the revision. The manager to the open offer should provide soft copies of the public announcement, the detailed public statement and the draft letter of offer in accordance with the specified specifications and the SEBI would upload the same on its website.

The SEBI should give its comments on the draft letter of offer as expeditiously as possible but not later than fifteen working days of its receipt and in the event of no comments being issued within this period, it would be deemed that the SEBI does not have comments to offer. However, in the event the SEBI has sought clarifications/additional information, the period for issuance of comments would be extended to the fifth working days from the date of receipt of satisfactory reply. If SEBI specifies any changes, the manager to the open offer and the acquirer should carry them out in the letter of offer before dispatch to the shareholders. In the case of competing offers, the SEBI should provide its comments on the draft letter of offer in respect of each competing offer on the same day. In case the disclosures in the draft letter of offer are inadequate, the SEBI may call for a revised letter of offer.

Provision of Escrow Within two working days prior to the date of the detailed public statement of the open offer, the acquirer should create an escrow account towards security for performance of his obligations and deposit amount as per the following scale: **(a)** on the first 500 crore rupees, 25 per cent of the consideration, **(b)** an additional amount equal to 10 per cent of the balance consideration.

Where, however, an offer is made conditional upon minimum level of acceptance, the higher of 100 per cent of the consideration payable in respect of the minimum level of acceptance or 50 per cent under the open offer should be deposited in cash in the escrow account. In case of an upward revision of the offer price/size, the value of the escrow amount should be computed on the revised consideration calculated at the revised offer price, and the additional amount brought into the escrow account prior to effecting the revision. The escrow account may be in the form of **(a)** cash at any bank; **(b)** bank guarantee issued in favour of the manager to the open offer; **(c)** deposit of frequently traded and freely transferable securities with appropriate margin. In case of escrow account by way of a bank guarantee/deposit of securities, the acquirer should also ensure that at least one per cent of the total payable consideration is in cash with a bank as a part of the escrow account. For the escrow account in the form of a cash deposit, the acquirer should empower the manager to the open offer to instruct the bank to issue a banker's cheque/demand draft/make payment of the amounts lying to the credit of the escrow account.

The escrow account in the form of a bank guarantee should be in favour of the manager to the open offer and kept valid throughout the offer period and for an additional period of 30 days after completion of payment of consideration to shareholders who have tendered their shares in acceptance of the open offer. Similarly, the acquirer should empower the manager to the open offer to realise the value of escrow account in the form of securities by sale or otherwise, and if there is any shortfall in the escrow account, he would be liable to make good such shortfall. The manager should not release the escrow account until the expiry of 30 days from the completion of payment of consideration to the concerned shareholders. In case of non-fulfilment of obligations by the acquirer, the SEBI may direct the manager to forfeit in full/part the escrow account/any amounts lying in the special escrow account.

The escrow account deposited with the bank in cash should be released only in the following manner: **(a)** the entire amount to the acquirer upon withdrawal of offer as certified by the manager to the open offer; **(b)** for transfer of an amount not exceeding 90 per cent of the escrow account to special escrow account (**discussed later**); **(c)** to the acquirer, the balance of the escrow account after transfer of cash to the special escrow account, on the expiry of 30 days from the completion of payment of consideration to the concerned shareholders; **(d)** the entire amount to the acquirer upon the expiry of 30 days from the completion of payment of consideration to the concerned shareholders, where the open offer is for exchange of shares/other secured instruments; **(e)** the entire amount to the manager to the open offer, in the event of forfeiture for non-fulfilment of any of the obligations, for distribution after deduction of expenses, if any, of registered market intermediaries associated with the open offer in the following manner: **(i)** one-third to the target company; **(ii)** one-third to the Investor Protection and Education Fund, and **(iii)** one-third to be distributed *pro rata* among the shareholders who have accepted the open offer.

Other Procedures Simultaneously with the filing of the draft letter of offer with the SEBI, the acquirer should send a copy to the target company at its registered office and to all the concerned stock exchanges. It should be dispatched to the shareholders whose names appear on the register of members of the target company as of the **identified date** (i.e. date falling on the tenth working prior to the commencement of the tendering period for the purpose of determining the shareholders to whom letter of offer would be sent), not later than seven working days from the receipt of comments from the SEBI or where no comments are offered within seven working days from the expiry of the period. However, where local laws/regulations of any jurisdiction outside India may expose the acquirer/the target company to material risk of civil, regulatory/criminal liabilities in the event the letter of offer in its final form were to be sent without material amendments or modifications into such jurisdiction, and the shareholders resident in such jurisdiction hold shares entitling them to less than 5 per cent of the voting rights of the target company, the acquirer may refrain from dispatch of the letter of offer into such jurisdiction. Moreover, every person holding shares, regardless of whether he held shares on the identified date or has not received the letter of offer, would be entitled to tender such shares in acceptance of the open offer. Simultaneously, the acquirer should send the letter of offer to the custodian of shares underlying depository receipts, if any, of the target company. Irrespective of whether a competing offer has been made, an acquirer may make upward revisions to the offer price/the number of shares sought to be acquired under the open offer, at any time prior to the commencement of the last three working days before the commencement of the tendering period. In case of any revision of the open offer (i.e. offer price/size), the acquirer should: **(a)** make corresponding increases to the amount kept in escrow account and make an announcement in respect of the revisions in all the newspapers in which the detailed public statement was made; and **(b)** simultaneously inform the SEBI, all the concerned stock exchanges and the target company at its registered office.

The acquirer should disclose during the offer period every acquisition made by him of any shares of the target company in the specified form to each of the concerned stock exchanges/ the target company at it registered office within 24 hours of the acquisition, and the stock exchanges should forthwith disseminate the information to the public. He should facilitate tendering of shares by the shareholders and its settlement through the SEBI specified stock exchange mechanism.

However, he would not acquire/sell any shares of the target company during the period between three working days prior to the commencement of, and until the expiry of, the tendering period.

The acquirer should issue an advertisement in the specified form one working day before the commencement of the tendering period, announcing the schedule of activities for the open offer, the status of statutory and other approvals, if any, whether for the acquisition attracting the obligation to make an open offer or for the open offer, unfulfilled conditions, if any, and their status, the procedure for tendering acceptances and such other specified material detail. The advertisement should be: **(a)** published in all the newspapers in which the detailed public statement was made; and **(b)** simultaneously sent to the SEBI, all the concerned stock exchanges and the target company at its registered office.

The tendering period should start within 12 working days from date of receipt of comments from the SEBI and remain open for 10 working days. Shareholders who have tendered shares in acceptance of the open offer would not be entitled to withdraw their acceptance during the tendering period.

The acquirer should, within 10 working days from the last date of the tendering period, complete all the legal requirements relating to the open offer including payment of consideration to the concerned shareholders. He would be responsible to pursue all required statutory approvals in order to complete the open offer without any default/neglect/delay. Where, however, the acquirer is unable to make the payment to the concerned shareholders within such period owing to non-receipt of statutory approvals, the SEBI may, where it is satisfied that such non-receipt was not attributable to any wilful default failure/neglect on the part of the acquirer to diligently pursue such approvals, grant extension of time for making payments, together with interest to the shareholders for the delay at the specified rate. Where the statutory approval extends to some but not all shareholders, the acquirer would have the option to make payment to shareholders in respect of whom no statutory approvals are required in order to complete the open offer.

The acquirer should issue a post-offer advertisement in the specified form within 5 working days after the offer period, giving details including aggregate number of shares tendered/accepted, date of payment of consideration. The advertisement should be: **(i)** published in all the newspapers in which the detailed public statement was made; and **(ii)** simultaneously sent to the SEB, all the concerned stock exchanges and the target company at its registered office.

Conditional Offer An acquirer may make an open offer conditional as to the minimum level of acceptance. Where, however, the open offer is pursuant to an agreement, the agreement should contain a condition to the effect that in the event the desired level of acceptance of the open offer is not received, the acquirer would not acquire any shares and the agreement attracting the obligation to make the open offer stand rescinded. In case of conditional offer, the acquirer should not acquire, during the offer period, any shares in the target company except under the open offer and any underlying agreement pursuant to which the open offer is made.

Conditional Offer is an open offer conditional as to the minimum level of acceptance.

Competing Offers Upon a public announcement of an open offer, any person would be entitled to a make a public announcement of an open offer within 15 working days of the date of the detailed public statement made by the acquirer. The open offer should be for such number of shares which when taken together with shares held by such acquirer would be at least equal to the holding of the acquirer who has made the first public announcement. Such open offer would not be regarded as a voluntary open offer. Every open offer and open offer first made would be regarded as competing offers.

Competing offers every open offer and open offer first made would be regarded as competing offers.

No person would be entitled to make a public announcement of an open offer enter into any transaction that would attract the obligation to make a public announcement of an open offer after 15 working days of the date of the detailed public announcement and until the expiry of the offer period for such open offer. Unless the open offer first made is conditional, an acquirer cannot make a competing offer conditional as to the minimum level of acceptances. A public announcement of an open offer to acquire shares, or enter into any transaction that would attract the obligation to make a public announcement of an open offer cannot be made until the expiry of the offer period where the open offer is **(a)** for acquisition of shares pursuant to disinvestment, **(b)** pursuant to a relaxation from strict compliance with the open offer process and other obligations granted by the SEBI. The schedule of activities and the tendering period for all competing offers should be carried out with identical timelines and the last date for tendering shares in acceptance of the every competing offer should stand revised to the last date for tendering shares in acceptance of the competing offer last made.

Upon the public announcement of the competing offers, an acquirer who had made a preceding competing offer would be entitled to revise his open offer with more favourable terms to the shareholders of the target company. The acquirers making the competing offers would be entitled to make upward revisions of the offer price at any time up to 3 working days prior to the commencement of the tendering period. Except for these variations, all the provisions of the SEBI code would apply to every competing offer.

Payment of Consideration In case of consideration payable in cash, the acquirer should open a special escrow account with a SEBI-registered banker to an issue and deposit therein, such sum as would, together with cash transferred to the escrow account, make up the entire sum due and payable to the shareholders as consideration payable under the open offer, and empower the manager to the offer to operate the special escrow account on his behalf. The acquirer should complete payment of consideration whether in the form of cash or by issue, exchange or transfer of securities, to the concerned shareholders, within 10 working days of the expiry of the tendering period. Unclaimed balances, if any, lying to the credit of the special escrow account at the end of 7 years from the date of deposit would be transferred to the Investor Protection and Education Fund.

Completion of Acquisition The acquirer should not complete the acquisition of shares or voting rights in, or control over, the target company, whether by way of subscription to shares or a purchase of shares attracting the obligation to make an open offer for acquiring shares, until the expiry of the offer period. In case of an offer made pursuant to a preferential allotment, the offer should be completed within 15 days from the date of passing of the resolution for preferential allotment. In case of delisting offer, the acquirer should complete the acquisition of shares only after making the public announcement regarding the success of the delisting proposal. Subject to the acquirer depositing in the escrow account, cash of an amount equal to 100 per cent of the consideration payable under the open offer assuming full acceptance of the open offer, the parties to such agreement may after the expiry of 21 working days from the date of detailed public statement, act upon the agreement and the acquirer may complete the acquisition of shares/voting rights in, or control over, the target company as contemplated.

The acquirer should complete the acquisition contracted under any agreement attracting the obligation to make an open offer not later than 26 weeks from the expiry of the offer period. In the event of any extraordinary and supervening circumstances rendering it impossible to complete the acquisition within this period, the SEBI may, for reasons to be published, may grant an extension of time by such period as it may deem fit in the interests of investors in securities/securities market.

Withdrawal of Open Offer An open offer once made can not be withdrawn except under any of the following circumstances: **(a)** Refusal of statutory approvals required for the open offer to acquire shares or for effecting the acquisitions attracting the obligation to make an open offer; **(b)** the acquirer, being a natural person, has died; **(c)** any condition stipulated in the agreement for acquisition attracting the obligation to make the open offer is not met for reasons outside the reasonable control of the acquirer, and such agreement is rescinded provided such conditions were specifically disclosed in the detailed public statement and the letter of offer. However, the acquirer cannot withdraw the open offer even if the proposed acquisition through the preferential issue is not successful; and **(d)** such circumstances, as in the opinion of the SEBI, merit withdrawal.

In case of withdrawal of the open offer, the acquirer should through the manager to the open offer, within two working days: **(a)** make an announcement in the same newspapers in which the public announcement was published, providing the grounds and reasons for withdrawal of the open offer; and **(b)** simultaneously inform in writing: **(i)** the SEBI, **(ii)** all the concerned stock exchanges, who should forthwith disseminate the information to the public, and **(iii)** the target company at its registered office.

Other Obligations The other obligations relate to: **(i)** directors of the target company, **(ii)** acquirer, **(iii)** target company, and **(iv)** manager to the offer.

Directors of the Target Company During the offer period, no person representing the acquirer should be appointed as director on the board of directors of the target company. After an initial period of 15 working days from the date of detailed public statement, appointment of persons representing him on the Board of Directors may, however, be effected in case the acquirer deposits in the escrow account, 100 per cent of the consideration payable under the open offer in cash. Where the acquirer has made conditional offer, no director representing him may be appointed to the Board of Directors of the target company during the offer period unless he has waived/attained such conditions and complies with the requirement of deposits cash in the escrow account.

In case of conditional offer, the acquirer, regardless of the size of the cash deposited in the escrow account, would not be entitled to appoint any director representing during the offer period. During the pendency of competing offers, regardless of the size of the cash deposited by an acquirer in the escrow account, there would be no induction of any new director to the Board of Directors of the target company. In case of death or incapacitation of any director, the vacancy may be filled by any person subject to approval by shareholders of the target company by way of a postal ballot. In the event the acquirer is already represented by a director, he would not participate in any deliberation of the Board of Directors of the target company/vote on any matter in relation to the open offer.

Obligations of the Acquirer Prior to making the public announcement, the acquirer should ensure that **(i)** firm financial arrangements have been made for fulfilling the payment obligations under the open offer and **(ii)** he is able to implement the open offer, subject to the necessary statutory approvals. In case he has not declared an intention in the detailed public statement and the letter of offer to alienate any material assets of the target company/its subsidiaries whether by way of sale, lease, encumbrance or otherwise outside the ordinary course of business, he would be debarred from causing such alienation after acquiring control for two years after the offer period. In the event the target company/its subsidiary(ies) is required to alienate the assets despite not expressing the intention to alienate by the acquirer, the alienation would require a special resolution passed by shareholders of the target company, by way of postal ballot and the notice for which should, *inter alia*, contain reasons as to why the alienation is necessary.

The acquirer should ensure that the contents of the public announcement, the detailed public statement, the letter of offer and the post-offer advertisement are true, fair and adequate in all material aspects and not misleading in any material particular, and are based on reliable sources, and state the source wherever necessary. He should not sell shares of the target company held by them, during the offer period. He would be jointly and severally responsible for fulfillment of applicable obligations.

Obligations of the Target Company Upon a public announcement of an open offer for acquiring shares of a target company being made, the Board of Directors of the target company should ensure that during the offer period, its business is conducted in the ordinary course consistent with past practice. Unless the approval of shareholders of the target company by way of a special resolution by postal ballot is obtained, the Board of Directors of the target company/any of its subsidiaries during the offer period would not **(A)** **(i)** alienate any material assets whether by way of sale, lease, encumbrance or otherwise or enter into any agreement; **(ii)** effect any material borrowings outside the ordinary course of business; **(B)** issue/allot any authorised but unissued securities entitling the holder to voting rights. However, the target company/its subsidiaries may issue/allot shares **(i)** **(a)** upon conversion of convertible securities issued prior to the public announcement of the open offer, in accordance with pre-determined terms of conversions, **(b)** pursuant to any public issue in respect of which the red herring prospectus has been filed with the Registrar of Companies prior to the public announcement of the open offer or **(c)** pursuant to any rights issue in respect of which the record date has been announced prior to the public announcement of the open offer **(C)** implement any buy-back of shares/effect any other change in the capital structure of the target company; **(D)** enter into, amend/terminate any material contracts to which the target company or any of its subsidiaries is a party, outside the ordinary course of business, whether such contract is with a related party, within the meaning of the term under applicable accounting principles, or with any other persons; and **(E)** accelerate any contingent vesting of a right of any person to whom the target company or any of its subsidiaries may have an obligation to acquire shares of the target company by way of employee stock options or otherwise.

In any general meeting of a subsidiary of the target company in respect of the above matters, the target company/its subsidiaries should vote in a manner consistent with the special resolution passed by the shareholders of the target company. The target company would be prohibited from fixing any record date for a corporate action on or after the third working day prior to the announcement of, and until the expiry of, the tendering period. It should furnish to the acquirer within two working days from the identified date, a list of shareholders as per the register of its members containing names, addresses, shareholding and folio number, in electric form and a list of persons whose applications for registration of transfer of shares are pending. The acquirer should, however, reimburse reasonable costs payable by the target company to external agencies in order to furnish such information.

Upon receipt of the detailed public statement, the Board of Directors of the target company should constitute a committee of independent directors to provide reasoned recommendations on the open offer, and the target company should publish them. The committee would be entitled to seek external professional advice at the expense of the target company. The committee should provide its written reasoned recommendations on the open offer to the shareholders of the target company which should be published in the specified form, at least two working days before the commencement of the tendering period, in the same newspaper where the public announcement of the open offer was published, and simultaneously, a copy of the same should be sent to: **(i)** the SEBI, **(ii)** all the concerned stock exchanges, who should forthwith disseminate the information to the public, and **(iii)** to the manger to the open offer, and where there are competing offers, to the manager to the open offer for every competing offer.

The Board of Directors of the target company should **(i)** facilitate the acquirer in verification of shares tendered in acceptance of the open offer, **(ii)** make available to all acquirers making competing offers, any information and co-operation provided to any acquirer who has made a competing offer.

Upon fulfilment by the acquirer of the required conditions, the Board of Directors of the target company should without any delay register the transfer of shares acquired by him in physical form, whether under the agreement or from open market purchases, or pursuant to the open offer.

Obligations of the Manager to the Open Offer Prior to public announcement being made, the manager to the open offer should ensure that **(a)** the acquirer is able to implement the open offer; and **(b)** firm arrangements for funds through verifiable means have been made by him to meet the payment obligations under the open offer. He should also ensure that the contents of the public announcement, the detailed public statement, the letter of offer and the post-offer advertisement are true, fair and adequate in all material aspects, not misleading in any material particular, are based on reliable sources, state the source wherever necessary, and are in compliance with the requirements under these regulations. Further, he should **(i)** furnish to the SEBI a due diligence certificate along with the draft letter of offer, **(ii)** ensure that market intermediaries engaged for the purposes of the open offer are SEBI-registered, **(iii)** exercise diligence, care and professional judgment to ensure compliance with these regulations, **(iv)** not deal on his own account in the shares of the target company during the offer period, **(v)** file a report with the SEBI within 15 working days from the expiry of the tendering period, in the specified form, confirming status of completion of various open offer requirements.

Disclosure of Shareholding and Control These relate to **(i)** disclosure related provisions, **(ii)** continual disclosures and **(iii)** disclosure of encumbered shares.

Disclosure-related Provisions The disclosures should be of the aggregate shareholding/voting rights of the acquirer/promoter of the target company/every person acting in concert with him. The acquisition/holding of any convertible security should also be regarded as shares and disclosed accordingly. Upon receipt of these disclosures, the stock exchange(s) should forthwith disseminate them.

Disclosure of Acquisition and Disposal The acquirers should disclose their aggregate shareholding and voting rights in the target company in the specified form. He should disclose every acquisition/

disposal of its shares of representing 2 per cent or more of the shares/voting rights in the specified form. These disclosures should be made within two working days of the receipt of intimation of allotment of shares/the acquisition of shares/voting rights in the target company to **(a)** every concerned stock exchange; and **(b)** the target company at its registered office.

Shares taken by way of encumbrance including pledge/lien or any such transaction should be treated as an acquisition while shares given upon release of encumbrance should be treated as a disposal, and disclosures should be made accordingly in the specified form. However, such requirement would not apply to a bank/public financial institution as pledgee in connection with a pledge of shares for securing indebtedness in the ordinary course of business.

Continual Disclosures Every person, who together with persons acting in concert with him, holds shares or voting rights entitling him to exercise 25 per cent or more of the voting rights, should disclose their aggregate shareholding and voting rights as of the thirty-first day of March, in such target company in the specified form. The promoter of should together with persons acting in concert with him, disclose their aggregate shareholding and voting rights as of the thirty-first of March, in such target company in the specified form. These disclosure should be made within seven working days from the end of each financial year to **(a)** every concerned stock exchange; and **(b)** the target company at its registered office.

Disclosure of Encumbered Shares The promoter of every target company should disclose details of their shares encumbered by him/persons acting in concert with him in the specified form. He should also disclose details of any invocation/release of encumbrance of share in the specified form. These disclosures should be made within seven working days from the creation/invocation/release of encumbrance to, **(a)** every concerned stock exchange; and **(b)** the target company at its registered office.

Miscellaneous *Power to Issue Direction* The SEBI may, in interest of investors in securities/securities market, issue such directions for violation of these regulations as it deems fit including: **(a)** Disinvestment of shares acquired; **(b)** Transfer of the shares, or any proceeds of a directed sale of shares, to the Investor Protection and Education Fund; **(c)** The target company/any depository not to give effect to any transfer of shares acquired; **(d)** The acquirer/any person acting in concert/any nominee or proxy not to exercise any voting or other rights attached to the shares acquired; **(e)** Debarring any person from accessing the capital market or dealing in securities for such period as may be directed, having regard to the nature and gravity of the violations; **(f)** The acquirer to make an open offer for acquiring shares of the target company at such offer price as determined by the SEBI; **(g)** The acquirer not to cause, and the target company not to effect, any disposal of assets of the target company or any of its subsidiaries contrary to the contents of the letter of offer, where the conditions set out are not met; **(h)** The acquirer who has failed to make an open offer or has delayed making of an open offer, to make the open offer and to pay interest at such rate as considered appropriate by the SEBI along with the offer price; **(i)** The acquirer who has failed to make payment of the open offer consideration to shareholders, not to make any open offer or enter into any transaction that would attract the obligation to make an open offer in respect of shares of any target company for such period as the SEBI may deem fit; **(j)** The acquirer who has made an open offer but has delayed making payment of the consideration to shareholders, to pay interest at such rate as considered appropriate by the SEBI for the delayed period; **(k)** Any person to cease and desist from exercising control acquired over any target company without complying with the specified requirements; **(l)** Divestiture of such number of shares as would result in the shareholding of an acquirer and persons acting in concert with him being limited to the maximum permissible non-public shareholding or below.

In any proceedings, the SEBI would comply with the principles of natural justice before issuing directions to any person. It may, for failure to carry out the requirements of these regulations by any registered intermediary, initiate appropriate proceedings in accordance with the applicable regulations.

Hostile Takeover

Strategies The acquirer company can use any of the following techniques aimed at taking over the target company.

Street Sweep This technique requires that the acquirer should accumulate large amounts of stock in a company before making an open offer. The advantage is that the target firm is left with no choice but to give in.

Bear Hug In this case, the acquirer puts pressure on the management of the target company by threatening to make an open offer. The board capitulates straightaway and agrees to a settlement with the acquirer for change of control.

Strategic Alliance This strategy involves disarming the opposition by offering a partnership rather than a buyout. The acquirer should assert control from within and takeover the target company.

Brand Power This implies entering into an alliance with powerful brands to displace the partner's brands and, as a result, buy out the weakened company.

Defensive Strategies The target company can also use one of the following strategies to defend itself against the attack mounted by the acquiring company in its bid for open market takeover.

Poison Pill This strategy involves issue of low price preferential shares to existing shareholders to enlarge the capital base. This would make hostile takeover too expensive.

Poison Put In this case, the target company can issue bonds that encourage holders to cash in at high prices. The resultant cash drainage would make the target unattractive.

Greenmail In this strategy, the target company should repurchase the shares cornered by the raider. The profits made by the raider are after all akin to blackmail and this would keep the raider at a distance from the target.

Pac-man Defence This strategy aims at the target company making a counter bid for the raider's company. This would force the raider to defend himself and consequently call off his raid.

White Knight In order to repel the move of the raider, the target company can make an appeal to a friendly company to buy the whole, or part, of the company. The understanding is that the friendly buyer promises not to dislodge the management of the target company.

White Squire This strategy is essentially the same as White Knight and involves sell out of shares to a company that is not interested in the takeover. As a consequence, the management of the target company retains its control over the company.

Evidently, hostile takeovers, as far as possible, should be avoided as they are more difficult to consummate; in other words, friendly takeovers are better forms of corporate restructuring.

LO 32.5 OTHER FORMS OF CORPORATE RESTRUCTURING

Financial restructuring, divestitures/demergers and buyouts are some of the other common forms used by firms for corporate restructuring. These forms of corporate restructuring are explained below.

Financial Restructuring

In the case of mergers/acquisitions/takeover and amalgamation types of corporate restructuring, the potential acquiring firm has to deal with the management and/or shareholders of the other firm(s). Financial restructuring, on the other hand, is carried out internally in the firm with the consent of its various stakeholders. This form of corporate restructuring is relatively more easy to put to ground.

Financial restructuring is a suitable mode of restructuring of corporate firms that have incurred/accumulated sizable losses for/over a number of years. As a sequel, the share capital of such firms, in many cases, gets substantially eroded/lost; in fact, in some cases, accumulated losses over the years may be more than share capital, causing negative net worth. Given such a dismal state of financial affairs, a vast majority of such firms are likely to have a dubious potential for liquidation. Can some of these firms be revived? Financial restructuring is one such a measure for the revival of only those firms that hold promise/prospects for better financial performance in the years to come. To achieve the desired objective, such firms warrant/merit a restart with a fresh balance sheet, which does not contain past accumulated losses and fictitious assets and shows share capital at its real/true worth.

Restructuring Scheme Financial restructuring is achieved by formulating an appropriate restructuring scheme involving a number of legal formalities (including consent of the court and consent of the affected stakeholders, say, creditors, lenders and shareholders). It is normal for equity shareholders to make the maximum sacrifice, followed by preference shares and debentureholders/lenders and creditors, respectively. The sacrifice is in terms of waiver of a part of the sum payable to various liability-holders. The sacrifice may be also be in terms of acceptance of new securities with a lower coupon rate, with a view to reduce the future financial burden on the firm. The arrangement may also take the form of conversion of debt into equity; sometimes, creditors, apart from reducing their claim, may also agree to convert their dues into securities to avert pressure of payment. As a result of all these measures, the firm may have better liquidity to work with. Thus, financial restructuring implies a significant change in the financial/capital structure of firms, leading to a change in the payment of fixed financial charges and change in the pattern of ownership and control.

In brief, financial restructuring (also referred to as internal reconstruction) aims at reducing the debt/payment burden of the firm. The aggregate sum resulting **(a)** from the reduction/waiver in the claims from various liability-holders and **(b)** profit accruing from the appreciation of assets such as land and buildings is then utilised to write off accumulated losses and fictitious assets (such as preliminary expenses and cost of issue of shares and debentures) and create provision for bad and doubtful debts and downward revaluation of certain assets, say, plant and machinery, if they are overstated. In practice, the financial restructuring scheme is drawn in such a way so that all the above requirements of write-off are duly met. The financial restructuring scheme is illustrated in Example 32.8.

Example **32.8**

Following is the balance sheet of Weak Limited as on March 31, current year

(₹ lakh)

Liabilities	*Amount*	*Assets*	*Amount*
Equity capital (5,00,000 shares)	500	Land and building	180
13% Preference shares (₹100 each)	100	Plant and machinery	220
12.5% Debentures	200	Furniture	30
Debenture interest payable	25	Stock	120
Bank loan	75	Sundry debtors	50
Trade creditors	300	Cash at bank	5
		Preliminary expenses	10
		Cost of issue of debentures	5
		Profit and loss account	580
	1,200		1,200

The company suffered heavy losses and was not getting on well. Now, it feels that the worst is over and that it holds the potential of earning profits in the future. To ensure better future functioning, the company adopts the following scheme of reconstruction:

(i) Equity shares are to be reduced to ₹25 per share, fully paid up.

(ii) Preference shares are to be reduced (with coupon rate of 11%) to equal number of shares of ₹50 each, fully paid up.

(iii) Debentureholders agree to forgo outstanding interest. They have also agreed to accept new debentures carrying 10 per cent interest.

(iv) Trade creditors have agreed to forgo 25 per cent of their existing claims.

(v) To make payment of the bank loan and augment the working capital, the company issues 5 lakh equity shares at ₹25 each; payable on application. The existing shareholders have agreed to subscribe to the new issue.

(vi) While land and building is to be revalued at ₹300 lakh, plant and machinery is to be written down to ₹175 lakh. A provision amounting to ₹5 lakh is to be made for bad and doubtful debts.

You are required to show the impact of financial restructuring/reconstruction. Also draw the new balance sheet assuming the scheme of reconstruction is executed.

Solution

Impact of Financial Restructuring (₹ lakh)

(I) Benefits to Weak Limited	
(a) Reduction of liabilities payable	
Reduction in equity share capital (5 lakh shares × ₹75 per share)	₹375
Reduction in preference share capital (1 lakh shares × ₹50 per share)	50
Waiver of outstanding debenture interest	25
Waiver from trade creditors (₹300 lakh × 0.25)	75
	525
(b) Revaluation of assets	
Appreciation of land and building (₹300 lakh – ₹180 lakh)	120
(c) Total sum available to write off fictitious assets and over-valued assets	645
(II) Amount (₹645 lakh) Utilised to Write off Losses, Fictitious Assets and Over-valued Assets	
Writing off profit and loss account	₹580
Cost of issue of debentures	5
Preliminary expenses	10
Provision for bad and doubtful debts	5
Revaluation of plant and machinery (₹220 lakh – ₹175 lakh)	45
	645

Balance Sheet of Weak Limited as at ... (After Reconstruction) *(₹ lakh)*

Liabilities	*Amount*	*Assets*		*Amount*
Equity capital (₹25 each)	250	Land and building		300
11% Preference shares (₹50 each)	50	Plant and machinery		175
10% Debentures	200	Furniture		30
Trade creditors	225	Stock		120
		Sundry debtors	₹50	
		Less: Provision	5	45
		Cash at bank		55*
	725			725

*Opening balance, ₹5 lakh + Sale proceeds from issue of new equity shares, ₹125 lakh – Payment of bank loan, ₹75 lakh.

In sum, financial restructuring is unique in nature and company specific. It is carried out, in practice, when all the stakeholders are prepared to sacrifice and are convinced that the restructured firm (reflecting true value of assets, capital and other significant financial parameters) can now be put back on the profit track. This type of corporate restructuring helps in the revival of firms that otherwise would have faced closure/liquidation.

Divestitures/Demergers

Unlike the merger in which all assets are sold, a **divestiture/demerger** involves selling of some of the assets only. These assets may be in the form of a plant, division, product line, subsidiary and so on. Although divestiture causes contraction from the perspective of selling firm, it may not, however, entail decrease in its profits. On the contrary, it is believed by the selling firm that its value will be enhanced by parting/divesting/demerging some of its assets/divisions/operating units (as they are either causing losses or yielding very low returns). By selling such unproductive/non-performing assets and utilising cash proceeds in expanding/rejuvenating other leftover assets/operating units, the firm is likely to augment the profits of the demerged/divesting firm. Evidently, the motive for demerger or divestiture is often positive. As Gitman aptly states, the motives for divestiture is to generate cash for the expansion of other product lines, to get rid of a poorly performing operation, to streamline the corporate firm, or to restructure the company's business consistent with its strategic goals[10].

> **Demerger (divestiture)** is a form of corporate restructuring which involves sale of only some assets of the firm.

> **Reverse synergy** implies that the assets/units which are demerged are of more worth to other firms than the firm itself.

Evidently, divestiture enables the selling firm to have a more lean and focussed operation. This, in turn, is likely to augment its efficiency as well as profitability and help in creating more value for its shareholders. In other words, it implies that the operating units are worth much more to other firms than to the firm itself. In technical terms, it is aptly referred to as **reverse synergy** in that the value of the parts is greater than the whole.

> **Reverse capital budgeting** is the capital budgeting in which cash inflows on account of demerger occur at time zero and the cash outflows are in terms of sacrifice associated with the transfer of the division/asset.

Financial Evaluation For the purpose of financial evaluation, the divestiture/demerger decision can be considered akin to **reverse capital budgeting** decision in that the selling firm receives cash by divesting an asset, say a division of the firm, and these cash inflows received are then compared with the present value of the CFAT sacrificed on account of parting of a division/asset. In other words, it has cash inflows in time zero period. For future years, it has been deprived of cash inflows after taxes (CFAT), which the division would have generated. Given the basic conceptual framework of capital budgeting, Format 32.3 contains the steps involved in assessing whether the divestiture decision is profitable for the selling firm or not.

FORMAT 32.3 Financial Evaluation of Divestiture/Demerger Decision

(a) Decrease in CFAT due to sale of division (for years 1,2......n)	______
(b) Multiply by appropriate present value factor (as per cost of capital) relevant to division (given its risk level)	______
(c) Decrease in present value of the selling firm ($a \times b$)	______
(d) *Less:* Present value of obligations related to the liabilities of the division (assuming liabilities are also transferred with the sale of a division which is normal)	______
(e) Present value lost due to sale of division ($c - d$)	______

The decision criterion is that the selling firm should go for divestiture/demerger, if its divestiture proceeds received from selling the division are more than the present value the demerged division otherwise would have provided; in case the present value lost due to sale of division is greater than the sale proceeds obtained from it, the firm should not go for divestiture/demerger.

Methods of Demerger/Divestiture Demerger/divestiture is normally accomplished either by an outright sale of an operating unit/division/asset to another firm or through a **spin-off**. A spin-off requires creation of a new, separate, corporate firm; the shares of the newly created legal entity are distributed on a *pro rata* basis to existing shareholders of the parent company; such a distribution enables the existing shareholders to maintain the same proportion of ownership in the newly created firm as they had in the original firm[11]. As a sequel, the newly created entity becomes an independent company, taking its own decisions and developing its own policies and strategies, which need not necessarily be the same as those of the parent company. In brief, the firm acts as a separate business entity. However, spin-off, like outright sale, does not bring any cash to the parent company.

Spin-off is a method for demerger through creation of a separate firm.

A variation of spin-off is the **split-up**. In broad terms, the split-up involves the breaking up of the entire firm in a series of spin-offs (in terms of newly created separate legal entities) so that the parent firm no longer exists and only the new offspring survive[12]. For instance, a corporate firm has 4 divisions, namely, A, B, C and D; a decision to split-up implies that four new corporate firms (with autonomous and separate legal status) are to be formed to takeover, say, one division each and the original corporate firm is to be wound up. Since demerged units are relatively smaller in size, they are logistically more conveniently managed. Therefore, it is expected that spin-offs and split-ups are likely to enhance efficiency and may prove instrumental in achieving better performance.

Split-up is a method for demerger through breaking-up of the firm in a series of spin-offs.

Annexure 4 below contains the salient features of the scheme of reverse merger of ICICI Ltd with ICICI Bank Ltd.

Annexure 4 Reverse Merger of ICICI Ltd with ICICI Bank Ltd

The ICICI Ltd was one of the leading development/public financial institutions [D/P FIs]. It had sponsored a large number of subsidiaries including the ICICI Bank Ltd. The RBI permitted D/P FIs to transform themselves into banks in 2002. As a bank, ICICI Ltd would have access to low-cost (demand) deposits and could offer a wide range of products and services and greater opportunities for earning non-fund-based income in the form of fee/commission. The ICICI Bank Ltd also considered various strategic alternatives in the context of the emerging competitive scenario in Indian banking. It identified a large capital base and size and scale of operations as key success factors. The ICICI Ltd and its two other subsidiaries, namely, ICICI Capital Services Ltd (ICICI Capital) and ICICI Personnel Financial Services Ltd (ICICI PFs) amalgamated in reserve merger with the ICICI Bank in view of its significant shareholding and the strong business synergies between them. As a financial institution, ICICI Ltd was offering a wide range of products and services to corporate and retail customers in India through a number of business operations, subsidiaries and affiliates. The ICICI PFs, a subsidiary of ICICI, was acting as a focal point for marketing, distribution and servicing the retail product portfolio of ICICI including auto/commercial vehicle loans, credit cards, consumer loans and so on. The ICICI Capital was engaged in sale and distribution of various financial and investment products like bonds, fixed deposits, Demat services, mutual funds and so on. The appointed date for the merger was March 30, 2002. The effective date of merger was May 3, 2002.

The (reverse) merger of ICICI Ltd and two of its subsidiaries with ICICI Bank has combined two organisations with complementary strengths and products and similar processes and operating structure. The merger has combined the large capital base of ICICI Ltd with strong deposit raising capacity of ICICI Bank, giving ICICI Bank improved ability to increase its market share in banking fee and commission while lowering the overall cost of funding through access to lower-cost retail deposits. The ICICI Bank would now be able to fully leverage the strong corporate relationship that ICICI has built seamlessly, providing the whole range of financial products and services to corporate clients. The merger has also resulted in the integration of the retail financial operations of the ICICI and its two merging subsidiaries and ICICI Banks into one entity, creating an optimum structure for the retail business and allowing the full range of assets and liability products to be offered to retail customers.

As per the scheme of amalgamation (reverse merger) approved by the High Court of Gujarat and the High Court of Mumbai in March/April 2002, the (consideration) exchange ratio for the merger was one fully paid-up equity share of ₹10 of ICICI Bank for two fully paid-up equity shares of the ICICI Ltd of the face value of ₹10 each. No shares were issued pursuant to the amalgamation of ICICI PFS and ICICI Capital. The exchange ratio was determined on the basis of a comprehensive valuation process incorporating international best practices, carried out by two separate financial advisors (JM Morgan Stanley and DSP Merril Lynch) and an independent accounting firm (Deloitte, Haskins and Sells).

The equity shares of the ICICI Bank held by ICICI Ltd were transferred to a trust, to be divested by appropriate placement. The proceeds of such divestment would accrue to the merged entity.

The ICICI Bank has issued to the holders of preference shares of ₹1 crore each of ICICI, one preference share of ₹1 crore fully-paid up on the same terms and conditions.

With respect to stock options issued by the ICICI to its Directors/employees, which have not been exercised/are outstanding, the options in ICICI Bank in the ratio of one equity share of ₹10 each for every two equity shares of ₹10 each granted in ICICI Ltd would be issued. The exercise price would be twice the price paid by the directors/employees for the exercise of ICICI stock options.

As both ICICI Ltd and ICICI Bank were listed in India and U.S. markets, effective communication to a wide range of investors was a critical part of the merger process. It was equally important to communicate the rationale for the merger to domestic and international institutional lenders and to rating agencies. The merger process was required to satisfy legal and regulatory procedures in India, as well as to comply with the U.S. Securities and Exchange Commission requirements under U.S. securities laws.

The merger also involved significant accounting complexities. In accordance with the best practices in accounting, the merger has been accounted for under the purchase method of accounting under the Indian GAAPs. Consequently, ICICI's assets have been fair-valued for their incorporation in the books of accounts. The fair value of ICICI's loan portfolio was determined by an independent valuer while its equity and related investment portfolio was fair-valued by determining its mark-to-market value. The total additional provisions and write-offs required to reflect the fair value of the ICICI's assets have de-risked the loan and investment portfolios and created a significant cushion in the balance sheet while maintaining healthy levels of capital adequacy.

The merger was approved by the shareholders of both companies in January 2002, by the Gujarat and Mumbai High Courts in March/April 2002.

Buyouts

Buyouts constitute yet another form of corporate restructuring. In the corporate world, **Management buyouts** (MBOs) are the more usual modes of acquisition. The MBO involves the sale of the existing firm to the management. The management may be from the same firm or may be form outside (entrepreneurs) or may assume a hybrid form (i.e., the management may be of the existing firm as well as from outside).

Management buyout is sale of the existing firm to the management.

In general, when the potential acquiring management team may not/does not have adequate financial resources of its own to pay the acquisition price, it seeks financial support from other sources, say, investors, institutions, venture funds, banks and so on. When finance is made/arranged by outside investors, it is normal for them to secure representation on the board of the corporate. In cases when debt forms a substantial part of the total financing from outsiders, the buyout transaction is appropriately referred to as a leveraged buyout (LBO). According to Emery and Finnerty, a **leveraged buyout** is an acquisition that is financed principally, sometime more than 90 per cent, by borrowing on a secured basis[13].

Leveraged buyout implies acquisition of a firm that is financed principally by borrowing on a secured basis.

Since LBOs cause substantial financial risk, it is desired that LBO acquisitions/ firms should have a relatively low degree of operating/business risk. LBOs will not be a suitable form of corporate restructuring if the acquired firm already has a high degree of business risk. Further, to ensure the success of LBO, it is imperative that the acquiring management/firm should carry out the exercise to determine the maximum level of debt it should go for, based on its cash generating capacity to service the debt in future. This exercise would enable the firm to determine the maximum degree of financial leverage it can employ in a buyout.

LO 32.6 MOTIVES AND ASSESSMENT OF MERGERS AND ACQUISITIONS PRACTICES IN INDIA

Mergers and acquisitions practices by corporate enterprises in India are summarized below:

- The market, usually, reacts positively to the mergers and acquisitions (M&A) announcements. Market starts reacting prior to the announcement. The moment the announcement information becomes public, investors start reacting and the stock price jumps high, providing positive abnormal returns to the investors. This reaction clearly indicates that investors perceive synergies in mergers and acquisitions and they appear to be beneficial for them.
- The acquisitions, financed with cash, experience higher returns than the acquisitions financed with stock. This could be a signal in favour of 'asymmetric information hypothesis and free cash flow hypothesis'. "Issuance of stock is not good news" as per the findings.
- Cross-border as well as domestic acquisitions have created value for shareholders of the acquiring company on the announcement. The results indicate that value creation is higher for cross-border acquisitions vis-a-vis domestic acquisitions. The acquisitions of targets from non-US developed market outperform the return from the acquisition of US targets.
- The acquirers of unlisted target firms experience higher returns than the acquirers of listed target firms. The acquirer earns when target remains as a wholly-owned subsidiary. In contrast, the acquirer shareholder loses when the target firm is absorbed with the operations of the acquiring firm.
- The primary motive of mergers in India has been to take advantage of synergies. Operating economies, increased market share and financial economies (lower risk leading to lower cost of capital) have been indicated in order of importance as the desired synergies to be gained through corporate mergers and acquisitions in India.

- M&A appear to have been financially beneficial for the acquiring companies. The findings suggest that profitability of acquiring firms has improved during post-M&A phase. Better management of liquidity position during the post-M&A period has also been observed.
- M&A has no impact on the leverage of acquiring firms after M&A.
- Operating profit margin based on sales has improved post-M&A. The significantly higher post-M&A operating margin indicates that the acquirers appear to have generated higher operating profit per unit net sales, post-M&A. The better operating margin seems to be due to the lower costs as a result of economies of scale.
- The efficiency of utilisation of assets does not appear to have improved (as revealed by total assets turnover ratio) post-M&A.

Source: Rani, N., Yadav, Surendra S. and Jain, P.K. (2016). *Mergers and Acquisitions: A Study of Financial Performance, Motives and Corporate Governance*, Springer Verlag, Singapore.

SUMMARY

LO 32.1

The growth of a firm can be achieved 'internally' either by developing new products and/or expanding the capacity of existing products or 'externally' by acquisitions, mergers, amalgamations, absorption and so on.

While a merger is a combination of two or more firms in which the resulting firm maintains the identity of one of the firms only, an amalgamation involves the combination of two or more firms to form a new firm. In the case of merger/absorption, the firm that has been acquired/absorbed is known as the target firm and the firm that acquires is known as the acquiring firm.

There are three types of mergers: (i) horizontal, (ii) vertical and (iii) conglomerate. Horizontal merger takes place when two or more firms dealing in similar lines of activity/business combine together. Vertical merger involves combination of two or more firms engaged in the various stages of production or distribution in the same business activity. Conglomerate merger is a combination of firms engaged in different/unrelated business activities.

The major economic advantages of a merger are: (i) economies of scale, (ii) synergy, (iii) fast growth, (iv) tax benefits and (v) diversification.

Synergy takes place as the combined value of the merged firm is likely to be greater than the sum of individual business entities. The combined value = value of acquiring firm, V_A + value of target firm, V_t + value of synergy, DV_{AT}.

In ascertaining the gains from the merger, costs associated with acquisition should be taken into account. Therefore, the net gain from the merger is equal to the difference between the value of synergy and costs: Net gain = DV_{AT} – costs.

Set-off and carry forward of losses of an acquiring firm with the firm having profits reduce the taxable income of the newly merged firm and, hence, the reduction of tax liability. Thus, a merger can provide tax benefits.

Merger suffers from certain weaknesses also, the major ones being: (i) the management of the two firms may not go along because of friction and (ii) the dissenting minority shareholders may cause problems.

LO 32.2	The financial framework of merger covers three inter-related aspects: (i) determining the firm's value, (ii) financing techniques in merger and (iii) analysis of the merger as a capital budgeting decision.
	The alternative approaches to value a firm are (i) book value, (ii) appraisal value, (iii) market value and (iv) earnings per share (EPS).
	The alternative methods of financing mergers/payment to the acquired company are: (i) ordinary share financing, (ii) debt and preference share financing, (iii) convertible securities, (iv) deferred payment plan and (v) tender offers.
	The extent of merger gains to be shared between the shareholders of the acquiring firm and the target firm depends on the exchange ratio. The ratio depends on the relative bargaining position of the two firms and the market reaction of the merger move. Normally, the exchange ratio is such in which the merger gains accrue to the shareholders of both firms.
	Merger as a capital budgeting decision involves the valuation of the target firm in terms of its potentials to generate incremental future free cash flows (FCFF) to the acquiring firm. These cash flows are then to be discounted at an appropriate rate that reflects the riskiness of the target firm's business. The cost of acquisition is deducted from the present value of FCFF. The merger proposal is financially viable in case the NPV is positive. The finance manager can use sensitivity analysis to have a range of NPV values within which the acquisition price may vary.
	Alternatively, the target firm can be valued according to the adjusted present value (APV) approach. The APV approach to value FCFF of target firm has two components: (i) the value of the target company if it were entirely equity financed discounting the FCFFs using the unlevered cost of equity and (ii) the value of impact of debt financing both in terms of tax shield and bankruptcy costs. The present value of tax shield is determined, discounting tax savings by pre-tax cost of debt. The incremental bankruptcy costs (due to debt financing) are subtracted. The proposal is financially viable in case the NPV is positive.
LO 32.3	The following are the major tax benefits available to the amalgamated/resulting company: (i) carry forward and set-off of business losses, unabsorbed depreciation, unabsorbed capital expenditure on scientific research and (ii) the expenditure on patents and copyrights, know how, family planning, preliminary expenses and so on not yet written off in the books of amalgamating/demerged company to be written off by the amalgamated/resulting company in the same number of balance instalments. Virtually all fiscal concessions/incentives/deductions available to the amalgamating/demerged company are also available to the amalgamated/resulting company.
	The tax concessions are also available to the amalgamating company. Several tax concessions are also available to the shareholders of the amalgamating as well as the demerged company.
LO 32.4	Although the economic considerations of mergers, amalgamations and acquisitions are similar, the legal procedures involved are different. While the mergers and amalgamations are governed by the Companies Act, the takeovers and acquisitions are regulated by the SEBI. The pre-security of combination is done by the CCI. The pre-entry scrutiny of combinations in India is conducted by the CCI under the Competition Act 2002. It is mandated upon its own knowledge or information to enquire within one year of its happening whether an acquisition/acquiring of control/amalgamation or merger has caused/is likely to cause an appreciable adverse effect on competition in India. It has issued regulation (2011) in respect of procedure regarding transactions of business relating to combinations. The main features of the regulation of combination under the Competition Act are: (i) regulation of combination, (ii) combination, (iii) conditions and (iv) procedure.

LO 32.4

- Any combination entered into by any person/enterprise which causes or is likely to cause an appreciable adverse effect on competition within the relevant market in India are void. Whether a combination would have the effect of/is likely to have appreciable adverse effect on competition in the relevant market, the CCI would have due regard to all/any of the factors listed below: (i) Actual/potential level of competition through imports in the market; (ii) Extent of barriers to entry to the market; (iii) Degree of countervailing power in the market; (iv) Likelihood of the combination resulting in the concerned parties being able to significantly and sustainably increase price/ profit margin; (v) Extent of effective competition likely to sustain the market; (vi) Extent to which substitutes are/likely to be available in the market; (vii) Market share in the relevant market of the concerned person/enterprise individually/jointly; (viii) Likelihood of the combination resulting in the removal of a vigours/effective competitor(s) in the market; (ix) Nature/extent of vertical integration in the market; (x) Possibility of a failing business; (xi) Nature/extent of innovation; (xii) Relative advantage by way of contribution to economic development by any combination having/likely to have appreciable adverse effect on competition; (xiii)The benefits of combination outweigh the adverse impact of combination.

The parties to combination should give notice to the CCI containing details of the proposed within 30 days of (a) approval of the merger/amalgamation by the Board of Directors, (b) execution of any agreement/other documents for acquisition/acquiring control. The combination would be effective after 210 days from the date of notice.

The conditions for pre-combination scrutiny by the CCI pertain to the value of assets and turnover. The acquirer and the concerned enterprise jointly have in (a) India assets and turnover exceeding ₹1,000 crore and ₹3,000 crore respectively, (b) India/outside India, the respective amounts are more than 500 million US dollars (including at least ₹500 crore in India), and 1,500 million US dollars (including at least ₹1,500 crore in India). The stipulations for the group to which the concerned enterprise belongs are that their joint holdings in India are/would be ₹4,000 crores (assets) and ₹12,000 crores (turnover). Such holdings in India/outside India should aggregate more than two billion US dollars (of which at least ₹500 crore in India) in terms of assets and six billion US dollars (including at least ₹1,500 crore in India0 in terms of turnover.

The main provisions of the Companies Act, 2013 relating to combination are contained in Section 230-32. Merger/Amalgamation can be by **(i)** absorption, **(ii)** formation of a new company. Merger by absorption involves the transfer of the undertaking, property and liabilities of the merging companies to another existing company. Their transfer to a new company is merger by formation of a new company.

Merger and amalgamation under the Companies Act requires mandatory sanction by the National Company Law Tribunal (NCLT).

The scheme/arrangement/proposal approved by three-fourths in value of creditors/members and sanctioned by the NCLT would be binding on the company and all creditors/members.

The procedural stipulations relate to **(i)** holding of meeting of creditors/members, **(ii)** agenda of the meeting, **(iii)** provision for the specified matter, **(iv)** filing of the copies of the NCLT order with the ROCs and **(v)** penalty for contravention of the prescribed procedures.

Takeovers imply acquisition of controlling interest in a company by another company. They can take three forms: (i) negotiated/friendly, (ii) open market/hostile and (iii) bail-out.

In the case of hostile takeover, the target company can use the following strategies to defend itself: (i) Poison Pill, (ii) Poison Put, (iii) Greenmail, (iv) Pac-man defence, (v) White Knight and (vi) White Squire.

LO 32.4

The corporate takeovers in India are governed by the Companies Act, listing agreements and SEBI code. The provisions of the Companies Act relate to acquisition of shares, restriction on acquisition and transfer of shares and so on. The takeover of companies listed on stock exchange is regulated by Clause 40–A and 40–B of the listing agreement. While Clause 40–A deals with conditions for continued listing, Clause 40–B contains the requirements to be met when a takeover offer is made.

The SEBI takeover code provides for the following: **(i)** Substantial Acquisition of Shares, Voting Rights/ Control, **(ii)** Open Offer Process, **(iii)** Other Obligations, **(iv)** Disclosures of Shareholding and Control, and **(v)** Miscellaneous.

Acquisition means directly/indirectly acquire/agree to acquire shares voting rights in, or control over, a target company. **Control** includes the right to appoint majority of directors or to control the management or policy decisions exercisable by a person(s) acting individually or in concert, directly/ indirectly, including by virtue of their shareholding/management rights/shareholders agreement/voting agreements or in any other manner. **Shares** means shares/security carrying voting rights including depository receipts carrying an entitlement to exercise voting rights. **Target company** means a company listed on a stock exchange. **Person acting in concert** means persons who, with a common objective/ purpose of acquisition of shares/voting rights in, or exercising control, over a target company, pursuant to a formal/informal agreement/understanding, directly/indirectly co-operate for acquisition of shares/ voting rights in, or exercise of control over, the target company. The persons falling within the following categories would be deemed to be persons acting in concert with other persons within the same category, unless the contrary is established: **(i)** a company, its holding company, subsidiary company and any company under the same management/control; **(ii)** a company, its directors, and any person entrusted with the management of the company; **(iii)** directors of companies referred to above and associates of such directors. **Associate** of a person means **(a)** any immediate relative, **(b)** trust of which the person/immediate relative is a trustee, **(c)** firm in which he/immediate relative is a partner, and **(d)** member of a Hindu Undivided Family of which he is a coparcener. **Immediate relative** means his spouse including parents/brothers/ sisters/children or of the spouse; **(iv)** promoters and members of the promoter group; **(v)** immediate relatives; **(vi)** a mutual fund, its sponsor, trustee, trustee company, and asset management company; **(vii)** a collective investment scheme and its collective investment management company, trustees and trustee company; **(viii)** a venture capital fund and its sponsor, trustees, trustee company and asset management company; **(viii-a)** an alternate investment fund and its sponsor/trustee/manager; **(ix)** a foreign institutional investor and its sub-accounts; **(x)** a merchant banker and its client, who is an acquirer; **(xi)** a portfolio manager and its client, who is an acquirer; **(xii)** banks, financial advisors and stock brokers of the acquirer, or of the company which is a holding company or subsidiary of the acquirer, and where the acquirer is an individual, of the immediate relative of such individual. However, a bank whose sole role is that of providing normal commercial banking services or activities in relation to an open offer under these regulations would be excluded;

(xiii) an investment company or fund and any person who has an interest in such investment company or fund as a shareholder or unitholder having not less than 10 per cent of the paid-up capital of the investment company or unit capital of the fund, and any other investment company or fund in which such person or his associate holds not less than 10 per cent of the paid-up capital of that investment company or unit capital of that fund.

LO 32.4

The main elements of the SEBI code relating to substantial acquisition of shares/voting rights/control are: **(i)** substantial acquisition of shares/voting rights, **(ii)** acquisition of control, **(iii)** indirect acquisition of shares/control, **(iv)** voluntary offer, **(v)** offer size, **(vi)** offer price, **(vii)** mode of payment, **(viii)** general exemptions, and **(ix)** exemptions by the SEBI.

The open offer for acquiring shares should be made at a price not lower than the price determined in the manner specified below:

1. **Direct Acquisition** In the case of direct acquisition and indirect **acquisition deemed to be direct acquisition** of shares, the offer price should be the highest of: **(a)** the highest negotiated price per share of the target company for any acquisition under the agreement attracting the obligation to make a public announcement of an open offer; **(b)** the **volume-weighted average** price (i.e. product of number of equity shares bought and price of each share divided by the number of shares bought) paid/payable for acquisitions, by the acquirer during the 52 two weeks immediately preceding the date of the public announcement; **(c)** the highest price paid/payable for any acquisition by the acquirer during the 26 weeks immediately preceding the date of the public announcement; **(d)** the **volume-weighted average market price** (i.e. product of number of shares traded on a stock exchange and price of each share divided by the total number of shares traded) of such shares for a period of 60 trading days immediately preceding the date of the public announcement as traded on the stock exchange where the maximum volume of trading in the shares of the target company are recorded during such period, provided such shares are **frequently traded**. Frequently traded shares mean shares in which the traded turnover on any stock exchange during 12-calendar months preceding the calendar month in which the public announcement is made is at least 10 per cent of the total shares of the target company; **(e)** where the shares are not frequently traded, the price determined by the acquirer and the manager to the open offer taking into account valuation parameters including, book value, comparable trading multiples, and such other parameters as are customary for valuation of shares of such companies; and **(f)** the per share value computed in case of indirect acquisition (**discussed later**).
2. **Indirect Acquisition Deemed Direct Acquisition** In the case of an indirect acquisition of shares, the offer price would be the highest of: **(a)** the highest negotiated price per share of the target company for any acquisition under the agreement attracting the obligation to make a public announcement; **(b)** the volume-weighted average price paid/payable for any acquisition, during the 52 weeks immediately preceding the earlier of, the date on which the primary acquisition is contracted, and the date on which the intention or the decision to make the primary acquisition is announced in the public domain; **(c)** the highest price paid/payable for any acquisition by the acquirer during the 26 weeks immediately preceding the earlier of, the date on which the primary acquisition is contracted, and the date on which the intention or the decision to make the primary acquisition is announced in the public domain; **(d)** the highest price paid/payable for any acquisition between the earlier of, the date on which the primary acquisition is contracted, and the date on which the intention or the decision to make the primary acquisition is announced in the public domain, and the date of the public announcement of the open offer for shares of the target company; **(e)** the volume-weighted average market price of the shares for a period of 60 days earlier of, the date on which the primary acquisition is contracted, and the date on which the intention or the decision to make the primary acquisition is announced in the public domain, as traded on the stock exchange where the maximum volume of trading in the shares of the target company are recorded during such period, provided such shares are frequently traded; and **(f)** the per share value in case of indirect acquisition (**discussed later**).

LO 32.4

3. In case the offer price is incapable of being determined under any of the parameters above, the offer price should be the fair price of shares of the target company to be determined by the acquire and the manager to the open offer taking into account valuation parameters including, book value, comparable trading multiples, and such other parameters as are customary for valuation of shares of such companies.
4. **Indirect Acquisition** In the case of an indirect acquisition and open offers, where the proportionate **(a)** net asset value of the target company as a percentage of the consolidated net asset value; **(b)** sales turnover of the target company as a percentage of the consolidated sales turnover; or **(c)** market capitalisation of the target company as a percentage of the enterprise value for the entity or business being acquired is in excess of 15 per cent, the acquirer would be required to compute and disclose, in the letter of offer, the per share value of the target company taken into account for the acquisition, along with a detailed description of the methodology adopted for such computation. The **market capitalisation** of the target company would be taken into account on the basis of the volume-weighted average market price of the shares on the stock exchange for a period of 60 trading days preceding the earlier of, the date on which the primary acquisition is contracted, and the date on which the intention or the decision to make the primary acquisition is announced in the public domain, as traded on the stock exchange where the maximum volume of trading in the shares of the target company are recorded during such period.
5. In respect of direct and indirect deemed direct acquisition, where the acquirer has any outstanding convertible instruments convertible into shares of the target company at a specific price, the price at which such instruments are to be converted into shares, would also be considered as a parameter. The price paid for shares of target company would include any price paid/agreed to be paid for the shares in the target company, in any form whatsoever, whether stated in the agreement for acquisition of shares or in any incidental, contemporaneous or collateral agreement, whether termed as control premium or as non-compete fees or otherwise.
6. Where the acquirer has acquired/agreed to acquire any shares in the target company during the **offer period** (i.e. period between the date of entering into formal/informal agreement to acquire shares/voting rights/control of a target company requiring public announcement and the date of public announcement and the date on which the payment of consideration to shareholders who have accepted the open offer is made or the date on which open offer is withdrawn) by subscription/purchase, at a price higher than the offer price, the offer price would stand revised to the highest price for any acquisition. However, no acquisition would be made after the third working day prior to the commencement and until the expiry of the tendering period.
7. The price parameters outlined above may be adjusted by the acquirer in consultation with the manager to the offer, for corporate actions such as issuances pursuant to rights issue, bonus issue, stock consolidations, stock splits, payment of dividend, de-mergers and reduction of capital, where the record date for effecting such corporate actions falls prior to three working days before the commencement of the tendering period. However, adjustment should be made for dividend declared if the per share dividend is more than 50 per cent higher than the average paid during the three financial years preceding the date of the public announcement.
8. Where the acquirer acquirers shares of the target company during the period of 26 weeks after the tendering period at a price higher than the offer price, he would pay the difference between the highest acquisition price and the offer price, to all the shareholders whose shares were accepted in the open offer, within 60 days from the date of such acquisition.

9. Where the open offer is subject to a minimum level of acceptances, the acquirer may indicate a lower price, but not be less than the price determined under this regulation, for acquiring all the acceptances despite the acceptance falling short of the indicated minimum level of acceptance, in the event the open offer does not receive the minimum acceptance.
10. In the case of any indirect acquisition, the offer price would stand enhanced by an amount equal to a sum determined at the rate of 10 per cent per annum for the period between the earlier of the date on which the primary acquisition is contracted or the date on which the intention or the decision to make the primary acquisition is announced in the public domain, and the date of the detailed public statement, provided such period is more than five working days.
11. The offer price for partly-paid-up shares should be computed as the difference between the offer price and the amount due towards calls-in-arrears including calls remaining unpaid with interest.
12. The offer price for equity shares carrying differential voting rights should be determined by the acquirer and the manager to the open offer with full disclosure of justification for the price so determined, being set out in the detailed public statement and the letter of offer. However, the price should not be lower than the amount determined by applying the percentage rate of premium that the offer price for the equity shares carrying full voting rights represents to the price parameter computed above to the volume-weighted average market price of the shares carrying differential voting rights in the aforesaid provisions, subject to shares carrying full voting rights and the shares carrying differential voting rights, both being frequently traded shares.
13. In the event of any of the price parameters not being available or denominated in Indian rupees, the conversion of such amount into Indian rupees would be effected at the exchange rate as prevailing on the date preceding the date of public announcement and the acquirer should set out the source of such exchange rate in the public announcement, the detailed public statement and the letter of offer.
14. The SEBI may, at the expense of the acquirer, require valuation of the shares by an independent merchant banker other than the manager to the open offer or an independent practicing chartered accountant having a minimum experience of 10 years.

LO 32.4

The main elements of the open offer process are: **(i)** manager to the offer, **(ii)** timing, **(iii)** publication, **(iv)** contents, **(v)** filing of letter with SEBI, **(vi)** provision of escrow, **(vii)** other procedures, **(viii)** conditional offer, **(ix)** competing offer, **(x)** payment of consideration, **(xi)** completion of acquisition, and **(xii)** withdrawal of open offer.

The other obligations relate to: **(i)** directors of the target company, **(ii)** acquirer, **(iii)** target company, and **(iv)** manager to the offer.

These relate to **(i)** disclosure related provisions, **(ii)** continual disclosures and **(iii)** disclosure of encumbered shares.

The SEBI may, in interest of investors in securities/securities market, issue such directions for violation of these regulations as it deems fit.

Activities related to expansion or contraction of a firm's operations or changes in its assets or financial or ownership structure are referred to as corporate restructuring. Its major forms other than mergers/amalgamation and takeovers/acquisitions are: (i) financial restructuring, (ii) divestitures/demergers and buyouts.

LO 32.5

Financial restructuring is carried out internally in the firm with the consent of its various stakeholders. It is suitable mode of restructuring for corporate firms that have accumulated sizable losses over a number of years but hold prospects for better financial performance in future. An appropriate financial restructuring scheme is formulated which enables the corporate to write-off past accumulated losses and fictitious assets and restart with a fresh balance sheet which shows its share capital as well as its assets at their real/true worth.

Divestitures/demergers involves selling of some segments of a business only in the form of a plant, division, product line, subsidiary and so on as they are either incurring losses or yielding very low returns. This enables the firm to have a more lean and focused operation. Besides, by selling the unproductive assets and utilising cash proceeds in expanding/rejuvenating other leftover assets/operating units, the firm is likely to augment the profits of the demerged firm/wealth for its shareholders. The concept of demerger is also known as reverse synergy in that the value of the parts is greater than that of the whole.

Divesture can take the following forms: (i) outright sale of an operating unit, (ii) spin-off, that is, creation of a new separate firm and (iii) split-up which involves the breaking-up of the entire firm in a number of new created separate legal entities.

The management buyouts (MBO) involves the sale of a existing firm to the management (from the same firm/from outside/hybrid form). The leveraged buyouts (LBO) takes place when debt forms a substantial part of total financing from outsiders. The LBO should be used by corporates which have a low degree of operating /business risk.

REFERENCES

1. Gitman, L J, *Principles of Managerial Finance,* Pearson Education Asia, Delhi, 2001, p. 779.
2. Koutsoyiannis, A *Non-Price Decisions—The Firm in a Modern Context,* Macmillan, London, 1982, p. 236.
3. *Ibid.*, p. 238.
4. Ramanujam, S *Mergers et al,* Tata McGraw-Hill Publishing Co. Ltd. New Delhi, 2000, p. 364.
5. For details of sensitivity analysis, refer to Chapter 3 of this book.
6. Copeland, T, *op. cit.,* p. 132.
7. Copeland, T, *op. cit.,* p. 147.
8. Copeland, T, *op. cit.,* p. 476.
9. Copeland, T, *op. cit.,* p. 477.
10. Gitman, L J, *op. cit.,* p. 787.
11. Weston, J Fred et al, *Mergers, Restructuring and Corporate Control,* Prentice-Hall of India, New Delhi, 1996, p. 6.
12. Weston, J Fred et al, *Ibid.*, p. 6.
13. Emery, D R and John D Finnerty, *Corporate Financial Management,* Prentice-Hall International, New Jersey, 1997, p. 911.

SOLVED PROBLEMS

P.32.1 The XYZ Ltd wants to acquire ABC Ltd by exchanging its 1.6 shares for every share of ABC Ltd. It anticipates to maintain the existing P/E ratio subsequent to the merger also. The relevant financial data are furnished below: LO 32.2 LOD E

	XYZ Ltd	ABC Ltd
Earnings after taxes (EAT) (₹)	15,00,000	4,50,000
Number of equity shares outstanding (N)	3,00,000	75,000
Market price per share (MPS) (₹)	35	40

(a) What is the exchange ratio based on market prices?
(b) What is pre-merger EPS and the P/E ratio for each company?
(c) What was the P/E ratio used in acquiring ABC Ltd.?
(d) What is EPS of XYZ Company after the acquisition?
(e) What is the expected market price per share of the merged company?

Solution

(a) Exchange ratio based on market prices: $= \dfrac{1.6 \times ₹35}{₹40} = 1.4$

(b) EPS and P/E ratio

Particulars	XYZ Ltd	ABC Ltd
(a) EAT (₹)	15,00,000	4,50,000
(b) N	3,00,000	75,000
(c) EPS (a)/(b) (₹)	5	6
(d) P/E ratio (MPS/EPS) (times)	7 (₹35/5)	6.67 (₹40/6)

(c) Implied P/E ratio in the acquisition of ABC Ltd:

$$\frac{\text{Market price of shares offered to XYZ}}{\text{Current EPS of ABC Ltd}} = \frac{₹56^{*}}{6} = 9.33 \text{ times } (^{*}1.6 \times ₹35 \text{ or } 1.4 \times ₹40)$$

(d) EPS of XYZ Company after merger: $\dfrac{₹15{,}00{,}000 + ₹4{,}50{,}000}{3{,}00{,}000 + 1{,}20{,}000} = ₹4.64$

(e) Expected market price after merger: ₹4.64 × 7 times = ₹32.48.

P.32.2 A Ltd wants to acquire T Ltd by exchanging 0.5 of its shares for each share of *T* Ltd. The relevant financial data are as follows: LO 32.2 LOD E

Particulars	A Ltd	T Ltd
EAT (₹)	18,00,000	3,60,000
Equity share outstanding	6,00,000	1,80,000
EPS (₹)	3	2
P/E ratio (times)	10	7
Market price per share (₹)	30	14

Required:

(a) What is the number of equity shares required to be issued by A Ltd for acquisition of T Ltd?
(b) What is the EPS of A Ltd after the acquisition?
(c) Determine the equivalent earnings per share of T Ltd.
(d) What is the expected market price per share of A Ltd after the acquisition, assuming its P/E multiple remains unchanged?
(e) Determine the market value of the merged firm.

Solution

(a) Number of shares = 1,80,000 × 0.5 = 90,000.

(b) EPS = $\frac{₹18,00,000 + ₹3,60,000}{6,00,000 + 90,000}$ = ₹3.13

(c) Equivalent EPS = ₹3.13 × 0.5 = ₹1.565.

(d) Expected Market price = ₹3.13 × 10 times = ₹31.30.

(e) Market value = ₹31.30 × 6,90,000 shares = ₹2,15,97,000

P.32.3 The following data concern companies *A* and *T*: LO 32.2 LOD M

Particulars	*Company A*	*Company B*
Earnings after taxes (₹)	1,40,000	37,500
Equity shares outstanding	20,000	7,500
EPS (₹)	7	5
P/E ratio (times)	10	8
Market price (₹)	70	40

Company A is the acquiring company, exchanging its one share for every 1.5 shares of B Ltd. Assume that company A expects to have the same earnings and P/E ratio after the merger as before (no synergy effect), show the extent of gain accruing to the shareholders of the two companies as a result of the merger. Are they better or worse off than they were before the merger?

Solution **EPS after the merger** = $\frac{₹1,40,000 + ₹37,500}{20,000 + 5,000}$ = ₹7.1.

Market price after the merger = ₹7.1 × 10 times = ₹71
Total market value = ₹71 × 25,000 = ₹17,75,000

Gains from the merger

Post-merger market value of the firm		₹17,75,000
Less: Pre-merger market value:		
Company A (20,000 × ₹70)	₹14,00,000	
Company T (7,500 × ₹40)	3,00,000	17,00,000
		75,000

Apportionment of gains among shareholders

Particulars	*Post-merger value*	*Pre-merger value*	*Difference*
Firm A	₹14,20,000*	₹14,00,000	₹20,000
Firm B	3,55,000**	3,00,000	55,000

*(20,000 × ₹71)
**(5,000 × ₹71)

Thus, the shareholders are better off after the merger.

P.32.4 (a) Assume every thing to be the same as provided in P.32.3. Determine the range of the minimum and maximum share exchange ratio between the two firms. Also provide confirmation of your answer. (b) Determine the exchange ratio when the gains from merger are to be shared equally. LO 32.2 LOD M

Solution

(a) (i) Determination of tolerable exchange ratio for shareholders of Firm A based on total gains accruing to shareholders of Firm B

(a) Total market value of the merged firm	₹17,75,000	
(b) *Less:* Pre-merger value/minimum post-merger value acceptable to shareholders of firm A	14,00,000	
(c) Maximum acceptable post-merger market value of Firm B	3,75,000	
(d) To maintain post-merger value of ₹14,00,000 of Firm A, pre-merger MPS of Firm A has to be	70	
(e) Number of equity issued required to be issued in firm A to have MPS of ₹70 and to have post-merger value of firm B at ₹3,75,000 (₹3,75,000/₹70)	5,357 app.	
(f) Existing number of equity shares outstanding of Firm B	7,500	
(g) Share exchange ratio (5,357/7,500)		0.714:1
For every 1 share of Firm B, 0.714 share will be issued in Firm A		

Confirmation

Combined earnings of the merged firm	₹1,77,500	
Divided by the total number of shares after the merger (20,000 + 5,357)	25,357	
Combined EPS after the merger (1,77,500/25,357)		7.00
MPS after the merger (₹7 × 10 P/E ratio)	70	
Total value of the post-merger firm (₹70 × ₹25,357)	17,74,990*	
Market value of shares for shareholders of Firm A (20,000 × ₹70) after the merger	14,00,000	
Market value of shares for shareholders of Firm A before the merger	14,00,000	
Gain to the shareholders of Firm A (₹14 lakh – ₹14 lakh)	Nil	
Market value of shares for shareholders of Firm B (5,357 × ₹70) after the merger	3,74,990	
Market value of shares for shareholders of Firm B before the merger	3,00,000	
Gain to the shareholders of Firm B (₹3,74,990 – ₹3,00,000)	74,990*	
Total gain from merger	75,000*	

*Difference of ₹10 in two sets of figures (₹75,000 – ₹74,990) and (₹17,75,000 – ₹17,74,990) is due to approximation in the number of shares determined (5,357).

(a) (ii) Determination of tolerable exchange ratio for shareholders of Firm B based on total gains accruing to shareholders of Firm A

(a) Total market value of the merged firm	₹17,75,000	
(b) *Less:* Pre-merger value/minimum post-merger value acceptable to shareholders of firm B	3,00,000	
(c) Maximum acceptable post-merger market value of Firm A	14,75,000	
(d) Divided by the number of existing equity shares of Firm A	20,000	
(e) Desired post-merger MPS (₹14,75,000/20,000 shares)	73.75	
(f) Number of equity issues required to be issued in Firm A to have MPS of ₹73.75 (given P/E ratio of 10 times) and to have postmerger value of ₹3,00,000 of Firm B (₹3,00,000/₹73.75)	4,068 shares app.	
(g) Existing number of equity shares outstanding of Firm B	5,000	
(h) Share exchange ratio (4,068/7,500)		0.5424:1
For every 1 share in firm B, 0.5424 share will be issued in firm A		

Confirmation

Combined earnings of the merged firm	₹1,77,500
Divided by the total number of shares after the merger (20,000 + 4,068)	24,068
Combined EPS after the merger (₹1,77,500/24,068)	7.375
MPS after the merger (₹7.375 × 10)	73.75
Total value of the post-merger firm (24,068 shares × ₹73.75)	17,75,015*
Market value of shares for shareholders of Firm *A* (20,000 shares × ₹73.75)	14,75,000
Market value of shares for shareholders of Firm *A* before the merger	14,00,000
Gain to the shareholders of Firm *A* (₹14,75,000 – ₹14,00,000)	75,000
Market value of shares for shareholders of Firm *B* (4,068 shares × ₹73.75)	₹3,00,015*
Market value of shares for shareholders of Firm *B* before the merger	3,00,000
Gain to the shareholders of Firm *B*	Nil/₹15*

*Difference of ₹15 in two sets of figures (₹17,75,015 and ₹17,75,000) and (₹3,00,015 and ₹3,00,000) is due to approximation in the number of shares determined 4,068.

Acceptable exchange ratios: Thus, the minimum and maximum shares exchange ratio are 0.5424:1 and 0.714 between the shares of Firm A and Firm B.

(b) Exchange ratio when gains are to be shared equally

Particulars	*Firm A*	*Firm B*
Market valuation (desired)	₹14,37,500	₹3,37,500
MPS (desired) (14,37,500/20,000)	71.88	71.88
Number of shares to be issued	–	4,695.33 (4,696)
Share exchange ratio (4,696/7,500)	–	0.63 : 1

For every one share in Firm B, 0.63 share will be issued in Firm A.

P.32.5 Sound Industries Limited (SI) is planning to purchase Not so Sound Industries Ltd. (NSS). SI has 5 lakh shares outstanding of ₹100 each, having the current market price per share (MPS) of ₹250. NSS has 2 lakh shares of ₹100 each, currently selling in the market at ₹170 per share. EPS are ₹32 and ₹24 for SI and NSS, respectively. LO 32.2 LOD M

Required

(a) Illustrate the impact of a merger on the EPS, assuming that the share exchange ratio is to be in the relative proportion of EPS of the two firms. Also determine the equivalent EPS after the merger with Firm NSS.

(b) The management of NSS has quoted a share exchange ratio of 1:1 for the merger to take place. Should SI accept this ratio, even through the price-earning ratio of SI Ltd. will remain unchanged after merger and no synergy accrues due to the merger. If not, what is the maximum ratio it should accept.

Solution

(a) Impact of merger on EPS (based on exchange ratio of ₹24/₹32 = 0.75)

Company	*Number of shares*	*EPS*	*Total EAT*
SI	5,00,000	₹32	₹1,60,00,000
NSS	2,00,000	24	48,00,000
Total post-merger earnings			2,08,00,000
Divided by the number of shares after the merger (5,00,000 + 1,50,000 i.e., 2,00,000 × 0.75)			6,50,000
Combined earnings per share			₹32
Shareholders of SI:			
EPS before the merger			32
EPS after the merger			32
Shareholders of NSS:			
EPS before the merger			24
Equivalent EPS after the merger (EPS after the merger × share exchange ratio) i.e., (₹32 × 0.75)			24

Thus, there is no change in effective EPS for shareholders of either of the firms.

(b) Effect of share exchange ratio of 1:1 on valuation of the firms *(in lakh)*

	Firm SI	*Firm NSS*
Pre-merger situation:		
EAT (₹)	160	48
Number of shares outstanding (N)	5	2
EPS (₹)	32	24
Market price per share (₹)	250	170
P/E ratio implicit (MPS/EPS) (times)	7.8125	7.0833
Total market value (N × MPS) (₹)	1,250	340
Post-merger situation:		
Combined EAT (₹)		208
Number of shares outstanding after additional shares of 2 lakh issued as shares exchange ratio is 1:1 (N)		7
EPSc (combined EAT/N) (₹)		208/7
P/E ratio (times)		7.8125
MPS (₹)		232.143
Total market value, MPS × Number of shares of merged firm		1,625
Gain from merger (₹1,625 lakh – ₹1,250 lakh – ₹340 lakh)		35
Gain to shareholders of firms		
Firm SI		
Pre-merger market value		1,250
Less: Post-merger market value (5 lakh shares × ₹232.143)		1,160.715
Loss to the shareholders		89.285
Firm NSS		
Post-merger market value (2 lakh shares × ₹232.143)		464.286
Less: Pre-merger market value		340.000
Gain to the shareholders		124.286

Evidently, the management of SI will not accept a share exchange ratio of 1: 1 as it reduces the wealth of its shareholders by ₹89.285 lakh. The maximum ratio likely to be acceptable to its management is (0.75 : 1) as calculated below.

Determination of acceptable share exchange ratio to Firm SI (based on total gains of ₹35 lakh accruing to Firm NSS) *(₹ lakh)*

Total market value of the merged firm	1,625
Less: Minimum post-merger value acceptable to SI	1,250
Post-merger market value of Firm NSS	375
Since post-merger value of Firm SI remains unchanged, it implies MPS of ₹250 is to remain intact. Therefore, the number of equity shares required to be issued in Firm SI to have a MPS of ₹250 and to have a post-merger value of ₹375 lakh for Firm NSS will be (₹375 lakh/₹250)	1,50,000
Existing number of equity shares outstanding in Firm NSS	2,00,000
Share exchange ratio (1,50,000/2,00,000)	0.75:1
For every 1 share in Firm NSS, 0.75 share will be issued in Firm SI. This is the maximum exchange ratio that may be acceptable to management of SI	

P.32.6 Company X wishes to takeover Company Y. The financial details of the two companies are as under: LO 32.2 LOD M

Particulars	*Company X*	*Company Y*
Equity shares (₹10 per share)	₹1,00,000	₹50,000
Share premium account	—	2,000
Profit & loss account	38,000	4,000
Preference shares	20,000	—
10% debentures	15,000	5,000
	1,73,000	61,000
Fixed assets	1,22,000	35,000
Net current assets	51,000	26,000
Maintainable annual profit (after tax) for equity shareholders	24,000	15,000
Market price per equity share	24	27
Price earning ratio	10	9

What offer do you think Company X could make to Company Y in terms of exchange ratio, based on **(a)** net asset value; **(b)** earning per share; and **(c)** market price per share? Which method would you prefer from Company X's point of view?

Solution

(a) Exchange ratio based on net asset value

Particulars	*Company X*	*Company Y*
Fixed assets	₹1,22,000	₹35,000
Net current assets	51,000	26,000
Total assets	1,73,000	61,000
Less: Preference shares	20,000	—
Less: 10% Debentures	15,000	5,000
Net assets	1,38,000	56,000
Divided by number of shares	10,000	5,000
Net assets per share	13.80	11.20

Exchange ratio = ₹11.20/₹13.80 = 0.8116

The shareholders of Company Y should get 0.8116 share of X for every share held by them.

(b) Exchange ratio based on earnings per share (EPS)

Particulars	*Company X*	*Company Y*
Earnings after taxes for equity-holders	₹24,000	₹15,000
Divided by number of shares	10,000	5,000
EPS	2.4	3

Exchange ratio = ₹3/₹2.4 = 1.25

The shareholders of Company Y should get 1.25 shares of Company X for every share held by them.

(c) Exchange ratio based on market price per share = ₹27/₹24 = 1.125

The shareholders of Company Y should get 1.125 shares of Company X for every share held by them.

The exchange ratio based on the net asset value is the best from Company X's point of view as on this basis it will be required to issue the minimum number of equity shares.

P.32.7 Firm A is planning to acquire Firm B. The relevant financial details of the two firms prior to the merger announcement are as follows: LO 32.2 LOD D

Particulars	Firm A	Firm B
Market price per share	₹75	₹30
Number of shares	10,00,000	5,00,000
Market value of the firm	7,50,00,000	1,50,00,000

The merger is expected to bring gains which have present value of ₹1.5 crore. Firm A offers 2,50,000 shares in exchange for 5 lakh shares to the shareholders of Firm B.

You are required to determine:

(a) total value of Firm AB (PVAB) after merger;

(b) gains to the shareholders of Firm A; and

(c) true cost of acquiring Firm B and net present value of the merger to Firm B.

Solution

(a) PV_{AB} = PV_A + PV_B + Present value gain from merger
= ₹7.5 crore + ₹1.5 crore + ₹1.5 crore
= ₹10.5 crore

(b) Number of shares after the merger = 10 lakh (A) + 2.5 Lakh (issued for shareholders of Firm B) = 12.5 lakh. The sumof ₹10.5 crore will be apportioned in the proportion of 4:1 between the shareholders of Firm A and B, that is, ₹8.4 crore and ₹2.1 crore respectively. The gain to firm A = ₹8.4 crore – ₹7.5 crore = ₹0.9 crore.

(c) Cost of acquiring Firm B is equal to the gain shared by the shareholders of Firm B, that is, (₹10.5 crore × 1/5 = ₹2.1 crore – ₹1.5 crore) = ₹0.6 crore.

P.32.8 A Ltd is considering takeover of B Ltd and C Ltd. The financial data for the three companies are as follows: LO 32.2 LOD M

Particulars	A Ltd	B Ltd	C Ltd
Equity share capital of ₹10 each (₹/million)	450	180	90
Earnings (₹/million)	90	18	18
Market price of each share (₹)	60	37	46

Calculate **(a)** Price-earnings (P/E) exchange ratios, and **(b)** Earnings per share of A Ltd after the acquisition of B Ltd and C Ltd separately. Will you recommend the merger of either/both of the companies? Justify your answer.

Solution

(a) Determination of P/E exchange ratio

Particulars	A Ltd	B Ltd	C Ltd
Total earnings (₹ million)	90	18	18
Number of equity shares (million)	45	18	9
EPS (₹)	2	1	2
MPS (₹)	60	37	46
P/E ratio (times)	30	37	23
P/E Exchange ratio	—	37/30	23/30

(b) EPS of A Ltd after the acquisition of B Ltd and C Ltd

	After the acquisition of	
	B Ltd	C Ltd
Total earnings after merger (₹ million)	108	108
Number of shares (million)	67.2	51.9
	45 + (18 × 37/30)	45 + (9 × 23/30)
Combined earnings (₹)	1.61	2.081

While there is an accretion in EPS on combining Firm C, there is a dilution in EPS on acquisition of Firm B. Therefore, merger with only company C is recommended.

P.32.9 Prospective Limited is contemplating taking over the business of Target Limited. The summarised balance sheet of Target Limited as on 31st March was as follows: **LO 32.2** LOD M

(₹ lakh)

Liabilities	*Amount*	*Assets*	*Amount*
Equity share capital (50 lakh @ ₹10)	500	Fixed assets:	
General reserve	250	Land and buildings	300
Profit and loss account	120	Plant and machinery	580
13% Debentures	100	Current assets:	
Current liabilities	30	Inventories	70
		Debtors	35
		Bank	15
	1,000		1,000

Additional information:

1. Prospective Limited agrees to takeover all the current assets at their book value but the fixed assets were to be revalued as under:
   Land and buildings: ₹500 lakh
   Plant and machinery: ₹500 lakh
   These sums apart, Prospective Limited is required to pay ₹50 lakh for goodwill.
2. Purchase consideration is to be paid as ₹130 lakh, in cash, to pay for 13% debentures and other liabilities, and the balance is to be paid in terms of shares of Prospective Limited.
3. Expected benefits (FCFF) accruing to Prospective limited. are as follows:

   (₹ lakh)

Year 1	*Year 2*	*Year 3*	*Year 4*	*Year 5*
₹200	₹300	₹260	₹200	₹100

   Further, it is estimated that the FCFF are expected to grow at 5 per cent per annum after 5 years.
4. Cost of capital for the purpose of analysis is to be 15 per cent.
   Suggest whether Prospective Limited is likely to benefit taking over Target Limited.

Solution

Financial evaluation of merger decision (₹ lakh)

(i) Cost of acquisition		
Fixed assets:		
Land and buildings	500	
Plant and machinery	500	
Goodwill	50	₹1,050

(Contd.)

(Contd.)

Current assets:		
Inventories	70	
Debtors	35	
Bank	15	120
		1,170

(ii) ₹1,170 lakh is payable as follows:

Cash payment to pay 13% Debentures and current liabilities	130
Shares of Prospective Limited (₹1,170 lakh – ₹130 lakh)	1,040

(iii) Present value of FCFF (Years 1 = 5) *(₹ lakh)*

Year-end	*FCFF*	*PV factor (0.15)*	*Total PV*
1	₹200	0.870	₹174.00
2	300	0.756	226.80
3	260	0.658	171.08
4	200	0.572	114.40
5	100	0.497	49.70
			735.98

(iv) PV of FCFF after the forecast period

TV5 = FCFF5 $(1 + g)/(K_e - g)$

= ₹100 (1.05)/(0.15 – 0.05) = ₹1,050 lakh

Present value = ₹1,050 lakh × 0.497 = ₹521.85 lakh

(v) Determination of net present value *(₹ lakh)*

Present value of FCFF (years 1 – 5)	₹735.98
Present value of FCFF subsequent to year 5	521.85
Total present value of benefits/FCFF	1,257.83
Less: Cost of acquisition	1,170.00
Net present value	87.83

Recommendation As the NPV is positive, acquisition of Target Limited is financially viable.

P.32.10 Balance sheet of XYZ Limited as on March 31 (current year) is as follows: LO 32.2 LOD M

(₹ lakh)

Liabilities	*Amount*	*Assets*	*Amount*
Equity share capital 10 lakh shares @ ₹20 each)	₹200	Plant and machinery	₹250
13% Debentures	100	Furniture and fittings	5
Retained earnings	50	Inventories	90
Creditors and other current liabilities	30	Debtors	25
		Bank balance	10
	380		380

(i) The company is to be absorbed by ABC Limited on the above date. The consideration for absorption is the discharge of debentures at a premium of 10 per cent, taking over the liability in respect of sundry creditors and other current liabilities and payment of ₹14 in cash and one share of ₹10 in ABC Limited, at the market value of ₹16 per share, in exchange for one share in XYZ Limited The cost of dissolution of ₹10 lakh is to be met by the purchasing company.

(ii) Expected incremental yearly free cash flows (FCFF) from acquisition for 5 years are as follows:

	(₹ lakh)
Year-end 1	₹100
2	135
3	175
4	200
5	80

(iii) The FCFF of XYZ Limited are expected to be constant after 5 years.

(iv) Cost of capital relevant for XYZ Limited cash flows is to be 14 per cent.

Based on the above information, comment on the financial soundness of ABC's decision regarding merger.

Solution

Financial analysis of merger decision

(i) Cost of acquisition (t = 0) *(₹ lakh)*

Equity share capital (10 lakh shares × ₹16)	₹160
Cash payment to shareholders (10 lakh shares × ₹14)	140
Redemption of 13% Debentures at 10% Premium	110
Payment required for creditors and other liabilities	30
Cost of dissolution	10
	450

(ii) PV of FCFF (years 1 – 5) *(₹ lakh)*

Year-end	*FCFF*	*PV factor (0.14)*	*Total PV*
1	₹100	0.877	₹87.70
2	135	0.769	103.81
3	175	0.675	118.12
4	200	0.592	118.40
5	80	0.519	41.52
			469.55

(iii) Present value of terminal sum related to FCFF after the forecast period

TV5 = FCFF5/k_0

= ₹80 lakh/0.14 = ₹571.429 lakh

PV of TV = ₹571.429 lakh × 0.519 = ₹296.57 lakh

(iv) Determination of net present value *(₹ lakh)*

PV of FCFF (years 1 – 5)	₹469.55
PV of FCFF (after year 5)	296.57
Total PV of FCFF	766.12
Less: Cost of acquisition	450.00
Net present value	316.12

Recommendation As the NPV is positive, acquisition of the target firm XYZ Limited is financially viable.

P.32.11 Excellent Limited, acquiring company, is interested in the acquisition of Pathetic Limited, target company. The management of Excellent Limited wants you to compute the maximum price it should be willing to pay to acquire Pathetic Limited as per adjusted present value approach. For the purpose, you have been provided with the following data: LO 32.2 LOD D

(i) As a result of acquisition, it is expected that the FCFF of Excellent Limited are likely to increase as follows for 6 years

	(₹ lakh)
Year – end 1	₹120
2	150
3	200
4	220
5	140
6	100

(ii) The FCFF of Pathetic Limited are expected to be constant after 6 years.
(iii) Unlevered cost of equity is 15 per cent.
(iv) 10% Debt (to the extent of ₹120 lakh) will finance part of acquisition cost. Debt will be reduced to ₹70 lakh at the end of year 6 by repaying ₹10 lakh at the end of the each year, commencing from year 1. Debt level is expected to remain at that level thereafter.
(v) Corporate tax rate is 35 per cent.
(vi) Advantage from debt is to be valued at cost of debt.
(vii) Bankruptcy costs are assumed to be zero.

Solution

(i) **PV of FCFF, discounted at unlevered cost of equity (k_u)** *(₹ lakh)*

Year-end	*FCFF*	*PV factor (0.15)*	*Total PV*
1	₹120	0.870	₹104.40
2	150	0.756	113.40
3	200	0.658	131.60
4	220	0.572	125.84
5	140	0.497	69.58
6	100	0.432	43.20
			588.02

(ii) **PV of FCFF after the explicit forecast period/terminal value**

$TV_6 = FCFF_6/k_u$ = ₹100 lakh/0.15 = ₹666.67 lakh
PV of terminal value = ₹666.67 lakh × 0.432 = ₹288.00 lakh

(iii) **(a) PV of tax shield, year 1 – 6** *(₹ lakh)*

Year-end	*Debt outstanding at year-end*	*Interest @ 10%*	*Tax shield (Interest × 0.35)*	*PV factor (0.10)*	*Total PV*
1	₹120	₹12	₹4.20	0.909	₹3.82
2	110	11	3.85	0.826	3.18
3	100	10	3.50	0.751	2.63
4	90	9	3.15	0.683	2.15
5	80	8	2.80	0.621	1.74
6	70	7	2.45	0.564	1.38
					14.90

(b)	PV of tax shield due to interest (on perpetual debt of ₹70 lakh)	(₹ lakh)
Amount of 10% Debt		₹70
Interest on debt (₹70 lakh × 10%)		7
Tax savings on interest (₹7 lakh × 0.35)		2.45
Present value of tax shield (₹2.45 lakh/0.10 = ₹24.50 lakh × 0.564)		13.82

(iv)	Value of Pathetic Limited as per APV	(₹ lakh)
Present value of FCFF (years 1 – 6)		₹588.02
Present value of FCFF after year 6		288
Present value of tax shield due to interest (₹14.90 lakh + ₹13.82 lakh)		28.72
Total adjusted present value		904.74

Recommendation Excellent Limited should be willing to pay ₹904.74 lakh as the maximum cost of acquiring Pathetic Limited.

P.32.12 The summarised balance sheet of Target Limited as at March 31 (current year is given below: **LO 32.2** LOD **D**

(₹ lakh)

Liabilities	Amount	Assets		Amount
Equity share capital (20 lakh shares @ ₹100 each)	₹2,000	Fixed assets		₹1,900
		Investments		100
11.5% Preference share capital	100	Current assets:		
Retained earnings	400	Inventories	₹500	
10.5% Debentures	300	Debtors	400	
Current liabilities	200	Bank	100	1,000
	3,000			3,000

Negotiations for takeover of T Limited result in its acquisition by A Limited. The purchase consideration consists of: (i) ₹300 lakh 11% debentures of A Limited for redeeming the 10.5% debentures of T Limited, (ii) ₹100 lakh 12% preference shares in A Ltd for the payment of the 11.5% preference shares capital of T Ltd, (iii) 20 lakh equity shares in A Limited to be issued at its current market price 150 and (iv) A Limited would meet dissolution expenses (estimated to cost ₹30 lakh).

(v) The following are projected incremental free cash flows (FCFF) expected from acquisition for 6 years

	(₹ lakh)
Year-end 1	₹450
2	600
3	780
4	900
5	650
6	350

(vi) The free cash flow of the target firm are expected to decline at 10 per cent per annum after 6 years.
(vii) After acquisition, investments are to be disposed off; they are expected to realise ₹120 lakh.
(viii) Current liabilities are expected to be settled at ₹190 lakh.
(ix) Given the risk complexion of target firm, cost of capital has been decided at 14 per cent.

Advise the company regarding financial feasibility of the acquisition.

Solution

(i) Cost of acquisition (t = 0) (₹ *lakh*)

Share capital (20 lakh shares × ₹150 per share)	₹3,000
12% Preference share capital	100
11% Debentures	300
Settlement of current liabilities	190
Dissolution expenses of target firm	30
Less: Cash proceeds from sale of investments	(120)
	3,500

(ii) Present value of FCFF (years 1 = 6) (₹ *lakh*)

Year-end	*FCFF*	*PV factor (0.14)*	*Total PV*
1	₹450	0.877	₹394.65
2	600	0.769	461.40
3	780	0.675	526.50
4	900	0.592	532.80
5	650	0.519	337.35
6	350	0.456	159.60
			2,412.30

(iii) PV of Terminal Value, that is, FCFF after the forecast period

TV6 = FCFF6 $(1 - g)/ (k_0 + g)$
= ₹350 lakh (1 – 0.10)/ (0.14 + 0.10) = ₹315 lakh/ 0.24 = ₹1,312.5 lakh

PV of TV = ₹1312.5 lakh × 0.456 = ₹598.5 lakh

(iv) Determination of net present value (₹ *lakh*)

Present value of FCFF (years 1 – 6)	₹2,412.30
Present value of FCFF subsequent to year 6	598.50
Total PV of FCFF	3010.80
Less: Cost of acquisition	3500.00
Net present value	(489.20)

Recommendation As the NPV is negative, acquisition of Target Limited is not financially viable.

P.32.13 Suppose, shareholders of Target Limited (of P. 33.12) agree to receive shares equivalent to their present net worth in A Limited. Does it make the decision of acquisition favourable? **LO 32.2** LOD **D**

Solution

(i) Cost of acquisition (*t* = 0) (₹ *lakh*)

Share capital (₹2,000 lakh) + Retained earnings (₹400 lakh) = ₹2,400 lakh net worth	
(16 lakh shares in *A* Ltd × ₹150 per share)	₹2,400
12% Preference share capital	100
11% Debentures	300
Settlement of current liabilities	190
Dissolution expenses of Target firm	30
Less: Cash proceeds from sale of investments	(120)
	2,900

(ii) Determination of net present value

	(₹ lakh)
Total PV of FCFF (computed in P.15.16)	₹3,010.80
Less: Cost of acquisition	2,900.00
Net present value	110.80

Recommendation As the NPV is positive, acquisition of Target Limited is now financially viable. Evidently, the decision of acquisition becomes favourable.

P33.14 A Ltd is contemplating to acquire T Ltd. The following data has been assembled in this connection: **LO 32.2** LOD **D**

Particulars	*A Ltd*	*T Ltd*
Earnings per share (EPS)	₹2	₹1
Expected growth in EPS	0.05	0.10
Number of equity shares outstanding (lakh)	10	3
Price per share	20	15

(i) If A Ltd acquires T Ltd on the basis of exchange of shares in proportion to their market values, what will the new EPS be?

(ii) Assuming no synergic gains, construct a schedule of EPS for the next 10 years with and without the acquisition. How long would it take to eliminate the dilution in EPS? Do you think the acquisition offer is attractive?

Solution

(i) Exchange ratio = Market price of shares of *T* Ltd /Market price of shares of A Ltd = ₹15/20 = 0.75.

Number of shares to be issued in *A* Ltd = 3,00,000 × 0.75 = 2,25,000.

EPS (new) = (₹2 × 10,00,000) + (₹1 × 3,00,000)/(10,00,000 + 2,25,000) = ₹1.88

(ii) Schedule of EPS with and without merger of A Ltd

Year	*A Ltd*		*T Ltd*		*AT Ltd (combined firm)*	
	Total EAT	*EPS*[a]	*Total EAT*	*EPS*[b]	*EATC*	*EPS*[c]
0	₹20,00,000	₹2.00	₹3,00,000	₹1.00	₹23,00,000	₹1.88
1	21,00,000	2.10	3,30,000	1.10	24,30,000	1.98
2	22,05,000	2.20	3,63,000	1.21	25,68,000	2.10
3	23,15,250	2.32	3,99,300	1.33	27,14,550	2.22
4	24,31,012	2.43	4,39,230	1.46	29,14,165	2.38
5	25,52,563	2.55	4,83,153	1.61	30,35,716	2.48
6	26,80,191	2.68	5,31,468	1.77	32,11,359	2.62
7	28,14,201	2.81	5,84,615	1.95	32,64,806	2.67
8	29,54,911	2.96	6,43,077	2.14	35,97,988	2.94
9	31,02,656	**3.10**	7,07,384	2.36	38,10,040	**3.11**
10	32,57,789	3.26	7,78,123	2.59	40,35,912	3.30

[a] EPS without acquisition
[b] EPS without acquisition
[c] EPS without acquisition

The dilution in EPS will be eliminated after 8 years. The acquisition does not seem to be an attractive proposition for A Ltd.

P33.15 The following are the financial statements for A Ltd and T Ltd for the current financial year. Both firms operate in the same industry.

LO 32.2 LOD D

Balance sheets

Particulars	*A Ltd*	*T Ltd*
Total current assets	₹14,00,000	₹10,00,000
Total fixed assets (net)	10,00,000	5,00,000
Total assets	24,00,000	15,00,000
Equity capital (of ₹10 each)	10,00,000	8,00,000
Retained earnings	2,00,000	—
14% Long-term debt	5,00,000	3,00,000
Total current liabilities	7,00,000	4,00,000
	24,00,000	15,00,000

Income statements

Net sales	₹34,50,000	₹17,00,000
Cost of goods sold	27,60,000	13,60,000
Gross profit	6,90,000	3,40,000
Operating expenses	2,96,923	1,45,692
Interest	70,000	42,000
Earnings before taxes (EBT)	3,23,077	1,52,308
Taxes (0.35)	1,13,077	53,308
Earnings after taxes (EAT)	2,10,000	99,000

Additional information:

Number of equity shares	1,00,000	80,000
Dividend payment (D/P) ratio	0.40	0.60
Market price per share (MPS)	₹40	₹15

Assume that the two firms are in the process of negotiating a merger through an exchange of equity shares. You have been asked to assist in establishing equitable exchange terms, and are required to:

(i) Decompose the share prices of both the companies into EPS and P/E components, and also segregate their EPS figures into return on equity (ROE) and book value or intrinsic value per share (BVPS) components.

(ii) Estimate future EPS growth rates for each firm.

(iii) Based on expected operating synergies, A Ltd estimates that the intrinsic value of T's equity share would be ₹20 per share on its acquisition. You are required to develop a range of justifiable equity share exchange ratios that can be offered by A Ltd to T Ltd's shareholders. Based on your analysis in parts (i) and (ii), would you expect the negotiated terms to be closer to the upper, or the lower exchange ratio limits? Why?

(iv) Calculate the post-merger EPS based on an exchange ratio of 0.4 : 1 being offered by *A* Ltd. Indicate the immediate EPS accretion or dilution, if any, that will occur for each group of shareholders.

(v) Based on a 0.4:1 exchange ratio, and assuming that *A*'s pre-merger P/E ratio will continue after the merger, estimate the post-merger market price. Show the resulting accretion or dilution in pre-merger market prices.

Solution

(i) Determination of EPS, P/E ratio, ROE and BVPS of A Ltd and T Ltd.

Particulars	*A Ltd*	*T Ltd*
EAT (₹)	2,10,000	99,000
N	1,00,000	80,000
EPS (EAT ÷ N) (₹)	2.10	1.24
Market price per share (MPS) (₹)	40	15
P/E ratio (MPS/EPS)	19.05	12.12
Equity funds (EF) (₹)	12,00,000	8,00,000
BVPS (EF ÷ N) (₹)	12	10
ROE (EAT ÷ EF)	0.175	0.1237

(ii) Growth rates in EPS

Retention ratio (1 – D/P ratio)	0.6	0.4
Growth rate (ROE × Retention ratio)	0.105	0.0495

(iii) Justifiable equity share exchange ratio

(a) Market price based = MPS_T/MPS_A = ₹15/₹40 = 0.375 : 1 (lower limit)

(b) Intrinsic value based = ₹20/40 = 0.5 : 1 (upper limit)

Since A Ltd has a higher EPS, ROE, P/E ratio, and higher EPS growth expectations, the negotiated terms would be expected to be closer to the lower limit, based on the existing share prices.

(iv) Post-merger EPS and other effects

Particulars	*A Ltd*	*T Ltd*	*Combined*
EAT (₹)	2,10,000	99,000	3,09,000
Shares outstanding	1,00,000	80,000	1,32,000*
EPS (₹)	2.10	1.24	2.34
EPS accretion or (dilution) (₹)	0.24	(0.30**)	—

(v) Post-merger market price and other effects

Particulars	*A Ltd*	*T Ltd*	*Combined*
EPS	₹2.10	₹1.24	₹2.34
P/E ratio	(×) 19.05	(×) 12.12	(×) 19.05
	40	15	44.60
MPS accretion	4.60	2.84***	

* 1,00,000 shares + (0.40 × 80,000) = 1,32,000 shares

** EPS claim per old share = ₹2.34 × 0.4 = ₹0.936

EPS dilution (₹1.24 – Re.0.936) = ₹0.304

***MPS claim per old share = ₹44.60 × 0.4 = ₹17.84

Less MPS per old share 15.00

2.84

P32.16 The following information is provided relating to the acquiring company Efficient Ltd., and the target company Healthy Ltd. **LO 32.2** LOD **D**

Particulars	*Efficient Ltd*	*Healthy Ltd*
Number of shares (face value. ₹10 each)	10.00 lakh	7.5 lakh
Market capitalisation	500.00 lakh	750.00 lakh
P/E ratio (times)	10.00	5.00
Reserves and surplus	300.00 lakh	165.00 lakh
Promoter's holding (number of shares)	4.75 lakh	5.00 lakh

The Board of Directors of both the companies have decided to give a fair deal to the shareholders and accordingly for swap ratio the weights are decided as 40 per cent, 25 per cent and 35 per cent respectively for earning, book value and market price of share of each company.

(i) Calculate the swap ratio and also calculate promoter's holding percentage after acquisition; **(ii)** What is the EPS of Efficient Ltd. after acquisition of Healthy Ltd.? **(iii)** What is expected market price per share and market capitalisation of Efficient Ltd. after acquisition, assuming P/E ratio of Firm Efficient Ltd. remains unchanged and (iii) Calculate free float market capitalisation of the merged firm.

Solution

(i) (a) Computation of EPS, book value per share and MPS

Particulars	*Efficient Ltd*	*Healthy Ltd*
1. Market capitalisation	₹500 lakh	₹750 lakh
2. Number of shares (face value of ₹10 each)	10 lakh	7.5 lakh
3. Market price per share (1/2)	₹50	₹100
4. Price-earnings ratio (times)	10	5
5. Earnings per share (3/4)	₹5	₹20
6. Total earnings after taxes (2 × 5)	50 lakh	150 lakh
7. Equity share capital (2 × ₹10)	100 lakh	75 lakh
8. Reserves and surplus	300 lakh	165 lakh
9. Equity funds (7 + 8)	400 lakh	240 lakh
10. Book value per share, BPS (9/2)	40	32

Determination of swap ratio

Particulars	*Ratio × weight = Total*
EPS (₹20:5)	4:1@ × 0.40 = 1.6
Book value (₹32:40)	0.8:1 × 0.25 = 0.2
Market price per share (₹100:50)	2:1 × 0.35 = 0.7
	2.5

@ Since EPS is 4 times of Healthy Ltd, 4 shares are required to be issued in Efficient Ltd. for every one share of Healthy Ltd; hence, the ratio is 4:1. Similarly, the other ratios are computed.

With a swap ratio is 2.5:1, for every 1 share of Healthy Ltd, 2.5 shares are to be issued in Efficient Ltd. Thus, the total number of shares to be issued to Healthy Ltd. is 7.5 lakh × 2.5 = 18.75 lakh shares.

Total number of shares in Efficient Ltd. (after acquisition) = (10 lakh existing shares + 18.75 lakh shares issued) = 28.75 lakh shares. The promoter's holding (%) after acquisition = number of shares held by promoters, 4.75 lakh + (2.5 × 5.00 lakh = 12.5 lakh) = 17.25 lakh/Total number of shares, 28.75 lakh = 60 per cent.

(ii) EPS after acquisition = Total earnings after acquisition/ Total number of shares after acquisition = ₹50 lakh + ₹150 lakh = ₹200 lakh/28.75 lakh = ₹6.956

(iii) Expected MPS = ₹6.956 × 10 times = ₹69.56

(iv) Free float market capitalisation (merged firm):

Total number of shares	28.75 lakh
Less shares held by promoters	17.25 lakh
Shares in the market	11.50 lakh
Multiplied by MPS	₹69.56
Free float market capitalisation	₹799.94 lakh

P.32.17 Mr. Ravi is a first generational entrepreneur. He had taken over the unorganised coal business- run in the family and organised into a well-respected firm in the region- doing better than the most companies operating in the same industry. The hard working man and his team of dedicated employees worked relentlessly for the growth of the firm. LO 32.5 LOD M

The company extracted coal from the coalmines, processed it into coke and charcoal and exported it to the energy hungry 'Western World'. The company had done very well during the period of 2002–2007 when the global economy was witnessing the steady growth. But due to the global recession of 2008 and the subsequent time, which followed, his firm witnessed a severe setback and has started to incur losses; its accumulated losses being ₹480 lakh as at March 31, 2014.

Although Mr. Ravi had a good business acumen (as his other two business companies were performing exceptionally well), he did not have the strong financial management background. Mr. Ravi, however, feels that the worst is over and the company would start earning profits. Given its present unsatisfactory state of financial affairs (as shown by its latest balance sheet), he apprehends that the firm would not be able to regain its past glory. While he was upset (at this juncture), he remembers his friend, Ankit, an MBA, who specialised in financial management. He, at present, is a leading consultant in Finance. He apprised him of the situation and sought his advice for future course of action.

Mr. Ankit asked for the current year's balance sheet of the coal processing company.

Balance Sheet of Coal Processing Company as at March 31, 2014

(*In ₹ Lakh*)

Liabilities	*Amount*	*Assets*	*Amount*
Equity shares (10,00,000 in number)	1,000	Land and building	360
12.5% Preference shares (₹100 each)	60	Plant and machinery	140
10% Debentures	600	Stock	590
Debenture interest payable	60	Debtors	170
10% Bank loan	160	Cash at bank	95
Trade creditors	100	Preliminary expenses	105
		Cost of issue of debentures	40
		Profit and loss account	480
	1,980		**1,980**

On further conversation with Mr. Ravi, Ankit was convinced that the future of the company looks bright. The company had decided to enter the domestic market- where the energy consumption was fast increasing because of the fast growth and also the Government had eased out the sector—making it possible for the company to expect nearly the same price for the upgraded quality of coke and charcoal.

Mr. Ankit, after looking at the balance sheet and analysing the future strategies of the company, was convinced that the firm is expected to make profits in future. He suggests that the fortune of the company can be turned around if the firm adopts the following measures for financial restructuring:

1. Equity shares are to be reduced by 65%, i.e. ₹35 per share, fully paid up. The company will also issue 7 lakh equity shares at ₹35 each to pay the bank loan and augment the working capital.
2. Preference shareholders are willing to accept new preference shares, carrying lower dividend of 11%.
3. Debentureholders have agreed to forgo the outstanding interest. They have also agreed to accept new debentures but at 9% interest payment.
4. Trade creditors have agreed to forgo 20% of their existing claims.

5. Fixed assets are to be revalued at:

(a) Land and building: ₹400 lakh

(b) Plant and machinery: ₹90 lakh

6. Stock is to be valued at ₹510 lakh.

7. Financial restructuring expenses are estimated at ₹15 lakh.

Show the impact of financial restructuring, drawing the new balance sheet after the scheme is executed. Do you agree with the suggestion provided by Ankit?

Solution

Impact of Financial Restructuring

(₹ in Lakh)

1. Benefits to company	
(a) Reduction of liabilities payable	
(i) Reduction in equity share capital (10 lakh shares × ₹65 per share)	₹650
(ii) Waiver of debentures interest	60
(iii) 20% waiver from trade creditors (20% of ₹100 lakh)	20
	730
(b) Revaluation of land and building (₹400 lakh – ₹360 lakh)	40
(c) Total sum available to write off fictitious and over-valued assets	**770**
2. Amount utilised to write off losses, fictitious assets, etc.	
(a) Writing off profit and loss account	₹480
(b) Preliminary expenses	105
(c) Cost of issue of debentures	40
(d) Decrease in stock (₹680 lakh – ₹600 lakh)	80
(e) Revaluation of plant and machinery (₹140 lakh – ₹90 lakh)	50
(f) Expenses incurred for restructuring	15
	770

Balance Sheet of Coal Processing Ltd. (After Reconstruction)

(₹ in Lakh)

Liabilities	*Amount*	*Assets*	*Amount*
Equity shares (17 lakh @ ₹35 each)	595	Land and building	400
11% Preference shares (₹100 each)	60	Plant and machinery	90
9% Debentures	600	Stock	510
Trade creditors	80	Debtors	170
		Cash at bank	165
	1335		**1335**

Financial restructuring is likely to help the company to improve its reputation in the market. Also, the company should be able to raise additional funds in future for business expansion plans. The company is advised to opt for financial restructuring (as suggested by Mr. Ankit).

P.32.18 A company has 4 divisions. Its one of the divisions is yielding low returns and has a trend of decline in sales. Therefore, its management is considering to sell it. For the purpose, the finance manager has been asked to determine the value at which it can be sold. He collates the following data to determine the sale value of the division.

LO 32.5 | LOD M

(i) The expected operating CFAT the division was to generate for next 5 years (economic useful life) are as follows:

Year	*Amount (in ₹ million)*
1	₹16
2	12
3	11
4	10
5	8

(ii) The expected salvage value of long-term assets at year-end 5 is ₹15 million

(iii) Release the working capital at year-end is ₹7 million.

(iv) Division's external liabilities at present (t = 0) is ₹5 million.

(v) Required rate of return is 12 per cent.

Assume that the buyer of the division would pay for external liabilities.

Solution

Financial evaluation to determine the value of division at which it can be sold.

(i) Expected PV of CFAT to be lost (Amount in ₹ millions)

Year	*CFAT*		*PV factor (12%)*	*Total PV*
1		₹16	0.893	₹14.29
2		12	0.797	9.56
3		11	0.712	7.83
4		10	0.636	6.36
5(a)		8	0.567	4.54
5(b)	Sale value of long-term assets	15	0.567	8.51
5(c)	Release of working capital	7	0.567	3.97
Total				55.06
PV lost due to sale of division				55.06
(ii) *Less:* External liabilities of the division				(5.00)
(iii) Sale value of division (i)-(ii)				50.06

Recommendation The management should not sell the division for a price of less than ₹50.06 million.

MINI CASES

32.C.1 Following are the financial statements for A Ltd and T Ltd for the current financial year. Both firms operate in the same industry.

Balance sheets

	A Ltd	*T Ltd*
Total current assets	₹14,00,000	₹10,00,000
Total fixed assets (net)	10,00,000	5,00,000
Total assets	24,00,000	15,00,000
Equity capital (of ₹10 each)	10,00,000	8,00,000
Retained earnings	2,00,000	—
14% Long-term debt	5,00,000	3,00,000
Total current liabilities	7,00,000	4,00,000
	24,00,000	15,00,000

Income statements

Net sales	₹34,50,000	₹17,00,000
Cost of goods sold	27,60,000	13,60,000
Gross profit	6,90,000	3,40,000
Operating expenses	2,96,923	1,45,692
Interest	70,000	42,000
Earnings before taxes (EBT)	3,23,077	1,52,308
Taxes (0.35)	1,13,077	53,308
Earnings after taxes (EAT)	2,10,000	99,000

Additional information:

Number of equity shares	1,00,000	80,000
Dividend payment (D/P) ratio	0.40	0.60
Market price per share (MPS)	₹40	₹15

Assume that the two firms are in the process of negotiating a merger through an exchange of equity shares. You have been asked to assist in establishing equitable exchange terms, and are required to:

(i) Decompose the share prices of both the companies into EPS and P/E components, and also segregate their EPS figures into return on equity (ROE) and book value or intrinsic value per share (BVPS) components.

(ii) Estimate future EPS growth rates for each firm.

(iii) Based on expected operating synergies, A Ltd estimates that the intrinsic value of T's equity share would be ₹20 per share on its acquisition. You are required to develop a range of justifiable equity share exchange ratios that can be offered by A Ltd to T Ltd's shareholders. Based on your analysis in parts (i) and (ii), would you expect the negotiated terms to be closer to the upper, or the lower exchange ratio limits? Why?

(iv) Calculate the post-merger EPS based on an exchange ratio of 0.4 : 1 being offered by A Ltd. Indicate the immediate EPS accretion or dilution, if any, that will occur for each group of shareholders.

(v) Based on a 0.4:1 exchange ratio, and assuming that A's pre-merger P/E ratio will continue after the merger, estimate the post-merger market price. Show the resulting accretion or dilution in pre-merger market prices.

Solution

(i) Determination of EPS, P/E ratio, ROE and BVPS of A Ltd and T Ltd

Particulars	*A Ltd*	*T Ltd*
EAT (₹)	2,10,000	99,000
N	1,00,000	80,000
EPS (EAT ÷ N) (₹)	2.10	1.24
Market price per share (MPS) (₹)	40	15
P/E ratio (MPS/EPS)	19.05	12.12
Equity funds (EF) (₹)	12,00,000	8,00,000
BVPS (EF ÷ N) (₹)	12	10
ROE (EAT ÷ EF)	0.175	0.1237

(ii) Growth rates in EPS

Retention ratio (1 – D/P ratio)	0.6	0.4
Growth rate (ROE × Retention ratio)	0.105	0.0495

(iii) Justifiable equity share exchange ratio

(a) Market price based = MPS_T/MPS_A = ₹15/₹40 = 0.375 : 1 (lower limit)
(b) Intrinsic value based = ₹20/40 = 0.5 : 1 (upper limit)

Since A Ltd has a higher EPS, ROE, P/E ratio, and higher EPS growth expectations, the negotiated terms would be expected to be closer to the lower limit, based on the existing share prices.

(iv) Post-merger EPS and other effects

	A Ltd	*T Ltd*	*Combined*
EAT (₹)	2,10,000	99,000	3,09,000
Shares outstanding	1,00,000	80,000	1,32,000*
EPS (₹)	2.10	1.24	2.34
EPS accretion or (dilution) (₹)	0.24	(0.30**)	—

(v) Post-merger market price and other effects

	A Ltd	*T Ltd*	*Combined*
EPS	₹2.10	₹1.24	₹2.34
P/E ratio	(×) 19.05	(×) 12.12	(×) 19.05
	40	15	44.60
MPS accretion	4.60	2.84***	

* 1,00,000 shares + (0.40 × 80,000) = 1,32,000 shares

** EPS claim per old share = ₹2.34 × 0.4 = ₹0.936
EPS dilution (₹1.24 – Re.0.936) = ₹0.304

***MPS claim per old share = ₹44.60 × 0.4 = ₹17.84
Less: MPS per old share 15.00
2.84

32.C.2 Expansion Ltd is a well-known brand in the country looking forward to diversify its product portfolio by acquiring another firm in the same industry. Stagnant Ltd is another firm in the country having popular brands in its product portfolio. Expansion Ltd is contemplating to acquire Stagnant Ltd. This acquisition is likely to add considerable value to Expansion Ltd with expanded client base. The management of Expansion Ltd. is keen to know if this acquisition is financially viable. Its CEO, Mr. Doordarshi Gupta, hires the best consultants in the Industry and asks his CFO, Prateek Dash, to evaluate the deal with the consultants in order to take a final call on the proposal of Expansion Ltd.

The following information is provided by the consultants about Stagnant Ltd:

The forecasted sales revenue of Stagnant Ltd for the next 7 years is given in the table below:

Year	*1*	*2*	*3*	*4*	*5*	*6*	*7*
Sales revenue (₹ million)	100	120	140	160	160	150	140

Balance sheet of Stagnant Ltd. as at March 31, 2014 is as follows

(₹ in million)

Liabilities	*Amount*	*Assets*	*Amount*
Share capital (10 lakh shares for ₹100 each)	100	Fixed assets:	
Reserves and surplus	30	Land and building	80
10% Debentures	20	Plant and machinery	90
Profit & loss	15	Patents	20
Trade creditors	80	Current assets:	
Provisions for taxes	5	Marketable securities (8 %)	5
		Inventory	45
		Debtors	5
		Cash and bank	5
	250		250

Additional Information:

(i) Variable expenses amount to 40 per cent of the sales revenue.

(ii) Fixed operating costs are estimated to be ₹20 million for the first 5 years and ₹24 million for next two years.

(iii) It would also be promoting its products by regular advertisement campaigns as per the product life cycle requirements. Estimated expenditure is given below:

Year	*1*	*2*	*3*	*4*	*5*	*6*	*7*
Expenditure (₹ million)	15	15	10	5	5	10	10

(iv) Plant and machinery are subject to 15 % rate of depreciation on written down value method.

(v) The company owns patents having useful life of 10 years and are subject to amortisation on the straight line basis.

(vi) The company has planned the following capital expenditure (incurred at the beginning of each year) for the next 7 years.

Year	*1*	*2*	*3*	*4*	*5*	*6*	*7*
Capital expenditure (₹ million)	15	20	25	20	30	25	20

(vii) Working capital in terms of Investment in current assets is estimated at 20 per cent of sales revenue.

(viii) Expected non-operating cash flow (including investment in marketable securities) in the initial year is ₹2.5 million.

(ix) Effective tax rate is 30 per cent and estimated cost of capital is 12 per cent.

(x) Free cash flows of the firm are expected to grow at 6 per cent after 7 years.

Balance sheet as at 31st March 2014 of the two firms operating in the same industry is as follows:

(Amounts in ₹ million)

Particulars	*Expansion Ltd.*	*Stagnant Ltd.*
Fixed assets	₹250	190
Current assets	100	60
Total assets	350	250
Equity capital	140	100
Reserves and surplus	50	30
10 % Debentures	25	20
Profit and loss Account	45	15
Total current liabilities	90	85
Total liabilities	350	250
Additional Information:		
EAT	20	10
P/E ratio	11	10

Purchase considerations (besides taking over current liabilities) consists of the following:

(i) Expansion Ltd would need to issue 6,00,000 (Exchange ratio: 0.6) at its current market price of ₹160,

(ii) Payment of ₹60 in cash per share issued,

(iii) Redemption of 10 per cent debentures at a premium of 10 per cent,

(Iv) Dissolution expenses are estimated at ₹15 million that would need to be taken into consideration

(v) Stagnant Ltd has a lawsuit pending against it which would require ₹50 million for its settlement in the coming years,

(vi) Market value of assets which would not be used after acquisition are worth ₹20 million.

The CFO, Prateek, decides to evaluate the deal as a capital budgeting decision. Prateek decides that in case the deal is viable, the most appropriate exchange ratio for the deal to materialise (at the current date), should also be provided for.

Solution

(i) Cost of acquisition *(t = 0)*

(₹ in million)

Payment to equity shareholders (6 lakh shares × 160)	96
Plus: Cash payment to equity shareholders (6 lakh shares × 60)	36
Plus: Payment to debentureholders	22
Plus: Payment for current liabilities	85
Plus: Dissolution expenses	15
Plus: Contingent liabilities	50
Less: Cash proceeds from sale of assets of Sunlife Pharma	(20)
Total	**284**

(ii) Present value of free cash flow for the period (year 1-7)

(Amount in ₹ million)

Particulars	*Year*						
	1	*2*	*3*	*4*	*5*	*6*	*7*
Sales revenue	100	120	140	160	160	150	140
Less:Variable cost	40	48	56	64	64	60	56
Fixed operating costs	20	20	20	20	20	24	24
Advertisement	15	15	10	5	5	10	10
Depreciation*	15.75	16.39	17.68	18.03	19.82	20.6	20.51
Amortization	2	2	2	2	2	2	2
EBIT	7.25	18.61	34.32	50.97	49.18	33.4	27.49
Less: Taxes (0.30)	2.17	5.58	10.30	15.29	14.75	10.02	8.24
NOPAT	5.08	13.03	24.02	35.68	34.43	23.38	19.25
Non-operating Income	2.5						
Add Depreciation	15.75	16.39	17.68	18.03	19.82	20.6	20.51
Add Amortisation	2	2	2	2	2	2	2
Gross cash flow	25.33	31.42	43.70	55.71	56.25	45.98	41.76
Less: Investment in (capital expenditure and current assets)**	0	0	28	24	30	23	18
Free cash flows(FCFF)	25.33	31.42	15.70	31.71	26.25	22.98	23.76
PV factor @12%	0.893	0.797	0.712	0.636	0.567	0.507	0.452
PV	22.63	25.04	11.18	20.17	14.89	11.65	10.74
Total present value							116.27

* Depreciation schedule is given in Working note I.

** Calculation for additional Investment is provided in the Working note II.

(iii) PV of free cash flows after the explicit forecast period of 7 years

$TV_7 = FCFF_7\ (1 + g)/(Ko\text{-}g)$

$= ₹23.753\text{million}\ (1 + 0.06)/(0.12 - 0.06) = ₹419.64 \text{ million}$

PV of TV = ₹419.64 million × 0.452 = ₹189.68 million

(iv) Determination of NPV

PV of free cash flows (years 1-7)	₹116.27 million
PV of free cash flows subsequent to year 7	189.68
Total PV of benefits/FCFF	305.95
Less: Cost of acquisition	284
Net present value	21.95

Recommendation As the NPV is positive, acquisition of Stagnant Ltd by Expansion Ltd is financially viable.

(v) Effect of merger on the market value of the combined firm.

Particulars	*Before Merger*		*After Merger*
	AB Pharma	*Sunlife Pharma*	*AB Pharma (Combined)*
EAT	₹2,00,00,000	₹1,00,00,000	₹3,00,00,000
Number of shares	14,00,000	10,00,000	20,00,000
P/E	11	10	11
EPS	14.54	10	15

(Contd.)

(*Contd.*)

MPS	160	100	165
Market value	₹22,40,00,000	₹10,00,00,000	₹33,00,00,000
Total MV		32,40,00,000	

Gain in market value after merger is ₹6 million. The minimum and maximum exchange ratio works out to be 0.625 and 0.6625***. So the EPS of the equity holders of both firms do not get diluted after the merger as is happening in the predetermined exchange ratio of 0.6.

(vi) Gain to the share-holders post-merger

Particulars	*Post-Merger*	
	Expansion Ltd.	*Stagnant Ltd.*
MPS	₹165	₹165
Market value	23,10,00,000	9,90,00,000
Gain to equityholders	70,00,000	(₹10,00,000)
Total gain	60,00,000	

***Calculation to determine the most the range of exchange ratio is shown in Working note III

Working Notes

I. Depreciation Schedule, Years 1-7

(Amount in ₹ million)

Year	*Depreciation base at the beginning of the year*	*Additions during the year*	*Total at the end of the year*	*Depreciation @15 %*
1	90	15	105	15.75
2	89.25	20	109.25	16.39
3	92.86	25	117.86	17.68
4	100.18	20	120.18	18.03
5	102.15	30	132.15	19.82
6	112.33	25	137.33	20.60
7	116.73	20	136.73	20.51

II. Determination of Investment [Capital Expenditure + Current Assets] Required, Years 1-7

(*Amount in ₹ million*)

Year	*Investment required*			*Existing investment in CA*	*Additional investments required*
	Capital expenditure	*Working capital*	*Total*		
1	15	20	35	60	Nil
2	20	24	44	45@	Nil
3	25	28	53	25@@	28
4	20	32	52	28	24
5	30	32	62	32	30
6	25	30	55	32	23
7	20	28	48	30	18

@ (₹60 million – ₹15 million capital expenditure); @@ (₹45 million – ₹20 capital expenditure)

III. Determination of exchange ratio range acceptable to both the companies

(a) The entire gain (₹6 million) from the merger goes to Expansion Ltd.

Post-merger value:

Expansion Ltd: ₹231 million
Stagnant Ltd: ₹100 million
The number of shares to be issued at market price of ₹160 so that the total market value of Stagnant Ltd remains at ₹100 million: 6,25,000
The number of shares already with Stagnant Ltd: 10,00,000
Therefore, the exchange ratio: 0.625

(b) If the entire gain (₹6 million) from the merger goes to Stagnant Ltd
Post-merger value:
Expansion Ltd: ₹224 million
Stagnant Ltd: ₹106 million
The number of shares to be issued at market price of ₹160 so that the total market value of Stagnant Ltd. is ₹106,000,000: 6,62,500
The number of shares already with Stagnant Ltd: 10, 00,000
Therefore, the exchange ratio: 0.6625
Acceptable range of exchange ratio is between 0.625 and 0.6625, for both the companies.

Scan the QR Code given at the end of chapter to access comprehensive cases.

REVIEW QUESTIONS

LOD: Easy

RQ.32.1 Provide the appropriate answers in the following: [LO 32.1,2]

(i) Merges can provide tax benefits in the case of set off and carry forward of losses. (True/False)

(ii) The cost of capital of a merged firm is different from both cost of capital of the acquiring firm and the target firm as synergy effects should be taken and risk complexion of both the firms changes on merger. (True/False)

(iii) In an amalgamation, the amalgamated company is entitled to carry forward accumulated losses as well as unabsorbed depreciation of the amalgamating company. (True/False)

(iv) Vertical merger is the merger of two firms which are involved
(a) in similar line of business (b) in different stages of distribution and production in same business activity (c) in different/unrelated business activities and (d) None of these

(v) Major advantages of merger are
(a) Tax benefits (b) Synergy (c) Economies of scale (d) All of these

(vi) The type of financing in which an initial payment (to the shareholders of acquired firm) is followed by additional payment in future years based on the target firm's increase in earnings is known as
(a) preference share financing (b) tender offer (c) deferred payment plan and (d) ordinary share financing.

(vii) The type of financing in which the purchaser approaches the shareholders directly instead of the management to acquire interest in acquired firm is known as
(a) preference share financing (b) tender offer (c) deferred payment plan and (d) ordinary share financing.

(viii) What is the terminal value of the firm if FCFF at the end of last year of explicit forecast period is ₹100 lakh. Cost of capital is 15% and growth rate of firm is constant at 5 per cent.
(a) ₹1000 lakh (b) ₹1050 lakh (c) ₹950 lakh and (d) None of these

(ix) Two firms A and B have earnings after taxes of ₹60,000 and ₹40,000 respectively, with identical EPS of ₹10. What will the EPS of the firm be after merger for share exchange ratio as 0.5:1,

where A acquires B?
(a) ₹10 (b) ₹15 (c) ₹12.5 and (d) ₹20

(x) Firm A acquires firm B, MPS of B is ₹20 and EPS is ₹5. For an exchange ratio of 1.5: 1, what was the P/E ratio used in acquiring B?
(a) 4 (b) 5 (c) 6 and (d) 2.67

[Answers: (i) True, (ii) True, (iii) True, (iv) b, (v) d, (vi) c, (vii) b, (viii) b, (ix) c, and (x) c.]

RQ.32.2 (a) What is a merger? Enumerate different types of mergers. What are the potential economic advantages from mergers? [LO 32.1]

(b) What synergies do exist in (a) horizontal mergers, (b) vertical mergers and (c) conglomerate mergers?

RQ.32.3 'Conglomerate firm shares tend to have a higher market value due to lower cost of capital'. Elucidate the statement. [LO 32.1]

RQ.32.4 AB Ltd wishes to acquire CD Ltd on the basis of an exchange ratio of 0.8. Other relevant financial data is as follows: [LO 32.2]

Particulars	*AB Ltd*	*CD Ltd*
Earnings after taxes (EAT)	₹1,00,000	₹20,000
Equity shares outstanding	50,000	20,000
Earnings per share (EPS)	2	1
Market price per share	20	8

(i) Determine the number of shares required to be issued by AB Ltd for acquisition of CD Ltd
(ii) What would be the exchange ratio if it is based on the market prices of shares of AB Ltd and CD Ltd?
(iii) What is the current price-earnings ratio of the two companies?
(iv) Assuming the earnings of each firm remains the same, what is the EPS after the acquisition?
(v) What is the equivalent EPS per share of CD Ltd?
(vi) Ascertain the gain to shareholders of both the companies (a) at 0.8 exchange ratio, and (b) an exchange ratio based on market price.

LOD: Medium

RQ.32.5 How are mergers financed? Analyse the impact of the various modes of finance on a company's EPS. [LO 32.2]

RQ.32.6 How are the expected gains from the merger shared between the acquiring and the acquired firms? Illustrate you answer with appropriate examples. [LO 32.2]

RQ.32.7 'The capital budgeting technique of evaluating a merger proposition is the most appropriate.' Elucidate the statement. [LO 32.2]

RQ.32.8 How are lower limit and upper limit of share exchange ratio between the acquiring company and the target company determined? Explain your answer with an appropriate numerical example. [LO 32.2]

RQ.32.9 What is corporate restructuring? State the major forms in which it can be carried out. [LO 32.5]

RQ.32.10 Distinguish between 'friendly takeover' and 'hostile takeover'. What strategies are adopted by the acquiring firm in the case of a hostile takeover? [LO 32.4]

RQ.32.11 What is a leveraged buyout (LBO)? What key points should be borne in mind in such an acquisition? [LO 32.5]

RQ.32.12 Describe the tax aspects related to amalgamations and demergers. [LO 32.3]

RQ.32.13 Discuss the legal process relating to approval of merger. [LO 32.4]

RQ.32.14 Examine the provisions of the Indian Companies Act governing corporate takeovers. [LO 32.4]

RQ.32.15 State the defences available to the target firm to prevent hostile takeover. [LO 32.4]

RQ.32.16 A Ltd has acquired T Ltd in the current year. T Ltd has its base year earnings of ₹15 lakh. At the time of merger, its equity shareholders received initial payment of 1 lakh shares of A Ltd. The market value of A Ltd's share is ₹100 per share and the P/E ratio is 10. As a part of the agreement, it has been also decided to pay to the shareholders of T Ltd on deferred payment basis for next 3 years; the payment is contingent to the realisation of the potential projected earnings after merger.

The projected post-merger earnings of T Ltd for next 3 years are ₹18 lakh, ₹20 lakh and ₹25 lakh respectively.

Assuming no change in the P/E ratio and share prices of T Ltd, determine the number of shares required to be issued to the shareholders of T Ltd during these years. [LO 32.2]

RQ.32.17 The Sick Company Ltd (SCL) has total accumulated losses of ₹25 lakh caused by operating losses of past several years. The Strong Ltd has acquired the SCL to use these losses and to diversify its operations. The Strong Ltd 's expected earnings before taxes are ₹20 lakh per year for the next 3 years.

Assuming these earnings are realised and setting off the losses is allowed under tax laws, determine the likely benefit to Strong Ltd, given corporate tax rate of 35 per cent and its cost of capital as 15 per cent. [LO 32.2]

RQ.32.18 Royal Industries Ltd (RIL) is considering a takeover of Supreme Industries Ltd (SIL). The earnings, number of outstanding equity shares and P/E ratios of the two companies are as follows: [LO 32.2]

Particulars	*Royal Industries Ltd*	*Supreme Industries Ltd*
Earnings after taxes (EAT)	₹20,00,000	₹10,00,000
Equity shares outstanding	10,00,000	10,00,000
Earnings per share (EPS)	2	1
P/E ratio (times)	10	5

(i) What is the market value of each company before merger?

(ii) Assume that the management of RIL estimates that the shareholders of SIL will accept an offer of one share of RIL for four shares of SIL. If there are no synergic effects, what is the market value of the post-merger RIL? What is the new price per share? Are the shareholders of RIL better or worse-off than they were before the merger?

(iii) Assume because of synergic effects, the management of RIL estimates that the earnings will increase by 10 per cent, what is the new post-merger EPS and price per share? Are the shareholders better or worse off than before the merger?

LOD: Difficult

RQ.32.19 What is the adjusted present value (APV) approach? How does it differ from the conventional net present value approach of evaluating a target firm? [LO 32.2]

RQ.32.20 What is financial restructuring? What are the key components of the financial restructuring scheme? Draw an appropriate financial restructuring scheme for a financially troubled firm. [LO 32.5]

RQ.32.21 What is demerger? What are the common methods used by firms to divest/demerge themselves off operating units? [LO 32.5]

RQ.32.22 Critically examine the SEBI takeover code. [LO 32.4]

RQ.32.23 Consider the following financial data of A Ltd and T Ltd just before the merger announcement of the latter by the former: [LO 32.2]

Particulars	*A Ltd*	*T Ltd*
Market price per share	₹150	₹30
Number of shares (in lakh)	10	6
Market value (MV) of the firm (in ₹lakh)	1,500	180

Determine the cost of merger:

(i) if A Ltd intends to pay ₹240 lakh in cash to T Ltd;

(ii) if A Ltd intends to offer its 1,60,000 shares in exchange of shares of T Ltd. Assume further, the merger is expected to generate cost savings with present value of ₹94.80 lakh. It is expected that these cost savings would push up the market price.

(**Note:** consider each case independently)

ANSWERS

32.4 **(i)** 16,000 shares,
(ii) 0.4:1,
(iii) P/E ratio 10 for AB Ltd. And 8 for CD Ltd.
(iv) ₹1.82 (when exchange ratio is 0.8) and ₹2.07 (when exchange ratio is 0.4),
(v) ₹1.45,
(vi) Loss ₹90,909 for shareholders of AB Ltd. and gain of ₹1,30,909 for shareholders of CD Ltd. (when exchange ratio is 0.8); Gain of ₹34.483 and of ₹5,517 for shareholders of AB Ltd. and Cd Ltd. (when exchange ratio is 0.4).

32.16 Year 1 (30,000 shares); Year 2 (50,000 shares); Year 3 (1,00,000 shares).

32.17 ₹7.4 lakh.

32.18 **(i)** ₹200 lakh (RIL), ₹50 lakh (SIL).
(ii) ₹300 lakh (Post-merger market value of RIL); ₹24 (MPS); Gain to the shareholders of RIL is ₹40 lakh due to merger.
(iii) EPS ₹2.64; the shareholders are better in post-merger situation.

32.23 **(i)** ₹60 lakh (ii) ₹64.80 lakh.

Scan the QR Code to access comprehensive solutions to all numerical review questions and additional material.

PART 10

INTERNATIONAL FINANCE

Chapter 33
FOREIGN EXCHANGE MARKETS AND DEALINGS

Chapter 34
FOREIGN EXCHANGE EXPOSURE AND RISK MANAGEMENT

Chapter 35
INTERNATIONAL FINANCIAL MANAGEMENT

International finance has assumed considerable significance in the context of the emerging financial scenario in India, in the wake of the globalisation of the Indian economy. Its important dimensions are comprehensively examined in Part 10 of the book. Chapter 33 discusses foreign exchange markets and dealings. Foreign exchange exposure and risk management are illustrated in Chapter 34, while international financial management, including important sources of international finance, is covered in Chapter 35.

CHAPTER 33

Foreign Exchange Markets and Dealings

LEARNING OBJECTIVES

LO 33.1	Present a broad view of the foreign exchange markets
LO 33.2	Explain the various types of foreign exchange rates (spot, forward and cross), direct and indirect quotations and spread and arbitrage processes in foreign exchange dealings
LO 33.3	Discuss the factors—inflation, interest, balance of payment, volume of international reserves and level of activity and employment—and theories that account for variation in exchange rates

INTRODUCTION

There is a growing tendency among business firms to operate in other countries. They set up their factories/subsidiaries abroad to seek new markets and develop products to cater to the needs and requirements of foreign markets; they raise capital from many countries. Being so, it is imperative for finance managers, in particular, and other managers, in general, to understand the processes and methods of dealings in foreign exchange markets.

This Chapter deals with the *modus operandi* of foreign exchange transactions in foreign exchange markets. First, it presents a broad overview of the foreign exchange markets. The foreign exchange dealings are covered in the subsequent discussion. The major determinants/select theories of exchange rates are also explained. The main points are summarised by way of recapitulation.

LO 33.1 FOREIGN EXCHANGE MARKETS

Different countries have different currencies and the settlement of all business transactions within a country is done/preferred in the local currency. The foreign exchange market provides a forum where the currency of one country is traded for the currency of another country. Suppose Air India has signed an agreement to buy/import aircrafts from a US based firm. Air India has to pay the US firm in American dollars. To do so, Air India has to purchase US dollars ($) in the foreign exchange market and pay the US firm. In case Air India buys aircrafts from a French firm, it would be required to purchase euros (€) from the foreign exchange market to make the payment. Thus, the requirement of foreign currency of the importer (Air India) hinges upon which country the imports are made from and/or the currency preferred by the exporter. While domestic currency is preferred by the exporters, in general, they may be willing to deal in the 'major' currencies (also referred to as 'hard' currencies) of the world. Included in this category are the US dollar (US $), the British pound sterling (£), Euro (€), the Japanese yen, and the Swiss franc (CHF). Apart from the payment of imports, foreign currency requirements may be traced to foreign direct investment and lendings also.

Foreign exchange (FE) markets deal with a large volume of funds as well as a large number of currencies (belonging to various countries). For this reason, they are not only worldwide markets but also the world's largest financial markets. Though there are foreign exchange markets in virtually all countries, London, New York and Tokyo are the nerve centres of foreign exchange activity. The large commercial/investment banks and central banks of the countries are the principal participants in the FE markets. In general, business firms do not operate on their own, they normally buy and sell currencies through a commercial bank. Likewise, as a strategy, commercial banks may sometimes engage/prefer the services of individual brokers to hide their identity as they apprehend that the disclosure of their names may unfavourably influence short-term quotes. For the same reason, importers, needing a large volume of funds may like to deal through brokers/commercial banks.

While the primary objective of commercial banks, investment bankers and brokers in dealing FE markets is *commercial* in nature, whether they deal on their own account or for their clients, the central bank's operations (say, in the case of India, the Reserve Bank of India) in the market are *regulatory* in nature. To put it differently, the principal central bank of the country intervenes in the FE market primarily to regulate the volatility of foreign exchange rates. Obviously, the objective of their operations in the FE markets is not to make profits. They intend to maintain the exchange rate of the domestic country in tune with the requirements of the national economy and Government policy. They intend to avoid a sudden appreciation or depreciation of the domestic currency as it may be against the interest of the domestic economy. This is achieved through the buying and selling of the foreign currency by the central bank of the country. For instance, the Reserve Bank of India, on many occasions in recent years, has sold US $ to augment their supply with a view to prevent a continuous decline in the value of Indian rupee *vis-à-vis* US $; likewise, it has purchased US $ many a time to weaken the Indian rupee, with a view to promote exports.

Most of the trading in the FE markets take place in the 'major' currencies stated earlier. All these currencies are fully convertible. There is an active market for these currencies in terms of the presence of a large number of buyers and sellers willing to execute foreign exchange dealings in these currencies; foreign exchange dealings primarily take place through telephone and fax messages. Therefore, the geographical existence of the foreign exchange markets does not have much relevance.

LO 33.2 FOREIGN EXCHANGE DEALINGS

We explain below the procedure of foreign exchange dealings—in terms of various types of exchange rates (spot, forward and cross), direct and indirect quotations and spread and arbitrage processes—to realise profits in the case of misalignment of exchange rates.

Exchange Rates

Different countries have different currencies and the different currencies have different values. Evidently, there is a need for rules for currency conversions for global business and investments.

The rate of conversion is the exchange rate. In other words, an **exchange rate** is the price of one country's currency expressed in terms of the currency of another country. For instance, a rate of ₹60 per US $ implies that one US dollar costs ₹60. To put it differently, US $0.01667 costs one rupee as 1/60 = $0.01667. Thus, there are two quotes: **(i)** Indian ₹60 = US $1 (Direct quote) and **(ii)** US $0.01667 = Indian ₹1 (Indirect quote). Both quotations reflect the same exchange/conversion rate and are reciprocal to each other.

Exchange rate is the price of one currency expressed in terms of the currency of another country.

Direct and Indirect Quotations A foreign exchange (FE) quotation can either be direct or indirect. A FE quotation is said to be **direct** when it is quoted/expressed in a manner that reflects the exchange of a specified number of domestic currency *vis-à-vis* 1 unit of foreign currency. In our preceding example, ₹60 = US $1 is a direct quotation for US $ in India. Likewise, ₹92.06 = British pound sterling £1, ₹70.94 = Euro €1, are direct FE quotes in India in that they indicate ₹92.06 and ₹70.94 are required to exchange one unit of £ and €1 respectively.

Direct quotation/European quotation is expressed in a manner that reflects the exchange of a specified number of domestic currencies vis-à-vis one unit of foreign currency.

The FE quotation is **indirect** when it is quoted in a manner that reflects the exchange of a specified number of foreign currency *vis-à-vis* 1 unit of local currency. In the above example, US $0.01667 = ₹1 is an indirect quotation in India. Likewise, £0.01076 = ₹ 1, €0.01409 = ₹ 1, are examples of indirect quotations in India.

Direct quotations are known as **European quotations** and indirect quotations as **American quotations**. Direct quotations are more easy to comprehend and are, hence, followed by a large number of countries, including India.

Indirect quotation/American quotation is expressed in a manner that reflects the exchange of a specified number of foreign currencies vis-à-vis one unit of local currency.

Two-way Quotations/Rates The FE rates explained above are single quote/rate. In practice, dealers quote two-way rates, one for buying the foreign currency (known as *bid price/rate*) and another for selling the foreign currency (referred to as *ask price/rate*). Since dealers expect profit in foreign exchange operations, the two prices obviously cannot be the same. Evidently, the dealer will buy the foreign currency at a lower rate and sell the foreign currency at a higher rate. For this reason, the 'bid' quote is at a lower rate and the 'ask' quote is a higher rate. The *quotations are always with respect to the dealer.*

The foreign exchange quotations contain two rates. By convention the first rate is the buying rate and selling rate is the second rate. For example, when a dealer in Mumbai quotes pound sterling £1 = ₹92.00 – ₹92.18, it implies that the dealer is prepared to buy British pound sterling at ₹92 and sell it at ₹92.18. Though we have taken the quote up to 2 decimal points, quotations in practice are normally made up to four decimal points for most of the currencies.

Spread Spread is the difference between the ask price and the bid price. The spread is affected by a number of factors. The currency involved, the volume of business and the market sentiments/rumours about the currency are the major variables reckoned by dealers/operators in the foreign exchange market. In case the currency involved is subject to higher volatility (say, the US $ in February-March 2003, on account of the US threat of war on Iraq), the dealer will obviously like to have a higher spread in his quote to compensate for the higher risk he assumes in such circumstances.

Spread is the difference between the ask price (sale price) and the bid price (purchase price).

Spread to the dealer is akin to the gross profit for a business firm, out of which he is to meet its establishment expenses. In percentage terms, spread can be expressed in terms of Equations 33.1 and 33.2.

Spread (per cent) = [(Ask price – Bid price)/Ask price] × 100 **(33.1)**

Spread (per cent) = [(Ask price – Bid price)/Bid price] × 100 **(33.2)**

In the above example of the £, the spread per cent is 0.19527, that is [(₹92.18 – ₹92.00)/ ₹92.18] × 100, when it is determined with reference to the ask price.

Prima facie, the spread (percentage) appears to be very low. Since the volume of business involved is substantial, the total gross return to the dealer (in absolute terms) may turn out to be attractive. Continuing with 0.19527 spread, if the dealer has a turnover of ₹100 million in a day, his gross spread will be ₹1,95,270, that is, (0.19527 × ₹100 million)/100.

Spot Rates and Forward Rates In discussing exchange rates, it is important to distinguish between spot exchange rates and forward exchange rates. *Spot exchange rates* are applicable to the purchase and sale of foreign exchange on an immediate delivery basis. Though the term 'immediate' gives an impression of instantaneous delivery, in practice, delivery actually takes place two days later. Suppose Air India has bought aircrafts. It is to convert Indian rupees into US $ or £ (depending on which country aircrafts have been bought from). In case the terms of payment are immediate, Air India is to arrange the spontaneous purchase of the required sum of US $/£ at the spot rate from the spot market. The **spot rate** is the rate of day on which the transaction has taken place, though the execution of transaction occurs within a maximum of two working days.

> **Spot rate** is the rate of exchange of the day on which the transaction has taken place and of the days the transaction is executed.

In contrast, **forward exchange rates** are applicable for the delivery of foreign exchange at a future date. If Air India is to make payment after 90 days, as per the credit terms from the US firm, it has two options available. First, do nothing to arrange foreign exchange payment; on the due date of payment (after 3 months), make purchases of the due sum of US $ from the spot market, at the spot rate prevailing at that point of time, and then remit the payment to the US firm. Second, Air India may wish to avoid the uncertainty of the exchange rate three months from now. In that case, Air India is to purchase the required US $ in the forward market at a forward exchange rate that is decided at the time of the agreement. The agreed forward rate is valid for settlement irrespective of the actual spot rate on the date of the maturity of the forward contract (that is, 90 days from today in the case of Air India). The delivery of US $ and the payment of Indian rupees takes place 90 days later, on the date of settlement. Thus, Air India has eliminated exchange risk by entering into a forward contract.

> **Forward exchange rates** is the rate of exchange applicable for delivery of foreign exchange at a future date.

The concept of **forward rates** is equally significant and relevant to the exporter/seller. The seller/exporter may/will like/prefer to be sure of the export/sale proceeds. Suppose, the Indian firm sells goods of the value of US $10 million on 6 months credit. To eliminate the uncertainty of the US $-rupee exchange rate, the Indian firm may enter into a contract of selling US $10 million six months from now. Consider Example 33.1.

***Example* 33.1**

On February 1, an Indian firm exports goods of the value of US $100 million on 6 months credit. On February 1, the six-month forward rate is ₹62 per US $. The firm agrees to sell US $100 million at ₹62 on August 1. By entering into such a contract, the Indian firm has assured itself of the receipt of (US $100 million × ₹62) ₹6,200 million, irrespective of the spot rate prevailing on that day. Suppose, the actual spot rate is ₹61 per US $ on August 1. The Indian firm has gained ₹100 million (₹6,200 million actual receipts minus ₹6,100 million that it otherwise would have obtained in absence of the forward rate contract). However, it should also be noted that the firm also runs the risk of potential loss in the event of the actual spot rate on August 1 turns out to be higher than ₹62. Let us assume that the actual spot rate is ₹62.2 on 1st August. The firm, in absence of the forward rate contract, would have received ₹6,220 million (US $100 million × ₹62.2); as a result, it would suffer a loss of ₹20 million (₹6,220 million – ₹6,200 million).

It is apparent from Example 33.1 that the forward rate contracts (which take place in the forward markets) eliminate exchange rate risk. The example also highlights that risk elimination is achieved at a cost in terms of the potential loss of less receipts (in the case of forward sale transaction) and more payments (in the case of forward purchase transactions). This happens when the actual spot rate on the date of settlement turns out to be unfavourable to the business firm hedging the risk.

Forward rate premium foreign currency is at premium when its forward rate is higher than spot rate.

In general, spot rates as well as forward rates have two way quotes, that is, the quotation contains both the buying rate and selling rate. Theoretically, forward rates can be for any number of months or even a fraction of a month. In practice, forward rates are normally quoted for one month, two months, three months, six months, nine months and twelve months.

Forward rate discount foreign currency is at discount when its spot rate is higher than the forward rate.

Finally, forward rates can be at a premium or discount. There is a very simple rule to ascertain whether the forward exchange rates are at a premium or discount. *The rule requires the comparison of the spot rate and forward rate.* In case the forward rates are higher than the spot rates, it implies that forward rates are at premium as more amount of domestic currency is required to be paid in future (to purchase y amount of foreign currency. On the contrary, if the forward rates are lower than the spot rates, it signals that the forward rates are at discount in that less amount of domestic currency is required in future (to purchase y amount of foreign currency). Forward rate premium or discount (in annualised percentage) *vis-à-vis* spot rate can be computed as per Equations 33.3 and 33.4.

$$\text{Premium} = \frac{\text{Forward rate} - \text{Spot rate}}{\text{Spot rate}} \times \frac{12 \text{ months}}{N} \qquad \textbf{(33.3)}$$

$$\text{Discount} = \frac{\text{Spot rate} - \text{Forward rate}}{\text{Spot rate}} \times \frac{12 \text{ months}}{N} \qquad \textbf{(33.4)}$$

where N refers to the number of months for which the forward contract has been made. Consider Example 33.2.

Example 33.2

From the data given below calculate forward premium or discount, as the case may be, of the £ in relation to the rupee.

	Spot	*1 month forward*	*3 months forward*	*6 months forward*
₹/£	₹92.1255/92.3279	₹92.4291/6523	₹91.7134/8906	₹93.1900/3200

Solution

Since 1 month forward rate and 6 months forward rate are higher than the spot rate, the British £ is at premium in these two periods. The premium amount is determined separately both for bid price and ask price. The first quote is the bid price and the second quote (after the slash) is the ask/offer/sell price. It is the normal way of quotation in foreign exchange markets.

Premium with Respect to Bid Price

$$1 \text{ month} = \left(\frac{₹92.4291 - ₹92.1255}{₹92.1255}\right) \times \frac{12}{1} \times 100 = 3.29 \text{ pre cent per annum}$$

$$6 \text{ months} = \left(\frac{₹93.1900 - ₹92.1255}{₹92.1255}\right) \times \frac{12}{6} \times 100 = 2.31 \text{ pre cent per annum}$$

Premium with Respect to Ask Price

$$1 \text{ month} = \left(\frac{₹92.6523 - ₹92.3279}{₹92.3279}\right) \times \frac{12}{1} \times 100 = 3.51 \text{ pre cent per annum}$$

$$6 \text{ months} = \left(\frac{₹93.3200 - ₹92.3279}{₹92.3279}\right) \times \frac{12}{6} \times 100 = 2.15 \text{ pre cent per annum}$$

In the case of 3 months forward, spot rates are higher than the forward rates, signalling that forward rates are at a discount.

Discount with Respect to Bid Price

$$3 \text{ months} = \left(\frac{₹92.1255 - ₹91.7134}{₹92.1255}\right) \times \frac{12}{3} \times 100 = 1.79 \text{ pre cent per annum}$$

Discount with Respect to Ask Price

$$\left(\frac{₹92.3279 - ₹91.8906}{₹92.3279}\right) \times \frac{12}{3} \times 100 = 1.89 \text{ pre cent per annum}$$

In Example 33.2, the British £ is at premium for one month and six months forward exchange deals. In other words, it implies that the Indian rupee is at a discount. Thus, when one currency (in the pair) is at a forward premium, it is imperative that the other currency is at a discount.

Example 33.2 shows the hybrid picture of the £ (both in terms of premium and discount). In general, forward premiums for longer time spans tend to be higher in view of enhanced risk with longer maturities.

Cross Rates When a direct quote of the home currency or any other currency (desired by dealer/corporate firm/bank) is not available in the forex market, it is computed with the help of exchange quotes of other pairs of currencies, known as **cross rates**. Thus, cross rates facilitate in deriving/determining exchange rates (both spot and forward) with respect to currencies that normally lack availability of direct quotes.

Cross rate is the rate of exchange of two currencies on the basis of exchange quotes of other pairs of currencies.

The US $ is the most actively traded currency in the world foreign exchange markets. On account of a dominant position of the US $, it is convention to quote exchange rates of most of the currencies in relation to the US dollar. Therefore, the US $ often acts as a benchmark currency to calculate exchange rates of other currencies. Though in the vast majority of cases, the US $ is normally the benchmark/intermediate/third currency, conceptually, the cross rate between two currencies can be determined/inferred using any other currency also (say £, €, ¥ and so on). Example 33.3 explains the concept of cross rates.

Example 33.3

Suppose an Indian importer is to pay to a New Zealand export firm in New Zealand dollars. Assume further that the direct quote of Indian rupee and New Zealand dollars is not available. Therefore, the exporter is to use the other two relevant quotes, namely, the New Zealand $/US $ and ₹/US $. These rates are as follows:

New Zealand $/US $: 1.2806 – 1.2816
Rupee/US $: 60.148 – 60.163

Determine the exchange rate between Indian rupee and New Zealand dollar.

Solution

Determination of ₹/New Zealand dollar exchange rate involves the following steps:

(i) The Indian importer is to buy US $ at the rate of ₹60.163 (when US $ are bought by the importer, the dealer say, the bank is selling US dollars and hence ₹60.163 is the relevant selling rate and not ₹60.148).

(ii) The Indian importer then sells the US \$ to buy New Zealand \$. When he sells the US \$, the dealer/bank buys US \$1 in exchange for New Zealand \$1.2806. In other words, the Indian importer gets New Zealand \$1.2806 by selling 1 US \$.

(iii) In sum, the Indian importer gets New Zealand \$1.2806 in exchange for Indian ₹60.163. Therefore, the rupee/New Zealand \$ exchange rate is (₹60.163/1.2806) = ₹46.9803/New Zealand \$.

Thus, ₹46.9803/New Zealand \$ is a cross rate, derived from the two sets of rates, namely, New Zealand \$/US \$ and rupee/US \$. Cross rates defined as a rate between a third pair of currencies, by using the rates of two pairs, in which one currency is common are derived rates.

₹46.9803/New Zealand \$ is the selling rate from the point of view of the dealer/bank. This provides one quote of the cross rate. To complete the quote, bid/buying rate is required. The buying rate would be derived as per the following steps:

(i) The dealer purchases one US \$ for ₹60.148.

(ii) The dealer sells one US \$ in exchange for 1.2816 New Zealand \$.

(iii) 1.2816 New Zealand \$ are equivalent to ₹60.148.

Accordingly, the rupee/New Zealand \$ buying rate is: ₹60.148/1.2816 = ₹46.9319

The complete quote is: Rupee/New Zealand \$ = ₹46.9319 – ₹46.9803.

The quote implies that the bank purchases New Zealand \$ at ₹46.9319 and sells it for ₹46.9803. The term 'cross' is used *literally* to determine bid rate and ask rate. For instance, bid rate is based on ₹60.163 and New Zealand \$1.2806 (it is one cross). Likewise, ask rate is based on ₹60.148 and New Zealand \$1.2816 (it is another cross). This is shown in Figure 33.1.

New Zealand \$/US \$	: 1.2806** – 1.2816*
Rupee/US \$	: 60.148* – 60.163**
Rupee/New Zealand \$	: 46.9319* – 46.9803**

FIGURE 33.1 Determination of Cross Rates

It is clear from Example 33.3 (summed up in Figure 33.1) that exchange rates for a third pair of currency can easily be derived, given two pairs of exchange rates. Conceptually, Equations 33.5 and 33.6 can be used to find the cross rates between two currencies, say B and C, if the rates between currencies A and B as well as A and C are given.

$$(B/C)_{bid} = (B/A)_{bid} \times (A/C)_{bid}, \text{ Where } (A/C)_{bid} = 1/(C/A)_{ask} \quad \textbf{(33.5)}$$

$$(B/C)_{ask} = (B/A)_{ask} \times (A/C)_{ask}, \text{ Where } (A/C)_{ask} = 1/(C/A)_{bid} \quad \textbf{(33.6)}$$

The concept is illustrated in Example 33.4.

Example 33.4

From the following rates, determine ₹/Canadian \$ exchange rate:

₹/US \$: ₹61.5642/61.8358

Canadian \$/US \$: 1.0949/1.0959

Solution

(₹/Canadian \$)$_{bid}$ = (₹/US \$)$_{bid}$ × (US \$/Canadian \$)$_{bid}$

= ₹61.5642 × 1/(1.0959*) = ₹56.1768

(* Since the question provides the rate in terms of Canadian \$/US \$, the equation warrants US \$/Canadian \$, the values get reversed to have denomination effect)

(₹/Canadian \$)$_{ask}$ = (₹/US \$)$_{ask}$ × (US \$/Canadian \$)$_{ask}$

= ₹61.8358 × 1/(1.0949) = ₹56.4762

₹/Canadian exchange rate is = ₹56.1768 – ₹56.4762.

In case the actual exchange rates are not in tune with cross rates, firms as well as dealers/bankers would like to switch over to markets offering them more favourable rates. Trading firms will benefit in terms of receiving more or paying less. On the other hand, non-equivalence of the two rates would provide a riskless arbitrage opportunity to dealers, bankers and arbitrageurs in forex markets. Eventually, the arbitrage process is likely to align actual and cross rates.

Arbitrage Process as a Means of Attaining Equilibrium on Spot Markets

Arbitrage is an act of buying currency in one market at a lower price and selling it in another at higher price resulting in equilibrium in exchange rates of different currencies.

The term **arbitrage** in the context of forex markets refers to an act of buying currency in one market (at lower price) and selling it in another (at higher price). Thus, the difference in exchange rates (in a specified pair of currencies) in two markets provides an opportunity to the operators/arbitrageurs in the market to earn profit without risk. As a result, equilibrium is restored in the exchange rates of currencies in different forex markets. The essence of the arbitrage process is to buy currencies from markets where prices are lower and sell in markets where prices are higher. In operational terms, the arbitrage process is essentially a balancing operation that does not allow the same currency to have varying rates in different forex markets on a sustainable basis.

In the context of spot markets, two types of arbitrages are plausible: **(i)** Geographical arbitrage and **(ii)** Triangular arbitrage. These are now briefly described.

Geographical Arbitrage As the name suggests, **geographical arbitrage** consists of buying currency from a forex market (say, London) where it is cheaper and sell in another forex market (say, Tokyo) where it is costly. Since geographical distance does not have much relevance in view of the fact that forex transactions primarily take place through telephone and fax messages, arbitrageurs will gain in buying at London and selling at Tokyo.

Geographical arbitrage is the buying of foreign currency from a foreign exchange market where it is cheaper and selling in another foreign exchange market where it is costly.

***Example* 33.5**

At two forex centres, the following rates with respect to US $ are quoted:

London	: ₹61.5730 – 61.6100
Tokyo	:₹61.6350 – 61.6675

Find out arbitrage possibilities for an arbitrageur who has ₹100 million.

Solution

The following *modus operandi*, will be deployed by the arbitrageur:

(i) He will buy US $ from the London forex market at the rate of ₹61.6100, as it is cheaper there compared to the Tokyo market (₹61.6675). He will obtain (₹100 million/₹61.6100) US $1,623,113.130 on conversion.

(ii) He will sell US $1,623,113.130 at the rate of ₹61.6350 per US $ and will obtain ₹100,040,577.76.

(iii) As a result of arbitrage, he will earn a profit of ₹40,577.76 (₹100,040,577.76 – ₹100 million) without any risk.

***Example* 33.6**

Assume the rate at London remains unchanged as stated in Example 33.5, but there is a change in the Tokyo rate.

London	: ₹61.5730 – 61.6100
Tokyo	: ₹61.6000 – 61.6450

Are there still any arbitrage gain possibilities for the arbitrageur of Example 33.5?

Solution

While, it is true that it is cheaper to buy US $ in London compared to Tokyo, there are no arbitrage gain possibilities as explained in the following steps:

(i) The Arbitrageur buys US $ at the London forex market at the rate of ₹61.6100.

(ii) He can sell US $ in the Tokyo market only at the lower rate of ₹61.6000. Thus, he loses. Clearly, there are no arbitrage gain possibilities. To have profits, the selling rate for an arbitrageur in one forex market should be higher than his buying rate. In other words, the differential in currency rates, *prima facie*, need not necessarily generate arbitrage gain.

Triangular arbitrage involves three foreign currencies involving three different foreign exchange markets.

Triangular Arbitrage As the name suggests, **triangular arbitrage** takes place when there are three currencies involving three markets. For this reason, triangular arbitrage is also known as a *three-point arbitrage*. Example 33.7 illustrates the concept of such an arbitrage.

***Example* 33.7**

The following are three quotes in three forex markets:

$1 = ₹62.2133 in Mumbai
£1 = ₹92.1125 in London
£1 = $1.5050 in New York

Are any arbitrage gains possible? Assume there are no transaction costs and the arbitrageur has US $1,000,000.

Solution

Arbitrage gains are possible since the cross rate between US $/British £ by using the rates at London and at Mumbai is different (₹92.1125/₹62.2133 = US $1.4805/£1) from that of New York ($1.5050). The arbitrageur can adopt the following steps to realise arbitrage gain.

(i) The arbitrageur will buy Indian rupees with US $1 million. The total proceeds he obtains is (₹62.2133 × $1 million US $) ₹62,213,300.

(ii) He converts Indian rupees in British £ at the London forex market. He receives (₹62,213,300/₹92.1125) £675,405.6181.

(iii) He then converts £675,405.6181 at the New York forex market. He obtains (£675,405.6181 × $1.5050) US $1,016,485.45

(iv) Thus, he has net gain of (US $1,016,485.45 – $1,000,000) US $16,485.45

To sum up the discussion, it can be said that the arbitrage process will set in whenever there are significant differences between cross rates and quoted rates and this process continues till there is a realignment between these rates.

Arbitrage in Forward Market

The concept of the arbitrage process is equally applicable in forward markets. In the case of spot markets, a mismatch between cross rates and quoted rates provides an opportunity for arbitrage gains. Similar arbitrage gain possibilities exist in forward markets also, in case the difference between the forward rate and the spot rate (in terms of premium or discount) is not matched by the interest rate differentials of the two currencies. Conceptually, interest rate differentials of the two currencies should be equal to the forward premium or discount on their exchange rates. Since the comparison is to be made with interest rate differentials, this kind of arbitrage is also appropriately referred to as **covered interest arbitrage**.

Example 33.8 explains the arbitrage in a forward market.

***Example* 33.8**

Determine arbitrage gain from the following data:

Spot rate	₹91.2/£
3 month forward rate	₹91.7/£
3 month interest rates:	
Rupees: 9%	
British £: 5%	

Assume ₹10 million borrowings or £200,000 (as the case may be) to explain your answer.

Solution

3 month forward rate of £ is higher (at ₹91.7) than the spot rate (₹91.2).
This implies that the £ is at premium.

$$\text{Premium (percentage)} = \left(\frac{₹91.7 - ₹91.2}{₹91.2}\right) \times \frac{12}{3} \times 100 = 2.19\%$$

Interest rate differential = 9% – 5% = 4%

Since interest rate differential (4%) and premium percentage (2.19%) do not match, there are arbitrage gain possibilities. An arbitrageur can take the following steps in this regard.

(i) The arbitrageur borrows £ 2,00,000 at 5 per cent for 3 months (he borrows in British currency, as it carries lower interest rate).

(ii) He then converts £ 2,00,000 at the spot rate of ₹91.2 in the spot market. He gets an amount of ₹1,82,40,000 (£ 2,00,000 × ₹91.2).

(iii) He invests ₹1,82,40,000 in the money market at 9 per cent interest per annum for 3 months. As a result of this investment, he obtains interest of ₹4,10,400 (₹1,82,40,000 × 3/12 × 9/100).

(iv) Total sum available with the arbitrageur, three months from now is ₹1,86,50,400 i.e. (₹1,82,40,000 amount invested + ₹4,10,400 interest).

(v) Since he would get ₹1,86,50,400 after 3 months, he will sell ₹1,86,50,400 forward at the rate of ₹91.7.

(vi) As a result of the forward deal, at the end of 3 months from now, he would get £ 2,03,384.9509, that is, (₹1,86,50,400/₹91.7).

(vii) He refunds £ 2,00,000 sum borrowed along with interest due on it. The refunded sum is £ 2,00,000 + £ 2,500 interest i.e., (£ 2,00,000 × 3/12 × 5/100) = £ 2,02,500.

(viii) Net gain is £ 2,03,384.9509 – £ 2,02,500 = £ 884.9509.

These arbitrage gain possibilities will cease to exist if the difference in forward rate and spot rate (in percentage terms) coincides with the interest rate differential (in percentage) of the two currencies. This principles is useful in determining/predicting forward rates (consider Example 33.9).

***Example* 33.9**

For facts in Example 33.8 as unchanged, determine the forward rate at which there will be no arbitrage gain possibilities.

Solution

Since the interest rate differential is 4 per cent, the forward premium differential should also be 4 per cent to have no arbitrage gain possibilities. Accordingly, the forward rate should fetch 4 per cent premium (on annual basis). The desired forward rate (on approximate basis) is determined as follows:

Spot rate	₹91.2
Add: 4% premium for 3 month period (₹91.2 × 4/100 × 3/12)	0.912
Forward rate	92.112*

*According to interest rate parity theory (as per equation 33.9), the forward rate will be ₹91.2 × 1.0225**/1.0125** = ₹92.1007; (** interest of 3 months)

At the forward rate of ₹92.1007/£ as per interest rate parity theory arbitrage gain possibility would come to an end. The verification table is as follows:

(i) to **(iv)** The steps **(i)** to **(iv)** are the same (**as in Example 33.8**).

(v) Since he would get ₹1,86,50,400 after three months, he will sell forward ₹1,86,50,400 at the rate of ₹92.1007.

(vi) At the end of 3 months he gets ₹1,86,50,400/₹92.1007 = £ 2,02,500.0895.

(vii) He refunds £ 2,00,000, the borrowed sum. On this, interest due is £ 2,500 (£ 2,00,000 × 3/12 × 5/100). Total sum refunded is £ 2,02,500.

(viii) Net gain is zero. (£ 0.0895 difference is due to approximation).

In contrast, if the interest rate differential is smaller than the forward discount, the arbitrageur would be benefitted by borrowing the currency that carries a higher interest rate and investing that currency in the money market that provides a lower interest rate. The concept is illustrated in Example 33.10.

***Example* 33.10**

Assume for Example 33.8 that the interest rate on the British £ is 6 per cent and on Indian rupee is 5 per cent and the 3 month forward rate is ₹90.60. Show the arbitrage process.

Solution

The British £ is at a forward discount of 2.631 per cent = $\left(\frac{₹91.20 - ₹90.60}{₹91.2} \times 100\right) \times \frac{12}{3}$

Interest rate differential is (6% – 5%) = 1 per cent

In view of the above disparity, there are arbitrage gain possibilities.

The arbitrageur is to adopt the following steps:

(i) The arbitrageur borrows £ 2,00,000 at 6 per cent for 3 months.

(ii) He converts £ 2,00,000 into rupees at the spot rate of ₹91.2, in the spot market. He gets an amount of ₹1,82,40,000 (£ 2,00,000 × ₹91.2).

(iii) He invests ₹1,82,40,000 in the money market at 5 per cent interest per annum for 3 months. After 3 months, he gets interest of ₹2,28,000, i.e., (₹1,82,40,000 × 5/100 × 3/12).

(iv) Total sum available at the end of 3 months is ₹1,84,68,000 (₹1,82,40,000 + 2,28,000).

(v) He sells forward ₹1,84,68,000 at the rate of ₹90.60.

(vi) At the end of 3 months he converts Indian Rupee and gets £ 2,03,841.0596 (₹1,84,68,000/₹90.6).

(vii) He refunds £ 2,00,000, the borrowed sum. On this, the interest due is £ 3,000 (£ 2,00,000 × 3/12 × 6/100). The total sum refunded is £ 2,03,000.

(viii) The net gain [£ 2,03,841.0596 – £ 2,03,000] = £ 841.0596.

Again at the forward equilibrium rate of ₹90.9753/£ as per interest rate parity theory (₹91.2 × 1.0125/1.015), there would be no arbitrage gain possible as shown below.

(**i** to **iv**) The steps **(i)** to **(iv)** remain the same.

(v) The arbitrageur sells forward ₹1,84,68,000 at the rate of ₹90.9753.

(vi) At the end of 3 months he converts Indian rupees and gets £ 2,03,000.1549 (₹1,84,68,000/₹90.9753).

(vii) He refunds £ 2,00,000, the borrowed sum plus £ 3,000 interest (£ 2,00,000 × 3/12 × 6/100). The total refunded sum is £ 203,000.

(viii) Net gain is zero (£ 0.1549 difference is due to approximation).

In sum, the arbitrage process helps in restoring/re-establishing the equilibrium both in the spot markets and forward markets.

LO 33.3 DETERMINANTS AND SELECT THEORIES OF EXCHANGE RATES

The preceding discussion has provided the *modus operandi* of dealing with foreign transactions primarily in terms of exchange rates. It has been observed that these rates vary between different currencies. The exchange rate values of some currencies (say of the British £, European €, US $) are significantly higher than those of others (say Japanese ¥ and Indian rupee). Why is it so? There are several political and economic factors that have a marked bearing on the determination of exchange rates of various currencies. We briefly explain the major factors/theories that account for variation in exchange rates of currencies of different countries. These factors are: **(i)** inflation rates, **(ii)** interest rates, **(iii)** balance of payment position, **(iv)** volume of international reserves and **(v)** level of activity and employment.

Inflation Rates

Differences in inflation rates between two countries are considered as the most important factor to explain the variation in exchange rates of two countries. In case the domestic inflation rate is greater than foreign inflation rate (prices of domestic goods are rising faster than the prices of foreign goods), it leads to more demand for foreign goods/imports (as they are relatively cheaper). This, in turn, leads to more demand for foreign exchange, making it costlier. In other words, there will be a relative decline in the value of domestic currency. This explanation has its genesis in the economic law of demand and supply.

In contrast, a lower domestic inflation rate will make domestic goods relatively cheaper. As a result, demand for exports will increase. This, in turn, will augment the supply of foreign exchange, resulting in lower price in relation to the domestic currency. In other words, domestic currency appreciates. In technical terms, the floating exchange rates are likely to vary in accordance with differing inflation rates in two countries.

Purchasing power parity theory is a theory according to which goods of equal value in different countries are equated through an exchange rate.

The **purchasing power parity (PPP) theory** provides the rationale for differences in exchange rates. The basic principle underlying this theory is that *goods of equal value in different countries are plausible to be equated through an exchange rate.* For instance, if a basket of goods in US costs \$10 and ₹600 in India, it is fair and equitable that the exchange rate between these currencies should be ₹60/\$1. In more comprehensive form, the PPP theory can be expressed as per Equation 33.7.

$$PPP_r = \text{Spot rate} \times (1 + r_h/1 + r_f) \quad \textbf{(33.7)}$$

$$PPP_r = \text{Spot rate} \times (P_h/P_f) \quad \textbf{(33.8)}$$

Where PPP_r = purchasing power rate; r_h and r_f are rates of inflation in the home country and foreign country, respectively; P_h and P_f represent the respective price indices of the home country and the foreign country. Consider Example 33.11.

***Example* 33.11**

Assume the spot rate between the Indian rupee and US \$ is ₹60 in year 1. In the first quarter of year 2, the price index of India is 108 and that of US is 102 (with year 1 as the base year, 100). Based on this data, determine the likely new exchange rate of the Indian rupee and US \$.

Solution

Exchange rate (₹/US \$) = ₹60 × (108/102) = ₹63.5294: US \$1

Since the inflation rate is relatively higher in India, the value of rupee *vis-à-vis* the US \$ declines. Thus, the PPP theory is very useful in explaining both existing exchange rates and future exchange rates. Essentially, it indicates that in countries that witness high inflation rates currency values decline more compared to the currencies of countries with lower inflation rates.

Interest Rates

Interest rate parity theory is a theory according to which the discount/premium of one currency in relation to another reflects the interest differentials between them.

Relative interest rates constitute the second major factor in determining exchange rates. For instance, if interest rates are relatively higher in US than in Japan, Japanese funds are likely to be attracted to the US as Japanese bankers/investors will earn higher yields by parking their funds in US than in investing in their own country. As a result, there will be a flight of capital funds from Japan to US; there will be more demand for US \$ in Japan, causing appreciation in the exchange rate of the US \$. In other words, more units of Japanese yen will be required to buy the same US \$; there would be a relative decline in the exchange value of Japanese ¥ *vis-à-vis* US \$.

Thus, the interest rate differentials in the two countries are likely to have a decisive influence on their exchange rates. This point was highlighted in the previous section when adjustment in the spot rate had been made pertaining to interest rate differentials of the two countries to predict the future forward rates (Example 33.9).

The economic premise of determining/predicting future forward rates of different currencies (based on differences in the interest rates) is derived from **the interest rate parity theory**. Basically, the theory states that the *premium or discount of one currency in relation to the other should reflect the interest rate differentials between the two currencies.* Forward rate, according to the theory, can be estimated as per Equation 33.9.

$$\text{Forward rate} = \text{Spot rate} \times \frac{(1 + I_h)}{(1 + I_f)} \quad \textbf{(33.9)}$$

Where I_f and I_h represent interest rates on foreign currency and home currency respectively.

It is very apparent from Equation 33.9 that foreign currency is to be at premium if it has a relatively lower interest rate *vis-à-vis* the home currency. On the other hand, foreign currency will be at a discount, in case interest rates are lower on home currency.

Balance of Payment Position

The structure of the balance of payments of a country also has a major impact on its exchange rate. In the event of the country running a big deficit or persistent deficit in its balance of payments, its currency is likely to be under pressure as deficits require payments in foreign currency. In the case of fixed exchange rates, therefore, persistent deficit mounts both internal and external pressures on the monetary authority to devalue the currency. Devaluation is expected to help in reducing imports (as foreign goods become more costly in view of the enhanced value of foreign currency) and in increasing exports (as the home currency becomes cheaper, which in turn makes the country's goods cheaper overseas). In a system of floating rates, persistent and big deficits are a forewarning signals of depreciation of the concerned country's currency.

In contrast, if the balance of payments of the country is having a favourable position in term of surpluses, the value of the currency of such a country appreciates/is likely to appreciate.

Volume of International Reserves/Foreign Exchange

The level of foreign exchange reserves (including gold) the Central Bank of the country/monetary authority possesses also has an impact on its currency exchange rate. In case the monetary authority feels that its currency is depreciating in the forex markets and has economic reasons to support/stabilise it, it may step in by releasing/selling foreign exchange out of its international reserves. Thus, sizeable reserves can contain the depreciation of home currency. In the case of inadequate reserves/foreign exchange, the monetary authority may find itself helpless/constrained to provide support to its currency. However, the monetary authority can "prop up" its currency only as long as it has foreign exchange reserves available.

Level of Activity and Employment

There is likely to be a positive impact by way of a higher level of economic activity and full employment on exchange rates. The low level of activity and low level of employment in the economy increases the probability of depreciation of its currency. In contrast, growing economies having a higher level of economic activity and employment have good potential and prospects of appreciation in the value of their currencies.

To sum up, all the above factors, taken together, have their impact on exchange rates. Low inflation rate, higher interest rates, surplus balance of payment position, possession of sizeable foreign exchange reserves and a higher level of economic activity have a positive impact in pushing up a country's exchange rates. In contrast, higher inflation rate, low interest rates, big/persistent deficit in the balance of payments, inadequate reserves with the monetary authority and a low level of economic activity tend to depreciate exchange rates.

SUMMARY

LO 33.1	Different countries have different currencies and the settlement of all business transactions within a country is required/preferred in the local currency. The foreign exchange (FE) market provides a forum where the currency of one country is traded for the currency of another country.
	The FE markets deal with a large volume of funds as well as a large number of currencies of various countries. The major FE markets are London, New York and Tokyo and the major currencies traded are the US dollar, British pound sterling, Euro and Japanese yen.
	Commercial banks and central banks of the countries are the major participants in the FE markets. Business firms normally buy and sell securities through authorised dealers, say, commercial banks or brokers.
	While the commercial banks and other participants in the FE markets operate on commercial principles, the operations of the central banks are primarily regulatory in nature.
LO 33.2	Different currencies have different values; they are traded at an exchange rate. An exchange rate is the price of one country's currency expressed in terms of the currency of another country.
	Foreign exchange rate/quotation can either be direct or indirect. It is said to be direct when it is expressed in a manner that reflects the exchange of a specified number of domestic currency (say, ₹60) for one unit of foreign currency (say, US \$). The FE quotation is indirect when it is quoted in a manner that reflects the exchange of a specified number of foreign currency (say, US \$0.01667) for one unit of local currency (say 1 rupee). Direct quotations are known as European quotations and indirect quotations as American.
	There are two-way rates for the FE quotations, one for buying the foreign currency (bid price) and another for its selling (ask price). Since dealers expect profit in foreign exchange operations, the bid price is lower than the ask price.
	The FE quotations are always with respect to the dealer. By convention, the first rate is the buying rate and the second rate is the selling rate (say ₹60.50 – ₹61.00 for US \$1). Quotations, in practice, are up to four decimal points.
	Spread is the difference between the bid price and the ask price. It is gross profit of a dealer, out of which it meets its business/establishment expenses.
	While spot exchange rates are applicable to the purchase and sale of foreign exchange on an immediate delivery basis (in practice delivery takes place two days later), the forward exchange rates are applicable for the delivery of foreign exchange at a future date (say, after 1 month/3 months/6 months and so on).
	Forward rates can be at a premium or discount. In case the forward rates are higher than the spot rates, the forward rates are at premium. The forward rates are at a discount when they are lower than the spot rates.
	When a direct quote of the home currency or any other desired currency is not available in the FE market, it is computed with the help of exchange quotes of other pairs of currencies, and is known as cross rates. Thus, cross rates facilitate computation of exchange rates of those currencies for which direct quotes are not available.
	Arbitrage refers to an act of buying foreign currency in one FE market at lower price and selling it in another at higher price. This difference in the exchange rates provides an opportunity to the arbitrageurs to earn profit without risk. As a result, equilibrium is restored in the exchange rates of currencies in different FE markets.
	Geographical arbitrage and triangular arbitrage are possible in spot markets. Geographical arbitrage consists of buying currency from a FE market where it is cheaper and selling it in another forex market where it is costly. Triangular/three-point arbitrage takes place when three currencies traded at three markets are involved.

LO 33.2	Covered interest arbitrage is feasible in forward markets. This is profitable when the difference between the forward rate and spot rate (in terms of premium or discount) is not matched by the interest rate differentials of the two currencies. In other words, when the difference in the forward and spot rates of the currencies involved coincides with their interest-rate differentials, arbitrage gain possibilities cease to exist.
LO 33.3	There are several factors that influence the determination of exchange rates of various currencies. The major factors are: (i) inflation rates, (ii) interest rates, (iii) balance of payment position, (iv) volume of international reserves and (v) level of activity and employment. Lower domestic inflation rate, higher interest rates, favourable balance of payment position, comfortable volume of international reserves (including gold) and the higher level of economic activity and full employment tend to appreciate exchange rates. In contrast, higher inflation rate, lower interest rates, big/persistent deficit in the balance of payment, inadequate/low foreign exchange reserves and a low level of economic activity tend to depreciate exchange rates.

REFERENCES

1. Yadav, Surendra, S *et al*, *Foreign Exchange Markets—Understanding Derivatives and Other Instruments*, New Delhi: Macmillan India, 2001, p. 56.
2. For the floating currencies, changes in the value of foreign exchange rates are called appreciation or depreciation; on the other hand, in the case of fixed currencies, changes in value are referred to as official revaluation or devaluation.
3. Rao, Ramesh K S, *Fundamentals of Financial Management*, New York: Macmillan Publishing Company, 1989, p. 734.

SOLVED PROBLEMS

P.33.1 The following rates appear in the foreign exchange market: LO 33.2 LOD E

	Spot rate	*2 Month forward*
₹/1 US $	₹60.75/61.06	₹61.5/62.00

(a) How many dollars should a firm sell to get ₹61.50 million after 2 months?
(b) How many rupees does the firm require to pay to obtain US $2,00,000 in the spot market?
(c) Assume the firm has US $50,000. How many rupees does the firm obtain in exchange for the US $?
(d) Are forward rates at premium or discount? Determine the percentages also.

Solution

(a) After 2 months, to get ₹61.50 million, the firm is to sell the US $. In other words, the dealer is buying dollars. As rates are always quoted from the point of view of the dealer, the dealer's buying of $ at ₹61.50 is relevant. Accordingly, the firm is required to pay US $1 million, i.e., (₹61.50 million/₹61.5).
(b) The firm is buying US $. To put it differently, the dealer is selling dollars As per the spot rate quotation, the dollar selling rate is ₹61.06. Accordingly, the firm is to pay ₹1,22,12,000, i.e., (US $2,00,000 × ₹61.06) to buy US $2,00,000.
(c) The firm is selling US $. The relevant spot exchange rate will be the buying rate from the point of view of the dealer; this rate is ₹60.75. Accordingly, the firm will receive ₹3,037,500 (US $50,000 × ₹60.75).
(d) Forward rates are at a premium as these rates are higher than the spot rate. The premium amount is determined separately both for the bid price and the ask price.

$$\left(\frac{\text{Forward rate} - \text{Spot rate}}{\text{Spot rate}}\right) \times \frac{12}{N} \times 100$$

Premium with respect to bid price:

$$\left(\frac{₹61.50 - ₹60.75}{₹60.75} \times \frac{12}{2} \times 100\right) = 7.40 \text{ per cent per annum}$$

Premium with respect to offer price:

$$\left(\frac{₹62 - ₹61.06}{₹61.06} \times \frac{12}{2} \times 100\right) = 9.23 \text{ per cent per annum}$$

P.33.2 Rates of the rupee and euro in the International market are US $0.0162 and US $1.2900, respectively. What direct quote of US dollar and euro will be provided by a forex dealer in India? **LO 33.2** LOD M

Solution As US $/₹= 0.0162, it implies US $0.0162 is equal to ₹1 [or 1 ₹ = US $0.0162]

Or, ₹/US $ = 1/0.0162 = ₹61.7283

So, direct quote of US $ in India will be ₹/US $: ₹61.7283

₹/US $ = 61.7283

US $/€ = 1.2900

₹/€ = ₹61.7283 × 1.2900 = ₹79.6295

So, a direct quote of € in India will be ₹/€ ₹79.6295.

P.33.3 Spot rate of Euro in New York is US $1.2800 and of the rupee is US $0.0163 **LO 33.2** LOD M

(a) What will the price of Euro be in India?

(b) If the euro is quoted in India as ₹78.65/€, what would you do to profit from the situation?

Solution In New York, spot rates are US $/€ = 1.2800 and US $/₹= 0.0163

(a) So, ₹/€ = (₹/US $) × (US $/€) = 1/0.0163 × 1.2800 = ₹78.527

So, a direct quote of the euro in India is ₹/€ ₹78.527

(b) As the direct quote of the euro in India is ₹78.65 (higher), it will be profitable to buy Euros using cross rates and sell to the dealer providing the direct quote. The following steps will be carried out to realise the arbitrage gain:

(i) Buy US $ for ₹1 million in New York. Total US $ obtained is ($0.0163 × ₹1 million) = US $16,300.

(ii) Convert these US $ into euros at New York, thus receiving (1/1.2800 × $16,300) = €12,734.375

(iii) Sell these euros in India to receive rupees. The proceeds will be (€12,734.375 × ₹78.65) = ₹10,01,558.593

Thus, there is a net gain of (₹10,01,558.593 – ₹10,00,000) = ₹1,558.593. In reality, the gain will be lower due to the transaction cost involved.

P.33.4 In the foreign exchange market the following information appears: **LO 33.2** LOD M

	Spot	*1 month forward*	*2 month forward*	*3 month forward*
1 British pound (£)	₹90.20/90.72	₹.80/.98	₹.60/.50	₹.30/.70

Determine forward rates for 1 month, 2 months and 3 months.

Solution Determination of forward rates

In case the forward margins are in the increasing order, they imply the forward rates are at a premium. Therefore, margins are added to the spot rate to compute the forward exchange rate. From the perusal of the data, the £ is at premium for 1 and 3 month forward deals. The computed forward rates are as follows:

	1 month		3 month	
Spot Rate	₹90.20/	₹90.72	₹90.20/	₹90.72
Margin	+ 0.80/	0.98	0.30/	0.70
	91.00/	91.70	90.5/	91.42

In contrast, decreasing margins indicate that the forward rates are at a discount. Therefore, these margins are deducted from the spot rate to compute forward rates. The British £ is at a discount for a 2 month deal. Its forward rate is computed below:

(Spot rate ₹90.20/₹90.72 – Margin ₹0.60/0.50) = ₹89.60/₹90.22

P.33.5 John is to pay £20,000 two months from today. Spot rate (ask) ₹1 = £0.0108. The rupee is likely to appreciate by 2% over two months. What is the likely forward rate? How much cash (in ₹) is likely to be paid by John to buy £20,000 after two months? **LO 33.2** LOD **M**

Solution Since the rupee is likely to appreciate, the rupee will be at a premium of 2 per cent. Therefore, the premium sum of 2 per cent is to be added to the existing spot rate to compute the likely forward rate (ask/sell).

(i) ₹1 = £0.0108 Spot rate + (£0.0108) 0.02 premium
= £0.0108 + £0.000216 = £0.01106

(ii) John is to pay ₹1,808,318.264, i.e., (£20,000/0.01106) to purchase £20,000.

P.33.6 An importer is to make payment of 1 million Thai baht to its trading partner in Bangkok. The currency quotes available are: **LO 33.2** LOD **E**

For dollar in India : ₹60.0843/60.0996
For dollar in Thailand : Thai baht 31.9400/31.9600

What is the amount of bill payable in terms of Indian rupees?

Solution As a direct quote of ₹/Thai baht is not available, the cross rate will be used by the importer to buy Thai baht.

₹/US $: ₹60.0843 – 60.0996
Thai baht/US $: 31.9400 – 31.9600

For cross rates, $(₹/\text{Thai baht})_{bid} = (₹/\text{US }\$)_{bid} \times (\text{US }\$/\text{Thai Baht})_{bid}$
$= 60.0843 \times 1/31.9600 = 1.8799$

And, $(₹/\text{Thai Baht})_{ask} = (₹/\text{US }\$)_{ask} \times (\text{US }\$/\text{Thai baht})_{ask}$
$= 60.0996 \times 1/31.9400 = 1.8816$

So the cross rate of ₹/Thai baht : 1.8799 – 1.8816.

As the importer is to buy 1 million Thai baht; his payment in rupees will be = 10,00,000 × 1.8816 = ₹18,81,600.

P.33.7 Shoe Company sells to a wholesaler in Singapore. The purchase price of a shipment is 50,000 Singapore dollar with a term of 90 days. Upon payment, the Shoe Company will convert the SGD to US dollars. The present spot rate for SGD per dollar is 1.31, whereas the 90 day forward rate is 1.30. **LO 33.2** LOD **D**

You are required to calculate and explain:

(i) If the Shoe Company were to hedge its foreign exchange risk, what would it do? What transactions are necessary?

(ii) Is the Singapore dollar at a forward premium or at a forward discount?

(iii) What is the implied differential in interest rate between the two countries? (Use interest rate parity assumption)

Solution

(i) In case the Shoe Company wishes to hedge its foreign exchange risk, it can opt for a forward contract. The spot rate for SGD/US $ is 1.31, that is, if the Shoe Company receives the payment of 50,000 SGD today then its equivalent dollar receipts are US \$38,167.938, that is, (50,000 SGD/1.31). By entering in the forward sale contract of selling SGD 50,000 at the rate of 1.30 SGD per \$, the company's dollar receipts are to be US \$38,461.538, i.e., (50,000 SGD/1.30). As a result, the company gains US \$293.600.

(ii) Spot rate is 1 US \$ = 1.31 SGD

1 SGD = 0.76335 US \$

90 day forward rate is 1 US \$ = 1.30 SGD

1 SGD = 0.769230 US \$

Since the US \$ forward rate is lower, it is at discount. In other words SGD is at premium.

$$\text{Premium of SGD (\%)} = \frac{\text{US \$0.76923} - \text{US \$0.76335}}{\text{US \$0.76335}} \times \frac{365}{90} \times 100 = 3.124 \text{ per cent per annum.}$$

(iii) The implied interest rate differential between the two countries is 3.124 per cent. According to the interest rate parity theory, forward rate is equivalent to spot rate + interest rate differential. Interest rates in Singapore are likely to be higher by 3.124 per cent compared to US.

P.33.8 Alert Limited is planning to import a multipurpose machine from Japan at a cost of 1680 lakh yen. The company can avail loans at 18 per cent interest per annum with quarterly rests with which it can import the machine. However, there is an offer from the Tokyo branch of an India based bank extending credit of 180 days at 2 per cent per annum against the opening of an irrevocable letter of credit. Other information is as follows: **LO 33.2** LOD M

(i) Present exchange rate ₹100 = 168 yen.

(ii) 180 days forward rate ₹100 = 170 yen.

(iii) Commission charges for letters of credit are at 2 per cent for 12 months.

Advise whether the offer from the foreign branch should be accepted?

Solution Alert Limited will accept the offer from the foreign branch only when it involves less cash outflows as compared to the domestic loan alternative. Given this as a financial framework for decision criterion, cash payments under both the alternatives are computed.

(a) Determination of cash payment under bank loan alternative

(i) Cost of multipurpose machine/borrowings (lakh)	¥1,680
(ii) Spot exchange rate	₹100 = ¥168
(iii) Bank loan required (¥1680 lakh/¥168) (assumed for 180 days as this period is equivalent to the credit period of the Tokyo branch) (in ₹lakh)	1,000
(iv) Interest for quarter 1 (₹1,000 lakh × 0.18 × 3/12) (in ₹lakh)	45
(v) Interest for quarter 2 (₹1,045 lakh × 0.18 × 3/12) (in ₹lakh)	47.025
(vi) Total cash payments (iii + iv + v) (after 180 days) (in ₹lakh)	1,092.025

(b) Determination of cash payment under letter of credit alternative

(i) Amount of borrowings (lakh)	¥1,680
(ii) Interest (¥1,680 lakh × 0.02 × 6/12) (in ₹lakh)	16.8
(iii) Commission charges (¥1,680 lakh × 0.02 × 6/12) (in ₹lakh)	16.8[1]
(iv) Total payment required (after 180 days) (in ₹lakh)	1,713.60
(v) Forward rate for 6 months ₹100 = ¥170	₹1 = ¥1.70
(vi) Indian rupees required to pay ¥1,713.6 lakh/1.70 (in ₹lakh)	1,008

(1) Assumption: Interest is not taken into account on commission that is due to be paid after 6 months as it is not normally subject to interest. However, if commission is subject to interest, there will be an additional interest of ₹16,800, i.e., (₹16.8 lakh × 0.02 × 6/12). As a result, total cash payments will be ₹1008.168 lakh (₹1008 lakh) + ₹16,800).

Recommendation Alert Limited is advised to avail an overseas offer as it causes less cash payments.

P.33.9 Calculate cross currency rate between €/£ (bid as well as ask), given the following spot exchange rates of 3 pair of currencies

LO 33.2 LOD D

₹/US $	: ₹61.25 – 61.94
₹/€	: 78.43 – 79.03
$/£	: $ 1.50 – 1.52

Solution Determination of €/£ exchange rate (bid quote)

$$(€/£)_{bid} = (€/₹)_{bid} \times (₹/\$)_{bid} \times (\$/£)_{bid}$$

As per equation, $(₹/\$)_{bid}$ and $(\$/£)_{bid}$ are available in the desired form; (€/₹) is not in desired form (its exchange rate is given as €/₹). To convert in the desired form €/₹ the values become ₹79.03 – ₹78.43. The rate to be determined is the unit of which can be purchased for 1 ₹1 euro was sold at ₹79.03 as per the quote provided. Therefore, 1 ₹ can purchase €1/79.30 = 0.01265. Substituting the values in equation, we have $(€/£)_{bid}$ = 0.01265 × 61.25 × 1.50 = 1.1622

Determination of €/£ exchange rate (ask quote)

$$(€/£)_{ask} = (€/₹)_{ask} \times (₹/\$)_{ask} \times (\$/£)_{bid}$$
$$= 1/78.43 = 0.01275 \times 61.94 \times 1.52 = 1.2003$$

P.33.10 If a direct quote of the euro in Delhi is ₹79 and if the transaction cost in buying or selling any currency is 1 per cent of the transaction amount, what is the range of possible direct quotes of the rupee in various EU countries?

LO 33.2 LOD E

Solution Direct quote of the euro in Delhi = ₹79/€. Let us say the direct quote of the rupee in a EU country is €q/₹, in an equilibrium condition, there should not be any possibility of arbitrage gain. If we convert ₹10,00,000 into euros in Delhi. We will receive ₹10,00,000 × 1/79 × 0.99 euro. Thus, the euro is converted back into the rupee using the quote in the EU country, this will give [10,00,000 × 1/79 × 0.99] × 1/q × 0.99 rupees.

For no arbitrage profit [10,00,000 × 1/79 × 0.99] × $1/q \times (0.99)^2$ < ₹10,00,000

$q > 0.0122$ **(i)**

Similarly, if we convert ₹10,00,000 in euros first in a EU country currency, we receive (10,00,000 × q × 0.99) euros. These euros exchanged for rupees in Delhi will fetch (10,00,000 × q × 0.99) × 79 × 0.99 rupees.

To avoid arbitrage profit 10,00,000 × q × 79 × $(0.99)^2$ < ₹10,00,000

or $q < 0.0129$ **(ii)**

So as it is evident from equations **(i)** and **(ii)** range is $0.0122 < q < 0.0129$

or €/₹ > 0.0122

and €/₹ < 0.0129

P.33.11 In the international monetary market, an international forward bid for December, 15 on a pound sterling future for delivery on the same day is US $1.4906. The contract size of the pound sterling is £62,500. How could the dealer use arbitrage in profit in this situation and how much profit is earned?

LO 33.2 LOD M

Solution The dealer can make arbitrage profit through the following steps:

(i) The dealer can purchase dollars from £62,500 in the international monetary market. He will obtain US $93,437.5, i.e., (£62,500 × 1.4906).

(ii) The dealer can sell US $93,437.5 in the future market at the rate of 1£ = US $1.4906. In other words, 1 US $ = 1/1.4906 = £0.67087.

(iii) On the date of settlement, the dealer will have = £62,684.415, i.e., (US $93,437.5 × £0.67087).

(iv) There is a gain of £62,684.415 – £62,500 = £184.415 to the dealer.

P.33.12 Are there any arbitrage gains possible from the spot exchange rates quoted at 3 different forex markets. There are no transaction costs and arbitrageur has 10 million US $.

LO 33.2 LOD D

\$1	= ₹61.50 in India
£1	= ₹90.62 in London
£1	= \$1.4901 in New York

Solution Arbitrage gains are possible since the cross rates between the US \$/British pound by using the rates at London and at Mumbai are different (₹90.62/61.50 = US \$1.4734/£1) from that of New York (US \$1.4901).

The arbitrageur can adopt the following steps to realise arbitrage gain.

(i) The arbitrageur will buy Indian rupees form 10 million US \$. The total proceeds he obtains is (₹61.50 × 10 million US \$) = ₹61,50,00,000.

(ii) He converts Indian rupees into British pounds at the London forex market. He receives (₹61,50,00,000/₹90.62) = £6,786,581.328.

(iii) He then converts £6,786,581.328 at the New York forex market. He obtains (£6,786,581.328 × US \$1.4901) = US \$10,112,684.83.

(iv) Thus, he has a net gain of (US \$10,112,684.83 – US \$10,000,000) = US \$112,684.83.

P.33.13 The following quotations are available to you: **LO 33.2** LOD D

by a bank in New York	: \$1.6012/£
by a bank in Hong Kong	: HKD7.75/\$
by a bank in London	: £0.0870/HKD

Is any triangular arbitrage possible?

Solution From a direct quote of New York and Hong Kong, the cross rate for £/HKD is £/HKD = £/\$ × \$/HKD = 1/1.6012 × 1/7.7500 or £/HKD = 0.0805. Since in the direct quote the HKD in London is £0.0870/HKD (different from 0.0805), triangular arbitrage is possible.

P.33.14 Are arbitrage gains possible from the following set of information to the arbitrageur? **LO 33.2** LOD M

Spot rate	: 61.88/\$
3 month forward rate	: ₹62.28/\$
3 month interest rates:	
₹	: 7% p a
\$	: 11% p a

Solution 3 month forward rate of the dollar is higher (at ₹62.28) than the spot rate (₹61.88). It implies that the dollar is at premium.

$$\text{Premium (percentage)} = \left(\frac{₹62.28 - ₹61.88}{₹61.88}\right) \times \frac{12}{3} \times 100 = 2.58\% \text{ per annum}$$

Interest rate differential = 11% – 7% = 4% per annum

Since interest rate differential (4%) and premium percentage (2.58%) do not match, there are arbitrage gain possibilities. An arbitrageur can take the following steps in this regard.

(i) Arbitrageur borrows, say, ₹100 million at 7 per cent for 3 months (he borrows in Indian currency as it carries lower interest rate).

(ii) He then converts ₹100 million in US \$ at the spot rate of ₹61.88 in the spot market. He gets an amount US \$1,616,031.02 (₹100 million/₹61.88).

(iii) He invests US \$1,616,031.02 in the money market at 11 per cent interest per annum for 3 months. As a result of this investment, he obtains the interest of US \$44,440.85 (\$1,616,031.02 × 3/12 × 11/100)

(iv) Total sum available with arbitrageur, 3 months from now is (US \$1,616,031.02 amount invested + US \$44,440.85 interest) = US \$1,660,471.87.

(v) Since he would get US \$1,660,471.87 after 3 months, he sells forward US \$1,660,471.87 at the rate of ₹62.28.

(vi) As a result of a forward deal, at the end of 3 months from now, he would get ₹10,34,14,188.266, i.e., (\$1,660,471.87 × 62.28).

(vii) He refunds the ₹100 million borrowed, along with interest due on it. The refunded sum is ₹100 million + ₹1,750,000 i.e. (₹100 million × 3/12 × 7/100) = ₹10,17,50,000.

(viii) Net gain is ₹10,34,14,188.266 – ₹10,17,50,000 = ₹16,64,188.266.

P.33.15 An Indian software company receives an order from an European union country. The buyer will pay in four quarterly instalments each of €0.5 million, starting from the end of the first quarter. The rates for euros in India is as follow:

LO 33.2 LOD M

Spot	*3 month forward*	*6 month forward*	*9 month forward*	*1 year forward*
₹78.40	₹78.20	₹77.95	₹77.80	₹77.75

If an Indian company hedges its foreign exchange rate risk in the forward market, how much revenue does it earn?

Solution

Indian software company will have the following income streams:

Instalment	*Euro income*	*Rate*	*Revenue*
1st quarter-end	€ 5,00,000	₹78.2/ €	₹3,91,00,000
2nd quarter-end	5,00,000	77.95/ €	3,89,75,000
3rd quarter-end	5,00,000	77.80/ €	3,89,00,000
4th quarter-end	5,00,000	77.75/ €	3,88,75,000
Total revenue income is			15,58,50,000

P.33.16 The following data (related to interest rates) is available from the forex market:

LO 33.3 LOD M

US 1 month treasury bill	: 2.50 – 2.55% p a
India 1 month treasury bill	: 6.75 – 6.80% p a

If the dollar spot rate in India is ₹61.5040/61.5054 per US $, find the no-arbitrage range of future prices for a 1 month dollar future.

Solution Let us assume the forward rate to be F. There are two possibilities for arbitrage.

(a) Borrow dollar, buy rupees, invest rupees, sell rupees in future.

(i) Borrows 1 dollar (@ 2.55%) and sell it in spot market to receive ₹61.5040.

(ii) Lends these rupees in money market to earn @ 6.75%. Thus, the future value after 1 month = 61.5040 (1 + 0.0675 × 1/12) = ₹61.8500.

(iii) Sells ₹61.8500 in future market (@ F) to receive dollars (61.8500 × 1/F).

(iv) As dollar 1 has been borrowed, after 1 month, the dollar to be returned is (1 × 0.0255 × 1/12). For a no arbitrage condition, dollars in (iii) must be less than dollar in (iv) or 61.8500 × 1/F < 1 × 0.0255 × 1/12 or F > 61.7185.

(b) Borrow rupees, buy dollar, invest in dollar, buy rupees in future.

(i) Borrows 1 ₹ (@ 6.80%) and sells it in spot market to receive US $1/61.5054 = US $0.0162.

(ii) Lends these US $0.0162 in money market @ 2.50%. After 1 month, it will fetch US $0.0162 (1 + 0.025 × 1/12).

(iii) Selling the dollar calculated in (ii) in the future market will provide ₹F × 0.0162 (1 + 0.025 × 1/12).

(iv) As 1 ₹ will be borrowed, so after 1 month the rupee to be returned is ₹(1 + 0.068 × 1/12).

For no arbitrage condition the rupee calculated in (iii) must be less than that in (iv) or F × 0.0162 (1 + 0.025 × 1/12) < (1 + 0.068 × 1/12) or F < 61.9491.

So the range in which forward prices will lie is ₹61.7185 < F < ₹61.9491.

P.33.17 The US inflation rate is expected to be 2 per cent annually and that of India is expected to be 6.5 per cent annually. The current spot rate of US $ in India is ₹59.4050/US $.

LO 33.3 LOD M

Find the expected rate of US $ in India after one year and after three years from now using purchase power theory of exchange rate.

Solution According to Purchase Power Parity, Forward rate = Spot rate $\left(\frac{1+R_H}{1+R_F}\right)^t$. Where R_H is the rate of inflation in the home country and R_F is rate of inflation in a foreign country during the year

$$\text{Forward rate} = ₹59.4050\left(\frac{1+0.065}{1+0.02}\right)^1 = ₹62.0258$$

or, Spot rate after one year = ₹62.0258/US $

$$\text{Spot rate after three years} = 59.4050\left(\frac{1+0.065}{1+0.02}\right)^3 = ₹67.4228/\text{US }\$$$

P.33.18 On April 1, 3 months interest rate in the US $ and UK are 6.5 per cent and 4.5 per cent per annum, respectively. The US $/UK £ spot rate is 0.6560. What would be the forward rate for £, for delivery on 30th June?

LO 33.3 LOD D

Solution Spot rate is US $0.6560/£

Using the interest rate parity relationship $S_1 = S_0\left[\frac{1+i_{nA}}{1+i_{nB}}\right]$

S_0 = Spot rate
S_1 = Future exchange rate
i_{na} = Nominal interest rate in country A (USA)
i_{nB} = Nominal interest rate in country B (UK)

$$S_1 = 0.6560\left[\frac{1+(0.0065\times 3/12)}{1+(0.045\times 3/12)}\right]$$

S_1 = 0.6560 × (1.01625/1.01125) = USD 0.6592 $/£

P33.19 An American importer has purchased goods worth euro 15,00,000. Payments are to be made after 6 months. The spot rate of Euro is US $ 1.2800/€. The American importer expects depreciation of the dollar against the euro in the coming months. A New York bank gives the 6 month forward rate as US$ 1.3381/€.

LO 33.3 LOD D

If the American importer makes use of the forward rate to hedge its currency risk, what is its loss or profit under following circumstances.

(a) Spot price of euro after 6 months is US$ 1.2800/€
(b) Spot price of euro after 6 months is US$ 1.3962/€
(c) Spot price of euro after 6 month is US$ 1.2000/€

Solution The importer will hedge his currency rate fluctuation exposure by hedging (buying euro) in the future market; the rate to be paid by him is US$ 1.3381/€, irrespective of what the rate will be in spot market after 6 months.

(a) If the rate in spot market after 6 months is US$ 1.2800/€, the importer suffers a loss due to forward contract = ($ 1.3381 – 1.2800) × 15,00,000 = €87,150.
(b) If the rate in the spot market after 6 months is US$ 1.3962/€, the importer gains due to the forward contract ($ 1.3962 – 1.3381) × 15,00,000 = €87,150.
(c) If the rate in the spot market after 6 months is US$ 1.2000/€, the importer suffers a loss (US$ 1.3381 – 1.2000) × 15,00,000 = € 2,07,150

P33.20 In March, 2018, the Multinational Industries makes the following assessment of dollar rates per British pound to prevail as on 1.9.2018:

LO 33.2 LOD M

$/Pound	*Probability*
1.50	0.15
1.60	0.20
1.70	0.25
1.80	0.20
1.90	0.20

(i) What is the expected spot rate for 1.9.2018?
(ii) If, as of March, 2018 the 6-month forward rate is \$ 1.70, should the firm sell forward its pound receivables due in September, 2018?

Solution

(i) Computation of expected spot rate (\$/pound) as on September 1, 2018

\$/Pound (X)	*Probability*	*Expected \$/Pound*
1.50	0.15	0.225
1.60	0.20	0.32
1.70	0.25	0.425
1.80	0.20	0.36
1.90	0.20	0.38
Expected spot rate (\$ for British pound)		1.71

(ii) Since the 6-month forward rate is lower (\$1.70) than the expected spot rate (\$1.71), it will be profitable for the firm not to sell forward its pounds receivables. By retaining pounds receivables, the firm is likely to get \$1.71 for each pound receivable *vis-à-vis* \$1.70 if it sells forward.

P33.21 A company operating in Japan has today effected sales to an Indian company, the payment being due 3 months from the date of invoice. The invoice amount is 108 lakh yen. At today's spot rate, it is equivalent to ₹60 lakh. It is anticipated that the exchange rate will decline by 10 per cent over the 3 months period and in order to protect the yen payments, the importer proposes to take appropriate action in the foreign exchange market. The 3 months forward rate is presently quoted as 1.75 yen per rupee. You are required to calculate the expected loss and to show how it can be hedged by a forward contract.

LO 33.2 LOD M

Solution

Computation of expected loss due to decline in exchange rate

Current spot rate of exchange is ₹1 = 1.8 yen, (108 lakh yen/₹60 lakh)	
Anticipated decline in exchange rate of Indian rupee is 10 per cent	
Expected spot rate of exchange after three months is 1.8 yen – (10% × 1.8 yen) = 1.62 yen per rupee	
Expected payment in Indian rupees after three months (108 lakh yen/1.62)	₹66,66,667
Less present cost of 108 lakh yen	60,00,000
Difference represents expected exchange loss	6,66,667

Computation of loss with forward contract

Payment in Indian rupees after three months under forward contract (108 lakh yen/1.75)	₹61,71,428.5
Less present cost of 108 lakh yen	60,00,000.0
Loss	1,71,428.5

Recommendation The company is advised to cover risk with forward contract in view of reduced exchange loss.

P33.22 You sold Hong Kong Dollar 1,00,00,000 value spot to your customer at ₹8.00 and covered yourself in London market on the same day, when the exchange rates were

LO 33.2 LOD M

US\$ 1 = H.K.\$ 7.7580 – 7.8920

Local inter bank market rates for US\$ were

Spot US\$ 1 = ₹61.70 – 61.85

Calculate cover rate and ascertain the profit or loss in the transaction. Ignore brokerage.

Solution **Cover rate:** For buying 1 US$ in the spot market, ₹61.85 are required. 1 US$ can be sold at London in exchange for HK $ 7.7580. The cover rate therefore will be:

₹61.85/7.7580 = ₹7.9724

Or 1 HK $ = ₹7.9724

Calculation of profit or loss in the transaction

Sale rate: 1 HK $	₹8.00
Cover rate: 1 HK $	7.9724
Profit per HK $	0.0276
Profit on the transaction (1,00,00,000 × 0.0276)	₹2,76,000

P33.23 Z Ltd (importing goods worth USD 2 million) requires 90 days to make the payment. The overseas supplier has offered a 60 days interest free credit period and for additional credit for 30 days interest is to be charged at 8% per annum. **LO 33.2,3** LOD D

The banker of Z Ltd offers a 30 days loan at 10% per annum and their quote for foreign exchange is as follows:

Spot 1 USD	₹62.50
60 days forward for 1 USD	63.10
90 days forward for 1 USD	63.50

You are required to evaluate the following options:

(i) Pay the supplier in 60 days, or **(ii)** Avail the supplier's offer of 90 days credit. Advise Z Ltd.

Solution

(i) Payment to supplier in 60 days

If the payment is made to supplier in 60 days, the applicable forward rate for 1 USD	₹63.10
Payment due	USD 2,000,000
Outflow in rupees (USD 2,000,000 × ₹63.10)	₹126,200,000
Add: Interest on loan for 30 days@10% p.a.	₹10,51,667
Total outflow	₹127,251,670

(ii) Payment to supplier in 90 days

Amount payable	USD 2,000,000
Add: Interest on credit period for 30 days @ 8% p.a.	USD 13,333
Total outflow in USD	USD 2,013,333
Applicable forward rate for 1 USD	₹63.50
Total outflow in ₹(USD 2,013,333 × ₹63.50)	₹127,846,646

Recommendation Alternative 1 is better as it entails lower cash outflow.

P33.24 A bank sold Hong Kong Dollars 40, 00,000 to its customer at spot price of ₹8.05 and covered itself in London Market on the same day, when the exchange rates were: US$ = HK$ 7.7500 – 7.7538 Local interbank market rates for US$ were: Spot US$ 1 = ₹62.50–63.00 **LO 33.2** LOD M

You are required to calculate rate and ascertain the gain or loss in the transaction. Ignore brokerage. You are to show the calculations for exchange rate up to four decimal points.

Solution

The bank (Dealer) covered itself by buying from the London market at market selling rate.

Rupee – US Dollar selling rate	₹63.00
US Dollar – Hong Kong Dollar	HK $ 7.7500
Rupee – Hong Kong cross rate (₹63.00/7.7500)	₹8.1290

Gain/Loss to the Bank

Amount received from customer (HK$ 40,00,000) × ₹8.05	₹3,22,00,000
Amount paid on cover deal (HK$ 40,00,000 × ₹8.1290)	₹3,25,16,000
Loss to bank	(₹3,16,000)

Alternative calculation: Loss to bank = 40,00,000 (₹8.05 – ₹8.1290) = ₹3,16,000

REVIEW QUESTIONS

LOD: Easy

RQ.33.1(a) Indicate whether the following statements are true or false: **[LO 33.1,2,3]**

(i) Foreign exchange is required by a country only to make payments for imports.

(ii) Business firms operate on their own in the foreign exchange market.

(iii) The role of a central bank in the foreign exchange market is commercial in nature.

(iv) Exchange rate is the price of one country's currency expressed in terms of the currency of another country.

(v) A foreign exchange quotation can be direct or indirect.

(vi) Spread is the difference between the ask price and the bid price.

(vii) Forward exchange rate is the rate of that day on which the transaction has taken place.

(viii) Cross rate is the rate of exchange of two currencies on the basis of exchange quotes of other pairs of currencies.

(ix) Foreign exchange quotations are always with respect to the customer.

(x) If the forward rates are higher than the spot rates, the forward rates are at discount.

[Answers: (i) False (ii) False (iii) False (iv) True (v) True (vi) True (vii) False (viii) True (ix) False (x) False]

(b) Fill in the blanks with the correct answer (out of the choices provided).

(i) A rate of ₹62 per U.S. dollar is an example of ____________ (direct/indirect) quotation.

(ii) Indirect quotations are known as ____________ (European/American) quotations.

(iii) Geographical arbitrage involves ____________ (two/three) currencies.

(iv) In countries that witness high inflation rates, currency values decline ____________ (more/less) compared to the currencies of countries with lower inflation rates.

(v) The spot and two month forward buying rates of US$ are ₹60.80 and ₹61.50 respectively. It implies that Rupee is quoting at a ____________ (premium/discount) in the forward market.

(vi) Given the spot rate of ₹89.00/£ and interest rate differential of 3 per cent between the two currencies, the 3 month forward rate should be ____________ (₹89.5675/£ or ₹89.6675/£) to eliminate any arbitrage gains.

(vii) If a foreign currency is to be at a premium in the forward market, it should have a relatively ____________ (higher/lower) interest rate vis-à-vis the home currency.

(viii) When a direct quote of the home currency or any other desired currency is not available in the foreign exchange market, it is computed with the help of ____________ (spot/forward/cross) rates.

(ix) The settlement of spot transactions in the foreign exchange markets occurs within a maximum period of ______________ (two/three) days.

(x) The rate at which a foreign exchange dealer is ready to sell a currency is called _____(bid/ask) rate.

[Answers: (i) direct (ii) American (iii) two (iv) more (v) discount (vi) ₹89.6675/£ (vii) lower (viii) cross (ix) two (x) ask]

RQ.33.2 What is the foreign exchange market? Why is such a market needed? Name a few major foreign exchange markets. [LO 33.1]

RQ.33.3 A forex dealer in India gives a quote for the US dollar as ₹60.9450 – 60.9577. [LO 33.2]

(a) An importer is looking to buy dollars to pay his import bill of US$ 10,000. How many rupees will be required to be paid to have US$ 10,000?

(b) An exporter receiving his export income of US$ 10,000 will receive How many rupees?

RQ.33.4 If in India the rate is ₹61.5320/61.5866 per US $, what will the direct quote of rupee be in New York? [LO 33.2]

LOD: Medium

RQ.33.5 What are spot and forward exchange rates? How do they differ from each other? [LO 33.2]

RQ.33.6 What is spread? Is it affected by the volatility of the currency? [LO 33.2]

RQ.33.7 What is the arbitrage process? What function does it serve in the context of foreign exchange markets? [LO 33.2]

RQ.33.8 Distinguish between geographical arbitrage and triangular arbitrage. [LO 33.2]

RQ.33.9 Explain in brief, the interest rate parity theory and purchasing power parity theory. What is their relevance in exchange rates? [LO 33.3]

RQ.33.10 What are the major determinants of exchange rates? [LO 33.3]

RQ.33.11 An Indian currency trader receives following currency quotes: [LO 33.2]

₹47.000/Singapore $ in Mumbai
₹60.3610/US $ in Mumbai

He checks rates at Singapore and he receives the rate as Singapore $ 1.2900/US$.

Assuming there are no transaction costs, how will the trader use this set of information for making profit?

RQ.33.12 The following are the various quotes for the US $ available in a bank in Mumbai. [LO 33.2]

Spot	*1 month forward*	*3 month forward*
₹60.9350/60.9550	325/375	520/580

Find the bid and ask rates and spread for all the quotes.

RQ.33.13 An Indian importer receives the following quotes of dollar from its banker. [LO 33.2]

Spot	: ₹61.3250
1 month forward	: ₹61.5230
6 month forward	: ₹62.1050

What is the discount/premium of the dollar forward prices?

RQ.33.14(a) The following is a direct quote of the dollar provided by a leading Indian bank. [LO 33.2]

Spot	*1 month forward*	*3 month forward*	*6 month forward*
₹60.6500/60.6620	35/30	60/45	30/38

What is the bid–ask rates for these quotes?

(b) If you are a small forex dealer and are required to provide forward rates for 2 month to a client, what forward bid-ask rate will you quote on the basis of rates provided in RQ 33.17(a)? [LO 33.2]

RQ.33.15 From the following data, at what forward rate will no arbitrage gain be possible: [LO 33.3]

₹61.00/$ (Spot)

6 *month interest rate*:

India : 7.5% per annum

US : 2.0% per annum

LOD: Difficult

RQ.33.16 Indicate whether forward exchange rates are normally at premium or discount compared to spot rates. How do you determine, such a discount or premium? Illustrate with an appropriate example. [LO 33.2]

RQ.33.17 What are cross rates? How are they determined? [LO 33.2]

RQ.33.18 State the situations in which riskless arbitrage opportunities are possible to the arbitrageur. Explain your answer with appropriate examples. [LO 33.2]

ANSWERS

RQ.33.3 **(a)** ₹4,79,550

(b) ₹4,79,450

RQ.33.4 The direct quote of rupee in New York (US $ / ₹) : 0.16236 – 0.16251

RQ.33.11 Arbitrage process will involve the following steps:

(i) Sell 1 million Singaporean $ and get rupees in Mumbai. The proceeds will be ₹10,00,000 × 47.00 = ₹4,70,00,000

(ii) Sell ₹4,70,00,000 in Mumbai and get US $. The proceeds will be US $ 4,70,00,000 × 1/60.3610 = US $ 7,78,648

(iii) Sell US $ 7,78,648 in Singapore to receive Singapore $ (7,78,648 × 1.2900) = Singapore $ 10,04,456

Thus, there is a gain of (Singapore $ 10,04,456 - $ 10,00,000) = Singapore $ 4,456.

RQ.33.12

Maturity	*Bid*	*Ask*	*Spread*
Spot	₹60.9350/$	₹60.9550/$	₹0.0200
1 month forward	60.9675/$	60.9925/$	0.0250
3 month forward	60.9870/$	61.013/$	0.0260

RQ.33.13 1 month forward premium 3.874% p.a.

6 month forward premium 2.5438% p.a.

RQ.33.14 **(a)**

Maturity	*Bid*	*Ask*
Spot	₹60.6500/$	₹60.6620/$
1 month forward	60.6475/$	60.6590/$
3 month forward	60.6440/$	60.6575/$
6 month forward	60.6520/$	60.6658/$

(b) Bid ₹60.6457; Ask ₹60.6582

Therefore, the 2 month forward rate will be ₹60.6457/$ – ₹60.6582/$

RQ.33.15 ₹61.83875/$

Scan the QR Code to access comprehensive solutions to all numerical review questions and additional material.

CHAPTER 34

Foreign Exchange Exposure and Risk Management

LEARNING OBJECTIVES	
LO 34.1	Explain the three types of exposures in international business—transaction exposure, translation exposure and economic exposure
LO 34.2	Describe the four external techniques—forward contracts, currency options, swaps and money market operations—of foreign exchange risk management
LO 34.3	Discuss the important internal hedging techniques to reduce foreign exchange risk exposure, namely, leading and lagging, invoice/billing in the desired currency, indexation clauses, sharing risk, shifting the manufacturing base, netting and reinvoicing centre
LO 34.4	Enumerate risk management practices in India

INTRODUCTION

Foreign exchange risk management (FERM) constitutes an integral part of all major corporate decisions to manage foreign exchange exposure, given the global business scenario in which business firms (in particular international companies and multinational companies) operate. Therefore, it is imperative that corporate firms are in the know of the various types of the foreign exchange risks they are exposed to as well as are fully conversant with the various important FERM techniques to deal with such risks. This Chapter discusses both these aspects. The major exposures faced by business firms in their international operations are discussed first. The techniques to hedge/cover foreign exchange risk, namely, currency market hedges and internal techniques are dealt in subsequent discussions. The chapter also enumerates risk management practices in India. The major points are summarised by way of recapitulation.

LO 34.1 TYPES OF EXPOSURE

Business firms, having international business operations, primarily encounter three types of exposure: (i) **transaction exposure**, (ii) **translation exposure** and (iii) **economic exposure**. They have been briefly explained below.

Transaction Exposure

Transaction exposure involves gain/loss arising out of the various types of transactions that require settlement in a foreign currency.

Transaction exposure is inherent in all foreign currency denominated contractual obligations/transactions. This involves gain or loss arising out of the various types of transactions that require settlement in a foreign currency. The transactions may relate to cross-border trade in terms of import or export of goods, the borrowing or lending in foreign currencies, domestic purchases and sales of goods and services of the foreign subsidiaries and the purchase of assets or take over of the liability involving foreign currency. The actual profit the firm earns or loss it suffers, of course, is known only at the time of settlement of these transactions.

A firm's balance sheet already contains several items reflecting transaction exposure; the notable items being debtors receivable in foreign currency, creditors payable in foreign currency, foreign loans and foreign investments. While it is true that transaction exposure is applicable to all these foreign transactions, it is usually employed in connection with foreign trade, that is, specific imports or exports on open account credit[1]. Example 34.1 illustrates transaction exposure.

***Example* 34.1**

Suppose an Indian firm imports goods from the US, invoiced at US $1 million. At the time of invoicing, the US dollar exchange rate was ₹61.4513. The payment is due after 4 months. During the intervening period, the Indian rupee weakens/and the exchange rate of the dollar appreciates to ₹61.9824. As a result, the Indian importer has a transaction loss to the extent of excess rupee payment required to purchase US $1 million. Now, the firm is to pay US $1 million × ₹61.4513 = ₹61.4513 million. After 4 months from now when it is to make payment on maturity, it will have to make higher payment at ₹61.9824 million, (US $1 million × ₹61.9824). Thus, the Indian firm suffers a transaction loss of ₹5,31,100, (₹61.9824 million – ₹61.4513 million).

In case the Indian rupee appreciates (or the US dollar weakens) to ₹61.1124, the Indian importer gains (in terms of the lower payment of Indian rupees); its equivalent rupee payment (of US $1 million) will be ₹61.1124 million. As a result, the firm has profit of ₹3,38,900, (₹61.4513 million – ₹61.1124 million).

Example 34.1 clearly demonstrates that the firm may not necessarily have losses from the transaction exposure; it may earn profits also. In fact, the international firms have a number of items in balance sheet at a point of time, on some of the items (say payments), it may suffer losses due to weakening of its home currency; it is then likely to gain on foreign currency receipts. However, in practice, the transaction exposure is associated with losses presumably due to the principle of conservatism.

Translation Exposure

Translation exposure results from the need to translate foreign currency assets/liabilities into local currency at the time of finalising accounts.

Translation exposure relates to the change in accounting income and balance sheet statements caused by the changes in exchange rates. These changes may take place by/at the time of finalisation of accounts compared to the time when the asset was purchased or liability was assumed. In other words, translation exposure results from the need to translate foreign currency assets or liabilities into the local currency at the time of finalising accounts. Example 34.2 illustrates the impact of translation exposure.

***Example* 34.2**

Suppose, an Indian corporate has taken a loan from a bank in the US to import plant and machinery worth US $10 million. When the import materalised, the exchange rate was ₹60.0. The imported plant and machinery in the books of the corporate would be shown at ₹60 × US $10 million = ₹60 crore and loan at ₹60 crore.

Assuming no change in the exchange rate, the corporate at the time of preparation of final accounts, will provide depreciation (say at 25 per cent) of ₹15 crore on the book value of ₹60 crore.

Let us assume further that the dollar exchange rate appreciates to ₹61. As a result, the book value of plant and machinery will change to ₹61 crore (₹61 × US $10 million); depreciation will increase to ₹15.25 crore (₹61 crore × 0.25), and the loan amount will also be revised upwards to ₹61 crore. Thus, there is a translation loss of ₹1 crore due to the increased value of loan. Besides, the higher book value of the plant and machinery causes higher depreciation, reducing the net profit.

Alternatively, translation losses (or gains) may not be reflected in the income statement. They may be shown separately under the head of 'translation adjustment' in the balance sheet, without affecting accounting income. This translation loss adjustment is to be carried out in the owners' equity account. The adjustment made to the owners' equity account is a better approach as the accounting income would not be diluted on account of translation losses or gains.

On account of varying ways of dealing with translation losses or gains, accounting practices vary in different countries and among business firms within a country. Whichever method is adopted to deal with translation losses/gains, it makes an impact on both the income statement and the balance sheet.

Economic Exposure

Economic exposure implies change in the value of a company that accompanies an unanticipated change in exchange rates.

Of all the three exposures, **economic exposure** is considered the most important as it has an impact on the valuation of a firm. It is defined as the **change in the value of a company that accompanies an unanticipated change in exchange rates**[2]. It is important to note that anticipated changes in exchange rates are already reflected in the market value of the company. For instance, when an Indian firm transacts business with an American firm, it has the expectation that the Indian rupee is likely to weaken *vis-à-vis* the US dollar. This weakening of the Indian rupee will not affect the market value (as it was anticipated, and hence already considered in valuation). However, in case the extent/margin of weakening is different from expected, it will have a bearing on the market value. The market value may enhance if the Indian rupee depreciates less than expected. In case, the Indian rupee weakens more than expected, it may entail erosion in the firm's market value. In brief, the unanticipated changes in exchange rates (favourable or unfavourable) are not accounted for in valuation and, hence, cause economic exposure.

Since economic exposure emanates from unanticipated changes, its measurement is not as precise and accurate as those of transaction and translation exposures; it involves subjectivity. Shapiro's definition of economic exposure provides the basis of its measurement. According to him, it is based on the extent to which the value of the firm—as measured by the present value of the expected future cash flows—will change when exchange rates change[3].

Symbolically, the firm has exposure risk when,

$$(\Delta\ PV/\Delta e) \neq \text{zero} \qquad \textbf{(34.1)}$$

Where, $\Delta\ PV$ is the change in the firm's present value associated with an exchange rate change (Δe). Thus, Equation 34.1 measures variability in the value of the firm due to uncertain exchange rate changes. Since the major parameter in determination of the PV is future cash flows, exposure risk clearly reflects the variability of the firm's future cash flows.

The transaction exposure also affects cash flow exposure (the importing firm is to make more payments in case the home currency depreciates). Should transaction exposure, then, not be a part of economic exposure? Shapiro recognises this and considers transaction exposure as a part of economic exposure. He classifies economic exposure into two components, namely, **transaction exposure** and **operating exposure**. Since transaction exposure is already explained, operating exposure will now be discussed.

Operating Exposure **Operating exposure** has an impact on the firm's future operating revenues, future operating costs and future operating cash flows. Clearly, operating exposure has a longer-term perspective. Given the fact that the firm is valued as a going concern entity, its future revenues and costs are likely to be affected by the exchange rate changes. In particular, it is true for all those business firms that deal in selling goods and services that are subject to foreign competition and/or uses inputs from abroad.

> **Operating exposure** has impact on firm's future operating revenue, costs and cash flows.

In case, the firm succeeds in passing on the impact of higher input costs (caused due to appreciation of foreign currency) fully by increasing the selling price, it does not have any operating risk exposure as its operating future cash flows are likely to remain unaffected. The less price elastic is the demand of the goods/services the firm deals in, the greater is the price flexibility it has to respond to exchange rate changes. Price elasticity in turn depends, *inter alia*, on the degree of competition and location of the key competitors. The more differentiated a firm's products are, the less competition it encounters and the greater is its ability to maintain its domestic currency prices, both at home and abroad[4]. Evidently, such firms have relatively less operating risk exposure. In contrast, firms that sell goods/services in a highly competitive market (in technical terms, have higher price elasticity of demand) run a higher operating risk exposure as they are constrained to pass on the impact of higher input costs (due to change in exchange rates) to the consumers.

Apart from supply and demand elasticities, the firm's ability to shift production and sourcing of inputs is another major factor affecting operating risk exposure. In operational terms, a firm having higher elasticity of substitution between home-country and foreign-country inputs or production is less susceptible to foreign exchange risk and hence encounters low operating risk exposure.

In brief, the firm's ability to adjust its cost structure and raise the prices of its products and services is the major determinant of its operating risk exposure.

Measurement of Economic Exposure Its measurement is a daunting task. A workable approach is suggested by Shapiro. The approach is based on an operational definition of the exchange risk encountered by a parent or one of its foreign subsidiaries. A company faces exchange risk to the extent that variations in the dollar value of the units' cash flows are correlated with variations in the nominal exchange rate[5]. This correlation is the same thing that a regression analysis seeks to provide. The relevant regression equation in this regard is:

$$\Delta CF_t = a + \beta \Delta EXCH_t + U_t \qquad \textbf{(34.2)}$$

Where, $\Delta CF_t = CF_t - CF_{t-1}$,

and CF_t equals the dollar value of total affiliate (parent) cash flows in period t.

$$\Delta EXCH_t - EXCH_t - EXCH_{t-1},$$

and $EXCH_t$ equals the average nominal exchange rate (dollar value of one unit of the foreign currency) during period t.

U = a random error term with mean 0.

Equation 34.2 provides three key parameters: **(i)** The foreign exchange beta coefficient (β) measures the sensitivity of dollar cash flows to exchange rate changes; **(ii)** the 't' statistic measures the statistical significance of the beta coefficient and **(iii)** the R^2 measures the fraction of cash flow variability explained by variations in exchange rates. The higher the value of β, the greater the impact of the change in exchange rates on the dollar value of cash flows. The firm is more exposed to exchange rate changes and has a higher degree of economic exposure. In contrast, a lower β value is indicative of the fact that the firm is less exposed to exchange rate changes and, hence, has less economic exposure. A larger 't' value implies a higher level of confidence in the value of the beta coefficient. In practice, while interpreting the result of the regression equation, it should be borne in mind that the past is representative of the future (as the past data is used to determine the values).

To sum up the discussion, it can be said that the firm can assess the economic exposure by predicting the future exchange rates and what impact such rates have on operating revenues, operating costs, operating profits and eventually operating cash flows. The greater is the susceptibility of operating cash flows to exchange rates changes, the greater is the economic exposure of the business firm, and *vice-versa.*

LO 34.2 FOREIGN EXCHANGE RISK MANAGEMENT—EXTERNAL TECHNIQUES

From an operational perspective, **foreign exchange risk** is defined as the possibility of loss to the business unit on account of unfavourable movement in foreign exchange rates. Foreign exchange risk management (FERM) is the process through which finance managers try to eliminate/reduce the adverse impact of unfavourable changes in the foreign exchange rates to a tolerable level. We describe below the four major external techniques of the FERM (also known as derivatives)* and money market operations. Derivatives are: **(i)** forward contracts, **(ii)** currency futures, **(iii)** currency options and **(iv)** swaps.

Foreign exchange risk is the possibility of loss on account of unfavourable movement in foreign exchange rates.

Forward Contracts

Forward exchange contracts (discussed in the previous chapter) are widely used by business firms to hedge against volatile/adverse exchange rates. Business firms enter into a forward contract (with authorised dealers of the forward exchange market, normally banks) to buy or sell foreign currency in exchange for home currency, normally at a specific future date, at a predetermined exchange conversion rate (known as forward rate). An Indian importer, who wishes to avoid foreign exchange risk, has to purchase the required foreign currency (say US $/British £) forward (for a period, say 90 days, when the payments are to be made). Likewise, an Indian exporter to US can enter into a forward exchange contract to sell US dollar to avoid the risk of depreciation of the dollar when he receives payment on maturity (say, 90 days hence). Forward exchange contracts enable firms to cover the foreign exchange risk. They are ideally suited for hedging transaction exposure.

A typical forward contract specifies the **(i)** contract amount, **(ii)** forward exchange rate, **(iii)** parties to the contract, **(iv)** the specified date of delivery, **(v)** name of foreign currencies involved in exchange and, **(vi)** terms and conditions for cancellation.

Futures contract is a standardised agreement to buy/sell a specified amount of foreign currency in future at some future date.

Currency Futures

Currency futures are closely related to forward contracts. These are more popularly known as *futures contracts* and are traded at the futures markets. A **futures contract** is a standardised agreement to buy or sell a pre-specified amount of foreign currency in the futures market at some specified future date between the parties to the contract.

---

*As per the L C Gupta Committee, "derivative means forward, futures or option contract of pre determined fixed duration, linked for the purpose of contract fulfillment to the value of specified real or financial asset or to index security".

Currency futures contracts/markets are for the major/hard currencies of the world, namely, the US $, the British £, the Euro €, the Singapore dollar, the Japanese Yen and the Canadian dollar.

Futures, being standardised contracts in nature, are traded on an organised exchange; the clearing house of the exchange operates as a link between the two parties of the contract, namely, the buyer and the seller. In other words, transactions are through the clearing house and the two parties do not deal directly between themselves.

While it is true that futures contracts are similar to the forward contracts in their objective of hedging foreign exchange risk of business firms, they differ in many significant ways.

Differences Between Forward Contracts and Future Contracts The major differences between the forward contracts and futures contracts are as follows:

(i) Nature and size of Contracts Futures contracts are standardised contracts in that dealings in such contracts are permissible in standard-size sums, say multiples of 1,25,000 Euros or 12.5 million yen. Apart from standard-size contracts, maturities are also standardised. In contrast, forward contracts are customised/tailor-made; such contracts can virtually be of any size or maturity.

(ii) Mode of Trading In the case of forward contracts, there is a direct link between the firm and the authorised dealer (normally a bank) both at the time of entering the contract and at the time of execution. On the other hand, the clearing house interposes between the two parties involved in futures contracts.

(iii) Liquidity The two positive features of futures contracts, namely, their standard-size and trading at clearing house of an organised exchange, provide them relatively more liquidity *vis-à-vis* forward contracts, which are neither standardised nor traded through organised futures markets. For this reason, the future markets are more liquid than the forward markets.

(iv) Deposits/Margins While futures contracts require guarantee deposits from the parties, no such deposits are needed for forward contracts. Besides, the futures contract necessitate valuation on a daily basis, meaning that gains and losses are noted (the practice is known as *marked-to-market*[6]). Valuation results in one of the parties becoming a gainer and the other a loser; while the loser has to deposit money to cover losses, the winner is entitled to the withdrawal of excess margin. Such an exercise is conspicuous by its absence in forward contracts as settlement between the parties concerned is made on the pre-specified date of maturity.

(v) Default Risk As a sequel to the deposit and margin requirements in the case of futures contracts, default risk is reduced to a marked extent in such contracts compared to forward contracts.

(vi) Actual Delivery Forward contracts are normally closed, involving actual delivery of foreign currency in exchange for home currency/or some other country currency (cross currency forward contracts). In contrast, very few futures contracts involve actual delivery; buyers and sellers normally reverse their positions to close the deal. Alternatively, the two parties simply settle the difference between the contracted price and the actual price with cash on the expiration date[7]. This implies that the seller cancels a contract by buying another contract and the buyer by selling the contract on the date of settlement.

Interest Rate Futures Apart from currency futures, interest rate futures represent another major technique available to business firms. *Interest rate futures* can be used to hedge/reduce risk of a rise in interest rates in the future. Example 34.3 illustrates the usefulness of interest rate futures.

***Example* 34.3**

Suppose IBM has taken a decision to build a new plant, estimated to cost US $100 million. It has been decided to finance it by 10-year bonds; the current coupon rate of interest on such bonds is 7 per cent. IBM does not need money for about 6 months. Of course, IBM can issue 7 per cent bonds now and can arrange funds. Since the money is not immediately needed, it would be invested in short-term securities, yielding an interest of less than 7 per cent, entailing loss.

Another alternative is that the IBM waits for 6 months to sell the bond issue. So far so good, if the interest rates remain unchanged at 7 per cent. In case, they move up higher than 7 per cent, the company will be required to pay higher interest on US $100 million for the 10 year period. Not surprisingly, IBM may find the building-up of the new plant with higher interest costs an unprofitable proposition.

Interest rate futures provide a solution to the IBM dilemma/or its worry pertaining to an increase in interest rates. IBM can have a futures contract to sell Treasury-bond futures 6 months hence to hedge its position [it is assumed that Treasury bonds (T-bonds) carry a rate of interest of 5 per cent]. Should interest rates rise, the value of T-bonds will decline (there is a negative correlation between interest rates and the value of bonds). As a result, it makes profit on the futures position. Of course, it has to pay higher interest on its bond issue, but it is partly compensated in terms of the profit it has earned by selling T-bonds. In the event of a decline of interest rates, it will suffer losses on its future position, but it would gain as it would pay a lower interest rate for all ten years. Thus, interest rate futures are useful derivatives to hedge/reduce the risk of a rise in the interest rates in future.

In view of the above, it is not surprising to find that forward contracts and futures contracts are widely used techniques of hedging risk. It has been estimated that more than 95 per cent of all transactions are designed as hedges, with banks and futures dealers serving as middlemen between hedging counterparties[8].

Currency Options

Forward contracts as well as futures contracts provide a hedge to firms against adverse movements in exchange rates. This is the major advantage of such financial instruments. However, at the same time, these contracts deprive firms of a chance to avail the benefits that may accrue due to favourable movements in foreign exchange rates. The reason for this is that the firm is under obligation to buy or sell currencies at pre-determined rates. This limitation of these contracts is the main reason for the genesis/emergence of currency options in forex markets.

Currency option *is a financial instrument that provides its holder a right but no obligation to buy or sell a pre-specified amount of a foreign currency at a pre-determined rate in the future (on a fixed maturity date/upto a certain period).* While the buyer of an option wants to avoid the risk of adverse changes in exchange rates, the seller of the option is prepared to assume the risk. Options are of two types, namely, call option and put option.

> **Currency option** provides its holder the right but not the obligation to buy/sell a specified amount of foreign currency at a specified rate upto a specified period.

Call Option In a call option the holder has the right to buy/call a specific currency at a specific price on a specific maturity date or within a specified period of time. However, the holder of the option is under no obligation to buy the currency. Such an option is to be exercised only when the actual price in the forex market, at the time of the exercising option, is more than the price specified in call option contract. To put it differently, the holder of the option obviously will not use the call option in case the actual currency price in the spot market, at the time of using the option, turns out to be lower than that specified in the call option contract.

Put Option A put option confers the right but no obligation to sell a specified amount of currency at a pre-fixed price on or up to a specified date. Obviously, put options will be exercised when the actual exchange rate on the date of maturity is lower than the rate specified in the put-option contract.

The option contracts place their holders in a very favourable/privileged position for the following two reasons: **(i)** they hedge foreign exchange risk of adverse movements in exchange rates and **(ii)** they retain the advantage of the favourable movement of exchange rates. Given the advantages of option contracts, the cost of currency option (which is limited to the amount of premium; it may be absolute sum but normally expressed as a percentage of the spot rate prevailing at the time of entering into a contract) seems to be worth incurring. In contrast, the seller of the option contract runs the risk of unlimited/substantial loss and the amount of premium he receives is income to him. Evidently, between the buyer and seller of call option contracts, the risk of a currency option seller is/seems to be relatively much higher than that of a buyer of such an option.

In view of high potential risk to the sellers of these currency options, option contracts are primarily dealt in the major currencies of the world that are actively traded in the over-the-counter (OTC) market. All the operations on the OTC option markets are carried out virtually round the clock. The buyer of the option pays the **option price** (referred to as *premium*) upfront at the time of entering an option contract with the seller of the option (known as the *writer of the option*). The predetermined price at which the buyer of the option (also called as the *holder of the option*) can exercise his option to buy/sell currency is called the **strike/exercise price**. When the option can be exercised only on the maturity date, it is called a **European option**; in contrast, when the option can be exercised on any date upto maturity, it is referred to as an **American option**. An option is said to be **in-money**, if its immediate exercise yields a positive value to its holder; in case the strike price is equal to the spot price, the option is said to be **at-money**; when option has no positive value, it is said **out-of-money**. Example 34.4 illustrates currency option.

***Example* 34.4**

An Indian importer is required to pay British £2 million to a UK company in 4 months time. To guard against the possible appreciation of the pound sterling, he buys an option by paying 2 per cent premium on the current prices. The spot rate is ₹90.50/£. The strike price is fixed at ₹91.32/£.

The Indian importer will need £2 million in 4 months. In case, the pound sterling appreciates against the rupee, the importer will have to spend a greater amount on buying £2 million (in rupees). Therefore, he buys a call option for the amount of £2 million. For this, he pays the premium up-front, which is: £2 million × ₹90.50 × 0.02 = ₹3.62 million.

Then the importer waits for 4 months. On the maturity date, his action will depend on the exchange rate of the £ *vis-à-vis* the rupee. There are three possibilities in this regard, namely £ appreciates, does not change and depreciates.

(i) Pound Sterling Appreciates If the pound sterling appreciates, say to ₹92.25/£, on the settlement date, the importer will exercise his call option and buy the required amount of pounds at the contract rate of ₹91.32/£. The total sum paid by importer is: (£2 million × ₹91.32) + Premium already paid = ₹182.64 million + ₹3.62 million = ₹186.26 million.

(ii) Pound Sterling Exchange rate does not Change This implies that the spot rate on the date of maturity is ₹91.32/£. Evidently, he is indifferent/neutral as he has to spend the same amount of Indian rupees whether he buys from the spot market or he executes call option contract; the premium amount has already been paid by him. Therefore, the total effective cash outflows in both the situations remain exactly identical at ₹186.26 million, that is, [(£2 million × ₹91.32) + Premium of ₹3.62 million already paid].

(iii) Pound Sterling Depreciates If the pound sterling depreciates and the actual spot rate is ₹90/£ on the settlement date, the importer will prefer to abandon the call option as it is economically cheaper to buy the required amount of pounds directly from the exchange market. His total cash outflow will be lower at ₹183.62 million, that is, (£2 million × ₹90) + Premium of ₹3.62 million, already paid.

Thus, it is clear that the importer is not to pay more than ₹186.26 million irrespective of the exchange rate of £ prevailing on the date of maturity. But he benefits from the favourable movement of the pound. Evidently, currency options are more ideally suited to hedge currency risks. Therefore, options markets represent a significant volume of transactions and they are developing at a fast pace.

An additional feature of currency options in that they can be repurchased or sold before the date of maturity (in the case of American type of options). The intrinsic value of an American call option is given by the positive difference between the spot rate and the exercise price; in the case of a European call option, the positive difference between the forward rate and exercise price yields the intrinsic value.

Intrinsic value (American option) = Spot rate – Exercise price **(34.3)**
Intrinsic value (European option) = Forward rate – Exercise price **(34.4)**

Of course, the option expires when it is either exercised or has attained maturity. Normally, it happens when the spot rate/forward rate is lower than the exercise price; otherwise holders of options will normally like to exercise their options if they carry positive intrinsic value.

Swaps

Swaps, as the name implies, are exchange/swap of debt obligations (interest and/or principal payments) between two parties. In general, currency swaps are arranged between two firms/parties through a bank. While it is true that swaps are not financing instruments (as the firms involved in swap contracts already have debt) they comfort the parties involved not only in terms of the desired currency involved in debt financing but also provide logistic convenience in making specified payments of interest and/or principal. Swaps are of two types, namely, interest swaps and currency swaps.

Interest Swaps **Interest swaps** involve exchange of interest obligations between two parties. Example 34.5 explains the *modus operandi* of interest swaps.

Interest swaps involve exchange of interest obligations between two parties.

***Example* 34.5**

Suppose, a US based party (Company X) has 10-year outstanding US $200 million bonds, with floating rate of interest. A French party (Company Y) also has 10 year outstanding US $200 million bonds. However, these bonds carry a fixed rate of interest. While both companies are to make a series of interest payments (annual/semi-annual basis) over the next 10 years, the interest payment stream is known/fixed in the case of Company Y and it varies in the case of Company X, as per the movements of interest rate changes.

Suppose further, Company X now has stable cash flows and, hence, it desires to have interest, which is non-varying/fixed. Unlike Company X, let us assume Company Y does not have stable cash flows; they are fluctuating in nature and move with the economy. Interest rates also move up or down with the economy. Therefore, its management feels it will be more appropriate to have a floating rate debt.

Interest rate swaps will obviously be ideal in these circumstances for both the companies. As a result of the swap, Company X is to make fixed interest payments (matching with its stable cash flow) and Company Y is to make fluctuating interest payments (consistent with its fluctuating earnings/cash flows).

Though both the companies, *prima facie*, find the interest rate swap catering to their preferences, yet in practice, one firm may be required to make payments to the other. For instance, payment may be necessitated if one of the two companies has a higher credit risk than the another; the weaker company is to make payments to the stronger company in a swap. Likewise, payments may be involved in the event of differences in the rate of interest of the two parties/firms involved in interest swaps.

Currency swaps involve exchange of debt obligation denominated in different currencies.

Currency Swaps **Currency swaps** involve two parties who agree to pay each other's debt obligations denominated in different currencies. Example 34.6 illustrates currency swaps.

Example **34.6**

Suppose Company B, a British firm, had issued £50 million pound-denominated bonds in the UK to fund an investment in France. Almost at the same time, Company F, a French firm, had issued £50 million of Euro-denominated bonds in France to make the investment in UK. Company B earns in Euros (€) but is required to make payments in the British pound. Likewise, Company F earns in pound but is to make payments in Euros. As a result, both the companies are exposed to foreign exchange risk. Foreign exchange risk exposure is eliminated for both the companies if they swap payment obligations. Company B pays in pound and Company F pays in Euros. Like interest rate swaps, extra payment may be involved from one company to another, depending on the creditworthiness of the company. The eventual risk of non-payment of bonds lies with the company that had initially issued the bonds. This apart, there may also be differences in the interest rates attached to these bonds, requiring compensation from one company to another.

Interest rate swaps are distinguished from currency swaps for the sake of comprehension only. In practice, currency swaps may also include interest rate swaps. Currency swaps involve three aspects: **(i)** parties involve exchange debt obligations in different currencies, **(ii)** each party agrees to pay the interest obligation of the other party and **(iii)** on maturity, principal amounts are exchanged at an exchange rate agreed in advance.

Money Market Operations

Apart from derivatives, foreign exchange risk can also be hedged through money market operations. The steps involved are as follows: **(i)** Determine the amount required in foreign currency, to be paid on specified date (say 3 months/4 months) from now. **(ii)** From an authorised dealer (say bank) ascertain the spot exchange rate at which it is selling the required foreign currency in exchange for home currency. **(iii)** Borrow home currency from the money market, at the prevailing interest rate. The quantum of borrowing should be in such a manner that can make the required foreign currency sums available on the date of payment (say, after 3 or 4 months). **(iv)** The borrowed funds are to be used to buy the required foreign currency from the forex spot market; once purchased, it is to be invested in forex money markets to yield interest in the desired foreign currency **(v)** As per steps **(iii)** and **(iv)**, the required amount of foreign currency to be purchased can be determined. These steps enable the firm to know the precise amount it will require to make payments of foreign currency on the date of maturity. Money-market operations serve an important hedging function in that uncertainty is resolved regarding the amount to be paid. Consider Example 34.7.

Example **34.7**

Suppose, an Indian importer is to make payment of US $1.1 million after 3 months. 3 months interest rates are: 4 per cent on the US dollar and 6 per cent on the Indian rupee. The current spot exchange rate of ₹/$ is ₹61.

The following steps will enable the Indian importer to know the precise amount he needs in Indian rupees to make a payment of US $1.1 million after 3 months.

(i) First of all, the Indian importer is to ascertain the amount of borrowings so that the borrowings along with interest earned on such funds can accumulate to US $1.1 million after 3 months. Let us say this amount is A. Equation 34.5 provides the required value.

$$A\,(1 + \text{rate} \times \text{time}) = \text{US } \$1.1 \text{ million} \quad (34.5)$$
$$A\,(1 + 0.04 \times 3/12) = \text{US } \$1.1 \text{ million}$$
$$A = \text{US } \$1.1 \text{ million}/1.01 = \text{US } \$1{,}089{,}108.91$$

(ii) The Indian importer has to then borrow a sum of ₹66,435,643.51 to purchase US$ 1,089,108.91 @ ₹61 from the spot market.

(iii) He will invest US $1,089,108.91 in the money market at 4 per cent rate of interest for a period of 3 months, yielding him US $1.1 million after 3 months, (US $1,089,108.91 × 0.04 × 3/12).

(iv) The accumulated sum of US $1.1 million will be paid by the Indian importer on the due date to the American export firm.

(v) The Indian importer would refund ₹66,435,643.51 along with 6 per cent interest after 3 months, to the Indian lender. The sum is ₹66,435,643.51 (1 + 0.06 × 3/12) = ₹67,432,178.16.

(vi) The Indian importer is to pay ₹67.43217816 million at the end of 3 months. To put it differently, he knows that his home currency cash outflow is ₹67.43217816 million, irrespective of the ₹/US dollar exchange rate, 3 months from now.

LO 34.3 FIRM—INTERNAL HEDGING TECHNIQUES

We explain below the major internal techniques that can be adopted by international and multinational companies (MNCs) to hedge/reduce their foreign exchange risk exposure. It is appropriate to designate these techniques as 'internal' in that corporate firms with international operations/MNCs and their subsidiaries can make use of these techniques independently, without the assistance of external agencies. The important internal hedging techniques are: **(i)** Leading and lagging, **(ii)** Invoicing/Billing in the desired currency, **(iii)** Indexation clauses,**(iv)** Sharing risk, **(v)** Shifting the manufacturing base, **(vi)** Netting and **(vii)** Reinvoicing centre.

Leading and Lagging

Sound international financial management practices warrant that the firms engaged in international operations should endeavour to have their assets in a strong currency and liabilities in a weak currency. This may be achieved with the help of the technique known as 'leading and lagging' (also called *leads* and *lags*) by adjusting the timing of receipts and payments (related to current account transactions). **Leading**, as its name implies, is taking the lead to collect from foreign currency designated debtors expeditiously before they are due (when the home currency is expected to strengthen) and to initiate lead to pay foreign currency designated creditors before their due date of payment (when depreciation/devaluation of the home currency is apprehended). Payment to creditors on maturity in such a situation will, obviously involve more cash outflow of home currency as the foreign currency is likely to become costlier. Likewise, when an upward movement of the home currency is expected, early receipts from foreign currency designated debtors will lead to higher home currency receipts.

Leading implies collection from designated debtors expeditiously foreign currency before due date.

In contrast, **lagging**, as the name implies, is delaying receipts from the foreign currency designated receivables whose currencies are likely to appreciate/strengthen and delaying foreign currency designated payables whose currencies are likely to depreciate/devalue/weaken. This makes financial sense on account of more receipts from debtors and less payment to creditors

Lagging implies delaying receipts from foreign currency designated receivables.

Therefore, to receive maximum receipts or make minimum payment, in appreciation-prone countries, accounts receivables are collected as soon as possible and payment of accounts payable is delayed as long as possible. The converse will hold true in depreciation-prone countries; debtors are collected as late as possible and creditors are paid as early as possible[9]. Example 34.8 illustrates the advantage of following such an approach.

***Example* 34.8**

Suppose, an Indian Company X imports and exports both to US and France. Assume further that Company X is to pay US $1 million for its imports after 2 months and is to receive € 0.5 million for exports due after 2 months. The current spot rates are ₹60/$ and ₹80/€. It is expected that the dollar exchange rate is likely to appreciate to ₹61 in about 2 months from now. Obviously, by preponing payment, Company X gains. Immediate payment will save ₹1 per US $ × US $1 million = ₹1 million (total savings). Payment after 1 month may be at the rate of ₹60.5 per US $; the determination exchange rate is based on interpolation, that is, the average price of ₹60 today and ₹61 after two months); the amount saved will be ₹0.5 × US $1 million = ₹5,00,000. There is a gain to Firm X due to lead in making early payment.

Assume that the € is likely to depreciate to ₹79.5, 2 months from now; Company X will initiate measures to collect € 0.5 million as early as possible; assuming its efforts enable him to collect after a month (based on interpolation technique, the € exchange rate is likely to be the average of ₹80 and ₹79.5 that is, ₹79.75. In rupee terms, its value is ₹79.75 × € 0.5 million = ₹39.875 million; the potential loss saved is ₹0.25 per € [(i.e., ₹79.75 – ₹79.50 likely € rate after two months)] multiplied by € 0.5 million = ₹1,25,000.

Example 34.8 clearly demonstrates the advantage of the 'leads and lags' approach to international firms. International firms/MNCs have substantial transaction/current account risk exposure in foreign currency designated accounts payable and accounts receivable; these accounts may relate to inter-company purchases and sales, dividends, interest receivable/payable, fees, royalties and so on.

Invoicing/Billing in Desired Currency

Invoicing sales as well as purchases in the home currency is an ideal method of hedging foreign exchange risk. Billing in home currency enables the firm to know the precise amount it is likely to receive from sales (exports) and likewise the exact amount it is to pay for purchases (imports). As a result, its foreign exchange risk is completely eliminated.

Although the method provides a natural hedge, it may not be operationally feasible to be used always and by all firms. Only firms having high demand for their products, across the world, and those having products with low price-elasticity, say petroleum products/with low competition/with less substitutes available, may be in a strong position with their counterparty to make them agree to receive/pay in their own home currency. This implies that the company should be in a very strong position to impose billing, either in its own domestic currency or currency of its choice, on the other party. In the current business world of globalisation, the number of such firms is decreasing. In fact, the vast majority of companies have to encounter competition on many fronts and, hence, it is likely to be a very daunting task for them to force the counter party to have billing in the currency of their choice. In sum, relatively few firms may enjoy 'hedge luxury' of this sort.

Indexation Clauses

Yet another technique of hedging risk is to provide clause (s) related to the export and import of goods and services between the two parties in contracts/agreements. Obviously, the terms and conditions included in the contract depend on the bargaining strengths of the parties involved. For instance, the exporter may be in a better bargaining position (on account of selling new technology or essential products like petroleum) to include a clause in a contract whereby prices are to be adjusted in such a manner that the adverse movement of foreign exchange rates is to be absorbed by the importer alone. In other words, prices are adjusted to take care of foreign exchange loss so that the exporter receives virtually the same amount in local currency; in such situations, the incidence of exchange rate loss is to be borne completely by the importer.

In contrast, if the buyer/importer happens to be in a strong bargaining position (as he is buying a competitive product having high price elasticity), he may succeed in pursuing the exporter to have a clause whereby prices are to be adjusted downwards to absorb losses due to unfavourable movement of exchange rates (i.e., the home currency depreciates or the currency of the exporting country appreciates). In such a situation, the foreign exchange risk is borne completely by the exporter. Such clauses are 'extreme' in nature; the indexation clause may be mild in nature stating changes in exchange rates, beyond which prices are to be adjusted (say above 5 per cent).

Sharing Risk

The indexation clauses illustrate the extreme positions/situations in which the entire incidence/loss of the unfavourable foreign exchange risk is shared by one of the parties only. In practice, the two parties may stipulate that loss incurred during the intervening period (the dates of contract and maturity) is to be shared between them in predetermined proportions. Risk-sharing techniques may be appropriate when the currency (currencies) involved in business deals are subject to abnormal rate of changes. Who bears a higher loss will depend on the bargaining positions of the two parties.

Shifting the Manufacturing Base

The use of such a technique is feasible for large MNCs having large financial resources and a large chain of subsidiaries operating around the world. In case an MNC has a production centre in one country and large sales in some another country, it may find it useful to have a new subsidiary set up or shift the existing one to a country where there are substantial sales of its products. As a result, there is built-in hedging of foreign exchange risk as the costs and revenues are then in the same currency.

Netting

It may not be uncommon among international companies to have mutual trading among themselves like multinational companies. Foreign exchange risk exposure of such companies can be substantially reduced if foreign designated receivables and payments among them are settled *on the net balance basis* (known as *netting*) instead of making two-way flows of money—one of receiving and another of paying. To have such a netting, it is important that the dates of settlement should match and the foreign currency involved should be the same for receipts and payments that are due.

Since the risk exposure is hedged for both parties, they try to match the maturity dates and currencies of sums receivable and payable between themselves.

Types of Netting Netting is of two types, namely, bilateral and multilateral. While netting involving two parties is referred to as *bilateral*, netting with more than two parties is called *multilateral*. Multilateral netting is practised among multinational corporations having subsidiaries whereas, bilateral netting is feasible between any two transacting companies.

Bilateral Netting Suppose Company X exports goods to Company Y for US \$2 million and imports goods worth US \$1.5 million from Company Y. Their dates of maturity are the same. Figure 34.1 shows the movement of funds between these two companies. The movement of funds with netting is exhibited in Figure 34.2.

In absence of netting, the total exposure of the two companies is US \$3.5 million (Figure 34.1); this exposure is reduced substantially to the net sum of US \$0.5 million, payable by Y to X.

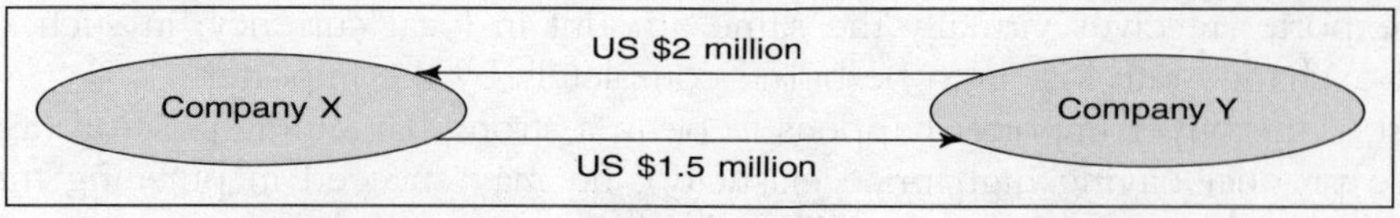

FIGURE 34.1 Normal Movement of Funds

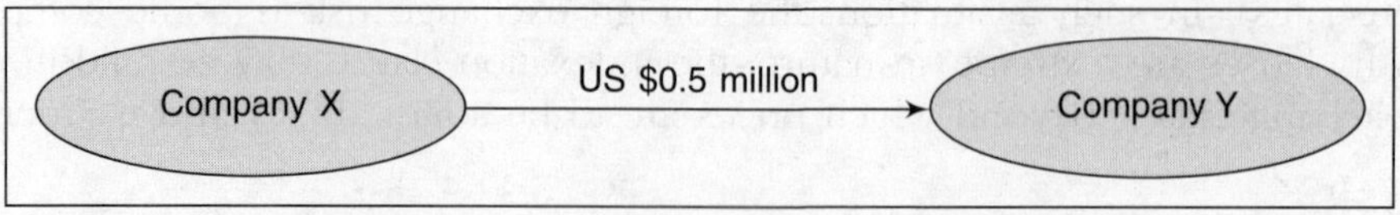

FIGURE 34.2 Movement of Funds with Netting

Multilateral Netting As stated above, multilateral netting involves netting of risk exposure among more than two companies. Normally such nettings are practised among a parent company and its subsidiaries. Figure 34.3 depicts the normal movement of funds between a parent company (P) and its four subsidiaries without netting.

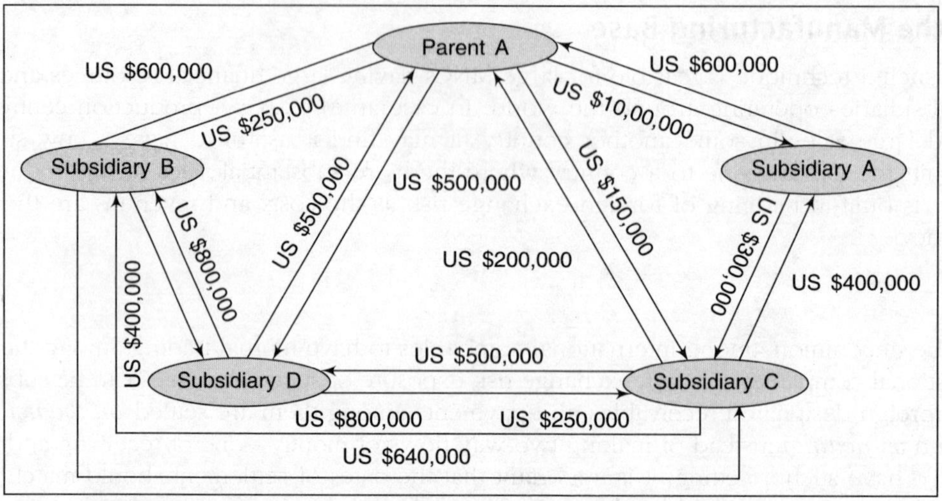

FIGURE 34.3 Normal Movement of Funds between Parent and Subsidiaries

The total risk exposure without netting is US $7,890,000. As a result of bilateral netting, as portrayed in Figure 34.4, the total risk exposure gets reduced to US $1,710,000.

Multilateral netting simplifies funds flow in that it requires only net amounts to be transferred. A further simplification is possible in such a manner that a company is either paying or receiving a net sum. As a result, the total risk exposure gets further reduced to US $1,410,000 (Figure 34.5).

Let us explain the procedure of arriving at the various amounts shown in Figure 34.5.

Procedure:

(i) Parent Company (P) is to pay Subsidiary A (Figure 34.4)	US $4,00,000
Subsidiary C is to pay Parent (Figure 34.4)	$50,000
Subsidiary C is to pay Subsidiary A (Figure 34.4)	$1,00,000
C's direct payables to A	$1,50,000

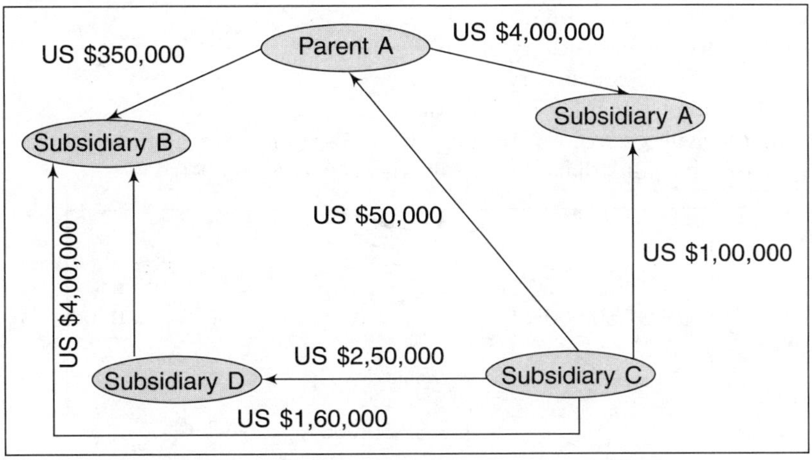

FIGURE 34.4 Movement of Funds with Bilateral Netting

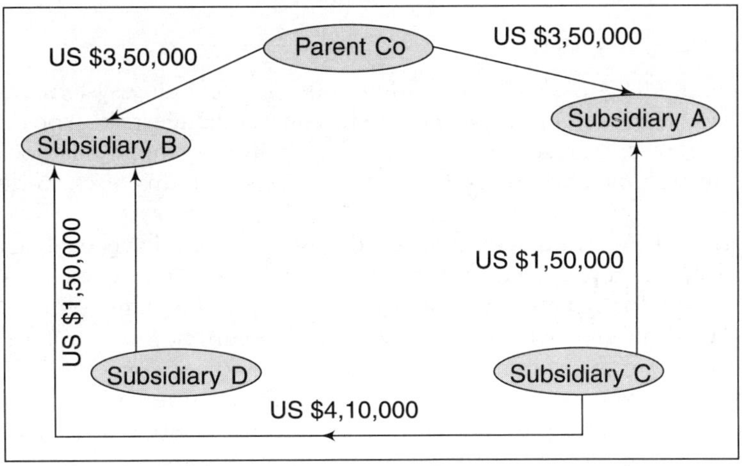

FIGURE 34.5 Movement of Funds subsequent to Multilateral Netting

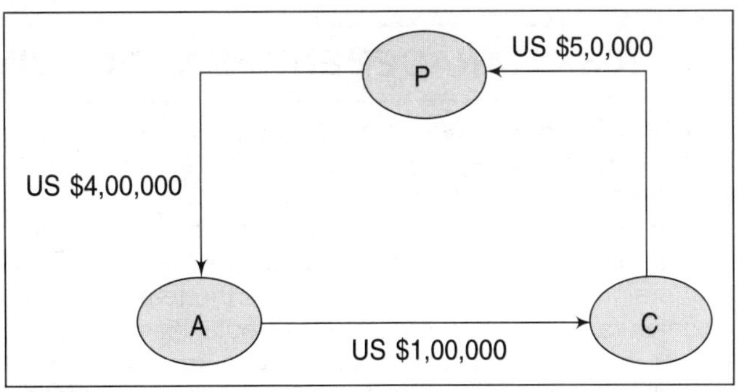

FIGURE 34.6 Net position of *P* and Subsidiaries *A* and *C*

Since P's receivables from C of US $50,000 are already paid to Subsidiary A, the net amount payable by P to A is US $350,000.

(ii) Subsidiary C is to pay Subsidiary D — US $2,50,000
Subsidiary C is to pay Subsidiary B — $1,60,000
Subsidiary D is to pay Subsidiary B — $4,00,000
Subsidiary C's direct payables to Subsidiary B — $4,10,000

Since D's receivables from Subsidiary C of $2,50,000 are already paid to subsidiary B, net amount payable by Subsidiary D to Subsidiary B is $1,50,000.

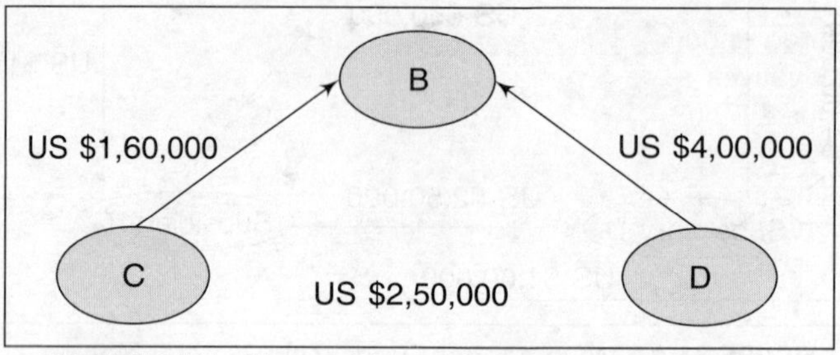

FIGURE 34.7 Net position of Subsidiaries *B*, *C* and *D*.

Reinvoicing Centre

The reinvoicing centre in MNCs is akin to a clearing house in a banking system. It may be beneficial for an MNC to create a separate centre to manage foreign exchange risk exposure. Such a centre, known as reinvoicing centre, is itself a subsidiary of the parent company; its location, for obvious reasons, is preferred in a country where exchange regulations, in terms of convertibility, repatriation and so on are the least constraining.

Subsidiaries are located in various countries of the world. They have dealings with clients and suppliers involving receipts and payments in currencies of various countries. Subsequent to the creation of a reinvoicing centre, the foreign currency invoices are made in the name of the rein-voicing centre by the subsidiaries. The centre receives the money in foreign currency, and in turn, makes payment/remittance of equivalent sum in national currency to the subsidiary concerned. Similarly, payments to various suppliers/lenders are made by the centre in foreign currency and it is reimbursed with an equivalent sum in the national currency from the concerned subsidiaries[10]. Being a centralised collection and payment centre of foreign currencies for all of its subsidiaries and affiliate companies, it not only helps in reducing the volume of foreign currency transfers but also hedging costs.

LO 34.4 RISK MANAGEMENT PRACTICES IN INDIA

- Minimising the variability in cash flows is the most emphasised objective of risk management.
- Firms are aware of the risk management techniques and an appreciably large proportion of them is using such techniques to manage various risks.
- All the risks are not managed equally. For instance, more than four-fifth of the firms manage the foreign exchange risk. Interest rate risk is managed by two-thirds, only two-fifths manage foreign exchange risk and foreign exchange translation risk is the least managed risk.
- The sample companies (as per survey of 2011–12) would like to reduce political or country risk by incorporating a risk premium in the cost of capital. Out of the various measures available, creating a joint venture with an enterprise of the host country is the most preferred one.
- In the case of anticipated depreciation of local currency, the sample companies sell local currency forward, invoice exports in foreign currency and import in local currency. In the case of anticipated appreciation, buying local currency forward and reducing local currency borrowings are the exchange risk management techniques adopted by the respondent firms.

- The sample companies use primarily netting and back-to-back swap techniques (from internal techniques of exchange risk management); as far as the use of external techniques is concerned, forwards are the most preferred, followed by currency swaps, currency options and currency futures.
- There are significant differences due to ownership in the use of risk management techniques. While private sector business group firms and public sector enterprises make greater use of foreign exchange transaction and interest rate risks, foreign controlled firms find it more useful to manage all risks except interest rate risk.
- 'Exposures are not large enough' is the most cited and prominent reason for not managing risks.
- Risks inherent in derivatives are a significant reason in making the firms desist from using risk management techniques. Moreover, the prominent barriers hindering the routine use of derivatives are monitoring and evaluating the risk of derivatives' pricing, valuing and accounting in conjunction with credit and liquidity risk.
- One-fifth of the firms perceive that the cost of hedging exceeds its benefits and, therefore, it is not beneficial for them to use risk management techniques.
- While a majority of the foreign controlled firms and private sector business group firms can be characterised as 'partial' hedgers, the majority of the public sector firms belong to the category of 'negligible' hedgers.
- The adoption of risk management techniques in India is still in infancy. The use of risk management techniques is likely to grow speedily with the active interest shown by regulatory bodies in propagating risk management techniques and making available various types of derivatives.

Sources: (i) Jain, P K, S S Yadav and A K Rastogi, "Risk Management Practices in Corporate Firms in India: A Comparative Study of Public Sector, Private Sector Business Houses and Foreign Controlled Firms", *Decision*, Vol. 36, No. 2, Aug. 2009, pp. 73-98 and (ii) Jain, P K, Shveta Singh and Surendra S Yadav, *Financial Management Practices: An Empirical Study of Indian Corporates*, Springer, New Delhi, 2013, Chapter 7.

SUMMARY

LO 34.1

The multinational corporates (MNCs) and other business firms, having global business operations primarily encounter three types of exposure: (i) transaction exposure, (ii) translation exposure and (iii) economic exposure.

Transaction exposure is inherent in all foreign currency denominated contractual obligations/transactions which require settlement in foreign currency. The notable items susceptible to translation exposure are debtors receivable in foreign currency, creditors payable in foreign currency, foreign loans and foreign investments. The profit (or loss) accruing to the business firm on these transactions is known at the time of their settlement.

Translation exposure results from the need to translate foreign currency assets or liabilities into the local currency at the time of finalising accounts. Translation profits (or losses) may either be reflected in the income statement or be shown in the balance sheet (under the head of 'translation adjustment' as a separate item or adjusted in the owners' equity account).

Economic exposure is defined as the change in the value of a firm due to unanticipated change in exchange rates. While favourable change in exchange rates enhances the value of a firm, unfavourable change may entail its erosion.

Shapiro classifies economic exposure into two components, namely, transaction exposure and operating exposure. Operating exposure has an impact on the firm's future operating revenues, future operating costs and future operating cash flows.

LO 34.1	The greater is the susceptibility of operating cash flows to exchange rate changes, the greater is the economic exposure of the business firm, or *vice versa.* The firm's ability to adjust its cost structure and raise the prices of its products and services (depending on supply and demand elasticities) is the major determinant of its operating risk exposure.
	Foreign exchange risk is defined as the possibility of loss to the business firm on account of unfavourable movement in foreign exchange rates.
	Foreign exchange risk management (FERM) is concerned with techniques (both external and internal) through which finance managers/firms try to eliminate/reduce the adverse impact of unfavourable changes in the foreign exchange rates.
LO 34.2	The major external techniques of the FERM are: (i) forward contracts, (ii) currency futures, (iii) currency options, (iv) swaps and (v) money market operations.
	Forward contracts are contracts between business firms and authorised dealers of the FE markets in which the firms undertake to buy or sell foreign currency in exchange for home currency, at a specific future date at a pre-agreed exchange rate. A typical forward contract contains the (i) contract amount, (ii) forward exchange rate, (iii) parties of the contract, (iv) specific date of delivery, (v) name of foreign currencies involved and (vi) terms and conditions for cancellation.
	A currency future/futures contract is a standardised agreement to buy or sell a pre-specified amount of foreign currency at some specified future date between the parties of the contract. Currency future contracts are normally in the hard currencies (say British £, US $, Japanese yen) of the world and are traded on an organised exchange.
	Although future contracts are similar to the forward contracts in their objective of hedging foreign exchange risk, they differ in many significant ways. These are: (i) nature and size of contracts, (ii) mode of trading, (iii) liquidity, (iv) deposits/margins, (v) default risk and (vi) actual delivery.
	Currency option is a financial instrument that provides its holder a right but no obligation to buy or sell a pre-specified amount of a foreign currency at a pre-determined rate in the future (on a fixed maturity date/upto a certain period). Options are of two types: (i) call option and (ii) put option.
	In a call option the holder has the right to buy (but is under no obligation to buy) a specific currency at a specific price on a specific maturity date or within a specified period of time. In contrast, a put option confers the right but no obligation to sell a specified amount of a specific currency at a pre-fixed price on or upto a specified date.
	Swaps are exchange of debt obligations (interest and/or principal payments) between two parties. These are of two types, namely, interest swaps and currency swaps. While interest swaps involve exchange of interest obligations between two parties, currency swaps involve two parties who agree to pay each other's debt obligations denominated in different currencies.
	Money market operations involve borrowing home currency by the business firm which will enable it to buy required foreign currency from the spot market. Once purchased, it is to be invested in the forex money markets in the desired foreign currency. The amount of home currency borrowed should be of the magnitude which will enable the firm to accumulate (after investment) such an amount of foreign currency which will enable it to make full payment on the date of maturity.
LO 34.3	The important internal hedging techniques of FERM are: (i) leading and lagging, (ii) invoicing/billing in the desired currency, (iii) indexation clauses, (iv) sharing risk, (v) shifting the manufacturing base, (vi) netting and (vii) reinvoicing center.
	'Leading' is taking the lead to collect debtors receivable in foreign currency before they are due (when the home currency is expected to strengthen) and to initiate lead to pay 'foreign' creditors before they are due for payment (when depreciation/devaluation of the home currency is apprehended). The strategy leads to higher home currency receipts and lower home currency payments. In contrast, lagging is delaying receipts from foreign currency designated receivables whose currencies are likely to appreciate and delaying payments of 'foreign' creditors whose currencies are likely to weaken.

LO 34.3

Instead of making two-way flows of money—one of receiving and another of paying, netting implies settlement on net basis. Netting is of two types: (i) bilateral and (ii) multilateral. While netting between two parties is referred to as bilateral, netting with more than two parties is called multilateral.

Reinvoicing center (normally a subsidiary of the parent company) is a centralised collection and payment center of foreign currencies for all of its subsidiaries and affiliate companies. It is located in such a country where the foreign exchange regulations primarily in terms of convertibility and repatriation are the least constraining. The Centre not only helps in red-ucing the volume of foreign currency transfers but also hedging costs.

REFERENCES

1. Van Horne, James C, *Financial Management and Policy*, Prentice Hall of India, New Delhi, 2000, p. 655.
2. Van Horne, James C, *op. cit.*, p 655.
3. Shapiro Alan C, *Multinational Financial Management*, 6th ed, John Wiley and Sons, New York, 2001, p. 317.
4. Shapiro, Alan C, *op. cit.*, p. 325.
5. Shapiro, Alan C, *op. cit.*, pp. 337–8.
6. Van Horne, James C, *op. cit.*, p. 665.
7. Brigham, E F and Joel F Houston, *Fundamentals of Financial Management* Harcourt Asia, Singapore: 2001, p. 803.
8. Brigham, E F and J F Houston, *op. cit.*, p. 804.
9. Gitman, L J, *Principles of Managerial Finance*, Pearson Education, New Delhi, 2001, p. 849.
10. Jain, P K *et al*, *International Financial Management*, Macmillan, New Delhi, 2001, p. 83.
11. *Report of Working Group on Rupee Derivatives*, Reserve Bank of India, Mumbai, January 2003.
12. Jain, P.K. et al, *Financial Management Practices: An Empirical Study of Indian Corporates*, Springer, New Delhi, 2013.

SOLVED PROBLEMS

P.34.1 An Indian exporter has sold handicrafts items to an American business house. The exporter will be receiving US $1,00,000 in 90 days. Premium for a dollar put option with a strike price of ₹62 and a 90 day settlement is ₹1. The exporter anticipates the spot rate after 90 days to be ₹60. Should the exporter hedge its account receivable in the option market? If the exporter is anticipating the spot rate to be ₹61.5 'or' ₹62.5 after 90 days, how would it effect the exporter's decision? LO 34.2 LOD M

Solution The Indian exporter will be buying a put option on the US $ to hedge against depreciation in the US $.

For settlement price of ₹60/US $

Option	Put
Strike	₹62/US $
Premium	1/US $
Settlement (expiration) rate	60

Benefit from put option = Max [(Strike rate – Expiration rate), 0] – Premium
= Max [(₹62/US $ – ₹60/US $),0] – ₹1/US $ = ₹1/US $

As there is benefit in owning the put, so the exporter should hedge using the put option.

Here, if exporter remains unhedged, it will receive ₹60,00,000 [₹60/US $ × US $100,000]. But with hedging using put option, the exporter receives at the end 90 days. ₹61,00,000 [₹62/US $ × US $1,00,000 – ₹1/US $ × US $1,00,000].

For settlement price of ₹61.50/US $.

Benefit from put option = Max [(₹62/US $ – ₹61.5/US $), 0] – ₹1/US $ = –₹0.5/US $

For settlement price of ₹62.50/US $

Benefit from put option = Max [(₹62/US $ – ₹62.50/US $), 0] – ₹1/US $ = –₹1/US $.

So, for anticipated price of ₹61.5/US $ or ₹62.5/US $, the exporter will not be hedging through a put option as that does not have positive benefit.

P.34.2 Mars Enterprises buys dollar futures contract to cover possible exchange losses on its import order denominated in US dollars. The firm has to put up an initial margin of ₹3,00,000. The maintenance margin imposed by the exchange is 70 per cent of initial margin. When would Mars Enterprises receive a margin call from its broker and what does Mars Enterprises have in such circumstances? **LO 34.2** LOD M

Solution If the spot rate for the US $ declines, the value of Mars Enterprises' future contract declines. As long as the decline is less than ₹90,000 (maintenance margin of 70 per cent is equal to ₹2,10,000), it does not need to put up any additional margin. When the cumulative decline in value comes to ₹90,001 and the margin account balance becomes ₹2,09,999. Mars Enterprises will receive a margin call from its brokerage firm. Under these circumstances, the company must restore the account to the initial level of ₹3,00,000. Otherwise, the exchange will sell out the future position of Mars Enterprises and return any remaining balance in the margin account.

P.34.3 A currency trader working at ONS capital management, expects higher volatility in the foreign exchange market owing to uncertain geopolitical situation. He expects the rupee to either appreciate by 2 per cent or depreciate by 2 per cent in comparison to the US $ in 30 days time. He assumes equal probability for the two scenarios. The currency quote machine installed at ONS capital management is flashing the following quotes: **LO 34.2** LOD D

Spot rate	₹61/US $
Future rate (for one month)	61.7650/US $
Call option (strike price ₹61, one month)	0.8900/US $
Put option (strike price ₹61, one month)	0.2000/US $

(a) What strategy should the currency trader adopt?

(b) If at the end of one month the spot rate is ₹62.35/US $, what is the return on investment?

Solution Spot rate = ₹61/US $: the spot rate after 30 days is

For 2 per cent appreciation in the rupee,
₹61/(1 + 0.02) = ₹59.8039/US $

For 2 per cent depreciation in the rupee
₹61/(1 – 0.02) = ₹62.2450/US $

So after 30 days the trader expects the spot rate (settlement rate for option or future) to be either ₹ 59.8039/US $ or ₹62.2450/US $.

To benefit from this expectation, the trader cannot use the futures market. Because if the trader takes a long position by buying futures at ₹61.7650/US $, it can earn only if the settlement rate is ₹62.2450/US $, whereas for a settlement rate of ₹59.8039 the trader will suffer loss. Similarly, if the trader takes a short position by selling futures, he can earn only if settlement rate is ₹59.8039, whereas he will loose if settlement rate is ₹62.2450/US $.

Also, buying only call or only put will not give profit in both expected settlement rate. Appropriate strategy for the trader at ONS capital management will be to buy call and simultaneously also buy put. As call will be providing profit for depreciation in rupees (settlement rate ₹62.2450/US $) and put will be providing profit for appreciation in rupees (settlement rate ₹59.8039/US $).

For a settlement rate of ₹62.2450/US $

Profit = Profit from call option + Profit from put option
{Max [(Settlement rate – Strike rate), 0] – Call premium} +

{Max [(Strike rate – Settlement rate), 0] – Put premium}

= {Max [(₹62.3500/US \$ – ₹61.000/US \$), 0] – ₹0.8900/US \$} +
{Max [(₹61.000/US \$ – ₹62.3500/US \$), 0] – ₹0.2000/US \$}
{₹1.35/US \$ – ₹0.89/US \$} + {0 – ₹0.2000/US \$}= ₹0.26/US \$.

Return on investment

Investment in buying a call and a put = ₹0.8900/US \$ + ₹0.2000/US \$ = ₹1.09/US \$.

So the return on investment = (0.26/1.09) × 100 = 23.85 per cent per month.

P.34.4 The corporate treasurer of a US multinational receives a fax on 21st February from its European subsidiary. The subsidiary will transfer € 10 million to the parent company on 16th August. The corporate treasurer decides to hedge the position using currency futures. The available spot and future rate of the Euro on the 21st February are:

LO 34.2 LOD M

Spot	*September future*	*December future*
US \$1.2800/€	US \$1.3283/€	US \$1.400/€

(a) What expiry month will be chosen for the future by the corporate treasurer?

(b) Will the corporate treasurer go long or short on the euro future?

(c) If the corporate treasurer plans to hedge through futures in the European currency market, will he buy or sell dollar futures?

(d) What is the unhedged and hedged outcome on 16th August, if the spot and futures rate on the 16th of August are as follows:

Spot	*September future*	*December future*
US \$1.2200/€	US \$1.2320/€	US \$1.3529/€

Solution

(a) The treasurer will choose the September future for hedging as it is the nearest expiry month from the date of euro receipt.

(b) The treasurer will go short on the euro future.

(c) He will buy a dollar future.

(d) If it remains unhedged.

In this case on 16th August, when the multinational will receive € 10 million, it will convert them in to dollars on an applicable spot rate of US \$1.2200/€.

So the US dollar proceeds = US \$12,200,000 (1.2200 × 1,00,00,000)

If hedged through future

As the settlement date is still far, the multinational has to convert its euro receipt using the spot market on 16th August and he will cover its short euro future position and receive the benefit.

The US dollar proceeds from the spot market = US \$12,200,000. US dollar profit from the futures market (US \$1.3283/€ – US \$1.2320/€) × 10,000,000 = US \$9,63,000. So the total US dollar proceeds = US\$1,31,63,000.

P.34.5 Company ABC and XYZ have been offered the following rates per annum on a ₹50.0 lakh five year loan.

LO 34.2 LOD M

	Fixed rate	*Floating rate*
Company ABC	9.0 %	Mibor + 0.3%
Company XYZ	10.8%	Mibor + 0.8%

Company ABC requires a floating rate loan. Company XYZ requires a fixed rate loan.

(a) How can the two companies enter into a swap arrangement in which each benefits equally?

(b) What risk could this arrangement generate?

Solution There is 1.8 per cent per annum differential between the fixed rate offered to the two companies and a 0.5 per cent per annum differential between the floating rates offered to the two companies. This provides the basis for swap. The total gain to the party from the swap is 1.8% in fixed rate to company ABC – 0.5% loss in higher payment of interest in floating rate by XYZ = 1.3 per cent per annum. Thus if the swap benefit has to be equally distributed (0.65%) between the two companies; swap will lead to an effective rate of MIBOR – 0.35 i.e., Mibor + 0.3 – 0.65% for Company ABC and 10.15% rate of interest for Company XYZ i.e. 10.80% – 0.65%.

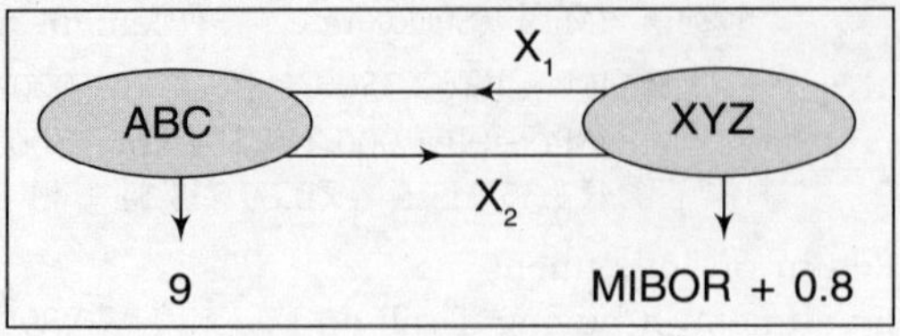

(a) Under swap arrangement, Company ABC will be borrowing from the fixed rate market and lending it to Company XYZ (say at X_1 is the rate of interest), similarly XYZ will be borrowing from the floating rate market and will lend that to Company ABC.

(b) The risk would include default risk on the part of the 2 swap parties.
There may also be liquidity risk in the event that one or both of the swaps may need to be reversed.
There may also be a country risk if one party is based overseas.

P.34.6 An Indian business house has decided to borrow US $ for its New York subsidiary. And an American multinational has made up its mind to borrow Indian rupees for its Indian subsidiary. The amount required by the two companies are the same at the current exchange rate. The companies have been quoted the following interest rates: **LO 34.2** LOD M

	On rupee loan in India	*On US $ loan in America*
Indian Company	9.0%	4.0%
American Company	9.5%	3.0%

Both the Indian business house and the American multinational carries out their banking operation through the same multinational bank. The multinational bank comes to know of the situation faced by the two companies and plans to design a swap. As the bank will be assuming all foreign exchange risk, it plans to receive total 50 basis points per annum and also plans to make the swap equally attractive to the two companies. What will the design of the swap be?

Solution On a rupee loan, the Indian company has absolute advantage of 0.5 per cent and the American company has absolute advantage of 1.0 per cent, so under the swap arrangement there will be benefit of 1.5 per cent. Since the bank requires 0.5 per cent, this leaves 1.0 per cent benefit to be shared. So, there will be 0.5 per cent gain for each, the Indian company and the US company.

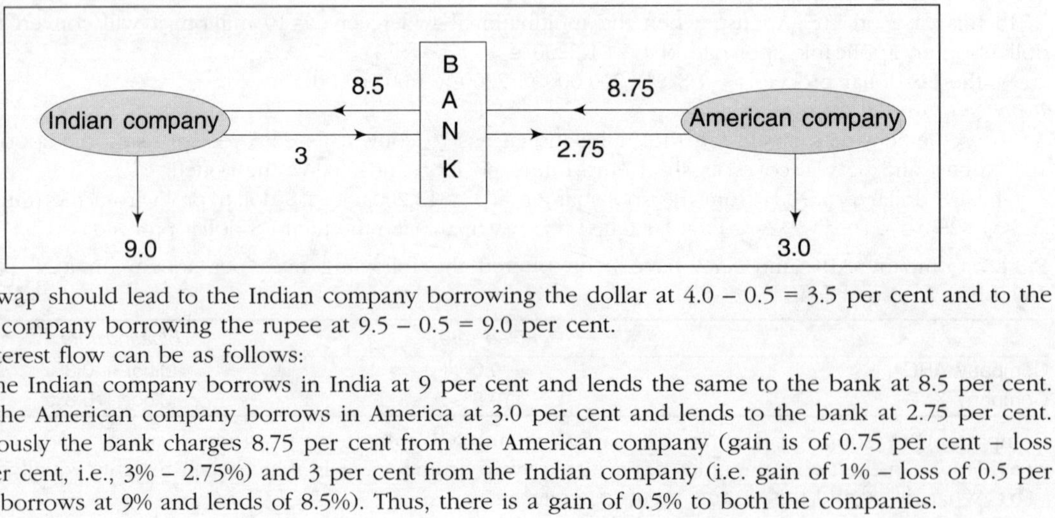

Thus swap should lead to the Indian company borrowing the dollar at 4.0 – 0.5 = 3.5 per cent and to the American company borrowing the rupee at 9.5 – 0.5 = 9.0 per cent.

The interest flow can be as follows:

Here the Indian company borrows in India at 9 per cent and lends the same to the bank at 8.5 per cent. Whereas the American company borrows in America at 3.0 per cent and lends to the bank at 2.75 per cent. Simultaneously the bank charges 8.75 per cent from the American company (gain is of 0.75 per cent – loss of 0.25 per cent, i.e., 3% – 2.75%) and 3 per cent from the Indian company (i.e. gain of 1% – loss of 0.5 per cent as it borrows at 9% and lends of 8.5%). Thus, there is a gain of 0.5% to both the companies.

P.34.7 Company ABC and XYZ face the following interest rate: LO 34.2 LOD D

	ABC	*XYZ*
US dollar (floating rate)	LIBOR + 0.5%	LIBOR + 2.5%
Japanese yen (fixed rate)	2%	2.25%

Assume that XYZ wants to borrow dollars at a floating rate of interest and ABC wants to borrow Japanese yen at a fixed rate of interest. A financial institution is planning to arrange a swap and requires a 75 basis point spread. If the swap is equally attractive to ABC and XYZ, what rate of interest will they end up paying?

Solution ABC has a higher comparative advantage in the floating rate US dollar market but wants to borrow in the fixed rate yen market. This provides the basis for a swap.

There is a 2 per cent per annum differential between the dollar rate offered to the two companies and a 0.25 per cent difference in yen rate offered to the two companies. Also, ABC has the advantage in absolute terms in both markets. So, the total gain to all parties from the swap is 2 – 0.25 = 1.75 per cent per annum as ABC company will raise in $ yielding gain of 2% and XYZ company will borrow in japanese yen causing loss of 0.25%. Since the bank gets 0.75 per cent per annum, the swap should make ABC and XYZ 0.5 per cent per annum benefit. This means the swap should lead to ABC borrowing the yen at 1.5 per cent per annum and to XYZ borrowing the dollar at LIBOR + 2 per cent per annum.

P.34.8 Drishti Electro Limited enjoys a very high rating in the Indian money market due to its strong financials and track record. Om Software Limited is a new but growing company. Drishti Electro and Om Software can obtain loans at the rate given below: LO 34.2 LOD D

	CD (Company Deposit) with fixed rate	*Mumbai inter-bank money market with variable rate*
Drishti Electronics Limited	T + 0.50	MIBOR + 0.10
Om Softwares Limited	T + 2.10	MIBOR + 0.60

Here T is the yield on 15-year government treasury bonds. Drishti Electronics Limited wants to take a loan at variable rate, while Om Software wants loan at fixed rate. The two companies approach a bank to design suitable swaps.

(a) If the bank wants to have a profit of 0.20 per cent to be contributed from the Om Software's (out of total profit of swap) share of swap benefit, what would be the two agreements that the bank will enter with these two companies?

(b) What are likely costs of debt to the two companies?

Solution Drishti Electronics has a comparative advantage in the fixed rate market of 1.6 per cent per annum but wants to take a loan at a variable rate. In the variable rate (floating rate) market the comparative advantage is 0.50 per cent. So, under swap arrangement there will be a total benefit of 1.6 – 0.5 = 1.1 per cent.

(a) Drishti Electronics will raise money from the fixed rate market and Om Software will raise money from the floating rate market. The bank will make an agreement with Drishti Electronics, under which the bank will borrow fixed rate money and will lend floating rate money. Similarly, the bank will make an agreement with Om Software for borrowing at floating rate and lending at fixed rate.

(b) As the total swap benefit is 1.1 per cent, 0.55 per cent benefit belongs to each party. The bank's share is 0.20 per cent of Om Software's share of benefit. As a result, Om Software's share of profit will decrease to 0.35 per cent per annum; Drishti Electronics's gain is 0.55 per cent per annum.

So, the likely cost of debt for Drishti Electronics will be MIBOR–0.45 per cent per annum and the cost of debt for Om Software will be (T + 1.75) per cent per annum.

P.34.9 Credit Bank Limited needs fixed rate funding. It plans to raise finance at the cost of a six month LIBOR + 1/4 per cent for £ 500 million, for 5 years. The bank is considering to enter into a swap of fixed rate at 6 per cent and receiving interest equivalent to a six month LIBOR. LO 34.2 LOD M

Set out the cash flows involved. What will the all-in-cost of funds to Credit Bank Limited be? Consider 6 months as exactly half a year.

Solution **(a)** Credit bank pays LIBOR + 0.25 per cent per annum for 5 years. Swap involves payment of 6 per cent per annum and receipts of LIBOR are 0.50.

Interest rates inflow	LIBOR
Interest rates outflow	(LIBOR + 0.25%) + 6%
So net interest payment	(LIBOR + 0.25%) + (6%) – LIBOR = 6.25 per cent per annum

Cash flows per six month period £ The 500 million × 6/12 × 6.25/100 = £ 15.625 million

P.34.10 The Airlines Company entered into an agreement with Airbus for buying the latest planes for a total value of Euro 100 million, payable after 6 months. The current spot exchange rate is INR 78/€. The Airlines Company cannot predict the exchange rate in the future. Can the Airlines Company hedge its foreign exchange risk using derivatives? Explain by examples. **LO 34.2** LOD E

Solution Yes. The Airlines Company can hedge its foreign exchange risk through the following methods:

(i) Forward Contract: The Airlines Company can enter into a forward contract (for a period of 6 months) for the full payment of € 100 million to hedge/reduce its foreign exchange risk. The given spot rate is ₹78/€, its liability is ₹7,800 million. The Airlines Company can enter into a forward contract with the bank to buy € forward, say, at the rate of ₹78.2/€. So the liability of the company is ₹7,820 million after 6 months. Suppose the actual exchange rate after 6 months turns out to be ₹78.5/€, in absence of such a forward contract, the liability would have been of ₹7,850 million. As a result, the Airline Company has reduced the risk and benefited by ₹30 million.

(ii) Foreign Currency Option: Risk can be hedged by having a call option. The call option holder will exercise the right only if it is beneficial for him. Airlines Company can purchase a 6 months call option at an agreed rate of, say, ₹78.5/€ plus a premium of 3 per cent. So, in this case the actual cost is ₹7,850 million × 1.03 = ₹8085.5 million.

Suppose at the end of 6 months the spot exchange rate turns out to be ₹79/€. Airlines Company will exercise its option and pay ₹78.5 per € and the total cost will be ₹8,085.5 million. In the open market one € will be available at ₹79 (Total outflow will be ₹7,900 million + premium already paid ₹235.5 million = ₹8135.5 million). So it is beneficial for him to exercise the option (the gain is ₹8135.5 million – ₹8085.5 million = ₹50 million).

Whether the company will opt for a forward contract (futures forward is also a possibility in case the amount of € 100 million is the standardised sum) or a call option will depend on the management's attitude towards risk. In case it is interested in hedging risk only, it would like to enter into a forward contract/futures contract (cash outflows are known with certainty irrespective of the Ff exchange rate on maturity). However, if the company wants to avail the advantage that may accrue due to the lowering of the Euro exchange rate, it will prefer to go for the call option.

P.34.11 A company operating in a country having the dollar as its unit of currency has invoiced sales to an Indian company today, the payment is due three months from the date of invoice. The invoice amount is US $16,500 and at today's spot rate of US $0.0165 per ₹1, it is equivalent to ₹10,00,000. It is anticipated that the exchange rate will decline by 5 per cent over the three month period and in order to protect the dollar proceeds, the importer proposes to take appropriate action through the foreign exchange market. **LO 34.2,3** LOD M

The three month forward rate is quoted as US $0.0160 per ₹1. You are required to calculate the expected loss and show how it can be hedged by a forward contract.

Solution Spot rate: ₹1 = US $0.0165

Three month forward rate: ₹1 = US $0.0160

Three month forward rate without forward contract is US $0.0165 × ₹0.95 = US $0.015675.

Calculation of expected loss without forward contract

Invoice amount is US $16,500, which is equal to ₹10,00,000, i.e. US $16,500/0.0165.

Payment due after three months is US \$16,500/0.015675 = ₹10,52,631.58
Expected loss is ₹10,52,631.58 – ₹10,00,000 = ₹52,631.58

Hedging of loss under forward contract

Payment at the time of import is US \$16,500, which is equal to ₹10,00,000
Payment due in three months is \$16,500/0.0160 = ₹10,31,250
Loss is ₹10,31,250 – ₹10,00,000 = ₹31,250

So, under the forward contract loss is hedged by 52,631.58 – 31,250 = ₹21,381.58.

P.34.12 X Limited, an Indian company, has an export exposure of 10 million yen value at September-end. The yen is not directly quoted against the rupee. The current spot rates are USD/INR = 61.79 and USD/JPY = 102.00. It is estimated that the yen will depreciate to 115 level and the rupee will depreciate against the dollar to ₹63.

LO 34.2 LOD M

Forward rate for September USD/Yen = 108 and USD/INR = 62.89.

You are required: **(i)** to calculate the expected loss if hedging is not done. How the position will change with the company taking forward cover? **(ii)** If the spot rate on 30th September was eventually US \$/¥ = 109 and USD/INR = 62.78, is the decision to take forward cover justified?

Solution Since a direct quote for yen and rupee is not given, it is to be calculated by cross currency exchange rates.

INR/USD × USD/JPY = INR/JPY
61.79/1 × 1/102.00 = 61.79/102.00 = 0.6057

Spot rate on the date of export = 1 yen = ₹0.6057
Estimated rate on September 1 yen = ₹0.5478 (63/115)
Actual rate on September [1 yen = ₹0.5760] i.e., (62.78/109)
Forward rate on September [1 yen = ₹0.5823] i.e., [62.89/108.0]

(i) Calculation of expected loss without hedging:
Value of exports at the time of export is ₹0.6057 × ¥10 million = ₹60,57,000.
Estimated payment to be received in September is ₹0.5478 × ¥10 million = ₹54,78,000.

Loss is ₹60,57,000 – ₹54,78,000 = ₹5,79,000

Hedging of loss under forward cover
Rupee value of exports (on the date of export) = ₹0.6057 × ¥10 million = ₹60,57,000.
Payment received under forward cover is ₹0.5823 × ¥10 million = ₹58,23,000.

Loss is ₹60,57,000 – ₹58,23,000 = ₹2,34,000.

By taking forward cover, loss of ₹3,45,000 (₹5,79,000 – 2,34,000) is reduced.

(ii) Since payment received under forward cover is higher at ₹58,23,000 *vis-a-vis* without any forward cover (₹57,60,000), the decision to take forward cover is justified.

P.34.13 A customer with whom the bank had entered into 3 months forward purchase contract for Swiss francs 10,000 at the rate of ₹62.25 comes to the bank after 2 months and requests cancellation of the contract. On this date, the rates prevailing are:

LO 34.2 LOD E

Spot	CHF 1 = ₹62.30	62.35
One month forward	62.45	62.52

Determine the amount of loss suffered by the customer due to cancellation of the contract.

Solution Since the customer finds the forward rate higher than the contract rate, at which he is to sell the Swiss francs (CHF) to the bank, he is suffering loss from the transaction. The loss amount will be equivalent to the difference of the one month forward price at which the customer would have purchased the CHF from the market (the relevant price is the selling price from the dealer's point of view, i.e., ₹62.52) and the contracted price of the bank is ₹62.25 multiplied by CHF 10,000. Total loss, therefore, is equivalent to ₹2,700 (₹62.52 – ₹62.25) × CHF 10,000.

P.34.14 Assume that in P34.13 the customer is a buyer of Swiss francs 10,000 at ₹62.25. Assume all rates remain unchanged, do you think the buyer would have cancelled the contract? LO 34.2 LOD E

Solution The buyer will not cancel the contract as it will be profitable from him to buy at ₹62.25 and sell at ₹62.45 (equivalent to the dealer's buying price). His gain will be ₹2,000, i.e., (₹62.45 – ₹62.25) × CHF 10,000.

P.34.15 A fixed rate currency swap has a remaining life of 12 months. It involves exchanging interest at 8 per cent on £10 million for interest at 6 per cent on US $20 million. If the swap rate were negotiated today, interest exchanged would be 4 per cent on the US $ and 6.5 per cent on pound sterling. The current exchange rate is US $1.6100/£. What is the value of the swap to the party paying pound sterling? LO 34.2 LOD M

Solution The swap involves exchanging the sterling interest of £10 million × 0.08 = £0.8 million for the dollar interest of $20 million × 0.06 = US $1.2 million. The principal amounts are also exchanged at the end of the swap's life.

So the value of the sterling bond underlying the swap is the present value of the sterling payment = (£10 million + £0.8 million)/1.065 = £10.14 million.

The value of dollar bond underlying the swap is = (US $20 million + US $1.2 million)/1.04 = US $20.38 million.

(a) Thus, the value of the swap to the party paying sterling is $20.38 – (£10.14 × 1.610) = $16.3254, i.e., US $4.0546 million.

P.34.16 An Indian importer purchases goods worth US $1,00,000. Payment is due in three months. The importer wants to hedge foreign exchange risk by using the money market. Money market data are as follows: LO 34.2 LOD M

Interest rate in the US money market for 3 months: 4% p a
Interest rate in the Indian money market for 3 months: 10% p a and spot rate of US $ is ₹62/$.

State all transactions the importer will undertake to hedge his risk.

Solution As the importer is to pay US $1,00,000 after 3 months, he would like to enter into a set of transactions that makes the rupee cost of this payment immune to exchange rate fluctuations. For this he will carry out the following transaction in the money market.

(a) He will invest the dollar amount (say x) in the US market in such quantity that he receives US $1,00,000 at the end of 3 months. Or

$$x(1 + 0.04 \times 3/12) = \text{US } \$1,00,000$$
$$1.01x = \text{US } \$1,00,000$$
$$x = \text{US } \$1,00,000/1.01 = \text{US } \$99,010.$$

(b) To invest US $99,010 in the US market, the importer will buy these US $ in the spot market. Rupees required to make this purchase = US $99.010 × ₹62 = ₹61,38,620.

(c) The importer is required to arrange through borrowings in Indian market (@ 10% p a). So, the importer will need to pay ₹61,38,620 (1 + 0.1 × 3/12) = ₹62,92,086 after 3 months.

Thus, whatever be the change in the spot rate over next 3 months the Indian importer is to pay ₹62,92,086 to pay its import bill of US $1,00,000.

P.34.17 ABC Textiles Limited places an order to buy textile machinery with an American company. As per the agreement, ABC Textiles Limited will be paying US $200,000 after 180 days. As the fluctuation in the spot rate of the US dollar over next 180 days will impact the rupee cost of import, the Board of ABCTextiles Limited asks its finance manager to collect data from the currency forward market, money market, currency option market etc. The board also asks a consultant to assess various possible dollar spot rates after six months. LO 34.2 LOD D

The various findings are as follows:

(a) Possible spot rate of dollar after six months, as estimated by the consultant, is ₹61.25, ₹61.75, ₹62, ₹62.50, ₹62.90.

(b) Spot rate of dollar as of today is ₹62/US $.

(c) 180 day forward rate of dollar as of today is ₹62.48/US $.

(d) Interest rates are as follows:

	India	*USA*
For 180 day deposit rate (per annum)	7.5%	1.5%
For 180 day borrowing rate (per annum)	8.0%	2.0%

(e) A call option on the dollar, which expires in 180 days, has an exercise price of ₹62/US $ and premium ₹0.52/US $.

(f) A put option on dollar, which expires in 180 days, has an exercise of ₹62/US $ and premium of ₹0.04/ US $.

Carry out a comparative analysis of the various outcomes (rupee cost of import) under the alternatives of (i) not hedging (ii) forward hedging (iii) money market hedging and (iv) option hedging.

Solution Comparison of hedging alternative for ABC Textiles Limited.

ABC Textiles will need to purchase US $2,00,000 to fulfill its import obligation. It will do so by making a purchase in the spot market after 180 days. ABC textiles rupee outgo in this circumstances will be:

Expected spot rate after 180 days	*Rupee outgo to purchase US $2,00,000*
₹61.25/US $	₹1,22,50,000
61.75/US $	1,23,50,000
62.00/US $	1,24,00,000
62.50/US $	1,25,00,000
62.90/US $	1,25,80,000

Forward hedge:

Rupees needed to buy US $2,00,000 with forward contract = US $2,00,000 × ₹62.48/US $ = ₹1,24,96,000.

Money market hedge

Borrow rupee, convert to US dollar, invest US dollar to receive US $2,00,000 in 180 days. Amount in US dollar to be invested = US $2,00,000/(1 + 0.015 × 180/360) = US $1,98,511.

Amount in rupees that need to converted into US dollar for investing = US $1,98,511 × ₹62/US $ = ₹1,23,07,682.

Interest and principal owed in rupee loan to be returned after 180 days = ₹1,23,07,682 (1 + 0.08 × 180/360) = ₹1,27,99,990.

So the rupee outgo for ABC Textiles will be ₹1,27,99,990.

Option hedge

Purchase call (assuming that the option is to be exercised on the day the US dollar are needed) exercised price is ₹62/US $; premium is ₹0.52/US $.

Possible spot rate after 180 days	*Premium per unit paid for option*	*Exercise option*	*Total price paid per unit*	*Total price paid for US $2,00,000*
₹61.25	₹0.52	No	₹61.77	₹1,23,54,000
61.75	0.52	No	62.27	1,24,54,000
62.00	0.52	No	62.52	1,25,04,000
62.50	0.52	Yes	62.52	1,25,04,000
62.90	0.52	Yes	62.52	1,25,04,000

P.34.18 Romesh Sharma is a currency trader for a large currency trading firm of USA, based in New Jersey. He expects the US dollar to depreciate against the euro. The current spot rate of the euro is US $ 1.300/€ and the premium on call and put options are as follows: **LO 34.2** LOD M

Strike: US$ 1.3280/€	*30 days*	*60 days*
Call option on the euro	0.085	0.100
Put option on the euro	0.110	0.135

(a) What should Romesh Sharma do to profit from his anticipation?

(b) What will the profit or loss be, if the rate on settlement date, after 30 days, is US $ 1.4728/€, and (i) Romesh Sharma has bought a 30 day call, (ii) Romesh Sharma has sold a 30 day put.

Solution

(a) As Romesh Sharma anticipates the US dollar to depreciate against the euro (appreciation of euro against the US dollar), he can be benefited either by buying a call option on euros or selling a put option on euros.

(b) (i) Profit from purchase of call

Profit from purchase of call for a strike price of US $ 1.3280/€, premium US $ 0.085/€ and settlement rate (expiration rate) of US $ 1.4728/€

= US $ (1.4728 – 1.3280)/€ – US $ 0.085/€ = US $ 0.0598/€

As the settlement rate is higher than the strike rate, Romesh Sharma will exercise the option.

(ii) Profit from sell of put

As the settlement rate (US $ 1.4728/€) is higher than the strike rate, this put option will not be exercised. So, for Romesh Sharma the premium that he received on selling (writing) the put option is his profit (US $ 0.110/€).

Selling an option entails high risk, but is used as a strategy by the currency trader when he is confident of his anticipation.

P.34.19 On January 28, 2018 an importer customer requested a bank to remit Singapore Dollar (SGD) 25,00,000 under an irrevocable LD. However, due to bank strikes, the bank could effect the remittance only on February 4, 2018. The interbank market rates were as follows: **LO 34.2** LOD M

	January 28	*February 4*
Mumbai US $ 1	₹60.85/60.90	60.91/60.97
London Pound 1	US$ 1.4940/1.4950	1.4865/1.4875
Pound 1	SGD 1.9175/1.9190	1.8990/1.9000

The bank wishes to retain an exchange margin of 0.125 per cent. How much does the customer stand to gain or lose due to the delay? (Calculate rate in multiples of .0001)

Solution

Since importer needs SGD, and the exchange rate of ₹/SGD is not given, we are to compute first the cross rate - (As the bank is selling so only ask prices are required)

$$[₹/SGD]_{ask} = [₹/\$]_{ask} \times [\$/SGD]_{ask}$$

Since, $[\$/SGD]_{ask}$ is not given, we will calculate it

$$[₹/SGD]_{ask} = [\$/£]_{ask} \times [£/SGD]_{ask}$$

For January 28, 2018:

$$[₹/SGD]_{ask} = 1.4950 \times \frac{1}{3.9175}$$

$$\Rightarrow \$0.7797/SGD$$

On February 4, 2018:

$$[₹/SGD]_{ask} = 1.4875 \times \frac{1}{1.8990}$$

⇒ \$0.78330/SGD

On January 28, Inter-bank rate:

$[₹/SGD]_{ask}$ = ₹60.90 × 0.7797
= ₹47.483/SGD

Rate to be charged from importer

SGD_1	₹47.4830
Plus exchange margin (0.125%)	0.0593
	₹47.5423

On February 4, Inter-bank rate:

$[₹/SGD]_{ask}$ = ₹60.97 × 0.7833
⇒ ₹47.7578/SGD

Rate to be charged from importer

SGD_1	₹47.7578
Plus exchange margin (0.125)	0.0597
	₹47.8175

Since on February 4, the SGD has appreciated, importer suffers loss.

Loss = (₹47.8175 – ₹47.5423) × 25,00,000 (SGD)
= ₹6,88,000

P.34.20 XYZ Limited borrows £15 million of six months LIBOR + 10.00% for a period of 24 months. The company anticipates a rise in LIBOR, hence, it proposes to buy a cap option from its bankers at the strike rate of 8.00%. The lump sum premium is 1.00% for the entire reset periods and the fixed rate of interest is 7.00% per annum. The actual position of LIBOR during the forthcoming reset period is as under:

LO 34.2,3 LOD D

Reset Period	1	2	3
LIBOR (%)	9.00	9.50	10.00

You are required to show how far interest rate risk is hedged through cap option. For calculation, work out figures at each stage up to four decimal points and amount nearest to £. It should form part of working notes.

Solution

Premium payable to bank:

$$P = \frac{R_p \times A}{\{(1/i) - [1/(i \times (1+i)^t)]\}} = \frac{0.01}{\{(1/0.035) - [1/(0.035 \times 1.035^4)]\}} \times £15{,}000{,}000$$

$$= £40{,}861$$

where

P = Premium
A = Principal amount
R_p = Rate of premium
i = Fixed rate of interest
t = Time period

Computation of net payment received from bank

Reset period	*Additional interest due to rise in interest rate*	*Amount received from bank*	*Premium paid to bank*	*Net amount received from bank*
1	£75,000	£75,000	£40,861	£34,139
2	£112,500	£112,500	£40,861	£71,639
3	£150,000	£150,000	£40,861	£109,139
Total	£337,500	£337,500	£122,583	£214,917

Thus, interest rate risk of £337,500 gets reduced by £214,917 by using cap option.

MINI CASES

34.C.1 The investment manager of a large Indian software company receives the following quotes from its foreign exchange broker.

US dollar spot rate : ₹60.75/US $

US dollar option quotation

Strike price	*Call*			*Put*		
	June	*September*	*December*	*June*	*September*	*December*
58.0000	3.0	—	—	—	—	—
58.5000	2.6	2.9	—	—	—	—
59.0000	2.0	2.3	2.45	0.2	—	—
59.5000	1.85	1.95	2.15	0.25	—	—
60.0000	1.25	1.85	2.00	0.70	0.90	—
60.5000	0.85	1.15	1.45	1.00	1.25	1.75
61.0000	0.50	0.74	0.89	1.59	1.92	2.50
61.5000	0.30	0.52	0.68	1.70	2.20	—
62.0000	0.15	—	—	1.90	—	—
62.5000	0.10	—	—	2.00	—	—
63.0000	0.08	—	—	2.30	—	—

What calculation will the investment manager make for following questions?

(a) What is the intrinsic value for the September 60.5 call option?

(b) What is the intrinsic value for the June 59 put option?

(c) What is the break-even exchange rate for the December 59.5 call and the December 61 put?

(d) If the December spot rate is expected to be ₹61.50/US $, which call option should be bought?

(e) The software company will receive its export income in December and the expected spot rate (in December) will be ₹59.5/US $, which put option should be bought?

Solution Intrinsic value of an option is the amount by which the option is in-the-money

For a call option, intrinsic value = Maximum [(Spot rate – Strike rate), 0]

For a put option, intrinsic value = Maximum [(Strike rate – Spot rate), 0]

(a) Intrinsic value for the September 60.5 call option

= Max [(₹60.75/US $ – ₹60.5/US $), 0] = Max [₹0.25/US $, 0] = ₹0.25/US $

(b) Intrinsic value for the June 59 put option

= Max [(₹59/US $ – ₹60.75/US $), 0]= Max [– (₹1.75/US $), 0] = 0

(c) The break-even exchange rate for the December 59.5 call on settlement date is ₹X/US $

So, the premium paid = ₹2.15/US $

profit from the call option = ₹(X – 59.5)/US $

at break-even, ₹(X – 59.5)/US $ = ₹2.15/US $

X = ₹61.65/US $

The break-even exchange rate for December 61 put is:

Premium paid = ₹2.50/US $

Profit from the put option = ₹(61 – X)/US $

At break-even, ₹(61 – X)/US $ = ₹2.50/US $

X = ₹58.5/US $

(d) For an expected spot rate of ₹61.5/US $, we need to find out profit from buying the December call option at various strike prices.

Gain from call option

= Max [(Settlement rate – Strike rate), 0] – Premium

= Value of option at expiration – Premium

Option	Strike price	Premium (A)	Option value at expiration (B)	Gain/Loss [B – A]
December call	₹59.00/US $	₹2.45/US $	₹2.50/US $	₹0.05/US $
December call	59.50/US $	2.15/US $	2.00/US $	– 0.15/US $
December call	60.00/US $	2.00/US $	1.50/US $	– 0.50/US $
December call	60.50/US $	1.45/US $	1.00/US $	– 0.45/US $
December call	61.00/US $	0.89/US $	0.50/US $	– 0.39/US $
December call	61.50/US $	0.68/US $	0.00/US $	– 0.68/US $

So, for the expected December spot price of ₹61.50/US $, the December call option of strike price ₹59.00/US $ should be bought.

(e) Gain from purchasing the December put option of various strikes, for which quotes are available, for an expiration price of ₹59.50/US $.

Option	Strike price	Premium (A)	Option value at expiration (B)	Gain/Loss [B – A]
December put	₹60.50/US $	₹1.75/US $	₹1/US $	– ₹0.75/US $
December put	61.00/US $	2.50/US $	1.50/US $	– 1.00/US $

As no gains accrue by purchasing the different December put available for the expected December expiration rate of ₹61.50/US $, the software company should not hedge through the put options.

REVIEW QUESTIONS

LOD: Easy

RQ.34.1 **(a)** Indicate whether the following statements are true or false: [LO 34.1,2,3]

(i) Exposure relating to the change in accounting income and balance sheet statements caused by changes in exchange rates is called Transaction exposure.

(ii) Change in the value of a company that accompanies an unanticipated change in exchange rates is called economic exposure.

(iii) Forward exchange contracts are traded on at an organised exchange.

(iv) Future contracts are carried out through direct dealings between parties.

(v) The benefits that accrue due to favourable movements in foreign exchange rates can be availed of by using currency options.

(vi) Firms engaged in international operations should endeavour to have their assets in a strong currency.

(vii) Leading and lagging is an internal technique of foreign exchange risk management.

(viii) Translation profits or losses must be reflected in the income statement.

(ix) In a call option, the holder has the right to sell (but is under no obligation to sell) a specific currency at a specific price on a specific maturity date or within a specified period of time.

(x) Currency swaps involve exchange of interest obligations between two parties.

[Answers: (i) False (ii) True (iii) False (iv) False (v) True (vi) True (vii) True (viii) False (ix) False (x) False]

(b) Fill in the blanks with the correct answer (out of the choices provided).

(i) Operating exposure to exchange rate changes has an impact on the firm's ________ (current/future) operating revenues, costs and cash flows.

(ii) The more differentiated a firm's products are, the ________ (more/less) is its operating exposure to exchange rate changes.

(iii) Forward contracts in currencies are closed by ________ (actual delivery of foreign currency/settlement of difference between the contracted and actual price.)

(iv) When the option can be exercised only on the maturity date, it is called an ________ (American/European) option.

(v) Operating exposure to exchange risk is ______________ (more/less) if the price elasticity of demand of the goods/services, the firm deals in is low.

(vi) If the immediate exercise of the option yields a positive value to the holder, the option is said to be ______________ (in/at) the money.

(vii) The practice of delaying receipts from the foreign currency designated receivables whose currencies are likely to appreciate and delaying foreign currency designated payables whose currencies are likely to depreciate is known as ______________ (leading/lagging).

(viii) Multilateral netting involves ______________ (two/more than two) parties.

(ix) A firm having a higher elasticity of substitution between home-country and foreign-country inputs or production is ______________ (more/less) susceptible to foreign exchange risk.

(x) Where an MNC firm having many foreign subsidiaries creates a reinvoicing centre, the invoices are made in the name of ______________ (subsidiaries/reinvoicing centre).

[Answers: (i) future (ii) less (iii) actual delivery of foreign currency (iv) European (v) less (vi) in (vii) lagging (viii) more than two (ix) less (x) reinvoicing centre]

RQ.34.2 What types of exchange exposures do international companies and multinational companies (MNCs) face? [LO 34.1]

RQ.34.3 What is 'strike price'? What is its relevance? [LO 34.2]

RQ.34.4 An Indian exporter sold goods to a US company. The receivables of 10 million dollars are due in 3 months. How can the exporter hedge this exposure by using a put option given the following information: [LO 34.2]

Strike price	₹61.10/$
Maturity	3 months
Premium	2 per cent
Current spot rate	₹61.50/$

Also state various possibilities regarding the use of the put option by him.

RQ.34.5 ABC Company is to pay 1 million Euro on 1st October in the current year. It wants to make sure that it does not pay too high in case Euro appreciates. It buys a call option by paying 3 per cent premium on the current price. The current rate is ₹78.10/€. The strike price is decided at ₹78.60/€. Determine the net price paid per Euro. Suppose on 1st October, the spot rate is ₹78.92. Will the company exercise its call option? [LO 34.2]

LOD: Medium

RQ.34.6 "Economic exposure implies the change in the value of a firm due to unanticipated change in exchange rates". Elaborate. [LO 34.1]

RQ.34.7 What are the major external techniques used in managing foreign exchange risk? Do you subscribe to the view that currency options are superior to other derivative financial instruments? Explain. [LO 34.3]

RQ.34.8 What are currency futures? In what major respects do they differ from forward contracts? [LO 34.2]

RQ.34.9 Distinguish between call and put options. Enumerate situations when the holder of such options would like to exercise his option. Use appropriate examples to explain your answer. [LO 34.2]

RQ.34.10 What are interest swaps and currency swaps? [LO 34.2]

RQ.34.11 Explain with examples how foreign exchange risk can be covered in the money market. [LO 34.2]

RQ.34.12 In case there are identical costs in a forward contract and a futures contract, which would you prefer and why? [LO 34.2]

RQ.34.13 What are the important internal techniques that can be used by MNCs to hedge their foreign exchange risk? [LO 34.3]

RQ.34.14 Explain the technique of 'Leads and Lags'. Enumerate situations, with examples, when it is the ideal technique of managing foreign exchange risk. [LO 34.3]

RQ.34.15 X Company Limited, an Indian company, is required to make a payment of 3 million US dollars after 6 months, against import of plant and machinery. What are the different alternatives to hedge against this foreign currency exposure. Give explanations. [LO 34.2,3]

RQ.34.16 Spot rate of the US dollar was ₹60.7650/US $ on February 28. And the call rate premium of the March (call option on the US dollar, with a strike ₹61/US $ and expiring on 28th March) was ₹0.2500/ US $. [LO 34.2]

(a) Is the call option in-the-money, at-the-money, or out-of-the-money?

(b) Compute the intrinsic value of the call.

(c) If the exchange rate settlement rate on 28th March is ₹61.3520, what is the percentage return on investment, if the investor has purchased a call on February 28.

Hint: As the settlement rate is higher than the strike rate, the call option will be exercised giving a value of (settlement rate – strike rate). And the premium is the cost incurred in buying the option.

Return on investment = (0.102/0.2500) × 100 = 40.8 per cent per month.

LOD: Difficult

RQ.34.17 Explain, with appropriate examples and figures, the technique of netting as a measure of covering foreign exchange risk. What are the prerequisites for using such a technique? Is it feasible to be used by MNCs only? [LO 34.3]

RQ.34.18 The "derivatives market in India is in its infancy". Elaborate. [LO 34.2]

RQ.34.19 Eureka Software is in the business of BPO (Business Process Outsourcing). The firm is run by three software engineers. For last three years, Eureka Software had been providing its services to a multinational firm based in UK for fixed every quarter-end revenue of £ 50,000. As the Indian rupee was consistently depreciating in respect to the pound, this fixed quarter-end revenue in pounds had an effect of increasing the revenue in rupee terms. So, the management never thought of foreign exchange risk exposure hedging. But during the last quarter the rupee revenue for Eureka Software was less than the previous quarter as the rupee appreciated during this time. This motivated the owners of Eureka Software to understand this risk and to neutralise it. Eureka Software's banker suggested that they hedge through currency forward or currency option. Understanding these hedging techniques, Eureka Software decides on option hedging (as forward hedging will not allow them profit in case of further depreciation in the rupee—because of which they have been benefited for so long—so they do not opt for the forward market route to hedge). [LO 34.2,3]

As Eureka Software's banker you are required to prepare a report on the rupee revenue possibility for various possible spot rates of the pound, for the next quarter.

(i) Current spot rate of the pound is ₹92/£.

(ii) Possible spot rate of the pound after 3 months	*Probability*
₹93.0/£	5%
92.5/£	10%
92.0/£	20%
91.5/£	20%
91.0/£	20%
90.5/£	15%
90.0/£	10%

(ii) A call option on the pound, which expires in 90 days, has an exercise price of ₹91.75/£ and premium of ₹0.80/£.

(iii) A put option on pound, which expires in 90 days, has an exercise price of ₹91.75/£ and premium of ₹0.55/£.

Also calculate the rupee revenue, if Eureka decides to remain unhedged.

ANSWERS

34.4 Exporter hedges risk by buying put option. He is to pay premium of ₹12.3 million. There are three possibilities: **(i)** US $ depreciates, **(ii)** US $ appreciates and **(iii)** its value is equal to strike price.

34.5 The company will not exercise call option. The net price paid per Euro is ₹81.2876.

34.15 The various methods available to X Company Limited are forward contract, foreign currency options and money market operations.

34.16 **(a)** Call option is out-of-money,
(b) zero,
(c) 40.8 per cent per month.

34.19

Spot rate (in ₹)	93	92.5	92	91.5	91.0	90.5	90.0
(i) Revenue (in ₹lakh)	46.5	46.25	46	45.75	45.50	45.25	45
(ii) Revenue (in ₹lakh)	46.225	45.975	45.720	45.6	45.6	45.6	45.6

Scan the QR Code to access comprehensive solutions to all numerical review questions and additional material.

CHAPTER

35 International Financial Management

LEARNING OBJECTIVES

LO 35.1	Explain multinational capital budgeting decisions—nature, difficulties and importance, data requirement, accounting for intangible benefits, cash flows at parent and subsidiary levels and expropriation and other political risks
LO 35.2	Discuss the computation of cost of capital for foreign investment projects
LO 35.3	Outline the adjusted present value approach to evaluation of foreign investment proposals
LO 35.4	Analyse the main components of multinational working capital management
LO 35.5	Examine the features of external commercial borrowings (ECBs) as a source of international finance in India
LO 35.6	Discuss another important source of international finance—Euro-issues
LO 35.7	Describe foreign currency exchangeable bonds

INTRODUCTION

The objective of this Chapter is to explain international financial management in terms of foreign/ multinational capital budgeting decisions, cost of capital, working capital and important sources of international finance. The focus is primarily on the distinguishing/special aspects related to the financial decisions of the multinational corporations (MNCs)/international firms since principles of financial management applicable to the domestic/local firms, by and large, do also apply to inter-national firms. In fact, the fundamental goal of international firms as well as MNCs matches with that of domestic firms, that is, maximisation of the wealth of shareholders. The Chapter first deals with foreign/ multinational capital budgeting decisions. The aspects related to cost of capital, adjusted presented value approach and working capital are discussed subsequently. The major international sources of finance in India, namely, external commercial borrowings and euro issues are also described. The foreign currency exchangeable bonds are covered in the subsequent discussion. The main points are summarised by way of recapitulation.

LO 35.1 MULTINATIONAL CAPITAL BUDGETING DECISIONS

Nature, Difficulties and Importance

Foreign capital budgeting decisions are beset with a variety of problems that are rarely encountered by domestic/local firms. The reason is that international firms have to deal with issues related to, among others, exchange rate risks, expropriation risk, blocked funds, foreign tax regulations, political risk and differences between basic business risks of foreign and domestic projects.[1] However, in spite of the complex problems of investing abroad, there is an increasing trend to set-up subsidiaries by MNCs and to have direct foreign investment by international firms in other countries. The major motivating factors for undertaking these investments are as follows: **(i)** Comparative cost advantage is a major factor in favour of foreign investments; **(ii)** Taxation is another vital economic/financial incentive to make such investments; **(iii)** Financial diversification, in terms of spreading the firm's risk over a wider range than just one nation, constitutes yet another economic motivation for multinational firms.[2]

Foreign capital budgeting projects/decisions are more difficult to evaluate than domestic capital budgeting projects. For operational purposes, there is a need to develop a *conceptual framework* that enables the set of factors mentioned above to be measured/reduced to a common denominator so that the various foreign investment projects under consideration can be evaluated on a uniform basis.

Data Requirement—Incremental/Relevant Cash Flows

The relevant data indicating *incremental cash outflows* to undertake foreign investment decisions are to be measured and so also the *incremental cash inflows* the foreign investment project is expected to yield during its projected economic useful life. These cash flows are to be discounted at an appropriate cost of capital to determine the net present value of the foreign capital budgeting project.

Incremental Cash Outflows These are incremental investment/capital outlays that can be conveniently, wholly and exclusively identified with the proposed foreign investment project. In the case of independent subsidiaries, maintaining independent books of accounts, preparing financial statements in the local currency of the country where the subsidiary is located, the determination of cash outflows (as well as cash inflows, discussed later) are akin to domestic capital budgeting decisions. Cash outflows are summarised in Format 35.1.

FORMAT 35.1 Cash Outflows

Cost of the proposed plant and equipment
Add: Shipping charges, custom duties, local transport etc
Add: Installation cost of plant and equipment
Add: Additional working capital requirement
Add: Cost of technology transfer
Add: Training cost of personnel (those required to work on the proposed plant), if any
Less: Sale proceeds (duly adjusted for taxes) from the existing plant and equipment (in case of replacement of existing technology/plant and equipment)

Incremental Cash Inflows After Taxes (CFAT) The determination of incremental CFAT is a daunting task for foreign capital budgeting projects in view of their more risky nature. Incremental cash inflows, like cash outflows, should be exclusively/wholly identifiable with the proposed project. For this purpose, it is very important to draw the distinction between the total CFAT, the proposed foreign investment project generates and incremental CFAT the firm eventually has. The major points of differences between the total and incremental cash flows are now explained.

Cannibalisation It implies the lost sales of the firm's existing product(s) on account of launching a new product (or on account of proposed foreign investment). This happens when an MNC builds a plant overseas in a country to which it was hitherto exporting. The proposed/new investment project's sales/profits should be reduced by the lost sales/earnings to the extent that the sales of a new product or plant just replace other corporate sales of a parent company. Thus, in the context of capital budgeting decisions, the effect of cannibalisation is equal to the profit on lost sales that otherwise would not have been lost had the new/proposed project not been undertaken. The sales that would have been lost irrespective of the proposed project, say on account of competition from other MNCs, should obviously, not be reckoned as an adverse effect/impact of cannibalisation.[3]

Cannibalisation implies lost sales of existing products of a multinational company on account of proposed foreign investment.

Sales Creation Sales creation means an increase in sales and is just the antithesis of cannibalisation. It has a favourable effect on cash flows. It is possible that the proposed investment project overseas may result in the additional sales of the existing products of the parent company. In such an event, incremental profits/cash inflows yielded by such additional sales should be attributed to the proposed investment project. Therefore, credit should be given to the proposed investment project on account of sales creation.

Sales creation implies increased sales on account of proposed foreign investment.

Opportunity Cost Opportunity cost (cost of the next best alternative foregone) constitutes yet another important factor to be reckoned with in this regard. For example, rent foregone on account of the use of the factory/office space in the proposed project should be considered as cost on account of the new project. The current market value of the land and building that are used for undertaking a new project should also be counted as the cost of the project.

Treatment of Fixed Overheads Only additional fixed overheads are to be considered for determining cash flows since existing overheads are to be incurred irrespective of the proposed investment project. In operational terms, the allocation of existing fixed overheads (either of parent or an MNC) should be excluded.

Fees and Royalties The proposed investment project should not be charged for various items such as legal counsel, management costs, training of personnel engaged by the subsidiary, by the parent and the like, (collectively referred to as fees and royalties) unless these costs are incurred additionally.

Accounting for Intangible Benefits

Besides quantifiable benefits, intangible benefits such as better quality, faster time to market, prompt and less error-prone order processing and higher customer satisfaction, and so on as these benefits hold the potential of having a favourable impact on corporate cash flows, even if they cannot be measured precisely should also be accounted for. Besides, many foreign projects can provide valuable learning experiences and sharpen competitive skills as they expose companies to tough foreign competition.[4] This, in turn, helps corporates to adapt their existing product(s) as well as develop new product(s); this is likely to have a favourable impact in terms of increased demand for its products in its own home country/market.

In brief, only incremental cash inflows after taxes accruing from investment abroad (by either setting up a new foreign subsidiary or expansion/diversification of existing subsidiary) should form a part of the capital budgeting exercise. The capital budgeting analysis based on total CFAT would overstate the profitability of the foreign project and run the risk of resulting in wrong decisions.

***Example* 35.1**

A US multinational is planning to set up a subsidiary in India (where hitherto it was exporting) in view of the growing demand for its product and the competition from other MNCs. The initial project cost (consisting of plant and machinery including installation) is estimated to be US dollar 400 million; working capital requirements are estimated at $50 million. The US multinational follows the straight-line method of depreciation.

At present, it is exporting 2 million units every year at a unit price of US dollar 80, its variable cost per unit being US dollar 40.

The finance manager of the firm has estimated, with respect to the project cost (measured in US dollars) as follows: (i) variable cost of production and sales, $20 per unit, (ii) additional fixed costs per annum at $30 million and the share of allocated fixed costs, $3 million, (iii) capacity of the plant set up in India is, to produce and sell 4 million units, (iv) the expected economic useful life of the plant is 5 years, with no salvage value, and (v) the firm's existing working capital investment in production and sales of 2 million units was $10 million.

In his report the finance manager also mentions that exports will decrease to 1.5 million units in case the firm does not open the subsidiary in view of the presence of competing MNCs that are in the process of setting up their subsidiaries in India.

The firm is subject to 35 per cent corporate tax rate and its required rate of return for such projects is 12 per cent. Assuming that there will be no variation in the exchange rate between the two countries and that all profits can be repatriated without withholding taxes, advise the US multinational regarding the financial viability of having a subsidiary in India.

Solution

Analysis of Financial Viability *(figures in million)*

(i) Incremental Cash Outflows:		
Cost of plant and machinery		$400
Add: Additional working capital ($50 million – Release of existing working capital, $10 million)		40
		440
(ii) Incremental Cash Inflows After Taxes (CFAT):		
(a) Generated by subsidiary (t = 1 – 5)		
Sales revenue (4 million units × $80)		320
Less: Costs:		
Variable costs (4 million units × $20)	$80	
Additional fixed costs	30	
Depreciation ($400 million/5 years)	80	190
Earnings before taxes		130
Less: Taxes (0.35)		45.5
Earnings after taxes		84.5
Add: Depreciation		80.0
CFAT (t = 1 – 4)		164.5
CFAT in 5th year		
Operating CFAT	$164.5	
Add: Release of working capital	40.0	204.5
(b) Generated by exports (t = 1 – 5)		
Sales revenue[a] (1.5 million units × $80)		$120
Less: Variable costs (1.5 million × $40)		60
Contribution before taxes		60
Less: Taxes (0.35)		21
Contribution after taxes/CFAT		39
(c) Incremental CFAT due to subsidiary ($164.5 million – $39 million)[(a) – (b)]		125.5

(iii) Determination of NPV ($ million)

Years	*CFAT*	*PV factor (0.12)*	*Total PV*
1 – 4	$125.5	3.037	$381.14
5	165.5[b]	0.567	93.84
Gross present value			474.98
Less: Incremental cash outflows			440.00
Net present value			34.98

(a) In future, in the event of not having subsidiary, exports are to produce/sell 1.5 million units only.
(b) $125.5 million + Recovery of working capital, $40 million.

Recommendation Since the NPV is positive, the firm is advised to go for its decision to set-up the subsidiary in India.

Cash Flows at Subsidiary and Parent Level

In foreign capital budgeting decisions, there may be a substantial difference between the cash flows of the project at the subsidiary level and the level of the parent firm. The difference arises primarily due to tax regulations (affecting repatriation to the parent), exchange controls, inflation as well as interest rates affecting the exchange rate and so on. The difference between the two sets of cash flows also arises on account of the fact that the parent company usually charges management fees, fees for technology transfer and royalties on production/sales from its subsidiary units. As per the incremental analysis, these expenses are ignored. However, in estimating the true profitability of the subsidiary unit, these expenses merit recognition as these are project expenses at the level of subsidiary. These project expenses constitute cash inflows/incomes at the parent level and, hence, need to be counted. In fact, the principle (as enunciated by Shapiro) can be any cash inflow back to the investor (parent company in the present context), should be taken into account in cash inflows for the purpose of determining NPV of the project. In respect of other incomes, the parent should value only those cash flows that are, or can be, repatriated net of any transfer costs (such as withholding taxes/other taxes) as these are the only accessible funds available to it.[5]

Assessing true profitability of an independent subsidiary company in terms of local currency where it is located, the determination of the CFAT is akin to a domestic project, as shown in Format 35.2. Cash inflows to the parent company are depicted in Format 35.3.

FORMAT 35.2 Cash Inflows After Taxes (CFAT) of Independent Subsidiary Company

Particulars	*Years* 1 2 ...N
Sales revenue	
Less: Variable costs	
Less: Additional fixed costs	
Less: Management fees charged by parent	
Less: Royalties for patents, licences, brands, etc charged by parent	
Less: Depreciation/amortisation	
Earnings before tax	
Less: Taxes	
Earnings after taxes	
Add: Depreciation/amortisation/non-cash expenses	

(*Contd.*)

(*Contd.*)

CFAT (operating)
Add: Salvage value of the plant, if any (nth year)
Add: Recovery or working capital (*n*th year or in earlier years)

FORMAT 35.3 Cash Inflows to the Parent Company

Particulars	*Years* 1 2 ...N
Dividends received	
Interest received	
Management fees	
Royalties received for patents, licences, brands, technology transfer, etc	
Terminal cash flows (net of all types of taxes) such as repatriation of sale proceeds of plant, release of working capital, blocked funds not paid due to exchange control restrictions, etc.	
Repayment of loan	
Increase in cash profits (after tax) due to increased export sales of other products at parent MNC	
Less: Decrease in cash profits (after taxes) due to decrease in export sales	

Apart from quantifiable benefits, there may be other intangible/indirect benefits that may improve/enhance the corporate's competitive position worldwide, contributing through increased sales of its other products. Sales accretion may also take place as the firm has a better knowledge of markets abroad. Though these benefits are non-quantifiable, they need to be reckoned, being strategic in nature, while evaluating foreign investment decisions. These qualitative benefits acquire added significance when the NPV of the project is either negligible/zero or negative by a marginal/small amount. In such situations, projects based on quantitative analysis is/may be rejected. Given the fact that non-quantifiable intangible benefits also contribute to cash flows (though non-measurable), the project that would otherwise have been rejected may be found worth accepting when such benefits are also taken into account.

Most of the items contained in Format 35.3 are self explanatory. However, aspects related to taxes, repatriation of profits/blocked funds and exchange rate risk deserve more explanation.

Impact of Taxes Since cash inflows after taxes are relevant, it is important to know when and what amount of taxes are payable on foreign earnings. These earnings are subject to tax at more than one 'stage' as per the tax laws in vogue in many countries. First of all, the taxes are levied on the subsidiary company by the local government of the country where it is located, as per the tax laws applicable to foreign companies[6]. In general, corporate tax rates of foreign companies are different from those of domestic companies.

Apart from corporate taxes, subsidiary companies may be required to pay withholding taxes on dividends remitted to the parent. These dividends, being the income of the parent company, may be further subject to tax in the country where the parent company is located. This causes *double taxation* [in fact, it tantamounts to *triple taxation* in that the affiliate of the parent company is taxed at two times already—one when it earns and another when it remits such earnings in the form of dividends; payment of taxes by the parent on dividends received is the third stage at which the same income earned (by the subsidiary) is taxed].

'Taxes at many stages' appears to be inequitable. Therefore, it is not uncommon for the governments of many countries to have special tax treaties to avoid/minimise the incidence of such heavy taxation on foreign subsidiaries/foreign earnings.

Granting *tax credit* is an alternative to special tax treaties. Under the tax credit system the tax laws of the country permit the adjustment of taxes already paid by the subsidiary unit (located in other country) either fully or partially against the tax liability of the parent; as a result, the incidence of tax is reduced. Tax credit adjustment is illustrated in Example 35.2.

***Example* 35.2**

Assume that a US multinational has its subsidiary in a country where its income is taxed at 20 per cent. Withholding tax rate is 5 per cent. Assume further that corporate firms in US are subject to tax of 35 per cent; however, corporate firms having their subsidiaries abroad are allowed tax credit.

Determine the amount of tax credit available to a subsidiary having remitted US $4 million after-tax earnings as dividends.

Solution

(i) The subsidiary's before-tax earnings (EBT) are equivalent to $5 million [i.e., $4 million/(1–tax rate 0.2)].

(ii) Taxes paid are ($5 million EBT × 0.20) = $1 million (corporate taxes). Withholding taxes paid are $4 million × 0.05 = $0.2 million. Thus, the total taxes paid are $1 million + $0.2 = 1.2 million.

(iii) In USA, the taxes on before-tax income of a subsidiary would have been ($5 million × 0.35) = $1.75 million, out of which, the subsidiary has already paid $1.2 million.

(iv) The tax liability of the US firm, after tax credit adjustment of $1.2 million, will be $0.55 million only ($1.75 million – $1.2 million).

The subsidiary has got tax credit for the entire amount of $1.2 million paid abroad. In case the tax rate is 40 per cent (applicable to subsidiary abroad), the tax credit allowed in the US would then have been limited to 35 per cent ($1.75 million only).

Repatriation of Profits It is not uncommon among third world countries to place restrictions on repatriation of profits, particularly in 'hard' currencies, in view of their limited foreign currency reserves. An equally important factor for restriction may be/is to make more funds available for development. As a result of such restrictions on the movement of foreign currency, the profits/funds available to the parent are reduced. This, in turn, may adversely affect the profitability of the foreign investment project, in particular when the currency of the country where the foreign investments are made is likely to depreciate.

To overcome the problem of blocked funds, MNCs and other international firms have innovated many ways/methods. The commonly used practices include transfer price adjustments on inter-corporate sales, loan repayments and fee and royalty adjustments. Instead of repatriating profits, subsidiary companies, adopt/prefer these methods to remit more funds to the parent. In general, the *modus operandi* of repatriation of funds through these ways is less restrictive.

In case the parent company intends to continue expanding the subsidiary's operations abroad (as they are profitable), repatriation restrictions on profits cease to be relevant as expansion of operation would require funds to be ploughed back in to the project instead of being remitted to the parent company.[7]

Exchange Rate Risk Exchange rate risk is yet another major factor affecting the profitability of foreign investment projects, particularly in the case of countries whose currencies are normally subject to depreciation/devaluation. Adverse exchange rates obviously decrease repatriable cash flows available to the parent in its own 'hard' currency and as a result it entails an unfavourable impact on the profitability of its foreign investment project as illustrated in Example 35.3.

***Example* 35.3**

Assume for **Example 35.1** that the exchange rate of ₹/US dollar during 0–1 year remains unchanged at ₹62/$. For the subsequent 4 years, it is forecasted that the rupee will depreciate vis-à-vis the US dollar by 2 per cent after the first year. As a result, the exchange rates for years 2–5 will be as follows:

Year 2	₹63.24 (₹62 × 1.02)
3	64.50 (63.24 × 1.02)
4	65.7948 (64.50 × 1.02)
5	67.1106 (65.7948 × 1.02)

Given the exchange rate of ₹62/$ in year 1, the equivalent Indian rupees of $125.5 million dollars will be ($125.5 million × ₹62) = ₹7781.0 million. This is the incremental operating CFAT in Indian currency, that the project is expected to generate in all the 5 years, as per Example 35.1 (given the assumption of no variation in exchange rate).

Assuming full repatriation every year, with no withholding taxes and full tax credit available in US, advise the US multinational regarding the financial viability of having a subsidiary in India.

Solution

Determination of NPV *(Amount in million)*

Year	*CFAT*	*Exchange rate (₹/$)*	*$ equivalent*	*PV factor (0.12)*	*Total PV*
1	₹7781	62.00	$125.50	0.893	$112.07
2	7781	63.24	123.04	0.797	98.06
3	7781	64.50	120.63	0.712	85.89
4	7781	65.7948	118.26	0.636	75.21
5	7781	67.1106	115.94	0.567	65.74
5	2480*	67.1106	36.95	0.567	20.95
Gross present value					457.92
Less: Cash outflows					440.00
Net present value					17.92

*Release of working capital will be equivalent to the working capital invested in Indian rupees in time zero period, that is, ($40 million at time zero period × ₹62 exchange rate = ₹2480 million); its conversion in dollars will be at the exchange rate of year 5.

Recommendation Since the NPV is positive at $17.92 million, the opening of a subsidiary in India continues to be financially viable.

Example 35.3 indicates that the NPV with the unfavourable exchange rate has come down by nearly 50 per cent (from $34.98 million to $17.92 million). By interpolation, it implies that the weakening of the Indian rupee at more than 4 per cent in relation to the US dollar would have resulted in negative NPV.

Example 35.3 is further modified to make it more realistic by incorporating withholding taxes on repatriation of profits (which may be partial).

In brief, the relevant cash inflows for evaluating international capital budgeting decisions are those that can be repatriated to the parent company. Format 35.4 contains the procedure of determining such relevant CFAT and NPV of the project.

FORMAT 35.4 Steps for Evaluating Foreign Capital Budgeting Decision from the Perspective of the Parent Company

1. Estimate cash outflows for undertaking foreign investment in the foreign currency (in which repatriation is to be made to the parent company)

2. Determine the expected incremental cash inflows after taxes (CFAT) in the currency of the country where the foreign investment is to be made/subsidiary is to be set up.
3. Determine the expected repatriation of CFAT/funds/profits as per the regulations of the country where foreign investment is made (say 60 per cent/70 per cent)
4. Deduct withholding tax from expected repatriation (as per step 3). The amount so determined is the sum available for repatriation to the parent company. In the terminal year, adjustments are to be carried out for payment of blocked funds, release of working capital (as shown in Example 35.4) and any other payment to be received by the parent.
5. Convert the expected CFAT (as per step 4), in foreign exchange equivalents (say $, £ or the currency of the parent), at the projected exchange rate.
6. Determine the NPV of the project of CFAT (as per step 5) by using the appropriate required rate of return/cost of capital, duly adjusted for the risk the proposed international project carries.
7. Accept the project if the NPV is positive; reject the project in case it is negative.

Example 35.4

Let us further assume that repatriation is allowed to the extent of 70 per cent of CFAT[8] in the first 4 years, accumulated arrears of blocked funds is allowed at the year-end 5 and withholding taxes are 10 per cent. Determine the feasibility of having a subsidiary company in India.

Solution

Determination of NPV *(Amount in million)*

Particulars	*Year 1*	*2*	*3*	*4*	*5*
1. CFAT	₹7781	₹7781	₹7781	₹7781	₹7781
2. *Less:* Retentions (0.3 for *t* = 1–4)	2334.3	2334.3	2334.3	2334.3	—
3. Repatriation made	5446.7	5446.7	5446.7	5446.7	7781
4. *Less:* Withholding taxes (0.10)	544.7	544.7	544.7	544.7	778.1
5. Accessible funds to parent	4902	4902	4902	4902	7002.9
6. *Add:* Repatriation of blocked funds**	—	—	—	—	8403.48
7. *Add:* Recovery of working capital	—	—	—	—	2480
8. ₹/$ Exchange rate	62	63.24	64.5	65.7948	67.1106
9. $ Equivalent (5/8)	$79.06	$77.51	$75.99	$74.50	$266.52
10. Multiply by PV factor (0.12)	0.893	0.797	0.712	0.636	0.567
11. Present value (9 × 10)	70.60	61.73	54.10	47.38	151.12
12. Total present value					384.93
13. *Less:* Cash outflows					440.00
14. Net present value					(55.07)

Recommendation Since the NPV is negative, a subsidiary in India is not financially viable for US multinational.

Working Note

****Repatriation of Blocked Funds, After Withholding Taxes** *(in million)*

Total CFAT (in years 1–4)	₹31,124
Less: Repatriation (0.70 × ₹31124 million)	21,786.8
Funds blocked	9,337.2
Less: Withholding taxes (0.10)	933.72
Funds repatriated (arrears of years 1–4) in year 5	8,403.48

The comprehensive Example 35.4 clearly brings to fore that the finance manager should take into consideration total taxes, extent of repatriation allowed, blocked funds and exchange rate to determine the funds accessible to the parent. The accessible funds should then form the basis of determining NPV to assess true profitability/the financial viability of the foreign investment project.

Expropriation and Other Political Risk

Political risk ranges from mild interference to complete confiscation of all assets of the MNC by the government in a foreign country.

Finally, expropriation risk merits consideration in foreign investment decisions as investment in a foreign country entails political risk. **Political risk** can range from mild interference to complete confiscation of all assets (referred to as outright expropriation). Included in interference are the laws warranting the employment of nationals at various positions, investment in environmental and social projects and restriction on the convertibility of currencies[9]. Political risk can also arise from other reasons. For instance, an incoming foreign government might not honour the previous government's agreement to permit convertibility or the foreign government might impose discriminatory/higher taxes, higher utility charges and so on.[10]

In view of the fact that political risk has a serious influence on the overall risk of a foreign investment project, it merits realistic assessment. The MNCs/international firms should try to ascertain, *inter-alia,* the stability of the government in power, prevailing political wind in case of the change of power, the likely attitude of a new government towards foreign investment, economic stability of the country, fairness and equatibility of the courts/judiciary. Answers to these questions should provide considerable insight into the political risk involved in the foreign investment. Based on these parameters, some companies categorise countries according to their political risk; they avoid investment in countries classified in the undesirable category, irrespective of the potentials of earning higher rates of return.[11]

Since political risk has a profound influence on foreign investment projects, MNCs/international firms evidently prefer investment in countries with stable governments, having stable economic policies and the least political risk of expropriation. Being so important, it should be incorporated in determining NPV. Shapiro has suggested three methods for this purpose. These are **(i)** shortening the minimum payback period, **(ii)** raising the required rate of return of the investment and **(iii)** adjusting cash flows (numerator) to reflect the specific impact of a given risk.[12] The third method can be appropriately used for evaluating foreign investment projects.

LO 35.2 COST OF CAPITAL

The cost of capital for foreign investment projects (like domestic capital budgeting projects) should be based on the weighted overage cost of long-term sources of finance. While computing the cost of capital, cash flows warrant adjustment not only for corporate taxes but also for foreign exchange risk, withholding taxes on repatriations made and so on. The determination of the WACC requires calculation of specific costs of different sources of long-term funds. The procedure of computing various sources of finance—**(i)** debt, **(ii)** preference shares, **(iii)** equity and **(iv)** retained earnings—is now explained.

Cost of Debt

The computation of cost of debt (k_d) is similar to the one used by domestic firms when subsidiary borrows in the host country. Consider Example 35.5.

***Example* 35.5**

The Indian subsidiary of an American MNC has raised ₹50 million to finance its investment requirements by issuing 8-year, 12 per cent debentures in the Indian market. While interest is to be paid annually, the debentures are to be redeemed at year-end 8, at 4 per cent premium. Flotation costs are estimated at 2 per cent. Assume that tax laws in India allow full amortisation of flotation costs in the first year itself, payment of premium in the year in which it is paid and corporate tax of 35 per cent. Determine the effective cost of debt of the Indian subsidiary.

Solution

Cost of debt is determined by solving the following equation:

$$CI_0 = \sum_{t=1}^{8} \frac{COI_t}{(1+k_d)^t} + \frac{COP_8}{(1+k_d)^8}$$

Where COI = Cash outflow of interest in years 1–8, duly adjusted for tax advantage, (₹50 million × 0.12 × 0.65) = ₹3.9 million.

COP_8 = Principal repayment in the year of maturity (t = 8) [₹50 million + 4 per cent premium, i.e., ₹2 million less tax advantage (₹2 million × 0.35) = ₹0.70 million = ₹51.3 million.]

CI_0 = Effective cash inflows/proceeds duly adjusted for flotation cost and tax shield on it as shown below:

(₹ million)

Amount of debentures		₹50.00
Less: Flotation costs (₹50 × 0.02)	₹1	
Tax advantage on flotation costs (₹1 × 0.35)	0.35	0.65
Effective cash proceeds received		49.35

$$\text{Therefore, ₹}49.35 = \sum_{t=1}^{8} \frac{₹3.9}{(1+k_d)^t} + \frac{₹51.3}{(1+k_d)^8}$$

k_d has two elements: (i) the after-tax cost of interest, that is, 12 per cent (1 – 0.35) = 7.8 per cent and (ii) flotation costs in raising funds and payment of premium on redemption of debentures, that is, ₹51.3 million – ₹49.35 million = ₹1.95 million. Evidently, k_d is to be higher than 7.8 per cent to take note of such costs.

While the determination of k_d involves a trial and error process, it is to be 7.8 per cent plus. For calculating how much that would be the rule is simple, ₹1.95 million (₹51.3 million – ₹49.35 million) is the cost of the ₹49.35 million funds that have been raised. It yields 4 per cent effective flotation cost. This 4 per cent is to be spread over in 8 years, which approximately is to 0.5 per cent each year. As a result, the k_d is to be 7.8 per cent + 0.5 per cent = 8.3 per cent. Accordingly, its precise value can be computed by interpolating two rates of discount, namely, 8 per cent and 9 per cent.

Determination of k_d at 8 Per cent and 9 Per cent *(₹ million)*

Years	Cash outflows	PV factor at (%)		Total PV at %	
		8	9	8	9
1 – 8	₹3.9	5.747	5.535	₹22.41	₹21.59
8	51.3	0.540	0.502	27.70	25.75
				50.11	47.34

$$k_d = 8\% + \left(\frac{₹50.11 - ₹49.35 = 0.76}{₹50.11 - ₹47.34 = 2.77}\right) = 8.27 \text{ per cent}$$

In case the subsidiary raises funds from the international markets and not from the host country where it is located, the k_d computation requires adjustment for variation in foreign ex-change rates. The cash outflows exercise should take into account the value of foreign currency (in which borrowings are made) with reference to the currency of the host country (known as the base currency). This is illustrated in Example 35.6.

Example 35.6

From the following facts pertaining to an Indian subsidiary of an American multinational, determine the effective cost of debt to the US parent MNC.

(i) Amount borrowed ₹3,000 million @ 11 per cent, for 6 years.
(ii) Flotation costs are estimated to be ₹12.85 million.
(iii) Interest is to be paid at the end of each year and the principal sum borrowed is to be returned at the end of 6th year.
(iv) Corporate tax applicable to the Indian subsidiary is 35 per cent.
(v) The rupee is expected to depreciate in relation to the US dollar at the rate of 2 per cent each year for 6 years; the current exchange rate of US dollar to the Indian rupee is ₹61.50.
(vi) For tax purposes, total flotation costs can be amortised at a uniform rate during 6 years

Solution

$$₹3{,}000 \text{ million} - ₹12.85 \text{ million} = \sum_{t=1}^{6} \frac{COI_t}{(1+k_d)^t} + \frac{COP_6}{(1+k_d)^6}$$

Where COI_t = Cash outflow on interest payments in time period (t = 1 – 6) after adjusting tax savings on interest payments and flotation costs in US dollars (taking the exchange rate into account).

COP_6 = Repayment of principal sum borrowed at year-end 6

Since cash outflows are to be in US dollars, proceeds of debt are also to be converted into US dollars, that is, (₹3,000 million – ₹12.85 million = ₹2987.15 million/₹61.50) = \$48.5715 million

Determination of Cash Outflows (\$) *(\$ million)*

Year	Cash outflows Interest (1 – 0.35) – Tax savings on flotation costs	Rate of exchange ₹/\$	Cash outflows
1	₹213.75[a]	62.73	\$3.4074
2	213.75	63.984	3.3406
3	213.75	65.264	3.2751
4	213.75	66.5695	3.2109
5	213.75	67.900	3.1480
6	3,213.75[b]	69.2589	46.4019

[a]₹3,000 million × 0.11 = ₹330 million (1 – 0.35) = ₹214.50 million – (Tax savings on flotation costs ₹12.85 million/6 years = ₹2.14 million × 0.35 = 0.75 million) = ₹213.75 million

[b]Includes principal payment at year-end 6 of ₹3,000 million

Based on cash outflows and cash inflows determined k_d will be given by the following equation (amount is in million).

$$\$48.5715 = \frac{\$3.4074}{(1 + k_d)^1} + \frac{\$3.3406}{(1 + k_d)^2} + \ldots + \frac{\$46.4019}{(1 + k_d)^6}$$

Solution of k_d involves trial and error. The hint of rate (k_d) can be inferred from total effective cost of interest paid each year (₹213.75 million) vis-à-vis the net proceeds of borrowings (₹2987.15 million). Based on these figures, k_d = ₹213.75 million/₹2987.15 million = 7.16 per cent. Since the Indian rupee depreciates at 2 per cent, k_d is to be lower as the US MNC gains in terms of a lower payment by 2 per cent of the US dollar. Therefore, the effective cost of debt (k_d) is likely to hover around 7.16 per cent minus 2 per cent = 5.16 per cent. Accordingly, the determination of k_d is attempted at 5 and 6 per cent rates of discount.

Determination of PV at 5 Per cent and 6 Per cent *($ million)*

Year	*Cash outflows*	*PV factor at*		*Total PV at*	
		5%	*6%*	*5%*	*6%*
1	$3.4074	0.952	0.943	3.2438	3.2131
2	3.3406	0.907	0.890	3.0299	2.9731
3	3.2757	0.864	0.840	2.8296	2.7510
4	3.2109	0.823	0.792	2.6425	2.5430
5	3.1480	0.784	0.747	2.4680	2.3515
6	46.4019	0.746	0.705	34.6158	32.7133
Total present value				48.8296	46.5450

$$\text{By interpolation, } k_d = 5\% + \left(\frac{\$48.8296 - 48.5715 = \$0.2581 \text{ million}}{\$48.8296 - 46.5450 = \$2.2846 \text{ million}}\right)$$

$$= 5\% + 0.11\% = 5.11 \text{ per cent.}$$

It may be observed that the computed value of effective cost of debt (5.11 per cent) is very close to the approximate value (5.16 per cent). In fact, the approximate basis of determining the cost of debt (k_d) itself is a measure for its determination, as shown in Equation 36.1.

$$k_d = k_i(1 - t)\ (1 - d)\ (1 + f) - d \qquad \textbf{(35.1)}$$

Where k_i = Coupon rate of interest; t = Corporate tax rate; f = Flotation costs (duly adjusted for taxes); d = Depreciation/devaluation rate of the currency in which borrowings are made with respect to the base currency (US dollar, in the present case). Based on Equation 36.1:

k_d = 11% (1 – 0.35) (1 – 0.02) (1 + 0.0015)* – 2%

= (11% × 0.65 × 0.98 × 1.0015) – 2% = 7.02% – 2% = 5.02%

* Flotation costs are 0.428 per cent; effective after tax flotation costs will be 0.428 per cent – Tax savings on 0.428 × 0.35 = 0.15 per cent.

Between 5.1 per cent and 5.02 per cent, 5.1 per cent value of k_d is precise. Equation 36.1 provides the approximate value. An approximate measure, however, is very useful in determining the precise value of k_d in that it provides a *benchmark rate(s)* at which the trial and error exercise can be worked.

Example 35.6 was based on the depreciation of the currency in which borrowings are made; the impact of such a depreciation in exchange rate has been reflected in a lower cost of debt. Therefore, it is likely to be financially cheaper for foreign companies to borrow in currencies that are likely to depreciate/devalue. In other words, borrowings should be avoided in currencies that are likely to appreciate or be revalued; appreciation in the exchange rate increases the effective cost of borrowings, as shown by Equation 36.2 and Example 35.7.

$$k_d = k_i(1 - t)\,(1 + r)\,(1 + f) + r \qquad \textbf{(35.2)}$$

Where r = appreciation/revaluation rate of the currency in which borrowings are made with respect to the base currency.

***Example* 35.7**

Assume for Example 35.6, that the Indian rupee is likely to appreciate by 2 per cent in relation to the US dollar, each year for 6 years. Determine the effective cost of debt to the US parent.

Solution

(i) k_d = 11% (1 – 0.35) (1 + 0.02) (1 + 0.0015) + 2%
= 7.16% + 2% = 9.16%

(ii) Determination of k_d, based on trial and error

(a) **Determination of Cash Outflows** *(₹& $ in million)*

Year	*Cash outflows**	*Rate of exchange ₹/$*	*Cash outflows*
1	₹213.75	₹60.27	$3.5465
2	213.75	59.064	3.6189
3	213.75	57.8833	3.6928
4	213.75	56.7256	3.7681
5	213.75	55.5911	3.8450
6	3,213.75	54.4792	58.9904

*Taken from solution of Example 35.6.

k_d is given by the following equation (amount is in million $)

$$\$48.5715 = \frac{\$3.5465}{(1+k_d)^1} + \frac{\$3.6189}{(1+k_d)^2} + \ldots + \frac{\$58.9904}{(1+k_d)^6}$$

(b) **Determination of PV at 9 Per Cent and 10 Per Cent** *($ million)*

Years	*Cash outflows*	*PV factor at*		*Total PV at*	
		9%	*10%*	*9%*	*10%*
1	$3.5465	0.917	0.909	$3.2521	$3.2238
2	3.6189	0.842	0.826	3.0471	2.9892
3	3.6928	0.772	0.751	2.8022	2.7260
4	3.7681	0.708	0.683	2.6678	2.5736
5	3.8450	0.650	0.621	2.4993	2.3877
6	58.9904	0.596	0.564	35.1583	33.2706
Gross present value				49.4268	47.1709

$$\text{By interpolation, } k_d = 10\% - \left(\frac{\$48.5715 - \$47.1709 = \$1.4006 \text{ million}}{\$49.4268 - \$47.1709 = \$2.2559 \text{ million}}\right)$$

$$k_d = 10\% - 0.62\% = 9.38 \text{ per cent}$$

The comparison of the effective cost of debt in Examples 36.6 and 36.7 is revealing in that the k_d is slightly less than double when exchange rate of the currency in which borrowings are made appreciates (k_d = 9.38 per cent); the corresponding value of k_d is 5.1 per cent when exchange rate depreciates.

In brief, the finance manager should take into account all the major factors, namely, exchange rate, rate of interest, corporate taxes, flotation costs, mode and timing of payment of interest as well as principal, tax laws applicable to exchange losses/gains, treatment of flotation costs and so on in determining k_d. For *the precise measurement of* k_d, *the IRR based approach should be preferred.*

Cost of Preference Shares

The computation of the cost of preference shares (k_p) is akin to the cost of debt. The stipulated/coupon rate of dividend on preference shares, like the interest on debt, constitutes the basis for the calculation of the cost of preference shares. However, unlike interest payments on debt, dividends payable on preference shares are not tax-deductible. Therefore, no adjustment is required for taxes while computing the cost of preference shares. In view of the non-availability of tax shields on dividends paid, k_p is higher than k_d.

The explicit cost of preference shares is the discount rate that equates the net proceeds of the sale of preference shares with the present value of the future preference dividends and principal repayments. The appropriate formula for determining k_p is given by Equation 35.3.

$$P_o(1-f) = \sum_{t=1}^{n} \frac{DP_t}{(1+k_p)^t} + \frac{P_n}{(1+k_p)^n} \tag{35.3}$$

Where P_o = Expected sale price of preference shares; f = Flotation cost as percentage of P_o; DP = Dividends paid on preference shares; P_n = Repayment of preference capital amount in the year of maturity.

***Example* 35.8**

A US MNC has its subsidiary in India. The subsidiary has issued 12 per cent preference shares of the face value of ₹100, to be redeemed at year-end 8. Flotation costs are expected to be 4 per cent; these costs can be amortised for tax purposes during the 8 years at a uniform rate. The corporate tax rate is 35 per cent. Determine the cost of preference shares from the perspective of the subsidiary.

Solution ₹96 $= \sum_{t=1}^{8} \frac{₹11.825^*}{(1+k_p)^t} + \frac{₹100}{(1+k_p)^8}$

*** Determination of Cash Outflows During Years 1–8**

Dividend payment	₹12.00
Less: Tax advantage on flotation cost [of ₹4/8 years = ₹ 0.5 @ 35%]	0.175
Effective dividend paid/cash outflows	11.825

Accordingly, k_p = ₹96 $= \sum_{t=1}^{8} \frac{₹11.825}{(1+k_p)^t} + \frac{₹100}{(1+k_p)^8}$

Given the rate of preference dividend of 12 per cent, the value of k_p is likely to be between 12 and 13 per cent.

Determination of PV at 12 Per Cent and 13 Per Cent

Year	*Effective cash outflows*	*PV factor at*		*Total PV at*	
		12%	*13%*	*12%*	*13%*
1 – 8	₹11.825	4.968	4.799	₹58.75	₹56.75
8	100.00	0.404	0.376	40.04	37.60
Total present value				98.79	94.35

$$k_p = 12\% + \left(\frac{₹98.79 - ₹96 = ₹2.79}{₹98.79 - ₹94.35 = ₹4.44}\right) = 12\% + 0.63\% = 12.63 \text{ per cent.}$$

Example 35.8 shows the computation of k_p when the foreign subsidiary raises funds in the currency of the country where it is located and payment of dividends as well as of principal repayments are to be made in Indian rupees.

In the event of a Indian subsidiary either raising preference share capital abroad or k_p is to be measured from the perspective of the US parent company, additional calculations in terms of adjustment for foreign exchange variations are required to determine the cost of preference shares. The treatment is akin to cost of debt. Consider Example 35.9.

***Example* 35.9**

Assume for Example 35.6 that the subsidiary has issued 12 per cent preference shares of ₹3,000 million for a 6 years period, with flotation costs of 3 per cent. Determine the effective cost of preference shares to the US parent.

Solution

(i) Determination of Cash Inflows	(₹ million)
Face value of 12 per cent preference shares	₹3,000
Less: Flotation costs (0.03 × ₹3,000 million)	90
Net proceeds received	2,910
Divided by ₹/$ exchange rate	61.50
US $ equivalent received	$47.3170

(ii) Determination of Cash Outflows (t = 1–8)	(₹ million)
Dividend payable on preference shares (0.12 × ₹3,000 million)	₹360
Less: Tax advantage on flotation costs (₹90 million/6 years = ₹15 million × 0.35)	5.25
Effective cash outflows	354.75

(iii) Determination of Cash Outflows in US $ *(million)*

Year	Effective cash outflows	Rate of exchange ₹/$	Cash outflows ($)
1	₹354.75	62.73	$5.6551
2	354.75	63.984	5.5443
3	354.75	65.264	5.4356
4	354.75	66.5695	5.3290
5	354.75	67.900	5.2246
6	3,354.75*	69.2589	48.4378

* Includes redemption sum of ₹3,000 million at year-end 6.

Based on Equation 35.3, k_p =

$$\$47.3170 = \frac{\$5.6551}{(1+k_p)^1} + \frac{\$5.5443}{(1+k_p)^2} + \ldots + \frac{\$48.4378}{(1+k_p)^6}$$

Like k_d, the approximate formula to determine k_p is provided by Equation 36.5.

$$= DP(1 - d)(1 + f) - d \quad \textbf{(35.4)}$$

$$= 12\%\ (1 - 0.02)\ (1 + 0.0195) - 2\%$$

$$= 11.99\% - 2\% = 9.99\% \text{ or } 10 \text{ per cent.}$$

The value of k_p is likely to be between 10 and 11 per cent.

Determination of PV at 10 Per Cent and 11 Per Cent *($ million)*

Year	*Cash outflows*	*PV factor at*		*Total PV at*	
		10%	*11%*	*10%*	*11%*
1	$5.6551	0.909	0.901	$5.1405	$5.0952
2	5.5443	0.826	0.812	4.5796	4.5019
3	5.4356	0.751	0.731	4.0821	3.9734
4	5.3290	0.683	0.659	3.6397	3.5118
5	5.2246	0.621	0.593	3.2444	3.0981
6	48.4378	0.564	0.535	27.3189	25.9142
Total present value				48.0052	46.0946

$$k_p = 10\% + \left(\frac{\$48.0052 \text{ million} - \$47.3170 \text{ million} = \$0.6882 \text{ million}}{\$48.0052 \text{ million} - \$46.0946 = \$1.9106 \text{ million}}\right)$$

$$= 10\% + 0.36\% = 10.36 \text{ per cent.}$$

In the event of the currency in which borrowings are made appreciating vis-à-vis the base currency (US dollar in the present context), Equation 36.5 provides the basis of determining the approximate value of k_p.

$$k_p = DP\,(1 + r)\,(1 + f) + r \tag{35.5}$$

***Example* 35.10**

Assume for Example 35.9 that the Indian rupee is likely to appreciate by 2 per cent each year in relation to US dollar, for 6 years. Determine the effective cost of preference shares from the point of view of the parent company.

$$k_p = 12\%\ (1 + 0.02)\ (1 + 0.0195) + 2\%$$
$$= 12.48\% + 2\% = 14.48 \text{ per cent}$$

Cost of Equity Capital

Two possible approaches can be employed to calculate the cost of equity capital are: **(i)** the dividend approach and **(ii)** the capital asset pricing model (CAPM) approach.

Dividend Approach According to this approach, the cost of equity capital is calculated on the basis of a required rate of return, in terms of the future dividends to be paid on the shares. Accordingly, k_e is defined as the discount rate that equates the present value of all expected future dividends per share with the net proceeds of the sale (or the current market price) of a share. In equation terms,

$$P_o\,(1 - f) = \sum_{t=1}^{n} \frac{D_1\,(1+g)^{t-1}}{(1+k_e)^t} \tag{35.6}$$

Where P_o = Current market price of the equity share, f = Flotation costs as a percentage of market price, and g = Growth in expected dividends

Simplifying Equation 35.6, we get

$$K_e = (D_1/P_o) + g \tag{35.7}$$

Equation 35.6, *inter-alia*, assumes that g is constant. This equation needs to be modified to take note of differing growth rates.

$$P_o = \sum_{t=1}^{n} \frac{D_0\,(1+g_n)^{t=1}}{(1+k_e)^t} + \sum_{t=n+1}^{\infty} \frac{D_n\,(1+g_c)^{t-1}}{(1+k_e)^t} \tag{35.8}$$

Where g_n = Rate of growth in earlier years and g_n = Constant growth in later years

***Example* 35.11**

The following information is available in respect of an Indian subsidiary of a US parent.

Current dividend per share is ₹2

Current market price per share is ₹75

Compound growth rates of dividends (%)	
1 – 5 years	15
6 – 10 years	10
11 years and beyond	5

Determine the cost of equity, assuming a fixed dividend pay out ratio.

Solution

The k_e would be obtained by solving for k_e in the following equation, as it is the case of different growth rates in expected dividends.

$$₹75 = \sum_{t=1}^{5} \frac{\text{Rs } 2\,(1.15)^t}{(1+k_e)^t} + \sum_{t=6}^{10} \frac{D_5\,(1.10)^{t-5}}{(1+k_e)^t} + \sum_{t=11}^{\infty} \frac{D_{10}\,(1.05)^{t-10}}{(1+k_e)^t}$$

The solution of the above equation gives the value of k_e equal to 9.5 per cent.

Capital Asset Pricing Model (CAPM) Approach[15] Another technique that can be used to estimate the cost of equity is the CAPM approach. According to CAPM approach, the k_e is a function of **(i)** the riskless rate of return (normally represented by the rate of return/yield available on long-term treasury bonds of the government of the country), **(ii)** market rate of return (average rate of return on market portfolio—represented in India, by say, the National Stock Exchange Index, NIFTY, and so on) and **(iii)** the beta is the measure of non-deversible/systematic risk. Symbolically,

$$K_e = R_f + b\,(R_m - R_f) \qquad \textbf{(35.9)}$$

Where R_f = Rate of return required on a risk-free investment; R_m = Rate of return expected on the market portfolio; b = Beta coefficient. The value of beta is measured as per Equation 36.10.

$$b = \frac{\text{Co-variance } (R_m, R_f)}{\text{Variance } R_m} \qquad \textbf{(35.10)}$$

The CAPM based equation of determining the cost of equity is in conformity with the basic finance theory related to risk and return, that is, the higher the risk, the higher the cost of equity, or vice versa. Clearly, this is a logical approach to determine k_e.

***Example* 35.12**

The British MNC's equity shares have a beta of 1.5, the British Treasury bonds yield a rate of return of 5 per cent and the return on the market portfolio is 11 per cent. Compute the cost of equity capital of the British multinational.

Solution

$$K_e = 5\%^* + 1.5\,(11\% - 5\%) = 14 \text{ per cent}$$

*Return on British Treasury bonds is a proxy of risk-free rate of return.

The value of beta of 1.5 means that the equity shares of the British multinational is more risky than the average market portfolio. Hence, the required rate of return expected by an equity investor is higher or the cost of equity is higher. It will obviously decrease with decrease in the value of beta. Assume, b is 0.9; k_e is lower at 10.4 per cent, that is, 5% + 0.9 (11% – 5%) = 10.4 per cent. The reason is that the equity securities of the British multinational are less risky than those of the market portfolio.

It is significant to note that foreign companies/MNCs, in general, may have a lower k_e than domestic companies due to the fact that they have access to several foreign capital markets to raise funds.

Cost of Retained Earnings

There is implicit cost of retained earnings i.e., the firm is implicitly required to earn on the retained earnings, at least equal to the rate that would have been earned by the shareholders, if they were distributed to them. Thus, retained earnings involve opportunity cost; the opportunity cost of retention of earnings is the rate of return that could be earned by investing the funds retained in investment opportunities that have the same degree of risk as that of the firm itself. In other words, the rate of return, the equityholders have been deprived of by allowing retentions with the corporate firm, is the cost of retained earnings (k_r). Accordingly, the cost of retained earnings (k_r) for all practical purposes is equal to the cost of equity. Gitman has appropriately referred retained earnings as un-issued equity shares. However, since raising funds through equity involves flotation costs, the k_r is marginally lower.

Apart from the adjustment for flotation costs, the cost of retained earnings in the context of foreign firms may require additional adjustment with respect to withholding taxes, as repatriation of dividends in most countries are subject to such taxes. As a result, k_r gets further reduced, as shown in Equation 35.11.

$$K_r = k_e (1 - wt) (1 - f) \qquad \textbf{(35.11)}$$

Where wt = Withholding taxes on earnings repatriated to the parent company and f = Flotation cost in percentage.

In case, transfer costs are also involved, k_r will be further lower.

$$k_e (1 - wt) (1 - f) (1 - c) \qquad \textbf{(35.12)}$$

Where c = Costs of transfer.

Computation of Overall Cost of Capital

The specific costs are combined together to obtain the overall/composite cost of capital/weighted average cost of capital. While market value weights are theoretically superior to book value weights, book value weights are operationally convenient and more often used in practice. The computation of the overall/weighted average cost of capital (k_o) is illustrated in Example 35.13.

***Example* 35.13**

Given below is the information related to the capital structure of a US based Indian subsidiary.

	Amount (₹ million)	*Specific cost (%)*
Equity share capital	900	15.0
12% Preference share capital	100	12.5
11% Debentures	400	7.5
Retained earnings	600	13.0

Determine the weighted average cost of capital (based on book value weights).

Solution

Computation of Weighted Average Cost of Capital

Source of capital	*Amount (₹ million)*	*Specific cost*	*Total cost (₹ million)*
Equity	900	0.15	135.0
12% Preference share capital	100	0.125	12.5
11% Debentures	400	0.075	30.0
Retained earnings	600	0.13	78.0
	2,000		255.5

K_o = (₹255.5 million/₹2,000 million) × 100 = 12.8 per cent.

LO 35.3 ADJUSTED PRESENT VALUE APPROACH

The concept of single discount rate (based on weighted average cost of capital) is appropriate if the risks are similar for all the foreign investment projects. However, projects with different risks are likely to have different debt capacities and, hence, warrant separate capital structures. For instance, projects with higher business risk (reflected in a high degree of operating leverage) should have equity dominated capital structure. In contrast, projects with lower business risk can afford more debt.

Apart from the varying risk profile of foreign projects, some foreign investments may carry project specific loans at concessional rates of interest. There may be other foreign capital budgeting projects that may require higher cost foreign funds due to home country exchange controls, higher political and economic risk and so on. Obviously, applying a single rate of discount (WACC) to evaluate capital budgeting proposals is not appropriate.

Adjusted present value is the total of present value of (1) cash flows after taxes, (2) interest tax shield and (3) any concessions /subsidies on interest costs.

An alternative approach to WACC is to discount cash flows at a rate that reflects only the business risks of the project[16]. The rate of discount is the *all equity rate* (explained in Chapter 32), to exclude the impact of debt on financing.

When an all equity rate (k_e*) is used as a discount rate in evaluating a capital budgeting proposal, the value of the project can be said to consist of the following three components: **(i)** the present value of CFAT, discounted at k_e*; **(ii)** the PV of interest tax shield and **(iii)** the PV of any subsidies/concessions on interest costs associated with project-specific financing[17]. The **adjusted present value** (APV) of the project is the sum of these three components, as shown in equation 35.13.

$$\text{APV} = \left[\sum_{t=1}^{n} \frac{CFAT_t}{(1+k_e^*)^t} + \sum_{t=1}^{n} \frac{TS_t}{(1+k_i)^t} + \sum_{t=1}^{n} \frac{S_t}{(1+k_i)^t}\right] - CO_o \qquad \textbf{(35.13)}$$

Where TS = Tax savings on interest, S = Value of interest subsidy,
K_i = Before-tax cost of debt, and CO_o = Initial capital cash outflows

In case the APV is positive, the project is worth accepting, otherwise, it merits rejection. It may be noted that the APV approach is similar to the NPV approach. However, the unique feature of the APV approach is that each project is assessed without reference to the firm's other investments and has its own required rate of return.

LO 35.4 MULTINATIONAL WORKING CAPITAL MANAGEMENT

The goals of working capital management in an MNC are the same as those of a domestic firm, that is, to manage the firm's current assets and liabilities in such a way that a satisfactory level of working capital is maintained. The discussion of the working capital management below is made with reference to: **(i)** cash management, **(ii)** credit management and **(iii)** inventory management.

Cash Management

Cash management is one of the key areas of working capital management. Its basic objective is to meet the payment schedule, that is, to have sufficient cash to meet the cash disbursement needs of the firm. In the normal course of business, firms are to make cash payments on a continuous and regular basis to suppliers of goods, employees, bankers and so on.

The importance of sufficient cash to meet the payment schedule can hardly be overemphasised. The major advantages are: **(i)** It helps in fostering good relations with trade creditors and suppliers of raw materials. **(ii)** Good relations are maintained with banks. **(iii)** It leads to a strong credit rating, which enables the firm to purchase goods on favourable terms and to maintain its line of credit with banks and other sources of credit, and **(iv)** Cash discounts can be availed.

Since large cash balances entail high financial costs, international firms/MNCs/foreign subsidiaries (like domestic firms) should maintain *adequate cash balances and not excessive cash balances.*

Like domestic firms, multinational companies can employ the following key cash management strategies to minimise the operating cash balance requirement: **(i)** speedy collection of accounts receivable (by using lock box system and electronic funds transfer); **(ii)** stretching accounts payable (without damaging its credit standing); **(iii)** shift cash as fast as possible from those parts of the business/foreign subsidiaries where it is not needed to those parts/places where it is needed (by using the netting system and currency centre concept). The first two strategies are self explanatory. The concept of currency centre is illustrated in Example 35.14.

Example 35.14

A US multinational has its subsidiaries in India, UK and China. The multinational optimises its inter-subsidiary cash flow using the netting system and currency centre located at its headquarters. Each subsidiary reports its payables to other subsidiaries, on the first day of each month, to the centre. In their report, these subsidiaries also intimate the funds available with them and expected requirement of funds for operations by it in that month.

The currency centre then issues instructions to the net-paying subsidiary on the fifth of each month, using the market exchange rate on that date. Also, the currency centre requires subsidiary companies to transfer their cash surplus to the currency centre. Deficit subsidiaries are asked to cover their temporary needs by drawing on their overdraft facilities with local banks.

Following is the summary of the report sent by three subsidiary companies on March 1.

Subsidiary	*Amounts due to other subsidiary*	*Funds available*	*Funds required for operation March 1–31*
Indian (₹)	£3,000,000 to UK subsidiary		
	CNY 4,000,000 to Chinese subsidiary	₹100,000,000	₹20,000,000
UK (£)	₹32,500,000 to Indian subsidiary		
	CNY 10,000,000 to Chinese subsidiary	£50,000	£2,000,000
China (CNY)	₹150,000,000 to Indian subsidiary		
	£2,000,000 to UK subsidiary	CNY 50,000,000	CNY 20,000,000

Spot exchange rate on March 5, are as follows:

$1 = ₹62.00
£1 = $1.50
$1 = CNY 7.00

(a) Design a netting system for all three subsidiary companies.
(b) Determine the total funds available to the currency centre for money market investment during March.
(c) Which subsidiary will be using local overdrafts and of what amount?

Solution

When positions are reported to the currency centre, the centre will convert these positions to US dollars using the spot exchange rate. The following matrix shows the amount due to and from one subsidiary to the other subsidiary in US dollars.

	Indian subsidiary	UK subsidiary	French subsidiary	Total payable
Indian subsidiary	—	4,500,000	571,428	5,071,428
UK subsidiary	524,194	—	1,428,571	1,952,765
French subsidiary	2,419,355	3,000,000	—	5,419,355
Total receivable	2,943,549	7,500,000	1,999,999	—

The matrix suggests that the Indian subsidiary as well as the Chinese subsidiary have higher total payables than total receivables; the UK subsidiary has higher receivable than payable. In view of these facts, the currency centre issues instructions to the Indian and Chinese subsidiaries to make the following payments to the UK subsidiary in pound sterling.

Indian subsidiary to UK subsidiary = $2,127,879 ($5,071,428–$2,943,549) or £1,418,586 ($2,127,879/$1.5)
French subsidiary to UK subsidiary = $3,419,356 ($5,419,355–$1,999,999) or £2,279,571 ($3,419,356/$1.5)
The following resources are available to the three subsidiary companies after the netting process

Subsidiary	*Currency*	*Total resources available*	*Funds required*	*Surplus or (deficit)*
Indian	₹	₹100,000,000 – 131,928,498@	₹20,000,000	(₹51,928,498)
UK	£	£50,000 + 3,698,157	£2,000,000	£1,748,157
Chinese	CNY	CNY 50,000,000 – 23,935,492	CNY 20,000,000	CNY 6,064,508

@($2,127,879 × ₹62)

As the Indian subsidiary has a net deficit of ₹51,928,498 for the month of March, it will use the local overdraft facility to tide over. The Chinese subsidiary has a surplus of CNY 6,064,508 (or $866,358) and the UK subsidiary has a surplus of £1,748,157 (or $2,622,236). The Chinese and UK subsidiary companies will transfer cash surplus to the centre. As a result, the currency centre will have $3,488,594 ($866,358 + $2,622,236) to carry out money market investment during March.

The temporarily idle cash balances need deployment in appropriate marketable securities to yield extra income. The MNC has also to hedge its undesirable cash and marketable securities against foreign exchange rate risks. This can be achieved by various foreign exchange rate hedging methods (explained in Chapter 35). Forward contracts are by far the most commonly used hedging technique. The other feasible techniques are borrowing or lending in different currencies, future contracts, options, interest rate swaps and currency swaps.

Credit Management

Multinational firms located in different countries compete for the same global export markets. Being so, it is imperative that they offer attractive/liberal credit terms to potential customers While the favourable credit terms are desirable to enhance sales and hence profits, MNCs should ensure that the risk/cost of default is lower than the incremental profits expected from such liberal credit terms because granting credit is more risky in the international context. In particular, such an exercise is required in the case of sales/exports to developing countries (given the risks associated with such sales and their lack of 'hard' currency). To minimise the risk, MNCs should seek the backing of their respective governments in extending credit.[18]

Risk also emanates from exchange rate fluctuations on account of time lag between when the sale is made and time when collections are made from debtors Hedging can reduce this type of risk, but at a cost. In general, cost incurred in hedging techniques (such as options, forward contracts) may outweigh the benefit. Therefore international firms should adopt the appropriate hedging technique(s) to minimise exchange rate risk, particularly with respect to export sales made to less developed countries, as their currencies are prone to depreciation/devaluation.

Finally, it will be useful to apply the "leads and lags" technique for advancing or delaying settlements, both in respect of debtors and creditors, as per the need (explained in Chapter 35).

Inventory Management

The task of inventory management in the case of multinational firms is more complex than that of domestic firms, particularly when foreign subsidiaries encounter the following situations:

(i) When a foreign subsidiary is located in a country having a high rate of inflation, it may be profitable, *prima-facie*, to accumulate more stocks than otherwise needed. However, carrying inventory involves costs, in particular, interest costs; such costs tend to be high in countries experiencing inflation. Therefore, MNCs should undertake a cost-benefit analysis before taking the decision of carrying more stocks. This becomes all the more important if foreign subsidiaries are located in politically unstable countries and run the threat/risk of expropriation of assets.

(ii) When the foreign subsidiary is located far from the market supplying the goods, the consideration will have to be given to potential delays in getting the goods from central storage locations to user locations, all around the world. There is a need to maintain both working stocks and safety stocks at each user location as well as at the strategic storage centres. The problem gets compounded in case the foreign subsidiaries are imposed with property taxes on assets, including inventories. In such cases the tax is on the holdings, on specific days, say, 31st December/31st March. Such rules then warrant that the foreign subsidiary should have a low inventory on these dates. To achieve that, it should hold safety stocks in different countries/locations at different times during the year[19]. Clearly, the problem of physical location of inventories is more acute in the case of foreign firms *vis-à-vis* domestic firms.

(iii) Finally, the MNC and its subsidiaries are to deal with, *inter-alia*, adverse exchange rate fluctuations, tariffs, non-tariff barriers, and other similar problems, generally when they are located in less developed nations.

LO 35.5 EXTERNAL COMMERCIAL BORROWINGS (ECBs)

External Commercial Borrowings (ECBs): ECBSs are commercial loans raised by eligible resident entities from recognised non-resident entities and should conform to parameters such as minimum maturity, permitted and non-permitted end-uses, maximum all-in-cost ceiling and so on. The parameters apply in totality and not on a standalone basis. The framework for raising loans through ECBs (ECB Framework) comprises the following three tracks: **Track I**: Medium term foreign currency denominated ECBs with minimum average maturity of 3-5 years. **Track II**: Long term foreign currency denominated ECBs with minimum average maturity of 10 years. **Track III**: Indian Rupee (INR) denominated ECBs with minimum average maturity of 3-5 years.

External commercial borrowings refer to commercial loans in the form of bank loans, buyer's credit, securities instruments, such as floating rate notes and fixed interest bonds availed from non-resistent lenders with minimum average maturity of 3 years.

Forms of ECBs

The ECB Framework enables permitted resident entities to borrow from recognized non-resident entities in the following forms: **(i)** Loans including bank loans,

(ii) Securitised instruments (e.g. floating rate notes and fixed rate bonds, non-convertible, optionally convertible or partially convertible preference shares / debentures), **(iii)** Buyers' credit, **(iv)** Suppliers' credit, **(v)** Foreign Currency Convertible Bonds (FCCBs), **(vi)** Financial lease and **(vii)** Foreign Currency Exchangeable Bonds (FCEBs). However, ECB framework is not applicable in respect of the investment in non-convertible debentures (NCDs) in India made by registered Foreign Portfolio Investors (FPIs).

Available Routes for Raising ECBs

The ECBs can be raised either under the automatic route or under the approval route. For the automatic route, the cases are examined by the Authorised Dealer Category-I (AD Category-I) banks. Under the approval route, the prospective borrowers are required to send their requests to the RBI through their ADs for examination. While the regulatory provisions are mostly similar, there are some differences in the form of amount of borrowing, eligibility of borrowers, permissible end-uses, and so on under the two routes. While all the above forms of borrowing can be raised both under the automatic and approval routes, FCEBs can be issued only under the approval route.

Parameters for ECBSs

The various parameters of raising loan under ECB framework are mentioned below:

Minimum Average Maturity Period: The minimum average maturities for the three tracks are:

Track I **(i)** 3 years for ECBs upto USD 50 million or its equivalent.

(ii) 5 years for ECBs beyond USD 50 million or its equivalent.

(iii) 5 years for eligible borrowers in infrastructure sector;non-banking financial companies-infrastructure finance companies (NBFC-IFCs); NBFCs-asset finance companies (NBFCs-AFCs); holding companies; and core investment companies (CISs) irrespective of the amount of borrowing;

(iv) 5 years for (FCCBs)/ (FCEBs) irrespective of the amount of borrowing. The call and put option for FCCBs would not be exercisable prior to 5 years.

Track II 10 years irrespective of the amount

Track III Same as under Track I.

Eligible Borrowers The list of entities eligible to raise ECBs under the three tracks is set out below: **Track I (i)** Companies in manufacturing and software development sectors, **(ii)** Shipping and airlines companies,**(iii)** Small Industries Development Bank of India (SIDBI), **(iv)** Units in Special Economic Zones (SEZs) **(v)** Export Import Bank of India (Exim Bank) (only under the approval route), **(vi)** Companies in infrastructure sector, Non-Banking Financial Companies - Infrastructure Finance Companies (NBFCIFCs), NBFCs-Asset Finance Companies (NBFC-AFCs), Holding Companies and Core Investment Companies (CICs), **(vii)** Housing Finance Companies regulated by the NHB, **(viii)** Port trusts.

Track II (i) All entities listed under Track I, **(ii)** Real Estate Investment Trusts (REITs) and Infrastructure Investment Trusts (INVITs) coming under the SEBI regulatory framework, **(iii)** Housing Finance Companies regulated by the NHB, **(iv)** Port trusts.

Track III (i) All entities listed under Track II, **(ii)** All Non-Banking Financial Companies (NBFCs) under the regulatory purview of the RBI, **(iii)** NBFCs-Micro Finance Institutions (NBFCs-MFIs), Not-for-Profit companies, societies, trusts and cooperatives, Non-Government Organisations (NGOs) which are engaged in micro-finance activities, **(iv)** Companies engaged in miscellaneous services, namely, research and development (R&D), training (other than educational institutes), companies supporting infrastructure, companies providing logistics services, **(v)** Developers of Special Economic Zones (SEZs)/ National Manufacturing and Investment Zones (NMIZs), **(vi)** HFCs regulated by the NHB, **(vii)** Port trusts.

Notes: Entities engaged in micro-finance activities to be eligible to raise ECB should have a (i) satisfactory borrowing relationship for at least three years with an AD Category I bank in India, and (ii) certificate of due diligence on 'fit and proper' status from the AD Category I bank.

Recognised Lenders/Investors: The list of recognised lenders / investors for the three tracks is as follows:

Track I: (i) International banks, **(ii)** International capital markets, **(iii)** Multilateral financial institutions (such as, IFC, ADB, etc.) / regional financial institutions and Government owned (either wholly or partially) financial institutions, **(iv)** Export credit agencies, **(v)** Suppliers of equipment, **(vi)** Foreign equity holders. **(vii)** Overseas long term investors such as: (a) Prudentially regulated financial entities; (b) Pension funds; (c) Insurance companies; (d) Sovereign Wealth Funds; (e) Financial institutions located in International Financial Services Centres in India and **(viii)** Overseas branches / subsidiaries of Indian banks.

Track II: All entities listed under Track I except overseas branches / subsidiaries of Indian banks.

Track III: All entities listed under Track I except overseas branches / subsidiaries of Indian banks. In case of NBFCs-MFIs, other eligible MFIs, not for profit companies and NGOs, ECBs can also be availed from overseas organisations and individuals*.

Notes:

- Overseas branches/subsidiaries of Indian banks can be lenders only under Track I. Further, their participation is subject to the prudential norms issued by the RBI.
- Overseas Organizations proposing to lend ECBs would have to furnish to the authorised dealer bank of the borrower a certificate of due diligence from an overseas bank, which, in turn, is subject to regulation of host-country regulators and such host country adheres to the Financial Action Task Force (FATF) guidelines on anti-money laundering (AML)/ combating the financing of terrorism (CFT). The certificate of due diligence should comprise the following: that **(i)** the lender maintains an account with the bank at least for a period of two years, **(ii)** the lending entity is organised as per the local laws and held in good esteem by the business/local community, and **(iii)** there is no criminal action pending against it.
- Individual lender has to obtain a certificate of due diligence from an overseas bank indicating that the lender maintains an account with the bank for at least a period of two years. Other evidence /documents such as audited statement of account and income tax return, which the overseas lender may furnish, need to be certified and forwarded by the overseas bank. Individual lenders from countries which do not adhere to FATF guidelines on AML / CFT are not eligible to extend ECBs.

All-in-Cost (AIC): The all-in-cost requirements for the three tracks are as under:

With a view to harmonising the provisions of foreign currency/rupee FCBs and RDBs, a uniform all-in cost ceiling of 450 basis points over the benchmark rate would be applicable. The benchmark rate would be 6 months USD LIBOR or applicable benchmark for respective currency, for Track I and Track II, while it would be the prevailing yield of GOI securities for corresponding maturity for Track III.

End-use Prescriptions The end-use prescriptions for ECBs raised under the three tracks are given in the following manner:

All the three categories of borrowers (Track I, II, and III) and not permitted to invest in (i) real estate/ purchase of land except when used for affordable housing/construction and development of SEZs/ industrial parks, integrated townships, (ii) capital market and (iii) equity shares. In addition, Tracks I and III borrowers cannot invest for (i) working capital/general corporate purposes, (ii) repayment of rupee loans except when raised from direct/indirect equity holders or from a group company and the loan is for a minimum average maturity of 5 years. Finally, all the three category of companies are prohibited from on-lending to entities for all the activities specified above.

Individual Limits: The individual limits refer to the amount of ECBs which can be raised in a financial year under the automatic route.

(i) The individual limits of ECBs that can be raised by eligible entities under the automatic route per financial year for all the three tracks are: (a) Up to USD 750 million or equivalent for the companies in infrastructure and manufacturing sectors, NBFC-IFCs, NBFC-AFCs, Holding Companies and Core Investment Companies(CICs); (b) Up to USD 200 million or equivalent for companies in software development sector; (c) Up to USD 100 million or equivalent for entities engaged in micro-finance activities; and (d) Up to USD 500 million or equivalent for remaining entities.

(ii) The ECB proposals beyond aforesaid limits will come under the approval route. For computation of individual limits under **Track III**, The exchange rate prevailing on the date of agreement should be taken into account.

(iii) In case the ECBs is raised from direct equity holder, the specified individual ECB limits will also be subject to ECBs liability: equity ratio requirement. For ECBs raised under the automatic route, the ECBs liability of the borrower (including all outstanding ECBSs and the proposed one) towards the foreign equity holder should not be more than four times of the equity contributed by the latter. For ECBs raised under the approval route, this ratio should not be more than 7:1. This ratio will not be applicable if total of all ECBs raised by an entity is up to USD 5 million or equivalent.

Notes: For the purpose of ECBs liability: equity ratio, the paid-up capital, free reserves (including the share premium received in foreign currency) as per the latest audited balance sheet can be reckoned for calculating the 'equity' of the foreign equity holder. Where there are more than one foreign equity holders in the borrowing company, the portion of the share premium in foreign currency brought in by the lender(s) concerned should only be considered for calculating the ratio.

Currency of Borrowing: The ECBs can be raised in any freely convertible foreign currency as well as in Indian rupees. In case of Rupee denominated ECBs, the non-resident lender, other than foreign equity holders, should mobilise Indian Rupees through swaps/outright sale undertaken through an AD Category-I bank in India. The change of currency of ECBs from one convertible foreign currency to any other convertible foreign currency as well as to INR is freely permitted. The change of currency from INR to any foreign currency is, however, not permitted. The change of currency of ECBs into INR can be at the exchange rate prevailing on the date of the agreement between the parties concerned for such change or at an exchange rate which is less than the rate prevailing on the date of agreement if consented to by the ECBs lender.

Hedging Requirements

The eligible borrowers should have a Board approved risk management policy and keep their ECBs exposure hedged 100 per cent at all times. Further, the designated AD Category-I bank should verify that 100 per cent hedging requirement is complied with during the currency of ECBs and report the position to RBI through ECBs returns. Also, the entities raising ECBs under the provisions of **Tracks I and II** should follow the guidelines for hedging issued by the concerned sectoral or prudential regulator in respect of foreign currency exposure.

Wherever hedging has been mandated by the RBI, the following should be ensured. The ECBs borrower will cover principal as well as coupon through financial hedges. The financial hedge for all exposures on account of ECBs should start from the time of each such exposure (i.e. the day liability is created in the books of the borrower). A minimum tenor of one year of financial hedge would be required with periodic rollover duly ensuring that the exposure on account of ECBs is not unhedged at any point during the currency of ECBs. The natural hedge, in lieu of financial hedge, will be considered only to the extent of offsetting projected cash flows / revenues in matching currency, net of all other projected outflows. An ECB may be considered naturally hedged if the offsetting exposure has the maturity/cash flow within the same accounting year. Any other arrangements/ structures, where revenues are indexed to foreign currency will not be considered as natural hedge.

Security for raising ECBs The AD Category-I banks are permitted to allow creation of charge on immovable assets, movable assets, financial securities and issue of corporate and/ or personal guarantees in favour of overseas lender / security trustee, to secure the ECBs to be raised / raised by the borrower, subject to satisfying themselves that: **(i)** the underlying ECBs is in compliance with the extant ECBs guidelines, **(ii)** there exists a security clause in the Loan Agreement requiring the ECBs borrower to create charge, in favour of overseas lender / security trustee, on immovable assets / movable assets / financial securities / issuance of corporate and / or personal guarantee, and **(iii)** No objection certificate, as applicable, from the existing lenders in India has been obtained.

Additional Conditions: Once the aforesaid stipulations are met, the AD Category-I bank may permit creation of charge on immovable assets, movable assets, financial securities and issue of corporate and / or personal guarantees, during the currency of the ECBs with security co-terminating with underlying ECBs, subject to the following:

Creation of Charge on Immovable Assets The arrangement should be subject to the following:

(i) The security should subject to provisions contained in the Foreign Exchange Management (Acquisition and Transfer of Immovable Property in India) Regulations, 2000,

(ii) The permission should not be construed as a permission to acquire immovable asset (property) in India, by the overseas lender/ security trustee,

(iii) In the event of enforcement / invocation of the charge, the immovable asset/ property will have to be sold only to a person resident in India and the sale proceeds repatriated to liquidate the outstanding ECBs.

Creation of Charge on Movable Assets In the event of enforcement/ invocation of the charge, the claim of the lender, whether the lender takes over the movable asset or otherwise, will be restricted to the outstanding claim against the ECBs. The encumbered movable assets may also be taken out of the country subject to getting 'No Objection Certificate' from domestic lender/s, if any.

Creation of Charge over Financial Securities The arrangements may be permitted subject to the following:

(i) Pledge of shares of the borrowing company held by the promoters as well as in domestic associate companies of the borrower is permitted. Pledge on other financial securities, namely, bonds and debentures, Government Securities, Government savings certificates, deposit receipts of securities and units of the Unit Trust of India or of any mutual funds, standing in the name of ECBs borrower/promoter, is also permitted,

(ii) In addition, security interest over all current and future loan assets and all current assets including cash and cash equivalents, including Rupee accounts of the borrower with ADs in India, standing in the name of the borrower/promoter, can be used as security for ECBs. The

Rupee accounts of the borrower/promoter can also be in the form of escrow arrangement or debt service reserve account,

(iii) In case of invocation of pledge, transfer of financial securities should be in accordance with the extant FDI/FII policy including provisions relating to sectoral cap and pricing as applicable read with the Foreign Exchange Management (Transfer or Issue of Security by a Person Resident outside India) Regulations, 2000.

Issue of Corporate or Personal Guarantee The arrangement should be subject to the following:

(i) A copy of Board resolution for the issue of corporate guarantee for the company issuing such guarantee, specifying name of the officials authorised to execute such guarantees on behalf of the company or in individual capacity should be obtained,

(ii) Specific requests from individuals to issue personal guarantee indicating details of the ECBs should be obtained,

(iii) The security shall be subject to provisions contained in the Foreign Exchange Management (Guarantees) Regulations, 2000, and

(iv) ECBs can be credit enhanced / guaranteed / insured by overseas party/ parties only if it/ they fulfil(s) the criteria of recognised lender under extant ECB guidelines.

Issuance of Guarantee

Issuance of guarantee, standby letter of credit, letter of undertaking or letter of comfort by Indian banks, All India Financial Institutions and NBFCs relating to ECB is not permitted. Further, they should not invest in FCCBs in any manner whatsoever.

Debt Equity Ratio

The ECB liability to equity ratio for ECBs raised from direct foreign equity holder under the automatic route would be 7 : 1 if the total of all ECBs raised by an entity exceeds USD 5 million or equivalent.

Parking of ECBs proceeds

The ECB proceeds are permitted to be parked abroad as well as domestically in the manner given below:

Parking of ECB Proceeds Abroad The ECB proceeds meant only for foreign currency expenditure can be parked abroad pending utilisation. Till utilisation, these funds can be invested in the following liquid assets: (a) deposits or Certificate of Deposit or other products offered by banks rated not less than **AA (–)** by Standard and Poor/ Fitch IBCA or Aa3 by Moody's; (b) Treasury bills and other monetary instruments of one year maturity having minimum rating as indicated above and (c) deposits with overseas branches/ subsidiaries of Indian banks abroad.

Parking of ECB Proceeds Domestically The ECB proceeds meant for Rupee expenditure should be repatriated immediately for credit to their Rupee accounts with AD Category I banks in India. The ECB borrowers are also allowed to park ECB proceeds in term deposits with AD Category I banks in India for a maximum period of 12 months. These term deposits should be kept in unencumbered position.

Conversion of ECBs into Equity

The conversion of ECBSs, including those which are matured but unpaid, into equity is permitted subject to the following conditions:

(i) The activity of the borrowing company is covered under the automatic route for Foreign Direct Investment (FDI) or approval, for foreign equity participation has been obtained as per the extant FDI policy;

(ii) The conversion, which should be with the lender's consent and without any additional cost, will not result in breach of applicable sector cap on the foreign equity holding;

(iii) The applicable pricing guidelines for shares are complied with;

(iv) The applicable reporting requirements are fulfilled; and

(v) If the borrower concerned has availed of other credit facilities from the Indian banking system, including overseas branches/subsidiaries, the applicable prudential guidelines issued by the RBI, including guidelines on restructuring are complied with; and

(vi) Consent of other lenders, if any, to the same borrower is available or at least information regarding conversions is exchanged with other lenders of the borrower.

Exchange Rate for Conversion of ECBs Dues into Equity: For conversion of ECBs dues into equity, the exchange rate prevailing on the date of the agreement between the parties concerned for such conversion or any lesser rate can be applied with a mutual agreement with the ECBs lender. The fair value of the equity shares to be issued should be worked out with reference to the date of conversion only.

LO 35.6 EURO ISSUES

As a part of globalising the Indian economy after 1991, Indian corporates are permitted to float their securities in, and raise funds from, the Euro markets. The two long-term primary instruments of Euro issues are Foreign Currency Convertible Bonds (FCCBs) and Global Depository Receipts/Certificates (GDRs)/American Depository Receipts/Certificates (ADRs). **A FCCB** means a bond subscribed by an non-resident in foreign currency and convertible into ordinary shares of the issuing company in India in any manner, wholly or in part, on the basis of any equity related warrants attached to the debt instruments. **A GDR/ADR** means any instrument in the form of a depository receipt/certificate, by whatever name called, created by the Overseas Depository Bank (ODB) outside India and issued to non-resident investors against the issue of ordinary shares or FCCBs of the issuing company. A bank authorised by the issuing company to issue GDRs/ADRs against the issue of FCCBs/ordinary shares of the issuing company is known as an ODB. The scheme for facilitating issue of FCCBs and ordinary shares through the GDR/ADR mechanism by Indian companies is discussed below.

Foreign currency convertible bonds are subscribed by a non-resident in a foreign currency and convertible into ordinary shares of the issuing company in India.

American/ Global depository receipts implies an instrument in the form of a depository receipt/ certificate issued to non-resident investors against the issue of ordinary shares of the issuing Indian company.

Eligibility for Issue of Convertible Bonds or Ordinary Shares of Issuing Company

An issuing company desirous of raising funds by issuing FCCBs or ordinary shares for equity issues through GDR/ADR is required to obtain the prior permission of the Department of Economic Affairs, Ministry of Finance, Government of India. It may sponsor an issue of ADRs/GDRs with an overseas depository against shares held by its shareholders, at a price determined by the lead manager with respect to disinvestment of their holdings by shareholders of Indian companies that are **(i)** listed in India, **(ii)** not listed in India, but listed overseas. Such a facility would be available *pari passu* to all categories of shareholders of the company whose shares are being sold in the ADR/GDR market overseas. An approved intermediary under the scheme would be an investment banker registered with the Securities and Exchange Commission in the USA, or under the Financial Services Authority in UK, or the appropriate regulatory authority in Germany, France, Singapore or in Japan. Such issues would need to conform to the foreign direct investment policy and other mandatory statutory requirements and detailed guidelines issued in this regard.

An Indian company which is not eligible to raise funds from the Indian capital including a company restrained by the SEBI from accessing the securities market would not be eligible to issue FCCBs and ordinary shares through GDRs. Unlisted Indian companies issuing GDRs/FCCBs should be simultaneously listed in the Indian stock exchange(s). However, if they have taken verifiable *effective steps* would be exempt from the requirement of simultaneous listing. ***Effective steps*** mean that **(1)** it has completed due diligence and filed offering circular in the overseas exchange(s), or **(2)** the approval of the overseas stock exchange(s) has been obtained, or, **(3)** the listing fee is paid, or **(4)** approval of the RBI for meeting issue-related expenses has been obtained. Private placement of issues, where no offering circular was placed before the overseas stock exchange(s), would not qualify for effective steps.

The issuing company should have a consistent track record of good performance (financial or Otherwise) for a minimum period of three years, on the basis of which an approval for finalising the issue structure would be issued to the company. On finalising the issue structure (discussed subsequently in this Section) in consultation with the lead manager to the issue, the issuing company should obtain the final approval from the Government for proceeding ahead with the issue.

FCCBs should be denominated in any convertible foreign currency and ordinary shares of an issuing company should be denominated in Indian rupees. The issued ordinary shares or bonds should be delivered to a DCB who would instruct the ODB to issue GDR/ADR certificates to non-resident investors against the shares or bonds held by it. A DCB means a banking company that acts as a custodian for ordinary shares/FCCBs of an Indian company, which are issued by it against GDRs/ADRs certificates. A GDR may be issued in negotiable form and may be listed on any international stock exchange for trading outside India. The provision of any law relating to the issue of capital by an Indian company would apply in relation to the issue of FCCBs or ordinary shares of an issuing company and it should obtain the necessary permission or exemption from the appropriate authority, under the relevant law, in this regard.

An Indian company which is not eligible to raise funds from the Indian capital market cannot issue FCCBs and ordinary shares through GDRs. Unlisted Indian companies issuing GDRs/FCCBs should be simultaneously listed in the Indian stock exchange(s). The OCBs (overseas corporate bodies) who are not eligible to invest in India through portfolio routes and entities prohibited by SEBI to buy/sell/deal in securities are not eligible to subscribe to FCCBs/ordinary shares through GDRs/ADRs.

Limits of Foreign Investment in the Issuing Company The ordinary shares and FCCBs issued against GDRs/ADRs should be treated as direct foreign investment in the issuing company. The aggregate of the foreign investment, made either directly or indirectly through GDR/ADR mechanism, should not exceed 51 per cent of the issue and the subscribed capital of the issuing company.

Issue Structure of the GDRs/ADRs A GDR/ADR may be issued for one or more underlying shares or bonds held with the domestic custodian bank (DCB). GDRs/FCCBs may be denominated in any freely convertible foreign currency. The ordinary shares underlying the GDRs and the shares issued upon conversion of the FCCBs should be denominated only in Indian currency. The following issues would be decided by the issuing company with the lead manager to the issue, namely: **(a)** public or private placement; **(b)** number of GDRs/ADRs to be issued; **(c)** the issue price. For listed companies: the pricing should not be less than the higher of the average of weekly high and low of the closing prices of the related shares quoted on the stock exchange during **(i)** the 6 months, **(ii)** the two weeks preceding the relevant date (i.e. the date 30 days prior to the date on which the meeting of the shareholders is held to consider the proposed issue). Companies issuing GDRs that have taken verifiable "effective steps" would be exempt from these requirements. For unlisted companies: the pricing should be in accordance with the RBI regulations. Listed companies going in for an offering in the domestic market and a simultaneous or immediately following on offering (i.e. within 30 days of domestic issue) through ADRs/GDRs issues wherein GDRs/ADRs are priced at/above the domestic price would be exempt from the above requirement. Such companies would have to take SEBI's approval for such issue which would specify the percentage to be offered in the domestic and ADR/GDR markets; **(d)** the rate of interest payable on FCCBs; and **(e)** the conversion price, coupon rate, and the pricing of the conversion options of the FCCBs. The conversion price of the FCCBs of listed companies should be similar to the issue price. They would be exempt from this requirement if they have taken the verifiable effective steps. The conversion price of FCCBs of unlisted companies should be in accordance with the RBI regulations. There would be no lock-in period for GDRs/ADRs. The pricing for listed companies as well as the conversion price of the FCCBs should not be less than the higher of the average of the weekly high and low of the closing prices of the related shares quoted in the stock exchange during **(i)** 2 weeks or **(ii)** 6 months preceding the relevant date (i.e. the date 30 days prior to the date on which the proposed issue is considered in the general meeting of the shareholders). The pricing for unlisted companies as well as the conversion price of the FCCBs should be according to the RBI regulations under FEMA.

Listing

The GDRs/ADRs may be listed on any of the overseas stock exchanges, or over the counter exchanges or through the book entry transfer system prevalent abroad. They may be purchased, possessed and freely transferable by a person who is a non-resident.

Transfer and Redemption

A non-resident holder of GDRs/ADRs may transfer them, or may ask the ODB to redeem them. In the case of redemption, the ODB should requires the DCB to get the corresponding underlying shares released in favour of the non-resident investor, for being sold directly on his behalf, or transferring them in the name of the non-resident in the books of account of the issuing company. The redeemed GDRs and underlying shares sold may be re-issued to the extent of such redemption and sale made in the domestic market. Such re-issuance should be in terms of the Foreign Exchange Management (Transfer or Issue of Security by a Person Resident Outside India) Regulations, 2000, as amended from time to time, and the guidelines issued in this regard. In case of redemption of the GDRs/ADRs into underlying shares, a request for the same should be transmitted by the ODB to the DCB in India, with a copy of the same being sent to the issuing company for information and record. On redemption, the cost of acquisition of the shares underlying the GDRs/ADRs would be reckoned as the cost on the date on which the ODB advises the DCB regarding redemption. The price of the ordinary shares of the issuing company prevailing in the Bombay Stock Exchange or the National Stock Exchange on the date of the advice of redemption should be taken as the cost of acquisition of the underlying ordinary shares. For the purpose of conversion of FCCBs, the cost of acquisition in the hands of non-resident investors would be the conversion price which is determined on the basis of the price of the shares at the Bombay Stock Exchange or the National Stock Exchange on the date of conversion into shares.

Taxation of Foreign Currency Convertible Bonds

Interest payments on bonds, until the conversion option is exercised, would be subject to deduction of tax at source at the rate of ten per cent. Tax on dividend on the converted portion of the FCCB would be subject to deduction of tax at source at the rate of ten per cent. Conversion of FCCBs into shares would not give rise to any capital gains liable to income tax in India. Transfer of FCCBs made outside India by a non-resident investor to another non-resident investor would not give rise to any capital gains liable to tax in India.

Taxation on Shares Issued Under GDR Mechanism

Under the provisions of the Income tax Act, income by way of dividend on shares issued under the GDR/ADR mechanism would be taxed at the rate of 10 per cent. The issuing company should transfer the net dividend payments after remitting tax at source to the ODB. On receipt of these payments, the ODB should distribute them to non-resident investors, proportionate to their holdings of GDRs/ADRs evidencing relevant shares. The holders may take credit for the tax deducted at source on the basis of certification by the ODB, if permitted by the country of their residence. All trading transactions of GDRs/ADRs outside India, among non-resident investors, would be free from any liability to income-tax in India on capital gains therefrom. If any capital gains arise from the transfer of the aforesaid shares in India to the non-resident investor, he would be liable to income tax under the provisions of the Income tax Act. If the aforesaid shares are held by the non-resident investor for a period of more than twelve months from the date of advice of their redemption by the ODB, the capital gains arising from the sale thereof would be treated as long-term capital gains and would be subject to income tax at the rate of 10 per cent under the provisions of Section 115-AC of the Income tax Act. If such shares are held for a period of less than twelve months from the date of redemption advice, the capital gains arising from the sale thereof would be treated as short-term capital gains and would be subject to tax at the normal rates of income tax applicable to non-residents under the provisions of the Income tax Act. After the redemption of GDRs/ADRs into underlying shares, during the period, if any, in which these shares are held by the redeeming non-resident foreign investor who has paid for them in foreign exchange at the time of its purchase, the rate of taxation of income by way of dividend on these shares would continue to be at the rate of 10 per cent, in accordance with Section 115-AC(1) of the Income tax Act. The long-term capital gains on the sale of these redeemed underlying shares held by non-resident investors in the domestic market would also be charged tax to the rate of 10 per cent, in accordance with the provisions of Section 115-AC(1). When the redeemed shares are sold on Indian stock exchanges against payment in rupees, these shares would go out of the purview of Section 115-AC of the Income tax Act and income therefrom would not be eligible for concessional tax treatment provided thereunder. After the transfer of shares, where consideration is in terms of rupees payment, normal tax rates would apply to the income arising or accruing from these shares. Deduction of tax at source on the amount of capital gains accruing from transfer of the shares would be made in accordance with Sections 195 and 196-C of the Income tax Act.

Application of Avoidance of Double Taxation Agreement in Case of Global/American Depository Receipts

During the period of fiduciary ownership of shares in the hands of the ODB, the provisions of Avoidance of Double Taxation Agreement, entered into by the Government of India with the country of residence of the ODB, would be applicable in the matter of taxation of income from dividends from underlying shares and interest on FCCBs. During the period, if any, when the redeemed underlying shares are held by the non-resident investor on transfer from the fiduciary ownership of the

ODB, before they are sold to resident purchasers, the Avoidance of Double Taxation Agreement entered into by the Government of India with the country of residence of the non-resident investor would be applicable in the matter of taxation of income from the dividends of the said underlying shares, or interest on FCCBs, or any capital gain arising out of transfer of underlying shares.

Gift Tax and Wealth Tax

Holding of GDRs/ADRs in the hands of non-resident investors and holding of the underlying shares by the ODB in a fiduciary capacity and the transfer of the GDRs/ADRs between non-resident investors and the ODB would be exempt from wealth tax under the Wealth tax Act, 1957, and from gift tax under the Gift tax Act, 1958.

LO 35.7 FOREIGN CURRENCY EXCHANGEABLE BONDS

A foreign currency exchangeable bond (FCEB) means a bond expressed in foreign currency, the principal and interest in respect of which is payable in foreign currency, issued by an Indian (issuing) company and subscribed to by a resident outside India and exchangeable into equity shares of another company (i.e. an **offered company** whose equity shares would be offered in exchange of the FCEB) in any manner either wholly or partly or on the basis of an equity related warrants attached to debt instruments. The main elements of the FCEB scheme, 2008 are discussed in this section.

FCEB means a bond expressed in foreign currency, the principal and interest in respect of which is payable in foreign currency, issued by an Indian (issuing) company and subscribed to by a person who is a resident outside India in foreign currency and exchangeable into equity shares of another company.

Eligibility Conditions

The issuing company should be part of the promoter group of the offered company and hold the equity shares being offered at the time of issuance of the FCEBs. The offered company should be a listed company engaged in a sector eligible **(i)** for FDI and **(ii)** to issue/avail of FCCBs/ECBs. An Indian company, which is not eligible to raise funds from the Indian securities market and has been restrained from accessing the securities market by the SEBI, cannot issue the FCEBs. The subscribers to the FCEBs should comply with the FDI policy and adhere to the sectoral caps at the time of issuance of the FCEBs. Prior approval of the FIPB, if required under the FDI policy, should be obtained. **Entities** prohibited to buy/sell/deal in securities by the SEBI are not eligible to subscribe to the FCEBs.

End-Use Requirements

The proceeds of the FCEBs may be invested by the issuing company in the promoter group companies who can use the proceeds in accordance with the end-user prescribed under the ECBs policy. (**These are discussed in section 5 of this chapter**). The investee promoter group company would not be able to utilise the proceeds/funds for investment in **(i)** the capital market, and **(ii)** real estate in India.

The issuing company may invest the proceeds of the FCEBs overseas by way of direct investment including in joint ventures/wholly owned subsidiaries subject to the guidelines in force in this respect.

Operational Procedure

The issuance of the FCEBs, which may be denominated in any freely convertible currency, would require the prior approval of the RBI.

All-in-Cost, Pricing and Maturity

The rate of interest payable on the FCEBs and the issue expenses incurred in foreign currency should be within the all-in-cost ceiling specified by the RBI under the ECBs policy. At the time of issuance of the FCEBs, the exchange price of the offered listed equity shares should not be less than the higher of the average of the weekly high and low of the closing prices of the shares of the offered company quoted on the stock exchange during the **(i)** six months, and **(ii)** two weeks preceding in the **relevant date**, that is, the date on which the Board of Directors of the issuing company passes the resolution authorising the issue of the FCEBs.

The minimum maturity of the FCEBs should be five years for redemption purposes. The exchange option can be exercised at any time before redemption. While exercising the option, the holders of the FCEBs should take delivery of the offered shares. Cash (net) settlement would not be permissible.

Mandatory Requirements

The issuing company should comply with the provisions of the Companies Act and obtain necessary approvals of its Board of Directors/shareholders, if necessary. Similarly, the offered company should also obtain the approval of its Board of Directors in favour of the FCEBs proposal of the issuing company. The issuing company should comply with all the applicable provisions of the SEBI Act/Rules/Regulations/Guidelines with respect to disclosures of their shareholding in the offered company. It should **(i)** not transfer/mortgage/offer as collateral/trade in the offered shares, and **(ii)** keep the offered shares free from all encumbrances from the date of issuance of the FCEBs till the date of exchange/redemption.

Retention/Deployment of Proceeds

The proceeds of the FCEBs should be retained and/or deployed overseas by the issuing/promoter group companies in accordance with the policy for the proceeds of the ECBs. The issuing company should ensure that the FCEB proceeds are used by the promoter group company(ies) only for the permitted end-uses prescribed under the ECB policy. It should also submit audit trail of end-uses of the proceeds to the RBI duly certified by the designated AD bank.

Taxation

The interest payments on the FCEBs, until the exchange option is exercised, would be subject to deduction of tax at source under the provisions of Section 115-AC (1) of the Income Tax Act. The tax on dividend on the exchange portion of the FCEBs would be in accordance with the provisions of Section 115-AC (1) of the Income Tax. The exchange of the FCEBs into shares would not give rise to any capital gains liable to tax in India. The transfer of the FCEBs made outside between investors resident outside India would also not give rise to any capital gains liable to tax in India.

SUMMARY

LO	Summary
LO 35.1	International financial management is concerned with decisions related to multinational capital budgeting, cost of capital, working capital and sources of international finance.
	Comparative cost advantage, financial diversification and tax/fiscal incentives are the major motivating factors for undertaking investment abroad by MNCs.
	Foreign capital budgeting decisions are to deal with a number of complex issues/problems such as exchange rate risks, expropriation risk, blocked funds, foreign tax regulations and political risk. Therefore, they are relatively more difficult decisions to evaluate vis-à-vis domestic investment decisions.
	Relevant data consisting of incremental cash outflows required to execute a foreign investment proposal and projected incremental cash inflows after taxes (CFAT) expected from the proposed foreign capital budgeting decision during its economic useful life are the major inputs for its evaluation.
	Since total CFAT tends to overstate profitability of the foreign investment proposal, it is important to draw distinction between the total CFAT such an investment proposal generates and the incremental CFAT, the firm eventually has. The difference between the two sets of CFAT may arise due to: (i) cannibalisation, (ii) sales accretion, (iii) opportunity cost, (iv) treatment of fixed overheads and (v) fees and royalties.
	Cannibalisation implies the lost sales of the firm's existing product(s) on account of proposed foreign investment. Accordingly, the adverse effect of cannibalisation in terms of lost profit due to lost sales is to be deducted from total CFAT to arrive at incremental CFAT. In contrast, the positive impact of increased profits due to sales accretion of the existing products of the parent company should be reckoned in determining incremental CFAT.
	While the allocation of the existing overheads and fees and royalties charged from the subsidiary by the parent merit exclusion, opportunity cost of existing resources used in undertaking a new investment proposal should be considered.
	In foreign capital budgeting decisions, there may be a substantial difference between the CFAT of the foreign investment project at the subsidiary level vis-à-vis that of the parent firm. The major factors causing the difference are: (i) double taxation of foreign income accruing to the parent company without giving any credit for corporate taxes as well as withholding taxes paid by the subsidiary company in the host country, (ii) exchange controls affecting repatriation of funds, (iii) inflation and interest rate differentials between the host country and the parent country affecting exchange rates, and so on. Being so, it is suggested that cash flows should be determined at the level of parent corporate firm as well as at subsidiary level separately.
	Political risk also has a profound influence on the overall risk of a foreign investment proposal. Political risk can range from mild interference to complete confiscation of all assets/or outright expropriation. In view of gravity of political risk, MNCs prefer investment in countries with stable governments, having stable economic policies and the least political risk of expropriation.
LO 35.2	Cost of capital (another major input) for foreign investment proposals (like domestic capital budgeting proposals) should be based on the weighted average cost of long-term sources of finance, namely, equity share capital, preference share capital, debentures, long-term loan/ debt and retained earnings. The weighted average (instead of simple average) is desired as the relative proportions of various sources of finance are different.
	While retained earnings have implicit costs, other sources of long-term finance have explicit costs.
	The explicit cost of any source of capital is the discount rate that equates the present value of the incremental cash inflows with the present value of its incremental cash outflows. In terms of equation:
	$CI_0 = \sum_{t=1}^{n} \frac{CO_t}{(1+k)^t}$

In the context of international finance, cash flows are to be adjusted for foreign exchange risk, flotation costs, corporate taxes, tax laws (regarding treatment of exchange losses and gains, withholding, repatriation of funds and amortisation of flotation costs), transfer costs involved in repatriation of funds, and so on.

LO 35.2

Cost of capital applicable to investment proposals of foreign subsidiaries should be based both on the origin of funds and risk involved in such proposals.

Retained earnings represent undistributed profits of the corporate firm belonging to equity shareholders. Being so, the cost of retained earnings is equivalent to the opportunity cost of investing these funds in a similar risk-class of companies by the shareholders themselves. However, in effect, it is lower than the cost of equity as is evident from the following equation:

$K_r = k_e (1 - Wt)(1 - f)$

The dividend approach and the capital asset pricing model (CAPM) approach are used to compute cost of equity (k_e). According to the dividend approach, k_e is defined as the discount rate that equates the present value of all expected dividends per share with the net proceeds of the sale/market price of share. In equation terms:

$$P_0 (1 - f) = \sum_{t=1}^{n} \frac{D_1 (1+g)^{t-1}}{(1+k_e)^t}$$

According to CAPM approach, the k_e is a function of (i) riskless rate of return (R_f), (ii) market rate of return (R_m) and (iii) beta. Symbolically,

$$K_e = R_f + b(R_m - R_f)$$

Where b = Covariance (R_m, R_f)/Variance R_m

Weighted average cost of capital (WACC/k_0), in equation terms is:

$$K_0 = k_e W_e + k_p W_p + k_d W_d + k_r W_r$$

While market value weights (W) are theoretically superior to book value weights, book value weights are operationally convenient and more often used in practice.

Applying a single rate of discount (k_0) to evaluate capital budgeting proposals is not appropriate in case the risks are different for various foreign investment proposals. Adjusted present value (APV) approach is an alternative approach to the WACC.

LO 35.3

According to the APV approach cash flows (CFAT) are to be discounted at an all equity rate (k_e*) that reflects only the business work so as to exclude the impact of debt financing. To this present value (PV) are added (i) the PV of interest tax shield (TS) and (ii) the PV of subsidies/concessions on interest costs (S_t) associated with project-specific financing. In terms of equation:

$$APV = \left[\sum_{t=1}^{n} \frac{CFAT_t}{(1+k_e^*)^t} + \sum_{t=1}^{n} \frac{TS_t}{(1+k_i)^t} + \sum_{t=1}^{n} \frac{S_t}{(1+k_i)^t} \right] - CO_0$$

LO 3.4

The basic objectives of cash management of the MNCs (like domestic firm) is to meet the cash disbursement needs of the firm and to minimise funds committed to cash balances. For the purpose, the MNCs, *inter-alia,* should instruct foreign subsidiaries to remit cash as fast as possible when it is not needed to those places where it is needed (by using the netting system and currency center concept).

MNCs should hedge its undesirable cash and marketable securities against foreign exchange rate risks. Forward contracts are by far the most commonly used hedging technique; others are borrowing or lending in different currencies, future contracts and options.

LO 3.4	In the context of credit management, the MNCs should ensure that (i) the risk/cost of default is lower than the incremental profits expected from granting credit, (ii) the risk from exchange rate fluctuations is hedged in particular for export credit sales to developing countries and (iii) the FERM technique ('leads and lags' indexation clause and others) are used as per the need.
	As far as inventory management is concerned, the MNCs (having subsidiaries all around the world) should maintain both working stocks and safety stocks at each user location as well as at the strategic storage centers. To ensure minimum payment of property taxes on assets (including inventories), it should hold safety stocks in different countries/locations at different times during the year.
LO 35.5	The Government of India permits Indian corporates to raise finance through external commercial borrowings (ECBs) only from internationally recognised sources. The ECBs include commercial bank loans, suppliers' credit securitised instruments such as floating rate notes (FRNs) and fixed rate bonds (FRBs) from non-resident lenders. The ECBs can be used for (i) investment, (ii) overseas client investment, (iii) first stage acquisition of shares in PSU disinvestments and (iv) lending to self-help groups/micro-finance. The RBI's operational guidelines relate to automatic route and approval route.
LO 35.6	Besides ECBs, Indian corporates are permitted to float their securities (known as euro issues) in the euro markets. There are two long-term euro issues: (i) Foreign Currency Bonds (FCCBs) and (ii) Global Depository Receipts (GDRs)/American Depositary Receipts (ADRs).
	A FCCB means a bond subscribed by a non-resident in foreign currency and convertible into ordinary shares of the issuing company in India, wholly or in part, on the basis of any equity related warrants attached to the debt instruments.
	A GDR/ADR means any instrument in the form of a depository receipt/certificate, created by the Overseas Depository Bank outside India and issued to non-resident investors against the issue of ordinary shares or FCCBs of the issuing company.
	Issue of FCCBs and ordinary shares through the GDR/ADR mechanism by Indian companies are to conform guidelines issued by the Government/RBI in this regard. Among others, the guidelines relate to (i) issue structure (i.e., the number of GDRs/ADRs to be issued, the issue price, the interest rate payable on FCCBs, conversion price, coupon rate, and so on), (ii) lis-ting, (iii) transfer and redemption, (iv) taxation.
LO 35.7	An Indian company can issue FCEB expressed in foreign currency the principal and interest in respect of which is payable in foreign currency and subscribed by a person who is resident outside India in foreign currency and exchangeable into equity shares of another company (i.e. offered company) in any manner, either wholly/partly or on the basis of any equity related warrants attached to a debt instrument.
	The proceeds of the FCEB may be invested by the issuing company in the promoter group companies which would use the proceeds in accordance with the end-users prescribed under the ECBs policy. They may also be invested overseas by way of direct investment including in JVs/WOS.
	The interest and the issue expenses should be within the all-in-cost ceiling specified by the RBI under the ECBs policy.
	The exchange price of the offered listed equity shares should not be less than the higher of the average of the weekly high and low of the closing prices quoted on the stock exchange during (i) six months, (ii) two weeks preceding the relevant date. The minimum maturity of the FCEB should be five years for redemption purposes.
	Interest payments on the FCEBs until the exchange option is exercised would be subject to deduction of tax at source. Tax on dividends on the exchanged portion of the FCEB would be in accordance with Section 115-AC(1) of the income-tax Act. The exchange of the FCEB into shares would not give rise to any capital gains tax.

REFERENCES

1. Shapiro, Alan C, *Multinational Financial Management*, John Wiley and Sons, New York: 2001, p. 718.
2. Rodriguez, R M and E E Carter, *International Financial Management*, Prentice Hall, New Jersey: 1984, p. 428.
3. Shapiro, Alan C, *op. cit.*, p. 720.
4. Shapiro, Alan C, *op. cit.*, p. 722.
5. Shapiro, Alan C, *op. cit.*, p. 725.
6. It is beyond the scope of this book to describe tax laws of various countries.
7. Rodriguez, R M and E E Carter, *op. cit.*, pp. 443–44.
8. From the perspective of financial management it is more logical to relate to CFAT as repatriation is not restricted to profits only.
9. Van Horne, James C, *Financial Management and Policy*, Prentice Hall of India, New Delhi: 2000, p. 653.
10. Emery, D R and John D Finnerty, *Corporate Financial Management*, Prentice Hall, New Jersey: 1997, pp. 984–5.
11. Van Horne, James C, *op. cit.*, p. 653.
12. Shapiro, Alan, C, *op. cit.*, p. 727. These methods have been explained in Chapter 3 of this book.
13. Porterfield, J T S, *Investment Decisions and Capital Costs*, Prentice Hall, Englewood Cliffs: 1965, p. 45.
14. Shapiro, Alan C, *op. cit.*, p. 724.
15. For details of CAPM, refer to Chapter 9 of this book.
16. Shapiro, Alan C, *op. cit.*, p. 724.
17. Shapiro, Alan C, *op. cit.*, p. 724.
18. Gitman, L J, *op. cit.*, p. 850.
19. Brigham, E F and J F Houston, *Fundamentals of Financial Management*, Harcourt Asia Pvt. Ltd., Singapore: 2001, pp. 861–2.

SOLVED PROBLEMS

P.35.1 A US MNC is planning to install a manufacturing unit to produce 5,00,000 units of an automobile component in India. Setting up of the manufacturing plant will involve an investment outlay of ₹50 million. The plant is expected to have a useful life of 5 years with ₹10 million salvage value. MNC will follow the straight-line method of depreciation. To support the running of business, working capital of ₹5 million, will have to be invested; variable cost of production and sales will be ₹20 per unit. Additional fixed cost per annum are estimated at ₹2 million. The forecasted selling price is ₹70 per unit. The MNC will be subjected to 40 per cent tax rate in India and its required rate of return is 15 per cent.

LO 35.1 LOD M

It is forecasted that the rupee will depreciate in relation to US dollar @ 3 per cent per annum, with an initial exchange rate of ₹58/$. Accordingly, the exchange rates for the relevant 5-year period of the project will be as follows:

Year	*Exchange rate*
0	₹58/$
1	59.74/$
2	61.53/$
3	65.80/$
4	67.24/$
5	69.26/$

Advise the MNC regarding the financial viability of the proposal.

Solution ***Financial viability of proposal (NPV method)***

I. Incremental cash outflow at $t = 0$	
Cost of the plant	₹50,000,000
Working capital	5,000,000
	55,000,000
Equivalent to \$ (₹55,000,000/₹58)	\$948,275
II. Incremental CFAT for year t = 1–5	
Sales revenue (500,000 × ₹70)	₹35,000,000
Less: Costs:	
Variable (500,000 × ₹20)	10,000,000
Fixed cost	2,000,000
Depreciation (₹40 million/5 years)	8,000,000
Earning before tax	15,00,000
Less: Taxes (0.40)	6,000,000
EAT	9,000,000
Add: Depreciation	8,000,000
CFAT (t = 1 to 5)	17,000,000
Additional CFAT in the 5th year	
Release of working capital	5,000,000
Salvage value of plant	10,000,000
	15,000,000

Conversion of rupees into \$

Year	*CFAT*	*Exchange rate*	*CFAT*
1	₹17,000,000	₹59.74/\$	\$284,566
2	17,000,000	61.53/\$	276,287
3	17,000,000	65.80/\$	258,358
4	17,000,000	67.24/\$	252,825
5	32,000,000	69.26/\$	462,027

III. Determination of NPV

Year	*CFAT (\$)*	*PV factor at 15 per cent*	*Total PV (\$)*
1	284,566	0.870	247,572
2	276,287	0.750	207,215
3	258,358	0.658	169,999
4	252,825	0.572	144,616
5	462,027	0.497	229,627
Gross present value			999,029
Less: Cash outflow			948,275
Net present value			50,754

IV. **Recommendation** Since the NPV is positive, the project should be accepted.

P.35.2 An Indian company is planning to set up a subsidiary in the US. The initial project cost is estimated to be US dollar 400 million; working capital requirements are estimated at US dollar 40 million. The Indian company follows the straight-line method of depreciation. **LO 35.1** LOD M

The finance manager of the Indian company estimated data in respect of the project as follows: (i) variable cost of production and sales \$25 per unit, (ii) fixed cost per annum are estimated at \$30 million (iii) plant will be producing and selling 50 million units at \$100 per unit and (iv) the expected economic useful life of the plant is 5 years with no salvage value.

The subsidiary of the Indian company is subject to 40 per cent corporate tax rate in the US and the required rate of return of such a project is 12 per cent. The current exchange rate between the two countries is ₹58/US dollar and the rupee is expected to depreciate by 3 per cent per annum for next five years.

The subsidiary will be allowed to repatriate 70 per cent of the CFAT every year along with the accumulated arrears of blocked funds at year-end 5, the withholding taxes are 10 per cent. The blocked funds will be invested in the USA money market by the subsidiary, earning 4 per cent (free of tax) per year.

Determine the feasibility of having a subsidiary company in the USA, assuming no tax liability in India on earnings received by the parent from the US subsidiary.

Solution

(i) Cash outflows (t = 0) *(figures in million)*

Cost of plant and machinery		$400
Working capital requirement		40
		440
Incremental cash outflow in rupees ($440 million × ₹58)		₹25,520

(ii) Cash inflows after taxes *(figures in million)*

Sales revenue (5.0 million units × $100)		500
Less: Costs:		
Variable cost (5.0 million units × $25)	$125	
Fixed cost	30	
Depreciation ($400 million/5 year)	80	235
Earning before taxes		265
Less: Taxes (0.40)		106
Earning after taxes		159
Add: Depreciation		80
CFAT (T = 1 – 4)		239
CFAT in 5th year:		
Operating CFAT	239	
Add: Release of working capital	40	279

Determination of NPV *(amount in million)*

Particulars	Year 1	2	3	4	5
Operating CFAT	$239	$239	$239	$239	$239
Less: Retention	71.7	71.7	71.7	71.7	–
Repatriation made	167.3	167.3	167.3	167.3	167.3
Less: Withholding tax	16.7	16.7	16.7	16.7	23.9
Accessible funds to parent	150.6	150.6	150.6	150.6	215.1
Add: Repatriation of blocked funds*	—	—	—	—	274
Add: Recovery of working capital	—	—	—	—	40
₹/$ exchange rate	59.74	61.53	65.80	67.24	69.26
Rupee equivalent	8,997	9,266	9,909	10,126	50,497
PV factor (0.12)	0.893	0.797	0.712	0.636	0.567
Present value	8,034	7,385	7,055	6,440	28,632
Total present value					57,546
Less: Cash outflow					25,520
Net present value					₹32,026

Recommendation Since the NPV is positive, having a subsidiary in the US is financially viable for the Indian company.

* *Repatriation of blocked funds after withholding taxes*

Future value in year 5 of blocked funds of 71.7 million each during $t = 1$ to 4 years invested at 4 per cent per year = 4.246 × 71.7 million = 304.44 million – 30.44 million withholding tax = 274 million.

P.35.3 A US based plastic manufacturer is considering a proposal to produce of high quality plastic glasses in India. The necessary equipment to manufacture the glasses would cost ₹1 lakh in India and it would last 5 years The tax relevant rate of depreciation is 25 per cent on written down value. The expected salvage value is ₹10,000. The glasses will be sold at ₹4 each. Fixed cost will be ₹25,000 each year and variable cost ₹2 per glass. The manufacturer estimates it will sell 75,000 glasses per year; tax rate in India is 35 per cent. The US manufacturer assumes 20 per cent cost of capital for such a project. Additional working requirement will be ₹50,000.

LO 35.1 LOD D

The US manufacturer will be allowed 100 per cent repatriation each year with a withholding tax rate of 10 per cent. Should the proposal of setting up a manufacturing unit in India be accepted by the US manufacturer? Spot and expected exchange rates are as follows:

Spot	₹60/$
Year-end 1	60
2	60
3	62
4	62
5	62

Solution

Cash outflow	
Cost of production equipment	₹1,00,000
Additional working capital	50,000
	1,50,000
Cash outflow in dollar (1 $ = ₹60)	$2,500

Determination of CFAT and NPV

Particulars	*Years*				
	1	*2*	*3*	*4*	*5*
Sales revenue (75,000 × ₹4)	₹3,00,000	₹3,00,000	₹3,00,000	₹3,00,000	₹3,00,000
Less: Costs:					
Variable cost (75,000 × ₹2)	1,50,000	1,50,000	1,50,000	1,50,000	1,50,000
Fixed cost	25,000	25,000	25,000	25,000	25,000
Depreciation	25,000	18,750	14,062	10,547	—
Earning before taxes	1,00,000	1,06,250	1,10,938	1,14,453	1,25,000
Less: Taxes	35,000	37,187	38,828	40,059	43,750
Earning after taxes	65,000	69,063	72,110	74,394	81,250
CFAT	90,000	87,813	86,172	84,941	81,250
Recovery of working capital					50,000
Salvage value					10,000
Tax benefit on short-term capital loss*					7,574
Withholding tax	9,000	8,781	8,617	8,494	14,882
Repatriated amount	81,000	79,032	77,556	76,447	1,33,942
Repatriated amount in dollar	$1,350	1,317	1,251	1,233	2,160
Multiplied by PV factor 0.20	0.833	0.694	0.579	0.482	0.402
Present value	1,125	914	724	594	868
Total present value (t = 1 – 5)					$4,225
Less: Cash outflow					2,500
Net present value					1,725

*(₹1,00,000 – ₹68,359, accumulated depreciation – ₹10,000, salvage value) × 0.35 = ₹7,574.

Recommendation As the NPV is positive the US manufacturer is advised to take up the proposal.

P.35.4 A USA based company is planning to set up a software development unit in India. Software developed at the Indian unit will be bought back by US parent at transfer price of US dollar 10 million. The unit will remain in existence in India for one year; as the software is expected to get developed within this time frame. LO 35.1 LOD E

The US based company will be subject to corporate tax of 30 per cent and withholding tax of 10 per cent in India and will not be eligible for tax credit in the US. The software developed will be sold in the US market for US dollar 12.0 million. Other estimates are as follows:

Rent for fully furnished unit with necessary hardware in India	₹15,00,000
Man power cost (80 software professional will be working for 10 hours each day)	₹400 per man hour
Administrative and other costs	12,00,000

Advise US company on financial viability of the project. The rupee-dollar rate is ₹60/$.

Solution

Proforma profit and loss account of the Indian software development unit.

Revenue		₹60,00,00,000
Less: Costs:		
Rent	₹15,00,000	
Manpower (₹400 × 80 × 10 × 365)	11,68,00,000	
Administrative and other costs	12,00,000	11,95,00,000
Earning before tax		48,05,00,000
Less: Tax		14,41,50,000
Earning after tax		33,63,50,000
Less: Withholding tax		3,36,35,000
Repatriation amount *(in rupees)*		30,27,15,000
Repatriation amount *(in dollars)*		$5.04 million

So the cost of developing software in India for the US based company is $5.04 million. And as the USA based Company is expected to sell the software in the US at $12.0 million, it is advised to develop the software in India.

P.35.5 The Indian subsidiary of an American multinational is planning to raise ₹100 million to finance its investment requirement by issuing 5 year bonds in the Indian market. The coupon rate of the bond will be 10 per cent, payable annually. The principal amount will be repaid at the end of the 5th year. The flotation cost is 5 per cent and the subsidiary is subject to 35 per cent tax in India. The current exchange rate is ₹58/US dollar and the rupee is expected to depreciate in relation to the US dollar at the rate of 3 per cent each year, for the next 5 years LO 35.2 LOD M

Determine the effective cost of debt to the US parent MNC. Assume tax laws in India allow full amortisation of flotation costs in the year in which it is incurred.

Solution

Cash inflow at $t = 0$

(i) Issue of debt		₹100 million
Less: Effective flotation cost (₹100 million × 0.05)	₹5 million	
Tax advantage on flotation cost (₹5 million × 0.35)	1.75	3.25
	96.75	
In dollar terms (₹96.75 million/₹58)		US $1,668,103

Cash Outflow

Year	Amount (in ₹ million) Interest	Tax advantage	Effective interest paid (cash outflows)	Exchange rate	Cash outflow in US dollar
1	₹10	₹3.5	₹6.5	₹59.74/US $	US $108,804
2	10	3.5	6.5	61.5322	105,635
3	10	3.5	6.5	63.3781	102,559
4	10	3.5	6.5	65.2795	99,571
5	10	3.5	6.5	67.2379	96,671
5	100*	—	—	69.2550	1,443,939

* Principal payment

So, if K_d is effective cost of debt, then

$$(CI)t = 0 = \frac{CO_1}{(1+k_d)^1} + \frac{CO_2}{(1+k_d)^2} + \frac{CO_3}{(1+k_d)^3} + \frac{CO_4}{(1+k_d)^4} + \frac{CO_5}{(1+k_d)^5}$$

$$\$1{,}668{,}103 = \frac{\$108{,}804}{(1+k_d)^1} + \frac{\$105{,}635}{(1+k_d)^2} + \frac{\$102{,}559}{(1+k_d)^3} + \frac{\$99{,}571}{(1+k_d)^4} + \frac{96{,}671}{(1+k_d)^5} + \frac{1{,}443{,}939}{(1+k_d)^5}$$

'or' K_d = 3.15 per cent.

P.35.6 An Indian company has borrowed $1 million at 5 per cent from the US market for two years. The Indian company has covered its debt exposure on the forward market. The rates are as follows: spot rate—₹61/US dollar, one year forward—₹61.50/US dollar and two year forward—₹62/US dollar. Interest is to be paid annually. The principal amount will be paid at the end of year two. The tax rate applicable for the company is 35 per cent. What is the effective cost of debt?

LO 35.2 LOD M

Solution

Cash inflow at (t = 0)

in dollars = $1,000,000 in rupees = ₹48,000,000

Cash Outflow

Year	Particulars	Dollar amount	Exchange rate	Rupee amount	Tax shield on interest	Net rupee outflow
1	Interest payment	$50,000	₹61.5/US dollar	₹3,075,000	₹10,76,250	₹19,98,750
2	Interest payment	50,000	62	3,100,000	10,85,000	20,15,000
2	Principal repayment	1,000,000	62	62,000,000	–	62,000,000

$$K_d = (CI)_{t=0} = \frac{CO_1}{(1+k_d)^1} + \frac{CO_2}{(1+k_d)^2}$$

$$₹61 \text{ million} = \frac{₹19{,}98{,}750}{(1+k_d)^1} + \frac{₹20{,}15{,}000}{(1+k_d)^2} + \frac{₹62{,}000{,}000}{(1+k_d)^2}$$

Or K_d = 2.75 per cent.

P.35.7 An Indian subsidiary of an American multinational borrows in India at the rate of 11 per cent. The subsidiary is subject to a tax rate of 35 per cent. The anticipated average annual devaluation of the Indian rupee in relation to US dollar is 2 per cent. Compute the cost of debt to the multinational.

LO 35.2 LOD E

Solution K_d $= K_i(1 - t)(1 - d) - d$

Where K_i = Interest/Coupon rate

t = Corporate tax rate
d = Expected currency depreciation
K_d = (0.11) (1 – 0.35) (1 – 0.02) – 0.02 = 0.05 or 5 per cent.

P.35.8 The liabilities in the balance sheet of a US based company are:

LO 35.2 LOD M

The cost of equity capital is 15 per cent and the cost of debt is 6 per cent in the US. The US based company is planning to start a subsidiary in India. The Indian subsidiary will be making an investment of ₹100 million. The interest rate in India is 10 per cent and the Indian rupee is expected to depreciate at the rate of 3 per cent per year. Tax rate in India is 35 per cent. The US company wants to maintain the capital structure of the Indian subsidiary in line with the parent's capital structure. What will be the cost of capital if the subsidiary is financed by the parent company and through Indian loans?

Owner's capital	US dollar 400 million
Debts	600
Total	1,000

Solution Debt and equity are in the proportion of 3:2 in the capital structure of the parent company. This implies that the Indian subsidiary will have ₹40 million of equity and ₹60 million of debt.

The cost of the equity capital is that of the parent, i.e., 15 per cent; the cost of debt would be 0.10 (1 – 0.35) (1 – 0.03) – 0.03 = 0.033 or 3.3 per cent.

So, the *weighted average cost of capital* would be: (15 × 40/100 + 3.3 × 60/100) = 7.98 per cent.

P.35.9 In year 1 a US based MNC floated an euro denominated bond issue in Europe with a coupon rate of 3 per cent, sold at par. In year 2 the euro appreciated against the US dollar by 2 per cent. What was the effective borrowing cost in year 2, given that the US based MNC has a marginal income tax rate of 40 per cent? If in year 1, the MNC could have sold a similar bond issued in the US (denominated in US dollar) at par with coupon rate of 4.5 per cent, which market could have afforded a lower borrowing cost?

LO 35.2 LOD M

Solution

(i) Effective borrowing cost in euro-denominated bonds
k_d = 3% (1 – 0.4) (1 + 0.02) + 2% = 3.836 per cent

(ii) Cost of the US bonds issued at par with a coupon rate of 4.5 per cent
(0.045) (1 – 0.4) = 0.027 or 2.7 per cent
Evidently, the US bond market would have afforded a lower borrowing cost.

P.35.10 ICM Computers Inc. has a subsidiary in country X producing computer components and it sells them to another subsidiary in country Y. The subsidiary in country Y uses those components to produce computers. The tax rate in country X is 40 per cent and in country Y, the tax rate is 20 per cent. The proforma income statement of the ICM subsidiaries are shown below:

LO 35.3 LOD D

ICM Computers income statement

Particulars	*Subsidiary X*	*Subsidiary Y*	*Consolidated figures*
Sales	$1,000,000	$2,500,000	$3,500,000
Cost of goods sold	500,000	1,000,000	1,500,000
Gross profit	500,000	1,500,000	2,000,000
Operating expenses	250,000	500,000	750,000
EBIT	250,000	1,000,000	1,250,000
Interest expenses	50,000	250,000	300,000
EBT	200,000	750,000	950,000
Taxes	80,000	150,000	230,000
EAT	120,000	600,000	720,000

If ICM Computers adjusts its transfer pricing policy so that sales by subsidiary X are reduced from $1,000,000 to $750,000, determine the effect on the net profit of ICM Computers from the two subsidiaries. Should ICM Computers go ahead with the proposal?

Solution If ICM Computers adjusts its transfer pricing policy, cost of goods of subsidiary Y will come down from $1,000,000 to $750,000 and the income statement (revised) will be as follows:

ICM Computers income statement

Particulars	*Subsidiary X*	*Subsidiary Y*	*Consolidated figures*
Sales	$750,000	$2,500,000	$3,250,000
Cost of goods sold	500,000	750,000	1,250,000
Gross profit	250,000	1,750,000	2,000,000
Operating expenses	250,000	500,000	750,000
EBIT	0	1,250,000	1,250,000
Interest expenses	50,000	250,000	300,000
EBT	(50,000)	1,000,000	950,000
Taxes	0	200,000	200,000
EAT	(50,000)	800,000	750,000

Recommendation Transfer pricing policy is beneficial as the total profit from the two subsidiaries is increased for ICM Computers.

REVIEW QUESTIONS

LOD: Easy

RQ.35.1(a) Indicate whether the following statements are true or false: [LO 35.1-6]

(i) International firms/MNCs and domestic firms are guided by the same fundamental goal, that is, maximisation of shareholders' wealth.

(ii) In multinational capital budgeting decisions, there is no distinction between the total CFAT that the new foreign investment project generates and the incremental CFAT the firm eventually has.

(iii) In determining the incremental cash inflows after tax for a new foreign capital budgeting proposal, the allocation of existing fixed overheads of the parent should be included.

(iv) Foreign exchange earnings are generally subject to tax at a single stage.

(v) The concept of single discount rate (based on weighted average cost of capital) is not appropriate for evaluating foreign projects subject to different risks.

(vi) Indian corporates can raise finance through ECBs only from recognised sources such as banks, export credit agencies etc.

(vii) Trusts and non-profit making organisations can raise finance through ECBs.

(viii) Funds raised through ECBs can be used for investment in the capital market.

(ix) The ordinary shares underlying the GDRs can be denominated in any freely convertible foreign currency.

[Answers: (i) True (ii) False (iii) False (iv) False (v) True (vi) True (vii) False (viii) False (ix) False]

(b) Fill in the blanks with the correct answer (out of the choices provided).

(i) Profitability from an investment in a country is adversely affected if the currency of that country is subject to (appreciation/depreciation).

(ii) Under the Adjusted Present Value Approach to evaluating foreign investment proposals, each project is assessed ____________ (with/without) reference to the firm's other investments.

(iii) When a foreign subsidiary is located in a country having a high rate of inflation, it is advisable to keep ____________ (more/less) stocks at that location.

(iv) Both working stocks and safety stocks should be kept at the location of a subsidiary that is ____________ (near to/far from) the market supplying the goods.

(v) A borrower can raise external commercial borrowings up to a maximum of ______________ (40/50 million dollars) under the automatic route.

(vi) Under the USD 100 million scheme of external commercial borrowing (ECB), all corporates and institutions are permitted to raise ECB up to USD 100 millions at a minimum simple maturity of ______________ (5/3) years.

(vii) Corporates which have foreign exchange earnings are permitted to raise ECB up to ______________ (twice/thrice) the average amount of annual exports during the previous three years, subject to a maximum of USD 200 millions.

(viii) ECBs of ______________ (six/eight) years average maturity and above are outside the ECB ceiling.

(ix) All infrastructure and greenfield projects are permitted to avail of ECB to the extent of ______________ (25/50) per cent of the total project cost, as appraised by a recognised financial institution.

(x) Approvals for short-term foreign currency loans with a maturity of less than three years are given by ______________ (Department of Economic Affairs/______________Reserve Bank Of India)

[Answers: (i) depreciation (ii) without (iii) more (iv) far from (v) 50 million dollars (vi) 3 years (vii) thrice (viii) eight (ix) 50 (x) Reserve Bank of India.]

RQ.35.2 Write short notes on the following: **[LO 35.5,6]**

(i) Foreign currency bonds (FCCBs)

(ii) Global Depository Receipts (GDRs)

(iii) Guidelines for disinvestment of shares by Indian companies in the overseas market.

RQ.35.3 An Indian software company having a subsidiary in the US borrows at 4 per cent in the US. If the US dollar is expected to appreciate by 2 per cent, what is the effective rate of interest for the Indian software company? **[LO 35.2]**

LOD: Medium

RQ.35.4 "Instead of total cash flows, incremental cash flows should be the basis of evaluating foreign capital budgeting projects". Elucidate the statement with suitable examples. **[LO 35.1]**

RQ.35.5 Explain the rationale of using weighted average cost of capital to evaluate foreign investments. Do you think it always provides the best results? **[LO 35.2]**

RQ.35.6 What is adjusted present value approach? Specify the situation(s) when APV approach provides better results than the NPV approach, based on WACC. **[LO 35.3]**

RQ.35.7 "We should avoid borrowing in a currency that is likely to appreciate". True or false? Explain. **[LO 35.2]**

RQ.35.8 In what respects are cash management, credit management and inventory management of a multinational enterprise different from those of a domestic company? **[LO 35.4]**

RQ.35.9 Describe in brief the main elements of the ECB (external commercial borrowings) guidelines currently in force in India. **[LO 35.5]**

RQ.35.10 The capital budget department of the ABC Inc. of the USA has developed the following data for the purpose of determining the financial feasibility of an investment proposal to be carried out in India. **[LO 35.1]**

(a) Purchase of land requires ₹3,00,000 to be paid at the time of purchase (t = 0) and two instalments of ₹2,00,000 each to be made at the end of the next 2 years (t = 1–2)

(b) Construction of the factory is to be completed in 2 years The contractor is to be paid ₹12,00,000 in two equal instalments at the end of year (t = 2–3); (c) Equipment cost to be incurred at the start of year 4 (t = 3) is ₹12,00,000; (d) Operations will begin at the start of year 5 (t = 4). It is expected that there will be a need for working capital investments. The details are: ₹3,00,000 accounts receivable; ₹15,00,000, inventories; current liabilities will also increase by ₹2,00,000.

Operations will begin in year 5 and will continue for 12 years, through year 16. The sales revenues and operating costs are assumed to come at the end of each year (t = 5 – 16). The following additional assumptions are made:

(a) The building and equipment will be depreciated over 12 years starting in year 5. After 12 years the factory building is estimated to have a salvage value of ₹6,00,000. The plant, however, is expected to have no salvage value. The company expects to sell the land at ₹8,00,000, when the plant is closed down. The company uses the straight-line method of depreciation and the same is allowed for tax purposes.

(b) Its cost of capital is 8 per cent.

(c) Annual sales are ₹28,00,000.

(d) Annual variable operating costs are ₹10,00,000.

(e) Annual fixed operating costs, excluding depreciation, are ₹2,00,000.

(f) The normal tax rate in India is 35 per cent.

(g) The company projects depreciation of the Indian rupee; to compensate for exchange rate loss, it adds a premium of 200 basis point on its cost of capital for any project to be carried out in India.

Should the company accept the project? Use the NPV method for the purpose of calculations.

RQ.35.11 Endalco Ltd. of India is planning to buy a small aluminum plant in the United States of America. The dollar cost of buying the aluminum plant is 50,000. Expected life of the plant is 5 years and it has no salvage value. The company uses the straight-line method of depreciation and the same is allowed for tax purposes. Estimated earning after taxes are $ 5,000 each year for 5 years.

[LO 35.1]

Dollar-Rupee rate is expected to be

Spot	₹62/$
After 1 year	62/$
After 2 year	62.5/$
After 3 year	62.5/$
After 4 year	62.5/$
After 5 year	63/$

Determine the IRR and payback period of the capital budgeting proposal. Will you accept the proposal if the required rate of return on such a project is 11 per cent?

LOD: Difficult

RQ.35.12 "A foreign capital budgeting project that is profitable from the point of view of a subsidiary is also profitable from the perspective of the parent." True or false? Explain. [LO 35.1]

RQ.35.13 Explain why a corporate finance manager would be unwise to follow a policy of always borrowing in a currency that offers the lowest rate of interest. [LO 35.2]

ANSWERS

35.3 Effective rate of interest is 6.8 per cent.

35.10 Company should accept the project (NPV ₹21,50,884).

35.11 **(i)** Project is profitable as IRR (15.54 per cent) is higher than required rate of return (11 per cent); **(ii)** Payback period is 3.3 years.

Scan the QR Code to access comprehensive solutions to all numerical review questions and additional material.

Appendices

TABLE A-1 The Compound Sum of One Rupee

Year	*1%*	*2%*	*3%*	*4%*	*5%*	*6%*	*7%*	*8%*	*9%*	*10%*
1	1.010	1.020	1.030	1.040	1.050	1.060	1.070	1.080	1.090	1.110
2	1.020	1.040	1.061	1.082	1.102	1.124	1.145	1.166	1.188	1.210
3	1.030	1.061	1.093	1.125	1.158	1.191	1.225	1.260	1.295	1.331
4	1.041	1.082	1.126	1.170	1.216	1.262	1.311	1.360	1.412	1.464
5	1.051	1.104	1.159	1.217	1.276	1.338	1.403	1.469	1.539	1.611
6	1.062	1.126	1.194	1.265	1.340	1.419	1.501	1.587	1.677	1.772
7	1.072	1.149	1.230	1.316	1.407	1.504	1.606	1.714	1.828	1.949
8	1.083	1.172	1.267	1.369	1.477	1.594	1.718	1.851	1.993	2.144
9	1.094	1.195	1.305	1.423	1.551	1.689	1.838	1.999	2.172	2.358
10	1.105	1.219	1.344	1.480	1.629	1.791	1.967	2.159	2.367	2.594
11	1.116	1.243	1.384	1.539	1.710	1.898	2.105	2.332	2.580	2.853
12	1.127	1.268	1.426	1.601	1.796	2.012	2.252	2.518	2.813	3.138
13	1.138	1.294	1.469	1.665	1.886	2.133	2.410	2.720	3.066	3.452
14	1.149	1.319	1.513	1.732	1.980	2.261	2.579	2.937	3.342	3.797
15	1.161	1.346	1.558	1.801	2.079	2.397	2.759	3.172	3.642	4.177
16	1.173	1.373	1.605	1.873	2.183	2.540	2.952	3.426	3.970	4.595
17	1.184	1.400	1.653	1.948	2.292	2.693	3.159	3.700	4.328	5.054
18	1.196	1.428	1.702	2.026	2.407	2.854	3.380	3.996	4.717	5.560
19	1.208	1.457	1.753	2.107	2.527	3.026	3.616	4.316	5.142	6.116
20	1.220	1.486	1.806	2.191	2.653	3.207	3.870	4.661	5.604	6.727
21	1.232	1.516	1.860	2.279	2.786	3.399	4.140	5.034	6.109	7.400
22	1.245	1.546	1.916	2.370	2.925	3.603	4.430	5.436	6.658	8.140
23	1.257	1.577	1.974	2.465	3.071	3.820	4.740	5.871	7.258	8.954
24	1.270	1.608	2.033	2.563	3.225	4.049	5.072	6.341	7.911	9.850
25	1.282	1.641	2.094	2.666	3.386	4.292	5.427	6.848	8.623	10.834
30	1.348	1.811	2.427	3.243	4.322	5.743	7.612	10.062	13.267	17.449
35	1.417	2.000	2.814	3.946	5.516	7.686	10.676	14.785	20.413	28.102
40	1.489	2.208	3.262	4.801	7.040	10.285	14.974	21.724	31.408	45.258
45	1.565	2.438	3.781	5.841	8.985	13.764	21.002	31.920	48.325	72.888
50	1.645	2.691	4.384	7.106	11.467	18.419	29.456	46.900	74.354	117.386

(*Contd.*)

TABLE A-1 The Compound Sum of One Rupeee *(Contd.)*

Year	*11%*	*12%*	*13%*	*14%*	*15%*	*16%*	*17%*	*18%*	*19%*	*20%**
1	1.110	1.120	1.130	1.140	1.150	1.160	1.170	1.180	1.190	1.200
2	1.232	1.254	1.277	1.300	1.322	1.346	1.369	1.392	1.416	1.440
3	1.368	1.405	1.443	1.482	1.521	1.561	1.602	1.643	1.685	1.728
4	1.518	1.574	1.630	1.689	1.749	1.811	1.874	1.939	2.005	2.074
5	1.685	1.762	1.842	1.925	2.011	2.100	2.192	2.288	2.386	2.488
6	1.870	1.974	2.082	2.195	2.313	2.436	2.565	2.700	2.840	2.986
7	2.076	2.211	2.353	2.502	2.660	2.826	3.001	3.185	3.379	3.583
8	2.305	2.476	2.658	2.853	3.059	3.278	3.511	3.759	4.021	4.300
9	2.558	2.773	3.004	3.252	3.518	3.803	4.108	4.435	4.785	5.160
10	2.839	3.106	3.395	3.707	4.046	4.411	4.807	5.234	5.695	6.192
11	3.152	3.479	3.836	4.226	4.652	5.117	5.624	6.176	6.777	7.430
12	3.498	3.896	4.334	4.818	5.350	5.936	6.580	7.288	8.064	8.916
13	3.883	4.363	4.898	5.492	6.153	6.886	7.699	8.599	9.596	10.699
14	4.310	4.887	5.535	6.261	7.076	7.987	9.007	10.147	11.420	12.839
15	4.785	5.474	6.254	7.138	8.137	9.265	10.539	11.974	13.589	15.407
16	5.311	6.130	7.067	8.137	9.358	10.748	12.330	14.129	16.171	18.488
17	5.895	6.866	7.986	9.276	10.761	12.468	14.426	16.672	19.244	22.186
18	6.543	7.690	9.024	10.575	12.375	14.462	16.879	19.673	22.900	26.623
19	7.263	8.613	10.197	12.055	14.232	16.776	19.748	23.214	27.251	31.948
20	8.062	9.646	11.523	13.743	16.366	19.461	23.105	27.393	32.429	38.337
21	8.949	10.804	13.021	15.667	18.821	22.574	27.033	32.323	38.591	237.373
22	9.933	12.100	14.713	17.861	21.644	26.186	31.629	38.141	45.923	55.205
23	11.026	12.552	16.626	20.361	24.891	30.376	37.005	45.007	54.648	66.247
24	12.239	15.178	18.788	23.212	28.625	35.236	43.296	53.108	65.031	79.496
25	13.585	17.000	21.230	26.461	32.918	40.874	50.656	62.667	77.387	95.395
30	22.892	29.960	39.115	50.949	66.210	85.849	111.061	143.367	184.672	237.373
35	38.574	52.799	72.066	98.097	133.172	180.311	243.495	327.988	440.691	590.657
40	64.999	93.049	132.776	188.876	267.856	378.715	533.846	750.353	1051.642	1469.740
45	109.527	163.985	244.629	363.662	538.752	795.429	1170.425	1716.619	2509.583	3657.176
50	184.559	288.996	450.711	700.197	1083.619	1670.669	2566.080	3927.189	5988.730	9100.191

*For compounded sum at rates between 21% and 40%, refer to website. The address is: www.mhhe.com/khan&jain5e

TABLE A-2 The Compound Value of an Annuity of One Rupee

Year	1%	2%	3%	4%	5%	6%	7%	8%	9%	10%
1	1.000	1.000	1.000	1.000	1.000	1.000	1.000	1.000	1.000	1.000
2	2.010	2.020	2.030	2.040	2.050	2.060	2.070	2.080	2.090	2.100
3	3.030	3.060	3.091	3.122	3.152	3.184	3.215	3.246	3.278	3.310
4	4.060	4.122	4.184	4.246	4.310	4.375	4.440	4.506	4.573	4.641
5	5.101	5.204	5.309	5.416	5.526	5.637	5.751	5.867	5.985	6.105
6	6.152	6.308	6.468	6.633	6.802	6.975	7.153	7.336	7.523	7.716
7	7.214	7.434	7.662	7.898	8.142	8.394	8.654	8.923	9.200	9.487
8	8.286	8.583	8.892	9.214	9.549	9.897	10.260	10.637	11.028	11.436
9	9.368	9.755	10.159	10.583	11.027	11.491	11.978	12.488	13.021	13.579
10	10.462	10.950	11.464	12.006	12.578	13.181	13.816	14.487	15.193	15.937
11	11.567	12.169	12.808	13.486	14.207	14.972	15.784	16.645	17.560	18.531
12	12.682	13.412	14.192	15.026	15.917	16.870	17.888	18.977	20.141	21.384
13	13.809	14.680	15.618	16.627	17.713	18.882	20.141	21.495	22.953	24.523
14	14.947	15.974	17.086	18.292	19.598	21.015	22.550	24.215	26.019	27.975
15	16.097	17.293	18.599	20.023	21.578	23.276	25.129	27.152	29.361	31.772
16	17.258	18.639	20.157	21.824	23.657	25.672	27.888	30.324	33.003	35.949
17	18.430	20.012	21.761	23.697	25.840	28.213	30.840	33.750	36.973	40.544
18	19.614	21.412	23.414	25.645	28.132	30.905	33.999	37.540	41.301	45.599
19	20.811	21.840	25.117	27.671	30.539	33.760	37.379	41.446	46.018	51.158
20	22.019	24.297	26.870	29.778	33.066	36.785	40.995	45.762	51.169	57.274
21	23.239	25.783	28.676	31.969	35.719	39.992	44.865	50.422	56.754	65.002
22	24.471	27.299	30.536	34.248	38.505	43.392	49.005	55.456	62.872	71.402
23	25.716	28.845	32.452	36.618	41.340	46.995	53.435	60.893	69.531	79.542
24	26.973	30.421	34.426	39.082	44.501	50.815	58.176	66.764	76.789	88.496
25	28.243	32.030	36.459	41.645	47.726	54.864	63.248	73.105	84.699	98.346
30	34.784	40.567	47.575	56.084	66.438	79.057	95.459	113.282	136.305	164.491
35	41.659	49.994	50.461	73.651	90.318	11.432	138.234	172.314	215.705	271.018
40	48.885	60.401	75.400	95.024	120.797	154.758	199.630	259.052	337.872	442.580
45	56.479	71.891	92.718	121.027	159.695	212.737	285.741	386.497	525.840	718.881
50	64.461	84.577	112.794	152.664	209.341	290.325	406.516	573.756	815.051	1163.865

(*Contd.*)

TABLE A-2 The Compound Value of an Annuity of One Rupee *(Contd.)*

Year	*11%*	*12%*	*13%*	*14%*	*15%*	*16%*	*17%*	*18%*	*19%*	*20%**
1	1.000	1.000	1.000	1.000	1.000	1.000	1.000	1.000	1.000	1.000
2	2.110	2.120	2.130	2.140	2.150	2.160	2.170	2.180	2.190	2.200
3	3.342	3.374	3.407	3.440	3.472	3.506	3.539	3.572	3.606	3.640
4	4.710	4.779	4.850	4.921	4.993	5.066	5.141	5.215	5.291	5.338
5	6.228	6.353	6.480	6.610	6.742	6.877	7.014	7.154	7.297	7.442
6	7.913	8.115	8.323	8.535	8.754	9.897	9.207	9.442	9.683	9.930
7	9.783	10.089	10.405	10.730	11.067	11.414	11.772	12.141	12.523	12.916
8	11.859	12.300	12.757	13.233	13.727	14.240	14.773	15.327	15.902	16.499
9	14.164	14.776	15.416	16.085	16.786	17.518	18.285	19.086	19.923	20.799
10	16.722	17.549	18.420	19.337	20.304	21.321	22.393	23.521	24.709	25.959
11	19.561	20.655	21.814	23.044	24.349	25.733	27.200	28.755	30.403	32.150
12	22.713	24.133	25.650	27.271	29.001	30.850	32.824	34.931	37.180	39.580
13	26.211	28.029	29.984	32.088	34.352	36.786	39.404	42.218	45.244	48.496
14	30.095	32.392	34.882	37.581	40.504	43.672	47.102	50.818	54.841	59.196
15	34.405	37.280	40.417	43.842	47.580	51.659	56.109	60.965	66.260	72.035
16	39.190	42.753	46.671	50.980	55.717	60.925	66.648	72.938	79.850	87.442
17	44.500	48.883	53.738	59.117	65.075	71.673	78.978	87.067	96.021	105.930
18	50.396	55.749	61.724	68.393	75.836	84.140	93.404	103.739	115.265	128.116
19	56.939	63.439	70.748	78.968	88.211	98.603	110.283	123.412	138.165	154.739
20	64.202	72.052	80.946	91.024	102.443	115.379	130.031	146.626	165.417	186.687
21	72.264	81.968	92.468	104.767	118.809	134.840	153.136	174.019	197.846	225.024
22	81.213	92.502	105.489	120.434	137.630	157.414	180.169	206.342	236.436	217.028
23	91.147	104.602	120.203	138.295	159.274	183.600	211.798	244.483	282.359	326.234
24	102.173	118.154	136.829	158.656	184.166	213.976	248.803	289.490	337.007	392.480
25	114.412	133.333	155.616	181.867	212.790	249.212	292.099	342.598	402.038	471.976
30	199.018	241.330	293.192	356.778	434.738	530.306	647.423	790.932	966.698	1181.865
35	341.583	431.658	546.663	693.552	881.152	1120.699	1426.448	1816.607	2314.173	2948.294
40	581.812	767.080	1013.667	1341.979	1779.048	2360.724	3134.412	4163.094	5529.711	7343.715
45	986.613	1358.208	1874.086	2590.464	3585.031	4965.191	6879.008	9531.258	13203.105	18280.914
50	1668.732	2399.975	3459.344	4994.301	7217.488	10435.449	15088.805	21812.273	31514.492	45496.094

*For compounded value of annuity at rates between 21% and 40%, refer to website. The address is: www.mhhe.com/khan&jain5e

TABLE A-3 The Present Value of One Rupee

Year	*1%*	*2%*	*3%*	*4%*	*5%*	*6%*	*7%*	*8%*	*9%*	*10%*
1	.990	.980	.971	.962	.952	.943	.935	.926	.917	.909
2	.980	.961	.943	.925	.907	.890	.873	.857	.842	.826
3	.971	.942	.915	.889	.864	.840	.816	.794	.772	.751
4	.961	.924	.888	.855	.823	.792	.763	.735	.708	.683
5	.951	.906	.863	.822	.784	.747	.713	.681	.650	.621
6	.942	.888	.837	.790	.746	.705	.666	.630	.596	.564
7	.933	.871	.813	.760	.711	.665	.623	.583	.547	.513
8	.923	.853	.789	.731	.677	.627	.582	.540	.502	.467
9	.914	.837	.766	.703	.645	.592	.544	.500	.460	.424
10	.905	.820	.744	.676	.614	.558	.508	.463	.422	.386
11	.896	.804	.722	.650	.585	.527	.475	.429	.388	.350
12	.887	.789	.701	.625	.557	.497	.444	.397	.356	.319
13	.879	.773	.681	.601	.530	.469	.415	.368	.326	.290
14	.870	.758	.661	.577	.505	.442	.388	.340	.299	.263
15	.861	.743	.642	.555	.481	.417	.362	.315	.275	.239
16	.853	.728	.623	.534	.458	.394	.339	.292	.252	.218
17	.844	.714	.605	.513	.436	.371	.317	.270	.231	.198
18	.836	.700	.587	.494	.416	.350	.296	.250	.212	.180
19	.828	.686	.570	.475	.396	.331	.227	.232	.194	.164
20	.820	.673	.554	.456	.377	.312	.258	.215	.178	.149
21	.811	.660	.538	.439	.359	.294	.242	.199	.164	.135
22	.803	.647	.522	.422	.342	.278	.226	.184	.150	.123
23	.795	.634	.507	.406	.326	.262	.211	.170	.138	.112
24	.788	.622	.492	.390	.310	.247	.197	.158	.126	.102
25	.780	.610	.478	.375	.295	.233	.184	.146	.116	.092
30	.742	.552	.412	.308	.231	.174	.131	.099	.075	.057
35	.706	.500	.355	.253	.181	.130	.094	.068	.049	.036
40	.672	.453	.307	.208	.142	.097	.067	.046	.032	.022
45	.639	.410	.264	.171	.111	.073	.048	.031	.021	.014
50	.806	.372	.228	.141	.087	.054	.034	.021	.013	.009

(Contd.)

TABLE A-3 The Present Value of One Rupee *(Contd.)*

Year	*11%*	*12%*	*13%*	*14%*	*15%*	*16%*	*17%*	*18%*	*19%*	*20%**
1	.901	.893	.885	.877	.870	.862	.855	.847	.840	.833
2	.812	.797	.783	.769	.756	.743	.731	.718	.706	.694
3	.731	.712	.693	.675	.658	.641	.624	.609	.593	.579
4	.659	.636	.613	.592	.572	.552	.534	.516	.499	.482
5	.593	.567	.543	.519	.497	.476	.456	.437	.419	.402
6	.535	.507	.480	.456	.432	.410	.390	.370	.352	.335
7	.482	.452	.425	.400	.376	.354	.333	.314	.296	.279
8	.434	.404	.376	.351	.327	.305	.285	.266	.249	.233
9	.391	.361	.333	.308	.284	.263	.243	.225	.209	.194
10	.352	.322	.295	.270	.247	.227	.208	.191	.176	.162
11	.317	.287	.261	.237	.215	.195	.178	.162	.148	.135
12	.286	.257	.231	.208	.187	.168	.152	.137	.124	.112
13	.258	.229	.204	.182	.163	.145	.130	.116	.104	.093
14	.232	.205	.181	.160	.141	.125	.111	.099	.088	.078
15	.209	.183	.160	.140	.123	.108	.095	.084	.074	.065
16	.188	.163	.141	.123	.107	.093	.081	.071	.062	.054
17	.170	.146	.125	.108	.093	.080	.069	.060	.052	.045
18	.153	.130	.111	.095	.081	.069	.059	.051	.044	.038
19	.138	.116	.098	.083	.070	.060	.051	.043	.037	.031
20	.124	.104	.087	.073	.061	.051	.043	.037	.031	.026
21	.112	.093	.077	.064	.053	.044	.037	.031	.026	.022
22	.101	.083	.068	.056	.046	.038	.032	.026	.022	.018
23	.091	.074	.060	.049	.040	.033	.027	.022	.018	.015
24	.082	.066	.053	.043	.035	.028	.023	.019	.015	.013
25	.074	.059	.047	.038	.030	.024	.020	.016	.013	.010
30	.044	.033	.026	.020	.015	.012	.009	.007	.005	.004
35	.026	.019	.014	.010	.008	.006	.004	.003	.002	.002
40	.015	.011	.008	.005	.004	.003	.002	.001	.001	.001
45	.009	.006	.004	.003	.002	.001	.001	.001	.000	.000
50	.005	.003	.002	.001	.001	.001	.000	.000	.000	.000

*For present value at rates between 21% and 40%, refer to website. The address is: www.mhhe.com/khan&jain5e

TABLE A-4 The Present Value of an Annuity of One Rupee

Year	*1%*	*2%*	*3%*	*4%*	*5%*	*6%*	*7%*	*8%*	*9%*	*10%*
1	.990	.980	.971	.962	.952	.943	.935	.926	.917	.909
2	1.970	1.942	1.913	1.886	1.859	1.833	1.808	1.783	1.759	1.736
3	2.941	2.884	2.829	2.775	2.723	2.673	2.624	2.577	2.531	2.487
4	3.902	3.808	3.717	3.630	3.546	3.465	3.387	3.312	3.240	3.170
5	4.853	4.713	4.580	4.452	4.329	4.212	4.100	3.993	3.890	3.791
6	5.795	5.601	5.417	5.242	5.076	4.917	4.767	4.623	4.486	4.355
7	6.728	6.472	6.230	6.002	5.786	5.582	5.389	5.206	5.033	4.868
8	7.652	7.326	7.020	6.733	6.463	6.210	5.971	5.747	5.535	5.335
9	8.566	8.162	7.786	7.435	7.108	6.802	6.515	6.247	5.995	5.759
10	9.471	8.983	8.530	8.111	7.722	7.360	7.024	6.710	6.418	6.145
11	10.368	9.787	9.253	8.760	8.306	7.887	7.499	7.139	6.805	6.495
12	11.255	10.575	9.954	9.385	8.863	8.384	7.943	7.536	7.161	6.814
13	12.134	11.348	10.635	9.986	9.394	8.853	8.358	7.904	7.487	7.103
14	13.004	12.106	11.296	10.563	9.899	9.295	8.746	8.244	7.786	7.367
15	13.865	12.849	11.938	11.118	10.380	9.712	9.108	8.560	8.061	7.606
16	14.718	13.578	12.561	11.652	10.838	10.106	9.447	8.851	8.313	7.824
17	15.562	14.292	13.166	12.166	11.274	10.477	9.763	9.122	8.544	8.022
18	16.398	14.992	13.754	12.659	11.690	10.828	10.059	9.372	8.756	8.201
19	17.226	15.679	14.324	13.134	12.085	11.158	10.336	9.604	8.950	8.365
20	18.046	16.352	14.878	13.590	12.462	11.470	10.594	9.818	9.129	8.514
21	18.857	17.011	15.415	14.029	12.821	11.764	10.836	10.017	9.292	8.649
22	19.661	17.658	15.937	14.451	13.163	12.042	11.061	10.201	9.442	8.772
23	20.456	18.292	16.444	14.857	13.489	12.303	11.272	10.371	9.580	8.883
24	21.244	18.914	16.936	15.247	13.799	12.550	11.469	10.529	9.707	8.985
25	22.023	19.524	17.413	15.622	14.094	12.783	11.654	10.675	9.823	9.077
30	25.808	22.397	19.601	17.292	15.373	13.765	12.409	11.258	10.274	9.427
35	29.409	24.999	21.487	18.665	16.374	14.498	12.948	11.655	10.567	9.644
40	32.835	27.356	23.115	19.793	17.159	15.046	12.332	11.925	10.757	9.779
45	36.095	29.490	24.519	20.720	17.774	15.456	13.606	12.108	10.881	9.863
50	39.197	31.424	25.730	21.482	18.256	15.762	13.801	12.234	10.962	9.915

(Contd.)

TABLE A-4 The Present Value of an Annuity of One Rupee *(Contd.)*

Year	*11%*	*12%*	*13%*	*14%*	*15%*	*16%*	*17%*	*18%*	*19%*	*20%**
1	.901	.893	.885	.877	.870	.862	.855	.847	.850	.833
2	1.713	1.690	1.668	1.647	1.626	1.605	1.585	1.566	1.547	1.528
3	2.444	2.402	2.361	2.322	2.283	2.246	2.210	2.174	2.140	2.106
4	3.102	3.037	2.974	2.914	2.855	2.798	2.743	2.690	2.639	2.589
5	3.696	3.605	3.517	3.433	3.352	3.274	3.199	3.127	3.058	2.991
6	4.231	4.111	3.998	3.889	3.784	3.685	3.589	3.498	3.410	3.326
7	4.712	4.564	4.423	4.288	4.160	4.039	3.922	3.812	3.706	3.605
8	5.146	4.968	4.799	4.639	4.487	4.344	4.207	4.078	3.954	3.837
9	5.537	5.328	5.132	4.946	4.772	4.607	4.451	4.303	4.163	4.031
10	5.889	5.650	5.426	5.216	5.019	4.833	4.659	4.494	4.339	4.192
11	6.207	5.938	5.687	5.453	5.234	5.029	4.836	4.656	4.487	4.327
12	6.492	6.194	5.918	5.660	5.421	5.197	4.988	4.793	4.611	4.439
13	6.750	6.424	6.122	5.842	5.583	5.342	5.118	4.910	4.715	4.533
14	6.982	6.628	5.303	6.002	5.724	5.468	5.229	5.008	4.802	4.611
15	7.191	6.811	6.462	6.142	5.847	5.575	5.324	5.092	4.876	4.675
16	7.379	6.974	6.604	6.265	5.954	5.669	5.405	5.162	4.938	4.730
17	7.549	7.120	6.729	6.373	6.047	5.749	5.475	5.222	4.990	4.775
18	7.702	7.250	6.840	6.467	6.128	5.818	5.534	5.273	5.033	4.812
19	7.839	7.366	6.938	6.550	6.198	5.877	5.585	5.316	5.070	4.843
20	7.963	7.469	7.024	6.623	6.259	5.929	5.628	5.353	5.101	4.870
21	8.075	7.562	7.102	6.687	6.312	5.973	5.665	5.384	5.127	4.891
22	8.176	7.645	7.170	6.743	6.359	6.011	5.696	5.410	5.149	4.909
23	8.266	7.718	7.230	6.792	6.399	6.044	6.723	5.432	5.167	4.925
24	8.348	7.784	7.283	6.835	6.434	6.073	5.747	5.451	5.182	4.937
25	8.422	7.843	7.330	6.873	6.464	6.097	5.766	5.467	5.195	4.948
30	8.694	8.055	7.496	7.003	6.566	6.177	5.829	5.517	5.235	4.979
35	8.855	8.176	7.586	7.070	6.617	6.215	5.858	5.539	5.251	4.992
40	8.951	8.244	7.634	7.105	6.642	6.233	5.871	5.548	5.258	4.997
45	9.008	8.283	7.661	7.123	6.654	6.242	5.877	5.552	5.261	4.999
50	9.042	8.305	7.675	7.133	6.661	6.246	5.880	5.554	5.262	4.999

*For present value of annuity at rates between 21% and 40%, refer to website. The address is: www.mhhe.com/khan&jain5e

Select Bibliography

Bierman, H and S Smidt, *The Capital Budgeting Decisions,* Macmillan, New York, 1992.

Bodie, Zvi et al, *Investments,* McGraw Hill Education, New Delhi, 2009.

Brealey, R A *et al., Principles of Corporate Finance,* McGraw Hill Education, New Delhi, 2014.

Brigham E F and J F Houston, *Fundamentals of Financial Management,* South Western/Cengage Learning India, New Delhi, 2012.

Copeland, Tom, et. al, *Valuation—Measuring and Managing the Value of Companies,* John Wiley & Sons, New York, 2000.

Damodaran Aswath, *Investment Valuation,* John Wiley & Sons, New York, 1996.

Dixit, Alok, Surendra S Yadav and P. K. Jain, *Derivative Markets in India: Trading, Pricing and Risk Management,* McGraw Hill Education, New Delhi, 2012.

Emery, D R and John D Finnerty, *Corporate Financial Management,* Prentice Hall, New Jersey, 1997.

Francis, Jack Clark, *Investments: Analysis and Management,* McGraw-Hill Education, New York, 1991.

Gitman, L J, *Principles of Managerial Finance,* Pearson Education, New Delhi, 2007.

Helfert, E H, *Techniques for Financial Analysis,* Irwin, Homewood, 1997.

Higgins, R C, *Analysis For Financial Management,* Irwin McGraw-Hill, Boston, 2012.

Jain, P K and Surendra S Yadav, *Financial Management Practices in Select Private Corporate Enterprises: A Comparative Study of India, Thailand and Singapore,* Hindustan Publishing Corporation, New Delhi, 2000.

Jain, P K, Josette Peyrard and Surendra S Yadav, *International Financial Management,* Macmillan India Ltd, New Delhi, 1998.

Jain, P K, Shveta Singh and Surendra Singh Yadav, *Financial Management Practices: An Empirical Study of Indian Corporates,* Springer, New Delhi, 2013.

Joy, O M, *Introduction to Financial Management,* Irwin, Homewood, 1997.

Khan, M Y, *Financial Services,* McGraw Hill Education, New Delhi, 2018.

Khan, M Y, *Indian Financial System,* McGraw Hill Education, New Delhi, 2018.

Khan, M Y and P K Jain, *Management Accounting,* McGraw Hill Education, New Delhi, 2018.

Koutsoyiannis, A, *Non-Price Decisions-The Firm in a Modern Contest,* Macmillan, London, 1995.

McMenamin, Jim, *Financial Management—An Introduction,* Oxford University Press, New Delhi, 2000.

Ramanujam, S *Mergers et. al,* Lexis Nexis, New Delhi, 2012.

Rani, N, et. al., *Mergers and Acquisitions: A Study of Financial Performance, Motives and Corporate Governance,* Springer, New Delhi, 2016.

Rao, R K S, *Financial Management-Concepts and Applications*, Macmillan, New York, 1992.

Ross, Stephen A, et. al, *Fundamentals of Corporate Finance,* Tata McGraw-Hill, New Delhi, 2012.

Shapiro, Alan C, *Multinational Financial Management,* John Wiley and Sons, New York, 2012.

Singh, Shweta, et. al., *Equity Market in India: Return, Risk and Price Multiples,* Springer, New Delhi, 2016.

Solomon, E and J J Pringle, *An Introduction to Financial Management,* Goodyear Publishing Co., Santa Monica Calif., 1977.

Solomon, E, *Theory of Financial Management,* Columbia University Press, New York, 1969.

Van Horne, J C, *Financial Management and Policy*, Prentice-Hall of India, New Delhi, 2002.

Weston J Fred et. al, *Mergers, Restructuring and Corporate Control,* Prentice-Hall of India, New Delhi, 2009.

Weston, J F, and E F Brigham, *Managerial Finance*, Holt, Rinehart and Winston, 1992.

White Gerald I, et. al, *The Analysis and Use of Financial Statements,* John Wiley & Sons, New York, 1998.

Yadav, Surendra S, et. al, *Foreign Exchange Markets—Understanding Derivatives and Other Instruments,* Macmillan India, New Delhi, 2001.

Index

Abandonment option 12.24
Accept-reject decision 9.6, 12.12
Accept-reject rule 12.14
Accounting for intangible benefits 35.3
Accruals 14.23
Acid-test/quick ratio 6.7
Acquisition/takeovers 32.33
Activity/efficiency ratios 6.26
Actual delivery 34.6
Additional sources of finance 25.8
Adjusted present value (APV) approach 32.16, 35.20
Administration of sales ledger 17.15
Administrator or servicer 23.18
Advantage of share repurchase 30.18
Advisory services 17.16
Agency costs 1.19
Agent and trustee 23.19
Aggregate amount 17.13
Algebraic approach 18.14
  for a new company 18.14
  for an existing company 18.15
Algebraic methods 7.2
All-in-cost (AIC) 35.25
All-in-cost, pricing and maturity 35.34
Alternative definition of financial leverage 18.9
Alternative definition of NWC 13.5
Analysis of credit information 15.7
Application of avoidance of double taxation agreement 35.32
Application of Black-Scholes option pricing formula to stock options 28.14
Application of Black-Scholes (BS) model 27.19
Application of the P/V/(C/V) ratio 7.14
Appraisal value 32.6
Approaches/methods of valuation 31.6
Arbitrage in forward market 33.11
Arbitrage pricing theory 3.28
Arbitrage process 19.14, 19.15, 33.10
AS-7: Statement of cash flows 5.13
Asset backed securities (ABS) 23.21
Asset characteristics 23.19
Asset-based approach to valuation 31.6
Assets turnover ratio 6.30
Assigning probability 12.4, 27.16
Assignment of receivables 17.22
Assignment of weights 11.19
Assumptions, definitions and symbols 19.2, 29.6
Attention hypothesis 30.15
Available routes for raising ECBs 35.24
Average rate of return 9.27
  accept-reject rule 9.28
  computation 9.27
  evaluation of ARR 9.28
Avoidance of early payments 14.22
Avoids conditionalities 25.8

Bad debts 32.20, 32.22
Bad debt expenses 15.4
Balance of payment position 33.15
Bank credit 17.3
Bankers' acceptances 14.26
Bankruptcy costs 19.20
  direct bankruptcy costs 19.20
  indirect bankruptcy costs 19.20
Basic bond valuation 4.3
  impact of maturity on bond value 4.4
  impact of required return on bond values 4.4
Basic propositions 19.11
Basic valuation model 4.2
Baumol model 14.6
Bear Hug 32.54
Behaviour of security market participants 1.19
Benefit associated with non-recourse factoring 17.19
Benefits associated with recourse factoring 17.19

Benefits of cash flow operation 5.14
Benefits of holding inventory 16.3
benefits in production 16.4
benefits in purchasing 16.4
benefits in sales 16.4
benefits in work-in-process 16.4
Beta 3.22
unlevering and relevering beta 3.23
Bills discounting 14.27
Bills purchased/discounted 17.3
Black-Scholes option pricing model/formulae 27.17, 28.12
Bonding expenditures 1.20
Bonus shares (stock dividend) 30.13
Book building 22.7
Book value 31.4, 32.6
Book value and market value weights 11.21
Book value approach 4.12
Book value per share 6.25
Brand power 32.54
Break-even analysis 7.2
applications 7.5
Break-even chart/volume cost profit (VCP) graph 7.10
Break-even lease rental 25.17, 25.19
BS formula 27.18
Budget—definition, meaning and purpose 8.2, 8.3
Bulk collection 14.28
Business cycle 13.14
Business general nature 13.13
Business losses
carry forward and set off 32.18
Business risk analysis 23.12
Buyback of CP 17.11
Buy-back of securities 30.20
Buyouts 32.60

Call and put provision 23.8
Call option 27.4, 34.7
boundaries 27.10
payoffs 27.9
Callable/puttable bonds/debentures/bond refunding 23.10
Calls and puts option 24.10
Cannibalisation 35.3
Capital asset pricing model (CAPM) 35.18, 3.19
approach 11.15
assumptions 3.20
elements of the model 3.20
Capital budgeting
difficulties 9.4
importance 9.4
meaning 9.3
nature 9.3
rationale 9.5
Capital expenditure on family planning 32.20
Capital expenditure ratio 6.17
Capital impairment rules 30.7
Capital market considerations 30.12
Capital market line 3.18
Capital rationing decision 9.6
Capital market perception 17.8
Capital structure theories 19.4
Cash and bank balances 13.18
Cash balances
factor determining 14.5
Cash break-even point 7.14
Cash budget: management tool 14.10
Cash collateral 23.17
Cash credit/overdrafts 17.3
Cash discount 15.9
Cash earnings per share 6.24
Cash 5.14
need 14.6
Cash equivalents 5.14
Cash flow 5.14, 23.19
determination 9.15
preparation of statement 5.5
Cash flow estimates 9.9
Cash flow pattern 9.9
conventional cash flows 9.9
non-conventional cash flows 9.9
Cash flows at subsidiary and parent level 35.5
Cash flows vs accounting profit 9.7
Cash management 35.20
basic strategies 14.16
objectives 14.4
techniques/processes 14.19
Cash management/conversion models 14.6
Cash substitution hypothesis 30.15
Cashflow analysis in recession 20.5
Cash-flow from operations ratio 6.11
Certainty-equivalent approach 12.13
Certificate of deposits (CDs) 17.13
Changes in cost of equity capital 19.8
Changes in ownership interests in subsidiaries 5.17
Changes in risk 4.14
Changes in sales and operating expenses 13.12
Changes in working capital 13.11
Cheque truncation 14.28
Cheque-encashment analysis 14.23
Claim on income and assets 23.8
Clientele effect 30.11
Coefficient of variation 3.5, 12.10
Collection costs 15.4
Collection methods 14.27
Collection policies 15.12
degree of collection effort 15.12
type of collection efforts 15.15
Combination and companies act 32.28
Combination and competition act 32.23
Combined cash management strategies 14.18
Combined effect 4.14
Combined leverage: total risk 18.20
Commercial paper 14.26, 17.9

Commissioned studies 26.10
Common conditions for public/rights issues 22.5
Common definition of NWC 13.4
Cost-of-carry model 28.6
Common size statements 6.40
Company
characteristics 20.13
Comparable riskless flow 12.14
Compounding
practical applications 2.18
Compulsory partly/fully convertible debentures 24.5
Computation
mechanics 11.21
Computation of overall cost of capital 11.18, 35.19
Computation of working capital 13.17
Concentration banking 14.20
Conceptual diversity 6.45
Conceptual framework of valuation 31.3
Conceptual framework 25.21, 32.1
Conditions for category I AIF 26.20
Conditions for category II AIFs 26.22
Conditions for category III AIFs 26.22
Conditions of certificate 26.19
Consequence of default 25.10
Constant dividend per share 30.3
Constant growth model/Gordon model 4.9
Constant payout ratio 30.4
Constant required returns 4.4
Constant valuation 19.28
Continuous price formation 21.8
Contribution margin approach 7.2
Conventional venture capitalist valuation method 26.5
Conversion of ECBs into equity 35.28
Conversion value (CV) 24.7
Convertibility 23.8, 24.3
Convertible debentures/bonds 24.4
eligibility for issue 35.29
Convertible debt 26.11
Corporate restructuring forms 32.55
Corporate taxes 19.18
Costs 15.2, 17.2
capital cost 15.2
collection cost 15.2
default cost 15.3
delinquency cost 15.2
Cost behaviour with change in volume 8.11
Cost considerations 13.7
Cost method 26.10
Cost of acquisition determination 32.14
Cost of additional investment 15.11, 15.12
Cost of capital 35.10
Cost of debt 11.5, 19.8, 35.11
Cost of equity capital 11.11, 35.17
Cost of marginal/incremental investment 15.6
Cost of perpetual debt 11.6
Cost of preference shares 11.9, 35.15
Cost of redeemable debt 11.7
Cost of redeemable preference capital 11.10
Cost of retained earnings 11.17, 35.19
Cost of services 17.16
Costs associated with recourse and non-recourse factoring 17.19
Costs of holding inventory 16.2
Covenants 23.2
negative 23.2
positive 23.3
Coverage ratio 6.15, 20.3
Creation of charge on immovable assets 35.27
Creation of charge over financial securities 35.27
Credit analysis 15.7
Credit control and credit restriction 17.16
Credit enhancement 23.17
Credit management 35.22
Credit period 15.10
Credit policy 13.14, 15.3
Credit rating 23.8
Credit standards 15.4
Credit terms 15.8
Credit trenching 23.17
Cross rates 33.8
Cumulative dividends 24.2
Currency futures 34.5
Currency of borrowing 35.26
Currency options 34.7
Current ratio 6.4
interpretation 6.5
rationale 6.5
Current share price 27.13

Data requirement 9.7, 35.2
Debenture redemption reserve (DRR) 23.7
Debentures/bonds/notes 23.7
Debt and preference shares financing 32.10
Debt equity ratio 35.28
Debt instruments 26.11, 26.7
Debt to total capital ratio 6.15
Debt-equity ratios 6.12
interpretation 6.13
Debtors 13.18
Debtors turnover ratio 6.8
Debt-service coverage ratio (DSCR) 6.17
Decision-tree approach 12.22
Deep discount bond (DDB) 23.9, 26.8
Default risk 34.6
Defensive-interval ratio 6.10
Deferred payment plan 32.11
Deferred taxes 5.16
Demerged company
meaning 32.21
Demerger
meaning 32.20
Deposits/margins 34.6
Depreciation 25.22
Depreciation policy 13.17
Direct and indirect quotations 33.5
Direct wages 13.19
Disclosure of shareholding and control 32.52
Discount/coupon rate 17.13
Disinvestments of equity/quasi-equity investments 26.14

Distributed risk 23.20
Distribution 21.10
Divestitures/demergers 32.57
Dividend approach 11.12, 35.17
Dividend capitalisation model 29.18
Dividend coverage ratio 6.16
Dividend payout (D/P) ratio 30.2
Dividend pay-out (D/P) ratio 6.25
Dividend per share (DPS) 6.25
Dividend policy 13.16
factors affecting 30.1
Dividend policy decision 1.9
Dividends 28.13, 5.16
Domestic lease 25.7
Double leverage 19.18
Duplicate certificate 17.14

Earnings and dividend yield 6.26
Earnings based approach to valuation 31.8
Earnings measure based on accounting 31.9
Earnings measure on cash flow basis (DCF approach) 31.12
Earnings per share (EPS) 6.24, 32.7
Earnings stability 30.9
Ebit-EPS analysis 18.10
Economic interdependence 21.7
Economic order quantity (EOQ) model 16.7
Economic value added (EVA) 1.17, 31.21
Economics of mergers 32.3
diversification 32.5
economies of scale 32.3
fast growth 32.4
synergy 32.3
tax benefits 32.4
Effect of changes in fixed costs 7.6
Effect of changes in variable costs 7.7
Effect of depreciation 9.11
Effect of indirect expenses 9.10
Effect of taxes 9.8
Effective and flat rates of interest 2.28
Effective rates of interest and discount 2.23
Efficient inventory-production management 14.18
Efficient portfolios 3.13
borrowing 3.16
margined short sales 3.14
one risk-free asset 3.15
Electronic banking 14.29
Electronic clearing service 14.28
Elements/preparation of cash budget 14.11
Eligible borrowers 35.24
Emerging role of finance managers in India 1.22
End-use prescriptions 35.25
Equation technique 7.4
Equilibrium formula 30.18
Equity instruments 26.6
Equity investments 26.10
Estimation of current liabilities 13.18
Evaluation 12.13, 23.8, 24.3, 26.13, 30.5
demerits 24.3
merits 24.3
Excess cash balance costs 14.5
Exchange rate risk 35.7
Exchange rates 33.4
determinants and select theories 33.13
Exercise price 24.8, 27.13
Exercise ratio 24.8
Exit of debt instruments 26.15
Expenditure on acquisition of patent rights or copy rights 32.19
Expenditure on prospecting of certain minerals 32.20
Expenditure on scientific research 32.19
Expenditure related to demerger 32.22
Expenses ratio 6.20
Explicit and implicit costs 11.4
Explicit statement of expectations 8.3
Exposure
economic exposure 34.3
transaction exposure 34.2
translation exposure 34.2
types 34.1
Extended CAPM 3.25
inflation 3.26
liquidity 3.26
taxes 3.25
External commercial borrowings (ECBs) 35.23
External credit enhancements 23.17

Factoring 17.14
Factoring in India 17.21
Fair value 31.5
Fair value method 31.20
Fallout of capital rationing 10.15
Fees and royalties 35.3
Finance and accounting 1.5
Finance and economics 1.4
Finance and other related disciplines 1.4, 1.6
Finance function 1.3
Finance lease and operating lease 25.3
Financial analysis 26.5
Financial appraisal 23.6
Financial assets 21.3
Financial budgets 8.5
cash budget 8.5
financial cash flows 8.6
operating cash flows 8.6
Financial cash flows 14.13
Financial evaluation 25.23, 32.57
Financial evaluation of leasing 25.10
Financial flows 20.7
Financial framework 32.5
Financial intermediaries 21.4
Financial lease limitations 25.10
Financial leverage 18.7
Financial manager key activities 1.9
Financial markets 21.4
capital market 21.5
money market 21.5
Financial performance measure 16.15
Financial risk analysis 23.13
Financial system 21.3
Financial terms 8.3
Financial/default risk 14.24

Financing activities 5.15
Financing decision 1.9
Financial management objectives 1.10
Financing nature 21.6
Financing of capital goods 25.8
Financing stages 26.3
Financing trade debts 17.15
Finished goods inventory 13.18
Firm
  internal hedging techniques 34.11
First Chicago method 26.6
Fixed costs 8.11
Fixed dividend 24.3
Flexibility in dividend payment 30.19
Flexibility in structuring of rentals 25.8
Flexibility option 12.25
Flexible budgets 8.10
Float 14.22
Floating rate bonds (FRBs) 23.10
Flotation costs 29.10
Foreign currency cash flows 5.16
Foreign currency exchangeable bonds 35.33
Foreign exchange dealings 33.4
Foreign exchange markets 33.3
Foreign exchange risk management 34.5
Format 17.14
Forms of credit 17.3
Forms of ECBs 35.23
Forward contracts 28.2, 34.5
  limitations 28.3
Framework of Indian CP market 17.9
Free cash flows to the firm (FCFF) 32.13
  determination of present value 32.14
Free of gift-tax 32.20
Full security 25.9
Fundamentals of equity shares 22.1
Funds committed to cash balances 14.4
Futures and options 28.10
Futures terminology 28.3
Futures/future contracts 28.3

Gain or loss 27.5
Geographical arbitrage 33.10
Gift tax and wealth tax 35.33
Going public/initial public offering/flotation 26.14
Gordon's model 29.17
Greenmail 32.54
Growth option 12.24
Growth prospects 30.9

Hands-holding nurturing 26.8
Hands-off nurturing 26.8
Hands-on nurturing 26.8
Hedging and conservative approaches 13.8, 13.9
Hedging approach 13.6
Hedging requirements 35.26
Higher credit standing 17.18
Hire-purchase finance 25.21
Hire-purchase vs instalment payment 25.22
Historical versus marginal weights 11.19
Historical weights 11.20
Homogeneity 23.20
Hostile takeover 1.19, 32.54
Hypothecation 17.4

Income notes 26.7
Increased valuation and decreased overall cost of capital 19.28
Incremental cash flow 9.8
Incremental cash inflows after taxes (CFAT) 35.2
Incremental cash outflows 35.2
Independent cash flows over time 12.16
Indexation clauses 34.12
Indian venture capital scenario 26.16
Individual limits 35.26
Inflation 30.12
  impact 6.44
Inflation and capital budgeting 10.15
Inflation rates 33.13
Innovative debt instruments 23.8
Insolvency 30.8
Instruments of securitisation 23.20
Insurance 23.17
Integrated analysis of ratios 6.31
Intercorporate deposits 14.27
Interest 5.16, 23.7
Interest coverage ratio 6.16
Interest rate futures 34.6
Interest rate risk 14.24
Interest rates 33.14
Inter-firm comparison 6.43
Internal credit enhancements 23.17
Internal rate of return (IRR) method 9.36
  accept-reject decision 9.37
  computation 9.37
  evaluation of IRR 9.40
Internal rate return (IRR) 25.12
In-the-money option 27.4
Intrinsic/economic value 31.4
Inventory (or stock) turnover ratio 6.27
Inventory management 35.23
Inventory turnover ratio 6.8
Investing activities 5.15
Investment company 26.13
Investment conditions and restrictions 26.19
Investment decision 1.8
  capital budgeting 1.8
  working capital management 1.8
Investment decisions affecting revenues 9.5
Investment decisions reducing costs 9.5
Investment nurturing/aftercare 26.8
Investments stages 26.10
Investment strategy 26.19
Investment trust 26.13
Investment/redemption 17.11
Investments in receivables 15.4
Investments in subsidiaries 5.17
Investor's risk preference 3.18
Investors 17.13, 23.18
Irrelevance of dividends 29.4
Issuance of guarantee 35.28
Issue mechanism 21.11
Issue of bonus shares 30.20
  completion 30.20
  conditions 30.20
  restrictions 30.20

Issue of corporate or personal guarantee 35.28
Issue of CP: credit enhancement limits 17.10
Issue procedure 22.4, 23.15, 23.21, 24.4, 30.20
Issue structure of the GDRs/ ADRs 35.30

Just-in time inventory/ production 16.14

Leading and lagging 34.11
Lease financing 25.1
Lease financing vs hire-purchase financing 25.22
Leasing
  limitations 25.10
Legal and procedural aspects of mergers/ amalgamations and acquisiton/takeovers 32.22
Letter of credit 17.4, 23.17
Leverage/capital structure ratios 6.11
Liability of debtor in case of micro/small enterprises 17.23
Liability of debtors 17.23
Lien 17.5
Limit of diversification gains 3.11
Limited liability 22.4
Limited partnership 26.12
Limits of foreign investment in the issuing company 35.30
Liquid assets 30.8
Liquidation 26.15
Liquidation value 31.4, 4.13
Liquidity 14.25, 34.6
Liquidity aspect: cash flow analysis 20.4
Liquidity hypothesis 30.15
Liquidity position 6.42
Liquidity ratios 6.3
Listing agreement 32.33
Loan repayment schedule for annuities 2.26
Loans 17.3
Loans/buy-backs 17.14
Lock-box system 14.20
Long-term solvency 6.43
Loss of residual value 25.10
Low cost 21.4
Maintenance of records 26.23
Making financing decisions 1.10
Making investment decisions 1.10
Management risk 23.13
Manager obligation 26.23
Managerial appraisal 23.6
Margin of safety 7.3
Marginal weights 11.19
Market appraisal 23.6
Market capitalisation size 3.27
Market forces 1.19
Market imperfection 29.10
Market place 21.8
Market portfolio 3.17
Market price of shares 19.10
Market price 19.6
Market risk 17.7
Market value 31.4, 32.6
Market value added approach (MVA) 31.20
Market value based approach to valuation 31.19
Market value of warrant (MVW) 24.9
Market value-based methods 26.10
Marketable securities 14.23
Marketable security alternatives 14.25
Markowitz diversification 3.12
Maturity 17.13, 23.2, 23.7
Measure of volume 8.11
Measurement of economic exposure 34.4
Measures of financial leverages 18.19
  stock terms 18.20
  flow terms 18.20
Meeting payments schedule 14.4
Mergers
  financing techniques 32.8
  types 32.2
    conglomerate merger 32.3
    horizontal merger 32.2
    vertical merger 32.2
Methods of demerger/ divestiture 32.58
Miller-Orr model 14.8
Minimum average maturity period 35.24
Minimum level of public shareholding 32.33
Minimum operating cash 14.17
Minimum size of issue and denominations 17.13
Mixed costs 8.11
Mode of compensation 26.13
Mode of issuance 17.11
Mode of payment 32.40
Mode of security 17.4
Mode of trading 34.6
Modification of original contract 17.23
Modified flexible budgets 8.12
Modigliani and Miller (MM) hypothesis 29.6
Modigliani-Miller (MM) approach 19.11
Money market mutual funds/liquid funds 14.27
Money market operations 34.10
Monitoring expenditures 1.19
Mortgage 17.5
Mortgage backed securities (MBS) 23.21
Motives for holding cash 14.2
  compensating motive 14.3
  precautionary motive 14.2
  speculative motive 14.3
  transaction motive 14.2
Multifactor linear model 3.28
Multinational capital budgeting decisions 35.2
Multinational working capital management 35.20
Multi-product firms (sales-mix) 7.8

Naïve diversification 3.12
Near vs distant dividend 29.12
Negotiable certificates of deposit (CDs) 14.25
Net income approach 19.4
Net operating income (NOI) approach 19.7
Net present value (NPV) method 9.34
Net present value of hire purchase plan [NPV (HPP)] 25.26
Net present value of lease plan [NPV (LP)] 25.26

Net present value vs. profitability index 10.12
Net profits 30.8
Net working capital 6.3
Netting 34.13
  types
    bilateral netting 34.13
    multilateral netting 34.14
New issues/primary market functions 21.9
New vs old securities 21.6
Nexus between savings and investment 21.8
No executory clauses 23.20
Non-cash transactions 5.17
Non-convertible debentures (NCDs) 26.7
Non-convertible debt 26.12
Non-financial performance measures 16.15
Non-operating cash flows 20.7
Normal probability distribution 12.18
Notice of assignment 17.22
NPV and IRR methods: differences 10.3
NPV and IRR: similarities 10.2
NPV vs. IRR methods 10.1
NPV, IRR, profitability index methods 10.1

Obligor(s) 23.18
Obsolescence risk 25.9
Obtaining credit information 15.7
    external 15.7
    internal 15.7
Offer for sale 21.12
Offshore investment company 26.13
Offshore unit trust 26.13
One-step optimisation 3.12
Open offer process 32.44
Operating activities 5.14, 5.15
Operating budgets 8.5
Operating cash flows 14.12, 20.6
Operating efficiency 6.43, 13.17
Operating leverage 18.4
Operating profit 7.6
Operations and resources 8.2
Opportunity cost 1.20, 35.3
Opportunity cost of funds 16.3
Optimal portfolio 3.19
Optimum capital structure 19.8
Option
  concept 27.3
  types 12.24, 27.3
Option payoffs 27.9
Option terminology 28.9
Option value (OV) 24.7
Option valuation
  factors influencing 27.12
Optionally convertible debentures 24.6
Options 24.10
Options payoffs 28.10
Options/options contracts 28.8
Order point problem 16.10
Ordinary share financing 32.9
Organisation of finance function 1.20
Orgler's model 14.9
Originator 23.18
Out-of-the-money option 27.4
Over-collateralisation 23.17
Owner's considerations 30.10
Ownership 25.22
Ownership preserved 25.8

Pac-man defence 32.54
Parameters for ECBSs 35.24
Parking of ECB proceeds abroad 35.28
Parking of ECB proceeds domestically 35.28
Parking of ECBs proceeds 35.28
Pass through certificates (PTCs) 23.20
Pay back method 9.29
    accept-reject criterion 9.30
    computation 9.29
    evaluation 9.30
Pay through security (PTS) 23.20
Payment of certificate 17.14
Payment outsourcing 14.29
Payoff for buyer of futures 28.4
Payoff for futures 28.4
Payoff for seller of futures 28.5
Payoff profile for buyer of call options 28.11
Payoff profile for buyer of put options 28.11
Payoff profile for seller of asset 28.11
Payoff profile for writer of put options 28.11
Payoff profile for writer to call options 28.11
Payoff profile of buyer of asset 28.11
Pecking-order theory 19.23
  implications 19.24
Perfect negative correlation 3.10
Perfect positive correlation 3.9
Performance measure 16.15
Performing financial analysis and planning 1.9
Periodic reports 26.10
Permanent and temporary working capital 13.11
Perpetual security 11.10
Placement memorandum 26.19
Placement method 21.12
Planning process 8.1
    goals 8.2
    objectives 8.1
    plans/budgets 8.2
    strategies 8.2
Plant visits 26.9
Pledge 17.5
Poison pill 32.54
Poison put 32.54
Policies related to current assets investment 13.5
    aggressive current assets investment policy 13.5
    moderate current assets investment policy 13.6
    relaxed current assets investment policy 13.5
Portfolio expected return 3.6
Portfolio risk (two-asset portfolio) 3.6
Portfolio risk and correlation 3.9
Portfolio selection 3.12
Post-dated cheque (PDC) management 14.28
Pound sterling exchange rate 34.8
  appreciates 34.8
  depreciates 34.9
Power to call for information 26.23

Power to issue direction 32.53
Precise measures of risk 12.9
Preference for current income 29.12
Preference share capital 24.1
Preferential issues 22.10
Preliminary expenses 32.20, 32.22
Preparation of cash budget 14.13
Preparation/types of budgets 8.5
Present value (PV)/discounted cash flow (DCF) 9.33
Present value calculations 12.14
Present value of an annuity payable PTHLY 2.25
Present value or discounting technique 2.11
Present value tables 2.12
Price earnings (P/E) ratio 31.10, 6.26
Price level changes 13.17
Price volatility of share 27.15
Price/earnings (P/E) multiples/ ratio 4.13
Price-earnings and market-to-book value ratios 3.27
Price-enhancing effect 30.19
Price-to-book value ratio 6.25
Pricing futures 28.5
Pricing index futures 28.6, 28.7
Pricing index options 28.13
Pricing options 28.12
Pricing stock futures 28.8
Pricing stock options 28.13
Principles of debtor protection 17.23
Prior claim on income/ assets 24.2
Probability distribution 3.3
 approach 12.16
Probability of stock-out 16.13
Procedure for action in case of default 26.25, 26.27
Procedure for grant of certificate 26.19
Procedure for issuance 17.11
Production cycle 13.13
Production policy 13.14
Profit level 13.16
Profit margin 6.19
 gross profit margin 6.19
 net profit margin 6.19
Profit on incremental sales 15.5
Profit/EPS maximisation decision criterion 1.12
 ambiguity 1.13
 quality of benefits 1.14
 timing of benefits 1.13
Profitability index (PI) or benefit-cost ratio (B/C ratio) 9.42
 accept-reject rule 9.43
 evaluation 9.43
Profitability ratios 6.18
 related to investments 6.22
 related to sales 6.18
Project appraisal 23.6
Project selection under capital rationing 10.12
Projects with unequal lives 10.5
Provision of collection facility 17.15
Public issues 22.6
 through prospectus 21.11
Put-and-call formulae 26.14
Put option 27.7
 payoffs 27.10

Qualified institutional placement 22.11

Rating agency 23.18
Rating methodology 23.12
Rating of debt instruments 23.11
Rating requirements 17.10
Rating symbols 23.14
Ratio analysis 6.2
 importance 6.42
 limitations 6.44
Rationale of time value of money 2.2
Raw materials inventory 13.18
Receivables (debtors) turnover ratio 6.28
Recognised lenders/ investors 35.25
Redeemability 24.2
Reduction of cost and expenses 17.18
Registration of alternative investment funds (AIFs) 26.16
Registration of assignments 17.23
Registration of factors 17.21
Regulation of combination 32.23
Reinvestment rate assumption 10.8
Reinvoicing centre 34.16
Relationship among financial decisions, return, risk and share values 4.13
Relationship between new issue market and stock exchange 21.5
Relevance of dividends 29.13
Repatriation of profits 35.7
Repayment schedule/loan amortisation 23.3
Replacement situation 9.20
Replacement value 31.5
Reporting cash flows 5.15
Repurchase (REPO) agreements 14.26
Reserve requirements 17.13
Reserves for shipping business 32.22
Residual claim on assets 22.2
Residual claim to income 22.2
Residual theory of dividends 29.4
Residual value of equity 19.8
Restructuring scheme 32.55
Resulting company meaning 32.21
Retention/deployment of proceeds 35.34
Return on assets (ROA) 6.22
Return on capital employed (ROCE) 6.23
Return on ordinary shareholders' equity 6.24
Return on shareholders' equity 6.23
Return on total shareholders' equity 6.23
Revenue multiplier method 26.6
Reverse stock splits 30.14
Right to control 22.2
Rights issue 21.13, 22.9
Rights of set-off of debtor 17.23
Risk
 definition 12.2
 description and measurement 12.2
Risk and real options 12.24

Risk and return of a single asset 3.2
Risk and return of portfolio 3.6
Risk and return 3.2
Risk consideration 13.8, 13.9
Risk evaluation approaches 12.11
Risk free interest rate 28.13
Risk perception 19.17
Risk-adjusted discount rate approach 12.11
Risk-free rate 3.22, 27.13
Risk-premium on market portfolio 3.22
Risk-return relationship 3.22

Safety stock 16.10
Sale and lease back 25.6
Sale of shares to entrepreneurs/ employees/earnout 26.14
Sales creation 35.3
Sales to a new investor/ takeout 26.15
Sales volume 15.4
Salvage value 31.5
Scenario analysis 12.6
Scope of financial management 1.7
Scoring and rating model of X bank 17.5
SEBI alternative investment funds regulation, 2012 26.16
SEBI foreign venture capital investors (FVCIs) regulations, 2000 26.25
SEBI regulations 30.21
  conditions 30.21
  open market 30.21
  panalties 30.22
  tender offer 30.21
SEBI substantial acquisition of shares and takeover code (SEBI takeover code) 32.34
Secured premium notes (SPNs) 23.9, 26.8
Securitisation process 23.16
Security for raising ECBs 35.27
Security market line (SML) 3.21
Security 17.14, 23.2, 23.8, 23.19
Selection of investment 26.3
Semi-annual and other compounding periods 2.5
  Semi-annual compounding 2.5
Semi-annual interest and bond values 4.7
Sensitivity analysis 3.2, 12.3
Share repurchase (share buyback) 30.17
Shareholder orientation in India 1.17
Sharing risk 34.13
Shifting the manufacturing base 34.13
Short costs 14.5
Short-cut method 15.6
Signalling effect 30.19
Signalling hypothesis 30.15
Signalling theory 19.22
Simulation 12.7
Single investor lease 25.6
Single proposal 9.15
Size of stock-out (units) 16.12
Size-disparity problem 10.3
Slowing disbursements 14.22
Small business investment company 26.13
Special decision budgets 8.10
Specified future period 8.3
Speedy cash collections 14.19
Spot rates and forward rates 33.6
Spread 33.5
Spread account 23.17
Spreadsheet solution 2.5–2.7, 2.9, 2.12, 2.14, 2.16, 2.18–2.22, 3.5, 3.8, 4.6, 4.8, 4.12
  compound sum of an annuity 2.10
  future/compounded value of a series of payments 2.8
  quarterly compounding 2.6
Stability of dividends 30.3
Stable rupee dividend 30.4
Standard deviation of return 3.4
Standard deviation 12.9
Stock exchange listing 21.7
Stock price 28.13
Stock/secondary markets/ exchanges
  functions 21.7
Straight debenture value (SDV) 24.6
Strategic alliance 32.54
Street sweep 32.54
Stretching accounts payable 14.17
Strike price 28.13
Stripped securities 23.21
Structural aspects 26.12
Structuring expenditure 1.20
Substantial acquisition of shares 32.34
Swaps 34.9
  interest swaps 34.9
  currency swaps 34.10
Synchronisation of cash flows 14.5

Takeover offer 32.34
Takeover 32.33
Tax advantage 30.19
Tax aspects of amalgamation 32.18
Tax aspects related to demergers 32.20
Tax benefit 25.10, 25.23
Tax concessions for demerged company 32.22
Tax concessions to amalgamated company 32.18, 32.20
Tax concessions to resulting company 32.21
Tax concessions to the shareholders of an amalgamating company 32.20
Tax concessions to the shareholders 32.22
Tax effect 9.10, 29.10
Taxes impact 35.6
Tax planning 20.13
Taxation of foreign currency convertible bonds 35.32
Taxation on shares issued under GDR mechanism 35.32
Taxes on income 5.16
Tax-timing hypothesis 30.15
Technical appraisal 23.6
Tender offer 32.12
Tender/book building method 21.11

Tenor 17.10
Term loans 23.2
  procedure 23.4
Terminal value method 9.41
  accept-reject rule 9.42
  evaluation 9.42
Theoretical framework 26.2
Theoretical value of warrant (TVW) 24.9
Third-party guarantee 23.17
Time to expiration 28.13
Time to expiration/maturity 27.14
Time-disparity problem 10.4
Timing of issue 20.12
Timing option 12.25
Total cashflow coverage ratio 6.17
Total fixed charge coverage ratio 6.16
Trade credit 17.1
Trade creditors 13.18
Trade in CDs 17.13
Trade sales 26.15
Trade-off approach 13.9
Trade-off theory 19.22
Trading and settlement 17.11
Trading on equity 25.10
Trading range hypothesis 30.15
Traditional techniques 9.27
Transaction and inconvenience costs 29.11
Transaction costs 19.18
Transfer and redemption 35.31
Treasury bills 14.25
Treatment of fixed overheads 35.3
Treatment of funds 1.6
Trend analysis 6.43
Trial and error (analytical) approach 16.8
Triangular arbitrage 33.11
Triggered amortisation 23.18
Trust indenture 23.7
Turnover ratio 6.8
Two-step optimisation 3.13
Two-way quotations/rates 33.5

Uncertainty and cash management 14.6
Under- and over-valued assets 3.23
Underpricing 29.13
Understatement of lessee's asset 25.10
Underwriting 21.10
Usefulness of statement of cash flows 5.4

Vagaries in the availability of raw material 13.15
Validity of CAPM 3.24
Valuation 24.5, 26.23
Valuation of bonds/debentures 4.3
Valuation of ordinary shares 4.8
Valuation of portfolio 26.10
Valuation of preference shares 4.8
Valuation of shares approaches 4.12
Value measurement approaches 31.20
Value of goodwill 31.5
Value of warrants 24.9
Variable costs 8.11
Variable growth model 4.10
VCP analysis 7.8
Volatility 28.13
Volume of international reserves/foreign exchange 33.15
Voting rights 24.3
Voting system 22.3

Walter's model 29.13
Warrants 24.7
Warrant premium 24.9
Wealth maximisation decision criterion 1.14
White knight 32.54
White squire 32.54
Winding-up 26.24
Working capital
  concepts and definitions 13.4
  determinants 13.13
  effect 9.14
  nature 13.3
  need 13.10
  planning 13.10
  term loans 17.4
Work-in-process (W/P) inventory 13.18

Yield 14.25
Yield to maturity (YTM) 4.6

Zero correlation 3.11
Zero growth model 4.9
Zero interest bonds/debentures (ZIB/D) 23.9
Zero working capital 13.5